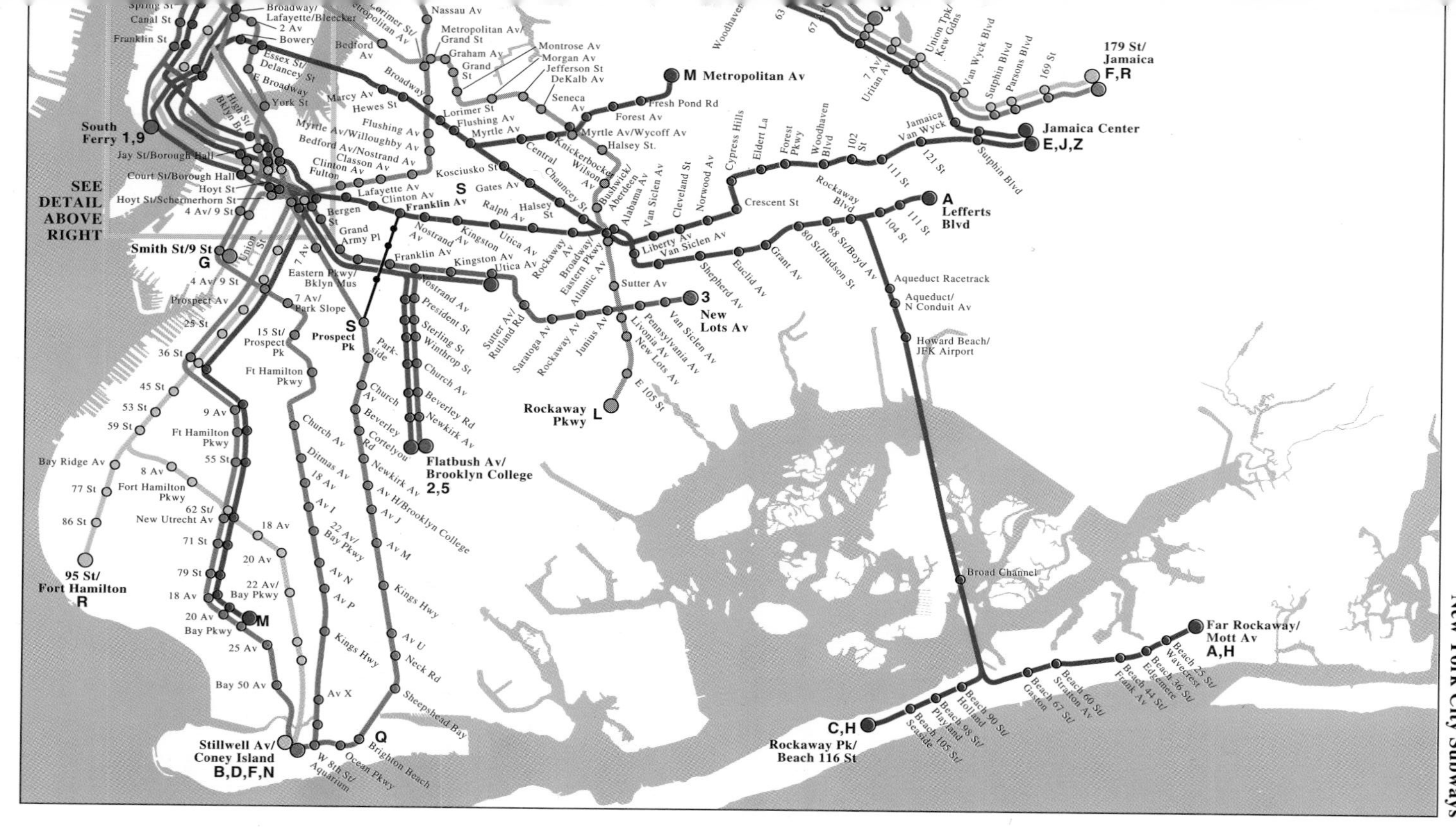
Far Rockaway/ Mott Av A,H
Beach 25 St/ Wavecrest
Beach 36 St/ Edgemere
Beach 44 St/ Frank Av
Beach 60 St/ Straiton Av
Beach 67 St/ Gaston
Beach 90 St/ Holland
Beach 98 St/ Playland
Beach 105 St/ Seaside
C,H Rockaway Pk/ Beach 116 St
Broad Channel
Howard Beach/ JFK Airport
Aqueduct/ N Conduit Av
Aqueduct Racetrack
A Lefferts Blvd
111 St
104 St
Rockaway Blvd
88 St/Boyd Av
80 St/Hudson St
Grant Av
Euclid Av
Shepherd Av
3 New Lots Av
Van Siclen Av
Pennsylvania Av
Livonia Av
New Lots Av
E 105 St
L Rockaway Pkwy
179 St/ Jamaica F,R
169 St
Parsons Blvd
Sutphin Blvd
Van Wyck Blvd
Union Tpk/ Kew Gdns
Jamaica Center E,J,Z
Sutphin Blvd
Jamaica Van Wyck
121 St
111 St
102 St
Woodhaven Blvd
Forest Pkwy
Elderts La
Cypress Hills
Crescent St
Norwood Av
Cleveland St
Van Siclen Av
Liberty Av
Van Siclen Av
M Metropolitan Av
Fresh Pond Rd
Forest Av
Myrtle Av/Wycoff Av
Halsey St.
Seneca Av
Knickerbocker Av
Wilson Av
Central Av
Alabama Av
Aberdeen
Bushwick/
Chauncey St
Halsey St
Gates Av
Kosciusko St
Montrose Av
Morgan Av
Jefferson St
DeKalb Av
Sutter Av
Atlantic Av
Eastern Pkwy/ Broadway
Rockaway Av
Junius Av
Rockaway Av
Saratoga Av
Sutter Av/ Rutland Rd
Ralph Av
Utica Av
Kingston Av
Nostrand Av
Franklin Av
S
Nassau Av
Metropolitan Av
Grand St
Graham Av
Grand St
Lorimer St
Flushing Av
Myrtle Av
Broadway
Flushing Av
Hewes St
Marcy Av
Myrtle Av/Willoughby Av
Bedford Av/Nostrand Av
Classon Av
Clinton Fulton
Lafayette Av
Clinton Av
Bergen St
Grand Army Pl
Eastern Pkwy/ Bklyn Mus
Nostrand Av
President St
Sterling St
Winthrop St
Church Av
Beverley Rd
Newkirk Av
Flatbush Av/ Brooklyn College 2,5
Prospect Pk
Parkside
Church Av
Beverley Rd
Cortelyou Rd
Newkirk Av
Av H/Brooklyn College
Av J
Av M
Kings Hwy
Av U
Neck Rd
Sheepshead Bay
Q Brighton Beach
Ocean Pkwy
W 8th St/ Aquarium
Stillwell Av/ Coney Island B,D,F,N
Church Av
Ditmas Av
18 Av
Av I
22 Av/ Bay Pkwy
Av N
Av P
Kings Hwy
Av X
7 Av
7 Av/ Park Slope
15 St/ Prospect Pk
Ft Hamilton Pkwy
9 Av
Ft Hamilton Pkwy
55 St
62 St/ New Utrecht Av
71 St
79 St
18 Av
20 Av
Bay Pkwy
25 Av
Bay 50 Av
18 Av
20 Av
22 Av/ Bay Pkwy
M
8 Av
Fort Hamilton Pkwy
Smith St/9 St G
4 Av/9 St
Prospect Av
25 St
36 St
45 St
53 St
59 St
Bay Ridge Av
77 St
86 St
95 St/ Fort Hamilton R
Union St
Hoyt St
Hoyt St/Schermerhorn St
4 Av/9 St
Court St/Borough Hall
Jay St/Borough Hall
High St/ Bklyn Br
York St
E Broadway
Essex St/ Delancey St
Bowery
Broadway/ Lafayette/Bleecker
2 Av
Canal St
Franklin St
Bedford Av
Lorimer St/ Metropolitan Av
South Ferry 1,9
SEE DETAIL ABOVE RIGHT

Downtown Manhattan

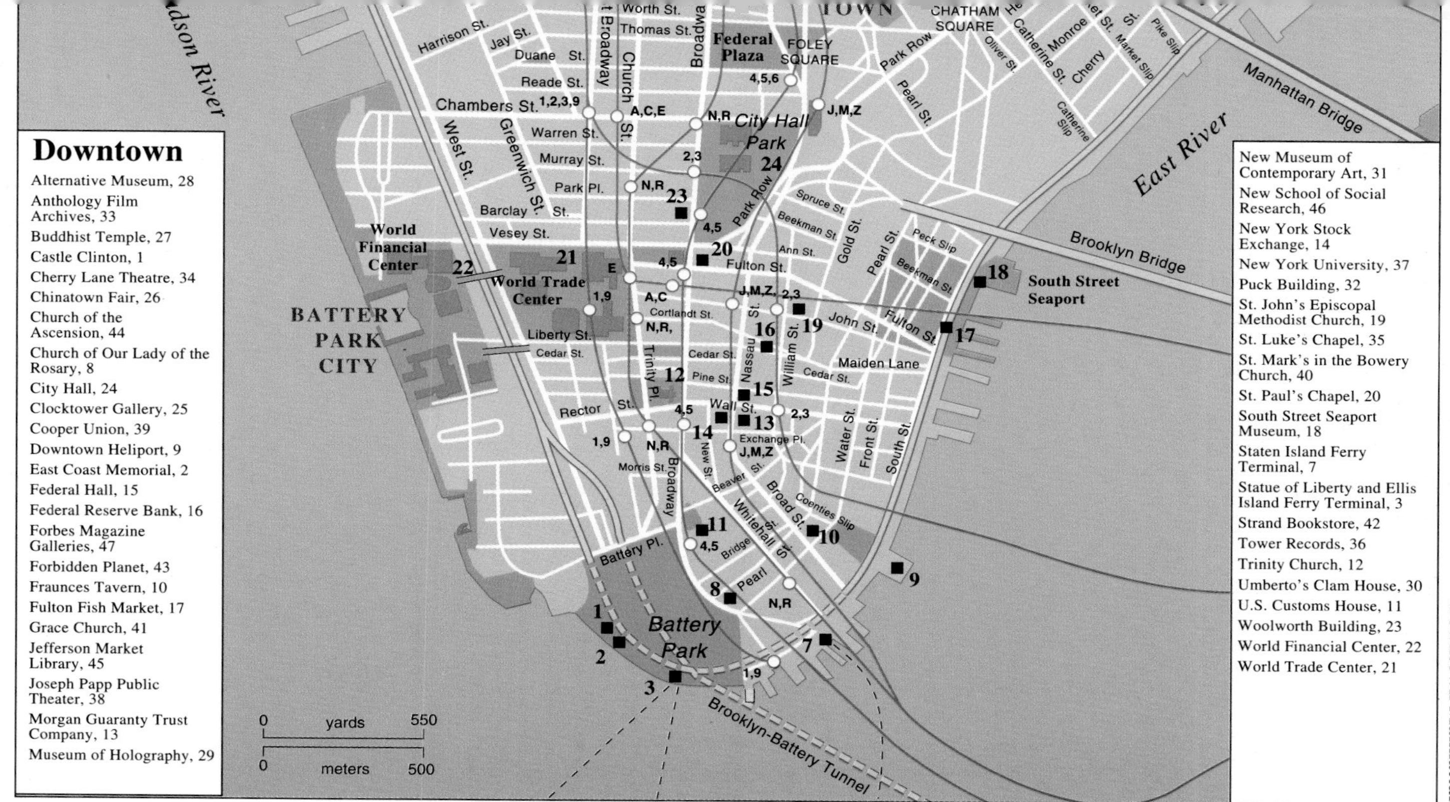
Downtown
Alternative Museum, 28
Anthology Film Archives, 33
Buddhist Temple, 27
Castle Clinton, 1
Cherry Lane Theatre, 34
Chinatown Fair, 26
Church of the Ascension, 44
Church of Our Lady of the Rosary, 8
City Hall, 24
Clocktower Gallery, 25
Cooper Union, 39
Downtown Heliport, 9
East Coast Memorial, 2
Federal Hall, 15
Federal Reserve Bank, 16
Forbes Magazine Galleries, 47
Forbidden Planet, 43
Fraunces Tavern, 10
Fulton Fish Market, 17
Grace Church, 41
Jefferson Market Library, 45
Joseph Papp Public Theater, 38
Morgan Guaranty Trust Company, 13
Museum of Holography, 29
New Museum of Contemporary Art, 31
New School of Social Research, 46
New York Stock Exchange, 14
New York University, 37
Puck Building, 32
St. John's Episcopal Methodist Church, 19
St. Luke's Chapel, 35
St. Mark's in the Bowery Church, 40
St. Paul's Chapel, 20
South Street Seaport Museum, 18
Staten Island Ferry Terminal, 7
Statue of Liberty and Ellis Island Ferry Terminal, 3
Strand Bookstore, 42
Tower Records, 36
Trinity Church, 12
Umberto's Clam House, 30
U.S. Customs House, 11
Woolworth Building, 23
World Financial Center, 22
World Trade Center, 21
East River
Manhattan Bridge
Brooklyn Bridge
Brooklyn-Battery Tunnel
South Street Seaport
Battery Park
BATTERY PARK CITY
World Financial Center
World Trade Center
City Hall Park
Federal Plaza
FOLEY SQUARE
CHATHAM SQUARE
0 yards 550
0 meters 500

Midtown Manhattan

Queensboro Bridge
East River
Queens-Midtown Tunnel
FDR Dr.
United Nations
TURTLE BAY
First Ave.
Second Ave.
Third Ave.
Lexington Ave.
Park Ave.
Madison Ave.
Fifth Ave.
Seventh Ave.
Broadway
Eighth Ave.
Ninth Ave.
Dyer Ave.
Tenth Ave.
Eleventh Ave.
Twelfth Ave.
E. 60th St.
E. 59th St.
E. 58th St.
E. 57th St.
E. 56th St.
E. 55th St.
E. 54th St.
E. 53rd St.
E. 52nd St.
E. 51st St.
E. 50th St.
E. 49th St.
E. 48th St.
E. 47th St.
E. 46th St.
E. 45th St.
E. 44th St.
E. 43rd St.
E. 42nd St.
E. 41st St.
E. 40th St.
E. 39th St.
E. 38th St.
E. 37th St.
E. 36th St.
E. 35th St.
E. 34th St.
E. 33rd St.
E. 32nd St.
W. 60th St.
W. 59th St.
W. 58th St.
W. 57th St.
W. 56th St.
W. 55th St.
W. 54th St.
W. 53rd St.
W. 52nd St.
W. 51st St.
W. 50th St.
W. 49th St.
W. 48th St.
W. 47th St.
W. 46th St.
W. 45th St.
W. 44th St.
W. 43rd St.
W. 42nd St.
W. 41st St.
W. 40th St.
W. 39th St.
W. 38th St.
W. 37th St.
W. 36th St.
W. 35th St.
W. 34th St.
W. 33rd St.
Citicorp Center
Grand Army Plaza
Central Park South
Carnegie Hall
Museum of Modern Art
Rockefeller Center
Grand Central Terminal
New York Public Library
Bryant Park
MURRAY HILL
Empire State Building
HERALD SQUARE
GARMENT DISTRICT
TIMES SQUARE
COLUMBUS CIRCLE
New York Convention & Visitors Bureau
Port Authority Bus Terminal
General Post Office
Lincoln Tunnel
HELL'S KITCHEN
N,R
4,5,6
B,Q
E,F
6
4,5,6,S
7
B,D,F,Q
B,D,E
1,2,3,9
C,E
A,C,E
A,B,C,D,1,2,3,9
1,2,3,N,R,9
B,D,F,Q,7
1 2 3 4 5 6 7 8 9 10 11 12 13 14 15 16 17 28 29 30 31 32 33 34 35 36 37 38 39 40 41 42 43 44 45 46 47 48 49 50 51 52 53 54 55 56 57 58 59 60 61 62 63 64 65 66 67 68

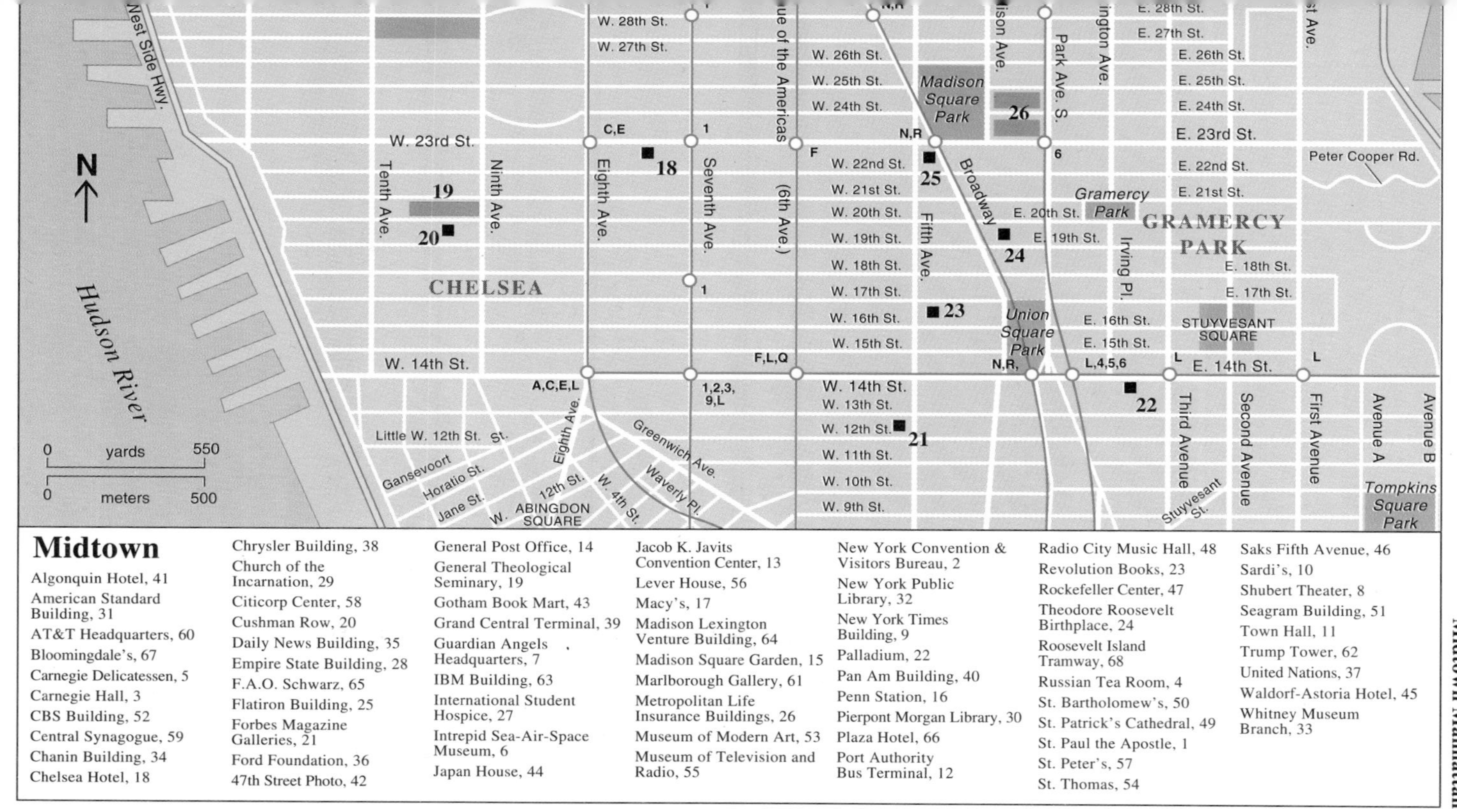

Midtown

Algonquin Hotel, 41
American Standard Building, 31
AT&T Headquarters, 60
Bloomingdale's, 67
Carnegie Delicatessen, 5
Carnegie Hall, 3
CBS Building, 52
Central Synagogue, 59
Chanin Building, 34
Chelsea Hotel, 18
Chrysler Building, 38
Church of the Incarnation, 29
Citicorp Center, 58
Cushman Row, 20
Daily News Building, 35
Empire State Building, 28
F.A.O. Schwarz, 65
Flatiron Building, 25
Forbes Magazine Galleries, 21
Ford Foundation, 36
47th Street Photo, 42
General Post Office, 14
General Theological Seminary, 19
Gotham Book Mart, 43
Grand Central Terminal, 39
Guardian Angels Headquarters, 7
IBM Building, 63
International Student Hospice, 27
Intrepid Sea-Air-Space Museum, 6
Japan House, 44
Jacob K. Javits Convention Center, 13
Lever House, 56
Macy's, 17
Madison Lexington Venture Building, 64
Madison Square Garden, 15
Marlborough Gallery, 61
Metropolitan Life Insurance Buildings, 26
Museum of Modern Art, 53
Museum of Television and Radio, 55
New York Convention & Visitors Bureau, 2
New York Public Library, 32
New York Times Building, 9
Palladium, 22
Pan Am Building, 40
Penn Station, 16
Pierpont Morgan Library, 30
Plaza Hotel, 66
Port Authority Bus Terminal, 12
Radio City Music Hall, 48
Revolution Books, 23
Rockefeller Center, 47
Theodore Roosevelt Birthplace, 24
Roosevelt Island Tramway, 68
Russian Tea Room, 4
St. Bartholomew's, 50
St. Patrick's Cathedral, 49
St. Paul the Apostle, 1
St. Peter's, 57
St. Thomas, 54
Saks Fifth Avenue, 46
Sardi's, 10
Shubert Theater, 8
Seagram Building, 51
Town Hall, 11
Trump Tower, 62
United Nations, 37
Waldorf-Astoria Hotel, 45
Whitney Museum Branch, 33

Uptown Manhattan

Uptown

American Museum of Natural History, 53
The Ansonia, 55
The Arsenal, 25
Asia Society, 14
Belvedere Castle, 36
Bethesda Fountain, 33
Blockhouse No. 1, 42
Bloomingdale's, 22
Bridle Path, 30
Cathedral of St. John the Divine, 47
Central Park Zoo, 24
Chess and Checkers House, 28
Children's Museum of Manhattan, 51
Children's Zoo, 26
China House, 19
Cleopatra's Needle, 38
Columbia University, 46
Conservatory Garden, 2
Cooper-Hewitt Museum, 7
The Dairy, 27
Dakota Apartments, 56
Delacorte Theater, 37
El Museo del Barrio, 1
Fordham University, 60
Frick Museum, 13
Gracie Mansion, 10
Grant's Tomb, 45
Great Lawn, 39
Guggenheim Museum, 9
Hayden Planetarium (at the American Museum of Natural History), 53
Hector Memorial, 50
Hotel des Artistes, 57
Hunter College, 16
International Center of Photography, 5
Jewish Museum, 6
The Juilliard School (at Lincoln Center), 59
Lincoln Center, 59
Loeb Boathouse, 34
Masjid Malcolm Shabazz , 43
Metropolitan Museum of Art, 11
Mt. Sinai Hospital, 4
Museum of American Folk Art, 58
Museum of American Illustration, 21
Museum of the City of New York, 3
National Academy of Design, 8
New York Convention & Visitors Bureau, 61
New York Historical Society, 54
New York Hospital, 15
Plaza Hotel, 23
Police Station (Central Park), 40
Rockefeller University, 20
7th Regiment Armory, 17
Shakespeare Garden, 35
Soldiers and Sailors Monument, 49
Strawberry Fields, 32
Studio Museum in Harlem, 44
Symphony Space, 48
Tavern on the Green, 31
Temple Emanu-El, 18
Tennis Courts, 41
Whitney Museum of American Art, 12
Wollman Rink, 29
Zabar's, 52

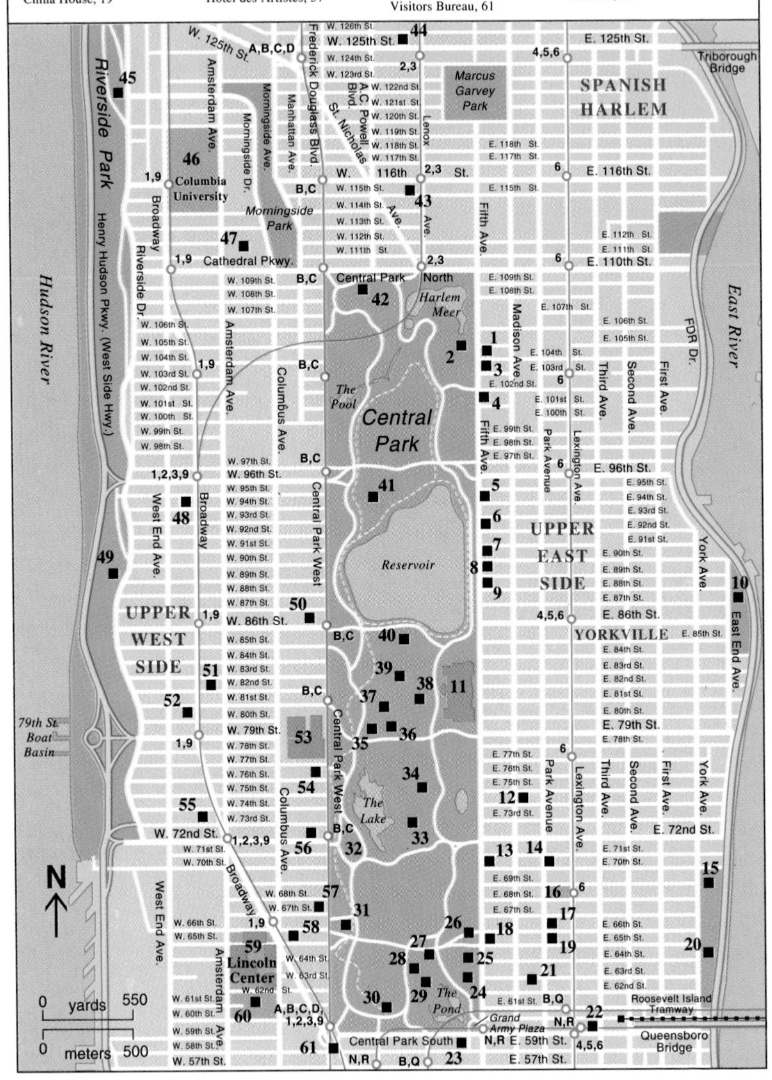

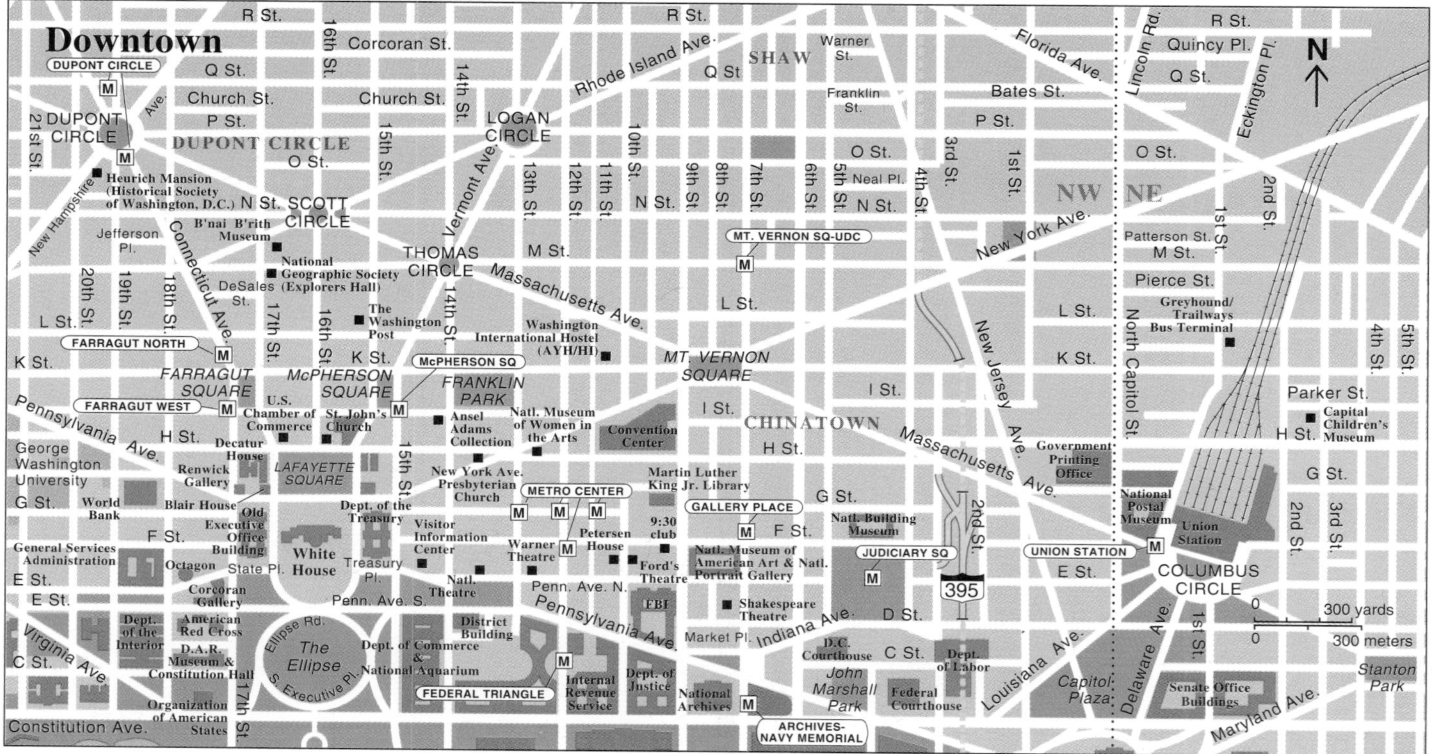
Downtown
N
0
300 yards
0
300 meters
DUPONT CIRCLE
LOGAN CIRCLE
SCOTT CIRCLE
THOMAS CIRCLE
COLUMBUS CIRCLE
SHAW
CHINATOWN
NW
NE
MT. VERNON SQUARE
FRANKLIN PARK
McPHERSON SQUARE
FARRAGUT SQUARE
LAFAYETTE SQUARE
The Ellipse
White House
Union Station
National Postal Museum
Government Printing Office
Capital Children's Museum
Greyhound/ Trailways Bus Terminal
Convention Center
Martin Luther King Jr. Library
Natl. Building Museum
Natl. Museum of American Art & Natl. Portrait Gallery
Shakespeare Theatre
Ford's Theatre
Petersen House
9:30 club
FBI
Dept. of Justice
National Archives
Internal Revenue Service
Dept. of Labor
Federal Courthouse
D.C. Courthouse
John Marshall Park
Senate Office Buildings
Capitol Plaza
Stanton Park
Natl. Museum of Women in the Arts
Ansel Adams Collection
New York Ave. Presbyterian Church
Washington International Hostel (AYH/HI)
The Washington Post
National Geographic Society (Explorers Hall)
B'nai B'rith Museum
Heurich Mansion (Historical Society of Washington, D.C.)
U.S. Chamber of Commerce
St. John's Church
Decatur House
Renwick Gallery
Blair House
Old Executive Office Building
Dept. of the Treasury
Visitor Information Center
Warner Theatre
Natl. Theatre
District Building
Dept. of Commerce & National Aquarium
Corcoran Gallery
Octagon
American Red Cross
D.A.R. Museum & Constitution Hall
Organization of American States
Dept. of the Interior
General Services Administration
World Bank
George Washington University
DUPONT CIRCLE
FARRAGUT NORTH
FARRAGUT WEST
McPHERSON SQ
METRO CENTER
GALLERY PLACE
MT. VERNON SQ-UDC
JUDICIARY SQ
UNION STATION
FEDERAL TRIANGLE
ARCHIVES-NAVY MEMORIAL
M
395
Pennsylvania Ave.
Massachusetts Ave.
Connecticut Ave.
New York Ave.
New Jersey Ave.
Rhode Island Ave.
Vermont Ave.
New Hampshire Ave.
Florida Ave.
Indiana Ave.
Louisiana Ave.
Delaware Ave.
Maryland Ave.
Virginia Ave.
Constitution Ave.
Penn. Ave. N.
Penn. Ave. S.
North Capitol St.
Lincoln Rd.
Eckington Pl.
Ellipse Rd.
S. Executive Pl.
State Pl.
Treasury Pl.
Market Pl.
Jefferson Pl.
DeSales St.
Neal Pl.
Patterson St.
Pierce St.
Parker St.
Quincy Pl.
Bates St.
Warner St.
Franklin St.
Corcoran St.
Church St.
R St.
Q St.
P St.
O St.
N St.
M St.
L St.
K St.
I St.
H St.
G St.
F St.
E St.
D St.
C St.
21st St.
20th St.
19th St.
18th St.
17th St.
16th St.
15th St.
14th St.
13th St.
12th St.
11th St.
10th St.
9th St.
8th St.
7th St.
6th St.
5th St.
4th St.
3rd St.
2nd St.
1st St.

Central Washington, D.C.

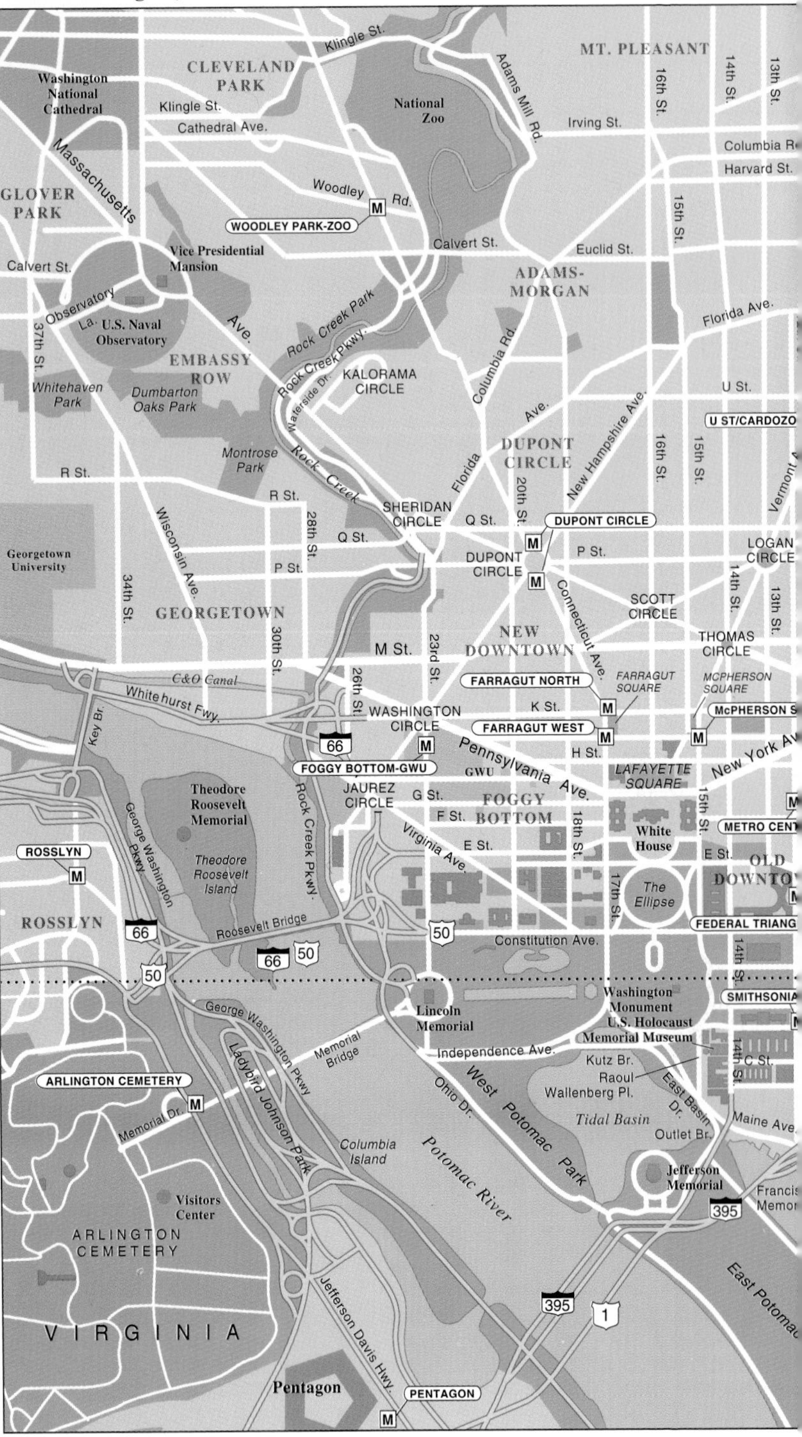

Klingle St.
MT. PLEASANT
CLEVELAND PARK
Washington National Cathedral
Klingle St.
Cathedral Ave.
National Zoo
Adams Mill Rd.
16th St.
14th St.
13th St.
Irving St.
Columbia Rd.
Harvard St.
Massachusetts
GLOVER PARK
Woodley Rd.
WOODLEY PARK-ZOO
15th St.
Calvert St.
Euclid St.
Vice Presidential Mansion
Calvert St.
ADAMS-MORGAN
Observatory La.
U.S. Naval Observatory
Ave.
Rock Creek Park
Florida Ave.
37th St.
EMBASSY ROW
Rock Creek Pkwy.
Waterside Dr.
KALORAMA CIRCLE
Columbia Rd.
Whitehaven Park
Dumbarton Oaks Park
U St.
Ave.
New Hampshire Ave.
U ST/CARDOZO
DUPONT CIRCLE
16th St.
15th St.
Montrose Park
Rock Creek
Florida
Vermont
R St.
R St.
Wisconsin Ave.
SHERIDAN CIRCLE
Q St.
20th St.
DUPONT CIRCLE
28th St.
Q St.
P St.
LOGAN CIRCLE
Georgetown University
P St.
DUPONT CIRCLE
34th St.
Connecticut Ave.
14th St.
13th St.
SCOTT CIRCLE
GEORGETOWN
30th St.
NEW DOWNTOWN
M St.
23rd St.
THOMAS CIRCLE
C&O Canal
FARRAGUT NORTH
FARRAGUT SQUARE
MCPHERSON SQUARE
26th St.
Whitehurst Fwy.
K St.
WASHINGTON CIRCLE
McPHERSON S
Key Br.
FARRAGUT WEST
66
Pennsylvania Ave.
H St.
New York Av
FOGGY BOTTOM-GWU
GWU
LAFAYETTE SQUARE
Theodore Roosevelt Memorial
JAUREZ CIRCLE
G St.
FOGGY BOTTOM
15th St.
Rock Creek Pkwy.
F St.
METRO CEN
George Washington Pkwy.
Theodore Roosevelt Island
Virginia Ave.
E St.
18th St.
White House
ROSSLYN
E St.
OLD DOWNTO
The Ellipse
17th St.
ROSSLYN
66
Roosevelt Bridge
50
FEDERAL TRIANG
Constitution Ave.
66
50
14th St.
50
Washington Monument
SMITHSONIA
Lincoln Memorial
U.S. Holocaust Memorial Museum
George Washington Pkwy
Memorial Bridge
Independence Ave.
Kutz Br.
C St.
14th St.
Ladybird Johnson Park
Raoul Wallenberg Pl.
ARLINGTON CEMETERY
Ohio Dr.
West Potomac Park
East Basin Dr.
Memorial Dr.
Tidal Basin
Maine Ave.
Columbia Island
Outlet Br.
Potomac River
Jefferson Memorial
Visitors Center
395
Francis Memor
ARLINGTON CEMETERY
East Potomac
Jefferson Davis Hwy.
395
1
VIRGINIA
Pentagon
PENTAGON

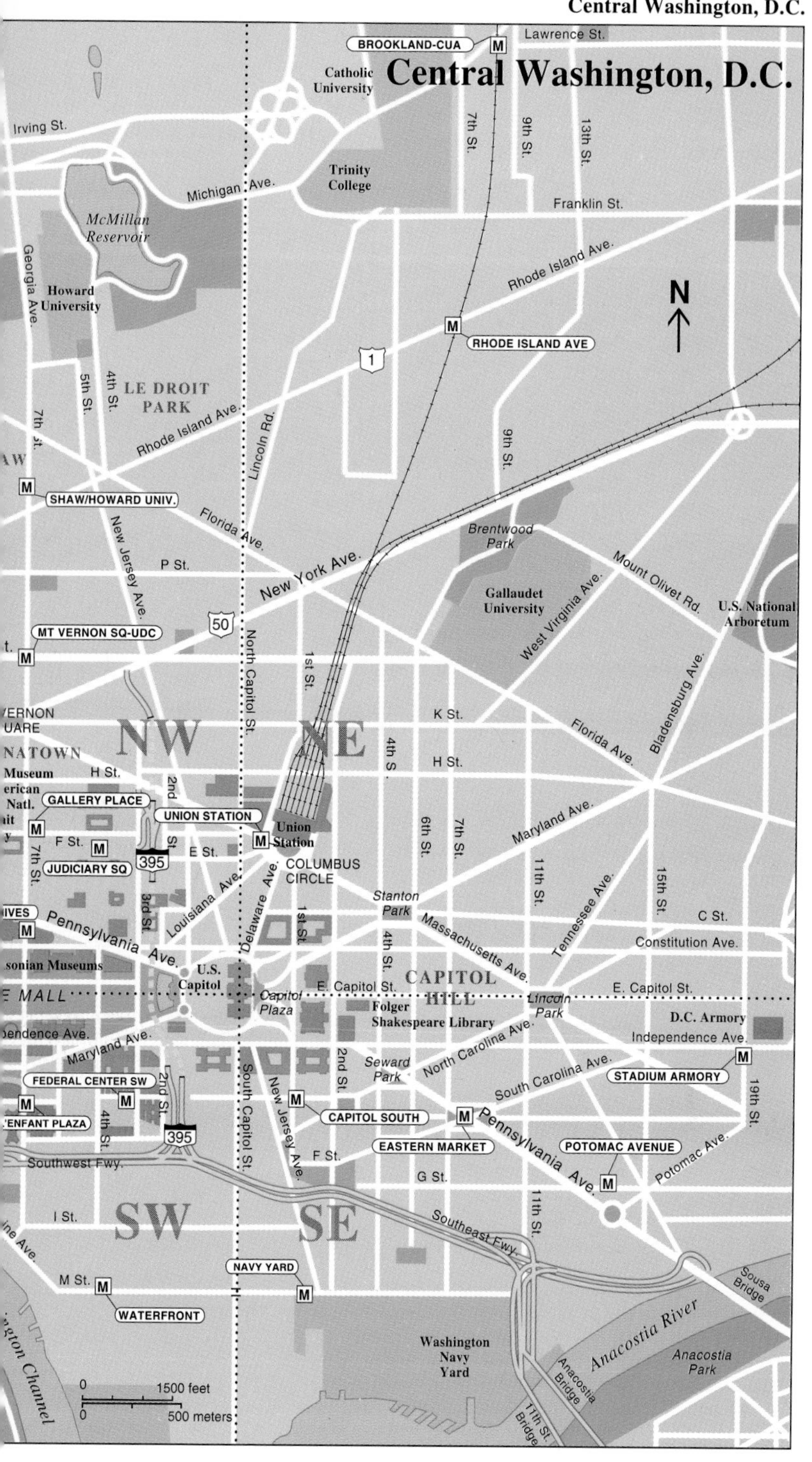
Central Washington, D.C.
BROOKLAND-CUA
Lawrence St.
Catholic University
Trinity College
Irving St.
Michigan Ave.
McMillan Reservoir
Howard University
Georgia Ave.
Franklin St.
7th St.
9th St.
13th St.
Rhode Island Ave.
RHODE ISLAND AVE
N
LE DROIT PARK
5th St.
4th St.
Lincoln Rd.
SHAW/HOWARD UNIV.
Florida Ave.
New Jersey Ave.
P St.
New York Ave.
Brentwood Park
Gallaudet University
West Virginia Ave.
Mount Olivet Rd.
U.S. National Arboretum
MT VERNON SQ-UDC
North Capitol St.
1st St.
Bladensburg Ave.
K St.
NW
NE
H St.
4th St.
GALLERY PLACE
UNION STATION
Union Station
2nd St.
F St.
E St.
JUDICIARY SQ
COLUMBUS CIRCLE
6th St.
Maryland Ave.
11th St.
15th St.
Louisiana Ave.
Delaware Ave.
Stanton Park
Massachusetts Ave.
Tennessee Ave.
C St.
Pennsylvania Ave.
3rd St.
Constitution Ave.
U.S. Capitol
Capitol Plaza
E. Capitol St.
CAPITOL HILL
Lincoln Park
Folger Shakespeare Library
D.C. Armory
Independence Ave.
North Carolina Ave.
South Carolina Ave.
STADIUM ARMORY
FEDERAL CENTER SW
Seward Park
2nd St.
South Capitol St.
New Jersey Ave.
CAPITOL SOUTH
EASTERN MARKET
19th St.
POTOMAC AVENUE
Potomac Ave.
395
Southwest Fwy.
F St.
G St.
I St.
SW
SE
Southeast Fwy.
NAVY YARD
M St.
WATERFRONT
Sousa Bridge
Anacostia River
Anacostia Park
Washington Navy Yard
Anacostia Bridge
11th St. Bridge
0 1500 feet
0 500 meters

The Mall Area, Washington, D.C.

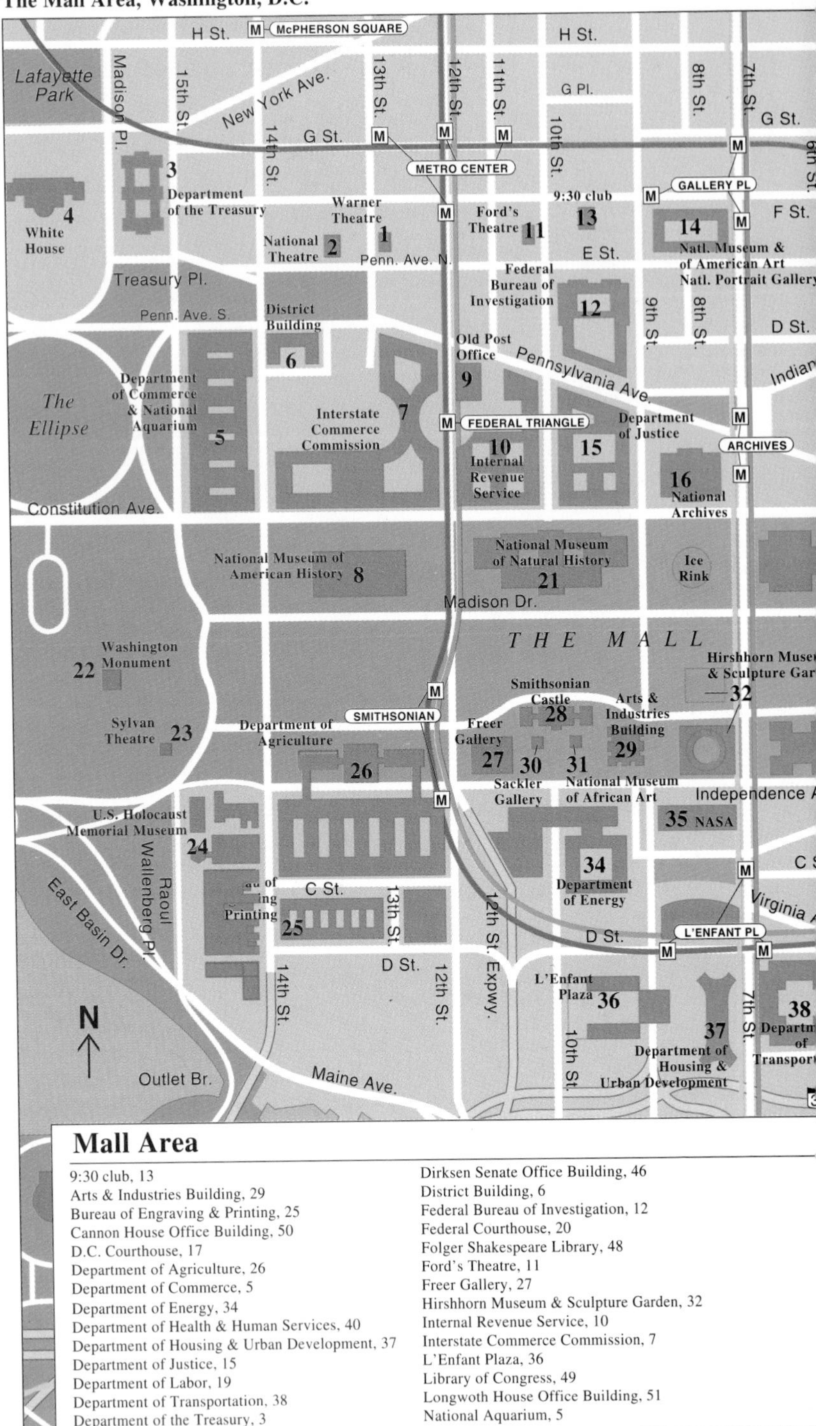

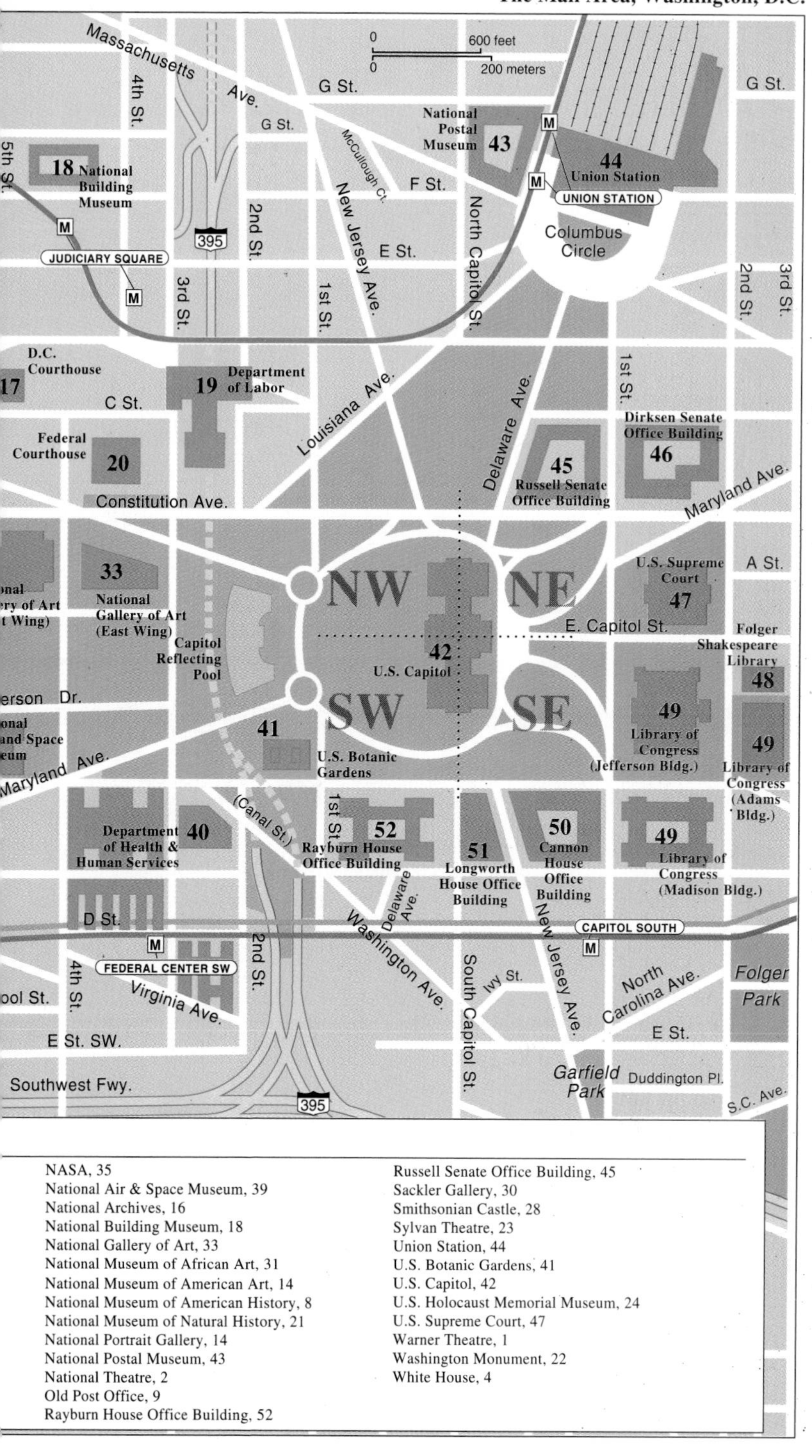

NASA, 35
National Air & Space Museum, 39
National Archives, 16
National Building Museum, 18
National Gallery of Art, 33
National Museum of African Art, 31
National Museum of American Art, 14
National Museum of American History, 8
National Museum of Natural History, 21
National Portrait Gallery, 14
National Postal Museum, 43
National Theatre, 2
Old Post Office, 9
Rayburn House Office Building, 52
Russell Senate Office Building, 45
Sackler Gallery, 30
Smithsonian Castle, 28
Sylvan Theatre, 23
Union Station, 44
U.S. Botanic Gardens, 41
U.S. Capitol, 42
U.S. Holocaust Memorial Museum, 24
U.S. Supreme Court, 47
Warner Theatre, 1
Washington Monument, 22
White House, 4

White House Area, Foggy Bottom, and Nearby Arlington

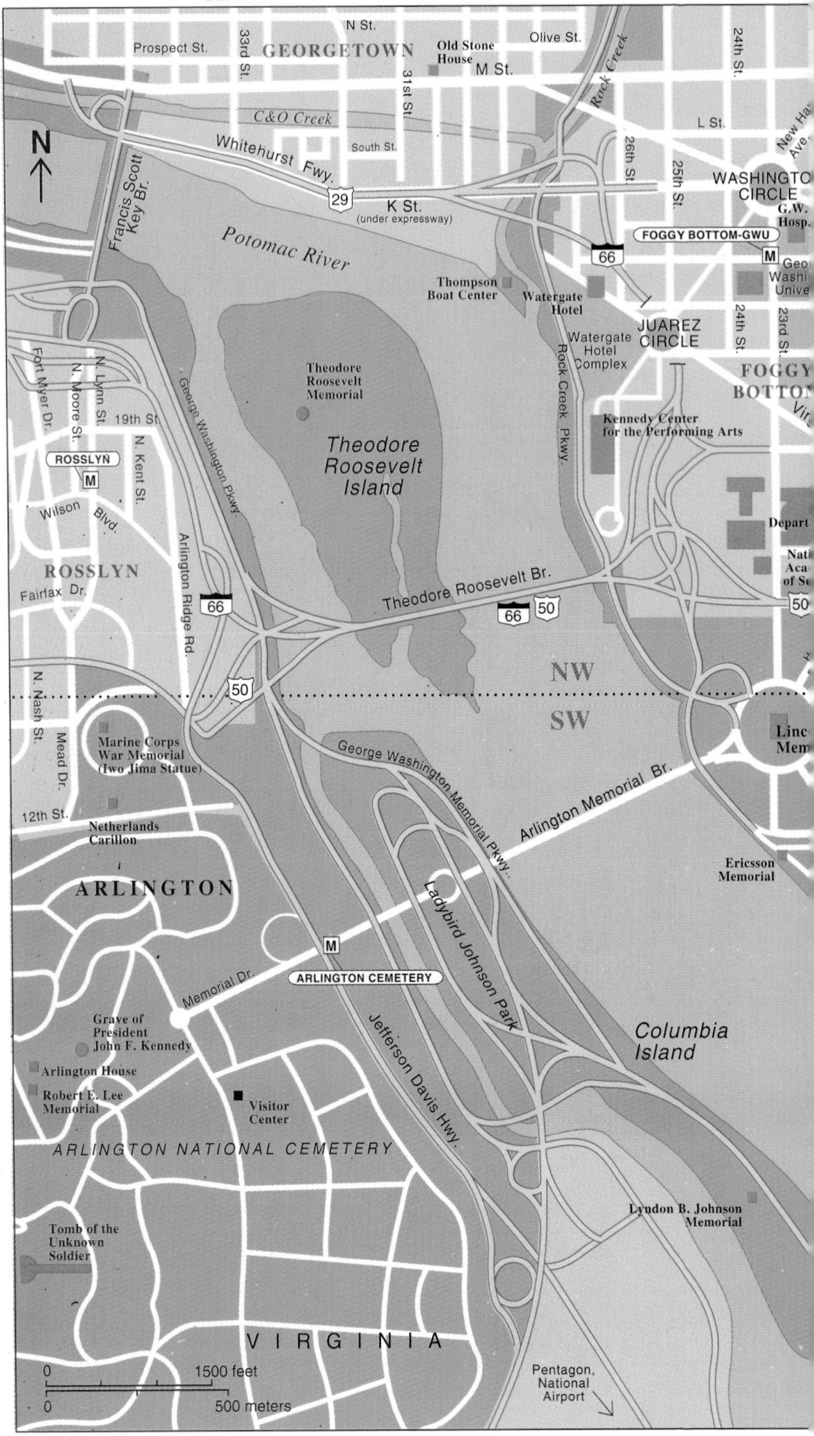

N St.
Prospect St.
33rd St.
GEORGETOWN
31st St.
Old Stone House
M St.
Olive St.
Rock Creek
24th St.
C&O Creek
L St.
New Hampshire Ave.
Whitehurst Fwy.
South St.
26th St.
25th St.
WASHINGTON CIRCLE
N
Francis Scott Key Br.
29
K St.
(under expressway)
G.W. Hosp.
FOGGY BOTTOM-GWU
M
Potomac River
66
Geo Washi Unive
Thompson Boat Center
Watergate Hotel
JUAREZ CIRCLE
24th St.
23rd St.
Watergate Hotel Complex
Fort Myer Dr.
N. Moore St.
N. Lynn St.
George Washington Pkwy.
Theodore Roosevelt Memorial
Rock Creek Pkwy.
FOGGY BOTTOM
Virginia
19th St.
N. Kent St.
Kennedy Center for the Performing Arts
ROSSLYN
M
Theodore Roosevelt Island
Wilson Blvd.
Depart
Arlington Ridge Rd.
ROSSLYN
Nati Aca of Sc
Fairfax Dr.
66
Theodore Roosevelt Br.
66
50
50
NW
N. Nash St.
50
SW
Mead Dr.
Marine Corps War Memorial (Iwo Jima Statue)
George Washington Memorial Pkwy.
Linc Mem
12th St.
Netherlands Carillon
Arlington Memorial Br.
Ericsson Memorial
ARLINGTON
Ladybird Johnson Park
M
Memorial Dr.
ARLINGTON CEMETERY
Jefferson Davis Hwy.
Columbia Island
Grave of President John F. Kennedy
Arlington House
Robert E. Lee Memorial
Visitor Center
ARLINGTON NATIONAL CEMETERY
Lyndon B. Johnson Memorial
Tomb of the Unknown Soldier
VIRGINIA
0
1500 feet
0
500 meters
Pentagon, National Airport

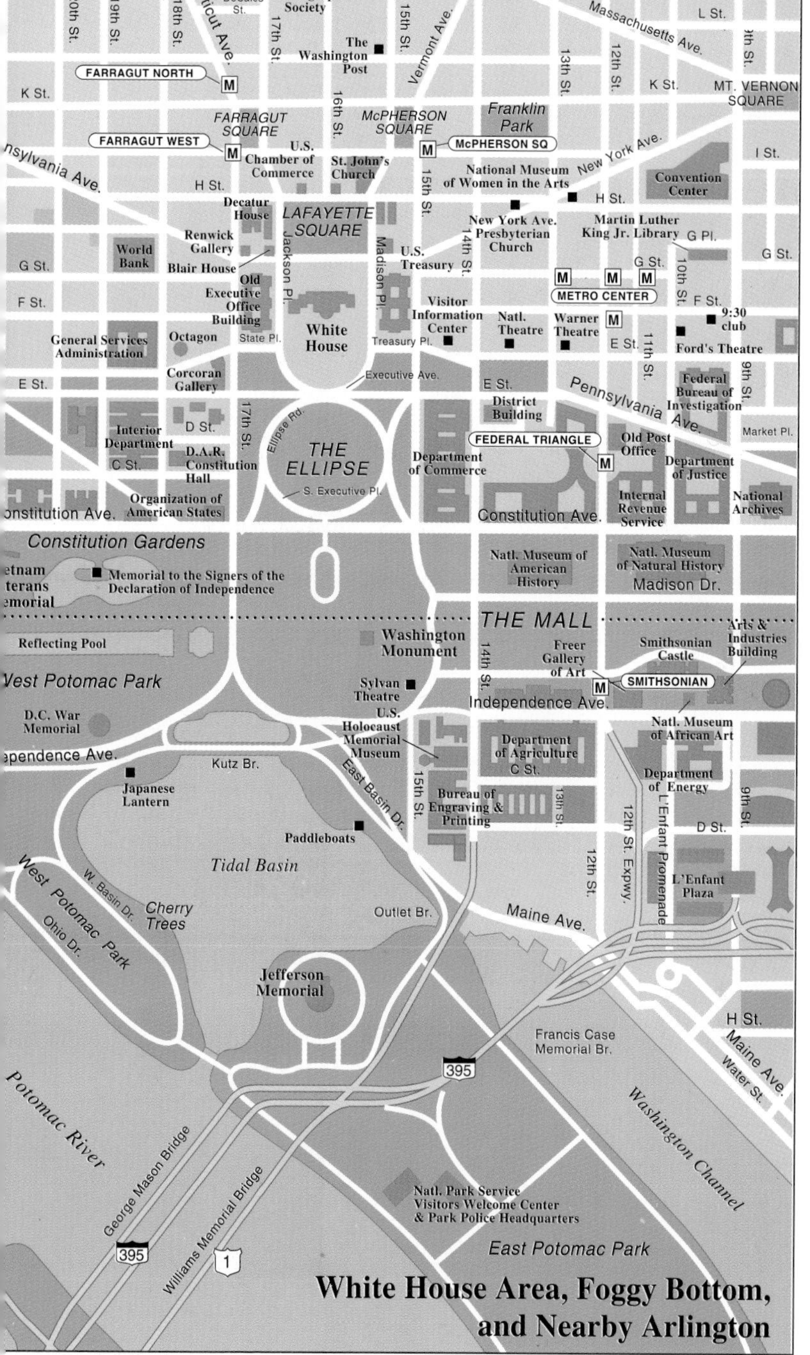

White House Area, Foggy Bottom, and Nearby Arlington

Metrorail System, Washington, D.C.

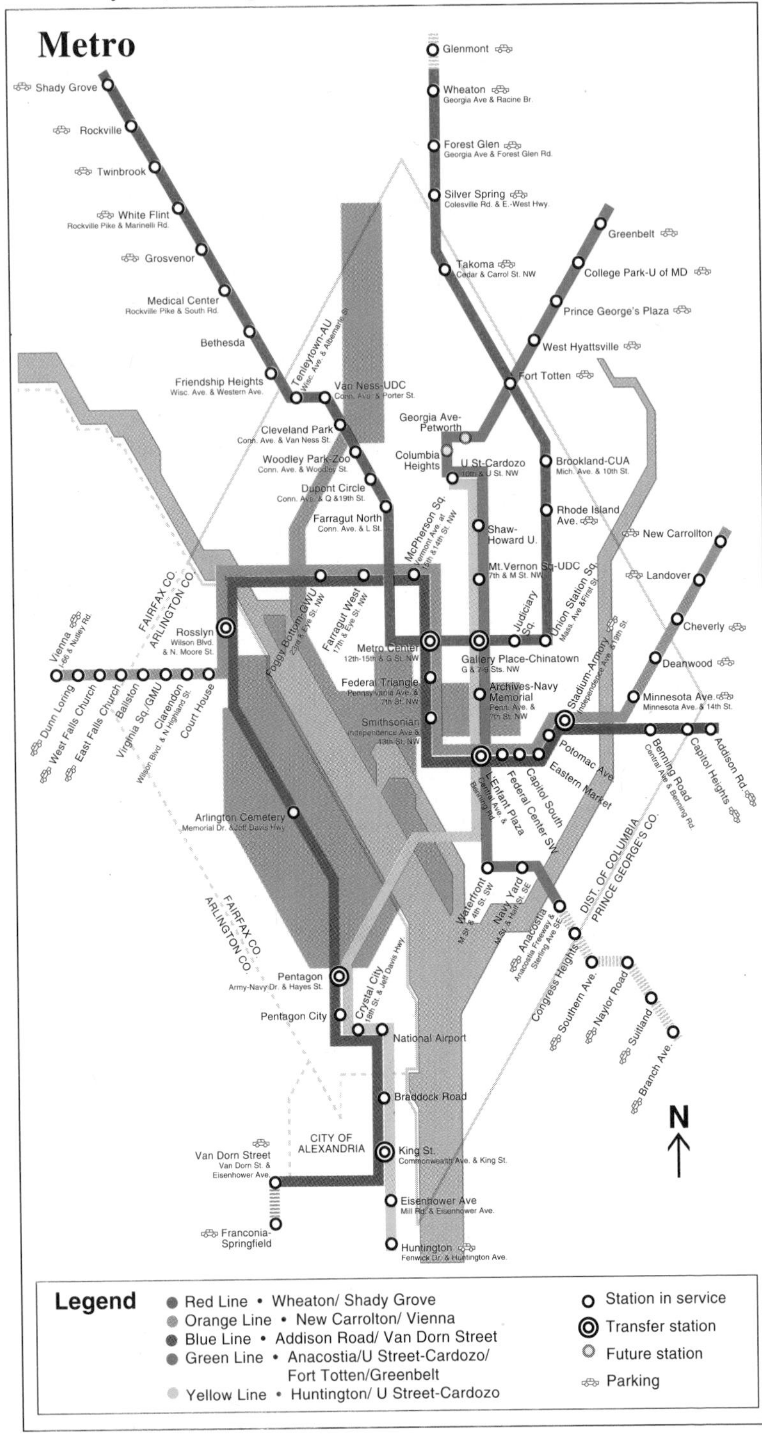

Metro
Glenmont
Wheaton
Georgia Ave & Racine Br.
Forest Glen
Georgia Ave & Forest Glen Rd.
Silver Spring
Colesville Rd. & E.-West Hwy.
Takoma
Cedar & Carrol St. NW
Greenbelt
College Park-U of MD
Prince George's Plaza
West Hyattsville
Fort Totten
Shady Grove
Rockville
Twinbrook
White Flint
Rockville Pike & Marinelli Rd.
Grosvenor
Medical Center
Rockville Pike & South Rd.
Bethesda
Friendship Heights
Wisc. Ave. & Western Ave.
Tenleytown-AU
Wisc. Ave. & Albemarle St.
Van Ness-UDC
Conn. Ave. & Porter St.
Cleveland Park
Conn. Ave. & Van Ness St.
Woodley Park-Zoo
Conn. Ave. & Woodley St.
Dupont Circle
Conn. Ave. & Q &19th St.
Farragut North
Conn. Ave. & L St.
Georgia Ave-Petworth
Columbia Heights
U St-Cardozo
10th & U St. NW
Brookland-CUA
Mich. Ave. & 10th St.
Rhode Island Ave.
Shaw-Howard U.
Mt.Vernon Sq-UDC
7th & M St. NW
New Carrollton
Landover
Cheverly
Deanwood
Minnesota Ave.
Minnesota Ave. & 14th St.
McPherson Sq.
Vermont Ave at I St. & 14th St. NW
Judiciary Sq.
Union Station Sq.
Mass. Ave & First St.
Stadium-Armory
Independence Ave. & 19th St.
Farragut West
17th & Eye St. NW
Foggy Bottom-GWU
23rd & Eye St. NW
Metro Center
12th-15th & G St. NW
Gallery Place-Chinatown
G & 7-9 Sts. NW
Federal Triangle
Pennsylvania Ave. & 7th St. NW
Archives-Navy Memorial
Penn. Ave. & 7th St. NW
Smithsonian
Independence Ave & 13th St. NW
FAIRFAX CO.
ARLINGTON CO.
Rosslyn
Wilson Blvd. & N. Moore St.
Vienna
I-66 & Nutley Rd.
Dunn Loring
West Falls Church
East Falls Church
Ballston
Virginia Sq./GMU
Clarendon
Wilson Blvd. & N Highland St.
Court House
L'Enfant Plaza
Federal Center SW
Capitol South
Eastern Market
Potomac Ave
Benning Road
Central Ave & Benning Rd.
Capitol Heights
Addison Rd.
Arlington Cemetery
Memorial Dr. & Jeff Davis Hwy
Waterfront
M St. & 4th St. SW
Navy Yard
M St. & Half St. SE
Anacostia
Anacostia Freeway & Sterling Ave SE
DIST. OF COLUMBIA
PRINCE GEORGE'S CO.
Congress Heights
Southern Ave.
Naylor Road
Suitland
Branch Ave.
FAIRFAX CO.
ARLINGTON CO.
Pentagon
Army-Navy Dr. & Hayes St.
Pentagon City
Crystal City
18th St. & Jeff Davis Hwy.
National Airport
Braddock Road
CITY OF ALEXANDRIA
King St.
Commonwealth Ave. & King St.
Van Dorn Street
Van Dorn St. & Eisenhower Ave.
Franconia-Springfield
Eisenhower Ave
Mill Rd. & Eisenhower Ave.
Huntington
Fenwick Dr. & Huntington Ave.
N
Legend
Red Line • Wheaton/ Shady Grove
Orange Line • New Carrolton/ Vienna
Blue Line • Addison Road/ Van Dorn Street
Green Line • Anacostia/U Street-Cardozo/ Fort Totten/Greenbelt
Yellow Line • Huntington/ U Street-Cardozo
Station in service
Transfer station
Future station
Parking

Let's Go:

USA

is the best book for anyone traveling on a budget. Here's why:

- **No other guidebook has as many budget listings.**

In the USA we list over 10,000 budget travel bargains. We tell you the cheapest way to get around, and where to get an inexpensive and satisfying meal once you've arrived. We give hundreds of money-saving tips that anyone can use, plus invaluable advice on discounts and deals for students, children, families, and senior travelers.

- **Let's Go researchers have to make it on their own.**

Our Harvard-Radcliffe researcher-writers travel on budgets as tight as your own—no expense accounts, no free hotel rooms.

- **Let's Go is completely revised each year.**

We don't just update the prices, we go back to the place. If a charming café has become an overpriced tourist trap, we'll replace the listing with a new and better one.

- **No other guidebook includes all this:**

Honest, engaging coverage of both the cities and the countryside; up-to-the-minute prices, directions, addresses, phone numbers, and opening hours; in-depth essays on local culture, history, and politics; comprehensive listings on transportation between and within regions and cities; straight advice on work and study, budget accommodations, sights, nightlife, and food; detailed city and regional maps; and much more.

- **Let's Go is for anyone who wants to see the USA on a budget.**

LET'S GO PUBLICATIONS

Let's Go: Alaska & The Pacific Northwest
Let's Go: Britain & Ireland
Let's Go: California
Let's Go: Central America
Let's Go: Eastern Europe
Let's Go: Europe
Let's Go: France
Let's Go: Germany
Let's Go: Greece & Turkey
Let's Go: Ireland
Let's Go: Israel & Egypt
Let's Go: Italy
Let's Go: London
Let's Go: Mexico
Let's Go: New York City
Let's Go: Paris
Let's Go: Rome
Let's Go: Southeast Asia
Let's Go: Spain & Portugal
Let's Go: Switzerland & Austria
Let's Go: USA
Let's Go: Washington, D.C.

Map Guides (coming March 1996)

Let's Go: Boston
Let's Go: London
Let's Go: New York City
Let's Go: Paris
Let's Go: San Francisco
Let's Go: Washington, D.C.

Let's Go

The Budget Guide to

USA

1996

Michelle C. Sullivan
Editor

Megan B. Callahan
Associate Editor

Edward Y. Park
Associate Editor

St. Martin's Press New York

HELPING LET'S GO

If you want to share your discoveries, suggestions, or corrections, please drop us a line. We read every piece of correspondence, whether a postcard, a 10-page e-mail, or a coconut. All suggestions are passed along to our researcher-writers. Please note that mail received after May 1996 may be too late for the 1997 book, but will be retained for the following edition. Address mail to:

Let's Go: USA
One Story Street
Cambridge, MA 02138
USA

Visit Let's Go at **http://www.letsgo.com,** or send e-mail to:

fanmail@letsgo.com
Subject: "Let's Go: USA"

In addition to the invaluable travel advice our readers share with us, many are kind enough to offer their services as researchers or editors. Unfortunately, the charter of Let's Go, Inc. enables us to employ only currently enrolled Harvard-Radcliffe students.

Map revisions pp. xvi-xvii, 95, 339, 393, 523, 797 by Let's Go, Inc.

Distributed outside the USA and Canada by Macmillan.

ISBN: 0-312-13557-2

First edition
10 9 8 7 6 5 4 3 2 1

Let's Go: USA is written by Let's Go Publications, One Story Street, Cambridge, MA 02138, USA.

Printed in the USA on recycled paper with biodegradable soy ink.

About Let's Go

THIRTY-SIX YEARS OF WISDOM

Back in 1960, a few students at Harvard University banded together to produce a 20-page pamphlet offering a collection of tips on budget travel in Europe. This modest, mimeographed packet was offered to passengers as an extra on their student charter flights to Europe. The following year, students traveling to Europe researched the first full-fledged edition of *Let's Go: Europe*, a pocket-sized book featuring irreverent write-ups of sights and a decidedly youthful slant. Throughout the 60s, our guides reflected the times; one section of the 1968 *Let's Go: Europe* discussed "Street Singing in Europe on No Dollars a Day," which we said "has very little to do with music." The 1969 guide to America led off with sound advice on San Francisco's Haight-Ashbury ("dig the scene"). During the 70s and 80s, we gradually added regional and city guides, and expanded coverage into the Middle East, Central America, and Asia.

We've seen a lot in 36 years. *Let's Go: Europe* is now the world's best-selling international guide, translated into seven languages. And our guides are still researched, written, and produced entirely by students who know first-hand how to see the world on the cheap. As the budget travel world expands, so does Let's Go. The first editions of *Let's Go: Central America* and *Let's Go: Southeast Asia* hit the shelves this year, and *Let's Go: India & Nepal* is right on their heels. Our useful new series of map guides combine concise city coverage with vivid fold-out maps. Our new guides bring our total number of titles, with their spirit of adventure and their honesty, accuracy, and editorial integrity, to 28.

HOW WE DO IT

Each guide is completely revised and updated every year by a well-traveled set of 200 students, who work on all aspects of each guide's development. Every winter, we recruit over 110 researchers and 50 editors to write our books anew. After several months of training, Researcher-Writers hit the road for seven weeks of exploration, from Anchorage to Ankara, Estonia to El Salvador, Iceland to Indonesia. Those hired possess a rare combination of budget travel sense, writing ability, stamina, and courage. Train strikes, stolen luggage, food poisoning, and irate tourist officials are all part of a day's work. Editors work from spring to fall, massaging copy written on Himalayan bus rides into witty yet informative prose. A student staff of typesetters, cartographers, publicists, and managers keeps our lively and sophisticated team together. In September, the collected efforts of the summer are delivered to our printer, who turns them into books in record time. And even as you read this, work on next year's editions is well underway.

WHY WE DO IT

At Let's Go, our goal is to give you a great vacation. We don't think of budget travel as the last recourse of the destitute; we believe that it's the only way to travel. Living cheaply and simply brings you closer to the real people and places you've been saving up to visit. Our book will ease your anxieties and answer your questions about the basics—to help you get off the beaten track and explore. Once you learn the ropes, we encourage you to put Let's Go away now and then to strike out on your own. As any seasoned traveler will tell you, the best discoveries are often those you make yourself. When you find something worth sharing, drop us a line. We're Let's Go Publications, One Story Street, Cambridge, MA 02138, USA (e-mail: LetsGo@delphi.com).

HAPPY TRAVELS!

Contents

Maps

Color Maps

Researcher-Writers

Ian Clark *Rocky Mountains*

Our own Taco Dude, Ian mosied through the Rocky Mountains, leaving a trail of Mexican joints and insightful prose. He braved hordes of tourists and tirelessly hiked the Rockies' daunting peaks and valleys to send back crisp copy and the best trail coverage that side of the Mississippi; we spent days dreaming of what he had seen. With an incisive mind, concise language, and a flair for finding mind-bending trivia, Ian's wry humor and thorough research were our mental joy.

Nick Corman *Arkansas, Louisiana, Mississippi, Texas*

Finder of a thousand pizza joints and IMAX theaters, Nick brought a touch of the bizarre to his route (check out the American Funeral Service Museum, p. 492). He came through car-rental confusion with flying colors, acquiring the (used) Nick-mobile, which he soon grew to love. ("I'd take a bullet for this car.") Well, Nick we'd take a bullet for one of your copy batches: clean, neat, illustrated, and chock full of blow-by-blow analyses from a culinary journey through the South.

Bridget Flynn *Connecticut (Hartford), Delaware, Massachusetts, Rhode Island Virginia (Virginia Beach), Maryland (Eastern Shore)*

Bridget's trip through Boston left us with a new understanding of our own home turf. Moving out of the city, Bridget brought us exciting yarns, tales, and lore from the coast, including a jailbird mayor, small-town pirates, and several anecdotes from her own exploits. After an enthusiastic jaunt through New England, Bridget lost herself in the Mid-Atlantic. We wish her well wherever she might be.

Mark Greif *Kentucky, New York (Catskills, Cooperstown, Niagara Falls, Ithaca and the Finger Lakes), Ohio, Ontario, Pennsylvania (Pittsburgh, Ohiopyle, Allegheny), Tennessee*

When Mark said he wanted to find American kitsch, we had no idea of the treasures he would discover—tattoos, gnomes, rural delicacies, 11 secret herbs and spices, and countless other oddities. Attacked by an angry grouse and a bout of road blues, Mark kept his wit and broke new ground in the Appalachians, lending his poetic touch to everything from Daniel Boone to Dollywood. Our clean-cut boy came back a hairy man in a spangled country jumpsuit—a dream come true.

Steven P. Janiak *Connecticut (New Haven, Mystic and the Coast), New Jersey, Pennsylvania*

Steve came fresh from his gig as Washington, DC editor for a cameo appearance in the role of RW, and we could not have asked for more. Though his time was short, his batch was long. Steve found amazing toys in Atlantic City, had a date at Foxwoods, and fell in love at Yale. A return researcher, Steve captured Philly's nightlife and barrelled through the Amish country, earning a big round of applause.

Karen Olsson *The Southwest*

Karen researched and rewrote the Southwest faster than you can say Aravaipa Canyon. She was the model of efficiency with a no-nonsense attitude and a nose for hard facts. With her WPA guide in hand, Karen eschewed tales of erosion to shed light on America's mythic view of the Southwest. On her day off, this recent graduate made news for buying beer on a Sunday in Santa Fe. We wish Karen, now employed in the big bad publishing world, all the best.

Amy Retzinger *The Great Plains*

Another news-maker, Amy waltzed through one of the longest-driving itineraries. Always willing to go the extra mile (or hundreds), she found beauty in the Badlands, Americana at Wall Drug, and her nemesis in Fargo. Along the way, Amy experienced a full range of down-home entertainment, as she powwowed, drove cattle, stopped for dinner with the Hudnalls in Nebraska, and took a moonlight tour of the base of Devils Tower. It was a wild ride to say the least.

Hannah Schott *Alabama, Florida, Georgia, North Carolina, South Carolina*
Hannah set out for the South with a vision of wrap-around porches and moss-covered trees and came back versed in coastline kitsch, tacky postcards, endless beaches, and Miami club couture. She scored a victory for budget travelers everywhere with a free pass to Disney, and finagled her way into the pressbox at a shuttle launch. Hannah's itinerary culminated in Georgia, where she soaked up the Olympic spirit and paid a visit to the land of R.E.M.

Jessica Seddon *The Great Lakes*
From urban Chicago to the vast, untrodden wilderness of Michigan's U.P., Jessica felled giants with her pen, rewriting and reorganizing everything in her path. Her voluminous copy, written with a pragmatic sensibility and a poetic eye, breathed life into the white beaches and rocky coasts of America's inland ocean. Jessica took no wine from strangers and no schtick from Frankenmuth; she was far too busy finding nightlife for the masses and making the Great Lakes greater.

Jason Sutherland *Atlantic Canada, Maine, New Hampshire, New York (Adirodacks, Lake Placid, Thousand Island Seaway), Ontario (Ottawa), Québec, Vermont*
Our native Canadian, Jason descended onto the Northeast like a bat out of hell. Nightlife listings multiplied as he zeroed in on the coolest parties and the cheapest beers with the brutal efficiency of a Carnot engine. Easily shrugging aside a run-in with a moose, the Bay of Fundy tides, and a kiss from a puffin, Jason made cutting insights into Canadian society, politics, and culture and instilled a vital new complexity into the Canada coverage. Newfoundler says, "Wa?"

Elizabeth Angell *Manhattan, Queens, Staten Island*
Carrie Ault *Lake Tahoe, Gold Country, Sacramento Valley and Cascades, North Coast, Reno*
Bruce Gottlieb *The Los Angeles Sprawl, San Diego, Santa Barbara, Cambria, San Simeon, Big Sur, San Luis Obispo*
Yeeyie Lieskovsky *Southern British Columbia, Alberta*
Luke Moland *Alaska, Northern British Columbia, the Yukon Territory*
Kevin Murphy *Manhattan, Westchester, Hoboken, the Bronx*
Maika Pollack *San Fancisco, Bay Area, Wine Country, Santa Cruz, Monterey, Carmel, Salinas*
Heather Phillips *Washington, Eugene, Northern Oregon Coast*
Jedediah Purdy *Alaska, Northern British Columbia*
Abigail Rezneck *Washington, DC, Annapolis*
Amina Runyan-Shefa *Manhattan, Brooklyn, Long Island*
Laurence Sacerdote *Oregon, Spokane, Southeastern Washington*
Liz Schoyer *The Desert, Sierra Nevada*
Raphael Sperry *Dalton Highway, Prudhoe Bay*
Matt Ware *Hawaii*
Erica Werner *Manhattan*
Clay West *Ciudad Juárez, Mexico, El Paso, TX*
Julie Zikherman *Washington, DC, Baltimore, Fairfax*

Acknowledgments

We thank the many people whose efforts went into creating this book: first and foremost, our unflagging researcher-writers, who deserve all the credit; Amelia, Sean, and Jeff, who infused USA 1995 with the spirit of the road; Haneen, who advised us wisely and edited us rigorously; Timur, for going beyond the call of duty in taking us on; James and Tim, the fourth and fifth members of Team USA; our regional contributors, James and Ted, Dan and Dave, Liz, and Steve, for doing their jobs (crunch, crunch) and for making the Domestic Room the social elite of the Let's Go corps; Mike and Eunice, who kept things running with unparalleled ease; Sean F.; Anne Chisholm; Jen and Kasia, who kept the troops happy; everyone who took an interest in their hometown coverage, including Patrick Chung for Canada, and Chuck, our Denver denizen; Sam and Amanda, who made sure everything was in its place (at least on paper); and Karlene Rosera and Linda Park. A special thanks goes to our on-the-spot instant R/Ws Steven P. Janiak, Steve Wotovich, and Julie Johnson. Several people made life on the road a little easier: Toby Pyle of Hostelling International, Mike and John of Merchants Car Rental, and everyone who respected the Let's Go press pass. Finally, we must thank Jill Liederman and the Letterman crew, for giving us our fifteen minutes (or was it seconds?).—**MCS, MBC, EYP**

My heartfelt thanks go to Megan, who blazed ever onward (even after I'd all but burned out), and Ed, who always had something extra up his sleeve; you guys taught me volumes this summer. Kudos to the USA R/Ws, who impress me constantly, both here and on the road. Thanks to Amelia who invited me into this mess and inspired me to take on the beast. Ravenhurst kept me sane with homey breakfasts and poolside chats, while Alexa put up with more Let's Go talk than any non-staffer ever should. I thank Danton for a rational ear and an idyllic escape, the DR for laffs, James for being the type of guy who makes a great R/W, and Chuck and Alex for the culinary adventures of the last days. Finally, I give my love to Mom, Dad, Mary, CiCi, and Rebecca; your trust and support keeps me going.—**MCS**

First and foremost, thanks to my parents, who have taken me on seven journeys across the U.S.A. To my brother, Michael, who always inspires me to work harder. Thanks to Michelle, for hiring me, and to Ed, for working with me. To my R/Ws: Amy, Bridget, Hannah, Karen, and Nick; for working so hard, and for writing so legibly. Special thanks to Amy; R/W, roommate, and friend. To Chris, Sarah, Drew, Reenah, and Alain, for caring at the end. Finally, to Jason, with my love.—**MBC**

My eternal thanks to Michelle and Megan for giving me just enough rope not to hang myself and spurring me on when I needed it most. Jason, Jessica, Ian, and Mark—you guys are über-R/Ws, and if I were ol' Joseph, I'd give you all Pulitzers. For my sanity, I am deeply indebted to all my friends, '80s cheese, rabid moose, and Bisque, King of Lobsters. Cin, life's a beach, and Nancy, you're all the things I've got to remember. Lastly, I owe everything to my brother Todd, who is always there, and to my parents, who sacrificed so much and gave me my life.—**EYP**

Staff

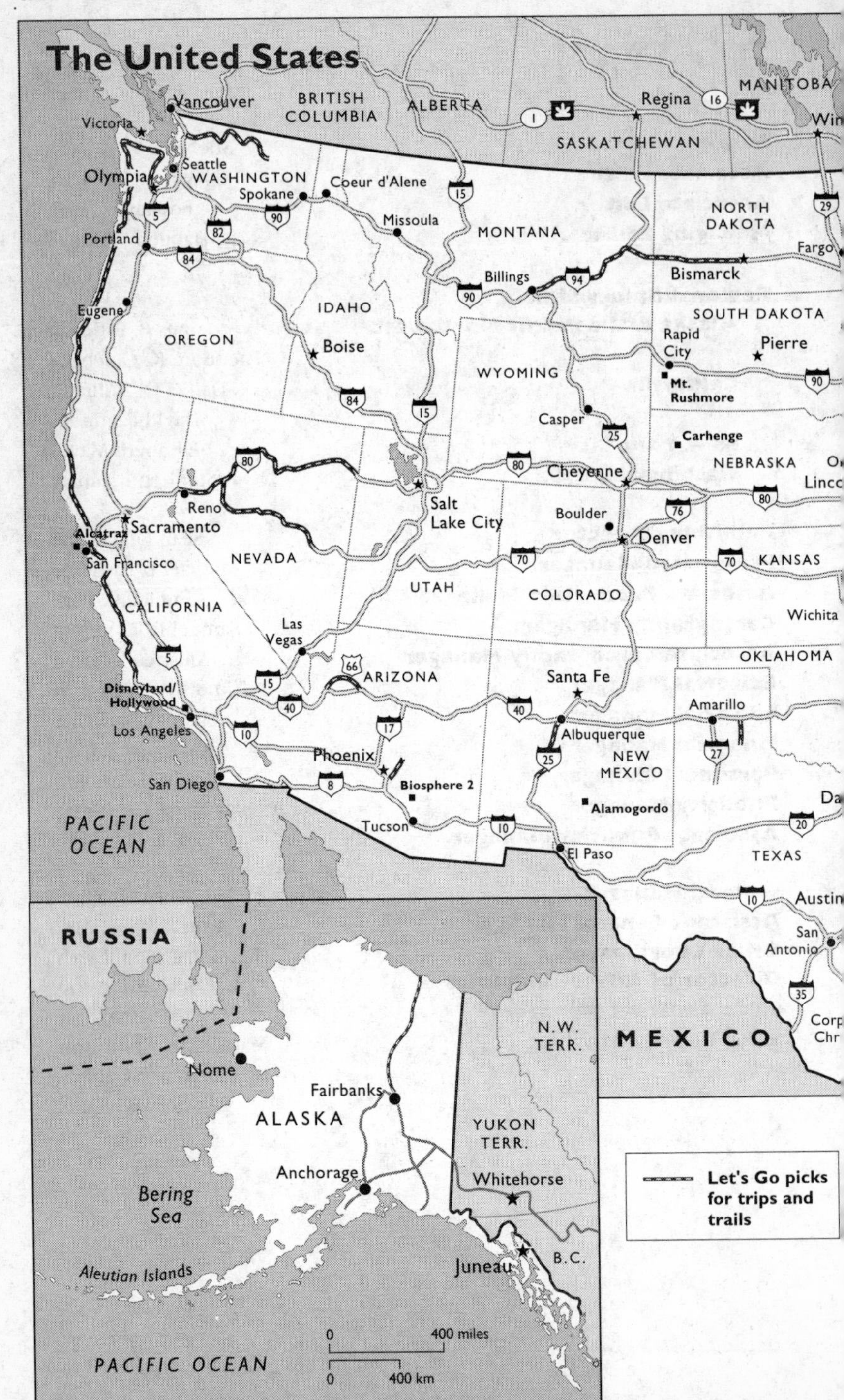
The United States
Vancouver
BRITISH COLUMBIA
ALBERTA
Regina
MANITOBA
SASKATCHEWAN
Victoria
Seattle
Olympia
WASHINGTON
Spokane
Coeur d'Alene
Missoula
MONTANA
NORTH DAKOTA
Fargo
Bismarck
Portland
Billings
Eugene
IDAHO
SOUTH DAKOTA
OREGON
Boise
Rapid City
Pierre
WYOMING
Mt. Rushmore
Casper
Carhenge
NEBRASKA
Cheyenne
Reno
Salt Lake City
Boulder
Sacramento
Alcatraz
Denver
San Francisco
NEVADA
KANSAS
UTAH
COLORADO
CALIFORNIA
Wichita
Las Vegas
OKLAHOMA
ARIZONA
Santa Fe
Disneyland/ Hollywood
Amarillo
Los Angeles
Albuquerque
Phoenix
NEW MEXICO
San Diego
Biosphere 2
Alamogordo
PACIFIC OCEAN
Tucson
El Paso
TEXAS
Austin
San Antonio
RUSSIA
N.W. TERR.
MEXICO
Nome
Fairbanks
ALASKA
YUKON TERR.
Anchorage
Whitehorse
Let's Go picks for trips and trails
Bering Sea
Juneau
B.C.
Aleutian Islands
0
400 miles
PACIFIC OCEAN
0
400 km

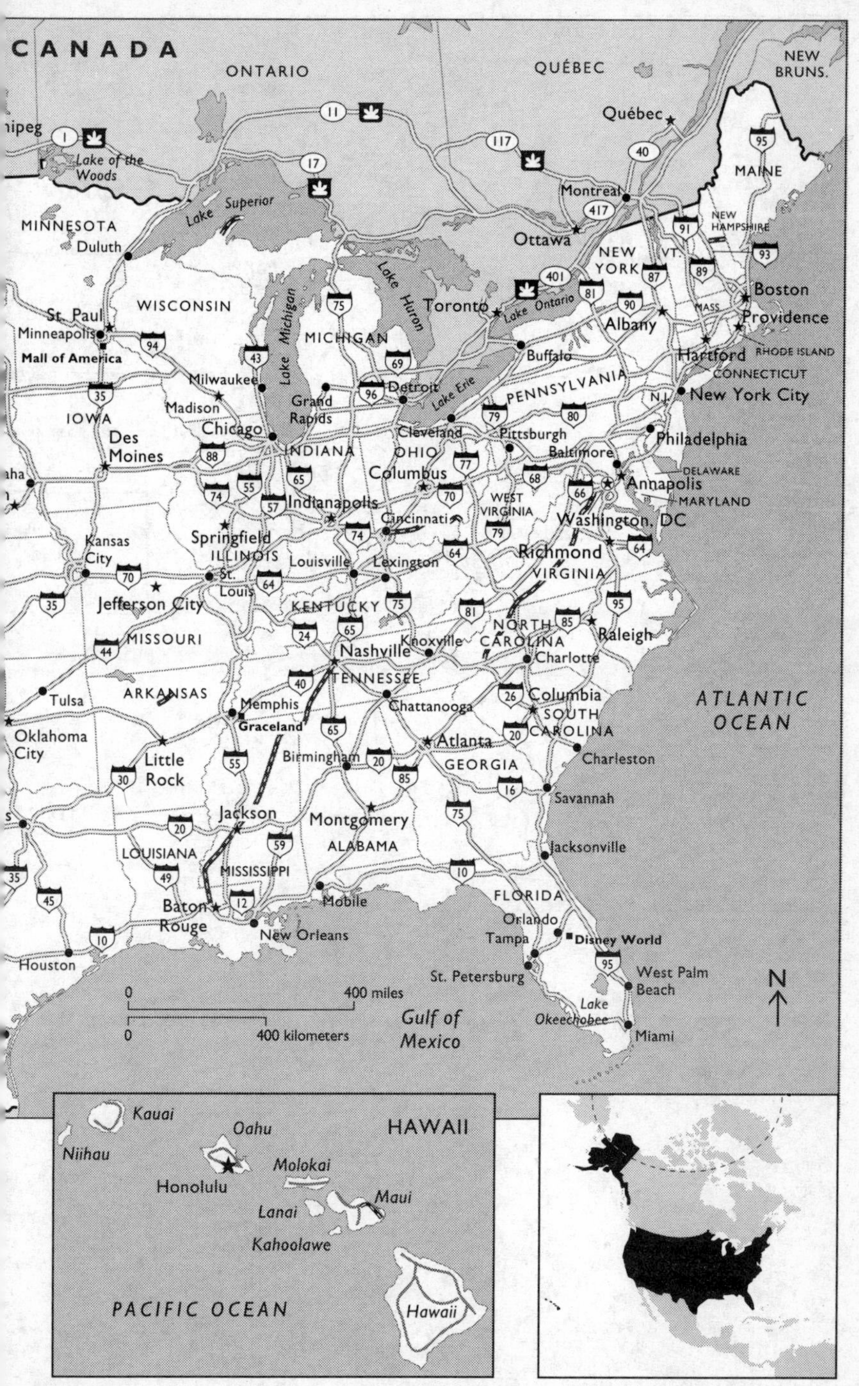
CANADA
ONTARIO
QUÉBEC
NEW BRUNS.
Québec
Lake of the Woods
Lake Superior
Montreal
Ottawa
MAINE
NEW HAMPSHIRE
VT.
NEW YORK
MASS
Boston
Providence
RHODE ISLAND
Toronto
Lake Ontario
Lake Huron
Lake Michigan
Albany
Hartford
CONNECTICUT
MINNESOTA
Duluth
WISCONSIN
St. Paul
Minneapolis
Mall of America
MICHIGAN
Buffalo
PENNSYLVANIA
N.J.
New York City
Milwaukee
Madison
Grand Rapids
Detroit
Lake Erie
IOWA
Des Moines
Chicago
INDIANA
OHIO
Cleveland
Pittsburgh
Philadelphia
Baltimore
DELAWARE
Annapolis
MARYLAND
Columbus
Indianapolis
WEST VIRGINIA
Washington, DC
Cincinnati
Springfield
ILLINOIS
Kansas City
Louisville
Lexington
Richmond
VIRGINIA
St. Louis
Jefferson City
KENTUCKY
MISSOURI
NORTH CAROLINA
Raleigh
Knoxville
Nashville
Charlotte
TENNESSEE
Tulsa
ARKANSAS
Memphis
Graceland
Chattanooga
Columbia
SOUTH CAROLINA
ATLANTIC OCEAN
Oklahoma City
Little Rock
Birmingham
Atlanta
GEORGIA
Charleston
Savannah
Jackson
Montgomery
ALABAMA
LOUISIANA
MISSISSIPPI
Jacksonville
Mobile
FLORIDA
Baton Rouge
New Orleans
Orlando
Tampa
Disney World
Houston
St. Petersburg
West Palm Beach
Lake Okeechobee
Miami
0
400 miles
0
400 kilometers
Gulf of Mexico
N
HAWAII
Kauai
Niihau
Oahu
Honolulu
Molokai
Maui
Lanai
Kahoolawe
Hawaii
PACIFIC OCEAN

BRITISH COLUMBIA
ALBERTA
SASKATCHEWAN
MANITOBA
WASHINGTON
Columbia River
THE PACIFIC NORTHWEST
OREGON
IDAHO
MONTANA
Missouri R.
THE ROCKY MOUNTAINS
NORTH DAKOTA
SOUTH DAKOTA
WYOMING
NEBRASKA
NEVADA
UTAH
THE SOUTHWEST
Sacramento R.
CALIFORNIA
Colorado R.
COLORADO
KANSAS
Arkansas R.
ARIZONA
NEW MEXICO
Rio Grande
OKLAH
Red River
TEXAS
PACIFIC OCEAN
MEXICO
RUSSIA
ALASKA
Yukon River
N.W. TERR.
YUKON TERR.
B.C.
Bering Sea
Aleutian Islands
PACIFIC OCEAN
0 400 miles
0 400 km
Kauai
Niihau
Oahu
Lanai
PACIFIC OCEAN
0 100 miles
0 100 km

USA National Park System

National Monuments
Black Canyon, CO, **37**
Canyon de Chelly, AZ, **32**
Colorado, CO, **40**
Devils Tower, WY, **49**
Dinosaur, CO, **41**
Gila Cliff Dwellings, NM, **17**
Great Sand Dunes, CO, **39**
Lassen Volcanic, CA, **9**
Little Bighorn, MT, **48**
Mt. Rushmore, SD, **51**
Natural Bridges, UT, **34**
Scotts Bluff, NE, **43**
Sunset Crater Volcanic, AZ, **25**
Walnut Canyon, AZ, **24**
White Sands, NM, **18**
Wupatki, AZ, **26**
Petroglyph, NM, **22**

National Parks
Acadia, ME, **71**
Arches, UT, **36**
Badlands, SD, **53**
Big Bend, TX, **20**
Bryce Canyon, UT, **30**
Canyonlands, UT, **35**
Capitol Reef, UT, **31**
Carlsbad Caverns, NM, **21**
Colonial, VA, **66**
Crater Lake, OR, **7**
Death Valley, CA, **13**
Denali, AK, **73**
Everglades, FL, **62**
Gates of the Arctic, AK, **72**
Glacier, MT, **5**
Grand Canyon, AZ, **27**
Grand Teton, WY, **45**
Great Smoky Mts., TN, **63**
Guadalupe Mts., TX, **19**
Haleakala, HI, **75**
Hot Springs, AR, **60**
Isle Royale, MI, **57**
Joshua Tree, CA, **15**
Kings Canyon, CA, **11**
Mammoth Cave, KY, **64**
Mesa Verde, CO, **33**
Mt. Rainier, WA, **4**
New River Gorge, WV, **65**
North Cascades, WA, **2**
Olympic, WA, **1**
Petrified Forest, AZ, **23**
Redwood, CA, **8**
Rocky Mt., CO, **42**
Saguaro, AZ, **16**
Sequoia, CA, **12**
Shenandoah, VA, **67**
Theodore Roosevelt, ND, **54**
Voyageurs, MN, **56**
Wind Cave, SD, **52**
Wrangell-St. Elias, AK, **74**
Yellowstone, WY, **46**
Yosemite, CA, **10**
Zion, UT, **29**

National Recreation Areas
Bighorn Canyon, MT, **47**
Hell's Canyon, OR, **6**
Lake Mead, NV, **28**
Ross Lake, WA, **3**
Santa Monica Mts., CA, **14**

National Forests
Allegheny, PA, **69**
Black Hills, SD, **50**
Chippewa, MN, **55**
Grand Mesa, CO, **38**
Manistee, MI, **58**
Medicine Bow, WY, **44**
Monongahela, WV, **68**
Ozark, AR, **59**
White Mts., NH, **70**

National Seashores
Padre Island, TX, **61**

How To Use This Book

The big disclaimer: this book does not contain everything there is to know about traveling in the USA. We went, we saw, we picked out the most helpful resources for travelers trying to see the U.S. on a tight budget, but we did not cover everything. Stray from our directions; see the sights between the places we mention—the U.S. is chock full of restaurants, inns, and roadside kitsch waiting to be found.

Let's Go: USA is divided into three parts. The first portion, **Essentials,** further splits in three. The chapter starts with information for planning a trip in the USA or Canada; this section includes details on necessary documents, entrance requirements, and exchange rates, a description of certain laws and customs, health and safety advice, packing tips, and travel advice addressed to the concerns of women, senior citizens, bisexuals, gays, and lesbians, disabled travelers, kosher Jews and vegetarians. Information on getting to the USA and Canada, including listings for budget travel agencies, comes next. Finally, look for advice on getting around (including descriptions of charter flights, ticket consolidators, and couriers), finding a bed, exploring the outdoors, and keeping in touch once you've arrived.

The **United States,** the book's second part, begins with a short chapter on **American Culture** and history and continues for most of the pages to come. Twelve chapters, named for geographic regions, make up the coverage of the 50 states. The regions run north to south and progress east to west in the following order: **New England, Mid-Atlantic, The South, Great Lakes, Great Plains, Texas, Rocky Mountains, The Southwest, The Pacific Northwest, California, Alaska,** and **Hawaii.** Within a chapter, the order of states advances toward the next region. Each state's text opens with the largest, or most accessible, destination and fans outward; large states, split into smaller areas, follow this pattern within each division. Look in the index for an alphabetized list of the destinations covered in each state.

The third section of the book contains locations in **Canada** which travelers often include in trips to the U.S. or make excursions from the U.S. to visit. Following a description of **Canadian Culture** and history, coverage of the 11 provinces runs from east to west: **Nova Scotia, Newfoundland and Labrador, New Brunswick, Prince Edward Island, Québec, Ontario,** the **Prairie Provinces, Alberta, British Columbia,** and the **Yukon Territory.** Entries within the provinces generally move away from the American border.

For all of the destinations in the USA and in Canda, we normally include **Accommodations, Camping, Food, Sights,** and **Entertainment.** Our **Practical Information** will help you get around, find help, and keep in touch; tourist offices provide further help and, often, free maps. **Near** sections include suggestions for daytrips.

If you intend to travel extensively in one area, consider buying one of our regional guides, *Let's Go: Alaska & the Pacific Northwest* and *Let's Go: California,* or one of our city guides, *Let's Go: New York City* and *Let's Go: Washington, D.C.*

A NOTE TO OUR READERS

The information for this book is gathered by Let's Go researchers during the summer months. Each listing is derived from the assigned researcher's opinion based upon his or her visit at a particular time. The opinions are expressed in a candid and forthright manner. Other travelers might disagree. Those traveling at a different time may have different experiences since prices, dates, hours, and conditions are always subject to change. You are urged to check beforehand to avoid inconvenience and surprises. Travel always involves a certain degree of risk, especially in low-cost areas. When traveling, especially on a budget, you should always take particular care to ensure your safety.

ESSENTIALS

PLANNING YOUR TRIP

■■■ PERFECT TIMING

Going to the right place at the right time makes a world of difference when traveling. In most of the U.S., **tourist season** is from **Memorial Day** to **Labor Day** (May 27 to Sept. 2 in 1996); expect things to be in full, camera-clicking swing. In the off-season, hotels might be cheaper and sights less crowded, but it's called the off-season for a reason—those sights you traveled so far to see might be closed. Call ahead to tourist offices for the scoop on local festivals. Remember holidays, when banks and offices frequently close. Check weather forecasts. You'll be glad you did.

OFFICIAL U.S. HOLIDAYS IN 1996

New Year's Day, Mon. Jan. 1; **Martin Luther King, Jr.'s Birthday,** Mon. Jan. 15; **Presidents Day,** Mon. Feb. 19 (observed); **Memorial Day,** Mon. May 27; **Independence Day,** Thurs. July 4; **Labor Day,** Mon. Sept. 2; **Columbus Day,** Mon. Oct. 14; **Veterans Day (Armistice Day),** Mon. Nov. 11 (observed); **Thanksgiving,** Thurs. Nov. 28; **Christmas Day,** Wed. Dec. 25.

OFFICIAL CANADIAN HOLIDAYS IN 1996

New Year's Day, Mon. Jan.1; **Easter Monday,** Mon. April 8; **Victoria Day,** Mon. May 20; **St. Jean,** Mon. June 24 (in Québec); **Canada Day,** Mon. July 1; **Thanksgiving,** Mon. Oct. 14; **Remembrance Day,** Mon. Nov. 11; **Christmas Day,** Wed. Dec. 25; **Boxing Day,** Thurs. Dec. 26.

WHERE'S THE PARTY?

New Year's Day (Jan. 1): Rose Bowl, Pasadena, CA; Orange Bowl, Miami, FL
St. Patrick's Day (Mar. 17): St. Pat's Day Parade, New York City, NY.
Mardi Gras (Feb. 13-20): New Orleans, LA; Mobile, AL.
Independence Day (July 4): fireworks everywhere!
Labor Day (Sept. 2): wherever the tourists are not.
Thanksgiving (Nov. 28): Macy's Parade, New York City, NY.
New Year's Eve (Dec. 31): Times Square, New York City, NY.

■■■ JUST THE FACTS, MA'AM

HITTING THE BOOKS

On the road, knowledge is power. The mail-order travel shops below offer books catering to special travel interests. Some sell travel supplies as well.

Adventurous Traveler Bookstore, P.O. Box 577, Hinesburg, VT 05461 (tel. and fax both 800-282-3963 or 802-482-3546; e-mail *books@atbook.com;* WWW *http://www.gorp.com/atbook.htm*). Specializes in outdoor adventure travel books and maps; the World Wide Web site offers extensive browsing opportunities.

Bon Voyage!, 2069 W. Bullard Ave., Fresno, CA 93711-1200 (800-995-9716, outside North America 209-447-8441, e-mail *70754.3511@compuserve.com*). Annual mail-order catalog offers products for travelers on any sort of budget. Books, travel accessories, luggage, electrical converters, maps, videos, more.

Travel Books & Language Center, 4931 Cordell Ave., Bethesda, MD 20814 (800-220-2665; fax 301-951-8546). Sells over 70,000 items, including books, cassettes, atlases, dictionaries, and maps (even beer maps of the U.S.).

Wide World Books and Maps, 1911 N. 45th St., Seattle, WA 98103 (206-634-3453; fax 634-0558; e-mail *travelbk@nwlink.com*). A good selection of travel guides, travel accessories, and hard-to-find maps.

LOST IN CYBERSPACE

On-line data services can be a gold mine for the prospective traveler looking to browse around for general information on an area, book airline reservations, or just chat with people thousands of miles away on the vast **Internet** computer network. Commercial services such as **America Online, CompuServe,** and **Prodigy** offer both Internet access and their own resources. To jump on the Information Highway, pick up a computer magazine and find one of the many advertisements which offers instructions for joining the rapidly expanding masses in cyberspace.

While navigating the Net is not extraordinarily difficult, the system's overwhelming size can make trying to find useful information troublesome. If you have **World Wide Web (WWW)** access, try one of the Web's search engines, such as **Webcrawler** (http://webcrawler.com); type in one or more keywords (e.g. "Boston travel") and the engine will generate a list of information headings. The **Student and Budget Travel Resource Guide** is among the best Web pages; it has links to the CIA world factbook, consular information sheets, state travel advisories, Amtrak train schedules, the Internet Guide to Hostelling, a subway navigator, a jet lag diet, and more (WWW: http://asa.ugl.lib.umich.edu/chdocs/travel/travel-guide.html, or send e-mail to travel-guide@umich.edu). **Rec-travel** (ftp.cc.umanitoba.ca), an archive containing travelogues and oodles more, can be reached on the Net via **FTP** (file transfer protocol). Try **newsgroups** and **mailing lists** if you're really in the mood to browse; unfortunately, their "signal-to-noise ratio" (the percentage of useful information) is often depressingly low. **IRC** (Internet Relay Chat) allows real-time typed conversation with users around the world; from most UNIX systems, type "irc" and then "/help newuser."

■■■ PENCIL PUSHIN' PAPERWORK

■ PASSPORTS

Be sure *before you leave* to photocopy the page of your passport that contains your photograph and identifying information; this will help prove your citizenship and facilitate the issuing of a new passport if your old one is **lost** or **stolen**. Carry this photocopy in a safe place apart from your passport, and leave another copy at home. Consulates recommend you also carry an expired passport or an official copy of your birth certificate. If you do lose your passport, notify the local police and the nearest embassy or consulate of your home government *immediately*. If you have the information that was on your passport, identification, and proof of citizenship, some consulates can issue a new passport within two days; of course, it may take weeks. In an emergency, ask for immediate temporary traveling papers which will permit you to return to your home country. Remember: your passport is a public document that belongs to your nation's government; you may have to surrender it to a foreign government official. If you don't get it back in a reasonable amount of time, inform the nearest embassy or consulate of your home country.

U.S. and Canadian citizens may cross the U.S.-Canada border with only proof of citizenship (e.g. a birth certificate or a voter's registration card, but **not** a driver's license). U.S. citizens under 18 need the written consent of a parent or guardian; Canadian citizens under 16 need notarized permission from both parents.

British citizens may apply for a passport in person at a passport office or by mail. Applications are available from main post offices (in Northern Ireland, from DSS offices). Passports cost UK£18 and are valid for 10 years (5 yrs. if under 16). Children under 16 may be included on a parent's passport. Processing usually takes 4-6 weeks. The London office offers same-day walk-in rush service; arrive early.

Irish citizens can apply for a passport by mail to either the Department of Foreign Affairs, Passport Office, Setanta Centre, Molesworth St., Dublin 2 (tel. (1) 671 1633), or the Passport Office, 1A South Mall, Cork (tel. (21) 627 2525). The new Passport Express service offers a two-week turnaround and is available through post offices for an extra IR£3. Passports cost IR£45 and are valid for 10 years. Citizens under 18 or over 65 can request a three-year passport that costs IR£10.

Australian citizens must apply for a passport in person at a post office, a passport office, or an Australian diplomatic mission overseas. Application fees are adjusted frequently. Call toll-free (in Australia) for more info (tel. 131 232).

New Zealand citizens should contact their local Link Centre, travel agent, or New Zealand representative for an application form, which must be completed and mailed to the New Zealand Passport Office, Documents of National Identity Division, Department of Internal Affairs, Box 10-526, Wellington (tel. (04) 474 81 00). Passports generally cost NZ$80 and are valid for 10 years. Standard processing time is 10 working days. Overseas citizens should send the application to the nearest embassy, high commission, or consulate that is authorized to issue passports.

South African citizens can apply for a passport at any Home Affairs Office. Two photos, either a birth certificate or an identity book, and the SAR38 fee must accompany a completed application. For further information, contact the nearest Department of Home Affairs Office.

■ EMBASSIES AND CONSULATES

U.S. EMBASSIES AND CONSULATES

U.S. Embassy in Australia, Moonah Place, Canberra, A.C.T. 2600 (tel. 011 61 6 270 5000); **in Canada**, 100 Wellington St., Ottawa, Ontario, K1P 5T1 (tel. (613) 238-5335); **in Ireland,** 42 Elgin Rd., Ballsbridge, Dublin (tel. 011 353 1 668 7122); **in New Zealand,** 29 Fitzherbert Terr., Thorndon, Wellington (tel. 011 64 4 472 2068); **in South Africa,** 877 Pretorius St., Arcadia 0083 (tel. 011 27 12 343 1048); **in United Kingdom,** 24/31 Grosvenor Sq., London W1A 1AE (tel. 011 44 71 499-9000).

U.S. Consulates in Australia, 59th Fl., MLC Centre, 19-29 Martin Place, Sydney NSW 2000 (tel. 011 612 373 9200); **in Canada,** 1155 Saint Alexandre St., Montreal, Quebec, H2Z 1Z2 (tel. (514) 398-9695); 1095 West Pender St., Vancouver, British Columbia V6E 2M6 (tel. (604) 685-4311); Tapachula 96, 22420 Tijuana, Baja California Norte (tel. 011 52 66 81 7400); **in New Zealand,** 4th Fl., Yorkshire General Bldg., corner of Shortland and O'Connell St., Auckland (tel. 011 64 9 303 2724); **in South Africa,** Broadway Industries Centre, Heerengracht, Foreshore (tel. 011 27 21 419 4822) **in United Kingdom,** 3 Regent Terr., Edinburgh EH7 5BW, Scotland (tel. 011 44 31 556 8315).

CANADIAN EMBASSIES AND CONSULATES

Canadian Embassy in Australia, Commonwealth Ave., Canberra ACT 2600 (tel. 011 61 6 273 3844); **in Ireland,** Canada House 65/68 St. Stephen's Green, Dublin 2 (tel. 011 353 1 78 19 88); **in New Zealand,** 61 Molesworth St., Thorndon, Wellington (tel. 011 64 4 473 9577); **in South Africa,** 5th Floor, Nedbank Plaza, Corner of Church and Beatrix St., Arcadia, Pretoria 0083, (tel. 011 27 12 324 3970); **in United Kingdom,** McDonald House, 1 Grosvenor Square, W1X 0AB (tel. 011 44 71 658 6600).

Canadian Consulates in Australia, Level 5 Quay West, 111 Harrington St., Sydney NSW, 2000 (tel. 011 612 364-3000); **in New Zealand,** Princes Court, 2 Princes St., Auckland (tel. 011 54 9 309 3690).

■ U.S. AND CANADIAN ENTRANCE REQUIREMENTS

Foreign visitors to the United States and Canada are required to have a **passport** and **visa/proof of intent to leave** (see Visas below). To visit Canada, you must be healthy and law-abiding, and demonstrate the ability to support yourself financially during your stay. A visa, stamped into a traveler's passport by the government of a host country, allows the bearer to stay in that country for a specified purpose and period of time. See Earning and Learning (p. 7) for information on specific types of visas. To obtain a U.S. visa, contact the nearest U.S. embassy or consulate.

U.S. VISAS

Travelers from certain nations may enter the U.S. without a visa through the **Visa Waiver Pilot Program.** Visitors qualify as long as they are traveling for business or pleasure, are staying for 90 days or less, have proof of intent to leave (e.g., a returning plane ticket) and a completed I-94W, and enter aboard particular air or sea carriers. Participating countries are Andorra, Austria, Belgium, Brunei, Denmark, Finland, France, Germany, Iceland, Ireland, Italy, Japan, Liechtenstein, Luxembourg, Monaco, the Netherlands, New Zealand, Norway, San Marino, Spain, Sweden, Switzerland, and the UK. Contact the nearest U.S. consulate for more information; countries are added frequently.

Most visitors obtain a **B-2,** or "pleasure tourist," visa, usually valid for six months. Don't lose your visa. If you do lose your I-94 form (arrival/departure certificate attached to your visa upon arrival), you can replace it at the nearest **U.S. Immigration and Naturalization Service** office, though it's very unlikely that the form will be replaced within the time of your stay. (If you lose your passport in the U.S., you must replace it through your country's embassy.) **Extensions** for visas (max. 6 months) require form I-539 as well as a $70 fee and are also granted by the INS. For a list of offices, write the INS Central Office, 425 I St. NW #5044, Washington, DC 20536 (202-514-4316). The **Center for International Business and Travel (CIBT),** 25 W. 43rd St., Ste. 1420, New York, NY 10036 (800-925-2428), secures travel visas to and from all possible countries (service charge varies).

CANADIAN VISAS

Citizens of Australia, Ireland, Mexico, New Zealand, the U.K., and the U.S., may enter Canada without visas, as long as they plan to stay for 90 days or less and carry proof of intent to leave. South Africans do need a visa to enter Canada. Citizens of all other countries should contact their Canadian consulate for more information

■ CUSTOMS

U.S. CUSTOMS

Passing customs should be routine, but take it seriously; don't joke around with customs officials or airport security personnel. It is illegal to transport perishable food like fruit and nuts, which may carry pests. In addition, officials may seize articles made from protected species, such as certain reptiles and the big cats. See To Your Health (p. 11) for information on carrying prescription drugs.

Duty free, you may bring the following into the U.S.: $200 in gifts; 200 cigarettes (1 carton) or 100 cigars; and personal belongings such as clothes and jewelry. Travelers ages 21 and over may also bring up to one liter of alcohol, although state laws may further restrict the amount of alcohol you can carry.

Money (cash or travelers checks) can be transported, but amounts over $10,000 must be reported. Customs officers may ask how much money you're carrying and your planned departure date in order to ensure that you'll be able to support yourself while in the U.S.

The **U.S. Customs Service,** 1301 Constitution Ave., N.W., Washington, D.C. 20229 (202-927-5580), publishes some helpful pamphlets. *Know Before You Go*

(KBYG) details everything the international traveler needs to know about customs requirements; *Pockets Hints* summarizes the most important data from KBYG. *Hints for Visitors* includes everything a foreign traveler visiting the U.S. for a year or less needs to know about customs requirements; *Customs Tips for Visitors,* available in more than a dozen languages, summarizes the most important information from *Hints for Visitors*.

CANADIAN CUSTOMS

Besides items of a personal nature that you plan to use in Canada during your visit, the following items may be brought in free of duty: either up to 1.1L of wine or liquor or a 24-pack of beer (as long you are of age in the province you are visiting), 50 cigars, 200 cigarettes, 1kg of manufactured tobacco, and gifts valued lass than CDN$60. As in the U.S., if you exceed the limited amounts, you will be asked to pay a fine. For detailed information on Canadian customs and booklets on other Canadian travel information, write Revenue Canada, Customs, Excise and Taxation, Communication Branch, Ottawa, Ont., Canada K1A 0L5 (613-957-0275; fax 957-9039).

■ INTERNATIONAL DRIVING PERMIT

Although not required in the U.S. or Canada, the International Driving Permit (IDP) can smooth out difficulties with American and Canadian police officers and serves as an additional piece of identification. A valid driver's license from your home country must always accompany the IDP. Your IDP must be issued in your own country before you depart; check with your national automobile association. Also make sure you have proper insurance (required by law). Some foreign driver's licenses are valid in the U.S. for up to one year; check before you leave.

■■■ THE COLOR OF MONEY

Staying in the cheapest accommodations possible and preparing your own food from time to time, expect to spend anywhere from $20 to $60 per person per day, depending on the local costs of living and your own needs. Transportation will increase these figures. Don't sacrifice your health or safety for a cheaper tab, though—no trip is fun if you're always hungry, tired, or getting mugged.

In the U.S., it is customary to **tip** waitstaff 15% on sit-down meals and cab drivers 15% on the fare. Tip more for unusually good service, less for unusually bad. At the airport, try to carry your own bags; porters expect a customary $1 per bag tip. Tipping is less compulsory in Canada, and a good tip signifies remarkable service. **Bargaining** is generally frowned upon and fruitless in the U.S. and in Canada.

The U.S. **sales tax** is the equivalent of the European Value-Added Tax. Expect to pay 4-10% depending on the item and the place; in most states, groceries are not taxed. *Let's Go* lists sales tax rates in the introduction to each state.

Prices tend to be higher in Canada than in the U.S., as are taxes; you'll quickly notice the 7% **goods and services tax (GST)** and an additional **sales tax** in some provinces. See the provincial introductions for info on local taxes. Oddly enough, you will find yourself being taxed on taxes; in Québec, for example, provincial sales tax of 6.75% is computed on the price including GST. Visitors can claim a rebate of the GST they pay on accommodations of less than one month and on most goods they buy and take home, so be sure to save your receipts and pick up a GST rebate form while in Canada. The total claim must be at least CDN$7 of GST (equal to $100 in purchases) and must be made within one year of the date on which you purchased the goods and/or accommodations for which you are claiming your rebate; further goods must be exported from Canada within 60 days of purchase. A brochure detailing restrictions is available from local tourist offices or through **Revenue Canada, Customs, Excise, and Taxation, Visitor's Rebate Program,** 275 Pope Rd., Summerside, Prince Edward Island, Canada C1N 6C6 (800-668-4748 in Canada, 613-991-3346 outside Canada). Québec and Manitoba offer refunds of provincial sales tax through this program, while Ontario, Nova Scotia, and Newfoundland require separate applications. Call the Provincial Tourist Information Centres for details (see Practical Information listing of each province). All prices in the Canada section of this book are listed in Canadian dollars unless otherwise noted.

Many Canadian shops, as well as vending machines and parking meters, accept U.S. coins at face value (which is a small loss for you). Many stores will even convert the price of your purchase for you, but they are under no legal obligation to offer you a fair exchange. During the past several years, the Canadian dollar has been worth roughly 20% less than the U.S. dollar.

■ THE MONEY-CHANGERS

Note: the following advice applies to Canada as well. You'll get better rates exchanging for U.S. dollars in the U.S. than at home, and wholesale rates offered at banks will be lower than those offered by other exchange agencies. Since you lose money with every transaction, convert in large sums. It's a good idea to buy enough U.S. dollars before you leave to last a couple of days; this prevents finding yourself stuck with no money upon an arrival after banking hours or on a holiday. If you are planning to visit a little-touristed area, where bank tellers may not recognize or be willing to exchange foreign currencies, carry U.S. dollars from early on. Most international airports in the U.S. have currency exchange booths.

THE GREENBACK (THE U.S. DOLLAR)

CDN$1 = US$.74	**US$1= CDN$1.35**
UK£1 = US$1.54	**US$1 = UK£0.65**
IR£1 = US$1.57	**US$1 = IR£0.63**
A$1 = US$0.74	**US$1 = A$1.35**
NZ$1 = US$0.65	**US$1 = NZ$1.55**

The main unit of currency in the U.S. is the **dollar;** the dollar is divided into 100 cents. The color of paper money is green in the U.S; bills come in denominations of $1, $5, $10, $20, $50, and $100. The U.S. has 1¢ (penny), 5¢ (nickel), 10¢ (dime), and 25¢ (quarter) coins.

THE LOONY (THE CANADIAN DOLLAR)

US$1 = CDN$1.35	**CDN$1 = US$0.74**
UK£1 = CDN$2.08	**CDN$1 = UK£0.48**
IR£1 = CDN$2.12	**CDN$1 = IR£0.47**
AUS$1 = CDN$1.00	**CDN$1 = AUS$1.00**
NZ$1 = CDN$0.88	**CDN$1 = NZ$1.15**

The main unit of currency in Canada is the **dollar,** which is identical to the U.S. dollar in name only. You will need to exchange money when you go over the border, although in many places you may use American currency. Paper money comes in denominations of $2, $5, $10, $20, $50, and $100, which are all the same size but color-coded by denomination. Coins come in denominations of 1¢, 5¢, 10¢, 25¢, and $1. Many years ago, the Canadian government phased out the $1 bill and replaced it with a $1 coin, known as the **loony** for the loon which graces its reverse.

■ TRAVELER'S CHECKS

Traveler's checks are the safest way to carry large sums of money; small denominations ($10 or $20) are safest and most convenient. Traveler's checks are widely accepted and refundable if lost or stolen, and some even come with perks such as travel insurance. Several agencies and banks sell traveler's checks (e.g. American Express or Bank of America), usually for a 1% commission. In less touristed regions, have some cash on hand; smaller establishments may not accept traveler's checks.

You should expect a fair amount of red tape and delay in the event of theft or loss of traveler's checks. To expedite the refund process, keep your check receipts separate from your checks and store them in a safe place or with a traveling companion; record check numbers when you cash them and leave a list of check numbers with someone at home; and ask for a list of refund centers when you buy your checks. Keep a separate supply of cash or traveler's checks for emergencies. Be sure never to countersign your checks until you're prepared to cash them.

American Express: in the **U.S. and Canada,** 800-221-7282; in the **U.K.,** (0800) 52 13 13; in **New Zealand,** (0800) 44 10 68; in **Australia,** (008) 25 19 02. Elsewhere, call U.S. collect 801-964-6665. Available in 11 currencies, American Express traveler's cheques are the most widely recognized worldwide and the easiest to replace if lost or stolen. Checks can be purchased at American Express Travel Service Offices, banks, and American Automobile Association offices (AAA members can buy the checks commission-free). Cardmembers can also purchase checks from American Express Dispensers at Travel Service Offices in airports or by phone (800-ORDER-TC/673-3782). **Cheques for Two** can be signed by either of two people traveling together.

Citicorp: in the **U.S. and Canada,** 800-645-6556; in the **U.K.,** (0171) 982 40 40; from elsewhere call U.S. collect 813-623-1709. Sells both Citicorp and Citicorp Visa traveler's checks in 6 currencies. Commission is 1-2% on check purchases. Checkholders are automatically enrolled for 45 days in Travel Assist Hotline (800-523-1199) which provides travelers with English speaking doctor, lawyer, and interpreter referrals as well as check refund assistance. Citicorp's World Courier Service guarantees hand-delivery of traveler's checks anywhere in the world.

Thomas Cook MasterCard: in the **U.S. and Canada,** 800-223-9920; elsewhere call U.S. collect 609-987-7300; in the **U.K.** call (0800) 622 101 toll-free or (1733) 502 995 collect. Offers checks in 12 currencies. Commission 1-2% for purchases. Buy the checks at a Thomas Cook office for potentially lower commissions.

Visa: In the U.S., call 800-227-6811; in the U.K. (0171) 937 8091; from anywhere else in the world call the U.S. collect at 212-858-8500. Sells traveler's checks by mail; call 800-235-7366 to order them.

■ PLASTIC

CREDIT CARDS

Credit cards are not accepted at many small, cheap locations where traveler's checks are welcomed, and pricey establishments which cheerfully accept them can quickly deplete your account. Still, credit cards can be invaluable in the U.S., and are sometimes expected or required (for example, many car rental agencies require that you have a credit card). Credit cards are also useful when an emergency, such as an unexpected hospital stay, leaves you temporarily without other resources. In addition, some cards carry services for users, which may range from personal or car rental insurance to emergency assistance. Major credit cards can be used to instantly extract cash advances from associated banks and ATM machines; this can be a great bargain for foreign travelers because credit card companies get the wholesale exchange rate, which is generally 5% better than the retail rate used by banks. Expect much higher interest rates for cash advances than for purchases.

MasterCard (outside North America, "EuroCard" or"Access") and **Visa** ("Carte Bleue" or "Barclaycard") are the most accepted. Both sell credit cards through banks. For lost or stolen cards: Visa, (800-336-8472); Mastercard, (800-999-0454).

American Express cards also work in some ATMs, as well as at AmEx offices and major airports. This card has a hefty annual fee ($55) but offers extensive travel-related services. For a lost or stolen card, call (800-CASH-NOW/528-4800).

ATM CARDS

There are tens of thousands of ATMs (automatic teller machines) everywhere in the U.S., offering 24-hour service in banks, airports, grocery stores, gas stations, etc.

ATMs allow you to withdraw cash from your bank account wherever you are, and happily get the same wholesale exchange rate as credit cards. Two major ATM networks in the U.S. are **Mastercard/Cirrus** (800-4-CIRRUS/424-7787) and **PLUS** (800-843-7587). Inquire at your bank about fees charged for ATM transactions.

■ MONEY FROM HOME

If you run out of money on the road, you can have more mailed to you in the form of traveler's checks bought in your name, a certified check, or through postal money orders, available at post offices (85¢ fee; $600 limit per order; cash only). Certified checks are redeemable at any bank, while postal money orders can be cashed at post offices upon display of two IDs (1 of which must be photo). Keep receipts, since money orders are refundable if lost. **Personal checks** from home will probably not be acceptable no matter how many forms of identification you have.

Wiring money can cost from around $15 (for domestic service) to $35 (international), depending on the bank, plus a fee ($7-15) for receiving the money. Once you've found a bank that will accept a wire, write or telegram your home bank with your account number, the name and address of the bank to receive the wire, and a routing number. Also notify the bank of the form of ID that the second bank should accept before paying the money. As a very last resort, consulates will wire home for you and deduct the cost from the money you receive.

Western Union (800-325-6000) is a classic and expensive service. You or someone else can phone in a credit card number or bring cash to a Western Union office for pick-up at another Western Union location. You will need ID to pick up money. Rates are $29 to send $250, $40 to send $500, and $50 to send $1000.

■■■ ALCOHOL AND DRUGS

You must be 21 to drink in the U.S. Even foreigners accustomed to observing no drinking age *will be carded* and will not be served without proper ID (preferably some government document; a driver's license suffices, but a passport is best). **In Canada, you must be 19,** except in Alberta, Manitoba, and Quebec, where you must be 18. Some areas of the United States are "dry," meaning they do not permit the sale of alcohol at all, while other places do not allow it to be sold on Sundays. Furthermore, some states require possession of a *liquor license.*

The possession or sale of marijuana, cocaine, LSD, and most opiates are serious crimes in the U.S. and Canada. For instructions on carrying prescription drugs, see To Your Health on p. 11.

■■■ STREET SMARTS

Trust your instincts. The obvious tourist is a tempting target; blend in as much as possible. Look like you know what you are doing and where you are going, even if you don't. Do not keep money in your back pocket or count your money in public. Do not keep anything precious in a fanny pack; use a neck pouch or money belt instead. Always keep an eye on your belongings; on trains and buses, put a leg through the straps of your bag if you can. Carry your purse against your body away from the street. Be aware of your surroundings; in cities, a single block can separate safe and unsafe areas. Watch for con artists. Do not respond or make eye contact with people who harass you. Carry a whistle to scare off attackers or attract attention. Finally, *never lose your cool or sense of adventure;* most people are Good.

In most places in the U.S. and Canada, **call 911 for emergency medical help, police, or fire** toll-free (you don't have to put a coin in the pay phone). In some rural areas, the 911 system has not yet been introduced; if 911 doesn't work, dial the **operator (0),** who will contact the appropriate emergency service.

■■■ TO YOUR HEALTH

BEFORE YOU GO

A compact **first-aid kit** should suffice for minor problems on the road. The following items are advisable: bandages of several sizes, aspirin, antiseptic soap or antibiotic cream, a thermometer with a sturdy case, a Swiss Army knife with tweezers, moleskin, a decongestant, motion sickness remedy, medicine for diarrhea or stomach problems, sunscreen, insect repellent, burn ointment, and an elastic bandage.

In your **passport** or other document, write the names of any people you wish to be contacted in case of a medical emergency and list any allergies or medical conditions of which doctors should be aware. Bring any **medication** you regularly take and may need while traveling, as well as a copy of the **prescription** and a statement of any preexisting medical conditions you may have, especially if you will be bringing insulin, syringes, or any narcotics into the USA or Canada. It is always a good idea to get a **check-up** before traveling, especially if you will be abroad for more than a month or two or if you will be hiking, camping, or visiting rural or unindustrialized regions. If you wear **glasses** or **contact lenses,** carry an extra prescription and arrange to have your doctor or a family member send a replacement pair in an emergency. If you wear contacts, be sure to carry a pair of glasses in case your eyes are tired or you lose a lens. The following organizations may be of some help:

American Red Cross, 61 Medford St., Somerville, MA 02143 (800-564-1234). Call to purchase the Red Cross's invaluable *First-Aid and Safety Handbook* ($14.95), The American Red Cross also offers many well-taught and inexpensive first-aid and CPR courses; contact your local American Red Cross office.

Medic Alert Foundation, P.O. Box 1009, Turlock, CA, 95381-1009 (24-hr. hotline 800-432-5378). For travelers with medical conditions that cannot be easily recognized (diabetes, epilepsy, heart conditions, allergies to antibiotics, etc.). Membership provides the internationally recognized Medic Alert Identification Tag and an annually updated wallet card. Lifetime membership begins at $35.

American Diabetes Association, 1660 Duke St., Alexandria, VA 22314 (800-232-3472). An excellent resource for diabetics.

Global Emergency Medical Services (GEMS), 2001 Westside Dr., Suite 120, Alpharetta, GA 30201 (800-860-1111). Subscribers have immediate 24-hr. access to an emergency room registered nurse with on-line access to your personal medical history, your primary physician, and a worldwide network of English-speaking medical providers.

AN OUNCE OF PREVENTION

Always eat well, drink lots of fluids, and get enough sleep. Keep some power chow handy, like trail mix, granola bars, bananas, or candy bars. *About 95% of headaches are caused by dehydration*—drink even if you're not thirsty. Pure water is best.

Many travelers experience fatigue, discomfort, or mild diarrhea upon arriving in a new area; allow time for your body to adjust before becoming worried. Travelers in high-altitude areas should expect some drowsiness and wait to adjust to the lower atmospheric oxygen levels before engaging in any strenuous activity; also, alcoholic beverages will have heightened effects. Of course, many real health problems are common on the road. If you suffer from any of these ailments in a severe form, seek medical help as soon as possible:

Diarrhea: Traveler's Diarrhea is common. Many people take over-the-counter remedies to counteract it (such as Pepto-Bismol or Immodium), but be aware that such remedies can complicate serious infections; if your diarrhea is severe, bloody, accompanied by fever or chills, or lasts more than a few days, seek medical help. The most dangerous side effect of any diarrhea is dehydration; a simple and effective anti-dehydration formula is 8oz. of water with a ½ tsp. of sugar or honey and a pinch of salt taken several times daily.

Frostbite: Skin affected by frostbite turns white, then waxy and cold. Victims should drink warm beverages, stay or get dry, and *gently and slowly* warm the frostbitten area with dry fabric or, better, with steady body contact. *Never rub frostbite;* the skin is easily damaged when frozen.

Giardia: Found in many rivers and lakes, giardia is a bacteria which causes gas, painful cramps, loss of appetite, and violent diarrhea; it can stay in your system for weeks. To protect yourself, bring your water to a rolling boil, or purify it with iodine tablets before drinking or cooking with it.

Insects: While insects can be annoying, they are rarely deadly. Wear long pants and long sleeves and buy a bednet for camping. When the weather allows, tuck your pants into your socks. Use an insect repellent which contains DEET, but use it sparingly (especially on children) and avoid areas with mucous membranes. Natural repellents, though not entirely effective, can be useful: taking vitamin B-12 or garlic pills regularly can eventually make you smelly to insects (of course, the latter may also make you smelly to people).

Heatstroke: In the early stages of heatstroke, sweating stops, body temperature rises, and an intense headache develops, which if untreated can be followed by mental confusion and, eventually, ultimately, death. Cool the victim off immediately with fruit juice or salted water, wet towels, and shade. In the desert, the body loses 1-2 gallons of water per day, so keep on drinking. Whether you're driving or hiking, *tote two gallons of water per person per day.* A hat, sunglasses, and a lightweight long-sleeve shirt can also help to keep you cool.

Hypothermia: Hypothermia results from exposure to cold and can occur even in the middle of the summer, especially in rainy or windy conditions or at night. The signs are easy to detect: body temperature drops rapidly, resulting in the failure to produce body heat; you may shiver, have poor coordination, feel exhausted, or have slurred speech, sleepiness, hallucinations, or amnesia. *Do not let victims of advanced hypothermia fall asleep*—their body temperatures will drop further, and if they lose consciousness they may die. To avoid hypothermia, keep dry and out of the wind. Dress in layers. Wool keeps insulating even when wet; pile fleece jackets and Gore-Tex raingear are also excellent choices. Never rely on cotton for warmth; this "death cloth" is absolutely useless when wet.

Poison Ivy, Poison Oak, Poison Sumac: These three-leafed plants secrete oils that can cause unbearable itchiness, hives, and sometimes inflammation of the infected areas. If you think you have come into contact with one of these plants, wash your skin in cold water and soap (heat dilates the pores, driving the poison deeper). If rashes occur, calamine lotion, topical cortisone (like Cortaid©), or antihistamines may stop the itching. *Never scratch the affected area;* this will only spread the oil to other locations. Some people have allergic reactions that cause serious asthma-like symptoms; find medical help if this occurs.

Rabies: Rabies may be a risk even in urban areas. If you are bitten by any animal, clean your wound thoroughly and seek medical help.

Sunburn: Carry sunscreen with you and apply it liberally and often. Sunscreens of SPF (sun protection factor) 20 are strong enough for the fairest skin; higher ratings generally won't help and are more expensive. If you do get sunburned, drinking more fluids than usual will cool you down and help your skin recover faster.

Ticks/Lyme Disease: Tick-borne diseases, such as Lyme disease, can be very serious. Lyme disease is a problem for hikers in the U.S., especially on the East Coast but also in parts of the West. Lyme is characterized by a circular rash of 2 inches or more which looks like a bull's-eye. Other symptoms are flu-like: fever, headache, fatigue, or aches and pains. Untreated, Lyme disease can lead to heart, joint, nervous system problems, or even death. There is no vaccine, but Lyme can be treated with antibiotics if caught early. Removing a tick within 24 hours greatly reduces the risk of infection. While hiking, periodically stop and check for ticks; check your neck and scalp with a fine-toothed comb. If you find a tick, grasp the tick's head parts with tweezers as close to your skin as possible and apply slow, steady traction. Do not attempt to get ticks out of your skin by burning them or coating them with nail polish remover or petroleum jelly.

AIDS, HIV and STDs: AIDS presents a particular threat, because it is untreatable and not as well understood as other sexually transmitted diseases (STDs); of the estimated 1 million people in the U.S. who are infected with HIV, the virus believed to be the cause of AIDS, 80% do not realize that they infected. In order to lessen your chances of contracting any STD, use a latex condom every time you have sex. Condoms are widely available in the U.S. and Canada, but it doesn't hurt to stock up before you set out. Opt for water-based lubricants over oil-based formulas which render latex useless in preventing viral transfer. The **U.S. Center for Disease Control** (800-342-2437) can provide more information.

■■■ EARNING AND LEARNING

Job leads often come from local residents, hostels, employment offices, and chambers of commerce. Temporary agencies often hire for non-secretarial placement as well as for standard typing assignments. Marketable skills, i.e. touch-typing, dictation, computer knowledge, and experience with children, will prove very helpful (even necessary) in your search for a temporary job. Consult local newspapers and bulletin boards on college campuses for job listings.

■ WORKING IN THE U.S.

Volunteer (unpaid) jobs are readily available almost everywhere in the U.S. Some jobs provide room and board in exchange for labor. The place to start getting specific information on the jungle of paperwork surrounding **work visas** is your nearest U.S. embassy or consulate. Write to **Council** (see Budget Travel Agencies, p. 21) for *Volunteer! The Comprehensive Guide to Voluntary Service in the U.S. and Abroad* ($12.95 plus postage). Council also runs a summer travel/work program designed to provide students with the opportunity to spend their summers working in the U.S.; university students from the following countries are eligible: **Australia,** NUS Services, 200 Faraday St., 1st floor, Carlton 3053 (tel. 61 3 348 1930); **Canada,** CFS, 243 College St., Suite 500, Toronto, Ontario, M5T 2Y1 (416-977-3703); **Costa Rica:** OTEC, P.O. Box 323-1002, Paseo de los Estudiantes, San Jose (tel. 506 22 08 66); **Dominican Republic,** Calle Luperon 51, esq. Hostos, Zona Colonial, 2nd floor, Santo Domingo (809-687-7005); **France,** Council, 1 place de l'Odeon, 75006 Paris (tel. 33 1 44 41 74 74); **Germany,** Council, Thomas Mann Strasse 33, 53111 Bonn 1 (tel. 49 228 659 746 7); **Ireland,** USIT, 19 Aston Quay, Dublin 2 (tel. 353 1 778 117); **Jamaica,** JOYST, 9 Eureka Crescent, Kingston 5 (809-929-5335); **New Zealand,** STS (NZ), 10 High St., 1st floor, Auckland (tel. 64 9 3099 723); **Spain,** Council, Carransa 7, 3-3 28004 Madrid (tel. 34 1 594 1886); **United Kingdom,** BUNAC, 16 Bowling Green Ln., Clerkenwell, London EC1R OBD (tel. 44 71 251 3472).

Foreign university-level students can get on-the-job technical training in fields such as engineering, computer science, agriculture, and natural and physical sciences from the **Association for International Practical Training,** which is the U.S. member of the **International Association for the Exchange of Students for Technical Experience (IAESTE).** You must apply through the IAESTE office at home; application deadlines vary. For more info, contact the local IAESTE or write to IAESTE, c/o AIPT, 10 Corporate Center, Suite 250, 10400 Little Patuxent Pkwy., Columbia, MD (410-997-2200). The **SCI-International Voluntary Service,** Rte. 2, Box 506B, Crozet, VA 22932 (804-823-1826), arranges placement in work camps in the U.S. for people over 16. Registration fees from $40 (U.S.) to $200 (former USSR).

U.S. WORK VISAS

You **must** apply for a work visa.Working or studying in the U.S. with only a B-2 (tourist) visa is grounds for deportation.

■ WORKING IN CANADA

Most of the organizations and the literature discussed above are not aimed solely at those interested in working in the U.S.; many of the same programs which arrange volunteer and work programs in the U.S. are also active in Canada. Contact individual organizations and write for the publications which interest you most. Travel CUTS (see Budget Travel Agencies p. 21) may also help you out.

CANADIAN WORK VISAS

If you intend to work in Canada, you will need an **Employment Authorization,** obtained before you enter the country; visitors ordinarily are not allowed to change status once they have arrived. A processing fee applies. Employment authorizations are only issued after it has been determined that qualified Canadian citizens and residents will not be adversely affected by the admission of a foreign worker. Your potential employer must contact the nearest **Canadian Employment Centre (CEC)** for approval of the employment offer. For more information, contact the consulate or embassy in your home country. Residents of the U.S., Greenland, and St. Pierre/Miquelon may apply for an Employment Authorization at a port of entry.

■ STUDY OPPORTUNITIES

If you are interested in studying in the U.S. or in Canada, there are a number of different paths you can take. One possibility is to enroll in a language education program, particularly if you are interested in a short-term stay. **World Learning, Inc.,** P.O. Box 676, Brattleboro, VT 05302-0676 (802-257-7751) runs the **International Students of English** program, which offers intensive language courses at select U.S. campuses. The price of a four-week program averages $1800.

An excellent source of information on studying in the U.S., Canada, and abroad is the **Institute of International Education (IIE)** (212-883-8200), which administers many exchange programs. IIE publishes *Academic Year Abroad,* which describes over 2100 semester and academic-year programs offered by U.S. and foreign institutions in Canada and overseas ($43 plus $4 shipping), and *Vacation Study Abroad,* with information on 1500 short-term programs including summer and language schools ($37 plus $4 shipping).

U.S. STUDENT VISAS

Foreign students who wish to study in the United States must apply for either a J-1 visa (for exchange students) or an F-1 visa (for full-time students enrolled in an academic or language program). To obtain a J-1, you must fill out an IAP-66 eligibility form, issued by the program in which you will enroll. Both are valid for the duration of stay, which includes the length of your particular program and a brief grace period thereafter. In order to extend a student visa, submit an I-538 form 15-60 days before your original departure date.

If you are studying in the U.S., you can take any on-campus job to help pay the bills once you have applied for a social security number and have completed an Employment Eligibility Form (I-9). If you are studying full-time in the U.S. on an F-1 visa, you can take any on-campus job provided you do not displace a U.S. resident. On-campus employment is limited to 20 hours per week while school is in session, but you may work full-time during vacation if you plan to return to school. For further information, contact the international students office at the institution you will be attending.

CANADIAN STUDENT VISAS

To study in Canada, you will need a **Student Authorization** in addition to any entry visa you may need. To obtain one, contact the nearest Canadian consulate or embassy. Be sure to apply well ahead of time; it can take up to six months, and there is a processing fee. You will also need to prove to the Canadian government that you are able to support yourself financially. A student authorization is good for one year. If you plan to stay longer, it is very important that you do not let it expire before you apply for renewal. Canadian immigration laws do permit full-time students to seek on-campus employment. For specifics, contact a Canadian Immigration Center (CIC) or consulate. Residents of the U.S., Greenland, and St. Pierre/Miquelon may apply for Student Authorization at a port of entry.

■■■ STUDENT TRAVEL

Many U.S. establishments will honor an ordinary university student ID for student discounts. Still, two main forms of student and youth identification are extremely useful, especially for the insurance packages that accompany them.

International Student Identity Card (ISIC) is $18. The 1996 card is valid from Sept. 1995-Dec. 1996. Present the card wherever you go, and ask about discounts even when none are advertised. Applicants must be attending secondary or post-secondary school on a full-time basis. The card provides accident insurance of up to $3000 as well as $100 per day of in-hospital care for up to 60 days. In addition, cardholders have access to a toll-free **Traveler's Assistance hotline** (800-626-2427 in U.S. and Canada, elsewhere call collect 713-267-2525) whose multilingual staff can provide help in medical, legal, and financial emergencies overseas. When you apply for the card, ask for a copy of the *International Student Identity Card Handbook,* which lists some available discounts. Most of the Budget Travel Agencies listed below (p. 21) issue the ISIC.

International Youth Discount Travel Card or **GO25 Card** is issued by the **Federation of International Youth Travel Organizations (FIYTO),** Bredgade 25H, 1260, Copenhagen K, Denmark, tel. 45 (33) 33 96 00; fax 45 (33) 93 96 76). Applicants must be 12-25. This 1-year card offers many of the same benefits as the ISIC, and most organizations that sell the ISIC also sell the GO25 Card. A brochure that lists discounts is free when you purchase the card. US$10, CDN$15, UK£5 (without travel insurance), US$16 (with insurance); prices subject to change.

■■■ WOMEN AND TRAVEL

Women exploring any area on their own often face heightened threats to personal safety. In all situations, it's best to trust your instincts; if you'd feel better somewhere else, move on. Hitchhiking is never safe for lone women, or even for women traveling in pairs. You may want to consider staying in hostels which offer single rooms which lock from the inside, YWCAs, or other establishments that offer rooms for women only. Stick to centrally located accommodations and avoid late-night treks or subway rides. Always carry change for the phone and extra money for a bus or taxi. Carry a whistle or airhorn on your keychain, and don't hesitate to use it in an emergency. These warnings and suggestions should not discourage women from traveling alone. Be adventurous, but avoid unnecessary risks.

The less you look like a tourist, the better off you'll be. Look as if you know where you're going (even when you don't) and consider approaching women or couples for directions if you're lost or feel uncomfortable. In general, dress conservatively, especially in rural areas. If you spend time in cities, you may be harassed no matter how you're dressed. Your best answer to verbal harassment is no answer at all (a reaction is what the harasser wants). Wearing a conspicuous wedding band may help prevent such incidents. Don't hesitate to seek out a police officer or a passerby if you are being harassed. *Let's Go* lists emergency numbers (including rape crisis lines) in the Practical Information listings of most cities.

The **National Organization for Women** has branches across the country and can refer women travelers to rape crisis centers and counseling services and provide lists of feminist events in the area. Main offices include 22 W 21st, 7th floor, **New York,** NY 10010 (212-807-0721); 1000 16th St. NW, Suite 700, **Washington, DC** 20036 (202-331-0066); and 3543 18th St., **San Francisco,** CA 94110 (415-861-8880).

Handbook For Women Travelers, by Maggie and Gemma Moss. Encyclopedic and well-written (UK£8.99). Order from Piaktus Books, 5 Windmill St., London W1P 1HF, tel. (0171) 631-0710.

Wander Women, 136 N. Grand Ave. #237, West Covina, CA 91791 (818-966-8857). A travel and adventure networking organization for women over 40. Publishes the newsletter *Journal 'n Footnotes*. Membership fee is $29 per year.

Women Going Places, a women's travel and resource guide emphasizing women-owned enterprises. Geared towards lesbians, but offers advice appropriate for all women. $14 from Inland Book Company, PO Box 12061, East Haven, CT 06512, (203-467-4257) or order from a local bookstore.

A Journey of One's Own, by Thalia Zepatos, (Eighth Mountain Press $14.95), The latest thing on the market, interesting and full of good advice, plus a specific and manageable bibliography of books and resources.

Places of Interest to Women, Ferrari Publications, PO Box 37887, Phoenix, AZ 85069 (602-863-2408), an annual guide for women (especially lesbians) traveling in the US, Canada, the Caribbean and Mexico ($8).

■■■ THE GOLDEN YEARS

Senior citizens are eligible for a wide range of discounts on transportation, museums, movies, theaters, concerts, restaurants, and accommodations. If you don't see a senior citizen price listed, ask and you may be delightfully surprised. See National Parks (p. 55) for information on discounts with the Golden Age Passport.

AARP (American Association of Retired Persons), 601 E St., NW, Washington, DC 20049 (202-434-2277). Members 50 and over receive benefits and services including the AARP Motoring Plan from AMOCO (800-334-3300) as well as discounts on lodging, car rental, and sight-seeing. Annual fee $8.00 per couple; lifetime membership $75.

National Council of Senior Citizens, 1331 F St. NW, Washington, DC 20004 (202-347-8800). Memberships are $12 a year, $30 for three years, or $150 for a lifetime. Individual or couple can receive hotel and auto rental discounts, a senior citizen newspaper, use of a discount travel agency, supplemental Medicare insurance (if you're over 65), and a mail-order prescription drug service.

Unbelievably Good Deals and Great Adventures That You Absolutely Can't Get Unless You're Over 50, by Joan Rattner Heilman. After you finish reading the title page, check inside for some great tips on senior discounts and the like. Contemporary Books, $7.95

Gateway Books, 2023 Clemens Rd., Oakland, CA 94602 (510-530-0299; fax 510-530-0497). Publishes *Get Up and Go: A Guide for the Mature Traveler* ($10.95). For credit card orders 800-669-0773.

■■■ BISEXUAL, GAY, AND LESBIAN TRAVELERS

Prejudice against bisexuals, gays, and lesbians still exists in the U.S. and Canada, but acceptance is growing. Still, in many areas, public displays of homosexual affection are illegal. Most major cities have large, active gay and lesbian communities.

Whenever available, *Let's Go* lists local gay and lesbian hotline numbers, which can provide counseling and social information for bisexual, gay, and lesbian visitors. *Let's Go* also lists local gay and lesbian hotspots whenever possible.

Giovanni's Room, 345 S. 12th St., Philadelphia, PA 19107 (215-923-2960; fax 215-923-0813). An international feminist, lesbian, and gay bookstore with mail-order service which carries many of the publications listed here.

Damron Travel Guides, PO Box 422458, San Francisco, CA 94142 (415-255-0404 or 800-462-6654). Publishers of the *Damron Address Book* ($13.95), which lists bars, restaurants, guest houses, and services in the United States, Canada, and Mexico which cater to gay men. The *Damron Road Atlas* ($12.95) contains color maps of 56 major U.S. and Canadian cities and gay and lesbian resorts and listings of bars and accommodations. *The Women's Traveller* ($10.95) includes maps of 50 major U.S. cities and lists bars, restaurants, accommodations, bookstores, and services catering to lesbians. Mail order available; add $5 shipping.

Spartacus International Gay Guides, published by Bruno Gmunder, Postfach 110729, D-10837 Berlin, Germany, tel. 49 (30) 615 00 30. Lists of bars, restaurants, hotels, and bookstores around the world catering to gay men. Also lists hotlines for gay men in various countries. Available in bookstores in the U.S. or by mail order from Giovanni's Room ($29.95).

Gayellow Pages, PO Box 533, Village Station, New York, NY 10014. An annually updated listing of accommodations, resorts, hotlines, and other items of interest to the gay traveler. USA/Canada edition $12.

Ferrari Publications, PO Box 37887, Phoenix, AZ 85069 (602-863-2408). Publishers of *Ferrari's Places of Interest* ($16), *Ferrari's Places for Men* ($15), *Ferrari's Places for Women* ($13), and *Inn Places: US and Worldwide Gay Accommodations* ($16). Available in bookstores, or by mail order (postage $4.50 for the first item, $1.00 for each additional item).

■■■ HANDI-CAPABLE TRAVELERS

Hotels and motels in the U.S. and Canada have become more and more accessible to disabled persons, and many attractions are trying to make exploring the outdoors more feasible. Call ahead to restaurants, hotels, parks, and other facilities to find out about the existence of ramps, the widths of doors, the dimensions of elevators, etc.

Hertz, Avis, and National **car rental agencies** have hand-controlled vehicles at some locations (see Renting p. 33). Amtrak **trains** and all **airlines** can better serve disabled passengers if notified in advance; tell the ticket agent when making reservations which services you'll need. Greyhound allows a traveler with disabilities and a companion to ride for the price of a single fare with a doctor's statement confirming a companion is necessary. Wheelchairs, seeing-eye dogs, and oxygen tanks are not deducted from your luggage allowance. See National Parks (p. 55) for information on discounts available with the Golden Access Passport.

American Foundation for the Blind, 11 Penn Plaza, New York, NY 10011, 212-502-7600, open Mon.-Fri. 8:30am-4:30pm. Provides information and services for the visually impaired. For a catalogue of products, contact Lighthouse Low-Vision Products (800-829-0500).

Facts on File, 460 Park Ave. S., New York, NY 10016 (212-683-2244). Publishers of *Access to the World* ($16.95), listing accommodations and sights with wheelchair access and aids for disabled travelers. Retail bookstores or by mail order.

Mobility International, USA (MIUSA), PO Box 10767, Eugene, OR 97440 (503-343-1284 voice and TDD; fax 503-343-6812). International headquarters in Britain, 228 Borough High St., London SE1 1JX, tel. 44 (071) 403 56 88. Information on travel programs, international work camps, accommodations, access guides, and organized tours for those with physical disabilities. Membership costs $20 per year, newsletter $10. They also sell *A World of Options: A Guide to International Educational Exchange, Community Service, and Travel for Persons with Disabilities* ($14, nonmembers $16, postpaid) and offer a series of courses on strategies for travelers with disabilities. Call for details.

MossRehab Hospital Travel Information Service, 1200 W. Tabor Rd., Philadelphia, PA 19141 (215-456-9603). Telephone information resource center on travel accessibility and other travel-related concerns for those with disabilities.

Twin Peaks Press, PO Box 129, Vancouver, WA 98666-0129 (360-694-2462, orders only MC and Visa 800-637-2256; fax 360-696-3210). Publishers of *Travel for the Disabled,* which provides travel tips, lists of accessible tourist attractions, and advice on other resources for disabled travelers ($19.95). Also publishes *Directory for Travel Agencies of the Disabled* ($19.95), *Wheelchair Vagabond*

($14.95), and *Directory of Accessible Van Rentals* ($9.95). Postage $3 for first book, $1.50 for each additional book.

Directions Unlimited, 720 North Bedford Rd., Bedford Hills, NY 10507 (800-533-5343, 914-241-1700; fax 914-241-0243). Specializes in arranging individual and group vacations, tours, and cruises for those with physical disabilities.

Flying Wheels Travel Service, PO Box 382, 143 W. Bridge St., Owatonna, MN 55060 (800-535-6790; fax 507-451-1685). Arranges international trips for groups or individuals in wheelchairs or with other sorts of limited mobility.

The Guided Tour Inc., Elkins Park House, Suite 114B, 7900 Old York Rd., Elkins Park, PA 19027-2339 (215-782-1370, 800-783-5841; fax 215-635-2637). Organizes travel and vacation programs for persons with developmental and physical challenges and those requiring renal dialysis. Call, fax, or write for a free brochure.

■■■ KOSHER AND VEGETARIAN TRAVELERS

Travelers who keep kosher should contact synagogues in larger cities for information on kosher restaurants; your own synagogue or college Hillel should have access to lists of Jewish institutions across the nation. If you are strict in your observance, consider preparing your own food on the road. The *Jewish Travel Guide* lists Jewish institutions, synagogues, and kosher restaurants in over 80 countries. It is available in the U.S. from Sepher-Hermon Press, 1265 46th St., Brooklyn, NY 11219 (718-972-9010; $12.95 plus $2.50 shipping), and in the UK from Ballantine-Mitchell Publishers, Newbury House 890-900, Eastern Ave., Newbury Park, Ilford, Essex IG2 7HH, tel. (0181) 599 8866; fax (0181) 599 0984.

Vegetarians should have no problem finding suitable cuisine. Most restaurants have vegetarian selections on their menus, and some cater specifically to vegetarians. *Let's Go* often notes restaurants with good vegetarian selections in city listings. The **North American Vegetarian Society,** PO Box 72, Dolgeville, NY 13329 (518-568-7970), sells several titles related to travel in the U.S. and Canada.

■■■ NUTS AND BOLTS

WEIGHTS AND MEASURES

Although the metric system has made considerable inroads into American business and science, the English system of weights and measures continues to prevail in the U.S. The following is a list of English units and their metric equivalents:

1 inch (in.) = 25 millimeters (mm)	1mm = 0.04 in.
1 foot (ft.) = 0.30 meter (m)	1m = a little less than 3 ft.
1 yard (yd.) = 0.92m	1m = 1.09 yd
1 mile (mi.) = 1.61 kilometers (km)	1km = 0.621 mi.
1 ounce (oz., mass) = 25 gram (g)	1g = 0.04 ounce
1 fluid ounce (fl. oz.; volume) = 29.6 milliliters (ml)	1ml = 0.34 fl. oz.
1 pound (lb.) = 0.45 kilograms (kg)	1kg = 2.2 lb.
1 liquid quart (qt.) = 0.94 liter (L)	1L = 1.057 qt.
1 U.S. gallon = 3.78L	1L = 0.27 U.S gallons

The U.S. uses the Fahrenheit temperature scale rather than the Centigrade (Celsius) scale. To convert Fahrenheit to Centigrade, subtract 32, then multiply by 5/9.

TIME ZONES

North Americans tell **time** on a 12-hour clock cycle. Hours before noon are "am" *(ante meridiem);* hours after noon are "pm" *(post meridiem).* Due to the easy confusion of 12pm and 12am, *Let's Go* uses "noon" and "midnight" instead. The four time zones in the continental U.S. are (east to west): **Eastern, Central, Mountain,** and **Pacific.** Canada contains these four, plus **Atlantic** and **Newfoundland** (½hr. ahead of Atlantic) to the east. **Alaska, Hawaii** and the **Aleutian Islands** have their own time zones. Most of the U.S. and all of Canada observe **daylight savings time** from the last Sunday in April (April 28th in 1996) to the last Sunday in October (Oct. 27th in 1996) by advancing clocks ahead one hour.

ELECTRICAL CURRENT

Electric outlets in North America provide current at 117 volts, 60 cycles (Hertz). Appliances designed for the European electrical system (220 volts) will not operate without a transformer and a plug adapter (this includes electric systems for disinfecting contact lenses). Transformers are sold to convert specific wattages (e.g. 0-50 watt transformers for razors and radios).

■■■ PACKING

Pack lightly...**that means you. Even if you have a car.** The more you bring, the more you have to worry about. If you'll be traveling on foot, before you leave, pack your bag, strap it on, and take it for a walk. At the slightest sign of heaviness, unpack something. A good general rule is to pack only what you absolutely need, then take half the clothes and more money than you thought you'd need. Packing doesn't have to be an ordeal; things that you didn't bring can usually be found along the way.

LUGGAGE

If you intend to do a lot of hiking, biking, and walking, you should have a **frame backpack.** Internal-frame packs are best for general traveling; they are flexible enough to follow you through contortions on twisting trails and crowded subways. An excellent choice is a conversion pack, an internal frame pack which converts easily to a suitcase. Backpacks with many compartments generally turn a large space into many unusable small spaces; use separate stuff-sacks instead. If you'll be doing extensive camping or hiking, you may want to consider an **external-frame** pack, which offers added support, distributes weight better, and allows for a sleeping bag to be strapped on. In any case, get a pack with a strong, padded hip belt to transfer weight from your shoulders to your legs. Remember, you get what you pay for; quality packs cost anywhere from $125-$300. When checking a backpack on a flight, tape down loose straps that can catch in the conveyer belt. Wrap sharper items in clothing so they won't stab you or puncture your luggage. Also, bringing a smaller bag in addition to your pack or suitcase allows you to leave your big bag in the hotel while you go sight-seeing.

DRESS FOR SUCCESS

The clothing you bring will, of course, depend on when and where in the U.S. you're planning to travel. In general, **dressing in layers** is best when traveling; if you're hot, peel off a shirt, and if you're cold, add a shirt or sweatshirt.

Summer: Stick to natural fibers and lightweight materials. Start with a few t-shirts; they take up virtually no space and you can wear a sweatshirt or sweater over them on a chilly night. Then pack a couple of pairs of shorts and jeans. Add underwear, socks, a towel, and swimwear.

ESSENTIALS

Winter: Add in heavier layers, including at least one that insulates while wet, such as polypropylene, polarfleece, or wool. Don't bring anything which requires elaborate laundering.

Rain: A rain poncho is cumbersome to wear, but light and compact to carry.

Footwear: For extensive walking, get good **athletic shoes** or **lace-up leather shoes.** Keds, Tevas, and Birkenstocks won't cut it. Leather-reinforced nylon **hiking boots** are good for general walking and essential for hiking: they're lightweight, rugged and dry quickly. A pair of light **flip-flops** provides protection against fungal floors. *Break in your shoes before you leave home.* Talcum powder in your shoes and on your feet can prevent sores, and moleskin is great for blisters. Two pairs of socks—light absorbent cotton inside and thick wool outside—will cushion feet, keep them dry, and help prevent blisters. In cold weather, replace the inner sock with a "stay-dry" liner such as polypropylene.

ETCETERA, ETCETERA, ETCETERA

Random Useful Stuff: umbrella, Ziploc bags (for damp clothes, soap, food), plastic trash bags (for rain protection), alarm clock, strike-anywhere matches, sun hat, sunglasses, needle and thread, safety pins, whistle, Walkman, pocketknife, notebook and pens, water bottle, tweezers, flashlight, string (makeshift clothesline and lashing material), clothespins, padlock, earplugs, compass, deodorant, razors, condoms, tampons, maps, an electrical transformer and plug adapter for North American outlets, a lead-lined pouch (for protecting film from airport x-rays).

Sleepsacks: If planning to stay in **youth hostels,** make the requisite sleepsack (instead of paying the hostel's linen charge). Fold a full size sheet in half the long way, then sew it closed along the open long side and one of the short sides.

GETTING THERE

BUDGET TRAVEL ORGANIZATIONS

Campus Travel, 52 Grosvenor Gardens, **London** SW1W OAG. A large supplier of student travel products in the U.K., with branches throughout the country. They supply student cards, flights, trains, boats, and a full range of related products and services. In London, telesales and bookings for Europe, tel. (0171) 730 3402; for North America, tel. (0171) 730 2101; worldwide, tel. (0171) 730 8111. In Manchester, tel. (0161) 273 1721. In Scotland, tel. (0131) 668 3303.

Council Travel (800-2-COUNCIL/226-8624), is a full-service travel agency specializing in student, youth, and budget travel. They offer discount airfares on scheduled airlines, railpasses, hosteling cards, low-cost accommodations, budget tours, travel gear, and international student (ISIC), youth (Go25) and teacher (ITIC) identity cards. Offices in most major U.S. cities, and a main office at 205 E. 42nd St., **New York,** NY 10017 (212-661-1450). Overseas offices include: 28A Poland St. (Oxford Circus), **London,** W1V 3DB, tel. (0171) 437 7767; 22 rue des Pyramides, 75001 **Paris,** tel. (1) 44 55 55 65; **Munich,** tel. (089) 39 50 22; **Tokyo,** tel. (3) 3581.5517; **Singapore,** tel. (65) 7387-066; **Bangkok,** tel. (66) 2-282-7705.

Let's Go Travel, Harvard Student Agencies, 53A Church St., **Cambridge,** MA 02138 (617-495-9649 or 800-5-LETS GO/553-8746). Offers railpasses, HI-AYH memberships, ISIC, ITIC, Go25 cards, guidebooks (including all *Let's Go* titles), maps, bargain flights, and a complete line of budget travel gear. All items available by mail; call or write for a catalog (or see the one inside this very book).

STA Travel, 6560 North Scottsdale Rd. #F100, Scottsdale, AZ 85253 (800-777-0112). Student and youth travel organization with offices around the world and 14 U.S. locations offering discount airfares (for travelers under 26 and full-time students under 32), railpasses, accommodations, tours, insurance, and ISIC. In the U.S.: 429 S. Dearborn St., **Chicago,** IL 60605 (312-786-9050); 4341 University Way NE, **Seattle,** WA 98105 (206-633-5000); 10 Downing St., **New York,** NY 10014 (212-477-7166); 297 Newbury St., **Boston,** MA 02115 (617-266-6014), 3730 Walnut St. **Philadelphia,** PA 19104 (215-382-2928); 2401 Pennsylvania Ave.,

TREK
AMERICA

Suite G, **Washington, DC** 20037 (202-887-0912); 7202 Melrose Ave., **Los Angeles,** CA 90046 (213-934-8722); 51 Grant Ave., **San Francisco,** CA 94108 (415-391-8407). **UK:** Priory House, 6 Wrights Ln., London W8 6TA, tel. (0171) 938 4711. **New Zealand:** 10 High St., Auckland, tel. (09) 309 9723. **Australia:** 224 Faraday St., Carlton, Melbourne VIC 3050, tel. (03) 347 6911.

Travel CUTS (Canadian University Travel Services, Ltd.), 187 College St., Toronto, Ont. M5T 1P7 (416-798-CUTS/2887; fax 979-8167). Offices across Canada. In the **U.K.,** 295-A Regent St., London W1R 7YA, tel. (0171) 637 31 61. Discounted European, South Pacific, and domestic flights; ISIC, Go25, and HI hostel cards; and discount travel passes. Special fares with valid ISIC or FIYTO cards. Free *Student Traveller* magazine, and info on Student Work Abroad Program (SWAP).

Usit, 19-21 Aston Quay, O'Connell Bridge, **Dublin** 2 (tel. (01) 679 88 33; fax 677 88 43). Sells ISIC, HI hostel cards and *Let's Go*. In addition to discounted student fares on scheduled flights, Usit books charter flights in the summer for some of the best flight deals going.

■■■ FROM EUROPE

Travelers from Europe will experience the least competition for inexpensive seats during the off-season. Peak-season rates generally take effect between mid-May and early June and run until mid-September. Don't count on getting a seat right away during these months. The worst crunch leaving Europe takes place from mid-June to early July; August is uniformly tight for returning flights. Take advantage of cheap off-season flights within Europe to reach an advantageous point of departure for North America. (London is a major connecting point for budget flights to the U.S.; New York City is often the destination.) To make your way out West, catch a coast-to-coast flight once you're in the U.S.

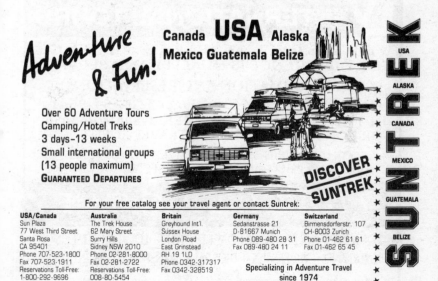

Charter companies, courier services, and ticket consolidators all offer low rates, but often come with restrictions or risks (see Winging It p. 27). Many major airlines

offer reduced-fare options, such as APEX (see p. 27) or youth fares, available only to persons under a certain age (often 24) within 72 hours of the flight's departure.

The lowest major airline fares for a round-trip ticket from Europe in July 1995: **British Airways** (London to NYC $673; 800-247-9297), **Continental** (London to Newark, NJ $810), **Northwest** (London to NYC $714), **TWA** (London to NYC $710), **United** (London to NYC $673; 800-538-2929). Smaller, budget airlines often undercut major carriers by offering bargain fares on regularly scheduled flights. Competition for seats on these smaller carriers can be fierce—book early. Other trans-Atlantic airlines include **Virgin Atlantic Airways** (London to NYC $714; 800-862-8621) and **IcelandAir** (London to NYC $708; 800-223-5500).

■■■ FROM ASIA, AFRICA, AND AUSTRALIA

Whereas European travelers may choose from a variety of regular reduced fares, Asian, Australian, and African travelers must rely on APEX (see p. 27). A good place to start searching for tickets is the local branch of an international budget travel agency (see Budget Travel Agencies p. 21). **STA Travel,** with offices in Sydney, Melbourne, and Auckland, is probably the largest international agency you will find.

Qantas (800-227-4500), **United,** and **Northwest** fly between Australia or New Zealand and the United States. Prices are roughly equivalent among the carriers; typical fare from Sydney to L.A. ranges $1250-1400 peak-season (April-early Jan.), and $1050-1300 off-season (late Jan.-March). Advance purchase fares from Australia have extremely tough restrictions. If you are uncertain about your plans, pay extra for an advance purchase ticket that has only a 50% penalty for cancellation. Many travelers from Australia and New Zealand take **Singapore Air** (800-742-3333) or other Far East-based carriers for the initial leg of their trip.

Delta Airlines (800-241-4141), **Japan Airlines** (800-525-3663), **Northwest** (800-225-2525) and **United Airlines** (800-538-2929) offer service from Japan. A round-trip ticket from Tokyo to L.A. usually ranges $2000-2500, although discounted fares may allow you to fly for as little as $1500. Round-trip fares from Hong Kong generally run $300-400 less than from Tokyo.

South African Airways (800-722-9675), **American** (800-433-7300), and **Northwest** (800-225-2525) connect South Africa with North America. Round-trip fares for the 16½-hour flight between Johannesberg and New York City ranged between $1375 (South African Airways) and $2153 (Northwest) in summer 1995.

ONCE THERE

■■■ EMBASSIES AND CONSULATES

FOREIGN EMBASSIES AND CONSULATES IN THE U.S.

Embassies in U.S.: Australia, 1601 Massachusetts Ave. NW, Washington, DC 20036 (202-797-3000); **Canada,** 501 Pennsylvania Ave. NW, Washington, DC 20001 (202-682-1740); **Ireland,** 2234 Massachusetts Ave. NW, Washington, DC 20008 (202-462-3939); **New Zealand,** 37 Observatory Circle NW, Washington, DC 20008 (202-328-4800); **South Africa,** 3051 Massachusetts Ave. NW, Washington, DC 20008 (202-232-4400); **United Kingdom,** 3100 Massachusetts Ave. NW, Washington, DC 20008 (202-462-1340).

Consulates in U.S.: Australia, 630/636 5th Ave., New York, NY 10020 (212-245-4000); 611 Larchmont Blvd., Los Angeles, CA 90004 (213-469-4300); **Canada,** 1251 Ave. of the Americas, Exxon Building, 16th Floor, New York, NY 10020 (212-596-1600), 300 S. Grand Ave., Suite 1000, Los Angeles, CA 90071 (213-687-7432); **Ireland,** 345 Park Ave., 17th Floor, New York, NY (212-319-2552), 655

Montgomery St., 9th Floor, San Francisco, CA 94111 (415-392-4214); **New Zealand,** 12400 Wilshire Blvd., 11th Floor, Los Angeles, CA 90024 (310-477-8241); **South Africa,** 333 E. 38th St., 9th Floor, New York, NY 10016 (212-213-4880), 50 N. La Clenga Blvd., Suite 300, Beverly Hills, CA 90211 (310-657-9200); **United Kingdom,** 845 3rd Ave., New York, NY 10022 (212-752-8400), Landmark II Building, 11766 Wilshire Blvd., Suite 400, Los Angeles, CA 90025 (213-385-7381).

FOREIGN EMBASSIES AND CONSULATES IN CANADA

Embassies in Canada: Australia, #710, 50 O'Connor St., Ottawa, Ontario K1P 6L2 (613-236-0841); **Ireland,** 170 Metcalfe St., Ottawa, Ontario K2P 1P3 (613-233-6281); **New Zealand,** #727, 99 Bank St., Ottawa, Ontario K1P 6G3 (613-238-5991); **Mexico,** 45 O'Connor St., Suite 1500, Ottawa, Ontario, K1P 1A4 (613-233-8988); **South Africa,** 15 Sussex Dr., Ottawa, Ontario K1M 1M8 (613-744-0330), **United Kingdom,** 80 Elgin St., Ottawa, Ontario K1P 5K7 (613-237-1530), **United States,** 100 Wellington St., Ottawa, Ontario K1P 5T1 (613-238-5335)

Consulates in Canada: Australia, 175 Bloor St. East, Toronto, Ontario M4W 3R8, (416-323-1155), 999 Canada Place, Vancouver, British Columbia V6C 3E1 (604-684-1856); **New Zealand,** 888 Dunsmuir St., Vancouver, British Columbia V6C 3K4 (604-684-7388); **South Africa,** 1, Place Ville Marie, Montreal, Québec H3B 4S3 (514-878-9217); **United Kingdom,** #901, 1155 University St., Montreal, Québec H3B 3A7 (514-866-5863), #800, 1111 Melville St., Vancouver, British Columbia V6E 3V6 (604-683-4421); **United States,** 2, Place Terrasse Dufferin, CP 939, Québec, Québec G1R 4T9 (418-692-2095), 1095 Pender St. West, Vancouver, British Columbia V6E 2M6 (604-685-4311).

■■■ GETTING AROUND

■ WINGING IT

When dealing with any commercial airline, buying in advance is best. Periodic **price wars** may lower prices in spring and early summer months, but they're are unpredictable; don't delay your purchase in hopes of catching one. To obtain the cheapest fare, buy a round-trip ticket, stay over at least one Saturday, and travel on off-peak days (Mon.-Thurs. morning) and off-peak hours (overnight **"red-eye"** flights can be cheaper and faster than primetime). Chances of receiving discount fares increase on competitive routes. Fees for changing flight dates range from $25 (for some domestic flights) to $150 (for many international flights). Most airlines allow children under two to fly free (on the lap of an adult).

Since travel peaks June to August and around holidays, reserve a seat several months in advance for these times. Call the airline the day before your departure to confirm your flight reservation, and get to the airport early to ensure you have a seat; airlines often overbook. (Of course, being "bumped" from a flight doesn't spell doom if your travel plans are flexible—you will probably leave on the next flight and receive a free ticket or cash bonus.)

The following programs, services, and fares may be helpful for planning a reasonably-priced airtrip, but always be wary of deals that seem too good to be true:

APEX (Advance Purchase Excursion Fare): The commercial carriers' lowest regular offer; specials advertised in newspapers may be cheaper, but have more restrictions and fewer seats. APEX fares provide you with confirmed reservations and often allow "open-jaw" tickets (landing and returning from different cities). Call as early as possible; these fares often require a two- to three-week advance purchase. Be sure to inquire about any restrictions on length of stay.

Frequent flyer tickets: It is not wise to buy frequent flyer tickets from others—it is standard policy on most commercial airlines to check a photo ID, and you could find yourself paying for a new, full-fare ticket.

Air Passes: Many major U.S. airlines offer special **Visit USA** air passes and fares to international travelers. You must purchase these passes in Europe, paying one price for a certain number of flight vouchers. Each voucher is good for one flight on an airline's domestic system; typically, all travel must be completed within 30-60 days. The point of departure and destination for each coupon must be specified at the time of purchase, and once in the U.S., changes carry a $50-$75 fee. Dates of travel may be changed once travel has begun, usually at no extra charge. **USAir** offers packages for the East coast (from $349) and for all 48 states (from around $400). **United, Continental, Delta, Air Ontario, Air BC,** and **TWA** sell vouchers as well. TWA's **Youth Travel Pak** offers a similar deal to students 14-24, including North Americans.

DOMESTIC CARRIERS

American Airlines (800-433-7300). In summer 1995, NYC to L.A. $358; L.A. to Honolulu $309, each requires a Saturday stay and max. stay of 30 days.

Continental Airlines (800-525-0280; fax 713-590-2150). In summer 1995, NYC to L.A. $358; L.A. to Honolulu $306; each with a Saturday stay, 7-day advance purchase, and a 30-day max. stay.

Air Canada (800-776-3000). Discounts for ages 12-24 on stand-by tickets for flights within Canada; still, advance-purchase tickets may be cheaper. In summer 1995, Montréal to Seattle $486; Montréal to Halifax $306; Montréal to Vancouver $362; Toronto to L.A. $478. All tickets are 14-day advance purchases with Saturday stay and max. stay of 30 days.

Southwest (800-435-9792). Baltimore to LA $358. As the name implies, this airline serves primarily the Southwestern United States. The "Friends Fly Free" package offers special low fares for two people traveling together between specific destinations at particular times.

Alaska Airlines (800-426-0333 for reservations). In summer 1995, Seattle to Anchorage $340; Juneau to Anchorage $99; each requiring a Saturday stay.

CHARTER FLIGHTS

Charters save you a lot of money on peak-season flights if you can be flexible. Companies reserve the right to change the dates of your flight or even cancel the flight a mere 48 hours in advance. Delays are not uncommon. Restrictions on the length of your trip and the timeframe for reservations may also apply. To be safe, get your ticket as early as possible, and arrive at the airport several hours before departure time. Think carefully when you book your departure and return dates; you will lose all or most of your money if you cancel your ticket. Prices and destinations can change markedly from season to season, so be sure to contact as many organizations as possible in order to get the best deal.

TICKET CONSOLIDATORS AND COURIERS

Consolidators sell unbooked commercial and charter airline seats for very low prices, but deals include some risks. Tickets are sold on a space-available basis which does not guarantee you a seat; you get priority over those flying stand-by but below regularly-booked passengers. The earlier you arrive at the airport the better, since passengers are seated in the order they checked in. Consolidators tend to be more reliable on domestic flights, both in getting you on the flight and in getting you exactly where you want to go. Flexibility of schedule and destination is often necessary, but all companies guarantee you a flight or a refund.

Courier travel works like this: you are a traveler seeking an inexpensive ticket to a particular location; the courier service is a company seeking to transport merchandise to a particular location. If your destinations and schedules coincide, the courier service will sell you a cheap ticket in exchange for the use of the luggage space which accompanies it. Courier services offer some great prices, but their schedules may be confining, and their luggage restrictions allow space for carry-on bags only. For a practical guide to the air courier scene, check out Kelly Monaghan's *Insider's Guide to Air Courier Bargains* ($14.95 plus $2.50 shipping), available from Upper Access Publishing (UAP), P.O. Box 457, Hinesburg, VT 05461 (800-356-9315), or consult the *Courier Air Travel Handbook* published by Bookmasters, Inc., P.O. Box 2039, Mansfield, OH 44905 (800-507-2665; 419-281-6883).

Now Voyager, 74 Varick St. #307, New York, NY 10013 (212-431-1616), does consolidation with reliability which rivals that of most charter companies (97% of customers get on flights the first time) and prices which are considerably lower. Also offers courier service: 70% off a ticket, but remember, only carry-on luggage. Subject to stays of very limited duration on round-trip flights. Flights originate primarily in NYC. (Phones open Mon.-Fri. 10am-5:30pm, Sat. noon-4:30pm, EST.)

Airhitch, 2641 Broadway Third Floor, New York, NY 10025 (800-326-2009 or 212-864-2000 on the East Coast; 800-397-1098 or 310-394-0550 on the West Coast), works to and from a greater number of cities than most other courier companies, but you must often list 2 or 3 cities within a given region to which you are willing to fly; Airhitch guarantees only that you will get to one of them. You must also give a range of three possible travel days on either end for domestic flights. Be sure to read *all* the fine print. The "USAhitch" program connects the northeastern United States with the West (NYC to Seattle or Baltimore to L.A. $129), and California to Hawaii ($129). Programs change frequently; call for the latest information. The Better Business Bureau of New York and Let's Go have received complaints about Airhitch; the company has recently changed ownership, but consumers should make careful inquiries. Delays of up to several days have been reported; if you are delayed, you could incur costs that outweigh savings.

Air Tech, 584 Broadway #1007, New York, NY 10012 (212-219-7000). Domestic travelers must give a 2-day travel window. Flights primarily from NYC (Boston departures possible). To: LA or San Francisco $129, and from Oct.-April, Florida $79. To Europe $169 with a 5-day window. Let's Go has received multiple complaints about delays, inaccurate information, and poor service associated with AirTech. Delays of up to several days have been reported; if you are delayed, you could incur costs that outweigh savings.

■ BY TRAIN

Locomotion is still one of the cheapest ways to tour the U.S. and Canada, but keep in mind that discounted air travel, particularly on longer trips, may be cheaper than train travel. *As with airlines, you can save lots of money by purchasing your tickets as far in advance as possible, so plan ahead and make reservations early.* It is essential to travel light on trains; not all stations will check your baggage.

Amtrak (800-872-7245) is the main provider of train service in the U.S. Most cities have Amtrak offices which directly sell tickets, but tickets must be bought through an agent in some small towns. **Discounts on full fares:** senior citizens (15% off); travelers with disabilities (25% off); children under 15 accompanied by a parent (50% off); children under age two (free); current members of the U.S. armed forces, active-duty veterans, and their dependents (20% off). Circle trips, and holiday packages can also save money. Call for up-to-date info and reservations. Amtrak also offers some **special packages:**

All-Aboard America: This fare divides the Continental U.S. into three regions—Eastern, Central, and Western. During the summer (June 16-Aug. 20), rates are $198 for travel within one region, $278 within and between two regions, and $338 among all three (rates for the remainder of the year, excepting late Dec., are $178, $238, and $278). The price includes travel with up to three stopovers within a 45-day period. The route may not be changed once travel has begun, though the times may be changed at no cost. Fares are subject to availability; make reservations for summer travel well in advance.

Air-Rail Travel Plan: Amtrak and United Airlines allow you to travel in one direction by train and return by plane, or to fly to a distant point and return home by train. The train portion of the journey can last up to 30 days and include up to 3 stopovers. The transcontinental plan, which allows coast-to-coast travel originating on either coast, sells for $605 during peak season (May 26-Sept. 18) and $516 off-season. The East Coast plan, which allows travel roughly as far west as Atlanta including destinations in Florida, Ohio, and Ontario, Canada, costs $417/$373. The West Coast plan, which allows travel roughly as far east as Tucson, AZ, including cities from Las Vegas to Seattle, sells for $407/$357. A multitude of variations are available; contact **Great American Vacations** (see below) for details.

USA Rail Pass: a discount option available only to those who aren't citizens of North America; allows unlimited travel and unlimited stops over a period of either 15 or 30 days. A 30-day nationwide travel pass sells for $425 during peak season (June 16-Aug. 20) and $339 during the off-season (except late Dec.); a 15-day nationwide pass is $340/$229. A 30-day pass limited to travel in the western region (as far east as Denver) is $255/209; the 15-day pass for the west is $225/$199; a 30-day pass to the eastern region (as far west as Chicago) is $255/$229; and the 15-day version is $200/$179.

Great American Vacations, 1220 Kensington, Oakbrook, IL 60521 (800-437-3441). An Amtrak-affiliated travel agency which offers packages in conjunction with airlines and hotel chains and, occasionally, discounts not to be found anywhere else. Programs vary throughout the year; call.

VIA Rail, Place Ville Marie, Lobby Level, Montreal, Québec H3B 2G6 (800-561-3949), is Amtrak's Canadian analogue. Regular fare tickets are discounted 40% with 7-day advance-purchase, and fares vary with seasons. **Discounts on full fares:** students, youths under 24, and seniors (10% off); children ages two to 11, accompanied by an adult (50% off); children under two (free on the lap of an adult). Reservations are required for first-class seats and sleeping car accommodations. Call for details. The **Canrail Pass** allows unlimited travel on 12 to 15 days within a 30-day period. Between early June and late September, a 12-day pass costs $420, senior citizens and youths under 24 pay $377. Off-season passes cost $287, seniors and youths pay $258. Add $35 For each additional day of travel desired.

■ BY BUS

Buses generally offer the most frequent and complete service between the cities and towns of the U.S. and Canada. Often a bus is the only way to reach smaller locales without a car. In rural areas and across open spaces, however, bus lines tend to be sparse. *Russell's Official National Motor Coach Guide* ($13.90 including postage) is an indispensable tool for constructing an itinerary. Updated each month, *Russell's Guide* contains schedules of literally every bus route (including Greyhound) between any two towns in the United States and Canada. Russell's also publishes two semiannual *Supplements,* one which includes a Directory of Bus Lines and Bus Stations ($5.75), and one which offers a series of Route Maps ($6.20). To order any of the above, write Russell's Guides, Inc., P.O. Box 278, Cedar Rapids, IA 52406 (319-364-6138; fax 319-364-4853).

Greyhound (800-231-2222), operates the largest number of routes the U.S., though local bus companies may provide more extensive services within specific regions. Schedule information is available at any Greyhound terminal or by calling the 800 number. Reserve with a credit card over the phone at least ten days in advance, and the ticket can be mailed anywhere in the U.S. Otherwise, reservations are available only up to 24 hours in advance. You can buy your ticket at the terminal, but arrive early. *Advance purchase is much cheaper, so make reservations early.* **Discounts on full fares:** senior citizens (15% off); children ages two to 11 (50% off); travelers with disabilities and their companions together ride for the price of one; active and retired U.S. military personnel and National Guard Reserves (with valid ID), and their spouses and dependents, may take a round-trip between any two points in the U.S. for $169. If **boarding at a remote "flag stop,"** be sure you know exactly where the bus stops. It's a good idea to call the nearest agency and let them know you'll be waiting and at what time. Catch the driver's attention by standing on the side of the road and flailing your arms wildly—better to be embarrassed than stranded. If a bus passes (usually because of overcrowding), a later less-crowded bus should stop. Whatever you stow in compartments underneath the bus should be clearly marked; be sure to get a claim check for it, and watch to make sure your luggage is on the same bus as you.

Ameripass: Allows unlimited travel for seven days ($259), 15 days ($459), or 30 days ($559). The pass takes effect the first day used. Before purchasing an Ameripass, total up the separate bus fares between towns to make sure that the pass is really more economical, or at least worth the unlimited flexibility it provides. **TNMO Coaches, Vermont Transit,** and **Continental Panhandle Line** are Greyhound subsidiaries, and as such will honor Ameripasses; actually most bus companies in the U.S. will do so, but check for specifics.

International Ameripass: For travelers from outside North America. Primarily peddled in foreign countries, they can also be purchased in either of Greyhound's International Offices, located in New York City and Los Angeles (800-246-8572). A 4-day pass is $89, 7-day pass $149, 15-day pass $209, 30-day pass $289.

Greyhound Lines of Canada (800-661-8747 in Canada or 403-265-9111 in the United States) is a Canadian bus company with no relation to Greyhound.

Green Tortoise, 494 Broadway, San Francisco, CA 94133 (415-956-7500 or 800-867-8647), has "hostels on wheels" in remodeled diesel buses done up for living and eating on the road; meals are prepared communally. Prices include transportation, sleeping space on the bus, and tours of the regions through which you pass. Deposits ($100 most trips) are generally required since space is tight. Trips run May to October. From Boston or New York to San Francisco (10-14 days, $299-349 plus $76-81 for food). There are also round-trip vacation loops that start and finish in San Francisco winding through Yosemite National Park, Northern California, Baja California, the Grand Canyon, or Alaska along the way. Prepare for an earthy trip; the buses have no toilets and little privacy. Reserve one to two months in advance; however, many trips have space available at departure.

East Coast Explorer (718-694-9667 or 800-610-2680 outside NYC) is a new, inexpensive way to tour the East Coast between NYC and Boston or Washington, DC. For $3-7 more than Greyhound, you and 13 other passengers will travel all day (10-11 hr.) on back roads stopping at historic sites. One trip per week runs in each direction between NYC and Washington, DC ($32), as between NYC and Boston ($29). The air-conditioned bus will pick up and drop off at most hostels and budget hotels. Reservations required.

■ BY CAR

Let's Go lists U.S. highways thus: "I" (as in "I-90") refers to Interstate highways, "U.S." (as in "U.S. 1") to United States highways, and "Rte." (as in "Rte. 7") to state and local highways. For Canadian highways, "TCH" refers to the Trans-Canada Highway, "Hwy." or "autoroute" refers to standard autoroutes.

HELP!

American Automobile Association (AAA), 1050 Hingham St., Rocklin, MA 02370 (800-AAA-HELP/800-222-4357). The best-known of the auto clubs. Offers free trip-planning services, roadmaps and guidebooks, discounts on car rentals, emergency road service anywhere in the U.S., free towing, and commission-free traveler's cheques from American Express. AAA has reciprocal agreements with the auto associations of many other countries which often provide you with full benefits while in the U.S. AAA membership fees are $54 for the first year with $40 annual renewal; $24 yearly for associate (a family member in household).

AMOCO Motor Club, P.O Box 9041, Des Moines, IA 50368 (800-334-3300). Services include trip planning and travel information, 24-hr. towing (free for 5mi. or back to the tower's garage), emergency road service, and car rental discounts. $50 annual membership enrolls you, your spouse, and your car. Premier membership ($75) entitles you to 50mi. free towing.

Mobil Auto Club, 200 N. Martingale Rd., Schaumbourg, IL 60174 (800-621-5581). Benefits include locksmith, towing (free up to 10mi.), roadside service, and car-rental discounts. $52 annual fee covers you and one person of your choice.

Montgomery Ward Auto Club, 200 N. Martingale Rd., Schaumbourg, IL 60173-2096 (800-621-5151). Provides locksmith services, roadside service, reimbursement for up to 80mi. of towing, and a stipend of up to $100 for lodging should you have to wait overnight for car repairs in a strange locale. $52 annual membership covers you and your spouse in any car. Youths (ages 16-23) $17.95 per year.

ON THE ROAD AGAIN...

Tune up the car before you leave, and make sure the tires are in good repair and have enough air. Get good maps; **Rand McNally's Road Atlas,** covering all of the USA and Canada, is one of the best (available at bookstores and gas stations, $8.95). A **compass** and a **car manual** can also be very useful.

In general, you should always carry a spare tire and jack, jumper cables, extra oil, flares, a flashlight, and blankets (in case you break down at night or in the winter). When traveling in the summer or in the desert bring 5 gallons of water for drinking and for the radiator. In extremely hot weather, use the air conditioner with restraint; if you see the car's temperature gauge climbing, turn it off. Turning the heater on full blast will help cool the engine. If radiator fluid is steaming, turn off the car for half an hour. *Never pour water over the engine to cool it.* Never lift a searing hot hood. In remote areas, remember to bring emergency food and water.

Gas in the U.S. runs about $1.25 per gallon (33¢ per litre), but prices vary widely according to state gasoline taxes. In Canada, gas costs CDN55-60¢ per litre (CDN$2-2.25 per gallon). **Sleeping in a car or van parked in the city is extremely dangerous**—even the most dedicated budget traveler should not consider it an option. **Be**

ESSENTIALS

sure to buckle up—seat belts are required by law in many regions of the U.S. and Canada. The **speed limit in the U.S.** is 55 mph in most places, but rural sections of major interstates may well be 65 mph (when posted). Heed the limit; not only does it save gas, but most local police forces and state troopers make frequent use of radar to catch speed demons. The **speed limit in Canada** is 100km/h.

HOW TO NAVIGATE THE INTERSTATES

In the 1950s, President Eisenhower envisioned an **interstate system,** a federally funded network of highways designed primarily to subsidize American commerce. His dream has been realized, and there is actually an easily comprehensible, consistent system for numbering interstates. Even-numbered interstates run east-west and odd ones run north-south, decreasing in number toward the south and the west. North-south routes begin on the West Coast with I-5 and end with I-95 on the East Coast. The southernmost east-west route is I-4 in Florida. The northernmost east-west route is I-94, stretching from Montana to Wisconsin. Three-digit numbers signify branches of other interstates (e.g., I-285 is a branch of I-85), often a bypass skirting around a large city.

RENTING

Although the cost of renting a car is often prohibitive for long distances, renting for local trips may be reasonable. **Auto rental agencies** fall into two categories: national companies with hundreds of branches, and local agencies which serve only one city or region.

National chains usually allow cars to be picked up in one city and dropped off in another (for a hefty charge). By calling a toll-free number you can reserve a reliable car anywhere in the country. Drawbacks include steep prices and high minimum ages for rentals (usually 25). If you're 21 or older and have a major credit card in your name, you may be able to rent where the minimum age would otherwise rule you out. **Alamo** (800-327-9633) rents to ages 21-24 with a major credit card for an additional $15 per day. **Avis** (800-331-1212) and **Hertz** (800-654-3131) enforce a minimum age of 25, unless the renter has a corporate account. Some branches of **Budget** (800-527-0700) rent to ages 21-24 with a credit card, but it's not the norm. Most **Dollar** (800-800-4000) branches and some **Thrifty** (800-367-2277 or 703-658-2200) locations allow ages 21-24 to rent for an additional daily fee of about $20. **Rent-A-Wreck** (800-421-7253) specializes in supplying vehicles that are past their prime for lower-than-average prices. Most branches rent to ages 21-24, but policies vary from agency to agency.

Most packages allow you a certain number of miles free before the usual charge of 30-40¢ a mile takes effect; if you'll be driving a long distance (a few hundred miles or more), ask for an unlimited-mileage package. When dealing with any car rental company, be sure to ask whether the price includes insurance against theft and collision. There may be an additional charge, the collision and damage waiver (CDW), which usually comes to about $12-15 per day. If you use **American Express** to rent the car, they will automatically cover the CDW; call AmEx's car division (800-338-1670) for more info.

BUYING

Adventures on Wheels, 41 Hwy 36, N. Middletown, NJ 07734 (908-583-8714; fax 583-8932) will sell domestic and international travelers a camper or station wagon, organize its registration and provide insurance, and guarantee that they will buy it back from you after you have finished your travels. Buy a camper for $6-8000, use it for 5-6 months, and sell it back for $4000-4500. The main office is in New York/New Jersey; there are other offices in Los Angeles, San Francisco, and Miami. Vehicles can be picked up at one office and dropped off at another.

AUTO TRANSPORT COMPANIES

These services match drivers with car owners who need cars moved from one city to another. Would-be travelers give the company their desired destination and the company finds a car which needs to go there. The only expenses are gas, tolls, and your own living expenses. Some companies insure their cars; with others, your security deposit covers any breakdowns or damage. You must be at least 21, have a valid license, and agree to drive about 400 mi. per day on a fairly direct route. Companies regularly inspect current and past job references, take your fingerprints, and require a cash bond. Cars are available between most points, although it's easiest to find cars for traveling from coast to coast; New York and Los Angeles are popular transfer points. If offered a car, look it over first. Think twice about accepting a gas guzzler since you'll be paying for the gas. With the company's approval you may be able to share the cost with several companions.

Auto Driveaway, 310 S. Michigan Ave., Chicago, IL 60604 (800-346-2277; fax 312-346-2277).

A. Anthony's Driveaway, 4391 NW 19th Ave., Pompano Beach, FL 33064 (305-970-7384; fax 305-970-3881).

Across America Driveaway, 3626 Calumet Ave., Hammond, IN 46320 (800-964-7874; 310-798-3377 in L.A.; 312-889-7737 in Chicago).

■ BY BICYCLE

Before you rush onto the byways of America pedaling furiously away on your banana-seat Huffy Desperado, remember that safe and secure cycling requires a quality helmet and lock. A good helmet costs about $40—much cheaper than critical head surgery. U-shaped **Kryptonite** or **Citadel** locks run about $30 and carry insurance against theft for one or two years if your bike is registered with the police.

There are a ton of publications that will help you get the most out of your bicycle. *Bicycle Gearing: A Practical Guide* ($9), available from **The Mountaineers Books,** 1011 SW Klickitat Way #107, Seattle, WA 98134 (800-553-4453), discusses in lay terms how bicycle gears work, covering everything you need to know in order to shift properly and get the maximum propulsion from the minimum exertion. *Anybody's Bike Book* ($9.95 plus $3.50 shipping), available from **10-Speed Press,** Box 7123, Berkeley, CA 94707, provides vital information on repair and maintenance during long-term bike sojourns. **Rodale Press,** 33 E. Minor St., Emmaus, PA 18098-0099 (610-967-5171), publishes a number of publications for the intrepid would-be cyclist. *Bike Touring* ($11, Sierra Club) discusses how to equip and plan a bicycle trip. **Umbrella Books,** a subsidiary of Epicenter Press, at P.O. Box 82368 Kenmore, WA 98028 (206-485-6822), sells a number of regional cycling guides, including *Bicycling the Oregon Coast,* by Robin Cody ($11), and *Alaska's Wilderness Highway, Traveling the Dalton Road,* by Mike Jensen.

Adventure Cycling Association, P.O. Box 8308-P, Missoula, MT 59807 (406-721-1776; fax 721-8754). A national, non-profit organization that researches and maps long-distance routes and organizes bike tours for members. Membership $45, $25 in the U.S., $35 in Canada and Mexico.

American Youth Hostels, 733 15th St., NW, Suite 840, Washington, DC 20005 (202-783-6161), offers group biking tours.

The Canadian Cycling Association, 1600 James Naismith Dr., #810, Gloucester, Ont. K1B 5N4 (613-748-5629; fax 748-5692; email *cycling@cdnsport.ca*). Distributes *The Canadian Cycling Association's Complete Guide to Bicycle Touring in Canada* (CDN$20), plus guides to specific regions of Canada, Alaska and the Pacific Coast. Also sells maps and books.

Backroads, 1516 Fifth St. Suite B131, Berkeley, CA 94710 (800-462-2848, fax 510-527-1444) offers tours in 21 states, including Alaska, Hawaii, California, New Mexico, and Maine. Travelers cycle from campsite to campsite; all prices include

■ MILEAGE CHART

	Atlanta	Boston	Chic.	Dallas	DC	Denver	L.A.	Miami	New O.	NYC	Phila.	Phnx.	St. L.	San F.	Seattle	Trnto.	Vanc.	Mont.
Atlanta		1108	717	783	632	1406	2366	653	474	886	778	1863	560	2492	2699	959	2825	1240
Boston	22 hr		996	1794	442	1990	3017	1533	1542	194	333	2697	1190	3111	3105	555	3242	326
Chicago	14 hr	20 hr		937	715	1023	2047	1237	928	807	767	1791	302	2145	2108	537	2245	537
Dallas	15 hr	35 hr	18 hr		1326	794	1450	1322	507	1576	1459	906	629	1740	2112	1457	2255	1763
DC	12 hr	10 hr	14 hr	24 hr		1700	2689	1043	1085	2375	139	2350	845	2840	2788	526	3292	665
Denver	27 hr	38 hr	20 hr	15 hr	29 hr		1026	2046	1341	1785	1759	790	860	1267	1313	1508	1458	1864
L.A.	45 hr	57 hr	39 hr	28 hr	55 hr	20 hr		2780	2005	2787	2723	371	1837	384	1141	2404	1285	2888
Miami	13 hr	30 hr	24 hr	26 hr	20 hr	39 hr	53 hr		856	1346	1214	2368	1197	3086	3368	1564	3505	1676
New O.	9 hr	31 hr	18 hr	10 hr	21 hr	26 hr	38 hr	17 hr		1332	1247	1535	677	2331	2639	1320	2561	1654
NYC	18 hr	4 hr	16 hr	31 hr	5 hr	35 hr	53 hr	26 hr	27 hr		104	2592	999	2923	2912	496	3085	386
Phila.	18 hr	6 hr	16 hr	19 hr	3 hr	33 hr	50 hr	23 hr	23 hr	2 hr		2511	904	2883	2872	503	3009	465
Phoenix	40 hr	49 hr	39 hr	19 hr	43 hr	17 hr	8 hr	47 hr	30 hr	45 hr	44 hr		1503	753	1510	2069	1654	2638
St. Louis	11 hr	23 hr	6 hr	13 hr	15 hr	17 hr	35 hr	23 hr	13 hr	19 hr	16 hr	32 hr		2113	2139	810	2276	1128
San Fran.	47 hr	60 hr	41 hr	47 hr	60 hr	33 hr	7 hr	59 hr	43 hr	56 hr	54 hr	15 hr	45 hr		807	2630	951	2985
Seattle	52 hr	59 hr	40 hr	40 hr	54 hr	25 hr	22 hr	65 hr	50 hr	55 hr	54 hr	28 hr	36 hr	16 hr		2623	146	2964
Toronto	21 hr	11 hr	10 hr	26 hr	11 hr	26 hr	48 hr	29 hr	13 hr	11 hr	13 hr	48 hr	14 hr	49 hr	48 hr		4563	655
Vancvr.	54 hr	61 hr	42 hr	43 hr	60 hr	27 hr	24 hr	67 hr	54 hr	57 hr	56 hr	30 hr	38 hr	18 hr	2 hr	53 hr		4861
Montreal	23 hr	6 hr	17 hr	28 hr	12 hr	39 hr	53 hr	32 hr	31 hr	7 hr	9 hr	53 hr	23 hr	56 hr	55 hr	7 hr	55 hr	

meals, guide services, maps and directions, and van support. Trips range from a weekend excursion ($199) to a 9-day extravaganza ($898).

■ BY MOTORCYCLE

It may be cheaper than car travel, but it takes a tenacious soul to endure a motorcycle tour. If you must carry a load, keep it low and forward where it won't distort the cycle's center of gravity. Fasten it either to the seat or over the rear axle in saddle or tank bags. Those considering a long journey should contact the **American Motorcyclist Association** (800-AMA-JOIN/262-5646), the linchpin of U.S. biker culture. A full membership ($29 per year) includes a subscription to the extremely informative *American Motorcyclist* magazine and a kick-ass patch for your riding jacket.

Of course, safety should be your primary concern. Motorcycles are incredibly vulnerable to crosswinds, drunk drivers, and the blind spots of cars and trucks. *Always ride defensively.* Dangers skyrocket at night; travel in the daytime. Wear the best helmet you can find; helmets are required by law in many states. For information on emergencies, get in touch with the **Motorcycling Safety Foundation,** 2 Jenner St., Suite 150, Irvine, CA 92718-3800 (800-447-4700). Americans should ask their State Departments of Motor Vehicles for a motorcycle operator's manual.

Americade is an enormous week-long annual touring rally. In 1996 it will be held June 3-8 in Lake George, NY. Registration is $50 per person for the week or $12 per day. Call 518-656-3696 to register.

■ BY THUMB

Let's Go urges you to consider the great risks and disadvantages of hitchhiking before thumbing it. Hitching means entrusting your life to a randomly selected person who happens to stop beside you on the road. While this may be comparatively safe in some areas of Europe and Australia, it is generally *not* so in the U.S. We do

NOT recommend it. We strongly urge you to find other means of transportation and to avoid situations where hitching is the only option.

■■■ ACCOMMODATIONS

So you wanna sleep? Wherever you go, try to make reservations ahead, especially if you plan to travel during peak tourist season. If you find yourself in truly dire financial straits, you can call the Traveler's Aid Society in some larger cities as a last resort; they will likely send you to a shelter. Local crisis hotlines may also be able to help.

HOTELS AND MOTELS

Many visitors centers, especially ones on interstates entering a state, have hotel coupons that can save you a bundle; if you don't see any, ask. Budget motels are usually clustered off a main highway several miles outside of town, but the carless may do better to try the hostels, YMCAs, YWCAs, and dorms downtown. The annually updated *National Directory of Budget Motels* ($6, plus $1.50 shipping), from **Pilot Books,** 103 Copper St., Babylon NY 11702 (516-422-2225 or 516-422-2227), covers over 2200 low-cost chain motels in the U.S. Pilot Books also offers *The Hotel/Motel Special Program and Discount Guide* ($6, plus $1.50 shipping), which lists hotels and motels offering special discounts and money-saving programs. Also look for the *State by State Guide to Budget Motels* ($12), from Marlor Press, Inc., 4304 Brigadoon Dr., St. Paul, MN 55126 (800-669-4908 or 612-484-4600; fax 612-490-1182).

Chains usually adhere to a level of cleanliness and comfort more consistent than locally operated budget competitors. The cellar-level price of a single is about $27. Some budget chains are **Motel 6** (505-891-6161), **Super 8 Motels** (800-800-8000, 605-229-8708; fax 605-229-8900), **Choice Hotels International** (800-453-4511), and **Best Western International** (800-528-1234, 602-957-5946; fax 602-957-5505).

ESSENTIALS

If you are addicted to expensive hotels, consider joining **Discount Travel International,** 25 E. Athens Ave., Ardmore, PA 19003 (610-645-9552; fax 610-645-9743). For an annual $45 membership fee, you and your household gain access to a clearinghouse of unsold hotel rooms in ritzier shacks such as Hiltons and Hyatts (as well as airline tickets, cruises, car rentals, etc.) which can save you as much as 50%.

HOSTELS

For cheap chummy lodgings, hostels can't be beat. Hostels are generally dorm-style accommodations where the sexes sleep apart, often in large rooms with bunk beds; some hostels allow families and couples to have private rooms. They often have kitchens and utensils for your use, and some have storage areas and laundry facilities. There can be drawbacks; some hostels close during certain daytime "lock-out" hours, have a curfew, require you to do chores, or impose a maximum stay. Fees range from $8 to $20 per night, hostels associated with one of the large hostel associations will often have lower rates for members. If you have Internet access, check out the **Internet Guide to Hostelling** (World Wide Web *http://hostels.com/rec-travel/hostels/,* or email *info@hostels.com* for more information). If you plan to stay in hostels, consider joining one of these associations:

Hostelling International-American Youth Hostels (HI-AYH), 733 15th St. NW, Suite 840, Washington, DC 20005 (202-783-6161, 800-444-6111; fax 202-783-6171). Maintains over 300 hostels in the U.S. and Canada. Basic rules (with much local variation): check-in 5-8pm, check-out by 9:30am, max. stay 3 days, no pets or alcohol allowed on the premises. Fees $5-22 per night. Memberships can be purchased from many budget travel agencies (see p. 21) or the national office in Washington, DC. 1-year membership $25, under 18 $10, over 54 $15, family cards $35; includes *Hostelling North America: The Official Guide to Hostels in Canada and the United States*. Reserve by letter, phone, fax, or through the

ESSENTIALS

International Booking Network (IBN), a computerized reservation system which lets you book from other HI hostels worldwide up to six months in advance.

Hostelling International-Canada (HI-C), 400-205 Catherine St., Ottawa, Ontario K2P 1C3, Canada (613-237-7884; fax 237-7868). The Canadian sister of HI-AYH. Maintains a network of 75 hostels throughout Canada.

Rucksackers North America, P.O. Box 90404, Santa Barbara, CA 20038 (301-469-5950).

BED AND BREAKFASTS

For a cozy alternative to impersonal hotel rooms, B&Bs (private homes with rooms available to travelers) range from the acceptable to the sublime. Hosts will sometimes go out of their way to be accommodating by accepting travelers with pets or by giving personalized tours. A home-cooked breakfast (and occasionally dinner) may be the best part of your stay; however, many B&Bs do not provide phones, TVs, or private bathrooms.

Several travel guides and reservation services specialize in B&Bs. Three of the more extensive guides are *Bed & Breakfast, USA* ($16), from Tourist House Associates, Inc., RR 1, Box 12-A, Greentown, PA 18426, *Complete Guide to Bed and Breakfasts, Inns and Guesthouses in the U.S. and Canada* ($16.95), available on CompuServe, enter "Go B&B," or from Lanier Publications, P.O. Box D, Petaluma, CA 94952 (707-763-0271; fax 763-5762; email *72662.1223@compuserve.com*), and *America's Wonderful Little Hotels and Inns: USA and Canada* (US$20, CAN$27). All three can be found in bookstores. The following services book rooms in B&Bs throughout the U.S. and Canada:

Bed and Breakfast International, P.O. Box 282910, San Francisco, CA 94128-2910 (800-872-4500 or 415-696-1690; fax 415-696-1699). Rates range $60-$150 per night per room and include breakfast; 2-night min. stay. Discounts for singles, families with children, and reservations over one week.

Bed and Breakfast: The National Network (TNN) of Reservation Services, Box 4616, Springfield, MA 01101(800-884-4288; fax 401-847-7309) can book reservations at over 7000 B&Bs throughout America and Canada.

YMCA AND YWCAS

Not all **Young Men's Christian Association (YMCA)** locations offer lodging; those that do are often located in urban downtowns, which can be convenient but a little gritty. YMCA rates are usually lower than a hotel's but higher than a hostel's and may include use of libraries, pools, and other facilities. Many YMCAs accept women and families, and some (as in Los Angeles) will not lodge people under 18 without parental permission. Payment for reservations must be made in advance, with a traveler's check (signed top and bottom), U.S. money order, certified check, Visa, or Mastercard. Key deposits are common; call the local YMCA in question for fee information. For information or reservation, write to **Y's Way to Travel,** 224 E. 47th St., New York, NY 10017 (212-308-2899; fax 212-308-3161).

Most **Young Women's Christian Associations (YWCAs)** accommodate only women. Nonmembers are often required to join when lodging. For more information, write **YWCA-USA,** 726 Broadway, New York, NY 10003 (212-614-2700). For Y's in **Canada,** contact the Montreal YMCA at 1450 Stanley St., Montreal, PQ H3A 2W6 (514-849-8393; fax 514-849-8017) or the Ottawa YWCA/YMCA at 180 Argyle Ave., Ottawa, Ont. K2P 1B7 (613-237-1320; fax 613-788-5095).

DORMS

In general, college campuses are good sources for information on things to do, places to stay, and possible rides out of town. Many **colleges and universities** open their residence halls to travelers when school is not in session—some do so even during term-time. These dorms are often close to the funky student areas and are usually very clean. No general policy covers all of these institutions, but rates tend to

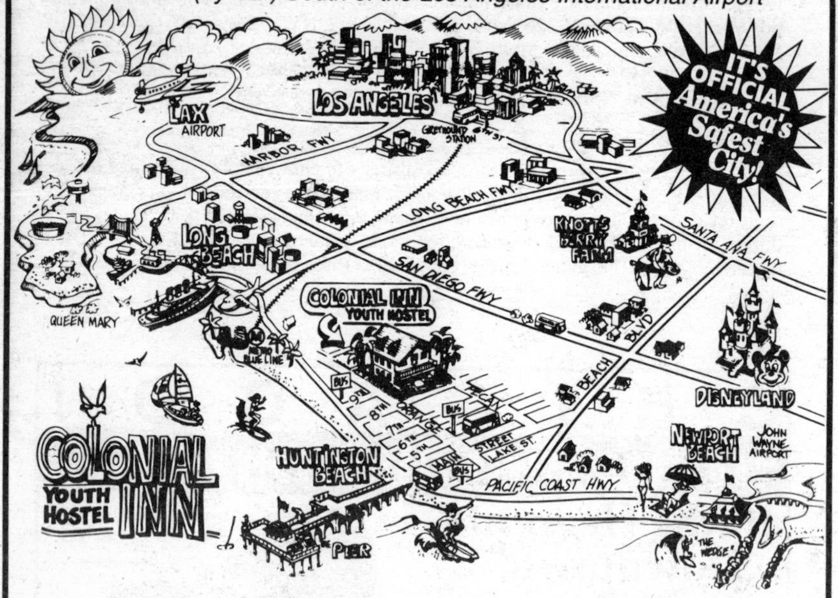

be low, and many offer free local calls. *Let's Go* lists colleges which rent dorm rooms among the accommodations for the appropriate cities. College dorms are popular with many travelers; reserve ahead.

NO PLACE LIKE HOMESTAYS

U.S. Servas Committee, 11 John St., Suite #407, New York, NY 10038-4009 (212-267-0252; fax 212-267-0292). **Servas** invites travelers to share life in homes in over 100 countries free of charge. Prospective travelers must submit an application with references, have an interview, and pay a membership fee of $55 (5 host lists with descriptions of hosts, $25).

Homestay/USA, 25 Bay State Rd., Boston, MA 02215 (800-327-4678 or 617-247-0350). World Learning's Homestay/USA coordinates three- to four-week homestays with U.S. families for international visitors over 14.

Home Exchange, PO Box 567, Northampton, MA 01061. Registry service links homeowners all over the USA, Britain, and Ireland. Subscribers (US$50 fee) list their homes in *Home Exchange Directory,* which is sent to all subscribers for the purpose of free exchange or rental.

Intervac U.S., International Home Exchange, PO Box 590504, San Francisco, CA 94159 (415-435-3497 or 800-756-HOME/4663, fax 415-435-7440). Part of a worldwide home-exchange network. Publishes four catalogs per year, containing more than 9400 homes in more than 36 countries. Members contact each other directly. $65 will get you three of the company's catalogs and inclusion of your own listing in one. Hospitality and rentals are also available.

International Home Rentals, PO Box 329, Middleburg, VA 22117 (800-221-9001 or 703-687-316; fax 703-687-3352). Has home rentals in Colorado, Connecticut, California, Florida, New York, South Carolina, Vermont, and Virginia.

ROUGHING IT: CAMPING

To Your Health (p. 11) and Everything But The Kitchen Sink (p. 19) both contain valuable advice for outdoor travelers.

Stayin' Alive

Stay warm, stay dry, stay hydrated. The vast majority of life-threatening wilderness problems stem from a failure to follow this advice. If you're going into an area that is not well-traveled or well-marked, let someone know where you're hiking and how long you intend to be out. *Never go camping or hiking by yourself for any significant time or distance.* On any hike, overnight or for the day, that will take you more than one mile from civilization, you should pack enough equipment to keep you alive in case of disaster: raingear, warm layers (not cotton!), a hat, mittens, a first-aid kit, high energy food, and water. Whether you're bound for a densely populated campground or deep wilderness, a good guide to outdoor survival is *How to Stay Alive in the Woods,* by Bradford Angier (Macmillan, $8). For information on outdoor ailments, such as rabies, giardia and insects, see An Ounce of Prevention (p. 11).

While safety from the environment is your main concern, you should also be concerned about safety from other people. Keep your gear nearby at all times; campgrounds can be ideal spots for thieves or worse. A well-lit and well-monitored campground can minimize this problem, but you should still be wary. Groups should try to stay together after dark.

It is also important to be concerned with your effect on the environment. Because firewood is scarce in popular parks, campers are asked to make small fires using only dead branches or brush; using a campstove is a safe way to cook. Check ahead to see if the park prohibits campfires altogether. To avoid digging a rain trench for your tent, pitch it on high, dry ground. Don't cut vegetation, and don't clear campsites. Make sure your campsite is at least 150 ft. from any water supply or body of water. If there are no toilet facilities, bury human waste at least four inches deep and 150 ft. or more from any water supply or campsite. Always pack your trash in a plastic bag and carry it with you until you reach the next trash can; burning and burying pollute the environment.

Bear Necessities

No matter how tame a bear appears, don't be fooled—they're wild and dangerous animals who are simply not intimidated by humans. As a basic rule of thumb, if you're close enough for a bear to be observing you, you're too close. Park rangers can tell you how to identify bear trails; don't camp on them! To avoid a grizzly experience, never feed a bear, or tempt it with such delectables as open trash cans. Keep your camp clean, and keep your trash high off the ground. Do not cook near where you sleep, and do not leave food lying around camp. Avoid indulging in greasy foods, especially bacon and ham. Bears are also attracted to perfume smells; do without cologne, scented soap, and hairspray while camping. Leave your packs empty and open on the ground so that a bear can nose through them without shredding them. When you sleep, don't even think about leaving food or any scented items (trash, toiletries) near your tent.

The best way to keep your toothpaste from becoming a condiment is to **bear-bag.** This amounts to hanging your delectables from a tree, out of reach of hungry paws. Seal food and waste in airtight plastic bags; place them in duffel bags, and hang them in a tree 10 ft. from the ground and five ft. from the trunk.

Always shine a flashlight when walking at night: the bears will clear out before you arrive if given sufficient warning. If you see a bear at a distance, calmly walk (don't run) in the other direction. If you stumble upon a bear cub, leave immediately, lest its over-protective mother stumble upon you. If you are attacked by a bear, get in a fetal position to protect yourself; put your arms over the back of your neck, and play dead. The aggressiveness of bears varies from region to region; always ask local rangers for details.

Equipment

At the core of your equipment is the **sleeping bag.** Your purchase should depend on the climate in which you plan to camp; sleeping bags are rated according to the lowest outdoor temperature at which they will still keep you warm. If a bag's rating is not a temperature but a seasonal description, keep in mind that "summer" translates to a rating of 30-40°F, "three-season" means 20°F, and "winter" means below 0°F. Bags are made either of down (warmer and lighter) or of synthetic material (cheaper, heavier, more durable, and warmer when wet). Low prices for good sleeping bags: $65-80 for a summer synthetic, $135-180 for a three-season synthetic, $170-225 for a three-season down bag, and upwards of $270-550 for a down winter-bag. **Sleeping bag pads** range from $15 to $30, while **air mattresses** go for $25-50.

When you select a **tent,** your major considerations should be shape and size. The easiest tents are free-standing, with their own frames and suspension systems. They set up quickly and require no staking (though staking adds security on windy days). Low profile dome tents are especially efficient; when pitched, their internal space is almost entirely usable, which means little unnecessary bulk. Be sure your tent has a rain fly. Good two-person tents start at about $135; $200 will fetch a four-person. Backpackers and cyclists prefer small, lightweight models (from $145). **Sierra Design,** 1255 Powell St., Emeryville, CA, 94608 (510-450-9555), sells excellent tents, including the two-person "Clip Flashlight" ($170) that weighs less than 4 lbs.

Other necessities include a **plastic groundcloth** to protect the tent floor and a **battery-operated lantern** (*never* gas). When camping in autumn, winter, or spring, bring along a "space blanket," an amazingly compact technological wonder that helps you retain your body heat ($3.50-13; doubles as a groundcloth). Large, collapsible **water sacks** will significantly improve your lot in primitive campgrounds. They weigh practically nothing when empty, but can get bulky. **Campstoves** come in all sizes, weights, and fuel types, but none are truly cheap ($30-85). Beware: stove gas can be heavy and bulky if you bring too much.

Whether buying or renting, finding sturdy yet inexpensive equipment is a must. Spend some time examining catalogs and talking to knowledgeable sales people. Many reputable mail-order firms have cheap rates, though buying locally means having someone there to tell you how to best use your equipment. In stores, look for last year's models; especially in the fall, prices can drop by as much as 50%.

Recreational Equipment, Inc. (REI), 6750 S. 228th St., Kent, WA 98032 (800-426-4840). Stocks a wide range of the latest in camping gear and holds great seasonal sales. Many items guaranteed for life (excluding normal wear and tear).

L.L. Bean, Freeport, ME 04033-0001 (800-341-4341). Supplies its own equipment and national-brand merchandise. 100% satisfaction guaranteed on all purchases.

Cabela's, Inc. 812 13th Ave., Sidney, NE 69160 (800-237-4444). Offers great prices on quality outdoor equipment.

Campmor, Inc. P.O. Box 700, Saddle River, NJ 07458 (800-526-4784). Tons of equipment at low prices. One-yr. guarantee on unused or defective merchandise.

Eastern Mountain Sports (EMS), One Vose Farm Rd., Peterborough, NH 03458 (603-924-7231). Stores nationwide provide excellent service and guaranteed customer satisfaction on all items sold. They don't have a catalog, and they generally don't take mail or phone orders; call the above number for the nearest branch.

Cheaper equipment can also be obtained on the used market, but make sure you know what you're buying. Consult want-ads and student bulletin boards, and take someone along who is knowledgeable. Spending a little more money up front may save money later because you won't have to replace equipment.

A good source of information on **recreational vehicles (RVs)** is the **Recreational Vehicle Industry Association,** P.O. Box 2999, 1896 Preston White Dr., Reston, VA 22090-0999 (703-620-6003). For information regarding RV camping publications and state campground associations, write to or call the **Go Camping America Committee,** P.O. Box 2669, Reston, VA 22090-0669 (800-47-SUNNY/78669).

■■■ LINES OF COMMUNICATION

U.S. MAIL

Offices of the **U.S. Postal Service** are usually open Monday to Friday from 9am to 5pm and sometimes on Saturday until about noon; branches in many larger cities open earlier and close later. All are closed on national holidays. If you don't want to make the trip to the post office, most **hotels** and **hostel owners** will send stamped postcards or letters home for you if you ask. Postal rates in the U.S.: **within the U.S.,** postcards 20¢, letters: 1oz. 32¢, 23¢ per additional ounce; **to Canada,** postcards 40¢, letters: ½oz. 46¢, 1oz. 52¢, 2oz. 72¢; **to Mexico,** postcards 35¢, letters: ½oz. 40¢; 1oz. 46¢, 40¢ per additional ounce; **overseas,** postcards 50¢, ½oz. 60¢, 1oz. $1, 40¢ per additional ounce. **Aerogrammes,** sheets that fold into envelopes and travel via air mail, are available at post offices for 50¢. Domestic mail generally takes 2-7 days; overseas mail, 2-14 days. Write **"AIR MAIL"** on the front of the envelope for speediest delivery.

If people want to get in touch with you, mail can be sent **General Delivery** to a city's main post office in the U.S. or Canada. Once a letter arrives it will be held for at least 10 days; it can be held for longer if such a request is clearly indicated on the front of the envelope. You should bring a passport or other ID to pick up General Delivery mail. Family and friends can send letters to you labeled like this:

Mr. Potato Head (underline last name for accurate filing)
c/o General Delivery
Main Post Office
Boise, ID 83707
USA (if from another country)

CANADIAN MAIL

Postcards and letters are charged at the same rate in Canada: **within Canada,** 30g 45¢, 31–100g 71¢; **to the U.S.,** 30g 52¢, 30-100g 77¢; **to other countries,** 20g 90¢, 21-50g $1.37, 51-100g $2.60. Letters take from three to eight working days to reach the U.S. and a week or two to get to an overseas address. Mailboxes in Canada are red and look something like space-age garbage chutes.

General Delivery (Poste Restante) mail can be sent to any post office and will be held for 15 days; it can be held for longer at the discretion of the Postmaster if such a request is clearly indicated on the front of the envelope. General Delivery letters should be labeled like this:

Micky van Sully (underline last name for accurate filing)
c/o General Delivery
Frederick Station C
1 Sesame St.
St. John's, NF A1C 5H1
CANADA (if from another country)

In both the U.S. and Canada, **American Express** offices will act as a mail service for cardholders if you contact them in advance. For information and a complete list of offices, call 800-528-4800 and ask for the *Traveler's Companion* booklet.

For speedy, reliable, and expensive mail, try **Federal Express** (800-238-5355 in the U.S. and Canada) or **DHL** (800-225-5345 in the U.S. and Canada).

TELEPHONES

Telephone numbers in the U.S. and Canada consist of a three-digit area code, a three-digit exchange, and a four-digit number, written as 123-456-7890. Numbers with an **800** area code are toll-free numbers. A quick guide:

Local calls: Dial the last 7 digits.

Long-distance calls within the U.S./Canada: 1 + area code + 7-digit number. Same area code calls are not always local; for long-distance calls within an area code: 1 + 7-digit number. For toll-free 800 numbers: 1 + 800 + 7-digit number.
International calls: Dial the universal international access code (011) followed the country code, the city code, and the local number. Country codes and city codes may sometimes be listed with a zero in front (e.g. 033 for France), but when using 011, drop successive zeros (e.g., 011-33). In some areas you will need to give the operator the number, who will then place the call for you.

Evening rates are considerably less than weekday rates (generally Sun.-Fri. 5-11pm); **night and weekend rates** are cheaper than evening rates (generally Mon.-Fri. 11pm-8am, all day Sat., and all day Sun. except 5-11pm).

Dialing **"0"** will get you the **operator,** who is omnipotent in all matters remotely connected with phones. To obtain local phone numbers for a specific place or to find area codes for other cities, call **directory assistance** at **411** or look in the local **white pages** telephone directory; for **long-distance directory assistance,** dial **1-(area code)-555-1212.** The **yellow pages,** published at the end of the white pages or in a separate book, will help you find general services (e.g. "canoe rental"). Federal, state, and local government listings (including **local consulates**) are provided in the **blue pages,** bundled with the white pages or at the end of the yellow/white pages directory. You can reach directory assistance and the operator free from any pay phone (no coin needed).

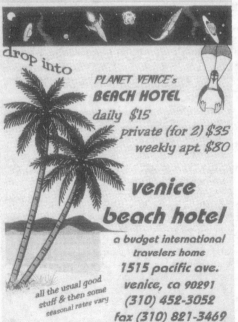

Pay phones are plentiful, most often stationed on street corners and in public areas. Put your coins (10-25¢ for a local call depending on the region) into the slot and before dialing. If there is no answer or if you get a busy signal, you will get your money back after hanging up, but if you connect with an answering machine the phone will gobble your coins. To make a long-distance direct call, simply dial the number, and an operator will tell you the cost for the first three minutes; deposit that amount in the coin slot. The operator or a recording will cut in when you must deposit more money. A rare type of pay phone can be found in some train stations which charges 25¢ for a one-minute call to anywhere in the continental U.S. If you are at a pay phone and don't have barrels of change, you can dial "0" for the operator and ask to place one of the following types of calls:

Collect call: If whoever picks up the phone call accepts the charges, he or she will be billed for the call. AT&T's collect service, 800-CALL-ATT, guarantees AT&T lines and rates for the call. The cheapest is MCI's new 800-COLLECT (205-5328) service, which offers a 20-44% discount off normal rates.

Person-to-person collect call: A little more expensive than a normal collect call, but a charge appears only if the person you wish to speak to is there (for example, if you want to speak to Michelle but not her parents).

Third-party billing: Bills the call to a third party. Have the number of the place you want to call and the number of the place you want to bill the call to (e.g., home).

Alternatively, you may want to consider getting a **calling card,** which is much cheaper. If you live in the U.S., contact **AT&T** (800-545-3117 within the U.S.) or **MCI** (800-444-3333) for more information. In other countries, call your local phone company. **In Canada,** contact Bell Canada's Canada Direct (800-561-8868), **in Australia,** contact Telsta Australia Direct (tel. 13 22 00); in **Ireland,** Telecom Eireann Ireland Direct (800 25 25 25); in **New Zealand,** Telecom New Zealand (123); in South Africa **Telkom South Africa** (0903); in the **U.K.,** British Telecom BT Direct (tel. (800) 34 51 44). Travelers with British Telecom, Telecom Eireann, New Zealand Telecom, Telkom South Africa, or Telecom Australia accounts at home can use special **access numbers** to place calls from the U.S. through their home systems. All companies except Telkom South Africa have different access numbers depending on whether their cooperative partner in the U.S. is AT&T, MCI, or Sprint. Access numbers are: British Telecom (800-445-5667 AT&T, 800-444-2162 MCI, 800-800-0008 Sprint); Telecom Eireann (800-562-6262 AT&T, 800-283-0353 MCI, 800-473-

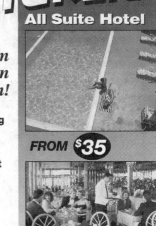

0353 Sprint); New Zealand Telecom (800-248-0064 AT&T, 800-666-5494 MCI, 800-949-7027 Sprint); Telecom Australia (800-682-2878 AT&T, 800-937-6822 MCI, 800-676-0061 Sprint); Telkom South Africa (800-949-7027).

TELEGRAMS

Sometimes cabling may be the only way to contact someone quickly (usually by the next day). Western Union (800-325-6000) delivers telegrams overseas and within the U.S. Foreign telegrams are more expensive and are usually priced on a per word basis. The minimum cost for a domestic, same day, hand-delivered telegram is $30.90 for 15 words. "Mailgrams" ($19 for 50 words) arrive on the next mail day.

■■■ NATIONAL PARKS

National Parks protect some of the most spectacular scenery in North America. Though their primary purpose is preservation, the parks also host recreational activities like ranger talks, guided hikes, skiing, and snowshoe expeditions. Generally, internal roads allow you to reach the interior and major sights even if you are not a hiker. For info on any facet of the national park system, contact the **National Park Service,** Office of Public Inquiries, P.O. Box 37127, Washington, DC 20013-7127 (202-208-4747). The **National Park Foundation**, 1850 K St. NW, Suite 210, Washington, DC 20006 (202-785-4500), distributes *The Complete Guide to America's National Parks* by mail-order ($13.95, plus $3 shipping).

Entrance fees vary. The larger and more popular parks charge a $3-10 entry fee for cars and sometimes a nominal fee for pedestrians and cyclists. The **Golden Eagle Passport** ($25), available at park entrances, allows entry into all national parks for one year. The **Golden Age Passport,** available to ages 62 and over, entitles the passport-holder's party to free park entry and a 50% discount on camping and boat-launching, along with a 50% discount on recreational fees for the passport holder (one-time fee $10). Persons eligible for federal benefits on account of disabilities can enjoy the same privileges with the **Golden Access Passport** (free). Golden Age and Golden Access Passports must be purchased at a park entrance with proof of age or federal eligibility, respectively. All passports are also valid at National Monuments, Forests, Wildlife Preserves, and other national recreation sites.

Most national parks have both backcountry and developed tent **camping;** some welcome RVs, and a few offer grand lodges. At the more popular parks in the U.S. and Canada, reservations are essential, available through **MISTIX** (800-365-2267 in U.S.; 619-452-8787 outside the U.S.). Lodges and indoor accommodations should be reserved months in advance. Campgrounds often observe first-come, first-camp policies. Arrive early; many campgrounds fill up by late morning. Some limit your stay and/or the number of people in a group.

Often less accessible and less crowded, **National Forests** provide a purist's alternative to parks. While some have recreation facilities, most are equipped only for primitive camping—pit toilets and no water are the norm. Entrance fees, when charged, are $6-7, but camping is generally free. Backpackers can take advantage of specially designated wilderness areas, which have regulations barring all vehicles; the necessary wilderness permits can be obtained at the U.S. Forest Service field office in the area. If you are interested in exploring a National Forest, call or write ahead for detailed maps; **National Forest Service,** U.S. Department of Agriculture, P.O. Box 96090, Washington, DC 20019-6090 (202-205-8333).

The U.S. Department of the Interior's **Bureau of Land Management (BLM)** offers a wide variety of outdoor recreation opportunities—including camping, hiking, mountain biking, rock climbing, river rafting, and wildlife viewing—on the 270 million acres it oversees in ten Western states and Alaska. These lands also contain hundreds of archaeological artifacts, such as ancient Indian cliff dwellings and rock art, and historic sites like ghost towns. For more information, write or call BLM Public Affairs, Washington D.C. 20240 (202-208-5717).

UNITED STATES

Reaching from below the Tropic of Cancer to above the Arctic Circle and handily spanning the North American continent, the United States is undeniably big. It is a country defined by open spaces and an amazing breadth of terrain. Above and beyond its physical presence, the culture of the U.S. creeps across the globe, making the country unavoidable as well. American culture has grown from the seed of a government dedicated to individualism in a land large enough to allow for every person's personal space. Through decades of open-door immigration, the United States has absorbed and integrated millions of immigrants (4 million foreign-born settlers arrived between 1830 and 1850 alone) to create the melting pot which now defines the population. In recent years, the country which knew no bounds has been forced to become acquainted with physical, social, and economic constraints to its growth. The individuals and groups who compose the country's diverse character chafe as they step into each other's space, but most will acknowledge that the conflict comes with the freedom.

Perhaps the best thing any visitor or any disenchanted American can do to regain hope in the whole experiment is to explore. Outside of the cities, the land that inspired this cross-continental adventure still awaits, and huge spaces assure us that there's still room to breathe and to move and to let each other do the same.

American Culture

HISTORY

IN THE BEGINNING

It is not known exactly when people first set foot in the Americas. Until recently, scientists estimated that the first Americans crossed the Bering Sea from Siberia on a land bridge during the last Ice Age, about 15,000 years ago. New archaeological digs show evidence of earlier habitation, but the validity of these sites is still questioned. It is certain that by 9000BC, scattered populations of hunter-gatherers lived in every corner of North America. These settlers showed remarkable adaptability to the North American environment; on the Plains, Native Americans hunted by forcing buffalo over ravines at places like Head-Smashed-In Buffalo Jump (p. 893), and in the West, Aleuts and Eskimos hunted whales and other sea mammals. By the time of European colonization, there were around a hundred major groups in nine cultural areas of North America.

EUROPEAN EXPLORATION AND COLONIZATION

The date of the first European exploration of North America is similarly disputed. The earliest Europeans to alight upon the "New World" were likely sea voyagers blown off course by storms. Two tales record the first deliberate explorations of North America; *The Saga of the Greenlanders* and *The Saga of Erik the Red* describe the travels of Icelanders who sailed to Greenland, and possibly as far south as northern New England, in 982AD. Northern Newfoundland was discovered and settled by the Vikings around the same time. But the most lasting "discovery" of the Americas occurred in 1492. Christopher Columbus found his voyage to the east blocked by Hispaniola in the Caribbean Sea. He believed he had reached the spice islands of the East Indies, and erroneously dubbed the inhabitants "Indians." Columbus's arrival launched one of the greatest cultural clashes in human history, a clash in which the Native Americans lost the ways of life they had developed.

Many Europeans came to the Americas in search of gold and silver; most were unsuccessful, but European colonization persisted. The Spanish boasted the most extensive American empire, based in South America but eventually spreading north into what are today New Mexico, Arizona, and Florida. St. Augustine (p. 323), founded in Florida in 1565, was the first permanent European settlement in the present-day United States. Meanwhile, the French and Dutch founded more modest empires to the north. It was the English, however, who most successfully settled the vast New World. After a few unsuccessful attempts, like the "lost colony" at Roanoke in North Carolina (p. 296), the English finally managed to establish a colony at Jamestown in 1607 (p. 247). The colonists struggled to survive in the New World. In 15 years, 8000 of the original 10,000 immigrants were dead. Luckily, friendly Powahatans introduced the colonists to a strain of Indian weed called tobacco, which achieved wild popularity in England. With an industry finally established, the economy improved, and the death rate fell. The Chesapeake Bay area became a land of opportunity for poor English; land was cheap, and passage to the New World could be paid for by indentured servitude. Not all labor was provided by indentured servants, however; the first African slaves were imported to Jamestown in 1619, and the slave trade became truly profitable in the later 17th century.

Not all English colonists sought wealth; many groups came to escape religious persecution, including the English Puritans. Finding life intolerable under the Stuart reign, they sought to realize their hopes for a godly community in the New World. In 1620, they landed in Provincetown (p. 113) (*not* Plymouth Rock, p. 109) in what is now Massachusetts. Native Americans helped them to survive in a harsh land and inspired one of the most treasured holidays in modern American culture, Thanksgiving. Though Britain's Empire grew to encompass 13 colonies along the eastern seaboard, the New England Puritans exerted a strong political and cultural influence until well after the Revolution.

CONSOLIDATION AND REVOLUTION

Throughout the first half of the 18th century, the English colonies expanded as people moved west into unsettled regions searching for more arable land. Valleys were settled, fields plowed, and babies born. A quarter-million settlers had grown into 2¼ million by 1775. The British colonies experienced growing pains as the French attempted to expand their nearby empire. Several military clashes resulted; the greatest of these encounters was the Seven Years War, known in the U.S. as the French and Indian War. From 1756 to 1763, English colonists and British troops fought the French and their Native American allies. The Native Americans fought with the French in return for their aid in inter-tribal conflicts. The British emerged victorious, and the 1763 Peace of Paris ceded French Canada to King George III, securing the colonies' boundaries from French incursion.

Enormous debts accompanied Britain's victory. Determined to make the colonists help pay the debts incurred in assuring their safety, the British government levied a number of taxes in the 1760s and early 1770s. The taxes were very unpopular; two of the most hated were the Stamp Act, which placed a tax on paper products and documents, and the tax on tea. The colonists felt they had a right to participate in decisions affecting their welfare, as they had grown accustomed to participating in colonial government, and they vigorously protested "taxation without representation." The British government repealed the Stamp Act in 1766, only to impose the Townshend Duties, tariffs on imported goods, a year later. Agitation over the taxes brought about the Boston Massacre in 1770 (p. 93). The Townshend Act was repealed, except for the tax on tea. The colonists threw a party to protest the tea tax—the Boston Tea Party in December of 1774—during which a group of colonists dressed as Native Americans dumped several shiploads of English tea into Boston Harbor. The British response, dubbed the Intolerable Acts, was swift and harsh. Boston was effectively placed under siege and filled to the brim with red-coated British soldiers. Armed rebellion ensued. On July 4, 1776, the Continental Congress formally issued the *Declaration of Independence,* announcing the thirteen colonies' desire to be free of British rule. Initially a guerilla army composed of home-spun militia known as Minutemen, the Continental forces eventually grew into an effective army under the leadership of George Washington. Despite many setbacks, the Continental forces prevailed, sealing their victory by vanquishing British General Lord Cornwallis at Yorktown, Virginia (p. 248) in 1781 with the help of the French fleet.

Until 1787, the newly independent states were governed by a loose confederation. This government proved unstable and problematic, so a Constitutional Convention was convened in Philadelphia (p. 193) to draw up a new plan which would provide for a stronger central government and a more powerful executive. The debates of the men who worked at this convention, known as the "Founding Fathers," resulted in the world's oldest written constitution. The document divides power between three separate branches of government—legislative, executive, and judicial. A system of checks and balances safeguard each branch against domination by any other. The first ten amendments were added immediately, so that all the states would ratify the document. These additions, known as the Bill of Rights, include the rights to free speech, freedom of the press, and freedom of religion. They are inalienable and cannot be infringed upon by the government. These rights have made a powerful imprint on the American character; all Americans know that these freedoms can not be denied them. The *Constitution* is open to interpretation, and also provides for its own amendment. This flexibility is its greatest strength; the *Constitution* has changed 26 times.

During the debate over the *Constitution*, the two-party system began to develop. The Federalists thought that the government should encourage economic growth by providing aid to capitalists. Their opposition, the Jeffersonians, believed that government should not interfere in economic matters, creating a truly free market. Over the years, the names of the parties have changed (they are now the Republicans and Democrats), but the issues are often the same.

ONWARD AND OUTWARD: MANIFEST DESTINY

With the original thirteen states under stable federal rule, America began to expand westward. In 1803, President Thomas Jefferson purchased the Louisiana Territory (¼ of the present-day United States) from Napoleon for less than 3¢ an acre. Curious about what lay in this tract and eager to tap the northwest fur trade, Jefferson sent explorers Meriwether Lewis and William Clark to chart the region. With the aid of a Native American woman called Sacajawea, they reached Seaside, Oregon in October, 1805. The work of Lewis and Clark strengthened American claims to the Oregon country, also claimed by Britain and Spain.

After the War of 1812 (a war over trade with Great Britain), the westward movement gained momentum. Manifest Destiny, a belief that the United States was destined by God to rule the continent, captured the ideological imagination of the era. Droves of people moved west in search of cheap, fertile land, and a new life. America's annexation of Texas led Mexico to declare war in 1846. After American forces were cut down at the Alamo (p. 531), the war gained a rallying cry and strength of purpose. The U.S. won in 1848, forcing Mexico to cede most of the southwest and California; $15 million bought 1 million square mi. The money quickly paid large dividends; settlers discovered gold in the California hills, and the gold rush was on.

White settlers continued moving west, requisitioning land rapidly. The Homestead Act of 1862, which distributed tracts of government land to those who would develop and live on that land, prompted the cultivation of the Great Plains. This large-scale settlement led to bloody battles with the Native Americans who had long inhabited these lands. Much of the legend of the Wild West revolves around stories of brave white settlers and stoic cowboys fending off attacks by Indians. These stories are largely distortions, created to justify the actions of the government in exploiting and displacing Native Americans. Nevertheless, expansion into wild frontier territory retains a significant place in America's self-image.

"A HOUSE DIVIDED"—THE CIVIL WAR

It became increasingly difficult for the United States to ease the tensions created by the existence of slavery within its borders. Although the *Declaration of Independence* nobly asserted that "all men are created equal," the *Constitution* allowed the slave trade to continue unrestricted for several years. Cultural, economic, and political differences divided North and South; slavery remained the basis of Southern agriculture, while the industrialized North was largely weaned from its dependence on slave labor by the mid-18th century. Compromises made while drawing up the *Constitution* were strained by westward expansion. The growing nation had to decide whether new territories would become free or slave states. The nation tried to work out its difficulties in laws like the Missouri Compromise of 1821, which legislated that all states north of latitude 36° 34' would be admitted to the Union as free states, except Missouri. Unfortunately, many did not want to compromise.

The 1860 election of Abraham Lincoln, who did not support the extension of slavery into the territories, pushed the southern states over the edge. South Carolina went first, seceding in late 1860. Twelve states (AL, AR, FL, GA, KY, LA, MS, MO, NC, TN, TX, and VA) followed in 1861. These states formed a Confederacy allowing greater autonomy and the freedom to pursue their agrarian, slave-based economy. For four years, the country endured a savage and bloody war, fought by the North to restore the Union, and by the South to be free of the North. The Civil War claimed more lives than any other war in U.S. history. Finally, the North's greater industrialization and population overcame the South, and on April 9, 1865, General Robert E. Lee, the commander of the southern army, surrendered to General Ulysses S. Grant, leader of the northern forces, at Appomatox Court House, Virginia. Lincoln had led the North to victory, but the price was high. He was assassinated on April 14 by a southern sympathizer. His legacy, the Thirteenth Amendment, ended slavery in 1865, but the fight for black equality is still being fought.

INDUSTRIALIZATION AND WORLD WAR I

The period after the war brought Reconstruction to the South, and Industrial Revolution to the North. For twelve years, troops were stationed in the South to suppress violence, regulate elections, and impose penalties for violation of federal law. As the South strained under the punishment inflicted by the North, the economy in the North flourished. Rapid investment by captains of industry such as George Vanderbilt, Andrew Carnegie, and John D. Rockefeller boosted the American economy and increased American influence abroad. This industrial expansion occurred at great cost to workers and farmers, and trade unions grew in response to poor working conditions and low wages. The 19th-century form of unabashed "free market" capitalism soon began to collapse under its own weight, as witnessed by the recessions of the 1890s and the 1930s. The superficial high which the U.S. rode in the decades leading up to the turn of the century is known as the Gilded Age.

Politically, the United States was coming of age. Through victory in the Spanish-American War in 1898, the United States acquired colonies in the Philippines, Puerto Rico, and Cuba. The imperial spirit was embodied in President Theodore Roosevelt, who assumed the office upon the assassination of President McKinley in 1901. Roosevelt also embraced another dominant turn-of-the century phenomenon: progressivism, a movement that sought to create a more just social order by attacking the corruption and monopolistic practices of big business. The efforts of the progressives resulted in such accomplishments as an increase in public works spending, the 1906 Pure Food and Drug Act, and the direct election of U.S. senators. These trends brought Democrat Woodrow Wilson to the White House in 1912. Wilson passed an economic reform program that was highlighted by the Clayton Anti-Trust Act and the establishment of the first peacetime income tax in American history. Wilson also created the National Park Service (p. 55) to protect the 40 national parks and monuments already in existence, and those to yet to be created.

The relative stability of the early years of the century was crushed beneath the steel weight of World War I. President Wilson overcame a strong isolationist sentiment among the people, and the United States eventually saw tardy but serious involvement in the war. When victory was won, Wilson was instrumental in drafting the peace, which included creation of the League of Nations, a forerunner of the United Nations. Domestic opposition prevented the U.S. from joining, and the League was a flop. Onerous terms imposed on Germany by the Versailles Treaty, which ended the war, would bear bitter fruit in the coming decades.

ROARING 20S, GREAT DEPRESSION, AND WORLD WAR II

Women were granted the right to vote in 1920 by the 19th Amendment to the *Constitution* and the 18th Amendment brought the prohibition of alcohol, a miserable failure of an amendment, introduced at a time when the nation wanted to celebrate its prosperity. Pro-business, Republican policies allowed American business to grow. President Calvin Coolidge proclaimed that the "business of America is business," and proceeded to assume an arch-indifference towards the operation of the economy. A general (if false) prosperity settled in and fueled an unprecedented fit of conspicuous consumption. The economic euphoria of the "Roaring 20s," however, was largely supported by overextended credit. The façade came tumbling down on Black Thursday, October 24, 1929, when the New York Stock Exchange crashed to the ground and launched the Great Depression. America suffered another harsh blow as the long-abused soil of the Great Plains literally blew away in one of the worst droughts in history, replacing the "bread basket" with a "dust bowl," and ruining thousands of farmers.

Under the firm hand of the reformer President Franklin D. Roosevelt, the United States began a decade-long recovery. His New Deal program created work for hundreds of thousands, building monuments, bridges, and parks with public funds through the Works Progress Administration (WPA). Farm prices were supported, plantings were centrally planned, and financial institutions (including the stock market) were put under federal jurisdiction. Agencies like the Tennessee Valley Authority supplied power to entire regions while private utility monopolies were broken up and placed under public regulation. Minimum wages were set, child labor was prohibited, and the Social Security Act brought the United States somewhat reluctantly into the era of the welfare state.

A crisis in foreign affairs gripped the national attention late in the decade. Hitler and his Nazi regime horrified the West; territorial gluttony in central Europe finally launched the second global war of the century. The Japanese attack on Pearl Harbor, Hawaii (p. 811) on December 7, 1941, a "day that will live in infamy" in the words of Roosevelt, unified the American people behind the allied cause. America entered World War II. The productive capacity of the nation's war-time economy was critical in assuring allied victory over the Axis powers. During the war, Hitler's regime systematically brutalized and exterminated most of the Jewish, gay, and mentally ill population of Germany and Poland. Many of those who survived later immigrated to the U.S. The war ended in Europe in April of 1945, when Hitler committed suicide. The war in the Pacific continued until August, when the United States dropped two newly developed nuclear bombs on Japan, killing 80,000 civilians. The war will always be remembered for the Holocaust, which killed 11 million Jews and "others," and for the United States' terrifying use of nuclear power.

COLD WAR AND THE NEW FRONTIER

Spared the war-time devastation of Europe and East Asia, the U.S. economy boomed in the post-war era, solidifying the status of the United States as the world's foremost economic and military power. But an ideological polarity was developing between America and the other nuclear power, the Soviet Union. Fears of Soviet expansion led to the Red Scare of the 1950s. Congressional committees saw communists everywhere; thousands of civil servants, writers, actors, and academics were blacklisted, and two American citizens, the Rosenbergs, were tried and sentenced to death during this time for allegedly selling nuclear secrets to the Soviets. Suspicion of communism had grown in the U.S. since the Russian Revolution in 1917, but the feverish intensity it gained during the Cold War ultimately led to American military involvement in the Korean and Vietnam Wars. Tensions between the U.S. and the USSR reached their peak during the Cuban Missile Crisis of 1962. President John Kennedy and Nikita Khrushchev brought the world to the brink of nuclear war in a showdown over the deployment of Soviet nuclear missiles in Cuba.

Despite the nuclear shadow, the early 1960s were characterized domestically by an optimism embodied in the President himself. Kennedy's Peace Corps, NASA's program to place Americans on the moon, and the "New Frontier" to eliminate poverty and racism all contributed to what many see as the nation's last period of large-scale activism. As the Vietnam conflict escalated, optimism waned; in 1963, optimism disappeared with Kennedy's assassination in Dallas (p. 516). As the 60s progressed, social unrest increased. The nation witnessed public protests against involvement in Vietnam and against the continuing discrimination against African-Americans. Dr. Martin Luther King, Jr. led peaceful demonstrations, marches, and sit-ins for civil rights. Unfortunately, these were often met with violence; civil rights activists were drenched with fire hoses, arrested, and sometimes even killed. Dr. King himself was assassinated in Memphis (p. 284) in 1968.

The second wave of the women's movement accompanied the civil rights movement. Sparked by Betty Friedan's landmark book, *The Feminine Mystique,* American women sought to change the delineation between men's and women's roles in society, demanding access to male-dominated professions and equal pay. The sexual revolution, fueled by the development of the birth control pill, brought a woman's right to choose to the forefront of national debate; the 1973 Supreme Court decision *Roe v. Wade* legalized abortion and began a battle between abortion opponents and pro-choice advocates that divides the nation today.

RECENT TIMES

In 1980, actor and former California governor Ronald Reagan was elected to the White House on a tidal wave of conservatism, and a materialistic ethic gripped the nation. College campuses became quieter and more conservative as graduates flocked to Wall Street to become investment bankers. Summing up the national mood, movie character Gordon Gekko (from Oliver Stone's *Wall Street*) declared "greed is good." Though the decade's conservatives did embrace certain right-wing social goals such as prayer in schools and the campaign against abortion, the Reagan Revolution was essentially economic. Reaganomics gave tax breaks to big business and the rich, spurred short term consumption, de-regulated Savings and Loans, and laid the ground work for economic disaster in the 1990s.

Today, America is dealing with a massive deficit, an insufficient education system, a crumbling infrastructure, and issues such as abortion, AIDS, gay rights, and racism. Hoping for change, Americans elected Democrat Bill Clinton to the presidency in 1992. The youngest elected president in the United States' history, Clinton promised a new era of government activism after years of laissez-faire rule. The promise of universal health care, the most ambitious of Clinton's policy goals, best captured the new attitude, but by 1995 health care legislation was dead. Clinton has had similar trouble achieving many of his goals.

■■■ GOVERNMENT AND POLITICS

The U.S. federal government has three branches, the executive, the legislative and the judicial. The executive branch is headed by the president and vice-president, who are elected every four years. The executive branch administers many federal agencies, which fall under the jurisdiction of 13 departments of the government. The heads of these 13 departments are known as the Cabinet. They aid the president in policy decisions.

The legislative branch has two arms, the House of Representatives and the Senate. In the House of Representatives, each state is allocated a number of seats proportional to its population. In the Senate, each state has two representatives. Both Senators and Representatives are directly elected by the people. Budget appropriations originate in the House of Representatives, but the Senate must concur. The Senate also approves presidential appointees and treaties with foreign governments.

The judicial branch consists of the Supreme Court of the United States and 90 district courts. The Supreme Court has nine justices, who are appointed to life terms by the President. These courts consider violations of federal law and certain civil cases. Decisions of the district courts may be appealed to one of the 12 appellate courts. Appellate court decisions may be appealed to the Supreme Court. In the U.S., the accused is innocent until proven guilty.

Elected representatives in the U.S. are usually members of the Republican or Democratic parties. The Republicans are conservative, or right-wing, while the Democrats are liberal, or to the left of the political spectrum. There are other small parties in the U.S., and it is also possible to run as an independent. H. Ross Perot recently made a run at the Presidency as an independent candidate. Politics in the U.S., however, have historically been dominated by the two parties.

■■■ ARCHITECTURE

Early settlers brought their native architectures to the Americas. Dutch, English, Spanish, and French influence meshed with native knowledge to shape the American landscape. The John Ward House in Salem (p. 107), has small windows and steep-pitched roofs that reflect the English medieval heritage prevalent in New England. In St. Augustine, Florida, the Castillo de San Marcos (p. 323) demonstrates traditional Spanish medieval building. The Spanish tradition became intertwined with that of the native pueblo in the southwest; for example, the Palace of the Governors in Santa Fe (p. 661) combines European order with native forms. The most important architectural movement of the early 18th century was Neoclassicism. Two of the best examples of this style are Monticello (p. 252), and the University of Virginia (p. 252), both designed by Thomas Jefferson. Many plantation homes in the south were built along these stylistic lines.

The 19th century was dominated by a romantic and eclectic architecture that drew from a spectrum of styles. In the middle of the century McKim, Mead, and White became the most important architectural firm in the U.S. These men brought the ideas of the Ecole des Beaux-Arts in Paris to the United States and applied classical style to the large buildings of the emerging American megalopolis. Their work can be seen at the Boston Public Library (p. 101) and the J. Pierpont Morgan Library in New York City (p. 154). At the same time, Frederick Law Olmstead achieved equivalent stature in landscape architecture. He sculpted New York's Central Park (p. 157) and the grounds of the Biltmore estate in Asheville, North Carolina (p. 295).

Louis Sullivan, the first modern architect, gave new form to the tall building in the late 19th century in Chicago (p. 423). Frank Lloyd Wright, Sullivan's student, was more interested in the home. His Fallingwater (p. 210) demonstrates his interest in integrating landscape and house. In the 1930s, skyscrapers rose to new heights; the Empire State Building (p. 154) grew thousands of feet into the sky. Mies van der Rohe next innovated the skyscraper by revealing the skeleton of steel and concrete. His Seagram Building in New York City (p. 156; built in the 1950s) is an elegant example. Eero Saarinen was a member of van der Rohe's school, but branched off to develop his own style, designing the TWA terminal at Kennedy Airport (p. 135). The most famous living American architect is I.M. Pei. His work includes the East Building of the National Gallery of Art (p. 231). A recent addition to the ranks of internationally renowned American architects is Frank Gehry; check out his copper-clad art center at the University of Toledo.

■■■ THE ARTS

LITERATURE

The first best-seller printed in America the *Bay Psalm Book,* was published in Cambridge in 1640. This, like much of the literature read and published in 17th- and 18th-century America, was religious in nature. The early 1800s saw the rise of works that told the tale of the strong, yet innocent American individual: Herman Melville's *Moby Dick,* Walt Whitman's *Leaves of Grass,* and Nathaniel Hawthorne's *Scarlet Letter* all revolved around characters made unique by the American experience. These works were contemporary to lyrical philosophical essays like Henry David Thoreau's *Walden* (written at Walden Pond, p. 108) and Ralph Waldo Emerson's *Self-Reliance*. While New England writers tried to portray a culture distinct from that of their European forebears, Midwestern humorists attempted to define the American character with larger-than-life tall tales set in the landscapes of the new continent. The most sophisticated practitioner of this genre was Mark Twain (who lived as a boy in Hannibal, Missouri, p. 501). His works, including the *Adventures of Huckleberry Finn,* explored coming-of-age on the Mississippi River. The pioneers also traveled farther west; authors like Willa Cather captured the stark beauty of the Plains.

The Industrial Revolution inspired works that portrayed the declining morals of society. Stephen Crane's *Maggie: A Girl of the Streets* captured the life of the tenement dwellers in the expanding cities, while Upton Sinclair's *The Jungle* portrayed the abominable conditions in the factories. The novels of Henry James and Edith Wharton showed how the other half lived, portraying the intricate mannerisms of late 19th century high society.

The early 20th century marked a reflective, self-centered movement in American literature. F. Scott Fitzgerald's works portray many restless individuals, financially secure, but empty inside. Many writers were caught in the tumult of the new century; some moved abroad in search of inner peace. This "lost generation" included Ernest Hemingway, William Faulkner, Eudora Welty, T.S. Eliot, Ezra Pound, Robert Frost, and Wallace Stevens. The 1920s also saw an important rise in black literature. Prefigured by the narratives of Fredrick Douglass, W.E.B. DuBois, and Booker T. Washington, the "Harlem Renaissance" matched the excitement of the Jazz Age with the works of Langston Hughes, Jean Toomer, and Zora Neale Hurston.

The Beatniks of the 50s, spearheaded by cult heroes Jack Kerouac and Allen Ginsberg, lived wildly through postwar America's dull conformity—Kerouac's *On the Road* (1955), though dated, nonetheless makes a fine companion to this guidebook for the contemporary road scholar.

Some of the greatest modern American novels have examined the tensions in American society. Books such as Ralph Ellison's *Invisible Man,* Richard Wright's *Black Boy,* Toni Morrison's *Beloved,* and Oliver LaFarge's portrayal of a Navajo youth, *Laughin' Boy,* all reflect this ongoing examination.

Please refer to the regional introductions for classics and newcomers associated with that region.

MUSIC

Although America is best known for its contribution to popular music—country, bluegrass, big band, jazz, blues, rock 'n roll, and rap—America has also nurtured classical composers of note, as well as some truly great classical musicians and ensembles. Leonard Bernstein, George Gershwin, Aaron Copland, and Charles Ives have made their marks on the international score, blending classical forms and American popular genres. Yo-Yo Ma, Joshua Bell, and Robert Levin are world-recognized players. Finally, the orchestras in most major cities range from excellent to world-renowned. The San Francisco Symphony, the New York Philharmonic, and the Philadelphia Orchestra (p. 201) are some of the best.

While classical music lives in the U.S., popular music flourishes. Jazz has been called America's classical music. The blues, ragtime, and military brass bands combined in New Orleans (p. 369) to create the music we call jazz. This music of the American soul has been sounded by greats like Louis Armstrong, Ella Fitzgerald, Miles Davis, Billie Holiday, Charlie Parker, John Coltrane, and Wynton Marsalis, to name a few. A baby of the blues, rock n' roll produced many of America's music icons—first Chubby Checker and Jerry Lee Lewis, and eventually the King of Rock, Elvis Presley (see Graceland, p. 283). Now, rock spans from punk (The Ramones) to grunge (Nirvana) to pop (Madonna and Michael Jackson).

FILM

American film has come a long way since viewers were first amazed by Thomas Edison's 30-second film of a galloping horse. Edison's technology was first used in peep shows, but the medium quickly developed more lofty goals. Today's movies are works of art (some more engaging than others), crafted by directors and actors, sometimes filled with stunning computer-generated special effects. The influence of the American movie industry is undisputed. Celebrated movies of each genre include: **sci-fi** (*Star Wars, Alien*), **adventure** (*Jurassic Park, Raiders of the Lost Ark*), **thriller** (*Psycho, Silence of the Lambs*), **drama** (*Casablanca, Citizen Kane*), **horror** (*Texas Chainsaw Massacre, Friday the 13th*), **cult** (*Easy Rider, The Rocky Horror Picture Show*), and the "most American of them all," the **western** (*True Grit, Unforgiven*).

VISUAL ART

The works of artists in the 19th century such as Thomas Cole and Winslow Homer expressed the beauty and power of the American continent. In the early twentieth century, Edward Hopper and Thomas Hart Benton explored the innocence and mythic values of the United States during its emergence as a superpower. The Abstract Expressionism of Arshile Gorky and Jackson Pollock displays both the swaggering confidence and frenetic insecurity of cold-war America. Pop Art, created by Jasper Johns, Robert Rauschenberg, Roy Lichtenstein, and Andy Warhol, satirizes the icons of American life and pop culture.

Since the 1890s, when Eastman-Kodak revolutionized the camera, photography has also provided a medium for American artists. Stieglitz's views of the city began a movement which realized the potential for art in a new method of framing the physical world. Photography became an excellent medium for artists concerned with social conditions. The Farm Security Administration (FSA), part of the WPA, paid photographers to document the Great Depression. Dorothea Lange and Walker Evans took photos which transcended this documentary purpose and can only be called art. American photographers have also used their medium to capture the beauty of the natural environment. Ansel Adams revealed the beauty of the National Parks with his black and white photographs, now immortalized in every poster store in America. Abstraction and surrealism have also worked their way into photography; Diane Arbus took pictures of "freaks," playing on the interaction of normality and abnormality to make her art. Robert Mapplethorpe framed nudes and flowers to create abstract forms.

Mapplethorpe's work also played with social conventions, especially the perceptions and manifestations of sexuality. His work often involves nudity and homoerotic imagery. When some Congressional members learned an exhibit of Mapplethorpe's work had been funded in part by the National Endowment for the Arts (NEA), a furor ensued, causing the Corcoran Gallery in Washington, DC (p. 234) to withdraw the exhibit from its gallery. Protesters had the last laugh, as they projected Mapplethorpe's photos on the side of the building, but the NEA has remained controversial, and with the new Republican Congress, faces serious budget cuts.

■■■ THE MEDIA

TELEVISION

There are television sets in almost 98% of U.S. homes, and the competition between the four national networks **(ABC, CBS, NBC,** and **Fox)** and cable television has led to an exponential growth in TV culture over the last few years. During prime time (8-11pm EST) you can find the most popular shows: the drama *ER,* the farcical yet popular *Melrose Place,* and *The Simpsons,* the wittiest animation ever to leave Springfield. On cable you'll discover around-the-clock channels offering news, sports, movies, kids' shows, or weather. Then there's **MTV,** whose dazzling display of calculatedly random visceral images affords a glimpse into the psyche of the North American under-30 set.

Most Americans watch television to find out what's happening in the news. The major networks all present "hard" news shows in the morning and evening hours. They also produce less serious shows, often referred to as "tabloid TV" (for their resemblance to the sensational newspapers of the same name). Twenty-four hour news coverage is available on **CNN,** a cable station. All the networks have politically moderate to liberal coverage. Perhaps the best, if underused, news programs in the U.S. are those on public television, or **PBS.** These programs are funded by viewer contributions and have no commercials (advertisements).

PRINT MEDIA

The most influential newspapers in the U.S. are the *New York Times, The Washington Post,* and the *Los Angeles Times.* These publications are all liberal in slant, and have wide distributions throughout the U.S. *The Christian Science Monitor* and the *Wall Street Journal* are well-respected conservative publications.

There are three major weekly newsmagazines. Liberal readers prefer *Time,* while conservatives favor *U.S. News & World Report.* A more moderate choice is *Newsweek.* Other widely-read magazines in the U.S. include *People,* which chronicles American gossip, *Spin,* focusing on the music industry, and the *New Yorker,* which combines New York happenings with short stories and essays on current events. Most European fashion magazines have an American counterpart. There are hundreds of other magazines aimed at audiences ranging from computer junkies to body builders. Find a good bookstore or newsstand and check them out.

■■■ THIS YEAR'S NEWS

Perhaps the most portentous change for American politics in 1995 was the takeover (in late 1994) of the American Congress by the Republican party. The Congress had been a Democratic stronghold since mid-century, but backlash from Clinton's inability to gain consensus for any major pieces of legislation drove voters away from the status quo, and a new leadership was born. Newt Gingrich, Speaker of the House, and spokesman for the "New Republicans," has just published a book, *To Renew America.* He originally accepted a $4.5 million advance for the book, although he later rescinded, and took a token $1 advance. He is currently under investigation by the House Ethics Committee due to the commission fiasco.

The American people experienced a great tragedy in 1995, with the bombing of the federal building in Oklahoma City (p. 509) on April 19, 1995. At this time three people have been charged with involvement in the crime.

For a year, the trial of O.J. Simpson for his alleged role in the murder of his ex-wife Nicole Brown and her companion Ron Goldman dominated the media, airing daily on television. On October 3, 1995, a jury acquitted O.J. on all counts. The tax-payers of Los Angeles paid more than $9 million for the trial.

On the lighter side, the entertainment industry proved that it has its own royalty, when the King of Rock's daughter, Lisa Marie Presley, married Michael Jackson, the King of Pop.

NEW ENGLAND

With a centuries-old commitment to education and an unending fascination with government, New England has counted itself an intellectual and political center for the nation since before the States were even United. Students and scholars from across the country funnel into New England's colleges each fall, and town meetings in many rural villages still evoke the feeling of public government which inspired the American colonists to create a nation so many years ago. The region supports countless historical attractions which commemorate every step in the formation of this nation as it broke with the old world.

Geographically, the region seems an unlikely cradle for any sort of civilization. Mountains wrinkle the land, while the soil at their feet lies barren. Mark Twain once said that if you don't like the weather in New England, you should wait 15 minutes; unpredictable at best, the region's climate can be particularly dismal in November, when winds blow in off the rocky shores bringing the harsh, wet winter, which lasts through to March. Be warned that everything from rivers to state campgrounds to tourist attractions may slow down or freeze up during these months.

Though the climate gave early settlers a tough time, today's visitors find adventure in the region's rough edges. New England's dramatic, salty coastline calls urbanites to spend their summers on the sand; the slopes of the Green and White Mountains, with their many rivers and lakes, inspire skiers, hikers, cyclists, and canoers. In the fall, the nation's most brilliant foliage bleeds and burns, transforming the entire region into a giant kaleidoscope.

New England Notes

Authors: Louisa May Alcott, Henry Adams, Emily Dickinson, Ralph W. Emerson, Robert Frost, Nathaniel Hawthorne, Henry James, Herman Melville, Henry D. Thoreau, John Updike, Thornton Wilder.
Artists: Winslow Homer, Mary Cassatt, Childe Hassan, Grandma Moses, John Singer Sargent, Andrew Wyeth, James Wilder.
Cuisine: Seafood, clam chowder, Boston baked beans, Yankee pot roast, oysters, lobsters, clambakes, cheddar cheese soup, maple syrup, pumpkin pie, Indian pudding, Maine blueberries, Ben & Jerry's.
Microbreweries: New England Brewing Co., New Haven, Acadia, Andrew's, Bar Harbor Brewing, D.L. Geary, Boston Beer Co., Ipswich, Massachusetts Bay, Middlesex, Old Harbor, Ould Newbury, Frank Jones, Catamount, Otter Creek, The Mountain Brewers.
Native Americans: Micmac, Massachusett, Penobscot, Abnaki, Pequot, Shamut, Iroquois.
Music: Boston Symphony Orchestra, Boston Pops, Boston, Aerosmith, Mighty Mighty Bosstones, Tracy Chapman.
Film and TV: *Love Story, Newhart, Wings.*
Climate: Cold.
Geography: Rocky.

Maine

Nearly a thousand years ago, Leif Ericson and his band of Viking explorers set foot on the coasts of Maine. Moose roamed as kings of the sprawling evergreen wilderness; the cry of the Maine coon cat echoed through towering mountains, and countless lobsters crawled in the ocean deep. A millennium has not changed much. Forests still cover nearly 90% of the land, an area larger than the entire neat stack of New England states below, and the inner reaches of the state stretch on for mile after uninhabited mile; the more populated shore areas embrace a harsh and jagged coastline. Rather than trying to conquer the wilderness like the urbanites to the south, the deeply independent Maine "Downeaster" has adapted to this rough wilderness with rugged pragmatism. The fierce beauty of the place has inspired such writers as Stephen King, Henry Wadsworth Longfellow, and Edna St. Vincent Millay, and beckons all to "Vacationland."

PRACTICAL INFORMATION

Capital: Augusta.

Maine Publicity Bureau: 325B Water St., Halowell (623-0363 or 800-533-9595). Send mail to P.O. Box 2300, Halowell 04347. **Bureau of Parks and Recreation,** State House Station #22 (1st floor Harlow Bldg.), Augusta 04333 (287-3821). **Maine Forest Service,** Bureau of Forestry, State House Station #22 (2nd floor Harlow Bldg.), Augusta 04333 (287-2791). All agencies open Mon.-Fri. 8am-5pm.

Time Zone: Eastern. **Postal Abbreviation:** ME

Sales Tax: 6%.

MAINE COAST

As the bird flies, the length of the Maine coast from Kittery to Lubec measures 228 mi., but if untangled, all of the convoluted inlets and rocky promontories would stretch out to a whopping 3478 mi. Fishing, the earliest business here, was later augmented by a vigorous shipbuilding industry; both traditions are still visible today. Unfortunately, rampant overfishing has catastrophically depleted the North Atlantic cod population and left fishermen wondering about the future of their livelihood. Lobsters are still plentiful, however, and lobster pounds are ubiquitous in coastal Maine; stop under one of the innumerable makeshift red wooden lobster signs which speckle the roadsides, set yourself down on a gray wooden bench and chow, but keep in mind that lobsters are tastiest before July, when most start to molt. Also be forewarned that lobster-poaching is treated seriously here; the color codings and designs on the buoy markers are as distinct as a cattle rancher's brand and serve the same purpose.

U.S. 1 hugs the coastline and strings the port towns together. Lesser roads and small ferry lines connect the remote villages and offshore islands. The best place for info is the **Maine Information Center** (439-1319), in Kittery, 3 mi. north of the Maine-New Hampshire bridge (open daily 8am-6pm; mid-Oct.-June daily 9am-5pm). **Greyhound** (800-231-2222) serves points between Portland and Bangor along I-95, the coastal town of Brunswick, and connecting routes to Boston. Reaching most coastal points of interest is virtually impossible by bus; a car or bike is necessary.

■■■ SOUTH OF PORTLAND

When the weather allows, biking may be the best way to travel Maine's rocky shores and spare yourself the aggravation of thick summer traffic. In **Biddeford,** 17 mi. south of Portland on U.S. 1, **Quinn's Bike and Fitness,** 140 U.S. 1, a.k.a. Elm St. (284-4632), rents 10-, 5-, and 3-speed bikes. ($10 per day, $30 per week, with $20 deposit; $1.25 lock rental; $6 helmet. Open Mon.-Thurs. and Sat. 9am-5:30pm, Fri. 9am-8pm.) You can get a copy of *25 Bicycle Tours in Maine* ($10) from the Portland Chamber of Commerce (see below).

A few minutes south on U.S. 1, you'll find the town of **Kennebunk,** and, several miles east on Rte. 35, its coastal counterpart **Kennebunkport.** If you want to bypass

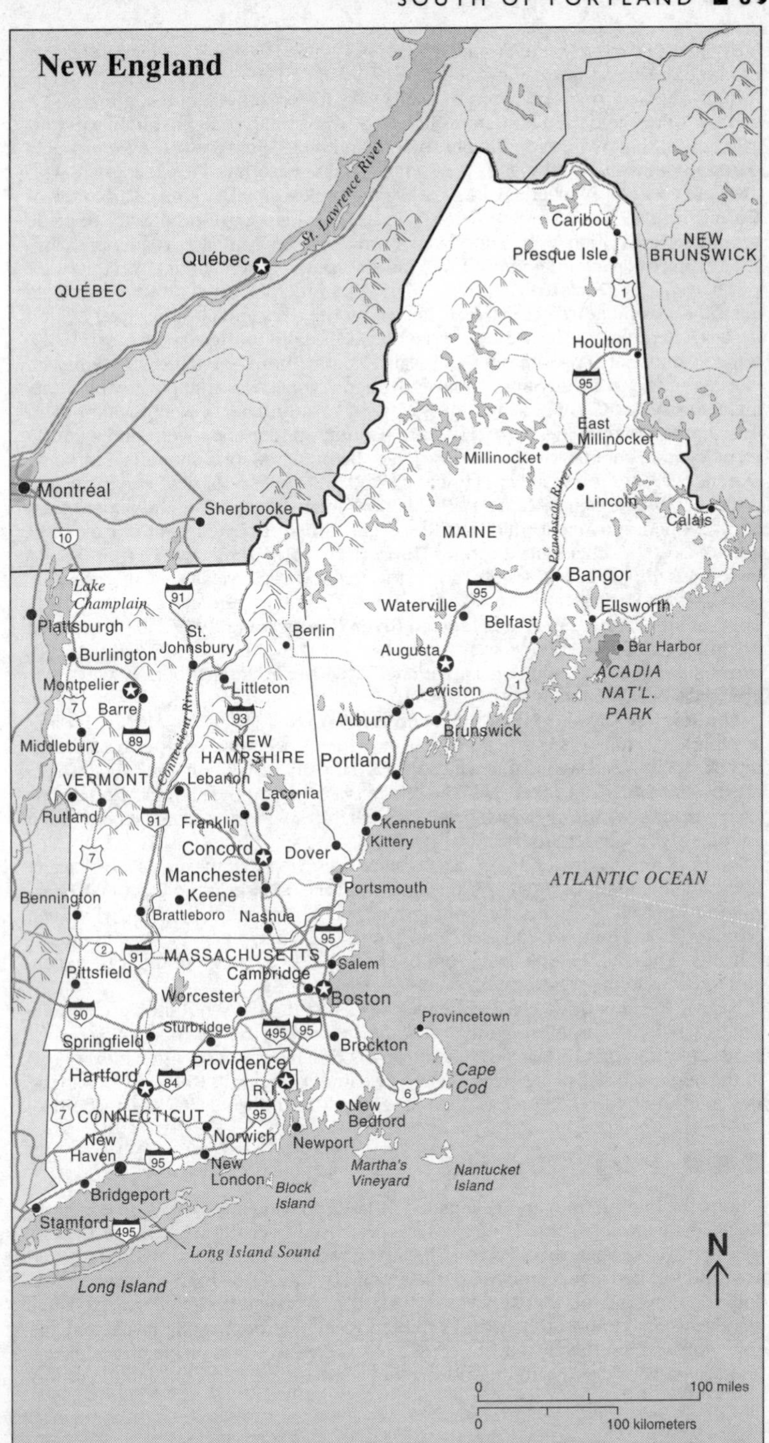
New England
St. Lawrence River
Québec
QUÉBEC
Montréal
Sherbrooke
NEW BRUNSWICK
Caribou
Presque Isle
Houlton
East Millinocket
Millinocket
Lincoln
Calais
MAINE
Penobscot River
Bangor
Ellsworth
Bar Harbor
ACADIA NAT'L. PARK
Belfast
Waterville
Augusta
Lewiston
Auburn
Brunswick
Portland
Kennebunk
Kittery
Dover
Portsmouth
Berlin
Littleton
NEW HAMPSHIRE
Laconia
Lebanon
Franklin
Concord
Manchester
Keene
Nashua
Lake Champlain
Plattsburgh
Burlington
St. Johnsbury
Montpelier
Barre
Middlebury
VERMONT
Connecticut River
Rutland
Bennington
Brattleboro
MASSACHUSETTS
Pittsfield
Cambridge
Salem
Boston
Worcester
Sturbridge
Springfield
Provincetown
Brockton
Cape Cod
Providence
R.I.
Hartford
CONNECTICUT
New Bedford
Norwich
Newport
New Haven
New London
Martha's Vineyard
Nantucket Island
Block Island
Bridgeport
Stamford
Long Island Sound
Long Island
ATLANTIC OCEAN
N
0
100 miles
0
100 kilometers

busy U.S. 1, take the Maine Turnpike south of Portland to exit 3, then take Fletcher St. east into Kennebunk.

Both of these towns are popular hideaways for wealthy authors and artists. A number of rare and used bookstores lines U.S. 1 just south of Kennebunk, while art galleries fill the town itself. The blue-blood (and blue-haired) resort of Kennebunkport grew reluctantly famous as the summer home of former President Bush, who owns an estate on Walker's Point. The **Kennebunk-Kennebunkport Chamber of Commerce,** 173 Port Road (967-0857), in Kennebunkport, distributes a free guide to area sights. (Open Mon.-Thurs. 9am-6pm, Fri. 9am-7pm, Sat. 10am-6pm, Sun. 11am-4pm; mid-Oct. to June, Mon.-Fri. 9am-5:30pm, weekend hours by request.)

The **Lobster Deck Restaurant** (967-5535), formerly located on Rt. 9 overlooking the Kennebunk Harbor, recently moved off the deck and into the water behind Bartley's Restaurant. This floating restaurant dishes out lobster dinners for $10-20. (Open Memorial Day-Columbus Day daily 11am-10pm.) Spending the night will make your trip to Kennebunk significantly more expensive; avoid poverty by camping. **Salty Acres Campground** (967-8623), 4½ mi. northeast of Kennebunkport on Rte. 9, offers swimming, a grocery store, laundry, phones, showers, and a convenient location about 1 mi. from the beaches. Be prepared for a communal camping experience; sites are small and closely packed. (300 sites $15, with electricity and water $20, full hookup $22; $8 per additional adult after 2; $2 per additional child after 2; open mid-May to mid-Oct. Reservations not accepted.) For cheap, fresh greens close by, check out **Patten's Berry Farm** (967-2418), where fruit (watermelon 39¢/lb.), vegetables, milk, bottled water, and eggs are all sold at reasonable prices (from Kennebunkport, take Rte. 9 to North St.; open May-Dec. daily 8am-6pm). A little farther out is the **Mousam River Campground** (985-2507), on Alfred Rd. just west of exit 3 off I-95 in West Kennebunk (115 sites $16, $15 with AAA; RV sites $20/$19; $4 per additional adult after 2, $3 per additional person age 13-17. Free showers. Open mid-May to mid-Oct.).

The **Rachel Carson National Wildlife Refuge** (646-9226, Mon.-Fri. 8am-4:30pm), a ½-mile off U.S. 1 on Rte. 9, provides a secluded escape from tourist throngs west. A self-guided trail winds through the salt marsh home of over 200 species of shorebirds and waterfowl. The refuge is a tribute to the naturalist and author who wrote *Silent Spring,* which helped launch the environmental movement (open daily sunrise to sunset; free).

South of Kennebunk on U.S. 1 lies **Ogunquit,** the home of the area's most beautiful beach; the long, sandy strip is a definite must-see. Stop in at the **Ogunquit Information Bureau,** on the left side of the road when driving south (646-2939; open Mon.-Fri. 11am-4pm, Sat.-Sun. 9am-5pm). In the summer, a vibrant gay community inhabits Ogunquit. **Moody**, just south of Ogunquit, hosts some of the least expensive lodgings in the region.

Nearby **Perkins Cove** charms the plaid socks off the polo-shirt crowd with boutiques hawking seashell sculptures. The two **Barnacle Billy's** (646-5575) restaurants, 20 yards apart on Oar Weed Road, practice an interesting division of labor. Go to the original for lobster, especially their delicious lobster rolls ($9), and look to the newer location for a fuller menu and full service. (Both open daily 11am-9:30pm.)

■■■ PORTLAND

During the July 4th fireworks celebration of 1866, a young boy playing on Portland's wharf inadvertently started a fire, which destroyed over three-fourths of the city before it was extinguished. Portland had to be rebuilt—for the fourth time (the old Portland fort had first been razed to the ground by Indians in 1632). Today, the Victorian reconstruction that survives in what is now called the Old Port Exchange stands in stark contrast to Portland's spirited youth culture. Despite its exciting history, Portland is relatively tourist-free; as a result, the city's reasonable prices make it an ideal base for daytrips to the surrounding coastal areas. Ferries run to the nearby

Casco Bay Islands; Sebago Lake provides sunning and water skiing opportunities; and Freeport, the outlet capital of the free world, offers ample budget shopping.

PRACTICAL INFORMATION

Tourist Office: Visitor Information Bureau, 305 Commercial St. (772-5800), at the corner of Center St. Open Mon.-Fri. 8am-6pm, Sat.-Sun. 10am-3pm; Oct. 16-May 14 Mon.-Fri. 9am-5pm, Sat.-Sun. 9am-6pm.

American Express: 480 Congress St. (772-8450). Open Mon.-Fri. 8:30am-5:30pm.

Buses: Concord Trailways, 161 Marginal Way (828-1151), a 15-min. walk from downtown. Office open daily 7am-8:30pm. To: Boston (6 per day, 2hr., $15); Bangor (3 per day, 2hrs., $20). Offers discounts on roundtrip fares for college students with ID. A local Metro Bus (8) will transport you from the station to downtown, but you must call (774-0351). **Greyhound/Vermont Trailways,** 950 Congress St. (772-6587 or 800-231-2222), on the western outskirts of town. Be cautious here at night. Take the Congress St. bus (1) to downtown. Office open daily 6am-6pm. To: Boston (7 per day, 2hrs., $26); Bangor (5 per day, 2hrs., $19).

Ferries: Prince of Fundy Cruises, P.O. Box 4216, 468 Commercial St. (800-341-7540 or 800-482-0955 in ME). Ferries to Yarmouth in southern Nova Scotia leave from the Portland Marine Terminal, on Commercial St. near the Million Dollar Bridge, May-late Oct. at 9pm. June 24-Sept. 20 $77, ages 5-14 $38.50; off season $57 and $28.50. Cars $98, off season $80. Reservations required. 50% off car fare on Tues. and Wed. Stay in HI Portland and get 10% off fares. See Sights for information on ferries to the Casco Bay Islands.

Public Transportation: Metro Bus (774-0351) offers service within and beyond the downtown area. Most routes run only noon-7pm. $1, seniors and disabled 50¢, under 6 free, transfers free.

Crisis Lines: Rape Crisis, 774-3613. **Crisis Intervention Hotline,** 800-660-8500. Both operate 24 hrs.

Emergency: 911.

Portland Police: 874-8300.

Post Office: 622 Congress St. (871-8449). Open Mon.-Fri. 8:30am-5pm, Sat. 9am-noon. The 125 Forest Ave. office (871-8410) handles passports. Open Mon.-Fri. 7:30am-7pm, Sat. 7:30am-5pm. **ZIP code:** 04104.

Area Code: 207.

Downtown sits near the bay, along Congress St. between State and Franklin St. A few blocks south lies the Old Port on Commercial and Fore St. These two districts contain most of the city's sights and attractions. I-295 (off I-95) forms the western boundary of downtown.

ACCOMMODATIONS AND CAMPING

Portland has some inexpensive accommodations, but prices jump during the summer season. You can always try exit 8 off I-95, where **Super 8** (854-1881) and other budget staples (singles around $40-45) proliferate.

Portland Youth Hostel (HI-AYH), 645 Congress St. (874-3281). Centrally located in a university dorm. 48 beds in clean doubles with bath and shower. After two years of operation, the staff is still energetic and eager to please; plans include locker space for storage during lockout (11am-3pm) and efforts to make this a "green" hostel. Check-in 5pm-midnight. Check-out 11am. $14, nonmembers $17. $5 linen deposit and $10 key deposit required. Reservations recommended.

The Inn at St. John, 939 Congress St. (773-6481). Reasonable prices in a comfortable inn make for a great alternative to the hostel. Tidy, tasteful singles ($25, with private bath $40) and doubles ($35/$45). Free local calls. Complimentary continental breakfast. Kitchen, laundry facilities, and bike storage available.

Hotel Everett, 51A Oak St. (773-7882), off Congress St. Central location. Check-in after 1pm. Check-out 11am. Old but tidy singles $38, with bath $43; doubles $49/

$53. Mid-Sept. to mid-June 10% cheaper. Weekly rates available. Reservations recommended in summer.

YWCA, 87 Spring St. (874-1130), downtown near the Civic Center. Women only. The small rooms verge on sterile, but the amiable atmosphere more than compensates. Fills up in summer. Check-out 11am. Singles $25, doubles $40. Lounge, pool, and kitchen (bring utensils). Phone in reservations with Visa or Mastercard.

YMCA, 70 Forest Ave. (874-1111), on the north side of Congress St., 1 block from the post office. Cash only. Men only. Check-in 11am-10pm. Singles $23 per night, $84 per week. Access to kitchen, pool, and exercise facilities. Key deposit $10.

Wassamki Springs, 855 Saco St. (839-4276), in Westbrook. Closest campground (15-min. drive) to Portland. Drive 6mi. west on Congress St. (becomes Rte. 22, then County Rd.), then turn right on Saco St. Full facilities plus a sandy beach. Flocks of migrant Winnebagos nest among cozy, fairly private sites that go right up to the lake. Sites $18 for 2 people, hookup $21, $4 per additional person; $2 additional for lakefront sites. 10% senior citizen discount. Showers 25¢. Reservations ($10 per day of stay) recommended 4-6 weeks in advance, especially July-Aug. Open May to mid-Oct.

FOOD

Life is de bubbles for seafood lovers in Portland. One of the nation's leaders in restaurants per capita, Portland loves to chop *le poisson* and make it taste nice, as well as to boil lobsters and sauté clams in ze spice. Do-it-yourselfers can buy raw (or still alive) seafood on the active port on Commercial St.

Raffles Café Bookstore, 555 Congress St. (761-3930), in the heart of downtown. Soothe both mind and body in this laid-back haunt. Enjoy breakfast, a light lunch (soups made from scratch $2, sandwiches $3-4), or scrumptious desserts ($1-2.50), then wander upstairs to browse books ranging from gay/lesbian/bisexual literature to philosophy. Occasionally reopens in the evenings for live music and poetry readings. Open Mon.-Tues. and Fri.-Sat. 8am-5:30pm, Wed.-Thurs. 8am-8pm, Sun. noon-5pm.

Seamen's Club, 375 Fore St. (772-7311), at Exchange St. in the Old Port with a harbor view. Top-notch seafood dining steeped in briny lore. Sandwiches $5-$7, dinner $9 and up. Fresh lobster year-round. Open Mon.-Thurs. 11am-10pm, Fri.-Sat. 11am-11pm, Sun. 10:30am-10pm.

Federal Spice, 225 Federal St. (774-6404), just off Congress St. It's new, it's hip, it's convenient, it's *hot.* Whips up cheap, bold home cooking in a hurry using spicy hot elements from Caribbean, South American, and Asian cuisine. Memorable selections from a health-smart menu all under $6. Eat in or take out. Wheelchair accessible.

Bella Bella, 606 Congress St. (780-1260). Specializes in ample servings of Italian specialties (entrees $7-10) served in a psychedelic flower-painted café. Open 5-10pm daily.

Silly's, 147 Cumberland Ave. (772-0360). Elvis, tinfoil ornaments, and pizza-shaped Christmas lights are highlights in this funky atmosphere. A solid menu featuring burgers ($3-4), pizza, shish kabobs ($4), and a damn good milkshake ($2) rewards the 15-min. walk from downtown. Open daily 10am-10pm.

SIGHTS

Many of Portland's most spectacular sights are to be found outside the city proper, along the rugged coast or on the beautiful, secluded islands a short ferry ride offshore. **Two Lights State Park** (799-5871), across the Million Dollar Bridge on State St. and south along Rte. 77 to Cape Elizabeth, is a wonderful place to picnic and relax; enjoy a rocky shore with a view of two lighthouses ($2, ages 5-11 50¢, seniors and under 5 free; open the week before Memorial Day-Labor Day daily 9am-sunset). **Casco Bay Lines** (774-7871), on State Pier near the corner of Commercial and Franklin, America's oldest ferry service, runs year-round to the nearby islands. Daily **ferries** depart approximately every hour (5:15am-midnight) for nearby **Peaks Island** ($4.50, seniors and ages 5-9 $2.25, under 5 free; bikes $3.40). On the island you can rent a bike at **Brad's Recycled Bike Shop,** 115 Island Ave. (766-5631), for $11 per day or $7.50 for 4 hrs. If your feet aren't up to pedaling, try the quiet, unpopulated beach on **Long Island** (departures daily 6am-9pm. $6.35, seniors and ages 5-9 $3.20; bikes just $4 extra). If you start at Long Island, you can island-hop by catching later ferries to other islands (same price as Peaks ferry). Getting to more than two islands will take all day, though; start early and pay close attention to the schedule.

You may feel the call of the sea the instant you arrive in Portland, but the city does have a full slate of activities for landlubbers. The **Portland Museum of Art,** 7 Congress Sq. (775-6148), at the intersection of Congress, High, and Free St., collects American art by notables such as John Singer Sargent and Winslow Homer (open Tues.-Wed. and Fri.-Sat. 10am-5pm, Thurs. 10am-9pm, Sun. noon-5pm. $6, seniors and students $5, ages 6-12 $1, under 6 free). Down the street at 487 Congress St., the **Wadsworth-Longfellow House** (879-0427), a museum of social history and U.S. literature, zeroes in on late 18th- and 19th-century antiques as well as on the life of the poet. Henry lived in the house from birth to his early twenties. (Tours every ½hr. $4, under 12 $1; purchase tickets at 489 Congress St. Open June-Oct. Tues.-Sun. 10am-4pm. Gallery and museum store also open Oct.-June Wed.-Sat. noon-4pm.)

ENTERTAINMENT AND NIGHTLIFE

After a not-so-brief respite, spanning back to its days as a Vaudeville venue, the **State Theater,** 609 Congress St. (879-1111; for tickets 879-1112) is back in business, presenting both concerts and theatrical productions. (Tickets $15-25. Info line open 24 hrs.; box office open Mon.-Fri. 9:30am-5pm, Sat. 10am-4pm, Sun. noon-showtime on performance days.) From early October to late April, the **Portland Symphony,** under the direction of Toschiyuki Shimada, also performs here. Call for details (773-8191, 800-639-2309 in ME and NH; 50% student discount for regular performances).

Traditionally held on the first Sunday in June, the **Old Port Festival** (772-6828) begins the summer with a bang, filling several blocks from Federal to Commercial St. with as many as 50,000 people. On summer afternoons, enjoy the **Noontime Performance Series** (772-6828), for which a variety of bands performs in Portland's Monument Square (late June-early July Mon.-Fri. noon-1:15pm). The **6-Alive Sidewalk Arts Festival** (828-6666), generally held around mid-August, lines Congress St. with booths featuring artists from all over the country.

For a taste of the hometown spirit, check out the **Portland Pirates,** Portland's own ice-kicking professional hockey team, at the Civic Center, 1 Civic Center Sq. (season runs Sept.-May; call 828-4665 for tickets; $8-13, under 12 and seniors ½-price). The **Portland Seadogs,** the local minor-league pro baseball team, takes the field from Apr. 6 to Sept. 4 at Hadlock Field on Park Ave. (tickets 874-9300; $4, under 16 and seniors $2).

After dark, head toward the Old Port area, especially **Fore Street** between Union and Exchange St., a stretch known as "the strip." **Gritty MacDuff's,** 396 Fore St. (772-2739), brews its own sweet beer for adoring locals. These tasty pints are worth the $2.50. (Open daily 11:30am-1am.) You'll find the atmosphere of an English pub around the corner at **Three Dollar Dewey's,** 446 Fore St. (772-3310), on the corner of Commercial and Union. Dewey's serves 65 varieties of beer and ale (30 on tap at $3), along with great chili and free popcorn (open Mon.-Sat. 11am-1am, Sun. noon-1am). **Brian Boru,** 57 Center St. (780-1506), provides a more mellow pub scene (open daily noon-1am). Try the Irish nachos ($5.50), or stop by on Sunday for a traditional Irish breakfast and chug $1.50 pints all day. Find info on Portland's sporadic jazz, blues, and club scene in the *Casco Bay Weekly*, a little gem free at most convenience stores.

■■■ NORTH OF PORTLAND

Much like the coastal region south of Portland, the north offers the traveler unforgettable beaches, windswept ocean vistas, and verdant forests—for a price. Lodging in L.L. Bean country isn't cheap, but camping or just passing through can give all the flavor, without the guilt of spending $70 at a hotel. Much of the region is unserviced by public transportation; but if you have a car, the drive along U.S. 1 offers a charming, unadulterated view of coastal Maine. Don't expect to speed through; congested traffic and winding roads make the drive up Maine's coast slow at times. Get a good map, and plan to move slowly.

Freeport About 20 mi. north of Portland on I-95, Freeport once garnered glory as the "birthplace of Maine;" the 1820 signing of documents declaring the state's independence from Massachusetts took place at the historic **Jameson Tavern,** 115 Main St. (865-4196). Dinner here will run you $12-22; lighter fare can be had in the tap room for $6-9. Freeport is now known as the factory outlet capital of the world, with over 100 downtown stores. The grandaddy of them all, **L.L. Bean,** began manufacturing Maine Hunting Shoes in Freeport in 1912. Bean sells everything from clothes epitomizing preppy *haute couture* to sturdy tenting gear. The factory outlet, 11 Depot St. (865-4761, ext. 2929), behind Bannister Shoes, is the place for bargains (open daily 8am-10pm). The retail store, 95 Main St. (865-4761 or 800-341-4341), stays open 24 hrs., 365 days a year. Only three events have ever caused the store to close (and only for a few hours each time): a nearby fire in the late 1980s, the death of President Kennedy, and the death of L.L. Bean founder Leon Leonwood (no wonder he went by L.L.) Bean.

Heading up to **Penobscot Bay** (not in the town of Penobscot) from factory-outlet-land, be sure to stop at **Moody's Diner** (832-7468), a haven for drivers on U.S. 1 in Waldoboro. Tourists and old salts have rubbed shoulders over fantastic food since business started in 1927. Burger $1.50, frappe $2.25. (Open Sun. 6am straight through Fri. 11:30pm, Sat. 5am-11:30pm.)

Camden In the summer, the khaki crowd flocks to friendly Camden, 100 mi. north of Portland, to dock their yachts alongside the tall-masted schooners in Penobscot Bay. Many of the cruises are out of the budgeteer's price range, but the Rockport-Camden-Lincolnville **Chamber of Commerce** (236-4404; outside ME 800-223-5459), on the public landing in Camden behind Cappy's Chowder House, can tell you which are most affordable. They also have information on a few rooms in local private homes for $30; otherwise, expect to pay $50 or more. (Open Mon.-Fri. 9am-5pm, Sat. 10am-4pm, Sun. noon-4pm.) Cheaper still, the **Camden Hills State Park** (287-3824; outside ME 800-332-1501), 1¼ mi. north of town on U.S. 1, is almost always full in July and August, but you can be fairly certain to get a site if you arrive before 2pm. This beautiful coastal retreat offers more than 25 mi. of trails, including one trail which leads up to **Mt. Battie** and has a harbor view. Make reservations by phone with a credit card. Showers are 25¢ and toilets are available. (Open May 15-Oct. 15. Day use $2. Sites $15, ME residents $11.)

Affordable to all and in the heart of downtown Camden is **Cappy's Chowder House,** 1 Main St. (236-2254), a kindly, comfortable hangout where great seafood draws tourists and townspeople alike (open daily 7:30am-midnight). Try the seafood pie ($8), made with scallops, shrimp, mussels, and clams. For lighter fare in a less crowded location, **The Harbor Café,** 1 Sharp's Wharf (236-6011), prepares excellent chowder ($2.50/cup), veggie pockets ($4.25), and salads; eat outside for a dockside view. (Open Mon.-Thurs. 9am-2:30pm and 5-9pm, Fri.-Sat. 9am-2:30pm and 5-10pm, Sun. 5-9pm).

The **Maine State Ferry Service** (789-5611), 5 mi. north of Camden in Lincolnville, takes you across the Bay to Isleboro Island (7-9 per day; round-trip $5, ages 5-11 $2, under 5 free, bike $3, car and driver $14). Don't miss the last return at 4:30pm, or you'll be stranded. The ferry also has an agency on U.S. 1 in **Rockland,** 517A Main St. (596-2202), that runs boats to North Haven, Vinalhaven, and Matinicus. Always confirm ahead of time; rates and schedules change with the weather.

Belfast Seventeen mi. north of Camden on U.S. 1, Belfast is "real life" coastal Maine at its best. The **Belfast Area Chamber of Commerce,** 31 Front St. (338-5900), on the water, can help you with planning (open mid-May to mid.-Oct. daily 10am-6pm). When the chamber is closed for the season, call the director, Jim Lovejoy, at home at the **Hiram Alden Inn,** 19 Church St. (338-2151). The inn is also Belfast's most affordable accommodation, and a luxurious one at that (singles $30, doubles $45, additional adult $10; breakfast included. Oct.16-May deduct $5 from room prices). Stroll by the waterfront and watch the fishing boats come in, or enjoy the innumerable antique sales, flea markets, and plain-old junk sales that line Rte. 1 in Belfast and the surrounding towns on summer weekends. **The Gothic,** 4 Main St. (338-4933), serves homemade baked goods and ice cream. If you're lucky, they'll have blueberry sorbet ($1.20) while you're in town. (Open Mon.-Wed. 8am-6pm, Thurs.-Sat. 8am-9pm.)

Deer Isle and Isle au Haut Fourteen mi. south of Blue Hill on Rte. 15 lies the picturesque, forested **Deer Isle,** connected to the mainland by a bridge. Off Main St. in Stoningham, at the southern tip of Deer Isle, the **Isle au Haut Company** runs boating excursions to the isolated **Isle au Haut**, a part of **Acadia National Park** ($18 round-trip, under 13 $9). The Industrial Revolution seems to have missed Isle au Haut; just as when French explorer Samuel Champlain first came to the island in 1604, walking is the primary mode of transportation here. There are only 4 mi. of paved trailways, and the only accommodations are the five lean-tos at **Duck Harbor Campground.** (Each lean-to holds up to 6 people. Sites $5. No showers; reservations necessary. Open mid-May to mid-Oct.) Be sure to take the boat to Duck Harbor (not Town Landing) unless the 5-mi. hike to the campground sounds appealing. Call or write **Acadia Park Headquarters,** P.O. Box 177, Bar Harbour 04609 (288-3338) for information.

■■■ MOUNT DESERT ISLAND

Despite its name, Mt. Desert Island is anything but deserted. During the summer, the island swarms with tourists lured by the thick forests and mountainous landscape. Roughly half of the island is covered by Acadia National Park, which harbors some of the last protected marine, mountain, and forest environments on the New England coast. To be the first person in the U.S. to see the sunrise, climb Cadillac Mountain just before dawn (4 or 4:30am in summer); then descend into the lively town of Bar Harbor, on Rte. 3 on the eastern side of the island, for your obligatory Maine lobster. Rte. 3 runs through Bar Harbor, becoming Mt. Desert St.; it and Cottage St. are the major east-west arteries. Rte. 102 circuits the western half of the island. Trips to the island's less-touristed towns provide a more relaxing, but also a more costly, visit.

PRACTICAL INFORMATION

Tourist Office: Acadia National Park Visitors Center (288-4932 or 288-5262), 3mi. north of Bar Harbor on Rte. 3. Open May-June and mid-Sept.-Oct. daily 8am-4:30pm; July-mid-Sept. daily 8am-6pm. **Park Headquarters** (288-3338), 3mi. west of Bar Harbor on Rte. 233. Open Oct.-May Mon.-Fri. 8am-4:30pm. **Bar Harbor Chamber of Commerce,** 93 Cottage St. (288-5103). Open Mon.-Fri. 8am-5pm. **Mount Desert Island Joint Chamber of Commerce** (288-3411), on Rte. 3 at the entrance to Thompson Island. Info on the whole island. Open July-Aug. daily 10am-8pm; May-June and Sept.-Oct. daily 10am-6pm. In the same building you'll find an **Acadia National Park Information Center** (288-9702). Open June-Sept. daily 9:30am-2:30pm.

Buses: Greyhound/ Vermont Transit (800-451-32922) leaves for Bangor daily at 6:45am in front of the Post Office, 55 Cottage St. ($8.50 June-Labor Day). Buy tickets at **Fox Run Travel,** 4 Kennebec St. (288-3366). Open Mon.-Fri. 8:30am-5pm.

Ferries: Beal & Bunker, from Northeast Harbor on the town dock (244-3575). To: Cranberry Islands (5-7 per day, 25min., $8, under 12 $4). Open Mon.-Fri. 8am-4:30pm for information. **Marine Atlantic** (288-3395 or 800-341-7981), Bar Harbor. To: Yarmouth, Nova Scotia (1 per day June 24-Columbus Day; call after Columbus Day for availability; 6hrs.; $39, seniors $29.50, ages 5-12 $20, car $51, bike $8.50; $3 port tax per person).

Bike Rental: Bar Harbor Bicycle Shop, 141 Cottage St. (288-3886). Mountain bikes $9 for 4hrs., $14 per day, $79 per week. Rentals include helmet, lock, and map. Driver's license, cash deposit, or credit card required. Open June to mid-Sept. daily 8am-8pm, mid-Sept. to mid-Dec. daily 8am-6pm.

National Park Canoe Rentals (244-5854), north end of Long Pond off Rte. 102. Canoes: 4-hr. am rental $18, 4-hr. pm $22, full day $28. Open May-Labor Day daily 8:30am-5pm.

Crisis Lines: Downeast Sexual Assault Helpline, 800-228-2470; **mental health crisis line,** 800-245-8889. Both 24 hrs.

Emergency: 911. **Acadia National Park Emergency,** 288-3369. **Mt. Desert Police,** 276-5111.

Post Office: 55 Cottage St. (288-3122), near downtown. Open Mon.-Fri. 8am-4:45pm, Sat. 9am-noon. **ZIP code:** 04609.

Area Code: 207.

ACCOMMODATIONS AND CAMPING

Grand hotels with grand prices remain from the island's exclusive resort days. Nevertheless, a few reasonable establishments can be found, particularly on Rte. 3 north of Bar Harbor. Camping exists throughout the island; most campgrounds line Rte. 198 and 102, well west of town.

Mt. Desert Island Hostel (HI-AYH), 27 Kennebec St., Bar Harbor (288-5587), behind the Episcopal Church, adjacent to the bus stop. Two large dorm rooms which accommodate 24 in cheery red-and-white bunks. Common room, full kitchen, and a perfect location. Organized activities include movie nights and comedy performances. Breakfast and dinner available ($3 each). Lockout 9am-5pm. Curfew 11pm. $12, nonmembers $15. Linen $1. Call 800-444-6111 for reservations; essential July-Aug. Open mid-June to Aug. 30.

Mt. Desert Island YWCA, 36 Mt. Desert St. (288-5008), Bar Harbor, near downtown. Office open daily 9am-10pm. Women only. Extensive common space, full kitchen, laundry. Dorm-style singles with hallway bath $25 per night, doubles $40; glassed-in porch with 7 beds $18 per bed. $25 key/security deposit. Fills quickly; make reservations early. Open only in summer.

Acadia Hotel, 20 Mt. Desert St. (288-5721), Bar Harbor. A sweet, homey place overlooking the park. TV, private bath. Room for 1 or 2 people $50-72 late June-early Sept.; $40-55 May-late June and early Sept.-Oct. Breakfast included.

White Birches Campground, (244-3797), Southwest Harbor, on Seal Cove Rd. 1½mi. west of Rte. 102. 60 wooded sites offer an escape from the touristy areas. $14 for up to 4 people, $18 with hookup; weekly $84/108; $2 per additional person. Free hot showers, stove, bathrooms. Open May 15-Oct. 15 daily 8:30am-10pm for check-in.

Acadia National Park Campgrounds: Blackwoods (288-3274), 5mi. south of Bar Harbor on Rte. 3. Over 300 sites. Mid-May to mid-June and mid-Sept. to mid-Oct. $12, mid-June to mid-Sept. $14, free mid-Sept. to mid-May. Reservations up to 8 weeks in advance; call 800-365-2267. **Seawall** (244-3600), Rte. 102A on the western side of the island, 4mi. south of Southwest Harbor. Station open May-Sept. daily 8am-8pm, first come, first served. Walk-in sites $8, drive-in $11. Both within a 10-min. walk of the ocean. Toilets but no showers or hookups. Privately owned public showers available nearby; bring quarters. No reservations.

FOOD, NIGHTLIFE, AND ENTERTAINMENT

Seafood is all the rage here. Lobster pounds sell the crustaceans cheaply; cooking them is the only problem. Our culinary consultants suggest a large fire and a pot of boiling water.

Beal's (244-7178 or 244-3202), Southwest Harbor, at the end of Clark Point Rd. The best price for lobster. Pick your own live crustacean from a tank ($7-8); Beal's does the rest. Dine on the dock with munchies and beverages from a nearby stand. Open daily 9am-8pm; Labor Day-May daily 9am-5pm.

Cottage St. Bakery and Deli, 59 Cottage St. (288-3010), Bar Harbor. Memorably delicious muffins (75¢), pancakes ($2.45), and breads (loaf $2.25-3.50) baked fresh on the premises. Open May-Oct. daily 6:30am-10pm.

Jordan's, 80 Cottage St. (288-3586), Bar Harbor. A blueberry smorgasbord specializing in muffins (6 for $3.50) and pancakes ($2.75). Their popular breakfast is served all day. Open daily 5am-2pm.

The Colonel's Deli Bakery and Restaurant, on Main St. in Northeast Harbor. The restaurant out back offers sandwiches so big you'll have to squash the fresh baked bread to get one into your mouth ($3-5). The desserts are unusual and delicious ($2-3). Open April-Oct. daily 6:30am-9pm.

Most after-dinner pleasures on the island are simple. For a treat, try **Ben and Bill's Chocolate Emporium,** 66 Main St. (288-3281), near Cottage, which boasts 48 flavors of homemade ice cream (cone $2) and enough luscious chocolates, fudges, and candy to challenge Willy Wonka (open March-Dec. daily 9:30am-11:30pm). **Benbow's Espresso Bar** (288-5271), at the **Alternative Market**, 99 Main St., features over 30 coffees roasted in-house (75¢-$2.50). Try the caramel mocha latte ($1.50). Seating is cramped, but the waterfront and park are one block away (open daily 7am-11pm; Oct. 7am-9pm; late Oct.-May 7:30am-6pm). **Geddy's Pub,** 19 Main St. (288-5077), is a three-tiered entertainment complex with a bar, sporadic live music, pool tables, and dancing. Dance to a DJ Friday and Saturday nights (no cover; open Apr.-Oct. daily noon-1am). Locals prefer the less-touristy **Lompoc Café & Brew Pub,** 36 Rodick St. (288-9392), off Cottage St., which features home-brewed *Bar Harbor Real Ale* ($2.50 for 12oz.) and live jazz, blues, Celtic, rock, or folk nightly (shows June-Sept. at 9pm, $1-2 cover charge; open May-Oct. 11:30am-1am). The art-deco **Criterion Theatre** (288-3441), on Cottage St., recently declared a national landmark, shows movies in the summer. (Shows daily 7:30pm. $6, under 12 $3.50, balcony seats $7. Box office open ½hr. before show.) Don't be discouraged by lines; the theater seats 891. Programs are available at the desk.

SIGHTS

Mt. Desert Island is shaped roughly like a lobster claw, 14 mi. long and 12 mi. wide. To the east on Rte. 3 lie Bar Harbor and Seal Harbor. South on Rte. 198 near the cleft is **Northeast Harbor,** and across Somes Sound, the only fjord in the continental U.S., on Rte. 102 is **Southwest Harbor,** where fishing and shipbuilding thrive without the taint of tacky tourism. **Bar Harbor** is by far the most crowded part of the island, sandwiched between the Blue Hill and Frenchmen Bays. Once a summer hamlet for the very wealthy, the town now welcomes a motley melange of R&R-seekers; the wealthy have fled to the more secluded Northeast and Seal Harbor.

The staff at the **Mt. Desert Oceanarium** (244-7330), at the end of Clark Pt. Rd. in Southwest Harbor, has forgotten more about the sea than most will ever know. All three of their facilities are located near Bar Harbor (lobster hatchery 288-2334, Salt Marsh Walk 288-5005; call for directions). The main museum, reminiscent of a grammar-school science fair, fascinates children and some adults. (Open mid-May to late Oct. Mon.-Sat. 9am-5pm. Ticket for all 3 facilities $9.50, ages 4-12 $7.50, under 4 free; inquire about individual rates.) Cruises head out to sea from a number of points on the island. In Bar Harbor, the **Frenchman Bay Co.,** 1 West St., Harbor Place (288-3322), offers sailing trips (2hr.; $14.75, ages 5-15 $10.75), lobster fishing, seal watching (1½hr.; $16.75, ages 5-15 $10.75, under 5 free), and whale watching trips (4hrs.; $26, ages 5-15 $18, under 5 free. Open May-Oct. Reservations recommended, especially for whale watching. Call for details or schedule.) The **Acadian Whale Watcher,** Golden Anchor Pier, West St. (288-9794, 288-9776, or 800-421-3307), has slightly lower prices, guarantees sightings on daylight trips, and offers food and a full bar on board. (53 trips per day, including sunset cruises; $25, seniors $20, ages 7-14 $14, under 7 free. Open mid-May to mid-Oct.) Bring extra clothing—the temperature can drop dramatically on the water.

Little Cranberry Island, out in the Atlantic Ocean south of Mt. Desert, has a spectacular view of Acadia and the area's cheapest uncooked lobster, which can be found at the fishers' co-op. From Northeast Harbor, the **Sea Princess Islesford Historical and Naturalist Cruise** (276-5352) runs past an osprey nesting site and several lobster buoys to the island. Watch for harbor seals, cormorants, or pilot whales on the cruise. The crew stops at the **Islesford Historical Museum,** in sight of Somes Sound. (Four cruises per day July-Aug., 1-3 per day May-June and Sept.-Columbus Day; 2-3hrs.; $10-12, ages 4-12 $7-8, under 4 free.)

Wildwood Stables (276-3622), along the Park Loop Rd. in Seal Harbor, lets tourists explore the island by horse (if indirectly) with one- and two-hour carriage tours through the park (1hr.; $10.50, seniors $9.50, ages 6-12 $6, ages 2-5 $3.50. 2hrs; $13.50/$12.50/$7/$4.50). Reservations are strongly suggested. No horses are available for rental on the island.

Acadia National Park The 33,000 acres that comprise **Acadia National Park** are a landlubber's dream, offering easy trails and challenging hikes which allow for an intimate exploration of Mt. Desert Island. More acres are available on the nearby **Schoodic Peninsula** and **Isle au Haut** to the west. Millionaire and expert horseman John D. Rockefeller, fearing the island would someday be overrun by cars, funded all of the park's 120 mi. of trails. These **carriage roads** make for easy walking, fun mountain biking, and pleasant carriage rides and are accessible to disabled persons.

Twenty-five trails offer more advanced hiking. Be realistic about your abilities here; the majority of injuries in the park occurs in hiking accidents. The handy *Biking and Hiking Guide to the Carriage Roads* (free), available at the visitors center, offers invaluable safety advice for some of the more labyrinthine trails. **Precipice Trail,** one of the most popular hikes, is closed June to late Aug. to accommodate nesting peregrine falcons. The 5-mi. **Eagle Lake Carriage Road** is graded for bicyclists. Touring the park by auto costs $5 per week, $2 per pedestrian or cyclist. Seniors can purchase a lifetime pass ($10), and disabled are admitted free.

About 4 mi. south of Bar Harbor on Rte. 3, **Park Loop Road** runs along the shore of the island, where great waves crash against steep granite cliffs. The sea comes into **Thunder Hole** with a bang at half-tide, sending plumes of spray high into the air and onto tourists. Swimming waters can be found in the relatively warm **Echo Lake** or at **Sand Beach,** both of which have lifeguards in the summer.

New Hampshire

"The Switzerland of America," New Hampshire bears little resemblance to the English county for which it is named. The White Mountains dominate the central and northern regions, while Mt. Washington, the highest point in the Appalachians (6288 ft.), surveys the Atlantic and five states. The first state to declare independence from Great Britain, New Hampshire still embraces an individualistic ideal; the state motto, "Live Free or Die," is emblazoned on every license plate. Today, eager hordes descend upon the state year-round, drawn by a wealth of wilderness activities and an abundance of tax-free outlet shopping.

PRACTICAL INFORMATION

Capital: Concord.

Office of Travel and Tourism: Box 856, Concord 03302 (603-271-2666, 800-262-6660, or 800-258-3608). A 24-hr. recording provides fall foliage reports, daily ski conditions, weekly snowmobile conditions, and weekly special events. Operators available Mon.-Fri. 8am-4pm. **Fish and Game Department,** 2 Hazen Dr., Concord 03301 (603-271-3421) provides information on hunting and fishing regulations and license fees. **U.S. Forest Service,** 719 Main St., Laconia (603-528-8721). Open Mon.-Fri. 8am-4:30pm. Mail to P.O. Box 638, Laconia 03247.

Time Zone: Eastern. **Postal Abbreviation:** NH

Sales Tax: 0%. Live Tax-Free or Die. 8% tax on rooms and meals.

■■■ WHITE MOUNTAINS

In the late 19th century, the White Mountains became an immensely popular summer retreat for wealthy New Englanders. Grand hotels peppered the rolling green landscape, and as many as 50 trains per day bore tourists through the region. The mountains are not quite as busy nor as fashionable these days, and hiking and skiing have mostly replaced train travel. Unfortunately, the economics of vacationing here have not changed nearly as drastically; affordable lodgings are as scarce as public transportation, and the notoriously unpredictable weather makes camping risky. The area is divided by passes between the mountains, which are called notches.

Getting There and Getting Around Boston makes a good starting point for trips into the White Mountains, but getting around the area itself can be problematic. **Concord Trailways** (228-3300 or 800-639-3317) runs from Boston's Peter Pan bus station, 555 Atlantic Ave., Boston, MA (617-426-8080), to Concord (Storrs St., 228-3300; open daily 5:15am-8pm, $11), Conway (First Stop store on Main St.; 447-8444; open daily 5:30am-10pm; $25), and Franconia (Kelly's Foodtown; 823-7795; open daily 9am-9pm; $26). **Vermont Transit** (800-451-3292) stops its Boston-to-Vermont buses in Concord at the Trailways terminal, 10 St. James Ave. (617-423-5810). The **Appalachian Mountains Club (AMC)** runs a **shuttle service** (466-2727) among points within the mountains. Consult **AMC's** *The Guide* for a complete map of routes and times; reservations are recommended for all stops and required for some. (Early June-early Oct. daily 8:45am-3:30pm. $6, nonmembers $8.) See Useful Organizations, below, for more AMC information. For **Trail and Weather Information** call the **Pinkham Notch Visitors Center** (466-2725), on Rte. 16 (open daily 6:30am-10pm). Regional **ZIP codes:** Franconia, 03580; Jackson, 03846; and Gorham, 03587; **area code:** 603.

Useful Organizations Travel information can be obtained at local travel offices or from the **White Mountain Attraction Center,** P.O. Box 10, N. Woodstock 03262 (745-8720), on Rte. 112 in North Woodstock. The main area office of the **U.S. Forest Service,** 719 Main St., Laconia 03247 (528-8721), lies south of the mountains. **Forest service ranger stations** dot the main highways through the forest: **Androscoggin** (466-2713), on Rte. 16, ½-mi. south of the U.S. 2 junction in Gorham (open Mon.-Fri. 8am-4:30pm); **Ammonoosuc** (869-2626), on Trudeau Rd. in Bethlehem west of U.S. 3 on U.S. 302 (open Mon.-Fri. 8am-4:30pm); and **Saco** (447-5448), on the Kancamangus Hwy. in Conway 100 yards off Rte. 16 (open daily 8am-4:30pm). Each station provides info on trail locations and conditions, and a free guide to the **backcountry facilities** in its area.

The **Appalachian Mountains Club (AMC)** has its main base in the mountains at the Pinkham Notch Visitors Center, on Rte. 16 between Gorham and Jackson (see Pinkham Notch, below). The area's primary supplier of information about camping, food, and lodging, the AMC also sells an assortment of camping and hiking accessories. The club runs two car-accessible lodgings in the White Mountains: **Joe Dodge Lodge** (see Pinkham Notch, below) and the **Crawford Hostel** (846-7773), adjoining the **Crawford Notch Depot,** east of Bretton Woods on U.S. 302. (Bunks for 24 people, toilets, metered showers, full kitchen. Bring a sleeping bag and food. Curfew 9:30pm. $10, nonmembers $15. Reservations recommended.) The Depot has trail guides, maps, food, camping necessities, film, and restrooms (open late May-Labor Day daily 9am-5pm). The AMC also operates a system of eight **huts,** spaced about a day's hike apart along the Appalachian Trail, inaccessible by car or by phone. Breakfast, dinner, or both must be taken with each night's lodging, and guests must provide their own sleeping bags or sheets. Meals at the huts, while not as good as those back at the lodge, are said to be ample and appetizing. (Bunk with 2 meals $50, child $20; nonmember $57/$27. $5 less without breakfast, $10 less without dinner.) All huts stay open for **full service** June-Oct.; **self-service rates** (caretaker in residence but no meals provided) are available at other times ($10, nonmembers $15; call for reservations). For all AMC information, consult AMC's *White Mountain Guide* (see below), available at its visitors centers.

Camping, Hiking, and Biking Camping is free in a number of backcountry areas throughout the **White Mountains National Forest (WMNF).** The forest allows neither camping nor fires above the tree line (approximately 4000 ft.), within 200 ft. of a trail, or within ¼ mi. of roads, huts, shelters, tent platforms, lakes, or streams. Rules vary depending on forest conditions; call the **U.S. Forest Service** (528-8721) before settling into a campsite. The Forest Service can also direct you to one of their 22 designated **campgrounds.** (Bathrooms and firewood usually available. Sites $10-14. Call 800-280-2267 two weeks in advance to reserve a site, especially July-Aug.; reservation fee $7.50).

If you intend to spend a lot of time in the area, and especially if you are planning to do some significant **hiking,** invest in the invaluable *AMC White Mountain Guide* ($17; available in most bookstores and huts). The guide includes full maps and descriptions of all trails in the mountains, with which you can pinpoint precisely where you are at any given time. When hiking, be careful and come prepared; many an unprepared hiker has died among the treacherous peaks, where weather conditions change at a moment's notice. Bring three layers of clothing in *all* seasons: one for wind, one for rain, and one for warmth. Beware of black flies, particularly in June. For general outdoor tips, see To Your Health (p. 11) and Roughing It (p. 47).

Next to hiking, **bicycling** is the best way to see the mountains close up. According to some bikers, the approach to the WMNF from the north is slightly less steep than others. Consult the *New Hampshire Bicycle* guide and map, available at information centers, the U.S. Forests Service's bike trail guides, or *30 Bicycle Tours in New Hampshire* ($11), available in local bookstores and outdoor equipment stores.

■ FRANCONIA NOTCH AREA

Formed by glacial movements which began during an ice age 400 million years ago, Franconia Notch is more than just old. Imposing granite cliffs, waterfalls, endless woodlands, and the famous rocky profile of the "Old Man of the Mountain" attract droves of summer campers. The nearest town, **Lincoln,** lies just south of I-93 where Rte. 112 becomes the scenic Kancamagus Hwy. From Lincoln, the Kancamagus Hwy. branches east 35 scenic mi. through the **Pemigewasset Wilderness** to Conway. Four-thousand-foot peaks rim the large basin, attracting many backpackers and skiers. South of the highway, trails head into the **Sandwich Ranges,** including **Mount Chocorua** (south along Rte. 16 near Ossippee), a dramatic peak and a favorite of 19th-century naturalist painters.

Sights and Activities The **Flume Visitors Center** (745-8391), off I-93 north of Lincoln, screens an excellent, free 15-min. film that acquaints visitors with the landscape (open daily 9am-6pm). While at the center, purchase tickets to **The Flume,** a 2-mi. nature walk over hills, through a covered bridge, and to a boardwalk over a fantastic gorge walled by 90-ft. granite cliffs ($6, ages 6-12 $3). A 9-mi. recreational **bike path** begins at the visitors center and runs through the park.

The westernmost of the notches, Franconia is best known for the **Old Man of the Mountain,** a 40-ft.-high human profile formed by five ledges of stone atop a 1200-ft. cliff north of The Flume. Nathaniel Hawthorne addressed this geological visage in his 1850 story "The Great Stone Face," and P.T. Barnum once offered to purchase the rock. Today, the Old Man is rather doddering; cables and turnbuckles support his forehead. **Profile Lake,** a 10-min. walk from the base of the Cannon Mountain Aerial Tramway, has the best view of the old fuddy duddy.

Unlike the Old Man, the **Great Cannon Cliff,** a 1000-ft. sheer drop into the cleft between **Mount Lafayette** and **Cannon Mountain,** beckons more than onlookers. Hands-on types test their technical skill and climb the cliff via the "Sticky Fingers" or "Meat Grinder" routes; less daring visitors opt to let the 80-passenger **Cannon Mountain Aerial Tramway** (823-5563) do the work. (Open daily 9am-4:30pm, Nov. to mid-April Sat.-Sun. 9am-4:30pm. $8, ages 6-12 $4; one-way $6.)

Myriad trails lead up into the mountains on both sides of the notch, providing excellent day hikes and spectacular views. Be prepared for severe weather, especially above 4000 ft. The **Lonesome Lake Trail,** a relatively easy hike, wends its way 1½ mi. from Lafayette Place to **Lonesome Lake,** where the AMC operates its westernmost summer hut (see White Mountains Useful Organizations, above). The **Greenleaf Trail** (2½mi.), which starts at the Aerial Tramway parking lot, and the **Old Bridle Path** (3mi.), from Lafayette Place, are much more ambitious; both lead up to the AMC's Greenleaf Hut near the summit of Mt. Lafayette overlooking Echo Lake, a favorite destination for sunset photographers. From Greenleaf, trudge the next 7½ mi. east along **Garfield Ridge** to the AMC's most remote hut, the Galehead. Hikes from this base can keep you occupied for days. A campsite on Garfield ridge costs $5; a number of other campsites, mainly lean-tos and tent platforms with no showers or toilets, scatter throughout the mountains. Most run $5 per night on a first come, first served basis, but many are free. Contact the U.S. Forest Service or consult the AMC's free two-page handout, *Backpacker Shelters, Tent sites, Campsites, and Cabins in the White Mountains.*

North of the south end of Franconia Notch, **The Basin,** a waterfall in the Pemigewasset River, drops into a 15-ft. granite pool. The Basin's walls, smoothed by 25,000 years of sandy scouring, seem almost too perfect to be natural. One of the park's most popular attractions, The Basin is fully wheelchair-accessible.

After any exertion, cool off at the lifeguard-protected **beach** on the northern shore of **Echo Lake State Park** (356-2672), just north of Franconia Notch (open daily mid-June to Sept. 9am-8pm; $2.50; under 12 and over 65 free).

Skiing Less renowned than the resorts of Mt. Washington Valley, the ski areas of Franconia Notch, collectively known as **Ski-93,** P.O. Box 517, Lincoln 13251 (745-8101 or 800-937-5493), offer multiple-area packages. **Loon Mountain** (745-8111), 3 mi. east of I-93 on Rt. 112, has a free beginner's rope tow and, by limiting lift-ticket sales, promises crowd-free skiing (lift tickets $36, Sat.-Sun. $43). For cross-country skiing plus some great downhill, try **Waterville Valley** (236-8311). **Cannon Mountain** (823-5563), in the Notch on I-93, sports decent slopes and the New England Ski Museum. (Lift tickets for either $36, Sat.-Sun. $41).

Camping **Lafayette Campground** (823-9513), is nestled smack in the middle of Franconia Notch. (Showers. Sites for 2 $16, $6 per additional person. Call ahead for reservations. Open mid-May to mid-Oct., weather permitting.) If Lafayette is full, try the more suburban **Fransted Campground** (823-5675), 1 mi. south of the village and 3 mi. north of the notch (showers, bathrooms; sites $13, on the river $16; open May-Columbus Day).

■ NORTH CONWAY

At first glance, North Conway, strung along the stretch of land shared by Rte. 16 and Rte. 302, seems like just another strip of motels and fast food joints on the way to somewhere else. Look again. This town, the largest city around, capitalizes on two of New Hampshire's most striking features: the taxes and the terrain. Factory outlet stores, including most major clothing labels, teem with voracious bargain-hunters, while mountain men and women crowd in the region's best outdoor equipment stores. A number of very good cross-country and downhill ski centers await nearby.

Accommodations and Food Four miles north of North Conway, the **Shamrock Village Hostel** (356-5153), on Rte. 16A in Intervale off Rte. 16/302, provides a bed, access to a kitchen and laundry facilities, and a free breakfast ($12, students and seniors $10); call ahead. The **Maple Leaf Motel** (356-5388), on Main St., south of the North Conway city park, has clean, spacious rooms for reasonable rates (singles $58, doubles $62; foliage and ski seasons $78/82; spring $30/34).

Breakfast and lunch spots line North Conway's Main St.; **Gunther's** (356-5200) serves up food devised by owner and cook George Gunther (meals $3-7, open daily 7am-2:30pm). The *après* crowd reconvenes at the pricey **Valley Square** (formerly Café Rubino), in the Eastern Slope Inn. (Nightly dinner specials $6-7. Dancing Fri.-Sat. Open Sun.-Thurs. 11:30am-midnight, Fri.-Sat. 11:30am-1am.)

Skiing and Outdoor Activities Though close to many ski areas, North Conway is proudest of its own local mountain, **Cranmore** (800-543-9206), which recently merged with **Attitash** (374-2368; both open mid-Dec. to April daily 9am-9pm). In 1996, the two resorts will offer combination lift tickets; call for prices. **Wildcat** (466-3326), known for having the area's largest lift capacity and a free novice skiing area, fronts Rte. 16 just south of Pinkham Notch State Park (lift tickets $25, Sat.-Sun. $37; under 23 $19/$22). All three areas offer special rates for groups and multi-day visitors; call ahead. During the summer, speed demons enjoy the **Alpine Slide** at Attitash, a wild ¾-mi. sled ride down the mountain to test the most adventurous souls. Purchase of a one-day pass ($16) includes unlimited rides on the alpine slide and nearby waterslides. (Open daily 9:30am-6pm.)

A number of stores in the North Conway area rent out quality skis and other outdoor equipment. For downhill skis, try **Joe Jones** (356-9411), in North Conway on Main St. at Mechanic. (Skis, boots and poles $15 for 1 day, $25 for 2 days. Open daily 9am-9pm; Sept.-Nov. and April-June Sun.-Thurs. 10am-8pm, Fri.-Sat. 9am-8pm.) **Eastern Mountain Sports (EMS)** (356-5433), on Main St. inside the Eastern Slope Inn, distributes free mountaineering pamphlets and books on the area, including *30 Bicycle Tours in New Hampshire* ($11). EMS also sells camping equipment and rents tents and sleeping bags. The knowledgeable staff can give assistance and recommendations for climbing and hiking in North Conway. (Open daily 9am-9pm; Oct.-May Sun.-Thurs. 9am-6pm, Fri.-Sat. 9am-9pm.)

■ PINKHAM NOTCH

Practical Information New Hampshire's easternmost notch lies in the shadow of Mt. Washington between Gorham and Jackson on Rte. 16. The home of AMC's main information center in the White Mountains, and the starting point for most trips up Mt. Washington, Pinkham Notch's practicality gets more publicity than its beauty, although both deserve renown. To get to Pinkham Notch from I-93 south, take exit 42 to U.S. 302E, then follow Rte. 116N to U.S. 2E to Rte. 16S. From I-93 north, take exit 32 onto Rte. 112E to Rte. 16N. AMC's **Pinkham Notch Visitors Center** (466-2725 or 466-2727 for reservations), 10 mi. north of Jackson on Rte. 16, is the area's best source of information on weather and trail conditions. The center also handles reservations at any of the AMC lodgings and sells the complete line of AMC books, trail maps ($3, weatherproofed $5), and camping and hiking accessories (open daily 6:30am-10pm).

Accommodations AMC's huts offer the best lodging on the mountain. At **Joe Dodge Lodge,** immediately behind the Pinkham Notch visitors center, get a comfy bunk with a delicious and sizeable breakfast and dinner. ($50, children $20; non-members $57/$27; $5 less without breakfast, $10 less without dinner. Lodging $5 more on Sat. and in Aug.) **Hermit's Lake Shelter,** situated about two hours up the Tuckerman Ravine Trail, has bathrooms but no shower and sleeps 72 people in eight lean-tos and three tent platforms ($7 per night; buy nightly passes at the visitors center). **Carter Notch Hut** lies to the east of the visitors center, a 4-mi. hike up the 19-mi. **Brook Trail.** Just 1½ mi. from Mt. Washington's summit sits **Lakes of the Clouds,** the largest (room for 90), highest, and most popular of the AMC's huts; additional sleeping space for six backpackers in its basement refuge room can be reserved from any other hut ($6 per night).

If all the AMC facilities are booked, head to the **Berkshire Manor,** 133 Main St. (466-2186), in Gorham. The outside appears somewhat dated, but inside, guests have access to a full kitchen, a spacious living room, cozy bedrooms, and hall bathrooms. (Singles $17, doubles $32.)

Mt. Washington From just behind the Pinkham Notch Visitors Center all the way up to the summit of Mt. Washington, **Tuckerman's Ravine Trail** takes four to five hours of steep hiking each way. Be careful—every year, Mt. Washington claims at least one life. A gorgeous day can suddenly turn into a chilling storm, with whipping winds and rumbling thunderclouds. It has never been warmer than 72°F atop Mt. Washington, and the average temperature on the peak is a bone-chilling 26.7°F. With an *average* wind speed of 35mph and gusts that have been measured up to an astounding 231mph, Mt. Washington ranks as the windiest place in the country by far. All risks aside, the climb *is* stellar, and the view well worth it. Motorists can take the **Mount Washington Auto Road** (466-3988), a paved and dirt road that winds 8 mi. to the summit. At the top, buy a bumper sticker boasting "This Car Climbed Mt. Washington"—it's certain to impress folks when you cruise back through town. The road begins at Glen House, a short distance north of the visitors center on Rte. 16. ($14 per car and driver, $5 per passenger, ages 5-12 $3. Road open mid-May to mid-Oct. daily 7:30am-6pm.) **Guided van tours** to the summit include a 30-minute presentation on the mountain's natural history ($18, ages 5-12 $10). On the summit you'll find an information center, a snack bar, a museum (466-3347), strong wind, and the **Mt. Washington Observatory** (466-3388; all open daily 6:30am-10pm).

Vermont

Perhaps no other state is as aptly named as Vermont. The lineage of the name extends back to Samuel de Champlain, who in 1609 dubbed the area "green mountain" in his native French (*vert mont*); the Green Mountain range shapes and defines Vermont, spanning the length of the state from north to south and covering most of its width as well. Over the past few decades, ex-urbanite yuppies have invaded, creating a tension between the original, pristine Vermont and the packaged Vermont of organic food stores and mountaineering shops. Happily, the former still seems to prevail; visitors can frolic in any of the 30 state forests, 80 state parks, or the mammoth 186,000-acre Green Mountain National Forest.

PRACTICAL INFORMATION

Capital: Montpelier.

Vermont Travel Division: 134 State St., Montpelier 05602 (802-828-3237). Open Mon.-Fri. 7:45am-4:30pm. **Department of Forests, Parks and Recreation,** 103 S. Main St., Waterbury 05676 (802-241-3670). Open Mon.-Fri. 8am-4:30pm. **Ver-**

mont Snowline (229-0531). 24-hr. recording on snow conditions Nov.-May. **Travel Division Fall Foliage Hotline** (828-3239). Fall leaf colors info Sept.-Oct.

Time Zone: Eastern. **Postal Abbreviation:** VT

Sales Tax: 5%; 7% on meals and lodgings.

SKIING

Twenty-four downhill resorts and 47 cross-country trail systems lace Vermont. For a free winter attractions packet, call the Vermont Travel Division (see Practical Information, above). Also contact **Vermont Ski Areas Association,** 26 State St., Montpelier 05601 (802-223-2439; open Mon.-Fri. 8am-4:30pm). The **Lake Champlain Regional Chamber of Commerce** (802-863-3489, ext. 203), P.O. Box 453, Burlington 05402 (open Mon.-Fri. 9am-5pm) has info on about the **"Burlington, Vermont Winter Fest Passport"** program, which offers a booklet of discounts on ski areas and activities for guests staying in certain accommodations.

Vermont's famous **downhill** ski resorts offer a great range of terrain and accommodations. Always inquire about shared rooms with bunks, which cost significantly less than private rooms. The better resorts include: **Killington** (802-773-1330 or 800-621-6867; 155 trails, 19 lifts, 6 mountains, and one of the most extensive snowmaking systems in the world); **Stratton** (802-297-2200 or 800-787-2886; 92 trails, 12 lifts); **Sugarbush** (802-583-2381 or 800-537-8427; 110 trails, 16 lifts, 2 mountains); **Stowe** (802-253-3000 or 800-253-4754; 47 trails, 10 lifts); **Middlebury College Snow Bowl** (802-388-4356; 14 trails; 3 lifts); and **Jay Peak** (802-988-2611 or 800-451-4449; 50 trails, 6 lifts). **Cross-country** resorts include the **Trapp Family Lodge,** Stowe (802-253-8511; lodging 800-826-7000; 60km of trails); **Mountain Meadows,** Killington (802-757-7077; 25km of trails); **Woodstock** (457-2114; 47km of trails); and **Sugarbush-Rossignol** (802-583-3333 or 800-451-4320; 25km of trails).

■■■ BURLINGTON

Tucked between Lake Champlain and the Green Mountains, the largest city in Vermont—a state known for its laid-back love of nature—successfully bridges the gap between the urban and the outdoors. Five colleges, including the University of Vermont (UVM), give the area a youthful, progressive flair; bead shops pop up next door to mainstream clothing stores without disrupting local harmony. Stroll along Church St. for a taste of the middle-class hippie atmosphere, which transcends its oxymoronic nature and colors the reality of this laid-back city.

PRACTICAL INFORMATION

Tourist Office: Lake Champlain Regional Chamber of Commerce, 60 Main St. (863-3489), provides free maps of the Burlington Bike Path and parks. Open Mon.-Fri. 8:30am-5pm, June-Oct. also Sat.-Sun. 10am-2pm. **Church St. Marketplace Information Gallery,** in a more central location at Church and Bank St. Open May 15-June Mon.-Sat. 11am-4pm; July to mid-Oct. daily 11am-5pm.

Trains: Amtrak, 29 Railroad Ave., Essex Jct. (879-7298 or 800-872-7245), 5mi. east of the center of Burlington on Rte. 15. To: Montreal (1 per day, 3hr., $19); New York (2 per day, 9¾hr., $63); White River Junction (1 per day, 2hr., $12). Station open daily 6am-6pm and 7-9pm. CCTA bus to downtown runs Mon.-Sat. every ½hr. 6am-9:30pm; 75¢.

Buses: Vermont Transit, 137 St. Paul St. (864-6811), at Main St. To: Boston ($45); Montreal ($22); White River Junction ($14.50); Middlebury ($7.50); Bennington ($19); Montpelier ($7.50); Albany ($34). Sept.-May 25% discount for students with ID. Connections made with Greyhound; Ameripasses accepted. Station open daily 7am-8pm; tickets sold 7:30am-8pm.

Public Transportation: Chittenden County Transit Authority (CCTA) (864-0211). Frequent, reliable service. Downtown hub at Cherry and Church St. Connections with Shelburne and other outlying areas. Buses operate every ½hr. Mon.-Sat. roughly 6:15am-9:20pm, depending on routes. Fare 75¢, seniors and disabled

35¢, under 18 50¢, under 5 free. **Special Services Transportation Agency,** 655-7880, has information and advice about travel for the disabled and elderly.

Bike Rental: Ski Rack, 85 Main St. (658-3313). Road bikes $8 per hr., $18 per day, $65 per week; mountain bikes $8/22/70. Helmet and lock included. Open Mon.-Thurs. 10am-8pm, Fri. 9am-9pm, Sat. 9am-6pm, Sun. 11am-5pm.

Crisis Lines: Women's Rape Crisis Center, 863-1236. **Crises Services of Chittenden County,** 863-2400. Both open 24 hrs.

Emergency: 911.

Post Office: 11 Elmwood Ave. (863-6033), at Pearl St. Open Mon.-Fri. 8am-5pm, Sat. 9am-noon. **ZIP code:** 05401. **Area code:** 802.

ACCOMMODATIONS AND CAMPING

Inquire at the Chamber of Commerce for a complete rundown on area accommodations. B&Bs are generally found in the outlying suburbs. Reasonably priced hotels and guest houses line **Shelburne Rd.** south of downtown. **Mrs. Farrell's Home Hostel (HI-AYH),** 27 Arlington (865-3730), lies 3 mi. from downtown, and is accessible by public transportation. By car, take Rte. 127N, turn left at North Ave. (not the Beaches), and look left for Heineburg after the third light. The six beds are split between a clean, comfortable basement and a lovely garden porch. The friendly, adventurous owner is sometimes hard to reach; call around 7-8am or 5-7pm in order to make an absolutely required reservation. (Free linens, showers, coffee, and bagels. Strict curfew 10pm. $15, nonmembers $17. Room accessible to the disabled available for summer.) Proprietor Bruce Howden created the original art that adorns the walls of the charming **Howden Cottage,** 32 N. Champlain (864-7198); he also bakes breakfast muffins at this B&B, and he recently added a solarium to boot. (Singles $39, doubles $49; mid-Oct. to mid-May $35/$45. Double bedrooms with a shared bath $45 year-round. Reservations by credit card recommended.)

North Beach Campsites (862-0942), on Institute Rd. only 1½ mi. north of town by North Ave., has access to a beach on Lake Champlain; take the "North Ave." bus from the main terminal on Saint Paul St. (67 sites. $14, with electricity $17, with full hookup $19. Vermont residents $4 less. Showers 25¢ per 5min. Beach free; closes 9pm. Open mid-May to mid-Sept.) You can have your MTV at **Shelburne Campground** (985-2540), on Shelburne Rd., 1 mi. north of Shelburne and 5 mi. south of Burlington by Rte. 7; buses to Shelburne South stop right next to the campground. (Pool, laundry facilities, free showers. Sites for 2 $16, with water and electricity $20, with full hookup $24; $2 per additional person. Open May-Oct.) See Near Burlington (below) for more camping options.

PHISH FOOD

Immortalized by ex-regulars Phish on their album *A Picture of Nectar,* **Nectar's,** 188 Main St. (658-4771), rocks with inexpensive food and nightly live music. (Famous fries $3. No cover. Open Mon.-Fri. 5:30am-2am, Sat. 7am-1am, Sun. 7am-2am.) Upstairs, **Club Metronome** (865-4563) ticks to a dance beat. **Sweetwater's,** 118 Church St. (864-9800), is a local favorite for soups ($2-4) and sandwiches ($4-5); try the Vermonter ($6; open daily 11:30am-10pm). **Henry's Diner,** 155 Bank St. (862-9010), has provided the ultimate American diner experience since 1925. Sandwiches run $2-4, full meals $5-10, and breakfast happens all day. (Open daily 6:30am-3:45pm.) The **Vermont Pub and Brewery,** 144 College St. (865-0500), at St. Paul's, offers affordable sandwiches, delicious homemade beers ($3 per pint), and English pub favorites like Cornish pasties (similar to a pot pie, $5). To learn more about Original Vermont Lager, go on the free brewery tour. (Tours Wed. 8pm, Sat. 4pm. Pub open Mon.-Thurs. and Sat. 11:30am-1am, Fri. 11:30am-2am, Sun. 11:30am-12:30am. Live entertainment June-Aug. Sat. 9:30pm.) Buy a bottle of wine for $4 in the odorific warehouse of the **Cheese Outlet,** 400 Pine St. (863-3968 or 800-447-1205; open daily 9am-7pm, Sun. 11am-5pm).

Top off any meal with the ultimate Vermont experience. Though the converted gas station has burned down, the first **Ben and Jerry's** (862-9620) still sits on its original site at 169 Cherry St., serving Cherry Garcia or Cookie Dough ice cream for $2 per cone (open Sun.-Thurs. 11am-11:30pm, Fri.-Sat. 11am-midnight).

SIGHTS AND ENTERTAINMENT

Despite its suburban appearance, Burlington offers lively cultural and artistic entertainment. The popular pedestrian mall at historic **Church Street Marketplace** provides a haven for tie-dye and ice-cream lovers and sells works by local artists. Amateur historians delight in Victorian **South Willard St.,** where you'll find **Champlain College** and the **University of Vermont** (656-3480), founded in 1797. **City Hall Park,** in the heart of downtown, and **Battery Street Park,** on Lake Champlain near the edge of downtown, are beautiful places to relax. The **Burlington Community Boathouse** (865-3377), at the base of College St. at Lake Champlain, rents sailboats ($25 per hr.) and rowboats ($5 per hr.) for a cruise on the lake (open mid-May to mid.-Sept. daily 9am-7pm).

The **Spirit of Ethan Allen** scenic cruise (862-9685) departs from Burlington's Perkins Pier at the bottom of Maple St. The boat cruises along the Vermont coast, giving passengers a close-up view of the famous Thrust Fault, which is not visible from land. (Late May to mid-Oct. daily 10am, noon, 2, and 4pm. $8, ages 3-11 $4. Call about the more costly Captain's Dinner and Sunset Cruises.)

The **Shelburne Museum** (985-3346), 7 mi. south of Burlington, in **Shelburne,** houses one of the best collections of Americana in the country. Beside 35 buildings transported from all over New England, 45-acre Shelburne has a covered bridge from Cambridge, MA and a steamboat and a lighthouse from Lake Champlain. Don't miss the Degas, Cassatt, Manet, Monet, Rembrandt, and Whistler paintings—a surprising find in the middle of rural Vermont. Tickets are valid for two consecutive days; you'll need the time to cover the mile-long exhibit. (Open daily 10am-5pm; mid-Oct. to mid-May by reservation. $17.50, students $10.50, ages 6-12 $6, under 6 free. AAA discount.) Five mi. farther south on U.S. 7, the **Vermont Wildflower Farm** (425-3500), has a seed shop and 6½ acres of wildflower gardens. (Open May-late Oct. daily 10am-5pm. $3, seniors and AAA members $2.50, under 12 free.)

The **Ethan Allen Homestead** (865-4556) rests northeast of Burlington on Rte. 127. In the 1780s, Allen, who forced the surrender of Fort Ticonderoga during the American Revolution and helped establish the state of Vermont, built his cabin in what is now the Winooski Valley Park. A multimedia show and tour give insight into the hero and his era. (Open Mon.-Sat. 10am-5pm, Sun. 1-5pm; Labor Day-late Oct. daily 1-5pm; late Oct. to mid-June Tues.-Sun. 1-5pm. Last tour 4:15. $3.50, seniors $3, ages 5-17 $2, under 5 free.)

Summer culture vultures won't want to miss the many festivities Burlington offers: the **Vermont Mozart Festival** (862-7352 or 800-639-9097) sends Bach, Beethoven, and Mozart to barns, farms, and meadows throughout the area (July 15-Aug. 5 in 1996); the **Discover Jazz Festival** (863-7992) features over 200 international and Vermont musicians early to mid-June in both free and ticketed performances; and the **Champlain Valley Folk Festival** (656-3311) entertains in early August. The Flynn Theatre Box Office, 153 Main St. (863-5966), handles sales for the Mozart and jazz performances (open Mon.-Fri. 10am-5pm, Sat. 11am-4pm).

■ NEAR BURLINGTON: CHAMPLAIN VALLEY

Lake Champlain, a 100-mi.-long lake between Vermont's Green Mountains and New York's Adirondacks, is often referred to as "Vermont's West Coast." **Lake Champlain Ferry** (864-9804), located on the dock at the bottom of King St., crosses from Burlington to Port Kent, NY and back. (Late June-Aug. daily 14 per day 7:15am-7:45pm; Sept. to mid-Oct. 8-11 per day 8am-5:30pm. $3, ages 6-12 $1, car $12. The trip takes 1hr.) Lake Champlain Ferry also sails from Grand Isle to Plattsburg, NY; and 14 mi. south of Burlington, from Charlotte, VT, to Essex, NY (either fare $2.75, ages 6-12 50¢, with car $6.75). Only the Grand Isle Ferry runs year-round.

Mt. Philo State Park (425-2390), 15 mi. south of Burlington on Rte. 7, offers pleasant camping and gorgeous views of the Champlain Valley; take the Vermont Transit bus from Burlington south along U.S. 7 toward Vergennes. (Open Memorial Day-Columbus Day daily 10am-sunset. 16 sites with no hookup $10. Lean-tos $14. Entrance fee $1.50, ages 4-14 $1.) The marsh of the **Missisquoi National Wildlife Refuge** sits at northern end of the Lake near Swanton, VT. Also in the north part of the Lake, **Burton Island State Park** (524-6353) is accessible only by ferry (8:30am-6:30pm) from Kill Kare State Park, 35 mi. north of Burlington and 3½ mi. southwest off U.S. 7 near St. Albans Bay. The campground has 42 tent sites ($11, $4 per additional person after 4) and 26 lean-tos ($15.50/$4). The state park on **Grand Isle** (372-4300), just off U.S. 2 north of Keeler Bay, also offers camping. (155 sites $12, $3 each additional person after 4. 34 lean-tos $16/$4. Open late May to mid-Oct.)

■■■ MIDDLEBURY

Unlike the many Vermont towns that seem to shy away from association with local colleges, Middlebury, "Vermont's Landmark College Town," welcomes the energy and culture stimulated by Middlebury College. The result is a traditional Vermont atmosphere tinged with vitality, historical attractions, and an active nightlife.

Practical Information Middlebury stretches along U.S. 7, 42 mi. south of Burlington. Ask the friendly staff at the **Addison County Chamber of Commerce,** 2 Court St. (388-7951), in the historic Gamaliel Painter House, for area information (open Mon.-Fri. 9am-5pm; in summer also Sat. 9am-2pm, Sun. 10am-2pm). **Vermont Transit** stops at Keeler's Gulf Station, 16 Court St. (388-4373), west of Main St. Buses run to Burlington (3 per day, 1hr., $7.50), Rutland (3 per day, 1½hr., $7.50), Albany (3 per day, 3hr., $28), and Boston (2 per day, 6hr., $42). (Open Mon.-Sat. 6am-10pm, Sun. 7am-9pm.) There is no public transportation in Middlebury, but the **Bike and Ski Touring Center,** 74 Main St. (388-6666), rents bikes on the cheap ($5 per day). Middlebury's **post office:** 10 Main St. (388-2681; open Mon.-Fri. 8am-5pm, Sat. 8am-12:30pm); **ZIP code:** 05753; **area code:** 802.

Accommodations and Camping Lodging does not come cheaply in Middlebury; prepare to trade in a few lesser vital organs for an extended stay. Middlebury's best budget accommodations chill several miles from the center of town. Linda and Paul Horn rent one room, complete with private bath and country decor, out of their charming **Horn Farnsworth House** (388-2300), 3 mi. north of town on Rte. 7 ($55, extra room for larger parties $25). The **Sugar House Motor Inn** (388-2770 or 388-4330), just south of the Horn Farnsworth House on Rte. 7, offers basic motel rooms (singles $35, doubles $45; prices jump to $90/95 during the turning of the leaves and Middlebury graduation). On the southern edge of Middlebury, the **Greystone Motel** (388-4935), 2 mi. south of the town center on Rte. 7, has 10 reasonably priced rooms (singles $45-50, doubles $55-60). Situated on a lake, **Branbury State Park** (247-5925), 7 mi. south on U.S. 7, then 4 mi. south on Rte. 53, takes care of camping and wet fun. (44 sites $12. Lean-tos $16. No hookups. Boat rentals $3-5 per day. Reservations recommended July-Aug. Open late May to mid-Oct.)

Food and Nightlife Middlebury's many fine restaurants cater chiefly to plump wallets, but the year-round presence of students assures the survival of cheaper places. **Calvi's,** 42 Main St. (388-4182), is an old-fashioned soda fountain with old-fashioned prices; try a cone of their homemade ice cream ($1.30; open Mon.-Sat. 8am-10pm; mid-Sept.-early June 8am-6pm.) Students also flock to **Mister Up's** (388-6724), on Bakery Ln. just off Main St., for an impressively eclectic menu, which includes eggplant rollatini ($8), sandwiches ($5-6), and an extensive salad bar ($6.50; open daily 11:30am-midnight). **Fire and Ice,** 26 Seymour St. (388-7166), down the hill from the Congregationalist Church downtown, quenches the appetites of students and locals with well-prepared American fare and a great salad/bread bar. (Open Tues.-Fri. 11:30am-9pm, Sat.-Sun. 11:30am-9:30pm. Entrees $9.90-$17.50; lunch menu $5-12.) **Noonie's Deli** (388-0014), in the Marbleworks building just behind Main St., makes terrific sandwiches on homemade bread ($4-5) and follows up with fresh baked desserts (open Mon.-Sat. 9am-8pm, Sun. 11am-7pm).

Thanks to the college, nightlife in town is surprisingly lively. Overlooking Otter Creek, the trendy **Woody's,** 5 Bakery Ln. (388-4182), off Main St., carves out delicious (if somewhat upscale) dishes and drinks. Lunch prices are reasonable ($4-7; open Mon.-Sat. 11:30am-midnight, Sun. 10:30am-3pm and 5-9:30pm). **Amigos,** 4 Merchants Row (388-3624), befriends weary travelers with Mexican food ($2.50-$12) and live local music Friday and Saturday 10pm-1am. Get happy with free spicy chicken wings 4-6pm Monday through Thursday. (Open Mon.-Sat. 11:30am-10pm, Sun. 4-9pm. Bar open nightly until midnight.)

Sights The **Vermont State Craft Center** (388-3177), at Frog Hollow, exhibits and sells the artistic productions of Vermonters (open Mon.-Sat. 9:30am-5:30pm, Sun. noon-5pm). The nearby **Sheldon Museum,** 1 Park St. (388-2117), houses an extensive and sometimes macabre collection of Americana, including a set of teeth extracted in the 19th century and a disturbingly well-preserved stuffed cat from the same period. Meow. (Open June.-Oct. Mon.-Fri. 10am-5pm, Sat. 10am-4pm; Nov.-May by appt. $2.50, students and seniors $2, under 12 50¢.) **Middlebury College** hosts year-round cultural events; the architecturally striking concert hall in the college **Arts Center,** just outside of town, resonates with a terrific concert series. Call the campus **box office** (388-3711, ext. 7469) for details on events sponsored by the college (open Tues.-Sat. 11am-4pm).

The **University of Vermont's Morgan Horse Farm** (388-2011), west of Middlebury on Rte. 23, 2 mi. from Rte. 125, conducts a pleasant, informative tour that won't bruise the behind; rides are not available. (Open May-Oct. daily 9am-4pm. $3.50, teenagers $2, under 12 free.)

■■■ STOWE

The village of Stowe winds gracefully up the side of Mount Mansfield (Vermont's highest peak, at 4393 ft.). Ostentatiously quaint, the town fancies itself an American skiing hotspot on par with its ritzier European counterparts. Stowe scoffs at the idea of being a bargain, but behind the façade, travelers can find some unbeatable values. Besides, no one can put a price on lush mountainous surroundings or the promise of a great downhill run.

Practical Information Stowe is 12 mi. north of I-89's exit 10, which is 27 mi. southwest of Burlington. The ski slopes lie along Rte. 108 northwest of Stowe. **Vermont Transit** only comes as close as **Vincent's Drug and Variety Store,** off Park Row in Waterbury, 10 mi. from Stowe (open Mon.-Fri. 8:30am-7pm, Sat. 8:30am-6pm, Sun. 9am-3pm). From there, **Lamoille County Taxi** (253-9433) will drive you to Stowe village for $17. In the winter, **The Stowe Trolley** (253-7585) runs on an irregular schedule between the important locations in the village (every 30min. 7:30-10:30am and 2-3pm, every hr. 11:30am-1:30pm; $1). In summer, the trolley does that tour thang (75-min. guided tours Mon., Wed., and Fri. 11am; $5).

In addition to providing information on area attractions, the **Stowe Area Association** (253-7321 or 800-247-8693), on Main St. in the center of the village, runs a free booking service for member hotels and restaurants. (Open Mon.-Fri. 9am-5pm, Sat.-Sun. 10am-5pm; in winter Mon.-Fri. 9am-9pm, Sat.-Sun. 10am-6pm.) The **Stowe Mountain Resort's** booking service (253-3000) provides the same service. Stowe's **post office:** 105 Depot St. (253-7521), off Main St. (open Mon.-Fri. 8:30am-5pm, Sat. 7am-4:30pm); **ZIP code:** 05672; **area code:** 802.

Accommodations and Camping The **Vermont State Ski Dorm** (253-4010), at the base of Mt. Mansfield, 7 mi. from town on Mountain Rd. (shuttles run to town during ski season), is Stowe's best lodging bargain by far. The manager will call town to get you special deals on bike, snowshoe, ski, in-line skate, and canoe rentals and make you a mean stack of pancakes; order ahead for breakfast ($4) and dinner ($6). (Beds $15, in ski season $20. Reserve by phone far in advance for ski and foliage seasons. Closed June-July.) The friendly, eccentric host of the **Golden Kitz** (253-4217 or 800-548-7568), Mountain Rd., treats her "lovies" like family—she's simply Divine. Complete with room for "flirty dancing," this lodge/motel offers parlor areas, an art studio, and bedrooms varying in theme and price. Call ahead. (Singles with shared bath $20-$30 in lowest season, $40-50 during Christmas week and fall foliage; doubles with private bath $40-46/$60-64. Multi-day packages available.) The committed budget traveler should ask for a "dungeon" double ($30).

Gold Brook Campground (253-7683), 1½ mi. south of the town center on Rte. 100, offers the experience of camping without all that wilderness stuff. (Showers, laundry, volleyball, badminton, horseshoes. Tent sites for 2 $14, with electrical hookup $16-21; $3 per each additional person.) **Smuggler's Notch State Park** (253-4014) keeps it simple with hot showers, tent sites, and lean-tos. (Sites for 4 $11, $3 per additional person up to 8; lean-tos $15/$4. Reservations recommended. Open May 20-Oct.10.)

At the **Depot Street Malt Shoppe,** 57 Depot St. (253-4269), visitors enjoy classic diner fare in an artfully recreated 50s soda shop (meals $3-8; open daily 11am-9pm). The **Sunset Grille and Tap Room** (253-9281), on Cottage Club Rd. off Mountain Rd., sells generous meals ($5-15) and a vast selection of domestic beers in a friendly, down-home barbecue restaurant and bar (open daily 11:30am-midnight).

Skiing and Activities Stowe's ski offerings consist of the **Stowe Mountain Resort** (253-3000 or 800-253-4754) and **Smuggler's Notch** (664-8851 or 800-451-8752). Both areas are expensive; lift tickets cost about $45 per day. Nearby, the hills are alive with the sound of the area's best cross-country skiing at the **Von Trapp Family Lodge** (yes, it *is* the family from *Sound of Music*) (253-8511), on Luce Hill Rd. The lodge also offers rentals and lessons. (Trail fee $10. Ski rentals $12. Lessons $14. Discounts for children.) **AJ's Ski and Sports** (253-4593), at the base of Mountain Rd., rents ski and snow equipment. (Skis, boots, and poles: downhill $18 per day, 2 days $32; cross-country $12/20; snowboard and boots $24 per day. 20% discount with 5-day advance reservations. Open daily 9am-6pm; Nov.-April 8am-6pm.)

In summer, Stowe's frenetic pace drops off—as do its prices. Rent mountain bikes ($6 per hr., $14 per ½day, $20 per day) and in-line skates ($6/$12/$18) at **Action Outfitters,** 2280 Mountain Rd. (253-7975; open daily 8am-6pm.) Stowe's 5½-mi. asphalt recreation path, perfect for cross-country skiing in the winter and biking, skating, or strolling in the summer, starts behind the Community Church and roughly parallels the Mountain Road's ascent.

Fly fisherfolk should head to the **Fly Rod Shop** (253-7346), 3 mi. south of Stowe on Rte. 100, to rent fly rods and reels ($12 per day) or rods with spinning reels ($6 per day) and to pick up the necessary **fishing licenses** (non-residents 3-day $18, season $35). The owner can show you how to tie a fly, or you can stick around for free

Ben & Jerry: Two Men, One Dream, and Lots of Chunks

In 1978, Ben Cohen and Jerry Greenfield enrolled in a Penn State correspondence course in ice cream making, converted a gas station into their first shop, and launched themselves on the road to the ice cream hall of fame. Today, **Ben and Jerry's Ice Cream Factory** (244-5641), a few miles north of Waterbury on Rte. 100, is a cow-spotted mecca for ice cream lovers. On a 20-minute tour of the facilities, taste the sweet success of the men who brought "Lemongrad" to Moscow and "Economic Chunk" to Wall Street ($1). The tour tells the history of the operation and showcases the policies which have given the company a reputation for social consciousness. And of course, there are samples. (Tours daily every 15min. 9am-9pm, Sept.-late June tours every 30 min. 9am-6pm.)

fly-fishing classes on the shop's own pond (April-Oct. Wed. 4-6pm, Sat. 9-10am). If you're looking to canoe on the nearby Lamoille River, visit **Umiak,** 1880 Mountain Rd. (253-2317), in Gale Farm Center; the store (its name is the Inuit word for "kayak") rents *umiaks* and canoes in the summer ($20 per ½day, $30 per day) and offers a full-day river trip for $20 (rental and transportation to the river included). Located in a rustic red barn on Mountain Rd., **Topnotch Stowe** (253-8585) offers 1-hour horseback riding tours (May-Nov. daily 11am, 1, and 3pm; $22).

The absence of any significant body of water doesn't stop the **Stowe Yacht Club** at the Commodore's Inn (253-7131), just south of the village on Rte. 100, from hosting a full summer racing season, albeit with remote controlled models. The races are free and public (May-Oct. Mon. and Wed. 5pm, Sun. 1pm).

■■■ WHITE RIVER JUNCTION

Named for its location at the confluence of the White and Connecticut Rivers, White River Junction was once the focus of railroad transportation in the northeastern U.S. Today, near the intersection of I-89 and I-91, the Junction preserves its status as a travel hub by serving as the bus center for most of Vermont. **Vermont Transit** (295-3011or 800-552-8737), on U.S. 5 adjoining the William Tally House Restaurant, makes connections to New York (3 per day, 8hr., $48), Burlington (4 per day, 2hr., $14.50), Montreal (1 per day, 5hr., $43), and smaller centers on a less regular basis (office open Sun.-Fri. 7am-8:30pm, Sat. 7am-5pm). **Amtrak** (800-872-7245), on Railroad Rd. (go figure) off N. Main St., rockets once per day to New York (7½hr., $54), Essex Junction (near Burlington; 2hr., $24), Montreal (4½hr., $58), and Philadelphia (9½hr., $60). (Open nightly 9:15pm-6am.)

If you must stay here, the **information booth,** at the intersection of Sykes and U.S. 5 off I-89 and 91 across from the bus station, will apprise you of any possible distractions (open June-Aug. Sat.-Sun. noon-5pm). In town, the **Chamber of Commerce,** 12 Gates St. (295-6200), just off S. Main, will inform you about Vermont at large (open Mon. 9:30am-4:30pm, Wed.-Fri. 9:30am-5pm; June-Aug. Fri.-Sat. 5-8pm also). White River's **post office:** 9 Main St. (295-2803; open Mon.-Fri. 8-10am and 3-5pm, Sat. 8-10am); **ZIP code:** 05001; **area code:** 802.

The best, and virtually only, bet for lodging is the old-style **Hotel Coolidge,** 17 S. Main St. (295-3118 or 800-622-1124), across the road from the retired Boston and Maine steam engine. From the bus station, walk to the right on U.S. 5 and down the hill past two stop lights (1mi.) into town. Renamed in honor of frequent guest "Silent Cal" Coolidge's pop, the Coolidge boasts neatly kept rooms at fair prices (economy singles from $32, doubles from $36). For a quick bite, stop at local favorite, the **Polkadot Restaurant,** 1 N. Main St. (295-9722). This authentic diner cooks up sandwiches ($1.50-4.50) and full sit-down meals (pork chop plate $5.50; open daily 5am-8pm). At the **Catamount Brewery,** 58 S. Main St. (296-2248), sample unpasteurized amber ale produced by British brewing methods. (Free tours Mon.-Sat. 11am, 1, 3pm, Sun. 1pm, 3pm. Open Mon.-Sat. 9am-5pm, Sun. noon-5pm.)

■■■ BRATTLEBORO

Southeast Vermont is often accused of living too much in its colonial past, but Brattleboro seems to be more a captive of the Age of Aquarius than the War for Independence. Whether camouflaged in Birkenstocks and tie-dye or adorned more conventionally, visitors feel right at home in this town, where the vibes are groovy and the organic produce is even better. Nature-worship peaks in the fall foliage season when a horde of tourists invades the area to take part in the ultimate earth fest.

Practical Information Get the *Brattleboro Main Street Walking Tour* and a detailed town map at the **Chamber of Commerce,** 180 Main St. (254-4565; open Mon.-Fri. 8:30am-5pm). In summer and in foliage season, an **information booth**

(257-1112), on the Town Common off Putney Rd., operates daily 9am-5pm. On the busiest summer weekends, an additional booth (257-4801) opens on Western Ave. just beyond the historic Creamery Bridge (open Thurs.-Sun. 10am-6pm). The **Amtrak** (800-835-8725) *Montrealer* train from New York City and Springfield, MA stops in Brattleboro, behind the museum on Vernon Rd. Trains go once daily to Montréal (6hr., $37), New York (5¼hr., $37), and Washington D.C. (10hr., $72). Arrange tickets and reservations at **Lyon Travel,** 10 Elliot St. (254-6033; open Mon.-Fri. 8:30am-5pm). **Greyhound** and **Vermont Transit** (254-6066) come into town at the parking lot behind the Citgo station at the U.S. 5/Rte. 9/I-91 junction on Putney Rd. (Open Mon.-Fri. 8am-5pm, Sat. 8am-12:15pm, Sun. 10:30am-12:15pm, 2-3:30pm, and 6-7pm.) Brattleboro is on Vermont Transit's Burlington-New York City route (to New York, 3 per day, $37). Other destinations include White River Junction (3 per day, 1½hr., $11.50), Burlington (3 per day, 3½hr., $26.50), Montreal (2 per day, 6½hr., $47), and Boston (1 per day, 3hr., $25). To get downtown from the bus station, take the **Brattleboro Town Bus** (257-1761), which stops in front of the station and runs on Putney Rd. to Main St., then goes up High St. to West Brattleboro (buses run Mon.-Fri. 6:30am-5:45pm; fare 75¢, students 25¢). Brattleboro's **post office:** 204 Main St. (254-4100; open Mon.-Fri. 9am-5pm, Sat. 9am-noon); **ZIP code:** 05301; **area code:** 802.

Accommodations and Camping Economy lodgings such as **Super 8** and **Motel 6** proliferate on Rte. 9 (singles generally $32-37). Renovated in the 1930s, the Art-Deco **Latchis Hotel** (254-6300), on the corner of Flat and Main St., rents decent rooms in an unbeatable location (singles $49-62, doubles $55-72). **West Village,** 480 Western Ave. (254-5610), about 3 mi. out of town on Rte. 9 in West Brattleboro, caters more to the long-term visitor. (Some rooms have kitchenette and microwave. Singles $40, doubles $45, weekly $160. No reservations more than 1 week in advance). If you're really short of cash, grab your bug repellent and flashlight and wander to the **Vagabond Hostel (HI-AYH)** (874-4096), 25 min. north on Rte. 30. The hostel offers decent bunks and extensive facilities, but not much lighting and many mosquitoes. (96 bunks, game room, kitchen. $12, nonmembers $15; group rates available. Open May 15-Nov. 16.) **Fort Dummer State Park** (254-2610) is 2 mi. south of town on U.S. 5; turn left on Fairground Ave. just before the I-91 interchange, and follow it around to South Main St. This "stupid" fort offers campsites with fireplaces, picnic tables, bathroom facilities, and a lean-to with disabled access. (Sites $10. Lean-tos $14. Firewood $2 per armload. Hot showers 25¢. Reservations accepted up to 21 days in advance for 2-day min. stay; $3 non-refundable reservation fee. Open May 21-Labor Day.) **Molly Stark State Park** (464-5460), 15 mi. west of town on Rte. 9., has much the same facilities. (Office open daily 10am-6pm. 24 sites $10; 11 lean-tos $14; RV sites without hookups $10. Hot showers 25¢. Reservations accepted up to 21 days in advance for 2-day min. stay; $3 non-refundable reservation fee. Open Memorial Day-Columbus Day.) About 40 mi. west near Bennington, the **Greenwood Lodge (HI-AYH)** rents bunks and private rooms in a 50-bed lodge in the **Prospect Cross-Country Ski Center** (442-2547; beds $14-19, private rooms for 1 or 2 $30-40; open May 20-Oct. 20). Camping is also available (sites $11.55, with hookup $13.65; $2.10 per additional person).

Food and Nightlife Just across Putney Rd. from the Connecticut River Safari, the **Marina Restaurant** (257-7563) overlooks the West River, offering a cool breeze and a beautiful view. Try the shrimp and chip basket ($4), or the garden burger ($3.50), and see why the locals rave. (Open Wed.-Sat. 4-10pm, Sun. 11am-2pm and 2:30pm-6:30pm.) **Common Ground,** 25 Eliot St. (257-0855), where the town's laid-back "granolas" cluster, supports organic farmers by featuring a wide range of affordable veggie dishes; have soup, salad, bread, and a beverage for $4.25, or a good ol' PB&J for $3 (open Mon. and Wed.-Sat. 11:30am-9pm, Sun. 10:30am-9pm). The **Backside Café,** 24 High St. (257-5056), inside the Mid-town Mall, serves delicious food in an artsy loft with rooftop dining. Breakfast features farm-fresh eggs cooked to perfection; later in the day, dive into a $6 pasta and herb salad or a $5 Mexican Chicken sandwich. (Open Mon. 7:30am-4pm, Tues.-Fri. 7:30am-4pm and 5-9pm, Sat. 8am-3pm, Sun. 10am-3pm; in winter, no lunch on Fri.) At the **Latchis Grill,** 6 Flat St. (254-4747), next to the Latchis Hotel (see Accommodations, above), patrons dine in inexpensive elegance and sample beer brewed on the premises by **Windham Brewery** (lunch and dinner $5-8; 7oz. beer sampler $1.75; open daily 11:30am-midnight). For locally grown fruits, vegetables, and cider, stop by the **farmers markets** (254-9657), on the Town Common on Main St. (open mid-June to mid-Sept. Sat. 10am-2pm), and on Western Ave. near the Creamery Bridge (open mid-May to mid-Oct. Wed. 3-6pm, Sat. 9am-2pm). At night, rock, blues, R&B, and reggae tunnel through the **Mole's Eye Café** (257-0771), at the corner of High and Main St. (Music Wed. and Fri.-Sat. 9pm. Cover Fri.-Sat. $3. Open Mon.-Fri. 11:30am-1am, Sat. 4pm-midnight or 1am.)

Entertainment Brattleboro chills at the confluence of the West and Connecticut Rivers, both of which can be explored by **canoe.** Rentals are available at **Connecticut River Safari** (257-5008 or 254-3908), on Putney Rd. just across the West River Bridge. (2-hr. min. rental $10, $15 per ½-day, $20 per day. Two not-necessarily-consecutive days $30. Open mid-May to Oct. daily 8:30am-6pm.)

The **Brattleboro Museum** and the **Brattleboro Art Center** (257-0124) reside in the old Union Railroad Station at the lower end of Main St. (Open mid-May to Oct. Tues.-Sun. noon-6pm. $2, students and seniors $1, under 18 free.) The **Windham Gallery,** 69 Main St. (257-1881), hosts local art openings on the first Friday of every month, as well as poetry readings and discussions by artists about their works. (Open Fri.-Sat. noon-8pm, Wed.-Thurs. and Sun. noon-4pm. $1 suggested donation.)

Brattleboro's internationally renowned **New England Bach Festival** (257-4526; Mon.-Fri. 9am-5pm for ticket info) runs throughout October, happily coinciding with the high season for fall foliage; plan your trip well in advance. Thousands cram the common for **Village Days,** the last weekend in July, and **Apple Days,** the last weekend in September, to browse through displays of local arts and crafts. Village Days also features the **Anything That Floats River Parade,** where man-made, non-motorized rafts (two kegs strung together will do) stop at nothing to win the race.

Massachusetts

Massachusetts sees itself as the intellectual center of the nation, and this belief is not entirely unfounded. From the 1636 establishment of Harvard, the oldest university in America, until today, Massachusetts has attracted countless intellectuals and literati. More than thinkers though, Massachusetts has attracted activists, including the men and women who fought the American Revolution. Today, the state remains rich in colonial and revolutionary history, while encouraging the ongoing pursuit of academics and liberal politics.

This little state also offers a large variety of cultural and scenic attractions. Boston, the revolutionary "cradle of liberty," has become an ethnically diverse urban center. Resplendent during the fall foliage season, the Berkshire Mountains fill western Massachusetts with a charm that attracts thousands of visitors. The seaside areas from Nantucket to Northern Bristol feature the stark oceanic beauty which first attracted settlers to the North American shore.

PRACTICAL INFORMATION

Capital: Boston.

Massachusetts Division of Tourism: Department of Commerce and Development, 100 Cambridge St., Boston 02202 (617-727-3201; 800-632-8038 for guides). Can send you a complimentary, comprehensive *Spirit of Massachusetts Guidebook* and direct you to regional resources. Open Mon.-Fri. 9am-5pm.

Time Zone: Eastern. **Postal Abbreviation:** MA

Sales Tax: 5%; 0% on clothing and pre-packaged food.

EASTERN MASSACHUSETTS

■■■ BOSTON

As one of the United States' oldest cities, Boston has deep roots in early America and a host of memorials and monuments to prove it. For a jam-packed tour of revolutionary landmarks and historic neighborhoods, the Freedom Trail winds its way through downtown Boston.

The Black Heritage Trail tells another story about this city which, despite an outspoken abolitionist history, has been torn by ethnic and racial controversy. Irish, East Asian, Portuguese, and African-American communities have found homes throughout the city, creating a sometimes uneasy cultural mosaic. Meanwhile a seasonal population of 100,000 college students tug the average age in Boston into the mid-20s. While most residents have a less Boston-centric view of the cosmos than Paul McCartney, who recently proclaimed the city "the hub of the universe," few would deny that Boston is an intriguing microcosm of the American melting pot.

PRACTICAL INFORMATION

Tourist Office: Boston Common Information Center, 147 Tremont St., Boston Common. T: Park St. A good place to start a tour of the city. Free maps and brochures of Boston, Freedom Trail maps ($1.50), and *The Official Guidebook to Boston* ($3), which has useful coupons. Open Mon.-Sat. 8:30am-5pm, Sun. 9am-5pm. **Boston Visitor's Information,** 800 Boylston St. (536-4100, ext. 280), in the Prudential Plaza's customer service booth. T: Prudential. Open Mon.-Fri. 8:30am-5pm, Sat. 10am-6pm, Sun. 11:30am-6pm. **National Historical Park Visitor's Center,** 15 State St. (242-5642). T: State. Info on historical sights and accommodations. Some rangers speak French and German. Open daily 9am-6pm; Sept.-May 9am-5pm.

Airport: Logan International (561-1800 or 800-235-6426), in East Boston. Easily accessible by public transport. The free **Massport Shuttle** connects all terminals with the "Airport" T-stop on the blue line. **City Transportation** (596-1177) runs shuttle buses between Logan and major downtown hotels ($8 one way, under 12 free; service daily every 30min. 7:15am-9:15pm). A **water shuttle** (330-8680) provides a more scenic journey to the downtown area. The shuttle runs from the airport to Rowes Wharf near the New England Aquarium and many hotels. Mon.-Fri. every 15min. 6am-8pm; Fri. every 30min. 8-11pm also; Sat. every 30min. 10am-11pm; Sun. every 30min. 10am-8pm. Taxi transport to downtown costs $15-20, depending on traffic. $8, seniors $4, under 12 free.

Trains: Amtrak (345-7442 or 800-872-7245), South Station, Atlantic Ave. and Summer St. T: South Station. Frequent daily service to: New York City (5hr., $39); Washington, DC (9hr., $55); Philadelphia (7hr., $55); Burlington, VT (12½hr., $99); Baltimore (8½hr., $55). Avoid travel on Fri. and Sun. to obtain the lowest fare. Station open daily 5:45am-10pm.

Buses: Greyhound (800-231-2222), inside South Station. T: South Station. To: New York City (13 per day, 4½hr., $25); Washington, DC (14 per day, 9½hr., $43); Philadelphia (13 per day, 7hr., $43); Baltimore (11 per day, 9hr., $43), and Burlington, VT (4 per day, 5hr., $45). **Vermont Transit** (802-862-9671), located in the same station. To: Burlington (3 per day, 5hr., $45). Station open 24 hrs. **Peter Pan,** 155 Atlantic Ave. (426-7838), across the street from South Station. T: South Station. Runs to Western Massachusetts and Albany, NY ($25), and connects to New York City via Hartford ($24). Station also houses **Concord Trailways** (800-

639-3317), which goes north to New Hampshire and Maine; Concord ($11) and Portland ($15). Both open daily 5:30am-12:30am. **Bonanza,** 145 Dartmouth St. (800-556-3815), in the Back Bay Railroad Station. T: Back Bay. Frequent daily service to Providence ($7.75); Fall River ($8); Newport ($13); Falmouth ($12); Woods Hole ($13). Open 24 hrs. **East Coast Explorer,** 245 Eighth Ave., NYC (718-694-9667, Mon.-Fri. 8-11pm), offers all-day, scenic budget bus trips between New York, Boston, and Washington DC.

Ferries: Bay State Cruises (723-7800) departs from Long Wharf; ticket sales in a red building across from the Marriot Hotel. T: Aquarium. Cruises Memorial Day-Labor Day daily on the hour 10am-4pm; Labor Day-Columbus Day call for schedule. To: George's Island ($6.50, under 13 and seniors $4.50); Provincetown ($29 same-day round trip).

Public Transportation: Massachusetts Bay Transportation Authority (MBTA), 722-3200 or 800-392-6100. The **subway** system, known as the "**T**," consists of the Red, Green, Blue, and Orange lines. "Inbound" trains run into the center of Boston, while "outbound" trains travel from the city into the outlying areas. Useful maps available at information centers and T-stops. Lines run daily 5:30am-12:30am. Fare 85¢, seniors 20¢, ages 5-11 40¢. Some automated T entrances in outlying areas require tokens and don't sell them; buy several tokens at a time and have them handy. **MBTA Bus** service covers the city and suburbs more closely than the subway. Fare, generally 60¢, may vary with destination. Bus schedules available at Park St. or Harvard Sq. T-stations. The **MBTA Commuter Rail** reaches suburbs and the North Shore, leaving from the North Station, Porter Sq., and South Station T-stops. A "T passport," sold at the Visitor's Center, offers discounts at local businesses and unlimited travel on all subway and bus lines and some commuter rail zones; only worthwhile for frequent users of public transportation. 1-day pass $5, 3-day $9, 7-day $18.

Taxis: Red Cab, 734-5000. Base fare $1.50; $2 per mi. **Checker Taxi,** 536-7000. Base fare $1.50, $2.10 per mi.

Car Rental: Merchants Rent a Car, 20 Rex Dr. (356-5656). T: Braintree. Rents to drivers 18 and over. Compact cars $27 per day, $168 per week, with unlimited mileage in New England. Under 21 25% surcharge per day. Customer must supply auto insurance or credit card with coverage. Open Mon.-Fri. 8am-6pm, Sat. 8am-noon. **Dollar Rent-a-Car** (569-5300), in Logan Airport. T: Airport. Rates vary daily depending on availability. Under 25 $20 surcharge per day. Must be 21 with major credit card. 10% AAA discount. Open Mon.-Fri. 7:30am-6pm, Sat.-Sun. 8am-4pm. Other offices throughout Boston, including the Sheraton Hotel (523-5098).

Bike Rental: Community Bike Shop, 496 Tremont St. (542-8623). $5 per hr., $20 per day (24 hrs.), $75 per week. Must have major credit card. Open Mon.-Fri. 9:30am-8pm, Sat. 9:30am-6pm., Sun. noon-5pm.

Crisis Lines: Rape Hotline, 492-7273. **Alcohol and Drug Hotline,** 445-1500. Both open 24 hrs. **Gay and Lesbian Helpline,** 267-9001. Open Mon.-Fri. 4-11pm, Sat.-Sun. 6-11pm.

Emergency: 911.

Post Office: 24 Dorchester Ave. (654-5327). Open Mon.-Fri. 8am-midnight, Sat. 8am-5pm, Sun. noon-5pm. **ZIP code:** 02205. **Area code:** 617.

Boston owes its layout as much to the clomping of colonial cows as to urban designers. Avoid driving—the public transportation system is excellent, parking expensive, and Boston drivers somewhat maniacal. Several outlying T-stops offer park-and-ride services. The North Quincy T-stop charges $2.50 per day. Alternatively, there is free parking on Memorial Dr. in Cambridge. If you do choose to drive, be defensive and alert; Boston's pedestrians can be as aggressive as its drivers. Finally, to avoid getting lost in Boston's labyrinth, ask for detailed directions wherever you go.

Let's Go's compendium **The Unofficial Guide to Life at Harvard** ($8) has the inside scoop and up-to-date listings for Boston/Cambridge area restaurants, history, entertainment, sights, transportation and services. Inquire at bookstores in Harvard Sq. (see Cambridge, below).

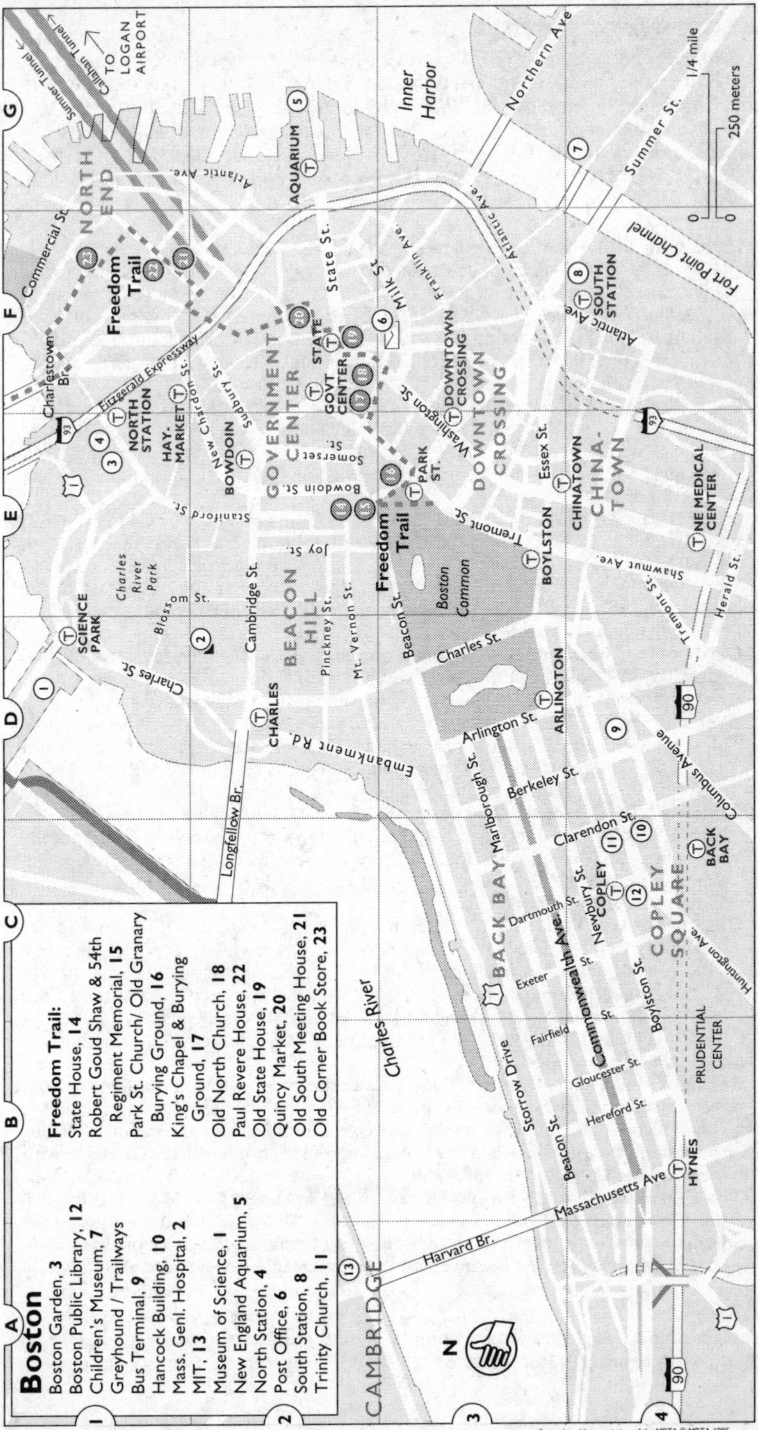

Boston

Boston Garden, **3**
Boston Public Library, **12**
Children's Museum, **7**
Greyhound / Trailways Bus Terminal, **9**
Hancock Building, **10**
Mass. Genl. Hospital, **2**
MIT, **13**
Museum of Science, **1**
New England Aquarium, **5**
North Station, **4**
Post Office, **6**
South Station, **8**
Trinity Church, **11**

Freedom Trail:
State House, **14**
Robert Goud Shaw & 54th Regiment Memorial, **15**
Park St. Church/ Old Granary Burying Ground, **16**
King's Chapel & Burying Ground, **17**
Old North Church, **18**
Paul Revere House, **22**
Old State House, **19**
Quincy Market, **20**
Old South Meeting House, **21**
Old Corner Book Store, **23**

ACCOMMODATIONS

Cheap accommodations are hard to come by in Boston. In September, Boston fills with parents depositing their college-bound children; in June parents help remove their graduated, unemployment-bound children. Reserve a room six months to a year in advance during those times. Those with cars should investigate the motels along highways in outlying areas. **Boston Reservations,** 1643 Beacon St. #23, Waban, 02168 (332-4199; fax 332-5751), presides over scores of Boston area accommodations (open Mon.-Fri. 9am-5pm; singles $60-110, doubles $80-150).

Hostelling International-Boston (HI-AYH), 12 Hemenway St. (536-9455). T: Hynes/ICA. This cheery, colorful hostel has clean but crowded rooms, some with sinks. Shared bath. Great location. Lockers, common rooms, cafeteria, kitchens, and laundry. Wheelchair-accessible. 190 beds in summer, 100 in winter. Planned activities nightly. Ask about discounts. Check-in 24 hrs. Check-out 11am. $15, nonmembers $18. Membership required in summer. Linen $2 plus a $5 deposit. Reservations highly recommended; IBN reservations available.

Back Bay Summer Hostel (HI-AYH), 519 Beacon St. (353-3294). T: Copley. Located in a pretty section of town, Back Bay picks up overflow from its sister in the Fenway. 100 beds. 5-day max. stay. Check-in 7-10am and 5pm-2am. Check-out 9:30am. $15, membership required. Reservations highly recommended. Open June 15-Aug 25.

Irish Embassy Hostel, 232 Friend St. (973-4841), above the Irish Embassy Pub. T: North Station. Small, clean, comfortable dorm rooms. 2 free barbecues per week and free admission to the pub; a lively place to stay and make friends. Common area with TV, kitchen. Check-in daily 9am-2pm and 5-9pm; otherwise ask in the pub. 24-hr access. 48 beds. $15; 1 private double $15 per person. Reservations recommended. Lockers free; lock rental $1. Linens free. No sleeping bags.

Garden Halls Residences, 260 Commonwealth Ave. (267-0079; fax 536-1735), in Back Bay. T: Copley. The rooms in these Boston brownstones are clean, bright, and attractively furnished. Outstanding location just a few blocks from Copley Sq. Vending machines, TV/VCR, laundry, microwaves, and linen service. Singles, doubles, triples, and quads; some private baths. Check-in 10am-4pm. $30 per person per night, $190 per week, $450 per month. Breakfast $3, dinner $5. Key and linen deposit $30. Reservations recommended.

Anthony's Town House, 1085 Beacon St. (566-3972), Brookline. T: Hawes, Green Line-C. Very convenient to the T-stop. 12 ornately furnished rooms for 20 guests, who range from trim professionals to scruffy backpackers. Check-out noon. Singles and doubles $30-66; mid.-Nov. to mid-March $5 less. Ask about weekly rates. Mention *Let's Go* for a 5% discount.

Greater Boston YMCA, 316 Huntington Ave. (536-7800). Down the street from Symphony Hall on Mass. Ave. T: Northeastern. Elegant lobby and friendly atmosphere, with access to cafeteria, pool, and recreational facilities. Must be 18. Shared hall bathroom. Breakfast included. Women accepted. Accessible to the disabled. 10-day max. stay. ID and luggage required for check-in. Office staffed 24 hrs. Check-out 11am. With HI-AYH ID singles $34, doubles $50, nonmembers $37.50/$55. Key deposit $5.

Berkeley Residence Club (YWCA), 40 Berkeley St. (482-8850). T: Arlington. Solid, clean, industrial accommodations for women only; men can visit the lobby. Grand piano, patio, pool, TV room, sun deck, laundry facilities, library. Hall baths. Some doubles with sinks are available. Singles $32, doubles $46. Cafeteria with breakfast for $2.50, dinner for $6.50.

The Farrington Inn, 23 Farrington Ave. (787-1860 or 800-767-5337), Allston Station. T: Harvard on Green Line-B, or bus #66. Call for driving directions. Functional rooms with local phone, parking, and breakfast. Most rooms have TVs. Shared baths. Somewhat inconvenient location. Singles $45-50, doubles $60.

FOOD

Boston ain't called Beantown for nothing. You can sample the real thing at **Durgin Park,** 340 Faneuil Hall Marketplace (227-2038; T: Government Center). Durgin was serving Yankee cuisine in Faneuil Hall (see Sights, below) long before the tourists arrived, and maintains its integrity with such delights as Indian pudding ($2.50) and Yankee Pot Roast ($7). Durgin Park's downstairs **Oyster Bar** highlights another Boston specialty with frequent seafood specials, including a modest lobster dinner for around $10. Find the city's celebrated seafood in the numerous (mostly expensive) seafood restaurants lining Boston Harbor by the wharf (T: Aquarium).

Beyond seafood and baked beans, Boston dishes out an impressive variety of international cuisines. The scent of garlic filters through the **North End** (T: Haymarket), where an endless array of Italian groceries, bakeries, cafés, and restaurants line Hanover and Salem St. **Café Vittoria,** 294 Hanover St. (227-7606), serves especially tasty cappuccino (open daily 8am-midnight). Chinese Fu dogs guard the entrance to **Chinatown** and watch over the countless delectable restaurants packed in behind the gates (T: Chinatown). It's easier to walk through the crowded streets, but if you're driving, Kneeland and Washington St. are two main arteries. A Sunday brunch of *Dim Sum* ("to point to the heart's desire") is an inexpensive Chinese tradition; try **The China Pearl,** 9 Tyler St. (426-4338), for a good variety ($2 each). The open-air stalls of **Haymarket** sell fresh produce, fish, fruits, cheeses, and pigs' eyes at well-below-supermarket prices. Get there early for the good stuff. (Indoor stores open daily dawn-dusk; outdoor stalls Fri.-Sat. only. T: Government Center or Haymarket.) Just up Congress St. from Haymarket, the restored **Quincy Market** houses a cornucopia of food booths peddling interesting but overpriced fare.

Addis Red Sea, 544 Tremont St. (426-8727). T: Back Bay. Walk 5 blocks south on Clarendon St. from the T-stop, then turn left on Tremont (10-min. walk). Boston's best Ethiopian, delicious cuisine served on *mesobs,* woven tables which support a communal platter. Entrees $6-10, but combination platters offer 5 dishes for $11-12 (the Winnie Mandela Combination Platter, $15, commemorates her visit to the restaurant). Open Mon.-Thurs. 5-10pm, Fri. 5pm-midnight, Sat. 3:30pm-midnight, Sun. 3:30-10pm.

No Name, 15½ Fish Pier (423-2705), on the waterfront. T: South Station, then a 15-min. walk. This hole-in-the-pier restaurant has been serving up some of the best fried seafood in Boston for 78 years; bigshots like the Kennedys and more obscure patrons from all walks of life swear by it. You'll get lots of fresh seafood (fresh scrod sandwich, $5) with no fuss and (almost) no bill. The harbor view allows you to watch tomorrow's dinner emerging from the boats. Entrees $5-15. Open daily 11am-10pm. No reservations.

Bob the Chef's, 604 Columbus Ave. (536-6204). T: Mass. Ave. From the T-stop, face the Prudential building, turn right and walk up Mass. Ave.; turn right onto Columbus Ave. Southern food that's unchallenged in Boston. Smokin' sweet potato pie ($2.50), and the chitterlings, fried fish, chicken livers, corn bread, and famed "glorifried chicken" have soul to spare. Vegetarians take caution! Entrees $7-10. Open Sun.-Thurs. 8am-10pm, Fri.-Sat. 8am-11pm.

Sultan's Kitchen, 72 Broad St. (728-2828). T: Downtown Crossing. Follow Chauncy St., which will become Arch St.; then turn right on Franklin St. and left on Broad St. Open for lunch only, this excellent Middle Eastern eatery (the first Turkish restaurant in Boston) has Turkish music, speedy service, and generous portions. 12-oz. soup with pita bread $2.85. Baba Ganoush salad $5.75. Open Mon.-Fri. 11am-5pm, Sat. 11am-3pm.

Ruby's, 280 Cambridge St. (367-3224). T: Charles. From the T-stop, walk toward the Holiday Inn with Mass. General Hospital on your left; it's on your right about 3 blocks down. Weekdays before 10am, you can "Beat the House" at this small Beacon Hill eatery; 2 eggs, home fries, and toast for 75¢. All-day breakfast is the star attraction, but "Dad's Dagwood" sandwich ($5.50) and burgers await those with afternoon appetites. Open Mon.-Thurs. 7am-9pm, Fri.-Sun. 8am-11pm.

Grand Chau Chow, 41-45 Beach St. (292-5166), in Chinatown. T: South Station. Follow Atlantic Ave. south to Beach St. There's no messing around about Grand Chau's Chow; wait in line, sit down, eat top-quality, award-winning Chinese food, pay, and leave. They pride themselves on seafood, but the chicken with cashews

($7) and the vegetarian Buddha's Delight ($5) are also excellent. Most dishes hover around $6. Huge portions. Open Sun.-Thurs. 10am-2am, Fri.-Sat. 10am-4am.

La Famiglia Giorgio's, 112 Salem St. (367-6711), in the North End. T: Haymarket. Notorious for serving two meals: the one you eat in the restaurant and the one you take home. Portions are enormous and tasty; the garden salad contains more than one head of lettuce. Lasagna $10. Chicken parmesan sandwich $7. Plenty of vegetarian options. Entrees $6-15. $8 minimum food purchase. Open daily 11am-11pm. No reservations; expect to wait, especially on weekends.

SIGHTS

The Freedom Trail

A great introduction to Boston's history lies along the red-painted line of the Freedom Trail, a 2½ mi. path through downtown Boston which passes many of the city's historic landmarks. Even on a trail dedicated to the land of the free, some sights charge admission; bring some money if you're bent on doing the whole thing. The National Park Service offers free guided tours of the trail's free attractions starting at their **visitors center,** 15 State St. (tours in summer daily on the hr. 10am-3pm).

The Freedom Trail begins at another **visitors center,** in **Boston Common** (T: Park St.). You can pick up maps here, in varying degrees of detail (free, $1.50, or $5). The trail runs uphill to the **Robert Gould Shaw and 54th Regiment Memorial,** on Beacon St. The memorial honors the first black regiment of the Union Army in the American Civil War and their Bostonian leader, all made famous by the movie *Glory*. The trail then crosses the street to the **State House** (free tours Mon.-Fri. every 30min. 10am-noon, every hr. noon-4pm; open Mon.-Fri. 9am-5pm). Next, the trail proceeds to the **Park Street Church** and passes the **Old Granary Burial Ground** on the way to **King's Chapel and Burial Ground,** on Tremont St. Boston's oldest Anglican church, the Chapel housed a congregation as early as 1688; more recently, the cemetery has come to house Governor Bradford and William Dawes (tours $1, students and seniors 50¢, under 12 free; open Mon.-Sat. 10am-4pm).

Closed for renovations until Spring of 1997, the **Old South Meeting House** (482-6439), was the site of the pre-party get together which set the mood for the Boston Tea Party. Formerly the seat of British government in Boston, the **Old State House** now serves as a museum and the next stop on the trail. (Open daily 9:30am-5pm; $3, students and seniors $2, ages 6-18 $1.50, under 6 free.) The trail proceeds past the site of the **Boston Massacre** and through **Faneuil Hall,** a former meeting hall and current mega-mall where the National Park Service operates a desk and conducts talks in the upstairs Great Hall (open daily 9am-5pm; talks every 30min.). As you head into the North End, the **Paul Revere House** (523-1676) is the next landmark on the path. (Open daily 9:30am-5:15pm; off season 9:30am-4:15pm; Jan.-March closed Mon. $2.50, students and seniors $2, ages 5-17 $1.) The **Old North Church** follows (open Mon.-Sat. 9am-5pm, Sun. services 9, 11am, and 4pm). **Copp's Hill Burial Ground** provides a resting place for lots of colonial Bostonians and a nice view of the Old North Church. Nearing its end, the Freedom Trail heads over the Charlestown Bridge to the **U.S.S. Constitution.** The *Constitution* is in dry-dock without masts until September 1995, but should be fully open for touring in 1996 (open daily 9:30-sunset). For more info call the Navy Yard Visitors Center at 242-5601. The final stop on the trail, the **Bunker Hill Monument,** isn't on loan from Washington. The fraudulent obelisk—nearby Breed's Hill was the real site of the battle in question—has a grand view of the city. Come prepared and do some stretches; the monument doubles as a Stairmaster (294 steps and no elevator). To return to Boston, follow the red line back over the bridge or hop on a water taxi from one of the piers near the *Constitution* (water taxis every 30min., every 15min. after 3:30pm. $1, exact change required).

Downtown

In 1634, early inhabitants designated the **Boston Common** (T: Park Street), now bounded by Tremont, Boylston, Charles, Beacon, and Park St., as a place to graze their cattle. These days, street vendors, not cows, live off the fat of this land. Though bustling in the daytime, the Common is dangerous at night—don't walk alone here after dark. Across from the Common on Charles St., the title characters from the children's book *Make Way for Ducklings* (immortalized in bronze) point the way to the **Public Gardens,** where peddle-powered **Swan Boats** (522-1966) glide around a quiet pond lined with shady willows. (T: Arlington. Boats open mid-April to mid-June daily 10am-4pm; mid-June-Labor Day 10am-5pm; Labor Day to mid-Sept. Mon.-Fri. noon-4pm, Sat.-Sun. 10am-4pm. $1.50, seniors $1.25, under 12 95¢.)

The city's neighborhoods cluster in a loose circle around the Common and Gardens. Directly above the Common lies **Beacon Hill,** an exclusive residential neighborhood originally settled by the Puritans. Significantly smaller today than when the Puritans resided here, the Hill gave tons of earth to fill in the marshes that are now the Back Bay (see Back Bay and Beyond, below). Art galleries, antique shops, and cafés line the cobblestone streets and brick sidewalks of the hill; Charles St. makes an especially nice setting for a stroll. The **State House** sits atop the Hill (see Freedom Trail, above). The **Harrison Gray Otis House,** 141 Cambridge St. (227-3956), is a Charles Bulfinch original. (Tours Tues.-Fri. on the hr. noon-4pm, Sat. 10am-4pm. $4, seniors $3.50, under 12 $2.) The nearby **Boston Athenaeum,** 10½ Beacon St. (227-0270), offers tours of its art gallery and print room, and of the collection, which contains over 700,000 books, including most of George Washington's library. (Free tours Tues. and Thurs. 3pm; reservations required. Open in summer Mon.-Fri. 9am-5:30pm; off season Sat. 9am-4pm also.)

The Black Heritage Trail begins at the **Boston African-American National Historic Site,** 46 Joy St. (742-1854; T: Park Street), where you can pick up a free map and visit the museum inside (open daily 10am-4pm; donation requested). Fourteen fascinating stops, each marked by a red, black, and green logo, make up the trail. Landmarks in the development of Boston's African-American community include North America's first black church, the **African Meeting House** (1805), the **Robert Gould Shaw and 54th Regiment Memorial** (see Freedom Trail, above), and the **Lewis and Harriet Hayden House,** a station on the Underground Railroad.

East of Beacon Hill on Cambridge St., the red brick plaza of **Government Center** (T: Government Center) surrounds the monstrous concrete **City Hall** (725-4000), designed by I.M. Pei (open to the public Mon.-Fri.). A few blocks south, its more aesthetically pleasing relative, the **Old State House,** 206 Washington St. (720-1713 or 720-3290; T: State), once rocked with a revolution (see Freedom Trail, above).

Set amidst Boston's business district, the pedestrian mall at **Downtown Crossing,** south of City Hall at Washington St. (T: Downtown Crossing), centers around **Filene's,** 426 Washington St., (357-2100), the mild-mannered department store that conceals the chaotic bargain-feeding frenzy that is **Filene's Basement.** Even if you don't plan to shop, check out the Basement—it's a cultural institution.

Southwest of the Common, Boston's **Chinatown** (T: Chinatown) demarcates itself with an arch and huge Foo dogs at its Beach St. entrance, and pagoda-style telephone booths and streetlamps throughout. Within this small area cluster many restaurants, food stores, and novelty shops; this is the place for good Chinese food, Chinese slippers, and 1000-year-old eggs. *Do not walk alone here at night.* Chinatown holds two big festivals each year. The first, **New Year,** usually celebrated on a Sunday in February, includes lion dances, fireworks, and Kung Fu exhibitions. The **August Moon Festival** honors a mythological pair of lovers at the time of the full moon, usually on the second or third Sunday in August. Call 542-2574 for details.

The east tip of Boston contains the historic **North End** (T: Haymarket). Now an Italian neighborhood, the city's oldest residential district overflows with windowboxes, Italian flags, fragrant pastry shops, créches, Sicilian restaurants, and Catholic churches. The most famous of the last, **Old St. Stephens Church,** 401 Hanover St. (523-1230), is the classic colonial brainchild of Charles Bulfinch. (Open daily

8:30am-5pm; services Mon.-Fri. 12:05pm, Sat. 5:15pm, Sun. 8:30 and 11am.) Down the street, the sweet-smelling **Peace Gardens** attempt to drown out the clamor of the North End with beautiful flora. (For more sights, see Freedom Trail, above.)

The Waterfront

The **waterfront area,** bounded by Atlantic and Commercial St., runs along Boston Harbor from South Station to the North End Park. Stroll down Commercial, Lewis, or Museum Wharf for a view of the harbor and a breath of sea air. The excellent **New England Aquarium** (973-5200; T: Aquarium), on Central Wharf at the Waterfront, presents cavorting penguins, giant sea turtles, and a bevy of briny beasts all in a 187,000 gallon tank. Dolphins and sea lions perform in the ship *Discovery,* moored alongside the Aquarium. Lines tend to be long on weekends; pass the time for free, watching harbor seals frolic in the tank outside. (Open Mon.-Wed. and Fri. 9am-5pm, Thurs. 9am-8pm, Sat.-Sun. and holidays 9am-6pm. $8.50, students and seniors $7.50, ages 3-11 $4.50; Thurs. after 4pm $1 off, seniors free Mon. noon-4:30pm.) The aquarium also offers **whale-watching cruises** (973-5277) from April to October. (Sightings guaranteed. Generally 2 trips daily; call for times. $24, students and seniors $19, ages 12-18 $17.50, ages 3-11 $16.50. Under 36" not allowed. Reservations suggested.) The **Bay State Cruise Company** (723-7800) conducts cheap lunch cruises of the harbor and longer cruises to the **Boston Harbor Islands** for a picnic or a tour of Civil War Fort Warren (see Practical Information, above).

Back Bay and Beyond

In **Back Bay,** north of the South End and west of Beacon Hill, three-story brownstone row houses line some of the only gridded streets in Boston. Originally the marshy, uninhabitable "back bay" on the Charles River, the area was filled in during the 19th century. Architectural styles progress chronologically through 19th-century popular design as you travel from east to west, reflecting the gradual process of filling in the marsh. Statues and benches punctuate the large, grassy median of **Commonwealth Ave.** ("Comm. Ave."). Boston's most flamboyant promenade, **Newbury St.** (T: Arlington, Copley, or Hynes/ICA). may inspire you to ask yourself some serious questions about your credit rating; the dozens of small art galleries, boutiques, bookstores, and cafés that line the street exude exclusivity and swank, and offer unparalleled people-watching. The riverside **Esplanade** (T: Charles) extends from the Longfellow Bridge to the Harvard Bridge, parallel to Newbury St. Boston's answer to the beach, the park fills with sun-seekers and sail-boaters in the summer. It may look nice, but don't go in the water. Pick up the bike path along the river and pedal to the posh suburb of **Wellesley** for a terrific afternoon ride.

Beyond Back Bay, west on Commonwealth Ave., the huge landmark **Citgo sign** watches over **Kenmore Sq.** (T: Kenmore). The area around Kenmore has more than its share of neon, with many of the city's most popular nightclubs hovering on **Landsdowne St.** (see Nightlife below). Near Kenmore Sq., the **Fenway** area contains some of the country's best museums. Ubiquitous landscaper Frederick Law Olmsted of Central Park fame designed the **Fens** area at the center of the Fenway as part of his "Emerald Necklace" vision for Boston. Though the necklace was never completed, the park remains a gem; fragrant rose gardens and neighborhood vegetable patches make perfect picnic turf. As you might well suspect, the Fenway also houses Fenway Park (see Curse of the Bambino below).

The rest of Olmsted's **Emerald Necklace Parks** make up a free five-hour walking tour given by the Boston Park Rangers (635-7383; tour reservations required). Visiting the parks individually—the Boston Common (T: Park St.; see Downtown, above), the Public Garden (T: Arlington; see Downtown, above), Commonwealth Avenue Mall (T: Arlington), Back Bay Fens (T: Kenmore), Muddy River, Olmsted Park, Jamaica Pond, the Arnold Arboretum (T: Arborway), and Franklin Park—requires a bit less time. Call the Park Rangers for info and directions.

Copley

In the Back Bay on commercial Boylston St., the handsome **Copley Sq.** (T: Copley) accommodates a range of seasonal activities, including summertime concerts, folk dancing, a food pavilion, and people-watching. The massive and imposing **Boston Public Library,** 666 Boylston St. (536-5400), serves as a permanent memorial to the hundreds of literati whose names are inscribed upon it. Relax on a bench or window seat overlooking the tranquil courtyard or in the vaulted reading room. The auditorium gives a program of lectures and films, and often displays collections of art. (Open Mon.-Thurs. 9am-9pm, Fri.-Sat. 9am-5pm.) Across the square next to I.M. Pei's Hancock Tower (see below), stands H.H. Richardson's Romanesque fantasy, **Trinity Church** (536-0944). Many consider Trinity, built in 1877, a masterpiece of U.S. church architecture—the interior justifies this opinion. (T: Copley. Open Mon.-Sat. 8am-6pm.) The ritzy mall on the corner is **Copley Place,** right next door to the renovated **Prudential Building.** The **Prudential Skywalk,** on the 50th floor of the Prudential Building, 800 Boylston St. (236-3318), grants a full 360° view from New Hampshire to the Cape. (T: Prudential. Open Mon.-Sat. 10am-10pm, Sun. noon-10pm. $2.75, students with ID, seniors, and children $1.75.) The **John Hancock Observatory,** 200 Clarendon St. (572-6429; 247-1977 for a recording; T: Copley or Back Bay), the tallest building in New England at 60 floors (740 ft.), also lets you take in the city skyline (open Mon.-Sat. 9am-10pm, Sun. 10am-10pm. $3.75, seniors and ages 5-17 $2.75). The partially gentrified **South End,** south of Copley, makes for good brownstone viewing and casual dining.

Two blocks down Massachusetts Ave. from Boylston St., the **Mother Church** of the **First Church of Christ, Scientist,** 1 Norway St. (450-2000), at Mass. Ave. and Huntington, headquarters the international movement founded in Boston by Mary Baker Eddy. A vast and imposing complex of buildings make up the church. Both the Mother Church and the smaller, older church out back can be seen by guided tour only. (Tours Tues.-Fri. every ½hr. 10am-4pm, Sun. 11:15am-2pm. Free.) Use the catwalk to pass through the **Mapparium,** a 30-ft.-wide stained-glass globe, in the Christian Science Publishing Society next door. The globe, built in the 1930s, features highly unusual acoustics; sound waves bounce off the sphere in any and all directions. Whisper in the ear of Pakistan while standing next to Surinam. (Tours Tues.-Fri. 9:30am-4pm. Sat. noon-4pm. Free.)

Museums

The free *Guide to Museums of Boston* has details on museums not mentioned here.

Museum of Fine Arts (MFA), 465 Huntington Ave. (267-9300), near Massachusetts Ave. T: Ruggles/Museum on Green line-E. Boston's most famous museum contains one of the world's finest collections of Asian ceramics, outstanding Egyptian art, a good showing of Impressionists, and superb American art. The two famous unfinished portraits of George and Martha Washington, begun by Gilbert Stuart in 1796, merit a gander. Open Tues. and Thurs.-Sat. 10am-4:45pm, Wed. 10am-9:45pm, Sun. 10am-5:45pm. West Wing only open Thurs.-Fri. 5-9:45pm. $8, students and seniors $6, ages 6-17 $3.50; free Wed. 4-9:45pm. West Wing only $5; Thurs.-Fri. evenings $6, students and seniors $5, ages 6-17 $3.

Isabella Stewart Gardner Museum, 280 Fenway (566-1401), a few hundred yards from the MFA. T: Ruggles/Museum. In what ranks as one of the greatest art heists in history, a 1990 break-in relieved the museum of works by Rembrandt, Vermeer, Dégas, and others. However, many masterpieces remain in Ms. Gardner's Venetian-style palace, and the courtyard garden soothes a weary traveler's soul. Open Tues.-Sun. 11am-5pm. Chamber music on 1st floor Sept.-June Sat. and Sun. afternoons. $7, students and seniors $5, under 12 free; Wed. students $3.

Museum of Science (723-2500), Science Park. T: Science Park. At the far east end of the Esplanade on the Charles River Dam. Contains, among other wonders, the largest "lightning machine" (a Van de Graaff generator, for all you science buffs) in the world. A multi-story roller-coaster for small metal balls explains energy states. Within the museum, the **Hayden Planetarium** features models, lectures, films, and laser and star shows; the **Mugar Omni Theatre** shows films on scientific subjects on a four-story-domed screen. Museum open Sun.-Thurs. 9am-5pm, Fri. 9am-9pm. Exhibits $8, seniors and ages 3-14 $6; Sept.-April Wed. 1-5pm free. Planetarium, laser show, and Omni each $7.50, seniors and ages 3-14 $5.50. Museum, Omni, and Planetarium $16, seniors and ages 3-14 $12.

Children's Museum, 300 Congress St. (426-8855), in south Boston on Museum Wharf. T: South Station. Follow the signs with milk bottles. Kids of all ages paw way-cool hands-on exhibits and learn a little something to boot. Open Sat.-Thurs. 10am-5pm, Fri. 10am-9pm; Sept.-June closed Mon. $7, seniors and ages 2-15 $6, age 1 $2, under 1 free; Fri. 5-9pm $1.

John F. Kennedy Presidential Library (929-4567), Columbia Point on Morrissey Blvd. in Dorchester. T: JFK/UMass; free MBTA shuttle to the U Mass campus and from the library. Dedicated "to all those who through the art of politics seek a new and better world." The looming white structure, designed by I.M. Pei, contains exhibits which trace President Kennedy's career from the campaign trail to his tragic death. Open daily 9am-5pm. $6, seniors $4, ages 6-16 $3, under 6 free.

Institute of Contemporary Art (ICA), 955 Boylston St. (266-5152). T: Hynes/ICA. Boston's lone outpost of the avant-garde attracts major contemporary artists while aggressively promoting lesser-known work. Their innovative, sometimes controversial exhibits change every 8 weeks. The museum also presents experimental theater, music, dance, and film. Prices vary; call for more info. Open Wed.-Thurs. noon-9pm, Fri.-Sun. noon-5pm. $5.25, students with ID $3.25, seniors and under 16 $2.25; free Thurs. 5-9pm.

ENTERTAINMENT

Musicians, dancers, actors, and *artistes* of every description reside in Boston. An unusually large and diverse community of **street performers** ("buskers") juggle steak knives, swallow torches, wax poetic, and sing folk tunes in the subways and squares of Boston and Cambridge. The *Boston Phoenix* and the "Calendar" section of Thursday's *Boston Globe* list activities for the coming week. Also check the free *Where: Boston* booklet available at the visitors center. What Boston doesn't have, Cambridge probably does (see Cambridge Entertainment and Nightlife, p. 106). **Bostix** (723-5181), a Ticketmaster outlet in Faneuil Hall and at Copley Sq. (at Boylston and Dartmouth St.), sells ½-price tickets to performing arts events starting at 11am on the day of performance. (Service charge $1.50-2.50 per ticket. Cash and traveler's checks only. Copley Sq. open Mon. 10am-6pm; both locations open Tues.-Sat. 10am-6pm, Sun. 11am-4pm.)

Actors in town cluster around Washington St. and Harrison Ave. in the **Theater District** (T: Boylston). The **Wang Center for the Performing Arts,** 270 Tremont St. (482-9393), produces theater, classical music, and opera in its gorgeous baroque complex. Here, the renowned **Boston Ballet** (695-6950), one of the nation's best, annually brings to life such classics as the *Nutcracker* and *Swan Lake.* The **Shubert Theater,** 265 Tremont St. (426-4520), hosts Broadway hits touring through Boston. Tickets for these and for shows at the **Charles Playhouse,** 74 Warrenton St. (426-6912) cost around $30.

The area's regional companies cost less and may provide a more interesting evening. Both the **New Theater,** 66 Marlborough St. (247-7388), and **Huntington Theater Co.,** 264 Huntington Ave. (266-7900; 266-0800 for box office), at Boston University, have solid artistic reputations (tickets $8-35). During termtime, affordable student theater goes up constantly; watch students tread the boards at **Tufts Theater Arena** (627-3493), the **BU Theater** (353-3320), the **MIT Drama Shop** (253-2908), and the **MIT Shakespeare Ensemble** (253-2903). For student musical performances, try the **New England Conservatory** (262-1120; box office 536-2412); the conservatory was temporarily closed for remodeling at press time, but performances should resume in November 1995.

The **Boston Symphony Orchestra,** 201 Mass. Ave. (266-1492; T: Symphony), at Huntington, holds its concert season from October to April ($20-57). Rush seats ($7) go on sale three hours before concerts. During July and August, the symphony takes a vacation at **Tanglewood** (413-637-5165), in western Massachusetts. Though difficult to reach by public transportation, Tanglewood defines music *en plein air*. Peter Pan (see Practical Information, above) buses to Lenox; from there, it's a 1½-mi. walk. Mid-May through July, while the BSO's away, the **Boston Pops Orchestra** (266-1492) plays in **Symphony Hall,** 301 Mass. Ave. (Box office and concert info 266-1200; open Mon.-Sat. 10am-6pm, Sun. 1-6pm on concert days. Recorded message 266-2378. Tickets $11-36.50.) You can also see the Pops at the **Hatch Shell** (727-9547) on the Esplanade any night in the first week of July; arrive early to sit within earshot of the orchestra (concert 8pm; free). On the **4th of July,** hundreds of thousands of patriotic thrillseekers pack the Esplanade to hear the Pops concert (broadcast by loudspeaker throughout the area) and watch the fireworks display. Arrive before noon for a seat on the Esplanade, although you can watch the fireworks from almost anywhere along the river.

The **Berklee Performance Center,** 136 Mass. Ave. (266-7455; box office 266-1400, ext. 261), an adjunct of the Berklee School of Music, holds concerts featuring students, faculty, and jazz and classical luminaries.

For information on other special events, such as the **St. Patrick's Day Parade** (March 17), **Patriot's Day** celebrations (April 8), the week-long **Boston Common Dairy Festival** (June), the **Boston Harbor Fest** (early July), the North End's **Festival of St. Anthony** (mid-August), and **First Night** (New Year's Eve), see the *Boston Phoenix* or *Globe* calendars.

Singing Beach, 40 minutes out of downtown, on the commuter line to Manchester-by-the-Sea (see Practical Information, above), gained its name from the sound made when you drag your feet through the sand. It's very cool. The beach charges a $1 entrance fee, but playing in the sand is free after that. You can swim too. Park your car in town and walk the ½ mi. to the beach. By car, take Rte. 127 to exit 16.

The Curse of the Bambino and Other Sports

Ever since the Red Sox traded Babe Ruth to the Yankees in 1918, Boston sports fans have learned to take the good with the bad. They have seen more basketball championships than any other city (16) but haven't boasted a World Series title in over 75 years. Yet through it all, they follow their teams with puritanical fervor. On summer nights, thousands of baseball fans make the pilgrimage to **Fenway Park** (T: Kenmore). Home of the infamous back wall known as the "Green Monster," Fenway is the nation's oldest Major League ballpark and center stage for the perennially heart-rending **Boston Red Sox** (box office 267-8661; open Mon.-Fri. 9am-5pm, Sat. 9:30am-2pm, or until game time if the team's in town) baseball club. At press time, the Sox were poised to win the American League Eastern Division; *Let's Go* can't predict the future, but remember, this is the team which, if given a chicken filet, would find a bone to choke on. Most grandstand tickets sell out far in advance, but bleacher seats are often available on game day.

The famous **Boston Garden** (T: North Station), located off the JFK Expressway between the West and North Ends, has been replaced by the FleetCenter (T: North Station). Call 624-1000 for FleetCenter info. The storied **Boston Celtics** basketball team (season Oct.-May; 227-3200 for info) and **Boston Bruins** hockey team (season Oct.-April; call 227-3200 for info) play here. A fair distance outside Boston, **Foxboro Stadium,** 16 Washington St., Foxboro, hosts the **New England Patriots** NFL team (season Sept.-Jan.; call 508-543-3900 for info). The stadium also stages concerts. Rail service to the games and some concerts runs from South Station; call for details.

In October, the **Head of the Charles** rowing regatta, the largest such single-day event in the world, attracts rowing clubs, baseball caps, and beer-stained college sweatshirts from across the country. The 3-mi. races begin at Boston University Bridge; the best vantage points are atop Weeks footbridge and Anderson Bridge near Harvard University. On the third Monday in April the 10,000 runners competing in the **Boston Marathon** battle Boston area boulevards and the infamous Heartbreak Hill. Call the **Massachusetts Division of Tourism** (727-3201) for details.

NIGHTLIFE

Remnants of the city's Puritan heritage temper Boston's nightlife ("blue laws" prohibit the sale of alcohol after certain hours and on Sundays), along with the lack of public transportation after midnight. Nearly all bars and most clubs close between 1 and 2am, and bar admittance for anyone under 21 is hard-won. Boston's local music scene runs the gamut from folk to funk; Beantown natives-gone-national include the Pixies, Aerosmith, Tracy Chapman, Dinosaur Jr., Lemonheads, Bobby Brown, and the Mighty Mighty Bosstones. Cruise down **Landsdowne St.** (T: Kenmore) and **Boylston Place** (T: Boylston) to find concentrated action. The weekly *Boston Phoenix* has comprehensive club and concert listings (out on Thurs.; $1.50). Call the *Phoenix* **club line** (859-3300) to hear about scheduled events at most clubs.

Avalon (262-2424), **Axis** (262-2437), **Venus de Milo** (421-9595), 5-13 Lansdowne St. T: Kenmore. Upscale 80s-style pre-yuppie, neo-punk/industrial, relentlessly techno and outrageously attired, respectively. All three open mid-week through the weekend 10pm-2am; exact hours for each vary, as does cover ($3-10). Axis and Venus have 18+ nights; call for details. Avalon stages live shows. Axis and Avalon join together for gay night on Sundays. Those over 21 can get in free (or for less, $0-8) from rowdy **Bill's Bar** (421-9678), next door to Venus.

Bull and Finch Pub, 84 Beacon St. (227-9605). T: Arlington. If you must see the bar that inspired *Cheers*, we can't stop you. Large crowds. The interior bears no resemblance to the set. Open Sun.-Fri. 11am-1:30am, Sat. 10am-1:30am.

Paradise, 967 Commonwealth Ave. (562-8800). T: Pleasant St. A young crowd flocks to this Back Bay spot for frequent live rock. Dancing on Sat. Most shows 18+. Cover about $8. Box office open Mon.-Sat. 3-7pm. Open daily 8pm-2am.

Wally's Café, 427 Mass Ave. (424-1408). T: bus #1 ("Dudley") to Columbus Ave. A great hole-in-the-wall bar frequented by Berklee School of Music's aspirants. Live music nightly; no cover. Open Mon.-Sat. 9am-2am, Sun. noon-2am.

Sticky Mike's, 21 Boylston Pl. (351-2583). T: Boylston. No pretensions at this blues joint—just live groups with names like D.D. and the Road Kings playing to an eclectic, somewhat older crowd. Cover $3-5. Open Tues.-Sat. 9pm-2am.

Sunset Grill and Tap, 130 Brighton Ave. (254-1331), in Allston. T: Harvard on Green line-B or bus #66 from the corner of Harvard St. and Brighton Ave. One of the country's largest selections of beer (over 400, more than 70 on tap). College students dig the buenos nachos ($7). Free late-night buffets Sun.-Tues. Open daily 11:30am-1am.

Nick's Comedy Stop, 100 Warrenton St. (482-0930), is funny. Jay Leno, who is not, got his start here. Mon.-Thurs., Sun. 8:30pm ($8), Fri.-Sat. 8:30 and 10:30pm ($12).

For those seeking the gay scene, **Coco's,** 965 Mass. Ave. (427-7807), clientele is predominantly women (cover $5; open Fri.-Sat. 9pm-2am). **Chaps** (266-7778), and **Club Café,** 209 Columbus Ave. (536-0966; T: Back Bay), are gay clubs. Club Café has a largely yuppie clientele, live music nightly, and no cover (open daily 4pm-2am, Sun. brunch 10am-3pm). Boston's favorite leather and Levi's bar, **Boston Ramrod,** 1254 Boylston St. (266-2986; T: Kenmore), behind Fenway Park on Boylston St., designates the last Saturday of the month Fetish Night—but why wait until then? (Cover Sun. $2. Open daily noon-2am.) Pick up a copy of *Bay Windows* for more information (available at many music stores).

■■■ CAMBRIDGE

Cambridge began its career as an intellectual and publishing center in the colonial era. Harvard, the nation's first university, was founded as a college of divinity here in 1636. Massachusetts Institute of Technology (MIT), founded in Boston in 1861, moved to Cambridge in 1916, giving the small city a second academic heavyweight. Today the city takes on the character of both universities. Bio-tech labs and computer science buildings radiate out from MIT through Kendall Sq. Harvard Sq. offers

Georgian buildings, stellar bookstores, coffee houses, street musicians, and excellent people-watching opportunities.

Practical Information Cambridge is best reached by a ten-minute T-ride outbound from the heart of Boston. The city's main artery, **Massachusetts Ave.** ("Mass. Ave."), parallels the Red Line, which makes stops at a series of squares along the avenue. The **Kendall Sq.** stop corresponds to MIT, just across the Mass. Ave. Bridge from Boston. The subway continues outbound through **Central Sq., Harvard Sq.,** and **Porter Sq.** The **Cambridge Discovery Booth** (497-1630), in Harvard Sq., has the best and most comprehensive information about Cambridge, as well as MBTA bus and subway schedules. Pick up the *Old Cambridge Walking Guide,* an excellent self-guided tour ($1.25); during the summer, ask about guided walking tours of Harvard and the surrounding area. (Open Mon.-Sat. 9am-5pm, Sun. 1-5pm.) Cambridge's **post office:** 770 Mass. Ave. (876-0620; open Mon.-Fri. 7:30am-6:45pm, Sat. 7:30am-2pm), in Central Sq.; **ZIP code:** 02139; **area code:** 617. See Boston Practical Information, above, for a complete listing of resources. For budget **accommodations,** turn around and go back to Boston.

Food Nightly, hundreds of college students renounce cafeteria fare and head to the funky eateries of Harvard Sq. Pick up the weekly *Square Deal,* usually thrust in your face by distributors near the T-stop, for coupons on local fare. The only 24-hr. eatery in Harvard Sq., the **Tasty Sandwich Shop,** 2 JFK St. (354-9016; T: Harvard) is more than just a 12-seater, fluorescent-lit, formica-countered, all-night diner—the Tasty is there for you, tonight and forever (entrees $2-6). **Jake and Earl's Dixie BBQ,** 1273 Cambridge St., Inman Sq. (491-7427), slops up masterfully spiced, award-winning barbecue with all the trimmings—coleslaw, baked beans, and a slice of watermelon ($7.25). Most folks go for the take-out option; Jake and Earl's is tiny. Take the bus #69 "Lechmere" from Harvard Sq.; look for the laughing pigs and the Elvis bust in the window. (Entrees $4-8. Cash only. Open daily 11:30am-11pm.) Between Harvard and Porter Sq., **Boca Grande,** 1728 Mass. Ave. (354-7400; T: Harvard or Porter, and a 10-min. walk), makes Mexican food to order right before your eyes, including enchiladas ($4), and spicy tamales ($4). The burritos grandes ($3.50) are certainly *grande,* but the bill stays *muy poco.* (Open Sun.-Wed. 10am-9pm, Thurs. 10am-9:30pm, Fri.-Sat. 10am-10pm.) The **Border Café,** 32 Church St. (864-6100), in Harvard Sq., has tasty, filling Tex-Mex and Cajun entrees ($5-13), and long lines. (Open Sun. noon-11pm, Mon.-Thurs. 11am-11pm, Fri.-Sat. 11am-midnight. No reservations.) Consistently voted the "Best Ice Cream in Boston," **Herrell's,** 15 Dunster St. (497-2179), in Harvard Sq., drowns the after-dinner crowd in lusciousness inside a former bank vault painted to resemble the watery depths (open Sun.-Thurs. noon-midnight, Fri.-Sat. 11-1am).

Sights **The Massachusetts Institute of Technology (MIT)** supports cutting edge work in the sciences. Campus tours (Mon.-Fri. 10am and 2pm) highlight the Chapel, designed by Eero Saarinen, and the impressive collection of modern outdoor sculpture which graces the grounds. Contact **MIT Information,** 77 Mass. Ave. (253-1000), for more information (open Mon.-Fri. 9am-5pm). The **MIT Museum,** 265 Mass. Ave. (253-4444), contains a slide rule collection and wonderful photography exhibits, including the famous stop-action photos of Harold Edgerton (open Tues.-Fri. 9am-5pm, Sat.-Sun. noon-5pm; $3, seniors $1, under 5 free).

In all its red brick-and-ivied dignity, **Harvard University,** farther down Mass. Ave. from Boston, finds space for nobel laureates, students from around the world, and, contrary to popular belief, the occasional party. The **Harvard University Information Center,** 1350 Mass. Ave. (495-1573), at Holyoke Center in Harvard Sq., distributes free guides to the university and its museums, and offers tours of the campus. (Tours Mon.-Fri. 10, 11:15am, 2 and 3:15pm, Sat. 11:15am, 2, and 3:15pm, Sun. 1:30 and 3:30pm; Sept.-May Mon.-Fri. 10am and 2pm, Sat. 2pm.) The university revolves around **Harvard Yard,** a grassy oasis amidst the Cantabridgian bustle. The Yard's eastern half holds classroom buildings, **Memorial Church,** and the **Harry Elkins Widener Memorial Library** (495-2411). Widener, named by Eleanor Widener for her son, who perished on the Titanic, stands as the largest academic library in the world, containing 4½ million of the university's 12 million books. To visit the library, you'll need a temporary pass from the library privileges office (495-4166) on the main floor (open Mon.-Fri. 9am-5pm). Some of the school's first buildings still grace the western half of the yard ("The Old Yard").

The most noted of Harvard's museums, the **Fogg Art Museum,** 32 Quincy St. (495-9400), gathers a considerable collection of works ranging from ancient Chinese jade to contemporary photography, as well as the largest Ingres collection outside of France. Across the street, the modern exterior of the **Arthur M. Sackler Museum,** 485 Broadway (495-9400), holds a rich collection of ancient Asian and Islamic art. The third of Harvard's art museums, the **Busch-Reisinger Museum,** 32 Quincy St. (495-9400), displays Northern and Central European sculpture, painting, and decorative arts. (All three open daily 10am-5pm. Admission to each $5, students $3, seniors $4; free Sat. mornings.) Peering down at the Fogg, Le Corbusier's guitar-shaped **Carpenter Center,** 24 Quincy St. (495-3251), shows student and professional work with especially strong photo exhibits and a great film series at the **Harvard Film Archives** (open Mon.-Sat. 9am-midnight, Sun. noon-10pm). The **Botanical Museum,** one of Harvard's several **Museums of Natural History,** 24 Oxford St. (495-3045), draws huge crowds to view the Ware collection of "glass flowers." A German glassblower and his son alone created these remarkably accurate, enlarged reproductions of over 840 plant species. (Open Mon.-Sat. 9am-4:30pm, Sun. 1-4:30pm. $4, students and seniors $3, ages 3-13 $1. Admission includes all the natural history museums.)

The restored **Longfellow House,** 105 Brattle St. (876-4491), now a National Historic Site, headquartered the Continental Army during the early stages of the Revolution. The poet Henry Wadsworth Longfellow, for whom the house is named, lived here later. The staff can give you info on other local historic sights. (Tours Wed.-Sat. 10:45am-4pm. $2, under 17 free.) The **Mt. Auburn Cemetery** (547-7105) lies about 1 mi. up the road at the end of Brattle St. The first botanical-garden/cemetery in the U.S. has 170 acres of beautifully landscaped grounds fertilized by Louis Agassiz, Charles Bulfinch, Dorothea Dix, Mary Baker Eddy, and H.W. Longfellow among others. Locals say it's the best birdwatching site in Cambridge.

Entertainment and Nightlife In warm weather, street musicians ranging from Andean folk singers to jazz trios staff every corner of Harvard Sq.

The **American Repertory Theater,** 64 Brattle St. (547-8300), in the Loeb Drama Center, produces shows from September through June. Planned 1995-96 productions include *The Tempest*, *A Long Day's Journey Into Night*, and *Tartuffe,* but don't expect the usual interpretation or staging. (Box office open daily 10am-5:30pm, until 7:30pm on show days. Tickets $19-45; student rush tickets, available ½hr. before shows, $12 cash only.)

Cambridge's many cafés attract crowds at all times of year for lunch or after-hours coffee. **Algiers Coffee House,** 40 Brattle St. (492-1557), has two beautiful floors of airy, wood-latticed seating, and exceptional food to boot. Enjoy an exotic coffee drink (about $3) or a falafel sandwich ($7). (Open Mon.-Thurs. 8am-midnight, Fri.-Sat. 8am-1am, Sun. 9am-midnight.)

If spending your evening discussing Proust over java doesn't sound appealing, Cambridge provides other options. The **Middle East,** 472 Mass. Ave. (354-8238), in Central Sq., a three-stage nirvana for the musically adventurous, books some of the best shows in the Boston area. Indie shows draw a somewhat alternateen audience. (Cover varies. Open Sun.-Wed. 11am-1am, Thurs.-Sat. 11:30am-2am.) Around the corner, **T.T. The Bear's Place,** 10 Brookline St. (492-0082), in Central Sq., brings really live, really loud rock bands to its intimate, seemingly makeshift stage (Cover $3-6. Open Mon.-Thurs. 8pm-1am, Fri.-Sun. noon-1am. 18+ welcome.) **Ryles,** 212 Hampshire St. (876-9330), in Inman Sq. accessible by bus #69, is a Boston jazz-scene standby with nightly live music and a jazz brunch on Sunday from noon to 4pm (open Sun.-Thurs. 5pm-1am, Fri.-Sat. 5pm-2am). Try **Johnny D's,** 17 Holland St. (776-9667; T: Davis), in neighboring Somerville, for more live music. For over 10 years, Little Joe Cook and his blues band have been packing the **Cantab Lounge,** 738 Mass. Ave. (354-2685), in Central Sq., with local fans and recently enlightened college students. (Cover Thurs. $3, Fri.-Sat. $5. Open Mon.-Wed. 8am-1am, Thurs.-Sat. 8am-2am, Sun. noon-1am.)

■■■ SALEM

Salem possesses a rich and varied history, witch stretches beyond the sensational **witch trials** of 1692. The city, once the sixth largest in the U.S., also features historic homes, a robust maritime heritage, and strong literary roots. Lodging in town is very expensive; plan your visit as a daytrip from Boston.

The **Witch Museum,** 19½ Washington Sq. (744-1692—note the numerology), gives a melodramatic but informative multi-media presentation that details the history of the trials. (Open July-Aug. daily 10am-7pm; Sept.-June 10am-5pm. $4, seniors $3.50, ages 6-14 $2.50.) Never actually a dungeon, the **Witch Dungeon,** 16 Lynde St. (741-3570), has re-enactments which amplify the toil and trouble of the proceedings. (Shows every 30min. $4, seniors $3.50, ages 6-14 $2.50. Open April-Dec. daily 10am-5pm.) Escape the sea of witch kitsch at the **Witch Trials Memorial,** off Charter St., where simple engraved stones commemorate the trials' victims.

Salem's **Peabody Museum** (745-1876; 745-9500 for recorded info), in East India Sq., recalls the port's former leading role in Atlantic whaling and merchant shipping. Ask for a free pass to the museum café and you can slip into the Oriental Garden, just beside the Museum on Liberty St. (Daily guided tour 2pm; in summer also 11am. Open Mon.-Wed. and Fri.-Sat. 10am-5pm, Thurs. 10am-8pm, Sun. noon-5pm; Nov.-Memorial Day closed Mon. $7, students and seniors $6, ages 6-16 $4, under 6 free.) The **Salem Maritime National Historic Site,** three wharves and several historic buildings by the waterfront on Derby St., deserves exploration. Derby Wharf is currently being restored, but you can still walk to the lighthouse on the end. Until 1917, federal officials, including Nathaniel Hawthorne, collected import duties at the **Customs House,** 174 Derby St., where the narrator of Hawthorne's novel claims to have found *The Scarlet Letter* (open daily 9am-6pm; off season 9am-5pm). Built in 1668, Salem's **House of Seven Gables,** 54 Turner St. (744-0991), became the "second most famous house in America" sometime after the release of Nathaniel Hawthorne's Gothic romance of the same name. The price is steeper than the famed roof, but the tour is thorough and informative. (Guided tour only. Open daily 9am-6pm; Sept.- June Mon.-Sat. 10am-4:30pm, Sun. noon-4:30pm. $6.50, ages 13-17 $4, ages 6-12 $3, under 6 free.)

Salem has two **information centers,** located at 2 New Liberty St. (740-1650; open daily 9am-6pm; Nov.-May 10am-5pm), and 174 Derby St. (740-1660; open daily 9am-6pm; Sept.-May 9am-5pm). Both provide a free map of Salem, but the New Liberty location shows a movie on three screens about Salem and Essex County. The town is packed during Halloween with a two-week-long festival called **Haunted Happenings;** book at least a year in advance. Salem, 20 mi. northeast of Boston, is accessible by the Rockport/Ipswich commuter train from North Station (722-3200; $2.50) or the bus #450 from Haymarket ($2.25). Salem's **area code:** 508.

■■■ LEXINGTON AND CONCORD

Lexington "Stand your ground. Don't fire unless fired upon, but if they mean to have a war, let it begin here," said Captain John Parker to the colonial Minutemen, on April 19, 1775. Although no one is certain who fired the first shot, the American Revolution did indeed erupt in downtown Lexington. The fateful command was issued from the **Buckman Tavern,** 1 Bedford St. (862-5598), which headquartered the Minutemen on the eve of their decisive battle. The tavern now dispenses information instead of ale, but has otherwise been restored to its 1775 appearance. The site of the fracas lies across the street at the **Battle Green** where a **Minuteman Statue** still watches over Lexington. The nearby **Hancock-Clarke House,** 36 Hancock St. (861-0928), and the **Munroe Tavern,** 1332 Mass. Ave. (674-9238), also played significant roles in the birth of the Revolution. (Must be seen on a 30-min. tour that runs continuously. House and Taverns open mid-April to Oct. Mon.-Sat. 10am-5pm, Sun. 1-5pm. $3 per site, ages 6-16 $1, under 6 free. Combination ticket $7/$2.) You can also survey an exhibit on the Revolution at the **Museum of Our National Heritage,** 33 Marrett Rd./Rte. 2A (861-6559), which emphasizes historical and popular American life (open Mon.-Sat. 10am-5pm, Sun. noon-5pm;disabled access; free). An excellent model and description of the Battle of Lexington decorates the **visitors center,** 1875 Mass. Ave. (862-1450), behind the Buckman Tavern (open May-Oct. daily 9am-5pm; Nov. 9am-3pm; Dec.-Feb. Mon.-Fri. 10am-2pm; March-April daily 9am-3pm). When the minutemen retreated from Lexington, they made their way to Concord via the **Battle Road;** the road now forms the spine of **Minuteman National Historical Park.** The **Battle Road Visitors Center** (862-7753), on Rte. 2A in Lexington distributes maps and screens a film that sets the stage for the Revolutionary War (open mid-April to Oct. daily 9am-5:30pm).

For those not traveling on horseback, the road from Boston to Lexington is easy. Drive straight up Mass. Ave. from Boston or Cambridge, or take your bike up the **Minuteman Commuter Bike Trail,** which runs right into downtown Lexington (access off Mass. Ave. in Arlington). MBTA buses from Alewife station in Cambridge run several times daily to Lexington (60¢). Lexington's **area code:** 617.

Concord Concord, the site of the second conflict of the American Revolution, is famous both for its military history and for its status as a 19th-century American intellectual center. Past **The Minuteman** and over the **Old North Bridge,** you'll find the spot where "the shot heard round the world" rang out. From the parking lot, a five-minute walk brings you to the **North Bridge Visitors Center,** 174 Liberty St. (369-6993), where rangers will gladly surrender hosts of pamphlets and brochures (open April-Oct. daily 9am-5:30pm, call for winter hrs.).

The Alcotts and the Hawthornes once inhabited **Wayside,** 455 Lexington Rd. (369-6975); now part of the **Minute Man National Historical Park,** the house is open for public viewing. (Guided tour only; tours leave on the hour. Open May-Oct. Thurs.-Tues. 10:30am-4:30pm. $3, under 17 free.) During the latter half of the 19th century, Ralph Waldo Emerson lived down the road, and the **Concord Museum** (369-9763), directly across the street from Wayside, houses a reconstruction of his study alongside Paul Revere's lantern and items from Henry David Thoreau's cabin. (Open Mon.-Sat 10am-5pm, Sun. 1-5pm; Jan.-March Mon.-Sat. 10am-4pm, Sun. 1-4pm. $6, students $3, seniors $5, under 18 $3.) Today, Emerson, Hawthorne, Alcott, and Thoreau all reside on "Author's Ridge" in the **Sleepy Hollow Cemetery** on Rte. 62, 3 blocks from the center of town.

Concord, 20 mi. north of Boston, is served by commuter rail (722-3200) trains from North Station ($2.75). Concord's **area code:** 508.

Walden Pond In 1845, Thoreau retreated 1½ mi. south of Concord on Rte. 126, "to live deliberately, to front only the essential facts of life." He did so and produced his famous *Walden.* The **Walden Pond State Reservation,** (369-3254), on Rte. 126, draws picnickers, swimmers, and boaters (open daily 5am-sunset; parking $2, daily in summer and Sat.-Sun. in spring). The Pond holds only 1000 visitors; call before coming out or risk being turned away. When Walden Pond swarms with crowds, head east from Concord center on Rte. 62 to another of Thoreau's haunts, **Great Meadows National Wildlife Refuge** (443-4661), on Monson Rd. (open daily dawn-dusk; free).

■■■ PLYMOUTH

Despite what American high school textbooks say, the Pilgrims did *not* first step ashore onto the New World at Plymouth—they first stopped at Provincetown, but left because the soil was inadequate. **Plymouth Rock** itself is a rather anti-climactically diminutive stone that has dubiously been identified as the actual rock on which the Pilgrims disembarked. Since that first Puritan foot was credited to the rock, it served as a symbol of liberty during the American Revolution, was moved three times, and was chipped away by tourists before landing at its current home beneath an extravagant portico on Water St., at the foot of North St.

On Warren Ave., **Plimoth Plantation** (746-1622), superbly recreates the Pilgrims's early settlement. In the **Pilgrim Village,** costumed actors play the roles of actual villagers carrying out their daily tasks, based on William Bradford's record of the year 1627. To make sure they know their stuff, the plantation sends a historian to England each summer to gather more information about each villager. (Open April-Nov. daily 9am-5pm. $18.50, students and seniors $16.50, ages 5-12 $11; good for 2 consecutive days.) The adjacent **Wampanoag Summer Encampment** represents a Native American village of the same period. Admission to the plantation includes entry to the **Mayflower II,** built in the 1950s to recapture the atmosphere of the original ship and docked off Water St. (Open July-Aug. daily 9am-7pm; Sept.-Nov. and April-June 9am-5pm. Mayflower only $5.75, ages 5-12 $3.75.) The nation's oldest museum in continuous existence, the **Pilgrim Hall Museum,** 75 Court St. (746-1620), houses Puritan crafts, furniture, books, paintings, and weapons (open daily 9:30am-4:30pm; $5, seniors $4, ages 5-12 $2.50).

When you feel bogged down in history, head for **Cranberry World,** 225 Water St. (747-2350), and celebrate one of the four indigenous American fruits (the others are the tomato, the blueberry, and the Concord grape). Exhibits, including a small cranberry bog in front of the museum, show how cranberries are grown, harvested, and sold. Cranberry juice flows freely. (Open May-Nov. 9:30am-5pm. Free.)

The **Plymouth Visitor's Information Center,** 130 Water St. (800-USA-1620/872-1620), gives out brochures, useful maps, and hotel and B&B info. (Open June-Aug. Sun.-Thurs. 9am-6pm, Fri.-Sat. 9am-7pm; Sept.-Nov. and April-May daily 9am-5pm.) Considering the proximity of Cape Cod's soft sand beaches, you may not want to spend more than a day here. The **Bunk and Bagel** (830-0914), has a cheerful, homey atmosphere and the cheapest beds in Plymouth by far. Both private rooms and hostel rooms come with a continental breakfast. (5-8 hostel beds with common bath. Office open daily 7-9:30am and 5-10pm. Hostel beds $15. Linens provided. Open May-Nov. Call for address and directions.) Majestic **Myles Standish Forest** (866-2526), 7 mi. south of Plymouth via Rte. 3, offers wooded ground for bedding down (sites $5, with showers $6).

CAPE COD

Henry David Thoreau once said: "At present [this coast] is wholly unknown to the fashionable world, and probably it will never be agreeable to them." Think again, Henry. In 1602, when English navigator and Jamestown colonist Bartholomew Gosnold landed on this peninsula in southeastern Massachusetts, he named it in honor of all the codfish he caught in the surrounding waters. In recent decades, tourists have replaced the cod. This small strip of land supports a diverse set of landscapes—long unbroken stretches of beach, salt marshes, hardwood forests, deep freshwater ponds carved by glaciers, and desert-like dunes sculpted by the wind. Thankfully, the Cape's natural landscape has been protected from the tide of commercialism by the establishment of the **Cape Cod National Seashore.** Blessed with an excellent hostel system, Cape Cod is a popular budget seaside getaway, used by many cross-country travelers as a resting place at the end of a tour of urban America. The Cape also serves as the gateway to **Martha's Vineyard** and **Nantucket.**

Terminology for locations on the cape is sometimes confusing. **Upper Cape** refers to the part of Cape Cod closer to the mainland, the most suburbanized and developed section of the Cape. Proceeding away from the mainland, you travel "down Cape" until you reach the **Lower Cape;** the National Seashore encompasses much of this area. Cape Cod resembles a bent arm, with **Woods Hole** at its armpit, **Chatham** at the elbow, and **Provincetown** at its clenched fist.

If you're up for some exercise, cycling is the best way to travel the Cape's gentle slopes. The park service can give you a free map of trails or sell you the detailed **Cape Cod Bike Book** ($2.50; available at most Cape bookstores). The 135-mi. **Boston-Cape Cod Bikeway** connects Boston to Provincetown at land's end. If you want to bike this route, pick up a bicycle trail map of the area, available at some bookstores and most bike shops. The trails which line either side of the **Cape Cod Canal** in the National Seashore rank among the country's most scenic, as does the 14-mi. **Cape Cod Rail Trail** from Dennis to Eastham. Cape Cod's **area code:** 508.

■■■ UPPER CAPE

Hyannis Hyannis is not the Cape Cod most people expect. JFK spent his summers on the beach in nearby Hyannisport, but the town itself sees more action as a transportation hub than as a scenic destination. Island ferries and buses to destinations throughout the Cape emanate from Hyannis; hop on one and get out of town—the Kennedys *aren't* going to meet you at the bus station.

The **Hyannis Area Chamber of Commerce,** 1481 Rte. 132 (775-2201), about 3 mi. up the road from the bus station, distributes the free *Hyannis Guidebook* and has accommodations listings and a campground guide for the whole cape. (Open Mon.-Thurs. 9am-5pm, Fri. 9am-7pm, Sat. 9am-4:30pm, Sun. 11am-3pm; Sept.-May closed Sun.) In an **emergency,** call 775-1212 for police or 775-2323 for the fire department or an ambulance. **ZIP code:** 02601.

Hyannis doesn't know the meaning of the phrase "budget accommodations." The closest affordable places to stay are the campgrounds near Sandwich (see below), about 15 mi. from Hyannis, and the hostel in Eastham (see Eastham, p. 112).

Hyannis is tattooed midway across the Cape's upper arm, 3 mi. south of U.S. 6 on Nantucket Sound. **Plymouth & Brockton** (775-5524) runs five Boston-to-Provincetown buses per day with ½-hr. layovers at the **Hyannis Bus Station,** 17 Elm St. (775-5524). Other stops include Plymouth, Sagamore, Yarmouth, Orleans, Wellfleet, and Truro. (To: Boston 3½hr., $10; Provincetown 1½hr., $9.) **Bonanza Bus Lines** (800-556-3815) operates a line through Providence, RI to New York City (6 per day, 6hr., $40). **Amtrak,** 252 Main St. (800-872-7245), sends a direct train from New York City to Hyannis on Friday, and one from Hyannis to New York on Sunday (6hr., $65). See the listings for Martha's Vineyard (p. 115) and Nantucket (p. 117) for info on ferry service to the islands.

Sandwich The oldest town on the Cape, Sandwich cultivates a charm unmatched by its neighbors on the upper part of the arm. The beauty and workmanship of Sandwich glass was made famous by the Boston & Sandwich Glass Company, founded in Sandwich in 1825. Though the original company is gone, you can still see Sandwich's master glassblowers shape works of art from blobs of molten sand; the artisans at **Pairpoint Crystal** (888-2344), on Rte. 6A just across the town border in Sagamore, do their thing Monday through Friday 8:30am-4:30pm (open Mon.-Sat. 9am-6pm, Sun. 10am-6pm; free). To enjoy the town's considerable collection of older pieces, tiptoe through the unparalleled menagerie at **The Sandwich Glass Museum,** 129 Main St. (888-0251), in Sandwich Center (open daily 9:30am-4:30pm; Nov.-March Wed.-Sun. 9:30am-4pm; $3, under 12 50¢).

The **Thornton W. Burgess Museum** (888-6870), on Water St., pays tribute to the Sandwich-born, self-taught naturalist who spun tales about Peter Cottontail and

Reddy Fox, among others. Take a gander at the herb garden outside—from one end, the outline mimics a "tussie-mussie" bouquet of flowers; from the other end it's Peter Cottontail's head. (Open Mon.-Sat. 10am-4pm, Sun. 1-4pm. Free; donations accepted.) Ask for directions to **The Green Briar Nature Center and Jam Kitchen,** 6 Discovery Rd. (888-6870), where you can wander through a briar patch and wildflower gardens. On Wednesdays and Saturdays, the center kitchen churns out jam before the eyes of hungry visitors. (Open Mon.-Sat. 10am-4pm, Sun. 1-4pm; Jan.-March Tues.-Sat. 10am-4pm. Free; donations accepted.) The best beach on the Upper Cape, **Sandy Neck Beach,** on Sandy Neck Rd. 3 mi. east of Sandwich off Rte. 6A, extends 6 mi. along Cape Cod Bay with beautifully polished egg-sized granite pebbles and verdant dunes. Hike only on marked trails; the plants are very fragile.

Across the Sagamore Bridge, **Scusset Beach** (888-0859), right on the canal near the junction of U.S. 6 and Rte. 3, offers fishing and camping, mostly for RVs (tent sites $6, with hookup $9; day use $2 per car). The **Shawme-Crowell State Forest** (888-0351), at Rte. 130 and U.S. 6, provides 280 wooded campsites with showers and campfires, but no hookups ($6, including parking at Scusset Beach; open April-late Nov.). **Peters Pond Park Campground** (477-1775), on Cotuit Rd. in south Sandwich, combines waterside sites with swimming, fishing, rowboat rentals ($15 per day), showers, and a grocery store (sites $18-32; open mid-April to mid-Oct).

Sandwich lies at the intersection of Rte. 6A and Rte. 130, about 13 mi. from Hyannis. The **Plymouth & Brockton** bus makes its closest stop in Sagamore, 3 mi. west. From Sandwich, the **Cape Cod Railroad** (771-3788), takes a scenic two-hour ride through cranberry bogs and marshes. (3 round-trips per day from Main and Center St. in Hyannis to the Cape Cod Canal. $11.50, ages 3-12 $7.50.)

■■■ LOWER CAPE

Cape Cod National Seashore As early as 1825, the Cape had suffered so much man-made damage that the town of Truro required local residents to plant beach grass and keep their cows off the dunes; the sea threatened to wash away the weakened dunes of the sandy town and make Provincetown an island. Further efforts toward conservation culminated in 1961 with the creation of the Cape Cod National Seashore, which includes much of the Lower Cape from Provincetown south to Chatham. Over 30 mi. of wide, soft, uninterrupted beaches lie under the tall clay cliffs and towering 19th-century lighthouses of this protected area. Thanks to conservationists, the area has largely escaped the boardwalk commercialism which afflicts most American seacoasts. Just a short walk away from the lifeguards, the sea of umbrellas and coolers fades into the distance. Hike one of the seashore's seldom used nature trails; the wide variety of habitats that huddle together on this narrow slice of land is truly impressive. Grassy dunes give way to forests as you move away from the water. Salt marshes play host to migrating and native waterfowl. When the waves or the crowds at the beach become too intense, warm, freshwater ponds, such as **Gull Pond** in Wellfleet, or **Pilgrim Lake** in Truro, are perfect for calm and secluded swimming.

Most beachgoers face one eternal question: ocean or bay. The ocean beaches attract with whistling winds and surging waves; the water on the bay side rests calmer and gets a bit warmer. The National Seashore oversees six beaches: **Coast Guard** and **Nauset Light** in Eastham; **Marconi** in Wellfleet; **Head of the Meadow** in Truro; **Race Point** and **Herring Cove** in Provincetown. (Parking at all beaches $5 per day, $15 per season; pedestrian and cyclist entrance $3.)

To park at any other beach, you'll need a town permit. Each town has a different beach-parking policy, but permits generally cost $25-30 per week, $75 per season, or $10 per day. Call the appropriate Town Hall before trying to get around the parking permit; beaches are sometimes miles from any other legal parking and police with tow trucks roam the area like vultures. On sunny days, parking lots fill up by 11am or earlier; it's often easier to rent a bike and ride in. Most town beaches do not require bikers and walkers to pay an entrance fee. Wellfleet and Truro stand out among the ocean beaches as great examples of the Cape's famous, endangered sand dunes. **Cahoon Hollow Beach** in Wellfleet separates itself from the rest with spectacular, cliff-like dunes, a particularly young crowd, and day parking.

Among the best of the seashore's nine self-guiding **nature trails,** the **Great Island Trail,** in Wellfleet, traces an 8-mi. loop through pine forests and grassy marshes and along a ridge with a view of the bay and Provincetown. The **Buttonbush Trail,** a ¼-mi. walk with braille guides and a guide rope for the blind, starts at the Salt Pond Visitors Center. Also inquire at the visitors center (see below) about the three park **bike trails:** Nauset Trail (1.6mi.), Head of the Meadow Trail (2mi.), and Province Lands Trail (5mi.).

Start your exploration at the **National Seashore's Salt Pond Visitors Center** (255-1301), at Salt Pond off U.S. 6 in Eastham (open daily 9am-6pm; Sept.-June 9am-4:30pm). The center offers info and advice on the whole seashore, as well as a free ten-minute film every ½ hour and a free museum with excellent exhibits on the Cape's human and natural history. Camping on the national seashore is *illegal*. See Eastham, Wellfleet, and Truro (below) for info on accommodations in the area.

Eastham The **Eastham Windmill,** on Rte. 6 at Samoset Rd. in Eastham, has had its nose to the grindstone since 1680. The windmill continues to function and demonstrates how the native American crop of corn was put to use by industrious Cape Codders. (Open July-Aug. Mon.-Sat. 10am-5pm, Sun. 1-5pm; free.) Off Rte. 6, **Fort Hill** grants a survey of Nauset Marsh and the surrounding forest and ocean, as well as the paths which access them. For a classic view of the dunes and sea, drive to **Nauset Light,** on Salt Pond Rd. Popular with Cape bikers, the **Mid-Cape Hostel (HI-AYH)** (255-2785) occupies a quiet, wooded spot in Eastham, convenient to the lower part of the Cape. The hostel has six cabins, a kitchen, and a relaxed atmosphere that attracts groups. On the Plymouth-Brockton bus to Provincetown, ask to be let off at the traffic circle in Orleans (not the Eastham stop). Walk out on the exit to Rock Harbor, turn right on Bridge Rd., and take a right onto Goody Hallet Rd. ½ mi. from U.S. 6; it takes about 15 minutes. (Office open daily 7:30-9:30am and 5-10:30pm. $12. Reservations essential July-Aug. Open mid-May to mid-Sept.) **Atlantic Oaks** (255-1457 or 800-332-2267) has about 100 tent and RV sites, a bath-house, playground, and basketball. (Office open daily 8am-9pm; off season 9am-6pm. Tent sites for 2 $22, with hookup $29; off season $16/$22. Open May-Nov.)

Wellfleet **Gull Pond,** off Gull Pond Rd. in Wellfleet, connected by a series of shallow channels to three more secluded ponds, provides the setting for some of the Cape's best paddling. From **Higgins Pond,** look for the home of the Wellfleet Oysterman; Thoreau based a chapter in *Cape Cod* on his stay there. In the spring, the **herring run** clogs the rivers of the Cape as the amorous creatures head inland to spawn, blindly ignoring the glut of potential mates swimming along with them. For an overnight stay, check out one of South Wellfleet's two **campgrounds: Maurice's** (349-2029) and **Paine's** (349-3007). Located right at the oceanfront at the end of Cahoon Hollow Rd. off U.S. 6, the **Beachcomber** (349-6055) serves foot-long hot dogs ($3.50), and burgers and fries ($6) to the bathing-suit-clad masses (open in summer daily noon-1am). The **Bayside Lobster Hut,** 91 Commercial St. (349-6333), lets you "see 'em swim." While it's questionable how inviting *that* is, cheap lobster ($12-19 by weight) and a casual setting with picnic tables are more certain enticements (open July-Aug. daily noon-10pm; Sept. and June 4:30-9pm).

Truro Built in 1827 and little-changed, the **First Congregation Parish of Truro** (United Church of Christ; 349-7735) transports visitors back to the 19th century; electricity was installed just 30 years ago, and the outhouse still serves in place of a new-fangled toilet. Take the Bridge Rd. exit off U.S. 6 and turn right onto Town Hall Rd. (Services Sun. 10am.) The picturesque **Cranberry Bog Trail,** North Pamet Rd., provides secluded, spectacular setting for a walk, criss-crossing the National Seashore; get a map at the National Seashore's Salt Pond Visitors Center (see above). At the far end of North Pamet Rd., the **Truro Hostel (HI-AYH)** (349-3889), 1½ mi. from a bus stop, offers an escape from the crowds with plenty of space, a large kitchen, lots of common space, great ocean views, and access to a secluded beach. (42 beds. Office open 7:30-10am and 5-10pm. $12, nonmembers $15. Reservations essential. Open late June-early Sept.) Several popular campgrounds nestle among the dwarf pines by the dunelands of North Truro, just 7 mi. southeast of Provincetown on U.S. 6; **North Truro Camping Area** (487-1847), on Highland Rd. ½ mi. east of U.S. 6., has small sandy sites, heated restrooms, hot showers, and free cable TV. (Sites for 2 $15, with water and electricity $20, full hookup $21; $7.50 per additional person.) Call **Horton's Park** (487-1220) or **North of Highland** (487-1191) for more sites in North Truro.

■■■ PROVINCETOWN

At Provincetown, Cape Cod ends and the wide Atlantic begins. The National Seashore protects two-thirds of "P-Town" as conservation land; the inhabited sliver touches the harbor on the south side of town. Still, Provincetown finds room for plenty of activity in that tiny space. Commercial St., the city's main drag, has seen the whalers of years past replaced by specialty shops, Portuguese bakeries, art galleries, nightclubs, and lots of people. For over a century, Provincetown has been known for its broad acceptance of many lifestyles, and a sizeable gay and lesbian community has flowered here. Over half the couples on the street are same-sex, and a walk here makes it quietly plain that homosexuality does not adhere to any stereotype of size, shape, color, or dress.

Practical Information Provincetown rests in the cupped hand at the end of the Cape Cod arm, 123 mi. from Boston by car or three hours by ferry across Massachusetts Bay. Parking spots are hard won, especially on cloudy days when the Cape's frustrated sun-worshippers flock to Provincetown. Follow the parking signs on **Bradford St.,** the town's auto-friendly thoroughfare, to dock your car for $5-7 per day, or try the lots off **Commercial St.,** parallel to Bradford St., closer to the action. Whale-watching boats, the Boston ferry, and buses depart from **MacMillan Wharf,** at the center of town, just down the hill from the Pilgrim Monument.

You'll find the **Provincetown Chamber of Commerce,** 307 Commercial St. (487-3424), on MacMillan Wharf. (Open July-Labor Day daily 9am-5pm; April to June and mid-Sept. to Nov. Mon.-Sat. 10am-4pm.) **Province Lands Visitors Center** (487-1256), Race Point Rd., has information on the national seashore and free guides to the nature and bike trails (open July-Aug. daily 9am-6pm; mid-April to June and Sept.-Nov. daily 9am-5pm). Hop on a **Plymouth and Brockton Bus** (746-0378), to Boston (in summer 4 per day, 4hr., $19) at the stop on MacMillan Wharf behind the Provincetown Chamber of Commerce (with schedules and information). **Bay State Cruises** (617-723-7800) sends a ferry to Boston (3hr., $16, $29 same-day round-trip); again, departures are made from the Chamber of Commerce. (Ferries mid-June to Labor Day daily; Memorial Day to mid-June and Labor Day-Columbus Day weekends only.) To get around in Provincetown and Herring Cove Beach, take the **Provincetown Shuttle Bus** (487-3353). One route travels the length of Bradford St.; the other goes from MacMillan Wharf to Herring Cove Beach. (Operates late June-early Sept. daily on the hour 8am-11pm; 10am-6pm for the beach. Fare $1.25, seniors 75¢.) Rented bikes from **Arnold's,** 329 Commercial St. (487-0844), are another workable mode of transport. ($2.50-3.50 per hr., 2-hr. min.; $10-15 per day. Deposit and ID required; credit cards accepted. Open daily 8:30am-5:30pm.) **Emergency:** 911. Provincetown's **post office:** 211 Commercial St. (487-0163; open Mon.-Fri. 8:30am-5pm, Sat. 9:30-11:30am); **ZIP code:** 02657. **Area code:** 508.

Accommodations and Camping Provincetown teems with expensive places to lay your head. Your most affordable option is the wonderful hostel 10 mi. away in nearby Truro (see Truro, above). In town, the cheapest beds can be found at **The Outermost Hostel (AAIH/Rucksackers),** 28 Winslow St. (487-4378), barely 100 yards from the Pilgrim monument. Thirty beds in five cramped cottages go for $14 each, including kitchen access and free parking. (Office open daily 8-10am and 6-10pm. Check-out 9:30am. Key deposit $5. Reservations recommended for weekends. Open mid-May to mid-Oct.) In the quiet east end of town, the **Cape Codder,** 570 Commercial St. (487-0131; call 9am-3pm or 9-11pm), welcomes you with archetypal Cape Cod decor, right down to the wicker furniture, and access to a private beach. (Singles and doubles $35-55; mid-Sept. to mid-June about $10 less. Morning tea included. Open May-Oct.) **Alice Dunham's Guest House,** 3 Dyer St. (487-3330), has four rooms (all named after squares on the Monopoly board) available upstairs in a cozy Victorian house near the beach and only a five-minute walk from the center of Provincetown. (Check-out 11am. Singles $38, doubles $48-52; rates variable on holidays. 1 free night per week of stay.)

Camping in Provincetown will cost you. The western part of **Coastal Acres Camping Court** (487-1700), a 1-mi. walk from the center of town, west on Bradford or Commercial St. and right on West Vine St., has over 100 crowded sites; try to snag one on the waterside. (Office open 24 hrs.; Sept.-June daily 8am-4pm and 8pm-9:30pm. Sites $20, with water and electricity $27. Open April-Oct.)

Food Sit-down meals in Provincetown cost a bundle; grab a bite at one of the Portuguese bakeries on Commercial St., or at a seafood shack on MacMillan Wharf. If you're hankerin' for a blue plate special, dine at **Dodie's Diner,** 401½ Commercial St. (487-3868), where they put together comforting meals like meatloaf ($8) and chicken-fried steak ($9) that would make a mother proud (entrees $7-10; open daily 8am-10pm). Since 1921, the **Mayflower Family Dining,** 300 Commercial St. (487-0121), has given visitors walls lined with ancient caricatures and a stomach lined with solid food. Try the Portuguese beef tips ($8), the Italian spaghetti ($4) or the crab cakes ($6; open daily 11:30am-10pm; cash only). **George's Pizza,** 275 Commercial St. (487-3744), serves up excellent deep-dish pizza. Gaze at the stars while eating your cheese pizza ($5) on the outdoor deck. (Open daily 11am-1am.)

Sights Provincetown has long been a refuge for artists and artisans; you can look but not touch at any of over 20 galleries—most are free and lie east of **MacMillan Wharf** on Commercial St. In general, galleries stay open in the afternoon and evening until 11pm, but take a two-hour break for dinner. Get the free *Provincetown Gallery Guide* for complete details. The kingpin of the artsy district, the **Provincetown Art Association and Museum,** 460 Commercial St. (487-1750), established in 1914, exhibits works by new Provincetown artists alongside the permanent 500-piece collection. (Open late June-Sept. daily noon-5pm and 7-9pm; call for winter hours. $3 suggested donation, seniors and children $1.)

Contrary to popular belief, the Pilgrims first landed at Provincetown, not Plymouth; they moved on after two weeks in search of more welcoming soil. The **Pilgrim Monument** (487-1310), on High Pole Hill, looms over Provincetown and commemorates that 17-day Puritan layover. The nation's tallest granite structure (255 ft.) also serves as a useful navigation aid to mariners. For a gorgeous panoramic view of the Cape, ascend the 255 ft. on stairs and ramps. The **Provincetown Museum,** at the tower's base, covers a broad swath of Cape history, from whaling artifacts to dollhouses. (Museum and monument open July-Aug. daily 9am-7pm; mid-March to June and Sept.-Oct. 9am-5pm. $5, ages 4-12 $3.) At the **Provincetown Heritage Museum,** 356 Commercial St. (487-0666), you can see a half scale model of a fishing schooner, complemented by paintings and other exhibits from Provincetown's past (open mid-June to mid-Oct. daily 10am-6pm; $3, under 12 free).

Entertainment and Nightlife Today, Provincetown seafarers carry telephoto lenses, not harpoons, when they go hunting for whales. **Whale-watch cruises** are some of P-town's most popular attractions. Several companies provide essentially the same service: riding out to the feeding waters in about 40 minutes, and cruising around them for about two hours. The companies claim that whales are sighted on 99% of the journeys. Tickets cost about $18; discount coupons can be found in most local publications. **Dolphin Fleet** (255-3857 or 800-826-9300), **Portuguese Princess** (487-2651 or 800-442-3188), and **Ranger V** (487-3322 or 800-992-9333), leave from and operate ticket booths on MacMillan Wharf, while **Superwhale** (800-942-5334) runs off Fisherman's Pier.

Back on *terra firma,* one of Provincetown's most entertaining attractions can be found sporadically at the corner of Commercial and Standish St., where, police officer extraordinaire Donald Thomas directs traffic to the rhythm of his whistle, whirling arms, and dancing feet.

Provincetown's nightlife is almost totally gay- and lesbian-oriented, but all are welcome. Most of the clubs and bars, on Commercial St., charge around $5, and shut down at 1am. Uninhibited dancing shakes the ground nightly for a mixed crowd at the **Backroom,** 247 Commercial St. (487-1430; cover $5; open 10pm-1am). Live music drives **Club Euro** in the Euro Island Grille, 258 Commercial St. (487-2505). Sway to live reggae on Saturdays. (Cover Sat. $2. Open May-Oct. daily 11am-2am.) Proud to be the "oldest gay bar on the seacoast," **Atlantic House,** 6 Masonic Ave. (487–3821), offers dancing and two bars (dancing cover $3-5; open daily 9pm-1am; bars open daily noon-1am). The town really rocks for **Carnival Week** in late August.

NEW ENGLAND

■■■ MARTHA'S VINEYARD

Martha's Vineyard provides a haven for many vacationing luminaries. From Princess Di to President Clinton, visitors seek out this secluded island for beach dunes, inland woods, pastel houses, and weathered cottages. "But," you might ask "how secluded is it?" Before the invention of the auto, over ¼ of the residents in Chilmark were born deaf and dumb due to intermarriage and resulting genetic defects.

Though the Vineyard was once left very much alone, it is now invaded every summer by hordes of travelers. Try coming in the fall, when the tourist season wanes and the foliage flares with autumnal hues. Seven communities comprise Martha's Vineyard. The western end of the island is called "up island," from the nautical days when sailors had to tack upwind to get there. The three largest towns, Oak Bluffs, Vineyard Haven, and Edgartown, are "down island" and have flatter terrain. Oak Bluffs and Edgartown are the only "wet" (alcohol-selling) towns on the island.

Oak Bluffs, 3mi. west of Vineyard Haven on State Rd., is the most youth-oriented of the Vineyard villages. Tour **Trinity Park** near the harbor and see the famous "Gingerbread Houses" (minutely detailed, elaborate pastel Victorian cottages), or Oak Bluffs' **Flying Horses Carousel** (693-9481), on Circuit Ave., the oldest in the nation (built in 1876), composed of 20 handcrafted horses with real horsehair (open daily 10am-10pm; fare $1). Ferries from Woods Hole dock here.

Edgartown, 7mi. south of Oak Bluffs, displays a waterfront cluster of stately Federal-style homes built for whaling captains. Skip the shops and stores and visit the town's historic sights maintained by **Dukes County Historical Society,** School and Cooke St. (627-4441; open Wed.-Fri. 1-4pm, Sat. 10am-4pm).

West Tisbury, 12mi. west of Edgartown on the West Tisbury-Edgartown Rd., grows the only vines on the Vineyard, at the **Chicama Vineyards,** on Stoney Hill Rd. (693-0309), off State Rd. Tours end in free tastings. (Open Jan.-April Fri.-Sat. 1-3pm; May Mon.-Sat. 1-4pm; June-Oct. Mon.-Sat. 11am-5pm, Sun. 1-5pm. Free.) The town supplies a well stocked general store.

Gay Head, 12mi. off West Tisbury, offers just about the best view in all of New England. The local Wampanoag frequently saved sailors whose ships wrecked on the breathtaking **Gay Head Cliffs.** The 100,000-year-old precipice contains a collage of clay in brilliant colors and supports one of five lighthouses on the island.

Menemsha and Chilmark, a little northeast of Gay Head, has good coastline and claims to be the only working fishing town on the island; tourists can fish off the pier or purchase lobster straight from the sea.

Vineyard Haven has more tacky t-shirt shops and fewer charming old homes than other towns. It is also the port for the Woods Hole ferry.

Practical Information Though small (30mi. across at its widest point), the Vineyard packs 15 beaches and a state forest in its bounds. A good free map and info are available at the **Martha's Vineyard Chamber of Commerce,** Beach Rd., Vineyard Haven (693-0085; open Mon.-Fri. 9am-5pm, Sat. 10am-6pm, Sun. 10am-2pm; Sept.-May Mon.-Fri. 9am-5pm) or write P.O. Box 1698, Vineyard Haven 02568.

Bonanza buses (800-556-3815) stop at the Ferry Terminal in Woods Hole and depart, via Bourne, for Boston (11 per day, 1¾hr., $12) and New York (5 per day, 6hr., $39). Most **taxis** are vans with negotiable fares; set a price before you get in. In Oak Bluffs, call 693-0037; in Edgartown, 627-4677; in Vineyard Haven, 693-3705. The **Island Transport** (693-1589 or 693-0058) runs shuttle buses between Vineyard Haven (Union St.), Oak Bluffs (Ocean Park), and Edgartown (Church St.) late June through August. (Daily every 15min. 10am-7pm, every 30min. 7-10am and 7pm-midnight. Vineyard Haven to: Oak Bluffs $1.50, $2 round-trip; Edgarton $2/$3.)

Ferries serve the island from Hyannis (778-2600 or 693-0112), New Bedford (997-1688), Falmouth (548-4800), and Nantucket (778-2600), but the shortest and cheapest ride, as well as the only one to transport cars, leaves from Woods Hole on Cape Cod. The **Steamship Authority** (477-8600) sends 13 boats per day on the 45-minute ride to Vineyard Haven and Oak Bluffs. (Ticket office open Mon.-Thurs. and Sat. 5am-9:45pm, Fri. and Sun 5am-10:45 pm. $4.75, ages 5-12 $2.40, bike $3, car $38; reservation necessary weeks in advance.) The ferry company has three parking lots ($7.50 per day) and shuttle service to the dock. The **Chappy "On Time" Ferry** (627-9427) connects Edgartown Town Dock and Chappaquidick Island. (Runs June to mid-Oct. daily 7:30-midnight; mid-Oct. to May reduced hours. Round-trip $1, car $4, bicycle $2.50, motorcycle $3.50.)

The Vineyard is designed for bicycles. Bring one or rent one at **Martha's Vineyard Scooter and Bike** (693-0782), at the Steamship Authority Dock in Vineyard Haven (open July-Aug. daily 8am-8pm; call for off season hours), or **Vineyard Bike and Moped** (693-4498), Circuit Ave. Exit in Oak Bluffs (open daily 9am-6pm), or **R.W. Cutler,** Main St., Edgartown (627-4052; open April 7-Oct. 15 daily 8am-6pm). All three charge $10-12 per day for a three-speed, $15-18 per day for a mountain bike or hybrid; a deposit may be required. R.W. Cutler has trail maps. Martha's Vineyard's **area code:** 508.

Accommodations and Camping America's first hostel, the fantastic **Martha's Vineyard Hostel (HI-AYH),** Edgartown-West Tisbury Rd., West Tisbury (693-2665), provides the 78 cheapest beds on the island. Located right next to the bike path, the hostel has a great kitchen with an illuminated stained glass hearth, a nice common space, and lots of recreational facilities. (Open April to mid-May 7-9:30am and 5-10:30pm. Curfew 11pm. Light chore required. $12, nonmembers $15. Linen $2. Reservations essential; IBN reservations available.) The Chamber of Commerce provides a list of inns and guest houses; all recommend reservations in July and August, especially for packed weekends. For relatively inexpensive rooms, try the **Sea Horse Guests** (693-0594), on Lambert's Cove Rd., West Tisbury (singles $45, doubles $50; open mid-May to mid-Oct.).

Martha's Vineyard Family Campground, 1¼ mi. from Vineyard Haven on Edgartown Rd. (693-3772), keeps 185 shaded sites in an oak tree forest. Groceries and metered showers are available nearby. (Sites for 2 $25; each additional person $9, ages 2-18 $2. Open mid-May to mid-Oct.) **Webb's Camping Area** (693-0233), Barnes Rd., Oak Bluffs, has 150 shaded and spacious sites. (Sites for 2 $26-28, depending on degree of privacy, with hookup $2 extra; each additional person $8, ages 5-17 $1. Open mid-May to mid-Sept.)

Food Cheap sandwich and lunch places speckle the Vineyard. Vineyard Haven and Oak Bluffs will best accommodate the traveler who watches the bottom line, though the options may not be so kind to the waistline. Fried-food shacks across the island sell clams, shrimp, and potatoes, which generally cost at least $15. **Shindigs,** 32 Kennebec Ave. (696-7727), in Oak Bluffs, serves generous portions of tasty BBQ ($6-7) and sandwiches ($4-7; open daily 10am-10pm). Prospective revelers should note that alcohol is tightly controlled on the Vineyard; again, Edgartown and Oak Bluffs are the only "wet" towns.

Considering the outdoor beauty, you may want to grab your food and run at one of a number of take-out joints. **Louis',** 102 State Rd. (693-3255), Vineyard Haven, serves take-out Italian food that won't break the bank. Try the fresh pasta with meat sauce ($4) or the vegetable calzone ($4.50; open Mon.-Thurs. 11am-8:30pm, Fri.-Sat. 11am-9pm, Sun. 4-8:30pm). Sample a range of creative and delicious pastries and breads (75¢-$3.50) at the **Black Dog Bakery** (693-4786), on Beach St. Exit in Vineyard Haven, but **for the love of God,** please don't buy another sweatshirt (open daily 5:30am-8pm). An island institution, **Mad Martha's** scoops out homemade ice cream and frozen yogurt. The main store (693-9151), on Circuit Ave. in Oak Bluffs (open daily 11am-midnight), is only one of eight throughout the island (2 more in Oak Bluffs). Several **farm stands** on the island sell inexpensive produce; the free chamber of commerce map shows their locations.

Sights Exploring the Vineyard should involve much more than zipping around on a moped. Take time to head out into the countryside, hit the beach, or trek down one of the area's great walking trails. **Felix Neck Wildlife Sanctuary** (627-4850), on the Edgartown-Vineyard Haven Rd., offers a variety of terrains and habitats for exploration (open daily 8am-sunset; off season closed Mon.; $3, seniors $1, under 12 $2). **Cedar Tree Neck** on the western shore harbors 250 acres of headland off Indian Hill Rd. with trails throughout, while the **Long Point** park in West Tisbury preserves 550 acres and a shore on the Tisbury Great Pond. The largest conservation area on the island, **Cape Pogue Wildlife Refuge and Wasque Reservation** (693-7662), floats on Chappaquiddick Island.

Two of the best beaches on the island, **South Beach,** at the end of Katama Rd. 3 mi. south of Edgartown, and **State Beach,** on Beach Rd. between Edgartown and Oak Bluffs, are free and open to the public. South boasts sizeable surf and an occasionally nasty undertow, while the warmer, gentler waters of State set the stage for parts of *Jaws,* the grandaddy of classic beach-horror films. For the best sunsets on the island stake out a spot at **Gay Head** or the **Manemsha Town Beach;** enjoy the sun's descent while dining on seafood from nearby stands.

■■■ NANTUCKET

Once the home of the biggest whaling port in the world, Nantucket saw one of its whaling ships, the *Essex,* rammed by a whale in 1820; the incident inspired Herman Melville's *Moby Dick*. Though Nantucket is today primarily a secluded outpost of privilege and establishment, it is possible to enjoy a stay on the island without holding up a convenience store to do so. You can always dig your toes into the Nantucket's 82 mi. of beach for free. If possible, visit during the last weeks of the tourist season, when prices drop. Only a few places stay open during the cold, rainy winter months, when awesome storms churn the slate-blue seas.

Practical Information The **visitor services center,** 25 Federal St. (228-0925), has a full complement of brochures and can help you find a place to stay (open Mon.-Sat. 9am-10pm, Sun. 9am-6pm). **Barrett's Bus Lines,** 20 Federal St. (228-0174 or 800-773-0174), opposite the visitors center, runs buses, on sunny days only, to Jetty's Beach (every ½hr. 10am-5pm, $1), Surfside Beach (hourly 10am-5pm), and Sconset (every hr. 10:10am-4:10pm, $3 round-trip, ages 5-12 $1.50). **Hyline** (778-2600) operates ferry service to Nantucket's Straight Wharf from Hyannis (6 per day, $11) and from Martha's Vineyard (mid-June to mid-Sept. 3 per day, $11). **Steamship Authority** (540-2022), docked at Steamboat Wharf on Nantucket, runs ferries from Hyannis only (6 per day, $10). Both charge $5 for bikes and take about two hours.

People say that hitchhiking is the best way to get around Nantucket. Those who prefer to pedal rent bikes at **Young's Bicycle Shop** (228-1151), Steamboat Wharf; mountain bikes and hybrids cost $20 per day. Young's distributes free, decent maps of the island; for an extended stay buy the $3 *Complete Map of Nantucket*. (Open daily 10am-8pm, Sept.-June 10am-6pm.) Nantucket's **area code:** 508.

Accommodations and Food **Nantucket Hostel (HI-AYH),** 31 Western Ave. (228-0433), sits surfside at Surfside Beach, 3½ mi. from town at the end of the Surfside Bike Path. (49 beds, full kitchen. Open daily 7:30-9:30am and 5-11pm. Curfew 11pm. Lockout 9:30am-5pm. $12, nonmembers $15. Linens $2. Reservations essential. Open late April to mid-Oct.) Right in the heart of Nantucket Town, **Nesbitt Inn,** 21 Broad St. (228-2446), offers 13 rooms, each with a sink and shared baths in this gorgeous Victorian guest house. The friendly, attentive owners make sure guests are comfortable with a common room and fireplace, a grill, a deck, kitchen access, and free continental breakfast. (Office open daily 7am-10pm. Check-in noon; check-out 11am. Singles $42, doubles $65, triples $85; Oct.-April $8-10 less. Reservations essential; deposit required.)

Nantucket restaurants don't know the meaning of the word budget. The standard entree runs about $12-14, but the frugal gourmet can still dine well. **Black Eyed Susan's,** 10 India St., offers a rotating breakfast and dinner menu with such interesting dishes as sourdough french toast with orange Jack Daniel's butter (full order $6.50, short $5). Banter with the chefs at no extra charge. (Breakfast daily 7am-1pm, dinner Fri.-Wed. 6-10pm. Reservations accepted.) Steal away to the **Brotherhood of Thieves,** 23 Broad St., a subterranean haven for those who don't like light to interfere with their meals. Down a jumbo sandwich ($4.50) and mellow out to the sounds of local bands Tuesday through Sunday nights. (Entrees $7-11; no credit cards or non-local checks. Open Mon. 11:30am-11pm, Tues.-Thurs. 11:30am-11pm, Fri.-Sat. 11:30am-midnight, Sun. noon-11pm.) To avoid restaurant prices altogether, buy groceries at the **A&P** (228-9756), on Commercial St. at Washington St. (open Mon.-Sat. 8am-10pm, Sun. 8am-8pm).

Sights and Activities The remarkable natural beauty of Nantucket is well protected; over 36% of the island's land can never be built upon. For a great **bike trip,** head east from Nantucket Town on Milestone Rd. and turn left onto any path that looks promising, and pedal in lush moors of heather, huckleberries, bayberries, and wild roses. **Sea Nantucket** (228-7499), at the end of Washington St. at the waterfront, will set you up in a rental **sea kayak** for an aquatic adventure ($25 for 4½hr.; open daily 8:30am-5:30pm). The boats aren't difficult to maneuver, but paddling works up a sweat. Take one out to a nearby salt marsh, or head across the harbor to one of the isolated beaches on the Coatue peninsula to enjoy a picnic undisturbed by other beachgoers. If you prefer to stand on the strand between land and sea, rent **surf fishing** equipment from **Barry Thurston's** (228-9595), at Harbor Sq. near the A&P (all necessary equipment $20 for 24hr.; open Mon.-Sat. 8am-9pm, Sun. 9am-6pm). The **Maria Mitchell Association,** 2 Vestal St. (228-5982), named after the nation's first female astronomer, leads nature classes and trips for children and operates an observatory. From mid-July to August, the observatory has open nights when the public can come and gaze at the stars ($2, children $1, family $5; call for observatory hours).

The fascinating **Nantucket Whaling Museum** (228-1736), Broad St. in Nantucket Town, recreates the old whaling community through exhibits on whales and the methods of whaling. Among other things, the museum contains a reconstructed candle shop and a complete whale skeleton. The **Museum of Nantucket History** (228-3889), in the Thomas Macy Warehouse, gives insight into the island's boom years as a whaling port and describes other island industries such as candlemaking and sheep raising. Catch a lecture by a genuine Nantucket old-timer. (Call for lecture times; $5, children $3. Both museums open early June to mid-Oct. daily 10am-5pm; late April-early June and mid-Oct. to early Dec. Sat.-Sun. 11am-3pm.) The best deal is a visitors pass which gets you into both museums and seven other historical sights run by the historical association ($8, children $4). Pick up a free copy of *Yesterday's Island* for listings of nature walks, concerts, lectures, art exhibitions, and more.

Rhode Island

Rhode Island, despite its diminutive stature (it's the smallest state in the Union), has always been a trendsetter. The first colony to declare independence from Great Britain became the first state to pass laws against slavery. Most Rhode Islanders are proud of their compact, non-conformist heritage. From founder Roger Williams, a religious outcast during colonial days, to Buddy Cianci, convicted felon and two-time mayor of Providence—he served one term while still on probation—Rhode Island has always lured a different crowd.

Though you can drive through the body of Rhode Island in 45 minutes, the state's 400 mi. coastline deserves a longer look. Small, provincial spots speckle the shores winding to Connecticut, and the inland roads remain quiet, unpaved thoroughfares lined with family fruit stands, marshes, and ponds.

PRACTICAL INFORMATION

Capital: Providence.

Rhode Island Department of Tourism: 7 Jackson Walkway, Providence 02903 (277-2601 or 800-556-2484). Open Mon.-Fri. 8:30am-4:30pm. **Division of Parks and Recreation,** 2321 Hartford Pike, Johnston 02919 (277-2632). Open Mon.-Fri. 8:30am-4pm.

Time Zone: Eastern. **Postal Abbreviation:** RI

Sales Tax: 7%.

■■■ PROVIDENCE

Like Rome, Providence sits aloft seven hills. Seven colleges inhabit these hills (including Brown and RISD), luring a community of students, artists, and academics to join the native working class and state representatives. Providence has cobbled sidewalks and colonial buildings, a college-town identity, and more than its share of bookstores and cafés. Head for the area around the colleges where students on tight budgets support a plethora of inexpensive restaurants and interesting shops.

Practical Information The state capitol and the downtown business district cluster just east of the intersection of I-95 and I-195. **Brown University** and the **Rhode Island School of Design (RISD)** (RIZZ-dee) sit atop of a steep hill, a 10-minute walk east of downtown. For a self-guided walking tour map and tourist literature, visit the **Greater Providence Convention and Visitors Bureau,** 30 Exchange Terrace (274-1636 or 800-233-1636), on the first floor, next to City Hall (open Mon.-Fri. 8:30am-5pm). The **Providence Preservation Society,** 21 Meeting St. (831-7440), at the foot of College Hill, gives detailed info on historic Providence (self-guided tour map $1, audio-cassette tour $5; open Mon.-Fri. 9am-5pm).

Amtrak operates from a gleaming white structure at 100 Gaspee St. (800-872-7245), behind the state capitol, a 10-minute walk from Brown or downtown. Trains set out for Boston (1hr., $8) and New York (4hr., $33-41) nine times per day. (Station open daily 5:30am-11:45pm.) **Greyhound** and **Bonanza,** 1 Bonanza Way (751-8800), off exit 25 of I-95, have frequent service to Boston (17 per day, 1hr., $7.75) and New York (7 per day, 4hr., $29). Bonanza accepts Ameripass.

(Station open 5am-midnight.) All buses make a stop at the Kennedy Plaza downtown, where Bonanza also has a ticket office (open daily 7am-6pm). **Rhode Island Public Transit Authority (RIPTA),** 265 Melrose St. (781-9400; 847-0209 from Newport; Mon.-Fri. 7am-7pm, Sat. 8am-6pm), runs an **information booth,** on Kennedy Plaza across from the visitors center, which provides in-person route and schedule assistance and free bus maps Monday to Friday 7am-6pm. RIPTA's service includes Newport ($2.50) and other points south. (Buses run daily 4:30am-1:30am; hours may vary by route. Fare 25¢ to $2.50; within Providence, generally 85¢; seniors ride free Mon.-Fri. 4:30-6am, 9am-3pm and 6pm-midnight, Sat.-Sun. all day. **Emergency:** 911. Providence's **post office:** 2 Exchange Terrace (421-4361; open Mon.-Fri. 7am-5:30pm, Sat. 8am-2pm); **ZIP code:** 02903; **area code:** 401.

Accommodations and Camping High downtown motel rates make Providence an expensive overnight stay, unless you have a friend at one of the local universities. Rooms book up far in advance for the graduation season in May and early June; don't expect any lit vacancy signs during that time. The stained-glass-windowed **International House of Rhode Island,** 8 Stimson Ave. (421-7181), near the Brown campus, has two comfortable rooms, but they're often full. Amenities include kitchen facilities, shared bath, TV, and a fridge. (2-night min. stay. Office open Mon.-Fri. 9:30am-5pm. Singles $45, students $30; doubles $50/$35; $5 off for stays of 5 nights or more. Reservations required.) The **New Yorker Motor Lodge,** 400 Newport Ave. (434-8000), in East Providence rents the cheapest rooms around. A typical motel, but the price is right (singles $40, doubles $44). The nearest campgrounds lie a 30-minute drive from downtown. One of the closest, **Colwell's Campground** (397-4614), provides showers and hookups for 75 sites on the shore of the Flat River Reservoir. From Providence, take I-95S to exit 10, then head west 8.5 mi. on Rte. 117 to Coventry. (Tent sites $10-15, depending on proximity to the waterfront.) If you really want to expose yourself to nature, try **Dyer Woods Nudist Campground,** 114 Johnson Rd. (397-3007), 3 mi. south of U.S. 6. Sixty nudist families live here year-round, but visitors can share the hot tub, sauna, volleyball, and badminton facilities. (12 sites $32. Day pass $22. Open May-Sept.)

Food Good food emanates from three areas in Providence: **Atwells Ave.** in the Italian district, on Federal Hill just west of downtown; **Thayer St.,** on College Hill to the east, home to off-beat student hangouts and ethnic restaurants; and the **Union St.** area, near downtown, with its beautiful old diners. **Geoff's,** 163 Benefit St. (751-2248), combines bread and ingredients in 60 different ways and names them all after stars like Buddy Ciani (sandwiches $4-6; open Mon.-Fri. 8am-10pm, Sat.-Sun. 10am-10pm). Sit down on a swivel stool for some good home cookin' at the **Seaplane Diner** (941-9547), on Allens Ave. Around "since Grandma was a girl," Seaplane has perfected cheap ($3.50-5.50) stick-to-your-ribs dinners. (Open Mon.-Tues. 5am-3pm, Wed. 5am-3pm and 4-8pm, Thurs. 5am-3pm, 4-8pm, and 11pm-4am, Fri. 5am-3pm, 4-8pm, and midnight-4am, Sat. 5am-1pm and midnight-4am.) **Louis' Family Restaurant,** 286 Brook St. (861-5225), has made the entire community its family with friendly service. Students swear by the prices and donate artwork for the walls in return. Try the famous #1 special; two eggs, homefries, toast, and coffee for $2.30. (Open daily 5:30am-3pm.)

Sights The most notable historic sights in Providence cluster around the 350-year-old neighborhood around **College Hill. Brown University,** established in 1764, includes several 18th-century buildings and provides the best information about the area. The **Office of Admissions,** housed in the historic **Carliss-Brackett House,** 45 Prospect St. (863-2378), gives free hour-long walking tours of the campus (tours daily 10, 11am, 1, 3, and 4pm; office open Mon.-Fri. 8am-4pm). In addition to founding Rhode Island, Roger Williams founded the *first* **First Baptist Church of America,** 75 N. Main St. (454-3418), built in 1775 (open Mon.-Fri. 9am-4pm; free). Down the hill, the **Rhode Island State Capitol** (277-2357) supports one of three free-standing marble domes in the world. (Free guided tours Mon.-Tues. and Thurs. 10 and 11am; reserve a spot months in advance. Free self-guide booklets available in room 218. Open Mon.-Fri. 8:30am-4:30pm.)

The nearby **RISD Museum of Art,** 224 Benefit St. (454-6500), gathers together a fine collection of Greek, Roman, Asian, and Impressionist art, as well as a gigantic 10th-century Japanese Buddha. (Open Wed.-Sat. noon-5pm; Sept.-June Tues.-Wed. and Fri.-Sat. 10:30am-5pm, Thurs. noon-8pm, Sun. 2-5pm. $2, seniors $1, ages 5-18 50¢.) The New England textile industry was born in 1793 when Samuel Slater used plans smuggled out of Britain to build the first water-powered factory in America. The **Slater Mill Historic Site** (725-8638), on Roosevelt Ave. in Pawtucket, preserves the fabric heritage with operating machinery. The mill must be seen on a tour that leaves every two hours. (Open June-Aug. Tues.-Sat. 10am-5pm, Sun. 1-5pm; March-May and Sept.-Dec. Sat.-Sun. 1-5pm. $5, under 12 $4.)

Entertainment and Nightlife The nationally acclaimed **Trinity Repertory Company,** 201 Washington St. (351-4242), offers $10 student rush tickets two hours before performances, except on Saturday (tickets $24-32). For splashier productions, contact the **Providence Performing Arts Center,** 220 Weybosset St. (421-2787), which hosts a variety of concerts and Broadway musicals. The **Cable Car Cinema and Café,** 204 S. Main St. (272-3970), shows artsy and foreign films in a kinder, gentler setting—recline on couches instead of regular seats (tickets $6).

If you're in the mood for a little hardball, check out the **Pawtucket Red Sox** (AAA farm team for their Boston big brothers) April through August in Pawtucket's McCoy Stadium, 1 Columbus Ave. (724-7300; box seats $5.50, seniors and under 12 $4.50; general admission $4/$3). Stock cars race at **Seekonk Speedway,** 1756 Fall River Ave. (336-8488), a few mi. east on Rte. 6 in Massachusetts ($15, under 13 $5).

Read the free *New Paper* (distributed Thurs.), the "Weekend" section of the *Friday Providence Journal,* or the *Providence Pheonix* for film, theater, and nightlife listings. Brownies, townies, and RISDs rock the night away at several hot spots throughout town. Mingle with the local artist community at **AS220,** 115 Empire St. (831-9327), a café/bar/gallery/performance space popular with local artists. (Cover $2-5. Open daily 11am-1am. Second floor gallery open Mon.-Fri. 9am-5pm; free.) **The Living Room,** 23 Rathbone St. (521-5200), hosts both dancing and live alternative bands (open Mon.-Thurs. 8pm-1am, Fri.-Sun. 8pm-2am). **Club Babyhead,** 73 Richmond St. (421-1698), is "loud, dark, and dirty"—what more could you ask for in an alternative club? The gay community favors **Gerardo's,** 1 Franklin Sq. (274-5560; cover Thurs.-Sat. $3; open Sun.-Thurs. 4pm-1am, Fri.-Sat. 4pm-2am).

■■■ NEWPORT

Money has always found its way into Newport. Once supported by slave trade profits, the town later became the summer home of society's elite and the site of some of the nation's most opulent mansions. The city's monied residents played the first game of polo in North America, hosted the America's Cup race for 35 years, and watched President Kennedy wed Jacqueline Bouvier. Today, the city attracts beautiful people (with deep pockets) from all over the world. For those with fewer funds, seasonal events such as the jazz and folk festivals are reason enough to visit. Keep in mind, though, that there's a 25-year waiting period to get a slip at the marina.

Practical Information **Newport County Convention and Visitors Bureau,** 23 America's Cup Ave. (849-8048 or 800-326-6030), in the Newport Gateway Center, offers free maps. Pick up *Best-Read Guide Newport* and *Newport This Week* for current listings. (Open Sun.-Thurs. 9am-5pm, Fri.-Sat. 9am-6pm.) **Bonanza Buses** (846-1820) depart from the center, as do the buses of **Rhode Island Public Transit Authority (RIPTA),** 1547 W. Main Rd. (847-0209; open daily 4:30am-8:30pm). RIPTA routes run daily 10am-7pm. Fare, generally 85¢, is free on most routes Monday to Friday 9am-3pm and 6-7pm, and all day Saturday and Sunday. RIPTA also heads north to Providence (1hr., $2.50) and points on Rte. 114. Rent bikes at **Ten Speed Spokes,** 18 Elm St. (847-5609)—surprisingly, there are no 10-speeds. (Mountain bikes $5 per hr., $25 per day. Must have credit card and photo ID. Open Mon.-Sat. 9:30am-6pm, Sun. 9:30am-5pm.) **Emergency:** 911. Newport's **post office:** 320 Thames St. (847-2329), opposite Perry Mill Market (open Mon.-Fri. 8:30am-5pm, Sat. 9am-1pm); **ZIP code:** 02840; **area code:** 401.

Accommodations, Camping, and Food Guest houses account for the bulk of Newport's accommodations. Most offer a bed and continental breakfast with colonial intimacy. Those willing to share a bathroom or forego a sea view might find a double for $65; singles are almost nonexistent. Be warned that many hotels and guest houses book solid two months in advance for summer weekends. When you're ready to blow your wad, **Bed and Breakfasts of Rhode Island, Inc.,** 580 Thames St. (849-1298), can make a reservation for you for $70-225 per night. **Campsites** await at **Fort Getty Recreation Area** (423-7264), on Conanicut Island. Walk to the nearby Fox Hill Salt Marsh for great birdwatching. (100 trailer sites; 20 year-round. 15-18 tent sites. Showers and beach access. Sites $17, hookup $22.)

Despite what you might expect, cheap food *does* exist in Newport. Most of Newport's restaurants line up on **Thames St.** A booth and some solid food beckon you to the **Franklin Spa,** 229 Spring St. Try the banana pancakes ($4) or lunch on the cajun chicken ($4; open Mon.-Sat. 6:30am-3pm, Sun. 6:30am-2pm). **Dry Dock Seafood,** 448 Thames St. (847-3974), fries 'em, and serves 'em with a minimum of fuss (entrees $6-11; open daily 11am-10pm). Shack up with some choice mollusks at **Flo's Clam Shack,** 4 Wave Ave. (847-8141), across from Newport Beach, or enjoy the clam product of your choice (fried clams $9) alongside a severely incapacitated lobster boat labeled the *S.S. Minnow* (open Thurs.-Sun. 11am-9pm).

Sights Newport takes "keeping up with the Joneses" to new heights. The Jones in question, George Noble Jones, built the first "summer cottage" here in 1839, thereby kicking off an extravagant string of palatial summer estates. A self-guided walking tour or a guided tour by the **Preservation Society of Newport,** 424 Bellevue Ave. (847-1000; open Mon.-Fri. 9am-5pm), will allow you to ogle the extravagance; purchase tickets at any mansion daily 10am-5pm. The 1765 **Wanton-Lyman Hazard House,** 17 Broadway (846-0813), the oldest standing house in Newport, has been restored in different period styles (open mid-June to Labor Day Thurs.-Sat. 10am-4pm, Sun. 1-4pm; $4). The father of William Mayes, a notorious Red Sea pirate, opened the **White Horse Tavern** (849-3600), on Marlborough and Farewell St., as a tavern in 1687, making it the oldest continuously operated drinking establishment in the country (beer $3-4). The oldest synagogue in the U.S., the beautifully restored Georgian **Touro Synagogue,** 85 Touro St. (847-4794), dates back to 1763. (Visits by free tour only. Tours mid-June to July 3 Sun. 1 and 2pm; July 4-Labor Day tours Sun.-Fri. every ½hr. 10am-4pm; please call for off season tour schedule.)

Die-hard tennis fans will feel right at home in Newport, where the **Tennis Hall of Fame,** 194 Bellevue Ave. (849-3990), hosts grass court tournaments and dedicates a museum to the game. (Open daily 10am-5pm. $6, under 16 $3, family $12.)

Newport's gorgeous beaches are frequently as crowded as the streets. The most popular, **First Beach** (848-6491), or Easton's Beach, on Memorial Blvd., features enchanting old beach houses and a carousel (open Memorial Day-Labor Day daily 8:30am-4pm; parking $7, weekends $10). Those who prefer hiking over dunes to sunbathing on them should try **Fort Adams State Park** (847-2400), south of town on Ocean Dr. 2½ mi. from Gateway Center, where visitors can also take advantage of showers, picnic areas, and two fishing piers (Entrance booth open Mon.-Fri. 7:30am-5pm, Sat.-Sun. 7:30am-6pm; park open sunrise to sunset. Parking $4). Good beaches also line Little Compton, Narragansett, and the shore between Watch Hill and Point Judith; for more details, consult the free *Ocean State Beach Guide,* available at the visitors center (see Practical Information above).

Entertainment In July and August, Newport gives lovers of classical, folk, and jazz each a festival to call their own. The oldest and best-known jazz festival in the world, the **Newport Jazz Festival** (847-3700, after May) has seen the likes of Duke Ellington, Count Basie, and many others; bring your beach chairs and coolers to Fort Adams State Park to join the fun in mid-August (Sat.-Sun. tickets $30, under 12 $12.50). The **Newport Music Festival** (846-1133; box office 849-0700), July 6-21 in 1996, attracts pianists, violinists, and other classical musicians from around the world for two weeks of concerts in the ballrooms and on the lawns of the mansions (box office open daily 9am-6pm; tickets $15-40). In August, folksingers such as Joan Baez and the Indigo Girls entertain at the legendary **Newport Folk Festival** (847-3709, June-Aug.), which runs two days, noon to dusk, rain or shine (tickets $28).

Newport's nightlife is easy to find. Down by the water, **Pelham East,** 2 Pelham St. (849-3888), at the corner of Thames, books bands for straight rock 'n' roll (live music nightly; cover Fri.-Sat. $5; open daily noon-1am). For an alternative scene, hop over to **Señor Frogg's,** 108 William St. (849-4747), across from the Tennis Hall of Fame (cover varies; open Wed.-Thurs. 8:30am-1pm, Fri.-Sun. 5pm-1am). **Bad Bob's** (848-9840) rocks the boat at Waite's Wharf with a DJ and live bands playing rock, soul, and reggae (cover $1-7; open June to mid.-Sept. Fri.-Mon. 7pm-midnight).

NEW ENGLAND

■ NEAR NEWPORT: BLOCK ISLAND

A popular daytrip 10 mi. southeast of Newport in the Atlantic, sand-blown **Block Island** possesses an untamed natural beauty. One quarter of the island is protected open space; local conservationists hope to increase that to 50%. From Old Harbor where the ferry lets you off (see below), a 4-mi. hike or bike ride brings you to the **National Wildlife Refuge,** a great spot to take a picnic. Two miles due south from Old Harbor, the **Mohegan Bluffs** invite the adventurous, cautious, and strong to wind their way down to the Atlantic waters 200 ft. below. High in the cliffs, the **Southeast Lighthouse** has warned fog-bound fisherfolk since 1875; its beacon shines the brightest of any on the Atlantic coast.

The **Block Island Chamber of Commerce** (466-2982) welcomes you at the ferry dock in Old Harbor Drawer D, Block Island 02807 (open daily 10am-4pm; mid-Oct. to mid-May Mon-Sat. 10am-4pm). Rhode Island rest stop info centers supply the free *Block Island Travel Planner.* **Cycling** is the ideal way to explore the tiny (7mi. by 3mi.) island; the **Old Harbor Bike Shop** (466-2029), to the left of the ferry exit, rents just about anything on wheels (10-speeds and mountain bikes $3 per hr., $15 per day; mopeds $15/$55; license required. Cars $60 per day; 20¢ per mi. Must be 21 with credit card. Insurance optional; $3 per day for mopeds, $10 per day for cars. Open daily 9am-7pm.) The **Interstate Navigation Co.** (783-4613) provides year-round **ferry service** to Block Island from Point Judith, RI (8-10 per day, off season 1-3 per day, 1¼hr., $6.60, under 12 $3.15, cars by reservation $20.25, bikes $1.75), and summer service from Newport, RI (late June-early Sept. 1 per day, 2hr., $6.45) and New London, CT (mid-June to mid-Sept. 1 per day, 2hr., $13.50). If possible, leave from Galilee State Pier in Point Judith for the most frequent, cheapest, and shortest ride. **Coast Guard:** 466-2462.

The island does not permit camping; make it a daytrip unless you're willing to shell out $60 or more for a room in a guest house. Most restaurants hover near the ferry dock in Old Harbor; several cluster at New Harbor one mi. inland.

Connecticut

Connecticut, the third smallest state in the Union, resembles a patchwork quilt, stitched from industrialized centers (like Hartford and New Haven), serene New

England villages, and lush woodland beauty. Perhaps it is this diversity that attracted such famous residents as Mark Twain, Harriet Beecher Stowe, Noah Webster, and Eugene O'Neill, and inspired the birth of the American Impressionist movement and the American musical—both Connecticut originals. Home to Yale University and the nation's first law school, Connecticut has an equally rich intellectual history. This doesn't mean that the people of Connecticut don't know how to let their hair down—hey, this is the state that brought the us the lollipop, the three-ring circus, frisbee, and one of the largest casinos in the western hemisphere.

PRACTICAL INFORMATION

Capital: Hartford.

Connecticut Vacation Center: 865 Brook St., Rocky Hill 06067 (800-282-6863). Call for vacation guides. **Department of Environmental Protection-State Parks Division,** 203-424-3015. Call for an application for a state parks and forests camping permit and brochures describing sites. Open Mon.-Fri. 8:30am-4:30pm. **Connecticut Forest and Park Association,** 16 Meriden Rd., Rockfall 06481 (203-346-2372), has outdoor activities info.

Time Zone: Eastern. **Postal Abbreviation:** CT

Sales Tax: 6%.

■■■ HARTFORD

Connecticut's capital has not always been law-abiding. In 1687, the English governor demanded the surrender of the charter that Charles II had granted Hartford 25 years before. Obstinate, Hartfordians hid the charter in a tree trunk until the infuriated governor returned to England. Today, a plaque marks the spot at Charter Oak Place. Sometime over these last three centuries, Hartford has grown into the world's insurance capital; the city's skyline is shaped by architectural wonders financed by some of the larger firms, including the monolithic oval of the Boat Building (America's first two-sided building).

Practical Information Hartford marks the intersection of I-91 and I-84. The **Greater Hartford Convention and Visitors Bureau** offices, at the Hartford Civic Center, 1 Civic Center Plaza (728-6789 or 800-446-7811), and on Main St. in the Pavilion (522-6766), both offer dozens of maps, booklets, and guides to local resorts, campgrounds, and historical sights (open Mon.-Fri. 10am-6pm, Sat. 10am-5pm). The **Greater Hartford Tourism District,** 1 Civic Center Plaza (520-4480 or 800-793-4480), can also help. For information on the streets, look for one of the red-capped and khaki-clad Hartford guides, all of whom are knowledgable about the history, services, events, and geography of the city. (Guides on duty Mon.-Sat. from mid-morning until late night. Guides have police radios.) In front of the Old State House, **Connecticut Transit's Information Center** (525-9181), at State and Market St., doles out helpful downtown maps and public transportation info (basic bus fare 95¢). Union Place is home to **Amtrak** (727-1776 or 800-872-7245), which runs eight trains daily both north and south (office open daily 5:30am-9pm), and **Peter Pan Trailways** (800-237-8747), which connects to New York (2½hr., $17) and Boston (2½hr., $16) 10 times each day (ticket office open daily 5:45am-10pm). **Greyhound** (800-231-2222), at Union Place, buses to New York (16 per day, 2½hr., $14) and to Boston (10 per day, 2½hr., $14; office open daily 7am-10:30pm). Hartford's **post office:** 141 Weston St. (524-6001; open Mon.-Fri. 7am-6pm, Sat. 7am-3pm); **ZIP code:** 06101; **area code:** 203.

Accommodations, Food, and Nightlife Within the city, the **YMCA,** 160 Jewell St. (522-4183), charges affordable rates and has a gym, a pool, a cafeteria, and racquet courts (singles $16.60, with private bath $21.60; no reservations accepted). Just north of Hartford, the sleepy **Windsor Home Hostel (HI-AYH)** (683-2847) resides in Connecticut's oldest town. Hostelers stay in four beds in rooms with 70s decor and share a bath, common area, and kitchen facilities. ($11-13. Call for required reservation; directions given upon confirmation.) The new **Mark Twain Hostel (HI-AYH),** 131 Tremont St. (523-7255), was set to open late in the summer of 1995; call for details. For camping enthusiasts who don't mind a 30-minute drive out of the city, **Burr Pond State Park** (379-0172), five minutes north of Torrington off Rte. 8 on Burr Mountain Rd., provides 40 wooded sites ($10) with showers and swimming (registration 8am-sunset).

Many delectable restaurants hover within a few blocks of the downtown area. The **Municipal Café,** 485 Main St. (278-4844; 527-5044 for entertainment info), at Elm, is a popular and friendly place to catch a good breakfast or lunch: the breakfast special means bacon, ham, or sausage with two eggs, toast, coffee or tea for $3.50. Hot dinners go for $6. At night, the "Muni" is big, big, big on the local music scene. (Bands Wed.-Thurs. and Sun. 8pm-1am, Fri.-Sat. 8pm-2am. Fri.-Sat. nights alcohol-free dance party 1:30-5am. Open daily for breakfast and lunch 7am-3:30pm, bar menu after 8pm.) **The Hartford Brewery, Ltd.,** 35 Pearl St. (246-2337), Connecticut's only brew-pub, serves up sandwiches ($5-7) and burgers ($7) and six freshly brewed beers (India Pale Ale $3.50). Brewery tours are available. (Open Mon.-Thurs. 11:30am-1am, Fri. 11:30am-2am, Sat. noon-2am.) Downtown, Hartford's oldest bar, the **Russian Lady,** 191 Ann St. (525-3003), has original antiques, from burnished wood counters to Tiffany lamps. Live modern music rocks this unlikely setting and the overpopulated mosh pit on the second floor. (Cover for the second floor $3-4. Open Wed.-Thurs. 5pm-1am, Fri. 5pm-2am, Sat. 7pm-2am, Sun. 7pm-1am.)

Sights Designed by Charles Bullfinch in 1796, the gold-domed **Old State House,** 800 Main St., housed the state government until 1914. Under renovation until Spring 1996, the State House has moved its historical exhibits to the **Renovation Headquarters** (522-6766), located across the plaza in the **Pavilion** (open Mon.-Fri. 10am-6pm, Sat. 10am-5pm). Call for an update. Thomas Hooker once preached across Main St. at the **Center Church and Ancient Burying Grounds,** 675 Main St.; the centuries-old tombstones of his descendants are in the graveyard.

A block or so west, park 'n' ride at **Bushnell Park,** supposedly the first public American park, on one of the country's few extant hand-crafted merry-go-rounds. The **Bushnell Park Carousel** (246-7739), built in 1914, spins 48 horses and two lovers' chariots to the tunes of a 1925 Wurlitzer Organ. (Open May-Aug. Tues.-Sun. 11am-5pm; April and Sept. Sat.-Sun. 11am-5pm. Admission 50¢.) Overlooking the park, the gold-domed (isn't everything?) **State Capitol,** 210 Capitol Ave. (240-0222), houses Lafayette's camp bed and a war-ravaged tree trunk from the Civil War Battle of Chickamauga, among other historic artifacts. Free one-hour tours begin at the west entrance of the neighboring **Legislative Office Building;** look for free parking behind the building. (Tours Mon.-Fri. 9:15am-2:15pm, Sat. tours from the capitol's SW entrance 10:15am-2:15pm.)

The **Wadsworth Atheneum,** 600 Main St. (278-2670), the oldest public art museum in the country, has absorbing collections of contemporary and Baroque art, including Monet, Renoir, Degas, and one of only three Caravaggios in the United States. (Tours Thurs. at 1pm and Sat.-Sun. noon-2pm. Open Tues.-Sun. 11am-5pm. $5, seniors and students $4, under 13 free; free Thurs., and Sat. before noon.)

Lovers of American literature won't want to miss the engaging tours at **Mark Twain House,** 351 Farmington Ave. (493-6411), and **Harriet Beecher Stowe House,** 79 Forest St. (525-9317), both just west of the city center on Farmington Ave.; from the Old State House take any "Farmington Ave." bus east. The rambling, richly colored Mark Twain Mansion housed the Missouri-born author for 17 years, during which Twain composed his masterpiece *Huckleberry Finn*. (Open Mon.-Sat. 9:30am-4pm, Sun. noon-4pm; Oct.-May closed Tues. $7.50, seniors $7, ages 6-12 $3.50.) Harriet Beecher Stowe lived next door on Nook Farm from 1873, after the publication of *Uncle Tom's Cabin*, until her death. (Open Mon.-Sat. 9:30am-4pm, Sun. noon-4pm; Oct.-May closed Mon. $6.50, seniors $6, ages 6-16 $2.75.)

Farther out Farmington Ave. in the colonial village of **Farmington,** the **Hill-Stead Museum,** 35 Mountain Rd. (677-9064), shows Impressionist masterpieces in a domestic setting. The Colonial Revival "country house," built by Alfred Pope specifically for the purpose of housing his Impressionist Collection, contains pieces by Manet, Monet, Degas, Cassat, and Whistler. (1-hr. guided tour only; Tues.-Sun. every ½hr. 10am-4pm. $6, students and seniors $5, ages 6-12 $3.)

Hockey enthusiasts enjoy catching the NHL's **Hartford Whalers** at the **Civic Center,** 242 Trumball St. (728-6637 or 800-WHALERS/942-5377; tickets $19-42).

■■■ NEW HAVEN

Simultaneously university town and depressed city, New Haven has gained a reputation as something of a battleground—academic types and a working-class population live uneasily side by side. Yalies tend to stick to their campus, widening the rift between town and gown. Every facet of life in the city, from architecture to safety, reflects this difference. While most of New Haven continues to decay, Yale has begun to renovate its neo-Gothic buildings and convert its concrete sidewalks to brick. Even as a revitalized coffeehouse and bar scene emerges around the university, however, Yalies must admit that New Haven is still no Harvard Square.

Practical Information New Haven lies at the intersection of I-95 and I-91, 40 mi. from Hartford. The **Greater New Haven Convention and Visitors Bureau,** 1 Long Wharf Dr. (777-8550 or 800-332-7829), provides free maps and current events info (open Mon.-Fri. 8:30am-5pm). For a weekly recorded events update, call 498-5050, ext. 1310. The **Yale Information Center,** Phelps Gateway, 344 College St. (432-2300), facing the Green, distributes free campus maps, a $1 walking guide, and *The Yale,* a guide to undergraduate life ($3.50), as well as bus maps and a New Haven bookstore guide. (Free 1-hr. tours Mon.-Fri. 10:30am and 2pm, Sat.-Sun. 1:30pm. Open Mon.-Fri. 9am-4:45pm, Sat.-Sun. 10am-4pm.) **Amtrak** (786-2888 or 800-872-7245), Union Station on Union Ave., runs out of a newly renovated station. Be careful; the area is unsafe at night. (To: New York City $25; Boston $31; Washington, DC $78; Mystic $18.) You may purchase tickets every day between 6am and 10pm. Also at Union Station, **Greyhound** (772-2470 or 800-231-2222) runs frequent service to New York ($13), Boston ($16), Providence ($16), and New London ($12). The ticket office is open daily 7:30am-8pm. Local **crisis lines** include the **Crisis Hotline,** 800-203-1234, and the **Gay Counseling Line,** 800-286-9900. New Haven's **area code:** 203.

At night, don't wander too far from the immediate downtown and campus areas; surrounding sections are notably less safe. New Haven is laid out in nine squares. Between **Yale University** and City Hall, **Green,** the central square, provides a pleasant escape from the hassles of city life. A small but thriving business district of bookstores, boutiques, cheap sandwich places, and other services catering to students and professors borders the Green.

Accommodations and Food Inexpensive accommodations are sparse in New Haven; the hunt quickens around Yale Parents Weekend (mid-Oct.) and commencement (early June). **Hotel Duncan,** 1151 Chapel St. (787-1273), contains the oldest elevator in CT and plush rooms with cable TV and mini fridges (singles $40, doubles $60; reservations recommended on weekends). Trusty **Motel 6** (469-0343), waits like an old friend at exit 8 off I-91 (singles $43, doubles $49). **Bed & Breakfast/Nutmeg,** 222 Girard Ave. (236-6698), in W. Hartford, reserves doubles ($35-45) in New Haven B&Bs (open Mon.-Fri. 9am-5pm). **Hammonasset Beach** (245-1817), 20 minutes from town, offers camping as close as it gets (sites $12).

The university's coffee-and-cigarette set haunt the mural-clad **Daily Caffe,** 316 Elm St. (776-5063), a psychedelic joint opened by a Yale Alum. Sandwiches start at $3.50. Top off your meal with the awesome chocolate mousse cake ($3) and a cup of joe. (Open Mon.-Sat. 7am-midnight, Sat.-Sun. 9am-midnight; Sept.-May Mon.-Sat.

7am-1am, Sat.-Sun. 9am-1am.) **Rainbow Gardens,** 1022 Chapel St. (777-2390), is a shiny, happy, veggie-friendly hangout with heart-shaped decor, good service, and great sandwiches ($4-7; open Mon.-Thurs. 9am-8pm, Fri. 9am-9pm, Sat. 10am-9pm, Sun. 10am-7pm). The ice cream ($1.90) at **Ashey's,** 278 York St. (863-3661), has been voted New Haven's best since 1983 (open Mon.-Thurs. 11am-11pm, Fri.-Sat. 11am-midnight, Sun. noon-11pm).

Sights Modeling their work on the colleges of Oxford, architects took great pains to artificially age the buildings on Yale's campus. Bricks were buried in different soils to give them that tarnished-by-the-centuries look; windows were shattered, and acid was sprayed, all to give Yale that wonderful going-to-shambles aura. James Gambel Rodgers, a firm believer in the sanctity of printed material, designed **Sterling Memorial Library** at 120 High St. (432-1775). The building looks much like a monastery; even the telephone booths are shaped like confessionals. Rodgers spared no expense in making Yale's library look "authentic," even decapitating the figurines on the library's exterior to replicate those at Oxford. (Open Mon.-Wed. and Fri. 8:30am-5pm, Thurs. 8:30am-10pm, Sat. 10am-5pm; Sept.-June Mon.-Thurs. 8:30am-midnight, Fri. 8:30am-5pm, Sat. 10am-5am, Sun. 1pm-midnight.)

The creator of the massive **Beinecke Rare Book and Manuscript Library,** 121 Wall St. (432-2977), decided to skip the windows. Instead, this intriguing modern structure is paneled with Vermont marble cut thin enough to be translucent; supposedly its volumes (including one Gutenberg Bible and an extensive collection of William Carlos Williams's writings) could survive a nuclear war. (Open Mon.-Fri. 8:30am-5pm, Sat. 10am-5pm.) On New Haven's own Wall St., between High and Yale St., take a moment to notice the Neo-Gothic gargoyles perched on the **Law School** building which portray cops and robbers.

Open since 1832, the **Yale University Art Gallery,** 1111 Chapel St. (432-0600), on the corner of York, claims to be the oldest university art museum in the Western Hemisphere. The university holds especially notable collections of John Trumbull paintings and Italian Renaissance works. (Open Sept.-July Tues.-Sat. 10am-4:45pm, Sun. 2-4:45pm. Free.) The **Peabody Museum of Natural History,** 170 Whitney Ave. (432-5050), at I-91's exit 3, houses Rudolph F. Zallinger's Pulitzer Prize-winning mural portraying the North American continent as it appeared 70 to 350 million years ago. Other exhibits range from Central American cultural artifacts to a dinosaur hall displaying the skeleton of a *brontosaurus.* (Open Mon.-Sat. 10am-5pm, Sun. noon-5pm. $5, over 64 and ages 3-15 $3.)

Entertainment and Nightlife Pick up a free copy of *The Advocate* to find out what's up in New Haven. Once a famous testing ground for Broadway-bound plays, New Haven's thespian community has scaled down in recent years. The **Schubert Theater,** 247 College St. (562-5666 or 800-228-6622), a significant figure in the town's on-stage tradition, still mounts shows (box office open Mon.-Fri. 10am-5pm, Sat. 11am-3pm). The **Yale Repertory Theater,** 222 York St. (432-1234), once turned out such illustrious alums as Meryl Streep, Glenn Close, and James Earl Jones and continues to produce excellent shows (open Oct.-May; tickets $10-30; ½-price student rush tickets on the day of a show). In summer, the city hosts concerts on the Green (787-8956), including free **New Haven Symphony** concerts (865-0831).

Toad's Place, 300 York St. (562-5694; 624-8623 for recorded info), has hosted gigs by Bob Dylan and the Stones and still stages great live shows. (Box office open daily 11am-6pm; buy tickets at the bar after 8pm. Bar open Sun.-Thurs. 8pm-1am, Fri.-Sat. 8pm-2am.) The **Anchor Bar,** 272 College St. (865-1512), off the Green, holds its ground with the area's best jukebox (bottled beer $2.50-3; open Mon.-Thurs. 11:30am-1am, Fri.-Sat. 11:30am-2am). Yalie jocks and fratboys get drunk on $2.50 beer at the **Union League Café,** 1032 Chapel St. (562-4299; open daily 5:30pm-2am). **Bar,** 254 Crown St. (495-8924), is anything but generic—*the* place for drinking, also *the* gay hotspot on Tuesdays (open daily 11:30am-2am).

MYSTIC AND THE CONNECTICUT COAST

Connecticut's coastal towns along the Long Island Sound were busy seaports in the days of Melville and Richard Henry Dana, but the dark, musty inns filled with tattooed sailors swapping sea journeys have been consigned to history. Today, the coast is important mainly as a resort and sailing base. **Mystic Seaport** (203-572-5315), 1 mi. south on Rte. 27 from I-95 at exit 95, commemorates the area's past with a maritime museum, tall ships, restored homes, shops, art and craft collections, and locals in funny costumes (open daily 9am-7pm; $18, over 60 $15, ages 6-15 $16). Seaport admission also entitles you to take a **Mystic River cruise** offered by **Sabino Charters** (203-572-5351) for a few dollars more. (30-min. trips mid-May to early Oct. daily on the hr. 11am-4pm. $3.50, ages 6-15 $2.50.) The hour-and-a-half evening excursions do not require museum admission (Runs mid-May to late Sept. daily 5pm; June 30-early Sept. Fri.-Sat. also 7pm. $8.50, ages 6-15 $7.)

Seals, penguins, and octopi share center stage with sharks and dolphins at **Mystic Aquarium,** 55 Coogan Blvd. (203-572-5955); take exit 90 from I-95 and follow the signs. (Open daily 9am-6pm; Labor Day-June 9am-5pm. $9.50, over 60 $8.50, ages 3-12 $6.50.) A little farther down the coast in **Waterford, Sunbeam Express** (203-443-7259) sails out to watch whales every summer Sunday, Tuesday, and Thursday from Capt. John's Dock at the Niantic River Bridge (departs 9am, returns 4pm; $30, over 62 $27, ages 4-12 $20). **New London** is the site of the U.S. **Coast Guard Academy** (203-444-8270), a five-minute drive up Rte. 32. Take a free tour through its museum (203-444-8511; open May-Oct. Mon.-Fri. 9am-4:30pm, Sat. 10am-5pm, Sun. noon-5pm) and, when it's in port, the cadet training vessel *U.S.S. Eagle.*

The **Tourist and Information Center,** Building 1d, Olde Mysticke Village, 06355 (536-1641), in **Olde Mysticke Village,** has oodles of information on area sights and accommodations (open Mon.-Sat. 9am-6:30pm, Sun. 9am-6pm). It may be difficult to secure cheap lodgings in tourist-infested Mystic; **Stonington** makes a more affordable base from which to explore the shore. If you plan to splurge on the pricey offerings in Mystic itself, call well ahead for reservations. The only cheap option in Mystic is **Seaport Campgrounds** (203-536-4044), on Rte. 184, 3 mi. from Mystic. (Tent sites for 2 adults and 2 children $25.50, with water and electricity $28.50; $4 per additional person; over 60 10% discount. Open mid-April to late Oct.) In Stonington, the **Sea Breeze Motel,** 812 Stonington Rd. (203-535-2843), rents big, clean rooms with A/C. (Singles $55, Fri.-Sun. $85; $10 per additional person; rates much lower in winter.) **Cove Ledge Resort Motel,** 368 Stonington Rd. (203-599-4130), has hardwood-floored rooms with A/C, TV, and an outdoor pool. (Singles $60, with microwave and fridge $80, doubles $70; Fri.-Sat. $5 more. Rates lower in winter.)

Though most people think of seafood when they think of coastal Connecticut, Mystic's most renowned eatery is **Mystic Pizza,** 56 W. Main St. (203-536-3737 or 536-3700). Since the popular 80s movie was filmed nearby, the pizza place has remodeled its façade to resemble the Hollywood set. (Unremarkable slices $2; small pizza $5; large $9.25. Open daily 10am-11pm; in winter until 10pm.) The popular

Foxwoods Resort Casino

Close to the Rhode Island border, Foxwoods (203-885-3000), the only casino complex in New England, wheels and deals on the land of the Pequots at the **Mashantucket Reservation;** take I-95 to exit 92, follow Rte. 2 west to **Ledyard,** and follow signs to the reservation. A shuttle whisks visitors between the enormous parking lot and the casino complex, where high-rollers play everything from slots to poker to blackjack to roulette. Take time to check out the informative exhibit on the Mashantucket Pequots, located beneath the waterfall at the main entrance. The casino has caused rifts within the Pequot community, as well as animosity from local whites who resent the recent success of their Pequot neighbors. Just goes to show, you can't buy happiness, even in America.

outdoor **Seaview Snack Bar,** 85 Greenmanville Ave. (203-572-0096), on the road to the Seaport, lives up to its name with a view of the sea. The service is fast, but expect lines around mealtimes. Gulp some chowder (cup $1.79, bowl $2.15), chow on a flounder sandwich ($3.60), or slurp some soft-serve ice cream (90¢). (Open March-Nov. Mon.-Thurs. 10am-10pm, Fri.-Sat. 10am-11pm.) **Trader Jacks,** 14 Holmes St. (572-8550), near downtown, pours $2 domestic beers. Happy hour (Mon.-Fri. 5-7pm) will have you smiling with ½-priced appetizers and 50¢ off all drinks. Frequent live music (no cover) will spice up your burger ($4.50). (Food daily 5pm-midnight. Last call for drinks Sun.-Thurs. 1am, Fri.-Sat. 2am.)

MID-ATLANTIC

Ranging up from the almost-Southern state of Virginia through the Eastern seaboard to New York, the mid-Atlantic states claim not only a large slice of the nation's population, but several of the nation's major historical, political, and economic centers. This region is home to every capital the U.S. has ever known; first settled in Philadelphia, PA, the U.S. government moved through Princeton, NJ, Annapolis, MD, Trenton, NJ, and New York City, before coming to rest in Washington, DC. During the Civil War, the mid-Atlantic even hosted the capital of the Confederacy, Richmond, VA. The legislative heart of the U.S., the area witnessed some of the war's bloodiest fighting, as it had in the American Revolution; today, countless historical attractions mark every step in the struggles. In addition to the region's central place in government and finance, two centuries of immigration have flooded the mid-Atlantic's shores to create a fun, crowded, ethnically diverse area which presents many of the challenges of preserving cultural variety while striving for national unity.

Though urban centers (and suburban sprawl) cover much of the mid-Atlantic, the great outdoors have survived. The celebrated Appalachian Trail meanders through the area. In northern New York, the Adirondacks make up the largest park in the U.S. outside of Alaska. Campers prance among pinecones in the untouched wilds of Pennsylvania's Allegheny Mountains, and wildlife refuges scattered along the coast protect birdlife and wild ponies alike.

Mid-Atlantic Morsels

Authors: Paul Auster, James F. Cooper, F. Scott Fitzgerald, Jay McInerney, Philip Roth, J.D. Salinger, Anne Tyler, Robert Penn Warren, Edith Wharton, E.B. White.
Artists: Hudson Valley School, Thomas Eakins, Charles Wilson Peale, Andy Warhol, Jasper Johns, Jackson Pollock.
Cuisine: Crabcakes, crab Imperial, Philadelphia cheesesteak, hoagies, Manhattan clam chowder, New York cheesecake, oyster pie, pepper pot, shoofly pie, soft pretzel, scrapple, Virginia ham, fried apples.
Microbreweries: Frederick Brewing Co., Oxford Brewing Co., Wild Goose Brewery, F.X. Matt, Buffalo, Woodstock, Pittsburgh, Jones, Latrobe, The Lion Inc., Straub, D.G. Yuangling, Arrowhead, Stoudt, Old Dominion, Potomac River.
Native Americans: Mahican, Delaware, Susquehannock, Nanticoke, Iroquois, Algonquin, Tutelo, Huron, Assateague.
Music: Crack the Sky, Counting Crows' lead singer, Dave Matthews Band, Beastie Boys, Boyz II Men, Manhattan Transfer.
Film and TV: *Rocky, The Exorcist, Philadelphia, Witness, Gettysburg, Dirty Dancing, The Virginian.*
Climate: Hot and muggy in summer, cold and rainy/snowy in winter.
Geography: Mountains, seashores.

New York

Surrounded by the beauty of New York's landscape, you may find it difficult to remember that smog and traffic exist. The cities that dot upstate New York have a sweet natural flavor that holds its own against the seedy core of the Big Apple. Whether in the crassly commercial Niagara Falls, the idyllic Finger Lakes, or in Albany (Albany?) you will have little doubt that nature is king in upstate New York.

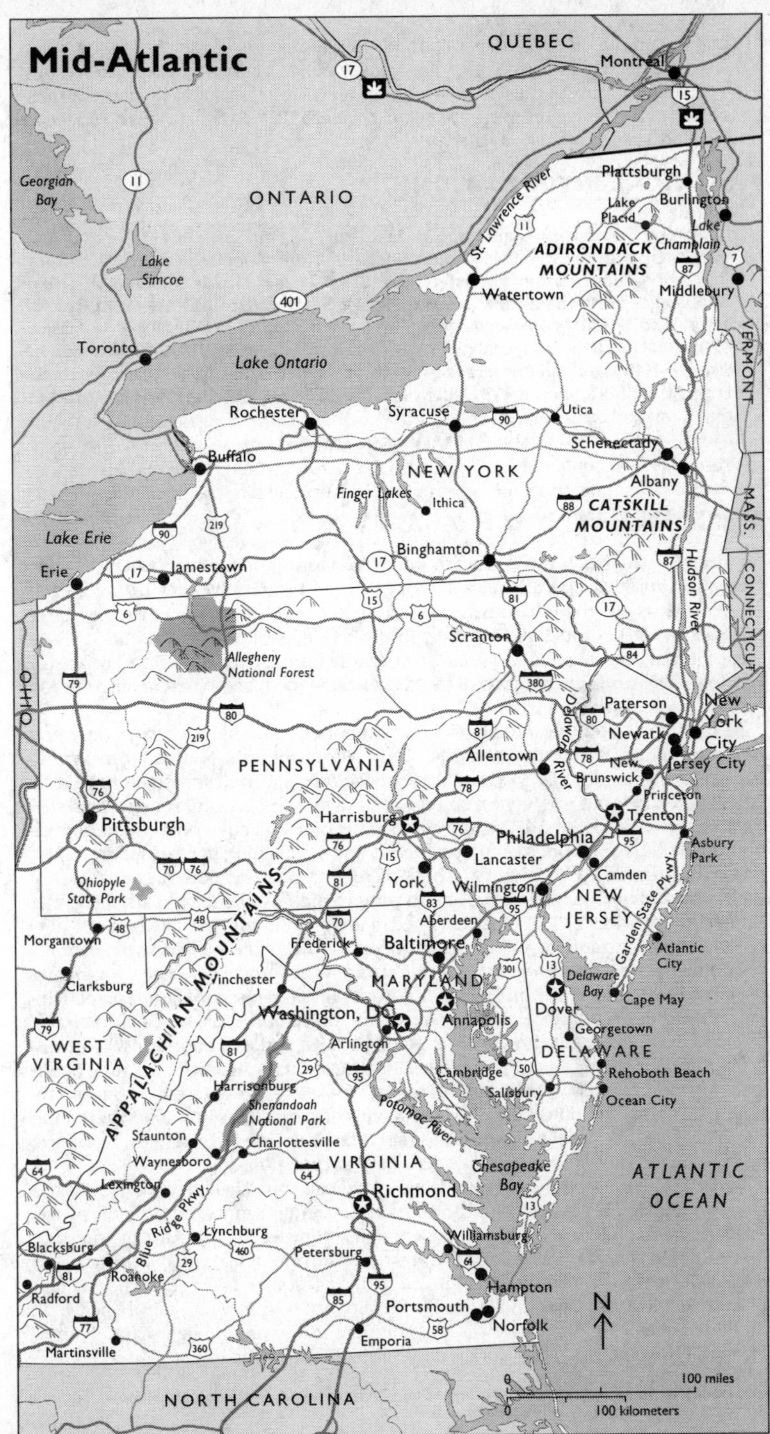

MID-ATLANTIC

The City, on the other hand, is an entirely different kettle of fish. According to Ed Koch, former mayor of New York: "This rural America thing. It's a joke." New York City, the eighth most populated city in the world, would claim to be grander than the other seven. With a diverse population, a spectacular skyline, towering financial power, and a range of cultural enterprises, New Yorkers may have a point.

PRACTICAL INFORMATION

Capital: Albany.

Division of Tourism: 1 Commerce Plaza, Albany 12245 (518-474-4116 or 800-225-5697). Operators available Mon.-Fri. 8:30am-5pm; voice mail system all other times. Excellent, comprehensive *I Love NY Travel Guide* includes disabled access and resource information. **New York State Office of Parks and Recreation and Historic Preservation,** Empire State Plaza, Agency Bldg. 1, Albany 12238-0001 (518-474-0456), has literature on camping and biking. The **Bureau of Preserve Protection and Management** of the **Division of Lands and Forests,** DEC, 50 Wolf Rd., Room 412, Albany 12233-4255 (518-457-7433) has information on hiking and canoeing.

Time Zone: Eastern. **Postal Abbreviation:** NY

Sales Tax: 8.25%.

■■■ NEW YORK CITY

Nowhere in America is the rhythm of urban life more pronounced than in the City. Crammed into tiny spaces, millions of people find themselves confronting each other every day. Perhaps because of the crush, people here are some of the loudest, pushiest, most neurotic, and loneliest in the world, though they may also be the most vibrant and talented as well. Much that is unique, attractive, and repulsive about the Big Apple is a function of the city's scale—too big, too heterogeneous, too jumbled, and too exciting.

In 1624, the Dutch West Indies Company founded a trading post; two years later, in a particularly shrewd transaction, Peter Minuit bought Manhattan from the natives for just under $24. Because the early colonists were less than enthralled by Dutch rule, they put up only token resistance when the British invaded the settlement in 1664. By the late 1770s the city had become an active port with a population of 20,000. New York's primary concern was maintaining that prosperity, and it reacted apathetically to the first whiffs of revolution. The new American Army understandably made no great efforts to protect the city and New York fell to the British in September of 1776 and remained in their hands until late November 1783.

Throughout turmoil, New York continued to grow, and emerged as the nation's pre-eminent city in the 19th century. Manhattan went vertical to house the growing population streaming in from Western Europe. Immigrants hoping to escape famine, persecution, and political unrest, faced the perils of the sea for the promise of America, landing on the shore of Ellis Island in New York Harbor. Post-WWII prosperity brought still more arrivals, especially African-Americans from the rural South and Hispanics from the Caribbean. However, by the 60s, crises in public transportation, education, and housing fanned the flames of ethnic tensions and fostered the rise of a criminal element. City officials raised taxes to improve services, but in the process drove away middle-class residents and corporations.

In the 80s, New York rebounded, but the tragically hip Wall Street of the 80s has faded to a gray 90s malaise, and the city once again confronts old problems—too many people, too little money, and not enough kindness. The first African-American mayor, David Dinkins, was elected in 1989 on a platform of harmonious growth, but this "melting pot" of New York continued to burn, smolder, and belch. The election of Rudy Giuliani as mayor in 1993 split the city once again along racial lines. Still, there are signs of life and renewed commitment in the urban blightscape. Former Mayor Ed Koch argues "New York is not a problem. New York is a stroke of genius."

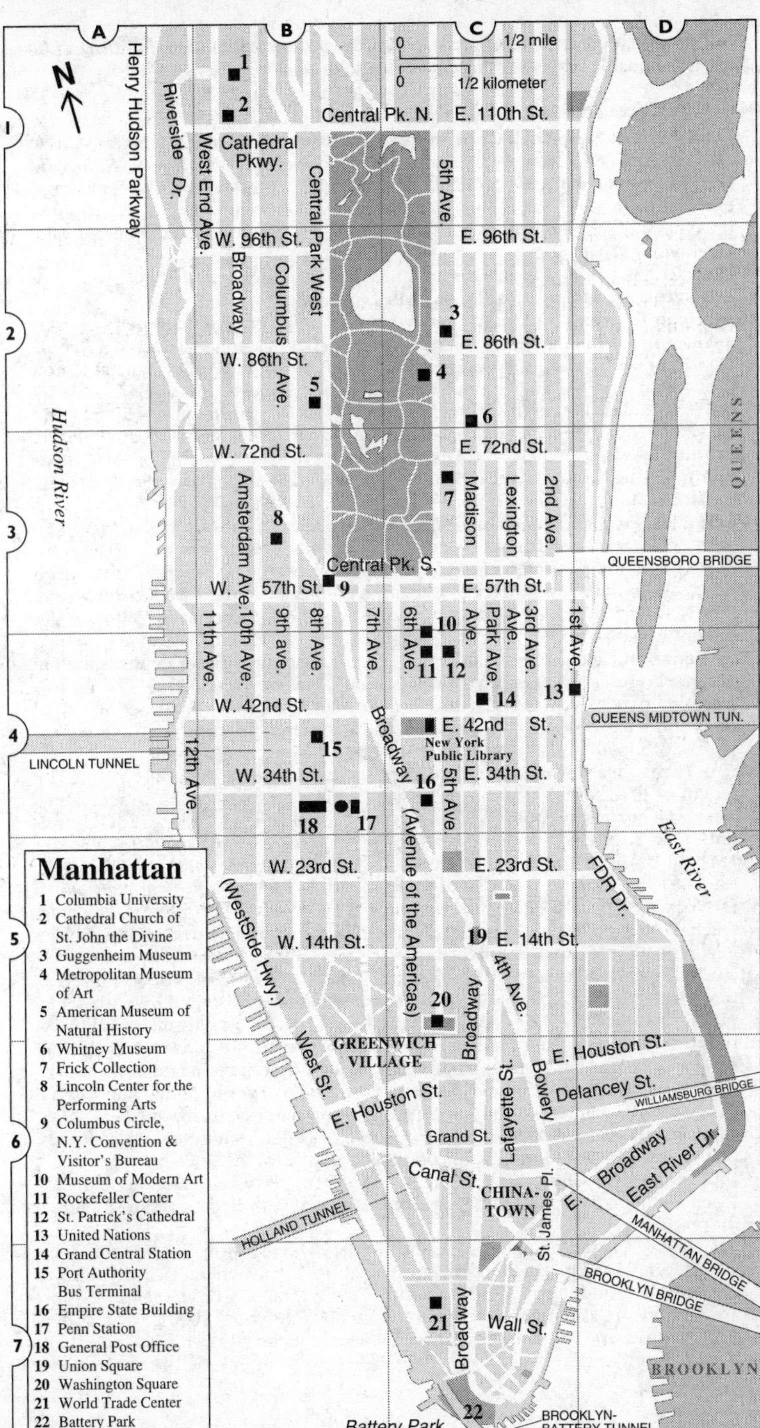
A
B
C
D
1
2
3
4
5
6
7
N
0 1/2 mile
0 1/2 kilometer
Central Pk. N.
E. 110th St.
Henry Hudson Parkway
Riverside Dr.
West End Ave.
Cathedral Pkwy.
Central Park West
5th Ave.
W. 96th St.
E. 96th St.
Broadway
Columbus Ave.
E. 86th St.
W. 86th St.
Hudson River
W. 72nd St.
E. 72nd St.
Madison
Lexington
2nd Ave.
Amsterdam Ave.
QUEENS
Central Pk. S.
QUEENSBORO BRIDGE
W. 57th St.
E. 57th St.
11th Ave.
10th Ave.
9th ave.
8th Ave.
7th Ave.
6th Ave.
Ave.
Park Ave.
3rd Ave.
1st Ave.
W. 42nd St.
E. 42nd St.
QUEENS MIDTOWN TUN.
LINCOLN TUNNEL
12th Ave.
New York Public Library
W. 34th St.
E. 34th St.
(Avenue of the Americas)
East River
W. 23rd St.
E. 23rd St.
FDR Dr.
(WestSide Hwy.)
W. 14th St.
E. 14th St.
4th Ave.
GREENWICH VILLAGE
West St.
E. Houston St.
Bowery
Delancey St.
WILLIAMSBURG BRIDGE
Grand St.
Lafayette St.
Canal St.
CHINA-TOWN
St. James Pl.
E. Broadway
East River Dr.
HOLLAND TUNNEL
MANHATTAN BRIDGE
BROOKLYN BRIDGE
Wall St.
BROOKLYN
Battery Park
BROOKLYN-BATTERY TUNNEL
Manhattan
1 Columbia University
2 Cathedral Church of St. John the Divine
3 Guggenheim Museum
4 Metropolitan Museum of Art
5 American Museum of Natural History
6 Whitney Museum
7 Frick Collection
8 Lincoln Center for the Performing Arts
9 Columbus Circle, N.Y. Convention & Visitor's Bureau
10 Museum of Modern Art
11 Rockefeller Center
12 St. Patrick's Cathedral
13 United Nations
14 Grand Central Station
15 Port Authority Bus Terminal
16 Empire State Building
17 Penn Station
18 General Post Office
19 Union Square
20 Washington Square
21 World Trade Center
22 Battery Park

For the ultimate coverage of New York City, see our city guide, *Let's Go: New York City*, available wherever fine books are sold.

PRACTICAL INFORMATION

Tourist Office: New York Convention and Visitors Bureau, 2 Columbus Circle (397-8222 or 484-1200), 59th St. and Broadway. Subway: #1, 9, A, B, C, or D to 59th St.-Columbus Circle. Multilingual staff helps with directions, hotel listings, entertainment ideas, safety tips, and descriptions of neighborhoods. Try to show up in person; the phone lines tend to be busy. Open Mon.-Fri. 9am-6pm, Sat.-Sun. and holidays 10am-3pm.

Police: 212-374-5000. Use this for inquiries that are not urgent. 24 hrs.

Consulates: See Embassies and Consulates (p. 25).

American Express: Multi-task agency providing tourists with traveler's checks, gift checks, cashing services, you name it. Branches in Manhattan include: **American Express Tower,** 200 Vesey St. (640-2000), near the World Financial Center (open Mon.-Fri. 9:30am-5:30pm); **Macy's Herald Square,** 151 W. 34th St. (695-8075), at Seventh Ave. inside Macy's (open Mon.-Sat. 10am-6pm); **150 E. 42nd St.** (687-3700), between Lexington and Third Ave. (open Mon.-Fri 9am-5pm); in **Bloomingdale's,** 59th St. and Lexington Ave. (705-3171; open Mon.-Sat. 10am-6pm); **822 Lexington Ave.** (758-6510), near 63rd St. (open Mon.-Fri. 9am-6pm, Sat. 10am-4pm).

Taxis: Most people in Manhattan hail yellow (licensed) cabs on the street: $1.50 base, 25¢ each one-fifth mi. or every 75 seconds; passengers pay for all tolls. Don't forget to tip. Ask for a receipt, which will have the taxi's ID number. This is necessary to trace lost articles or to make a complaint to the **Taxi Commission,** 221 W. 41st St. (221-8294). For radio-dispatched cabs, check the Yellow Pages under "Taxicabs."

Car Rental: All agencies have min. age requirements and ask for deposits. Call in advance to reserve, especially near weekends. **Nationwide,** 220 E. 9th St. (867-1234), between Second and Third Ave. Reputable nationwide chain. Mid-sized domestic sedan $59 per day, $289 per week, 150 free mi. per day, 1000 free mi. per week. Open Mon.-Fri. 8am-6pm. Must be 23 with a major credit card.

Auto Transport Companies: New York serves as a major departure point. The length of time for application processing varies; these 2 process immediately. Nearly all agencies require references and a refundable cash deposit. **Dependable Car Services,** 801 E. Edgar Rd., Linden, NJ (840-6262 or 908-474-8080). Must be 21, have 3 personal references, and a valid license without major violations. $150-200 deposit. Open Mon.-Fri. 8:30am-4:30pm, Sat. 9am-1pm. **Auto Driveaway,** 264 W. 35th St., Suite 500 (967-2344); 33-70 Prince St., Flushing, Queens (718-762-3800). Must be 21, with 2 local references and a valid driver's license. $250 deposit, $10 application fee. Open Mon.-Fri. 9am-5pm.

Bicycle Rentals: Bike and Fitness, 242 E. 79th St. (249-9344), near Second Ave., rents 3-speeds for $3 per hr., $10.50 per day; mountain bikes and rollerblades $6 per hr., $20 per day. $20 deposit required for 3-speeds, $40 for mountain bikes, plus driver's license and credit card. Overnight rentals ($8 plus cash deposit of $100 or $250). 2-hr. min. Open Mon.-Fri. 9:30am-8pm, Sat.-Sun. 9am-7pm. May-Oct. weekdays 10am-3pm and 7-10pm and from Fri. 7pm to Mon. 6am, Central Park closes its main loops to cars, allowing bicycles to rule its roads.

Help Lines: Crime Victim's Hotline, 577-7777; 24-hr. counseling and referrals. **Sex Crimes Report Line,** New York Police Dept., 267-7273; 24-hrs.

Walk-in Medical Clinic, 57 E. 34th St. (683-1010), between Park and Madison. Open Mon.-Fri. 8am-6pm, Sat. 10am-2pm. Affiliated with Beth Israel Hospital.

Emergency: 911.

Post Office: Central branch, 421 Eighth Ave. (967-8585 Mon.-Fri. 8:30am-5pm), across from Madison Square Garden (open 24 hrs.). For General Delivery, mail to and use the entrance at 390 Ninth Ave. C.O.D.s, money orders, and passport applications are also processed at some branches. **ZIP code:** 10001. **Area codes:** 212 (Manhattan); 718 (Brooklyn, Bronx, Queens, Staten Island.)

GETTING THERE

Plane Three airports service the New York Metro Region. **John F. Kennedy Airport (JFK)** (718-244-4444), 12 mi. from Midtown in southern Queens, is the largest, handling most international flights. **LaGuardia Airport** (718-533-3400), 6 mi. from Midtown in northwestern Queens, is the smallest, offering domestic flights and air shuttles. **Newark International Airport** (201-961-6000 or 201-762-5100), 12 mi. from Midtown in Newark, NJ, offers both domestic and international flights at better budget fares (though getting to and from Newark can be expensive).

JFK to midtown Manhattan can easily be covered by public transportation. Catch a brown and white JFK long-term parking lot bus from any airport terminal (every 15min.) to the **Howard Beach-JFK subway station,** where you can take the A train to the city (1hr.). Or you can take one of the city buses (Q10 or Q3; $1.25, exact change required) into Queens. The Q10 and Q3 connect with subway lines to Manhattan. Ask the bus driver where to get off, and make sure you know which subway line you want. The **Carey Airport Express** (718-632-0500), a private line, runs between JFK and Grand Central Station and the Port Authority Terminal (leaves every 30min. 5am-1am, 1hr., $13). A cab from JFK costs around $35.

LaGuardia can be reached from Manhattan two ways. If you have extra time and light luggage, you can take the MTA Q33 bus ($1.25, exact change or token) to the 74th St./Broadway/Roosevelt Ave./Jackson Hts. subway stop in Queens, and from there, take the #7, E, F, G or R train into Manhattan ($1.25). Allow at least 90 minutes travel time. The second option, the Carey bus, stops at Grand Central Station and the Port Authority Terminal (every half-hour, 30min., $9). A cab from LaGuardia costs around $25 and can easily be split with other passengers.

Newark Airport to Manhattan takes about as long as from JFK. **New Jersey Transit (NJTA)** (201-762-5100 or 212-629-8767) runs a fast, efficient bus (NJTA #300) between the airport and Port Authority every 15 minutes during the day, less often at night ($7). For the same fare, the **Olympia Trails Coach** (212-964-6233) travels between the airport and either Grand Central or the World Trade Center (every 20-30min. daily 5am-11pm; 25-60min. depending on traffic; $7).

Bus **Greyhound** (800-231-2222) grooves out of their major Northeastern hub, the **Port Authority Terminal,** 41st. St. and Eighth Ave. (435-7000; Subway: A, C, or E to 42nd St.-Port Authority). Be careful—with so many tourists, there are plenty of scam artists around. *This neighborhood is especially unsafe at night.* Avoid the terminal's bathrooms at all times. To: Boston (4½hr., $26); Philadelphia (2hr., $12); Washington, DC (4½hr., $26); Montréal (8hr., $70). **East Coast Explorer,** 245 Eighth Ave. (718-694-9667), offers budget full-day, scenic bus trips between New York, Boston, and Washington DC (NYC to Boston $29, to Washington $32).

Train Train service in New York runs primarily through two stations. On the East side, **Grand Central Station,** 42nd St. and Park Ave. (Subway: #4, 5, 6, 7, or S to 42nd St./Grand Central), handles **Metro-North** (532-4900 or 800-638-7646) commuter lines to Connecticut and New York suburbs. Longer routes run from the West Side's **Penn Station,** 33rd St. and Eighth Ave. (Subway: #1, 2, 3, 9, A, C, or E to 34th St./Penn Station), courtesy of **Amtrak** (582-6875 or 800-872-7245), serving most major cities in the U.S., especially in the Northeast. (Washington, DC, 4hr., $52). The **Long Island Railroad (LIRR)** (718-822-5477), and **NJ Transit** (201-762-5100) also chug from Penn Station to New Jersey. Nearby at 33rd St. and Sixth Ave, you can catch a **PATH** train to New Jersey as well (435-7000 or 800-234-7284, Mon.-Fri. 8am-5pm).

Car From New Jersey there are three ways to reach the city. The **George Washington Bridge,** which crosses the Hudson River into northern Manhattan, gives easy access to either Harlem River Dr. or the West Side Hwy. From the N.J. Turnpike you'll probably end up going through Weehawken, N.J. at the **Lincoln Tunnel,** which exits in Midtown in the West 40s. The **Holland Tunnel** connects to lower

Manhattan, exiting into the SoHo and TriBeCa area. Coming from New England or Connecticut on I-95, follow signs for the **Triboro Bridge.** From there get onto FDR Dr., which runs along the east side of Manhattan and exits onto city streets every 10 blocks or so. Another option is to look for the **Willis Avenue Bridge exit** on I-95 to avoid the toll, and enter Manhattan north on the FDR Drive.

Hitchhiking is illegal in New York state and cops strictly enforce the law within NYC. *Hitching in and around New York City is suicidal.* Don't do it.

ORIENTATION

Five **boroughs** comprise New York City: Brooklyn, the Bronx, Queens, Staten Island, and Manhattan. For all its notoriety, **Manhattan** Island's length is only half that of a marathon; 13 mi. long and 2.5 mi. wide, it houses the third largest population of the five boroughs, after Brooklyn and Queens. Though small, Manhattan has all the advantages; it is surrounded by water and adjacent to the other four boroughs. **Queens,** the largest and most ethnically diverse of the boroughs, beckons to the east of midtown Manhattan. **Brooklyn** lies due south of Queens. **Staten Island,** to the south of Manhattan, has remained defiantly residential, like the suburban communities of outer Long Island. North of Manhattan nests the **Bronx,** the only borough connected by land to the rest of the U.S., home of the lovely suburb Riverdale as well as New York's most depressed area, the South Bronx.

Manhattan's Neighborhoods

Glimpsed from the window of an approaching plane, New York City can seem a monolithic concrete jungle. Up close, New York breaks down into manageable neighborhoods, each with history and personality. Boundaries between these neighborhoods can often be abrupt.

The city began at the southern tip of Manhattan, in the area around **Battery Park** where the first Dutch settlers made their homes. The nearby harbor, now jazzed up by the **South Street Seaport** tourist magnet, provided the growing city with the commercial opportunities that helped it to succeed. Historic Manhattan, however, lies in the shadows of the imposing financial buildings around **Wall St.** and the civic offices around **City Hall.** A little farther north, neighborhoods rich in the cultures brought by late 19th-century immigrants rub elbows below Houston Street—**Little Italy, Chinatown,** and the southern blocks of the **Lower East Side.** Formerly the home of Eastern European and Russian Jews, Delancey and Elizabeth Streets now offer pasta and silks. To the west lies the newly fashionable **TriBeCa** ("Triangle Below Canal St."). **SoHo** (for "South of Houston"), a former warehouse district west of Little Italy, now shelters a pocket of art studios and galleries. Above SoHo thrives **Greenwich Village,** where jumbled streets, trendy shops, and cafés have for decades been home to intense political and artistic activity.

A few blocks north of Greenwich Village, stretching across the west teens and twenties, lies **Chelsea,** the late artist Andy Warhol's favorite hangout and former home of Dylan Thomas and Arthur Miller. East of Chelsea, presiding over the East River, is **Gramercy Park,** a pastoral collection of elegant brownstones immortalized in Edith Wharton's *Age of Innocence.* **Midtown Manhattan** towers from 34th to 59th St., where traditional and controversial new skyscrapers share the skies, supporting over a million elevated offices. Here department stores outfit New York while the nearby **Theater District** attempts to entertain the world, or at least people who like musicals. North of Midtown, **Central Park** slices Manhattan into East and West. On the **Upper West Side,** the gracious museums and residences of Central Park West neighbor the chic boutiques and sidewalk cafés of Columbus Ave. On the **Upper East Side,** the galleries and museums scattered among the elegant apartments of Fifth and Park Ave. create an even more rarefied atmosphere.

Above 97th St., the Upper East Side's opulence ends with a whimper where commuter trains emerge from the tunnel and the *barrio* begins. Above 110th St. on the Upper West Side sits majestic **Columbia University** (founded as King's College in 1754), an urban member of the Ivy League. The communities of **Harlem** and **Morn-**

ingside Heights produced the Harlem Renaissance of black artists and writers in the 1920s and the revolutionary Black Power movement of the 1960s. Now torn by crime, these areas are historically interesting, but not to be explored after dark. **Washington Heights,** just north of St. Nicholas Park, is home to Fort Tryon Park, the Medieval Cloisters museum, and a community of Old World immigrants.

Manhattan's Street Plan

New York's east/west division refers to an address's location in relation to the two borders of Central Park—**Fifth Ave.** on the east side and **Central Park West** on the west. Below 59th St. where the park ends, the West Side begins at the western half of Fifth Ave. **Midtown** presides between 34th and 59th St. **Uptown** (59th St. and *up*) refers to the area north of Midtown. **Downtown** (34th St. and *down*) means the area south of Midtown. **Streets run east-west. Avenues run north-south.**

Manhattan's grid makes calculating distances fairly easy. **Four streets are equivalent to one avenue.** Numbers also increase from south to north along the avenues, but you always should ask for a cross street when getting an avenue address. This plan does not work in Greenwich Village or in lower Manhattan; you must get a good map and ask directions.

GETTING AROUND

(For info on Taxis and Biking, see Practical Information.) Get a free subway map from station token booths or the visitors bureau, which also has a free street map (see Practical Information above). For a more detailed program of interborough travel, find a Manhattan Yellow Pages, which contains detailed subway, PATH, and bus maps. In the city, the round-the-clock staff at the **NYC Transit Information Bureau** (718-330-1234) dispenses subway and bus info.

Subways The fare for **Metropolitan Transit Authority (MTA)** subways and buses is $1.25; groups of four or more may find cabs cheaper for short rides. Once underground you may transfer to any train without restrictions. Most buses have access ramps, but steep stairs make subway transit more difficult for disabled people. Call for specifics on public transportation Mon.-Fri 9am-5pm (see Practical Information, above).

In crowded stations (notably those around 42nd St.), pickpockets find plenty of work; in deserted stations, more violent crimes can occur. *Always watch yourself and your belongings.* Try to stay in lit areas near a transit cop or token clerk. When boarding the train, make sure to pick a car with a number of other passengers on it—for long subway rides, the conductor's car is usually the best idea.

For safety, avoid riding the subways between 11pm and 7am, especially above E. 96th St. and W. 120th St. and outside Manhattan. Riding the subway at night is dangerous—don't ride alone. During rush-hour you'll be fortunate to find air, let alone seating: on an average morning, more commuters take the E and the F than use the entire rapid-transit system of Chicago (the nation's second-largest system). Buy several tokens at once at the booth or, preferably, at the new token-vending machines now at most stations (you'll not only avoid a long line, but you'll be able to use any station—some token booths close at night.)

Buses The **Metropolitan Transit Authority (MTA)** also runs buses for $1.25 a ride. Because buses sit in traffic, during the day they often take twice as long as subways, but they also stay relatively safe, clean—and are always windowed. They'll also probably get you closer to your destination, since they stop roughly every two blocks and run crosstown (east-west), as well as uptown and downtown (north-south), unlike the subway which mostly travels north-south. The MTA transfer system provides north-south bus riders with a slip for a free east-west bus ride, or vice-versa. Just ask the driver for a transfer slip when you pay. Ring when you want to get off. A yellow-painted curb indicates bus stops, but you're better off looking for the blue signpost announcing the bus number or for a glass-walled shelter displaying a map of the bus's route and a schedule of arrival times. Either exact change or a subway token is required; drivers will not accept dollar bills.

ACCOMMODATIONS

If you know someone who knows someone who lives in New York—get that person's phone number. The cost of living in New York is out of sight. Don't expect to fall into a hotel; if you do, odds are it will be a pit. At true full-service establishments, a night will cost you around $125 plus the hefty 14.25% hotel tax. Some choices are available for under $60 a night, but it depends on your priorities. People traveling alone may want to spend more to stay in a safer neighborhood. The outgoing may prefer a crowded budget-style place; honeymooning couples may not.

Hostels and Student Organizations

New York International HI-AYH Hostel, 891 Amsterdam Ave. (932-2300; fax 932-2574), at 103rd St. Subway: #1, 9, B, or C to 102nd St. Located in a block-long, landmark building, this is the largest hostel in the U.S., with 90 dorm-style rooms and 480 beds. Shares site with the **CIEE Student Center** (666-3619), an information depot for travelers, as well as a Council Travel office. Members' kitchens and dining rooms, laundry machines ($1), TV lounges, and an outdoor garden. Walking tours and outings. Secure storage area and individual lockers. 7-night max. stay in summer. Open 24 hrs. Check-in any time, check-out 11am (late check-out fee $5). No curfew. Members $22-25 per night, nonmembers $25-28. Family room $66. Groups of 4-10 may get private rooms; groups of 10 or above definitely will. Linen rental $3. Towel $2. Excellent wheelchair access.

International Student Center, 38 W. 88th St. (787-7706; fax 580-9283), between Central Park West and Columbus Ave. Subway: B or C to 86th St. Open only to foreigners (but not Canadians) aged 20-30; you must show a foreign passport or valid visa to be admitted. A once-gracious, welcoming brownstone. Single-sex, no-frills bunk rooms. Large basement TV lounge. 5-day max. stay when full in the summer, 7-day max the rest of the year. Open daily 8am-11pm. No curfew. $12. Key deposit $10. No reservations, and generally full in summers, but call by 10pm for a bed, and they'll hold it for you for two hours. Call before your arrival.

Sugar Hill International House, 722 Saint Nicholas Ave. (926-7030; fax 283-0108), at 146th St. Subway: A, B, C, or D to 145th St. Located on Sugar Hill in Harlem, across from the subway station. Reassuring, lively neighborhood. Converted brownstone with huge, well-lit, comfortable rooms. 2-10 people per room in bunkbeds. Staff is friendly and helpful, with a vast knowledge of NYC and the Harlem area. Facilities include kitchens, TV, stereo, and paperback library. Beautiful garden in back. All-female room available. Check-in 9am-10pm. 24-hr access. $12-14 per person. Call in advance. The owners of Sugar Hill also run the new 4-floor hostel next door at 730 Saint Nicholas Ave., the **Blue Rabbit Hostel** (491-3892 or 800-610-2030). Similar to the Sugar Hill, but with more doubles and more privacy. Backyard garden, friendly cats, common room, kitchen. Amazingly spacious rooms. Check-in 9am-10pm. $12-14; $14-16 for a private room. Call in advance.

Banana Bungalow (AAIH/Rucksackers), 250 W. 77th St. (800-6-HOSTEL/646-7835 or 769-2441; fax 877-5733), between Broadway and 11th Ave. Subway: #1 or 9 to 79th St. Walk two blocks south and turn right. A continually expanding and renovating hostel, with sun deck on the top floor, tropical-themed lounge/kitchen, and dorm-style rooms sleeping 4-7; some rooms have private baths. Beds $12-15. Reservations recommended. Wheelchair access.

De Hirsch Residence, 1395 Lexington Ave. (415-5650 or 800-858-4692; fax 415-5578), at 92nd St. Subway: #6 to 96th St. Affiliated with the 92nd St. YMHA/YWHA. Some of the largest, cleanest, and most convenient housing in the city. Hall bathrooms, kitchens, and laundry machines on every other; a collegiate feel. Single-sex floors, strictly enforced. A/C available for $3 per day or $45 per month. Access to the many facilities of the 92nd St. Y—free Nautilus and reduced rates for concerts. Organized activities such as walking tours of New York. Singles $294 per week ($42 per night); beds in doubles $210 per week ($30 per night).

3-day min. stay. Application required at least a month in advance; must be a student or working in the city, and must supply references. Wheelchair access.

International Student Hospice, 154 E. 33rd St. (228-7470), between Lexington and Third Ave. Subway: #6 to 33rd St. Up a flight of stairs in an inconspicuous converted brownstone with a brass plaque reading "I.S.H." Homey hostel with helpful owner exudes friendliness and community. Populated by a predominantly European crowd of backpackers. Good location in Murray Hill. Twenty very small rooms with bunk beds bursting with antiques, Old World memorabilia, and clunky oak night tables. The ceilings are crumbling and the stairs slant precariously, but the house is slowly being restored by residents. Rooms for 2-4 people and hall bathroom. Large common room, lounge, and enough dusty books to last a summer. Strict midnight curfew. $25 per night, with some weekly discounts.

Big Apple Hostel (AAIH/Rucksackers), 119th W. 45th St. (302-2603), between Sixth and Seventh Ave. Subway: #1, 2, 3, 9, N, or R to 42nd St.; or B, D, or E to Seventh Ave. Centrally located, this hostel offers clean, comfortable, carpeted rooms, full kitchen, back deck, luggage room, grill for barbecuing, a few common rooms, and laundry facilities. Passport nominally required; Americans accepted with out-of-state photo ID. Open 24 hrs. Bunk in dorm-style room with shared bath $20. Lockers in some rooms; bring a lock. Free coffee and tea in the kitchen. No reservations July-Aug., but they'll hold a bed if you call on the day you want to arrive. Reservations accepted Sept.-June; make them a few weeks in advance.

Chelsea International Hostel (AAIH/Rucksackers), 251 W. 20th St. (647-0010), between Seventh and Eighth Ave. Subway: #1, 9, C, or E to 23rd St. The congenial staff at this new 47-bed hostel offers their guests free beer and pizza on Wed. nights, and free beer (bring your own pizza) on Sun. Located in south Chelsea on a block with a police precinct, this hostel is fairly safe. Adequate 4-person dorm rooms $18 per bed; private rooms $35. Reservations recommended; call ahead.

Gershwin Hotel, 3 E. 27th St. (545-8000; fax 684-5546), between Fifth and Madison Ave. Subway: N or R to 28th St. Colorful sculptures and European travelers congregate in this recently renovated hotel, while a rooftop terrace beckons to sun-seekers. Out-of-state or foreign passport required. Free tea and coffee. 24-hr. reception. Check-out 11am. No curfew. 4-bed dorms $20 per bed. Private rooms are also available: doubles $65-82, triples $82-99. Continental breakfast $2.50.

Mid-City Hostel, 608 Eighth Ave. (704-0562), between 39th and 40th St. on the 3rd and 4th floors. Subway: #1, 2, 3, 9, N, or R to 42nd St.-Seventh Ave.; or A, C, or E to 42nd St.-Ninth Ave. No sign: just look for the street number on the small door. Lively neighborhood. Brick walls, skylights, and wooden beams across the ceiling. Caters to an international backpacking crowd—a passport and ticket out of the country are required. Small breakfast included. 7-day max. stay in summer. Lockout noon-6pm. Curfew Sun.-Thurs. midnight, Fri.-Sat. 1am. Bunk in dorm-style room with shared bath $18; Oct.-late June $15. Reservations are required and should be made far in advance for summer. Strictly no smoking.

Chelsea Center Hostel, 313 W. 29th St. (643-0214), between Eighth and Ninth Ave. Subway: #1, 2, 3, 9, A, C, E to 34th St. Knowledgeable staff will give advice in multiple languages (including Gaelic). 22 bunks in a low-ceilinged room make for a slightly cramped setup. Two showers. Tiny backyard garden, replete with ivy and a picnic table. Check in anytime, but lockout 11am-5pm. Dorm beds $20 in summer, $18 in winter, light breakfast included. Blankets and sheets provided as well. Be sure to call ahead; usually full in summer.

Uptown Hostel, 239 Lenox/Malcolm X Ave. (666-0559), at 122nd St. Bunk beds, sparkling clean and comfy rooms, and spacious hall bathrooms. $12 a night. Call 1-2 weeks in advance in summer, and at least 2 days in advance any other time.

YMCA—Vanderbilt, 224 E. 47th St. (756-9600; fax 752-0210), between Second and Third Ave. Subway: #6 to 51st St. or E, F to Lexington-Third Ave. Five blocks from Grand Central Station. Convenient and well-run, with vigilant security. Clean, brightly lit lobby bustles with internationals touting internal-frame backpacks. Rooms are quite small, and bathroom-to-people ratio is pretty low, but lodgers can use the copious athletic facilities (Stairmasters, aerobics classes, Nautilus machines, pool, and sauna), safe-deposit boxes, and guided tours of the city. No NYC residents. Five shuttles per day to the airports. Check-in 1-6pm; after

6pm must have major credit card to check in. Check-out at noon, but luggage storage until departure ($1/bag). Singles $47, doubles $59, quad $103. Key deposit $10 (refundable). Make reservations a week or two in advance and guarantee them with a deposit.

Hotels

Carlton Arms Hotel, 160 E. 25th St. (684-8337 or 679-0680), between Lexington and Third Ave. Subway: #6 to 23rd St. Stay inside a submarine and peer through windows at the lost city of Atlantis or stow your clothes in a dresser suspended on an astroturf wall. Each room has been designed in a different motif by a different avant-garde artist. The decoration doesn't completely obscure the age of these budget rooms, or their lack of air, but does provide distractions. Singles $49, with bath $57, doubles $62/$69, triples $74/$84. Pay for 7 or more nights up front and get a 10% discount. Make reservations for summer at least two months in advance. Substantial discounts for students and foreign travelers.

Roger Williams Hotel, 28 E. 31st St. (684-7500, reservations 800-637-9773; fax 576-4343), at Madison Ave. in pleasant Murray Hill neighborhood. Subway: #6 to 33rd St. This hotel, with its spacious, clean rooms, should suit your every need (though the elevator's tiny). Small refrigerators in each room. All rooms with toilet, bath, cable TV, phone, stove, and kitchenette. 24-hr. security. Singles $65, doubles $70, two twin beds $75, triples $80, and quads $90. Approximately 15% off regular rates with student ID, except for June through mid-July.

Portland Square Hotel, 132 W. 47th St. (382-0600 or 800-388-8988; fax 382-0684), between Sixth and Seventh Ave. Subway: B, D, F, or Q to 50th St.-Sixth Ave. Rooms are carpeted, clean, and entirely comfortable, with A/C and cable TV, but the hotel's main asset is its great location. Attracts mostly foreigners. Singles with shared bath $40, with private bath $65, doubles $89, triples $94, quads $99.

Herald Square Hotel, 19 W. 31st St. (279-4017 or 800-727-1888, fax 643-9208), at Fifth Ave. Subway: B, D, F, N, or R to 34th St. In the original Beaux Arts home (built in 1893) of Life magazine. Work by some of America's most noted illustrators adorns the lobby, halls, and rooms. Tiny, clean, newly renovated rooms with color TV, small refrigerators, phones, and A/C. Singles with shared bath $45, with private bath $55, doubles $60, with 2 beds $85. International students get a 10% discount. Reservations recommended.

Pioneer Hotel, 341 Broome St. (226-1482), between Elizabeth St. and the Bowery. Located between Little Italy and the Lower East Side in a century-old (but recently renovated) building. Close to the nightlife of SoHo and the East Village. NYU film students shoot their film projects in this hotel's classic rooms. All rooms have TVs. Public telephones in the lobby. Singles $33, with A/C $39, doubles $45/$53, with bath $57. Singles also rent for $200 for the week

Pickwick Arms Hotel, 230 E. 51st St. (355-0300 or 800-PICKWIK/742-5945, fax 755-5029), between Second and Third Ave. Subway: #6 to 51st St.; or E, F to Lexington-Third Ave. Business types congregate in this well-located mid-sized hotel. Chandeliered marble lobby filled with the silken strains of Top 40 Muzak contrasts with tiny rooms and microscopic hall bathrooms. Roof garden, airport service available. Check-in 2pm; check-out 1pm. Singles $45, with shared bath $55. Doubles with one bed and bath $95, two beds $105. Studios (double bed and sofa, with up to four people) $110. Additional person in room $12. Reservations recommended.

Hotel Wolcott, 4 W. 31st St. (268-2900; fax 563-0096), between Fifth and Sixth Ave. Subway: B, D, F, N, or R to 34th St. An ornately mirrored and marbled entrance hall leads into this inexpensive, newly renovated hotel. New furniture and carpeting, cable TV, and A/C. Singles $70, doubles $75, triples $85. Reservations recommended at least a month in advance for summer.

Washington Square Hotel, 103 Waverly Pl. (777-9515 or 800-222-0418; fax 979-8373), at MacDougal St. Subway: A, B, C, D, E, F, or Q to W. 4th St. Fantastic location. Glitzy marble and brass lobby, with a cool medieval gate in front. TV, A/C, and key-card entry to individual rooms. Recent additions include a restaurant/bar, lounge, and exercise room. Clean and comfortable; friendly and multilingual staff.

Singles $70, doubles $99 with two twin beds $107, quads $128. Reservation required 2-3 weeks in advance.

Hotel Iroquois, 49 W. 44th St. (840-3080 or 800-332-7220; fax 398-1754), near Fifth Ave. Subway: B, D, or F to 47th St.-Rockefeller Ctr. Slightly worn but spacious rooms in an old pre-war building. This hotel once hosted James Dean and is now the stop of choice for Greenpeace and other environmental activists when in town. Check-out noon. Singles and doubles $75-100. Suites (up to 5 people) $125-150. Student discounts available, and prices negotiable during winter. Reservations advisable a few weeks in advance in the summer.

Mansfield Hotel, 12 W. 44th St. (944-6050 or 800-255-5167; fax 764-4477), at Fifth Ave. Subway: B, D, or F to 47th St.-Rockefeller Ctr. A dignified establishment housed in a turn-of-the-century building with comfortable leather couches in the lobby and beautiful oak doors in the hallways. Rooms have recently been renovated; the new ones have new lighting, paint, and furniture, and some of the larger ones have whirlpool tubs. Specifically request a renovated room when making reservations (1 month in advance for summer). Check-out noon. Singles and doubles $145, triples and quads $160. Large suites $195 for 5 or 6 people. Ask about student discounts.

Hotel Grand Union, 34 E. 32nd St. (683-5890; fax 689-7397), between Madison and Park Ave. Subway: #6 to 33rd St. Centrally located and reasonably priced. Large, comfy rooms equipped with cable TV, phone, A/C, a mini-fridge, and full bathroom. Friendly, 24-hr. security. Singles $60-70, doubles $65-90, two-room suite from $105. Major credit cards accepted.

FOOD

This city takes its food seriously. New York will dazzle you with its culinary bounty, serving the needs of its diverse (and hungry) population. Ranging from mom-and-pop diners to elegant five-star restaurants, the food offered here will suit all appetites and pocketbooks. New York's restaurants do more than the United Nations to promote international goodwill and cross-cultural exchanges. City dining spans the globe, with eateries ranging from sushi bars to wild combinations like Afghani/Italian and Mexican/Lebanese. Listed below are some choice places divided by neighborhood, but feel free to explore and take a bite out of the Big Apple yourself.

East Midtown

East Midtown teems with restaurants. Around noon to 2pm, the many delis and cafés become swamped with harried junior executives trying to eat quickly and get back to work. The 50s on **Second Ave.** and the area immediately surrounding Grand Central Station are filled with good, cheap fare. You might also check out grocery stores, such as the **Food Emporium,** 969 Second Ave. (593-2224), between 51st and 52nd, **D'Agostino,** Third Ave. (684-3133), between 35th and 36th, or **Associated Group Grocers,** 1396 Second Ave., between E. 48th and E. 49th St. This part of town has many public spaces (plazas, lobbies, parks) to picnic; try **Greenacre Park,** 51st St. between Second and Third; **Paley Park,** 53rd St. between Fifth and Madison; or the **United Nations Plaza,** 48th St. at First Ave.

Dosanko, 423 Madison Ave. (688-8575), at E. 47th St. Very cheap, very fast, and very good Japanese food. Get the ramen ($5.30-7, depending on the toppings). Sit-down a few blocks up at 217 E. 59th St. (752-3936), between Second and Third Ave. Open Mon.-Fri. 11:30am-10pm, Sat.-Sun. noon-8pm.

Maria Caffè, 973 Second Ave. (832-9053; fax 750-7125), between E. 51st and E. 52nd St. Pastries and pizzas made on the premises, and an incredible combo deal—$5 for pasta, salad, roll, and drink (daily 11am-3pm). Pita pizza $1.25, chicken cacciatore $6.50/lb. Open daily 8am-9pm.

Oysters Bar and Restaurant (490-6650), in Grand Central Station. Excellent seafood for the weary traveler. The prices are a little high, but the chowder is a great deal—$3.25 for a huge bowl. Open Mon.-Fri. 11:30am-9:30pm.

West Midtown

Your best bets here are generally along Eighth Ave. between 34th and 59th St. in the area known as **Hell's Kitchen.** Although once deserving of its name, this area has given birth to an array of ethnic restaurants. The area's cheapest meals are of the **fast food** variety, on the east side of **Seventh Ave.** between 33rd and 34th Those with deeper pockets should take a meal on **Restaurant Row,** on 46th St. between Eighth and Ninth Ave., which offers a solid block of dining primarily to a pre-theater crowd (arriving after 8pm will make getting a table easier).

Ariana Afghan Kebab, 769 Ninth Ave. (307-1612 or 262-2323), between 52nd and 53rd St. This family-run restaurant serves up excellent Afghani food. Try the beef *tikka kebab,* chunks of beef marinated and cooked over wood charcoal, served with rice, bread, and salad ($7), or the *aushak,* leek-filled dumplings topped with yogurt and a spicy meat sauce. Open Mon.-Sat. noon-10pm.

Bali Nusa Indah, 651 Ninth Ave. (765-6500), between 45th and 46th St. Great Burmese food served in plentiful portions. The fried rice noodles with shrimp and chicken ($7) are a favorite, and the lunch specials, served with salad topped with a warm, spicy peanut dressing ($5, served daily 11:30am-4pm), are a great bargain. Try the mango ice cream for dessert ($2.50). Open daily 11:30am-10:30pm.

Carnegie Delicatessen, 854 Seventh Ave. (757-2245), at 55th St. Eat elbow-to-elbow at long tables, and chomp on free dill pickles. The "Woody Allen," an incredible pastrami and corned beef sandwich, could easily stuff two people ($12.45). Don't leave without trying the sinfully rich cheesecake topped with strawberries, blueberries, or cherries ($5.45). Open daily 6:30am-4am.

Lower Midtown and Chelsea

Straddling the extremes, the lower Midtown dining scene is neither fast-food commercial nor *haute cuisine* trendy. East of Fifth Ave. on **Lexington Ave.,** Pakistani and Indian restaurants battle for customers. Liberally sprinkled throughout, Korean corner shops that are equal parts grocery and buffet offer hot and cold salad bars.

Finding food in Chelsea isn't always easy. Good food tends not to be cheap, and cheap food is rarely good. The neighborhood is dotted with fake-retro diners that offer unexceptional $6 hamburgers and $7 omelettes. The best offerings are the products of the large Mexican and Central American community in the southern section of the neighborhood. **Eighth Ave.** provides the best restaurant browsing.

Jai-ya, 396 Third Ave. (889-1330), at 28th St. Thai and other Asian food that the critics rave over, with three different degrees of spiciness, from mild to "help-me-I'm-on-fire." *Pad thai* $8. Another location at 81-11 Broadway in Elmhurst, Queens. Open daily Mon.-Fri. 11:30am-midnight, Sat. noon-midnight, Sun. 5pm-midnight.

Daphne's Hibiscus, 243 E. 14th St. (505-1180 and 505-1247), between Second and Third Ave. A Caribbean restaurant whose ambience and decor transport you to Jamaica. Try the chicken cooked in coconut milk ($11), the jerk pork ($9), or the patties (meat-filled pastries). Most entrees $7.50-9.50. Open Tues.-Thurs. 11am-11pm, Fri. 11am-midnight, Sat.-Sun. 4pm-midnight.

Zen Palate, 34 E. Union Sq. (614-9345), across from the park. Gourmet veggie food, with an Asian twist. Stir-fried rice fettucini ($6.50). Moo shu, Mexican style ($7.45). Delivery available in limited range. Open Mon.-Sat. 11am-11pm, Sun. noon-10:30pm.

Kitchen, 218 Eighth Ave. (243-4433), near 21st St. A take-out kitchen specializing in Mexican food, with hot red peppers dangling from the ceiling. All food to go; there's no dining room. Burrito stuffed with pinto beans, rice, and green salsa ($5.70). Open daily 11:30am-10:30pm.

Utopia-W-Restaurant, 338 Eighth Ave. (807-8052), at 27th St. Located in the boxy shadow of the Fashion Institute of Technology, this is the school's chic diner, populated by the equally chic student body. Heavy-duty meaty burgers on toasted buns (cheeseburger with fries $5). Dinner often comes with a complimentary glass of wine. Open daily 6am-9:30pm.

Upper East Side

Meals on the Upper East Side descend in price as you move east from **Fifth Ave.'s** glitzy, overpriced museum cafés towards **Lexington, Third** and **Second Ave.** Hot dog hounds shouldn't miss the 100% beef "better than filet mignon" $1.50 franks and exotic fruit drinks at **Papaya King** (369-0648), at 179 E. 86th St. off Third Ave. (open Sun.-Thurs. 8am-1am, Fri.-Sat. 9am-3am). Visitors aiming to experience the classic New York bagel should try **H&H East** (734-7441), at 1551 Second Ave. between 80th and 81st St. Open 24 hours, H&H still uses a century-old formula to send you to bagel heaven. But don't feel confined to restaurant dining; grocery stores, delis, and bakeries speckle every block. You can buy provisions here and picnic in Central Park.

Barking Dog Luncheonette, 1678 Third Ave. (832-1800), at 94th St. As the staff shirts command, "SIT–STAY!" and satisfy your hunger pangs with helpings fit for the biggest dog on the block. Breakfast special ($4.25), with two eggs, hash browns, and a choice of bacon or sausage biscuit. Burger platter ($6.50). Admire the dog-related paraphernalia adorning the walls during your meal. Real canines should enjoy the "dog bar" water trough outside. Open daily 8am-11pm.

Brother Jimmy's BBQ, 1461 First Ave. (545-7427), at 76th St. This greasy-chops Carolina kitchen serves up plenty of delicious BBQ and a healthy dose of southern hospitality, including free margaritas with dinner Mon. nights. Ribs $13, with 2 side dishes and corn bread. Sandwiches, for the less strong, $6-7. Kitchen open Sun.-Thurs. 5pm-midnight, Fri.-Sat. 11am-1am. Bar open "until you finish your last drink" or until 4am.

Tang Tang Noodles and More, 1328 Third Ave. (249-2102/3/4), at 76th St. Cheap, hot, tasty Chinese noodles and dumplings. Not one noodle dish over $5.75—most around $5. Dense crowds but lightning-quick service. Open Sun.-Thurs. 11am-11pm, Fri.-Sat. 11:30am-11:15pm.

EJ's Luncheonette, 1271 Third Ave. (472-0600), at 73rd St. Eternally crowded; huge portions of good food. Blueberry-strawberry buttermilk pancakes $6.50. Hamburgers also a great deal ($5.75, fries included). Open Mon.-Thurs. 8am-11pm, Fri.-Sat. 8am-midnight, Sun. 8am-10:30pm.

MID-ATLANTIC

Upper West Side

Unlike many other New York neighborhoods, the Upper West Side lacks a definitive typology of restaurants. Cheap pizza joints often neighbor chic eateries; street vendors hawk sausages in the shadow of pricey specialty stores. **Columbus Ave.** provides lots of options within a budgeters realm. Wander down the tempting aisles of **Zabar's,** 2245 Broadway (787-2002), at 81st St., the gourmet deli and grocery that never ends. The original **H&H Bagels,** 2239 Broadway (595-8000), at 80th St., bakes the best bagels in NYC (a noble title) all day, every day. Get a hot one.

La Caridad, 2199 Broadway (874-2780), at 78th St. Feed yourself and a pack of burros with one entree at this successful Chinese-Spanish hybrid. *Arroz con pollo* (¼-chicken with yellow rice) $5.55. Fast-food ambience, but so what? Lunch and dinner rushes cause lines. Open Mon.-Sat. 11:30am-1am, Sun. 11:30am-10:30pm.

Mingala West, 325 Amsterdam Ave. (873-0787), at 75th St. Burmese cooking uses rice noodles, peanut sauces, coconuts, and curries. Generous $5 lunch specials Mon.-Fri. noon-4pm; $6-9 "light meal" samplers 4:30-6:30pm. Open Mon.-Thurs. noon-11pm, Fri.-Sat. noon-midnight.

Café La Fortuna, 69 W. 71st St. (724-5846), at Columbus Ave. Delicious Italian pastries, coffees, and sandwiches served in a dark grotto of a café. A definite local favorite; high school swingers sit in clumps and wish they could smoke, scholars stretch out with books and papers at corner tables, and families bring their children out on the back patio. Try the delicious iced cappuccino served with Italian chocolate ice ($3.50). Open Sun.-Thurs. noon-midnight, Fri.-Sat. noon-1:30am.

Dallas BBQ, 27 W. 72nd St. (873-2004), between Columbus and Central Park West. Authentic Texas-style chicken and ribs on the same bill as tasty tempura and homey chicken soup. Big breakfast featuring 50¢ coffee. Look for early-bird specials throughout the year. ½-lb. burger $5, bowl of Texas-style chili $4 per bowl. Open Sun.-Thurs. noon-midnight, Fri.-Sat. noon-1am.

Morningside Heights and Harlem

The cafés and restaurants in Morningside Heights cater to Columbia students, faculty, and their families. This usually means that hours run late and the price range fits that of a starving student. But college students aren't without discernment; the old-style coffeeshops and restaurants serve up delicious food with atmosphere.

Mill Korean Restaurant, 2895 Broadway (864-6137), at 112th St. Traditional, freshly prepared Korean food. Lunch specials Mon.-Fri. 11am-3pm ($5-7). Complete dinners with side dishes ($7-10). Try the fiery stir-fried squid ($8 at dinner, $5.50 at lunch). Open daily 10:30am-10:30pm.

Tom's Restaurant, 2880 Broadway (864-6137), at 112th St. "Doo-doo-doo-doo..." Suzanne Vega wrote that darn catchy tune about this diner. Greasy burgers for $3-5, dinner under $6.50. This place is a neighborhood mainstay. Open Mon.-Wed. 6am-1:30am and from Thurs. 6am-Sun. 1:30am. "Doo-doo-doo-doo..."

The Hungarian Pastry Shop, 1030 Amsterdam Ave. (866-4230), at 111th St. The West Side's worst-kept secret. Plain, friendly, Boho pastry shop. Eclairs, cake slices, and other goodies all around $2. Fine coffee, too ($1.30). Open Mon.-Sat. 8am-11:15pm, Sun. 8am-10pm.

MID-ATLANTIC

Greenwich Village

Whatever your take on the West Village's bohemian authenticity, it's undeniable that all the free-floating artistic angst does result in many creative (and inexpensive) food venues. The aggressive and entertaining street life makes stumbling around and deciding where to go almost as much fun as eating. Try the major avenues for cheap, decent food. The European-style bistros of **Bleecker St.** and **MacDougal St.**, south of Washington Square Park, have perfected the homey "antique" look. You can't eat inside the **Murray Cheese Shop,** 257 Bleecker St. (243-3289; open Mon.-Sat. 8am-7pm, Sun. 9am-5pm), at Cornelia St., but the 400-plus kinds of cheese justify a picnic. Try the camembert in rosemary and sage ($4), and get the bread next door at **A. Zito Bread.** Late night in the Village is a unique New York treat: as the sky grows dark, the streets quicken. Explore twisting side streets and alleyways where you can drop into a jazz club or join Off-Broadway theater-goers as they settle down over a burger and a beer to write their own reviews. Or ditch the high life and slump down 8th St. to **Sixth Ave.** to find some of the best pizza in the city.

Cucina Stagionale, 275 Bleecker St. (924-2707), at Jones St. Unpretentious Italian dining in a pretty environment. Packed with locals on weekends—the lines reach the street at times. Sample the soft *calimari* in spicy red sauce ($6) or the pasta *putanesca* ($7) to realize why. Pasta dishes $6-8; veal, chicken, and fish dishes $8-10. Open Sun.-Thurs. noon-midnight, Fri.-Sat. noon-1am.

Olive Tree Café, 117 MacDougal St. (254-3480), north of Bleecker St. Middle Eastern food complemented by endless stimulation. If you get bored by the old movies on the wide screen, rent chess, backgammon, and Scrabble sets ($1), doodle with colored chalk on the slate tables, or sit on the patio and survey the Village nightlife. Falafel $2.50, chicken kebab platter with salad, rice pilaf, and vegetable $7.50. Open Sun.-Thurs. 11am-3am, Fri.-Sat. 11am-5am.

Elephant and Castle, 68 Greenwich Ave. (243-1400), near Seventh Ave. Their motto is *"J'adore les omelettes,"* and boy, are those omelettes adorable ($5.50-7.50). The apple, cheddar, and walnut creation, the spinach-cheddar combo, and all the rest of the strange omelette mixtures are a tad unnerving, but well worth a try. Open Mon.-Thurs. 8:30am-midnight, Fri. 8:30am-1am, Sat. 10am-1am, Sun. 10am-midnight.

Tea and Sympathy, 108 Greenwich Ave. (807-8329), between Jane and W. 13th St. An English tea house—high tea, cream tea, and good old-fashioned British cuisine. Filled with kitschy teacups and salt shakers, fading photos of English families, and beautiful chipped china. Afternoon tea (the whole shebang—

sandwiches, tea, scones) $11, cream tea (tea, scones, and jam) $6, shepherds pie $6.75. Open Mon.-Fri. 11:30am-10pm, Sat. 10am-10pm, Sun. 10am-9pm.

Caffè Reggio, 119 MacDougal St. (475-9557), south of W. 3rd St. Celebs, wannabes, and students crowd the oldest café in the Village. Open since 1927, this place showcases busts and madonnas in every corner and pours a mean cup of cappuccino ($2.25). Choose from a wide selection of pastries ($2.50-3.50). Open Sun.-Thurs. 10am-2am, Fri.-Sat. 10am-4am.

SoHo and TriBeCa

In SoHo, food, like life, is all about image. Most of the restaurants here tend to be preoccupied with decor, and most aim to serve a stylishly healthful cuisine.The image lifestyle, however, takes money, so don't be surprised if you find it hard to get a cheap meal. Often the best deal in SoHo is brunch, when the neighborhood shows its most good-natured front.

Dining in TriBeCa is generally a much funkier (and blessedly cheaper) experience than in chic SoHo. The restaurants here have a dressed-down, folksy, flea marketish flavor. TriBeCa is much more industrial than SoHo, and restaurants are often hidden like little oases among the hulking warehouses and decaying buildings.

Yaffa's Tea Room, 19 Harrison St. (274-9403), near Greenwich St. Wide selection of delicious sandwiches ($7.50) and entrees ($7-15). Brunch served daily 8:30am-5pm (omelettes and main selections $4.50-6.50, pastries $4-6). High tea ($15, reservations required) served daily 2-6pm, and includes a "savory course," fresh baked scones, dessert sampler, and a pot of tea. Open daily 8:30am-midnight. The attached bar/restaurant, at the corner of Greenwich St., is a little less subdued. Bar is open nightly until 4am.

Bell Caffè, 310 Spring St. (334-2355), between Hudson and Greenwich. This low-key restaurant in an old bell factory (hence the name) may be off the beaten path, but there are good reasons to walk the extra blocks. Bell serves up good-sized portions of an "ethno-healthy" cuisine, including "Spring Street Rolls" made with shrimp, ginger, port vinaigrette, and couscous. Enjoy free live music nightly and monthly receptions for the new art that goes up on the restaurant's walls. Outdoor seating. Open Sun.-Thurs. noon-2am, Fri.-Sat. noon-4am.

Abyssinia, 35 Grand St. (226-5959), at Thompson St. Terrific Ethiopian restaurant with low-to-the-ground, hand-carved stools at tables made of woven fibers akin to wicker. Scoop up the food with pieces of dense and spongy *injara* bread. Vegetarian entrees $6-8, meat dishes $8.50-12. The *azefa wotólentils*—red onions, garlic ginger, and hot green peppers, served cold—is great in the summer. Open Mon.-Thurs. 6-11pm, Fri. 6pm-midnight, Sat. 1pm-midnight, Sun. 1-11pm.

East Village, Lower East Side, and Alphabet City

Culinary cultures clash on the lower end of the East Side, where pasty-faced punks and starving artists dine alongside an older generation conversing in Polish, Hungarian, and Yiddish. The neighborhood took in the huddled masses, and, in return, immigrant culture after immigrant culture has left its mark in the form of cheap restaurants. **First** and **Second Ave.** are the best for restaurant-exploring, and sidewalk cafés and bars line **Avenue A.** Check out **6th St.** between First and Second Ave., a block composed of several Indian restaurants offering $3 lunch specials. For kosher eating, head on down to the Lower East Side south of East Houston St. **Kossar's Hot Bialys,** 367 Grand St. at Essex St. (473-4810; open 24 hrs.), makes bialys that recall the heyday of the Lower East Side.

Dojo Restaurant, 24 St. Mark's Pl. (674-9821), between Second and Third Ave. One of the most popular restaurants and hangouts in the East Village, and rightly so. Offers an incredible variety of healthful, delicious, and inexplicably inexpensive food. Tasty soyburgers with brown rice and salad $3.20. Spinach and pita sandwich with assorted veggies $2.95. Outdoor tables allow for interaction with slick passers-by. New location (same menu) on Washington Square South. Open Sun.-Thurs. 11am-1am, Fri.-Sat. 11am-2am.

Veselka, 144 Second Ave. (228-9682), at 9th St. Down-to-earth, soup-and-bread, Polish-Ukrainian joint. Enormous menu includes about 10 varieties of soups, as well as salads, blintzes, meats, and other Eastern European fare. Blintzes $3.25, soup $1.95 a cup (try the sumptuous chicken noodle). Combination special gets you soup, salad, stuffed cabbage, and four melt-in-your-mouth *pirogi* ($7.75). Open 24 hrs.

Pink Pony Café, 174 Ludlow St., between E. Houston and Stanton St. Self-consciously hip café/ice cream parlor/bookshop catering to the Lower East Side artist set. A great place to study, read, or write over an espresso ($1.50). Several shelves of second-hand books for sale or perusal, tending toward the trashy spy thriller genre. Comfy chairs and couches and a pool table in the back room. Open Sun.-Thurs. 9:30am-midnight, Fri.-Sat. 9:30am-4am.

Second Ave. Delicatessen, 156 Second Ave. (677-0606), at 10th St. The definitive New York deli, established in 1954. People come into the city just to be snubbed by the waiters here. Strictly kosher, and proudly so. Have pastrami (reputed to be the best in the city) or tongue on rye bread for $7.50, a fabulous burger deluxe for $7, or chicken soup for $3. Note the Hollywood-style star plaques embedded in the sidewalk outside; this was once the heart of the Yiddish theater district. Open Sun.-Thurs. 8am-midnight, Fri.-Sat. 8am-2am.

Ratner's Restaurant, 138 Delancey St. (677-5588), just west of the Manhattan Bridge. The most famous of the kosher restaurants, partly because of its frozen-food line. In odd contrast to its run-down surroundings, this place is large, shiny, and popular. Jewish dietary laws are strictly followed and only dairy food is served—but oy vey! Such matzo brei! ($8.95) Also feast on fruit blintzes and sour cream ($9) or simmering vegetarian soups ($4). Open Sun.-Thurs. 6am-midnight, Fri. 6am-3pm, Sat. sundown-2am.

Chinatown

If you're looking for cheap, authentic Asian fare, join the crowds that push through the narrow, chaotic streets of one of the oldest Chinatowns in the U.S. The neighborhood's 200-plus restaurants cook up some of the best Chinese, Thai, and Vietnamese cooking around. Once-predominantly Cantonese cooking has now burgeoned into different cuisines from the various regions of China: hot and spicy Hunan or Szechuan, the sweet and mildly spiced seafood of Soochow, or the hearty and filling fare of Beijing. Cantonese *dim sum* is still a Sunday afternoon tradition, when waiters roll carts filled with assorted dishes of bite-sized goodies up and down the aisles. Simply point at what you want (beware of "Chinese Bubblegum," a euphemism for tripe), and at the end of the meal, the empty dishes on your table are tallied up. For dessert, check out the **Chinatown Ice Cream Factory,** 65 Bayard St. (608-4171), at Mott St., for flavors like lychee, mango, ginger, red bean, and green tea. (Open Mon.-Thurs. 11:30am-11pm, Fri. and Sun. 11:30am-11:30pm, Sat. 11:30am-midnight.)

Excellent Dumpling House, 111 Lafayette St. (219-0212 or 219-0213), at Canal St. True to its name, this restaurant offers absolutely terrific vegetarian and meat dumplings fried, steamed, or boiled ($4 for 8 large pieces). Also great pan-fried noodles ($5-6.50) and huge bowls of noodle soups (mostly $3.50-4). Lunch specials (served Mon.-Fri. 11am-3pm) include entrees such as shredded pork with garlic sauce or chicken with black bean sauce, choice of soup, and fried rice and a wonton (all specials $5.50). Open daily 11am-9pm.

House of Vegetarian, 68 Mott St. (226-6572), between Canal and Bayard St. Faux chicken, faux beef, faux lamb, and faux fish comprise the huge menu, made from soy and wheat by-products. Try *lo mein* (with 3 kinds of mushrooms, $6.75) or gluten with black bean sauce ($7). Most entrees $6-10. An ice-cold lotus seed or lychee drink ($2) hits the spot on hot summer days. Open daily 11am-11pm.

HSF (Hee Sheung Fung), 46 Bowery (374-1319), just south of Canal St. Well-known for its fantastic *dim sum* (served daily 7:30am-5pm) and for its "Hot Pot buffet." The Hot Pot is a sort of Asian equivalent to fondue, in which a huge pot of boiling broth is placed on the table with a platter of more than 50 raw ingredients for dipping. Ingredients are unlimited ($18 per person). Range of other entrees as well($7.50-17), including delicacies like prawns in Yushan garlic sauce ($13). Open daily 7:30am-5am.

New Lung Fong Bakery, 41 Mott St. (233-7447), at Bayard St. The "New" refers to the eating area installed toward the back. An amazingly cheap selection of pastries (all 40-75¢ each). Almond cookies 50¢, pineapple sponge cake 50¢, chicken rolls 60¢, ham and cheese or sausage buns 50¢. Open daily 8am-9pm.

Foul Play?

The **Chinatown Fair,** 8 Mott St., features old-school video games and one clever chicken. Take on the fair's resident chicken genius. For 50¢, the fowl in question will engage you in an arduous battle of wits, tic-tac-toe style. Don't write off the bird just yet—remember, this is its livelihood. When we say that the Chinatown Fair chicken is tough to beat, we're not kidding.One disgruntled sore loser, upon falling to the mighty bird, was overheard to remark: "I'm not normally so terrible at tic-tac-toe—the chicken confused me." Hmmm. Keep that cockiness to yourself; you just might walk away a loser.

Little Italy

A chunk of Naples seems to have migrated to this lively yet very compact quarter roughly bounded by Canal, Lafayette, Houston St., and the Bowery. **Mulberry St.** is the main drag and the appetite avenue of Little Italy. Stroll here after 7pm to catch street life, but arrive earlier to get one of the better tables. For the sake of variety and thrift, dine at a restaurant but get your just desserts at a café.

Ballato, 55 E. Houston St. (274-8881), at Mott St. Although clearly cross-bred with SoHo style, Ballato serves impeccable southern Italian cooking to a small crowd of couples, tourists, and college students. Pasta $9-11.50. *Antipasti* $5.50-8. *Prix fixe* dinner (Sun.-Fri. 4-6:30pm, Sat. 5-6:30pm; $14.50) includes three courses. Open Mon.-Fri. noon-11pm; Sat. 4pm-midnight, Sun. 4pm-11pm.

La Mela, 167 Mulberry St. (431-9493), between Broome and Grand St. If Little Italy believed in cult restaurants, La Mela would be the kingpin. Rambunctious outdoor seating in their backyard, complete with a guitar-touting bard. A wide assortment of pasta and *gnocchi* ($6.50-10), along with a large number of entrees ($12-15). Always specials; the waiters love to shout. Open daily noon-11pm.

Caffè Roma, 385 Broome St. (226-8413), at Mulberry St. A good *caffè* gets better with time. A full-fledged saloon in the 1890s, Roma has kept its original styling intact. The pastries and coffee prove as refined as the setting. Try the neapolitan *cannoli* or the *baba au rhum* ($1.50 to take out, $2.25 to eat in). Potent espresso $1.60; obligatory cappuccino, with a tiara of foamed milk, $2.40. Open daily 8am-midnight.

Financial District

Lower Manhattan is luncheon heaven to sharply-clad Wall St. brokers and bankers—it offers cheap food prepared lightning-fast at ultra-low prices and always available as take-out. Bargain-basement cafeterias here can fill you up with everything from gazpacho to Italian sausages. Fast-food joints pepper Broadway near Dey and John St. just a few feet from the overpriced offerings of the Main Concourse of the World Trade Center. In the summer, ethnic food pushcarts form a solid wall along Broadway between Cedar and Liberty St.

Zigolini's, 66 Pearl St. (425-7171), at Coenties Alley. One of the few places in the area where indoor air-conditioned seating abounds, this authentically Italian restaurant serves huge and filling sandwiches ($5-7), as well as some great pasta dishes. Open Mon.-Fri. 7am-7pm.

Frank's Papaya, 192 Broadway (693-2763), at John St. Excellent value, quick service. Very close to the World Trade Center. Hot dog 70¢. Breakfast (egg, ham, cheese, coffee) $1.50. Open Mon.-Sat. 5:30am-10pm, Sun. 5:30am-5:30pm.

Hamburger Harry's, 157 Chambers St. (267-4446), between West and Greenwich St. Gourmet burgers for the connoisseur: 7-oz. patty broiled over applewood with exotic toppings like avocado, alfalfa sprouts, chili, salsa, and bernaise sauce ($6, with red slaw and fries or potato salad $8). Regular burger $4, nacho cheese fries $3. Open daily 11:30am-10pm.

Brooklyn

Ethnic flavor changes every two blocks in Brooklyn. **Brooklyn Heights** offers nouvelle cuisine, but specializes in pita bread and *baba ghanoush.* **Williamsburg** is dotted with kosher and cheap Italian restaurants, **Greenpoint** is a borscht-lover's paradise, and **Flatbush** serves up Jamaican and other West Indian cuisine. Brooklyn now has its own Chinatown in Sunset Park.

Primorski Restaurant, 282 Brighton Beach Ave. (718-891-3111), between Brighton Beach 2nd St. and Brighton Beach 3rd St. Subway: D or Q to Brighton Beach, then four blocks east on Brighton Beach Ave. Populated by Russian-speaking Brooklynites, this restaurant serves some of the best Ukrainian borscht ($2.25) in the Western hemisphere in an atmosphere of gritty Slavic decadence. Eminently affordable lunch special (Mon.-Fri. 11am-5pm, Sat.-Sun. 11am-4pm; $4)—your choice among three soups and about 15 entrees, bread, salad, and coffee or tea. At night, prices rise as the disco ball begins to spin. Nightly entertainment, including "live disco music." Open daily 11am-2am.

Nathan's (718-946-2206), Surf and Stillwell Ave., on Coney Island. Subway: B, D, F, or N to Coney Island. Across from the subway stop. Nathan Handwerker's crunchy dogs have become nationally famous since their debut in 1922, and are now sold in franchises of the restaurant and in supermarkets. A classic frank at this crowded place—the original Nathan's—sells for $1.85. Unique, absurdly plump, crinkle-cut french fries ($1.59) have the taste of fresh-cut potatoes. Open Sun.-Thurs. 8am-4am, Fri.-Sat. 8am-5am.

Tom's Restaurant, 782 Washington Ave. (718-636-9738), at Sterling Pl. Subway: #2 or 3 to Brooklyn Museum. Walk a ½-block east to Washington St. and then 1½ blocks north. A quintessential Brooklyn breakfast place—an old-time luncheonette complete with a soda fountain and 50s-style hyper-friendly service. Two eggs with fries or grits, toast, and coffee or tea $1.95. Famous golden challah french toast $2.75. Breakfast served all day. Open Mon.-Sat. 6:30am-4pm.

Moroccan Star, 205 Atlantic Ave. (718-643-0800), in Brooklyn Heights. Subway: #2, 3, 4, 5, M, or R to Borough Hall, then down 4 blocks on Court St. A fixture in the local Arab community. Try the *pastello,* a delicate semi-sweet chicken pie with almonds ($8.75, lunch $6). Open Sun. noon-10pm, Tues.-Thurs. 10am-11pm, Fri.-Sat. 11am-11pm.

Junior's, 986 Flatbush Ave. Extension (718-852-5257), across the Manhattan Bridge at De Kalb St. Subway: #2, 3, 4, 5, B, D, M, N, Q, or R to Atlantic Ave. Lit up like a jukebox, Junior's feeds classic roast beef and brisket to hordes of loyals. Brisket sandwich $6.25, dinner specials $10. Satisfy a cheesecake craving here (plain slice $3.50). Open Sun.-Thurs. 6:30am-12:30am, Fri.-Sat. 6:30am-2am.

Queens

With nearly every ethnic group represented in Queens, this often overlooked borough offers visitors authentic and reasonably priced international cuisine away from Manhattan's urban neighborhoods. **Astoria** specializes in discount shopping and cheap eats. Take the G or R train to Steinway St. and Broadway and start browsing—the pickings are good in every direction. In **Flushing,** excellent Chinese, Japanese, and Korean restaurants flourish, often making use of authentic ingredients such as skatefish, squid, and tripe. **Bell Blvd.** in Bayside, out east near the Nassau border, is the center of Queens nightlife for the young, white, and semi-affluent; on most weekends you can find crowds of natives bar-hopping here. **Jamaica Ave.** in downtown Jamaica and **Linden Blvd.** in neighboring St. Albans are lined with restaurants specializing in African-American and West Indian food.

Pastrami King, 124-24 Queens Blvd. (718-263-1717), near 82nd Ave., in Kew Gardens. Subway: E or F to Union Tpke./Kew Gardens. Exit station following sign that says "Courthouse" and "Q10 bus;" then go left following the sign to the north side of Queens Blvd.; it's 2 blocks ahead and across the street. The home-cured pastrami and corned beef are among the best in New York. Take out a sprawling, 3-inch-thick pastrami on rye for $7, or eat in at one of the back tables. Open Tues.-Sun. 9:30am-11pm.

Uncle George's, 33-19 Broadway, Astoria (718-626-0593), at 33rd St. Subway: N to Broadway, then 2 blocks east; or G or R to Steinway St., then 4 blocks west. This popular Greek restaurant serves inexpensive and hearty Greek delicacies around the clock. Almost all entrees are under $10; try the roast leg of lamb with potatoes ($8). Excellent Greek salad with feta cheese ($6). Open 24 hrs.

Jack 'n' Jill's, 187-29 Linden Blvd., St. Albans (718-723-9344), near Mexico St. Subway: E, J, or Z to Jamaica Ctr., then the Q4 bus to St. Albans and Linden Blvd.; ask to be let off at Farmers Blvd. and then backtrack 1 block. This small and sparsely decorated restaurant serves up great Southern BBQ. 4-piece rib dinner $9; BBQ'd ½-chicken $3.50—both served with choice of 2 sides such as greens, string beans, black-eyed peas, or candied yams. Try the peach cobbler ($1.50) for dessert. Open Mon.-Sat. noon-9pm, Sun. noon-6pm.

The Bronx

When Italian immigrants settled the Bronx, they brought their recipes and a tradition of hearty communal dining. While much of the Bronx is a culinary disaster zone, the New York *cognoscenti* soon discovered the few oases along **Arthur Ave.** With a sexy interior, and inviting outdoor tables, **Egidio Pastry Shop,** 622 E. 187th St., makes the best *gelato* in the Bronx.

Mario's, 2342 Arthur Ave. (718-584-1188), near 186th St. A neighborhood fixture for five generations, Mario's appears in the pages of Puzo's *Godfather*. Celebrities still pass through, among them the starting lineups for the Yankees and Giants. Try *spiedini alla romana,* a deep-fried sandwich made with anchovy sauce and mozzarella ($8). Notorious for pizza too. Traditional pasta $9.50-11.50, *antipasti* $5.50. Open Sun. and Tues.-Thurs. noon-10:30pm, Fri.-Sat. noon-midnight.

Ann & Tony's, 2407 Arthur Ave. (718-933-1469), at 187th St. Typical of Arthur Ave., this bistro may specialize in comfortable, no-frills decor, but unlike most restaurants in the area, Ann & Tony's has specials for dinner that run as low as $6, salad included. For lunch, sandwiches begin at $5. Open Mon.-Thurs. 11am-10pm, Fri. 11am-11pm, Sat. 1pm-midnight, Sun. 1-9pm.

SIGHTS

You can tell tourists in New York City from a mile away—they're all looking up. The internationally famous New York skyline is deceiving and elusive; while it can be seen miles away, the tallest skyscraper seems like just another building when you're standing next to it. This sightseeing quandary may explain why many New Yorkers have never visited some of the major sights in their hometown. In this densely-packed city, even the most mind-boggling landmarks became backdrops for everyday life. The beauty of New York City goes beyond its museums, parks, and sights. In New York you can get anything you could want, need, or dream of within a few city blocks. Explore, explore, explore. The city moves faster than we do—there will always be something new around the corner. Seeing New York takes a lifetime.

Lower Manhattan

The southern tip of Manhattan is a jumbled collection of cobblestones and financial powerhouses. The Wall St. area is the densest in all New York, though Wall St. itself measures less than a ½-mile long. This narrow state of affairs has driven the neighborhood into the air, creating one of the highest concentrations of skyscrapers in the world. With density comes history: lower Manhattan was the first part of the island to be settled by Europeans, and many of the city's historically significant sights lie in the concrete canyons here. Its crooked streets serve as a reminder of what New York City was like before it grew up and tidied out into a neat grid.

Battery Park, named for a battery of guns that the British stored there from 1683 to 1687, is now a chaotic chunk of green forming the southernmost toenail of Manhattan Island. The #1 and 9 trains to South Ferry terminate at the southeastern tip of the park; the #4 and 5 stop at Bowling Green, just off the northern tip. On weekends the park is often mobbed with people on their way to the Liberty and Ellis Island ferries, which depart from here.

Once the northern border of the New Amsterdam settlement, **Wall St.** takes its name from the wall built in 1653 to shield the Dutch colony from a British invasion from the north. By the early 19th century, the area was the financial capital of the United States. At Wall and Broad St. meet **Federal Hall** (825-6888), the original City Hall, where the trial of John Peter Zenger helped to establish freedom of the press in 1735. On the southwest corner of Wall and Broad St. stands the current home of the **New York Stock Exchange** (656-5168; open to the public Mon.-Fri. 9:15am-4pm). The Stock Exchange was first created as a marketplace for handling the $80 million in U.S. bonds that were issued in 1789 and 1790 to pay Revolutionary War debts. Arrive early in the morning, preferably before 9am, because tickets usually run out by1pm. The observation gallery that overlooks the exchange's zoo-like main trading floor draws many observers.

Around the corner, at the end of Wall St., rises the seemingly ancient **Trinity Church** (602-0800). Its Gothic spire was the tallest structure in the city when first erected in 1846. The vaulted interior feels positively medieval.

Walk up Broadway to Liberty Park, and in the distance you'll see the twin towers of the city's tallest buildings, the **World Trade Center.** Two World Trade Center has an **observation deck** (435-7377) on the 107th floor. (Open daily June-Sept. 9:30am-11:30pm, Oct.-May 9:30am-9:30pm. $6, seniors $3.50, children $2.)

Farther north on Broadway, City Hall Park and **City Hall** serve as the focus of the city's administration. The Colonial chateau-style structure, completed in 1811, may be the finest piece of architecture in the city. North of the park, at 111 Centre St., between Leonard and White St., sits the **Criminal Court Building.** You can sit in on every kind of trial from misdemeanor to murder here—visit the clerk's office in Room 150 for a schedule of what's taking place where, or call 374-6261.

One of the most sublime and ornate commercial buildings in the world, the Gothic **Woolworth Building,** towers at 233 Broadway, off the southern tip of the park. Erected in 1913 by F.W. Woolworth to house the offices of his corner-store empire, it stood as the world's tallest until the Chrysler Building opened in 1930. Gothic arches and flourishes litter the lobby of this five-and-dime Versailles, including a caricature of Woolworth himself counting change. A block and a half farther south on Broadway, **St. Paul's Chapel** was inspired by London's St. Martin-in-the-Fields. St. Paul's is Manhattan's oldest public building in continuous use. For information on the chapel, call the office of the Trinity Museum (602-0773; chapel open Mon.-Fri. 9am-3pm, Sun. 7am-3pm).

Turn left off Broadway onto Fulton St. and head to the **South Street Seaport.** New York's shipping industry thrived here for most of the 19th century. The process of revitalization recently turned the historic district, in all its fishy and foul-smelling glory, into the ritzy South Street Seaport complex; an 18th-century market, graceful galleries, seafaring schooners, and **Pier 16,** a shopping mall and food court. At the end of Fulton St., as the river comes suddenly into view, so does the smell of dead fish pass through your nostrils. The stench comes from the **Fulton Fish Market,** the largest fresh-fish mart in the country, hidden right on South St. on the other side of the overpass. Those who can stomach wriggling scaly things might be interested in the behind-the-scenes tour of the market given some Thursday. mornings June to Oct. (market opens at 4am). The Pier 16 kiosk, the main ticket booth for the seaport, is open from 10am to 7pm (open 1hr. later on summer weekends).

The Statue of Liberty and Ellis Island

The renovated **Statue of Liberty** (363-3200) remembers decades of immigrant crossings. The statue was given by the French in 1886 as a sign of goodwill. Since it has stood at the entrance to New York Harbor, the Statue of Liberty has welcomed millions of immigrants to America. Today, the statue welcomes tourists galore, as everyone and their sixteen cousins make the ferry voyage to Liberty Island. The other ferry stop is **Ellis Island.** Once the processing center for the 15 million Europeans who came to the U.S via New York, Ellis Island was shut down after the large waves of immigration were over. Recently redone, Ellis Island now houses an excellent **museum** telling the tale of many Americans' ancestors. (Ferries leave for Liberty Island from Battery Park every ½-hr. Mon.-Fri. 9am-3:30pm, Sat.-Sun. 9am-4:30pm. Last ferry back at 7pm, Sept.-June 5:15pm. Ferry information 269-5755. $7, seniors $5, ages 3-17 $3, under 2 free.)

Lower East Side

Down below Houston lurks the trendily seedy Lower East Side, where old-timers rub shoulders with heroin dealers and hip twentysomethings. Two million Jews swelled the population of the Lower East Side in the 20 years before World War I; immigrants still live in the Lower East Side, though now they are mostly Asian and Hispanic. Chinatown has expanded across the Bowery and along the stretch of East Broadway, one of the district's main thoroughfares. A lot of East Village-type artists and musicians have recently moved in as well, especially near Houston St., but despite the influx of artists, a down-at-heel element remains.

Despite the population shift, remnants of the Jewish ghetto that inspired Jacob Riis's compelling work *How the Other Half Lives* still remain. New York's oldest synagogue building, the red-painted **Congregation Anshe Chesed** at 172-176 Norfolk St., just off Stanton St., now houses a Hispanic social service organization. Further down Norfolk, at #60 between Grand and Broome St., sits the **Beth Hamedrash Hagadol Synagogue,** the best-preserved of the Lower East Side houses of worship. From Grand St., follow Essex St. three blocks south to **East Broadway.** This street epitomizes the Lower East Side's flux of cultures. You will find Buddhist prayer centers next to (mostly boarded up) Jewish religious supply stores, and the offices of several Jewish civic organizations.

The area around Orchard and Delancey Streets is one of Manhattan's bargain shopping centers. At 97 Orchard St., between Broome and Delancey St., you can visit the **Lower East Side Tenement Museum** (431-0233), a preserved tenement house of the type that proliferated in this neighborhood in the early part of the century. Buy tickets for a slide show, video, and guided tour at 90 Orchard St., at the corner of Broome St. (Tours are conducted Tues.-Fri. at 1, 2, and 3pm, and Sat.-Sun. every 45min. 11am-4:15pm. $7, students and seniors $6). The museum gallery at 90 Orchard St. (open Tues.-Sun. 11am-5pm) offers free exhibits and photographs documenting Jewish life on the Lower East Side. Guided historical walking tours depart from the corner at 90 Orchard St. on Saturday and Sunday

SoHo and TriBeCa

SoHo ("SOuth of HOw-ston Street") is bounded by Houston St., Canal, Lafayette, and Sullivan St. The architecture here is American Industrial (1860-1890), notable for its cast-iron façades. While its roots are industrial, its inhabitants are New York's prospering artistic community. Here, **galleries** reign supreme and experimental theaters and designer clothing stores fill the voids. This is a great place for star-gazing, too, but don't bother celebrities—they really don't like that.

Greene St. offers the best of SoHo's lofty architecture. Genuine starving artists hang out in **TriBeCa** ("Triangle Below Canal St."), an area bounded by Chambers St., Broadway, Canal St., and the West Side Highway. Admire the cast-iron edifices lining White St., Thomas St., and Broadway, the 19th-century Federal-style buildings on Harrison St., and the shops, galleries, and bars on Church and Reade St.

Greenwich Village and Washington Square Park

Located between Chelsea and SoHo on the lower West side of Manhattan, Greenwich Village (or, more simply put, "the Village") and its residents have defied convention for almost two centuries. Greenwich Village is the nexus of New York bohemia and counter-culture capital of the East Coast. In direct contrast to the orderly, skyscraper encrusted streets of greater Manhattan, narrow thoroughfares meander haphazardly through the Village without regard to artificial grids. Tall buildings give way to brownstones of varying ages and architectural styles. Village residents embody the alternative spectrum, with punks, hippies, ravers, rastas, guppies, goths, beatniks, and virtually every other imaginable group coexisting amidst a myriad of cafés, bars, shops, and theaters.

The bulk of Greenwich Village lies west of Sixth Ave. The West Village boasts an eclectic summer street life and excellent nightlife. The area has a large and visible gay community around **Sheridan Sq.** These are the home waters of the Guppie (Gay Urban Professional), and many gay males and lesbians shop, eat, and live here. **Christopher St.,** the main byway, swims in novelty restaurants and specialty shops. (Subway: #1 or 9 to Christopher St./Sheridan Sq.) A few street signs refer to Christopher St. as "Stonewall Place," alluding to the **Stonewall Inn,** the club where police raids in 1969 prompted riots that sparked the U.S. gay rights movement

Washington Square Park beats at the heart of the Village, as it has since the district's days as a suburb. (Subway: A, B, C, D, E, F, or Q to W. 4th St./Washington Sq.) The marshland here served first as a colonial cemetery, but in the 1820s the area was converted into a park and parade ground. Soon chi-chi residences made the area the center of New York's social scene. Society has long since gone north, and **New York University** has moved in. The country's largest private university and one of the city's biggest landowners (along with the city government, the Catholic Church, and Columbia University), NYU has dispersed its buildings and eccentric students throughout the Village.

In the late 1970s and early 80s Washington Square Park became a base for low-level drug dealers and a rough resident scene. The mid-80s saw a noisy clean-up campaign that has made the park fairly safe and allowed a more diverse cast of characters to return. Today musicians play, misunderstood teenagers congregate, dealers mutter cryptic code words, homeless people try to sleep, and children romp in the playground. In the southwest corner of the park, a dozen perpetual games of chess clock their ways toward checkmate while circles of youths engage in hours of hacky-sacking. The fountain in the center of the park provides an amphitheater for comics and musicians of widely varying degrees of talent.

On the south side of Washington Square Park, at 133 MacDougal St., find the dislocated **Provincetown Playhouse,** a theatrical landmark. Originally based on Cape Cod, the Provincetown Players were joined by the young Eugene O'Neill in 1916 and went on to premiere many of his works. Farther south on MacDougal are the Village's finest coffeehouses, which saw their glory days in the 1950s when beatnik heroes and coffee-bean connoisseurs Jack Kerouac and Allen Ginsberg attended jazz-accompanied poetry readings at **Le Figaro** and **Café Borgia.** These sidewalk cafés still provide some of the best coffee and people-watching in the city.

The north side of the park, called **The Row,** showcases a stretch of elegant Federal-style brick residences built largely in the 1830s. Up Fifth Ave., at the corner of 10th St., the **Church of the Ascension,** a fine 1841 Gothic church, with a notable altar and stained-glass windows, looks heavenward (open daily noon-2pm and 5-7pm). **The Pen and Brush Club,** located at 16 E. 10th St., was founded to promote female intelligentsia networking; Pearl Buck, Eleanor Roosevelt, Marianne Moore, and muckraker Ida Tarbell counted among its members.

At Fifth Ave. and 11th St. **The Salmagundi Club,** New York's oldest club for artists, has sheltered the sensitive since the 1870s. The club's building is the sole remaining mansion from the area's heyday. (Open during exhibitions. Call 255-7740 for details.) **Forbes Magazine Galleries** (206-5548), dominate the corner of Fifth

Ave. and 12th St. The galleries present eccentric Malcolm Forbes's vast collection of *stuff.* (Open Tues.-Sat. 10am-4pm. Free.)

East Village and Alphabet City

The East Village, a comparatively new creation, was carved out of the Bowery and the Lower East Side as rents in the West Village soared and its residents sought accommodations elsewhere. Allen Ginsberg, Jack Kerouac, and William Burroughs all eschewed the Village establishment to develop their junked-up "beat" sensibility east of Washington Square Park. A fun but touristy stretch of Broadway runs through the Village, marking the western boundary.

One of the world's most famous bookstores, the **Strand,** at the corner of 12th St. and Broadway, bills itself as the "largest used bookstore in the world" with over two million books on 8 mi. of shelves. John Jacob Astor constructed the **Joseph Papp Public Theatre,** 425 Lafayette St. (598-7150), in 1853 to serve as the city's first free library. In 1967, Joseph Papp's **New York Shakespeare Festival** converted the building to its current use as a theatrical center.

The intersection of **Astor Place** (at the juncture of Lafayette, Fourth Ave., Astor Pl., and E. 8th St.) is distinguished by a sculpture of a large black cube balanced on its corner. Astor Place prominently features the rear of the **Cooper Union Foundation Building,** 41 Cooper Sq. (254-6300), built in 1859 to house the Cooper Union for the Advancement of Science and Art, a tuition-free technical and design school founded by the self-educated industrialist Peter Cooper. The school's free lecture series has hosted almost every notable American since the mid-19th century. Cooper Union was the first college intended for the underprivileged and the first college to offer free adult-education classes. Across from a church at 156 Second Ave., stands a famous Jewish landmark, the **Second Avenue Deli** (677-0606). This is all that remains of the "Yiddish Rialto," the stretch of Second Ave. between Houston and 14th St. that comprised the Yiddish theater district in the early part of this century. The Stars of David embedded in the sidewalk in front of the restaurant contain the names of some of the great actors and actresses who spent their lives entertaining the poor Jewish immigrants of the city. (See Lower East Side Food).

St. Mark's Place, running from Third Ave. at 8th St. down to Tompkins Square Park, is the geographical and spiritual center of the East Village. In the 1960s, the street was the Haight-Ashbury of the East Coast, full of pot-smoking flower children waiting for the next concert at the Electric Circus. In the late 1970s it became the King's Rd. of New York, as mohawked youths hassled the passers-by from the brownstone steps of Astor Place. Things are changing again: a Gap store sells its color-me-matching combos across the street from a shop stocking "You Make Me Sick" T-shirts. Many Villagers now shun the commercialized and crowded street.

In **Alphabet City,** east of First Ave., south of 14th St., and north of Houston, the avenues run out of numbers and adopt letters. This part of the East Village has so far escaped the escalating yuppification that has claimed much of St. Mark's Place; during the area's heyday in the 60s, Jimi Hendrix would play open-air shows to bright-eyed Love Children. There has been a great deal of drug-related crime in the recent past, although the community has done an admirable job of making the area livable. Alphabet City is generally safe during the day, and the addictive nightlife on Avenue A ensures some protection there, but try to avoid straying east of Avenue B at night. Alphabet City's extremist Boho activism has made the neighborhood chronically ungovernable; a few years ago, police officers set off a riot when they attempted to forcibly evict a band of the homeless and their supporters in **Tompkins Square Park,** at E. 7th St. and Ave. A. The park has just reopened after a two-year hiatus, and still serves as a psycho-geographical epicenter for many a churlish misfit.

Lower Midtown and Chelsea

Madison Ave. ends at 27th St. and **Madison Square Park.** The park, opened in 1847, originally served as a public cemetery. The area near the park sparkles with funky architectural gems. Another member of the "I-used-to-be-the-world's-tallest-building" club—the eminently photogenic **Flatiron Building** sits off the southwest corner of the park. Often considered the world's first skyscraper, it was originally named the Fuller Building, but its dramatic wedge shape, imposed by the intersection of Broadway, Fifth Ave., 22nd St., and 23rd St., quickly earned it its current *nom de plume.* St. Martin's Press, publisher of such fine books as *Let's Go: USA,* currently occupies roughly half the famed building's space.

A few blocks away, **Union Square** (so named because it was a union of two main roads), between Broadway and Park Ave. South, and 17th and 14th St., sizzled with High Society intrigue before the Civil War. Early in this century, the name gained dual significance when the neighborhood became a focal point of New York's Socialist movement, which held its May Day celebrations in **Union Square Park.** Later, the workers and everyone else abandoned the park to drug dealers and derelicts, but in 1989 the city attempted to reclaim it. The park is now pleasant and safe, though not necessarily pristine. The scents of herbs and fresh bread waft through the park every Wednesday, Friday, and Saturday, courtesy of the **Union Square Greenmarket.** Farmers and bakers from all over the region come here to hawk their produce, jellies, and baked goods.

Home to some of the most fashionable clubs, bars, and restaurants in the city, **Chelsea** has lately witnessed something of a rebirth. A large and visible gay and lesbian community and an increasing artsy-yuppie population have given the area, west of Fifth Ave. between 14th and 30th St., the flavor of a lower-rent West Village. The historic **Hotel Chelsea,** 222 W. 23rd St. between Seventh and Eighth Ave., has sheltered many a suicidal artist, most famously Sid Vicious of the Sex Pistols. Edie Sedgwick made stops here between Warhol films before torching the place with a cigarette. Countless writers, as the plaques outside attest, spent their days searching for inspiration and mail in the lobby. Arthur Miller, Vladimir Nabokov, and Dylan Thomas all sojourned here. Chelsea's **flower district,** on 28th St. between Sixth and Seventh Ave., blooms most colorfully during the wee hours of the morning.

East Midtown and Fifth Avenue

The Empire State Building, on Fifth Ave. between 33rd and 34th St. (736-3100), has style. It retains its place in the hearts and minds of New Yorkers even though it is no longer the tallest building in the U.S., or even the tallest building in New York (stood up by the twin towers of the World Trade Center). It doesn't even have the best looks (the Chrysler building is more delicate, the Woolworth more ornate). But the Empire State remains New York's best-known and best-loved landmark and dominates the postcards, the movies, and the skyline. The limestone and granite structure, with glistening ribbons of stainless steel, stretches 1454 ft. into the sky; its 73 elevators run through 2 mi. of shafts; the nighttime view from the top will leave you gasping. The Empire State was among the first of the truly spectacular skyscrapers, benefiting from innovations like Eiffel's pioneering work with steel frames and Otis's perfection of the "safety elevator." In Midtown it towers in relative solitude, away from the forest of monoliths that has grown around Wall St. (Observatory open daily 9:30am-midnight, tickets sold until 11:30pm. $4, children and seniors $2.) You can walk from Penn and Grand Central Stations. The nearest subway stations are at 34th St. (subway: B, D, F, N, Q, and R), 33rd St. (#6), and 28th St. (R).

In the **Pierpont Morgan Library,** 29 E. 36th St. (685-0610), at Madison Ave., the J. Pierpont Morgan clan developed the concept of the book as fetish object. With regular exhibitions and lots and lots of books inside, this Low Renaissance-style *palazzo* attracts many book lovers. (Subway: #6 to 33rd St. Open Tues.-Sat. 10:30am-5pm, Sun. 1-5pm. Suggested contribution $5, students and seniors $3. Free tours on various topics Tues.-Fri. 2:30pm.)

The **New York Public Library** (661-7220) reposes on the west side of Fifth Ave. between 40th and 42nd St., near Bryant Park. On sunny afternoons, throngs of people perch on the marble steps, while the mighty lions Patience and Fortitude dutifully keep watch. This is the world's seventh-largest research library; witness the immense third-floor reading room. (Free tours Tues.-Sat. 12:30 and 2:30pm. Open Mon. and Thurs.-Sat. 10am-6pm, Tues.-Wed. 11am-7:30pm.)

Spread out against the back of the library along 42nd St. to Sixth Ave. **Bryant Park** soothes with large, grassy, tree-rimmed expanses. The stage that sits at the head of the park's big, grassy field plays host to a variety of free cultural events throughout the summer, including screenings of classic films, jazz concerts, and live comedy. Call 397-8222 for an up-to-date schedule of events.

To the east along 42nd St., **Grand Central Terminal** sits where Park Ave. would be, between Madison and Lexington Ave. A former transportation hub where dazed tourists first got a glimpse of the glorious city, Grand Central has since been partially supplanted by Penn Station and the Wright Brothers, but it maintains its dignity. The massive Beaux Arts front, with the famed 13-ft. clock, gives way to the Main Concourse, a huge lobby area. Constellations are depicted on the sweeping, arched expanse of green roof, while egg-shaped ribbed chandeliers light the secondary apses to the sides. (Free tours Wed. at 12:30pm from the Chemical Bank in the Main Concourse and Fri. from the Phillip Morris building across the street.)

The New York skyline would be incomplete without the familiar Art Deco headdress of the **Chrysler Building,** at 42nd St.and Lexington Ave., built by William Van Allen as an ode to the automobile and topped by a spire modeled on a radiator grille. When completed in 1929, this elegantly seductive building stood as the world's tallest. The Empire State Building topped it a year later. East on 42nd St. about 1½ blocks, between Park and Second Ave., stands the **Daily News Building** home to the country's first successful tabloid. The paper and building supposedly served as the inspiration for the *Daily Planet* of Superman fame. A gigantic rotating globe, which still features East Germany, Yugoslavia, and the U.S.S.R., dominates the lobby.

If you feel an urgent need to get out of the city, head for the **United Nations Building** (963-4475), which appears to be located along New York's First Ave. between 42nd and 48th St. However, this area is international territory and operates outside of the laws and jurisdiction of the U.S. Outside, a multicultural rose garden and a statuary park provide a lovely view of the East River. Inside, go through security check and work your way to the back of the lobby for the informative tours of the **General Assembly. (Visitor's entrance** at First Ave. and 46th St. Daily tours about 45min., leaving every 15min. 9:15am-4:45pm, available in 20 languages. $6.50, seniors over 60 and students $4.50, under 16 $3.50.) You must take the tour to get past the lobby. Sometimes free tickets to G.A. sessions can be obtained when the U.N. is in session (Oct.-May); call 963-1234.

Between 48th and 51st St. and Fifth and Sixth Ave. stretches **Rockefeller Center,** a monument to the conjunction of business and art. On Fifth Ave., between 49th and 50th St., the famous gold-leaf statue of Prometheus sprawls on a ledge of the sunken **Tower Plaza** while jet streams of water pulse around it. The Plaza serves as an open-air café in the spring and summer and as a world-famous ice-skating rink in the winter. The 70-story **RCA Building,** seated at Sixth Ave., remains the most accomplished artistic creation in this complex. Every chair in the building sits less than 28 feet from natural light. The **NBC Television Network** makes its headquarters here, allowing you to take a behind-the-scenes look at their operations. The network offers an hour-long tour which traces the history of NBC, from their first radio broadcast in 1926 through the heyday of TV programming in the 50s and 60s. The tour visits the studios of *Conan O'Brien* and the infamous 8H studio, home of *Saturday Night Live.* (Tours run every 15min. Mon.-Sat 9:30am-4:30pm. $8.25.)

Despite an illustrious history and a wealth of Art Deco treasures, **Radio City Music Hall** (632-4041) was almost demolished in 1979 to make way for new office high-rises. However, the public rallied and the place was declared a national landmark. First opened in 1932, at the corner of Sixth Ave. and 51st St., the 5874-seat theater remains the largest in the world. The brainchild of Roxy Rothafel (originator of the Rockettes), it was originally intended as a variety showcase. Yet the hall functioned primarily as a movie theater; over 650 feature films debuted here from 1933 to 1979, including *King Kong, Breakfast at Tiffany's,* and *Doctor Zhivago.* The

Rockettes, Radio City's chorus line, still dance on. Tours of the great hall are given daily 10am-5pm ($12, children 6 and under $6).

At 25 W. 52nd St., the **Museum of Television and Radio** (621-6800) works almost entirely as a "viewing museum," allowing visitors to attend scheduled screenings in one of its theaters or to choose and enjoy privately a TV or radio show from its library of 60,000. Continue over a block down W. 53rd St. towards Sixth Ave. and take in masterpieces in the **American Craft Museum** and the **Museum of Modern Art** (see Museums). Rest your tired feet with a visit to the sculpture garden of MoMA, and contemplate the works of Rodin, Renoir, Miró, Lipschitz, and Picasso.

St. Patrick's Cathedral (753-2261), New York's most famous church and the largest Catholic cathedral in America, stands at 51st St. and Fifth Ave. Designed by James Renwick, the structure captures the essence of great European cathedrals like Reims and Cologne yet retains its own spirit. The twin spires on the Fifth Ave. façade stretch 330 ft. into the air.

One of the monuments to modern architecture, Ludwig Mies Van der Rohe's dark and gracious **Seagram Building** looms over 375 Park Ave., between 52nd and 53rd St. Pure skyscraper, fronted by a plaza and two fountains, the Seagram stands as a paragon of the austere International Style. Van der Rohe envisioned it as an oasis from the tight canyon of skyscrapers on Park Ave.

The stores on Fifth Ave. from Rockefeller Center to Central Park are the ritziest in the city. Take time to worship at the shrines to capitalism. At **Tiffany & Co.** (755-8000), get rid of the mean reds; everything from jewelry to housewares shines, especially the window displayed, which can be art in themselves, especially around Christmas (open Mon.-Wed. and Fri.-Sat. 10am-5:30pm, Thurs. 10am-7:30pm). **F.A.O. Schwarz,** 767 Fifth Ave. (644-9400) at 58th St. impresses kids and adults with one of the world's largest toy stores, including complex Lego constructions, life-sized stuffed animals, and a separate annex exclusively for Barbie dolls. (Open Mon.-Wed. and Fri.-Sat. 10am-7pm, Thurs. 10am-8pm, Sun. noon-6pm.)

On Fifth Ave. and 59th St., at the southeast corner of Central Park, sits the legendary **Plaza Hotel,** built in 1907 at the then-astronomical cost of $12.5 million. Its 18-story, 800-room French Renaissance interior flaunts five marble staircases, countless ludicrously named suites, and a two-story Grand Ballroom. Past guests and residents have included Frank Lloyd Wright, the Beatles, F. Scott Fitzgerald, and, of course, the eminent Eloise. *Let's Go* recommends the $15,000-per-night suite.

West Midtown

Pennsylvania Station, at 33th St. and Seventh Ave., is one of the less engrossing pieces of architecture in West Midtown, but, as a major subway stop and train terminal, it can at least claim to be functional. (Subway: #1, 2, 3, 9, A, C, or E to 34th St./Penn Station). The original Penn Station, a classical marble building modeled on the Roman Baths of Caracalla, was demolished in the 60s. The railway tracks were then covered with the equally uninspiring **Madison Square Garden** complex. Facing the Garden at 421 Eighth Ave., New York's immense main post office, the **James A. Farley Building,** luxuriates in its 10001 ZIP code. A lengthy swath of Corinthian columns muscles broadly across the front, and a 280-ft. frieze tops the broad portico with the motto of the U.S. Postal Service: "Neither snow nor rain nor heat nor gloom of night stays these couriers from the swift completion of their appointed rounds."

East on 34th St., between Seventh Ave. and Broadway, stands monolithic **Macy's** (695-4400). This giant, which occupies a full city block, was recently forced to relinquish its title as the "World's Largest Department Store" and change its billing to the "World's Finest Department Store" when a new store in Germany was built one square foot larger. With nine floors (plus a lower level) and some two million sq. ft. of merchandise, Macy's has come a long way since 1857, when it grossed $11.06 on its first day of business. Recently, however, it was forced to revisit its humble roots when it filed for bankruptcy, and its fate still remains uncertain. The store sponsors the **Macy's Thanksgiving Day Parade,** a New York tradition buoyed by helium-filled 10-story Snoopies, marching bands, floats, and general hoopla. (Open Mon.

and Thurs.-Fri. 10am-8:30pm, Tues.-Wed. and Sat. 10am-7pm, Sun. 11am-6pm. Subway: #1, 2, 3, or 9 to Penn Station; or B, D, F, N, Q, or R to 34th St.)

The streets of **Times Square** flicker at the intersection of 42nd St. and Broadway. Still considered the dark and seedy core of the Big Apple by most New Yorkers, the Square has worked hard in the past few years to improve its image. Robberies have decreased by 40%, pick-pocketing and purse-snatching by 43%, and the number of area porn shops has plummeted by more than 100 from its late-70s climax of 140. The historic Victory Theater is undergoing restoration and will be the site of a new children's theater, and Disney has big plans for the aging New Amsterdam Theater, where the Ziegfield Follies performed their original chorus line routine for more than twenty years. Still, Times Square is Times Square. Teens continue to roam about in search of fake IDs, hustlers wait eagerly to scam suckers, and every New Year's Eve, millions booze and schmooze and watch an electronic ball drop. One-and-a-half million people pass through Times Square every day. Lots of subway lines stop in the square (#1, 2, 3, 7, 9, and A, C, E, N, R, S).

On 42nd St. between Ninth and Tenth Ave. lies **Theater Row,** a block of renovated Broadway theaters that many consider the heart of American theater. The nearby **Theater District** stretches from 41st to 57th St. along Broadway, Eighth Ave., and the streets which connect them. Approximately 37 theaters remain active, most of them grouped around 45th St.

How do you get to **Carnegie Hall?** Practice, practice, practice. At 57th St. and Seventh Ave.; the hall was founded in 1891 and remains New York's foremost soundstage. Tchaikovsky, Caruso, Toscanini, and Bernstein have played Carnegie, as have the Beatles and the Rolling Stones. Other notable events from Carnegie's playlist include the world premiere of Dvorâk's *Symphony No. 9 (From the New World)* on December 16, 1893, and a lecture by Albert Einstein in 1934. Carnegie Hall almost faced the wrecking ball in the 50s, but outraged citizens managed to stop the impending destruction through special legislation in 1960. (Tours are given Mon., Tues., Thurs. and Fri. at 11:30am, 2, and 3pm. $6, students and seniors $5; call 903-9790 for more info.) Carnegie Hall's **museum** displays artifacts and memorabilia from its illustrious century of existence (open daily 11am-4:30pm; free).

MID-ATLANTIC

Upper East Side

The Golden Age of the East Side society epic began in the 1860s and progressed until the outbreak of World War I. Scores of wealthy people moved into the area and refused to budge, even during the Great Depression when armies of the unemployed pitched their tents across the way in Central Park. These days parades, millionaires, and unbearably slow buses share Fifth Ave. Upper Fifth Ave. is home to **Museum Mile,** which includes the **Metropolitan,** the **Guggenheim,** the **ICP,** the **Cooper-Hewitt,** and the **Jewish Museum,** among others (see Museums).

The Upper East Side, drips with money along the length of the Park. Start your journey at 59th St. and Third Ave., where **Bloomingdale's** sits in regal splendor. **Madison Ave.** graces New York with luxurious boutiques and most of the country's advertising agencies. **Park Ave.,** the street that time forgot, maintains a regal austerity with gracious buildings and landscaped medians. **Gracie Mansion,** at the north end of Carl Schurz Park, between 84th and 90th St. along East End Ave., has been the residence of every New York mayor since Fiorello LaGuardia moved in during World War II. Now Rudolph Giuliani occupies this hottest of hot seats. (Tours Wed.; suggested admission $3, seniors $2. To make a reservation for a tour, call 570-4751.)

Central Park

Central Park rolls from Grand Army Plaza all the way up to 110th St. between Fifth and Eighth Ave. Twenty years of construction turned these 843 acres, laid out by Frederick Law Olmsted and Calvert Vaux in 1850-60, into a compressed sequence of infinite landscapes. The park contains lakes, ponds, fountains, skating rinks, ball fields, tennis courts, a castle, an outdoor theater, a bandshell, and two zoos.

The Park may be roughly divided between north and south at the main reservoir; the southern section affords more intimate settings, serene lakes, and graceful promenades, while the northern end has a few ragged edges. Nearly 1400 species of trees, shrubs, and flowers grow here, the work of distinguished horticulturist Ignaz Anton Pilat. When you wander amidst the shrubbery, look to the nearest lamppost for guidance and check the small metal four-digit plaque bolted to it. The first two digits tell you what street you're nearest (e.g., 89), and the second two whether you're on the east or west side of the Park (even numbers mean east, an odd west). In an emergency, call the **24-hr. Park Hotline** from boxes in the park (570-4820).

At the renovated **Central Park Wildlife Center** (861-6030), Fifth Ave. at 64th St., the monkeys effortlessly ape their visitors. (Open April-Oct. Mon.-Fri. 10am-5pm, Sat.-Sun. 10:30am-5:30pm; Nov.-March daily 10am-4:30pm. Last entry ½-hr. before closing. $2.50, seniors $1.25, ages 3-12 50¢.)

The Dairy building now houses the **Central Park Reception Center** (794-6564). Pick up the free map of Central Park and the seasonal list of events. (Open Tues.-Thurs. and Sat.-Sun. 11am-5pm, Fri. 1-5pm; Nov.-Feb. Tues.-Thurs. and Sat.-Sun. 11am-4pm, Fri. 1-4pm.) The **Wollman Skating Rink** (517-4800) doubles as a **miniature golf course** in late spring. (Ice- or roller-skating $6, seniors and children $3, plus $5 skate rental or $7 in-line skate rental; 9-hole mini-golf $5, kids $2.50; bank-shot $6, kids $3; discounts for combining activities. Whole megillah open Mon. 10am-5pm, Tues. 10am-9:30pm, Wed.-Thurs. 10am-6pm and 7:30-9:30pm, Fri.-Sat. 10am-11pm, Sun. 10am-9:30pm.)

The **Friedsam Memorial Carousel** (879-0244) turns at 65th St. west of Center Dr. The 58-horsepower carousel was brought from Coney Island and fully restored in 1983. (Open Mon.-Fri. 10:30am-5pm, Sat.-Sun. 10:30am-6pm. Thanksgiving to mid-March Sun. 10:30am-4:30pm. 90¢.) Directly north of the Carousel, **Sheep Meadow** grows from about 66th to 69th St. on the western side of the Park. This is the largest chunk of greensward, exemplifying the pastoral ideals of the Park's designers. It is not uncommon to join a stranger's game of frisbee, but ask first. Spreading out to the west, the **Lake** provides a dramatic patch of blue in the heart of the City. The 1954 **Loeb Boathouse** (517-2233) supplies all necessary romantic nautical equipment. (Open daily late March-Nov. Mon.-Fri. noon-5pm, Sat.-Sun. 10am-5:30pm, weather permitting. Rowboats $10 per hr., $20 deposit.)

Strawberry Fields was sculpted by Yoko Ono as a memorial to John Lennon. The Fields are located to the west of the Lake at 72nd St. and West Dr., directly across from the Dakota Apartments where Lennon was assassinated and where Ono still lives. Ono battled valiantly for this space against city-council members who had planned a Bing Crosby memorial on the same spot. Picnickers and 161 varieties of plants now bloom over the rolling hills around the star-shaped "Imagine" mosaic on sunny spring days. On John Lennon's birthday on October 9, in one of the largest unofficial Park events, thousands gather here to remember, or imagine, the legend.

The **Swedish Cottage Marionette Theater** (988-9093), at the base of Vista Rock near the 79th St. Transverse, puts on regular puppet shows (Sat. noon and 3pm; $5, children $4). Climb the hill to the round wooden space of the **Delacorte Theater,** which hosts the wildly popular **Shakespeare in the Park** series each midsummer. These plays often feature celebrities and are always free. Come early: the theater seats only 1936 lucky souls (see Theater). Large concerts often take place north of the theater, on the **Great Lawn.** Paul Simon sang here, the Stonewall 25 marchers rallied here, *Pocahontas* premiered here, and the New York Philharmonic and the Metropolitan Opera Company frequently give free summer performances here.

Upper West Side

Broadway leads uptown to **Columbus Circle,** 59th St. and Broadway, the symbolic entrance to the Upper West Side and the end of Midtown. A statue of Christopher marks the border. One of the Circle's landmarks, the **New York Coliseum,** has been relatively empty since the construction of the **Javits Center** in 1990.

Broadway intersects Columbus Ave. at **Lincoln Center,** the cultural hub of the city, between 62nd and 66th St. The seven facilities that constitute Lincoln Center—Avery Fisher Hall, the New York State Theater, the Metropolitan Opera House, the Library and Museum of Performing Arts, the Vivian Beaumont Theater, The Walter Reade Theater, and the Juilliard School of Music—accommodate over 13,000 spectators at a time. At night, the Metropolitan Opera House lights up, making its chandeliers and huge Chagall murals visible through its glass-panel façade. **Columbus Ave.** leads to the **Museum of Natural History** (see museums). **Broadway** pulses with energy all day (and all night) long. The Upper West Side is covered with residential brownstones, scenic enough for a pleasant (and free) stroll. See Upper West Side food section for info on **Zabar's,** a sight as well as a store.

Harlem

Half a million people are packed into the 3 sq. mi. of greater Harlem. On the East Side above 96th St. lies **Spanish Harlem,** known as El Barrio ("the neighborhood"), and on the West Side lies Harlem proper, stretching from 110th to 155th St. Columbia University controls the area, west of Morningside Ave. and south of 125th St., more commonly known as **Morningside Heights.** On the West Side, from 125th to 160th St., much of the cultural and social life of the area takes place in **Central Harlem.** To the far north, from 160th St. to 220th St., **Washington Heights** and **Inwood** are areas populated by thriving Dominican and Jewish communities. All these neighborhoods heat up with street activity, not always of the wholesome variety; visit Harlem during the day or go there with someone who knows the area. If you lack street wisdom or can't find your own guide, opt for a commercial tour.

Do not let Harlem's problems overshadow its positive aspects. Although an extremely poor neighborhood, it is culturally rich; and, contrary to popular opinion, much of it is relatively safe. Known to locals as the "city within the City," Harlem is considered by many to be the black capital of the Western world. Over the years Harlem has often been viewed as the archetype of America's frayed cities—you won't believe that hype after you've visited. The 1920s were Harlem's Renaissance; a thriving scene of artists, writers, and scholars lived fast and loose, producing cultural masterworks in the process. The Cotton Club and the Apollo Theater, along with numerous other jazz clubs, were on the musical vanguard, while Langston Hughes and Zora Neale Hurston changed the face of literature.

Columbia University, chartered in 1754, huddles between Morningside Dr. and Broadway, 114th and 120th St. Now co-ed, Columbia also has cross-registration across the street with all-female **Barnard College** (call 854-2842 for info or a tour).

The **Cathedral of St. John the Divine** (316-7540), along Amsterdam Ave. between 110th and 113th, promises to be the world's largest cathedral when finished. Construction, begun in 1812, continues and should not be completed for another century or two. Near Columbia, at 120th St. and Riverside Dr., is the **Riverside Church.** The observation deck in the tower commands an amazing view of the bells within and the expanse of the Hudson River and Riverside Park below. You can hear concerts on the world's largest carillon (74 bells), a gift of John D. Rockefeller, Jr. (Tours of the tower given Sun. 12:30pm; call for tickets. Open Mon.-Sat. 9am-4:30pm, Sun. service 10:45am.) Diagonally across Riverside Dr. lies **Grant's Tomb** (666-1640). Once a popular monument, it now attracts only a few brave souls willing to make the hike. (Open daily 9am-5pm. Free.)

125th St., also known as Martin Luther King, Jr. Blvd., spans the heart of traditional Harlem. Fast-food joints, jazz bars, and the **Apollo Theater** (222-0992, box office 749-5838) keep the street humming day and night. 125th St. has recently experienced a resurgence. Off 125th St., at 328 Lenox Ave., **Sylvia's** (966-0660) has magnetized New York for 22 years with enticing soul-food dishes (open Mon.-Sat. 7am-10pm, Sun. 1-7pm). The silver dome of the **Masjid Malcolm Shabazz,** where Malcolm X was once a minister, glitters on 116th St. and Lenox Ave. (visit Fri. at 1pm and Sun. at 10am for services and information, or call 662-2200).

In Washington Heights, north of 155th St., the **George Washington Bridge** has spanned the Hudson since 1931, connecting New York with New Jersey.

Brooklyn

When romantics ponder Brooklyn, they conjure up images of the rough stickball players who grew up to become the Brooklyn Dodgers. What goes on in Brooklyn tends to happen on the streets and out of doors, whether it's neighborhood banter, baseball games in the park, ethnic festivals, or gang violence. The Dutch originally settled the borough in the 17th century. When asked to join New York in 1833, Brooklyn refused, saying that the two cities shared no interests except common waterways. Not until 1898 did Brooklyn decide, in a close vote, to become a borough of New York City. The visitors bureau (see Practical Information, above) publishes an excellent free guide to Brooklyn's rich historical past that outlines 10 walking tours of the borough.

The Brooklyn Bridge spans the East River from lower Manhattan to Brooklyn. Built in 1883, the bridge was one of the greatest engineering feats of the 19th century. The 1-mi. walk along the pedestrian path (make sure to walk on the left side, as the right is reserved for bicycles) will show you why every New York poet feels compelled to write at least one verse about it, why photographers snap the bridge's airy spider-web cables, and why people jump off. Once on the bridge, you can look straight up at the cables and Gothic arches. To get to the entrance on Park Row, walk a couple of blocks west from the East River to the city hall area. Plaques on the bridge towers commemorate John Augustus Roebling, its builder, who, along with 20 of his workers, died during its construction.

Head south on Henry St. after the Brooklyn Bridge, then turn right on Clark St. toward the river for a synapse-shorting view of Manhattan. Many prize-winning photographs have been taken from the **Brooklyn Promenade,** overlooking the southern tip of Manhattan and New York Harbor. George Washington's headquarters during the Battle of Long Island, now-posh **Brooklyn Heights** has hosted many authors, from Walt Whitman to Norman Mailer, with beautiful old brownstones, tree-lined streets, and proximity to Manhattan. Continuing south, you'll find **Atlantic Ave.,** home to a large Arab community. Atlantic runs from the river to Flatbush Ave. At the Flatbush Ave. Extension, pick up the **Fulton St.** pedestrian mall.

Williamsburg, several blocks north of downtown Brooklyn, has retained its Hasidic Jewish culture. The quarter encloses Broadway, Bedford, and Union Ave. It closes on *shabbat* (Saturday), the Jewish holy day.

Prospect Park, designed by Frederick Law Olmsted in the mid-1800s, was supposedly his favorite creation. He was even more pleased with it than with his Manhattan project—Central Park. At the north corner of the park **Grand Army Plaza** provides an island in the midst of the borough's busiest thoroughfares, designed to shield surrounding apartment buildings from traffic. (Subway: 2 or 3 to Grand Army Plaza.) The nearby **Botanic Gardens** (718-622-4433) seem more secluded and include a lovely rose garden. (Open Tues.-Fri. 8am-6pm, Sat.-Sun. and holidays 10am-6pm; Oct.-March Tues.-Fri. 8am-4:30pm, Sat.-Sun. and holidays 10am-4:30pm. Free). The mammoth **Brooklyn Museum** (718-638-5000) rests behind the gardens (open Wed.-Sun. 10am-5pm; suggested donation $4, students $2, seniors $1.50).

Both a body of water (really part of the Atlantic) and a mass of land, **Sheepshead Bay** lies on the southern edge of Brooklyn. Walk along Emmons Ave. and peruse menus for daily seafood specials. Nearby **Brighton Beach,** nicknamed "Little Odessa by the Sea," has been homeland to Russian emigrés since the turn of the century. (Subway: D or Q.)

Once a resort for the City's elite, made accessible to the rest of the Apple because of the subway, fading **Coney Island** still warrants a visit. The **Boardwalk,** once one of the most seductive of Brooklyn's charms, now squeaks nostalgically as tourists are jostled by roughnecks. Enjoy a hot dog and crinkle-cut fries at historic **Nathan's,** Surf and Sitwell Ave. The **Cyclone,** 834 Surf Ave. (718-266-3434), at W. 10th St., built in 1927, was once the most terrifying roller coaster ride in the world. Hurtle through the 100-second-long screamer; with nine hills of rickety wooden tracks the ride's well worth $3. (Open mid-June to Labor Day daily noon-midnight; Easter weekend to mid-June Fri.-Sun. noon-midnight.) Go meet a walrus, dolphin, sea lion, shark, or other ocean critter in the tanks of the **New York Aquarium,** (718-265-3400), Surf and West 8th. (Open Mon.-Fri. 10am-5pm, Sat.-Sun. 10am-7pm; in winter daily 10am-5pm; holidays 10am-7pm. $6.75, seniors and children $2).

Queens

In this urban suburbia, the American melting pot bubbles away with a more than 30% foreign-born population. Immigrants from Korea, China, India, and the West Indies rapidly sort themselves out into neighborhoods where they try to maintain the memory of their homeland while living "the American Dream."

Queens is easily New York's largest borough, covering over a third of the city's total area. You need to understand Queens's kaleidoscope of communities to understand the borough. If you visit only one place in Queens, let it be **Flushing.** Here you will find some of the most important colonial neighborhood landmarks, a bustling downtown, and the largest rose garden in the Northeast. (Subway: #7 to Main St., Flushing.) Nearby **Flushing Meadows-Corona Park** was the site of the 1964-1965 World's Fair, and now holds Shea Stadium (home of the Mets) and several museums.

The Bronx

While the media presents "Da Bronx" as a crime-ravaged husk, the borough offers its few tourists over 2000 acres of parkland, a great zoo, turn-of-the-century riverfront mansions, grand boulevards evocative of Europe, and thriving ethnic neighborhoods, including a Little Italy to shame its counterpart to the south. If you're not heading for Yankee Stadium, stay out of the **South Bronx** unless you're in a car and with someone who knows the area.

The most obvious reason to come to the Bronx is the **Bronx Zoo/Wildlife Conservation Park** (718-367-1010 or 718-220-5100), also known as the New York Zoological Society. The largest urban zoo in the United States, it houses over 4000 animals. You can explore the zoo on foot or ride like the king of the jungle aboard the Safari Train, which runs between the elephant house and Wild Asia ($1). Soar into the air for a funky cool view of the zoo from the **Skyfari** aerial tramway that runs between Wild Asia and the Children's Zoo (one-way $2, children $1). The **Bengali Express Monorail** glides round Wild Asia (20min.; $2). If you find the pace too hurried, saddle up a camel in the Wild Asia area ($3). Call 220-5142 three weeks in advance to reserve a place on a **walking tour.** Pamphlets containing self-guided tours are available at the Zoo Center for 75¢. Parts of the zoo close down during the winter (Nov.-April). (Open Mon.-Fri. 10am-5pm, Sat.-Sun. 10am-5:30pm; Nov.-Jan. daily 10am-4:30pm; $6.75, seniors and children $3; free Wed. For disabled-access, call 718-220-5188. Subway: #2 or 5 to E. Tremont Ave.)

North across East Fordham Rd. from the zoo, the **New York Botanical Garden** (718-817-8705) sprawls over snatches of forest and virgin waterways. (Garden grounds open Tues.-Sun. 10am-7pm; Nov.-March 10am-6pm. Suggested donation $3, seniors, students, and children $1. Parking $4. Subway: #4 or D to Bedford Park Blvd. and Bx26 bus 8 blocks east.)

Wave Hill, 675 W. 252nd St. (718-549-2055), in Riverdale, was home to Samuel Clemens (Mark Twain) and Teddy Roosevelt. Picnic in the world-famous gardens with an astonishing view of the Hudson and the Palisades. (Gardens open June to mid-Oct. Tues. and Thurs.-Sun. 9am-5:30pm, Wed. 9:30am-dusk; mid-Oct.-May Wed.-Sun. 10am-4:30pm. Tues.-Fri. free, Sat.-Sun. $4, students and seniors $2.).

The **Museum of Bronx History** (881-8900), at Bainbridge Ave. and 208th St. (Subway: D to 205th St., or #4 to Mosholu Pkwy. Walk 4 blocks east on 210th St. and then south a block) is run by the Bronx Historical Society on the premises of the landmark Valentine-Varian House. The museum presents historical narratives explaining the borough of the Bronx. (Open Sat. 10am-4pm, Sun. 1-5pm, $2.)

Staten Island

Getting there is half the fun. At 50¢ (round-trip), the half-hour ferry ride from Manhattan's Battery Park to Staten Island is as unforgettable as it is inexpensive. Or you can drive from Brooklyn over the **Verrazano-Narrows Bridge,** the world's second-longest (4260 ft.) suspension span. Because of the hills and the distances (and some very dangerous neighborhoods in between), it's a bad idea to walk from one site to the next. Make sure to plan your excursion with the bus schedule in mind.

The most concentrated number of sights on the island cluster around the beautiful 19th-century **Snug Harbor Cultural Center,** at 1000 Richmond Terrace. Picnic and see its catch: the **Newhouse Center for Contemporary Art** (718-448-2500), a small gallery displaying American art with an indoor/outdoor sculpture show in the summer (open Wed.-Sun. noon-5pm; free), the **Staten Island Children's Museum** (718-273-2060), with participation exhibits for the five- to 12-year-old in you (open Tues.-Sun. noon-5pm; $3), and the **Staten Island Botanical Gardens.**

Live Free or Die

The Staten Island secession movement is a lot more serious than one might think. Virtually every municipal election on the island in recent memory has included the petition to make New York City four boroughs instead of five. When one referendum showed that a majority of residents wanted to leave the Big Apple, the Borough President, Guy Molinari, got so excited that he set up four cannons, pointed them at each of the other four boroughs, and fired off a round. "Just warning shots," he said. Brooklyn, Manhattan, Queens, and the Bronx did not return fire.

MUSEUMS AND GALLERIES

For museum and gallery listings consult the following publications: *New Yorker* (the most accurate and extensive listing), *New York,* the Friday *New York Times* (in the Weekend section), the *Quarterly Calendar,* (available free at any visitors bureau), and *Gallery Guide,* found in local galleries. Most museums and all galleries close on Mondays, and are jam-packed on the weekends. Many museums require a "donation" in place of an admission fee—you can give less than the suggested amount. Most museums are free one weeknight; call ahead to confirm.

Major Collections

Metropolitan Museum of Art, (879-5500), Fifth Ave. at 82nd St. Subway: 4, 5, 6 to 86th St. If you see only one, see this. The largest in the Western Hemisphere, the Met's art collection encompasses 3.3 million works from almost every period through Impressionism; particularly strong in Egyptian and non-Western sculpture and European painting. Contemplate infinity in the secluded Japanese Rock Garden. When blockbuster exhibits tour the world they usually stop at the Met—get tickets in advance through Ticketron. Open Sun. and Tues.-Thurs. 9:30am-5:15pm, Fri.-Sat. 9:30am-8:45pm. Donation $7, students and seniors $3.50.

Museum of Modern Art (MoMA), 11 W. 53rd St. (708-9400), off Fifth Ave. in Midtown. Subway: E or F to Fifth Ave./53rd St. One of the most extensive contemporary (post-Impressionist) collections in the world, founded in 1929 by scholar Alfred Barr in response to the Met's reluctance to embrace modern art. Cesar Pelli's structural glass additions flood the masterpieces with natural light. See Monet's sublime *Water Lily* room, and many Picassos. Gorgeous sculpture garden. Open Sat.-Tues. 11am-6pm, Thurs.-Fri. noon-8:30pm. $8, students and seniors $5, under 16 free. Films require free tickets in advance. Pay-what-you-wish Thurs.-Fri. 5:30-8:30pm.

American Museum of Natural History (769-5100), Central Park West, at 79th to 81st St. Subway: B or C to 81st St. The largest science museum in the world, in a suitably imposing Romanesque structure. Newly reopened dinosaur exhibit is worth the lines you'll inevitably face. Locals recommend seeing things from a new perspective by lying down under the whale in the Ocean Life room. Open

Sun.-Thurs. 10am-5:45pm, Fri.-Sat. 10am-8:45pm. Donation $6, students and seniors $4, children $3. Free Fri.-Sat. 5-8:45pm. The museum also houses **Nature-max** (769-5650), a cinematic extravaganza on a huge movie screen (4 stories). $6, students and seniors $5, children $3, Fri.-Sat. double features $7.50, children $4. The **Hayden Planetarium** (769-5700) offers multi-media presentations. Seasonal celestial light shows twinkle in the dome of its **Theater of the Stars,** accompanied by astronomy lectures. Admission $5, seniors and students $4, kids $2.50. Electrify your senses with the theater's Laser Floyd or Laser Grunge.

Guggenheim Museum, 1071 Fifth Ave. and 89th St. (423-3500). Many have called this controversial construction a giant turnip, Frank Lloyd Wright's joke on the Big Apple. The museum closed from 1990-92 while a ten-story "tower gallery" sprouted behind the original structure, allowing the museum to show more of its rich permanent collection of mostly 20th-century art. Open Sun.-Wed. 10am-6pm, Fri.-Sat. 10am-8pm. $7, students and seniors $4, under 12 free. Pay what you wish Fri. 6-8pm. Two-day pass to this museum and **Guggenheim Museum SoHo,** 575 Broadway (423-3500) at Prince St. Open Sun. and Wed.-Fri. 11am-6pm, Sat. 11am-8pm. $5, students and seniors $3, and children under 12 free.

Whitney Museum of American Art, 945 Madison Ave. (570-3676), at 75th St. Subway: #6 to 77th St. Futuristic fortress featuring the largest collection of 20th-century American art in the world, with works by Hopper, Soyer, de Kooning, Motherwell, Warhol, and Calder. Controversial political art has infiltrated what was once a bastion of high-modernism, with food, trash, and video becoming accepted media. Open Wed. 11am-6pm, Thurs. 1-8pm, Fri.-Sun. 11am-6pm. $7, students and seniors $5, under 12 free. Thurs. 6-8pm $3.50.

Cooper-Hewitt Museum, 2 E. 91st St. (860-6868), at Fifth Ave. Subway: #4, 5 or 6 to 86th St. Andrew Carnegie's majestic, Georgian mansion now houses the Smithsonian Institution's National Museum of Design. The playful special exhibits, focus on such topics as doghouses and the history of the pop-up book. Open Tues. 10am-9pm, Wed.-Sat. 10am-5pm, Sun. noon-5pm. $3, students and seniors $1.50, under 12 free. Free Tues. 5-9pm.

The Frick Collection, 1 E. 70th St. (288-0700), at Fifth Ave. Subway: #6 to 68th St. Robber-baron Henry Clay Frick left his house and art collection to the city, and the museum retains the elegance of his French "Classic Eclectic" château. Impressive grounds. The Living Hall displays 17th-century furniture, Persian rugs, Holbein portraits, and paintings by El Greco, Rembrandt, Velázquez, and Titian. Relax in a courtyard inhabited by elegant statues surrounding the garden pool and fountain. Open Tues.-Sat. 10am-6pm, Sun. 1-6pm. $3.50, students and seniors $3. Ages under 10 not allowed, under 16 must be accompanied by an adult.

Smaller and Specialized Collections

American Craft Museum, 40 W. 53rd St. (956-3535), across from MoMA. Subway: E or F to Fifth Ave.-53rd St. Offering more than quilts, this museum revises the notion of crafts with its modern media, including metal and plastic. Open Tues. 10am-8pm, Wed.-Sun. 10am-5pm. $5, students and seniors $2.50.

The Cloisters (923-3700), Fort Tryon Park, upper Manhattan. Subway: A through Harlem to 190th St.; or take the M4 bus that departs from the Met. This monastery, built from pieces of 12th- and 13th-century French and Spanish cloisters, was assembled at John D. Rockefeller's behest by Charles Collens in 1938 as a setting for the Met's medieval art collection. Highlights include the Unicorn Tapestries, the Cuxa Cloister, and the Treasury, with 15th-century playing cards. Museum tours Tues.-Fri. 3pm, Sun. noon, in winter Wed. 3pm. Open Tues.-Sun. 9:30am-5:15pm. Donation $6, students and seniors $3 (includes admission to the Metropolitan Museum of Art).

International Center of Photography, 1130 Fifth Ave. (860-1777), at 94th St. Subway: #6 to 96th St. Housed in a landmark townhouse built in 1914 for *New Republic* founder Willard Straight. The foremost exhibitor of photography in the city, and a gathering-place for its practitioners. Historical, thematic, contemporary, and experimental works, running from fine art to photo-journalism. Midtown branch at 1133 Sixth Ave. (768-4680), at 43rd St. Both open Tues. 11am-8pm, Wed.-Sun. 11am-6pm. $4, students and seniors $2.50.

Intrepid Sea-Air-Space Museum, Pier 86 (245-0072), at 46th St. and Twelfth Ave. Bus: M42 or M50 to W. 46th St. One ticket admits you to the veteran World War II and Vietnam War aircraft carrier *Intrepid,* the Vietnam War destroyer *Edson,* the only publicly displayed guided-missile submarine, *Growler,* and the lightship *Nantucket.* A breathtaking wide-screen flick puts the viewer on a flight deck as jets take off and land. The Iraqi tanks parked near the gift shop were captured in the Gulf War. Open daily 10am-5pm; Labor Day-Memorial Day Mon.-Fri. 10am-5pm. $10, seniors $7.50, ages 6-11 $5.50.

Jacques Marchais Center of Tibetan Art, 338 Lighthouse Ave. (718-987-3478), Staten Island. Take bus S74 from Staten Island Ferry to Lighthouse Ave., turn right and walk up the hill. One of the finest Tibetan collections in the U.S. Exuding serenity, the center replicates a Tibetan temple set amid sculpture gardens. Open April-Nov. Wed.-Sun. 1-5pm. $3, seniors $2.50, children $1.

The Jewish Museum, 1109 Fifth Ave. (423-3200), at 92nd St. Subway: #6 to 96th St. Over 14,000 works detail the Jewish experience throughout history. Open Sun.-Mon. and Wed.-Thurs. 11am-5:45pm, Tues. 11am-8pm. $6, students and seniors $4, under 12 free; Tues. pay what you wish after 5pm.

The Museum for African Art, 593 Broadway (966-1313), between Houston and Prince St. in SoHo. Subway: N or R to Prince and Broadway. Formerly the Center for African Art, the museum has changed its name and expanded to feature two major exhibits of stunning African and African-American art. Open Tues.-Fri. 10am-5:30pm, Sat.-Sun. noon-6pm. $4, students and seniors with ID $2.

El Museo del Barrio, 1230 Fifth Ave. (831-7272), at 104th St. Subway: #6 to 103rd St. El Museo del Barrio is the only museum in the U.S. devoted exclusively to the art and culture of Puerto Rico and Latin America. Open Wed.-Sun. 11am-5pm. Suggested contribution $4, students and seniors $2.

Museum of the City of New York (534-1672), 103rd St. and Fifth Ave. next door to El Museo del Barrio. Subway: #6 to 103rd St. Premier museum chronicling New York City presents the city's story from the 16th century to the present through historical paintings, Currier and Ives prints, period rooms and artifacts. Open Wed.-Sat. 10am-5pm, Sun. 1-5pm. Contribution requested.

Museum of Television and Radio, 25 W. 52nd St. (621-6600), between Fifth and Sixth Ave. Subway: B, D, F, Q to Rockefeller Center; E or F to 53rd St. Boob tube relics and memorabilia, as well as over 50,000 programs in the museum's permanent collection. With admission you can watch or listen to anything from the *Twilight Zone* to *Saturday Night Live.* Open Tues.-Wed. and Fri.-Sun. noon-6pm, Thurs. noon-8pm. $6, students $4, seniors and children $3.

National Museum of the American Indian, 1 Bowling Green (668-6624), in the U.S. Customs House. Subway: #4 or 5 to Bowling Green. This newly re-opened museum exhibits the best of the Smithsonian's vast collection of Native American artifacts, in galleries and exhibitions designed by Native American artists and craftsmen as well as historians. Also shows works by contemporary artists. Open daily 10am-5pm. Free.

New Museum of Contemporary Art, 583 Broadway (219-1355), between Prince and Houston St. Subway: R to Prince, #6 to Bleecker, or B, D or F to Broadway/Lafayette. Dedicated to the destruction of the canon and of conventional ideas of "art," supports the hottest, the newest, and the most controversial. Many works deal with politics of identity—sexual, racial, and ethnic. Once a month, an artist sits in the front window and converses with passers-by. Open Wed.-Fri. and Sun. noon-6pm, Sat. noon-8pm. $3.50, students, seniors, and artists $2.50, children under 12 free; Sat. 6-8pm free.

ENTERTAINMENT AND NIGHTLIFE

New York's incomparable nightlife presents the traveler with a welcome problem: finding the "right show" from among the city's dizzyingly broad options. New York's cultural activity does not revolve around a nuclear institution; instead, hundreds of independent venues compete for attention and credibility, each claiming greater artistry than the others but all equally (well, nearly equally) responsible for New York's premiere cultural status. **Publications** with especially noteworthy sections on nightlife include the *Village Voice, New York* magazine, and the Sunday edition of the *New York Times.* The most comprehensive survey of the current theater scene can be found in *The New Yorker.* An **entertainment hotline** (360-3456; 24 hrs.) covers weekly activities by both borough and genre.

Only a short train ride away, **Hoboken, NJ** hosts happening nightlife (see Maxwells below) as well as a trendy, less expensive bar scene. For longer NYC stays, it's worth the foray, if only to see the tremendous skyline view from across the Hudson. To get to Hoboken, take the B, D, F, N, Q, or R train to 34th St., then the PATH train ($1) to the 1st stop in Hoboken. (The PATH train also leaves from the 23rd and 14th St. stations of the F train, as well as from its own stations at 9th St./Sixth Ave. and Christopher St./Greenwich St.)

Theater

Broadway is currently undergoing a revival—ticket sales are booming, and mainstream musicals are receiving more than their fair share of attention. Broadway tickets cost about $50 each when purchased through regular channels. **TKTS** (768-1818 for recorded info) sells half-price tickets to many Broadway shows on the same day of the performance. TKTS has a booth in the middle of Duffy Square (the northern part of Times Square, at 47th and Broadway). TKTS tickets are usually about $25 each plus a $2.50 service charge per ticket. (Tickets are sold Mon.-Sat. 3-8pm for evening performances, Wed. and Sat. 10am-2pm for matinees, and Sun. noon-8pm for matinees and evening performances.) For information on shows and ticket availability, call the **NYC/ON STAGE hotline** at 768-1818. **Ticketmaster** (307-7171) deals in everything from Broadway shows to mud-truck races; they charge at least $2 more than other outlets, but take most major credit cards. *Listings,* a weekly guide to entertainment in Manhattan ($1), has listings of Broadway, Off-Broadway, and Off-Off-Broadway shows.

Off-Broadway theaters have between 100 and 499 seats; only Broadway houses have over 500. Off-Broadway houses frequently offer more offbeat or quirky shows, with shorter runs. Occasionally these shows have long runs or make the jump to Broadway houses. Tickets cost $10-20. The best of the Off-Broadway houses huddle in the Sheridan Square area of the West Village. TKTS also sells tickets for the larger Off-Broadway houses. **Off-Off-Broadway** means cheaper, younger theaters.

For years, the **Joseph Papp Public Theater,** 425 Lafayette St. (598-7150), was inextricably linked with its namesake founder, one of the city's leading producers. The theater recently produced an exhaustive and exhausting Shakespeare Marathon, every single one of the Bard's plays was shown down to *Timon of Athens.* Tickets cost $15-35. About one-quarter of the seats are sold for $10 on the day of performance (starting at 6pm for evening performances and 1pm for matinees). Papp also founded **Shakespeare in the Park** (861-7277), a New York summer tradition. From June through August, two Shakespeare plays are presented at the **Delacorte Theater** in Central Park, near the 81st St. entrance on the Upper West Side, just north of the main road. Tickets are free, but lines form early. Call for info.

Movies

If Hollywood is *the* place to make films, New York City is *the* place to see them. Most movies open in New York weeks before they're distributed across the country, and the response of Manhattan audiences and critics can shape a film's success or failure nationwide. Dozens of revival houses show motion picture classics, and independent filmmakers from around the reel world come to New York to flaunt their work. Big-screen fanatics should check out the cavernous **Ziegfeld,** 141 W. 54th St. (765-7600), one of the largest screens left in America, which shows first-run films. **MoviePhone** (777-FILM/3456) allows you to reserve tickets for most major movie-houses and pick them up at showtime from the theater's automated ticket dispenser; you charge the ticket price plus a small fee over the phone. **The Kitchen,** 512 W. 19th St. (255-5793), between Tenth and Eleventh Ave., (subway: C or E to 23rd St.), is a world-renowned showcase for the off-beat from New York-based struggling artists (prices vary). See eight screens of alternative (not quite underground) cinema at the **Angelika Film Center,** 18 W. Houston St. (995-2000), at Mercer St. (subway: #6 to Bleecker St. or B, D, F, or Q to Broadway-Lafayette). The café upstairs has excellent espresso. **Anthology Film Archives,** 32 Second Ave. (505-5181) at E. 2nd St. Subway: F to Second Ave., is a forum for independent filmmaking. The **New York International Film Festival** packs 'em in every October; check the *Voice* or the *Times* for dates and times.

Opera and Dance

You can do it all at **Lincoln Center** (875-5000), New York's one-stop shopping mall for high-culture consumers; there's usually opera or dance at one of its many venues. Write Lincoln Center Plaza, NYC 10023, or drop by its Performing Arts Library (870-1930) for a full schedule and a press kit as long as the *Ring* cycle. The **Metropolitan Opera Company** (362-6000), opera's premier outfit, plays on a Lincoln Center stage as big as a football field. Regular tickets run as high as $100—go for the upper balcony (around $15; the cheapest seats have an obstructed view), unless you're prone to vertigo. You can stand in the orchestra ($14) along with the opera freakazoids, or all the way back in the Family Circle ($15). (Regular season runs Sept.-April Mon.-Sat.; box office open Mon.-Sat. 10am-8pm, Sun. noon-6pm.) In the summer, watch for free concerts in city parks (362-6000).

At right angles to the Met, the **New York City Opera** (870-5570) has a new sound under the direction of Christopher Keene. "City" now has a split season (Sept.-Nov. and March-April) and keeps its ticket prices low year-round ($15-73). For rush tickets, call the night before and wait in line the morning of. In July, look for free performances by the **New York Grand Opera** (360-2777) at Central Park Summerstage every Wednesday night. Check the papers for performances of the old warhorses by the **Amato Opera Company,** 319 Bowery (228-8200; Sept.-May). Music schools often stage opera as well; see Music for further details.

The New York State Theater (870-5570) is home to the late, great George Balanchine's **New York City Ballet,** the country's oldest and most famous dance company. Decent tickets for the *Nutcracker* in December sell out almost immediately. (Performances Nov.-Feb. and April-June. Tickets $12-57, standing room $8.) The **American Ballet Theater** (477-3030), under Mikhail Baryshnikov's guidance, dances at the Met every May and June (tickets $16-95). The **Alvin Ailey American Dance Theater** (767-0940) bases its repertoire of modern dance on jazz, spirituals, and contemporary music. Often on the road, it always performs at the **City Center** in December. Tickets ($15-40) can be difficult to obtain. Write or call the City Center, 131 W. 55th St. (581-7907), weeks in advance. Look for ½-price tickets at the Bryant Park ticket booth (see below). The **Joyce Theater,** 175 Eighth Ave. (242-0800), between 18th and 19th St., has experimental dance troupes (tickets $15-40).

Other companies include the **Martha Graham Dance Co.,** 316 E. 63rd St. (832-9166), performing original Graham pieces during its October New York season, and the **Merce Cunningham Dance Company** (255-8240), of John Cage fame. Half-price tickets for many music and dance events can be purchased on the day of performance at the **Bryant Park** ticket booth, 42nd St. (382-2323), between Fifth and Sixth Ave. (Open Tues.-Sun. noon-2pm and 3-7pm; cash and traveler's checks only.) Concert tickets to Monday shows are available on the preceding Sunday.

Classical Music

Begin with the ample listings in the *New York Times, The New Yorker,* or *New York* magazine. Remember that many events, like outdoor music, are seasonal.

The **Lincoln Center Halls** have a wide, year-round selection of concerts. The **Great Performers Series,** featuring famous and foreign musicians, packs the Avery Fisher and Alice Tully Halls and the Walter Reade Theater from October until May (call 721-6500; tickets from $11). **Avery Fisher Hall** (875-5030; wheelchair accessible) paints the town ecstatic with its annual **Mostly Mozart Festival.** Show up early; there are usually pre-concert recitals beginning one hour before the main concert which are free to ticketholders. The festival runs from July to August, with tickets to individual events costing $12-30. The **New York Philharmonic** (875-5656) begins its regular season in mid-September (tickets $10-60; call 721-6500 Mon.-Sat. 10am-8pm, Sun. noon-8pm). Students and seniors can sometimes get $5 tickets; call ahead (Tues.-Thurs. only). Anyone can get $10 tickets for the odd morning rehearsal; again, call ahead. For a couple of weeks in late June, Kurt Masur and friends lead the posse at **free concerts** (875-5709) on the Great Lawn in Central Park, in Prospect Park in Brooklyn, in Van Cortland Park in the Bronx, and elsewhere. Free outdoor events at Lincoln Center occur all summer; call 875-4000.

Carnegie Hall (247-7800), Seventh Ave. at 57th St., is still the favorite coming-out locale of musical debutantes (box office open Mon.-Sat. 11am-6pm, Sun. noon-6pm; tickets $10-60). One of the best ways for the budget traveler to absorb New York musical culture is to visit a **music school.** Except for opera and ballet productions ($5- 12), concerts at the following schools are free and frequent: The **Juilliard School of Music,** Lincoln Center (769-7406), the **Mannes School of Music** (580-0210), and the **Manhattan School of Music** (749-2802).

Jazz Joints

The **JVC Jazz Festival** (787-2020) blows into the city in June. All-star performances have included Ray Charles and Mel Torme. Tickets go on sale in early May.

Apollo Theatre, 253 W. 125th St. (749-5838, box office 864-0372), between Frederick Douglass Blvd. and Adam Clayton Powell Blvd. Subway: #1, 2, 3, or 9 to 125th St. Historic Harlem landmark has heard Duke Ellington, Count Basie, Ella Fitzgerald, and Billie Holliday. Legendary Amateur Night (where the audience boos acts off the stage, à la *Gong Show*) $5.

Augie's, 2751 Broadway (864-9834), between 105th and 106th St. Subway: #1 or 9 to 103rd St. Jazz until 3am. Quality musicians and an unpretentious crowd. No cover; $3 drink min., $5 Fri.-Sat. Sets start around 10pm. Open daily 6pm-4am.

Birdland, 2745 Broadway (749-2228), at 105th St. Subway: #1 or 9 to 103rd St. Good food and top jazz. Cover Fri.-Sat $5 plus $5 min. per set at bar, $10/$15 at tables; Sun.-Thurs. $5 plus $5 min. per set at tables; no cover at bar. No cover for brunch Sun. noon-4pm. Open Mon.-Sat. 4pm-4am, Sun. noon-4pm and 5pm-4am. First set nightly at 9pm.

Blue Note, 131 W. 3rd St. (475-8592), near MacDougal St. Subway: A, B, C, D, E, F, or Q to Washington Sq. The Carnegie Hall of jazz clubs. Now a commercialized concert space with crowded tables and a sedate audience. Often books top performers. Sets Sun.-Thurs. 9 and 11:30pm, Fri.-Sat. 9, 11:30pm, and 1:30am.

Village Vanguard, 178 Seventh Ave. (255-4037), south of 11th St. Subway: #1, 2, 3, or 9 to 14th St. A windowless, wedge-shaped cavern, as old and hip as jazz itself. Every Mon. the Vanguard Orchestra unleashes its torrential Big Band sound at 10pm and midnight. Cover Sun.-Thurs. $12 plus $8 min., Fri.-Sat. $15 plus $8 min. Sets Sun.-Thurs. 9:30 and 11:30pm, Fri.-Sat. 9:30, 11:30pm, and 1am.

Clubs

In addition to the venues listed below, check the *Village Voice* for shows at the **Bottom Line** (228-7880), the **Cooler** (229-0785), the **Knitting Factory** (219-3055), and **Wetlands** (966-4225), all fine clubs for live music of all varieties.

CBGB/OMFUG (CBGB's), 313 Bowery (982-4052), at Bleecker St. Subway: #6 to Bleecker St. The initials stand for "country, bluegrass, blues, and other music for uplifting gourmandizers," but everyone knows that since 1976 this club has been all about punk rock. Blondie and the Talking Heads got their starts here, and the club continues to be *the* place to see great alternative rock. Shows nightly at around 8pm, Sun. (often hardcore) matinee at 3pm. Cover $5-10.

Maxwell's, 1039 Washington St. (201-798-4064), in nearby Hoboken, NJ. Subway: B, D, F, N, Q, or R to 34th St., then PATH train ($1), or simply take the PATH train ($1) to the Hoboken stop; walk down Washington to 11th St. High-quality underground rockers from America and abroad have plied their trade in the back room of a Hoboken restaurant for about 15 years. Cover $5-10; shows sometimes sell out, so get tix in advance from Maxwell's or Ticketmaster.

Mercury Lounge, 217 E. Houston St. (260-4700), at Ave. A. Subway: F to 2nd Ave.-E. Houston St. The Mercury has attracted an amazing number of big-name acts to its fairly small-time room, running the gamut from folk to noise to pop. Past standouts have included Lenny Kravitz, Morphine, They Might Be Giants, and Bikini Kill. Music nightly; cover usually $5-15.

Bars

The White Horse Tavern, 567 Hudson St. (243-9260), at W. 11th St. Dylan Thomas drank himself to death here. Boisterous crowd pays a strange and twisted homage to the poet. Beer $4, ½-price during happy hr. Open Sun.-Thurs. 11am-2am, Fri.-Sat. 11am-4am.

The Ear Inn, 326 Spring St. (226-9060), near the Hudson. Established in 1817 and once a big bohemian/activist hangout, this bar now tends to the TriBeCa young-and-wistful crowd. Mellow jazz and blues at low volume so as not to stem the flow of conversation. Appetizers and salads $2-6. Food served from 11am-4:30pm and 6pm-1am. Bar open till 4am.

10th Street Lounge, 212 E. 10th St. (473-5252), between Second and Third Ave. Chic East Village hotspot favored by an artsy young crowd. Dim red lighting and music ranging from reggae to hip-hop lure them to this inconspicuous, unmarked hole-in-the-wall. Thurs.-Sat. evenings have a $10 cover. Open daily until 3am.

The Shark Bar, 307 Amsterdam Ave. (496-6600), at 75th. Classy and enjoyable bar and soul-food restaurant. After-work crowd nurses stiff drinks. Live jazz Tues. with a $5 cover; "gospel brunch" Sat. 12:30 and 2pm (no cover). Beer from $3. Open Mon.-Wed. 5:30pm-midnight, Thurs.-Sat. 5:30pm-1am, Sun. 5:30-11pm.

Max Fish, 178 Ludlow St. (529-3959), at Houston St. in the Lower East Side. The crowd is hip, if a bit pretentious, and the all-CD jukebox is easily the best in town: The Fall, The Minutemen, and Superchunk. Beer $2.50. Open daily 5:30pm-4am.

Polly Esther's, 21 E. 8th St. (979-1970), near University Pl. Grab those bell bottoms and platform shoes—it's a bar dedicated to the 1970s! Beer $3. Two-for-one happy hour 1-9pm on weekdays and 1-7pm on weekends. Open Mon.-Fri. 11am-2am, Sat.-Sun. 11am-4am. Another location at 249 W. 26th St. (929-4782).

McSorley's Old Ale House, 15 E. 7th St. (473-9148), at Third Ave. One of the oldest bars in the city, McSorley's has hosted Abe Lincoln, the Roosevelts, and John Kennedy since it opened in 1854. Great selection of beers. Open Mon.-Sat. 11am-1am, Sun. 1pm-1am.

The Westend Gate, 2911 Broadway (662-8830), between 113th and 114th St. Subway: #1 or 9 to 116th St. Once frequented by Kerouac, now a hangout for the Columbia set. Small dance room with rock and funk bands in the back—bands every Fri.-Sat. night (cover $5 and up). Cheap pitchers with a great beer selection. Food served until 11pm. Open daily 11:30am-2am.

Dance Clubs

Tunnel, 220 Twelfth Ave. (695-7292), near 28th St. Subway: C or E to 23rd St. Immense club; 3 floors packed with 2 dance floors, lounges, glass-walled live shows, and a skateboarding cage. Enough room for a multitude of parties in this labyrinthine club. Cover $20. Open Fri.-Sat.; Sat. nights are gay.

Webster Hall, 125 E. 11th St. (353-1600), between Third and Fourth Ave. Subway: #4, 5, 6, N, or R to Union Sq.-14th St. Walk 3 blocks south and a block east. New and popular club offers dancing, a reggae room and a coffee shop. "Psychedelic Thursdays" often feature live bands. Cover $5-15. Open Wed.-Sat. 10pm-4am.

Limelight, 47 W. 20th St. (807-7850), at Sixth Ave. Subway: F or R to 23rd St. Huge club in a converted church. Several rooms for dancing. Big suburban crowd. Men may have trouble getting in without women. Queer Wed. and Fri. nights. Sun. night is live heavy metal. Cover $15, but look for discount fliers everywhere.

Nell's, 246 W. 14th St. (675-1567), between Seventh and Eighth Ave. Subway: #1, 2, 3, or 9 to 14th St. A legendary hotspot; some faithful admirers hang on even through its decline. Dingy neighborhood belies the opulence of the huge Victorian-style sitting room inside. Angular dance floor downstairs. Not a gay club, but a popular gay spot. Cover Mon.-Wed. $7, Thurs.-Sun. $15. Open daily 10pm-4am.

Palladium, 126 E. 14th St. (473-7171), at Third Ave. Subway: #4, 5, 6, L, N, or R to 14th St. Once Madonna and her friends set the pace, now big hair has replaced big crowds. But the music is still good and the space is still cool. Look in Village stores for discount invites. Cover $20. Open Fri.-Sat. 10pm-4am.

Gay and Lesbian Clubs

Clit Club, 432 W. 14th St. (529-3300), at Washington St. This is *the* place to be for young, beautiful, queer grrls. Host Julie throws the hottest party around every Fri. night. Cover $3 before 11pm, $5 after 11pm. Doors open at 9:30pm.

Jackie 60, 432 W. 14th St. (366-5680), at Washington St. Drag queens and sometimes celebrity crowd. Cover $10. Open at 10pm.

Uncle Charlie's, 56 Greenwich Ave. (255-8787), at Perry St. Subway: #1 or 9 to Christopher St. Biggest and best-known gay club in the city. Guppies galore. Women welcome, but few come. Open daily 4pm-4am.

The Pyramid, 101 Ave. A (420-1590), at 6th St. Subway: #6 to Astor Pl. Also known by its street address, this dance club mixes gay, lesbian, and straight folks. Vibrant drag scene. Fri. is straight night. Cover $5-10. Open daily 9pm-4am.

Hipster Hangouts and Must-Sees

Nuyorican Poets Café, 236 E. 3rd St. (505-8183), between Ave. B and Ave. C. Subway: F to Second Ave. Walk 3 blocks north and 3 blocks east. New York's leading venue for the currently in-vogue "poetry slams" and spoken word performances. Cover $5-10.

Collective Unconscious, 28 Ave. B (505-8991), between 2nd and 3rd St. Subway: F to Second Ave. Walk 3 blocks east and 2 blocks north. Plays, rock shows, and other performances (cover usually $5-7). Open-mike night Sun. at 9pm ($3). Ongoing serial play on Sat. at 8pm ($5). Bring your own refreshments.

Blue Man Group-Tubes, 434 Lafayette St. (254-4370), at the Astor Place Theater. Not a hangout, but a hilarious off-Broadway show with a cult following. Definitely worth the ticket price.

Giant Step and **Soul Kitchen,** mobile parties that move from club to club, drawing ardent followers of their funk-jazz-hip-hop hybrid. Check the *Voice* for locations and dates.

Sports

While most cities would be content to field a major-league team in each big-time sport, New York opts for the Noah's Ark approach: two baseball teams, two hockey teams, and two NFL football teams. In addition to local teams' regularly scheduled games, New York hosts a number of celebrated world-class events. Get tickets three months in advance for the prestigious **U. S. Open** (718-760-6200; tickets from $12), held in late August and early September at the USTA Tennis Center in Flushing Meadows, Queens. On the third Sunday in October, two million spectators witness the 22,000 runners of the **New York City Marathon** (only 16,000 finish). The race begins on the Verrazzano Bridge and ends at Central Park's Tavern on the Green.

On the **baseball** diamond, the **New York Mets** bat at **Shea Stadium** in Queens (718-507-8499; tickets $6.50-15). The legendary but mortal **New York Yankees** play ball at Yankee Stadium in the Bronx (293-6000; tickets $6.50-17). Both the **New York Giants** and the **Jets** play **football** across the river at **Giants Stadium** (201-935-3900) in East Rutherford, NJ. Tickets start at $25. The **New York Knickerbockers** (that's the Knicks to you) dribble the **basketball** at **Madison Square Garden** (465-6751, 751-6130 off season; tickets from $12). The **New York Rangers** play **hockey** at **Madison Square Garden** (465-6741 or 308-6977); the **New York Islanders** hang their skates at the **Nassau Coliseum** (516-794-9300), Uniondale, Long Island. Tickets begin at $12 and $14, respectively.

■■■ LONG ISLAND

For some, Long Island evokes images of sprawling suburbia dotted with malls and office parks; others see it as the retreat for privileged New Yorkers, a summer refuge of white sand and open spaces. Yet between the malls and beaches lie both vital cultural centers and pockets of poverty. Although the New York City boroughs of Brooklyn and Queens are technically part of the island, practically speaking, Nassau and Suffolk Counties constitute the real Long Island. East of the Queens-Nassau line, people back the Islanders, not the Rangers, and they enjoy their role as neighbor to the great metropolis. The Hamptons, on the South Fork, are mainly ritzy summer homes. The North Fork is home to many farms. Besides great beaches, Long Island offers good camping just outside the City. The Long Island Expressway (LIE, officially State Highway 495), stretches 73 exits over 85 mi. from Manhattan to Riverhead. Traffic jams are seemingly incessant on the expressway during rush hour (which basically lasts from 7am-midnight). Many Islanders commute to the city by train, but the sights of Long Island are most easily accessible by car.

PRACTICAL INFORMATION

Get Long Island info at the **Long Island Convention and Visitors Bureau** (794-4222), which operates a visitors booth on the LIE South between Exits 51 and 52 in Commack, and on the Southern State Pkwy. between exits 13 and 14. The Island's main public transportation, **Long Island Railroad (LIRR)** (822-5477), has five central lines. Depending on how far you want to go, peak fares range from $4.25 to 14, and off-peak fares range from $3 to 9.50. Call for connection directions from NYC subways. Daytime bus service is provided by **Long Island Bus** in Queens, Nassau, and western Suffolk (542-0100, bus information 766-6722). The routes are complex and irregular—make sure you confirm your destination with the driver. (Fare $1.50, crossing into Queens an additional 50¢, transfers 25¢. Disabled travelers and senior citizens pay ½-fare.) The S-92 bus of **Suffolk Transit** (852-5200) loops back and forth between the tips of the north and south forks, with nine runs daily, most of them between East Hampton and Orient Point. Call to confirm stops and schedules. (Open Mon.-Fri. 8am-4:30pm.) The route also connects with the LIRR at Riverhead, where the forks meet. (No service Sun. Fare $1.50, transfers 25¢, senior and the disabled 50¢, under 5 free.) **Hampton Express** (212-861-6800, on Long Island 286-4600) runs to and through the South Fork, while **Sunrise Express** (800-527-7709, in Suffolk 477-1200) covers the North Fork. Long Island's **area code:** 516.

ACCOMMODATIONS AND CAMPING

Finding a place to stay on the island can be daunting. Daytrippers in Nassau would do best to return to the city. Suffolk County provides a wider variety of mostly touristy accommodations. In Montauk, sleep at **Montauket,** Tuthill Rd. (668-5992). Follow the Montauk Hwy. to Montauk; at the traffic circle take Edgemere, then left onto Fleming, then another left. Make reservations for summer weekends starting March 1—it fills up quickly. (Doubles $35, with private bath $40.) For **camping,** dig your trenches at **Battle Row** (572-8690), in Bethpage, Nassau. Eight tent sites, and 50 trailer sites are available on first come, first served basis. Electricity, restrooms, showers, grills, and a playground available. (Tent sites $8.50, trailer sites $15.) Also try **Heckscher Park** (581-4433 or 800-456-2267), in East Islip, Suffolk. Take LIE exit 53 and go south on the Sagtikos State Pkwy. Follow signs onto the Southern State Pkwy. east, and follow this as it turns south and becomes the Heckscher Spur Pkwy. The Park is at the end of the Pkwy. The state-run facility has 69 tent and trailer sites, restrooms, showers, food, grills, a pool, and a beach. ($12.50 for the first night and $11 per additional night. Make reservations at least 7 days in advance. Open May-Sept.) **Wildwood Park** (929-4314 or 800-456-2267), at Wading River. LIE exit 68 and go north onto Rte. 46 (Wm. Floyd Pkwy.). Follow it to its end and go right (east) on Rte. 25A. Follow the signs from there. The former estate of Charles and John Arbuckle, multi-millionaire coffee dealers, has 300 tent sites and 80 trailer sites with full hook-ups, restrooms, showers, food, and a beach. (Sites $11.50 first night and $10 each additional night; sites with a concrete platform $12.50/11. Reservations urged for summer weekends and must be made at least a week in advance). **A Reasonable Alternative, Inc.** (928-4034), offers rooms in private homes all along the shores of Nassau and Suffolk (singles or doubles $50-100).

SIGHTS

Nassau At **Old Westbury Gardens** (333-0048), on Old Westbury Rd., nature overwhelms architecture. The elegant house, modeled after 19th-century English country manors, sits in the shadow of its surroundings of gardens and tall evergreens. A vast rose garden adjoins a number of stunning theme gardens. (Open Wed.-Mon. 10am-5pm. House and garden $10, seniors $7, children $6. Take LIE to Exit 39S (Glen Cove Rd.), turn right on Old Westbury Rd., and continue ¼ mi.)

Jones Beach State Park (785-1600) is the best compromise between convenience and crowd for city daytrippers. There are nearly 2500 acres of beachfront here and the parking area accommodates 23,000 cars. Only 40 minutes from the city, Jones Beach packs in the crowds during the summer months. Along the 1½-mi. boardwalk you can find deck games, roller-skating, miniature golf, basketball, and nightly dancing. The **Marine Theater** in the park hosts big-name rock concerts. There are eight different bathing areas on the rough Atlantic Ocean and the calmer Zach's Bay, plus a number of beaches restricted to residents of certain towns in Nassau County. In the summer take the LIRR to Freeport or Wantaugh, where you can get a bus to the beach. Call 212-739-4200 or 212-526-0900 for information. **Recreation Lines** (718-788-8000) provides bus service straight from mid-Manhattan. If you are driving, take the LIE east to the Northern State Pkwy., go east to the Meadowbrook (or Wantaugh) Pkwy., and then south to Jones Beach.

Suffolk The peaceful villages of Suffolk County, only a few hours's drive from Manhattan, are New York's version of the tradition-steeped towns of New England. Many of Suffolk's colonial roots have been successfully preserved, and the county offers some fine colonial house-museums. Salty old towns, full of shady streets—refreshing retreats from the din of New York—line the lazy coast.

After shopping at the **Walt Whitman Mall,** the nearby **Walt Whitman's Birthplace,** 246 Old Walt Whitman Rd. (427-5240), will seem a more appropriate memorial to the great American poet. (Open Wed.-Fri. 1-4pm, Sat.-Sun. 10am-4pm. Free. Take LIE to Exit 49N, drive 1¾ mi. on Rte. 110, and left on Old Walt Whitman Rd.)

Fire Island A 32-mi.-long barrier island buffering the South Shore from the roaring waters of the Atlantic, Fire Island has both summer communities and federally protected wilderness. Cars are allowed only on the easternmost and westernmost tips of the island; there are no streets, only "walks." Fire Island was a hip counterculture spot during the 60s and still maintains a laid-back atmosphere. The **Fire Island National Seashore** (289-4810 for the headquarters in Patchogue) is the main draw here, and in summer it offers fishing, clamming, and guided nature walks. The facilities at **Sailor's Haven** (just west of the Cherry Grove community) include a marina, a nature trail, and a famous beach. Similar facilities at **Watch Hill** (597-6455) include a 20-unit **campground,** where reservations are required. **Smith Point West,** on the eastern tip of the island, has a small visitor information center and a nature trail with disabled access (281-3010; center open daily 9am-5pm). Here you can spot horseshoe crabs, whitetail deer, and monarch butterflies, which flit across the country every year to winter in Baja California. **Wilderness camping** is available near Smith Point West on Fire Island. Camping is free but requires a hike of about 1½ mi. to get into the camping area. You must pick up a permit from Smith Point Visitors Center (281-3010; open daily 9am-5pm) on the day you go down. To get to Smith Point, take exit 68, head south, and follow the signs.

The **Sunken Forest,** so called because of its location down behind the dunes, is another of the Island's natural wonders. Located directly west of Sailor's Haven, its soils support an unusual and attractive combination of gnarled holly, sassafras, and poison ivy. From the summit of the dunes, you can see the forest's trees laced together in a hulky, uninterrupted mesh.

To get to Fire Island from **Bay Shore** (665-3600), ferries sail to Fair Harbor, Ocean Beach, Ocean Bay Park, Saltaire, and Kismet (round-trip fare $10.50, children under 12 $5). From **Sayville** (589-8980), ferries leave for Sailor's Haven (round-trip fare $8, children under 12 $4.50) and Cherry Grove and Fire Island Pines (round-trip fare for either $10, children under 12 $5). From **Patchogue** (475-1665), ferries go to Davis Park and Watch Hill (round-trip to either $10, children under 12 $5.50). LIRR stations lie within a short distance of the three ferry terminals, making access from New York City relatively simple. (All ferries May-Nov.)

Wine Country Long Island does not readily conjure up images of plump winegrapes just waiting to be plucked by epicurean Islanders. But a visit to one of the North Fork's 40 vineyards can be a pleasant and interesting surprise. The wineries and vineyards here produce the best Chardonnay, Cabernet Sauvignon, Merlot, Pinot Noir, and Riesling in New York State. Many of the Island wineries offer free tours and tastings. To get to there, take the LIE to Exit 73, then Rte. 58, which becomes Rte. 25 (Main Rd.). North of and parallel to Rte. 25, Rte. 48 (North Rd. or Middle Rd.), claims a number of wineries. Road signs announce tours and tastings. Of note is **Palmer Vineyards,** 108 Sound Ave. (722-9463), in Riverhead. Take a self-guided tour of the most advanced equipment on the Island and see a tasting room with an interior assembled from two 18th-century English pubs.

MID-ATLANTIC

Hamptons Composed of **West, South, Bridge,** and **East Hampton,** this area is famous for its ritzy homes for rich New Yorkers who "summer" and great beaches. Each town offers a quaint Main St. with shops, restaurants, and good people watching in the summer. Historians and sadists should check out the **Southampton Historical Museum** (283-2494), located near the center of town at the corner of Meeting House Ln. and Main St. Start with the pillory, where thieves and those *accused* of adultery were publicly flayed. Or try your neck in the stocks, the clever device used to humiliate (and hurt) the drunkards and disrespectful children. (Open in summer Tues.-Sun. 11am-5pm. $2, ages 6-11 50¢. Take Rte. 27E to Southampton Center.) The **Guild Hall Museum,** 158 Main St. (324-0806), in East Hampton, specializes in well-known artists of the eastern Island region, from the late-19th century to the present. (Open daily 11am-5pm; Sept.-May Wed.-Sun. 11am-5pm. $2.) The East Hampton beach is known as being one of the most beautiful in the world.

East Hampton Bowl, 71 Montauk Hwy. (324-1950), just west of East Hampton, is a spot for nightlife: the bowling alley and attached bar stay open until at least midnight every night, and Saturday nights feature "Rock-'n'-Bowl." (Bowling $3.40 per game; shoe rental $2.)

Sag Harbor Out on the South Fork's north shore droops Sag Harbor, one of the best-kept secrets of Long Island. Founded in 1707, this port used to be more important than New York Harbor since its deep shore made for easy navigation. The legacy of Sag Harbor's former grandeur survives in the second-largest collection of Colonial buildings in the U.S., and in the cemeteries lined with the gravestones of Revolutionary soldiers and sailors. Check out the **Sag Harbor Whaling Museum** (725-0770). Enter the museum through the jawbones of a whale. Note the antique 1864 washing-machine and the excellent scrimshaw collection. (Open May-Sept. Mon.-Sat. 10am-5pm, Sun. 1-5pm. $3, children $1. Call for tours.)

Montauk At the easternmost tip of the South Fork, Montauk is one of the most popular destinations on Long Island. The trip from Manhattan takes four hours by car. Take the LIE to Exit 70 (Manorville), then go south to Sunrise Hwy. (Rte. 27), which becomes Montauk Hwy., and drive east.

The **Montauk Point Lighthouse and Museum** (668-2544) is the high point of a trip here. The 86-ft. structure went up by special order of President George Washington. On a clear day, you should climb the 138 spiralling steps to the top, where you can see across the Long Island Sound to Connecticut and Rhode Island. The best seasons for viewing are spring and fall; the thick summer air can haze over the view. But even on a foggy day, you may want to climb up to see if you can spot the *Will o' the Wisp,* a ghostly clipper ship sometimes sighted on hazy days under full sail with a lantern hanging from its mast. Experts claim that the ship is a mirage resulting from the presence of phosphorus in the atmosphere. (Open May-June and Oct.-Nov. Sat.-Sun. 10:30am-4pm; June-Sept. daily 10:30am-6pm; Sept.-Oct. Fri.-Mon. 10:30am-5pm. $2.50, children $1, plus parking $3.)

Try **Viking** (668-5700) or **Lazybones'** (668-5671) for half-day fishing cruises ($20-25). **Okeanos Whale Watch Cruise** (728-4522) offers excellent six-hour trips for spotting fin, minke, and humpback whales ($30 and up).

Shelter Island Shelter Island bobs in the protected body of water between the north and south forks. Accessible by ferry or by private boat, this island of about 12 sq. mi. offers wonderful beaches (locals tend to favor Wades Beach and Hay Beach) and a serene sense of removal from the intrusions of the city. A detailed map of the island is available from most inns and other places of business. **The Belle Crest House,** 163 North Ferry Rd. (749-2041), in Shelter Island Heights just up the hill from the north ferry, is a beautiful old country home with large rooms—a great spot for a romantic getaway. (From May 1-Oct. 31: Mon.-Thurs. doubles $65-70 with shared bath, $95 with private bath; Fri.-Sun. $80 and $165. 2-night min. for summer weekends. Off season rates dip as low as $45.) **North Fork: Greenport Ferry** (749-0139), North Ferry Rd., on the dock, takes passenger and driver for $6.50, round-trip $7, each additional passenger $1, walk-on (without a car) $1. Ferries run daily every 15 minutes, with the first ferry leaving Greenport at 6am and the last ferry departing the island at 11:45pm. **South Fork: North Haven Ferry** (749-1200), 3 mi. north of Sag Harbor on Rte. 114, on the dock, takes car and driver for $6 one-way, $6.50 round-trip, additional passengers $1 each, walk-ons $1 round-trip. Ferries run daily at approximately 10 minute intervals from 6am to 1:45am.

■■■ CATSKILLS

When Rip Van Winkle chose a napping place, he couldn't have found a more peaceful spot than the Catskill Mountains. Captivating city folk even before they were celebrated in Washington Irving's short stories, these lovely mountains are home to quiet villages, sparkling streams, and miles of hiking and skiing trails, all of which can be found in the state-managed Catskill Preserve. Those who prefer rock-and-roll to rocks and trees can visit the site of Woodstock, the concert that rocked the nation and cast a purple haze on this region in 1969.

Practical Information **Adirondack Pine Hill Trailways** provides excellent service through the Catskills. The main stop is in **Kingston,** at 400 Washington Ave. on the corner of Front St. (914-331-0744 or 800-858-8555). Buses run to New York City (11 per day, 2 hr., $18.50; same-day round-trip $25 or $35, depending on day). Other stops in the area include Woodstock, Pine Hill, Saugerties, and Hunter; each connects with New York City, Albany, and Utica. (Ticket office open Mon.-Fri. 5:30am-11pm; Sat.-Sun. 6:30am-11pm.) The **Ulster County Public Information Office,** 244 Fair St., 5th Floor (914-331-9300, ext. 436 or 800-342-5826), six blocks from Kingston bus station, has a helpful travel guide and a list of Catskill hiking trails (open Mon.-Fri. 9am-5pm). Four stationary **tourist cabooses** dispense info at the traffic circle in Kingston, on Rte. 28 in Shandaken, on Rte. 209 in Ellenville, and on Rte. 9W in Milton (open in summer Fri.-Sun; hours vary depending on volunteer availability). Rest stop **visitors centers** along I-87 can advise you on area sights.

■ CATSKILL FOREST PRESERVE

The 250,000-acre **Catskill Forest Preserve** contains many small towns which host travelers looking for outdoor adventure. The required permits for **fishing** (non-NY residents, 5 days $20) are available in any sporting goods store. Ranger stations distribute free permits for **back-country camping** necessary for stays of more than three days. Though trails are maintained year-round, lean-tos are sometimes dilapidated and crowded. Always boil or treat water with chemicals, and remember to pack out your garbage. For more information on fishing, hunting, or environmental issues, call the **Department of Environmental Conservation** (914-256-3000). **Adirondack Trailways** buses from Kingston service most trail heads— drivers will let you out anywhere along secondary bus routes.

Accessible by bus from Kingston, **Phoenicia** is a fine place to anchor a trip to the Catskills. The **Esopus River,** to the west, has great trout fishing, and **The Town Tinker,** 10 Bridge St. (914-688-5553), rents inner-tubes for summertime river-riding. (Inner-tubes $7 per day, with a seat $10. Driver's license or $15 required as a deposit. Transportation $3. Life jackets provided. Open May-Sept. daily 9am-6pm; last rental 4:30pm.) Artifacts from the late-19th-century glory days of the steam engine fill the **Empire State Railway Museum** (914-688-7501), on High St. off Rte. 28; a restored 1910 locomotive will eventually run on the tracks of the former Ulster and Delaware here (open weekends and holidays 10am-6pm). At the 65-ft. **Sundance Rappel Tower** (914-688-5640), Rte. 214, visitors climb up and return to earth the hard way. (4 levels of lessons; beginner, 3-4hr., $20. Lessons only held when a group of 4 is present. Reservations required.)

Take a detour and stop in at the town of **Woodstock,** between Phoenicia and Kingston. Though a haven for artists and writers since the turn of the century, Woodstock is best known for the concert which bore its name, an event which actually took place in nearby Saugerties. Since then, the tie-dyed legacy has faded, and Woodstock has become an expensive, touristy place. When your Woodstock pilgrimage goes bust, soothe your soul and chant your mantra at the **Zen Mountain Monastery,** S. Plank Rd., P.O. Box 197, Mt. Tremper 12457 (914-688-2228), a few mi. from Woodstock off 28N from Mt. Tremper. (Beginning meditation instruction free Wed. 7:30pm, $5 Sun. 9am-1pm; weekend and week-long retreats from $175.)

What is now **Historic Kingston** was once a defensive stockade built by Peter Stuyvesant; stroll down Wall St., Fair St., or North Front St. and defend yourself against the cutesy shops that have taken its place. Live out your childhood firefighting fantasies at the **Volunteer Fireman's Hall and Museum,** 265 Fair St. (914-331-0866; open Apr.-Oct. Fri. 11am-3pm, Sat. 10am-4pm; call for Wed. and Thurs. hours June-Aug.). Head to the **Woodstock Brewing Company,** 20 James St. (914-331-2810), for a taste of beer brewed right in the Hudson Valley. Nat Collins, the owner and brewmaster, will give you a free tour and tasting in his, the state's only, complete microbrewery (tours Sat. 1pm, call for details).

Accommodations and Camping Huddle around the fire and shiver to ghost stories at any of the **state campgrounds.** Reservations (800-456-2267) are vital during the summer, especially Thursdays through Sundays. (Sites $9-12; $1.50 registration fee; phone reservation fee $7; $2 more for partial hook-up. Open May-Sept.) The **Office of Parks** (518-474-0456) distributes brochures on the campgrounds. **North Lake/South Lake** (518-589-5058), Rte. 23A 3 mi. northeast of Haines Falls, rents canoes ($15 per day) and features two lakes, a waterfall, hiking, and 219 campsites ($15, reserve 7 days in advance; day use $5). **Kenneth L. Wilson** (914-679-7020), a 4-mi. hike from the Bearsville bus stop, has well-wooded campsites ($11), showers, a pond-front beach, and a family atmosphere. A bit more primitive, **Woodland Valley** (914-688-7647), 5 mi. southeast of Phoenicia, does have flush toilets and showers, and sits on a good 16-mi. hiking trail (sites $9).

If the thought of sleeping outside in the land of the headless horseman makes your blood run cold, you can take refuge in a giant room with cable TV at the **Super**

8 Motel, 487 Washington Ave. (914-338-3078), in Kingston two blocks from the bus station. (Singles from $49, doubles from $58; senior discounts available. Reserve for summer weekends.) In Phoenicia, the **Cobblestone Motel** (914-688-7871), on Rte. 214, has an outdoor pool and well worn but very clean rooms (singles $44, doubles $50, rooms with kitchenette $55). Countless other motels, motor inns, inns, economy cabins, etc. line Rte. 28 between Kingston and Phoenicia. For a true bargain, follow Rte. 28 off the beaten path to the **Belleayre Hostel** (914-254-4200). Bunks and private rooms, in a rustic setting not far from Phoenicia, all have sinks and radios and access to a kitchen, a picnic area, and sporting equipment. Call ahead for directions. (Bunks in summer $9, in winter $12. Private rooms $20/$25. Efficiency cabins for up to 4 $35/$45.)

■■■ ALBANY

Although the English took Albany in 1664, the city was actually founded in 1614 as a trading post for the Dutch West Indies Company; established six years before the Pilgrims landed on the New England shore, it is the oldest continuous European settlement in the original 13 colonies. Today, Albany, New York's state capital since 1797, is the site of the largest state government in the nation and can justly claim the status of a major northeastern transportation hub. Even so, the city once named Fort Orange has never matched the growth of its southern sibling, the Big Apple, and the quaint multicolored streets, inexplicably named for birds—Dove, Lark, Peacock—make comparing Albany to New York City like trying to compare...oh, never mind.

Practical Information The **Albany Visitors Center,** 25 Quackenbush Sq. (434-5132), at Clinton Ave. and Broadway, runs trolley tours on Thursdays and Fridays July through September ($4, seniors and kids $2) and free guided walking tours on Saturdays June through September; call for times. **Amtrak,** 555 East St. (462-5763 or 800-872-7245), in Rensselaer across the Hudson from downtown Albany, has service to New York City (6-8 per day, 2½hr., $31) and Buffalo (3 per day, 5hr., $71), and offers discounts for advance purchase (open Mon.-Fri. 5:30am-11pm, Sat.-Sun. 6am-midnight). **Greyhound,** 34 Hamilton St. (434-8095 or 800-231-2222), runs buses to Utica (1½hr., $13), Syracuse (3hr., $18), Rochester (4hr., $31), and Buffalo (5hr., $35), with substantial student discounts. *Be careful in this area at night.* (Station open 6am-1am.) Across the street, **Adirondack Trailways,** 360 Broadway (436-9651), connects to other upstate locales: Lake George (3-5 per day, 2hr., $9); Lake Placid (1-2 per day, 4hr., $22); Tupper Lake (1 per day, 4hr., $27). Discounts for students and seniors are available for some routes. (Open daily 5:30am-11pm.) For local travel, the **Capital District Transportation Authority (CDTA)** (482-8822) serves Albany, Troy, and Schenectady (fare $1). The main office gives out info, and schedules are available at the Amtrak and Trailways stations. Albany's **post office:** 30 Old Karner Rd. (452-2499; open Mon.-Fri. 8:30am-6pm, Sat. 9am-2pm); **ZIP code:** 12212. **Area code:** 518.

Accommodations and Food The **College of Saint Rose,** Lima Hall, 366 Western Ave., has large rooms and clean bathrooms in dorms on a safe campus. The dining hall is open for use, and rooms with kitchen facilities are available. (Singles $35, shared doubles $25 per person. For reservations contact Tonita Nagle at Student Affairs, Box 114, 432 Western Ave.; 454-5171, after hours 454-5150. Open May 15-Aug. 15 daily 8:30am-4:30pm.) Spectacular accommodations in a safe neighborhood come with a sizable discount for HI-AYH members at **Pine Haven Bed & Breakfast,** 531 Western Ave. (482-1574). Look for a big Victorian house at the convergence of Madison and Western Ave.; parking is in the rear. (Members $25, $10 each additional; nonmembers singles $49, doubles $64.) Nearby Schenectady (accessible via CDTA) provides a couple of reasonable rooming options. The **YWCA,** 44 Washington Ave. (374-3394), rents single rooms to women only ($20). Men can walk around the corner to the small, sweaty rooms of the **YMCA,** 13 State

St. (374-9139); it's a last resort ($21.50; reservations encouraged). To get to either "Y" from Albany, take bus #55 or drive Rte.5. **Thompson's Lake State Park** (872-1674), on Rte. 157 4 mi. north of East Berne, has the area's closest outdoor living (18mi. southwest of Albany). Expect 140 primitive sites ($10) and some natural perks, including nearby fishing, hiking trails, and a swimming beach.

The hill above downtown Albany is stocked with affordable eats. **Shades of Green,** 185½ Lark St. (434-1830), located in a small nook near Western Ave., serves delicious vegetarian cuisine; wash down your Tempeh Reuben ($4.25) with a cool fruit or vegetable shake ($3; open Mon.-Sat. 11am-6pm). Around the corner at **Torino Café** (434-3540), downtown office workers stain their ties eating Veal Marsala ($7.75) and spaghetti with red or white clam sauce ($6.75; open daily 8am-9pm or later, by the whim of the owner). Students and other locals foment pacifist revolution while slurping *pasta e fagioli* ($5.50) and biting into bagel melts ($3) uptown at **Mother Earth's Café,** 217 Western Ave. (434-0944), at Quail St.; live music, poetry readings, and plays provide radical entertainment every night (open daily 11am-11pm; no cover). To cruise for more restaurants, walk along Lark St. While you're there, surprise and delight Mom with an "I love Let's Go" **tattoo** from **Irezumi, Ink,** 274 Lark St. (432-1905; open daily 11am-11pm).

Sights Albany offers about a day's worth of sight-seeing activity. The **Rockefeller Empire State Plaza,** on State St., is a $1.9 billion towering, modernist Stonehenge. It houses state offices and any sort of store or service one might want, including a **bus terminal,** a **post office,** cleaners, a cafeteria, and the **New York State Museum** (474-5877). In addition to exhibits on state history, the museum displays an original set for "Sesame Street" (open Wed.-Mon. 10am-5pm; $2 suggested donation). Hanging throughout the Plaza concourse, across from the museum, the **Empire State Collection** features works by innovative New York School artists such as Jackson Pollock, Mark Rothko, and David Smith (concourse level open daily 6am-11pm; tours by appointment; free). Don't be alarmed by the huge flying saucer at one end of the Plaza; it's just the **Empire Center for the Performing Arts** (473-1845), a venue for theater, dance, and tasty concerts (box office open Mon.-Fri. 10am-5pm, Sat. noon-3pm). For a bird's-eye view of Albany, visit the observation deck on the 42nd floor of the **Corning Tower** (open Mon.-Fri. 9am-4pm).

The architectural landscape of the rest of the city is more traditional. Within walking distance of the Plaza, on Washington Ave., you'll find **City Hall,** 24 Eagle St. (434-5100; open Mon.-Fri. 8am-5pm, Wed. until 8pm; free tours by appointment), and the gothic **Capitol Building** (474-2418; free tours on the hr. Mon.-Fri. 9am-4pm, Sat.-Sun. 10am-4pm); architect H.H. Richardson designed both. George Washington and Benjamin Franklin dined with colonial statesman Philip Schuyler at the elegant **Schuyler (SKY-ler) Mansion,** 32 Catherine St. (434-0834; open April-Oct. Wed.-Sun. 10am-5pm; free, although admission may be charged soon). Founded in 1642 and rebuilt in 1798, the **First Church in Albany** (463-4449), at Orange and N. Pearl St., houses the oldest known pulpit and weather vane in America (open Mon.-Fri. 8:30am-3:30pm).

Bounded by State St. and Madison Ave. north of downtown, **Washington Park** has tennis courts, paddle boats, and plenty of room for celebrations and performances. In early May, music, dancing, food, and street-scrubbing accompany a colorful show of Albany's Dutch heritage during the **Tulip Festival** (434-2032). The **Park Playhouse** (434-2035) stages free musical theater in the park from July to mid-August. On Thursdays during the summer, come **Alive at Five** (434-2032) with the sound of free concerts at the **Tercentennial Plaza,** across from Fleet Bank on Broadway. For a list of events, call the **Albany Alive Line** (434-1217, ext. 409).

Home to the **Albany Roverats** and **Firebirds, Knickerbocker Arena,** 51 South Pearl St. (487-2000), also hosts large musical shows and sporting events (call Ticketmaster at 476-1000 for info on events). Bikers should check out the **Mohawk-Hudson Bikeway,** which passes along old railroad grades and canal towpaths as it weaves through the capital area (maps available at the visitors center).

■■■ COOPERSTOWN

To an earlier generation, Cooperstown evoked images of James Fenimore Cooper's frontiersman hero, Leatherstocking, who roamed the woods around the gleaming waters of Lake Otsego. Today, Cooperstown recalls a different source of American legend—baseball. Tourists file in every summer to visit the Baseball Hall of Fame, buy baseball memorabilia, eat in baseball-theme restaurants, and sleep in baseball-theme motels. Fortunately for the tepid fan, baseball's mecca is surrounded by rural beauty and some of New York state's best (non-baseball) rural tourist attractions.

Practical Information Cooperstown is accessible from I-90 and I-88 via Rte. 28. Street parking is rare in Cooperstown; your best bets are the three free parking lots just outside of town: near the Fenimore House, on Rte. 28 south of Cooperstown, and on Glen Ave. at Maple St. Take a **trolley** into town from any of these lots (runs July-Sept. daily 8:30am-9pm; weekends only Memorial Day-June and Labor Day-Columbus Day; all-day pass $1.50). **Adirondack Trailways** (800-225-6815) picks up at Chestnut and Elm St. for two trips per day to New York City (6 hr., $40). The **Cooperstown Area Chamber of Commerce,** 31 Chestnut St. (547-9983), on Rte. 80 near Main St., has maps, brochures, and accommodation listings and can make reservations (open Mon.-Sat. 10am-4:45pm). Cooperstown's **post office:** 40 Main St. (547-2311; open Mon.-Fri. 8:30am-5pm, Sat. 9:30am-1pm); **ZIP code:** 13326. **Area code:** 607.

Accommodations and Food The Chamber of Commerce will help out, but summertime lodging in Cooperstown seems to require the salary of a Major Leaguer (or the salary of a manager); fortunately, there are alternatives to endless negotiation. If it's not full, try **Lindsay House,** 56 Chestnut St. (547-5618), a B&B near the center of town. As long as he lives, proprietor and bluegrass guitar picker Doug Lindsay vows he will provide a haven for the budget traveler (rooms from $25). Otherwise, camping will help you avoid Chapter 11. **Glimmerglass State Park,** RD2 Box 580, 8 mi. north of Cooperstown on Rte. 31 (a.k.a. Main St. in Cooperstown) on the east side of Lake Otsego, has 35 pristine campsites in a gorgeous lakeside park. Swimming, fishing, and boating reward daytime visitors from 11am-7pm. (Sites $11.50; showers, dumping station, handicapped access; no hookups. Register Sun.-Wed. 8am-9pm, Thurs.-Sat. 8am-11pm. Call 547-8662 or 800-456-2267 for reservations and a heinous $7 service charge.) **Shadowbrook,** RD2 Box 646, Cooperstown (264-8431), 10 mi. north on Rte. 31, offers reasonable sites, a safe atmosphere, a pool, and a pond. (Sites $19, electricity and water $22; showers and laundry facilities. Office open daily 9am-9pm; make reservations for summer weekends.) **KOA,** P.O. Box 786, Cooperstown (315-858-0236 or 800-562-3402), 20 minutes from Cooperstown on Rte. 20, accommodates families with kids' facilities, a pool, and nighttime entertainment. (Sites $18, hookup $25, cabins $35. Office open Mon.-Fri. 8am-8pm, Sat.-Sun. 8am-9pm; nighttime registration possible. Fills up in summer.)

For hearty grub, sidle into **Black Bart's BBQ,** 64 Main St. (547-5656), across from the Baseball Hall of Fame, a bad-ass Tex-Mex restaurant whose burritos ($5.50), BBQ (half-chicken $7), and hydroponically grown greens "ain't for sissies." (Open Wed.-Thurs. and Sun. 11am-3pm, Fri. 11am-8pm, Sat. 11am-9pm; soon to have Mon. and Tues. hours.) A Cooperstown institution, **Schneider's Bakery,** 157 Main St. (547-9631), has been serving locals since 1887; try the delicious "old-fashioneds," donuts which are less sweet and greasy than their conventional cousins (38¢), or the equally spectacular onion rolls (25¢; open Mon.-Sat. 6:30am-5:30pm).

Take me out to the **National Baseball Hall of Fame and Museum** (547-7200) on Main St., an enormous monument to America's favorite pastime. In addition to memorabilia from the immortals—including the bat with which Babe Ruth hit his famous "called shot" home run in the 1932 World Series—the museum displays a moving multimedia tribute to the sport and a history that traces baseball's roots back to ancient Egyptian religious ceremonies (sure). The annual ceremonies for new inductees are held in **Cooper Park,** next to the building (July or Aug.; call ahead). There are special exhibits for hearing- and visually impaired fans. (Open daily 9am-9pm; Oct.-April 9am-5pm. $9.50, ages 7-15 $4, under 7 free.)

Aficionados of American culture should also see the **Corvette Americana Hall of Fame** (547-4135), on Rte. 28 4½ mi. south of Cooperstown—probably the only place you'll ever see two 1963 Corvettes framed by a backdrop depicting the Lost Continent of Atlantis. The museum features 'Vettes through the years, including the car used in the movie *Death Race 2000.* Simply the coolest. (Open July-Labor Day Mon.-Sat. 10am-9pm, Sun 10am-6pm; day after Labor Day-June daily 10am-6pm. $8.95, seniors and kids discounted, under 9 free.)

■■■ ITHACA AND FINGER LAKES

According to Iroquois legend, the Great Spirit laid his hand upon the earth, and the impression of his fingers made the Finger Lakes: Canandaigua, Keuka, Seneca, Cayuga, Owasco, and Skaneateles, among others. Others credit the glaciers of the last Ice Age for these formations. Regardless of their origins, the results are spectacular; visitors can stand beneath waterfalls in Ithaca's gorgeous gorges or gorge themselves on another of nature's divine liquids—the rich wine of the Finger Lakes Region's acclaimed vineyards.

PRACTICAL INFORMATION

The **Ithaca/Tompkins County Convention and Visitors Bureau,** 904 E. Shore Dr., Ithaca 14850 (272-1313 or 800-284-8422), has the best map of the area ($3.50), complete hotel and B&B listings, and a zillion brochures on upstate New York. (Open daily 9am-6pm; Labor Day to mid-Oct. 9am-5pm; mid-Oct. to Memorial Day Mon.-Fri. 9am-5pm.) Get a copy of the *Finger Lakes Travel Guide* from **The Finger Lakes Association,** 309 Lake St., Penn Yan 14527 (315-536-7488 or 800-548-4386). **Ithaca Bus Terminal** (272-7930; open Mon.-Sat 7am-6pm, Sun. noon-5pm), W. State and N. Fulton St., houses **Short Line** and **Greyhound** (800-231-2222), with service to New York City (8 per day, $33), Philadelphia (3 per day, $46), and Buffalo (3 per day, $17-20). **Tomtran (Tompkins County Transportation Services Project)** (277-7433) is your only choice for getting out to the Finger Lakes without wheels, with coverage of Trumansburg (northwest of Ithaca on Rte. 96) and Lansing Village (north of Ithaca on Rte. 13). Buses stop at Ithaca Commons, westbound on Seneca St. and eastbound on Green. (60¢, more distant zones $1.25. Buses run Mon.-Fri.) Rent a bike from **Pedal Away,** 700 W. Buffalo St. (272-5425), ¼ mi. from the commons ($20 per day; open Mon.-Fri. 10am-8pm, Sat. 10am-5pm, Sun. 11am-4pm). **Emergency:** 911. Ithaca's **post office:** 213 N. Tioga St. (272-5455), at E. Buffalo (open Mon.-Fri. 8:30am-5pm, Sat. 8:30am-1pm); **ZIP code:** 14850; **area code:** 607.

ACCOMMODATIONS AND CAMPING

Podunk House Hostel (387-9277), on Podunk Rd. in Trumansburg about 8mi. northwest of Ithaca. Take Rte. 96 north, turn left on Cold Springs Rd., and proceed until it ends at Podunk Rd.; or take Tomtran Mon.-Fri. Venture into the land of Oz, the friendly hostel-owner. Finnish sauna fired up periodically; if you miss it, the serenity of this 30-acre farm will relax your body. Chilly mountain creek and hiking trails accessible. 9 beds in the loft of a homestead barn. No kitchen; refrigerator and hot plate only. $6; linen $1.50. Call ahead 7am-9pm. Open April-Oct.

The Wonderland Motel, 654 Elmira Rd. (272-5252). Follow the talking white rabbit saying "I'm late! I'm late! For a very important date!" down Rte. 13 south. Outdoor pool, A/C, HBO, free coffee & danish breakfast and local calls. Family atmosphere. Singles from $36, doubles from $45; in winter $30/$36.

Elmshade Guest House, 402 S. Albany St. (273-1707), at Center St. 3 blocks from the Ithaca Commons. From the bus station, walk up State St. and turn right onto Albany St. Impeccably clean, well-decorated, good-sized rooms with shared bath.

You'll feel like a guest at a rich relative's house. Cable TV in every room, refrigerator, microwave in hall. Singles from $25, doubles $50. Morning coffee, rolls, and fruit included. Reservations recommended.

Three of the nearby state parks which offer camping are **Robert H. Treman** (273-3440), on Rte. 327 off Rte. 13, **Buttermilk Falls** (273-5761), and **Tanghennoch Falls** (387-6739), north on Rte. 89. (Sites $10-12; $1.50 walk-on fee or $7 reservation fee by calling 800-456-2267. Cabins $94 per week.) The brochure *Finger Lakes State Parks* describes the location and services of all area state parks; pick it up from any tourist office or park, or contact the **Finger Lakes State Park Region,** 2221 Taughannock Park Rd., P.O. Box 1055, Trumansburg 14886 (387-7041). Whatever your plans, reserve ahead; summer weekends often fill up.

FOOD AND NIGHTLIFE

Restaurants in Ithaca cluster along Aurora St. and in Ithaca Commons and Collegetown. The *Ithaca Dining Guide* pamphlet from the Tompkins County Visitors Center (see above) lists more options.

Moosewood Restaurant, 210 N. Cayuga (273-9610), at Seneca St. The legendary vegetarian collective and home of the *Moosewood Cookbook.* Long-time veggies genuflect before Moosewood's ever-changing menu of yummy meals. Lunch $5; dinner $9-11. Open in summer Mon.-Sat. 11:30am-4pm and 6-9pm, Sun. 6-9pm; off season Mon.-Thurs. 11:30am-4pm and 5:30-8pm, Fri.-Sat. 11:30am-4pm and 5:30-9pm, Sun. 5:30-8pm. No reservations.

Joe's Restaurant, 602 W. Buffalo St. (273-2693), at Rte. 13 (Meadow St.), a 10-min. walk from Ithaca Commons. This is a *big* student spot. Original Art Deco interior dates from 1932. Italian and American entrees ($7-15) come with Joe's much beloved bottomless salad. Open daily 4-10pm.

Just a Taste, 116 N. Aurora (277-9463), near Ithaca Commons. Taste an extensive selection of fine wines (2½oz. $1.75-3.75), 80 beers, and tempting *tapas,* Spanish "little dishes" ($2.50-5.25). Individual pizzas from $3.50. Entrees $9-12. Open Mon.-Sun. 11:30am-3:30pm, Sun.-Thurs. 5:30-10pm, Fri.-Sat. 5:30-11pm.

Rongovian Embassy to the USA ("The Rongo") (387-3334), on Rte. 96 on the main strip in Trumansburg about 10mi. from Ithaca; worth the drive. Seek asylum in amazing Mexican entrees at this classic restaurant/bar, and plot a trip to "Beefree," "Nearvarna," or "Freelonch" on their huge wall map. Dinners $8-12; try the *Pescado Verde.* Tacos $2.75. Mug of beer $1.50. Open Tues.-Thurs. and Sun. 5-9pm, Fri.-Sat. 5-10pm; bar open Tues.-Sun. 4pm-1am. Bands Wed.-Sat.; cover $5.

Station Restaurant, 806 W. Buffalo (272-2609), in a plushly renovated train station, registered as a National Historical Landmark. Pasta, poultry, and seafood specials $9-14. Open Mon.-Sat. 4-9:30pm, Sun. noon-8:30pm.

The area near Cornell called **Collegetown,** centering on College Ave., harbors student hangouts and access to a romantic path along the gorge. Maintain your Bohemian cachet in smoky, red-walled **Stella's,** 403 College Ave. (277-8731), one café that wears its pretension well. Try your Italian soda ($1.65) with heavy cream. (Open daily 7:30am-1:30am.) Skulk down to **The Haunt,** 114 W. Green St. (273-3355), for live bands, an infamous Saturday night 80s dance party, and 75¢ pint specials Mondays and Tuesdays during the summer (admits ages 18+).

SIGHTS AND ENTERTAINMENT

Ithaca **Cornell University,** youngest of the Ivy League schools, sits on a *steep* hill in downtown Ithaca. Stop by the **Information and Referral Center** in the Day Hall Lobby for info on campus sights and activities (254-4636; open Mon.-Sat. 8am-5pm). The strangely pleasing cement edifice rising from the top of the hill houses Cornell's **Herbert F. Johnson Museum of Art** (255-6464), at the corner of University and Central. The small, intense collection of European and American painting and sculpture includes works by Giacommetti, Matisse, O'Keeffe, deKooning, and Thomas

Hart Benton; the rooftop sculpture garden has a magnificent view of Ithaca. (Open Tues.-Sun. 10am-5pm; free; wheelchair accessible.) **Ithaca College** (274-3011 for campus info), located on South Hill, also offers more campus-style entertainment.

Discriminating moviegoers should head to the **Cornell Cinema,** 104 Willard Straight Hall (255-3522), at the College; its programming and prices will thrill even the most jaded art-house movie junkie (tickets $4.50). The **State Theatre,** 109 W. State St. (273-1037 or 274-2781), hosts concerts and movies in a vintage 1926 faux Spanish castle/movie palace. The architect, legend has it, went insane shortly after the completion of its construction. (Movies Mon.-Fri. 1-10:30pm, Sat.-Sun. 2-10:30pm; $6, seniors and children $4. Concerts $10-20.)

Finger Lakes The fertile soil of the Finger Lakes area has made this region the heart of New York's wine industry. The three designated **wine trails** provide opportunites for wine tasting and vineyard touring; locals say that the fall harvest is the best time to visit. All of the area's vineyards and eight wineries lie on the **Cayuga Trail,** located along Rte. 89 between Seneca Falls and Trumansburg; call the Ithaca/Tomkins County Convention and Visitors Bureau for details (see Practical Information above). For information on the **Seneca Trail,** 14 wineries split into those on the east side of the lake (Rte. 414) and those on the west side (Rte. 14), or the **Keuka Trail,** seven wineries along Rte. 54 and Rte. 76, contact The Finger Lakes Association (see Practical Information above). Some wineries offer free picnic facilities, and all conduct free tours and tastings, though several require purchase of a glass ($1.50-2). **Americana Vineyards Winery,** 4367 East Covert Rd., Interlaken (387-6801), ferments 2 mi. from Trumansburg, accessible by Greyhound; if you're driving, take Rte. 96 or 89 north of Trumansburg to E. Covert Rd. A family of four operates this winery from grape-picking to bottle-corking; one of them will give you a personal tour and free tasting. Pick up a bottle for about $5. (Open May-Oct. Mon.-Sat. 10am-5pm, Sun. noon-5pm; April and Nov.-Dec. weekends only.) Held in late August, the annual **Finger Lakes Wine Festival,** P.O. Box 145, Fayette 13065 (869-9962 or 800-747-NOSE/6673), offers wines from over 30 vineyards ($15).

In the Lakes region, a car provides the easiest transportation, but biking and hiking allow for better appreciation of nature. The **Finger Lakes State Park Region** (see Camping above) distributes free maps and advice. Write the **Finger Lakes Trail Conference,** P.O. Box 18048, Rochester 14618 (716-288-7191), for 85¢ maps of the **Finger Lakes Trail,** an east-west footpath from the Catskills to the Allegheny Mountains. The 555-mi. trail and its 260 mi. of branch trails link several state parks, most with camping facilities. In the immediate Ithaca area, **Buttermilk Falls** (273-5761), on Rte. 13, and **Robert H. Treman** (273-3440), on Rte. 327, offer swimming, hiking, and astonishingly beautiful waterfalls (park entrance $4).

Seneca Falls saw the birth of the women's rights movement at the 1848 Seneca Falls Convention. Elizabeth Cady Stanton and Amelia Bloomer, two leading suffragists who lived in the town, organized the meeting of those seeking the vote for women; today, the **Women's Rights National Historical Park** commemorates their efforts. Begin at the **visitors center,** 136 Fall St. (315-568-2991; open daily 9am-5pm). Free talks and walking tours are scheduled June through September; guided tours of the **Elizabeth Cady Stanton House** happen daily year-round (1 per hr. 1-4pm, Oct.-May 2pm only). The **National Women's Hall of Fame,** 76 Fall St. (315-568-8060), commemorates outstanding U.S. women with photographs and biographies (open Mon.-Sat. 9:30am-5pm, Sun. noon-4pm; $3, students and seniors $1.50).

The town of **Corning,** home to the Corning Glass Works, awaits 40 mi. outside Ithaca on Rte. 17W off Rte. 13S. Watch glassworkers blow glass at the **Corning Glass Center,** 151 Centerway (607-974-2000), which chronicles the 3500-year history of glass-making with over 20,000 pieces—sopranos beware! (Open daily 9am-8pm; Sept.-June 9am-5pm. $7, seniors $6, under 18 $5.) The nearby **Rockwell Museum,** 111 Cedar St., Rte. 17 (607-937-5386), shows pieces by Frederick Carder (founder of the Steuben Glass Work) and an excellent collection of American Western art (open Mon.-Sat. 10am-5pm, Sun. noon-5pm; $4, seniors $3.60, youth $2).

■■■ NIAGARA FALLS

One of the seven natural wonders of the world, Niagara Falls also claims the title of one of the world's largest sources of hydro-electric power. Originally, 5½ billion gallons of water tumbled over the falls every hour; now, ¾ of this volume is diverted to supply the United States and Canada with power. Coincidentally, the work by hydro-electricians to regulate water flow has slowed the erosion which was rapidly eating away at the falls. It is believed that the falls now move back at a rate of 1 ft. per decade, down from 6 ft. per year. Admired not only for their beauty, the Falls have attracted thrill-seeking barrel-riders since 1901, when 63-year-old Annie Taylor successfully completed the drop. Modern day adventurers beware—heavy fines are levied for barrel attempts, and as park officials note, "chances for survival are slim."

PRACTICAL INFORMATION

Tourist Office: Niagara Falls Convention and Visitors Bureau, 310 4th St., Niagara Falls, NY 14302 (285-2400 or 800-421-5223; 24-hr. Niagara City Events Line 285-8711). Open daily 9am-5pm. To receive the excellent *Niagara USA* travel guide by mail, call 800-338-7890. An **information center** (284-2000) adjoins the bus station on 4th and Niagara St., a 10-min. walk from the Falls; free 1-hr. parking. Open daily 8am-8pm, mid-Sept. to mid-May daily 9am-5pm. The state runs the **Niagara Reservation State Park Visitors Center** (278-1796), right in front of the Falls' observation deck; the entrance is marked by a garden. Open daily 8am-10pm; Oct.-Dec. 8am-8pm, mid-Nov. to Dec. (during the **Festival of Lights,** see p. 183) 8am-10pm; Dec.-April 8am-6:30pm. **Niagara Falls Canada Visitor and Convention Bureau,** 5433 Victoria Ave., Niagara Falls, Ont. L2E 3L1 (905-356-6061), has info on the Canadian side. Open Mon.-Fri. 8:30am-8pm, Sat.-Sun. 10am-8pm; off season Mon.-Fri. 9am-5pm. **Ontario Travel Information Center,** 5355 Stanley Ave. (905-358-3221), at Rte. 420, provides tourism info for the province.

Trains: Amtrak (285-4224 or 800-872-7245), at 27th St. and Lockport 1 block east of Hyde Park Blvd. Take #52 bus to Falls/Downtown. To: New York City (2-3 per day, $50); Toronto (1 per day, $18). Open Thurs.-Mon. 6:20am-11:30pm, Tues.-Wed. 6:20am-3pm. Closed daily 10:45-11:30am for lunch.

Buses: Niagara Falls Bus Terminal (282-1331), 4th and Niagara St., sells **Greyhound** tickets for use in Buffalo. Open Mon.-Fri. 8am-4pm. To get a bus in Buffalo, take bus #40 from the Niagara Falls bus terminal to the **Buffalo Transportation Center,** 181 Ellicott St. (800-231-2222; 12-17 per day, 1hr., $1.70). To: New York City (9 per day, 8hr., $67); Boston (4 per day, 12hr., $82); Chicago (6 per day, 12hr., $86); Rochester (8 per day, 2hr., $8); and Albany (5 per day, 7hr., $31). Open daily 6:30am-11:45pm.

Public Transportation: Niagara Frontier Metro Transit System, 343 4th St. (285-9319), provides local city transit and free maps of bus routes; schedules available at bus station. Fare $1.25. **ITA Buffalo Shuttle** (800-551-9369) provides service from Niagara Falls info center and major hotels to Buffalo Airport ($15).

Taxis: Rainbow Taxicab, 282-3221. **United Cab,** 285-9331. Both charge $1.50 base fee, $1.50 per additional mi. A taxi from Buffalo Airport to Niagara costs $40.

Emergency: 911.

Post Office: 615 Main St. (285-7561). Open Mon.-Fri. 7:30am-5pm, Sat. 9am-2pm. **ZIP code:** 14302. **Area code:** 716 (NY), 905 (Ontario).

Niagara Falls falls in both the U.S. and Canada; addresses given here are in NY, unless otherwise noted. Visitors approaching Niagara Falls, NY should take U.S. 190 to the Robert Moses Pkwy., or else skirt the tolls (but suffer traffic and commercialism) by taking exit 3 to Rte. 62. In town, Niagara St. is the main east-west artery, ending in the west at Rainbow Bridge, which crosses to Canada (pedestrian crossings 25¢, cars 75¢). Numbered north-south streets increase towards the east. Outside of town, stores, restaurants, and motels line Rte. 62 (Niagara Falls Blvd.). The gorgeous state park which includes Falls Park lies at the west edge of the city. Parking in town is plentiful; most lots near the Falls charge $3; but you can park in an equivalent spot for less on streets bordering the park. The free parking lot on Goat Island fills early.

MID-ATLANTIC

ACCOMMODATIONS AND CAMPING

Niagara Falls International Hostel (HI-C), 4699 Zimmerman Ave., Niagara Falls, Ont. (357-0770). Pleasant brick Tudor building in a nice neighborhood close to the Falls, about 2 blocks from the bus station and VIA Rail. 50 beds; can be cramped when full. Family rooms, laundry facilities, and parking available. Bike rentals $12 per day. Young, friendly managers lead bike trips and hikes along the Niagara gorge. Office open 9-11am and 5-11:30pm; kitchen and lounge open all day. Check-out 11am. CDN$12, nonmembers CDN$16.28. CDN50¢ returned for doing morning chore. Linen CDN$1. Reservations recommended.

Niagara Falls International Hostel (HI-AYH), 1101 Ferry Ave. (282-3700). From bus station, walk east on Niagara St., turn left on Memorial Pkwy.; the hostel is at the corner of Ferry Ave. Walking from the falls, avoid the area on Ferry Ave., between 4th and 5th St., particularly at night. 44 beds, kitchen, TV lounge, limited parking. Owners will shuttle you to airport, train, or bus station on request; rate depends on group size. Bike rentals $10 per day. The daily Sunset Tour runs by the Power Project to Fort Niagara State Park, where the sun sets over Lake Ontario (weather and interest permitting, $4). Family rooms available. Check-in 7:30-9:30am and 4-11pm. Lockout 9:30am-4pm. Curfew 11:30pm; lights out midnight. Required sleep sack $1.50. $13, in winter $11; nonmembers $16/$14. Reservations essential. Closed for Christmas holidays mid-Dec. to early Jan.

Olde Niagara House, 610 4th St. (285-9408). A country B&B just 4 blocks from the falls. Free pickup at the Amtrak or bus station. Rooms come with a delicious, hearty breakfast. Rooms $45-55, in winter $35-45; student singles $25-35/$20-25. Per person rates available, $15.

YMCA, 1317 Portage Rd. (285-8491), a 20-min. walk from the Falls; at night take bus #54 from Main St. 58 beds; 24-hr. check-in. Fee includes use of full YMCA facilities; no laundry. Dorm rooms for men only; singles $25, key deposit $10. Men and women can sleep on mats in the gym, $15.

Four Mile Creek State Park (745-3802), on Robert Moses Pkwy. in the Ft. Niagara Area about 15mi. from downtown, 4mi. east of Youngstown. Affordable camping in sparsely wooded sites ($11) at the edge of Lake Ontario. Hiking and fishing on the premises. Showers. Reserve in advance.

Niagara Glen-View Tent & Trailer Park, 3950 Victoria Ave., Niagara Falls, Ont. (800-263-2570). The closest sites to the Falls, but bare and unwooded; hiking trail across the street. Ice, showers, laundry facilities, and a pool. Shuttle from driveway to the bottom of Clifton Hill every ½hr. during the day. Office open daily 8am-11pm. CDN$24.75, with full hookup CDN$31.25. Open May to mid-Oct.

FOOD

Chomp options are slim here. The flagship restaurants of Niagara's pricey **Little Italy** have seen better days. Fortunately, there are a few other places which aren't over the Falls. One popular spot, **The Press Box Bar,** 324 Niagara St. (284-5447), between 3rd and 4th St., lets patrons leave their mark by adding a dollar bill to the several thousand taped to the wall; every winter the owner takes them down and gives them to a cancer-fighting charity. Monday to Wednesday go for the spaghetti special (99¢, meatballs 25¢ each); otherwise, burgers ($1.75) and the trademark Porterhouse steak ($8.50) are good bets. (Food served Sun.-Thurs. 11am-11pm, Fri.-Sat. 11am-midnight; bar open Mon.-Thurs. 10am-2am, Fri.-Sat. 10am-3am, Sun. noon-2am.) **Sinatra's Sunrise Diner,** 829 Main St. (284-0959), serves genuine diner cuisine just a few blocks from the Falls (2 eggs and toast 99¢, sandwiches $2-4; open Mon.-Thurs. 7am-8pm, Fri.-Sat. 7am-10pm, Sun. 7am-3pm). For a bite on the Canadian side, there's **Simon's Restaurant,** 4116 Bridge St., Niagara Falls, Ont. (356-5310), across from the whirlpool bridge, the oldest restaurant in Niagara Falls. Enjoy big breakfasts with giant homemade muffins (CDN 74¢) or hearty diner dinners. (Open Mon.-Sat. 5:30am-9pm, Sun. 5:30am-3pm.) Farther inland, locals chow on pancakes, hot sandwiches, and full-meal specials (CDN$4-7) at **Basell's Restaurant,** 4880 Victoria Ave., Niagara Falls, Ont. (356-5310; open daily 6am-11pm). Near the Falls and the Clifton Hill area, run home to **Mama Leone Restaurant,** 5705 Victoria

Ave., Niagara Falls, Ont. (357-5220), for award-winning Northern Italian cuisine (CDN$7-10; open daily noon-11pm).

SIGHTS AND ENTERTAINMENT

The natural Canadian-U.S. border at the Niagara River divides the attractions at the Falls. Either side can be seen in an afternoon. As early as the 1870s, gaudy commercialism had overrun the Falls; officials on the American side responded in 1885 by making the immediate vicinity a state reservation park, the nation's first. Thus, though tourist snares abound on both sides, they're less rampant on the American shore. Stick to the official sights and you'll get more for your money.

From late November to early January, Niagara Falls holds the annual **Festival of Lights.** Bright bulbs line the trees and create brilliant, animated, outdoor scenes. The illumination of the falls caps the spectacle. This year, the Canadian festival (800-461-5373) includes Disney performances, a country music night, and a car show. For festival info on the U.S. side, call 800-338-7890.

American Side **Niagara Wonders** (278-1792), a 20-minute movie on the Falls, plays in the info center. (Shows in summer daily on the hr. 10am-8pm; in fall Wed.-Sun. 10am-6pm; in spring daily 10am-6pm. $2, ages 6-12 $1.) The **Maid of the Mist Tour** (284-8897) consists of a 30-minute boat ride to the foot of both Falls; don't bring anything that isn't waterproof. (Tours in summer daily every 15min. 9:15am-8pm; in fall and spring 10am-5pm. $7.75 plus 50¢ elevator fee, ages 6-12 $4.25, under 6 free.) The **Viewmobile** (278-1730), an open-sided people transporter, does a guided tour of the park, including stops at Goat Island, the brink of the falls, the visitors center, Schoellkopf's Museum, and the Aquarium. (Tours in summer daily every 15min. 10am-8pm, in winter 10am-6:30pm. $3.50, children $2.50.) The Viewmobile will drop off passengers on Goat Island for the **Caves of the Wind Tour,** which outfits visitors with yellow raincoats for a thrilling body-soaking ride to the base of the Bridal Veil Falls. Adventurous souls can climb to the Hurricane Deck to test their nerve. **Schoellkopf's Geological Museum** (278-1780), in Prospect Park, depicts the birth of the Falls with slide shows every ½ hour. (Open daily 9:30am-7pm; Labor Day-Oct. 10am-5pm; Nov.-Memorial Day Thurs.-Sun. 10am-5pm. 50¢.) The **Master Pass** (278-1796), available at the park visitors' center, covers admission to the theater, Maid of the Mist, the Viewmobile, the observation tower, Caves of the Wind, and the geological museum, as well as parking ($15, kids $10).

Outside the park, sharks, penguins, otters, and performing sea lions strut their stuff at the **Aquarium,** 701 Whirlpool St. (285-3575; open daily 9am-5pm, Labor Day-Memorial Day 9am-7pm; $6.25, ages 4-12 $4.25). Continuing north, the **Niagara Power Project,** 5777 Lewiston Rd. (285-3211, ext. 6660), features interactive demonstrations, short videos, and displays on energy, hydropower, and local history (free); take Robert Moses Pkwy. north to Rte. 104. While you're there, stop at the fishing platform and catch salmon, trout, or bass for dinner. (Open daily 9am-6pm; Labor Day-June 10am-5pm.) The 200-acre state **Artpark** (800-659-PARK/7275), at the foot of 4th St., focuses on visual and performing arts, with a variety of workshops, classes, and demonstrations. The theater presents opera, pops concerts, and blues and jazz festivals (tix $26-30; open July-Aug. Tues.-Sun; call for schedule).

The French, British, and American flags have all flown over **Old Fort Niagara** (745-7611), a French castle built in 1726 to guard the entrance to the Niagara River; follow Robert Moses Pkwy. north from Niagara Falls. (Open daily 9am-6:30pm; Labor Day-Dec. and April-May 9am-4:30pm; Jan.-Mar. 9am-5:30pm. $6, seniors $4.75, ages 6-12 $3.75.) **The Turtle (American Center for the Living Arts),** 25 Rainbow Blvd. South (284-2427), between Winter Garden and the river, boasts an impressive collection of regional Iroquois arts and crafts. (Open daily 9am-6pm; Oct.-April Tues.-Fri. 9am-5pm, Sat.-Sun. noon-5pm. $3.50, seniors $3, students and kids $2.) Wander into **Artisans Alley,** 10 Rainbow Blvd. (282-0196), at 1st St., to see the works of over 600 American craftsmen (open daily 10am-9pm, Jan.-April Mon.-Sat. 10am-5pm, Sun. noon-5pm; free). The 4-time AFC Champ/Super Bowl bust **Buf-**

falo Bills, Ticket Office, One Bills Dr., Orchard Park 14127 (649-0015 for ticket info) play at Rich Stadium in Orchard Park, south of the Falls (season Sept.-Dec.).

Canadian Side On the Canadian side of Niagara Falls (across Rainbow Bridge), **Queen Victoria Park** provides the best view of Horseshoe Falls. The falls are illuminated for three hours every night, starting one hour after sunset. Parking is expensive (CDN$8). Once you park, air-conditioned buses called **People Movers** (357-9340) will take you through the 19-mi. area on the Canadian side of the Falls, stopping at points of interest along the way. (Early May to mid-Oct. Mon.-Fri. 10am-6pm, Sat.-Sun. 10am-10pm. CDN$4, children CDN$2.) You can save a buck by using **Park & Ride:** park at Rapids View, at the south end of Niagara Pkwy., and take People Movers from there (CDN$11). **Skylon Tower,** 5200 Robinson St. (356-2651), has the highest view of the Falls at 775 ft.; on a clear day you can see as far as Toronto (CDN$6.75, kids CDN$3.75). Its 552-ft. **Observation Deck** (CDN 75¢) offers an unhindered view of the falls (open daily 8am-11pm, in winter 8am-9pm). Canada's version of the Master Pass, the **Explorer's Passport** (CDN$13.25, children CDN$6.65), includes passage to **Journey Behind the Falls** (354-1551), a gripping tour behind the rushing waters of Horseshoe Falls (CDN$5.50, children CDN$2.75), to **Great Gorge Adventure** (374-1221), a descent into the Niagara River Rapids (open late April-late Oct.; CDN$4.50, children CDN$2.25), and to the **Spanish Aero Car** (354-5711), an aerial cable ride over the turbulent whirlpool waters (open mid-March to Oct.; CDN$4.75, children CDN$2.40). Throw People Movers service into the bargain, and you get the **Explorer's Passport Plus** (adults CDN$16.85, children CDN$8.45). The **Falls Incline Railway** (356-0943) transports visitors between Table Rock Scenic Tunnels and the Falls view location (CDN 75¢).

The **Niagara Falls Brewing Company,** 6863 Lundy's Lane (374-1166), hosts free touring and tasting (open daily 10am-6pm). **Vincor International** (formerly Brights Winery), 4887 Dorchester Rd. (357-2400), is Canada's oldest and largest winery. (Tours Mon.-Sat. 10:30am, 2pm, and 3:30pm, Sun. 2 and 3:30pm; Nov.-April Mon.-Fri. 2pm, Sat.-Sun. 2 and 3:30pm. CDN$2 to taste 4 wines.) Bikers, rollerbladers, and leisurely walkers enjoy the 56km **Niagara River Recreation Trail,** which runs from Ft. Erie to Ft. George and passes many interesting historical and geological sights.

For the happy few who realize that tourist commercialism can be as much a thing of beauty as any natural wonder, Niagara Falls offers the delightfully tasteless **Clifton Hill,** a collection of wax museums, funhouses, and other overpriced freak shows. One jewel in this tourist strip's crown, **Ripley's Believe It or Not Museum,** 4960 Clifton Hill (356-2238), displays such wonders as wax models of unicorn men and a genuine shrunken head (CDN $7, seniors $5.50, kids CDN$3.40, under 5 free).

NORTHERN NEW YORK

■■■ THE ADIRONDACKS

In 1892, the New York State legislature demonstrated uncommon foresight in establishing the **Adirondacks State Park**—the largest U.S. park outside Alaska and one of the few places left where hikers can spend days without seeing another soul. In recent years, unfortunately, pollution and development have left a harsh imprint; acid rain has damaged the tree and fish populations, especially in the fragile high-altitude environments, and tourist meccas like **Lake George** have continued to expand rapidly. Despite these urban intrusions, much of the area retains the beauty visitors have enjoyed for over a century.

Of the six million acres in the Adirondacks Park, 40% are open to the public, offering an unsurpassed range of outdoor activities. Whether hiking, snow-shoeing, or cross-country skiing, the 2000 mi. of trails that traverse the forest provide spectacular mountain scenery. Canoers paddle through an interlocking network of lakes and streams, while mountain climbers conquer **Mt. Marcy,** the state's highest peak (5344 ft.) and skiers take advantage of a dozen well-known alpine centers. **Lake Placid** hosted the winter Olympics in 1932 and 1980, and frequently welcomes national and international sports competitions. **Tupper Lake** and Lake George have carnivals every January and February; Tupper also hosts the Tin Man Triathlon in mid-July. In September, the hot air balloons of the Adirondack Balloon Festival in paint the sky over Glens Falls.

Practical Information The **Adirondack Mountain Club (ADK)** is the best source of information on hiking and other outdoor activities in the region. In its 74th year, the ADK has over 22,000 members and offices at RR3, Box 3055, Lake George 12845 (668-4447), and at Adirondak Loj Rd., P.O. Box 867, Lake Placid 12946 (523-3441; open Sat.-Thurs. 8am-8pm, Fri. 8am-10pm). Call the Lake Placid number for information on outdoors skills classes such as canoeing, rock climbing, whitewater kayaking, and wilderness medicine. For the latest backcountry info, visit ADK's **High Peaks Information Center,** 3 mi. south of Lake Placid on Rte. 73, then 5 mi. down Adirondack Loj Rd. The center also has washrooms (open daily 8am-7pm) and sells basic outdoor equipment, trail snacks, and the club's extremely helpful guides to the mountains ($18). Rock climbers should consult the experienced mountaineers at the **Mountaineer** (576-2281), in Keene Valley between I-87 and Lake Placid on Rte. 73. Snowshoes rent for $15 per day; ice-climbing equipment (boots and crampons) goes for $20 per day. (Open Mon.-Fri. 9am-5:30pm, Sat. 8am-5:30pm, Sun. 10am-5:30pm.) The ADK and the Mountaineer are better equipped to give you details, but the **State Office of Parks and Recreation,** Agency Bldg. 1, Empire State Place, Albany 12238 (474-0456), can provide basic information on the conditions and concerns of backwoods travel.

Adirondacks Trailways serves the Adirondacks with frequent stops along I-87. From Albany, buses go to Lake Placid, Tupper Lake, and Lake George. From the Lake George bus stop at the Mobil station, 320 Canada St. (668-9511; 800-858-8555 for bus info), buses set out for Lake Placid (1 per day, $13), Albany (1 per day, $9.75), and New York City ($37.50). The gas station may close Dec.-May but buses still run. (Open June-Nov. Mon.-Wed. 7am-10pm, Thurs. 7am-midnight, Fri.-Sun. 7am-2am.) Adirondacks' **area code:** 518.

Accommodations and Camping Two lodges near Lake Placid are also run by the ADK. The **Adirondak Loj** (523-3441), 8 mi. east of Lake Placid off Rte. 73, fills a beautiful log cabin on Heart Lake with comfortable bunk facilities and a family atmosphere. Guests can swim, fish, canoe, and use rowboats on the premises (canoe or boat rental $5). In winter, explore the wilderness trails on rented snowshoes ($15 per day) or cross-country skis ($20 per day). (B&B $30, with dinner $41; linen included. Tent sites for 2 $14, in winter $8, $1.50 per additional person; lean-tos for 2 $16/$12/$2.50.) Call ahead for weekends and peak holiday seasons. For an even better mix of rustic comfort and wilderness experience, hike 3½ mi. to the **John's Brook Lodge** from the closest trailhead, in Keene Valley (call the Adirondak Loj for reservations); from Lake Placid, follow Rte. 73 15 mi. through Keene to Keene Valley and turn right at the Ausable Inn. The hike runs slightly uphill, but the meal which awaits you justifies the effort; the staff packs in groceries every day and cooks on a gas stove. A great place to meet friendly New Yorkers, John's Brook is no secret; beds fill completely on weekends. Make reservations at least one day in advance for dinner, longer for a weekend. Bring sheets or a sleeping bag. (B&B $26, with dinner $37. Lean-tos $10. Open mid-June to early Sept. Memorial Day-June 12 and Labor Day-Columbus Day, bunks $9, Fri.-Sat. $12; full kitchen access.)

If ADK facilities are too pricey, try the **High Peaks Base Camp,** P.O. Box 91, Upper Jay 12987 (946-2133), a charming restaurant/lodge/campground just a 20-min. drive from Lake Placid; take Rte. 86 E. to Wilmington, turn right on Fox Farm Rd. (just before the Hungry Trout Tackle Shop), then go right 2½ mi. on Springfield

Rd. You'll get a bed for the night for $15 or $18 (Fri.-Sat.) and a huge breakfast in the morning. Sometimes rides can be arranged from Keene; call ahead. (Free hot showers. Check-in until 10pm; later with reservations. Tent sites $5; $3 per additional person. Cabins for 4 $30.) **Free camping** is easy to come by. Always inquire about the location of free trailside shelters before you plan a hike in the forest. Better still, camp for free anywhere on public land in the **backcountry** as long as you are at least 150 ft. away from a trail, road, water source, or campground and below 4000 ft. in altitude. The State Office of Parks and Recreation (see Practical Information, above) has more details.

In **Lake George,** 45 mi. south of the junction of Rte. 73 and I-87, off of I-87's exit 22, the basement of **St. James Episcopal Church Hall,** P.O. Box 176, Lake George 12845 (668-2634), on Montcalm St. at Ottawa a few blocks from the lake, doubles as the **Lake George Youth Hostel (HI-AYH).** From the bus terminal, walk south 1 block to Montcalm, turn right, and go 1 block to Ottawa; you'll find a slightly musty bunkroom and a decent kitchen behind an HI-AYH sign in the parking lot. (Check-in 5-9pm; later only with reservations. Curfew 10pm. $10, nonmembers $13. Sleep-sack required; rental $1. Open late May-early Sept.; spring and fall by reservation.)

■■■ LAKE PLACID

Home of the Olympic Winter Games in both 1932 and 1980, Lake Placid keeps the memory and the dream of Olympic glory alive. World-class athletes train year-round in the town's extensive sporting facilities, lending an international flavor which distinguishes Lake Placid from its Adirondack neighbors. The natural setting of the Adirondack High Peaks Region draws droves of hikers and backpackers each year.

Practical Information Lake Placid sits at the intersection of Rte. 86 and Rte. 73. The town's Olympic past has left its mark; the **Olympic Regional Development Authority,** 216 Main St., Olympic Center (523-1655 or 800-462-6236), operates the sporting facilities and sells tickets for self-guided tours. (Available July to mid-Oct daily 9am-4pm. $16, seniors and children 6-12 $12, under 6 free.) Information on food, lodging, and area attractions can be obtained from the **Lake Placid-Essex County Visitors Bureau** (523-2445), also in Olympic Center (open Mon.-Sat. 9am-5pm, Sun. 9am-4pm). **Adirondack Trailways** (523-4309 for bus info) stops at the **326 Main St. Deli,** and has extensive service in the area. Buses run to New York City (1 per day, $49.50) and Lake George (1 per day, $13). For **weather** info, call 523-1363 or 523-3518. Lake Placid's **post office:** 201 Main St. (523-3071; open Mon.-Fri. 9am-5pm, Sat. 8:30am-2pm); **ZIP code:** 12946; **area code:** 518.

Accommodations, Camping, and Food As long as you avoid the resorts on the west end of town, both accommodations and food can be had cheaply in Lake Placid. The **White Sled** (523-9314; on Rte. 73 between the Sports Complex and the ski jumps) is the best bargain around: for $17 you get a comfortable, clean bed in the bunkhouse, which includes a full kitchen, a spacious living room with TV, and a quiet setting to collect your thoughts. **Meadowbrook State Park** (891-4351), 5 mi. west on Rte. 86 in Ray Brook, and **Wilmington Notch State Campground** (946-7172), off Rte. 86 between Wilmington and Lake Placid, have the area's nearest campsites. Both offer sites without hookups which accommodate two tents and up to six people ($10 first night, $9 per additional night).

In Lake Placid Village, **Main St.** offers reasonably priced pickings to suit any palate. The lunch buffet (Mon.-Sat. noon-2pm) at the **Hilton Hotel,** 1 Mirror Lake Dr. (523-4411), includes a sandwich and all-you-can-eat soup and salad ($5.25). At the **Black Bear Restaurant,** 157 Main St. (523-9886), enjoy a $5 lunch special and a $2.75 Saranac lager (the Adirondack's own beer) in the company of stuffed animals (bottomless java 80¢; open Sun.-Thurs. 6:30am-10pm, Fri.-Sat. 24 hrs.). **The Cottage,** 5 Mirror Lake Dr. (523-9845), serves up sandwiches, salads ($4-6), and Lake Placid's best views of Mirror Lake, where the U.S. canoe and kayaking teams practice (food daily 11:30am-9pm; bar open daily 11:30am-1am). **Mud Puddles,** 3 School St. (523-4446), below the speed skating rink, is a splash with the pop music crowd (open Wed.-Sun. 9pm-3am; cover $1.50).

Sights You can't miss the 70 and 90m runs of the Olympic ski jumps which, along with the **Kodak Sports Park,** make up the **Olympic Jumping Complex,** just outside of town on Rte. 73. The $7 admission fee includes a chairlift and elevator ride to the top of the spectator towers, where you can catch summer (June to mid-Oct.) jumpers flipping and sailing into a swimming pool. (Open daily 9am-5pm, Sept.-June 9am-4pm.) Three mi. farther along Rte. 73, the **Olympic Sports Complex** (523-4436) at Mt. Van Hoevenberg has a summer trolley that coasts to the top of the bobsled run ($3, mid-June to mid-Oct.). In the winter, you can bobsled down the Olympic run ($25), or try the luge ($10; open Dec.-March Tues.-Sun. 1-3pm). Contact the Olympic Regional Development Authority (see above) for a tour of the facilities.

The west branch of the **Ausable River,** just east of Lake Placid, lures anglers to its shores. **Fishing licenses** (5-day $20, season $35; resident 3-day $6, season $14) are sold at **Town Hall,** 301 Main St. (523-2162), or **Jones Outfitters,** 37 Main St. (523-3468). Jones rents the necessary equipment as well, including rod, reel, line, tackle, and bait (package $15 per day; open daily 9am-6pm). The **Fishing Hotline** (891-5413) plays an in-depth recording with straight talk on fishing hotspots.

■■■ THOUSAND ISLAND SEAWAY

The Thousand Island region of St. Lawrence Seaway spans 100 mi. from the mouth of Lake Ontario to the first of the many man-made locks on the St. Lawrence River. Some 250 wooded islands and countless rocky shoals make navigation tricky in this area. Locals divide people into two groups: those who *have* hit a shoal and those who *will* hit a shoal. But don't let this dire prediction deter you; not only is the Thousand Island region a fisherman's paradise, with some of the world's best bass and muskie catch, it's the only area in the nation with a salad dressing named after it.

Practical Information The Thousand Islands region hugs the coast just two hours from Syracuse by way of I-81 N. **Clayton, Alexandria Bay,** and **Cape Vincent** are the main cities in the area. For Welleslet Island, Alexandria Bay, and the eastern 500 islands, stay on I-81 until you reach Rte. 12E. For Clayton and points west, take exit 47 and follow Rte. 12 until you reach 12E. Write or visit the **Clayton Chamber of Commerce,** 510 Riverside Dr., Clayton 13624 (686-3771), for the *Clayton Vacation Guide* and the *Thousand Islands Seaway Region Travel Guide* (both free; open daily 9am-4pm). The **Alexandria Bay Chamber of Commerce,** Market St., Alexandria Bay 13607 (482-9531), is just off James St. on the right (open daily 9am-5pm; in winter Mon.-Tues. and Thurs.-Sat. 9am-5pm). The **Cape Vincent Chamber of Commerce** (654-2481) receives mail and visitors at James St., Cape Vincent 13618, by the ferry landing (open Sun.-Mon. 10am-4pm, Tues.-Sat. 9am-5pm). Access the region by bus with **Greyhound,** 540 State St., Watertown (788-8110). Two buses run daily to New York City (8½hr., $48), Syracuse (1¾ hr., $13), and Albany (5½ hr., $33). From the same station, **Thousand Islands Bus Lines** (287-2782) leaves for Alexandria Bay and Clayton Monday to Friday at 1pm ($5.60 to Alexandria, $3.55 to Clayton); return trips leave Clayton from the **Nutshell Florist,** 234 James St. (686-5791), at 8:45am, and Alexandria from the **Dockside Cafe,** 17 Market St. (482-9849), at 8:30am. (Station open 9:15am-2:30pm and 6-8pm.)

Clayton's **post office:** 236 John St. (686-3311; open Mon.-Fri. 9am-5pm, Sat. 9am-noon); **ZIP code:** 13624. Alexandria Bay's **post office:** 13 Bethune St (482-9521; open Mon.-Fri. 8:30am-5:30pm, Sat. 8:30am-1pm); **ZIP code:** 13607. Cape Vincent's **post office:** 360 Broadway St. (654-2424; open Mon.-Fri. 8:30am-1pm, 2-5:30pm); **ZIP code:** 13618. Thousand Island's **area code:** 315.

Accommodations and Camping George and Jean Couglar lovingly care for the idyllic **Tibbetts Point Lighthouse Hostel (HI-AYH),** RR1 Box 330 (654-3450), on the western edge of the seaway on Cape Vincent, situated where Lake Ontario meets the St. Lawrence River. Take Rte. 12E into town, turn left on Broadway, and follow the river until the road ends. There is no public transportation to Cape Vincent, but with enough advance notice, George or Jean will pick you up in Clayton. (2 houses with 31 beds. Full kitchen with microwave. Check-in 5-10pm. Curfew 11pm. $10, nonmembers $13. Linen $1. Open May 15-Oct. 25.) **Burnham Point State Park** (654-2324), on Rte. 12E 4 mi. east of Cape Vincent and 11 mi. west of Clayton, sports 50 tent sites and boat docking facilities. (No showers. Sites for up to 2 tents and 6 people $9, with hookup $12.50. Open Memorial Day-Labor Day daily 8am-9pm.) **Keewaydin State Park** (482-3331), just south of Alexandria Bay, maintains 41 sites along the St. Lawrence River. Campers have free access to an Olympic-size swimming pool. (Showers available. $11.50 first night, $10 per additional night. No hookups. Open Memorial Day-Labor Day.)

Exploring the Seaway Any of the small towns that dot Rte. 12 will serve as a fine base for exploring the region, though Clayton and Cape Vincent tend to be less expensive than Alexandria Bay. **Uncle Sam Boat Tours,** 604 Riverside Dr. (686-3511), in Clayton, and on James St. in Alexandria Bay (482-2611), gives a good look at most of the islands and the plush estates situated atop them. (2¼-hr. tours April-Dec. daily. From Clayton $12.50, children 4-12 $7.25. From Alexandria Bay $11.50, children 4-12 $6.25. Seniors $1 off.) Tours highlight **Heart Island** and its famous **Boldt Castle** (482-9724 or 800-847-526) and make unlimited stops so that visitors can get off and stay as long as they would like before being picked up; they do not cover the price of admission to the castle. George Boldt, former owner of New York City's elegant Waldorf-Astoria Hotel, financed this six-story replica of a Rhineland castle as a gift for his wife, who died before its completion. In his grief, Boldt stopped construction on the 365-bedroom, 52-bathroom behemoth, which remains unfinished today. After extensive renovations, this exorbitant monument is now open to the public. (Open May-Oct. $3.25, seniors $2.75, ages 6-12, $1.75.) In Clayton, **French Creek Marina,** 98 Wahl St. (686-3621), rents 14-ft. fishing boats ($45 per day) and pontoon boats ($110 per day), launches boats ($5), and provides overnight docking ($15 per night). **O'Brien's U-Drive Boat Rentals,** 51 Walton St. (482-9548), handles boat rentals in Alexandria Bay with 16-ft. fishing boats ($60 per day, $100 deposit) and 18-ft. runabouts ($150 per day, $300 deposit; open April-Oct.; mechanic on duty daily). In Cape Vincent, **Sunset Trailer Park** (654-2482), 2 mi. beyond town on 12E, offers motor boats ($40 per day); convenient to Tibbets Point Hostel (see above).

Fishing licenses (5-day $20, season $35; resident 3-day $6, season $14) are available at sporting goods stores or at the **Town Clerk's Office,** 405 Riverside Dr., Clay ton (686-3512; open Mon.-Fri. 9am-noon and 1-4pm). No local store rents equipment; bring your own rods and reels or plan to buy them.

New Jersey

New Jersey was once called the Garden State for a reason, but with the advent of suburbia (NJ serves both New York City and Philadelphia), and tax-free shopping (giving rise to outlets and major mall country), travelers who refuse to get off the interstates envision the state as a conglomeration of belching chemical plants and ocean beaches strewn with garbage and gamblers. This picture, however, belies the state's quieter delights (off the highway). A closer look reveals that there is more to New Jersey than commuters, chemicals, and craps; the interior blooms with countless fields of corn, tomatoes, and peaches, while quiet sandy beaches outline the southern tip of the state. New Jersey also shelters quiet hamlets, the Pine Barrens forest, and two world-class universities: Rutgers and Princeton. Certainly, Atlantic City continues its gaudy existence, and the New Jersey Turnpike remains the zone of the road warrior, but those who stray from the path will be pleasantly surprised.

PRACTICAL INFORMATION

Capital: Trenton.
State Division of Tourism: CN 826, Trenton 08625 (609-292-2470). **New Jersey Department of Environmental Protection and Energy, State Park Service,** 401 East State St., Trenton, 08625-0404.
Time Zone: Eastern. **Postal Abbreviation:** NJ
Sales Tax: 6%; no tax on clothing.

■■■ ATLANTIC CITY

For over 50 years, coffee-table high rollers have been struggling for control of the likes of St. James Place and Ventnor Avenue. When these thoroughfares were immortalized in *Monopoly,* Atlantic City was a beachside hotspot tops among resort towns, frequented by wealthy families like the Vanderbilts and the Girards. The opulence has since faded; with the rise of competition from Florida resorts, the community chest closed, and Atlantic City suffered decades of decline. Then, with the legalization of gambling in 1976, casinos rose from the rubble of Boardwalk. Velvet-lined temples of tackiness now blight the beach, drawing international jet-setters and small-time slot-players alike.

PRACTICAL INFORMATION

Tourist Office: Atlantic City Convention Center and Visitors Bureau, 2314 Pacific Ave. (499-7130 or 800-262-7395); main entrance on the Boardwalk between Mississippi and Florida Ave. Home of the Miss America Pageant. Also a booth on the Boardwalk at Mississippi Ave. Personal assistance daily 9am-5pm; leaflets available 24 hrs.
Tours: Gray Line Tours, 900 Eighth Ave., New York City (397-2600), between 53rd and 54th St. Several daily round-trip excursions to Atlantic City (3hr., $21, on weekends $23). Redeemable your ticket receipt for up to $15 in cash, chips, or food from a casino when you arrive. Caesar's, the Taj Mahal, and TropWorld have the best offers ($15 in cold, flexible cash). The bus drops you off at the designated casino and picks you up three hours later.
Trains: Amtrak (800-872-7245), at Kirkman Blvd. near Michigan Ave. Follow Kirkman to its end, bear right, and follow the signs. To: New York (1 per day, 2½hr., $28). Open Sun.-Fri. 9:30am-7:40pm, Sat. 9:30am-10pm.
Buses: Greyhound (345-6617 or 800-231-2222), in the **Atlantic City Municipal Bus Terminal,** at Arkansas and Arctic Ave. Buses every hr. to New York (2½hr., $20). **New Jersey Transit** (800-582-5946) operates from the same station. Service to New York City daily every hr. 6am-10pm ($21). Both bus lines offer casino-sponsored round-trip discounts, including cash back in Atlantic City; Bally's has a particularly good deal—you get your full fare ($15) back in quarters upon arrival. Terminal open 24 hrs.
Public Transportation: A **yellow tram** runs continuously. Fare $2, all-day pass $5. **Jitneys** run up and down Pacific Ave. 24 hrs.; $1.25. **NJ Transit** buses up and down Atlantic Ave. Fare $1.
Crisis Lines: Rape and Abuse Hotline, 646-6767. **Gambling Abuse,** 800-GAMBLER/800-426-2537. Both 24 hrs. **AIDS Hotline,** 800-281-2437. Open Mon.-Fri. 9am-5pm.
Emergency: 911.
Post Office: (345-4212), at Martin Luther King and Pacific Ave. Open Mon.-Fri. 8:30am-6pm, Sat. 8:30am-noon. **ZIP code:** 08401. **Area code:** 609.

Atlantic City lies about half-way down New Jersey's coast, accessible via the **Garden State Pkwy.** and the **Atlantic City Expwy.,** and easily reached by train from Philadelphia and New York. Atlantic City's attractions cluster on and around the Boardwalk, which runs east-west along the Atlantic Ocean. Running parallel to the Boardwalk, Pacific and Atlantic Ave. offer cheap restaurants, hotels, and convenience stores. Atlantic Ave. can be dangerous after dark, and any street farther out can be dangerous even by day.

Getting around Atlantic City is easy on foot. **Parking** at the Sands Hotel is free, but "for patrons only"; go spend a dollar at the slots after enjoying this little-known convenience. If you want to park at a **lot,** park as close to the boardwalk as possible. It'll run about $5-7 per hour, but the $3 lots several blocks away offer dubious security.

ACCOMMODATIONS AND CAMPING

Large, red-carpeted beachfront hotels have bumped smaller operators a few streets back. Smaller hotels along **Pacific Ave.,** 1 block from the Boardwalk, charge about $60-95 in the summer. Reserve ahead, especially on weekends. Many hotels lower their rates mid-week and in the winter when water temperature and gambling fervor drop significantly. Rooms in guest houses are reasonably priced, though facilities can be dismal. If you have a car it pays to stay in **Absecon,** about 8 mi. from Atlantic City; exit 40 from the Garden Sate Pkwy. leads to Rte. 30 and cheap rooms.

Inn of the Irish Pub, 164 St. James Pl. (344-9063), near the Ramada Tower, just off the Boardwalk. Big, clean, pretty rooms, decorated with antiques. No TVs, phone, or A/C, but the summer breeze from the beach keeps things cool. Some rooms have a view of the sea. Plush lobby with TV and pay phone. Coin-op laundry in hotel next door. Singles with shared bath $29, with private bath $51.40, doubles $45.80/$80. Breakfast and dinner $10, children $8. Key deposit $5.

Hotel Cassino, 28 Georgia Ave. (344-0747), at Pacific Ave. behind Trump Plaza. Slightly run-down, but clean, cheap, and family-run. Small gaudy green and orange-painted rooms with shared bath. Rates negotiable. Singles $25-35, doubles $30-45. Key deposit $10. Open May-early Nov.

American Lodge, 232 E. White Horse Pike (800-452-4050), ½mi. east of the Garden State Pkwy. from exit 40. Large, clean rooms with king-sized beds, cable, and A/C. Singles $35, with a jacuzzi $45; $5 per additional person.

Birch Grove Park Campground (641-3778), on Mill Rd. in Northfield. About 6mi. from Atlantic City, off Rte. 9. 50 sites. Attractive and secluded. Sites for 4 $15, with hookup $20. Reservations recommended July-Aug.

FOOD

After you cash in your chips, visit a **casino buffet** for a cheap meal (about $10 for dinner; $6-7 for lunch), but don't expect gourmet quality. The cheapest casino buffet in town is on the sixth floor of the **Claridge;** all-you-can-eat for breakfast goes for $3.77, lunch and dinner cost $4.72. Yes, the town does provide higher-quality meals in a less noxious atmosphere. For a complete rundown of local dining, pick up a copy of *TV Atlantic Magazine, At the Shore,* or *Whoot* (all free) from a hotel lobby, restaurant, or local store.

An inviting pub with a century's worth of Irish memorabilia draped on the walls, the **Inn of the Irish Pub,** 164 St. James Pl. (345-9613), serves hearty, modestly priced dishes such as deep-fried crab cakes ($4.25), honey-dipped chicken ($4.25), and Dublin beef stew ($5). The lunch special (Mon.-Fri. 11am-2pm) gets you a preselected sandwich and cup of soup for $2. (Open 24 hrs.) Frank Sinatra is rumored to have the immense subs ($4.50-9) from **White House Sub Shop** (345-1564 or 345-8599), at Mississippi and Arctic Ave., flown to him while he's on tour (open Mon.-Sat. 10am-midnight, Sun. 11am-midnight). For renowned Italian food, including the best pizza in town, hit **Tony's Baltimore Grille,** 2800 Atlantic Ave. (345-5766), at Iowa Ave. (pasta around $5; pizza $5-8; open daily 11am-3am, bar open 24 hrs.). For a traditional oceanside dessert, try custard ice cream or saltwater taffy, both available from vendors along the Boardwalk. **Custard and Snackcups,** between South

Carolina and Ocean Ave. (345-5151), makes 37 flavors of soft-serve ice-cream and yogurt, ranging from peach to pineapple to tutti-frutti. (Cones $2.25. Open Sun.-Thurs. 10am-midnight, Fri.-Sat. 10am-3am.)

CAINO, THE BOARDWALK, AND BEACHES

You don't have to spend a penny to enjoy yourself in Atlantic City's casinos; their vast, plush interiors and spotless marble bathrooms can entertain a resourceful and voyeuristic budget traveler for hours. Watch the blue-haired ladies shove quarter after quarter in the slot machines with a vacant, zombie-like stare. Open nearly all the time, casinos lack windows and clocks, denying you the time cues that signal the hours slipping away; keep your eyes on your watch or you'll have spent five hours and five digits before you know what hit you. To curb inevitable losses, stick to the cheaper games—blackjack and slot machines—stay away from the cash machines. If you're on a really tight budget, the **5¢ slots,** available only at Trump Plaza, TropWorld, Bally's Grand, and Taj Mahal (see below), will allow you to gamble for hours on less than $10. The minimum gambling age of 21 is strictly enforced.

All of the casinos on the Boardwalk fall within a dice toss of one another. The farthest south is **TropWorld** (340-4000), at Iowa Ave., and the farthest north is **Showboat** (343-4000), at States Ave. If you liked *Aladdin,* you'll love the **Taj Mahal** (449-1000), at Pennsylvania Ave. Donald Trump's huge and glittering jewel is too out there (and too large) to be missed—it was missed payments on this tasteless tallboy that cast the financier into his billion-dollar tailspin. It will feel like *Monopoly* when you realize Trump owns three other hotel casinos in the city: **Trump Plaza** (441-6000) and **Trump Regency** (344-4000) on the Boardwalk, and **Trump Castle** (441-2000) at the Marina. The outdoor Caesar at **Caesar's Boardwalk Resort and Casino** (348-4411) at Arkansas Ave., has moved indoors, replaced by a kneeling Roman gladiator heralding the entrance to **Planet Hollywood.** Come, see, and conquer at the only casino with 25¢ video blackjack, and play slots at the feet of a huge **Statue of David.** The **Sands** (441-4000) at Indiana Ave. goes for a more "natural" effect with a decor of huge, ostentatious pink and green seashells.

There's something for everyone in Atlantic City, thanks to the Boardwalk. Those under 21 (or those tired of the endless cycle of winning and losing), **gamble for prizes** at one of the many arcades that line the Boardwalk. It feels like real gambling, but the teddy bear in the window is easier to get than the grand prize at a resort. The **Steel Pier,** an extension in front of the Taj Mahal, has the usual amusement park standbys: roller coaster, ferris wheel, tilt-a-whirl, carousel, kiddie rides, and many a game of "skill." Rides cost $1.50-3 each (open in summer daily noon-midnight; call the Taj Mahal for winter hours).

When you tire of spending money, check out the **beach.** Though older couples, families, and defunct gamblers often litter the dunes, the sand and water are generally clean, and a nice breeze blows over a beautiful view of the ocean. **Ventnor City,** just west of Atlantic City, has quieter shores.

■■■ CAPE MAY

Cape May lies at the southern extreme of New Jersey's coastline. The quiet community passed on the rampant boardwalk commercialism adopted by many other beachfront towns and relies only on sand, surf, tree-lined avenues, and 19th-century cottages to draw crowds of older visitors and young couples.

Practical Information Despite its geographic isolation, Cape May can be accessed easily. By car from the north, Cape May is literally the end of the road—follow the toll-heavy **Garden State Pkwy.** south as far as it goes, watch for signs to Center City, and you'll end up on Lafayette St. From the south, take a 70-minute **ferry** from Lewes, DE (302-645-6346) to Cape May (886-9699; 800-643-3779 for recorded schedule info). In summer months, 13 to 16 ferries cross daily; the rets of the year, expect only five to nine per day. ($18 per vehicle and driver, Dec.-March

$15. Passengers $4.50, $8.50 round-trip; ages 6-12 $2.25, motorcyclists $15, bicyclists $8.) Take a **shuttle** to the ferry from the Cape May Bus Depot ($1). The **Welcome Center,** 405 Lafayette St. (884-9562), provides a wagonload of friendly info about Cape May, and free hotlines to B&Bs (open daily 9am-4:30pm). As its name indicates, the **Chamber of Commerce and Bus Depot,** 609 Lafayette St. (884-5508), near Ocean St. across from the Acme, provides tourist info and a local stop for **New Jersey Transit** (800-582-5946; 800-772-2222 in northern NJ). Buses run to Atlantic City (2hr., $3.50), Philadelphia (3hr., $13.50), and New York City (4½hr., $27). (Open Mon.-Fri. 9am-8pm, Sat. 9am-5pm; mid-Oct. to mid-May Mon.-Thurs. 9am-5pm, Fri. 9am-8pm.) Pick up wheeled transportation at the **Village Bike Shop** (884-8500), Washington and Ocean St. right off the mall. Ask about the four-person tandem bike. (One-seaters $3.50 per hr., $9 per day. Open daily 7am-6pm.) But no riding on the beach! Cape May's **post office:** 700 Washington St. (884-3578; open Mon.-Fri. 9am-5pm, Sat. 9am-noon); **ZIP code:** 08204; **area code:** 609.

Accommodations and Camping Look for specials on hotel rooms along Beach Dr., or try one of the many seaside homes which now take in nightly guests. The homes cater to the B&B set with comfortable rooms for $60-100 per night. Still, some reasonable inns persevere. The **Clinton Hotel,** 202 Perry St. (844-3993; 516-799-8889 in winter), at Lafayette St., has decent-sized singles ($25-30) and doubles ($35-40) with a shared bath (16 rooms; reservations recommended; open mid-June to Sept.). Next door, the **Parris Inn,** 204 Perry St. (884-8015 or 884-6363), near Lafayette St., rents simple rooms, some of which have private baths. (Singles $45-55, Fri.-Sat.$85-95; doubles $75/$125. Ask for the 10% *Let's Go* discount.)

Campgrounds line U.S. 9 south of Atlantic City. Sleep under the stars at, **Cold Springs Campground,** 541 New England Rd. (884-8717; 450 fairly private sites; $16.50, with hookup $20; open May to mid-Oct.), or the slightly ritzier **Cape Island Campground,** 709 U.S. 9 (884-5777), with a pool, a store, and athletic facilities (sites with water and electricity $26, full hookup $31; open May to mid-Dec.).

Food Cape May's cheapest food is the pizza and burger fare along **Beach Ave.;** you'll have to shell out a lot of clams for a sit-down meal. Bustles with pedestrians shopping for fudge and saltwater taffy, the **Washington St. Mall** supports a couple of popular food stores and eateries. At the corner of Washington and Perry St., the **Cape May Popcorn Factory,** 43 Perry St. (898-1315 or 800-453-4855), has the largest selection of flavored popcorn ($2-3) you're likely to find anywhere (open daily 10am-5pm; Jan.-March Sat.-Sun. 10am-4pm). **The Ugly Mug,** 426 Washington St. Mall (884-3459), serves a dozen ugly clams for half as many dollars. Chowda goes for $2 a cup or $2.30 a bowl. (Open Mon.-Sat. 11am-2am, Sun. noon-2am. Food served until 11pm.) With live bands nightly, **Carney's,** 401 Beach Ave. (884-4424), proclaims itself the "best bar in town." Chase your sandwich ($6-8) with a $1.75 mug of beer. (Food served Mon.-Sat. 11:30am-10pm, Sun. noon-10pm. Bar open daily until 2:30am; off season until 2am.) One of the most popular pubs in southern Jersey, **The Shire,** 315 Washington St. Mall (884-4700), just off Perry St., pour $2 domestic drafts for a lively crowd while live music plays nightly. (No cover; 2-drink min. while the bands play. Open Mon.-Sat. 10am-2am, Sun. noon-2am.)

Hitting the Beach Fine beaches bless the entire Jersey shore, but the sands of Cape May literally glisten, dotted with the famous Cape May diamonds (actually quartz pebbles that glow when cut and polished). When you unroll your beach towel on a city-protected beach (off Beach Ave.), make sure you have the **beach tag** required for beachgoers over 12 from June to September between 10am and 5pm each day. Pick up a tag from the vendors roaming the shore (daily $4, weekly $9, seasonal $15). For more info, call the Beach Tag Office (884-9522).

The **Mid-Atlantic Center for the Arts,** 1048 Washington St. (884-5404), offers many tours and activities. Pick up *This Week in Cape May* in any of the public buildings or stores for a detailed listing. (Guided walking and trolley tours $5, ages 3-12

$2.50.) The beacon of the **Cape May Light House** in **Cape May Point State Park** (884-2159), west of town at the end of the point, guides tourists, not ships. A199-step climb to the top of the lighthouse, built in 1859, offers a magnificent panorama of the New Jersey and Delaware shore. ($3.50, ages 2-12 $1. Park open 8am-dusk.)

Due to prevailing winds and geographic location, hundreds of thousands of birds make a pit stop in Cape May every year on their way to greener pastures. The **Cape May Bird Observatory,** 707 E. Lake Dr. (884-2736), on Cape May Point, serves as the information center for this "bird watching mecca of North America." They distribute bird maps and information, and run field trips and workshops. (Open Tues.-Sun. 9am-5pm. Recorded birding hotline, 884-2661.) **Shore Shot Speedboats** (884-6161) motors tourists around the Cape daily at 11am, 2, and 4:30pm ($8, under 3 free). Boats depart from Miss Chris Marina, at 2nd Ave. and Wilson Dr.

Pennsylvania

Driven to protect his fellow Quakers from persecution, William Penn, Jr. petitioned the English crown for a slice of North America in 1680. King Charles II owed the Penns a considerable sum of money, so in 1681 he granted the Quakers a vast tract of land between present-day Maryland and New York. By making his colony a bastion of religious tolerance, Penn attracted all types of settlers, and Pennsylvania's towns flourished. The site of the First Continental Congress, the birthplace of the *Declaration of Independence,* and the country's first capital was soon overshadowed, however—New York City rapidly grew into the nation's most important commercial center, and Washington, DC became the national capital.

But Pennsylvania, a state accustomed to revolution, has rallied in the face of adversity. In 1976, Philadelphia groomed its historic shrines for the nation's bicentennial celebration, and they have remained immaculate. Pittsburgh, a city once dirty enough to fool streetlights into burning during the day, has also initiated a cultural renaissance. Between the two cities, Pennsylvania's landscape, from the farms of Lancaster County to the deep river gorges of the Allegheny Plateau, retains much of the natural beauty that the area's first colonists discovered centuries ago.

PRACTICAL INFORMATION

Capital: Harrisburg.

Pennsylvania Travel & Tourism: 453 Forum Bldg., Harrisburg 17120 (800-237-4363). Info on hotels, restaurants, and sights. **Bureau of State Parks,** Rachel Carson State Office Bldg., 400 Market St., Harrisburg 17108 (717-787-8800). The detailed *Recreational Guide* is available at no charge from all visitors centers.

Time Zone: Eastern. **Postal Abbreviation:** PA

Sales Tax: 6%.

■■■ PHILADELPHIA

The first capital of the United States, Philly has a strong and proud patriotic history. Textbooks will tell you of the pivotal role the city played in forging the fledgling nation; both the *Declaration of Independence* and the *Constitution* were drafted here. But look beyond the historic red brick and cracked Liberty Bell, and you'll find sophistication. Part large metropolis, part small city, Philadelphia has the museums, concert halls, galleries, and universities of a world-class urban center, and a throbbing club scene to complement the star-spangled historic district.

PRACTICAL INFORMATION

Tourist Office: 1525 John F. Kennedy Blvd. (636-1666), at 16th St. Pick up a free *Philadelphia Visitor's Guide* and the *Philadelphia Quarterly Calendar of Events.* Open daily 9am-6pm; Labor Day-Memorial Day daily 9am-5pm. **National Park Service Visitors Center** (597-8974, 627-1776 for recording), between Chestnut and Walnut St. Info on **Independence Park,** including maps, schedules, and the film *Independence* (shown daily 9:30am-4pm). Also has the above brochures. Open daily 9am-6pm; Sept.-June 9am-5pm. Tour assistance for non-English-speaking and disabled travelers. **Gay Switchboard,** 546-7100. Provides info Sun.-Tues. 7-10pm, Wed.-Sat. 6-11pm.

Airport: Philadelphia International (24-hr info line 492-3181), 8mi. southwest of Center City on I-76. The 20-min. **SEPTA Airport Rail Line** runs from Center City to the airport. Trains leave 30th St. Station, Suburban Station, and Market East daily every 30min. 5:25am-11:25pm; $5 at window, $7 on train. Last train from airport 12:10am. **Airport Limelight Limousine** (342-5557) will deliver you to a hotel or a specific address downtown ($8 per person). Taxi downtown $20.

Trains: Amtrak, 30th St. Station (349-2153 or 800-872-7245), at 30th and Market St., in University City. To: New York (19 per day, 2hr., $30-39); Boston (9 per day, 7hr., $55-75); Washington, DC (19 per day, 2¼hr., $28); Pittsburgh (2 per day, 8hr., $67). Office open Mon.-Fri. 5:10am-10:45pm, Sat.-Sun. 6:10am-10:45pm. Station open 24 hrs. To get to NYC, take the SEPTA commuter train to Trenton, NJ ($5), then hop on a New Jersey Transit train to NYC through Newark ($8-9).

Buses: Greyhound (931-4075 or 800-231-2222), 10th and Filbert St., 1 block north of Market near the 10th and Market St. subway/commuter rail stop in the heart of Philadelphia. To: New York (21 per day, 3hr., $13); Boston (18 per day, 9¾hr., $39); Baltimore (8 per day, 2½hr., $12); Washington, DC (10 per day, 3-4hr., $16); Pittsburgh (9 per day, 6¾hr., $29); Atlantic City (12 per day, 2½hr., $10). Station open daily 7am-1am. **New Jersey Transit** (569-3752), in the same station. To: Atlantic City (1½hr., $10); Ocean City (2hr., $10.60), and other points on the New Jersey Shore. Operates Mon.-Wed. 6am-9:30pm, Thurs.-Sun. 6am-10:30pm.

Public Transportation: Southeastern Pennsylvania Transportation Authority (SEPTA), 580-7800. Extensive bus and rail service to the suburbs. Buses serve the 5-county area; most operate 5am-2am, some all night. Two major subway routes: the east-west **Market St. line** (including 30th St. Station and the historic area) and the north-south **Broad St. line** (including the stadium complex in south Philadelphia). *The subway is unsafe after dark,* but buses are usually okay. Subway connects with commuter rails—the Main Line local runs through the western suburb of Paoli ($3.75); SEPTA runs north to Trenton, NJ ($5). Pick up a SEPTA system map ($3) and a good street map at any subway stop. Fare $1.60, 2 tokens for $2.30, transfers 40¢. Unlimited all-day pass for buses and subway $5.

Taxis: Yellow Cab, 922-8400. **United Cab,** 238-9500. $1.80 base, $1.80 per mi.

Car Rental: Courtesy Rent-a-Car, 7704 Westchester Pike (446-6200). $19 per day with unlimited mi. Must be 21 with major credit card. **Budget** (492-9400), at 21st and Market St. Downtown and easy to find, but more expensive. $38 per day with unlimited mi. Drivers must be 24.

Crisis Lines: Suicide and Crisis Intervention, 686-4420. **Youth Crisis Line,** 800-448-4663. Both 24 hrs. **Gay Switchboard,** 546-7100. Accepts calls Sun.-Tues. 7-10pm, Wed.-Sat. 6-11pm.

Emergency: 911.

Post Office: 2970 Market St. (895-8000), at 30th St. across from the Amtrak station. Open Mon.-Fri. 9am-5pm. **ZIP code:** 19104. **Area code:** 215.

William Penn, Jr., a survivor of London's great fire in the 1660s, planned his city as a logical and easily accessible grid of wide streets. The north-south streets ascend numerically from the **Delaware River,** flowing near **Penn's Landing** and **Independence Hall** on the east side, to the **Schuylkill River** (pronounced SKOO-kill) on the west. The first street is **Front;** the others follow consecutively from 2 to 69. **Center City** runs from 8th Street to the Schuylkill River. From north to south, the primary streets are Race, Arch, JFK, Market, Chestnut, and South. The intersection of Broad (14th St.) and Market marks the focal point of Center City. The **Historic District**

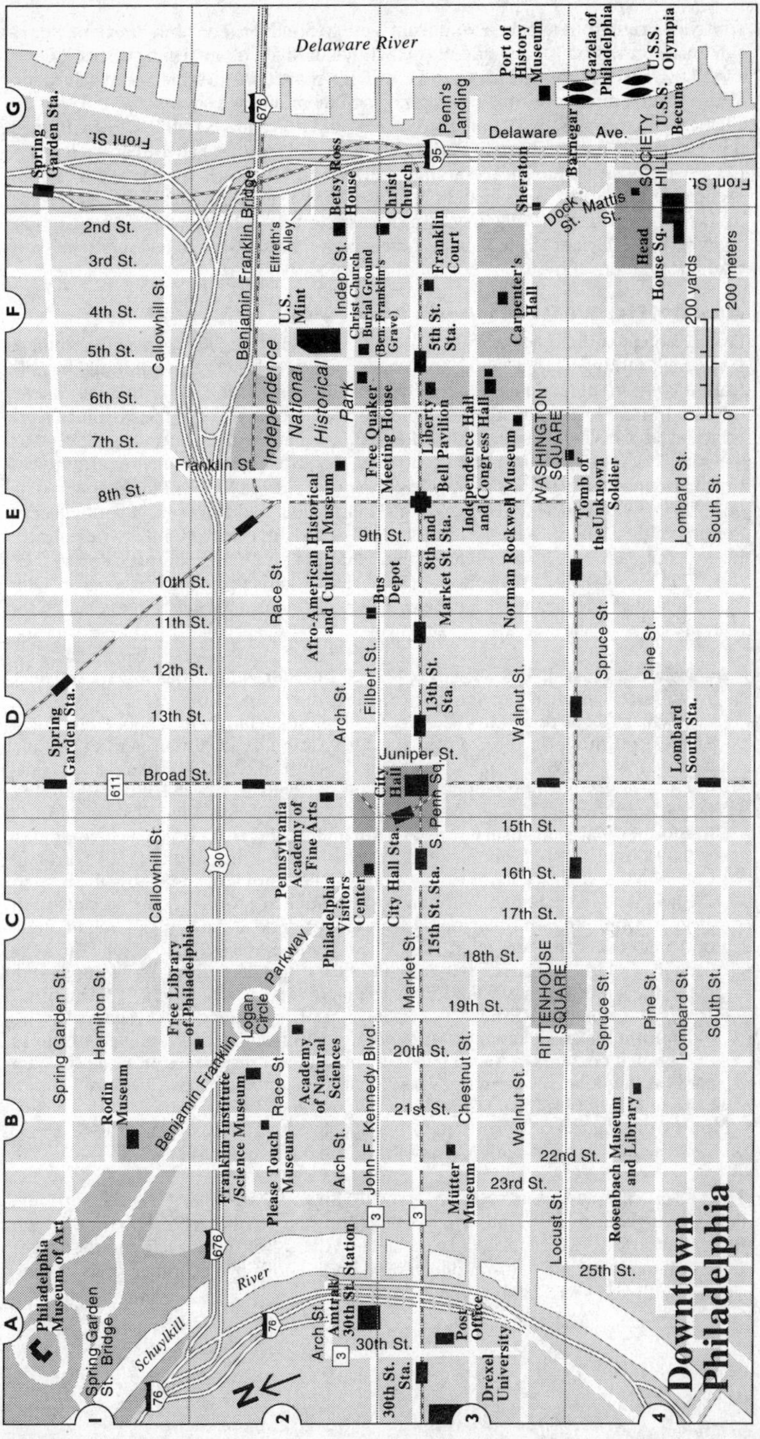

MID-ATLANTIC

stretches from Front to 8th St. and from Vine to South St. The **University of Pennsylvania** sprawls on the far side of the Schuylkill River, about 1 mi. west of Center City. **University City** includes the Penn/Drexel area west of the Schuylkill River. When getting directions, make sure they include numbered streets.

Due to the proliferation of one-way streets and horrendous traffic, **driving** is not a good way to get around town. Parking in Philly will cost you an arm and a leg. Try the city-run **Visitors Parking** (entrance on Dock and Walnut). The $1.50 per ½-hour is crazy, but the value kicks in at 24 hrs. for $9. If you lose your ticket, it's $9 no matter how long you stay. Philly's system of **buses** and its **subway** will take you almost anywhere you'll want to go. Pick up transit maps at the visitor info center (see Practical Information, above).

ACCOMMODATIONS AND CAMPING

Luxury hotels saturate downtown Philadelphia, so anything inexpensive is popular. If you make arrangements even a few days in advance, however, you should be able to find comfortable lodging close to Center City for under $50. With a car, check out the motels located near the airport at exit 9A on I-95 for the absolute least expensive rooms in the area. **Bed and Breakfast Center City,** 1804 Pine St., 19103 (735-1137 or 800-354-8401), will rent you a room ($45-85) or find you a room in a private home. **Bed & Breakfast Connections/Bed & Breakfast of Philadelphia** (610-687-3565), in Devon, PA, also books in Philadelphia and throughout southeastern Pennsylvania. (Singles $40-75, doubles $45-80. Make reservations a week ahead. Best to call 9am-7pm.) The **Philadelphia Naturist and Work Camp Center,** P.O. Box 4755 (634-7057; call Fri.-Sat. 8-11pm), rents rooms to foreign visitors ($5 with light breakfast) and arranges free room and board on nearby farms in exchange for daily chores.

Bank Street Hostel, 32 S. Bank St. (922-0222 or 800-392-4678). Subway: 2nd St. A great hostel in a great location in the historic district. A/C, big-screen TV and VCR in lobby, free coffee and tea, laundry facilities, a kitchen, a free pool table, and a musical morning wakeup. From the bus station, walk down Market St.; it's between 2nd and 3rd. Super-convenient to South St., Penn's Landing, and Chinatown. Like-new facilities. Single-sex dorms. 54 beds. Lockout 10am-4:30pm, but they'll hold baggage. Curfew Sun.-Thurs. 12:30am, Fri.-Sat. 1am. $15. Linen $2.

Chamounix Mansion International Youth Hostel (HI-AYH) (878-3676 or 800-379-0017), in West Fairmount Park. Take bus #38 from Market St. to Ford and Cranston Rd., follow Ford to Chamounix St., then turn left, and follow the road to the hostel (about a 20-min. walk). A hostel-deluxe in a former country estate with clean, beautifully furnished rooms with lots of perks—showers, a kitchen, coin-op laundry, a nice chess table, and a piano. Some basic groceries for sale. Very friendly, helpful staff. Free parking. 44 beds. Check-in 8-11am and 4:30pm-midnight. Lockout 11am-4:30pm. Curfew midnight. $10, nonmembers $13. Linen $2.

Old First Reformed Church (922-4566), at 4th and Race St. in Center City, 1 block from the Independence Mall and 4 blocks from Penn's Landing. A historic church that converts its social hall to a youth hostel that sleeps around 30. Foam pads on the floor, showers. Ages 18-26 only. 3-night max. stay. Check-in 5-10pm. Curfew 11pm. $11. Breakfast included. Open June 30-Sept. 4.

Motel 6, 43 Industrial Hwy. (610-521-6650), in Essington, exit 9A off I-95. Clean, large, standard rooms with A/C and cable. Singles $46, doubles $50.

The closest camping lies across the Delaware River in New Jersey. Try the **Timberline Campground,** 117 Timber Ln., Clarksboro, NJ 08020 (609-423-6677), 15 mi. from Center City. Take U.S. 295S to exit 18B (Clarksboro), turn left and then right onto Cohawkin Rd.; go ½-mi. and turn right on Friendship Rd. Timber Ln. is 1 block on the right. (Sites $17, with hookup $22.)

FOOD

Philly phood is phantastic—this is a city that likes to eat, and eat well. If you do nothing else in this city, try a **cheesesteak, hoagie,** or **soft pretzel,** all Philly specialities. Cheap food fills the carts of the ubiquitous city street vendors, and eateries gather in several specific areas: very hip **South St.,** between Front and 7th; **Sansom St.,** between 17th and 18th; and **2nd St.,** between Chestnut and Market. An abundance of inexpensive places serving cheap eats fill **Chinatown,** bounded by 11th, 8th, Arch, and Vine St., near downtown, and **South Philadelphia.** The quintessential Philly Cheesesteak can be found at **Pat's Steaks** (468-1546), 12th and Passyunk in South Philly, a big cheese in the world of steaks and worth the trek. A basic cheesesteak costs $4.75. (Call for directions; open 24 hrs.) In **University City,** west of the Schuylkill River, Drexel and Penn Universities support many student hangouts.

For fresh fruit, suckling pigs, fish heads, live chickens, and some other foodstuffs that you probably won't ever need, visit the **Italian Market,** on 9th St. below Christian St. The **Reading Terminal Market** (922-2317), at 12th and Arch St., is by far the best place to go for lunch in Center City. Since 1893, food stands have clustered in the indoor market selling fresh produce and meats. (Open Mon.-Sat. 8am-6pm.)

Historic District

Famous 4th St. Delicatessen (922-3274), 4th and Bainbridge St. A Philadelphia landmark since 1923. They have pickels from a barrel ($1.80), egg creams from a soda fountain ($1.50), knishes ($1.50), matzos ($5), and a devoted following. Open Mon.-Sat. 7am-6pm, Sun. 7am-4pm.

DiNardo's, 312 Race St. (925-5115). Savory seafood dishes popular with the locals. Get 1lb. of sauteed garlic crabs for $9. Entrees $12.50-$15.25. Chowder $2.75. Lunch is cheaper—fried clams $6, broiled monkfish $9. Open Mon.-Thurs. 11am-10pm, Fri.-Sat. 11am-11pm, Sun. 3-9pm.

Rib-It, 52 S. 2nd St. (568-1555). Claims to have the best ribs in Philly ($9-12). All-you-can-eat ribfest Mon.-Wed. until 10pm ($16). Burgers $6. Brick, polished wood, and stained glass give this joint a classy feel. Open Mon.-Thurs. noon-11pm, Fri.-Sat. noon-1am, Sun. noon-10:30pm.

Center City

Rangoon, 145 N. 9th St. (829-8939), Chinatown. This intimate restaurant serves intensely wonderful Burmese cuisine. The proprietor nourishes a love of good food, low prices, and spice. Entrees $4-10, most around $6.50. Open Mon.-Thurs. 11:30am-3pm and 5-10pm, Fri. 11:30am-10pm, Sat. 1-10pm, Sun. 1-9pm.

Seafood Unlimited, 270 S. 20th St. (732-3663), at Spruce. Very fresh (still has scales) seafood $7-12. Open Mon.-Thurs. 9am-9pm, Fri.-Sat. 9am-10pm.

Harmony, 135 N. 9th St. (627-4520), Chinatown. The chefs in this small, popular establishment masterfully dupe carnivores with a variety of meatless Chinese dishes, including imitation beef, poultry, seafood, and pork. Most entrees $7-8. Open Sun.-Thurs. 11:30am-10:30pm, Fri.-Sat. 11:30am-midnight.

Lee's Hoagie House, 44 S. 17th St. (564-1264). Authentic hoagies ($3.75-6) since 1953. The 3-ft. hoagie ($39) is an all-day affair. Open Mon.-Fri. 10:30am-6pm, Sat. 10:30am-5pm.

University City

Smoky Joe's, 210 S. 40th St. (222-0770), between Locust and Walnut. An unofficial branch of Penn, "smokes" has been giving students a place to hang out for over 50 years. Try Rosie's Homemade Chili or an 8-oz. burger (each $4). Occasional live music. Open daily 11am-2am.

Tandoor India Restaurant, 106 S. 40th St. (222-7122). Northern Indian cuisine straight from the clay oven. All-you-can-eat lunch buffet ($6), dinner buffet ($9). 20% student discount. Open for lunch daily noon-3pm; for dinner Mon.-Thurs. 4:30-10pm.

Le Bus, 3402 Sansom St. (387-3800). Eclectic gourmet college food? You'll think you have stumbled into the dining hall when you have to grab a tray, but good food awaits. Sandwiches $3-5.50; entrees $6-8. Open June-Aug. Mon.-Fri. 7:30am-9pm; Sept.-May Mon.-Fri. 7:30am-10pm, Sat. 9am-10pm, Sun. 10am-10pm.

Abner's Cheesesteaks (662-0100), at 38th and Chestnut. The Philly Buster means a cheesesteak or hoagie, a 24-oz. soda, and cheese fries for $5.49. Open Mon.-Thurs. 11am-midnight, Fri.-Sat. 11am-3am, Sun. 11am-11pm.

SIGHTS

Independence Hall and The Historic District

The buildings of the **Independence National Historical Park** (597-8974), bounded by Market, Walnut, 2nd, and 6th St. (open daily 9am-6pm; Sept.-May 9am-5pm; free), witnessed many landmark events in U.S. history. The **visitors center** makes a good starting point. The grandiose building across the street is the **First Bank of the U.S.** Located at Chestnut and 4th St., the **Second Bank of the U.S.** presents a stunning example of Greek Revival architecture. Arguably one of the most beautiful buildings in Philly, the Bank now displays the Park's portrait gallery. Notice the weathered, ancient look of the colossal pillars, despite their relative youth; cut across the grain by unskilled prison labor, the marble has aged considerably. Delegates signed the *Declaration of Independence* in 1776 and, in 1787, drafted and signed the 1787 *Constitution* in **Independence Hall,** between 5th and 6th St. on Chestnut. Arrive before 11am in the summer to avoid a long line for tours. (Free guided tours daily every 15-20min.) The U.S. Congress first assembled in nearby **Congress Hall** (free self-guided tours available); its predecessor, the First Continental Congress, convened in **Carpenters' Hall,** in the middle of the block bounded by 3rd, 4th, Walnut and Chestnut St. (open Tues.-Sun. 10am-4pm). North of Independence Hall, the **Liberty Bell Pavilion** houses one of America's most famous symbols. The cracked **Liberty Bell** once tolled for presidents but now rests silent.

MID-ATLANTIC

The remainder of the park contains preserved residential and commercial buildings of the Revolutionary era. To the north, Ben Franklin's home presides over **Franklin Court,** on Market between 3rd and 4th St. The home contains an underground museum, a 20-minute movie, and phones which allow you to confer with long-dead political luminaries. (Open daily 9am-5pm. Free.) At nearby **Washington Sq.,** an eternal flame commemorates the **Tomb of the Unknown Soldier** of the Revolutionary War. Philadelphia's branch of the **U.S. Mint** (597-7350), 5th and Arch St. across from Independence Hall, offers a self-guided tour to explain the mechanized coin-making procedure. No free samples here. (Open daily 9am-4:30pm; Sept.-April Mon.-Fri. 9am-4:30pm; May-June Mon.-Sat. 9am-4:30pm. Free.)

Just behind Independence Hall the **Norman Rockwell Museum** (922-4345), 6th and Sansom St., exhibits many of the artist's *Saturday Evening Post* covers (open Mon.-Sat. 10am-4pm, Sun. 11am-4pm. $2, seniors $1.50, under 12 free). Walk onto the **Benjamin Franklin Bridge,** a powder-blue marvel near the mint just off Race and 5th, to observe boat traffic on the Delaware and get a great view of both Philadelphia and Camden, NJ. It's bound to make you wonder exactly how safe it is to put so much faith in engineers—not for those with vertigo.

In 1723, a penniless Ben Franklin arrived in Philadelphia and walked along **Elfreth's Alley,** tucked away near 2nd and Arch St., allegedly "the oldest street in America." Betsy Ross supposedly sewed the first flag of the original 13 states at the tiny **Betsy Ross House** (627-5343), on Arch near 3rd St. (open Tues.-Sun. 10am-5pm; $1 donation requested, kids 50¢). Two Quaker meeting houses grace the streets of Phildadelphia; the original **Free Quaker Meeting House** (923-6777), at 5th and Arch St., and a new one at 4th and Arch St. (open Tues.-Sat. 10am-4pm, Sun. noon-4pm). **Christ Church** (922-1695), on 2nd near Market, served the Quakers who sought a more fashionable way of life. Ben Franklin lies buried in the nearby **Christ Church cemetery,** at 5th and Arch St.

Mikveh Israel (922-5446), the first Jewish congregation of Philadelphia, has a burial ground on Spruce near 8th St. The **Afro-American Historical and Cultural Museum** (574-0381), 7th and Arch St., was the first U.S. museum devoted solely to the history of African-Americans. (Open Tues.-Sat. 10am-5pm, Sun. noon-6pm. $4, seniors, students, handicapped, and children $2.)

On the corner of 8th and Race St., the Pennsylvania College of Podiatric Medicine contains the **Shoe Museum** (625-5243). This 6th-floor collection contains footwear fashions from the famous feet of Reggie Jackson, Lady Bird Johnson, Dr. J, Nancy Reagan, and more. (Tours Wed. and Fri. 9am-5pm, by appointment only.) Near the Shoe Museum, the **Tattoo Museum,** 3216 Kensington Ave. (426-9477), has historical artifacts and useless tattooing information written all over it (freaky and free).

Society Hill proper begins where the park ends, on Walnut St. between Front and 7th St. Federal-style townhouses dating back 300 years line the picturesque cobblestone walks illuminated by old-fashioned streetlights. **Head House Sq.,** 2nd and Pine St., held a marketplace in 1745 and now houses restaurants, boutiques, and craft shops. An outdoor flea market moves in on summer weekends.

South of Head House Sq., the **Mario Lanza Museum,** 416 Queen St. (468-3623), enshrines a collection of artifacts and memorabilia from the life of opera singer Mario Lanza (Mon.-Fri. 10am-3:30pm; disabled access; free; free parking). Even farther south, the **Mummer's Museum** (336-3050), 2nd and Washington Ave., gives you a peek inside the closets of the construction workers, policemen, and others who follow the tradition of Philly's mummers, dressing in feathers and sequins for a bizarre New Year's Day parade. (Open Tues.-Sat. 9:30am-5pm, Sun. noon-5pm. $2.50, seniors and under 12 $2.)

Located on the Delaware River, **Penn's Landing** (923-8181) is the largest freshwater port in the world. Docked here you'll find the *Gazela,* a three-masted, 178-ft. Portuguese square rigger built in 1883; the *U.S.S. Olympia,* Commodore Dewey's flagship during the Spanish-American War (922-1898; tours daily 10am-5pm; $5, children $2); and the *U.S.S. Becuna,* a WWII submarine. Jump on the **Penn's Landing Trolley** (627-0807), Delaware Ave. between Catharine and Race St., for a 20-minute tour along the waterfront (Thurs.-Sun. 11am-dusk; $1.50, under 12 75¢).

Center City

Center City, the area bounded by 12th, 23rd, Vine, and Pine St., bustles with activity. An ornate structure of granite and marble with 20-ft.-thick foundation walls, **City Hall** (686-1776), at Broad and Market St., is the nation's largest municipal building. Until 1908, it also reigned as the tallest building in the U.S., with the help of the 37-ft. statue of William Penn, Jr. on top. A municipal statute prohibited building higher than the top of Penn's hat until Reagan-era entrepreneurs overturned the law in the mid-80s, finally launching Philadelphia into the skyscraper era. You can share Billy's outlook on things by taking an elevator up to the **tower** (686-9074) for a commanding view of the city. (Tower open Mon.-Fri. 10am-3pm. Last elevator 2:45pm. Call ahead for tickets or you may have to wait. Free.) The **Pennsylvania Academy of Fine Arts** (972-7600), Broad and Cherry St., the country's first art school and one of its first museums, has an extensive collection of American and British art, including works by Charles Wilson Peale, Thomas Eakins, Winslow Homer, and some contemporary artists. (Open Tues. and Thurs.-Sat. 10am-5pm, Wed. 10am-7:30pm, Sun. 11am-5pm. Tours daily 12:15 and 2pm. $6, students and seniors $5, under 5 free; free Wed. 5-7:30pm.) Across from City Hall the **Masonic Temple,** 1 N. Broad St. (988-1917), contains numerous halls of various architectural styles. (Must be seen on a 45-min. tour. Mon.-Fri. 10, 11am, 1, 2, and 3pm, Sat. 10, and 11am. Free.)

Just south of **Rittenhouse Square,** the **Rosenbach Museum and Library,** 2010 Delancey St. (732-1600), houses rare manuscripts and paintings, including some of the earliest-known copies of Cervantes' *Don Quixote,* the original manuscript of James Joyce's *Ulysses,* and the original *Yankee Doodle Dandy.* (Open Sept.-July Tues.-Sun. 11am-4pm. Guided tours $3.50, students, over 62, and children $2.50. Exhibitions only $2.) Ben Franklin founded the **Library Company of Philadelphia,** 1314 Locust St. (546-3181), near 13th St., over 250 years ago so that colonists could order books from England; the club's members still pay for books from the mother country today (open Mon.-Fri. 9am-4:45pm; free).

Benjamin Franklin Parkway

Nicknamed "America's Champs-Elysées," the Benjamin Franklin Pkwy. cuts a wide, diagonal deviation from William Penn's original grid of city streets. Built in the 1920s, this tree- and flag-lined street connects Center City with Fairmount Park and the Schuylkill River. The street is flanked by elegant architecture, including the twin buildings at Logan Sq., 19th and Ben Franklin Pkwy., which house the **Free Library of Philadelphia** and the **Municipal Court.**

The fantastic **Science Center** in the **Franklin Institute** (448-1200), at 20th and Ben Franklin Pkwy., amazes visitors with four floors of gadgets and games depicting the intricacies of space, time, motion, and the human body. The 20-ft. **Benjamin Franklin National Memorial** statue divines lightning at the entrance. In 1990, to commemorate the 200th anniversary of Franklin's death, the Institute unveiled the **Futures Center;** glimpse life in the 21st century including simulated zero gravity and a timely set of exhibits on the changing global environment. (Futures Center open Mon.-Wed. 9:30am-5pm, Thurs.-Sat. 9:30am-9pm. Sun. 9:30am-6pm; Science Center daily 9:30am-5pm. Admission to both $9.50, over 62 and ages 4-11 $8.50.) The **Omniverse Theater** provides 180° and 4½ stories of optical oohs and aahs. (Shows on the hr. Mon.-Wed. 10am-4pm, Thurs. 10am-4pm and 7-8pm, Fri.-10am-4pm and 7-9pm, Sat. 5 and 7-9pm, Sun. 5-6pm. $7.50, seniors and kids $6.50.) **Fels Planetarium** boasts an advanced computer-driven system that projects a simulation of life billions of years beyond ours. Drop in for a groovy rock music and multi-colored laser show on Friday or Saturday night; call for details. (Shows daily every hr. 11:15am-4:15pm. $7.50, seniors and kids $6.50. Exhibits and a show $12, seniors and kids $10.50; exhibits and both shows $14.50/$12.50.)

A casting of the *Gates of Hell* outside the **Rodin Museum** (563-1948), 22nd St., guards the portal of the most complete collection of the artist's works this side of the Seine, including one of the gazillion versions of *The Thinker* (open Tues.-Sun. 10am-5pm; $1 donation). Try your hand at the sensuous **Please Touch Museum,** 210 N. 21st St. (963-0666), designed specifically for grabby kids under eight (open daily 9am-6pm; Labor Day-Memorial Day 9am-4:30pm; $7, under 1 free).

The **Academy of Natural Sciences** (299-1000), 19th and Ben Franklin Pkwy., showcases an exhibit of precious gems and a 65-million-year-old dinosaur skeleton. (Open Mon.-Fri. 10am-4:30pm, Sat.-Sun. and holidays 10am-5pm; $6.50, over 64 $6, ages 4-12 $5.) Farther down 26th St., the **Philadelphia Museum of Art** (763-8100) holds one of the world's major art collections, including Rubens's *Prometheus Bound,* Picasso's *Three Musicians,* and Duchamp's *Nude Descending a Staircase,* as well as extensive Asian, Egyptian, and decorative art collections. (Open Tues. and Thurs.-Sun. 10am-5pm, Wed. 10am-8:45pm. $7, over 61 and ages 5-18 $4; free Sun. 10am-1pm.) Three blocks from the museum, **Eastern State Penitentiary** (236-7236), on Fairmount Ave. at 22nd St., once a revolutionary institution in the system of criminal punishment and rehabilitation, conducts tours of the solitary quarters which prisoners inhabited many years ago. Tours include an exhibit of artwork addressing life in confinement in various media. (Open mid-May to early Sept. Thurs.-Sun. 10am-7pm; early Sept.-Oct. Sat.-Sun. 10am-7pm. $7, seniors $6, ages 7-18 $3.) The **Free Library of Philadelphia** (686-5322) scores with a library of orchestral music and one of the nation's largest rare book collections. (Open Mon.-Wed. 9am-9pm, Thurs.-Fri. 9am-6pm, Sat. 9am-5pm; Oct.-May also Sun. 1-5pm.)

Covered with bike trails and picnic areas, **Fairmount Park** sprawls behind the Philadelphia Museum of Art on both sides of the Schuylkill River. At night, look for the faces which appear in the lights of **Boathouse Row,** where the shells of local crew teams are kept. In the northern arm of Fairmount Park trails leave the Schuylkill and wind along secluded Wissahickon Creek for 5 mi. The **Horticultural Center** (685-0096; open daily 9am-3pm), off Belmont Ave., blooms with greenhouses, Japanese gardens, and periodic flower shows (grounds open daily 9am-6pm; Oct.-May 9am-5pm; $2 suggested donation).

West Philadelphia (University City)

The **University of Pennsylvania (UPenn)** and **Drexel University,** located across the Schuylkill from Center City, reside in West Philadelphia within easy walking distance of the 30th St. Station. The Penn campus provides a cloistered retreat of green lawns, red-brick quadrangles, and rarefied air. Ritzy shops line Chestnut St. and boisterous fraternities line Spruce; warm weather brings out a variety of street vendors along the Drexel and Penn borders. Enter the Penn campus at 34th and Walnut, where you'll be greeted by a statue of Benjamin Franklin, who founded the university in 1740. Some of the area surrounding University City is not the safest—try not to travel alone or at night.

Discover magazine calls Penn's large and elegantly landscaped **University Museum of Archeology and Anthropology** (898-4000), 33rd and Spruce St., one of the world's ten best science museums. Peruse the outstanding East Asian art collection under the beautiful stone-and-glass rotunda, and stop to puzzle over the museum's Egyptian mummy and 12-ton sphinx. (Open June-Aug. Tues.-Sat. 10am-4:30pm; Sept.-May Tues.-Sat. 10am-4:30pm, Sun. 1-5pm. $5, students and over 62 $2.50.) In 1965, Andy Warhol had his first one-man show at the **Institute of Contemporary Art** (898-7108), 36th and Walnut St., and the gallery has stayed on the cutting edge to this day. (Open Thurs.-Sun. 10am-5pm, Wed. 10am-7pm. $3, students, seniors, and children $1, under 12 free; free Sun. 10am-noon.)

ENTERTAINMENT

The Academy of Music (893-1930), Broad and Locust St., modeled after Milan's *La Scala,* houses the **Philadelphia Orchestra.** Formerly under the direction of the late Eugene Ormandy, now under Wolfgang Sawallisch, the orchestra, among the nation's best, performs September through May. General admission tickets ($5) go on sale at the Locust St. entrance 45 minutes before Friday and Saturday concerts; check with the box office for availability. (Regular tickets $15-78.)

The **Mann Music Center** (878-7707), on George's Hill near 52nd St. and Parkside Ave. in Fairmount Park, hosts summer Philadelphia Orchestra concerts and jazz and rock events with 5000 seats under cover and 10,000 on outdoor benches and lawns. June through August, pick up free lawn tickets for the orchestra from the visitors center at 16th St. and JFK Blvd. on the day of a performance. (See Practical Information, above.) For the big-name shows, sit just outside the theater and soak in the sounds gratis (real seats $12-35). The **Robin Hood Dell East** (477-8810), Strawberry Mansion Dr. in Fairmount Park, brings in top names in pop, jazz, gospel, and ethnic dance in July and August. The Philadelphia Orchestra holds several free performances here in summer, and as many as 30,000 people gather on the lawn. Inquire at the visitors center (636-1666) about upcoming events.

More free concerts fill summer evenings at **Penn's Landing** (923-8181; see Sights, above). During the school year, the outstanding students of the **Curtis Institute of Music,** 1726 Locust St. (893-5279), give free concerts on Mondays, Wednesdays, and Fridays at 8pm (concerts mid-Oct to April). **Merriam Theater,** 250 S. Broad St., Center City (732-5446), stages a variety of dance, musical, and comedy performances September through May. The **Old City,** Chestnut to Vine and Front to 4th St., comes alive on the first Friday of every month (Oct.-June) for the fantastic **First Friday** celebration. The streets fill with people and the music of live bands, as the area's many art galleries open their doors, enticing visitors with offers of free food.

Philly's four professional sports teams play a short ride away on the Broad St. subway line. The **Phillies** (baseball; 463-1000) and **Eagles** (football; 463-5500) hold games at **Veterans Stadium,** Broad St. and Pattison Ave., while the **Spectrum,** across the street, houses the **76ers** (basketball; 339-7676) and the **Flyers** (hockey; 755-9700). General admission tickets for baseball and hockey run from $5 to $20; football and basketball tickets cost more ($15-50).

NIGHTLIFE

Check Friday's weekend magazine section in the Philadelphia *Inquirer* for entertainment listings. Free at newsstands and markets, *City Paper,* distributed on Thursdays, and the *Philadelphia Weekly,* distributed on Wednesdays, have weekly listings of city events. *Au Courant* and *PGN* (75¢), gay and lesbian weekly newspapers, list and advertise events throughout the Delaware Valley region. Along **South St.,** clubs dance and live music plays on weekends. Many pubs line 2nd St. near Chestnut, close to the Bank St. Hostel. **Columbus Blvd.,** running along Penn's Landing, has recently become a local hotspot, with tons of nightclubs and restaurants; a great place to stroll on a warm summer night. Most bars and clubs catering to gay clientele congregate along Camac St., S. 12th St., and S. 13th St.

Khyber Pass Pub, 56 S. 2nd St. (440-9683). One of Philly's best live music venues, bringing in a variety of alternative bands. Cover varies. Open daily noon-2am.

Trocadero (923-ROCK/7625), 10th and Arch St. Nationally known live bands perform to a mostly college-aged crowd. Cover around $6-16. Advance tickets through Ticketmaster. Doors usually open around 9pm.

Gothum, 800 Columbus Blvd. (928-9319). Hardcore dancing to an acid techno beat. Oldies night Mon. Cover Mon. and Thurs. $5, Fri.-Sat. $10. Open Mon. and Fri. 5pm-2am, Thurs. 7pm-2am, Sat. 8pm-2am.

Cat Man Du, 417 Columbus Blvd. (629-7400). A hopping bar with nightly live music. Drafts $2.75. Cover Mon.-Thurs. after 8:30pm $5, Fri.-Sat. $7, Sun. $2, after 5pm $5. Open daily noon-2am.

Middle East, 126 Chestnut St. (922-1003). 3 huge floors, each with a different band. Drafts $2.50-3. Cover Fri.-Sat. $3-18 depending on show. Comedy Sat. 8pm ($10). Open Mon.-Sat. 5pm-2am, Sun. 5pm-midnight.

Xero, 613 S. 4th St. (629-0565). Popular twentysomething bar with $2.50 drafts and $3.25 rails. Happy hour Fri.-Sat. 7-10:30pm includes 75¢ drafts and free wings until 9pm. All-you-can-drink Thurs.; cover $7. Open Mon.-Wed. 5pm-2am, Thurs.-Fri. 4pm-2am, Sat.-Sun. 2pm-2am.

Mako's Retired Surfer, 301 South St. (625-3820). Super-eclectic crowd at the busiest bar on South St. Drafts $1.75. Happy hour, Mon.-Fri. 10pm-midnight, brings $1.25 drafts and $2.25 domestic bottles. Kitchen open daily until 1:30pm. Open Mon.-Tues. 2pm-2am, Wed.-Sun. noon-2am.

Woody's, 202 S. 13th St. (545-1893). A good-looking, young, gay male crowd grind Tues.-Wed. and Fri.-Sat. Cover after 10pm $5. Open daily 11am-2am.

Hepburn's, 254 S. 12th St. (545-8088). A lesbian bar with $2 drafts. Dance upstairs Tues.-Sun. after 10pm; cover $5. Open daily 4pm-2am.

■ NEAR PHILADELPHIA: VALLEY FORGE

American troops during the Revolutionary War waged a fierce battle at Valley Forge, but not against the British; during the winter of 1777-78, the 12,000 men under General George Washington's command spent agonizing months fighting starvation, bitter cold, and disease. Only 8000 survived. Nonetheless, inspired by Washington's fierce spirit and the news of an American alliance with France, the troops left Valley Forge stronger and better trained. They went on to win victories in New Jersey, to reoccupy Philadelphia, and to become a free and independent nation.

Valley Forge National Historic Park encompasses over 3600 acres (open daily 6am-10pm). Self-guided tours begin at the **visitors center** (610-783-1077), which also features a museum and film (15-min. shows twice per hr. 9am-4:30pm; center open daily 9am-5pm). The tour visits Washington's headquarters, reconstructed soldier huts and fortifications, and the Grand Parade Ground where the army drilled. Admission to the historic buildings, such as **Washington's headquarters,** costs $2 (under 17 free), but the grounds of the park are free to all. Audio tapes rent for $8. The park has three picnic areas, but no camping; the visitors center distributes a list of nearby campgrounds. A 5-mi. bike trail winds through the hills of the park.

To get to Valley Forge, take the Schuylkill Expwy. westbound from Philadelphia for about 12 mi. Get off at the Valley Forge exit, then take Rte. 202S for 1 mi. and

Rte. 422W for 1½ mi. to another Valley Forge exit. SEPTA (see Philadelphia Practical Information, above) runs buses to the visitors center Monday through Friday only; catch #125 at 16th and JFK ($3.10).

■■■ LANCASTER COUNTY

The Amish, the Mennonites, and the Brethren, three groups of German Anabaptists who fled persecution in Deutschland (thus the misnomer "Pennsylvania Dutch" by confused locals), sought freedom to pursue their own religion in the rolling countryside of Lancaster County. They successfully escaped censor, but they have not escaped attention. Thousands of visitors flock to this pastoral area every year to glimpse a way of life that eschews modern conveniences like motorized vehicles, electricity, and The Gap, in favor of modest amenities.

PRACTICAL INFORMATION

Tourist Office: Lancaster Chamber of Commerce and Industry, 100 Queen St. (397-3531 or 800-735-2629), in the Southern Market Center. Pick up guided walking tours of Lancaster City (April-Oct. Mon.-Sat. 10am and 1:30pm, Sun. and holidays 10, 11am, and 1:30pm; $4, kids $3) or buy a self-guided booklet ($1.50). To reserve a tour off season call 653-8225 or 394-2339. Open Mon.-Fri. 8:30am-5pm. **Pennsylvania Dutch Visitors Bureau Information Center,** 501 Greenfield Rd. (299-8901), on the east side of Lancaster City just off Rte. 30. Walls of brochures and free phone lines to most area inns and campsites. Open Mon.-Sat. 8am-6pm, Sun. 8am-5pm; Sept.-May daily 9am-5pm. **Mennonite Information Center,** 2209 Millstream Rd. (299-0954), just off Rte. 30. Guides for a 2-hr. tour $23; call for times. Open Mon.-Sat. 8am-5pm.

Trains: Amtrak, 53 McGovern Ave. (291-5080 or 800-872-7245), in Lancaster City. To: Philadelphia (4-7 per day, 1¼hr., $9).

Buses: Capitol Trailways, 22 W. Clay St. (397-4861). 3 buses per day between Lancaster City and Philadelphia (2hr., $12.35). Open daily 7am-4:45pm.

Public Transportation: Red Rose Transit, 45 Erick Rd. (397-4246). Service around Lancaster and the surrounding countryside. Pick up route maps at the office. Base fare $1, over 65 free Mon.-Fri.9am-3:30pm, after 6:30pm, and all day on weekends. Lancaster City to Intercourse $1.65.

Post Office: 1400 Harrisburg Pike (396-6900). Open Mon.-Fri. 7:30am-7pm, Sat. 9am-2pm. **ZIP code:** Lancaster City, 17604. **Area code:** 717.

Lancaster County covers a huge area. It's difficult to get around without a car; but Red Rose Transit (see above) can shuttle between major sights. If you drive, pick up a map at one of the visitors centers; you will probably get lost on the confusing county roads. Still, veering off U.S. 30 to explore the sideroads is the best way to see the area. If you like to know where you are, drive along Rte. 340 or pay a guide from one of the visitors centers to show you around. You always thought **Intercourse** would lead to **Paradise,** and on the country roads of Lancaster County, it does. All addresses given here are found in Lancaster City, unless noted.

ACCOMMODATIONS AND CAMPING

Hundreds of hotels and B&Bs cluster in this area. Stop by a visitors center (see Practical Information, above) for help in finding a room. About the only thing to outnumber cows in this countryside is **campgrounds;** there's little difference between them, so choose the location you like best.

Pennsylvania Dutch Motel, 2275 N. Reading Rd. (336-5559), at exit 21 off Pennsylvania Turnpike. Big clean rooms with cable and A/C. Friendly hostess has written directions to major sights. Singles $42, doubles $46; Nov.-March $8-10 less.

Conestoga Wagon Motel (286-5061), Rte. 23E in Morgantown. Spotless rooms with cable TV, A/C, and free local calls. Singles $40, doubles $45; $5 each additional person.

MID-ATLANTIC

Old Millstream Camping Manor, 2249 U.S. 30E (299-2314). The closest year-round facility, 4mi. east of Lancaster City. Office open daily 8am-8pm. Sites $17, with hookup $20. Reservations recommended.

Roamers Retreat, 5005 Lincoln Hwy. (442-4287 or 800-525-5605), off U.S. 30, 7½mi. east of Rte. 896. Sites $18, with hookup $20. Call for reservations. Open April-Oct.

Shady Grove, 264 W. Swartzville Rd. (215-484-4225), on Rte. 272 at Rte. 897. 80 sites. With electricity $16, with full hookup $18. Write for information at P.O. Box 28, Adamstown 19501.

FOOD

A good alternative to high priced "family-style" restaurants exists at **farmers markets** which dot the roadways. Don't miss the **Central Market,** in Lancaster City at the northwest corner of Penn Sq., a huge food bazaar which has provided inexpensive meats, cheeses, vegetables, and sandwiches since 1899 (open Tues. and Fri. 6am-4:30pm, Sat. 6am-2pm). Many fun and inexpensive restaurants surround the market. The huge **Farmers Market** complex in Bird-in-the-Hand, on Rte. 340, charges more than the Amish road stands, but is centralized and has parking (open daily 8:30am-5:30pm). If you'd like to stuff yourself with "real" German cuisine and have some cash, try any of the restaurants on Rte. 340 in Bird-in-Hand which offers all-you-can-eat meals for $12-16. **The Amish Barn,** 3029 Old Philadelphia Pike (768-8886), makes your plate bottomless for $13 (kids $5; open daily 7:30am-9pm). Lancaster City cooks up more varied fare. **Isaac's,** 44 N. Queen St. (394-5544), in the Central Mall, creates imaginative sandwiches with avian names ($4-6; open daily 10am-9pm). If you try nothing else in Lancaster, sample a **whoopie pie** (75¢).

SIGHTS

The **People's Place** (768-7171), on Main St./Rte. 340, in Intercourse, 11 mi. east of Lancaster City, spans an entire block with bookstores, craft shops, and an art gallery. The film *Who Are the Amish* runs every half hour 9:30am-5pm. (Film $3.50, under 12 $1.75. Open Mon.-Sat. 9:30am-9:30pm; Labor Day-Memorial Day 9:30am-5pm.) If you have questions, seek out friendly locals at the Mennonite Information Center (see Practical Information, above), which shows another film, *Portraits of Our Heritage and Faith.* **Amish World,** also in Intercourse, has charming hands-on exhibits on Amish and Mennonite life, from barn-raising to hat-styles ($6.50, children $3.25). There is nothing cooler than a postcard that says "I am in Intercourse, having a good time, and wishing you were here." Hell, send us one.

County seat **Lancaster City,** in the heart of Dutch country, has clean, red-brick row houses huddled around historic **Penn Sq.** The **Quilt Museum** (768-7171), on Main St. in Intercourse, has a lovely patchwork of Amish quilts. (Open Mon.-Sat. 9am-5pm; $4, under 13 $2.)

Hershey's Candyland

Milton S. Hershey, a Mennonite resident of eastern Pennsylvania, discovered how to mass market chocolate, previously a rare and expensive luxury. Today the company that bears his name operates the world's largest chocolate factory, in **Hershey,** about 45 minutes from Lancaster. East of town at **Hersheypark** (800-HERSHEY/437-7439), the **Chocolate World Visitors Center** (534-4900) presents a free, automated tour through a simulated chocolate factory. After the tour visitors emerge into a pavilion full of chocolate cookies, discounted chocolate candy, and fashionable Hershey sportswear. Beware: to take this "free" tour, you must pay $4 to park in a Hershey lot. (Open Sun.-Fri. 9am-10pm, Sat. 9am-7:45pm; Labor Day to mid-June daily 9am-5pm.) Hersheypark's **amusement center** (534-3900) has heart-stopping rides and short lines. Don't miss the Sidewinder, the Comet, or the SooperdooperLooper. (Open late May-early Sept. daily 10am-10pm. $25, over 55 and ages 3-8 $16.) **Trailways** (397-4861) provides transportation from Lancaster City to Hershey (1 per day, 2½hr., $8.15).

MID-ATLANTIC

■■■ GETTYSBURG

In early July of 1863, Union and Confederate forces met at Gettysburg in one of the bloodiest and most decisive battles of the Civil War. The ultimate victory of the Union forces dealt a dire blow to the hopes of the South, but the victory exacted a horrible price: over 50,000 casualties. Four months later, President Lincoln arrived in Gettysburg to dedicate the **Gettysburg National Cemetery** (many Union soldiers lie buried where they fell) and to give "a few appropriate remarks." Lincoln emphasized the preservation of the union in a speech that, though only two minutes long, was a watershed in American history. Lincoln's *Gettysburg Address,* and the brutality of the battle which preceded it, have made Gettysburg the most famous battlefield in America. Each year thousands of visitors head for these Pennsylvania fields, heeding the President's call to "resolve that these dead shall not have died in vain."

For a great overview of the area, take a high-speed elevator up the 300-ft. **National Tower** (334-6754; open Easter-Aug. daily 9am-6:30pm; Sept.-Nov. 9am-5:30pm; $4.90, seniors $4.35, ages 6-15 $2.65). The **Cyclorama Center,** across from the tower, holds the second draft of Lincoln's speech, exhibits, a 20-minute film on the battle, and, of course, the cyclorama, a 356x26-ft. mural depicting this turning point in the Civil War. A sound and light show runs every 30 minutes. (Open daily 9am-5pm. $2, seniors $1.50, under 15 free.)

Before attacking Gettysburg's Civil War memorabilia, get your bearings at the **National Military Park Visitors Information Center** (334-1124), 1 mi. south of town on Taneytown Rd. (open daily 8am-6pm; Labor Day-Memorial Day 8am-5pm). Drive the 18-mi. **self-guided auto tour** on your own, letting the free map navigate you through the monuments and landmarks, or pay a park guide to show you the sights (2-hr. tour $25). Rangers lead free guided walking tours. The visitors center also houses a 750-sq.-foot **electric map;** areas light up in coordination with a taped narration bringing the great sweep of the battle into brighter focus ($2, over 61 $1.50, under 15 free). You can rent a **bike** at Artillery Ridge campground (see below; $4 per hr., $10 half day, $16 full day). Gettysburg's **area code:** 717.

The **Gettysburg Travel Council,** 35 Carlisle St. (334-6274), in Lincoln Sq., stocks a full line of motel brochures, as well as maps and information on local sights (open daily 9am-5pm). For cheap, large rooms with A/C, try **Cleveland's Motel** (334-3473), located just off U.S. 15 about 2 mi. from the park (singles $30, doubles $45; Sept.-April rates drop). The closest hostel is 20 mi. away; follow Rte. 34N to Rte. 233. Next to the entrance of **Pine Grove Furnace State Park,** the incredibly large and luxurious **Ironmasters Mansion Hostel (HI-AYH)** (717-486-7585), has 44 beds in a gorgeous area, close to swimming, fishing, and hiking—even a sliver of the Appalachian Trail. Play a game of pool or volleyball, and work out the kinks in the jacuzzi. Marvel at the life-sized chess set. (Open 7:30-9:30am and 5-10pm. $10, non-members $13.) **Artillery Ridge,** 610 Taneytown Rd. (334-1288), 1 mi. south on Rte. 134, maintains campsites with access to showers, a riding stable, laundry facilities, and a pool (sites for 2 $12.50, with hookup $17; open April-Nov.).

The candle-lit **Springhouse Tavern,** 89 Steinwehr Ave. (334-2100), hides in the basement of the **Dobben House,** Gettysburg's first building (c. 1776) and an Underground Railroad shelter for runaway slaves during the Civil War. Create your own grilled burger ($6) or try "Mason's Mile High" ($6.25), a double-decker with ham, roast beef, and turkey (open daily 11:30am-9pm). **Food for Thought,** 46 Baltimore St. (337-2221), serves huge salads, sandwiches, and other organic fare. (Meals $2.50-5.25; open Tues.-Thurs. 8:30am-9pm, Fri.-Sat. 8:30am-11pm, Sun. 10am-6pm.)

When the Union and the Confederacy decided to lock horns here, they didn't have the traveler in mind. Inaccessible by Greyhound or Amtrak, Gettysburg is in south-central PA, off U.S. 15 about 30 mi. south of Harrisburg.

■■■ PITTSBURGH

Charles Dickens called this city "Hell with the lid off" for a reason. As late as the 1950s, smoke from area steel mills made street lamps essential even during the day. Thankfully, the decline of the steel industry has meant cleaner air and rivers, and a recent renaissance in Pittsburgh's economy has produced a brighter urban landscape; private-public partnerships have created shiny new architecture like Phillip Johnson's Pittsburgh Plate Glass Building, a gothic black-glass cathedral. Throughout these renewals, Pittsburgh's individual neighborhoods have maintained strong and diverse identities; Oakland, Southside, and the Strip District vie for visitors' attention as much as downtown. Admittedly, some of the old, sooty Pittsburgh lives on in the suburbs; but one need only ride up the Duquesne Incline and view downtown from atop Mount Washington to see how thoroughly Pittsburgh has entered a new age—and to understand why locals are so justly proud of "The 'Burgh."

PRACTICAL INFORMATION

Tourist Office: Pittsburgh Convention and Visitors Bureau, 4 Gateway Center (281-7711), downtown in a little glass building on Liberty Ave. across from the Hilton. Unfortunately, their city maps only cover downtown. Open Mon.-Fri. 9:30am-5pm, Sat.-Sun. 9:30am-3pm; Nov.-April closed Sun.

Airport: Pittsburgh International (472-3525), 15mi. west of downtown by I-279 and Rte. 60 in Findlay Township. **Airline Transportation Company** (471-2250) runs shuttles to downtown (daily every 30min. 6am-7pm, every hr. 7-10pm; $12, $20 round-trip), Oakland (Mon.-Fri. every hr. 9am-9pm, Sat.-Sun. every 2hr. 9am-9pm; $21 round-trip), and Monroeville (daily every 2hr. 6am-2pm, every hr. 2pm-7pm; $32 round-trip).

Trains: Amtrak, 1100 Liberty Ave. (471-6170; 800-872-7245 for reservations), at Grant on the northern edge of downtown next to Greyhound and the post office. Safe and very clean inside, but be careful walking from here to the city center at night. To: Philadelphia (7hr., $67); Chicago (9hr., $84). Open 24 hrs.; ticket office closes for meals Mon.-Fri. 5:15-6:15am and 8-9pm, Sat.-Sun. 12:30-1:30pm.

Buses: Greyhound, (391-2300 or 800-231-2222), on 11th St. at Liberty Ave. near Amtrak. Large and fairly clean, with police on duty. To: Philadelphia (7hr., $42), Chicago (12hr., $62). Station and ticket office open 24 hrs.

Public Transportation: Port Authority of Allegheny County (PAT) (442-2000 for general info). Within the Golden Triangle: bus fare free until 7pm, 75¢ after 7pm; subway (between the 3 downtown stops) free. Beyond the Triangle: bus fare $1.25, weekend all-day pass $3; subway $1.25-1.60. Schedules and maps at most subway stations and in the Community Interest section of the yellow pages.

Taxis: Peoples Cab, 681-3131. $1.40 base fare, $1.40 per mi.

Car Rental: Rent-A-Wreck, 101 Hargrove St. (488-3440), 1 block from Liberty tunnels. $28 per day with 50 free mi.; 18¢ per additional mi. Must be 21 with major credit card or $200-300 cash deposit. Open daily 8am-8pm; in winter 8am-6pm.

Crisis Lines: Rape Action Hotline, 765-2731. Open 24 hrs.

Emergency: 911.

Post Office: (642-4475 or 642-4476; 642-4478 for general delivery), at 7th and Grant St. Open Mon.-Fri. 6am-6pm, Sat. 6am-2:30pm. **ZIP code:** 15219. **Area code:** 412.

Pittsburgh's downtown, the **Golden Triangle,** is shaped by two rivers—the Allegheny to the north, and the Monongahela to the south—which flow together to form a third, the Ohio. Streets in the Triangle parallel to the Monongahela number 1 through 7. The **University of Pittsburgh** and **Carnegie-Mellon University** can be found east of the Triangle in **Oakland.** With one of the lowest crime rates in the nation for a city of its size, Pittsburgh is fairly safe, even downtown at night.

ACCOMMODATIONS AND CAMPING

More a hotel than a hostel, **Point Park College,** 201 Wood St. (392-3824), at Blvd. of the Allies 8 blocks from the Greyhound Station, provides clean rooms, some of which have private baths, to college students with ID and HI-AYH members. There's no kitchen, but the third-floor cafeteria serves an all-you-can-eat breakfast ($4) 7-9:30am daily. (3-day max stay. Office open daily 8am-4pm. Check-in until 11pm; tell the guards you're a hosteler. $15; linen included. Reservations recommended. Open May 15-Aug. 15.) A 30-minute (11-mi.) drive from downtown, the **Red Roof Inn,** 6404 Stubenville Pike (787-7870), south on I-279 past the Rte. 22/Rte. 30 junction at the Moon Run exit., offers all the comforts of a clean, quiet chain motel. (Check-in 24 hrs. Check out by noon. Singles $41, doubles $48. In summer, reserve more than a week in advance.) **Pittsburgh North Campground,** 6610 Mars Rd., Cranberry Township 16066 (776-1150), has the area's closest camping, 20 minutes from downtown; take I-79 to the Mars exit. (110 campsites; showers, swimming. Tent sites for 2 $17, hook-up $23; $3 per extra adult, $2 per extra child.)

FOOD

Aside from the pizza joints and bars downtown, **Oakland** is the best place to look for a good, inexpensive meal. Collegiate watering holes and cafés pack **Forbes Ave.** around the University of Pittsburgh, while colorful eateries and shops line **Walnut St.** in Shadyside and **East Carson St.** in South Side. The **Strip District** on Penn Ave. between 16th and 22nd St. (north of downtown along the Allegheny) bustles with Italian, Greek, and Asian cuisine, vendors, grocers, and craftsmen. On Saturday mornings, fresh produce, fresh fish, and fresh street performers vie for business.

Original Hot Dog Shops, Inc., 3901 Forbes Ave. (687-8327), at Bouquet St. in Oakland. A rowdy (actually, very rowdy), greasy Pittsburgh institution with lots and lots of fries, burgers, dogs, and pizza. Call it "the O" like a local. 16" pizza $4. Open Sun.-Wed. 10am-3:30am, Thurs. 10am-4:30am, Fri.-Sat. 10am-5am.

Beehive Coffeehouse and Theater, 3807 Forbes Ave. (683-HIVE/4483), just steps from the "O." A quirky coffeehouse brimming with cool wall paintings, cool staff, cool clientele, and hot cappuccino ($2.10). The theater in the back features current films. Poetry and an occasional open-mike improv night buzz upstairs. Mon.-Fri. 7am-midnight; Sat.-Sun. 8am-midnight. Another location in Southside, 1327 E. Carson St. (488-HIVE/4483).

The Elbow Room, 5744 Ellsworth Ave. (441-5222), in Shadyside. The relaxed clientele take advantage of garden seating, free refills, and Crayolas for the tablecloths. Spicy chicken sandwiches ($6) and a hybrid southwest/front parlor decor make it worth the trip. Open Sun.-Thurs. 11am-midnight, Fri.-Sat. 11am-1am.

Harris' Grill-A Cafe, 5747 Ellsworth Ave. (363-0833), across the street from The Elbow Room. Chomp on inexpensive Greek specialties ($3-9) beneath the European-style umbrellas on the outdoor deck. Open daily 11:30am-2am.

SIGHTS

The **Golden Triangle** is home to **Point State Park** and its famous 200-ft. fountain. A ride up the **Duquesne Incline,** 1220 Grandview Ave. (381-1665), in the South Side, affords a spectacular view of the city ($2, ages 6-11 $1, under 6 free). The **Fort Pitt Blockhouse and Museum** (281-9285), in the park, dates back to the French and Indian War (open Wed.-Sat. 10am-4:30pm, Sun. noon-4:30pm. $4, seniors $3, kids $2). About 3 mi. east along the Blvd. of the Allies in Schenley Park, **Phipps Conservatory** (622-6915; ext. 6958 for tour reservations), conserves 2½ acres of happiness for the flower fanatic. (Open Tues.-Sun. 9am-5pm. $4, students and seniors $3, ages 2-12 $2; $1 more for shows.) Founded in 1787, the **University of Pittsburgh** (621-4141; 648-9402 for tours) stands in the shadow of the 42-story **Cathedral of Learning** (624-6000) at Bigelow Blvd. between Forbes and 5th Ave. The "cathedral," an academic building dedicated in 1934, features 23 "nationality classrooms" designed and decorated by artisans from Pittsburgh's many ethnic traditions. **Carn-**

egie-Mellon University (268-2000) welcomes scholars right down the street on Forbes Ave.

The **Andy Warhol Museum,** 117 Sandusky St. (237-8300), on the North Side, houses seven floors of the Pittsburgh native's material, from Pop portraits of Marilyn, Jackie, and Grace to continuous screenings of films with titles like *Blowjob* and *Sleep*. (Open Wed. and Sun. 11am-6pm, Thurs.-Sat. 11am-8pm. $5, students and children $3, seniors $4.) A 20-minute walk farther into the North Side, **The Mattress Factory,** 500 Sampsonia Way (231-3169), is actually a modern art museum (very sneaky!) which specializes in temporary site-specific installations that surround and engage the audience; don't miss the three spectacular permanent exhibits by James Turrell, the mythic light-worker (open Tues.-Sat. 10am-5pm, Sun. 1-5pm; free).

Two of America's greatest financial legends, Andrew Carnegie and Henry Clay Frick, made their fortunes in Pittsburgh; today, their bequests enrich the city's cultural fortune. Carnegie's most spectacular gift, **The Carnegie,** 4400 Forbes Ave. (622-3131; 622-3289 for guided tours), across the street from the Cathedral of Learning (take any bus to Oakland), comprises both an art museum and a natural history collection. Five hundred famous dinosaur specimens stalk the natural history section, including an 84-ft. giant dubbed *Diplodocus Carnegii* (the things money will buy...). The modern art wing hosts an impressive collection of Impressionist, Post-Impressionist, and 20th-century work. (Open Tues.-Sat. 10am-5pm, Sun. 1-5pm. $5, students and children $3, seniors $4.) Though most people know Henry Clay Frick for his art collection in New York, the **Frick Art Museum,** 7227 Reynolds St., Point Breeze (371-0600), 20 minutes from downtown, displays some of his earlier, less famous acquisitions; the permanent collection contains Italian, Flemish, and French works from the 13th to 18th centuries. Call about chamber music concerts October through April. (Open Tues.-Sat. 10am-5:30pm, Sun. noon-6pm. Free.)

The tropical **National Aviary** (323-7234) lies across the river to the west of Allegheny Sq.; take bus #16D or the Ft. Duquesne bridge (open daily 9am-4:30pm; $4, seniors $3, under 12 $2.50).

ENTERTAINMENT AND NIGHTLIFE

Most restaurants and shops carry the weekly *In Pittsburgh,* a great source for free, up-to-date entertainment listings, nightclubs, and racy personals. The internationally acclaimed **Pittsburgh Symphony Orchestra** (392-4900) performs September through May at **Heinz Hall,** 600 Penn Ave., downtown, and gives free outdoor concerts on summer evenings in Point State Park. The **Pittsburgh Public Theater** (321-9800) is quite renowned, but charges a pretty penny (performances Oct.-July; tickets $25.50-$34.50). Visitors with fewer (or uglier) pennies should check out both the professional and student productions at the **Three Rivers Shakespeare Festival** (624-0933), at the University of Pittsburgh's Steven Foster Memorial Theater, near Forbes Ave. and Bigelow Blvd. in Oakland. (Performances late May to mid-August. Box office 624-7529; open Tues.-Sat. 11am-8pm, Sun. noon-3pm. Tickets $7-16, $1 discount for students and seniors.)

North across the Allegheny, four-time Super Bowl champs the **Steelers** (323-1200) and baseball's **Pirates** (800-289-2827) play ball at **Three Rivers Stadium.**

Punk rockers, blues mavens, and anyone else over 21 looking for a relaxing place to sit down with a bottled beer ($1.85) mark the passage of time at **The Decade,** 223 Atwood St. (682-1211), in Oakland. Live music starts at 10pm nightly. (Open Mon.-Fri. 9am-2am, Sat. 11am-2am, Sun. 1pm-2am.) **The Metropol,** 1600 Smallman St. (261-4512), in the Strip District, fills a spacious warehouse with raving natives and other dancing species (cover $2-15; doors generally open 8-9pm).

■■■ ALLEGHENY

Heaven for hikers and those who prefer Nature unsullied and non-commercial, the **Allegheny National Forest** encompasses half a million acres of virgin woodland in northwest Pennsylvania. While fishing, hunting, mountain/trail biking, and cross-country skiing opportunities make it an outdoor-lover's ideal year-round vacation destination, its location—only 20 mi. from I-80 at its southern border—makes it also an excellent stopover for car-weary travelers looking for some sylvan R&R.

Practical Information The forest divides into four quadrants, each with its own ranger station providing forest maps (the best costs $3) and info about activities and facilities within the region. **NE: Bradford Ranger District** (362-4613), on Rte. 59 west of Marshburg (open Mon.-Fri. 7am-4:30pm, Sat.-Sun. 9am-5:30pm). **NW: Sheffield Ranger District** (968-3232), on U.S. 6 (open Mon.-Fri. 8am-4:30pm, Sat. 10am-4pm). **SE: Ridgway Ranger District** (776-6172), on Montmorenci Rd. (open Mon.-Fri. 8am-4:30pm). **SW: Marienville Ranger District** (927-6628), on Rte. 66 (open Mon.-Fri. 7:30am-4pm, Sat. 8am-4:30pm). For general forest info call the Bradford ranger station or write to **Forest Service,** USDA, P.O. Box 847, Warren 16365. When driving in the forest, be very careful during wet weather; about half the region is served only by dirt roads. Allegheny's **area code:** 814.

Accommodations and Camping From whatever direction you approach the Allegheny Forest, you'll encounter a small community near the park that offers groceries and accommodations. **Ridgway,** 25 mi. from I-80's exit 16 at the southeast corner, and **Warren,** on the northeastern fringe of the forest at the U.S. 6/U.S. 62 junction, provide comparable services. The forest administers 16 **campgrounds;** 10 stay open year-round, albeit with no services in the winter (sites $7-11, depending on location and time of year; parking fee $3). **Red Ridge, Dew, Kiasutha,** and **Heart's Content** are the most popular areas. You can call 800-280-2267 to reserve sites (reservation fee $7.50), although half are allotted on a first-come, first-served basis. You don't need a site to crash in the Allegheny; stay 1500 ft. from a major road or body of water and you can partake of **free backcountry camping** anywhere. There are also five free boat- or hiking-accessible camping sites along the 95-mi. shore of the Allegheny Reservoir (see below) which do not require reservations or a permit (fresh water, toilets, no showers).

Sights and Activities Each summer, the **Allegheny Reservoir,** located in the northern section of the forest, is stocked with fish and then with tourists who enjoy fishing, boating, swimming, or touring the **Kinzua Dam. Allegheny Outfitters** (723-1203), on Rte. 6 in Warren next to the Allegheny River Motel, handles canoe rentals for the reservoir and the Allegheny River ($18 per day; open Mon.-Fri. by appt., Sat.-Sun. 9am-5pm). **Kinzua Boat Rentals and Marina** (726-1650), 4 mi. east of Kinzua Dam on Rte. 59, rents canoes ($5.50 per hr., $20 per day), rowboats ($5.50/$20), and motorboats ($12/$50; open Memorial Day-Sept. daily 8am-8pm). **Fisherfolk** should dial the 24-hr. fishing hotline for lake conditions (726-0164). **Hikers** will find the free pamphlet describing the forest's 10 trails quite helpful. Twelve mi. of trails meander through the wildlife refuge at **Buzzard Swamp,** near Marienville; no motor vehicles are permitted.

■■■ OHIOPYLE

Lifted by steep hills and cut by cascading rivers, southwest Pennsylvania encompasses some of the loveliest forests in the East. Native Americans dubbed this region "Ohiopehhle" ("white frothy water") for the grand Youghiogheny River Gorge (pronounced yock-a-gay-nee—"The Yock" to locals), now the focal point of Pennsylvania's **Ohiopyle State Park.** The park's 19,000 acres offer hiking, fishing, hunting, whitewater rafting, and a variety of winter activities. The latest addition to the banks of the Yock, a gravelled bike trail that winds 28 mi. north from the town of Confluence to Connellsville, was converted from a riverside railroad bed. Recently named one of the 19 best walks in the world, the trail is just one section of the "rails to trails" project that will eventually connect Pittsburgh and Washington, DC.

Practical Information Ohiopyle borders on Rte. 381, 64 mi. southeast of Pittsburgh via Rte. 51 and U.S. 40. The **Park Information Center,** P.O. Box 105 (329-8591), lies just off Rte. 381 on Dinnerbell Rd. (open daily 8am-4pm; Nov.-April Mon.-Fri. 8am-4pm). To receive a free booklet on the Laurel Highlands region, which includes Ohiopyle, call 800-925-7669. **Greyhound** serves **Uniontown,** a large town 20 mi. to the west on U.S. 40., from Pittsburgh (2 per day, 1½hr., $11). Ohiopyle's **post office:** 47 E. Fayette St. (438-2522; open Mon.-Fri. 8am-6pm, Sat. 8am-noon); **ZIP code:** 15470; **area code:** 412.

Accommodations and Camping Motels around Ohiopyle are few and far between, but the excellent **Ohiopyle State Park Hostel (HI-AYH),** P.O. Box 99 (329-4476), on Ferncliffe Rd., sits right in the center of town off Rte. 381. Bob Utz has 24 bunks, a kitchen, a great yard, a washer and dryer, and an extreme fondness for chess—unbeatable. (Check-in 6-9pm. $9, nonmembers $12.) Just down the street, **Falls Market and Overnight Inn,** P.O. Box 101 (329-4973), rents surprisingly nice singles ($25) and doubles ($40) with shared baths (laundry facilities, fridge, access to TV/VCR). The downstairs store has groceries and a restaurant/snackbar (burgers $1.65; pancakes $2.25; open daily 7am-9pm). There are 226 **campsites** in Ohiopyle (PA residents $9, out-of-staters $11; $3 reservation fee). The park recommends calling at least 30 days in advance for summer weekend reservations.

The Yock Throngs of tourists come each year to raft Ohiopyle's 8-mi.-long class III rapids. Some of the best whitewater rafting in the East, the rapids take about five hours to conquer. Four outfitters front Rte. 381 in "downtown" Ohiopyle: **White Water Adventurers** (800-992-7238), **Wilderness Voyageurs** (800-272-4141), **Laurel Highlands River Tours** (800-472-3846), and **Mountain Streams and Trails** (800-245-4090). The price for a guided trip on the Yock varies dramatically ($28-57 per person per day), depending on the season, day of the week, and difficulty. If you're an experienced river rat (or if you just happen to *enjoy* flipping boats), any of the above companies will rent you equipment. (Rafts about $11-14 per person; canoes $20; "duckies"—inflatable kayaks—about $20-25.) **Bike rental** prices vary with bike styles (generally $3-4 per hr.). In order to float just about anything on the river, you must get a **launch permit** (Mon.-Fri. free; weekend passes $2.50, call at least 30 days in advance) at the Park Information Center (see above). You'll also need a $2 token for the park shuttle-bus which will return you to the launch area. The market in the Falls Market and Overnight Inn (see above) sells the **fishing licenses** required in the park (PA residents $12.50, senior residents $2.50, 5-day tourist passes $20.50).

Near Ohiopyle **Fallingwater** (329-8501), 8 mi. north of Ohiopyle on Rte. 381, is a cantilevered masterpiece by the father of modern architecture, Frank Lloyd Wright. Designed in 1936 for the wealthy Kaufmann family and perched over a waterfall, "the most famous private residence ever built" blends into the surrounding terrain, creating a stunning effect—better than *Cats*. The house can only be seen on a one-hour guided tour; make reservations. (Open Tues.-Sun. 10am-4pm; Nov.-March weekends only. Tours Tues.-Fri. $8, students $6, ages 9-18 with parents $5; Sat.-Sun. $12/$8/$6. Children under 9 must be left in child care, $2 per hr.)

Fort Necessity National Battlefield, on U.S. 40 near Rte. 381, is a replica of the original fort built by George Washington. In July 1754, young George, then of the British army, was trounced in a sneak attack on Fort Necessity that left commanding officer General Braddock dead and began the French and Indian War. Check out the fort's **Visitors Information Center** (329-5512) for more info (open daily 8:30am-6:30pm; Labor Day-Memorial Day 10:30am-5pm). Entrance to the park costs $2; those under 17 get in free. **Braddock's Grave** lies 1 mi. northwest of the fort on U.S. 40. Another mi. down the road the singular **Museum of Early American Farm Machines and Very Old Horse Saddles with a History** (438-4500) exhibits rusted and zany Americana strewn about a motel lawn.

Delaware

Delaware, a small state with the feel of a small town, comes as a welcome sanctuary from the sprawling cities of the upper east coast. Delaware's particular charm is well represented by the story of the state bug, the ladybug, adopted in 1974 after an ardent campaign by elementary school children. Quiet seaside communities and rolling dunes lure vacationers to Delaware from all along the country's eastern shores.

PRACTICAL INFORMATION

Capital: Dover.

State Visitors Service: P.O. Box 1401, 99 King's Hwy., Dover 19903 (800-282-8667 in DE, 800-441-8846 outside DE). Open Mon.-Fri. 8am-4:30pm. **Division of Fish and Wildlife,** P.O. Box 1401, 89 King's Hwy., Dover 19903 (739-5297).

Time Zone: Eastern. **Postal Abbreviation:** DE

Sales Tax: 8% on accommodations, 2.75% on motorized vehicles. 0% on everything else; you gotta love it.

■■■ DELAWARE SEASHORE

Lewes Founded in 1613 by the Zwaanendael colony from Hoorn, Holland, **Lewes** (LOO-IS) touts itself as Delaware's first town. More than 350 years later, the town is still just a sleepy burg on the Delaware Bay. Lewes' history and its calm shores attract an annual influx of antique hunters and vacationing families, who seek a safe retreat from the rough Atlantic waters. The atmosphere in Lewes is upscale and reserved, but well-kept beaches and welcoming natives make the town inviting for budget travelers as well.

The **Lewes Chamber of Commerce** (302-645-8078) operates out of the Fisher Martin House on King's Hwy. (open Mon.-Fri. 10am-4pm, Sat.-Sun. 10am-2pm). East of Lewes, on the Atlantic Ocean, the secluded **Cape Henlopen State Park** (302-645-8983) is home to a seabird nesting colony, sparkling white "walking dunes," and a beach with a bathhouse. ($5 per car, bikes and walkers free; open daily 8am-sunset.) Sandy campsites are available on a first-come, first-served basis. (302-645-2103; sites $15; open April-Oct.) Enjoy a sandwich ($2-4) and a fat-free, caffeine-free Vanilla Dream ($1.25) at the aromatic **Oby Lee Coffee Roasters and Café,** in the **Lewes Bake Shoppe,** 124 2nd St. (open Sun.-Fri. 7:30am-10pm, Sat. 7:30am-11pm).

Carolina Trailways (302-227-7223 in Rehoboth for ticket info) serves Lewes, from the Ace Hardware on Rte. 1, with buses to Washington, DC (3½hr., $31), Baltimore (3½hr., $27), and Philadelphia (4hr., $29). Lewes makes up one end of the 70-minute **Cape May, NJ/Lewes, DE Ferry** route (Lewes terminal 302-645-6313). The Delaware Resort Transit (DRT) **shuttle bus** (302-226-2001 for schedules) runs from the ferry terminal, through Lewes, and to Rehoboth and Dewey Beach, approximately every ½-hr. (Memorial Day-Labor Day daily 7am-4am. $1 all day.)

Rehoboth Beach A youthful gay minority has found a home in **Rehoboth Beach,** leaving its mark both on the town's social life and its business activities. Unlike some towns which simply host a gay social scene, Rehoboth is fostering a settled gay community. Of course, visitors of all orientations come to Rehoboth to tan, mix, and mingle on summer weekends at the beach. Follow Rehoboth Ave. until it hits the water at Rehoboth Beach, or follow Rte. 1 south to **Dewey Beach.**

For more info, visit the **Rehoboth Beach Chamber of Commerce,** next to the lighthouse at 501 Rehoboth Ave. (800-441-1329 or 227-2233; open Mon.-Fri. 9am-5pm, Sat. 9am-noon). Rehoboth's **post office:** 179 Rehoboth Ave. (227-8406; open

Mon.-Fri. 9am-5pm, Sat. 8:30am-12:30pm); Lewes and Rehoboth's **ZIP code:** 19971; **area code:** 302.

For inexpensive lodging, try **The Abbey Inn,** 31 Maryland Ave. (227-7023), where a local and a conversation await you on the porch. Call for reservations at least one week in advance, especially in summer. (2-day min. stay. Singles from $32, doubles from $40; 15% surcharge on weekends.) **The Whitson,** 30 Maryland Ave. (227-7966), sits right across from The Abbey, and offers plush rooms for a bit more money. (2-day min. stay on weekends, 3 on holidays. Singles $43-53, doubles $58-63.) Located just one block from the boardwalk, **The Lord Baltimore,** 16 Baltimore Ave. (227-2855), has clean, antiquated, almost beachfront rooms, TV and A/C. (Singles and doubles $30-65. Call ahead; it's popular.) The **Big Oaks Family Campground,** P.O. Box 53 (645-6838), sprawls at the intersection of Rte. 1 and 270. The campground itself is secluded but the sites are open. (Sites with hookup $21.50.)

Practice your French and enjoy a Grand Marnier crepe ($4) at **Cafe Papillion,** 42 Rehoboth Ave. (227-7568), in the Penny Lane Mall. The croissant sandwiches (about $5) are wicked good. (Open Mon.-Fri. 8am-midnight, Sat.-Sun. 9am-midnight). **Thrasher's** has served fries and only fries, in enormous paper tubs ($3-6) for over 60 years. Don't expect ketchup; these fries come with vinegar and salt. Locations on both sides of the main drag, at 7 and 26 Rehoboth Ave., make it easy to find. (Open daily 11am-11pm.) The **Blue Moon,** 35 Baltimore Ave. (227-6515), rises at 4pm daily and rocks a predominantly gay crowd until 1am (no cover). Live music, Irish on the weekends and rock during the week, awaits at **Irish Eyes,** 15 Wilmington Ave. (open Mon.-Fri. 5pm-1am, Sat.-Sun. noon-1am).

Carolina Trailways, 251 Rehoboth Ave. (227-7223), runs through Rehoboth Beach. Buses go to: Washington, DC (3½ hr., $31), Baltimore (3½ hr., $27), and Philadelphia (4 hr., $29). To get around within Rehoboth, use the DRT **shuttle bus** (226-2001), which runs from the ferry terminal in Lewes to Rehoboth and Dewey Beach, approximately every ½-hr. (Memorial Day-Labor Day daily 7am-4am. $1 all day.)

Maryland

Once upon a time, the Chesapeake Bay, a picturesque, shellfish-rich estuary, ruled the Maryland economy. On the rural eastern shore, small-town Marylanders captured crabs and raised tobacco. Across the bay in Baltimore, workers ate the crabs, loaded ships, and ran factories. Then the federal government expanded, industry shrank, and Maryland's economy moved to the Baltimore-Washington Parkway. Suburbs grew up and down the corridor, Baltimore cleaned up its smokestack act and the state acquired a new, liberal urbanity. As DC's homogenized commuter suburbs break the limits of Maryland's Montgomery and Prince Georges counties, Baltimore revels in its polyglot character while Annapolis, the capital, stays small-town.

PRACTICAL INFORMATION

Capital: Annapolis.

Office of Tourism: 217 E. Redwood St., Baltimore 21202 (410-333-6611 or 800-534-1036). **Forest and Parks Service,** Dept. of Natural Resources, Tawes State Office Building, Annapolis 21401 (410-974-3771; Mon.-Fri. 8am-4:30pm).

Time Zone: Eastern. **Postal Abbreviation:** MD

Sales Tax: 5%.

■■■ BALTIMORE

Baltimore impresses the visitor with long rows of townhouses, as even, regular, and expensive as gold teeth in a broad smile. The city has always focused on the sea—

Maryland's famous crabs are everywhere, plastered on buildings, windows, posters, and billboards while the modern, industrial harbor reminds visitors of the city's distinguished past and glorious present: historic stone drawbridges compete with new steel structures and the old Baltimore & Ohio Railroad contrasts with the sleek glass windowed skyline. Modern Baltimore forms Maryland's urban core while old-time, shirtsleeve Bawlmer endures in the quiet limelight of Anne Tyler's novels and John Waters's films. After gaping at the National Aquarium's array of rays, be sure to explore the rest of Baltimore—the local events, the neighborhoods, and the people.

PRACTICAL INFORMATION

Tourist Office: Baltimore Area Visitors Centers, 300 W. Pratt St. (837-INFO/4636 or 800-282-6632), at S. Howard St. 4 blocks from Harborplace. Pick up a map and a *Quick City Guide,* a quarterly glossy with excellent maps and entertainment listings. Open daily 9am-5:30pm.

Airport: Baltimore-Washington International (BWI) (859-7111). On I-195 off the Baltimore-Washington Expressway (I-295), about 10mi. south of the city center. Take MTA bus #17 to the N. Linthicumlight rail station. Airport shuttles (859-0800) to hotels run daily every ½hr. 6am-midnight ($10 to downtown Baltimore). For DC, shuttles leave every 1½hr. between 7am-8:30pm (Sat. every 2½hr. from 8:30am-6:30pm) and drop passengers off at 16th and K St. NW ($14). Trains from BWI Airport run to Baltimore ($5); MARC trains are considerably cheaper ($3) but also slower and only run Mon.-Fri. Trains to Washington, DC $10; MARC $4.50. BWI train office 672-6167.

Trains: Amtrak, Penn Station, 1500 N. Charles St. (800-872-7245), at Mt. Royal Ave. Easily accessible by bus #3, or 11 from Charles Station downtown. Trains run about every ½hr. to: New York ($49-67, Metroliner $91); Washington, DC ($12, Metroliner $17); Philadelphia ($26, Metroliner $44). Ticket window open daily 5:30am-9:30pm, self-serve machines open 24 hrs. (credit card only).

Buses: Greyhound, (800-231-2222) downtown at 210 W. Fayette St. (752-0868), near N. Howard St.; also at 5625 O'Donnell St. (744-9311), 3mi. east of downtown near I-95. Frequent buses to: New York ($23.50); Washington, DC ($6); Philadelphia ($12). Open 24 hrs.

Public Transportation: Mass Transit Administration (MTA), 300 W. Lexington St. (333-3434 or 800-543-9809), near N. Howard St. Bus and rapid-rail service to most major sights in the city; service to outlying areas is more complicated. Bus #17 serves the airport. Some buses run 24 hrs. **Metro** operates Mon.-Fri. 5am-midnight, Sat. 6am-midnight. Base fare for bus and metro $1.25; transfers 10¢. The **Water Taxi** (563-3901) makes stops every 8-18 min. at the harbor museums, Harborplace, Fell's Point, and more. Full-day pass $2-3.25.

Crisis Lines: Suicide Hotline, 531-6677. **Sexual Assault and Domestic Violence Center,** 828-6390. **Gay and Lesbian Information,** 837-8888.

Emergency: 911.

Post Office: 900 E. Fayette St. (655-9832; open Mon.-Fri. 7:30am-9pm, Sat. 8:30am-5pm). **ZIP code:** 21233. **Area code:** 410.

Baltimore dangles in central Maryland, 100 mi. south of Philadelphia and about 150 mi. up the Chesapeake Bay from the Atlantic Ocean. The Jones Falls Expressway (I-83) splits the city from the south at the Inner Harbor, while the Baltimore Beltway (I-695) circles it. I-95 cuts across the southwest corner of the city.

Baltimore is plagued by one-way streets. **Baltimore St.** (runs east across the Inner Harbor) and **Charles St.** (running north from the west side of the Harbor) divide the city into quarters. Streets parallel to Baltimore St. get "West" or "East" tacked onto their names, depending on their side of Charles St. Streets are dubbed "North" or "South" according to their relation to Baltimore St.

ACCOMMODATIONS AND CAMPING

Baltimore International Youth Hostel (HI-AYH), 17 W. Mulberry St. (576-8880), at Cathedral St. Near bus and Amtrak terminals. Take MTA bus #3, 11, or 18. Elegant, centrally located 19th-century brownstone provides 48 beds in dorms. Kitchen, laundry, and lounge with baby grand piano. Friendly managers are a great source of information about Baltimore. Don't walk in the area alone at night. 3-night max. stay, longer with manager's approval. Lockout noon-5pm. Curfew 11pm, but house keys available for rent ($2). Chores required. $13, non-members $16. Reservations recommended, especially in the summer.

Duke's Motel, 7905 Pulaski Hwy. (686-0400), in Rosedale off the Beltway. Don't worry about the bulletproof glass in the front office—all the motels around here have it. Simple, clean rooms and the best deal on the otherwise undesirable Pulaski Hwy. motel strip. Suitable only for people with cars. Cable TV. Singles $41, doubles $46. $2 key deposit and ID required.

Capitol KOA, 768 Cecil Ave. (923-2771; fax 923-3169), near Millersville. 18mi. from Baltimore, 25mi. to DC. Sites $22, full hookup $29.75. Rates less in the off-season. Free shuttle to the MARC ($6.75 to Baltimore). Open April-Nov.

FOOD

Virginia may be for lovers, but Maryland is for crabs; every eatery serves **crab cakes.** The Light Street Pavilion at **Harborplace** (332-4191), at Pratt and Light St., has multifarious foodstuffs to suit every tourist—hence the long lines. **Phillips'** serves some of the best crabcakes in Baltimore; buy them cheaper from the cafeteria-style Phillips' Express line. (Harborplace open Mon.-Sat. 10am-9pm, Sun. 10am-6pm.) **Lexington Market,** 400 W. Lexington at Eutaw St., provides an endless variety of produce, fresh meat, and seafood, often at cheaper prices (open Mon.-Sat. 8:30am-6pm; take the subway to Lexington Station or bus #7).

Bertha's Dining Room, 734 S. Broadway (327-5795), at Lancaster. Obey the bumper stickers and "Eat Bertha's Mussels." Gorge yourself on the black-shelled bivalves ($7.50) while sitting at butcher-block tables, and don't miss the chunky veggie mussel chowder (cup $1.75). Locals of all ages crowd in to hear jazz bands Mon.-Wed. and Fri.-Sat. nights. Twelve kinds of beer and ale ($1.50-6). Kitchen open Sun.-Thurs. 11:30am-11pm, Fri.-Sat. 11:30am-midnight. Bar until 2am.

Obrycki's, 1727 E. Pratt St. (732-6399), near Broadway; take bus #7 or 10. Some of Balto's best crabs served every and any way—steamed, broiled, sauteed, or in crab cakes for $20-46 per dozen depending on size. Expect lines on weekends. Don't walk here alone at night. Open Mon.-Sat. noon-11pm, Sun. noon-9:30pm.

Hellmands, 806 N. Charles St. (752-0311). Don't let the white linen on the tables frighten you: nary an item on the menu is over $10. Acclaimed by local magazines as one of the ten best restaurants in the city, exquisite Afghan dishes will make your mouth water. Open Sun.-Thurs. 5-10pm, Fri.-Sat. 5-11pm.

Haussner's, 3242 Eastern Ave. (410-327-8365), at S. Clinton; take bus #10. An East Baltimore institution. 700 original oil paintings crowd the huge dining room. Central European cuisine like fresh pig knuckle and *sauerbraten* (meat stewed in vinegar and juices) $10.60, sandwiches $3.75-12; big portions. Try the famous strawberry pie ($3.65), or get other freshly baked goods to go. Long pants preferred after 3pm; lines for dinner on weekends. Open Tues.-Sat. 11am-10pm.

SIGHTS

The **National Aquarium,** Pier 3, 501 E. Pratt St. (576-3800), makes the whole Inner Harbor worthwhile. Multi-level exhibits and tanks show off rare fish, big fish, red fish, and blue fish along with the biology and ecology of oceans, rivers, and rainforests. The Children's Cove (level 4) lets visitors handle intertidal marine animals. (Open March-Oct. Sun.-Thurs. 9am-6pm, Fri.-Sat. 9am-8pm; Nov.-Feb. Sat.-Thurs. 10am-5pm, Fri. 10am-8pm. $11.50, seniors $9.50, ages 3-11 $7.50, under 3 free; Oct.-March Fri. 5-8pm $3.50.)

Several ships bob in the harbor, among them the **U.S.S. Constellation** (539-1797), the first commissioned U.S. Navy ship, which sailed from 1797 until 1945, serving in the War of 1812, the Civil War, and as flagship of the Pacific Fleet during WWII. The *Constellation* will probably spend part of 1995 in dry dock for much-needed repairs; call to see if it may be visited. (Open daily 10am-5pm; winter 10am-4pm. $2.50, seniors $2, ages 6-15 $1, military $1, under 6 free.) Also moored in the harbor are the submarine *U.S.S. Torsk,* the lightship *Chesapeake,* and the Coast Guard cutter *Taney.* These vessels make up the **Baltimore Maritime Museum** at Piers 3 and 4. (396-3453; open Mon.-Fri. 10am-5pm, Fri.-Sat. 9:30am-6pm; winter Fri.-Sun. 9:30am-5pm. $4.50, seniors $4, under 13 $1.75, active military free.)

At the Inner Harbor's far edge lurks the **Maryland Science Center,** 601 Light St. (685-5225), where kids can learn chemistry and physics through hands-on games. The IMAX Theater's 5-story screen stuns audiences. On summer weekends, come in the morning while lines are short. (Open Mon.-Thurs. 10am-5pm, Fri.-Sun. 10am-7:30pm; Sept.-May Mon.-Fri. 10am-5pm, Sat.-Sun. 10am-6pm. $8.50, ages 4-17, seniors and military $6.50, under 3 free. IMAX schedule posted as you enter.)

The **Baltimore Museum of Art** (396-7100), N. Charles and 31st St., exhibits a fine collection of modern art (including pieces by Andy Warhol), and paintings and sculpture by Matisse, Picasso, Renoir and Van Gogh. Two adjacent sculpture gardens highlight 20th-century works and make wonderful picnic grounds. The museum's **Baltimore Film Forum** shows classic and current American, foreign, and independent films (Thurs.-Fri. 8pm, $5, students and seniors $4); get schedules at the museum or call 889-1993. (Open Wed.-Fri. 10am-4pm, Sat.-Sun. 11am-6pm. $5.50, students and seniors $3.50, ages 7-18 $1.50, under 7 free; Thurs. free.)

Baltimore's best museum, the **Walters Art Gallery,** 600 N. Charles St. (547-9000), at Centre, keeps one of the largest private collections in the world, spanning 50 centuries. The museum's apex is the Ancient Art collection (level 2); its seven marble sarcophagi with intricate relief carvings are of a type found in only two known collections (the other is the National Museum in Rome). Other high points are the Italian works and Impressionists, including Manet's *At the Café* and Monet's *Springtime,* as well as rare early Buddhist sculptures from China and Japanese decorative arts of the late 18th and 19th centuries. (Open Tues.-Sun. 11am-5pm. $4, seniors $3, students and kids under 18 free; Sat. free before noon.)

Fort McHenry National Monument (962-4290) at the foot of E. Fort Ave. off Rte. 2 (Hanover St.) and Lawrence Ave. (take bus #1), commemorates the victory against the British in the War of 1812. The battle inspired Francis Scott Key to write the "Star Spangled Banner," but the flag isn't still there (it's in the Smithsonian now). (Open daily 8am-8pm; Sept.-May 8am-5pm. $2, seniors and under 17 free.)

Once a station for the Baltimore & Ohio Railroad, the **B&O Railroad Museum,** 901 W. Pratt St. (752-2490; take bus #31), looks out on train tracks where dining cars, Pullman sleepers, and mail cars park themselves for your touring frenzy. The Roundhouse captures historic trains and a replica of the 1829 "Tom Thumb," the first American steam-driven locomotive. Don't miss the extensive model train display. (Open daily 10am-5pm. $6, seniors $5, ages 5-12 $3, under 5 free. Train rides on weekends for an additional $2.)

Baltimore also holds the **Babe Ruth Birthplace and Baltimore Orioles Museum,** 216 Emory St. (727-1539; open daily 10am-5pm, Nov.-March 10am-4pm;

Cognac and Roses

A short-lived, moustached, opium-addicted 1830s author, Edgar Allan Poe virtually invented the horror tale and the detective story. His most famous works include *The Tell-Tale Heart.* You probably won't hear a beating heart at the **Edgar Allan Poe Grave** where the divine Edgar sleeps evermore in the Westminster Churchyard (706-7228), at Fayette and Greene St. (Guided tours every 1st and 3rd Fri. evening at 6:30pm and Sat. morning at 10am. Reservations required. Tour $4, seniors and under 13 $2.) Every year on the anniversary of Poe's death (Oct. 7, 1849), a mysterious visitor dressed in black decorates his grave with cognac and roses. (Cemetery open during daylight hours.) Edgar Allan Poe came into this world at the **Edgar Allan Poe House** (396-7932), in a somewhat seedy area at 203 N. Amity St., near Saratoga St. (bus #15 or 23). The tour ushers Poe-heads through the writer's biography and around the tell-tale original furniture. (Open Wed.-Sat. noon-3:45pm; Aug.-Sept. Sat. noon-3:45pm. $3, under 13 $1.)

$5, seniors $3.50, ages 5-16 $2, under 4 free). The sparkling new **Oriole Park at Camden Yards** (547-6234) sits just west of the Inner Harbor at Eutaw and Camden St. (Tours leave hourly Mon.-Fri. 11am-2pm, Sat. 10am-2pm, Sun. at 12:30pm and 1-3pm. $5, seniors and kids under 12 $4.)

To get a feel for Baltimore's historic districts, take bus #7 or 10 from Pratt St. to Abermarle St. and see **Little Italy,** or ride the same buses to Broadway and walk four blocks to **Fells Point.** The neighborhood around Abermarle, Fawn, and High St. is still predominantly Italian, even if the restaurant clientele has diversified; many of the brownstones have been in the same family for generations. Fell's Point recalls the past with cobblestone streets, quaint shops and historic pubs.

ENTERTAINMENT AND NIGHTLIFE

The **Showcase of Nations Ethnic Festivals** (837-4636 or 800-282-632) celebrates Baltimore's ethnic neighborhoods with a different culture each week June-Sept. Most events are at **Festival Hall,** W. Pratt and Sharp St. The **Pier Six Concert Pavilion** (625-4230) at Pier 6 at the Inner Harbor presents big-name musical acts at night from late July to Sept. Get tickets at the Mechanic Theatre Box Office between October and May, and at the pavilion or through TeleCharge (625-1400, 800-638-2444) during the summer ($15-30). Sit on Pier 5, near Harborplace, and overhear the music for free. The **Left Bank Jazz Society** (466-0600) sponsors jazz shows from September and May; call for schedules and information. The **Theatre Project,** 45 W. Preston St. near Maryland St. (752-8558), experiments with theater, poetry, music, and/or dance Wednesday to Saturday at 8pm and Sunday at 3pm ($5-14). Box office open Tues. noon-5pm, Wed.-Sat. 1-9pm, Sun. noon-4pm. The beloved **Baltimore Orioles** now play at their new stadium at Camden Yards, just a few blocks from the Inner Harbor at the corner of Russell and Camden St. Bawlmer holds its breath for the yearly ups and downs of the Os with an attention very few cities can equal. For **drinking and dancing**, try the following bars and clubs.

Baltimore Brewing Co., 104 Albermarle St. (837-5000), west of the Inner Harbor on the outskirts of Little Italy. Brewmaster Theo de Groen has captured the hearts and livers of Baltimoreans with his original and distinctive lagers, brewed right on the premises in the large brass tuns that loom behind the bar. Happy hour Mon.-Fri 4-7pm with $2 beer. Open Mon.-Thurs. 11am-11pm, Fri.-Sat. 11am-midnight.

8 X 10, 10 E. Cross St. (625-2000). As the name implies, this bar is *small*. But, it's overflowing with locals who come to hear progressive live rock every night. Cover ranges $8-12. Open Mon. and Wed.-Sat. 9pm-2am.

Hammerjacks, 1101 S. Howard St. (659-7625). The place in Baltimore for big bands. Tickets, shows, and showtimes vary. Call for information.

Orpheus, 1003 E. Praits St. (276-5599). Art Deco club with serious dancin' goin' on. Tues. is Rave Night with a $7 cover; Thurs. is Gothic Night with a $5 cover, Fri. is house with a $5 cover, Sat. is 70s, 80s, 90s dance mix with a $3 cover; Sun. is 18+ with an open bar and $6 cover. Open Thurs.-Sat. 10pm-2am.

Cat's Eye Pub, 1730 Thames St. (276-9866), in Fells Point. *Playboy* thinks this is the best bar in Fells Point, and so do the regulars who pack it every night for live blues, jazz, folk, or traditional Irish music. No cover, but drink prices rise when the band strikes up. Over 25 drafts and 60 bottled beers. Bands every night and twice Sat.-Sun. Happy hour 4-7pm. Open daily 1pm-2am.

The Hippo, 1 W. Eager St. (547-0069). Baltimore's largest and most popular gay bar, with pool tables, videos, and a packed dance floor. Cover Thurs.-Fri. $3, Sat. $5. Saloon open daily 3pm-2am. Dance bar open Wed.-Sat. 10pm-2am. Video bar open Thurs.-Sat. 10pm-2am.

■■■ ANNAPOLIS

Walking the fine line between nostalgia and anachronism, the capital of Maryland boasts an historic waterfront, narrow streets flanked by 18th-century brick antique shops, and peaceful docks. Settled in 1649, Annapolis's Georgian townhouses once held Colonial aristocrats (and their slaves). It was here that the 1783-1784 Continental Congress ratified the *Treaty of Paris,* and the city made headlines again in 1790 during its stint as temporary capital of the U.S.

Practical Information Annapolis lies southeast of U.S. 50 (also known as U.S. 301) 30 mi. east of Washington, DC and 30 mi. south of Baltimore. From DC, take U.S. 50E. (In DC, U.S. 50 begins at New York Ave.) From Baltimore, follow Rte. 2S to U.S. 50W, cross the Severn River Bridge, then take Rowe Blvd. **Greyhound/Trailways** buses (800-231-2222) connect Annapolis with DC (2 per day, 1hr., $7.50) and with towns on the far side of the Chesapeake Bay. Baltimore's **Mass Transit Administration** (539-5000) links Baltimore with Annapolis. (Express bus #210 runs Mon.-Fri., 1hr., $2.85. Local bus #14 daily, 90min., $2.25. Call for times.) The **Annapolis Department of Public Transportation,** 160 Duke of Gloucester St. (263-7964), operates a web of buses connecting the historic district with the rest of town (Mon.-Sat. 5:30am-10pm, Sun. 8am-7pm). The **Annapolis and Anne Arundel County Conference & Visitors Bureau,** 26 West St. (268-8687) has brochures and information (open daily 9am-5pm). **Information desks** field questions at the State House (841-3810; open daily 10am-5pm). The city extends south and east from two landmarks: Church Circle and State Circle. School St., in a blatantly unconstitutional move, connects Church and State. Maryland Ave. runs from the State House to the Naval Academy. Main St., where food and entertainment sources congregate, starts at Church Circle and ends at the docks. Those lost in Annapolis can reorient themselves by looking for the State House dome or St. Anne's spire. Annapolis is compact and easily walkable; save yourself a headache by **parking** in a lot or garage ($4-10). For **emergencies** dial 911; the **area code** is 410.

Accommodations and Food Hostels and motels are few. The visitors information centers have brochures for B&Bs and hotels. Reserve in advance, especially in summer. **Amanda's Bed and Breakfast Regional Reservation Service** (225-0001 or 900-899-7533; open Mon.-Fri. 8:30am-5:30pm, Sat. 8:30am-noon), can help arrange accommodations. Rates fluctuate depending on demand: ask around and sound like you need convincing. **Middleton Tavern,** 2 Market Space (263-3323) at Randall St., was established in 1750 and frequented by members of the Continental Congress. Try a little of Maryland's specialty: seafood lasagna ($8) or oysters from the raw bar (until 1am). Nightly music accompanies marine delights. (Open Mon.-Fri. 11:30am-2am, Sat.-Sun. 11am-2am. Food served until midnight.) **Chick & Ruth's Delly,** 165 Main St. (269-6737) offers dishes satirically named after politicians. Try a foot-long cheeseburger ($3) or a kosher dish. (Open 24 hrs.)

Sights and Nightlife The Corinthian-columned **State House** offers maps and houses the state legislature, a fine silver collection, and other exhibits. *The Treaty of Paris* was signed here on January 14, 1874. (Open daily 9am-5pm; free tours 11am and 3pm.) Restaurants and tacky tourist shops line the waterfront at **City Dock,** where Naval Academy ships ply the waters and civilian yachtsmen congregate. Main St., full of tiny shops and eateries, stretches from here back up to Church Circle. Stop by the **Maritime Museum,** 77 Main St. (268-5576), at Compromise St., before heading up to the circle (open daily 9am-5pm). From Church Circle, walk along College Ave. past St. John's St. to find **St. John's College** (founded in 1696). The **U.S. Naval Academy** squats at the end of King George St. Tours begin at the **Armel-Leftwich Visitors Center** (263-6933), inside the academy gates at the end of King George St. (call for times; $5, students $3, over 62 $4). Sailors flock to **Marmadukes's Pub** (269-5420), 7th Ave. at 3rd, on Wednesday nights to watch videos of their races (weekend piano bar, cover $3; open daily 11:30am-2am). **Buddy's Late Night Annapolis,** 30 Hudson St. (266-5888) is the only dance club in town (cover after 10pm; Wed.-Thurs. $3, Fri.-Sat. $6; open Wed.-Sat. 8:30pm-2am).

■■■ EASTERN SHORE

The long arm of land known as the Eastern Shore is claimed by Maryland in the north and Virginia in the south. Though the Chesapeake Bay is the only physical divide between the Eastern Shore and its mother states, the gulf between these areas is cultural as well. The Eastern Shore harbors a lifestyle last found in most of Virginia and Maryland decades ago. Peaceful hamlets and expansive fields punctuate the forests and dunes of this tranquil landscape. Here, tractors are more common than commuters on the roads, and wild ponies still go unpenned. For more information, contact the MD and VA visitors information centers.

Assateague, MD and Chincoteague, VA Local legend has it that horses first came to Assateague Island by swimming ashore after escaping a sinking Spanish galleon. Though less romantic, a more likely story is that a few centuries ago, several miserly mainland farmers put their horses out to graze on Assateague to avoid taxes and fencing expenses. Whatever their origins, the descendents of Assateague's original horses, the famous wild ponies, now roam free across the unspoiled beaches and forests of the island.

Assateague Island is divided into three parts. The **Assateague State Park** (410-641-2120), Rte. 611 in southeast Maryland, is a 2-mi. stretch of picnic areas, beaches, hot-water bathhouses, and campsites. (Park open daily April-Oct. 8am-sunset. $2 per person for day use, seniors free. Campsite registration 8am-11pm. Sites $20; reservations available only in one-week blocks, Sat.-Sat.) The **Assateague Island National Seashore** claims most of the long sandbar north and south of the park and has its own campground (sites $10, Nov.-mid-May $8) and beaches. The **ranger station** (410-641-3030) here distributes free back country camping permits, but only before 2pm; get there early. The **Barrier Island Visitors Center** (410-641-1441), Rte. 611, provides an introduction to the park and gives day-use information. (Visitors center open daily 9am-5pm. $4 entrance fee per car.) Meander down one of the ½-mile nature trails—the Forest Trail offers the best viewing tower, but the Marsh Trail (ironically) has fewer mosquitoes. Bring plenty of insect repellent. The mosquitoes are bad. Very bad. Bring gallons.

The **Chincoteague National Wildlife Refuge** stretches across the Virginia side of the island. This refuge provides a temporary home for the threatened migratory peregrine falcon, a half million Canadian and snow geese, and the beautiful Chincoteague ponies. During slack tide, on the last Wednesday in July, the wild ponies are herded together and made to swim from Assateague Island to Chincoteague Island, where, on the following day, the local fire department auctions off the foals. The adults swim back to Assateague and reproduce, providing next year's crop of ponies. The best time of year for pony sightings on Assateague Island is in mid-July, just before the sale. To get more information on the refuge, swing by the **Chincoteague Refuge Visitor Contact Station,** on the island (804-336-6122; open daily 9am-5pm). The **Wildlife Loop** begins in the visitor's center parking lot and provides your best chance to see the ponies (open 5am-sunset; open to cars 3pm-sunset).

To get to Assateague Island, take **Carolina Trailways** (410-289-9307) to Ocean City, via daily express or local routes from Greyhound stations in Baltimore ($22) and Washington, DC ($36.50). From Ocean City, take a taxi to Assateague (289-1313; about $20). Carolina Trailways also buses from Salisbury, MD, and Norfolk, VA, stopping on U.S. 13 at **T's Corner** (804-824-5935), 11 mi. from Chincoteague. For more area info, call or write to **Chincoteague Chamber of Commerce,** P.O. Box 258 (6733 Maddox Blvd.), Chincoteague, VA 23336 (804-336-6161; open summer daily 9am-4:30pm, after Labor Day Mon.-Sat. 9am-4:30pm).

■■■ OCEAN CITY

Ocean City is a lot like a kiddie pool. It's shallow and plastic, but can be fun if you're the right age. This 10-mile strip of land packs endless bars, all-you-can-eat buffets, hotels, mini-golf courses, and tourists into a thin region between the Atlantic Ocean and the Assawoman Bay. Tourism is the town's only industry; in-season the population swells from 12,000 to 300,000, with a large migratory population of "June bugs," high school seniors that descend in swarms in the week after graduation. If you dig flashing lights, lots of action, and beer, this is the place to go. But if go-carts and boardwalks make you itch, head for quieter shores.

Practical Information Ocean City runs north-south with numbered streets connecting the ocean to the bay. A good first stop is the **Ocean City Visitor's Center** (800-626-2326), 40th St. in the Convention Center (open Mon.-Thurs. 8am-5pm, Fri. 8am-6pm, Sat. 9am-5:30pm, Sun. 9am-5pm; Sept.-May daily 8:30am-5:30pm). **Carolina Trailways** (289-9307), at 2nd St. and Philadelphia Ave., sends seven buses per day to Baltimore (3hr., $22) and Washington DC (4hr., $36.50). (Station open daily 7am-8am and 10am-5pm; Sept.-May 10am-3pm.) Once in town, **the bus** (723-1607) is by far the best way to get around ($1 unlimited riding for the day). The bus runs 24 hrs. and travels the length of the town. **Parking** in Ocean City is a nightmare. If you have a car, you can park free during the day at the Convention Center, 40th St., or try to find a spot on the street. If you're in town for more than one day, get up early one morning and claim a free spot on the street. Ocean City's **post office:** 408 N. Philadelphia Ave. at 5th St. (289-7819; open Mon.-Fri. 9am-5pm, Sat. 9am-noon); **ZIP code:** 21842; **area code:** 410.

Accommodations and Food If you're going to stay in Ocean City, make every effort to secure a room at the **Summer Place Youth Hostel,** 104 Dorchester St. (289-4542), in the south end of town. This exceptional establishment houses two hip proprietors and tasteful southwestern decor, and gives you more bang for your buck than you're likely to find at most hostels anywhere. Private rooms come with access to kitchen, TV, common areas, deck, hammock, and grill. ($18 per person; no lockout, shared bath, reservations helpful but not required; open April-Oct.) If the hostel's full, try **Whispering Sands** (289-5759), 45th St. oceanside. The amenable owner rents out rooms, complete with kitchen access, to students for $15. (Open May-Oct.) You can also pitch a tent at **Assateague National Seashore** (641-1441) or **Assateague State Park** (641-2120). See Eastern Shore (p. 218) for details.

Dining in Ocean City is a glutton's delight. The streets are lined with seemingly identical restaurants hosting all-you-can-eat specials. Be sure to try Maryland's specialty: crabs. Locals favor **The Crab Bag** (250-3337), at 130th and Coastal Hwy., oceanside. It may look like a shanty, but the all-you-can-eat crabs ($15) are unbeatable. There's not much seating; plan to take out. (Open daily 4-9pm.) Pick up anything you could ever possibly want or need at the massive **Food Lion** (524-9039), on 120th St., bayside (open daily 6am-midnight).

Sights and Entertainment Ocean City's star attraction is its **beach,** and a beautiful beach it is. It runs the entire 10 mi. length of town and is wide and sandy the entire way. It's free and open 6am-10pm. You might have better luck avoiding the crush of beach-goers if you go uptown, away from the boardwalk. Volleyball, surfing, fishing, tanning, and flexing are favorite beach activities. When the sun goes down, hard-earned tans are put to work at Ocean City's league of bars and nightclubs. The most popular of the bunch is **Seacrets** (524-4900), on 49th St., bayside. This huge complex brings a taste of Jamaica to the mid-Atlantic. Barefoot barflies wander between floats to the strains of reggae. There are live bands every night. (Cover $3-5. Open Mon.-Sat. 11am-2am, Sun. noon-2am.) Seek refuge from the meat market at **Macky's Bayside Bar & Grill,** 5309 Coastal Hwy. (723-5565), bayside (no, really), behind Tio Gringo's. Macky's offers an all-wood interior and the opportunity to rub elbows with the locals (Open daily 11:30am-2am.)

Washington, DC

Despite urban problems, Washington's strange experiment—an infant nation building a capital from scratch—has matured into one of America's most interesting, and consequently most visited, cities. Somewhere between political powerhouse, sleepy Southern town, and decaying metropolis lies DC's impressive, intimidating, but entertaining and ultimately distinctive character.

After winning independence from Great Britain in 1783, the United States was faced with the challenge of finding a home for its fledgling government. Both Northern and Southern states wanted the capital on their turf. The final location—100 sq. mi. pinched from Virginia and Maryland—was a compromise resulting in what President Kennedy later termed "a city of Northern charm and Southern efficiency."

Nineteenth-century Washington was a "city of magnificent distances"—a smattering of slave markets, elegant government buildings, and boarding houses along the absurdly large-scale avenues designed by French engineer Pierre L'Enfant. The city had hardly begun to expand when the British torched it in 1814; a post-war vote to give up and move the capital failed in Congress by just eight votes. Washington continued to grow, but so did its problems—a port city squeezed between two plantation states, the district was a logical first stop for slave traders, whose shackled cargo awaited sale on the Mall and near the White House. Foreign diplomats were properly disgusted. The Civil War altered this forever, transforming Washington from the Union's embarrassing appendix to its jugular vein.

During the 1960s, Washington hosted a series of demonstrations advocating civil rights and condemning America's role in Vietnam. Martin Luther King, Jr. delivered his "I Have a Dream" speech in 1963 to 250,000 people of all races gathered on the Mall. In 1968, an anti-war gathering ringed the Pentagon with chants and shouts. Later the same year, riots touched off by King's assassination torched parts of the city; some blocks still await rebuilding. 1993 saw the inauguration of Bill Clinton, America's first baby boomer president.

Most travelers come to Washington to be impressed and slightly intimidated by its elaborate monuments, museums, and monolithic edifices. Just blocks from the tourist-infested Mall, DC communities—yuppie, gay, Latino, black—dwell and prosper, separate from the goings-on of government. From the bars and businesses around Dupont Circle and the ethnic delights of Adams-Morgan to the college crowds in Georgetown, Washington's second city has more to offer than downtown can display and more to see than any tour guide will show you.

For more in-depth radical and hip Washington, DC budget coverage, see *Let's Go: Washington, D.C.*, available from the coolest booksellers everywhere.

PRACTICAL INFORMATION

Tourist Office: Washington, DC Convention and Visitors Association (WCVA), 1212 New York Ave., Ste. 600 NW (789-7000). Does not expect walk-ins. Write or call for copies of *The DC Visitor's Guide and Visitor Map* and a calendar of events. **Meridian International Center,** 1630 Crescent Pl. NW (667-6800). Near Adams-Morgan. Call or write for brochures in a variety of languages. Office open Mon.-Fri. 9am-5pm.

Embassies: Please see our section on Embassies and Consulates (p. 25).

Airport: National Airport (703-419-8000). It's best to fly here from within the U.S., since National is on the Metro and closer to Washington. Metro: National Airport, then walk or take a shuttle. Taxi $10-15 from downtown. **Dulles International Airport** (703-419-8000) is Washington's international airport and much further away; some domestic flights also land here. Taxi to Dulles over $40. No Metro near the airport, but the **Dulles Express Bus** (703-685-1400) runs from the West Falls Church Metro every 20-30min. ($8 one-way; Mon.-Fri. 6am-10:30pm, Sat-Sun. 7:30am-10:30pm; last bus from Metro 11pm). The **Washington Flyer**

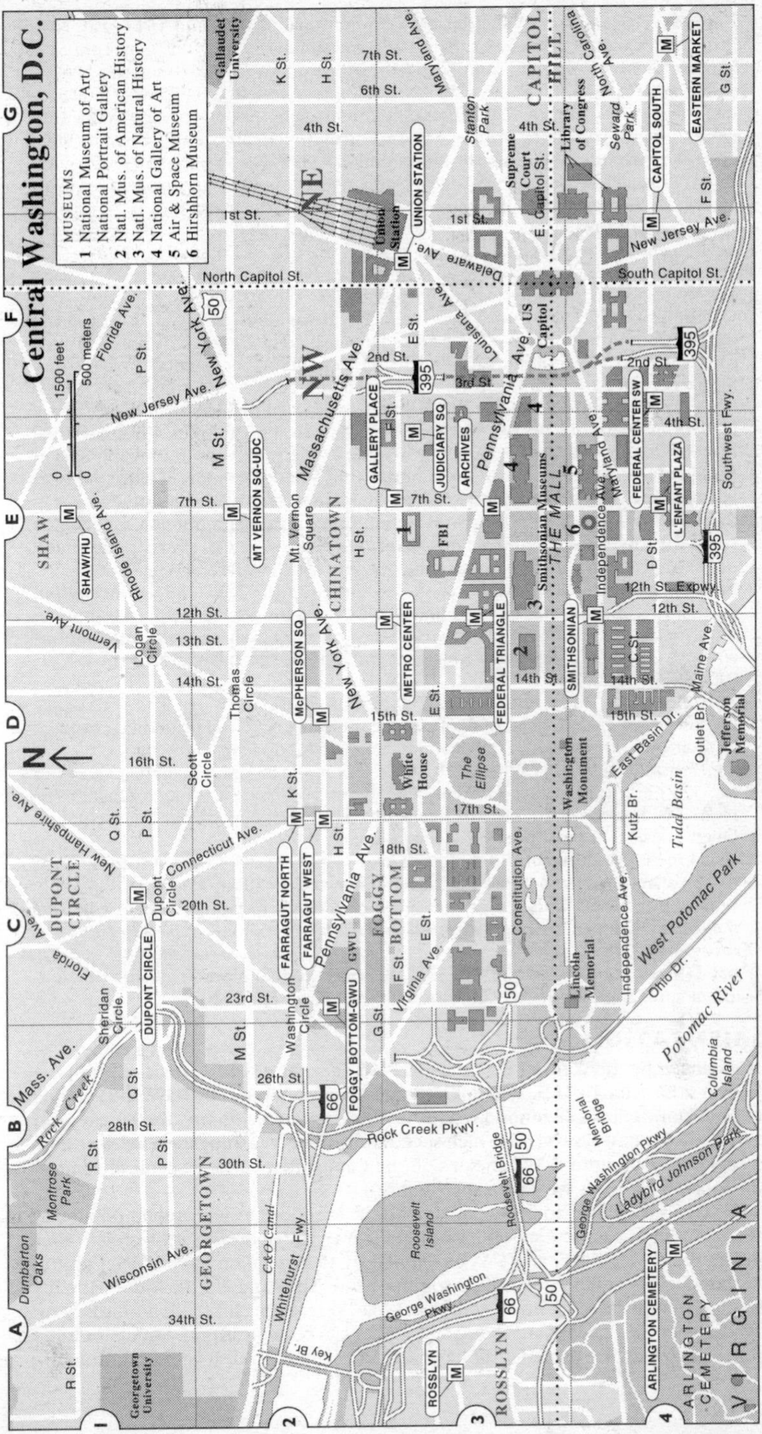

Central Washington, D.C.

MUSEUMS
1 National Museum of Art/
National Portrait Gallery
2 Natl. Mus. of American History
3 Natl. Mus. of Natural History
4 National Gallery of Art
5 Air & Space Museum
6 Hirshhorn Museum

Express, (703-685-1400) shuttles between National, Dulles, and 1517 K St. NW. Buses run roughly every ½-hr. 6am-10:30pm Mon.-Fri., every hr. 6am-1pm Sat.-Sun. National one-way $8, round-trip $14; Dulles one-way $16, round-trip $26.

Trains: Amtrak, Union Station, 50 Massachusetts Ave. NE (484-7540 or 800-872-7245; 800-523-8720 for Metroliner). Frequent daily service to: New York City (3½hr., $51); Baltimore (45min., $12); Philadelphia (2hr., $28); Boston (9hr., $55). Less frequent service to: Richmond ($21); Williamsburg ($21); Virginia Beach ($31). **MARC** (800-325-7245), Maryland's commuter rail, also leaves Union Station for Baltimore ($5.25), Harper's Ferry, and Martinsburg, WV.

Buses: Greyhound, 1005 1st St. NE (800-231-2222) at L St., in a rather decrepit neighborhood. To: Philadelphia ($16); New York City ($25); Baltimore ($7).

Public Transportation: Metrorail, 600 5th St. NW, (637-7000; open daily 6am-11:30pm). Clean, quiet, carpeted trains with A/C; the system is nearly crime-free. Computerized fare card must be bought from machines. If you plan to use the Metro several times, buy a $10 or more farecard; you will get a 5% bonus. Trains run daily 5:30am-midnight. Fare $1.10-3.25, depending on distance traveled; during peak-hour $1-$3.15. **Flash Pass** allows unlimited bus (and sometimes Metro) rides for 2-weeks ($20-34). **1-day Metro pass** $5. To make a bus transfer, get a pass from machines on the platform *before* boarding the train. The extensive **Metrobus** (same address, phone, and hours as Metrorail) system reliably serves Georgetown, downtown, and the suburbs. Fare $1.10. A comprehensive bus map is available from the main Metro office.

Taxis: Yellow Cab (544-1212). Fares are not based on a meter but on a map which splits the city into five zones and 27 subzones. Zone prices are fixed; ask how much the fare will be at the beginning of your trip. Max. fare within DC $10.20.

Car Rental: Easi Car Rentals, 2485 S. Glebe Rd. (703-521-0188), in Arlington. From $15 per day, plus 10¢ per mi. Weekly rates from $105, with 200 free mi. Must be 21 or older with major credit card or $300 cash deposit. Reservations advised. Open Mon.-Fri. 9am-7pm, Sat. 9am-2pm. **Bargain Buggies Rent-a-Car,** 912 N. Lincoln St. (703-841-0000), in Arlington. $20 per day and 10¢ per mi.; $110 per week (local rental) with 200 free mi. Must be 18 or older with major credit card or cash deposit of $250. Those under 21 need full insurance coverage of their own. Open Mon.-Fri. 8am-7pm, Sat.10am-6pm, Sun. 11am-5pm.

Bike Rental: Big Wheel Bikes, 315 7th St. SE (543-1600). Mountain bikes $15 per hr., $25 per business day; 3-hr. min. For an extra $5, you can keep the bike overnight. Major credit card, driver's license, or $150 cash deposit per bike required. Open Tues.-Fri. 11am-7pm, Sat. 10am-6pm, Sun. 11am-5pm.

Crisis Lines: Washington Post News Line: 334-9000 (everything you could want to know about what's going on in DC). **Gay and Lesbian Hotline:** 833-3234. 7pm-11pm. **Rape Crisis Center:** 333-7273. **Information, Protection, and Advocacy Center for Handicapped Individuals:** 966-8081, TDD 966-2500.

Emergency: 911.

Post Office: 900 Brentwood Rd. NE (682-9595). Open Mon.-Fri. 8am-8pm, Sat. 10am-6pm, Sun. noon-6pm. **ZIP code:** 20090. **Area code:** 202.

ORIENTATION

DC is ringed by the **Capital Beltway,** or I-495 (except where it's part of I-95); the Beltway is bisected by **U.S. 1,** and is intruded upon via Virginia by **I-395. I-95** shoots up from Florida, links Richmond, VA, to Washington and Baltimore, then rockets up the East Coast past Boston. The high-speed **Baltimore-Washington Parkway** connects DC to Baltimore. **I-595** trickles off the Capital Beltway and scenically east to Annapolis. **I-66** heads west through Virginia.

The city is roughly diamond-shaped, with the four tips of the diamond pointed at the four compass directions, and the street names and addresses split up into four quadrants: NW, NE, SE, and SW, as defined by their relation to the U.S. Capitol, Washington's geographic as well as spiritual heart. The names of the four quadrants distinguish otherwise identical addresses—pay very, *very* close attention to them. DC designer Pierre L'Enfant's basic street plan is a rectilinear grid. Streets running from east to west are named in alphabetical order running north and south from the

Capitol, from two A Streets two blocks apart (nearest the Capitol) out to two W Streets dozens of blocks apart. (There is no A or B St. in NW and SW, and no J St. anywhere.) After W St., east-west streets take on two-syllable names, then three-syllable names, then (at the north end of NW) names of trees and flowers in alphabetical order (roughly—some letters get repeated, and others skipped entirely). Streets running north-south get numbers (1st St., 2nd St., etc.). Numbered and lettered streets sometimes disappear for a block, then keep going as if nothing happened. Addresses on lettered streets indicate the numbered cross street (1100 D St. SE will be between 11th and 12th St.). State-named avenues radiate outward from the U.S. Capitol or the White House. The city added streets as the U.S. added states, and ultimately acquired avenues named for all 50. (Well, almost. CA has a "street" instead.)

Some **major roads** are **Pennsylvania Ave.,** which runs SE-NE from Anacostia to Capitol Hill to the Capitol, through downtown, past the White House (#1600), and ends finally at 28th and M St. NW in Georgetown; **Connecticut Ave.,** which runs north-northwest from the White House through Dupont Circle and past the Zoo; **Wisconsin Ave.,** north from Georgetown past the Cathedral to Friendship Heights; **16th St. NW,** which zooms from the White House north through offices, townhouses, Adams-Morgan, and Mt. Pleasant; **K St. NW,** a major artery downtown; **Constitution and Independence Ave.,** just north and south of the Mall; **Massachusetts Ave.,** from American University past the Cathedral, then through Dupont and Old Downtown to Capitol Hill; **New York Ave.,** whose principal arm runs from the White House through NE; and high-speed **North Capitol St.**

MID-ATLANTIC

Neighborhoods

Over 600,000 residents inhabit the federal city and more than double that number live in suburban areas surounding the city. Black, white, Asian, Hispanic, gay, bisexual, straight, Democrats, and Republicans are all well-represented. Escape the touristy **Mall** to get a true feel for the city. **Capitol Hill** extends east from the Capitol; its townhouses and bars mix white- and blue-collar locals with legislation-minded pols. The area south of the Mall, begins with federal offices all the way to the **Navy Yard,** which then give way to clubs and bars, and terminates at the **waterfront.** North of the Mall, **Old Downtown** goes about its business accompanied by **Foggy Bottom** (sometimes called the "West End") on the other side of the White House and **Farragut** around K St. west of 15th St. NW. **Georgetown** draws crowds and sucks away bucks nightly at its center at Wisconsin and M St. NW. Business and pleasure, embassies and streetlife, and a huge gay scene converge around **Dupont Circle;** east of 16th St. the Dupont Circle character changes to struggling **Logan Circle,** then to the clubby **Shaw/U District** (once the home of African-American power and culture in DC), and finally to Howard University and **LeDroit Park,** an early residence for Washington's African-American elite. North of Dupont and east of Rock Creek Park, **Adams-Morgan,** reigns as multicultural and hippy center of the capitol. The neighborhood experienced a flood of Mexican and El Salvadorean immigration in the late 80s, and now boasts a mix of Hispanic, Caribbean, and international coolness that any city would envy. West of the park begins **Upper Northwest,** a big stretch of spread-out, mostly residential territory that includes the National Zoo and the Cathedral. Across the Anacostia River, the **Southeast** (including **Anacostia**), has been damaged and further isolated by poverty, crack, and guns.

Any big city can be unsafe. Neighborhoods to take particular note of are Shaw/U District, the Theater District east of Dupont Circle, and any place southeast of the Mall. Use common sense at all times: walk on busy, well-lit streets whenever possible, and don't go out alone at night. DC's cheap taxi rates make a ride home after dining, clubbing, or taking in a show a more affordable option for anybody.

ACCOMMODATIONS

Business hotels discount deeply and swell with tourists on summer weekends. Hostels, guest houses, and university dormitories get particularly packed; reservations are a good idea. Check the *New York Times* Sunday Travel section for summer weekend deals before you go. DC automatically adds an **13% occupancy surcharge** and another **$1.50 per room per night** to your bill. Prices listed below *do not* include taxes, unless otherwise noted. **Bed & Breakfast Accommodations, Ltd.,** P.O. Box 12011, Washington, DC 20005 (328-3510; fax 332-3885), reserves rooms in private homes (singles start at $45, doubles at $55; $15 per additional person).

Washington International Hostel (HI-AYH), 1009 11 St. NW 20001 (737-2333). Metro: Metro Center; take the 11th St. exit, then walk 3 blocks north. International travelers appreciate the college-aged staff, bunk beds, bulletin boards, kitchen, and common rooms. Rooms with A/C hold 4-12 beds, accessible by elevator. Lockers, game room, and laundry facilities. Be careful northeast of here. Open 24 hrs. $18, nonmembers $21. Telephone reservations recommended; written reservations must be received 3 weeks in advance. Wheelchair accessible.

Simpkins' Bed & Breakfast, 1601 19th St. NW (387-1328), at the corner of Q in the heart of Dupont Circle. Metro: Dupont Circle. Unbeatable location. No curfew or lockout. For travelers carrying passports (U.S. or foreign). Shared-room rates are $15 for a single bed, $20 for double bed, or $25 total for double occupancy of a double bed; private single $40, private double $50. Linen $5, or BYO. Pre-paid reservations required. Without passport or public-interest affiliation, rates are 100% higher, but breakfast is included. Reserve 2-3 weeks ahead.

Kalorama Guest House at Kalorama Park, 1854 Mintwood Place NW (667-6369) and **at Woodley Park,** 2700 Cathedral Ave. NW (328-0860). Metro (both): Woodley Park-Zoo. Well-run, impeccably decorated guest rooms in Victorian townhouses; the first is in the upscale western slice of Adams-Morgan near Rock Creek Park, the second in a high-class neighborhood near the zoo. Both have laundry facilities and free local calls. Free continental breakfast. Mintwood location also has a fireplace and refrigerator space. Office open Mon.-Fri. 8am-8pm, Sat.-Sun. 8:30am-7pm. Rooms with shared bath $40-65, $5 per additional person. Rooms with private baths $55-85. Reserve 1-2 weeks in advance.

Hereford House, 604 South Carolina Ave. SE (543-0102). Metro: Eastern Market. British-style B&B in a Capitol Hill townhouse. Quietly charming B&B. Two shared baths, laundry, A/C, fridge, garden patio. Singles $40-50, doubles $55-60. Senior discount. Reservations recommended.

Allen Lee Hotel, 2224 F St. NW (331-1224 or 800-462-0186), near 23rd St. and George Washington University. Metro: Foggy Bottom-GWU. Rooms vary widely in size, furnishings, and state of repair. Singles $28, with private bath $35. Doubles $35/$45. Twins $37/$49. Reserve a few days in advance in summer.

Adams Inn, 1744 Lanier Place NW (745-3600 or 800-578-6807), near Ontario Rd. behind the Columbia Rd. 2 blocks from the center of Adams-Morgan. Metro: Woodley Park-Zoo, then a 12-min. walk; or bus #42 to Columbia Rd. from Dupont Cir. Elaborate and elegant Victorian townhouses. Patio, coin laundry facilities, and pay phones. TV in common room. Office open Mon.-Sat. 8am-9pm, Sun. 1-9pm. Shared-bath singles $45, private bath $60; doubles $55/70. Breakfast included. Weekly singles with shared bath $220, with private bath $275; doubles $295/350. 10% discount with ISIC Card. Prices include taxes.

Tabard Inn, 1739 N St. NW (785-1277; fax 785-6173), at 17th St. Metro: Dupont Circle. Romantic inn offers complimentary breakfast in a maze of darkened lounges. Singles $59-79, with private bath $99-135. Each additional person $12

Connecticut Woodley Guest House, 2647 Woodley Rd. NW (667-0218). Metro: Woodley Park-Zoo. Modest furnishings in threadbare yet tidy rooms. Free parking. Office open daily 7:30am-midnight. Singles with shared bath $39-43, private bath $49-56; doubles $45-48/54-61. Group, family, and long-term rates available.

Davis House, 1822 R St. NW (232-3196; fax 232-3197), near 19th St. Metro: Dupont Circle. Charming and spacious wood-floored building. Common room, sun room, patio, fridge, and microwave. Accepts international visitors, staff of Quaker organizations, and "representatives of other organizations working on peace and justice concerns." Other visitors occasionally accepted on a same-day, space-available basis. Office open daily 8am-10pm. Shared singles $30, private singles $35. Doubles $60 (with hall bath). One night's deposit required. Reserve early. No credit cards.

Brickskeller Inn, 1523 22nd St. NW (293-1885), between P and Q St. Metro: Dupont Circle. Small, clean rooms, usually with private sinks and shared hall bathrooms. Some rooms with private bath, A/C, and TV. Singles from $35-65, doubles from $45-65. Weekly: singles from $150, doubles from $225. Taxes included.

Swiss Inn, 1204 Massachusetts Ave. NW (371-1816 or 800-955-7947). Metro: Metro Center. 4 blocks from Metro Center; close to downtown. 7 clean, quiet studio apartments with refrigerator, private bath, high ceilings, kitchenettes, and A/C. Free local phone calls and laundry. Parking $5 per day weekdays (free weekends), or call the managers from the bus stop, Metro station, or downtown airport terminal and they'll come pick you up. Singles and doubles $98. Weekly rates: singles and doubles $78 per night. 20% discount for travel-club members (including HI-AYH), *Let's Go* readers, and adults over 59.

HoJo Inn, 600 New York Ave. NE (546-9200; fax 546-6348). Metro: Union Station. A ½-hr.walk from the Metro; take N. Capitol St., then turn right on New York Ave. A cab ride is safer than walking. Clean rooms with A/C and TV. Outdoor pool and free continental breakfast. Singles and doubles range $47-98. 10% discount for seniors and military types.

University Dorms: Georgetown University Summer Housing: Contact G.U. Office of Housing and Conferences Services, Georgetown University 20057 (687-4560). Metro: Foggy Bottom and a 10-min. walk. Available only for summer educational pursuits; they gladly take college-aged interns but *will not house self-declared tourists.* Housing is single-sex. 3-week min. stay. Singles $18, with A/C $19. Available early June-early Aug. **American University Summer Housing:** Write to 407 Butler Pavilion, 4400 Massachusetts Ave. NW 20016-8039, attn.: Housing Management (885-2669). Metro: Tenleytown-AU. Simple dorm rooms with A/C for students and interns (late May-mid-Aug). 3-week min. stay. Doubles with hall bathrooms $105 per week per person; triples $84 per week per person. Valid ID from any university and full payment for stay must be presented at check-in. $300 deposit required. Reserve early for check-in dates in early June; after that you can call 24 hrs. ahead and get a room if the dorms aren't full. **Howard University Housing** (806-5661 or 806-5653) has hostel-like rates for interns and students in DC for the summer. Singles $14, with A/C $18. Rooms available June 1-July 31. Call and ask for Rev. James Coleman.

Cherry Hill Park, 9800 Cherry Hill Rd. (301-937-7116) in Maryland. Metrobus from the Metrorail runs to and from the grounds every 30min., every 15min. during rush hour. Call for directions by car. The closest campground to Washington. Most of the 400 sites are for RVs. Cable hookup available; coin-operated laundry; heated swimming pool with whirlpool and sauna. Pets allowed. Tent site $25; RV site with electricity, water, and sewer $33. Extra person $2. $25 deposit required. Reserve at least 5 days ahead (call 9am-8pm). Seniors, AAA, military, and KOA members 10% discount.

FOOD

DC makes up for its days as a "sleepy Southern town" with a kaleidoscope of international restaurants. Smithsonian-goers should plan to eat dinner far away from the triceratops and the biplanes; visitors to the Mall get stuffed at mediocre institutional cafeterias mere blocks from the respectable food on Capitol Hill. You can eat for $4 or eat well for $7 at many places in DC. It's an open secret among interns that **happy hours** provide the cheapest dinners in Washington. Bars desperate to attract early-evening drinkers set up plates, platters, and tables of free appetizers; the best concentrate on Capitol Hill or south of Dupont Circle.

Capitol Hill

Head's, 400 1st St. SE (546-4545). On the corner of D St., right across from the Capitol South Metro stop. Washingtonian magazine thinks proprietor Nelson Head prepares the best barbecue in the District, and the bustling crowds at lunch and dinner seem to agree. This place is so popular with Congressfolk and their staffs that it keeps a few TVs tuned to C-SPAN at all times. If you see diners rush out mid-bite, you know a vote has been called in the House or Senate. Barbecued pork, beef, or chicken sandwiches $6, platters $7. Open Mon.-Sat. 11:30am-1am (kitchen closes at 10:30pm). Closed Sun. during the summer.

The Market Lunch, 225 7th St. SE (547-8444), in the Eastern Market complex. Metro: Eastern Market. Hailed by newspapers around DC as one of the best deals in town. Strong smells of fish and fresh meat waft over a dozen stools. Crab cakes ($6-9) are the local specialty, but the Blue Bucks (buckwheat blueberry pancakes $3) draw the crowds. Open Tues.-Sat. 7:30am-2:30pm.

Misha's Deli, 210 7th St. SE (547-5858), north of Pennsylvania Ave. on 7th St. Metro: Eastern Market. Inexpensive, authentic Russian and Eastern European food. Admire the posters of past and present Soviet leaders (the scorecard: Gorbachev 2, Yeltsin 1, Lenin 1). Ah, the Republic. Tasty knishes just $2, blintzes $1.75. Plenty of meats, cheeses, and breads. Borscht $2-2.50; wide array of sweets and desserts. Open Mon.-Fri. 8am-7:30pm, Sat. 7am-6pm, Sun. 9am-5pm.

Chinatown

Burma Restaurant, upstairs at 740 6th St. NW (638-1280). If you can't choose among the repetitive menus at Chinatown's restaurants, make it your mission at Burma to try the *Kauswe Thoke,* rice noodles with ground shrimp, fried onion, cilantro, hot pepper, garlic, and fresh lemon juice ($7.50), or anything served in the *Kotang* sauce, made from sesame, soya, cilantro, ginger, garlic, onions, and lemon juice. Most entrees go for $8, and all the noodle dishes are $7.50. Open for lunch Mon.-Fri. 11am-3pm, dinner daily 6pm-10:30pm.

White House Area/Foggy Bottom

DJ's, 2145 G St. NW (429-0230), near 22nd St. Metro: Foggy Bottom-GWU. Chef tosses out Italian, Chinese, American, and Middle Eastern fare at record speed. Cafeteria-style diner, packed with collegians. Entrees under $5. Veggie options. Open Mon.-Thurs. 7:15am-8:30pm, Fri. 7:15am-5:30pm, Sat. 10am-2:30pm.

Georgetown

Aditi, 3299 M St. NW (625-6825), at 33rd St. The Sanskrit name translates as "creative power" or "abundance;" here it means great food. Vegetarian entrees, $5-8. Meat dishes $8-14. Open Mon.-Thurs. 11:30am-2:30pm and 5:30-10pm, Fri.-Sat. 11:30am-2:30pm and 5:30-10:30pm, Sun. noon-2:30pm and 5:30-10pm.

Booeymonger, 3265 Prospect St. NW (333-4810), at Potomac St. Georgetown students stop by for breakfast ($3 for the special) or a quick 'n' tasty, giant sandwich (like the Pita Pan and Tuna Turner) for under $5. The $6 dinner special includes a specialty sandwich, soda, and choice of salad or soup. Free coffee refills (until 11am) to jump-start your weekday morning. Open daily 8am-midnight.

Paolo's, 1303 Wisconsin Ave. NW (333-7353), near N St. Huge, elegant Italian dishes well worth the price (pasta $10-17, pizza $7-10, other entrees $13-17). Open Sun.-Thurs. 11:30am-1am, Fri.-Sat. 11:30am-2am.

Sarinah, 1338 Wisconsin Ave. NW (337-2955), near O St. Charge through the inauspicious doorway and you'll find yourself downstairs in a tropical jungle: broad-leaved potted plants, pulpy wooden fruits, and colorful statuettes. Delicious Indonesian food includes skewered lamb, beef, chicken, or shrimp with spicy sauces ($9-10), and vegetarian entrees ($7-8). Long list of exotic desserts ($3.25-4.25). Open Tues.-Sat. noon-3pm and 6-10:30pm, Sun. 6-10:30pm.

Zed's Ethiopian Cuisine, 3318 M St. NW (333-4710), near 33rd St. Award-winning cuisine. Eat with your hands without embarrassment in the company of youthful, savvy clientele. Appetizers $4. Entrees $6-12. $5 weekday lunch specials. On a level with the Ethiopian fare in Adams-Morgan. Open daily 11am-11pm.

Farragut

The Star of Siam, 1136 19th St. NW (785-2839), between L and M St. Metro: Farragut West or Farragut North. This critically-acclaimed restaurant is a favorite of both business folk and true connoisseurs. Try the *Gang Keo-Wan,* or green curry with chicken or beef, coconut milk, bamboo shoots, eggplant, and green beans ($7.50 lunch, $8.50 dinner), and raise the temperature of the roof of your mouth to a whole new level. Open Mon.-Sat. 11:30am-11pm, Sun. 5-10pm.

Tokyo Terrace, 1025 Vermont Ave. NW (628-7304), near K St. Metro: McPherson Square. Join every other sushi-lover in Farragut for an inexpensive Japanese lunch fast-food-style. The "Sushi Deluxe" (6 California rolls, 2 *futomaki*, and 2 *inari*) is only $5.25. Just $9.75, or $5 for children will buy you all-you-can-eat sushi rolls plus salad, vegetable roll, and miso soup on Fri. 6-9pm and Sat. noon-9pm. Open Mon.-Thurs. 9am-7:30pm, Fri. 9am-9pm, Sat. noon-9pm.

Dupont Circle

City Lights of China, 1731 Connecticut Ave. NW (265-6688), between R and S St. Probably the District's best Chinese restaurant, City Lights serves carefully prepared Szechuan-Hunan standards ($9-22, most at the low end) and widely acclaimed house specialities, like the crispy fried shredded beef ($13). Try the steamed dumplings with chives and pork to start ($4.50). Open Mon.-Thurs. 11:30am-10:30pm, Fri. 11:30am-11pm, Sat. noon-11pm, Sun. noon-10:30pm.

Food for Thought, 1738 Connecticut Ave. NW (797-1095). Casual coffeehouse atmosphere attracts alternative youth, and veggie dishes satisfy the healthiest appetites. Evening sets by local acoustic musicians add a Bohemian touch; open mike every Mon. 9-11:30pm. Bulletin boards announce everything from rallies to beach parties to rides to LA. Pool table upstairs. Great chunky gazpacho ($2.95 a cup). Lunch combos with soup or salad $4.75-6.75 (Mon.-Fri. until 4:30pm), dinner $6-10. Open Mon. 11:30am-3pm and 5pm-12:30am; Tues.-Thurs. 11:30am-12:30am, Fri. 11:30am-2am, Sat. noon-2am, Sun. 4pm-12:30am.

Pizzeria Paradiso, 2029 P St. NW (223-1245), near 21st St. The lines are permanently long most nights, but wouldn't you expect them to be for the best pizza in the city? The toppings are tasty and traditional—basil, prosciutto, capers—but the crispy crust is the real star around here. Sides include the tangy *panzanella* (Tuscan bread and vegetable salad) and elegant salads. Open Mon.-Thurs. 11am-11pm, Fri.-Sat. 11am-midnight, Sun. noon-10pm.

The Pop Stop, 1513 17th St. NW (328-0880), near P St. The price of a cup of coffee buys you several hours in the easy chairs upstairs at the hippest of DC cafés. Or why not settle in for some serious people-watching on the streetside patio? The structural diversity attracts a diverse crowd, though it's weighted toward the local, gay, and young; many stop by on their way to or from bars and clubs. The café serves a wide range of coffee drinks ($1-3) and a handful of sandwiches (with chips $4). Open Sun.-Thurs. 7:30am-2am, Fri.-Sat. 7:30am-4am.

Skewers, 1633 P St. NW (387-7400, delivery 546-8646), near 17th St. Defies the neighborhood tendency towards multiethnic menus and sticks exclusively to Middle Eastern fare; coupled with its tapestry-hung, pottery-filled interior, the result is authenticity. Chicken kabob and 2 side dishes, $7. Open Sun.-Thurs. 11am-11pm, Fri.-Sat. 11am-midnight.

Soho Tea & Coffee, 2150 P St. NW (463-7646). Directly en route to any of the bars or clubs near P St. west of the Circle. This hip new coffeehouse benefits from its strategic location, drawing crowds of bar-and-club-hoppers in the wee hours of the morning, and serving a steady stream of patrons, gay and straight, all day long. Try a veggie bowl ($4.25) or a sandwich ($5.25). Espresso $1.25-3.50. Admire the artwork on the walls or watch passers-by. Open daily 6am-4am.

Zorba's Café, 1612 20th St. NW (387-8555), near Connecticut Ave., by the Q St. entrance to the Dupont Circle Metro. Mediterranean folk music played for the indoor and outdoor customers enjoying popular Greek food. The restaurant is self-service; place your order with the cashier inside. Try the *yero* plate ($5.40). Open Mon.-Wed. 11am-11:30pm, Thurs.-Sat. 11am-2:30am, Sun. noon-10:30pm.

Shaw/U District

Ben's Chili Bowl, 1213 U St. NW (667-0909), at 13th St. Metro: U St.-Cardozo. The self-declared "Home of the Famous Chili Dog," this venerable (30-year-old) neighborhood hangout got a facelift a few years ago, with a jukebox, smooth counters, and a molded ceiling to prove it. Spicy homemade chili—on a chili dog (served with onion, mustard, and potato chips, $2), on a half-smoke ($2.75), or on a ¼-lb. burger ($2.25). Die-hards eat it plain: small bowl $1.90, large bowl $2.55. Open Mon.-Thurs. 6am-2am, Fri.-Sat. 6am-3am, Sun. noon-8pm.

Florida Avenue Grill, 1100 Florida Ave. NW (265-1586), at 11th St. From the U St.-Cardozo Metro stop, walk east on U to 11th St., then walk north up 11th St. to Florida Ave. or take the Metrobus that runs up 11th St. Small, enduring (since 1944) diner once fed Black leaders and famous entertainers. Awesome Southern-style food: breakfast with salmon cakes or spicy half-smoked sausage, grits, apples, or southern biscuits ($2-6). Lunch and dinner dishes served with choice of 2 vegetables ($6.50-9). Open Tues.-Sat. 6am-9pm.

Adams-Morgan

The Islander, 1762 Columbia Rd. NW (234-4955), easy to miss above a jewelry store. Some of the best food in DC. Small Trinidadian and Caribbean restaurant has been winning regulars for over 15 years with its exotic but unpretentious cuisine. Consider curried goat or Calypso chicken (each $8.50). 9 kinds of *roti* (thin pancakes stuffed with vegetables/meat) are a bargain for $3.50-7. Appetizers $1.50-3. Wash it all down with sweet ginger beer ($1.50). Open Mon. 5-10pm, Tues.-Thurs. noon-10pm, Fri.-Sat. noon-11pm. Closed Mon. in summer.

Meskerem, 2434 18th St. NW (462-4100), near Columbia Rd. Fine Ethiopian cuisine in a beautiful setting. Cheery yellow 3-level interior incorporates an upstairs dining gallery with Ethiopian woven tables and a view of the diners below. Lunch entrees $7.25-11, dinner $9-12. Open daily noon-midnight.

Mixtec, 1792 Columbia Rd. NW (332-1011), near 18th St. A cheap, friendly, and refreshing bastion of authentic Mexican food. 2 bright rooms wear neat paper lanterns and wooden Mexican chairs, while a neon window-sign flashes the specialty, *tacos al carbon.* The $3 version consists of 2 small tortillas filled with beef and served with 3 kinds of garnish. Mixtec makes a mind-bending chicken *mole,* too ($9). Entrees $7-8. Open Sun.-Thurs. 10am-10pm, Fri.-Sat. 10am-1am.

Red Sea, 2463 18th St. NW (483-5000), near Columbia Rd. The first of Adams-Morgan's famous Ethiopian restaurants and still among the best. The red-painted exterior is weather-beaten but enticing. Use the traditional pancake bread, *injera,* to scoop up spicy lamb, beef, chicken, and vegetable *wats*. Entrees $7-9. Open Sun.-Thurs. 11:45am-11pm, Fri.-Sat. 11:45am-midnight.

Upper Northwest

Cactus Cantina, 3300 Wisconsin Ave. NW (686-7222), at Macomb St. near the Cathedral. Metro: Tenleytown, then Metrobus #30, 32, 34, or 36 towards Georgetown. How fresh is the food here? The kitchen doesn't even own a can opener and the salsa is no more than 30min. old when it arrives at your table. A local hangout with great food. Try the exceptional Tex-Mex standards, like the enchiladas ($7.50 for 3), or order something from the mesquite-fired grill ($9.50-20). Open Sun.-Thurs. 11:30am-11pm, Fri.-Sat. 11:30am-midnight.

Faccia Luna, 2400 Wisconsin Ave. NW (337-3132), at Glover Park. Pizza-crust connoisseurs, this is your Mecca, your Delhi, your Jerusalem. Forget pepperoni and top it with eggplant, spinach, or pesto. Don't even think about asking for tuna. Basic 10-in. pie $6.05, 12-in. $8.30, 14-in. $9.95, and 16-in. $11.50. Toppings extra. Open Sun.-Thurs. 11:30am-11pm, Fri.-Sat. 11:30am-midnight.

Rocklands, 2418 Wisconsin Ave. NW (333-2558), at Glover Park. South Carolina/Florida-style tangy grilled barbecue. Quarter-rack of pork ribs $4.50, BBQ pork sandwich $4. Raid owner John Snedden's shelf of some 100 different hot sauces; sample as extensively as your mouth will permit. Open Mon.-Sat. 11:30am-10pm, Sun. 11am-10pm.

SIGHTS

Every first-time visitor is compelled to go to the Capitol and the Smithsonian. But away from the grassy expanses of the manicured Mall, the rest of DC is a veritable thicket of art museums, ethnic communities, parks, public events, and nightlife. Adams-Morgan, Dupont Circle, Connecticut Ave., and Georgetown are all good bets for those sick of the standard tourist circuit.

If you're pressed for time, however, or like riding around in unusal vehicles, **Tourmobile Sight-seeing,** 1000 Ohio Drive SW, near the Washington Monument

(554-7950 or 554-5100 for recorded info) offers one of the most popular standard tours (9am-6:30pm, mid-Sept. to mid-March 9:30am-4:30pm; standard 18-sight loop $9, ages 3-11 $5; buy tickets from booth or drivers). **Scandal Tours** (783-7212) schleps tourists from one place of infamy to the next, including Gary Hart's townhouse, Watergate, and the Vista Hotel, where Mayor Barry was captured smoking crack on film (75min., $27). Capitol Entertainment Services (636-9203) specializes in a **Black History Tour** through Lincoln Park, Anacostia, and the Frederick Douglass home. (Tours begin at area hotels. 3hr.; $22, children 5-12 $12.)

Capitol Hill

The scale and style of the **U.S. Capitol** (224-3121) still evoke the power of the republic. (Metro: Capitol South.) The **East Front** faces the Supreme Court; from Jackson (1829) to Carter (1977), most Presidents were inaugurated here. For Reagan's 1981 inauguration, Congress moved the ceremony to the newly fixed-up **West Front,** overlooking the Mall. If there's light in the dome at night, Congress is still meeting. The public East Front entrance brings you into the 180-ft.-high **rotunda.** You can get a **map** from the tour desk here (free guided **tours** begin here daily every 20min. 9am-3:45pm). Downstairs, ceremony and confusion reign in the **crypt** area; most of the functioning rooms are upstairs. For a spectacle, but little insight, climb to the **House and Senate visitors galleries.** Americans should request a gallery pass (valid for the whole 2-year session of Congress) from the office of their representative, delegate, or senator. Foreign nationals may get one-day passes by presenting a passport, driver's licence, or birth certificate (or photocopies thereof) at the desk immediately outside the House visitors gallery (for a House pass) or at the "Appointments desk" located at the extreme North End of the main hallway of the crypt level (for a Senate pass). Expect to see a few bored-looking elected officials failing to listen to the person on the podium who is probably speaking only for benefit of home-district cable TV viewers. The real business of Congress is conducted in **committee hearings.** Most are open to the public; check the *Washington Post's* "Today in Congress" box for times and locations. The free **Capitol subway** shuttles between the basement of the Capitol and the House and Senate office buildings; a buzzer and flashing red lights signals an imminent vote. (Open daily 9am-4:30pm, Memorial Day-Labor Day daily 8am-8pm.)

The nine justices of the **Supreme Court,** 1 1st St. NE (479-3000), across from the East Front of the Capitol building, are the final interpreters of the U.S. Constitution (Metro: Capitol South or Union Station). Oral arguments are open to the public; show up early (before 8:30am) to be seated, or walk through the standing gallery to hear 5 minutes of the argument. (Court is in session Oct.-June Mon.-Wed. 10am-3pm for 2 weeks each month.) The *Washington Post's* A-section can tell you what case is up. Hoof through the courtroom itself when the Justices are on vacation. Brief lectures cover the history, duties, and architecture of the court and its building (every hr. on the ½-hr. 9:30am-3:30pm). (Open Mon.-Fri. 9am-4:30pm. Free.)

The **Library of Congress,** 1st St. SE (707-5000; recorded events schedule 707-8000), between East Capitol and Independence Ave. (Metro: Capitol South), is the world's largest library, with 26 million books and over 80 million other holdings occupying three buildings: the 1897 Beaux Arts Jefferson Building; the 1939 Adams Building across 2nd St.; and the 1980 Madison Building. The entire collection, including rare items, is open to those of college age or older with a legitimate research purpose, but anyone can take the tour (irregular hours), which starts in the Madison Building lobby. After a brief film, the tour scuttles through tunnels to the Jefferson Building, which is otherwise closed for renovations. The octagonal Main Reading Room, under a spectacular dome, remains open to scholars despite renovations. (Most reading rooms open Mon.-Fri. 8:30am-9:30pm, Sat. 8:30am-6pm.)

Folger Shakespeare Library, 201 East Capitol St. SE (544-4600), houses the world's largest collection of Shakespeareana (about 275,000 books and manuscripts); you can see the Great Hall exhibition gallery and the theater, which imitates the Elizabethan Inns of Court indoor theaters where Shakespeare's company performed. The Folger also sponsors readings, lectures, and concerts such as the PEN/Faulkner poetry and fiction readings and the Folger Consort, a chamber music group specializing in Renaissance music. (Exhibits open Mon.-Sat. 10am-4pm; library open Mon.-Fri. 8:45am-4:45pm.) Stop for a rest in the authentic Elizabethan **"knot" garden,** on the building's 3rd St. side.

The trains run on time at **Union Station,** 50 Massachusetts Ave. NE (371-9441), 2 blocks north of the Capitol (Metro: Union Station). Colonnades, archways, and huge domed ceilings equate Burnham's Washington with imperial Rome; today the station is a spotless ornament in the crown of capitalism, with a food court, chic stores, and mall rats aplenty (shops open Mon.-Sat. 10am-9pm, Sun. noon-6pm).

Directly west of Union Station is the **National Postal Museum,** 1st St. and Massachusetts Ave. NE (357-2700), on the lower level of the City Post Office (Metro: Union Station). The Smithsonian's collection of stamps and other philatelic materials was relocated here in July 1993. The collection includes such postal floatsam as airmail planes hung from the ceiling in the 90-ft.-high atrium, half of a fake mustache used by a train robber, goofy mail boxes, and the letter-carrier uniform worn by everyone's favorite oedipal oddity, Cliff Claven in TV's "Cheers." (Open daily 10am-5:30pm. Free.) Northeast of Union Station is the red-brick **Capital Children's Museum,** 800 3rd St. NE (675-4125; Metro: Union Station). Touch and feel every exhibit in this huge interactive experiment of a museum; walk through the life-sized cave, learn how a printing press works, grind and brew your own hot chocolate, or wander through the room-sized maze. Or just watch cartoons. (Open daily 10am-5pm. $6, under 2 free. All kids must be accompanied by an adult.)

The **Sewall-Belmont House,** 144 Constitution Ave. NE (546-3989; Metro: Union Station), one of the oldest houses in DC and headquarters of the National Woman's Party, now houses a museum of the U.S. women's movement. (Open Tues.-Fri. 11am-3pm, Sat.-Sun. noon-4pm; ring the bell, as tours are unscheduled. Free.)

Southeast

Three museums and a boardable destroyer stay ship-shape among the booms at the **Washington Navy Yard,** at 9th and M St. SE (Metro: Navy Yard). The best of the lot, the **Navy Museum,** Building 76 (433-4882), should buoy anyone let down by the admire-but-don't-touch Air & Space Museum on the Mall. Climb inside the space capsule, play human cannonball inside huge ship guns, jam yourself into a bathysphere used to explore the sea floor, or give orders on the bridge. (Open Mon.-Fri. 9am-5pm, Sat.-Sun. 10am-5pm; Sept.-May Mon.-Fri. 9am-4pm, Sat.-Sun. 10am-5pm.) Tour the **U.S.S. Barry,** a decommissioned destroyer, docked a few steps from the Navy Museum. The **Marine Corps Historical Museum,** Building 58 (433-3534), marches through Marine Corps time from the American Revolution to the present, touting the actions, guns, uniforms, swords, and other memorabilia of marines from the halls of Montezuma to the shores of Kuwait (Complex open April-Sept. Tues.-Sun. 10am-5pm, Oct.-March 10am-4pm. Free.).

After the Civil War, one-acre plots sold by the Freedmen's Bureau drew freed slaves to **Anacostia.** *Use caution in this neighborhood.* Despite the opening of the Anacostia Metro, this neglected neighborhood remains largely unattractive to tourists, despite community struggles to overcome drug-related violence. If you prefer exploring on foot, do so here only during the day and with a friend or two. The **Anacostia Museum,** 1901 Fort Place SE (357-2700), focuses on African-American history and culture. (Take the W-1 or W-2 bus from Howard Rd. near the Metro Station to Fort Place.) Pick up a flyer at the Smithsonian Castle to see what's showing at the museum. (Open daily 10am-5pm; free.)

Museums on the Mall

The **Smithsonian** is the catalogued attic of the United States. The world's largest museum complex stretches out along Washington's longest lawn, **the Mall. Constitution Ave.** (on the north) and **Independence Ave.** (on the south) fence the double row of museums. All Smithsonian museums are free and wheelchair-accessible;

all offer written guides in various languages. For all Smithsonian museums, call 357-2700, TDD 357-1729; for info on tours, concerts, lectures, and films, call 357-2020. Take the Metro to the Smithsonian stop to reach the following museums.

The National Museum of American History, Henry Ford said "History is bunk." This museum thinks history is junk—several centuries' worth of machines, textiles, photographs, vehicles, harmonicas, hats, and uncategorizable American detritus reside here. When the Smithsonian inherits a quirky artifact of popular history, like Dorothy's slippers from *The Wizard of Oz* or Archie Bunker's chair, it usually ends up here. The original "Star Spangled Banner" hangs behind Foucault's pendulum. Open daily 10am-6:30pm; Sept.-May daily 10am-5:30pm.

The Museum of Natural History, This golden-domed, neoclassical museum considers the earth and its life in 2½ big, crowded floors of exhibits. Inside, the largest African elephant ever "captured" (i.e., killed) stands under dome-filtered sunshine. Dinosaur skeletons dwarf it in a nearby gallery. Upstairs, cases of naturally-occurring crystals (including glow-in-the-dark rocks) make the final plush room of cut gems anticlimactic, despite the famously cursed Hope Diamond. The Insect Zoo pleases with an array of live creepy-crawlies, from cockroaches to walking sticks. Open daily 10am-6:30pm; Sept.-May daily 10am-5:30pm.

The National Gallery of Art: West Building (737-4215), houses and hangs its jumble of pre-1900 art in a domed marble temple to Western Tradition, including important works by El Greco, Raphael, Rembrandt, Vermeer, and Monet. Leonardo da Vinci's earliest surviving portrait, Ginevra de' Benci, the only da Vinci in the U.S., hangs amongst a fine collection of Italian Renaissance Art. Other highlights include a bevy of French Impressionist pieces, a hall of Dutch masters, Jan Van Eyck's The Annunciation, and works by John Singer Sargent, George Bellows, and Winslow Homer. Open Mon.-Sat. 10am-5pm, Sun. 11am-6pm.

The National Gallery Of Art: East Building (737-4215), houses the museum's plentiful 20th-century collection in I. M. Pei's celebrated spacious, sunlit structure. The National Gallery owns works by a veritable parade of modern artists, including Picasso, Matisse, Mondrian, Miró, Magritte, Pollock, Warhol, Lichtenstein, and Rothko. Don't expect to see all of them, however; the East Building constantly rearranges, closes, opens, and remodels parts of itself for temporary exhibits. Open Mon.-Sat. 10am-5pm, Sun. 11am-6pm.

The National Air and Space Museum, gigantic, and the world's most popular museum to boot, with 7.5 million visitors per year. Airplanes and space vehicles dangle from the ceiling; the Wright brothers' biplane in the entrance gallery looks intimidated by all its younger kin. The space-age atrium holds a moon rock, worn smooth by two decades of tourists' fingertips. Walk through the Skylab space station, the Apollo XI command module, and a DC-7. A full-scale lunar lander has touched down outside the cafeteria. A new exhibit entitled "Where Next, Columbus?" brings a historical perspective to issues dealing with space-exploration, while another gallery test-flies the *U.S.S. Enterprise* from *Star Trek*. The gift shop is a blast. IMAX movies on Langley Theater's 5-story screen are so realistic that some viewers suffer motion sickness. Films 9:30am-6:45pm. Tickets $3.25, students, and seniors, and kids $2; available at the box office on the ground floor. Open daily 10am-6:30pm; Sept.-June daily 10am-5:30pm.

Hirshhorn Museum and Sculpture Garden, This four-story, slide-carousel-shaped brown building has outraged traditionalists since 1966. Each floor consists of 2 concentric circles, an outer ring of rooms and paintings, and an inner corridor of sculptures. The Hirshhorn's best shows feature art since 1960; no other gallery or museum in Washington even pretends to keep up with the Hirshhorn's avant-garde paintings, mind-bending sculptures, and mixed-media installations. The museum claims the world's most comprehensive set of 19th- and 20th-century Western sculpture, including small works by Rodin and Giacometti. Outdoor sculpture shines in the museum's courtyard. Museum open daily 10am-5:30pm. Sculpture Garden open daily 7:30am-dusk.

The Arts and Industries Building, is an exhibition of an exhibition, the 1876 Centennial Exhibition of American technology in Philadelphia. Pause for the exterior: a polychromatic, multi-style chaos of gables, arches, rails, shingles, and bricks.

Inside, furniture and candy-making equipment congregate near the Mall entrance; further back, heavy machinery will delight steam fans. Open daily 10am-5:30pm.

The National Museum of African Art, underground at 950 Independence Ave. SW (357-4600), displays artifacts from Sub-Saharan Africa such as masks, textiles, ceremonial figures, and fascinating musical instruments like a harp made partly of pangolin scales. One permanent display contains bronzes from what is today Nigeria; another focuses on pottery. Open daily 10am-5:30pm.

The Arthur M. Sackler Gallery, underground at 1050 Independence Ave. SW (357-2041), showcases an extensive collection of art from China, South and Southeast Asia, and Persia, including illuminated manuscripts; Chinese and Japanese painting; jade miniatures; carvings and friezes from Egypt, Phoenicia, and Sumeria; Hindu statues; and the Sackler Library. Open daily 10am-5:30pm.

The Freer Gallery of Art, is the small pearl on a Mall-encircling necklace of big, showy gems. The Freer displays Asian and Asian-influenced art, including Chinese bronzes, precious manuscripts, jade carvings, and James McNeill Whistler's opulent *Peacock Room.* Open daily 10am-5:30pm. Free tours at 1:30pm.

The U.S. Holocaust Memorial Museum, 100 Raoul Wallenberg Place SW (488-0400). The entrance is not on the Mall. Houses displays that move beyond historical narrative, and puts the Holocaust on a personal level. The permanent exhibit chronicles the rise of Nazism, the events leading up to the war in Europe, and the history of anti-semitism. Still photos and dioramas depict barbaric Nazi "medical" experiments, Jews being rounded up and sent to concentration camps, then being exterminated in gas chambers or at gunpoint. Films show Soviet, British, and American troops entering the concentration camps, shocked by the mass graves and emaciated prisoners they encounter. Tapes bear the testimony of Holocaust survivors. "The Hall of Remembrance" contains an eternal flame. The main exhibit is not recommended for children under 12, but the exhibit "Daniel's Story: Remember the Children" was designed for younger folk. This museum draws immense crowds; get in line by 9am to acquire same-day tickets. (Open daily 10am-5:30pm. Free.)

On and Around the Mall: Monuments and Stuff

The **Washington Monument** (Metro: Smithsonian) is a vertical altar to America's first president. The stairs up the monument were a famous (and strenuous) tourist exercise until the Park Service closed them after heart attacks (on the way up) and vandalism (on the way down). The experts say the thing could withstand a super-tornado blowing at 145 mi. per hour. At the top, tiny windows offer lookout points. The line takes 45 minutes to circle the monument; people with disabilities can bypass it. (Open daily 8am-midnight; Sept.-March daily 9am-5pm. Free.) The **Reflecting Pool** reflects Washington's obelisk in 7 million gallons of lit-up water 24 hrs. a day—if you lean far enough over, it might reflect you too.

Maya Ying Lin, who designed the **Vietnam Veterans Memorial,** south of Constitution Ave. at 22nd St. NW (Metro: Foggy Bottom/GWU), called it "a rift in the earth—a long, polished black stone wall, emerging from and receding into the earth." 58,132 Americans died in Vietnam, and each of their names is chiseled onto the memorial's stark black edifice. Books at both ends of the structure serve as indexes to the memorial's numbered panels. Families and veterans come here to ponder and to mourn; many make rubbings of their loved ones' names from the walls. (Open 24 hrs.)

Anyone with a penny already knows what the **Lincoln Memorial** looks like, at the west end of the Mall (Metro: Smithsonian or Foggy Bottom/GWU); the design copies the rectangular grandeur of Athens' Parthenon. From these steps, Martin Luther King, Jr. gave his "I Have a Dream" speech to the 1963 March on Washington. Daniel Chester French's seated Lincoln presides over the memorial from the inside, keeping watch over protesters and Fourth of July fireworks. You can read his Gettysburg address on the wall to the left of the statue. Climbing the 19-ft. president is a federal offense; a camera will catch you if the rangers don't. (Open 24 hrs.)

Dedicated in July 1995, the 19 colossal polished steel statues (14 Army men, 3 Marines, a Navy Medic, and an Air Force officer) of the **Korean War Memorial** trudge up a hill, rifles in hand, an eternal expression of weariness mixed with fear frozen upon their faces. A black granite wall with over 2000 sandblasted photographic images from this forgotten war in which 54,000 Americans lost their lives stands nearby. One edge of the wall extends into a shallow pool of water, a symbol of the Korean peninsula. The memorial is at the west end of the Mall, near Lincoln.

A 19-ft. hollow bronze Thomas Jefferson stands enshrined in the domed, open-air rotunda of the **Jefferson Memorial,** surrounded by massive ionic columns. The memorial's design pays tribute to Jefferson's home, Monticello, which he designed. Interior walls quote from Jefferson's writings: the *Declaration of Independence,* the *Virginia Statute of Religious Freedom, Notes on Virginia,* and an 1815 letter. (Open 24 hrs.) The memorial overlooks the **Tidal Basin,** where pedalboats ripple in and out of the memorial's shadow. (Metro: L'Enfant Plaza.)

South of the Mall, exotic foliage from all continents and climates vegetates inside and outside the **U.S. Botanical Garden** (225-7099), 1st St. and Maryland Ave. SW (Metro: Federal Center SW). Cacti, bromeliads, and other plants flourish indoors. (Open daily 9am–5pm. 40-min. guided tours at 10am and 2pm; call ahead.) Further west, the **Bureau of Engraving and Printing** (a.k.a. the Mint) (662-2000), 14th St. and C St. SW, offers cramped tours of the presses that annually print over $20 billion worth of money and stamps. Money-love has made this the area's longest line; arrive mega-early or expect to grow old while you wait. (Open Mon.-Fri. 9am-2pm; free.

MID-ATLANTIC

Downtown and North of the Mall

It's only proper that an architectural marvel should house the **National Building Museum** (272-2448) which towers above F St. NW between 4th and 5th St. (Metro: Judiciary Square). Montgomery Meigs's Italian-inspired edifice remains one of Washington's most beautiful; the Great Hall could hold a 15-story building. "Washington: Symbol and City," one of the NBM's first permanent exhibits, covers DC architecture. Other highlights include rejected designs for the Washington Monument and the chance to design your own Capitol Hill rowhouse. (Open Mon.-Sat. 10am-4pm, Sun. noon-4pm. Tours Mon.-Fri. 12:30pm, Sat.-Sun. 12:30, 1:30pm. Free.)

The **National Museum of American Art** and the **National Portrait Gallery** (357-2700) share the Old Patent Office Building, a neoclassical edifice 2 blocks long (American Art entrance at 8th and G St., Portrait Gallery entrance at 8th and F; Metro: Gallery Place-Chinatown). The NMAA's corridors contain a diverse collection of major 19th- and 20th-century painters, as well as folk and ethnic artists. DC janitor James Hampton stayed up nights in an unheated garage for 15 years to create the *Throne of the Third Heaven of the Nations' Millennium General Assembly,* to the right of the main entrance. "Art of the American West" puts the U.S.'s westward expansion in perspective, while Edward Hopper competes with the abstractions of Franz Kline on the third floor. (Open daily 10am-5:30pm; tours Mon.-Fri. noon, Sat.-Sun. 2pm. Free.) The wide range of media, periods, styles, and people represented make the National Portrait Gallery a museum of the American character (open daily 10am-5:30pm; tours daily 10:15am, 1:15pm, and by request. Free).

The U.S.'s founding documents can still be found at the **National Archives** (501-5000, guided tours 501-5205), 8th St. and Constitution Ave. NW (Metro: Archives-Navy Memorial). Visitors line up outside to view the original *Declaration of Independence, U.S. Constitution,* and *Bill of Rights.* Humidity-controlled, helium-filled glass cases preserve and exhibit all three documents in the central rotunda. Also on display is H. Ross Perot's 13th-century copy of the *Magna Carta* (insert your own joke here). (Exhibit area open daily 10am-9pm, Sept.-March 10am-5:30pm. Free.) The **Federal Bureau of Investigation** (324-3000) still hunts spies, enemies of the state, and interstate felons with undiminished vigor. Tour lines form on the beige-but-brutal J. Edgar Hoover building's outdoor plaza (tour entrance from 10th St. NW at Pennsylvania Ave.; Metro: Federal Triangle or Archives-Navy Memorial). Real FBI agents sport walkie-talkies as they speed you through gangsta paraphernalia and photos, confiscated drugs, gun displays, and mugshots of the nation's 10 most wanted criminals. John Dillinger's death mask hangs alongside his machine gun. At the tour's end, a marksman shreds cardboard evildoers; tellingly, the mostly American audience applauds vigorously. (Tours Mon.-Fri 8:45am-4:15pm; free.)

"Sic semper tyrannis!" shouted assassin John Wilkes Booth after shooting President Abraham Lincoln during a performance at **Ford's Theatre,** 511 10th St. NW (426-6924; Metro: Metro Center). National Park rangers narrate the events of the April 14, 1865 assassination. (Open daily 9am-5pm; talks every hr. 9am-noon and 2-5pm; Feb.-June every 30min. Free.) The **Old Post Office** (606-8691, TDD 606-8694), at Pennsylvania Ave. and 12th St. NW, sheathes a shopping mall in architectural wonder (Metro: Federal Triangle). Its arched windows, conical turrets, and 315-ft. clock tower rebuke its sleeker contemporary neighbors. The National Park Service can show you around the clock tower; the view from the top may be DC's best. (Tower open 8am-10:45pm; mid-Sept. to mid-April 10am-6pm. Shops open Mon.-Sat. 10am-8pm, Sun. noon-6pm.)

The **National Museum of Women in the Arts,** 1250 New York Ave. NW (783-5000; Metro: Metro Center), houses works by the likes of Mary Cassatt, Georgia O'Keeffe, Lilla Cabot Perry, Frida Kahlo, and Alma Thomas in a former Masonic Temple. The hunt for the museum's permanent collection, which begins on the third floor, is something like an initiation rite. (Open Mon.-Sat. 10am-5pm, Sun. noon-5pm. Suggested donation $3, students, seniors, and kids $2.)

White House and Foggy Bottom

The **White House,** 1600 Pennsylvania Ave. NW (456-7041), isn't Versailles; the President's house, with its simple columns and expansive lawns, seems a compromise between patrician lavishness and democratic simplicity. The President's personal staff works in the West Wing, while the First Lady's cohort occupies the East Wing. Get a free ticket for a short tour at the ticket booth at the northeast corner of the **Ellipse,** the park due south of the White House. Get in line for a ticket *before 7:30am;* expect a 2½ hour wait afterwards. (Tours Tues.-Sat. 10am-noon; tickets distributed starting at 8am.) American citizens can arrange a better tour of the White House through their Congressperson. Sometimes it's hard to tell the homeless, the political demonstrators, and the statues apart in **Lafayette Park,** across Pennsylvania Ave. from the White House. All three are more-or-less permanent presences.

At 17th St. and Pennsylvania Ave. NW, the **Renwick Gallery** (357-1300) is filled with "American crafts" (Metro: Farragut West). The first floor's temporary exhibits often show fascinating mixed-media sculptures and constructions by important contemporary artists. (Open daily 10am-5:30pm. Free.) Once housed in the Renwick's mansion, the **Corcoran Gallery** (638-3211) is now in much larger quarters on 17th St. between E St. and New York Ave. NW (Metro: Farragut West). The Corcoran shows off American artists like John Singer Sargent, Mary Cassatt, and Winslow Homer. Thomas Cole's 1841 *Return from the Tournament* provides an air of romance. The gallery's temporary exhibits seek the cutting edge of contemporary art. (Open Mon., Wed. and Fri.-Sun. 10am-5pm, Thurs. 10am-9pm. Suggested donation $3, families $5, students and seniors $1, under 12 free.)

The **Organization of American States** (458-3000, museum/gallery 458-6016), at 17th St. and Constitution Ave. NW, across the street from the southwest corner of the Ellipse, is a Latin American extravaganza: dappled sunlight engulfs its air-conditioned center, where a fountain gurgles over greenery. The patio's tiles copy traditional pre-Colombian designs. The OAS holds formal sessions which welcome tourists. During parades, the OAS locks up so that would-be snipers have no opportunity to take advantage of its strategic rooftop position. (Metro: Farragut West.)

The **National Academy of Sciences** (334-2000), 21st and C St. NW, holds scientific and medical exhibits. Pay homage to the statue of Albert Einstein outside, and note that the man who formulated the Theory of Relativity seems to be wearing Tevas. (Open Mon.-Fri. 8:30am-5pm.)

Above Rock Creek Parkway, the **John F. Kennedy Center for the Performing Arts** (tickets and info 467-4600; entrance off 25th St. and New Hampshire Ave. NW) rises like a marble sarcophagus (Metro: Foggy Bottom-GWU). Built in the late 60s, the center boasts four major stages and a film theater. The flag-decked Hall of States and Hall of Nations lead to the Grand Foyer, which could swallow the Washington Monument with room to spare. A rather unsavory 7-ft. bronze bust of JFK stares up and away at 18 Swedish chandeliers. In the Opera House, snowflake-shaped chandeliers require 1735 electric light bulbs. The terrace has an unbeatable view of the Potomac. (Open daily 10am-11pm. Tours 10am-1pm. Free.)

Georgetown

When Archbishop John Carroll learned where the new capital would be built, he rushed to found **Georgetown University** (main entrance at 37th and O St.), which opened in 1789 as the U.S.'s first Catholic institution of higher learning. Students live, study, and party together in the townhouses lining the streets near the university. Georgetown's basketball team, the **Hoyas,** are perennial contenders for the national college championship. Buy tickets through Ticketmaster (432-7328), the campus Ticket Office (687-4692), or Athletic Department (687-2449).

Philip Johnson's 1963 gallery, **Dumbarton Oaks,** 1703 32nd St. NW (recorded info 338-8278, tour info 342-3212), between R and S St., holds a collection of beautifully-displayed carvings, tools, and other art from the Aztec and Mayan civilizations. In 1944, the Dumbarton Oaks Conference, held in the Music Room, helped write the United Nations charter. (Collections open Tues.-Sun. 2-5pm; "suggested contribution" $1.) Save at least one hour for the Edenic gardens (open daily 2-6pm, Nov.-March 2-5pm; $3, seniors and kids $2; Nov.-March free).

Retired from commercial use since the 1800s, the **Chesapeake & Ohio Canal** (301-299-3613) extends 185 mi. from Georgetown to Cumberland, MD. The benches under the trees around 30th St. make a prime city lunch spot.

No Way Down

When Kevin Costner, in the movie *No Way Out,* escaped Pentagon nasties by racing deep into the bowels of the "Georgetown Metro," DC audiences laughed out loud. Persistent rumors claim that the Georgetown Citizens' Association vetoed a Georgetown Metro stop, illogically voting to clog their streets with other people's autos just to keep away carless proletarians. In fact, a Georgetown subway would have posed a prohibitive engineering problem—a 90-degree turn in an underground tunnel just at the water's edge.

Dupont Circle

Dupont Circle used to be called Washington's most diverse neighborhood; then it turned expensive and Adams-Morgan turned cool. Nevertheless, the Circle and its environs remain a haven for Washington's artsy, international, and gay communities. Unless otherwise stated, the closest Metro to these sites is Dupont Circle. Massachusetts Ave. between Dupont Circle and Observatory Circle is also called **Embassy Row**. Identify an embassy by the national coat-of-arms or flag out front. The **Art Gallery District** is bounded by Connecticut Ave. on the east, Florida Ave. on the west, and Q St. to the south. More than 25 galleries (most of them on R St.) exhibit here. Call 232-3610 for more information.

The **Phillips Collection,** 1600 21st St. (387-2151), at Q St. NW, was the first museum of modern art in the U.S. Everyone gapes at Auguste Renoir's masterpiece *Luncheon of the Boating Party,* in the Renoir room. Among the other few permanent exhibitions are the Rothko room and the Klee room. A stroll up the annex and down through original mansion is a delightful parade of Delacroix, Matisses, Van Goghs, Mondrians, Degas, Miros, Gris, Kandinskys, Turners, Courbets, Daumiers, Prendergasts, O'Keefes, and Hoppers—to name a few. (Open Tues.-Sat. 10am-5pm, Sun. noon-7pm. Sat.-Sun. $6.50, students and seniors $3.25, required Sat.-Sun. and suggested Tues.-Fri. Under 18 free.)

The **Bethune Museum and Archives,** 1318 Vermont Ave. NW (332-1233; Metro: McPherson Square), chronicles the life of leader and civil rights activist Mary

McLeod Bethune. (Open Mon.-Sat. 10am-4pm; Sept.-June Mon.-Fri. 10am-4pm. Archives open by appointment. Free.) The pensive **B'nai B'rith Klutznick National Jewish Museum,** 1640 Rhode Island Ave. NW (857-6583; Metro: Farragut North) contains the nation's first statement enunciating America's commitment to religious and ethnic toleration. (Open Sun.-Fri. 10am-4:30pm, except Jewish holidays. Suggested donation $2, students, seniors, and children $1). **Anderson House,** 2118 Massachusetts Ave. NW (785-2040), retains the robber-baron decadence of U.S. ambassador Larz Anderson, who built it in 1902-5. The Society of the Cincinnati makes this mansion its home base. (Open Tues.-Sat. 1-4pm. Free.) Flags line the entrance to the **Islamic Center,** 2551 Massachusetts Ave. NW (332-8343), a brilliant white building whose stunning designs stretch to the tips of its spired ceilings. No shorts; women must cover their heads and wear sleeved clothing (no short skirts). (Open daily 10:30am-5pm. Donation requested.)

On the corner of M St. and 17th St. NW, the **National Geographic Society Explorer's Hall** (857-7588, group tours 857-7689; Metro: Farragut North) conquers the first floor of its pin-striped building. The museum proffers interactive films, a live parrot, a miniature tornado that you can touch, a huge globe, and fascinating changing exhibits, often by *National Geographic* magazine's best photographers. For $3, get a *National Geographic* cover made with your face on it. (Open Mon.-Sat. 9am-5pm, Sun. 10am-5pm. Wheelchair access. Free.)

Upper Northwest

Legend has it that "pandemonium" entered the vernacular when the first giant pandas left China for **Washington's National Zoological Park** (673-4800) as a gift from Mao to Nixon. After years of unsuccessful attempts to birth a baby panda in captivity, Ling-Ling died tragically; her sexually frustrated life-mate Hsing-Hsing remains in the Panda House. The zoo spreads east from Connecticut Ave. a few blocks uphill from the Woodley Park-Zoo Metro; follow the crowds to the entrance at 3000 Connecticut Ave. NW. Forested paths—sometimes very steep—and flat walks near the entrance pass plenty of outdoor exhibits in fields and cages, which visitors seeking the big attractions often ignore. Valley Trail (marked with blue bird tracks) connects the bird and sealife exhibits, while the red Olmsted Walk (marked with elephant feet) links land-animal houses. (Grounds open daily 8am-8pm, Oct. 16-April 14 8am-6pm; buildings daily 9am-6pm, Sept. 16-April 9am-4:30pm. Free.)

The **Washington National Cathedral** (537-6200, recording 364-6616), at Massachusetts and Wisconsin Ave. NW (Metro: Tenleytown, then take the #30, 32, 34 or 36 bus toward Georgetown; or walk up Cathedral Ave. from the equidistant Woodley Park-Zoo Metro), took over 80 years (1907-90) to build, though the cathedral's interior spaces have been in use for decades. Rev. Martin Luther King, Jr. preached his last Sunday sermon from the Canterbury pulpit; more recently, the Dalai Lama spoke here. Take the elevator to the Pilgrim Observation Gallery and see Washington from the highest vantage point in the city (open daily 10am-3:15pm). Angels, gargoyles, and grotesques glower outside. (Open Mon.-Fri. 10am-9pm, Sat. 10am-4:30pm, Sun. 12:30-4pm; Sept.-April Mon.-Sat. 10am-4:30pm, Sun. 12:30-4pm. Free.) The **National Arboretum** (245-2726), 24th and R St. NE (Metro: Stadium-Armory, then a B2 bus), is the U.S.'s living library of trees and flowers. Experts go berserk over the arboretum's world-class stock of *bonsai* (dwarf trees). Azaleas and azalea-watchers clog the place each spring. Be careful in the surrounding area; come in a car, if possible. (Open daily 8am-5pm; July-March Mon.-Fri. 8am-5pm, Sat.-Sun. 10am-5pm. Bonsai collection open daily 10am-3:30pm. Free.)

Bonsai!!

Love of the bonsai has engendered an international network of fanciers, cultivators, and weirdos: in July 1991, a mysterious thief nabbed a $1000 bonsai from the Arboretum and then returned it three days later in improved condition—it had been pruned rather expertly. Go figure.

Arlington, VA and Alexandria, VA

The silence of **Arlington National Cemetery** (Metro: Arlington Cemetery) honors those who sacrificed their lives in war. The 612 acres of hills and tree-lined avenues hold the bodies of U.S. military veterans from five-star generals to unknown soldiers. Before you enter the main gate, get a map from the visitors center. The Kennedy Gravesites hold both President John F. Kennedy and his brother, Robert F. Kennedy, newly joined by Jacqueline Kennedy Onassis. The Eternal Flame flickers above JFK's simple memorial stone. The Tomb of the Unknowns honors all servicemen who died fighting for the United States and is guarded by delegations from the Army's Third Infantry (changing of the guard every ½-hr., Oct.-March every hr. on the hr.). Robert E. Lee's home **Arlington House,** overlooks the cemetery. Enter the pastel-peach mansion at the front door; tours are self-guided. Head down Custis Walk in front of Arlington House and exit the cemetery through Weitzel Gate to get to the **Iwo Jima Memorial,** based on Joe Rosenthal's Pulitzer Prize-winning photo of six Marines straining to raise the U.S. flag on Mount Suribachi. (Cemetery open daily 8am-7pm, Oct.-March daily 8am-5pm.)

The **Pentagon,** the world's largest office building, shows just how huge a military bureaucracy can get (Metro: Pentagon). To take the guided tour, sign in, walk through a metal detector, get X-rayed, and show proper photo identification (passports for non-U.S. citizens). The guide keeps the pace of the tour so brisk that it's like a military music video. (Call 695-1776 for tour info. Tours every ½-hr. Mon.-Fri. 9:30am-3:30pm, Oct.-May no tours at 10:30am, 1:30, and 3pm. Free.)

Old Town Alexandria (Metro: King St.) has cobblestoned streets, bricked sidewalks, over 1000 restored old facades, tall ships and quaint shops. Come here to shop, stroll, and dine. A newly renovated info center, the **Lyceum,** 201 S. Washington St. (703-838-4994) shows exhibitions and audio-visual presentations on historic Alexandria. (Open Mon.-Sat. 10am-5pm, Sun. 1-5pm.) George Washington and Robert E. Lee prayed at **Christ Church,** 119 N. Washington St. (703-549-1450) at Cameron St., a red brick Colonial building with a domed steeple. Restored to its 18th-century good looks, **Gadsby's Tavern,** 134 N. Royal St. (838-4242), allows you to see how budget travelers did it 200 years ago (when as many as 4 people would be assigned to a bed). (Open Oct.-March Tues.-Sat. 10am-4pm, Sun. 1-4pm. Admission $3, children 11-17 $1.) See one of America's first indoor kitchens at **Robert E. Lee's Boyhood Home,** 607 Oronoco St. (548-8454), near Asaph St. (open Mon.-Sat. 10am-4pm, Sun. 1-4pm; $3, students 10-17 $1). The **George Washington Masonic National Memorial,** 101 Callahan Dr. (683-2007) has a museum and a lofty Greek-temple-style portico that supports a steep pyramid (Open daily 9am-5pm).

Mount Vernon (703-780-2000), in Fairfax County, VA was George Washington's final estate. (Metro: Huntington, then take the Fairfax Connector 101 bus at the north end of the station; call 703-339-7200 for info). To drive, take the Beltway (I-495) to the George Washington Parkway and follow it to Mount Vernon. A key to the Bastille, a gift from the Marquis de Lafayette, is on display in the main hall. Upstairs, see the bedroom of George and Martha Washington. A gravel path outside leads to their tomb. The graveless "slave burial ground" is nearby. The estate also has 18th-century gardens; its fields once grew corn, wheat, tobacco, and marijuana. (Open daily 8am-5pm, Sept.-Oct. and March 9am-5pm, Nov.-Feb. 9am-4pm. $7, over 61 $6, ages 6-11 $3.)

ENTERTAINMENT AND NIGHTLIFE

On the nation's birthday, the capital throws an all day bash. Morning activities include the reading of the Declaration of Independence from the steps of the National Archives. A Fourth of July parade (789-7000) crowds Constitution Ave. at noon (but arrive by 11:30am for a good view). The National Symphony plays on the Capitol's West Lawn from 8pm on, and at 9:20 fireworks begin exploding over the Mall. Arrive before 6:30pm and spread your blanket facing the Lincoln Memorial for the best view.

Theater and Movies

At 25th St. and New Hampshire Ave., the **Kennedy Center's** (416-8000) has zillions of performing-arts spaces. Tickets get expensive ($10-65), but most productions offer ½-price tickets the day of performance to students, seniors, military, and handicapped persons; call 467-4600 for details. Free events dot the Kennedy calendar. The **National Theatre,** 1321 Pennsylvania Ave. NW (628-6161; Metro: Metro Center or Federal Triangle) produces big-name, big-budget theater often with visitors from Broadway, and the ticket prices reflect it ($35-65). ½-priced tickets available for students, seniors (over 64), military, and the disabled Tuesday and Wednesday and for Sunday matinees. The prestigious **Shakespeare Theater,** 450 7th St. NW (box office 393-2700; Metro: Archives-Navy Memorial), at the Lansburgh on Pennsylvania Ave., puts on...Shakespeare. Call for ticket prices, show times, and discounts for students and seniors. Standing-room tickets ($10) are available two hours before curtain. Thespians thrive in Washington's **14th St. theater district,** where tiny repertory companies explore and experiment with truly enjoyable results. *City Paper* provides great coverage of this scene. **Woolly Mammoth,** 1401 Church St. NW (393-3939), **Studio Theater,** 1333 P St. NW (332-3300), and **The Source Theater,** 1835 14th St. NW (462-1073), all hang out in this borderline neighborhood near Dupont Circle (tickets $16-29; call for info on student discounts). Take a taxi home after the show.

Biograph, 2819 M St. NW (333-2696), in Georgetown, shows first-run independents, foreign films, and classics. Film festivals are frequent; the eclectic is the norm. ($6, seniors and children $3.) **Key Theatre,** 1222 Wisconsin Ave. NW (333-5100), near Prospect St. (1 block north of M St.) features first-run art films. Subtitled foreign films, too. ($6.50, over 65 $4, children $3, matinees $3.50.)

Classical Music

DC is home to the well-respected **National Symphony Orchestra,** which performs in the **Kennedy Center.** Tickets are normally expensive ($18-45), but ½-price tickets are available (see above). The NSO also gives concerts in celebration of Memorial Day, the Fourth of July, and Labor Day. The **Washington Opera** (416-7890) also calls the Kennedy Center home. For a schedule of free events, call 467-4600. Check the *Washington Post's* "Weekend" section for information.

Jazz Joints

A free lunchtime summer jazz series takes place downtown at the **Corcoran Gallery** (638-3211), 17th St. between E St. and New York Ave. NW, in the Hammer Auditorium every Wed. at 12:30pm. (Metro: Farragut West.)

Madame's Organ, 2003 18th St. NW (667-5370), near Florida Ave. in Adams-Morgan. The neon sign above the door shouts "Sorry, we're open" and in flows an eclectic clientele. Pink walls, dark red lighting, and wolf skin greet patrons. Live music nearly every night; Sat. reserved for "a DJ from outer space." Cover around $3. Drafts $2.50, drinks $3.50. Open Sun.-Thurs. 6pm-2am, Fri.-Sat. 6pm-3am.

Vegas Lounge, 1415 P St. NW (483-3971), 4 blocks east of Dupont Circle. Metro: Dupont Circle. Tiny tables, dim red lights, and a devoted crowd. Professional jam sessions Tues.-Wed. (otherwise known as "open mike nights," but these guys play like pros) and bands Thurs.-Sat. (cover $5-9) churn out an assortment of styles the manager, "Dr. Blues", enthusiastically describes as Chicago-meets-New Orleans. Happy hour Tues.-Sat. offers $1 off beers. Be careful in this area at night. Open Tues.-Thurs. 7pm-2am, Fri.-Sat. 7pm-3am.

Clubs and Bars

If you don't mind a young crowd, squeeze into a *local* rock-and-roll show; the DC punk scene is, or at least was, one of the nation's finest. To see what's up with local bands, check *City Paper.* The newest of DC's live music venues, colossal **Capitol Ballroom,** 1015 Half St. SE (703-549-7625; Metro: Navy Yard) boasts an impressive line-up of big-name alternative bands and small-name, big-draw local groups. Tickets $10-20, available from Ticketmaster (432-SEAT/7328). Doors open at 7pm. In summer on Saturday and Sunday, jazz and R&B shows occupy the outdoor **Carter-Barron Amphitheater** (426-6837), in Rock Creek Park up 16th St. and Colorado Ave. NW (tickets about $13.50). From late June to August, rock, punk, and metal preempt soccer-playing at **Fort Reno Park** (282-0018 or 619-7225), at Chesapeake and Belt St. NW above Wisconsin Ave. (Metro: Tenley Circle.)

9:30 club, 930 F St. NW (393-0930 or 638-2008). Metro: Metro Center. DC's most established local and alternative rock venue. Occasionally $3 to see 3 local bands; $5-20 for nationally known acts, which often sell out weeks in advance. Cash-only box office open Mon.-Thurs. 1-6pm, 11pm if there's a show, Fri. 1-11:30pm, Sat. 9-11:30pm, Sun. 7:30-11pm. Tickets also available from Ticketmaster (432-7328). Door time Sun.-Thurs. 7:30pm-midnight, Fri.-Sat. 9pm-2am. Under 21 admitted.

The Tombs, 1226 36th St. NW (337-6668), at Prospect St. Recognize the bar? Designers for the movie *St. Elmo's Fire* based a stage set on it. Georgetown students as well as some high profile clientele (Clinton, Chris O'Donnell) drop in for burgers and beer. $3 cover on Tues. nights (live music) and Sun. nights (DJ and dancing). Mixed drinks $3.25 and up. Open Mon.-Thurs. 11:30am-2am, Fri 11:30am-3am, Sat. 11am-3am, Sun. 9:30am-2am.

The Bayou, 3135 K St. NW (333-2897), in Georgetown; take any #30 Metrobus to M St. and walk 2 blocks down Wisconsin Ave. Bands on their way up and bands on their way down. Music varies from metal to jazz. Comedy at 6:30pm Sat. Most shows 18+; the rest all ages. Cover $3-20. Open Sun.-Thurs. 8pm-1:30am, Fri. 8pm-2:30am, Sat. 6:30pm-2:30am, but call ahead; no band means no Bayou.

15 Minutes, 1030 15th St. NW (408-1855), between K and L St. Metro: McPherson Square or Farragut North. Mostly bar on weekdays becomes mostly dance club on weekends. All nights officially 21+. Thurs.-Sat. live bands, DJ and dancing the rest of the time. $6 cover on weekends, varies on weekdays. Tickets for some popular bands can be purchased through Ticketmaster (432-7328). Open Mon.-Thurs. 4:30pm-2am, Fri. 4:30pm-3am, Sat. 8pm-3am.

Crow Bar, 1006 20th St. NW (223-2972). Metro: Farragut North or Farragut West. Everyone from bikers to business types. Stop by for the house brew, Crow Beer ($3.75), space-age dance room "Forbidden Planet" (open Thurs.-Sat. 9pm-close), or just for the off-beat decor. Two floors and a game room. Open Mon.-Thurs. 11:30am-1:45am, Fri. 11:30am-2:45am, Sat. noon-2:45am, Sun. noon-1:45am.

Brickskeller, 1523 22nd St. NW (293-1885), between P and Q St. Metro: Dupont Circle. *THE* place for beer. 600 brews—the world's largest beer selection. Go down under with a Van Diemens lager from Australia ($4.50), mate, or try the saloon's original "beer-tails": mixed drinks made with beer. Must be 21. Open Mon.-Thurs. 11:30am-2am, Fri. 11:30am-3am, Sat. 6pm-3am, Sun. 6pm-2am.

Planet Fred, 1221 Connecticut Ave. NW (331-3733 or 466-2336). Between the craters, neon spacescape, and lava lamps decking the walls, a trip to Planet Fred may feel like an alien experience. Occasional live bands pack in wall-to-wall punks; "Female Trouble" every other Sun. is an ever-popular lesbian dance party. Thurs. is DJ dancing and $10 all-you-can-drink; Fri-Sat. $5 cover for dancing. Daily happy hour (5-8pm). Open Sun.-Thurs. 11:30am-2am, Fri. 11:30am-3am, Sat. 8pm-3am.

Asylum in Exile, 1210 U St. NW (319-9353; 232-9354 for info.). Metro: U St.-Cardozo. An alternative to DC's bigger and badder band clubs. Asylum tends to book lesser known live musicians. Bands Wed.-Fri. with acoustic music on Wed. and no cover. $3 cover on Thurs., $5 on Fri. Nightly happy hour 8-11pm, with varying $2 pints. 18+. Open Sun.-Thurs. 8pm-2am, Fri.-Sat. 8pm-3am.

Oxford Tavern "Zoo Bar," 3000 Connecticut Ave. NW (232-4225), across the street from the zoo. Metro: Woodley Park-Zoo. Washington's oldest saloon with a cheery wildlife mural and a bright neon subtitle. They say the first time you come in here is the last time you'll be a stranger. Happy hour Mon.-Fri. 3-7pm with $1.50 drafts. A DJ plays on Fri. nights, and live jazz, rock, and blues bands hold forth Tues.-Thurs. and Sat. Open Sun.-Thurs. 10:30am-2am, Fri.-Sat. 10:30am-3am.

Bardo, 2000 Wilson Blvd. (527-9399). Metro: Court House. 1 block east (downhill) from the Metro. Twentysomething haunt is the self-proclaimed "largest microbrewery on the continent." Happy hour weekdays before 8pm and all day Sun. with $1.50 mugs of Bardo beer. Billiard room with 24 tables opens daily at 5pm. Free brewery tours, Thurs. 7pm. Open Mon.-Fri. 11:30am-2am, Sat. 1pm-2am, Sun. 4:30pm-2am. Free parking.

Dance Clubs

Tracks, 1111 1st St. SE (448-3320). Metro: Navy Yard. The hottest dance club in DC. Two dance floors, three bars, a patio, an outdoor volleyball court, and a set of bleachers overlooking the main dance floor (all packed into an old warehouse) ensure that there's something for every club goer to do. Thurs. is college night: $5 cover and open bar 9-10:30pm. Fri.'s music is deep house with no cover 8-9pm, $5-7 9-11pm, $8-10 after 11pm. Sat. is gay. Secured parking nearby. Open Thurs. 9pm, Fri.-Sat. 8pm, Sun. 4pm. No set closing time. Always 18Ğ.

Fifth Colvmn, 915 F St. NW (393-3632), near 9th St. Metro: Gallery Place-Chinatown. Euro-crowd brings serious soul into the trendy 90s. The artist-formerly-called-Prince has been spotted here. Bright lights and bold colors make this bank-turned-nightclub a museum of cool culture. The basement offers an alternative scene with a music selection to match.Cover $5-10. Open Mon. 9pm-2am, Tues. and Thurs. 10pm-2am, Wed. 10pm-2:30am, Fri.-Sat. 10pm-3am.

The Insect Club, 625 E St. NW (347-8884). Metro: Gallery Place-Chinatown. The Insect Club crawls with plastic, painted, and paper maché bugs and swarms with barflies. Happy hour (Mon.-Fri. 5-8pm) draws interns for $1.50 domestic drafts; on Fri. these specials last until 10pm. Thurs. has a $10 cover for all-you-can-drink 9pm-1am with DJ dancing; Fri.-Sat. bring a $5 cover for DJ hip hop, reggae, rock, and retro. Open Mon.-Thurs. 5pm-2am, Fri.-Sat. 5pm-3am.

Winston's, 3295 M St. NW (333-3150), near 33rd St. So many men, so little hair. Marines and Navy soldiers come for R&R. Georgetown, American, and George Washington University guys crowd in too. A happenin' dance scene every night of the week. No sleeveless shirts. 18Ğ. $2 cover weeknights, $5 weekends. Beer $1.50-3. Mixed drinks $3-4. Open Sun.-Thurs. 8pm-2am, Fri.-Sat. 8pm-3am.

Bent, upstairs at 1344 U St. NW (986-6364), near 13th St. Metro: U St.-Cardozo. Look for the big Dalí clocks melting off the roof. Silver walls sweat with disco dancing in riotus retro fashion. Happy hour Thurs.-Fri. 6-9pm with free fondue and salsa and $1.50 Rolling Rocks. Cover $2-7 Open Wed. 9pm-2am, Thurs. 6pm-2am, Fri. 6pm-3am, Sat. 9pm-3am, Sun. 9pm-2am.

Club Heaven and **Club Hell,** 2327 18th St. NW (667-4355), near Columbia Rd. Hell is every high schooler's dream of a New York café and bar. Heaven sports a scuffed wood floor, comfy couches, a small bar, and 3 TVs, but the dance floor throbs to pounding beats. 80s dance party in Heaven on Thurs. with $4 cover. No cover other nights. Domestic beer $3; $1 off during happy hour (daily 6-8:30pm in Hell). Dancing starts about 10pm. Heaven open Sun.-Thurs. 10pm-2am, Fri.-Sat. 10pm-3am. Hell open Tues.-Thurs. 9pm-2am, Fri.-Sat. 6pm-3am

Gay Bars and Clubs

The *Washington Blade* is the best source of gay news, reviews, and club listings; published every Friday, it's available in virtually every storefront in Dupont Circle. **Tracks,** 111 First St. SE (488-3320; Metro: Navy Yard) becomes *the* hottest gay dance club in DC on Sat. nights. See Dance Clubs above for more info.

The Circle Bar, 1629 Connecticut Ave. NW (462-5575). A 3-in-1 social emporium with a ground-floor restaurant, a top-floor bar, and an underground dance club. All three draw a young, professional, racially mixed crowd. Happy hour Mon.-Fri. 5-9pm, Sat.-Sun. happy hour 11am-10pm. Wednesday is ladies' night. Open Sun.-Thurs. 11am-2am, Fri.-Sat. 11am-3am.

Fraternity House, at 2122 P St. rear NW (223-4917), in the alley between 21st and 22nd St. Strobe lights, disco balls, videos, and hard-core house beats pump and flicker as the guys dance the night away. Happy hour (Mon.-Fri. 4-9pm) features $1.50 domestic beer. Downstairs cover Mon., Wed., Thurs. $3; cover Fri.-Sat. $4. Open Mon. 4pm-3am, Tues.-Wed. 4pm-2am, Thurs. 4pm-4am, Fri. 4pm-5am, Sat. 8pm-5am, Sun. 8pm-2am.

Badlands, 1415 22nd St. NW (296-0505), near P St. Enter the peach-colored monolith of a building where a young crowd serious about dancing moves to the beat of Top 40, dance, and house music. Tues. is ½-price night; a $2 cover goes to charity. Thurs. is college night; cover is $3. Cover Fri.-Sat. $5. Expect to wait in line Fri.-Sat. Open Sun.-Thurs. 9pm-2am, Fri.-Sat. 9pm-2:45am.

J.R.'s, 1519 17th St. NW (328-0090). Upscale brick and varnished-wood bar with a DJ in a choir stall overlooking the tank of "guppies" (gay urban professionals). Happy hour Mon.-Fri. 2-8pm: $2 domestic bottled beer, Sat. noon-8pm and Sun. all day: 75¢ vodka. A relaxed neighborhood bar by day, at night it becomes *the* place for S&M (stand and model). Mon.-Thurs. 2pm-2am, Fri. 2pm-3am, Sat. noon-3am, Sun. noon-2am.

Hung Jury, 1819 H St. NW (279-3212). Metro: Farragut West. Lesbians from all over DC from thirtysomething couples to singles scoping the scene spend their weekend nights bopping to Top 40. $5 cover. Men must be accompanied by a woman to enter; gay men are admitted but occasionally must "prove" they're gay. Open Fri.-Sat. 9pm-3:30am.

Sports

Opportunities for sports addicts abound in the DC area. The **Georgetown Hoyas** (basketball) pack the **USAir Arena** (formerly the Capital Centre). The Hoyas won it all in 1987. Their professional counterparts, the **Bullets,** also fire away here, as do the **Capitals** (hockey). (Call USAir Arena at 301-350-3400, located between Landover Rd. and Central Ave. in Landover, MD. Take the Beltway (I-95) to exits 15A or 17A and follow signs.) The **Redskins** won the Super Bowl in 1982, 1987, and 1992, and fans flock religiously to **RFK Stadium** to see them. Purchase preseason tickets through the Redskins' ticket office (546-2222). Just dream about regular season tix. Call the **Department of Recreation** (673-7660 or 673-7671) for info on public pools, biking and hiking trails, jogging, and ice skating.

What's a Hoya?

Georgetown teams are called Hoyas, which supposedly derives from the old, half-Greek, half-Latin cheer *hoya saxta,* "what rocks," developed back when students were forced to study both languages. Tour leaders on campus further test the gullibility of prospective students by explaining that the correct answer to the question: "What's a *Hoya*?" is "Yes." Famous Hoyas have included pro basketball player Patrick Ewing, New York prelate John Cardinal O'Connor, Supreme Court Justice Antonin Scalia, and Senate Majority Leader George Mitchell (D-Maine). The basketball team, perennial contender for the national college title (they won in 1984), plays at the USAir Arena in Landover, MD, since crowds are far too large for a college gym. (Call 301-350-3400 for information.) Purchase tickets through Ticketmaster (432-7328) or through the campus Ticket Office (687-4692) or Athletic Department (687-2449).

Virginia

If Virginia seems obsessed with its past, it has good reason: the white settlement of North America, the shameful legacy of the slave trade, American independence, the aristocratic farsightedness of the early United States, and even the Civil War might all be said to have their roots in Virginia. English colonists founded Jamestown in 1607; the New World's first black slaves joined them unwillingly 12 years later. While George Washington was still battling Native Americans in the French and Indian War, Thomas Jefferson wrote about religious and political freedom in the colonial capital, lavish Williamsburg. Virginian James Madison traveled to Philadelphia in 1787 with drafts of the *Constitution,* and Virginian George Mason led the campaign for a Bill of Rights. Meanwhile, eastern Virginia's Tidewater aristocracy dominated the state for a century with its rigid, refined culture of slave-dependent plantations—a culture that exploded during the Civil War, when Union and Confederate armies pushed one another around the state on the way to Appomattox.

Virginia has mostly left the Old South it once led, but a host of Confederate street names, Robert E. Lee parks, fixed-up plantations, and battlefields exhibit to excess its antebellum days. In Richmond, where Patrick Henry boomed, "Give me liberty or give me death," nostalgia and horror compete in the Confederate Museum. Nostalgia climaxes in Colonial Williamsburg, where guides in 18th-century dress show sweating tourists around the restored capital.

PRACTICAL INFORMATION

Capital: Richmond.

Virginia Division of Tourism: 901 E. Byrd St., 19th Floor, Richmond 23219 (804-786-4484 or 800-VISIT-VA/847-4882). **Division of State Parks,** 203 Governor St., Richmond 23219 (804-786-1712).

Time Zone: Eastern. **Postal Abbreviation:** VA

Sales Tax: 4.5%.

■■■ RICHMOND

Once the capital of the rebel Confederacy, Richmond is by no means reluctant to display its history. Civil War leaders Robert E. Lee and Stonewall Jackson are worshipped through Richmond's numerous museums and restored homes, which showcase anything and everything Confederate. But Richmond is not mired in its own history; with districts like the sprawling, beautiful Fan and formerly industrial Shockoe Bottom, this state capital shows its kinder 20th-century face.

PRACTICAL INFORMATION

Tourist Office: Richmond Visitors Center, 1710 Robin Hood Rd. (358-5511), exit 78 off I-95/64, in a converted train depot. Helpful 6-min. video introduces the city's attractions. Walking tours and maps of downtown and the metro region. Can also arrange for same-day discounted accommodations. Open Memorial Day-Labor Day daily 9am-7pm; off season 9am-5pm.

Trains: Amtrak, far away at 7519 Staple Mills Rd. (264-9194, 800-872-7245). To: Washington, DC (4 per day, 2hr., $18-23); Williamsburg (8 per day, 1¼hr., $9-10); Virginia Beach (2 per day, 3hr., $16-19); New York City (8 per day, 7hr., $81); Baltimore (5 per day, 3hr., $26-31); Philadelphia (5 per day, 4¾hr., $38-48). Taxi fare to downtown $12. Open 24 hrs.

Buses: Greyhound, 2910 N. Boulevard (254-5910 or 800-231-2222). 2 blocks from downtown; take GRTC bus #24 north. To: Washington, DC (16 per day, 2½hr., $10); Charlottesville (2 per day, 1½hr., $18); Williamsburg (8 per day, 1hr., $9); Baltimore (8 per day, 3½hr., $22); Philadelphia (9 per day, 7hr., $40).

Public Transportation: Greater Richmond Transit Co., 101 S. Davis Ave. (358-4782). Buses serve most of Richmond infrequently, downtown frequently; most leave from Broad St. downtown. Bus #24 goes south to Broad St. and downtown. Fare $1.15, transfers 15¢. Seniors 50¢ during off-peak hours. Free trolleys provide dependable, if limited, service to downtown and Shockoe Slip daily 10am-4pm, with an extended Shockoe Slip schedule 5pm-midnight.

Taxis: Colonial Cab (264-7960); Town and Country Taxi (271-2211).

Crisis Lines: Traveler's Aid, 643-0279 or 648-1767. **Rape Crisis Hotline,** 643-0888. **Psychiatric Crisis Intervention,** 648-9224. **Gay Information,** 353-3626. **AIDS/HIV Info.,** 359-4783. Mon.-Fri. 8am-6pm, Sat. noon-5pm, Sun. noon-8pm.

Emergency: 911.

Post Office: 1801 Brook Rd. (775-6133). Open Mon.-Fri. 7am-6pm, Sat. 10am-1pm. **ZIP code:** 23219. **Area code:** 804.

Richmond is divided into several regions with interesting names. **Carytown** is an upscale district in the northwest between Thompson St. and the Boulevard. The **Fan** neighborhood, bounded by the Boulevard, I-95, Monument Ave., and Virginia Commonwealth University, holds many of Richmond's oldest homes and is named after its dubious resemblance to a lady's fan. **Jackson Ward,** in the heart of downtown, and **Shockoe Slip** and **Shockoe Bottom** farther to the east, are more urban sections of town. **Broad St.,** not Main St., is the city's central artery, and the numbered streets that cross it increase from west to east.

ACCOMMODATIONS AND CAMPING

Budget motels in Richmond cluster on **Williamsburg Rd.,** on the edge of town, and along **Midlothian Turnpike,** south of the James River; public transport to these areas is infrequent at best. As usual, the farther away from downtown you stay, the less you pay. The visitors center can reserve accommodations at a discount.

Massad House Hotel, 11 N. 4th St. (648-2893), 4 blocks from the capitol, near town. Shuttles guests via a 1940s elevator to clean, spacious rooms with shower, A/C, and TV. The only inexpensive rooms downtown. Singles $38, doubles $40.

Cadillac Motel, 11418 Washington Hwy. (798-4049), 10mi. from the city. Take I-95 to exit 89. Offers sparse but economical rooms. Singles $38, doubles $45.

Red Carpet Inn, 5215 W. Broad St. (288-4011), 3mi. from the center of town; take Bus #6. Offers grand (by motel standards) but slightly faded rooms and a pool/health club. Singles $42, doubles $46.

Pocahontas State Park, 10301 Beach Rd. (796-4255), 10mi. south on Rte. 10 and Rte. 655 in Chesterfield. Offers showers, biking, boating, lakes, and a huge pool. Sites $10.50. No hookups. Pool admission $2.25, ages 3-12 $1.75. Open year-round. Free reservations at 225-3867 or 800-933-7275.

MID-ATLANTIC

FOOD

As both a college town and an old Southern capital, Richmond offers cheap student eateries and affordable down-home fare. At the **farmers market,** outdoors at N. 17th and E. Main St., pick up fresh fruit, vegetables, meat, and maybe even a pot swine. For the student haunts, head for the area around **Virginia Commonwealth University (VCU),** just west of downtown. For fried apples, grits, and cornbread, make your way downtown.

Coppola's, 2900 W. Cary St. (359-6969). A popular deli and food mart crowded with happy people and Italian food. Dinners ($5-7) and fantastic sandwiches ($3-6). Outdoor seating available. Open Mon.-Wed. 10am-8pm, Thurs.-Sat. 10am-9pm.

3rd St. Diner (788-4750), at the corner of 3rd and Main, is a taste of Richmond day or night. Enjoy the $2.25 breakfast special (2 eggs, biscuit or toast, and homefries, grits, or Virginia fried apples) on the mint-green balcony. Old-time locals served by tattooed waitresses in combat boots. Open 24 hrs.

Texas-Wisconsin Border Café, 1501 W. Main St. (355-2907). Stetson-sporting stuffed steer survey a selection of specialties ranging from salsa to *sauerkraut.* At night the café becomes a popular bar. Lunches and dinners $4-8. Open daily 11am-2am.

The Ocean Restaurant, 414 E. Main St. (643-9485), serves excellent, filling breakfasts and lunches. All items under $5. Open Mon.-Fri. 6:30am-3pm, Sat. 9am-3pm.

Bottom's Up, 1700 Dock St., at the corner of 17th and Cary. Popular hangout serves the best pizza in Richmond ($8 will feed two) and will ply you with drinks. Open Sun.-Wed. 11am-11pm, Thurs. 11am-midnight, Fri.-Sat. 11am-2am.

SIGHTS

Ever since Patrick Henry declared "Give me liberty or give me death" in Richmond's **St. John's Church,** 2401 E. Broad St. (648-5015), this river city has been quoting, remembering, and bronzing its heroes. Sundays in summer at 2pm, actors re-create the famous 1775 speech. You must take a tour to see the church. (Tours Mon.-Sat.

10am-3:30pm, Sun. 1-3:30pm; $3, seniors $2, students under 18 $1.) The Thomas Jefferson-designed **State Capitol,** at 9th and Grace St. (786-4344), is a Neoclassical masterpiece that served as the home of the Confederate government during the Civil War and today houses the only statue for which George Washington posed (open daily 9am-5pm; Dec.-March Mon.-Sat. 9am-5pm, Sun. 1-5pm). For a trip down Richmond's memory lane, follow Franklin Ave. from the capitol until it becomes **Monument Ave.,** a boulevard lined with trees, gracious old houses, and towering statues of Confederate heroes. Robert E. Lee faces his beloved South; Stonewall Jackson scowls at the Yankees.

The **Court End** district stretches north and east of the capitol to Clay and College St. and guards Richmond's most distinctive historical sights. The **Museum of the Confederacy,** 1201 E. Clay St. (649-1861), possesses the world's largest collection of Confederate artifacts. The main floor leads visitors through the military history of the Great War of Northern Aggression; the basement displays guns and flags of the Confederacy; the top floor houses temporary exhibits on such topics as slave life in the antebellum South. The museum also runs one-hour tours through the **White House of the Confederacy** next door (ask at the museum desk). Statues of Tragedy, Comedy, and Irony grace the White House's front door. (Museum open Mon.-Sat. 10am-5pm, Sun. 1-5pm; tours of the White House Mon., Wed., and Fri.-Sat. 10:30am-4:30pm, Tues. and Thurs. 11:30am-4:30pm, Sun. 1:15-4:30pm. Admission to museum $5, students $3, seniors $4, under 6 free; for the White House $5.50/ $3.50/$4.50; for both: $8/$3.50/$5.)

The **Valentine Museum,** 1015 E. Clay St. (649-0711), enamors visitors with exhibits on local and Southern social and cultural history. Admission price includes a tour of the recently renovated **Wickham-Valentine House** next door. (Museum open Mon.-Sat. 10am-5pm, Sun. noon-5pm; house tours on the hr., 10am-4pm. $5, students and seniors $4, ages 7-12 $3.) Combination tickets to the Museum of the Confederacy, White House of the Confederacy, Valentine Museum, and **John Marshall House**—all within easy walking distance of each other—are $11, students and seniors $10, ages 7-12 $5 (tickets available at any of the sights). John Marshall House, at 818 E. Marshall St. (648-7998), is open Tues.-Sat. 10am-5pm, Sun. 1-5pm.

East of the Capitol, follow your tell-tale heart to the **Edgar Allan Poe Museum,** 1914 E. Main St. (648-5523). Poe memorabilia stuffs five buildings, including the **Stone House,** the oldest extant structure within the original city boundaries. (Open Tues.-Sat. 10am-4pm, Sun.-Mon. 1-4pm. $5, students $3, seniors $4.)

Four blocks from the intersection of Monument Ave. and North Blvd. reposes the Southeast's largest art museum, the **Virginia Museum of Fine Arts,** 2800 Grove Ave. (367-0844). An exhibit of Fabergé eggs made for the Russian czars stands out among the museum's collections. (Open Tues.-Sat. 11am-5pm, Thurs. 11am-8pm in the North Wing Galleries, Sun. 1-5pm; $4 donation requested).

The **Maggie L. Walker National Historic Site,** 110½ E. Leigh St. (780-1380), commemorates the life of an ex-slave's gifted daughter. Physically disabled, Walker fought for black women's rights and succeeded as founder and president of a bank. (Tours Wed.-Sun. 9am-5pm. Free.) The **Black History Museum and Cultural Center of Virginia,** 00 (yes, 00) Clay St. (780-9093), showcases rotating exhibits. (Open Tues. and Thurs.-Sat. 11am-4pm. $2, children $1.)

To the west lies the hands-on **Science Museum of Virginia,** 2500 W. Broad St. (367-1080). The museum houses the **Universe Theater,** which doubles as a planetarium and an Omni theater. (Museum open Mon.-Fri. 9:30am-5pm, Sat. 9:30am-9pm, Sun. noon-5pm. Planetarium and Omni shows daily; call for times. $4.50, seniors and ages 4-17 $4. $2-3 extra for shows.)

The **Shockoe Slip** district from Main, Canal, and Cary St. between 10th and 14th St. features fancy shops in restored and newly painted warehouses, but few bargains. **Cary St.,** from the Boulevard to Thompson St., is crowded with vintage clothing stores, antique boutiques, and entertaining crowds.

ENTERTAINMENT AND NIGHTLIFE

One of Richmond's most entertaining and delightful diversions is the marvelous old **Byrd Theater,** 2908 W. Cary St. (353-9911). Buy your ticket from a tuxedoed agent, then get ushered into an opulent, chandeliered theater and treated to a pre-movie concert, played on an ornate and cavernous Wurlitzer organ that rises out of the floor. All shows 99¢; on Saturdays the balcony opens for $1 extra. **Free concerts** abound near the farmers market at N. 17th and E. Main St. in the summer; check *Style Weekly,* a free magazine available at the visitors center. Nightlife enlivens Shockoe Slip and sprinkles itself in a less hectic manner throughout the Fan.

The **Tobacco Company Club,** 1201 E. Cary St. (782-9555), smokes with top 40 music (open Tues.-Sat. 8pm-2am). **Matt's British Pub and Comedy Club,** at 1045 12th St. (643-5653), pours out a bit of Brit wit Friday at 8 and 10:30pm and Saturday at 8 and 11pm. Microbrews and drafts from $3, rails $3.40. (Open Mon.-Sat. 1:30pm-2am, Sun. 4pm-2am.) The **Penny Lane Pub,** 207 N. 7th St. (780-1682) plays to the Irish crowd; an authentic Irish tavern with traditional live Irish music on Friday and local bands other nights (open Mon.-Sat. 11am-2am, Sun. 4pm-2am). **Flood Zone,** 11 S. 18th St. (643-6006), south of Shockoe Slip, hosts both big-name and off-beat rock bands (ticket office open Tues.-Fri. 10am-6pm; $6-20). **Paramyd,** 1008 North Blvd. (358-3838), one of Richmond's few gay bars, turns into a dance club on weekends (happy hour Mon.-Fri. 6-9pm, drafts $2; Fri.-Sat. cover varies, Sun. $4).

■■■ WILLIAMSBURG

At the end of the 17th century, when women were women and men wore wigs, Williamsburg was the capital of Virginia. During the Revolutionary War, the capital moved to Richmond, along with much of Williamsburg's grandeur. The depressed city was rescued in 1926 by John D. Rockefeller, Jr. who showered the troubled spots with money and restored a large chunk of the historical district. Today, street-side performers, evenings of 18th-century theater, and militia reviews are part of everyday business in Williamsburg. However, though the ex-capital claims to be a faithfully restored version of its 18th-century self, visitors will never see dirt roads, open sewers, or African slaves.

Williamsburg also prides itself on **William and Mary,** the second-oldest college in the United States. Outside Williamsburg, Virginia's other big tourist sights (**Jamestown, Yorktown,** and **Busch Gardens**) lie in wait.

PRACTICAL INFORMATION

Tourist Office: Williamsburg Area Convention & Visitors Bureau, 201 Penniman Rd. (253-0192), ½mi. northwest of the transportation center. Open Mon.-Fri. 8:30am-5pm. **Tourist Visitors Center,** 102 Information Dr. (800-447-8679), 1 mi. northeast of the train station. Tickets and transportation to Colonial Williamsburg. Maps and guides to historic district, including a guide for the disabled, upstairs. Information on prices and discounts on Virginia sights available downstairs. Open daily 8:30am-8pm.

Trains: Amtrak, 408 N. Boundary St. across from the fire station at the end of the road (229-8750 or 800-872-7245). To: New York (1 per day, 7½hr., $56); Washington, DC (1 per day, 3½hr., $26); Philadelphia (1 per day, 6hr., $40); Baltimore (1 per day, 6hr., $30); Richmond (3 per day, 1½hr, $9); and Virginia Beach (2 per day, 2hr., $12). Open Fri.-Mon. 7:15am-9:30pm, Tues.-Thurs. 7:15am-2:45pm.

Buses: Greyhound/Trailways, 408 N. Boundary St. (229-1460). To: Richmond (7 per day, 1hr., $9); Norfolk (8 per day, 2hr., $13); Washington, DC (7 per day, 4hr., $35). Ticket office open Mon.-Fri. 8:30am-6pm, Sat.-Sun. 8:30am-2pm.

Public Transportation: James City County Transit (JCCT), (220-1621). Service along Rte. 60, from Merchants Sq. in the Historic District west to Williamsburg Pottery or east past Busch Gardens. Operates Mon.-Sat. 6:15am-6:20pm. Fare $1 plus 25¢ per zone-change; exact change required.

Bike Rentals: Bikes Unlimited, 759 Scotland St. (229-4620), rents for $10 per day, with $5 deposit (includes lock). Open Mon.-Fri. 9am-7pm, Sat. 9am-5pm, Sun. noon-4pm.
Taxis: Williamsburg Limousine Service (877-0279). To Busch Gardens or Carter's Grove $8 round-trip. To Jamestown and Yorktown $15 round-trip.
Emergency: 911.
Post Office: 425 N. Boundary St. (229-4668). Open Mon.-Fri. 8am-5pm, Sat. 10am-2pm. **ZIP code:** 23185. **Area code:** 804.

Williamsburg lies some 50 mi. southeast of Richmond between **Jamestown** (10mi. away) and **Yorktown** (14mi. away). The Colonial Parkway, which connects the three towns, has no commercial buildings along its route, helping to preserve an unspoiled atmosphere.

ACCOMMODATIONS AND CAMPING

Budget motels line Rte. 60W and Rte. 31S. Avoid the hotels operated by the Colonial Williamsburg Foundation; they're expensive. A cheaper, friendlier, and more comfortable alternative is guest house. Some don't require reservations, but all expect you to call ahead and most expect customers to behave like houseguests.

Only five minutes from the historic district, **Lewis Guest House,** 809 Lafayette St. (229-6116), rents several comfortable rooms, including the upstairs unit with private entrance, kitchen, and bath as a single (for $25) or double (for $30). A few doors down is the **Carter Guest House,** 903 Lafayette St. (229-1117). Two spacious rooms, each with two beds and a shared bath. (Singles $25, doubles $26-30.) Be forewarned: Mrs. Carter will not let unmarried men and women sleep in the same bed. Hotels close to the historic district, especially chain- or foundation-owned hotels, do not come cheap. The **Southern Inn,** 1220 Richmond Rd. (229-8913), a 10-minute walk from William & Mary, has clean, ordinary rooms with colonial-looking façades and a pool. (Singles $30-35, doubles $35-40.) **Anvil Campgrounds,** 5243 Moretown Rd. (565-2300), 3 mi. north of the Colonial Williamsburg Information Center on Rte. 60, boasts 73 shaded sites, a swimming pool, bathhouse, recreational hall, and store. (Sites $17.50, with hookup $24.50.)

The closest hostel, **Sangraal-by-the-Sea Youth Hostel (HI-AYH),** Rte. 626 (776-6500), near Urbanna, is 30 mi. away. It does provide rides to bus or train stations during business hours, but don't expect a daily ride to Williamsburg. ($15, nonmembers $18.)

EATING AND DRINKING

Avoid the authentic-looking "taverns"—most are packed with sweaty tourists and priced accordingly. For a fraction of the price, you can still enjoy a colonial culinary experience by fixing a picnic with food from the **Williamsburg Shopping Center,** at the intersection of Richmond Rd. and Lafayette St. Rte. 60. The center also contains a bevy of fast-food places and far more pancake houses than any sane person might expect.

Greenleafe Café, 465 Scotland St. (220-3405), next door to Paul's Deli. Always mellow, Greenleafe cultivates a subdued atmosphere while serving sandwiches and salads ($3.50-5.50) and swaying on Tues. (after 9pm; cover $2) to the quiet sounds of live folk music. The café's slogan is "Life's too short to drink bad beer." You won't get any here: 15 yummy brews on tap ($3 per pint, $3.25 for bottles). Locals and students eat at a 20% discount. Open daily 9am-2am.
Beethoven's Inn, 467 Merrimac Trail (229-7069). Great sandwiches, subs, and other light fare with music-related names. Try the Titanic Sub, a combination of turkey, roast beef, grilled veggies, and feta cheese ($5.50). Play a variety of board games while you wait for your food. Open Mon.-Sat. 11am-9pm, Sun. noon-8pm.
Paul's Deli Restaurant and Pizza, 761 Scotland St. (229-8976), a lively summer hangout for errant, leftover William and Mary students, sells crisp stromboli for 2 ($6.15-9) and filling subs ($4-5). Great jukebox. Open daily 11am-2am.

The Old Chickahominy House, 1211 Jamestown Rd. (229-4689), rests over a mile from the historic district. Share the antiques and dried-flower decor with pewter-haired locals whose ancestors survived "Starvation Winter" in Jamestown. Miss Melinda's "complete luncheon" of Virginia ham served on hot biscuits, fruit salad, a slice of delectable homemade pie, and iced tea or coffee will fill you up for hours ($5). Expect a 20- to 30-min. wait for lunch. Open daily 8:30-10:15am and 11:30am-2:15pm.

SIGHTS

Unless you plan to apply to W&M, you've probably come to see the restored gardens and buildings, crafts, tours, and costumed actors in the historic district also known as **Colonial Williamsburg.** The Colonial Williamsburg Foundation (CWF) owns nearly everything in the historic district, from the **Governor's Palace** to the lemonade stands and even most of the houses marked "private home." A **Patriot's Pass** allows two days of unlimited admission to sights (good for 1 year; $30, ages 6-12 $18). A one-day **Basic Admission Ticket** allows unlimited admission for one day ($25, kids 6-12 $15). Buy them at the **CWF Visitors Center** (220-7645). Open daily 8:30am-8pm.

"Doing" the historic district without a ticket definitely saves money; for no charge you can walk the streets, ogle the buildings, march behind the fife-and-drum corps, lock yourself in the stocks, and even use the restrooms. Some old-time shops that actually sell goods—notably **McKenzie Apothecary,** by the Palace Green—are open to the public. Two of the buildings on the CWF map, the **Wren Building** and the **Bruton Parish Church**—are made to look like regular exhibits but in fact are free. Outdoor events, including a mid-day cannon-firing, are listed in the weekly *Visitor's Companion,* given away to ticket-holders—many of whom conveniently leave it where non-ticket-holders can pick it up.

Take one of the **guided walking tours** trampling Colonial Williamsburg night and day. The fascinating "Other Half" tour relates the experience of Africans and African-Americans (tours March-Sept.; separate ticket ostensibly required).

Those willing to pay shouldn't miss the **Governor's Palace,** on the Palace Green. This mansion housed the appointed governors of the Virginia colony until the last one fled in 1775. Reconstructed Colonial sidearms and ceremonial sabers line the reconstructed walls, and the extensive gardens include a hedge maze. (Open daily 9am-5pm. Separate admission $17.) Most sights in town are open 9:30am-5:30pm; a complete list of hours is provided in the *Visitor's Companion.*

Spreading west from the corner of Richmond and Jamestown Rd., the other focal point of Williamsburg, **The College of William & Mary,** is the second-oldest college in the U.S. Chartered in 1693, the college educated Presidents Jefferson, Monroe, and Tyler. The **Sir Christopher Wren Building,** also restored with Rockefeller money, is the oldest classroom building in the country. Nearby, the shops at **Merchant Square** sprawl a hair's breadth from the historic district. Park here and walk straight into the restored town proper.

■ NEAR WILLIAMSBURG

Jamestown and Yorktown At the **Jamestown National Historic Site** you'll see the remains of the first permanent English settlement (1607) as well as exhibits explaining colonial life. At the **visitors center** (229-1733), skip the hokey film and catch a 30-minute "living history" walking tour (free with admission to the site), on which a guide portraying one of the colonists describes the Jamestown way of life. Among other sights, you'll visit the **Old Church Tower,** built in 1639 and the only 17th-century structure still standing. Also featured is a statue of **Pocahontas.** Call ahead for tour info. since "living history" guides get occasional off-days. After the tour, you may want to explore on your own. You can rent a 45-minute **audio tape** ($2) and drive or hike the 5-mi. **Island Loop Route** through woodlands and marsh. In the remains of the settlement itself, archeologists work to uncover the original site of the triangular **Jamestown fort.** The National Historic Site is open daily 9am-

6pm; off season 8am-5:30pm. The park opens and closes a half hour before the visitors center. (Entrance fee $8 per car, $3 per hiker or bicyclist.)

Sniff around at the nearby **Jamestown Settlement** (229-1607), a museum commemorating the settlement with changing exhibits, a reconstruction of James Fort, a Native American village, and full-scale replicas of the three ships that brought the original settlers to Jamestown in 1607. The 20-minute "dramatic film" lives up to its name and fills tourists in on the settlement's history, including an embarrassed treatment of settler relations with the indigenous Powhatan tribe. (Open daily 9am-5pm. $9, ages 6-12 $4.25.)

The British defeat at **Yorktown** signaled the end of the Revolutionary War. British General Charles Lord Cornwallis and his men seized the town for use as a port in 1781, but were stranded when the French fleet blocked the sea approaches. Colonists and French troops attacked and the British soldiers surrendered, dealing a devastating blow to the British cause. The Yorktown branch of **Colonial National Park** (898-3400) vividly recreates this last significant battle of the war with an engaging film, dioramas, and a smart-looking electric map (behind the information center). Take a 7-mi. automobile journey around the battlefield; you can rent a tape and recorder for $2 at the visitors center to listen to while you drive (**visitors center** open daily 8:30am-6pm; last tape rented at 5pm). The **Yorktown Victory Center** (887-1776), one block from Rte. 17 on Rte. 238, offers a museum brimming with Revolutionary War items and an intriguing "living history" exhibit: in an encampment in front of the center, a troop of soldiers from the Continental Army of 1781 takes a well-deserved break from active combat. (Open daily 9am-5pm. $6.75, ages 6-12 $3.25.)

Williamsburg Limousine (877-0279) will shuttle a group of at least four people (at $19.50 per person) to both Jamestown and Yorktown. The unlined **Colonial Parkway** to both Jamestown and Yorktown also makes a beautiful biking route.

James River Plantations Built near the water to facilitate the planters' commercial and social lives, these country houses buttressed the slave-holding Virginia aristocracy. Tour guides at **Carter's Grove Plantation** (229-1000), 6 mi. east of Williamsburg on Rte. 60, show off the restored house and fields. The last owners doubled the size of the original 18th-century building while trying to keep its colonial "feel." The complex also includes reconstructed 18th-century slave quarters and, in front of the house, an archaeological dig. The **Winthrop Rockefeller Archaeological Museum,** built unobtrusively into a hillside, provides a fascinating case-study look at archaeology. (Plantation open Tues.-Sun. 9am-5pm; Nov.-Dec. 9am-4pm. Museum and slave quarters open March-Dec. Tues.-Sun. 9am-5pm. $13, ages 6-12 $9, free with CWF Patriot's Pass. Call for info.) **Williamsburg Limousine** (877-0279) offers daily round-trip tours to **Carter's Grove Plantation** ($8). If you can, **bike** from South England St. in Williamsburg along the one-way, 7-mi., wooded **Carter's Grove Country Road** (road open Tues.-Sun. 8:30am-4pm; Nov.-Dec. 8:30am-3pm).

Berkeley Plantation (829-6018), halfway between Richmond and Williamsburg on Rte. 5, claims to have had the first Thanksgiving in 1613, saw the birth of President William Henry Harrison, and hosted Union Soldiers in 1862; one of them wrote the famous bugle tune *Taps.* (For more on Thanksgiving controversies, see The Plymouth Conspiracy p. 542.) Pause at the terraced box-wood gardens which stretch from the original 1726 brick building to the river. (House open daily 9am-6pm; grounds open daily 8am-5pm. House and grounds $8.50, seniors $6.65, ages 6-12 $9. Grounds only $5, seniors $3.60, ages 6-16 $2.50.)

Busch Gardens, the Anheuser Busch Brewery, and Water Country: USA When you've filled your colonial quotient, head to **Busch Gardens: The Old Country** (253-3350), 3 mi. east of Williamsburg on Rte. 60. You'll be flung, splashed, and throttled by the various shows and rides. Each section of the park represents a different European nation; trains and sky-cars connect the sections. Recently opened is **Escape from Pompeii,** a water coaster ride. Williamsburg

Limousine serves Busch Gardens (see Williamsburg Practical Information above). (Open April-mid-June daily 10am-7pm; mid-June-Aug. Sun.-Fri. 10am-10pm, Sat. 10am-midnight; Sept.-Oct. daily 10am-7pm. $29, ages 3-6 $24. $5 off after 5pm. Parking $4.) A free monorail from Busch Gardens takes you to the **Anheuser-Busch Brewery** (253-3036). The Brewery is under renovation through 1996; call ahead to see if any tours are being given. Even if you can't get into the actual brewery, you can still get **two free cups of Busch beer** at the **Hospitality Center.** Accessible from I-64. (Open daily 10am-4pm. Free.) Owned and operated by Busch Gardens (and about 2 mi. away) is **Water Country: USA,** a mammoth water park to end all water parks. (Open weekends in May and June-Sept 10am-dusk. $20, ages 3-6 $16. After 3pm, $12 for all.)

■■■ VIRGINIA BEACH

After years of attracting a cruising college crowd, Virginia Beach is shedding its playground image and evolving into a family-oriented vacation spot. While the beach and boardwalk still draw hundreds of students, nightlife venues are being systematically pushed off the main drag by the town's inhabitants; residents of Virginia Beach have become so concerned about crime and youthful irreverence that they recently had security cameras installed on the boardwalk. However, be assured that Virginia Beach is no retirement community; it remains a beach town, with the usual menagerie of surf shops, fast-food joints, hotels, and motels, which often fill seaside towns.

PRACTICAL INFORMATION

Tourist Office: Virginia Beach Visitors Center, 22nd St. and Parks Ave. (437-4888 or 800-446-8038). Information on budget accommodations and area sights, as well as the Virginia Beach Bikeway Map. Open daily 9am-8pm; Labor Day-Memorial Day 9am-5pm.

Trains: Amtrak, (245-3589 or 800-872-7245). Nearest station, in Newport News, provides free 45-min. bus service to and from the Radisson Hotel at 19th St. and Pavilion Dr. in Virginia Beach, but you must have a train ticket to get on the bus. To: Washington, DC (6hr., $42); New York City (10hr., $85); Philadelphia (8½hr., $70); Baltimore (7hr., $49); Richmond (4hr., $18); Williamsburg (2hr., $13).

Buses: Greyhound, 1017 Laskin Rd. (422-2998 or 800-231-2222). Connects with MD via the Bridge Tunnel. To: Washington, DC (6½hr., $35); Richmond (3½hr., $23); Williamsburg (2½ hrs., $14).

Public Transportation: Virginia Beach Transit/Trolley Information Center (428-3388) provides info on area transportation and tours, including trolleys, buses, and ferries. The **Atlantic Avenue Trolley** runs from Rudee Inlet to 42nd St. (in summer daily noon-midnight; 50¢, seniors and disabled 25¢). Other trolleys run along the boardwalk, the North Seashore, and to Lynnhaven Mall.

Bike/Moped Rental: Atlantic Convenient Mart (491-6143), at 28th St. and Atlantic Ave. Bikes $3 per hr., $13 per day. In-line skates $5 per hr., $15 per day. Open daily 7am-midnight. **Moped Rentals, Inc.,** 21st St. and Pacific Ave. Mopeds $23.50 per 1½hr. Open in summer daily 10am-midnight.

Emergency: 911.

Post Office: (428-2821), 24th St. and Atlantic Ave. Open Mon.-Fri. 8am-4:30pm. **ZIP code:** 23458. **Area code:** 804.

Virginia Beach is hard to get to, but easy to get around. Drivers from the north can take I-64 east from Richmond through the Bay Bridge Tunnel into Norfolk, then get on Rte. 44 (the Virginia Beach-Norfolk Expressway; toll 25¢), which will deliver them straight to 22nd St. and the beach. In Virginia Beach east-west streets are numbered; north-south avenues parallel the beach.

ACCOMMODATIONS

The number of motels in Virginia Beach is unreasonably high; unfortunately, so are most of the rates. Atlantic Ave. and Pacific Ave. buzz with activity during the summer and boast the most desirable hotels; reserve as far in advance as possible. If you're traveling in a group, look for "efficiency rate" apartments, which are rented cheaply by the week.

Angie's Guest Cottage-Bed and Breakfast and HI-AYH Hostel, 302 24th St. (428-4690), ranks as the best place to stay on the entire Virginia Coast. Barbara Yates (a.k.a. "Angie") and her team welcome guests with exceptional warmth. (Check-in 10am-9pm. Memorial Day-Labor Day $11, nonmembers $14. Off-season: $8.50, nonmembers $11.50. Overflow camping at off-season rates. Kitchen and lockers available. Linen $2. Reservations helpful, but not required. Open April 1-Oct. 1, March with reservations.) In the bed and breakfast, breakfast is (duh) included (doubles $48-72). Accommodations at the **Ocean Palms Motel** (428-8362), 30th St. and Arctic Ave., consist of two-room apartments with refrigerators ($30-45 per night). Right next door, the **Cherry Motel,** 2903 Arctic Ave. (428-3911), rents tidy one- and two-bedroom apartments by the week, each with four beds and a kitchen. (May 15-June 15 1-bedroom $300, 2-bedroom $375; June 16-Labor Day $375/$525.)

Camp at the **Seashore State Park** (481-2131, reservations 490-3939), about 8 mi. north of town on U.S. 60, where choice sites go for $19. Because of its desirable location amid sand dunes and cypress trees, the park is very popular; call two to three weeks ahead (during business hours) for reservations. (Park open 8am-dusk. Take the North Seashore Trolley.) **KOA,** 1240 General Booth Blvd. (428-1444 or 800-665-8420), runs a quiet campground with open sites and free bus service to the beach and boardwalk. The campground may be hard to find; keep your eyes peeled for the red and yellow KOA sign. (Sites $24, with electricity $26, with full hook-up $33; comfortable and spacious 1-room cabins $46.)

FOOD AND NIGHTLIFE

Junk-food aficionados will love Virginia Beach, thanks to the jumble of fast-food joints along the boardwalk and the major thoroughfares. Beyond the neon glare, **The Jewish Mother,** 3108 Pacific Ave. (422-5430), dotes on her customers with quiche, omelettes, crepes ($5-9), deli sandwiches ($4-6), and desserts ($2-4). At night the restaurant becomes a popular (and cheap) bar with live music. The grill stays open until 2 or 3am on the weekends, feeding the "lush rush," an influx of drunkards who appear when other bars shut down. (Cover $3-5; no cover for "ladies" on Thurs. Open Sun.-Thurs. 9am-2am, Fri.-Sat. 9am-3am.) **The Raven,** 1200 Atlantic Ave. (425-1200), lays out tasty seafood and steaks in a tinted-glass greenhouse, or outdoors when it's warm. (Sandwiches and burgers $5-7, dinners $12-17. Open daily 11:30am-2am.) **Giovanni's Pasta Pizza Palace,** 2006 Atlantic Ave. (425-1575), serves tasty Italian pastas, pizzas, and hot grinders. (Lunches and dinners $5-8. Open daily noon-11pm.)

For organic produce and vegetarian goodies try **The Heritage Store,** 314 Laskin Ave. (428-0100). The Garden Burger is particularly tasty ($5). (Open Mon.-Sat. 10am-7pm, Sun. noon-6pm.) At 31st St. (Luskin Rd.) and Baltic Ave., the **Farm Fresh Supermarket** salad bar, stocked with fresh fruit and pastas ($3 per lb.), is a cheap alternative (open 24 hrs.).

In darkness the beach becomes a haunt for lovers. **Chicho's** (422-6011), on Atlantic Ave. between 20th and 21st St., is one hot spot left from the days when bars clustered near the water. (Dress code: T-shirts, shorts, tight dresses, tanned skin.) Bartenders shout to one another while videos of surfing competitions and bungee jumping play on screens above their heads and hopeful patrons ogle their neighbors. (Open Mon.-Fri. 5pm-2am, Sat.-Sun. 1pm-2am; no cover charge.) Increasingly, the bar scene has retreated from the main arteries to places like **H_2O,** 1069 19th St. (425-5684). Massive columns filled with burbling blue water flank the walls and give the club the atmosphere of a posh, tasteful fish tank. Mingle with other tanned and well-groomed fishes for a $3-5 cover. (Open daily 11am-3pm for lunch, 5pm-10pm for dinner, 5pm-2am for drinks. Live DJ and a dance floor.) Across the way, **The Bayou,** 1900 Pavilion Dr. (422-8900), on the first floor of the Radisson Hotel will drown you in the deafening sounds of live alternative bands five nights a week (cover $3-5; open daily 6pm-2am).

■■■ CHARLOTTESVILLE

The renowned jack-of-all trades Thomas Jefferson, when writing his own epitaph, was careful to point out his role as "father of the University of Virginia." The college he founded dominates Charlottesville economically, geographically, and culturally, supporting a community of writers such as Pulitzer Prize-winning poet Rita Dove—not to mention a community of pubs. Visitors are steered to Monticello, the cleverly constructed Neoclassical mansion Jefferson designed. Even the friendly, hip, and down-to-earth population of the Blue Ridge foothills town seems to embody the third U.S. President's dream of a well-informed, culturally aware citizenry which chooses to live close to the land.

PRACTICAL INFORMATION

Tourist Office: Chamber of Commerce, 415 E. Market St. (295-3141), within walking distance of Amtrak, Greyhound, and historic downtown. Open Mon.-Fri. 9am-5pm. **Charlottesville/Albermarle Convention and Visitors Bureau,** P.O. Box 161 (977-1783), Rte. 20 near I-64. Take bus #8 ("Piedmont College") from 5th and Market St. They can make same day accommodation arrangements at a discounted rate. Discounted combo tickets to Monticello, Michie Tavern, and Ash Lawn-Highland ($17; seniors $15.50, under 12 $7.50). Open daily 9:30am-4:45pm. Students answer questions and distribute brochures in **Newcomb Hall** (924-3363), on campus. Open daily 8am-10pm. The larger **University Center** (924-7166) is off U.S. 250 west—follow the signs. Transport schedules, entertainment guides, and hints on budget accommodations. Campus maps. Open 24 hrs.

Campus Police: Dial 4-7166 on a UVA campus phone.

Trains: Amtrak, 810 W. Main St. (296-4559 or 800-872-7245), 7 blocks from downtown. To: Washington, DC (1-2 per day, 3hr., $25); New York City (1-2 per day, 7-8hr., $92); Baltimore (1 per day, $42); Philadelphia ($62). Open daily 5:30am-9pm.

Buses: Greyhound, 310 W. Main St. (295-5131 or 800-231-2222), within 3 blocks of historic downtown. To: Richmond (1 per day, $17); Washington, DC (2 per day, 3hr., $29); Norfolk (1 per day, 4hr., $32). Open Mon.-Sat. 7am-8:30pm, Sun. noon-8:30pm.

Public Transportation: Charlottesville Transit Service (296-7433). Bus service within city limits, including most hotels and UVA campus locations. Maps available at both info centers, the Chamber of Commerce, and the UVA student center. Buses operate Mon.-Sat. 6:30am-6:30pm. Fare 60¢, seniors and disabled 30¢, under 6 free. The more frequent University of Virginia buses hypothetically require UVA ID but the merely studious-looking usually ride free.

Taxis: Yellow Cab, 295-4131. 25¢ first sixth mi., $1.50 each additional mi. To Monticello $8.

Crisis Lines: Region 10 Community Services Hotline, 972-1800. **Lesbian and Gay Hotline,** 971-4942. UVA-affiliated and open Mon.-Thurs. 5-9pm.

Emergency: 911.

Post Office: 513 E. Main St. (978-7610). Open Mon.-Fri. 8:30am-5pm, Sat. 10am-1pm. **ZIP code:** 22902. **Area code:** 804.

Charlottesville streets number east to west, using compass directions; 5th St. N.W. is 10 blocks from (and parallel to) 5th St. N.E. Streets running east-west across the numbered streets are neither parallel nor logically named. Charlottesville has two downtowns: one on the west side near the university called **The Corner,** and **Historic Downtown,** about a mile east. The two are connected by **University Ave.,** running east-west, which becomes **Main St.** after the Corner ends at a bridge.

ACCOMMODATIONS AND CAMPING

Budget accommodations are scarce in C-ville. Try **Budget Inn,** 140 Emmet St./U.S. 29 (293-5141), near the university (the name says it all). 40 comfortable, hotel-quality rooms with TV and A/C. (Office open 8am-midnight. Singles $33, doubles $36; $1 off in winter; each additional person $5. Senior discounts.) **Econo Lodge,** 400 Emmet St. (296-2104) has 60 typical rooms and a pool (office open 24 hrs.; singles $39, doubles $46). **Charlottesville KOA Kampground,** (296-9881 or 800-336-9881) stakes out on Rte. 708. Take 29S to Rte. 708; the campground's on the left. All campsites are shaded. Recreation hall with video games, a pavilion, and a pool (open Mon.-Sat. 10am-8pm). Fishing (not wading or swimming) is allowed. (Check-in after noon, check-out before noon. Sites $17, hook-up $23. Open March 15-Nov. 15.)

GRUB

The Corner neighborhood near UVA has bookstores and countless cheap eats, with good Southern grub in C-ville's unpretentious diners. **The Hardware Store,** 316 E. Main St. (977-1518), near the middle of the outdoor "mall," revels in a slightly offbeat atmosphere: beers served in glass boots, and condiments in toolboxes. An American grille with an eclectic set of entrees, from *ratatouille gratinée* ($5.75) to crêpes both sweet ($2-5) and savory ($6-7). Sandwiches from $3-7. (Open Mon.-Thurs. 11am-9pm, Fri.-Sat. 11am-10pm.) **Macado's,** 1505 University Ave. (971-3558) has great sandwiches ($4-5), a handful of entrees ($5-7), homemade desserts, and long hours. Upstairs is a rockin' bar where Edgar Allen Poe once lived. Amontillado is the specialty of the house ($5). (Open Sun.-Thurs. 9am-1am, Fri.-Sat. 9am-2am.) **Littlejohn's,** University Ave. (977-0588) 24-hr. deli has answered the prayers of many UVA students-cum-late-night eaters with great sandwiches ($3-6). Finally, stop by **Coupe DeVille's,** 9 Elliewood Ave. (77-3966). College students cross the road for the half-rotisserie chicken ($6.50). (Open Mon.-Fri. 11:30am-2pm and 5:30-10pm, Sat. 5:30-10pm. Pub only Mon.-Sat. 10pm-2am.)

SIGHTS

Most activity on the spacious **University of Virginia (UVA)** campus clusters around the **Lawn** and fraternity-lined **Rugby Rd.** Jefferson watched the University being built through his telescope at Monticello, and you can return the gaze with a glimpse of Monticello from the Lawn, a terraced green carpet that is one of the prettiest spots in American academia. Professors live in the Lawn's pavilions; Jefferson decorated each with a different style of ornamentation. Lawn tours, led by students, leave from the Rotunda on the hour from 10am-4pm; self-guided tour maps are provided for those who prefer to find their own way. **The Rotunda** (924-7969) once housed a bell that was shot for the crime of waking students up too early. (Free tours given daily, call for times. Open daily 9am-4:45pm.) The **Bayley Art Museum** (924-3592), Rugby Rd., features visiting exhibits and a small permanent collection including one of Rodin's castings of *The Kiss* (open Tues.-Sun. 1-5pm).

The **Downtown Mall,** about five blocks off E. Main St., is a brick thoroughfare lined with restaurants and shops catering to a diverse crowd. A kiosk near the fountain in the center of the mall has posters with club schedules.

Jefferson oversaw every stage of the development of his beloved home **Monticello** (984-9800), and the house reflects the personality of its creator. Monticello is a Neoclassical jewel loaded with fascinating innovations collected or conceived by Jefferson. A unique all-weather passage links the kitchen with the dining room so that neither rain nor snow nor gloom of night could keep dinner from its appointed rounds, and an indoor compass registers wind direction using a weathervane on the roof. The grounds, cleverly laid out, afford good strolling and views. There is often a hefty wait for the house tour, but you can explore the grounds in the interim. Arrive before 9am to beat the heat and crowds. (Open daily March-Oct. 8am-5pm; Nov.-Feb. 9am-4:30pm. Tickets $8, seniors $7, ages 6-11 $4, students $3 Nov.-Feb., $1.)

Ashlawn (293-9539), the 500-acre plantation home of President James Monroe, is minutes away (take a right turn to Rte. 795). Jefferson assisted with the building of

Ashlawn as well, but made the front door short so that Monroe was always obliged to bow to his neighbor at Monticello. (Open daily 9am-6pm; Nov.-Feb. 10am-5pm. Tour $6, seniors $5.50, ages 6-11 $3.)

Down the road from Monticello on Rte. 53 is **Michie** (Mick-ee) **Tavern** (977-1234), a 200 year-old establishment with an operating grist mill and a general store (open daily 9am-5pm; tours $5, under 6 $1). **The Ordinary,** located in the tavern, serves up a fixed buffet of fried chicken, beans, cornbread, and other dishes ($9.50, ages 6-11 $4). Eat outside in good weather. (Open daily 11:15am-3:30pm; Nov.-April 11:30am-3pm.) To visit these sites at a discount price, purchase the President's Pass at the Charlottesville/Albemarle Convention and Visitors Bureau (see Practical Information above).

ENTERTAINMENT AND NIGHTLIFE

The town loves jazz, likes rock, and has quite a few pubs. Around the Downtown Mall, ubiquitous posters and the free *Charlottesville Review* can tell you who plays where and when. In the **Box Gardens** behind Ashlawn, from June to August, English-language opera and musical theater highlight the **Summer Festival of the Arts** (293-4500, open Tues.-Sun. 10am-5pm; call for shows and ticket prices). Ashlawn hosts **Music at Twilight** on Wednesday evenings ($10, students $6, seniors $9), including New Orleans jazz, Cajun music, blues, and swing.

At night, take it to **The Max,** 12 11St. SW (295-6299). One of the largest and most popular bars in the city has a Top-40 DJ on Tuesday and dancing (cover: men 21+ $4, women 18+ $3). On Wednesday learn two-steppin' with free lessons until 9:30pm ($4 cover). The weekend brings live bands (and a $5 cover for men). Drafts are $1.85. (Open Tues., and Thurs.-Sat. 8pm-2am, Wed. 7pm-midnight.) The **Outback Lodge,** 917 Preston Ave. (979-7211), plays with a pool table and foosball. Live music sounds Wednesday through Saturday (cover around $10).

■■■ SHENANDOAH

Shenandoah National Park was one of the U.S.'s first attempts at large-scale restoration. Before Congress established a national park here in 1926, the land was occupied by rocky formations and resourceful but reclusive mountain folk. Today, residents include not-so-reclusive deer, bears, and other critters who make their home in the lush forest that has reclaimed the area. Fields have given way to forest, transforming the park into a spectacular ridgetop preserve. A trip along its spine via Skyline Dr. allows glimpses of the Blue Ridge Mountains, the fertile plains below, and quite possibly some of the park's furry and inquisitive inhabitants.

Shenandoah's natural beauty comes in the form of sweeping vistas and an abundance of wildlife. On clear days, drivers and hikers can look out over miles of unspoiled ridges and treetops, home to more plant species than all of Europe. In the summer, the cool mountain air offers a respite from Virginia's oppressive heat and humidity. Early in June, mountain laurel blooms in the highlands. In the fall, Skyline Dr. and its lodges are choked with tourists who come to enjoy the magnificent fall foliage. The narrow park stretches almost 75 mi. along the Blue Ridge Mountains, parallel to and south of the wilder George Washington National Forest.

Practical Information Rockfish Gap, at the southern end of the park, is only 25 mi. west of Charlottesville on Rte. 64. You can also drive to Shenandoah from Washington, DC; take Rte. 66W to U.S. 340S to Front Royal. **Greyhound** (800-231-2222) sends buses once per morning from Washington, DC to Waynesboro, near the park's southern entrance ($40), but no bus or train serves Front Royal, at the park's northern extreme.

The **Dickey Ridge Visitors Center** at Mile 4.6 (635-3566), serves the north entrance with daily interpretative programs (open April-Nov. daily 9am-5pm). The **Byrd Visitors Center,** Mile 51 (999-3283), in the center of the park features a movie and a museum which explain the history of the Blue Ridge Range and its mountain culture (open April-Oct. daily 9am-5pm). Both stations offer changing exhibits on the park, free pamphlets detailing short hikes, daily posted weather updates, and ranger-led nature hikes. When planning to stay more than a day, purchase the *Park Guide* ($2), a booklet containing all the park regulations, trail lists, and a description of the area's geological history. Another good guide which doubles as a souvenir is *Exploring Shenandoah National Park* ($2). For general park information call 999-2243 (daily 8am-4:30pm), or 999-3500 for a 24-hr. recorded message. Write for info at: Superintendent, Park Headquarters, Shenandoah National Park, Rte. 4, P.O. Box 348, Luray 22835. In the park, call 800-732-0911 in an **emergency,** or contact the nearest ranger. Shenandoah's **area code:** 540.

Shenandoah's technicolor mountains—bluish peaks covered with deciduous flora in the summer, streaked with brilliant reds, oranges, and yellows in the fall—can be ogled from overlooks along **Skyline Dr.,** which runs 105 mi. south from Front Royal to Rockfish Gap. (Miles along Skyline Dr. are measured north to south, beginning at Front Royal.) The overlooks provide picnic areas for hikers; map boards also carry data about trail conditions. The drive closes during and following bad weather. Most facilities also hibernate in the winter. (Entrance $5 per vehicle, $3 per hiker, biker, or bus passenger, disabled persons free; pass good for 7 days.)

Accommodations and Camping The **Bear's Den HI-AYH** (554-8708), located 35 mi. north of Shenandoah on Rte. 601S, provides a woodsy stone lodge for travelers with two 10-bed dorm rooms and a room with one double bed and two bunk beds. Drivers should exit from Rte. 7 onto Rte. 601S and go about ½ mi., turn right at the stone-gate entrance, and proceed up the hostel driveway for another ½ mi. No bus or train service is available. The hostel has a dining room, kitchen, on-site parking, and a laundry room. Ask the staff for activities information. (Check-in 5-10pm. Check-out 9:30am. Front gate locked and quiet hrs. begin at 10pm. $12, non-members $15. Camping $6 per person. Reservations recommended; write Bear's Den AYH/HI, Postal Route 1, Box 288, Bluemont 22012.)

The park maintains two affordable lodges with motel-esque rooms in cabin-esque exteriors. **Skyland** (999-2211or 800-999-4714), Mile 42 on Skyline Dr., offers brown and green wood-furnished cabins ($43-77, $5 more in Oct.; open April-Oct.) and slightly more upscale motel rooms ($78-82; open April-Nov.). **Lewis Mountain,** Mile 57 (999-2255 or 800-999-4714), also gets cabin fever with a set of its own ($52-55, $7 more in Oct.). Reservations are necessary, up to six months in advance.

The park service maintains three major campgrounds: **Big Meadows** (Mile 51); **Lewis Mountain** (Mile 58); and **Loft Mountain** (Mile 80). All have stores, laundry facilities, and showers (no hookups). Heavily wooded and uncluttered by mobile homes, Lewis Mountain makes for the happiest tenters. Sites at Lewis Mountain and Loft Mountain $12, at Big Meadows $12, $14 with reservation. Reservations possible only at Big Meadows (800-365-2267). Call a visitors center (see Practical Information above) to check availability.

Backcountry camping is free, but you must obtain a permit at a park entrance, visitors center, ranger station, or the **park headquarters** (see Practical Information above) halfway between Thornton Gap and Luray on U.S. 211. Since open fires are prohibited, bring cold food or a stove; boil water or bring your own because some creeks are oozing with microscopic beasties. Illegal camping carries a hefty fine. Hikers on the **Appalachian Trail** can make use of primitive open shelters, three-sided structures with stone fireplaces, which are strewn along the trail at approximately 7-mi. intervals. At full shelters, campers often will move over to make room for a new arrival. These shelters are reserved for hikers with three or more nights in different locations stamped on their camping permits; casual hikers are banned from them. $1 per night donation. The **Potomac Appalachian Trail Club (PATC)** maintains five cabins in back-country areas of the park. You must reserve in advance by writing to the club at 118 Park St., SE, Vienna 22180 (242-0693), and bring lanterns and food. The cabins contain bunk beds, water, and stoves. (Sun.-Thurs. $3 per person, Fri.-Sat. $14 per group; one member in party must be 21.)

Hikes and Activities The **Appalachian Trail** runs the length of the park. Trail maps and the PATC guide can be obtained at the visitors center (see Practical Information above). The PATC puts out three different topographical maps (each $5) of three different parts of the park. When purchased as a package, the maps come with a trail guide, descriptions, and suggestions for budgeting time ($16). Brochures that cover the popular hikes are available for free. Overnight hikers should keep in mind the unpredictability of mountain weather. Be sure to get the park services package of brochures and advice before a long hike.

Old Rag Mountain, 5 mi. from Mile 45, is 3291 ft.—not an intimidating summit—but the 7.2-mi. loop up the mountain is deceptively difficult. This six- to eight-hour hike is steep, involves scrambling over and between granite, and at many points flaunts disappointing "false summits." Bring lots of water, energy food, and chutzpah. Camping is banned above 2800 ft. The **Whiteoak Canyon Trail** beckons from its own parking lot at Mile 42.6. The trail to the canyon is easy; the waterfalls and trout-filled streams below are spectacular. Waysides vend five-day fishing licenses ($7). From Whiteoak Canyon, the **Limberlost** trail slithers into a hemlock forest. At Mile 51.4, **Lewis Spring Falls Trail** takes only ¾-mi. to reach a gorgeous array of falls—the closest to Skyline Dr. in the whole park. The trail descends farther (about an hour's walk) to the base of the falls, where water drops 80 ft. over the crumbling stone of an ancient lava flow. **Hogback Overlook,** from Mile 20.8 to Mile 21, bristles with easy hikes and idyllic views of the smooth Shenandoah River and Valley. At **Dark Hollow Falls,** Mile 50.7, a 1½-mi. hike takes you to the base of scenic cascades.

Take a break from hiking or driving at one of Shenandoah's seven **picnic areas,** located at Dickey Ridge (Mile 5), Elkwallow (Mile 24), Pinnacles (Mile 37), Big Meadows (Mile 51), Lewis Mountain (Mile 58), South River (Mile 63) and Loft Mountain (Mile 80). All have tables, fireplaces, water fountains, and comfort stations. When you forget to pack a picnic basket, swing by the **Panorama Restaurant** (999-2265 or 800-999-4714), at Mile 31.5, for a meal and a view. (Sandwiches $3-5, entrees $5-12. Open April-Nov. daily 9am-5:30pm.)

MID-ATLANTIC

■ BLUE RIDGE PARKWAY

If you don't believe that the best things in life are free, a drive along the 469-mi. Blue Ridge Parkway could change your mind. Continuous with **Skyline Dr.,** the Parkway runs through Virginia and North Carolina, connecting the **Shenandoah** (see above) and **Great Smoky Mountains National Parks** (p. 278). From Shenandoah, the road winds south through Virginia's **George Washington National Forest,** between Waynesboro and Roanoke. Every bit as scenic as Skyline Dr., the Blue Ridge Parkway also remains much wilder and less crowded. Don't expect to get anywhere fast, though—the speed limit is 45mph and the morning mist will slow you further.

The forest beckons motorists off the road with spacious campgrounds, canoeing routes, and the clear mountain water of **Sherando Lake** (Mile 16). Nature trails range from the **Mountain Farm Trail** (Mile 5.9), a 20-minute hike to a reconstructed homestead, to the **Rock Castle Gorge Trail** (Mile 167), a three-hour excursion. **Humpback Rocks** (Mile 5.8) is an easy hike with a spectacular view. While die-hards venture onto the **Appalachian Trail,** which meanders in scenic style all the way to Georgia, those not interested in hiking can visit the mountain farm at **Mabry Mill** (Mile 176.1) or purchase local crafts at **Crabtree Meadows** (Mile 339). The Park Service hosts a variety of ranger-led interpretive activities, and any of the visitors centers can give you info on the trails (see below).

For general info on the parkway, call the **Blue Ridge Parkway Information Line** (704-298-0398) or contact **Blue Ridge Parkway Headquarters,** 400 BB&T Bldg., Asheville, NC 28801 (704-271-4779). The park service in Roanoke (703-857-2490) or Montebello (703-377-2377) can provide additional details. Eleven **visitors centers** line the parkway at Miles 5.8, 63.8, 86, 169, 217.5, 294, 304.5, 316.4, 331, 364.6, and 382, and there are seven stands where you can pick up brochures. The centers, located at entry points where major highways intersect the Blue Ridge, offer various exhibits, programs, and information facilities along with the free, helpful Milepost guide. (Most open May-Oct. daily 9am-5pm.) In an **emergency** call 800-727-5928 anywhere in VA or NC; be sure to give your location to the nearest mile.

The **Blue Ridge Country HI-AYH Hostel,** Rte. 2, P.O. Box 449, Galax 24333 (703-236-4962), just 100 ft. from the Parkway at Mile 214, houses 22 beds in a reproduction of a 1690 colonial building (lockout 9:30am-5pm, curfew 11pm; $12, nonmembers $15; open Feb.-Dec.). Parkway travelers can also lodge in hostels in Asheville, NC (p. 294) and Boone, NC (p. 291). Each of the nine **campgrounds** along the Parkway, located at Miles 61, 86, 120, 167, 239, 297, 316, 339, and 408, has water and restrooms ($9, no reservations). Contact the Parkway for info on free backcountry and winter camping.

The cities and villages along the Blue Ridge Parkway offer a range of accommodations. For a complete listing, pick up a Blue Ridge Parkway Directory at a visitors center. The communities listed allow easy access to the Parkway and many have attractions of their own. For info on bus access to the major towns around the Parkway, contact **Greyhound,** at 26 Salem Ave. S.W., Roanoke (540-343-7885 or 800-231-2222; open daily 6-10:30am, 11am-5:30pm, 6:30-9:30pm) or at the station in Charlottesville (see Charlottesville Practical Information, p. 251). Buses run to and from Richmond, Waynesboro, and Lexington; one bus per day serves Buchanan and the Natural Bridge between Roanoke and Lexington.

■ OUTSIDE THE PARK

The **Shenandoah Caverns** (477-3115) tout an iridescent panoply of stalactites and stalagmites, with Rainbow Lake and the amusing Capitol Dome among the imitative underground formations prospering in the year-round 56°F air. Take U.S. 211 to Newmarket, get on I-81 North, go 4 mi. to the Shenandoah Caverns exit, and follow the signs for the caverns—not the town of the same name. (Accessible to disabled persons. $8, ages 8-14 $4, under 8 free. Open mid-April to mid-June and Labor Day-Oct. 9am-6pm; other times 9am-5pm.) **Skyline Caverns** (635-4545 or 800-635-4599) in Front Royal built a reputation on its anthodites, whose white spikes defy gravity and grow in all directions at the rate of an inch every seven thousand years. The caverns are 15 minutes from the junction of Skyline Dr. and U.S. 211. (Open mid-June to Aug. daily 9am-6pm; spring and fall Mon.-Fri. 9am-5pm, Sat.-Sun. 9am-6pm; winter daily 9am-4pm. $10, ages 6-12 $5, under 7 free.) If a scenic paddle floats your boat, contact the **Downriver Canoe Co.,** Rte. 613 (Indian Hollow Rd.), Bentonville (635-5526). Trips stretch from 3 mi. to 120-plus mi. From Skyline Dr. Mile 20 follow U.S 211W for 8 mi., then north onto U.S. 340, 14 mi. to Bentonville. Turn right onto Rte. 613 and go 1 mi. (Prices vary with length of trip. 3-mi. trips $29 per canoe; 3-day trip $122 per canoe. 25% discount weekdays.)

West Virginia

Geography and history have colluded to keep West Virginia among the poorest and most isolated states in the Union. The Appalachians, at their highest and most rugged, physically wall off the state, while mining in West Virginia has been synonymous with the worst excesses of industrial capitalism. Still, West Virginia has had proud moments. The state was formed during the Civil War when the Virginia counties which remained loyal to the Union shunned the Confederacy. Having suffered in the mines, West Virginians also helped start the American Labor movement.

With the decline of heavy industry in the last 30 years, West Virginia has turned to another resource—abundant natural beauty. Thanks to great skiing, hiking, and fishing, and the best whitewater rafting in the east, tourism has become one of the state's main sources of employment and revenue. West Virginians remain people of sturdy character, and in the face of irrepressible tourism, hold firmly their traditional, early 20th-century values and lifestyles.

PRACTICAL INFORMATION

Capital: Charleston.
Department of Tourism: 1900 Kanawah Blvd. E., Bldg. 6, #B564, Charleston 25305 (304-348-2286 or 800-CALL-WVA/225-5982). **Division of Parks and Recreation,** State Capitol Complex, Bldg. 3, #714, Charleston 25305 (304-558-2764). **U.S. Forest Service Supervisor's Office,** 200 Sycamore St., Elkins 26241 (304-636-1800).
Time Zone: Eastern. **Postal Abbreviation:** WV
Sales Tax: 6%.

■■■ HARPER'S FERRY

Harper's Ferry's stunning location—at the junction of the Potomac and Shenandoah rivers—has time and again provided a beautiful backdrop to the events of history. This town witnessed John Brown's famous 1859 raid on the U.S. Armory—an attempt to start a war to liberate the slaves. (Although he failed to end slavery and paid for his actions with his life, Brown's raid fanned the smoldering fires which soon blazed into the Civil War.) No longer a revolutionary hotbed, Harper's Ferry today provides excellent hiking, biking, canoeing, rafting, and surveying nature's beauty. Thomas Jefferson called the view from a Harper's Ferry overlook "worth a voyage across the Atlantic," and while that may seem a strong statement, if you're already across it's certainly worth the journey.

Practical Information Harper's Ferry can be reached from the north via U.S. 340S from Frederick, MD. From the south, take U.S. 340N from Front Royal. The **visitors center** (304-535-6298) rests just inside the park entrance off U.S. 340. Park rangers at the visitors center provide free 45- to 60-minute tours, daily from 10:30am to 4pm throughout the summer. Keep your ears open for summer evening programs. (Open daily 8am-5pm, Memorial Day-Labor Day 8am-6pm. Admission fee $5 per car, $3 per hiker or bicyclist; good for 7 consecutive days.) If you drive, park near the visitors center; you'll get ticketed any closer to town. The shuttle bus between the parking lot and town shuttles every 15 minutes. The **West Virginia Welcome Center** (535-2482), across the street from the entrance to Harper's Ferry, is unaffiliated with the town but has great info for in-state travelers on accommodations, restaurants, and activities such as white-water rafting. (Open daily 9am-5pm.) For further park information write Harper's Ferry National Historical Park, P.O. Box 65, Harper's Ferry 25425 or call 304-535-6223. **Amtrak** (800-872-7245) goes to Harper's Ferry (station is on Potomac St.) from Washington, DC in the afternoon and returns to DC in the morning. Reservations required ($15 one-way, $24 round-trip, depending on availability). The **Maryland Rail Commuter (MARC)** (800-325-7245) trains offer a cheaper and more frequent rail-ride; Monday through Friday trains run to Union Station in DC and 3 return to Harper's Ferry. ($6.75, seniors, disabled travelers, and ages 5-15 $3.50. Ticket office open Mon., Wed., Fri. 6am-9pm, Tues. and Thurs. 5am-8pm. You can also buy tickets on the train, $3 extra if ticket window open.) The closest **Greyhound** bus stations are half-hour drives away in Winchester, VA, and Frederick, MD. **Emergency:** 911 or contact a ranger at 304-535-6455.

Accommodations and Camping Hikers can try the **Harper's Ferry HI-AYH Hostel,** 19123 Sandy Hook Rd. (301-834-7652), at Keep Tryst Rd. in Knoxville, MD, for cheap accommodations. You could meet a rugged through-hiker or two about halfway along their 2020-mi. Appalachian Trail odyssey. This renovated auction house, high above the Potomac, has 36 beds in two dormitory rooms. Train service is available to Harper's Ferry, 2 mi. from the hostel, and Brunswick, 3 mi. away. (Limited parking. 3-night max. stay. Check-in 7:30am-9am and 5-9pm. Lockout 9:30am-5pm. Curfew 11pm. $9, nonmembers $12. Sleepsack $2. Camping $4 per member or ATC hiker, $7 per nonmember; includes use of hostel kitchen and bathrooms. 50% reservation deposit.) The **Hillside Motel,** 340 Keep Tryst Rd. (301-834-8144) in Knoxville, MD, has 19 rooms (singles $30, doubles $35).

You can **camp** along the C&O Canal, where sites lie 5 mi. apart, or in one of the five Maryland state-park campgrounds within 30 mi. of Harper's Ferry. **Greenbrier State Park** (301-791-4767) lies a few miles north of Boonsboro on Rte. 66 between exits 35 and 42 on I-70 ($16; open April-Nov.). Far closer is the commercial **Camp Resort,** Rte. 3, Box 1300 (304-535-6895), adjacent to the entrance to Harper's Ferry National Park (sites for 2 $25, with water and electric $28; each additional person $4, under 17 $2; registration fee $3 per person). They also rent cabins ($75, 2-room cabin sleeps eight).

Hikes and Activities The bus from the parking lot near the visitors center stops at **Shenandoah St.** Browse through the renovated blacksmith's shop and wince as the blacksmith hammers at real iron fired in a furnace. A ready-made clothing store, and general store contain replicas of 19th-century goods. Guides in period costume explain the vagaries of the Industrial Revolution. A turn onto High St. reveals many of Harper's Ferry's most interesting exhibits. **Black Voices from Harper's Ferry,** on the corner of High and Shenandoah St., is an exhibit on the history of local African-Americans from their lives as slaves to their acceptance as students at Storer University. Also on High St., the **Civil War Story** chronicles the town's role in the national conflict through displays and a 20-foot time line.

High St. also offers more "olde time" crafts, West Virginia t-shirts, and books on Harper's Ferry than should be legal. The restaurants here are also predictable; walk down Potomac St. instead. Here you'll find the **Back Street Café** (304-725-8019), which doubles as a burger joint (burgers and hot dogs under $2.25) and an offbeat guide service; "Ghost Tours" of the town are offered weekend nights. (Tours May-Nov. Fri.-Sun. 8pm; reservations recommended in Oct.; $2. Call and ask for Shirley. Café open daily 10am-5pm.) A few three-speed bikes are for rent near the Back Street Café ($3 per hr. and $15 per day).

Stairs on High St. climb uphill, following the Appalachian Trail to **Upper Harper's Ferry.** The route passes **Harper's House,** the restored home of town founder Robert Harper, **St. Peter's Church,** where a sagacious pastor flew the Union Jack during the Civil War to protect the church, and **Jefferson's Rock,** where you-know-who had his Atlantic crossing inspiration.

While Harper's Ferry's history attracts many visitors, its natural beauty shouldn't be overlooked. The **Maryland Heights Trail** offers some of the best views in the Blue Ridge Mountains and winds past cliffs worthy of experienced rock climbers. Climbers must register at the visitors center. The **Bolivar Heights Trail** follows a Civil War battle line and features trailside exhibits and a 3-gun battery. The **Appalachian Trail Conference Headquarters** (304-535-6331), at the corner of Washington and Jackson St., offers catalogs to its members featuring good deals on hiking books, as well as trail information and a maildrop for hikers. (Open May-Oct. Mon.-Fri. 9am-5pm, Sat.-Sun. 9am-4pm; Nov. to mid-May Mon.-Fri. 9am-5pm. Membership $25, students and seniors $18. Write to ATC Headquarters, P.O. Box 807, Harper's Ferry 25425 or call.) The less adventurous can stroll along the **Chesapeake & Ohio Canal Towpath,** off the end of Shenandoah St. and over the bridge. The Towpath is also popular with bikers.

Antietam National Battlefield After skirmishing at Harper's Ferry, Civil War soldiers fought in the bloodiest one-day battle of the War at Antietam, a few miles north. On September 17, 1862, 12,410 Union and 10,700 Confederate soldiers lost their lives as Confederate General Robert E. Lee tried and failed to overcome the army of Union General George B. McClellan. McClellan's typical failure to follow the retreating Confederates and crush them decisively tainted the victory, but the nominal Union triumph provided President Lincoln with the opportunity to issue the Emancipation Proclamation, freeing all slaves in those states still in rebellion against the United States on January 1, 1863. The **visitors center** (301-432-5124) has a museum of artifacts used in the battle, free maps for self-guided tours of the battlefield, tapes for rent ($5) with a detailed account of the battle, and an introductory film (film 9am-5pm on the hr.; center open daily May-Sept. 8:30am-6pm, Oct.-April 8:30am-5pm; battlefield entrance $2, family $4). To get to Antietam from Harper's Ferry, take Rte. 340N to Rte. 67 heading toward Boonsboro. Stay on Rte. 67N until you reach Rte. 65; follow 65 to Antietam.

■■■ NEW RIVER GORGE

The New River Gorge is a mixture of raw beauty, raw resources, and raw power. One of the oldest rivers in the world, the New River cuts a narrow gouge in the Appalachian Mountains, leaving valley walls which tower an average of 1000 ft. above the white waters. Industrialists bled the region until coal and timber virtually disappeared in the early and middle parts of this century. The **New River Gorge National Park** now protects the area and oversees the fishing, climbing, canoeing, mountain biking, and world-class rafting that go on in the gorge. There are a number of excellent hiking trails in the park; among them, the **Kaymoor Trail** runs 2 mi. into the abandoned town and mines of Kaymoor. The park operates three visitors centers: **Canyon Rim,** (574-2115), off Rte. 19 near Fayetteville at the northern extreme of the park; **Grandview,** (763-3715), Rte. 9 near Beckley; **Hinton,** (466-0417), Rte. 20. Canyon Rim has the most extensive resources, with info on all activities in the park, including free, detailed hiking guides, and an 11-minute slide presentation that's not to be missed. (Canyon Rim and Grandview open daily 9am-8pm; Sept.-May 9am-5pm. Hinton open daily 9am-5pm; Sept.-May Sat.-Sun 9am-5pm.)

The area's main draw, **whitewater rafting,** has become one of the state's leading industries. A general information service at 800-225-5982 can connect you to some of the nearly 20 outfitters who operate on the New River and the nearby Gauley River. **American Whitewater Tours,** P.O. Box 1168, Oak Hill 25901 (800-787-3982), on Rte. 19 in Fayetteville, runs all-day trips on the New River (Mon.-Fri. $68, Sat. $88). In the summer, **New River Rafting,** P.O. Box 249, Glen Jean 25846 (800-639-7238), does ½-day New River trips (3-3½hr.; Mon.-Fri. $39, Sat. $49). The company also runs trips on the rowdier **Gauley River,** which is only open six weeks in the fall. An express trip on the Upper Gauley (for experienced rafters only) covers some of the country's wildest whitewater (trips Mon. and Fri. $59), while the lower Gauley makes a mellow all-day trip (trips Mon.-Fri. $59, Sat.-Sun. $69). The visitors center distributes a complete list of outfitters.

Where Rte. 19 crosses the river at the park's northern end, the engineered grace of the **New River Gorge Bridge** complements the natural beauty of the gorge itself; take a walk down to the overlook at the Canyon Rim Visitors Center for a good gander. On **Bridge Day,** the third Saturday of October, you can walk across the bridge and parachute off it. Old time coal miners lead you down into an actual mine at the **Beckly Exhibition Coal Mine** (256-1747), New River Park in Beckley (open April-Oct. daily 10am-5:30pm; $6.50, seniors $5.50, ages 4-12 $3, under 4 free). However, the **Fayette Airport** (574-1035), Nickellville Rd. in Fayetteville, offers the park's best attraction for your non-outdoorsman's dollar. The airport, built, owned, and operated by "five dollar" Frank, houses the small planes in which Frank gives fearless travelers in groups of two or three ten-minute tours of the gorge ($5 per person). Frank, a self-described Hillbilly #1, will give you his unique perspective on local politics and foreign policy or recite poetry (his own or requests). Frequent fliers know better than to look at the gas guage during the trip. (Open daily 8:30am-8pm, weather permitting.)

Camping abounds in the area. Many of the raft companies operate private campgrounds and four public campgrounds are scattered in the general area. The most central, **Babcock State Park** (800-225-5982), Rte. 41 south of U.S. 60, 15 mi. west of Rainelle, has shaded, sometimes slanted sites ($11, with water and electric $14). **Greyhound** stops in Beckley, at 105 Third Ave. (253-8333 or 800-231-2222; open Mon.-Fri. 7-11am and 4-8pm, Sat.-Sun. 7-9am and 4-8pm). **Amtrak** (253-6651 or 800-872-7245) serves Prince, on Rte. 41N. (Trains Sun., Wed., and Fri. Open Sun., Wed., and Fri. 9am-1pm and 7-9:30pm, Thurs. and Sat. 7am-2:30pm.) **Area code:** 304.

■■■ MONONGAHELA

Popular with canoers and spelunkers, mammoth **Monongahela National Forest** supports deer, bears, wild turkeys, and magnificent limestone caverns. Over 500 campsites and 600 mi. of well-maintained hiking trails lure additional outdoor adventurers to this camping mecca, where much of West Virginia's most scenic country can be experienced, relatively unspoiled by noisy crowds. Each of the forest's six districts comes complete with its own campground and recreation area; the forest **Supervisor's Office,** Monongahela National Forest, 200 Sycamore St., Elkins 26241-3962 (636-1800), distributes a full list of sites and fees (open Mon.-Fri. 8am-4:45pm). Established sites run $7-15, but the adventurous can sleep in the backcountry for free. If you're going into the backcountry, drop by the **Cranberry Visitor's Center** (653-4826), at the junction of Rte. 150 and Rte. 39/55; they like to know you're out there. (Open daily 9am-5pm; Sept.-Nov. and Jan.-May Sat.-Sun. 10am-4pm, during foliage time daily 9am-5pm.) The forest's **Lake Sherwood Area** (536-3660), 25 mi. north of I-64 on Rte. 92 in the south of the Forest, offers fishing, hunting, swimming, hiking, and boating, as well as campgrounds, but few roving Merry Men to spoil your stay; the campsites often fill on summer weekends (2-week max. stay; sites $10). **Cranberry Mountain** (846-2695), in the Gauley district approximately 6 mi. west of U.S. 219 on Rte. 39/55, has hiking trails through cranberry bogs and campsites for $5 and $8. The forest's slightly more civilized option, the **Middle Mountain Cabins** (456-3335), on Rte. 10, features fireplaces, kitchen facilities, drinking water, and resident field mice. Three cabins, which sleep a total of 11 people, rent as a group regardless of the number of cabins in use. (1-week max. stay. $30 per night, $168 per week. Open May-Oct.)

The only public transportation in the forest area comes into White Sulphur Springs at the forest's southern tip. **Greyhound** (800-231-2222) has a flag stop at the Village Inn, 38 W. Main St. (536-2323; 1 eastbound and 1 westbound bus per day). **Amtrak** (800-872-7245) stops trains at an unmanned station on W. Main St., across from the Greenbriar, on Sunday, Wednesday, and Friday (To: Washington, DC $51; Charlottesville, VA $28). The Monongahela National Forest's **area code:** 304.

THE SOUTH

The American South has always fought to maintain a unique identity in the face of the more economically powerful North. That tension, of course, produced the bloodiest war in the nation's history. Now North and South battle through stereotypes and conventional wisdom. Today's South has adopted the industry and urbanity of the North while retaining notions of hospitality, an easy-going pace, and a *carpe diem* philosophy. The rapid economic growth of the southern metropoli—Atlanta, Nashville, Charlotte, Orlando, and New Orleans—has disproved the Northern stereotypes of rednecks, racists, and impoverished hayseeds. The cities have infused much of the region with a modern flavor. But the past lingers on for good, in the genuine warmth of southern hospitality, and for bad, in the division of wealth beneath whites and blacks.

This region's history and culture, a mélange of Native American, Anglo, African, French, and Spanish, are reflected in its architecture, cuisine, language, and people. Landscapes vary equally. Nature blessed the region with overwhelming mountains, lush marshlands, sparkling beaches and fertile lands. From the Atlantic's Sea Islands to the rolling Ozarks, the Gulf's bayous to the Mississippi Delta, the South's beauty will awe, entice and enchant.

Southern Snippets

Authors: Maya Angelou, Kate Chopin, Ralph Ellison, William Faulkner, Zora Neale Hurston, Harper Lee, Margaret Mitchell, Toni Morrison, Flannery O'Connor, Alice Walker, Eudora Welty, Tennessee Williams, Richard Wright.
Artists: Ralph Earl, William Aiken Walker, James Rosenquist, Howard Finster.
Cuisine: Hopping John, southern fried chicken, spareribs, spoon bread, key lime pie, pecan pie, chess pie, greens, hushpuppies, grits, peanut soup, red rice, jambalya, chitlins, fritters, muffuletta, po'boy, Kentucky Burgoo, ale-8-one.
Microbreweries: The Florida Brewery, Beach Brewing, Birmingham, Oldenberg, Dixie, Abita, Rikenjaks, Bohannon Brewing Co.
Native Americans: Algonquian, Catawba, Seminole, Calusa, Creek, Choctaw, Chickasaw, Cherokee, Natchez, Biloxi, Shawnee. The Trail of Tears begins here, for more on this trail, see p. 509.
Music: Jazz, Country, Grand Ole' Opry, Garth Brooks, Alabama, R.E.M., B-52s, Lynyrd Skynyrd, Allman Brothers, Elvis, Dolly Parton.
Film and TV: *Steel Magnolias, Gone with the Wind, Designing Women.*
Climate: Hot and muggy.
Geography: Coastal, marsh and inland waters, mountains.

Kentucky

Legendary for the duels, feuds, and stubborn frontier spirit of its earlier inhabitants (such as Daniel Boone, for whom almost everything in the state is named), Kentucky presents a gentler face to travelers. Kick back, take a shot of local bourbon, grab a plate of burgoo (a spicy meat stew), and relax amidst rolling hills and bluegrass. These days, Kentuckians' fire erupts on the highways—they aren't ungracious, but they do drive *fast.* Of course, the most respected mode of transportation in the state remains the horse; Louisvillle ignores its vibrant cultural scene and active nightlife for a full week at Derby time, and Lexington devotes much of its most beau-

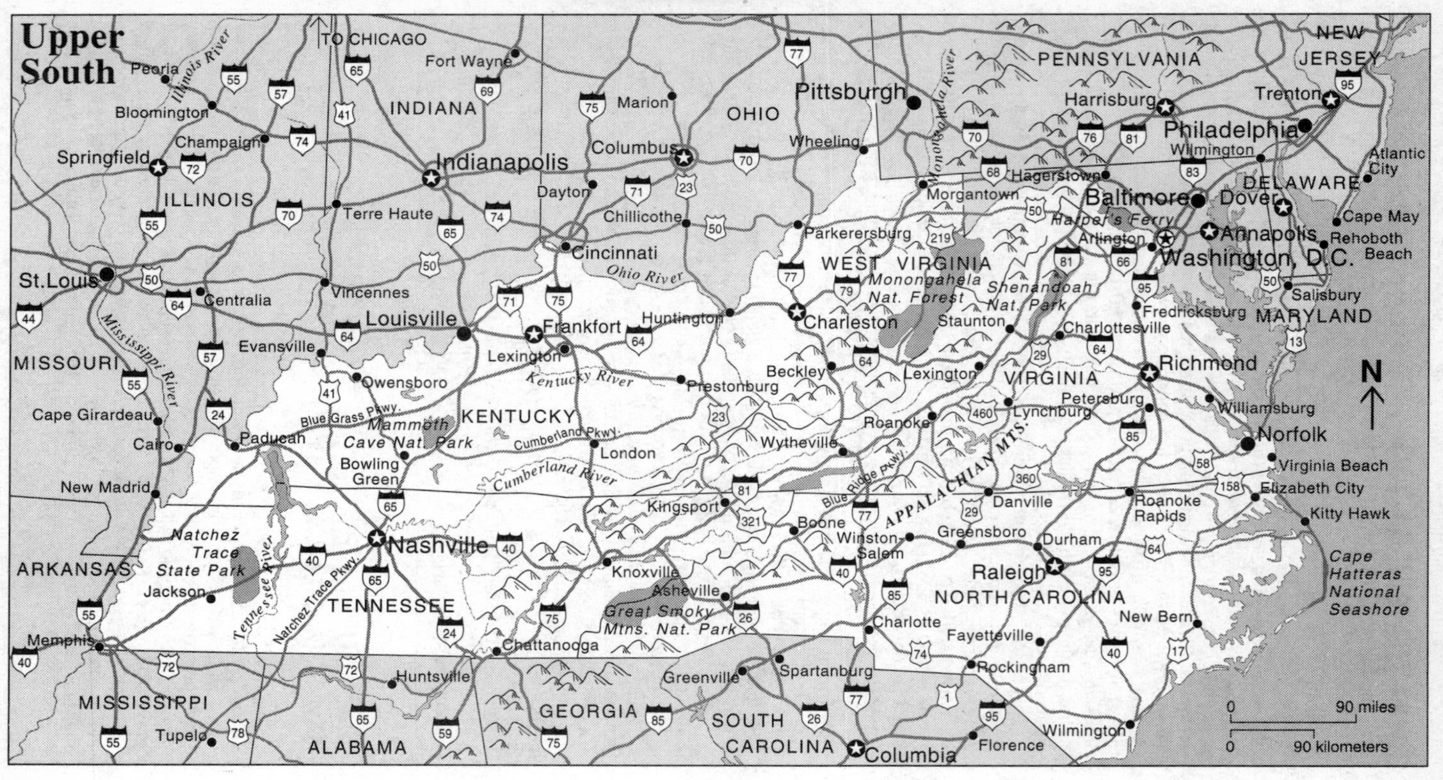
Upper South
TO CHICAGO
N
0 90 miles
0 90 kilometers
ILLINOIS
INDIANA
OHIO
PENNSYLVANIA
NEW JERSEY
DELAWARE
MARYLAND
WEST VIRGINIA
VIRGINIA
KENTUCKY
MISSOURI
ARKANSAS
TENNESSEE
NORTH CAROLINA
SOUTH CAROLINA
GEORGIA
ALABAMA
MISSISSIPPI
Peoria
Illinois River
Bloomington
Champaign
Springfield
Fort Wayne
Marion
Indianapolis
Columbus
Dayton
Terre Haute
Chillicothe
Cincinnati
Ohio River
Pittsburgh
Wheeling
Monongahela River
Harrisburg
Trenton
Philadelphia
Wilmington
Atlantic City
Hagerstown
Baltimore
Dover
Cape May
Annapolis
Rehoboth Beach
Washington, D.C.
Arlington
Harper's Ferry
Salisbury
Morgantown
Parkerersburg
Monongahela Nat. Forest
Shenandoah Nat. Park
Fredricksburg
Charleston
Staunton
Charlottesville
Richmond
St. Louis
Centralia
Vincennes
Louisville
Frankfort
Huntington
Lexington
Evansville
Owensboro
Kentucky River
Prestonburg
Beckley
Lexington
Petersburg
Williamsburg
Lynchburg
Roanoke
Norfolk
Virginia Beach
Elizabeth City
Kitty Hawk
Mississippi River
Cape Girardeau
Cairo
Paducah
Blue Grass Pkwy.
Mammoth Cave Nat. Park
Cumberland Pkwy.
Bowling Green
London
Cumberland River
Wytheville
Blue Ridge Pkwy.
APPALACHIAN MTS.
Danville
Roanoke Rapids
New Madrid
Kingsport
Boone
Winston-Salem
Greensboro
Durham
Raleigh
Natchez Trace State Park
Nashville
Tennessee River
Natchez Trace Pkwy.
Knoxville
Asheville
Great Smoky Mtns. Nat. Park
Jackson
Memphis
Chattanooga
Charlotte
Fayetteville
New Bern
Cape Hatteras National Seashore
Huntsville
Greenville
Spartanburg
Rockingham
Tupelo
Columbia
Florence
Wilmington

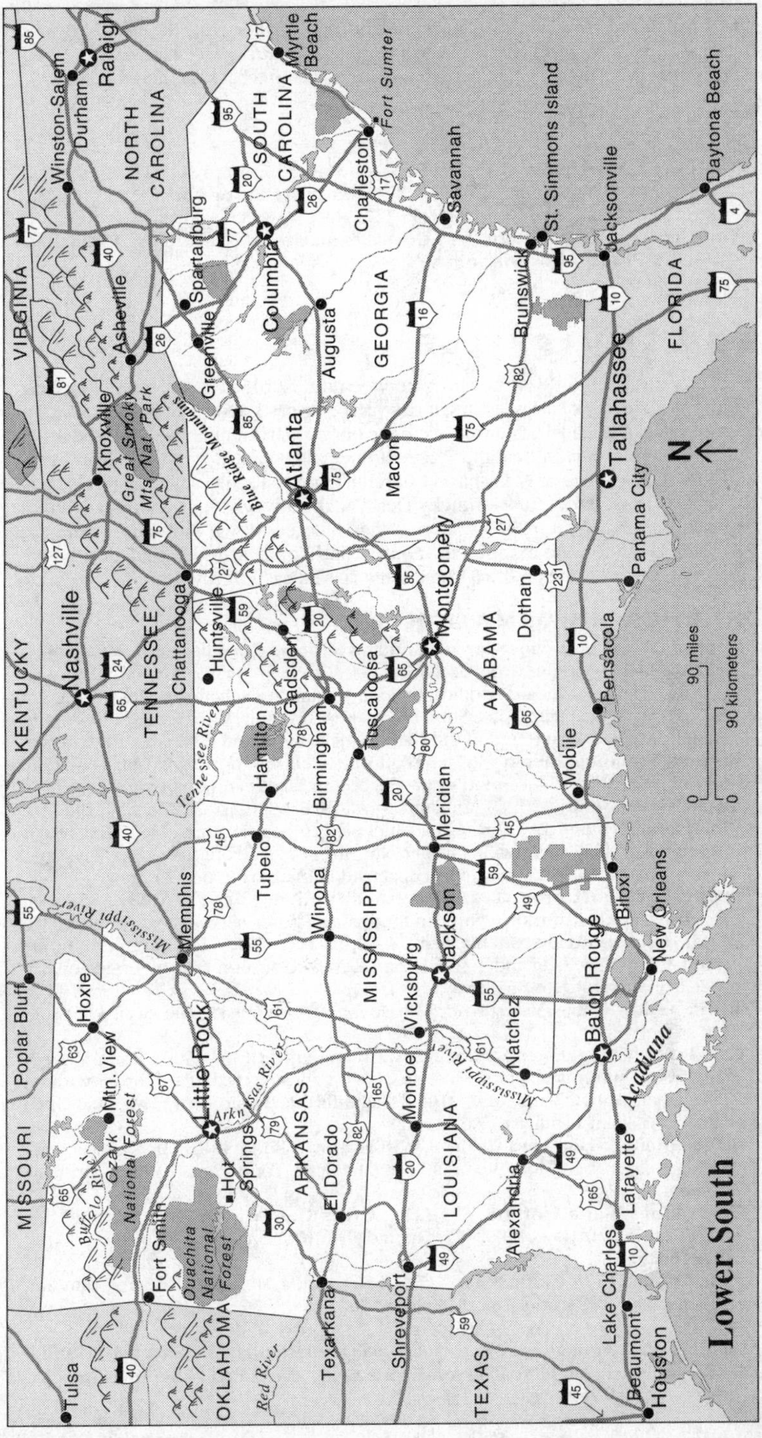

Lower South

MISSOURI
KENTUCKY
VIRGINIA
NORTH CAROLINA
SOUTH CAROLINA
TENNESSEE
ARKANSAS
MISSISSIPPI
ALABAMA
GEORGIA
FLORIDA
LOUISIANA
TEXAS
OKLAHOMA

Tulsa
Fort Smith
Poplar Bluff
Hoxie
Mtn. View
Little Rock
Hot Springs
El Dorado
Texarkana
Shreveport
Monroe
Alexandria
Lafayette
Lake Charles
Beaumont
Houston
Baton Rouge
New Orleans
Natchez
Vicksburg
Jackson
Winona
Memphis
Tupelo
Meridian
Biloxi
Hamilton
Birmingham
Tuscaloosa
Gadsden
Huntsville
Montgomery
Mobile
Pensacola
Dothan
Panama City
Tallahassee
Jacksonville
Daytona Beach
St. Simmons Island
Brunswick
Savannah
Macon
Atlanta
Augusta
Columbia
Charleston
Fort Sumter
Myrtle Beach
Greenville
Spartanburg
Asheville
Knoxville
Chattanooga
Nashville
Winston-Salem
Durham
Raleigh

Ozark National Forest
Ouachita National Forest
Great Smoky Mts. Nat. Park
Blue Ridge Mountains
Buffalo River
Arkansas River
Red River
Mississippi River
Tennessee River
Acadiana

N

0 90 miles
0 90 kilometers

THE SOUTH

tiful farmland to breeding champion racehorses. Farther east, the Daniel Boone National Forest preserves the virgin woods of the Kentucky Highlands, where trailblazers first discovered a route across the mountains to what was then the West.

PRACTICAL INFORMATION

Capital: Frankfort.
Kentucky Department of Travel Development: 500 Mero St., #2200, Frankfort 40601 (502-564-4930 or 800-225-8747). **Kentucky State Parks,** 500 Mero St., 10th Floor, Frankfort 40601 (800-255-7275).
Time Zones: Mostly Eastern; *Let's Go* makes note of areas in Central (1hr. behind Eastern). **Postal Abbreviation:** KY
Sales Tax: 6%.

■■■ LOUISVILLE

Perched on the Ohio River, hovering between the North and the South, Louisville (LOU-uh-vul) feels like a town caught between two pasts. One past has left a legacy of smokestacks, meat-packing yards, and the occasional crumbling edifice; the other still entices visitors with beautiful Victorian neighborhoods, ornate cast-iron buildings, and the elegance of twin-spired Churchill Downs. Each year, the nation's most prestigious horse race, the Kentucky Derby, caps a week-long extravaganza that draws more than half a million visitors. When it comes down to the big event, the party stands still for one thunderous moment and Kentuckians become deadly serious; many fortunes ride on the $15 million wagered each Derby Day.

PRACTICAL INFORMATION

Tourist Office: Louisville Convention and Visitors Bureau, 400 S. 1st St. (584-2121; 800-633-3384 outside Louisville; 800-626-5646 outside KY), at Liberty St. downtown. The standard goodies, including some bus schedules. Open Mon.-Fri. 8:30am-5pm, Sat. 9am-4pm, Sun. 11am-4pm. Brochures available at booths in Standiford Field airport and in the Galleria Mall, at 4th and Liberty St. downtown.
Airport: Standiford Field (367-4636), 15min. south of downtown on I-65. Take bus #2 into the city. **Airspeed of an European Swallow:** I don't know. Aaah!
Buses: Greyhound, 720 W. Muhammad Ali Blvd. (800-231-2222), at 7th St. To: Indianapolis (8 per day, 2hr., $21); Cincinnati (6 per day, 2hr., $18); Chicago (8 per day, 6hr., $57); Nashville (12 per day, 3hr., $29); Lexington (1 per day, 2hr., $13.50). Lockers $1 first day, $3 per each additional day. Open 24 hrs.
Public Transportation: Transit Authority River City (TARC), 585-1234. Extensive system of thoroughly air-conditioned buses serves most of the metro area; buses run daily roughly 5am-11:30pm. Fare 75¢, $1 during peak hours (Mon.-Fri. 6:30-8:30am and 3:30-5:30pm). Disabled access. Trolley service on 4th Ave. from River Rd. to Broadway (10¢).
Taxis: Yellow Cab, 636-5511. $1.50 base fare ($1.80 outside the city), $1.50 per mi. 24 hrs.
Car Rental: Budget Rent-a-Car, 4330 Crittenden Dr. (363-4300). From $50 per day, from $30 on weekends. Must be 21 with a major credit card, or 25 without one. Open daily 6:30am-9pm. Also at Standiford Field airport (336-3360). Open Sun.-Fri. 6:30am-11pm, Sat. 7am-11pm.
Bicycle Rental: Highland Cycle, 1737 Bardstown Rd. (458-7832). $4.25 per hr., $15 per day. Open Mon.-Wed. and Fri. 9am-8pm, Thurs. 9am-5:30pm, Sat. 9am-4:30pm.
Crisis Lines: Rape Hotline, 581-7273. **Crisis Center,** 589-4313. Both 24 hrs. **Gay/Lesbian Hotline,** 897-2475. Open daily 6-10pm.
Emergency: 911.
Post Office: 1420 Gardner Ln. (454-1650). Open Mon.-Fri. 7:30am-7pm, Sat. 7:30am-1pm. **ZIP code:** 40231. **Area code:** 502.

Major highways through the city include **I-65** (north-south expressway), **I-71,** and **I-64.** The easily-accessible **Watterson Expressway,** also called I-264, rings the city, while the **Gene Snyder Freeway** (I-265) circles farther out. The central downtown area is defined by **Main St.** and **Broadway** running north-south, and **Preston Hwy.** and **19th St.** running east-west. The **West End,** beyond 20th St., has a reputation for being a rough neighborhood.

Aside from theater and riverfront attractions, much of the activity in Louisville takes place outside the city center; thankfully, the bus system goes to all the major areas. Call TARC (see above) for help when the written schedules gets confusing.

ACCOMMODATIONS AND CAMPING

Though easy to find, accommodations in downtown Louisville are not particularly cheap. For a bargain, try the budget motels on I-65 near the airport or head to **Newburg** (6mi. away) or **Bardstown** (39mi. away; see South of Louisville, p. 267). To get Derby-Week lodging, make reservations at least six months to a year in advance and prepare to pay big bucks; the Visitors Bureau (see Practical Information above) will help after March 13. **Kentucky Homes Bed and Breakfast** (635-7341) arranges stays in private homes from $65; call seven to 10 days ahead.

Red Roof Inn, 4704 Preston Hwy. (968-0151), off I-65 at exit 130, 1mi. from the airport and 15min. from downtown; accessible by TARC. Small, *nice* rooms in a swell motel but a drab neighborhood. A/C, cable TV, free local calls. Singles $37, doubles $52.

Collier's Motor Court, 4812 Bardstown Rd. (499-1238), south of I-264, 30min. from downtown by car; TARC buses serve this area. Inconvenient, but well-maintained and cheap. Singles $31, doubles $36.

Junction Inn, 3304 Bardstown Rd. (456-2861), near I-264 in the middle of a heavy traffic zone. Slightly shabby, aging rooms in a decent location. Cable TV, free local calls. Singles $26, Fri.-Sat. $33; doubles $33/$36.

KOA, 900 Marriot Dr., Clarksville, IN (812-282-4474), across the river from downtown. Follow I-65 north across the bridge and take the Stansifer Ave. exit. Grim, paved camping, but *very* convenient to downtown. Grocery, playground, free use of the next door motel's pool, mini golf, and fishing lake. Sites for 2 $17, with hookup $22.50; each additional person $4, under 18 $2.50. Kabins for 2 $31.

FOOD

Louisville's chefs whip up a wide variety of cuisines, though good budget fare can be hard to find in the heart of downtown. **Bardstown Rd.** offers easy access to cafés, budget eateries, and local and global cuisine, while **Frankfort Rd.** is rapidly becoming Bardstown-ized with restaurants and chi-chi cafés of its own. Downtown, **Theatre Sq.** provides plenty of good lunch options.

Ramsi's Café on the World, 1293 Bardstown Rd. (451-0700). This classy, intimate restaurant peddles "ethnic non-regional cuisine" to a mix of hipsters and local families. Good vegetarian and gourmet-ish options. Chipolte con Queso $4; salad Nicoise $6.50. Entrees $5-9. Open Mon.-Thurs. 11am-1am, Fri.-Sat. 11am-2am, Sun. 3-11pm.

Mark's Feed Store, 1514 Bardstown Rd. (458-1570). Award-winning barbecue served up on the cheap. If the weather's fine, eat on the patio with the metal pigs. Bodacious Burgoo and Bar-B-Q combo $5; pork sandwich $3.50; large ½ basket of onion straws $1.79. Open Sun.-Thurs. 11am-10pm, Fri.-Sat. 11am-11pm.

Stevens & Stevens and **Ditto's,** 1114 Bardstown Rd. Stevens & Stevens (584-DELI/3354) serves movie-themed deli goods such as the Woody Allen (pastrami on rye with hot mustard $4). Open Tues.-Sat. 10am-7pm. Dittos (581-9129) does it up yuppie-style with dark woods, tasty Florentine Pizza ($6), and Sunday brunch. Open Mon.-Thurs. 11am-11pm, Fri.-Sat. 11am-midnight, Sun. 9am-10pm.

Cafe Kilimanjaro (583-4332), in Theater Sq. Jamaican, Ethiopian, and international cuisine, plus live world music Fri.-Sat. 10:30pm-3am. Jamaican Jerk Chicken lunch special $4.75. Open Mon. 11am-3pm, Tues.-Thurs. 11am-3pm and 4-9pm, Fri.-Sat. 11am-3pm and 5-10:30pm.

Twice Told, 1604 Bardstown Rd. (456-0507). Vegetarian options to relieve your hunger and serious coffee in a Bohemian coffeehouse atmosphere to mess with your head. Entertainment nightly 9pm; Mon. jazz or comedy, Tues. poetry slams, Wed. open mike. Cover $2. Open in summer Sun.-Thurs. 10am-1am, Fri.-Sat. 10am-2am; off season Sun.-Thurs. 10am-midnight, Fri.-Sat. 10am-1am.

NOT JUST A ONE-HORSE TOWN

The **Highlands** strip runs along Baxter/Bardstown and is bounded by Broadway and Trevilian Way on the south. Buses #17, 23, and 44 can all take you to this "anti-mall" of largely unfranchised (o.k., so *nothing* can escape fast-food), independent businesses. Cafés, pizza pubs, antique shops, record stores, and other enticements beckon to strollers. There's even a cyberestablishment, **Diverse Media,** 1609 Bardstown Rd. (473-0644), which allows you to surf the 'Net (15min. 25¢; open Mon.-Fri. 11am-7pm, Sat.-Sun. 2-7pm). **Old Louisville,** between downtown and the university, harbors interesting Victorian architecture; it also has a high crime rate. Farther south, in University of Louisville territory (take bus #2 or 4), the **J.B. Speed Art Museum,** 2035 S. 3rd St. (636-2893), houses an impressive collection of Dutch paintings and tapestries, Renaissance and contemporary art, and a sculpture court (open Tues.-Sat. 10am-4pm, Sun. noon-5pm; free; parking $2). Call the **Louisville Visual Arts Association** at 896-2146 for info on local artists' shows and events. (Open Mon.-Fri. 9am-5pm, Sat. 9am-3pm, Sun. noon-4pm.)

The **Belle of Louisville** (574-2355), an authentic stern-wheeler, floats at 4th St. and River Rd. (2-hr. cruises depart from Riverfront Plaza late May-early Sept. Tues.-Sun. 2pm; sunset cruises Tues. and Thurs. 7pm; nighttime dance cruise Sat. 8:30-11:30pm. Boarding begins 1hr. before departure; arrive early, especially in July. $8, seniors $7, under 13 $4; dance cruise $12.)

Downtown, the **Louisville Science Center,** 727 W. Main St. (561-6103), presents hands-on exhibits and larger-than-life IMAX movies. (Open Mon.-Thurs. 10am-5pm, Fri.-Sat. 10am-9pm, Sun. noon-5pm. $6.75, seniors and kids $5.25; includes IMAX.)

Lovers of American kitsch will find a treat at the **Harlan Sanders Museum,** Kentucky Fried Chicken International Headquarters, 1441 Gardiner Ln. (456-8607), off the Watterson Expwy. (I-264) at Newburg Rd. S. The smell of fried chicken permeates this monument to the honorary Colonel who, with his pressure cooker, secret recipe of 11 herbs and spices, and trademark white suit, brought chicken to the masses. His autobiography, *Life As I Have Known It Has Been Finger Lickin' Good,* is on display but, sadly, *not* for sale. (Open Mon.-Thurs. 8am-5pm, Fri. 8am-3pm.)

Across the river in Jeffersonville, IN, the **Hillerich and Bradsby Co.,** 1525 Charleston-New Albany Rd. (585-5229), 4 mi. north of Louisville, manufactures the famous "Louisville Slugger" baseball bat. Go north on I-65, exit to Rte. 131, and turn east. (Tours Mon.-Fri. on the hr. 8am-4pm. Free.) As of July 1995, the company had plans to move the plant and museum to their rightful place in Louisville; call for details.

ENTERTAINMENT AND NIGHTLIFE

The **Kentucky Center for the Arts,** 5 Riverfront Plaza (tickets and info 584-7777 or 800-775-7777), off Main St., hosts the **Louisville Orchestra** and other major productions (open Mon.-Sat. 9am-6pm, Sun. noon-5pm). The **Lonesome Pines** series showcases indigenous Kentucky music, including bluegrass, as well as national jazz and various eccentric acts (ticket prices vary; student discounts available). Downtown, **Actors Theater,** 316 W. Main St. (584-1265), a Tony award-winning repertory company, gives evening performances (8pm) and some matinees from September through mid-June. (Box office open Mon.-Fri. 9am-5pm. Tickets from $15; student and senior rush tickets 15min. before each show $7.) Bring a picnic dinner to the **Kentucky Shakespeare Festival** (583-8738), in Central Park, which takes place over eight summer weekends starting in early June (performances 8pm).

Butchertown Pub, 1335 Story Ave. (583-2242), presents three stages of alternative music and blues from local and national bands (cover $0-4; open Mon. 4-11:30pm, Tues. 4pm-1am, Wed.-Sat. 4pm-2am). A multi-faceted entertainment machine, **The Brewery,** 426 Baxter Ave. (583-3420), hosts folks like Collective Soul and Toad the Wet Sprocket. When there's no show hang out on the Brewery's four volleyball courts or catch the monthly boxing night. (Cover for live shows only. Open Sun.-Thurs. 11am-2am, Fri.-Sat. 11am-4am.) **Phoenix Hill Tavern,** 644 Baxter Ave. (589-4957), cooks with nightly blues, rock, and reggae on four stages including a deck and a roof garden (cover $2-3; open Wed.-Thurs. and Sat. 8pm-4am, Fri. 5pm-4am). Members of the Techno Alliance take heart; **Sparks,** 104 W. Main St. (587-8566), throbs 'til the early morn (cover Fri.-Sat. $3-5, Sun. $3; open daily 10pm-4am). For gay nightlife, check out **The Connection** entertainment complex, 120 S. Floyd St. (585-5752; cover $2-5).

HORSIN' AROUND

Even if you miss the Kentucky Derby, make a visit to **Churchill Downs,** 700 Central Ave. (636-4400), 3 mi. south of downtown; take bus #4 ("4th St.") to Central Ave. You don't have to bet to admire the twin spires, the colonial columns, the gardens, and the sheer scale of the track—but it sure does make things exciting. (Races April-July 1 Wed.-Fri. 3-7pm, Sat.-Sun. 1-5:30pm; Oct.-Nov. Tues.-Sun. 1-5pm. Grandstand seats $2, clubhouse $3.50, reserved clubhouse $5.50. Grounds open in racing season daily 10am-4pm. Parking $2.)

The **Kentucky Derby Festival** parties with balloon and steamboat races, concerts, and parades for a full week before climaxing in the prestigious **Run for the Roses** on the first Saturday in May. A one- to five-year waiting list stands between you and a ticket for the Derby ($20-30), but never fear; on Derby morning, tickets are sold for standing-room-only spots in the grandstand or infield. Get in line early for good seats lest the other 80,000 spectators get there first. Amazingly, no one is turned away. The **Kentucky Derby Museum** (637-1111), at Churchill Downs, offers a slide presentation on a 360° screen, tours of the stadium, profiles of famous stables and trainers (including the African-Americans who dominated racing early on), a simulated horse-race for betting practice, and tips on exactly what makes a horse a "sure thing." (Open daily 9am-5pm. $4, seniors $3, ages 5-12 $1.50, under 5 free.)

When you get tired of spectating, go for a trail ride at **Iroquois Riding Stable,** 5216 New Cut Rd. (363-9159); take 3rd St. south to Southern Pkwy. or ride bus #4 or #6 to Iroquois Park (open May-Sept. 10am-8pm; $10 per hr.).

■ SOUTH OF LOUISVILLE

Bardstown Kentucky's second-oldest city hosts **The Stephen Foster Story** (800-626-1563 or 348-5971), a mawkish, heavily-promoted outdoor musical about America's first major songwriter, the author of "My Old Kentucky Home." (Mid-June to Labor Day Tues.-Sun. 8:30pm, indoor matinee Sat. 2:30pm. $12, under 13 $6.)

In 1791, Kentucky Baptist Reverend Elijah Craig left a fire unattended while heating oak boards to make a barrel for his aging whiskey. The boards were charred but Rev. Craig carried on. Bourbon was born in that first charred wood barrel, and Bardstown became the "Bourbon Capital of the World." Ninety percent of the nation's bourbon hails from Kentucky, and 60% of that is distilled in Nelson and Bullitt Counties. At **Jim Beam's American Outpost** (543-9877), 15 mi. west of Bardstown in Clermont off Rte. 245, Jim Beam's grandson, "master distiller emeritus" Booker Noe, narrates a film about bourbon. Don't miss the free lemonade, coffee, and sampler bourbon candies. From Louisville, take I-65 south to exit 112, then Rte. 245 east for 1½ mi. (Open Mon.-Sat. 9am-4:30pm, Sun. 1-4pm. Free.) You can't actually tour Beam's huge distillery, but **Maker's Mark Distillery** (865-2099), 19 mi. southeast of Bardstown in Loretto, will show you how bourbon was made in the 19th century (sorry, no Funky Bunch). Take Rte. 49 south to Rte. 52 east. (Tours Mon.-Sat. on the ½hr. 10:30am-3:30pm, Sun. on the hr. 1:30-3:30pm; Jan.-Feb. Mon.-Fri. only. Free.) Neither site has a license to sell its liquors. **Bardstown Visitors Center,** 107 E. Stephen Foster Ave. (348-4877 or 800-638-4877), gives a free one-hour tour, taking visitors by **My Old Kentucky Home** and **Heaven Hill Distillery** in an open-air trolley. (Tours in summer daily 9:30am, 11am, 1:30pm, and 3pm; visitors center open Mon.-Sat. 8am-7pm, Sun. noon-5pm; Nov.-Mar. Mon.-Sat. 8am-5pm.)

Abraham Lincoln's Birthplace Near Hodgenville 45 mi. south of Louisville on U.S. 31 east, this national historic site marks the birthplace of the 16th president. From Louisville, take I-65 down to Rte. 61; public transportation does not serve the area. Fifty-six steps representing the 56 years of Lincoln's tragically shortened life lead up to a stone monument sheltering the small log cabin. Only a few of the Lincoln logs in the walls are believed to be original. A plodding 18-min. film describes Lincoln's ties to Kentucky. (358-3137; open June-Aug. daily 8am-6:45pm; Labor Day-Oct. and May 8am-5:45pm; Nov.-April 8am-4:45pm. Free.)

Mammoth Cave Hundreds of enormous caves and narrow passageways cut through **Mammoth Cave National Park** (758-2328 or 800-967-2283), 80 mi. south of Louisville off I-65, then west on Rte. 70. Mammoth Cave comprises the world's longest network of cavern corridors—over 325 mi. in length. Start your exploration at the **visitors center** (open in summer daily 7:30am-7:30pm; off season 7:30am-5:30pm). Devoted spelunkers should try the 6-hr. "Wild Cave Tour" during the summer (must be 16; $31); less ambitious types generally take the two-hour, 2-mi. historical walking tour ($5.50, seniors $3.25, ages 6-15 $3, under 5 free). Ninety-minute tours accommodate disabled visitors ($4). The caves stay at 54°F year-round; bring a sweater. **Greyhound** comes only as close as **Cave City,** just east of I-65 on Rte. 70. **Time Zone:** Central (1hr. behind Eastern).

■■■ LEXINGTON

Lexington, Kentucky's second-largest city, revels in its Southern heritage. Even recent growth spurts have left the city with the atmosphere of a town. Historic mansions show through the skyscrapers downtown, and a 20-minute drive from the city will set you squarely in bluegrass country. Like the rest of Kentucky, Lexington has horse-fever; the Kentucky Horse Park gets top billing, while shopping complexes and small industries at the outskirts of town share space with 150-odd quaint, green horse farms. These farms have nurtured such equine greats as Citation, Lucky Debonair, Seattle Slew, and Whirlaway, giving good reason for the city's passion.

PRACTICAL INFORMATION

Tourist Office: Greater Lexington Convention and Visitors Bureau, 301 E. Vine St. (233-1221 or 800-848-1224), at Rose St. Open Mon.-Fri. 8:30am-6pm, Sat. 10am-5pm.

Airport: Blue Grass Field, 4000 Versailles Rd. (255-7218). Serves regional and some national carriers; it is often easier to fly to Louisville's Standiford Field.

Buses: Greyhound, 477 New Circle Rd. N.W. (299-8804 or 800-231-2222); take Lex-Tran bus #6 downtown. To: Louisville (1 per day, 1¾hr., $19); Cincinnati (4 per day, 1hr., $18); Knoxville (4 per day, 3hr., $39). Open daily 7:30am-11:00pm.

Public Transportation: Lex-Tran, 109 W. London Ave. (253-4636). Buses leave from the **Transit Center,** 220 W. Vine St., between Limestone and Quality. Modest system serves the university and city outskirts. Bus service is erratic. Buses run 6:15am-6:15pm; evening service on some routes until 10pm. Fare 80¢, transfers free. **WHEELS** (233-3433) provides transportation for those with disabilities. 24-hr. notice required. Open Mon.-Fri. 6:30am-11pm, Sat. 6:30-8pm.

Taxis: Lexington Yellow Cab, 231-8294. $1.90 base fare, $1.60 per mi. 24 hrs.

Crisis Lines: Crisis Intervention, 233-0444. **Rape Crisis,** 253-2511. Both 24 hrs. **AIDS Volunteers of Lexington,** 254-2865. Open Mon.-Fri. 9am-5:30pm.

Emergency: 911.

Post Office: 1088 Nandino Blvd. (231-6700); take bus #1 ("Georgetown"). Open Mon.-Fri. 8am-5pm, Sat. 9am-1pm. General delivery to 111 Barr St. (254-6156). Open Mon.-Fri. 8am-4:30pm. **ZIP code:** 40511. **Area code:** 606.

New Circle Rd. (Rte. 4/U.S. 60 bypass) loops the city, intersecting with many roads that connect the downtown district to the surrounding towns. **High, Vine,** and **Main St.** running east-west and **Limestone St.** and **Broadway** running north-south provide the best routes through downtown.

ACCOMMODATIONS AND CAMPING

A concentration of horse-related wealth in the Lexington area pushes accommodation prices up. The cheapest places lurk outside the city, beyond New Circle Rd. **Dial-A-Accommodations,** 301 E. Vine St. (233-1221 or 800-848-1224), can help you find a room, especially during busy times (open Mon.-Fri. 8:30am-6pm, Sat. 10am-6pm, Sun. noon-5pm; off season reduced hours).

Econo Lodge, 925 Newton Pike (231-6300), 5min. from downtown. Giant rooms, bathtubs, HBO, outdoor pool, free local calls, and some refrigerators. Singles from $30, doubles from $35; $5 per additional person. AAA and seniors discount.

Microtel, 2240 Buena Vista Dr. (299-9600), near I-75 and Winchester Rd. Pleasant, new motel rooms. Singles $35, doubles $40.

Bryan Station Inn, 273 New Circle Rd. (299-4162); take bus #4 or Limestone St. north from downtown and turn right onto Rte. 4. Clean rooms on a motel/fast-food strip. No phones. Must be 21. Singles $32, doubles $34; Fri.-Sat. higher.

Kimball House Motel, 267 S. Limestone St. (252-9565), between downtown and the university. Look for the grungy sign and peeling paint, and step into a mid-20th century timewarp. Parking in back. No phones in rooms. Ask specifically for one of the 1st-floor singles (no A/C, shared bath) which go for $28; they often fill by late afternoon. Otherwise, singles from $34, doubles $38. Key deposit $5.

Kentucky Horse Park Campground, 4089 Ironworks Pike (233-43030), 10mi. north of I-75. Great camping plus laundry, showers, tennis, basketball and volleyball courts, swimming pool, and a free shuttle to the KY Horse Park and Museum next door (see Horses and Seasonal Events). Wide open tent sites, but the 200 RV sites have a good mix of shade and lawn. 2-wk. max stay. Sites $11, with hookup $15. Senior discounts available.

FOOD AND NIGHTLIFE

Ramsey's, 496 E. High St. (259-2708). Real Southern grease. Vegetarians beware: even the vegetables are cooked with pork parts, though the menu *is* newly sensitive to veggies' needs. 1 meat and 3 vegetables $8.50; 4 vegetable dishes $5.75. Sandwiches under $5. Open Sun.-Mon. 11am-11pm, Tues.-Sat. 11am-1pm.

Alfalfa Restaurant, 557 S. Limestone St. (253-0014), across from Memorial Hall at the university; take bus #9. Menu of fantastic international and veggie meals changes nightly. Complete dinners with salad and bread under $10. Filling soups and salads from $2. Live jazz, folk, etc. Fri.-Sat. 8-10pm; no cover. Open for lunch Mon.-Fri. 11am-2pm and 3-5:30pm, Sat.-Sun. 10am-2pm. Dinner Tues.-Thurs. 5:30-9pm, Fri.-Sat. 5:30-10pm.

Parkette Drive-In, 1216 New Circle Rd. (254-8723). Drive-up, 50s-style eatery with bargain food, but no rollerskating waitresses. Giant "Poor Boy" burger plate $2.50; chicken box with 3 pieces, gravy, fries, cole slaw, and roll $4.10. A few booths inside give carless folks an equal opportunity to join in the nostalgia. Open Mon.-Thurs. 11am-11pm, Fri.-Sat. 11am-1am.

Everybody's Natural Foods and Deli, 503 Euclid Ave. (255-4162). A pleasant health-food store which sets out a few tables and serves excellent gazpacho, sandwiches ($2.75-3.65), and a daily lunch special ($4.75). Veggie delight $3.65; fruit smoothies $2.75. Open Mon.-Fri. 8am-8pm, Sun. noon-5pm.

Lexington's nightlife surpasses most expectations for a town its size. For current entertainment info, read the "Weekender" section of Friday's *Herald-Leader.* **Sundance** and **The Brewery,** both at 509 W. Main St. (255-2822), provide a lively country and western bar and music scene (both open daily 8am-1am). Stand-up comics do their thing at **Comedy off Broadway,** 3199 Nicholsville Rd. (271-5653), at Lexington Green Mall (call for details). **The Bar,** 224 E. Main St. (255-1551), a popular disco cabaret/lounge complex, caters to gays and lesbians. (Cover Fri. $4, Sat. $5. Must be 21. Lounge open Mon.-Sat. 4pm-1am; disco open Mon.-Thurs. 10pm-1am, Fri. 10pm-2am, Sat. 10pm-3:30am.) **The Wrocklage,** 361 W. Short St. (231-7655), stages alternative and punk rock, and even some all-ages shows. For a bit o' the Irish, stop in at **Lynagh's Pub** and **Club** (259-9944), in University Plaza at Woodland and Euclid St. The pub offers superior burgers ($4.35; open Mon.-Sat. 11am-1am, Sun. noon-11pm), while the club has music next door (cover from $3; open Tues.-Sat. 8pm-1am). Meet the university's frat and sorority set at **Two Keys Tavern,** 333 S. Limestone (254-5000), where there's comedy on Tuesday and bands Wednesday through Saturday (open Mon.-Sat. 11am-1am, Sun. 11am-11pm).

SIGHTS

To escape the stifling swamp conditions farther south, antebellum plantation owners built beautiful summer retreats in milder Lexington. The most attractive of these stately houses preen only a few blocks northeast of the town center in the **Gratz Park** area near the old public library. Wrap-around porches, wooden minarets, stone foundations, and rose-covered trellises distinguish these old estates from the neighborhood's newer homes. The **Hunt Morgan House,** 201 N. Mill St. (253-0362), stands at the end of the park across from the old library. Built in 1814 by John Wesley Hunt, the first millionaire west of the Alleghenies, the house witnessed the birth of Thomas Hunt Morgan, who won a 1933 Nobel Prize for proving the existence of the gene. The house's most colorful inhabitant, however, was Confederate General John Hunt Morgan who, pursued by Union troops, rode his horse up the front steps and into the house, leaned down to kiss his mother, and rode out the back door. (Tours Tues.-Sat. 10am-4pm, Sun. 2-5pm. $5, under 12 $2.) Ironically, Mary Todd, the future wife of Abraham Lincoln, grew up just five blocks away in the **Mary Todd Lincoln House,** 578 W. Main St. (233-9999); you can see the house on a one-hour tour (open April-Dec. 15 Tues.-Sat. 10am-4pm; last tour 3:15pm; $4, ages 6-12 $2). Senator Henry Clay and John Hunt Morgan now lie buried at the **Lexington Cemetery,** 833 W. Main St. (255-5522; open daily 8am-5pm; free). During his lifetime, Clay resided at **Ashland,** 120 Sycamore Rd. (266-8581), a 20-acre estate across town at the corner of Sycamore and Richmond Rd.; take the "Woodhall" bus. (Open Tues.-Sat. 10am-4:30pm, Sun. 1-4:30pm. 1-hr. tours $5, students $3, ages 6-12 $2.)

In Victorian Sq. on the west side of downtown, the **Lexington Children's Museum,** 401 W. Main St. (258-3255), puts kids in a variety of simulated contexts for fun and covert education. (Open Mon.-Fri. 10am-6pm, Sat. 10am-5pm, Sun. 1-5pm; early Sept.-late May closed Mon. Kids 2-17 $2, grown-ups $3, seniors $2.)

The **University of Kentucky** (257-3595) gives free campus tours in a double-decker bus called "Old Blue" (Mon.-Fri. 12:15pm; walking tours Mon.-Fri. 10am and 2pm). The university specializes in architecture and (surprise!) equine medicine.

HORSES

Lexington horse farms are among the most beautiful places on earth. Visit the home of 1977 Triple Crown winner Seattle Slew, **Three Chimneys Farm** (873-7053), at Rte. 1 and Old Frankfort Pike 4 mi. from I-64 and 8½ mi. from New Circle Rd. (tours daily 10am and 1pm, by appointment only). **Kentucky Horse Park,** 4089 Ironworks Pike (233-4303), 10 mi. north at exit 120 off I-75, has full facilities for equestrians, a museum, a film, and the Man O' War Monument, and rates a visit despite the touristy herds. (Open daily 9am-5pm. $10, ages 7-12 $5; live horse shows and horse-drawn vehicle tours included.) For one weekend in early June, thousands flock to the park for the **Festival of the Bluegrass** (846-4995). Every April, the **Keeneland Race Track,** 4201 Versailles Rd. (254-3412 or 800-456-3412), west on U.S. 60, holds the final prep race for the Kentucky Derby (races Oct. and April; post time 1pm; $2.50; workouts open to the public). At **Red Mile Harness Track,** 847 S. Broadway (255-0752; take bus #3 on S. Broadway), the crowds run the gamut from wholesome families to seasoned gamblers. (Races April-June and late Sept.-early Oct.; in spring post time 7:30pm, in fall 1pm. $3; programs $2; parking free. Morning workouts 7:30am-noon; open to the public in racing season.) The **Lexington Junior League Horse Show** (252-1893), the largest outdoor show in the nation, unfolds its pageantry at the Red Mile during the week of July 14-21 in 1996.

■ NEAR LEXINGTON

The Shakers, a 19th-century celibate religious sect, practiced the simple life at **Shaker Village** (734-5411), about 25 mi. southwest of Lexington and north of Harrodsburg on U.S. 68. The 5000-acre farm features 27 restored Shaker buildings; a tour includes demonstrations of everything from making apple butter to coopering (barrel-making). Riverboat excursions on the Kentucky River can be added into the deal. (Open daily 9am-6pm. $8.50, students 12-17 $4, ages 6-11 $2; with river trip $14/$7.50/$5.50. Oct.-Mar. reduced hours and prices.)

Harrodsburg, the oldest permanent English settlement west of the Alleghenies, nestles 32 mi. southwest of Lexington on U.S. 68. Relive the legacy of Fort Harrod, founded in 1774, at **Old Fort Harrod State Park,** S. College St., P.O. Box 156 (734-3314), an active replica in which craftspeople clothed in 18th-century garb demonstrate skills like blacksmithing and quilting. (Open 8:30am-5:30pm; off season 8am-4:30pm. $3.50, ages 6-12 $2. Mid-June to Aug. the fort itself stays open until 8pm.) Pick up a tour booklet for historic downtown Harrodsburg at the **visitors center** (606-734-2364), on the corner of U.S. 68 and Main (open Mon.-Fri. 8:30am-4:30pm).

In **Richmond,** exit 95 off I-75, the elegant Georgian/Italianate mansion **White Hall** (623-9178) was the home of the abolitionist (not the boxer) Cassius M. Clay, cousin of Senator Henry Clay. (45-min. guided tours only. Open April-Oct. daily 9am-4:30pm; Labor Day-Oct. Wed.-Sun. only; open briefly in winter for Christmas celebration. $3, under 13 $2.50, under 6 free.) A re-creation of one of Daniel Boone's forts, **Fort Boonesborough State Park** (527-3131), also in Richmond, has samples of 18th-century crafts, a small museum collection, and films about the pioneers. (Open April-Aug. daily 9am-5:30pm; Sept.-Oct. Wed.-Sun. 9am-5:30pm. $4, ages 6-12 $2.50, under 6 free. Combination White Hall/Boonesborough tickets available.)

THE SOUTH

■■■ DANIEL BOONE NATIONAL FOREST

The **Daniel Boone National Forest** cuts a vast green swath through Kentucky's Eastern Highlands. Enclosing 670,000 acres of mountains and valleys, the forest is layered with a gorgeous tangle of chestnut, oak, hemlock, and pine, as well as pristine lakes, waterfalls, and extraordinary natural bridges. This is Bluegrass country, where seasoned backpackers and Lexington's day-trippers still find the heart of old Appalachia deep in the forest—though, by some reports, you're less likely these days to stumble onto feuding Hatfields and McCoys than into some farmer's hidden field of marijuana, reputedly Kentucky's #1 cash crop.

Practical Information Seven U.S. Forest Service Ranger Districts administer the National Forest. Ranger offices in each district offer help, brochures, and trail maps for the regions, including info on which portions of the 254-mi. **Sheltowee Trace,** the forest's most significant trail, pass through their districts. **Stanton Ranger District,** 705 W. College Ave., Stanton (663-2852), includes the Red River Gorge and Natural Bridge. To the north, **Morehead Ranger District,** 2375 KY 801 S. (784-5624), includes Cave Run Lake; for tourist info, contact the **Morehead Tourism Commission,** 168 E. Main St., Morehead 40351 (784-6221). To the south, **London Ranger District** (864-4163 or 864-4164), with an office on U.S. 25S, covers Laurel River Lake, close to **Cumberland Falls;** Laurel River Lake's **visitors center** (878-6900 or 800-348-0095) is at exit 41 off I-75 (open Mon-Sat. 9am-5pm). For forest-wide info contact the Forest Supervisor, 1700 Bypass Rd., Winchester 40391 (745-3100). **Greyhound** (800-231-2222) serves several towns in the Forest with buses to and from Lexington, KY: Morehead, on Rte. 32 at Pine Crest Lane (1 per day, 1hr., $16); London, at the London Shopping Center by Wal-Mart (3 per day, 1½hr., $17); Corbin, off Rte. 25E and Rte. 77 at exit 29 off I-75 (4 per day, 2hr., $19). **Emergency:** 911. **Area code:** 606.

Stanton Ranger District **Natural Bridge,** off Rte. 11, is the area's absolute must-see site. It takes a hike through the forest to reach the bridge, but the expansive view which awaits at the top of the bridge's vast span proves more than enough. The **Red River Gorge** area contains some of the most varied and ecologically rich terrain in this part of the country, as well as the sandstone cliffs and rock bridges immortalized in song and square dance. From Slade, a drive around the loop of scenic Rte. 715 shows off the area to its best advantage. The circuit runs through the single-lane **Nada Tunnel,** an old railroad tunnel cut directly through the rock (scary as hell!), and past the restored **Gladie Historic Site Log House,** which illuminates turn-of-the-century rural logging life. Along the way, it takes in buffalo, curving mountain roads, forests, and picturesque wooden and metal bridges. If you don't mind driving down a 3-mi. gravel road, make a stop at the beautiful **Rock Bridge,** down Rock Bridge Rd. near the junction of Rte. 715 and Rte. 15, the only natural bridge in this area with water flowing beneath it. Route 715 also provides access to the protected 13,300-acre **Clifty Wilderness,** but no motor vehicles, motorized equipment, or bicycles are permitted.

Slade, 52 mi. southeast of Lexington (take I-64 to Mountain Pkwy.), makes a good base for a tour of this portion of the forest. A red **tourist caboose** run by the **Natural Bridge/Powell County Chamber of Commerce** (663-9229) sits at the Slade exit off Mountain Pkwy. The town itself contains almost nothing except the forest and the lavish **Natural Bridge State Resort Park,** 2135 Natural Bridge Rd. (663-2214 or 800-325-1710), off Rte. 11. Avoid the park's pricey lodge, and patronize its **campgrounds: Whittletown,** with 40 well-shaded sites; and **Middle Fork,** with 39 more-open sites. (Sites for 2 with hookup $12; $1 per additional adult, under 17 free. Primitive camping $8.50.) Off Rte. 15, **Koomer Ridge** offers wooded primitive camping (sites $6, double sites $10). You can also pitch a tent anywhere in the forest, as long as you stay more than 300 ft. from roads or marked trails; use common sense. Those who prefer the great indoors should lay down their burdens in one of the large, clean, dimly-lit rooms at **Lil Abners** (663-5384), 2½ mi. from Red River Gorge on Rte. 11 in Slade (singles $44, doubles $49).

While wandering this part of the state, be sure to try **Ale-8-1** ("A Late One"), the local soft drink in the tall green bottle and the regional staple of soup beans and cornbread. Good restaurants are hard to come by, but many **general stores** peddle cheap, filling sandwiches; the particularly well-stocked **Pine Ridge General Store,** 6023 Rte. 15 (668-3498), near the Koomer Ridge campground, has ham & cheese sandwiches ($1.85) and 12" pizzas ($7; open Sun.-Thurs. 8am-10pm, Fri.-Sat. 8am-midnight). In nearby Stanton, **Bruen's Restaurant,** on Sipple St. at exit 22 off Mountain Pkwy., makes fine greasy spoon fare in an authentic down-home atmosphere. Breakfast is served all day; have two eggs, bacon, and a biscuit with gravy for just $2.55. (Cheeseburger $1.50. Open Sun.-Thurs. 4:30am-9pm, Fri.-Sat. 4:30am-10pm).

London Ranger District For boating, fishing, hiking, and just plain hanging out, try **Laurel River Lake. Camping** is available at two spacious and densely wooded Forest Service campgrounds on the lake, both off Rte. 1193 and adjacent to marinas: **Grove** (528-6156), with 52 sites; and **Holly Bay** (878-8134), with 90 sites (all sites have hookups; sites for 6 $12, for 12 $18). Visitors to giant **Cumberland Falls,** 18 mi. west of Corbin on Rte. 90—"The Niagara of the South"—camp at the state park which surrounds the falls (528-4121; 50 sites with hookup $8.50; open Apr.-Oct.). If you stay, check out the falls' famous moonbows. **Sheltowee Trace Outfitters** (800-541-RAFT/7238), in Parker's Lake behind Holiday Motor Lodge at Hwy. 90, 1 mi. west of the state park, arranges guided, six-hour whitewater rafting trips down the area's Class III rapids ($40, ages 5-12 $30). Unguided canoe trips ($20 per person) and the 30-minute **Rainbow Mist** boat trip to the falls provide less harrowing options (Rainbow Mist early July-Labor Day Fri.-Sun. 10am-6pm; $4, under 13 $3).

■■■ CUMBERLAND GAP

Stretching from Maine to Georgia, the majestic Appalachian Mountain Range proved a formidable obstacle to the movement of early American settlers, but not to buffalo; by following herds of buffalo, Native Americans learned of the Cumberland Gap, a natural break in the mountains which allows passage to the west. Frontiersman Daniel Boone became famous when he blazed the Wilderness Trail through the Gap in 1775, thereby opening the west to colonization. Today, the **Cumberland Gap National Historic Park,** best reached by U.S. 25E from Kentucky or U.S. 58 from Virginia, sits on 20,000 acres shared by Kentucky, Virginia, and Tennessee. The Cumberland Gap **visitors center** (606-248-2817), on U.S. 25E in Middleboro, KY, presents displays, a film, and a brief slide presentation on the history of the Gap. (Park and center open daily 8am-6pm; Labor Day-Memorial Day Mon.-Fri. 9am-5pm.) The Park's 160-site **campground,** on U.S. 58 in Virginia, almost never fills (hot showers; primitive sites $8). Backcountry camping requires a free permit from the visitors center. For more information on the park, contact the Superintendent, Cumberland Gap National Historic Park, Box 1848, Middleboro, KY 40965.

Tennessee

THE SOUTH

Sloping from the majestic Great Smoky Mountains to the verdant Mississippi lowlands, Tennessee makes and breaks stereotypes with the smooth ease of a Jack Daniels. The last state to secede from the Union and the first to rejoin, Tennessee is noticeably free of the antebellum plantations that blanket the other Southern states. Industry—commercial machinery, chemicals, electronics, and the world's largest Bible-producing business—not agriculture, drives this economy. Meanwhile, music fuels the state's artistic life; country-western twangs from Nashville, while the blues wail out in Memphis.

PRACTICAL INFORMATION

Capital: Nashville.

Visitor Information: Tennessee Dept. of Tourist Development, P.O. Box 23170, Nashville 37202 (741-2158). Open Mon.-Fri. 8am-4:30pm. **Tennessee State Parks Information,** 401 Church St., L & N Tower, 7th floor, Nashville 37243 (800-421-6683).

Time Zones: Eastern and Central (1hr. behind Eastern); *Let's Go* makes note of areas which lie in Central. **Postal Abbreviation:** TN

Sales Tax: 7.75-9%, by county.

■■■ NASHVILLE

Long-forgotten Francis Nash is one of only four Revolutionary War heroes honored with U.S. city names (Washington, Wayne, and Knox are the others), but his tenuous foothold in history pales in comparison to Nashville's notoriety as the banjo pickin', foot stompin' capital of country music. Large, eclectic, and unapologetically heterogeneous, Tennessee's capital is not only the home of the Country Music Hall of Fame, but also a slick financial hub ("the Wall Street of the South"). The city also headquarters the Southern Baptists and finds room for centers of fine arts and higher learning such as Fisk University and Vanderbilt.

PRACTICAL INFORMATION

Tourist Office: Nashville Area Convention and Visitors Bureau, 161 4th Ave. N. (259-4700), between Commerce and Church St. downtown. Ask for the free *Music City Vacation Guide*. Information booth in main lobby open Mon.-Fri. 8am-5pm. **Nashville Tourist Information Center** (259-4747), I-65 at exit 85, James Robertson Pkwy., ½mi. east of the capitol just over the bridge; take bus #3 "Meridian" east on Broadway. Complete maps marked with attractions. Open daily 8am-8pm. **Gay and Lesbian Switchboard,** 297-0008. Opens nightly 5pm.

Airport: Metropolitan (275-1675), 8mi. south of downtown. Bus fare downtown totals $1.40 with a transfer. An airport shuttle (275-1180) operates out of major downtown hotels ($8, $15 round-trip). Taxis downtown run $15-17.

Buses: Greyhound, 200 8th Ave. S. (255-1691 or 800-231-2222), at Broadway downtown. Borders on a rough and rowdy neighborhood, but the station is bright. To: Memphis (6 per day, 4-5hr., $30); Chattanooga (6 per day, 3hr., $21); Birmingham (5 per day, 3½hr., $30); Knoxville (6 per day, 3hr., $33); Louisville (10 per day, 3½hr., $33). Open 24 hrs.

Public Transportation: Metropolitan Transit Authority (MTA) (862-5950). Buses operate Mon.-Fri. 5am-midnight, less frequent service Sat.-Sun. Fare $1.30, transfers 10¢. MTA runs 2 **tourist trolleys** from Riverfront Park and Downtown Circle daily every 10-15min. 11am to early evening (90¢).

Taxis: Nashville Cab, 242-7070. 90¢ base fare, $1.50 per mi. 24 hrs.

Car Rental: Alamo Rent-A-Car (800-327-9633), at the airport. $36 per day, on weekends $16 per day. Under 25 surcharge $20 per day.

Crisis Lines: Crisis Line, 244-7444. **Rape Hotline,** 256-8526. Both 24 hrs.

Emergency: 911.

Post Office: 901 Broadway (255-9447 or 255-9451), across from the Park Plaza Hotel and next to Union Station. Open Mon.-Fri. 7:30am-7pm, Sat. 9am-2pm. **ZIP code:** 37202. **Area code:** 615.

Nashville's streets are fickle, often interrupted by curving parkways and one-ways. Names change constantly and without warning; **Broadway,** the main east-west thoroughfare, melts into **West End Ave.** just outside downtown at Vanderbilt and I-40, and later becomes **Hillsboro Pike.** Downtown, numbered avenues run north-south, parallel to the Cumberland River. The curve of **James Robertson Pkwy.** encloses the north end, becoming **Main St.** on the other side of the river (later **Gallatin Pike**) and **McGavock St.** at the south end. The area south of Broadway between 2nd and 7th Ave. and the region north of James Robertson Pkwy. are both unsafe at night.

ACCOMMODATIONS AND CAMPING

Finding a room in Nashville isn't difficult, just expensive. Make reservations well in advance, especially for weekend stays (which take an even bigger toll on the wallet). Budget motels concentrate around **W. Trinity Ln.** and **Brick Church Pike,** off I-65 at exit 87B. Dirt-cheap hotels inhabit the area around **Dickerson Rd.** and **Murfreesboro,** but the neighborhood is seedy at best. Closer to downtown (but still seedy), several motels huddle on **Interstate Dr.** just over the Woodland St. Bridge.

The Cumberland Inn, 150 W. Trinity Ln., (226-1600), exit 87A off I-65N north of downtown. Cheerful rooms with bright, modern furnishings, HBO, laundry facilities, and a free continental breakfast. Unlimited local calls $1 per day. No pets. Singles $30, doubles $38; Fri.-Sat. $35/$48.

Hallmark Inn, 309 W. Trinity Ln. (800-251-3294). Comfortable, well-kept rooms, with cable TV, free continental breakfast, and a pool. Singles $28-38, doubles $38-58. Another location on Dickerson Rd. (356-6005).

Motel 6, 4 locations. 311 W. Trinity Ln. (227-9696), at exit 87B off I-65; 323 Cartwright St., Goodlettsville (859-9674), off Long Hollow Pike west from I-65; 95 Wallace Rd. (333-9933), off exit 56 from I-24; 420 Metroplex Dr. (833-8887), near the airport. Decent rooms with stall showers, HBO, outdoor pool, free local calls. Singles $30, doubles $34. Under 18 free with parents. Wallace and Metroplex locations are slightly ritzier and more expensive.

The Liberty Inn, 2400 Brick Church Pike (228-2567). Stall showers only. Singles $30, doubles $42; Fri.-Sat. $42/nonexistent—no, we don't understand either.

Two campgrounds lie within the range of public transportation near Opryland USA; by car, take Briley Pkwy. north to McGavock Pike and exit west onto Music Valley Dr. **Nashville Holiday Travel Park,** 2572 Music Valley Dr. (889-4225), provides a wooded area for tenting and densely packed RV sites (sites for 2 $16, with hookup $25; $4 per additional person over age 11). **Opryland KOA,** 2626 Music Valley Dr. (889-0282), has 50 tent sites ($18) and tons of crowded sites with hookups ($29); perks include a pool and live summer music. To leave the achy breaky crowds behind, camp 25 min. north of Opryland at the nice **Nashville KOA,** 708 N. Dickerson Rd., Goodlettsville (859-0075), on exit 97 off I-65 (sites $15, with hookup $18).

FOOD

In Nashville, music even influences the local delicacies; pick up a Goo-Goo Cluster (peanuts, pecans, chocolate, caramel, and marshmallow), sold at practically any store, and you'll bite into the initials of the Grand Ole Opry. Nashville's other finger-lickin' traditions, barbecue or fried chicken followed by pecan pie, are no less sinful. Restaurants for collegiate tastes and budgets cram West End Ave. and the 2000 block of Elliston Pl., near Vanderbilt.

Slice of Life, 1811 Division St. (329-2525), next to music studios. Hang out with country musicians and celebs (visitors include ZZ Top and Lily Tomlin) in this cool yuppie hangout. Features fresh bread, wholesome Tex-Mex, and macrobiotic foods like 16-bean gumbo. Dinner entrees $7-11; lunches $5-7. Giant cookies and muffins ($1.25) steam in the bakery. Open Mon. 7am-4pm, Tues.-Thurs. 7am-9pm, Fri. 7am-10pm, Sat. 8am-10pm, Sun. 8am-4pm.

Calypso, 2424 Elliston Pl. (321-3878), near Vanderbilt, also at 4910 Thoroughbred, Brentwood (370-8033). Lively, fresh, and easy on the pocket. Tasty Caribbean food: Jamaican chicken $5; corn and coconut muffins $1.35. Open Mon.-Thurs. and Sat. 11am-9pm, Fri. 11am-10pm, Sun. noon-8pm.

Iguana, 1910 Belcourt (383-8920). Iguana does it right—good food, great service, and *the best* chicken fajitas, hands-down, no questions asked ($10). Young crowd, outdoor deck. Open Mon.-Fri. 11am-2am, Sat.-Sun. 5pm-2am.

The World's End, 1713 Church St. (329-3480). It's the end of the world as we know it, and I feel like a burger or a salad ($5-8), or maybe a beer ($2.50). Huge, airy gay restaurant and bar. Open Sun.-Thurs. 4pm-12:30am, Fri.-Sat. 4pm-1:30am.

International Market, 2010-B Belmont Blvd. (297-4453). This Asian grocery and its large Thai buffet (each dish $1.50) get crowded at lunch. Pad Thai $4.50. Open daily 10:30am-9pm.

SIGHTS

Music Row, home of Nashville's signature industry, centers around Division and Demonbreun St. from 16th to 19th Ave. S., bounded to the south by Grand Ave. (take bus #3 to 17th Ave. and walk south). After surviving the mobs outside the must-see **Country Music Hall of Fame,** 4 Music Sq. E. (256-1639), at Division St., you can marvel at classic memorabilia such as Elvis's "solid gold" Cadillac and 24-karat gold piano, evocative photos from the early days of country music, and aggressively colored costumes from more recent performances. Though Tennessee is the birthplace of bluegrass, the Hall of Fame shows off Cajun, cowboy, western-swing, and honky-tonk styles of country music as well. Admission includes a tour of RCA's historic **Studio B,** where stars like Dolly Parton and Chet Atkins—not to mention The King—recorded their first hits. (Hall of Fame open Mon.-Sat. 8am-6pm, Sun. 9am-5pm. $8, ages 6-16 $3, under 6 free.) When you get inspired enough to record your own hit, the **Recording Studio of America,** 1510 Division St. (254-1282), underneath the **Barbara Mandrell Country Museum,** lets you karaoke and record popular country and pop tunes with 24-track backgrounds (open Sun.-Thurs. 9am-6pm, Fri.-Sat. 9am-8pm; audio $15, video $25). See Elvis' evergreen Cadillac and special exhibit cars like the Batmobile at **World Famous Car Collectors' Hall of Fame,** 1534 Demonbreun St. (255-6804; open daily 8am-9pm; $5, ages 4-11 $3.25).

Nashville's pride and joy awaits in **Centennial Park,** a 15-minute walk west along West End Ave. from Music Row. The "Athens of the South" boasts a full-scale replica of the **Parthenon** (862-8431), complete with a towering Athena surrounded by her fellow Olympians. Originally built as a temporary exhibit for the Tennessee Centennial in 1897, the Parthenon met with such Olympian success that the model was rebuilt to last. The Nashville Parthenon also houses the **Cowan Collection of American Paintings** in its first floor galleries, a refreshing but erratic selection of 19th- and early 20th-century American art. (Open Tues.-Sat. 9am-4:30pm, Sun. 12:30-4pm. $2.50, seniors and kids $1.25, under 4 free.) But soft! what light on yonder Parthenon steps breaks? It's **Shakespeare-in-the-Park,** performed in mid-July and August. The **Upper Room Chapel Museum,** 1908 Grand Ave. (340-7207), also in the park area off 21st Ave. S., houses a spectacular 20-ft. floor-to-ceiling stained glass window with over 9000 pieces of glass (open Mon.-Fri. 8am-4:30pm; free, but $2 contribution recommended).

A downtown stroll reveals more of Nashville's eclectic architecture. **Union Station Hotel,** 1001 Broadway (726-1001), next to the post office, displays a full stained-glass arched ceiling and evokes the glamour of turn-of-the-century railroad travel with old-time schedules and clocks. **Ryman Auditorium,** a.k.a. "the Mother Church of Country Music," 116 5th Ave. N. (254-1445), off Broadway at 5th, housed a tabernacle and the Grand Ole Opry in previous incarnations (tours daily 8:30am-4pm; $5, ages 4-11 $2). Up 2nd Ave. from Broadway, the **Market St.** area, now gentrified with restaurants and nightspots, features the cast-iron and masonry façades of handsome late 19th-century commercial buildings.

The **Tennessee State Capitol** (741-0830), a comely Greek Revival structure atop the hill on Charlotte Ave. next to downtown, offers, among other things, free guided tours of the tomb of James Knox Polk (tours hourly Mon.-Fri. 9-11am and 1-3pm). Across the street, the **Tennessee State Museum,** 505 Deaderick (741-2692), depicts the history of Tennessee from the early Native American era to the time of "overlander" pioneers; imaginative and interactive displays enhance the sometimes whitewashed version of Tennessee history. A new War Memorial Building recounts America's wartime history from the Spanish-American War through World War II. (Open Tues.-Sat. 10am-5pm, Sun. 1-5pm. Free.)

The **Museum of Tobacco Art and History,** 800 Harrison St. (271-2349), off 8th Ave., pays tribute to Tennessee's most important crop. From a dual-purpose Indian pipe/tomahawk (a slow and a quick way to death) to giant glass-blown pipes, the museum's exhibits expound upon the unexpectedly captivating history of tobacco, pipes, and cigars. (Open Mon.-Sat. 9am-4pm. Free.)

Fisk University's **Van Vechten Gallery** (329-8543), at the corner of Jackson St. and D.B. Todd Blvd. off Jefferson St., exhibits a small but distinguished collection of art by Picasso, Renoir, and Cezanne among others. The gallery also displays African sculpture and many works by Alfred Steiglitz and Georgia O'Keeffe. (Open Tues.-Fri. 10am-5pm, Sat.-Sun. 1-5pm. Free, but donations accepted.)

If you tire of the downtown area, rest at the **Cheekwood Museum of Art** and **Tennessee Botanical Gardens** (356-8000), 7 mi. southwest of town on Forest Park Dr.; take bus #3 ("West End/Belle Meade") from downtown to Belle Meade Blvd. and Page Rd. The leisurely, well-kept Japanese rose and English-style gardens are a welcome change from Nashville glitz. (Open Mon.-Sat. 9am-5pm, Sun. noon-5pm. $5, students and seniors $4, ages 6-17 $2, under 6 free. Tea daily 3-5pm; $6.50.) The nearby **Belle Meade Mansion,** 5025 Harding Rd. (356-0501), dubbed "The Queen of Tennessee Plantations," offers a second respite. This 1853 plantation has the works: gorgeous grounds, smokehouse, dollhouse, and dairy (most buildings open to tours). Belle Meade was also the site of the nation's first thoroughbred and Tennessee walking-horse breeding farm. (Two great tours per hr., led by guides in period costume; last tour 4pm. Open Mon.-Sat. 9am-5pm, Sun. 1-5pm. $6, ages 6-12 $2.)

Andrew Jackson's beautiful manor house, the **Hermitage,** 4580 Rachel's Ln. (889-2941), off exit 221 from I-40, sits atop 625 gloriously shaded acres 13 mi. from downtown Nashville. Admission includes a terrific 15-min. film, a museum, access to the house and grounds, and a visit to nearby Tulip Grove Mansion and church. Allow yourself 1½ to two hours for the whole shebang; it's worth it. One of the city's more popular attractions, the Hermitage gets crowded in the summer. (Open daily 9am-5pm. $7.50, seniors $6.50, kids 6-12 $4.)

ENTERTAINMENT AND NIGHTLIFE

Opryland USA, 2808 Opryland Dr., Rm. 4787, Nashville 37214 (889-6611 for info), exit 11 off Briley Pkwy., cross-pollinates Las Vegas schmaltz and Disneyland purity (or maybe vice versa) with the best in country music thrown in the middle. This amusement park contains all the requisite family attractions, from the outlandish new Hangman roller coaster to a state fair midway, but the music sets it apart: Opryland stages a dozen slickly produced live music spectaculars daily. Tune your radio to 580AM for more info. (Open April-May Sat.-Sun.; May-early Oct. daily; call for changing hours. $28, ages 4-11 $18; 2 days $38. Celebrity concert series $15-22.) The **Grand Ole Opry,** setting for America's longest-running radio show, moved here from the town center in 1976. *The* place to hear country music, the Opry howls every Friday and Saturday night ($16.50); matinees are held on various days during peak tourist season (April-Oct. Tues. and Thurs. 3pm; $14.50). Call or write to Opryland for reservations. Check the Friday *Tennessean* for a list of performers.

Set aside the first weekend in June for the outdoor **Summer Lights** downtown, when top rock, jazz, reggae, classical, and (of course) country performers all jam simultaneously (performances Mon.-Thurs. 4pm-12:30am). For information on **Nashville Symphony** tickets and performances, call Ticketmaster (741-2787).

Whether it's a corner honky-tonk joint or the Grand Ole Opry, Nashville offers a wealth of opportunities to hear country and western, jazz, rock, bluegrass, and folk. The Nashville *Key,* available at the chamber of commerce, opens many entertainment doors. Comprehensive listings for all live music and events in the area can be found in free copies of *Nashville Scene,* or in the Thursday or Friday *Tennessean*. Pick up *Bone* for more music info, and *Q (Query)* for gay and lesbian news and listings. Muse over these publications plus many more at **Moskós,** 2204-B Elliston Place (327-2658), a newsstand and muncheonette (sandwiches $4-5.25; open Mon.-Fri. 7am-midnight, Sat. 8am-midnight, Sun. 8:30am-midnight).

Blue Bird Café, 4104 Hillsboro Rd. (383-1461), in Green Hills. This famous bird sings original country, blues, and folk; Garth Brooks got his start here. Women traveling solo will feel safe in this mellow, clean-cut establishment. Dinners of salads and sandwiches ($4-6.50) until 11pm. Early shows 7pm; cover begins around 9:30pm ($4-7). Open Mon.-Sat. 5:30pm-1am, Sun. 6pm-midnight.

Tootsie's Orchid Lounge, 422 Broadway (726-0463). For years, owner Tootsie Bess lent money to struggling musicians until they shot to stardom on the Grand Ole Opry. These days, the Lounge still has good C&W music and affordable drinks (domestic beer $2.25). Women should think twice about braving the sometimes rowdy bar alone at night. Open Mon.-Sat. 9:30am-3am, Sun. noon-3am.

Lucy's Record Shop, 1707 Church St. (321-0882), vends wicked vinyl during the day to the same young crowd that shows up for indie, national, and local shows at night. Cover $5. All ages welcome.

Station Inn, 402 12th Ave. S. (255-3307). World-renowned bluegrass. Music starts 9pm. Cover $4-6. Open Tues.-Sun. 7pm-late. Free Sun. night open jam session.

Ace of Clubs, 114 2nd Ave. S. (254-2237), in a huge downtown warehouse. Packs 'em in Mon.-Thurs. for live blues and rock, Fri.-Sat for retro and disco. Cover after 9pm $5. The party really starts after 11pm, and lasts til 2:45am.

The Connection, 901 Cowen St. (726-8718). Nashville's top gay club, imported from—Louisville? Anyway, high-energy dance music! Open Wed.-Sun. 6pm-3am.

■■■ CHATTANOOGA

Chattanooga, a thriving city snuggled against the Tennessee River, cultivates more than its dominant choo-choo image. The city that began as a trading post in 1815 has kept its commercial tradition, evolving into a major factory outlet center. **Hunter Museum of Art,** 10 Bluff View (423-267-0968), houses the South's most complete American art collection alongside impressive traveling exhibits (open Tues.-Sat. 10am-4:30pm, Sun. 1-4:30pm; $5, students $3, seniors $4, ages 3-12 $2.50). The **riverwalk** pathway connects the museum to the **Tennessee Aquarium** (423-265-0695 or 800-322-3344), on Ross's Landing, one of the world's largest aquariums (2 living forests, 5 stories, 7000 animals), with a focus on freshwater life and regional rivers. (Open Mon.-Fri. 10am-6pm, Sat.-Sun. 10am-8pm; Oct.-April daily 10am-6pm. $9.75, ages 3-11 $5.25.) The **artsline** (756-2787) gives 24-hr. info on current cultural offerings.

A few miles outside Chattanooga the world's steepest passenger railway, the **Incline** ($7, ages 3-12 $4), takes passengers up a ridiculous 72.7-degree grade, to **Lookout Mountain,** where seven states can be seen on a clear day. Atop and around the mountain are several attractions, from the **Battles for Chattanooga Museum** (423-821-2812; open daily sunup to sundown; $4, children $2), to an **alpine slide** (423-825-5666; call for hours; $4.25, ages 7-12 $3.75). Also on Lookout Mountain, **Rock City Gardens** (706-820-2531), attracts families and hardcore aficionados of kitsch with subterranean black-lit gnome dioramas and Mother Goose theme areas built around several interesting rock formations. (Open daily 8am-sundown; Labor Day-Memorial Day 8:30am-sundown; $9, ages 3-12 $5.) Purchase tickets for all these sights at the space-age **visitors center,** 2 Broad St. (800-322-3344; open daily 8:30am-5:30pm), next to the Aquarium.

Budget motels congregate on the highways coming into the city and on **Broad St.** at the base of Lookout Mountain. **Holiday Trav-l-Park,** 2131 Mack Smith Rd. (423-891-9766), in Rossville ½ mi. off I-755 at the East Ridge exit, enlivens sites for tents and RVs with a Civil War theme (2-person site $12.50, with hookup $16.50). Two nearby lakes, Chickamauga and Nickajack, are equipped with **campgrounds.**

A **free shuttle** scuttles from the Chattanooga Choo Choo Holiday Inn to the Aquarium, with stops on every block. (Runs Mon.-Sat. 7am-9:45pm, Sun. 10am-8pm; off season hrs. shorter. Summer service to Lookout Mountain $1, children 50¢.)

■■■ GREAT SMOKY MOUNTAINS

The largest wilderness area in the eastern U.S., the **Great Smoky Mountains National Park** encompasses a half-million acres of gray-green Appalachian peaks bounded on either side by misty North Carolina and Tennessee valleys. This park welcomes more visitors per year than any other National Park. Bears, wild hogs, white-tailed deer, groundhogs, wild turkeys, and more than 1500 species of flowering plants make their homes here despite the human invasion. Whispering conifer forests line the mountain ridges at elevations of over 6000 ft. Rhododendrons burst into their full glory in June and July; by mid-October the sloping mountains become a giant crazy-quilt of color.

Practical Information Start any exploration of the area with a visit to one of the park's three visitors centers: **Sugarlands** (423-436-1200), on Newfound Gap Rd., 2 mi. south of Gatlinburg, TN, next to the park's headquarters; **Cades Cove** (423-436-1275), on Little River Rd. 7 mi. southwest of Townsend, TN, and 15 mi. southwest of Sugarland in the park's western valley; and **Oconaluftee Visitors Center** (704-497-1900), 4 mi. north of Cherokee, NC, which serves travelers entering the park from the Blue Ridge Parkway and all points south and east. The standard park service brochure provides the best driving map of the region. Be sure to ask for *The Smokies Guide,* a newspaper detailing the park's tours, lectures, activities and changing natural graces. All the visitors centers have the same hours (daily 8am-

7pm, Sept.-Nov. and March-April 8am-6pm; Dec.-Feb. 8am-4:30pm). The park's **information line** (423-436-1200; open daily 8:30am-4:30pm) links all three visitors centers. Park **emergency** can be reached at 423-436-1230.

Sleeping and Eating After a Long Day of Hiking Ten campgrounds lie scattered throughout the park, each with tent sites, limited trailer space, water, tables, and comfort stations (no showers or hookups). **Smokemont, Elkmont,** and **Cades Cove** accept reservations (sites $11); the rest are first come, first served (sites $6-11). In summer, RV drivers or those who wish to stay at one of the campgrounds near the main roads should reserve at least eight weeks in advance (800-365-2267).

Motels lining Rte. 441 and Rte. 321 decrease in price with distance from the park. Small motels also cluster in both **Cherokee** and **Gatlinburg.** Prices vary wildly depending on the season and the economy; in general, Cherokee motels are cheaper ($35+) and Gatlinburg motels are nicer ($45+); prices soar to even greater heights on weekends. But fear not, brave heart; two hostels service the park. **Smoky Mountain Ranch Camp (HI-AYH),** 3248 Manis Rd. (429-8563 or 800-851-6715), a perfectly terrific hostel, nestles in the mountains between Pigeon Forge and Cades Cove. Crash at the top of the hill in the comfortable hostel dorm with A/C and cable TV, or down below in the barn with a VCR and a kicking stereo; either way, savor hippie communal life in Tennessee comfort. ($13.25, nonmembers $15. Linen included.) Closer to Gatlinburg, **Bell's Wa-Floy Retreat,** 3610 East Pkwy. (423-436-5575), 10 mi. east of Gatlinburg on Rte. 321. From Gatlinburg proper, catch the east-bound trolley (25¢) to the end of the line; from there, hop, skip, or jump the 5 mi. to Wa-Floy. The lovely grounds of this Christian retreat community envelop a pool, tennis courts, meditation area, chapel, and bubbling brook. Friendly proprietor Mrs. Floy Bell recites poetry and rents spaces in dark apartment-style buildings. (Check-in before 10pm. HI-AYH members $10, nonmembers $12 first night, $8 each additional. Linens $1. Reservations required.) If you're on your way to North Carolina, Nantahala National Forest offers beds in Bryson City, NC (see p. 296).

Sights and Activities Over 900 mi. of hiking trails and 170 mi. of road meander through the park. Rangers at the visitors centers will help you devise a trip appropriate to your ability. Some of the most popular trails wind 5 mi. to **Rainbow Falls,** 4 mi. to **Chimney Tops,** and 2½ mi. to **Laurel Falls.** To hike off the marked trails, you'll need a free backcountry camping permit at a park visitors center. Wherever you go, bring water and DON'T FEED THE BEARS. For gorgeous scenery without the sweat, drive the 11-mi. **Cades Cove** loop, which circles the vestiges of a mountain community that occupied the area from the 1850s to the 1920s, before the park took over; a $1 guide is available at the entrance to the loop. In the summer, grist is ground at the 1876 **Mingus Mill,** on Newfound Gap Rd. 1 mi. north of the Oconaluftee visitors center. **Mountain Farm Museum,** right next to the Oconaluftee center, re-creates a turn-of-the-century settlement, including a blacksmith shop and a corncrib. (Both sights free and open visitors center's hours.)

Dollywood

A mythical American village created by Dolly Parton in the Tennessee hills, **Dollywood,** 1020 Dollywood Ln. (800-365-5996), dominates Pigeon Forge, celebrating the cultural legacy of the East Tennessee Mountains and the country songmistress herself (famous for some mountainous topography of her own). In Dolly's world, craftspeople demonstrate their skills and sell their wares, thirty rides offer thrills and chills, and and country favorites perform. While Dolly asserts that she wants to preserve the culture of the Tennessee Mountains, she alsos seems to want you to pay to come again: Dollywood's motto is "Create Memories Worth Repeating." Generally open May-Oct. 10am-6pm, but hours change constantly. Call for hours and special events like the Smoky Mountain Christmas. $24, over 59 $21, ages 4-11 $16.

■■■ KNOXVILLE

Settled as a frontier outpost in the years after the Revolution and named for Washington's Secretary of War Henry Knox, the former capital of Tennessee hosted the 1982 World's Fair (which attracted 10 million visitors) and continues to welcome the 26,000 students of the University of Tennessee. A pleasant day-trip away from the stunning Smoky Mountains Knoxville, hemmed by vast lakes created by the Tennessee Valley Authority, offers friendly, whistle-clean urbanity and hopping nightlife for city slickers looking for a taste of the outdoors.

Practical Information The downtown stretches north from the Tennessee River, bordered by **Henley St.,** and the **World's Fair Park,** to the west. The University of Tennessee, student hangouts, restaurants, bars, shopping, and sights, revolve around it. The highly visible **Sunsphere** within the park houses **Knoxville Visitor's Information,** 810 Clinch Ave. (523-2316; open Mon.-Fri. 8:30am-5pm). **Greyhound,** 100 Magnolia Ave. (522-5144 or 800-231-2222), at Central St., hightails to Nashville (3 per day, 2hr., $31), Chattanooga (3 per day, 2½hr., $19), and Lexington (4 per day, 3½hr., $38). Public transportation is provided by **KAT** (637-3000); buses run from 6:15am to 6:15pm or later, depending on day of the week and route (fare $1, transfers 20¢). Knoxville's main **post office:** 1237 E. Wisegarber Rd. (558-4502), at Middlebrook Pike (Mon.-Fri. 8am-4:30pm); **ZIP code:** 37950; **area code:** 423.

Accommodations, Food, and Nightlife Many not-quite-budget motels string along the interstates (I-75 and I-40) approaching the city. **Red Roof Inn North,** 5640 Merchants Center Blvd. (689-7100), at exit 108 off I-75, offers tidy, standard rooms with cable TV (singles $32, doubles $39). If **camping** is your game, head to **KOA North,** 908 E. Racoon Valley Rd. (947-9776), at exit 117 off I-75; closer to the city than most other campgrounds. (28 tent sites and plenty for RVs. $13, with hookup $15.75.)

Known for good parties and a little crime, **The Fort,** the set of numbered cross-streets west of World's Fair Park, houses the majority of students from the **University of Tennessee** (campus info 974-1000, Mon.-Fri. 7:45am-6pm). **The Strip,** the stretch of Cumberland Ave. separating The Fort from campus proper, offers student hangouts, bars, and restaurants. **Falafel Hut,** 601 15th St. (522-4963), the middle eastern brother of Jabba and a major center of collegiate hipsters, cooks a few blocks off The Strip; slobber over the lentil soup ($1.69) or a falafel sandwich ($2.55; open Mon.-Thurs. 9am-9pm, Fri.-Sat. 9am-10pm, Sun. 11am-9pm). **Longbranch Saloon,** 1848 Cumberland Ave. (546-9914), rustles up a casual, neighborhood-bar beer-pool-and-dark-wood-atmosphere (no chaps and spurs) and a mellow twentysomething crowd. Take a domestic bottle ($1.75) or draft ($1.25) out to the patio in nice weather. (Open daily 3pm-3am).

Market Sq., a popular pedestrian plaza to the east of World's Fair Park, offers restaurants, fountains, and shade. **Mercury Theater,** 28 Market Sq. (637-8634), hosts punkish and alternative bands. The other center of chowing, browsing, and carousing, **Old City,** spreads north up Central St. **Java,** 109½ S. Central St. (525-1600), in the middle of Old City, serves up steaming cups of you-know-what ($1.25, refills 25¢), slices of amazing cake ($3.50), and thick, funky atmosphere (open Sun.-Thurs. 8am-11pm, Fri.-Sat. 9am-1am). Two clubs duke it out for the title of Soul Central in Knoxville: **Bullfrog's,** 131 S. Central (673-0411), plays reggae, while **Lucille's,** 106 N. Central (546-3742), dishes out jazz. **The Underground,** 214 W. Jackson Ave. (525-3675), a dance club, houses the **Boiler Room,** an intimidating after-hours club that keeps things cooking until the wee hours. (Underground open Mon.-Wed. and Fri.-Sat. 10am-3am; Boiler open Sat.-Sun. mornings 1am-6am.) For goings-on around town, pick up a free *Metro Pulse.*

Sights Knoxville offers about a day's worth of sightseeing. **World's Fair Park** makes a fine stroll with a reflecting pool, grassy expanses, a playground, and more national flags than sands through the hourglass—so are the Days of our Lives. Within the park, the **Knoxville Museum of Art,** 1050 World's Fair Park Dr. (525-6101), houses changing exhibits of high caliber. (Open Tues.-Thurs. 10am-5pm, Fri. 10am-9pm, Sat. 10am-5pm, Sun. 11:30am-5pm. Most exhibits free.) **Blount Mansion,** 200 W. Hill (525-2375), a National Historic Landmark, was the 1792 frame house of governor William Blount (pronounced as if there were no "o"—as in "M. Poirot, it seems the victim was struck with a Blount object"). One-hour tours of the period-furnished home leave on the hour; last tour at 4pm. (Open Mar.-Oct. Tues.-Sat. 9:30am-5pm, Sun. 2-5pm; Nov.-Feb. Tues.-Fri. 9:30am-5pm. $4, ages 6-12 $2.) Nearby, the **James White Fort,** 205 E. Hill Ave. (525-6514), still preserves portions of the original stockade built in 1786 by Knoxville's first citizen and founder. (Must be seen on tour; tours run continuously until 3:30pm; open Mon.-Sat. 9:30am-4:30pm; $4, children $2.) The small **Museum of East Tennessee History,** 600 Market St. (544-5732), at Clinch, will fill you with wonder. The museum covers the cultural history of East Tennessee from its founding to the World's Fair. (Open Tues.-Sat. 10am-4pm, Sun. 1-5pm. $3, students $2, seniors $2.50, under 6 free.) Picnickers will appreciate **Kirch Park,** across the street, a tiny perfectly manicured oasis of green in the midst of downtown (open 8am-9pm; Oct.-March Mon-Fri. 8am-6pm, Sun. 8am-4pm).

For a taste of down-home Appalachia, visit the **Farmer's Market** (524-3276), 15 mi. from downtown on I-640 off exit 8. The pavilion peddles local produce, plants, jams and jellies, arts and crafts, ice cream, soft pretzels, and more. Don't leave the area without visiting the **Museum of Appalachia** (494-7680 or 494-0514), 16 mi. north of Knoxville on I-75 at exit 22 in **Norris.** The "museum" is actually a vast village with authentic houses, barns, a school, livestock—even jail cells. In the display barn, don't miss the incredible story of Brother Harrison Mayes, the evangelist who planted signs advertising God in all 50 states and hoped to land one on the moon. The museum avoids schmaltz and fustiness; if you want a sense of what real Appalachian life was like, this is it. For Pete's sake, go! (Open daily dawn to dusk year-round except Christmas Day. $6, ages 6-15 $4, under 6 free.)

■■■ MEMPHIS

Follow the sound of soulful melodies up the "Blues Route," Highway 61, to the southwestern corner of Tennessee, and Memphis, home of the blues and the birthplace of rock 'n' roll. Decades after W.C. Handy published a blues piece on legendary Beale St. in 1912, Elvis Presley (also a Memphian) became the "King of Rock 'n' Roll" with the help of his gyrating pelvis and amazingly versatile voice. Though the King may be dead, his image lives on throughout the city. Every year roadtrippers from around the country make a pilgrimage to the mecca of tack—Graceland, Elvis's former home.

PRACTICAL INFORMATION

Tourist Office: Visitor Information Center, 340 Beale St. (543-5333 or 800-447-8278), 2 blocks south on 2nd St. and 2 blocks east of the Greyhound station on Beale. Open Mon.-Sat. 9am-6pm, Sun. noon-6pm; Nov.-March Mon.-Sat. 9am-5pm.

Airport: Memphis International, 2491 Winchester Rd. (922-8000), south of the southern loop of I-240. Taxi fare to the city $16—negotiate in advance. Hotel express **shuttles** (922-8238) cost $8 (service 8:20am-11pm). Public transport to and from the airport $1.10, service is sporadic and the trip is tough for a traveler unfamiliar with the area.

Trains: Amtrak, 545 S. Main St. (526-0052 or 800-872-7245), at Calhoun on the southern edge of downtown. *Take a taxi—the area is very unsafe* even during the day. To: New Orleans (5 per week, 8hr., $75); Chicago (5 per week, 10½hr., $100). Call for station hrs.

Buses: Greyhound, 203 Union Ave. (523-1184 or 800-231-2222), at 4th St. downtown. Unsafe area at night, but it beats the Amtrak station. To: Nashville (12 per day, 3¾hr., $29); Chattanooga (6 per day, 2-4hr., $20); Jackson (9 per day, 4hr., $32); Gatlinburg (2 per day, 10hr.; call for prices). Open Mon.-Fri. 7am-8:30pm, Sat.-Sun. 7am-3:30pm.

Public Transportation: Memphis Area Transit Authority (MATA) (274-6282), corner of Union and Main. Extensive bus routes cover most suburbs, but don't run very frequently. The two major downtown stops are at the intersections of Front and Jefferson St., and 2nd St. and Madison Ave.; the major routes run on Front, 2nd, and 3rd St. Starts running Mon.-Fri. 7am, Sat.-Sun. 10am; ends from 6pm-11pm, depending on route. Fare $1.10, transfers 10¢. Refurbished 19th-century Portuguese **trolley** cars (run by MATA) cruise Main St. Mon.-Thurs. 6:30am-9pm., Fri. 6:30am-1am, Sat. 9:30am-1am, Sun. 10am-6pm. 50¢.

Taxis: Yellow Cab, 526-2121. $2.35 first mi., $1.10 each additional mi. 24 hrs.

Crisis Lines: Crisis Line, 274-7477. **Sexual Assault Crisis,** 528-2161. **Gay/Lesbian Switchboard,** 728-4297. **HIV/AIDS Switchboard,** 278-2437.

Time Zone: Central (1hr. behind Eastern).

Emergency: 911.

Post Office: 555 3rd St. (521-2186). Open Mon.-Fri.8:30am-5:30pm, Sat. 10am-2pm. **ZIP code:** 38101. **Area code:** 901.

Downtown, named avenues run east-west and numbered ones north-south. **Madison Ave.** divides north and south addresses. Two main thoroughfares, **Poplar** and **Union Ave.,** pierce the heart of the city from the east; 2nd and 3rd St. arrive from the south. **I-240** and **I-55** encircle the city. **Bellevue** becomes **Elvis Presley Blvd.** and leads you straight to Graceland. If traveling by car, take advantage of the free, unmetered parking along the river.

SINCE M'BABY LEFT ME, I FOUND A NEW PLACE T'DWELL

Memphis offers a fine hostel (the budget traveler's best option), and not much else. A few downtown motels have prices in the budget range; otherwise, more distant lodgings are available near Graceland at Elvis Presley Blvd. and Brooks Rd. During the celebration of the earth-shattering days of Elvis's birth (Jan. 8) and death (Aug. 15), book way in advance. The visitors center has a thorough listing of lodgings. Contact **Bed and Breakfast in Memphis,** P.O. Box 41621, Memphis 38174 (726-5920; 800-336-2087 for reservations), for guest rooms in Memphian homes. Spanish-speaking hosts are available (singles and doubles $65-145).

Lowenstein-Long House/Castle Hostelry (AAIH/Rucksackers), 217 N. Waldran (527-7174), parking lot at 1084 Poplar. Take bus #50 from 3rd St. Good location, but somewhat sketchy neighborhood a drawback for those without cars. Beautiful grounds surround an elegant Victorian mansion. Women's rooms on the 3rd floor are pleasant and homey; mens' rooms out back can be a bit less neat. $12; stay 3 nights, get 1 free. Pretty private doubles $33. Camping on lawn out back, $6 per person; includes access to kitchen and bath. Work (when available) can be exchanged for price of stay. Towels $1, laundry $2. Key deposit $20.

Motel 6, 1117 E. Brooks Rd. (346-0992), near intersection of Elvis and Brooks Rd. close to Graceland. HBO, pool, and small, clean rooms with stall showers and free local calls. $32, two adults $38, under 18 free.

Hernando Inn, 900 E. Commerce St. (601-429-7811), just across the Mississippi border in Hernando (about 15mi. south of Memphis). Take exit 280 of I-55. Must be 21. Singles $38, doubles $42; prices may vary. $2 key deposit, $5 remote deposit.

Memphis/Graceland KOA, 3691 Elvis Presley Blvd. (396-7125), location right next door to Graceland, makes up for the lack of trees and privacy. Sites $19, with hookup $25.

Memphis South Campground, 460 Byhalia Rd., Hernando, MS (601-429-1878). 15mi. south, at exit 280 off I-55 in Mississippi. Relaxing, verdant pastures. Pool and laundry. Tent sites $12, with water and wattage $15, with full hookup $17.

MEALS FIT FOR THE KING

In Memphis, barbecue is as common as rhinestone-studded jumpsuits; the city even hosts the World Championship Barbecue Cooking Contest in May. But don't fret if gnawing on ribs isn't your thing—Memphis has plenty of other Southern-style restaurants with down-home favorites like fried chicken, catfish, chitlins, and grits.

The Rendezvous (523-2746), Downtown Alley, in the alley across from the Peabody Hotel off Union St. between the Ramada and Days Inn. A Memphis legend, serving large portions of ribs ($6.50-10), and cheaper sandwiches ($3-4). Open Tues.-Thurs. 4:30pm-midnight, Fri.-Sat. noon-midnight.

The North End, 346 N. Main St. (526-0319 or 527-3663), at Jackson St. downtown. A happening place specializing in tamales, wild rice, stuffed potatoes, and creole dishes ($3-8). Rabbit-food alternatives to BBQ. Entrees $3-10. Hot fudge pie known as "sex on a plate," $3.25. Happy Hour daily 4-7pm. Live music starts at 10:30pm Wed.-Sun. with a $2 cover. Open daily 10:30am-3am.

Jake's Place, 356 N. Main St. (527-2799), next door to The North End, offers pizza and sandwiches ($4-7). Crazy huge hot fudge pie $3.50. Open daily 11am-2am.

P and H Café, 1532 Madison Ave. (726-0906). The initials aptly stand for Poor and Hungry. "The beer joint of your dreams" serves huge burgers and grill food ($3-5) to students and locals; try the patty melt with grilled onions ($3). Waitresses are a friendly Memphis institution. During Death Week in Aug., P and H hosts the infamous "Dead Elvis Ball." Local bands occasionally play Sat. nights (music starts around 9pm, cover $3-5). Open Mon.-Fri. 11am-3am, Sat. 5pm-3am.

Corky's, 5259 Poplar Ave. (685-9744), about 25min. from downtown. Nationally famous BBQ, very popular with the locals and justifiably so. Top-notch BBQ dinner and ribs served with baked beans, cole slaw, and bread ($6-9). Scrumptious pies and cobbler. Arrive early and expect to wait, or use the drive-thru. Corky's mails ribs overnight anywhere in the continental U.S.: call 800-9-CORKYS/926-7597. Open Mon.-Thurs. 11am-10pm, Fri.-Sat. 11am-10:30pm, Sun. 11am-10pm.

Jim Neely's Interstate BBQ, 2265 S. 3rd St. (775-2304). Hoppin', heapin' pig and cow sandwiches shellacked with sauces containing "herbs a lot of people never heard of" for under $5. Pork BBQ sandwich $3.50; small order of ribs $6.50. BBQ spaghetti with pork sauce; 12oz. for $2. Open Mon.-Thurs. 11am-11pm, Fri.-Sat. 11am-2pm, Sun. noon-10pm.

Squash Blossom Market, 1720 Poplar Ave. (725-4823). Truly an island; this upscale health food store (with tasty café in back) seems a little out of place in a city dripping with sauces, grease, and above all, meat. Veggie delights about $4 during Sun. brunch. Open Mon.-Fri. 9am-9pm, Sat. 9am-8pm, Sun. 11am-6pm.

Front St. Delicatessen, 77 S. Front St. (522-8943). Lunchtime streetside deli in the heart of downtown. There's almost no room inside; patio dining in sunny weather. Sandwiches $2.50-$3.50. Open Mon.-Fri. 8am-4pm, Sat. 11am-3pm.

Western Steakhouse, 1298 Madison (725-9896), slaps down some fine hearty beef. The back corner was graced by the King. Grilled cheese $2.25-$4.50. Live music Fri. and Sat. nights. Open Tues.-Sun. 4pm-midnight.

MEMPHIS MUSIC AND MARVELS

Elvis Sightings: Graceland

You'll laugh. You'll cry. You'll want to see it again and again. Bow down before **Graceland** (332-3322 or 800-238-2000), or rather "GRACE-lin," as the tour guides drawl, Elvis Presley's home and the paragon of Americana that every Memphis visitor must see. Unfortunately, any desire to learn about the man, to share his dream, or to feel his music requires the ability to transcend the mansion's crowd-control methods and required audio-tape tour, to reach beyond the tacky commercialism and ignore the employees who seem to adhere to the Elvis motto "Taking Care of Business in a Flash." Still you'll never forget the mirrored ceilings, carpeted walls, and yellow-and-orange decor of Elvis' 1974 renovations; by tour's end, even those who aren't die-hard Elvis fans may be genuinely moved. Elvis bought the mansion when he was only 22, and his daughter Lisa Marie inherited it. Be sure to gawk at the Trophy Building where hundreds of gold and platinum records line the wall. The list of exhibits is crazy: a collection of guns includes his favorite turquoise-handled Colt 45. The King and his court are buried next door in the **Meditation Gardens,** where you can seek enlightenment while reciting a mantra to the tune of "You're So Square." (Ticket office open 7:30am-6pm; Labor Day-Memorial Day 8:30am-5pm. Attractions open 2 hrs. after ticket office closes. Nov.-Feb. mansion closed on Tues. $9, seniors $8.10, ages 5-12 $5.)

If you love him tender, love him true, visit several Elvis museums, and several more Elvis souvenir shops. The **Elvis Presley Automobile Museum** houses a score of pink and purple Elvis-mobiles in a huge hall, whilean indoor drive-in movie theater shows clips from 31 Elvis movies ($5, seniors $4.50, ages 5-12 $2.75). A free 20-minute film, *Walk a Mile in My Shoes,* with performance footage contrasts the early (otherwise known as slim) years with the later ones. **Elvis's Airplanes** features—you got it—the two Elvis planes: the *Lisa Marie* (named for the Elvis daughter) and the tiny *Hound Dog II* Jetstar ($4.50, seniors $4.05, children $2.75). The **Sincerely Elvis** exhibit glimpses into Elvis's private side; see the books he read, the shirts he wore, and home movies with his wife Priscilla ($2.75). The **Platinum Tour Package** discounts admission to the mansion and all attractions ($17, seniors $15.30, ages 5-12 $11). Take bus #13 "Lauderdale/Elvis Presley" from 3rd and Union to Graceland.

Every year on the week of August 15 (the date of Elvis' death), millions of the King's cortege get all shook up for **Elvis Week,** an extended celebration that includes a pilgrimage to his junior high school and a candlelight vigil. You can also make the bus trip to the two-room house in **Tupelo, MS** where it all began. The days surrounding his birthday (Jan. 8) also see some Kingly activities.

THE SOUTH

Facing the Music: The Blues, B.B. King, and more...

Long before Sam Phillips and the tiny **Sun Studio,** 706 Union Ave. (521-0664), first produced Elvis, Jerry Lee Lewis, U2, and Bonnie Raitt, historic **Beale St.** saw the invention of the blues (30-min. studio tours every hr. on the ½hr. Open daily 9am-6:30pm; Oct.-April 10am-6pm. $7.50, under 13 free.) The **W.C. Handy Home and Museum,** 352 Beale St. (527-3427), exhibits the music and photographs of the man, the myth, the legend who first put a blues melody to paper (open Mon.-Sat. 10am-6pm, Sun. noon-6pm; $2, students $1). Of course, Memphis music history includes the soul hits of the Stax label and rockers like Big Star as well as the blues; the **Memphis Music Hall of Fame,** 97 S. 2nd St. (525-4007), showcases the city's music history from 1945 to the 1970s (open Mon.-Sat. 10am-6pm, Sun. noon-6pm), while the **Beale Street Blues Museum,** 329 Beale St. (527-6008), sings the blues story from the slavery to the 1940s. (Same summer hours as Hall of Fame; winter Mon.-Sat. 11am-5pm. Each $5, under 13 $2). The **Center for Southern Folklore,** 130 Beale St. (525-3655), documents various aspects of music history, including a tribute to Memphis's WDIA—the nation's first all-black radio station. Notables like B.B. King and Rufus Thomas began their musical careers on these airwaves (open daily 10am-8pm; free). Call the center for info on the **Music and Heritage Festival,** which fills the Main St. Mall downtown during the 3rd weekend of July. Gospel, country, blues, and jazz accompany dance troupes and craft booths. Some booths offer oral histories on everything from life on the Mississippi to playing in segregated baseball leagues. (Open 11am–11pm. Free.)

...and still more: Civil Rights, Mud, and Miscellany

The **National Civil Rights Museum,** housed at the site of Martin Luther King, Jr.'s assassination at **Lorraine Motel,** 450 Mulberry St. (521-9699), at 2nd St., serves as a reminder of the suffering African-Americans have endured and a tribute to their courage. A 10-minute movie, graphic photographs of lynching victims, live footage, and life-size exhibits vividly trace the progress of the Civil Rights Movement. (Open Mon.-Sat. 10am-6pm, Sun. 1-6pm; in winter Mon. and Wed.-Sat. 10am-5pm, Sun. 1-5pm. $5, students with ID and seniors $4, ages 6-12 $3; free Mon. 3-5pm.)

Mud Island (576-7241), a quick monorail ride over the picturesque Mississippi, has it all: a museum, the renowned World War II B-17 **Memphis Belle,** and a five-block scale model of the Mississippi River you can swim in or stroll along. In the summer, visitors can swim in the enormous pool posing as the Gulf of Mexico at the mouth of the Mississippi River sculpture. Free tours of the Riverwalk and Memphis Belle Pavilion run several times daily. Thursday evenings on the island are free; arrive before 6pm and catch the sunset. (Call for hours. Entrance to the island $2. Parking $3.) At the **Mississippi River Museum,** 125 N. Front St. (576-7241), spy on a Union ironclad gunboat from the lookout of a Confederate bluff, or relax to the blues in the Yellow Dog Café (museum and grounds $6, seniors and under 12 $4).

On the waterfront, you won't be able to miss the 32-story, six-acre **Great American Pyramid** (526-5177), which houses a 20,000-seat arena. Tours cover the "Entertainment Hallway" and a University of Memphis basketball locker room. (Open Mon.-Sat. 10am-4pm, Sun. noon-5pm $3.75, seniors and under 13 $2.75.)

A. Schwab, 163 Beale St. (523-9782), a small department store run by the same family since 1876, still offers old-fashioned bargains. A "museum" of relics-never-sold gathers dust on the mezzanine floor, including an array of voodoo potions, elixirs, and powders. Elvis bought some of his flashier ensembles here. (Free guided tours. Open Mon.-Sat. 9am-5pm.) Next door on Beale St., the **Memphis Police Museum** (528-2370) summons visitors to gawk at 150-years-worth of confiscated drugs, homemade weapons, and officer uniforms (open 24 hrs.; free).

The Pink Palace Museum and Planetarium, 3050 Central Ave. (320-6320), which is, by the way, gray, details the natural history of the mid-South and expounds upon the development of Memphis; check out the sharp and sparkling crystal and mineral collection or experience the vertigo of the IMAX theater. (Open Mon.-Wed. 9am-4pm, Thurs. 9am-8pm, Fri. 9am-9pm, Sat. 10am-9pm, Sun. noon-5pm. $5.50, seniors $5, ages 3-12 $3.50. Call for IMAX times: $5.50/$5/$4. Planetarium: $3/$2.50/$2.) On the corner of Central Ave. and Hollywood the **Children's Museum,** 2525 Central Ave. (320-3170), stands ready to entertain the kids (open Tues.-Sat. 9am-5pm, Sun. noon-5pm; $5, seniors $4, under 13 $4).

Victorian Village consists of 18 mansions in various stages of restoration and preservation. **Mallory-Neeley House,** 652 Adams Ave. (523-1484), one of the village's mansions which is open to the public, was built in the mid-19th century. Most of its original furniture remains intact for visitors to see. (40-min. tour $4, seniors and students $3, under 5 free. Last tour 3:30pm. Open Tues.-Sat. 10am-4pm, Sun. 1-4pm.) French Victorian architecture and an antique/textile collection live on in **Woodruff-Fontaine House,** 680 Adams Ave. (526-1469; open Mon.-Sat. 10am-3:30pm, Sun. 1-3:30pm; $5, students $2, seniors $4). **Magevney House,** 198 Adams Ave. (526-4464), once held the clapboard cottage of Eugene Magevney, who helped establish Memphis's first public schools. (Open Tues.-Sat. 10am-4pm; Labor Day-Memorial Day Mon.-Fri. 10am-2pm, Sat. 10am-4pm. Free. Reservations required.)

Memphis has almost as many parks as museums, each offering a slightly different natural setting. Brilliant wildflowers and a marvelous heinz of roses (57 varieties) bloom and grow forever at the **Memphis Botanical Garden,** 750 Cherry Rd. (685-1566), in Audubon Park off Park Ave. (Open Tues.-Sat. 9am-sunset, Sun. 11am-6pm. $2, ages 6-17 $1.) Across the street, the **Dixon Galleries and Garden,** 4339 Park Ave. (761-5250), flaunts its manicured landscape and collection of European art. (Open Tues.-Sat. 10am-5pm, Sun. 1-5pm. $5, students $3, seniors $4, ages 1-12 $1; free Tues. 12:30-6pm. Mon. only the gardens are open, and admission is ½ the above prices.) **Lichterman Nature Center,** 1680 Lynfield (767-7322), is a 65-acre wildscape with virgin forests and wildlife and a picnic area (open Tues.-Sat. 9:30am-5pm, Sun. 1-5pm. $2, students ages 4-18 and seniors $1).

The **C.H. Nash Museum-Chucalissa,** 1987 Indian Village Dr. (785-3160), recaptures the past of America's earliest residents with its reconstructed prehistoric village and historical and archaeological museum. Take Winchester, which becomes Mitchell, which becomes Indian Village Dr. in T.O. Fuller State Park. Local Choctaw Native Americans sell pottery and beaded jewelry. The Museum and Village will be closed for part of 1996 for renovations; call before visiting for further info. (Open Tues.-Sat. 9am-4:30pm, Sun. 1-5pm. $3, children $2.)

Rubber Ducky, you make...wait, those ducks are real!

William Faulkner once said of Memphis that "the Delta meets in the lobby of the **Peabody Hotel,**" 149 Union St. (529-4000), in the heart of downtown. While you're there, gobble the Peabody Cheesecake with Strawberry Sauce ($4). Every day at 11am and 5pm, the hotel rolls out the red carpet and the **ducks** that live in its indoor fountain waddle about the premises with a piano accompaniment.

ARE YOU LONESOME TONIGHT?

If you don't know what to do while you're in Memphis, the visitors center's *Key* magazine, the free *Memphis Flyer,* or the "Playbook" section of the Friday morning *Memphis Commercial Appeal* can tell you what's goin' down 'round town. Also, swing by **Sun Café,** 710 Union Ave. (521-0664), adjacent to the Sun Studios, for a tall, cool glass of lemonade ($1.75) and a talk with the young waiters and cashiers about what to do (open daily 9am-7pm; Sept.-May 10am-6pm).

Beale St. sways with the most happening, hip nightlife. Blues waft up and down the street; save a few bucks by buying a drink at one of the many outdoor stands and meandering from doorway to doorway, park to park. **B.B. King's Blues Club,** 143 Beale St. (527-5464), where the club's namesake still makes appearances, happily mixes young and old, tourist and native. Wash down a catfish sandwich ($7) with a beer ($3). (Cover $4-10; when B.B. himself plays $30. Open daily from 11:30am-til the show stops.) **Rum Boogie Café,** 182 Beale St. (528-0150), presents a friendly, relaxed atmosphere and honest homegrown blues to a touristy crowd. Check out the celebrity guitars on the wall, including blues great Willie Dixon's. (Cover $5. Full menu; domestic beer $2.50. Open daily 11:30am-very late.) For pool, **Peoples,** 323 Beale St. (523-7627), racks 'em up from noon until at least 2am (tables $7.35, Fri.-Sat. $8.40). **Silky O'Sullivan's,** 183 Beale St. (522-9596), is a big Irish bar behind the façade of an almost completely razed historic landmark. Outside, chill out with the goats and munch on burgers ($4-6) to the tune of LOUD piano music or blues emanating from next door. (Cover Fri.-Sat. $3. Open Mon. 6pm-2:30am, Tues.-Thurs. 3pm-2:30am, Fri.-Sat. noon-5am, Sun.-noon-2:30am.)

Up, up, and away to the **Daily Planet,** 3439 Park Ave. (327-1270), where live bands play everything from rock to country (open Tues.-Sun. 5pm-2am). For a collegiate atmosphere, try the Highland St. strip near Memphis State University, with hopping bars like **Newby's,** 539 S. Highland St. (452-8408), which has backgammon tables and hosts rock and blues (music Fri.-Sat. around 10:30pm; domestic beer $2.25). Just up the street from Sun Studio **"616,"** 600 Marshall (526-6552), has a huge dance floor, local and national bands, and occasional 10¢ longnecks. (Cover around $8). A hot gay spot, **J. Wags,** 1268 Madison (725-1909) has been open 24 hrs. since way back. (All-you-can-drink beer busts 10pm-3am $4. Live music Fri.-Sat. Drag shows Fri.-Sat. at 1:30am.)

The majestic **Orpheum Theater,** 203 S. Main St. (525-3000), shows classic movies on summer weekends along with an organ prelude and a cartoon ($5, seniors and under 13 $4). The grand old theater, with 15-ft.-high chandeliers and a pipe organ, also has occasional live music (box office open Mon.-Fri. 9am-5pm and before shows). **Memphis in May** (525-4611) celebrates through the month with concerts, art exhibits, food contests, and sports events. Make hotel reservations early. The **Memphis Chicks** (who are, by the way, men), 800 Home Run Ln. (272-1687), near Libertyland, are a big hit with fans of Southern League baseball. ($5, box seats $6; $2 off for seniors and under 13. Call Ticketmaster or the box office Mon.-Fri. 9am-5pm and on game days.)

North Carolina

North Carolina can be split into three neat regions: down-to-earth mountain culture in the west, mellow sophistication in the Research Triangle of the central piedmont area, and placid coastal towns in the east. Often untouched by development, the state's natural beauty is a presence throughout.

Confederate soldiers from Mississippi first called their allies from North Carolina Tar Heels after they failed to maintain their position in the face of Union troops, meaning that they forgot to tar their heels in order to really stick to their ground. North Carolina adopted the nickname turning the insult into a source of pride; while they may have faltered in body, they remained tenacious in spirit.

PRACTICAL INFORMATION

Capital: Raleigh.

Travel and Tourism Division: 430 N. Salisbury St., Raleigh 27611 (919-733-4171 or 800-847-4862). **Department of Natural Resources and Community Development,** Division of Parks and Recreation, P.O. Box 27687, Raleigh 27611 (919-733-4181).

Time Zone: Eastern. **Postal Abbreviation:** NC

Sales Tax: 6%.

■■■ THE RESEARCH TRIANGLE

Large universities and their students dominate the cities of the research triangle. **Raleigh,** the state capital, is an easygoing, historic town, boasting a thriving art community and providing a home for North Carolina State University (NC State). **Durham,** formerly a major tobacco producer, now, ironically, devotes its time to medicine supporting multiple hospitals and diet clinics. Duke University, one of the most prestigious schools in the nation, adds a share of PhDs to Durham's doctoral mix. The nation's first state university, the University of North Carolina (UNC), can be found just 20 mi. down the road in **Chapel Hill.** College culture predominates here—a sea of bicycles provide environment-friendly student transport, and the Hill's music scene thrives, with several bands starting to receive national attention.

PRACTICAL INFORMATION

Tourist Office: Raleigh Capitol Area Visitors Center, 301 N. Blount St. (733-3456). Walk-in info only. Open Mon.-Fri. 8am-5pm, Sat. 9am-5pm, Sun. 1-5pm. **Durham Convention Center and Visitors Bureau,** 101 E. Morgan St. (687-0288). Open Mon.-Fri. 8:30am-5pm, Sat. 10am-2pm. **Chapel Hill Chamber of Commerce,** 104 S. Estes Dr. (967-7075). Open Mon.-Fri. 9am-5pm.

Airport: Raleigh-Durham International (460-1383), 15mi. northwest of Raleigh on U.S. 70. Many hotels and rental car agencies provide free airport limousine service if you have reservations. **Airport Information Assistance,** in the main lobby of Terminal A and near the baggage claim of Terminal C.

Trains: Amtrak, 320 W. Cabarrus, Raleigh (833-7594 or 800-872-7245). To: Washington, DC (2 per day, 6hr., $50); Richmond (2 per day, 4hr., $39); Miami (1 per day, 17hr., $149). Open daily 4:45am-10pm.

Buses: Greyhound (800-231-2222) has a station in each city. **In Raleigh,** 314 W. Jones St. (834-8275). To: Durham (5 per day, 35min., $7); Chapel Hill (4 per day, 80min., $8); Richmond (4 per day, 3-4hr., $34); North Charleston (3 per day, 8hr., $46). Open daily 7am-12:30am. **In Durham,** 820 W. Morgan St. (687-4800), 1 block off Chapel Hill St. downtown, 2½ mi. northeast of Duke University. To: Chapel Hill (4 per day, 35min., $3.40); Washington, DC (3 per day, 6hr., $49). Open daily 7am-11:30pm. **In Chapel Hill,** 311 W. Franklin St. (942-3356), 2 blocks from the UNC campus. Open Mon.-Thurs. 8:30am-4:20pm, Fri. 8:30am-6:30pm, Sat.-Sun. 8:30am-4:20pm.

Public Transportation: Capital Area Transit, Raleigh (828-7228). Buses run Mon.-Sat., fewer on Sat. Fare 50¢. **Duke Power Company Transit Service,** Durham (688-4587). Most routes start downtown at the corner of Main and Morgan St. on the loop. Operates daily; hours vary for each route. Fare 60¢, transfers 10¢. **Chapel Hill Transit,** Chapel Hill (968-2769). Operates Mon.-Fri. 6am-6pm. Fare 60¢, on campus 30¢.

Taxis: Safety Taxi, 832-8800. **Cardinal Cab,** 828-3228. Both charge $1.35, plus $1.50 each mi. 24-hr. service.

Crisis Line: Rape Crisis, 828-3005. Operates 24 hrs.

Emergency: 911.

Post Office: In Raleigh, 311 New Bern Ave. (420-5333). Open Mon.-Fri. 8am-5:30pm, Sat. 8am-noon; **ZIP code:** 27611. **In Durham,** 323 E. Chapel Hill St. (683-1976). Open Mon.-Fri. 7:30am-5pm; **ZIP code:** 27701. **In Chapel Hill,** 179 E. Franklin St. (967-6297). Open Mon.-Fri. 8:30am-5:30pm, Sat. 8:30am-noon; **ZIP code:** 27514. **Area code:** 919.

ACCOMMODATIONS AND CAMPING

Carolina-Duke Motor Inn (286-0771 or 800-438-1158), I-85 at Guess Rd. in Durham. Clean rooms with wood furnishings, A/C, and heat. Access to swimming pool and laundry facilities. Free Movie Channel, local calls, local maps, and shuttle to Duke Medical Center on the main campus. Singles $29, doubles $33; $3 each additional person. 10% discount for *Let's Go* users, seniors, and AAA members. Next door, the **Wabash Express** (286-0020) serves cheap, filling breakfasts (6 pancakes for $2.75) in an old railway car. Sat.-Sun. 8-11am.

Red Roof Inns, 3250 Maitland Dr. (231-0200 or 800-THE-ROOF/843-7663; fax 231-0228), off U.S. 64E. Large, clean rooms with sitting areas. Disabled access, coded keys, free local calls, cable TV, A/C, and heat. Singles $35, doubles $39.

Clairmont (828-5151), on S. Saunders St. off I-40. Clean, mid-sized rooms. Cable TV, 5 free local calls, A/C, heat, and 24-hr. free coffee and juice. Singles or doubles $43. 10% discount for AAA members.

Umstead State Park (787-3033), 2mi. northwest of Raleigh, on U.S. 70. Tent and trailer sites in pristine woodland. Large lake for fishing, hiking, and horseback riding. Open 8am-9pm; Sept.-May shorter hours. Closed to camping Mon.-Wed. Sites $9; no hookups.

FOOD

The restaurants near the universities are well-suited to budget travelers. In Raleigh, **Hillsborough Street,** across from NC State, has a wide array of inexpensive restaurants and bakeries staffed largely by students; the same is true of **Franklin Street** in Chapel Hill and, to a lesser degree, of **9th Street** in Durham. The **WellSpring Grocery,** at the Ridgewood Shopping Center on Wade Ave. in Raleigh (286-2290), 737 9th St. in Durham, and at Franklin and Elliott St. in Chapel Hill, sells organic fruits and vegetables and whole grain baked goods (open daily 9am-9pm).

Mecca Restaurant, 13 E. Martin St., Raleigh (832-5714). A local favorite since 1930. Sit at the counter or in small wooden booths. Sandwiches $2-4, burgers $3-5. Open Mon.-Fri. 7am-7pm.

Side Street, 225 N. Bloodworth St., Raleigh (828-4927), at E. Lane St. 3 blocks from the capitol. A classy place with antique furniture, botanical prints, flowered table settings, and wholesome sandwiches; salads too. All selections under $5. Open Mon.-Sat. 11am-3pm and 5-9pm, Sun. 11am-8pm.

Clyde Cooper's Barbeque, 109 E. Davie, Raleigh (832-7614), 1 block east of the Fayetteville Street Mall downtown. Beckons you to "Eat Mo' Pig" NC-style. Locals favor the baby back ribs ($5.25 per lb.) and the barbeque chicken ($5.25). Open Mon.-Sat. 10am-6pm.

The Ninth Street Bakery Shop, 776 9th St., Durham (286-0303). More than a bakery; sandwiches from $3. Try the dense bran or blueberry muffins (baked goods start at 45¢). Weekend nights see vegan and seafood dinners 5:30-9pm and acoustic music 8-11pm. Open Mon.-Thurs. 7am-6pm, Fri. 7am-11pm, Sat. 8am-11pm, Sun. 8am-4pm.

Francesca's Dessert Café, 709 9th St., Durham (286-4177). Locals satisfy sweet-cravings here, with homemade ice cream and gourmet cakes (Kahlua Espresso Pound Cake or Chocolate Raspberry Decadence) served on shiny black marble tables. Open Sun.-Thurs. 11:30am-11:30pm, Fri.-Sat. 11:30am-midnight.

Ramshead Rath-Skeller, 157-A E. Franklin St., Chapel Hill (942-5158), directly across from UNC. A student hang-out featuring pizza, sandwiches, and hot Apple Pie Louise. Ships' mastheads, German beer steins, and old Italian wine bottles adorn 6 dining rooms with names like the Rat Trap Lounge. "Reverend" Jim Cotton, here since 1947, may cook your steak. Meals $7-8. Open Mon.-Thurs. 11am-2:30pm and 5-9:30pm, Fri.-Sat. 11am-2:30pm and 5-10:30pm, Sun. 11am-10pm.

Skylight Exchange, 405½ W. Rosemary St., Chapel Hill (933-5550). An eclectic den where used books and records are sold, as well as sandwiches ($2-3). Live music on weekends makes it an effortlessly hip hangout. Open Sun.-Thurs. 11am-11pm, Fri-Sat. 11am-midnight.

SIGHTS AND ENTERTAINMENT

Raleigh's historical attractions are a welcome break from the academic pursuits of the research triangle. The **capitol building,** in Union Square at Edenton and Salisbury St., was built in 1840. (Open Mon.-Fri. 8am-5pm, Sat. 9am-5pm, Sun. 1-5pm. Tours available for large groups. Free.) Across from the capitol, the **North Carolina Museum of History,** 1 E. Edenton St. (715-0200), exhibits memorabilia from the earliest settlement to the present (open Tues.-Sat. 9am-5pm, Sun. 1-6pm; free). Pick up a brochure at the visitors center for a self-guided tour of the beautifully renovated 19th-century homes of **Historic Oakwood** and **Oakwood Cemetery,** where Confederate soldiers and prominent Raleigh citizens are buried. Across the street and around the corner at Bicentennial Square, the **Museum of Natural Sciences** (733-7450) displays fossils, gems, and animal exhibits including a live 17-ft. Burmese python named George (open Mon.-Sat. 9am-5pm, Sun. 1-5pm; free). The **North Carolina Museum of Art,** 2110 Blue Ridge Blvd. (833-1935), off I-40 (Wade Ave. exit), has eight galleries, containing works by Raphael, Botticelli, Rubens, Monet, Wyeth, and O'Keeffe, as well as artifacts from ancient Egypt. (Tours Tues.-Sun. 1:30pm. Open Tues.-Thurs. 9am-5pm, Fri. 9am-9pm, Sat. 9am-5pm, Sun. 11am-6pm. Free.) To see local artists in action, visit the galleries and craft shops of the **Moore Square Art District** (828-4555), which occupies a 3-block radius around Moore Square. **Mordecai Historic Park,** 1 Mimosa St. (834-4844), recreates 19th-century life in Raleigh on the grounds of an antebellum plantation ($3).

Duke University is Durham's main draw, and the **admissions office,** 2138 Campus Dr. (684-3214), doubles as a visitors center (open Mon.-Fri. 8am-5pm, Sat. 9am-1pm). **Duke Chapel** (684-2921), in the center of the university, has more than a million pieces of stained glass depicting almost 900 figures in 77 windows. Show up around lunchtime, and you might catch a free personal concert on the Duke Memorial Organ inside. (Open July-Aug. daily 8am-8pm, Sept.-June 8am-10pm.) The walkway to the left of the chapel leads to the **Bryan Center,** Duke's labyrinthine student center, with a gift shop, a café, a small art gallery, and an **info desk.** The **Sarah Duke Gardens** (684-3698), near West Campus on Anderson St., have over 15 acres of landscaping and tiered flower beds (open daily 8am-dusk). Take the free Duke campus shuttle bus to East Campus, where the **Duke Museum of Art** (684-5135) hangs a small but impressive collection, which is especially strong in Italian and Dutch oils, classical sculptures, and African art (open Tues.-Fri. 9am-5pm, Sat. 11am-2pm, Sun. 2-5pm; free). Also take time to enjoy Duke's 7700-acre **forest** (682-9319), with more than 30 mi. of trails and drivable roads.

The **Duke Homestead,** 2828 Duke Homestead Rd. (477-5498), is on the other side of Durham, up Guess Rd. Washington Duke started his tobacco business on this beautiful estate and went on, with the help of his sons, to endow what would become Duke University. (Open Mon.-Sat. 9am-5pm, Sun. 1-5pm; Nov.-March Tues.-Sat. 10am-4pm, Sun. 1-4pm. Free.)

Once you've checked out the area's past, enjoy the present-day entertainment supplied by **University of North Carolina** (962-2211), in Chapel Hill. The university's Smith Center (a.k.a. the Dean Dome) hosts sporting events and concerts; call for further information. Until 1975, astronauts practiced celestial navigation at the university's **Morehead Planetarium** (962-1236), which houses a rare Zeiss Star projector. The planetarium puts up six different shows per year, each of which involves a combination of films and Zeiss projections. These shows are conceived and produced while you watch. (Open Sun.-Fri. 12:30-5pm and 7-9:45pm, Sat. 10am-5pm and 7-9:45pm. $3.50, students, seniors, and children $2.50.)

Pick up a free copy of the *Spectator* and *Independent* weekly magazines, available at most restaurants, bookstores, and hotels, for complete listings of the Triangle's concerts, guest lectures, exhibits, and nightlife. Students frequent bars along **9th Street** in Durham, and **Franklin Street** in Chapel Hill, but to hear the emerging Chapel Hill and national talent, go to the **Cat's Cradle,** 300 E. Main St., Carroboro (967-9053), the quasi-legendary rock club where R.E.M. and Pearl Jam once played (inexpensive cover).

The **Durham Bulls** (688-8211), a class-A farm team for the Atlanta Braves, became famous after the 1988 movie *Bull Durham* was filmed in their ballpark. You can still see them play here when the season is right. (Reserved tickets $5.25, general admission $4.25, students, seniors, and under 18 $3.25.)

■■■ CHARLOTTE

In 1799, a fortunate fellow happened upon a gold nugget in the town of Charlotte. It was exactly the kind of nugget you wouldn't want to stub your toe on—basically, a 17-pound nugget. Mines sprung up, prospectors poured in, and gold speculation boomed. The rush lasted about 50 years, until folks in California began finding smaller nuggets in larger quantities. The 19th-century mines are gone, but Charlotte, which began as a village on the Catawba Indian trade route, is now the largest city in the Carolinas and the nation's third largest banking center.

Practical Information **INFO Charlotte,** 330 S. Tryon St. (331-2700 or 800-231-4636), awaits uptown for brochure-browsing. Free parking off 2nd St. (Open Mon.-Fri. 8:30am-5pm, Sat. 10am-4pm, Sun. 1-4pm.) Heed the "All Aboard" at **Amtrak,** 1914 N. Tryon St. (376-4416 or 800-872-7245), or ride **Greyhound,** 601 W. Trade St. (372-0456 or 800-231-2222). Both are open 24 hrs. **Charlotte Transit,** 901 N. Davidson St. (336-3366), runs local buses (80¢, $1.15 for outlying areas; transfers free). In an **emergency,** call 911. Charlotte's **post office:** 201 N. McDowell (333-5135; open Mon.-Fri. 7am-5:30pm); **ZIP code:** 28202; **area code:** 704.

Accommodations and Food Charlotte's budget motels thrive off I-85, exit 41, around Sugar Creek Rd. and the I-85 Service Rd. **Red Roof Inn** (596-8222), I-85 at Sugar Creek Rd., has large rooms, new wood furniture, A/C, heat, cable TV, free local calls and coffee, and daily papers (singles $34, doubles $39). Nearby **Continental Inn,** 1100 Sugar Creek Rd. (597-8100) has nicely furnished new rooms with A/C and cable TV, but you must be 21 or older to stay (singles $33, doubles $45).

South from uptown, the **Dilworth** neighborhood cooks with a generous number of independent restaurants serving everything from ethnic cuisine to pizza and pub fare. Part yuppie, part gay, and continuously upbeat, the area and its residents are well-heeled; yet there are places which won't turn away, or bankrupt, unwashed backpackers. At **300 East,** 300 East Blvd. (332-6507), you can eat at a table under the trees outside or inside in a big wooden booth. (Entrees $10-12, sandwiches $5-6, baked stuffed potatoes $6; open Mon.-Thurs. 11:30am-10:30pm, Fri.-Sat. 11:30am-midnight, Sun. 11am-10pm.) **Café 521,** 521 N. College St. (377-9100), is a coffeehouse with a killer euro image and outstanding lunchtime fare ($4-6). Portions are small, but everything comes with free bread and olive oil to dip it in. (Open Tues.-Fri. 11:30am-3:30pm and 5pm-1am, Sat.-Mon. 5pm-1am; bar closes nightly 2am.) The **Charlotte Regional Farmer's Market,** 1801 Yorkmont Rd. (357-1269), hawks local produce, baked goods, and crafts year-round (Tues.-Sat. 8am-6pm).

Sights, Entertainment, and Nightlife The **Mint Museum of Art,** 2730 Randolph Rd. (337-2000), a 5-min. drive from uptown, is particularly proud of its pottery, porcelain, and American art collections. (Open Tues. 10am-10pm, Wed.-Sat. 10am-5pm, Sun. noon-5pm. Guided tours daily 2pm. $4, under 13 free; free Tues. after 5pm.) The **Discovery Place,** 301 N. Tryon St. (845-6664 or 800-935-0553), draws crowds with its hands-on science and technology museum, OmniMax theater, and planetarium. (Open Mon.-Sat. 9am-6pm, Sun. 1-6pm; Sept.-May Mon.-Fri. 9am-5pm, Sat. 9am-6pm, Sun. 1-6pm. Exhibit halls, OmniMax, or planetarium $5.50, seniors and ages 6-12 $4.50, ages 3-5 $2.75; any two $7.50/$6.50/$4.50.)

Paramount's Carowinds Entertainments Complex (588-2600 or 800-888-4FUN/4386), 10 mi. south of Charlotte off exit 90 from I-77, is an amusement park which pays tribute to *Wayne's World* with the "Hurler" roller coaster. (Open June-Aug. Mon.-Fri. 10am-8pm, Sat.-Sun. 10am-10pm; March-May and Sept. Sat.-Sun. 10am-8pm. $25, seniors and ages 4-6 $13.50, under 4 free. Parking $3.)

Jazz Charlotte (332-0126) provides free outdoor music—jazz, blues, R&B, and gospel—uptown during the second weekend in September. The **Charlotte Knights** play minor league baseball April through July at Knights Castle (357-8071) off I-77S at exit 88 (tickets $5, seniors and children $3.50).

For nightlife, arts, and entertainment listings, grab a free copy of *Creative Loafing* or *Break* in one of Charlotte's shops or restaurants. The **Moon Room,** 433 S. Tryon St. (342-2003), has live music on weekends and occasionally explodes into bohemian funkiness with Thursday theme-nights; watch for Poetry Night and Psychic Night (open Thurs. 5:30-11:30pm, Fri.-Sat. 5:30pm-1am). Slake your thirst with homemade brew from **Dilworth Brewing Co.,** 1301 East Blvd. (377-2739), where local rock and blues plays on weekends. Hearty pub food ($4-6; Thurs. all-you-can-eat spaghetti $7). **Heretics/Aardvark,** 5600 Old Concord Rd. (596-1342), has local talent on-stage and all ages in the crowd. Late night dancing is provided by **The Edge,** 4369 S. Tryon St. (525-3343), a "progressive dance complex" with nights like Disco Hump and College Quake. Arrive before 11pm for a short line and a low cover (Open Fri.-Sat. until 4am). Call about occasional all-age live music shows.

CAROLINA MOUNTAINS

The sharp ridges and rolling slopes of the southern Appalachian range create some of the most spectacular scenery in the Southeast. At one time, North Carolina's verdant highlands provided a refuge for the country's rich and privileged; the Vanderbilts owned a large portion of the 500,000-acre Pisgah National Forest, which they willed to the U.S. government. Today the western Blue Ridge, Great Smoky, Black, Craggy, Pisgah, and Balsam Mountains beckon budget travelers with campsites and inexpensive youth hostels and ski lodges. Enjoy the area's rugged wilderness while backpacking, canoeing, rafting, mountain biking, cross-country skiing, or just driving the **Blue Ridge Parkway** (p. 255).

The Blue Ridge Mountains divide into two areas. The north area is the **High Country,** which includes the territory between Boone and Asheville, 100 mi. to the southwest. The south includes the **Great Smoky Mountains National Park** (see p. 278) and the **Nanatahala National Forest.**

■■■ BOONE AND BLOWING ROCK

Nestled among the breathtaking mountains of the High Country, **Boone,** named for frontiersman Daniel Boone, has two faces. Tourist attractions such as Mast General Store, Tweetsie Railroad, and the many antiques shops lure young and old to eat family-style, flatten coins on railroad ties, and, of course, shop. But this small town lives year-round, populated by locals and the students of **Appalachian State University (ASU).** Downtown beckons with a soda fountain and numerous student hangouts. **Blowing Rock,** 7 mi. south at the entrance to the Blue Ridge Parkway, is a folk artists' colony. The rock which blows overhangs **Johns River Gorge;** chuck a piece of paper (biodegradable, please) over the edge, and it will blow right back at you.

PRACTICAL INFORMATION

Tourist Office: Boone Area Chamber of Commerce, 208 Howard St. (264-2225 or 800-852-9506), has info on accommodations and sights. Turn from Rte. 321S onto River St., drive behind the university, turn right onto Depot St., then take the first left onto Howard St. Open Mon.-Fri. 9am-5pm. The **Blowing Rock Chamber of Commerce** (295-7851) is on Main St. Open Mon.-Sat. 9am-5pm. **North Carolina High Country Host Visitor Center,** 1700 Blowing Rock Rd. (264-1299 or 800-438-7500), distributes the *High Country Host Area Travel Guide,* an informative, detailed map of the area, and the *Blue Ridge Parkway Directory,* a mile-by-mile description of services and attractions located on or near the Parkway. Open daily 9am-5pm.

Buses: Greyhound (800-231-2222). Call for pick-ups at a stop in Hickory, NC.

Public Transportation: Boone AppalCart, 274 Winkler's Creek Rd. (264-2278). Local bus and van service with 3 main routes: Red links downtown Boone with ASU and motels and restaurants on Blowing Rock Rd.; Green serves Rte. 421; Crosstown runs between ASU and the marketplace. Red route every hr. Mon.-Fri. 7am-6:30pm; Green Mon.-Fri. 7am-7pm; crosstown Mon.-Fri. 6:30am-11pm, Sat. 9am-8pm. Fare 50¢. AppalCart goes to Blowing Rock Town Hall twice daily.

Taxis: Boone Taxi (264-9322). $6 flat rate. Open Mon.-Thurs. 7am-midnight, Fri.-Sat. 7am-3am. Call ahead for an earlier pick-up.

Bike Rental: Magic Cycles, 208 Faculty St. (265-2211), behind the Blockbuster in Boone. $10 per ½day, $20 per day. Open Mon.-Sat. 10am-6pm, Sun. noon-4pm.

Emergency: 911. **National Park Service/Blue Ridge Parkway Emergency,** 800-727-5928.

Post Office: 637 Blowing Rock Rd. (264-3813), and 678 W. King St. (262-1171). Both open Mon.-Fri. 9am-5pm, Sat. 9am-noon. Lobby at Blowing Rock Rd. sells stamps until 10pm. **ZIP code:** 28607. **Area code:** 704.

ACCOMMODATIONS, CAMPING, AND FOOD

Catering primarily to vacationing families, the area fronts more than its share of expensive motels and B&Bs. Scratch the surface, though, and you'll find enough inexpensive rooms and campsites to keep you comfy.

Blowing Rock Assembly Grounds, P.O. Box 2530, Blowing Rock (295-7813), near the Blue Ridge Pkwy., has clean hostel rooms, shared bathrooms, sports facilities, and a cheap cafeteria, all in a gorgeous setting with access to hiking trails. Call for a pick-up, or follow Rte. 321S from Boone (left at the Shoppes on the Pkwy. onto Possum Hollow Rd., left at the first stop sign, left at the golf course). "BRAG" is primarily a retreat for religious groups. (Reception daily 9am-5pm. Check-in 4pm, check-out noon. $14, motel-like rooms in new building $40. Package rates available. Reservations required.)

Most inexpensive hotels are concentrated along **Blowing Rock Rd.** (Rte. 321) or Rte. 105. The red-brick **Red Carpet Inn** (264-2457 or 800-443-7179) has spacious rooms that come with TV/VCR, A/C, heat, a playground, and a pool. Prices vary drastically with seasonal availability; call ahead. Some holiday weekends have a two-night minimum stay. (Singles around $53, doubles $57. Reservations recommended.) The **Boone Trail Motel,** 820 E. King St./U.S. 421 (264-8839), south of downtown, has brightly painted rooms with quaint country baskets to hold the TP. (Singles $25, doubles $30; Fri.-Sat. $35/$38.) The **High Country Inn,** 1785 Rte. 105 (264-1000 or 800-334-5605), has a pool, a jacuzzi, a sauna, and an exercise room, in addition to standard-sized, comfortable rooms with two double beds. (Check-in 4pm, check-out 11am. Singles $39, doubles $42; Fri.-Sat. $59/$62. Ask about seasonal prices. Breakfast and dinner packages available.)

Boone and **Pisgah National Forest** offer developed and well-equipped **campsites** as well as **primitive camping** options for those looking to rough it. Along the Blue

Ridge Pkwy., spectacular tent sites ($9) are available at the **Julian Price Campground,** Mile 297 (963-5911); sites around Loop A are on a lake. **Linville Falls,** Mile 316 (963-5911), and **Crabtree Meadows,** Mile 340 (675-4444; open May-Oct.), are your other options. If you're willing to drive to Tennessee, cabins in **Roan Mountain State Park** (615-772-3314) sleep six comfortably and come furnished, with linens and cooking utensils ($65, Fri.-Sat. $85; weekly $430). The state park has a pool, tennis facilities, and smaller crowds than the campgrounds on the parkway.

Route 321 boasts countless fast-food options and family-style eateries. College students and professors alike hang out on **West King Street** (U.S. 441/221). **Our Daily Bread,** 627 West King St. (264-0173), offers sandwiches, salads, and super vegetarian specials for $3-5 (open Mon.-Fri. 8am-6:30pm, Sat. 9am-5pm). The **Daniel Boone Inn** (264-8657), at the Rte. 321/421 junction, does hefty, sit-down, all-you-can-eat meals, country-style (open daily 11am-9pm for dinner, $10; also Sat.-Sun. 8am-11am for breakfast, $6). Choose a soup ($2) from five or six made daily at **Piccadeli's,** 2161 Blowing Rock Rd. (262-3500), or build your own deli sandwich ($4-5) with all the fixin's (open Sun.-Thurs. 11am-10pm, Fri.-Sat. 11am-10:30pm). The **Appalachian Soda Shop,** 516 West King St. (262-1500), gives you an awful lot of grease at a low, low price (huge, juicy burgers $2-4; open Mon.-Sat. 11am-5pm).

SIGHTS AND ENTERTAINMENT

Horn in the West (264-2120) dramatizes the American Revolution as it was fought in the south Appalachians in an open-air amphitheater located near Boone off Rte. 105. (Shows late June-late Aug. Tues.-Sun. 8:30pm. $9-12, under 13 ½-price; group rates upon request. Reservations recommended.) Adjacent to the theater, the **Daniel Boone Native Gardens** celebrate mountain foliage, and the **Hickory Ridge Homestead** documents 18th-century mountain life. **An Appalachian Summer** (800-843-2787) is a month-long festival of high-caliber music, art, theater, and dance sponsored by ASU. Held May through September, Roan Mountain's **"Summer in the Park"** festival features cloggers and storytellers; call the **Roan Mountain Visitors Center** (615-772-3314 or 615-772-3303) for info.

In Blowing Rock, stop by **Parkway Craft Center,** Mile 294 Blue Ridge Pkwy. (295-7938), 2 mi. south of Blowing Rock Village in the Cone Manor House, where members of the Southern Highland Handicraft Guild demonstrate their skills and sell their crafts (open daily 9am-6pm). The craft center is on the grounds of the **Moses H. Cone Memorial Park,** 3600 acres of shaded walking trails and magnificent views, including a picture-postcard view of Bass Lake. Check the **National Park Service** desk in the center for a copy of *This Week's Activities.* (Open May-Oct. daily 9am-5:30pm; free.) Guided horseback rides from **Blowing Rock Stables** (295-7847) let you tour the park without hoofing it yourself. To find the stables, get off the Blue Ridge Pkwy. at the Blowing Rock sign, turn left onto Yonahlossee Rd. and look for the "Blowing Rock Stables" sign on the right. (Open March-Dec. daily 9am-4pm. 1-hr. tour $20, 2-hr. $35. No kids under 9 permitted. Call 1 day in advance to reserve.) The **Cosmic Coffee House** (295-4762), N. Main St., shows local artwork and hosts local bands several times a month, all the while brewing coffee that's "out-of-this-world" (open Mon.-Sat. 8am-11pm, Sun. 9am-9pm).

Hikers should arm themselves with the invaluable, large-scale map *100 Favorite Trails* ($3.50). **Edge of the World,** P.O. Box 1137, Banner Elk (898-9550), on Rte. 184 downtown, is a complete outdoor equipment and clothing store which rents equipment and gives regional hiking information. The staff also lead day-long backpacking, whitewater canoeing, spelunking, and rock climbing trips throughout the High Country for about $65. (Open Sun.-Thurs. 9am-6pm, Fri.-Sat. 9am-10pm.)

Downhill skiers enjoy the Southeast's largest concentration of alpine resorts, with four found in the Boone/Blowing Rock/Banner Elk area: **Appalachian Ski Mountain,** P.O. Box 106, Blowing Rock 28605 (800-322-2373; lift tickets $26, Sat.-Sun. $36; rentals $11/$13), off U.S. 221/321; **Ski Beech,** 1007 Beech Mt. Pkwy., Beech Mountain 28604 (387-2011 or 800-438-2093; lift tickets $25, Sat.-Sun. $34; rentals $12/$16); **Ski Hawknest,** Town of Seven Devils, 1800 Skyland Dr. (963-6561 or 800-822-

4295; lift tickets $20, Sat.-Sun. $33; rentals $12/$14); and **Sugar Mountain,** P.O. Box 369, Banner Elk (898-4521; lift tickets $25, Sat.-Sun. $39; rentals $12/$15). It's best to call ahead to the resort for specific ski package prices. The Boone AppalCart (264-2278) runs a **shuttle** in winter to Sugar Mountain and Ski Beech; call after December for routes. Call the High Country Host (264-1299) for **ski reports.**

The 5-mi. auto road to **Grandfather Mountain** (800-468-7325) provides an unparalleled view of the entire High Country area. At the top, a private park features a 1-mi.-high suspension bridge; a museum displaying minerals, birds, and plants indigenous to North Carolina; and a small zoo ($9, ages 4-12 $5, under 4 free). To hike or camp on Grandfather Mt. requires a permit, available at the Grandfather Mt. Country Store on Rte. 221 or at the park entrance (day use $4, camping $8). Pick up a trail map at the entrance to learn which trails are available for overnight use, and inform the **Backcountry Manager,** Grandfather Mt., Linville 28646, of your plans. (Mountain open daily 8am-7:30pm; Dec.-March 8am-5pm, weather permitting.)

■■■ ASHEVILLE

The hazy blue mountains, deep valleys, spectacular waterfalls, and plunging gorges draw a diverse crowd to this Appalachian Mountain hub while the students of the University of North Carolina at Asheville (UNC-Asheville), a thriving gay and lesbian community, nature lovers, and artists provide a human landscape to complement the terrain. While natural beauty prevails, the Biltmore Estate, nearby Cherokee museums and cultural exhibitions, and year-round festivals keep tourists busy. Asheville's craggy vistas are best seen from the Blue Ridge Pkwy.

PRACTICAL INFORMATION

Tourist Office: Chamber of Commerce, 151 Haywood St. (258-3858 or 800-257-1300 in NC), off I-240 on the northwest end of downtown; just follow the frequent signs. Ask at the desk for detailed city and transit route maps and *The Asheville Urban Trail* guide. Open Mon.-Fri. 8:30am-5:30pm, Sat.-Sun. 9am-5pm.

Buses: Greyhound, 2 Tunnel Rd. (253-5353 or 800-231-2222), 2mi. east of downtown, near the Beaucatcher Tunnel. Asheville Transit buses #13 and #14 run to and from downtown every ½hr.; last bus 5:50pm. To: Charlotte (4 per day, 3hr., $26); Knoxville (6 per day, 3hr., $23); Atlanta (1 per day, 7hr., $39). Open Mon.-Fri. 8am-5:30pm, Sat. 8-11:30am and 3-5:30pm.

Public Transportation: Asheville Transit, 360 W. Haywood (253-5691). Bus service within city limits. All routes converge on Pritchard Park downtown. Operates Mon.-Fri. (and some Sat.) 5:30am-7pm, most at ½-hr. intervals. Fare 60¢, transfers 10¢. Discounts for seniors, disabled, and multi-fare tickets.

Crisis Line: Rape Crisis, 255-7576.

Emergency: 911.

Post Office: 33 Coxe Ave. (257-4112), at Patton Ave. Open Mon.-Fri. 7:30am-5:30pm, Sat. 9am-noon. **ZIP code:** 28802. **Area code:** 704.

ACCOMMODATIONS AND CAMPING

Asheville's many reasonably priced motels cluster in two spots—several independents lie on **Merrimon Ave.** near downtown (bus #2), and **Tunnel Rd.,** east of downtown, sports many chains (bus #4 or #12). The **American Court Motel,** 85 Merrimon Ave. (253-4427 or 800-233-3582), has bright, cozy, well-kept rooms with cable, A/C, a pool, and a laundromat (singles $40, doubles $46; AAA discount). **In Town Motor Lodge,** 100 Tunnel Rd. (252-1811), provides light, clean rooms with cable, A/C, a pool, and free local calls (singles $27, doubles $32; Sat.-Sun. $32/$39). The **Down Town Motel,** 65 Merrimon Ave. (253-9841), just north of the I-240 expressway (bus #2), offers cable, A/C, and large rooms a 10-min. walk from downtown (singles $38, doubles $40; multi-night discounts possible). If you dug Lincoln Logs as a kid, you'll love **Log Cabin Motor Court,** 330 Weaverville Hwy. (645-6546). Take Rte. 240 to Rte.19/23/70N to New Bridge exit, turn right, then left at the light; 1 mi. down on the right. Each log cabin has ruffled curtains, TV, heat, and pool access. (Single $31, double $35; with kitchen $6 more and 2-day min. stay.)

With the Blue Ridge Pkwy., Pisgah National Forest, and the Great Smokies easily accessible by car, campsites are far from scarce. Close to town, **Bear Creek RV Park and Campground,** 81 S. Bear Creek Rd. (253-0798), takes the camp out of camping with a pool, laundry facilities, groceries, and a game room. Take I-40 exit 47, and look for the sign. (RV sites with hookup $25.) The nearest campground in the National Forest, **Powhatan** (667-8429), 12 mi. southwest of Asheville off Rte. 191, has wooded sites on an 8-acre trout lake, with hiking trails and a swimming lake to entertain you (gates close 10pm; $10, no hookups; open May 15-Oct.).

FOOD

You'll find the greasy links of most major fast-food chains on **Tunnel Rd.** and **Biltmore Ave.** The **Western North Carolina Farmers Market** (253-1691), at the intersection of I-40 and Rte. 191 near I-26, sells fresh produce and crafts. Take bus #16 to I-40, then walk ½mi. (Open daily 8am-6pm.)

Malaprops Bookstore/Café, 61 Haywood St. (254-6734 or 800-441-9829), downtown in the basement of the bookstore. Gourmet coffees, bagels, and great smells emanate throughout. Check out the scintillating readings upstairs and the Malaprops staff art on the walls. Open Mon.-Thurs. 9am-8pm, Fri.-Sat. 9am-10pm, Sun. noon-6pm.

Beanstreets, 3 Broadway (255-8180). Quality art hangs next to protruding fake body parts in this swank café. Excellent breakfasts of Belgian waffles, blueberry scones ($1.50), and crunchy granola with fruit ($2.50). Open Mon.-Tues. 8am-6pm, Wed.-Sat. 8am-midnight, Sun. 9am-3pm.

Five Points Restaurant, 258 Broadway (252-8030), at Chestnut 2 blocks from Merrimon Ave. and close to motels. This unremarkable-looking diner can't be beat for home-cookin'. So inexpensive your jaw will drop; full dinners (entree, salad, and two veggies) $3-5, sandwiches from $1.70. Open Mon.-Fri. 6am-8pm, Sat. 6am-5pm.

Superette, 78 Patton Ave. (254-0255), in the heart of downtown, serves good, fast, cheap Middle Eastern food. Salads from $1.50, sandwiches $2.50-$3.50. Open Mon.-Fri. 8am-5pm, Sat. 10am-4pm.

SIGHTS AND ENTERTAINMENT

Two free weekly papers, *Mountain Express* and *Community Connections,* feature entertainment listings; pick them up to find out what's going on around town.

Elvis's Southern mansion, Graceland, has nothing on the Vanderbilt family's **Biltmore Estate,** 1 North Pack Sq. (255-1700 or 800-543-2961), three blocks north of I-40's exit 50. The ostentatious abode was built in the 1890s and remains the largest private home in America. A tour of this French Renaissance castle can take all day if it's crowded; try to arrive early. The self-guided tour winds through some of the 250 rooms, around the indoor pool, through a bowling alley, into rooms lined with Sargent paintings and Dürer prints, and through the immense rare-book libraries. Tours of the surrounding gardens, designed by Central Park planner Frederick Law Olmsted, and of the Biltmore winery (with sour-wine tasting for those 21 and over) are included in the hefty admission price. (Open daily 9am-5pm; winery opens Mon.-Sat. 11am, Sun. 1pm. $25, ages 10-15 $19, under 9 free; Nov.-Dec. $2-3 more to defray the cost of Christmas decorations.)

Past travelers Henry Ford, Thomas Edison, and F. Scott Fitzgerald all stayed in the towering **Grove Park Inn** (252-2711), on Macon St. off Charlotte St. Look for the bright red-tile roof peeking through the trees. The still-operating hotel, made of stone quarried from the surrounding mountains, is expensive lodging but cheap sightseeing with early-20th-century furniture and fireplaces so immense you can walk into them. Next door is the **Estes-Winn Memorial Museum,** which houses about 20 vintage automobiles ranging from a Model T Ford to a 1959 Edsel. Check out the 1922 candy-red America La France fire engine. (Open Mon.-Sat. 10am-5pm, Sun. 1-5pm. Free.)

The **Thomas Wolfe Memorial,** 48 Spruce St. (253-8304), between Woodfin and Walnut St., site of the novelist's boyhood home, was a boarding house run by his mother, perhaps the inspiration for the guest house in Wolfe's novel *Look Homeward, Angel.* (Open Mon.-Sat. 9am-5pm, Sun. 1-5pm; hours vary in winter. Tours every ½hr. $1, students and children 50¢.) Wolfe currently resides at the **Riverside Cemetery,** Birch St. off Montford Ave. north of I-240, along with O. Henry.

Asheville's artistic tradition extends beyond literature; visit the **Folk Art Center,** Mile 382 Blue Ridge Pkwy. (704-298-7928), east of Asheville and north of U.S. 70, to see the outstanding work of the Southern Highland Handicraft Guild (open daily 9am-5pm; free). The Center's **Guild Fair** fills the Asheville Civic Center, off I-240 on Haywood St., with craft demonstrations, dancing, and music for one weekend in mid-July. Both the Center and the chamber of commerce have details.

Scrutinizing observers may catch the next Colorado Rockies' baseball star at **McCormick Field** (258-0428), at the intersection of Biltmore Ave. and S. Charlotte St. ($4, students with ID $3.50, ages 3-12 $2.50).

■ NEAR ASHEVILLE: NANTAHALA NATIONAL FOREST

The **Cherokee Indian Reservation** (800-438-1601) lies on about 30 mi. outside Asheville on U.S. 441. "Unto these Hills," an outdoor drama, retells the story of the Cherokees and climaxes with a moving re-enactment of the Trail of Tears (June-Aug., Mon.-Sat 8pm; $9, children $5); also from May to October, the reservation offers a guided tour of a re-created mid-18th century Native American village ($9, children $5). At the **Museum of the Cherokee Indian** (704-497-3481), on Drama Rd. off U.S. 441, hear the Cherokee language spoken, view artifacts and films, and learn about the past and the present of the Cherokee. Fascinating and well worth a visit. (Open Mon.-Sat. 9am-8pm, Sun. 9am-5pm; Sept. to mid-June daily 9am-5pm. $4, under 13 $2.) The **Cherokee Visitors Center** (800-438-1601), on U.S. 441, is open daily from 9am-5pm.

The bustling **Nantahala Outdoor Center (NOC),** 13077 Hwy. 19 W., Bryson City, NC (704-488-2175), 13 mi. southwest of Bryson City on U.S. 19/74 just south of GSM Park, beckons with cheap beds and the great outdoors. (Bunks in simple wooden cabins as well as fairly large-sized motel rooms with kitchenettes. Showers, kitchen, laundry facilities. $11. Call ahead.) The NOC's whitewater rafting expeditions are pricey, but you can rent your own raft for a frothy trip down the Nantahala River. (Sun.-Fri. $15, Sat. $22. 1-person inflatable "duckies" $27 weekdays, $30 on Sat. Group rates available. Higher prices on July-Aug. Prices include transportation to site and all necessary equipment.) The NOC also offers trips with slightly higher price tags on the **Ocoee, Nolichucky, Chattoga,** and **French Broad Rivers.** If you're a Gremlin, skip the river and hike a thousandth of the 2144-mi. **Appalachian Trail;** the NOC staff will assist if you need help charting an appropriate daytrip. After a full day of rafting, drink in the heavenly smell of freshly baked bread at **Maxwell's Bakery** (704-586-5046), Dillsboro exit off U.S. 74 (hours depend on season). In Cherokee, **My Grandma's** (704-497-9801), U.S. 19 and U.S. 441, serves up home-cookin' at down-low prices ($2-4; open daily from 7am, closing hours vary).

CAROLINA COAST

■■■ OUTER BANKS

Mystery and adventure have long been the spice of life on this coast. England's first attempt to colonize North America ended in 1590 with the peculiar disappearance of Sir Walter Raleigh's Roanoke Island settlement. In the early 18th century, Blackbeard called Ocracoke home, until a savvy serviceman struck him down at Pamlico Sound. Over 600 ships have foundered on the Banks' southern shores, but don't blame the weather. Early inhabitants of Nags Head would string lanterns over their horses' necks and walk them along the beach; convinced that the lights signified boats safe in harbor, captains crashed their ships on the shore trying to make port. The townspeople looted these vessels; their scheme earned the town its name.

Today, the Outer Banks descend from touristy beach towns southward into heavenly wilderness. Highly developed Bodie Island, on the Outer Banks' northern end, includes the towns of Nags Head, Kitty Hawk (the site of the Wright Brothers' first flight in 1903), and Kill Devil Hills. Crowds become less overpowering as you travel south on Rte. 12 through magnificent wildlife preserves and across Hatteras Inlet to Ocracoke Island and its isolated beaches.

PRACTICAL INFORMATION

Tourist Office: Aycock Brown Visitors Center (261-4644), off U.S. 158 across the Wright Memorial Bridge on Bodie Island. Information on lodging and picnic areas; National Park Service schedules. Open daily 8:30am-6:30pm; in winter 9am-5pm. **Cape Hatteras National Seashore Information Centers: Bodie Island** (441-5711), Rte. 12 at Bodie Island Lighthouse. **Ocracoke Island** (928-4531), next to the ferry terminal at the south end of the island. Information on ferries, camping, lighthouses, and wild ponies. Both open Easter-Columbus Day daily 9am-5pm. **Hatteras Island** (995-4474), Rte. 12 at Cape Hatteras Lighthouse. Camping info and special programs. Open daily 9am-5pm.

Ferries: Toll ferries run to Ocracoke (800-345-1665) from **Cedar Island** (800-856-0343; 4-8 per day, 2¼hr.), east of New Bern on U.S. 70, and from **Swan Quarter** (800-773-1094), on the north side of Pamlico. $1, $10 per car (reserve ahead), $2 per biker. Free ferries cross Hatteras Inlet between Hatteras and Ocracoke (daily 5am-11pm, 40min.). Call 800-BY-FERRY/293-3779 for all ferry times.

Taxis: Beach Cab (441-2500), serves Bodie Island and Manteo. $1.50 first mi., $1.20 each additional.

Car Rental: U-Save Auto Rental (800-685-9938), 1mi. north of Wright Memorial Bridge in Point Harbor. $25 per day with 50 free mi. 15¢ each additional mi. Drivers must be 21 with Mastercard, Visa, or $250 cash deposit. Open Mon.-Fri. 8am-6:30pm, Sat. 8am-2pm.

Bike Rental: Pony Island Motel (928-4411). $2 per hr., $10 per day. Open daily 8am-dusk. **Slushie Stand** (928-1878). $4 first hr., $1 per hr. thereafter; $12 for 24 hrs. Open daily 9am-dusk. Both on Rte. 12, Ocracoke Island.

Emergency: 911.

ZIP codes: Manteo 27954, Nags Head 27959, Ocracoke 27960, Kill Devil Hills 27948, Kitty Hawk 27949. **Area code:** 919.

Four narrow islands strung along half the length of the North Carolina coast comprise the Outer Banks. In the north, **Bodie Island** is accessible via U.S. 158 from Elizabeth, NC, and Norfolk, VA. **Roanoke Island** lies between Bodie and the mainland on U.S. 64 and includes the town of **Manteo. Hatteras Island,** connected to Bodie by a bridge, stretches like a great sandy elbow. **Ocracoke Island,** the southernmost island, is linked to Hatteras Island and to towns on the mainland by ferry. **Cape Hatteras National Seashore** encompasses Hatteras, Ocracoke, and the southern end of Bodie Island. On Bodie Island, U.S. 158 and Rte. 12 run parallel to each other until the north edge of the preserve. After that, Rte. 12 (also called Beach Rd.) continues south, stringing together Bodie and Hatteras. Addresses on Bodie Island are determined by their distance in miles from the Wright Memorial Bridge.

Nags Head and Ocracoke lie 76 mi. apart, and public transportation is virtually nonexistent. Hitching, though common, is not recommended, and may require lengthy waits. The flat terrain makes hiking and biking pleasant, but the Outer Banks' ferocious traffic calls for extra caution.

ACCOMMODATIONS AND CAMPING

Most motels cling to Rte. 12 on crowded Bodie Island; for more privacy, try **Ocracoke.** On all three islands, rooming rates are highest from Memorial Day to Labor Day. Reserve seven to 10 days ahead for weeknights and up to a month in advance for weekends. Rangers advise campers to bring extra-long tent spikes, because of the loose dirt, and tents with extra-fine screens, to keep out flea-sized, biting "no-see-ums." Strong insect repellent is also helpful. Sleeping on the beach is illegal.

Kill Devil Hills

The Ebbtide, Mile 10, Beach Rd. (441-4913). A family place with spruced up, wholesome rooms. Cable TV, A/C, heat, refrigerator, microwave, and pool. Sets you on the "inside track" for local activities. Singles or doubles $49-95; off season $29-70. 99¢ breakfast. Open March-Oct.

Nettlewood Motel, Mile 7, Beach Rd. (441-5039), on both sides of the highway. Private beach access. Bright, clean, cozy rooms. TV, A/C, heat, refrigerator, and pool. Singles or doubles $46-65; off season $30-35. Free night for week-long stays.

Manteo

Scarborough Inn (473-3979), U.S. 64/264. Romantic inn with 4-poster canopy beds, flowered linens, and wrap-around porches. Telephone, A/C, heat, refrigerator, continental breakfast and free use of bicycles. One queen bed $50, 2 queen beds $55, 1 king bed $60. Off season $10 less.

Ocracoke

Sand Dollar Motel (928-5571), off Rte. 12. Turn right at the Pony Island Inn, right again at the Back Porch Restaurant, and left at the Edwards Motel. Accommodating owner makes you feel at home in this breezy, quiet, immaculate motel. One queen bed $55, 2 queen beds $65. Off season $40/$45. Open April-Thanksgiving.

Edwards Motel (928-4801), off Rte. 12 by the Back Porch Restaurant. Bright assortment of rooms, all with TV, A/C, and heat. Fish-cleaning facilities on premises. Two double beds, or 1 double and 1 single, $45, off season $40; 2 double beds and 1 single, with refrigerator and screened porch $52/$45; efficiencies $62/$58; cottages $75-85/$71-77.

Three oceanside **campgrounds** on Cape Hatteras National Seashore are open Memorial Day to Labor Day: **Cape Point** (in Buxton) and **Frisco,** near the elbow of Hatteras Island, and **Ocracoke,** in the middle of Ocracoke Island. **Oregon Inlet,** on the southern tip of Bodie Island, opens in mid-April. All have restrooms, cold running water, and grills. All sites (except Ocracoke's) cost $12, and are rented on a first-come, first-served basis. Ocracoke sites ($13) can be reserved by calling 800-365-CAMP/2267. For info, contact **Cape Hatteras National Seashore,** Rte. 1, P.O. Box 675, Manteo, NC 27954 (473-2111).

SIGHTS AND ACTIVITIES

The **Wright Brothers National Memorial,** Mile 8, U.S. 158 (441-7430), marks the spot where Orville and Wilbur Wright made the world's first sustained, controlled power flight on December 17, 1903. You can see models of their planes, hear a detailed account of the day of the first flight, and view the dramatic monument dedicated to the brothers in 1932. (Open daily 9am-6pm; in winter 9am-5pm. Presentations every hr. 10am-5pm. $2 per person, $4 per car. See National Parks p. 55 for details on discount Passports.) In nearby **Jockey's Ridge State Park** (441-7132), home of the East Coast's largest sand dunes, hang-gliders soar in the sky that Wilbur and Orville first navigated. Open daily 8am-9pm.

On **Roanoke Island,** the **Fort Raleigh National Historic Site,** off U.S. 64, offers several attractions in one park. *The Lost Colony* (473-3414 or 800-488-5012), the longest-running outdoor drama in the U.S., has been performed here since 1937. (Early June-late Aug., Mon.-Fri. and Sun. 8:30pm. $12, seniors and military $11, under 12 $6. Bring insect repellent.) In the **Elizabethan Gardens** (473-3234), antique statues and fountains punctuate a beautiful display of flowers, herbs, and trees. (Open early June-late Aug. daily 9am-8pm; off season 9am-dusk. $3, under 12 free.) **Fort Raleigh** (473-5772) is a reconstructed 1585 battery—basically a pile of dirt. The nearby **visitors center** contains a tiny museum and shows a short film recalling the earliest days of English activity in North America. (Open Mon.-Fri. and Sun. 9am-8pm, Sat. 9am-6pm. Free.) Horseshoe crabs and marine monsters await at the Shark, Skate, and Ray Gallery of the **North Carolina Aquarium** (473-3493), 1 mi. west of U.S. 64. A full slate of educational programs keeps it lively. (Open Mon.-Sat. 9am-5pm, Sun. 1-5pm. $3, seniors $2, ages 6-17 $1.)

Majestic **lighthouses** dot the Outer Banks, and **Cape Hatteras,** run by the Cape Hatteras National seashore, is North America's tallest at 208 ft. (Open for climbing Labor Day-Columbus Day daily 9:30am-4pm, weather permitting. Free.) Special programs at the Hatteras Island Visitor Center in Buxton include **Maritime Woods Walk** (Mon. 2pm) and **Morning Bird Walk** (Wed. 7:30am). At **Soundside Snorkel,** park rangers teach visitors to snorkel (duh); bring sneakers and a swimsuit. (Thurs. 2:30pm. To participate in this program, you must enter a lottery on Wed. at 4:15pm at the Cape Hatteras Visitors Center.)

South Carolina

The first state to secede from the Union in 1860, South Carolina continues to take great pride in its Confederate history; Civil War monuments dot virtually every public green or city square, and Confederate "patriots" periodically protest legislative efforts to remove the Confederate flag from the state flag.

However, the timber of the state is generally more laid-back than this would suggest. The capital, Columbia, is slow-paced with little to see—it was demolished during the Civil War along with everything else in Sherman's path. Charleston was spared, and despite nature's repeated assaults, still boasts stately, antebellum style. You may need to do the Charleston for a few days to take in the city's flavor. Those who slow to South Carolina's languid pace find that this state preserves a grace and charm which often render the rituals of daily life more enjoyable.

PRACTICAL INFORMATION

Capital: Columbia.

Department of Parks, Recreation, and Tourism: Edgar A. Brown Bldg., 1205 Pendleton St. #106, Columbia 29021 (803-734-0122). **U.S. Forest Service,** 4931 Broad River Rd., Columbia 29210 (803-561-4000).

Time Zone: Eastern. **Postal Abbreviation:** SC

Sales Tax: 6%.

■■■ CHARLESTON

Dukes, barons, and earls once presided over Charleston's great coastal plantations, building an extensive, now historic, downtown district. In recent years natural disasters, including five fires and 10 hurricanes—the most recent in 1989—have necessitated repeated rebuilding in the city. New storefronts and tree stumps mix with beautifully refurbished antebellum homes, old churches, and hidden gardens. The area also offers access to the nearby Atlantic coastal islands. While you're in Charleston, try to meet the locals, some of the friendliest you'll find in the South.

PRACTICAL INFORMATION

Tourist Office: Charleston Visitors Center, 375 Meeting St. (853-8000), across from Charleston Museum. Walking tour map ($4.50) has historical info and good directions. *Forever Charleston* film gives an overview of the city past and present ($2.50, children $1). Open daily 8:30am-7:30pm, off season 8:30am-5:30pm.

Trains: Amtrak, 4565 Gaynor Ave. (744-8263 or 800-872-7245), 8mi. west of downtown. One train per day to: Richmond (8hr., $90); Savannah (2hr., $28); Washington, DC (8hr., $108). Open daily 4:15am-noon and 1:30-8:30pm.

Buses: Greyhound, 601 W. Trade St. (372-0456 or 800-231-2222), in N. Charleston near I-26. Try to avoid this area at night. To: Savannah (2 per day, 3hr., $27); Charlotte (2 per day, 6hr., $40). The SCE&G "Dorchester/Waylyn" bus goes to town from the station. Return on the "Navy Yard: 5 Mile Dorchester Rd." bus; there are two "Navy Yard" buses, so be sure to take this one. Open daily 24 hrs.

Public Transportation: South Carolina Electric and Gas Company (SCE&G) City Bus Service, 3664 Leeds Ave. (747-0922). Operates Mon.-Sat. 5:30am-midnight. Fare 75¢. **Downtown Area Shuttle (DASH)** operates Mon.-Fri. 8am-5pm. Fare 75¢, transfers to other SCE&G buses free.

Car Rental: Thrifty Car Rental, 3565 W. Montague Ave. (552-7531 or 800-367-2277). $30 per day with unlimited mi. Must be 21 with major credit card. Under 25 surcharge $9 per day. Open daily 5:30am-11:30pm.

Bike Rental: The Bicycle Shoppe, 280 Meeting St. (722-8168). $3 per hr., $15 per day. Open Mon.-Sat. 9am-8pm, Sun. 1-5pm.

Taxis: North Area Taxi, 554-7575. Base fare $2.50 per person per zone.

Crisis Lines: Hotline, 744-4357. General counseling and information on transient accommodations. **People Against Rape,** 722-7273. Both operate 24 hrs.

Emergency: 911.

Post Office: 83 Broad St. (577-0690). Open Mon.-Fri. 8:30am-5:30pm, Sat. 9:30am-2pm. **ZIP code:** 29402. **Area code:** 803.

Old Charleston lies at the southernmost point of the mile-wide peninsula below **Calhoun Street. Meeting, King,** and **East Bay St.** are major north-south routes through the city. North of Calhoun St. runs the **Savannah Hwy. (U.S. 17).**

ACCOMMODATIONS AND CAMPING

Motel rooms in historic downtown Charleston are expensive. Cheap motels are a few mi. out of the city or across the Ashley River on U.S. 17S—not a practical option for those without cars. The best budget option in town is the **Rutledge Victoria Inn,** 114 Rutledge Ave. (722-7551), a beautiful historic home with shared rooms and free coffee or tea in summer (May 15-Aug.) and discount rooms with shared bath and full continental breakfast off season. (Lockout 10:30am-4:30pm. $20 per person first day, $15 each additional day; Sept.-May 15 $50. Only 6 beds; call ahead for reservations.) **Motel 6,** 2058 Savannah Hwy. (556-5144), 4 mi. out of town, is clean and pleasant but far from downtown and frequently filled; call ahead in summer (singles $28, additional person $6).

There are several inexpensive campgrounds in the Charleston area, including **The Campground at James Island County Park** (795-9884 or 800-743-7275). Take U.S. 17S to Rte. 171 and follow the signs. This spectacular park offers full hookups in addition to 16 acres of lakes, miles of bicycle and walking trails, and a small water park. (Tent sites, in limited number, $13; full hookup $20.) **Oak Plantation Campground** (766-5936), 8 mi. south on U.S. 17, has 350 sites and a free shuttle to the visitors center (office open daily 7:30am-9pm; sites $10, with hookup $15.40).

FOOD AND NIGHTLIFE

Hyman's Seafood Company, 215 Meeting St. (723-6000). Kudos to the proprietor, who manages to serve 15-25 different kinds of fresh fish daily ($8). The snow crabs ($10) are a must for shellfish-lovers. Open daily 11am-11pm.

Henry's, 54 N. Market St. (723-4363), at Anson. The oldest restaurant in town, and a local favorite. Not cheap, but the food is worth it, especially the grilled shrimp ($8). Open Mon.-Wed. 11:30am-10:30pm, Thurs.-Sun. 11:30am-1am. The bar upstairs has good live jazz and beer. Happy hour Mon.-Fri. 4-7pm; "ladies night" Wed. Open Mon.-Fri. 4pm-2am, Sat.-Sun. noon-2am.

T-Bonz Gill and Grill, 80 N. Market St. (517-2511). From T-bone to stir-fry, all in an open-beam building in the historic district. Popular Tues. night live music. Lunch or dinner $3-12. Potato with chili $2.95. Open daily 11am-midnight.

Baker Café, 214 King St. (577-2694). Serves gourmet sandwiches (blackened grouper with cayenne tartar sauce) and eggs just about any way imaginable ($6-8). Open Mon.-Fri. 8am-late afternoon and Sat.-Sun. 9am-late afternoon. Lunch starts at 11:30am.

Craig Cafeteria (953-5539), corner of St. Philip and George St., the place to chow in Chaz. Serves all-you-can-eat buffets at Charleston College. In summer, breakfast (9-11am, $4.25), lunch (noon-2pm, $4.50), dinner (4:30-6:30pm, $4.75); during the school year, breakfast 7-9am, lunch 11am-2pm, and dinner 4:30-6:30pm.

Locals rarely dance the Charleston anymore, and the city's nightlife suffers for it. Before going out, pick up a free copy of *Poor Richard's Omnibus,* available at grocery stores and street corners all over town, for listings of concerts and other events. Most bars and clubs are in the **Market St.** area. The **Music Farm,** 32 Ann St. (853-3276), has everything from rave to disco to live bands (hours and cover vary; call ahead). Find eclectic live music at the **Acme Bar and Grill,** 5 Faber St. (577-7383; Sun. and Tues. 8pm-3am, Wed. and Sat. 8pm-2am, Thurs.-Fri. 8pm-wee hours).

SIGHTS AND ENTERTAINMENT

Charleston's ancient homes, historical monuments, churches, galleries, and gardens can be seen by foot, car, bus, boat, trolley, or carriage; ask about organized tours at the visitors center. The 2-hr. **Gray Line Water Tours** (722-1112) boat trip is not only longer but less expensive than most others (daily 10am, 12:30pm, and 3pm; $9.50, ages 6-11 $4.75; reservations recommended).

The open-air **City Market,** downtown at Meeting St., has a deal on everything from porcelain sea lions to handwoven sweetgrass baskets (daily 9:30am-sunset).

Gibbes Museum of Art, 135 Meeting St. (722-2706), displays a fine collection of portraits by prominent American artists (open Sun.-Mon. 1-5pm, Tues.-Sat. 10am-5pm; $5, students and seniors $4, under 13 $3). Founded in 1773, the **Charleston Museum,** 360 Meeting St. (722-2996), maintains collections ranging from natural history specimens to old sheet music (open Mon.-Sat. 9am-5pm, Sun. 1-5pm). Charleston's mansions are very pricey, so a good bet is the package deal with the Charleston Museum. A combination ticket is available for the museum and two historic homes within easy walking distance: the 18th-century **Heyward-Washington House,** 87 Church St., and the **Joseph Manigault House,** 350 Meeting St. The Washington House includes the only 18th-century kitchen open to the public in Charleston—hope they hide those dirty dishes. (Both homes open Mon.-Sat. 10am-5pm, Sun. 1-5pm. Museum and two homes $15, children $5; call the museum for individual prices.) For a look at how Charleston's wealthy merchant class lived in the early 19th century, visit the **Nathaniel Russell House,** 51 Meeting St. (724-8481), where a magnificent staircase spirals from floor to floor without visible support. (Open Mon.-Sat. 10am-5pm; Sun. 2-5pm.) The **Edmonston-Allston House,** 21 E. Battery St. (722-7171), looks out over the harbor. (Open Sun.-Mon. 1:30-4:40pm, Tues.-Sat. 10am-4:40pm. Tours every 10min. ending at 4:40pm. 1 house $5, both $8.)

The Battery offers a good view of the harbor and **Fort Sumter,** where an attack by rebel forces on April 12, 1861 touched off the Civil War. Over seven million pounds of metal were fired against the fort before it was finally abandoned in February, 1865. If you feel you must walk the sacred ground, call **Fort Sumter Tours** (722-1691). Boat tours leave several times daily from the Municipal Marina, at the foot of Calhoun St. and Lockwood Blvd. ($9.50, ages 6-12 $4.75). They also offers tours to **Patriots' Point,** the world's largest naval and maritime museum, where you can walk the decks of the massive retired U.S. aircraft carrier *Yorktown* or stroke the destroyer *Laffey's* huge fore and aft cannons. Touring the ships will take several hours ($9, under 12 $4.50).

One of several majestic plantations in the area, the 300-year-old **Magnolia Plantation and Magnolia Gardens** (571-1266), 10 mi. out of town on Rte. 61 off U.S. 17, treats visitors to 50 acres of gorgeous gardens with 900 varieties of camellia and 250 varieties of azalea. Get lost in the hedge maze. If you've seen some of the homes in the city, you may want to skip the manor house, but do consider renting bicycles or canoes ($2 per hr.) to explore the neighboring swamp and bird sanctuary. (Open daily 8am-5pm. $9, seniors, military, and AAA $8, ages 13-19 $7, ages 4-12 $4.)

From mid-March to mid-April, the **Festival of Houses and Gardens** (723-1623) celebrates Charleston's architecture and traditions; many private homes open their doors to the public (10 houses $25). Music, theater, dance, and opera fill the city during **Spoleto Festival U.S.A.** (800-255-4659) in late May and early June ($7-86). The **Charleston Maritime Festival** (800-221-5273) in mid-September celebrates America's water heritage with parades, artists, and a regatta. During **Christmas in Charleston** (853-8000), private homes and buildings offer tours, people sell crafts, and the Nutcracker Suite dances on; many motels offer special reduced rates.

■■■ COLUMBIA

One of America's first planned cities, Columbia sprang up in 1786 when Charleston's bureaucrats decided their territory needed a proper capital. Surveyors found some land by the Congaree River, and soon more than 1000 people had poured in. The students of the University of South Carolina (USC) now call the city home. In many ways, Columbia's college-town flavor overshadows its state politics, but the bronze stars on the State House, which mark General Sherman's cannonball strikes, indicate strong links to a Confederate past not soon forgotten.

PRACTICAL INFORMATION

Tourist Office: Columbia Metropolitan Convention and Visitors Bureau, 1012 Gervais St. (254-0479). Pick up maps for self-guided walking tours of *Historic Columbia* or *African-American Historic Sites in Columbia*. Open Mon.-Fri. 9am-5pm, Sat. 10am-4pm, Sun. 1-5pm. **University of South Carolina Information Desk,** 1400 Green St. (777-3196), inside Russell House Union, 2nd floor, stocks maps, shuttle schedules, and the low-down on campus events. Open Mon.-Thurs 8:30am-9pm, Fri. 8:30am-5pm; schoolyear Mon.-Fri. 9am-midnight.

Airport: Columbia Metropolitan Airport, 3000 Aviation Way (822-5010). Taxis to downtown run $10-$12.

Trains: Amtrak, 850 Pulaski St. (252-8246 or 800-872-7245). One per day to: Washington, DC (10hr., $104); Miami (13hr., $124); Savannah (2hr., $36). Open daily 10am-6pm. Northbound train departs 1:36am, southbound 12:53am.

Buses: Greyhound, 2015 Gervais St. (256-6465 or 800-231-2222), at Harden about 1mi. east of the capital. To: Charlotte (4 per day, 2hr., $18); Atlanta (6 per day, 5hr., $43). Most buses running along the East Coast stop here. Open 24 hrs.

Public Transportation: South Carolina Electric and Gas (SCE&G) (748-3019). Local buses 75¢. Most routes start from the transfer depot at Assembly and Gervais St.

Crisis Lines: Helpline of the Midlands, 790-4357. **Rape Crisis,** 771-7273. Both 24 hrs.

Emergency: 911.

Post Office: 1601 Assembly St. (733-4643). Open Mon.-Fri. 7:30am-5pm. **ZIP code:** 29202. **Area code:** 803.

The **Congaree River** marks the west edge of the city. **Assembly** and **Sumter St.** are the major north-south arteries downtown; **Gervais** and **Calhoun St.** cut east-west.

ACCOMMODATIONS, CAMPING, AND FOOD

Just outside of downtown across the Congaree River, a number of inexpensive motels line **I-26** and **I-77.** One is **Masters Inn Economy** (791-5850 or 800-633-3434); off I-26E at exit 113, take a left then an immediate right onto Frontage Rd. Fresh paint, free local calls, a pool, and cable TV brighten these disabled accessible rooms. (Singles $24, doubles $28.) On the same road, try **Knights Inn** (794-0222), where rooms stenciled with castle scenes keep the knight theme going. All rooms have refrigerators, microwaves, cable TV, A/C, heat, and access to a pool. (Singles $28, doubles $30.) The **Sesquicentennial State Park** (788-2706) has a lake for swimming and 87 wooded sites with electricity and water (gate closes 9pm; $13). Public transportation does not serve the park; take I-20 to the Two Notch Rd./Rte. 1 exit and head northeast for 4 mi.

The **Five Points** business district, at the junction of Harden, Devine, and Blossom St. ("Veterans Hospital" bus from downtown), caters to Columbia's large student population with bars, nightclubs, and coffeehouses. **Groucho's,** 611 Harden St. (799-5708), in the heart of Five Points, is both a Columbia institution and an anomaly—a New York-style Jewish deli. (Large sandwiches $4-6. Open Mon.-Wed. 11am-4:30pm, Thurs.-Fri. 11am-9pm, Sat. 11am-4pm.) **Adriana's,** 721 Saluda Ave. (799-7595), serves a super selection of Italian ice cream (massive serving $1.60), coffees, and homemade Italian pastries. Students and locals frequent USC's renowned deli **Stuffy's Famous,** 629 S. Main St. (771-4098), down Main St. from the State House (cheeseburger, fries, and iced tea $3.45). Happy hour (Mon.-Fri. 4-7pm) means 15¢ wings. (Open Mon.-Fri. 10am-11pm, Sat. 11am-11pm, Sun. noon-10pm.) The **Columbia State Farmers Market** (253-4041), Bluff Rd. across from the USC Football Stadium, is a good place to stock up on fresh Carolina peaches, melons, and, of course, peanuts (open Mon.-Sat. 6am-9pm).

SIGHTS AND ENTERTAINMENT

One of the finest zoos in the country, **Riverbanks Zoo and Garden** (779-8730), on I-26 at Greystone Blvd. northwest of downtown, shows visitors a rainforest, a desert, an undersea kingdom, and a southern farm. Over 2000 animals roam in open habitats. (Open Mon.-Fri. 9am-4pm, Sat.-Sun. 9am-5pm. $5.75, students $3.50, seniors $3.25, ages 3-12 $3.)

Columbia's 18th-century elegance remains intact at the **Robert Mills Historic House and Park,** 1616 Blanding St. (252-1770), three blocks east of Sumter St. One of America's first federal architects, Mills designed the Washington Monument and 30 of South Carolina's public buildings. His Neoclassical home is said to be haunted. Across the street at #1615, the **Hampton-Preston Mansion** (252-0938) not only served as headquarters for Sherman's Union forces during the Civil War, but also once housed Confederate general Wade Hampton. (Both open Tues.-Sat. 10:15am-3:15pm, Sun. 1:15-4:15pm. Tours $3, students $1.50, under 6 free.) The **South Carolina State Museum,** 301 Gervais St. (737-4595), beside the Gervais St. Bridge, is in the historic Columbia Mills building. Exhibits include a prehistoric great white shark—far more impressive than its modern cousin. (Open Mon.-Sat. 10am-5pm, Sun. 1-5pm. $4, students with ID and seniors $3, ages 6-17 $1.50, under 6 free.)

Stroll through the USC **Horseshoe,** at the junction of College and Sumter St., to admire the university's oldest buildings, which date from the early 19th century. The **McKissick Museum** (777-7251), at the top of the Horseshoe, shows scientific exhibits, pottery, and selections from the university's extensive collection of Twentieth Century-Fox newsreels. (Open Mon.-Fri. 9am-4pm, Sat.-Sun. 1-5pm. Free.)

Finlay Park, behind the post office on Assembly and Laurel St., a large, manicured city park with playing fields, fountains, and swinging benches, makes a romantic setting for a picnic dinner or lunch break. (Closes daily 11pm.)

■■■ MYRTLE BEACH AND THE GRAND STRAND

Stretching 60 mi. from Little River near the North Carolina border to the tidelands of historic Georgetown, the Grand Strand is a long, wide ribbon of land covered with beaches, tourists, restaurants, and small villages. In the middle of it all basks Myrtle Beach, full of mini-golf courses, tennis courts, water parks, and white sand. During spring break and in early June, Myrtle Beach (especially North Myrtle Beach) becomes jam-packed with leering, sun-burned students who revel in the area's commercialism and the call of the deep blue.

The pace slows significantly south of Myrtle Beach. **Murrell's Inlet,** a quaint port stocked with good seafood, and **Pawley's Island** are both dominated by private homes. **Georgetown,** once one of the South's most important port cities, retains its history in white-pillared homes on 18th-century rice and indigo plantations.

PRACTICAL INFORMATION

Tourist Office: Myrtle Beach Chamber of Commerce, 1200 Oak St. (626-7444), provides area info including entertainment listings, coupons, and details on accommodations. Open Mon.-Fri. 8:30am-5pm, Sat. 9am-5pm, Sun. noon-5pm.

Buses: Greyhound, 508 9th Ave. N. (448-2471 or 800-231-2222). Open daily 8:30am-1pm and 3-7:30pm.

Public Transportation: Costal Rapid Public Transit (CRPTA) (626-9138) does minimal busing. Local 75¢; Conway to Myrtle Beach $1.25.

Bike Rental: The Bike Shoppe, 711 Broadway (448-5335). Mountain bikes $2.50 per hr., $15 per day. License or credit card required. Open daily 8am-6pm.

Emergency: 911.

Post Office: 505 N. Kings Hwy. (626-9533). Open Mon.-Fri. 8:30am-5pm, Sat. 9am-1pm. **ZIP code:** 29577. **Area code:** 803.

U.S. 17, also called **Kings Hwy.,** runs north-south through the entire Grand Strand. In Myrtle Beach, **Ocean Blvd.** parallels Rte. 17, lined with pricier motels and hotels and reasonably priced restaurants. **Rte. 501** runs west towards Conway, U.S. 95, and, more importantly, the popular factory outlet stores. Unless otherwise stated, addresses on the Grand Strand are for Myrtle Beach.

ACCOMMODATIONS AND CAMPING

Couples and families take over in summer, Myrtle Beach's most expensive season. In fact, many motels and campgrounds accept only families or couples. Cheap motels lurk just west of the beach in the 3rd St. area or on U.S. 17. Prices plunge October through March when they need your business; you can often bargain for a lower hotel rate. A free n'easy way to find the most economical rooms is to call the **Beach Hotel and Motel Reservation Service,** 1551 21st Ave. N. Suite #20 (626-7477 or 800-626-7477). For the best deals, ask for the "second row" string of hotels across the street from the ocean front. (Open daily 8am-8pm.) The Grand Strand has been called the "camping capital of the world;" Myrtle Beach alone is laden with nine campgrounds and two state parks.

Sea Banks Motor Inn, 2200 S. Ocean Blvd. (448-2434 or 800-523-0603), across the street from the ocean. Family-run establishment with laundry facilities, a pool, beach access, new carpet, large windows, and TV. Some rooms have balconies. Rooms with 1 double bed from $23 (March and Sept.-Oct.) to $39 (in summer).

Lazy G Motel, 405 27th Ave. N. (448-6333 or 800-633-2163), has 2-bed efficiency apartments with full mini-kitchens, attractive decor, TV, A/C, a pool, and heat. From $23 (mid-Oct.-mid-March) to $61 (in summer).

Grand Strand Motel, 1804 S. Ocean Blvd. (448-1461 or 800-433-1461). Similar to Sea Banks. Small rooms with 1 double bed for 2 adults from $53 (in summer) to $18 (in winter). Golf packages available.

Myrtle Beach State Park Campground (238-5325), 3mi. south of town off U.S. 17 across from the air force base. 350 sites with full hookup on 312 acres of unspoiled land with a cool beach, fishing, a pool, and a nature trail. Showers and bathrooms are close by. Office open Mon.-Fri. 9am-5pm, Sat.-Sun. 11am-noon and 4-5pm. $16, Oct.-March $11. First come, first served; call ahead.

Huntington Beach State Park Campground (237-4440), 5mi. south of Murrell's Inlet on U.S. 17. A diverse natural environment with lagoons, salt marshes, and, of course, a beach. 127 sites with full hookup and convenient showers and rest rooms. Office open Mon.-Fri. 9am-5pm, Sat.-Sun. 11am-noon. $17, Oct.-March $11. Call ahead for reservations; it fills very quickly.

ALL-YOU-CAN-EAT

Over 1600 restaurants, serving anything you can imagine, can be found (or, can't be missed) on the Grand Strand. Massive, family-style, all-you-can-eat joints await at every traffic light. Seafood is best on Murrell's Inlet, while Ocean Blvd. and Hwy. 17 offer endless steakhouses, fast food joints, and buffets.

River City Café, 404 21st Ave. N. (448-1990), also on Business 17 in Murrell's Inlet, serves juicy burgers ($2.95), homemade fries, beer, and free peanuts (toss the shells on the floor) in a fun, collegiate atmosphere. Open daily 11am-10pm.

Mammy's Kitchen (448-7242), 11th Ave. N. at King's Hwy., grills up a breakfast deal and a half—hashbrowns, toast, eggs, and bacon for $2.19. Open daily 7am-noon and 4:30-9:30pm.

The Filling Station, (626-9435) Hwy. 17 at 17th Ave. N., and on the Alabama Theater side of Bearfoot Landing (272-7034). One great menu idea: all-you-can-eat pizza, soup, sandwich bar, and dessert. Fill 'er up at lunch ($5) or dinner ($7). Children eat for $2-3, including drink.

SIGHTS AND ENTERTAINMENT

The cheapest and most amusing entertainment here is people-watching. Families, newlyweds, foreigners, and students flock to this incredibly popular area to lie out, eat out, and live American beach culture. The boulevard and the length of the beach are called the **strand.** Cruising it at night is a must, but be careful—it's illegal. Look for signs that read: "You may not cross this point more than twice in 2 hours."

White sand beaches and refreshing water are Myrtle Beach's classic attractions. The mind-boggling number of golf and mini-golf courses (45!) and amusement and water parks (13!) could make the Las Vegas Strip seem tasteful. The largest of the amusement parks is the **Myrtle Beach Pavilion** (448-6456), on Ocean Blvd. and 9th Ave. N. (Open daily 1pm-midnight. Unlimited rides $18.25, under 42" $11.75. Individual tickets 50¢; rides use 2-7 tickets, depending on the number of loops, droops, and spins.) The **Myrtle Waves Water Park** (448-1026), 10th Ave. N and Hwy. 17 by-pass, will water-log you with 30 water rides, including the world's largest tubular slide (open daily 10am-7pm; $16, under 42" $10).

Oddly, Myrtle Beach is a mecca for country music shows. The **Gatlin Brothers Theater** (236-8500), Hwy. 501 at Waccamaw, features the Gatlins themselves or other well-known country favorites ($21.95, under 12 $9.95). The **Carolina Opry** (238-8888), at Business 17 and the Hwy. 17 Bypass, is a country spectacular with over 20 musicians ($21, under 12 $7). The **Alabama Theater at Barefoot Landing,** 4750 U.S. 17S (272-1111), has it all—singin', swingin', and comedy, complete with an aptly named production called the American Pride Show (Mon.-Sat. 8pm; $17, ages 3-11 $7; reservations required).

The area's nightclubs slam every night of the week. Pick up free copies of *Beachcomber* and *Kicks* at the Chamber of Commerce for upcoming events. **Studebakers,** 2000 N. Kings Hwy. (626-3855), is a casual, young (18 and up) hang-out with a 50s theme and a lifeguard stand by the dance floor. Contests and theme nights are held often; call for details. (Open nightly 8pm-2am. Cover $8-10.) **2001,** 920 Lake Arrowhead Rd. (449-9434), in Restaurant Row, is three clubs in one: a contemporary country club, a "shag" club, and a high energy dance club. (Open Mon.-Fri. 8pm-3am, Sat.-Sun. 8pm-2am. Live entertainment Thurs.-Sat. Cover $6-8.) Grand Strand fests include the **Canadian-American Days Festival** in mid-March, the huge **Sun Fun Festival** in early June, and **Christmas** partying starting in November.

Georgia

From the North Georgia mountains to the coastal plains and swamps, Georgia thrives on such alliterative industries as paper products, popcorn, peanuts, pecans, peaches, poultry, and politicians. President Jimmy Carter's hometown and the only house ever owned by President Franklin D. Roosevelt both stand on red Georgia clay. Coca-Cola was invented here in 1886; since then, it has gone on to carbonate and caffeinate the world over. Ted Turner and CNN have brought world news and folks from all over the globe, making the capital a diverse, sophisticated metropolis.

In 1996, Atlanta will play host to the Olympic Games. Sharing the spotlight are coastal Savannah, a city with stately, romantic antebellum homes and colonial city blocks, and Athens, home of the Bulldogs and REM. The state blooms in the spring, glistens in the summer, and mellows in the autumn, all the while welcoming y'all with peachy Southern hospitality. Stay here long and you'll *never* be able to shake Georgia from your mind.

PRACTICAL INFORMATION

Capital: Atlanta.

Department of Industry and Trade, Tourist Division, 285 Peachtree St., Atlanta 30301 (656-3590), across from Atlanta Convention and Visitors Bureau. Write for or pick up the comprehensive *Georgia Travel Guide.* Open Mon.-Fri. 8am-5pm. **Department of Natural Resources,** 205 Butler St. SE, Atlanta 30334 (800-542-7275; 404-656-3530 in GA). **U.S. Forest Service,** 1720 Peachtree Rd. NW, Atlanta 30367 (347-2384), has info on the Chattahoochee and Oconee National Forests. Open Mon.-Fri. 10am-4:30pm.

Time Zone: Eastern. **Postal Abbreviation:** GA

Sales Tax: 4-6%, depending on county.

■■■ ATLANTA

Unlike other southern cities which define themselves by their Civil War past, Atlanta defines itself in terms of its ever-expanding present. A nationwide economic powerhouse, Atlanta contains the offices of 400 of the Fortune 500 companies, including the headquarters of Coca-Cola and CNN. Nineteen institutions of higher learning, including Georgia Tech, Morehouse College, Spelman College, and Emory University, call "Hotlanta" home. This prosperity has diluted Atlanta's Old South flavor, and an influx of Northerners, Californians, the third-largest gay population in the U.S., and a host of ethnicities contribute to the city's cosmopolitan air.

As host of the 1996 summer Olympics, Atlanta burns with Olympic fever. Clocks count down the days to go until July 19, 1996, and the city is besieged by new construction at nearly every turn. Rumors circulate that tickets and hotel rooms are already gone, but budget travelers need not despair. There are several free Olympic events, hostels who are expanding capacity, and other places (e.g., Birmingham, Athens, Savannah) that will host less crowded Olympic events. As the first Olympics ever to be held in the South arrives, Atlantans, Georgians, and Southerners alike hope that, if just for a few weeks, the entire world will be "y'all."

PRACTICAL INFORMATION

Tourist Office: Atlanta Convention and Visitors Bureau, 233 Peachtree St. NE, #200 (521-6600), Peachtree Center, 20th floor of Harris Tower, downtown; stop by to pick up a free copy of *Atlanta and Georgia Visitors' Guide.* Open Mon.-Fri. 10am-5pm. Also at **Underground Atlanta** (577-2148), Pyror and Alabama St. Open Mon.-Sat. 10am-6pm, Sun. noon-6pm. **Gay Center Help Line,** 892-0661. Open daily 6-11pm. Center located at 71 12th St. (876-5372). Provides community info and short-term counseling.

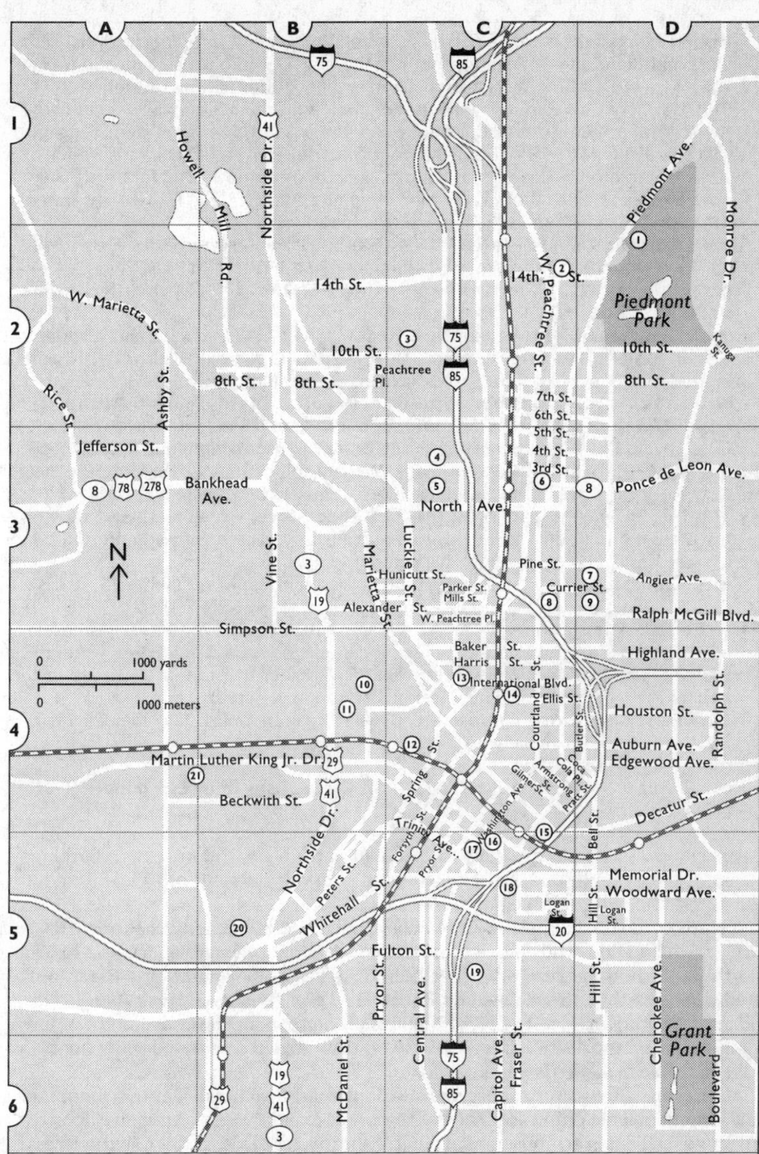

Downtown Atlanta

1 Atlanta Botanical Garden
2 Peachtree Community Playhouse
3 Alexander Memorial Coliseum
4 Georgia Institute of Technology
5 Grant Field / Bobby Dodd Stadium
6 Fox Theatre
7 Exhibition & SciTrek Museum
8 Civic Center
9 Atlantic Civic 3 Center
10 World Congress Center
11 Georgia Dome
12 CNN Center
13 Greyhoun Bus Depot
14 Peachtree Center
15 Georgia State University
16 State Capitol
17 City Hall
18 Georgia Dept. of Archives & History
19 Atlanta Fulton County Stadium
20 Spelman College
21 Clark Atlanta University

THE SOUTH

Airport: Hartsfield International (222-6688 for general info; international services and flight info 530-2081), south of the city. Get phone assistance in 6 languages at the **Calling Assistance Center** in the international terminal (873-6170). MARTA (see Public Transportation, below) is the easiest way to get downtown, with 15-min. rides departing every 8min. daily 5am-1am, with baggage space available ($1.25). **Atlanta Airport Shuttle** (524-3400) runs vans from the airport to midtown, downtown, Emory, and Lenox Sq. ($8-12). **Northside Airport Express** (768-7600) serves Stone Mountain, Marietta, and Dunwoody. Buses run daily 5:30am-10pm ($15-30). Taxi to downtown $15.

Train: Amtrak, 1688 Peachtree St. NW (881-3061), 3mi. north of downtown at I-85. Take bus #23 to and from the "Arts Center" MARTA station. To: New York (1 per day, 19hr., $147); New Orleans (3 per week, 11hr., $95). Open daily 6:30am-9:45pm.

Buses: Greyhound, 81 International Blvd. NW (584-1728), 1 block from Peachtree Center. MARTA: Peachtree Center. To: New York (11 per day, 17hr., $89); Washington, DC (11 per day, 13hr., $89); Savannah (4 per day, 6hr., $51). Open 24 hrs.

Public Transportation: Metropolitan Atlanta Rapid Transit Authority (MARTA) (848-4711; schedule info Mon.-Fri. 6am-10pm, Sat.-Sun. 8am-4pm). Combined rail and bus system serves virtually all area attractions and hotels. Operates Mon.-Sat. 5am-1:30am, Sun. 6am-12:30am in most areas. Fare $1.50 exact change, or buy a token at station machines; transfers free. Unlimited weekly pass $11. Pick up a system map at the **MARTA Ride Store,** Five Points Station downtown, or at one of the satellite visitors bureaus. If you get confused, just find the nearest MARTA courtesy phone in each rail station.

Taxis: Checker, 351-1111. $2 per person downtown. **Rapid,** 222-9888. $1.50 base fare, $1.20 per mi. 24 hrs.

Car Rental: Atlanta Rent-a-Car, 3185 Camp Creek Pkwy. (763-1160), just inside I-285 3mi. east of the airport. 9 other locations in the area including Cheshire Bridge Rd. and I-85, 1mi. west of the Lindberg Center Railstop. $20 per day, 100 free mi., 19¢ per additional mi. Must be 21 with major credit card.

Help Lines: Rape Crisis Counseling, 616-4861. Open 24 hrs. **Gay Center Help Line,** 892-0661. Open daily 6-11pm.

Emergency: 911.

Post Office: 3900 Crown Rd. (768-4126). Open 10am-4pm. **ZIP code:** 30321. **Area code:** 404.

Atlanta sprawls across the northwest quadrant of the state, 150 mi. east of Birmingham, AL and 113 mi. south of Chattanooga, TN, at the junctures of I-75, I-85, and I-20. I-285 ("the perimeter") circumscribes the city.

Getting around is confusing—*everything* seems to be named Peachtree. However, of the 40-odd roads bearing that name, only one, **Peachtree St.,** is a major north-south thoroughfare; other north-south roads are **Spring St.** and **Piedmont Ave.** Major east-west roads include **Ponce De León Ave.** and **North Ave.** In the heart of downtown—west of I-75/85, south of International Blvd. and north of the capitol, around the district known as Five Points—angled streets and shopping plazas run amok, making navigation difficult.

Most tourists frequent **Underground Atlanta** and **Peachtree Center,** shopping and entertainment complexes. The **Midtown** area (from Ponce de Leon Ave. to 26th St.) holds Atlanta's art museums. Directly southwest of downtown is the **West End**—a black residential area and the city's oldest historical quarter. North of Auburn Ave. lies the **Little Five Points** (L5P) district, which brims with galleries, theaters, bookstores, and a plethora of restaurants and nightclubs.

OLYMPIC INFORMATION

Information changes quickly; call 224-1996 for the most current facts (open Mon.-Sat. 10am-9:30pm, Sun. noon-6pm). The games will run from July 19 through August 4. **Tickets** range in price from $6-600, with the average around $40. **Archery** (from $11), **track cycling** (from $27) and **shooting** (from $22) are some of the least likely to be sold out. With their multiple sessions, locations, and very large seating capacities, **baseball** (from $7) and **soccer** ($20) are also decent bets. For up-to-the-minute **ticket information,** call 744-1996; ask for the ticket request form, which includes a **schedule** for the 1996 games. Tickets will be sold by mail until December 1; after that, tickets will be sold by phone. Non-U.S. residents should contact their National Olympic Committee to inquire about purchasing tickets in their country. If you missed the ticket rush but refuse to miss the Olympics, several metro-area events, such as the **marathon, racewalking,** and **road-cycling** events, are free of charge. Also, consider watching the **soccer** matches at Birmingham's Legion Field (800-923-1996 for tickets) and **yachting** on Savannah's Wassaw Sound, whose distance from Atlanta offers a more peaceful arena for Olympic mania.

Most events are located within a 1½-mi. radius, the imaginary **Olympic Ring.** There will be no parking at Olympic Ring venues; you must ride Olympic transportation—a combination of MARTA trains, a fleet of 1000 buses, and new walkways. The **Olympic Stadium** is located between Capitol Ave. and I-85 (C5). The **Olympic Center** is located near the intersection of Marietta and Simpson St. (B4).

Finally, the Olympics will be accompanied by a slew of cultural activities, part of a planned **Cultural Olympiad.** The **1996 Olympic Arts Festival** will highlight the artistic and cultural life of the south. Nightly concerts will play in Olympic Park, featuring artists such as Willie Nelson, James Brown, and Lynyrd Skynyrd. World-class international and regional theater troupes will present premieres by Sam Shepard and Pearl Cleage. A budget traveler's dream, **The Festival of the American South** will celebrate artists and craftspeople from the nine-state region in a huge, free outdoor festival in Olympic Park.

ACCOMMODATIONS AND CAMPING

> **Stop!** What date is it? If it is between July 19 and August 4, 1996, turn around and go back where you came from. The Olympics are here! Everything is sold out! And don't say we didn't warn you.

If you're an international student and plan to stay for more than a few days, check with the **International Youth Travel Program (IYTP)** (212-206-7307), you're cheapest bet besides the hostels. Travelers should pick up coupon books like *Look at Atlanta Now* at the convention and visitors bureau (see Practical Information), which will also help locate a single for a reasonable price. **Bed and Breakfast Atlanta,** 1801 Piedmont Ave. NE (875-9672; call Mon.-Fri. 9am-noon or 2-5pm), offers singles from $50 and doubles from $55-65 in over 80 establishments.

Expect rates to double during the Olympics. Many accommodations are already sold out. The Olympic committee has bought a heap of rooms, and will dole them out to ticket holders. If you're really desperate, the committee has an officially sanctioned central reservation number for private homes, which range from $120 per night upwards to thousands of dollars per night; call 455-0081.

Hostelling International Atlanta (HI-AYH), 223 Ponce de Leon Ave. (875-9449). From MARTA: North Ave. station, exit onto Ponce de Leon, about 3½ blocks east on the corner of Myrtle St. Part of a converted Victorian B&B in the middle of historic downtown. Clean, dorm-style rooms ½mi. from the Olympic village. Kitchen and showers at no charge. No sleeping bags allowed, but they distribute free blankets. A/C. Free local calls and rides to city sights in van. Luggage storage $1. Free city map, and occasional free passes to city attractions. Free coffee and doughnuts 8-10am. No curfew, but if out past midnight, you need a combination for the lock. $13.25, nonmembers $16.25. Linens $1. Sheets $1. Reservations recommended. The hostel began accepting reservations for the Olympics on July 1, 1995. This rate is $39 per night, and you must reserve for a full week; for HI-AYH members only.

Atlanta Dream Hostel, 222 E. Howard Ave., Decatur 30030 (370-0380 or 800-DREAM96/373-2696 for reservations only). From MARTA: Decatur, go right on Church St. for 2 blocks and then left on Howard. Located in a very safe neighborhood yet convenient to downtown. A funky communal joint complete with 2 peacocks, a bus that serves as an Elvis shrine, and a biergarten, it is a hostel for the adventurous soul. *Un vrai poème bohème.* Showers, kitchen, TV, free linen, and free local calls. Reception daily 8am-11pm; no curfew. Dorm rooms with roomy wooden bunks $12. Two creative private rooms available—one in a converted limousine $28. John Makar, the owner, claims he will make many improvements before the Olympics. He plans to buy the building next door; allowing him to house 100 people indoors at a rate around $30. Another 150 will be able to sleep under a huge circus tent. They will begin accepting reservations for the Olympics on Jan. 1, 1996.

Economy Inns of America, 3092 Presidential Pkwy (454-8373), exit Chamblee Tucker Rd. off I-85. Large rooms with king-size beds available, satellite TV and pool. 1-4 people $30 weekdays, $40 weekends. Sold out for the Olympics.

Motel 6, 3 perimeter locations: 3585 Chamblee Tucker Rd. (455-8000) in Chamblee, exit 27 off I-285; 6015 Oakbrook Pkwy. (446-2311), in Norcross, exit 37 off I-85; and 2565 Weseley Chapel Rd. (288-6911), in Decatur, exit 36 off I-20. Spacious and immaculate rooms. Each location offers free movie channel, free local calls, A/C, pool. Under 18 stay free with their parents. All locations $34, $6 per additional person. Sold out for the Olympics.

Atlanta Midtown Manor, 811 Piedmont Ave., NE (872-5846). Six Victorian houses located in a safe spot, convenient to downtown. Lovely rooms with floral shams, big round windows, A/C, TV. Free coffee and doughnuts. Singles $30-40, doubles $45-85.

Villager Lodge, 144 14th St. NW (873-4171). A fence separates you from the highway. Tidy rooms in a dark decor. Chinese restaurant. Optional phone ($10 deposit); local calls 30¢. Laundry facilities. Pool. Singles $40, doubles $48. Key deposit $5. Sold out for the Olympics.

Red Roof Inn, 1960 Druid Hills (321-1653), exit 31 off I-85, offers rooms with clean, modern decor and a pleasant tree-cloistered location. Convenient to downtown. Look carefully for the sign; it's partially hidden by branches. Singles $40, doubles $54. Sold out for the Olympics.

Stone Mountain Family Campground (498-5710), on U.S. 78, 16mi. east of town. Exit 30B off I-285, or subway to Avondale then "Stone Mountain" bus. Part of state park system. Gorgeous sites, most on the lake. Tent sites $15. RV sites with hookup $16, full hookup $17. Entrance fee $6 per car. Presently taking names and numbers for Olympics reservations.

KOA South Atlanta (957-2610), on Mt. Olive Rd. in McDonough, exit 72 off I-75. Showers, pool, laundry, and fishing pond on the premises. Tent sites with water $16, full hookup $23. Sold out for the Olympics. You can also try **KOA North Atlanta,** 2000 Old U.S. 41 (427-2406), in Kennesaw 3mi. west of Six Flags Amusement Parks.

FOOD

From Russian to Ethiopian, al fresco to underground, Atlanta dining provides a ample treats to tantalize your tastebuds. But since y'all are here you may want to savor some home-style cookin'. Some favorite dishes to sample include fried chicken, black-eyed peas, okra, sweet-potato pie, and mustard greens. Dip a hunk of cornbread into "pot likker," water used to cook greens. For a cheap breakfast, you can't beat the Atlanta-based **Krispy Kreme Doughnuts** whose baked delights are a Southern institution. Eat 'em hot! The factory store is at 295 Ponce de Leon Ave. NE (876-7307; open 24 hrs.).

The internationally inclined food shopper should take the subway to Avondale and then the "Stone Mountain" bus to the **Dekalb County Farmers Market,** 3000 E. Ponce De Leon Ave. (377-6400), where the famished can run the gustatory gamut from Chinese to Middle Eastern and everything in between (open daily 9am-9pm). For heaps of fresh fruit and vegetables in the middle of nowhere, head for the 146 acres of **Atlanta's State Farmers Market,** 16 Forest Pkwy. (366-6910), exit 78 off I-75S; take the "Farmers Market" bus from the airport (open daily 9am-5pm).

Bridgetown Grill, 1156 Euclid Ave. (653-0110), in L5P. Reggae and salsa make for a hopping hole in the wall. Jerk chicken dinner ($8). Open Sun.-Thurs. 11:30am-10:30pm, Fri.-Sat. 11:30am-midnight.

The Varsity, 61 North Ave. NW (881-1706), at I-85. Take MARTA to North Ave. station. The world's largest drive-in. Best known for chili dogs ($1-2) and the greasiest onion rings in the South ($1.10). Ice cream cones (90¢). Open Sun.-Thurs. 7am-12:30am, Fri.-Sat. 7am-2am.

Crescent Moon, 254 W. Ponce de Leon (377-5623). A heavenly and healthful breakfast spot. Luscious Belgian waffle pancakes ($2.50), or try the Elvis: seasoned potatoes with smoked chicken, mozzarella, and 2 scrambled eggs ($4.50). Whopping portions. Open for lunch Mon.-Fri. 7:30-10:45am and 11am-3pm, for dinner Tues.-Sat. 5:30-10pm. Weekend brunch 8am-2:30pm.

Nicola's, 1602 Lavista Rd. NE (325-2524), cooks, bakes, and dishes up the most savory and authentic Lebanese cuisine in Atlanta ($5-10). Look for raw kibby, a Lebanese delicacy, on Sat. nights. Open daily 5:30-10:30pm.

Mary Mac's Tea Room, 224 Ponce De Leon Ave. (876-1800) at Myrtle NE. Take the "Georgia Tech" bus north. 40s atmosphere with amazing cinnamon rolls and peach cobbler ($1). Entrees $6. Open Mon.-Fri. 11am-3pm, 5-9pm, Sat. 5-9pm, Sun. 11am-3pm.

The Beautiful Restaurant, 397 Auburn Ave. (505-0271), where Southern cooked soul food warms the body and mind. Dinner under $5, vegetarian platter $2.50. Open daily 7am-8:30pm.

Everybody's, 1040 N. Highland Ave. (873-4545). Locals love the mouth-watering pizza and Italian dishes. Large pie $10.50. Open Mon.-Thurs. 11:30am-11pm, Fri.-Sat. 11:30am-1am and Sun. noon-11pm.

Tortillas, 774 Ponce de Leon Ave. (892-3493). Student crowd munches dirt-cheap (and thoroughly yummy) Mexican. Try the upstairs patio for open air eating. Big vegetarian burritos $2. Soft taco with chicken $3. Open daily 11am-11pm.

Manuel's Tavern, 602 N. Highland Ave. (525-3447), prime spot between L5P and Virginia-Highlands. Chicken salad melt $4.50. Jimmy and Rosalyn Carter are regulars. Open Mon.-Sat. 10:30am-2am, Sun. 3-11pm.

Eat Your Vegetables Café, 438 Moreland Ave. NE (523-2671), in the L5P area. Vegetarian entrees $7-8, including macrobiotic dinner special. Open Mon.-Thurs. 11:30am-10pm, Fri. 11:30am-10:30pm, Sat. 11am-10:30pm, Sun. 11am-3pm.

Touch of India, 962 Peachtree St. (876-7777) and 2065 Piedmont Rd. (876-7775). 3-course lunch buffet $7. Dinners $8-10. Open Mon.-Sat. 11:30am-2:30pm and 5:30-10:30pm.

SIGHTS

Downtown and Around

Atlanta's sights may seem scattered, but the effort it takes to find them usually pays off. The **Atlanta Preservation Center,** 156 7th St. NE (876-2040), offers ten walking tours of popular areas from March through November: Fox Theatre District, West End and the Wren's Nest, Historic Downtown, Miss Daisy's Druid Hills, Inman Park, Underground and Capitol area, Ansley Park, Sweet Auburn (MLK District), Piedmont Park, and Vine City; the 1½-hour Fox Theatre tour is given year-round ($5, students $3, seniors $4; call for more info). Of course, you can just hop on MARTA and take in the sights on your own.

Reverend Dr. Martin Luther King, Jr.'s birthplace, church, and grave are all part of a 23-acre **Martin Luther King, Jr. National Historic Site.** The **birthplace of MLK** offers guided tours (331-3920) starting every ½ hour from 522 Auburn Ave. (open daily 9am-7:30pm; in winter 9am-5pm). **Ebenezer Baptist Church,** 407 Auburn Ave. (688-7263), the church where Martin Luther King, Jr. was pastor from 1960 to 1968, now serves as a visitors center for the National Park Service (open Mon.-Sat. 9:30am-4:30pm, Sun. 2-4pm). Plaques lining Sweet Auburn point out the Queen Anne architecture and eminent past residents of this historically African-American neighborhood. King's **grave** rests at the **Martin Luther King Center for Nonviolent Social Exchange,** 449 Auburn Ave. NE (524-1956); take bus #3 from Five Points.

The center also holds a collection of King's personal effects and shows a film about his life. (Open daily 9am-8pm; Nov.-March 9am-5:30pm. Entrance and film free.)

The APEX Museum, 135 Auburn Ave. (521-2739), recognizes the cultural heritage of the African-Americans who helped build this country as slaves and as freemen. (Open Tues.-Sat. 10am-5pm; in Feb. only Sun. 1-5pm. $3, students $2, seniors and under 5 free.)

South of the MLK Historic District, Margaret Mitchell and golfer Bobby Jones are buried in **Oakland Cemetery,** 248 Oakland Ave. SE (874-1743); take bus #3 (visitors center open Mon.-Fri. 9am-5pm; free). True fans of Rhett Butler and Scarlett O'Hara should also visit the Margaret Mitchell Room in the **Atlanta-Fulton Public Library,** 1 Margaret Mitchell (730-1700). The collection of memorabilia includes autographed copies of her famous novel. (Open Mon.-Thurs. 9am-9pm, Fri.-Sat. 9am-6pm, Sun. 2-6pm.) On the corner of 10th and Crescent, you can see the dilapidated three-story house where Mitchell used to live.

In **Grant Park,** directly south of Oakland Cemetery and Cherokee Ave., a 100-year-old **Cyclorama** (624-1071), a massive panoramic painting (42ft. high and 358ft. around), recreates the 1864 Battle of Atlanta with 3D sound and light effects. (Open daily 9:20am-5:30pm; Oct.-May 9:20am-4:30pm. $5, students and seniors $4, ages 6-12 $3.) Next door, **Zoo Atlanta,** 800 Cherokee Ave. SE (624-5600), mounts displays stressing conservation and environmental awareness. Among the special exhibits are the Masai Mara, Sumatran Tiger Forest, and the Ford African Rain Forest. (Open daily 10am-4:30pm, until 5:30pm on weekends during Daylight Savings Time. $7.50, seniors $6.75, ages 3-11 $5, under 3 free.)

High-tech "Hotlanta" reigns with multinational business powerhouses situated in the business section of **Five Points District. Turner Broadcasting System** offers an insider's peek with its **Cable News Network (CNN) Studio Tour** (827-2300), at corner of Techwood Dr. and Marietta St. Witness anchorfolk broadcasting live while writers toil in the background. Take MARTA west to the Omni/Dome/GWCC Station at W1. (45-min. tours given on the ½hr. Open daily 9am-6pm. $6, seniors $4, ages 5-12 $3.50.)

Redeveloped **Underground Atlanta** gets down with six subterranean blocks filled with over 120 shops, restaurants, and night spots behind restored 19th-century Victorian storefronts. Descend at the entrance beside the Five Points subway station. (Shops open Mon.-Sat. 10am-9:30pm, Sun. noon-6pm. Bars and restaurants open later.) **Atlanta Heritage Row,** 55 Upper Alabama St. (584-7879), Underground, documents the city's past and looks into the future with exhibits and films (open Tues.-Sat. 10am-5pm, Sun. 1-5pm; $2). Adjacent to the shopping complex, the **World of Coca-Cola Pavilion,** 55 Martin Luther King, Jr. Dr. (676-5151), highlights "the real thing's" humble beginnings in Atlanta, in a $15 million facility. Over 1000 artifacts and interactive displays tell the powerhouse's tale. (Open Mon.-Sat. 10am-8:30pm, Sun. noon-5pm. $3.50, seniors $3, ages 6-12 $2.50.)

The politically minded revel in the **Georgia State Capitol** (656-2844; take the MARTA to Georgia State, then 1 block south), Capitol Hill at Washington St. (tours Mon.-Fri. on the hr. 10am-2pm except noon; open Mon.-Fri. 8am-5pm, Sat. 10am-4pm, Sun. noon-4pm; free). Farther out, the **Carter Presidential Center,** 1 Copenhill (331-3942), north of Little Five Points, documents the Carter Administration (1977-1981) through exhibits and films. Take bus #16 to Cleburne Ave. (Open Mon.-Sat. 9am-4:45pm, Sun. noon-4:45pm. $4, seniors $3, under 16 free.)

In the **West End**—Atlanta's oldest neighborhood, dating from 1835—discover the **Wren's Nest,** 1050 R.D. Abernathy Blvd. (753-8535), home to Joel Chandler Harris, who popularized the African folktale trickster Br'er Rabbit through the stereotypical slave character Uncle Remus. Take bus #71 from West End Station South. (Tours $4, teens and seniors $3, ages 4-12 $2. ½-hr. storytelling June-Aug. 11:30am, 12:30, 1:30pm; Sept.-May Sat. 2pm; $2 extra. Open Tues.-Sat. 10am-4pm, Sun. 1-4pm.) The **Hammonds House,** 503 Peeples St. SW (752-8730), displays a fantastic collection of African-American and Haitian art. Take bus #67 from West End Station South to the corner of Oak and Peeples. (Open Tues.-Fri. 10am-6pm, Sat.-Sun. 1-

5pm. $2, students and seniors $1.) Built by slave-born Alonzo F. Herndon, the **Herndon Home,** 587 University Place NW (581-9813), a 1910 Beaux Arts Classical mansion, deserves a look; take bus #3 from Five Points station to the corner of Martin Luther King, Jr. Dr. and Maple, and walk one block north. Herndon, a prominent barber, became Atlanta's wealthiest African-American in the early 1900s. View the house's original furnishings, glass and silver collections, and family photographs. (Free tours every hr. Open Tues.-Sat. 10am-4pm.)

North of Midtown

Piedmont Park sprawls around the 60-acre **Atlanta Botanical Garden** (876-5859), Piedmont Ave. at the Prado. Stroll through five acres of landscaped gardens, a 15-acre hardwood forest with walking trails, and an exhibition hall. The **Dorothy Chapman Fugua Conservatory** houses hundreds of species of rare tropical plants; take bus #36 "North Decatur" from the Arts Center subway stop (open Tues.-Sun. 9am-7pm; $6, students $3, seniors $5; Thurs. free after 1pm).

Near the park, **Scitrek** (The Science and Technology Museum of Atlanta), 395 Piedmont Ave. NE (522-5000), houses over 100 interactive exhibits for all ages making it one of the top ten science centers in the country. Take bus #2 from North Ave. Station. (Open Tues.-Sat. 10am-5pm, Sun. noon-5pm; call for summer hours. $6.50, students and seniors $4.25.)

Just to the west of Piedmont Park, the **Woodruff Arts Center,** 1280 Peachtree St. NE (733-4200; take the subway to Arts Center), contains the **High Museum of Art** (733-HIGH/4444), Richard Meier's award-winning building of glass, steel, and white porcelain. In 1996, the museum will hang a one-time-only collection of 100 masterpieces from around the world in celebration of the 1996 Olympics. (Open Tues.-Sat. 10am-5pm, Sun. noon-5pm. $6, students with ID and seniors $4, children $2; free Thurs. 1-5pm.) The museum branch at **Georgia-Pacific Center** (577-6940), 1 block south of Peachtree Center Station, houses folk art and photography galleries (open Mon.-Sat. 10am-5pm; free).

The **Center for Puppetry Arts,** 1404 Spring St. NW (873-0398 or 873-3391 for tickets), at 18th St., has a museum featuring Wayland Flower's "Madame," traditional Punch and Judy figures, and some of Jim Henson's original Muppets. (Museum open Mon.-Sat. 9am-5pm. $5.75, students and seniors $4.75, ages 2-13 $2. Shows $5.50, ages 2-13 $4.50; museum free with show tickets.)

A drive through **Buckhead** (north of midtown and Piedmont Park off Peachtree near W. Paces Ferry Rd.) uncovers the "Beverly Hills of Atlanta"—the sprawling mansions of Coca-Cola CEOs and the like. This area is also a hub of local grub and grog (see Entertainment below). One of the most exquisite residences in the Southeast, the Greek Revival **Governor's Mansion,** 391 W. Paces Ferry Rd. (261-1776), has elaborate gardens and furniture from the Federal period. Take bus #40 "West Paces Ferry" from Linbergh Station. (Free tours Tues.-Thurs. 10-11:30am.) In the same neighborhood, discover the **Atlanta History Center/Buckhead,** 130 W. Paces Ferry Rd. NW (814-4000). On the grounds are the **Swan House,** a lavish Anglo-Palladian Revival home, and the **Tullie Smith House,** an antebellum farmhouse. Don't miss the intriguing *"Atlanta Resurgens"* exhibit. The **New Museum of Atlanta History** features a fine Civil War Gallery. (Open Mon.-Sat. 9am-5:30pm, Sun. noon-5:30pm. $7, students and seniors $5, ages 6-17 $4, under 6 free.)

East of Midtown

A respite from the city is available at **Stone Mountain Park** (498-5698), 16 mi. east on U.S. 78, where a fabulous Confederate Memorial is carved into the world's largest mass of granite. The "Mount Rushmore of the South" features Jefferson Davis, Robert E. Lee, and Stonewall Jackson and measures 90 ft. by 190 ft. Surrounded by a 3200-acre recreational area and historic park, the mountain dwarfs the enormous statue. Check out the dazzling laser show on the side of the mountain every summer night at 9:30pm (free). Take bus #120 "Stone Mountain" from the Avondale subway stop (buses leave Mon.-Fri. only at 4:30 and 7:50pm). (Park gates open daily 6am-midnight; attractions open daily 10am-9pm, off season 10am-5:30pm. $6 per car. Admission to beach complex $4.)

The **Fernbank Museum of Natural History,** 767 Clifton Rd. NE (370-0960), near Ponce de Leon Ave., has a 65-acre forest, a display of the Apollo 6 command module, and an IMAX theater, among other exhibits. (Open Mon.-Thurs., Sat. 10am-5pm, Fri. 10am-9pm, Sun. noon-5pm. Museum or IMAX theater $5.50, students and over 61 $4.50, ages 3-12 $4; both $9.50/$8.50/$6.50.)

ENTERTAINMENT AND NIGHTLIFE

For sure-fire fun in Atlanta, buy a MARTA pass (see Practical Information above) and pick up one of the city's free publications on music and events. *Creative Loafing, Music Atlanta,* the *Hudspeth Report,* or "Leisure" in the Friday edition of the *Atlanta Journal* will all give you the low-down. *Southern Voice* has complete listings on gay and lesbian news and nightclubs throughout Atlanta; stop by **Charls,** 419 Moreland Ave. NE (524-0304), for your free copy (open Mon.-Thurs. 10:30am-6:30pm, Fri.-Sat. 10:30am-10pm, Sun. noon-6pm). Look for free summer concerts in Atlanta's parks.

The excellent **Woodruff Arts Center,** 1280 Peachtree St. NE (892-2414), houses the Atlanta Symphony, the Alliance Theater Company, Atlanta College of Art, and the High Museum of Art. For more plays and movies, check the Moorish and Egyptian Revival Movie Palace, the **Fox Theatre,** 660 Peachtree St. (881-2100), or the **Atlanta Civic Center,** 395 Piedmont St. (523-6275), home to the Atlanta ballet.

Six Flags, 7561 Flags Rd. SW (948-9290), at I-20W, one of the largest theme amusement parks in the nation, includes several rollercoasters and a plethora of rides. Take bus #201 "Six Flags" from Hightower Station. (Open Memorial Day-Labor Day Sun.-Thurs. 10am-10pm, Fri.-Sat. 10am-midnight. Open weekends rest of year. 1-day admission $28, ages 3-9, $19; 2-day pass for adults or kids $33; be sure to check local grocery stores and soda cans for discounts.)

THE SOUTH

For drink or dance, hotspots center in **Little Five Points; Virginia Highlands,** a trendy, hip neighborhood east of downtown; **Buckhead;** and **Underground Atlanta.** A college-age crowd usually fills Little Five Points; many head for **The Point,** 420 Moreland Ave. (659-3522) where live music plays all the time (cover $3-6; open Mon.-Fri. 4pm-4am, Sat. 1pm-3am, Sun. 1pm-4am). For blues, go to **Blind Willie's,** 828 N. Highland Ave. NE (873-2583), a dim, usually packed club with Cajun food and occasional big name acts (live music 8pm-3am; cover $5-10; open daily at 8pm). In Virginia Highlands, big name acts using assumed names try out new material at the **Dark Horse Tavern,** 816 N. Highland Ave. (873-3607; music starts downstairs 10pm; cover free-$8; open daily 6pm-'til). For a laid-back and often international crowd, move next door to **Limerick Junction Pub,** 822 N. Highland Ave. (874-7147), where contagious Irish music jigs nightly (open daily 5pm-2am).

For dancing, nearby **Oxygen,** 3065 Peachtree St. (816-6522), at Bolling Way will leave you breathless. DJs spin an alternative, techno, and industrial mix nightly. (Cover $7. Ladies' night Thurs. Open Mon.-Sat. 9pm-4am.) Cool off with a 60-oz. industrial strength goblet margarita at **Lu Lu's Bait Shack,** 3057 Peachtree St. (262-5220; open Sun.-Thurs. 5-11pm, Fri.-Sat. 5pm-4am).

Kenny's Alley, a street in The Underground, is composed solely of bars—a blues club, a dance emporium, a jazz bar, a country/western place, a New Orleans-style daiquiri bar, and an oldies dancing spot. Towards downtown, **Masquerade,** 695 North Ave. NE (577-8026), occupies an original turn-of-the-century mill. The bar has three different levels: heaven, with live dance music; purgatory, a more laid-back coffee house; and hell, offering techno and industrial. A recently added outside dance space provides dancing with lights and celestial views. (Cover $4-8 or more, depending on band. Open Wed.-Sun. 9pm-4am. 18+.) **Backstreet,** 845 Peachtree St. NE (873-1986), a 24-hr., hot, gay dance spot, prides itself on being straight-friendly. The bar picks a different theme for every night; disco rules on Wednesdays. (Extra-special hoppin' X-rated drag cabaret Thurs.-Sun. at midnight. Cover Mon.-Thurs. $2, Fri. $5, Sat. $7, Sun. $3.)

■■■ ATHENS

Home to over 30,000 University of Georgia (UGA) students and the host for '96 Olympic soccer, Athens challenges its Hellenic namesake in cultural prowess. History and legend aside, Athens has nurtured a prolific music scene—REM, the B-52s, Love Tractor, and Pylon, to name a few.

Practical Information Situated 70 mi. northeast of Atlanta, Athens can be reached from I-85 via U.S. 316 (exit 4), which runs into U.S. 29. Two blocks north of the UGA campus is the **Athens Welcome Center,** 280 E. Dougherty St. (353-1820), located in the Church-Brumby House, the city's oldest surviving residence (open Tues.-Sat. 10am-5pm and Sun. 2-5pm). The **Athens Transit System** (613-3430) runs buses every half hour on the hour (Mon.-Fri. 6am-7pm, Sat. 7:30am-7pm). Schedules are available at the Welcome Center, City Hall at College and Hancock Ave., and the bus garage on Pound St. and Prince Ave. (Fare 75¢, children and seniors 35¢.) The **Athens-Atlanta Airport** (767-2000 or 800-354-7874) offers commuter shuttles six times a day to Atlanta for $25 (open 24 hrs.). **Greyhound,** 222 W. Broad St. (549-2255 or 800-231-2222), has service to Atlanta (3 per day, 2hr., $13). (Station open daily 7:30am-9pm.) The **Rape Crisis Line** (353-1912) takes calls 7pm to 7am daily. The **health center** (546-5526) is open by appointment (Mon.-Fri. 8:30am-4:15pm). **Post office:** 575 Olympic Dr. (613-2695; open Mon.-Fri. 8:30am-5pm); **ZIP code:** 30601; **area code:** 706.

Accommodations, Camping, and Sights The **Downtowner Motor Inn,** 1196 S. Milledge Ave. (549-2626), has affordable rooms in 70s colors near campus with A/C, continental breakfast, TV, and pool (singles $34, doubles $38). Twelve mi. from Athens lies the **Hawkes-Nest Guesthouse,** 1760 McRee Mill Rd. (769-0563), a delightful and romantic love shack with a single bed, clawfoot tub, TV, and a loft capable of sleeping two. ($4 for A/C. $10, groups of 1-4 $16. Call the friendly owners for required reservations and directions). A full-service campground with secluded sites, **Pine Lake RV Campground,** Rte. 186 (769-5486), in nearby Bishop, has full hookups and fishing lakes. Do a little night swimming. (Tent sites $12.50, RV sites for 1 or 2 people $16.50). They are almost booked for the Olympics ($28/$42).

For a walking tour of Athens's historical neighborhood pick up a copy of *Athens of Old* at the Welcome Center. For an in-depth look at Athens old and new take the two-hour **Classic City Tour.** This fascinating driving tour tells the stories of the antebellum homes, the Civil War, and the University of Georgia. (Tours leave from the Welcome Center Tues.-Sat. 11am and 2pm, Sun. 2pm. $8.50. Reservations 208-8687.) You'll see more than a thumbnail sketch at the **Georgia Museum of Art,** in historic North University Campus off Jackson St. (542-3255). The museum houses a collection of over 7000 works. (Open Mon.-Sat. 9am-5pm, Sun. 1-5pm. Free.) Look for the flowers of Guatemala at the **State Botanical Gardens of Georgia,** 2450 S. Milledge Ave. (542-1244), a paradise for aesthete and botanist alike (open daily 8am-sunset; free). Some bizarre Athenian sights include a double-barreled cannon at City Hall Plaza that never worked and the **"The Tree That Owns Itself."** Prof. W.H. Jackson deeded that the white oak standing at the corner of Dearling and Finley streets should own itself and its 8-ft. radius of shade. The original oak died in 1942 but was reborn from one of its own acorns.

Food and Nightlife Make an orange crush at **Guaranteed,** 167 E. Broad St. (208-0962), where you become the "juicemaster." Mix standard fruits with special additions (like bee pollen, $1) for a tasty treat ($2.50). Creative vegetarian creations ($3-6) round out the menu. (Open Sun.-Thurs. 9am-10pm and Fri.-Sat. 9am-11pm.) The **Last Resort Grill,** 174 W. Clayton St. (549-0810), serves up massive quesadillas piled with fresh veggies ($3; open Sun.-Fri. 11am-3pm 5-10pm, Sat. 11am-3pm 5-11pm.) **The Grit,** 199 Prince Ave. (543-6592), serves up a variety of grits as well as super-healthy meals. Eat a bagel grilled with olive oil and herbs ($2), or try the excellent Middle Eastern food. All dinners go for less than $5. (Open Mon.-Fri. 11am-10pm and Sat.-Sun. brunch 10am-3pm and dinner 5-10pm.)

Those on an REM pilgrimage must check out the **40 Watt Club,** 285 W. Washington St. (549-7871), where the group started out and where many bands today try to follow their lead (open daily 10am-3am). The **Georgia Theatre** (549-9918), at the corner of Lumpkin and Clayton St., attracts shiny, happy people with southern R&B ($5 cover; open daily 4pm-'til). With Guinness on tap and a smoke-free zone on the second floor, even Michael Stipes hangs out at **The Globe,** 199 N. Lumpkin St. (353-4721; open Mon.-Sat. 4pm-1am).

■■■ SAVANNAH

In February 1733, General James Oglethorpe and a rag-tag band of 120 colonists founded the state of Georgia at Tamacraw Bluff on the Savannah River; the city of Savannah was born. When the price of cotton crashed at the turn of the century, many of the homes and warehouses along River St. fell into disrepair, and the townhouses and mansions that lined Savannah's boulevards became boarding houses or rubble. In the mid-1950s, a group of seven concerned women mobilized to restore the downtown area and preserve its numerous Federalist and English Regency houses as historic monuments. Today, broad streets, four historic forts, and trees dripping with Spanish moss enhance the city's classic Southern aura. Savannah has long rivaled the history and beauty of cities like New Orleans and Charleston while remaining relatively untouristed. Of course, things can always change; Forrest-Gump-mania has brought devotees to a certain bench in Chippewa Square, and Savannah will serve as the site for boating and yachting events during the 1996 Olympic Summer Games.

PRACTICAL INFORMATION

Tourist Office: Savannah Visitors Center, 301 Martin Luther King, Jr. Blvd. (944-0456), at Liberty St. in a lavish former train station. Excellent free maps and guides. 15-min. slide show about Savannah past and present (every ½hr.; $1, ages 6-12 50¢). Open Mon.-Fri. 8:30am-5pm, Sat.-Sun. 9am-5pm. The **Savannah History Museum,** in the same building, has exhibits depicting the city's history (duh). Open daily 9am-5pm. $3, students and seniors $2.50, ages 6-12 $1.75.

Trains: Amtrak, 2611 Seaboard Coastline Dr. (234-2611 or 800-872-7245), 4mi. out of the city. Taxis to town run about $5. To: Charleston, SC (1 per day, 2hr., $28); Washington, DC (2 per day, 11hr., $138). Open 3:30pm-7:30am.

Buses: Greyhound, 610 W. Oglethorpe Ave. (232-2135 or 800-231-2222), near downtown. To: Jacksonville (8 per day, 3hr., $19); Columbia, SC (4 per day, 4-6hr., $35); Washington, DC (5 per day, 12hr., $89). Open daily 5:30am-1:30am.

Public Transportation: Chatham Area Transit (CAT) (233-5767). Operates daily 6am-midnight. Fare 50¢, transfers 5¢; one-day passes $1.50. **C&H Bus,** 530 Montgomery St. (232-7099). From the civic center to Tybee Beach in summer 8:15am, 1:30pm, and 3:30pm; returns 9:25am, 2:30pm, and 4:30pm. Fare $1.75.

Taxis: Adam Cab (927-7466). 60¢ initial fee, $1.20 per mi.

Crisis Line: Rape Crisis Center, 233-7273. 24 hrs.

Emergency: 911.

Post Office: 2 N. Fahm St. (235-4646). Open Mon.-Fri. 8:30am-5pm. **ZIP code:** 31402. **Area code:** 912.

Savannah rests on the coast of Georgia at the mouth of the **Savannah River,** which runs north of the city along the border with South Carolina. Charleston, SC lies 100 mi. up the coast; Brunswick, GA is 90 mi. to the south. The city stretches south from bluffs overlooking the river. The restored 2½-square-mi. **downtown historic district,** bordered by East Broad, Martin Luther King, Jr. Blvd., Gwinnett Street, and the river, is best explored on foot. **Tybee Island,** Savannah's beach, 18 mi. east on U.S. 80 and Rte. 26, makes a fine daytrip but not an overnight. Try to visit at the beginning of spring, the most beautiful season in Savannah.

ACCOMMODATIONS AND CAMPING

The **downtown** motels cluster near the historic area, visitors center, and Greyhound station. Do not stray south of Gwinnett St.; the historic district quickly deteriorates into an unsafe and seedy area. For those with cars, **Ogeechee Rd. (U.S. 17)** has several independently owned budget options.

Savannah International Youth Hostel, 304 E. Hall St. (236-7744), 2 blocks from the historic district 2 blocks east of Forsyth Park. Far and away the best deal in town. Located in a restored Victorian mansion with a kitchen, laundry facilities, and table-top games. Flexible 3-night max. stay. Check-in 7:30-10am and 5-10pm; call the friendly manager, Brian, for late check-in. Lockout 10am-5pm; no curfew. Dorm beds $11.50, private rooms $25. The hostel will be closed Jan.-Feb. 1996.

Bed and Breakfast Inn, 117 W. Gordon St. (238-0518), at Chatham Sq. in the historic district. 10 rooms decorated with antiques, poster beds, and oriental rugs. All have TV, A/C, phones, and full southern breakfast; some with shared bath. Singles $35, doubles $49. Add $10 on weekends. Reservations requested.

Fort McAllister State Park (727-2339), ½hr. south of downtown off Rte. 144; take exit 15 off I-95. Wooded sites with water and electricity, some with a water view. Office open daily 8am-5pm. Check-in before 10pm. Sites $12. Parking $2.

Skidaway Island State Park (598-2300), 13mi. southeast of downtown off Diamond Causeway. Inaccessible by public transportation. Follow Liberty St. east from downtown until it becomes Wheaton St.; turn right on Waters Ave. and follow it to the Diamond Causeway. Generally more noisy and crowded than Fort McAllister. Bathrooms and heated showers. Check-in before 10pm. Sites $17, additional nights $15; off season $15/$12.

FOOD AND NIGHTLIFE

Olympia Café, 5 E. River St. (233-3131), on the river. Great Greek specialities, including salads and pizzas. Lunch or dinner $5-13. Open Sun.-Thurs. 10am-10pm, Fri.-Sat. 10am-midnight.

Mrs. Wilkes Boarding House, 107 W. Jones St. (232-5997), is truly a southern institution. Sit with friendly strangers around a large table and help yourself to luscious fried chicken, sweet potatoes, spinach, beans, and spaghetti that Grandma made. All you can eat (and then some) $8. Open Mon.-Fri. 11:30am-3pm. No sign; just join the line. Get there early; the wait can be up to 2 hr.

606 East Café, 319 W. Congress St. (233-2887). A world of jungle scenes, wacky cartoon characters, and little hanging lights awaits in this hand-painted bistro. Gourmet food for lunch or dinner $4-13. Open Mon.-Wed. 11am-10pm, Thurs.-Sat. 11am-2am with live music.

Clary's Café, 404 Abercorn St. (233-0402). A local family spot since 1903 with a famous weekend brunch and friendly service. Malted waffle $3.50. Open Mon.-Fri. 6:30am-4pm and 5-10pm, Sat. 8am-4pm and 5pm-midnight, Sun. 8am-2pm.

Try the waterfront area **(River St.)** for budget meals in a pub-like atmosphere. **Kevin Barry's Irish Pub,** 117 W. River St. (233-9626), offers live Irish folk music (Wed.-Sun. after 8:30pm; $2 cover), as well as cheap drinks during happy hour. For a drink that will keep you on your ear for days, check out **Wet Willies,** 101 E. River St. (233-5650), with its casual dining, young folks, and irresistible frozen daiquiris (open Sun.-Thurs. 11am-1am, Fri.-Sat. 11am-2am). Local college students usually hang out at **City Market,** where an array of shops, restaurants, and bars are clustered. One hot spot is **Malone's Bar and Grill,** 27 Barnard St. (234-3059), with dancing, drinks, live jazz, and rock Thursday through Sunday nights (open daily 11am-2am; happy hour daily 5-8pm, "ladies" night Wed.-Thurs.). Hustlers will enjoy **B&B Billiards,** 411 W. Congress St. (233-7116), which recently won a city renovation prize for transforming a five-and-dime warehouse into an airy brick nightspot. B&B is just as proud of its 10 new Gandi pool tables and 80+ types of beer. (Open Mon.-Sat. 4pm-3am. Happy hour daily 4-8pm; free pool Tues.)

SIGHTS AND EVENTS

In addition to restored antebellum houses, the downtown area includes over 20 small parks and gardens. Scads of bus, horse carriage, and van tours ($7-12) leave every 10-15 min. from outside the visitors center (see Practical Information above); ask inside for details. The **Historic Savannah Foundation,** 210 Broughton St. (233-7703), gives a tour through **Gray Line Tours** (233-3597 for reservations; $14).

Savannah's best-known historic houses are the **Davenport House,** 324 E. State St. (236-8097), on Columbia Square, and the **Owens-Thomas House,** 124 Abercorn St. (233-9743), a block away on Oglethorpe Square. The Owens-Thomas House is one of the best examples of Federalist architecture in the U.S. (Open Tues.-Sat. 10am-4:30pm, Sun. 2-4:30pm. Last tour 4:30pm. $5, students $3, under 13 $2.) The Davenport House, earmarked to be razed for a parking lot, was saved in 1955; the event marked the birth of the Historic Savannah Foundation and its efforts to restore the city. There are guided tours of the first floor every ½ hour; explore the third floor at your leisure. (Open Mon.-Wed. and Fri.-Sat. 10am-4:30pm, Sun. 10am-4pm. Last tour 4pm. $5.) The **Green Meldrim House,** 1 W. Maco St. (233-3845), on Madison Sq., is a Gothic revival mansion which served as one of General Sherman's headquarters throughout the Civil War (open Tues. and Thurs.-Sat. 10am-4pm; $4, students $2). The **Telfair Mansion and Art Museum,** 121 Bernard St. (232-1177), displays a distinguished collection of decorative arts in an English Regency house. (Open Tues.-Sat. 10am-5pm, Sun. 2-5pm. $3, students and seniors $1, ages 6-12 50¢, under 6 free.)

Lovers of Thin Mints, Do-si-dos, and, of course, Savannahs, should make a pilgrimage to the **Juliette Gordon Low Girl Scout National Center,** 142 Bull St. (233-4501), near Wright Square. The Scouts' founder was born here on Halloween 1860, which may explain the Girl Scouts' door-to-door treat-selling technique. The "cookie shrine" contains an interesting collection of Girl Scout memorabilia. (Open Mon.-Tues. and Thurs.-Sat. 10am-4pm, Sun. 12:30-4:30pm. $4, under 18 $3; discounts for AAA, groups, and Girl Scouts.)

The **Negro Heritage Trail** visits African-American historic sights from the days of slavery to the present. The Savannah branch of the **Association for the Study of Afro-American Life and History,** King-Tisdell Cottage, Negro Heritage Trail, 514 E. Harris St. (234-8000), conducts three different tours, which begin at the visitors center. (Mon.-Fri. 1 and 3pm, Sat.-Sun. 10am, 1pm, and 3pm. $10, under 13 $5.)

Savannah's four forts once protected the city's port from Spanish, British, and other invaders. The most interesting, **Fort Pulaski National Monument** (786-5787), 15 mi. east of Savannah on U.S. 80 and Rte. 26, marks the Civil War battle site where rifled cannons first pummeled walls, making Pulaski and similar forts obsolete. (Open daily 8:30am-6:30pm, off season 8:30am-5:30pm. $2, $4 maximum per car, over 62 free with Golden Age Passport, under 16 free.) Built in the early 1800s, **Fort Jackson** (232-3945), also along U.S. 80 and Rte. 26, contains exhibits on the American Revolution, the War of 1812, and the Civil War (open daily 9am-5:30pm; $2, students and seniors $1.50). Both make quick detours on a daytrip to Tybee Beach.

Special events in Savannah include the **Hidden Garden of Historic Savannah** (238-0248), in mid-April, when private walled gardens are opened to the public. The free, three-day **St. Patrick's Day Weekend Music Fest** (232-4903) blares jazz, blues, and rock 'n' roll from noon to midnight, Friday to Sunday in the City Market.

■■■ BRUNSWICK AND ENVIRONS

Brunswick Beyond the unique hostel and nearby beaches, laid-back Brunswick is of little interest to the traveler who expects more than a relaxing layover between destinations. The fantastic **Hostel in the Forest** (264-9738, 265-0220, or 638-2623) is located 9 mi. west of Brunswick on U.S. 82. Take I-95 to exit 6 and travel west on U.S. 82/84 about 1½ mi. until you see a white-lettered wooden sign set back in the trees along the eastbound lane, just past a small convenience store. The hostel sits ½ mi. back from the highway; every effort is made to keep the area surrounding the complex of geodesic domes and treehouses as natural as possible. Try to stay in one of the three treehouses at the hostel, each complete with a 25-sq.-ft. picture window, ceiling fan, and a spacious double bed. Bring insect repellent in the summertime; mosquitoes and yellow, biting flies abound. In addition, there is a natural swimming pool made from a diverted stream, complete with a rope swing and a teepee sweat lodge. The atmosphere is communal, and a few residents seem to be permanent. The low-key managers will shuttle you to the Brunswick Greyhound station for $3; they can usually be convinced to make daytrips to Savannah, the Okefenokee Swamp, and the coastal islands. (No lockout, no curfew, and few rules. $9; linens $2.)

Twin Oaks Pit Barbecue, 2618 Norwick St. (265-3131), 8 blocks from downtown Brunswick across from the Southern Bell building, features a chicken-and-pork combination ($6). The breaded french fries ($1) are deep fried and deeeeelicious. (Open Mon.-Fri. 10am-8:30pm, Sat. 10am-10pm.)

Greyhound, 1101 Glouchester St. (265-2800; open Mon.-Sat. 7:30am-6:30pm), offers service to Jacksonville (4 per day, 1½hr., $17) and Savannah (4 per day, 1½hr., $14). Brunswick's **area code:** 912.

Okefenokee Swamp The **Okefenokee Swamp Park,** 5700 Okefenokee Swamp Park Rd. (912-283-0583), on U.S. 1, 8 mi. south of Waycross, is a haven for snoozing alligators, snakes, and birds. Admission includes interpretive talks, a 25-min. guided boat trip, a ½-mi. wilderness walkway leading to a 90-ft. observation tower, and reptile exhibits ($10, ages 5-11 $7). Come and walk on water, or at least over it on a boardwalk directly on the swamp. Adventurers can take their chances renting a canoe ($9 per day, must be 18 or with an adult). Be ready to wring some serious muck out of your socks if you capsize. (Open daily 9am-6:30pm; off season 9am-5:30pm.)

Golden Isles The Golden Isles, **St. Simon's Island, Jekyll Island,** and **Sea Island,** have miles of white sand beaches. **Cumberland Island National Seashore,** near the isles, is 16 mi. of salt marsh, live-oak forest, and sand dunes laced with trails and a few decaying mansions. Phone reservations (882-4335, Mon.-Fri. 10am-4pm) are necessary for overnight visits (primitive camping only). The effort is rewarded with seclusion; you can walk all day on these beaches without seeing another person. Sites are also available on a stand-by basis 15 min. before ferry departures to Cumberland Island. The **ferry** leaves from St. Mary's, on the mainland at the terminus of Rte. 40 at the Florida border. (45min. In summer daily 9 and 11:45 am, returning 10:15am and 4:45pm; off season Thurs.-Mon. only. $10, children $6.)

Florida

Ponce de León landed on the Florida coast in 1513, in search of the elusive Fountain of Youth. Although the multitudes who flock to Florida today aren't desperately seeking fountains, many find their youth restored in the Sunshine State—whether they're dazzled by Orlando's fantasia Disney World or bronzed by the sun on the state's seductive beaches. Droves of senior citizens also migrate to Florida, where they thrive in comfortable retirement communities, leaving one to wonder whether the unpolluted, sun-warmed air isn't just as good as Ponce de León's fabled magical elixir. Although he never found the legendary Fountain of Youth, Ponce de León did live to age 61, twice the expected life span at that time.

But a dark shadow hangs over this land of the winter sun. Anything as attractive as Florida is bound to draw hordes of people, the nemesis of natural beauty. Florida's population boom has strained the state's resources; commercial strips and tremendous development in some areas have turned pristine beaches into tourist traps. Nevertheless, it is possible to find a deserted spot on this peninsula, and natural beauty survives in the Everglades

PRACTICAL INFORMATION

Capital: Tallahassee.

Florida Division of Tourism: 126 W. Van Buren St., Tallahassee 32399-2000 (904-487-1462). **Department of Environmental Protection—Division of Recreation and Parks,** 3900 Commonwealth Blvd. #506, Tallahassee 32399-3000 (904-488-9872).

Time Zones: Mostly Eastern; Central (1hr. behind Eastern) in the westernmost parts of the panhandle. **Postal Abbreviation:** FL

Sales Tax: 6%.

■■■ JACKSONVILLE

Originally known as "Cowford" because the British believed that cows could wade across the 90-ft.-deep St. Johns River here, Jacksonville was renamed in 1822 for General Andrew Jackson. The river has proven to be less of an impediment to growth than it was to cows; the nation's largest city, by square mileage, Jacksonville now crosses the St. Johns and stretches well beyond. The city draws visitors and residents with its mild climate and abundant beaches; travelers looking for the eternal Florida beach-party should move on down the coast.

Practical Information **I-95** runs through downtown leading across the Fuller Warren Bridge to the beaches. **Main St.** is the main north-south route through downtown; **Union St.** crosses east-west. To find the beaches, take Beach Blvd. from I-95 until you hit Rte. A1A and slide into the sand.

The **Jacksonville and the Beaches Convention & Visitors Bureau,** 3 Independent Dr. (798-9120), provides maps, brochures, and accommodations coupons (open Mon.-Fri. 9am-5pm). Fly into **Jacksonville International** (741-4902), off I-95 from exit 127B; a cab downtown will cost $19-21. **Amtrak,** 3570 Clifford Ln. (766-5108 or 800-872-7245), off I-95 at the 20th St. exit, sends trains to Orlando (3hr., $32) and Washington, DC (13hr., $139) two or three times per day (open daily 5am-10pm). **Greyhound,** 10 N. Pearl St. (356-9976 or 800-231-2222), connects Jacksonville with Orlando (6 per day, 3hr., $23) and Atlanta (8 per day, 6hr., $39) by bus (open daily 24 hrs.). **Jacksonville Transportation Authority** (630-3100) operates in-town buses from 5:30am-midnight daily (hours vary somewhat by route; fare 60¢, to the beach $1.10; no transfers). If you want to cab it, **Gator City Taxi and Shuttle Service,** 5320 Springfield Blvd. (355-8294), will take you where you need to go ($1.25 base fare, $1.25 per mi.; open daily 24 hrs.). Drive your very own **Thrifty** rental car, 1617 Airport Entrance Rd. (741-4366 or 800-367-2277), from $22 per day (unlimited mi.). People ages 21 to 24 must have a credit card and pay a $9 surcharge per day. **Rape Crisis** (355-7273), answers calls 24 hrs. **Emergency:** 911. Jacksonville's **post office:** 1100 King's Rd. (359-2838; open Mon.-Fri. 7am-7pm and Sat. 8:30am-2:30pm); **ZIP code:** 32203; **area code:** 904.

Accommodations and Camping Most budget chains offer inexpensive rooms at locations near the airport (see Practical Information, above), off I-95. **Admiral Benbow Inn,** 14691 Duval Rd. (741-4254 or 800-451-1986), I-95 and Airport Rd. exit 127, rents large rooms with a medieval motif, cable TV, and A/C; non-smoking and wheelchair-accessible rooms are available (singles $29.50, doubles $36.50). In an excellent location right on Jacksonville Beach, **Eastwinds Motel,** 1505 1st St. S. (249-3858; fax 249-4549), offers a wide variety of rooms. (1 queen-sized bed $43, 3-room suite with kitchen for up to 7 $94. In fall and winter $20 less, in spring $10 less.)

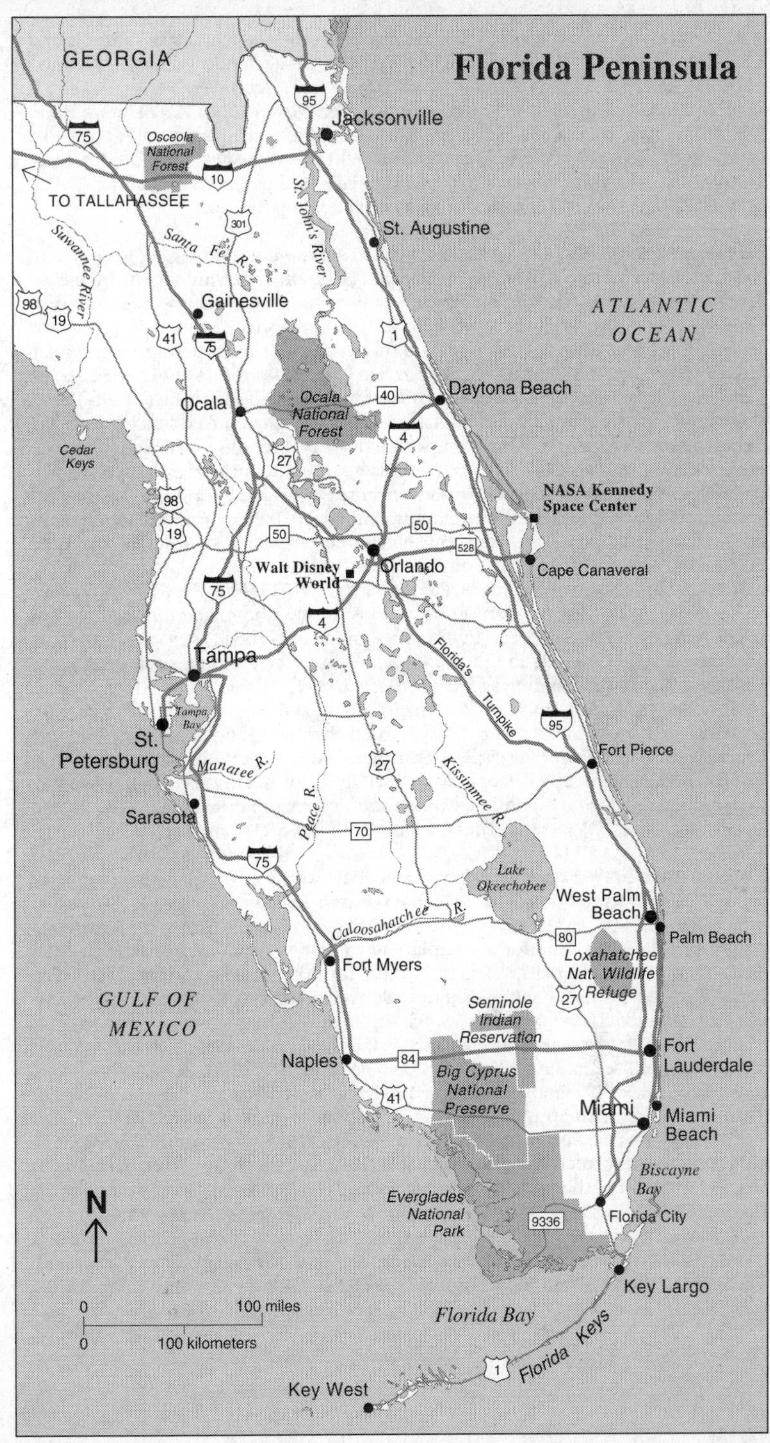
Florida Peninsula
GEORGIA
Jacksonville
Osceola National Forest
TO TALLAHASSEE
Suwannee River
Santa Fe R.
St. John's River
St. Augustine
Gainesville
ATLANTIC OCEAN
Ocala
Ocala National Forest
Daytona Beach
Cedar Keys
NASA Kennedy Space Center
Walt Disney World
Orlando
Cape Canaveral
Tampa
Tampa Bay
St. Petersburg
Manatee R.
Florida's Turnpike
Fort Pierce
Kissimmee R.
Peace R.
Sarasota
Lake Okeechobee
West Palm Beach
Palm Beach
Caloosahatchee R.
Fort Myers
Loxahatchee Nat. Wildlife Refuge
GULF OF MEXICO
Seminole Indian Reservation
Naples
Fort Lauderdale
Big Cyprus National Preserve
Miami
Miami Beach
Biscayne Bay
Everglades National Park
Florida City
Key Largo
Florida Bay
Florida Keys
Key West
N
0 100 miles
0 100 kilometers
75
95
10
301
98
19
41
1
40
4
27
50
528
70
80
84
9336

THE SOUTH

Across the street from the Atlantic and its white sandy beach, **Little Talbot Island State Park,** 12157 Heckscher Dr. (251-2320), has 40 sites under palmetto trees and oaks. Take I-95S to Rte. A1A and go north. (Sites with electricity $18; in winter $7; ½-price for senior or disabled FL residents. Open March-Sept.) **K.A. Hanna Park,** 500 Wonderwood Dr. (249-4700), has mountain bike trails, hiking, and access to a beach with lifeguard service, in addition to 300 wooded sites with full hookups. Hop on Rte. A1A going north and follow the signs to Mayport Naval Station. (Office open daily 8am-sunset. Tent sites $10, with full hookup $13.50.)

Food and Nightlife **Five Points,** located south of downtown on Park St. and **the Landing,** a dining and shopping extravaganza on Independent Dr. by the St. Johns River, swarms with dining options. In Five Points, try **Heartworks Gallery & Café,** 820 Lomax St. (355-6210), off Park St. Vegetarian specials (such as the famous "carrot dog") and killer desserts spice up this small café behind an even smaller gallery ($3-5.50; open Mon.-Sat. 11am-3pm, also Fri. 6-10pm for dinner specials). A Jacksonville institution, **The Old South Restaurant,** 3058 Beach Blvd. (396-1920), skips the fancy stuff and attracts a local crowd with homecooked lunches and dinners. The menu varies daily but always includes an entree (fried chicken, meatloaf, etc.) and two veggies ($5). Try the chocolate ice box pie ($1) for dessert. (Open daily 11am-9pm.) **The Pizza Italian Restaurant,** 1053 Park St. (289-1059), serves up a mean red sauce (the secret is cinnamon) and quality Italian meals. All lunch items come in at or under $4. (For dinner, chicken parmigiana with a side of spaghetti $6.35. Open Mon.-Thurs. 11am-9pm, Fri. 11am-10pm.)

Nightlife in Jacksonville sprawls like the city itself. **The Milk Bar,** 128 W. Adams St. (356-6455), downtown, houses two clubs in one: the main club features live music and DJs, while the Green Room (open Mon. and Fri.-Sat.) plays jazz and funk. The crowd is as varied as the tunes. (Open Mon., Wed., and Fri.-Sun. 9pm-3am.) Also downtown, the **Landing's** (353-1188) courtyard has a series of different music performers; call for information. Modern art murals and other splashes of paint have transformed an old theater into **Club 5,** 1028 Park St. (356-5555), in Five Points (open Wed.-Thurs. 9am-3am, Fri.-Sat. 9am-4am). Near the beach, the **Ragtime Tap Room and Brewery,** 207 Atlantic Blvd. (241-7877), at Atlantic Beach, has live jazz music Thursday through Sunday. Come for a dessert (gold brick sundae $3), and stay for the tunes. (Open Sun.-Thurs. 11am-11pm, Fri.-Sat. 11am-1:30am.)

Sights and Entertainment Jacksonville spares the wallet with a couple of top-notch free attractions. **The Anheuser-Busch Brewery Tour,** 111 Busch Dr. (751-8118), off I-95, explains both the brewing process and the history of the company and still leaves time for a complimentary tasting (open Mon.-Sat. 9am-4pm; free). One of the first plantations in Florida, the **Kingsley Plantation,** 11676 Palmetto Ave., off Rte. A1A, includes unusually well-preserved slave quarters and several historical exhibits (open daily 9am-5pm; free).

The Cummer Museum of Art & Gardens, 829 Riverside Ave. (356-6857), shows a collection of Western art dating to 2000BC. In the gardens, planted in the 1920s, look for an oak with a limbspan of over 150 ft. (Open Tues. 10am-9:30pm, Wed.-Fri. 10am-4pm, Sat. noon-5pm, Sun. 2-5pm. $3, children $1.50.) Interactive hands-on exhibits at **The Museum of Science and History,** 1025 Museum Cir. (396-7062), cover a range of subjects from the history of Native Americans on the St. Johns River to the functions of the body. (Open Mon.-Fri. 10am-5pm, Sat. 10am-6pm, Sun. 1-6pm. $5, seniors and ages 4-12 $3. Get 2-for-1 admission with their brochure.)

For three days in October, the **Jacksonville Jazz Festival** (353-7770; call for exact dates) attracts large crowds with a piano competition, live performances, and food. Throughout the year, pick up a copy of *Folio Weekly* for the dirt on weekly events.

■■■ ST. AUGUSTINE

Spanish adventurer Juan Ponce de León founded St. Augustine in 1565, making it the first European colony in North America and the oldest continuous settlement in the United States. Thanks to preservation efforts, much of St. Augustine's Spanish flavor remains intact. Unlike most towns on Florida's east coast, beaches do not define the character of St. Augustine; small crowds, historic sights, and friendly people invite visitors to relax and settle in for a rejuvenating stay.

Practical Information St. Augustine has no public transportation; fortunately, most points of interest lie within walking distance of one another. The major east-west axis, **King St.** runs along the river and crosses the bay to the beaches. **St. George St.,** also east-west, contains most of the shops and many sights in St. Augustine but does not permit vehicular traffic. **San Marco Ave.** and **Cordova St.** travel north-south. The **Visitors Center,** 10 Castillo (825-1000), at San Marco Ave. (from the Greyhound station, walk north on Ribeira, then right on Orange), gives out the free *Chamber of Commerce Map,* and a comprehensive city guide. A worthwhile (it took 7 years to research) 52-minute video presentation gives visitors a glimpse of life in early St. Augustine ($3, students $2; open daily 8am-7:30pm; off season 8:30am-5:30pm). **Greyhound,** 100 Malaga St. (829-6401 or 800-231-222), has service to Jacksonville (45min., $10) and Daytona Beach (1hr., $12) six times per day (open daily 7:30am-8:30pm). **Ancient City Taxi** (824-8161) can take you from the bus station to San Marco Ave. for about $2. For **Rape Crisis** counseling, call 355-7273 (open 24 hrs.). **Emergency:** 911. St. Augustine's **post office:** 99 King St. (829-8716), at Martin Luther King Ave. (open Mon.-Tues. and Thurs.-Fri. 8:30am-5pm, Wed. 8:30am-3:30pm, Sat. 10am-1pm); **ZIP code:** 32084; **area code:** 904.

Accommodations and Camping The immaculate **St. Augustine Hostel (HI-AYH),** 32 Treasury St. (808-1999), at Charlotte 6 blocks from the bus station, offers large dorm-style rooms, oversized bunk beds, A/C, a kitchen, a common area, and a roof garden. Call the welcoming manager Jean to make special arrangements for arrivals outside of open hours. (Open for reservations daily 8-10am and 5-10pm. No curfew; get a combination for the lock. Beds $12. Linens $2.) The **American Inn,** 42 San Marco Ave. (829-2292), near the visitors center, rents spacious rooms with new carpets, two double beds, TV, and A/C, in a location convenient to the restaurants and historic sights (singles $25, doubles $30). Just over the Bridge of Lions, east of the historic district, the **Seabreeze Motel,** 208 Anastasia Blvd. (829-8122), features clean rooms with 2 double beds, A/C, cable TV, and a pool (singles $28, doubles $30). For a real treat, splurge on the **St. Francis Inn,** 279 Saint George (824-6068), a charming 16-room inn with a jungle of flowers, a tucked-away pool, and much of its original 18th–century interior. Juice and iced tea are served free all day, along with sangria in the summer and sherry in the winter. (Free use of bikes. Rooms from $55. Cottage for 4 with kitchen and living room $160, $12 per additional person. Free continental breakfast.)

A nearby salt run and the Atlantic provide opportunities for great windsurfing, fishing, swimming, and surfing near the campground of the **Anastasia State Recreation Area** (461-2033), on Rte. A1A, 4 mi. south of the historic district. From town, cross the Bridge of Lions and turn left just beyond the Alligator Farm. (Office open daily 8am-8pm. Sites $15; Oct.-Feb. $12. Make reservations.)

Food and Nightlife The bustle of daytime tourists and abundance of budget eateries make lunch in St. Augustine's historic district a delight. Stroll **St. George St.** and check the daily specials scrawled on blackboards outside each restaurant; locals prefer the spots clustered at the southern end of St. George St. near King St. An expedition along Anastasia Blvd. should unearth good meals for under $6. Seafood-lovers go for the large surf 'n' turf dinners ($15) at **Captain Jack's,** 410 Anastasia Blvd. (829-6846), or the local and house specialty: fried shrimp ($8; open Mon.-Fri.

11:30am-9pm, Sat.-Sun. noon-9pm). Have a delicious fruit shake or sandwich and check out the local artwork hanging in cozy **Café Camacho,** 11-C Aviles St. (824-7030), 1 block from Saint George St. in the historic district. Vegetarian dishes and daily breakfast and lunch specials run $5-6. (Open daily 8am-9pm.) **The Bunnery Café,** 35 Hypolita St. (829-6166), serves enormous cinnamon rolls ($1.29) on an outdoor patio; ask for icing, and they'll heap it on until you say the magic word. (8-in. cookies 80¢; sandwiches $3; open daily 9am-5:30pm). A combination museum, luncheonette, and bookstore, the **St. George Pharmacy and Restaurant,** 121 Saint George St. (829-5929), puts together cheap sandwiches (from $2.50) and dinners (from $3) in an old-fashioned soda fountain setting. Try the grilled cheese with a thick chocolate malt. (For breakfast, 1 egg, bacon, grits, toast or biscuit, and jelly $2. Open daily 7:30am-5pm.) The sandwich and juice counter (open Mon.-Sat. 10am-3pm) at **New Dawn,** 110 Anastasia Blvd. (824-1337), a health-conscious grocery store, makes delicious vegetarian sandwiches, including the savory tofu salad surprise ($3.75; banana smoothies $2.75; store open Mon.-Sat. 9am-5:30pm).

St. Augustine supports an impressive array of bars. Pick up a copy of the *Today Tonight* newspaper, available at most grocery and convenience stores, for a complete listing of current concerts and events. In the restored area, try the **Milltop,** 19½ Saint George St. (829-2329), a tiny bar situated above an old mill. Local string musicians play on the tiny stage (no cover; music daily 11am-midnight). **Panama Hattie's,** 361 A1A/Beach Blvd. (471-2255), on St. Augustine Beach, caters to the post-college crowd with live music Friday to Sunday during July and August and dancing on the upstairs deck (no cover; open daily 1pm-midnight). The new hot spot for the young beach crowd, **The Oasis Deck and Restaurant,** 4000 A1A/Beach Blvd. (471-3424), schedules nightly live entertainment and happy hours (happiness Mon.-Fri. 4-7pm; open daily 6:30am-1am). Hang out with the locals at **Scarlett O'Hara's,** 70 Hypolita St. (824-6535), at Cordova St., where the barbecue chicken sandwiches ($4.50) are juicy and filling and the drinks flow ample and cool. Live entertainment begins at 9pm Tuesday through Saturday. (Happy hour Mon.-Fri. 5:30-6:30pm "Ladies" nights Tues. and Thurs. Cover Fri.-Sat. $1. Open daily 11:30am-1am.)

Sights and Entertainment The historic district centers on **Saint George St.,** beginning at the Gates of the City near the visitors center and running south past Cadiz St. and the Oldest Store. Visit the **Spanish Quarter** (825-6830), a living museum which includes Gallegos House, on Saint George St., and the rest of St. Augustine's authentically restored 18th-century neighborhood. Artisans and villagers in period costumes describe the customs and crafts of the Spanish New World. (Open daily 9am-5pm. $5, students and ages 6-18 $2.50, seniors $3.75.) The oldest masonry fortress in the continental U.S., **Castillo de San Marcos National Monument,** 1 Castillo Dr. (829-6506), off San Marco Ave., has 14-ft. thick walls built of coquina, the local shellrock. Inside the fort itself, a four-pointed star complete with drawbridge and murky moat, you'll find a museum, a large courtyard surrounded by guardrooms, livery quarters for the garrison, a jail, a chapel, and the original cannon brought overseas by the Spanish. A cannon-firing ceremony occurs four times per day on weekends. (Open daily 8:45am-4pm. $2, over 62 and under 16 free.)

For twenty years, St. Augustine was the end of the line—the railroad line, that is. Swarms of wealthy Northerners escaped to railroad-owner Henry Flagler's Ponce de León Hotel, at King and Cordova St. The hotel, decorated entirely by Tiffany and outfitted with electricity by Edison himself (the first hotel to feature this luxury), is now **Flagler College.** In the summer, the college lies deserted, but students enliven the campus and the town during the school year. On summer days, free 20- to 25-minute tours pass through some of the recently restored rooms in the old hotel; go, if only to see the exquisite stained glass windows. (Tours daily on the hr. 10am-4pm.) In 1947, Chicago publisher and art-lover Otto Lightner converted the Alcazar Hotel, across the street, into the **Lightner Museum** (824-2874), to hold an impressive collection of cut, blown, and burnished glass, as well as old clothing and numerous oddities including nun and monk beer steins (open daily 9am-5pm; $4, college students with ID and ages 12-18 $1).

Being the oldest continuous settlement in the U.S. entails having some of the oldest stuff in the U.S. The self-described **Oldest House,** 14 Saint Francis St. (824-2872), has been occupied continuously since its construction in the 1600s (open daily 9am-5pm; $5, students $2.50, seniors $4.50). The **Oldest Store Museum,** 4 Artillery Ln. (829-9729), holds over 100,000 odds and ends from the 18th and 19th centuries (open Mon.-Sat. 9am-5pm, Sun. noon-5pm; $4, ages 6-12 $1.50).

Six blocks north of the info center, **La Leche Shrine and Mission of Nombre de Dios,** 27 Ocean St. (824-2809), held the first Catholic service in the U.S. on September 8, 1565. Soaring over the moss- and vine-covered structure, a 208-ft. steel cross commemorates the founding of the city. (Open daily 7am-8pm; Sept.-June 7am-6pm. Mass Mon.-Fri. 8:30am, Sat. 6pm, Sun. 8am. Admission by donation.) No trip to St. Augustine would be complete without a trek to the **Fountain of Youth,** 155 Magnolia Ave. (829-3168); go right on Williams St. from San Marco Ave. and continue a few blocks past Nombre de Dios (open daily 9am-5pm; $4, seniors $3, ages 6-12 $1.50). Not only can you drink from the spring that Ponce de León thought would give him eternal youth, you can marvel at a statue of the explorer which doesn't age. Look around while you're there; Magnolia Ave., lined with huge oaks and hanging Spanish moss, is heralded as one of the prettiest streets in America.

St. Augustine Sight-Seeing Trains, 170 San Marcos Ave. (829-6545), offer a variety of city tours (1-8hr.; open daily 8:30am-4:30pm). The one-hour tour ($10, ages 6-12 $5), gives a good introduction to the city starting at the front of the visitors center (see Practical Information, above). All tours allow stop-off privileges to the various attractions. **Colée Sight-Seeing Carriage Tours** (829-2818) begin near the entrance to the fort, take about an hour, and cover the historic area of the city (open daily 8:30am-10pm; $10, ages 4-11 $5). The **Victory II Scenic Cruise Ships** (824-1806) navigate the emerald Matanzas River from the City Yacht Pier, a block south of the Bridge of Lions (leaves 11am, 1, 2:45, 4:30, 6:45, and 8:30pm; $7.50, under 12 $3).

On Anastasia Island, at **St. Augustine Amphitheater,** south on Rte. A1A, Paul Green's *Cross and Sword,* Florida's official state play, tells St. Augustine's story with a large cast, a booming cannon, and swordfights ($12, students and ages 6-12 $6).

■■■ DAYTONA BEACH

Daytona's 500-ft.-wide beach is the city's *raison d'être.* During spring break, students from practically every college in the country come here to get a head start on summer. The beach itself resembles a traffic jam; dozens of cars, motorcycles, and rental dune buggies crawl along the hot sand. During any season, hundreds of cars roll along the beach within feet of sunbathers, or cruise the Atlantic Avenue strip. If you're looking for scenery in Daytona Beach, go a few miles north to picturesque Ormond Beach. If not, slap on some sunblock and enjoy.

Practical Information Daytona Beach lies 53 mi. northeast of Orlando and 90 mi. south of Jacksonville. **Atlantic Ave.,** or **Rte. A1A,** crawls with budget motels, surf shops, and bars in **Beachside,** the main strip of land. **East International Speedway Blvd.** (U.S. 92) divides Atlantic Ave. north-south. Pay attention when hunting down street addresses; numbers on north-south streets are not consecutive through various towns. To avoid the gridlock on the beach, arrive early (6 or 7am) and leave early (3pm or so). You'll pay $5 to drive onto the beach (permitted from sunrise to sunset), and police strictly enforce the 10mph speed limit. Free parking is plentiful during most of the year, but difficult during peak seasons.

For tourist info, visit **The Daytona Beach Area Convention and Visitors Bureau,** 126 E. Orange Ave. (255-0415 or 800-854-1234), at the chamber of commerce on City Island (open Mon.-Fri. 9am-5pm). Flights into Daytona arrive at the **Daytona Beach International Airport,** 700 Catalina Dr. (248-8069). **Amtrak,** 2491 Old New York Ave., Deland (734-2322 or 800-872-7245), 24 mi. west on Rte. 92, makes tracks to Miami (1-2 per day, 8hr., $50; open daily 7:45am-6:45pm). **Greyhound** buses come and go from 138 S. Ridgewood Ave. (255-7076 or 800-231-2222), 4 mi. west of the beach (open daily 8am-10pm). **Voltran Transit Co.** (761-7700), at the corner of Palmetto and 2nd Ave. on the mainland, operates local buses (Service Mon.-Sat. 5:30am-6:30pm; 75¢, transfers free; free system maps available at hotels.) **A&A Cab Co.** (253-2522) charges $1.80 for the first ½ mi. and $1.20 per additional mi. Rent an **Alamo** car (255-1511 or 800-327-9633) at the airport. A subcompact costs $25 per day or $109 per week with unlimited mileage. (Free drop-off in Jacksonville or Ft. Lauderdale. Must be 21 with credit card. Under 25 surcharge $20 per day.) Reach the 24-hr. **Rape Crisis and Sexual Abuse** line at 254-4106. **Emergency:** 911. Daytona Beach's **post office:** 220 N. Beach St. (253-5166; open Mon.-Fri. 8am-5pm. Sat. 9am-noon); **ZIP code:** 32176; **area code:** 904.

Accommodations and Camping Almost all of Daytona's accommodations front **Atlantic Ave. (Rte. A1A),** either on the beach or across the street; those off the beach offer the best deals. During spring break and big race weekends, even the worst hotels become overpriced. Don't plan to sleep on these well-patrolled shores. Look for cheaper, quieter hotels along **Ridgewood Ave.** In summer and fall, prices plunge; most hotels offer special deals in June. **Daytona Beach International Youth Hostel (AAIH/Rucksackers),** 140 S. Atlantic Ave. (258-6937), 1 block north of E. International Speedway Blvd., provides 100 beds, A/C, TV, kitchen facilities, and a recreation room in close proximity to the beach. Don't expect luxury. A crowd of international students usually fills the place. (With HI-AYH card $12, without $16. Weekly $70. Lockers $1-2. Key deposit $5.) If you have a few extra dollars, the **Camellia Motel,** 1055 N. Atlantic Ave. (252-9963), across the street from the beach, is well worth the money. The maternal manager oversees cozy, bright rooms, with phones, free local calls, cable TV, and A/C; rooms with kitchens cost an extra $5. (Singles and doubles $25; $5 per additional person. During spring break singles $60; $10 per additional person.) The **Rio Beach Motel,** 843 S. Atlantic Ave. (253-6564), has large rooms decorated in dark plums and greens. Cable TV, A/C, a swimming pool, and a prime location directly on the ocean make it even better (singles and doubles $27; during spring break $60-70).

Camping options await at **Tomoka State Park,** 2099 N. Beach St. (676-4050), 8 mi. north of Daytona and 70 minutes from Disney World. Take bus #3 "North Ridgewood" to Domicilio and walk 2 mi. north. You'll find 97 sites located under tropical foliage near a salt marsh, along with nature trails, a museum, and lots of shade. (Open daily 8am-7:45pm. Sites $15; Oct.-Feb. $8.) **Nova Family Campground,** 1190 Herbet St. (767-0095 or 800-551-0036), in Port Orange south of Daytona Beach 10 minutes from the shore, comes through for the RVers with shady hookup-equipped sites, a grocery store, and a swimming pool. Take bus #7 or 15 from downtown or from the beach. (Open Sun.-Thurs. 8am-7pm, Fri.-Sat. 8am-8pm. Sites $17, with hookup $20. Open sites posted after hours; register the next day.)

Food "If it swims...we have it," boasts **B&B Fisheries,** 715 E. International Speedway Blvd. (252-6542). Take out broiled flounder or sea trout lunches for under $5.15, or lobster specials for under $10. (Open Mon.-Fri. 11am-8:30pm, Sat. 4-8:30pm. Take-out service Mon.-Sat. 11:30am-8:30pm.) If you're (not) in the mood, the **Oyster Pub,** 555 Seabreeze Blvd. (253-6600), will do you right. Sit at the huge square bar where locals eat hearty meat sandwiches ($3-5) and slurp raw oysters ($3-19, depending on size) all day long. (Happy hour from 4-7pm. Open daily 11:30am-3am.) **St. Regis Bar and Restaurant,** 509 Seabreeze Blvd. (252-8743), in a historic home, is a good break from budget fare. Eat an eclectic array of edibles (dinner $9-22) on the cool veranda, while listening to live saxophone and jazz (Fri.-Sat. 8pm-midnight). Happy hour 5-7pm means free hors d'oeuvres, $1 drafts, and $2.50 mixed drinks. (Open Tues.-Thurs. 5-10pm, Fri.-Sat. 5-11pm.)

Entertainment and Nightlife When you grow tired of the languid pace of the beach, race off to the **Daytona International Speedway,** 1801 W. International Blvd. (254-2700 for general info; 253-RACE/7223 for race tickets). **Speed Week,** February 11-18, consists of the **Daytona 500** (Feb. 18; Daytona 500 1996 is already sold out), the **Goody's 300** (Feb. 17), and the **ARCA World Championship Race** (Feb. 11); tickets range from $70-135. The **Daytona Racefest** and the **Pepsi 400 NASCAR Winston Cup Series** kick into gear on July 6 (tickets $20-45) and during the first weekend in March, respectively. Motorcycle Week culminates with the **Daytona 200 Motorcycle Classic** (tickets $30). The speedway houses a huge collection of racing memorabilia and early racing films and conducts 30-minute tours on days with no races (tours daily 9am-5pm; $5, children $2).

During spring break, concerts, hotel-sponsored parties, and other events cater to students questing for fun. News about these transient events and parties travels fastest by word of mouth, but check the *Calendar of Events* and *SEE Daytona Beach,* available at the Chamber of Commerce for a starting point. On more mellow nights, head to the boardwalk where you can play volleyball, pinball, listen to music at the Oceanfront Bandshell, or park (ahem) on the beach until 1am for $3.

As if you needed more outlets for sin, you sickos—fine, have two spring break hotspots, **600 North Attitudes,** 600 N. Atlantic Ave. (255-4471), and **Kokomos,** 100 North Atlantic Ave. (254-8200), on the beach. **Razzel's,** 611 Seabreeze Blvd. (257-6236), dazzles all ages from 18 up (cover $3-8). At **Finky's,** 600 Grandview (255-5093), the motto says it all: "I got kinky at..." Cover varies ($0-5) depending on the time of year, as does the music selection (top 40 dance to country).

■■■ ORLANDO: THE LAND OF AMUSEMENT PARKS

Shaquille O'Neal may stand over 7 ft. tall and weigh in at over 300 lbs., but the biggest character in Orlando is still a mouse—that's Mickey to you. Millions annually descend on this central Florida city for just one reason: **Disney World,** the most popular tourist attraction on earth. When Walt Disney selected the area south of Orlando as the place for the sequel to California's Disneyland, he had no idea what would follow. Disney has since augmented the Magic Kingdom with the Epcot Center and the Disney-MGM Studios theme park, while a plethora of parasitic attractions, such as expensive water parks, have come to scavenge the leftovers of Disney tourism. Be warned: this land of illusions offers many ways to blow your dough; it's generally best to spend your time and money at Disney first.

PRACTICAL INFORMATION

Tourist Office: Orlando-Orange County Convention and Visitors Bureau, 8445 International Dr. (363-5871), several mi. southwest of downtown at the Mercado (Spanish-style mall); take bus #8 and ask the driver to make the stop. Maps and info on nearly all of the area's attractions, plus free bus system maps. Open daily 8am-8pm.

Airport: Orlando International Airport, 1 Airport Blvd. (825-2001), from the Airport take Rte. 436N, exit to Rte. 528W (the B-line Expwy.), then go east on I-4 to the exits for downtown. City bus #11 makes the trip for 75¢. **Mears Motor Shuttle,** 324 W. Gore St. (423-5566), has a booth at the airport for transportation to most hotels, including Plantation Manor (see Accommodations, below). Also runs from most hotels to Disney ($7-14); call 1 day in advance to reserve a seat. Open 24 hrs.

Trains: Amtrak, 1400 Sligh Blvd. (843-7611 or 800-872-7245), 3 blocks east of I-4; take S. Orange Ave., turn west on Columbia, then right on Sligh. To: Tampa (1 per day, 2hr., $19); Jacksonville (3 per day, 3hr., $30). Open 7am-6pm.

Buses: Greyhound, 555 N. Magruder Blvd. (292-3424 for 24-hr. fare and ticket info or 800-231-2222) across from John Young Pkwy. To: Tampa (7 per day, 3hr., $14); Jacksonville (7 per day, 4hr., $23). Station open 24 hrs. **Gray Line Tours**

(859-4211) offers bus transport to Busch Gardens (see p. 351). Round-trip $49 plus admission, ages 3-9 $43. Pick-up at most major hotels.

Public Transportation: LYNX, 7800 W. Central Blvd. (841-8240; Mon.-Fri. 6:30am-6:30pm, Sat. 7:30am-6pm, Sun. 8am-4pm). Buses operate daily 6am-9pm. Fare 75¢, under 18 25¢, transfers 10¢. Downtown terminal at Central and Pine St., 1 block west of Orange Ave. and 1 block east of I-4. Schedules available at most shopping malls, banks, and at the downtown terminal. Serves the airport (bus #11 at side A, level 1), Sea World, and Wet 'n' Wild.

Taxis: Yellow Cab, 422-4455. $2.75 first mi., $1.50 per additional mi. 24 hrs.

Car Rental: Alamo, 8200 McCoy Rd. (857-8200 or 800-327-9633), near the airport. $37 per day, $120 per week. Under 25 surcharge $20 per day. Open 24 hrs. Must have a major credit card.

Crisis Lines: Rape Hotline, 740-5408, and **Crisis Information,** 425-2624. 24 hrs.

Emergency: 911.

Post Office: 46 E. Robinson St. (843-5673), at Magnolia downtown. Open Mon.-Fri. 8am-5pm, Sat. 9am-noon. **ZIP code:** 32801. **Area code:** 407.

Orlando lies at the center of hundreds of small lakes and amusement parks. **Lake Eola** is in the center of the city, east of I-4 and south of Colonial Dr. Streets divide north-south by **Rte. 17-92 (Orange Blossom Trail)** and east-west by **Colonial Dr.** Supposedly an east-west expressway, I-4 actually runs north-south through the center of town. To reach either downtown youth hostel (see Accommodations, below) by car, take the Robinson St. exit and turn right. **Disney World** and **Sea World** await 15 to 20 mi. south of downtown on I-4; **Cypress Gardens** is 30 mi. south of Disney off U.S. 27 near Winter Haven. Most hotels offer shuttle service to Disney. City buses and Gray Line serve some parks as does Mears Motor Shuttle (see above).

ACCOMMODATIONS AND CAMPING

Orlando does not cater to the budget traveler. Prices for hotel rooms rise exponentially as you approach Disney World; plan to stay in a hostel or in downtown Orlando. Reservations are prudent, especially December to January, March to April, late June to August and on holidays.

Orlando International Youth Hostel at Plantation Manor (HI-AYH), 227 N. Eola Dr. (843-8888), at E. Robinson, downtown on the east shore of Lake Eola. Porch, TV room, A/C, kitchen facilities. Rooms sleep 4-8. The friendly managers will take you to the Disney park of your choice for $10 round-trip. Must be a member or have non-U.S. passport to stay; there may be exceptions if they're not full. 3-day max. stay. Curfew 1am. $10. Private rooms $25. Breakfast $2. Linen $2. Key deposit $5. Usually full July-Oct.; make reservations.

Hostelling International-Orlando Resort (HI-AYH), 4840 W. Irlo Bronson Memorial Hwy./Rte. 192 (396-8282), in Kissimmee. Brand-new hostel in the process of changing over from the Lake View Motel; look for the Lake View marquee. Super-clean rooms with new wooden bunk beds, A/C, pool, lake, and transportation to Disney ($12-14). Presently there is a small common area with TV and a kitchen, but renovations should make them larger and add a BBQ site. Office open 24 hrs. $13, nonmembers $16. Private rooms $10 extra. Ages 6-17 ½-price, under 6 free. Linens $1. Reservations recommended.

Sun Motel, 5020 W. Irlo Bronson Memorial Hwy./Rte. 192 (396-6666 or 800-541-2674), in Kissimmee. Very reasonable considering its proximity to Disney World (4mi.). Pretty rooms with floral bedspreads, cable TV, phone, pool, and A/C. Singles $45, doubles $70; off season $25/$28.

Disney's All-Star Resorts (934-7639), in Disney World. Not exactly cheap, but a great deal if you're in a group, and came to Orlando to see Disney. Amazingly large cowboy boots and football helmets decorate large courtyards. Pools, A/C, phone, refrigerator ($5 extra per day), food court, free parking, free Disney transportation. $69-79 for 2 adults and 2 kids, $8 for each additional adult up to four.

KOA, 447 W. Irlo Bronson Memorial Hwy. (Rte. 192) (396-2400 or 800-331-1453), in Kissimmee. Spacious sites with lots of trees, a pool, tennis courts, and a store (open 7am-11pm). Even in season you're bound to get a site, but arrive early. Free buses twice per day to Disney. Office open 24 hrs. Tent sites with hookup for 2 $22, kamping kabins with A/C for 2 $38; $4 per additional person up to 4.

Stage Stop Campground, 700 W. Rte. 50 (656-8000), 8mi. north of Disney in Winter Garden. Take exit 267 off the Florida Turnpike N, then follow Rte. 50W. Family campground with a game room, a pool, laundry facilities, and many long-term residents. Office open daily 8am-8:30pm. 248 sites (tent or RV) with full hookup $17; weekly $102.

Orlando has two municipal campgrounds, **Turkey Lake Park,** 3401 S. Hiawassee Rd. (299-5581), near Universal Studios (open daily 9:30am-7pm; sites with water and electricity $14.32, with full hookup $16.50), and **Moss Park,** 12901 Moss Park Rd. (273-2327), 10 mi. from the airport (open daily 8am-8pm; tent sites $11, with water and electricity $14; park entrance $1). In **Kissimmee,** a few mi. east of Disney World along U.S. 192, look for **South Port Park,** 2001 South Port Rd. (open daily 6am-6pm; tent sites $12, with water and electricity $14, with full hookup $15).

FOOD

Lilia's Grilled Delight, 3150 S. Orange Ave. (851-9087), 2 blocks south of Michigan St. 5min. from the downtown business district. Small, modestly decorated Polynesian restaurant—one of the best-kept secrets in town. Don't pass up the Huli Huli Chicken, a twice baked delight (½ chicken $6). Lunch $4-6. Dinner $5-9. Open Mon.-Fri. 11am-9pm, Sat. noon-9pm.

Bakely's, 345 W. Fairbanks Ave. (645-5767), in Winter Park. Take I-4 to Fairbanks Ave. exit. The variety at this restaurant/bake shop is as large as the portions. Lasagna with salad and bread $7. Save room for the six-layer Boston Cream cake ($3). Open Sun.-Thurs. 7am-11pm, Fri.-Sat. 7am-midnight.

Thai House, 2101 E. Colonial Dr. (898-0820). A small and charming family-run restaurant crowded with locals. The house specialty, Thai House Fried Rice, sizzles with a combination of pork, chicken, beef, shrimp, veggies, and spices ($7). Healthy portions for $5.50-8.50 (duck and seafood $9-15). Open Mon.-Fri. 11am-2:30pm and 5-9:30pm, Sat.-Sun noon-2pm and 5-10pm.

Clarkie's Restaurant, 3110 S. Orange Ave. (859-1690). Serves up simple "Mom" food for under $5. Early Bird breakfast special: 2 eggs, grits, and toast or biscuit, $1.29 until 8am. Every kind of sandwich imaginable. Open Mon.-Fri. 6am-2:30pm, Sat. 6am-noon, Sun. 7am-1pm.

Francesco's Ristorante Italiano, 4920 W. Irlo Bronson Memorial Hwy./Rte. 192 (396-0889). Dine beneath Chianti bottles while Sinatra tunes croon in the background. Large portions of pasta, steak, or seafood complete with salad bar and bread $7-14. Open daily 7:30am-11pm.

ENTERTAINMENT AND NIGHTLIFE

Improvisational comedy shows will keep you in stitches at the **SAK Theater,** 45 E. Church St. (648-0001; shows Tues. 9pm, Wed.-Thurs. 8 and 9:45pm, Fri.-Sat. 7:30, 9:30, and 11:30pm, Fri.-Sat. $11, with FL ID $9, students or military $7).

The **Church Street Station,** 129 W. Church St. (422-2434), downtown on the corner of Church and Garland St., is a slick, block-long entertainment, shopping, and restaurant complex (open 11am-2am). Inside, boogie down and enjoy 5¢ beers (Wed. 6:30-7:30pm) at **Phineas Phogg's Balloon Works** (21+). For $16, you can see the three theme shows: **Rosie O'Grady's,** the most popular, features Dixieland music and can-can dancers; **Cheyenne Saloon and Opera House** has a country and western show; while rock rules at the **Orchid Garden Ballroom.** Exploring **Orange Ave.,** downtown, should turn up less expensive nightlife. Several good bars and clubs have live music and dancing at reasonable prices. At **yab-yum,** 25 Wall St. Plaza (422-3322), they sell 20 brands of cigarettes and almost as many coffees. (Live entertainment Tues.-Sat. Open Sun.-Thurs. 8am-1am, Fri.-Sat. 8am-2:30am.)

■ DISNEY WORLD

Disney: the mother of all amusement parks, a sprawling three-park labyrinth of kiddie rides, movie sets, and futuristic world displays. If bigger is better, Disney World wins the prize for best park in the U.S. by a mile (824-4321, for info daily 8am-10pm). Disney World contains three sections: the **Magic Kingdom,** with seven theme regions; the **Epcot Center,** part science fair, part World's Fair; and **Disney-MGM Studios,** a pseudo movie- and TV-studio with Magic Kingdom-style rides. All three cluster a few mi. from each other in the town of **Lake Buena Vista,** 20 mi. west of Orlando via I-4.

The one-day entrance fee of $37 (ages 3-9 $30) admits you to *one* of the three parks, and allows you to leave and return to the same park later in the day. A four-day **Value Pass** ($124, ages 3-9 $97) covers one day at each park, plus an extra day at one of them. A four-day **Park-Hopper Pass** ($137, ages 3-9 $109) buys admission to all three parks for all four days. The five-day **World-Hopper Pass** ($186, ages 3-9 $148), includes admission to all other Disney attractions (see below). Both "Hopper" passes allow for unlimited transportation between attractions on the Disney monorail, boats, buses, and trains. Multi-day passes need not be used on consecutive days and they *never* expire. Disney attractions that charge separate admissions (unless you have a World-Hopper Pass) include **River Country** ($14.75, ages 3-9 $11.50), **Discovery Island** ($10, ages 3-9 $5.50), **Typhoon Lagoon** ($22.50, ages 3-9 $17), **Pleasure Island** ($15.95, over 18 only, unless with adult), and **Blizzard Beach** ($22.50, ages 3-9 $17). For descriptions, see Other Disney Attractions below.

Disney World opens its gates 365 days a year, but hours fluctuate with the season. Expect the parks to open at 9am and close at 8pm; these hours are often extended. The parks get busy during the summer when school is out, but the enormously crowded "peak times" are Christmas, Thanksgiving, spring break, and the month around Easter; more people visit between Christmas and New Year's than at any other time of year. The crowd hits the main gates at 10am; arrive before the 9am opening time and seek out your favorite rides or exhibits before noon. During peak periods (and often during the rest of the year), Disney World actually opens earlier than the stated time for guests staying at Disney resorts. To avoid the crowds, begin the day at the rear of a park and work your way to the front. You'll be able to see the distant attractions while the masses cram the lines for those near the entrance. If you have extremely limited time, though, go on your "must-see" rides in spite of the lines. Persevere through dinner time (5:30-8pm), when a lot of cranky kids head home. Regardless of tactics, you'll often have to wait anywhere from 45 minutes to two hours at big attractions.

Mears Motor Shuttle offers transport from most hotels to Disney (see Practical Information, above). Major hotels and some campgrounds provide their own shuttles for guests. **Cyclists** can store their bikes at Epcot free of charge.

Magic Kingdom Seven "lands" comprise the Magic Kingdom. Enter on **Main Street, USA,** to capture the essence of turn-of-the-century hometown U.S. The architects employed "forced perspective" here, building the ground floor of the shops 9/10 of the normal size and making the second and third stories progressively smaller. Walt describes his vision in the "Walt Disney Movie" at the Hospitality House, to the right as you emerge from under the railroad station. The Main Street Cinema shows some great old silent films. Late in the afternoon, the "Mickey Mania Parade" down Main Street gives you a chance to see all the Disney characters, or find shorter lines at the more crowded attractions. Near the entrance, you'll find a steam train that huffs and puffs its way across the seven different lands.

Tomorrowland just received a neon and stainless steel facelift which skyrocketed it out of the space-race days of the 70s and into a futuristic intergalactic nation, **XS. Alien Encounter,** the newest Magic Kingdom attraction, chills without spins or drops, creating suspense in pitch blackness. The very cool indoor roller coaster

Space Mountain still proves the high point of this section, if not the whole park, and absolutely merits the lengthy wait.

The golden-spired Cinderella Castle marks the gateway to **Fantasyland,** where you'll find Dumbo the Elephant and a twirling teacup ride. Two classic rides, **Peter Pan's Flight** and **Snow White's Adventures** capture the original charm of the park; the evil Queen scares children like no one else. You know the song, so see what it means at **It's A Small World,** a saccharine but endearing boat tour celebrating the children of the world. Be warned, you may never, ever, get this tune out of your head. Killer A/C makes it a good bet for a hot day.

Liberty Square and **Frontierland** devote their resources to U.S. history and a celebration of Mark Twain. History buffs will enjoy the recently updated Hall of Presidents (President Clinton makes a cameo, Maya Angelou narrates), which focuses on our nation's quest for equality. Adventurers should catch the rickety, runaway **Big Thunder Mountain Railroad** rollercoaster or the truly dope **Splash Mountain,** which takes you on a voyage with Br'er Rabbit and leaves you chilled inside and out. Spooky and dorky, **Haunted Mansion** is a classic with a quick line. Also be sure to stop and watch the entertaining animatronics at the **Country Bear Jamboree,** or take a steamboat ride or canoe trip and rest your feet.

Adventureland romanticizes unexplored regions of the world. **The Jungle Cruise** takes a tongue-in-cheek tour through tropical waterways populated by not-so-authentic-looking wildlife. **Pirates of the Caribbean** explores caves where animated buccaneers spar, swig, and sing. The Swiss Family Robinson tree house, a replica of the eternally shipwrecked family's home, captures all the clever tricks the family used to survive.

Epcot Center In 1966, Walt dreamed up an "Experimental Prototype Community Of Tomorrow" (EPCOT) never intended to be completed, evolving constantly to incorporate new ideas from U.S. technology—a self-sufficient, futuristic utopia. At present, Epcot splits into **Future World** and **World Showcase.** For smaller crowds, visit the former in the evening and the latter in the morning.

The 180-ft.-high trademark geosphere which forms the entrance to Future World houses the **Spaceship Earth** attraction, where visitors board a "time machine" for a tour through the evolution of communications. At the **Wonders of Life, Body Wars** takes its visitors on a tour of the human body (with the help of a simulator) and tells us all where babies come from in a movie called "The Making of Me." **The Land** presents **The Circle of Life,** a live-action/animated film about the environment with characters from *The Lion King.* Fish, sharks, and manatees inhabit the re-created coral reef in **The Living Seas.** The immensely popular **Journey Into Imagination** pavilion recently replaced Michael Jackson's film "Captain Eo" with "Honey I Shrunk the Audience" which boasts stellar 3D effects. The **World of Motion** traces the evolution of transportation, and the **Universe of Energy** explains the history of energy (in a somewhat outdated fashion, since it lionizes the Alaskan port of Valdez—site of the 1989 Exxon oil spill).

The **World Showcase** consists of a series of international pavilions surrounding an artificial lake. An architectural style or monument, as well as typical food and crafts, represent each country. People in indigenous costumes perform dances, theatrical skits, and other "cultural" entertainment at each country's pavilion. Before setting out around the lake, pick up a schedule of daily events at **Epcot Center Information** in Earth Station. The two 360° films made in China and Canada and the 180° film made in France rate among the best of the attractions; each includes spectacular landscapes, some national history, and an insider's look at the people of each country. **The American Adventure** gives a very enthusiastic and patriotic interpretation of American history. Save your pesos by shopping at Pier 1 rather than the marked-up Mexican marketplace. Norwegian life must be more exciting than the fishing, sailing, and oil exploring shown by the boat ride in the Norway Pavilion—but hey, it's the only ride in the World Showcase. Every night at 9pm (Sat. 10pm)

Epcot presents a magnificent show called **Illuminations,** with music from the represented nations accompanied by dancing, lights, and fireworks.

The World Showcase pavilions specialize in regional cuisine. At the **Restaurant Marrakesh** in the Moroccan Pavilion head chef Lahsen Abrache cooks delicious *brewat* (spicy minced beef fried in pastry) and *bastilla* (sweet and slightly spicy pie). A belly dancer performs in the restaurant every evening. (Lunch $10-15. Dinner $15-20.) The Mexican, French, and Italian pavilions serve up excellent food at similar prices. If you plan to eat a sit-down meal in the park, make reservations first thing in the morning at the Earth Station World Key Terminal, behind Spaceship Earth. The regional cafés (no reservations required) present cheaper options, but no real bargains. Unfortunately, all the food at Disney is hopelessly overpriced—hot dogs go for $4.50! Eat outside "the World" to save your money for Goofy-eared hats.

Disney-MGM Studios Disney-MGM Studios set out to create a "living movie set," and they seem to have succeeded. Many familiar Disney characters stroll through the park, as do a host of characters dressed as directors, starlets, gossip columnists, and fans. Events such as stunt shows and mini-theatricals take place continually. And, every day, a different has-been star leads a parade across Hollywood Blvd.

The Twilight Zone Tower of Terror climbs 13 flights in an old-time Hollywood hotel; when the cable snaps, the fastest ride at Disney begins. **The Great Movie Ride,** inside the Chinese Theater, takes you on a simple but nostalgic trip through old and favorite films. Sites such as **Superstar Television,** which projects audience members alongside TV stars in classics like "I Love Lucy," and the **Monster Sound Show,** which asks volunteers to add special effects to a short movie, get the spectators involved in the process. One of the two biggest attractions at this park, the **Indiana Jones Epic Stunt Spectacular** lets you watch stuntmen and volunteers pull off amazing moves. The other biggie, the **Star Tours** ride, based on Star Wars, simulates turbulance or a space cargo ship caught in laser crossfire.

Other Disney Attractions For those who didn't get enough amusement at the three main parks, Disney also offers several other attractions on its grounds with different themes and separate admissions (see Disney World above). The newest, **Blizzard Beach,** one of several water parks, was built on the premise of a melting mountain. Ride a ski-lift to the peak of Mount Gushmore and take the fastest waterslide in the world (Summit Plummet) down the 120-ft. descent. **Typhoon Lagoon,** a 50-acre water park, centers around the world's largest wave-making pool and the 7-ft. waves it creates. Besides eight water slides, the lagoon has a creek on which you can take a low-key inner-tube ride, an anomaly at Disney, and a saltwater coral reef stocked with tropical fish and harmless sharks. Built to resemble a swimming hole, **River Country** offers water slides, rope swings, and plenty of room to swim. Parks fill up early on hot days, and you might get turned away. Across Bay Lake from River Country is **Discovery Island,** a zoological park. Those seeking more (relatively) sinful excitations should head to **Pleasure Island** when the sun goes down. Disney attempts to draw students and the thirtysomething set with this conglomeration of theme nightclubs—country, comedy, live rock, and jazz. Those over 18 roam freely; those under 18 can enter only if they stay with their guardians.

■ OTHER ATTRACTIONS

Sea World One of the country's largest marine parks, **Sea World** (407-351-3600), 19 mi. southwest of Orlando off I-4 at Rte. 528, makes a splash with shows featuring marine mammals such as whales, dolphins, sea lions, seals, and otters; all in all, the attractions should take about six hours to see. Though the Seal and Otter Show and the Baywatch water-ski show are enjoyable, the killer whales Baby Shamu and Baby Namu get the big raves. Not only do they share the stage (or pool) with two beautiful white whales and two Orcas, they actually mix it up with trainers and give the trainers rides on their snouts. Visitors to the park gravitate towards Shamu

Stadium before the show; arrive early to get a seat. After the outdoor fun, visit the air-conditioned **Nautilus Theater** for a musical devoted to sea myths starring human characters in costume. The smallest crowds come in February and from September to October. Most hotel brochure displays and hostels have coupons for $2-3 off regular admission. Take bus #8. (Guided tours $6, children $5. Open daily 8:30am-10pm; off season daily 9am-10pm. $38, ages 3-9 $32. Sky Tower ride $3 extra.)

Cypress Gardens Cypress Gardens (813-324-2111) lies southwest of Orlando in Winter Haven; take I-4 southwest to Rte. 27S, then Rte. 540W. The botanical gardens feature over 8000 varieties of plants and flowers with winding walkways and electric boat rides for touring. The plants, flowers, and sculptured mini-gardens of the "The Gardens of the World" depict the horticultural styles of many countries and periods. Despite all the pretty flowers, the daily water-ski shows attract the biggest crowds and the loudest applause (daily 10am, noon, 2, and 4pm). Look for coupons at motels and visitors centers. (Open daily 9:30am-5:30pm; in winter 9am-7pm. $27, ages 3-9 $18). **Greyhound** stops here once a day on its Tampa-West Palm Beach schedule ($20 from Tampa to Cypress Gardens).

Universal Studios Florida Opened in 1990, Universal Studios (363-8000) combines an amusement park with a working film studio. Rides take on movie themes: **Kongfrontation,** in which a 35-ft. King Kong roughhouses with your cable car; the **E.T. Adventure** bike ride; and **Back to the Future...The Ride,** which utilizes seven-story OmniMax surround screens and spectacular special effects.

Since the park also makes films, celebrity-sightings are common. The studio recently produced *Apollo 13, Schindler's List,* and *Jurassic Park* (look for a display of dinosaurs from the film). You may recognize a number of Universal's back-lot locations at the park—Hollywood, Central Park, Beverly Hills, and the infamous Bates Motel from *Psycho.* Nickelodeon TV programs are in continuous production. Take I-4 to exit 29 or 30B. (Open Mon.-Sat. 9am-10pm, Sun. 9am-9pm; off season daily 9am-7pm. $37, ages 3-9 $30.)

■■■ COCOA BEACH AND CAPE CANAVERAL

Known primarily for rocket launches, space shuttle blast-offs, and **NASA's** enormous space center complex, the "Space Coast" also has uncrowded golden beaches and vast wildlife preserves. Even during spring break, the place remains placid; most vacationers and sunbathers here are Florida or Space Coast residents.

The Cocoa Beach area, 50 mi. east of Orlando, consists of mainland towns Cocoa and Rockledge, oceanfront towns Cocoa Beach and Cape Canaveral, and Merritt Island in between. **Route A1A** runs through Cocoa Beach and Cape Canaveral, while **North Atlantic Ave.** parallels the beach. The **Cocoa Beach Chamber of Commerce,** 400 Fortenberry Rd. (459-2200; open Mon.-Fri 8:30am-5pm), on Merritt Island, and the **Brevard County Tourist Development Council** (455-1309 or 800-872-1969; open Mon.-Fri. 8:30am-5pm, Sat. 8:30am-noon), at Kennedy Space Center, provide area info. **Greyhound,** 302 Main St. (636-3917), services Cocoa, 8 mi. inland. **Space Coast Area Transit** (633-1878), runs a shuttle with at least one stop in each town, and another route which covers the coast (fare $1; transfers free). From the bus station, a **taxi** to Cocoa Beach costs $15-20 (call **Yellow Cab,** 636-7017). **The Cocoa Shuttle** (784-3831) connects Cocoa Beach with Orlando International Airport, Disney World ($75 round-trip for 1 or 2), and the Kennedy Space Center ($45 round-trip for 1 or 2). Make reservations three days in advance. **Area code:** 407.

Accommodations, Camping, and Food Across from the beach, the **Luna Sea,** 3185 N. Atlantic Ave. (783-0500 or 800-586-2732), has tastefully decorated rooms with refrigerators, A/C, pool access, and a large continental breakfast (singles $30-38; Jan.-March $42; $4 per additional person). If you need a place to spend the night between bus connections, walk right behind the Greyhound station to the **Dixie Motel,** 301 Forrest Ave. (632-1600), 1 block east of U.S. 1, where there are big, clean rooms with tile floors, pastel decor and A/C, plus a swimming pool (singles $30, doubles $35; key deposit $10). Pitch your tent at scenic **Jetty Park Campgrounds,** 400 E. Jetty Rd. (868-1108), right on the beach in Cape Canaveral. (Sites $13.50, with hookup $18.50. Reservations recommended before shuttle launches.) **Herbie K's Diner,** 2080 N. Atlantic Ave. (783-6740), south of Motel 6, serves mac and cheese or chicken pot pie ($4-7) in a shiny chrome reproduction of a 50s diner, while waitresses in saddle shoes dance choreographed numbers to classic tunes (open Sun.-Thurs. 6am-10pm, Fri.-Sat. 24 hrs).

Beam Me Up, Scotty All of NASA's shuttle flights take off from the **Kennedy Space Center,** 18 mi. north of Cocoa Beach. If you don't have a car, you can reach Kennedy via **Gray Line Tours** (422-0744; $39 round-trip and admission). The Center's **Spaceport USA** (452-2121 for information) provides a huge welcoming center for visitors and two different two-hour bus tours of the complex. The **red tour** takes you around the space sites, while the **blue tour** visits Cape Canaveral Air Force Station. There are also three IMAX films projected on 5½-story screens: *The Blue Planet* addresses environmental issues, *The Dream is Alive* tells the story of human and robotic space exploration, and *Destiny in Space* is about—you guessed it—space. (Tours depart daily every 15min. 9:45am-6pm. $7, ages 3-11 $4. Movie tickets $4, ages 3-11 $2). Buy tickets to tours and IMAX movies immediately upon arriving at the complex to avoid a long line; the center itself is free, as are movies at the Spaceport Theater. The **Rocket Garden** and the **Astronauts Memorial,** the newest national memorial in the country, also deserve a visit (open daily 9am-8:30pm; in winter 9am-6pm; in spring and fall 9am-7:30pm). The **NASA Pkwy.,** site of the visitors center, is accessible only by car via State Rd. 405; from Cocoa Beach, take Rte. A1AN until it turns west into Rte. 528, then follow Rte. 3N to the Spaceport. With NASA's ambitious launch schedules, you may have a chance to watch the space shuttles *Endeavor, Columbia, Atlantis,* or *Discovery* thunder off into the blue skies above the cape. In Florida, call 800-KSC-INFO/572-4636 for **launch information** or send your name and address to the Public Affairs Office, PA-PASS, Kennedy Space Center 32899, for a viewing pass.

Surrounding the NASA complex, the marshy **Merritt Island Wildlife Refuge** (861-0667) stirs with deer, sea turtles, alligators, and eagles (open daily sunrise-sunset). Just north of Merritt Island, **Canaveral National Seashore** (867-2805), encompasses 67,000 acres of undeveloped beach and dunes, home to more than 300 species of birds and mammals. (Take Rte. 406E off U.S. 1 in Titusville. Open daily 6am-sunset. Closed 3 days before and 1 day after NASA launches.)

■■■ FORT LAUDERDALE

Fort Lauderdale's gleaming white sands stretch 23 mi. down Florida's east coast, but it is the water that dominates the city's landscape. Dubbed the "Venice of America," Fort Lauderdale supports an intricate intra-coastal waterway with over 165 mi. of navigable waters. Numerous inlets cut streets in two, carrying luxury yachts and serving as an arena for countless water sports. If marine activities don't float your boat, the number two activity in ritzy Fort Lauderdale is shopping. Join the ranks at Sawgrass Mills, the world's largest outlet mall, or window shop on Los Olas Blvd.

PRACTICAL INFORMATION

Tourist Office: Greater Fort Lauderdale Convention and Visitors Bureau, 200 E. Los Olas Blvd., #1500 (765-4466), in the Sentinel Building. Friendly advice and pamphlets galore. For published information, call 1-800-222-SUNY/7869. The

Chamber of Commerce, 512 NE 3rd Ave. (462-6000), 3 blocks off Federal Hwy. at 5th St. Pick up the free *Visitor's Guide.* Open Mon.-Fri. 8am-5pm.

Airport: Fort Lauderdale/Hollywood International (359-6100), 3½mi. south of downtown on U.S. 1, at exits 26 and 27 on I-95.

Trains: Amtrak, 200 SW 21st Terrace (587-6692 or 800-872-7245), just west of I-95 ¼mi. south of Broward Blvd. Take bus #9, 10, or 81 from downtown. To: Miami (2 per day, 45min., $7); Orlando (1 per day, 4hr., $48). Open daily 6:45am-6:45pm.

Buses: Greyhound, 515 NE 3rd St. (764-6551 or 800-231-2222), 3 blocks north of Broward Blvd. downtown. *Be careful in this unsavory location; especially unfriendly at night.* To: Orlando (8 per day, 4½hr., $34); Daytona Beach (6 per day, 6hr., $45); Miami (12 per day, 1hr., $5). Open 24 hrs.

Public Transportation: Broward County Transit (BCT) (357-8400; Mon.-Fri. 7am-8:30pm, Sat. 7am-8pm, Sun. 8:30am-5pm). Most routes go to the terminal at the corner of 1st St. NW and 1st Ave. NW, downtown. Operates daily 6am-9pm, every ½hr. on most routes. Fare 85¢, students (grades 6-12) with ID 40¢, seniors 40¢; transfers 10¢. 7-day passes $8; available at beachfront hotels. Pick up a handy system map at the terminal. **Tri-Rail** (728-8445 or 800-872-7245) connects West Palm Beach, Fort Lauderdale, and Miami. Trains run Mon.-Sat. 5am-midnight, Sun. 8am-8pm. Pick up schedules at the airport or at Tri-Rail stops. Fare $3, students and seniors with ID $1.50.

Taxis: Yellow Cab, 565-5400. Open 24 hrs. **Public Service Taxi,** 587-9090. Open daily 7:30am-6:30pm. Both charge $3.65 base fare, $1.40 per mi.

Car Rental: Alamo, 2601 S. Federal Hwy. (525-4713 or 800-327-9633). $23 per day with unlimited mi., $70 per week. Free drop-off in Daytona and Miami; shuttle to airport $3. Must be 21 with credit card deposit of $50 per day or $200 per week. Under 25 surcharge $20 per day.

Bike Rental: Mike's Cyclery, 5429 N. Federal Hwy. (493-5277). A variety of bicycles $15 per day, $40 per week. Credit card deposit required; amount varies according to bike. Open Mon.-Fri. 10am-7pm, Sat. 10am-5pm.

Crisis Lines: Crisis Hotline, 746-2756. Open 24 hrs.

Emergency: 911.

Post office: 1900 W. Oakland Park Blvd. (527-2028). Open Mon.-Fri. 7:30am-7pm, Sat. 8:30am-2pm. **ZIP code:** 33310. **Area code:** 305.

North-south **I-95** connects West Palm Beach, Fort Lauderdale, and Miami. **Rte. 84/I-75** (Alligator Alley) slithers 100 mi. west from Fort Lauderdale across the Everglades to Naples and other small cities on the Gulf Coast of Southern Florida. Fort Lauderdale is bigger than it looks—and it looks huge. The city extends westward from its 23 mi. of beach to encompass nearly 450 sq. mi. of land area. Roads come in two categories: streets and boulevards (east-west) and avenues (north-south). All are labeled NW, NE, SW, or SE according to their quadrant. **Broward Blvd.** divides the city east-west, **Andrews Ave.** cuts north-south. The unpleasant downtown centers around the intersection of **Federal Hwy. (U.S. 1)** and **Las Olas Blvd.,** about 2 mi. west of the oceanfront. Between downtown and the waterfront, yachts fill the ritzy inlets of the **Intracoastal Waterway. The strip** (variously called Rte. A1A, N. Atlantic Blvd., 17th St. Causeway, Ocean Blvd., and Seabreeze Blvd.) runs along the beach for 4 mi. between **Oakland Park Blvd.** to the north and Las Olas Blvd. to the south. Las Olas Blvd. has pricey shopping. **Sunrise Blvd.** offers shopping malls; while both degenerate into ugly commercial strips west of downtown.

ACCOMMODATIONS AND CAMPING

Hotel prices vary from slightly unreasonable to absolutely ridiculous, increasing exponentially as you approach prime beachfront and spring break. High season runs from mid-February to early April. Investigate package deals at the slightly worse-for-wear hotels along the strip in Fort Lauderdale. Many hotels offer off-season deals for under $35. Small motels crowd each other 1 or 2 blocks off the beach area, many with tiny kitchenettes; look along **Birch Rd.,** 1 block from Rte. A1A. **The Broward County Hotel and Motel Association,** 2701 E. Sunrise Blvd. (561-9333), provides a free directory of area hotels (open Mon.-Fri. 9am-5pm). Scan the *Fort Lauderdale News* and the Broward Section of the *Miami Herald* for occasional listings by local residents who rent rooms to tourists in spring. Sleeping on the well-patrolled beaches is illegal and virtually impossible between 9pm and sunrise.

Fort Lauderdale Youth Hostel, Sol-y-Mar (AAIH/Rucksackers), 2839 Vistamar St. (305-566-1023 or 565-1419). A nice hostel with plenty of amenities, an excellent location in a wooded area near the beach, and proximity to the clubs. 80 beds. Cable TV and refrigerator in every room. Common kitchen, entertainment room with big screen TV, and a pool. Wild but friendly monkeys make regular appearances out back. Arrangements can be made for transportation to most area locations. Ask about discounts on car rentals. Open 7am-midnight. Beds $12. Reservations recommended.

HI-International House (HI-AYH), 3811 N. Ocean Blvd. (568-1615). Take bus #10 to Coral Ridge Mall, then pick up bus #72 east; it will stop at the hostel. 1 block from beach. Rooms with 4-6 beds, showers, A/C, cable TV, and kitchen that opens onto a pool. Dive trips offered for guests with SCUBA certification $35-70. 96 beds. $12, nonmembers $15. Private rooms $33. Linen $2. Key deposit $5.

Floyd's Hostel/Crew House, (462-0631 or 800-444-5825); call ahead for address. A home-like hostel catering to international travelers and boat crews. 10 beds (6 bedrooms, 4 bathrooms), three separate kitchen and living room areas, and a quiet, friendly atmosphere. Free rice, tea, sugar, local calls, linens, laundry facilities, and pick-up service from bus station or airport. Open 24 hrs. Beds $10.

Estoril Apartments, 2648 NE 32nd St. (563-3840; 800-548-9398 reservations only; fax 568-0286). From downtown, take bus #20, 10, 55, or 72 to Coral Ridge Shopping Center and walk 2 blocks east on Oakland; a 10-min. walk to the beach. Students can probably persuade the proprietors to pick them up from the bus station or airport. Very clean rooms with A/C, TV, and small kitchenette in some rooms. Pool and barbecue. Office closes 11pm. Singles $29, $6 per additional person; Jan.-April $43-49/$10. 10% discount for *Let's Go* users and AAA. Reservations recommended.

Quiet Waters County Park, 6601 N. Powerline Rd. (a.k.a. SW 9th Ave. in Pompano Beach) (360-1315), 10mi. north of Oakland Park Blvd. off I-95's exit 37B. Take Hillsboro Blvd. west to Powerline Rd. From downtown, take bus #14. Fully equipped campsites (tent, mattresses, cooler, grill, canoe) for up to 6 people, all by the lake ("don't feed the gators!"). Normal water sports and see-it-to-believe-it 8-person "boatless water skiing" at the end of a cable. No electricity. No RVs. Check-in 2-6pm. Sites $17, Fri.-Sat. $25. $20 refundable deposit.

FOOD

The clubs along the strip offer massive quantities of free grub during happy hour: surfboard-sized platters of wieners, chips, and hors d'oeuvres, or all-you-can-eat pizza and buffets. However, these bars have hefty cover charges (from $5) and expect you to buy a drink once you're there (from $2). The quality of the cuisine often serves to remind you of the difference between a restaurant and a bar. For "real" food, try **La Spada's,** 4346 Seagrape Dr. (776-7893)—best and biggest subs in southern Florida. The foot-long Italian sub ($6.50) is an absolute must. (Open Mon.-Sat. 10am-8pm, Sun. 11am-8pm.) Popular with locals since 1951, **Tina's Spaghetti House,** 2110 S. Federal Hwy. (522-9943), just south of 17th St. (take bus #1 from downtown), has authentic red-checked tablecloths, hefty oak furniture, and bibs. Lunch specials run $4-5, while a spaghetti dinner costs $6-7. (Open Mon.-Thurs. 11:30am-10pm, Fri. 11:30am-11pm, Sat. 4-11pm.) In an aggressively marine decor, **Southport Raw Bar,** 1536 Cordova Rd. (525-2526), by the 17th St. Causeway behind the Southport Mall (take bus #40 from the strip or #30 from downtown), serves spicy conch chowder ($2.50) and fried shrimp ($7). Try the tasty custom sandwiches. (Open Mon.-Fri. 11am-2am, Sat. 11am-3am, Sun. noon-2am.)

SIN, SIGHTS, AND ACTIVITIES

Fort Lauderdale offers all kinds of licit and illicit entertainment. Planes flying over the beach hawk hedonistic happy hours at local watering holes. Students frequent the night spots on the A1A strip along the beach—emphasis on "strip." When going out, bring a driver's license or a passport as proof of age; most bars and nightclubs won't accept college IDs. Be warned that this is *not* the place for cappuccino and conversation; expect nude jello wrestling and similarly lubricated entertainment.

For those who prefer garbed service, several popular nightspots line N. Atlantic Blvd. next to the beach. Hit **Banana Joe's on the Beach,** 837 N. Atlantic Blvd. (565-4446), at Sunrise and Rte. A1A, a tiny little bar directly on the beach, for happy hour Monday through Friday 5-8pm. (Open Mon.-Sat. 7am-2am, Sun. noon-2am. Kitchen open 11:30am-7pm.) For off-the-beach entertainment, Fort Lauderdale's hotspot is **Crocco's World Class Sports Bar,** 3339 N. Federal Hwy. (566-2406). Built in an old movie theater, this gargantuan club has lines out the door almost every night. (Cover varies. Open Mon. 8pm-2am, Thurs.-Sat. 8pm-2am.) **Mombasa Bay,** 3051 NE 32nd Ave. (561-8220), on the Intracoastal Waterway, charges no cover, but requires that everyone be 21 when there's live music. (Happy hour daily 4-7pm. Live jazz Wed., R&B Thurs., reggae Fri.-Mon.; music starts 9:30pm. Open Mon.-Fri. 4pm-2am, Sat. 11:30am-3am, Sun. 11:30am-2am.)

For daytime entertainment, take a tour of Fort Lauderdale's waterways aboard the **Jungle Queen,** located at the **Bahia Mar Yacht Center** (462-5596), on Rte. A1A 3 blocks south of Las Olas Blvd. (3-hr. tours daily 10am, 2, and 7pm; $7.50, children $5). The **Water Taxi,** 651 Seabreeze Blvd. (467-6677), offers a different way to get around town and a fun place to dine in style. ($3, under 12 $1.50. All day, unlimited service $14/$7. Call 10min. before desired pick-up.) **Water Sports Unlimited,** 301 Seabreeze Blvd. (467-1316), on the beach, rents equipment for a variety of water sports including wave runners ($45 per ½hr., $70 per hr.) and motor boats ($40 per hour, $89-129 for 4hr.). Parasailing trips let you take a broader view of the whole beach scene ($42 per ride). Landlubbers can get closer to nature with a visit to **Butterfly World,** 3400 W. Sample Rd. (977-4400), just west of the Florida Turnpike in Coconut Creek, 3 acres of tropical gardens with thousands of live butterflies (open Mon.-Sat. 9am-5pm, Sun. 1-5pm; $9.95, ages 4-12 $5).

■■■ MIAMI

Long a hot spot for stars and a popular setting for TV shows and movies, Miami's Latin heart pulses to the beat of the largest Cuban population outside of Cuba. Only 7½ sq. mi., Miami Beach has an unbelievable number of hotels, which can accommodate three times the city's usual population. Tourists lie-and-fry by day, then dance the night away. Many small cultural communities distinguish Miami's residential areas: Little Havana, a well-established Cuban community; Coconut Grove, an eclectic community of wealthy intellectuals; placid, well-to-do Coral Gables (one of the country's earliest planned cities); and the African-American communities of Liberty City and Overtown. Wherever you find yourself in Miami, a knowledge of Spanish is always helpful and sometimes necessary.

PRACTICAL INFORMATION

Tourist Office: A tourist **information booth,** 401 Biscayne Blvd. (C5; 539-2980) outside of Bayside Marketplace, downtown, has free maps and advice. Open daily 10am-6:30pm. **Coconut Grove Chamber of Commerce,** 2820 McFarlane Ave. (B6; 444-7270). Mountains of maps and advice. Open Mon.-Fri. 9am-5pm. **Greater Miami Convention and Visitors Bureau,** 701 Brickell Ave. (C5; 539-3000 or 800-283-2707 outside Miami), 27th floor of the Barnett Bank building downtown. Open Mon.-Fri. 8am-6pm. **Gay Community Hotline,** 759-3661.

Airport: Miami International (A4; 871-7000), located at Le Jeune Rd. and NW 36th Ave., 7mi. northwest of downtown. Bus #20 is the most direct public transportation into downtown, but bus #3 is also an option; from there, take bus C or

K to South Miami Beach. The airport's **information booth** doles out helpful maps of Miami and the Public Transportation systems.

Trains: Amtrak, 8303 NW 37th Ave. (A3; 835-1223 or 800-872-7245), not far from the Northside station of Metrorail. Bus L goes directly to Lincoln Rd. Mall in South Miami Beach. To: Orlando (2 per day, 5hr., $54); New Orleans (3 per week, 11hr., $158); Charleston (1 per day, 12hr., $125). Station open daily 6:15am-7:15pm.

Buses: Greyhound, Miami Station, 4111 NW 27th St. (B4; 871-1810). To: Atlanta (6 per day, 16hr., $69); Orlando (8 per day, 6hr. $33); Fort Lauderdale (16 per day, 1hr., $4). Station open 24 hrs. A cheaper service to Key West and Orlando departs several times weekly from the main HI youth hostel. Call 534-2988 for more info.

Public Transportation: Metro Dade Transportation (638-6700; 6am-11pm for info.) Complex system; buses tend to be quite tardy. The extensive **Metrobus** network converges downtown; most long bus trips transfer in this area. Lettered bus routes A through X serve Miami Beach. After dark, some stops are patrolled by police (indicated with a sign). Buses run daily 4:30am-2am. Fare $1.25; transfers 25¢, to Metrorail 50¢. The futuristic **Metrorail** elevated trains service downtown. Fare $1.25, rail to bus transfers 50¢. The **Metromover** loop downtown, which runs 6am-midnight, is linked to the Metrorail stations. Fare 25¢, free if transferring from Metrorail. **Tri-Rail** (800-872-7245) connects Miami, Ft. Lauderdale, and West Palm Beach. Trains run Mon.-Sat. 5am-9:30pm. Fare $3, daily $5, weekly $18; students and seniors 50% off.

Taxis: Yellow Cab, 444-4444. Double double your pleasure with **Metro Taxi,** 888-8888. Both $1.10 base fare and $1.75 per mile.

Car Rental: Value Rent-a-Car, 2401 Collins Ave. (D4; 532-8257 or 800-327-2501), Miami Beach. $34 per day, $170 per week; unlimited free mi. Open daily 8am-6pm. Also at the **airport,** 2875 NW Le Jeune Rd. (A4; 871-6761). $17 per day, $85 per week; unlimited free mi. Open 24 hrs. At both locations, you must be 21+ with a credit card; under 25 surcharge $5 per day.

Auto Transport Company: Dependable Car Travel, 162 Sunny Isles Blvd. (945-4104). A free service. Must be 21 with $200 deposit and passport and foreign license. Call a week in advance. Open Mon.-Fri. 8:30am-5pm, Sat. 8:30am-noon.

Bike Rental: Miami Beach Bicycle Center, 923 W. 39th St. (D4; 531-4161), Miami Beach. $5 for 1hr., $3 per additional hr.; $15 per day; $40 per week. Must be 18 with credit card or $100 deposit. Open Mon.-Fri. 9:30am-6pm, Sat. 9:30am-6pm. **Dade Cycle Shop,** 3216 Grand Ave. (B6; 443-6075), Coconut Grove. $4-8 per hr., $17-30 per day. Must have $100 deposit, driver's license, or credit card. Open daily 10:30am-5:30pm.

Crisis Lines: Crisis Hotline, 358-4357. **Rape Treatment Center and Hotline,** 1611 NW 12th Ave. (585-6949). Both 24 hrs.

Emergency: 911.

Post Office: 500 NW 2nd Ave. (C5; 371-2911). Open Mon.-Fri. 8:30am-5pm, Sat. 8:30am-12:30pm. **ZIP code:** 33101. **Area code:** 305.

ORIENTATION

Three highways criss-cross the Miami area. **I-95,** the most direct route north-south, hits **U.S. 1 (Dixie Hwy.)** just south of **downtown.** U.S. 1 runs to the Everglades entrance at Florida City and then continues as the Overseas Hwy. to Key West. **Rte. 836,** a major east-west artery through town, connects I-95 to **Florida's Turnpike,** passing the airport in between. If you're headed to Florida City, take Rte. 36 and the Turnpike to avoid the traffic on Rte. 1.

Several four-lane causeways connect Miami to **Miami Beach.** The most useful is **MacArthur Causeway,** which becomes 5th St. in Miami Beach. Numbered streets run east-west across the island, increasing towards the north. The main north-south drag is **Collins Ave.** (or A1A). In South Miami Beach, north-south **Washington Ave.,** one block to the west of Collins, is the main commercial strip, while **Ocean Ave.,** on the waterfront, lies one block east. To get to **Key Biscayne,** you must take the **Rickenbacker Causeway** (toll).

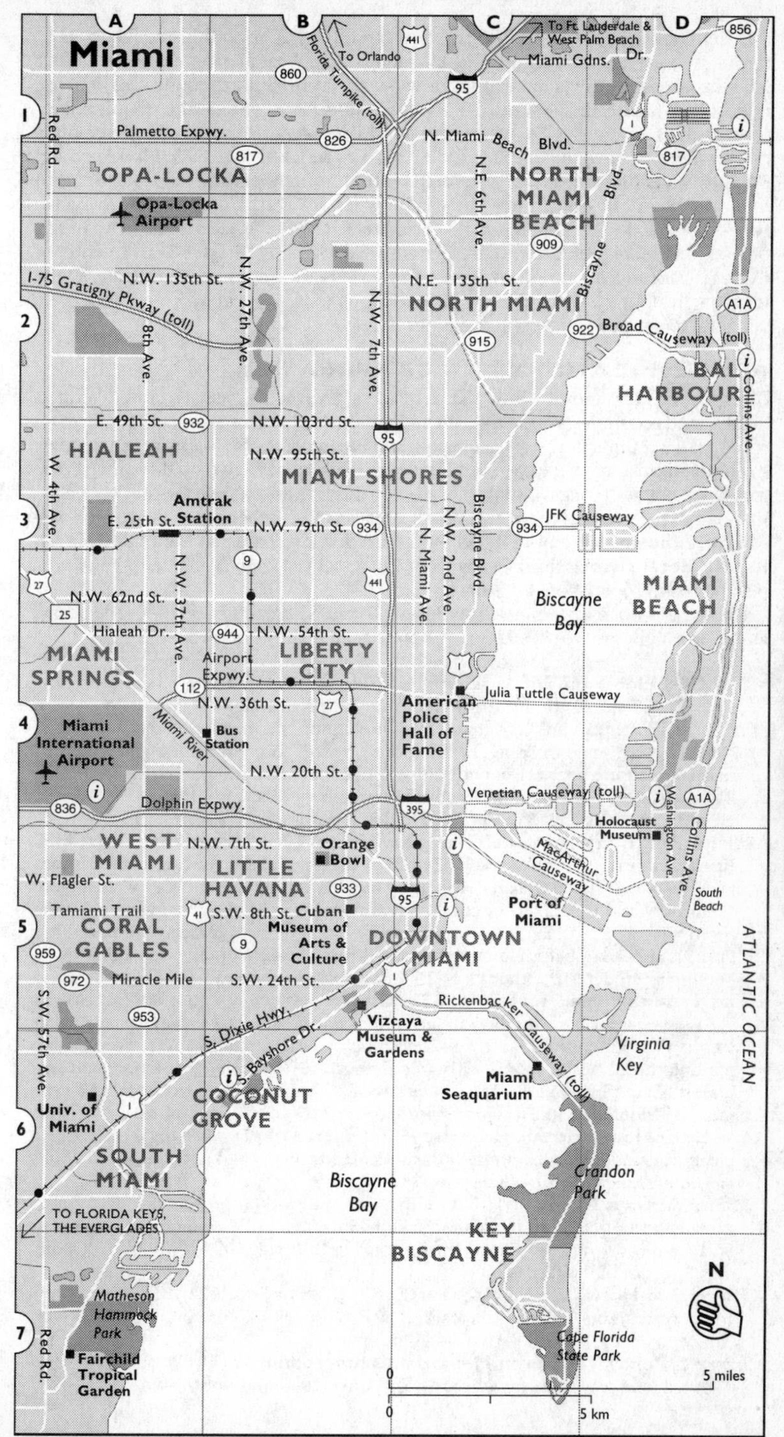
Miami
A
B
C
D
1
2
3
4
5
6
7
To Orlando
To Ft. Lauderdale & West Palm Beach
Florida Turnpike (toll)
Miami Gdns. Dr.
Palmetto Expwy.
N. Miami Beach Blvd.
OPA-LOCKA
Opa-Locka Airport
NORTH MIAMI BEACH
N.E. 6th Ave.
Biscayne Blvd.
N.W. 135th St.
N.E. 135th St.
I-75 Gratigny Pkway (toll)
NORTH MIAMI
Broad Causeway (toll)
8th Ave.
N.W. 27th Ave.
N.W. 7th Ave.
BAL HARBOUR
Collins Ave.
E. 49th St.
N.W. 103rd St.
HIALEAH
N.W. 95th St.
MIAMI SHORES
W. 4th Ave.
Amtrak Station
E. 25th St.
N.W. 79th St.
JFK Causeway
N.W. 37th Ave.
N. Miami Ave.
N.W. 2nd Ave.
Biscayne Blvd.
N.W. 62nd St.
Biscayne Bay
MIAMI BEACH
Hialeah Dr.
N.W. 54th St.
MIAMI SPRINGS
Airport Expwy.
LIBERTY CITY
N.W. 36th St.
Julia Tuttle Causeway
American Police Hall of Fame
Miami International Airport
Miami River
Bus Station
N.W. 20th St.
Venetian Causeway (toll)
Washington Ave.
Dolphin Expwy.
Holocaust Museum
WEST MIAMI
N.W. 7th St.
Orange Bowl
LITTLE HAVANA
MacArthur Causeway
W. Flagler St.
Collins Ave.
Tamiami Trail
S.W. 8th St.
Cuban Museum of Arts & Culture
Port of Miami
South Beach
CORAL GABLES
DOWNTOWN MIAMI
Miracle Mile
S.W. 24th St.
Rickenbacker Causeway (toll)
ATLANTIC OCEAN
S. Dixie Hwy.
Vizcaya Museum & Gardens
S.W. 57th Ave.
S. Bayshore Dr.
Virginia Key
Miami Seaquarium
Univ. of Miami
COCONUT GROVE
SOUTH MIAMI
Biscayne Bay
Crandon Park
TO FLORIDA KEYS, THE EVERGLADES
KEY BISCAYNE
N
Matheson Hammock Park
Red Rd.
Fairchild Tropical Garden
Cape Florida State Park
0
5 miles
5 km
856
441
860
95
826
817
909
A1A
922
915
932
934
9
27
25
944
112
836
395
933
41
959
972
953
1

When looking for street addresses, pay careful attention to the systematic street layout; it's *very* easy to confuse North Miami Beach, West Miami, Miami Beach, and Miami addresses. Streets in Miami run east-west, avenues north-south, and both are numbered. Miami divides into NE, NW, SE, and SW sections; the dividing lines (downtown) are **Flagler St.** (east-west) and **Miami Ave.** (north-south). Some numbered streets and avenues also have names—e.g., Le Jeune Rd. is SW 42nd Ave., and SW 40th St. is Bird Rd. Try to get a map with both numbers and names in order to minimize headaches. **Little Havana** lies between SW 12th and SW 27th Ave; take bus #3, 11, 14, 15, 17, 25, or 37. The **Calle Ocho** (SW 8th St.) lies at the heart of this district; one block north, the corresponding section of **W. Flagler St.** is a center of Cuban business. In Miami, knowledge of Spanish is always a plus. Coordinates in the text key locations to *Let's Go's* **map. Parking** is expensive in Miami—beware the vengeful meter maids ticketing round the clock.

ACCOMMODATIONS AND CAMPING

Cheap rooms abound in South Miami Beach's Art Deco hotels. For safety, convenience, and security, stay north of 5th St. Finding a "pullmanette" (in 1940s lingo), a room with a refrigerator, stove, and sink, and buying groceries will save you money. In South Florida, many inexpensive hotels are likely to have two- to three-inch cockroaches ("palmetto bugs"), so try not to take them as absolute indicators of quality. In general, high season for Miami Beach runs late December to mid-March; off season, when rooms are empty, hotel clerks are quick to bargain. The **Miami Beach Resort Hotel Association,** 407 Lincoln Rd. #10G (531-3553), can help you find a place to crash (open Mon.-Fri. 9am-4:30pm).

Camping is not allowed in Miami Beach. Those who can't bear to put their tents aside for a night or two should head to one of the nearby national parks.

The Clay Hotel and International Hostel (HI-AYH), 1438 Washington Ave. (D5; 534-2988), in the historic Clay Hotel in the heart of the Art Deco district, near nightlife; take bus C from downtown. Explore the halls and archways of this Mediterranean-style building. International crowd. Kitchen, laundry facilities, TV room, and a ride board. 180 beds; most rooms have 4. 2 rooms share a bathroom. 24-hr. A/C. No curfew. Members $9, nonmembers $14 Dec.-March $11/$15. Singles $24, doubles $33. Key deposit $5. IBN reservations available.

Miami Beach International Travelers Hostel (9th Street Hostel) (AAIH/Rucksackers), 236 9th St. (D5; 534-0268), at Washington Ave; from the airport, take bus J to 41st and Indian Creek, then transfer to bus C to 9th and Washington. Central location. Relaxed international atmosphere. Kitchen, laundry, common room with TV. 29 clean, comfortable rooms (max. 4 people), all with A/C (after 9pm) and private bath. No curfew. Hostel rooms $12 with any hostelling membership or student ID; otherwise $14. Private singles or doubles $31.

The Tropics Hotel/Hostel, 1550 Collins Ave. (D4; 531-0361; fax 531-8676), across the street from the beach. From the airport, take bus J to 41st St., transfer to bus C to Lincoln Rd. and walk one block south on Collins Ave. Free on-site parking. Clean hostel rooms with 4 beds, A/C, private baths, telephone, and free linens. No curfew. $14. Private rooms have A/C, cable TV, and free local calls; singles $36, doubles $40; Dec.-Mar. $46/$50.

Sea Deck Hotel and Apartments, 1530 Collins Ave. (D4; 538-4361). Cozy and clean pullmanettes with pretty floral bedspreads open onto a lush tropical courtyard. Pullmanettes $39, efficiencies $49.

Miami Airways Motel, 5001 NW 36th St. (A4; 883-4700 or 800-824-9910), near the airport but far from the action; take I-95 to Rte. 112W, which runs into 36th St. Free airport pickup. Clean, small rooms with breakfast, A/C, pool, HBO. Singles $36, doubles $42.

Miami Sun Hotel, 226 NE 1st Ave. (C5; 375-0786 or 800-322-0786). Near downtown, restaurants, and Bayside Marketplace. 88 spacious, comfortable rooms with Art-Deco decor. Cable TV, phones. All rooms $35.

Larry & Penny Thompson Memorial Campground, 12451 SW 184th St. (232-1049), a long way from anywhere. By car, drive 20-30min. south along Dixie Hwy.

Pretty grounds with 240 sites in a grove of mango trees. Laundry, store, and all facilities, plus artificial lake with swimming beach, beautiful park, and waterslides. Lake open daily 10am-5pm; for further info, call 255-8251. Office open daily 8am-7pm but takes late arrivals. Sites with full hookup $17, weekly $90.

FOOD

If you eat nothing else in Miami, be sure to try Cuban food. Specialties include *media noche* sandwiches (a sort of Cuban club sandwich on a soft roll, heated and compressed); *mamey,* a bright red ice cream concoction; rich *frijoles negros* (black beans); and *picadillo* (shredded beef and peas in tomato sauce, served with white rice). For Cuban sweets, seek out a *dulcería,* and punctuate your rambles around town with thimble-sized shots of strong, sweet *café cubano* (around 25¢).

Cheap restaurants are not common in Miami Beach, but an array of fresh bakeries and fruit stands can sustain you with melons, mangoes, papayas, tomatoes, and carrots for under $3 a day.

The Versailles, 3555 SW 8th St. (C4; 444-0240). Massive dining room, seemingly packed with Little Havana's entire population. Good Cuban fare. Breakfast $2-4, lunches from $2.50; entrees about $10. Open daily 8am-2am.

11th St. Diner, 1065 Washington Ave. (D5; 534-6373), at 11th St. A vintage diner with all the trimmings: soda fountain, straw dispensers, and an ancient Coca-Cola clock. Serves breakfast at all hours ($2-4), all sorts of sandwiches ($2.50-6), and grill items. Also a bar. Open daily 24 hrs.

King's Ice Cream, 1831 SW 8th St., a.k.a. Calle Ocho (B5; 643-1842). Tropical fruit *helado* (ice cream) flavors include coconut (served in its own shell), *mamey,* and banana ($2). Also try *churros* (thin Spanish donuts, 10 for $1), or *café cubano* (10¢). Open Mon.-Sat. 10am-11pm, Sun. 1pm-1am.

Flamingo Restaurant, 1454 Washington Ave. (D5; 673-4302), down the street from the Clay hostel. Friendly service, all in Spanish. Peck at the grilled chicken with pinto beans and rice ($5.50). Open Mon.-Sat. 7am-7:30pm.

Irish House (D5; 534-5667), at 14th St. and Alton Rd. in Miami Beach. A favorite hangout for local journalists, politicos and beach-goers. Noted for buffalo wings ($3.50) and cheeseburgers ($4.50). Open Mon.-Sat. 11am-2am, Sun. 5pm-2am.

La Rumba, 2008 Collins Ave. (D4; 534-0522), between 20th and 21st St. in Miami Beach. Noisy fun and tremendous portions of good Cuban food. Try their *arroz con pollo* (chicken with yellow rice, $6.50). Open daily 7:30am-midnight.

SIGHTS

The beach is hot, but if you get burned, you can cool down at the **Seaquarium,** 4400 Rickenbacker Causeway (C6; 361-5703), just minutes from downtown in Virginia Key; take bus B from downtown toward Key Biscayne. Lolita, the killer whale, livens the obligatory array of dolphins and sharks. (Open daily 9:30am-6pm; ticket office closes 4:30pm. $18, ages 3-12 $13, police officers $1.)

Between 6th and 23rd St. (D5), **South Miami Beach** (or just South Beach) teems with hundreds of hotels and apartments whose sun-faded pastel façades conform to 1920s ideals of a tropical paradise. An unusual mixture of people populates the area, including large retired and first-generation Latin communities. Tours of the **historic district** by foot (Sat. 10:30am, $6) or by bike (Sun. 10:30am; $5, rental $5 extra) are available; call 672-2014 for info. The new **Holocaust Memorial,** 1933-45 Meridian Ave. (D5; 538-1663), Miami Beach, remembers the six million Jews who perished in World War II through sculpture and historical displays (open daily 9am-9pm; free).

On the waterfront downtown, Miami's sleek **Bayside** shopping complex (C5), bursts with expensive shops, exotic food booths, and live reggae or *salsa* on Friday and Saturday nights. Near Bayside, visit the **American Police Hall of Fame and Museum,** 3801 Biscayne Blvd. (C4; 573-0070), and learn more than you ever wanted to know about the police; exhibits feature execution equipment, "specialty" cars, and jail cell replicas (open daily 10am-5:30pm; $6, seniors and ages 6-11 $3).

In **Little Havana,** the exhibits at the **Cuban Museum of Arts and Culture,** 1300 SW 12th Ave. (B5; 858-8006), reflect the bright colors and rhythms of Cuban art; take bus #27 (open Wed.-Sun. 10am-3pm; donation required). At **La Gloria Cubana,** 1106 SW 8th St. (B5; 858-4162), the art of Cuban-style cigar manufacture lives on (open Mon.-Fri. 8am-6pm, Sat. 9am-4pm; free). In early March, **Caranaval Miami,** the largest Hispanic festival in the U.S., fills 23 blocks of Calle Ocho with salsa, music, and the longest conga-line in the world.

On the bayfront between the Grove and downtown stands the **Vizcaya Museum and Gardens,** 3251 S. Miami Ave. (B5; 250-9133); take bus #1 or the Metrorail to Vizcaya. Surrounded by 10 acres of lush gardens, this 70-room Italianate mansion, built in 1916 by International Harvester heir James Deering, houses an array of European antiques. (Open Tues.-Fri. 11am-4:30pm, Sat.-Sun. 10am-4:30pm; last admission 4:30pm. $4, ages 6-12 $1.60.) Screaming kids congest the **Museum of Science** and its **Planetarium,** 3280 S. Miami Ave. (B5; 854-4247, show info 854-2222) across the street from Vizcaya (open daily 10am-6pm; $6, seniors and ages 3-12 $4; shows $6 extra). Farther south in Coral Gables, the largest tropical botanical garden in the world, the **Fairchild Tropic Garden,** 10901 Old Cutler Rd., (A7; 667-1651), **Coral Gables,** covers 83 acres and features winding paths, a rain forest, a sunken garden, and a narrated train tour (open daily 9:30am-4:30pm; $7, under 13 free).

ENTERTAINMENT AND NIGHTLIFE

For the latest word on Miami entertainment, check the *Miami-South Florida Magazine;* the "Living Today," "Lively Arts," and Friday "Weekend" sections of the *Miami Herald;* or the *Miami New Times,* which comes out every Tuesday and can be found for free on street corners and in alleyways or for a little more in establishments in Miami Beach. **Performing Arts and Community Education (PACE)** manages more than 400 concerts each year (jazz, rock, soul, dixieland, reggae, *salsa,* and bluegrass), most of which are free.

The nightlife in the Art Deco district of South Miami Beach follows the Latin rhythms of the area—the party starts *late* (usually after midnight) and continues until well after sunrise. Gawk at models and stars while eating dinner at one of Ocean Blvd.'s open cafés and bars, then head down to Washington Ave. between 6th and 7th St. for some serious fun. Remember to put on your dancing shoes (literally)—these clubs have dress codes, and everyone dresses to the nines. The coolest of the cool, **Bash,** 655 Washington Ave. (D5; 538-2274), stands out among its neighbors; the large inside dance floor grooves to dance music while the courtyard in back jams to the ocean beat of reggae (cover $10, Sun. free; open Wed.-Sun. 10pm-5am). On the same strip, things heat up at **Chili Pepper,** 621 Washington Ave. (D5; 531-9661; no cover; open Tues.-Sun. 9pm-5am) and **Jessie's,** 615 Washington Ave. (D5; 538-6688; open Sun.-Wed. 10am-4am, Thurs.-Sat. 10am-5am).

For those with dance fever, boogie on Sunday night to 70s and 80s music on the huge multi-level dance floor of the **Cameo Theater,** 1445 Washington Ave. (D5; 532-0922 for showtimes and prices), at Española Way. The theater also rocks with national acts such as Peter Frampton, the Caifanes, and the Beastie Boys. (Cover $5-10. Open Fri.-Sun. 11pm-5am.) Arrive before midnight to dodge the cover and the huge line at the **Groove Jet,** 323 23rd St. (D4; 532-2002). The front room of this massive dance hall rocks to popular dance tracks while the back room mellows out with blues and funk. (Women 18+, men 21+. Cover midnight-2am $5, Fri.-Sat. $7. Open Thurs.-Tues. 10pm-5am.) For gay nightlife, check out **Warsaw Ballroom,** 1450 Collins Ave. (D5; 531-4555), Miami Beach, where frequent theme nights (e.g., bubble bath night) liven up the two dance floors (happy hour 4-9pm; no cover before 11pm; open Wed.-Sun. 4pm-5am). **Diamante,** 1771 West Ave. (D5; 538-5567), at 18th and Alton Rd., pumps chemical music Fridays and jammin' tunes always over a two-floor dance club. Thursday is straight night and Saturday is gay night, but anyone is welcome any night. (Cover before midnight $5, after $10. Open Thurs.-Sat. 10pm-5am.)

EVERGLADES REGION AND FLORIDA KEYS

■■■ EVERGLADES

Encompassing the entire tip of Florida and spearing into Florida Bay, **Everglades National Park,** the next largest national park after Yellowstone, spans 1.6 million acres of one of the most beautiful and fragile ecosystems in the world. Vast prairies of sawgrass spike through broad expanses of shallow water, creating the famed "river of grass," while tangled mazes of mangrove swamps wind up the western coast. To the south, delicate coral reefs lie below the shimmering blue waters of the bay. A host of species found nowhere else in the world inhabits these lands and waters: American alligators, sea turtles, and various birds and fishes, as well as the endangered Florida panther, Florida manatee, and American crocodile. Today, man-made activities threaten to destroy this unique environment, and the entire Everglades environment perches precariously on the edge of extinction.

Practical Information If you visit in the summertime, expect to get eaten alive by swarming mosquitoes. Visit the park in winter or spring, when heat, humidity, storms, and bugs are at a minimum and when wildlife congregates in shrinking pools of evaporating water. Whenever you go, be sure to bring mosquito repellent. There are three primary roads into the park, each of which is self-contained and separate from the others. Guarding the eastern section, the **Main Visitor Center,** 40001 Rte. 9336, Homestead 33034 (305-242-7700), lies on **Rte. 9336** just inside the park (open daily 8am-5pm). Rte. 9336 cuts 40 mi. through the park past campgrounds, trailheads, and canoe waterways to the heavily developed **Flamingo** outpost resort. At the northern end of the park off U.S. 41 (Tamiami Trail), the **Shark Valley Visitors Center** provides access to a 15-mi. loop that can be seen by foot, bike, or a two-hour tram. (Tram tours Christmas-April daily every hr. 8:30am-4:30pm. $8, seniors $7.20, under 12 $4. Reservations recommended; call 305-221-8455.) The **Gulf Coast Visitors Center** (813-695-2591), near Everglades City in the northwestern end of the park, provides access to the 99-mi. Wilderness Waterway, which winds down to Flamingo. **Park headquarters** (305-247-7272) is a fount of information and also handles **emergencies.** The park **entrance fee** is $5 per car and good for 7 days; Shark Valley admission is $4 per car, $2 for bike or on foot. For **radio information** on the park, tune your radio to AM1610.

THE SOUTH

Accommodations Outside the eastern entrance to the park, Homestead and Florida City offer some cheap options along Rte. 997. In Flamingo, **Flamingo Lodge** (305-253-2241) offers large rooms with A/C, TV, private baths, pool, and a great bay view (singles and doubles $65, Nov.-Dec. and April $82, Jan.-March $96). A few first-come first-served park **campgrounds** line Rte. 9336; all have drinking water, grills, dump sites, and restrooms, but none have RV hookups (sites free in summer, in winter $8). **Backcountry camping** is accessible by foot or by bicycle, but primarily by boat; most sites are on chickees, wooden platforms elevated above mangrove swamps. The required permits are available at the Flamingo and Everglades City ranger stations. Park campgrounds fill rapidly from December to April, so get there early. If the park campgrounds are full, try **Chekkia,** SW 237th Ave. (305-247-7272), off Rte. 997, with 20 secluded sites, restrooms, showers, water, and a dump station, as well as a swimming lake and fishing (free, Oct.-May $8).

Near the northwestern entrance, motels, RV parks, and campgrounds scatter around Everglades City. The **Barron River Villa, Marina, and RV Park** (813-695-3591) has 67 RV sites, 29 on the river (full hookup $16, on river $18; Oct.-April $22/$27); they also manage cute motel rooms with TV and A/C (single or double $37, Dec. 15-April 30 $47). **Glades Haven RV Park** (813-695-2746), overlooking Chokoloskee Bay near the Gulf Coast Ranger Station, has 54 sites with shower facilities, full hookups, cable hookups, marina, and dock (tent sites $15, RV $20).

Sights Plentiful fishing, hiking, canoeing, biking, and wilderness observation opportunities exist in the park. Avoid swimming; hungry alligators, sharks, and barracuda patrol the waters. From November to April, the park sponsors amphitheater programs, canoe trips, and ranger-guided Swamp Tromps. Numerous trailheads lie off Rte. 9336; the ½-mi. **Mahogany Hammock Trail** passes the largest mahogany tree in the U.S., and the ¼-mi. **Pahayokee Overlook Trail** leads to a broad vista of grasslands and water. But water, not land, rules the park, and if you really want to experience the Everglades, start paddling. **Canoe trails** wind from Rte. 9336; the **Nine Mile Pond** canoe loop passes through alligator ponds, mazes of mangrove trees, and open sawgrass areas (allow 3-4 hr.), while the **Hell's Bay Canoe Trail** threads through mangrove swamps past primitive campsites like **Lard Can.** Among other places, canoe rental is available at the **Flamingo Marina** (305-253-2241; $7 per hr., $20 per ½-day, $25 per day) in Flamingo. From the Gulf Coast Visitor Center, explore the area's 10,000 islands and see a **manatee** from a boat or canoe (1½-hr. guided boat tour $12, ages 6-12 $5.50). Cruises into Florida Bay are offered daily at the Flamingo Marina; catch the 1½-hr. **Sunset Cruise** to end your day at the park ($8.50, ages 6-12 $4.50, under 6 free).

■ NEAR EVERGLADES: BIG CYPRESS

Covering over 2400 sq. mi. of southwestern Florida, a third of which is patched with stands of cypress trees, **Big Cypress National Preserve** provides the freshwater supply crucial to the Everglades's survival. During the summer, deluges flood the reserve; this water slowly drains south through Everglades National Park into the Gulf of Mexico due to the land's average downward slope of two inches per mi.

U.S. 41 (Tamiami Trail) slices through the preserve. The **Loop Road Scenic Dr.** is a 26-mi. detour from U.S. 41 through the eastern half of the park; autos can pass year-round, but watch for potholes. The **Florida National Scenic Trail,** a wet but popular trek that takes hikers through 31 mi through wetlands, starts from **Big Cypress National Preserve Visitors Center,** HCR 61, Box 11, Ochopee, FL 33943 (941-695-4111), which is bypassed by Loop Road on U.S. 41. No **entrance fee** is charged for the preserve. Several **free, primitive campgrounds** dot the park. **Monument Lake** and **Dona Drive,** along U.S. 41, boast potable water and picnic tables; **Burns Lake,** also along U.S. 41, sports good fishing and abundant wildlife. If you crave TV and hot showers, **Trail Lakes Campground** (813-695-2275), on U.S. 41 at the western end of the park in Ochopee, is the only campground in the preserve with electricity, water, a bathhouse, and laundry facilities (tent sites $10, hookup $12). For accommodations just outside the preserve or for other sights near the preserve, check with the **Everglades City Chamber of Commerce** (813-695-3941).

■■■ FLORIDA KEYS

While descriptions of the Florida Keys's tropical weather, crystal blue waters, and fiery orange sunsets may bring to mind a deserted paradise, there are few places where capitalism runs more rampant; bustling tourist centers, bronzed bodies, and countless cars jam the Keys from tip to toe. But to get away from it all, just take a dive. Millions of colorful fish flash through gardens of coral off the coast; here, scuba divers and snorkelers can find peace and relative solitude. Approximately 6 mi. offshore from the Keys, these corals form a 100-yd.-wide barrier reef running from Key Largo south to Key West, hiding hundreds of wrecked ships loaded with legendary lost treasure. Contrary to popular belief, there are few sharks.

The **Overseas Highway (U.S. 1)** bridges the divide between the Keys and the southern tip of Florida, stitching the islands together. **Mile markers** section the highway and replace street addresses. The first marker, Mile 126 in Florida City, begins the countdown to zero. **Greyhound** runs buses to the Keys from Miami ($27), stopping in Perrine (flag down the bus from U.S. 1), Homestead (247-2040), Key Largo (451-2908), Marathon (743-3488), Big Pine Key (872-4022), and Key

West (296-9072). If you need to get off at a particular mile marker, most bus drivers can be convinced to stop at the side of the road. Biking along U.S. 1 across the swamps between Florida City and Key Largo is treacherous due to fast cars and narrow shoulders; bring your bike on the bus.

■ KEY LARGO

Baby why don't we go…Past the thick swamps and crocodile marshland of the Everglades, Key Largo opens the door to these Caribbean-esque islands. Dubbed "long island" by Spanish explorers, this 30-mi. island is the largest of the Florida Keys, but the carless shouldn't worry; everything of importance lies within a 6-mi. range. With 120-ft. visibility, the gin-clear waters off Key Largo are one of its biggest attractions; John Pennekamp State Park protects the longest reef in the western hemisphere (178 nautical sq. mi.), which begins just off the coast. Twenty ft. down, an underwater statue of Jesus (meant to symbolize "peace for mankind") blesses all those who explore these depths. Fishing, swimming, and glass-bottom boats offer recreation without total submersion.

Practical Information The **Key Largo Chamber of Commerce/Florida Keys Welcome Center,** Mile 106 (451-1414), is stuffed with information; look for a large turquoise awning at 106 Plaza (open daily 9am-6pm). The dramatic mailroom scene from Bogart and Bacall's *Key Largo* was filmed at the **post office:** Mile 100 (451-3155; open Mon.-Fri. 8am-4:30pm); **ZIP code:** 33037; **area code:** 305.

Accommodations, Camping, and Food The **Hungry Pelican,** Mile 99.5 (451-3576), boasts beautiful bougainvillea vines, tropical birds in the trees, and tidy, cozy rooms and cottages with double beds ($45-100, $10 for extra person). The **Sea Trail Motel,** Mile 98.6 (852-8001), has clean rooms with tile floors, A/C, TV and refrigerator ($30, in winter $35, extra person $5). Reservations are a must for the popular **John Pennekamp State Park Campground** (see below); the sites are clean, convenient, and well worth the effort required to obtain them ($24, with electric $26). If you can't get a reservation there, the crowded but well-run **Key Largo Kampground,** Mile 101.5 (451-1431 or 800-KAMP-OUT/526-7688), behind Tradewinds shopping plaza, manages 170 RV and tent sites, a heated pool, a game room, a laundry, a bath house, and a marina with boat ramp (waterfront sites available; $18-38, extra person $3). The **Calusa Camp Resort,** Mile 101.5 (451-0232 or 800-457-CAMP/2267), on the bay side, has 400 sites (some waterfront), a pool, tennis courts, two bathhouses, and a marina ($25-31, extra person $3).

The 99-beer selection at **Crack'd Conch,** Mile 105 (451-0732), can quench any thirst. Chase your beer with an entire key lime pie ($8.50), once called "the secret to world peace and the alignment of the planets." (Open Thurs.-Tues. noon-10pm.) **The Italian Fisherman,** Mile 104 (451-4471), has it all—fine food and a spectacular view of Florida Bay. Formerly an illegal gambling casino, this restaurant was the locale for some scenes from *Key Largo.* (Lunch $4-8, dinner $7-15. Open daily 11am-10pm.) Other scenes from *Key Largo* were filmed at the **Caribbean Club,** Mile 104 (451-9970), a friendly local bar; snapshots of Bogart and Bacall grace the walls (beer $1.50, drinks $2; live rock and reggae Thurs.-Sun.; open daily 7am-4am).

John Pennekamp State Park The nation's first underwater sanctuary, Key Largo's **John Pennekamp State Park,** Mile 102.5 (451-1202), 60 mi. from Miami, safeguards a 120-sq.-mi. stretch of coral reef that runs the length of the Florida Keys (park admission $3.25 for driver, 50¢ per extra passenger up to 8). The park's **visitor center** (451-1202), about ¼ mi. past the entrance gate, provides maps of the reefs, information on boat and snorkeling tours, three aquariums, and introductory films on the park (open daily 8am-5pm). To see the reefs, visitors must take a boat or rent their own. **Boat rentals** (451-1621), unfortunately, are rather expensive (19' motor boat; 2-hr. min.; $25 per hr, $80 for 4 hr.; refundable deposit required; call for reservations). **Scuba trips** (9:30am and 1:30pm) are $37 per person for a two-tank dive. A **snorkeling tour** also allows you to experience the underwater quiet (2½ hr. total, 1½ hr. water time; tours 9am, noon, and 3pm; $25, under 18 $20). If you're up for a longer snorkeling tour, ask about the combined sailing/snorkeling trip, which takes about half a day and costs a little more than snorkel alone. To get a crystal clear view of the reefs without wetting your feet, take a **Glass Bottom Boat Tour** (451-1621), which leaves from the park shore at mile 102.5 (daily 9:15am, 12:15, and 3pm; $14, under 12 $9, for 9:15am tour 2 children free with an adult).

■ KEY WEST

This is the end of the road. Key West boasts the southernmost point of the continental U.S. at the end of Rte. 1 and dips farther into the Gulf of Mexico than much of the Bahamas. Due to the ocean breezes, the island is cooler than mainland Florida in summer and much warmer in winter; when searching for a year-round tropical paradise in the U.S., you can do no better. Key West's balmy weather once drew authors such as Ernest Hemingway, Tennessee Williams, Elizabeth Bishop, and Robert Frost; today, an easygoing diversity continues to attract a new generation of writers, artists, recluses, adventurers, and eccentrics, along with an out and swinging gay population. Visitors stream into the town, filling the small island to capacity. Still, Key West's charm shines through the gaggles of scooter-riding teenagers; walk around the historic district, or take to the advantage of the best that the island has to offer: the ocean that surrounds it.

PRACTICAL INFORMATION

Tourist Office: Key West Chamber of Commerce, 402 Wall St. (294-2587 or 800-527-8539), in old Mallory Sq. Dispenses the useful *Guide to the Florida Keys,* as well as a list of popular gay accommodations. Open daily 8:30am-5pm. **Key West Welcome Center,** 3840 N. Roosevelt Blvd. (296-4444 or 800-284-4482), just north of the intersection of U.S. 1 and Roosevelt Blvd. Arranges housing, theater tickets, and reef trips if you call in advance. Open daily 9am-7pm.

Airport: Key West International Airport (296-5439), on the southeast corner of the island. No public bus service.

Buses: Greyhound, 615½ Duval St. (296-9072). In an alley behind Antonio's restaurant. To: Miami (3 per day, 4½hr., $27). Open daily 7:30am-7:30pm.

Public Transportation: Key West Port and Transit Authority (292-8161), City Hall. One bus ("Old Town") runs clockwise around the island and Stock Island; the other ("Mallory St.") runs counterclockwise. Service Mon.-Sat. 6:35am-10:15pm, Sun. 6:35am-10:35pm. Fare 75¢, students and seniors 35¢. Pick up a good free map from the Chamber of Commerce (see above) or any bus driver. **Disabled Transportation,** 292-3515.

Taxis: Keys Taxi, 296-6666. Not divisible by 3. $1.40 base fare, $1.75 per mi.

Car Rental: Alamo, 2839 N. Roosevelt Blvd. (294-6675 or 800-327-9633), near the airport. $20 per day, $110 per week. Must be 21 with major credit card. Under 25 surcharge $20 per day. Miami drop-off free.

Moped/Bike Rental: Keys Moped & Scooter, Inc., 523 Truman Ave. (294-0399). $18 for 9am-5pm, $23 for 24 hrs. Open daily 9am-6pm. **Key West Hostel,** 718 South St. (296-5719). $4 per day, $30 per week. Credit card and deposit required. Open daily 9am-10pm.

Crisis Line: 296-4357, everything from general info to crises. 24 hrs.

Emergency: 911.

Post Office: 400 Whitehead St. (294-2557), 1 block west of Duval at Eaton. Open Mon.-Fri. 8:30am-5pm. **ZIP code:** 33040. **Area code:** 305.

Key West lies at the end of U.S. 1, 155 mi. southwest of Miami (3-3½hr.). Divided into two sectors, the eastern part of the island, known as **New Town,** harbors tract houses, chain motels, shopping malls, and the airport. Beautiful old conch houses clutter **Old Town,** on the west below White St. **Duval St.** is the main north-south thoroughfare in Old Town, **Truman Ave.** the major east-west route.

ACCOMMODATIONS AND CAMPING

Key West remains packed virtually year-round, with a lull of sorts from mid-September to mid-December; even then, don't expect to find a room for less than $40. Good rooms at the nicer hotels go for up to $400 per day, especially during the winter holidays. Try to bed down in **Old Key West;** the beautiful, 19th-century clapboard houses capture the flavor of the Keys. Some of the guest houses in the Old Town are for gay men exclusively. *Do not park overnight on the bridges*—this is illegal and dangerous.

Key West Hostel, 718 South St. (296-5719), at Sea Shell Motel in Old Key West, 3 blocks east of Duval St. Call for airport or bus station pick-up. Rooms with 4-8 beds, shared bath. A/C runs only late at night. Kitchen open until 9pm. Office open daily 9am-10pm. Check in 24 hrs. No curfew. With HI-AYH membership card $13, otherwise $16; Dec.-Apr. $14/$18. Key deposit $5. Motel rooms $45, in winter $50-100. Call ahead to check availability; also call for late arrival.

Caribbean House, 226 Petronia St. (296-1600 or 800-543-4518), at Thomas St. in Bahama Village. Caribbean-style rooms with cool tile floors, A/C, cable TV, fridge, and ceiling fans. Comfy double beds. Free continental breakfast. The management may be able to place you in a completely furnished Caribbean cottage (sleeps 6) or an unfurnished low-rent apartment for comfortable summer living. Rooms $39, cottage $59; winter $69/$79-89. First come, first served (no reservations); rooms are usually available.

Wicker Guesthouse, 913 Duval St. (296-4275 or 800-880-4275). Excellent location on the main drag. Individually decorated rooms with pastel decor and hardwood floors. TV, ceiling fans; some rooms have A/C. Kitchen and pool access. Single or double room with shared bath, $45-69; Christmas to Easter $60-90.

Eden House, 1015 Fleming St. (296-6868 or 800-533-5397). Bright, clean, friendly hotel with very nice rooms, just 5 short blocks from downtown. Cool rooms with private or shared bath, some with balconies. Pool, jacuzzi and kitchen. Join other guests for free happy hour by the pool, daily 4-5pm. $50-70, winter $80-125.

Boyd's Campground, 6401 Maloney Ave. (294-1465), at Mile 5. 12 acres on the ocean. Full facilities, including showers. $25, in winter $31; each additional person $5. Waterfront sites $5 extra. Water and electricity $5, A/C or heat $5.

FOOD AND NIGHTLIFE

Expensive restaurants line festive **Duval St.** Side streets offer lower prices and fewer crowds. Sell your soul and stock up on supplies at **Fausto's Food Palace,** 522 Fleming St. (296-5663), the best darn grocery store in Old Town (open Mon.-Sat. 8am-8pm, Sun. 8am-7pm). When it was a pool hall, Hemingway used to drink beer and referee boxing matches at **Blue Heaven Fruit Market,** 729 Thomas St. (296-8666), 1 block from the Caribbean House. Today, Blue Heaven serves healthy breakfasts (75¢ to $7.50) and plenty of vegetarian for lunch ($3-8) and dinner ($6.50-15; open daily 8am-10:30pm). You won't have to bait a hook at **Angler's,** 3618 N. Roosevelt Blvd. (294-4717), which serves huge (pre-cooked) seafood platters and inexpensive lunches and entrees; lunch $4-7, dinners $6-22 (open daily 11am-10pm, and Fri.-Sat. 11am-11pm). People-watch from the outside tables at **Gringo's Cantina,** 509½ Duval St. (294-9215), which slaps down large Mexican platters at reasonable prices ($4.25-11; open daily 11am-midnight). Finally, don't leave Key West without having a sliver of **key lime pie,** available everywhere.

Nightlife in Key West revs up at 11pm and winds down very late. **Captain Tony's Saloon,** 428 Greene St. (294-1838), the oldest bar in Key West, still chugs away; Tony Tarracino, the owner, usually shows up at 9pm (open Mon.-Thurs. 10am-1am, Fri.-Sat. 10am-2am, Sun. noon-1am). Originally located in Havana, **Sloppy Joe's,** 201 Duval St. (294-5717), at Greene, moved to Key West when Castro rose to power. Reputedly one of "Papa" Hemingway's preferred watering holes, the bar's usual frenzy heightens during the Hemingway Days Festival in mid-July. (Drafts $2.50. R&B day and night. Open daily 9am-4am.) If you're feeling lucky, punk, try **Rick's/Durty Harry's,** 208 Duval St. (296-4890). This place rocks, especially when the

Terry Cassidy Band plays (Tues.-Sat. 5-11pm); live rock plays daily in the backroom from 3pm. (House specials include $1.50 drafts. Open daily 11am-4am.)

SIGHTS AND ENTERTAINMENT

Check out the daily *Key West Citizen* (sold in front of the post office) and the weekly *Solares Hill* (available at the Key West Chamber of Commerce) for the latest in Key West entertainment. Most tourists take to Key West's streets aboard a bike or moped, but tours are available. The **Conch Tour Train** (294-5161) provides a fascinating 1½-hr. narrated ride through Old Town, leaving from Mallory Sq. at 3840 N. or from Roosevelt Blvd. next to the Quality Inn (runs daily 9am-4:30pm; $14, ages 4-12 $6). **Old Town Trolley** (296-6688) runs a similar tour, but you can get on and off throughout the day at 14 stops (full tour 1¾ hr.; $15, ages 4-12 $6).

The glass-bottomed boat *Fireball* takes two-hour cruises to the reefs and back (296-6293; tickets $19, ages 3-12 $2.50). One of a few cruise specialists, the **Coral Princess Fleet,** 700 Front St. (296-3287), offers snorkeling trips daily at 10am, 1:30, and 5pm with free instruction for beginners ($20; open daily 8:30am-6:30pm). For a landlubber's view of the fish of Key West, the **Key West Aquarium,** 1 Whitehead St. (296-2051), in Mallory Square, offers a 50,000 gallon Atlantic shore exhibit as well as a touch pool and shark feedings ($6.50, students, seniors, and military $5.50, ages 8-15 $3.50, under 8 free; open daily 10am-6pm).

"Papa" wrote *For Whom the Bell Tolls* and *A Farewell to Arms* at the **Hemingway House,** 907 Whitehead St. (294-1575), off Olivia St. Take a tour, or traipse through on your own. About 50 cats (descendants of Hemingway's cats) prowl the grounds; ask the tour guides their names. (House open daily 9am-5pm. $6.50, ages 6-12 $2.50.) The **Audubon House,** 205 Whitehead St. (294-2116), built in the early 1800s, houses some fine antiques and a collection of the works of ornithologist John James Audubon (open daily 9:30am-5pm; $7, ages 6-12 $2). Down Whitehead St., past Hemingway House, you'll come to the **southernmost point** in the continental U.S. and the nearby **Southernmost Beach.** A small, conical monument and a few conchshell hawkers mark the spot, along with a few hustlers who might offer to take your picture; beware, they may not give your camera back until you pay them. **Mel Fisher's Treasure Exhibit,** 200 Greene St. (294-2633), glitters with glorious gold; Fisher discovered the sunken treasures from the shipwrecked Spanish vessel *Atocha.* A *National Geographic* film is included in the entrance fee. (Open daily 9:30am-5pm. $5, students $4, ages 6-11 $1.50). The **Monroe County Beach,** off Atlantic Ave., has an old pier allowing access past the weed line. The **Old U.S. Naval Air Station** offers deep water swimming on Truman Beach ($1). Known as the "Oldest House," the **Wrecker's Museum,** 322 Duval St. (294-9502), occupies a home built in 1829. The museum details the colorful history of wrecking; a "wrecker" was a daring sea captan who risked life and limb for the promise of money and adventure. (Open daily 10am-4pm. $3, under 12 $2.50.) A paragon of Cuban architecture, the **San Carlos Institute,** 516 Duval St., built in 1871, houses a research center for Hispanic studies. The **Haitian Art Company,** 600 Frances St. (296-8932), six blocks east of Duval, explodes with vivid Haitian artworks (open daily 10am-6pm; free). Sunset connoisseurs will enjoy the view from **Mallory Square Dock.** Magicians, street entertainers, and hawkers of tacky wares work the crowd, while swimmers and speedboaters show off; the crowd always cheers when the sun slips into the Gulf with a blazing red farewell.

Every October (Oct. 18-27 in 1996), the entire population turns out in astounding costumes for the week-long **Fantasy Fest,** which culminates in an extravagant parade. In April (April 19-20 in 1996), the **Conch Republic** celebrates with bed races (don't ask). **Old Island Days** (Jan. to March) features art exhibits, a conch shell-blowing contest, and the blessing of the shrimp fleet.

GULF COAST

■■■ TAMPA

Even with perfect weather year-round and some of Florida's most beautiful beaches nearby, Tampa has managed to avoid the plastic pink flamingos and alligator beach floats of its Atlantic Coast counterparts. The city's existence doesn't hinge on tourism; a relatively young city, Tampa is one of the nation's fastest growing cities and largest ports, containing thriving financial, industrial, and artistic communities. While this cosmopolitan flair strips the city of the crazily diverse party-til-you-drop spunk of West Palm Beach and Miami, it also makes Tampa a less tacky, more peaceful vacation destination.

PRACTICAL INFORMATION

Tourist Office: Tampa/Hillsborough Convention and Visitors Association, 111 Madison St. (223-1111 or 800-826-8358). Open Mon.-Sat. 9am-5pm.

Airport: Tampa International, (870-8700), 5 mi. west of downtown. HARTline bus #30 runs between the airport and downtown Tampa. **The Limo Inc.** (572-1111 or 800-282-6817) offers schmantzy 24-hr. service from the airport to the city and to all the beaches between Ft. De Soto and Clearwater ($13). Make reservations 24 hrs. in advance.

Trains: Amtrak, 601 Nebraska Ave. (221-7600 or 800-872-7245), at Twiggs St. 1 block north of Kennedy. Open daily 7:30am-6pm. Trains to: Orlando (2 per day, 2hr., $19); Miami (1 per day, 6hr., $50). No trains run south from Tampa. There is no direct train link between Tampa and St. Petersburg.

Buses: Greyhound, 610 E. Polk St. (229-2174 or 800-231-2222), next to Burger King downtown. To: Atlanta (7 per day, 12hr., $49); Orlando (6 per day, 2½hr., $44). Open 24 hrs.

Public Transportation: Hillsborough Area Regional Transit (HARTline), 254-4278. Fare $1, transfers 10¢. The **Tamp Town Ferry** has pick-up and drop-off points throughout downtown. $6 round-trip.

Crisis Lines: Rape Crisis, 238-8821. 24 hrs. **AIDS,** 800-352-2437.

Emergency: 911.

Post Office: 5201 W. Spruce Rd. (879-1600), at the airport. Open 24 hrs. **ZIP code:** 33601. **Area code:** 813.

Tampa divides into quarters with **Florida Ave.** running north-south and **Kennedy Blvd.,** which becomes **Frank Adams Dr.** (Rte. 60), running east-west. Numbered streets run north-south and numbered streets run east-west. **Ybor City,** Tampa's Latin Quarter, is bounded roughly by 22nd St., Nebraska Ave., 5th Ave., and Columbus Dr. *Be careful not to stray more than two blocks north or south of 7th Ave. since the area can be extremely dangerous, even during the daytime.* You can reach Tampa on I-75 from the north, or I-4 from the east. Some dangerous areas exist near Ybor City (see Sights, below).

ACCOMMODATIONS AND CAMPING

Inexpensive, convenient lodgings are rare in Tampa. You may want to consider St. Petersburg's somewhat cheaper and less chain-based accommodations (see below).

Motel 6, 333 E. Fowler Ave. (932-4948), off I-275 near Busch Gardens. On the northern outskirts of Tampa, 30mi. from the beach. Big, clean rooms with free local calls, A/C, and pool. Singles $25; each additional person $4.

Budget Host, 3110 W. Hillborough Ave. (876-8673), near the airport and Busch Gardens. 33 small rooms with A/C, cable TV, pool. Singles $28, doubles $30.

Gram's Place Bed & Breakfast, 3109 N. Ola Ave. (221-0596), 2mi. from Ybor City; from I-275, take Martin Luther King Blvd. west to Ola Ave., and take a left on Ola. Gram's Place is an eclectic Key West style B&B dedicated to keeping the music and spirit of Gram Parsons alive. This artistic haven features a friendly owner, jacuzzi, sundeck, courtyard, cable TV, and continental breakfast. Rooms $45. 10% Let's Go discount. Rates negotiable depending upon occupancy.

Americana Inn, 321 E. Fletcher Ave. (933-4545) 3mi. from Busch Gardens in northwest Tampa; from I-275, take the Fletcher exit west. Clean rooms, most with fridge and stove. Pool and cable TV. Regular rates (up to 4 people) Sun.-Thurs. $30, Fri.-Sat. $35-40. $5 discount for college students, seniors, military, and AAA depending upon availability.

Friendship Inn, 2500 E. Busch Blvd. (933-3958). Very close to Busch Gardens. Well-kept rooms with cable TV and A/C. Pool. Singles $32, doubles $38.

FOOD AND NIGHTLIFE

Cheap Cuban and Spanish establishments dot Tampa; for the best deals, try black bean soup, gazpacho, or Cuban bread. **Ybor City** houses the best and cheapest food around; **JD's,** 2029 E. 7th Ave. (247-9683), in Ybor City (take bus #12), creates soups, sandwiches, and Cuban dishes in a roomy, low-key restaurant; get breakfast for $2.50, lunch for $4 (open Mon.-Fri. 9am-2pm). Downtown, **The Loading Dock,** 100 Madison St. (223-6905), hoists sandwiches like "flatbed" or "forklift" ($3-5; open Mon.-Fri. 8am-8pm, Sat. 10:30am-2:30pm). Make your own pasta combinations at **The Spaghetti Warehouse** (248-1720), at 9th and 13th St. in Ybor Sq. ($6-8; open Mon.-Sat. 11am-11pm, Sun 11am-10pm).

A frothy cold one is never far away in Tampa; most hotels have beachside bars or tiki huts where you can enjoy a drink while watching a brilliant red sunset. The extremely popular **Yucatan Liquor Stand,** 4811 W. Cypress (289-8454), also known as the "Yucatan Pick-up Stand," has a spacious bar, a tiki bar, and volleyball courts. Weeknight happy hour (4-9pm) brings 99¢ margaritas. (Open Mon.-Fri. 4pm-3am, Sat.-Sun. 6pm-3am.)

SIGHTS AND ACTIVITIES

Ybor City expanded rapidly after Vincent Martínez Ybor moved his cigar factories here from Key West in 1886. Although cigar manufacturing has since been mechanized, some people still roll cigars by hand and sell them for $1 in **Ybor Sq.,** 1901 13th St. (247-4497), an upscale retail complex converted from three 19th-century cigar factories (open Mon.-Sat. 9:30am-5:30pm, Sun. noon-5:30pm). **Ybor City State Museum,** 1818 9th Ave. (247-6323), at 21st St., traces the development of Ybor City, Tampa, the cigar industry, and Cuban migration (open Tues.-Sat. 9am-noon and 1-5pm; 50¢). Aside from the square, the Ybor City area has remained relatively unsullied by Tampa's rapid urban growth; **East 7th Ave.** serves up old-time jazz and Cuban cuisine. Buses #5, 12, and 18 run to Ybor City from downtown.

Before the Spanish-American War, Teddy Roosevelt trained his Rough Riders in the backyard of the Moorish **Tampa Bay Hotel,** 401 W. Kennedy Blvd., now part of the University of Tampa. Built in 1891, the hotel once epitomized fashionable Florida coast motels. Gaze in awe at the **Henry B. Plant Museum** (254-1891), in a wing of a University of Tampa building. The exhibits, which include Victorian furniture and Wedgewood pottery, pale in comparison to the museum, a no-holds-barred orgy of rococo architecture. (Tours at 1:30pm. Open Tues.-Sat. 10am-4pm, Sun. noon-4pm. $3, kids $1.)

Downtown, the **Tampa Museum of Art,** 600 N. Ashley Dr. (274-8130), houses a noted collection of ancient Greek and Roman works as well as a series of changing exhibitions. (Open Mon.-Sat. 10am-5pm, Wed. 10am-9pm, Sun. 1-5pm. $5, students with ID and seniors $4, ages 6-18 $3; free Sun. and Wed. 5-9pm.) Across from the University of South Florida, north of downtown, the **Museum of Science and Industry (MOSI),** 4801 E. Fowler Ave. (987-6300), features a simulated hurricane and an OmniMax. (Open Sun.-Thurs. 9am-5pm, Fri.-Sat. 9am-9pm, extended hours July and Aug. $8, students and seniors $7, ages 2-12 $5.) The **Museum of African American Art,** 1308 N. Marion St. (272-2466), features the art history and culture of the classical Barnett-Aden collection (open Tues.-Sat. 10am-4:30pm and Sun. 1-4:30pm; $3, seniors and under 12 $2). Tampa's newest attraction is the **Florida Aquarium,** 701 Channelside Dr. (273-4000). Mash your face to the glass for a *tête-á-tête* with fish from Florida's wetlands, bays and beaches, coral reefs and offshore areas (open daily 9am-6pm; $14, seniors and ages 13-18 $13, ages 3-12 $7).

For serious amusement-park fun among African wildlife, descend into **Busch Gardens—The Dark Continent,** E. 3000 Busch Blvd. (987-5171), at NE 40th St.; take I-275 to Busch Blvd., or bus #5 from downtown. Throw your stomach for a loop on Kumba, the largest drop (143ft.) in the world, or observe giraffes, zebras, ostriches, and antelope roaming freely across the park's 60-acre plain; trains, boats, and walkways cater to the tamer crowd. Busch Gardens has two of an estimated 50 white Bengal tigers in existence. (Open daily 9am-8pm; off season daily 9:30am-6pm. $35, parking $3.) Inside the park, you can take advantage of the generous **Anheuser-Busch Hospitality House** without feeling guilty, but you must stand in line for each beer, with a two-drink limit. If the Dark Continent sears you, you can cool off at **Adventure Island,** 4500 Bougainvillea Ave. (987-5660), a 13-acre water theme park about ¼ mi. northeast of Busch Gardens ($19, under 48" $17; open 9am-7pm, winter 10am-5pm).

"Day-O! Day-O! Daylight come and me wanna go home." Banana boats from South and Central America unload and tally their cargo every day at the **waterfront** docks on 139 Twiggs St., near 13th St. and Kennedy Blvd. Every year in February the *Jose Gasparilla,* a fully rigged pirate ship loaded with hundreds of exuberant "pirates," invades Tampa and kicks off a month of parades and festivals, such as the **Gasparilla Sidewalk Art Festival** (223-7000). Pick up a copy of the visitors guide for current info on various other events and festivals.

■■■ ST. PETERSBURG AND CLEARWATER

Twenty-two mi. southwest of Tampa, across the bay, St. Petersburg caters to a relaxed, attractive community made up of retirees and young singles alike. The town enjoys 28 mi. of soft white beaches, emerald water, melt-your-heart sunsets, and approximately 361 days of sunshine yearly. The sun'll come out, tomorrow...

PRACTICAL INFORMATION

Tourist Office: St. Petersburg Area Chamber of Commerce, 100 2nd Ave. N. (821-4069). Open Mon.-Fri. 9am-5pm. **The Pier Information Center,** 800 2nd Ave. NE (821-6164). Open Mon.-Sat. 10am-7:30pm, Sun. 11am-6pm.

Airport: St. Petersburg Clearwater International (539-7491) sits right across the bay from Tampa. **The Limo Inc.** (572-1111 or 800-282-6817) offers 24-hr. service from the airport to the city and to all the beaches between Ft. De Soto and Clearwater ($10.50). Make reservations 24 hrs. in advance.

Trains: Amtrak, 3101 37th Ave. N. (522-9475 or 800-872-7245). Open 8:15am-7pm. There is no direct train between Amtrak and St. Petersburg, but Amtrak will transport you from Tampa to St. Petersburg by bus ($5). Amtrak runs a free shuttle to Clearwater from Tampa for its passengers; the bus drops off in Clearwater at 657 Court St. (441-1793), at E. Ave. While Clearwater is inaccessible by train from Tampa, it can be reached from other Florida cities.

Buses: Greyhound, 180 9th St. N. (898-1496), downtown St. Petersburg. To: Panama City (1 per day, 9hr., $57); Clearwater (2 per day, ½hr., $7). Open 6:15am-11:30pm. In Clearwater: 2111 Gulf-to-Bay Blvd. (796-7315). Open 6am-8pm.

Public Transportation: Pinnellas Suncoast Transit Authority (PSTA), 530-9911. Most routes depart from Williams Park at 1st Ave. N. and 3rd St. N. Fare $1, transfers free. To reach Tampa, take express bus #100 from downtown to the Gateway Mall ($1.50). A free shuttle loops through downtown.

Crisis Line: Rape Crisis, 344-5555. 24 hrs.

Emergency: 911.

Post Office: 3135 1st Ave. N. (323-6516). Open daily 24 hrs. **ZIP code:** 33737. **Area code:** 813.

In St. Petersburg, **Central Ave.** runs east-west. **34th St. (U.S. 19)** cuts north-south through the city and links up with the **Sunshine-Skyway Bridge,** connecting St. Pete with the Bradenton-Sarasota area to the south. The St. Pete beachfront is a chain of barrier islands accessible by bridges on the far west side of town, and extends from **Sand Key Beach** in the north to **Pass-a-Grille Beach** in the south. Many towns on the islands offer quiet beaches and reasonably priced hotels and restaurants. From north to south, these towns include: **Belleair, Indian Rocks Beach, Madiera Beach, Treasure Island,** and **St. Pete Beach.** The stretch of beach past the **Don Cesar Hotel** (luxury resort-cum-pink monstrosity recently declared a historical landmark) in St. Pete Beach and Pass-a-Grille Beach have the best sand, a devoted following, and less pedestrian and motor traffic. The town of **Clearwater,** connected by toll bridge to Sand Key in St. Petersburg, at the far north end of this island coastline, offers beaches, pricey motels and resorts, and not much else.

ACCOMMODATIONS AND CAMPING

St. Petersburg and Clearwater offer two hostels as well as many cheap motels lining 4th St. N. and U.S. 19 in St. Pete. Some establishments advertise singles for as little as $20, but these tend to be very worn-down. To avoid the worst neighborhoods, stay on the north end of 4th St. and the south end of U.S. 19. Several inexpensive motels cluster along the St. Pete beach.

St. Petersburg Youth Hostel, 326 1st Ave. N. (822-4141), downtown in the McCarthy Hotel. Bunk rooms for a maximum of 4 people with in-suite bathrooms. Common room with kitchen, TV, A/C. 11pm curfew. $11 with any youth hostel card or student ID. $2 linen fee. Hostel rooms are available Nov.-May.; in the summer, rent historic hotel rooms with A/C and private baths for $15.

Clearwater Beach International Hostel (AAIH/Rucksakers), 606 Bay Esplanade Ave. (443-1211), directly on the coast in the nearby city of Clearwater; by car take Rte. 60W to Clearwater Beach, or catch the free bus from the Tampa Amtrak station to Clearwater Beach. (Clearwater has its own Amtrak and Greyhound stations for more direct arrivals.) Just 2 blocks from a superb white-sand beach. Kitchen, common room, free bikes and tennis rackets, ping pong. Bunk in shared room. $11, nonmembers $13. Linen $2. Private rooms with kitchens $35.

Grant Motel, 9046 4th St. N. (576-1369), 4mi. north of town on U.S. 92. Rooms with ruffled pillow shams and A/C; most have a fridge. Beautifully landscaped grounds. Pool. Singles and doubles $30; Jan.to mid-April singles $39, doubles $43.

Kentucky Motel, 4246 4th St. N. (526-7373). A little out of place, but hey. Large, clean rooms with friendly owners, cable TV, refrigerator in each room, and free postcards. Singles $24, doubles $28. Jan.-March $10 more.

Treasure Island Motel, 10315 Gulf Blvd. (367-3055), across the street from beach. Big rooms with A/C, fridges, and color TV. Pool. Singles and doubles $35, Jan.-Feb. $52/$53; each additional person $4. Pirates not allowed.

Fort De Soto State Park (866-2662), composed of five islands at the southern end of a long chain of keys and islands, has the best camping with 233 wooded, private sites (no alcohol; 2-day min. stay; front gate locked at 9pm; curfew 10pm; $16.50). From January to April, you may want to make a reservation in person at the St. Petersburg County Building, 150 5th St. N. #125, or at least call ahead (582-7738). A wildlife sanctuary, the park also makes a great oceanside picnic spot.

FOOD AND NIGHTLIFE

St. Petersburg's cheap, health-conscious restaurants cater to its retired population, and generally close by 8 or 9pm. Hungry night owls should glide to St. Pete Beach and 4th St. If you're itching for crabs, try **Crabby Bills,** 5100 Gulf Blvd. (360-8858), near Indian Rocks Beach; order 6 blue crabs ($5.50) from a cheap, extensive menu in an ultra-casual atmosphere. (Open Mon.-Thurs. 11am-10pm, Fri.-Sat. 11am-11pm, Sun. noon-10pm; another location at 6445 4th St. N.) For more crabs, head to **Tangelo's Bar and Grille,** 226 1st Ave. NE (894-1695), which serves tasty crab burgers

($5) and gazpacho soup ($2; open Mon.-Sat. 11am-9pm). If you've had enough of those damned crabs, **Beach Nutts,** 9600 W. Gulf Blvd. (367-7427), Treasure Island, doesn't have much of a selection, but oh! what an atmosphere; the restaurant lies on the beach, and bands plays every night (live reggae Sat.-Sun. 4-8pm; open daily 9am-2am). **Club Detroit** (896-1244), a block away from the St. Pete hostel at 1st Ave N. and 1st St., offers great live music and $2 drafts (open Thurs.-Sat. 9am-2am).

SIGHTS AND ACTIVITIES

Pass-a-Grille Beach may be the nicest, but its parking meters gobble quarters like Pac-Man in Vegas. For free parking, drive to the **Municipal Beach** at Treasure Island, accessible from Rte. 699 via Treasure Island Causeway.

If the world turns surreal under St. Pete's eternal sun, the **Salvador Dalí Museum,** 1000 3rd St. S. (823-3767), in Poynter Park on the Bayboro Harbor waterfront, will make things better. The museum contains the world's most comprehensive collection of Dalí works and memorabilia—94 oil paintings, 1300 graphics, and juvenalia from a 14-year-old Dalí. (45-min. tours five times daily. Open Tues.-Sat. 9:30am-5:30pm, Sun.-Mon. noon-5:30pm. $5, students and seniors $4, under 10 free.) For alligator-wrestling thrills, climb down into the **Sunken Gardens,** 1825 4th St. N. (896-3186), home of over 7000 varieties of exotic flowers and plants (open daily 10am-5pm; $14, ages 3-11 $8). **Great Explorations,** 1120 4th St. S. (821-8885), allows you to fondle six areas of exhibits; test your strength at the **Body Shop,** where you can compare your muscles' scores with scores taken from around the country (open Mon.-Sat. 10am-5pm, Sun. noon-5pm; $5, seniors $4.50, ages 4-17 $4). **The Pier** (821-6164), at the end of 2nd Ave. NE, downtown, extends into Tampa Bay from St. Pete, ending in a five-story inverted pyramid complex that contains a shopping center, aquarium, restaurants and bars. (Open Mon.-Thurs. 10am-9pm, Fri.-Sat. 10am-10pm, Sun. 11am-7pm; bars and restaurants open later. Free trolley service from the parking area.)

■■■ PANAMA CITY BEACH

Move over, Daytona—you're no longer "where the boys are." Suntan oil is the perfume of choice at Panama City Beach, the latest fad in spring break hotspots and a boldly rising meat market mecca. Here, along miles of snow-white beach, nearly bare bodies bask between a Gulf and a party place. Still, PCB is not always a den of iniquity; while most attractions cater to the spring-break beer and bikini mob, the Brady Bunch crowd claims its turf during the summer.

Practical Information After crossing Hathaway Bridge, Rte. 98 splits. Everything centers on **Front Beach Rd.,** also known as **The Strip** or **Miracle Mile.** To bypass the hubbub, take some of the smaller roads off Rte. 98. **Panama City Beach Convention and Visitors Bureau,** 12015 Front Beach Rd. (233-5070 or 800-PCBEACH/722-3224) will cram you with info (open daily 8am-5pm). **Panama City Beach Trolley** (234-3459) shuttles along the beach, making various flag stops ($3 per day or $1 one-way; open Mon.-Sat. 9am-7pm). Taxis run on a grid system; fares increase as you move away from Harrison Ave. **AAA Taxi** (785-0533) or **Yellowcab** (763-4691) will take you from the airport to The Strip for $16. The **Domestic Violence and Rape Crisis Hotline** is 763-0706; **Crisis and Mental Health Emergency Hotline,** 769-9481; both are open 24 hrs. **Emergency** is 911. Panama City's **post office:** 275 Rte. 79 (234-8888; open Mon.-Fri. 8:30am-5pm, Sat. 8:30am-12:30pm); **ZIP code:** 32407; **area code:** 904.

Accommodations and Camping Depending on the time of year and strip location, rates range from can-do to outrageous. High season runs from the end of April until early September; rates drop in fall and winter. **La Brisa Inn,** 9424 Front Beach Rd. (235-1122 or 800-523-4369), off the beach, has spacious rooms with two double beds and free coffee, doughnuts, and local calls (singles or doubles $50-60;

off season, singles $28). **The Reef,** 12011 Front Beach Rd. (234-3396 or 800-847-7286), near the visitors center, has large rooms with bright decor, many with bay views (kitchens, TV, A/C available; singles $50-65, Sept.-April ½ price). **Sea Breeze Motel,** 16810 Front Beach Rd. (234-3348), offers small rooms across the street from the beach; Cable TV, A/C, a pool, and reasonable rates will blow you away (single bed for 1 or 2 people $40, off season $20).

Camp on the beach at **St. Andrews State Recreation Area,** 4415 Thomas Dr. (233-5140), 3 mi. east of PCB on Rte. 392. Call ahead (up to 60 days) for reservations at this popular campground to grab private sites right on the water beneath tall pine trees. Half of the 176 sites can be reserved. (Sites $15; on the water with electricity $19.) **Panama City Beach KOA,** 8800 Thomas Dr. (234-5731), two blocks south of Rte. 98 on the Gulf, but not beachside, maintains 114 sites with showers, laundry, and a pool (tent sites with water $19, full hookup $23; winter $14/$18).

Food and Nightlife Buffets stuff The Strip. **JP's Restaurant and Bar,** 4701 Front Beach Rd. (769-3711), serves homemade specialties in abundant portions (fettuccini and clams $9; open Mon.-Sat. 11am-10:30pm). **The Pickle Patch,** 5700 Thomas Dr. (235-2000), concocts delicious Greek cuisine in a homey atmosphere; $4 pita sandwiches for lunch and $6 plates for dinner (open daily 8am-8pm). **Captain Anderson's Restaurant,** 5551 N. Lagoon Dr. (234-2225), off Thomas Dr., has a rep for superb seafood and a panoramic view (dinners $9-20; open daily 4-10pm).

Cruisers and those who hope to be cruised will find a home on meat-market Miracle Mile. At **Spinnaker,** 8795 Thomas Dr. (234-7892), dive into the massive club's pool, visit one of the several clubs inside, or join one of the daily hot body contests; on the side, listen to major music acts (cover varies; open daily 10am-4pm). The largest club in the U.S. (capacity 8000), **Club LaVela,** 8813 Thomas Dr. (235-1061), jams on multiple dance floors to just about every kind of music (including national acts) all night. "Ladies" make out with no cover and free drinks on Thursday night; call for other frequent specials, including daily wet T-shirt, bikini, and hot bod contests. (Cover $3-25. Open daily 10am-4am.) **Salty's Beach Bar,** 11073 Front Beach Rd. (234-1913), attracts a more laid-back crowd with nautical decor and live music every night (cover Fri.-Sat. $2; open 11am-2am).

Sights and Entertainment Over a thousand acres of gators, nature trails, and beaches make up the **St. Andrews State Recreation Area** (see Accommodations, above; open daily 8:30am-sunset; $2.35 per car). Take a glass-bottom boat trip to **Shell Island** from **Treasure Island Marina** (234-8944), on Thomas Dr. (3-hr. trips at 9am, 1 and 4:30pm; $10, under 13 $6). The **Museum of the Man in the Sea,** 17314 Back Beach Rd. (235-4101), explores the ocean deep (open daily 9am-5pm; $4, seniors $3.60, ages 6-16 $2). Daredevils bungee jump, parasail, and scuba dive every day here. Check out the **Miracle Strip Amusement Park** (234-5810; open Mon.-Fri. 6-11:30pm Sat. 1-11:30pm, Sun. 5-11pm; $17), adjacent to the **Shipwreck Island Water Park,** 2000 Front Beach Rd. (234-0368; admission to both parks $27). Nearby **Alvin's Magic Mountain Mall,** 12010 Front Beach Rd. (234-3048), houses sharks and alligators in a 30,000-gallon tank (open daily 9am-11pm).

Alabama

The "Heart of Dixie" has matured since the 1960s, when Governor George Wallace fought a vicious campaign opposing African-American advancement. During decades of internal racial strife, Alabama's bigotry forged dynamic civil rights leaders like Reverend Dr. Martin Luther King, Jr., whose legendary patience and fortitude helped to spawn the first real changes in race relations. The most compelling reasons to visit Alabama today are the monuments and legacies of this divided past, from the poignant statues in Birmingham's Kelly Ingram Park commemorating the struggles of the 1950s and 1960s to Booker T. Washington's pioneering Tuskegee Institute, now a university.

PRACTICAL INFORMATION

Capital: Montgomery.

Alabama Bureau of Tourism and Travel: 401 Adams Ave. (334-242-4169; 800-252-2262 outside AL). Open Mon.-Fri. 8am-5pm. **Travel Council,** 702 Oliver Rd. #254, Montgomery 36117 (334-271-0050). Open Mon.-Fri. 8am-5pm. **Division of Parks,** 64 N. Union St., Montgomery 36130 (800-252-7275). Open daily 8:30am-4:30pm.

Time Zone: Central (1hr. behind Eastern). **Postal Abbreviation:** AL

Sales Tax: 4% plus county tax.

■■■ MONTGOMERY

While Montgomery, the first capital of the Confederacy, is linked strongly to the history of the Old South, the city also played a key role in the birth of the New South. In 1955, local authorities arrested Rosa Parks, an African-American, because she refused to give up her bus seat; a local minister named Dr. Martin Luther King, Jr. responded by calling a famed boycott. The nation took notice of his nonviolent approach to gaining equal rights for African-Americans, igniting a movement that forever changed the face of race relations and a dream that continues to this day.

PRACTICAL INFORMATION

Tourist Office: Visitor Information Center, 401 Madison Ave. (262-0013). Open Mon.-Sat. 9am-4pm, Sun. noon-4pm. **Chamber of Commerce,** 401 Adams Ave. (242-4670). Open Mon.-Fri. 9am-4pm. For further info on events in the city (and endless fun), call the Chamber of Commerce's 24-hr. **FunPhone** (240-9447).

Buses: Greyhound, 210 S. Court St. (834-1288 or 800-231-2222), south of downtown. From Court Sq. Fountain on Washington St., take a left on Court St. and 2 blocks ahead. To: Mobile (8 per day, 3hr., $27); Atlanta (9 per day, 3-5hr., $29); Tuskegee (7 per day, 1hr., $8). Open 24 hrs.

Trains: Amtrak, 335 Coosa St. (277-9400), in Riverfront Park; Coosa St. is downtown at Madison and Bibb. Take Coosa across the railroad tracks; the stop is on your left. Limited bus service to connecting cities of Atlanta, Pensacola, and New Orleans. Open Mon.-Fri. 9am-6pm, Sat. 10am-4pm.

Public Transportation: Montgomery Area Transit System (MATS), 701 N. McDonough St. (262-7321). Operates throughout the metropolitan area Mon.-Sat. 5am-5pm. Fare $1, transfers 10¢.

Taxis: Yellow Cab, 262-5225. $1.50 first mi., $1.10 each additional mi. 24 hrs.

Crisis Lines: Council Against Rape, 286-5987. **Help-A-Crisis,** 279-7837. Both open 24 hrs.

Emergency: 911.

Post Office: 135 Catoma St. (244-7576). Open Mon.-Fri. 7am-5:30pm, Sat. 8am-noon. **ZIP code:** 36104. **Area code:** 334.

Downtown Montgomery follows a grid pattern: **Madison Ave.** and **Dexter Ave.** are the major east-west routes; **Perry St.** and **Lawrence St.** run north-south.

ACCOMMODATIONS AND FOOD

Centrally located and well-maintained, two budget motels serve the downtown area: the comfortable and newly renovated **Town Plaza,** 743 Madison Ave. (269-1561), at N. Ripley St. near the visitors center (singles $22, doubles $26), and **Capitol Inn,** 205 N. Goldthwaite St. (265-0541), at Heron St. near the bus station, with spacious, clean rooms overlooking the city and a pool (singles $30, doubles $39). Those with a car will find it easy to procure accommodations; **I-65's** exit 168 overflows with cheap beds. **The Inn South,** 4243 Inn South Ave. (288-7999), has nicely decorated rooms and a lobby with a grand double staircase and chandelier (singles $29, doubles $35). **Red Carpet Inn,** 1015 W. South Blvd. (281-6111), counters with large rooms with cable TV (singles $25, doubles $29). For an alternative to these inns, contact **Bed and Breakfast Inns Montgomery,** P.O. Box 1026, Montgomery 36101 (264-0056). For the camping crowd, **Fort Toulouse Jackson Park** (205-567-3002), 7 mi. north of Montgomery on Rte. 6 off U.S. 231 has 39 rustic sites with water and electricity in beautiful woods (tents $6, RVs $8).

A 70-year-old Montgomery institution, **Chris's Hot Dogs,** 138 Dexter Ave. (265-6850), has a carnivorous following. This small diner serves stuffed-silly hot dogs (under $2) and thick Brunswick stew ($1.65; open Mon.-Thurs. 8:30am-7pm, Fri. 8:30am-8pm, Sat. 10am-7pm). **Martha's Place,** 458 Sayre St. (263-9135), a new but soon-to-be-legendary, family-run, down-home restaurant serves a daily country-style lunch (entree, 2 veggies, lemonade and dessert $5.50) and a Sunday buffet ($6.50; open Mon.-Fri. 11am-3pm, Fri. 5-9pm, Sun. brunch 11am-3pm). At **The China Bowl,** 701 Madison Ave. (832-4004), 2 blocks from the Town Plaza Motel, large portions include a daily special of one entree, fried rice, egg roll, chicken wing, and a fried wonton for $4.20; take-out is available (open Mon.-Thurs. 11am-9pm, Fri. 11am-9:30pm). For a great snack, make your way over to the **Montgomery State Farmers Market** (242-5350), at the corner of Federal Dr. (U.S. 231) and Coliseum Blvd., and snag a bag of peaches for a buck (open spring and summer daily 7am-6pm). For a more filling meal, there is never an empty seat for the Southern cooking at **The State Market Cafeteria,** 1659 Federal Dr., which serves free iced tea with every inexpensive meal ($3-5; open Sun.-Fri. 5am-2pm).

SIGHTS AND ENTERTAINMENT

Maya Lin, the architect who designed the Vietnam Memorial in Washington, DC also designed Montgomery's newest sight, the **Civil Rights Memorial,** 400 Washington Ave. (264-0268), at Hull St. This dramatically minimalist tribute remembers 40 of the men, women, and children who died fighting for civil rights. The outdoor monument bears names and dates of significant events on a circular black marble table over which water continuously flows; a wall frames the table with Martin Luther King, Jr.'s words, "Until justice rolls down like waters and righteousness like a mighty stream." (Open 24 hrs. Free.)

The legacy of African-American activism and faith lives on one block away at the 112-year-old **Dexter Avenue King Memorial Baptist Church,** 454 Dexter Ave. (263-3970), where King first preached. Here, Reverend King and other Civil Rights leaders organized the 1955 Montgomery bus boycott; 10 years later, King led a nationwide Civil Rights march past the church to the capitol building. The basement mural chronicles King's role in the nation's struggle during the 1950s and 60s. (Tours Mon.-Thurs. 10am and 2pm, Fri. 10am, Sat. every hr. from 9am-2pm. Free.)

Old Alabama Town, 310 N. Hull St. (240-4500), at Madison, encompasses a historic district of 19th-century buildings 3 blocks north of the church. The complex includes a pioneer homestead, an 1892 grocery, a schoolhouse, and an early African-American church. Renowned Alabama storyteller Kathryn Tucker Windham artfully recounts her family's past as she leads you through the quaint, reconstructed village. (Open Mon.-Sat. 9am-3:30pm, last tour at 3pm; Sun. 1-3:30pm. $5, ages 6-18 $3.)

The **State Capitol** (242-3935), Bainbridge St. at Dexter Ave., has recently reopened after years of renovations (open Mon.-Sat. 9am-4pm for free, self-guided tours; make an appointment for a guide; free). The nearby **Alabama State Archives and History Museum,** 624 Washington Ave. (242-4363) exhibits many Native American artifacts along with early military swords and medals. **Grandma's Attic** lets you try on antique furs and play with antique sewing machines and typewriters in a wooden-frame attic replica (open Mon.-Fri. 8am-5pm, Sat. 9am-5pm; free). Next door to the Archives, the elegant **First White House of the Confederacy,** 644 Washington Ave. (242-1861), contains many original furnishings from Jefferson Davis's presidency (open Mon.-Fri. 8am-4:30pm; free). Another restored home of interest, the **F. Scott and Zelda Fitzgerald Museum,** 919 Felder Ave. (264-4222), off Carter Hill Rd., contains a few of her paintings and some of his original manuscripts, as well as their strangely monogrammed bath towels. Zelda, originally from Montgomery, lived here with F. Scott from October 1931 to April 1932. (Open Wed.-Fri. 10am-2pm, Sat.-Sun. 1-5pm. Free.)

Country music fans might want to join the droves who make daily pilgrimages to the **Hank Williams Memorial,** 1304 Upper Wetumpka Rd. (262-0804), located in the Oakwood Cemetery Annex off Upper Wetumpka Rd. near dowtown. A stone cowboy hat rests upon the grave, flanked by oversized music notes and other memorabilia. (Open Mon.-Fri. 10am-4pm.) For more live entertainment, turn to the renowned **Alabama Shakespeare Festival,** (800-841-4ASF) staged at the **State Theatre** on the grounds of the 250-acre private estate, **Wynton M. Blount Cultural Park;** take East Blvd. 15 minutes southeast of the downtown area onto Woodmere Rd. The theater also stages Broadway shows and other plays. (Tickets $7-$23. Open rehearsals $10. Box office open daily 10am-6pm.). Nearby, off Woodmere Blvd., the **Montgomery Museum of Fine Arts,** 1 Museum Dr. (244-5700), houses a substantial collection of 19th- and 20th-century paintings and graphics, as well as ARTWORKS, a hands-on gallery and art studio for children (open Tues.-Wed. and Fri-Sat. 10am-5pm, Thurs. 10am-9pm, Sun. noon-5pm; free).

Montgomery shuts down fairly early, but if you're in the mood for some blues and beers, try **1048,** 1048 E. Fairview Ave. (834-1048), near Woodley Ave. (open Mon.-Sat. 6pm until the cow walks in the door), or **Sinclair's,** 1051 Fairview Ave. (834-7462; open Mon-Thurs. 11am-10pm, Fri.-Sat. 11am-11pm).

■ NEAR MONTGOMERY: TUSKEGEE

After Reconstruction, Southern states still segregated and disenfranchised "emancipated" African-Americans. Booker T. Washington, a former slave, believed that blacks could best combat repression and racism by educating themselves and learning a trade, as opposed to pursuing the classical, more erudite education which W.E.B. Dubois proposed. Therefore, the curriculum at the college Washington founded, **Tuskegee Institute,** revolved around such practical endeavors as agriculture and carpentry, with students constructing almost all of the campus buildings. Washington raised money for the college by giving lectures on social structure across the country. Artist, teacher, and scientist **George Washington Carver** became head of the Agricultural Department at Tuskegee, where he discovered many practical uses for the peanut, including axle grease and peanut butter.

Today, a more academically oriented Tuskegee University fills 160 buildings on 1500 acres and offers a wide range of subjects; the buildings of Washington's original institute comprise a national historical site. A walking tour of the campus begins near the entrance to the university at the **Carver Museum;** the **Visitor Orientation Center** (334-727-3200) is inside (both open daily 9am-5pm; free). Down the street from the museum on old Montgomery Rd. lies **The Oaks,** a restored version of Washington's home. Free tours from the museum begin on the hour.

For a filling, delicious, and inexpensive meal after your tour, just cross the street from campus to **Thomas Reed's Chicken Coop,** 527 Old Montgomery Rd. (334-727-3841). Chicken is sold by the piece or as a full dinner (all under $5)—and you *will* lick your fingers, unless you're feeling stubborn (open daily 10am-5pm).

To get to Tuskegee, take I-85 toward Atlanta and exit at Rte. 81 south. Turn right at the intersection of Rte. 81 and Old Montgomery Rd. onto Rte. 126. **Greyhound** (334-727-1290 or 800-231-2222) also runs frequently from Montgomery (1hr., $9).

■■■ BIRMINGHAM

Like its English namesake, Birmingham sits on soil rich in coal, iron ore, and limestone—responsible for its lightning transformation into a premier steel industry center. No longer an industrial town, the University of Alabama now employs the majority of the city's workers; with the fires out, an easy, cosmopolitan version of Southern charm and hospitality have kicked in, visible in the city's art festivals and museums. Still, there is a dark side to the city's recent history. Birmingham has been "A Place of Revolution and Reconciliation," trying in recent decades to heal the wounds left by Eugene "Bull" Connor, firehoses, bombings, and police dogs, whose images were spread all over the American news media during the civil rights protests of the early 1960s.

PRACTICAL INFORMATION

Tourist Office: Birmingham Visitors Center, 1200 University Blvd. (458-8001), at 12 St., I-65 exit 259. Maps, calendars, and coupons for accommodations. Open Mon.-Sat. 8:30am-5pm, Sun. 1-5pm. Another location on the lower level of **Birmingham Municipal Airport** (458-8002). Open daily 7:45am-10pm. **Greater Birmingham Convention and Visitors Bureau,** 2200 9th Ave. N., 3rd floor (252-9825), downtown. Open Mon.-Fri. 8:30am-5pm.

Trains: Amtrak, 1819 Morris Ave. (324-3033 or 800-872-7245). To: Atlanta (3 per week, 5hr., $33); New Orleans (3 per week, 7hr., $68).

Buses: Greyhound, 619 N. 19th St. (251-3210 or 800-231-2222). To: Montgomery (8 per day, 2hr., $15); Mobile (8 per day, 8hr., $39); Atlanta (6 per day, 2-3hr., $22). Open 24 hrs.

Public Transportation: Metropolitan Area Express (MAX), 322-7701. Runs Mon.-Sat. 5am-5pm. Fare $1. **Downtown Area Runabout Transit (DART),** 252-0101. Runs Mon.-Fri. 10am-4pm. Fare 25¢.

Taxi: Yellow Cab, 252-1131. $3 base fare, $1.20 per additional mi.

Crisis Lines: Crisis Center, 323-7777. Open 24 hrs.

Emergency: 911.

Post Office: 351 24th St. N. (521-0209). Open Mon.-Fri. 24 hrs. Closes Sat. 4:30am and reopens Mon 4:30am. **ZIP code:** 35203. **Area code:** 205.

The downtown area grid system has avenues running east-west and streets running north-south. Each numbered avenue has a north and a south. Major cultural and government buildings surround **Linn Park,** located between 19th and 21st St. N. on 7th Ave. N. The **University of Alabama in Birmingham (UAB)** extends along University Blvd. (8th Ave. S.) from 11th to 20th St.

ACCOMMODATIONS AND CAMPING

Royal Inn, 821 20th St. S. (252-8041), 2 blocks from UAB hospital. Large, clean rooms and tasteful decor in a convenient location. Pool. Singles and doubles $35.

Ranchhouse Inn, 2125 7th Ave. S. (322-0691). Near busy bars and restaurants. Pleasant rooms with cable TV and wood paneling. Local calls 25¢ each. Singles $30, doubles $36.

Masters Inn Economy, 1011 9th Ave. SW (424-9690), take exit 108 off U.S. 11. Large, clean rooms with new furniture, cable TV, A/C and heat. Free doughnuts and coffee. Pool. Singles $24, doubles $28.

Oak Mountain State Park (620-2527), 15mi. south of Birmingham off I-65 in Pelham (exit 246). Alabama's largest state park with nearly 10,000 heavily forested acres. Horseback rides, golf, hiking, and an 85-acre lake. Sites for 1-4 $8.50, with full hookup $15.

FOOD

Barbecue remains the local specialty, although more ethnic variations have sprung up downtown. The best places to eat cheaply (and meet young people) are at **Five Points South,** located at the intersection of Highland Ave. and 20th St. S. Choose from pesto pizza with sun-dried tomatoes ($3 per slice) at **Cosmo's Pizza,** 2012 Magnolia Ave. (930-9971; open Mon.-Thurs. 11am-11pm, Fri.-Sat. noon-midnight, Sun. noon-10pm), or health-conscious veggie lunches and groceries at **The Golden Temple,** 1901 11th Ave. S. (933-6333; open Mon.-Fri. 8:30am-7pm, Sat. 9:30am-5:30pm, Sun. noon-5:30pm; kitchen open Mon.-Sat. 11:30am-2pm).

Ollie's, 515 University Blvd. (324-9485), near Green Springs Hwy. Bible Belt dining in an enormous circular 50s-style building. Pamphlets shout "Is there really a Hell?" while you lustfully consume your beef. BBQ sandwich $2, homemade pie $1.50. Diet plates available. Open Mon. 10am-3pm, Tues.-Sat. 10am-8am.

The Mill, 1035 20th St. S. (939-3001), sits at the center of Five Points South, serving tasty pizzas ($6-8) and sandwiches ($5-6). Microbrewery, bakery, and restaurant in one, this sidewalk café/restaurant/bar will sate any gastronomic need. Live entertainment Wed.-Sat. (cover on weekends $2). Open daily 11am-midnight.

Bogue's, 3028 Clairmont Ave. (254-9780). A short-order diner with true, delicious Southern fare (cheese omelette and biscuit $3). Always busy weekend mornings. Open Mon.-Fri. 6am-2pm, Sat.-Sun. 6-11:30am.

Café Bottega, 2240 Highland Ave. S. (939-1000). High-ceilinged and sophisticated, this café serves fresh bread to dip in olive oil and Italian specialties brimming with fresh vegetables and herbs. Marinated pasta with sweet peas and mint $5.25. Entrees $5-12. Open Mon.-Sat. 11am-11pm. Bar open until "everyone goes home."

SIGHTS

Part of Birmingham's efforts at reconciliation have culminated in the **Black Heritage Tour** of the downtown area. The **Birmingham Civil Rights Institute,** 520 16th St. N. (328-9696), at 6th Ave. N., rivals the museum in Memphis (see Memphis, p. 284) in thoroughness, and surpasses it in visual and audio evocations, depictions, and footage of African-American history and the turbulent events of the Civil Rights Movement. The Institute intends to display exhibits on human rights across the globe and to serve as a research facility open to the public. A trip to Birmingham would be incomplete without tour. (Open Tues.-Sat. 10am-6pm, Sun. 1-5pm. $3, students $1.) Other significant sights include the **Sixteenth Street Baptist Church,** 1530 6th Ave. N. (251-9402), at 16th St. N. (in the lower level), where four African-American girls died in a September 1963 bombing by white segregationists after a protest push which culminated in Dr. Martin Luther King Jr.'s "Letter From a Birmingham Jail" (open Tues.-Fri. 9am-4pm). The deaths spurred many protests in nearby **Kelly-Ingram Park,** corner of 6th Ave. and 16th St., where a bronze statue of Dr. Martin Luther King, Jr. and sculptures portraying the brutality and hope of the civil rights demonstrations now grace the green lawns.

Remnants of Birmingham's steel industry are best viewed at the gigantic **Sloss Furnaces National Historic Landmark** (324-1911), adjacent to the 2nd Ave. N. viaduct off 32nd St. downtown. Though the blast furnaces closed 20 years ago, they stand as the only preserved example of 20th-century iron-smelting in the world. Ballet and drama performances and music concerts are often held here at night. (Open Tues.-Sat. 10am-4pm, Sun. noon-4pm; free guided tours Sat.-Sun. at 1, 2, and 3pm.) To anthropomorphize the steel industry, Birmingham cast **Vulcan** (Roman god of the forge), who overwhelms the skyline as the largest cast-iron statue in the world. Visitors can watch over the city from its observation deck. The Vulcan's glowing torch burns red when a car fatality has occurred that day, green when none occur. (Open daily 8am-10:30pm. $1, under 7 free.)

The **Alabama Sports Hall of Fame** (323-6665), corner of Civic Center Blvd. and 22nd St. N., honors the careers of outstanding sportsmen like Bear Byrant, Jesse Owens, Joe Louis, Joe Namath, and Willie Mays (open Mon.-Sat. 9am-5pm, Sun. 1-5pm. $5, students and seniors $3). A few blocks down from the Hall of Fame **Linn Park** refreshes visitors, and sits across from the **Birmingham Museum of Art,** 2000 8th Ave. N. (254-2565). The museum displays U.S. paintings and English Wedgewood ceramics, as well as a superb collection of African textiles and sculptures. (Open Tues.-Sat. 10am-5pm, Sun. noon-5pm. Free.)

For a breather from the downtown scene, revel in the marvelously sculpted grounds of the **Birmingham Botanical Gardens,** 2612 Lane Park Rd. (879-1227), whose spectacular floral displays, elegant Japanese gardens, and enormous greenhouse vegetate on 68 acres (open daily dawn-dusk; free).

Antebellum **Arlington,** 331 Cotton Ave. (780-5656), southwest of downtown, houses a fine array of Southern decorative arts from the 19th century. Go west on

1st Ave. N., which becomes Cotton Ave., to reach the stately white **Greek Revival** building, which also hosts craft fairs throughout the year. (Open Tues.-Sat. 10am-4pm, Sun. 1-4pm. $3, ages 6-18 $2.)

To learn more about the geology of the area, visit the **Red Mountain Museum and Cut,** 2230 22nd St. S. (933-4104). You can wander a walkway above the highway to see different levels of rock formation inside Red Mountain. The museum indoors has various exhibits on the prehistoric inhabitants of Alabama. (Open Mon.-Fri. 9am-5pm, Sat. 10am-4pm, Sun. 1-4pm. $2.)

ENTERTAINMENT AND NIGHTLIFE

Historic **Alabama Theater,** 1817 3rd Ave. N. (251-0418), shows old movies on occasional weekends throughout the year; their organ, the "Mighty Wurlitzer," entertains the audience before each showing ($4, seniors $3, under 12 $2). Pick up a free copy of *Fun and Stuff* or see the "Kudzu" in the Friday edition of *The Birmingham Post Herald* for listings of all movies, plays, and clubs in the area.

Music lovers lucky or smart enough to visit Birmingham in the middle of June for **City Stages** (251-1272) will hear everything from country to gospel to big name rock groups, with headliners like James Brown, the Indigo Girls, and George Jones. The three-day festival also includes food, crafts, and children's activities. (Daily pass $15, weekend pass $20.)

Nightclubs concentrate in **Five Points South (Southside).** On cool summer nights many people grab outdoor tables in front of their favorite bars or hang out by the fountain. Use caution here, and avoid parking or walking in dark alleys near the square. For the hippest licks year-round check out **The Nick,** 2514 10th Ave. S. (322-7550). The poster-covered exterior says it clear and proud: "the Nick...rocks." (Cover $2-5. Open Mon.-Sat. Live music nightly.) **Louie Louie's,** 2001 Highland Ave. (933-2778), at 21st St., has good cheap drinks and tunes; live bands play Wednesday, Friday, and Saturday, and disco plays on Thursday (Tues.-Thurs. 75¢ cans and $1 drinks; open Tues.-Sat. 7pm-'til). **The Burly Earl,** 2109 7th Ave. S. (322-5848), specializes in fried finger-foods and local acoustic, blues, and rock sounds; sandwiches are $3-5. (Wed.-Thurs. live folk from 8:30pm-midnight; Fri.-Sat. rock bands 9:30pm-2am. Restaurant open Mon.-Thurs. 10am-midnight, bar open until midnight; Fri.-Sat. 10am-1am, bar open until 2am.)

Olympic soccer games, including the quarterfinals and a small opening ceremony, will take place at Birmingham's **Legion Field** July 20-28, 1996. Officials do not anticipate selling out. (Tickets $20-30; call 933-1996 or 800-923-1996.)

■■■ MOBILE

Since its founding in 1702, French, Spanish, English, Sovereign Alabama, Confederate and American flags have flown over Mobile (mo-BEEL). This historical diversity manifests itself in the city's varied architectures; antebellum mansions, Italianate dwellings, Spanish and French historical forts, and Victorian homes line azalea-edged streets. The faded splendor of some of these buildings tell of a time in the not-so-distant past when cotton was king—the last slave ship unloaded its human cargo as late as 1859. Today, Mobile offers a laid-back and untouristed version of New Orleans; the site of the first Mardi Gras, the city continues to hold Fat Tuesday without the visiting hordes and MTV that plague its cajun brother.

PRACTICAL INFORMATION

Tourist Office: Fort Condé Information Center, 150 S. Royal St. (434-7304), in a reconstructed French fort near Government St. Open daily 8am-5pm.

Trains: Amtrak, 11 Government St. (432-4052 or 800-872-7245). The "Gulf Breeze" blows from Mobile to New York via bus service to Birmingham or Atlanta. To: New Orleans (3 per week, 16hr., $45). Ticket office open Mon.-Thurs. 6am-10pm, Fri. 6am-2:30pm, Sat. 11:30pm-8:30am, Sun. 2am-10pm.

Buses: Greyhound, 2545 Government St. (478-9793 or 800-231-2222), at S. Conception downtown. To: Montgomery (8 per day, 4hr., $27); New Orleans (10 per day, 3hr., $24); Birmingham (7 per day, 6hr., $39). Open 24 hrs.

Public Transportation: Mobile Transit Authority (MTA), 344-5656. Major depots are at Bienville Sq., St. Joseph, and Dauphin St. Operates Mon.-Sat. 5am-7pm. Fare $1, seniors and disabled 50¢, transfers 10¢.

Taxis: Yellow Cab, 476-7711. $1.30 base fare, $1.20 per additional mi.

Crisis Lines: Rape Crisis, 473-7273. **Crisis Counseling,** 666-7900. Both 24 hrs.

Emergency: 911.

Post Office: 250 Saint Joseph St. (694-5917). Open Mon.-Fri. 7am-5pm, Sat. 9am-4pm. **ZIP code:** 36601. **Area code:** 334.

The downtown district fronts the Mobile River. **Dauphin St.** and **Government Blvd.** (U.S. 90), which becomes Government St. downtown, are the major east-west routes. **Royal St.** and **St. Joseph St.** are the north-south byways. Some of Mobile's major attractions lie outside downtown. The *U.S.S. Alabama* is off the causeway (I-10) leading out of the city; **Dauphin Island** is 30 mi. south.

ACCOMMODATIONS AND CAMPING

Accommodations are both reasonable and accessible, but stop first at the Fort Condé Information Center (see above); they can make reservations for you at a 10-15% discount. **Family Inns,** 900 S. Beltline Rd. (344-5500), I-65 at Airport Blvd., sports new carpets, firm beds, and general comfort (singles $27, doubles $36). **Motel 6,** 400 Beltline Hwy. (343-8448), has large, dark rooms with tidy furnishings and shag carpets (free movie channel, pool; 1 person $32, each additional person $5). **I-10 Kampground,** 6430 Theodore Dawes Rd. E. (653-9816), lies 7½ mi. west on I-10 (exit 13 and turn south). The kampground is not accessible by public transportation. (Pool, kiddie playground, laundry, and bath facilities. Tent sites $12; RVs $16, full hookup $17; each additional person $1.)

FOOD AND NIGHTLIFE

Mobile's Gulf location means fresh seafood and Southern-style cookin'. Next to the *U.S.S. Alabama* and choice fishing spots, **Argiro's,** 1320 Battleship Pkwy. (626-1060), provides cheap hot dogs and sandwiches ($2-5) and Southern specialties such as fried catfish in a quick-stop deli (open Mon.-Sat. 8am-4pm). **Dreamland,** 3314 Old Shell Rd. (479-9898), has two things on the menu: whole slab or half slab. That's ribs, y'all, smoked right there. (Open Mon.-Thurs. 10am-10pm, Fri.-Sat. 10am-midnight, Sun. 11am-9pm.) The **Lumber Yard,** 2617 Dauphin St. (471-4609), saws off healthy sandwiches, salads and pizzas, and a full-service bar with happy hour 4-7pm daily. ($1 domestic drafts; open daily 11am-1am). **Judge Roy Bean's** (626-9988), off Old Hwy. 98 in Daphne, offers a unique experience. Multiple tin-roofed buildings inhabited by cats and a goat make up this ramshackle bar; come on a Sunday when the courtyard opens its raw bar, frozen drink bar, and food bar, and things get really strange. Live rock music (including frequent appearances by Jimmy Buffet) plays daily. (Open Tues.-Sun. 4:30pm-'til.) Cheap beer ($1 and up), 10 pool tables, and mega-subs ($3) make **Solomon's,** 5753 Old Shell Rd. (344-0380), the quintessential beer and pool college hangout (open 24 hrs.). **Hayley's,** 278 Dauphin St. (433-4970), an alternative bar/hangout, adorns its tables with peaceful messages (beer $1.50, jello shots $1; open daily 3pm-3am). For after-hours dancing, **Exit,** 9 N. Jackson off Dauphin St. (433-9979), pulses until morning (open Wed.-Sat. 2am-'til).

SIGHTS

Mobile encompasses four historic districts: **Church St., DeTonti Square, Old Dauphin Way,** and **Oakleigh Garden.** Each offers an array of architectural styles. The information center provides maps for walking or driving tours of these areas. **Gray Line of Mobile** (432-2228) leads tours which get you there and back to most sights.

Church St. divides into east and west subdistricts. The homes in the venerable **Church St. East District** showcase popular U.S. architectural styles of the mid to late 19th century, including Federal, Greek Revival, Queen Anne, and Victorian. While on Church St., pass through the **Spanish Plaza,** at Hamilton and Government St., which honors Mobile's sibling city—Málaga, Spain—while recalling Spain's early presence in Mobile. **Christ Episcopal Church,** 114 St. Emanuel St. (433-1842), sits opposite the tourist office at Fort Condé. Dedicated in 1842, the church contains beautiful German, Italian, and Tiffany stained glass windows. Call the office (weekdays 8am-4pm) or wander in when the church opens on weekends (Sunday services at 8 and 10am). The intriguingly named **Phoenix Fire Museum,** 203 S. Claiborne St. (434-7554), displays several antique fire engines including an 1898 steam-powered one (open Tues.-Sat. 10am-5pm, Sun. 1-5pm; free).

In the **DeTonti Historical District,** north of downtown, tour the restored **Richards-DAR House,** 256 North Joachim St. (434-7320); the stained glass and rococo chandeliers blend beautifully with the antebellum Italianate architecture and ornate "Iron Lace" (tours $3, children $1; open Tues.-Sat. 10am-4pm, Sun. 1-4pm). Brick townhouses with wrought-iron balconies fill the rest of the district.

Oakleigh, 350 Oakleigh Place (432-1281), off Government St., reigns as one of Mobile's grande dames, with a cantilevered staircase and enormous windows that open onto all the balconies upstairs. Inside, a museum contains furnishings of the early Victorian, Empire, and Regency periods. (Tours every ½hr.; last tour at 3:30pm. Open Mon.-Sat. 10am-4pm, Sun. 2-4pm. $5, students $2, seniors $4.50, ages 6-18 $1.) Also tour the **Bragg-Mitchell,** 1906 Spring Hill Ave. (471-6364; open Mon.-Fri. 10am-4pm, Sat. 1-4pm) and **Conde-Charlotte,** 104 Theatre St. (432-4722; open Tues.-Sat. 10am-4pm), the former residences of cotton brokers and river pilots. (Package tour available at the visitors center; $10 for four house museums.)

The **Mobile Museum of Art,** 4850 Museum Dr. (343-2667), displays some fascinating African-American art (open Tues.-Sun. 10am-5pm; free). The **Exploreum,** 1906 Springhill Ave. (476-6873), offers hands-on scientific diversions geared to children (open Tues.-Fri. 9am-5pm, Sat.-Sun. 1-5pm; $3, ages 2-17 $2).

The battleship *U.S.S. Alabama,* permanently moored at **Battleship Park** (433-2703), fought in every major battle in the Pacific during World War II. The park is at the entrance of the Bankhead Tunnel, 2½ mi. east of town on I-10. The famous submarine *U.S.S. Drum* berthed along the port side of this intriguing ship. (Open daily 8am-sunset. Admission to both vessels $6, ages 6-11 $3.50. Parking $2.)

Bellingrath Gardens, 12401 Bellingrath Gardens Rd. (973-2217), exit 15A off I-10, includes some of the premier gardens in the U.S. The lush landscaped grounds feature a formal rose garden and Asian-American garden. Plants bloom year round, but March to November offer the most spectacular displays. (Open daily 8am-sunset. Home and gardens $14, ages 5-11 $10. Gardens only $7/$5.)

Mobile's calendar gets crowded in February. Locals await the blooming of the 27 mi. **Azalea Trail** in February and March, and on February 20, 1996 Mobile's **Mardi Gras** will fill the streets. Enjoy parades, floats, costumes and "throws" of the oldest (and, some say, best) Fat Tuesday around.

Mississippi

The siege of Vicksburg and the near-destruction of Jackson during the Civil War left Mississippi devastated; in many ways, the state has never fully recovered. Perhaps more than any other state, Mississippi is known for economic turmoil—the average income in Mississippi is the lowest in the nation—and racial strife. In the 1960s, whites in Mississippi reacted to the black civil rights movement with riots and violence. The racial balance remains strained at times, despite the undeniable importance of African-Americans to Mississippi's cultural heritage. Black musicians brought blues riffs from Mississippi up Rte. 61, the "Blues Highway" (see below), to Memphis, Chicago, and the world.

Those with no interest in music can still appreciate the towering willows which hang elegantly over the flat countryside. The great physical beauty of the "Magnolia State," has inspired an impressive literary heritage; writers William Faulkner, Eudora Welty, Tennessee Williams, and Richard Wright all called Mississippi home.

PRACTICAL INFORMATION

Capital: Jackson.

Division of Tourism: 1301 Walter Siller Bldg., 550 High St. (359-3414 or 800-927-6378). Open Mon.-Fri. 8am-5pm. **Bureau of Parks and Recreation,** P.O. Box 10600, Jackson 39209.

Time Zone: Central (1hr. behind Eastern). **Postal Abbreviation:** MS

Sales Tax: 7-8%.

Rte. 61: The Blues Highway

The sun-scorched length of **Highway 61** winds through the small-towns of the Mississippi River Delta. Blues greats Bessie Smith, W.C. Handy, Muddy Waters, and John Lee Hooker rolled down this route bringing this music to Memphis. Once the home of W.C. Handy, **Clarksdale,** 60 mi. south of Memphis, now pays tribute to the "Father of the Blues" with the **Delta Blues Museum,** 114 Delta Ave. (601-624-4461). Already chock full of photos, paintings, recordings, and books on blues artists, the museum now features an exhibit on the roots of popular American music. (Open Mon.-Fri. 9am-5:30pm, Sat. 10am-5pm. Free; donations are appreciated.) For live laments, mosey down to one of Clarksdale's juke joints. **Red's South End Disco,** 395 Sunflower St. (601-627-3166), on the corner of Sunflower and Martin Luther King, Jr. St., doesn't have a sign; it's the inside that counts (open Mon.-Fri. 8pm-1am, Sat.-Sun. 1pm-1am). During the first week of August, Clarksdale sponsors a rollicking **blues festival** (601-624-4461).

■■■ JACKSON

A sleepy Deep South town, Mississippi's commercial and political capital offers travelers a glimpse into life below the Mason-Dixon line without the usual plastic tourist traps. North Jackson's lush homes and plush country clubs epitomize traditional southern living, while shaded campsites, cool reservoirs, national forests, and Native American burial mounds invite exploration only minutes away.

PRACTICAL INFORMATION

Tourist Office: Visitor Information Center, 1150 Lakeland Dr. (981-0019), off I-55's Lakeland East exit. Open Mon.-Sat. 9am-5pm. **Convention and Visitors Bureau,** 921 N. President St. (960-1891), downtown. Open Mon.-Fri. 8:30am-5pm.

Airport: Jackson Municipal (932-2859), east of downtown off I-20. Cab fare to downtown costs about $15.

Trains: Amtrak, 300 W. Capitol St. (355-6350 or 800-872-7245). The neighborhood is deserted at night. To: Memphis (5 per week, 4hr., $46); New Orleans (5 per week, 4hr., $42). Open daily 8:30am-7pm. Walk downtown via Capitol St.

Buses: Greyhound, 201 S. Jefferson (353-6342 or 800-231-2222). *Be cautious walking in the area at night.* To: Dallas (5 per day, 10hr., $64); Montgomery (3 per day, 7hr., $46); Memphis (5 per day, 4½hr., $32); New Orleans (4 per day, 4½hr., $34). Open 24 hrs.

Public Transportation: Jackson Transit System (JATRAN), 948-3840. Limited service Mon.-Fri. 5am-7pm, Sat. 7am-6pm. Fare 75¢, transfers free. Bus schedules and maps posted at most bus stops and available at JATRAN headquarters, 1025 Terry Rd. (open Mon.-Fri. 8am-4:30pm).

Taxis: City Cab, 355-8319. $1.10 base fare, $1 per mi.
Crisis Lines: First Call for Help, 352-4357. **Rape Hotline,** 982-7273. Both 24 hrs.
Emergency: 911.
Post Office: 401 E. South St. (968-1612). Open Mon.-Fri. 7am-6pm, Sat. 8am-noon. **ZIP code:** 39201. **Area code:** 601.

Downtown, just west of I-55, is bordered on the north by **High St.,** on the south by **Tombigbee St.,** and on the west by **Farish St.** North-south **State St.** bisects the city.

ACCOMMODATIONS AND CAMPING

At Jackson hotels, price varies with proximity and comfort; if you have a car, head for the motels along I-20 and I-55. Expect to pay $25-30 for decent accommodations in the area, unless you go the bargain route and camp.

Sun 'n' Sand Motel, 401 N. Lamar St. (354-2501), downtown. Large, newly-renovated rooms in 50s orange 'n' aqua—there's even a Polynesian room. Cable TV, a pool, and an in-house barber shop. Lounge/restaurant in motel serves a $5 lunch buffet. Singles $30, doubles $35; $5 per additional person.

Admiral Benbow Inn, 905 N. State St. (948-4161), downtown. Large, comfortable rooms. Frequent $29 specials on rooms that the management admits are a bit drab: cracked paint, stained carpet, etc. Otherwise, singles and doubles $33-48.

Parkside Inn, 3720 I-55N (982-1122), at exit 98B, close to downtown. Plain, worn rooms with full amenities: pool, cable TV, restaurant/lounge, free local calls. Singles $29-32, doubles $35.

Timberlake Campgrounds, 143 Timberlake Dr. (992-9100). Stays busy throughout the summer. Pool, video games, tennis courts, playground. Tent sites $9, with full hookup $14.

FOOD AND NIGHTLIFE

A waterfall trickles from the 2nd floor of the converted smokehouse where **The Iron Horse Grill,** 320 W. Pearl St. (355-8419), at Gallatin, serves its Tex-Mex specialties ($8-11). Steak and seafood can be had for a bit more cash. (Open Mon.-Thurs. 11am-10pm, Fri.-Sat. 11am-11pm.) A 31-year Jackson institution, **Primo's,** 4330 N. State St. (982-2064), fills a spacious, quasi-romantic dining room with candlelight, jazz, and open-faced prime rib sandwiches ($8; open Mon.-Sat. 11am-10pm). Be prepared to wait in line during the lunch rush at **The Elite Café,** 141 E. Capitol (352-5606); the plate lunch specials (with 2 veggies and bread, under $5.10) make it worth the wait (dinner slightly pricier; open Mon.-Fri. 7am-9:30pm, Sat. 5-9:30pm).

For a list of weekend events in Jackson, pick up a copy of the *Clarion-Ledger* on Thursday. **Hal & Mal's Restaurant and Oyster Bar,** 200 Commerce St. (948-0888), stages live music, from reggae to innovative rock, in a converted warehouse. (Bands Fri.-Sat. Cover $0-12. Restaurant open Mon.-Thurs. 11am-9pm, Fri. 11am-1am, Sat. 5pm-1am; bar open Fri.-Sat. until 1am.) **Cups,** 2757 Old Canton Rd. (362-7422), caters to an artsy collegiate crowd craving cappuccino and conversation (open Mon.-Thurs. 7am-10pm, Fri. 7am-midnight, Sat. 8am-midnight, Sun. 9am-10pm).

SIGHTS AND ENTERTAINMENT

Built in 1840, the **Old State Capitol** (359-6920), at the intersection of Capitol and State St., houses an excellent museum of Mississippi's turbulent history, including artifacts from original Native American settlements and documentaries on the Civil Rights Movement (open Mon.-Fri. 8am-5pm, Sat. 9:30am-4:30pm, Sun. 12:30-4:30pm; free). The **War Memorial Building,** 120 S. State St. (354-7207), tells a gruesome story of American wars and the Mississippians who fought, distinguished themselves, and often died in them (open Mon.-Fri. 8am-4:30pm; free). A tour of the **Governor's Mansion,** 300 E. Capitol St. (359-3175), gives an enlightening introduction to Mississippi politics. Because the governor still lives here, the touring hours are slim. (Tours Mon.-Fri. every ½-hr. 9:30-11am; free.) During the siege of Jackson in 1863, General Sherman occupied an antebellum cottage called **The Oaks,** 823 N. Jefferson St. (353-9339; open Tues.-Sat. 10am-4pm, Sun. 1:30-4pm; $2, students $1).

Though rich in history, Jackson hardly neglects the wonders of the present. The state legislature's currently resides in the beautiful **New State Capitol** (359-3114), at Mississippi and Congress, completed in 1903. A huge restoration project preserved the *beaux arts* grandeur of the building, complete with a gold-leaf eagle perched on the capitol dome, carnival-like colors, and strings of lights which brighten the spacious interior. (Guided 1-hr. tours Mon.-Fri. 9, 10, 11am, 1:30, 2:30, and 3:30pm. Open Mon.-Fri. 8am-5pm. Free.) For more priceless beauty, the **Mississippi Arts Center,** 201 E. Pascagoula (960-1515), at Lamar St., has a fabulous collection of Americana and a fun participatory Impression Gallery for kids (open Tues.-Sun. noon-5pm; $3, children $2; students free Tues. and Thurs.). Next door, the **Russell C. Davis Planetarium,** 201 E. Pascagoula (960-1550), ranks among the most stellar worldwide. (Shows Tues.-Sat. 7:30pm, Sat.-Sun. 2 and 4pm. Laser shows Thurs.-Sat. 8:30pm, Sat.-Sun. 3pm. $4, under 13 $2.50.)

Learn about the struggles and achievements of Mississippi's African-Americans at the **Smith-Robertson Museum and Cultural Center,** 528 Bloom St. (960-1457), directly behind the Sun 'n' Sand Motel. This large museum once housed the state's first African-American public school; *Black Boy* author Richard Wright attended until the eighth grade. Now it displays folk art, photographs, and excellent exhibits on the Civil Rights Movement, particularly on the role of African-American women in Mississippi. (Open Mon.-Fri. 9am-5pm, Sat. 9am-noon, Sun. 2-5pm. $1, children 50¢.) Every Labor Day, the surrounding neighborhood celebrates African-American culture through art, theater, and food at the **Farish Street Festival** (960-1891).

Though a bit out of the way, the **Museum of the Southern Jewish Experience** (885-6042), 40 mi. south of Jackson at the UAHC Henry S. Jacobs Camp in Utica, is the only museum in the country that focuses on southern Jewry. Among other exhibits, a staggering map of the South shows where synagogues stood in the 18th and 19th centuries, but no longer operate due to the shrinking population of observant Jews in the area. (Call for directions and tour info. $3, seniors and kids $1.50.)

■■■ VICKSBURG

Vicksburg's verdant hills and prime Mississippi River location made it the focus of much strategic planning during the Civil War. President Abraham Lincoln called the town the "key," and maintained that the war "can never be brought to a close until that key is in our pocket." The Confederates' "Gibraltar of the South" fell to Union forces on July 4, 1863, after valiantly resisting a 47-day bombardment. The loss hit the city hard: Vicksburg refused to hold any 4th of July celebrations until the late 1940s. Today, Vicksburg embraces and doesn't shy away from its history. Downtown, 19th-century mansions house museums and Civil War monuments dominate the urban landscape. Lush parks give the city a relaxed, pastoral feel.

Practical Information You'll need a car to see most of Vicksburg. The bus station, the information center, downtown, and the far end of the sprawling military park mark the city's extremes. The **Tourist Information Center** (636-9421 or 800-221-3536), across the street from the park, has a helpful local map with info and locations for Vicksburg's sights (open daily 8am-5pm; in winter 9am-4pm). **Greyhound** (636-1230 or 800-231-2222) rides from a station inconveniently located at 1295 S. Frontage Rd. (open daily 7am-8:30pm). The **Rape and Sexual Assault Service** (638-0031) takes calls 24 hrs. Vicksburg's **post office:** (636-1822), on U.S. 61 at Pemberton Blvd. (open Mon.-Fri. 8:30am-5pm, Sat. 9am-noon); **ZIP code:** 39180; **area code:** 601.

Accommodations, Food, and Nightlife Inexpensive accommodations come easy in Vicksburg, except during the military park's July Fourth weekend battle reenactment (see below). One of the best deals in town, the **Beechwood Motel,**

4449 Rte. 80E (636-2271), offers cable and newly furnished rooms (singles $30, doubles $35). Rooms at the **Hillcrest Motel,** 40 Hwy. 80E (638-1491), come with plastic furniture and pool access (singles $24, doubles $28). Most hotels cluster near the park; don't expect to stay downtown, unless you choose the **Dixiana Motel,** 4033 Washington St. (636-9876; rooms $25-35). **River City RV Park,** 211 Miller St. (631-0388), provides 66 RV hookups, a pool, a gameroom, and a playground (sites $17).

While downtown, chow down at the **Burger Village,** 1220 Washington St. (638-0202), where a good meal comes in at under $5 (open Mon.-Thurs. 9am-6pm, Fri.-Sat. 9am-7pm). The popular **New Orleans Café,** 1100 Washington St. (638-8182), serves mouth-watering sandwiches (under $6), delectable Cajun specialties, seafood, and more (specials $6-16; open Mon.-Thurs. 11am-10pm, Fri.-Sat. 11am-2am). On weekends, the café's **Other Side Lounge** hosts live bands and a crowd of locals (open Fri.-Sat. 5:30pm-2am). Across the street, **Miller's Still Lounge,** 1101 Washington St. (638-8661), is a real Southern watering hole with blues and rock bands Thursday through Sunday (no cover; open Tues.-Sat. noon-2am, Sun. 5pm-2am).

Sights Memorials and markers of combat sites riddle the grassy 1700-acre **Vicksburg National Military Park** (636-0583; 800-221-3536 outside MS). The park blockades the eastern and northern edges of the city, with its entrance and visitors center on Clay St., about 1 mi. west of I-20's exit 4 (center open daily 8am-5pm; park open 7am-8pm). Driving through ($4 per car), you have three options: guide yourself with a free map available at the entrance, rent an informative cassette tape to guide you ($4.50), or have a real live person get in your car and take you through the sights ($20). Within the park, be sure to visit the **U.S.S. Cairo Museum** (636-2199). The Union boat, sunk in 1862, contains countless artifacts salvaged in the early 1960s (open daily 9:30am-6pm; off season 8am-5pm; free with park fee). Many consider the **Old Courthouse Museum,** 1008 Cherry St. (636-0741), one of the South's finest Civil War museums. During the siege of Vicksburg in 1863, Confederate troops used the cupola as a signal station and held Union prisoners in the upstairs courtroom. (Open Mon.-Sat. 8:30am-5pm, Sun. 1:30-5pm; early Oct.-early April Mon.-Sat. 8:30am-4:30pm, Sun. 1:30-4:30pm. $2, seniors $1.50, under 18 $1.)

Control of the mighty Mississippi River continues to preoccupy the military. A free tour, with or without a guide, of the **U.S. Army Engineer Waterways Experiment Station,** 3909 Halls Ferry Rd. (634-2502), the largest in the nation, explains the role of the Mississippi River in urban and rural development and the functions of locks and dams. A scale model of the dam system of Niagara Falls occupies the floor of one entire room. (Guided tours daily 10am and 2pm. Open daily 7:45am-4:15pm. Free.) Taste the lighter side of Vicksburg history, 2 blocks away, at the **Museum of Coca-Cola History and Memorabilia** and the **Biedenharn Candy Company,** 1107 Washington St. (638-6514), which first bottled the soft drink. The two-room museum displays Coke memorabilia from as far back as 1894, but, considering it takes 10 minutes to look around, the price is a bit steep. The museum does sell tasty Coke floats, along with over 100 different Coca-Cola items. (Open Mon.-Sat. 9am-5pm, Sun. 1:30-4:30pm. $1.75, under 12 $1.25.) Across the street from the Coke museum, a man known as **Johnny Reb** carves foot-tall caricatures of Civil War luminaries at a shop inside **Wilson's Hardware,** 1108 Washington St. (636-7602). Anyone who visits Vicksburg should go see Johnny's work. (Open daily 9am-5pm.)

Vicksburg's finest contribution to the historical home circuit, the **Martha Vick House,** 1300 Grove St. (638-7036), was home to the daughter of the city's founder,

It's not easy being green...

The creator of the Muppets, Jim Henson, hung his hat in **Greenville,** 90 mi. north of Vicksburg. His fuzzy, original creations (including the Swedish Chef and Chester the Rat) live on at the **Jim Henson Museum** (686-2687), intersection of Rte. 82 and S. Deer Creek, 7 mi. east in **Leland.** (Open Memorial Day-Labor Day Mon.-Fri. 10am-4pm, Sat.-Sun. 1-5pm. Free, but donations are appreciated.)

Reverend Newitt Vick (open Mon.-Sat. 9am-5pm. $5, under 12 free). The **Holidays Washateria and Lanes,** 2900 Clay St. (636-9682), on Rte. 80 near the river and Riverfront Park, shines with the sparkle of classic Americana—it's a bowling alley, a pool room, and a laundromat all in one! Bowl a game ($1.75 per person) and clean your socks (wash 75¢; dry 25¢) at the same time. (Open Mon.-Fri. 9am-11pm, Sat. 10am-midnight, Sun. 1-10pm.)

■■■ NATCHEZ

Around the turn of the 19th century, Natchez stood out as one of the wealthiest settlements on the Mississippi. Of the thirteen millionaires in Mississippi at the time, eleven had their cotton plantations here; the custom was to build a manor on the Mississippi side of the River, and till the soil on the Louisiana side. After the Civil War, the cotton-based economy of the South crumbled and the days of the mansion-building-magnates passed. Many of the homes remain, however, allowing visitors to Natchez the opportunity to gaze at elegant dwellings from a vanished era.

Practical Information Housed in an antique-filled home, the **Mississippi Welcome Center,** 370 Sergeant Prentiss Dr. (442-5849), does its thing with southern hospitality. Pick up maps, discount books, suggested tours, and even let them book your hotel. (Open daily 8am-8pm; Labor Day-Memorial Day 8am-5pm.) Make connections to Vicksburg (1 per day, 1hr., $14) and New Orleans (2 per day, 3hr., $35) at the **Natchez Bus Station,** 103 Lower Woodville Rd. (445-5291; open Mon.-Sat. 8am-5:30pm, Sun. 2-5pm). In-town transportation is available from **Natchez Ford Rental** (445-0060) for $38 per day plus 20¢ per mi. (must be 21 with major credit card or $250 cash deposit). The **Natchez Bicycling Center,** 334 Main St. (446-7794), rents vehicles of the two-wheeled variety. ($7.50 for 1-3hr., $10 for 3-5hr., $14 for all day. Must be 14 or accompanied by an adult 18 or older. Open Tues.-Fri. 10am-3pm, Sat. 10am-4pm; other times by appointment.) Natchez's **post office:** 214 N. Canal St. (442-4361; open Mon.-Fri. 8:30am-5pm, Sat. 10am-2pm); **ZIP code:** 39120; **area code:** 601.

Accommodations and Food The intersection of Rte. 61 and Highland Blvd. supports lots of good quality, cheap rooms. **Scottish Inns,** 40 Sgt. Prentiss Dr. (442-9141 or 800-251-1962), has spacious, clean rooms with wood furniture (singles $33, doubles $38). Just down the road, the **Days Inn,** 109 Highway 61 S. (800-524-4892), rents chain-motel singles for $42 and doubles for $47; call for possible discounts. Campers should settle in at the secluded **campground** in **Natchez State Park** (442-2658), less than 10 mi. north of Natchez on U.S. 61 in Stanton. The park has 22 sites, six with full RV hookup ($11) and the rest for less-evolved camping ($6).

A multitude of cafés and diners serve budget eats in Natchez. **Cock of the Walk,** 200 N. Broadway (446-8920), earns its title and stature with spicy catfish and baked potatoes. (Catfish fillet $9. Open Mon.-Thurs. 5-9pm, Fri.-Sat. 5-10pm, Sun. 5-8pm.) At the corner of Washington and Canal St., **Depot Deli** (442-6500) puts together po'boys ($5) and other deli-style sandwiches on a huge porch with live music (open daily 10am-5pm). Try regional specialties such as Cajun boudin sausage, chili, peanut butter pie, and Gringo Pie (tamales with cheese, onions, and jalapeno peppers, $5) at **Fat Mama's Tamales,** 500 S. Canal St. (442-4548). The "knock-you-naked" margarita ($3.25) is a perfect way to wash it all down. (Open Mon.-Wed. 11am-7pm, Thurs.-Sat. 11am-9pm, Sun. noon-5pm.)

Sights **Natchez Pilgrimage Tours,** P.O. Box 347 (446-6631 or 800-647-6742), on the corner of Canal St. and State St., supervises tours of the restored manors left from Natchez's "white gold" days. Pick up free tour schedules, maps, and pamphlets, or their guidebook ($5) which details the histories of the homes. (Open Mon.-Sat. 9am-5pm, Sun. 12:30-5pm.) While the individual houses sell tour tickets ($5), Pilgrimage Tours offers discount packages for multiple manors (3 houses $14,

4 houses $17, 5 houses $19; children ½-price). For a faster view of the city and the mansion exteriors, Pilgrimage Tours also sells tickets for a 35-minute horse-drawn-carriage tour ($8) and a 55-minute air-conditioned bus tour ($10).

The largest octagonal house in America, **Longwood,** 140 Lower Woodville Rd. (442-5193), astounds visitors with its creative, elaborate decor and imaginative floor-plan. Yet, the six-story edifice, designed to be an "Arabian palace," remains unfinished; the builders, hired from the North, abandoned work at the beginning of the Civil War to fight for the Union. They never returned, and their discarded tools and undisturbed crates still lie as they were left. (Tours every 20min. Open daily 9am-4:30pm.) **Stanton Hall,** 401 High St. (442-6282), on the other hand, arose under the direction of local Natchez architects and artisans. Completed in 1857, the mansion regales the visitor with French mirrors, Italian marble mantels, and specially-cut chandeliers. (Tours every ½-hr. Open daily 9am-4:30pm.)

For centuries before the rise of such opulence, the Natchez Indians flourished on this fertile land. The arrival of the French incited fighting in the 1720s and 1730s, and French military successes brought an end to the thriving Natchez community. The **Grand Village of the Natchez Indians,** 400 Jefferson Davis Blvd. (446-6502), pays homage to the tribe with a museum that documents their history and culture. The museum sits atop one of several huge tribal burial mounds which dominate the area. When the Great Sun, or chief, of the tribe died, his wife and others who so desired were strangled and buried in the same mound; the house of the chief's successor was then built on top. (Open Mon.-Sat. 9am-5pm, Sun. 1:30-5pm. Free.)

The first educational institution in the Mississippi Territory, historic **Jefferson College** (442-2901), 6 mi. east of Natchez off U.S. 61 near U.S. 84E, hosted the treason trial of Aaron Burr, Vice-President under Thomas Jefferson, in 1807. Fortunately for Burr, the judges couldn't be found for sentencing; Burr escaped into the night and was later acquitted in Virginia. (Grounds open daily sunrise-sunset. Buildings open Mon.-Sat. 9am-5pm, Sun. 1-5pm. Free.)

Combining history with natural beauty, the **Natchez Trace Parkway** leads north from Natchez to Nashville, TN. The Parkway rambles through lush forests, swamps, and shady countryside, passing through historic landmarks and a beautiful national park along the way. The Mississippi River floats nearby, a gentle companion in the sleepy, scenic South.

Louisiana

Legend has it that after exploring the Mississippi River valley in 1682, Frenchman René-Robert Cavalier stuck a cross in the ground and proclaimed the land "Louisiane," in honor of Louis XIV. The name remained, although King Louis' ownership of the region did not. For a little more than a century after Cavalier's journey, the area was tossed around (sometimes forcibly, sometimes secretly) between France, England, and Spain before arriving in the hands of Thomas Jefferson and the United States in 1803. Each successive reign lured a new group of settlers searching for a tolerant government: Spaniards came from the Canary Islands, French Acadians from Nova Scotia created Acadiana (see p. 381), and U.S. ownership attracted whites and free blacks from the West Indies. The descendants of these diverse populations mix and mingle here today—in Louisiana you'll find folks wailing the blues on one side of town and dancing to zydeco on the other, or a family cooking up pecan pie and chicken-fried steak while a neighbor's gumbo simmers next door.

PRACTICAL INFORMATION

Capital: Baton Rouge.

Louisiana Office of Tourism: P.O. Box 94291, Baton Rouge 70804-9421 (504-342-8119 or 800-633-6970). Open Mon.-Fri. 9am-5pm. **Office of State Parks,** P.O. Box 44426, Baton Rouge 70804. Open Mon.-Fri. 9am-5pm.
Time Zone: Central (1hr. behind Eastern). **Postal Abbreviation:** LA
Sales Tax: 8%.

■■■ NEW ORLEANS

New Orleans stands as a country unto itself. Originally explored by the French, *La Nouvelle Orleans* was secretly ceded to the Spanish in 1762 (the citizens didn't realize until four years later). Spain returned the city to France just in time for Thomas Jefferson to purchase it in 1803. N'Awlins stayed faithful, and in 1812, Louisiana was admitted to the Union. Multiculturalism rules here; Spanish courtyards, Victorian verandas, Acadian jambalaya, Caribbean Gumbo, and French beignets mix and mingle to create an atmosphere unlike any other. Don't try to place the local accent—it's a combination found nowhere else. Similarly unique, New Orleans's internationally-renowned jazz fuses African rhythms and modern brass.

New Orleans loves to party, and come late February there's no escaping the month-long celebration of Mardi Gras, the apotheosis of the city's already festive atmosphere. Anxious to accrue as much sin as spirit and flesh will allow before Lent, perfect strangers, in all stages of undress, embrace each other, ostensibly to acquire multi-colored beads and doubloons. The "city that care forgot" promenades, shuffles, sings, and swigs until Ash Wednesday. Afterwards, the soulful jazz melodies play on, comforting those who have forsaken drunken cavorting for the next 40 long and Lenten days. The New Orleans Jazz and Heritage Festival provides a post-Lenten party that rivals the excitement of Mardi Gras but stays a bit more mature.

PRACTICAL INFORMATION

Tourist Office: Write or call ahead to the very helpful **New Orleans/Louisiana Tourist Center,** 529 St. Ann (F.Q. C3; 568-5661), at Jackson Sq. in the French Quarter. Free city and walking tour maps. Open daily 10am-6pm. **Greater New Orleans Tourist and Convention Commission,** 1520 Sugar Bowl Dr., New Orleans 70112 (N.O. C3; 566-5011), on the main floor of the Superdome. Open Mon.-Fri. 9am-5pm.

Airport: Moisant International (464-0831), 15mi. west of the city. Cab fare to the Quarter is set at $21 for 2 people. **Louisiana Transit Authority** (737-9611; open 8:30am-4:30pm) runs to downtown at Elk and Tulane Ave. (approx. 45min.); Mon.-Sat. every hr. 6am-6pm; $1.10 in exact change. Pick-up on the upper level, near the exit ramp.

Trains: Amtrak, Good morning America, how are ya! 1001 Loyola Ave. (F.Q. B1; 528-1610 or 800-872-7245), in the Union Passenger Terminal a 10-min. walk to Canal St. via Elk. To: Houston (3 per week, 8hr., $73); Jackson (5 per week, 4hr., $42); Atlanta (3 per week, 12hr., $95). Station open 24 hrs.; ticket office open Mon., Wed., and Fri. 5am-8pm, Tues., Thurs., and Sun. 8am-11pm, Sat. 8am-8pm. Dontcha ya' know me, I'm your native son.

Buses: Greyhound, 1001 Loyola Ave. (F.Q. B1; 524-7571 or 800-231-2222), in Union Passenger Terminal. To: Austin (5 per day, 13hr., $79); Baton Rouge (8 per day, 1½hr., $13). Open 24 hrs.

Public Transportation: Regional Transit Authority (RTA), 700 Plaza Dr. (569-2700, for 24-hr. route information). Most buses pass Canal St., at the edge of the French Quarter. Major buses and streetcars run 24 hrs. Fare $1, seniors and disabled passengers 40¢; transfers 10¢. 1-day passes $4, 3-day passes $8. Office has bus schedules and transit info; open Mon.-Fri. 8:30am-5pm.

Those with an eastern accent: It's not pronounced (NU or-LEEEEns); elide the first two syllables; work on (NOHR-lens)—like *nor*-mal.

Taxis: United Cabs, 522-9771. **Checker Yellow Cabs,** 943-2411. $2.10 base fare, $1.20 per mi. 75¢ per additional person.

Car Rental: Budget, 1317 Canal St. (F.Q. B1; 467-2277), and 4 other locations. $37 per day with 100 free mi. Must be 25 with credit card. Open daily 7:30am-5:30pm. Reservations suggested.

Bike Rental: Michael's, 622 Frenchmen St. (N.O. C2; 945-9505), a few blocks west of the Quarter. $3.50 per hr., $12.50 per day, weekly rates available. Car racks available. Must have major credit card for deposit. Open Mon.-Sat. 10am-7pm, Sun. 10am-5pm.

Crisis Lines: Crisis Line, 523-2673. **Rape Hotline,** 483-8888. Both 24 hrs.

Emergency: 911.

Post Office: 701 Loyola Ave. (F.Q. A2; 589-1111 or 589-1112), near the Union Passenger Terminal. Open Mon.-Fri. 8am-6pm, Sat. 8am-noon. **ZIP code:** 70113. **Area code:** 504.

ORIENTATION

New Orleans, though fairly small, can be very confusing. The city's main streets follow the curve of the **Mississippi River,** hence the nickname "the crescent city." Directions from locals show further watery influences—lakeside means north, referring to **Lake Ponchartrain,** and riverside means south. Uptown lies to the west, up river; downtown lies down river. Many streets run only one way; watch out for drivers who make U-turns to cross intersections. Tourists flock to the small **French Quarter (Vieux Carré),** bounded by the Mississippi River, **Canal St., Esplanade Ave.,** and **Rampart St.** downtown. Streets in the Quarter follow a grid pattern, making foot travel easy. The best way to get downtown fast, the St. Charles Streetcar, runs 24 hrs. between the Quarter and areas uptown ($1). Streetcars goes out to **Lee**

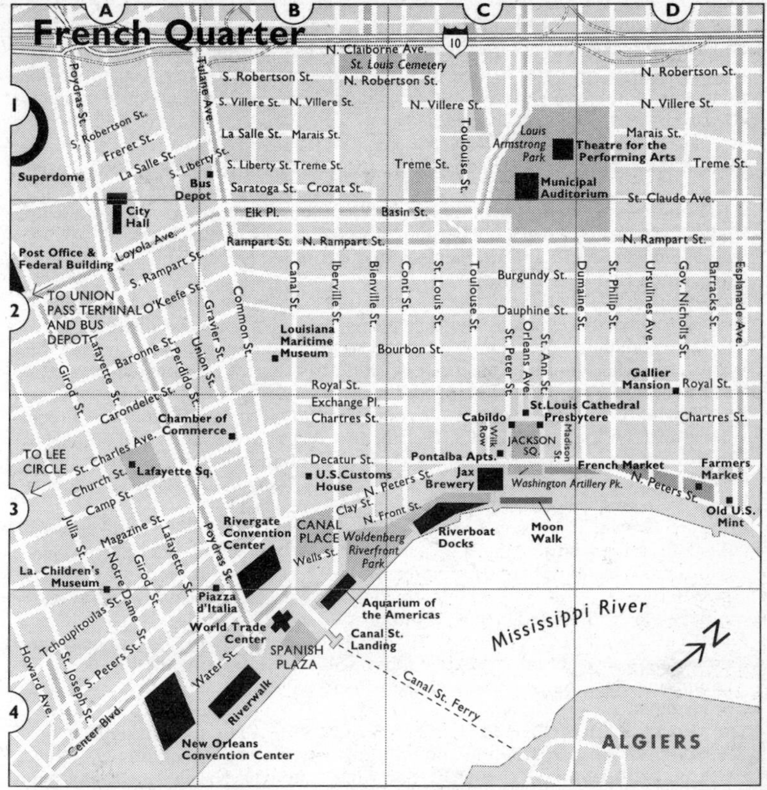

Circle at **Howard Ave.** (a convenient spot for shoppers to get off), through **Audubon Park,** and up **South Carrollton Ave.** Buses to all parts of the city pass by Canal St. at the edge of the Quarter. The **Garden District** is situated west of downtown.

New Orleans struggles to play down its high murder and crime rates, but avoid areas where you feel at all uncomfortable; do not walk around alone at night anywhere in this city. The tenement areas directly to the north of the French Quarter and directly northwest of Lee Circle pose particular threats to personal safety. At night, even quaint-looking side streets in the Quarter can be dangerous—stick to busy, well-lit roads and look as little like a tourist as possible (don't wear shorts). Take a cab to your lodgings when returning from the Quarter late at night. African and African-American travelers should be aware that racial tensions exist in the city.

Coordinates in the text match locations in New Orleans to their locations on *Let's Go's* **maps** of the city. Map coordinates preceded by "N.O." denote placement the New Orleans map; those preceded by "F.Q." are keyed to the French Quarter map.

Parking in New Orleans is easier than driving in it. To park near the French Quarter for as long as you like, head for the residential area around **Marigny St.** and **Royal St.,** where many streets have no meters and no restrictions.

ACCOMMODATIONS

Finding inexpensive yet decent rooms in the French Quarter is as difficult as finding a sober person on Mardi Gras; luckily, other parts of the city compensate for the dearth of cheap lodging downtown. Several **hostels** pepper the area and cater to the young and almost penniless, as do **B&Bs** near the Garden District.

Accommodations for **Mardi Gras** get booked up to a year in advance, and **The Jazz Festival** makes budget rooms reasonably scarce. During peak times, proprietors will rent out any extra space—be sure you know what you're paying for. Rates tend to sink in June and early December when accommodations become desperate for business; try to negotiate a deal.

Marquette House New Orleans International Hostel (HI-AYH), 2253 Carondelet St. (N.O. C3; 523-3014). The cleanest hosteling experience in New Orleans. 160 new, comfy beds. Clean, homey kitchens and study rooms. Exceptionally quiet for a hostel. No alcohol permitted; smoking only in the courtyard. $12.50, nonmembers $15.50. Private rooms with queen-sized bed and pull-out sofa $39/$45. Linen $2.50. Key deposit $5.

India House, 124 S. Lopez St. (N.O. B2; 821-1904). If you've come to New Orleans for its bawdy entertainment, this bohemian haunt is party central. Spacious, comfortable common room with pictures and artwork from past visitors covering the walls. Late check-out time (1pm) designed for those with "morning grogginess." $12 per night. Free linens. Key deposit $5.

St. Charles Guest House, 1748 Prytania St. (N.O. C3; 523-6556). In a serene neighborhood near the Garden District and St. Charles streetcar. A big three-building complex with 38 rooms. Lovely pool and sunbathing deck, with (recorded) classical music. Small backpacker's singles with no A/C $15-25. Rooms with 1 queen-sized bed or 2 twins $45-65. Free breakfast.

Longpre House, 1726 Prytania St. (N.O. C3; 581-4540), in a 154-year-old house 1 block off the streetcar route; a 25-min. walk from the Quarter. Attracts travelers with a relaxed atmosphere. Free coffee. Dorm check-in 8am-10pm, after 11am for private rooms. Dorms $16, with international passport or student ID $12. Singles and doubles with shared bath $35, with private scrub-a-dub $40.

Hotel LaSalle, 1113 Canal St. (N.O. B1; 523-5831 or 800-521-9450), 4 blocks from Bourbon St. downtown. Attractive lobby with coffee on an antique sideboard around the clock. Singles $29, with bath $49; doubles $39/$59. Reservations recommended.

Old World Inn, 1330 Prytania St. (N.O. C3; 566-1330). A clean, comfortable house with multi-colored carpeting and painting-covered walls. The owners (New Orleans natives) can tell you what's hot, what's not, what's safe, what isn't. Complimentary breakfast. Singles $30, with bath $49; doubles $49/$55.

Prytania Inn, 1415 Prytania St. (N.O. C3; 566-1515). Includes 3 restored 19th-century homes about 5 blocks from each other; stay in St. Vincent's if you can. Reasonable prices, multilingual staff (German, French, Italian, Spanish, and Japanese spoken). Singles $30-45, doubles $35-55. Breakfast $5; served Mon.-Fri. 8-10am, Sat.-Sun. 8-10:30am.

CAMPING

The few campgrounds near New Orleans are tough to reach via public transportation. Travelers with wheels, however, have several options.

KOA West, 11129 Jefferson Hwy., River Ridge 70123 (467-1792), off I-10; RTA bus transport available. Shuttle to French Quarter ($3) leaves 9am and returns 4pm. Pool, laundry facilities. Bathrooms new and very clean. Tent sites for 2 $22, with full hookup $26.

St. Bernard State Park, P.O. Box 534, Violet 70092 (682-2101), 18mi. southeast of New Orleans; take Rte. 46S and go right on Rte. 39. Nearest public transport to New Orleans ½mi. away. Registration until 8pm, weekends 10pm. 51 sites $12.

Willow Mar Travel Park, 10910 Chef Menteur Hwy. (242-6611; 800-788-6787 outside LA), 3mi. east of the junction of I-10 and U.S. 90 (Chef Menteur Hwy.). Near public transport into the city. Pool, showers, and laundry facilities. Sites $12, with full hookup $16.

Parc D'Orleans Travel Park, 7676 Chef Menteur Hwy. (241-3167 or 800-535-2598), near the intersection of U.S. 90 and I-10. 71 small but orderly sites and a pool. Sites with water and electricity $14, with full hookup $16.

FOOD

New Orleans has more restaurants per capita than any major city in the world outside of Paris. In addition to the international options which entice hungry visitors, the city offers a long list of regional specialties which have evolved from the combination of Acadian, Spanish, Italian, African-American, and Native American ethnic cuisines. Here, the Acadian hot, spicy, **Cajun** culinary style—like a good stew—has a bit of everything thrown in. **Jambalaya**—a jumble of rice, shrimp, oysters, and ham or chicken mixed with spices—and the stew-like African **gumbo** grace practically every menu in New Orleans. A southern breakfast of grits, eggs, bacon, and corn bread satisfies even the most ardent eaters. **Creole cuisine,** a mixture of Spanish, French, and Carribean is famous for red beans and rice, **po'boys** (a french-bread sandwich filled with sliced meat, particularly seafood, and vegetables), and shrimp or crawfish **étouffé.** The daring go to **Ralph & Kacoos Seafood Restaurant,** 519 Toulouse St. (F.Q. C3; 522-5226), order the **crawfish,** and eat it the way the locals do: tear off the head and suck out the tasty juices. (Hey, when in Rome…) Finally, you may *not* leave New Orleans without dining on **beignets** and **café au lait** (or milk with a dash of coffee) at the world-famous, 1862 **Café du Monde** (see below).

Some of the best and cheapest **Creole pralines** ($1) come from **Laura's Candies,** 600 Conti (F.Q. C3; 525-3880; open daily 9am-7pm), and 155 Royal St. (F.Q. B2; 525-3886; open daily 9am-5pm). The **French Market** (F.Q. D3), between Decatur and N. Peters St. on the east side of the French Quarter, sells pricey fresh vegetables and everything else under the sun.

If the eats in the Quarter prove too trendy, touristy, or tough on your budget, take a jaunt down **Magazine St.,** where cafés, antique stores, and book fairs spill onto the sidewalk, or catch a streetcar uptown to the **Tulane University** (N.O. B3) area for some late-night grub and collegiate character.

French Quarter

Acme Oyster House, 724 Iberville (F.Q. B2; 522-5973). Slurp fresh oysters shucked before your eyes (6 for $3.75, 12 for $6.50) or sit at the red checkered tables for a good ol' po'boy ($5-6). Open Mon.-Sat. 11am-10pm, Sun. noon-7pm.

Café du Monde, 200 Decatur St. (F.Q. D3; 587-0835), near the French Market. The consummate people-watching paradise since 1862. The café really only does two things—café au lait ($1) and hot beignets ($1)—but boy, oh boy, they sure crank them out. Absolutely delicious. Open 24 hrs. To take home some of that chickory coffee visit the **Café du Monde Gift Shop,** 1039 Decatur St., (581-2914 or 800-772-2927). 15oz. of the grind $4.50. Open daily 9:30am-6pm.

Central Grocery, 923 Decatur St. (F.Q. C3; 523-1620). Try an authentic **muffuletta** at the place that invented them. A half ($3.75) serves 1, and a whole ($7) serves 2 or some big, hairy guy. Open Mon.-Sat. 8am-5:30pm, Sun. 9am-5:30pm.

Olde N'awlins Cookery, 729 Conti (F.Q. C2; 529-3663), between Bourbon and Royal. Scrumptious crawfish étouffé $15.50; sincere turtle soup $4. Entrees $14-19, but well worth it. Open daily 11am-11pm.

Gumbo Shop, 630 St. Peter (F.Q. C2; 525-1486). Sit under a broad-leafed palm and savor a bowl of seafood okra gumbo or chicken andouille gumbo (each $5.50). Entrees $5.50-15. Expect a line. Recipes available. Open daily 11am-11pm.

Croissant d'Or, 617 Ursuline St. (F.Q. D3; 524-4663). The historic building was the first ice cream parlor in New Orleans. Delicious, reasonably-priced French pastries. Carré Mocca and Chocolate Mousse each $1.75. Open daily 7am-5pm.

Country Flame, 620 Iberville St. (F.Q. B3; 528-1138). No, it's not a country-western bar; it's a terrific Mexican restaurant with very low prices (2 tacos $2.25) and a laid-back atmosphere. Dig those cafeteria-style plastic plates. Open Mon.-Thurs. 11am-10pm, Fri.-Sun. 11am-1am.

Mama Rosa's, 616 North Rampart (F.Q. C2; 523-5546). Locals croon in praise over this Italian ristorante and gay hangout. Rosa's pizza was recently rated one of the nine best in the country by *People Magazine*…a true stamp of fine American dining. 14" cheese pie $9.25. Open Tues.-Thurs. 10:30am-10:30pm, Fri.-Sun. 10:30am-11:30pm.

Outside The Quarter

Mother's Restaurant, 401 Poydras St. (F.Q. A3; 523-9656), 4 blocks southwest of Bourbon St. Serving up roast beef and ham po'boys ($6-9) to locals for almost half a century. Try the crawfish or shrimp *étouffé* omelette ($8). Tremendous entrees $6-15. Open Mon.-Sat. 5am-10pm, Sun. 7am-10pm.

Pie in the Sky, 1818 Magazine St. (N.O. B4; 522-6291). Artwork by locals hangs on the pastel walls of this very hip, very tasty pizza joint. A traditional cheese pie goes for $10, but it's far more fun to make creative topping choices. Great salads and focaccia sandwiches too. Open Mon.-Sat. 11:30am-11pm, Sun. noon-10pm.

All Natural, 5517 Magazine St. (N.O. B4; 891-2651). This friendly neighborhood health store cooks up fabulous and healthy sandwiches, pizzas, and hot specials ($3-5). Probably the only place in the world which serves vegetarian jambalaya (with salad $5) and rye grass juice. Open Mon.-Sat. 10am-8pm, Sun. 9am-6pm.

Café Atchafalaya, 901 Louisiana Ave. (N.O. C4; 891-5271). Take the "Magazine St." bus. A cozy, homestyle restaurant with mouth-watering food. Simple dishes like red beans and rice ($6) or lamb chops will make you cry for joy, and question the cooking at home. You can't go wrong. Cobblers galore. Open Tues.-Thurs. 11:30am-2pm and 5:30-9pm, Fri. 11:30am-2pm and 5:30-10pm, Sat. 8:30am-2pm and 5:30-10pm, Sun. 8:30am-2pm.

Tee Eva's, 4430 Magazine St. (N.O. B4; 899-8350). Tee attracts locals with peerless pies and sizzlin' soul food. 3-in. sweet potato, cream cheese pecan, or plain pecan pie $1.25. Large 9-in. pies $8-12, by order only. Soul food lunches change daily ($5). Open daily 11am-8pm.

Dunbar's, 4927 Freret St. (N.O. C3; 899-0734), at Robert St. Breakfast, lunch, and dinner soul-food style. Sit next to the Tulane football team and gorge yourself on cabbage and candied yams or all-you-can-eat red beans and chicken (each $4). Kind of a risky area; go when the sun shines. Open Mon.-Sat. 7am-9pm.

Franky and Johnny's, 321 Arabella (N.O. B4; 899-9146), southwest of downtown towards Tulane off Tchoupitoulas St. A hole-in-the-wall with great onion rings ($3.50) and boiled crawfish (2 lbs. $4, Nov.-June). Open Mon.-Thurs. 11am-11pm, Fri.-Sat. 11am-midnight, Sun. 11am-10pm.

Camellia Grill, 626 S. Carrollton Ave. (N.O. A3; 866-9573). Take the St. Charles streetcar away from the Quarter to the Tulane area. One of the finest diners in America and the safest, best, late-night bet. Have the chef's special omelette ($7) or partake of the pecan pie ($2.45). Expect a wait on weekend mornings. Open Sun.-Wed. 8am-1am, Thurs.-Sat. 8am-2am.

Uglesich's, 1238 Baronne St. (N.O. C3; 523-8571). Their spicy, local dishes will certainly curl your toes. Off the beaten path, but well worth the trip. Family-owned and managed since 1924. Gumbo $4.75. Bring your wallet; entrees can get pricey. Open Mon.-Fri. 9:30am-4pm.

SIGHTS

French Quarter

Allow yourself *at least* a full day (some take a lifetime) in the Quarter. The oldest section of the city is famous for its ornate wrought-iron balconies, French, Spanish, and uniquely New Orleans architecture, and a joyous atmosphere. Known as the **Vieux Carré** (view-ca-RAY), meaning Old Square, the historic district of New Orleans offers interesting used book and record stores, museums, and about a zillion tourist shops. The farther you get from **Bourbon St.,** the more clearly you'll hear the variety of street musicians. Stroll down **Royal St.** to **Madame Lalaurie's "haunted house,"** at 1140 Royal (F.Q. D2), a socialite's mansion in which firefighters discovered slaves chained and tortured in the attic. A mob ran Madame Lalaurie out of town, but rumor has it that the screams of slaves can still be heard. The residential section down **Dumaine St.** features less intriguing but equally pretty houses.

The heart of the Quarter beats at **Jackson Sq.,** (F.Q. C3) centered around a bronze equestrian statue of General Andrew Jackson, victor of the Battle of New Orleans. While the square jumps and jives with artists, mimes, musicians, psychics, magicians, and con artists, the **St. Louis Cathedral,** 615 Pere Anoine Alley (525-9585), presides at its head (cathedral tours every Mon.-Fri. 15-20min. 9am-5pm). The historic **French Market** (F.Q. D3; 522-2621) takes up several city blocks just northeast of Jackson Sq. Vendors sell everything from watermelons to earrings. If you want touristy t-shirts that say "New Orleans" they'll have them, but the market is not a recently-conceived tourist trap. On the contrary, the French Market has been operating in the same spot since 1791—long before tacky shorts, laminated maps, and disposable cameras. (Open daily 9am-8pm.) Stop in at the market's **visitors center** (596-3424), on Dumaine St. at the river (open daily 9am-6pm).

The **Jean Lafitte National Historical Park and Preserve,** 916-918 North Peters (589-2636), headquartered in the back section of the French Market at Dumaine and St. Phillip St., recognizes the rich cultural heritage of the French Quarter. The park conducts free 90-minute walking tours, which emphasize aspects of New Orleans's cultural, ethnic, and environmental history, through the Quarter (daily 10:30, 11:30am, and 2:30pm) and into the Garden District (2:30pm; reservations required). Call ahead for specific info.

Though the Park Service no longer leads tours of the city's cemeteries (these areas have been deemed unsafe), the **New Orleans Historic Voodoo Museum,** 724 Dumaine St. (F.Q. C2; 523-7685), continues to bring visitors foul in heart and experienced with the evil eye right onto local burial grounds (tours $12-18; museum open daily 10am-dusk; admission $5.35). Tourists of pure heart should opt for the **Hidden Treasures Cemetery Tour** (529-4507), which visits New Orleans's original St. Louis cemetery #1. Tours ($12) last about an hour and depart at 9am daily from The Ultimate Coffee Shop, 417 Bienville St. (B3; 524-7417). Free coffee for those who live to see the next sunrise.

At the very southwest corner of the Quarter, the **Aquarium of the Americas** (F.Q. B4; 861-2538), Waldenberg Park by the World Trade Center, houses an amazing collection of sealife and birds. Among the 500 species you'll see black-footed penguins, endangered sea turtles, and the world's only white alligators. The steamboat **John Audubon** (586-8777) shuttles between the aquarium and the Audubon Zoo. (see below) four times each day. (From the aquarium 10am, noon, 2, and 4pm; from the zoo 11am, 1, 3, and 5pm; $9.50, children $4.75; round-trip $12.50/$6.25; package tours including cruise, zoo, and aquarium from $26.50/$13.25.).

Before You Die, Read This:

Being dead in New Orleans has always been a problem. Because the city lies 4 to 6 ft. below sea level, a 6-ft. hole in the earth fills up with 5 ft. of water. Coffins used to literally **float in the graves,** while cemetery workers pushed them down with long wooden poles. One early solution was to **bore holes in the coffins,** allowing them to sink. Unfortunately, the sight of a drowning coffin coupled with the **awful gargling sound** of its immersion proved too much for the squeamish families of the departed. Burial soon became passé, and stiffs were laid to rest in beautiful raised stone tombs. Miles and miles of **creepy, cool marble tombs** now fill the city's graveyards and its ghost stories.

Outside The Quarter

If you're not sure there's more to New Orleans than the French Quarter, take in the city from the 31st floor of the **World Trade Center,** 2 Canal St. (F.Q. B4; 525-2185), in the southernmost corner of the Quarter, at the "foot of Canal St." where the riverboats dock ($2, seniors $1.50, ages 6-12 $1; open daily 9am-5pm). The **Riverwalk** (F.Q. B4), a multi-million dollar conglomeration of overpriced shops originally built as a venue for the 1984 World's Fair, ambles through this area overlooking the port. Combining entertainment and a cooking lesson with an unbeatable meal, the **Cookin' Cajun New Orleans Cooking School,** 116 Riverwalk (586-8832), prepares Cajun or Creole creations before your eyes for your edification and consumption. Call ahead for the menu of the day, or just drop by and sample one of their 18 hot sauces. (Open Mon.-Sat. 11am-1pm. 2-hr. class $15.) For a 25-minute view of the

Mississippi River and a bite of African-American history, take the free **Canal Street Ferry** to Algiers Point (F.Q. D4); Algiers of old housed many of New Orleans's free people of color (ferry runs until about 9pm).

Relatively new in the downtown area, the **Warehouse Arts District,** (F.Q. A3, A4), on Julia St. between Commerce and Baronne, contains revitalized warehouse buildings which house contemporary art galleries inside historic architecture. Exhibits range from Southern folk art to experimental sculpture. Individual galleries distribute maps of the area. The **Contemporary Arts Center,** 900 Camp St. (N.O. C3; 523-1216), in an old brick building with a modern glass and chrome façade, mounts exhibits ranging from the cryptic to the puzzling; at least the architecture within is amazing and reasonably easy to appreciate. (Open Mon.-Sat. 10am-5pm, Sun. 11am-5pm. $3, students and seniors $2, under 12 free.)

Though much of the Crescent City's fame derives from the **Vieux Carré,** areas uptown have their fair share of beauty and action. The streetcar named "Desire" saw its day long ago, but the **St. Charles Streetcar** still runs west of the French Quarter, passing some of the city's finest buildings, including the elegant, mint-condition 19th-century homes along **St. Charles Ave.** ($1). Fans of fancy living should disembark in the **Garden District** (N.O. C3), an opulent neighborhood between Jackson and Louisiana Ave. The legacies of French, Italian, Spanish, and American architecture create an extraordinary combination of structures, colors, ironworks, and, of course, exquisite gardens. Watch for houses raised several feet above the ground for protection from the swamp on which New Orleans stands.

The St. Charles Streetcar eventually makes its way to **Audubon Park** (N.O. B4), across from Tulane University. Designed by Frederick Law Olmsted—the architect who planned New York City's Central Park—Audubon contains lagoons, statues, stables, and the awesome and award-winning **Audubon Zoo** (N.O. A4; 861-2537), where the world's only white alligators (wait a second...) swim in a re-created Louisiana swamp. A free museum shuttle glides from the park entrance (streetcar stop #36) to the zoo. (Zoo open daily 9:30am-5pm. $7.75, seniors and ages 2-12 $3.75.)

One of the most unique sights in the New Orleans area, the coastal wetlands along Lake Salvador make up a segment of the **Jean Lafitte National Historical Park** called the **Barataria Preserve,** 7400 Hwy. 45 (589-2330), off the West Bank Expwy. across the Mississippi River down Barataria Blvd. (Rte. 45). The only park-sponsored tour through the swamp leaves, on foot, at 1:15 every day (free). Countless commercial boat tours operate outside and around the park; **Bayou Segnette Swamp Tours** (561-8244) does its 2-hr. bit for $20 per person, $12 for children. They'll pick you up from your hotel for an extra $20. Tour times change seasonally; call for details.

Museums

Louisiana State Museum, P.O. Box 2448 (568-6968), oversees 4 separate museums: the **Old U.S. Mint,** 400 Esplanade (F.Q. D3); the **Cabildo,** 701 Chartres St. (F.Q. C3); **Presbytère,** 751 Chartres St. (F.Q. C3); and **1850 House,** 523 St. Ann St. (F.Q. C3). All four contain artifacts, papers, and other changing exhibits on the history of Louisiana and New Orleans. The Old U.S. Mint is particularly interesting, focusing not on currency (as you might expect) but on the history of jazz and the lives of jazz greats like Louis "Satchmo" Armstrong. All open Tues.-Sun. 9am-5pm. Pass to 1 $4/$3; pass to all 4 $10, seniors $7.50; under 13 free.

New Orleans Museum of Art (N.O. B2; 488-2631), in City Park. Take the Esplanade bus from Canal and Rampart St. This magnificent museum houses the arts of North and South America, a small collection of local decorative arts, opulent works by the jeweler Fabergé, and a strong collection of French paintings with work by Degas. Guided tours available. Open Tues.-Sat. 10am-5pm, Sun. 1-5pm. $6, seniors and ages 2-17 $3; free to LA residents with valid ID Thurs. 10am-noon.

Historic New Orleans Collection, 533 Royal St. (F.Q. C2; 523-4662). Extensive facilities and 2 guided tours. The History Tour explores New Orleans's past, while the interesting Williams Residence Tour showcases the eclectic home furnishings of the collection's founders General and Mrs. L. Kemper Williams. Downstairs gallery displays changing exhibits. Tours 10, 11am, 2, and 3pm; each $2. Gallery open Tues.-Sat. 10am-4:45pm; free.

Musée Conti Wax Museum, 917 Conti St. (F.Q. C2; 525-2605). One of the world's finest houses of wax. The voodoo display and haunted dungeon are perennial favorites, along with the mock-up of Madame Lalaurie's torture attic. Open daily 10am-5pm; except Mardi Gras. $5.75, seniors $5.25, under 17 $3.50.

Confederate Museum, 929 Camp St. (N.O. C3; 523-4522), in a brownstone just west of Lee Circle. An extensive collection of Civil War records and artifacts. Warning: they root for the South. Open Mon.-Sat. 10am-4pm. $4, under 16 $2.

K&B Plaza, 1055 St. Charles Ave. (N.O. C3; 568-5661), on Lee Circle. Houses an outstanding contemporary collection of art and sculpture from the Virlane Foundation, including sculpture by Henry Moore, mobiles by Alexander Calder, and a bust by Renoir. Open Mon.-Fri. 8am-5pm. Sculpture garden open 24 hrs. Free.

Louisiana Children's Museum, 420 Julia St. (F.Q. A3; 523-STAR/7827). Invites kids to play and learn, as they star in their own news shows, pretend to be streetcar drivers, or shop in a re-created mini-mart. Lots of cool, fun options. Kids under 12 must be accompanied by an adult. Open Mon.-Sat. 9:30am-5:30pm; Labor Day-Memorial Day Tues.-Sat. 9:30am-5:30pm, Sun. noon-5:30pm. $4, under 1 free.

Louisiana Nature and Science Center, 11000 Lake Forest Blvd. (246-5672). Trail walks, exhibits, planetarium and laser shows, and 86 acres of natural wildlife preserve in Joe Brown Memorial Park. Hard to reach without a car, but a wonderful escape from the debauchery of the French Quarter. Open Tues.-Fri. 9am-5pm, Sat. 10am-5pm, Sun. noon-5pm. $4, children $2.

Historic Homes and Plantations

Called the "Great Showplace of New Orleans," **Longue Vue House and Gardens,** 7 Bamboo Rd. (N.O. B2; 488-5488), off Metairie Rd., epitomizes the grand Southern estate with its lavish furnishings and opulent decor. The breathtaking sculpted gardens date back to the turn of the century. Take the Metairie Rd. exit off I-10 and pause for a peek at the 85-ft.-tall monument among the raised tombs in the Metairie Cemetery on the way. (Tours available in English, French, Spanish, Italian, and Japanese. Open Mon.-Sat. 10am-4:30pm, Sun. 1-5pm. $7, students $3, seniors $6, under 5 free; gardens only $3, students $1.) **River Rd.** curves along the Mississippi River across from downtown New Orleans, accessing several plantations preserved from the 19th century; pick up a copy of *Great River Road Plantation Parade: A River of Riches* at the New Orleans or Baton Rouge visitors centers for a good map and descriptions of the houses. Frequent free ferries cross the river at Plaquemines, White Castle, and between Lutcher and Vacherie. With each charging an individual entrance fee, a tour of all the privately-owned plantations would be quite expensive. Those below are listed in order from New Orleans to Baton Rouge.

Hermann-Grima Historic House, 820 St. Louis St. (F.Q. C2; 525-5661). Built in 1831, the house exemplifies early American influence on New Orleans architecture, replete with a large central hall, guillotine windows, a fan-lit entrance, and the original parterre beds. On Thurs. October-May trained volunteer cooks prepare meals from recipes of the period; call for details. Open Mon.-Sat. 10am-4pm; last tour 3:30pm. $5, students $4, seniors $4, ages 8-18 $4, under 7 free.

Gallier House Museum, 1118-1132 Royal St. (F.Q. D2; 523-6722). The elegantly restored residence of James Gallier, Jr., New Orleans's most famous architect, brings alive the taste and lifestyle of the extremely wealthy in the 1860s. Tours every ½hr.; last tour 4pm. Open Mon.-Sat. 10am-4:30pm. $4, students and seniors $3, children $2.25.

San Francisco Plantation House (535-2341), Rte. 44 2mi. north of Reserve 42mi. from New Orleans on the east bank of the Mississippi. Beautifully maintained plantation built in 1856. Laid out in the old Creole style with the main living room on the 2nd floor. The three-color exterior is restrained compared to the ceilings. Tours daily 10am-4pm. $7, ages 12-17 $4, ages 6-11 $2.75.

Houmas House, 40136 Rte. 942 (522-2262), in Burnside just over halfway to Baton Rouge on the west bank of the Mississippi. Setting for the movie *Hush,*

Hush, Sweet Charlotte, starring Bette Davis and Olivia DeHavilland. Built in two sections: the rear constructed in the last quarter of the 18th century and the Greek Revival mansion in front built in 1840. Beautiful gardens and furnishings. "Southern Belle" guides lead tours in authentic antebellum dress. Open daily 10am-5pm; Nov.-Jan. 10am-4pm. $7, ages 13-17 $5, ages 6-12 $3.50.

Nottoway (545-2730), Rte. 405, between Bayou Goula and White Castle, 18mi. south of Baton Rouge on the southern bank of the Mississippi. Largest plantation home in the South; often called the "White Castle of Louisiana." An incredible 64-room mansion with 22 columns, a large ballroom, and a 3-story stairway. The first choice of David O. Selznick for filming *Gone with the Wind,* but the owners frankly didn't give a damn and simply wouldn't allow it. Open daily 9am-5pm. Admission and 1-hr. guided tour $8, under 13 $3.

ENTERTAINMENT AND NIGHTLIFE

If you've come to New Orleans to take advantage of drinking laws which let those over 18 buy and guzzle booze, you're about a year too late. Ever since the nation adopted the "21 or older" law, Louisiana had held out, creating its own liquor laws even if it meant losing out on federal highway funds. In the summer of 1995, the state legislature finally gave in—officially, *you now have to be 21 to buy and drink alcoholic beverages in Louisiana.*

Needless to say, life in New Orleans is and will always be a party. On any night of the week, at any time of the year, the masses converge on **Bourbon St.,** to drift in and out of bars and shop for a romantic interlude. Unfortunately, the many bars and clubs on Bourbon tend toward the sleazy and clothing optional. After exploring the more traditional jazz, blues, and brass sound of the Quarter, survey the rest of the city for less tourist-oriented bands playing to a more local clientele. Check *Off Beat* or the Friday *Times-Picayune* to find out who's playing where. The movements of New Orleans's large gay community fill the pages of *Impact* and *Ambush,* both available at **Faubourg Marigny Books,** 600 Frenchmen St. (N.O. C2; 943-9875), to find out what's happening and where to go. (Open Mon.-Fri. 10am-8pm, Sat.-Sun. 10am-6pm.)

Born at the turn of the century in **Armstrong Park,** traditional New Orleans jazz still wails every night of the week at the tiny, dim, historic **Preservation Hall,** 726 Saint Peter St. (F.Q. C2; 523-8939); expect jazz in its most fundamental element. Arrive early or be prepared for a lengthy wait in line, poor visibility, and sweaty standing-room only ($3). The Hall does not sell food or beverages. Doors open at 8pm; music begins at 8:30pm and goes on until midnight. If you don't get a seat, wait outside and listen for free.

Keep your ears open for **Cajun** and **zydeco** bands who use accordions, wash-boards, triangles, and drums to perform hot dance tunes (true locals two-step expertly) and sappy waltzes. Anyone who thinks couple-dancing went out in the 50s should try a *fais do-do,* a lengthy, wonderfully energetic traditional dance; just grab a partner and throw yourself into the rhythm. The locally based **Radiators** do it up real spicy-like in a rock-cajun-zydeco style.

Festivals

New Orleans's Mardi Gras celebration is the biggest party of the year, a world-renowned, epic bout of lascivious debauchery that fills the three weeks leading up to Ash Wednesday. Parades, gala, balls, and general revelry take the streets, as tourists pour in by the planeful (flights into the city book up months in advance along with hotel rooms). In 1996, the day before Ash Wednesday, Fat Tuesday (literally *Mardi Gras*), falls on February 20; the biggest parades and the bulk of the partying will take place during the week of February 13-20. Remember: when it comes time to traffic in beads, anything goes, and a trade which sounds too good to be true probably carries some unspoken conditions.

The ever-expanding annual **New Orleans Jazz and Heritage Festival** (522-4786), April 26 to May 5 in 1996, attracts 4000 musicians from around the country to the city's fairgrounds. The likes of Aretha Franklin, Bob Dylan, Patti LaBelle, and Wynton

Marsalis have graced this slightly "classier" fest, where music plays simultaneously on 11 stages in the midst of a huge Cajun food and crafts festival. The biggest names perform evening riverboat concerts. Exhilarating and fun, the festival grows more zoo-like each year. Book a room early.

New Orleans's festivals go beyond the biggies. From the **Tennessee Williams Literary Festival** (March 21-24) to the **Gumbo Festival** (Oct. 11-12), you're likely to find a celebration of something year-round. Call the Tourist Convention Commission (see Practical Information, above) for further info.

Nightlife in the French Quarter

Bars in New Orleans stay open late, and few keep a strict schedule; in general, they open around 11am and close around 3am. Some places go the $3-5-per-drink route, but most blocks feature at least one establishment with cheap draft beer and Hurricanes, sweet drinks made of juice and rum. Beware of overly forward strangers and pickpockets, and always bring ID—the party's fun, but the law is enforced.

Pat O'Brien's, 718 Saint Peter St. (F.Q. C2; 525-4823). The busiest bar and best in the French Quarter, bursting with happy (read: drunk) tourists. Listen to the piano in one room, mix with local students in another, or lounge near the fountain in the courtyard. Home of the original Hurricane; purchase your first in a souvenir glass ($7). Open Sun.-Thurs. 10:30am-4am, Fri.-Sat. 10:30am-5am.

The Old Absinthe House, 240 Bourbon St. (F.Q. B2; 525-8108). Reputed to be the oldest bar in the U.S., opened in 1807. The House has irrigated the likes of Mark Twain, Franklin D. Roosevelt, the Rolling Stones, and Humphrey Bogart. Bet you've never heard those four names together in the same sentence! Reasonably priced drinks for the French Quarter. The Absinthe Frappe re-invents the infamous drink with anisette or Pernod liqueur ($4.75). Open daily 11am-2am.

House of Blues, 225 Decatur St. (F.Q. B3; 529-BLUE/2583). A sprawling complex with a large music/dance hall, and a balcony and bar which overlook the action. The restaurant serves everything from veggie pasta ($8) to Bayou Voodoo smothered chicken in Dixie's blackened voodoo beer (phew...$11). Cover $5-25; folks like Clapton get the big bucks. Concerts daily 8pm; stop by or call for the upcoming schedule. Restaurant open Sun.-Thurs. 11am-midnight, Fri.-Sat. 11am-2am.

The Napoleon House, 500 Chartres St. (F.Q. C3; 524-9752). Located on the ground floor of the Old Girod House, which was built as an exile home for Napoleon in a plan to spirit him away from St. Helena. Movie buffs take note: the bar set the scene for one of the opening clips in Oliver Stones's "fictional documentary" *JFK.* New Orleans fare $3-9. Open Mon.-Thurs. 11am-midnight, Fri.-Sat. 11am-1am, Sun. 11am-7pm.

Bourbon Pub/Parade, 801 Bourbon St. (F.Q. C2; 529-2107). This gay dance bar sponsors a "tea dance" on Sun. with all the beer you can drink for $5. Dancing nightly 9pm until you run out of gas. Open 24 hrs.

Rubyfruit Jungle, 640 Frenchmen St. (N.O. C2; 947-4000). The biggest lesbian bar in New Orleans. High-energy music on weekends; other days usually have special themes. Mon. is seafood boil night (shrimp, crawfish, and a pitcher of beer $5), and Tues. is country/western. Open Mon.-Fri. 4pm-4am, Sat.-Sun. 3pm-4am.

Nightlife Outside The Quarter

Mid City Lanes, 4133 S. Carrolton Ave. (N.O. B3; 482-3133), at Tulane Ave. "Home of Rock n' Bowl;" bowling alley by day, dance club by night. (Don't worry, you can bowl at night too.) Featuring local zydeco, blues, and rock n' roll, this is where the locals party. Thurs. is wild zydeco night. Music Wed.-Thurs. 9:30pm, Fri.-Sat. 10pm; cover $5-7. Pick up a *Rock n' Bowlletin* for specific band info (and a list of the regulars' birthdays). Lanes Sun.-Thurs. $8 per hr., Sat.-Sun. $10 per hr.

Cooter Brown's Tavern and Oyster Bar, 509 S. Carrolton Ave. (N.O. A3; 866-9104). Sporting a very mainstream-young-singles crowd, this blues bar lofts over 200 beers including a 3-liter Belgian ale for $60. Ground cow on a bun too ($4-7). Open Sun.-Mon. 11am-2am, Tues.-Thurs. 11am-3am, Fri-Sat. 11am-4am.

Checkpoint Charlie's, 501 Esplanade (F.Q. D3; 947-0979), in the Marigny. Grunges it up like the best of Seattle. Do your laundry while you listen to live rockin' music 7 nights a week. No cover. Open 24 hrs.

Tipitina's, 501 Napoleon Ave. (N.O. B4; 895-8477; 897-3943 for concert info). This famous establishment attracts both the best local bands and some big national names. The Neville Brothers, John Goodman, and Harry Connick Jr. stop in regularly. Favorite bar of late jazz pianist and scholar Professor Longhair; his bust now graces the front hall. Cover $4-15; call ahead for times and prices.

Maple Leaf Bar, 8316 Oak St. (N.O. B3; 866-9359), near Tulane University. The best local dance bar offers zydeco and Cajun music; everyone does the two-step. Poetry readings Sun. 3pm. The party starts Sun.-Thurs. at 10pm, Fri.-Sat. at 10:30pm. Cover $3-5. Open daily 3pm-4am.

F&M Patio Bar, 4841 Tchoupitoulas St. (N.O. B4; 895-6784), near Napolean. Mellow twentysomethings mix with doctors, lawyers, and ne'er-do-wells. Serves food after 6pm, mostly fajitas ($3) and burgers ($4.25). Open Mon.-Thurs. 1pm-4am, Fri. 1pm-6am, Sat. 3pm-6am, Sun. 3pm-4am.

Ms. Mae's, 5535 Magazine St. (N.O. B4; 891-9974). The cheapest beer in town, possibly the world. Long-neck $1.25; mixed drinks $1-2. Hosts a frat-style college crowd at night, with locals and "older groups" during the day. Open 24 hrs.

Michaul's, 840 St. Charles Ave. (N.O. C3; 522-5517). A huge floor for Cajun dancing; they'll even teach you how. In the evenings they teach for 30min., then dance for 30min.—alternating all night long. No cover. Open Mon.-Fri. 5pm-11pm, Sat. 6pm-midnight, Sun. 6pm-10pm.

Snug Harbor, 626 Frenchmen St. (N.O. C2; 949-0696), just east of the Quarter near Decatur St. Shows nightly 9 and 11pm. Regulars include Charmaine Neville, Amasa Miller, and Ellis Marsalis. The cover is steep ($6-14), but Mon. evening with Ms. Neville is worth it. Listen for soulful music from the bar in the front room. Bar open daily 5pm-2am; restaurant open Sun.-Thurs. 5-11pm, Fri.-Sat. 5pm-midnight

■■■ BATON ROUGE

Once a tall cypress tree marking the boundary between rival Native American tribes, Baton Rouge ("red stick") has grown to be the capital of Louisiana. State politics have shaped the character of this city, once the home of "Kingfish" Huey P. Long—a Depression-era populist demagogue who, until his assassination, was considered Franklin D. Roosevelt's biggest political threat. Though politics remain important, today the rhythm and pace of this port city are defined by a state within the state: **Louisiana State University (LSU).** The downtown area of Baton Rouge has enough urban attractions to satisfy only the easily-pleased tourist. For the party-happy young visitor who can't make it to New Orleans, however, the sprawling campus of the state university offers cheap eateries, quite a few bars, and a few more bars. Enjoy.

Practical Information The **State Capitol Visitors Center** (342-7317), hands out info on the first floor of the State Capitol; get off I-110 on U.S. 61, go west to 3rd St., then go north to the sky-scraping capitol (open Mon.-Fri. 8am-4pm). For more resources, stop by the **Baton Rouge Convention and Visitors Bureau,** 730 North Blvd. (383-1825; open Mon.-Fri. 8am-5pm). A short walk from downtown, **Greyhound,** 1253 Florida Blvd. (800-231-2222), at 13th St., sends buses to New Orleans (10 per day, 2hr., $15) and Lafayette (9 per day, 1hr., $12). Be careful; the area is unsafe at night. (Station and ticket booth open 24 hrs.) **Capital City Transportation** (336-0821), has its main terminal at 22nd and Florida Blvd. The service to LSU is decent; otherwise, buses tend to be unreliable or infrequent. (Runs Mon.-Sat. 6:30am-6:30pm. Fare $1, transfers 25¢.) **Crisis Intervention/Suicide Prevention Center** (924-3900) and **Rape Crisis** (383-7273) both operate 24 hrs. In an **emergency,** call 911. Baton Rouge's **post office:** 750 Florida Blvd. (381-0713), off River Rd. (open Mon.-Fri. 8:30am-5pm, Sat. 9am-noon); **ZIP code:** 70821; **area code:** 504.

Downtown Baton Rouge is clearly defined by a combination of waterways and interstates: to the north lies **Capitol Lake** and to the west lies the ubiquitous **Mississippi River.** The rest of town is squared off by **I-10** and its off-shoot, **I-110.** Try to avoid the area known as "the bottom," if you value your own; the area of streets named after presidents down on Highland Rd. is also quite dangerous at night.

Accommodations and Camping For those who need or want to stay downtown, **The General Lafayette Inn,** 427 Lafayette St. (387-0421), has clean rooms with free local calls and a view of the Mississippi River (and the parking lot, just don't look down; singles $32, doubles $42). **Motel 6,** 10445 Rieger Rd. (291-4912), at exit 163 off I-10, throws you no surprises—cookie-cutter rooms, good security, soft beds, hard water, cable TV, and a pool (singles $32, doubles $38). The **KOA Campground,** 7628 Vincent Rd. (664-7281), 12 mi. east of Baton Rouge (take the Denham Springs exit off I-12), keeps sites well-maintained, along with clean facilities and a big pool (sites for 2 $15.50, with hookup $21.50).

Food and Nightlife Near LSU, on and around **Highland Rd.,** you'll find all the sustenance you need. **Louie's Café,** 209 W. State (246-8221), a 24-hr. grill, serves fabulous stir-fried vegetable omelettes around the clock ($5). Behind Louie's on the corner of Chimes and Highland Rd., **The Bayou,** 124 W. Chimes (346-1765), a local favorite, set the stage for the bar scene from *Sex, Lies, and Videotape.* The smoky, sweaty pool hall fills with students regularly. (Open Mon.-Sat. 5pm-2am; in winter 2pm-2am.) When you want a place good enough for your parents, try **The Chimes,** 3357 Highland Rd. (383-1754), a big ol' restaurant and bar with more than 120 different beers. Louisiana Alligator, farm-raised, marinated, and fried, served with dijon mustard sauce goes for $6—do you dare? (Open Mon.-Fri. 11:30am-2am, Sat. 11am-2am, Sun 11am-midnight.) Downtown, you can't miss the **Frostop Drive-In,** 402 Government (344-1179); the giant frothy root beer mug spinning on a post outside advertises delicious root beer floats ($2) crafted with homemade root beer inside. (Sandwiches $1-3. Open Mon.-Fri. 10am-8pm, Sat. 11am-8pm, Sun. 11am-6pm.)

Sights In a move reminiscent of Ramses II, Huey Long ordered the building of the unique **Louisiana State Capitol** (342-7317), a magnificent, modern skyscraper, completed over a mere 14 months in 1931 and 32. The front lobby alone merits a visit, but visitors should also go up to the free 27th-floor observation deck (open daily 8am-4pm). While remarkable architecturally, the building is also a powerful affirmation of the staying power of Long's personality; in a back corridor, look for the bullet holes near the plaque which suggests the possible site of his assassination, and stop to see the statue out front under which Long is buried.

The **LSU Rural Life Museum,** 4600 Essen Ln. (765-2437), take the Essen exit off I-10, recreates everyday life in pre-industrial Louisiana. The authentically furnished shops, cabins, and storage houses adjoin meticulously-kept rose and azalea gardens. (Open daily 8:30am-5pm. $5, seniors $4, ages 5-11 $3.)

The restored French Creole **Magnolia Mound Plantation,** 2161 Nicholson Dr. (343-4955), completed in 1791, offers a view of plantation life which pre-dates the sprawling mansions of the "Gone with the Wind" genre. (Open Tues.-Sat. 10am-4pm, Sun. 1-4pm; last tour 3:20pm. $3.50, students $1.50, seniors $2.50.) Just south of downtown, the **Beauregard District** boasts Baton Rouge's share of typically ornate antebellum homes; walk down North Blvd. from the Old State Capitol to the Visitors Bureau to take in the beauty of this neighborhood.

ACADIANA

Throughout the early eighteenth century, the English government in Nova Scotia became increasingly jealous of the prosperity of French settlers *(Acadiens)* and deeply offended by their refusal to swear allegiance to the British Crown. During the war with France in 1755, British frustration and hatred peaked; they rounded up the Acadians and deported them by the shipload in what came to be called the *le Grand Dérangement,* "the Great Upheaval." Of 7,000 Acadians who went to sea, one-third died of small pox and hunger on the ships. Those who survived sought refuge along the Atlantic Coast in places like Massachusetts and South Carolina. As French Catholics they were met with fear and suspicion, and most were forced into indentured servitude. The Acadians soon realized that freedom waited only in the French territory of Louisiana. The "Cajuns" of St. Martin, Lafayette, Iberia, and St. Mary parishes are descended from these settlers.

Several factors have threatened Acadian culture since the relocation. In the 1920s, Louisiana passed laws forcing Acadian schoolchildren to speak English. Later, during the oil boom of the 1970s and 80s, oil executives and developers envisioned the Acadian center of Lafayette (see below) as the Houston of Louisiana and threatened to flood the town and its neighbors with mass culture. Still, the proud people of southern Louisiana have resisted homogenization; today, the state is officially bilingual and a state agency preserves Acadian French in schools and in the media. "Cajun Country" spans the south of the state, from Houma in the east to the Texas border in the west. Mostly bayou and swampland, this unique natural environment has shaped Cajun culture.

■■■ LAFAYETTE

The undeniable capital of Acadiana, Lafayette is the perfect place to try some boiled crawfish or dance the two-step to a fiddle and accordion. Though the city's French roots can get lost in the chain motels and service roads which have come with its growth, there is no question that the Cajuns still own the surrounding countryside, where zydeco music heats up dance floors every night of the week and locals go on answering their phones with a proud *bon jour.*

PRACTICAL INFORMATION

Tourist Office: Lafayette Parish Tourist Information Bureau, 1400 Evangeline Thruway (232-3808), will swamp you with information. Open Mon.-Fri. 8:30am-5pm, Sat.-Sun. 9am-5pm.

Trains: Amtrak, 133 E. Grant St. (800-231-2222). 3 trains per week to: New Orleans (4hr., $29); Houston (5hr., $52); San Antonio (9hr., $81). The station does not sell tickets; buy in advance from **Bass Travel,** 1603 W. Pinhook Rd. (237-2177 or 800-777-7371; open Mon.-Fri. 8:30am-5pm), or another travel agent.

Buses: Greyhound, 315 Lee Ave. (235-1541 or 800-872-7245). To: New Orleans (7 per day, 3½hr., $19); Baton Rouge (7 per day, 1hr., $11); New Iberia (2 per day, ½hr., $6) and other small towns. Open 24 hrs.

Public Transportation: Lafayette Bus System, 400 Dorset Rd. (261-8570). Infrequent service Mon.-Sat. Fare 45¢, seniors and disabled 20¢, ages 5-12 30¢.

Taxis: Yellow/Checker Cab Inc., 237-6196. Runs on zones; from the bus or train station to downtown $4.

Car Rental: Thrifty Rent-a-Car, 401 E. Pinhook Rd. (237-1282). $25 per day with 100 free mi. Must be 25 with major credit card. Open Mon.-Fri. 7:30am-6pm, Sat.-Sun. 8am-5pm.

Crisis Line: Rape Crisis Center, 233-7273. Open Mon.-Fri. 8:30am-4:30pm.

Post Office: 1105 Moss St. (269-4800). Open Mon.-Fri. 8am-5:30pm, Sat. 8am-12:30pm. **ZIP code:** 70501. **Area code:** 318.

Lafayette stands at Louisiana's crossroads. **I-10** leads east to New Orleans (130mi.) and west to Lake Charles (76mi.); **U.S. 90** heads south to New Iberia (20mi.) and the Atchafalaya Basin; **U.S. 167** runs north into central Louisiana. The **Evangeline Thruway** runs north-south, splitting Lafayette in half. (The name comes from Henry Wadsworth Longfellow's epic poem, *Evangeline,* which portrays the plight of two ill-fated Acadian lovers who are separated on their wedding day in *le Grand Dérangement.*) You'll need a car to explore Acadiana and the Gulf Coast bayou country.

ACCOMMODATIONS AND CAMPING

Inexpensive chains and local hotels line the **Evangeline Thruway. Travel Host Inn South,** 1314 N. Evangeline Thruway (233-2090 or 800-671-1466), has large, attractive rooms, with cable TV, a pool, and a convenient location (singles $29, doubles $34). The ample but plain-looking rooms at **Super 8,** 2224 N. Evangeline Thruway (232-8826 or 800-800-8000), come with access to a pool and a stunning view of the highway (singles $27, doubles $35). Off the main drag, the **Travelodge Lafayette,** 1101 W. Pinhook Rd. (234-7402), complements rooms with free breakfast, free local calls, and an in-room coffee maker and beans (single $38, double $43). Steal a glimpse at the raised marble crypts in the graveyard off Pinhook.

One close area campground, **Acadiana Park Campground,** 1201 E. Alexander (261-8388), off Louisiana, includes tennis courts and a soccer field. (Office open Mon.-Thurs. 9am-5pm, Fri.-Sat. 8am-8pm, Sun. 9am-5pm. Sites with full hookup $8.) The lakeside **KOA Lafayette** (235-2739), 5 mi. west of town on I-10 at exit 97, has a komplete store, a mini-golf kourse, and a kool pool. (Office open daily 7:30am-8:30pm; tent sites $15.50, with water and electricity $20, with full hookup $21.50.)

FOOD AND NIGHTLIFE

Cajun restaurants with live music and dancing have popped up all over Lafayette. Unfortunately, they cater to a tourist crowd with a substantial budget. **Mulates** (MYOO-lots), 325 Mills Ave. (332-4648), near Breaux Bridge, calls itself the most famous Cajun restaurant in the world, and the autographs on the door corroborate its claim. Have them whip up some fried alligator ($5) or the special catfish ($14. Music nightly 7:30-10pm, also Sat.-Sun. noon-2pm. Open Mon.-Sat. 7am-10:30pm, Sun. 11am-11pm.) In central Lafayette, **Chris' Po'Boys,** with four locations including 1941 Moss St. (237-1095), and 631 Jefferson St. (234-1696), offers seafood platters ($7) and—you guessed it—po'boys ($4-5; open Mon.-Thurs. 10:30am-8:30pm, Fri. 10:30am-9:30pm, Sat. 11am-9pm). **Randol's,** 2320 Kaliste Saloom Rd. (981-7080), romps with live music nightly, and doubles as a restaurant (open Sun.-Thurs. 5-10pm, Fri.-Sat. 5-10:30pm). **Prejeans,** 3480 U.S. 167N (896-3247), may be hard to find (take Frontage Rd. which parallels Evangeline Rd.), but it sho' is good for savory Cajun food (dinners $8-12) and nightly music and dancing (7pm). Check out the 14-ft. alligator by the entrance. (Open Mon.-Thurs. 11am-9:30pm, Fri.-Sat. 11am-11pm, Sun. 11am-10pm.) Pick up a copy of *The Times,* available at restaurants and gas stations, to find out about what's going on; Lafayette has a surprising variety of after-hours entertainment.

THE SOUTH

SIGHTS AND ENTERTAINMENT

First-time visitors to Lafayette should start at the **Acadian Cultural Center,** 501 Fisher Rd. (232-0789), which features a 40-min. documentary, *The Cajun Way: Echos of Acadia,* as well as a terrific exhibit on the exodus and migration of these French settlers (shows every hr. on the hr.; open daily 8am-5pm; free). The re-creation of an Acadian settlement at **Vermilionville,** 1600 Surrey St. (233-4077 or 800-992-2968), entertains as it educates with music, crafts, food, and dancing (open daily 10am-5pm; $8, seniors $6.50, ages 6-18 $5). Unlike the grandiose mansions which populate the South, **Acadian Village,** 200 Greenleaf Rd. (981-2364 or 800-962-9133), offers a look at the unpretentious homes of common 19th-century Acadian settlers. Rumor has it that a petting zoo is on the way, but for now, uncaged peacocks, ducks, and chickens happily frolic around the village. Take U.S. 167N, turn right on Ridge Rd., then left on Mouton, and follow the signs. (Open daily 10am-5pm. $5.50, seniors $4.50, children $2.50.)

Check out **St. John's Cathedral Oak,** in the yard of St. John's Cathedral, 914 St. John St. This 450-year-old tree—one of the largest in the U.S.—shades the entire lawn with gargantuan, spidery limbs which spread 210 ft.; the weight of a single limb is estimated at 72 tons. (Free.) The **Lafayette Museum,** 1122 Lafayette St. (234-2208), exhibits heirlooms, antiques, and Mardi Gras costumes (open Tues.-Sat. 9am-5pm, Sun. 3-5pm; $3, students and children $1, seniors $2).

Lafayette kicks off spring and fall weekends with **Downtown Alive!** (268-5566), a series of free concerts which features everything from new wave to Cajun and zydeco (April-June and Sept.-Nov. Fri. 5:30pm). The **Festival International de Louisiane** (232-8086), April 23-28 in 1996, highlights the music, visual arts, and cuisine of southwest Louisiana in a francophone tribute to the region. **New Evangeline Downs** (896-7223 or 800-256-1234), on I-49N, has opened the gates for Lafayette's newest attraction, fast-paced thoroughbred racing. (Races April-Aug. Mon. and Thurs.-Fri. 6:45pm. $2, $4.50 for a seat. Minimum bet $2.)

The Atchafalaya Basin

If you're driving through south-central Louisiana, you're probably driving over America's largest swamp, the Atchafalaya (a-CHAH-fa-LIE-a) Basin. The **Atchafalaya Freeway** (I-10 between Lafayette and Baton Rouge) crosses 32 mi. of swamp and cypress trees. To get down and dirty in the muck, exit at Henderson, 15 mi. east of Lafayette, and follow the signs to **McGee's Landing,** 1337 Henderson Rd. (228-2384). This operation sends four 1½-hour **boat tours** into the Basin each day. (Tours daily 10am and 1, 3, and 5pm. $9, seniors $8, under 12 $5.)

■■■ NEW IBERIA AND ENVIRONS

While Lafayette was being invaded by oil magnates eager to build a Louisiana oil-business center, New Iberia kept right on about the daily business of being a picturesque bayou town. Though the area's attractions aren't numerous, several give visitors a better feel for the unique conditions of life on the bayou.

Unlike the many plantations which made fortunes from cotton, most plantations in southern Louisiana grew sugarcane. Most of these plantations are still private property, but **Shadows on the Teche,** 317 E. Main St. (318-369-6446), at the Rte. 14/Rte. 82 junction, welcomes visitors. A Southern aristocrat saved the plantation's crumbling mansion, built in 1831, from neglect after the Civil War. (Open daily 9am-5pm. $6, ages 6-11 $3.) A lone chimney protrudes from the lake next to **Live Oak Gardens,** 5505 Rip Van Winkle Rd. (318-365-3332), marking the existence of a mansion which was devoured by a whirlpool in 1980. Today, peaceful gardens and scenic boat tours belie the area's tempestuous past. (Open daily 9am-5pm. $10, children $5.) **Avery Island,** 7 mi. away on Rte. 329 off Rte. 90 (50¢ toll to enter the island), sizzles with the world-famous **Tabasco Pepper Sauce factory,** where the McIlhenny family has produced the famous condiment for nearly a century. Guided tours include a sample taste. *OOOOOeeeeeee!!!!* (Open Mon.-Fri. 9am-4pm, Sat. 9am-noon. Free.) Nearby the **Jungle Gardens** (318-369-6243) inhabit 250 acres developed in the 19th century to shelter waterways, herons, egrets, alligators, and an 800-year-old statue of the Buddha (open daily 9am-5:30pm; $5.25, children $3.75). Before you leave New Iberia, be sure to take a one-hour **Airboat Tour** (318-229-4457) of the shallow water swamps and bayous of Lake Fausse Pointe. Look for snowy egrets, alligators, and the large, edible nutria rat. (Open Feb.-Oct. Tues.-Sun. $10. Call for directions and required reservations.)

Primitive campsites are available at **Atchafalaya Delta Wildlife Area** at the mouth of the Atchafalaya River in St. Mary Parish. The preserve, which encompasses bayous, potholes, high and low marshes, and some dry ground, can only be accessed by boat launch from Morgan City, near the Bayou Boeuf locks. To reach the boat launch, take Hwy. 90 from Lafayette to the town of Berwick. In Berwick, take a right at the traffic light, then a right at the end of the road. Follow the levy to the public boat launch. To enter the area, you will need a fishing license, a hunting license, or a "Wild Louisiana" stamp; all three can be found at a sheriff's office, or anyplace hunting and fishing licenses are sold. Call the **Department of Wildlife and Fisheries** (318-369-3807) for more information.

New Iberia lies 21 mi. southeast of Lafayette on U.S. 90. See the **Iberia Parish Tourist Commission,** 2704 Rte. 14 (318-365-8246; open daily 9am-5pm), or the **Greater Iberia Chamber of Commerce,** 111 W. Main St. (318-364-1836; open Mon.-Fri. 9am-5pm), for maps. **Amtrak** (800-872-7245) stops in New Iberia, at an unstaffed station off Washington St., on the way between New Orleans and Lafayette. Three trains per week set out in each direction, for Lafayette (30min., $6) and New Orleans (3hr., $28). **Greyhound** (318-364-8571 or 800-231-2222) pulls into town at 101 Perry St. Buses run to Morgan City (1 per day, 1hr., $9), New Orleans (1 per day, 4hr., $23), and Lafayette (2 per day, 40min., $6). (Open Mon.-Fri. 7:30am-5:30pm, Sat.-Sun. 7:30am-12:30pm.)

Arkansas

As you zip over the Mississippi River heading west into Arkansas, the landscape spreads into expansive green fields that sparkle with the last rain. "The Natural State," as Arkansas license plates proclaim it, lives up to its boast, encompassing the ascents of the Ozarks, the clear waters of Hot Springs, and miles of highway twisting through lush pine forests.

As varied as Arkansas geography may be, one theme unites the entire state: Bill…er, President Clinton. Museums and exhibits, billboards, and posters everywhere celebrate and recount the life of this native son done good. Some folks here simply disdain the man ("I didn't vote for the dope from Hope," reads one bumper-sticker), but most wallow in praise for the Prez who (we must always remember) was once just a little lad from Arkansas. The November election will determine who's in the majority.

PRACTICAL INFORMATION

Capital: Little Rock.
Arkansas Department of Parks and Tourism: 1 Capitol Mall, Little Rock 72201 (501-682-7777 or 800-NATURAL/628-8725). Open Mon.-Fri. 8am-5pm.
Time Zone: Central (1hr. behind Eastern). **Postal Abbreviation:** AR
Sales Tax: 5-6.5%.

■■■ LITTLE ROCK

Trouble swept Little Rock in 1957 when it became the focus of a nationwide civil rights controversy. Governor Orval Faubus led a violent segregationist movement, using state troops to prevent nine black students from enrolling at Central High School. This event marked one of the first attempts to test the school integration mandate set by the Supreme Court's *Brown v. Board of Education* decision and displayed the ferocity of southern opposition to integration. In the end, the U.S. government stood by the court; the students entered school under protection from federal troops sent by President Eisenhower. Racial tension has cooled considerably since then, and Little Rock is slowly becoming a more integrated community with a modest collection of historical attractions.

PRACTICAL INFORMATION

Tourist Office: Little Rock Convention and Visitors Bureau, 100 W. Markham St. (376-4781 or 800-844-4781), next door to the Excelsior Hotel. Open Mon.-Fri. 8:30am-5pm. Also try **Arkansas Dept. of Parks and Tourism** (directly above).

Airport: Little Rock Regional (372-3430), 5 mi. east of downtown off I-440. Easily accessible from downtown (by bus 80¢, by Black and White Cab about $10).

Trains: Amtrak, Union Station, 1400 W. Markham St. (372-6841 or 800-872-7245), at Victory St. Three trains per week to: St. Louis (7hr., $74); Dallas (9hr., $81); Malvern, 20mi. east of Hot Springs (1hr., $11). Open Mon. and Wed. 6am-10pm, Tues. and Thurs. 6am-2pm and 5pm-1am, Fri.-Sat. 6am-2pm, Sun. 5pm-1am.

Buses: Greyhound, 118 E. Washington St. (372-1871 or 800-231-2222), across the river in North Little Rock. Use the walkway over the bridge to get downtown. To: St. Louis (2 per day, 7hr., $59); New Orleans (5 per day, 14hr., $69); Memphis (16 per day, 2hr., $21). Ticket prices higher on weekends. Discount of 25% for 14-day advance-purchase. Open 24 hrs.

Public Transportation: Central Arkansas Transit (375-1163). Little Rock has a fairly comprehensive local transport system (but no evening hours), with 21 bus routes running through the city Mon.-Sat. 6am-6pm. Maps available at the **Sterling Department Store** (375-8181), at 6th and Center St.

Taxis: Black and White Cabs, 374-0333. $1.10 initial fee; $1 per mi.

Car Rental: Budget Car and Truck Rental (375-5521 or 800-527-0700), at the airport, does its thing for $37.50 per day, with 150 free mi.; $175 per week, with 1000 free mi. 25¢ per additional mi. Must be 21; under 25 surcharge $5 per day. Open Sun.-Fri. 6am-11:30pm, Sat. 7am-10pm.

Crisis Lines: Rape Crisis, 663-3334. Open 24 hrs. **First Call for Help,** 376-4567. Open Mon.-Fri. 8am-5pm.

Emergency: 911.

Post Office: 600 E. Capitol (375-5155). Open Mon.-Fri. 7am-5:30pm. **ZIP code:** 72201. **Area code:** 501.

Downtown Little Rock is relatively grid-like, although the order deteriorates as you move away from the heart of the city. **Broadway** and **Main St.** are the major north-south arteries running to and from the river. **Markham St.** and all streets numbered 1 to 36 run east-west. **Third St.** turns into **W. Markham St.** as it moves west.

ACCOMMODATIONS

Inexpensive motels in Little Rock tend to cluster around **I-30,** next to downtown, and **University Ave.** at the intersection of I-630 and I-430, a 5- to 10-min. drive from downtown. A few motels in town are cheaper but shabbier.

Master's Inn Economy (372-4392 or 800-633-3434), I-30 (exit 140) and 9th St., *almost* in downtown. Locations in North Little Rock as well. Spacious, well-lit rooms with a lovely pool, a restaurant, and even room service. Just one catch: you must be 21 to rent. Singles $26, $6 per extra person; under 18 free with adult.

Mark 4000 Motel, 4000 W. Markham St. (664-0950). The exterior may be a bit dingy, but the recently renovated rooms boast a comfortable and attractive decor. Be careful at night in the surrounding neighborhood. Singles $29, doubles $36.

Little Rock Inn, 601 S. Center St. (376-8301), at 6th St. half a block from downtown. Primarily a residential hotel, the Inn rents spacious but worn rooms without TV or phone. $33 per night for 1-2 people, $75-90 per week with $20 security deposit. Call 2 days ahead.

KOA Campground (758-4598), on Crystal Hill Rd. in North Little Rock, 7mi. from downtown between exit 12 on I-430 and exit 148 on I-48. Well-kept grounds with 100 sites (some more public than others). You can "rough it" outdoors by the pool (sites $19, with hookup $25, kabins $28).

FOOD AND NIGHTLIFE

Vino's, 923 W. 7th St. (375-8466), at Chester St., the only micro-brewery in Little Rock, gives Italian food a good name and a good price (pizza 95¢ a slice, calzones $5). This youthful hangout is also a mecca for the night owl—weekends bring live music, poetry, plays, and film showings ($5). Open Mon.-Wed. 11am-10pm, Thurs.-Fri. 11am-midnight, Sat. noon-midnight.

Juanita's, 1300 S. Main St. (372-1228), at 13th St. Scrumptious Mexican food, on the pricey side (dinner $8-12) but wonderfully prepared. Even if the food's beyond your budget, the nightly live music may not be; call or stop by for a jam-packed schedule. Open Mon. 11am-2:30pm, Tues.-Fri. 11am-2:30pm and 5:30-10:30pm, Sat. noon-10:30pm, Sun. 5:30-9pm.

Wallace Grill Café, 103 Main St. (372-3111), near the visitors center. Generous portions of rib-stickin' cuisine. BLT $1.70, fried catfish $5.25. Open Mon.-Fri. 6am-2:30pm, Sat. 6am-noon.

Olde World Pizza, 1706 Markham Blvd. (374-5504), will put anything from Yellow Squash to Smoked Turkey on your pie ($6-6.75). Though it has tablecloths, the atmosphere is relaxed. Open Mon.-Thurs. 11am-10pm, Sat.-Sun. 11am-11pm.

The Minute Man, 322 Broadway (375-0392). If it were a chain, you could call it McTaco Bell. Good, cheap, greasy food. Open Mon.-Fri., 10:30am-9pm, Sat. 11am-8pm.

Backstreet, 1021 Jessie Rd. (664-2744), near Cantrell and Riverfront Rd., is a large complex, housing several gay and lesbian bars: **701** for women, **501** for men (rock and disco in each), and **Miss Kitty's,** which plays country 'n western. Cover $3. Open daily 9pm-5am.

Discovery (664-4784), next door to Backstreet. A big, loud, heavy-dancing gay bar, home to the Ms. Gay America pageant. Cover $3. Open Thurs.-Sat. 9pm-5am.

SIGHTS

Tourists can visit the legendary "Little Rock" at **Riverfront Park,** a pleasant place for a walk along the Arkansas River. Pay close attention; the rock has had a long, hard life and is (oddly enough) *little* and quite easy to miss. For quick access, cut through the back of the Excelsior Hotel at Markham and Center St. The town celebrates its waterway with arts, crafts, bands, food, and a fireworks display at **Riverfest** (376-4781 for info), on the last evening of Memorial Day weekend (admission $1). Just a block or so north of Riverfront Park, the **Decorative Arts Museum** (372-4000), 7th and Rock St., displays innovative silverware and furniture designs which demonstrate that art can be functional. (Open Mon.-Sat. 10am-5pm, Sun. noon-5pm. Tours Wed. noon, Sun. 1:30pm. Free.) One block from the visitors bureau sits the refined **Old State House,** 300 W. Markham St. (324-9685), which served as the capitol from 1836 until the ceiling collapsed during a legislative session in 1899. The restored building now displays the gowns of first ladies, and an exhibit devoted to President Clinton. (Open Mon.-Sat. 9am-5pm, Sun. 1-5pm. $2, students grades K-12 25¢; free Mon.) The functioning **state capitol** (682-5080), at the west end of Capitol St., may look familiar—it's a replica of the U.S. Capitol in Washington, DC. Take a self-guided tour or call in advance to schedule a free 30- to 40-min. guided tour. (Open Mon.-Fri. 9am-4pm.) To get an idea of the Clintons' pre-Presidential lifestyle, swing by the **Governor's Mansion,** S. Center at 18th St. in the middle of a gorgeous historic district. The **Arkansas Territorial Restoration,** 200 E. Third St. (324-9351), gives visitors a look at everyday life in 19th-century Little Rock through tours of four restored buildings including an old-fashioned print shop. Though long (1 hr.), the tours are fascinating. (Open Mon.-Sat. 9am-5pm, Sun. 1-5pm. Tours begin every hr. on the hr.; last tour 4pm. $2, seniors $1, children 50¢; free 1st Sun. of the month.)

On the eastern edge of town lounges **MacArthur Park,** elegant home to the **Museum of Science and History** (324-9231). Particularly suited to kids, the museum houses exhibits on Arkansas history and wildlife, including a walk-through bear cave and an entire room of stuffed birds. (Open Mon.-Sat. 9am-4:30pm, Sun. 1-4:30pm. $1, seniors and under 12 50¢; free Mon.) Next door the **Arkansas Art Center** (372-4000) features outstanding collections by both European masters and contemporary artists (open Mon.-Sat. 10am-5pm, Sun. noon-5pm; free). Northwest of the state capitol off I-30 at Fair Park Blvd., **War Memorial Park** houses the 40-acre **Little Rock Zoo,** 1 Jonesboro Dr. (666-2406), where animals are kept in areas which simulate their natural habitats (open daily 9am-5pm; $3, under 12 $1).

The **Toltec Mounds State Park** (961-9442), 15 mi. east of North Little Rock on Rte. 386, brings you back to 700AD, when the Mounds were a political and religious center for the Plum Bayou Native Americans. (Open Tues.-Sat. 8am-5pm, Sun. noon-5pm. 1-hr. guided tours, every ½hr. starting at 9:30am. $2.64, children $1.32.)

■■■ THE OZARKS

Stretching from southern Missouri to northern Arkansas, the stunning **Ozark Mountains** gently ripple through the land, with a splendor matched only by that of the crystalline caves beneath them. Highways have bridged the natural boundaries that long isolated the lives and customs of American mountain natives, but the simple Ozark lifestyle survives in spite of the tourist trade.

Take caution when driving; the scenic highways which traverse these tall mountains expose curving, twisting danger as well as great beauty. Few buses venture into the area, and hitching is *not* recommended. Drivers should follow U.S. 71, or Rtes. 7 or 23 for best access and jaw-dropping views. Eureka Springs to Huntsville on Rte. 23 south is an especially scenic 1-hr. drive, and U.S. 62 east or west from Eureka Springs has some attractive stretches of road. Contact the **Arkansas Department of Parks and Tourism** (see Arkansas Practical Information p. 385) for info on camping, hiking, and canoeing.

MOUNTAIN VIEW

Despite the commercialism gradually seeping into Mountain View (Shop at Wal-Mart!), the village remains refreshingly unpretentious, authentically Ozark, and rather small (pop. 2400). Nearly every day, locals gather on a street corner to make music with hammered dulcimers, fiddles and guitars. Visit the Ozark Folk Center for a more contained taste of Ozark charm.

First and foremost, know that Mountain View is a dry county; beware of people selling renegade booze. Mountain View's **Chamber of Commerce** (269-8068) is located on Main St. (open Mon.-Sat. 8am-5pm). Pick up one of their essential and easy-to-read maps. **Rental cars** are available at **Lackey Motors Car Rental** (269-3211), at the corner of Main St. and Peabody Ave. Must be 23, with a credit card in your name if you're under 25. ($25 per day plus 25¢ per mi.; open Mon.-Sat. 8am-5pm.) The **Mental Health and Rape Crisis Hotline** (800-592-9503) and **Crisis Intervention** (800-542-1031) are both open 24 hrs. In **emergencies,** dial 911. Mountain View's **post office** (269-3520), is moving to a new location this year; **ZIP code:** 72560. **Area code:** 501.

Mountain View offers countless lodging options for the budget traveler. The **Mountain View Motel,** 407 E. Main St. (269-3209), is a particularly good deal, with 18 clean rooms sporting hot pots of free coffee (singles $26, doubles $32). The owners of the **Wildflower Bed & Breakfast** (800-591-4879), on the northeast corner of the courthouse square, are particularly hospitable; they happily welcome even those travelers who lack a Southern drawl. Eight rooms with soft blue carpeting, several windows and antique desks lead off a common hallway. (Singles $37, doubles $42. Reservations recommended.) Small cottages with modern amenities (A/C, cable TV) cluster at the **Dry Creek Lodge** (269-3871 or 800-264-3655), spur 382 off Rte. 5 within the Ozark Folk Center (single or double, $45-50).

Because Mountain View lies only 14 mi. south of the Ozark National Forest, the cheapest way to stay in the area is free **camping.** Pitching a tent anywhere within the forest is free and legal (and usually safe) as long as the campsite does not block any road, path, or thoroughfare. Campgrounds around the Blanchard Springs caverns, off Rte. 14N about 20 min. from Mountain View, include **Blanchard Springs Recreation Area** (32 sites, $8), **Gunner Pool Recreation Area** (27 sites, $5), and **Barkshed Recreation Area** (5 sites, free, but beware young idlers who bring their drink and wickedness). For more information about camping in the areas, contact the **Sylamore Ranger District** of the National Forest, P.O. Box 1279, Mountain View, 72560 (757-2211).

Some of the best lunches in town come from **The Hearthstone Bakery** (269-3297), inside the Wildflower Bed & Breakfast, which satisfies meat-eaters (Chinese Smoked Chicken Salad on Cold Sesame Noodles…mmm… $5) and vegetarians alike (Santa Fe Black Bean Salad $5). The **Catfish House** (269-3820), Rte. 14 to School Dr. to Senior Dr., dishes up (you guessed it!) deep-fried catfish ($8) in an old school complex. Thursday through Saturday, $16 pays for dinner and a hoedown with banjo and fiddle music, "Ozark humor" (read: lots of outhouse jokes), and clogging. (Open daily 4-9pm.) Locals swear by **Tommy's Famous...a pizzeria** (269-FAST/3278), about ½mi. west of the courthouse square on Rte. 66. A small pie goes for $6; calzones start at $7. (Open Wed.-Sat. 3-10pm, Sun. 3-7pm.)

Ozark culture thrives undiluted on the lush grounds of the **Ozark Folk Center** (269-3851), just min. north of Mountain View off Rte. 9N. The center recreates a mountain village and showcases the cabin crafts, music, and lore of the Ozarks. Among the 20 artisans practicing their trades in the **Crafts Forum** are a blacksmith, a basket weaver, a potter, a gunsmith, and a furniture maker. Visitors can taste biscuits and cornbread baked fresh in an antique kitchen (free), or dip their own candles in the chandler's shop (50¢). Musicians fiddle, pluck, and strum in the auditorium at lunchtime and nightly (shows at 7:30pm), while dancers implore the audience to jig and clog along. (Open May-Oct. daily 10am-5pm. Crafts area $6.50, ages 6-12 $3.75. Evening musical performances $7, ages 6-12 $4.50. Combination tickets and family rates available.) The center's seasonal events include the **Arkansas Folk Festival,** (April 19-21, 1996), the **Annual Dulcimer Jamboree** (April 26-28, 1996), **Banjo Weekend** in late May, and the **National Fiddle Championships** (Nov. 1-3, 1996). Revel in the musical charisma of triple Grammy Award winner Jimmy Driftwood, the quintessential Ozark artist, at the **Jimmy Driftwood Barn and Folk Museum** (269-8042), also on Rte. 9N (shows Fri. and Sun. 7:30pm; free). Then, when you're ready to learn everything there is to know about the dulcimer, travel up Rte. 9N to the **Dulcimer Shoppe,** P.O. Box 1230 (269-4313). Visitors can watch craftsmen fashion these mellow music makers and even hammer a few strings themselves. (Open Mon.-Fri. 9am-5pm, Sat. 10am-5pm.)

Fishing along the **White River** is one of many popular outdoor diversions in the area around Mountain View. Non-residents can purchase a 3-day **fishing license** ($10) from Wal-Mart, 314 Sylamore Ave. (269-4395). To experience the Ozarks from the saddle, contact **OK Trading Post** (585-2217), 3½ mi. west of the Rte. 5/9/14 junction (horse rentals $10 per hour). Daytrips from Mountain View to the **Buffalo River** (45min. northwest) are excellent for canoeing. **Crockett's Country Store and Canoe Rental** (800-355-6111), at the Rte. 14/27 junction in Harriet, can provide picnic lunches (about $5 per person), boats ($25), and maps of the waterways (life jackets and paddles come with boats; open daily 6am until the Crocketts go to bed). The **Blanchard Springs Caverns** (757-2211), on the south border of the Ozark Forest, glisten with exquisite cave formations and glassy, cool springs. Guided trails navigate the caverns (frequent 45-min. tours; last tour about 1hr. before closing); Blanchard has some great outdoor trails as well. (Open daily 9am-6:30pm; Nov.-March Wed.-Sun. 9:30am-4:30pm. $8, with Golden Age Passports and ages 6-15 $4.)

EUREKA SPRINGS

In the early 19th century, the native Osage spread reports of a wonderful spring with magical healing powers. Settlers quickly came to the site and established a small town from which they sold bottles of the miraculous water. Today, the tiny town in northwest Arkansas is filled with ritzy boutiques and Victorian buildings painted in the gaudy colors of citrus fruits. Tourists still come in droves, but no longer to experience the waters (they go to Hot Springs for that); Eureka's main attraction is the **Great Passion Play** (253-9200 or 800-882-PLAY/7529), off U.S. 62 on Passion Play Rd., modeled after Germany's *Oberammergau* Passion Play. Featuring a cast of 250 actors and countless live animals, this seasonal event built on piety, holy water, and slick marketing has drawn more than five million visitors to its depiction of Jesus Christ's life and death. Even if you miss the show, you can't miss the **Christ of the Ozarks** statue, seven stories of the messianic schtick used in the set. (Performances April 26-Oct. 26 Tues.-Wed. and Fri.-Sun. 8:30pm. Disabled access seating provided; sign language interpretation available on request. $12-13, ages 4-11 ½-price. For reservations write P.O. Box 471, Eureka Springs 72632.)

For info on the town and the play, visit the **chamber of commerce** (253-8737 or 800-643-3546), on U.S. 62 just north of Rte. 23 (open Mon.-Sat. 9am-5:30pm, Sun. 9am-5pm; Nov.-April Mon.-Fri. 9am-5pm). A **trolley** (253-9572) runs to the play, local churches, and the downtown historic loop (April-Labor Day daily 9am-7pm; Labor Day-Oct. Sun.-Thurs. 9am-5pm, Fri.-Sat. 9am-7pm. $3.50 per day for 1 route, kids under 7 free). Eureka's **post office:** 101 Spring St. (253-9850), on the loop (open Mon.-Fri. 8:15am-4:15pm, Sat. 10am-noon); **ZIP code:** 72632. **Area code:** 501.

Eureka Springs has more hotel beds than it does residents, and rates change almost daily. The **Frontier Motel** (253-9508), on Rte. 62E 1 mi. east of the Passion Play entrance, rents clean rooms with wooden-paneled walls and shaggy brown carpets (singles and doubles $32, two beds $38). Prices drop on Mondays and Thursdays, when Passion Players take a break. **Kettle Campgrounds** (253-9100), on Rte. 62 at the east edge of town, has 14 tent sites and 66 RV hook-ups ($10/15) as well as a brand-new pool. Reservations recommended.

The town is filled with tourist-oriented restaurants. Get away from the fast food and tourist glitz at the **Chuck Wagon,** 84 S. Main St. (253-5629), which serves "sandwiches stacked like Mae West" ($3.25-$5.50) on a cozy patio jutting over a cliff (open Tues.-Sat. 11am-5pm). After your meal, head downstairs, take off your hat, and stay a while at the **Wagon Wheel** (253-9934), a beer-drinker's, country-western bar decorated with antiques (open Mon.-Fri. 10am-2am, Sat. 10am-midnight).

■■■ HOT SPRINGS

Despite tourist traps like alligator farms, wax museums, and ubiquitous gift shops, the town of Hot Springs delivers precisely what it advertises—cleansing, soothing relaxation. Once you've bathed in the coils of these 143° springs, you'll realize why everybody, even the federal government (see below for info on **Hot Springs National Park**), got in on the bathhouse craze of the 20s.

Practical Information Before touring Hot Springs, stop by the **visitors center,** 600 Central St. (321-2277, 800-772-2489, or 800-543-2284), downtown at Reserve St., and pick up the free *Hot Springs Pipeline* (open daily 9:30am-5pm). Hot Springs's **post office:** 100 Reserve St. (623-7703), at the corner of Central in the Federal Reserve Building; **ZIP code:** 71901. **Area code:** 501.

Accommodations, Camping, and Food Hot Springs has ample lodging, and the best deals can be found on the side streets off Central Ave., the town's main drag. The motels clustered along Rte. 7 and 88 have similar prices, but rates rise for the tourist season (Feb.-Aug.). Walk into a fairy tale at the **Best Motel,** 630 Ouachita (624-5736), which has gingerbread-like cabins organized around a small pool (singles $25, doubles $35). Those who can forsake the cuteness might look next door at the **Holiday Motel,** 642 Ouchita (624-9317; singles $24, doubles $26). The **Margarete Motel,** 217 Fountain St., offers an excellent deal on large rooms with kitchenettes (singles $26, doubles $34). Rooms at the **Parkway Motel,** 815 Park Ave. (624-2551), start at $22. Some rooms have microwaves, but, more importantly, all have "Sleep-Ease" to gently vibrate you to sleep (25¢ for 15min.).

The closest **campgrounds** are at **Gulpha Gorge** (624-3383 for info and emergencies), part of Hot Springs National Park; follow Rte. 70 to 70B about 3 mi. northeast of town (sites $8, seniors $4; no hookups, no showers). **Shore Line RV Park,** 5321 Central Ave. (525-1902), just south of town on Lake Hamilton, has full RV hookups, a pool, restrooms, showers, laundry facilities, and space for houseboats (sites $12 per day, $72 per week).

Snack on *beignets* (3 for 90¢) and *café au lait* (95¢) at **Café New Orleans,** 210 Central Ave. (624-3200). At dinnertime, the café serves New Orleans's best, including po'boys ($4.25-6) and seafood selections ($5-10). (Open Sun.-Thurs. 11am-8pm, Fri.-Sat. 11am-9pm.) **Granny's Kitchen,** 322 Central Ave. (624-6183), cooks up good ol' country food (plate lunches $4), with old-fashioned Americana lining the walls and huge model planes hanging from the ceiling. **Magee's Cafe,** 362 Central Ave. (623-4091), costs a bit more (dinners $5-8), but serves a fabulous chicken-fried steak ($7); try the Mississippi mud pie ($2) for dessert (open Sun.-Thurs. 8:30am-10pm, Fri.-Sat. 8:30am-midnight). Wherever you dine, just remember to drink the water—after all, that's what made Hot Springs famous.

Sights and Entertainment Let the baths begin! The **Buckstaff** (623-2308), in "Bathhouse Row" on Central Ave., retains the dignity and elegance of Hot Springs's heyday in the 1920s. (Open Mon.-Fri. 7-11:45am and 1:30-3pm, Sat. 7-11:45am. Bath $11.50, whirlpool $1.50 extra; massage $11.75.) Around the corner is the rather unconventional **Hot Springs Health Spa,** N. 500 Reserve (321-9664); not only does the spa offer the only coed baths in town (yes, suits are required!), but you can stay as long as you like and meander among many baths. Note the late hours. (Open daily 9am-9pm. Bath $11; massage $11-13.) The **Downtowner,** 135 Central Ave., gives the town's cheapest hands-on, full treatment baths with no difference in quality. (Open Mon.-Fri. 7-11:30am and 1:30-3:30pm, Sat. 7-11:30am and 2-4:30pm; closed Wed. afternoon. Bath $9.50, whirlpool $1.50 extra; massage $10.)

For info on **Hot Springs National Park,** contact the **Fordyce Bathhouse Visitors Center,** 369 Central Ave. (623-3383, TTD 624-2308), which distributes a handy guide listing the hours and prices of all the baths in town and a chart helpful for disabled and hearing-impaired visitors. The Center also has two self-guided tours: one on the history of the local baths, and one on the rise of President Clinton, who grew up in Hot Springs. (Open daily 9am-6pm.) Diehard sightseers should take the amphibious **National Park Duck Tour** (321-2911 or 800-682-7044), which leaves from 418 Central Ave. seven times a day to travel through Hot Springs and out into Lake Hamilton ($8.50, seniors $8, kids $5.50).

Hot Springs's natural beauty is unmistakable. You can gaze up at the green-peaked mountains as you cruise Lake Hamilton on the **Belle of Hot Springs,** 5200 Central Hwy. (525-4438), during a 1-hr. narrated tour alongside the Ouachita Mountains and Lake Hamilton mansions (trips in summer daily 1 and 3pm; $8.50, children $4.25). In town, the **Mountain Valley Spring Water Company,** 150 Central Ave. (623-6671 or 800-643-1501), offers free samples and tours of its national headquarters (open Mon.-Fri. 9am-5pm, Sat.-Sun. 10am-4pm). From the **Hot Springs Mountain Observatory Tower** (623-6035), located in the national park (turn off Central Ave. onto Fountain St. and follow the signs), you can view the beautiful panorama of the surrounding mountains and lakes. (Open May 16-Labor Day daily 9am-9pm, day after Labor Day-Oct. and March-May 15 9am-6pm, Nov.-Feb. 9am-5pm. $2.75, ages 5-11 $1.75, under 5 free.) Simpler (cheaper) pleasures await at **Whittington Park,** on Whittington St. off Central Ave., where shops and bathhouses give way to an expanse of trees, grass, and shaded picnic tables.

Family entertainment fills Hot Springs's nights. **The Famous Bath House Show,** 701 Central Ave. (623-1415), features just about every type of music around. (Show dates and times are sporadic; call for details. $9.45, under 13 $5; reservations recommended.) The **Music Mountain Jamboree,** 2720 Albert Pike, also U.S. 270W (767-3841), is a short drive out of town. Family-style country music shows take place here Monday through Saturday in summer and at various times throughout the rest of the year. (Shows at 8pm. $9, children $4.50; reservations recommended.))

Leaving Arkansas: Texarkana

Texarkana straddles the border between Texas and Arkansas; stand on the median of **State Line Ave.,** and you'll have a foot in each state. The **Texarkana Historical Museum,** 219 State Line Ave. (903-793-4831), has exhibits on the area's Native Americans and Texarkana's most famous entertainer, the father of ragtime, **Scott Joplin** (open Tues.-Sat. 10am-4pm; $1, kids 50¢). Maps and information on sights in Texarkana are available at the **Arkansas Tourist Information Center** (501-772-4301), off I-30E between exits 1 and 2 (open daily 8am-6pm).

GREAT LAKES

The world has glaciers to thank for this Midwestern freshwater paradise. During the Ice Age, massive sheets of ice flowed from the north, doing the work of countless bulldozers as they plowed the earth, carving out huge lake basins. At the end of the Ice Age, the glaciers receded and melted, leaving flat expanses of rich topsoil, numerous small pools, and five inland seas. These lands have yielded billions of bushels of grain and vegetables, acres of timber, and countless tons of iron and copper ore; the lakes have been the region's lifeline. Together, the Great Lakes comprise 15% of the earth's drinkable freshwater supply and an invaluable network of transport arteries for the surrounding states.

Lake Superior is the largest freshwater lake in the world, and its unpopulated, scenic coasts dance with one of the only significant wolf populations left in the lower 48 states. Lake Michigan proclaims itself a sports lover's paradise and delivers, with swimming, sailing, deep-water fishing, and sugar-fine sand dunes. Lake Erie has suffered the most from industrial pollution, but thanks to vigilant citizens and strict regulations, the shallowest Great Lake is gradually reclaiming its former beauty. The first Great Lake to be seen by Europeans, Lake Huron ironically lags behind in development, though not in size or recreational potential. The runt of the bunch, Lake Ontario still covers an area larger than New Jersey.

People have been drawn to the fertile plains and deep forests of the Great Lakes since prehistoric times. Today, the Great Lakes region's water and wilderness attract hostel and camping crowds, who revel in discovering areas that the talons of "progress" have never reached. The sophisticated urban traveler should not despair, however—Minneapolis/St. Paul has all the artsy panache of any coastal metropolis, while urban Chicago stands out as the focal point of Midwestern activity with world-class music, architecture, and cuisine.

Great Lakes Goodies

Authors: Sherwood Anderson, Theodore Dreiser, Ernest Hemingway, Garrison Keillor, Elmore Leonard, Carl Sandburg, Upton Sinclair.
Artists: Jim Dine, Charles Schulz.
Cuisine: Red meat, deep dish pizza, five-way chili, pasties, sour cream raisin pie, persimmon pudding.
Microbreweries: Detroit & Mackinac Brewery Ltd., Frankenmuth Brewery, Chicago, Golden Prairie, Pavichevich, Evansville, Indianapolis, Kalamazoo, August Schell, Cold Spring, Minnesota, Pete's, James Page, Summit, Hudepohl-Schoenling, Columbus, Joseph Huber, Jacob Leinenkugel, Stevens Point, Capital, Lakefront, Sprecher Brewing Co.
Native Americans: Erie, Miami, Illinois, Dakota, Santee, Winnebago, Fox, Menominee, Potawatomi.
Music: Jazz, blues, Muddy Waters, Chicago, Prince, Afghan Whigs, Hüsker Dü, The Replacements, John Cougar Mellencamp.
Film and TV: *The Blues Brothers, The Untouchables, Chicago Hope, Family Ties, Mary Tyler Moore, Coach, David Letterman* (he used to do the weather in Indianapolis), *WKRP in Cincinnati, Fantasy Island.*
Climate: Lake-effect snow.
Geography: Lakeshore.

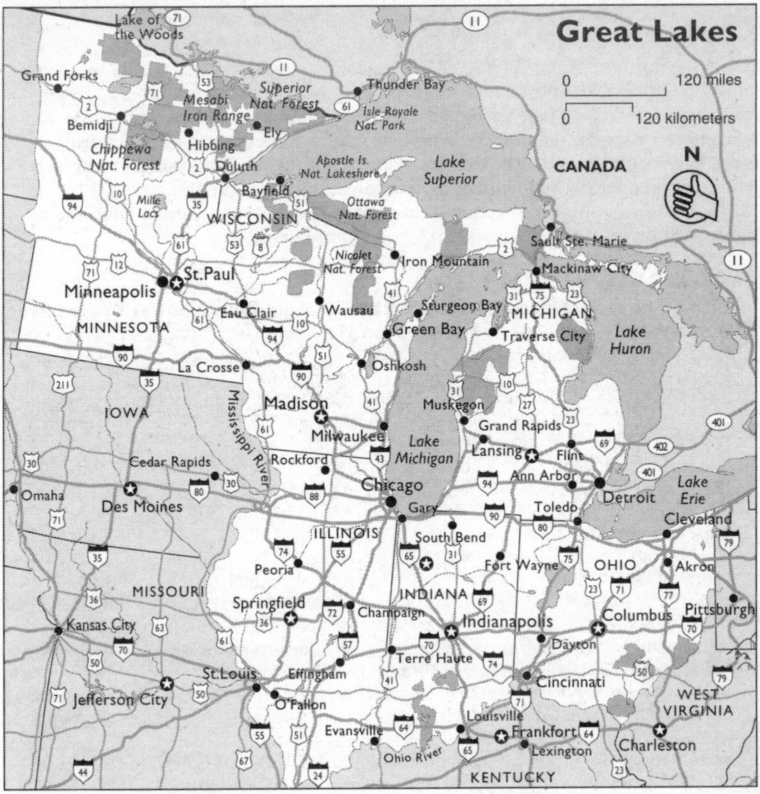

Ohio

Contrary to popular belief, Ohio is not Iowa, Idaho, all cornfields, or grimy and industrial; it *is* the only state south of Lake Erie that borders Michigan and starts with an "O." Eons ago, the glaciers that carved out the Great Lakes flattened the northern half of the state, creating perfect farmland that is today patched with cornfields and soybean plants. The southern half, spared the bulldozing, still rolls with endless wooded hills. Columbus sits just north of the abrupt line dividing the regions. The state's other two metropoli, mortal enemies Cincinnati and Cleveland, lie on opposite ends of the state. Not only unexpectedly diverse, Ohio is innovative, as evidenced by the state beverage, tomato juice—until popularized in Reynoldsburg, a Columbus suburb, tomatoes were thought poisonous and inedible.

PRACTICAL INFORMATION

Capital: Columbus.

State Office of Travel and Tourism: 77 S. High St., P.O. Box 1001, Columbus 43215 (614-466-8844). **Greater Columbus Convention and Visitors Bureau,** 1 Columbus Bldg., 10 W. Broad St., #1300, Columbus 43215 (614-221-2489 or 800-234-4386). Open Mon.-Fri. 8am-5pm. **Ohio Tourism Line:** 800-282-5393.

Time Zone: Eastern. **Postal Abbreviation:** OH

Sales Tax: 5.5%.

■■■ CLEVELAND

"Just drive north until the sky and all the buildings turn gray. Then you're in Cleveland." The critic who uttered this quote, hoping to achieve the "city cliché" honors normally reserved for Mark Twain, has remained obscure, much like any praise for beleaguered Cleveland—until recently. Despite a sometimes gloomy landscape, things have begun to look up; the city's old warehouses on the Cuyahoga River have been reworked into raving nightclubs, and the much-anticipated Rock and Roll Hall of Fame is finally open. With skillful management, Cleveland should continue its transformation from a popular joke to a pop culture haven.

PRACTICAL INFORMATION

Tourist Office: Cleveland Convention and Visitors Bureau, 3100 Tower City Center (621-4110 or 800-321-1001), on the 31st floor of Terminal Tower at Public Sq. Free maps. Write for the *Greater Cleveland Official Visitors Guide* for info on any conceivable attraction. Open Mon.-Fri. 8:30am-5pm.

Airport: Cleveland Hopkins International (265-6030), 10mi. west of downtown in Brookpark. Take RTA's airport rapid transit line #66X ("Red Line") to Terminal Tower ($1.50).

Trains: Amtrak, 200 Cleveland Memorial Shoreway N.E. (696-5115 or 800-872-7245), across from Municipal Stadium east of City Hall. To: New York City (1 per day, 11hr., $101); Chicago (2 per day, 6hr., $76). Open nightly 11pm-3:30pm.

Buses: Greyhound, 1465 Chester Ave. (781-0520 or 800-231-2222), at E. 14th St. 7 blocks from Terminal Tower. Near RTA bus lines. To: New York City ($6 per day, 11hr., $61); Chicago (8 per day, 7½hr., $32); Pittsburgh (10 per day, 3hr., $19).

Public Transportation: Regional Transit Authority (RTA), 315 Euclid Ave. (566-5074; 24-hr. **answerline** 621-9500), across from Woolworth's. Bus lines, connecting with Rapid Transit trains, provide transport to most of the metropolitan area. Service daily 4:30am-midnight; call the answerline for info on "owl" after-midnight service. Train fare $1.50. Bus fare $1.25, express $1.50; ask the driver for free transfer tickets when you get on. Office open Mon.-Fri. 7am-6pm with system schedules.

Taxis: Yellow Cab, 623-1550; **Americab,** 429-1111. Both $1.50 base fare, $1.20 per mile. Both 24 hrs. The wonders of government regulation!

Crisis Line: Rape Crisis Line, 391-3912. Open 24 hrs.

Emergency: 911.

Post Office: 2400 Orange Ave. (443-4199; 443-4096 after 5pm). Open Mon.-Fri. 8am-7pm. **ZIP code:** 44101. **Area code:** 216.

Terminal Tower in **Public Sq.** cleaves the land into east and west. North-south streets are number away from Terminal Tower with east-west prefixes; e.g. E. 18th St. is 18 blocks east of the Tower. To reach Public Sq. from **I-90** or **I-71,** follow the Ontario Ave./Broadway exit. From **I-77,** take the 9th St. exit to Euclid Ave., which runs into Public Sq. From the Amtrak station, follow **Lakeside Ave.** to **Ontario Ave.,** which leads to the tower. Almost all RTA trains and buses run downtown.

ACCOMMODATIONS AND CAMPING

With hotel taxes (not included in the prices listed below) as high as 14.5%, pickings are slim for good budget lodging in Cleveland. If you know your plans well in advance, **Cleveland Private Lodgings,** P.O. Box 18590, Cleveland 44118 (321-3213), can place you in a home around the city for as little as $35. (All arrangements must be made through the office; leave 2-3 weeks for a letter of confirmation. Call Mon.-Fri.; messages will be promptly returned.) Otherwise, travelers with cars should head for the suburbs, where prices tend to be lower. The great though somewhat distant **Stanford House Hostel (HI-AYH),** 6093 Stanford Rd. (467-8711), 22 mi. south of Cleveland in Peninsula off exit 12 from I-80 (take bus #77F to its last stop at Ridgefield Holiday Inn and buck up for a 5-mi. walk), occupies a beautifully restored 19th-century Greek Revival farmhouse in the Cuyahoga Valley National Recreation Area. Hiking and bike trails await nearby. (30 beds. 1-week max. stay.

Check-in 5-10pm. Curfew 11pm. Everybody pays $10. Reservations recommended.) **Cross Country Inn,** 7233 Eagle Rd. (243-2277), 20 minutes from downtown, is one of many on a strip of chain motels in Middleburg Heights. (A/C, cable, free local calls. Singles $36, plus an insane 14.5% tax; doubles $48+tax. 25% senior discount.)

Woodside Lake Park, 2256 Frost Rd. (626-4251), off I-480 in Streetsboro 40 minutes east of downtown, has 300 wooded and unwooded sites. (Sites for 2 $18, with electricity $19; $2 per extra person, ages 3-17 75¢. Reserve in summer.)

FOOD

Cleveland's culinary delights hide in tiny neighborhoods surrounding the downtown area. To satiate a craving for hot corned beef, step into one of the dozens of delis in the city center. Italian cafés and restaurants cluster in Little Italy around **Mayfield Rd.** For fine food, cool shops, and a healthy dose of hipness, slouch toward nearby Coventry Rd. Over 100 vendors hawk produce, meat, cheese and other groceries at the indoor-outdoor **West Side Market,** 1995 W. 25th St. (771-8885), at Lorain Ave. (open Mon. and Wed. 7am-4pm, Fri.-Sat. 7am-6pm).

Contemplate a stairway leading into the ceiling and a psychedelic VW bug clock while sipping cappuccino ($2) or munching on a deli sandwich ($4-5) at downtown hipster hang-out **Brewed Awakenings,** 1859 Prospect Ave. (696-5530), 15 minutes by sneaker from Terminal Tower (open Mon.-Fri. 7am-6pm, Sat. 9am-3pm). Tommy and the groovy health-conscious staff of **Tommy's,** 182 Coventry Rd. (321-7757), up the hill from University Circle (take bus #9X east to Mayfield and Coventry Rd.), whip up scrumptious natural and vegetarian cuisine. Of course, you can also dodge all that health stuff and sock your gut with a Brownie Monster ($1.75; open Mon.-Thurs. 7:30am-10pm, Fri.-Sat. 7:30am-11pm, Sun. 9am-10pm). **Mama Santa's,** 12305 Mayfield Rd. (421-2159), in Little Italy just east of University Circle, serves Sicilian food in a dark, authentic, no-frills setting. (Medium pizza $3.70; spaghetti $4.50. Open Mon.-Thurs. 10:30am-11:45pm, Fri.-Sat. 10:30am-12:45am.)

SIGHTS AND ENTERTAINMENT

Downtown Cleveland has escaped the plight of other Great Lakes cities, such as Detroit and Erie, with a new baseball diamond, the first-class mall in Terminal Tower, and a rockin' new museum—cash is flowing in, and life is good. **The Rock and Roll Hall of Fame,** 1 T Plaza (781-7625), finally opened on Labor Day, 1995; call for a description of current exhibits. (Open Sept. 5-Memorial Day Tues. and Thurs.-Sun. 10am-5:30pm, Wed. 10am-9pm; call for summer hours.) **Cleveland Lakefront State Park** (881-8141), a 14-mi.-long park 2 mi. west of downtown accessible from Lake Ave. or Cleveland Memorial Shoreway, includes a beach with great swimming and waterfront picnic areas (7mi. from downtown).

Seventy-five cultural institutions cluster in **University Circle,** 4 mi. east of the city. Check with the helpful visitors bureau (see Practical Information above) for details on museums, live music, and drama. The world-class **Cleveland Museum of Art,** 11150 East Blvd. (421-7340), exhibits fine French and American Impressionist paintings, as well as a version of Rodin's "The Thinker." A beautiful plaza and pond face the museum. (Open Tues. and Thurs.-Fri. 10am-5:45pm, Wed. 10am-9:45pm, Sat. 9am-4:45pm, Sun. noon-5:45pm. Free.) Nearby, the **Cleveland Museum of Natural History,** 7 Wade Oval Dr. (231-4600), displays the only existing skull of the fearsome Pygmy Tyrant *(Nanatyrannus)* in all its malignant smallness. (Open Mon.-Sat. 10am-5pm, Sun. noon-5pm. $6, students, seniors, and ages 5-17 $4, under 4 free; free Tues. and Thurs. 3-5pm.)

The **Cleveland Orchestra,** one of the nation's best, bows, plucks, and blows in University Circle at **Severance Hall,** 11001 Euclid Ave. (231-7300; tickets $14-26). In the summer, the orchestra moves to **Blossom Music Center,** 1145 W. Steels Corners Rd., Cuyahoga Falls (920-8040), about 45 minutes south of the city (lawn seating $12-14). In a nice area east of University Circle, the **Dobama Theatre,** 1846 Coventry Rd. (932-6838), Cleveland Hts., gives terrific, inexpensive (up to $15) performances in an intimate atmosphere. *Though University Circle is generally safe, some nearby areas get a little rough, especially at night.*

Playhouse Square Center, 1519 Euclid Ave. (771-4444), a 10-minute walk east of Terminal Tower, is the third-largest performing arts center in the nation. Inside, the **State Theater** hosts the **Cleveland Opera** (575-0900) and the famous **Cleveland Ballet** (621-2260) from October to June.

The **Cleveland Indians** play baseball at beautiful Jacobs Field (861-1200; tickets $4-18), while the **Cavaliers** hoop it up at the Arena (420-2000; tickets $10-31). In the fall, catch the orange-helmeted **Browns** in all their gridiron glory at Municipal Stadium (696-3800; tickets from $17).

NIGHTLIFE

A great deal of Cleveland's nightlife is focused in the **Flats,** the former industrial core of the city along both banks of the Cuyahoga River. Numerous nightclubs and restaurants, some with a family atmosphere, populate the northernmost section of the Flats just west of Public Square. On weekend nights, expect large crowds and larger traffic jams. Listen to live music and watch the sunset from the deck at **Rumrunners,** 1124 Old River Rd. (696-6070), on the east side of the river. (Draft beer $2. 18+ welcome. Cover $5; for those over 21, the cover includes 1 drink. Open Thurs. 7pm-2am, Fri. 4pm-2:30am, Sat.-Sun. 1pm-2:30am.) **Fagan's,** 996 Old River Rd. (241-6116), looks like a South Florida beach resort, not a den of iniquity which trains hungry English waifs to pickpocket. "Please, Sir. Can I have some sandwiches for $6-9 or entrees starting at $11?" "Yes, son, you can, but please tell your friends not to dance on the gorgeous riverside deck." (Bands nightly. Cover Sat.-Sun. $2-3. Open Sun.-Thurs. 11am-midnight, Fri.-Sat. 11am-2am.) Happy memories of a childhood rec-room return in **The Basement,** 1078 Old River Rd. (344-0001), three floors of 60s-retro theme rooms and paraphernalia. (Domestic beer $2.25. Happy hour with $1.50 drinks daily 7-9pm. Open Sun.-Thurs. 7pm-2:30am, Fri.-Sat. 5pm-2am.) Gays and lesbians plot a course to **The Grid,** 1281 W. 9th St. (623-0113), near the East Flats. Come to relax in the comfortable bar and stay for the high-tech dance floor. (Bottled beer $2.25. Open daily 4pm-2:30am.)

Several other clubs front the boardwalk on the west side of the river. **Shooters,** 1148 Main Ave. (861-6900), a huge bar and restaurant with a smashing view of the river and Lake Erie, occasionally books major acts for an all-ages audience. Avoid the restaurant (dinners $11-20—ouch!) and take your drink to the in-deck pool. (No cover. Open daily 11:30am-1:30am.) Hard-core rockers should steer clear of the Flats and head for Coventry, where the **Grog Shop,** 1765 Coventry Rd. (321-5588), brings in local and national acts for their entertainment.

■ NEAR CLEVELAND

The "best amusement park in the world," **Cedar Point Amusement Park** (419-627-2350), off U.S. 6, 65 mi. west of Cleveland in **Sandusky,** earns superlatives over and over. Basically, it's just cool as all hell. Eleven rollercoasters, from the world's highest and fastest inverted rollercoasters (riders are suspended from above) to a "training coaster" for kids, offer a grand old adrenaline rush for all. Stick around for the patriotic laser light show which takes the sky on summer nights at 10pm. (Open mid-May to mid-Sept. daily 10am-10pm; closes in May 8pm and on summer weekends midnight. $27, seniors $16, kids over 3 and under 48" $10.) The Lake Erie Coast around Sandusky is lined with numerous 50s-era roadside "amusements." **Train-O-Rama,** 6732 E. Harbor Rd. (419-734-5856), in Marblehead, consists of 1½ mi. of miniature track through a miniature landscape with towns, villages, ski slopes, waterfalls, airports, monorails, and more. (Open Mon.-Sat. 10am-6pm, Sun. 1-6pm; Labor Day-Memorial Day call for hours. $3.50, ages 4-11 $2.50.)

Sea World, 1100 Sea World Dr. (562-8101 or 800-63-SHAMU/637-4268), 30 mi. south of Cleveland off Rte. 43 at Rte. 91, presents Shark Encounter—sequel to the less menacing Penguin Encounter—along with numerous other aquatic exhibits.

(Open in summer daily 10am-11pm; off season call for hours. $24, ages 3-11 $19. Reduced prices on summer nights; senior discounts. Parking $3.)

Are you ready for some football? The **Pro Football Hall of Fame,** 2121 George Halas Dr. N.W. (456-8207), 60 mi. south of Cleveland in Canton, honors the pigskin greats; take exit 107a at the junction of I-77 and U.S. 62. (Open daily 9am-8pm, Labor Day-Memorial Day 9am-5pm. $7, seniors $3.50, and ages 6-14 $3.)

The Amish communities of **Holmes County** make an interesting day-trip a bit farther south. In **Berlin,** 70 mi. south of Cleveland on I-77 and 17 pastoral mi. west on Rte. 39, the **Amish Farm** (893-2951) sheds some light on Amish life with slide presentations, tours, and demonstrations of non-electrical appliances ($2.25, children $1), and buggy rides ($2.75; open April-Oct. Mon.-Fri. 10am-5pm, Sat. 10am-6pm).

■■■ COLUMBUS

Recently, rapid growth, a huge suburban sprawl, and some gerrymandering have pushed Columbus's population beyond that of Cincinnati or Cleveland. The main drag, High St., heads north from the towering office complexes of downtown, through the lively galleries and gay community in the Short North, and finally to the collegiate coolness of Ohio State University (OSU), the largest university in the country with over 60,000 students. Columbus is America without glitz, smog, pretension, or fame—the clean, wholesome land of *Family Ties* (Bexley, a Columbus suburb, was the model for the hit sitcom) and suburbanization.

Practical Information The **Greater Columbus Visitors Center** (221-2263 or 800-345-4386) is on the second floor of **City Center Mall** downtown. **Greyhound,** 111 E. Town St. (221-2389 or 800-231-2222), offers service from downtown to Cincinnati (10 per day, 2hr., $16), Cleveland (12 per day, 2½hr., $19), Chicago (5 per day, 7-10hr., $35). The **Central Ohio Transit Authority (COTA),** 177 S. High St. (228-1776; Mon.-Fri. 8:30am-5:30pm), runs in-town transportation until 11pm or midnight (fare $1, express $1.35). Columbus's **area code:** 614.

Accommodations and Food In the summer, when OSU students have vacated, check around the campus for apartment houses which advertise for cheap temporary rentals. Another resource, **Greater Columbus Bed & Breakfast Cooperative** (444-8488 or 800-383-7839) offers B&Bs in a wide radius around Columbus ($35 and up). The **Heart of Ohio Hostel (HI-AYH),** 95 E. 12th Ave. (294-7157), 1 block from OSU, has outstanding facilities, including a piano and a kitchen with an espresso machine, in a house designed by Frank Lloyd Wright. The management conducts numerous organized activities—biking, hiking, rock climbing, and more—and gives a free night's stay to anyone who puts on a one-hour concert. (Check-in 5-11pm. Curfew 11pm. $8, nonmembers $11. Weekly rates available.)

High St. features scads of tasty budget restaurants. **Bernie's Bagels and Deli,** 1896 N. High St. (291-3448), offers a variety of sandwiches in a dark punk-rock cellar atmosphere ($3-6); live shows play in the adjoining Bernie's Distillery. (See Nightlife below. Open Mon.-Tues. 8:30am-1am, Wed.-Fri. 8:30am-2am, Sat. 9:30am-2am, Sun. 9:30am-1am; in summer closed Sun.) **Bermuda Onion Delicatessen,** 660 N. High St. (221-6296), specializes in sandwiches ($4-7), such as grilled provolone on challah with herb mayo, sprouts, and tomato (open Mon.-Fri. 8am-4pm, Sat.-Sun. 8am-5pm). A small and well-loved Middle Eastern restaurant/grocery, **Firdous,** 1538 N. High St. (299-1844), makes tasty hummus plates ($5), fresh falafel, and shish-kebabs (open Mon.-Thurs. 10am-9pm, Fri.-Sat. 10am-10pm, Sun. noon-8pm).

Sights **Ohio State University (OSU)** looms 2 mi. north of downtown. On campus, the well-respected, heavily endowed, and architecturally outstanding **Wexner Center for the Arts** (292-3535; box office 292-2354, open Mon.-Fri. 9am-5pm), on N. High St. at 15th Ave., shows avant-garde exhibits and films and hosts progressive music, dance, and other performances. The bookstore (292-1807) carries an exhaustive selection of art books and gifts. (Exhibits open Tues. and Thurs.-Fri. 10am-6pm, Wed. and Sat. 10am-8pm, Sun. noon-5pm. Free.)

In 1991, the **Columbus Museum of Art,** 480 E. Broad St. (221-6801), acquired the Sirak Collection of Impressionist and European Modernist works. (Open Tues.-Wed. and Fri.-Sun. 10am-5:30pm, Thurs. 10am-8:30pm. Suggested donation $3, students and seniors $2.) Frazzle your hair and shock your friends with the static electricity ball at the **Center of Science and Industry (COSI),** 280 E. Broad St. (288-COSI/2674), ½ mi. west of I-71. (Open Mon.-Sat. 10am-5pm, Sun. noon-5:30pm. $6, seniors and ages 2-12 $4, ages 13-18 $5.) Look across the street to see the very first link in the **Wendy's** restaurant chain. Just west, James Thurber's childhood home, the **Thurber House,** 77 Jefferson Ave. (464-1032), is decorated with cartoons by the famous author and *New Yorker* cartoonist (open daily noon-4pm; free).

The expansive **Franklin Park Conservatory,** 1777 E. Broad St. (645-8733), has a mammoth collection of self-contained plant environments including rain forests, deserts, and Himalayan mountains. (Open Tues.-Sun. 10am-5pm, Wed. 10am-8pm. $4, students and seniors $3, kids $2.)

South of Capitol Square, the **German Village,** first settled in 1843, is now the largest privately-funded historical restoration in the U.S., full of stately brick homes and old-style beer halls. At **Schmidt's Sausage Haus,** 240 E. Kossuth St. (444-6808), the oom-pah band **Schnickelfritz** leads polkas at 8pm nightly; between dances, try a plate of homemade sausage ($7; open Sun.-Thurs. 11am-10pm, Fri.-Sat. 11am-midnight). On only one magical day each year, the last Sunday in June, visitors can tour everything in the village. Call or stop by the **German Village Society,** 588 S. 3rd St. (221-8888; open Mon.-Fri. 9am-4pm, Sat. 10am-2pm, Sun. noon-4pm).

Entertainment and Nightlife Four free weekly papers, *The Other Paper, Columbus Alive, The Guardian,* and *Moo,* available in many shops and restaurants, list arts and entertainment options. On the first Saturday night of each month, Columbus hosts the roaming art-party known as **The Gallery Hop;** galleries in the Short North display new exhibitions while socialites and art collectors admire the works (and each other) far into the night. A good place to start hopping is **Gallery V,** 694 N. High St. (228-8955), which exhibits contemporary paintings, sculptures, and works in less common media (open Tues.-Sat. 11am-5pm). The **Riley Hawk Galleries,** 642 N. High St. (228-6554), rank among the world's finest for glass sculpture (open Tues.-Sat. 11am-5pm, Sun. 1-4pm).

When you O.D. on art, Columbus has a sure cure: rock 'n' roll. Bar bands are a Columbus mainstay; it's hard to find a bar that *doesn't* have live music on the weekend. For rock, blues, and more, head to **Stache's,** 2404 N. High St. (263-5318). Bigger national acts stop at the **Newport,** 1722 N. High St. **Bernie's Distillery,** 1896 N. High St. (291-3448), intoxicates with 75 imported beers (domestic beer $1.75) and pounding live music all week (cover Fri.-Sat. $1). The once-industrial **Brewery District** now houses bunches of bars. **High Beck,** 564 S. High St. (224-0886), grooves to rock and R&B, while **Hosters Brewing Co.,** 550 S. High St. (228-6066), at Livingston, attracts locals with homemade brew. **Paradigm,** 163 N. High St. (464-2100), provides house, tribal, acid jazz, and thumping club fare (Tues.-Sat.). Music enthusiasts should browse **Used Kids** or **Magnolia Thunderpussy,** both on High St. near the OSU campus, for some of the best used CD and cassette bargains in the nation.

On more mellow evenings, many Columbians (Columbusians?) head for the cafés. **Insomnia,** 1728 N. High St. (421-1234), near the OSU campus, serves up sweet caffeine in a homey atmosphere (if your home is filled with Bohemian students) with couches, board games, and a gas pump (iced flavored coffee $1). **Cup O' Joe,** 627 S. 3rd St. (221-1563), in German Village, adorns itself with a cubist Cup O' Joe interpretation on one wall and futuristic lamps, and a deliciously high level of pretention. Try the $2.50 Mocha Joe. (Open Mon.-Wed., Thurs. 7am-11pm, Fri. 7am-10pm, Sat. 8am-1am, Sun. 8am-10pm.)

■ NEAR COLUMBUS

A one-hour drive south of Columbus, the area around **Chillicothe** features several interesting attractions. Three mi. north of town on Rte. 14, the **Hopewell Culture National Historic Park** (774-1125) swells with 24 enigmatic Hopewell burial mounds spread over 13 acres. The adjoining museum elucidates theories about Hopewell society based upon the mounds' configuration and shows a 17-minute video. (Museum open daily 8am-5pm; grounds open dawn-dusk. Entrance $4 per car, $2 per pedestrian, seniors and under 17 free.) Check with park officials for info on other nearby mounds. From mid-June to early September, the Sugarloaf Mountain Amphitheatre, 7 mi. northeast of Chillicothe, presents **Tecumseh** (775-0700), a drama re-enacting the life and death of the Shawnee leader (shows Mon.-Sat. 8pm; tickets Mon.-Thurs. $11, Fri.-Sat. $13; under 11 $6). A $3.50 behind-the-scenes tour, available hourly 2-5pm, will answer your questions about how the stunt men dive headfirst off the 21-ft. cliff. At **Scioto Trail State Park** (663-2125), 10 mi. south of Chillicothe off U.S. 23, a ¼-mi. walk leads to free 24-hr. walk-in **camping** behind Stuart Lake; no walk means crashing at the designated sites ($7, with electricity $11).

From Columbus, take U.S. 33 and then some very hilly, winding roads down to the stunning **Hocking Hills State Park,** 30 mi. east of Chillicothe; follow the signs. Waterfalls, gorges, cliffs, and "caves"—cavernous overhangs gouged in the rock by ancient rivers—scar the rugged terrain within the park. The park's main attraction is **Old Man's Cave** (385-6165), off Rte. 64, which takes its name from a hermit who lived, died, and was buried there in the 1800s. Be careful when exploring the cave area itself, especially in wet weather or in winter; people have died after slipping and falling. Old Man's Cave offers **camping** (primitive camping $5; sites with pool $6, with electricity and pool—don't try this at home!—$11).

■■■ CINCINNATI

Longfellow called it the "Queen City of the West." However, the winged pigs which guard the entrance to downtown's Sawyer Point Park recall a different moniker bestowed on Cincinnati by more prosaic folk—"Porkopolis." In the 1850s, the city led the planet in pork-packing. Today, the frontier has long ago moved on to parts west, and pigs no longer snort through the streets; Cincinnati instead parades an excellent collection of museums, a pleasantly designed waterfront, and a jillion parks. Hidden in a valley surrounded by seven rolling hills and the Ohio River, Cincinnati seems to defy its isolation with prosperity.

PRACTICAL INFORMATION

Tourist Office: Cincinnati Convention and Visitors Bureau, 300 W. 6th St. (621-2142 or 800-246-2987). Open Mon.-Fri. 8:45am-5pm. Pick up the *Official Visitors Guide.* Also try the **Information Booth** in Fountain Sq. Open Mon.-Sat. 9am-5pm. **Info Line,** 528-9400. Lists plays, opera, and symphonies.

Airport: Greater Cincinnati International, in Kentucky, 13mi. south of Cincinnati. **Jetport Express** (606-767-3702) shuttles to downtown ($10).

Trains: Amtrak, 1301 Western Ave. (651-3337 or 800-872-7245), in Museum Center at Union Terminal. To: Indianapolis (3 per week, 3hr., $32); Chicago (3 per week, 8hr., $64). Open Mon. 9:30am-5pm, Tues.-Fri. 9:30am-5pm and 11pm-6:30am, Sat.-Sun. 11pm-6:30am. Avoid the neighborhood north of the station.

Buses: Greyhound, 1005 Gilbert Ave. (352-6041 or 800-231-2222), just past the intersection of E. Court and Broadway. To: Indianapolis (4 per day, 2-3hr., $19); Louisville (12 per day, 2hr., $19); Cleveland (10 per day, 4-6hr., $36); Columbus (12 per day, 2-3hr., $16). Open daily 7:30am-6:30am. Tickets 24 hrs.

Public Transportation: Queen City Metro, 122 W. Fifth St. (621-4455; Mon.-Fri. 6:30am-6pm, Sat. 8am-5pm). Most buses run out of Government Sq., at 5th and Main St., to outlying communities. Rush-hour fare 80¢, other times 65¢, Sat.-Sun. 50¢; to suburbs 30¢ extra. Office has schedules and info.

Taxi: Yellow Cab, 241-2100. $1.50 base fare, $1.20 per mi. 24 hrs.

Crisis Lines: Rape Crisis Center, 216 E. 9th St. (381-5610), downtown. 24 hrs. **Gay/Lesbian Community Switchboard:** 651-0070. Open Mon.-Fri. 7am-11pm, Sat.-Sun. noon-7pm.
Emergency: 911.
Post Office: 525 Vine St. (684-5667), located in the Skywalk. Open Mon.-Fri. 8am-5pm, Sat. 8am-1pm. **ZIP code:** 45202. **Area code:** 513; Kentucky suburbs 606.

The downtown business community centers on **Fountain Sq.,** on E. 5th at Vine St. Cross streets are numbered and designated East or West, by their relation to Vine St. **Riverfront Stadium,** the **Serpentine Wall,** and the **Riverwalk** are down by the river. The **University of Cincinnati** spreads out from Clifton, north of the city.

ACCOMMODATIONS AND CAMPING

Sometimes, life doesn't go your way. Sometimes, you just have to take what you can get. Sometimes, the selection of accommodations in a city just...

College of Mount St. Joseph, 5701 Delhi Rd. (244-4327 or 244-4373), about 8mi. west of downtown off U.S. 50; take bus #32. A few immaculate rooms in a quiet, remote location available year-round; call ahead. Sinks in rooms, baths in the hall, lounge, no A/C. Singles $15, doubles $20; rates may rise. Cafeteria lunch $3.50.

Super 8 Motel, 11335 Chester Rd. (772-3140), in Sharonville 30min. from downtown. Cheery, luxurious accommodations in a safe and unusually pleasant motel district. A/C, cable TV, HBO, outdoor pool and free local calls. Singles or doubles $49; prices rise on weekends. AAA and AARP discounts.

Yogi Bear's Camp Resort, 5688 Kings Island Dr. (800-832-1133), off I-71 exit 25 at Mason. 350 pricey sites for 2 $25, with full hookup $38. Cabins for 2 $50. $5 per extra adult, $3.50 per extra child. Pool, playground. Within a stone's throw of Kings Island amusement park. Reservations recommended.

Rose Gardens Resort—KOA Campgrounds (606-428-2000), off I-75 at exit 166, 30mi. south of Cincinnati. 100 sites, some overlooking a small pond. Tent sites with hook-up $16. Cabins with water and electricity $25. Paddleboats $3 per hr.

GREAT LAKES

FOOD

The city that gave us the first soap opera, the first baseball franchise (the Redlegs), and the Heimlich maneuver presents its great culinary contribution—**Cincinnati chili.** Although this mixture of meat sauce, spaghetti, and cheese is an all-pervasive ritual in local culture, somehow, no other city seems to have caught this gastronomical wave. Chili is cheap; antacid tablets cost extra.

Skyline Chili, everywhere. 65 locations in Cincinnati, including 643 Vine St. (241-2020), at 6th St. Better than other chains. The secret ingredient has been debated for years; some say chocolate, but curry is more likely. 5-way jumbo chili $4.90, cheese coney (hot dog) $1.15. Open Mon.-Fri. 10:30am-7pm, Sat. 11am-3pm.

Graeter's, 41 E. 4th St. (381-0653), between Walnut and Vine St. downtown, and 10 other locations. Since 1870, Graeter's has been pleasing sweet-toothed locals with candy and ice cream made with giant chocolate chips. (Not very) small cone $1.25, with chips $1.30. Open Mon.-Sat. 7am-6pm.

Izzy's, 819 Elm St. (721-4241), also 610 Main St. This unpretentious deli, founded in 1901, is a Cincinnati institution. Overstuffed sandwiches $3-4. Addictive potato pancakes (99¢ each, and worth every penny). Izzy's famous Reuben $5. Open Mon.-Fri. 8am-10pm, Sat. 10am-5pm; Main St. location open Mon.-Sat. 7am-9pm.

Mulane's, 723 Race St. (381-1331). A streetside café and restaurant with terrific vegetarian food. Out-of-this world meatless entrees (lunch $5-6, dinner $7-8) and hearty salads. Live music weekly. Chicken or ham can be added to entrees for $2. Open Mon.-Thurs. 11:30am-11pm, Fri. 11:30am-midnight, Sat. 5pm-midnight.

Kaldi's, 1204-6 Main St. (241-3070). Get hep, hepcat. Grab a book from the shelf, nurse a cup of Kaldi's blend java ($1.25, or $2 to render it bottomless), and git hit in your soul, daddy-o. This café also serves healthy entrees, sandwiches, and salads. Sausage & Cheese Soufflé $5. Live jazz Thurs.-Sun. 9pm; local alternative or bluegrass music Mon. and Wed.; poetry readings Sat. or Sun. Open Mon.-Thurs. 8am-1am, Fri. 8am-2:30am, Sat. 10am-2:30am, Sun. 10am-1am.

SIGHTS

Downtown Cincinnati orbits around the **Tyler Davidson Fountain,** a florid 19th-century masterpiece and an ideal spot to people-watch. If you squint, you can almost see Les Nesman rushing to WKRP to deliver the daily hog report. Check out the expansive gardens at **Proctor and Gamble Plaza,** just east of Fountain Sq., or walk along **Fountain Square South,** a shopping and business complex connected by a series of second-floor skywalks. In the square, the observation deck at the top of **Carew Tower** provides the best view in the city. When the visual stimuli exhaust you, prick up your ears for a free concert in front of the fountain, presented by **Downtown Council** (579-3191; open Mon.-Fri. 8:30am-5pm).

Close to Fountain Sq., the **Contemporary Arts Center,** 115 E. 5th St., 2nd floor (345-8500), near Walnut St., carries a strong reputation in the national arts community. In 1990, the Center was indicted for showing Robert Mapplethorpe's photographic works, in an incident which touched off the national controversy over the NEA. Exhibits change frequently; call about current shows and evening films, music, and multimedia performances. (Open Mon.-Sat. 10am-5pm, Sun. 1-5pm. $2, seniors and students $1, under 13 free; free Mon.) Also downtown, the **Taft Museum,** 316 Pike St. (241-0343), has a beautiful collection of painted enamels, as well as pieces by Rembrandt and Whistler. (Open Mon.-Tues. and Thurs.-Sat. 10am-5pm, Sun. 1-5pm. $3, seniors and students $1.)

Cincinnati's answer to Paradise is **Eden Park,** northeast of downtown; take bus #49 to Eden Park Dr. The **Krohn Conservatory** (421-5707), one of the largest public greenhouses in the world, presents an indoor Eden (open daily 10am-5pm; $2, seniors and under 18 $1). The collections at the **Cincinnati Art Museum** (721-5204), within the park, span 5000 years, including musical instruments and Near Eastern artifacts. (Open Tues.-Sat. 10am-5pm, Sun. 11am-5pm. $5, students and seniors $4, under 17 free.)

Union Terminal, 1031 Western Ave. (287-7000 or 800-733-2077), 1 mi. west of downtown near the Ezzard Charles Dr. exit off I-75 (take bus #1), functions more as a museum than as a bus terminal. A fine example of Art Deco architecture, the building boasts the world's largest permanent half-dome. Inside, cool down in an Ice-Age world of simulated glaciers at the **Museum of Natural History** (287-7020), or investigate a carefully constructed artificial cavern, which features a colony of real live bats. On the other side of the dome, the **Cincinnati Historical Society,** 1301 Western Ave. (287-7030), in Museum Center, houses exhibits on Cincinnati history and an **Omnimax Theater** (287-7081; call for showtimes). (Both museums open Mon.-Sat. 9am-5pm, Sun. 11am-6pm. 1 museum $5, ages 3-12 $3; both museums $8/$4; Omnimax $6/$4; all 3 $12/$7.)

ENTERTAINMENT AND NIGHTLIFE

Pick up the free newspapers *City Beat* and *Everybody's News* for happenings around town. The cliff-hanging communities on the steep streets of **Mt. Adams** support a vivacious arts and entertainment industry. Perched on its own wooded hill, the **Playhouse in the Park,** 962 Mt. Adams Circle (421-3888), does theater-in-the-round with a remarkable range of dramatic style. (Performances mid-Sept. to June Tues.-Sun. Tickets $19-31; student and senior rush 15min. before show $12.)

The University of Cincinnati's **Conservatory of Music** (556-9430) gives free pops concerts, as well as classical recitals. A tad more upscale, the **Music Hall,** 1243 Elm St. (721-8222), hosts the **Cincinnati Symphony Orchestra** (381-3300) September through May (tickets $10-40). The orchestra's summer season (June-July) takes place at **Riverbend,** near Coney Island (tickets $12.50-29). The **Cincinnati Ballet Company** (621-5219; performances Oct.-May; tickets $9-48) and **Cincinnati Opera** (241-2742; limited summer schedule; tickets $15-60) perform in the Music Hall as well. For updates, call **Dial the Arts** (751-2787).

Escape the highbrow and beat the summer heat in the world's largest recirculating pool at **Coney Island,** 6201 Kellogg Ave. (232-8230), off I-275 at the Kellogg Ave. exit. Other amusements include waterslides, rides, and an 18-hole miniature golf course on which each hole replicates one of the famous holes on the PGA tour. (Pool open daily 10am-8pm; rides Mon.-Fri. noon-9pm, Sat.-Sun. 11am-9pm. Pool only $11, seniors and ages 4-11 $9; rides only $7/$7; both $15/$13.) **Summerfair** (531-0050), an art extravaganza, takes over the park for the first weekend in June.

Cincinnati's fanatical fans watch baseball's **Reds** (421-4510; tickets $6.50-11.50, day of game $3.50) and football's **Bengals** (621-3550; tickets $30) in **Riverfront Stadium,** 100 Broadway. The **Riverfront Coliseum** (241-1818), a Cincinnati landmark, hosts other sports events and concerts year-round.

At the beginning of September, **Riverfest** (352-4001) memorializes the roles of the river and steamboats in Cincinnati's history. The city basks in its German heritage during **Oktoberfest-Zinzinnati** (579-3191), held the third weekend in September. For more info on festivals, contact the Convention and Visitors Bureau (see Practical Information above).

Overlooking downtown from the east, Mt. Adams harbors Cincinnati's most active nightlife. For a drink that will transport you back to the 19th century, try Cincinnati's oldest tavern, **Arnold's,** 210 E. 8th St. (421-6234), between Main St. and Sycamore downtown. After 9pm, Arnold's does that ragtime, traditional jazz, bluegrass, and swing thing; wash down a Thai chicken sandwich ($5.75) with a draft beer (domestic $1.25) and sit a spell. (Open Mon.-Fri. 11am-1am, Sat. 4pm-1am). Antique toys adorn the inside of **Blind Lemon,** 936 Hatch St. (241-3885), at St. Gregory St. in Mt. Adams, while live jazz and blues fill the courtyard. (Domestic draft $2. Music daily 9:30pm; no cover. Open Mon.Fri. 5pm-2:30am, Sat. 3pm-2:30am, Sun. 3-8:30pm.) **Main Street Brewery,** 1203 Main St. (665-HOPS/4677), downtown, pours homebrewed Main Street Ale (pint $3) for crowds of youngish locals who come to be seen in this new hotspot (open Mon.-Thurs. 11am-11pm, Fri.-Sat. 11am-midnight, Sun. noon-11pm).

■ NEAR CINCINNATI

If you can't get to California's Napa or Sonoma Valleys, the next best thing may be **Meiers Wine Cellars,** 6955 Plainfield Pike (891-2900); take I-71 to exit 12 or I-75 to Galbraith Rd. Free tours of Ohio's oldest and largest winery give you a chance to observe the entire wine-making operation and taste the fermented fruits of the labor. (Tours June-Oct. Mon.-Sat. every hr. 10am-3pm; Nov.-May by appointment.)

The town of **Mason,** 24 mi. north of Cincinnati off I-71 at exit #24, beckons with **Paramount's Kings Island** (800-288-0808), an amusement park which cages **The Beast,** the world's longest wooden rollercoaster. Do you remember the now-classic 1974 Brady Bunch episodes in which the kids lost Mike Brady's architectural plans? Well, all the wild shenanigans took place at Kings Island. Admission to the park entitles you to unlimited rides and attractions and the opportunity to buy expensive food. Lines shrink after dark. (Open May 27-Sept. 4 Sun.-Fri. 10am-10pm, Sat. 10am-11pm. $27, seniors and ages 3-6 $16. Parking $4.)

Michigan

Michigan's developed Lower Peninsula paws the Great Lakes like a huge mitten, while its pristine and oft-ignored Upper Peninsula hangs above, quietly nursing moose and a famed population of wolves. Together, they define over 3000 mi. of coastline along four of the Great Lakes; their shores have the feel of an ocean coast— uniquely blended with the fresh water of the lakes—in the heart of America. Dunes, beaches, forests, and over 11,000 smaller inland lakes add to Michigan's coastal character; and the state, whose once-booming automotive industry now fills only a shadow of its former stature, is starting to make waves as a natural getaway.

PRACTICAL INFORMATION

Capital: Lansing.

Michigan Travel Bureau: 333 S. Capitol Suite F, Lansing 48909 (517-335-1876 or 800-543-2937). Gives out info on the week's events and festivals. **Department of Natural Resources,** Information Services Center, P.O. Box 30028, Lansing 48909 (517-373-1270). Offers info on state parks, forests, campsites, and other facilities. Entry to all state parks requires a motor vehicle permit; $4 per day, $20 annually. Call 800-543-2937, for reservations at any state park campground.

Time Zones: Eastern, except a small sliver of the western Upper Peninsula which lies in Central (1hr. behind Eastern). All of *Let's Go's* Michigan coverage lies within Eastern. **Postal Abbreviation:** MI

Sales Tax: 6%.

■■■ DETROIT

An author recently proclaimed Detroit "America's first Third-World city"; indeed, the city has witnessed a quarter-century of hardship. In the 60s, as the country grooved to Motown's beat, the city erupted with some of the era's most violent race riots. Massive white flight to the suburbs has been the norm ever since; the population has more than halved since 1967, turning some neighborhoods into ghost towns. The decline of the auto industry in the late 70s added unemployment to the city's slate of problems, causing frustration, violence, and hopelessness among its residents.

The five gleaming towers of the riverside Renaissance Center symbolize the hope of a city-wide comeback. Aggressive tourist media focuses attention on Detroit's attractions: Michigan's largest and most comprehensive museums, a fascinating ethnic history, and the still-visible (though soot-blackened and slightly crumbling) architectural evidence of the city's former grandeur. Detroit may no longer be the city it once was, but it does its best to present an attractive face to the world.

PRACTICAL INFORMATION

Tourist Office: Detroit Convention and Visitors Bureau, 100 Renaissance Center, #126 (567-1170 or 800-338-7648). Pick up the free *Metro Detroit Visitors Guide.* Open Mon.-Fri. 9am-5pm, Sat. 10am-5pm, Sun. noon-5pm; call after hours for a recorded list of entertainment events.

Airport: Detroit Metropolitan (942-3550 or 800-351-5466), 2mi. west of downtown off I-94 at Merriman Rd. in Romulus. **Commuter Transportation Company** (941-3252) runs shuttles downtown (45min.; $13), stopping at major hotels such as the Shorecrest Motor Inn (see Accommodations, below). Daily on the hour 7am-midnight. Make reservations. A taxi to downtown costs $25.

Trains: Amtrak, 11 W. Baltimore (873-3442 or 800-872-7245), at Woodward. To: Chicago (3 per day, 5hr., $31); New York (1 per day, 16hr., $112). Open daily 6am-11:30pm. For Canadian destinations, you must go through **VIA Rail,** 298 Walker Rd., Windsor, Ont. (800-561-3949), across the river in Canada.

Buses: Greyhound, 1001 Howard St. (961-8011 or 800-231-2222). At night, the area is deserted and not very safe. To: Chicago (7 per day, 7hr., $25); St. Louis (7 per day, 13-15hr., $49). Station open 24 hrs.; ticket office open daily 6:30am-1am.

Public Transportation: Detroit Department of Transportation (DOT), 1301 E. Warren (925-4910; 933-1300 for customer service). Carefully policed public transport system serves downtown, with limited service to the suburbs. Many buses stop service at midnight. Fare $1.25, transfers 25¢. **DOT Attractions Shuttle** (259-8726), shuttles tourists to the metro area's most popular sights 10am-7:45pm. All-day ticket $4. **People Mover,** Detroit Transportation Corporation, 150 Michigan Ave. (800-541-RAIL/7245). Ultramodern elevated tramway circles the Central Business District on a 2.7-mi. loop; worth a ride just for the view.

Runs Mon.-Thurs. 7am-11pm, Fri. 7am-midnight, Sat. 9am-midnight, Sun. noon-8pm. Fare 50¢. **Southeastern Michigan Area Regional Transit (SMART),** 962-5515. Bus service to the suburbs. Fare $1-2.50, transfers 10¢. Get free maps of the system at the office on the first floor of First National Bank at Woodward and Fort. Buses run 4am-midnight. All-day pass $1.50. **Tunnel Bus,** 519-944-4111. Transport from Detroit to downtown Windsor, Ont. Fare $1.50. **Detroit Trolley,** 933-1300 or 933-8020. Runs daily 7am-5pm, weather permitting. Fare 50¢.

Taxis: Checker Cab, 963-7000. Flat fee $1.40 per mi.

Car Rental: Thrifty Rent-a-Car, 29111 Wick Rd. (946-7830), in Romulus. $35 per day, $185 per week; unlimited mi. in Michigan and neighboring states. Optional insurance $9. Must be 21 with credit card. Under 25 surcharge $10 per day.

Crisis Lines: 24-hr. Crisis Hotline, 224-7000. **Sexual Abuse Helpline,** 800-551-0008 or 800-234-0038. 24 hrs. **Gay and Lesbian Switchboard Line,** 398-4297. Sun.-Fri. 4:30-11pm.

Emergency: 911.

Post Office: 201 Michigan (965-1719) handles general delivery; Open Mon.-Fri. 7:45am-5pm, Sat. 7:45am-noon. **ZIP code:** 48226. **Area code:** 313, 810 (just a little north). All numbers are in area code 313 unless otherwise noted.

Detroit lies on the Detroit River, which connects Lakes Erie and St. Clair. South across the river, the town of **Windsor, Ont.,** can be reached by tunnel just west of the Renaissance Center, or by the Ambassador Bridge, 3500 Toledo St. Detroit is a tough town—it was the fictional setting for *Robocop*—but you shouldn't encounter trouble during the day, especially within the People Mover loop.

Detroit's streets form a grid. The **Mile Roads** run east-west as major arteries. **Eight Mile Rd.** is the city's northern boundary and the beginning of the suburbs. **Woodward Ave.** heads northwest from downtown, dividing city and suburbs into "east side" and "west side." **Gratiot Ave.** flares out northeast from downtown, while **Grand River Ave.** shoots west. **I-94** and **I-75** pass through downtown. For a particularly helpful map, check the pull-out in the *Detroit Metro Visitor's Guide.*

ACCOMMODATIONS AND CAMPING

Detroit's suburbs harbor cheap chain motels, especially near the airport in Romulus. The *Detroit Metro Visitor's Guide* lists accommodations by area and includes price ranges. Devoted campers should resign themselves to a 45-min.-plus commute to the city if they insist on communing with nature.

Metro Inn-Detroit Metro Airport, 8230 Merriman Rd., Romulus (729-7600). Free airport shuttle and health club. Clean, cheap rooms from $25.

The Villager Lodge-Detroit Metro Airport, 8500 Wichham Rd., Romulus (595-1990). Clean rooms and free airport shuttle. Rooms from $30.

Park Avenue Hotel (HI-AYH), 2305 Park Ave. (961-8310), at Montcalm 1 block west behind the Fox Theater and the police academy. *Do not walk in this area alone at night.* 3 sparkling rooms, 13 wooden beds, a lounge, TV, laundry facilities, parking on the street or in a guarded lot ($1; during showtimes $5), and delicatessen on the 1st floor. Bring a lock for the lockers, and have your own linen. Check-in 24 hrs., but preferred before 11pm. Beds $12, nonmembers $14. Private rooms for 1 or 2 $20. Full apartments from $75 per week.

Shorecrest Motor Inn, 1316 E. Jefferson Ave. (800-992-9616), downtown 3 blocks east of Renaissance Center north of nightlife in Rivertown. TV, phones (local calls 50¢), A/C, refrigerators in clean rooms. Single $48, 2-bed double $54.

Country Grandma's Home Hostel (HI-AYH) (753-4901), in New Boston about halfway between Detroit and Ann Arbor, inaccessible by public transportation. The best place to stay if you have a car. This small, friendly 10-bed hostel features a kitchen and on-site parking. Beds $10, nonmembers $12.

Algonac State Park (765-5605; 465-2160 Nov. to mid-April), on the shore of the Detroit River 55mi. from downtown; take I-94E, then Rte. 29N. Watch the big ships cruise the river at night, carrying cargo to and from Detroit, the country's fifth largest port. Two campgrounds: 76 inland sites $10, 220 riverview sites $14. All have electricity. Vehicle permits $4.

FOOD AND NIGHTLIFE

Although many of the restaurants downtown have migrated to the suburbs, the budget traveler still has some in-town dining options. **Greektown,** at the Greektown People Mover stop, has Greek restaurants and excellent bakeries on Monroe St., all on 1 block near Beaubien St. Locals favor **Cyprus Taverna,** 579 Monroe St. (961-1550), for Greek cuisine (open Sun.-Thurs. 11am-2am, Fri.-Sat. 11am-3:30am). Once a tannery, **Trapper's Alley** (963-5445), in Greektown, has been converted into a four-story mall of food and retail shops (open Mon.-Thurs. 10am-9pm, Fri.-Sat. 10am-midnight, Sun. noon-11pm). **Mexican Town,** a lively neighborhood south of Tiger Stadium, has some terrific restaurants (see Xochimilco below), but be somewhat wary in the surrounding area. The summer **Mexicantown Mercado** (842-0450), at 21st St. and Bagley, has Hispanic arts, crafts, imports, entertainment, and a children's program (open late June-Aug. Sun. 10am-4pm). **Hamtramck,** a Polish neighborhood northeast of Detroit, serves up old-fashioned pirogies and such. East of the Renaissance Center in the old warehouse district, **Rivertown** hosts some of the city's best nightlife, though it is safest not to loiter in the streets. No budget traveler should miss the **Eastern Market** (833-1560), at Gratiot Ave. and Russell St., an 11-acre smorgasbord with almost every edible imaginable (open Mon.-Sat. 7am-4pm).

Xochimilco, 3409 Bagley St. (843-0179); from downtown, take the "Baker St." bus to Lafayette and Washington Blvd. Chefs from Mexico give customers an authentic and inexpensive experience. 3 meat tacos, 3 enchiladas, or 3 burritos with rice and beans $4.75-5. Free chips and salsa. Open daily 11am-4am. No reservations on weekends; come early.

Soup Kitchen Saloon, 1585 Franklin St. (259-1374). Once home to a speakeasy and brothel, this Rivertown building now features the best live blues music in town. Fresh seafood, steaks, and cajun. BBQ catfish $11, seafood creole $7.50, at lunch. 12 beers on tap and over 25 bottled. Shows Fri.-Sat.; cover varies. Open Mon.-Thurs. 11am-midnight, Fri. 11am-2am, Sat. 4pm-2am, Sun. 4pm-midnight.

The Clique Restaurant, 1326 East Jefferson St. (259-0922). Heralded city-wide for fast service and fabulous breakfasts, served all day. French toast $2.75; 3-egg omelette $4.50. Open Mon.-Fri. 6am-10pm, Sat.-Sun. 7am-10pm.

Union Street, 4145 Woodward St. (831-3965). Spicy, mouthwatering cuisine in a popular mid-town beer hall. Rasta wings with hellfire sauce are very popular ($7.25). Although Union Street itself is nice, be careful in the surrounding area. Open Mon.-Thurs. 11am-midnight, Fri. 11am-1am, Sat.-Sun. 4pm-1am.

For the latest in nightlife, pick up a free copy of *Orbit* in record stores and restaurants. *Between the Lines,* also free, has entertainment info for lesbians, gays, and bisexuals. **St. Andrew's Hall,** 431 E. Congress (961-MELT/6358), hosts local and national alternative acts (shows Fri.-Sun.; usually 17+, sometimes all ages). **Shelter,** the dance club downstairs, draws crowds on non-concert nights (advance tickets sold through Ticketmaster, 810-645-6666; $7-10). Take advantage of Ontario's lower drinking age (19) at the **Zoo Club,** 800 Wellington (519-258-2582) in Windsor. Those with too much cash can rid themselves of the burden with three floors of gambling at **The Windsor Casino,** 445 Riverside Dr. (800-991-7777; open 24 hrs.).

SIGHTS

For a reason to visit Detroit, look no farther than the colossal **Henry Ford Museum & Greenfield Village,** 20900 Oakwood Blvd. (271-1620; 271-1976 for 24-hr. info), off I-94 in nearby Dearborn; take SMART bus #200 or 250. The 12-acre museum showcases a comprehensive exhibit of the importance of the automobile in America, including the limousine in which President Kennedy was murdered and the Apollo mission's Lunar Rover. Over 80 historic edifices from around the country have been moved to **Greenfield Village,** next to the museum; visit the workshop of the Wright Brothers or the factory where Thomas Edison researched. (Both open daily 9am-5pm. Museum or village $12.50, seniors $11.50, ages 5-12 $6.25. Combination ticket valid 2 consecutive days $22, ages 5-12 $11.) The most impressive of the auto barons' mansions, **Fisher Mansion and Bhaktiredanta Cultural Center,** 383 Lenox Ave. (331-6740), houses India-centered cultural exhibits within an ornate stone, marble, and carved wood structure leafed with over 200 ounces of gold. By a strange twist of fate, the center and mansion were co-founded by Henry Ford's grandson and United Auto Workers President Walter Reuther's daughter. (Tours Fri.-Sun. 12:30, 2, 3:30, and 6pm. $6, seniors and students $5, under 13 $4.)

Detroit makes an effort to lure people to its **Cultural Center,** at Woodward and Warren St. (take bus #53 or the Attractions Shuttle)—and it's worth the time to take the bait. In the area, one of the nation's finest art museums, the **Detroit Institute of Arts,** 5200 Woodward (833-7900), houses Van Gogh's "Self-Portrait" and the nation's largest historic puppet collection (open Wed.-Fri. 11am-4pm, Sat.-Sun. 11am-5pm; suggested donation $4, children $1). Explore the history of the African experience in America at the **Museum of African American History,** 301 Frederick Douglass Rd. (833-9800; open Wed.-Sat. 9:30am-5pm, Sun. 1-5pm; suggested donation $2, kids $1). Succumb to vertigo at the Omnimax theater in the **Detroit Science Center,** 5020 John R. St. (577-8400; open Mon.-Fri. 10am-2pm, Sat.-Sun. 10:30am-6pm; $6.50, seniors free, children $4.50).

Downtown Detroit can be seen in about a day. The futuristic, gleaming, steel-and-glass **Renaissance Center** strikes a shocking contrast to the downtown wasteland. A five-towered complex of office, hotel, and retail space, the Ren Cen encloses a maze of concrete walkways and spiraling stairs; the **World of Ford** on level two reminds visitors of Detroit's heyday as the center of an auto empire. A ride to the top of the 73-story **Westin Hotel,** the tallest hotel in North America, creates an opportunity to contrast the historical view with the city of today. (Tours $3. Open Sun.-Thurs. 11am-11pm, Fri.-Sat. 11am-1:30am. For general Ren Cen info call 568-5600; tour information 341-6810; lines open daily 9am-5pm.)

Although Berry Gordy's Motown Record Company has moved to Los Angeles, the **Motown Museum,** 2648 W. Grand Blvd. (875-2264), preserves its memories. Downstairs, shop around the primitive studio in which the Jackson Five, Marvin Gaye, Smokey Robinson, and Diana Ross recorded their tunes. (Open Mon. noon-5pm, Tues.-Sat. 10am-5pm, Sun. 2-5pm. $6, seniors $5, ages 12-18 $4, under 12 $3.) The museum lies east of Rosa Parks Blvd. about 1 mi. west of the Lodge Freeway (Rte. 10); take the "Dexter Avenue" bus or the Attractions Shuttle from downtown.

The **Holocaust Memorial Center,** 6602 W. Maple Rd., West Bloomfield (810-661-0840), provides a historical and educational memorial to the victims of the Nazis. The museum's collection of rare documentaries and propaganda films, an invaluable resource for those studying the Holocaust, has made it an important research center as well. (Tours Sun. 1pm. Open Sun.-Thurs. 10am-3:30pm. Free.)

One of Detroit's favorite escapes, **Belle Island** (267-7121), 3 mi. from downtown via the MacArthur Bridge, maintains many attractions: a conservatory, a nature center, an aquarium, and a small zoo for animal lovers with short attention spans.

ENTERTAINMENT

Newly renovated and restored, Detroit's theater district, around Woodward and Columbia, is witnessing a cultural revival. The **Fox Theater,** 2211 Woodward Ave. (396-7600), near Grand Circus Park, features high-profile performances (drama, comedy, and musicals) and some Broadway shows. The nation's largest movie theater hall, the Fox also shows epic films occasionally. (Box office open Mon.-Fri. 10am-6pm. Tickets $25-100, movies under $10.) The **State Theater,** 2115 Woodward Ave. (961-5450; 810-932-3643 for event information), brings in a variety of popular concerts, including big-name rockers like Björk, and dancing. **Orchestra Hall,** 3711 Woodward Ave. (962-1000), at Parsons St., houses the Detroit Symphony Orchestra. The **Masonic Temple,** 500 Temple Ave. (832-2322; box office open 10am-5:45pm), presents Broadway plays and concerts in a classic gothic building.

Pick up a copy of the weekly *Metro Times* for complete entertainment listings. Call **Ticketmaster** (645-6666) for concert tickets.

Detroit's numerous festivals draw millions of visitors. Jazz fans jet to Hart Plaza during Labor Day weekend for the four-day **Montreux-Detroit Jazz Festival** (963-7622). With more than 70 acts on three stages and mountains of international food at the World Food Court, it's the largest free jazz festival on the continent. The nation's oldest state fair, **Michigan State Fair** (368-1000 or 369-8250), at Eight Mile Rd. and Woodward, gathers together bake-offs, art exhibits, and livestock for 10 days of fun in late August and early September. A two-week extravaganza in late June, the international **Freedom Festival** (923-7400), held jointly with Windsor, Ontario, celebrates the friendship between the U.S. and Canada. North America's largest annual fireworks display takes place over the Detroit River near the Renaissance Center, marking the birthdays of both nations. The **Concours d'Elegance** (810-370-3140) exhibits elegant classic cars at the Meadow Brook Hall during the first weekend in August. In January, the gee-whiz **North American International Auto Show** (224-1010 or 886-6750) showcases the new models, prototypes, and concept cars from manufacturers around the world in the Cobo Center, One Washington Blvd. The **Detroit Grand Prix** (393-7749) zooms by for three days in June as the streets of Belle Isle are transformed into a race course. The **Spirit of Detroit Thunderfest APBA Gold Cup** (259-7760), the speedboat equivalent of the Indy 500, churns the waters of the Detroit River in early June. Detroit's **African World Festival** (833-9800) brings over a million people to Hart Plaza in mid-August for an open-air market and free reggae, jazz, blues, and gospel concerts.

The Detroit **Pistons** shoot hoops at the Palace of Auburn Hills, 3777 Lapeer Rd., Auburn Hills (810-377-8600). Hockey's **Red Wings,** face off in the Joe Louis Arena, 600 Civic Center Dr. (567-6000). The **Tigers** catch fly balls at Tiger Stadium, on Michigan and Trumball Ave. (962-4000). The **Lions** punt, pass, and tackle at the Pontiac Silverdome, 1200 Featherstone Rd., Pontiac (810-335-4151). For tickets to any sporting events, call **Ticketmaster** (645-6666).

■■■ ANN ARBOR

Named after Ann Rumsey and Ann Allen, wives of two of the area's early pioneers (who supposedly enjoyed sitting under grape arbors), Ann Arbor has certainly made tracks. In 1837 the University of Michigan moved to town. Since then, this gargantuan, well-respected institution has created a hip collage of leftists, granolas, yuppies, and middle America.

PRACTICAL INFORMATION

Tourist Office: Ann Arbor Convention and Visitors Bureau, 120 W. Huron St. (995-7281), at Ashley. Has info on the city and the University of Michigan. Open Mon.-Fri. 8:30am-5pm.

Trains: Amtrak, 325 Depot St. (994-4906 or 800-872-7245). To: Chicago (3 per day, 4½hr., $31); Detroit (3 per day, 1hr., $11). Station open daily 6:30am-10:30pm; tickets sold 6:30am-midnight.

Buses: Greyhound, 116 W. Huron St. (662-5511). To: Detroit (6 per day, 1-1½hr., $6); Chicago (4 per day, 5hr., $25). Office open Mon.-Sat. 9am-6:30pm.

Public Transportation: Ann Arbor Transportation Authority (AATA), Blake Transit Center, 331 South 4th Ave. (996-0400 or 973-6500). Service in Ann Arbor and a few neighboring towns. Buses run Mon.-Fri. 6:45am-10:15pm, Sat.-Sun. 8am-6:15pm. Fare 75¢, seniors and students 35¢. Station open Mon.-Fri. 7:30am-9:30pm, Sat. noon-6:15pm. AATA's **Nightride,** 663-3888. Safe door-to-door transportation 11pm-6am. Call to book a trip; average wait 20min. Fare $2 per person, regardless of distance. **Commuter Transportation Company,** 941-9391 or

800-488-7433. Frequent shuttle service between Ann Arbor and Detroit Metro Airport. Vans depart Ann Arbor 5am-7pm; return 7am-midnight. $14.50, $27 round-trip. Door-to-door service for up to 4 $39; reserve at least 2 days in advance.

Car Rental: Campus Auto Rental, 202 S. Division St. (761-3768). $29 per day with 150 free mi., $145 per week with 1000 free mi.; 20¢ per additional mi. Optional insurance $9. Open Mon.-Fri. 8am-6pm, Sat.-Sun. 9am-1pm.

Crisis Lines: Sexual assault crisis line, 483-7273. **U. Michigan sexual assault line,** 936-3333. Both 24 hrs. **Gay crisis line,** 662-1977. Open Mon.-Fri. 9am-7pm. **U. Michigan gay/lesbian hotline,** 763-4186.

Most important thing in the world: Happiness.

Emergency: 911.

Post office: 2075 W. Stadium Blvd. (665-1100; open Mon.-Fri. 7:30am-5pm). **ZIP code:** 48106. **Area code:** 313.

Ann Arbor's streets usually lie in a neat grid, but watch out for the slant of Packard and Detroit St. **Main St.** divides the town east-west and **Huron St.** cuts it north-south. The central campus of the University of Michigan, where restaurants cluster, lies four blocks east of Main St., south of E. Huron (a 5-min. walk from downtown). Although street meter parking is plentiful, invisible authorities ticket ruthlessly.

ACCOMMODATIONS

Expensive hotels, motels, and B&Bs dominate Ann Arbor due to the many business travelers and sports fans flocking to the town. Reasonable rates can be found at discount chains farther out of town or in Ypsilanti southeast of town along I-94. The **Embassy Hotel,** 200 E. Huron (662-7100), at Fourth Ave., offers clean singles for $25 and doubles for $30. During the summer, the University of Michigan rents rooms in **Bursley Hall,** 1931 Duffield St. (763-1140), in North Campus, for $30 (parking in nearby lot $3.50 per day, free local calls, no A/C). The **YMCA,** 350 S. Fifth Ave. (663-0536), provides basic singles with shared bath for 80 men and 20 women (check-out 11am; $28, weekly or monthly rentals available; key deposit $5). With seven campgrounds within a 20-mi. radius of Ann Arbor, **camping** is a very accessible option; call the campground offices of the **Pinckney Recreation Area,** 8555 Silver Hill, Pinckney (426-4913; open Mon.-Thurs. 8am-4:30pm, Fri.-Sat. 8am-8:30pm, Sun. 8am-6:30pm), or the **Waterloo Recreation Area,** 16345 McClure Rd., Chelsea (475-8307; open daily 8am-noon and 1-5pm).

FOOD AND NIGHTLIFE

Where there are students, there are cheap eats; restaurants cram the sidewalks of **State St.** and **S. University St.** Purchase fresh produce straight from the growers at the **farmers market,** 315 Detroit St. (761-1078), at Kerrytown (open May-Dec. Wed. and Sat. 7am-3pm; Jan.-April Sat. 8am-3pm). The readers of *Ann Arbor News* voted **Cottage Inn Pizza,** 512 E. William St. (663-3379), at Thompson St., the "best pizza," and the dinner lines to back them up. (Pasta $4-7; pizza $7-14. Open Mon.-Thurs. 11am-midnight, Fri.-Sat. 11am-1am, Sun. noon-midnight. Also at 927 Maiden Lane, 995-9101; 2301 W. Stadium, 663-0228; 2900 S. State, 663-4500.) Locals seek out **Del Rio,** 122 W. Washington (761-2530), at Ashley, for cheap burgers and Mexican food (burritos $2.50). A vestige of a fast-dying Ann Arbor tradition, Del Rio's employees manage the business cooperatively. (Free jazz Sunday nights. Open Mon.-Fri. 11:30am-2am, Sat. noon-2am, Sun. 5:30am-2am.) **Angelo's,** 1100 Catherine St. (761-8996), gains its fame for hearty breakfasts; the thick, heavenly raisin bread will do you right ($4.50; open Mon.-Fri. 6am-4pm, Sat. 6am-2pm, Sun. 7am-2pm).

The Blind Pig, 208 S. First St. (996-8555), showcases the rock-'n-roll, reggae, and blues offerings of local bands and acts from all over the country (cover $3-4). Happy hour on Friday means no cover 6-8:30pm (Open Tues.-Sat. until 2am.) **Green Room,** 206 W. Michigan (482-8830), in Ypsilanti, peddles coffee and entertainment, including open mic nights, to folks of all ages (cover varies; open Mon.-Sat. 6am-midnight). **Rick's American Café,** 611 Church St. (996-2747), plays Ann Arbor's blues, with live music and a packed dance floor almost nightly (19+, Tues. 18+; cover varies; open daily). The **Bird of Paradise,** 207 S. Ashley (662-8310), sings with live jazz every night; the big names come on Fridays and Saturdays (cover usually $3). **The Nectarine,** 510 F. Liberty (994-5436), offers DJ-controlled dance music, with gay nights on Tuesdays and Fridays. Though few clubs target a gay audience as The Nectarine does, many of Ann Arbor's clubs cater to mixed crowds.

SIGHTS AND ENTERTAINMENT

The university offers a handful of free museums which merit a walk-through. A small but impressive collection of artworks from around the world fills the **University of Michigan Arts Museum (UMAM),** 525 S. State St. (764-0395), at the corner of University St. (open Tues.-Sat. 10am-5pm, Sun. 1-5pm). Just down the street, the **Kelsey Museum of Archaeology,** 434 S. State St. (764-9304), presents pieces recovered from digs in the Middle East, Greece, and Italy. (Open Tues.-Fri. 11am-4pm, Sat.-Sun. 1-4pm; Sept.-April Mon.-Fri. 9am-4pm, Sat.-Sun. 1-4pm.) The **University of Michigan Exhibit Museum of Natural History,** 1109 Geddes Ave. (763-6085), at Washtenaw, displays a Hall of Evolution and other exhibits on Michigan wildlife, astronomy, and rocks; within, the **Planetarium** (764-0478 or 763-6085) projects star-gazing weekend entertainment ($2.50). (Museum open Mon.-Sat. 9am-5pm, Sun. 1-5pm.) Outside the University at the **Ann Arbor Hands-On Museum,** 219 E. Huron (995-5437), exhibits are designed to be felt, turned, touched, and pushed. (Open Tues.-Fri. 10am-5:30pm, Sat. 10am-5pm, Sun. 1-5pm. $4, seniors, students, and children $2.50.) Numerous local artists display their creations at the **artisan market,** 315 Detroit St. (open May-Dec. Sun. 11am-4pm).

The monthlies *Current, Agenda, Weekender Entertainment,* and the weekly *Metrotimes,* all free and available in restaurants, corner kiosks, music stores, and elsewhere, print up-to-date entertainment listings. For classical music contact the **University Musical Society** (764-2538), in the Burton Memorial Clock Tower at N. University and Thouper; the society sponsors 40 to 50 professional concerts per season (tickets $10-50; open Mon.-Fri. 10am-5pm). Ann Arbor prides itself on live jazz; call the University Activities Office (763-1107) for info.

As tens of thousands of students depart for the summer (and rents plummet), locals indulge in a little celebrating. During late July, thousands pack the city to view the work of nearly 600 artists at the **Ann Arbor Summer Art Fair** (995-7281). The **Ann Arbor Summer Festival** (747-2278) draws crowds from mid-June to early July for a collection of humorous dance and theater productions, as well as musical performances ranging from jazz to country to classical. Outdoor movies top off the festivities every night at **Top of the Park,** on top of the Heath Service Building on Fletcher St. The **county events hotline** (930-6300) has info on all these events.

■■■ GRAND RAPIDS

From its humble beginning as one among many fur trading posts, Grand Rapids worked hard to distinguish itself from its neighbors. While many towns opted for tourist chic with quaint, old-fashioned looks, Grand Rapids plowed ahead to become a city of concrete, pavement, and tall buildings. The city has gone on to further distinguish itself by claiming a couple of notable American firsts; Grand Rapids was the first city to put fluoride in its drinking water, and also earns distinction as the city that produced America's first (and only) unelected president, Gerald Ford.

Practical Information Most of Grand Rapids' streets are neatly gridded; **Division St.** divides the city east-west. For general area info, head to the **Grand Rapids-Kent County Convention and Visitors Bureau,** 140 Monroe Center NW, #300 (459-8287 or 800-678-9859; open Mon.-Fri. 10am-5:30pm, Sat. 10am-2pm), or the **West Michigan Tourist Association,** 136 E. Fulton (456-8557; open Mon.-Fri. 8:45am-5pm). Grand Rapids serves as a transportation hub for Western Michigan, providing **Greyhound,** 190 Wealthy St. (456-1707), connections to the surrounding area as well as further afield. Detroit (4 per day, 3½hr., $21), and Chicago (5 per day,

4½hr., $24) can be easily reached from Grand Rapids. (Open daily 6:40am-10pm.) **Amtrak** (800-872-7245), at Wealthy and Market, has service to the south and west, including Chicago (1 per day, 3½hr., $29). The station only opens when trains pass through. For eastern service, travelers have to get to the Kalamazoo Station, 459 N. Burdick St., Kalamazoo, 50 mi. south of Grand Rapids on Rte. 131., where trains leave for Detroit (3 per day, 3hr., $42-56). (Station open daily 9am-9pm.) **Grand Rapids Transit Authority (GRATA),** 333 Wealthy St. (776-1100), sends buses throughout the city and suburbs (buses run Mon.-Fri. 6am-6pm, Sat. 9:30am-9:30pm; fare $1.25, 10-ride pass $7). **Yellow Cab** (458-4100) will get you where you want to go ($1.45 base fare, $1.35 per mi.; 24 hrs.). In a crisis, call the **Suicide, Drug, Alcohol, and Crisis Line,** 336-3535. **Emergency:** 911. Grand Rapids's **post office:** 225 Michigan Ave. NW (776-1519; open Mon.-Fri. 8:30am-6pm, Sat. 8am-noon); **ZIP code:** 49503; **area code:** 616.

Accommodations and Food Most of the cheaper motels cluster south of the city along Division and 28th St. The **Grand Rapids Motel,** 35 28th St. SE (956-6601), formerly a Howard Johnson's, has an indoor pool, A/C, and cable TV (singles $30, doubles $33). Women are out of luck at the **YMCA,** 33 Library St. N.E. (458-1141), within walking distance of downtown ($20 the first night, $10 each additional night). The *West Michigan Travel Planner* includes listings to help campers choose among the many area campgrounds; write or call the West Michigan Tourist Association (see Practical Information, above) for a copy. The *MARVAC RV and Campsite Guide* and the *Michigan Campground Directory* list state and private sites; inquire at the visitors bureau.

Grand Rapids' most popular Mexican food comes from the **Beltline Bar and Café,** 16 28th St. SE (245-0494). Enormous plates of tacos go for $5.50, and burritos start at $5. (Open Mon.-Tues. 7am-midnight, Wed.-Sat. 7am-1am, Sun. noon-10:30pm.) **Pietro's Back Door Pizzeria,** 2780 Birchcrest Dr. (452-3228), off 28th St. SE, serves delicious wood-fired pizza with a wide array of gourmet toppings ($5-9). The *ristorante* in front concocts higher-end Italian food ($7.50-12). (Open Mon.-Thurs. 11:30am-1:30pm and 5-10pm; Fri. 11:30am-1:30pm and 5-11pm; Sun. noon-10pm; pizzeria Mon.-Thurs. 11:30am-2pm, Sun. 4-10pm.) Head to the **Grand Rapids Brewing Company,** 3689 28th St. SE (285-5970), for burgers ($5.50), pasta, and "handcrafted" house beers ($2.75 per pint). Tours are available upon request. (Open Mon.-Thurs. 11am-10pm, bar until midnight; Fri.-Sat. 11am-11pm, bar until 1am; Sun. 1-10pm, bar until 11pm.) The **Four Friends Coffehouse,** 136 Monroe Center (456-5356), has the usual cappuccino, espresso, and semi-artsy atmosphere, plus good muffins ($2) and live music on Saturdays. (Open Mon.-Wed. 7am-8pm, Thurs. 7am-10pm, Fri. 7am-midnight, Sat. 10am-midnight.)

Sights, Festivals, and Nightlife The **Van Andel Museum Center,** 272 Pearl St. NW (456-3977), houses the **Grand Rapids Public Museum,** a showcase for marvels such as the world's largest whale skeleton, a 50-animal carousel (which you can ride), and a planetarium (open daily 9am-5pm; $5, seniors $4, ages 3-17 $2; planetarium $1.50). The **Gerald R. Ford Museum,** 303 Pearl St. NW (451-9263), records the life and turbulent times of Grand Rapids's favorite native son. Above and beyond showcasing a respectable collection of art, the **Grand Rapids Art Museum,** 155 N. Division St. (459-4677), makes an effort to get children's attention with a special tour map designed to keep them occupied and engaged. (Open Sun. and Tues. noon-4pm, Wed. and Fri.-Sat. 10am-4pm, Thurs. 10am-9pm. $3, students with ID $1, seniors $1.50.) The largest year-round conservatory in Michigan, the **Frederik Meijer Gardens** (957-1580), at the intersection of Beltline and Bradford St., keeps over 70 bronze sculptures among numerous tropical plants spread out over 70 acres of wetlands (open daily 9am-6pm; $3.50, seniors $3, ages 5-13 $1.50).

Grand Rapids hosts a number of free ethnic festivals, each lasting two to three days: the **Afro-American Festival** in mid-July; the **Festa Italiana** in mid-August; the

Polish Festival in late August; the **Hispanic Festival** in September; and the German **Oktoberfest.** For more information on any of the festivals, call 456-3361.

For detailed listings on events and nightlife in Grand Rapids, swipe a free copy of *On the Town* or *In the City,* both available just about everywhere—shops, restaurants, kiosks, etc. The 24-hr. **Fun Line** (439-8629) saves you the trouble of reading. Dance clubs overshadow other forms of nightlife in Grand Rapids; **The Reptile House,** 139 S. Division St. (242-9955), showcases very loud alternative bands Wednesday through Friday and dances Tuesdays and Saturdays (some weekdays 18+, on weekends 21+). The largest dance club in Grand Rapids, **The Orbit Room** (942-1328), at E. Beltline and 28th St., packs in up to 1200 gyrating bodies for nightly music ranging from alternative to top 40 to disco to—country? (Wed. 18+, other nights 19+ until 11pm; open Wed., Fri., and Sat.-Sun.). **The Anchor,** 447 Bridge St. (774-7177), is your basic bar, filled with locals and relatively cheap drinks.

■■■ LAKE MICHIGAN SHORE

With dunes of sugary sand, superb fishing, abundant fruit harvests, and deep winter snows, the eastern shore of Lake Michigan has been a vacationer's dreamland for over a century. The coastline stretches 350 mi. north from the Indiana border to the Mackinaw Bridge; its southern end comes within a scant two hours from downtown Chicago. The freighters that once powered the rise of Chicago still steam along, but have long since been usurped by pleasure boats that mob the coast.

Many of the region's attractions nestle in small coastal towns, which cluster around **Grand Traverse Bay** in the north. Coastal accommodations can be exorbitantly expensive; for cheaper lodging, head inland. **Traverse City,** at the south tip of the bay, is famous as the "cherry capital of the world," and fishing is best in the **Au Sable** and **Manistee Rivers.** However, the rich **Mackinac Island Fudge,** sold in numerous specialty shops, seems to have the biggest pull on tourists ("fudgies" to locals; see Mackinac Island, p. 414). The main north-south route along the coast is **U.S. 31.** Numerous detours twist closer to the shoreline, providing an excellent way to explore the coast. The **West Michigan Tourist Association,** 136 E. Fulton, Grand Rapids 49503 (456-8557), hands out free literature on the area (open Mon.-Fri. 8:45am-5pm). The entire Lake Michigan Shore's **area code:** 616.

■ SOUTHERN MICHIGAN SHORE

Holland Southwest of Grand Rapids off I-196, Holland was founded in 1847 by Dutch religious dissenters and remained mostly Dutch until well into the 20th century. Today the town cashes in on its heritage with a wooden shoe factory (396-6513), at U.S. 31 and 16th St.; **Windmill Island** (396-5433), at 7th St. and Lincoln Ave.; the **Holland Museum,** 310 W. 10th St. (392-9084); **Veldheer Tulip Gardens,** 12755 Quincy St. (399-1900); a recreated **Dutch Village** (396-1475), U.S. 31 at James St.; and a **Dutch Winter Fest** (396-4221), in late November/early December. The attractions (admission $1-4) attempt to paint a picture of life as it was once lived here, but a simple stroll around downtown will give any visitor a sense of how this tightly-knit community has survived and how it continues to function today. The **Wooden Shoe Motel** (392-8521), U.S. 31 Bypass at 16th St., rents single rooms starting at $49 (doubles $54), with a **putt-putt** course out back (before 5pm $2, after 5pm $4; weekends $3). For more info visit the **Holland Convention and Visitors Bureau,** 100 E. 8th St. (396-4221 or 800-968-8590; open Mon.-Fri. 9am-5pm). **Greyhound,** 171 Lincoln Ave. (396-8664), runs through Holland to Detroit (3 per day, 4hr., $24), and Chicago (3 per day, 8hr., $22). (Open Mon.-Fri. 7:45am-4pm.)

Grand Haven Several miles of fine sugary sand shift on the shore at Grand Haven, 25 mi. west of Grand Rapids off I-96, perhaps the best beach on Lake Michigan. The sand sticks to everything, so pure that auto manufacturers use it to make cores and molds for engine parts. A cement "boardwalk" connects the beach to the small downtown, where action centers on Washington St. **Butch's Beach Burritos,** 726 S. Harbor Ave. (842-3690), has burritos, chili dogs, and other greasy beach fare ($2-5; open May-Sept. 11am-9pm). The **Bij De Zee Motel,** 1030 Harbor Ave. (846-7431), may look a little ramshackle, but it's right across from the beach and one of the cheapest places around (rooms from $40; some have kitchenettes). State Parks such as **Muskegon** (744-3480) and **Hoffmaster** (798-3711) line the coast between Saugatuck and Muskegon. Campground sites run $10-14.

■ CENTRAL MICHIGAN SHORE

Manistee and Interlochen **Manistee** beckons tourists with Victorian shtick. The **A.H. Lyman Store,** 425 River St. (723-5531), has been transformed into a museum celebrating the area's ethnic heritage and history (open Mon.-Sat. 10am-5pm; Oct.-May Tues.-Sat. 10am-5pm). **Manistee National Forest** has copious camping (sites $5-9) with hookup or primitive sites. Most areas are open year-round except when closed by snowfall; for information on camping, hiking, canoeing, and the late June/early July **National Forest Festival,** call the **Manistee Ranger Station,** 1658 Manistee Hwy. (723-2211 or 800-999-7677; open Mon.-Fri. 8am-5pm) or the **Cadillac District Ranger Office** (775-8539), on Rte. 55, 4 mi. west of Cadillac (open Sat. 8am-noon). The **Riverside Motel,** 520 Water St. (723-3554), has dock space for boaters (rooms $45-70; in winter around $35). Cheaper lodgings lie in the small towns along Rte. 22 north of Manistee (from $33). The **Manistee County Chamber of Commerce,** 11 Congress St. (723-2575), has pamphlets on local attractions.

A little south, the **Lake Michigan Car Ferry** (800-841-4243) shuttles people and cars between **Ludington** and Manitowoc, WI (4-hr. trips, 2 each way per day July-Aug.; in spring and fall 1 per day. $35, seniors $32, ages 5-15 $15, cars $45.)

The renowned **Interlochen Center for the Arts** (276-6230), in **Interlochen,** 17 mi. south of Traverse City on Rte. 137, trains talented young artists in classical music, dance, theater, creative writing, etc. Here, the **International Arts Festival,** held year-round, has attracted the likes of Yo Yo Ma, Itzhak Perlman, the Boston Pops, the Emerson String Quartet, and Willie Nelson; faculty and students also put on top-notch concerts in the various arts throughout the year. (Box office open in summer Mon. 9am-4:30pm, Tues.-Sat. 9am-8:30pm, Sun. 11:15am-8:30pm; reduced hours off season. Tickets $5 for student performances, from $10 for professional; student and senior discounts available.) **Interlochen State Park** offers recreation and camping nearby (sites $8, with electricity and showers $10; daily vehicle permit $4); for directions and information, contact the ranger office (800-543-2937; open 8am-5pm), 1 mi. south of Interlochen along Rte. 137.

Sleeping Bear Dunes The Sleeping Bear Dunes doze along the western shores of the Leelanau Peninsula. According to legend, the mammoth sand dunes, 20 mi. west of Traverse City on Rte. 72, are a sleeping mother bear, waiting for her cubs—the **Manitou Islands**—to finish a swim across the lake. Local legend does not explain why the cubs didn't just take the ferry that services the islands from Leland. **Manitou Island Transit** (256-9061) makes daily trips to South Manitou and ventures three times per week to the larger, wilder North Manitou (check-in 9:30am; round-trip $18, under 12 $13). Camping is free on both islands with a required permit (available at the visitors center); the Manitou islands do not permit cars.

The **Sleeping Bear Dunes National Lakeshore** (326-5134), of which the islands are one part, also includes 25 mi. of lakeshore on the mainland. When the glaciers lumbered to a halt and melted, mountains of fine sand were left behind, creating a landscape that looks like a cross between an ocean coast and a desert. You can be king of the sandhill at **Dune Climb,** 5 mi. north of Empire on Rte. 109, but to reach an *absolutely gorgeous* sandy beach, hike 2.8 strenuous mi. over sandy hills along one of Dune Climb's trails. The less adventurous motor to an overlook along the **Pierce Stocking Scenic Drive,** off Rte. 109 just north of Empire, where they can run down a 450-ft. sand cliff to the cool water below (open mid-May to mid-Oct.

daily 9am-10pm). For maps and info on the numerous cross-country skiing, hiking, and mountain biking trails, call the National Parks Service **visitors center** (326-5134), on Rte. 72 in Empire (open daily 9am-6pm; mid-Oct. to May 9:30am-4pm).

The **Platte River** (at the southern end) and the **Crystal River** (near Glen Arbor at the northern end) are great for canoeing or floating. **Riverside Canoes,** 5042 Scenic Hwy., Honor (325-5622), off Rte. 22 at the Platte River Bridge, will equip you with an inner tube ($4-6 for 1hr., $8-10 for 2hr.), canoe ($22-26), kayak ($13), or paddle board ($10). Sleeping Bear Dunes has four campgrounds: **DH Day** (334-4634), in Glen Arbor, with 88 primitive sites ($8); **Platte River** (325-5881), in Honor, with 179 sites and showers ($10, with electricity $15); and two free backcountry campsites accessible by 1½-mi. trails (no reservations; required permit available at the visitors center or at either developed campground).

Traverse City In summer, vacationers head to Traverse City for its sandy beaches and annual **Cherry Festival** (947-4230), held the first full week in July. The Traverse City area produces 50% of the nation's sweet and tart cherries—and they won't let you forget it. In early to mid-July, five orchards near Traverse City let you pick your own cherries, including **Amon Orchards** (938-9160), 10 mi. east on U.S. 31 (open 8am-7pm). The nearby sparkling bay and ancient sand dunes make this region a Great Lakes paradise, though a crowded and expensive one. In summer, swimming, boating, and scuba diving focus on **Grand Traverse Bay;** free beaches and public access sites speckle the shore of the bay. Explore the coastline of the **Leelanau Peninsula,** between Grand Traverse Bay and Lake Michigan, on scenic **Rte. 22.** Get to **Leland,** a charming one-time fishing village which now launches the Manitou Island ferries (see Sleeping Bear Dunes, above), via M22. For local events and entertainment, pick up the weekly *Traverse City Record-Eagle Summer Magazine,* available in corner kiosks around the city.

There are many **campgrounds** around Traverse City—in state parks, the National Lakeshore (see Sleeping Bear Dunes, above), and various townships. The West Michigan Tourist Association's guide gives a comprehensive list of public and private sites and the tourist bureau has a helpful *Camping* pamphlet. State parks usually charge $10-14, but national forests are the best deal at $5-8. **Northwestern Michigan Community College,** East Hall, 1701 E. Front St. (922-1406), has the cheapest beds in the city. (1 bedroom $25, additional person $35; 2-room suite with bathroom $50. Nearby parking is accessible via College Dr. Open late June-Aug. Reservations recommended.) The **Shoestring Resort** (946-7935), 10 mi. east of town at the intersection of Garfield and River Rd., has one- and two-bedroom cabins with A/C and TV starting at $25, $35 during peak season; some have kitchens.

The **Traverse City Convention and Visitors Bureau,** 415 Munson Ave./U.S. 31N, #200 (800-940-1120 or 947-1120), on the second floor of the brick Delta Center, dispenses the helpful *Traverse City Guide* (open Mon.-Fri. 9am-5pm). **Indian Trails** and **Greyhound,** 3233 Cass Rd. (946-5180), tie Traverse City to Detroit (2 per day, 7½hr., $31) and to the Upper Peninsula via St. Ignace (1 per day, 2½hr., $16). The **Bay Area Transportation Authority** (941-2324) runs buses once per hour on scheduled routes, every 20 minutes within the city (fare $1.50; daily pass $3). Traverse City's **post office:** 202 S. Union St. (946-9616; open Mon.-Fri. 8am-5pm); **ZIP code:** 49684.

■ NORTHERN MICHIGAN SHORE

Charlevoix and Petoskey Situated on the ½-mi.-wide ribbon of land between Lake Michigan and Lake Charlevoix, the stretch of coast near Charlevoix (SHAR-le-voy), north of Traverse City by U.S. 31, served as the setting for some of Hemingway's Nick Adams stories. The town now attracts more tourists than it did in Hemingway's time; downstaters triple Charlevoix's population in summer. In Charlevoix the Beautiful, sailing is king. Join in the tacking and jibing on a two-hour afternoon or evening cruise on the **Appledor** (547-0024; $24, kids $11). For visitor info, head to the **Charlevoix Chamber of Commerce,** 408 Bridge St. (547-2101; open Mon.-Fri. 9am-5pm, Sat. 10am-5pm). Lodging rarely comes cheap in this resort-oriented area, but reasonably priced camping, RV stations, and cottages are available at **Uhrick's Lincoln Log Motel and Campground,** 800 Petoskey Ave. (547-4881), on U.S. 31 (tent sites $10, with full hookup $15; cottages from $30).

Petoskey, 18 mi. north of Charlevoix, gains notoriety for its **Petoskey Stones**, fossilized coral from an ancient sea which can now be found heaped along the lakeshores. For information on beaches and other attractions, including canoeing, orchards, and walking tours, contact the **Petoskey Regional Chamber of Commerce,** 401 E. Mitchell (347-4150 or 800-845-2828; open summer Mon.-Fri. 8:30am-5pm, Sat. 10am-3pm, Sun. noon-4pm; mid-Oct. to May Mon.-Fri. 9am-5pm). Greyhound affiliate **Indian Trails** (517-725-5105 or 800-292-3831 in MI) stops at the **Bookstop,** 301 W. Mitchell (347-4400; open Mon.-Sat. 8am-5:30pm), and buses once daily to St. Ignace ($8) and Detroit ($39).

North Central Michigan College, 1515 Howard St. (348-6611; 348-6612 for reservations), lets single dorm rooms within a suite. (Rooms $22.50, for 2 $28, 4-person suite $48. Linens provided. Reservations highly recommended.) Petoskey's **Gaslight District,** 1 block from the Chamber of Commerce, features local crafts and foods in period shops. Hop on the **Grain Train Natural Foods Co-op,** 421 Howard St. (347-2381), for soy pizza and a slate of ever-changing delectables ($2.50-3.50; deli open Mon.-Thurs. 9am-7pm, Fri. 9am-8pm, Sat. 9am-5pm, Sun. 11am-5pm). **Petoskey State Park,** 2 mi. east of town off Rte. 31 (347-2311), offers 190 modern campsites (sites $13; $4 vehicle fee) on Little Traverse Bay.

North of Petoskey, **Rte. 119** winds along the lakeside through tunnels of trees, combining the scenic surrounding of a hiking trail with the comfort of a smooth auto road. In Cross Village, **Legs Inn** (526-2281), the only restaurant for miles, serves Polish entrees ($9-16) amidst fantastic Native American decor. (Live blues, folk, reggae, polka, etc. Wed.-Sun. Cover Sat.-Sun. $4. Open daily 11am-10pm.)

Straits of Mackinac Never say "mackinACK"; in the Land of the Great Turtle (as early native Americans called it), Mackinac and Mackinaw are both pronounced "mackinAW." Colonial **Fort Michilimackinac** still guards the straits between Lake Michigan and Lake Superior, as tourists, not troops, flock to **Mackinaw City,** the town that grew up around the fort. Along with Fort Michilimackinac, **Fort Mackinac** (on Mackinac Island) and **Historic Mill Creek** (3½mi. south of Mackinac on Rte. 23), form the trio of **State Historic Parks** (436-5563). (All open mid-June to Labor Day daily 9am-6pm; Labor Day-Oct. and mid-May to mid-June 10am-4pm. Each park $6.50, ages 6-12 $4, family $20; season pass to all three $12.50, kids $7.50.)

Pick up brochures at the **Mackinaw City Chamber of Commerce,** 706 S. Huron (436-5574; open Mon.-Fri. 9am-7:30pm, Sat. 9am-4pm, Sun. 9am-1pm; off season Mon.-Fri. 9am-2pm) or the **Michigan Dept. of Transportation Welcome and Travel Information Center** (436-5566), on Nicolet Ave. off I-75 (free reservation service; open daily 8am-8pm; off season 9am-5pm). **Indian Trails** bus lines (517-725-5105 or 800-292-3831 in MI) has a flag stop at the Big Boy restaurant on Nicolet Ave. One bus runs north and one south each day; buy tickets at the next station.

Campers can hunker down at **Mackinaw Mill Creek Campground** (436-5584), 3 mi. south of town on Rte 23; most of its 600 sites lie near the lake (sites $11.25, with full hookup $13.25). Sites at the **Wilderness State Park** (436-5381), 11 mi. west on Wilderness Park Dr., come with showers and electricity ($14). Look south of town along Rte. 31 for cheap indoor lodging; **Flamingo Hotel,** 13959 Mackinaw Terrace (436-8751), has a heated outdoor pool and clean, air-conditioned rooms (singles $35, doubles $40, triples $45; off season $22/$24/$28).

On **Mackinac Island,** tourists visit **Fort Mackinac** (906-847-3328), Victorian homes, and the **Grand Hotel** (906-847-3331). Connoisseurs will immediately recognize the island as the birthplace of **Mackinack Fudge,** sold in shops all over the Michigan coastline. Lodging is never cheap on the island, but the Grand Hotel carries the cost (and elegance) to an extreme; the average double goes for $390 per night. For $5 you can lurk on the estate grounds (daily 9am-5:30pm), for $10 you can dangle your feet in the pool, and for $15 you can even set foot on the tennis courts. Horse-drawn **carriages** cart guests all over the island (906-847-3325; open daily 8:30am-5pm; $11.50, ages 4-11 $6). **Saddle horses** ($20 per hr.) and **bikes** ($3-4 per hr.) are also available. Encompassing 80% of the island, **Mackinac Island State Park** features a circular 8.2-mi. shoreline road for biking and hiking (free). Pick up the invaluable *Mackinac Island Locator Map and Business Directory* ($1) at the **Mackinac Island Chamber of Commerce** (906-847-3783; open in summer daily 8:30am-7pm; off-season hours vary). Three competing **ferry lines** leave Mackinaw City and St. Ignace with overlapping schedules; during the summer, a ferry leaves every 15 minutes 8am-8pm ($11.50 round-trip, ages 5-12 $6.50, bike passage $3-4). Cars are not allowed on the island.

■■■ UPPER PENINSULA

A multi-million-acre forestland bordered by three of the world's largest lakes, Michigan's Upper Peninsula (U.P.) must be counted among the most scenic and unspoiled stretches of land in the Great Lakes region. But in 1837, after Congress decided in favor of Ohio in the fight over Toledo, Michigan only grudgingly accepted this "wasteland to the north" in the unpopular deal which gave the territory statehood. From the start, Michigan made the most of the land, laying waste to huge tracts of forests destined for the treeless Great Plains and the fireplaces of Chicago. In the past century, however, the forests have been protected and returned to their former grandeur, while the U.P.'s extensive natural resources, spectacular waterfalls, and miles of coastline have won over the hearts of most Michiganites.

Only 24,000 people live in the U.P.'s largest town, Marquette; the region is a paradise for fishing, camping, hiking, snowmobiling, and getting away from it all. Hikers enjoy numerous treks, including Michigan's 875 mi. of the **North Country Trail,** a national scenic trail which extends from New York to North Dakota. (Contact the North Country Trail Association, P.O. Box 311, White Cloud 49349, for details.) A vibrant spectrum of foliage makes autumn a beautiful time to hike the U.P.; in the winter, skiers replace hikers. Half a dozen rivers beckon canoers to the area as well; those who heed the call of the rapids should contact the **Michigan Recreational Canoe Association,** P.O. Box 668, Indian River 49749 (616-238-7868).

Welcome centers guard the U.P. at its six main entry points: **Ironwood,** 801 W. Cloverland Dr. (932-3330); **Iron Mountain,** 618 Stephenson Ave. (774-4201); **Menominee,** 1343 10th Ave. (863-6496); **St. Ignace** (643-6979), on I-75N; **Sault-Ste. Marie,** 1001 Eureka St. (632-8242); and **Marquette,** 2201 U.S. 41S (249-9066). (All generally open daily 9am-5pm.) Pick up their invaluable *Upper Peninsula Travel Planner.* Write to the **U.S. Forestry Service,** 2727 N. Lincoln Rd., Escanaba 49829 (786-4062), for help planning a trip into the wilderness, or contact **Upper Peninsula Travel and Recreation Association** (800-562-7134; open Mon.-Fri. 8am-4:30pm). Upper Peninsula's **area code:** 906.

The peninsula has 200 **campgrounds,** including those at both national forests (call 800-543-2937 for reservations). Sleep with your dogs or bring extra blankets; temperatures in these parts drop to 40°F even in July. Outside the major tourist towns, motel rooms start around $24. For regional cuisine, indulge in the Friday night **fish-fry:** all-you-can-eat perch, walleye, or whitefish buffets available in nearly every restaurant in every town for about $7-10. The local ethnic specialty is a meat pie, imported by Cornish miners in the 19th century, called a **pastie** (PASS-tee).

The U.P.'s isolation and large distances make travel very difficult without a car. **Greyhound** (632-8643 or 800-800-2814) has just three routes: Sault-Ste. Marie to St. Ignace and points south; St. Ignace to Rapid River, Iron Mountain, and Ironwood along U.S. 2; and Calumet south to Marquette, Rapid River, and Green Bay on U.S. 41. (All routes run once per day.) Carless travelers should rent in one of the gateway cities (Green Bay in the west or Grand Rapids in the east), or bike the area.

Sault Ste. Marie and the Eastern U.P. A 21-ft. falls on the St. Mary's River connects—and separates—Lake Huron and Lake Superior. Native Americans simply carried their canoes around the rapids, but a 1000-ft. freighter needs a little more help; in 1855, entrepreneurs built the first lock at Sault Ste. Marie (the "SOO"). Now the busiest in the world, the city's four locks float over 12,000 ships annually. The **Locks Park Historic Walkway** parallels the water for 1 mi. On the waterfront at the end of Johnston St., the *Valley Camp* (632-3658), a 1917 steam-powered freighter, has been converted into the Great Lakes' largest maritime museum. (Open July-Aug. daily 9am-9pm; mid-May to June and Sept. to mid-Oct. 10am-6pm; $6, seniors $5.45, ages 6-16 $3.50.) Just up the block from the water, the concrete **Tower of History,** 326 E. Portage St. (632-3658), offers a panoramic view of the locks, bridges, and ships (open May 15-Oct. 15 daily 10am-6pm; $3, seniors $2.50, kids 6-16 $1.75). The U.S. Army Corps of Engineers, which operates the locks, maintains a good **visitors center,** 10 Portage St. (632-0888; open mid-May to early Nov.; in summer daily 6am-11pm; in spring and fall 8am-10pm). Ask for info on boat and train tours of the locks. The city's best lodging deals crowd the **I-75 Business Spur. Buck's Motel,** 3501 I-75 Business Spur (632-1173), has clean, fresh-smelling, relatively cheap rooms with TV and phones, but no A/C, for $30-47.

A bit west of the city, frolic and camp in the eastern branch of the **Hiawatha National Forest** (786-4062; no showers, water hookups available; sites $6-10; no reservations). For more modern camping, try **Tahquamenon Falls State Park** (492-3415), a 90-min. drive west from the city through the Forest (many sites with hookup; sites $6-10, $4 vehicle permit required; reservations recommended). Canoe and rowboat rentals can be found at Lower Falls. To the north of Tahquamenon, over 500 shipwrecks lie off **Whitefish Point.** Today protected as the **Underwater Preserve,** P.O. Box 64, Paradise 49768 (492-3927), the wrecks afford divers an opportunity to search for **sunken treasure.** The **Great Lakes Shipwreck Historical Museum** (635-1742) grippingly documents this "Graveyard of the Great Lakes" (open mid-May to mid-Oct. daily 10am-6pm; $5, ages 6-18 $3.50, families $16).

Middle of the Peninsula The western branch of the **Hiawatha National Forest** dominates the middle of the Peninsula, offering limitless wilderness activities and infinite campsites (pit toilets, water hookups available, no showers; sites $4-10; no reservations). In the west branch, **Munising** has access to the forest and to **Pictured Rocks National Lakeshore,** where water saturated with copper, manganese, and iron oxide has painted the cliffs with multicolored bands. **Pictured Rocks Boat Cruise** (387-2379) gives the best view (tours $19, under 12 $9.50). The Forest and Lakeshore share a **visitors center** (lakeshore 387-3700; forest 387-2512), at the intersection of Rte. 28 and H58 in Munising (open daily 8am-6pm). From Munising, H58—an oft-bumpy, unpaved gem of a road—weaves along the lakeshore past numerous trailheads and campsites. Free permits for backcountry camping are available from the Munising visitors center or from the **Grand Sable Visitors Center** (494-2660), 1 mi. west of Grand Marais on H58 (open mid-June to mid-Sept. daily 9am-7pm, mid-May to mid-June 9am-5pm). Stroll, birdwatch, or collect smooth stones along the shore at **Twelve Mile Beach** and **Grand Sable Dunes;** swim if you're fond of ice water. For more-than-a-tent shelter, the **Poplar Bluff Cabins** (452-6271), has rooms with a view and a kitchen (from $35 per cottage; open May-Nov.); go 12 mi. east of Munising on Rte. 28, and head 6 mi. south from Shingleton on M94.

Equidistant from the north and south coasts and a little east of Hiawatha's west branch, the **Seney National Wildlife Refuge** (586-9851), off Rte. 77, shelters 95,000 acres for over 250 species of birds and mammals. The 7-mi. **Marshland Wildlife Drive,** a self-guided auto tour, includes loon and eagle observation decks; the best times for viewing wildlife are early morning and early evening. The refuge also offers hiking, cross-country skiing, biking, canoeing, and fishing opportunities. (Open mid-May to mid-Oct. dawn to dusk.) Before you fish, get a required state **fishing permit** ($20 per day, residents $9; available at any convenience store, grocery, or tackle shop).

At the bottom of the peninsula, don't miss **Big Spring** (341-2355), called Kitch-iti-kipi ("mirror of heaven") by Native Americans, at **Palms Book State Park.** Take a self-operated raft to watch plump trout play among billowing clouds of silt in a forest of ancient tree trunks in the 45-ft.-deep, 200-ft.-wide spring (open daily 9am-7pm). Nearby **Indian Lake State Park** offers scenic camping (sites $12). Farther south, the **Fayette State Historic Park** (644-2603) features the historic site of the town of Fayette and a preserved ghost town (open mid-May to mid-Oct. daily 9am-7pm). The park also handles camping (no showers; $8), scuba diving, hiking, and boat tours past the limestone cliffs of **Snail Shell Harbor** (boats depart continuously from the townsite dock; $6, kids $4). All state parks require a $4 vehicle permit.

Keweenaw Peninsula In 1840, Dr. Douglas Houghton's mineralogical survey of the Keweenaw Peninsula, a curved finger of land on the U.P.'s northwest corner, incited a copper mining rush which sent the area booming. When mining petered out around 1969, the land was left barren and exploited. Today, reforestation and government support have helped Copper Country find new life as a tourist destination. Every year, 250 in. of snow fall on the towering pines, smooth-stone beaches, and low mountains of Keweenaw. Visitors ski, snowshoe, and snowmobile through the winter and enjoy the gorgeous green coasts in the summer.

At the base of the peninsula, along the shore of Lake Superior, **Porcupine Mountain Wilderness State Park** (885-5275), affectionately known as "The Porkies," offers **campsites** (hookups available; $6-10, depending on facilities), **cabins** (sleeps 2-8; $30), and beautiful hiking trails. The **visitors center,** near the junction of M-107 and South Boundary Rd., provides brochures and camping permits (open in summer daily 10am-6pm). Created in 1992, **Keweenaw National Historical Park** comprises a decentralized collection of historic sites and museums throughout the peninsula which showcase the industry and prosperity of the Copper Age; contact the **Keweenaw Tourism Council,** P.O. Box 336, Houghton 49931 (337-4579 or 800-338-7982) for details. In the heart of Keweenaw, the **Houghton Visitor Center,** 326 Sheldon St. (482-5240), has info on the entire peninsula (open Mon.-Sat. 8am-5pm).

Off the tip of the peninsula, the **Keweenaw Underwater Preserve** offers divers a museum of wrecks ranging from a Coast Guard Cutter (100ft. down) to a wooden sidewheel steamer (20ft.). The **Narcosis Corner Dive Shop,** 474 Third St. (337-3156), in Calumet, deals in rentals, charters, and air fills (½-day dives $40-50).

The **Brockway Mountain Drive,** between Eagle Harbor and Copper Harbor, rises 1337 ft. above sea level, providing postcard views of Lake Superior and inland forests along with some roller-coaster driving. The northernmost town in Michigan, **Copper Harbor** functions as the main gateway to **Isle Royale National Park** (see below). The **Norland Motel** (289-4815), near the mouth of U.S. 41 north of Copper Harbor, perks up their rooms with TV and fridge ($28-40). **Johnson's Restaurant and Bakery** (289-4595), in Copper Harbor, serves outstanding donuts (45¢) as well as breakfast ($3-5), burgers ($3-4), and hearty dinners ($8-12; open daily 8am-9pm). The **Keweenaw Adventure Company,** 64 Manganese St. (289-4303), can make all your wilderness dreams come true with dog sled rides ($10 per person), adventure packages (sea kayaking, hiking, biking), bike rentals ($10 for 5hr.), and more.

■■■ ISLE ROYALE

Around the turn of the century, moose swam from the Canadian coast to this pristine 45-mi.-long, 10-mi.-wide island. With no natural predators, the animals overran the land and quickly overpopulated it—then came the wolves. Today, wild animals are the island's only permanent inhabitants; the fisherfolk who once lived here left or died off after the island was designated **Isle Royale National Park** in 1940. For backcountry seclusion, this is the real McCoy—where the wild things are; no cars, phones, or medical services pamper visitors on the island. Come prepared.

Practical Information Despite the fact that it's closer to the Ontario and Minnesota mainlands, Isle Royale is part of Michigan. Accessible only by boat, the park has its **headquarters** on the Upper Peninsula, in **Houghton,** at 800 E. Lakeshore Dr., 49931 (906-482-0984; open Mon.-Sat. 8am-4:30pm). The headquarters operates a 6½-hour ferry to the island (call for schedules; $85 round-trip, under 12 $40), while **Isle Royale Ferry Service,** The Dock, Copper Harbor (906-289-4437; off season at 108 Center St., Hancock, 906-482-4950), makes 4½-hour trips from Copper Harbor (call for schedule; $68 round-trip, under 12 $34). Both ferries land at **Rock Harbor.** For access to other parts of the island, take any of several shuttles from Rock Harbor or leave from **Grand Portage, MN;** the **Grand Portage-Isle Royale Transportation Line Inc.,** 1507 N. First St., Superior, WI (715-392-2100), sends a boat to Windigo, which makes stops at trailheads around the island before reaching Rock Harbor six hours later. (Call for schedules; $80 round-trip to Rock Harbor, under 12 $50; fares to other points vary.) On the island, the park's **ranger stations** include **Windigo** on the west tip; **Rock Harbor,** the most developed, on the east tip; and **Malone Bay,** midway between Windigo and Rock Harbor on the south shore.

Camping, Accommodations, and Food Scattered **campgrounds** cover the island; required free permits are available at any ranger station. Some sites have three-sided, screened-in shelters (88 total) which go quickly on a first come, first served basis; bring your own tent just in case. Nights are always frigid (mid-40s°F in June), and biting bugs peak in June and July; bring warm clothes and insect repellent. Intestinal bacteria, tapeworms, and giardia lurk in the waters of Isle Royale; use a .4-micron filter or boil water for at least two minutes. Purified water is available at Rock Harbor and Windigo. Very few places on the island permit fires; bring a small campstove. The **Rock Harbor Lodge** (906-337-4993) controls most of the island's commercial activity; the store carries a decent selection of overpriced food and camping staples. The lodge and associated cabins are the only indoor accommodations on the island (from $60 per person, double occupancy).

Activities Streams, lakes, and 170 mi. of trails traverse the park. The **Greenstone Ridge Trail,** the main artery of the trail system, follows the backbone of the island from Rock Harbor Lodge, passing through several spectacular vistas. Serious backpackers will want to conquer the **Minong Ridge Trail,** which runs parallel to the Greenstone Trail to the north for 30 mi. from McCargoe Cove to Windigo; the remains of early Native Americans' shallow copper mines lie along the trail. Shorter hikes near Rock Harbor include **Scoville Point,** a 4.2-mi. loop out onto a small peninsula, and **Suzy's Cave,** a 3.8-mi. loop to an inland sea arch. Contact the park office for information on cruises, evening programs, and ranger-led interpretive walks.

Canoeing and **kayaking** allow access to otherwise unreachable parts of the island, and both Rock Harbor and Windigo have **boat** and **canoe rental** outfitters. (Motors $12 for ½day, $20 per day. Boats and canoes $10.50 for ½day, $18 per day.) **Scuba divers** explore shipwrecks in the treacherous reefs off the northeast and west ends of the island; all divers must register at the park's office. Bring filled tanks; there are no publicly available air compressors. The only charter services for Isle Royale operate out of Grand Portage, MN: **Royal Diver, Inc.** (218-475-2316). On Lake Superior, a Michigan **fishing license** is required.

Indiana

The seemingly endless cornfields of southern Indiana's Appalachian foothills give way to expansive plains in the industrialized north. Here, Gary's smokestacks spew black clouds over the waters of Lake Michigan, and urban travel hubs have earned the state its official nickname, "The Crossroads of America." The origin of Indiana's unofficial nickname, "The Hoosier State," is less certain; some speculate that it is a corruption of the pioneers' call to visitors at the door—"Who's there?"—while others claim that it spread from Louisville, where labor contractor Samuel Hoosier preferred to hire Indiana workers over Kentucky laborers. Whatever the nickname's derivation, Indiana's Hoosiers are generally considered a no-nonsense Midwestern breed. The Indiana General Assembly once nearly passed a law to make the official value of pi three instead of 3.14etc., just for the sake of simplicity; more recently, the pragmatic people of Indianapolis laughed a meteorologist named David Letterman out of town for forecasting hail "the size of canned hams."

PRACTICAL INFORMATION

Capital: Indianapolis.

Indiana Division of Tourism: 1 N. Capitol #700, Indianapolis 46204 (800-289-6646). **Division of State Parks,** 402 W. Washington #W-298, Indianapolis 46204 (232-4125).

Time Zones: Confusing. Mostly Eastern; Central near Gary in the northwest and Evansville in the southwest. Only the parts of the state near Louisville, KY and Cincinnati, OH observe daylight savings time. **Postal Abbreviation:** IN

Sales Tax: 5%; 10% hotel tax.

■■■ INDIANAPOLIS

Flat, dusty expanses of corn surround this calm Midwestern metropolis. Folks shop and work all day among downtown's skyscrapers and drive home to sprawling suburbs in the evening. Life moves at an amble here—until May. Then, an army of 350,000 spectators and countless crewmembers overruns the city, and the winged wheel of the Indianapolis 500 rises above clouds of turbocharged exhaust to claim its throne. Gentlemen, start your engines…and the city goes into a frenzy as modern-day chariots of fire strain toward the finish for a $7.5 million winner's purse.

PRACTICAL INFORMATION

Visitor Information: Indianapolis City Center, 201 S. Capital St. (237-5200), in the Pan Am Plaza across from the Hoosier Dome. Has a helpful model of the city; press marked buttons to light up tourist attractions. Open Mon.-Fri. 10am-5:30pm, Sat. 10am-4pm, Sun. noon-5pm. Also try 800-233-INDY/4639.

Airport: Indianapolis International (487-7243), 7mi. southwest of downtown off I-465, exit 11B. To get to the city center, take bus #9 ("West Washington"), American Trailways ($6), or a cab ($7-9).

Trains: Amtrak, 350 S. Illinois (263-0550 or 800-872-7245), behind Union Station. Trains travel east-west only. To: Chicago (4 per week, 4½hr., from $32), Washington, DC (3 per week, 19hr., from $118). Station hours vary daily; call ahead.

Buses: Greyhound, 127 N. Capital Ave. (800-231-2222), downtown at E. Ohio St. 1 block from Monument Circle. To: Chicago (9 per day, 4hr., $32), Cincinnati (4 per day, 2hr., $19). Open 24 hrs. **American Trailways** (635-4000) operates out of the Amtrak station and serves cities within the state. To: Bloomington (4 per day, 1hr., $23), airport (4 per day, 15min., $6). Open daily 7am-11pm.

Public Transportation: Metro Bus, 36 N. Delaware St. (635-3344), across from City County building. Open Mon.-Fri. 7:30am-5:30pm. Fare 75¢, rush hour (Mon.-Fri. 6-9am and 3-6pm) $1. Service to the Speedway area 25¢ extra. Transfers 25¢. Patchy coverage of outlying areas. For disabled service, call 632-3000.

Taxis: Barrington Cab (786-7994), $1.25 first mi., 72¢ each additional. **Yellow Cab** (487-7777), $2.70 first mi., $1.80 each additional.

Car Rental: Thrifty, 5860 Fortune Circle West (636-5622), at the airport. Daily $37 with 225 free mi. Weekly $134 with 1500 free mi. Must be 21 with major credit card. If under 25 add $5 daily. Open Sun.-Fri. 6am-11pm, Sat. 7am-10pm.

Emergency: 911 or 236-3000.

Post Office: 125 W. South St. (464-6000), across from Amtrak. Open Mon.-Fri. 8am-4:30pm. **ZIP code:** 46206. **Area code:** 317.

The city is laid out in concentric circles, with a dense central cluster of skyscrapers and low-lying outskirts. The very center of Indianapolis is just south of **Monument Circle** at the intersection of **Washington St.** (U.S. 40) and **Meridian St.** Washington St. divides the city north-south; Meridian St. east-west. **I-465** circles the city and provides access to downtown. **I-70** cuts through the city east-west and passes by the Speedway. Plentiful 2-hr. meter parking can be found along the edges of the downtown area, and there are numerous indoor and outdoor lots ($5-8 per day) in the center, especially along **Ohio St.**

ACCOMMODATIONS AND CAMPING

Budget motels line the **I-465 beltway,** 5 mi. from downtown. Their concentration and prices increase in the west, near the Speedway. Make reservations a year in advance for the Indy 500, and expect to pay inflated rates throughout May.

Fall Creek YMCA, 860 W. 10th St. (634-2478), just north of downtown. Small rooms have minimal furniture, but resources make them ideal; access to a pool, a gym, athletic and laundry facilities, and free parking included. 86 rooms for men, 10 for women. Singles $25, with bath $35; weekly $70/$80, students $58. Call for availability and reservations as early as possible.

Motel 6 (293-3220) I-465 at Exit 16A, 3mi. from the Indy Speedway and 10mi. from downtown, or take the #13 bus. Clean, bright rooms and an outdoor pool. Singles $31, doubles $37. Fills up fast; call for reservations, especially on weekends.

American Inn North, 7202 E. 82nd St. (849-6910), 20min. north of downtown just outside I-465. Clean though worn rooms and suites. All have kitchenettes; coin-op laundry on-site. Singles from $23, family room for up to 4 $40.

Medical Tower Inn, 1633 N. Capitol Ave. (925-9831), an easy 5-min. drive from downtown. One- and 2-room setups with standard hotel florals and a decent view of the city. Singles $43, doubles $58; students $41/$54. $10 each additional.

Indiana State Fairgrounds Campgrounds, 1202 E. 38th St. (927-7510). If you want to get close to nature, go elsewhere. 170 sod and gravel sites, most along the edge of a vast parking lot. Sites $10.50, full hookup $12.60. Especially busy during the state fair in mid-Aug. (Aug. 7-18 in 1996).

FOOD

Ethnic food stands, produce markets, and knick-knack sellers fill the spacious **City Market,** 222 E. Market St., in a renovated 19th-century building. **Union Station,** 39 Jackson Pl. (267-0070), a 13-acre refurbished rail depot 4 blocks south of Monument Circle near the Hoosier Dome, is crowded with shops, dance clubs, bars, hotels, and restaurants; at the Trackside Food Court and Market on the second floor, vendors hawk a variety of eats (entrees average $2.50-5).

Bazbeaux Pizza, 334 Massachusetts Ave. (636-7662), and 832 E. Westfields Blvd. (255-5712). Indianapolis's favorite pizza either downtown or at Broad Ripple. The Xchoupitoulas pizza is a cajun masterpiece. Construct your own culinary wonder ($5-18) from a choice of 53 toppings. Open Mon.-Thurs. 11am-10pm, Fri. 11am-11pm, Sat. noon-11pm, Sun. 4:30-10pm.

Mezza Luna, 927 Broad Ripple Ave. (255-9300). Mediterranean food served in a stucco building with a streetside terrace. A local favorite for gourmet pizza—toppings range from goat cheese to smoked salmon to sauerkraut. Dinner entrees $10-15; lunch specials from $5. Open daily 11am-2:45pm; Mon.-Thurs. 4-9:45pm, Fri.-Sat. 4-10:45pm, Sun. 4-8:45pm.

Acapulco Joe's, 365 N. Illinois (637-5160). The first Mexican restaurant in Indianapolis greets its guests with a perplexing sign saying: "Acapulco Joe's has sold over 5 million tacos—do you realize that represents *over 6 pounds of ground beef?*" Heavy on flavor, atmosphere, and popularity. Entrees up to $7.65. Open Mon.-Thurs. 7am-9pm, Fri.-Sat. 7am-10pm.

SIGHTS

Gold chandeliers and a majestic stained glass dome grace the marbled interior of the **State House** (232-3131), between Capitol and Senate St. near W. Washington St.; self-guided tour brochures are available inside (open daily 8am-5pm, main floor only Sat.-Sun.). The **Eiteljorg Museum of American Indian and Western Art,** 500 W. Washington St. (636-9378), houses a large collection of works from the original Taos artists' colony (open Tues.-Sat. 10am-5pm, Sun. noon-5pm; $5, students $3.50, seniors $4.50). About a 5-min. drive from the Eiteljorg, the seemingly cageless **Indianapolis Zoo,** 1200 W. Washington St. (630-2001), has one of the world's largest enclosed whale and dolphin pavilions (open daily 9am-5pm; $9, seniors $6.50, ages 3-12 $5.50, under 3 free).

Farther from the city center, but well worth a visit, is the **Indianapolis Museum of Art,** 1200 W. 38th St. (923-1331). The museum's beautifully landscaped, 152-acre grounds offer nature trails, art pavilions, the Eli Lily Botanical Garden, a greenhouse, and a theater. Visit the third floor of the **Krannert Pavilion** for interactive modern art installations. (Open Mon.-Wed. and Fri. 10am-5pm, Thurs. 10am-8:30pm, Sun. noon-5pm. Free. Special exhibits $3; free Thurs.) Dig for fossils, speed through the cosmos, or explore a maze at the **Children's Museum,** 3000 N. Meridian St. (924-5437), one of the country's largest (open daily 10am-5pm; closed Mon. Sept.-Feb.)

ENTERTAINMENT AND NIGHTLIFE

In its heyday, the **Walker Theatre,** 617 Indiana Ave. (236-2009, 236-2087 for tickets), a 15-min. walk northwest of downtown, booked jazz greats Louis Armstrong and Dinah Washington. Local and national artists still perform here as part of the weekly **Jazz on the Avenue** series (Fri. 6-10pm) and the annual **Jazz Festival** (3rd week in Aug.). The theater, erected in 1927 with stunning Egyptian and African decor, commemorates Madame Walker, an African-American beautician who invented the straightening comb and became America's first self-made woman millionaire. The **Indianapolis Symphony Orchestra,** 45 Monument Circle (box office 639-4300 or 800-366-8457), handles refined entertainment in classical style. The **Indianapolis Opera,** 250 E. 38th St. (283-3531, tickets 921-6444), and the **Indianapolis Repertory Theatre,** 140 W. Washington St. (635-5252; tickets $6-30, student rush 1hr. before show $6), both perform September through May. Contact the **Arts Council Office,** 47 S. Pennsylvania St. (631-3301 or 800-865-ARTS/2787), for the schedules of other performance groups in the area.

By day an outlying cluster of art galleries, bead shops, and record shops, the **Broad Ripple** area (6mi. north of downtown at College Ave. and 62nd St.) transforms after dark into a nightlife mecca for anyone under 40. The party fills the clubs and bars and spills out onto the sidewalks and side streets off Broad Ripple Ave. until about 1am on weekdays and 3am on weekends. Check out **O.P.T.,** 829 Broad Ripple Ave., for pool tables and a juke box, or chug nightly drink specials and sing an inebriated "Love Me Tender" to pictures of Elvis at **Rock Lobster,** 820 Broad Ripple Ave. (257-9001). **The Patio,** 6308 Guilford Ave. (255-2828), and **The Vogue,** 6259 N. College Ave. (255-2828), are music clubs featuring local and mid-size national acts, respectively. The Patio has free dancing on Wednesday nights which attracts a 20-25% gay crowd. (Cover $2-7, more for big names). After the clubs close, make a run for tacos ($1.75) and burritos ($3) at **Páco's Cantina,** 737 Broad Ripple Ave. (251-6200; open until 4am or later, by the owner's whim).

GO, SPEED RACER, GO!

Most of the year, the **Indianapolis Motor Speedway,** 4790 W. 16th St. (481-8500), off I-465 at the Speedway exit (bus #25), lies dormant and waiting, as tourists ride buses around the 2½-mi. track ($2). The adjacent **Speedway Museum** (484-6747) houses Indy's Hall of Fame (open daily 9am-5pm; $2, under 17 free).

The country's passion for fast cars reaches a fevered pitch during the **500 Festival** (636-4556), a month of parades, a mini-marathon, and lots of hoopla leading up to the day when 33 aerodynamic race cars, specially designed not to go airborne, jet around the track at speeds exceeding 225mph. The festivities begin with time trials the two weekends in mid-May preceding the race and culminate with the bang of the **Indianapolis 500** starter's gun on the Sunday of Memorial Day Weekend (weather permitting). Think ahead; tickets for a race go on sale the day after the previous year's race and are usually sold out within a week (from $30; call the Speedway for an order form, available in April). NASCAR's **Brickyard 400** (800-822-4639) sends stockcars zooming down the speedway in early August.

■ NEAR INDIANAPOLIS

Wolves and bison roam under researchers' supervision at **Wolf Park** (567-2265), on Jefferson St. in Battle Ground, IN (1hr. north of Indianapolis on I-65). Let the werewolf within you howl with the pack on Fridays at 7:30pm, or sit in suspense as the wolves and bison mingle in uneasy harmony on Sundays at 1pm. (Open daily 1-5pm, open later Fri. for the wolf howl. Mon.-Sat. $4, Sun. $5, under 14 free.)

■■■ BLOOMINGTON

Home to 35,000 students and five-time national college basketball champions, the Hoosiers, Indiana University (IU) has left its mark on this rural community; record shops, cafés, and bead stores cluster on the east side of town where bicycle-riders weave between frat boys and punks. The areas west of College St. remain immune to student influence; drive south a few minutes to enjoy the scenic beauty of farmland and Lake Monroe.

Practical Information Bloomington is south of Indianapolis on Rte. 37; **N. Walnut** and **College St.** are the main thoroughfares running north-south in town. The **visitors center** is located at 2855 N. Walnut St. (334-8900 or 800-800-0037; open Mon.-Fri. 8am-5pm, Sat. 9am-4pm, Sun. 10am-3pm; 24-hr. brochure area). Buses from **American Trailways,** 535 N. Walnut (332-1522), four blocks from the center of downtown, connect Bloomington to Chicago (4 per day, 6hr., round-trip $88) and Indianapolis (4 per day, 1hr., round-trip $23; open Mon.-Sat. 4:30am-5:30pm, Sun. during bus times only). **Bloomington Transit** transports the public on seven routes. Service is infrequent; call 332-5688 for info (50¢, seniors and kids 5-17 25¢). Call **Yellow Cab** (336-4100) for a taxi. Bloomington's **post office:** Fourth St., two blocks east of Walnut St. (open Mon.-Fri. 8am-6pm, Sat. 8am-1pm); **ZIP code:** 47401; **area code:** 812.

Accommodations, Food, and Nightlife Budget hotels cluster around the intersection of N. Walnut St. and Rte. 46. Just west of town off Rte. 46 stands the beautiful brick **Bauer House,** 4595 N. Maple Grove Rd. (336-4383). In this family-run B&B, $50 will secure a room that sleeps up to four and a country breakfast prepared by Mrs. Bauer. (Open May-Oct. Reservations recommended, especially around the beginning and end of the school year.) **Motel 6,** 1800 N. Walnut St. (332-0820), offers clean, spacious rooms, a pool, free local calls, and free HBO (singles $30, doubles $36). The **Lake Monroe Village Campgrounds,** 8107 S. Fairfax Rd. (824-2267), 8 mi. south of Bloomington, allows campers to choose a spot on 60 wooded acres and throws in free showers and a pool (sites $16, hookup $23, log cabins for 2 $42).

The **Downtown Square** of Bloomington holds a wealth of restaurants in a two-block radius, most on Kirkwood Ave. near College and W. Walnut St. Laugh the hemp cheese ($1 per oz.) off your Mondo Burrito ($3.50) at **The Laughing Planet Café,** 322 E. Kirkwood Ave. (323-CAFE/2233), where they whip up "whole foods in a hurry" (open daily 11am-9pm). A half block west of the square, the **Irish Lion,** 212 5th St. (336-9076), serves pub grub (leg of lamb $4.85), full entrees (ballydebob halibut $13), and famous half-yard glasses of beer ($5; open Sun.-Thurs. 11am-midnight, Fri.-Sat. 11am-1am). Enter a hall of mirrors at **Snow Lion,** 113 S. Grant St. (336-

0835), just off Kirkwood Ave., to sample Tibetan cuisine (lunch $3.75, entrees $7.50; open Mon.-Sat. 11:30am-2pm, daily 5-10pm). Why are these restaurants both named Lion? We could tell you, but then we'd have to kill you. Cheap eateries multiply on the east end of town. **Jiffy-Treet,** 425 E. Kirkwood Ave. (332-3502), produces homemade ice-cream; the strawberry sherbert is dreamy (1 scoop $1.09).

Beer and alternative rock are the milk and ambrosia of college students, and IU is no exception. Taste 80 beers brewed from Jamaica to Japan at **The Crazy Horse,** 214 W. Kirkwood (336-8877; open Mon.-Thurs. 11am-1am, Fri.-Sat. 11am-2am, Sun. 11am-midnight). **Mars,** 479 N. Walnut St. (336-6277 concert line), is the planet for big-name regional and mid-size national acts; **Bluebird,** 216 N. Walnut St. (336-2473), stages local acts, and **Second Story,** 201 S. College Ave. (336-5827) hosts alternative groups. **Rhino's,** 225½ S. Walnut St. (333-3430) has lesser-known acts and accepts people under 21, unlike the others. Check bulletin boards on the east side of town for concert flyers

Sights IU's **Art Museum,** Fine Arts Plaza, E. 7th St. (855-5445), maintains an excellent collection including a rather likeable Dada enclave and surrealist works by Marcel Duchamp and Man Ray (open Wed.-Thurs. and Sat. 10am-5pm, Fri. 10am-8pm, Sun. noon-5pm; free). Browse three floors of old valuables downtown at the **Antique Mall,** 311 W. 7th St. (332-2290; open Mon.-Thurs. and Sat. 10am-5pm, Fri. 10am-8pm, Sun. noon-5pm). The cool waters and calm breezes of **Lake Monroe,** 10 mi. south of town, make for a relaxing end to a hard day of sight-seeing. Labor Day Weekend, the 4th St. **Festival of the Arts and Crafts** (800-800-0037) draws hundreds of Midwestern artisans to Bloomington. In June, **A Taste of Bloomington** gathers local bands and food from local restaurants together under a single tent while festival-goers eat their hearts out.

Illinois

Four cities exemplify Illinois's diversity. Cairo, at the southern tip of the state, is so-called for its resemblance to the fertile Nile River Valley. All of Illinois farms here, and ranks second only to Iowa in the production of corn. To the north, Collinsville's Cahokia Mounds, the largest pre-historic Native American city north of Mexico, reveal Illinois' Native American heritage; the state's name derives from a word in the Illinois tribe meaning "warrior." Lincoln-worship centers around Springfield, the capital, but every Illinois license plate bears the motto "Land of Lincoln." Finally, the Midwest's ubiquitous cornfields come to an abrupt halt in the industrial north, where suits trade corn futures, pork bellies, and soybeans behind Chicago's jungle of polished steel and glass.

PRACTICAL INFORMATION

Capital: Springfield.
Office of Tourism: 620 E. Adams St., Springfield 62701 (217-782-7500).
Time Zone: Central (1hr. behind Eastern). **Postal Abbreviation:** IL
Sales Tax: 6.25%-8.75%, depending on city.

■■■ CHICAGO

Over two centuries ago, Checagon ("place of the wild onion" to its early Native American inhabitants) occupied a reeking marsh at the southern tip of Lake Michigan. Railroads and canals built in the mid-1800s formed a commercial center for farmers seeking to trade cattle and crops for cash. Freight depots, stockyards, and refrigerator cars multiplied, and Chicago became the nation's slaughterhouse, horrifyingly depicted in Upton Sinclair's *The Jungle* in 1906. At the turn of the century, millions of immigrants flooded the city to meet demand for labor, creating a few vast fortunes and countless broken dreams. Machine politics ruled the slums with an iron fist, giving way to the alcohol-smuggling Mafia during the Prohibition era.

As time wore on, trading commodities displaced cattle slaughter as the city's mainstay, and narrow steel tracks gave way to the wide concrete runways of O'Hare, the world's busiest airport. Chicago began to export authors—Studs Terkel, Theodore Dreiser, and Ernest Hemingway to name a few—along with its Cracker Jacks and canned hams. Today, the city prides itself on its status as an extremely diverse world-class metropolis. Its neighborhoods shelter many ethnic communities, and feature the work of Frank Lloyd Wright, Mies van der Rohe, and Louis Sullivan, as well as the art of Picasso, Chagall, and Joan Miró; its orchestra and museums are first-rate. The University of Chicago employs more Nobel Laureates than any other university in the world. The "City in a Garden" (its current motto), once a humble onion patch by the lake, has come into its own.

PRACTICAL INFORMATION

Tourist Office: Call or write the **Chicago Office of Tourism,** 78 E. Washington St. 60602 (B4; 744-2400 or 800-487-2446). Open Mon.-Fri. 10am-6pm, Sat. 10am-5pm, Sun. noon-5pm. Another location a few min. north at 806 Michigan Ave. The **Chicago Visitor Information Center,** 163 E. Pearson (C3; 467-7114), in the Water Tower Pumping Station. Open Mon.-Fri. 9:30am-6pm, Sat. 10am-6pm, Sun. 11am-5pm. The **Chicago Cultural Center,** 77 E. Randolph St. at Michigan Ave. (B4), has info on Chicago's ethnic groups. Open Mon.-Fri. 10am-6pm, Sat. 10am-5pm, Sun. noon-5pm.

Police: 744-4000 (non-emergency).

Consulates: Canada, 180 N. Stetson Ave. (B4; 616-1860); **Ireland,** 400 N. Michigan Ave. (B4; 337-1868); **U.K.,** 33 N. Dearborn St. (B4; 346-1810). Hours vary, though most are open at least Mon.-Fri. 8am-5pm; call ahead.

Airports: O'Hare International (686-2200), off I-90. Inventor of the layover, the holding pattern and the headache; flights depart every 40-46 seconds. Depending on traffic, a trip between downtown and O'Hare can take up to 2hr. The **Rapid Train** runs between the Airport El station and downtown ($1.50); the ride takes 40min-1hr. **Midway Airport** (767-0500), on the western edge of the South Side, often offers less expensive flights. To get downtown, take the El orange line from the Midway stop. Lockers $1 per day. **Continental Air Transport** (454-7800 or 800-972-7000) connects both airports to downtown hotels and convenient, central downtown locations. From O'Hare: runs every 30min. (5am-10:30pm) from each baggage terminal. The ride takes 60-75min., and costs $13.75. From Midway: runs every hr., 25min. after the hr., and costs $9.75 (6:25am-8:25pm).

Trains: Amtrak, Union Station, 225 S. Canal (A5; 558-1075 or 800-872-7245), at Adams St. west of the Loop. Take the El to State and Adams, then walk 7 blocks west on Adams. Amtrak's main hub may look familiar; it was the backdrop for the final baby-buggy scene of *The Untouchables.* To: Milwaukee (4 per day, 1½hr., $25); Detroit (2 per day, 6½hr., $31); New York (2 per day, 18½hr., $128). Station open 24 hrs.; tickets sold daily 6am-9pm. Lockers $1 per day.

Buses: Greyhound, 630 W. Harrison St. (800-231-2222), at Jefferson and Desplaines. Take the El to Linton. *The* hub of the central U.S. Also home base for several smaller companies covering the Midwest. To: Detroit (10 per day, 8hr., $25); Milwaukee (14 per day, 2hr., $12); St. Louis (7 per day, 5-8hr., $29). Station open 24 hrs., ticket office open Mon.-Fri. 5am-2:30pm, Sat.-Sun. 6am-10am.

Taxis: Yellow Cab, 829-4222. **Flash Cab,** 561-1444. **American United Cab,** 248-7600. Average fare $1.50 for flag drop, $1.20 per mi.

Car Rental: Dollar Rent-a-Car (800-800-4000), at O'Hare and Midway; P.O. Box 66181, 60666. $47 per day, $135 per week; Under 25 surcharge $12 per day. **Thrifty Car Rental** (800-367-2277), at O'Hare and Midway. $35 per day, $129 per week, $9 for liability insurance. Under 25 surcharge $10 per day. 100 free mi. per day, 15¢ per additional mi. Must be 21 with major credit card for both.

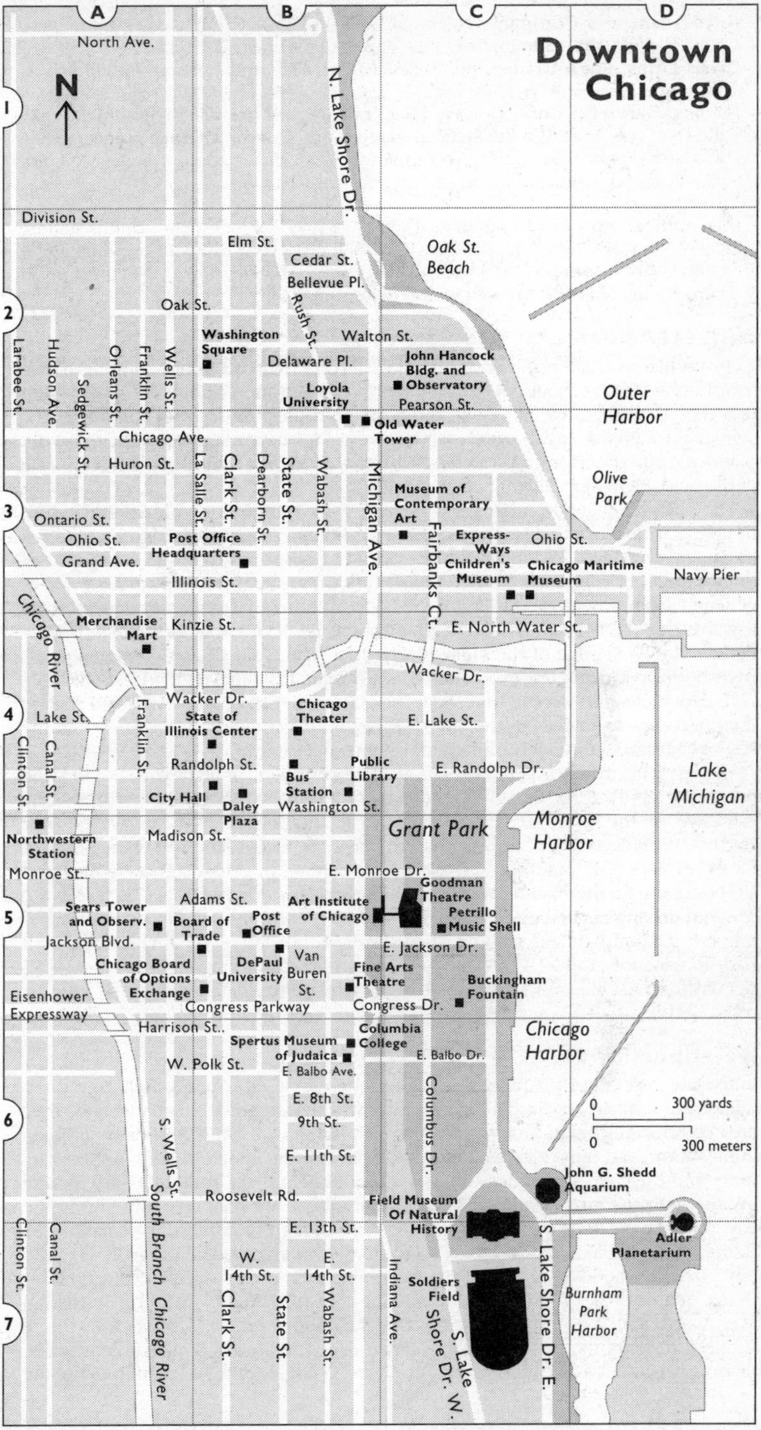

Downtown Chicago

A B C D
1 2 3 4 5 6 7
N

North Ave.
N. Lake Shore Dr.
Division St.
Elm St.
Cedar St.
Bellevue Pl.
Oak St.
Oak St. Beach
Rush St.
Walton St.
Washington Square
Delaware Pl.
John Hancock Bldg. and Observatory
Loyola University
Pearson St.
Outer Harbor
Larabee St.
Hudson Ave.
Sedgewick St.
Orleans St.
Franklin St.
Wells St.
Old Water Tower
Chicago Ave.
Huron St.
La Salle St.
Clark St.
Dearborn St.
State St.
Wabash St.
Michigan Ave.
Museum of Contemporary Art
Olive Park
Ontario St.
Ohio St.
Grand Ave.
Post Office Headquarters
Fairbanks Ct.
Express-Ways Children's Museum
Chicago Maritime Museum
Navy Pier
Illinois St.
Chicago River
Merchandise Mart
Kinzie St.
E. North Water St.
Wacker Dr.
Lake St.
Franklin St.
State of Illinois Center
Chicago Theater
E. Lake St.
Clinton St.
Canal St.
Randolph St.
Public Library
E. Randolph Dr.
Lake Michigan
Bus Station
City Hall
Daley Plaza
Washington St.
Northwestern Station
Madison St.
Grant Park
Monroe Harbor
Monroe St.
E. Monroe Dr.
Goodman Theatre
Adams St.
Art Institute of Chicago
Petrillo Music Shell
Sears Tower and Observ.
Board of Trade
Post Office
Jackson Blvd.
E. Jackson Dr.
Van Buren St.
Chicago Board of Options Exchange
DePaul University
Fine Arts Theatre
Buckingham Fountain
Eisenhower Expressway
Congress Parkway
Congress Dr.
Harrison St.
Columbia College
Chicago Harbor
Spertus Museum of Judaica
E. Balbo Dr.
W. Polk St.
E. Balbo Ave.
E. 8th St.
9th St.
E. 11th St.
Columbus Dr.
0 300 yards
0 300 meters
S. Wells St.
South Branch Chicago River
Roosevelt Rd.
Field Museum Of Natural History
John G. Shedd Aquarium
E. 13th St.
Adler Planetarium
W. 14th St.
E. 14th St.
Indiana Ave.
Soldiers Field
S. Lake Shore Dr. W.
S. Lake Shore Dr. E.
Burnham Park Harbor

GREAT LAKES

Auto Transport Company: National U-Drive, 3626 Calumet Ave., Hammond, IN (219-852-0134). 20min. from the Loop. Call for rates.

Crisis Lines: Rape Crisis Line, 708-872-7799. **Gay and Lesbian Hotline/Anti Violence Project,** 871-2273. Both 24 hrs.

Medical Services: Cook County Hospital, 1835 W. Harrison (633-6000). Take the Congress A train to the Medical Center Stop. **Doctor's Office Center,** 3245 N. Halsted Ave. (528-5005). Non-emergencies. Call for appointments Mon.-Fri. 9am-7pm, Sat. 9am-2pm.

Emergency: 911.

Post Office: 433 W. Van Buren St. (B5; 697-6497), 2 blocks from Union Station. Open Mon.-Fri. 7am-9pm, Sat. 8am-5pm. Self-service available 24 hrs. **ZIP code:** 60607. **Area code:** 312 (Chicago), 708 (outside the city limits). Numbers given here are in area code 312 unless otherwise noted.

ORIENTATION

Chicago has overtaken the entire northeastern corner of Illinois, running north-south along 29 mi. of southwest Lake Michigan shorefront. The city sits at the center of a web of interstates, rail lines, and airplane routes; most cross-country traffic swings through the city. A good map is essential for navigating Chicago; it was not planned on an orderly grid. *Streetwise Chicago,* available at many bookstores, is one of the best; Rand McNally publishes a similar map.

The one area that you *must* know is the **Loop,** Chicago's downtown and hub of the public transportation system. The Loop is bounded by the Chicago River to the north and west, Lake Michigan to the east, and Roosevelt Rd. to the south. Attractions within the Loop have been keyed to *Let's Go's* **map.** Directions in *Let's Go* are generally from downtown. South of the Loop, numbered east-west streets increase towards the south; many ethnic neighborhoods lie in this area. Lasalle Dr. loosely defines the west edge of the **Near North** area. The **Gold Coast** shimmers on N. Lakeshore Dr. **Lincoln Park** is bounded by Clark St., Lincoln Ave., and Halstead. Lincoln Park melts into **Wrigleyville,** near the 300s of N. Clark and N. Halstead St., and then becomes **Lakeview,** in the 4000s. For more information on the Loop and the rest of Chicago, see Neighborhoods and Sights (below).

The city's north side is generally safe at all times, though at night you should avoid the area around Cabrini Green (bounded by W. Armitage Ave. on the north, W. Chicago Ave. on the south., Sedgwick on the west, and Halsted on the east). The west side of the Chicago River (north and south branches) is also unsafe at night. South of the Loop, especially south of Cermak Rd., be careful. In general, know where you are going and go there; don't wander around aimlessly or ignorantly.

Avoid **driving** in the city as much as possible. Daytrippers can leave their cars in one of the suburban subway lots for 24 hrs. ($1.75). There are a half-dozen such park-and-ride lots; call CTA (see above) for information. Parking downtown costs $8 per day for most lots; most residential areas in the north side have street parking for residents only (look for signs).

Neighborhoods

In the late 19th century, Chicago's slaughterhouses, factories, and warehouses drew millions of immigrants from all areas of the world; the ethnic neighborhoods they created remain, though their borders have shifted due to gentrification, continued immigration, and university-building. Some have disintegrated, leaving only restaurants and businesses behind. Chicago's ethnic neighborhoods offer fascinating insights into the city's history and personality. Most are relatively safe during the day, but take a cab or get very good directions at night. For more information see Katherine Rodeglier's article *Ethnic Chicago,* which gives a detailed analysis of the city's neighborhoods (available at the Cultural Center; see Practical Information).

The center of the **Chinese** community lies out of the Loop, at Cermak Rd. and Wentworth Ave. New Chinatown, north of the Loop at Argyle St. offers a few more Chinese restaurants, but is mainly **Vietnamese.** The area of Argyle St. east of N. Broadway is known as Little Saigon. The **German** community has scattered, but the beer halls, restaurants, and shops in the 3000s and 4000s of N. Lincoln Ave. bear witness to their presence. The former residents of **Greektown** have moved to the suburbs, but S. Halsted St., just west of the Loop, offers a wide variety of Greek restaurants. **Little Italy** fell prey to the University of Illinois at Chicago (UIC), but a shadow of the old neighborhood remains along W. Taylor St. west of the UIC campus. The **Jewish** community leaves its mark on Devon Ave. from Western Ave. to the Chicago River. The area near Midway Airport is home to much of Chicago's **Lithuanian** population, one of the world's largest. The **Pilsen** neighborhood, south of downtown around 18th-44th St., offers a slice of **Mexico.** Quell your hunger for Polish sausage along N. Milwaukee Ave. between blocks 2800 and 3100; Chicago's **Polish** population ranks as one of the largest outside of Warsaw. **Andersonville,** along Clark St. north of Foster Ave., is the historic center of the **Swedish** community, though immigrants from Asia and the Middle East have settled here in recent years. The golden dome of Sts. Volodymyr and Olha Ukrainian Catholic Church (739 N. Oakley Ave.) marks the **Ukrainian Village.**

GETTING AROUND

The **Chicago Transit Authority (CTA),** 7th floor, Merchandise Mart, 350 N. Wells (836-7000), runs rapid transit trains, subways, and buses. The **elevated rapid transit train** system, called the **El,** bounds the major downtown section of the city, known as the **Loop.** Some downtown routes run underground, but are still referred to as the El. The El operates 24 hrs., but late-night service is infrequent and unsafe in many areas; stick with the crowds. Also, some buses do not run all night; call CTA for schedules and routes. CTA maps are available at many stations and the Water Tower Information Center (see Practical Information, above). The CTA map is your best friend; it includes a "Quick Ride" Guide with instructions to major attractions from downtown. Since buses and trains are everywhere, deciphering the map is worth the trouble. Don't just step blindly onto a train; many are express trains, and often different routes run along the same tracks. Train fare is $1.50; bus fare is $1.25, $1.50 6-10am and 3-7pm. Remember to get a transfer (30¢) from bus drivers or when you enter the El stop, which will get you up to two more rides on different routes during the following two hours. Ten tokens good for one train or bus ride each at any time of day cost $12.50. Buy token rolls at *some* stations, many supermarkets, and at the "Check Cashed" storefronts with the yellow sign; these places also carry $18.50 weekly passes (valid Sun.-Sat.) or $72 monthly passes.

METRA operates a vast commuter rail network; 11 rail lines and four downtown stations send trains snaking out into suburbs north, west, and south. (Free schedules and maps at their office at 547 W. Jackson. Route information, 322-6777 Mon.-Fri. 8am-5pm, 836-7000 evenings and weekends. Fare $1.75-5, depending on distance.) **PACE** (836-7000) is the suburban bus system.

ACCOMMODATIONS

A cheap, convenient bed awaits you at one of Chicago's hostels. If you have a car, you can also try the moderately priced motels on Lincoln Ave. Motel chains have locations off the interstates, about an hour's drive from downtown; they're inconvenient and expensive ($35 and up), but are a reliable option for late night arrivals. **Chicago Bed and Breakfast,** P.O. Box 14088, Chicago 60614 (951-0085), runs a referral service with over 150 rooms of varying prices throughout the city and outlying areas. None have parking, but the majority are near public transit; street parking is occasionally available. (2-night min. stay. Singles from $65, doubles from $75. Reservations required; a few weeks in advance is best.)

Chicago International Hostel, 6318 N. Winthrop (262-1011). Take the Howard St. northbound train to Loyola Station; walk 2 blocks south on Sheridan Rd., 1 block east on Sheridan Rd. (the road zigs) to Winthrop, and ½ block south. Bland but sunny and clean rooms in a safe location near the lake, beaches, and many fast food joints, but a 30-min. train ride from the Loop. Free parking in rear. Kitchen, laundry. Bike rental $8 per day. 4-6 beds per room. Check in 7-11am, 4pm-2am. Lockout 11am-4pm. $13, double with bath $40. Lockers $1. Key deposit $5. Reservations recommended.

Eleanor Residence, 1550 N. Dearborn Pkwy. (664-8245). Fantastic location near Lincoln Park and Gold Coast, majestic common room and lobby, clean single rooms. *Women over 18 only.* $34 with breakfast. Large dinner $5. Reserve at least 1 day in advance; 1-night deposit required.

Chicago Summer Hostel (HI-AYH), 731 S. Plymouth Ct. (327-5350). Close to downtown and the Lake. Clean, light, dorm-style housing filled with international students. Kitchen, laundry, exercise rooms, ride-sharing board. 2-3 beds per room; suites have 2-3 bedrooms, a bathroom, and a living room. $14, nonmembers $17. Private double $45. Open mid-June to early Sept.

International House (HI-AYH), 1414 E. 59th St. (753-2270), Hyde Park, off Lake Shore Dr. Take the Illinois Central Railroad (10-20min.) to 59th St. and walk ½ block west. Part of the University of Chicago. Isolated from the rest of the city; the neighborhood can be dangerous at night. Clean, monk-like singles filled mostly by permanent residents. Cheap cafeteria with soothing outdoor courtyard. Shared bath, linens provided. $16, nonmembers $31. Reservations recommended. Open year-round.

Hotel Cass, 640 N. Wabash (B3; 787-4030), just north of the Loop. Take subway to State or Grand St. Convenient location; clean rooms with wood trim. No parking. A/C and laundry room. Singles $50, doubles $55. $5 discount with ISIC (see p. 15). Key deposit $5. Reservations recommended.

Arlington House (AAIH/Rucksackers), 616 Arlington Pl. (929-5380 or 800-467-8355). Take the El to Fullerton, walk 2 blocks east, left on Orchard, then right on Arlington Place. The rooms are more than offset by the ideal location in Lincoln Park, near the center of nightlife. Free parking in the street if you can find it. Laundry room, kitchenette. Dorm-style rooms with 4, 6, or 10 beds. Open 24 hrs. $13, nonmembers $16. Linen $2.

Hotel Wacker, 111 W. Huron (A3; 787-1386), Near North Side. Insert your own joke, you lecherous swine. A large green sign on the corner of N. Clark and W. Huron and maps in the tourist office make this place easy to find. Clean, old-fashioned rooms. Convenient to downtown, no parking, TV, A/C, phone. 24-hr. check-in. Singles $40, doubles $45. Weekly $210-225. Key and linen deposit $5.

Leaning Tower YMCA, 6300 W. Touhy, Niles 60714 (708-647-8222). From the Harvard St. El stop, take bus #290; 1hr. from the Loop. Inaccessible by public transport evenings and Sundays. Look for a half-scale replica of the Leaning Tower of Pisa (it's a water tower). Private baths, cafeteria. Use of YMCA facilities, including swimming pool and gym. Both men and women welcome. Must be over 21. Free parking. Singles $32, doubles $35. Key deposit $5. Call ahead for summer reservations.

Acres Motel, 5600 N. Lincoln Ave (561-7777), at Bryn Mawr Ave., offers free parking and singles or doubles for $35.

FOOD

See "Neighborhoods" to find specific ethnic cuisine. For further inspiration, *Chicago* magazine includes an extensive restaurant guide which is cross-indexed by price, cuisine, and quality. The monthly magazine can usually be picked up at tourist offices; ask at the desk.

Pizza

Chicago's pizza is known 'round the world. Try it standard-style, with the cheese on top, or stuffed, with toppings in the middle of the crust. Mmmm!

Pizzeria Uno, 29 E. Ohio (B3; 321-1000), and **Due,** 619 N. Wabash (943-2400). The newspaper clippings on the wall may look like any other Uno's, but this is where the delicious legacy of cheese, tomato, and deep-dish pizza began. Lines are long, and pizza takes 45min. to prepare. Same menu at younger sister Due (right up the street), with a terrace and more room than Uno's. Pizzas $5-18. Uno open Mon.-Fri. 11:30am-1am, Sat. 11:30am-2am, Sun. 11:30am-11:30pm. Due open Sun.-Thurs. 11:30am-1:30am, Fri. 11:30am-2:30am, Sat. noon-2:30am.

Giordano's, 747 N. Rush St. (B2; 951-0747). The downtown location is only one of 35 Giordano's in the Chicago area. The stuffed pizza is worth the 35-min. wait. Call ahead to get your pizza cooking. Pizzas $4-18. Lunch specials $5. Open Sun.-Thurs. noon-midnight, Fri.-Sat. 11am-1am.

The Loop

Heaven on Seven, 111 N. Wabash (B4; 263-6443). On the 7th floor of the Garland Building. The mantlepiece painted with vegetables, alligators, and crabs means you're getting closer to Cajun nirvana. The line is long, but hell, the gumbo ($7-12) is great. Cash only. Open Mon.-Fri. 7am-5pm, Sat. 7am-3pm.

The Berghoff, 17 W. Adams (B5; 427-3170). Dark, cavernous German restaurant filled with lunching traders. Bratwurst $4.75, beer stein $2.25. Open Mon.-Thurs. 11am-9:30pm, Fri. 11:30am-9:30pm, Sat. noon-10pm.

Morry's Old Fashioned Deli, 345 S. Dearborn (B5; 922-2932). Serves everything from beer to omelettes, large salads ($5-6), and burgers ($4). Come for the pickles on every table. Open Mon.-Fri. 7am-7pm, Sat. 8am-5pm.

Near North

Billy Goat's Tavern, 430 N. Michigan (B4; 222-1525), underground on lower Michigan Ave. Descend through a seeming subway entrance in front of the Tribune building. The gruff service was the inspiration for the legendary *Saturday Night Live* "Cheezborger, cheezborger—no Coke, Pepsi" greasy spoon. Cheezborgers $2.40. Butt in anytime Mon.-Sat. 10am-midnight, Sun. 11am-2am.

The Original A-1, 401 E. Illinois (D3; 644-0300), in North Pier. A haven for the homesick Texan. No mere hamburgers; try a Durango burger ($6.50) instead. Open Mon.-Fri. 11:30am-10pm, Sat. noon-midnight, Sun. noon-9pm.

New Chinatown, Little Saigon

Mekong, 4953 N. Broadway (271-0206), at Argyle St. Busy, spotless Vietnamese restaurant. All-you-can eat lunch buffet $5 (Mon.-Fri. 11am-2:30pm). Tasty soups $3.50-4. Open Sun.-Thurs. 10am-10pm, Fri.-Sat. 10am-11pm.

Gin Go Gae, 5433 N. Lincoln Ave. (334-3894). Korean cuisine popular with locals. *Be bim bob,* steamed rice with marinated beef, spinach, kimchee, and an egg, $7.25. *Mashisuh* (delicious). Lunch specials $6. Open daily 11am-10:30pm.

Chinatown

Hong Min, 221 W. Cermak (842-5026). El: Cermak. Attention paid to the food, *not* the furnishings—unlike some Chinese restaurants nearby. Duck of West Lake $10, steamed whitefish $7. Open daily 10am-2am.

Three Happiness, 2130 S. Wentworth Ave. (791-1228). Don't worry, be happy, happy, happy. Gulping fish greet you at the door; a dragon and crowds wait upstairs. Dim sum $1.75 (served Mon.-Fri. 10am-2pm, Sat.-Sun. 10am-3pm). Open Mon.-Thurs. 10am-midnight, Fri.-Sat. 10am-1am, Sun. 10am-10pm. Not connected to the smaller 3 Happiness restaurant across the street.

Little Italy

What is left of Little Italy can by reached by taking the El to UIC, then walking west on Taylor St. or taking bus #37.

The Rosebud, 1500 W. Taylor (942-1117). Small, dark restaurant serves huge portions of pasta. Lunch specials $7-9, dinner from $9. Free parking, reservations recommended. Open for lunch Mon.-Fri. 11am-3pm; dinner Mon.-Thurs. 5-10:30pm, Fri.-Sat. 5:30-11:30pm.

Al's Italian Beef, 1079 W. Taylor St. (226-4717), at Aberdeen near Little Italy; also at 169 W. Ontario. Churns out top-notch Italian beef, reddish with lots of spices. Join the crowd standing at the formica counter. Italian beef sandwich $3.30. Open Mon.-Sat. 9am-1am.

Mario's Italian Lemonade, 1074 W. Taylor St., across from Al's. A classic neighborhood stand that churns out sensational Italian ices (70¢-$4.50) in flavors ranging from cantaloupe to cherry. Open mid-May to mid-Sept. 10am-midnight.

Greektown

The Parthenon, 314 S. Halsted St. (726-2407). Don't look for the golden ratio in the architecture here. The staff converses in volleys of Greek, the murals and hangings transport you to the Mediterranean, and the food wins top awards. The Greek Feast, a family-style dinner, includes everything from *saganaki* to *baklava.* ($12.25). Open daily 11am-1am.

Greek Islands, 200 S. Halsted (782-9855). Stroll under the grape leaf awning and sit down at a blue-checked table for magnificent food. No reservations, so expect a ¾- to 1-hr. wait on weekends. Daily special $7-9. Open daily 11am-midnight.

North Side/Lincoln Park

Jada's, 1909 N. Lincoln Ave. (280-2326). Nondescript decor focuses attention on excellent Thai food. Most dishes can be cooked without meat. Entrees $5-8. Open Mon. 5-10pm, Tues.-Sat. 5-11pm, Sun. 4-10pm.

Potbelly's, 2264 N. Lincoln (528-1405). Could be named for the stoves scattered around the deli or your stomach when you leave. 50s-style decor with wooden booths. Subs $3.29. Open daily 11am-11pm.

Kopi, A Traveller's Café, 5317 N. Clark (989-5674). A 10-min. walk from the Berwyn El, 4 blocks west on Berwyn. Peruse a travel guide over a few cups of java or just sit back and appreciate the art. Open Mon.-Thurs. 8am-11pm, Fri. 8am-midnight, Sat. 9am-midnight, Sun. 10am-11pm.

Café Ba-Ba-Reeba!, 2024 N. Halsted (935-5000). Well marked by the colorful, glowing façade. Hearty Spanish cuisine with subtle spices; try the *paella valenciana* ($10.25) under clumps of hanging garlic or people-watch on the outdoor terrace. Open for lunch Tues.-Sat. 11:30am-2:30pm; open for dinner Mon.-Thurs. 5:30-11pm, Fri. 5:30pm-midnight, Sat. 5pm-midnight, Sun. 5:30-10:30pm.

Café Voltaire, 3231 N. Clark (528-3136). Named for the Zurich hangout of James Joyce, Picasso, and friends, this high-minded coffeehouse struggles to match the legend. Underground performance space (cover $3-10) for aspiring intellectuals. Grain-based planet burgers $6. Open Sun.-Thurs. 11am-1am, Fri.-Sat. 11am-3am.

The Bourgeois Pig, 748 Fullerton Ave. (883-5282). Quiet, soothing coffee shop with faux marble tables and board games. Cappuccino $1.75, scones $1.45. Open Mon.-Thurs. 6:30am-11pm, Fri. 6:30am-12pm, Sat. 8am-midnight, Sun. 8am-11pm.

Downtown

Wishbone, 1001 W. Washington (850-2663). Take bus #20 "Madison" to Morgan St. A southern cuisine extravaganza in a converted tire warehouse, with cornbread and banana bread on every table. Homemade pies $7. Mon.-Fri. sit-down breakfast 7-11am, cafeteria-style lunch 11:30am-2pm, dinner Mon. 5-8pm, Tues.-Fri 5-10:30pm.; brunch Sat.-Sun. 8am-2:30pm.

Frontera Grill, 445 N. Clark (661-1434). Avant-Tex-Mex for yuppies. The piñatas inside are worth seeing. Entrees $10-17. Open Tues.-Sat. after 9am.

SIGHTS

Chicago's "sights" range from well-publicized museums to undiscovered back streets, from beaches and parks to towering skyscrapers. Begin with the tourist brochures, the bus tours, and the downtown area, but remember that they reveal only a fraction of Chicago. Walk north of the Magnificent Mile, south of the Loop, and west of the river; venture out on the El and the buses, and enjoy Chicago in all of its splendor—but be careful and use common sense.

Museums

Each of Chicago's major museums admits visitors free at least one day per week. The "Big Five"—The Art Institute of Chicago, the Museum of Science and Technology, and the closely clumped Lakefront Museums (Shedd Aquarium, Adler Planetarium, and the Field Museum of Natural History)—exhibit everything from Monet to mummies to marine mammals. A handful of smaller collections represent diverse ethnic groups and professional interests. Pick up brochures at the tourist information office (see Practical Information).

The Art Institute of Chicago, 111 S. Michigan Ave. (C5; 443-3600), at Adams St. in Grant Park. The city's premier art museum. Four millennia of art from China, Africa, Europe, and beyond. The Institute's Impressionist and Post-Impressionist collections win international acclaim. Highlight tour daily 2pm. Open Mon. and Wed.-Fri. 10:30am-4:30pm, Tues. 10:30am-8pm, Sat. 10am-5pm, Sun. and holidays noon-5pm. Donation of any amount required (5¢ if you want); free Tues.

Museum of Science and Industry, 5700 S. Lake Shore Dr. (684-1414), housed in the only building left from the 1893 World's Columbian Exposition. In Hyde Park; take bus #6 "Jeffrey Express" to 57th St. Hands-on exhibits ensure a crowd of grabby kids. Highlights include the Apollo 8 command module, a German submarine, a life-sized replica of a coal mine, and an exhibit on learning disabilities. OmniMax Theatre shows; call for showtimes and prices. Open Sun.-Thurs. 9:30am-5:30pm, Fri. 9:30am-9pm; Labor Day-Memorial Day Mon.-Fri. 9:30am-4pm, Sat.-Sun. 9:30am-5:30pm. $5, seniors $4, ages 5-12 $2; free Thurs.

Field Museum of Natural History (C7; 922-9410), Roosevelt Rd. at Lake Shore Dr. in Grant Park. Take bus #146 from State St. Geological, anthropological, botanical, and zoological exhibits. Don't miss the Egyptian mummies, the Native American Halls, the Hall of Gems, and the dinosaur display. Open daily 9am-5pm. $4, students, seniors, and ages 3-17 $2.50, families $13; free Thurs.

The Adler Planetarium, 1300 S. Lake Shore Dr. (D7; 322-0300), in Grant Park. Discover your weight on Mars, read the news from space, and examine astronomy tools of the past. Don't forget the spectacular Skyshow. Open daily 9am-5pm, Fri. until 9pm. Skyshow daily 10am, 1, 2, 3, and 4pm; also Fri. 6, 7, and 8pm. $4, seniors and ages 4-17 $2; free Tues.

Shedd Aquarium, 1200 S. Lake Shore Dr. (C6; 939-2438), in Grant Park. The world's largest indoor aquarium with over 6600 species of fresh and saltwater fish in 206 tanks. The Oceanarium features small whales, dolphins, seals, and other marine mammals. Check out the Pacific Ocean exhibit, complete with simulated crashing waves. Parking available. Open daily 9am-6pm; Labor Day-Memorial Day Mon.-Fri. 9am-5pm, Sat.-Sun. 9am-6pm; will be closed Jan. 1-12 in 1996. Feedings Mon.-Fri. 11am and 2pm. Combined admission to Oceanarium and Aquarium $8, seniors and ages 3-11 $6; Thurs. Aquarium free, Oceanarium ½-price. Buy weekend tickets in advance through Hot Tix or Ticketmaster.

The Oriental Institute, 1155 E. 58th St. (702-9521), take bus #6 "Jeffrey Express" to the University of Chicago campus. Houses an extraordinary collection of ancient Near Eastern art and archeological treasures. Open Tues. and Thurs.-Sat. 10am-4pm, Wed. 10am-8:30pm, Sun. noon-4pm. Free.

The Museum of Contemporary Art, 237 E. Ontario (C3; 280-5161). Exhibits change often. One gallery is devoted to local artists. Open Tues.-Sat. 10am-5pm, Sun. noon-5pm. $5, students and seniors $2.50; free Tues.

Chicago Historical Society (B1; 642-4600), N. Clark St. at North Ave. A research center for scholars with a good museum open to the public. Founded in 1856, 19 years after the city was incorporated, to record events, like a kid who keeps a diary for future biographers. Permanent exhibit on America in the age of Lincoln, plus changing exhibits. Open Mon.-Sat. 9:30am-4:30pm, Sun. noon-5pm. $3, students and seniors $2; free Mon. Library and reading room closed Sun.-Mon.

Terra Museum of American Art, 666 N. Michigan Ave. (B3; 664-3939), at Eric St. Excellent collection of American art from colonial times to the present, with a focus on 19th-century American Impressionism. Free tours Tues.-Sun. noon and 2pm. Open Tues. noon-8pm, Wed.-Sat. 10am-5pm, Sun. noon-5pm. Suggested donation $3, seniors $2, under 14, teachers, and students with ID free; free Tues.

Museum of Broadcast Communications (B4; 629-6000), at Michigan and Washington. Celebrate couch-potato culture with exhibits on America's pastime: zonking out with the tube. Open Mon.-Sat. 10am-4:30pm, Sun. noon-5pm. Free.

The Loop

When Mrs. O'Leary's cow kicked over a lantern and started the Great Fire of 1871, Chicago's downtown flamed into a pile of ashes. The city rebuilt with a vengeance, turning the functional into the fabulous to create one of the most concentrated clusters of architectural treasures in the world.

The downtown area, hemmed in by the Chicago River and Lake Michigan, had no choice but to spring up rather than out. Take a few hours to explore this street museum either alone or on a **walking tour** organized by the Chicago Architectural Foundation. Tours start from the foundation's bookstore/gift shop at 224 S. Michigan Ave. (922-3432). Learn to recognize Louis Sullivan's arch, the Chicago window, and Mies van der Rohe's revolutionary skyscrapers. Two two-hour tours are offered: one of early skyscrapers, another of modern. ($10 for one, $15 for both.)

Long ago, the city's traders developed the concept of a graded commodity; a bag of wheat, once evaluated, can then be treated as a currency unit. Today, the three exchanges barter within a few blocks. You can watch the frantic trading of Midwestern farm goods at the world's oldest and largest commodity, the **Futures Exchange** or the **Chicago Board of Options Exchange,** both located in **The Board of Trade Building,** 400 S. LaSalle (435-3590); just look for Ceres, the grain goddess, towering 609 ft. above street level. (Tours Mon.-Fri. 9:15am, every ½hr. 10am-12:30pm. Open Mon.-Fri. 9am-2pm. Free.) The third exchange is the **Chicago Mercantile Exchange,** 30 S. Wacker (930-8249), at Madison.

In the late 19th century, Sears and Roebuck, along with competitor Montgomery Ward, created the mail-order catalog business, undercutting many small general stores and permanently altering the face of American merchandising. Today, although the catalog business has faded, the **Sears Tower,** 233 W. Walker (875-9696) remains; more than an office building, at 1707 ft., it stands as a monument to the insatiable lust of the American consumer. Cars become peaceful, orderly ants viewed from the top of this, the tallest building in the world. (Open 9am-11pm, Oct.-Feb. 9am-10pm. $6.50, seniors $4.75, children $3.25, families $18. Lines can be long.) **The First National Bank Building and Plaza** rises about 2 blocks northeast at the corner of Clark and Monroe St. The world's largest bank building compels your gaze skyward with its diagonal slope. Marc Chagall's vivid mosaic, *The Four Seasons,* lines the block and sets off a public space often used for concerts and lunchtime entertainment. At the corner of Clark and Washington St. 2 blocks north, **Chicago Temple,** the world's tallest church, sends its steeples toward heaven.

State and Madison, the most famous intersection of "State Street that great street," forms the focal point of the Chicago street grid. Louis Sullivan's **Carson Pirie Scott** store building is adorned with exquisite ironwork and the famous extra-large Chicago window. Sullivan's other masterpiece, the **Auditorium Building,** awaits several blocks south at the corner of Congress and Michigan. Beautiful design and flawless acoustics highlight this Chicago landmark.

Chicago is decorated with one of the country's premier collections of outdoor sculpture. Large, abstract designs punctuate many downtown corners. The Picasso at the foot of the **Daley Center Plaza,** Washington and Dearborn (346-3278), enjoys the greatest fame. Free entertainment plays at noon on summer weekdays in the plaza. Across the street rests Joan Miró's *Chicago,* the sculptor's gift to the city. A great Debuffet sculpture sits across the way in front of the **State of Illinois Building.** The building is a postmodern version of a town square designed by Helmut Jahn in 1985; take the elevator all the way up, where there is a thrilling (and free) view of the sloping atrium, circular floors, and hundreds of employees at work. A few years ago, the city held a contest to design a building costing less than $144 million in honor of the late mayor; the result is the **Harold Washington Library Center,** 400 S. State St. (747-4300), a researcher's dream and an architectural delight. (Tours Mon.-Sat. noon and 2pm; Sun. 2pm. Open Mon. 9am-7pm, Tues. and Thurs. 11am-7pm, Wed., Fri.-Sat. 9am-5pm.)

Near North

The city's ritziest district lies above the Loop along the lake, just past the Michigan Ave. Bridge. A hotly contested international design competition in the 1920s resulted in the **Tribune Tower,** 435 N. Michigan Ave., a Gothic skyscraper which overlooks this stretch. Chicago's largest newspaper, *The Chicago Tribune,* writes here; quotations exalting the freedom of the press adorn the inside lobby. Roam the 8.5 mi. corridors of **Merchandise Mart** (A4; 644-4664; entrances on N. Wells and Kinzie), the largest commercial building in the world, 25 stories high and two city blocks long. The first two floors are a mall open to the public; the rest of the building contains showrooms where design professionals converge to choose home and office furnishings—everything for a building from kitchen products to restroom signs. (Public tours Mon.-Fri. noon. $8, students over 15 and seniors $7.)

Chicago's showy **Magnificent Mile,** a row of glitzy shops along N. Michigan Ave. between Grand Ave. and Division St., can put a magnificent drain on the wallet. Several of these retail stores, including Banana Republic and Crate & Barrel, were designed by the country's foremost architects. The **Chicago Water Tower** and **Pumping Station** (467-7114) hide among the ritzy stores at the corner of Michigan and Pearson Ave. Built in 1867, these two structures survived the Great Chicago Fire. The pumping station houses the multimedia show *Here's Chicago* and a tourist center (see Practical Information, above). Across the street, expensive and trendy stores pack **Water Tower Place,** the first urban shopping mall in the U.S.

Beautiful old mansions and apartment buildings line the **Gold Coast,** comprised of the streets between the Water Tower and Lincoln Park along Lakeshore Dr. This area has long glittered as the elite residential enclave of the city. Early industrialists and city founders made their homes here, and lately many families have moved back from the suburbs. Lake Michigan and Oak St. Beach shine a few blocks east.

Urban renewal has made **Lincoln Park,** a neighborhood just west of the park which bears the same name, a popular choice for upscale residents. Bounded by Armitage to the south and Diversey Ave. to the north, lakeside Lincoln Park offers recreation and nightlife, with beautiful harbors and parks. Cafés, bookstores, and nightlife pack its tree-lined streets; some of Chicago's liveliest clubs and restaurants lie in the area around Clark St., Lincoln Ave., and N. Halsted.

The bells of St. Michael's Church ring in **Old Town,** a neighborhood where eclectic galleries, shops, and nightspots crowd gentrified streets. Absorb the architectural atmosphere while strolling the W. Menomonee and W. Eugenie St. area. In early June, the **Old Town Art Fair** attracts artists and craftsmen from across the country. (Take bus #151 to Lincoln Park and walk south down Clark or Wells St.)

North Side

North of Diversey Ave., the streets of Lincoln Park become increasingly diverse. Supermarket shopping plazas alternate with tiny markets and vintage clothing stores, while apartment towers and hotels spring up between aging two-story houses. In this ethnic no man's land, you can find a Polish diner next to a Korean restaurant or a Mongolian eatery across the street from a Mexican bar.

Though they finally lost their battle against night baseball in 1988, Wrigleyville residents remain fiercely loyal to the Chicago Cubs. Just east of Graceland, at the corner of Clark and Addison, tiny, ivy-covered **Wrigley Field** at 1060 W. Addison (see Sports) is the North Side's most famous institution—well worth a pilgrimage for the serious or simply curious baseball fan, as well as for the *Blues Brothers* nut who wants to visit the famous pair's falsified address. After a game, walk along Clark St., one of the city's busiest nightlife districts, where restaurants, sports bars, and music clubs abound. Explore the neighborhood, window shop in the funk, junk, and 70s revival stores. Wrigleyville and Lakeview, around the 3000s and 4000s of N. Clark St. and N. Halsted, are the city's most concentrated gay areas.

Near West Side

The **Near West Side,** bounded by the Chicago River to the east and Ogden Ave. to the west, assembles a fascinating variety of tiny ethnic enclaves. Farther out, however, looms the West Side, one of the most dismal slums in the nation. Dangerous neighborhoods lie alongside safe ones, so always be aware of your location. Greektown, several blocks of authentic restaurants (north of the Eisenhower on Halsted), draws people from all over the city.

A few blocks down Halsted (take the #8 Halsted bus), Jane Addams devoted her life to historic **Hull House.** This settlement house bears witness to Chicago's role in turn-of-the-century reform movements. Although the house no longer offers social services, painstaking restoration has made the **Hull House Museum,** 800 S. Halsted (413-5353), a fascinating part of a visit to Chicago. (Open Mon.-Fri. 10am-4pm, Sun. noon-5pm. Free.) The **Ukrainian Village,** centered at Chicago and Western, is no longer dominated by ethnic Ukrainians, but you can still visit the **Ukrainian National Museum,** 2453 W. Chicago Ave. (421-8020; open Thurs.-Sun. 11am-4pm; donations suggested).

Hyde Park and the University of Chicago

Seven mi. south of the Loop along the lake, the **University of Chicago's** (702-9192) beautiful campus dominates the **Hyde Park** neighborhood; get there via the METRA South Shore Line. A former retreat for the city's artists and musicians, the park's community underwent urban renewal in the 50s and now provides an island of intellectualism in a sea of dangerous neighborhoods. University police "aggressively patrol" the area bounded by 51st St. to the north, Lakeshore Dr. to the east, 61th St. to the south, and Cottage Grove to the west, but don't test the edges of these boundaries. Lakeside Burnham Park, to the east of campus, is relatively safe during the day but dangerous at night.

On campus, U. of Chicago's architecture ranges from knobby, gnarled, twisted Gothic to neo-streamlined high-octane Gothic. Frank Lloyd Wright's famous **Robie House,** 5757 S. Woodlawn (702-8374), at the corner of 58th St., blends into the surrounding trees; a seminal representative of Wright's Prairie School, which sought to integrate house with environment, its low horizontal lines now house university offices. Tours depart daily at noon ($3, students and seniors $1 on Sun.). The **Oriental Institute, Museum of Science and Industry,** and **DuSable Museum of African-American History** (see Museums) are all in or border on Hyde Park. From the Loop, take bus #6 "Jefferson Express" or the METRA Electric Line from the Randolph St. Station south to 59th St.

Oak Park

Oak Park sprouts 10 mi. west of downtown on the Eisenhower Expwy. (I-290). In his quest to integrate architecture with nature, Frank Lloyd Wright endowed the community with 25 of his spectacular homes and buildings; don't miss the **Frank Lloyd Wright House and Studio,** 951 Chicago Ave., with his beautiful 1898 workplace. The park's **visitors center,** 158 Forest Ave. (708-848-1500), offers maps, guidebooks, and tours of the house and environs. (45-min. tours of the house Mon.-Fri. 11am, 1, 3pm, Sat.-Sun. every 15min. 11am-4pm. 1-hr. self-guided tours of Wright's other homes in Oak Park can be accomplished with a map and audio cassette available daily 10am-3pm, or a tour guide will take you through Sat.-Sun. 10:30am, noon, and 2pm. All three types of tours $6, seniors and under 18 $4; combination interior/exterior tour tickets $9/$7. Open daily 10am-5pm.)

Outdoors

A string of lakefront parks fringes the area between Chicago proper and Lake Michigan. On a sunny afternoon, a cavalcade of sunbathers, dog walkers, roller skaters, and skateboarders storm the shore, yet everyone still has room to stake out a private little piece of paradise. The two major parks, both close to downtown, are Lincoln and Grant, operated by the Recreation Department (294-2200). **Lincoln Park,** which extends across 5 mi. of lakefront on the north side of town, rolls in the style of a 19th-century English park: winding paths, natural groves of trees, and asymmetrical open spaces. The **Lincoln Park Conservatory** (249-4770) encloses fauna from desert to jungle environments under its glass palace (open daily 9am-5pm; free).

Grant Park, covering 14 blocks of lakefront east of Michigan Ave., follows the 19th-century French park style: symmetrical, ordered, with squared corners, a fountain in the center, and wide promenades. The **Petrillo Music Shell** hosts free summer concerts here; contact the **Grant Park Concert Society,** 520 S. Michigan Ave. (819-0614). Bathe in the colored lights that illuminate **Buckingham Fountain** each night from 9-11pm. The **Field Museum of Natural History, Shedd Aquarium,** and **Adler Planetarium** beckon museum-hoppers to the southern end of the park (if you don't want to walk the mile from the fountain, take bus #146), while the **Art Institute** lies to the northwest (see Museums).

On the north side, Lake Michigan lures swimmers to **Lincoln Park Beach** and **Oak St. Beach.** Popular swimming spots, both attract sun worshippers as well. The rock ledges are restricted areas, and swimming from them is illegal. Although the beaches are patrolled 9am-9:30pm, they are unsafe after dark. Call the Chicago Parks District (747-2200) for further information.

Farther Out

In 1885, George Pullman, inventor of the sleeping car, wanted to create a model working environment so that his Palace Car Company employees would be "healthier, happier, and more productive." The town of **Pullman,** the result of this quest, grew up 14 mi. southeast of downtown, and was considered the nation's ideal community until a celebrated strike in 1894. As the centerpiece of the town, Pullman built **Hotel Florence,** 1111 S. Forrestville Ave. (785-8181); today, the hotel houses a museum and conducts tours of the Pullman Historic District. (Tours leave the hotel on the first Sun. of each month May-Oct. at 12:30 and 1pm. $4, students and seniors $3. By car, take I-94 to W. 111th St.; by train, take the Illinois Central Gulf Railroad to 111th St. and Pullman or the METRA Rock Island Line to 111th St. 20min.)

In **Wilmette,** the **Baha'i House of Worship** (708-256-4400), at Shendan Rd. and Linden Ave., tops out with an 11-sided Near Eastern-styled dome modeled on the House of Worship in Haifa, Israel (open daily 10am-10pm; Oct.-May 10am-5pm; services daily 12:15pm). The **Chicago Botanic Garden** (708-835-5440), on Lake Cook Rd. ½ mi. east of Edens Expwy., pampers vegetation 25 mi. from downtown (open daily 8am-sunset; parking $4 per car, includes admission). Spend a cheery, exhausting day at **Six Flags Great America** (708-249-1776), I-94 at Route 132 E., Gurnee, IL, the largest amusement park in the Midwest. (Open daily 10am-10pm; shortened hours in spring and fall. $29.50, over 59 $14.75, ages 4-10 $24.50; 2-day pass, not necessarily consecutive, $35.) At **Arlington International Racetrack** (708-255-4300), Rte. 53 at Euclid, Arlington Heights, watch thoroughbred racing at cheap (or bank-breaking) prices; it's up to you and the betting windows.

Steamboat Gambling has been embraced by the Midwest as a way to avoid anti-betting laws. The action centers in Joliet, IL. Roll the bones on **Empress River Cruises,** 2300 Empress Dr. (708-345-6789), Rte. 6 off I-55 and I-80, (departs six times daily; Mon.-Fri. morning $2, afternoon $5; Sat.-Sun. $10) or **Harrah's Casino Cruises** (800-342-7724), which accommodates over 1000 "guests."

ENTERTAINMENT

To stay on top of Chicago events, grab a copy of the free weekly *Chicago Reader,* published Thursdays, available in many bars, record stores, and restaurants. The *Reader* reviews all major shows, with show times and ticket prices. *Chicago* magazine has exhaustive club listings, theater reviews, and complete listings of music, dance, and opera performances throughout the city. The Friday edition of the *Chicago Tribune* includes a section with full music, theater, and cultural listings.

Theater

One of the foremost theater centers of North America, Chicago also makes a home for Improv and the Improvorgy. The city's 150+ theaters show everything from blockbuster musicals to off-color parodies. Downtown theaters cluster around the intersection of Diversey, Belmont, and Halsted (just west of the Loop), and around Michigan Ave. and Madison Ave. (B5). Smaller, community-based theaters scatter throughout the city. The "Off-Loop" theaters on the North Side specialize in original drama, with tickets usually $17 and under.

Victory Gardens Theater, 2257 N. Lincoln Ave. (871-3000). 3 theater spaces. Drama by Chicago playwrights. Tickets $23-28. Box office open 10am-8pm.

Center Theatre, 1346 W. Devon Ave. (508-5422). Solid, mainstream work. Tickets vary show to show ($10-20). Box office hours vary; usually open noon-5pm.

Annoyance Theatre, 3747 N. Clark (929-6200). Original works that play off pop culture, 7 different shows per week. Often participatory comedy. Tickets ($7-10) sold just before showtime, usually 8 or 9pm.

Bailiwick Repertory, 1225 W. Belmont Ave. (327-5252), in the Theatre building. A mainstage and experimental studio space. Tickets from $6. Box office open Wed. noon-6pm, Thurs.-Sun. noon-showtime.

Live Bait Theatre, 3914 N. Clark St. (871-1212). Shows with titles like *Food, Fun, & Dead Relatives* and *Mass Murder II.* Launched a multi-play *Tribute to Jackie* (Onassis, that is). Tickets $6-12. Box office open Mon.-Fri. noon-5pm.

Most theater tickets are expensive, though you can get half-price tickets on the day of performance at **Hot Tix Booths,** 108 N. State St. (977-1755), or at the 6th level of 700 N. Michigan Ave. Buy in person only. Show up 15-20 minutes before the booth opens for first dibs. (Open Mon.-Fri. 10am-7pm, Sat. 10am-6pm, Sun noon-5pm.) Phone **Curtain Call** (977-1755) for information on ticket availability, schedules, and Hot Tix booths. **Ticket Master** (559-0200) supplies tickets for many theaters.

Famous theaters come with famous prices. **Steppenwolf Theater,** 1650 N. Halsted (335-1650), is where David fucking Mamet got his goddamn start. (Tickets $25-33; ½-price after 5pm Tues.-Fri., after noon Sat.-Sun. Box office open Sun.-Mon. 11am-5pm, Tues.-Fri. 11am-8pm, Sat. 11am-9pm.) The **Goodman Theatre,** 200 S. Columbus Dr. (443-3800), also presents consistently good original works. (Tickets around $28, ½-price after 6pm, or after 1pm for matinee Box office open 10am-5pm, 10am-8pm show nights, usually Sat.-Sun.). **Shubert Theater,** 22 W. Monroe St. (902-1500), presents big-name Broadway touring productions; tickets vary with show popularity ($25-70; box office open Sun.-Fri. 10am-6pm, Sat. 10am-4pm).

Comedy

Chicago boasts a giggle of comedy clubs. The most famous, **Second City,** 1616 N. Wells St. (337-3992), satirically spoofs Chicago life and politics. Second City graduated Bill Murray and late greats John Candy, John Belushi, and Gilda Radner, among others. Most nights a free improv session follows the show. **Second City ETC.** (642-8189) offers yet more comedy next door. (Shows Mon.-Thurs. 8:30pm, Fri.-Sat. 8 and 11pm, Sun. 8pm. Tickets $10-15, Mon. $5. Box office hours for both daily 10:30am-10pm. Reservations recommended; during the week you can often get in if you show up 1hr. early.) The big names drop by and make it up as they go along at **The Improv,** 504 N. Wells (782-6387). (Shows Sun. and Thurs. 8pm, Fri.-Sat. 7, 9:30pm, and midnight; but season varies, so call ahead. Tickets $10-13.50.)

Dance, Classical Music, and Opera

Chicago philanthropists built the network of high-priced, high-art performance center of this metropolis. Ballet, comedy, live theater, and musicals perform at **Auditorium Theater,** 50 E. Congress Pkwy. (922-2110). From October to May, the **Chicago Symphony Orchestra,** conducted by Daniel Barenboim, resonates at **Orchestra Hall,** 220 S. Michigan Ave. (435-6666). **Ballet Chicago** (251-8838) pirouettes in theaters throughout Chicago (performance times vary; tickets $20-32). The

Lyric Opera of Chicago performs from September to February at the **Civic Opera House,** 20 N. Wacker Dr. (332-2244). While these places may suck your wallet dry, the **Grant Park Music Festival** affords the budget traveler a taste of the classical for free; from mid-June to late August, the acclaimed **Grant Park Symphony Orchestra** plays a few free evening concerts a week at the Grant Park Petrillo Music Shell (usually Wed.-Sun.; schedule varies; call 819-0614 for details).

Seasonal Events

Like Chicago's architecture, the city celebrates summer on a grand scale. The **Taste of Chicago** festival cooks the eight days up through July Fourth; 70 restaurants set up booths with endless samples in Grant Park while crowds chomp to the blast of big name bands (free entry, food tickets 50¢ each). The first week in June, the **Blues Festival** celebrates the city's soulful, gritty music; the **Chicago Gospel Festival** hums and hollers in mid-June; and Nashville moves north for the **Country Music Festival** at the end of June. The **¡Viva! Chicago** Latin music festival swings in late August, and the **Chicago Jazz Festival** scats Labor Day weekend. All festivals center at the Grant Park Petrillo Music Shell. Call the Mayor's Office Special Events Hotline (744-3370 or 800-487-2446) for more info on all six free events.

Chicago also offers several free summer festivals on the lakeshore, including the **Air and Water Show** in late August, when Lake Shore Park, Lake Shore Dr., and Chicago Ave. witness several days of boat races, parades, hang gliding, and stunt flying, as well as aerial acrobatics by the fabulously precise Blue Angels. In mid-July, the **Chicago to Mackinac Island Yacht Race** begins in the Monroe St. harbor.

The regionally famous **Ravinia Festival** (728-4642), in the northern suburb of Highland Park, runs from late June to early September. The Chicago Symphony Orchestra, ballet troupes, folk and jazz musicians, and comedians perform throughout the festival's 14-week season. (Shows Mon.-Sat. 8pm, Sun. 7pm. Lawn seats $7; other tickets $15-35.) Round-trip on the train (METRA) costs about $7; the festival runs charter buses for $12. The bus ride takes 1½ hours each way.

Sports

The National League's **Cubs** play baseball at Wrigley Field, at Clark St. and Addison (831-2827), one of the few ballparks in America that has retained the early grace and intimate feel of the game; it's definitely worth a visit, especially for international visitors who haven't seen a baseball game (tickets $8-19). The **White Sox,** Chicago's American League team, swing on the South Side at the new Comiskey Park, 333 W. 35th St. (tickets, $4-18; 924-1000). Da **Bears** play football at Soldier's Field Stadium, McFetridge Dr. and S. Lakeshore Dr. (708-615-BEAR/2327). The **Blackhawks** hockey team skates and da **Bulls** basketball team slam-dunks at the **United Center,** 1901 W. Madison (Blackhawks 455-4500, tickets $15-75; Bulls 943-5800, tickets $15-30), known fondly as "the house that Michael Jordan built." Beware of scalpers who illegally sell tickets at inflated prices outside of sports events. For current sports events, call **Sports Information** (976-1313).

NIGHTLIFE

"Sweet home Chicago" takes pride in the innumerable blues performers who have played here. Jazz, folk, reggae, and punk clubs throbulate all over the **North Side. Bucktown,** west of Halsted St. in North Chicago, stays open late with bucking bars and dance clubs. Aspiring pick-up artists swing over to Rush and Division, an intersection that has replaced the stockyards as one of the biggest **meat markets** in the world. To get away from the crowds, head to a little neighborhood spot for atmosphere. Full of bars, cafés, and bistros, **Lincoln Park** is influenced by singles and young married couples, as well as by the gay scene. For more raging, raving, and discoing, there are plenty of clubs in River N., in Riverwest, and on Fulton St.

Blues

B.L.U.E.S., 2519 N. Halsted St. (528-1012); El to Fullerton, then take the west-bound bus "Fullerton." Cramped, but the music is unbeatable. Success here led to larger relative **B.L.U.E.S. etcetera,** 1124 W. Belmont Ave. (525-8989); El to Belmont, then 3 blocks west on Belmont. The place for huge names: Albert King, Bo Diddley, Dr. John, and Wolfman Washington have played here. Live music every night 9pm-1:30am. Cover for both places Mon.-Thurs. $5, Fri. $7, Sat. $8.

Kingston Mines, 2548 N. Halsted St. (477-4646). Grooving with live blues daily, this local favorite is fast becoming a tourist theme park: buses outside, T-shirts inside, and crowds. A legend with many believers. Music starts at 9:30pm. Cover Sun.-Thurs. $8, Fri.-Sat. $10. Open Sun.-Fri. 8pm-4am, Sat. until 5am.

Cabaret Metro, 3730 N. Clark (549-0203). Live alternative and alternateen music, ranging from local bands to Soul Asylum and Tom Jones. 18+; occasionally all ages are welcome upstairs. Downstairs, the **Smart Bar** (549-4140) is 21+. Cover $5-13. Opening times vary (around 10pm); closes around 5am on weekends.

Shelter, 564 W. Fulton (528-5500). Club kids immersed in pulsating rhythms and lava lamps congregate on several dance floors. Cover $8-10. Opens around 10pm and raves until the wee hours.

Wild Hare & Singing Armadillo Frog Sanctuary, 3350 N. Clark (327-0800), El to Addison. Near Wrigley Field. Live Rastafarian bands play to a swaying, bobbing mass of twenty-somethings. Cover $3-5, Mon.-Tues. free. Open daily until 2-3am.

Butch McGuires, 20 W. Division St. (337-9080), at Rush St. Originator of the singles bar. Owner estimates that "over 6500 couples have met here over 23 million glasses of beer and gotten married" since 1961—he's a little fuzzier on divorce statistics. Once on Rush St.; check out the other area hangouts. Drinks $2-5. Open Sun.-Thurs. 9:30am-2am, Fri. 10am-4am, Sat. 10am-5am.

Jazz Showcase, 636 S. Michigan (427-4846), in the Blackstone Hotel downtown. #1 choice for serious jazz. Big names heat up with impromptu jam sessions during the jazz festival. No smoking. Music Tues.-Thurs. 8 and 10pm, Fri.-Sat. 9 and 11pm, Sun. 4 and 8pm. Cover Tues.-Thurs. $12, Fri.-Sat. $15. Closing time varies.

Zebra Lounge, 1220 N. State St. (642-5140). Small piano bar lined with zebra skins and dark wood. Mostly thirty-somethings, but younger and older visitors drop in. Live music Mon.-Sat. at 9:30pm. Open Sun.-Thurs. 2pm-2am, Fri.-Sat. 2pm-3am.

Melvin B.'s, 1114 N. State St. (751-9897). "I built this place for people to have fun," says the owner. Obviously popular, in a prime downtown location with a pleasant outdoor terrace. Open Sun.-Thurs. 11am-2am, Fri.-Sat. 11am-3am. Wander next door to the **Cactus Cantina** to do battle with their margaritas. En garde.

Roscoe's Bar and Café, 3354 N. Halsted. (281-3355). Primarily gay clientele, but all are welcome. Roscoe's has it all: a pool room, garden terrace, dance floor, even a clairvoyant. Occasional live performances. $10 Long Island Iced Tea pitchers. on Sun. Open Sun.-Fri. until 2am, Sat. until 3am.

■■■ SPRINGFIELD

In 1837, amidst charges of logrolling and corruption, Springfield replaced Vandalia as the capital of Illinois. Vandalia's defenders accused Abraham Lincoln and other Springfield legislators of underhanded vote-currying, but supporters of relocation pointed out the convenience of Springfield's relatively central location.

Practical Information The **Springfield Convention and Visitors Bureau,** 109 N. 7th St. (789-2360 or 800-545-7300), will give you a detailed street map for your stroll through Lincolnland (open Mon.-Fri. 8am-4:30pm, Sat. 8am-3pm). Write ahead to request an exhaustive info packet. Springfield is accessible via **Amtrak** (753-2013 or 800-872-7245), at 3rd and Washington St. near downtown. Trains run to Chicago (3-4 per day, 4hr., $34) and St. Louis (3 per day, 2½hr., $21). (Open daily 6am-9:30pm.) **Greyhound** has a station at 2351 S. Dirksen Pkwy. (544-8466), on the eastern edge of town. Walk or take a cab to the nearby shopping center, where you can catch bus #10. Roll to Chicago (5 per day, 5hr., $24), Indianapolis (4 per day, 2hr., $23), or St. Louis (3 per day, 5hr., $54). (Open Mon-Fri. 9am-8pm, Sat. 9am-

1pm. Lockers $1 per day.) **Springfield Mass Transit District,** 928 S. 9th St. (522-5531), shuttles around town. Pick up maps at transit headquarters, most banks, or at the Illinois State Museum. (Buses operate Mon.-Sat. 6am-6pm. Fare 50¢, transfers free.) For taxi service, try **Lincoln Yellow Cab** (523-4545 or 522-7766; $1.25 base, $1.50 per mi.). Springfield's **post office:** 2105 E. Cook St. (788-7200; open Mon.-Fri. 7:30am-5:30pm, Sat. 8am-3pm), at Wheeler St.; **ZIP code:** 62703; **area code:** 217.

Accommodations and Camping Cheap accommodations await off I-55 and U.S. 36 on Dirksen Pkwy., but bus service from downtown is limited. More expensive downtown hotels may be booked solid on weekdays when the legislature is in session, but ask the visitors bureau (see Practical Information above) about finding reasonable weekend packages. Make reservations as early as possible for holiday weekends and during the State Fair in mid-August.

The **Dirksen Inn Motel,** 900 N. Dirksen Pkwy. (522-4900; take bus #3 "Bergen Park" to Milton and Elm St. then walk a few blocks east) has clean, pleasant rooms, comfy beds, and refrigerators (office open 24 hrs.; singles $28, doubles $30). **Shady Rest Motel,** 1518 N. 30th St. (544-5485), just of Dirksen Pkwy north of town, beckons with relatively clean rooms for a rock-bottom price (singles $20, doubles $22). **Best Rest Inn,** 700 N. Dirksen Pkwy. (522-7961) offers full-sized beds, free local calls, and cable TV (singles $24, doubles $26). **Mister Lincoln's Campground,** 3045 Stanton Ave. (529-8206), next to the car dealership 4 mi. southeast of downtown, has free showers, a field for tents ($7 per person, kids under 15 free), cabins (for 2 with A/C $23), and a large area for RVs (full hookup $17). Take bus #10.

Food and Nightlife Although they may look more like what ends up on horseshoes than horseshoes, Horseshoe sandwiches—a Springfield original—are tasty concoctions of ham on prairie toast smothered with cheese sauce and french fries. When Lincoln-looking makes you hungry, head to the **Vinegar Hill Mall** area (southeast of downtown, at 1st and Cook St.) for a variety of moderately priced restaurants. In the mall, the **Capitol City Brewery Bar and Grill** (753-5720) cooks up lunch specials and homemade brew; daily specials include 50¢ homemade lagers on Wednesdays. (Open Mon. 11am-2pm, Tues.-Fri. 11am-1am, Sat. noon-1am; stops serving food at 9pm.) Later at night, **The Atrium** (753-5710) merges with the Capitol City Brewery to provide a full-fledged dance-floor disco-ball entertainment complex. DJs play on weekdays, bands on weekends. (21+; cover $5.)

Farther north, across from the old state capitol, **The Feed Store,** 516 E. Adam S. St. (528-3355), has homemade soup, deli sandwiches ($2.75-4.50), and a no-choice special—sandwich, soup, and drink for $4.65 (open Mon.-Sat. 11am-3pm). **Saputo's,** 801 E. Munroe at 8th St. (522-0105), 2 blocks from Lincoln's home, dishes up tasty southern Italian cuisine. Try the baked lasagna (for lunch $4.75; for dinner $10. Open Mon.-Fri. 10:30am-midnight, Sat. 5pm-midnight, Sun. 5-10pm.)

Sights Springfield makes money by re-creating Lincoln's life, and it does so zealously. Park the car and walk from sight to sight, retracing the steps of the man himself (or so they keep telling you). Happily, all Lincoln sights are free. Call 800-545-7300 to verify site hours (winter weather often forces curtailed hours). The **Lincoln Home Visitors Center,** 426 S. 8th St. (492-4150), at Jackson, shows an 18-minute film on "Mr. Lincoln's Springfield" and doles out free tickets to see the **Lincoln Home** (492-4150), the only one Abe ever owned and the main Springfield attraction, sitting at 8th and Jackson in a restored 19th-century neighborhood. (10-min. tours every 5-10min. from the front of the house. Open daily 8am-8pm; in winter 8:30am-5pm. Arrive early to avoid the crowds. Free.)

A few blocks northwest, at 6th and Adams right before the Old State Capitol, the **Lincoln-Herndon Law Offices** (785-7289) let visitors see how Lincoln spent a day at the office, before the Presidency (open for tours only daily 9am-5pm; last tour at 4; donation suggested). Around the corner and to the left, across from the Downtown Mall, sits the magnificent limestone **Old State Capitol** (785-7691). In 1858,

Lincoln delivered his stirring and prophetic "House Divided" speech here, warning that the nation's contradictory pro-slavery and abolitionist government risked dissolution. The rotunda houses a display of the manuscript copy of Lincoln's "Gettysburg Address." The capitol also witnessed the famous Lincoln-Douglas debates which catapulted Lincoln to national prominence. (Tours daily. Open daily 9am-5pm. Donation suggested.) Opened in 1877, the **New State Capitol** (782-2099), 4 blocks away at 2nd and Capitol, engrosses with murals of Illinois pioneer history and an intricately designed dome. Sneak a closer peek at the façade through the free sidewalk telescopes in front of the building. (Tours Mon.-Fri. 8:30am-4pm, Sat.-Sun. 9am-3:30pm. Building open Mon.-Fri. 8am-4pm, Sat.-Sun. first floor only 9am-3:30pm.) Enter at 1500 Monument Ave., north of town, to view the **Lincoln Tomb** (782-2717), at Oak Ridge Cemetery; Lincoln, his wife, and three sons rest here (open daily 9am-5pm).

If Lincoln-mania begins to bring you down, walk to the **Dana-Thomas House,** 301 E. Lawrence Ave. (782-6776), 6 blocks south of the Old State Capitol. Built in 1902, the stunning and well-preserved home was one of Wright's early experiments in Prairie Style and still features original Frank fixtures. (1-hr. tours every 15-20min.; $3, children $1; open Wed.-Sun. 9am-5pm.) The **Illinois State Museum** (782-7386), Spring and Edwards St., houses contemporary Illinois art and displays on the area's Native American inhabitants (open Mon.-Sat. 8:30am-5pm, Sun. noon-5pm; free).

With 66 bells, the **Thomas Rees Carillon** (753-6219), in **Washington Park Botanical Gardens** (753-6228), rings true as the third largest carillon in the world, and one of the few to offer visitors a view of the bells and playing mechanism (tours June-Aug. Tues.-Sun. noon-sunset; also spring and fall weekends). Springfield's renowned Fourth of July shebang, called (surprise!) **Lincolnfest,** more than doubles the town's population with fireworks and plenty of patriotism.

Wisconsin

Oceans of milk and beer flood the Great Lake's most wholesome party state. French fur trappers first explored this area in search of lucrative furry creatures; later, miners burrowed homes in the hills during the 1820s lead rush (earning them the nickname "badgers") and hearty Norsemen set to clearing vast woodlands. By the time the forests had fallen and the mines had been exhausted, German immigrant farmers had planted rolling fields of barley amidst the state's 15,000 lakes and made Wisconsin the beer capital of the nation. Today, visitors to "America's Dairyland" flock past cheese-filled country stores to delight in the ocean-like vistas of Door County, as well as the ethnic fêtes (and less refined beer bashes) of Madison and Milwaukee.

PRACTICAL INFORMATION

Capital: Madison.
Division of Tourism: 123 W. Washington St., P.O. Box 7606, Madison 53707 (608-266-2161, 608-266-6797, or 800-372-2737; 800-432-8748 out of state).
Time Zone: Central (1hr. behind Eastern). **Postal Abbreviation:** WI
Sales Tax: 5½%.

■■■ MILWAUKEE

A mecca of drink and festivals, Milwaukee is a city given to celebration. The influx of immigrants, especially German and Irish, gave the city its reputation for *gemütlichkeit* (hospitality). The ethnic communities take turns throwing city-wide parties each summer weekend; some bars even curtail weekend activities in the summer, realizing that the crowds will be at the fiestas. The city's notorious beer industry adds to the melee, supplying the city's more than 1500 bars and taverns with as much brew as anyone could ever need. Aside from merrymaking, Milwaukee's attractions include top-notch museums, beautiful German-inspired architecture, delicious frozen custard, and a long expanse of scenic lakeshore.

PRACTICAL INFORMATION

Tourist Office: Greater Milwaukee Convention and Visitors Bureau, 510 W. Kilbourne (273-7222, 273-3950, or 800-231-0903), downtown. Open Mon.-Fri. 8am-5pm; in summer also Sat. 9am-4pm. Another location in Grand Avenue Mall at 3rd St. Open Mon.-Fri. 10am-8pm, Sat. 10am-7pm, Sun. 11am-5pm. Pick up a copy of *Greater Milwaukee Official Visitor's Guide.*

Airport: General Mitchell International, 5300 S. Howell Ave. (747-5300). Take bus #80 from 6th St. downtown (30min.). **Limousine Service,** 769-9100 or 800-236-5450. 24-hr. pick-up and drop-off from most downtown hotels with reservation. $7.50, round-trip $14.

Trains: Amtrak, 433 W. St. Paul Ave. (271-0840 or 800-872-7245), at 5th St. 3 blocks from the bus terminal. Fairly safe during the day, less so at night. To: Chicago (4 per day, 2hr., $25); St. Paul (1 per day, 5hr., $71). Ticket office open Mon.-Sat. 5:30am-9pm, Sun. 7am-9pm.

Buses: Greyhound, 606 N. 7th St. (800-231-2222), off W. Michigan St. downtown. To: Chicago (16 per day, 2hr., $12); Minneapolis (6 per day, 7½hr., $47). Station open 24 hrs.; ticket office open daily 6:30am-11:15pm. **Wisconsin Coach** (544-6503 or 542-8861), in the Greyhound terminal services southeast Wisconsin. **Badger Bus,** 635 N. 7th St. (276-7490), across the street, burrows to Madison (6 per day, 1½hr., $9). Open daily 6:30am-10pm. Neither station is very safe at night.

Public Transportation: Milwaukee County Transit System, 1942 N. 17th St. (344-6711). Efficient service in the metro area. Most lines run 4:30am-2am. Fare $1.25, seniors with Medicare card 60¢. Weekly pass $9.25. Free maps at the library or at the Grand Ave. Mall info center. Call for schedules.

Taxi: City Veteran Taxi, 291-8080. $1.75 base fare, $1.50 per mi., 50¢ per additional passenger.

Car Rental: Sensible Car Rental, 5150 S. 27th St. (282-1080). $26 per day with 200 free mi.; 20¢ per additional mi. Insurance $7 per day. Must be 22 with a credit card or $500 deposit. Weekend specials. Free airport pickup. Open Mon.-Fri. 9am-9pm, Sat. 9am-6pm.

Auto Transport Company: Auto Driveaway Co., 9039A W. National Ave. (327-5252), in West Allis. Must be 21 with good driving record. $250 cash deposit refunded at destination; driver pays for gas. Call in advance for availability. Open Mon.-Fri. 8am-5pm, Sat. 8-10am.

Crisis Lines: Crisis Intervention, 257-7222. **Rape Crisis Line,** 542-3828. Both 24 hrs. **Gay People's Union Hotline,** 562-7010. Open daily 7-10pm.

Emergency: 911.

Post Office: 345 W. St. Paul Ave. (291-2544), south along 4th Ave. from downtown next to the Amtrak station. Open Mon.-Fri. 7:30am-8pm. **ZIP code:** 53203. **Area code:** 414.

Most north-south streets are numbered, increasing from Lake Michigan toward the west. Downtown Milwaukee lies between **Lake Michigan** and 10th St. Addresses increase north and south from **Wisconsin Ave.,** the center of east-west travel.

ACCOMMODATIONS

Downtown lodging options tend toward the pricey; travelers with cars should head out to the city's two hostels. **Bed and Breakfast of Milwaukee** (277-8066) finds rooms in local B&Bs (from $55).

University of Wisconsin at Milwaukee (UWM), Sandburg Halls, 3400 N. Maryland Ave. (229-4065 or 299-6123). Take bus #30 north to Hartford St. Convenient to nightlife and east-side restaurants. Laundry facilities, cafeteria, free local calls. No kitchen. Singles with shared bath $24, doubles $32. Clean, bland suites with bath divided into single and double bedrooms: 4 beds $56, 5 beds $66. Parking $5 for 24 hrs. 2-day advance reservations required. Open June-Aug. 15.

Hotel Wisconsin, 720 N. 3rd St. (271-4900), across from the Grand Avenue Mall. 250 large, floral rooms with private bath, and cable TV at a convenient downtown location. Free parking. Singles $59, students with ID $39, doubles $64; $8 per additional adult. Key deposit $5. Make reservations early.

Wellspring Hostel (HI-AYH), 4382 Hickory Rd., Newburg (675-6755), take I-43N to Rte. 33W to Newburg; Hickory Rd. intersects Newburg's Main St. The setting, on a riverside vegetable farm, is worth the 45-min. drive north of the city; 25 beds, kitchen, on-site parking. Office open daily 8am-8pm. $12, nonmembers $15. Private room with bath $37.50. Reservations required.

Red Barn Hostel (HI-AYH), 6750 W. Loomis Rd. (529-3299), in Greendale 13mi. southwest of downtown via Rte. 894; take the Loomis exit. Public transportation takes forever and barely comes within a mile, not worth it without a car. Cool, dark rooms with stone walls on the bottom floor of an enormous red barn. Full kitchen, no laundry facilities, campground-quality bathroom. Check-in 5-10pm. $10, nonmembers $13. Open May-Oct.

Belmont Hotel, 751 N. 4th St. (271-5880), at Wells downtown. Mainly a residential hotel with an exceptional location. The surrounding neighborhood is not as safe at night. Gaudy 70s-style singles $28, with private bath $34. Key deposit $3.

Wisconsin State Fair Park's RV Park (266-7035), just off Rte. 94 at 84th St. Showers, toilets, electricity, dump station, and 24-hr. police patrol. No tents. 7-day max. stay. Check-in 2pm. Sites $14. Reservations and 50% deposit required.

FOOD

Milwaukee is a premier town for food and drink. German brewery masterminds took a gold liquid that has been around since 4000BC, industrialized it with refrigeration, glass bottles, cans, and lots of PR, and made **beer** available to all. Milwaukeeans take advantage of their proximity to Lake Michigan with a local favorite called the Friday night **fish fry.** To finish things off, French ice cream, better known as **frozen custard,** is this dairy state's renowned treat; stands throughout the city vend specialties like Snow Job and Grand Marnier Blueberry Crisp.

For Italian restaurants, look on **Brady St.** You'll find heavy Polish influences in the **South Side. East Side** eateries are a little more cosmopolitan, and good Mexican food sambas at S. 16th St. and National.

Bangkok Orchid, 2239 N. Prospect Ave. (223-3333), 1 block south of North Ave. A local favorite for Thai food. Entrees $6-13; soups $2-3 per cup. Open Mon.-Fri. 4-10pm, Sat. 4-11pm, Sun. 4-9pm.

Abu's Jerusalem of the Gold, 1978 N. Farwell (277-0485), at Lafayette on the East Side. A tiny corner restaurant with tapestries, trinkets, and tasty Middle Eastern delights for herbivore and carnivore alike. *Miklube* (rice and vegetables with secret spices) with bread, salad, hummus, and tabouli. Rosewater lemonade 85¢. Open Mon.-Thurs. 11:30am-9pm, Fri.-Sat. 11:30am-11pm, Sun. noon-9pm.

John Hawk's Pub, 100 E. Washington Ave. (272-3199). A riverside terrace and gleaming oak bar complement the wide range of traditional British pub fare. Try the fish fry (2-piece basket $5.25). Live jazz Sat. 9pm; no cover. Open Sun.-Thurs. 10am-10:30pm, Fri.-Sat. 10am-2am.

Leon's, 3131 S. 27th St. (383-1784). Straight out of *Grease* (minus the roller-skating waitresses). Great frozen custard; 2 scoops $1. Hot dog 95¢. Open Sun.-Thurs. 11am-midnight, Fri. 11am-12:30am, Sat. 11am-1am.

La Casita, 2014 N. Farwell Ave. (277-1177). A wide range of Mexican food served at simple wooden tables. Eat inside the brightly colored walls or on the crowded outside patio. Entrees $5-8. Open Mon. 5-10:30pm, Tues.-Thurs. 11:30am-10:30pm, Fri.-Sat. 11:30am-midnight, Sun. 4:30-10:30pm; Sept.-Mar. Tues.-Thurs. 11:30am-9:30pm, Fri.-Sat. 11:30am-11pm, Sun. 4:30-10:30pm.

SIGHTS

Although many of Milwaukee's breweries have left, the city's name still conjures up images of a cold one. No visit to the city would be complete without a look at the yeast in action. **The Miller Brewery,** 4251 W. State St. (931-2337), the corporate giant that produces 43 million barrels of beer annually, offers free one-hour tours with free samples. (2 tours per hr. Mon.-Sat. 10am-3:30pm. Under 19 must be accompanied by adult.) **Pabst Brewing Company,** 915 W. Juneau Ave. (223-3709), offers free 35- to 40-minute tours with free tastings in a magnificent stone courtyard (on the hr. Mon.-Fri., 10am-3pm, Sat. 10am-2pm; Sept.-May closed Sat.). The **Lakefront Brewery,** 818 E. Chambers St. (372-8800), produces four year-round beers and several seasonal specials including pumpkin beer and cherry lager (tours Sat. 1:30, 2:30, and 3:30pm; $3—$1 goes to Vietnam Veterans Memorial).

The **Milwaukee County Transit System** (344-6711) runs four-hour **bus tours** with stops at a brewery (Pabst or Miller) and several of Milwaukee's many beautiful churches. (Tours leave the Grand Ave. 2nd St. entrance mid-June to Aug. Mon.-Sat. 12:15pm. $11, seniors and under 12 $8.) **Historic Milwaukee, Inc.** (277-7795), P.O. Box 2132, offers walking tours focusing on ethnic heritage, original settlements, and architecture ($4, students $2). Tours include **St. Josaphat's Basilica,** 2333 S. 6th St. (645-5623), a turn-of-the-century landmark with a dome larger than the Taj Mahal's (doors open daily 10am-2pm; call to arrange a visit at other times).

A road warrior's nirvana, **Harley-Davidson Inc.,** 11700 W. Capitol Dr. (342-4680), gives one-hour tours of its engine and transmission facility. (Mon.-Fri. 9, 10:30am, and 12:30pm, but there are many exceptions; call ahead. Reservations required for groups larger than 7.)

Several excellent museums grace the city of Milwaukee. The **Milwaukee Public Museum,** 800 W. Wells St. (278-2700; 278-2702 for recorded info), at N. 8th St., attracts visitors with numerous exhibits including dinosaur bones, a replicated Costa Rican rainforest, and a re-created European village. (Open daily 9am-5pm. $5.50, students with ID and ages 4-17 $3.50, seniors $4.50. Parking available.) The lakefront **Milwaukee Art Museum,** 750 N. Lincoln Memorial Dr. (224-3200), in the War Memorial Building, houses Haitian art, 19th-century German art, and American sculpture and painting, including two of Warhol's soup cans. (Open Tues.-Wed. and Fri.-Sat. 10am-5pm, Thurs. noon-9pm, Sun. noon-5pm. $4, students, seniors, and disabled $2. Park free along the Lincoln Memorial Dr., or pay $2 to use the Museum lot.) The **Charles Allis Art Museum,** 1801 N. Prospect Ave. (278-8295), at Royal Ave. 1 block north of Brady (take bus #30 or 31), houses a fine collection of Chinese, Japanese, Korean, Persian, Greek, and Roman artifacts, as well as American and European furniture in an English Tudor mansion (open Wed. 1-5pm and 7-9pm, Thurs.-Sun. 1-5pm; $2). The stone-and-ivy **Milwaukee County Historical Center,** 910 N. Old World 3rd St. (273-8288), details the early years of the city (open Mon.-Fri. 9:30am-5pm, Sat. noon-5pm, Sun. noon-5pm; free).

Better known as "The Domes," the **Mitchell Park Horticultural Conservatory,** 524 S. Layton Blvd. (649-9800), at 27th St., recreates a desert and a rain forest and mounts seasonal displays in a series of three seven-story conical glass domes. (Open daily 9am-5pm. $2.50; students, seniors, and disabled $1.25. Take bus #10 west to 27th St., then #27 south to Layton.) At the **Milwaukee County Zoo,** 10001 W. Bluemound Rd. (256-5412), 4 mi. west of the conservatory (take bus #10 west from Wisconsin St. downtown), zebras and cheetahs eye each other across a moat in the only predator-prey exhibit in the U.S.; also look for black rhinos and trumpeter swans. Admission covers many of the shows. (Open Mon.-Sat. 9am-5pm, Sun. 9am-6pm; Oct.-April daily 9am-4:30pm. $6, ages 3-12 $4. Parking $4.) The **Boerner Botanical Gardens,** 5879 S. 92nd St. (425-1130), in Whitnall Park between Grange and Rawsen St., boasts billions of beautiful blossoms (open May-Oct. daily 8am-sunset; free). County parks line much of Milwaukee's waterfront, providing free recreational areas and trails. **High Roller Bike and Skate Rental** (273-1343), at McKinley Marina in Veteran's Park, has in-line skates ($5 per hr.) and bikes ($7 per hr.) for your rental enjoyment (open daily 10am-8pm, weather permitting; must be over 18 with ID).

Ice skaters pirouette at **Pettit National Ice Center,** 500 S. 84th St. (266-0100), by the State Fairgrounds (about $2; hours vary).

ENTERTAINMENT

The modern white stone **Performing Art Center (PAC),** 929 N. Water St. (273-7206 or 800-472-4458), across the river from Pére Marquette Park, hosts the **Milwaukee Symphony Orchestra, First Stage Milwaukee,** a ballet company, and the **Florentine Opera Company.** (Symphony tickets $9-50; ballet and symphony offer ½-price student and senior tickets on the day of any show.) Throughout the summer, the PAC's Peck Pavilion hosts **Rainbow Summer** (273-7206), a series of free lunchtime concerts which run the spectrum from jazz and bluegrass to country (Mon.-Fri. noon-1:15pm). **The Milwaukee Repertory Theater,** 108 East Wells St. (224-9490), features three stages of contemporary, classical, cabaret, and holiday shows from September to May (tickets $8-26; ½-price student rush tickets available ½hr. before shows). On summer Thursdays, **Jazz in the Park** (271-1416) presents free concerts in East Town's Cathedral Square Park, at N. Jackson St. between Wells and Kilbourn St. In Pére Marquette Park, by the river between State and Kilbourn, **River Flicks** (286-5700) screens free movies at dusk every Thursday in August.

Milwaukee is festival-happy, throwing a different city-wide party almost every summer weekend. **Summerfest** (273-3378; 800-837-3378 outside Milwaukee), the largest and most lavish, lasts over 11 days in late June and early July; daily life halts as a potpourri of big-name musical acts, culinary specialities, and an arts and crafts bazaar take over Maier Festival Park. (see below). Milwaukeeans line the streets for **The Great Circus Parade** (273-7877), in mid-July, an authentic re-creation of turn-of-the-century processions with trained animals, daredevils, costumed performers, and 75 original wagons. In early August (1-11 in 1996) the **Wisconsin State Fair** (266-7000) rolls into the fairgrounds toting big-name entertainment, 12 stages, exhibits, contests, rides, fireworks, and a pie-baking contest ($5, seniors and disabled $4, under 11 free). Ethnic festivals fill almost every weekend in a Milwaukee summer; the most popular are **Polishfest** (529-2140), in mid-June; **Asian Moon** (332-6544), in mid-June; **Festa Italiana** (223-2180), in mid-July; **Bastille Days** (271-1416), near Bastille Day (July 14); **German Fest** (464-9444), in late July ($6, under 12 free); **Mexican Fiesta** (383-7066), in late August; and **Indian Summer Fest** (774-7119), in early September. Pick up a copy of the free weekly entertainment magazine, *Downtown Edition,* for the full scoop on festivals and other events.

The **Milwaukee Brewers** baseball team play at **County Stadium,** at the interchange of I-94 and Rte. 41 (933-9000 or 800-933-7890), as do the pigskin-tossing **Green Bay Packers** (342-2717) for some of their home games. The **Milwaukee Bucks** (227-0500), the local basketball team, and the **Marquette University Warriors** (288-7127) lock horns with opponents at Bradley Center, 1001 N. 4th St. (227-0700), where the **Milwaukee Admirals** (227-0550) slam pucks in the winter.

NIGHTLIFE

Even with over 15,000 lakes, it sometimes seems there's more beer than water flowing in Wisconsin. Milwaukee never lacks for *something* to do after sundown. Though downtown gets a little seedy at night, the area along **Water St.** between Juneau and Highland offers slightly yuppified bars and street life. **North Ave.,** on the east side near UW Campus, borders another convenient cluster of bars and clubs around the **N. Farwell St.** intersection.

Safehouse, 779 N. Front St. (271-2007), across from the Pabst Theater downtown. Come in from the cold and enter a truly bizarre world of spy hideouts, James Bond music, mata hari outposts, and drinks with names like Rahab the Harlot. A brass plate labeled "International Exports, Ltd." marks the entrance. Draft beer (code name: "liquid gold") $1.50; simple dinners $8-12. Cover $1-2. Open Mon.-Thurs. 11:30am-1:30am, Fri.-Sat. 11:30am-2am, Sun. 4pm-midnight.

Von Trier's, 2235 N. Farwell (272-1775), at North. Murals, beer steins, and deer antlers crowd the walls and ceilings of this small, overwhelmingly German establishment. 20 beers on tap (mostly imported) and 74 in bottles ($2.50-5), along with numerous hot drinks and coffees. Service in the lavish interior or on a large outdoor patio. Open Sun.-Thurs. 4pm-1:30am, Fri. Sat. 4pm-2am.

ESO_2, 1905 E. North Ave. (278-8118). Flashing lights and alternative dance mixes shower down on a large, ventilated dance floor. 21+. Cover usually $2.

Dance, Dance, Dance, part of **Lacage,** 801 S. 2nd Ave. (383-8330), caters to a 20s-30s gay clientele, but all are welcome. Videos accompany dance mixes by the Pet Shop Boys and others. Cover Fri.-Sat. $3.50. Open daily 9pm-2:30am.

Café Melange, 720 Old World 3rd St. (291-9889), in the Hotel Wisconsin. Diverse entertainment includes jazz, blues, and Latin music ensembles, Mon. poetry readings, open mike nights, and tap dance. No live acts on summer weekends, when the festivals take over. Opens Mon.-Sat. 11am-11pm, Sun. 5pm-11pm; open until 1am when bands play.

■■■ MADISON

The capitol crowns one of Madison's hilltops, while the University of Wisconsin presides over the other; together, the two determine the character of Madison. Sandwiched between Lake Mendota and Lake Monona, Madison holds her head high as a staid capital city and boogies down as an exuberant college town. Twenty-something culture (coffee shops, used clothing stores, record shops, endless rows of apartments, bicycle paths on the streets) dominates the area without completely edging out Wisconsin-centered museums and senators in suits.

Practical Information The **Greater Madison Convention and Visitors Bureau,** 615 E. Washington Ave. (255-2537 or 800-373-6376), provides travel info (open Mon.-Fri. 8am-5pm). **Greyhound,** 2 S. Bedford St. (257-3050 or 800-231-2222), buses to Chicago (5 per day, 3-5hr., $15) and Milwaukee (4 per day, 1hr., $9). The station is open daily from 5:45am-10pm. **Madison Metro Transit System,** 1101 E. Washington Ave. (266-4466), offers efficient service through downtown, UW campus, and surrounding areas. ($1; free Mon.-Sat. 10am-3pm within the capitol and UW campus.) **Post office:** 3902 Milwaukee Ave. (246-1249; open Mon. 7:30am-7pm, Tues.-Fri. 7:30am-6pm, Sat. 8:30am-2pm); **ZIP code:** 53714; **area code:** 608.

Accommodations and Camping Budget hotels cluster along Hwy. 151 (E. Washington Ave.) east of downtown. Prices average $30-35, but **Select Inn,** 4845 Haynes Rd. (249-1815), near the junction of I-90 and Hwy. 151, offers large rooms from $26 with cable TV, A/C, free continental breakfast, and free local calls. The **Short Course Dorms,** 105 Agricultural Hall (262-2270), on the UW campus, sometimes have rooms in summer (pay phone in hall, shared bath, linen service; singles $25, doubles $36). Also on campus, the **Wisconsin Center Guest House,** 610 Langdon St. (256-2621) costs a bit more (indoor pool, radio, TV; doubles $44; free breakfast). **Campers** should head south on Hwy. 90 to Stoughton, where **Lake Kegonsa State Park,** 2405 Door Creek Rd. (873-9695), has 80 sites (½ reserved for walk-ins) in a wooded area ½ mi. from the beach. (Brand new showers, flush toilets. Wisconsin residents weekdays $7, weekends $9; non-residents $9/$11.)

Food and Nightlife Good restaurants pepper Madison, but the biggest cluster lies near the University. **State St.** hosts a wide variety of cheap restaurants, both chains and Madison originals. **Dotty Dumpling's Dowry,** 116 N. Fairchild (255-3175), prides itself on award-winning burgers ($3.65, veggie burger $3.80), eaten under hanging wooden canoes and other eclectic adornments (open Mon.-Wed. 11am-10pm, Thurs.-Sat. 11am-midnight, Sun. noon-8:30pm). **Himal Chuli,** 318 State St. (251-9225), offers *tarkari, dal,* and other Nepali favorites for very low prices—a full meal goes for around $5 (open Mon.-Sat. 11am-9pm). **Taqueria Gila Monster,**

106 King St. (225-6425), stomps out low-fat, high-flavor Mexican food with flair; try the catfish and cactus fillings in your two enchiladas ($3; open Mon.-Sat. 11am-10pm). At **Crystal's Corner Bar,** 1302 Williamson St. (256-2953), down a draught beer ($1.10-2) and jam to live bands, usually blues. (Music Thurs. 9:30pm and Sat. 10:15pm; cover $5.40. Open Mon.-Thurs. 11am-2am, Fri.-Sat. 11am-2:30am, Sun. noon-2am.) For the scoop on bands, movies, plays, and other nightlife, get down with the university-sponsored info line (225-INFO/4636), updated daily. Farmers markets surround Madison, but farm-fresh produce can be also found at **Capitol Sq.** (563-5031; Apr.-Nov. Sat. 6am-2pm).

Sights and Entertainment Between the university and the capitol area, Madison offers many options for intelligent sight-seeing. The imposing **State Capitol** (266-0382), in Capitol Square at the center of downtown, boasts beautiful ceiling frescoes and the only granite dome in the U.S. (Free guided tours from the ground floor info desk Mon.-Sat on the hr. 9-11am and 1-4pm, Sun. on the hr. 1-4pm. Open daily 6am-8pm.) Also on Capitol Sq., the **Wisconsin Veterans Museum,** 30 W. Mifflin St. (264-6086), honors Wisconsin soldiers who served the nation during the 19th and 20th centuries (open Tues.-Sat. 9:30am-4:30pm; also April-Sept. Sun. noon-4pm; free). The **State Historical Museum,** 30 N. Carroll St. (264-6555) explores the history of Wisconsin's Native American population (open Tues.-Sat. 10am-5pm, Sun. noon-5pm; free). The **Madison Art Center** (257-0158) exhibits modern and contemporary art and hosts traveling exhibitions. (Open Tues.-Thurs. 11am-5pm, Fri. 11am-9pm, Sat. 10am-5pm, Sun. 1-5pm; most exhibits free).

The **Madison Civic Center,** 211 State St. (266-6550), stages many of the city's arts and entertainment performances; mainly during the winter. Call for details (office open Mon.-Fri. 8am-4:30pm). **Madison Repertory Theatre,** 122 State St., #201 (256-0029), performs classic and contemporary musical productions in the **Isthmus Playhouse** at the Civic Center or at UW's **Mitchell Theater** (performance times vary; tickets $16.50-$19.50). For the latest on the entertainment scene, pick up a free copy of the weekly *Isthmus* (printed Thurs.).

A few noteworthy museums grace **University of Wisconsin,** one of the best public universities in the U.S.; highlights include the **Geology Museum,** 215 W. Dayton (262-2399; open Mon.-Fri. 8:30am-4:30pm, Sat. 9am-noon) and the **Elvehjem Museum of Art,** 800 University Ave. (263-2246; open daily 9am-5pm; free). Also part of UW, the outdoor **Olbrich Botanical Gardens** and indoor **Bolz Conservatory,** 3330 Atwood Ave. (246-4550), offer a plethora of plants. Inside the conservatory dome, free-flying birds, waterfalls, and tropical plants ignore the Wisconsin weather. (Gardens open daily 8am-8pm; Sept.-May Mon.-Sat. 8am-5pm, Sun. 9am-5pm. Free. Conservatory open Mon.-Sat. 10am-4pm, Sun. 10am-5pm. $1, ages 6-18 50¢, under 5 free; free Wed. and Sat. 10am-noon.) For more information on any UW attraction, visit the **UW Visitors Center** at the corner of Observatory Dr. and N. Park St., on the west side of the Memorial Union.

Come one, come all to the spectacular **Circus World Museum,** 426 Water St. (356-8341; 356-0800 for recorded info), a 45-min. drive from Madison in Baraboo (take exit 106 off I-90/94). This former home of the Ringling Brothers Circus continues the fun-loving, clown-filled, ooh-aah! tradition of the big top with an elephant barn, flea circus paraphernalia, and more. (Shows throughout the day. Open May-Sept. 5 daily 9am-6pm, some nights until 10pm. $11, seniors $10, ages 3-12 $6; after 4pm $7, kids $4.) **Family Land** (254-7766), off Hwy. 12 at Wisconsin Dells just north of Baraboo, splashes with the world's fastest and steepest water slide, a wave pool, a miniature golf course, and other wholesome water park fun ($15, water park alone $10). East of Madison, **House on the Rock,** 5754 Hwy. 23 (935-3639), in Spring Green, offers spectacular views of the Wyoming Valley from the vertiginous glass-walled Infinity Room, as well as a 40-acre complex of gardens, fantastic architecture, and displays. (Open daily 9am-7:45pm; last tickets sold at 5pm. Tickets $13.50, ages 7-12 $8.40, ages 4-6 $3.50, under 4 free.)

■■■ DOOR COUNTY

Door County's 250 mi. of coastline, ten lighthouses, rocky shores, and sandy beaches give the peninsula the atmosphere of a New England seashore. Lake Michigan reinforces the comparison, sending ocean-like waves and riptides to pound the windy eastern shore. With miles of bike paths, acres of orchards, and stunning scenery, Door County, much like the towns of the Atlantic coast, swings open to visitors on a summer-oriented seasonal schedule.

Practical Information **Door County Chamber of Commerce,** 6443 Green Bay Rd. (743-4456 or 800-52-RELAX), on Rte. 42/57 entering Sturgeon Bay, has free brochures for every village on the peninsula as well as biking maps. Outside, a free **Triphone** allows you to call hotels, restaurants, police, a weather line, and a fishing hotline. (Open Mon.-Fri. 8:30am-5pm, Sat.-Sun. 10am-4pm; Nov.-May. Mon.-Fri. 8:30am-4:30pm.) Look for a visitors center in each of the other villages as well. Public transportation comes only as close as **Green Bay,** 50 mi. southwest of Sturgeon Bay, where **Greyhound** has a station at 800 Cedar (414-432-4883; open Mon.-Fri. 6:30am-5:15pm, Sat. 6:30am-noon, Sun. 9am-noon). In Green Bay, rent a car from **Advantage,** 1629 Velp (414-497-2152), 3 mi. from the Greyhound station. ($14 per day, $89 per week; 10¢ per mi.; insurance $5. Must be 25 with credit card. Open Mon.-Fri. 8:30am-5:30pm, Sat. 8am-3pm.) **Emergency:** 911. Door County's **post office:** 359 Louisiana (743-2681), at 4th St. in Sturgeon Bay (open Mon.-Fri. 8:30am-5pm, Sat. 9:30am-noon); **ZIP code:** 54235; **area code:** 414.

Door County truly begins north of **Sturgeon Bay,** where Rte. 42 and 57 converge and then split again—Rte. 57 running up the eastern coast of the peninsula, Rte. 42 up the western side. The peninsula juts out 200 mi. northeast of Madison and 150 mi. north of Milwaukee, with no land access except via Sturgeon Bay. Summer (especially July and August) is high season in Door County's 12 villages. The county is less developed and more traditional the farther north you go and less commercialized in the east; **Fish Creek, Sister Bay,** and **Ephraim,** the county's largest towns, lie on the west side of the peninsula. Anywhere in the area, temperatures can dip to 40°F at night, even in July; dress warmly.

Accommodations and Camping Pricey resorts, hotels, and motels crowd Rte. 42 and Rte. 57 ($60 and up in summer). Camping is as plentiful, and much cheaper. Reserve for July and August as far in advance as possible. The **Camp-Tel Family Campground,** 8164 Hwy. 42 (868-3278), 1 mi. north of Egg Harbor, offers tent sites, as well as tiny A-frame cabins, each with two sets of bunks, a loft, heat, and electricity (sites for 2 $14, A-frame $28; each additional adult $5). **Billerbecks,** 9864 Hidden Spring Rd., Ephraim (854-2528), off Rte. 42, close to the beach, accepts guests in three clean, beautiful rooms filled with antique furniture (shared bath; rooms $24-27). The **Century Farm Motel** (854-4069), on Rte. 57, 3 mi. south of Sister Bay, gives visitors a choice of themes—southwestern, cows, honeymoon, and more (A/C, TV, private bath; cabins for 2 $45, for 4 $55, for 5 $65). One thousand Barbies, 600 animated store window mannequins, 35 cars, and a bevy of gnome statues grace the premises of the **Chal-A Motel,** 3910 Rte. 42/57 (743-6788), 3 mi. north of the bridge in Sturgeon Bay. Need we say more? (July-Aug. singles $44, doubles $44; Nov. to mid-May $24/$29; mid-May to June $29/$34.)

Four out of the area's five **state parks** (all except Whitefish Dunes State Park) provide space for camping ($12, Wisconsin residents $10). All state parks require a motor vehicle permit ($6 per day, $24 annually). **Peninsula State Park,** P.O. Box 218, Fish Creek 54212 (868-3258), by Fish Creek village on Rte. 42, contains the largest of the campgrounds (469 sites), with showers and flush toilets, 20 mi. of shoreline, a golf course, a spectacular view from Eagle Tower, and 17 mi. of hiking trails. Make reservations well in advance (i.e. 6 months), or come in person and put your name on the waiting list for one of the 127 walk-in sites. **Potawatomi State Park,** 3740 Park Dr., Sturgeon Bay 54235 (746-2890), just outside Sturgeon Bay off

Rte. 42/57, maintains 125 campsites, half of which are open to walk-ins; write to make reservations for the other half. **Newport State Park** (854-2500), is a wildlife preserve at the tip of the peninsula, 7 mi. from Ellison Bay off Rte. 42. Although it permits entrance to vehicles, all 16 of its sites are accessible only by hiking. To get to **Rock Island State Park** (847-2235), take the ferry from Gill's Rock to Washington Island (see Sights and Activities below), and another ferry (847-2252; $6 round-trip, campers with gear $7) to Rock Island (40 sites; open mid-April to mid-Nov.). **Path of Pines,** 3709 Hwy. F (868-3332), 1 mi. east of the ever-packed Peninsula off Rte. 42 in Fish Creek, one of many private campgrounds, rents 91 quiet, scenic sites (showers, laundry facilities; tent sites $14, with hookup $19; Fri.-Sat. $3 extra).

Food and Drink Many people come to Door County just for **fishboils,** not trout-blemishes, but a Scandinavian tradition dating back to 19th-century lumberjacks. Cooks toss potatoes, onions, and whitefish into an enormous kettle over a wood fire. To remove the fish oil from the top of the water, the boilmaster (often imported from Scandinavia) judges the proper time to throw kerosene into the fire, producing a massive fireball; the cauldron boils over signalling chow time—it's much better than it sounds. Most fishboils conclude with a big slice of cherry pie, another county tradition. Door County's best-known fishboils take place at **Edgewater Restaurant** (854-4034), in Ephraim (June Mon.-Sat. 6 and 7:45pm; July-Aug Mon.-Sat. 5:30, 6:45, and 8pm; $12.50, under 12 $8.50; reservations recommended), and **The Viking** (854-2998), in Ellison Bay (mid-May to Oct. every ½hr. 4:30-8pm; $10.50, under 12 $7.50). **Sandpiper,** in Bailey's Harbor off Rte. 57, does an outdoor fishboil for $8.50. (July-Aug. daily 6 and 7pm boilover; Sept.-Oct. and mid-May to June Tues., Fri., Sat. 5:30 and 6:30pm boilover.) **Al Johnson's Swedish Restaurant** (854-2626), in Sister Bay on Rte. 42 down the hill and 2 blocks past the information center on the right, has excellent Swedish food ($8-17), waitstaff in traditional Swedish dress, and goats who dine daily on the thick sod roof (open daily 6am-9pm; in winter Mon.-Sat. 6am-8pm, Sun. 7am-8pm). **Bayside Tavern** (868-3441), on Rte. 42 in Fish Creek, serves serious burgers ($2.50-3.50) and a delicious Friday perch fry ($8). At night, it's a crowded bar with live entertainment on Mondays (cover $2) and open-mic Wednesdays. (Open Sun.-Thurs. 11am-2am, Fri.-Sat. 11am-2:30pm.)

Sights and Activities Biking is the best way to take in the breathtaking scenery the lighthouses, rocks, and white sand beaches of Door's 250-mi. coastline; ask for free bike maps at tourist offices. **Whitefish Dunes State Park** heaps high with sand dunes, hiking/biking/skiing trails, and a well-kept wildlife preserve (open daily 8am-8pm; vehicle permit $6 per day). Just north on Cave Point Rd. off Rte. 57, **Cave Point County Park** stirs the soul with some of the most stunning views on the peninsula (open daily 6am-9pm; free). At Jacksonport, **Lakeside Park,** immortalized in song by the rock band *Rush,* offers a wide, sandy expanse of beach backed by a shady park and playground (open daily 6am-9pm; free). South of Bailey's Harbor off Rte. 57, follow Kangaroo Lake Rd. to **Kangaroo Lake,** the largest of the eight inland lakes on this thin peninsula; circle the lake to find your own secluded swimming spot in waters warmer than Lake Michigan's. The scenic trail at **Ridges Sanctuary** (839-2802), north of Bailey's Harbor off County Rte. Q, leads to an abandoned lighthouse (open Mon.-Sat. 9am-4pm, Sun. 1-4pm; free). At **Peninsula State Park,** in Fish Creek, visitors ride mopeds and bicycles along 20 mi. of shoreline road, rent boats, and sunbathe at **Nicolet Beach.** At the top of **Eagle Tower,** 1 mi. and 110 steps up from the beach, you can see clear across the lake to Michigan (open daily 6am-11pm; vehicle permit $6 per day). At the park entrance, **Edge of Park Bike Rentals,** 4007 Hwy. 41, (868-3344), rents six-speed bikes ($5 per hr., $20 per day) and mopeds ($22 per hr.). For more satisfying hiking than Peninsula offers, try **Newport State Park,** 6 mi. east of Ellison Bay on Newport Dr. off Rte. 42. The park also encompasses an expansive 3000-ft. swimming beach and 13 mi. of shoreline on Lake Michigan and inland Europe Lake (no vehicles).

There's more to Door County than parks. Two free **Maritime Museums** document the water industries of the Great Lakes: one at **Gills Rock** (743-5958; open June-Sept. Mon.-Sat 10am-4pm, Sun. 1-4pm; Oct. weekends) and another at **Sturgeon Bay** (743-8139; open May weekends; June-Oct. Sun.-Thurs. 10am-4pm, Fri.-Sat. 10am-8pm). If water doesn't float your boat, **Door Peninsula Winery,** 5806 Rte. 42, Sturgeon Bay (743-7431 or 800-551-5049), enjoins you to partake of another liquid (15-20min. tours and tastes in summer daily 9am-6pm; off season 9am-5pm). The **Peninsula Players** (868-3287), off Rte. 42 in Fish Creek, are America's oldest professional resident summer theater (shows in summer Tues.-Fri.; call for details). The shipping and packing town of **Green Bay,** the largest city anywhere near Door County, gives a home to the aptly named (and oldest) NFL team, the **Green Bay Packers** (496-5719 for tickets; $24-28). The city also packs pollution, noise, and industry, as well as plenty of bars and a little gambling; **The Oneida Bingo and Casino** (414-497-8118), County Rte. GG southwest of downtown, antes up with 1300 slot machines open 24 hrs. seven days a week and 47 blackjack tables open 10am-4am (18+ only). The **National Railroad Museum,** 2285 S. Broadway, Green Bay (414-435-7245), exhibits, yes, trains. (Open May-Oct. daily 9am-5pm; $6, ages 6-15 $3).

■■■ APOSTLE ISLANDS

Long ago, pious Frenchmen mistakenly believed that there were only 12 islands off the coast of Wisconsin and named these bodies the Apostle Islands. Over the years, this beautiful area has been variously claimed by Native Americans, loggers, quarrymen, and fishmen. Today, a National Lakeshore protects twenty-one of the islands, as well as a 12-mi. stretch of mainland shore; summer tourists visit the islands's caves by the thousands, camping on the unspoiled sandstone bluffs and foraging for wild blueberries and raspberries.

Practical Information All Apostle Islands excursions begin in the sleepy mainland town of **Bayfield,** in northwest Wisconsin on the Lake Superior coast. The nearest **bus** station, 101 2nd St., **Ashland** (682-4010), 22 mi. southeast of Bayfield on U.S. 2, has service to Duluth (1per day, 1½hr., $15). The **Bay Area Rural Transit (BART),** 300 Industrial Park Rd., Ashland (682-9664), offers a shuttle to Bayfield (4 per day; Mon.-Fri. 7am-3:30pm; $1.80, students $1.50, seniors $1.10). The **Bayfield Chamber of Commerce,** 42 S. Broad St. (779-3335 or 800-447-4094), has helpful info on the area and a listing of accommodations with price and availability (open Mon.-Sat. 9am-5pm, Sun. 10am-2pm). **National Lakeshore Headquarters Visitors Center,** 410 Washington Ave. (779-3397), distributes hiking and camping info along with free **camping** permits for 19 of the 22 islands; many sites are primitive (open daily 8am-6pm; in winter Mon.-Fri. 8am-4:30pm). For the latest assessment of the area's unpredictable **weather,** call 682-8333. The Apostle Islands's and Bayfield's **area code:** 715.

Accommodations, Camping, and Food The **Frostman Home,** 24 N. 3rd St., Bayfield (779-3239), puts visitors in three spotless and comfortable rooms (two with lake views) for $25 each (open mid-June to mid-Sept.). **The Seagull Bay Motel** (779-5558), off Rte. 13 at 7th St. in Bayfield, offers large, clean rooms and some kitchenettes (from $41; mid-Oct. to mid-May $23). To arrange a stay in a guesthouse ($25-200), inquire at the chamber of commerce (see Practical Information). **Dalrymple Park** (779-5712), ¼ mi. north of town on Rte. 13, offers 30 **campsites** under tall pines on the Lake (no showers; $7, with electricity $8; no reservations). **Apostle Islands View Campground** (779-5524), ½ mi. south of Bayfield on County Rd. J off Rte. 13, lives up to its name with modern sites which overlook the islands. (Showers 25¢. Sites $12, with hookup $15, with hookup and cable $19. Reservations recommended a month in advance for July-Aug.)

In early summer, Bayfield's baskets overflow with berry pies. **Maggie's,** 257 Maypenny Ave. (779-5641), prepares burgers ($5) and various gourmet specials in flamingo-filled decor (open daily 6am-midnight; Nov.-April Sun.-Thurs. 11am-9pm, Fri.-Sat. 11am-10pm). Crack **Martha's Pie Safe and Pantry** (779-5355), at Rittenhouse Ave. and 3rd St., for mouthwatering slices of pie—rhubarb, fudge, apple, lemon, pecan, and many more ($2.50-$3; open Sun.-Wed. 9am-6pm, Thurs.-Sat. 9am-9pm; off-season hours vary). **Greunke's Restaurant,** 17 Rittenhouse Ave. (779-5480), at 1st St., specializes in huge, cheap diner-style breakfasts ($3-5) by day and holds locally famous fishboils on summer nights at 6:30 and 7:30pm ($11, kids $7).

Getting Around and Activities Though often overshadowed by Bayfield and Madeline Island (see below), the other 21 islands have subtle charms of their own. The sandstone quarries of Basswood and Hermit Islands, as well as the abandoned logging and fishing camps on some of the other islands, serve as mute reminders of a more vigorous era. The restored **lighthouses** on Sand, Raspberry, Michigan, Outer, and Devils Islands offer spectacular views of the surrounding country. Sea caves, carved out by thousands of years of winds and water, pocket the shores of several islands; a few on Devil's Island are large enough to explore by boat. The narrated three-hour cruises organized by the **Apostle Islands Cruise Service** (779-3925 or 800-323-7619) allow visitors a chance to see all of these sights without paying the exorbitant prices charged by other companies (tours depart the Bayfield City Dock mid-May to mid-Oct. daily 10am; $20, kids $9). From late June to mid-August, the cruise service runs an inter-island shuttle that delivers campers and lighthouse-o-philes to their destinations. The best **beach** on the mainland is just south of Bayfield along Rte. 13, near Sioux Flats; watch for a poorly marked path to the left about 7 or 8 mi. out of town. Due to the extreme cold, **swimming** in Lake Superior can be quite uncomfortable.

Not just a base town for the islands, Bayfield is the proud home of some awfully good apples. The town comes vibrantly alive in early October for the **Apple Festival.** For fresh-picked orchard taste, make your way to the **Bayfield Apple Company** (779-5700), on Betzold Rd. (open Sept.-Jan. daily 9am-6pm).

Madeline Island A few hundred years ago, the Chippewa came to **Madeline Island** from the Atlantic in search of the *megis shell,* a light in the sky that was purported to bring prosperity and health. Today, the island maintains a more natural allure, as thousands of visitors each summer seek the clean and sandy beaches of this relaxing retreat. Towards the end of the day, head to **Sunset Bay** on the island's north side and see why the bay got its name. The **Indian Burial Ground,** 1 mi. south of La Pointe, looks a little scruffy, but among the tufts of grass lie the graves of Chief Great Buffalo and other early settlers. **Madeline Island Bus Tours** (747-2051) offers two-hour tours of the island. (June 18-24 daily 10:30am and 1pm; June 25 to mid-Aug. 10:30am, 1, and 3:15pm; $6.75, ages 6-11 $3.75.)

With only about five streets, Madeline Island is easy to navigate by foot, bike, or car. The **Madeline Island Chamber of Commerce** (747-2801), on Main St., can be especially helpful in finding accommodations (open daily 10am-4pm). **Madeline Island Ferry Line** (747-2051 or 747-6801) shuttles between Bayfield and **La Pointe,** on Madeline Island. (20-min. summer ferries daily every 30min. 7am-11pm. $3, ages 6-11 $1.75, bikes $1.50, cars $6.75. March-June and Sept.-Dec. ferries run less frequently and prices drop. See Getting Around, above, for more ferry info.) During the winter (Jan.-March), people make the crossing by windsled, snowmobile, foot, or car. Rent a moped at **Motion to Go,** 102 Lake View Pl. (747-6585), about 1 block from the ferry. ($10 per hr., $45 per day. Mountain bikes $5/$18. Open mid-May to early Oct. 10am-8pm.) La Pointe's **post office:** (747-3712), just off the dock on Madeline Island (open Mon.-Fri. 9am-4:20pm, Sat. 9:30am-12:50pm); **ZIP code:** 54850.

Rooms in the area disappear during the summer; call ahead for reservations. The **Madeline Island Motel** (747-3000) has clean rooms named for personalities in the island's history (singles $51, doubles $56; May-June and Labor Day-Nov. $41/ $45; Dec.-April all rooms $31). Madeline Island has two campgrounds. **Big Bay Town Park** (747-6913), 6½ mi. from La Pointe out Big Bay Rd., sits right next to beautiful Big Bay Lagoon (sites $9, with electricity $16). Across the lagoon, **Big Bay State Park** (747-6425; Bayfield office 779-3346) doesn't question why the body of water isn't just named Big Lagoon or Big Bay; it just goes quietly about its business, renting 55 primitive sites ($9-12; daily vehicle permit $6, $4 for Wisconsinites). Sites can be reserved by mail for an extra $3. The **Island Café** (747-6555), 1 block to the right from the ferry exit, serves big meals, good lunches ($3-7), and many vegetarian dishes. The whitefish and trout meals ($9.50) are dinner classics. (Open daily 8am-10:30pm.) Treat a growling tummy to good shortcake ($3), a relaxed atmosphere, and a view of the lake at the **Beach Club** (747-3955), just off the ferry in La Pointe (open in summer daily 6:30am-1am, food only until 10pm).

Minnesota

Overwhelming expanses of isolated wilderness blanket most of northern Minnesota It is a land that spawns giants in the imagination; Mesabi of Native American legends, and Paul Bunyan and his blue ox Babe in more recent lore. In the south, the Twin Cities produce proud urban giants of their own, in defiance of the north's raw nature; pop star Prince casts a purple shadow over his hometown, and the Pillsbury Doughboy chuckles for the world. Hee, hee...

PRACTICAL INFORMATION

Capital: St. Paul.
Minnesota Office of Tourism: 100 Metro Sq., 121 7th Pl. E., St. Paul 55101-2112 (612-296-5029 or 800-657-3700). Open Mon.-Fri. 9am-4:30pm.
Time Zone: Central (1hr. behind Eastern). **Postal Abbreviation:** MN
Sales Tax: 6.5-7%.

■■■ MINNEAPOLIS AND ST. PAUL

In the beginning, there was Pig's Eye. The rebel squatter settlement, quickly renamed St. Paul, was not long an only child; across the river, St. Anthony Falls powered the flour and lumber mills of rising Minneapolis ("water city"). Not to be outdone, St. Paul set out to become a shipping center and steamboat depot—the Twin Cities were born, joined by proximity but markedly different in character. St. Paul enjoys ethnic diversity (German, Irish, Polish, Italian) among historical sights and striking architecture, while predominantly Scandinavian Minneapolis leads a fast-paced urban existence marked by colleges and towering skyscrapers.

PRACTICAL INFORMATION

Tourist Office: Minneapolis Convention and Visitors Association, 40 S. 7th St. (348-2453; open Mon.-Fri. 8am-5:30pm), and in the **City Center Shopping Area,** 2nd level skyway (open Mon.-Fri. 10am-8pm, Sat. 10am-6pm, Sun. noon-5pm). For info by mail, write the Visitors Bureau at 4000 Multifoods Tower, 33 S. 6th St., 55402. **St. Paul Convention and Visitors Bureau,** 101 Northwest Center, 55 E. 5th St. (297-6985 or 800-627-6101). Open Mon.-Fri. 8am-5pm. For 24-hr. info on local events, call **Cityline** (645-6060) and **The Connection** (922-9000). **Gay-Lesbian Information Line,** 822-0127. Open 9am-5pm.
Airport: Twin Cities International, south of the cities on I-494 in Bloomington (726-8100). Take bus #7 to Washington Ave. in Minneapolis or bus #54 to St. Paul. **Airport Express** (726-6400) shuttles to the downtowns and some hotels about

every 15min. 5am-midnight; departs from lower level near baggage claim. To St. Paul $8, to Minneapolis $10. Taxis charge $17 to St. Paul, $20 to Minneapolis.

Trains: Amtrak, 730 Transfer Rd. (800-872-7245), on the east bank off University Ave. SE, between the Twin Cities. Fair distance from both downtowns. Bus #7 runs to St. Paul, #16 connects to both downtowns. To: Chicago (1 per day, 7½hr., $74); Milwaukee (1 per day, 6hr., $71). Open daily 6am-12:30am.

Buses: Greyhound: In **Minneapolis,** 29 9th St. (371-3325), at 1st Ave. N. Very convenient. To: Chicago (11 per day, 9-11hr., $52); Milwaukee (9 per day, 7hr., $47). Open 24 hrs. with security. In **St. Paul** (222-0509), at 7th St. and St. Peter 3 blocks east of the Civic Center. In a somewhat unsafe area. 5 buses per day to: Chicago (8-12hr., $52), Milwaukee (6-10hr., $47). Open daily 5:30am-9:30pm.

Public Transportation: Metropolitan Transit Commission, 560 6th Ave. N. (349-7700; 373-3333 for automated schedule info and directions). Buses service both cities Mon.-Fri. 6am-11pm, Sat.-Sun. 7am-11pm; some buses operate 4:30am-12:45am, others shut down earlier. Peak fare (Mon.-Fri. 6-9am and 3:30-6:30pm) $1.25, off peak $1, under 18 25¢; off-peak express 50¢ extra. Bus #16 connects the 2 downtowns (50min.); bus #94 freeway express is much faster (25-30min.). **University of Minnesota Bus,** 625-9000. Buses run 7am-9pm. Free for students to campus locations. Off-campus routes 35¢-$1.20, depending on distance.

Car Rental: Affordable Rent-A-Car, 6405 Cedar Ave. S. (861-7545), Minneapolis, near the airport. Used cars from $26 per day with 150 free mi.; 22¢ per additional mi. Weekly from $149. Must be 23 with major credit card. Open Mon.-Fri. 9am-6pm, Sat. 11am-3pm. **Thrifty Car Rental,** 160 E. 5th St. (227-7690). $30-46 with 150 free mi., $159 per week with 1000 free mi.; 20¢ each additional mi. Must be 21 with major credit card. Under 25 surcharge $10 per day.

Taxis: In Minneapolis, **Yellow Taxi,** 824-4444. In St. Paul, **Yellow Cab,** 222-4433. Both charge $1.75 base fare, $1.30 per mi.

Crisis Lines: Crime Victim Center, 822 S. 3rd St., St. Paul (340-5400). **Rape/Sexual Assault Line,** 825-4357. Both open 24 hrs. **Gay-Lesbian Helpline,** 822-8661 or 800-800-0907. Open Mon.-Fri. noon-midnight, Sat. 4pm-midnight.

Emergency: 911.

Post Office: In **Minneapolis** (349-4957), 1st St. and Marquette Ave. next to the Mississippi River. Open Mon.-Fri. 7am-11pm, Sat. 9am-1pm. **ZIP code:** 55401. In **St. Paul,** 180 E. Kellogg Blvd. (293-3011). Open Mon.-Fri. 8am-6pm, Sat.-Sun. 8:30am-1pm. **ZIP code:** 55101. **Area code:** 612.

A loopy net of interstates covers the entire Minneapolis/St. Paul area. **I-94** connects the downtowns. **I-35** (north-south) splits in the Twin Cities, with **I-35W** serving Minneapolis and **I-35E** serving St. Paul—here's where things get tricky; buy a map (the ones in tourist brochures aren't very helpful) and pay attention. Curves and one-way streets tangle both of the downtown areas; even the numbered grids in the cities are skewed, making north-south and east-west designations tricky. In Minneapolis, **Hennepin Ave.** cuts diagonally across northwest downtown, dividing streets (running "east-west") into **N.** and **S.;** Avenues (running "north-south") begin numbering at Hennepin and increase both towards the southeast (**S.**) and towards the northwest (**N.**). Just east of Hennepin, **Nicollet Mall** runs north-south. Across the river from downtown, avenues and streets are designated **N.E.** or **S.E.** Hennepin runs northeast across the river and southwest across I-94 to **Lake St.** near **Lake Calhoun.** Lake St. beelines east across the river, where it becomes St. Paul's **Marshall Ave. Summit Ave.** parallels Marshall a little to the south, and **Grand Ave.** runs one block south of Summit. **Snelling Ave.,** a major north-south thoroughfare, intersects all three midway between the downtowns. **W. 7th St.** (a.k.a. **Fort Rd.**) runs northeast along the river through downtown St. Paul. **Skyways,** a second-story tunnel system, connect more than ten square blocks of buildings in each downtown area, protecting workers and pedestrians from the winter cold.

ACCOMMODATIONS AND CAMPING

Cost, safety, and cleanliness tend to go hand-in-hand-in-hand in the Twin Cities, with a few notable exceptions. The visitors bureaus have useful lists of **B&Bs,** while the

Downtown St. Paul
Mississippi St.
L'Orent St.
Empire St.
Penn Ave.
Arch St.
Jackson St.
Arch St.
Winter St.
Park St.
Rice St.
Como Ave.
University Ave.
Capitol Hts.
Jackson St.
University Ave.
State Capitol
Constitution Ave.
Columbus Ave.
E. 12th St.
Ireland Blvd.
TO MINNEAPOLIS
Pine St.
Broadway
E. 10th St.
E. 9th St.
E. 8th St.
E. 7th St.
Wall St.
Wacouta St.
Sibley St.
Kellogg Blvd.
Union Depot
7th Pl.
E. 7th St.
E. 6th St.
Robert St.
Minnesota St.
Cedar St.
St.
5th St.
E. 4th St.
Arts & Science Center
Minnesota History Center
Science Museum
St. Peter St.
Market St.
Landmark Center
Washington
Ordway Music Theatre
W. 6th St.
Cathedral of Paul
James J. Hill House
Summit Ave.
Chestnut St.
Walnut St.
Sherman St.
Exchange St.
Ryan Ave.
Hill St.
Eagle St.
Wabasha St.
Mississippi River
W. 7th St.

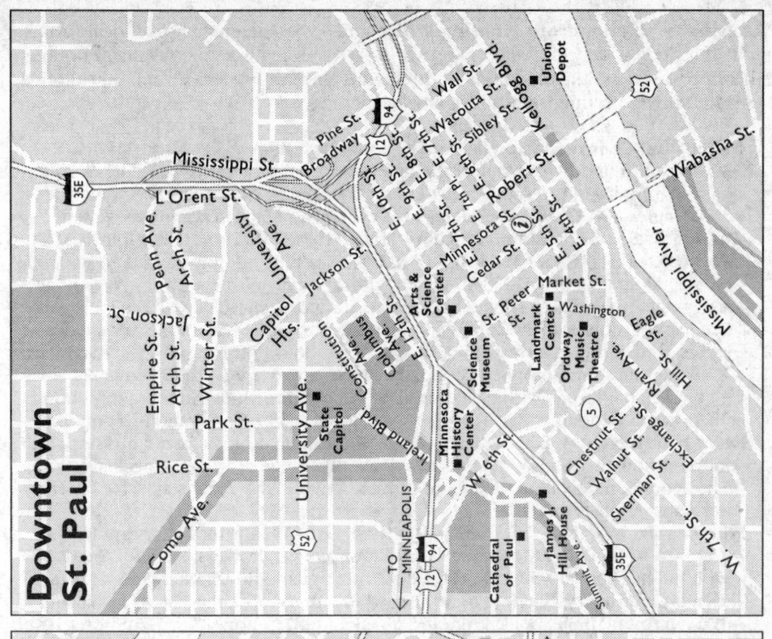

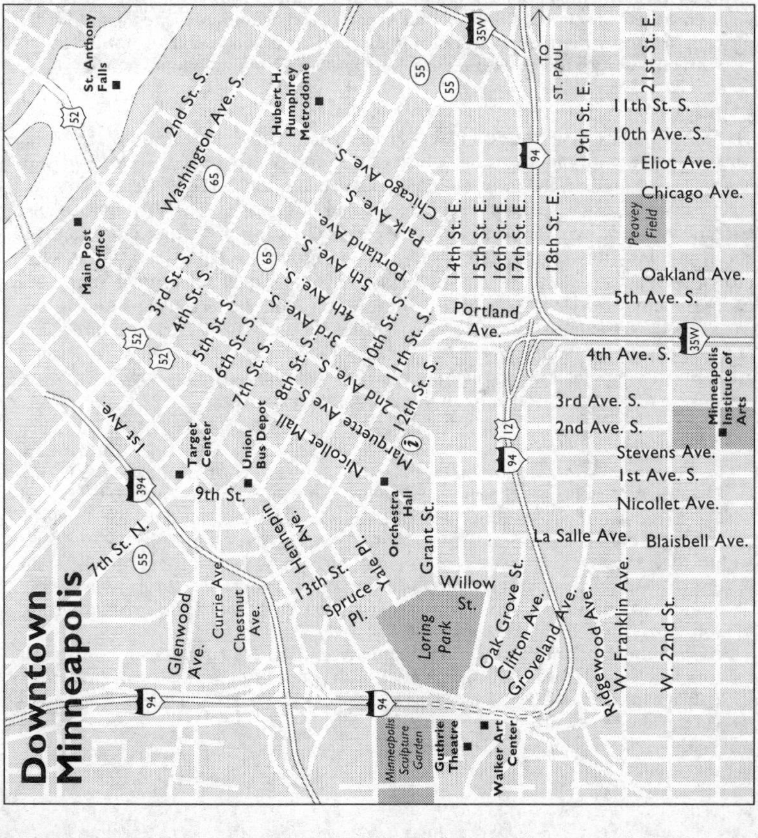

Downtown Minneapolis
St. Anthony Falls
2nd St. S.
Washington Ave. S.
Hubert H. Humphrey Metrodome
TO ST. PAUL
Main Post Office
3rd St. S.
4th St. S.
5th St. S.
6th St. S.
7th St. S.
8th St. S.
10th St. S.
11th St. S.
12th St. S.
Chicago Ave. S.
Park Ave. S.
Portland Ave.
5th Ave. S.
4th Ave. S.
3rd Ave. S.
2nd Ave. S.
Marquette Ave S.
Nicollet Mall
1st Ave.
Target Center
Union Bus Depot
9th St.
7th St. N.
Hennepin Ave.
Orchestra Hall
Grant St.
13th St.
Yale Pl.
Spruce Pl.
Willow St.
Loring Park
Glenwood Ave.
Currie Ave.
Chestnut Ave.
Oak Grove St.
Clifton Ave.
Groveland Ave.
Ridgewood Ave.
W. Franklin Ave.
W. 22nd St.
Minneapolis Sculpture Garden
Guthrie Theatre
Walker Art Center
14th St. E.
15th St. E.
16th St. E.
17th St. E.
18th St. E.
19th St. E.
21st St. E.
Portland Ave.
11th St. S.
10th Ave. S.
Eliot Ave.
Chicago Ave.
Peavey Field
Oakland Ave.
5th Ave. S.
4th Ave. S.
3rd Ave. S.
2nd Ave. S.
Minneapolis Institute of Arts
Stevens Ave.
1st Ave. S.
Nicollet Ave.
La Salle Ave.
Blaisbell Ave.

University of Minnesota Housing Office (624-2994) keeps a list of local rooms which rent on a daily ($13-45) or weekly basis. Camping is an inconvenient option; the closest state park camping is in the **Hennepin Park** system 25 mi. outside the city, and private campgrounds lie about 15 mi. out.

City of Lakes International House, 2400 Stevens Ave. S., Minneapolis (871-3210), south of downtown near the Institute of Arts. Owner gives suggestions for bars (happy hours), restaurants, etc. Free local calls. Afternoon check-out. Beds $14; singles $28, 2 available. Linen $3. Key deposit $5. Reservations required.

College of St. Catherine, Caecilian Hall (HI-AYH), 2004 Randolph Ave., St. Paul (690-6604). Take I-35E south from I-94, exit at Randolph St., and go west 17 blocks; or St. Paul bus #14. Simple, quiet dorm rooms near the river in a generally safe residential neighborhood. Shared bath, laundry, kitchenette. Free local calls. Singles $14, doubles $26, triples $33. 2-week max. stay. Open June to mid-Aug.

Evelo's Bed and Breakfast, 2301 Bryant Ave., South Minneapolis (374-9656), a 15-min. walk from uptown; take bus #17 from downtown. Friendly owners have 3 comfortable rooms with elegant wallpaper and furnishings in a beautiful house filled with Victorian artifacts. Singles $40, doubles $50. Reservations required.

Kaz's Home Hostel (822-8286), in South Minneapolis 1 block from a bus stop; call for directions. 1 frilly room, 2 beds, and an adjoining bathroom. Check-in 5-9pm. Check-out 9am. Lockout 9am-5pm. Curfew 11pm. 3-day max. stay. $10. Reservations absolutely required.

Minneapolis Northwest I-94 KOA (420-2255), 15mi. north of Minneapolis. Take Rte. 30W (I-94 exit 213) to Rte. 101N. Pool, sauna, showers. Sites for 2 $17.50, with full hookup $19.50, cabins for 2 $27; $2 per additional adult, kids $1.

Town and Country Campground, 12630 Boone Ave. S. (445-1756), 15mi. south of downtown Minneapolis. From I-35W, take Rte. 13S until it turns into Rte. 101, then go left on Zimran Rd. to Boone Ave. 65. Well-maintained sites with laundry facilities and a pool; quiet, but clearly close to an urban area. Sites for 2 $14.50, with electricity $18.50, with full hookup $20.50; $1 per additional person.

FOOD

The Twin Cities' love of music and art carries over into their culinary choices—look for small cafés with nightly music, plush chairs, and poetry readings. **Uptown** Minneapolis, centered on the intersection of Lake St. and the 2900s of Hennepin Ave., has plenty of funky restaurants and bars without high prices. The **Warehouse District,** near downtown Minneapolis, and **Victoria Crossing,** at Victoria and Grand St. about midway between Snelling Ave. and downtown St. Paul, serve the dessert crowd with lavish pastries (a meal in themselves). Near the University of Minnesota campus, **Dinkytown** (on the same side of the river) and the **West Bank** (across the river, hence the name) cater to student appetites with many dark and intriguing low-end places. **St. Paul Farmers Market** (227-6856) sells fresh produce and baked goods in varying locations throughout the city, including its main downtown location, every day except Monday; call for times and locations.

Minneapolis

The Loring Café, 1624 Harmon Pl. (332-1617), next to Loring Park and the Loring Theater. A truly beautiful 3-room café with stone walls, arches, indoor trees, and live music wafting from above. Pricey for dinner ($15-26), but great for drinks or late-night coffee. Open Sun.-Thurs. 11am-11pm, Fri.-Sat. 11am-2am.

Mud Pie, 2549 Lyndale Ave. S. (872-9435), at 26th. A wide variety of vegetarian dishes with Mexican and Middle Eastern accents. Don't miss the famous veggie burger ($4.75). Open Mon.-Thurs. 11am-10pm, Fri. 11am-11pm, Sat. 8am-11pm, Sun. 8am-10pm. Breakfast served Sat.-Sun. only.

Urban Bean Coffeehouse, 2717 Hennepin Ave. (872-1419). Relax in a soft plush armchair, gaze at the fish (in a tank filled with water from the Red Sea!), and enjoy a great cappuccino ($1.85). Live jazz and singers Thurs.-Fri.; no cover. Open Sun.-Thurs. 7am-11pm, Fri.-Sat. 7am-midnight.

Jitters, 1026 Nicollet Mall (333-8511). A cheerful, brightly painted coffeehouse with formica tables and, well, unique lamps. Great coffee. Sat.-Sun. omelettes $5.25; Sun. waffle bar $5. Open Mon.-Fri. 6:30am-1am, Sat.-Sun. 8am-1am.

A&J Gem Cafe, 2827½ Hennepin Ave. (874-1225). Twenty-something slackers and families crowd this diner for cheap, delicious breakfasts (omelettes $4-5), sandwiches, and burgers. Open daily 6am-2am.

Annie's Parlor, 313 14th Ave. S.E. (379-0744), in Dinkytown; 406 Cedar Ave. (339-6207), in the West Bank; 2916 Hennepin Ave. (825-4455), uptown. Neon lighting casts a soft pink glow over delicious hamburgers ($3.50-4.50). Open Mon.-Thurs. 11am-11pm, Fri.-Sat. 11am-12:30am, Sun. 11am-10pm.

St. Paul

Café Latté, 850 Grand Ave. (224-5687), near Victoria Crossing. Enormous pastries and a steaming milk drink called Hot Moo ($1.85) overshadow the soups and sandwiches ($3-5); the Swedish Hot Moo is especially good. The long line moves quickly. Open Mon.-Thurs. 10am-11pm, Fri. 10am-midnight, Sat. 9am-midnight, Sun. 9am-10pm.

Table of Contents and **Hungry Mind Bookstore,** 1648 Grand Ave. (699-6595), near Snelling Ave., and another, slightly dressier location with a bar in Minneapolis, 1310 Hennepin Ave. (339-1133). An excellent gourmet café. Try the wafer-crust pizza ($5). Open Mon.-Thurs. 9am-10pm, Fri.-Sat. 9am-11:30pm (bar in Minneapolis until 1am), Sun. 10am-6pm (in Minneapolis until 10pm).

Mickey's Dining Car, 36 W. 7th St. (222-5633), kitty-corner to the Greyhound station. Delicious, greasy, 24-hr. diner food. Steak and eggs from $5; pancakes $2.30.

Ciatti's, 850 Grand Ave. (292-9942). A popular Italian restaurant next to Café Latté. Fettucine Alfredo $10. Open Mon.-Thurs. 11am-10pm, Fri.-Sat. 11am-11pm, Sun. 10am-2pm and 2:30-10pm.

SIGHTS

Minneapolis

Situated in the land of 10,000 lakes, Minneapolis boasts three of its own clumped together a couple miles southwest of downtown; take bus #28. Ringed by stately mansions, **Lake of the Isles** is an excellent place to meet Canadian geese. **Lake Calhoun,** on the west end of Lake St. south of Lake of the Isles, is a hectic social and recreational hotspot. Located in a more residential neighborhood, **Lake Harriet** features tiny paddleboats and a stage with occasional free concerts. The city keeps up 28 mi. of lakeside trails for strolling, biking, etc. Rent roller- and in-line **skates** at **Rolling Soles,** 1700 W. Lake St. (823-5711; both $6 per hr., $12 per day; open Mon.-Fri. 10am-9pm, Sat.-Sun. 9am-9pm; weather permitting). **Calhoun Cycle Center** (827-8231), across the street, rents out **bikes.** ($5 per hr., $12.50 for ½day, $20 per day. Must have credit card and drivers license. Open daily 9am-9pm.) At the northeast corner of Lake Calhoun, the **Minneapolis Park and Recreation Board** (661-4875; 348-5364 for canoe info) handles **canoe** rentals ($5.50 per hr.).

Home to two of the country's premiere art museums, Minneapolis is an art hub. The **Minneapolis Institute of Arts,** 2400 3rd Ave. S. (870-3131; take bus #9), south of downtown, displays an outstanding collection of international art including the world-famous *Doryphoros*, a Roman sculpture of a perfectly proportioned man (open Tues.-Sat. 10am-5pm, Thurs. 10am-9pm, Sun. noon-5pm; free). The **Walker Art Center,** 725 Vineland Place (375-7622), a few blocks southwest of downtown, draws thousands with daring exhibits by Lichtenstein and Warhol. (Open Tues.-Sat. 10am-5pm, Thurs. 10am-8pm, Sun. 11am-5pm. $4, students with ID, seniors, and ages 12-18 $3; free Thurs. and first Sat. of the month.) Next to the Walker, the beautiful **Minneapolis Sculpture Garden,** the largest urban sculpture garden in the U.S., contains dozens of sculptures and a fountain in a maze of landscaped trees and flowers. To find a sure cure for absolutely anything, stop by the **Museum of Questionable Medical Devices,** 219 Main St. S.E. (379-4046), north of the river near St. Anthony Falls. The Solorama Bedboard (meant to cure brain tumors) and phrenological equipment (phrenologists measure head bumps to determine personality) are among the more respectable highlights of the collection. (Open Tues.-Thurs. 5-9pm, Fri. 5-10pm, Sat. noon-10pm. Donations requested.)

The Twin Cities exist because of the Mississippi River, and you can get a good look at the Mighty Miss from several points in town. Off Portland Ave., **Stone Arch Bridge** offers a scenic view of **St. Anthony Falls;** several miles downstream, Minnehaha Park (take bus #7 from Hennepin Ave. downtown) lets you to take a gander at the **Minnehaha Falls,** immortalized in Longfellow's *Song of Hiawatha*. The visitors center at the **Upper St. Anthony Lock and Dam** (332-3660), at Portland Ave. and West River Pkwy., provides a great view and a helpful explanation of the locks (under renovation from July 1995; expected 1996 hours: April-Dec. daily 9am-dusk).

St. Paul

St. Paul's history and architecture are its greatest appeals. West of downtown along **Summit Ave.,** the nation's longest continuous stretch of Victorian homes, built on the tracks of an old railroad, include a former home of American novelist **F. Scott Fitzgerald,** the Governor's Mansion, and the home of railroad magnate **James J. Hill,** 240 Summit Ave. (297-2555; 1¼-hr. tours Wed.-Sat. every ½hr. 10am-3:30pm; $4, seniors $3, ages 6-15 $2). Overlooking the capitol on Summit Ave. stands **St. Paul's Cathedral,** 239 Selby Ave. (228-1766), a scaled-down version of St. Peter's in Rome. (Mass daily 7:30am, also Thurs.-Tues. 5:15pm; open Thurs.-Tues. 7:30am-5:45pm.) Battle fieldtripping schoolchildren to see the golden horses atop the ornate **State Capitol** (296-3962 or 297-1503), at Cedar and Aurora St. (Tours on the hr. Mon.-Fri. 9am-4pm, Sat. 10am-3pm, Sun. 1-3pm. Open Mon.-Fri. 9am-5pm, Sat. 10am-4pm, Sun. 1-4pm.) The nearby **Minnesota History Center,** 345 Kellogg Blvd. W. (296-1430), an organization older than the state itself, houses three exhibit galleries on Minnesota history, as well as a café and gift shop (open Tues.-Sat. 10am-5pm, Thurs. 10am-9pm, Sun. noon-5pm; free). The society also runs a re-creation of life in the fur-trapping era at **Fort Snelling** (725-2413), far to the southwest at the intersection of Rte. 5 and 55, where elaborately costumed artisans, soldiers, and guides lead you through the 18th-century French fort. (Infantry drills daily 11:30am and 2:30pm. Open Mon.-Sat. 10am-5pm, Sun. noon-5pm. $4, seniors $3, ages 6-15 $2.) The historic **Landmark Center,** 75 W. 5th St. (292-3225), a grandly restored 1894 Federal Court building replete with towers and turrets, contains the **Minnesota Museum of Art** along with a collection of pianos, a concert hall, and four restored courtrooms. The museum keeps other collections in the **Jemne Building,** at St. Peter and Kellogg Blvd. (Museum open Tues.-Sat. 11am-4pm, Thurs. 11am-7:30pm, Sun. 1-5pm.) The **Science Museum,** 30 E. 10th St. (221-9454), near Exchange and Wabasha St., features displays on everything from paleontology to your own backyard, as well as an **OmniMax** theater. (Museum open Mon.-Fri. 9:30am-9pm, Sat. 9am-9pm, Sun. 10am-9pm. Museum only $5, seniors and under 13 $4; Omni only $6/$5; both $7/$6.)

Shop 'Til You Drop

About 10 min. south of downtown, **Mall of America,** 60 E. Broadway, Bloomington (883-8800), corrals an indoor rollercoaster, a ferris wheel, a minigolf course, and 2 mi. of stores in the largest mall in America. Shop until the funds run out, then try your luck panning for gold. Watch out: mind-boggling consumerism can be exhausting even when it's fun. (Take I-35E south to I-494W to the 24th Ave. exit; follow the signs. Open Mon.-Sat. 10am-9:30pm, Sun. 11am-7pm.)

ENTERTAINMENT

Second only to New York in number of theaters per capita, the Twin Cities bring musicals, comedy, opera, and experimental drama to the masses. The Twin Cities are filled with parks, and almost all feature free evening concerts in the summer; for information on dates and locations, check at one of the visitors centers. The thriving alternative, pop, and classical music scene fills out the wide arrange of entertainment options. For general information on the local music scene and other events, pick up the free and extremely useful *City Pages* or *Twin Cities Reader*, available throughout the cities.

Guthrie Theater, 725 Vineland Pl., Minneapolis (377-2224), adjacent to the Walker Art Center just off Hennepin Ave., stands out in the theater world, running shows from June to March. (Box office open Mon.-Sat. 9am-8pm, Sun. 11am-7pm. Tickets $10-40; rush tickets 10min. before show $10, line starts 1-1½hr. before show.) For family-oriented shows, try the **Children's Theater Company** (874-0400), at 3rd Ave. at 24th S. next to the Minneapolis Institute of Arts. (Season Sept.-June. Box office open Mon.-Sat. 9am-4pm. Tickets $9.50-24, seniors, students, and children $9-16; rush tickets 15min. before show $8.) For experimental theater, try the **Theatre de la jeune lune** ("Theater of the young moon"), which performs (in English) at the **Loring Playhouse,** 1645 Hennepin Ave. (333-6200; tickets $9-19, depending on day), and the **Illusion Theater,** 528 Hennepin Ave., 8th floor (338-8371; tickets $10). The **Penumbra Theatre Company,** 270 N. Kent St., St. Paul (224-3180), is Minnesota's only professional African-American theater company (box office open Mon.-Fri. 11am-4pm).

Dudley Riggs's **Brave New Workshop,** 2605 Hennepin Ave. (332-6620), stages consistently good musical comedy shows in an intimate club. (Box office open Mon. 5-8pm, Fri. 4-10pm, Sat. 4pm-12:30am, Sun. 4-9pm. Call for performance times. Tickets $12-15.) The **Comedy Gallery,** 219 Main St., S.E., Minneapolis, and **Galtier Plaza,** 175 E. 5th St., St. Paul (331-5653; tickets $5) feature stand-up comedians for 21+ audiences.

The Twin Cities' music scene offers everything from the opera to Paisley. **Sommerfest,** a month-long celebration of Viennese music performed by the **Minnesota Orchestra,** marks the high point of the cities' classical scene during July and August; **Orchestra Hall,** 1111 Nicollet Mall, Minneapolis (371-5656), downtown, hosts the event. (Box office open Mon.-Sat. 10am-6pm. Tickets $11-46; rush tickets for students with ID 30min. before show $6.75.) Nearby **Peavey Plaza,** in Nicollet Mall, holds free coffee concerts. The **St. Paul Chamber Orchestra,** the **Schubert Club,** and the **Minnesota Opera Company** all perform at St. Paul's glass-and-brick **Ordway Music Theater,** 345 Washington St. (224-4222; box office open Mon.-Sat. 10am-9pm; tickets $10-50). The man formerly known as **Prince** emerged from local status to make his mark on the world. Today, his state-of-the-art **Paisley Park** studio complex outside the city draws bands from all over to the Great White North.

The Twin Cities' festivals span the seasons. In January, the 10-day **St. Paul Winter Carnival,** near the state capitol, cures cabin fever with ice sculptures, ice fishing, parades, and skating contests. June brings the 12-day **Fringe Festival** (770-2233) for the performing arts (tickets $4-5). On July 4, St. Paul celebrates **Taste of Minnesota** on the Capitol Mall. Following the Fourth, the nine-day **Minneapolis Aquatennial** begins, with concerts, parades, art exhibits, and kids dripping sno-cones on their shirts. (Call **The Connection,** 922-9000, for information on all of these events.) During late August and early September, spend a day at the **Minnesota State Fair,** at Snelling and Como, or the **Renaissance Festival** (445-7361) in Shakopee, MN.

The **Hubert H. Humphrey Metrodome,** 501 Chicago Ave. S. (332-0386), in downtown Minneapolis, houses the **Minnesota Twins,** the Twin Cities' baseball team, and the **Minnesota Vikings,** the resident football team. The **Timberwolves** kindle basketball hardwood at the **Target Center,** 600 1st Ave. (673-0900).

NIGHTLIFE

Minneapolis' vibrant youth culture spawns most of the Twin Cities' clubs and bars. The post-punk scene thrives in the Land of 10,000 Aches: **Soul Asylum** and **Hüsker Dü,** as well as the best bar band in the world, **The Replacements,** rocked here before it all went big (or bad). Nightlife blooms on **Hennepin Ave.,** around the **University of Minnesota Minneapolis,** and across the river on the **West Bank** (bounded on the west by I-35W and to the south by I-94), especially on **Cedar Ave.** The Twin

Cities card hard, even for cigarettes, so carry your ID with you. After 1am, many clubs open their doors to the 18+ crowd; call clubs for specifics.

Ground Zero, 15 4th St. N.E. (378-5115), off Hennepin just north of the river, is a local fave, mushrooming with live music on Wednesdays, techno and dance other nights; Thursdays mean bondage and go-go (open until 1am). Prince's old court—**First Avenue and 7th St. Entry,** 701 First Ave. N. (332-1775), downtown, rocks with live music several nights a week for older folk; even Prince turns up occasionally (cover $1-5, for concerts $7-18; open Mon.-Sat. 8pm-1am). In the West Bank on 4th St. at Cedar Ave., the **400 Bar** (332-2903) features kicking live music nightly on a miniscule stage; acts range from local garage bands to national acts like Mazzy Star or the Rembrandts (cover Fri.-Sat. $2-5; open daily noon-1am). **Red Sea,** 316 Cedar Ave. (333-1644), has live reggae nightly and serves Ethiopian food and ethnic burgers ($4-5) until 11pm; bar closes at 1am. Try the **Uptown Bar and Café,** 3018 Hennepin (823-4719), near Lake Calhoun, for live music with high and low-profile bands and a great breakfast served until 8pm (shows around 10:30pm; weekend cover varies; open 8am-1am). **The Gay 90s** (333-7755), on Hennpin at 4th St., is a popular gay nightspot (open daily 8pm-3am). The top floor of the **Mall of America** (see p. 456) invites bar-hopping after the screaming kids have gone to bed; stop at **Fat Tuesdays** for drinks and move on from there. In St. Paul, **O'Gara's Garage,** 164 N. Snelling Ave. (644-3333), jams with big bands and jazz nightly in the Irish-theme front bar (no cover); live alternative and dance music plays in the back Fridays and Saturdays (cover $2; open daily until 1am; 21+ after 8pm).

■■■ DULUTH

With the world's longest dock line at 49 mi., Duluth claims the crown as King of the Great Lake ports. The city's glory days as an iron-ore shipping center have not been forgotten; the flagship of U.S. Steel's steampowered fleet floats in the harbor, while the massive Glensheen mansion (built with iron dollars) sits in splendor on the hill. Although shipping continues, Duluth increasingly hopes to become not only a gateway to the northern wilderness, but a vacation destination in itself; sculpture gardens, convention centers, and elaborate festivals vie with excursion outfitters in the pea soup fog and extreme cold.

Practical Information Four locations distribute tourist literature and maps in Duluth: **Convention and Visitors Bureau,** 100 Lake Place Dr. (722-4011), at Endion Station in Canal Park (open Mon.-Fri. 8:30am-5pm); the **Summer Visitors Center** (722-6024), at Vista dock on Harbor Dr. (open mid-May to mid-June and Labor Day to mid-Oct. daily 8:30am-7pm); **Holiday Center,** 207 W. Superior St. (open Mon.-Fri. 9am-5:15pm); **The Depot,** 506 W. Michigan St. (727-8025; open daily 10am-5pm; mid-Oct. to April Mon.-Sat. 10am-5pm, Sun. 1-5pm). **Greyhound,** 2212 W. Superior (722-5591; 722-6193 for recorded information; 800-231-2222), stops 2 mi. west of downtown; take bus #9 "Piedmont" from downtown and walk 1 block. Buses run to Milwaukee (3 per day, 10hr., $70) and St. Paul (3 per day, 2hr., $19). Buy tickets daily 6:45am-7pm. The **Duluth Transit Authority,** 2402 W. Michigan St. (722-7283), sends buses throughout the city (peak fare Mon.-Fri. 7-9am and 2:30-6pm $1, high-school students 75¢; off peak 50¢). Tourist mover extraordinaire, **Port Town Trolley** (722-7283), serves the downtown area, canal park, and the waterfront (runs Memorial Day-Labor Day daily 11am-7pm and Sept. weekends; 50¢). Local help lines include the **24-hour Sexual Assault Crisis Line** (726-1931) and the **Gay/Lesbian Resource Line** (722-4903; open daily 9am–7pm, otherwise leave a message). Duluth's **post office:** 2800 W. Michigan St. (723-2590), 6 blocks west and 1 block south of the Greyhound station (open Mon.-Fri. 8am-4:30pm, Sat. 10am-12:30pm); **ZIP code:** 55806; **area code:** 218.

Accommodations and Camping Duluth motels depend on the summer migration of North Shore-bound tourists for their livelihood. Rates rise and rooms fill during the warm months; call as far ahead as possible. The **College of St. Scholastica,** 1200 Kenwood Ave. (723-6396, ask for the housing director), rents out large, quiet dorm rooms with free local phone calls, kitchen access, and laundry facilities, from early June to mid-August (singles $18, doubles $36; reservations recommended). Group rates and week-long apartment rentals can be arranged. The **Willard Munger Inn,** 7408 Grand Ave. (624-4814 or 800-982-2453), at the base of Sprint Mountain across from the zoo, offers clean, comfortable rooms, some with kitchenettes (singles $30-41, doubles $39-49). Some relatively reasonable motels line **London Rd.,** west of downtown; try the **Chalet Motel,** 1801 London Rd. (728-4238 or 800-235-2957. Singles $32-41, doubles $42-51, 3 double beds $48-69, depending on season and owner's mood). The luxury of a large game room/bar/restaurant enhances the campsites at **Buffalo Valley** (624-9901), 15 mi. from Duluth off I-35S at exit 245. (Showers, bathrooms. 24-hr. patrol. Open 11am-1am; Sept.-May 3pm-1am. Sites $10, with hookup $14.) **Jay Cooke State Park** (384-4610), southwest of Duluth off exit 242 of I-35, has 80 campsites (21 with electricity), 50 mi. of hiking trails, 12 mi. of snowmobile trails, and 32 mi. for cross-country skiing, all among the tall trees of the dramatic St. Louis River valley. (Open daily 9am-9pm. $12, with electricity $14.50; Oct.-June, $10/$12.50. Vehicle permit $4.) **Spirit Mountain,** 9500 Spirit Mountain Pl. (628-2891 or 800-642-6377), near the ski resort of the same name, stretches skyward 10 mi. south on I-35 off exit 249 (beautiful, spacious sites $12, with electricity $15, with electricity and water $17).

Food The restored **Fitger's Brewery Complex,** 600 E. Superior St. (722-8826 or 800-726-2982), and the **Canal Park** region south from downtown along **Lake Ave.,** feature plenty of pleasant eateries, both chains and local. The **DeWitt-Seitz Marketplace,** on the south end of Canal St., has a number of slightly pricier restaurants for a variety of palates. **Hacienda del Sol,** 319 E. Superior St. (722-7296), drums up cheap, original Mexican recipes and occasional live music and poetry readings (entrees $4-6; open Mon.-Thurs. 11am-11pm, Fri.-Sat. 11am-midnight). In a mildly campy cottage overlooking the lake, **Sir Benedict's Tavern on the Lake,** 805 E. Superior St. (728-1192), serves soups ($2-4) and sandwiches ($4-6) with an English flair, as well as a wide variety of imported and microbrewery beers ($2-3). Those under 21 are not admitted without parents. (Live music Wed.-Thurs. free; open Mon.-Tues. 11am-midnight, Wed.-Sat. 11am-12:20am, Sun. 11am-11pm; in winter Mon.-Tues. 11am-11pm, Wed.-Sat. 11am-midnight; Sun. 11am-10pm.) The **Blue Note Café,** 357 Canal Park Dr. (727-6549), creates delicious sandwiches ($4-5) in a moody coffeehouse setting. (Live music Thurs.-Sat. 8-11pm; in winter Wed. 6-8pm and Fri.-Sat. 8-11pm. Open Mon.-Thurs. 9am-9pm, Fri.-Sat. 9am-11pm, Sun. 9am-6pm; in winter Mon.-Thurs. 9am-6pm, Fri.-Sat. 9am-11pm, Sun. 9am-5pm.) **Grandma's** restaurant and entertainment complex usurps nearly the entire wharf at the south end of Lake Ave. Inside, the saloon and deli serve sandwiches and pub fare, **Mickey's Grill** specializes in steaks, and the **Sports Garden** combines dining with full-court basketball, pool, arcade, and other games.

Sights and Entertainment Duluth's proximity to majestic Lake Superior is its biggest draw; many visitors just head right down to **Waterfront Canal Park** and watch the big ships go by. Call the **Boatwatcher's Hotline** (722-6489) for up-to-the-minute info on ship movements in the area. Accompanied by deafening horn blasts, the unique **Aerial Lift Bridge** climbs 138 ft. in 55 seconds to allow vessels to pass through the world's largest inland harbor; late afternoon is prime viewing time. Within **Canal Park,** the **Marine Museum** (727-2497), run by the U.S. Army Corps of Engineers, presents extensive exhibits on commercial shipping in Lake Superior. (Open daily 10am-9pm; early Sept. to mid-Dec. Mon.-Fri. 10am-4:30pm; mid-Dec to March Fri.-Sun. 10am-4:30pm; April-May Mon.-Fri. 10am-4:30pm, Sat.-Sun. 10am-6pm. Free.) International sculpture and art celebrating Duluth's sister cities in Sweden, Ontario, Russia, and Japan line the paths of the park. It's well worth a stroll;

pick up a free walking tour brochure at any information center. Across the Aerial Lift bridge, **Park Point** provides excellent swimming areas and sandy beaches.

The **Ore Docks Observation Platform,** part of the Duluth, Missabe, and Iron Range Railway Co., extends out into the harbor, allowing for outstanding views of the shiploading process and the harbor itself. The **Willard Munger State Trail** links West Duluth to Jay Cooke State Park, providing 14 scenic mi. of paved riding area for bikes and skates. To explore the trail, rent bikes or in-line skates from the Willard Munger Inn (see Accommodations, above; each $8 per ½day, $12 per day). For panoramic views of the city and harbor, visit **Skyline Pkwy.,** a 30-mi. road rising 600 ft. above the shoreline. A birdwatcher's paradise awaits at **Hawk Ridge,** 4 mi. north of downtown off Skyline Pkway. In order to avoid flying over open water, hawks steer their migration over Duluth; in September and October they fly past this bluff in flocks. The five-story stone octagonal **Enger Tower,** on Skyline Pkwy. at 18th Ave. W., rises from the highest land in Duluth; the nearby Japanese flower gardens make a beautiful picnic area.

A 39-room neo-Jacobean mansion built on wealth created by iron-shipping, **Glensheen,** 3300 London Rd. (724-8864), north towards the outskirts of town, gets even more interesting if you ask the tour guides where the double-murder, which reputedly occurred in the house during the early 1970s, actually took place. (Hours vary. $8, seniors and ages 12-15 $7, ages 6-11 $4, family $25. Grounds only $4. Make reservations for large groups up to 2 weeks in advance.) For further evidence of Duluth's shipping past, take a tour of the most visited ship on the Great Lakes, the steamer **William A. Irvin** (722-7876 or 722-5573), downtown on the waterfront (tours June-Sept. daily 9am-6pm; call for spring and fall times. $6, ages 3-11 $3.50).

The **Tweed Museum of Art** (726-8222), at the University of Minnesota-Duluth, maintains a collection of European and American paintings and mounts over 40 changing exhibits annually (open Tues. 9am-8pm, Wed.-Fri. 9am-4:30pm, Sat.-Sun. 1-5pm; free). Duluth's cultural calendar centers around **The Depot,** 506 W. Michigan St. (727-8025), an old converted Amtrak station that houses several museums and four performing arts groups. Among the museums, the **Lake Superior Museum of Transportation** stands out, displaying antique locomotives restored to shining splendor by retired railway workers. (Open daily 10am-5pm; mid-Oct. to April Mon.-Sat. 10am-5pm, Sun. 1-5pm. $5 includes all museums in The Depot; families $15, ages 3-11 $3.) The **Duluth-Superior Symphony Orchestra** (727-7560, Mon.-Fri. 8:30am-4:30pm; tickets $16-24, student rush $6.50), **Duluth Ballet, Duluth Playhouse,** and **Matinee Musicale** all strut their stuff in The Depot.

On the waterfront, **Bayfront Park** hosts many events and festivals, including the **Fourthfest** (July 4, of course) and the **Bayfront Blues Festival** in mid-August.

■■■ CHIPPEWA

Gleaming white stands of birch lace the Norway pine forests of the **Chippewa National Forest.** Home to the highest density of breeding bald eagles in the continental U.S., the forest sees these proud birds soaring over the Mississippi River between Cass Lake and Lake Winnie from mid-March to November. Wetlands and lakes usurp nearly half of the forest land, providing ample opportunities for canoeing and watersports. The national forest shares territory with the **Leech Lake Indian Reservation,** home to 4560 members of the Minnesota Chippewa tribe, the fourth largest tribe in the U.S.; the Chippewa migrated from the Atlantic coast in the 1700s, displacing the Sioux. In the mid-1800s, the government seized most of the Chippewa's land and set up reservations like Leech Lake.

Despite the huge statue of Paul Bunyan and Babe the Blue Ox in the parking lot of the visitors center in **Bemidji** (to the northwest), **Walker,** a smaller town on Leech Lake, makes a better gateway to the national forest with all the requisite wilderness activities and easier navigation. Travelers can find information at the **Leech Lake Area Chamber of Commerce** (547-1313 or 800-833-1118) on Rte. 371 downtown (open Mon.-Fri. 8am-4:30pm). The **Forest Office** (547-1044; superintendent 335-

Travel Gear

Supreme Convertible back-pack/carry-on suitcase with innovative hideaway suspension and parallel stay internal frame. Includes leather trim, lumbar support pad, torso and waist adjustments, and a dual pocket detachable daypack. Waterproof Cordura nylon, lifetime guarantee. 4400 cubic inches, 14" x 26" x 14". Black, Hunter, or Navy. *As seen on cover in Hunter.* $175

Backpack/Suitcase Hideaway suspension with an internal frame turns this backpack into a carry-on suitcase. Detachable daypack makes it three bags in one. Lightweight and versatile, Waterproof Cordura nylon, lifetime guarantee. 3750 cubic inches, 14" x 24" x 11". Black, Hunter, or Navy. *As seen on cover in Navy.* $130

Padded Toiletry Kit Large padded main compartment to protect contents. Mesh lid pocket with metal hook to hang kit on a towel rod or bathroom hook. Features two separate small outside pockets and detachable mirror. 9" x 4 3/4" x 4 1/4". Black, Evergreen, or Blue. *As seen on cover in Blue.* $20

Departure Pouch Great for travel or everyday use. Features a multitude of inside pockets to store passport, tickets, and monies. Includes see-thru mesh pocket, pen slots, and gusseted compartment. Can be worn over shoulder, around neck, or cinched around the waist. 6" x 12". Black, Evergreen, or Blue. *As seen on cover in Black.* $16

Padded Travel Pouch Main zipper compartment is padded to protect a compact camera or mini binoculars. Carries as a belt pouch, or use 1" strap to convert into waist or shoulder pack. Front flap is secured by a quick release closure. 6" x 9" x 3". Black, Evergreen, or Blue. *As seen on cover in Evergreen.* $26

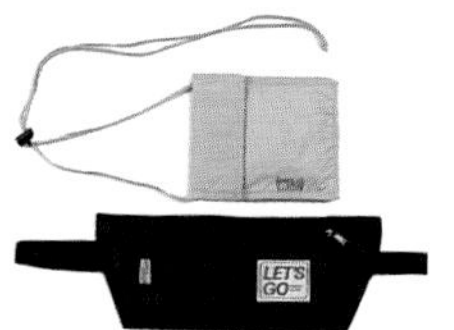

Undercover Neckpouch Ripstop nylon with a soft Cambrelle back. Three pockets. 5 1/4" x 6 1/2". Lifetime guarantee. Black or Tan. $9.95

Undercover Waistpouch Ripstop nylon with a soft Cambrelle back. Two pockets. 4 3/4" x 12" with adjustable waistband. Lifetime guarantee. Black or Tan. $9.95

*Prices and availability of products are subject to change.

1-800-5-LETS GO

Discounted Airfares

Available on international flights all over the world. Domestic fares too! For prices and reservations, call 1-800-5-LETS GO.

1996 International ID Cards

Provides discounts on accommodations, airfares, tourist attractions, rental cars and more! Also includes basic accident and medical insurance. Instructions for ordering are located on the next page, at top of order form.

International Student ID Card (ISIC)....................$18
International Teacher ID Card (ITIC)....................$19
International Youth ID Card (GO25)...............$18

Hostelling Essentials

1996-97 Hostelling Membership: Often required at international hostels. Cardholders usually receive first preference and discounts. Must have a U.S. address to apply.

Adult (ages 18-55)...$25
Youth (under 18)..$10
Senior and Family memberships also available.Please call.

Sleepsack: Required at all hostels. Two thin sheets sewn together (78" x 30") with 18" pillow pocket. Durable poly/cotton. Washable, folds into pouch size..$13.95

1996 International Youth Hostel Guide (IYHG): Contains essential information about the 4000 hostels located in Europe and the Mediterranean. $10.95

Travel Guides

Let's Go Travel Guides: The bible of the budget traveler! All 22 titles available.

Europe • USA & Canada................................$18.99

Regional & Country Guides (please specify)....$16.99
Alaska & The Pacific Northwest • Austria & Switzerland • Britain & Ireland • California & Hawaii • Central America • Eastern Europe • France • Germany • Greece & Turkey • Ireland • Israel & Egypt • Italy • Mexico • Southeast Asia • Spain & Portugal

City Guides (please specify)..........................$15.99
London • New York City • Paris • Rome • Washington, DC.

Let's Go Map Guides: New item for 1996! Includes fold-out maps and up to 40 pages of text!

City Maps (please specify) $7.95
Boston • London • New York City • Paris • San Francisco • Washington, DC

Eurail Passes

The most convenient and affordable way to travel in Europe. Save up to 70% off the cost of individual tickets.

Prices listed are 1995 prices. 1996 prices were not available at time of publishing; prices are expected to increase 5% to 6% and are subject to change. Please call before ordering to verify prices.

Eurailpass (First Class): Unlimited train travel for a specified duration of time. Accepted in 17 countries.

15 days..$498
21 days..$648
1 month..$798
2 months..$1098
3 months..$1398

Eurail Flexipass (First Class): Individual travel days that can be used at your convenience within a two month period.

Any 5 days in 2 months................................$348
Any 10 days in 2 months.............................$560
Any 15 days in 2 months.............................$740

Eurail Youthpass (Second Class): The same advantages of the Eurailpass but for those travelers who will be under 26 years old by the first date of the travel on the train.

15 days..$398
1 month..$578
2 months..$1078

Eurail Youth Flexipass (Second Class): The convenience of the Eurail Flexipass but for those travelers who will be under 26 years old by the first date of the travel on the train.

Any 5 days in 2 months................................$225
Any 10 days in 2 months.............................$398
Any 15 days in 2 months.............................$540

Europass: Offers the option of purchasing travel days within a two month period for 3, 4, or 5 country combinations for the following countries: France • Germany • Italy • Spain • Switzerland. Associate countries can also be added. Call for more details.

Regional and Country Passes and **Point-to-Point Tickets** also available. Call for more details.

1-800-5-LETS GO

Order Form

Please print or type. Incomplete applications will not be processed.

International Student/Teacher Identity Card (ISIC/ITIC) (ages 12 and up) enclose:

1. Proof of status (letter from registrar or administrator, proof of tuition payment, or copy of student/faculty ID card. FULL-TIME only.)
2. One picture (1 1/2" x 2") signed on the reverse side.
3. Proof of birthdate (copy of passport, birth certificate, or driver's license).

GO25 card (ages 12-25) enclose:

1. Proof of birthdate (copy of passport, birth certificate, or driver's license).
2. One picture (1 1/2" x 2") signed on the reverse side.

Last Name　　First Name　　Date of Birth

Street　　*We do not ship to P.O. Boxes.*

City　　State　　Zip Code

Phone (very important!)　　Citizenship (Country)

School/College　　Date of Travel

Description, Size	Color	Quantity	Unit Price	Total Price

Shipping & Handling		
Domestic	Total Merchandise Price	
If order totals ....add	Shipping and Handling (See box at left)	
up to $30.00.......................$4	Add $10 for Rush, $20 for Overnight	
$30.01-100.00....................$6	MA Residents (Add 5% sales tax on gear & books)	
over $100.00......................$8	**Total**	
add additional $5 for AK & HI		
International		
via Federal Express............$30	From which Let's Go Guide are you ordering?	

Master Card/Visa/Amex Order
cardholder name________
card number________
expiration date________

Allow 2-3 weeks for delivery. Rush orders guaranteed within one week of our receipt.

Make check or money order payable to:

Let's Go Travel

53A Church Street • Cambridge, MA 02138 • USA

1-800-5-LETS GO

8600), just east of town on Rte. 371, has the dirt on outdoor activities (open Mon.-Fri. 7:30am-5pm). **Greyhound** (722-5591) runs from Minneapolis to Walker (1 per day, 5½ hr., $35), stopping at the **Lake View Laundrette** (547-9585), 1st and Michigan St. just east of the Chamber of Commerce. A south-bound bus leaves daily at 8:30am, a north-bound at 3:30pm; purchase tickets at the next station. Chippewa National Forest Area's **area code:** 218.

Camping—cheap, plentiful, and available in various degrees of modernity—is the way to stay. For info on forest campgrounds, over 400 of which are free, contact the forest office. North of Walker, billboards for private campgrounds string along the edges of Rte. 371; **Camper Landing, Inc.** (335-9941), County Road 92, stands out, offering quiet, scenic sites along Leech Lake ($12, with hookup $14). Indoors, **Barley's Resort** (547-1464), 4½ mi. north off Kabekona Bay Rd., rents comfortable cabins with full kitchens starting at $470 per week for four people; reserve early. The cabins at **Stoney Point Resort** (335-6311 or 800-332-6311), 16 mi. east of town on Rte. 2, sleep up to eight people; prices start at $78 per day for a four-person cabin. Tent and RV sites run $12-15 depending on degree of hookup.

M I double-S I double-S I double-P I

Step across the mighty Mississippi at its source, officially (and cleverly!) known as the **Beginning of the Mississippi,** at **Lake Itasca State Park,** 30 mi. west of Chippewa National Forest on Rte. 200. The park office (266-3654), through the north entrance and down County Rd. 38, has info on camping (office open daily 8am-4:30pm; park open daily 8am-10pm; ranger on call after hours). Located in a renovated building, the comfortable **Mississippi Headwaters HI-AYH Hostel** (266-3415), includes 34 beds with some four-bed rooms for families. The hostel stays open in the winter to facilitate access to the park's excellent cross-country skiing. (2-night min. stay on certain weekends. Check-in Sun.-Thurs. 5-10pm, Fri.-Sat. 5-11pm. Check-out Mon.-Fri. 10am, Sat.-Sun. 1pm. Memorial Day-Labor Day and winter weekends $13, nonmembers $16; otherwise $11/14. Key deposit $5. Linen $2-4.) In the park, **Itasca Sports Rental** (266-3654, ext. 150) offers mountain bikes ($3.50 per hr., $20 per day), canoes ($3/$18), and 6-h.p. motorboats ($12 for 2 hr., $30 per day; open May-Oct. daily 7am-9pm).

■■■ THE IRON RANGE

Long before the presence of mere humans, the giant Mesabi roamed through northern Minnesota, creating lakes with every step. When he grew tired and lay down to sleep, the earth slowly covered him and formed mountains. According to Native American legend, he would awake after a snowless winter. Well, the snowless winter of 1890 did not wake him; it did, however, coincide with the discovery of iron in the hills. Miners rushed to the area, and their excavations made rust-red caverns along the edges of the pristine Border Waters Canoe Access Wilderness along the U.S.-Canada border. **Route 169** runs from Grand Rapids 120 mi. northeast to Ely through defunct, tourable mines as well as Minnesota's inescapable wilderness.

Grand Rapids Toto, I don't think we're in Kansas anymore. The former home of **Judy Garland,** this small paper mill town stands at the southwest corner of the Iron Range, offering a convenient starting point for a trip through the mines. The town celebrates its native daughter with its own Yellow Brick Road, and the **Judy Garland Historical Center,** 10 5th St. NW, (218-326-6431), in the Central School (open Memorial Day-Labor Day Mon.-Sat. 10am-5pm, Sun. 11am-4pm). The **Judy Garland Festival** (218-326-6431) throws a party each year around her birthday on June 10. See a re-created turn-of-the-century mining camp at the **Forest History Center,** 2609 Country Rd. 76 (218-327-4482), off Rte. 2W or Rte. 169S. ($4, seniors $3, ages 6-15 $2. Open mid-May to mid-Oct. Mon.-Sat. 10am-5pm, Sun. noon-5pm; interpretive center and trails also open mid-Oct. to mid-May daily noon-4pm.)

Grand Rapids's cheapest, most convenient lodging awaits at the **Motel Americana,** 1915 Rte. 2W (218-326-0369 or 800-533-5148; singles $25, doubles $29; most rooms have refrigerators). **Prairie Lake Campground,** 400 Wabana Rd. (218-326-8486), 6½ mi. north of town on Rte. 38, has a nice, shady waterfront location with showers, flush toilets, and canoe/paddleboat rentals (tent sites $9.75, with varying degrees of hookup $11.75-$15.75).

To get to Grand Rapids, click your heels together three times and say "There's no place like home..." or just settle on a **Greyhound** bus from Duluth ($15.40) or Minneapolis ($29). Buses stop at the **Redding Bus Depot** (218-326-37226), on Fourth St. next to Variety Cleaners (open daily 9-11am, 1-3pm). **Arrowhead Transit,** 308 2nd Ave. NE (326-3505), serves the local area, with fares from 50¢ to $1.25.

A little northeast of Grand Rapids in **Calumet,** drop in at the **Hill Mine Annex State Park** (247-7215), a now-retired intact natural iron ore pit mine. An exceptional 90min. tour brings visitors through the buildings and shops and all the way into the 500-ft.-deep mine, where guides who once worked this mine relive their experience for visitors. The $5 admission is money well spent (ages 5-12 $3).

Hibbings and Chisholm The answer, my friend, is blowing in **Hibbing,** the hometown of Robert Zimmerman (a.k.a. **Bob Dylan**). Don't miss the largest open-pit ore mine in the area, **Hull Rust Mahoning Mine** (262-4900); take Third Ave. E. to the north until it ends (open mid-May to Sept. daily 9am-7pm). Greyhound spent its puppyhood here as a transport for miners in the Hibbing area; carless travelers in particular may wish to pay tribute at the **Greyhound Bus Origin Center** (262-3895), at 23rd St. and 5th Ave. E., where exhibits include model buses and a zillion bus cartoons (open mid-May to Sept. Mon.-Sat. 9am-5pm; $1, ages 6-12 50¢). Flags from around the world fly on the **Longyear Lake Bridge of Peace,** which connects Hibbings to **Chisholm,** home to **Ironworld USA** (254-3321 or 800-372-6437), a mining theme park which contains displays on the area's ethnic groups. (Open Memorial Day-Labor Day daily 10am-7pm. $6.50, seniors $5.50, ages 7-17 $4.50.) **Adams House,** 201 E. 23rd St. (263-9742), lets double rooms in a beautiful Tudor-style B&B for $43. **Forest Heights,** 2240 E. 25th St. (263-5782), offers camping (tents $6, RVs $12; showers $1.50). The **Hibbing Chamber of Commerce** is at 211 East Howard St. (218-262-3895; open Mon.-Fri. 8am-5pm).

In **Eveleth,** 20 mi. east, the **U.S. Hockey Hall of Fame** (744-5167), at Rte. 53 and Trick Ave., honors the hockey greats of Eveleth and elsewhere (open Mon.-Sat. 9am-5pm, Sun. 11am-5pm; $3, ages 13-17 $2, ages 6-12 $1.75).

Soudan and Ely Plunge into the **Soudan Underground Mine** (753-2245), in Soudan on Rte. 1, where visitors take a 90-minute tour to the 17th level of digging, ½ mi. beneath the earth's surface. (Tours Memorial Day-Labor Day every ½ hr. 9:30am-4pm; off season by reservation. $5, ages 5-12 $3, plus $4 state park vehicle fee. Gates open until 6pm; off season by reservation.) Next to the mine, **McKinley Park Campground** (753-5921) rents semi-private campsites overlooking gorgeous Vermilion lake (sites $10, with hookup $11.50).

Serving as a launching pad both into the **Boundary Waters Canoe Area Wilderness (BWCAW)** and the Iron Range, **Ely** supports its share of wilderness outfitters. Head to the **Chamber of Commerce,** 1600 E. Sheridan St. (365-6123 or 800-777-7281), for BWCAW permits and brochures on various guides. (Open in summer Mon.-Sat. 9am-6pm, Sun. noon-4pm; off season Mon.-Fri. 9am-5pm.) The **International Wolf Center,** 1396 Rte. 169 (365-4685), has informative displays on the history, habitat, and behaviors of these creatures. (Open daily 9am-7pm; Sept. to mid-Oct. and May-June 9am-5pm; mid-Oct. to April Tues. and Fri.-Sat. 10am-5pm, Sun. 10am-3pm. $4, seniors and ages 6-12 $2.50.) Next door, The **Dorothy Molter Museum** (365-4451), honors the "Root Beer Lady of Knife Lake." Not only was Ms. Molter the last year-round resident of the BWCAW, but she brewed eleven to twelve *thousand* bottles of root beer each year. (Open May-Sept. daily 10am-6pm. $2, children $1.) **Shagawa Sam's,** 60 W. Lakeview Pl. (365-6757), Ely, has a tidy loft full of bunks for $10 per night, including linen and showers, plus some campsites and cabins (tent sites $6, RV sites $10, $1.50 each for water and electricity; cabin for 4 $60-65). While in town, let the **Chocolate Moose,** 101 N. Central (356-6343), a favorite of locals and canoeists alike, tempt you with blueberry pancakes ($4). A BBQ with ribs ($10) and chicken ($9.25) takes over on Friday and Saturday nights (open daily 6am-9pm, ice cream until 10pm; breakfast served 6-11am).

■■■ LAKE SUPERIOR NORTH SHORE

Rte. 61 Although the true Lake Superior North Shore extends 646 mi. from Duluth, MN to Sault Ste. Marie, ONT, **Rte. 61 (North Shore Dr.),** hugging the coast from Duluth to Grand Portage, gives travelers an abbreviated but by no means diluted version of the journey. Boat-dragging trucks and family-filled campers chug along past the endless expanse of steel-blue water that appears through each break in the trees. Small, touristy fishing towns separate the 31,000-sq.-mi. inland sea (comprising 10% of the world's freshwater surface area) from the moose, bear, and wolves inland. The kamping kabins, cottages, and luxurious resorts that flank the roadside fill up fast in summer; make reservations early. Remember to bring warm clothes; temperatures can drop into the low 40s (°F) at night in summer.

Most towns along the shore maintain a visitors information center. The **Lake County Information Center** (218-834-4005 or 800-554-2116), 30 mi. from Duluth up Rte. 61 in Two Harbors, has lodging guides and information for each town along the MN stretch of the North Shore. (Open mid-May to mid-Oct. Mon.-Thurs. 10am-6pm, Fri-Sat. 10am-8pm, Sun. noon-4pm.) **Happy Trails** runs one bus per day up the shore from the **Duluth Greyhound Station,** 2122 W. Superior St. (218-722-5591; open daily 7am-9pm); to Grand Marais ($28).

Boundary Waters Canoe Area Wilderness (BWCAW) At its northern end, Rte. 61 runs along BWCAW, a designated wilderness comprising 1.2 million acres of lakes, streams, and forests (including part of **Superior National Forest**) in which no man-made improvements—phones, roads, electricity, private dwellings—are allowed. Within the BWCAW, small waterways and portages string together 1100 lakes, allowing virtually limitless "canoe-camping." Running northwest from **Grand Marais,** the 60-mi., paved **Gunflint Trail** (County Rd. 12) is the only developed road offering access to the wilderness; resorts and outfitters gather around this lone strip of civilization. The BWCAW permits the use of motorized boats only at Seagull Lake, at the far end of the trail.

The **Tip of the Arrowhead Visitors Information Center** (218-387-2524), off Rte. 61 in Grand Marais, has information on the BWCAW and the Minnesota portion of the North Shore (open in summer Mon.-Sat. 8:30am-7pm, Sun. 11am-7pm; call for winter hours). The **Gunflint Ranger Station** (218-387-2451), ¼ mi. south of town, distributes the permits required to enter the BWCAW from May to September (open in summer daily 6am-6pm).

At the end of the Gunflint Trail, the well-kept cabins of **"Spirit of the Land" Island Hostel (HI-AYH)** (218-388-2241 or 800-454-2922), float on an island in Seagull Lake. **Wilderness Canoe Base,** which leads canoe trips and summer island camps for various groups, administers the hostel. Call from Grand Marais to arrange a boat pick-up. (Full kitchen, outhouses. Beds $13, Fri.-Sun. $15, nonmembers $15/$17. Meals $4-6. Hot showers $2. Saunas $3. Closed Nov. and April.) Closer to civilization, the pine-paneled **Cobblestone Cabins** (218-663-7957), off Rte. 61 in Tofte, come with access to a cobblestone beach and a woodburning sauna (cabins for 1-12 $40-85; some have kitchenettes). The elegant **Naniboujou Lodge** (218-387-2688), 15 mi. northeast of Grand Marais on Rte. 61, offers summer/fall family rates on rooms with shared baths ($50, doubles $65). Cheap and popular with the fishermen, **South of the Border Café,** 4 W. Rte. 61 (218-387-1505), in Grand Marais, specializes in huge breakfasts and satisfying, greasy food. The bluefin herring sandwich (fried, of course) will run you $2.75. (Open daily 5am-2pm.)

■■■ VOYAGEURS

Voyageurs National Park sits on Minnesota's boundary with Ontario, accessible almost solely by boat. Named for the French-Canadian fur traders who once traversed this area, the park invites today's voyagers to leave the auto-dominated world and push off into the longest inland lake waterway on the continent. While some hiking trails exist, boats and canoes provide most transportation within the park; in the winter, when ice freezes to more than 1½ ft. thick, it is frequently possible to drive through plowed parts of the park. Preservation efforts have kept the area much as it was in the late 18th century, and wolves, bear, deer, and moose roam freely. Remember that undeveloped often means uncontrolled; water should be boiled for at least two minutes before consumption. Many fish in these waters contain mercury. Lyme-disease-bearing ticks have been found in the area as well; visitors should take precautions. (For more details, see To Your Health, p. 11.)

The park can be accessed through **Crane Lake, Ash River,** or **Kabetogama Lake,** all of which lie east of Rte. 53, or through **International Falls,** at the northern tip of Rte. 53 just below Ft. Frances, Ontario. Outside the park, call **Crane Lake Visitor and Tourism Bureau,** 7238 Handberg Rd. (993-2234 or 800-362-7405; Mon.-Fri. 9am-5pm), or visit the **International Falls Visitors and Convention Bureau**, 200 Fourth St. (800-325-5766; open daily 8am-5pm). Within the park, three visitors centers serve tourists: **Rainy Lake** (286-5258), 12 mi. east of International Falls at the end of Rte. 11; **Ash River** (374-3221), 7 mi. west of Rte. 53 on Rte. 129, then 4 mi. north (open mid-May to Aug. daily 10am-5pm; closed for road construction, scheduled to re-open in June 1996); and **Kabetogama Lake** (875-2111), 1 mi. east of Rte. 53, then follow the signs (open mid-May to Sept. daily 9am-5pm). In addition to free walks and programs, both Rainy Lake and Kabetogama Lake arrange **cruises** ($8-32.50; call Rainy Lake at 286-5470 or Kabetogama at 875-2111 for more info). Voyageur's **area code:** 218.

Many of the park's numerous **campsites** are accessible only by water. Car-accessible sites can be found in state forest campgrounds, including **Wooden Frog** (757-3274), about 4 mi. from Kabetogama Visitors Center Rd. 122, and **Ash River** (757-3274), 3 mi. from the visitors center and 2 mi. east on Rte. 129 ($7, no showers). Only five minutes from International Falls, **International Voyageurs RV Campground** (283-4679), off Rte. 53 south of town, offers decent camping—cheap sites, showers, and laundry facilities. What more could you want? (Sites $8, with full hook-up $12.) **Rocky Pine Campground** (286-3500), lies 9 mi. east of town (showers, toilets; sites $10). For a roof and a bed, try the **Hilltop Motel** (283-2505 or 800-322-6671), Rte. 53 in International Falls (singles $32, Fri.-Sat. $44; doubles $34/$45). No phones or TVs spoil the rooms of **Lakeview Motel,** 7533 Gold Coast Rd. (993-2398; 749-3635 in winter), in Crane Lake by the shore (doubles $35, triples $39).

International Falls, the "Icebox of the Nation" and the inspiration for **Rocky and Bullwinkle's** hometown Frostbite Falls, hosts a few non-park attractions. The state's largest prehistoric burial ground, **Grand Mound History Center** (279-3332), 17 mi. west of town on Hwy. 11, supposedly dates from 200BC. (Open May-Aug. Mon.-Sat. 10am-5pm; Sept.-Oct. Sat. 10am-4pm, Sun. noon-4pm. Free.) **Smokey Bear Park,** home of a 22-ft.-tall thermometer and the 26-ft., 82-ton giant who asks you to help fight forest fires, rounds out the offerings with some lighter entertainment.

GREAT PLAINS

Between the big cities of the East and West Coasts, the Rocky Mountains and the Great Lakes, lies the Heartland of the United States—a vast land of prairies and farms, less developed and less appreciated than the rest of the country. Here, open sky stretches from horizon to horizon, unbroken by mountain, forest, or skyscraper. Grasses and grains paint the land green and gold; the plains breadbasket feeds the country and much of the world.

A young America suddenly acquired these lands west of the Mississippi when Thomas Jefferson purchased the Louisiana Territory from France. Over time, the plains spawned legends of the pioneers and cowboys who sought to conquer the frontier, and of the Native Americans who sought to defend it. With the Homestead Act of 1862, the land-hungry settlers who invaded the area as farmers realized that the Great Plains were prize farmlands, not just a flat barrier to cross en route to the fertile valleys of the West Coast. The act and the new transcontinental railroad brought bloody struggles over land rights, and later over slavery; they also began an economic boom that lasted until a drought during the Great Depression transformed the region into a devastated Dust Bowl. Modern farming techniques have since reclaimed the soil, and the heartland now produces most of the nation's grain and livestock; cities such as Des Moines, Omaha, and Dodge City thrive on the trade of farm commodities.

Despite the touch of man, the land still rules here, and the most staggering sights in the region are the work of nature—the Badlands of the Dakotas, the prairies of North Dakota, the vast caverns of Missouri, the rolling hills of Iowa, the Willa Cather Memorial Prairie in Nebraska, and the rising Black Hills, which mark the transition from plains to mountains. The mighty Missouri and Mississippi Rivers trace their way through the thriving small towns of America, while "amber waves of grain" quietly reign among the greatest of American symbols.

People on the Plains

Authors: Willa Cather *(My Ántonia)*, Louise Erdich, Mari Sandoz, John Steinbeck, Mark Twain, Ian Frazier *(The Great Plains)*.
Artists: Thomas Hart Benton, John Stuart Curry, Grant Wood.
Cuisine: red meat and potatoes, freshwater fish, pan-fried chicken.
Microbreweries: Dubuque, Dallas County, Millstream, Miracle Brewing Co.
Native Americans: Cheyenne, Sioux, Kansas, Pawnee, Arapaho, Crow, Dakota, Iowa, Missouri, Kansa, Osage, Kiowa, Omaha.
Music: Jazz, Blues, Kansas.
Film and TV: *Boys Town, The Grapes of Wrath, Field of Dreams, Little House on the Prairie, The Wizard of Oz, Oklahoma!*
Climate: Summer thunderstorms and heat, winter is very cold.
Geography: Flat.

North Dakota

An early visitor to the site of present-day Fargo declared, "It's a beautiful land, but I doubt that human beings will ever live here." Posterity begs to differ. The stark, haunting lands that so intimidated early settlers found an audience, and the territory became a state along with South Dakota on November 2, 1889. Ultimately, the momentous event did not go off without confusion—because Benjamin Harrison concealed the names when he signed the two bills, both Dakotas claim to be the 39th state.

North Dakota has remained largely isolated. In the western half, the colorful buttes of the Badlands rise in desolate beauty, while in the eastern half, mind-numbing flatness and emptiness rule; the 110 mi. of Rte. 46 from U.S. 81 to Rte. 30 is the longest stretch of highway in the U.S. without a single curve.

PRACTICAL INFORMATION

Capital: Bismarck.
Tourism Department: 604 East Blvd., Bismarck 58505 (701-328-2525 or 800-437-2077). **Parks and Recreation Department,** 1424 W. Century Ave. #202, Bismarck 58502 (701-221-5357). Both open Mon.-Fri. 8am-5pm.
Time Zones: Mostly Central (1hr. behind Eastern). *Let's Go* makes note of areas in Mountain (2hr. behind Eastern). **Postal Abbreviation:** ND
Sales Tax: 6%.

■■■ FARGO

In the 1880s, easy divorce laws and a large concentration of lawyers made Fargo a premier divorce destination; unhappy couples from all over the U.S. and Europe traveled to Fargo for a ten-minute divorce. Though Fargo is no longer the favored site for a quickie divorce, people still pass through at a rapid pace.

Amtrak, 402 4th St. N (232-2197 or 800-872-7245), chugs four trains per week to Minneapolis (5hr, $53) and Williston (8hr., $69). (Open nightly midnight-7am, Fri. also 8am-3:30pm.) **Greyhound,** 402 Northern Pacific (N.P.) Ave. (293-1222 or 800-231-2222), lopes to Minneapolis (5 per day, 4-7hr., $32) and Bismarck (3 per day, 5hr., $28). (Open daily 6am-6pm and 10:30pm-4am; closed Sun. 8am-1pm.)

Fargo's **Main Ave.** runs east-west and intersects **I-29, University Dr.,** and **Broadway.** If you find Fargo just *too much,* sort things out at the **Fargo-Moorhead Convention and Visitors Bureau,** 2001 44th St. SW (282-3653 or 800-235-7654; open daily 7am-9pm, Sept.-April daily 8am-6pm). For help, dial the 24-hr. **Crisis Line,** 232-4357. Fargo's **post office:** 657 2nd Ave. N (241-6100; open Mon.-Fri. 7:30am-5:30pm, Sat. 8am-2pm); **ZIP code:** 58103; **area code:** 701.

Cheap chain motels line I-29 and 13th Ave. **The Sunset Motel,** 731 W. Main (800-252-2207), in West Fargo, shines with huge rooms, a spa, and an indoor pool with a two-story waterslide. Call early on weekends. (Singles $22, doubles $35; kitchenettes $5 extra.) **Moorhead State University** (218-236-2231) rents rooms with linens and phones in Ballard Hall, just north of 9th Ave. on 14th St. (check-in 24 hrs., $10 per person) **Lindenwood Park** (232-3987), at 17th Ave. and 5th St. S, offers campsites close to the peaceful Red River and the not-so-peaceful train tracks ($8, with hookup $14). **Old Broadway,** 22 Broadway (237-6161), serves as the ubiquitous midwestern microbrewery, serving burgers ($5-10), and beer cheese soup ($3). After 11pm it's a popular nightspot. (Open Mon.-Sat. 11am-1am.) **Pannekoeken,** 3340 13th Ave. SW (237-3569), has incredible Dutch oven-baked pancakes ($5-6; open Sun.-Thurs. 6am-11pm, Fri.-Sat. 6am-midnight). At night, NDSU students descend upon the bars along Broadway near Northern Pacific Ave.

The **Heritage Hjemkomst Interpretive Center,** 202 1st Ave. N (218-233-5604), in Moorhead, displays traveling exhibits from around the world as well as a 76-ft. hand-built replica of a Viking ship. (Open Mon.-Sat. 9am-5pm, Thurs. 9am-9pm; Sun. noon-5pm. $3.50, ages 5-17 $1.50.) In mid-July, the **Red River Valley Fair** (800-456-6408), off Main Ave. in West Fargo, brings live music and carnival rides to Fargo.

■■■ THEODORE ROOSEVELT

Theodore Roosevelt appreciated the beauty of the Badlands' red- and brown-hued lunar-like formations so much that he bought a ranch here. He came here to find

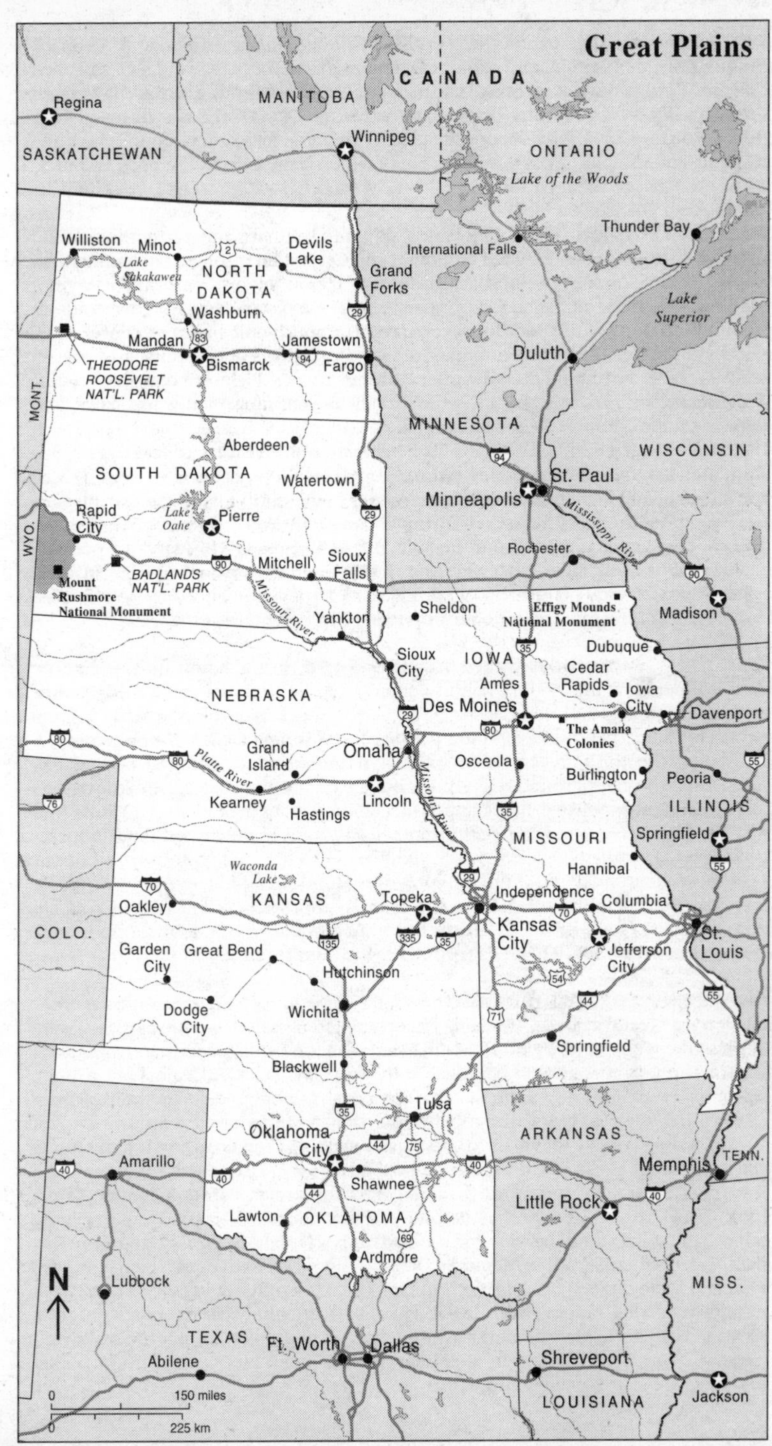

GREAT PLAINS

spiritual renewal after his mother and his wife died on the same day. Horseback riding, big-game hunting, and cattle ranching in this unforgiving land so influenced the pre-White House Roosevelt that he later claimed, "I never would have been President if it weren't for my experiences in North Dakota." Today's visitor to **Theodore Roosevelt National Park** can achieve the same inspiration among the quiet canyons and dramatic rocky outcroppings which have earned the park the nickname "rough-rider country."

Practical Information The park is split into southern and northern units and bisected by the border between Mountain and Central time zones. The entrance to the better-developed south unit is just north of I-94 in the historic frontier town of **Medora.** The **park entrance fee** ($4 per vehicle, $2 per pedestrian) covers admission to both units of the park for seven days. The **south unit's visitors center** (623-4466), in Medora, maintains a mini-museum; see Teddy's guns, spurs, and old letters, as well as a beautiful film of winter Badlands scenes. Pick up a copy of *Frontier Fragments,* the park newspaper, which has listings of ranger-led walks, talks, and demonstrations. (Open daily 8am-8pm; Sept. to mid-June 8am-4:30pm.) The **south unit's emergency** number is 623-4379. The **north unit's visitors center** (842-2333) dispenses free overnight camping permits (open May-Sept. daily 9am-5:30pm). Call the ranger at 842-2137 in case of an **emergency** in the north unit. For more information, write to Theodore Roosevelt National Park, P.O. Box 7, Medora 58645-0007. **Greyhound** serves Medora from the Sully Inn, with buses to Bismarck (3 per day, 3½hr., $21) and Billings (2 per day, 6hr., $43). Medora's **post office:** 355 3rd Ave. (open Mon.-Fri. 8am-noon, 12:30-4:30pm, Sat. 8:15-9:45am); **zip code:** 58645; **area code:** 701. **South Unit Time Zone:** Mountain (2hr. behind Eastern).

Camping, Accommodations, and Food In the south unit, get a free camping permit at the Medora visitors center or try the **Cottonwood Campgrounds** in the park (toilets and running water; sites $8). Check in at the north unit visitors center for a free overnight camping permit, or try **Squaw Creek Campground,** 5 mi. west of the north unit entrance (toilets and running water; sites $8). During mating season, the campground is a popular buffalo night-spot—just so you know.

You can find expensive, non-camping accommodations in Medora. The **Sully Inn,** 401 Broadway (623-4455), offers tiny and clean rooms at the lowest rates in town, plus free local calls (singles $25-$35, doubles $30-$40). Teddy Roosevelt himself was known to bunk down at the **Rough Riders Hotel** (623-4444, ext. 297), at 3rd St. and 3rd Ave. The hotel's restaurant serves pasta, sandwiches, and burgers (buffalo and otherwise) for $5-$7. Say "Hi" to the stuffed buffalo in the lobby. (Open mid-June to Labor Day Sun.-Thurs. 7am-9pm, Fri.-Sat. 7am-10pm.)

Sights and Entertainment The south unit features a 36-mi. **scenic automobile loop,** a great way to see the park; many hiking trails start from the loop and wander into the wilderness. **Wind Canyon,** located on the loop, is a constantly mutating canyon formed by winds blowing against the soft clay. The **Coal Vein Trail,** a ¾-mi. self-guided tour, follows a seam of lignite coal that caught fire here and burned from 1951 to 1977. For 26 years, the smoking, glowing vein was a tourist attraction; park visitors would come to gawk or to roast marshmallows. The fire's out, but the tour's still interesting. The U.S.'s third largest **petrified forest** lies a day's hike into the park; if you prefer to drive, ask at the visitors center for a map. **Painted Canyon Overlook,** 7 mi. east of Medora, has its own **visitors center** (575-4020), with picnic tables, and a breathtaking view of the Badlands. (Open Memorial Day-Labor Day daily 8am-6pm; mid-April to Memorial Day and Labor Day to mid-Nov. 8am-4:30pm.) **Peaceful Valley Ranch** (623-4496), 7 mi. into the park, offers a variety of horseback riding excursions, ranging from 1¼-hr. ($12) to overnight. Near the ranch, go for a swim in the lazy **Little Missouri**—warm, shallow, and quiet. **Rough Rider Adventures** (623-4808), on 3rd St. in Medora, rents mountain bikes ($15 for 4hr.; open mid-June to Labor Day daily 8am-8pm).

The less-visited **north unit** of the park is 75 mi. from the south unit on U.S. 85. Most of the land is wilderness, resulting in virtually unlimited backcountry hiking possibilities. Be careful not to surprise the buffalo; one ranger advises singing while hiking so they can hear you coming. The **Caprock Coulee Trail** journeys through prairie, river valley, mountain ridge, and juniper forest, all in the space of 4 mi.

In Medora, the **Museum of the Badlands** (623-4451), on 3rd and Main St., exhibits Plains Indians' artifacts and local natural history (open mid-May to Labor Day daily 9am-8pm; $2.50, ages 6-16 $1). The popular **Medora Musical** (623-4444), in the Burning Hills Amphitheater west of town, stages different shows nightly at 8:30pm from early June through early September. Featured attractions may range from "The Flaming Idiots" to "Arneberg's Sensational Canines," depending on your luck. Tickets ($13-14.50, students grades 1-12 $7.50-8.50) are available at the **Harold Schafer Heritage Center** (623-4444), on 4th St.

South Dakota

From the forested granite crags of the Black Hills to the glacial lakes of the northeast, the Coyote State has more to offer than casual passers-by might expect. WALL DRUG. In fact, with only ten people per sq. mi., South Dakota has the highest ratio of sights-to-people in all of the Great Plains. Colossal man-made attractions like Mount Rushmore National Monument and the Crazy Horse Memorial compete with stunning natural spectacles such as the Black Hills and the Badlands, making tourism the state's largest industry after agriculture. WALL DRUG. Camera-toting tourists in search of nature have brought both dollars and development to South Dakota, which struggles to keep its balance between natural beauty and neon signs.

YOU ARE NOW ONLY TWO PAGES FROM WALL DRUG.

PRACTICAL INFORMATION

Capital: Pierre.

Division of Tourism: 711 E. Wells St., Pierre 57051 (773-3301 or 800-732-5682). Open Mon.-Fri. 8am-5pm. **U.S. Forest Service,** 330 Mt. Rushmore Rd., Custer 57730 (673-4853). Open Mon.-Fri. 7:30am-4:30pm. **Division of Parks and Recreation,** 523 E. Capitol Ave., Foss Building, Pierre 57501 (773-3371); has information on state parks and campgrounds. Open Mon.-Fri. 8am-noon and 1-5pm.

Time Zones: Mostly Mountain (2hr. behind Eastern). *Let's Go* makes note of areas in Central (1hr. behind Eastern). **Postal Abbreviation:** SD

Sales Tax: 4-7%, depending on the city.

■■■ SIOUX FALLS

Sioux Falls is like a nice guy. Some will take this description to mean "boring," but those who value the quiet, friendly, and clean-cut will understand that "nice" truly is a compliment. As the largest city in the upper Midwest, many pass through Sioux Falls, but the city can't be appreciated from the inside of the Greyhound station. The downtown is sprinkled with historic buildings of pink quartzite, and the city is ringed by a series of riverside parks connected by bike trails.

You can visit the city's namesake rapids at **Falls Park,** just north of downtown on Falls Park Dr. The **Old Courthouse Museum** (367-4210), at 6th and Main, houses interesting exhibits on local history (open Mon.-Sat. 9am-5pm, Sun. 1-5pm; free). The **Pettigrew Home and Museum** (339-7097), at 8th and Duluth, displays artifacts collected from all over the world by Richard F. Pettigrew, South Dakota's first full-term U.S. Senator (open Tues.-Fri. 9am-noon and 1-5pm, Sat. 9am-5pm, Sun. 1-5pm;

free). Hike, bike, or skate on the **Sioux River Greenway Recreation Trail,** which rings the city from Falls Park in the northeast to the Elmwood golf course in the northwest. Legend says that in order to escape the law, Jesse James made a 20-ft. leap on horseback across **Devil's Gulch** in **Garretson,** 20 mi. northeast of Sioux Falls; take Rte. 11 10 mi. north from I-90 (open summer daily 9am-7pm; free).

Main St. divides the city east-west, but **Minnesota Ave.** is the major north-south thoroughfare. **10th** and **12th St.** intersect them; 10th connects with **I-229** in the east and 12th connects with **I-29** in the west. The **Chamber of Commerce,** 200 N. Phillips (336-1620), at 8th, provides free city maps (open Mon.-Fri. 8am-5pm). **Greyhound,** 301 N. Dakota Ave. (336-0885; open daily 7:30am-5pm and 9-9:20pm) bolts to Minneapolis (1 per day, 6hr., $40), Omaha (2 per day, 4hr., $35), and Rapid City (1 per day, 8hr., $97). Flag a **Yellow Cab** (336-1616; $1.50 base fare, $1.25 per mi.). **Time zone:** Central. Sioux Falls's **post office:** 320 S. Second St. (357-5000; open Mon.-Fri. 7:30am-5:30pm, Sat. 8am-1pm); **ZIP code:** 57101; **area code:** 605.

Every national motel chain has a location in this popular stopover; take your pick along I-29. If you see and mention one of the billboards that advertise $26 singles, **Excel Inn,** 1300 W. Russell St. (331-5800), at exit 81 off I-29, will give you that rate; otherwise, singles are $32-34 (doubles $37-40). The slightly dog-eared **Albert House,** 333 N. Phillips (336-1680), offers cheap rooms downtown (singles $24, doubles $29). There are a number of state parks nearby, but you can camp for free at **Split Rock City Park,** 20 mi. northeast in Garretson. From I-90E, exit north to Rte. 11 (Corson) and drive 10 mi. to Garretson; turn right at the sign for Devil's Gulch, and it will be on your left before the tracks. Sites have pit toilets and drinking water.

Every city needs a trendy downtown brewery, and the **Sioux Falls Brewing Co.,** 431 N. Phillips (332-4847) fits the bill. Grab a slice of buffalo pie (cheesecake with stout beer and dark chocolate) with your sandwich, burger, or salad ($5-8; open Mon.-Thurs. 11am-midnight, Fri.-Sat. 11am-2am, Sun. 1-9pm). **Minerva's,** 301 S. Phillips (334-0386), has upscale sandwiches, pasta, and a great salad bar ($6-7.50), but pricey dinners ($10-12; open Mon.-Fri. 11am-2:30pm and 5:30-10pm, Sat. 11am-2:30pm and 5-11pm). **Metro Mix,** 215 S. Phillips (338-2698), a coffeehouse with $3-5 sandwiches by day, transforms into a DJ'd club by night; live blues, dance, or jazz play Friday and Saturday nights (cover varies).

■■■ THE BADLANDS

Some 60 million years ago, when much of the Great Plains was under water, tectonic shifts thrust up the Rockies and the Black Hills. Mountain streams deposited silt from these nascent highlands into the area now known as the Badlands, capturing and fossilizing the remains of wildlife that once wandered these flood plains in layer after pink layer. Erosion has carved spires and steep gullies into the earth, creating a landscape that contrasts sharply with the prairies of eastern South Dakota and perhaps with the rest of the world. The Sioux first called these arid and treacherous formations "Mako Sica," or "bad land;" General Alfred Sully—the opposition—called them "hell with the fires out."

Practical Information **Badlands National Park** smolders about 50 mi. east of Rapid City on I-90. Begin a driving tour at either end of Rte. 240, which winds through the wilderness in a 32-mi. detour off I-90. The **Ben Reifel Visitors Center** (433-5361; open daily 7am-8pm; Sept.-May hours vary), 5 mi. inside the park's northeastern entrance, is much more convenient than **White River Visitors Center** (455-2878; open May 31-Sept. 9am-5pm), 55 mi. to the southwest off Rte. 27 in the park's less-visited southern section. Both visitors centers have potable water. The **entrance fee,** collected at the visitors centers, is $5 per car, $2 per person. **Jack Rabbit Buses,** 333 6th St. (348-3300), leaves Rapid City for Wall at 11:30am ($22.80). The Badlands experience extreme temperatures in midsummer and winter; but late spring and fall offer pleasant weather and fewer insects. Always watch (and listen) for rattlesnakes. For **emergencies,** call 433-5361. **Area code:** 605.

Accommodations, Food, and Camping **Welsh's Motel** (279-2271), located near the beginning of Rte. 240 in Wall at exit 110 off I-90, has clean, comfy rooms (singles $40, doubles $52). Next to the visitors center inside the park, **Cedar Pass Lodge** (433-5460), rents air-conditioned cabins with showers (singles $41, doubles $45; $4 per additional person; open mid-April to mid-Oct.). At the lodge's mid-priced **restaurant** (the only one in the park), brave diners try the **buffalo burger** ($3.45); it's basically a hamburger, but try it anyway (open April-Sept. daily 6:45am-8:30pm; off season hours vary). Two campgrounds lie within the park. **Cedar Pass Campground,** just south of the Ben Reifel Visitors Center, has sites with water and restrooms ($8). It fills up by afternoon in summer; get there early. At **Sage Creek Campground,** 11 mi. from the Pinnacles entrance south of Wall, you can sleep in an open field for free; no toilets, no water, and no fires—but what do you expect for nothing? Pitch your tent ½ mi. from the road and out of sight to enjoy a more intimate introduction to this austere landscape through **backcountry camping** (no campfires allowed). Wherever you sleep, don't cozy up to the bison; especially in spring, nervous mothers can become just a shade too overprotective.

Sights and Activities The 244,000-acre park protects large tracts of prairie as well as stark rock formations. The Reifel Visitors Center has a video on the Badlands, as well as a wealth of information on nearby parks, camping, and activities. Park rangers offer free stargazing programs, evening slide shows (call for times), and nature walks. Try one of the 1½-hr. walks from the Cedar Pass amphitheater (8am and 6pm)—you may find Oligocene fossils at your feet.

To hike through the Badlands on your own, pick up a trail guide from one of the visitors centers. Try the short but steep **Saddle Pass Trail** or the less hilly **Castle Trail** (10mi. round-trip). Overnight hikers should ask for **backcountry camping** information. If you'd rather drive than hike, **Rte. 240** runs past scenic vistas such as the **Seabed Jungle Overlook,** where red and yellow formations relieve the ubiquitous bleached rose. Rte. 240 also runs past the trailheads of the **Door, Window,** and **Notch Trails,** all brief excursions into the Badlands terrain. The gravel **Sage Creek Rim Rd.,** west of Rte. 240, has fewer people and more animals; highlights are **Roberts Prairie Dog Town** and the park's herd of 400 bison. It is easy to lose your bearings in this territory, so consult with a ranger or tote a map.

Have you dug Wall Drug?

There is almost no way to visit the Badlands without being importuned by advertisements from **Wall Drug,** 510 Main St., Wall (605-279-2175); a towering monument to the success of saturation advertising. After seeing billboards for Wall Drug from as far as 500 mi. away, travelers feel obligated to make a stop in Wall to see what all the ruckus is about, much as they must have done 60 years ago when Wall enticed parched Plains travelers with free water. The "drug store" itself is now a conglomeration of shops, containing Old West memorabilia, kitschy souvenirs, and numerous photo opportunities with statues of oversized animals. (Open daily 6am-10pm; mid-Sept. to April daily 6:30am-6pm.) All in all the town is just another brick in the...well, forget it.

BLACK HILLS REGION

The Black Hills, named for the dark hue that distance lends the green pines covering the hills, have long been considered sacred by the Sioux. The Treaty of 1868 gave the Black Hills and the rest of South Dakota west of the Missouri River to the tribe, then when gold was discovered during the rush of 1877-79, the U.S. government snatched back the land. The neighboring monuments of Mt. Rushmore (a national monument) and Crazy Horse (an independent project) strikingly illustrate the clash of the two cultures that revere these hills. Today, white residents dominate the area, which contains a trove of natural treasures including Custer State Park, Wind Cave National Park, Jewel Cave National Monument, and the Black Hills National Forest.

I-90 skirts the northern border of the Black Hills from Spearfish in the west to Rapid City in the east; **U.S. 385** twists from Hot Springs in the south to Deadwood in the North. The interconnecting road system through the hills covers beautiful territory, but the roads are difficult to navigate without a good map; pick up one for free almost anywhere in the area. Don't expect to get anywhere fast—these convoluted roads will hold you to half the speed of the interstate.

Take advantage of the excellent and informative **Grayline** tours (605-342-4461); tickets can be purchased at Rapid City motels, hotels, and campgrounds. Make reservations, or call one hour before departure; they will pick you up at your motel. Tour #1 is the most complete Black Hills tour, with stops at Mt. Rushmore, Black Hills National Forest, Custer State Park, Needles Highway, and the Crazy Horse Memorial (mid-May to mid-Oct. daily, 8hr., $30).

■■■ BLACK HILLS FOREST

The majority of the land in the Black Hills area is part of the National Forest. Like other national forests, the Black Hills exercise the "multiple use" principle; mining, logging, ranching, and tourism all take place in close proximity. "Don't-miss" attractions like reptile farms and Flintstone Campgrounds lurk around every bend in the Black Hills's narrow, sinuous roads. The close proximity of area attractions allows travelers to use **Spearfish, Hot Springs,** or **Rapid City** as a base to explore the monuments and parks. The forest itself provides unlimited opportunities for backcountry hiking and camping, as well as park-run campgrounds and private tent sites. Contact the **Black Hills National Forest Visitor Center** (605-343-8755), on I-385 at Pactola Lake, for details on backcountry camping (open Memorial Day-Labor Day Sun.-Fri. 8am-6pm, Sat. 8am-7pm).

Camping **Backcountry camping** in the national forest is free; disappear down one of the many dirt roads (make sure it isn't somebody's driveway), stay 1 mi. away from any campground or visitors center, don't park on the side of the road, don't build a campfire, and you're set. Watch for poison ivy and afternoon thundershowers. The most popular state-run campgrounds include **Bear Gulch** and **Pactola,** on the Pactola Reservoir just south of the junction of Rte. 44 and U.S. 385 (sites $12), and **Sheridan Lake,** 5 mi. northeast of Hill City on U.S. 385 (sites $13). All campgrounds are quiet and wooded, offering fishing, swimming, and pit toilets, but no hookups. Sheridan Lake also has ranger talks Saturday nights at 7:30pm. National forest campsites can and should be reserved by calling 800-280-CAMP/2267. For more info and a $3 topographical map, contact the visitors center (see above). The Black Hills National Forest extends into Wyoming, with a ranger station (307-283-1361; open Mon.-Fri. 8am-5pm) in Sundance. The Wyoming side of the forest permits campfires, allows horses in more areas, and draws fewer visitors.

■■■ MOUNT RUSHMORE

Americans are known the world over for their never-ending quest for the biggest and the best. Nowhere is this more evident than at **Mount Rushmore National Monument.** South Dakota historian Doane Robinson originally conceived this "shrine of democracy" in 1923 as a memorial for local Western heroes like Lewis and Clark and Kit Carson; sculptor Gutzon Borglum finally chose the four presidents. Borglum initially encountered opposition from those who felt the work of God could not be improved, but the tenacious sculptor defended the project's size, insisting that "there is not a monument in this country as big as a snuff box." Work progressed slowly through the Depression, and a great setback occurred when the nearly completed face of Thomas Jefferson had to be blasted off Washington's right side and moved to his left due to insufficient granite. In 1941, the 60-ft. heads of George Washington, Thomas Jefferson, Theodore Roosevelt, and Abraham Lincoln were completed; work ceased as the U.S. entered World War II. The planned 465-ft.-tall bodies were never completed, but the millions of visitors who come here every year don't seem to mind.

From Rapid City, take U.S. 16 and 16A to Keystone and Rte. 244 up to the mountain. Parking is free, but there will be a $5 per car charge after October 1996 (optional free parking farther away). The **visitors center** (605-574-4104) has exhibits and wheelchairs (open daily 8am-10pm; Labor Day-Memorial Day daily 8am-5pm). Ranger talks and walks are available in the summer from 10am to 4pm. **Borglum's Studio** holds a plaster model of the carving, as well as his tools and plans (open daily 9am-5pm). From Memorial Day to Labor Day, the **Mount Rushmore Memorial Amphitheater** hosts a monument-lighting program; a patriotic speech and slide show commence at 9pm, and light floods the monument 9:30-10:30pm.

The **Hill City-Mount Rushmore KOA** (605-574-2525 or 800-233-4331), lies 5 mi. west of Mount Rushmore on Rte. 244. With kabins ($35-40) come the use of showers, stoves, a heated pool, laundry facilities, free shuttle service to Mount Rushmore, movies, hayrides, and volleyball—it's not really like camping anymore, is it? Make reservations early. (Kampsites for 2 $20, with water and electricity $26.)

■■■ CRAZY HORSE MEMORIAL

If you thought Mount Rushmore was big, think again. The Crazy Horse Memorial is a wonder-of-the-world in progress; an entire mountain will metamorphose into a 563-ft.-high memorial sculpture of the great Lakota war-leader Crazy Horse. A fiercely independent battle-tactician Crazy Horse fought against the U.S. government to protect his people's land, rights, and pride; he was stabbed in the back (literally) by an American soldier in 1877 under a flag of truce.

The project was initiated by Lakota Chief Henry Standing Bear in response to nearby Mount Rushmore to let "the white man know the red man has heroes, too." The memorial stands as a bittersweet reminder that one year before Crazy Horse died the U.S. took back the Black Hills, which they had promised to the Sioux. The project began in 1947 and receives no government funding of any kind; the sculptor, Korczak Ziolkowski, believed in the American spirit of free enterprise and went solo for years, twice refusing $10 million in federal funding. Crazy Horse's face and part of his arm are now visible; eventually, his entire torso and his head will be carved into the mountain, and the site will contain a university, a medical training center, and a museum. The Memorial, 17 mi. southwest of Mount Rushmore on U.S. 16/385, includes the **Indian Museum of North America** as well as the mountain statue; don't miss the impressive 10-min. slide show. (Open daily 6:30am-9pm; Oct.-April 8am-dusk. $6, $15 per carload, under 6 free. AAA discount.) For information or to make a tax-deductible donation, write to Crazy Horse Memorial, Crazy Horse, SD 57730-9506, or call 605-673-4681.

■■■ CUSTER STATE PARK

Peter Norbeck, governor of South Dakota during the late 1910s, loved to hike among the thin, towering rock formations that haunt the area south of Sylvan Lake and Mt. Rushmore. In order to preserve the area, he created Custer State Park. The spectacular **Needles Hwy.** (Rte. 87) within the park follows his favorite hiking route; Norbeck designed this road to be especially narrow and winding so that newcomers could experience the pleasures of discovery. The highway does not have guard rails, so slow and cautious driving is essential; watch out for mountain goats and bighorn sheep. Custer's biggest attraction is its herd of 1500 **buffalo,** which can best be seen near dawn or dusk wandering near **Wildlife Loop Rd.;** If you're "lucky," they'll come right up to your car. For information, contact HC 83, P.O. Box 70, Custer SD 57730 (605-255-4515; open Mon.-Fri. 7:30am-5pm). The park's **entrance fee** is $3 per person, $8 per carload for a 7-day pass. At the entrance, ask for a copy of *Tatanka* (Lakota for "bison"), the informative Custer State Park newspaper. The **Peter Norbeck Visitor Center** (605-255-4464), on U.S. 16A 1 mi. west of the State Game Lodge, serves as the park's information center. (Open Memorial Day-Labor Day daily 8am-8pm, Labor Day-Oct. 9am-5pm, May-Memorial Day 9am-5pm). All seven park **campgrounds** charge $8-11 per night; most have showers and restrooms. About half of the park's 323 sites are reservable (800-710-2267), and the entire park fills by about 1pm in the summer. Food and concessions are available at all four park lodges, but the local general stores in Custer, Hermosa, or Keystone generally charge less.

You can hike, fish, ride horses, paddle boats, or canoe at popular **Sylvan Lake** (605-574-2561), on Needles Hwy. (kayak rental $3.50 per person per ½hr.). Horse rides are available at **Blue Bell Lodge** (605-255-4531; stable 255-4571) on Rte. 87 about 8 mi. from the south entrance ($14 per hr., under 12 $12). Rent mountain bikes ($7.50 per hr.) at the **State Game Lodge** (605-255-4541), on U.S. 16A near the visitors center. All lakes and streams permit fishing, with a daily license ($6; 5-day nonresident license $14). Summer trout fishing is the best; call for limitations on the number of fish you can keep. Rental equipment is available at the four area lodges.

■■■ WIND CAVE AND JEWEL CAVE

In the cavern-riddled Black Hills, the subterranean scenery often rivals that aboveground. Private concessionaires will attempt to lure you into the holes in their backyards, but the government owns the area's prime underground real estate: **Wind Cave National Park** (605-745-4600), adjacent to Custer State Park on U.S. 385, and **Jewel Cave National Monument** (605-673-2288), 14 mi. west of Custer on Rte. 16. There is no public transportation to the caves. Bring a sweater on all tours—Jewel Cave remains a constant 47°F, Wind Cave 53°F.

Wind Cave Wind Cave was discovered in 1881 by Tom Bingham, who heard the sound of air rushing out of the cave's single tiny natural entrance—the wind was so strong it knocked his hat off. Air whooshes forcefully in and out of the cave due to outside pressure changes, and when Tom went back to show his friends the cave, his hat got sucked in. The cave is known for its "boxwork," a honeycomb-like lattice of calcite that covers the cave walls. There are five **tours,** all of which have more than 150 stairs. The **Garden of Eden Tour** is the least strenuous (1hr.; 6 per day, 8:40am-5:30pm; $3, seniors and ages 6-15 $1.50). The **Natural Entrance Tour** passes the original opening to the cave (1¼hr.; on the hour 9am-6pm; $5, seniors and ages 6-15 $2.50). The **Caving Tour** is limited to 10 people ages 16 and over (4-hr. tours depart 1pm; $15, seniors $7.50; reservations required). In the afternoon, all tours fill about an hour ahead of time, so buy tickets early and come back later. For info, contact Wind Cave National Park, RR1, Box 190-WCNP, Hot Springs 57747 (605-745-4600; open June to mid-Aug. daily 8am-7pm; winter hours vary).

Jewel Cave In striking contrast to nearby Wind Cave's boxwork, the walls of this sprawling underground labyrinth (the second longest cave in the U.S.) are covered with a layer of gray calcite crystal—hence the name. The ½-mi. **Scenic Tour** takes you over 723 stairs every half hour between 8:30am-5:30pm (in winter only 1 per day; $5, ages 6-15 $2.50). Make reservations for the 4-hr. **Spelunking Tour,** limited to 10 people ages 16 and over, and be sure to wear sturdy foot gear (summer Sun., Tues., Thurs., and Sat. 12:30pm; $15). For more info, contact the **visitors center** (605-638-2288; open daily 8am-7pm, mid-Oct. to mid-May 8am-4pm).

■■■ RAPID CITY

Rapid City's location in southwest South Dakota makes it an ideal base from which to explore the Black Hills and the Badlands; every summer the area welcomes about 3 million tourists, over 40 times the city's permanent population. Come here for a roof and a hot meal, then head to the nearby parks and monuments.

Practical Information The main east-west roads, **St. Joseph, Kansas City,** and **Main** (also **business loop 90**) are right next to each other. **Mount Rushmore Rd.** (also Rte. 16) is the main north-south route. Pick up a free map at most motels or at the **Rapid City Chamber of Commerce and Visitors Information Center,** 444 Mt. Rushmore Rd. N., in the Civic Center. (Visitors Information 348-2015; open mid-May to mid-Oct. daily 7:30am-6pm. Chamber of Commerce 343-1744, open Mon.-Fri. 8am-5pm. Racks in lobby other times.) **Jack Rabbit Lines** scurries east from the **Milo Barber Transportation Center,** 333 6th St. (348-3300), downtown, with one bus daily to Pierre (3hr., $52) and Sioux Falls (8hr., $97). **Powder River Lines,** also in the center, services Wyoming and Montana, running once per day to Billings (9hr., $54) and Cheyenne (8½hr., $65). (Station open Mon.-Fri. 8am-5pm, Sat. 10am-5pm, Sun. 10am-noon and 2-5pm.) **Public transportation** (394-6631) runs buses 6am-6pm (fare $1, seniors 50¢). Call for specific routes. Bus transportation is available by reservation for disabled travelers; call 24 hrs. in advance. (Office open Mon.-Fri. 8am-4pm.) The **Rape and Assault Victims Helpline** (341-4808) is open 24 hrs. **Emergency** is 911. **Time zone:** Mountain (2hr. behind Eastern); Rapid City's **post office:** 500 East Blvd. (394-8600), several blocks east of downtown (open Mon.-Fri. 8am-5pm, Sat. 9am-12:30pm); **ZIP code:** 57701; **area code:** 605.

Accommodations Rapid City accommodations are *considerably* more expensive during the summer. Make reservations; budget motels often fill up weeks in advance, especially during the first 2 weeks in August when nearby Sturgis hosts its annual motorcycle rally. The **Rapid City YMCA Hostel,** 815 Kansas City St. (342-8538), 1 block south of Main at Mt. Rushmore, has eight male and eight female beds with a possible private room for families. Check in at the **YMCA;** the hostel occupies the building next door. If the Y is closed, call Tobie, the friendly manager, at 394-5434—he'll take good care of you. Access to the YMCA's pool, gym, and game rooms is free. (Must have hostel card or passport. Open 4pm-10am. Curfew at 11pm. Cots $10, children $5; $5 to sleep on the floor if they're full. Linen $5.) Downtown motels are pricey, but the budget traveler with a car can find solace on E. North St. near I-90. The **Ranch House Motel,** 202 E. North St. (341-0785), has rooms with fridges and microwaves, but no phones (July-Aug. singles $32.50, doubles $45). A few blocks east, the **Tradewinds Motel,** 420 E. North St. (342-4153), offers a little more (pool, free local calls) for a little more (June-Aug. singles $40-65, doubles $55-75). Camping is available at Badlands National Park (p. 471), Black Hills National Forest (p. 472), and Custer State Park (p. 473).

Food and Nightlife **Sixth St. Bakery and Delicatessen,** 516 6th St. (342-6660), next to the $1.50 cinema, serves up delectable sandwiches ($3.50-4), biscuits (65¢), croissants, and espresso. (Open Mon.-Fri. 6:30am-8pm, Sat. 7am-8pm, Sun. 9am-6pm; in winter Mon.-Sat. 7am-6pm, Sun. 10am-4pm.) **Remington's,** 603 Omaha St. (348-4160), doesn't shave as close as a blade or your money back—it memorializes the late great cowboy and sculptor Frederic Remington and serves fine sandwiches, burgers, steak and chicken ($4.50-$11; open Mon.-Thurs. 11am-10:30pm, Fri.-Sat. 11am-11:30pm, Sun. 4:30pm-10pm).

Nightlife lines **Main St.** between 6th and Mt. Rushmore St. For a beer as black as the Hills, toss back a Rushmore Stout ($2.75) at the **Firehouse Brewing Co.,** 610 Main St. (348-1915), *the* bar in Rapid City. Located in a restored 1915 firehouse, the company brews 12 beers in-house and serves up sandwiches, burgers, pasta ($5-10), and occasional live music in the summer. (Open Mon.-Thurs. 10am-midnight,

Fri.-Sat. 11am-2am, Sun. 4-10pm.) The **Atomic Café,** 515 7th St. (399-1922), mushrooms with alternative and punk "most nights" in a laid-back atmosphere; sip a cappucino ($1-2.25) or try the "Atomic Bomb" ($4.50), four shots of espresso that will detonate in your stomach (cover varies; open Mon.-Thurs. 8am-midnight, Fri.-Sat. 9am-2am, Sun. 9am-10pm). For boot-stompin', knee-slappin' country-western music and dancing, head to **Boot Hill,** 526 Main St. (343-1931), where bands perform nightly (occasional $2 cover Fri.-Sat.; open Mon.-Sat. 1pm-2am).

Sights and Entertainment If you have a car, pick up a map of the **Rapid City Circle Tour** at the Civic Center; the route leads you to numerous free attractions and includes a jaunt up Skyline Dr. for a bird's-eye view of the city. All of the tour's museums can be reached on foot: **The Museum of Geology** (free) and the children's **Museum in Motion** ($2), both at 501 E. St. Joseph St. (394-2467); the **Dahl Fine Arts Center** (394-4101; free), at 7th and Quincy St.; and the **Sioux Indian Museum** (348-0557) and **Pioneer Museum** (394-6099), at 515 W. Blvd. (both free). On July 12, 13, and 14 in 1996, Rapid City's **Pow Wow** at the Civic Center will offer traditional Native American crafts at much-lower-than-a-gift-shop prices.

The Sturgis Rally and Races

During the first full week in August, nearby Sturgis, 30 mi. northwest of Rapid City on I-90, holds its annual motorcycle Rally and Races (347-6570). The event brings in 100,000 bikers who compete in races, display custom and vintage bikes, and vie for the "rattiest bike" title. The event packs all the highways and motels within a 50-mi. radius (especially Rapid City); plan ahead if you're traveling in the area. Expect traffic jams. For info, contact the Rally (605-347-2556) or the **Chamber of Commerce,** P.O. Box 504, Sturgis 57785, at exit 32 off I-90.

■■■ SPEARFISH, LEAD, AND DEADWOOD

Spearfish Located on the northwest edge of the Black Hills, Spearfish makes a good base for exploring more expensive Lead and Deadwood. Nearby, the lovely **Spearfish Canyon Scenic Byway** (U.S. 14A) winds through 18 mi. of forest along Spearfish Creek passing one of the sites where *Dances with Wolves* was filmed (marked by a small sign 2mi. west of U.S. 14A on Rte. 222).

For free maps and help with hiking plans stop by the **Spearfish Ranger Station,** 2014 N. Main St. (605-642-4622; open Mon.-Fri. 8am-5pm, Sat. 7am-3pm). The **Chamber of Commerce,** 115 E. Hudson St. (800-626-8013), lies just east of Main St. (Open Mon.-Fri. 8am-7pm, Sat. 10am-3pm, Sun. noon-7pm; in winter Mon.-Fri. 8am-5pm.) The weary traveler can rest at **Bell's Motor Lodge** (605-642-3812), on Main St. at the east edge of town, with free local calls, TV, and a pool (singles $34, doubles $48; open May-Sept.). The **Canyon Gateway Hotel** (605-642-3402 or 800-281-3402), ½ mi. south of town on U.S. 14A, offers cozy rooms with hardwood paneling (singles $34, doubles $37.50). Two mi. past the poorly-marked *Dances with Wolves* site on Rte. 222, two National Forest campgrounds offer pit toilets, picnic tables, and the sweet smell of Ponderosa pine nestled among the hills: **Rod and Gun Campground** (sites $5), and further west, **Timon Campground** (sites $7).

The vaguely Mediterranean **Bay Leaf Café,** 126 W. Hudson (605-642-5462), right off Main St., serves salads, sandwiches, and veggie dishes ($3-12; jazz and blues piano Fri.-Sat. 8pm; open daily 7am-10pm; Sept.-May 8am-9pm). Lunch on the lawn of **Lown House Restaurant** (605-642-5663), at 5th and Jackson, or feast on the sandwiches, burgers, and steaks ($3-10) inside the 1893 mansion (open daily 7am-9pm; Labor Day-Memorial Day 9am-7pm).

Lead About 20 mi. from Spearfish on U.S. 14A lies Lead (LEED), an old 1870s gold rush town. The longest continuously operated gold mine in the world, the **Home-**

stake Mine, 160 W. Main St. (605-584-3110), continues to produce almost 1000 oz. of gold daily. If you want to view the surface operations, take a one-hour bus tour of the **Open Cut,** a huge chasm where a mountain once stood—it's not very exciting. (Tours $4, ages 6-18 $3. Open June-Aug. Mon.-Fri. 8am-5pm, Sat.-Sun. 10am-5pm. Winter hours vary.) See a good re-creation of operations 1½ mi. beneath the surface, or pan for gold at **Black Hills Mining Museum,** 323 W. Main St. (605-584-1605). (Tours $3.78, students $2.70; open mid-May to Sept. daily 9am-5pm; $3.75.)

Deadwood Continue down Main St. from Lead for 3 mi. and you'll find yourself in Deadwood. Gunslingers **Wild Bill Hickock** and **Calamity Jane** sauntered into town during the height of the Gold Rush. Bill stayed just long enough—two months—to spend an eternity here; Deadwood is home to **Saloon #10,** 657 Main St. (605-578-3346) where legend has it that he was shot holding aces and eights, the infamous "dead man's hand." But every summer Bill has more lives than 60 cats; the shooting is morbidly re-enacted on location four times per day from Memorial Day to Labor Day. The main attraction in Deadwood is **gambling,** with casinos lining **Main St.** The **Midnight Star,** 677 Main St. (800-999-6482), owned by Kevin Costner, displays memorabilia from his cinematic exploits among the slot machines (open *all* the time). Budget digs are scarce in Deadwood; stay in nearby Spearfish or Rapid City, or try **Wild Bill's Campground** (605-578-2800), on Rte. 385 about 5 mi. south of Lead and Deadwood (sites $12.50, with water and hookup $14.50). Wild Bill's also has two large cabins with kitchenettes ($45) and free shuttles to Deadwood. **Mama Leon's,** 638 Main St. (605-578-2440), in the rear of the Lucky Wrangler Casino, dishes up shockingly cheap Italian ($3-6) among familiar red-checkered tablecloths and candles in chianti bottles (open Mon.-Sat. noon-10pm).

■■■ HOT SPRINGS

Located on scenic **U.S. 385,** the well-to-do once flocked from the four corners to bathe in the mineral waters of this quaint town. Today, Hot Springs is just about the only town in the Black Hills untouched by glitz and neon; its charming pink sandstone buildings and less expensive lodgings make it a good base from which to explore the southern Black Hills. Wind Cave National Park lies just outside of town, but plan to give Hot Springs's sights a few hours before you head for the hills. For information, stop at the **visitors center,** 801 S. 6th St. (745-6974 or 800-325-6991), on U.S. 385, which runs right through downtown (open May-Oct. daily 8am-8pm).

The Sioux and Cheyenne used to fight over possession of the 87°F spring here; in 1890, a public pool was erected at the spring. Zip down the waterslide at **Evan's Plunge** (745-5165), on U.S. 385, into the world's largest naturally heated pool (open June-Aug. daily 5:30am-10pm; winter hours vary; $7, ages 3-12 $5). **Kidney Spring,** just to the right of the waterfall near U.S.385 and Minnekahta Ave., is rumored to have healing powers; drink from the public fountain at the gazebo or bring a jug and take some of the mineral water home.

Wooly mammoths were sucked into a sinkhole and fossilized near Hot Springs about 26,000 years ago; see their bones at the **Mammoth Site** (745-6017), on the U.S. 18 bypass (½-hr. tours $4.25, seniors $4, ages 6-12 $2.50. Open daily 8am-8pm; winter hours vary.) About 15 mi. south of Hot Springs on Rte. 71, 300 wild mustangs roam the **Black Hills Wild Horse Sanctuary** (800-252-6652). Two-hour tours run daily Memorial Day through Labor Day (tours $15, seniors $13.50, under 13 $7.50; open daily dawn to dusk).

At the **Historic Log Cabin Motel** (745-5166), on U.S. 385 at the north edge of town, cabins come in all shapes and sizes; visitors can partake of the communal outdoor hot tub (no phones; some have kitchenettes; singles $39, doubles $49). **Hide Away Cabins,** 442 S. Chicago St. (745-5683), on U.S. 385, has rooms tucked away in the proprietors' backyard next to the flower garden (singles $27, doubles with kitchenettes around $40). For cheap eats (including a $3.65 buffalo burger), head to the generic but friendly **Black Hills Family Restaurant,** 745 Battle Mountain Ave. (745-3737), across from Evan's Plunge (open daily 6am-9pm; in winter 7am-7pm).

Iowa

"Boring" Iowa bears the brunt of the nation's jokes about farming, corn, and rednecks; Iowa Hawkeyes prefer the word "quiet." It's a fine distinction, and you'll have to get off I-80 to understand it. Along old country roads you can find fields of dreams, bridges of Madison County, and the scenic Loess Hills in the west; created by wind-blown quartz silt, the hills are a geological rarity found only in Iowa and China. Iowa preserves its European heritage in the small towns that keep German, Dutch, and Swedish traditions alive. Of course, Iowa's farming reputation can't be ignored; Iowa contains ¼ of all U.S. Grade A farmland, and the familiar farmers of *American Gothic* were painted by native son Grant Wood. Clearly, Iowa can be proud. This year, Iowa will be particularly cocky as it celebrates its 150th birthday in a year-long party from December 28,1995 to December 28, 1996.

PRACTICAL INFORMATION

Capital: Des Moines.

Iowa Department of Economic Development: 200 E. Grand Ave., Des Moines 50309 (515-242-4705 or 800-345-4692).

Time Zone: Central (1hr. behind Eastern). **Postal Abbreviation:** IA

Sales Tax: 5%.

■■■ DES MOINES

French explorers originally named the Des Moines river the "Rivière des Moingouenas," for a local Native American tribe, but then shortened the name to "Rivière des Moings." Because of its identical pronunciation (mwan), later French settlers mistakenly called the river and city by a name much more familiar to them: Des Moines (of the monks). Today, Des Moines (pronounced "da moyne") shows neither Native American nor monastic influence, but rather the imprint of the agricultural state that spawned it. The World Pork Expo is a red letter event on the Iowan calendar and the city goes hog-wild for the Iowa State Fair every August. Des Moines also boasts a great art museum and hosts many local festivals and events.

PRACTICAL INFORMATION

Tourist Office: Greater Des Moines Convention and Visitors Bureau, 2 Ruan Center, #222 (800-451-2625), at 6th and Locust in the skywalk. Open Mon.-Fri. 8:30am-5pm. For upcoming events, call 830-1451. **Gay and Lesbian Resource Center,** 522 11th St. (281-0634).

Airport: Des Moines International (256-5195), Fleur Dr. at Army Post Rd., about 5mi. southwest of downtown; take bus #8 "Havens." Taxi $10 to downtown.

Buses: Greyhound, 1107 Keosauqua Way (800-231-2222), at 12th St. just northwest of downtown; take bus #4 "Urbandale." To: Iowa City (6 per day, 2hr., $18); Omaha (8 per day, 2hr., $24); St. Louis (3 per day, 10hr., $40-69). Tickets sold daily 7am-midnight. Open 24 hrs.

Public Transportation: Metropolitan Transit Authority (MTA), 1100 MTA Lane (283-8100), just south of the 9th St. viaduct. Open Mon.-Fri. 8am-5pm. Buses run Mon.-Sat. approx. 6am-6pm. Fare 75¢, transfers 5¢. Routes converge at 6th and Walnut St. Get maps at the MTA office or any Dahl's market.

Taxis: Yellow Cab, 243-1111. $1.40 base fare, $1.20 per mi.

Car Rental: Budget (287-2612), at the airport. $21 weekend, $32 weekdays with 150 free mi. per day; 25¢ per additional mi. Must be 21 with major credit card. Under 25 surcharge $10 per day. Open Sun.-Fri. 6am-11pm, Sat. 6am-10pm.

Crisis Lines: Rape/Sexual Assault Line, 288-1750. Open 24 hrs. **Suicide Hotline,** 244-1010. **Red Cross Crisis Line,** 244-1000. Both Mon.-Fri. 3pm-8am, weekends 24 hrs.

Emergency: 911.

Post Office: 1165 2nd Ave. (283-7505), downtown just north of I-235. Open Mon.-Fri. 7:30am-5:30pm. **ZIP code:** 50318. **Area code:** 515.

Des Moines idles at the junction of I-35 and I-80. Numbered streets run north-south, named streets east-west. Numbering begins at the **Des Moines River** and increases as you move east or west; **Grand Ave.** divides addresses north-south. Other east-west thoroughfares are **Locust St.,** and, moving north, **University Ave.** (home to Drake University), **Hickman Rd.,** and **Euclid/Douglas Ave.** Most downtown buildings are connected by the **Skywalk,** a series of passages above the street, so many Des Moines businesspeople never have to go outdoors—except to smoke.

ACCOMMODATIONS AND CAMPING

Finding cheap accommodation in Des Moines is usually no problem, though you should make reservations for visits in August, when the State Fair comes to town, and during high school sports tournament season in March. Several cheap motels cluster around **I-80** and **Merle Hay Rd.,** 5 mi. northwest of downtown. Take bus #4 "Urbandale" or #6 "West 9th" from downtown.

YMCA, 101 Locust St. (288-2424), at 1st St. downtown on the west bank of the river. Convenient location. Small, somewhat clean rooms with a communal bathroom. Lounge, laundry, athletic facilities, including pool. Men only. Singles $19.70, $72 per week. Key deposit $5. Call ahead; it fills quickly.

YWCA, 717 Grand Ave. (244-8961), across from the Marriott Hotel downtown in a fairly safe area. Moderately clean dorm-style rooms with access to lounge, kitchen, laundry, and pool. All rooms have two beds; its main purpose is to provide social services and emergency shelter. Women (and boys under 12) only. $8 per day, $44 per week. $7 for use of pool and facilities. Call ahead; it books up.

Village Inn, 1348 E. Euclid (265-1674), at 14th St. E, offers large, recently-renovated rooms. Take bus #4 "E. 14th." Singles $30, doubles $37.

Iowa State Fairgrounds Campgrounds, E. 30th St. (262-3111), at Grand Ave. Take bus #1 "Fairgrounds" to the Grand Ave. gate and follow Grand straight east through the park. Sites have water and electricity. No fires. $8 per vehicle; fee collected in the morning. At fairtime in August, the place books well in advance. Open mid-May to mid-Oct.

FOOD

Good eating tends to congregate on **Court Ave.** downtown, or in antique-filled **Historic Valley Junction** in West Des Moines, on 5th St. south of Grand.

The Tavern, 205 5th St. (255-9827), in Historic Valley Junction, has the best pizza around—and everyone knows it, so you'll have to wait your turn. Pizzas with toppings from "bacon cheeseburger" to "taco fiesta" range $9-12.50. Open Mon.-Thurs. 11am-11pm, Fri.-Sat. 11am-midnight, Sun. noon-10pm.

Stella's Blue Sky Diner, 400 Locust St. (246-1953), at the Skywalk level in the Capital Square Mall. Loud waitresses serve up meatloaf and burgers 50s-style. Have an order of Neutron Fries ($2) and a malt ($2); ask for it "Stella's way"—do you feel lucky? Open Mon.-Fri. 6:30am-6pm, Sat. 8am-6pm.

Billy Joe's Pitcher Show, 1701 25th (224-1709), at University in West Des Moines. A combination restaurant and movie theater. Waitresses serve beer and pizza ($4.50-8.50) while you watch the flick ($3, before 6pm $2). 4-5 shows per day, 12:30-9pm; call for exact times.

The Iowa Machine Shed, 1151 Hickman Rd. (270-6818), in Urbandale. The highest-volume restaurant in all of Iowa, cracks 3600 eggs every week. The overall-clad waitstaff serves sandwiches ($4-5) beef, pork, and ham entrees ($8-10). Open Mon.-Sat. 6am-10pm, Sun. 7am-9pm.

SIGHTS

The most elaborate of all the state capitols, the copper- and gold-domed **state capitol** (281-5591), on E. 12th St. across the river and up Grand Ave., sports an 18-ft. long scale model of the battleship *U.S.S. Iowa* in the lobby; take bus #5 "E. 6th and 9th St.," #1 "Fairgrounds," #4 "E. 14th," or #7 "Walker." (Free tours Memorial Day-Labor Day Mon.-Sat. every ½hr. 9:30am-3pm; call for winter hours. Building open Mon.-Fri. 6am-5:30pm, Sat.-Sun. 8am-4pm.) Farther downhill, the modern **Iowa State Historical Museum and Archives,** 600 E. Locust (281-5111), houses displays on Iowa's natural, industrial, and social history, including an exhibit addressing the environmental overdevelopment of Iowa and the disappearance of the prairie. Take any bus that goes to the capitol. (Open Tues.-Sat. 9am-4:30pm, Sun. noon-4:30pm. Free.) The geodesic greenhouse dome of the **Botanical Center,** 909 E. River Dr. (242-2934), just north of I-235 and the capitol, encompasses a desert, rainforest, and bonsai exhibit. (Open Mon.-Thurs. 10am-6pm, Fri. 10am-9pm, Sat.-Sun. 10am-5pm. $1.50, ages 6-17 50¢, under 6 free.)

Most cultural sights cluster west of downtown on Grand Ave. The **Des Moines Art Center,** 4700 Grand Ave. (277-4405), draws raves for its modern art collection as well as for its architecture; Eero Saarinen, I. M. Pei, and Richard Meier contributed to the design of the museum. Check out the statue *Pegasus and Man* in the courtyard; the museum planned to market a wine with the statue as their logo, but the Bureau of Alcohol, Tobacco, and Firearms said they would have to put shorts on the figure. Take bus #1 "West Des Moines." (Open Tues.-Wed. and Fri.-Sat. 11am-5pm, Thurs. 11am-9pm, Sun. noon-5pm. $2, students and seniors $1; free until 1pm and all day Thurs.) Only a few blocks south of the Art Center on 45th St., the **Science Center of Iowa,** 4500 Grand Ave. (274-6868), dazzles with simulated space shuttle flights, laser shows, and computer-generated planetarium shows (open Mon.-Sat. 10am-5pm, Sun. noon-5pm; $5, seniors $3, ages 3-12 $2.50). Historic **Jordan House,** 2001 Fuller Rd. (225-1286), east of Grand, was once a stop on the Underground Railroad (open May-Oct. Wed. and Sat. 1-4pm, Sun. 2-5pm; $2, children 50¢).

Ten mi. northwest of downtown in Urbandale, **Living History Farms** (278-5286) at Hickman Rd. and 111th St., sets the standard for re-created pioneer villages. (Last tour 2hr. before closing. Open May to mid-Oct. Mon.-Sat. 9am-5pm, Sun. 11am-6pm. $7, seniors $6, ages 4-16 $4.) In **Indianola,** 12 mi. south on U.S. 69, the **National Balloon Museum,** 1601 N. Jefferson (961-3714), holds the annual **National Balloon Classic** with hot-air balloons from all over the world. (Classic held in July, call for exact dates. Museum open Mon.-Fri. 9am-4pm, Sat. 10am-4pm, Sun. 1-4pm.)

ENTERTAINMENT AND NIGHTLIFE

The **Civic Center,** 221 Walnut St. (243-1109), sponsors theater and concerts; call for information. For lots of free event listings, pick up a copy of *Cityview,* the free local weekly paper. The **Iowa State Fair,** one of the largest in the U.S., captivates Des Moines for ten days during the middle of August (8-18 in 1996) with prize cows, crafts, cakes, and corn ($5 per day); for the low-down, write to State House, 400 E. 14th St., Des Moines 50319-0198. From May to September, Des Moinians gather for **Seniom Sed** (Des Moines spelled backwards), a city-wide block party held Fridays from 4:45 to 7pm at Nollen Plaza downtown. **Jazz in July** (280-3222) presents a series of free jazz concerts at various places around the city nearly every day of the month; pick up a schedule at area restaurants or the visitors bureau. **Pella,** 41 mi. east of Des Moines on Rte. 163, blooms in May with its annual **Tulip Time** festival (628-4311; May 9-11 in 1996), with traditional Dutch dancing, a parade, concerts, and *klokkenspel* performances.

Court Ave., in the southeast corner of downtown, is a yuppified warehouse district packed with a variety of trendy restaurants and bars. Come to **Papa's Planet,** 208 3rd St. (284-0901), a young, loud club with two dance floors and a patio with outdoor pool tables (21+; live music Wed., Fri. Sat.; cover $2; open Wed.-Sat. 7pm-2am). **Java Joe's,** 214 4th St. (288-JAVA/5282), sells coffee from such exotic locales as Kenya and Sumatra ($1-2) and plays live folk or world music Thursday to Saturday. (Cover Fri.-Sat. $3. Open Mon.-Thurs. 7:30am-11pm, Fri.-Sat. 7:30am-1am, Sun. 9am-11pm.) For laughs, hop over to **Noodles Comedy Club,** 310 Court St. (243-2195; performances Fri.-Sat. 8 and 10pm; $6; reservations recommended). **The Garden,** 112 SE 4th St. (243-3965), is a friendly gay and lesbian dance bar. (Free beer Sat. 8-10pm. Drag shows Sunday 10pm. Cover Thurs.-Sat. $2-3. Open daily 4pm-2am.)

■■■ IOWA CITY

Iowa City, the staid capital of Iowa until 1857, is now a classic college town and a mecca of liberalism in a conservative state. The main University of Iowa campus fills the city with hordes of students who support a large number of bars, frozen yogurt stands, and street musicians. Each autumn weekend, hordes of Iowans make a pilgrimage to the city to cheer on the University's football team, the Hawkeyes.

Practical Information Iowa City lies on I-80 about 112 mi. east of Des Moines. North-south **Madison** and **Gilbert** and east-west **Market** and **Burlington** bound the downtown. The **Convention and Visitors Bureau,** 408 1st Ave. (800-283-6592), sits across the river in Coralville off U.S. 6 (open Mon.-Fri. 8am-5pm, Sat.-Sun. 10am-4pm). Downtown, public transportation is run by **Iowa City Transit** (356-1130). Buses runs Monday to Friday 6am-10:30pm, Saturday 6am-7:30pm (fare 50¢, off-peak hours seniors 25¢). The free **Cambus** runs all over campus and downtown. The University of Iowa's **Campus Information Center** (335-3055), in the **Iowa Memorial Union** at Madison and Market, has area information (reduced hours in summer; open termtime Mon.-Sat. 8am-9pm, Sun. noon-4pm). **Greyhound** and **Burlington Trailways** are both located at 404 E. College St. (337-2127 or 800-231-2222), at Gilbert. Buses head out for Des Moines (6 per day, 2-4hr., $18), Chicago (6 per day, 5hr., $34), and St. Louis (2 per day, 9-13hr., $55). (Station open Mon.-Fri. 8am-7:30pm, Sat.-Sun. 12:30pm-7:30pm.) **Help lines** include the **24-hr. Crisis Line** (335-0140), **Rape Crisis** (335-6000), and **Gayline** (335-3877; open termtime Tues.-Thurs. 8-9pm). Iowa City's **post office:** 400 S. Clinton St. (354-1560; open Mon.-Fri. 8:30am-5pm, Sat. 9:30am-1pm); **ZIP code:** 52240; **area code:** 319.

Accommodations, Camping, and Food Cheap motels line U.S. 6 in **Coralville,** 2 mi. west of downtown at exit 242 off I-80. Skip the chains, and choose the last of a dying breed: the **Blue Top Motel** (351-0900), at 5th St. and 10th Ave. in Coralville (take Coralville Express bus "B" to the Post Office), rents ten homey, inexpensive white cottages on five acres of manicured lawns (singles $29, doubles $37, with kitchen $44). Less expensive, but very much a hole-in-the-wall, the **Wesley House Hostel (HI-AYH),** 120 N. Dubuque St. (338-1179), at Jefferson, crams seven beds into two small rooms. (Check-in 7-10pm, Sat. 7-9pm. Check-out 9am. Strict curfew 10pm. $12, nonmembers $24.) **Kent Park Campgrounds** (645-2315), 9 mi. west on U.S. 6, manages 86 secluded first come, first served sites in a pretty area near a lake ($4, with electricity $8).

Downtown invites the budget traveler with good, cheap restaurants and bars; at the open-air **Pedestrian Mall,** on College and Dubuque St., you can eat and shop among the melodies of street musicians. In the mall, **Gringo's,** 115 E. College St. (338-3000), slaps down Mexican dishes ($4.50-8) and all-you-can-eat buffets Mondays ($7) and Tuesdays ($5) from 5 to 8pm (open Mon.-Thurs. 11am-10pm, Fri.-Sat. 11am-11pm, Sun. 11:30am-10pm). A college favorite, **Micky's Irish Pub,** 11 S. Dubuque St. (338-6860), will rock your world with salads, mickwiches, and burgers ($5-8; open Mon.-Fri. 11am-10pm, Sat.-Sun. 7am-10pm). Play pool at **Vito's,** 118 E. College St. (338-1393), in the Pedestrian Mall, while they craft pizzas ($10-13), pastas ($6-8), and drinks (open daily 11am-9pm).

Sights, Entertainment, and Nightlife Iowa City's main attraction, the **Old Capitol** building (335-0548), at Capitol and Iowa St., has been restored almost beyond recognition (open Mon.-Sat. 10am-3pm, Sun. noon-4pm; free). The capitol is the focal point of the **Pentacrest,** a five-building formation with a center green perfect for hanging out. One of the five buildings, the **Museum of Natural History** (335-0480), at Jefferson and Clinton, displays killer dioramas on the Native Americans of Iowa (open Mon.-Sat. 9:30am-4:30pm, Sun. 12:30-4:30pm; free). Although it may sound strange, the **University of Iowa Hospitals and Clinics** (335-0480), on Hawkins Dr. in Coralville, feels more like Disney World than a sick ward; it features free concerts, an in-house museum, and an extensive collection of art sprinkled throughout its corridors. Enter at the main entrance and take elevator D to the eighth floor **Medical Museum** (open Mon.-Fri. 8am-5pm, Sat.-Sun. 1-4pm). **Hancher Auditorium** (800-426-2437), North Riverside Dr., hosts top-notch performances; ask for student and senior discounts.

Bars and nightspots cover the downtown. Local jazz, folk, and blues play Thursdays through Saturdays at 9:30pm in **The Sanctuary,** 405 S. Gilbert (351-5692), a cozy, wood-paneled restaurant and bar with 111 beers (cover varies; open daily 4pm-2am). **The Union Bar and Grill,** 121 E. College St. (339-7713), brags that it's the "biggest damn bar in the Big Ten" (open Tues.-Sat 7pm-2am).

■■■ AMANA COLONIES

In 1714, German fundamentalists disillusioned with the established church formed the Community of True Inspiration. Facing persecution at home, they fled to the U.S. in 1843, settling near Buffalo, NY until their community grew too large. They migrated again—this time to the rich lands along the Iowa River, where they founded the Amana Colonies (Amana means "to remain true"), where they lived a quiet, communal lifestyle. Eventually, they became tired of the sacrifices required to maintain the community, and in 1932 they went capitalist. Some members joined to form the Amana Society, Inc., which now owns most of the area's land and mills; another member started the hugely successful Amana Refrigeration Co. Unlike the Amish, the Inspirationists did not believe that technology or material wealth obstructed personal piety. Although the colonies have become a large tourist attraction, most of the stores are run by colonists' descendents (and some former commune members themselves), and many are still active in the Church.

Practical Information The Amana Colonies lie 5 mi. north of I-80, clustered around the intersection of U.S. 6, Rte. 220, and U.S. 151. From Iowa City, take U.S. 6 west to U.S. 151; from Des Moines, take exit 225 off I-80 north on U.S. 151. Until 1994, there were no addresses in the colonies, only place names. The main thoroughfare, the **Amana Trail,** runs off U.S. 151 and goes through all seven villages; signs off this road point to the main attractions. **Main Amana** is the largest and most touristy town; farther out, the smaller villages offer a taste of earlier times. There is no public transportation in the Colonies. The **Amana Colonies Visitors Center** (800-245-5465), just west of Amana on Rte. 220, provides free calls to area motels and B&Bs (open Mon.-Sat. 9am-5pm, Sun. 10am-5pm; call for winter hours). A private car **caravan tour** (622-6178) covering six villages begins from the visitors center every Saturday at 10am (3hr., $8, ages 6-12 $4; covers all admission fees). Throughout the colonies, look for the helpful *Guide Map.* Main Amana's **post office:** 4015 G St. (622-3019), off U.S. 151 (open Mon.-Fri. 7:30-11am and noon-4:30pm, Sat. 8-9:30am); **ZIP code:** 52203; **area code:** 319.

Accommodations and Camping Most lodging options consist of pricey but personal B&Bs ($40-60); call from the visitors center. At the **Guest House**

Motor Inn (622-3599), on 47th Ave. in downtown Main Amana, rooms in a 135-year-old former communal kitchen have charming quilts on the beds (singles $37, doubles $43). **Sudbury Court Motel** (642-5411), 7 mi. west of the colonies on U.S. 6 at M St. in Marengo, offers large, cheap rooms in a quiet location (singles $24, doubles $29). Camp at the **Amana Community Park,** on 27th Ave. in Middle Amana (call visitors center for info; no showers; sites $3 per vehicle, with hookup $4.50).

Food Restaurants throughout the colonies serve huge portions of heavy food family-style. **Ox Yoke Inn** (800-233-3441), on 220th Trail in Main Amana, has the most extensive German menu around; family-style lunch ($6-9) and dinner ($9-12) come with shared salad, cottage cheese, sauerkraut, bread, vegetables, and potatoes (open Mon.-Sat. 11am-8pm, Sun. 9am-7pm). Middle Amana's **Hahn's Hearth Oven Bakery** (622-3439), at 25th and J St., sells the scrumptious products of the colonies' only functional open-hearth oven. (Open April-Oct. Tues.-Sat. 7am to sell-out, usually around 4:30pm; Nov.-Dec. and March Wed. and Sat. only.) Sample some dandelion wine at the **Heritage Wine and Cheese Haus** (622-3564), in Main Amana, which brims with local goods and free samples (open Mon.-Wed. 9am-6pm, Thurs.-Sat. 9am-7pm, Sun. 9am-6pm).

Sights The **Amana Heritage Society** (622-3567) operates four museums in the area: Museum of Amana History, Communal Kitchen and Cooper Shop Museum, Communal Agriculture Museum, and Community Church. A combination ticket can be purchased for all four sights. The **Museum of Amana History** (622-3567), on 220th Trail in Main Amana, helps explain what life was like for the colonists with restored buildings and a super-cool slide show. (Open mid-April to mid-Nov. Mon.-Sat. 10am-5pm, Sun. noon-5pm. $3, ages 8-17 $1.) Near the **Amana Refrigeration Plant,** in Middle Amana, tour the **Communal Kitchen Museum** (622-3567), the former site of all local food preparation (open May-Oct. Mon.-Sat. 9am-5pm, Sun. noon-5pm; $1.50, kids 75¢). **Mini Americana** (622-3058), in South Amana on 220th trail, has a quirky exhibit of American history in miniature; the entire collection was built by a man named Henry Moore (not the sculptor) and is run by his family (open daily April-Oct. 9am-5pm; $3, grades 7-12 $1.50, grades 1-6 75¢). The **High Amana Store** (622-3797), at 13th and G St., hasn't changed its interior or the friendliness of its service since 1857 (usually open daily 10am-5pm, less in winter).

Nebraska

Early travelers on the Oregon and Mormon trails rushed through Nebraska on their way towards western gold and greenery. Accustomed to the forested hills of New England, these pioneers nicknamed Nebraska Territory the "Great American Desert," mistakenly believing that if trees did not grow here, neither would crops. Eventually, they caught on, and began to abandon their westward journeys to farm the fertile Nebraskan soil. Their settlements drove out the native tribes of Sioux and Pawnee, who had long understood the value of Nebraska's land. But neither these property-minded settlements, which have since grown into cities, nor the tourists who drive past Scotts Bluff in air-conditioned autos can truly master the land: "We come and go, but the land is always here," philosophized Willa Cather, "and the people who love it and understand it are the people who own it—for a little while."

PRACTICAL INFORMATION

Capital: Lincoln.

Tourist Information: Nebraska Department of Economic Development, P.O. Box 94666, Lincoln 68509 (402-471-3796 or 800-228-4307). Open Mon.-Fri. 8am-

5pm. **Nebraska Game and Parks Commission,** 2200 N. 33rd St., Lincoln 68503 (471-0641). Open Mon.-Fri. 8am-5pm.

Time Zone: Central (1hr. behind Eastern). **Postal Abbreviation:** NE

Sales Tax: 5%.

■■■ OMAHA

Omaha is not the type of place one associates with "Nebraska." The birthplace of Gerald Ford, Malcolm X, and Boys Town, Omaha's diversity and urbanity shock the traveler lulled by miles of monotonous cornfields. From the quiet streetside cafés of the Old Market to the jumping gay clubs at 16th and Leavenworth, Omaha offers cosmopolitan glitz with midwestern manners, combining world-class museums and restaurants with the native friendliness of a Nebraska small town.

PRACTICAL INFORMATION

Tourist Office: Greater Omaha Convention and Visitors Bureau, 6800 Mercy Rd., #202 (800-332-1819). Open Mon.-Fri. 8:30am-4:30pm. The **Visitors Center** (595-3990), at 10th and Deer Park by the zoo, is much easier to find; get off I-80 at 13th St. Open daily 8am-5pm; Nov.-Feb. Mon.-Fri. 8am-5pm. **Events Hotline,** 444-6800. **Gay and Lesbian Hotline,** 558-5303.

Trains: Amtrak, 1003 S. 9th St. (800-872-7245), at Pacific. To: Chicago (1 per day, 9½hr., $103); Denver (1 per day, 8hr., $108). Open daily 10:30pm-7:30am, Mon.-Sat. 7:30-11:15am and 12:30-4pm.

Buses: Greyhound, 1601 Jackson (800-231-2222). To: Des Moines (9 per day, 2-3hr., $25); Cheyenne (3 per day, 9-11hr., $67); Kansas City (2 per day, 4-6hr., $36); Sioux Falls (2 per day, 3-4hr., $35). Open 24 hrs.

Public Transportation: Metro Area Transit (MAT), 2222 Cumming St. (341-0800). Open Mon.-Fri. 8am-4:30pm. Schedules available at the Park Fair Mall, at 16th and Douglas near the Greyhound station, and the library at 14th and Farnam. Fare 90¢, transfers 5¢.

Taxis: Happy Cab, 339-0110. $1.80 first mi., $1.25 per additional mi. 24 hrs.

Car Rental: Cheepers Rent-a-Car, 7700 L St. (331-8586). $19 per day with 100 free mi.; $25 per day with 300 free mi., 20¢ per additional mi. Must be 21 and have a major credit card as well as a personal liability policy. Open Mon.-Fri. 7:30am-8pm, Sat. 8:30am-3pm.

Crisis Lines: Rape Crisis, 345-7273. **Suicide Hotline,** 449-4650. Both 24 hrs.

Emergency: 911.

Post Office: 1124 Pacific St. (348-2895). Open Mon.-Fri. 8am-6pm, Sat. 8am-noon. **ZIP code:** 68108. **Area code:** 402.

Numbered north-south streets begin at the river and go west; named roads run east-west. **Dodge St.** (Rte. 6) divides the city north-south. At night, avoid N. 24th St.

ACCOMMODATIONS AND CAMPING

Many budget motels lie off I-80 at the L or 84th St. exits 6½ mi. southwest of downtown. Buses #11, 21, and 55 service the area.

YMCA, 430 S. 20th St. (341-1600) at Howard. Plain, basic rooms. Co-ed by floor. Microwave. Men's and women's singles $9.41-11.41. Linen provided. Key deposit $10. $3.50 extra to use athletic facilities. Call ahead; if they have no more women's rooms, speak to John Fitzgerald—he may be able to set you up.

Excel Inn, 2211 Douglas St. (345-9565). Downtown location is ideal for the carless. Newly remodeled rooms in a slightly frayed neighborhood. Singles $25, doubles $31, with kitchenette $38. Stay 4 nights, and the next 3 nights are free.

Bellevue Campground (291-3379), Haworth Park, on the Missouri River 10mi. south of downtown at Rte. 370. Take the infrequent bus "Bellevue" from 17th and Dodge to Mission and Franklin, and walk down Mission. Sites are paved with concrete, but there are enough trees to eliminate that trailer park feel. Showers, toilets, shelters. Open daily 6am-10pm; quiet stragglers can enter after hours. Sites $5, with hookup $9.

FOOD

Once a warehouse area, the **Old Market,** on Jones, Howard, and Harney St. between 10th and 13th, now has cobblestone streets with hopping shops, restaurants, and bars. While you're there, visit the erie **Fountain of the Furies,** "Greek avengers of patricide and disrespect of ancestors," in a dim alcove across from Trini's (see below). Late May through early October, local growers stage a **Farmers Market** (345-5401), Saturdays from 8am to 12:30pm at 11th and Jackson St.

Trini's, 1020 Howard St. (346-8400), in the Old Market inside the "Passageway" on Howard. Authentic Mexican and vegetarian food. The elegant candlelight grotto makes for an exquisitely romantic dining experience. Dinner $2.50-7. Open Mon.-Thurs. 11:30am-10pm, Fri.-Sat. 11:30am-11pm.

The Jones Street Brewery, 1316 Jones St. (344-3858). A trendy, clean-cut microbrewery that serves soups, salads, and the "Need a Brew Burger," with jalapeños and hot sauce ($7). Live music on weekends; cover varies. Open Mon.-Thurs. 11:30am-11pm, Fri.-Sat. 11:30am-midnight, Sun. 2-10pm.

The Bohemian Café, 1406 S. 13th St. (342-9838), in South Omaha's old Slavic neighborhood. Caters to the slightly older crowd with meaty German and Czech fare accompanied by onions and potatoes ($6-8). Open daily 11am-10pm.

Joe Tess' Place, 5424 S. 24th St. (731-7278), at U St. in South Omaha; take the bus from Farnam and 16th. Renowned for its fresh, fried carp and catfish. Admire the albino carp for sale in the fountain—they're a paler version of your dinner. Entrees $3-7. Open Sun.-Thurs. 11am-10pm, Fri.-Sat. 11am-11pm.

SIGHTS

Omaha's **Joslyn Art Museum,** 2200 Dodge St. (342-3300), a monumental Art Deco masterpiece, presents an exterior of pink Georgian marble and an interior decorated with 30 different types of the stone. It contains an excellent collection of 19th- and 20th-century European and American art. From mid-July to mid-August, the museum hosts free "Jazz on the Green" concerts each Thursday from 7 to 9pm. (Open Tues.-Sat. 10am-5pm, Thurs. until 8pm, Sun. noon-5pm. $4, seniors and ages 5-11 $2; free Sat. 10am-noon.) The grand **Union Pacific Railroad Station** houses the **Western Heritage Museum,** 801 S. 10th St. (444-5071), which in turn houses a huge exhibit on historic life in Nebraska. The museum will be closed from January to June of 1996 for renovations. (Open Mon.-Sat. 10am-5pm, Sun. 1-5pm; Labor Day-Memorial Day closed Mon. $3, seniors $2.50, ages 5-12 $2.)

The largest indoor jungle in the world has made the amazing **Henry Doorly Zoo,** 3701 S. 10th St. (733-8401), at Deer Park Blvd. (or exit at 13th St. off I-80), the number one tourist attraction between Chicago and Denver. At the Kingdom of the Seas Aquarium, brown sharks swim above the glass-enclosed walkway. (Open Mon.-Sat. 9:30am-5pm, Sun. 9:30am-6pm, Labor Day-Memorial Day daily 9:30am-5pm. $7, seniors $5.50, ages 5-11 $3.50.)

In 1917, Father Edward Flanagan founded **Boys Town** (498-1140), west of Omaha at West Dodge and 132nd St., as a home for troubled and neglected boys. Made famous by the 1938 Spencer Tracy movie of the same name, Boys Town has become a popular tourist attraction and still provides a home to more than 550 boys and girls. Visits are free; guided tours take place hourly from 9am-4pm. (Visitors center open daily 9am-5:30pm; Sept.-April 9am-4:30pm.)

ENTERTAINMENT AND NIGHTLIFE

In late June and early July, **Shakespeare on the Green** (280-2391) stages free performances in Elmwood Park, on 60th and Dodge, Sunday through Thursday at 8pm. The **Omaha Symphony** (342-3560) plays at the **Orpheum Theatre,** 409 S. 16th St. (Sept.-May usually Thurs.-Sun.; call for specific dates and times; tickets $10-32). **Omaha's Magic Theater,** 325 S. 16th St. (346-1227; call Mon.-Fri. 9am-4pm), devotes itself to the development of new American musicals (evening performances Mon.-Sat. tickets $12, children $7).

Punk and progressive folk have found a niche at the several area universities; check the window of the **Antiquarian Bookstore,** at 1215 Harney, in the Old Market, for the scoop on shows. Several good bars cluster nearby. **The Dubliner,** 1205 Harney (342-5887), stages live traditional Irish music Friday and Saturday nights (cover varies). **Downtown Grounds,** 1117 Jackson St. (342-1654), grinds with live music in a tragically hip coffeehouse. (Double mocha $3. Live music Fri.-Sat. and Mon.; cover Fri.-Sat $2. Open Mon.-Thurs. 9am-10pm, Fri. 9am-midnight, Sat. 8am-midnight, Sun. 10am-10pm.) A string of gay bars hover within a block of 16th and Leavenworth. One of the most popular, **The Max,** 1417 Jackson (346-4110; no sign outside), caters to men and women with five bars, a disco dance floor, DJ, fountains, and patio (cover Fri.-Sat. $3; open daily 4pm-1am).

■■■ LINCOLN

Friendly folk, cool nightlife, a renovated downtown, and the University of Nebraska endow Lincoln (christened in 1867 after the President) with the culture and entertainment options of a city and the atmosphere of a small town. In its breathtaking capitol building, the "Tower on the Plains," Lincoln houses the only unicameral (one-house) state legislature in the U.S. The state switched from two houses during the Great Depression in order to save money and avoid red tape; today, the Nebraskan government is considered a model of efficiency.

PRACTICAL INFORMATION

Tourist Office: Lincoln Convention and Visitors Bureau, 1221 N St., #320 (434-5335 or 800-423-8212). Open Mon.-Fri. 8am-4:45pm.

Airport: Lincoln Airport (474-2770), 5mi. northwest of downtown on Cornhusker Hwy. A taxi to downtown costs about $10.

Trains: Amtrak, 201 N. 7th St. (476-1295 or 800-872-7245). Once daily to: Omaha (1hr., $14); Denver (7½hr., $106); Chicago (10½hr., $111); Kansas City (6½hr., $46). Open nightly 11:30pm-7am; Mon.-Wed. also 7:30-11am and 12:30-4pm.

Buses: Greyhound, 940 P St. (474-1071 or 800-231-2222), close to downtown and city campus. To: Omaha (4 per day, 1hr., $12); Chicago (4 per day, 12-14hr., $71); Kansas City (3 per day, 6½hr., $41); Denver (3 per day, 9-11hr., $67). Open Mon.-Fri. 8:30am-5:30pm, Sat. 9am-5pm.

Public Transportation: Star Trans, 710 J St. (476-1234). Schedules are available on the bus, at many downtown locations, and at the office. Buses run Mon.-Sat. 6am-6pm. Fare 75¢, seniors with Medicare card 35¢, ages 5-11 40¢.

Taxis: Husker Cabs, Inc., 447-4111. $1.75 initial fee, $1.60 per mi. 24 hrs.

Car Rental: U-Save Auto Rental, 2240 Q St. (477-5236), at 23rd St. $20 per day with 150 free mi.; 9¢ per additional mi.; $132 per week. Must be 21. $100 deposit.

Bike Rental: Blue's Bike & Fitness Center, 427 S. 13th (435-2322), at K St. Bikes $8 ½-day, $12 per day. Credit card deposit required. Open Mon.-Thurs. 9am-7pm, Fri. 9am-6pm, Sat. 9am-5pm, Sun. noon-4pm.

Quadratic Formula: $(-b\pm\sqrt{(b^2-4ac)})/(2a)$.

Crisis Lines: Crisis Line, 475-5171. **Rape Crisis Line,** 475-7273. Both 24 hrs. **University of Nebraska Gay/Lesbian Resource Center,** 472-5644.

Emergency: 911.

Post Office: 700 R St. (473-1695). Open Mon.-Fri. 7:30am-6pm, Sat. 9am-noon. **ZIP code:** 68501. **Area code:** 402.

Getting around Lincoln is as easy as A,B,C, 1,2,3, cha cha cha. Numbered streets increase as you go west; lettered streets progress through the alphabet as you go north. **O St.** is the main east-west drag, splitting the town north-south. **R St.** runs along the south side of the **University of Nebraska-Lincoln (UNL)** campus. **Cornhusker Hwy. (U.S. 6)** shears the northwest edge of Lincoln.

ACCOMMODATIONS AND CAMPING

There are few inexpensive motels in downtown Lincoln; most abound east of downtown around the 5600 block of **Cornhusker Hwy.** The **Town House Motel,** 1744 M St. (800-279-1744), at 18th only 5 blocks from the downtown campus, has sweet suites with full kitchen, bath, living room, a pull-out sofabed, and cable TV (silverware and parking included; singles $39, doubles $44). The city's only hostel is the small, ministry-run **Cornerstone Hostel (HI-AYH),** 640 N. 16th St. (476-0355 or 476-0926), at Vine, located in the basement of a church in the university's downtown campus. Take the #4 bus; from the Greyhound station, walk 7 blocks east to 16th, then 5 blocks north. (2 single-sex rooms; 3 beds for women, 5 for men. Shower, full kitchen, laundry facilities. Free parking. Curfew 11pm. $8, nonmembers $10. Free linen.) **UNL** (472-3561) rents some rooms when school is not in session; sheets, towels, and blankets are included (singles $17, doubles $11.50 per person). **The Great Plains Budget Host Inn,** 2732 O St. (476-3253 or 800-288-8499), has large rooms with fridges and coffeemakers; take bus #9 "O St. Shuttle" (free parking; singles $34, doubles $42; free continental breakfast). The **Nebraska State Fair Park Campground,** 2402 N. 14th St. (473-4287), offers a convenient location and a parking-lot atmosphere; take bus #7 "Belmont." (Site for 2 $10, with electricity $12, with full hookup $15; $1 per additional person. Open mid-April to Nov. 1.)

FOOD AND NIGHTLIFE

A dandy collegiate hangout, the **Nebraska Union** (472-2181), on 14th and R on campus, has cheap and speedy food, a post office, an ATM, and a bank (hours vary, but usually in summer Mon.-Fri. 7am-5pm, academic year daily 7am-11pm). **Historic Haymarket,** 7th to 9th and O to R St., is a newly renovated warehouse district near the train tracks, with cafés, bars, several restaurants and a **farmers market** (434-6900; open mid-May to mid-Oct. Sat. 8am-12:30pm). All downtown buses connect at 11th & O St., 2 blocks east of Historic Haymarket. Every renovated warehouse district has its yuppie brewery, and **Lazlo's Brewery and Grill,** 710 P St. (474-BEER/2337), is the oldest brewery in Nebraska, founded in 1991; chow down on salads, sandwiches, burgers, steak, and chicken entrees for $5-15 (open Mon.-Sat. 11am-1am, Sun. 11am-10pm). Cheap bars and eateries cluster downtown between N and P from 12th to 15th St. Bop on into the **Rock 'n' Roll Runza,** 210 N. 14th St. (474-2030) for roller-skating waitstaff, foot-long chili cheese dogs ($5), and the ultimate diner experience. (Open Mon.-Thurs. 10:30am-10:30pm, Fri.-Sat. 10:30am-midnight, Sun. 10am-10pm; "unless we want to close early.") **Valentino's,** 232 N. 13th St. (475-1501), a regional chain with roots in Lincoln, offers inexpensive Italian pizza and pasta ($3-10). Locals come to sample from six different all-you-can-eat buffets—pizza, pasta, dessert, and more. ($5, after 4pm $7. Open Sun.-Thurs. 11am-10pm, Fri.-Sat. 11am-midnight.) **The Coffee House,** 1324 P St. (477-6611), provides that near-a-university, espresso-induced intellectual-conversation kind of atmosphere (coffee 75¢-$1.25; open Mon.-Sat. 7am-midnight, Sun 11am-midnight).

Nightspots abound in Lincoln, particularly of the sports-bar variety; locals always take time to celebrate Nebraska football, Lincoln's pride and joy. For the biggest names in Lincoln's live music scene, try **The Zoo Bar,** 136 N. 14th St. (435-8754). Cover varies, as does the music, but the emphasis is blues; *good* blues—Kansas City's famed Grand Emporium was patterned on this place. (Must be 21. Fri. 5-7pm cover $1. Open Mon.-Fri. 3pm-1am, Sat. noon-1am.) **The Panic,** 200 S. 18th St. (435-8764), at N St., is a great gay dance/video/patio bar (open Mon.-Fri. 4pm-1am, Sat.-Sun. 1pm-1am). And now for something completely different... **Sidetracks Tavern,** 935 O St. (435-9171). Sing along with house band Joyce, Paul, and Fred—they play everything, and everyone joins in the ruckus (Fri.-Sat. 7pm-1am).

SIGHTS AND ENTERTAINMENT

The "Tower on the Plains," the 400-ft. **Nebraska State Capitol Building** (471-0448), 14th at K St., an unofficial architectural wonder of the world, wows with its streamlined exterior and detailed interior. Its mosaic floor is reminiscent of a Native American blanket. Even more remarkable, the building was completely paid for at its dedication (to the tune of $9.8 million). Take the elevator to the 14th floor for a view of the city. (Tours June-Aug. Mon.-Fri. every 30min.; Sept.-May daily every hr. Open Mon.-Fri. 8am-5pm, Sat. 10am-5pm, Sun. 1-5pm. Free, 'cause it's paid for.)

The **Museum of Nebraska History** (471-4754), 15th and P St., has a phenomenal, moving exhibit on the history of the Plains Indians (open Mon.-Sat. 9am-5pm, Sun. 1:30-5pm; free). The **University of Nebraska State Museum** at **Morrill Hall** (472-6302), 14th and U St., houses an amazing fossil collection that includes the largest mounted mammoth in any American museum (open Mon.-Sat. 9:30am-4:30pm, Sun. 1:30-4:30pm; requested donation $1). In the same building, the **Mueller Planetarium** (472-2641) lights up the ceiling with several shows daily and laser shows Fridays and Saturdays (call for times; planetarium $3, students and under 13 $2; laser shows $5/$2). An extensive sculpture garden surrounds the Phillip Johnson-designed **Sheldon Memorial Art Gallery** (472-2461), 12th and R St.; inside a Pop art collection by Warhol stands out along with several other excellent exhibits (open Tues.-Wed. 10am-5pm, Thurs.-Sat. 10am-5pm and 7-9pm, Sun. 2-9pm; free). **Antelope Park** stretches from 23rd and N St. just southeast of campus to 33rd and Sheridan Blvd. Open sunrise to midnight year-round, the park contains a golf course, botanical gardens, and jogging and biking trails. Many couples marry among the lily ponds of the **Sunken Gardens,** at 27th and D St.

■■■ SCOTTS BLUFF

The beautiful clay and sandstone highlands of **Scotts Bluff National Monument** were landmarks for people traveling the **Oregon Trail** in the 1840s. For some time the bluff was too dangerous to pass through, but in the 1850s a single-file wagon trail was opened through narrow **Mitchell's Pass,** where traffic wore deep marks in the sandstone. Evidence of the early pioneers can still be seen today on the ½-mi. stretch of the original Oregon Trail preserved at the pass. The **visitors center** (308-436-4340), at the entrance on Rte. 92, will tell you of the mysterious death of Hiram Scott, the fur trader who gave the Bluffs their name (open daily 8am-8pm, in winter 8am-5pm; $4 per carload, $2 per pedestrian). To get to the top of the bluffs, hike the strenuous **Saddle Rock Trail** (1.6 mi. each way) or motor up **Summit Dr.** At the top, there are **nature trails** and a magnificent view. Take U.S. 26 to Rte. 92; the monument is on Rte. 92 about 2 mi. west of **Gering** (*not* in the town of Scottsbluff).

For a cheap bed, try **Circle S Lodge** (308-436-2157), on Rte. 92 in Gering (singles $26, doubles $33). The **Oregon Trail Park** (308-436-5096, ext. 838), at 10th and D St. in Gering, across from a public park, offers campsites with a distant view of the Bluffs (12 sites $8, hookup available). Twenty mi. east on Rte. 92, the 525-ft. spire of **Chimney Rock,** visible from more than 30 mi. away, is another familiar landmark for travelers on the Oregon Trail. A gravel road leads from Rte. 92 to within ½ mi. of it. For more information, contact the Scotts Bluff National Monument.

Carhenge—Unofficial Monument to Let's Go: USA

Driving through the low plains and small bluffs of western Nebraska, things begin to look the same. Suddenly, a preternatural power sweeps the horizon as you come in view of the ultimate shrine to bizarre on-the-road Americana—Carhenge. Made up of 36 old cars painted gray, this bizarre sculpture has the same orientation and dimensions as Stonehenge in England. Jim Reinders, creator and guru to travel guide writers in Cambridge seeking quirky spirituality, wants to be buried here someday. When asked why he built it, Reinders replied, "plane, loqui deprehendi," or "clearly, I spoke to be understood." This wonder of the cornhuskers can be found 2 mi. north on U.S. 385 from **Alliance,** NE. If you need to recenter your karma for the night, try the **Rainbow Lodge,** 614 W. 3rd St./U.S. 385 (308-762-4980; singles $27, doubles $35).

Kansas

The geographic center of the contiguous U.S., Kansas has been a major link in the nation's chain since the 1820s. Families on the Oregon and Santa Fe Trails drove their wagons west in search of new homes, while cowboys on the Chisholm Trail drove their longhorns north in search of railroads and good times. Cowtowns such as Abilene and Dodge City were happy to oblige; these rip-roaring meccas of gambling and drinking made legends of lawmen like "Wild Bill" Hickok and Wyatt Earp. The influx of settlers resulted in fierce battles over land, as whites forced Native Americans to move into the arid regions farther west. More grueling feuds over Kansas's slavery status (Kansas joined the Union as a free state in 1861) gave rise to the term "Bleeding Kansas." The wound has healed, and Kansas today presents a peaceful blend of kitschy tourist attractions—the Kansas Teachers' Hall of Fame in Dodge City or the World's Largest Hand-Dug Well in Greensburg—and farmland. Highway signs subtly remind travelers that "every Kansas farmer feeds 75 people—and *you.*"

PRACTICAL INFORMATION

Capital: Topeka.
Division of Travel and Tourism: 700 SW Harrison, #1300, Topeka 66603-3712 (800-2KANSAS/252-6727). Open Mon.-Fri. 10am-6pm. **Kansas Wildlife and Parks,** 900 Jackson Ave., #502N, Topeka 66612 (913-296-2281).
Time Zone: Central (1hr. behind Eastern). **Postal Abbreviation:** KS
Sales Tax: 4.9%.

■■■ WICHITA

In 1541, Coronado came to the site of present-day Wichita in search of the mythical gold-laden city Quivira. Upon arriving, he was so disappointed that he had his guide strangled for misleading him. The largest city in Kansas (yes, the rest are even smaller), Wichita is *the* place for airplane manufacturing: Lear, Boeing, Beech, and Cessna all have factories in town. Much of the downtown is painfully suburban in its tree-lined stillness. However, as the Old Town area gets revamped, bars and cafés there party farther and farther into the Kansas night.

Practical Information The **Convention and Visitors Bureau,** dispenses info at 100 S. Main St. (265-2800), on the corner of Douglas Ave. (open Mon.-Fri. 8am-5pm). The closest **Amtrak** station, 414 Main St. (283-7533 or 800-872-7245), in the town of Newton, 25 mi. north of Wichita, sends one (very early) train for Kansas City (4hr., $54) and Albuquerque (12hr., $136) each day (ticket office open Wed.-Fri. 7:30am-4pm). **Hutchinson Shuttle** (800-288-3342), provides transport to and from the Newton Amtrak Station for $15 (to Newton Mon.-Fri. 1pm; return Mon.-Fri. 10:45am). **Greyhound,** 312 S. Broadway (265-7711 or 800-231-2222), barks 2 blocks east of Main St. (open daily 3:15am-7pm). Buses serve Kansas City (3 per day, 5hr., $34), Denver (2 per day, 14hr., $59-67), and Dodge City (1 per day, 3hr., $24). **WMTA,** 214 S. Topeka (265-7221), handles in-town transportation. (Buses Mon.-Fri. 6:20am-6:20pm, Sat. 7:20am-5:20pm. Fare 85¢, seniors 40¢, ages 6-17 55¢; transfers 20¢. Station open Mon.-Fri. 6am-6:30pm, Sat. 7am-5:30pm.) In the summer a **trolley** (25¢) runs from downtown to Old Town during lunch hours (Mon.-Fri. 11am-3:30pm) and from downtown to Old Town and the museums on the river on Saturdays (10am-3:40pm). **Thrifty Rent-A-Car,** 8619 W. Kellogg (721-9552), puts you in a car for $35 per day (250 free mi., 29¢ each additional mi.) or $145 per week (2000 free mi.). You must be 21; ages 21 to 24 pay a $5-per-day surcharge (open daily 6:30am-10pm). **Emergency:** 911. Wichita's **post office:** 330 W. Second St.

(262-6245), at Waco (open Mon.-Fri. 7am-5:30pm, Sat. 7am-1pm; lobby open 24 hrs.); **ZIP code:** 67202; **area code:** 316.

Wichita lies on I-35, 170 mi. north of Oklahoma City and about 200 mi. southwest of Kansas City. Small and quiet, downtown makes for easy walking or parking. **Main St.** is the major north-south artery. **Douglas Ave.** divides the numbered east-west streets to the north from the named east-west streets to the south. Many downtown businesses have moved out along **Kellogg Ave. (U.S. 54),** the main east-west route.

Accommodations and Chow Wichita offers up a bounty of cheap hotels. South Broadway has plenty of mom-and-pop places, but be wary of the neighborhood. The chains line E. and W. Kellogg Ave. 5 to 8 mi. from downtown. Only ten blocks from downtown, the **Mark 8 Inn,** 1130 N. Broadway (265-4679), hits the mark with a nice neighborhood, clean rooms, free local calls, and fridges (singles $27, each additional person $3; no checks). The **Royal Lodge,** 320 E. Kellogg Ave. (263-8877), near downtown and the bus station, has funky 60s furniture and cable TV (singles $25, doubles $30; key deposit $5; no checks). **Blasi Campgrounds,** 11209 W. U.S. 54 (722-2681), about 8 mi. west of downtown, features a pool, tennis courts, and a small fishing pond in a next-to-the-highway setting. (Tent sites or full hookups $14.45; weekly rates, AAA, and AARP discounts available.)

Wichita is flavored with *meat*!!! If you eat only one slab of meat in Wichita, make it a slab from **Doc's Steakhouse,** 1515 N. Broadway (264-4735), where the most expensive entree, a 17-oz. T-bone, is only $9. (Open Mon.-Thurs. 11:30am-9:30pm, Fri. 11:30am-10pm, Sat. 4-10pm.) Doc's brother Ted opened a small drug store in South Dakota sometime in the 1930s, and he'd like you to know that, from Doc's, it's "676 mi. to Wall Drug" (for more on this roadside legend see p. 471). Veggie-philes get their fill on Chinese and Vietnamese dishes ($4.50-7) at **Saigon Oriental Restaurant,** 1103 N. Broadway (262-8134; open Sun.-Thurs. 10am-9pm, Fri.-Sat. 10am-10pm). In the **Old Town** area, at Douglas Ave. and Washington St., revitalized warehouses now house breweries and restaurants; many have live music on weekends. **Station Square** (263-1950), at Mead St. and Douglas Ave., combines two restaurants, two bars, and an outdoor barbecue grill, for cuisine and atmosphere ranging from 50s-diner-style to fajitas and 'ritas (live jazz and oldies Fri.-Sat.; open Sun.-Thurs. 11am-midnight, Fri.-Sat. 11am-2am).

Sights The museums of the **Museums-on-the-River** series are located within a few blocks of each other; take the trolley or bus #12 ("Riverside"), then walk. **Old Cowtown,** 1871 Sim Park Dr. (264-0671), walks you through the rough and tumble cattle days of the 1870s with an open-air history exhibit. (Open Mon.-Sat. 10am-5pm, Sun. noon-5pm; Nov.-Feb. weekends only. $5, seniors $4.50, ages 6-12 $2, under 6 free.) Across the way, **Botanica,** 701 Amidon (264-0448), presents an interesting and colorful series of gardens. (Open Mon.-Wed. 9am-8pm, Thurs.-Sat. 9am-5pm, Sun 1-5pm; Sept.-Dec. Mon.-Sat. 9am-5pm, Sun. 1-5pm; Jan.-March Mon.-Fri. 9am-5pm; April Mon.-Sat. 9am-5pm, Sun. 1-5pm. $3, students $2; Jan.-March. free) The **Mid-America All-Indian Center and Museum,** 650 N. Seneca (262-5221), just down the road, showcases traditional and modern works by Native American artists. The late Blackbear Bosin's awe-inspiring sculpture, *Keeper of the Plains,* stands guard over the grounds. (Open Mon.-Sat. 10am-5pm, Sun. 1-5pm. $2, ages 6-12 $1, under 6 free.) The **Mid-America All-Indian Intertribal Powwow** surrounds the museum with traditional dancing, foods, arts, and crafts during the last weekend in July. The **Wichita Art Museum,** 619 Stockman Dr. (268-4921), exhibits American art including works by Mary Cassatt, Winslow Homer, and Edward Hopper, as well as an interactive gallery for kids (open Tues.-Sat. 10am-5pm, Sun. 12-5pm; free).

Fifty-three sculptures adorn the campus of the **Wichita State University,** at N. Hillside and 17th St. (take the "East 17th" bus); the collection includes pieces by Rodin, Moore, Nevelson, and Hepworth. Get free sculpture maps at the **Edwin A. Ulrich Museum of Art** office (689-3664), in the McKnight Arts Center, also on campus, and admire the gigantic glass mosaic mural by Joan Miró which forms one wall of the building (call for hours; free). Just north of campus, the **Center for the Improvement of Human Functioning,** 3100 N. Hillside (682-3100), on the "N. Hillside-Oliver Loop" bus route, features a 40-ft. pyramid, used for reflection and receptions, with the world's largest FDA food pyramid painted on its side. Tours of the biochemical research station include a chance to "de-stress" mind, body, and soul by hurling clay skeet pigeons at a wall (tours daily 1:30pm; $4).

Wichita parties at the **River Festival** (May 10-19 in 1996), when concerts, sporting events, and culinary delights line the rivers ($2). The **Winfield Bluegrass Festival** (221-3250), 45 minutes southeast of Wichita on U.S. 77, will draw big-name artists for a long weekend of folk fun September 19-22, 1996.

■■■ LAWRENCE

In the 1850s, travelers weary of the Oregon Trail were attracted by the lush, hilly lands of eastern Kansas. Lawrence was founded by travelers who had had enough. Tired voyagers now enjoy the cafés and lively bars supported by the students of the **University of Kansas.** The university's **Museum of Anthropology** (864-4245), right across from their (not-so-exciting) Museum of Natural History, features traveling exhibits on American culture (open Mon.-Sat. 9am-5pm, Sun. 1-5pm; free). The **Spencer Museum of Art** (864-4710), on campus at 14th and Mississippi, has an extensive collection of Asian art. (Open Tues.-Wed. and Fri.-Sat. 8:30am-5pm, Thurs. 8:30am-8pm, Sun. noon-5pm. Free.) Students and professionals present plays and concerts at the **Lied Center** (864-ARTS/2787), at 15th and Iowa (box office open Mon.-Fri. noon-5:30pm). **Liberty Hall,** 644 Massachusetts St. (749-1972), rents videos, hosts concerts, and shows artsy and independent flicks in an ornate theater, complete with constellations twinkling on the ceiling. Chat with the employees to find out what's happening in town.

The **Convention and Visitors Bureau** (865-4411), at 8th and Vermont, has more local info (open Mon.-Fri. 8:30am-5pm). The **Greyhound** station can be found at 2447 W. 6th St. (843-5622). Lawrence's **area code:** 913.

If you need to spend the night, a slew of motels settle on 6th St. The **Westminster Inn,** 2525 W. 6th St. (841-8410), looks like a charming English lodge and has a swimming pool ($36 singles, $46 doubles). The **College Motel,** 1703 W. 6th St. (843-0131), has large, clean, phoneless rooms and a pool (rooms $30-40). Pitch your tent at **Clinton Lake Campground** (843-7665), 4 mi. west of town on 23rd St., and take advantage of fishing, hiking, and swimming in beautiful Clinton Lake State Park (tent and RV sites with hookup $10).

Fast food hangs out on 23rd St., Iowa St., and 6th St. Massachusetts St. is home to the funkier coffeehouses and bars. **Full Moon Café,** 803 Massachusetts St. (832-0444), feeds the hip and the hippie alike with tofu burgers ($4.25), falafel ($4.35), and meat dishes with an international theme. (Free live music Tues.-Wed. 8:30pm, Thurs.-Sat. 10pm. Open Tues.-Sat. 11am-midnight.) The **Paradise Café,** 728 Massachusetts St. (842-5199), specializes in good old American breakfasts (served until 2:30pm), lunches, and dinners. The pancakes of the day ($3) taste as good as this place smells. Dinners (burgers, salads, or steaks) range from $4.75 to $13. (Live jazz Thurs. 11pm; cover $1. Open Mon.-Sat. 6:30am-2:30pm and 5-10pm, Sun. 8am-2:30pm.) Watch 'em make brew, then try it at **The Freestate Brewery Co.,** 636 Massachusetts St. (843-4555), the oldest legal brewery in Kansas. Chase your beer with sandwiches, gumbo, or pasta. (Meals $4-9. Free live acoustic and jazz June-Aug. Thurs.-Fri. 7pm. Open Mon.-Sat. 11am-midnight, Sun. noon-11pm.) Live rock and

Geographic Center of the U.S.

Have you ever wanted to be the center of the action? Go 2 mi. northwest of **Lebanon,** KS. Sit by the stone monument and feel special—the entire contiguous U.S. is revolving around you.

reggae crowd **The Bottleneck,** 737 New Hampshire (842-5483; cover $3-15; open Mon.-Sat. 3pm-2am).

■■■ DODGE CITY

Legend haunts Dodge City, the "wickedest little city in America." Originally, soldiers built Fort Dodge with the hope that annihilating the buffalo would thereby annihilate the Native Americans. Rapidly, the city grew from the influx of buffalo hunters and the travelers on the Santa Fe Trail. By 1879, the buffalo were gone (over 3 million had been slaughtered), the railroad had arrived, and Dodge City had switched to cattle herding. With more gunfighters, prostitutes, and other lawless types than there are pages in this god-forsaken book, chaos reigned; at one time **Front St.,** the main drag, had a saloon for every 50 citizens. Legendary lawmen Wyatt Earp and Bat Masterson earned their fame cleaning up the streets of Dodge City. The city eventually burned, and has been replaced with a highly polished, touristy re-creation.

Saunter on down to the **Boot Hill Museum** (227-8188), at Front St. and 5th Ave., a block-long complex re-creating the Boot Hill cemetery and Front St. as they looked in the 1870s. A 1903 Santa Fe locomotive stands among the saloons, barber shops, and the restored and furnished **Hardesty House,** a rancher's Gothic Revival home. (Admission to the complex $5.50, seniors and ages 7-17 $5. Open daily 8am-8pm.) Across from Boot Hill, the **Wax Museum,** 603 5th Ave. (225-7311), also houses the **Kansas Teachers' Hall of Fame** (no kidding! open Mon.-Sat. 8am-6pm, Sun. 1-5pm; $2, ages 6-13 $1.25). Walk down 2nd Ave. to Front St. to check out **"El Capitan,"** an enormous longhorn cattle statue which commemorates the cattle drives of the 1870s. Today, longhorn cattle lumber through town only during **Dodge City Days** (225-2244), July 26-August 4, 1996, when the city reminisces with a huge festival.

Dodge City Convention and Visitors Dept., P.O. Box 1474, 67801 (225-8186), has additional info on the festival and rodeo. Their office is upstairs from the **Chamber of Commerce** (227-3119), at 4th Ave. and Spruce (open Mon.-Fri 9am-5pm). On the lawn outside, stop and see the town memorial **sculpture garden,** carved by the late dentist O.H. Simpson. The Dodge City attractions are all very walkable, but to go beyond the immediate downtown, call the **Minibus Transportation System** (225-8119), and they will pick you up for free within the city limits (operates Mon.-Fri. 9am-4pm; $1 donation requested). Dodge City's **area code:** 316.

On the east end of town, the **Western Inn Motel,** 2523 E. Wyatt Earp Blvd. (225-3000), offers large rooms, a pool, a restaurant, and free local calls (singles $33, doubles $40). Most other motels tucker out about 4 mi. west along Wyatt Earp Blvd. (U.S. 50 outside of town). Dodge City's campgrounds are adequate but none too scenic. The dusty **Gunsmoke Campground** (227-8247) on W. U.S. 50, 3 mi. west of Boot Hill, has a pool, an ice cream parlour, and an office that looks like a saloon (sites for 2 $11, with hookup $15; each additional person $1.50). The **Water Sports Campground,** 500 Cherry St. (225-9003), 10 blocks south of Front St. on 2nd Ave., has lakeside sites for fishing and swimming (sites for 2 $13, with full hookup $15, A/C $2 extra). Customers' crayon drawings line the walls at the comfortable **West Side Grill,** 2001 W. Wyatt Earp Blvd. (225-3100), where fajitas, burgers, and fish entrees run $3.50 to $10. (Open Mon. 5-10pm, Tues.-Thurs. 11am-10pm, Fri.-Sat. 11am-11pm, Sun. 11:30am-9pm.) **Peppercorn's,** 1301 W. Wyatt Earp Blvd. (225-2335), rustles up sandwiches and salads ($2-4.50) as well as steaks ($6.50-14) in a dark bar-like atmosphere. (Open Mon.-Thurs. 11am-midnight, Fri.-Sat. 11am-1am, Sun. 3pm-midnight; bar open Mon.-Sat. 11am-2am.)

North of the Oklahoma panhandle, Dodge City rides 150 mi. west of Wichita and 310 mi. east of Colorado Springs on U.S. 50. **Amtrak** (800-872-7245) runs out of the **Santa Fe Station,** a century-old national historic landmark at Central and Wyatt Earp Blvd.; contact a travel agent for tickets. One train goes to Chicago (8hr., $77) and Albuquerque (9hr., $112) each day. **TNM&O/Greyhound,** 2301 N. Central (227-9547 or 800-231-2222), in the Total Gas station at Plaza St., sends one bus per day to Wichita (3hr., $23.50), Denver (9hr., $51), and Oklahoma City (7½hr., $47).

Missouri

Pro-slavery Missouri applied for statehood in 1818, but, due to Congressional fears about upsetting the balance of free and slave states, was forced to wait. In 1821, Maine chose to enter the Union as a free state, evening the score and allowing for the admission of both. Missouri's troubled entry into the Union and its Civil War-era status as a border state were harbingers of its future ambiguity. Perhaps because it is so close to the center of the country, Missouri defies regional stereotyping: the rural landscape of the Great Plains, bustling cities like those to the east, Midwestern friendliness, and the slightest hint of a southern drawl combine to create a state which transcends its borders.

Missouri's patchwork geography further complicates characterization. In the north, near Iowa, amber waves of grain undulate. Along the Mississippi, towering bluffs inscribed with Native American pictographs evoke western canyonlands. Farther inland, spelunkers enjoy some of the world's largest limestone caves—made famous by Tom Sawyer and Becky Thatcher. In the south, the ancient and underrated Ozarks ripple into Arkansas.

PRACTICAL INFORMATION

Capital: Jefferson City.

Missouri Division of Tourism: Department MT-90, P.O. Box 1055, Jefferson City 65102 (314-751-4133). Open Mon.-Fri. 8am-5pm. **Missouri Department of Natural Resources,** Division of State Parks, 205 Jefferson St., Jefferson City 65101 (800-334-6946). Open Mon.-Fri. 8am-5pm.

Time Zone: Central (1hr. behind Eastern). **Postal Abbreviation:** MO

Sales Tax: 6.225%.

■■■ ST. LOUIS

In the early 1700s, Pierre Laclede set up a trading post directly below the junction of the Mississippi, Missouri, and Illinois rivers. A natural stopover, the "River City" of St. Louis gained prominence as the U.S. raced into the west. Today, Eero Saarinen's magnificent Gateway Arch, a silvery beacon to visitors and a landmark of America's westward expansion, gleams over one of America's largest inland trading ports.

St. Louis, Memphis, and New Orleans have together been dubbed "America's Music Corridor." In the early 1900s, showboats carrying ragtime and brassy Dixieland jazz bands regularly traveled between Chicago and New Orleans; the music floated through St. Louis and left the city addicted. St. Louis contributed to the development of the blues and saw the birth of ragtime during Scott Joplin's years in the city. The music of America continues to thrive in St. Louis's bars and clubs.

PRACTICAL INFORMATION

Tourist Office: St. Louis Visitors Center, 308 Washington Ave. (241-1764). Open daily 9:30am-4:30pm. Other locations at the **airport** and **America's Center** (342-5041), at 7th and Washington. Open Mon.-Fri. 9am-5pm, Sat.-Sun. 10am-2pm. The free booklet *Where: St. Louis* has the best maps around.

Airport: Lambert-St. Louis International (426-8000), 12mi. northwest of the city on I-70. Hub for **TWA.** MetroLink provides easy access to downtown ($1). A few westbound Greyhound buses stop at the airport.

Trains: Amtrak, 550 S. 16th St. (331-3301 or 800-872-7245), 2 blocks south of Kiel Center. To: Chicago (3 per day, 6hr., $40-50); Kansas City (1 per day, 5½hr., $53). Open daily 6:30am-12:30am.

Buses: Greyhound, 1450 N. 13th St. (621-3682 or 800-231-2222), at Cass Ave. Bi-State bus #30 takes less than 10min. from downtown. To: Chicago (6 per day, 6hr., $29), Kansas City (4 per day, 5hr., $35). Open 24 hrs.

Public Transportation: Bi-State (231-2345). Extensive daily service; infrequent during off-peak hours. Maps and schedules available at the Bi-State Development Agency, 707 N. 1st St. (on Laclede's Landing) or the reference desk of the public library at 13th and Olive St. **MetroLink,** the light-rail system, runs from 5th and Missouri in East St. Louis to Lambert Airport Mon.-Fri. 5am-1:30am, Sat. 5am-1:20am, Sun. 5:30am-12:30am. Travel is free in the "Ride Free Zone" (from Laclede's Landing to Union Station) Mon.-Fri. 10am-3pm. Metrolink or bus fare $1, transfers 10¢; seniors 50¢/5¢. 1-day passes $3, 3-day passes $7; available at Metrolink stations. **Shuttle Bug** is a small bus painted like a ladybug which cruises around Forest Park and the Central West End. All day fare (until 6pm) $1.

Taxis: County Cab, 991-5300. $1.45 initial fee, $1.10 per mi. **Yellow Cab,** 991-1200. $1 initial fee, $1.20 per mi. Both open 24 hrs.

Crisis Lines: Rape Crisis, 531-2003. **Suicide Hotline,** 647-4357. Both open 24 hrs. **Gay and Lesbian Hotline,** 367-0084. Open daily 6-10pm.

Emergency: 911.

Post Office: 1720 Market St. (436-4458). Open Mon.-Fri. 7am-8pm, Sat. 8am-3pm. **ZIP code:** 63155. **Area code:** 314 (in MO), 618 (in IL); in text, 314 unless noted.

I-44, I-55, I-64, and I-70 meet in St. Louis. The city is bounded on the west by I-170 and circled farther out by I-270. **U.S. 40/I-64** runs east-west through the entire metropolitan area. Downtown, **Market Street** divides the city north-south. Numbered streets run parallel to the river, increasing to the west. The historic **Soulard** district borders the river south of downtown. **Forest Park** and **University City,** home to **Washington University,** lie west from downtown; the Italian neighborhood called **The Hill** is south of these. Parking comes easy; wide streets allow for lots of meters, and private lots are cheap ($1-5). The city's dangerous sections include **East St. Louis** (across the river in IL), the **Near South Side,** and most of the **North Side.**

ACCOMMODATIONS AND CAMPING

Budget lodging is generally located several miles from downtown. For chain motels, try **Lindbergh Blvd. (Rte. 67)** near the airport or the area north of the I-70/I-270 junction in **Bridgeton,** 5 mi. beyond the airport. **Watson Rd.** (old Rte. 66 in South County) is littered with cheap motels southwest of where it merges with Chippewa; take bus #11 ("Chippewa-Sunset Hills") or #20 ("Cherokee-Sunset Hills"). **Bed and breakfasts** (singles from $50, doubles from $60) are listed in the **Visitors Guide,** free at visitor's centers and many hotels.

Huckleberry Finn Youth Hostel (HI-AYH), 1904-1906 S. 12th St. (241-0076), 2 blocks north of Russell Blvd. in the Soulard District. From downtown, take bus #73 ("Carondelet"), or walk south on Broadway to Russell Blvd. and over (30-40min.). Don't walk on Tucker; the hostel is *just* past an unsafe neighborhood. Full kitchen, free parking, and friendly staff. Dorm-style rooms with 5-9 beds. Outdoor lockers. Office open daily 8-10am and 6-10pm. Check-out 9:30am. $14, nonmembers $17. Linen $2 for stay.

Overland Trail Bed & Breakfast, 9626 Midland Blvd., Overland (427-3918), a 20-min. drive from downtown. Get off Lindbergh Blvd. (Rte. 67) at Midland and go east 2mi.; it's 6 blocks past Ashby Rd. on the right. Bob and Helen Clark lovingly run this 3-room B&B, dishing up orange-spice pancakes and hazelnut coffee for breakfast. Check-in by 9:30pm. Single with shared bath $25, double $35; with private bath, refrigerator, and microwave $35/$45. Single $55 per week. Cash only.

Washington University (935-4637), Eliot Hall at the corner of Big Bend and Forsyth Blvd. Buses #91 and 93 take 40min. from downtown. Small, spartan dorm rooms with A/C, free local calls, and laundry; near Mallinkrodt student center. Singles $18, doubles $32. Reservations recommended. Open late May-early Aug.

Comfort Inn, 2750 Plaza Way (949-8700), a 20-min. drive from downtown in St. Charles. Go south on First Capitol Dr. (off Rte. 70 just west of the Missouri River) and turn right on the service road; the Inn is on the left. Free airport and St. Charles Casino shuttles, local calls, and breakfast, plus a swimming pool. Laundry facilities ($1.50 per load). Ask for the "hostel rate" ($25 per person).

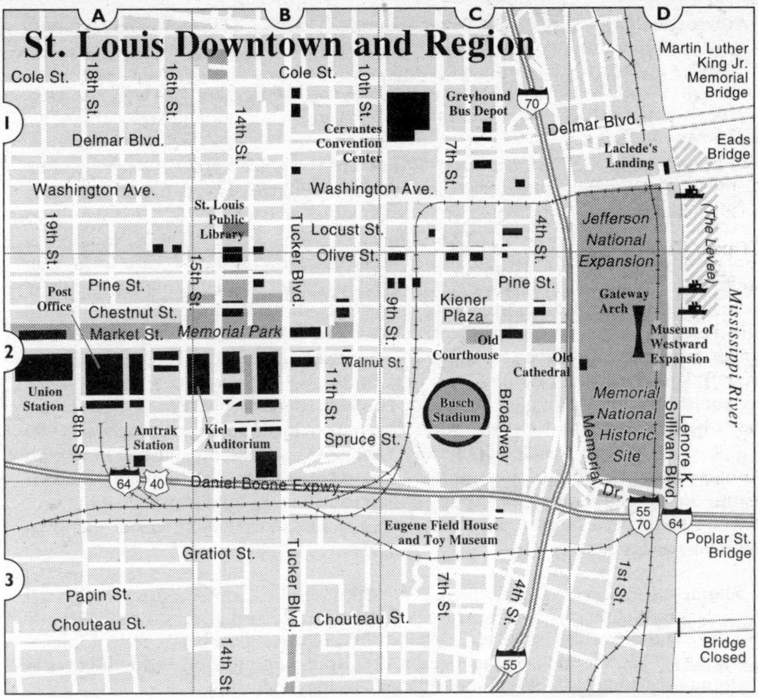

St. Louis Downtown and Region

A B C D
1 2 3

Cole St.
18th St.
16th St.
14th St.
10th St.
Greyhound Bus Depot
70
Martin Luther King Jr. Memorial Bridge
Delmar Blvd.
Cervantes Convention Center
7th St.
Laclede's Landing
Eads Bridge
Washington Ave.
St. Louis Public Library
19th St.
Tucker Blvd.
Locust St.
Olive St.
4th St.
Jefferson National Expansion
(The Levee)
Mississippi River
15th St.
Pine St.
Post Office
Chestnut St.
9th St.
Kiener Plaza
Gateway Arch
Market St.
Memorial Park
Old Courthouse
Museum of Westward Expansion
Walnut St.
Old Cathedral
11th St.
Union Station
Busch Stadium
Broadway
Memorial National Historic Site
Lenore K. Sullivan Blvd.
Amtrak Station
Kiel Auditorium
Spruce St.
Memorial Dr.
64
40
Daniel Boone Expwy.
55
70
64
Eugene Field House and Toy Museum
Poplar St. Bridge
Gratiot St.
1st St.
Papin St.
Chouteau St.
Bridge Closed
55

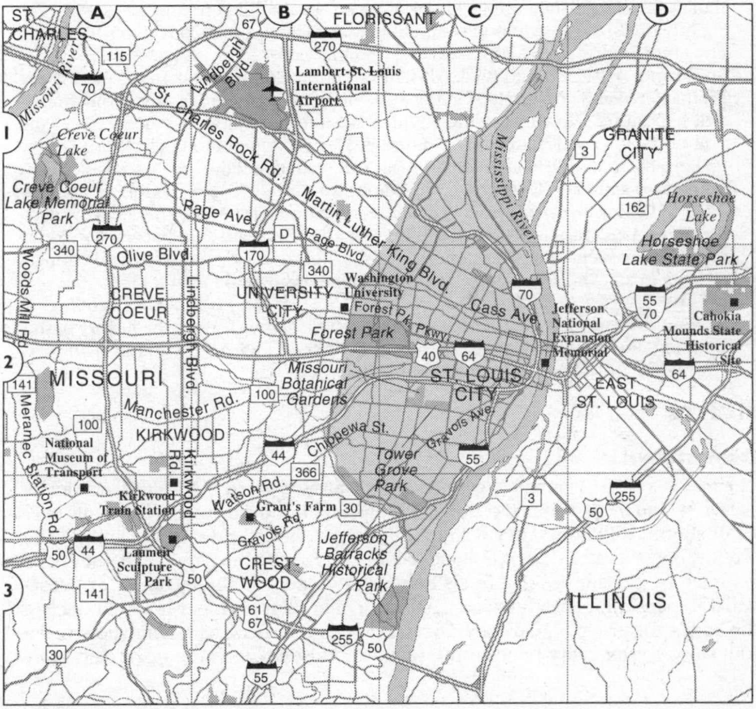

ST CHARLES
67
FLORISSANT
270
115
Missouri River
70
Lindbergh Blvd.
Lambert-St. Louis International Airport
St. Charles Rock Rd.
Creve Coeur Lake
GRANITE CITY
3
Mississippi River
Creve Coeur Lake Memorial Park
Martin Luther King Blvd.
162
Horseshoe Lake
Page Ave.
Horseshoe Lake State Park
270
D
Page Blvd.
340
Olive Blvd.
170
340
Washington University
Woods Mill Rd
CREVE COEUR
Lindbergh Blvd.
UNIVERSITY CITY
70
Cass Ave.
Jefferson National Expansion Memorial
55
70
Cahokia Mounds State Historical Site
Forest Pk. Pkwy.
Forest Park
40
64
141
MISSOURI
Missouri Botanical Gardens
ST. LOUIS CITY
EAST ST. LOUIS
64
Meramec Station Rd
100
Manchester Rd.
Gravois Ave.
100
KIRKWOOD
Chippewa St.
National Museum of Transport
44
55
Kirkwood Rd
Tower Grove Park
366
Watson Rd.
3
255
Kirkwood Train Station
Grant's Farm
30
50
Gravois Rd.
50
44
Jefferson Barracks Historical Park
Laumeir Sculpture Park
CREST-WOOD
50
141
ILLINOIS
61
67
255
50
30
55

GREAT PLAINS

Horseshoe Lake State Park Campgrounds, 3321 Rte. 111 (618-931-0270), off I-70 in Granite City, IL near Cahokia Mounds. In a secluded area near a lake. Fish from your car for bass, bluegill, and catfish; check out the live-bait vending machine. No electricity or water. Park closes daily 10pm. Sites $7. Open Apr.-Oct.

FOOD

I'm hungry; skip the big silver arch. Where are the golden arches? Because of St. Louis's many historical and ethnic districts, the difference of a few blocks can mean vastly different food styles. For beer, outdoor tables, and live music, often without a cover charge, head to **Laclede's Landing** (241-5875), a collection of restaurants, bars, and dance clubs housed in 19th-century buildings on the riverfront. Once an industrial wasteland, the Landing is now a hot nightspot (closed to minors midnight-6am). To get there, walk north along the river from the Gateway Arch, or toward the river on Washington St. The **Central West End** offers coffeehouses and outdoor cafés; a slew of impressive restaurants await just north of Lindell Blvd. along **Euclid Ave.** Take Metrolink to "Central West End" and walk north, or catch the Shuttlebug. St. Louis's historic Italian neighborhood, **The Hill,** southwest of downtown and just northwest of Tower Grove Park, produces plenty of inexpensive pasta; take bus #99 ("Lafayette"). Cheap Thai, Phillipine, and Vietnamese restaurants spice up the **South Grand** area, at Grand Blvd. just south of Tower Grove Park. The hip intellectual set hangs out on **University City Loop** (not actually a loop, but Delmar Blvd. west of Skinker Blvd.), which features coffeehouses and a mixed bag of American and international restaurants.

Blueberry Hill, 6504 Delmar Blvd. (727-0880), on the Loop. A touristy rock-n-roll restaurant similar to the Hard Rock—but cool. Record covers, Howdy-Doody toys, and a world-class jukebox charm the premises. Live bands Fri.-Sat. nights (cover $3-5) and Mon. nights (free). After 4pm, you must be 16 to enter; after 9pm, 21. Open Mon.-Sat. 11am-1:30am, Sun. 11am-midnight.

Cunnetto's, 5453 Magnolia (781-1135), on The Hill. This universally acclaimed Italian favorite dishes up 30 kinds of pasta, veal, chicken, and steak ($7-12). Slightly dressy. Expect a long wait. Open Mon.-Thurs. 11am-2pm and 5-10:30pm, Fri. 11am-2pm and 5-11:30pm; Sat. 5-11:30pm.

Pho Grand, 3191 S. Grand Blvd. (664-7435), in the South Grand area. Voted "Best Vietnamese" and "Best Value" in the St. Louis area. If you order soup, your waiter will let you try it before adding cilantro, basil leaves, and hot sauce; "yes," you will nod, "it's even better now." Entrees $3-4.50. Open Mon. and Wed.-Thurs. 9:30am-11pm, Fri. 9:30am-midnight, Sat.-Sun. 9am-midnight.

Ted Drewe's Frozen Custard, 6726 Chippewa (481-2652), on old Rte. 66. Also at 4224 S. Grand Blvd. The place for the summertime St. Louis experience; frozen custard is very popular here. Get in line for the chocolate-chip banana concrete; toppings are blended, as in a concrete mixer, but the ice cream stays hard enough to hang in an overturned cup ($2). Open Feb.-Dec. daily 11am-midnight.

The Old Spaghetti Factory, 727 N. 1st St. (621-0276), on Laclede's Landing. A link in the chain, sure, but here it's an institution. Menus feature the history of the building and the funky artifacts inside. Dinners $4.25-7. Open Mon.-Thurs. 5-10pm, Fri. 5-11:30pm, Sat. 4-11:30pm, Sun. 3:30-11pm.

SIGHTS

Downtown

The nation's tallest monument at 630 ft., the **Gateway Arch** (425-4465), on Memorial Dr. within the **Jefferson National Expansion Memorial,** towers gracefully over all of southern Illinois. After waiting one to two hours, ride up the arch in the world's only elevator that runs along half of an inverted catenary curve, the shape assumed by a chain hanging freely between two points. The **Museum of Westward Expansion,** beneath the arch, shows a ½-hr. film once per hour chronicling the arch's construction; **Odyssey Theater** arches your neck with films shown on a four-story screen every hour on the ½ hour. (Museum and arch open daily 8am-

10pm; in winter 9am-6pm. Tickets for 1 attraction $5, children $2; 2 attractions $7.50/$3; 3 attractions $9.50/$3.50; all 4 $11/$4.) View St. Louis from the water with **Gateway Riverboat Cruises** (621-4040); one-hour tours leave from the docks in front of the arch (cruises daily every 1½hr. 11am-3:30am; $7.50, ages 3-12 $3.50).

Within walking distance is the **Old Courthouse,** 11 N. 4th St. (425-4468), across the highway from the arch. Here, in 1847, Dred Scott sued for freedom from slavery (open daily 8am-4:30pm; tour hours vary; free). The **Old Cathedral,** 209 Walnut St. (231-3250), St. Louis' oldest church, still holds masses daily. The museum is around the corner (open daily 10am-4:30pm; 25¢).

North of the arch, on the riverfront, **Laclede's Landing** was the birthplace of St. Louis in 1764. The cobblestone streets of this district are bordered by restaurants, bars, and two museums. If you don't know what an Algerian hook is (but might like to), visit the Chamber of Horrors in the **Wax Museum,** 720 N. 2nd St. (241-1155). Here's your chance to meet famous people, if not in the flesh, at least in the tallow. (Open Mon.-Sat. 10am-10pm, Sun. noon-8pm. $4, ages 6-12 $3.) Play Space Invaders, Pac-Man, Donkey Kong, and other classics (25¢) at the **National Video Game and Coin-Op Museum,** 801 N. 2nd St. (621-2900), which charts the rise of video games and pinball machines (open Mon.-Sat. 10am-10pm, Sun. noon-8pm; free).

Stroll down the lane to the **National Bowling Hall of Fame and Museum,** 111 Stadium Plaza (231-6340), across from Busch Stadium. This well-organized museum is lined with funny panels on the history and development of bowling, with titles like "real men play quills and throw cheeses." For $2 you can play four frames in the old-fashioned lanes downstairs. (Open Mon.-Sat. 9am-5pm, Sun. noon-5pm; baseball game days until 7pm. $5, ages 5-12 $2.50.) Historic **Union Station,** at 18th and Market St. 1 mi. west of downtown ("Levee" bus), houses a shopping mall, food court, and entertainment center within its magnificent structure. The Entertainer lives on at the **Scott Joplin House,** 12580 Rott Rd. (821-1209), just west of downtown at Geyer Rd., where the ragtime legend lived and composed from 1901 to 1903.

South and Southwest of Downtown

Soulard is bounded by I-55 and Seventh St.; walk south on Broadway or 7th St. from downtown, or take bus #73 ("Carondelet"). The city proclaimed this area a historic district in the early 70s, because it once housed German and East European immigrants, many of whom worked in the breweries. Young couples and families are revitalizing the area, without displacing the older generation of immigrants. The historic district surrounds the **Soulard Farmers Market,** 730 Carroll St. (622-4180), on 7th St., which claims a more than 200-yr. tradition but *still* has fresh produce (open daily around 6am-5pm; hours vary among merchants). The end of 12th St. features the largest brewery in the world, the **Anheuser-Busch Brewery,** 1127 Pestalozzi St. (577-2626), at 12th and Lynch St. Take bus #40 ("Broadway") south from downtown. During the 70-min. tour, you'll watch the beer-making process from barley to bottling, meet the famous Clydesdale horses, and have a chance to sample Anheuser-Busch beers. Don't get too excited about the free brew, bucko—you'll get booted after 15 min. (Tours in summer Mon.-Sat. 9am-5pm; off season 9am-4pm. Get free tickets at the office.) A few blocks southwest of the brewery, Cherokee Street's **Antique Row** is filled with antiques and used bookstores.

The internationally acclaimed **Missouri Botanical Gardens,** 4344 Shaw Blvd. (800-642-8842), north of Tower Grove Park, thrive on grounds left by botanist Henry Shaw. From downtown, take I-44 west by car or catch bus #99 ("Lafayette") at 4th and Locust St.; get off at Shaw Blvd. and Tower Grove Ave. The gardens display flora and fauna from all over the globe; the Japanese Garden is guaranteed to soothe the weary budget traveler. (Open Memorial Day-Labor Day daily 9am-8pm; off season 9am-5pm. $3, seniors $1.50, under 12 free; free Wed. and Sat. until noon.) Much farther out this way, late President Ulysses S. once lived on **Grant's Farm,** 10501 Gravois Rd. (843-1700). Take I-55 to Reavis Barracks Rd., turn right onto Gravois Rd., then left onto the farm. Now an Anheuser Busch-owned wildlife preserve and Clydesdale stomping and breeding ground, the farm offers visitors a train ride, animal shows, and free beer in the historic Baurnhof area. (Open June-Aug. Tues.-Sun. 9am-3pm; other times vary. Call for reservations.)

Laumeier Sculpture Park, 12580 Rott Rd. (821-1209), awaits discovery 12 mi. southwest of downtown off the Lindbergh Blvd. exit of I-44. Quiet trails and contemporary sculpture grace 118 partially wooded acres. Beverly Pepper's Cromlech Glen combines nature, art, and utility to create a charmed space in a shapely glen with modest spruce- and pine-log stairs emerging from its grassy surface. Continuous exhibitions of contemporary art can be found inside the museum. (Park open daily 8am-30min. after sunset; museum Tues.-Sat. 10am-5pm, Sun. noon-5pm. Free.)

West of Downtown

West of downtown, **Forest Park,** the country's largest urban park, was home to the 1904 World's Fair and St. Louis Exposition, where ice cream cones and hot dogs decorated kids' faces for the first time ever. Take MetroLink to Forest Park or Central West End, then catch the Shuttle Bug, which stops at all the important sights. The park contains two museums, a zoo, a planetarium, a 12,000-seat amphitheater, a grand canal, and countless picnic areas, pathways, and flying golf balls. The **St. Louis Science Center,** 5050 Oakland Ave. (289-4444), in the park's south corner, has lots of hands-on exhibits, an OmniMax, and a planetarium. Learn how a laser printer works, watch an old Star Trek episode, practice surgery, or use police radars to clock the unusually high speeds of cars on I-40. (Museum open Sun.-Thurs. 9:30am-5pm, Fri.-Sat. 9:30am-9pm; free. Call for show schedules and prices.) Marlin Perkins, the late, great host of TV's *Wild Kingdom,* turned the **St. Louis Zoo** (781-0900) into a world-class institution. You can even view computer-generated images of future human evolutionary stages (no, they don't all look like Kate Moss) at the "Living World" exhibit. (Open Wed.-Mon. 9am-5pm, Tues. 9am-8pm; Labor Day-Memorial Day daily 9am-5pm. Free.) The **History Museum** (746-4599), at Lindell Blvd. and DeBaliviere Ave. just north of the park, is filled with U.S. memorabilia, including an exhibit devoted to Charles Lindbergh's flight across the Atlantic in the *Spirit of St. Louis* (open Tues.-Sun. 9:30am-5pm; free). Atop **Art Hill,** just to the southwest, an equestrian statue of France's Louis IX, the city's namesake and the only Louis of France to achieve sainthood, beckons with his raised sword toward the **St. Louis Art Museum** (721-0072), which contains masterpieces of Asian, Renaissance, and Impressionist art (open Tues. 1:30-8:30pm, Wed.-Sun. 10am-5pm; free except for special exhibits).

From Forest Park, head north a few blocks to gawk at the lavish residential sections of the **Central West End,** where every house is a turn-of-the-century version of a French château or Tudor mansion. The **Cathedral of St. Louis,** 4431 Lindell Blvd. (533-0544) is a strange amalgam of Romanesque, Byzantine, Gothic, and Baroque styles. Gold-flecked mosaics depict 19th-century church history in Missouri. Take bus #93 ("Lindell") from downtown, or walk from the Central West End MetroLink stop. (Open daily 7am-8pm, Labor Day-Memorial Day 7am-5pm. Guided tours Mon.-Fri. 10am-3pm, Sun. after the noon Mass; $2.)

Northwest of Forest Park, **Washington University** makes things lively with a vibrant campus. The **Washington University Gallery of Art** (935-5490), in Steinberg Hall at the corner of Skinker and Forsyth Blvd., has a diverse collection including a few Warhols. Conrad Atkinson's *Critical Mats* proffers an inviting welcome to "the seductiveness of the end of the world." (Open during the school year Mon-.Fri. 10am-5pm, Sat.-Sun. 1-5pm. Free.)

The KATY Trail State Park (800-334-6946) is an old 1890's railroad route that has been converted into a hiking and biking trail. The 138 miles pass towering bluffs, wetlands, and wildlife that even Lewis and Clark stopped to admire. The route begins in St. Charles and ends in Kansas City. Recent flooding has damaged much of the trail; repair crews are working, but exercise caution.

ENTERTAINMENT

Founded in 1880, the **St. Louis Symphony Orchestra** is one of the country's finest. **Powell Hall,** 718 N. Grand Blvd. (534-1700), houses the 101-member orchestra in acoustic and visual splendor. Take bus #97 to Grand Blvd. or MetroLink to Grand Station and walk north. (Performances Sept.-May Thurs. 8pm, Fri.-Sat. 8:30pm, Sun. 3 and 7:30pm. Box office open Mon.-Sat. 9am-5pm and before performances. Tickets $13-59; student and senior rush tickets ½-price the day of the show.)

St. Louis offers theater-goers many choices. The outdoor **Municipal Opera** (361-1900), the "Muny," performs tour productions of hit musicals on summer nights in Forest Park. The back rows provide 1456 free seats on a first come, first served basis. The gates open at 7pm for 8:15pm shows; get there even earlier for popular shows and bring a picnic. (Tickets $6-40.) Other productions are regularly staged by the **St. Louis Black Repertory,** 634 N. Grand Blvd. (534-3807), and the **Repertory Theatre of St. Louis,** 130 Edgar Rd. (968-4925). Call for current show information. Renovated and reopened in 1982, the **Fox Theatre** (534-1678) was originally a 1930s movie palace. Tour the Fox or pay a little more for Broadway shows, classic films, or Las Vegas, country, or rock stars. (Tours Tues., Thurs., and Sat. at 10:30am. $2.50, under 12 $1.50; call for reservations.) The recently renovated **Tivoli Theatre,** 6350 Delmar Blvd. (862-1100) shows arty and lesser-known releases.

A recent St. Louis ordinance allows gambling on the rivers, and the **Casino Queen** (800-777-0777) claims "the loosest slots in town." (10 cruises daily leave on odd-numbered hours from the riverfront near the arch. Admission $2-4; parking free.)

Six Flags over Mid-America (938-4800) is a popular area amusement park, located 30 min. southwest of St. Louis on I-44 at Exit 261 (hours vary by season; $28, seniors $14, ages 3-11 $23). The **St. Louis Cardinals** (421-3060) play ball downtown at **Busch Stadium** April through October (tickets $5-14). **Blues** hockey games (622-2500) slice ice at the **Kiel Center** at 14th St. and Clark Ave.

NIGHTLIFE

With the city's jazzy history, music rules the night in St. Louis. The *Riverfront Times* (free at many bars and clubs) and the *Get Out* section of the Post-Dispatch list weekly entertainment. For seasonal events, check *St. Louis Magazine,* published annually, or the comprehensive calendar distributed at the tourist office.

Bars and restaurants featuring jazz, blues, and reggae fill **Laclede's Landing.** In the summer, bars take turns sponsoring "block parties," with outdoor food, drink, music, and dancing in the streets. Weekends see hordes of St. Louis University (SLU, pronounced "slew") students descending on the waterfront. Try **Kennedy's Second Street Co.,** 612 N. 2nd St. (421-3655), for cheap food (burgers $3.25-5.25) and assorted local bands. (Open Mon.-Fri. 11:30am-3am, Sat.-Sun. 1pm-3am. Acoustic act 7pm, free with dinner. 21+ show 10:30pm, usually progressive rock; may have a cover.) **Tasmania,** 118 Morgan (621-1160), features late-night dancing. Women drink free on Tuesday and Thursday before 1am. (Open Mon.-Sat. 9pm-3am.) **Mississippi Nights,** 914 N. 1st St. (421-3853), hosts big local and national bands (box office open Mon.-Fri. 11am-6pm).

Historic **Soulard's** pubs and bars make it another groovy nightspot. **McGurk's** (776-8309), at 12th and Russell, has live Irish music nightly (open Mon.-Fri. 11am-1:30am, Sat. noon-1:30am, Sun. 1pm-midnight; no cover). Soulard is also quite gay-friendly; **Clementine's,** 2001 Menard (664-7869), houses both a crowded restaurant and St. Louis's oldest gay bar (est. 1978). Sandwiches and entrees run $4.50-9.50. (Open Mon.-Fri. 10am-1:30am, Sat. 8am-1:30am, Sun. 11am-midnight.) Watch goldfish swim in a pond at **1860's Hard Shell Café & Bar,** 1860 S. 9th St. (231-1860). The restaurant is pricey (sandwiches $5-6, seafood $10-16); come later for nightly live music with no cover in the bar. (Restaurant open Sun.-Thurs. 11am-11pm, Fri.-Sat. 11am-midnight. Music Mon.-Sat. 9pm-1am, Sun. 7:30-11:30pm.)

The bohemian **Loop** parties hardy as students and intellectual-types flock to the coffeehouses and bars of Delmar Blvd. for outdoor dining, conversation, and occasional music. **Brandt's Market & Café,** 6525 Delmar Blvd. (726-3663), may be too hip to believe—it can't decide whether to be a gourmet or health food store, a café, or a coffeehouse. They even spin discs or have live music at night—jazz, folk, who knows? *Puttanesca* pizza and other entrees run $5-10 and are served *late.*

■ NEAR ST. LOUIS

Cahokia Mounds State Historic Site Fifteen minutes from the city in Collinsville, IL (8mi. east of downtown on I-55/70 to Rte. 111), over 120 earthen mounds mark the site of the city of Cahokia, an extremely advanced Native American settlement inhabited from 700 to 1500AD. The mounds, which now comprise the Cahokia Mounds State Historic Site, were built as foundations and protection for important buildings. The construction required the builders to carry over 15 million loads of dirt on their backs; the largest, **Monk's Mound,** took 300 years to complete. The Cahokians, at one time a community of 20,000, faced the same problems of pollution, overcrowding, and depletion of resources that we do today—which might help explain their mysterious disappearance. The **Interpretive Center** (618-346-5160) has a life-sized diorama and a free 15-minute movie illustrating this "City of the Sun" (shows every hr. 10am-4pm; center open daily 9am-5pm). Celebrate equinoxes and solstices at **Woodhenge,** a solar calendar much like Britain's stone one, at dawn on the Sunday closest to the big day. (Site open daily 8am-dusk. Free.)

St. Charles The starting point for Lewis and Clark's 1804 exploration of the Louisiana Purchase lies just 20 minutes from downtown St. Louis in the town of St. Charles. The **Lewis & Clark Center,** 701 Riverside Dr. (947-3199), tells all about the five days the explorers spent here in May 1804 (open daily 10:30am-4:30pm; $1, children 50¢). Nestled along the Missouri River, St. Charles now supports numerous antique shops and cafés, which make it a peaceful place to spend a day. Relax with high tea at **Lord Winston Ltd.'s** Victorian tea room. The owners dress in period costumes and assume the personae of "Lord and Lady Winston" to transport you back to 1850s England. (Tea and scones $4.50. Open daily 11am-6pm.)

Other attractions lend themselves to not-so-peaceful days: outdoor festivals, riverboat gambling, and the **Goldenrod Showboat,** 1000 Riverside Dr. (946-2020), the nation's last surviving showboat and the inspiration for the musical (shows Wed.-Sun. $21-30; box office open Mon.-Sat. 9am-5pm, Sun. noon-7pm).

St. Charles marks the starting point of **KATY Trail State Park** (800-334-6946), an 1890s railroad route which has been converted into a hiking and biking trail. The 200-mi. trail includes towering bluffs, wetlands, and wildlife (which even Lewis and Clark stopped to admire) on the way to Kansas City. Call for info on portions of the trail which remain unfinished. Various places along S. Main St. rent bicycles; **The Touring Cyclist,** 104 S. Main St. (949-9630), is open daily 9am-6pm.

To reach the St. Charles historic area, take I-70W and exit north at 5th St. A right on Boonslick Rd. takes you a few block to S. Main St., the main drag. The **Visitors Bureau** is at 230 W. Main (800-366-2427; open Mon.-Fri. 8am-5pm, Sat. 10am-5pm).

Lewis and Clark National Historic Trail

Commissioned by President Thomas Jefferson in 1804, Meriwether Lewis and William Clark set off from Missouri to reach the Pacific. Two years later they reached the mouth of the Columbia River in Oregon. You can trace the steps of these two intrepid adventurers up the Missouri River and across the Rocky Mountains on marked highways, water routes, and hiking trails which follow the explorers' outbound and return routes for over 3700 mi. For more information, write the National Park Service, 700 Rayovac Dr., Suite 100, Madison, WI 53711.

■■■ HANNIBAL

Hannibal hugs the Mississippi River 100 mi. west of Springfield, IL and 100 mi. northwest of St. Louis. Founded in 1819, the town remained a sleepy village until Samuel Clemens (a.k.a. Mark Twain) roused the world's attention to his boyhood home by making it the setting of *The Adventures of Tom Sawyer.* Today, tourists flock to Hannibal like gullible boys to a white-washed fence.

Practical Information The **Hannibal Visitors and Convention Bureau,** 505 N. Third (221-2477), offers info and free local calls (open Memorial Day-Labor Day Mon.-Sat. 8am-6:30pm, Sun. 8am-5pm; call for off season hours). Hannibal is serviced by **Trailways Bus Lines,** 308 Mark Twain Ave. (221-0033), in the Citgo Station (open daily 5:30am-1:30am). A northbound bus leaves daily at 6am for Sioux City, IA (5½hr., $60) and a southbound bus at 9:30pm for St. Louis (2hr., $24). Hannibal's **post office:** 801 Broadway (221-0957; open Mon.-Fri. 8:30am-5pm, Sat. 8:30am-noon); **ZIP code:** 63401. **Area code:** 314.

Lean-Tos and Apple Cores Chain motels swarm about Hannibal, particularly on **Mark Twain Ave.** (Rte. 36) and on **U.S. 61** near the Rte. 36 junction. Numerous **bed and breakfasts** are located downtown, but these tend to be costlier (singles $50, doubles $60). Shiny and familiar, the newly redone **Howard Johnson Lodge,** 3603 McMasters Ave. (221-7950), at the U.S. 36/61 junction, is probably the best deal in town, especially for students (A/C, pool; singles $40-45, doubles $50-55, students $32/$48). The **Mark Twain Cave Campgrounds,** P.O. Box 913 (221-1656), adjacent to the cave 1 mi. south of Hannibal on Rte. 79, are cheery and family-oriented, but not too secluded ($11, full hookup $15; $1.50 per person after 2). **Injun Joe Campground** (985-3581), 5 mi. south of Hannibal on U.S. 61, lures a young crowd with mini-golf, go-carts, an arcade, and a water slide ($12, with water and electric $13.50, with full hookup $14.50, $1 per person after 2). Sidestep Hannibal's unending fast food options with a sandwich ($4) or one of 99 dreamy cheesecakes at **The Café** (221-3355), on North St. near the waterfront (open Mon.-Sat. 8am-3pm). For an unparalleled view of the mighty Mississippi, dine outside at the **Riverview Café** (221-8292), 1 mi. south of town on Rte. 79 at Sawyer's Creek (entrees $5-13; open daily 11am-10pm).

Jumping Frogs and Riverboats The **Mark Twain Boyhood Home and Museum** and **Museum Annex,** 208 Hill St. (221-9010), highlight the downtown **historic district** with restored rooms and an assortment of memorabilia from the writer's life. Across the street, the **Pilaster House** and **Clemens Law Office** complete the experience. (Open daily 8am-6pm, in spring and fall 8am-5pm, Jan.-Feb. 10am-4pm. All 5 sites $4, ages 6-12 $2, under 6 free.) **The Mark Twain Riverboat Co.** (221-3222), Center St. Landing, steams down the Mississippi for a 1-hr. sightseeing cruise. (Memorial Day-Labor Day 3 per day, May and Sept.-Oct. 1 per day. $7.50, ages 3-12 $4.50; dinner cruises $24.95/$15.95.) The **Mark Twain Cave** (221-1656), 1 mi. south of Hannibal on Hwy. 79, is the one Twain explored as a boy (open daily 8am-8pm, Nov.-Feb. 9am-5pm. 1-hr. tour $9, ages 4-12 $4.50, under 4 free). Nearby **Cameron Cave** provides a slightly longer and far spookier lantern tour ($11, ages 4-12 $5.50). In early July, 100,000 fans converge on Hannibal for the fence-painting, frog-jumping fun of the **Tom Sawyer Days** festival (July 2-7 in 1996).

■■■ KANSAS CITY

With over 200 public fountains and more miles of boulevard than Paris, Kansas City has a reputation for a heavy European influence. Nevertheless, this city can't hide its Heartland roots; Kansas City has twice been voted "Barbeque Capital of the World" and is considered a key player in the development of jazz. When Prohibition stifled many of the nation's parties in the 1930s, booze continued to flow here; KC's alcohol-induced nightlife brought jazz musicians from all over the country, and their music flourished. The Kansas City of today maintains its big bad blues-and-jazz rep in a metropolis spanning two states: the highly-suburbanized half in Kansas (KCKS) and the quicker-paced commercial half in Missouri (KCMO).

PRACTICAL INFORMATION

Tourist Office: Convention and Visitors Bureau of Greater Kansas City, 1100 Main St., #2550 (221-5242 or 800-767-7700), in the City Center Square Building downtown. Pick up *An Official Visitor's Guide to Kansas City.* Open Mon.-Fri. 8:30am-5pm.

Airport: Kansas City International (243-5237), 18mi. northwest of KC off I-29. **KCI Shuttle** (243-5000) departs every 30-45min., servicing downtown (KCMO), Westport, Overland Park, Mission, and Lenexa; $11-15. Taxi fare from airport to downtown about $21-23.

Trains: Amtrak, 2200 Main St. (421-3622 or 800-872-7245), at Grand Ave. directly across from Crown Center. 1 per day to: St. Louis (5½hr., $53); Chicago (8hr., $77). Open 24 hrs.

Buses: Greyhound, 1101 N. Troost (221-2835 or 800-231-2222). To: St. Louis (7 per day, 4-5hr., $37); Chicago (5 per day, 10-15hr., $51). Open daily 5:30am-12:30am.

Public Transportation: Kansas City Area Transportation Authority (Metro) (221-0660 for info; Mon.-Fri. 6am-6pm). Excellent downtown coverage. Fare 90¢, $1 for KCKS, $1.20 for Independence; seniors ½-price with Medicare card. Free transfers; free return receipt available downtown. Pick up maps and schedules at headquarters or on buses. Buses run Mon.-Fri. 7am-5:30pm. The **trolley** (221-3399) loops from downtown to the City Market, Crown Center, Westport, and Country Club Plaza March-Dec. Mon.-Sat. 10am-10pm, Sun. noon-6pm; holiday hours vary. $4 for all day, seniors and ages 6-12 $3.

Taxis: Yellow Cab, 471-5000. $1.30 base fare, $1.10 per mi. 24 hrs.

Car Rental: Thrifty Car Rental, 2001 Baltimore (842-8550 or 800-367-2277), 1 block west of 20th and Main St. $26 per day, with unlimited mi. within state. Under 25 surcharge $5 per day. Must be 21 with a major credit card. Open Mon.-Fri. 8am-8pm, Sat.-Sun. 9am-4pm. Free shuttle from the airport will take you to location at 11530 N.W. Prairie View Rd. (464-5670).

Crisis Line: 822-7272. 24 hrs.

Emergency: 911.

Post Office: 315 W. Pershing Rd. (374-9275), at Broadway. Open Mon.-Fri. 8am-6:30pm, Sat. 9am-noon. **ZIP code:** 64108. **Area codes:** 816 in Missouri, 913 in Kansas. Phone numbers given here lie in 816 area code unless otherwise noted.

The KC metropolitan area sprawls across two states, and travel may take a while, particularly without a car. Most sights worth visiting in KC lie south of downtown on the Missouri side; all listings are for Kansas City, MO unless otherwise indicated. Although parking around town is not as easy as in many midwestern towns, there are lots that charge $4 or less per day. KCMO is laid out on a grid with numbered streets running east-west and named streets running north-south. **Main St.** divides the city east-west.

ACCOMMODATIONS AND CAMPING

Kansas City can usually accommodate anyone who needs a room, but if there's a big convention and the Royals are in town, the whole city may be booked; call ahead. The least expensive lodgings are near the interstate highways, especially I-70. Downtown, most hotels are either expensive, uninhabitable, or unsafe—sometimes all three. Most in KCKS require a car. The Westport area is lively, but prices can be steep. **Bed and Breakfast Kansas City** (913-888-3636) has over 40 listings at inns and homes throughout the city ($50 and up).

American Inn (800-90-LODGE/905-6343) has several locations off I-70. Despite the gaudy red, white, and blue neon façade, the rooms inside are large, cheap, and good-lookin'. The low prices advertised on signs are usually limited to a handful of rooms that go quickly; you'll probably have to pay a few dollars more. All have outdoor pools. There are locations on Woods Chapel Rd. (228-1080), 16 mi. east on I-70 off exit 18 (singles $29, doubles $36); Noland Rd. (373-8300), 12 mi. east on I-70 off exit 12 ($34/$39); and 78th St. (299-2999), just east of the intersection of I-70 and Rte.-435 in Kansas ($25/$36).

Lake Jacomo (229-8980), 22 mi. southeast of KC, has forested campsites, fishing, swimming, and a darn cool dam across the street (sites $10, with full hookup $15). Take I-470 south to Colbern, then go east on Colbern for 2 mi. to the Lake.

FOOD

Kansas City rustles up a herd of meaty, juicy barbecue restaurants that serve unusually tangy ribs. If midwestern meat dishes don't float your boat, the **Westport** area, at Westport Rd. and Broadway just south of 39th, sports eclectic menus, cafés, and coffeehouses. For fresh produce year-round, visit the large and exceptional **city market,** at 5th and Walnut St. in the River Quay area. Saturday and Wednesday are the busy days, although scattered shops stay open all week. (Open Mon.-Fri. 8am-4pm, Sat. 6am-6pm, Sun. noon-4pm.)

Strouds, 1015 E. 85th St. (333-2132), at Troost, 2mi. north of the Holmes exit off I-435; also at 5410 N. Oak Ridge Rd. (454-9600). Sign proclaims: "We choke our own chickens," but you won't choke on the famous fried chicken with cinnamon rolls, biscuits, and honey. Enormous dinners ($4.25-13) in a weathered wooden hut crammed between the train tracks and an overpass. Open Mon.-Thurs. 5-10pm, Fri. 11am-11pm, Sat. 2-11pm, Sun. 11am-10pm.

Arthur Bryant's, 1727 Brooklyn St. (231-1123). Take the Brooklyn exit off I-70 and turn right. Down-home, sloppy BBQ. The thin, orange, almost granular sauce is a spectacular blend of southern and western influences. A monstrous and messy sandwich is $5.45—choose beef, ham, pork, or turkey, but don't wear anything fancy. Open Mon.-Thurs. 10am-9:30pm, Fri.-Sat. 10am-10pm, Sun. 10am-8:30pm.

Californos, 4124 Pennsylvania (531-7878), in Westport. Salads, gourmet pizza, and grilled salmon sandwiches run $6.50-10 in Californo's converted 1903 trolley garage. Open Mon.-Thurs. 11am-3pm and 5-10pm, Fri.-Sat. 11am-3pm and 5-11pm, Sun. 1-8pm.

SIGHTS

For a taste of KC's masterpieces, try the **Nelson-Atkins Museum of Art,** 4525 Oak (751-1278 or 561-4000), at 45th 3 blocks east of Country Club Plaza. The museum contains one of the best East Asian art collections worldwide. (Free tours Tues.-Sat. 10:30, 11am, 1, and 2pm; Sun. 1:30, 2, 2:30 and 3pm. Open Tues.-Thurs. 10am-4pm, Fri. 10am-9pm, Sat. 10am-5pm, Sun. 1-5pm. $4, students $2, ages 6-18 $1; free Sat.) **Black Archives of Mid-America,** 2033 Vine (483-1300), holds a large and fine collection of paintings and sculpture by African-American artists (take the "Indiana" bus; open Mon.-Fri. 9am-4:30pm; $2, under 18 50¢).

A few blocks to the west at 47th and Southwest Trafficway, **Country Club Plaza** (753-0100), known as "the plaza," is the oldest and perhaps most picturesque shopping center in the U.S. Modeled after buildings in Seville, Spain, the plaza boasts fountains, sculptures, hand-painted tiles, and the reliefs of grinning gargoyles. You can pick up a free guide to the architecture at many shops and motels. A Country Club Plaza bus runs downtown until 11pm.

Crown Center, 2450 Grand Ave. (274-8444), sits 2 mi. north of the Plaza at Pershing; take bus #40, 56, or 57, or any trolley from downtown. The center, headquarters of Hallmark Cards, houses a maze of restaurants and shops, plus the **Coterie Theatre** (474-6552) and KC's only public outdoor ice skating rink, the **Ice Terrace** (274-8444; open Nov.-April daily 10am-9pm; $5, prices may change). From mid-June to July, Crown Center has **Free Concerts in the Park** (274-8444) every Friday at 7pm. Picnic or run through a huge fountain designed for exactly that purpose—you can't have more fun on a hot summer night with your clothes on. To the west stands **Liberty Memorial,** 100 W. 26th St. (221-1918), a tribute to those who died in World War I. The memorial is closed indefinitely due to structural problems.

Nearby **Independence,** Missouri, a 15-minute drive east of KC, may have more claims to fame than KC; it's the hometown of former president Harry Truman, the starting point of the California, Oregon, and Santa Fe trails, and now, the world headquarters of the **Reorganized Church of Jesus Christ of Latter Day Saints** (532-3030), at River and Walnut St. Inspired by the chambered nautilus, the computer-designed building is a bizarre and beautiful seashell that spirals up nearly 200 ft. The interior is equally impressive, containing art representing the church's worldwide following as well as an enormous pipe organ. (Tours on the ½hr. Mon.-Sat. 9-11:30am and 1-4:30pm, Sun. 1-4:30pm. Organ recital daily 3:30pm. Free.) The town of Independence is accessible by bus #24 "Independence." Its **Department of Tourism,** 111 E. Maple (325-7111), can provide more information (open Mon.-Fri. 8am-5pm).

ENTERTAINMENT AND NIGHTLIFE

The **Missouri Repertory Theatre** (235-2700), at 50th and Oak, stages American classics. (Tickets $17-32. Box office open Mon.-Fri. 10am-5pm, Sat.-Sun. noon-5pm, when shows are running.) Huck Finn wanna-bes can take a one-hour cruise on the **Missouri River Queen** (281-5300 or 800-373-0027), at the Lewis & Clark viaduct (boards daily 2pm; $7, seniors $6.30, ages 3-13 $3.50). For more entertainment news, pick up a free copy of the *New Times* at area restaurants and bars.

Sports fans will be pierced to the heart by **Arrowhead Stadium,** at I-70 and Blue Ridge Cutoff, home to football's **Chiefs** (931-3300 or 800-676-5488; tickets $26-35). Next door, the water-fountained wonder of **Kauffman Stadium** (800-422-1969), houses the **Royals** baseball team (tickets $6-14, Mon. and Thurs. $4.50). A stadium express bus runs from downtown on game days.

In the 20s, Kansas City played hot spot to the nation's best jazz. Count Basie and his "Kansas City Sound" reigned at the River City bars, while Charlie "Bird" Parker spread his wings and soared in the open environment. Stop by the **Grand Emporium,** 3832 Main St. (531-7557), twice voted the #1 blues night club in the U.S., to hear live jazz Fridays and Saturdays; weekdays feature rock, blues, and reggae bands (cover ranges $3-15; open Mon.-Sat. 10am-3am, Sun. noon-3am). A few blocks west, noisy nightspots pack the restored **Westport** area (756-2789), near Broadway and Westport Rd. ½ mi. north of Country Club Plaza (see Sights above). **Kiki's Bon-Ton Maison,** 1515 Westport Rd. (931-9417), features KC's best in-house soul band (Wed. 9-11pm and Sat. 10:30pm) and whips up cajun food with bayou flavor (jambalaya and crawfish $9-13; sandwiches $6). Kiki's also hosts the annual Crawfish Festival around the last weekend in May. (Open Mon.-Thurs. 11am-10pm, Fri. 11am-11pm, Sat. 11am-1:30am, Sun. 11:30am-8pm.) Big names in jazz and blues show up at the club downstairs from the ritzy **Plaza III Steakhouse,** 4749 Pennsylvania (753-0000), at Country Club Plaza. (Cover varies; Fri.-Sat. $4. Restaurant open Mon.-Thurs. 5:30-10pm, Fri.-Sat. 5:30-11pm, Sun. 5-10pm. Club open Wed.-Sat. 8:30pm-12:30am.) **The Edge,** 323 W. 8th St. (221-8900), is a popular gay bar and dance club (cover varies; open Mon.-Thurs. 9pm-3am, Fri.-Sat. 8pm-3am).

■■■ LAKE OF THE OZARKS

In 1929, Union Electric began construction of a dam across the Osage River, 50 miles southwest of Jefferson City in the Ozark hills. By 1931, the river had backed up to create a 617 billion gallon reservoir with 1375 mi. of shoreline—at the time, the world's largest man-made lake. A popular tourist spot, Lake of the Ozarks now reflects its man-made origins in man-made motels, go-karts, and helicopter rides. Most restaurants and motels cluster around the U.S. 54 in **Camdenton, Lake Ozark,** and **Osage Beach.** The best-known piece of the Lake area, **The Strip** is a ½-mile conglomeration of bumper cars and souvenir stands on Business Rte. 54 in Lake Ozark near the Bagnell Dam ("where it all began"). The Strip dazzles the eye and the pocketbook and challenges the intrepid vacationer to seek out the scenic beauty which survives in the areas away from highway.

The state parks provide the cheapest and most beautiful opportunities for boating, fishing, and swimming. The state's largest park, **Lake of the Ozarks State Park,** off U.S. 54 in Osage Beach, offers a wide range of activities, including horseback rides ($12 per hour; call 314-348-6670 for reservations). Unusual land formations and a romantic history have brought fame to **Ha Ha Tonka State Park** (314-346-2986), off U.S. 54 in Camdenton. The topography here, called "karst," resulted from water which percolated through the underlying rock to create caves, sinkholes, underground streams, and natural bridges. Captivated by this area, Robert Snyder, a prominent Kansas City businessman, set out to build a magnificent 60-room castle here. In 1906, one year after construction began, Snyder was killed in Kansas City's first fatal car accident. The castle was eventually completed, only to burn down in 1942; its stark ruins add to the mysterious beauty of the park.

The **Lake Area Chamber of Commerce** (800-451-4117), across from the Howard Johnson's at U.S. 54 and Business Rte. 54 in Osage Beach, has all the usual info on eating and sleeping. Due to tourist demand, even the shabbiest roadside motels, clamoring for attention along U.S. 54, run $35-50 per night and fill on weekends. The **Heritage Inn** (314-348-3600), on U.S. 54 just east of the Glaze Bridge in Osage Beach, while similar to its peers in price, stands out for its swimming pool, boat launch, and excellent view of the lake. Rooms have small refrigerators, but no phones. Like many motels here, prices rise for the weekend. (Singles $32-42, doubles $40-50; open Mar.-Oct.) To avoid the Osage Beach scene altogether, stay across the bridge in quieter Camdenton. Try the **Ramblewood Inn Bed and Breakfast,** 402 Panoramic Dr. (314-346-3410); take U.S. 54 a few blocks west of its intersection with Rte. 5 to Panoramic Dr. Host Mary Massey has a meticulously decorated house yet manages to make you feel right at home while serving a four-course breakfast on crystal and china. (Single $45, double $50, 2 rooms $85. Cash or check only. No children allowed.) **Lake of the Ozarks State Park** (314-348-2694), off U.S. 54 in Osage Beach, offers lakeside sites, but don't expect too much serenity—powerboats and jet-skis rule the lake (sites $6, with electricity $12). Call ahead if possible—they can book up—and watch out for the tricky gravel road on the way in.

Restaurants here, like lodgings, generally fall into two categories: expensive or tacky. The **Thunder Mountain Country Inn** (314-346-6369), on Bridal Cave Rd. in Camdenton, proves the exception to the rule. Take Rte. 5 north from U.S. 54 and turn left at the entrance to Bridal Cave (yes, it's down there). Come at sunset for a breathtaking view and a touch of class—in a region not often so touched. Matronly waitresses serve German and American cuisine, ranging from salads and sandwiches ($4-6) to five kinds of schnitzel ($12-17); "the chef's a little 'crabby' today appetizer," served with fresh blackberries on the side, is especially tasty (Open Feb.-Dec. Tues.-Fri. 11am-9pm-ish, Sat. 4:30pm-"til we close.")

■■■ BRANSON

The tourists, the shops, and the inns congregate in Branson for one reason: the music. Branson has become *the* place for country musicians to set up house and theater in the 90s. The **Grand Palace,** 2700 W. Rte. 76 (334-7263 or 800-5-PALACE/572-5223), hears from big names like Vince Gill and Billy Ray Cyrus when they blow through town. (Shows April-Dec. $15-26, ages 4-11 $5.75-10; except for limited engagements.) Japanese performer Shoji Tabuchi may not be a household name, but he's the most popular show in town. See him fiddle, sing, and crack jokes at none other than the **Shoji Tabuchi Show,** 3620 Shepherd of the Hills Expwy. (334-7469), near Rte. 76 a.k.a., Country Music Blvd. (shows March-Dec.; $26, children $17; senior discount available). Ever wonder what happened to the Osmond Brothers? Wonder no longer—they're still jammin' in the **Osmond Family Theater** (336-6100), at the intersection of Rte. 76 and Rte. 165 (shows May-Dec.; $19, under 13 $7). These are a mere smattering of the full repertoire. Others include the **Andy**

Williams' Show (334-4500), the **Mel Tillis Show** (335-6635), and **Presley's** (334-4874), for a bit of Ozark humor. **Dolly Parton's Dixie Stampede** (800-520-5544), on Rte. 76 across from the Silver Fountain Inn, a one-of-a-kind combination dinner theater and rodeo, should be the hot ticket in 1996 (dine ringside for $26.50, ages 4-11 $15.50). Call the Chamber of Commerce (see below) for exact dates and prices of all shows; they are subject to change.

If country music isn't your *thang* and you're in Branson anyway, never fear—this is the Ozarks, after all. **Table Rock Lake, Lake Taneycomo,** and a criss-crossing system of streams and creeks are perfect for canoeing, fishing, or just splashing along the shoreline. Try renting equipment at the state parks, or the **Indian Point Boat Dock** (338-2891), at the end of Indian Point Rd. You can get fishing boats ($15 per hour), jet-skis, pontoon boats, and others, as long as you have a driver's license. Follow Rte. 76W for 5 mi. past the Strip and turn left on Indian Point Rd.

The **Branson Chamber of Commerce** (334-4136), at the Rte. 248/65 junction, has brochures and a computer/telephone system which can help arrange your whole stay (open Mon.-Fri. 8am-7pm, Sat. 8am-5pm, Sun. 11am-4pm). For crisis help, call the **Missouri Victim Center** at 889-4357. **Emergency:** 911. Branson's **post office:** 327 S. Commercial St. (334-3366), off Main St. (open Mon.-Fri. 8:30am-5pm, Sat. 9am-1pm); **ZIP code:** 65616; **area code:** 417.

Motels along Rte. 76 tend to be cheap; for tasteful, inexpensive motels, try Rte. 265, 4 mi. west of the Strip. The **Storybrook Inn** (338-2344), on Rte. 265 just south of Rte. 76, provides cheery, newly-renovated rooms with no phones (singles $35, doubles $40). **Indian Point** (338-2121), at the end of Indian Point Rd. south of Rte. 76, one of many campgrounds on Table Rock Lake run by the Corps of Engineers, has lakeside sites with swimming access and use of the boat launch (2-day min. stay.; check-in by 9pm; sites $10, with electricity $13; open May-Oct.).

A few charming local restaurants stave off the fast-food invasion in the older section of town, on Rte. 76 near Business Rte. 65. For an art-deco combination of old and new, visit the **Uptown Café** (336-3535), at Rte. 76 and 165, a nouveau diner with a mirrored-and-purple facade and an all-you-can-eat breakfast buffet (daily 7:30-10:30am) for $5. Dinner entrees, such as chicken-fried steak and burgers range from $3.75 to $12.50. (Open daily 7:30am-midnight.)

Greyhound (800-321-2222) runs two buses per day to Springfield (1hr., $9), Kansas City (5½hr., $40-45), and Memphis (6-8hr., $52). Buses pick up and drop off from the **Branson Welcome Center,** 1911 Main St. (Rte. 76 in the old downtown). The center is open Monday to Friday 9am-6pm and Saturday 9am-noon.

Oklahoma

Between 1838 and 1839, President Andrew Jackson ordered the forced relocation of "The Five Civilized Tribes" from the southern states to the designated Oklahoma Indian Territory, in a tragic march which came to be known as the "Trail of Tears" (see below). The survivors rebuilt their tribes in Oklahoma, only to be moved again in 1889 to make way for whites rushing to stake claims on newly opened settlement lands. (Homesteaders who slipped in and claimed plots before the first official land run were called "sooners"—Oklahoma's nickname ever since.) Ironically, when the territory was admitted to the Union in 1907, it adopted a Choctaw name; Oklahoma means "land of the red man." Despite the serious mistreatment of the Native Americans, many streets carry Indian names, and cultural life seems to center around Native American heritage and experiences. There are re-enactments and interpretations of the Trail of Tears throughout Oklahoma, and the world's largest collection of western American art in Tulsa features 250,000 Native American artifacts.

Visitors expecting a brown dustbowl of a state à la *The Grapes of Wrath* will be happily disappointed—thanks to improvements in farming technology, Oklahoma's rolling red hills are blanketed with green grass and crops.

PRACTICAL INFORMATION

Capital: Oklahoma City.
Oklahoma Tourism and Recreation Department: 500 Will Rogers Bldg., Oklahoma City 73105 (800-652-6552), in the capitol. Open daily 8am-8pm.
Driving: Oklahoma does not honor the International Driver's Permit.
Time Zone: Central (1hr. behind Eastern). **Postal Abbreviation:** OK
Sales Tax: 7.65%.

■■■ TULSA

First settled by Creeks arriving from the "Trail of Tears," Tulsa's location on the banks of the Arkansas River made it a logical trading outpost for Native Americans and Europeans. The discovery of huge oil deposits in the 1920s transformed the city into the oil capital of America. Today, Tulsa's Art Deco skyscrapers, French villas, and Georgian mansions, as well as its Native American population (the second largest among U.S. metropolitan areas) reflect its varied heritage—it's this diversity that lends Tulsa its status as the "cultural capital of Oklahoma."

PRACTICAL INFORMATION

Tourist Office: Convention and Visitors Division, Metropolitan Tulsa Chamber of Commerce, 616 S. Boston (585-1201 or 800-558-3311). Open Mon.-Fri. 8am-5pm. **Gay Information Line,** 743-4297. Lists gay bars and social groups in Tulsa. Open daily 8am-10pm.
Buses: Greyhound, 317 S. Detroit (800-231-2222). To: Oklahoma City (7 per day, 2hr., $17); St. Louis (4 per day, 7½-9½hr., $71); Kansas City (3 per day, 5hr., $38); Dallas (8 per day, 7hr., $34). Open 24 hrs.
Public Transportation: Metropolitan Tulsa Transit Authority, 510 S. Rockford (582-2100). Buses run 5am-7pm. Fare 75¢, transfers 5¢, seniors and disabled (disabled card available at bus offices) 35¢, ages 5-18 60¢, under 5 free with adult. Maps and schedules, though not always reliable, are available at the main office (open Mon.-Fri. 8am-5pm), and at any library.
Taxis: Yellow Cab, 582-6161. $2.25 base fare, $1 per mi., $1 per extra passenger.
Car Rental: Thrifty, 1506 N. Memorial Dr. (838-3333). $29 per day, $165 per week; unlimited mileage. Must be 21 with major credit card; under 25 surcharge $10 per day. Open 24 hrs. The state of Oklahoma does not honor the International Driver's Permit.
Bike Rental: River Trail Bicycles, 6861 S. Peoria (481-1818). 5-speeds $4 per hr., $12 per day. In-line skates $5 per hr., $10 per day. Open Mon.-Thurs. 10am-7pm, Fri.-Sat. 10am-8pm, Sun. 11am-7pm. Credit card deposit required.
Crisis Line: 583-HELP/4357. For info, referral, or crisis intervention. Open 24 hrs.
Emergency: 911.
Post Office: 333 W. 4th St. (599-6800). Open Mon.-Fri. 8:30am-5pm. **ZIP code:** 74101. **Area code:** 918.

Tulsa sections off into 1-sq.-mi. quadrants. Downtown lies at the intersection of **Main St.** (north-south) and **Admiral Blvd.** (east-west). Numbered streets lie in increasing order as you move north or south from Admiral. Named streets run north-south in alphabetical order. Those named after western cities are west of Main St.; eastern cities to the east. Every time the alphabetical order reaches the end, the cycle begins again. Always note whether an address is north, south, east, or west.

ACCOMMODATIONS AND CAMPING

The downtown motels are generally unclean and unsafe, especially north of 244 near the airport. For more options, try the budget motels which crowd I-44 and I-

244. Skelly Dr., which runs along I-44 to exit 222, where I-44 and I-244 meet, features many motels of the non-chain variety; take bus #17 ("Southwest Blvd."). Downtown, the **Executive Inn,** 416 W. 6th St. (584-4461), right across from the police station and a bustling diner, gives you cook-it-yourself kitchenettes (singles $40, doubles $49). The **Georgetown Plaza Motel,** 8502 E. 27th St. (622-6616), off I-44 at 31st and Memorial St., has free local calls and cable (singles $24, doubles $30). The **Tulsa Inn,** 5554 S. 48th W. Ave. (446-1600), rents sparkling singles with free local calls (singles $23, doubles $33).

The **KOA Kampground,** 193 East Ave. (266-4227), ½ mi. west of I-44's exit 240A, makes the outdoors less rough with a pool, laundry facilities, showers, and a game room (office open 8am-8pm; sites for 2 $15, with hookup $17). More picturesque, but less convenient, the **Heyburn State Park** (247-6695), 20 mi. southwest of the city off I-44 at Rte. 33, provides lovely sites on Heyburn Lake. (Fishing, free swimming, and bike rentals. Tent sites $6; RVs sites $8, with electric $11.)

FOOD AND NIGHTLIFE

Many downtown restaurants cater to the lunching businesspeople in the area, closing at 3pm on weekdays and 1pm on Saturdays. **Nelson's Buffeteria,** 514 S. Boston (584-9969), takes you on a sentimental journey to Tulsa's past. Operating since 1929 and now run by Nelson Jr., this old-style diner's walls are blanketed with mid-American memorabilia. Try a blue plate special (two scrambled eggs, hash browns, biscuit and gravy $2.50) or the famous chicken-fried steak ($4.50). Ask for extra gravy. (Open Mon.-Fri. 6am-2:30pm.) For that old Rte. 66 feel, visit the **Metro Diner,** 3001 E. 11th St. (592-2616). The back end of a '57 Chevy greets you at the door. Salads, sandwiches, burgers, and pasta from $4-8. Kids eat free Monday nights. (Open Sun.-Thurs. 8am-10pm, Fri.-Sat. 8am-11pm.)

For up-to-date stats on arts and entertainment, pick up a free copy of *Urban Tulsa* at local restaurants. At night, head to the bars on Cherry St., an area on 15th St. east of Peoria lined with restaurants and antique shops, or to those in the 30s along S. Peoria. The **Blue Rose Café,** 3421 S. Peoria (742-3873), has great, cheap food (burgers $3-6) and an outdoor patio equipped with a misting machine. *Tulsa People Magazine* voted it runner-up in the "Best Place to Ride Your Harley" division. (Must be 21 at all times. Live blues and rock Sun.-Thurs. 9pm; no cover. Open daily 11am-2am.) The intersection of 18th and Boston makes noises in the night as well; the college crowd flocks to **Hoffbraü,** 1738 Boston (583-9520), "the snob-free, dork-free, band and brewski place to be." (Burgers, sandwiches, Tex-Mex entrees $5-7. Must be 21. Local bands Fri.-Sat. 10pm; cover varies. Open Mon.-Thurs. 11am-10pm, Fri. 11am-2am, Sat. 5pm-2am.)

SIGHTS AND ENTERTAINMENT

The ultra-modern, gold-mirrored architecture of **Oral Roberts University,** 7777 S. Lewis (495-6161), rises out of an Oklahoma plain about 6 mi. south of downtown Tulsa between Lewis and Harvard Ave.; take bus #9. In 1964, Oral had a dream in which God commanded him to "Build Me A University," and Tulsa's most-frequented tourist attraction was born. The 80-ft.-high sculpture of praying hands which guards the campus, and the hordes of believers flocking to visit, catapult the university beyond the realm of mere kitsch. Free **campus tours** (495-6807) for prospective students. (Visitors center open Mon.-Sat. 10:30am-4:30pm, Sun. 1-5pm.)

The **Fenster Museum of Jewish Art,** 1223 E. 17th Pl. (582-3732), housed in B'nai Emunah Synagogue, contains an unexpected and impressive collection of Judaica dating from 2000 BC to the present (open Sun.-Thurs. 10am-4pm; free). The **Philbrook Art Center,** 2727 S. Rockford Rd. (749-7941), combines a collection of Native American pottery and artifacts with Renaissance art in the Renaissance villa of an oil baron. (Open Tues.-Wed. and Fri.-Sat. 10am-5pm, Thurs. 10am-8pm, Sun. 11am-5pm. $4, students and seniors $2, under 13 free.) Take bus #5 ("Peoria") from downtown for both museums. Perched atop an Osage foothill 2 mi. northwest of downtown (take bus #47), the **Thomas Gilcrease Museum,** 1400 Gilcrease

Museum Rd. (596-2700), houses the world's largest collection of western American art. Designed as an anthropological study of North America from pre-history to present, the museum holds 250,000 Native American artifacts and 10,000 paintings and sculptures by artists such as Remington and Russell. (Open Tues.-Wed. and Fri.-Sat. 9am-5pm, Thurs. 9am-8pm, Sun. 1-5pm. $3 donation requested.)

Rodgers and Hammerstein's *Oklahoma!* continues its run under the stars at the **Discoveryland Amphitheater** (245-6552), 10 mi. west of Tulsa on 41st St., accessible only by car. The musical commemorates the suffering of Okie farmers in the 19th century, and the showstopper "Oklahoma" has been adopted as the state song. (Shows June-Aug. Mon.-Sat. 8pm. Mon.-Thurs. $12, seniors $11, under 12 $5; Fri.-Sat. $14, seniors $13, under 12 $5.) Arrive early for the pre-show barbecue, starting at 5pm ($7, seniors $6.50, children $5). For more cultural enlightenment, the **Tulsa Ballet** (585-2573), acclaimed as one of America's finest regional troupes, dances at the **Performing Arts Center** (596-7111), at 3rd and Cincinnati St. (Box office open Mon.-Fri. 10am-5:30pm, Sat. 10am-3pm.) The **Tulsa Philharmonic** (747-7445), and **Tulsa Opera** (582-4035), also perform at the PAC; the Philharmonic harmonizes most weekends September through May ($8-35), while the Opera stages three productions per year. Call for exact dates.

Tulsa shines during annual events like the **International Mayfest** (582-6435). This outdoor food, arts, and performance festival takes place in downtown Tulsa, (May 16-19 in 1996). The **Pow-Wow** (744-1113), June 7-9 in 1996, at the Tulsa Fairground Pavilion, attracts Native Americans from dozens of tribes for a three-day festival of food, arts and crafts, and nightly dancing contests which visitors may attend ($2, seniors $1, under 10 free.)

■ NEAR TULSA: TAHLEQUAH

A moving commemoration of Native American heritage, the **"Trail of Tears" Drama** re-enacts the Cherokees' tragic march, in **Tahlequah,** 66 mi. east of Tulsa on Rte. 51. The Cherokees' western capital, Tahlequah marks the end of the tribe's forced movement west; see below for more on the history of their journey. (Performances June-Aug. Tues.-Sat. 8pm. $9, children $4.50. For tickets, call 456-6007, or write P.O. Box 515, Tahlequah 74465; reservations recommended.) Visitors to Tahlequah can explore the **Tsa-La-Gi village,** a recreation of a 16th-century Cherokee settlement and the **Cherokee National Museum.** (Village tours May-Aug. Mon.-Sat. 10am-5pm, Sun. 1-5pm. $4, children $2. Museum open Mon.-Sat. 10am-8pm, Sun. 1pm-5pm; in winter Mon.-Sat. 10am-5pm, Sun. 1-5pm. $2.75, children $1.50).

Trail of Tears National Historic Trail

President Andrew Jackson ignored a Supreme Court proclamation when he forced 16,000 Cherokee Indians to march from North Carolina, Tennessee, Georgia, and Alabama to the Indian Territories. Many walked the trail at gunpoint, and by the end tens of thousands had died of hunger and disease. The Historic Trail, established in December of 1987, commemorates this journey. Though the trail is still under construction, an auto route follows as closely as possible the northern land trail taken by many of the Indians. For more information, contact Trail of Tears National Historic Trail, Southwest Region, National Park Service, P.O. Box 728, Santa Fe, NM 87504 (505-988-6888).

■■■ OKLAHOMA CITY

At noon on April 22, 1889, a gunshot sent settlers scrambling into Oklahoma Territory to claim land. By sundown, Oklahoma City, set strategically on the tracks of the Santa Fe Railroad, had a population of over 10,000 homesteaders. The 1928 discovery of oil modernized the city, and elegant homes rose with the oil derricks. Oklahoma City plodded along fairly peacefully for the next 70 years until the quiet was shattered on April 19, 1995, when a bomb at the Alfred R. Murrah federal office building exploded; 168 people died as a result. A large portion of Oklahoma City was damaged in the blast which shocked and confused the nation.

PRACTICAL INFORMATION

Tourist Office: Chamber of Commerce Tourist Information, 123 Park Ave. (278-8900), at Broadway. Open Mon.-Fri. 8:30am-5pm.

Airport: Will Rogers Memorial (680-3200), southwest of downtown. **World Coach,** 3800 S. Meridian (685-2638), has 24-hr. van service to downtown ($9 for 1 person; $3 per additional person). A taxi downtown costs $14.

Buses: Greyhound, 427 W. Sheridan Ave. (235-6425 or 800-231-2222), at Walker. Take city bus #4, 5, 6, 8, or 10. *In a rough area.* To: Tulsa (7 per day, 2hr., $17); Dallas (4 per day, 5hr., $32); and Kansas City (6 per day, 10hr., $68). Open 24 hrs.

Public Transportation: Oklahoma Metro Transit, offices at Union Station, 300 S.W. 7th (235-RIDE/7433; open Mon.-Fri. 7am-5pm). Bus service Mon.-Sat. approximately 6am-6pm. All routes radiate from the station at Reno and Gaylord St., but don't expect to find a schedule here (or on the buses, for that matter)—they're hidden at the Union Station office (50¢). Route numbers vary depending on the direction of travel. Fare 75¢, seniors and ages 6-17 35¢.

Taxis: Yellow Cab, 232-6161. $2.50 base, $1.25 per mi, $1 per extra passenger. 24 hrs.

Car Rental: Dub Richardson Ford Rent-a-Car, 2930 N.W. 39th Expwy. (946-9288). Used cars $27 per day with unlimited in-state mileage; 25¢ per additional mi. Must be 21 with major credit card. Open Mon.-Fri. 8am-6pm, Sat. 8:30am-noon. The state of Oklahoma does not honor the International Driver's Permit.

Bike Rental: Miller's Bicycle Distribution, 3350 W. Main (360-3838), at I-35. 10-speeds and mountain bikes $5 per day, $54 per month. In-line skates $10 per day. Open Mon.-Sat. 10am-8pm, Sun. 1-6pm. May ask for a credit card deposit.

Crisis Lines: Contact, 848-2273. For referrals or crisis intervention. **Rape Crisis,** 943-7273. Both open 24 hrs.

Emergency: 911.

Post Office: 320 S.W. 5th St. (278-6300). Open Mon.-Fri. 8:30am-5:30pm, Sat. 9am-noon. Emergency window open 24 hrs. **ZIP code:** 73125. **Area code:** 405.

Main St. divides the town north-south, while Broadway splits it east-west. Almost all of the city's attractions are outside the city center, but the all-encompassing Metro Transit reaches them. Use caution with public transportation, especially downtown after dark. Easy parking makes driving the best way to go.

ACCOMMODATIONS AND CAMPING

Accommodations in downtown OKC are scarce (even more so since the bombing). **The Economy Inn,** 501 N.W. 5th St. (235-7455), though downtown near the epicenter, remains open for business (cable TV; singles $25, doubles $35). The interstates offer a much wider selection of inexpensive motels, usually chains. However, not all motels of the same chain are identical, as evidenced by the positively luxurious **Motel 6** at 4200 W. I-40 (947-6550), at Meridian (take bus #11 or #38). Palatial rooms come with access to a pool and a spa. (Singles $32, doubles $38.) This intersection is loaded with chains, including another **Motel 6** ($2 cheaper, no spa).

Oklahoma City has two accessible campgrounds. **RCA,** 12115 Northeast Expwy. (478-0278), next to Frontier City Amusement Park 10 mi. north of the city on I-35, has a pool, laundry room, showers, and lots of fast-food restaurants nearby (open 8am-9pm; sites $12.50, with full hookup $16). Much prettier (and much farther from an amusement park), a state-run campground roosts on Lake Thunderbird, 30 mi. south of OKC at **Little River State Park** (360-3572). Take I-40 East to Choctaw Rd., then south until the road ends, and make a left. Swim or fish in the lake or hike the cliffs for a view. (Showers available. Open 8am-5pm. Tent sites $6, in area with gate attendant $7; RV sites $11/$12. Seniors from 16 participating states and disabled travelers ½-price.)

FOOD AND NIGHTLIFE

Oklahoma City contains the largest feeder cattle market in the U.S., and **beef** tops most menus. Aside from the turn-of-the-century warehouses which have been converted into yuppified eating and drinking establishments, most places downtown close early in the afternoon after they've served business lunchers. **Cattleman's Steak House,** 1309 S. Agnew (236-0416), 1 block from the stockyards, (est. 1910) may be a classy restaurant today, but its colorful past includes a stint as a prohibition-era speakeasy. Steaks range from chopped sirloin ($7) to USDA prime ($18). (Open Sun.-Thurs. 6am-10pm, Fri.-Sat. 6am-midnight.) Behind an old western movie façade, **Yippie Yi Yo Café,** 4723 N. Western (542-5282), serves coffee ($1-3) in an artsy interior. (Open Mon.-Wed. 7am-7pm, Thurs.-Fri. 7am-11pm, Sat. 8am-11pm, Sun. 9am-3pm.) **Sweeney's Deli,** 900 N. Broadway (232-2510), is one of the few downtown places that stays up late. Enjoy a tasty dish in a friendly atmosphere; if you play enough pool here, everyone really *will* know your name. (Sandwiches $3-4; burgers $2.20. Open Mon.-Fri. 11am-11pm.)

Nightlife in Oklahoma City is as rare as the elusive jackalope. For ideas, pick up a copy of the *Oklahoma Gazette,* or try the Bricktown district on Sheridan Ave.; many area restaurants have live music after dark. At the **Bricktown Brewery** (232-BREW/2739), at Sheridan Ave. and Oklahoma St., you can watch the beer brew while dining on burgers, salads, and chicken dishes ($5-9). The second floor houses a bonanza of bar games, as well as live music. Cover depends on the band—most are local rock/alternative acts, but big names like Dave Matthews have been known to show up. (Must be 21. Live music Tues. and Fri.-Sat. 8pm. Open Tues.-Sat. 11am-1am, Sun.-Mon. 11am-midnight). For good dancing, the **Wreck Room at The Habana Inn** (525-7610), at 39th and Barnes opens its doors Thursday through Saturday (cover $3/$5/$7; open 10pm-5am).

SIGHTS AND ENTERTAINMENT

Monday morning is *the* time to visit the **Oklahoma City Stockyards,** 2500 Exchange Ave. (235-8675), the busiest in the world; cattle auctions (Mon.-Tues.) begin at 8am and sometimes last into the night. Visitors enter free of charge via a calfwalk over pens, leading from the parking lot east of the auction house. (Take bus #12 from the terminal to Agnew and Exchange.) James Earle Fraser's *The End of the Trail,* commemorates the plight of Native Americans along the "Trail of Tears." Ironically, the sculpture of a man slumped over an exhausted pony graces the **National Cowboy Hall of Fame and Western Heritage Center,** 1700 N.E. 63rd St. (478-2250), which celebrates the pistol-packin' frontiersmen who displaced the Cherokees. (Take bus #22 from downtown. Open daily 8:30am-6pm; Labor Day-Memorial Day 9am-5pm. $6.50, seniors $5.50, ages 6-12 $3.25.)

The **Kirkpatrick Center Museum Complex,** 2100 N.E. 52nd St. (427-5461), feels like an educational amusement park. A mall-like complex houses a pastiche of eight separate museums. Highlights are the **Air and Space Museum, International Photography Hall of Fame, Red Earth Indian Center,** and the **Omniplex,** a hands-on science museum with free planetarium shows. (Take bus #22. Open Mon.-Sat. 9am-6pm, Sun. noon-6pm; Labor Day-Memorial Day Mon.-Fri. 9:30am-5pm, Sat. 9am-6pm, Sun. noon-6pm. Admission to all 8 museums $6, seniors $4, ages 3-12 $3.50, under 3 free.) Check out **Myriad Botanical Gardens** (297-3995), at Reno and Robinson. The **Crystal Bridge** is a glass-enclosed cylinder 70 feet in diameter containing both a desert and a rainforest, while still functioning as a bridge over a small lake. (Open daily 9am-6pm; $3, seniors $2, ages 4-12 $1.25. Outdoor gardens open daily 6am-11pm; free.) The **Oklahoma Opry,** 404 W. Commerce (632-8322), is home to a posse of country music stars (regular performances Sat. 8pm; $7, seniors $6, kids $2.50-3.50). The **Festival of the Arts** (236-1426), held at Myriad Gardens (April 23-28 in 1996), highlights visual, culinary, and performing arts. The **Red Earth** festival (427-5228), June 7-9, 1996, is the country's largest celebration of Native America; the Myriad Convention Center hosts intense dance competitions in which dancers from tribes all over perform for prize money (ticket prices vary).

Texas

Spanning an area as wide as Wisconsin to Montana and as long as North Carolina to Key West, Texas is more like its own country than a state. In fact, after revolting against the Spanish in 1821, the Republic of Texas stood alone until 1845, when it entered the Union as the 28th state. The state's unofficial motto proclaims that "everything is bigger in Texas," and "everything" certainly includes wide-brimmed hats, boat-sized American autos, and toweringly tall urban ranchers who seem ready and willing to conquer the frontier and fight for independence all over again.

Cotton, cattle, and oil built the Texan fortune, but the state's growing technology and tourism industries form the building blocks of the state's future. Texan cities welcome visitors with cosmopolitan diversity and a unique culture which relies heavily on Mexican influence. The flavor of Texas's southern neighbor is unmistakable in the state's architecture, place names, and cuisine. Regional dishes, like most of Texan culture, profit from the state's age-old Mexican heritage.

Texas Tidbits

Authors: Cormac McCarthy, James Michener *(Texas),* Nelson Algeren *(A Walk on the Wild Side),* Katherine Anne Porter.

Artists: Jerry Bywaters, Otis Dozier, Florence McClung, James Surls.

Cuisine: Tex-Mex, barbecue, hot links (spicy Texan sausages broiled over a barbecue), jerky, *menudo* (stew of tripe and corn meal), chicken fried steak, longhorn beef, Mexican pastries.

Microbreweries: Pearl Brewing Company, Spoetzl, Selis, Hill Country, Texas Brewing, Shiner Bock Brewing Co.

Native Americans: Tonkawa, Atakapa, Wichita, Apache, Comanche.

Music: Country-western, Buddy Holly, Stevie Ray Vaughn, ZZ Top, Edie Brickell, Lyle Lovett, Tripping Daisy.

Film and TV: *Dazed and Confused, Slacker, Debbie Does Dallas, Fandango, The Last Picture Show, Dallas, Paris, Texas.*

Climate: Hot and dry. **Best Time to Visit:** Not summer.

Geography: Desert, hill country, pine woods in east Texas.

PRACTICAL INFORMATION

Capital: Austin.

Texas Division of Tourism: P.O. Box 12728, Austin 78711-2728 (800-888-8839). **Texas Travel Information Center** (800-452-9292) helps visitors plan trips (open daily 8am-9pm). **U.S. Forest Service,** 701 N. First St., Lufkin 75901 (409-639-8501). **Texas Parks and Wildlife Dept.,** Austin Headquarters Complex, 4200 Smith School Rd., Austin 78744 (512-389-4800 or 800-792-1112).

Time Zones: Mostly Central (1hr. behind Eastern); *Let's Go* makes note of areas in Mountain (2hr. behind Eastern). **Postal Abbreviation:** TX

Sales Tax: 6-8%.

DALLAS

Dallas mixes a little country, a little rock 'n' roll, rancher-businessmen, and cowgirl cheerleaders together in a "metroplex" mishmash of skyscrapers, neon lights, modern shopping malls, and miles upon miles of suburbs. In 1841 founding father John Neely Bryan, an ambitious Irish immigrant, built a tiny little loghouse outpost in the hope that one day it would grow into a bustling inland port on the Trinity River. Over time, the river, a raging torrent at times and a dusty little trickle at others, proved too unpredictable. This by no means hindered Dallas's development; the city rose to prominence in the 1870s when a major north-south railroad crossed a

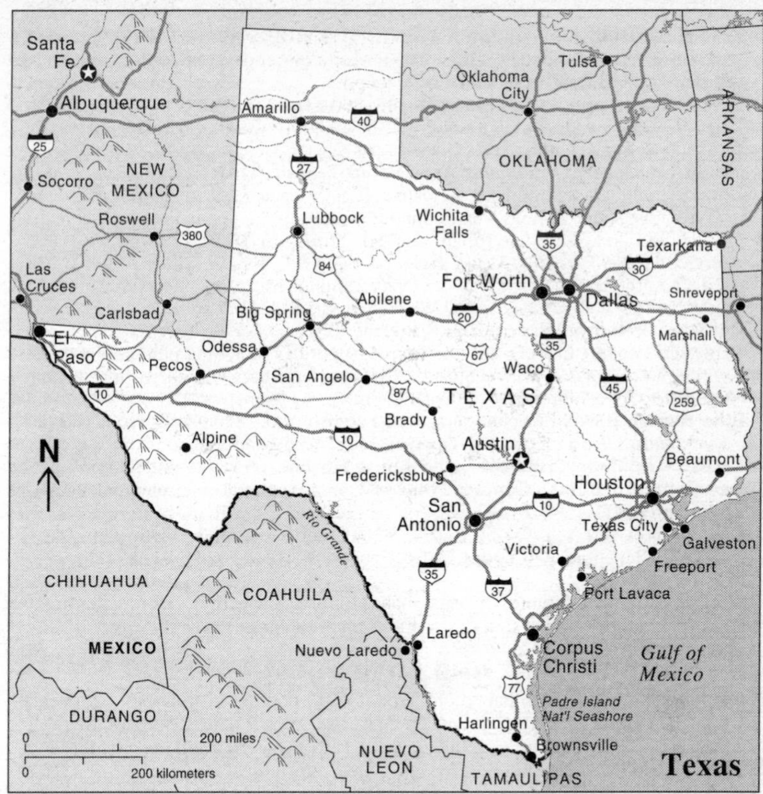

transcontinental line just south of town, and waves of settlers rode in on the rails to swell the population. Now the eighth-largest city in the United States, Dallas has since attracted flocks of immigrants from the Far East and Latin America who see the city as far more than a rail stop. While the city's legendary preoccupation with commerce remains evident, recent campaigns for historic preservation have restored many run-down urban areas to their pre-petro glory.

PRACTICAL INFORMATION

Tourist Office: Dallas Convention and Visitors Bureau, 1201 Elm St. (B2; 746-6700), in the Renaissance Tower. Provides a slew of maps and brochures. Open Mon.-Fri. 8am-5pm. The bureau also oversees two **visitors centers:** 1303 Commerce St. (B3; 746-6603; open Mon.-Thurs. 8am-5:30pm, Fri. 8am-5pm, Sat. 9am-5pm, Sun. noon-5pm) and 603 Munger St. (B2; 880-0405), in the West End Market Place (open Mon.-Sat. 11am-8pm, Sun. noon-8pm). The **Dallas Gay and Lesbian Alliance,** 2701 Reagan (528-4233), provides commmunity info. Open Mon.-Fri. 9am-9pm, Sat. 10am-6pm, Sun. noon-6pm. **Special Events Info Line,** 746-6679. 24 hrs. **Internet Surfers:** contact http://www.pic.net/cityview/dallas.html for info on local clubs, restaurants, museums, concerts, etc.

Airport: Dallas-Ft. Worth International (574-8888), 17mi. northwest of downtown; take bus #409. **Love Field** (670-6080; take bus #39) has mostly intra-Texas flights. To get downtown from either airport, take the **Super Shuttle,** 729 E. Dallas Rd. (817-329-2000; in terminal, dial 02 on service phone located at ground transport services). Shuttle to downtown from DFW $15, from Love Field $11. 24-hr. service. Taxi to downtown from DFW $25, from Love Field $15.

Trains: Amtrak, 400 S. Houston Ave. (B3; 653-1101 or 800-872-7245), in Union Station. To: L.A. (3 per day, 42hr., $217); Austin (3 per day, 6hr., $36); Little Rock (3 per day, 7½hr., $81). Open daily 9am-6pm.

Buses: Greyhound, 205 S. Lamar St. (B3; 800-231-2222), 3 blocks east of Union Station. To: New Orleans (12 per day, 13hr., $69); Houston (9 per day, 5hr., $25); Austin (12 per day, 4hr., $23). Open 24 hrs.

Public Transportation: Dallas Area Rapid Transit (DART), 1401 Pacific Ave. (B2; 979-1111; open Mon.-Fri. 8:30am-4:45pm). Routes radiate from downtown; serves most suburbs. Runs 5am-midnight; to suburbs 5am-8pm. Fare $1. Get maps at Elm and Ervay St. office (open Mon.-Fri. 7am-6pm). DART's downtown Dallas service **Hop-a-Bus** (979-1111), has a park-and-ride system. Three routes (blue, red, and green) run Mon.-Fri. about every 10min. Fare 25¢; transfers free.

Taxis: Yellow Cab Co., 426-6262. $2.70 first mi., $1.20 per additional mi.

Car Rental: Rent-a-Wreck, 2025 S. Buckner Blvd. (800-398-2544). Extremely reliable service. Late-model used cars from $19 per day including unlimited mileage within 100mi. of downtown. Must be 18. Cash deposits accepted. Airport pick-up available. Open 9am-6pm, Sat. 9am-3:30pm.

Bike Rental: Bicycle Exchange, 11716 Ferguson Rd. (270-9269). From $60 per week. Must have a credit card. Open Mon.-Fri. 9am-7pm, Sat. 9am-5pm.

Crisis Lines: Rape Crisis and Child Abuse Hotline, 653-8740. **Suicide and Crisis Center,** 828-1000. **Contact 214,** 233-2233, for general counseling. All 24 hrs.

Emergency: 911.

Post Office: 400 N. Ervay St. (C2; 953-3045), near Bryan St. downtown. Open Mon.-Fri. 8am-6pm. **ZIP code:** 75201; General Delivery, 75221. **Area code:** 214.

The compactness of downtown Dallas makes for easy navigation. Coordinates in the text key locations in Dallas to their locations on *Let's Go's* **map** of the city.

ACCOMMODATIONS AND CAMPING

Cheap lodging of the non-chain-motel type doesn't come easy in Dallas; big events such as the Cotton Bowl (Jan. 1) and the State Fair in October exacerbate the problem. Look on **U.S. 75 (Central Expwy.), I-635 (LBJ Freeway),** and in the suburbs of **Irving, Mesquite,** and **Arlington,** for inexpensive motels. If you can afford it, **Bed and Breakfast Texas Style,** 4224 W. Red Bird Ln. (298-5433 or 298-8586; daily 8:30am-4:30pm), will place you in a nice home, usually near town, with friendly residents who are anxious to make y'all as comfortable as possible. It's an especially good deal for groups of two. (Singles from $50, doubles from $60.) The **Delux Inn,** 3817 Rte. 80E (681-0044), takes care of those with tighter wallets. All 133 units have key-card locks, A/C, and free HBO and ESPN. (Singles $20, doubles $25; each additional person $2. Free continental breakfast.) No matter where you find yourself, one of Dallas's 13 **Motel 6** locations (800-440-6000) should be nearby (singles $30).

Tent campers should take I-35E to exit 460 and follow signs to the **KOA Kampground,** 7100 S. Stemmons Rd. (817-497-3353), in Denton, for shady sites, free firewood, and a public hot tub and sauna (office open daily 8am-9pm. Tent sites for 2 $18, with full hookup $24). **Sandy Lake Campground,** 1915 Sandy Lake Rd. (242-6808), has a grocery store, a game room, two laundries, and 270 trailer sites ripe for RVs. Take I-635 to I-35E and get off at exit 444. (Office open Mon.-Fri. 7:30am-8pm, Sat. 8am-8pm, Sun. 1-6pm. RV sites $15-19, depending on vehicle size.)

FOOD

Cheap 'n' cheesy taco joints spring from every crack in the sidewalk here. For the low-down on more diverse dining, pick up the Friday weekend guide of the *Dallas Morning News.* The **West End Marketplace,** 603 Munger St. (B2; 748-4801), has fast Tex-Mex food amidst a variety of touristy shops, while gourmet restaurants and low-priced authentic barbecue joints hang near **Greenville Ave.** In this desert of beef, **Farmers Produce Market,** 1010 S. Pearl Expwy. (D3), between Pearl and Central Expwy. near I-30, is a veggie oasis (open daily 5am-6pm).

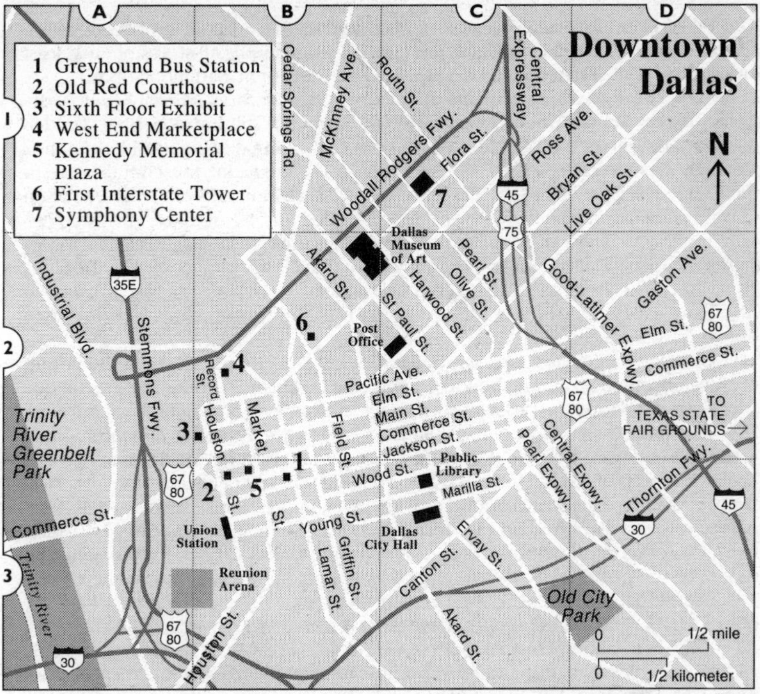

Downtown Dallas

1 Greyhound Bus Station
2 Old Red Courthouse
3 Sixth Floor Exhibit
4 West End Marketplace
5 Kennedy Memorial Plaza
6 First Interstate Tower
7 Symphony Center

Snuffer's, 3526 Greenville Ave. (826-6850). Good burgers ($4.25) surrounded by cacti, peppy music, a nice all-wood interior, friendly service, and a fun crowd. The miraculous cheddar fries ($4) send cholesterol levels soaring. Other dishes $5-7. Cash bar. Open daily 11am-2am.

Bubba's, 6617 Hillcrest Ave. (373-6527). A remodeled, 50s-style diner near the heart of SMU. Awful good fried chicken and chicken-fried steak dinners $5-6. Open daily 6:30am-10pm.

Terilli's, 2815 Greenville Ave. (827-3993). A sexy atmosphere with low-lit lamps and some of the best jazz in Dallas. The goal is "creative Italian," with terrific antipasto and vegetarian dishes. Try the veggie lasagna ($9), and wash it down with a specialty martini ($5.50). Open daily 11:30am-2am.

Sonny Bryan's Smokehouse, 302 N. Market St. (B2; 744-1610). Located at the threshold of the historic West End, this landmark defines Dallas BBQ. Try 1 meat on a bun ($6) or combine all 7 smokehouse delicacies ($14). Some vegetables available. Open Mon.-Thurs. 11am-10pm, Fri.-Sat. 11am-11pm, Sun. noon-9pm.

Tony Roma's, 310 Market St. (B2; 748-6959). Famous for meaty baby-back ribs. A 1-room restaurant with red brick walls, lots o' plants, and small clay pigs on almost every window sill. Always crowded. Ribs $7-8. Open Mon.-Thurs. 11am-11pm, Fri. 11am-midnight, Sat. 11:30am-midnight, Sun. 11:30am-10pm.

SIGHTS

A replica of the 1841 log cabin of **John Neely Bryan,** the City's founder, sits in the very heart of the city at Elm and Market St. Encircled by the present-day downtown, historic Dallas can easily be seen on a walking tour. Ride to the top of the **Reunion Tower,** 300 Reunion Blvd. (A3; 651-1234), 50 stories above the street, to get a feel for the city before you start walking (open Sun.-Thurs. 10am-10pm, Fri.-Sat. 9am-midnight; $2, seniors and kids $1).

An underground walkway at the bottom of Reunion Tower leads to the adjoining **Union Station,** 400 S. Houston Ave. (B2), one of the city's few grand old buildings.

The **West End Historic District and Marketplace** (B2), full of broad sidewalks, funky shops, restaurants, and bars, lies north of the station. (All stores open at least Mon. and Fri.-Sat. 11am-midnight, Tues.-Thurs. 11am-10pm, Sun. noon-6pm.)

Two blocks down and six flights up on Elm St., the notorious **Sixth Floor** of the former **Texas School Book Depository** (B2; 653-6666) still leaves people wondering how Lee Harvey Oswald could have fired the shot that killed President John F. Kennedy on November 22, 1963. This floor, now a fascinating museum devoted to the Kennedy legacy, traces the dramatic and macabre moments of the assassination in various media. (Open daily 9am-6pm. Self-guided tour $4, ages 6-8 $2. Audio cassette rental $2.) Below the depository, Elm St. runs through **Dealey Plaza,** a national landmark and site of the infamous grassy knoll, which the limo passed as the shots were fired. The area hasn't changed much and still bears an eerie resemblance to Abraham Zapruder's film of the assassination. Philip Johnson's **Memorial to Kennedy,** looms nearby, at Market and Main St.

Frightening gargoyles adorn the **Dallas County Courthouse** (B3), on the corner of Houston and Main St. The building gained the nickname "Old Red" for its unique Pecos red sandstone. Just east, at the corner of Ross Ave. and Field St., stands Dallas's most impressive skyscraper, **The First Interstate Tower** (B2), a multi-sided prism which towers above a glistening water garden. Farther east on Ross Ave. the **Dallas Museum of Art,** 1717 N. Harwood St. (B2; 922-1200), anchors the new **Arts District** with its excellent collections of Egyptian, impressionist, modern, and decorative art (open Tues.-Wed. 11am-4pm, Thurs.-Fri. 11am-9pm, Sat.-Sun. 11am-5pm; free). Closer to the downtown area, the imposing **Dallas City Hall,** 100 Marilla St. (C3; 670-3957), at Ervay St., was designed by the ubiquitous I.M. "Everywhere" Pei.

Almost 35 late-19th-century buildings from around Dallas (including a dentists' office, a bank, and a schoolhouse) have been restored and moved to **Old City Park** (D3; 421-5141), about 9 blocks south of City Hall on Ervay St. at Gano. Pack a picnic and eat at the city's oldest and most popular recreation area and lunch spot. (Park open daily 9am-6pm. Exhibit buildings open Tues.-Sat. 10am-4pm, Sun. noon-4pm. $5, seniors $4, children $2, families $12; free Mon. when exhibits are closed.)

Home to the state fair (Sept.-Oct.) since 1886, **Fair Park's** (890-2911) 30s art deco architecture, southeast of downtown on 2nd Ave., has gained national landmark status. The 277-acre park hosts the Cotton Bowl, and during the fair **Big Tex,** the 52-ft. smiling cowboy float, stands over the land Texas-tall. Inside the park, the **Dallas Aquarium** (670-8443) features swimming beasts that range from the ugly (although very edible) catfish to the fluorescent red empress. (Shark feedings Wed., Fri., and Sun. 2:30pm. Open daily 9am-4:30pm. $2, children $1.) The **Science Place** (428-5555) has toddlerish hands-on exhibits, as well as a special "What's happening to me?" exhibit geared toward adolescents (open daily 9:30am-5:30pm; $6, seniors and ages 3-12 $3, under 3 free). Other attractions include the **Museum of Natural History** (670-8457; open Mon.-Sat. 9am-5pm, Sun. 11am-5:30pm; $3, students and seniors $2, under 12 $1, under 3 free); the **African-American Museum** (565-9026), a multi-media collection of folk art and sculpture (open Tues.-Thurs. noon-5pm, Fri. noon-9pm, Sat. 10am-5pm, Sun. 1-5pm; free); and the **Dallas Horticulture Center** (428-7476; open Tues.-Sat. 10am-5pm, Sun. 1-5pm; free).

Nearby **White Rock Lake** provides a safe haven for walkers, bikers, and in-line skaters. On the east shore of the lake, resplendent flowers and trees bloom and grow throughout the 66-acre **Dallas Arboretum,** 8525 Garland Rd. (327-8263). Take the #60N bus from downtown. (Open daily 10am-5pm. $6, ages 6-12 $3.) To gaze upon Dallas's mansions, drive up the **Swiss Avenue Historic District** or through the streets of the **Highland Park** area.

ENTERTAINMENT

Most Dallas establishments cater to the night owl; restaurants, bars, and fast food joints typically stay open until 2am. The free weekly *Dallas Observer* (out Wed.) can help you assess your entertainment options. The **Shakespeare in the Park** festival (497-1526), at Samuel-Grand Park just northeast of State Fair Park, presents two free plays every summer (July-Aug.); each runs about two weeks. At Fair Park, the **Music Hall** (565-1116) showcases **Dallas Summer Musicals** (421-0662; 691-7200 for tickets) June through October (tickets $5-45; call 696-HALF/4253 for ½-price tickets on performance days). The **Dallas Opera** (443-1043) takes residence November to February (tickets $20-95). The **Dallas Symphony Orchestra** (692-0203) plays in the new **Morton H. Meyerson Symphony Center,** at Pearl and Flora St. (C1) in the arts district. Take in a show if only to hear the world-class acoustics. (Tickets $12-50.)

Six Flags Over Texas (817-640-8900), 15 mi. from downtown off I-30 in Arlington between Dallas and Fort Worth, maintains the original link in the nationwide amusement park chain. Admission buys unlimited access to over 100 rides and attractions, but these thrills don't come cheap—look for discounts on soda cans and in grocery stores. (Opens June-Labor Day daily 10am; Labor Day-Dec. and March-May opens Sat.-Sun. 10am. Closing times vary. $25, over 55 or under 4 ft. $19.)

In Dallas, the moral order is God, country, and the **Cowboys.** Football devotees flock to **Cowboys Stadium** at the junction of Loop 12 and Rte. 183, west of Dallas in **Irving** (579-5000 for tickets; open Mon.-Fri. 9am-4pm). Sports fans will also want to visit the **Ballpark in Arlington,** 1000 Ballpark Way (817-273-5100), home of the Texas **Rangers** (ticket office open Mon.-Fri. 9am-6pm, Sat. 10am-4pm).

NIGHTLIFE

For alternative nightlife, head to **Deep Ellum,** east of the downtown. Eighties bohemians revitalized the area, which had been a blues haven for the likes of Blind Lemon Jefferson, Lightnin' Hopkins, and Robert Johnson in the 20s. Like almost everything in Dallas, it's commercial, but enjoyable. **Trees,** 2709 Elm St. (C2; 748-5009), recently rated the best live music venue in the city by the *Dallas Morning News,* occupies a converted warehouse with a loft full of pool tables. Bands tend to be alternative groups. (Cover $2-10; 17+. Open daily 9pm-2am.) **Club Dada,** 2720 Elm St. (C2; 744-3232), former haunt of Edie Brickell, has added an outdoor patio and live local acts. Twentysomethings with pierced parts and ponytails come out in droves. (Cover Thurs.-Sat. $3-5. Open daily 8pm-2am.) For more info on Deep Ellum, call the **What's Up Line** (747-DEEP/3337).

The trendy **West End** packs eight clubs into **Dallas Alley,** 2019 N. Lamar (B2; 988-0581), under one single cover charge ($3-5). Inside, **Alley Cats** entertains with dueling piano sing-alongs, while **Paragon** plays Euro-tech music for dancing. The **Outback Pub** (761-9355) and **Dick's Last Resort** (747-0001), both at 1701 N. Market (B2), are popular with locals for having no cover, good beer selections, and raucous crowds (both open daily 11am-2am). On weekends (occasionally during the week) bands perform free concerts out on the red brick marketplace.

Greenville Ave. provides a refreshing change from the downtown crowds. **Poor David's Pub,** 1924 Greenville Ave. (821-9891), stages live music ranging from Irish folk tunes to reggae. Music is the main, and only, event: if there's no group booked, Poor David's just doesn't open. (Open Mon.-Sat. 7:30pm-2am. Tickets available after 5pm at the door; $3-20, cash only.) A classic R&B bar, the **Greenville Bar and Grill,** 2821 Greenville Ave. (823-6691), has dollar beers Monday through Friday 4-7pm (open daily 11am-2am). More popular nightspots line **Yale Blvd.,** home of Southern Methodist University's fraternity row. **Green Elephant,** 5612 Yale Blvd. (750-6625), a pseudo-60s extravaganza complete with lava lamps and tacky tapestries appears to be the bar of choice (open daily 11pm-2am). Many gay clubs rock north of downtown, in **Oak Lawn.** Among the more notable is **Roundup,** 3912 Cedar Springs Rd. (B1; 522-9611), at Throckmorton, a huge cover-free country and western bar which up to 1500 on weekends. Check out the shuffle board, pool tables, and game room for fun. (Open Wed.-Sun. 8pm-2am.)

■ NEAR DALLAS: FORT WORTH

If Dallas is the last Eastern city, Fort Worth is undoubtedly the first Western one. The historic **Stockyard District** (817-625-9715), 40 minutes west on I-30, provides a worthwhile daytrip and some raw Texan entertainment. At the corner of N. Main and E. Exchange Ave., the Stockyards host weekly rodeos (817-625-1025; April-Sept. 17 Sat. 8pm; $8) and **Pawnee Bill's Wild West Show** (817-625-1025; Sat. 2 and 4:30pm), which features sharpshooting, bulldoggin', and a stagecoach robbery. At night, head for **Billy Bob's,** 2520 Rodeo Plaza (817-624-7117), in the Yards. At 100,000 sq. ft., the place bills itself as the world's largest honky tonk, with a bull ring, a BBQ restaurant, pool tables, video games, a country and western dance club, and 42 bar stations. On one night alone, during a Hank Williams, Jr. concert, Billy Bob's sold 16,000 bottles of beer. (Professional bull-riding Fri.-Sat. 9 and 10pm. Free Texas Waltz lessons Thurs. 7-8pm. Cover $1, Sun.-Thurs. after 6pm $3, Fri.-Sat. $5.50-$8.50. Open Mon.-Sat. 11am-2am, Sun. noon-2am.)

The **Tarantula** steam train (800-952-5717), takes riders on a short journey in and around Stockyards Station, a marketplace of shops and restaurants developed from abandoned hog and sheep holding pens. The train leaves from 2318 S. 8th Ave. and 140 E. Exchange Ave.; the schedule changes seasonally. ($6, seniors $5, under 12 $3; round-trip $10/$8/$5.50.) The stockyards also hosts the **Chisholm Trail Round-Up,** a three-day jamboree, June 14-16 in 1996, commemorating the heroism of cowhands who led the long cattle drive to Kansas during the Civil War. During the event, check out the **Hog and Armadillo Races** (625-7005); grandfather and grandson work together blowing at the beast to make it move. For more on the Stockyards, go to the **visitor information center,** 130 Exchange Ave. (624-4741) and grab a copy of the *Stockyards Gazette* (open Mon.-Sat. 10am-5pm, Sun noon-6pm).

Down Rodeo Plaza, a walk on **Exchange Ave.** provides a window on the wild west. For decades, after cattlemen sold their livestock at the stockyards, they mosied down this street with cash in their pockets looking for entertainment. The trip still offers a plethora of saloons, restaurants, stores, and gambling parlors. Since 1906, a favorite stopping point has been the **White Elephant Saloon,** 106 E. Exchange Ave. (624-1887), with rough-hewn wood, brass footrails and photos of Old Fort Worth covering the walls.

■■■ AUSTIN

If the "Lone Star State" still inspires images of rough 'n' tumble cattle ranchers riding on horses across the plains, Austin does everything it can to put the stereotype to rest. Here, high-tech whiz-kids start Fortune 500 computer companies, artists make and sell exotic handicrafts, and bankers don sneakers for midday exercise on the city's downtown greenbelts. Austin's conspicuous student population keeps this small metropolis youthful and energetic; a thriving slacker population around the University of Texas campus makes dyed hair and pierced noses far more common than cowboy boots or 10-gallon hats. Though the city struggles to live up to its ambitious boast—"Live Music Capital of the World"—Austin undoubtedly sports a funky, rowdy nightlife.

PRACTICAL INFORMATION

Tourist Office: Austin Convention Center/Visitor Information, 201 E. 2nd St. (474-5171 or 800-926-2282). Open Mon.-Fri. 8:30am-5pm, Sat. 9am-5pm, Sun. 10am-5pm. **University of Texas Information Center,** 471-3434. **Texas Parks and Wildlife,** 4200 Smith School Rd. 78744 (389-4800 or 800-792-1112), has info on camping outside Austin. Open Mon.-Fri. 8am-5pm.

Airport: Robert Mueller Municipal, 4600 Manor Rd. (480-9091), 4mi. northeast of downtown. Taxi to downtown $12-14.

Trains: Amtrak, 250 N. Lamar Blvd. (476-5684 or 800-872-7245). To: Dallas (3 per week, 6hr., $36); San Antonio (3 per week, 3hr., $16; continues to Houston); El Paso (3 per week, 10hr., $129). Ticket office open Sun.-Thurs. 8am-10:30pm, Fri. 8am-5:30pm, Sat. 1-10:30pm.

Buses: Greyhound, 916 E. Koenig (800-231-2222), several mi. north of downtown off I-35. Easily accessible by public transportation. Bus #15 stops across the street and runs downtown. To: San Antonio (12 per day, 1½hr., $14); Houston (7 per day, 4hr., $19); Dallas (14 per day, 5hr., $23). Open 24 hrs.

Public Transportation: Capitol Metro, 2910 E. 5th St. (474-1200 or 800-474-1201; info line open Mon.-Fri. 6am-10pm, Sat. 6am-8pm, Sun. 7am-6pm). Fare 50¢, students, seniors, kids, and disabled 25¢. Maps and schedules available at the office (Mon.-Fri. 8am-5pm) or at the green kiosk at 5th and Congress. The **'dillo bus service** (474-1200) connects major downtown points; green trolleys run Mon.-Fri. every 15min. 6:30am-7pm, every 50min. 7pm-9pm (free). Park for free in the 'dillo lot at the City Coliseum at Bouldin and Barton Springs. The **University of Texas Shuttle Bus** serves the campus area. Officially only for UT affiliates, but drivers rarely ask for ID.

Taxis: Yellow Cab, 472-1111. $1.50 base fare, $1.50 per mi.

Car Rental: Rent-A-Wreck, 6820 Guadalupe (454-8621). $25 per day; 50 free mi. with cash deposit, 100 free mi. with credit card; 25¢ per additional mi. Open Mon.-Fri. 8am-7pm, Sat. 9am-5pm. Must be 18; under 21 surcharge $10 per day.

Bike Rental: Bicycle Sports Shop, 1426 Toomey St. (477-3472), at Jesse. $10 for 2hr., $14 for 3-5hr., $20 for full day (overnight $10 extra), $26 for 24hr., $44 for 48hr., $16 per day for 3 or more days, $50 per week. $100 cash or credit card deposit required; American Express not accepted. Open Mon.-Fri. 10am-7pm, Sat. 9am-6pm, Sun. noon-5pm. **Austin Adventure Company,** 706 B. Simonetti Dr. (209-6880). $14 for 2hr. Also conducts 2-3-hr. city bicycle tours ($30) and full-day off-road mountain bike tours in and around Austin ($40-65). Van pick-up available. Reservations required; call and leave a message.

Crisis Lines: Crisis Intervention Hotline, 472-4357. **Austin Rape Crisis Center Hotline,** 440-7273. Both 24 hrs. **Outyouth Gay/Lesbian Helpline,** 326-1234 or 800-96-YOUTH/969-6884, for referrals and counseling. Open daily 5:30-9:30pm.

Emergency: 911.

Post Office: 209 W. 19th St. (929-1253). Open Mon.-Fri. 7am-6:30pm, Sat. 8am-3pm. **ZIP code:** 78701. **Area code:** 512.

UT students inhabit central **Guadalupe St.** ("The Drag"), where numerous music stores and cheap restaurants thrive on their business. The state capitol governs the area a few blocks to the southeast. South of the dome, **Congress Ave.** features upscale eateries and classy shops. A plethora of bars and live-music clubs front **6th St.** giving Austin its nickname ("live music capital of the world"); some of the nightlife, however, has headed to the **Warehouse Area,** around 4th St., west of Congress. Away from the urban gridiron, **Town Lake** offers a verdant haven for the town's joggers, rowers, and cyclists.

ACCOMMODATIONS AND CAMPING

Cheap accommodations lie along **I-35,** running north and south of Austin. In town, three co-ops, run by college houses at UT, rent rooms to hostelers, which include three meals per day. The co-ops work on a first come, first served basis and welcome everyone. Patrons have access to all their facilities including a fully-stocked kitchen. Unfortunately, UT houses are open only from May to August.

Austin International Youth Hostel (HI-AYH), 2200 S. Lakeshore Blvd. (444-2294 or 800-725-2331), about 3mi. from downtown. From the Greyhound station, take bus #7 "Duval" to Lakeshore Blvd. and walk about ½mi. From I-35E, exit at Riverside, head east, and turn left at Lakeshore Blvd. Extremely clean, well-kept hostel with a sprawling common room which overlooks Town Lake. Waterbeds available on request. Kitchen, with a convenient cubby for each guest; located near grocery store. Barrack-style, single-sex rooms. No curfew. $12, nonmembers $15. No sleeping bags allowed; linen rental $1. Open daily 9-11am, 5-10pm.

Taos Hall, 2612 Guadalupe (474-6905), at 27th St. The third of the UT co-ops. You're most likely to get a private room here. Stay for dinner, and the friendly residents will give you a welcoming round of applause; stay a week, and they'll vote you a member. Three meals and a bed $15.

21st St. Co-op, 707 W. 21st St. (476-1857). From the bus stop take bus #39 on Airport St. to Koenig and Burnet, transfer to the #3 South, and ride to Nueces St.; walk 2 blocks west. Carpeted suites with A/C and a common room and bathroom on each floor. $10 per person, plus $5 for three meals and kitchen access. Fills up rapidly in summer.

The Goodall Wooten, 2112 Guadalupe (472-1343). The "Woo" has private rooms with small fridges and access to a TV room, laundry facilities, and basketball courts. Office open 9am-5pm and 8pm-midnight. Singles $20, doubles $25. Linen $5. Call ahead.

Motel 6, 8010 N. I-35 (837-9890 or 800-440-6000), 5mi. from downtown and Lake Austin; from I-35S take exit 240A (Rundberg Ln.) and follow Frontage Rd. 112 units, a pool, new A/C, and free local calls. Even if they're booked, show up at 6pm and you might get a room. Singles $32, doubles $38. Reservations necessary, particularly on weekends.

Pearl Street Co-op, 2000 Pearl St. (476-9478). Large, clean, sparsely furnished rooms. Laundry facilities, kitchen, and a beautiful courtyard pool. Open, friendly atmosphere. Rooms include 3 square meals, shared bath, and access to TV/VCR room. 2-week max. stay. Singles $13, doubles $17.

A 15- to 45-minute drive separates Austin and the nearest **campgrounds.** The **Austin Capitol KOA** (444-6322 or 800-284-0206), 6 mi. south of the city along I-35, offers a pool, a game room, laundry facilities, a grocery, and a playground. (Tent sites with water and electricity $24, with full hookup $27; $3 per additional person over 17. Cabins for 4 $34, for 6 $44.) A large preserve in the bend of the Colorado River, **Emma Long Metropolitan Park,** 1706 City Park Rd. (346-1831), has sites with hookups, a boat ramp, and a concession stand. Take I-35 north to its junction with Rte. 222 at City Park Rd.; the park is 6½ mi. west. (Open 7am-10pm. Entrance $3, on weekends $5. Sites $6, with water and electricity $10. Dumpster nearby.)

FOOD

Scores of fast-food joints line the west side of the UT campus on **Guadalupe St.** another area clusters around **Sixth St.,** south of the capitol; here the battle for happy hour business rages with unique intensity, and competitors employ such deadly weapons as three-for-one drink specials and free *hors d'oeuvres.* Though a bit removed from downtown, **Barton Springs Rd.** offers a diverse selection of inexpensive restaurants, including Mexican and Texas-style barbecue joints. The **Warehouse District** has safe bets for seafood or Italian chow.

Threadgill's, 6416 N. Lamar St. (451-5440). A legend in Austin since 1933, serving up southern soul food with the best of 'em. Creaky wooden floors, slow-moving ceiling fans and antique beer signs set the stage. When former governor Ann Richards needed a caterer for her 60th birthday, she called Threadgill's. Southern fried chicken with all the veggies you can eat $7. Open 11am-10pm.

Ruby's BBQ, 512 W. 29th St. (477-1651). Possibly the best (and that means messiest) barbecue in all of Austin. Wood-burning brick pit stoves in the back yard cook the beef and chicken for hours on end. The owners demand only farm-raised, grass-fed cows, none of that steroid crap. A grampus of a brisket sandwich goes for $3.55. Open Sun.-Thurs. 11am-midnight, Fri.-Sat. 11am-4am.

Trudy's Texas Star, 409 W. 30th St. (477-2935). Fine Tex-Mex dinner entrees $5.25-8, and a fantastic array of margaritas. Famous for *migas,* a corn tortilla soufflé ($4). Pleasant outdoor porch bar with picnic tables open until 2am nightly. Open Mon.-Thurs. 7am-midnight, Fri.-Sat. 7am-2am, Sun. 8am-midnight.

Mongolian BBQ, 117 San Jacinto Blvd. (476-3938), at 2nd St. Create your own stir-fry. Lunch $5, dinner $7; all-you-can-eat $2 extra. No added cost for herbivores. Open Mon.-Fri. 11am-3pm and 5-9:30pm, Sat. 11:30am-3:30pm and 5-10pm.

Sholz Garden, 1607 San Jacinto Blvd. (477-4171), near the capitol. An Austin landmark recognized by the legislature for "epitomizing the finest traditions of the German heritage of our state." German only in name, though—great chicken fried steaks and Tex-Mex meals $5-6. Live country-rock music. Open Mon.-Thurs. 11am-midnight, Fri.-Sat. 11am-2am.

Quackenbush's, 2120 Guadalupe St. (472-4477), at 21st St. A café/deli popular with UT students for espresso and other stylish drinks ($1-2.50). Expect lots of intense-looking intellectuals pontificating on their latest theories. Open Mon.-Fri. 7am-11pm, Sat.-Sun. 8am-11pm.

Insomnia's, 2222 Guadalupe St. (474-5730). Gourmet coffee drinks served all day and all night amidst metal chairs, amoeba-shaped glass tables, and cement floors. Oh, so chic. Cup of espresso $1. Open 24 hrs.

SIGHTS

Not to be outdone by Washington, DC, Texans built their **state capitol** (463-0063), at Congress Ave. and 11th St., 7 ft. higher than the national one. (Free tours every 15min. Mon.-Fri. 8:30am-4:30pm, Sat. 9:30am-4:30pm, Sun. 12:30-4:30pm. Open daily 7am-10pm.) The **Capitol Complex Visitors Center,** 112 E. 11th St. (463-8586), is located in the southeast corner of the capitol grounds (open Tues.-Fri. 9am-5pm, Sat. 10am-5pm). Governor Hogg and his daughter Ima (Ura was just a myth) once lived across the street in the **Governor's Mansion** (463-5516), 11th and Colorado St., built in 1856 (free tours Mon.-Fri. every 20min. 10-11:40am).

Both the wealthiest public university in the country, with an annual budget of almost a billion dollars, and the second largest university in the country, with over 50,000 students, the **University of Texas at Austin (UT)** forms the backbone of Austin's cultural life. The campus has two **visitors information centers,** one in Sid Richardson Hall, 2313 Red River St. (471-6498), and the other in the Nowtony building (471-1420), at I-35 and Martin Luther King, Jr. Blvd. (both open daily 8am-4:30pm). Campus tours leave from the base of the Tower (Mon.-Sat. 11am and 2pm); campus highlights include the **Lyndon B. Johnson Library and Museum,** 2313 Red River St. (482-5279), which houses 35 million documents (open daily 9am-5pm; free) and the **Harry Ransom Center** (471-8944), which hoards a copy of the Gutenberg Bible along with a vast collection of manuscripts and letters penned by Virginia Woolf, James Joyce, William Faulkner, D.H. Lawrence, and Evelyn Waugh (open Mon.-Sat. 9am-5pm, Sun. noon-5pm; free).

The **Austin Museum of Art at Laguna Gloria,** 3809 W. 35th St. (458-8191), 8 mi. from the capitol in a Mediterranean-villa lookalike, blends art, architecture, and nature. The rolling grounds overlook **Lake Austin,** while the museum displays 20th-century artwork and hosts **Fiesta Laguna Gloria,** a May arts and crafts festival, with inexpensive evening concerts and plays. Take bus #21. (Group tours Aug.-June by appointment. Open Tues.-Wed. and Fri.-Sat. 10am-5pm, Thurs. 10am-9pm, Sun. 1-5pm. $2, students and seniors $1, under 16 free; free Thurs.)

On hot afternoons, Austinites zip to riverside **Zilker Park,** 2201 Barton Springs Rd., just south of the Colorado River. Flanked by walnut and pecan trees, **Barton Springs Pool** (476-9044), a natural spring-fed swimming hole in the park, stretches 1000 ft. long and 200 ft. wide with wooden decks. Beware: the pool's temperature rarely rises above 60°F. Get away from the crowd and avoid the park fee by walking upstream and swimming at any spot that looks nice. (Hours vary seasonally. In general, the park is open 9am-8pm with a lifeguard present; you may swim without supervision before and after these hours. $2, Sat.-Sun. $2.25, ages 12-17 50¢, under 12 25¢.) The **Shoppe at Barton Springs** (476-6922), overlooking the lake, sells sundries and rents floats for $2 per hour (open Mon.-Fri. 10:30am-7pm, Sat. 9:30am-8pm, Sun. 11:30am-7pm). For more fun and sun, drive to **Windy Point,** on Comanche Rd. 3 mi. west off the I-620 intersection, a picturesque sandy park on **Lake Travis,** and try your hand (and body) at windsurfing or scuba-diving.

Just before dusk, head to the Congress Ave. Bridge and watch for the massive swarm of Mexican free-tail **bats** that emerge from their roosts to feed on the night's mosquitoes. When the bridge was reconstructed in 1980, the engineers unintentionally created crevices which formed ideal homes for the migrating bat colony. The city began exterminating the night-flying creatures until **Bat Conservation**

International (327-9721) moved to Austin to educate people about bats' harmlessness and the benefits of their presence (the bats eat up to 30,000lbs. of insects each night). Today, the bats are among the biggest tourist attractions in Austin. The colony, seen from mid-March to November, reaches its peak in July, after the babies are born when the population climbs to around 1.5 million.

NIGHTLIFE

Nashville may be the queen of country music, but Austin is a renegade, funky princess with suitors including Willie Nelson, Waylon Jennings, and Stevie Earle. On weekends fans from around the city and nearby towns converge to swing to the music on **Sixth St.,** an area bespeckled with warehouse nightclubs, fancy bars, a tattoo workshop, and an Oriental massage parlor. The *Weekly Austin Chronicle* provides detailed listings of current music performances, shows, and movies.

Famous for its blues, **Antone's,** 2915 Guadalupe St. (474-5314), at 29th St., features all types of sounds and draws names the likes of Stevie Ray Vaughan, B.B. King, and Muddy Waters from time to time. (All ages welcome. Shows at 10pm. Cover $3-6. Open daily 8pm-2am.) The self-effacing name of **Hole in the Wall,** 2538 Guadalupe St. (472-5599), at 28th St., disguises another renowned music spot which features college-alternative bands, and an occasional country and western or hard-core group. By day, the Hole is a sports bar with the requisite pool tables in the back. (Music every night. Cover $3-5. Open 11-2am, Sat.-Sun. noon-2am.) On campus, the **Cactus Café** (471-8228), 24th and Guadalupe St. in the Texas Union, hosts different musicians almost every night. Specializing in folk rock, and the "New Country" sound which came out of Austin, the Cactus gave Lyle Lovett his start. (Cover $2-15. Hours vary; usually 9am-1am.)

In the Sixth St. area, the **Chicago House,** 607 Trinity (473-2542), off 6th St., plays a different tune on weekends and hosts the occasional poetry readings. ($7, students and seniors $6; open Mon.-Sat. 5pm-2am, Thurs. 8pm-2am). For raunchy Texas-style rock 'n' roll and cheap beer, try **Joe's Generic Bar,** 315 E. 6th St. (480-0171; open daily 11am until the wayward crawl home; no cover). One of the biggest and best nightclubs on 6th St., **Toulouse's,** 402 E. 6th St. (478-0766), boasts up to five stages of live music on the weekends. Professionals opt for the relaxed outside patio acoustic music, while raucous teenagers congregate inside for the "rougher" tunes. A karaoke machine upstairs spins vocal-free orchestrations every night at 10pm. (Cover $1-4. Open Mon.-Fri. 5pm-2am, Sat. 7pm-2am, Sun. 8pm-2am.) **Paradox,** 311 E. 5th St. (469-7615), at Trinity, a warehouse-style dance club with retro-80s music, draws lots of twentysomethings (cover $3; open 9pm-4am; 17+). **404,** 404 Colorado (476-8297), is the city's most popular gay dance club ($5, under 21 $10; open Thurs.-Sun. 10pm-til people stop dancing).

For a quiet evening in Austin, visit the sophisticated **Copper Tank Brewing Company,** 504 Trinity St. (478-8444), probably the city's best microbrewery. On Wednesday a pint of any of the freshly-brewed beers costs just 90¢—normally $3. (Open Mon.-Fri. 11am-2am, Sat.-Sun. 3pm-2am.)

Where have all the hippies gone?

About 15 mi. northwest of downtown Austin, **Hippie Hollow,** 7000 Comanche Trail (266-1644), provides the only public area for nude swimming and sunbathing in Texas. The water of beautiful **Lake Travis** floats in the heart of Texas Hill Country, as everyone gets back to nature. Take Mopac (Loop 1) north to the exit for F.M. 2222. Follow 2222 west and turn onto Oasis Bluff. (Must be over 17 to enter. Entrance in summer and spring $5 per car; otherwise free.)

■■■ HOUSTON

Houston was born when two brothers from the east, Augustus and John Allen, bought 2000 acres of land on the Buffalo Bayou in 1836. As the story goes, Augustus

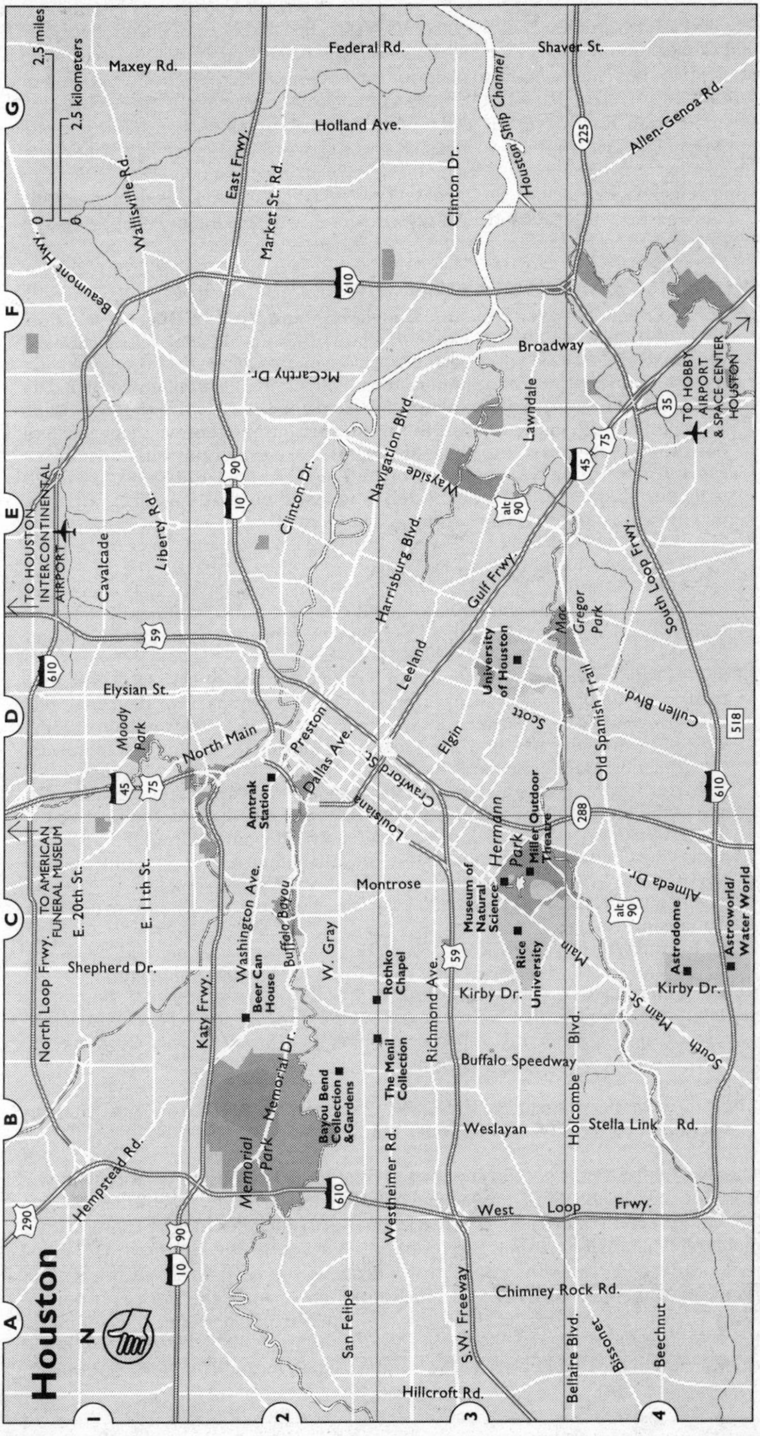

Houston

N

0 — 2.5 miles
0 — 2.5 kilometers

A B C D E F G
1 2 3 4

North Loop Frwy.
Hempstead Rd.
Beaumont Hwy.
Wallisville Rd.
Maxey Rd.
Federal Rd.
Shaver St.
Holland Ave.
East Frwy.
Marker St. Rd.
Clinton Dr.
Houston Ship Channel
Allen-Genoa Rd.
McCarthy Dr.
Broadway
Lawndale
Navigation Blvd.
Wayside
Harrisburg Blvd.
Leeland
Gulf Frwy.
Cavalcade
Liberty Rd.
TO HOUSTON INTERCONTINENTAL AIRPORT
TO HOBBY AIRPORT & SPACE CENTER HOUSTON
TO AMERICAN FUNERAL MUSEUM
Elysian St.
Moody Park
North Main
E. 20th St.
E. 11th St.
Shepherd Dr.
Katy Frwy.
Washington Ave.
Amtrak Station
Preston
Dallas Ave.
Crawford St.
Louisiana
Elgin
Scott
University of Houston
Mac Gregor Park
Old Spanish Trail
Cullen Blvd.
South Loop Frwy.
Buffalo Bayou
Beer Can House
W. Gray
Montrose
Rothko Chapel
The Menil Collection
Richmond Ave.
Museum of Natural Science
Hermann Park
Miller Outdoor Theatre
Rice University
Main
Almeda Dr.
Astrodome
Astroworld/ Water World
Kirby Dr.
South Main St.
Memorial Dr.
Memorial Park
Bayou Bend Collection &Gardens
Westheimer Rd.
Buffalo Speedway
Weslayan
Holcombe Blvd.
Stella Link Rd.
West Loop Frwy.
S.W. Freeway
Chimney Rock Rd.
San Felipe
Hillcroft Rd.
Bellaire Blvd.
Bissonet
Beechnut
10 45 59 75 90 225 288 290 518 610 35 alt 90

TEXAS

stepped ashore at what is now called Allen's landing, drew a knife from his girdle and walked south, slicing through the weeds the path which would become Main St. Despite the Allens' elaborate plans for the city—first sketched out on the top of Augustus's stovepipe hat—Houston has come into its own only in the last half-century, due primarily to its status as the petrochemical capital of the nation. The 4th-most-populated city in the U.S., Houston sprawls over 5436 sq. mi. In recent years, the city has actively cultivated opera, theater, ballet, and museums, in an attempt to combat its image as a culturally-devoid oil city. While Houston lacks natural beauty, it compensates with glass and steel skyscrapers that reflect the dazzling Texas sun and skies.

PRACTICAL INFORMATION

Tourist Office: Greater Houston Convention and Visitors Bureau, 801 Congress St. (D2; 227-3100), at Milam St. downtown. **Gay and Lesbian Switchboard of Houston** (529-3211) distributes entertainment info. Open daily 3pm-midnight.

Airport: Houston Intercontinental (230-3000), 25mi. north of downtown. Get to city center via **Airport Express** (523-8888) buses daily every 30min. 7am-11:30pm ($15-17, under 12 $5). **Hobby Airport,** just west of I-45, 9mi. south of downtown. Take bus #73 to Texas Med. Center, then catch any bus downtown.

Trains: Amtrak, 902 Washington Ave. (D2; 224-1577 or 800-872-7245), in a rough neighborhood. During the day, catch a bus west on Washington (away from downtown) to Houston Ave.; at night, call a cab. To: San Antonio (3 per week, 5hr., $44); New Orleans (3 per week, 8hr., $73). Station and ticket office open Sat.-Wed. 7am-midnight, Thurs.-Fri. 7am-6pm.

Buses: Greyhound, 2121 S. Main St. (D2; 759-6565 or 800-231-2222), on or near local bus routes. Late-night arrivals should call a cab—this is an unsafe area. To: Dallas (9 per day, 5hr., $25); Santa Fe (5 per day, 24hr., $99); San Antonio (10 per day, 4hr., $21). Open 24 hrs. Lockers $1.

Public Transportation: Metropolitan Transit Authority (METRO Bus System) (635-4000; Mon.-Fri. 8am-11pm, Sat.-Sun. 8am-8pm). Provides good, reliable service anywhere between NASA (15mi. southeast of town) and Katy (25mi. west of town). Operates Mon.-Fri. 5am-10pm, Sat.-Sun. 8am-8pm; less frequently on weekends. Maps available at the Houston Public Library, 500 McKinney (236-1313), at Bagby St. (open Mon.-Fri. 9am-9pm, Sat. 9am-6pm, Sun. 2-6pm), or at any of the Metro Rides Stores: 813 Dallas Ave. and 405 Main St. (open Mon.-Fri. 9:30am-5:30pm); 1709 Dryden (open Mon.-Fri. 7:45am-5:45pm); Sharpstown Mall, 7500 Bellaire Blvd. (open Mon.-Sat. 10am-5pm). Fare $1; students and seniors (with $2 ID, available at Metro Ride stores) 25¢.

Taxis: Yellow Cab, 236-1111. $2.70 base fare, $1.35 per mi. *Be sure* to ask for a flat rate in advance.

Car Rental: Alamo (800-327-9633), at Hobby Airport. $31 per day, $119 per week. Must be 21 with major credit card. Open daily 5:30am-midnight.

Crisis Lines: Crisis Center Hotline, 228-1505. **Rape Crisis,** 528-7273. Both open 24 hrs. **Gay and Lesbian Switchboard of Houston,** 529-3211. For counseling or medical and legal referrals. Open daily 3pm-midnight. **Women's Center Hotline,** 528-2121. Open daily 9am-9pm.

Emergency: 911.

Post Office: 401 Franklin St. (D2; 227-1474). Open Mon.-Fri. 6am-7pm, Sat 8am-noon. **ZIP code:** 77052. **Area code:** 713.

Though the flat Texan terrain supports several mini-downtowns, true downtown Houston, a squarish grid of interlocking one-way streets, borders the **Buffalo Bayou** at the intersection of I-10 and I-45. **The Loop (I-610)** encircles the city center with a radius of 6 mi. Anything inside The Loop is easily accessible by car or bus. The shopping district of **Westheimer Blvd.** grows ritzier as you head west. Nearby, restaurants and shops line **Kirby Dr.** and **Richmond Ave.;** while the upper portion of Kirby Dr. winds past some of Houston's most spectacular mansions. *Be careful in the south and east areas of Houston which contain some risky neighborhoods.* Coordinates in the text key places in Houston to their locations on *Let's Go's* **map.**

ACCOMMODATIONS AND CAMPING

Houston has plenty of cheap motels southwest of downtown along the **Katy Freeway (I-10W),** but better, more convenient rooms can be found along **South Main St.** Singles dip to $26, doubles to $30. Remember though, these parts of town can be quite dangerous at night. (Bus #8 goes down S. Main; #119 and #72, "Westview," go out along the Katy Freeway.) If you're stuck, there's always **Motel 6...**

Perry House, Houston International Hostel (HI-AYH), 5302 Crawford St. (D3; 523-1009), at Oakdale St. In a nice residential neighborhood near Hermann Park. From the Greyhound station, take bus #8 or #9 south to Southmore St. (you'll see a Bank of Houston); walk 5 blocks east to Crawford St. and 1 block south to Oakdale St. 30 beds in 5 spacious rooms; well-equipped kitchen available for all guests. A chore is required, but you can pick it. Lock-out 10am-5pm; you can hang out in the lobby during lock-out. Beds $11.25, nonmembers $14.25. Linen $1.50.

YMCA, 1600 Louisiana Ave. (D2; 659-8501), between Pease and Leeland St. Good downtown location only blocks from Greyhound. Tiny cubicle-rooms with daily maid service, TV, and common bath—some floors are substantially nicer than others (read: ask to see your room before accepting). Singles $17.45. Key deposit $5. Another branch, 7903 South Loop (643-4396), is farther out but less expensive. Take Bus #50 at Broadway. Singles $14. Key deposit $10.

The Roadrunner, 8500 S. Main St. (C4; 666-4971). One of 2 locations in Houston. Friendly, helpful management, cable TV, mini-pool, and free coffee, local calls, and ACME catalogs. Large, well-furnished rooms, but be careful of falling rock formations. Singles $24, doubles $30. Meep! Meep!

One campground graces the Houston area; it's in the boondocks, inaccessible by METRO Bus. **KOA Houston North,** 1620 Peachleaf (442-3700), has sites with access to a pool and showers. From I-45, go east on Beltway 8N, then turn right on Aldine-Westfield Rd., and then right again on Peachleaf (tent sites for 2 $16, with electricity $18, full hookup $20; $2 per additional adult).

FOOD

Houston's port has witnessed the arrival of many immigrants (today the city's Indochinese population is the second largest in the nation), and its restaurants reflect this diversity. Houston's cuisine mingles Mexican, Greek, Cajun, and Vietnamese food. Look for reasonably priced restaurants along the chain-laden streets of **Westheimer** and **Richmond Ave.,** especially where they intersect with **Fountainview.** Houston has two **Chinatowns:** a district south of the George R. Brown Convention Center and a newer area on **Bellaire Blvd.** called **DiHo.**

Goode Company BBQ, 5109 Kirby Dr. (C3; 522-2530), near Bissonet. This might be the best (and most popular) BBQ in Texas, with a honky-tonk atmosphere to match. Check out the "bully bags" (bull scrotums) hanging above the cash register, and the jackalope mounted over the feeding line; expect to wait. *No hay pollo aquí.* Sandwiches $3; dinner $6-9. Open daily 11am-10pm.

Barry's Pizza and Italian Diner, 6003 Richmond Ave. (A3; 266-8692). Pizzeria in a log cabinesqe building, replete with wooden beams and red brick chimney. Good menu for veggies: spinach canneloni $6; a 13" cheese pizza pie $7. Open Mon.-Fri. 11am-11pm, Sat.-Sun. noon-11pm.

Cadillac Bar, 1802 N. Shepherd Dr. (C2; 862-2020), at the Katy Freeway (I-10) northwest of downtown; take bus #75, change to #26 at Shepherd Dr. and Allen Pkwy. Wild, fun, authentic Mexican food. Tacos and enchiladas $5-10; heartier entrees $7-15. Drinks with sexy names $4. Open Mon.-Thurs. 10am-10:30pm, Sat. noon-midnight, Sun. noon-10pm.

Luther's Bar-B-Q, 8777 S. Main St. (C4; 432-1107). One of 11 locations in the Houston area. Good Texas BBQ entrees ($5-7) with all-you-can-eat side dishes. Open Sun.-Thurs. 11am-10pm, Fri.-Sat. 11am-11pm.

Magnolia Bar & Grill, 6000 Richmond Ave. (A3; 781-2607). An upscale but reasonable Cajun seafood restaurant (chicken creole $9). The constant and varied crowd attests to the quality of the food and the relaxed, welcoming atmosphere. Open Mon.-Thurs. 11am-10pm, Fri.-Sat. 11am-11pm, Sun. 10:30am-10pm.

Van Loc, 3010 Milam St. (C3; 528-6441), at Elgin. Yummy Vietnamese and Chinese food (entrees $5-8). Have a lunch special for dinner and eat cheaper ($3-4). Open daily 9am-midnight.

SIGHTS

Central downtown is a shopper's subterranean paradise. Hundreds of shops and restaurants line the **Houston Tunnel System** (D2), which connects all the major buildings in downtown Houston, extending from the Civic Center to the Tenneco Building and the Hyatt Regency. On hot days, duck into the air-conditioned passageways via any major building or hotel. To navigate the tunnels, pick up a map ($1.50) at the Public Library, Pennzoil Place, Texas Commerce Bank, the Hyatt Regency, or call Tunnel Walks at 840-9255. (Tunnels open daily 7am-6pm.)

The collection of 17th- to 19th-century American decorative art at **Bayou Bend Museum of Americana,** 1 Westcott St. (639-7750), in **Memorial Park,** is an antique-lover's dream. The collection, housed in the mansion of millionaire Ima Hogg (we *swear*), daughter of turn-of-the-century Texas governor Jim "Boss" Hogg, includes some of the more obscure Remington paintings. (90-min. tours every 15min. Open Tues.-Fri. 10am-1pm. $10, seniors $8.50, ages 10-18 $5, under 10 not admitted. Gardens open Tues.-Sat. 10am-5pm, Sun. 1-5pm. $3, under 11 free.)

Most of Houston's museums lie 3 to 4 mi. southwest of downtown, and within a few blocks of the northern edge of beautifully landscaped **Hermann Park** (C3). On Main St. near the park, the **Houston Museum of Natural Science** (C3; 639-4600) offers a splendid display of gems and minerals, permanent exhibits on petroleum, a hands-on gallery geared toward grabby children, and a planetarium and IMAX theater. Inside the museum's **Cockrell Butterfly Centre,** a tropical paradise of 80°, you'll find yourself surrounded by more than 2000 butterflies; wear bright colors to attract them, and they will flutter your way, searching for nectar. (Hours for each part of the museum change seasonally; call for details. Exhibits $3, seniors and under 12 $2; IMAX $9/$6; Planetarium $2/$1.50; Butterfly Center $3/$2.) The **Museum of Fine Arts,** 1001 Bissonet (C3; 639-7300), adjoins the north side of Hermann Park. Designed by Mies van der Rohe, the museum boasts a collection of Impressionist and post-Impressionist art, as well as a slew of Remingtons. (Open Tues.-Wed. and Fri.-Sat. 10am-5pm, Thurs. 10am-9pm, Sun. 12:15-6pm. $3, students and seniors $1.50; free Thurs.) Across the street, the **Contemporary Arts Museum,** 5216 Montrose St. (C3; 526-0773), has multi-media exhibits. (Open Tues.-Wed. and Fri.-Sat. 10am-5pm, Thurs. 10am-9pm, Sun. noon-5pm. $3 suggested donation.) The park grounds also encompass sports facilities, a kiddie train, a Japanese garden, and the Miller Outdoor Theater (see Entertainment, below).

About 1 mi. north of the park, three of Houston's highly acclaimed art museums are located within a block of one another. The **de Menil Collection,** 1515 Sul Ross (C3; 525-9400), includes an eclectic assortment of Byzantine and medieval art and 20th-century European and American paintings and sculpture. Be sure to see Magritte's work in the surrealism exhibit. (Open Wed.-Sun. 11am-7pm. Free.) The recently built **Cy Twombly Gallery,** 1501 Branard (C3), is a permanent collection of work by the American artist...(drum roll, please)...Cy Twombly, whose minimalist art may elicit the common "I could have done that" response. Italian architect Renzo Piano designed the building with its dazzling sky roof. (Open Wed.-Sun. 11am-7pm. Free.) A block away, the **Rothko Chapel,** 3900 Yupon (C3; 524-9839), houses some of the artist's paintings. Fans of modern art will delight in Rothko's ultra-simplicity; others will wonder where the paintings are (open daily 10am-6pm).

Fans of folk art or booze should drive by **Beer Can House,** 222 Malone (B2). Adorned with 50,000 beer cans, strings of beer-can tops, and a beer-can fence, the house was built by the late John Mikovisch, a retired upholsterer from the Southern Pacific Railroad. Conveniently, there's an **Anheuser-Busch Brewery,** 775 Gellhorn

Rd. (F2; 670-1695), in town to satisfy any cravings which result from your visit; the free self-guided tour ends with a complimentary drink (open Mon.-Sat. 9am-4pm).

If you've got a car and a morbid sense of interest, head to the **American Funeral Service Museum,** 415 Barren Springs Dr. (876-3063 or 800-238-8861); from I-45, exit at Airtex, go west to Ella Blvd., turn right, and proceed to Barren Springs. The museum aims to "bring the history and facts behind our funeral service customs into the non-threatening light of day." It contains countless elaborate and ornate coffins. Yes, it is a bit eerie, but also extremely interesting: check out the chicken-shaped caskets designed by die-hard farmers. (Open Mon.-Sat. 10am-4pm, Sun. noon-4pm. $5, seniors and under 12 $3.)

The **San Jacinto Battleground State Historical Park** (479-2431), 21 mi. east on Rte. 225 and 3 mi. north on Rte. 134, stands as the most important monument to Lone Star independence; the battle which brought Texas independence from Mexico was fought on this site on April 21, 1836. The **museum** in the Park celebrates Texas history with a dramatic multi-image presentation which employs 42 projectors. Ride to the top of the 50-story-high **San Jacinto Monument** (479-2421) for a view of the area. (Both open daily 9am-6pm. Slide show $3.50, seniors $3, under 12 $1; elevator to top of monument $2.50/$2/$1; combo ticket $5.50/$4.50/$2.75.)

The city's most popular attraction, **Space Center Houston,** 1601 NASA Rd. 1 (224-2100 or 800-972-0369), is not only expensive but far from downtown; take I-45 south to NASA Rd. exit, then head east 3 mi. The active Mission Control Center here still serves as HQ for modern-day Major Toms; when astronauts ask, "Do you read me, Houston?" these folks answer. The complex also houses models of Gemini, Apollo, and Mercury as well as countless galleries and hands-on exhibits: you too can try to land the space shuttle on a computer simulator! (Open daily 9am-7pm; Labor Day to Memorial Day Mon.-Fri. 10am-5pm, Sat.-Sun. 10am-7pm. $12, ages 4-11 $8.50, under 4 free. Parking $3.)

ENTERTAINMENT AND NIGHTLIFE

Jones Hall, 615 Louisiana Blvd. (D2), provides the stage for most of Houston's high-brow entertainment. The **Houston Symphony Orchestra** (227-ARTS/2787) performs here September through May (tickets $10-60); between October and May, the **Houston Grand Opera** (546-0200) produces seven operas in the space (tickets $15-125; 50% student discount available at noon on the day of the show). In the summer, take advantage of the **Miller Outdoor Theater** (D2; 520-3290), in Hermann Park. The symphony, opera, and ballet companies and various professional theaters stage free concerts on the hillside most evenings April to October; the annual **Shakespeare Festival** struts and frets upon the stage from late July to early August. For an events update call 520-3292. The downtown **Alley Theater,** 615 Texas Ave. (D2; 228-8421), puts on Broadway-caliber productions at moderate prices (tickets $25-45; 50% student rush discount the day of the show).

The **Astrodome,** Loop 610 at Kirby Dr. (C4; 799-9555), the first mammoth indoor arena of its kind, is the home of the **Oilers** (799-1000) and the **Astros** (526-1709). Unfortunately, for the price of the tour, you're better off paying admission to a game; call for schedules and prices. (Tours daily 11am, 1, and 3pm. $4, seniors and students $3, under 7 free. Parking $4.)

Much of Houston's nightlife centers around a strip of **Richmond Ave.** (A3-B3), between Hillcroft and Chimney Rock. Dance to trash disco and early 80s with local college students at the very chic, very dress-code-enforced **Blue Planet,** 6367 Richmond Ave. (A3; 978-5913). No baseball caps, no t-shirts, no sneakers. (Open Tues.-Fri. 6pm-2am, Sat.-Sun. 8pm-2am.) **Sam's Place,** 5710 Richmond Ave. (A3; 781-1605), is your typical spring-break-style Texas hangout. On Sunday afternoons, a band plays outdoors (5-10pm), and various booths proffer different beers. (Happy Hour Mon.-Fri. 2-9pm. "Ladies" get 1 free drink on Wed. Open Mon.-Sat. 11am-2am, Sun. noon-2am.) Rub elbows with venture capitalists and post-punks alike in the distinctly English atmosphere of **The Ale House,** 2425 W. Alabama (B3; 521-2333), at Kirby. The bi-level bar and beer garden offers over 130 brands of beer, some rather costly ($3-4). Upstairs you'll find old-time rock n' roll or the blues on Sat. nights. (Open Mon.-Sat. 11am-2am, Sun. noon-2am.) Listen to live jazz at **Cody's Jazz Bar and Grill,** 2540 University Blvd. (C3; 520-5660; open Tues.-Thurs. 4pm-1am, Fri. 4pm-2am, Sat. 6pm-2am).

■■■ GALVESTON ISLAND

The narrow, sandy island of **Galveston** (pop. 65,000), 50 mi. southeast of Houston on I-45, meets the beach resort quotas for t-shirt shops, ice cream stands, and video arcades, but redeems itself with beautiful vintage homes, antique shops, and even a few deserted beaches. In the 19th century, Galveston was the "Queen of the Gulf," Texas's most prominent port and wealthiest city. Yet the shipping industry could not be protected from the refocus of commerce which resulted from the completion of the Houston Ship Channel in 1914. Wealthy residents packed up for the mainland, leaving austere mansions behind to adorn the defunct port city.

Practical Information Galveston's streets follow a grid; lettered avenues (A to U) run north-south, while numbered streets run east-west, with **Seawall** following the southern coastline. Most routes have two names; Avenue J and Broadway, for example, are the same street. The **Strand Visitors Center,** 2016 Strand St. (765-7834; open daily 9:30am-6pm) and the **Galveston Island Convention and Visitors Bureau,** 2106 Seawall Blvd. (736-4311; open daily 9am-5pm), provide info about island activities. **Greyhound** affiliate, **Texas Bus Lines,** 714 25th St. (765-7731), provides transportation to Houston (4 per day, 1½hr., $11; open daily 8am-7pm). **Emergency** is 911. Galveston's **post office:** 601 25th St. (763-1527; open Mon.-Fri. 8:30am-5pm, Sat. 9am-12:30pm); **ZIP code:** 77550; **area code:** 409.

Accommodations and Food Accommodation prices in Galveston fluctuate by season, rising to exorbitant heights during holidays and weekends. Money-minded folk should avoid lodging on the island; instead, make Galveston a daytrip from Houston. Nevertheless, RVs can find a reasonable resting place at any of several parks on the island. The closest to downtown, the **Bayou Haven Travel Park,** 6310 Heards Ln. (744-2837), off 61st St., is located on a peaceful waterfront with laundry facilities and bug-free restrooms and showers. (Sites for 2 with full hookup $14, waterfront sites $17; $3 per additional person.) **Galveston Island State Park** (737-1222), on 13½ Mile Rd., 6 mi. southwest of Galveston on FM3005 (it's not a radio station, it's a road—a continuation of Seawall Blvd.), rents sites for tents (sites $12, plus $5 entrance fee per vehicle).

Seafood and traditional Texas barbecue are bountiful in Galveston, especially along Seawall Blvd. and Strand St. **Hill's Pier 19** (763-7087), on the wharf at 20th St., serves seafood in a sprawling restaurant with tables upstairs, downstairs, inside and outside, as well as a comfortable cash bar. It's not cheap—a bowl of shrimp gumbo goes for $5. (Open Mon.-Fri. 11am-9pm, Sat.-Sun. 11am-10pm.) The restaurant also has an in-house fish market, which makes things more affordable but less immediately edible (catfish $2.50/lb., flounder $3.75/lb.). A popular place, **El Nopalito,** 614 42nd St. (763-9815), sports cheap Mexican breakfasts and lunches. The early afternoon closing time makes sense, given that the area is somewhat seedy. (Entrees $3.75-5. Open Mon.-Fri. 6:30am-2pm, Sat.-Sun 6:30am-4pm.) After a day at the beach, indulge your sweet tooth with a cherry phosphate ($1) at **LaKing's Confectionery,** 2323 Strand St. (762-6100), a large, old-fashioned ice cream and candy parlor (open Mon.-Fri. 10am-9pm, Sat. 10am-10pm, Sun. 10am-9pm).

Sights and Activities Galveston recently spent more than six million dollars to clean up and restore its shoreline—the money was well spent; finding a beautiful beach is as easy as strolling along the seawall and picking a spot. The only beach in Galveston which permits alcoholic beverages, **Apfel Park,** on the far eastern edge of the island, attracts young partiers like flies. A more family-oriented atmosphere can be found at **Stewart Beach,** near 4th and Seawall, where a water slide keeps kids entertained. Three **Beach Pocket Parks** lie on the west end of the island, east of Pirates Beach, each with bathrooms, showers, playgrounds, and a concession stand. (Car entry for each of these beaches $5.)

Strand St., near the northern coastline, between 20th and 25th St., is a national landmark, with over 50 Victorian buildings which house a range of cafés, restaurants, gift shops, and clothing stores. The **Galveston Island Trolley** shuttles between the seawall beach area and the posh historic section of Strand St. (30-min., Oct.-April every hr. on the ½-hr.; $4, seniors and children $3). Pick up the trolley and trolley tickets at either visitors center (see Practical Information, above). While in Galveston, stop in at **Moody Gardens** (744-1745); head up 81st from Seawall and you'll run right into it. The area, though filled with a collection of touristy spas and restaurants, makes room for a 10-story glass pyramid which encloses a tropical rainforest, 2000 exotic species of flora and fauna, and a 3D **IMAX Theater** with a six-story high screen. (Rainforest and IMAX open daily 10am-9pm; Nov.-Feb. Mon.-Thurs. 10am-6pm, Fri.-Sun. 10am-9pm. $6 each.)

■■■ SAN ANTONIO

Texas propaganda claims that every Texan has two homes—his own and San Antonio. The skyline may be dominated by soaring modern office buildings, but no Texan city seems more determined to preserve its rich heritage than San Antone. Founded in 1691 by Spanish missionaries, the city is home to the magnificent Alamo, historic Missions, and La Villita, once a village for San Antonio's original settlers and now a workshop for local artisans. Though both Native Americans and Germans have at one time claimed San Antonio as their own, Spanish-speakers (55% of the population) today outnumber any other group and the city's food, architecture, and language reflect their influence. San Antonio is just 150 mi. from the Mexican border at Laredo on the most traveled route between the U.S. and Mexico.

PRACTICAL INFORMATION

Tourist Office: 317 Alamo Plaza (270-8748), downtown across from the Alamo. Open daily 8:30am-6pm. **Lesbian Info San Antonio,** 828-5472. Open 24 hrs.

Airport: San Antonio International, 9800 Airport Blvd. (821-3411), north of town accessible by I-410 and U.S. 281. Bus #2 ("Airport") connects the airport to downtown at Market and Alamo. **Star Shuttle Service** (341-6000) travels to several locations near downtown for $6. Cab fare $14.

Trains: Amtrak, 1174 E. Commerce St. (223-3226 or 800-872-7245), off the I-37 E. Commerce St. exit. To: Houston (3 per day, 4½hr., $44); Dallas (3 per day, 8hr., $44); Austin (3 per day, 2½hr., $16). Closed daily 6:30-10:30pm only.

Buses: Greyhound, 500 N. Saint Mary's St. (800-231-2222). To: Houston (10 per day, 4hr., $21); Dallas (16 per day, 8hr., $32). Lockers $1. Open 24 hrs.

Public Transportation: VIA Metropolitan Transit, 800 W. Myrtle (227-2020; open Mon.-Sat. 6am-8pm, Sun. 8am-8pm), between Commerce and Houston. Buses operate daily 5am-10pm, but many routes stop at 5pm. Inconvenient service to outlying areas. Fare 40¢ (plus zone changes), express 75¢. VIA operates two **"cultural tour"** routes: Rte. 7 stops include the Zoo, McNay Art Museum, Witte Museum, Pioneer Hall, S.A. Botanical Gardens, and Alamo Plaza; Rte. 40 hits La Villita, Love Star Brewery, and the missions. "On-and-off" passes ($2), available at 112 Soledad. Cheap (25¢), dependable, and frequent old-fashioned **streetcars** operate downtown at varying hours.

Taxis: Yellow Cab, 226-4242. $2.90 for first mi., $1.30 per additional mi.

Car Rental: Chuck's Rent-A-Clunker, 3249 S.W. Military Dr. (922-9464). $18 per day with 100 free mi., vans $35 per day. Must be 19 with credit card or cash deposit. Open Mon.-Fri. 8am-7pm, Sat. 9am-6pm, Sun. 10am-6pm.

Crisis Lines: Rape Crisis Center, 349-7273. 24 hrs. Open Mon.-Fri. 8:30am-noon and 1-4pm. **Presa Community Service Center,** 532-5295, referrals and transport for elderly and disabled.

Emergency: 911.

Post Office: 615 E. Houston (227-3399), 1 block from the Alamo. Open Mon.-Fri. 8:30am-5:30pm. **ZIP code:** 78205. **Area code:** 210.

ACCOMMODATIONS AND CAMPING

In a city this popular, downtown hotel managers have no reason to keep prices low. Furthermore, San Antonio's dearth of rivers and lakes makes for few good campsites. For cheap motels, try **Roosevelt Ave.,** an extension of St. Mary's, and **Fredericksburg Rd.** Inexpensive motels also clutter **Broadway** between downtown and Brackenridge Park. Drivers should follow **I-35N** to find cheaper and often safer accommodations within 15 mi. of town.

Bullis House Inn San Antonio International Hostel (HI-AYH), 621 Pierce St. (223-9426), 2mi. northeast of the Alamo across from Fort Sam Houston. From the bus station, walk ½ block east on Pecan St. to Navarro St.; take bus #11 or #15 to Grayson and New Braunfels; walk west 2 blocks. A friendly hostel in a quiet neighborhood. Pool, kitchen. Fills quickly in summer. Office open daily 7:30-11pm. $13, nonmembers $16. Private rooms for 1 or 2 $30, nonmembers from $34. Sheets $2.

Elmira Motor Inn, 1126 E. Elmira (222-9463), about 3 blocks east of St. Mary's a little over 1mi. north of downtown; take bus #8 and get off at Elmira St. Very large, well-furnished rooms—the cleanest you'll get at this price. Women and single travelers should not wander the neighborhood late at night. TV, 5 free local calls, and A/C (with in-room control). Very caring management. 1 king-sized or 2 double beds for 1 or 2 $34. Key deposit $2.

El Tejas Motel, 2727 Roosevelt Ave. (533-7123), at E. South Cross 3mi. south of downtown near the missions; take bus #42. A less-than-enticing exterior, hides big, clean rooms with old-fashioned furniture. Singles $25-28, doubles $32-36.

Navarro Hotel, 116 Navarro St. (223-8453). Great location in the heart of town with free parking and A/C. Some rooms have cracked plaster and most are irregularly shaped. Singles $27, with bath $37; doubles $45, with or without bath.

Alamo KOA, 602 Gembler Rd. (224-9296), 6mi. from downtown; take bus #24 ("Industrial Park") from the corner of Houston and Alamo downtown. Beautiful, well-kept grounds with lots of shade. Each site has a BBQ grill and patio. Showers, laundry facilities, A/C, pool, playground, movies. Open daily 7:30am-10:30pm. Sites for 2 $16, with full hookup $20; $2 per additional person over age 3.

Traveler's World RV Park, 2617 Roosevelt Ave. (532-8310 or 800-755-8310), at South Cross 3mi. south of downtown. Large sites with tables and benches. Showers, laundry facilities, pool, hot tub, playground. Next to a golf course and restaurants. Open Mon.-Sat. 8am-7pm, Sun. 9am-6pm. Tent sites for 2 $15, RV sites $20; $2 per additional person.

FOOD

Explore the area east of S. Alamo and S. Saint Mary's St. for the best Mexican food and BBQ. Expensive cafés and restaurants cram the **River Walk**—breakfast alone could clean you out, if you don't settle for a muffin and coffee. **Pig Stand** (227-1691) diners offer decent, cheap food all over this part of Texas; the branch at 801 S. Presa, off S. Alamo, stays open 24 hrs. **Taco Cabana** does the best fast-food Mexican in the area, with many locations across downtown. Visit the one at 101 Alamo Plaza (224-6158), at Commerce, any time (open 24 hrs.). North of town, many Asian restaurants line **Broadway** across from Brackenridge. The **Farmers Market** (207-8596), near Market Sq., sells produce, Mexican chiles, candy, and spices. Come late in the day when prices drop and vendors are willing to haggle. (Open daily 10am-8pm; Sept.-May daily 10am-6pm.)

Josephine St. Steaks/Whiskey, 400 Josephine St. (224-6169), at McAllister. Away from the more touristy spots along the River Walk. Josephine's specializes in Texan steaks, but offers an assortment of chicken, seafood, and pork dishes (entrees $5-11). Great home-baked desserts; try the carrot cake or cookie pie (each $2.50). Open Mon.-Thurs. 11am-10pm, Fri.-Sat. 11am-11pm.

Rio Rio Cantina, 421 E. Commerce (CAN-TINA/226-8462). Funky upscale Mexican in a fancy, shaka-shaka setting. Order up a huge naked José Iguana ($8.50)—a 27 oz. combo of every alcohol they've got, and a splash of refreshing 7Up. Enchiladas go for $9. After you eat, check out Iggy, the live iguana on the premises. Open Sun.-Thurs. 11am-11pm., Fri.-Sat. 11am-midnight.

Earl Abel's, 4220 Broadway (822-3358). A professional organist for silent movies, Mr. Abel found himself out of work once the "talkies" hit the silver screen; he opened this classy diner in 1933; his family still runs the operation. Bacon, eggs, hash browns, and toast $4.25. Open daily 6:30am-1am. Breakfast until 11am.

Hung Fong Chinese and American Restaurant, 3624 Broadway (822-9211), at Queen Anne 2mi. north of downtown; take bus #14 or #9. The oldest Chinese restaurant in San Antonio. Consistently good and crowded. Big portions $5-7. Open Mon.-Thurs. 11am-10:30pm, Fri. 11am-11:30pm, Sat. 11:30am-11:30pm, Sun. 11:30am-10:30pm.

SIGHTS

Much of historic San Antonio lies in the present-day downtown and surrounding areas. The city may seem diffuse, but almost every major site or park is within a few miles of downtown and accessible by public transportation. The VIA Transit "cultural tour" routes focus on specific sets of sights (see Practical Information, above).

The Missions

The five missions along the San Antonio River once formed the soul of San Antonio; the city preserves their remains in the **San Antonio Missions National Historical Park.** To reach the missions, follow the blue-and-white "Mission Trail" signs beginning on S. Saint Mary's St. downtown. **San Antonio City Tours** (520-8687), at the Alamo's visitors center on Crockett St., offers ½-day ($25) and full-day ($39) tours of the city. Bus #42 stops right in front of Mission San José, within walking distance of Mission Concepción. (All missions open daily 9am-6pm; Sept.-May 8am-5pm. For general info on the missions, call 229-5701.) Every Saturday morning, a national park ranger leads a 10-mi. round-trip **bike tour** (229-4700) from Mission San José along the historic corridor. The tours are free, but you must provide your own bike. Call ahead for tour availability and more information.

Mission Concepción, 807 Mission Rd. (229-5732), 4mi. south of the Alamo off E. Mitchell St. The oldest unrestored church in North America (1731) and active in the parish. Traces of the once-colorful frescoes are still visible.

Mission San José, 6539 San José Dr. (229-4770). The "Queen of the Missions" (1720). Has its own irrigation system, a gorgeous sculpted rose window, and numerous restored buildings. The largest of San Antonio's missions, it best conveys the self-sufficiency of these institutions. 4 Catholic services held each Sun. (including a noon "Mariachi Mass").

Mission San Juan Capistrano, 9102 Graf (229-5734), at Ashley, and **Mission San Francisco de la Espada,** 10040 Espada Rd. (627-2021), both off Roosevelt Ave., 10mi. south of downtown as the Texas swallows fly. Smaller and simpler than the others, these two missions best evoke the isolation of such outposts.

Remember the Alamo!

"Be silent, friend, here heroes died to blaze a trail for other men." Disobeying orders to retreat with their cannons, the defenders of the Alamo, outnumbered 20 to one, held off the Mexican army for 12 days. Then, on the morning of the 13th day, the Mexicans commenced the infamous *deguello* (throat-cutting). Forty-six days later General Sam Houston's small army defeated the Mexicans at San Jacinto amidst cries of "Remember the Alamo!" These days, phalanxes of tourists attack the **Alamo** (225-1391), at the center of Alamo Plaza near Houston and Alamo St., and sno-cone vendors are the only defenders. A single chapel and barracks, preserved by the state, are all that remain of the former Spanish mission. (Open daily 9am-6:30pm; Labor Day-Memorial Day Mon.-Sat. 9am-6:30pm, Sun. 9am-5:30pm.) The **Long Barracks Museum and Library,** 315 Alamo Plaza, houses Alamo memorabilia (open Mon.-Sat. 9am-6:30pm). Next door, the **Clara Driscoll Theater** shows an historical documentary, entitled "The Battle of the Alamo," every 20 minutes (Mon.-Sat. 9am-5:30pm).

Southwest of the Alamo, black signs indicate access points to the **Paseo del Río (River Walk),** a series of well-patrolled shaded stone pathways which follow a winding canal built by the Works Progress Administration in the 1930s. Lined with picturesque gardens, shops, and cafés, and connecting most of the major downtown sights, the River Walk is the hub of San Antonio's nightlife. **River Tour Boats,** 430 E. Commerce St. (222-1701) offers a 35- to 40-minute narrated boat tour along the Paseo del Rio ($3, under 4ft. $1). The **Alamo IMAX Theater** (225-4629), in Rivercenter Mall, shows "The Price of Freedom," a 45-minute docudrama Alamo film, on its six-story screen (7 shows 9am-6pm; $6.40, under 11 $4.25). A few blocks south, **La Villita,** 418 Villita (207-8610), a cluster of 27 restored buildings, houses restaurants, crafts shops, and art studios (open daily 10am-6pm).

The site of the 1968 World's Fair, **HemisFair Plaza,** on S. Alamo, draws tourists to browse through the surrounding restaurants, museums, and historic houses, and for special events. The **Tower of the Americas,** 600 Hemisphere Park (207-8615), rises 750 ft. above the dusty plains, dominating the meager skyline. Get a view of the city from the observation deck on top (open daily 8am-11pm; $2.50, seniors $1.25, ages 4-11 $1). The free museums in the plaza include the **Institute of Texan Cultures,** 801 S. Bowie (558-2300), at Durango, with exhibits on the 27 ethnic and cultural groups who first settled Texas and lots of touchable stuff for kids (open Tues.-Sun. 9am-5pm; parking $2), and the **Mexican Cultural Institute,** 600 HemisFair Park (227-0123; open Tues.-Fri. 10am-5pm, Sat.-Sun. 11am-5pm).

Directly behind **City Hall,** between Commerce and Dolorosa St. at Laredo, the **Spanish Governor's Palace,** 105 Plaza de Armas (224-0601), built in 1772, displays Spanish Colonial style architecture with carved doors and an enclosed patio and garden (open Mon.-Sat. 9am-5pm, Sun. 10am-5pm; $1, under 14 50¢, under 7 free).

Home to the San Antonio **Spurs** and the world's largest retractable seating system, the **Alamodome,** 100 Montana (207-3600), at Hoefgen St. downtown, resembles a Mississippi riverboat. Park at the south entrance in Lot A. (Tours Tues.-Sat. 10am, 1 and 3pm, except during scheduled events. $3, under 12 $1.50.)

For a self-guided tour of downtown, hop on an **old-fashioned street car** (25¢; see Practical Information, above), and spend at least an hour tooting by the sites. The purple-line street car has a more extensive route that stretches from the Alamo to the Spanish Governor's Mansion to La Villita.

San Antonio North and South

Head to **Brackenridge Park,** 3500 N. Saint Mary's St. (734-5401), 5 mi. north of the Alamo, for a day of unusual sight-seeing; from downtown, take bus #8. The 343-acre showground includes playgrounds, a miniature train, an aerial tramway ($4), and a Japanese garden. (Open Mon.-Fri. 9am-5pm, Sat.-Sun. 9am-5:30pm.) Directly across the street, the **San Antonio Zoo,** 3903 N. Saint Mary's St. (734-7183), one of the country's largest, houses over 3500 animals from 800 species in reproductions of their natural settings, including an extensive African mammal exhibit. (Open daily 9:30am-6:30pm; Nov.-March 9:30am-5pm. $6, seniors $4, ages 3-11 $4.) Nearby **Pioneer Hall,** 3805 N. Broadway (822-9011), contains a splendid collection of artifacts, documents, portraits, and cowboy accessories which chronicle early Texas history (open Tues.-Sun. 10am-5pm; Sept.-April Wed.-Sun. 11am-4pm. $1, ages 6-12 25¢). Next door, the **Witte Museum**, 3801 Broadway (820-2111), attempts to explain Texas wildlife and anthropology with everything from dinosaur bones to rock art. (Open Mon. and Wed.-Sat. 10am-5pm, Tues. 10am-9pm, Sun. noon-5pm; off season Tues. 10am-5pm. $4, seniors $2, ages 4-11 $1.75; free Tues. 3-9pm.)

The **San Antonio Museum of Art,** 200 W. Jones Ave. (978-8100), just north of the city center, fills the towers, turrets, and spacious rooms of the restored Lone Star

Brewery building with Texan furniture and pre-Columbian, Native American, Spanish Colonial, and Mexican folk art. (Open Mon. and Wed.-Sat. 10am-5pm, Tues. 3-9pm, Sun. noon-5pm. $4, college students with ID and seniors $2, ages 4-11 $1.75; free Tues. Free parking.) The former estate of Marion Koogler McNay, the **McNay Art Museum,** 6000 N. New Braunfels (824-5368), displays a large collection of post-Impressionist European art. Sculpted fountains and meticulous landscaping invite lingering in the inner courtyard. (Open Tues.-Sat. 10am-5pm, Sun. noon-5pm. Free.)

The **Lone Star Brewing Company,** 600 Lone Star Blvd. (226-8301), resides about 2 mi. south of the city. Trigger-happy Albert Friedrich accumulated 3500 animal heads, horns, and antlers before he opened the Buckhorn in 1887. What better place to put them than in his bar? Now you can pity his prey and sample some beer on hourly tours. (Open daily 9:30am-5pm. $5, seniors $4, ages 6-12 $1.75.)

For intoxicating natural beauty, visit **Natural Bridge Caverns,** 26495 Natural Bridge Caverns Rd. (651-6101); take I-35N to exit 75 and follow the signs. Discovered 36 years ago, the caverns's phallic rock formations will knock your socks off. (1¼-hr. tours every ½hr. Open daily 9am-6pm. $7, ages 3-11 $5.)

Take U.S. 90 to Rte. 151W then follow the signs to **Sea World of Texas** (523-3611) for a visit with killer whale Shamu. (Hours vary widely; call ahead. Generally open 10am-6pm; later in summer. $26, seniors $22, ages 3-11 $18, under 3 free.)

ENTERTAINMENT AND NIGHTLIFE

During the last 10 days of April, **Fiesta San Antonio** ushers in spring with concerts, parades, and plenty of Tex-Mex to commemorate the victory at San Jacinto and honor the heroes at the Alamo. On May 13-19, the **15th Tejano Conjunto Festival** will celebrate and study the regional music of South Texas (call 271-3151 for info).

For fun after dark any time, any season, stroll down the **River Walk.** Peruse the Friday *Express* or the weekly *Current* which will guide you to concerts and entertainment. The biggest dance club on the river, **Acapulco Sam's,** 212 College St. (212-SAMS/7267), features a top 40s and Reggae discothèque on one level and live rock 'n' roll music on another (music nightly 9:30pm; cover around $4; open Wed.-Sun. 6pm-2am). For authentic *tejano* music, a Mexican and country amalgam, head to **Cadillac Bar,** 212 S. Flores (223-5533), where a different *tejano* band whips the huge crowd (anywhere from 500-1000 people) into a cheering and dancing frenzy every weeknight (open Mon.-Fri. 11am-11pm, Sat. 5pm-11pm). Right around the corner from the Alamo, the **Bonahm Exchange,** 411 Bonahm (271-3811), San Antonio's biggest gay dance club, plays high-energy music with some house and techno thrown in. A younger, more mixed crowd comes on Wednesday. (Open Mon.-Fri. 4pm-2:30am, Sat.-Sun. 8pm-4am.) Some of the best blues in the city plays at **Jim Cullum's Landing,** 123 Losoya (222-1234), in the Hyatt downtown. The music starts at 9pm and goes until around 2am. A jazz quartet performs on Sunday nights.

An old hangout of scruffy but lovable country music star Willie Nelson, **Floore's Country Store,** 14464 Old Bandera Rd. (695-8827), toward the northwest outskirts of town, invites you to kick up your heels on the large cement platform outside

How many words can YOU make from Schlitterbahn?

The entire local economy of the town of New Braunfels depends on one dough-nut-shaped object: the innertube. Almost two million visitors per year come to this town, hoping only to spend a day floating along the pea-green waters of the spring-fed Comal River. **Rockin' "R" River Rides,** 193 S. Liberty (210-620-6262), will drop you off upstream with a lifejacket and a trusty tube and pick you up downstream 1½ hours later. (Open May-Sept. Mon.-Fri. 9am-7pm, Sat.-Sun. 8:30am-8pm. Tube rentals $8, $25 deposit required.) If the Comal don't float your boat, head for the chlorinated waters of **Schlitterbahn,** 400 N. Liberty (210-625-2351), a 65-acre extravaganza of a waterpark with 17 water slides, nine tube chutes, and five giant hot tubs. (Open late May-late Aug.; call for hours, which change constantly. $20, ages 3-11 $16.)

every Friday night 8pm-midnight. (Cover $5-15. Open Mon.-Thurs. 11am-8pm, Fri. 11am-midnight, Sat. 3pm-1am, Sun. 3-11pm; in winter free dancing Sun. 6-10pm.)

■■■ CORPUS CHRISTI

After you've taken in all of Corpus Christi's sights—in other words, after about half an hour—you may wonder what you're doing in the town named for the "body of Christ." Once you hit the beach, you'll understand why this area is divine.

Practical Information Touristy Corpus Christi (pop. 257,000) follows **Shoreline Dr.,** which borders the Gulf Coast, 1 mi. east of the downtown business district. The **Convention and Visitors Bureau,** 1201 N. Shoreline (882-5603 or 800-678-6232; open Mon.-Fri. 8:30am-5pm), where I-37 meets the water, has piles of pamphlets, bus schedules, and local maps, as does the **Corpus Christi Museum,** 1900 N. Chaparral (883-2862; open daily 10am-6pm). **Greyhound,** 702 N. Chaparral (882-2516 or 800-231-2222; open daily 8:30am-3am), at Starr downtown, goes to Dallas (3 per day, 8½-10½hr., $38), Houston (4 per day, 4½hr., $21), and Austin (2 per day, 5-6hr., $29). **Regional Transit Authority (The "B")** (289-2600) runs buses on a varying schedule; pick up route maps and schedules at the visitors bureau or at "B" headquarters, 1812 S. Alameda (open Mon.-Fri. 8am-5pm). City Hall, Port Ayers, and Six Points serve as central transfer points. (Fare 50¢; students, seniors, kids, and disabled 25¢, 10¢ during off-peak hours. Sat. all buses 25¢.) **The Corpus Christi Beach Connector** follows the shoreline and stops at the aquarium daily 6:40am-6:30pm (same fares as buses). If you need help, call **Bay View Hospital** (993-9700) for counselling and crisis service, or the **Battered Women and Rape Victims Shelter** (881-8888); both stay open 24 hrs. **Emergency:** 911. Corpus Christi's **post office:** 809 Nueces Bay Blvd. (886-2200; open Mon.-Fri. 7:30am-5:30pm, Sat. 8am-1pm); **ZIP code:** 78469; **area code:** 512.

Accommodations, Food, and Nightlife Cheap accommodations are scarce downtown. Posh hotels and expensive motels take up much of the scenic and convenient shoreline. For the best motel bargains, drive several miles south on Leopard St. (take bus #27) or I-37 (take #27 Express). The rooms at **Ecomotel,** 6033 Leopard St. (289-1116; exit I-37 at Corn Products Rd., head south, and take a left on Leopard St.), have A/C, ceiling fans, ample furniture, cable TV, and "massago-beds"—an excellent deal (singles $28, doubles $39). Eat at the on-site Mexican restaurant. Overshadowed by a plethora of expensive lodgings, the **Sand and Sea Budget Inn,** 1013 N. Shoreline Dr. (882-6518), 5 blocks from the Greyhound station across from the visitors bureau, rents brick-walled rooms with TV and sliding glass doors. Make reservations in advance for weekends and holidays. (Singles $24, doubles $35, with a bay view $45.) Campers should head for the **Padre Island National Seashore** or **Mustang State Park** (see Padre Island National Seashore, below). **Nueces River City Park** (241-1464), off I-37N from exit 16, has free tent sites and three-day RV permits, but no showers and only portable restrooms.

The mixed population and seaside locale of Corpus Christi have resulted in a wide range of cuisine. Restaurants of the non-chain type can be found on the "south side" of the city, around **Staples St.** and **S. Padre Island Dr.** The **Water St. Seafood Company,** 309 N. Water St. (882-8683), sells moderate to pricey edible marine life, such as deep fried Gulf oysters ($8) and shrimp and pasta salad ($5.50). Yum! (Open Sun.-Thurs. 11am-10pm, Fri.-Sat. 11am-11pm.) **Howard's BBQ,** 120 N. Water St. (882-1200), shells out a beef and sausage plate, an all-you-can-graze salad bar, and a drink for $5 (open Mon.-Fri. 11am-3pm). **Buckets Sports Bar & Grill,** 227 N. Water St. (883-7776), takes care of near-sighted folk who need a TV fix; every table has its own television set *clooooose* up. The eclectic menu sports American, Cajun, Italian, and Mexican dishes. (Hamburger $3.50; chef's salad $6. Open daily 11am-2am.) The city shuts down early, but several clubs manage to survive on **Water St.;** the **Yucatan Beach Club,** 208 N. Water St. (888-6800), visibly marked with a fluorescent blue and pink exterior, stages live nightly music, usually rock 'n' roll or reggae (cover $3; open daily 5pm-2am).

Sights Corpus Christi's most significant sight is the shoreline, bordered by miles of wide sidewalks with graduated steps down to the water. Overpriced seaside restaurants, sail and shrimp boats, and hungry seagulls overrun the piers. Feeding the birds produces a Hitchcockian swarm; wear a hat and prepare to run for your life. Almost all of the beaches on **N. Shoreline Dr.** allow swimming; just follow the signs, or call the Beach Services (949-7023) for directions.

Just offshore floats the aircraft carrier **U.S.S. Lexington,** a World War II relic now open to the public. In her day, the "Lady Lex" set more records than any carrier in the history of naval aviation. Be sure to check out the soldiers' quarters—you won't complain about small hostel rooms ever again. (Open daily 9am-6pm. $7, seniors and active military personnel $5, children $3.75.) Built by the government of Spain in 1992, the **Columbus Fleet,** Dock One (883-1862), under the Harbor Bridge, commemorates the 500th anniversary of Columbus's historic voyage with replicas of the *Niña,* the *Pinta,* and the *Santa María* (open daily 10am-5pm; $5, ages 2-12 $2.50). To eke out a little culture after a day in the sun, the **Art Museum of South Texas,** 1902 N. Shoreline (884-3844), at the north end of Shoreline Dr., is your only option. The collection changes every six to eight weeks; past exhibits have featured the works of Matisse, Remington, and Ansel Adams. (Open Tues.-Sat. 10am-5pm, Sun. 1-5pm. $3, students $2, ages 2-12 $1.) The **Texas Jazz Festival** (883-4500) jams for three days in early July, drawing hundreds of musicians and thousands of fans from around the country (most performances free).

■■■ PADRE ISLAND

With over 60 mi. of perfectly preserved beaches, dunes, and wildlife refuge land, the **Padre Island National Seashore (PINS)** is a flawless gem sandwiched between the condos and tourists of North Padre Island and the spring break hordes of South Padre Island. The seashore provides excellent opportunities for windsurfing, swimming, or even surf-fishing—an 850-lb. shark was once caught at the southern, more deserted, end of the island. Entry into PINS costs $4; however, beautiful, uncrowded **North Beach** (15mi. from Corpus Christi) lies just before the checkpoint where fees are collected. Five mi. south of the entrance station, **Malaquite Beach** makes your day on the sand as easy as possible with picnic tables, restrooms, and a concession which rents everything you could need (inner tubes $2 per hr., chairs $1 per hr., boogie boards $2.50 per hr.). The **Malaquite Visitors Center** (512-949-8068), has maps, exhibits, videos, and wildlife guidebooks (open daily 9am-6pm; Sept.-May 9am-4pm).

Visitors with four-wheel-drive and a penchant for solitude should make the 60 mi. trek to the **Mansfield Cut,** the most remote and untraveled area of the seashore; loose sands prevent most vehicles from venturing far onto the beach. If you decide to go, be sure to tell the folks at the **Malaquite Ranger Station** (512-949-8173), 3½ mi. south of the park entrance; they handle first aid and emergency assistance for all of the National Seashore, and they like to know who's out there.

Camping on the beach at PINS means falling asleep to the crashing of waves on the sand; if you're not careful, morning may mean waking up to the slurping noise of thousands of mosquitoes sucking you dry—bring insect repellant. The **PINS Campground** (512-949-8173), less than 1 mi. north of the visitors center, consists of an asphalt area for RVs, restrooms, and cold-rinse showers—no soap is permitted on PINS. Primitive camping occupies a 5-mi. section of beach (tent and RV sites $5). Wherever vehicles can go, camping is free. Near the national seashore, the **Balli County Park** (512-949-8121), on Park Rd. 22, 3½ mi. from the JFK Causeway, provides running water, electricity, and hot showers for campers. (3-day max. stay. Sites with water and electricity $10. Key deposit $5.) Those who value creature comforts should head a few mi. farther north to the **Mustang State Park Camp-**

ground (512-749-5246), on Park Rd. 53, 6 mi. from the JFK Causeway, for electricity, running water, dump stations, restrooms, hot showers, and picnic tables. (Entry fee $5. Tent sites $7; with water and electricity $12. RVs must reserve ahead.)

Motorists enter the PINS via the JFK Causeway, from the Flour Bluff area of Corpus Christi. PINS is difficult to reach by Corpus Christi's **public bus** transportation. Corpus Christi bus #29 (Mon.-Fri. 8:45am and 1:45pm, 50¢) takes you to the tip of the Padre Isles (get off at Padre Isles Park-n-Ride near the H-E-B supermarket); from there, it's a 15-mi. hike to PINS. **Yellow Checker Cab Co.** (see Corpus Christi Practical Information, above) offers a special rate for groups of four going from the Greyhound bus station in Corpus Christi to PINS ($25).

WESTERN TEXAS

On the far side of the Río Pecos lies a region whose stereotypical Texan character verges on self-parody. This is the stomping ground of Pecos Bill—the mythical cowpoke who was raised by coyotes and grew to lasso a tornado. The land here was colonized in the days of the Republic of Texas, during an era when the "law west of the Pecos" meant a rough mix of vigilante violence and frontier gunslinger machismo. The border city of El Paso, and its Chihuahuan neighbor, Ciudad Juárez, beckon way, *wayyyy* out west—700 mi. from the Louisiana border—while Big Bend National Park dips down into the desert cradled by a curve in the Río Grande.

■■■ AMARILLO

Amarillo, named for the yellow clay of a nearby lake, opened for business as a railroad construction camp in 1887 and, within a decade, became the nation's largest cattle-shipping market. For years, the economy depended largely on the meat industry. Then, the discovery of oil in the 1920s gave Amarillo's economy a kick, and "black gold" translated into enormous wealth for all involved. More recently, the city has gotten a boost from a relatively new industry—tourism. Amarillo successfully lures visitors to taste and experience the old west with chuck wagon rides through the flat plains and an impressive collection of museums which celebrate the culture of the bygone western frontier.

Practical Information Amarillo sprawls at the intersection of I-27, I-40, and U.S. 287/87; you'll need a car to explore. Rte. 335 (the Loop) encircles the city; Amarillo Blvd. (Historic Rte. 66) runs east-west, parallel to I-40. The **Texas Travel Info Center,** 9400 I-40E (335-1441), at exit 76, opens daily 8am-5pm. The **Amarillo Convention and Visitors Bureau,** 1000 S. Polk (374-1497 or 800-692-1338), at 10th St., distributes more specific info (open Mon.-Fri. 8am-5pm). **Amarillo International Airport,** 10801 Airport Blvd. (335-1671), sits about 7 mi. east of downtown off I-40. Cab fare to the hotels on I-40 averages $4-6, to downtown $12-13. Go **Greyhound** from 700 S. Tyler (374-5371), to Lubbock (3 per day, 3hr., $20), Albuquerque (6 per day, 5hr., $50), or Santa Fe (5 per day, 7½hr., $52). The station is open 24 hrs. In town, buses from **Amarillo City Transit** (378-3094) operate Monday through Saturday, every ½ hour 6am to 6pm; fare is 60¢. Ride like a king with **Royal Cab Co.** (376-4276; $1.30 base fare, $1 per mi). **Emergency:** 911. Amarillo's **post office:** 505 E. 9th Ave. (379-2148), in Downtown Station at Buchanan St. (open Mon.-Fri. 7:30am-5pm); **ZIP code:** 79105; **area code:** 806.

Accommodations, Camping, and Food Cheap motels lurk on the outskirts of town on I-40; be prepared to pay more as you near the downtown area. **Camelot Inn,** 2508 I-40E (373-3600), at exit 72A, a pink castle-like hotel with big, recently-renovated rooms and shiny wood furniture, ranks among the best of the I-40 offerings (single $28, double $35; no extra charge for 3 or 4 people). **Motel 6**

(800-440-6000) has two locations along I-40 off exit 72B (singles $28, doubles $34). Pitch your tent at the **KOA Kampground,** 111 Folsom St. (335-1792), 6 mi. east of downtown; take I-40 to exit 75, go north 2 mi. to Hwy. 60, then east 1 mi. The campground has a large pool, a basketball court, free morning coffee, and shady sites (open 7am-10pm, Labor Day to Memorial Day 8am-8pm; sites $16, full hookup $21).

Beef is what's for dinner at **The Big Texan** (372-6000 or 800-657-7177) at the Lakeside exit of I-40. Signs for miles around remind you that anyone who can eat a 72-oz. steak in an hour gets it free; the defeated pay $50. To date 23,342 have tried, but only 4,619 have succeeded (19.7%). The portions are as big as the state, but the bill won't whip you. Try the $3 rattlesnake appetizer. (Burgers $5-10; Texas steaks $12-22. Open daily 10:30am-10:30pm. Free Texas Opry concerts Tues.; reservations required.) To give your arteries a rest, eat at the **Back to Eden Deli,** 2425 I-40W (353-7476), in Wolfin Sq., which specializes in health food and veggie dishes. The salad bar ($5.95 per lb.) surpasses expectations with leafy lettuce, mung beans and red lentils. (Open Mon.-Sat. 9am-5:30pm.)

Big Texan Women

Our intrepid researcher-writer reports that women are statistically more successful in their attempts to consume the Big Texan's 72-oz. monster steak (see Food above). While 3977 of the 21,347 men who have tried (18.6%) have succeeded, 642 of only 1995 women (32.1%) have conquered the cow. Remember: "Whatever women do they must do twice as well as men to be thought half as good. Luckily, this is not difficult." —Charlotte Whitton, mayor of Ottawa, Ontario

Sights and Entertainment The outstanding **Panhandle-Plains Historical Museums,** 2401 4th Ave. (656-2244), in nearby Canyon, has fossils, an old drilling rig, and exhibits galore about local history and geology (open Mon.-Sat. 9am-5pm, Sun. 1-6pm; free). The **Amarillo Zoo** (378-3000) spreads over 20 acres of open prairie with bison, roadrunners, and other Texas fauna. Take the Thompson Park exit on U.S. 287. (Open Tues.-Sun. 11am-7pm. Free.) The **American Quarter Horse Heritage Center and Museum,** 2601 I-40E (376-5181), at exit 72A, explores horse racing's cowboy origins, with additional exhibits on all things equine (open Mon.-Sat. 10am-5pm, Sun. noon-5pm; $4, over 54 $3.50, ages 6-18 $2.50, under 6 free). Amarillo celebrates its location, on top of the world's largest supply of helium, with the six-story stainless steel **Helium Monument,** 1200 Strait Dr. (355-4547). When the structure was erected in 1968, several contributors volunteered to put common items inside it to make a time capsule. One of the items is a $10 savings account deposit in an Oklahoma City bank which, when the monument is opened in 2968, will be worth over $1,000,000,000,000,000,000 (one quintillion dollars!) payable to the U.S. Treasury. Get in some ropin', ridin', and brandin' at Figure 3 Ranch's **Cowboy Morning** (800-658-2613; $19, $14.50 for cowpokes; reservations required). The fee includes a wagon-ride to Palo Duro Canyon, a sausage, eggs, 'n' biscuit breakfast served out of a chuck wagon, and lessons in various cowboyish activities (horseback riding, branding, cow-chip throwing, etc.) In early August, mosey over to the **Civic Center** (378-4297), at 3rd and Buchanan, for **Old West Days,** a city-wide game of cops and robbers.

■ PALO DURO CANYON STATE PARK

Rightly known as the "Grand Canyon of Texas," Palo Duro covers 16,000 acres of jaw-dropping beauty. The canyon—1200 ft. from rim to rugged floor—exposes red, yellow, and brown cliffs which are truly awesome. The park is 23 mi. south of Amarillo; take I-27 to exit 106 and head east on Rte. 217 (from the south, get off I-27 at exit 103). The **Visitor/Interpretive Center** (806-488-2227), just inside the park, has maps of hiking trails and information on all park activities (park and center open daily 7am-10pm). The park charges an entrance fee of $5 per vehicle.

The pleasant 16-mi. scenic drive through the park provides many photo opportunities for the auto-inclined. If you want to experience the canyon from the saddle, **Goodnight Riding Stables** (806-488-2331), about 1 mi. into the park on the scenic drive, will rent you a horse/saddle/hard-hat combo for $9 per hour. **Goodnight Trading Post** (806-488-2760), also on the scenic drive, has a souvenir shop, a terrific restaurant (sliced BBQ sandwich $3.50), and mountain bikes to rent ($6.50 per hr.). Particularly good for kids, the **Sad Monkey Railroad** (800-687-2222) offers a ½-hour lecture tour in a miniature, narrow-gauge choo-choo train ($3, under 6 free). Rangers allow and encourage **backcountry hiking** in Palo Duro. Most hikers can manage the 5-mi. **Lighthouse Trail,** but only experienced hikers should consider the rugged 9-mi. **Running Trail.** Temperatures in the canyon frequently climb to 100°F; *always* take at least two quarts of water on your hike.

Backcountry camping is allowed in designated areas; primitive sites go for $13, RV hookup costs you $17. (Call 512-389-8900 for recommended reservations.)

Set in the heart of the park, Pulitzer Prize-winner Paul Green's musical drama **Texas,** Box 268, Canyon 79015 (806-655-2181 for tickets), takes the stage under the stars in an outdoor amphitheater (mid-June to mid-Aug. Mon.-Sat. 8:30pm).

■■■ LUBBOCK

Lubbock seems a stage set for a city rather than a real one. Nevertheless, for an afternoon of mindless meandering and an inexpensive overnight stay, this travel hub will treat you right—a few decent sights help pass the time, and the inordinately low rates of many local motels let you rest in peace. Although no passenger trains service Lubbock, there is a **TNM&O Coach station** at (get ready, all you superstitious folks) **1313 13th St.** (765-6641), with buses leaving for Amarillo (3 per day, 2½hr., $20), Oklahoma City (4 per day, 7-11hr., $61), and Dallas (2 per day, 7hr., $50).

The laid-back **Convention & Tourism Bureau of Lubbock,** 1120 14th St. (747-5232 or 800-692-4035), at Avenue K, gives out a **13**-page brochure on all of Lubbock's accommodations, attractions, and annual events (open Mon.-Fri. 8am-5pm). Lubbock's **Citibus Transportation** (762-0111) offers **13** routes which stay predominately within Loop 289. Maps are available at the main transfer center, 801 Broadway, at Avenue H. (Buses run Mon.-Fri. every ½hr. and Sat. every hr. 6am-7pm.) **Enterprise Car Rental,** 1911 Avenue Q (765-0622), at 19th St., has mid-sized automobiles for those who need wheels. ($34 per day, $168 per week; unlimited mi. within Texas, New Mexico and Oklahoma. Must be 21 with major credit card. Open Mon.-Fri. 8am-6pm, Sat. 9am-1pm.) **Yellow Cab** (765-7777) handles taxi service ($1.50 base fare, $1.10 per mi.). **Emergency:** 911. Lubbock's **post office:** 411 Avenue L (open Mon.-Fri. 8:30am-5pm); **ZIP code:** 79408; **area code:** 806.

Good motels congregate around the intersection of I-87 and Slaton Hwy. **The Circus Inn,** 150 Slaton Rd. (745-2515), has well-kept grounds with hedges, a nice pool, and terrific rooms which would cost as much as $200 in a big city. Most have carpeted bathrooms and desks with cushioned chairs. (Queen-sized bed for 1 $23, for 2 $26; two double beds for 2 $30.) Lubbock **KOA Kampground,** 5502 Country Rd. 6300 (762-8653), off U.S. 84W 2½ mi. west of Loop 289, provides just about everything except privacy: indoor heated pool and hot tub, 24-hr. laundry facilities, playground, ping-pong tables, and basketball courts. (Open daily 8am-8pm. Sites $15, full RV hookup $18.) For good Texas BBQ, head to **Stubb's,** 620 19th St. (747-4777). Pictures of cowfolk in ten-gallon hats hang over customers in matching headgear. All recipes concocted by the 6-ft.-5-in., 230-lb. Christopher B. "Stubbs." (Bar-B-Q Burger $3.50. Open daily 11am-10pm.)

The **Ranching Heritage Center** (742-2490), 4th St. and Indiana, tells the story of Panhandle ranching through 33 authentic structures moved onto a 15-acre site; the center emphasizes the evolution of ranch architecture from single-room log cabins and line camps to the stylish Queen Anne houses fashionable at the turn of the century. (Open Mon.-Sat. 10am-5pm, Sun. 1-5pm.) The exhibits at the **Science Spectrum,** 2579 S. Loop 289 (745-2525), between Indiana and University Ave., may be lame, but the *very cool* 58-ft. dome theater shows movies on space, volcanoes, and other earthy stuff (shows 11am, 1, 3, 4, 6, and 7pm; $5.50, ages 3-18 $4.50).

■■■ GUADALUPE MOUNTAINS

The Guadalupe Mountains rise out of the vast Texas desert to reach heights of unexplored grandeur. Early westbound pioneers avoided the area, fearful of the climate and the Mescalero Apaches who controlled the range. By the 1800s, when the Apaches had been driven out, only a few homesteaders and *guano* miners inhabited this rugged region. **Guadalupe Mountains National Park** covers 86,000 acres of desert, canyons, and highlands. Passing tourists will want to stop for the park's most renowned sights: **El Capitán,** a 2000-ft. limestone cliff, and **Guadalupe Peak,** the highest point in Texas at 8749 ft. Less hurried travelers should take the time to explore. With over 70 mi. of trails, the mountains promise challenging desert hikes for those willing to journey to this remote area. **Carlsbad, NM,** 55 mi. northeast, makes a good base town with several cheap motels, campgrounds, and restaurants.

Most major trails begin at the Headquarters Visitors Center (below). Guadalupe Peak presents a difficult three- to five-hour hike, depending on your mountaineering ability. Allow a full day to hike to the spring-fed stream of **McKittrick Canyon** or to **The Bowl,** a stunning high-country forest of Douglas fir and Ponderosa pine. The 2½-mi., 1½-hour **Spring Trail** leads from the **Frijole Ranch,** about 1 mi. north of the visitors center, to a mountain spring. The trail leading to the historic Pratt Cabin in the Canyon begins at the **McKittrick Visitors Center,** off U.S. 62/180. Free backcountry hiking is also permitted.

The **Headquarters Visitors Center** (828-3251) lies right off U.S. 62/180. (Open daily 7am-6pm; Sept.-May 8am-4:30pm. After-hours info posted on the bulletin board outside.) For more park info, get in touch with Guadalupe Mountains National Park, HC60, Box 400, Salt Flat 79847 (828-3251). **Emergency:** 911. Guadalupe's **area code:** 915. Guadalupe Mountains National Park sets its clocks to **Mountain time zone** (2hr. behind Eastern).

The park's two campgrounds, **Pine Springs Campgrounds** (828-3251), on the highway just past the headquarters, and **Dog Canyon Campground** (505-981-2418), just south of the New Mexico border at the north end of the park, have water and restrooms, but lack hookups and showers (sites $6). Dog Canyon is accessible only by a 72-mi. drive from Carlsbad, NM on Rte. 137.

The park's lack of development may be a bonus for backpackers, but it makes daily existence tough. Bring water for even the shortest, most casual hike. There is no gas in the park; fill up ahead of time. *Hundreds of people run out of gas every season, so gas up before you enter the park.* Guadalupe Park is 120 mi. east of El Paso. **TNM&O Coaches** (505-887-1108), an affiliate of **Greyhound,** runs along U.S. 62/180 between Carlsbad, NM and El Paso, making flag stops at Carlsbad Caverns National Park (p. 670) and Guadalupe Mountains National Park en route (Carlsbad to Guadalupe $11, $21 round-trip). Buses stop at the Headquarters Visitors Center.

■■■ EL PASO

In its disparate architectural landscape, modern El Paso combines the elements of an oversized strip mall and a Mexican mission town. A city caught between two states, two countries, and two languages, El Paso suffers from a bona fide identity crisis. The largest of the U.S. border towns, El Paso grew up in the 17th century, a stop-over on an important east-west wagon route that trailed the Río Grande though "the pass" *(el paso)* between the Rockies and the Sierra Madres. As Spain extended its reach into the New World, El Paso became a center for missionary activity; missions from the period of Spanish colonization can still be seen today. More recently, the city has been dominated by Fort Bliss, the largest air defense base in the West, and the Biggs Army Airfield.

PRACTICAL INFORMATION

Tourist Office: El Paso Tourist Information Center, 1 Civic Center Plaza (544-0062), next to the Chamber of Commerce at the intersection of Santa Fe and San Francisco St. Easily identifiable by the thin, water-filled moat which surrounds it. Well-stocked with brochures; sells tickets for the **El Paso-Juárez Trolley Co.** (544-0061; 544-0062 for reservations), which conducts day-long tours across the border leaving on the hr. from the Convention Center ($10, ages 6-13 $8, under 6 free; trolleys run 10am-5pm, Nov.-March 9am-4pm).

Mexican Consulate: 910 E. San Antonio St. (533-4082), on the corner of San Antonio and Virginia St. Dispenses **tourist cards.** Open Mon.-Fri. 9am-4:30pm.

Currency Exchange: Valuta, 307 E. Paisano (544-1152). Conveniently near the border. Open 24 hrs.

AmEx Office: 3100 N. Mesa St. (532-8900). Open Mon.-Fri. 8am-5pm.

Airport: El Paso International Airport, northeast of the city center. Take Sun Metro bus #33 from the traffic island outside the air terminal building, across from the Delta ticket window to or from St. Jacinto Plaza. **K.C. Express Shuttle Service** does air-conditioned bus service to downtown starting at $6 (operates Sun.-Thurs. 4am-midnight, Fri.-Sat. 4am-3pm).

Trains: Amtrak, 700 San Francisco St. (545-2247 or 800-872-7245). Open Mon., Wed., and Sat. 11am-6:30pm, Tues., Thurs., and Sun. 9am-5pm.

Buses: Greyhound, 201 San Antonio (532-2365 or 800-231-2222), across from the Civic Center between Santa Fe and Chihuahua St. Daily buses to New York ($99), L.A. ($35), Dallas, and Phoenix. Lockers up to 6hr. $2, 6-24hr. $4. Open 24 hrs.

Public Transportation: Sun Metro (533-3333) departs from San Jacinto Plaza, at Main and Oregon St. Fare 85¢, students and children 40¢, seniors 20¢.

Taxis: Yellow Cab, 533-3433. $1.20 base fare, $1.50 per mi. Wheelchair service.

Car Rental: Dollar Rent-A-Car (778-5445 or 800-800-4000). $33 per day, $143 per week with unlimited free mi. $11 extra for travel into Mexico; must stay within 10mi. of Juárez. Must be 21 with major credit card; under 25 surcharge $10 per day. Open 24 hrs.

Crisis Lines: Crisis Hotline, 779-1800. Open 24 hrs. **Lambda,** 562-4217. Gay and lesbian line with info 24 hrs. and counseling Mon., Wed., and Fri. 7-9pm.

Hospital: Providence Memorial Hospital (577-6011). Open 24 hrs. For immunizations, visit **El Paso City County Health District,** 222 S. Campbell St. (543-3560); when approaching the Mexican border, turn left on Paisano St. and walk 3 blocks. Immunizations (by appointment, Wed. only) are not required to enter Mexico, but are recommended. Open Mon.-Fri. 8am-5pm.

Emergency: 911.

Post Office: 219 E. Mills (775-7563). Open Mon.-Fri. 9am-5pm, Sat. 8am-noon. **ZIP code:** 79910. **Area code:** 915. To call **Ciudad Juárez,** dial 011-52-16, followed by the local number.

Time Zone: Mountain (2hr. behind Eastern.)

Approach El Paso from the east or west on **I-10** and from the north or south on **U.S. 54.** The intrusion of the Río Grande and the Franklin Mountains makes El Paso unusually confusing; get a map to get oriented. Near most hotels and restaurants, **San Jacinto Plaza** is right in the thick of things. **Santa Fe St.** runs north-south dividing El Paso into east and west; **San Antonio St.** crosses east-west dividing the city north and south. Tourists should be wary of the streets between San Antonio and the border late at night.

ACCOMMODATIONS

The area's cheapest rooms lurk across the border in Juárez, but downtown El Paso has more appealing options. Budget hotels cluster around the center of town, near Main St. and San Jacinto Plaza. The **Gateway Hotel,** 104 S. Stanton St. (532-2611; fax 533-8100), at S. Stanton and San Antonio St.—a stone's throw from San Jacinto

Plaza, is a favorite stop for middle-class Mexicans. Speak Spanish to get respect and a large, immaculate room, tastefully furnished with a large bed and equipped with a private bathroom. (A/C upstairs. Check-out 4pm. Singles $21, with TV $28; doubles $27/$31; doubles with king-sized bed $32/$33. Parking $1.50 for 24 hrs. Reservations accepted up to 5 days in advance, except during festivals and holidays.) The **Gardner Hotel/Hostel (HI-AYH),** 311 E. Franklin (532-3661), is two blocks up Mesa St. from San Jacinto Park; walk 1 block north to Franklin, turn right, and head east 1½ blocks. This 75-year-old establishment features small, clean, inexpensive singles and dorm rooms, along with larger doubles. Hostelers stay in four-person dorm rooms with shared bathrooms and access to a beautiful, spacious kitchen, a common room, and a comfy basement with plenty of couches for lounging. Hotel rooms include color cable TV and phones. The management takes extreme care regarding security concerns. (Reception open 24 hrs. Hostel check-out 10am; hotel check-out 1pm. Dorm beds $12.50, nonmembers $15.50; singles with small bed and no bath $22.50; larger singles with better furnishings $27.50, with bath $35; doubles up to $40. Lockers 75¢, 4 or more days 50¢ per day. Linen $2.)

FOOD AND NIGHTLIFE

El Paso is a hybrid species with North American and Mexican ancestors. Well known *gringo* chains coexist with small mom-and-pop restaurants. Residents of the city claim to have the best Mexican food anywhere, and *cocina mexicana* does indeed dominate the culinary scene; burritos are the undisputed local specialty. Attention vegetarians: tasty meatless options such as bean burritos and *chiles rellenos* may contain animal lard.

Luby's Restaurant (533-5042), at Texas and Campbell St. A local favorite, with a bustling atmosphere and inexpensive fare. Pick up food on a cafeteria-style line and chow in the well-lit dining area. Lunch or dinner $2.85-4.35. For breakfast, try a waffle with fresh fruit ($1.49). Open Mon.-Sat. 7:30-10am and 10:30am-6pm.

Big Bun, 500 N. Stanton St. (533-3926). Serves inexpensive tacos, burritos. and hefty burgers (99¢) with salsa on the side. Refills at the soda machine 45¢. Breakfast burritos $1-2; deli sandwiches $2-3. Open Mon.-Sat. 7am-7pm.

The Tap Bar and Restaurant, 408 E. San Antonio St. (546-9049), near Stanton St. Breakfast means excellent *huevos rancheros* ($3). For lunch or dinner, the Mexican Plate #1 (tacos, *chiles rellenos,* enchilada, rice, beans, and nachos for $4.50) surpasses its generic title in taste. Neon lights on the tiny dance floor light the place at night. Live *mariachis* every Sat. night (10:30-11:30pm) and sports on a big-screen TV. One of the only places open after 7pm, outlasting even McDonald's. Full bar with endless varieties of beer. Open daily 7am-2am.

For nightlife, check out the **Cadillac Bar,** 1170 Sunmount (779-5881; open daily 6pm-2am). Downtown, **The Old Plantation,** 219 S. Ochoa (533-6055), offers gay nightlife at a dance club and bar (open Thurs.-Sun. 8pm-2am). Juárez (see below) provides a rowdier scene with ubiquitous nightlife and no minimum drinking age.

SIGHTS AND ENTERTAINMENT

The majority of visitors to El Paso are either stopping off on the long drive through the desert or heading south to Ciudad Juárez and beyond. Nevertheless, downtown El Paso has more to offer than just a stop-over. For a whirlwind tour of the city and its southern neighbor, hop aboard the hourly El Paso-Juárez Trolley Co. **tour trolley** (see Practical Information above).

Historic **San Jacinto Plaza** swarms with men and women of all ages. Street musicians play music which hearkens to the days when *conquistadores* and cavalry filled El Paso. South of the square, on **El Paso St.,** hundreds of locals dash into stores in search of new bargains; here, a pair of Wranglers can be had for as little as $10. To take in a commanding view of El Paso, Juárez, and the Sierra Madres, head northeast of downtown to Rim Rd. (which becomes Scenic Dr.), then to **Murchinson Park,** at the base of the mountains. The Franklin Mountains to the north form the southern tip of the Rockies.

El Paso hosts the **Southwestern Livestock Show & Rodeo** (532-1401) in February and the **World's Finals Rodeo** (545-1188) in November. Fear not: El Paso's celebrations transcend its country-western roots. The city also boasts the **First Thanksgiving Reenactment** (El Paso claims to have hosted the first Thanksgiving and harbors a deep resentment for Plymouth, MA) and the **Sun Bowl Parade** (533-4916 or 800-915-BOWL/2695) at the **University of Texas at El Paso (UTEP).**

April through August, the **El Paso Diablos** (755-2000), pride of the fabled Texas League, play the best minor-league baseball around at Cohen Stadium, 9700 Gateway North; call for game times. To reach the stadium, take bus #41 or #42 as far north as possible and walk the rest of the way; ask the driver for directions.

The Plymouth Conspiracy

Take that turkey out of the oven: contrary to popular belief—if El Paso has any say in it—those straight-laced Plymouth pilgrims did not celebrate the first Thanksgiving on the North American continent. Residents of El Paso wistfully recount the story of Don Juan de Oñate, a Spanish noble who, in January 1598, led a caravan of colonists north from Santa Barbara, Mexico (near the city of Chihuahua). The procession plodded through the desert, subsisting on roots, berries, and water from cacti until, on April 20, 1598, (nearly a quarter-century before the Mayflower even set sail), the colonists reached the Río Grande. They rested in the soothing river valley, and on April 30, Don Juan asked his people to don their finest duds for a feast in celebration of their safe arrival. Soon after, they continued to what is presently Santa Fe, New Mexico.

■ NEAR EL PASO: CIUDAD JUÁREZ

Though only the narrow Río Grande separates Ciudad Juárez (founded in 1581 by Spanish explorers) from El Paso, the trip into Mexico seems like a step into another dimension. Visitors are immediately bombarded by commotion on all sides and treated to a feast of bright paint and neon. In the face of American business and bands of carousing *gringos,* Mexican culture has withdrawn to the city's cathedral square and Parque Chamizal, a pleasant respite from the industrial production centers and poor residential areas that dot most of the cityscape.

To reach the border from El Paso, take the north-south bus (25¢) to the **Santa Fe Bridge,** its last stop before turning around. Do not confuse the inexpensive bus with the costly trolley. Two pedestrian and motor roads cross the Río Grande: **El Paso St.,** an overcrowded one-way street, and **Santa Fe St.,** a parallel road lined with Western-wear stores and decent restaurants. Entry to Mexico is 25¢ and the return trip costs 30¢. When entering by foot, walk to the right side of the Santa Fe Bridge and pay the quarter to cross. Daytrippers should be prepared to flash their documents of citizenship in order to pass in and out of Mexico. If you're one of those people who always breaks off the short end of the wishbone, you may get your bag searched by a guard; although most people don't even have to show ID. If you have questions about crossings, call the **transit police** (tel. 12-31-97 or 14-17-04).

Practical Information Go left from the Santa Fe Bridge to find the **Coordinación de Turismo** (tel. 14-06-07), Malecón and Francisco Villa in the gray Unidad Administrativa Municipal building. The amiable English-speaking staff has few truly helpful brochures. In Juárez, banks congregate near the bus station, on Juárez St., and on 16 de Septiembre. Most display their rates outside. One of the biggest, **Comisiones San Luis** (tel. 14-20-33), at 16 de Septiembre and Juárez, accepts traveler's checks (open Mon.-Thurs. 9am-9pm, Fri.-Sat. 9am-9:15pm, Sun. 9am-6:15pm). **Chequerama** (tel. 12-35-99), at Unión and Juárez, also takes traveler's checks (open Mon.-Sat. 10am-7pm). In an **emergency,** dial 06.

Old Juárez, immediately adjoining the Santa Fe and Stanton bridges, can be covered on foot. Most city buses leave from the intersection of Insurgentes and Francisco Villa or thereabouts; always ask where the bus is going and tell the driver your destination. Taxis are available downtown, but fees are steep; set a price before getting in. The "Ruta 8" bus goes from *el centro* to the Americanized ProNaf for 1.20 pesos; taxis charge 30 times as much. During the day, Juárez is relatively safe for alert travelers. At night, however, women should not walk alone or in dark places; everyone should avoid the area more than 2 blocks west of Avenida Juárez.

Accommodations, Food, and Nightlife In Juárez, a typical cheap hotel meets only minimal standards and charges some of the highest "budget" rates in Mexico. Inexpensive lodging can be found along Avenida Juárez; pricier places are located in the ProNaf area. **Hotel del Río,** 488 Juárez (tel. 12-37-76), is worth the climb upstairs for large, simple, clean rooms with comfortably thick beds, A/C, and color TVs. Room service and parking are available. (Check-out 1pm. Singles, doubles, or tightly-squeezed triples US$20. AmEx, MC accepted.)

Expect a long quest for food that will not cause a bacteriological mutiny in a *gringo* belly; the prudent beat a path to Av. Juárez and Lerdo or to the ProNaf center. Weak-stomached travelers should avoid shacks. In general, *mariscos* (shellfish) are overpriced and less than fresh in Juárez. **Cafetería El Coyote Inválido,** Juárez 615 at Colón (tel. 14-27-27), offers a bustling, clean, American-diner atmosphere. Come for the A/C alone. Hamburgers go for 14.50 pesos; an array of Mexican plates run 14-20 pesos. Dark and spacious, **Restaurant/Bar Villa Española,** Juárez 614 (tel. 12-02-38), gets lively at night. Three cheers for *agua purificada*. (*Chilaques* 9 pesos, enchiladas 10.80 pesos. Open daily noon-2am. AmEx accepted.)

Many of the countless drinking establishments in Juárez are unsavory, and some of the savory ones can become dangerous; stick to the glutted strip along Av. Juárez or in the ProNaf area. **Mr. Fog Bar,** Juárez Nte. 140 (tel. 14-29-48), is a popular spot for roving Americans looking for a weekend of excitement south of the border. A cartoon crocodile adorns the mirrored walls of this dark watering hole. (Dance floor in back. Beer 7 pesos, liquor 6 pesos. Open daily 11am-1am.)

Sights and Entertainment In *el centro* stands the **Aduana Fronteriza** (tel. 12-47-07), where Juárez and 16 de Septiembre cross. Built in 1889 as a trading outpost and later used for customs, it is now home to the **Museo Histórico de la Ex-Aduana,** which features exhibits on the region's history during the Mexican Revolution (museum open Tues.-Sun. 10am-5pm; free). At the ProNaf center, the **Museo de Arte e Historia** (tel. 16-74-14) displays Mexican art from the past and present (open Tues.-Sun. 11am-6pm; .75 pesos, students free). Also at the ProNaf center, the **Centro Artesanal** sells handmade goods at maximum prices; haggle and the prices will change.

The *toro* and the *matador* battle in traditional bullfights on occasional evenings during the summer at the **Plaza Monumental de Toros,** Paseo Triunfo de la República and López Mateos (tel. 13-16-56 or 13-11-82). General admission seating begins at 25 pesos, in the shade 40 pesos (under 13 free). Call for dates and times. The **Lienzo de Charro,** on Av. Charro off República (tel. 27-05-55), also conducts bullfights and a *charreada* (rodeo) on Sunday afternoons during the summer.

For more information on Ciudad Juárez and border towns, see *Let's Go: Mexico.*

■■■ BIG BEND

Roadrunners, coyotes, wild pigs, mountain lions, and 350 species of birds make their home in **Big Bend National Park,** a 700,000-acre tract that lies in the curve of the Río Grande. Spectacular canyons, vast stretches of the **Chihuahuan Desert,** and the **Chisos Mountains** occupy this literally and figuratively far-out spot.

Practical Information Big Bend may be the most isolated spot you'll ever encounter. *You can only reach the park by car* via Rte. 118 or U.S. 385. There are few gas stations along the way; fill your tank before you leave urban areas. The **park headquarters** (915-477-2251) is at **Panther Junction,** about 26 mi. inside the park (open daily 8am-6pm; vehicle pass $5 per week). For info, write the Superintendent, Big Bend National Park, P.O. Box 129, 79834. The **Texas Travel Information Center** (800-452-9292) provides info on the park and helps visitors plan excursions (open daily 8am-9pm). Other **ranger stations** are located at Río Grande Village, Persimmon Gap, and Chisos Basin (all open Nov.-April daily 8am-4pm; Persimmon Gap open year-round). **Amtrak** (800-872-7245) serves the town of **Alpine,** 70 mi. north of Big Bend. **Emergency:** 915-477-2251 until 6pm; afterwards call 911.

Accommodations and Food The expensive **Chisos Mountain Lodge** (915-477-2291), 10 mi. from park headquarters, offers the only motel-style lodging within the park (singles $59, doubles $67; $11 per additional person). There are also lodges, equipped with showers and baths but no A/C (singles $56, doubles $66; $11 per additional person), and stone cottages which come with three double beds (1 or 2 people $70; $11 per additional person). Reservations are a must; the lodge often gets booked up to a year in advance. The restaurant and coffee shop at the lodge charge $5-12 for entrees (open daily 7am-8pm). Cheaper motels line Rte. 118 and Rte. 170 near Terlingua and Lajitas, 21 and 28 mi. from park headquarters, respectively. **Groceries, gas,** and green monkeys are available in Panther Junction, Río Grande Village, and the Chisos Basin at Castolon. The Río Grande Village Store has the park's only public **shower** (5min. 75¢).

Stay in **Terlingua, TX,** if you plan to spend more than a day at the Park. Terlingua, named for the three languages spoken in the town in the late 1800s (English, Spanish, and a Native American dialect), is accessible from Road 170 in Study Butte, about 35 mi. from park headquarters but only 7 mi. from the park's western entrance. The **Easter Egg Valley Motel** (915-371-2430) provides a good alternative to park sites (singles $36, doubles $43). Farther up Road 170, the **Starlight Theatre Bar and Grill** (915-371-2326) has large portions of cheap food ($3-8) and free live music (open daily 5:30pm-midnight).

Hiking, Rafting, and Camping Before you venture into the park, make sure you have plenty of water. If your stay is brief, take the 43-mi. **scenic drive** to Santa Elena Canyon; watch for flash floods. Park rangers at the visitors center can suggest other hikes and sights. The **Lost Mine Trail,** a 3-hr. hike up a peak in the Chisos, leads to an amazing summit-top view of the desert and the Sierra de Carmen in Mexico. Another easy walk ambles through the **Santa Elena Canyon** along the Río Grande. The canyon walls rise as high as 1000 ft. over the banks of the river. Four companies offer **river trips** down the 133-mi. stretch of the Río Grande owned by the park. **Far-Flung Adventures** (800-359-4138), next door to the Starlight Theatre Bar and Grill in Terlingua (see above), organizes one- to seven-day trips. A one-day trip to Santa Elena averages $100; call for exact prices. Park headquarters (see above) has more information on rafting and canoeing.

Designated **campsites** within the park are allotted on a first come, first served basis. **Chisos Basin** and **Río Grande Village** offer sites with restrooms and flush toilets ($5), while **Cottonwood** has water and pit toilets ($3). In summer, the sites in Chisos Basin are the best (and coolest) by far. In the park's peak season (Nov.-April) Río Grande Village fills first. Get to either campground early; sites fill quickly. For overnight backcountry camping or free sites along the hiking trails, obtain a free **backcountry permit** at the park headquarters.

ROCKY MOUNTAINS

The abrupt escarpment of the Rocky Mountains provides stark and menacing geographic contrast to the Great Plains to the east and the searing deserts to the west. Created by immense tectonic forces some sixty-five million years ago, the Rockies mark a vast wrinkle in the North American continent; sculpted by wind, water, and glaciers over eons, their weathered peaks extend 3000 mi. from northern Alberta to central New Mexico and soar to altitudes exceeding 2½ vertical miles. Humans stumble and cars overheat while ascending the mountains, pausing between gasps to explore low-lying brushlands and thick pine and aspen forests ruled by grizzly bears and lynx, all before reaching the cool, thin air above the treeline, where Rocky Mountain goats and bighorn sheep graze on flowers and grasses. Less welcoming to life are the harsh tundra and packed snow which blanket the peaks year-round.

Although the whole of the Rocky Mountain area supports less than five percent of the U.S. population, millions throng every year to its spectacular national parks and forests. The Waterton-Glacier International Peace Park straddles Montana's border with Alberta; Wyoming and Colorado are landlords to Yellowstone and Rocky Mountain National Parks; and Idaho encompasses two backcountry regions, as well as countless acres of state and national forests. The Continental Divide follows the spine of the Rocky Mountains; all rivers east of this boundary flow east to the Mississippi, all rivers west to the Pacific.

Rocky Mountain Morsels

Authors: James Crumbley, A.B. Guthrie, Jr., Norman MacLean, Pam Houston.
Artists: Ansel Adams.
Cuisine: Elk and buffalo steaks, potatoes, Rocky Mountain oysters.
Microbreweries: Avery, Rockies, Lone Wolfe, Bristol, Pikes Peak, Bradway, Lonetree, Tabernash, Durango, H.C. Berger, New Belgium, Odell, Golden City, Irons, Left Hand, Silver Plume, Beier, Coeur d'Alene, Sun Valley, Bayern, Kessler, Milestown, Spanish Peaks, Whitefish, Otto Brothers Brewing Co.
Native Americans: Ute, Cheyenne, Arapaho, Apache, Comanche, Blackfoot, Nez Perce, Shoshone, Crow, Sioux, Chippewa-Cree, Salish-Koolenai, Oglala.
Music: Country, Steven Stills, Big Head Todd & the Monsters, The Samples, John Denver, Sister Smith, C.W. McCall.
Film and TV: *A River Runs Through It, Mork and Mindy, Dynasty.*
Climate: Cool and dry.
Geography: Mountains.

Idaho

Chiseled from the harsh Rockies, Idaho is the only state never to have had a foreign flag fly above it. Snow-capped mountains in central Idaho tower above a rocky, sparsely populated landscape. To the south, world-famous potatoes thrive; to the north, dense pine forests envelop clear, cold lakes; to the west, frothing rivers snake violently through Hell's Canyon, the deepest gorge in North America, and spill over Shoshone Falls, a descent longer than the fall from Niagara. Time stands still in this pristine land; little has changed since Lewis and Clark explored the territory in 1805. The landscape remains largely free of heavy industry, and Idaho's motto—*Esto perpetua,* Latin for "It is Forever"— suggests that nothing will change anytime soon.

PRACTICAL INFORMATION

Capital: Boise.

Idaho Information Line: 800-635-7820. **Boise Convention and Visitors Bureau** (344-7777), corner of 9th and Idaho, 2nd floor. Open daily 8:30am-5pm. **Parks and Recreation Department,** 5657 Warm Springs Ave., Boise (334-4199). **Idaho Outfitters and Guide Association,** P.O. Box 95, Boise 83701 (342-1438). Info on companies leading whitewater, packhorse, and backpacking expeditions in the state. Free vacation directories.

Time Zones: Mountain and Pacific. The dividing line runs east-west across the state with the Salmon River.

Postal Abbreviation: ID

Sales tax: 5%.

■■■ BOISE

Small and hip, Boise is a verdant residential oasis in the state's dry southern plateau. The easy, small-town familiarity of the residents, numerous grassy parks, and airy shopping plazas make for a relaxing way-station on a cross-country jaunt. Most of the city's sights lie between the capitol and I-84, a few miles south; you can manage pretty well on foot.

Practical Information The **visitor's center,** 850 W. Front St. (388-0711) at the Boise Center Mall, dispenses tourist tips. **Amtrak** (800-872-7245) serves Boise from the beautiful Spanish-mission-style **Morrison-Knudsen Depot,** 2601 Eastover Terr. (336-5992), easily visible from Capitol Blvd. Trains run to Salt Lake City (3 per week, 8hr., $70), Portland (3 per week, 10hr., $83), and Seattle (3 per week, 14hr., $111). **Greyhound** zips along I-84 from its terminal at 1212 W. Bannock (343-3681), a few blocks west of downtown. Portland (3 per day, 8-10hr., $39), Seattle (2 per day, 14hr., $49), and Missoula (1 per day, $85) are popular connections. **Boise Urban Stages** (336-1010) runs several routes through the city, with maps available from any bus driver and displayed at each stop. (Buses operate Mon.-Fri. 5:15am-8:45pm, Sat. 6:45am-6:45pm. Fare 75¢, seniors 35¢.) **McU's Sports,** 822 W. Jefferson (342-7734), rents in-line skates ($5 per hr., $15 per day, $20 overnight) and mountain bikes ($14 per ½ day, $22 per day) as well as equipment for sports of all seasons. Boise's main **post office:** 770 S. 13th St. (383-4211; open Mon.-Fri. 7:30am-5:30pm, Sat. 10am-2pm); **ZIP code:** 83707; **area code:** 208.

Accommodations and Camping Finding lodging in Boise is harsh; neither the YMCA nor the YWCA provide rooms, and even the cheapest hotels charge more than $20 per night. The more reasonable places tend to fill quickly, so make reservations. The friendly **Boisean,** 1300 S. Capitol Ave. (343-3645 or 800-365-3645), has spacious, clean rooms and a helpful staff (singles $32, doubles $38-47; $6 per additional person). The **Sun Liner Motel,** 3933 Chinden Ave. (344-7647), offers plain, air-conditioned singles for $30. The **Boise National Forest** office, 5493 Warm Springs Rd. (364-4241), provides info about campgrounds in the forest; the nearest one to Boise is 16 mi. north. They also sell maps ($3) and permits for mushroom foraging ($5 per day). (Open Mon.-Fri. 7:30-4:30pm). Other campgrounds include **Boise KOA Kampground,** 7300 S. Federal Way (345-7673; sites $18.50, full hookup $23.50); **Americana Kampground,** 3600 American Terrace Blvd. (344-5733; 90 sites, $17); and **Fiesta Park,** 11101 Fairview Ave. (375-8207; sites $16, with partial hookup $18.50, with full hookup $19.50).

Food and Nightlife Mr. Potatohead doesn't rule Boise food. The downtown area, centered around 6th and Main St., is bustling with lunchtime delis, coffee shops, ethnic cuisine and several stylish bistros. **Moon's Kitchen,** 815 W. Bannock St. (385-0472) is a local tradition. (Soup and sandwich special $4.50. Huge breakfast $2.75. Open Mon.-Fri. 7am-3pm, Sat. 8am-3pm.) A more innovative menu and tast-

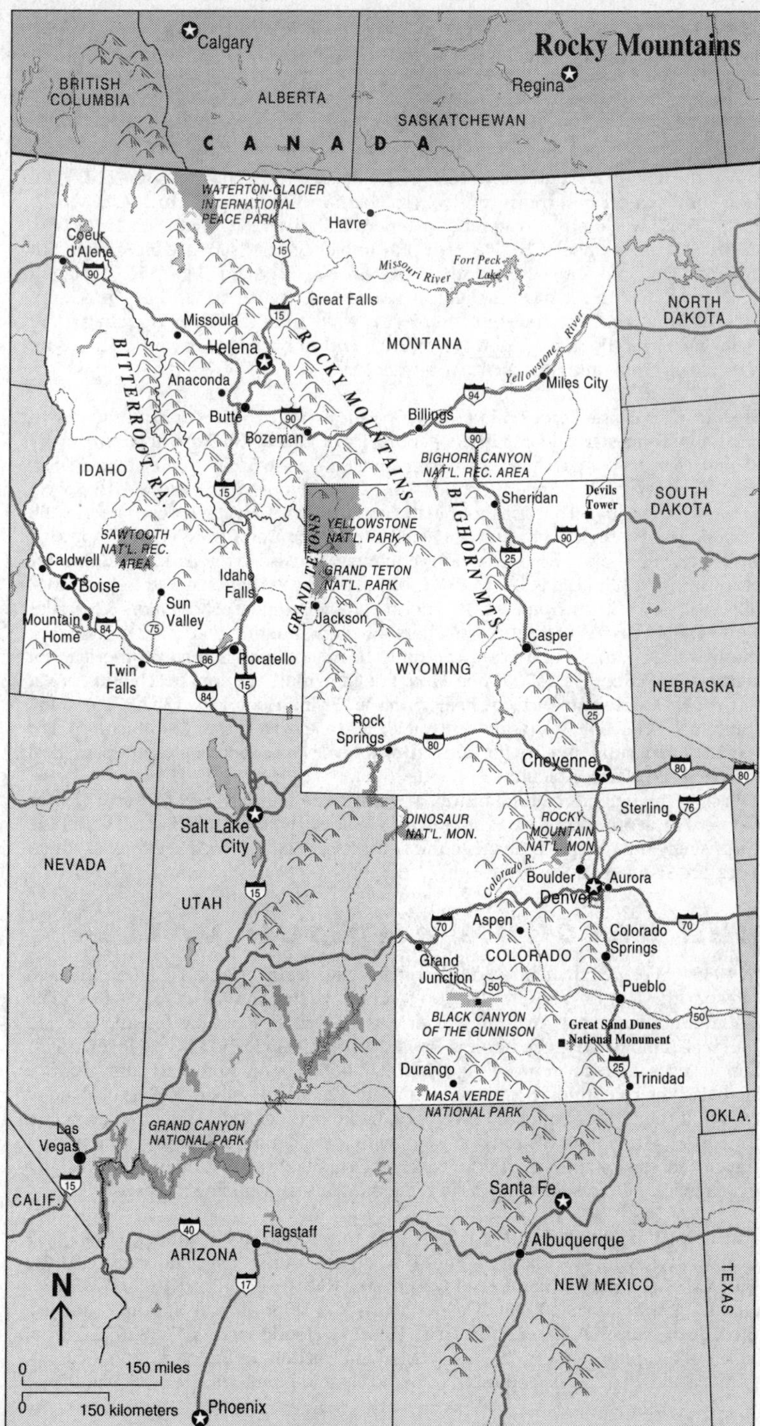
Rocky Mountains
Calgary
Regina
BRITISH COLUMBIA
ALBERTA
SASKATCHEWAN
CANADA
WATERTON-GLACIER INTERNATIONAL PEACE PARK
Havre
Coeur d'Alene
Fort Peck Lake
Missouri River
Great Falls
NORTH DAKOTA
Missoula
Helena
ROCKY MOUNTAINS
MONTANA
BITTERROOT RA.
Yellowstone River
Miles City
Anaconda
Butte
Billings
Bozeman
BIGHORN CANYON NAT'L. REC. AREA
IDAHO
Sheridan
Devils Tower
SOUTH DAKOTA
YELLOWSTONE NAT'L. PARK
BIGHORN MTS.
SAWTOOTH NAT'L. REC. AREA
GRAND TETONS
GRAND TETON NAT'L. PARK
Caldwell
Boise
Idaho Falls
Sun Valley
Jackson
Mountain Home
Casper
Pocatello
WYOMING
Twin Falls
NEBRASKA
Rock Springs
Cheyenne
Sterling
Salt Lake City
DINOSAUR NAT'L. MON.
ROCKY MOUNTAIN NAT'L. MON
NEVADA
Colorado R.
Boulder
Aurora
Denver
UTAH
Aspen
Colorado Springs
Grand Junction
COLORADO
Pueblo
BLACK CANYON OF THE GUNNISON
Great Sand Dunes National Monument
Durango
Trinidad
MASA VERDE NATIONAL PARK
OKLA.
GRAND CANYON NATIONAL PARK
Las Vegas
Santa Fe
CALIF.
Flagstaff
Albuquerque
ARIZONA
NEW MEXICO
TEXAS
N
0 150 miles
0 150 kilometers
Phoenix

ier sandwiches can be found at the **Raintree Deli,** 210 North Capitol Blvd. (336-4611), where half a sandwich is $3 and a stuffed baked potato will cost you $4 (open Mon.-Fri. 9am-3:30pm). **The Beanery,** 107 8th St. (342-3456), carves up slow-roasted meats and serves them with bread, mashed potatoes, carrots, and a side salad for $5-6. (Open Mon.-Tues. 11am-9pm, Wed.-Fri. 11am-10pm, Sat. 11:30am-10pm, Sun. 11:30am-9pm.) Long live *Casablanca* at the combination restaurant and movie theater **Rick's Café American/The Flicks,** 646 Fulton St. (342-4222). The food comes in huge portions ($6-13). (Kitchen open 5-9:30pm. Movies daily 5, 7, and 9:45pm; weekends and summer matinees daily 1pm. $6, double feature $7.50, students, seniors, under 12 $3.75.) For pub ambience, stroll along Main St. from 5th to Capitol and check out the bar scene—**Hannah's,** 621 Main (345-7557), is a good choice with live music most nights (open Tues.-Fri. 3pm-2am, Sat.-Sun. 5pm-2am). Treat all your senses to the smoky funk that wafts from the **Blues Bouquet,** 1010 Main St. (345-6605). Have a pint ($1.25-2.25) and sit back for live music Tues.-Sun. (Open daily 5pm until the blues take a walk.)

Sights The **Boise Tour Train** (342-4796) shows you 75 sites around the city in one hour. Tours start and end in the parking lot of **Julia Davis Park,** departing every 75 min. (5 tours per day, Mon.-Sat. 10am-3pm, Sun. noon-5pm, evening tour Fri.-Sat. 7pm; Sept.-May Wed.-Sun. afternoons only. $6, seniors $5.50, ages 3-12 $3.50. Arrive 15min. early.) To learn about Idaho and the Old West at your own pace, walk through the **Historical Museum** (334-2120), in Julia Davis Park. (Open Mon.-Sat. 9am-5pm, Sun. 1-5pm. Free, donations encouraged.) Also in the park, the **Boise Art Museum,** 670 Julia Davis Dr. (345-8330), displays international and local works. (Open Tues.-Fri. 10am-5pm, Sat.-Sun. noon-5pm. $3, students and seniors $2, grades 1-12 $1, under 6 free; free the first Thurs. of every month.) Take a self-guided tour through the country's only **state capitol** to be heated with natural geothermal hot water (tour office 334-2470; open Mon.-Fri. 8am-5pm). Raptors perch and dive at the **World Center for Birds of Prey,** 5666 W. Flying Hook Lane (362-3716), 6 mi. south of I-84 on Cole Rd. You must call ahead to arrange a tour ($4 donation). For more back-to-nature fun, try the 22-mi. **Boise River Greenbelt,** a pleasant path ideal for a leisurely walk or picnic.

Bask in the region's cultural history at the **Basque Museum and Cultural Center** (343-2671), at 6th and Grove St. in downtown Boise, where you'll find out about the surprisingly rich Basque heritage in the Great Basin and the Western Rockies (open Tues.-Fri. 10am-4pm, Sat. 11am-3pm).

■■■ KETCHUM AND SUN VALLEY

In 1935, Union Pacific heir Averill Harriman sent Austrian Count Felix Schaffgotsch to scour the U.S. for a site to develop a ski resort area rivaling Europe's best. The Count dismissed Aspen, reasoning its air was too thin for East Coasters, and selected the small mining and sheep herding town of Ketchum in Idaho's Wood River Valley. Sun Valley is the fancy resort village Harriman built one mi. from Ketchum to entice such dashing celebrities as Ernest Hemingway, Claudette Colbert, and Errol Flynn to "rough it" amid the manicured ski slopes, haute cuisine, and nightly orchestra performances. An imported East-coast yacht-club feel still tinges Ketchum. The budget traveler should escape the artificial tans and fashionable stores and head for the gorgeous trails and lakes that abound in the mountains surrounding the valley.

Practical Information The best time to visit the area is during "slack" (late Oct.-Thanksgiving and May-early June), when the tourists magically vanish. At the **Sun Valley/Ketchum Chamber of Commerce** (800-634-3347), at 4th and Main St., Ketchum, a helpful staff shines (open daily 9am-5pm; off season hours shorter). **Sawtooth National Recreation Area (SNRA) Headquarters** (726-7672), 8 mi. north of Ketchum off Rte. 75, has detailed information on the recreation area, hot springs, and area forests and trails. (Open daily mid-June to mid-Sept. 8:30am-5pm;

off season Mon.-Fri. 8am-4:30pm, Sat.-Sun. 9am-4:30pm.) Ketchum's **post office:** 301 1st Ave. (726-5161; open Mon.-Fri. 8:30am-5:30pm, Sat. 11am-1pm); **ZIP code:** 83340; **area code:** 208.

Camping and Food Prices here are for the Trumps. From early June to mid-October, **camping** is the best option for cheap sleep. Sack out for free at the nearby **Sawtooth National Forest** (2 locations with 6 sites each). **Boundary** campground, with restrooms and drinking water, is 3 mi. northeast of town on Trail Creek Rd. Two mi. further on the right, **Corral Creek Rd.,** scatters its isolated sites along a rushing brook (no services). Up Rte. 75 into **Sawtooth National Recreation Area (SNRA)** (727-5013) lie several campgrounds; the cheapest are **Murdock** (8 sites) and **Caribou** (10 sites), which cost $3.25 and are respectively 2 and 4 mi. beyond the SNRA headquarters. Water for these sites is available at the North Fork Dump Site. **North Fork** (26 sites) and **Wood River** (31 sites), 7 and 10 mi. north of Ketchum, respectively, each charge $8.50. **Easley campground and pool,** 5 mi. west of the SNRA headquarters and 12 mi. northwest of Ketchum, has 50¢ showers.

Ketchum's small confines bulge with over 65 restaurants, many of which serve inexpensive, well-prepared grub. **The Hot Dog Adventure Co.,** 210 N. Main (726-0017), offers a cosmopolitan selection of hot dogs ($3) and mouthmelting steak fries ($1.75) at urban hours (daily noon-2am). Have this book and eat it too (along with coffee and a pastry) at the **Main St. Bookcafé,** 211 Main St. (726-3700; open daily 10am-10pm; mid-Sept. to May Wed.-Sat. 10am-10pm, Sun.-Tues. 10am-6pm). Find HUGE food at **Mama Inez** (726-4213), at 7th and Warm Springs, including bean burritos ($2.30) and beef enchiladas ($6; open Mon.-Sat. 11:30am-2pm and 5:30-10pm, Sun. 5-10pm). **Starwood Bakery** takes pride in fresh breads, muffins, and salads; $5.25 buys a deli sandwich, side salad, and chips (open Mon.-Fri. 6:30am-6pm, Sat. 6:30am-5pm, Sun. 8am-5pm).

Hemingway would have liked the dollar mixed drinks nights (Tues. and Sun.) now held at his old haunt, **Whisky Jacques,** 209 N. Main St. (726-5297; open daily 4pm-2am).

The Outdoors and Hot Springs The hills of Ketchum have more natural **hot springs** than any spot in the Rockies except Yellowstone; bathing is free and uncrowded in most of the springs. Like the ghost towns of the surrounding mountains, many springs can be reached only by foot. For books and guidance, inquire at the **Elephant's Perch,** 280 East Ave. (726-3497), off Sun Valley Rd. (open daily 9am-6pm) or at SNRA headquarters. Elephant's Perch is also the best source for mountain bike rentals and trail info. (Bikes $12 per ½-day, $18 per day.)

Two of the more accessible, non-commercial springs are **Warfield Hot Springs** on Warm Springs Creek, 11 mi. west of Ketchum on Warm Springs Rd., and **Russian John Hot Springs,** 8 mi. north of the SNRA headquarters on Rte. 75, just west of the highway. For the best information on fishing conditions and licenses, as well as equipment rentals (fly rods $12 per day), stop by **Silver Creek Outfitters,** 500 N. Main St. (726-5282 or 800-726-5282; open daily 8am-6pm). The fly-fishing bible, *Curtis Creek Manifesto,* is available here ($7).

■■■ CRATERS OF THE MOON

Astronauts once trained at the unearthly **Craters of the Moon National Monument,** an elevated lava field that rises darkly from fertile rolling plains 70 mi. southeast of Sun Valley on U.S. 20/26/93. Windswept and deathly quiet, the stark, twisted lava formations dominate sparse vegetation, a reminder of the volcanic eruptions that occurred here as recently as 2000 years ago.

Park admission is $4 per car, $2 per individual, and the bizarre black campsites cost $10 (51 sites without hookup). Wood fires are prohibited but charcoal fires are permitted. You can also camp for free in adjacent **Bureau of Land Management** land. The park's sites often fill by 4pm in summer. Unmarked sites are free with a free backcountry permit. **Echo Crater,** accessible by a 4-mi. hike, is the most frequented of these sites. Other comfortable sites are hard to find; the first explorers couldn't sleep in the lava fields for lack of bearable places to bed down.

The **visitors center** (527-3257), just off U.S. 20/26/93, has displays and videotapes on the process of lava formation, and printed guides for hikes to all points of interest within the park. They also distribute backcountry camping permits. Rangers lead evening strolls and programs at the campground amphitheater (daily mid-June to mid-Sept.). (Center open daily 8am-6pm; off season 8am-4:30pm.) Explore nearby **lava tubes,** caves formed when a surface layer of lava hardened and the rest of the molten rock drained out, creating a tunnel. Bring sturdy shoes and a flashlight. From nearby Arco, Blackfoot, or Pocatello you can connect with **Greyhound**. There is, however, neither transportation to the national monument nor food available when you get there.

■■■ SAWTOOTH

Rough mountains pack the 756,000 acres of natural land in **Sawtooth National Recreation Area (SNRA)**. Home to the **Sawtooth** and **White Cloud Mountains** in the north and the **Smokey** and **Boulder ranges** in the south, the area is surrounded by four national forests, encompassing the headwaters of five of Idaho's major rivers. If you have a car, be sure to pause at the **Galena Overlook,** 25 mi. north of Ketchum on Rte. 75; the 8701-ft. peak provides an excellent introductory view of the region.

Practical Information The small town of **Stanley,** located at the intersection of Hwy. 21 and Hwy. 75, serves as a northern base for exploring Sawtooth; **Ketchum** (see above) is a southern base. **SNRA Headquarters** (726-7672), 53 mi. south of Stanley and 8 mi. north of Ketchum off Rte. 75, has the most detailed information on the park. The building itself mimics the peaks of the Boulder mountains. (Open daily 8:30am-5pm; mid-Sept. to mid-June Mon.-Fri. 8am-4:30pm, Sat.-Sun. 9am-4:30pm.) Stop by the **Stanley Chamber of Commerce** (774-3411), on Rte. 21 in Stanley for info about services in town and the park (open daily 9am-6pm; winter hours vary). Topographical maps ($2.50) and various trail books are available at McCoy's Tackle (see below) and at the **Stanley Ranger Station** (774-3000), 3 mi. south of Stanley on Rte. 75 (open Mon.-Fri. 8am-5pm, Sat.-Sun. 8:30am-4:30pm). The **Redfish Visitors Center** (774-3376) lies 5 mi. south and 2 mi. west of Stanley near the **Redfish Lake Lodge** (774-3536; both open June 19-Sept. 2 Thurs.-Sun. 10am-5pm). All the info centers have maps of the Sawtooths ($3) and free taped auto tours of the impressive Ketchum-Stanley trip on Rte. 75. Stanley's **post office:** (774-2230) is on Ace of Diamonds St. (open Mon.-Fri. 8am-noon, 1-5pm); **ZIP code:** 83278; **area code:** 208.

Accommodations, Camping, and Food In the heart of Stanley on Ace of Diamonds St., the **Sawtooth Hotel and Café** (774-9947) is a colorful, comfortable place to rest after a wilderness sojourn (singles $27, with private bath $40; doubles $30/$47). More scenic is **McGowan's Resort** (800-447-8141 or 774-2290), 1 mi. down Rte. 75 in Lower Stanley. Hand-built cabins ($50-95; Sept.-early June $40-75) here sit directly on the banks of the Salmon River, house up to six people each, and usually contain kitchenettes. They also offer a terrific view of the Sawtooths and unmatched hospitality. Campgrounds line Rte. 75; clusters are at **Redfish Lake** at the base of the Sawtooths at **Stanley Lake** farther north on Rte. 75; at **Alturas Lake** in the Smokies; at **Salmon River Canyon** along the Salmon to the east of Stanley; and at the **Wood River Corridor** farther south on Rte. 75. Each cluster has at least three campgrounds: Redfish Lake (177 sites), Stanley Lake (128 sites), and Salmon River (89 sites) have the most sites. Sites at Redfish are $10.50, most others are $8.50. Most operate on a first come, first served basis. The two campgrounds on nearby Little Redfish Lake are the best spots for trailers. There are also a few prime sites that can be reserved, such as Point (at Redfish), which has its own beach; call

800-280-CAMP/2267. For general info on all campgrounds call the SNRA Headquarters (727-5013). Overflow camping, primitive but free, is available in several spots. Two good areas are **Redfish Overflow,** just off Rte. 75, and **Decker Flats,** just north of 4th of July Rd. on Rte. 75.

The Great Outdoors **Hiking, boating,** and **fishing** are unsurpassed in all four of the SNRA's little-known ranges. Redfish Lake is the source of many trails; try the popular, leisurely hikes up to Fishhook Creek and Bench Lakes. The long, gentle loop around **Yellow Belly, Toxaway,** and **Petit Lakes** is an easy overnight suitable for novices. Two mi. northwest of Stanley on Rte. 21, take the 3-mi. Iron Creek Rd. which leads to the trailhead of the **Sawtooth Lake Hike;** this 5½-mi. trail is steep but well-worn, and not overly difficult if you stop to rest. Bionic hikers can try the steep 4-mi. hike to **Casino Lakes,** which begins at the **Broadway Creek** trailhead southeast of Stanley. The 18-mi. **Fisher-Creek-Williams Creek Loop** is a woodsy **mountain bike trail** that winds past the old Aztec Mine. Many more specifics on all trails are found in the *SNRA Guide* available at all area ranger stations. (Groups of 10-20 need free wilderness permits for sojourning into the wilderness area on the western side of the SNRA. Always remember to keep fires small and within existing rings.) For additional hiking info, consult the detailed topographic maps in any of Margaret Fuller's **Trail Guides** ($13 for the Sawtooths and White Cloud guide), available at SNRA headquarters and McCoy's Tackle Shop (see below). Stock up on eats for the trail at the **Mountain Village Grocery Store** (774-3350; open daily 7am-9pm).

In the heat of summer, cold rivers beg for **fishing, canoeing,** or **whitewater rafting. McCoy's Tackle Shop** (774-3377), on Ace of Diamonds St. in Stanley, rents gear, sells a full range of outdoor equipment, and has a gift shop (spinning rod $6 per day, $27 per 6 days; open daily 8am-8pm). **Sawtooth Rentals** (774-3409), ¼ mi. south of the Rte. 21-Rte. 75 junction, lends vehicles for every terrain. (Mountain bikes $15-25 per day, kayaks $25 per day for a single or $35 for a double, rafts $15 per person per day, snowmobiles $100 per day.) The **Redfish Lake Lodge Marina** (774-3536) rents paddleboats ($4-5 per ½ hr.), canoes ($5 per hr., $15 per ½ day, $25 per day), and outboards ($10 per hr., $33.50 for ½ day, $60 per day; open in summer daily 7am-9pm). **The River Company** (800-398-0346), based in Ketchum with an office in Stanley (774-3444) arranges expert whitewater rafting and floating trips. Full day trips ($80) feature gourmet campfire cuisine; ½-day trips are $50. (Ketchum office open late May-early Sept. 8am-6pm; Stanley office open in summer 7am-11pm).

The most inexpensive way to enjoy the SNRA waters is to visit the **hot springs** just east of Stanley. Watch for the rising steam on the roadside, often a sign of hot water. **Sunbeam Hot Springs,** 13 mi. from town, is the best of the batch. Be sure to bring a bucket or cooler to the stone bathhouse; you'll need to add about 20 gallons of cold Salmon River water before you can get into these hot pools (120-130°F). The SNRA headquarters has information on all hot springs in the area.

For evening entertainment, try **Casanova Jack's Rod and Gun Club** (774-9920); Casanova Jack will fill your gullet with a burger ($5.25 with fries) and steal your heart. On Thursday through Saturday nights, the spacious halls fill with live music and local crowds. (Open daily 11am-2am or later.)

■■■ COEUR D'ALENE

When French and English fur traders passed through northern Idaho in the late 1800s, they attempted to trade with the local Native Americans, who weren't interested. The trappers' french-speaking Iroquois guides dubbed the dismissive natives "people with pointed hearts," which the trappers shortened to "hearts of awls"—Coeur d'Alene. The gaggles of tourists can do little to mar the rustic beauty of this spot. No matter how many people clutter the beaches near the tastefully developed resort town, the deep blue waters of Lake Coeur d'Alene offer a serene escape.

Practical Information Get info at the **visitors center** (664-0587), at the corner of First and Sherman Ave. (open Mon.-Fri. 9am-5pm, Sat.-Sun. 10am-3pm). The **bus station** lies at 1527 Northwest Blvd. (664-3343), 1 mi. north of the lake (open daily 8am-8pm). **Greyhound** serves Boise (1 per day, 11hrs., $55), Spokane (3 per day, 45min., $9.75), Lewiston (2 per day, 3hrs., $30), and Missoula (3 per day, 4hrs., $34). **U-Save Auto Rental,** 302 Northwest Blvd. (664-1712), does the car rental thang. ($22 per day with 150 free mi, 20¢ per additional mi. Open Mon.-Fri. 8am-6pm, Sat. 8am-3pm, Sun. 10am-4pm.) For help in a personal crisis, call **Crisis Services** at 664-1443 (24 hrs.). Coeur d'Alene's **post office:** 111 N. 7th St. (664-8126), 5 blocks east of the Chamber of Commerce off Sherman Ave. (open Mon.-Fri. 8:30am-5pm); **ZIP code:** 83814; **area code:** 208.

Accommodations, Camping, and Food Cheap lodgings are hard to find in this unpretentiously touristy resort town. Try the motels on Sherman Ave., on the eastern outskirts of the city. **Star Motel,** 1516 E. Sherman Ave. (664-5035), fits phones and TVs with HBO in its tidy cubicles (singles $30, doubles $35-40). Across the street, **Budget Saver Motel,** 1519 Sherman Ave. (667-9505), competes with roomier accommodations (singles $35, doubles $42-47; late Sept.-early June $30/$37-40). Near Silver Mt., about 35 mi. east of Coeur d'Alene, the **Kellogg International Hostel,** 834 W. McKinley Ave. (783-4171), has laundry facilities, TV, VCR, and 30 beds. (April-Oct. $10; Nov.-March $12.)

Camping is the way to go for cheap lodging in Coeur d'Alene. There are five **campgrounds** within 20 mi. of Coeur d'Alene. **Robin Hood RV Park,** 703 Lincoln Way (664-2306), lies within walking distance of downtown and just a few blocks from a swimmable beach (sites $15.50; showers, laundry, hookups, no evil sheriffs). There are a few first come, first served national forest campgrounds in the area: popular **Beauty Creek,** 10 mi. south from Robin Hood along the lake; **Honeysuckle Campground,** 25 mi. northeast, with 9 sites; and **Bell Bay,** on Lake Coeur d'Alene (off U.S. 95 south, then 14mi. to Forest Service Rd. 545), with 26 sites and good fishing. All sites cost $8 and have access to potable water and pit toilets; the campgrounds are generally open May through September. Call the **Fernan Ranger District Office** (769-3000), for details on these and other forest campgrounds (open Mon.-Fri. 7:30am-4pm). **Farragut State Park** (683-2425), 20 mi. north on U.S. 95, is an extremely popular 4000-acre park dotted with hiking trails and beaches along Lake Pend Oreille (pon-do-RAY). (Sites $9, with hookup $12. $2 day-use fee for motor vehicles. Open late May-early Oct.)

Coeur d'Alene has oysters aplenty. If you like your snacks to come without shells, sit at the sidewalk tables at the "Wake up and Live" **Java Café,** 324 Sherman Ave. (667-0010); sip gourmet coffee, eat confetti eggs for breakfast ($3.50), or gourmet pizza for lunch ($4-5; open Mon.-Sat. 7am-11pm, Sun. 7am-6pm). Create your own sandwich ($4.25) at **Spooner's,** 215 Sherman Ave. (667-7666); ice cream will set you back $1-3 (open daily 7:30am-10pm; off season 7am-6pm). Revere the scorching power of the chile and the heroism of **Taco Dude,** 415 Sherman Ave. (666-9043). Only the pain of the *muy* hot salsa will keep you from laughing at the ridiculous anthropomorphic chili figures on the wall. (Tacos, etc. $1.25-$5. Open Sun.-Thurs. 11am-9pm, Fri.-Sat. 11am-10pm.) **Down the Street,** 1613 E. Sherman Ave. (765-3868) neatly serves up crispy homefries and fresh biscuits and gravy as part of its $2-5 breakfasts.

Sights and Activities The lake is Coeur d'Alene's *raison d'être.* Hike 2 mi. up **Tubbs Hill** to a scenic vantage point, or head for the **Coeur d'Alene Resort** and walk along the **world's longest floating boardwalk** (3300 ft.). You can tour the lake on a **Lake Coeur d'Alene Cruise** (765-4000) and see the world's only floating golf green. (Departs from the downtown dock May-Sept. 1:30, 3:30, and 5:30pm; 90 min.; $10.75, seniors $9.75, kids $5.75.) Rent a canoe from **Eagle Enterprises** (664-1175), at the city dock, to explore the lake ($7 per hr., $20 per ½ day, $35 first whole day, $15 per day thereafter). A 3-mi. bike/foot path follows the lake shore.

Four Seasons Outfitting, 200 Sherman Ave. (765-2863), organizes horse rides ($13 first 45min., $36 for 3hr.) and a variety of other expensive outdoor activities. Call in advance.

■ NEAR COEUR D'ALENE

Look 55 mi. east of Coeur d'Alene on I-90 for the **Wallace Mining Museum,** 509 Bank St. (556-1592), which features turn-of-the-century mining equipment (open daily 8am-8pm; off season hours vary. $1.50, seniors $1, kiddies 50¢). Next door, take the **Sierra Silver Mine Tour** (752-5151) through a depleted silver mine. (1-hr. tours May-Sept. daily every 30min. 9am-4pm; July-Aug. 9am-6pm. $7, seniors and under 12 $6.) Peek at Wallace's once-rollicking nightlife at the **Oasis Bordello Museum,** 605 Cedar St. (753-0801), an old-fashioned brothel-turned-museum with elaborate displays of lingerie that will stimulate the serious historian's imagination (½-hr. tours $4). Ride the **world's longest gondola** up Silver Mountain from Kellogg, 20 mi. north of Coeur d'Alene on U.S. 95. The gondola can transport mountain bikes. (783-1111; $10, students and seniors $8, kids under 6 free; chairlift rides $2.) "Rise and dine" packages (gondola ride and dinner) are also popular. (Open mid-May to early Oct. Mon.-Thurs. 10am-6pm, Fri.-Sat. 10am-10pm, Sun. 10am-9pm.)

Montana

Despite the recent acquisition of large amounts of acreage by such Eastern celebrities as Ted Turner, Tom Brokaw, and Liz Claiborne, Montana still has 25 million acres of national forest and public lands. In Big Sky country, the populations of elk, deer, and pronghorn antelope outnumber the humans. Cattle ranches bespeckle the plains of the east, while grizzlies and glaciers grace the Rockies of the western regions. Copious fishing lakes, 500 species of wildlife (not including millions of insect types), and thousands of ski trails make Montana a nature-lover's paradise.

PRACTICAL INFORMATION

Capital: Helena.

Travel Montana: P.O. Box 200533, Helena 59620 (406-444-2654 in MT or 800-541-1447). Write for a free *Montana Travel Planner.* **National Forest Information,** Northern Region, Federal Bldg., 200 E. Broadway, Box 7669, Missoula 59801 (406-329-3511). Gay and lesbian tourists can contact **PRIDE!,** P.O. Box 775, Helena 59624 (406-442-9322), for info on Montana gay community activities.

Time Zone: Mountain (2hr. behind Eastern). **Postal Abbreviation:** MT

Sales Tax: 0%.

■■■ BILLINGS

The railstop town founded by Northern Pacific Railroad president Fredrick Billings in 1882 still rumbles with the passage of freight trains. Despite heavy development Billings retains a deserted feel; strip malls and chains punctuate the sparse, industrial atmosphere, and sights are few and far between. Located at the junction of I-90 and I-94, Billings has become more of a stopover than a destination. Both **Greyhound** and **Rimrock Trailways** operate from 2502 1st Ave. N. (245-5116); buses run to Bozeman (4 per day, $19), Missoula (3 per day, $41), Bismarck (3 per day, $57.50), Seattle (3 per day, $105), and Cheyenne (2 per day, $99). The station is open 24 hrs.

Street names in Billings are confusing; three streets may have the same name, distinguished only by direction. Invest in a $1 city map at the Chamber of Commerce's **visitors center,** 815 S. 27th St. (252-4016); while you're there, check out the electronic map which highlights good hiking and fishing areas (open daily 8:30am-7:30pm, off season 8:30am-5pm). Montana State University's **Lambda Alliance** (657-2951) has info on local gay and lesbian activities. See the town, or leave quickly, in a car from **Rent-a-Wreck,** 5002 Laurel Rd. (252-0219). Rentals start at $28.50 per day or $185 per week (less in winter), with 100 free mi. per day and a 19¢ charge per additional mi. (Must be 21 with credit card and liability insurance. Open Mon.-Fri. 8am-5:30pm, Sat. 9am-2pm, Sun. by appt.) Billings's **post office:** 2200 Grant Rd. (657-5732; open Mon.-Fri. 8am-5:30pm); **ZIP code:** 59108; **area code:** 406.

Billings offers a generic potluck of accommodations. The **Picture Court,** 5146 Laurel Rd. (252-8478), rents cozy, well-kept, affordable rooms with A/C and TV (check-out 10:30am; singles $29, doubles $35). Though the **Rainbow Motel,** 421 St. Johns (259-4949), is inexpensive, women and lone travelers should be advised that it is not in the safest part of town. (A/C, TV, laundry facilities; pot of gold not included. Singles $25, doubles $35; weekly rooms with kitchenettes $120.) **Motel 6** has two locations here, 5400 Midland Rd. (252-0093) and 5353 Midland Rd. (248-7551); they charge the same rates, but the former has a pool. (Check-out noon. Singles $33, doubles $39, 3rd or 4th person $3, under 18 free; AARP discount 10%.)

You can try your luck at slot machines in a number of downtown hamburger and pizza joints, but the strips outside of town have more interesting food. Allow **Dos Machos** (652-2020), 24th St. W. at Phyllis, or 1233 N. 7th St. (259-1980), to test your stomach capacity with a crowded combination plate of such Mexican favorites as tacos and enchiladas ($6-8). Celebrate your clean plate with an $11 pitcher of margaritas. (Open Mon.-Sat. 11am-10pm, Sun 9am-9pm). **Khanthaly's Laotian Cuisine,** 1301 Grand Ave. (259-7252), serves tasty Southeast Asian fast food (fried rice noodles, spring rolls, etc.) at rates more likely to be found in Laos than the U.S. ($1-4; open Mon.-Sat. 11am-9pm, Sun. noon-8pm). **The Happy Diner,** 1045 Grand Ave. (248-5100), has burgers from $2.15 and pie slices for $1.60 (open Mon.-Thurs. 11am-10pm, Fri.-Sat. 11am-10:30pm).

The creations of Montana artists evoke the ranging, independent spirit of the West at the **Yellowstone Art Center,** 401 N. 27th St. (256-6804; open Tues.-Wed. and Fri.-Sun. 10am-5pm, Thurs. 10am-8pm; free). The outdoor recreation department at **Montana State University,** 2522 Normal Ave. (657-2882, line open Mon.-Fri. noon-6pm), offers canoeing classes and other outdoor activities; continue up the hill on Normal Ave. for a fantastic view of Billings and the surrounding valley. Look for the **Billings Summer Fair** the third weekend in July.

■■■ BOZEMAN

Wedged between the Bridger and Madison Mountains, Bozeman keeps on growing in Montana's broad Gallatin River Valley. The valley, originally settled by farmers who sold food to Northern Pacific Railroad employees living in the neighboring town of Elliston, now supplies food to a large portion of southern Montana. The presence of Montana State University makes Bozeman more accommodating to young wanderers and latter-day hippies than most Montana towns.

Practical Information The **Bozeman Area Chamber of Commerce,** 1205 E. Main St. (586-5421), provides ample info on local events (open Mon.-Fri. 8am-5pm). **Lambda Alliance** (994-4551) has local gay and lesbian info and an advocacy group. **Greyhound** and **RimRock Stages** serve Bozeman from 625 N. 7th St. (587-3110). Greyhound runs to Butte (3 per day, 1½hr., $13) and Billings (4 per day, 3hr., $19). RimRock buses to Helena (1 per day, 2hr., $14) and Missoula (3 per day, 5hr., $26). (Open Mon.-Fri. 7:30-11:30am, 12:30-5:30pm, and 8:30-10pm, Sat. 7:30-11:30am, 3:30-5:30pm, and 8:30-10pm, Sun. and holidays 7:30-9:15am, 3;30-5:30pm, and 8:30-10pm.) **Rent-a-Wreck,** 112 N. Tracey St. (587-4551), will put you in a well-worn auto for $29 per day. (100 free mi., 18¢ each additional mi. Must be 21 with major credit card. Open Mon.-Fri. 8am-6pm, Sat. 8am-5pm, Sun. by appt.)

Bozeman's **post office:** 32 E. Babcock St. (586-1508; open Mon.-Fri. 9am-5pm); **ZIP code:** 59715; **area code:** 406.

Accommodations Summer travelers in Bozeman support a number of budget motels along Main St. and on 7th Ave. north of Main. The **Sacajawea International Backpackers Hostel,** 405 West Olive St. (586-4659), offers travelers showers, laundry facilities, a full kitchen, and transportation to trailheads. There are only 10 beds ($10, kids $5); call ahead. Owners can give advice on where to eat, drink, hang out, and hike; they even rent bikes (½ day $6, full day $10). The **Ranch House Motel,** 1201 E. Main St. (587-4278), has free cable TV and A/C (singles $26, doubles $31-36; in winter $22/$27-32). For a bit more, the **Alpine Lodge,** 1017 E. Main St. (586-0356), provides clean, small rooms with soft carpets and venetian blinds (singles $30, doubles $42; cabins with kitchen $55, in winter $45).

Food and a Museum Whole sandwiches at **The Pickle Barrel,** 809 W. College (587-2411), consist of giant loaves of fresh sourdough bread stuffed with succulent deli meats and fresh vegetables. Ask the friendly collegiate behind the counter for a hefty half sandwich ($4; open daily 10:30am-10pm; in winter 11am-10:30pm). **Brandi's,** 717 N. 7th (587-3848), has a great breakfast deal: two hotcakes for 50¢ or 2 eggs, hash browns, and toast for $1, with free coffee to boot (open 8am-9:30pm; breakfast 8am-noon). Hang out with the locals and create your own delicious deep-dish pizza (from $11.50) at **McKenzie's River Pizza** (587-0055), on E. Main St. (open Mon.-Sat. 11:30am-10pm, Sun 5-9pm). The **Haufbrau,** 22 S. 8th Ave. (587-4931), serves grilled delights (burger with fries and salad $3.30) at well-worn, carved wooden tables or at the bar. Wash down your meal with a pint of draft (10 beers on tap; pints $1.25-2.50, pitchers $6-9) and sit back for the nightly performance by a local musician. Led Zeppelin's Robert Plant recommends the Black Dog Ale at **Spanish Peaks Brewery,** 1290 N. 19th Ave. (585-2296). Pints are $2.50, and a sampler of all their beers goes for $5—try the honey-raspberry (mmm!).

Yogi, Smokey, and a number of scarier, grizzlier bears prowl the halls of the **Museum of the Rockies,** 600 W. Kagy Blvd. (994-2251), immediately south of the MSU campus. Combining big-city quality with small-town charm, the museum contains a number of immaculately explained exhibits. The impressive dinosaur halls alone justify the visit; see the bones of the largest T. Rex ever found (excavated in Montana) and the world's only extant Triceratops family (actually, three scarily convincing life-sized robots). (Open 8am-8pm; Labor Day-Memorial Day Mon.-Sat. 9am-5pm, Sun. 12:30pm-5pm.)

Fishing Surrounded by three renowned trout-fishing rivers—Yellowstone, Madison, and Gardiner—the small town of **Livingston,** about 20 mi. east of Bozeman off I-90, is an angler's heaven. The **Yellowstone Angler** (222-7130), located ½ mi. south of Livingston on U.S. 89, rents and sells fishing gear and wear (rod and reel rental $15, waders $15, inner tubes $20), provides licenses ($15 for 2 days), and answers queries about fishing conditions (open Mon.-Sat. 7am-6pm, Sun. 7am-5pm; Oct.-March Mon.-Sat. 7am-5pm). After a day of fly fishing, cast a line to **Livingston's Bar and Grill,** 130 N. Main St. (222-7909), where vast quantities of imported and domestic beer cheer up even the most luckless fisherfolk (open Mon.-Sat. 11:30am-11pm, Sun. 4-11pm).

■■■ LITTLE BIG HORN

Little Big Horn National Monument, 60 mi. southeast of Billings off I-90 on the Crow Reservation, marks the site of the United State's Seventh Cavalry's defeat at the hands of Sioux and Cheyenne warriors. George Armstrong Custer and his 225 men made their last stand here on June 25, 1876; the defeat was a grave setback in the U.S. government's efforts to deny the Native Americans of the Northern Plains the land ceded to them by the Laramie treaty. The recent renaming of the monument, formerly known as the Custer Battlefield Monument, signifies the U.S. government's admission that Custer acted purely offensively. White stone graves mark where the U.S soldiers fell; a somber stone monument, engraved with the names of the dead, covers the mass grave site where the soldiers are actually buried. The locations of Sioux casualties are not known, since their families and fellow warriors removed the bodies from the battlefield almost immediately. A 5-mi. self-guided audio tour ($10) will narrate you through the battle movements of both sides; you can also see the park on a 45-min. bus tour ($4, kids $3). The **visitors center** (638-2621) contains a modest museum including a small movie theater, an electronic map of the battlefield, and displays of the weapons used in the battle. (Museum and visitors center open daily 8am-8pm; in fall 8am-6pm; in winter 8am-4:30pm. Free. Monument open daily 8am-7:30pm. Entrance $4 per car, $2 per person.)

■■■ MISSOULA

Home to the University of Montana, Missoula is Montana's most happening college town. The Clark Fork River ripples through the mountains of western Montana here as nature-lovers, artists, and students rub elbows with ranchers. Health food and used bookstores complement a selection of funky delis and restaurants downtown.

Practical Information Traveling within Missoula is easy thanks to reliable city **buses** (721-3333; buses operate Mon.-Fri. 6am-7pm, Sat. 9:30am-6pm; fare 50¢). The **Missoula Chamber of Commerce,** 825 E. Front St. (543-6623), at Van Buren, provides bus schedules. (Open Mon.-Fri. 8:30am-7pm, Sat.-Sun 10am-5pm; Labor Day-Memorial Day daily 8:30am-5pm.) **Greyhound,** 1660 W. Broadway (549-2339), shuffles off to Bozeman (4 per day, 5hr., $26) and Spokane (3 per day, 3½hr., $35); **Intermountain Transportation** serves Whitefish (1 per day, 3½hr., $18), and **Rim-Rock Stages** buses to Helena (1 per day, 2½hr., $17) from the same terminal. **Enterprise Rent-a-Car,** 2201 W. Broadway (721-1888), rents year-old autos for low prices. ($27 per day with 150 free mi., 21¢ each additional mi.; rates go down in winter. Must be 21. Credit card deposit required.) The **Rape Crisis Line** (543-7606) is open 24 hrs. **Lambda Alliance** (523-5567) handles bisexual, gay, and lesbian advocacy. Missoula's **post office:** 1100 W. Kent (329-2200), at Brooks and South St. (open Mon.-Fri. 8am-6pm, Sat. 9am-1pm); **ZIP code:** 59801; **area code:** 406.

Accommodations Spend your nights in Missoula at the **Birchwood Hostel,** 600 S. Orange St. (728-9799), 13 blocks east of the bus station on Broadway, then 8 blocks south on Orange. The spacious, immaculate dorm rooms sleep 22. Laundry, kitchen, and bike storage facilities are available, and the friendly owner knows the area. (Open daily 5-10pm. HI members and cyclists $8, otherwise $9. Closed for 2 weeks in late Dec.) Cheap lodgings cluster along Broadway; check the quieter east end for a place to stay. Descend into the **Canyon Motel,** 1015 E. Broadway (543-4069 or 543-7251), for a roomy, comfortable, wood-paneled feel (A/C, cable TV; singles $25, doubles $30-35). **The Downtown Motel,** 502 E. Broadway (549-5191), has sunny rooms (singles $31, doubles $38-43). The year-round **Outpost Campground** (549-2016), 2 mi. north of I-90 on U.S. 93, provides showers, laundry facilities, and scattered woodsy shade (sites for 2 $10, with hookup $12).

Food and Nightlife Missoula's dining scene offers more than the West's usual steak and potatoes. Great, thrifty eateries line the downtown area, particularly between Broadway and Railroad St. and north of the Clark Fork River; a few more places lurk about the perimeter of the university campus south of the river. Many a Montana grizzly eats and thinks at the **Food for Thought Café,** 540 Daly Ave., where creative sandwiches, salads, and veggie dishes run $3-6 (open daily 7am-10pm). Every breakfast dish you ever imagined is under $5 at the **Old Town Café,** 127 W. Alder St. (728-9742); most can be sprinkled with salsa, granola, or simple salt and pepper, depending on your taste (open daily 6am-5pm). Both a restaurant and a natural food store, **Torrey's,** 1916 Brooks St. (721-2510), serves health food at absurdly low prices; seafood stir-fry $3.50. (Restaurant open Mon.-Sat. 11:30am-8:30pm; store open Mon.-Sat. 10am-8:30pm.) If you'd rather be happy than healthy, try the retro 1950s atmosphere of the **Uptown Diner** (542-2449), on Higgins near Main St. downtown. The rich creamy shakes and specialty ice cream dishes ($1.75-$3.75) from the fountain will overwhelm you. (Open Mon.-Sat. 7am-9pm, Sun. 8am-9pm.)

Discerning palates wash down cheap, filling bar food with pilsner, amber, and dark brews of Bayern beer from the **Iron Horse Brew Pub,** 100 W. Railroad Ave. (728-8866), at Higgins Ave. S. (open daily noon-midnight). For a larger selection and a rowdier crowd, try one of the 50 beers on tap at **Rhinoceros (Rhino's),** 158 Ryman Ave. (721-6061), a local favorite (open daily 11am-2am).

Outdoor Activities The outdoors are Missoula's greatest attraction. Located at the intersection of the Trans-America and the Great Parks bicycle routes, the town swarms with cycling enthusiasts. **Adventure Cycling,** 150 E. Pine St. (721-1776) can provide info about bike trails in the area, and **New Era Bicycles,** 741 S. Higgins (728-2080), can help you join the pack with a rental. ($15 for 24 hrs.; leave credit card for deposit. Open Mon.-Thurs. 9am-6pm, Fri. 9am-7pm, Sat. 10am-6pm.)

Other popular Missoula diversions include skiing, rafting, backpacking, and hiking. For specific information or equipment rentals, stop by area outdoor shops such as **Trailhead,** 110 E. Pine St. (543-6966), at Higgins St. Although priority goes to University of Montana students, tourists can sometimes take part in day hikes, overnight trips, and classes on outdoor activities organized by the outdoor program of the **University of Montana Department of Recreation** (243-5172), at Field House 116 (open Mon.-Fri. 9am-5pm, Sat. 9am-1pm). The **Rattlesnake Wilderness National Recreation Area,** a few mi. northeast of town off the Van Buren St. exit from I-90, makes for a great day of hiking. Wilderness maps ($3) are available from the **U.S. Forest Service Information Office,** 200 E. Broadway (329-3511; open Mon.-Fri. 7:30am-4pm). The Clark Fork, Blackfoot, and Bitterroot Rivers overflow with opportunities for float trips. The **Montana State Regional Parks and Wildlife Office,** 3201 Spurgin Rd. (542-5500), sells float maps ($3.50; open Mon.-Fri. 8am-5pm). For rafting trips to a time when the continent thing wasn't so complicated, visit **Pangaea Expeditions,** 180 S. 3rd (721-7719; $15 for 2hr., $25 per ½ day, $45 per day).

The **Historical Museum at Fort Missoula** (728-3476) on Fort Rd. off Reserve St., conducts exhibits and lectures on forestry, agriculture, mining, and community life. (Open Tues.-Sat. 10am-5pm, Sun. noon-5pm; Labor Day-Memorial Day Tues.-Sun. noon-5pm.) Missoula's hottest sight is the **Aerial Fire Depot Visitors Center** (329-4934), 7 mi. west of town on Broadway (Rte. 10, past the airport), where you'll learn to appreciate the courage aerial firefighters need in order to jump into flaming, roadless forests. (Open daily 8:30am-5pm; Oct.-April by appointment for large groups. Tours May.-Sept. every hr. except noon-1pm. Free.) The first Friday of every month occasions a touch of Missoula culture with open houses in all of the local museums and galleries (15 total); artists are present at some.

■ FROM MISSOULA TO GLACIER

The **Miracle of America Museum,** off U.S. 93 between Missoula and Glacier before you enter the town of **Polson,** houses one of the greatest collections of Americana in the country. Look for the reconstructed general store, saddlery shop, barber shop, and gas station among the jumbled collection of classic American kitsch. (Open April-Sept. Mon.-Sat. 8am-5pm, Sun. 2-6pm; any other time by chance or appointment. $2.) The **National Bison Range,** about 40 mi. north of Missoula on U.S. 93, was established in 1908 to protect bison. Before they were hunted to near-extinction, 50 million of these animals roamed the plains; the range is home to 300-500 of the imposing creatures today, as well as several other indigenous life forms. (Range open 7am-9:30pm, ranger office open 8am-4:30pm. Free.)

■■■ WATERTON-GLACIER PEACE PARK

Waterton-Glacier transcends international boundaries to encompass one of the most strikingly beautiful portions of the Rockies. Symbolizing the peace between the United States and Canada, the park provides sanctuary for many endangered bears, bighorn sheep, moose, mountain goats, and now the grey wolf.

Technically one park, Waterton-Glacier is, for all practical purposes, two distinct areas: the small **Waterton Lakes National Park** in Alberta, and the enormous **Glacier National Park** in Montana. Each park charges its own admission fee (in Glacier, $5 per week; in Waterton Lakes, CDN$5 per day, CDN$10 for 4 days), and you must go through customs to pass from one to the other. Several **border crossings** pepper the park: **Chief Mountain** at Rte. 17 (open May 19-May 31 9am-6pm; June 1-Sept. 17 7am-10pm; closed Sept. 18 to mid-May in 1996); **Piegan/Carway** at U.S. 89 (year-round daily 7am-11pm); **Trail Creek** at North Fork Rd. (open June-Oct. daily 9am-5pm); and **Roosville** on U.S. 93 (open year-round 24 hrs).

Since snow melt is an unpredictable process, the parks are usually in full operation only from late May to early September. To find out which areas of the park, hotels, and campsites will be open when you visit, contact the headquarters of either Waterton (403-859-2203) or Glacier (406-888-5441). The *Waterton Glacier Guide* has dates and times of trail, campground, and border crossing openings.

■ GLACIER, MT

Practical Information Glacier's layout is simple: one road enters through West Glacier on the west side, and three roads enter from the east at Many Glacier, St. Mary, and Two Medicine. West Glacier and St. Mary serve as the two main points of entry into the park, connected by **Going-to-the-Sun Road** ("The Sun"), the only road traversing the park. **U.S. 2** runs between West and East Glacier along 82 mi. of the southern park border. Look for the "Goat Lick" signs off Rte. 2 near **Walton.** Mountain goats often descend to the lick for a salt fix in June and July.

Ask about trail and campsite availability and local weather and wildlife conditions at any of the three visitors centers. **St. Mary** (732-4424) guards the east entrance of the park. (Open daily late May to mid-June 8am-5pm; mid-June to early Sept. 8am-9pm; Sept. 8am-5pm.) **Apgar** aids at the west entrance. (Open daily late April to mid-June 8am-5pm; mid-June to early Sept. 8am-8pm; Sept. 8am-5pm; Oct. 8am-4:30pm; after Oct. 31 open only on weekends.) A third visitor's center graces **Logan Pass** on Going-to-the-Sun Rd. (Open early to mid-June daily 9am-5pm; mid- to late June 9am-6pm; early July to mid-Sept. 9am-8pm.)

Amtrak (226-4452 or 800-872-7245) traces a dramatic route along the south edge of the park. Daily trains chug to West Glacier from Whitefish ($7), Seattle ($126), and Spokane ($63); Amtrak also runs from East Glacier to Chicago ($213) and Minneapolis ($189). **Rimrock Stages** (862-6700) is the only bus line that comes near the park (Kalispell). As with most of the Rockies, a car is the most convenient mode of transport, particularly within the park. **Rent-a-Wreck** rents used cars from two locations in the area: in Kalispell, 2425 U.S. 2 E. (755-4555; $30 per day); in East Glacier, at the Sears Motel (226-9293; $50 per day). Both locations offer 100 free mi. per day, and charge 20¢ for each additional mile. At both locations, you must be 21 with a major credit card. Glacier's post office: Lake McDonald Lodge, in the park (open Mon.-Fri. 9am-3:45pm); **ZIP code:** 59921; **area code:** 406.

Accommodations and Food Staying indoors within Glacier is absurd and expensive. **Glacier Park, Inc.** handles all lodging within the park and provides only the **Swiftcurrent Motor Inn** (732-5531), in Many Glacier Valley, for budget travelers. The Swiftcurrent has cabins without bathrooms for $26, or with two bedrooms for $35 (open mid-June to mid-Sept.). Motel rooms are available, but they cost twice as much. All advance reservations can be made through the distant offices of **Gla-**

cier Park, Inc., 925 Dial Corporate Center, Phoenix, AZ 85077-0928 (602-207-6000). Last-minute (1-2 days) reservations can be made at East Glacier Park (406-226-9311). Other than the Swiftcurrent, the company operates seven pricier lodges which open and close on a staggered schedule.

On the west side of the park, the cozy **North Fork Hostel** (888-5241), at the end of Beaver Dr. in **Polebridge,** makes an ideal base for exploring some of Glacier's most pristine areas. The bumpy 12-mi. trip up the dirt road is preparation for the propane and kerosene lamps, wood stoves, and outhouses which provide creature comforts at the hostel. (Dorm beds $12, $10 after 2 nights. Cabins $26. Linen $2. Log homes $35, weekly $200). The **Polebridge Mercantile Store** will replenish depleted supplies. A slice of homemade pie or a beer to revive flagged spirits can be had at the **Northern Lights Saloon** (open 4-9pm for food and 9-12pm for drinks). East of the town of Hungry Horse, the **Mountain Meadow RV Park and Campground** (387-9125), 9 mi. from the park entrance off U.S. 2, has 56 secluded sites, hot showers, and a stocked trout pond (tent sites $10, with hookup $16-19).

In the east, excellent, affordable lodging can be found just across the park border in **East Glacier,** on U.S. 2, 30 mi. south of the St. Mary entrance and about 5 mi. south of the Two Medicine entrance. **Brownies Grocery (HI-AYH),** 1020 Rte. 49 (226-4426), in East Glacier, has a yummy bakery and comfortable dorms in what is rumored to have once been a brothel. Rent bunks ($11, nonmembers $13), private rooms (singles $15, nonmembers $18; doubles $20/$23), or a family room (sleeps 4-6; $30). Next door, the **Whistle Stop Café** is an oasis of local gourmet creations (Huckleberry French Toast $5) made with fresh ingredients and individual flair. The **Backpacker's Inn Hostel,** 29 Dawson Ave. (226-9392), offers 20 clean beds, hot showers, and the invaluable advice of owners Pat and Renée Schur for only $8 per night (bring a sleeping bag or rent one for $1).

Camping Camping is a cheaper and more scenic alternative to indoor accommodations. All developed campsites are available on a first come, first camped basis; the most popular sites fill by noon. However, "Campground Full" signs sometimes stay up for days on end; look carefully for empty sites. All 10 campgrounds accessible by car are easy to find. Just follow the map distributed at the park entrance. **Sprague Creek** on Lake McDonald has 25 peaceful sites near the lake; arrive early to avoid those near the road. **Bowman Lake** (48 sites) and **Kintla Lake** (13 sites) rarely fill and offer scenic, lakeside sites. Neither has flush toilets, but they're the cheapest thing going ($8); the rest of the campgrounds cost $10 and you can flush to your little heart's content. **Two Medicine,** at the southeast corner of the park nearer to East Glacier, has 99 sites. **Apgar** (196 sites) and **Fish Creek** (180 sites) are in the southwest corner, near Lake McDonald. Some sites at Sprague, Apgar, and Avalanche remain reserved for bicyclists and pedestrians; trailers are prohibited. Campgrounds without running water in the surrounding national forests offer sites for $5. Check at the Apgar or St. Mary visitors centers for up-to-date information on conditions and vacancies at established campgrounds. Weather and the grizzlies adjust the operating dates at their whim.

In Touch with Nature *There are bears out there. Familiarize yourself with the precautions necessary to avoid a run-in with a bear; consult rangers for advice. We're serious.* **Backcountry trips** are the best way to appreciate the mountain scenery and the wildlife which make Glacier famous. The **Highline Trail** from Logan Pass is a good day hike through prime bighorn sheep and mountain goat territory, although locals consider it too crowded. The visitors center's free *Nature with a Naturalist* pamphlet has a hiking map marked with distances and backcountry campsites. All backcountry campers must obtain in person a free wilderness permit from a visitors center or ranger station no more than 24 hrs. in advance; backcountry camping is allowed only at designated campgrounds. The **Two Medicine** area in the southeast corner of the park is well traveled, while the treks to

Kintla Lake and **Numa Lake** reward you with fantastic views of nearby peaks. **Belly River** is an isolated and pretty spot to stake a tent for an overnight wilderness stay.

Going-to-the-Sun Rd. runs a beautiful 52-mi. course through the park. Even on cloudy days, the constantly changing views of the peaks will have you struggling to keep your eyes on the road. Snow clogs the road until June, so check with rangers for exact opening dates. All vehicles must be under 21 ft. long and under 8 ft. wide.

Although "The Sun" is a popular **bike route,** only experienced cyclists with appropriate gear and legs of titanium should attempt this grueling ride. The sometimes nonexistent shoulder of the road creates a hazardous situation for cyclists: in the summer (June 15-Sept. 2), bike traffic is prohibited 11am-4pm from the Apgar turn-off at the west end of Lake McDonald to Sprague Creek, and from Logan Creek to Logan Pass. The east side of the park has no such restrictions. Bikes are not permitted on any hiking trails. **Equestrian** explorers should check to make sure trails are open; fines for riding on closed trails are steep.

While in Glacier, don't overlook the interpretive programs offered through the park. Ask about **jammers,** the red tour buses that snake around the park ($2-30); there are also regular shuttles for hikers ($2-14) that tour the length of The Sun. Get a schedule at any visitors center. Visitors centers also provide the day's menu of guided hikes, lectures, bird-watching walks, and children's programs.

Boating and Fishing **Boat tours** explore all of Glacier's large lakes. Tours leave from **Lake McDonald** (4-5 per day, 1hr., $7, ages 4-12 $3.50) and **Two Medicine** (5 per day, 45min., $6.50/$3.25). The tours from **St. Mary** (90min.) and **Many Glacier** (75min.) provide access to Glacier's backcountry (from St. Mary $8.50/$4.25; from Many Glacier $8/$4). The $7 sunset cruise proves a great way to see this quotidian phenomenon which doesn't commence until about 10pm in the middle of the summer. Call Lake McDonald (888-5727), Many Glacier (732-4480), or St. Mary (732-4430) for information. **Glacier Raft Co.** (888-5454 or 800-332-9995), in West Glacier, hawks full- and half-day trips down the middle fork of the Flathead River. A full-day trip (lunch included) costs $62, under 13 $33; ½-day trips ($32/$21) leave in the morning and the afternoon. Call for reservations.

Rent **rowboats** ($6 per hr., $30 per 10 hr.) at Lake McDonald, Many Glacier and Two Medicine; **canoes** ($6.50 per hr.) at Many Glacier, Two Medicine, and Apgar; and **outboards** ($11 per hr., $55 per 10 hr.) at Lake McDonald. All require a $50 deposit. Fishing is excellent in the park—cutthroat trout, lake trout, and even the rare Arctic Grayling challenge the angler's skill and patience. No permit is required—just be familiar with the rules, as explained in the pamphlet *Fishing Regulations,* available at all visitors centers. Right outside the park, however, on Blackfoot Indian land, you need a special permit, and anywhere else in Montana you need a Montana permit.

■ WATERTON LAKES, AB

Only a fraction of the size of its Montana neighbor, Waterton Lakes National Park offers spectacular scenery and activities without the crowds that plague Glacier during the peak months of July and August.

Practical Information The only road from Waterton's park entrance leads 5 mi. south to **Waterton.** On the way, grab a copy of the *Waterton-Glacier Guide* at the **Waterton Visitor Center,** 215 Mountain View Rd. (859-2224), 5 mi. inside the park (open daily 8am-8pm; mid-May to June daily 10am-5:30pm). Rent **bikes** from **Pat's Texaco and Cycle Rental,** Mount View Rd., Waterton townsite (859-2266; mountain bikes $5.50 per hr.; $27 per day; damage deposit $20). In a medical **emergency,** call an **ambulance** (859-2636). The **police station** (859-2244) is on Waterton Ave. at Cameron Falls Dr. Waterton's **post office**: Fountain Ave. at Windflower (open Mon., Wed., and Fri. 8:30am-4:30pm, Tues. and Thurs. 8:30am-4pm); **postal code**: T0K 2M0; **area code:** 403.

Accommodations, Camping, and Food As you enter the park, marvel at the enormous **Prince of Wales Hotel** (859-2231 or 602-207-6000), where you can have tea while maintaining a proper distance from the common townsite. Pitch a tent at one of the park's three campgrounds. **Crandell** (sites $12), on Red Rock Canyon Rd., and **Belly River** (sites $9), on Chief Mountain Hwy., are cheaper and farther removed from the hustle and bustle characteristic of townsite life. **Backcountry camping** is $5 per site and requires a permit from the visitor center (see above) or from **Park Headquarters and Information,** Waterton Lakes National Park, 215 Mount View Rd., Waterton AB T0K 2M0 (859-2224; open Mon.-Fri. 8am-4pm). The backcountry campsites are rarely full, and several, including beautiful **Crandell Lake,** are less than an hour's walk from the trailhead.

If you prefer to stay indoors, head straight for the **Mountain View Bed and Breakfast,** Box 82, Mountain View, AB T0K 1N0 (653-1882), 20km east of the park on Hwy. 5, where you'll enjoy comfy beds, true down-home hospitality, and a hearty breakfast, including homemade bread. (Singles $25, doubles $45.) Don Anderson, the owner, also runs a fishing guide service and can supply you with gear. Don will keep you entertained and educated with stories of more than 50 years of living in the area. If you insist on having a bed in Waterton, drop by the **Waterton Pharmacy,** on Waterton Ave. (859-2335), and ask to sleep in one of the nine rooms of the **Stanley Hotel** (singles or doubles $45; no shower or private bath).

Waterton is sorely lacking in budget restaurants; the most attractive option in the townsite is **Zum's,** 116B Waterton Ave. (859-2388), which serves good cheeseburgers on a pleasant patio for $3.50 (open daily 8am-9pm). Stock up on dried meat and granola at the **Rocky Mountain Foodmart** (859-2526) on Windflower Ave. (open daily 8am-10pm). Nothing gets cheaper by being trucked out to Waterton. Buy your groceries outside the park for substantial savings.

Outdoors If you've brought only hiking boots to Waterton, you can set out on the **International Lakeside Hike,** which leads along the west shore of Upper Waterton Lake and delivers you to Montana some 5 mi. after leaving the town. The **Crypt Lake Trail,** voted Canada's best hike in 1981, leads past waterfalls in a narrow canyon, and through a 20m natural tunnel bored through the mountainside to arrive after 4 mi. at icy, green Crypt Lake, which straddles the international border. To get to the trailhead, you must take the **water taxi** run by the **Waterton Shoreline Cruises** (859-2362). The boat runs twice a day ($10, ages 4-12 $5). The marina also runs a 2-hr. boat tour of Upper Waterton Lake ($16, ages 13-17 $12, ages 4-12 $8; open mid-May to mid-Sept.).

Anglers will appreciate Waterton's **fishing.** Fishing in the park requires a **license** ($4 per day, $6 per week, $13 per year), available from the park offices, campgrounds, wardens, and service stations in the area. Lake trout cruise the depths of **Cameron** and **Waterton Lakes,** while northern pike prowl the weedy channels of **Lower Waterton Lake** and **Maskinonge Lake.** Most of the backcountry lakes and creeks support populations of rainbow and brook trout. Try the nameless creek that spills from Cameron Lake about 200m to the east of the parking lot, or hike 1.5km in to Crandell Lake for plentiful, hungry fish. You can rent a **rowboat, paddleboat,** or **canoe** at Cameron Lake for $8 per hour. **Alpine Stables** (859-2462, in winter 403-653-2449), 2½ mi. north of the townsite, conducts trail rides of varying lengths. (1-hr. ride $15, all-day $77).

In the evening, take in a free **interpretive program** at the **Falls** or **Crandell Theatre.** These interesting programs change yearly and have funky titles, like *Bearying the Myths,* which offers straight talk about bears. There are programs daily in summer at 8:30pm; contact the visitor center for schedule information.

Wyoming

The ninth-largest state in the Union, Wyoming is also the least populated. This is a place where men wear cowboy hats and boots for *real,* and livestock outnumber citizens. Yet this rugged land was more than just a frontier during westward expansion; it was the first state to grant women the right to vote without later repealing it. With the country's first national monument (Devils Tower) and first national park (Yellowstone) within its borders, Wyoming has everything you'd want to see in a state in the Rockies: a Frontier Days festival, national parks, spectacular mountain ranges, breath-taking panoramas, and, of course, cattle and beer.

PRACTICAL INFORMATION

Capital: Cheyenne.

Wyoming Information and Division of Tourism, I-25 and College Dr., Cheyenne 82002 (307-777-7777; 800-225-5996 outside WY; open daily 8am-5pm). Write for the free *Wyoming Vacation Guide.* **Department of Commerce, State Parks and Historic Sites Division,** 2301 Central Ave., Cheyenne 82002 (307-777-6323). Information on Wyoming's 10 state parks. Open Mon.-Fri. 8am-5pm. **Game and Fish Department,** 5400 Bishop Blvd., Cheyenne 82006 (307-777-4600). Open Mon.-Fri. 8am-5pm.

Time Zone: Mountain (2hr. behind Eastern). **Postal Abbreviation:** WY

Sales Tax: 6%.

■■■ YELLOWSTONE

Six hundred thousand years ago, intense volcanic activity fueled a catastrophic eruption that spewed out nearly 35 trillion cubic feet of debris, creating the central basin of what is now **Yellowstone National Park.** Although these geologic engines have downshifted, they still power boiling, sulfuric pits, steaming geysers, and smelly mudpots. John Colter's descriptions of his 1807 explorations of this earthly inferno inspired fifty years of popular stories about "Colter's Hell." By 1872, popular opinion had swayed and President Grant declared Yellowstone a national park, the world's first. Today, Yellowstone's natural beauty is cluttered with cars, RVs, and thousands of snapshot-shooting, finger-pointing tourists. Still, in the backcountry, away from the crowds and geothermic anomalies that line the roads, you can survey the bears, elk, moose, wolves, bison, and bighorn sheep that thrive in the park's quieter peaks and valleys. In 1988, a blaze charred a third of Yellowstone; rangers have set up exhibits throughout the park to explain the fire's effects.

PRACTICAL INFORMATION

Tourist Office: Most regions in this vast park have their own center/station. The district rangers have a good deal of autonomy in making regulations for hiking and camping, so check in at each area. All centers have backcountry permits and guides for the disabled, or a partner ranger station that does. Each center's display focuses on the attributes of its region of the park: **Albright Visitors Center** at **Mammoth Hot Springs** (344-2263), natural and human history; **Grant Village** (242-2650), wilderness; **Old Faithful/Madison** (545-2750), geysers; **Fishing Bridge** (242-2450), wildlife and Yellowstone Lake; **Canyon** (242-2550), natural history and history of the canyon area. All stations are open Memorial Day to Labor Day daily 8am-7pm; Nov.-Memorial Day 9am-5pm; call for hours between Labor Day and Nov. The **Norris** (344-2812) station houses the park museum. Open Memorial Day-Labor Day daily 9am-6pm, Nov.-late May 9am-5pm. **Tower/Roosevelt Ranger Station** (344-7746) has temporary exhibits. Open daily 8am-5pm. *Yellowstone Today,* the park's activities guide, has a thorough listing of tours and programs. For general park information, campground availability, and emergencies call or write the Superintendent, Mammoth Hot Springs, Yellowstone National Park 82190 (344-7381). Headquarters open Mon.-Fri. 9am-5pm. **West Yellowstone Chamber of Commerce,** 100 Yellowstone Ave., West Yellowstone, MT 59758 (406-646-7701). Located 2 blocks west of the park entrance. Open daily 8am-8pm; Labor Day-Memorial Day 8am-5pm.

Tours: TW Services, Inc. (344-7311, TDD 344-5395). 9-hr. bus tours of the lower portion of the park leave daily from lodges ($25, ages 12-16 $12, under 12 free). Similar tours of the northern region leave from Canyon Lodge, Lake Hotel, and Fishing Bridge RV Park ($17-22). Full-day tours around the park's figure-eight road system also available, leaving from Gardiner, MT and Mammoth Hot Springs ($25, ages 12-16 $12). Individual legs of this network of tour loops can get you as far as the Grand Tetons or Jackson, but the system is inefficient and costs much more than it's worth.

Buses: Greyhound (800-231-2222). No local office; pick-up at Chamber of Commerce at West Yellowstone. To: Bozeman (1 per day, 2hr., $13); Salt Lake City (1 per day, 9hr., $49).

Car Rental: Big Sky Car Rental, 429 Yellowstone Ave., West Yellowstone, MT (406-646-9564 or 800-426-7669). $30 per day, unlimited mi. Must be 21 with a credit card or passport. Open Mon.-Sat. 8am-5pm, Sun. 8am-noon; Nov.-April hours vary.

Bike Rental: Yellowstone Bicycles, 132 Madison Ave., West Yellowstone, MT (406-646-7815). Mountain bikes $3.50 per hr., $12.50 per ½ day, $18.50 per day; with helmet and water bottle. Open daily 8:30am-9:30pm; Nov.-April 10am-8pm.

Horse Rides: TW Services, Inc. (344-7311). From Mammoth Hot Springs Hotel, Roosevelt Lodge, Canyon Lodge. Late May-early Sept. $15 per hr., $24 for 2hr.

Radio Information: Tune to 1610AM for park information.

Medical Services: Lake Clinic, Pharmacy, and **Hospital** (242-7241) at Lake Hotel. Clinic open late May-mid-Sept. daily 8:30am-8:30pm. Emergency Room open May-Sept. 24 hrs. **Old Faithful Clinic,** at Old Faithful Inn (545-7325), open early May to mid-Oct. daily 8:30am-5pm; closed Thurs. and Fri. May 5-27 and Sept. 15-Oct. 22. **Mammoth Hot Springs Clinic** (344-7965), open daily 8:30am-5pm; Sept.-July Mon.-Fri. 8:30am-5pm. You can always contact a ranger at 344-7381.

Emergency: 911.

Post Offices: Mammoth Hot Springs (334-7764), near the park headquarters. Open Mon.-Fri. 8:30am-5pm. **ZIP code:** 82190. In **West Yellowstone, MT,** 17 Madison Ave. (406-646-7704). Open Mon.-Fri. 8:30am-5pm. **ZIP code:** 59758. **Area codes:** 307 (in the park), 406 (in West Yellowstone and Gardiner). Unless otherwise listed, phone numbers have a 307 area code.

The bulk of Yellowstone National Park lies in the northwest corner of Wyoming, with slivers slicing into Montana and Idaho. **West Yellowstone, MT,** at the park's western entrance, and **Gardiner, MT,** at the northern entrance, are the most developed and expensive towns along the edge of the park. For a rustic stay, venture northeast to **Cooke City, MT.** The northeast entrance to the park leads to U.S. 212, a gorgeous stretch of road known as **Beartooth Highway,** which climbs to **Beartooth Pass** at 11,000 ft. and descends to **Red Lodge,** a former mining town. (Road open summer only because of heavy snowfall; ask at the chamber of commerce for exact dates.) The eastern entrance to the park from Cody is via Rte. 14/20. The southern entry to the park is through Grand Teton National Park.

The park's **entrance fee** is $10 for cars, $4 for pedestrians and bikers. The pass is good for one week at Yellowstone and Grand Teton National Parks.

Yellowstone's roads circulate its millions of visitors in a rough figure-eight configuration, with side roads branching off to park entrances and some of the lesser-known sites. The major natural wonders which make the park famous (e.g. Old Faithful) dot the Upper and Lower Loops. Construction and renovation of roads are planned for the next 80 years; call ahead to find out which sections will be closed during your visit. It's unwise to bike or walk around the deserted roads at night, since you may risk startling large wild animals. The best time to see the animals is at dawn or dusk. When they're out, traffic stops and cars pull over. Approaching any wild beast at any time is illegal and extremely unsafe, and those who don't remain at least 25 yds. from moody and unpredictable bison or moose and 100 yds. from bears risk being mauled or gored to death. For more tips on avoiding fisticuffs with a bear, see Bear Necessities, p. 47. Another danger is falling trees; dead trees can fall into a campsite or road with little or no warning. Near thermal areas, stay on marked trails, because "scalding water can ruin your vacation."

The park's high season extends from about June 15 to September 15. If you visit during this period expect large crowds, clogged roads and motels, and campsites filled to capacity.

ACCOMMODATIONS AND FOOD

Camping is far cheaper, but cabin-seekers will find many options within the park. Standard hotel and motel rooms for the nature-weary also abound, but if you plan to keep your budget in line, stick to the towns near the park's entry-points.

In The Park

TW Services (344-7311) controls all accommodations within the park with an iron fist, using a secret code for budget cabins: "Roughrider" means no bath, no facilities; "Frontier" means with bath, somewhat furnished; "Eggplant Jello" means you are probably delirious. All cabins or rooms should be reserved well in advance of the June to September tourist season. Be very choosy when buying food in the park, as the restaurants, snack bars, and cafeterias are quite expensive. If possible, stick to the **general stores** at each lodging location (open daily 7:30am-10pm).

Old Faithful Inn and Lodge, near the west Yellowstone entrance. Pleasant Roughrider cabins with sink ($21), "Economy" cabins (toilet and sink, $28), and Frontier cabins ($34). Well-appointed hotel rooms from $44, with private bath $62.

Roosevelt Lodge, in the northwest corner. A favorite campsite of Roughrider Teddy Roosevelt. Provides the cheapest and most scenic indoor accommodations around. Rustic shelters $21, each with a wood-burning stove (bring your own bedding and towel). Also Roughrider cabins ($24, bring your own towel) and more spacious "family" cabins with toilet ($39).

Mammoth Hot Springs, 18mi. west of Roosevelt area, near the north entrance. Unremarkable budget cabins $30. Frontier cabins from $59.

Lake Yellowstone Hotel and Cabins, near the south entrance. Overpriced, but very close to the lake. Spacious, frontier cabins $59.

Canyon Village, middle of the figure eight of the park loop, is less authentic and more expensive than Roosevelt Lodge's cabins, but slightly closer to the popular Old Faithful area. Frontier cabins $45. Roomier "Western" cabins $80.

West Yellowstone, MT

West Yellowstone International Hostel (AAIH/Rucksackers), 139 Yellowstone Ave. (406-646-7745 or 800-838-7745 outside MT), at the Madison Hotel and Motel. Friendly manager presides over old but clean, wood-adorned hotel. Hostel honors all memberships. Slightly crowded rooms; no kitchen. $15, nonmembers $17. Singles $24, with bath $37; doubles with bath $37-42. Rooms $2 cheaper in the spring. Open May 27 to mid-Oct.

Alpine Motel, 120 Madison (406-646-7544). Clean rooms with cable TV, a pool, and hand-crafted bed frames. Singles $45, doubles $47-59; off season $3 less.

Traveler's Lodge, 225 Yellowstone Ave. (406-646-9561). Comfortable, large rooms; ask for one away from the hot tub. Singles $58, off season $40; doubles $70. $5 discount if you rent a car from them (see Practical Information, above).

Gardiner, MT

Located about 90 minutes northeast of West Yellowstone, Gardiner served as the original entrance to the park and is smaller, friendlier, and less tacky than its neighbor. Pick a bundle of inexpensive food at **Food Farm,** 710 Scott St. W. (406-848-7524), across from the Super 8, or lasso some chow at the **Food Round-Up Gro-**

cery Store, 107 Dunraven St., W. Yellowstone (406-646-7501). Hearty Mexican favorites are served by **Señor Frog and Taco Tootie's,** down U.S. 89 near Park Ave., with beans and rice for $4. Tacos are 50¢.

The Town Café and Motel (406-848-7322), on Park St. across from the park's northern entrance. Pleasant, wood-paneled, carpeted rooms. TVs and baths but no showers or phones. Singles with kitchen $38, doubles $48.

Hillcrest Cottages (406-848-7353), on U.S. 89 near the crossing of the Yellowstone River. Singles with kitchen $45, doubles $50-56; $6 each additional adult, $3 each under 12.

Wilson's Yellowstone River Motel, 14 Park St. (406-848-7303). Large, well-decorated rooms, friendly manager. Singles $50, doubles $59; off season $45/$54.

Cooke City, MT

Cooke City is located at the northeast corner of the park. The Nez Perce slipped right by the U.S. cavalry here, Lewis and Clark deemed the area impassible, and many tourists today still miss the cheap lodging and **Joan and Bill's Family Restaurant** (406-838-2280), at 214 Rte. 212, which dishes out mean plates of homefries, $4 soup-sandwich specials, and $3-6 breakfast combos (open daily 6am-9:45pm).

After a day of tracking Yogi Bear, sniff out the bright, airy tent cabins at the **Yellowstone Yurt Hostel** (800-364-6242), at the corner of W. Broadway and Montana St., a quiet relief from the tourist traps which generally encrust the park. Cozy bunks, showers, and a kitchen are at your disposal for $10 a night. Check in before 9pm; call ahead if coming later. Ask about the shuttle to Bozeman, MT. You can also rest at the eastern end of town (there's only one street in Cooke, Rte. 212) at **Antler's Lodge** (406-838-2432), a renovated U.S. Cavalry outpost where Teddy Roosevelt once stayed. (Singles $35, doubles $45; larger cabins for families equipped with kitchens from $55.)

CAMPING

Sites can be reserved at five of Yellowstone's 12 developed campgrounds. TW Recreational Services controls **Canyon, Grant Village, Madison** (all $12.50), and **Fishing Bridge RV** ($20). Reservations can be made up to a year in advance or on the same day (307-344-3711), but sites tend to fill early. Madison (292 sites; open May-Oct.) fills by 11am. Canyon may have sites until 4pm. **Bridge Bay Campground** (420 sites; open late May to mid-Sept.) sits on treeless and non-scenic MISTIX turf, and accepts reservations up to eight weeks in advance (800-365-2267 or 619-452-5956).

Seven campgrounds provide first come, first served sites ($8-12). During summer, most of these campgrounds fill by 10am. Arrive very early, especially on weekends and holidays. Bring a stove or plan to search for or buy firewood. Two of the most beautiful and tranquil areas are **Slough Creek Campground** (29 sites, 10mi. northeast of Tower Junction; open late May-Oct.) and **Pebble Creek Campground,** 36 sites, 15 mi. farther down the same road (no RVs; open mid-June to early Sept.). Both offer relatively uncrowded spots and have good fishing. You can also try **Canyon Village,** with 208 sites on pine-tree-laden Lewis Lake. The popular and scenic campground at **Norris** (116 sites; open May-Sept.) fills early (by 11am), while others, such as **Pebble Creek** and **Lewis Lake** (10mi. from the southern entrance; 85 sites; open June-Oct.) may have sites until 4pm. **Indian Creek** (75 sites; open mid-June to mid-Sept.) and **Mammoth** (85 sites; open year-round) campgrounds are none too scenic. Except for **Mammoth Campground,** all camping areas close in winter. If all sites are full, try the $8 campgrounds outside the park in the **Gallatin National Forest** to the northwest. Good sites line U.S. 20, 287, 191, and 89. Call the Park Headquarters (344-7381) for info on any of Yellowstone's campgrounds.

The campgrounds at Grant, Fishing Bridge, and Canyon all have coin laundries and pay showers ($2, 50¢ for towel, 25¢ for soap). The lodges at Mammoth and Old Faithful have no laundry facilities but have showers for $2.

More than 95% (almost two million acres) of the park is backcountry. To venture overnight into the wilds of Yellowstone, you must obtain a free **wilderness permit** from a ranger station or visitors center. Pity the fool who doesn't consult a ranger before embarking on a trail; rangers can give instructions on which trails and campgrounds to avoid due to bears, ice, and other natural hindrances. Other backcountry regulations include sanitation rules, pet and firearms restrictions, campfire permits, and firewood rules. The more popular areas fill up in high season, but you can reserve a permit in person up to 48 hours in advance; campfire permits are not required, but ask if fires at your site are allowed.

SIGHTS AND ACTIVITIES

For mountains of cash, **TW Services** will sell you tours, horseback rides, and chuckwagon dinners until the cows come home. But given enough time, your eyes and feet will do a better job than TW's tours, and you won't have to sell your firstborn. The main attractions all feature informative self-guiding tour pamphlets with maps (25¢). All are accessible from the road by wooden or paved walkways, usually extending ¼ to 1½ mi. through the various natural phenomena. All of the walkways are partially wheelchair-accessible, until they connect with longer hiking trails.

Like spaghetti sauce on a very hot range, where steam pressure builds up at the bottom and explodes through the surface, ruining your shirt, groundwater is superheated by rocks and explodes through holes in the earth's crust in the form of a **geyser.** The geysers that made Yellowstone famous are clustered on the western side of the park near the West Yellowstone entrance. The duration of the explosion depends on how much water is in the hole and the heat of the steam. **Old Faithful,** while neither the largest, the highest, nor the most regular geyser, is certainly the most popular; it gushes in the **Upper Geyser Basin,** 16 mi. south of **Madison Junction** where the entry road splits north-south. Since its discovery in 1870, the granddaddy of geysers has consistently erupted with a whoosh of spray and steam (5000-8000 gallons worth) every 30 to 120 minutes. Enjoy other geysers as well as elk in the surrounding **Firehole Valley.** Swimming in any hot springs or geysers is prohibited, but you can swim in the **Firehole River,** three-quarters of the way up Firehole Canyon Drive (turn south just after Madison Jct.), or in the **Boiling River,** 2½ mi. north of Mammoth, which is not really hot enough to cook ramen, let alone pasta. Still, do not swim alone, and beware of strong currents.

From Old Faithful, take the easy 1½-mi. walk to **Morning Glory Pool,** a park favorite, or head 8 mi. north to the **Lower Geyser Basin,** where examples of all four types of geothermal activity (geysers, mudpots, hot springs, and fumaroles) steam, bubble, and spray together in a cacophonous symphony. Farther north, 14 mi. past Madison, is the **Norris Geyser Basin,** the setting for **Echinus,** a park gem. About every hour, this geyser slowly mounts its furious display from a clear basin of water. Its neighbor, **Steamboat,** is the largest geyser in the world, topping 400 feet and erupting for up to 20 minutes. Its huge emissions used to occur about once a year. This steamer currently toots on an erratic schedule, however; its last enormous eruption occurred on October 2, 1991.

Whether you're waiting for geysers to erupt or watching them shoot skyward, don't go too close, as the crust of earth around a geyser is only 2 ft. thick, and the Surgeon General has determined that falling into a boiling sulfuric pit *may* be hazardous to your health. Pets are not allowed in the basin. Check out the squirrel-type animals roaming around without much fur to understand why.

Shifting water sources, malleable limestone deposits, and temperature-sensitive, multicolored bacterial growth create the most rapidly changing natural structure in the park, the hot spring terraces at **Mammoth Hot Springs,** 20 mi. to the north. Ask a local ranger where the most active springs are on the day of your visit. Also ask about area trails, which feature some of the park's best wildlife viewing.

The east side's featured attraction, the **Grand Canyon of the Yellowstone,** wears rusty red-orange colors created by hot water acting on the volcanic rock. For a close-up view of the mighty Lower Falls, hike down the short but steep **Uncle Tom's**

Trail. To survey the canyon from a broader vista, try **Artist Point** on the south rim or **Lookout Point** on the northern rim. All along the canyon's 19-mi. rim, keep an eye out for bighorn sheep; at dawn or dusk the bear-viewing area (at the intersection of Northern Rim and Tower roads) should be loaded with opportunities to use your binoculars.

Yellowstone Lake, 16 mi. south of the Canyon's rim at the southeastern corner of the park, contains tons o' trout but requires a Yellowstone **fishing permit,** available at visitors centers. ($5 per week; 12-15 must get a free permit, under 12 may fish without a permit.) Catch a few and have the chef fry them for you in the Lake Yellowstone Hotel Dining Room. Some other lakes and streams allow catch-and-release fishing only. The **Hamilton Store** (242-7326), at Bridge Bay Dock, rents spinning rods ($7.50 per day, $20 deposit; open late May to mid-Sept. daily 7:30am-9pm). The expensive **Lake Yellowstone Hotel,** built in 1891 and renovated in 1989, merits a visit, if only for the magnificent view of the lake through the lobby's large windows. Walks around the lake are scenic and serene rather than strenuous. Nearby **Mud Volcano,** close to Yellowstone Lake, features seething, warping sulfuric earth and the **Dragon's Mouth,** a vociferous steaming hole that early explorers reportedly heard all the way from Yellowstone River. You'll smell it from that far away for sure.

Over 1200 mi. of trails crisscross the park, but many are poorly marked. Rangers of any visitor center are glad to recommend an array of **hikes** in their specific area for explorers of all levels. Most of the spectacular sights in the park are accessible by car, but only a hike will get you up close and personal with the multilayered petrified forest of **Specimen Ridge** and the geyser basins at **Shoshone** and **Heart Lake. Cascade Corner,** in the southwest, is a lovely area accessible by trails from Bechler. The already spectacular view from the summit of **Mt. Washburn,** between the **Canyon** and **Tower** areas, is enhanced when surveyed from the telescope inside the old fire lookout station. The **North Trail** is a mild incline; the **South Trail** is steeper. Trails in the **Tower-Roosevelt** area in the northeast of the park provides some of the most abundant wildlife watching. When planning a hike, pick up a topographical trail map ($7) at any visitors center and ask a ranger to describe forks in the trail. Allow yourself extra time (at least 1hr. per day) in case you lose the trail.

Federal Wolf Packs

In January 1995, after years of public debate, the federal government began to reintroduce gray wolves into the greater Yellowstone ecosystem. Before the program, the last known wolves in Yellowstone were killed in 1929 as part of a federally funded bounty hunt to eradicate the predators. Local and state response to the federal initiative has been mixed. Many ranchers have violently denounced the reappearance of wolves, fearing the wolves will kill livestock. Others hail the program as the first step in a return to a complete ecosystem. Montana's State Senate and House of Representatives responded with a caustic joint resolution that made their position clear: "Now, therefore, be it resolved that if the United States government is successful in its efforts to reintroduce wolves into the Yellowstone Park ecosystem, the U.S. Congress be urged to take the steps necessary to ensure that wolves are also reintroduced into every other ecosystem and region of the United States, including Central Park in New York City, the Presidio in San Francisco, and Washington, DC."

■■■ GRAND TETON

When French fur trappers first peered into Wyoming's wilderness from the eastern border of Idaho, they found themselves facing three craggy peaks, each over 12,000 ft. In an attempt to make the rugged landscape seem more trapper-friendly, they dubbed the mutant mountains "Les Trois Tetons," French for "the three tits." When they found that these triple nipples had numerous smaller companions, they named the entire range "Les Grands Tetons." Today the snowy heights of **Grand Teton**

National Park delight modern hikers and cyclists with miles of strenuous trails. The less adventurous will appreciate the rugged appearance of the Tetons; the lofty pinnacles and glistening glaciers are stunning even from below.

PRACTICAL INFORMATION

Tourist Offices: Moose (733-3399), Teton Park Rd. at the southern tip of the park. Open June-early Sept. daily 8am-7pm; early-Sept.-May 8am-5pm. **Jenny Lake** (739-3392), next to the Jenny Lake Campground. Open June-early Sept. daily 8am-7pm. **Colter Bay** (739-3594), on Jackson Lake in the north part of the park. Open early June-early Sept. daily 8am-8pm; May and early Sept.-early Oct. 8am-5pm. Park info brochures available in Braille, French, German, Japanese, Spanish, Hebrew. Topographical maps ($4, waterproof $7). Pick up the free *Teewinot* newspaper at entrance or at the visitors center for a list of park activities, lodgings, and facilities. For general info contact the **Park Headquarters** (739-3600 or 733-3300) or write Superintendent Grand Teton National Park, P.O. Drawer 170, Moose 83012. Office at the Moose Visitors Center.

Police: Sheriff's office, 733-2331

Equipment Rental: Venture Sports (733-3307), at Dornan's in Moose. Adult mountain bikes $6 per hr., $24 per day; kids $4/$14; includes helmet. Canoes $18.50 ½ day, $30 full day; kayaks $20/$40. Open daily 9am-6pm. Credit card or deposit required. **Fish-Moose** (733-3699), next to Venture Sports, rents spinning rods for $10 per day. Open late May to mid-Sept. daily 8am-6pm.

Park Information and Weather and Road Conditions: 733-3611. 24-hr. recording. **Wyoming Highway Info Center,** 733-3316 (winter only).

Medical Services: Grand Teton Medical Clinic, Jackson Lake Lodge (543-2514, after hours 733-8002), near the Chevron. Open late May to mid-Oct. daily 10am-6pm. In dire emergency, contact **St. John's Hospital** (733-3636), in Jackson.

Emergency: 911. Also 733-3301 or 543-2581.

Post Office: In **Moose** (733-3336), across from the Park HQ. Open Mon.-Fri. 8:45am-1pm and 1:30-5pm, Sat. 9-10:30am. **ZIP code:** 83012. **Area code:** 307.

The national park occupies most of the space between Jackson to the south and Yellowstone National Park to the north. **Rockefeller Pkwy.** connects the two parks and is open year-round. The park is directly accessible from all directions except the west, as those poor French trappers found out centuries ago. The park **entrance fee** is $10 per car, $4 per pedestrian or bicycle, $5 per family (non-motorized), under 16 (non-motorized) free. The pass is good for 7 days in both the Tetons and Yellowstone. There are several recreational areas; the most developed is **Colter Bay,** the most beautiful is **Jenny Lake** (sorry, no swimmy in the Jenny). For a cool, secluded dip, drive north to the **Lizard Creek Campground** and grab one of the highly prized lakeside camping spots.

CAMPING

To stay in the Tetons without emptying your savings account, find a tent and pitch it. Call 739-3603 for camping information. The park service maintains five campgrounds, all first come, first served (sites $10). All have restrooms, cold water, fire rings, dump stations, and picnic tables. RVs are welcome in all but the Jenny Lake area, but there are no hookups. Large groups can go to Colter Bay and Gros Ventre; all others allow a maximum of six people and one vehicle per site. With 49 quiet, woodsy sights, Jenny Lake is the most popular; *arrive early.* **Lizard Creek,** convenient to Yellowstone, has 60 coveted, secluded sites at the north end of the park. At **Signal Mountain,** a few miles south of Colter Bay, the 86 sites are a bit closer together and are usually full by 10am. **Colter Bay,** with 310 sites, showers, a grocery store, and a laundromat, is usually full by noon. **Gros Ventre,** 360 sites on the park's southern border, is the best bet if you arrive late. The maximum stay at Jenny Lake is seven days, at all others 14 days. Reservations are required for camping groups.

To feed your hungry RV water, sewer, and electricity try **Colter Bay RV Park,** which has 112 sites with full hookup, a grocery store, and eateries. (Sites $22; May

12-June 12 and Sept. 4-25 $17. Showers $2. Reserve through Grand Teton Lodge Co., 733-2811 or 543-2855.) Five mi. north of Grand Teton and 2 mi. south of Yellowstone on Rte. 89, **Flagg Ranch Village Camping** has 100 quickly filled RV sites with full hookups, groceries, and eateries. (1 or 2 adults $23; $1 per additional person. Reserve through Flagg Ranch Village, 543-2861 or 800-443-2311).

For **backcountry camping,** reserve a spot in a camping zone in a mountain canyon or on the shores of a lake by submitting an itinerary to the **permit office,** Grand Teton National Park, Moose HQ, Attn: Permits, P.O. Box 170, Moose 83012 (739-3309), from January 1 to May 15. Still, two-thirds of all spots are available first come, first served; get a permit up to 24 hours before setting out at the Moose, Colter Bay, or Jenny Lake visitors center (see Practical Information). Camping is unrestricted in some off-trail backcountry areas (though you must have a permit). Wood fires are not permitted above 7000 ft.; check with rangers about fires in the lower regions. The weather can be severe, even in the summer. All backcountry campers should take precautions.

ACCOMMODATIONS AND FOOD

The Grand Teton Lodge Co. (543-2855 or 800-628-9988 outside WY) runs both of the Colter Bay accommodations, which are open late May through early October. **Colter Bay Tent Cabins** (543-2855) are the cheapest, but you don't want to be here when the temperature drops. You might as well camp; the "cabins" are canvas shelters with dusty floors, wood-burning stoves, tables, and 4-person bunks. Sleeping bags, wood, and ice chests are available for rent. (66 cabins for 1 or 2 $22; $2.50 per additional person. Cots $4. Restrooms and $2 showers nearby. Office open June-early Sept. daily 7am-10pm.) **Colter Bay Log Cabins** (543-2855) maintains 208 quaint log cabins near Jackson Lake. (Room with semi-private bath $27, with private bath $55-77. 2-room cabins with bath $79-99. Open mid-May to late Sept.) Reservations are recommended. Make them up to a year in advance for any Grand Teton Lodge establishment through the Reservations Manager, Grand Teton Lodge Co., P.O. Box 240, Moran 83013; deposits are often required. **Flagg Ranch Village,** P.O. Box 187, Moran 83013 (543-2861 or 800-443-2311), lies on the Snake River, near the south entrance to Yellowstone. The brand-spanking new cabins are a good deal for a group. (Cabin for 2 $104, for 3-4 $109). For accommodations outside the park, see Jackson (p. 571).

The best way to eat in the Tetons is to bring your own grub. If this isn't possible, stick to whatever non-perishables you can pick up at the **Flagg Ranch Grocery Store** (543-2861 or 800-443-2311; open daily 7am-10pm; reduced winter hours) at Flagg Ranch (see Camping, above), or **Dornan's Grocery** in Moose (733-2415; open daily 8am-8pm, in winter 8am-6pm). In Jackson, stock up on provisions at **Albertson's** supermarket (733-5950; open daily 6am-midnight), on Broadway.

SIGHTS AND ACTIVITIES

While Yellowstone wows visitors with geysers and mudpots, Grand Teton's geology boasts some of the most scenic mountains in the U.S., if not the world. The youngest mountain range in North America, the Tetons stand alone, almost without foothills, providing hikers, climbers, rafters, and sightseers with vistas not found in more weathered peaks. The Grandest Teton rises 13,771 ft. above sea level.

Jenny Lake's tranquility overcomes the steady tramp of its many visitors. **Cascade Canyon Trail,** one of the least arduous and most popular hikes in the park, begins at the far end of the lake; to get there, hike the 2-mi. trail around the lake or rely on **Teton Boating** (733-2703), which shuttles across the lake every 20 minutes 8am-6pm ($3.25, ages 7-12 $2.25, under 7 free) and rents boats ($10 for the first hr., $7 per additional hr., $45 per day). Free trail guides are available near the visitors center at the trailhead. The **Hidden Falls Waterfall** plunges ½ mi. from the trail entrance; only the lonely can trek 6¾ mi. further to **Lake Solitude.**

Other **hiking trails** abound. The 4-mi. walk from Colter Bay to **Hermitage Point** is popular for the scope of wildlife it encounters. The **Amphitheater Lake Trail,** beginning just south of Jenny Lake at the Lupine Meadows parking lot, takes you 4.8 breathtaking mi. to one of the park's glacial lakes. Those who were bighorn sheep in past lives can butt horns with **Static Peak Divide,** a steep 15-mi. trail up 4020 ft. from the Death Canyon trailhead (4½mi. south of Moose visitors center) which offers some of the best lookouts in the park. All visitors centers (see Practical Information above) provide pamphlets about the day hikes and sell the *Teton Trails* guide ($5). **National Park Tours** (733-4325) offers tours as well. (Open 7am-9pm; Prices vary greatly depending on where you want to start. Reservations required.)

For a leisurely afternoon on Jackson Lake, **Signal Mountain Marina** (543-2831) rents boats. (Rowboats and canoes $8 per hr., $30 for 4hr., $55 for 8hr.; motorboats $15/$60/$90; water-ski boats $45/$150/$220 plus gas and oil; pontoons $40/$125/ $175. Open early May to mid-Oct. daily 8am-7pm.) **Colter Bay Marina** has a somewhat smaller variety of boats at similar prices (open daily 7am-8pm; rentals stop at 6pm). **Grand Teton Lodge Co.** (733-2811 or 543-2811) can also take you on scenic Snake River float trips within the park (10½-mi. ½-day trip $30, ages 6-12 $16; with lunch $35/$25; with supper $40/$30). **Triangle X Float Trips** (733-5500) can float you on a 5-mi. river trip for less ($20, under 13 $15). **Fishing** in the park's lakes, rivers, and streams is excellent. A Wyoming license ($5) is required; get one in Jackson, at Moose General Store, at Signal Mt., at Colter Bay, in Flagg Ranch, or at Dornan's (see Accommodations and Food, above). **Horseback riding** is available through the Grand Teton Lodge Co. (1½-5hr. rides; $17-40 per person).

The **American Indian Art Museum** (739-3594), next to the Colter Bay Visitors Center, offers an extensive private collection of Native American artwork, artifacts, movies, and workshops (open June-Sept. daily 8am-7pm; late May and late Sept. daily 8am-5pm; free). During July and August you can see Cheyenne, Cherokee, Apache, and Sioux dances at Jackson Lake Lodge (Fri. 8:30pm). At the **Moose** and **Colter Bay Visitors Centers,** June through September, rangers lead a variety of activities aimed at educating visitors about such subjects as the ecology, geology, wildlife, and history of the Tetons. For exact times, check the *Teewinot,* a free magazine available at the visitors centers (see Practical Information, above).

In the **winter** all hiking trails and the unploughed sections of Teton Park Road are open to **cross-country skiers.** Pick up the trail map *Winter in the Tetons* or the *Teewinot* at the Moose Visitors Center. From January through March, naturalists lead **snowshoe hikes** from the Moose Visitors Center (739-3300; snowshoes distributed free). Call for reservations. **Snowmobiling** along the park's well-powdered trails and up into Yellowstone is a noisy but popular winter activity; grab a map and guide at the Jackson Chamber of Commerce, 10 mi. south of Moose. For a *steep* fee you can rent snowmobiles at **Signal Mt. Lodge, Flagg Ranch Village,** or down in **Jackson;** an additional $10 registration fee is required for all snowmobile use in the park. A well-developed snowmobile trail runs from Moran to Flagg Ranch. The Colter Bay and Moose parking lots are available for RVs and cars. All **campgrounds** close in winter, but **backcountry snow camping** (only for those who know what they're doing) is allowed with a free permit from the Moose visitors center. Check with a ranger station for current weather conditions (many early trappers **froze to death** in the 10-ft. drifts) and avalanche danger, and let them know where you're going.

■■■ JACKSON

Jackson Hole—called a hole rather than a valley due to its high elevation—describes the valley bounded by the Teton and Gros Ventre ranges. Nearby Jackson is a ski village gone ballistic. By winter Wyoming's only ski resort town, by summer a major whitewater rafting center drawing three *million* tourists from around the globe, Jackson's snug confines are packed with expensive shops and eateries. The outdoorsy folk who make their living off the year-round tourism are Jackson's saving grace, offering a dollop of Western charm in a sea of out-of-state license plates. Although a sliver of the area's beauty can be seen from town, striking out into the nearby Tetons or onto the Snake River—whether by foot, boat, horse, or llama—yields a richer experience.

PRACTICAL INFORMATION

Tourist Office: Jackson Hole Area Chamber of Commerce, 532 N. Cache St. (733-3316), in a modern, wooden split-level with grass on the roof. A crucial information stop. Open daily 8am-8pm; mid-Sept. to Mid-June daily 8am-5pm. **Bridger-Teton National Forest Headquarters,** 340 N. Cache St. (739-5500), 2 blocks south of the chamber of commerce. Paper maps $3.75, waterproof $5. Open Mon-Fri. 8am-5:30pm, Sat. 8am-4:30pm; late Sept.-late May Mon.-Fri. 8:30am-4:30pm.

Tours: Grayline Tours, 332 N. Glenwood St. (733-4325). Full-day tours of Grand Teton National Park ($36) and Yellowstone National Park lower loop ($39). Call for reservations. Tour picks up at hotels. Office takes calls 9am-9pm.

Public Transportation: Jackson START (733-4521). $1 per ride, $2 out of the county; free for over 65 and under 9. **Grand Teton Lodge Co.** (733-2811) runs a shuttle twice daily in summer to Jackson Lake Lodge ($10).

Car Rental: Rent-A-Wreck, 1050 U.S. 89 (733-5014). $24 per day, $140 per week; 150 free mi. per day, 1000 free mi. weekly, 20¢ each additional mi. Must be 21 with credit card; over 25 need credit card or $300 cash deposit. Must stay within 500mi. of Jackson. Open daily 8am-6pm.

Equipment Rental: Hoback Sports, 40 S. Millward (733-5335). A complete, professional outdoor sports store. Mountain bikes $11 for 2hr., $22 for 24 hrs.; lower rates for longer rentals. Skis, boots, and poles $13 per ½ day, $16 per day. Open peak summer daily 9am-7pm; peak winter daily 8am-9pm; off season daily 9am-7pm. Must have drivers license or credit card. **Skinny Skis,** 65 W. Deloney St. (733-6094). Cross country skis $8 per ½ day, $12 per day; in-line skates $12 per day; camping equipment also available. Major credit card or deposit for value of equipment (from $300-500) required. Open daily 9am-8pm.

Weather and Road Conditions: Weather Line, 733-1731. 24-hr. recording. **Road Information,** Nov.-April 733-9966, outside WY 800-442-7850.

Crisis Lines: Rape Crisis Line, 733-7466.

Emergency: 911.

Post Office: 220 W. Pearl St. (733-3650), 2 blocks east of Cache St. Open Mon.-Fri. 8:30am-5pm, Sat. 9am-2pm. **ZIP code:** 83001. **Area code:** 307.

The southern route into Jackson, U.S. 191/I-80, becomes W. Broadway. The highway continues along Broadway, becoming Cache St. as it veers north into Grand Teton Park and eventually reaches Yellowstone, 70 mi. to the north. The intersection of Broadway and Cache St. at **Town Square Park** marks the center of town. The Jackson Hole ski resort draws snow bunnies to **Teton Village,** 12 mi. to the north via Rte. 22 and Teton Village Rd.

ACCOMMODATIONS AND CAMPING

Jackson's constant influx of tourists ensures that if you don't book ahead, rooms will be small and expensive at best and non-existent at worst. Fortunately, you can sleep affordably in one of two local hostels. **The Hostel X,** P.O. Box 546, Teton Village 83025 (733-3415), near the ski slopes 12 mi. northwest of Jackson, is a budgetary oasis among the wallet-parching condos and lodges of Teton Village and a favorite of skiers because of its location. It has a game room, a TV room, a ski waxing room, a nursery room, and nightly movies in winter. Accommodations range from dorm-style rooms to private rooms. (4 beds in dorm rooms. In summer honors HI-AYH cards. $15, nonmembers $18, $37 for 2 nonmembers, $47 for 3 or 4. In winter, no member discount, $43 for 1 or 2, $56 for 3 or 4.) **The Bunkhouse,** 215 N. Cache St. (733-3668), in the basement of the Anvil Motel, has a lounge, kitchenette, laundromat, ski storage, and, as the name implies, one large but quiet sleeping room with comfortable bunks ($18; linens included). **The Pioneer,** 325 N. Cache St. (733-3673), offers lovely rooms with teddy bears and stupendous hand-made quilts during the summer (singles $70, doubles $80; off peak $45/$50).

While it doesn't offer scenery, Jackson's campground, the **Wagon Wheel Village,** 435 N. Cache St. (733-4588), welcomes tents and RVs on a first come, first served basis (35 sites; $15, RVs $20). Cheaper sites and more pleasant surroundings are available in the **Bridger-Teton National Forest** (800-342-2267) surrounding Jackson. Drive toward Alpine Junction on U.S. 26/89 to find spots. (Sites $5-7, no showers.) The map at the chamber of commerce has a complete list of campgrounds.

FOOD

The Bunnery, 130 N. Cache St. (733-5474), in the "Hole-in-the-Wall" mall, has hearty breakfasts; two eggs, homefries, chili, cheese, and sprouts go for $5.25, and lunch sandwiches cost $4-6 (open daily 7am-9:30pm; mid-Sept. to late May 7am-3:30pm). When the moon hits your eye, climb **Mountain High Pizza Pie,** 120 W. Broadway (733-3646; 10" pie $6; open daily 11am-midnight; in winter 11am-10pm). Chow down on barbecued chicken and spare ribs ($8) at the unglamorous but popular **Bubba's,** 515 W. Broadway (733-2288). They don't take reservations, so come early. (Open daily 7am-10pm.) What the **LeJay's Sportsmen Café** (733-3110), at the corner of Glenwood and Pearl, lacks in legitimate athletes, it makes up for in a good, cheap, greasy menu (burgers and sandwiches with fries $3-6) and a lively, wrangler-meets-bohemian atmosphere (open 24 hrs.). At a ½-pound each, muffins ($1.25-1.65) come fully loaded at **Bombers** (739-2295) in the Grand Teton Plaza. (Sandwiches $4-6. Open Mon. 6:30am-3pm, Tues.-Fri. 6:30am-10pm, Sat. 7am-10pm, Sun. 7am-3pm.) For fresh, tasty bagels seek out **Pearl St. Bagels,** 145 W. Pearl St. (739-1218; open daily 7am-4pm) at the corner of Glenwood and Pearl. Sit back with steak 'n potatoes and appreciate cowboy yodeling at the **Bar J Chuckwagon** (733-3370) supper and western show on Teton Village Rd. ($13, under 8 $4.50, lap-sized free).

OUTDOOR ADVENTURES

Whitewater rafting draws over 100,000 city slickers and backwoods folk to Jackson between May 15 and Labor Day. **Mad River Boat Trips,** 1060 S. Hwy. 89/U.S. 89 (733-6203 or 800-458-7238) 25 mi. from Jackson, offers one of the cheaper whitewater and scenic raft trips. (8mi. trip $23, with dinner $28; smaller boats, "bigger action" $28/$33. Trips leave from 9:30am-3:30pm.) **Lone Eagle Expeditions** (377-1090) also gives you a meal on your 8-mi. raft trip. (Breakfast and lunch trips $23 per person; afternoon and evening dinner trips $33 per person.) **Black Diamond Llamas,** Star Route Box 11-G (733-2877), offers hikes in the company of these South American furry friends (they carry your packs; $50 day hike with meals, $135 per day overnight). Cheaper thrills include a lift 10,452 ft. up Rendez-Vous Mountain on the **Jackson Hole Aerial Tram.** (733-2292. Office open daily 9am-7pm; early Sept.-late May 9am-5pm. $14, seniors $12, ages 13-17 $7, ages 6-12 $5; coupons in local newspapers.) In winter, the **Jackson Hole Ski Resort** (733-2292) at Teton Village offers challenging slopes, including the steepest terrain accessible by lift in the U.S.

ENTERTAINMENT AND NIGHTLIFE

Cultural activities in Jackson fall into two camps—the rowdy, foot-stomping Western celebrations and the more sedate presentations of music and art. Every summer evening except Sunday, the Town Sq. hosts a kitschy episode of the **Longest-Running Shoot-Out in the World.** On Friday evenings at 6:30pm, you can do-si-do and swing your partner at the **Teton Twirlers Square Dance** (733-5269 or 543-2825) on Snow King Rd. in the fair building on the rodeo grounds ($2.50). At the end of May, the town celebrates the opening of the **Jackson Hole Rodeo** (733-2805; open Memorial Day-Labor Day Wed. and Sat. 8pm; tickets $7, ages 4-12 $4.50, under 4 free, family rate $21). The **Grand Teton Music Festival** (733-1128) blows and bows in Teton Village in mid-July and August. (Chamber music Tues.-Thurs. 8pm, festival orchestra Fri. and Sat. 8pm. $15-25, 40% student discount. Reserve in advance.) On Memorial Day, the town bursts its britches as tourists, locals, and nearby Native American tribes pour in for the dances and parades of **Old West Days.** In the second half of September, the **Jackson Hole Fall Arts Festival** attracts crafters, paint-

THUMBS UP FROM LET'S GO

With pen and notebook in hand, a change of underwear in our backpacks, and a budget as tight as your own, we spent the summer roaming the globe in search of travel bargains.

We've put the best of our discoveries into the book you're now holding. Our researchers hit the road for seven weeks of exploration, from Anchorage to Ankara, Estonia to El Salvador, Iceland to Indonesia. Editors work from spring to fall, massaging copy written on Himalayan bus rides into witty yet informative prose. A brand-new edition of each guide hits the shelves every year, only months after it is researched, so you know you're getting the most reliable, up-to-date, and comprehensive information available.

We're an indispensable companion, but the best discoveries are often those you make yourself. When you find something worth sharing, drop us a line. We're Let's Go Publications, One Story Street, Cambridge, MA 02138, USA (e-mail: LetsGo@delphi.com). Good luck, and happy travels!

Photo: R. Olken

ers, dancers, actors, and musicians to town. Discover the fine points of brewing from the knowledgeable owner of **Otto Brothers Brewery** (733-9000), in downtown Wilson on North St. Free tours include a sample of his unique homemade products, such as "Moose Juice Stout." (Open Mon.-Fri. 8am-8pm, Sat.-Sun. 4-8pm.)

Live moosic, food, and frolicking fill the labyrinthine complex of the **Mangy Moose** (733-4913), in Teton Village (dinner daily 5:30-10:30pm, bar open 10pm-2am; 21+). Thursday brings popular disco night to tiny Wilson at the **Stagecoach Bar** (733-4407) on Rte. 22. Shed your sequins (or wear them again) and don a cowboy hat for the country-music dancing on Sunday. (Open Mon.-Sat. 10am-2am, Sun. noon-10pm.) For local ales, head to the **Jackson Hole Pub and Brewery,** 265 Millward St. (739-2337), Wyoming's first brew-pub; the "Zonkers Stout" will put hair on your chest (pints $3, pitchers $10), while the pasta, sandwiches, and pizzas ($7-12) will fill your tummy (open Mon.-Thurs. until midnight, Fri.-Sat. until 1am, Sun. until 10pm). Western saddles serve as bar stools at the **Million Dollar Cowboy Bar,** 25 N. Cache St. (733-2207), Town Sq. This Jackson institution caters to tourists, but attracts some rodeo goers and local cowboys. (Live music Mon.-Sat. 9pm-2am. Cover $5-10 after 8pm. Open Mon.-Sat. 10am-2am, Sun. noon-10pm.)

■■■ BIGHORN MOUNTAINS

The Bighorns erupt from the hilly pasture land of northern Wyoming, a dramatic backdrop to the grazing cattle and sprawling ranch houses at their feet. In the 1860s, violent clashes broke out here between incoming settlers and the Sioux, who were defending their traditional hunting grounds. Cavalry posts such as Fort Phil Kearny (on U.S. 87 between Buffalo and Sheridan) could do little to protect the settlers; the war reached a climax when 81 settlers were killed in the Fetterman Massacre. Now peaceful, visitors can hike through the woods or follow **scenic highways U.S. 14** and **U.S. 16** to waterfalls, layers of prehistoric rock, and the mysterious, ancient **Medicine Wheel** stone formation, which had even the earliest Native Americans guessing. For sheer solitude, poke your head above **Cloud Peak Wilderness** in the **Bighorn National Forest.** To get to **Cloud Peak,** a 13,175-ft. summit in the range, most hikers enter at **West Tensleep,** accessible from the town of **Tensleep** on the western slope, 55 mi. west of Buffalo on U.S. 16. Tensleep was so named because it took the Sioux 10 sleeps to travel from there to their main winter camps. You must register at major trailheads to enter the Cloud Peak area. The most convenient access to the wilderness area is from the trailheads near U.S. 16, 25 mi. west of Buffalo. From the **Hunter Corrals** trailhead, move to beautiful **Seven Brothers Lake,** an ideal base for dayhikes into the high peaks beyond. You can also enter the wilderness area from U.S. 14 from **Sheridan** in the north. Check with a forest office to find out about more out-of-the-way treks, and always check on local conditions with a ranger before any hike.

Campgrounds fill the forest (sites $8-10). Near the Buffalo entrance, **Crazy Woman** has six first come, first served sites (25mi. from Buffalo on U.S. 16; open mid-May to late Sept.; elevation 7600ft.), while **Lost Cabin,** 28mi. from Buffalo on U.S. 16 and 8200 ft. up, furnishes 14 sites with water and toilets (14-day max. stay; call 800-280-CAMP/2267; open mid-May to late Oct.). Both boast magnificent scenery, as do **Cabin Creek** and **Porcupine** campgrounds near Sheridan. You can spend one night (and one night only!) free just off Coffeen St. in Sheridan's grassy **Washington Park.** Camping is also available along the Bighorn River at Afterbay, Two Leggins, Bighorn, and Mallards Landing.

■■■ CODY

William F. "Buffalo Bill" Cody was more than a Pony Express rider, scout, hunter, sportsman, and entrepreneur. Buffalo Bill started "Buffalo Bill's Wild West Show," an extravaganza that catapulted the image of the cowboy into the world's imagination.

Cody's show traveled all over the U.S. and Europe, even attracting the attention of royalty and statesmen. Founded in 1896 by Cody, this "wild west" town still hasn't come down off that cowboy high.

The **Buffalo Bill Historical Center,** 720 Sheridan Ave. (587-4771), is known affectionately as the "Smithsonian of the West." The center is actually four museums under one roof: **The Buffalo Bill Museum** documents the life of you-know-who; the **Whitney Gallery of Western Art** shows off Western paintings, including a few Russells and Remingtons; the **Plains Indian Museum** contains several exhibits about its namesake group; and the **Cody Firearms Museum** shows off the rifles that the white man brought here—the world's largest collection of American firearms. (Open June-Aug. daily 7am-8pm, May and Sept. 8am-8pm, April and Oct. 8am-5pm, March and Nov. Tues.-Sun. 10am-3pm. $8, students 13-21 $4, seniors $6.50, ages 6-12 $2, under 5 free.) From June through August, Cody turns into "The Rodeo Capital of the World" with one every night at 8:30 (587-5155; tickets $7-9, ages 7-12 $4-6). On July 2nd, 3rd, and 4th the **Cody Stampede** rough-rides on into town (587-5155, $11). For fun without the bullshit, drive about 6 mi. west on Rte. 20/14/16 towards Yellowstone and see the mighty **Buffalo Bill Dam** (325ft.), which was the highest dam in the world at the time of its completion in 1910. Anyone passing through Cody should stop at the **Irma Hotel and Restaurant,** 1192 Sheridan Ave. (587-4221), originally owned by Buffalo Bill and named after his youngest daughter. Don't miss the original cherrywood bar, sent as a gift from Queen Victoria. (Open daily 6am-10pm, Oct.-March 6am-9pm.)

Cody lies at the junction of Rte. 120 and Rte. 14. The eastern entrance to Yellowstone Park is 53 mi. to the west; the Montana border is about 40 mi. north on Rte. 120; and the foot of the Bighorns lies 90 mi. to the east. The town's main street is **Sheridan Ave.** Otherwise, the streets running east-west have names, those running north-south are numbered. The friendly **Chamber of Commerce,** 836 Sheridan Ave. (587-2297), can give you the lowdown (open Mon.-Sat. 8am-7pm, Sun. 10am-3pm). **Rent-a-Wreck,** 2515 Grable Hwy. (527-4993 or 800-452-0396) rents cars for $20 with 100 free mi. per day; you must be 21 with major credit card. Call ahead. Cody's **post office:** 1301 Stampede Ave. (527-7161; open Mon.-Fri. 8am-5:30pm, Sat. 9am-noon); **ZIP code:** 82414; **area code:** 307.

There is a veritable slew of budget hotels which fill up quickly in the summertime when the livin' is easy. The **Skyline Motel,** 1919 17th St. (587-4201), has some decent, clean rooms, cable TV, a pool, and a restaurant (summer singles from $46, doubles from $54; winter $28/$32). **Rainbow Park Motel,** 1136 17th St. (587-6251 or 800-341-8000), has cable TV and laundry. (Summer singles $39, doubles $56; off season $25-29/$32-39; $3 per additional person). **The Gateway Campground** (587-2561), ½ mi. north of the Buffalo Historical Center on Yellowstone Highway, has 74 tidy sites (tent sites $10; hookup available).

Though it may seem suspicious under the dim lights, the grub at the 24-hr. **Granny's,** 1550 Sheridan Ave. (587-4829), is trustworthy, even tasty (sandwich specials served all day, $3-6). **Patsy Ann's Pastry and Ladle,** 1243 Beck Ave. (527-6297), will toss a freshly baked bun on your plate, add honey and butter for only two bits (that's 25¢), or serve you pastries, muffins, and lunch sandwiches (eight to sixteen bits; open Mon.-Sat. 6:30am-3pm).

■■■ BUFFALO

Not touristy enough to be a trap, not small enough for wayward travelers to feel like unwanted outsiders, Buffalo, at the crossroads of I-90 and I-25, is a charming, laid-back, friendly town and a perfect base for exploring the Bighorn Mountains.

Absorb some of the character of the Old West in the elegant, entertaining rooms of the **Occidental Hotel,** 10 N. Main St. (684-2788), which opened its doors as the town hall in 1880 (open daily 10:30am-4:30pm and 6-8pm; free). If you're hankerin' after a bit o' frontier history, visit **The Jim Gatchell Museum of the West,** 10 Fort St. (684-9331; open daily 9am-8pm; Sept.-Nov. 9am-5pm; $2, under 18 free), or the museum and outdoor exhibits at the former site of **Fort Phil Kearny** (684-7629), on U.S. 87 between Buffalo and Sheridan (open daily 8am-6pm; mid-Oct. to mid-May Wed.-Sun. noon-4pm; $2, students $1). In nearby **Sheridan** Buffalo Bill Cody used to sit on the porch of the once luxurious **Sheridan Inn,** at 5th and Broadway, as he interviewed cowboy hopefuls for his *Wild West Show.* The Inn now gives tours ($3, seniors $2, under 12 free).

The **Buffalo Chamber of Commerce,** 55 N. Main St. (684-5544 or 800-227-5122), is at your service for town info (open June-Aug. Mon-Sat. 8am-6pm; May and Sept. Mon.-Fri. 8am-6pm; Nov.-April Mon.-Fri. 8:30am-4:30pm). The **U.S. Forest Service Offices,** 300 Spruce St. (684-7981), will answer questions about the Buffalo District of the Bighorns and sell you a road/trail map of the area for three greenbacks (open Mon.-Sat. 8am-4:30pm). There is no bus service in Buffalo; travel by **Greyhound** from either Sheridan or Gillette. In Sheridan, buses leave twice daily for Billings (3hr., $27) and Cheyenne (7hr., $45), from 1700 E. Hwy. 14/16 (office open daily 5:30am-5pm and 6:30-7:30pm). At **Alabam's,** 421 Fort St. (684-7452), you can buy topographical maps ($2.50), hunting, fishing, and camping supplies, and **fishing licenses** (1 day $5, 5 days $20; open daily Mon.-Sat. 8am-6pm, Sun. 8am-5pm). Buffalo's **post office:** 193 S. Main St. (684-7063; open Mon.-Fri. 8:30am-5pm, Sat. 10am-noon); **ZIP code:** 82801; **area code:** 307.

In Buffalo, budget motels line Main St. (Rte. 90) and Fort St. The **Mountain View Motel,** 545 Fort St. (684-2881), keeps appealing pine cabins with TV, A/C, and heating (singles $34, doubles $40; winter $24/$30; big cabin with 3 double rooms $56, with kitchen $60). Next door, the **Z-Bar Motel** (684-5535 or 800-341-8000) has HBO, refrigerators or kitchens, and A/C (singles $37, doubles $45; Nov-April $29/36; kitchen $5 extra; reservations recommended). Fer grub, the **Stagecoach Inn,** 845 Fort St. (684-2507), cooks up huge, hearty meals and miraculous bread spitfire fast for $9-12 (open Mon.-Fri. 11:30am-2:30pm and 5-9pm, Sat. 5-9pm). **Dash Inn,** 620 E. Hart St. (684-7930), dips in with scrumptious fried chicken (2 pieces $3.75; open Tues.-Sun. 11am-9:30pm; in winter 11am-8:30pm).

■■■ DEVILS TOWER

A Native American legend tells of seven sisters who were playing with their little brother when the boy turned into a bear and began to chase them. Terrified, the girls ran to a tree stump and prayed for help. The stump grew high into the sky, where the girls became the stars of the Big Dipper. The bear, infuriated, scraped the now-massive stump with his claws. Others tell of a core of fiery magma that shot up without breaking the surface sixty million years ago, and of centuries of wind, rain, and snow that eroded the surrounding sandstone, leaving a stunning spire. Still others, not of this world, have used the stone obelisk as a landing strip (*Close Encounters of the Third Kind).* The massive, stump-like column that figures so prominently in the myths of Native Americans, geologists, and space aliens is the centerpiece of **Devils Tower National Monument** in northeastern Wyoming.

The **entrance fee** to Devils Tower is $4 per car, $2 per pedestrian. The only way to get to the top is by climbing; nearly 6000 people attempt it yearly. Those interested in making the climb must register with a ranger at the **visitors center** (307-467-5283), 3 mi. from the entrance (open Memorial Day-Labor Day daily 8am-7:45pm; Labor Day-Oct. 8am-5pm). There are more than 220 established routes with names such as "Liken' Lichen" and "The Route of All Evil"—check out the list at the visitors center for a good laugh. Cool **climbing demos** are given outside the visitors center from Memorial Day to Labor Day at 11am and 4pm. Park officials ask that you refrain voluntarily from climbing the tower in June out of respect for the Native American ceremonies taking place there. For ground hikers, several **hiking trails** provide an excellent view of the Tower; the most popular 1.3-mi. **Tower Trail** loops the monument. The park maintains a **campground** near the red banks of the Belle Fourche River. (Water, bathrooms, fireplaces, picnic tables, no showers. Sites $8. Open April-Oct.) **KOA** (307-467-5395), also on a scenic location near the river, camps right next to the park entrance ($15, with full hookup $20; cabins $28). To reach the monument from I-90, take U.S. 14 25 mi. north to Rte. 24.

■■■ CASPER

In its frontier heyday, Casper hosted mountain men, Mormons, friendly ghosts, Shoshone, and Sioux as they ventured west. Eight pioneer trails intersected near Casper, including the famed Oregon, Bozeman, and Pony Express trails. The convergence of those famous paths lives on in the minds of those who call Casper by its nicknames, "the Hub" and "the Heart of Big Wyoming"—they also seem to have forgotten that most of those trailblazers kept on going.

Casper's pride and joy is **Fort Caspar,** 4001 Ft. Casper Rd. (235-8462), a reconstruction of an old army fort on the western side of town. (Open Mon.-Fri. 9am-6pm, Sat. 9am-5pm, Sun. noon-5pm; mid-Sept. to mid-May Mon.-Fri. 9am-5pm, Sun. 1-4pm. Free.) The **Nicolayson Art Museum,** 400 E. Collins Dr. (235-5247), explores the aesthetics of the old and new west with such exhibits as a bison made of rusted auto parts and old tires (open Tues.-Sun. 10am-5pm, Thurs. until 8pm; $2, under 12 $1). A few mi. southeast of town on Rte. 251, **Lookout Point** (on top of **Casper Mountain**) and **Muddy Mountain** (6mi. farther) provide the best vantage points from which to survey the terrain. **Devil's Kitchen** (also called **Hell's Half-Acre**), 45 mi. west of Casper on U.S. 20/26, is a 320-acre bowl filled with hundreds of crazy colorful spires and caves; camping is available nearby. In early August, the week-long **Central Wyoming Fair and Rodeo,** 1700 Fairgrounds Rd. (235-5775), keeps the town excited with parades, livestock shows, and rodeos.

The **Casper Area Convention and Visitors Bureau,** 500 N. Center St. (234-5311 or 800-852-1889; fax 265-2643), will load you down with helpful info on camping and a fine street map (open Mon.-Fri. 8am-6pm, Sat.-Sun. 9am-6pm). **Powder River Transportation Services,** (266-1904; 800-433-2093 outside WY), at I-25 and Center St. in the Parkway Plaza Hotel, #1159, sends one bus per day to Buffalo (4hr., $21), Sheridan (5hr., $26), and Rapid City (overnight, $44). Two buses per day trundle to Cheyenne (3hr., $30) and Billings (6hr., $45). (Ticket office open daily 6-10:30am, 11:30am-5pm.) **Casper Affordable Used Car Rental,** 131 E. 5th St. (237-1733), rents affordable used cars. ($27 per day with 50 free mi., $179 per week with 350 free mi.; 18¢ per additional mi. Must be 22 with $200 or credit card deposit. Open Mon.-Fri. 8am-5:30pm.) Casper's main **post office:** 411 N. Forest St. (266-4000; open Mon.-Fri. 8:30am-5pm); **ZIP code:** 82601; **area code:** 307.

Unforgiven drifters can bunk down at **The Royal Inn,** 440 E. A St. (234-3501). The management has been known to pick up pale riders from the bus station. (Outdoor heated pool, cable TV; fridge, microwave for $4. Singles $25, doubles $32.) Camp at **Fort Caspar Campground,** 4205 W. 13th St. (234-3260; tents $11, full hookup $16.50); **Casper Mountain Campground** (237-8098), south of Casper on Rte. 251. (sites $5); or **Alcova Lake Campground** (237-7052), a popular recreation area with beaches 35 mi. southwest of Casper on County Rd. 407 off Rte. 220 (tents $6, hookup $15). Perk up at the **Daily Grind Coffeehouse,** 328 E. A St. (234-7332), with dozens of caffeinated beverages ($1.25), omelettes ($3), and sandwiches (open Mon.-Sat. 8am-4pm; Sept.-May Mon.-Sat. 8am-8pm). Make a run from Casper's border into neighboring Mills's **Café José's,** 522 SW Wyoming Blvd. (266-1414), for traditional Mexican dishes at south-of-the-border prices ($3-6; open Mon.-Sat. 11am-2pm, 5-9pm). Lunch specials (from $3.75) will enchant you at Casper's ancient Chinese secret, **The Peking Restaurant,** 333 E. A St. (266-2207; open Mon.-Thurs. 5-8pm, Fri.-Sat. 5-9pm).

■■■ CHEYENNE

Originally the name of the Native American tribe that roamed the wilderness of the region, "Cheyenne" was considered a prime candidate for the name of the Wyoming Territory. The moniker was struck down by vigilant Senator Sherman, who pointed out that the pronunciation of Cheyenne closely resembled that of the French word *chienne* meaning, er, "female dog."

Practical Information Check with the **Cheyenne Area Convention and Visitors Bureau,** 309 W. Lincolnway (778-3133; 800-426-5009 outside WY), just west of Capitol Ave., or the **Wyoming Information and Division of Tourism** (777-7777; 800-225-5996 outside WY; open daily 8am-5pm), at I-25 and College Drive, for accommodation and restaurant listings (open daily 8am-6pm; in winter Mon.-Fri. 8am-5pm). There is no **Amtrak** station in Cheyenne, although there is an unstaffed drop-off point in the lobby of the Plains Hotel (see Accommodations, below); from there a shuttle bus runs to the **Borie** train stop, 15 minutes away. Trains chug three times per week to Denver (2½hr., $22) and Chicago (13½hr., $182). Reservations are required for trains from Borie. (Open daily 9:30am-5:30pm.) **Greyhound,** 120 N. Greely Hwy. (634-7744), near College Ave., makes daily trips to Salt Lake City (9hr., $60), Chicago (24hr., $129), Laramie (1hr., $9), Rock Springs (5hr., $50), and Denver (3hr., $21). (Station open daily 10am-12:30pm and midnight-4am; hours subject to change.) **Powder River Transportation** (635-1327), in the Greyhound terminal, honors Greyhound passes on daily runs to Rapid City (10hr., $65), Casper (4hr., $35), and Billings (12hr., $70). The **Rape Crisis Line** (637-SAFE/7233) is open 24 hrs. **Emergency** is 911. Cheyenne's **post office:** 4800 Converse Ave. (772-6580; open Mon.-Fri. 7:30am-5:30pm, Sat. 7am-1pm); **ZIP code:** 82009; **area code:** 307.

Accommodations and Camping It's not hard to land a cheap room here among the plains and pioneers unless your visit coincides with Wyoming's enormous hootenanny **Frontier Days,** the last full week of July (see Sights and Entertainment, below). Beware of doubling rates and disappearing rooms in the days approaching this week.

Many budget motels line **Lincolnway** (U.S. 30). **Plains Hotel,** 1600 Central Ave. (638-3311), offers cavernous, retro-stylish rooms with marble sinks, HBO, and phones in grand-lobbied splendor (singles $30, doubles $37; $5 per additional person). The **Guest Ranch Motel,** 1100 W. 16th St. (634-2137), a short hike west from the bus stop, has large, tidy rooms with cable, phones, shower, and bath (singles with 1 queen bed $27, doubles $33-38). **The Ranger Motel,** 909 W. 16th St. (634-7995), lets small, beige rooms with phone and TV (singles $25, doubles $28). For **campers,** spots blanket the **AB Campground,** 1503 W. College Rd. (634-7035; laundry, game room; 130 sites $12, full hookup $15). You might also try **Curt Gowdy State Park,** 1319 Hynds Lodge Rd. (632-7946), 23 mi. west of Cheyenne on Rte. 210. This year-round park has shade, scenery, 280 sites, fishing, hiking, an archery range, and land for horseback riding—B.Y.O. horse. (Entrance fee $2; out-of-state visitors $3; sites $4 per night.)

Food and Nightlife Cheyenne's eateries won't garnish your plate with exotic culinary concoctions, but several do justice to the hearty meat 'n' potatoes fare. **Lexie's Café,** 216 E. 17th St. (638-8912), has cheerful cottage-style decor featuring wicker chairs and flowers. Its menu includes filling breakfast combos ($3-4), towering stacks of pancakes ($3), and huge burgers ($4). Float on in to the **Driftwood Café,** 200 E. 18th (634-5304), for some home cookin'; try the daily pies and specials ($5 and under) concocted in the diner's small kitchen (open Mon.-Fri. 7am-4pm).

Those weary of the deer and antelope can play in **Joe Pages Bookstore and Coffeehouse,** 207 W. 17th St. (778-7134 or 800-338-7428), which offers occasional live music and poetry readings. A country night spot for the over-21 crowd, **The Cheyenne Club,** 1617 Capitol Ave. (635-7777) hosts live bands nightly at 9pm. When you want to guzzle, look for a pink elephant above **D.T.'s Liquor and Lounge,** 2121 E. Lincolnway (632-3458; open Mon.-Sat. 7am-2am, Sun. noon-10pm).

Festivals and Sights If you're within 500 mi. of Cheyenne during the last week in July, make every possible effort to attend the **Cheyenne Frontier Days,** nine days of non-stop Western hoopla. The town doubles in size as anyone worth a grain of Western salt comes to see the world's oldest and largest outdoor rodeo competition and partake of the free pancake breakfasts (every other day in the parking lot across from the chamber of commerce), parades, and square dancing. For information, contact Cheyenne Frontier Days, P.O. Box 2477, Cheyenne 82003 (800-227-6336; fax 778-7229; open Mon.-Fri. 9am-5pm). Throughout June and July in Cheyenne, a "gunfight is always possible," and the **Cheyenne Gunslingers** (635-1028) make it happen on schedule at W. 16th and Carey St. (Mon.-Fri. 6pm, Sat. noon). The **Wyoming State Capitol Building** (777-7220), at the base of Capitol Ave. on 24th St., shows off stained glass windows and yellowed photographs. (Free 1½-hr. tours twice daily. Open Mon.-Fri. 8am-5pm, Sat. 9am-5pm, Sept.-April Mon.-Fri. 8am-5pm.) Thrifty coyotes can scavenge the **Bargain Barn Flea Market,** 2112 Snyder Ave. (635-2844), which clutters its expansive floor with an eclectic collection of antiques, furniture, toys, and Western memorabilia (open Mon.-Sat. 10am-6pm, Sun. noon-5pm).

■ WEST OF CHEYENNE

Laramie Laramie, the hoppin' home to the University of Wyoming (the state's only four-year college), serves up collegiate coffee shop chic with cowboy grit. Drifters can get a dose of youthful spirit in town and then relax in nearby Medicine Bow National Forest or Curt Gowdy State Park. From Cheyenne, take the **"Happy Jack Road" (Rte. 210)** for the cow-filled scenic tour, or Rte. 80W for expedience. Laramie does its darndest to bring its rough and rugged 19th-century history back to life in **Wyoming Territorial Park,** 975 Snowy Range Rd. (800-845-2287); although the shops, dramatic re-creations, and jug bands are geared toward young'uns, the **Wyoming Territorial Prison** (hourly guided tours) and the **National U.S. Marshals Museum** offer a fascinating glimpse into outlaw history. (Open mid-June to mid-Aug. daily 9:30am-6pm; May and Sept. hours vary. $8, seniors $7.50, ages 9-12 $6, under 9 free.) During the first week of July, Laramie hosts **Jubilee Days** (800-445-5303). All day, broncs and steers buck and twist in the rodeo ($8, under 12 $4); when the sun sets, townfolk kick up their heels in street dances, filled with hearty barbecue and healthy doses of Western spirit(s). For the lowdown on sights, festivals, and outdoor activities (skiing, snowmobiling, biking, and hiking) in the area, drop by the **chamber of commerce,** 800 S. 3rd St. (307-745-7339 or 800-445-5303; open Mon.-Fri. 8am-5pm). Laramie's **post office:** 152 N. 5th St. (307-742-2109; open Mon.-Fri. 8am-5pm, Sat. 9am-1pm).

Ranger Hotel, 453 N. 3rd St. (307-742-6677), patrols downtown. (Phone, HBO, A/C, fridge, microwave. Singles $29, doubles $33; in winter $27/$31). The sprawling **Motel 8** complex, 501 Boswell (307-745-4856), contains large rooms for your motel comfort (A/C, pool; singles $27, doubles $30). Lined with hotels and fast food, **3rd St.** leads south into the heart of town, crossing **Ivinson** and **Grand St.;** both burst with student hangouts. **Jeffrey's Restaurant,** 123 Ivinson St. (307-742-7046), proffers heavenly homemade bread, fresh pasta dishes ($5-7), deli items, and mouth-watering dessert specialties (open Mon.-Sat. 11am-11pm). Next door, **Jeffrey's Too** builds similarly succulent sandwiches ($3-4; open daily 7am-8pm). The air in **The Home Bakery and Café,** 304 S. 2nd St. (307-742-2721), is musty with fresh flour and 100 years of bakery tradition (baked goods 40¢-$2.50; daily sandwich specials $3). **Wild Willie's,** 303 S. 3rd St. (307-721-4779), hops with a variety of music styles (live music Thurs.-Sat.; open daily 4pm-2am). Both students and Harleys steer their way into the **Buckhorn Bar,** 114 Ivinson St. (307-742-3554), a popular neighborhood hangout which features live music Sunday nights (open Mon.-Sat. 6pm-2am, Sun. noon-10pm).

Medicine Bow Legend has it that **Medicine Bow National Forest's** name derives from two practices Native Americans associated with the area; medicinal powwows and bow-making from the mahogany of the forest. The forest is not heavily touristed, which renders its serene lakes and tranquil trails all the more powerful. The **Snowy Range Scenic Byway (Rte. 130)** runs 29 mi. through the forest, climbing the **Snowy Mountain Range** to elevations nearing two vertical miles. Several trails and campgrounds are accessible from Rte. 130, including the challenging **Medicine Bow Trail,** which climbs 4.5 boulder-strewn mi. to **Medicine Bow Peak** (12,013ft.), the highest point in the forest. Nearby **Silver Lake** offers 19 first come, first served sites ($7). A little east, **Nash Fork** is another of several ideal, untrampled camp settings (27 first come, first served sites $7). **Brooklyn Lake** (17 first come, first served sites $7), also on the east side of the forest, offers fishing and access to the lonely 8.2-mi. **Sheep Lake Trail,** as well as to the short, rolling **Glacier Lake Trail.** A drive up **Kennaday Peak** (10,810ft.), at the end of Forest Rd. 215 off Rte. 130 in the northeast, takes you to an impressive vista of the park's forest from a restored fire lookout tower. All 23 of the park's developed campgrounds are open only in the summer and have toilets, but none have electric hookups or showers. Reservations for some campgrounds are available (800-280-2267; $7.50 reservation fee). During winter, 24 downhill and many cross-country ski trails slalom through the park. Two visitors centers flank the park on Rte. 130: **The Bush Creek Ranger District Office** (307-326-5258), near the west entrance (open daily 7:30am-4:30pm; Sept.-May Mon.-Fri. 730am-4:30pm); and the **Centennial Visitor Center** (307-742-6023), 1 mi. west of Centennial at the east entrance (open daily 9:30am-5pm).

Saratoga On the far side of Medicine Bow from Laramie, Saratoga, like its New York sister, is known for its **hot mineral springs,** located at the end of E. Walnut Ave. off Rte. 130 (open 24 hrs., free). After curing your aches, head to the **North Platte River** and do some **fishing.** No full-moon discounts, but the nearby **Hotel Wolf,** 101 E. Bridge St. (307-326-5525), a renovated Victorian inn, is still a howlin' good deal (singles $30, doubles $37). Next door to the Wolf, find lotsa ice cream ($1.35) and coffee specialties ($1-3) at **Lollypops,** 107 E. Bridge St. (307-326-5020). **Classic Knead Bakery,** 113 W. Bridge St. (326-8932), works wonders with dough; delicious cinnamon rolls ($1), donuts (50¢), breads, pastries, and homemade soups will fill your tummy (open Tues.-Sat. 6am-2:30pm).

Colorado

The citizens of Colorado are rightly proud of their state's thin air, in which golf balls fly farther, eggs take longer to cook, and visitors tend to lose their breath while just getting out of bed. Oxygen-deprivation also lures athletes looking to loosen their lungs for a competitive edge, but most hikers, skiers, and climbers instead worship Colorado for its peaks, which give rise to enclaves such as Grand Junction and Crested Butte. Meanwhile, Denver—the country's highest capital—serves as the hub for the entire Rocky Mountain region, providing both an ideal resting place for cross-country travelers and a "culture fix" for those heading to the mountains. Colorado's extraordinary heights are balanced by its equally spectacular depths; for millions of years, the Gunnison and Colorado Rivers have been etching such natural wonders as the Black Canyon and the Colorado National Monument. Early settlers mined Colorado for its silver and gold, the U.S. military burrowed enormous intelligence installations into the mountains around Colorado Springs, but most travelers dig their feet into the state's soil simply to get down and dirty with Mother Nature.

PRACTICAL INFORMATION

Capital: Denver.

The Colorado Board of Tourism: CTTA, P.O. Box 3924, Englewood 80155 (800-265-6723). Call the local chamber of commerce in the area you plan to visit. **U.S. Forest Service,** Rocky Mountain Region, 740 Sims St., Lakewood 80225 (303-275-5350). Free tour maps; forest maps $3. Open Mon.-Fri. 7:30am-4:30pm. **Ski Country USA,** 1560 Broadway #1440, Denver 80202 (303-837-0793; open Mon.-Fri. 8am-5pm; recorded message 831-7669). **National Park Service,** 12795 W. Alameda Pkwy., P.O. Box 25287, Denver 80255 (969-2000). For reservations for Rocky Mountain National Park, call MISTIX at 800-365-2267. Open Mon.-Fri. 7:30am-4:15pm. **Colorado State Parks and Recreation,** 1313 Sherman St. #618, Denver 80203 (303-866-3437). Guide to state parks and metro area trail guide. Open Mon.-Fri. 8am-5pm. For reservations for any Colorado state park, call 470-1144 or 800-678-2267.

Time Zone: Mountain (2hr. behind Eastern). **Postal Abbreviation:** CO

Sales Tax: 3%.

■■■ DENVER

In 1858, the discovery of gold in the Rocky Mountains brought a rush of eager miners to northern Colorado. After the excruciating trek through the plains, the desperadoes set up camps for a breather (of thin, high-altitude air) and a stiff shot of whiskey before heading west into "them thar hills." In 1860, two of the camps consolidated to form a town named after then-governor of Kansas Territory James W. Denver. Between 1863 and 1867, Denver and nearby Golden played a political tug-of-war for the title of state capital. Today, Golden makes a lot of beer, while Denver, the "Queen City of the Plains," has become the Rockies's largest and fastest growing metropolis, serving as the commercial and cultural nexus of the region. Recent completion of one of the world's largest airports and the debut of a new Major League baseball team have catapulted the "Mile High City" into the national limelight. The city has doubled in population since 1960 and continues to attract diversity—ski bums, sophisticated city-slickers from the coasts, and, of course, old-time cowpokes. The gold may be depleted, but Denver retains its best asset—a combination of harmlessly charming urban sophistication and the laid-back attitude of the West.

PRACTICAL INFORMATION

Tourist Office: Denver Metro Convention and Visitors Bureau, 225 W. Colfax Ave. (892-1112 or 892-1505), near Civic Center Park just south of the capitol. Open Mon.-Sat. 8am-5pm, Sun. 10am-2pm; in winter Mon.-Fri. 8am-5pm, Sat. 9am-1pm. Pick up a free copy of the comprehensive *Denver Official Visitors Guide.* **Big John's Information Center,** 1055 19th St. (892-1505 or 892-1112), at the Greyhound station. Big John, an ex-professional basketball player, enthusiastically offers info on hosteling and activities in Colorado. Stop by for information on tours around Denver and daytrips to the mountains. Open Mon.-Sat. 7-10am and 1-3pm. **16th St. Ticket Bus,** in the 16th St. Mall at Curtis St. Double-decker bus with visitor information, ½-price tickets to local theater performances, and RTD bus info. Open Mon.-Fri. 10am-6pm, Sat. 11am-3pm.

Tours: Gray Line Tours (289-2841), at the bus station, runs tours daily in summer to Rocky Mountain National Park (10hr.; $39, under 12 $29); the U.S. Air Force Academy (10hr.; $57, under 12 $29); year-round tours of Denver include Mountain Parks (3½hr.; $20, under 12 $10); and the city (2½hr.; $17, under 12 $9).

Airports: Denver International (342-2000), 25mi. northeast of downtown off I-70. Various shuttles run from the airport to downtown Denver and to ski resorts in the area. From the main terminal, **Airporter** (333-5833 or 800-355-5833) and **DASH** (342-5454 or 800-525-3177) both shuttle to downtown hotels (35min.-1hr., $15). Public **buses** also run downtown (4:38am-12:50am, 45-50min., $6). A **taxi** downtown costs about $35-45. Call ground transportation (342-4059) for info on more shuttles serving the greater Denver area.

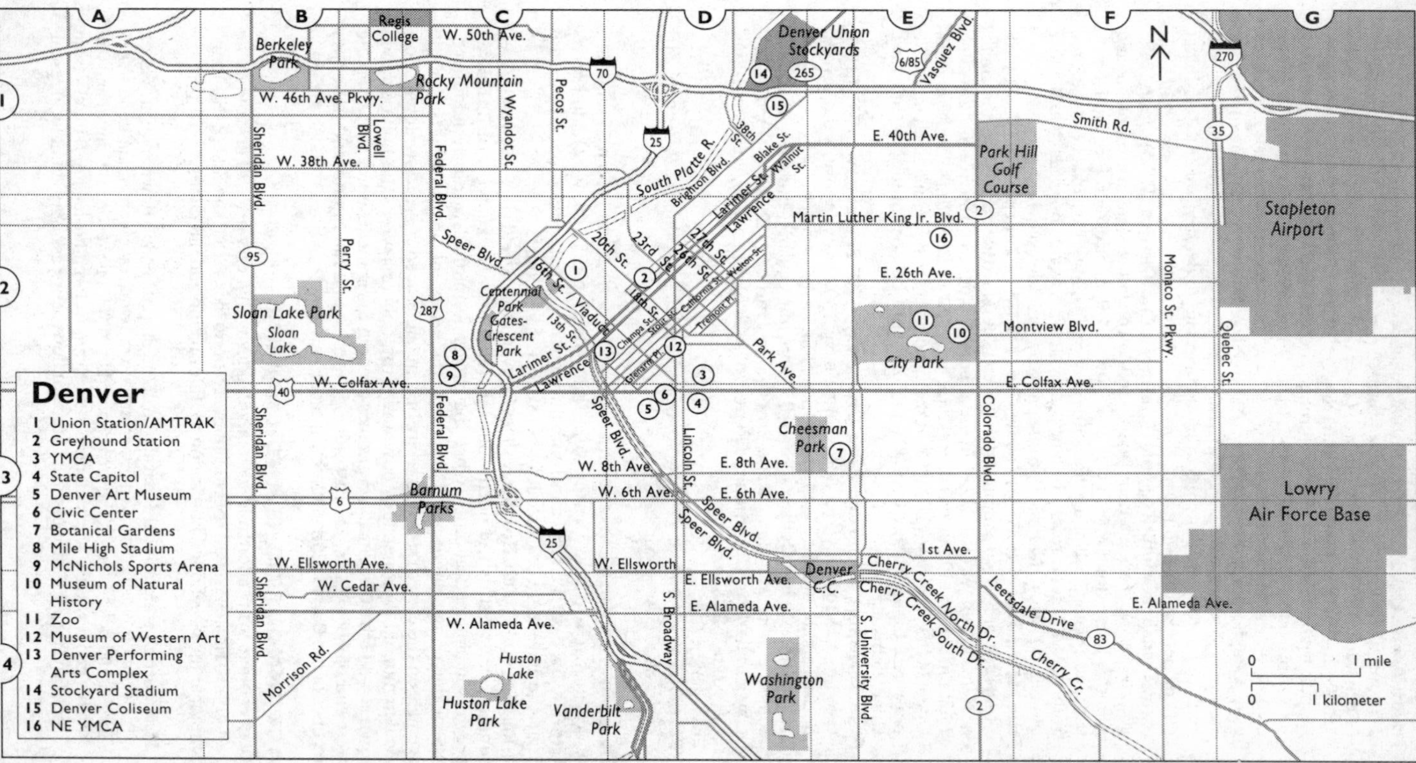
Denver
1 Union Station/AMTRAK
2 Greyhound Station
3 YMCA
4 State Capitol
5 Denver Art Museum
6 Civic Center
7 Botanical Gardens
8 Mile High Stadium
9 McNichols Sports Arena
10 Museum of Natural History
11 Zoo
12 Museum of Western Art
13 Denver Performing Arts Complex
14 Stockyard Stadium
15 Denver Coliseum
16 NE YMCA
0 1 mile
0 1 kilometer
N
A
B
C
D
E
F
G
1
2
3
4
Berkeley Park
Regis College
W. 50th Ave.
Rocky Mountain Park
W. 46th Ave. Pkwy.
Lowell Blvd.
Wyandot St.
Pecos St.
Denver Union Stockyards
Vasquez Blvd.
Smith Rd.
E. 40th Ave.
Park Hill Golf Course
Stapleton Airport
W. 38th Ave.
Sheridan Blvd.
Federal Blvd.
South Platte R.
Brighton Blvd.
38th St.
Blake St.
Walnut St.
Larimer St.
Lawrence
Martin Luther King Jr. Blvd.
Speer Blvd.
Perry St.
20th St.
23rd St.
26th St.
27th St.
Welton St.
E. 26th Ave.
Monaco St. Pkwy.
Quebec St.
Centennial Park
Gates-Crescent Park
16th St. / Viaduct
13th St.
14th St.
California St.
Stout St.
Champa St.
Tremont Pl.
Glenarm Pl.
Sloan Lake Park
Sloan Lake
Larimer St.
Park Ave.
City Park
Montview Blvd.
W. Colfax Ave.
E. Colfax Ave.
Cheesman Park
Lincoln St.
Colorado Blvd.
W. 8th Ave.
E. 8th Ave.
W. 6th Ave.
E. 6th Ave.
Barnum Parks
Lowry Air Force Base
1st Ave.
W. Ellsworth Ave.
W. Ellsworth
Denver C.C.
Cherry Creek North Dr.
Cherry Creek South Dr.
Leetsdale Drive
E. Ellsworth Ave.
W. Cedar Ave.
E. Alameda Ave.
W. Alameda Ave.
S. Broadway
S. University Blvd.
Cherry Cr.
Morrison Rd.
Huston Lake
Huston Lake Park
Vanderbilt Park
Washington Park
70
25
270
35
6/85
265
95
287
40
6
83
2

Trains: Amtrak, Union Station, 1701 Wynkoop St. (534-2812 or 800-872-7245) at 17th and Wynkoop. To: Colorado Springs (2 per day, 2hr., $15.25); Salt Lake City (4 per week, 13½hr., $109); Chicago (1 per day, 19hr., $161). Ticket office open 7am-9pm. The **Río Grande Ski Train,** 555 17th St. (296-4754), leaves from Amtrak Union Station and treks through the Rockies, stopping in Winter Park (Dec.-April only). Departs Denver 7:15am, Winter Park 4:15pm (2hr., $30 round-trip).

Buses: Greyhound, 1055 E. 19th St. (293-6550 or 800-231-2222), downtown. To: Santa Fe (4 per day, 8½-9hr., $66), Salt Lake City (5 per day, 10-13hr., $54), St. Louis (4 per day, 12-19hr., $93), Colorado Springs (5 per day, 2hr., $9.75). Ticket office open 6am-11:30pm.

Public Transportation: Regional Transportation District (RTD), 1600 Blake St. (299-6000). Service within Denver and to Longmont, Evergreen, Golden, and suburbs. Route hours vary; many shut down by 9pm or earlier. Fare Mon.-Fri. 6-9am and 4-6pm $1; all other times 50¢; over 65 15¢. Must have exact change. Free 16th St. Mall Shuttle covers 14 blocks downtown. Over 20 buses daily to Boulder (50min., $2.50). Call Mon.-Fri. 6am-8pm, Sat.-Sun. 8am-8pm. Bus maps $1.

Taxi: Metro Taxi (333-3333); **Yellow Cab** (777-7777); **Zone Cab** (444-8888). All $1.40 base fare, $1.40 per mi. Phone numbers designed for the memory impaired.

Car Rental: Budget (341-2277), in the airport. $29 per day, 100 free mi., 20¢ each additional mi.; $139 per week, 1000 free mi. Must be 25 with major credit card. Open 24 hrs. **Thrifty** (342-9400), in the airport. $33 per day, unlimited mi.; $170 per week. Under 25 surcharge $10 per day. Must be 21 with major credit card. Open 24 hrs.

Auto Transport Company: Auto Driveaway, 5777 E. Evans Ave. (757-1211); take bus #21 to Holly and Evans. Must have $300 cash deposit, valid drivers license, and be at least 21. $10 fee. Open Mon.-Fri. 8:30am-5pm.

Crisis Lines: Crisis Center (756-8485). Open irregularly, but there is usually someone there 9am-10pm. **Rape Emergency Hotline** (322-7273). Open 24 hrs. **Gay and Lesbian Community Center** (831-6268). Open Mon.-Fri. 10am-10pm, Sat. 10am-7pm, Sun. 1-4pm.

Emergency: 911.

Post Office: 951 20th St. (297-6000). Open Mon-Fri. 9am-5pm, Sat. 9am-noon. **ZIP code:** 80202. **Area code:** 303.

During rush hour, traffic sits at a virtual standstill along I-25 until about 15 mi. south of downtown. I-70 links Denver with Grand Junction (250 mi. west) and Kansas City (600 mi. east). Rte. 285 cuts south through the central Rockies, opening up the Saguache and Sangre de Cristo Ranges to easy exploration.

Running north-south, **Broadway** slices Denver into east and west. **Ellsworth Ave.,** running east-west, is the north-south dividing line. Streets west of Broadway progress in alphabetical order, while the streets north of Ellsworth are numbered. Streets downtown run diagonal to those in the rest of the metropolis. Many of the avenues on the eastern side of the city become numbered *streets* downtown. Most even-numbered thoroughfares downtown run only east-west. The hub of downtown is the **16th Street Mall.** Few crimes occur in the immediate area, but avoid the west end of Colfax Ave., the east side of town beyond the capitol, and the upper reaches of the **Barrio** (25th-34th St.) at night.

ACCOMMODATIONS AND CAMPING

Denver offers many affordable accommodations within easy reach of downtown by foot or bus. Hostelers with specific interests (or no ideas at all) should ask "Big John" Schrant at the Greyhound bus station for information and directions.

Melbourne International Hostel, 607 22nd St. (292-6386), downtown at Welton St., yet a bit outside the well-traversed downtown area—women and lone travelers should be cautious in the area. Owned by WWII pilot Leonard Schmitt and run by his nephew Gary, the Melbourne is a clean, well-run hostel, just 6 blocks from the 16th St. Mall. Office in the laundromat downstairs; ask Gary about local restaurants and music clubs. Every room has a fridge; communal kitchen. Check-in 7am-midnight. No curfew. Dorms $10, nonmembers $13; private rooms $18/21; couples $24/27. Sheet rental $2. Key deposit $10. Make reservations for June-Oct.

Denver International Youth Hostel (AAIH/Rucksackers), 630 E. 16th Ave. (832-9996), 10 blocks east of the bus station, 7 blocks east of downtown. The hostel is outside the well-traversed area; women and lone travelers should be cautious in the area. Take AB or DIA bus to Market St., 1 block away, or take free 16th St. shuttle to Circle St. station at Broadway and walk 6 blocks east on 16th Ave. 120 beds in dorm-style rooms. Kitchen, laundry facilities and communal fridge. Office open daily 8-10am and 5-10:30pm. Not the tidiest place around, but the price is right—$7.60, $1 discount with a copy of *Let's Go.* Sheet rental $1. Call to arrange arrival plans. "Professor K's" 110-mi. full-day tour of Denver and the surrounding mountains leaves from the hostel Mon.-Sat. at 9:15am ($12).

Franklin House B&B, 1620 Franklin St. (331-9106). Homey, cozy European-style inn within walking distance of downtown. Clean, spacious rooms. Free breakfast. Not for late-night arrivals; check in before 10pm. Check-out 11am. Singles $22, doubles $32, with private bath $42. $10 for each additional person.

YMCA, 25 E. 16th St. (861-8300) at Lincoln St. Divided into 3 sections for men, women, and families. Laundry and TV rooms. Singles from $22.50 per day, $90 per week; doubles from $42/$179. Prices rise depending on how communal you want your bath to be. Key deposit $12.

Two state parks lie in the Denver metro area. **Cherry Creek State Park** (699-3860) has 102 sites ($7, with electricity $10; daily entrance fee $4; $6.75 reservation fee); take I-25 to exit 200, then go west on Rte. 225 for about ½ mi. and turn south on Parker Rd. **Chatfield State Park** (791-7275) maintains 153 well-developed sites ($7, with electricity $10; daily entrance fee $3); take I-25 or U.S. 85 south, turn west on Rte. 470, and then go south on Wadsworth Rd. A little farther away, to the city's northwest, **Golden Gate Canyon State Park** offers 35 primitive year-round sites at its Aspen Meadows campground (sites $6, daily entrance fee $3); take I-70 west to 6th Ave., take 6th Ave. west towards Central City to Rte. 119, and go north 19 mi. The Metro-Regional offices of the **Colorado Division of Parks and Recreation** (791-1957) has detailed information on all sites (open Mon.-Fri. 8am-5pm). For reservations for any Colorado state park, call 470-1144 or 800-678-2267.

FOOD

Downtown Denver is great for inexpensive Mexican and Southwestern food. Eat *al fresco* and people-watch at the cafés along the **16th St. Mall. Larimer Sq.,** southwest of the mall on Larimer St, has several more gourmet eateries. **Sakura Sq.,** at 19th St. and Larimer, offers Japanese cuisine in restaurants and a market. Along with sports bars and grills, trendy restaurants cluster around **LoDo,** around the new Coors Stadium. Colorado's distance from the ocean may make you wonder about *Rocky Mountain oysters;* this salty-sweet delicacy and other buffalo-meat specialties can be found at the **Denver Buffalo Company,** 1109 Lincoln St. (832-0080).

The Market, 1445 Larimer Sq. (534-5140), downtown. Popular with a young, artsy, not-quite-bohemian crowd that people-watches alongside suits and hippies. Cappuccino $2, sandwiches $4-5, exotic salads $5-8 per lb. Open Mon.-Thurs. 6am-11pm, Fri.-Sat. 6am-midnight, Sun. 7:30am-6pm.

City Spirit Café, 1434 Blake St. (575-0022), a few blocks from the north end of the 16th St. Mall. Flamboyant decor with waitstaff to match. Serves delicious salads ($6), vegetarian dishes (try the City Smart Burrito, $6.25), and fresh desserts. Acid jazz on Tues. nights. Open Tues., Fri., Sat. 11am-2am; other days 11am-midnight.

Mead St. Station, 3625 W. 32nd Ave. (433-2138). Take bus #32 between Mead and Lowell. A slightly artsy pub for locals north of the city. Try the scrumptious homemade pies ($3) or the vegetarian MacGregor sandwich ($5). Live music Mon. and Wed. nights. Open Tues.-Sat. 11am-midnight, Sun. 2pm-10pm, Mon. 4pm-midnight; kitchen closes Mon.-Thurs. 10pm, Fri.-Sat. 11pm, Sun. 9pm.

El Tacos Del Mexico, 714 Santa Fe (629-3926). Explore the wondrous *carnitas* burrito for a zesty Mexican treat, or bite into one big beef burrito ($3.50). Open Sun.-Thurs. 8am-10pm, Fri.-Sat. 8am-2am.

Wynkoop Brewery, 1634 18th St. (297-2700), at Wynkoop across from Union Station. An American pub in a renovated warehouse dedicated to brewing and serving beer (pint $3), Alfalfa mead, homemade root beer, and lunch and dinner, too (burgers $6). Pool tables upstairs. Happy hour 3-6pm, $1.50 pints. Brewery open Mon.-Sat. 11am-2am, Sun. 11am-midnight. Free brewery tours Sat. 1-5pm.

Mercury Café, 2199 California (294-9258). Just across from the Melbourne Hostel. Inside is decorated like an old tea parlor. Homebaked wheat bread and reasonably priced lunch and dinner items. 10-oz. sirloin with bread and vegetable $10. Tues.-Fri. 11:30am-2:30pm and 5:30pm-2am, Sat.-Sun. 9am-3pm and 5:30pm-2am. Nightly events include live bands, open stage, and poetry readings until 2am.

Reese Coffee House, 1435 Curtis St. (534-4304) between 14th and 15th. In the basement of an apartment building across from the Denver Performing Arts Complex. Sandwiches $3-6. Good, cheap breakfast served 24 hrs.

Mexican Madness

Denver has more Mexican-food restaurants than you could shake a tamale at, but there's special reason to make a trip out to **Casa Bonita,** 6715 W. Colfax (232-5115), in Lakewood near Sheraton Blvd. A one-of-a-kind, boggle-the-mind Denver tradition for over 20 years, this converted department store is most likely the only indoor restaurant in the world where you can scarf honey-filled *sopapillas,* listen to roaming mariachi bands, explore a dark, scary, dragon-infested cave, and watch cliff-divers plunge 30 feet into deep pools below. Come during lunchtime for smaller crowds; bring the grandparents, and make sure the kiddies get to cash in their toy-exchangeable "Monkey Money." (Open daily 11am-9:30pm.)

SIGHTS

Denver's mild, dry climate and 300 days of sunshine promise pleasant days (sorry, no money-back guarantees). The **Denver Metro Visitors Bureau,** (see Practical Information above) across from the U.S. Mint, is a good place to plan tours in the city or to the mountains. One of the best deals around is the **Cultural Connection Trolley** (299-6000), where $3 takes you to over 20 of the city's main attractions. The 1-hr. tour runs daily every 20 min. from 9:30am to 5:30pm; buy your tickets from the driver. The tour begins at the **Denver Performing Arts Complex** (follow the arches to the end of Curtis, at 14th St.), but can be picked up near any of the attractions or the visitors bureas; look for the green and red sign. The fare entitles you to a full day of transportation, so feel free to get off at any or all of the sights.

A modern reminder of Colorado's old silver mining days, the **U.S. Mint,** 320 W. Colfax (844-3582), issues U.S. coins with a small "D" for Denver embossed beneath the date. Shake your money-maker while strutting by a million-dollar pile of gold bars, or jam to the deafening roar of countless machines churning out a total of 20 million shiny coins per day. No, they do not give free samples. Arrive early; summer lines often reach around the block. (Free 15-min. tours every 15-20min. in summer and every 30min. in winter Mon.-Fri. 8am-2:45pm, sales Mon.-Fri. 8am-3:30pm. Tickets must be bought in person the day of the tour; get there before 11am.)

Don't be surprised if the 15th step on the west side of the **State Capitol Building** (866-2604) is crowded—it sits exactly 5280 ft. (1 mi.) above sea level. The gallery under the 24-karat-gold-covered dome gives a great view of the Rocky Mountains. Free tours pass the Senate and House of Representatives chambers. (Tours every 30-40min.; summer Mon.-Sat. 9:30am-5:30pm, winter Mon.-Fri. 9:30am-2pm.)

Just a few blocks from the capitol and the U.S. Mint stands the **Denver Art Museum,** 100 W. 14th Ave. (640-2793), which houses a world-class collection of Native American art. Architect Gio Ponti designed this six-story "vertical" museum in order to accommodate totem poles and period architecture. The fabulous third floor of pre-Columbian art of the Americas resembles an archaeological excavation site with temples, huts, and idols. Call for info on special exhibits. (Open Tues.-Sat. 10am-5pm, Sun. noon-5pm. $3, seniors and students $1.50, free Sat.) Housed in the Navarre Building, the **Museum of Western Art,** 1727 Tremont Place (296-1880), holds a stellar collection of Russell, Benton, O'Keeffe, and Wood paintings and drawings (open Tues.-Sat. 10am-4:30pm; $3, students and seniors $2). Gawk at the tunnel connecting this one-time brothel to the **Brown Palace,** across the street at 321 17th St. (297-3111), a historic grand hotel that once hosted presidents, generals, and movie stars. Get posh in the beautiful atrium lobby. **The Black American West Museum and Heritage Center,** 3091 California St. (292-2566), presents a side of frontier history unexplored by John Wayne movies and textbooks; learn, for example, that one-third of all cowboys were African-American (open Mon.-Fri. 10am-5pm, Sat.-Sun. noon-5pm; $3, students and seniors $2).

The **Natural History Museum,** 2001 Colorado Blvd. (370-6357), in massive and central City Park, presents life-like wildlife sculptures and dioramas (open daily 9am-5pm, summer Fri. until 9pm; $4.50, seniors and ages 4-12 $2.50). The Natural History Museum complex includes the **Gates Planetarium,** with Led Zeppelin and Pink Floyd laser shows and an **IMAX theater** (370-6300; call for shows, times and current prices).

Red Rocks Amphitheater and Park, 12 mi. southwest of Denver on I-70 at the Morrison exit, is carved into red sandstone. As the sun sets over the city, even the best performers have to compete with the view behind them. (For tickets call Ticketmaster 830-8497 Mon.-Fri. 9am-9pm, Sat.-Sun. 9am-8pm, or Tele-Seat at 800-444-SEAT/7328 Mon.-Sat. 6am-7pm, Sun. 7am-4pm. Park admission free. Shows $25-45.)

West of Denver in nearby Golden, bite the silver bullet at the **Coors Brewery** (277-2337), 3rd and Ford St. (free 30-min. tours every 20-30min. Mon.-Sat. 10am-4pm). Gray Line (see Practical Information) runs buses to Golden.

For outdoor enthusiasts, Denver has more public parks per sq. mi. than any other city, providing prime space for bicycling, walking, or lolling about in the sun; **Cheesman Park** (take bus #10) offers a view of the snow-capped peaks of the Rockies. Call 698-4900 for further information on Denver Parks. Nearby state parks also offer recreation; see Accommodations and Camping (above) for directions. Check with the **Colorado Division of Parks and Outdoor Recreation** (866-3437; open Mon.-Fri. 8am-5pm). From June to September, head to **Mt. Evans** for a wilder park experience; take I-70 from Golden to Idaho Springs, and then pick up Rte. 103 south over the summit of **Mt. Evans** (14,260ft.).

ENTERTAINMENT AND NIGHTLIFE

Every January, Denver hosts the world's largest rodeo, the **National Western Stock Show** (297-1166). Here, cowfolk compete for prize money while over 10,000 head of cattle compete for "Best of Breed." Hop on a rip snortin' bull, or purchase any combination of shiny spurs, day-glo necklaces, and leather whips. In the last weekend of August, **A Taste of Colorado** features a large outdoor celebration with food vendors and local bands at Civic Center Park, near the capitol.

Denver's long-awaited baseball team, the **Colorado Rockies** (ROC-KIES/702-5437), loft home runs out of shiny new **Coors Field,** at 20th and Blake (tickets $8, $1 on game day to sit in the Rock Pile). In the fall, the **Denver Broncos** (433-7466) put on the blitz at **Mile High Stadium,** as Broncoitis spreads throughout the state. Pan for Denver's NBA team, the **Nuggets,** at **McNichols Arena** (572-4703).

Denver's local restaurants and bars cater to a college-age and slightly older singles crowd. Pick up a copy of *Westword* for the word on the downtown club scene and local events. At **Muddy's Java Café,** 2200 Champa St. (298-1631), eat dinner while listening to live music or reading a novel from their downstairs bookstore; then, after a long night of partying or reading James Joyce, contemplate their very early morning breakfast (jazz Tues., Fri., Sat.; open Sun.-Thurs. 11am-3am, Fri.-Sat. 11am-4am). A local favorite, **My Brother's Bar,** 2376 15th St. (455-9991), at Platte, replaces sports TV and pool tables with a friendly, chatty atmosphere. (Domestic draft $2.75, imported $3.75. Live music every Sat.; free classical concert the first

Mon. of summer months. No cover.) The "Hill of the Grasshopper," **El Chapultepec** (295-9126), 20th and Market St., is an authentic hole-in-the-wall with jazz be-bopping nightly 9pm-1am (one drink min. per set; open daily 7am-2am). **Charlie's,** 900 E. Colfax (839-8890), at Emerson, is a popular gay bar which swings with country and western dancing. **Metro Express,** 314 E. 13th St. (894-0668), another gay nightspot, hosts a non-alcoholic youth night on Thurs. for the 21-and-under crowd.

■ MOUNTAIN RESORTS NEAR DENVER

Summit County Skiers, hikers, and mountain bikers can tap into a sportman's paradise in the six towns of Summit County, about 55 mi. west of Denver on I-70. All six towns fall under the jurisdiction of the **Summit County Chamber of Commerce,** 110 Summit Blvd., P.O. Box 214, Frisco 80443 (303-668-5800 or 303-668-2051), which provides information on current area events (open Mon.-Fri. 9am-5pm). **Breckenridge, Dillon, Copper Mountain, Keystone, Frisco,** and **Silverthorne** provide respite from the expensive and adulterated resorts of Aspen and Vail, and are popular with skiers and outdoorspeople from in-state. The **Summit Stage** shuttle bus provides a free ride to and from any Summit County towns.

The **Alpen Hütte (HI-AYH),** 471 Rainbow Dr. (970-468-6336), in Silverthorn, offers welcoming hosts, a familial atmosphere, and a plethora of year-round outdoor activities. Greyhound (from Denver) and Summit Stage both stop outside the door. (Free ski storage; mountain bike rental. On-site parking. Office open 7am-noon and 4pm-midnight, located across the street in a huge recreation center. Lockout 9:30am-3:30pm. Curfew midnight. $10 per day. $10, nonmembers $12; winter $20-22/$23-25. Lockers $5. Free sheets and towels. Reservations recommended.) Several forest service campgrounds lie nearby; for instant seclusion, wing to **Eagle's Nest Wilderness.** For more information, contact **Dillon Ranger District Office,** 680 Blue River Parkway (970-468-5400).

Fashionable **Breckenridge** lies a little south of Silverton. Despite the many expensive restaurants and stores, you can still find reasonably priced accommodations at the **Fireside Inn,** 114 N. French St. (970-453-6456), parallel to and two blocks east of Main St. The indoor hot-tub is great for *apres-ski.* (Dormitory $15, private rooms $45-65; in winter $27/$80-130. Reservations deposit—the first two nights lodging—due within 10 days of reservation; balance is due thirty days before your arrival. Closed in May.) To cut costs on ski gear, books, and anything else, try the **The Near Gnu** (970-453-6026), on the north end of Main St.

Winter Park The closest major ski resort to Denver (68 mi. northwest on U.S. 40), Winter Park slaloms among delicious-smelling mountain pines, surrounded by 600 sq. mi. of skiing, hiking, and biking trails. The **Winter Park Mary Jane Ski Area** (800-453-2525) has information on skiing. The **Winter Park-Fraser Valley Chamber of Commerce,** 78841 U.S. 40 (303-726-4118 or 800-903-7275), provides information about a diverse range of outdoor activities (open daily 8am-6pm). **Timber Rafting** offers an all-day rafting trip ($37 for hostelers, includes transportation and lunch). The **Alpine Slide,** at 1½ mi. long, is Colorado's longest. (Open early June-early Sept. daily 10am-6pm; late Sept. Sat.-Sun. 10am-6pm. $6, seniors and children $4). You and your bike can ride the **Zephyr Express** chairlift to challenging trails. (Open mid-June to early Sept. and weekends through late Sept. 10am-5pm. Full-day pass $16). Every Saturday at 6pm in July and August, get trampled underfoot at the **High Country Stampede Rodeo** at the John Work Arena, west of Fraser on County Road 73 (adults $6, children $3).

On the town's southern boundary, the energetic Polly and Bill run the **Winter Park Hostel (HI-AYH)** (303-726-5356), 2½ blocks from the Greyhound stop and 2 mi. from Amtrak (free shuttle if you call ahead). The hostel is made up of a cheery, homey village of converted trailer units, each with its own kitchen, bathroom, and living area. In winter, free shuttles run to the ski area and supermarket. Hostelers save money on bike and ski rentals, raft trips, and restaurants. (Check-in 8am-noon and 4-8pm. May-Oct. $8, nonmembers $10; Nov.-April $13/$16. Private singles add $3; private doubles available. Linens $2. Closed April 15-June 15. Call for reservations.) **Le Ski Lab,** 7894 U.S. 40 (303-726-9841), conveniently next door, offers discounts for hostelers (mountain bikes $12.50 per day; ski rentals $8.50 per day). The fresh sandwiches at **Rudi's Deli** (303-726-8955), at Park Plaza on U.S. 40, are double-diamond, mogul-sized (half sandwich, soup, and drink $5; open June-Sept. 11am-5pm, otherwise 8am-8pm). Reach into **Cookie Jar** (303-726-9832), on Cooper Creek Way, for a fantastically fattening array of sweets.

The chamber of commerce (see above) also serves as the **Greyhound** depot (2 buses per day from Denver, 2hr., $10). The nearest **Amtrak** station is in Fraser (726-8816). **Home James Transportation Services** (303-726-5060 or 800-451-4844) runs door-to-door shuttles to and from Denver Airport. (Daily mid-April to mid-Nov.; 6 per day mid-Nov. to mid-Dec. and early April; 11 per day mid-Dec. to April 1. $33, round-trip $64. Call ahead for reservations.) From December to April, the **Río Grande Ski Train** (303-296-4754) leaves from Denver's Union Station for Winter Park. (Mid-Dec. to early April Sat.-Sun. 7:15am, arrive Winter Park 9:30am; depart Winter park 4:15pm. Round-trip $30).

■■■ BOULDER

Almost painfully hip, Boulder lends itself to the pursuit of both higher knowledge and better karma. It is home to both the central branch of the University of Colorado (CU) and the only accredited Buddhist university in the U.S., the Naropa Institute. Only here can you take summer poetry and mantra workshops lead by Beat guru Allen Ginsberg at the Jack Kerouac School of Disembodied Poets.

Boulder is an aesthetic and athletic mecca. The nearby Flatiron Mountains, rising up in charcoal-colored slabs on the western horizon, beckon rock climbers, while a system of paths make Boulder one of the most bike- and pedestrian-friendly areas around. For those motorists seeking a pacific retreat into nature, Boulder is *on the road* (Colorado Rte. 36) to Rocky Mountain National Park.

PRACTICAL INFORMATION

Tourist Office: Boulder Chamber of Commerce/Visitors Service, 2440 Pearl St. (442-1044), at Folsom about 10 blocks from downtown. Take bus #200. Open Mon.-Fri. 8:30am-5pm. **University of Colorado Information** (492-6161), 2nd floor of University Memorial Center (UMC) student union at Broadway and 16th. Campus maps. Open Mon.-Thurs. 7am-11pm, Fri.-Sat. 7am-midnight, Sun. 11am-11pm; termtime open Sun.-Thurs. 7am-midnight, Fri.-Sat. 7am-1am. The **CU Ride Board,** UMC 1st floor, advertises lots of rides and lots of riders—even in summer.

Public Transportation: Boulder Transit Center (299-6000), 14th and Walnut St. Routes to Denver and Longmont as well as intra-city routes. Buses run Mon.-Fri. 6am-8pm, Sat.-Sun. 8am-8pm. Fare 60¢. To Nederland ("N" bus) and Lyons ("Y" bus) $1.50; to Golden ("G" bus) and to Boulder Foothills or Denver ("T" or "FH" bus) $2.50. Several other lines link up with the Denver system (see Denver Practical Information). Get a $1 bus map at the terminal.

Taxis: Boulder Yellow Cab (442-2277). $1.50 base fare, $1.20 per mi.

Car Rental: Budget Rent-a-Car, 1545 28th St. (444-9054), near the Clarion Harvest House. $45 per day with 100 free mi., 20¢ each added mi.; $200 per week. Must be 25 with major credit card. Open Mon.-Fri. 8am-6pm, Sat.-Sun. 8am-3pm.

Bike Rental: University Bicycles, 839 Pearl St. (444-4196), downtown. Rents mountain bikes $14 per 4 hr., $18 per 8 hr., $24 overnight, with helmet and lock; 6-speeds $10/$12/$15. Open Mon.-Fri. 9am-7pm, Sat.-Sun. 10am-6pm.

Crisis Lines: Rape Crisis, 443-7300. 24 hrs. **Crisis Line,** 447-1665, for general counseling. 24 hrs. **Lesbian, Bisexual, Gay Transgender Alliance,** 492-8567; no regular hours during summer, but a recorded message has info. **Boulder Campus Gay, Lesbian, and Bisexual Resource Center,** 492-2966.

Emergency: 911.

Post Office: 1905 15th St. (938-1100), at Walnut across from the RTD terminal. Open Mon.-Fri. 7:30am-5:30pm, Sat. 10am-2pm. **ZIP code:** 80302. **Area code:** 303.

Boulder (pop. 83,000) is a small, manageable city. The most developed part of Boulder lies between **Broadway** (Rte. 93) and **28th St.** (Rte. 36), two busy streets running parallel to each other north-south through the city. **Baseline Rd.,** which connects the Flatirons with the eastern plains, and **Canyon Blvd.** (Rte. 7), which follows the scenic Boulder Canyon up into the mountains, border the main part of the **University of Colorado** (CU) campus. The school's surroundings are known locally as **The Hill.** The pedestrian-only **Pearl St. Mall,** between 11th and 15th St., is the center of hip life in Boulder. Most east-west roads have names, while north-south streets have numbers; Broadway is a conspicuous exception.

ACCOMMODATIONS AND CAMPING

After spending your money at the Pearl St. Mall on tofu and yogurt, you may find yourself strapped for cash and without a room—Boulder doesn't offer many inexpensive places to spend the night. In summer, you can rely on the hostel.

Boulder International Youth Hostel (AAIH/Rucksackers), 1107 12th St. (442-0522), two blocks west of the CU campus and 15min. south of the RTD station. From Denver take the A or B bus as close to College Ave. as possible. Located in the heart of CU housing and frats, the BIYH is a loud, youthful place. Shared hall bathrooms, kitchen, laundry, TV. Lockout for dorms 10am-5pm. Curfew Sun.-Thurs. 1am, Fri.- Sat. 2:30am. $12, CO residents $15; $1 *Let's Go* discount. Private singles $25 per night, $135 per week, doubles $30/$170. Shower and towels $5. Linen $4. Key deposit $5.

Chautauqua Association (442-3282), off Baseline Rd., turn at the Chautauqua Park sign and follow Kinnikinic to the administrative office, or take bus #203. Set at the foot of the Flatirons. Stay in one of their lodges in a suite (2-person $43, 4-person $55), or in a private cottage with a kitchen (4-night min. stay; 4-person $46; 10-person $91). Make reservations months in advance.

The Boulder Mountain Lodge, 91 Four Mile Canyon Dr. (444-0882), 3mi. west on Canyon Rd. near creekside bike and foot trails. Pay phone. 2 hot tubs and seasonal pool are a nice plus. 25 campsites. 2-week max. stay. Check-in after 10am. 3-person sites with or without hookup $14, $2 each additional person; $80 per week. Total vehicle length cannot exceed 25ft.

Camping information for **Arapahoe/Roosevelt National Forest** is available from the **Forest Service Station** at 2995 Baseline Rd. #10 , Boulder 80303 (444-6600), at 32nd St. (open Mon.-Fri. 8am-5pm). Several campgrounds are available: **Kelly Dahl** (46 sites), 3 mi. south of Nederland on Rte. 119; **Rainbow Lakes** (18 sites), 6 mi. north of Nederland on Rte. 72 and 5 mi. west on unmaintained Arapahoe Glacier Rd. (no water; campground open late May to mid-Sept.). **Peaceful Valley** (15 sites) and **Camp Dick** (34 sites), both north on Rte. 72, offer cross-country skiing in the winter; first come, first served. All sites are $9 except Rainbow Lakes ($5). For reservations, call 800-280-CAMP/2267.

FOOD AND HANGOUTS

The streets on The Hill surrounding CU and those along the Pearl St. Mall burst with good eateries, natural foods markets, cafés, and colorful bars, as well as bedraggled teens looking to supplement their parental allowance with the spare change of hapless travelers. Many more restaurants and bars line Baseline Rd. Boulder has more restaurants for vegetarians than for carnivores. For an abundance of fresh produce and homemade breads and pies, head for the **Boulder County Farmer's Market** (494-4997), at 13th and Canyon; get there early (open May-Oct. Wed. 11am-4pm, Sat. 8am-2pm).

The Sink, 1165 13th St. (444-7465). When the word went out in 1989 that the Sink had reopened, throngs of former "Sink Rats" commenced their pilgrimage back to Boulder; the restaurant still awaits the return of its former janitor, Robert Redford, who quit his job and headed out to California back in the late 50s. Burgers $3.50. Vegetarian and Mexican specialties, too. Call for info on live music (Tues. and Fri.). Open Mon.-Sun. 11am-2am; food served until 10pm.

The Mediterranean Restaurant, 1002 Walnut St. (444-5335), mixes regional dishes and ingredients in a classy, sunny setting. Spaghetti with shrimp, chicken cordon bleu, or souvlaki for $6. Open Mon.-Fri. 11:30am-2:30pm, Sun.-Thurs. 5-10pm, Fri.-Sat. 5-11pm.

The Deli Zone, 1091 13th St. (449-6952), builds huge meat-and-veggie sandwiches that transgress zoning restrictions without sacrificing quality ($3-6). Open Mon.-Wed. 7:30am-9pm, Thurs.-Fri. 7:30am-3am, Sat. 9am-3am, Sun. 9am-8pm.

Mountain Sun Pub and Brewery, 1535 Pearl St. (546-0886). A 21-tap salute to microbreweries near and far, plus burgers ($4), veggie selections, and pizza. Open Mon.-Sat. 11:30am-1am, Sun. 2pm-midnight.

Boulder Salad Co., 2595 Canyon Blvd. (447-8272), revamps the cafeteria concept far beyond your wildest dreams. Giant platters full of salads, pastas, and grains settle onto your tray. All-you-can eat lunch buffet $5, dinner $7-8. Open Mon.-Sat. 11am-9pm, Sun. 11am-8:30pm. Seniors 10% off, under 12 ½-price.

SIGHTS AND ENTERTAINMENT

The Boulder Museum of Contemporary Art, 1750 13th St. (443-2122), focuses on contemporary regional art (open Tues.-Fri. 11am-5pm, Sat. 9am-5pm, Sun. noon-5pm; free). The intimate and impressive **Leanin' Tree Museum,** 6055 Longbow Dr. (530-1442), presents an interesting array of Western art and sculpture (open Mon.-Fri. 8am-4:30pm, Sat. 10am-4pm; free). Writers give readings at the small **Naropa Institute,** 2130 Arapahoe Ave. (444-0202), or tune-up your karma via mediation (open daily 9am-5pm). The **Rockies Brewing Company,** 2880 Wilderness Place (444-8448), between 30th St. and Foothills Pkwy., offers tours and free beer (25-min. tours Mon.-Sat. at 2pm; open Mon.-Sat. 11am-10pm).

University of Colorado intellectuals collaborate with wayward poets and back-to-nature crunchers to find innovative things to do. Check out the perennially outrageous street scene on the Mall and the Hill and watch the university's kiosks for the scoop on downtown happenings. The **University Memorial Center** (492-6161), at Euclid and Broadway, is an event hub (open Mon.-Sat. 10am-6pm). On the third floor, its **Cultural Events Board** (492-3228) has the latest word on all CU-sponsored activities. CU's **Muenzinger Auditorium** (492-1531), near Folsom and Colorado Ave., and the **Boulder Public Library,** 1000 Canyon Rd. (441-3197), both screen international and art films; call for times and prices (library doesn't screen in Aug.). From June to mid-August, the **Colorado Shakespeare Festival** (492-0554) suffers the slings and arrows of outrageous fortune (previews $9, tickets $12-34; student discounts available). The **Chautauqua Association** (442-3282) hosts the **Colorado Music Festival** (449-2413) from mid-July to August (tickets $6-32). During the second week of September, tunes wail at the **Boulder Blues Festival** (443-5858; $10-15). The **Parks and Recreation Department,** 3198 N. Broadway (441-3400) sponsors free summer performances in local parks; dance, classical and modern music, and children's theater are staples (open Mon.-Fri. 8am-5pm). **Running** and **biking** competitions dominate the Boulder sports scene. Call the **Boulder Roadrunners** (499-2061; open daily 9am-6pm).

Flatiron Mountains Rising up from Green Mountain, the Flatirons offer countless opportunities for walking, hiking, and biking. Take a stroll or cycle along **Boulder Creek Path,** a beautiful strip of park that lines the creek for 15 mi. Farther back in the mountains lie treacherous, less accessible rocky outcroppings. Trails weave through the 6000-acre **Boulder Mountain Park,** beginning from several sites on the western side of town. **Flagstaff Rd.** winds its way to the top of the mountains from the far western end of Baseline Rd. The **Boulder Creek Canyon,** accessible from Rte. 119, offers splendid rocky scenery. Nearby **Eldorado Canyon,** as well as the Flatirons themselves, has some of the best **rock climbing** in the world.

■■■ ROCKY MOUNTAIN PARK

Of all the U.S. national parks, **Rocky Mountain National Park** is closest to heaven. A full third of the park lies above treeline, with some peaks piercing the sky at over 14,000 ft.; here, among the clouds, arctic winds whip through a craggy landscape carpeted with tundra and blessed with vibrant natural beauty. The failure to find precious metal in these mountains in the late 1800s, and the area's subsequent designation as a national park in 1915, have allowed the park's delicate ecosystem to escape industrialization. Today, visitors mob the park, which has become the ultimate playground for the large surrounding populace.

Northwest of Denver, the mountain wilds are made accessible by tourist towns on the park's borders and by **Trail Ridge Rd. (U.S. 34),** the highest continuously paved road in the U.S., which runs 45 mi. west through the park from **Estes Park** to **Grand Lake.** The Ute shied away from **Grand Lake,** believing that mists rising from its surface were the spirits of rafters who had drowned in a storm. This glacial lake and its namesake town now serve as a quiet base from which to explore the park's less traversed but equally stunning western side.

PRACTICAL INFORMATION

Tourist Office: Park Headquarters and Visitors Center (586-1206), 2½mi. west of Estes Park on Rte. 36 at the Beaver Meadows entrance to the park. Call for park info or to make sure the Trail Ridge Rd. is open. Headquarters and visitors center open daily 8am-9pm; late Aug. to mid-June 8am-5pm. **Kawuneeche Visitors Center** (627-3471), just outside the park's western entrance 1¼ mi. north of Grand Lake. Open 7am-7pm, Labor Day-June daily 8am-4:30pm. **Moraine Park Visitors Center and Museum** (586-3777), on the Bear Lake Rd. Open April-late Sept. daily 9am-5pm. **Alpine Visitors Center,** at the crest of Trail Ridge Rd. Great view of the tundra from the back window. Open Memorial Day to the closing day for Trail Ridge Rd. (mid-Oct.) daily 9am-5pm. **Lily Lake Visitors Center,** 6 mi. south of Park Headquarters on Rte. 7. Open mid-June to early Sept. daily 9am-4:30pm. **Estes Park Chamber of Commerce,** P.O. Box 3050, Estes Park 80517 (586-4431 or 800-443-7837), at 500 Big Thompson Hwy. slightly east of downtown. Open daily 8am-8pm, in winter 8am-5pm. **Grand Lake Area Chamber of Commerce,** 14700 U.S. 34 (627-3402 or 800-531-1019), at the park's west entrance. Open daily 9am-5pm; mid-Oct. to mid-May Fri.-Sun. 10am-4pm.

Police: Estes Park police, 586-4465. **Grand Lake police,** 627-3322.

Horse Rental: Sombrero Ranch, 1895 Big Thompson Rd. (586-4577), in Estes Park 2mi. from downtown on U.S. 34E, and on Grand Ave. in Grand Lake (627-3514). 1hr. $17; 2hr. $28. Breakfast ride (7am, $25) includes a 2-hr. ride and huge breakfast. Call ahead. 10% HI discount. Both locations open daily 7am-5:30pm.

Equipment Rental: Colorado Wilderness Sports, 358 Elkhorn Ave. (586-6548), in Estes Park. Fly rods $12 per day; waders $15 per day; and spinning rods $10 per day. Open daily 9am-8pm.

Weather and Road Conditions: 586-1333 in park; 586-9561 out of park. Recorded messages.

Emergency: 911. **Park Emergency,** 586-1399 or 586-1206.

Post Offices: Grand Lake, 520 Center Dr. (627-3340). Open Mon.-Fri. 8:30am-5pm; **ZIP code:** 80447. **Estes Park,** 215 W. Riverside Dr. (586-8177). Open Mon.-Fri. 8:30am-5:30pm, Sat. 10am-2pm. **ZIP code:** 80517. **Area code:** 970.

You can reach the National Park most easily from Boulder via U.S. 36 or from Loveland up the Big Thompson Canyon via U.S. 34. In Boulder the entrance to U.S. 36 lies at 28th and Baseline Rd. To get to Estes Park from Boulder, call the **Hostel Hauler** (586-3688) before 9pm and arrange a shuttle ($12, $20 round-trip).

From the eastern side, loop through U.S. 36, pick up Trail Ridge Rd. (U.S. 34), take U.S. 40 south, and bullet back along the interstates. From the west, when Trail Ridge Rd. is closed (Oct.-May), you can drive U.S. 40 over spectacular **Berthoud Pass** to I-70, then Rtes. 119 and 72 north to the park (140mi.). One of the most scenic entrances, Rte. 7 approaches the park from the southeast, accessing the **Wild Basin Trailhead,** the start of some glorious hikes. The park entrance **fee** is $5 per vehicle, $3 per biker or pedestrian, under 17 free. The pass is valid for seven days.

ACCOMMODATIONS

Although Estes Park and Grand Lake have an overabundance of expensive lodges and motels, there are few good deals on indoor beds near the national park, especially in winter when the hostels close down.

Estes Park

H Bar G Ranch Hostel (HI-AYH), 3500 H Bar G Rd., P.O. Box 1260, Estes Park 80517 (586-3688; fax 586-5004). Turn on Dry Gulch Rd., 1mi. north of town next to the lake; at H Bar G Rd., turn right to get to the hostel. Spectacular view of the forest and prime location; this converted ranch could be a luxury resort. Instead, its hillside cabins, warm lodge, tennis court, rec room, and kitchen shelter up to 100 hostelers. Proprieter Lou drives into town or the park entrance at 7:30am and retrieves guests from the chamber of commerce in the afternoon. Members only. $8. Car rental $26 per day. Open late May to mid-Sept. Call ahead.

The Colorado Mountain School, 351 Moraine Ave. (586-5758). Tidy dorm-style accommodations open to travelers unless already booked by mountain-climbing students. Wood bunks with comfortable mattresses, linens, and shower ($2). Check-out 10am. 20 beds total, $16. Reservations recommended at least 1 week in advance. Open daily 9am-5pm.

YMCA of the Rockies, 2515 Tunnel Rd., Estes Park Center 80511 (586-3341), 2mi. south of the park headquarters on Rte. 66 and 5mi. from the chamber of commerce. It's fun to stay at the Y-M-C-A; extensive facilities on the 1400-acre complex, as well as daily hikes and other events. Great for kids. Caters to large groups. 4-person cabin with kitchen and bath from $49. 5-person lodge $43. Guest membership $3, families $5. Call way ahead; they take reservations for members in early March, nonmembers in early April; booked for the summer by mid-May.

Grand Lake

Grand Lake draws fewer crowds than Estes Park in the summer. Though inaccessible without a car in the winter, the town offers hair-raising snowmobile and cross-country routes. Ask at the visitors center about seasonal events. Camp on the shores of adjacent **Shadow Mountain Lake** (81 sites) and **Lake Granby** (148 sites). Both charge $10 for a site and have toilets and water; call 800-280-2267 for reservations.

Shadowcliff Hostel (HI-AYH), P.O. Box 658, Grand Lake 80447 (627-9220). Leaving the western entrance to the park, turn left into Grand Lake, then take the left fork ¼mi. into town on W. Portal Rd.; their sign is ¾mi. down the road to the left. Hand-built pine lodge perched on a cliff with a stunning view of the lake. Roaring brook lulls up to 14 hostelers to sleep. Hiking trails nearby. Kitchen. Hall showers. $8, nonmembers $10. Private doubles $28, $4 per additional person. 3 cabins sleep 6-8; all have fireplaces, stoves, refrigerators, and private bath (6-day min. stay). For 5 people $55 per night; $4 per additional person. Open June-Oct.

Sunset Motel, 505 Grand Ave. (627-3318). Friendly owners plus cozy rooms equals a warm stay. Singles $40, doubles $45-55; in winter $45-55/$35-45.

Bluebird Motel, 30 River Dr. (627-9314). Spiffy little rooms with spotted carpet, fluffy pink curtains, TV, and fridges. Singles $40, doubles $49-55; rates go down $5 in winter.

CAMPING

Sites fill up right quick in summer; call ahead or arrive early. Make reservations from eight to 12 weeks in advance through **DESTINET,** 9450 Carroll Park Dr., San Diego, CA 92121 (586-1206 or 800-365-2267). There is a seven-day maximum stay at all campgrounds except Long's Peak (3 days). There is a $10 fee for all reservations, regardless of group size or length of stay.

National Park Campgrounds: Moraine Park (5½mi. from Estes; 247 sites) and **Glacier Basin** (9mi. from Estes; 150 sites). Both require reservations in summer. Sites at both $12. Both open May 29-Sept. 6. The other three are first come, first served. **Aspenglen,** 5mi. west of Estes Park near the Fall River entrance, has 56 sites ($10) and is open May 8-Sept. 30. **Longs Peak,** 11mi. south of Estes Park and 1mi. off Rte. 7, takes campers year-round (26 tent-only sites $10; in winter, no water, no charge). **Timber Creek** (10mi. north of Grand Lake—the only campground on the western side of the park) is open year-round and has 100 sites ($10; in winter, no water, no charge). **Spring Lake Handicamp** (586-1242 for info and reservations; daily 7am-7pm.), 7mi. from Estes Park Headquarters, at Sprague Lake Picnic Area, is the park's backcountry campsite for the disabled.

Backcountry camping: Offices at **Park Headquarters** (586-1242) and **Kawuneeche Visitors Center** (627-3471), on the western side of the park at Grand Lake. Open daily 7am-7pm. Get reservations at these offices or write Backcountry Permits, Rocky Mountain National Park, Estes Park 80517 (586-1242). Many areas are in no-fire zones; bring a campstove if you plan to cook.

Olive Ridge Campground, 15mi. south of Estes Park on Rte. 7, in Roosevelt National Forest. Elevation: 8350ft.; do not come unless you can handle the rarified air. 56 first come, first served sites. $9. Reservations available. Open mid-May to late Oct. Contact the **Arapaho-Roosevelt National Forest Visitors Center,** 1311 S. College Ave. (498-2770), in Ft. Collins. Open Mon.-Fri. 8am-5pm.

Indian Peaks Wilderness, just south of the park, jointly administered by Arapaho and Roosevelt National Forests. Permit required for backcountry camping during the summer. On the east slope, contact the **Boulder Ranger District,** 2995 Baseline Rd. #110 (303-444-6600). Open Mon.-Fri. 8am-5pm. Backcountry permits for Indian Peaks ($5) are available here or at **Coast to Coast Hardware** (303-258-3132), 17mi. west of Boulder off Rte. 119 in Nederland. Open daily 8am-8pm. On the west slope, contact the **Sulphur Ranger District,** 62429 Hwy. 40 (887-3331) in Granby. Open daily 8am-5pm; Sept.-May Mon.-Fri. 8am-5pm.

FOOD

Both towns near the park have good restaurants and several grocery stores where you can stock up on trail snacks. Look for "bulk foods" at **Safeway** in Estes's Stanley Village Mall across from the chamber of commerce.

Mountain Home Café (586-6624), 2 buildings to the right of Safeway, across from the Chamber of Commerce. Try Mike's waffles (from $2), made from scratch and served all day long. Open Mon.-Sat. 7am-8pm, Sun. 8am-8pm.

Village Pizza, 543 Thomson Ave. (580-6031), near Stanley Village Mall. Carbo-depleted mountain-hoppers can load up on $5-6 pasta specials with garlic bread and side salad. Open Wed.-Sun. 11am-10pm.

Poppy's, 832 Elkhorn Ave. (586-8282), in Barlow Plaza. Serves fresh individual-sized pizzas ($3) in a genteel fast-food atmosphere. 15" pizza $10-12, subs $4-7, all-you-can-eat salad/soup bar $6. Open Sun.-Fri. 11am-8pm, Sat. 11am-9pm.

Casa del Sol, 825 Grand Ave. (627-8382). Serves its filling homemade Mexican specialties in trios: 3 chicken enchiladas $4.85; 3 beef-and-bean tostadas $4.30. Free chips and salsa. Open daily 11am-9pm.

The Terrace Inn, 813 Grand Ave. (627-3079), in Grand Lake. Good homemade grub. Debby's special Italian sauce and huge fluffy pancakes ($4) are definite favorites. Open in summer Sun.-Fri. 8am-9pm, Sat. 8am-10pm.

SIGHTS AND ACTIVITIES

The star of this park is **Trail Ridge Rd.** (U.S. 34), a 50-mi. stretch that takes you up 12,183 ft. above seal level into frigid tundra. The round-trip drive takes three hours by car, 12 hours by bicycle (if you have buns of steel and abs of iron). The road is closed Oct.-May for obvious reasons. For a closer look at the fragile environment, walk from roadside to the **Forest Canyon Overlook,** or take the ½-hour **Tundra Trail** round-trip. **Old Fall River Rd.,** a one-way dirt road going from east to west merging with Trail Ridge Rd. at the alpine center, basks in even more impressive scenery, but there are sharp cliffs and tight switchbacks along the road (normally open July-Sept.; call Park Headquarters; see Practical Information above).

Rangers can help plan a **hike** to suit your interests and abilities. Since the trailheads in the park are already high, just a few hours of hiking will bring you into unbeatable alpine scenery along the Continental Divide. The 12,000- to 14,000-ft. altitudes can make your lungs feel like they're wrapped in rubber bands; give your brain and body enough time to adjust before starting up the higher trails. Some easy trails include the 3.6-mi. round-trip from Wild Basin Ranger Station to **Calypso Cascades** and the 2.8-mi. round-trip from the Long Peaks Ranger Station to **Eugenia Mine.** From the nearby **Glacier Gorge Junction** trailhead, take a short hike to **Mills Lake** or walk 3 mi. to the **Loch.**

From Grand Lake, a trek into the scenic and remote **North** or **East Inlets** should leave camera-toting crowds behind. Rugged mountaineers can hike to the superlative **Lake Nanita** (leave from North Inlet); the trail ascends 2240 ft. over the course of 11 mi. through pristine wilderness. From East Inlet, hike the 7 mi. to Lake Verna if you still feel strong. Plump trout swim in both wooded valleys, offering excellent fishing. The park's gem, prominent **Longs Peak** (14,255ft.), dominates the eastern slope. The peak's monumental east face, a 2000-ft. vertical wall known simply as the **Diamond,** is the most challenging rock-climbing face in Colorado.

You can also traverse the park on a mountain bike. **Colorado Bicycling Adventures,** 184 E. Elkhorn, Estes (586-4241 or 800-607-8765), rents bikes. ($5 per hr., $9 per 2hr., $15 per ½-day, $20 per day. Helmets included. 10% hosteler discounts.) Guided mountain bike tours are also offered (2hr. tour $20, 4hr. $35, ½-day $45-65; open daily 10am-9pm; off season 10am-5pm).

During the summer, the three major campgrounds (Moraine Park, Glacier Basin, and Aspenglen) have nightly amphitheater programs that examine the park's ecology. The visitors centers have information on these and on many ranger-led interpretive activities, including nature walks, birding expeditions, and artist's forays.

■■■ ASPEN

A world-renowned asylum for musicians and skiers, Aspen looms as the budget traveler's worst nightmare. In this upper-class playground, where shoppers exclaim "I'll take it!" without asking how much, low-budget living is a distant vision. To catch Aspen on the semi-cheap, stay in **Glenwood Springs** (40mi. north on Rte. 82; see p. 594) and make a daytrip here, or camp in the surrounding national forests.

Skiing is the main attraction in Aspen. The hills surrounding town contain four ski areas: **Aspen Mountain, Aspen Highlands, Buttermilk Mountain,** and **Snowmass Ski Area** (925-1220 or 800-525-6200). The resorts sell interchangeable lift tickets ($50, ages over 70 free, kids $29, under 6 free). The **Glenwood Springs Hostel** (see Glenwood Springs, p. 594) offers a $36 full-day package for Aspen which includes lift ticket, transportation, skis, and ski clothes on the cutting edge of fashion. In the summer, ride the **Silver Queen Gondola** (925-1220) to the top of the Aspen mountains (open daily 9:30am-4pm; $15, ages 13-19 $9, over 70 and under 13 free). **Hiking** in the Maroon Bells and Elk Mountains is permitted when the snow isn't too deep. Aspen's most famous event, the **Aspen Music Festival** (925-9042), holds sway over the town from late June to August. Free bus transportation goes from Rubey

Park downtown to "the Tent," south of town, before and after all concerts. (Tickets $15-50; Sun. rehearsals $8; free lawn seating.)

Pick up the free *Traveler's Guide* magazine at the **visitors center,** 320 E. Hyman Ave. (open daily 9am-7pm; winter 9am-5pm). For info on hikes and **camping** within 15 mi. of Aspen, contact the **Aspen Ranger District,** 806 W. Hallam (925-3445; **weather/avalanche info** 920-1664). They also sell a map ($3) of the area. (Open daily 8am-4:30pm, Sept.-May Mon.-Fri. 8am-4:30pm). Aspen's **area code:** 970.

If you insist on staying here, you'll have to bite the bullet and reach deep into shallow pockets. The **Little Red Ski Haüs,** 118 E. Cooper (925-3333), lies two blocks west of downtown in a cozy Victorian-style B&B (summer from $24 per person for a quad with shared bath, winter from $42 per person). The **St. Moritz Lodge,** 344 W. Hyman Ave. (925-3220 or 800-817-2069), charms ski bums with a pool, jacuzzi, hot tub, plus fridges and microwaves in rooms (dorm beds in summer $20, in early and late winter $25, peak winter from $39). Unless six ft. of snow cover the ground, try **camping** in the one of the many **National Forest Campgrounds** within 15 mi. of Aspen; both reservable and first come, first served sites scatter just west of Aspen on Maroon Rd. and southest of Aspen on Rte. 82. (3-5 day max. stay. Sites fill before noon. Open June-early Sept. Reserve by calling 800-280-2267). Free backcountry camping is also available. Contact the Aspen Ranger District for more info.

The Main Street Bakery, 201 E. Main St. (925-6446), creates gourmet soups ($4-6), homemade granola with fruit ($4.25), and three-grain pancakes ($4-5; open Mon.-Sat. 7am-9pm, Sun. 7am-4pm.) The **In and Out House,** 233 E. Main St. (925-6647), is just that—a virtual revolving door of customers in an outhouse-sized space. They offer huge sandwiches on fresh-baked bread ($2-5; open Mon.-Fri. 8am-5pm, Sat. 9am-4pm, Sun. 10am-4pm). Even if you can't afford the slopes, you can probably buy a beer. The **Flying Dog Brew Pub,** 424 E. Cooper Ave. (925-7464), just a few blocks down, is a mini-brewery serving American food; try a five-beer sampler for $3.75 (open Mon.-Sun. 11:30am-10pm). **The Red Onion,** 420 E. Cooper (925-9043), has a long, narrow bar and retaurant as well as a streetfront patio. Happy hour (daily 4-6pm) features selected ½-price appetizers. (Open daily 11am-10pm.) Mi casa es **Su Casa,** 315 E. Hyman (920-1488), which serves a range of Mexican fare (lunches $5-8, dinners $10-15) and entertains with a bar and pool tables (open daily 11:30am-3pm and 5:30-10pm). Off Rte. 82 towards Glenwood Springs, you'll find **Woody Creek Tavern,** 2 Woody Creek Pl. (923-4585), with hefty burgers ($6.50) and great Mexican specialties (open daily 11:30am-10pm).

■■■ GLENWOOD SPRINGS

Glenwood Springs, 40 mi. north on Colorado Rte. 82, is a smarter choice than Aspen for the budget traveler. Renowned for its steaming hot springs and vapor caves, Glenwood is sprinkled with budget-friendly markets, cafés, pool/dance halls, and a great hostel. The **Aspen/Glenwood Bus** shuttles between between Aspen and Glenwood several times daily. (Last bus leaves Glenwood at 3:15pm, Aspen at 5:15pm. $5 one-way, children and seniors $4, within Glenwood $1.) Contact **Glenwood Springs Chamber Resort Association,** 1102 Grand Ave. (945-6589), for more town info. (Open Mon.-Fri. 8:30am-5pm, Sat.-Sun. 9am-3pm; Sept.-May Mon.-Fri. 8:30am-5pm.) Glenwood Springs's **area code:** 970.

Nearby **Glenwood Hot Springs Pool,** 401 N. River Rd. (945-7131 or 800-537-7946), located in a huge resort complex and maintained at 90°F year-round, is the world's largest outdoor hot springs pool. (Open daily 7:30am-10pm; but call ahead. Day pass $6.50, after 9pm $4.75; ages 3-12 $4.25/$3.75.) Just one block from the large pools, the **Yampah Spa and Vapor Caves,** 709 E. 6th St. (945-0667), enjoys hot mineral waters that create a relaxing 115°F heat ($7.75, hostelers $3.75; open daily 9am-9pm). Ski at **Sunlight,** 10901 County Rd. 117 (945-7491 or 800-445-7931), 10 mi. west of town. (4-5 lifts. Hostelers Mon.-Fri. $17, Sat.-Sun. $21 per day. Cross-country skiing trail pass $4. Downhill rentals for hostelers $10.)

Within walking distance of the springs, you'll find the **Glenwood Springs Hostel (HI-AYH),** 1021 Grand Ave. (945-8545 or 800-9-HOSTEL/946-7835), consisting of a spacious former Victorian home and a newer building next door. Hostelers can ski at Sunlight, get big discounts at Aspen or Vail, go white-water rafting ($22), go with Gary on a hiking or spelunking expedition ($16), and rent equipment (mountain bikes $14 per day). (Free pickup from train/bus stations. Free pasta, rice, potatoes, and Rocky Mountain Oysters. No curfew. Lockout 10am-4pm. $10, $12 for deluxe dorms, $18 for private single, $24 for a private double. Linen included.) The Victorian B&B next door is **Adducci's Inn,** 1023 Grand Ave. (945-9341). *Let's Go*-toting guests get $28-65 singles, $38-65 doubles; otherwise slightly higher. (Prices are negotiable according to room availability. Includes morning breakfast and evening wine. Hot tub. Free pick-up from bus and train stations. $10 per additional person.) Cheap motels line the main drag of 6th St.

For a good, cheap breakfast or lunch, try the **Daily Bread Café and Bakery,** 729 Grand Ave. (945-6253; open Mon.-Fri. 7am-2pm, Sat. 8am-2pm, Sun. 8am-noon). Sit among the plants in dreamy **Avalon,** 1022 Grand Ave. (928-0731), and watch the chef chop, whip, and fry up one of many fruity and vegetarian dishes. (Granola, fruit, and yogurt $5; 2 pancakes $3.25; lunch sandwiches $4-6. Open Mon.-Sat. 7am-4pm, until 10pm for coffee and pastry; Sun. 8am-2:30pm.) **Doc Holliday's,** 724 Grand Ave. (945-9050), is the place for burgers ($6). Weekdays 5-7pm, the Doc offers dollar drafts and food. (Open daily 10am-2am.)

The **Amtrak** station thinks it can at 413 7th St. (945-9563 or 800-872-7245), chugging once per day to Denver (6½hr., $54) and Salt Lake City (9hr., $84). (Station open daily 9am-5pm. Ticket office open daily 9:30am-4:30pm.) **Greyhound** runs from 118 W. 6th St. (945-8501). Five buses run daily to Denver (3½hr., $18) and Grand Junction (2 hr., $8). (Open Mon.-Fri. 7am-2pm and 4-5:30pm, Sat. 8am-2pm.)

■■■ GRAND JUNCTION

Grand Junction gets its hyperbolic name from its seat at the confluence of the Colorado and Gunnison Rivers and the conjunction-junction of the Río Grande and Denver Railroads. This city serves as a base from which to explore **Colorado National Monument, Grand Mesa,** the Gunnison Valley, and the western San Juans.

Several wineries ferment in town, while a few museums enlighten. **Dinosaur Valley,** an extension of the **Museum of Western Colorado** (242-0971), is located at 362 Main St. Moving and growling dinosaurs entertain children, while displays of serious paleontological research cater to adults (open daily 9am-5:30pm; Sept.-May Tues.-Sat. 10am-4:30pm; $4, ages 2-12 $2.50). For "a playground for the mind" that roars at you with robotic dinos and shakes you up with simulated earthquakes, descend into **Devil's Canyon Science & Learning Center,** 550 Crossroads Ct. (858-7282), 13 mi. west in Fruita (open daily 8:30am-7pm; Sept-May 9am-5pm. $5, over 54 or under 13 $3.50).

The **Grand Junction Visitor and Convention Bureau,** 740 Horizon Dr. (244-1480) has area information; ask about their weekly lecture and slide show programs which highlight the history and culture of southwest Colorado (open daily 8:30am-8pm, late Sept.-early May 8:30am-5pm). Many Grand Junction sites are difficult to get to without a car. **Enterprise Car Rental,** 406 S. 5th St. (242-8103), rents compact cars for $27 per day, $140 per week, with unlimited mileage within Colorado, 24¢ per mi. outside; you must be 21. Grand Junction's **post office:** 241 N. 4th St. (244-3401; open Mon.-Fri. 8am-5:30pm, Sat. 9am-12:30pm); **ZIP code:** 81502; **area code:** 970.

Grand Junction's chief attribute is its location among several natural wonders. Fortunately, the smooth-running **Melrose Hotel (HI-AYH),** 337 Colorado Ave. (242-9636 or 800-430-4555), between 3rd and 4th St., is poised to guide travelers to almost all natural wonders and to direct hostelers to the best deals in town. Owners Marcus and Sabrina will make you feel at home and direct you to the best deals in town. Marcus's tours to Arches National Park (see p. 626), Colorado National Monument (p. 596), Grand Mesa (p. 596), and Black Canyon (p. 601) are a must, taking you off tourist paths for serious sightseeing (individual excursions $25-35; all four trips $75). In winter, $25 will buy a day trip to Powderhorn, which includes a lift ticket, skis, boots, poles, clothes, and transportation. Just hope the Melrose hostel doesn't explode at the end of the season. (Kitchen facilities. Dorms $10, including light breakfast. Singles $22.50, with private bath $27.50; doubles $26, with TV and private bath $32.50. Call for winter rates.) **Lé Master Motel,** 2858 North Ave. (243-3230), has singles for $29, doubles for $32. Camp in **Highline State Park** (858-7208), 24 mi. from town and 7 mi. north of exit 15 on I-70 (fishing access, restrooms; 25 sites $10), or **Island Acres State Park** (464-0548), 12 mi. east on the banks of the Colorado River (32 sites $9, plus $3 day pass to enter the park).

The **Rockslide Restaurant and Brew Pub,** 401 S. Main (245-2111), has chipped in to the avalanche of micro-breweries covering the nation; the home-brewed Big Bear Stout is $3 per pint. (Generous 10-in. pizza $6.75. Free pub grub during happy hour, 4-6pm. Open Mon.-Fri. 11am-10pm, Sat.-Sun. 8am-11pm; bar open daily 11am-11pm.) **Dos Hombres Restaurant,** 421 Brach Dr. (242-8861), just south of Broadway (Rte. 340) on the southern bank of the Colorado River, serves great Mexican food in a casual setting. (Combination dinners $4-7. Open daily 11am-10pm.) For all the fixins', head to **City Market,** 1909 N. 1st St. (243-0842; open 24 hrs.).

Grand Junction lies at the intersection of U.S. 50 and U.S. 6 in northwestern Colorado. Denver is 228 mi. to the east; Salt Lake City 240 mi. to the west. The **Greyhound station,** 230 S. 5th St. (242-6012), has service to Denver (5 per day, 5½hr., $24), Durango (1 per day, 4hr., $26), Salt Lake City (1 per day, 6hr., $42), and Los Angeles (5 per day, 15hr., $85). (Open Mon.-Fri. 3am-10pm, Sat.-Sun. 3-8am and 11am-10pm.) **Amtrak,** 337 S. 1st St. (241-2733 or 800-872-7245), chugs once a day to Denver (8hr., $72) and Salt Lake City (5½hr., $69). (Open daily 10am-6pm.)

■■■ COLORADO MONUMENT

Colorado National Monument is a 32-sq.-mi. sculpture of steep cliff faces, canyon walls, and obelisk-like spires wrought by the forces of gravity, wind, and water. A ride along 23-mi. **Rim Rock Dr.** treats the visitor to eerie red skeletal formations, bubble-like white boulders, and piles of compressed red rock that mimic giant stacks of flapjacks. **Window Rock Trail,** an easy ¼-mi. walk from the visitor's center, gives a sweeping view of Monument Canyon. **Otto's Trail** (¼mi.) provides a dramatic view of many monoliths. The trail is named for John Otto, who fell in love with the area and built 10 of the park's 14 trails, then lobbied President Taft for two years to make the park a National Monument. The **Monument Canyon** trail drops 6 mi. down into the canyon and gives a dwarfing perspective of many stunning formations from below. Check in at the monument **headquarters and visitors center** (970-858-3617), near the campground on the Fruita side (open daily 8am-7pm; off season 8am-4:30pm). No camping permit is needed. **Saddlehorn Campground** offers 80 campsites in the monument on a first come, first served basis, with picnic tables, grills, and restrooms (sites $8). The **Bureau of Land Management,** 2815 Horizon (970-244-3000; open Mon.-Fri. 7:30am-4:30pm), across from the airport, maintains three free primitive campgrounds near **Glade Park** at Mud Springs. Bring your own water. **Little Dolores Fall,** 3 mi. west of Mud Springs, has fishing and swimming. The monument charges an admission fee of $4 per vehicle, $2 per cyclist or hiker, and is free for the disabled and seniors.

■■■ GRAND MESA

Grand Mesa, "the great table," is the world's largest flat-top mountain, looming 50 mi. east of Grand Junction (by road). Dominating the landscape for miles around, Grand Mesa has long been subject to speculation. A Native American story tells how the Mesa's many lakes were formed by fragments of a serpent torn to bits by a mad mother eagle who believed her young to be inside the serpent's belly. Recently, geologists have estimated that a 300-ft.-thick lava flow covered the entire region 6000 million years ago, and the Mesa is the only portion to have endured erosion.

Whatever the Mesa's origin, this area is rife with outdoor attractions, including fine **backcountry hiking.** To reach Grand Mesa from Grand Junction, take I-70 eastbound to Plateau Creek, where Rte. 65 cuts off for the long climb through spruce trees to the top of the mesa. Near the top is the Land's End turn-off, which leads to the very edge of Grand Mesa, some 12 mi. down a well-maintained dirt road (closed in winter). On a clear day, you can see halfway across Utah. The higher areas of the Mesa remain cool into summer, so be sure to bring a sweater and long pants.

The Mesa not only has an excellent view, but excellent camping as well. The district **forest service,** 764 Horizon Dr. (970-242-8211), in Grand Junction, has maps ($3) and info on the **campsites** they maintain on the Mesa (open Mon.-Fri. 8am-5pm). **Island Lake** (41 sites, $8) and **Ward Lake** (27 sites, $9) are both on the water and have good fishing; **Jumbo** (26 site,s $9), **Little Bear** (37 sites, $9), and **Cottonwood** (42 sites, $7) are good, large campgrounds; **Crag Crest** (11 sites, $8) and **Spruce Grove** (16 sites, $8) are smaller and more intimate; **Eggleston** (6 sites, $7) is for group camping; and there are also 10 free campgrounds. Call the visitors center (856-4153) for more info on any site. **Vega State Park** (970-487-3407), 12 mi. east of Colbran off Rte. 330, offers 140 campsites in the high country. (Park entrance fee $3 per vehicle; sites $6 per night.)

The **Alexander Lake Lodge** (970-856-6700), off scenic Rte. 65, is a good place to stop if you're cold, tired, or hungry. This old hunting lodge serves up burgers ($5), pasta dinners with salad and bread ($9), and hot cocoa to warm you up (restaurant open Wed.-Sun. 8am-9pm). The Lodge also runs a general store and rents out 17 cabins. (Most have kitchenettes. Mon.-Thurs. $40, Fri.-Sun. $55; $10 more for each additional person.) The stable (970-856-7323) across the street offers horseback riding for $18 per hour. Motor boats are available at $9 per hour. There are over 300 lakes boiling with rainbow trout around the Mesa.

■■■ COLORADO SPRINGS

Surrounded by outstanding natural beauty, Colorado Springs reaches for the sky. Long ago, legend has it, gods hurled down the bodies of the Ute Indian's enemies from above, thus creating the hypnotizing Garden of the Gods. In 1859, pioneers rushed towards towering Pikes Peak when gold was discovered in the area, crying "Pikes Peak or Bust!" Today, the United States Olympic Team, housed in Colorado Springs, are the ones looking for gold, while jets from United States Air Force Academy streak through wisps of clouds overhead.

PRACTICAL INFORMATION

Tourist Office: Colorado Springs Convention and Visitors Bureau, 104 S. Cascade #104, 80903 (635-7506 or 800-368-4748), at Colorado Ave. Pick up the *Colorado Springs Pikes Peak Region Official Visitors Guide* and the city bus map. Open Mon.-Fri. 8:30am-5:30pm, Sat.-Sun. 8:30am-5pm; Nov.-March Mon.-Fri. 8:30am-5pm.

Tours: Gray Line Tours, 3704 Colorado Ave. (633-1747 or 800-345-8197), at the Garden of the Gods Campgrounds. Trips to the U.S. Air Force Academy and Garden of the Gods (4hr., $18, under 13 $9), Pikes Peak (4hr., $25, under 13 $15). Also offers a 10mi. whitewater rafting trip (7hr., includes lunch, $55, under 13 $35; must weigh at least 50 lbs). Office open daily 7am-10pm.

Buses: Greyhound, 120 S. Weber St. (635-1505). To: Denver (7 per day, 1¾hr., $10); Pueblo (5 per day, 50min., $6.25); Albuquerque (4 per day, 7-9hr., $60). Tickets sold daily 5:15am-9:30pm.

Public Transportation: Colorado Springs City Bus Service, 125 E. Kiowa (475-9733) at Nevada, 3 blocks from the Greyhound station. Serves the city itself, Widefield, Manitou Springs, Fort Carson, Garden of the Gods, and Peterson AFB. Service Mon.-Sat. 5:45am-6:15pm every ½hr., evening service 6-10pm every hr.

Fare 75¢, seniors and kids 35¢, under 6 free; long trips 25¢ extra. Exact change required.

Taxis: Yellow Cab, 634-5000. $1.65 base fare, $1.35 per mi.

Car Rental: Ugly Duckling, 2021 E. Platte (634-1914). From $20 per day, $108 per week. 100 free mi. per day. Open Mon.-Fri. 9am-5:30pm, Sat. 9am-1pm. Must stay in Colorado and be 21 with major credit card or $250 deposit.

Crisis Lines: Crisis Emergency Services, 635-7000. 24 hrs. **Rape Crisis Line,** 444-7563 (day), 444-7000 (night).

Road Conditions: 635-7623 (recording).

Emergency: 911.

Post Office: 201 Pikes Peak Ave. (570-5336), at Nevada Ave. Open Mon.-Fri. 7:30am-5:30pm, Sat. 7:30am-1pm. **ZIP code:** 80903. **Area code:** 719.

Colorado Springs is laid out in a grid of broad thoroughfares. The mountains are to the west. **Nevada Ave.** is the main north-south strip, known for its bars and restaurants. **Colorado Ave.** is the east-west axis, which connects with **U.S. 24** on the city's west side. **I-25** from Denver plows through downtown. East of Nevada Ave., there are basically only residential homes and large shopping centers. The streets west of Nevada are numbered, increasing as you move west.

ACCOMMODATIONS AND CAMPING

Avoid the mostly shabby motels along Nevada Ave. If the youth hostel fails you, head for a nearby campground or the establishments along W. Pikes Peak Ave. and W. Colorado Ave.

Garden of the Gods Youth Hostel and Campground (HI-AYH), 3704 W. Colorado Ave. (475-9450 or 800-248-9451). Take bus #1 west to 37th St. Stealth hostel: twelve 4-bunk shanties hidden behind the massive 300-site campground. Showers and bathrooms shared with campground. Spare but clean facilities. Bunkrooms are not heated; bring your sleeping bag! Swimming pool, jacuzzi, laundry; no kitchen. Members only, $10. Linen $2. Open April-Oct.

Apache Court Motel, 3401 W. Pikes Peak Ave. (471-9440). Take bus #1 west down Colorado Ave. to 34th St. and walk 1 block north. Pink adobe rooms. A/C, TV, hot tub. Singles $33-35 for one person, $40-45 for two, doubles $54-59 for two. $5 each additional person. Prices lower in winter. No pets.

Amarillo Motel, 2801 W. Colorado Ave. (635-8539). Take bus #1 west down Colorado Ave. to 28th St. Ask for rooms in the older National Historic Register section. Bunker-like rooms lack windows, but have kitchens and TV. Laundry available. Singles $32-40, doubles $38-45. Sept.-May rooms $5 cheaper.

Located inside the city limits, the four-star **Garden of the Gods Campground** (see hostel above) is better for RVs than tents; most of the sites are on a gravel parking lot. Enjoy flapjack breakfasts (Sun.) or coffee and doughnuts (3-person sites $22, $2 for each extra person, hookup $23, full hookup $25). Several **Pike National Forest** campgrounds lie in the mountains flanking Pikes Peak (generally open May-Sept.), but no local transportation serves this area. Campgrounds clutter Rte. 67 5-10 mi. north of **Woodland Park,** which is 18 mi. northwest of the Springs on U.S. 24. Others fringe U.S. 24 near the town of Lake George, 50 mi. west of the Springs. (All sites $8-10.) You can always camp off any road on national forest property for free if you are at least 150 yds. from a road or stream.The **Forest Service Office,** 601 S. Weber (636-1602), has maps ($3) of the area (open Mon.-Fri. 8am-4:30pm). Farther afield, you can camp in the **Eleven Mile State Recreation Area** (748-3401 or 800-678-2267), which surrounds a reservoir, off a spur road from U.S. 24 near Lake George (showers; sites $6, electricity $10; entrance fee $3). As a last resort, try the **Peak View Campground,** 4954 N. Nevada Ave. (598-1545; 2-person sites $16, water and electricity $16.50, full hookup $18-19).

FOOD AND NIGHTLIFE

Students and the young-at-heart perch among outdoor tables in front of the cafés and restaurants that line Tejon Ave. north of Colorado Ave. **Poor Richard's Restaurant,** 332 North Tejon (632-7721), is the local coffeehouse/college hangout, serving pizza ($1.95 per slice; $9.50 per pie) and veggie food (open daily 11am-10pm). Next door, the popular street tables of **Boulder Street Coffee Roasters** (577-4291) heat up with caffeinated drinks and sinful desserts (open daily 6:30am-midnight). **La Baguette,** 2417 W. Colorado Ave. (577-4818), bakes bread and melts fondues a sight better than you might expect in a place so far from Paris. Soup and roll go for $3.75; filling fondue, apple, and loaf for $6. (Open Mon.-Sat. 7am-6pm, Sun. 6am-5pm.) Big crowds gather at **Henri's,** 2427 W. Colorado Ave. (634-9031), for fantastic margaritas and Mexican food, such as $3 meat-and-cheese enchiladas (open Tues.-Sat. 11:30am-10pm, Sun. noon-10pm). Spend a fun, hokey evening at the **Flying W Ranch,** 3330 Chuckwagon Rd. (598-4000 or 800-232-3599), where you chomp a huge chuckwagon supper while watching a Wild West show. ($13 includes show and dinner, kids under 8 $7. Oct.-May Fri.-Sat. nights only; closed Jan.-Feb.) The **Dublin House,** 1850 Dominion Way (528-1704), at Academy St., is a popular sports bar with occasional live tunes (open Mon.-Thurs. 4pm-2am, Fri.-Sun. 11am-2am; no cover).

SIGHTS

Pike's Peak From any part of the town, one can't help noticing the 14,110-ft. summit of Pikes Peak on the western horizon. You can climb the peak via the 13-mi. **Barr Burro Trail;** the trailhead is in Manitou Springs by the "Manitou Incline" sign (bus #1 to Ruxton). Don't despair if you don't reach the top—explorer Zebulon Pike never reached it either, and they named the whole mountain after him. Otherwise, pay the fee to drive up the **Pikes Peak Highway** (684-9383), administered by the Colorado Department of Public Works. (Open June-Sept. 7am-7pm; Apr.-May and Sept.-Oct. 9am-3pm, weather permitting. $5, ages 6-11 $2.) Five mi. west in Manitou Springs, you can also reserve a seat on the **Pikes Peak Cog Railway,** 515 Ruxton Ave. (685-5401), which takes you to the top from May to early October daily between 8am and 5:20pm, with departures every 80 minutes. (Call for times in May, Sept. and Oct. Round-trip $21, ages 5-11 $9.50, under 5 free if held on lap.) From the summit, Kansas, the Sangre de Cristo Mountains, and the Continental Divide unfold before you. This lofty view inspired Kathy Lee Bates to write "America the Beautiful." Expect cold weather. Roads often remain icy through the summer.

Garden of the Gods City Park Frolic in the 300-million-year-old "Garden of the Gods," 1401 Recreation Way (578-6640). Once the red-rock basin of an inland sea, it was lifted by tectonic forces. To get there, take Colorado Ave. to 30th St. and then head north on Ridge Rd. A slick new **visitors center,** 1805 N. 30th St. (634-6666), gives a 45-min. tram tour that putters about the park's natural formations and historic sights ($2). A walk around the four trail loops is free; the 1-mi. central garden trail shows the most in the shortest distance and is wheelchair-accessible. The park contains many secluded picnic and hiking areas. The oft-photographed "balanced rock" is at the park's south entrance. The best vantage point for pictures is from Mesa Rd., off 30th St.

Cave of the Winds For more adventurous hiking, head for the contorted caverns of the Cave of the Winds (685-5444) on Rte. 24, 6 mi. west of exit 141 off I-25 (guided tours daily every 15min. 9am-10pm; April 10am-5pm; $8, ages 6-15 $4). Just above Manitou Springs on Rte. 24 lies the **Manitou Cliff Dwellings Museum** (685-5242 or 685-5394) on the U.S. 24 bypass, where you can wander through a pueblo of ancient Anasazi buildings dating from 1100-1300AD. (Open daily June-Aug. 9am-8pm; hours vary in off season. $4.50, seniors $3.50, ages 7-11 $2.50.)

Going for the Gold and Aiming High Watch Olympic hopefuls at the **U.S. Olympic Complex,** 750 E. Boulder St. (578-4644), at I-25 exit 156A; take bus #1 east to Farragut. Every ½ hr., the complex offers 1¼-hr. tours that include a tear-jerking film. (Open Mon.-Sat. 9am-5pm, Sun. 10am-4pm; off season Mon.-Sat. 9am-4pm, Sun. noon-4pm.) Earlier searches for gold are recorded at the **Pioneers' Museum,** downtown at 215 S. Tejon St. (578-6650), which recounts the settling of Colorado Springs, and includes a display on the techniques and instruments of a pioneer doctor (open Tues.-Sat. 10am-5pm, Sun. 1-5pm; free). Get your own yellow chunk at the **Western Museum of Mining and Industry,** 1025 N. Gate Rd. (488-0880), where you can learn how to pan for gold. (Open Mon.-Sat. 9am-4pm, Sun. noon-4pm. $5, students and seniors $4, under 13 $2. Closed Dec.-Feb.)

Hosting over a million visitors yearly, the most popular attraction in the area is the **United States Air Force Academy,** 12 mi. north of town off I-25 exit 156B. Its chapel (472-4515) is constructed of aluminum, steel, and other materials used in building airplanes (open Mon.-Sat. 9am-5pm, Sun. 1-5pm). On weekdays during the school year, cadets gather at 12:10pm near the chapel for the cadet lunch formation (i.e., to eat). The **visitors center** (472-2555 or 472-2025) has self-guided tour maps, info on special events, and a 14-min. movie every ½-hr. (open daily 9am-6pm).

Ground Zero

Buried in a hollowed-out cave 1800 ft. below Cheyenne Mountain, the **North American Air Defense Command Headquarters (NORAD)** (554-2241) was designed to survive even a direct nuclear hit. Call way ahead for tour reservations; security clearance takes six months,. A 3-mi. tunnel leads to this center, which monitors every plane in the sky. The **Peterson Air Force Base,** on the east side of the city, houses a **visitors center** and the **Edward J. Peterson Space Command Museum** (556-4915; open Tues.-Fri. 8:30am-4:30pm, Sat. 9:30am-4:30pm; free).

■■■ GREAT SAND DUNES

When Colorado's mountains all begin to look the same, make a path to the **Great Sand Dunes National Monument** at the northwest edge of the **San Luis Valley.** There, a sea of 700-ft. sand dunes, representing thousands of years of wind-blown accumulation, laps silently at the base of the **Sangre de Cristo Range.** The progress of the dunes through passes in the range is checked by the shallow **Medano Creek;** visitors can wade across the creek when it flows (April to mid-July). Those with four-wheelers can motor over the **Medano Pass Primitive Road.** The best way to enjoy the dunes is to just plow on in; but beware the intense afternoon heat. At the southern boundary of the monument, the **Oasis** complex (719-378-2222) offers four-wheel-drive tours that huff over Medano Pass Primitive Road to the nether regions of the dunes (2 tours daily; 2hr.; $14, ages 5-11 $8).

Rangers preside over daily activities. Full schedules are at the **visitors center** (719-378-2312), ½ mi. past the entrance gate. (Open daily 9am-6pm, Labor Day-Memorial Day 8am-5pm. Entrance fee for vehicles $4, pedestrians and bikers $2.) For more info contact the Superintendent, Great Sand Dunes National Monument, Mosca, CO 81146 (719-378-2312). For **emergencies** within the park, call 911.

Pinyon Flats (719-378-2312) is the monument's primitive, cactus-covered **campground.** Bring mosquito repellent in June. (88 first come, first served sites $8; arrive by early afternoon to be safe. Group sites reservable, $2 per person, $25 min.) Get free **backcountry camping** permits for the dunes from the visitors center. If the park's sites are full, Oasis (see above) will quench your needs with with showers, two-person sites ($10, with hookup $15; each additional person $2.50), and cabins or tepees ($25 for 2 people). **San Luis State Park** (719-378-2020), 8 mi. away in Mosca, has showers and 51 electrical sites ($10; $3 vehicle entrance fee; closed in winter). For info on nearby National Forest Campgrounds (all sites $8), contact the

Río Grande National Forest Service Office, 1803 W. U.S. 160, Monte Vista, CO 81144 (719-274-5193).

Great Sand Dunes National Monument drifts 32 mi. northeast of Alamosa and 112 mi. west of Pueblo on Rte. 150 off U.S. 160. **Greyhound** sends one bus per day from Denver to Alamosa, 32 mi. from the monument (5½hr., $36, see Denver: Practical Information, above). The depot in Alamosa is at 8480 Stockton St. (719-589-8558; open Mon.-Fri. 10am-5pm, Sat.-Sun. 4-5pm). From Alamosa, however, there is no public transportation to the monument.

SAN JUAN MOUNTAINS

Ask Coloradans about their favorite mountain retreats, and they'll most likely name a peak, lake, stream, or town in the San Juan Range of southwestern Colorado. Four **national forests**—the **Uncompahgre** (un-cum-PAH-gray), the **Gunnison,** the **San Juan,** and the **Río Grande**—encircle this sprawling range. **Durango** is an ideal base camp for forays into these mountains. Northeast of Durango, the **Weminuche Wilderness** tempts the hardy backpacker with a vast expanse of rugged terrain where wide, sweeping vistas stretch for mile upon mile. Get maps and info on hiking in the San Juans from **Pine Needle Mountaineering,** Main Mall, Durango 81301 (970-247-8728; open Mon.-Sat. 9am-6pm, Sun. 10am-5pm; maps $4).

The San Juan area is easily accessible on U.S. 50, which is traveled by hundreds of thousands of tourists each summer. **Greyhound** serves the area, but very poorly; traveling by car is the best option in this region. On a happier note, the San Juans are loaded with HI-AYH hostels and campgrounds, making them one of the more economical places to visit in Colorado.

■■■ BLACK CANYON

Native American parents used to tell their children that the light-colored strands of molten material streaking through the walls of the Black Canyon were the hair of a blond woman—and that if they got too close to the edge they would get tangled in it and fall. With or without folklore, the edge of **Black Canyon of the Gunnison National Monument** is a staggering place. The Gunnison River gouged out the 53-mi.-long canyon over a period of 2 million years, crafting a steep 2500-ft.-deep gorge dominated by inky shadows (hence black); the Empire State Building, if placed at the bottom of the river, would reach barely halfway up the canyon walls.

Practical Information The Black Canyon lies 60 mi. southeast of Grand Junction. The **South Rim** is accessible via Rte. 347 off U.S. 50; the less touristed **North Rim,** which has arguably better views, lies at the end of a gravel country road off Rte. 92 from Crawford. The Canyon has two **visitors centers**—one on the South Rim (249-1915; open daily 8am-6pm), and another on the North Rim (open May-Sept. daily 8am-6pm). **Montrose,** on U.S. 50, houses the **administrative offices** for the canyon at 2233 E. Main St. (249-7036; open Mon.-Fri. 8am-4:30pm; reduced hours off season). **Greyhound** serves Montrose at 132 N. 1st St. (249-6673), and **Gunnison,** 55 mi. east, at the Gunnison county airport, 711 Rio Grande (641-0060). Fare between Gunnison and Montrose is $12; the bus will drop you off at the junction of U.S. 50 and Rte. 347, 6 mi. from the canyon. **Western Express Taxi** (249-8880) will drive you to the canyon from Montrose for about $30. Montrose's **visitors center** assists at 2490 S. Townsend Ave. (249-1726; open May-Oct. Mon.-Sat. 9am-7pm, Sun. 9am-5pm). Montrose's **ZIP code:** 81401; **area code:** 970.

Accommodations and Food Many inexpensive motels line **Main St. /U.S. 30. The Traveler's B&B Inn,** 502 S. First (249-3472), parallel to Main St., lets simple, cozy rooms with TV and breakfast (singles $30, doubles $35; with private bath $35/

$40). **The Log Cabin Motel,** 1034 E. Main St. (249-7610), toward the end of town closest to the Monument, offers clean rooms (singles $32, doubles $34; $4 less in winter). **Starvin' Arvin's,** 1320 S. Townsend Ave. (249-7787), serves generous breakfasts all day; feast on 3-egg omelettes with hashbrowns and hotcakes ($5; open daily 6am-10pm). The **Stockmen's Café and Bar,** 320 E. Main St. (249-9946), serves Mexican and western food (sandwiches $3-6; open Sun.-Tues. and Thurs. 7am-10pm, Fri.-Sat. 7am-midnight).

Exploring the Black Canyon The 8-mi. scenic drive along the South Rim boasts spectacular **Chasm View,** where you can peer 2000 ft. down a sheer vertical drop; **Painted Wall,** 56 yds. away, is the highest cliff in Colorado and is over a billion years old. Inspired hikers can descend to the bottom of the canyon; the least difficult trail (more like a controlled fall), **Gunnison Route,** drops 1800 ft. over a distance of 1 mi. The hike up is a *tad* more difficult. At certain points you must hoist yourself up on a chain in order to gain ground. Suffice it to say, this hike is not to be undertaken lightly. Free **backcountry permits** are required for sub-rim adventurers and are available at the South Rim visitors center. Get advice from a ranger before any descent. Easier hikes stick to the rims. On the North Rim, the **North Vista Trail** to **Exclamation Point** (3mi. round-trip) punctuates a leisurely walk with several dizzying canyon views. On the South Rim, **Warner Point Nature Trail** is a ½-mi. loop that affords a great view of surrounding mountain ranges. The visitors center offers guided nature walks (½hr.-1½hr.). Free narrated evening programs are given at the park's entrance daily in summer at 8:45pm. (Park entrance fee $4 per car charged only on the South Rim.)

Each rim has one **campground.** The North Rim has 13 sites, the South Rim has 102 sites (pit toilets, charcoal grills, water available; sites at both $8, open May-Nov.). Since wood gathering is not allowed, bring your own wood/charcoal or pick some up at the **Information/Gift Shop** at the turn-off to the park from U.S. 50 (open May to mid-Nov.). Call the National Park Service (249-7036) in Montrose or the South Rim visitor center (see above) for details.

For **picnics,** head to the tables of **Crystal Dam** via the long, winding, *steep* E. Portal Rd. off S. Rim Rd. just before South Rim Campground, which leads to a gorgeous setting on the Gunnison River (no vehicles longer than 22ft. allowed).

The **Ute Indian Museum,** 17253 Chipeta Dr. (249-3098), a few mi. south of Montrose on U.S. 550, has exhibits on the Bear Dance and the bilingual letters of Southern Ute chief Ouray. (Open mid-May to Aug. Mon.-Fri. 9am-6pm, Sat. 10am-5pm, Sun. 1-5pm; in Sept. closed Mon.-Tues. $2.50, over 64 $2, ages 6-16 $1.50.)

■ NEAR GUNNISON: CRESTED BUTTE

Crested Butte (CREST-ed BYOOT, not Crusty Butt you meddling kids), 27 mi. north of **Gunnison** on Rte. 135, was once a mining town. Luckily for snow bunnies, the coal was exhausted by the 1950s, and Crested Butte is now frequented by skiers and mountain bikers. **Mt. Crested Butte,** 3 mi. north, lies in the middle of a broad valley, completely dominating the area. During the winter, **Mt. Crested Butte Resort** (800-544-8448) offers great trails, racing, ski schools, and snowboarding. (Free skiing early to mid-April and mid-Nov. to mid-Dec.; some lodging/ski packages are also available. Call for details.) The resort also offers endless activities such as **dog-sled** tours (641-1636), **fondue** parties (349-2211), and **hot air balloon** rides (349-6712). During the summer, the main activities are hiking, camping, and biking on the mountain and in Gunnison National Forest.

The **Crested Butte Chamber of Commerce** (349-6438 or 800-545-4505) awaits queries at 6th and Eliot St. (open daily 9am-5pm). From the chamber of commerce, take a free **shuttle** (349-5616) to the mountain (every 15min. late May-late Sept., in winter when snow is around). Crested Butte's **post office:** on Elk Ave. (349-5568; open Mon.-Fri. 8am-4:30pm, Sat. 9am-1pm); **ZIP Code:** 81224; **area code:** 970.

You'll have as much luck finding budget lodging in Crested Butte as you will striking a major vein of gold; call the Crested Butte lodging hotline at 800-215-2226. **Gunnison National Forest's** office, 216 N. Colorado (641-0471), Gunnison, has info on a plethora of campgrounds. Within the forest are the **Lake Irwin Campground** (32 sites, $8), the **Cement Creek Campground** (13 sites, $7), and the **Almont Campground** (10 sites, $7).

Brick Oven Pizza, 313 3rd St. (349-5044), dishes out authentic NY- and Chicago-style pizzas from a small window; big slices go for $1.75-$2. (Open Mon.-Thurs. 11am-midnight, Fri.-Sat. 11:30am-2:30am, Sun. 11:30am-10pm.) **Stefanie's Country Store** serves burgers ($3.50), savory lunch specials, and homemade pies (open Mon.-Fri. 7am-6pm, Sat. 8am-6pm, Sun. 9am-2pm; winter hours vary). **The Crested Butte Brewery,** 226 Elk Ave. (349-5026), features homemade beers such as the famed "Rodeo Stout" (pint $2.75) as well as BBQ, Tex-Mex fare, and live music (open daily 11am-10pm).

■■■ TELLURIDE

Site of the first bank Butch Cassidy ever robbed (the San Miguel), Telluride has a history right out of a 1930s black-and-white film. Prizefighter Jack Dempsey used to wash dishes in the Athenian Senate, a popular saloon/brothel that frequently required Dempsey to double as bouncer between plates. The **Sheridan Theatre** (see below) hosted actresses Sarah Bernhardt and Lillian Gish on cross-country theater tours. Presidential candidate William Jennings Bryan delivered his "Cross of Gold" speech in silver-scooping Telluride from the front balcony of the Sheridan Hotel. Not so rare (especially after its devaluation) was the silver that attracted all the less aesthetically inclined hoodlums to Telluride in the first place. Today, skiers, hikers, and vacationers come to Telluride to put gold and silver *into* these mountains; the town is gaining popularity and may become the Aspen of the future. Still, a small-town feeling prevails; rocking chairs sit on the porches of lightly painted, wood-shingled houses, and dogs are tied to storefront porches.

Practical Information The **visitors center** is upstairs at Rose's, near the entrance to town at demonic 666 W. Colorado Ave. (728-3041 or 800-525-3455; open Mon.-Fri. 9am-9pm, Sat.-Sun. 9am-6pm). Telluride is only accessible by car, on U.S. 550 or Rte. 145. The closest Greyhound stop is in Montrose, 132 N. 1st St. (249-6673), a 60-mi. drive. Telluride's **post office:** 101 E. Colorado Ave. (728-3900; open Mon.-Fri. 9am-5pm, Sat. 10am-noon); **ZIP code:** 81435; **area code:** 970.

Accommodations, Food, and Nightlife If you're visiting Telluride for a festival, bring a sleeping bag; the cost of a bed is outrageous. The **Oak Street Inn,** 134 N. Oak St. (728-3383), offers dorm-style lodging complete with a sauna. (Singles with shared bath $39, doubles $53, triples $67, quads $80. Showers $3. More expensive during festivals.) **Camp** at the east end of town in a town-operated facility with water, restrooms, and showers (728-3071; 2-week max. stay; 46 sites; $8, except during festivals). **Sunshine,** 6 mi. southwest on Rte. 145 toward Cortez, is a developed national forest campground (2-week max. stay; 14 sites, $8). For info on all **National Forest Campgrounds**, call the Forest Service (327-4261). Several free primitive sites huddle nearby, accessible by jeep roads. During festival times, you can crash almost anywhere; hot showers are available at the local high school ($2).

Baked in Telluride, 127 S. Fir St. (728-4775), has enough rich coffee and delicious pastry, pizza, salad, and 50¢-bagels to get you through a festival weekend even if you *are* baked in Telluride (open daily 5:30am-10pm). For delicious Italian fare, head to **Eddie's Café,** 300 W. Colorado (728-5335), for eight-inch pizzas ($5) and hefty pasta entrees ($8-12; open daily 11:30am-10pm). Good breakfasts hide out at **Sofio's Mexican Café,** 110 E. Colorado (728-4882). Most breakfast items start at $4. (Open daily 7am-11:30am for breakfast; 5:30-10pm for dinner.)

Sample live world-beat music and international bar food (from $5) at **One World Café,** 114 E. Colorado Ave. (728-5530; open daily 11:30am-1:30am; cover $3-5 after 9pm). Chug one of ten beers on tap at **The House, A Tavern,** 131 N. Fir St. (728-6207), where many college-students-gone-ski-bums hang out (drafts $2-4; happy hour 4-7pm, 75¢ off all beers). The cool, conversational **Last Dollar Saloon,** 100 E. Colorado (728-4800), near Pine, will take your last buck and smile (bottled beer $2-3). Although the continental cuisine is expensive, the welcoming bar at **Leimgruber's,** 573 W. Pacific Ave. (728-4663), is "the place to be for aprés-ski."

Festivals and Activities The quality and number of summer arts festivals seem staggering when you consider that only 1500 people call the town home. For general festival information, contact the visitors center (see above). While get-togethers occur just about every weekend in summer and fall, the most renowned is the **Bluegrass Festival** (800-624-2422) in late June—in recent years the likes of James Taylor and the Indigo Girls have attracted crowds of 19,000, although capacity is limited to 10,000 (tickets $30-45 per night). Telluride also hosts a **Talking Gourds** poetry fest (327-4767 or email *goodtimes@infozone.telluride.co.usa*) and a **Jazz Celebration** (first weekend in Aug.), among others. Music festivals seem to jam all over town, all day, and deep into the night. The **Telluride International Film Festival** (603-643-1255) on Labor Day weekend draws actors and directors from all over the globe, including Jodie Foster and Daryl Hannah. It premiered such films as *The Crying Game* and *The Piano.* For some festivals, you can volunteer to usher, set up chairs, or perform other tasks in exchange for tickets.

Biking, hiking, and backpacking opportunities are endless; ghost towns and lakes are tucked behind mountain crags. For an enjoyable day hike, trek up the San Miguel River Canyon to **Bridal Veil Falls,** which is visible from Telluride; drive to the end of Rte. 145 and hike the steep dirt road to the waterfall.

In winter, even self-proclaimed atheists can be spied crossing themselves before hitting the "Spiral Stairs" and the "Plunge," two of the Rockies' most gut-wrenching ski runs. For more info, contact the **Telluride Ski Resort,** P.O. Box 307, Telluride 81435 (728-3856). For a copy of the *Skier Services Brochure* contact the visitors center (see above). A free shuttle connects the mountain village with the rest of the town; pick up a current schedule at the visitors center. **Paragon Ski and Sport,** 213 W. Colorado Ave. (728-4525), rents camping supplies, bikes, skis and boots ($15 per day), and roller blades. (Open daily 9am-7:30pm; winter daily 8am-9pm.)

■■■ DURANGO

As Will Rogers once put it, Durango is "out of the way and glad of it." Despite its popularity as a tourist destination, Durango retains a relaxed atmosphere. Come here to see Mesa Verde and to raft down the Animas River.

Practical Information Durango parks at the intersection of U.S. 160 and U.S. 150. Streets run perpendicular to avenues, but everyone calls Main Ave. "Main Street." The **Durango Area Chamber Resort Association,** 111 S. Camino del Rio (247-0312 or 800-525-8855), across from Gateway Dr., is extremely helpful and will answer questions about camping. (Open Mon.-Sat. 8am-7pm, Sun. 10am-4pm; winter Mon.-Sat. 8am-5pm, Sun. 10am-4pm.) **Greyhound,** 275 E. 8th Ave. (259-2755), runs once per day to Grand Junction (6hr., $35), Denver (12hr., $56), and Albuquerque (5hr., $35). (Open Mon.-Fri. 7:30am-noon and 3:30-5pm, Sat. 7:30am-noon; Sun. and holidays 7:30-10am.) The **Durango Lift** (259-5438) provides hourly bus service beginning at Main Ave. and Earl St. (8am-5:15pm, 75¢). **Emergency** is 911. Durango's **post office:** 222 W. 8th St. (247-3434; open Mon.-Fri. 8:30am-5:30pm, Sat. 9am-1pm); **ZIP code:** 81301; **area code:** 970.

Accommodations, Food, and Nightlife **Durango Youth Hostel,** 543 E. 2nd Ave. (247-9905), only 1 block from downtown, has simple bunks and kitchen facilities in a large converted house that still retains a cozy home-like feel. Ask the owners about local cafés, hangouts, and activities. (Check-in 7-10am and 5-10pm. Check-out 7-10am. $10.) Prices for other accommodations change rapidly in Durango; check ahead with the chamber resort association (see above). The lowest price for a summer double is about $40. Even **Budget Inn,** 3077 Main Ave. (247-5222), charges a lot for its spacious rooms—but it does have a nice pool and hot tub (one bed $48-52, two beds $64-69; winter $29-32/$35-40). **Cottonwood Camper Park,** on U.S. 160 (247-1977), ½ mi. west of town, is the closest campground to the train station (2-person site $14, full hookup $18; $2 per each additional person).

Although **Silverton,** 47 mi. north on U.S. 550, is a less popular (read: cheaper) vacation spot than Durango, this small mining town lies at the base of some of the most beautiful mountains and hiking trails in the area. The **Teller House Hotel,** 1250 Greene St. (387-5423 or 800-342-4338), next to the French Bakery (which provides the hotel's complimentary breakfast), has comfy rooms in a well-maintained 1896 hotel. (Singles $25, with bath $37; doubles $31/$47, $8 per additional person.) Silverton is at the end of the Durango & Silverton RR (see below).

For fixins', head to **City Market** on U.S. 550 one block down 9th St., or at 3130 Main St. (both open 24 hrs). Eat breakfast with locals at **Carver's Bakery and Brewpub,** 1022 Main Ave. (259-2545), which has good bread, breakfast specials ($2-4.50), fresh pasta ($5-7), and vegetarian dishes. Pints of home-brewed beer cost $3, pitchers $8. (Open Mon.-Sat. 6:30am-10pm, Sun. 6am-1pm.) **Farquhart's,** 725 Main Ave. (247-5442), serves up a hearty burrito plate for $6.50, along with the best live music in town (Wed.-Sun. rock, world beat, and reggae; $5 cover; open daily 11am-2am). Bohemians blend their own vapors with those wafting from the aromatic **Steaming Bean Coffee Co.,** 915 Main. Ave. (385-7901), where cakes, pastries, and coffees go for $1-3; soup-and-sandwich specials are $4 (open daily 6:30am-11pm).

Activities Winter is Durango's busiest season, when nearby **Purgatory Resort** (247-9000), 27 mi. north on U.S. 550, hosts skiers of all levels. (Lift tickets $39, 1 free child under 12 per adult.) When the heat is on, trade in your skis for a sled and test out the **Alpine Slide** (under 6 must ride with an adult; open summer daily 9:30am-6pm; $4, July to mid-Aug. $7); or, take a **Scenic Chairlift Ride** ($3-5).

Durango is best known for the **Durango and Silverton Narrow Gauge Train,** 479 Main St. (247-2733), which runs along the Animas River Valley to the glistening old town of **Silverton.** Old-fashioned, 100% coal-fed locomotives wheeze and cough through the San Juans, making a 2-hr. stop in Silverton before returning to Durango. (Trains at 7:30, 8:30, 8:15, and 10:10am; 8-9hr.; $43; ages 5-11 $21.50.) From mid-July to mid-August, you can buy a one-way train ticket ($28.45) and return on a bus (1½hr., whole trip $42.70) which connects with the 8:30am train. The train can also drop off **backpackers** at various scenic points along the route and pick them up on return trips; call for more info on this service. (Office open daily June to mid-Aug. 6am-8pm, May and mid-Aug. to Oct. 7am-7pm; Nov.-May 8am-5pm.)

The entire Durango area is engulfed by **San Juan National Forest,** the headquarters of which are located in Durango (247-4874)—call for information on hiking and camping in the forest. In particular, backpackers planning trips in the massive **Weminuche Wilderness** northeast of Durango should contact the office. For river rafting, **Rivers West,** 520 Main St. (259-5077), has good rates (1hr. $12, 2hr. $19; kids 20% off; open daily 8am-9pm). **Durango Rivertrippers,** 720 Main St. (259-0289), also organizes trips (2hr. $19, for kids $14; 4hr. $29/$20; open daily 8am-9pm). Biking gear is available from **Hassle Free Sports,** 2615 Main St. (259-3874 or 800-835-3800). Bikes rent at $10 for ½ day, $25 per day. (Open Mon.-Sat. 8:30am-6pm, Sun. 10:30am-5pm. Must have driver's license and major credit card.)

■ NEAR DURANGO: PAGOSA SPRINGS

The Ute people—the first to discover the waters of Pagosa—believed that the springs were a gift of the Great Spirit. Pagosa Springs, the hottest and largest in the world, bubble from the San Juan Mountains 62 mi. east of Durango on Rte. 160. The principal **hot baths** are located in two motels: **Spring Inn,** 165 Hot Springs Blvd. (264-4168; outside baths $6.50; open 24 hrs.), and **Spa Motel,** 317 Hot Springs Blvd. (264-5910; $7.50 for outdoor pool and indoor hot tub; open 8am-9pm daily; must be 18). **Chimney Rock Archeological Area** (883-5359), 20 mi. west of Pagosa Springs on U.S. 160 and Rte. 151S, contains the ruins of a high-mesa Anasazi village. (2-hr. guided tour from May 15-Sept. 30 at 9:30, 10:30am, 1, and 2pm. $3, under 12 $2.) Ski at **Wolf Creek**, 20 mi. east of Pagosa, which claims to have the most snow in Colorado (lift tickets $32, under 13 $20; rates subject to change.) For fishing, hiking, and camping, contact the San Juan National Forest (247-4874; see Durango: Activities, above). The **visitors center** (264-2360) sits at the intersection of San Juan St. and Hot Springs Blvd. (open Mon.-Sat. 8am-5pm, Sun. 1-5pm; in winter daily 9am-5pm). Except for the occasional mudslide and stampede, there is no public transportation in Pagosa Springs.

Lodging here won't break you. The **Sky View Motel** (263-5803), 1 mi. west of town on Rte. 160, offers singles with cable TV for $35, doubles for $40-45, and quads for $50. **Harvey's Motel,** 157 Pagosa St. (264-5715), one block from downtown, has cozy wood-paneled rooms with TVs and phones (singles $38-40, doubles $40-45). The **High Country Lodge** (264-4181) lies 3 mi. east on Rte. 160. (Singles $47, cabin for 1 $60. For both, $5 each additional person up to 4. In winter $5 less.)

The **Moose River Pub,** 20 Village Dr. (731-5451), serves up southwestern-style chop-lickin' goodies (open Mon.-Fri. 11am-2pm and 5-9pm, Sat. 5-9pm). **The Hogs Breath Saloon,** 157 Navajo Trail Dr. (731-2626), near Rte. 160W, features country western dancing (Fri.-Sat.) and a surf 'n' turf menu (entrees $8-10; open daily 11am-10pm). The award-winning green chili stew ($4) at the **Rolling Pin Bakery Café,** 214 Pagosa St. (274-2255), gets your attention with its unique combo of spices, chili, and chicken. Big breakfast flapjacks ($4) and sandwiches ($4-6) can cool your palate. (Open Mon.-Thurs. and Sat. 7am-2pm, Fri. 7:30am-5:30pm.)

■■■ MESA VERDE

Mesa Verde—literally, "green table"—rises from the deserts of southwestern Colorado, its flat top noticeably friendlier to vegetation than the dry lands below. Fourteen hundred years ago, Native American tribes began to cultivate the area now known as **Mesa Verde National Park.** These people—today called the Anasazi, or "ancient ones"—constructed a series of elaborate cliff dwellings beneath the overhanging sandstone shelves surrounding the mesa. Then, around 1275AD, 700 years after their ancestors had arrived, the Anasazi abruptly and mysteriously vanished, leaving behind their eerie and starkly beautiful dwellings.

The southern portion of the park divides into the **Chapin Mesa** and the **Wetherill Mesa.** To get an overview of the Anasazi lifestyle, visit the **Chapin Mesa Museum** (529-4475) at the south end of the park (open daily 8am-6:30pm; in winter 8am-5pm). Rangers lead tours to **Cliff Palace,** the largest cliff dwelling in North America, and **Balcony House** (open summer only), a 40-room dwelling 600 ft. above the floor of the Soda Canyon (tours depart every ½hr. 9am-6pm from the visitors center; $1). **Step House,** on Weatherill Mesa, is one of the better-preserved ruins, as is **Spruce Tree House,** near the museum.

The Far View Lodge (see below) offers two half-day bus tours. One departs from the Lodge at 9am and visits Spruce Tree House; the second departs at 1pm and runs to Cliff Palace. The Lodge also offers a full-day tour, which departs at 9:30am and visits both sites. Be sure to arrive at least ½ hour before the tour departs. (½-day tours $15, under 12 $8. Full day $19/$8. No reservations.) **Mesa Verde Tours** (259-4818 or 800-626-2066) picks up travelers in Durango or Cortez for a 9-hr. bus tour of the park, leaving at 8:30am ($60, entry fees and one special tour included; under 12 $30.) Bring a lunch and make reservations the night before, as tours fill up.

The park's main entrance is off U.S. 160, 36 mi. from Durango and 10 mi. from **Cortez.** The **entrance fee** is $5 for vehicles, $3 for pedestrian and bikers. The **Far**

View Visitors Center (529-4543), 20 mi. from the gate on the main road, publishes a comprehensive visitors guide with up-to-date and complete listings on park walks, drives, and trails (open summer daily 8am-5pm). During the winter, head to the museum (see above) or the **Colorado Welcome Center/Cortez Chamber of Commerce,** 928 E. Main (800-253-1616 or 565-3414), in Cortez, where you'll find the *Mesa Verde Country Visitors Guide* (open daily 8am-6pm; winter 8am-5pm). Since sights in the park lie up to 40 mi. apart, a car is helpful. For **emergencies,** call 529-4469. Mesa Verde's **ZIP code:** 81330; **area code:** 970.

Mesa Verde's only lodging, **Far View Lodge** (529-4421), across from the visitors center, is extremely expensive (from $70), but a few nearby motels can put you up for under $30. Try the **Ute Mountain Motel,** 531 S. Broadway (565-8507), in Cortez. (singles from $34, doubles from $42; winter $24/$28-34). **North Broadway Motel,** 510 N. Broadway (565-2481), stocks its small rooms with AC, TV, fridge, microwave, and a big bath (singles $30, doubles $35; in winter $23/$28). The nearby **Durango Hostel** (see Durango Accommodations, p. 604) has cheap beds. The only camping in Mesa Verde is 4 mi. inside the park at **Morfield Campground** (529-4400; off season 533-7731). The third-largest national park campground in America *has never been full* and boasts some beautiful, secluded sites. (Actually, it technically filled once, in 1989. Whatever. 450 sites $8, full hookup $16. Showers 75¢ for 5min.)

Four Corners

New Mexico, Arizona, Utah, and **Colorado** meet at an unnaturally neat intersection about 40 mi. northwest of **Shiprock,** NM, on the Navajo Reservation. **Four Corners** epitomizes American ideas about land; these state borders were drawn along scientifically determined lines of longitude and latitude, with no regard for natural boundaries. There isn't much to see, but die-hard tourists derive perverse thrills out of getting down on all fours and putting a limb in each state—a good story for a cocktail party. (Open daily dawn-dusk; $1.)

THE SOUTHWEST

Thomas Jefferson sent Meriwether Lewis on an exploratory expedition through the new Louisiana Territory, with instructions to investigate the region, its resources, the Indian populations, and to find a live mastodon. With the creature, Jefferson hoped to prove to European scientists that American creatures were just as large and powerful as those on other continents. The West—and in particular the Southwest—has always provided fodder for American myths such as the equation of size and quality. The area has led a double life as both a physical territory and a romantically-imagined land of savages, outlaws, and buffalo, settled by dint of American courage and ingenuity. In reality, Americans have played only a small part in the history of the region. The Anasazi of the 10th and 11th centuries were the first to discover that the arid lands of the Southwest could support an advanced agrarian civilization. The Navajo, Apache, and Pueblo nations later migrated into the region, sharing the land with descendents of the Anasazi, the Hopi. Today, reservation lands and ruins mark both the current and ancient presence of these peoples.

Spanish conquest began with the 16th-century forays of explorers based in Mexico, and continued at the hands of Catholic missionaries, who attempted to organize the Indians into a society of Christian village-dwellers. The United States first laid claim to parts of the Southwest with the 1803 Louisiana Purchase. The idealistic hope for a western "empire of liberty," where Americans could live the virtuous farm life, motivated further expansion, until the 1853 Gadsen Purchase set the last boundaries of today's Southwest. Since then, the individualist mythology of the region—of the lone gunslinger, the courageous lawman, and the rugged pioneer—has flourished. Ironically, in the past 200 years the American West has relied more than any other region on federal aid and bureaucracy and has become the country's most urban section, measuring by the percentage of the population living in urban areas. Nonetheless, explorers and cowboys continue to excite the national imagination in a way that the Bureau of Land Management never will.

The Southwest's natural grandeur lures visitors and keeps Kodak in business. The vastness of the desert and its peculiar colors—of red rock, sandstone, scrub brush, and pale sky—invite contemplation; farther north, Utah's mountains offer equally breathtaking vistas. The steel blue of the Superstition peaks, the rainbow expanse of the Painted Desert, the deep gorges of the Grand Canyon, the murky depths of Carlsbad Caverns, and the red stone arches and twisted spires of southern Utah and northern Arizona inspire awe and await exploration.

Southwestern Scenes

Authors: Barbara Kingsolver, Willa Cather *(Death Comes to the Archbishop)*, Edward Abbey, Tony Hillerman, Sandra Cisneros.
Artists: Georgia O'Keeffe, R.C. Gorman, Oscar Burninghouse, Dorothy Smith.
Cuisine: Essentially an adaptation of Mexican dishes. Chile con carne, tortillas, refried beans, enchiladas, tamales, and sopapillas. Navajo dishes such as the sheepherder sandwich and fry-bread.
Microbreweries: Electric Dave Brewery, Black Mountain, Russell, Santa Fe, and Schirf Brewing Co.
Native Americans: Apache, Anasazi, Hopi, Navajo, Pueblo, Sinagua, Ute, Zuni.
Music: Santa Fe Opera, country-western, Tex-Mex, Gin Blossoms, Giant Sand, Linda Ronstadt.
Film and TV: Most John Wayne films, *Thelma and Louise, Raising Arizona.*
Climate: Hot and dry.
Geography: Desert.

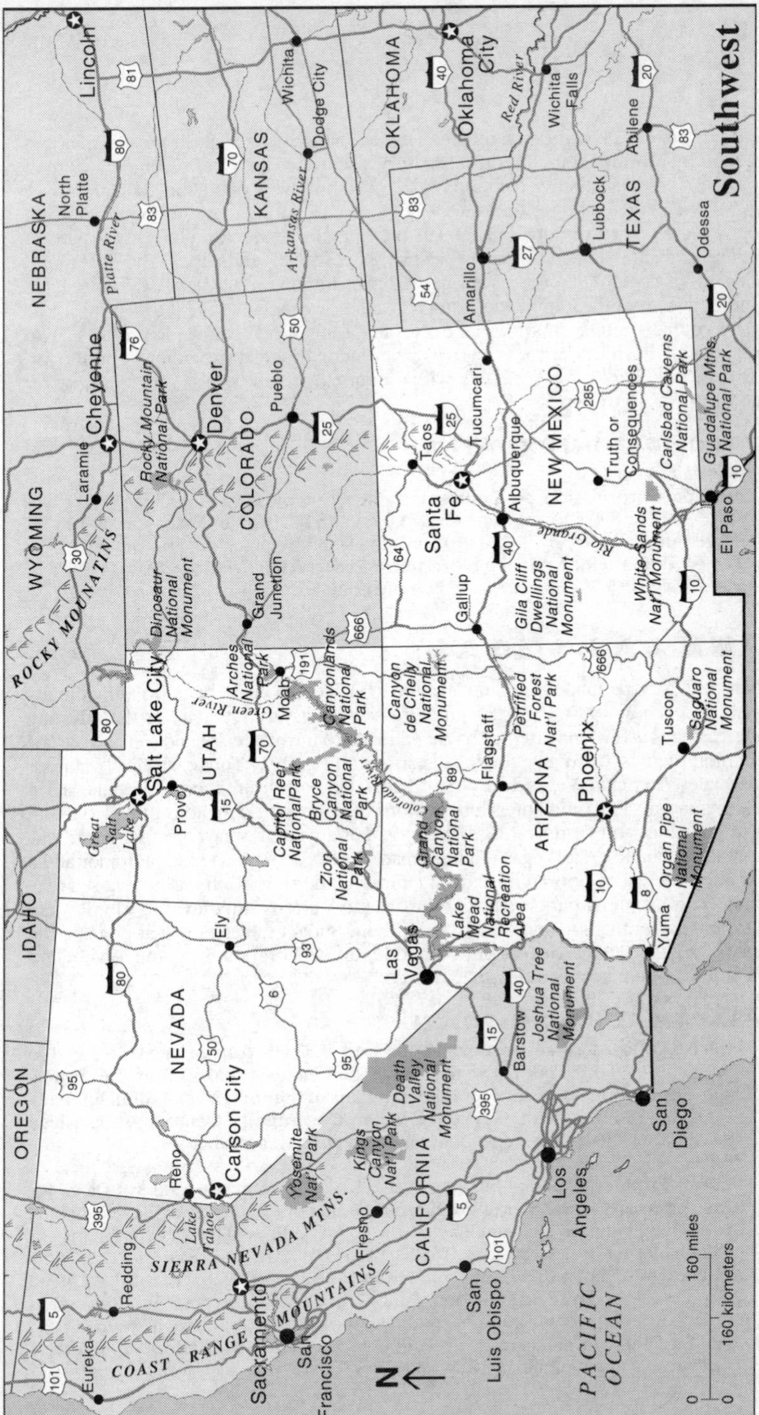
Southwest
NEBRASKA
WYOMING
IDAHO
OREGON
NEVADA
UTAH
COLORADO
KANSAS
OKLAHOMA
TEXAS
NEW MEXICO
ARIZONA
CALIFORNIA
PACIFIC OCEAN
ROCKY MOUNTAINS
SIERRA NEVADA MTNS.
COAST RANGE MOUNTAINS
Lincoln
North Platte
Platte River
Cheyenne
Laramie
Rocky Mountain National Park
Denver
Pueblo
Wichita
Dodge City
Arkansas River
Oklahoma City
Red River
Wichita Falls
Abilene
Lubbock
Amarillo
Odessa
Tucumcari
Taos
Santa Fe
Albuquerque
Truth or Consequences
Carlsbad Caverns National Park
Guadalupe Mtns. National Park
El Paso
White Sands Nat'l Monument
Rio Grande
Gallup
Gila Cliff Dwellings National Monument
Dinosaur National Monument
Grand Junction
Arches National Park
Moab
Green River
Canyonlands National Park
Canyon de Chelly National Monument
Petrified Forest Nat'l Park
Flagstaff
Phoenix
Tuscon
Saguaro National Monument
Organ Pipe National Monument
Yuma
Salt Lake City
Great Salt Lake
Provo
Capitol Reef National Park
Bryce Canyon National Park
Zion National Park
Colorado River
Grand Canyon National Park
Lake Mead National Recreation Area
Las Vegas
Ely
Joshua Tree National Monument
Barstow
Death Valley National Monument
Carson City
Reno
Lake Tahoe
Yosemite Nat'l Park
Kings Canyon Nat'l Park
Fresno
Los Angeles
San Diego
San Luis Obispo
Redding
Eureka
Sacramento
San Francisco
N
160 miles
160 kilometers
0
0
80
81
70
83
76
50
25
40
20
27
54
285
10
30
64
666
191
89
15
93
6
95
395
5
101
8

Nevada

Nevada once walked the straight and narrow. Explored by Spanish missionaries and settled by Mormons, the Nevada Territory's scorched expanses seemed a perfect place for ascetics to strive for moral uplift. The discovery of gold in 1850 and silver in 1859 changed all that; the state was won over permanently to the worship of filthy lucre. When the precious metals ran out, Nevadans shirked most vestiges of virtue, and gambling and marriage-licensing became big industries. The final moral cataclysms came when the state legalized prostitution on a county by county basis and built a crooning lounge idol named Wayne Newton.

Of course, there *is* another side to Nevada. Lake Mead National Recreation Area, only 25 mi. from Las Vegas, is an oasis in stunning desert surroundings, and the forested slopes of Lake Tahoe, shared with California, provide serene resort retreats for an escape from the cities.

PRACTICAL INFORMATION

Capital: Carson City.

Nevada Commission on Tourism: Capitol Complex, Carson City 89710 (702-687-4322 or 800-NEVADA8/638-2328). **Nevada Division of State Parks,** 123 W. Nye Lane, Carson City 89710 (702-687-4384). Both open Mon.-Fri. 8am-5pm.

Time Zone: Pacific (3hr. behind Eastern). **Postal Abbreviation:** NV

Sales Tax: 6.75-7%; 8% room tax, in some counties.

■■■ LAS VEGAS

Not until Nevada made gambling legal in 1931 did Las Vegas begin to attract many visitors; even in 1940, the WPA guide to Nevada assured its readers that, despite increasing tourism, "no attempt has been made to introduce pseudo-romantic architectural themes, or to give artificial glamour and gaiety." Today, artificial glamour and gaiety dominate Vegas. Old West dreams of quick wealth meet the capitalist service-economy, as casino-hotels lure millions of visitors (and millions of dollars) with slot machines and Disneyesque attractions. For anyone dismayed by American culture at its gaudiest, Las Vegas is a nightmare; for those with a sense of humor and a healthy interest in pop culture, it's a fantasy come true. Each casino is a self-contained amusement park with its own theme—circus, medieval castle, Roman empire, ancient Egypt, and on and on and on. Budget travelers will appreciate the city's bargains; all-you-can-eat buffets and luxurious hotel rooms come at unbelievable prices, and most entertainment is free.

PRACTICAL INFORMATION

Tourist Office: Las Vegas Convention and Visitors Authority, 3150 Paradise Rd. (892-7575 or 892-0711), at the Convention Center, 4 blocks from the Strip by the Hilton. Up-to-date info on hotel bargains and buffets. Open Mon.-Fri. 8am-6pm, Sat.-Sun. 8am-5pm. **Gay and Lesbian Community Center,** 912 E. Sahara Ave. (733-9800). Hours dependent on volunteer staff availability.

Police: 795-3111.

Tours: Gambler's special bus tours leave L.A., San Francisco, and San Diego for Las Vegas early in the morning and return at night or the next day. Prices include everything but food and gambling. Ask at tourist offices in the departure cities or call casinos for info. **Gray Line,** 1550 S. Industrial Rd. (384-1234). Mini City Tours (1 per day, ½-day, $17.50). Bus tours from Las Vegas to: Hoover Dam/Lake Mead Express (2 per day, 8am and noon, 5hr., $18); Grand Canyon's South Rim (spans 2 days, 1 night's lodging and park admission included; 3 per week, Mon., Wed., and Fri. 7am; with single room $147, double $111, triple or quad $99; runs March-Oct.; reservations required). **Ray and Ross Tours,** 300 W. Owens St. (646-4661

or 800-338-8111). To: Hoover Dam (1 per day, 6hr., $18); Hoover Dam/Lake Mead (1 per day, 7hr., $32); other locations. Pick-up and drop-off at most hotels.

Airport: McCarran International (261-5743), at the southeast end of the Strip. Main terminal on Paradise Rd. Within walking distance of University of Nevada campus. Vans to hotels on the Strip and downtown $5; taxi to downtown $23.

Trains: Amtrak, 1 N. Main St. (386-6896 or 800-872-7245), in the Union Plaza Hotel. To: L.A. (3 per week, 8hr., $68); San Francisco (daily, 13hr., $120). Ticket office open daily 6am-7:30pm.

Buses: Greyhound, 200 S. Main St. (382-2292 or 800-231-2222), at Carson Ave. downtown. To: L.A. (10 per day, 5hr., $37); San Francisco (10 per day, 15hr., $52). Ticket office and terminal open daily 5am-1am.

Public Transportation: Citizens Area Transit (CAT), 228-7433. Route #301 serves downtown and the Strip 24 hrs. Route #302 serves the airport. Both are $1.50, seniors and under 18 50¢; other routes $1, 50¢. Routes other than #301 operate daily 5:30am-1:30am.

Taxis: Yellow, Checker and **Star Taxis** (873-2000). $2.20 initial fee, $1.50 per mi. Cabs run 24 hrs.

Car Rental: Rebel Rent-a-Car, 5021 Swenson (597-0427 or 800-372-1981). From $20 per day, with unlimited mi. within Clark County. Must be 21 with major credit card; under 25 surcharge $15 per day. Insurance $13 per day. Discounts in tourist publications.

Tying the Knot: Marriage License Bureau, 200 S. 3rd St. (455-3156). Must be 18 or obtain parental consent. Open Mon.-Thurs. 8am-midnight, Fri. 8am-Sun. midnight. $35, cash only.

Crisis Lines: Rape Crisis Center Hotline, 366-1640. **Gamblers Anonymous,** 385-7732. 24 hrs. **Suicide Prevention:** 731-2990. 24 hrs.
Emergency: 911.
Post Office: 301 E. Stewart (385-8944). Open Mon.-Fri. 9am-5pm, Sat. 9am-1pm; general delivery Mon.-Fri. 10am-3pm; **ZIP code:** 89114. **Area code:** 702.

Getting to Vegas from Los Angeles involves a straight, 300-mi. shot on I-15. From Arizona, take I-40 west to Kingman and then U.S. 93/95 north. Las Vegas has two major casino areas. The **downtown** area, around Fremont and 2nd St., is foot-friendly; casinos cluster close together, and some of the sidewalks are even carpeted (man, oh man). The other main area, known as the **Strip,** is a collection of mammoth casinos on both sides of **Las Vegas Boulevard South.** Other casinos lie on Paradise Blvd., parallel to Las Vegas Blvd. As in any city where money reigns supreme, many areas of Las Vegas are unsafe. Always stay on brightly lit pathways and do not wander too far from the major casinos and hotels. The neighborhoods just north and west of downtown can be especially dangerous.

For those under 18, Las Vegas has a **curfew.** Persons aged 14 to 18 are not allowed unaccompanied in public places from midnight to 5am; those under 14 from 10pm to 5am. On weekends, no one under 18 is allowed on the Strip or in other designated areas from 9pm to 5am, unless accompanied by an adult.

ACCOMMODATIONS

Make reservations as far in advance as possible. Coming to town on a Friday or Saturday night without reservations is flirting with disaster. Even though Vegas has over 90,000 rooms, most hotels fill on weekend nights. If you get stuck call the **Room Reservations Hotline** (800-332-5333). Remember too, the earlier you reserve, the better chance you have of snagging a special rate. Room rates at most hotels in Vegas fluctuate all the time; many hotels use two rate ranges—one for week nights, the other weekend nights. In addition, a room that costs $20 during a promotion can cost hundreds during a convention. Check local publications such as *What's On In Las Vegas, Today in Las Vegas, Vegas Visitor, Casino Player, Tour Guide Magazine,* and *Insider Viewpoint of Las Vegas* for discounts and coupons; they are all free and available at visitors centers, hotels, and attractions.

The **Strip** hotels are the center of the action and within walking distance of each other. Cheap motels line **Fremont St.,** from downtown south. Another option, if you have a car, is to stay at one of the hotel-casinos in Jean, NV (approximately 30mi. south on I-15, near the California border). These tend to be less crowded and cheaper than the in-town hotels. Try the **Goldstrike** (477-5000), off I-15 at exit 12.

Las Vegas International Hostel (AAIH/Rucksackers), 1208 Las Vegas Blvd. South (385-9955). Spartan rooms with A/C and an extremely helpful staff. Free breakfast. Ride board in kitchen. Tours to Zion, Bryce, and Grand Canyon (3 days, $125). Office open daily 7am-11pm. Check-out 7-10am. Shared room and bath $9, private room and shared bath $20. Rates lower Dec.-March. Key deposit $5.

Gold Spike, 400 E. Ogden Ave. (384-8444), a few blocks from Fremont St. at the corner of Las Vegas Blvd. and Ogden Ave. downtown. 109 rooms at a fixed $22.

Nevada Palace, 5255 Boulder Hwy. (458-8810), a quick *drive* from the Strip and downtown. 220 rooms. Sun.-Thurs. $30, Fri.-Sat. $50, barring conventions.

Circus Circus, 2880 Las Vegas Blvd. South (734-0410 or 800-634-3450). A major hotel-casino (2800 rooms) with great prices. Rooms with TV and A/C for 1-4 people. Sun.-Thurs. $29-69, Fri.-Sat. $59-99, holidays $65-125. Roll-away bed $7. In summer, fills 2-3 months in advance for weeknights, 3-4 months for weekends.

Excalibur, 3850 Las Vegas Blvd. South (597-7777 or 800-937-7777). A giant white castle of a hotel-casino with over 4000 rooms. Guests are paged as "Lady" or "Lord," as they beat the medieval thing into the ground again and again. Sun-Thurs. $39-60, Fri.-Sat. $79-90.

Stardust, 3000 Las Vegas Blvd. South (732-6111 or 800-824-6033). A hotel-casino with 2300 rooms. Sun.-Thurs. $36-150, Fri.-Sat. $60-150.

CAMPING

Lake Mead National Recreation Area (293-8906), 25mi. south of town on U.S. 93/95. Sites $8, with hookup $14-18. See Lake Mead (p. 614) for details.

KOA Las Vegas (451-5527). Take U.S. 93/95 south to the Boulder exit and turn left. Free casino shuttle. Pool, laundry facilities, slots, and video poker. Sites $22; with hookup $26, A/C $3 extra.

Circusland RV Park, 500 Circus Circus Dr. (734-0410), a part of the Circus Circus hotel on the strip. Laundry facilities, showers, pool, jacuzzi, and convenience store. Sun.-Thurs. $13, Fri.-Sat. $17.

BUFFET BONANZA

Almost every hotel-casino in Vegas courts tourists with cheap all-you-can-eat invitations, but expect cafeteria-quality food and long lines at peak hours. Alcoholic drinks in most casinos cost 75¢-$1 or come free to those who look like they're playing. Scores of low-priced restaurants are located a short drive west from the Strip, particularly along **Decatur Boulevard.**

Circus Circus, 2800 Las Vegas Blvd. South (734-0410). One of the cheapest buffets in town; breakfast $3 (6-11:30am), brunch $4 (noon-4pm), dinner $5 (4:30-11pm).

Excalibur, 3850 Las Vegas Blvd. South (597-7777), has the Roundtable Buffet; breakfast $4 (7-11am), lunch $5 (11am-4pm), dinner $6 (4-10pm).

Luxor, 3900 Las Vegas Blvd. South (262-4000), goes a bit classier (within the buffet spectrum) with the Manhattan Buffet; breakfast $4.50 (7:30-11am), lunch $5.50 (11am-4pm), dinner $7.50 (4-11pm).

Treasure Island, 3300 Las Vegas Blvd. South (894-7111). A couple bucks more for elegance and a choice of American, Italian, or Chinese; breakfast $5 (7-10:45am), lunch $7 (11am-3:45pm), dinner $9 (4-11pm). Lower prices for children.

Rincon Criollo, 1145 Las Vegas Blvd. South (388-1906), near the youth hostel. When you're sick of the buffet scene, dine on filling Cuban food beneath a wall-sized photograph of palm trees. Hot sandwiches $3.50-4.50. Meals (meat, rice, and beans) $6.50-8. Open Tues.-Sun. noon-10pm.

CA$INO-HOPPING AND NIGHTLIFE

Gambling is illegal for those under 21. Hotels and most casinos give out "funbooks," with alluring gambling coupons which allow you to buy $50 in chips for $5. Do not bring more money than you're prepared to lose cheerfully. And always remember: *in the long run, you will almost definitely lose money.* Keep your wallet in your front pocket, and beware of the thieves who prowl casinos to nab big winnings from unwary jubilants. Most casinos offer free gambling lessons; more patient dealers may offer a tip or two (in exchange for one from you). Casinos, nightclubs, and wedding chapels stay open 24 hrs.

Caesar's Palace, 3570 Las Vegas Blvd. South (731-7110), is one of the glitziest casinos in town. Marble statues grace the hallways and lobby, as actors dressed in Roman garb wander the casino day and night posing for pictures and uttering proclamations. In the **Festival Fountain show,** statues move, talk, battle, and shout amid a fantastic laser-light show—ah, the decorum of old Rome (shows every hr., daily 10am-11pm). Next door, **Mirage,** 3400 Las Vegas Blvd. South (791-7111), includes among its attractions a Dolphin habitat (admission $3), an indoor tropical rain forest, and, outside, a "volcano" that erupts in fountains and flames every ½ hr. (daily 8pm-1am), barring bad weather. At **Treasure Island,** 3300 Las Vegas Blvd. South (894-7111), pirates battle with cannons staged on giant wooden ships in a "bay" on the Strip (every 1½hr., daily 4:30pm-midnight). **Luxor,** 3900 Las Vegas Blvd. South (262-4000), has boat rides through the Nile River and the hotel lobby (every 20min., daily 9am-12:30am; $4). Also inside, the **King Tut Tomb and Museum** houses replicas of the artifacts uncovered at the king's grave (open daily 9am-11pm; $3). The hotel's three, 3-D **holographic films,** *Search of the Obelisk, Luxor Live,* and *The Theater of Time* have dazzling special effects ($4 each). The **MGM Grand,** 3799 Las

Vegas Blvd. South (891-1111), offers a Hollywood theme, with special attention to the *Wizard of Oz*, and an amusement park across the street from the casino (park open daily 10am-10pm; $17, seniors $9, ages 4-12 $10). **Circus Circus,** 2880 Las Vegas Blvd. South (734-0410), attempts to cultivate a (dysfunctional) family atmosphere; while parents run to the card tables and slot machines downstairs, their children spend their quarters upstairs on the souped-up carnival midway and in the titanic video game arcade. Two stories above the casino floor, tightrope-walkers, fire-eaters, and rather impressive acrobats perform (11am-midnight). Within the hotel complex the **Grand Slam Canyon** is a Grand Canyon theme park with a rollercoaster and other rides—all enclosed in a glass shell. (Open Sun.-Thurs. 10am-10pm, Fri.-Sat. 10am-midnight. Admission and 2 small rides $4, seniors and under 3 free; additional rides $2-4. Unlimited rides $14, ages 3-9 $10.) **Excalibur,** 3850 Las Vegas Blvd. South (800-937-7777), has a medieval England theme which may make you nostalgic for the Black Plague. There are more, but you get the idea.

Extra bucks will buy you a seat at a made-in-the-USA phenomenon—the **Vegas spectacular.** These stunning casino-sponsored productions happen twice per night and feature marvels such as waterfalls, explosions, fireworks, and casts of thousands (including animals). You can also see Broadway plays and musicals, ice revues, and individual entertainers in concert. Some "production shows" are topless; most are tasteless. For a show by one of the musical stars, such as Diana Ross or Frank Sinatra, who haunt the city, you may have to fork over $40 or more. "Revues" featuring imitations of (generally deceased) performers are far more reasonable. But, why pay? You can't turn around in Las Vegas without bumping into an aspiring Elvis clone, or perhaps the real Elvis, pursuing anonymity in the brilliant disguise of an Elvis impersonator. Some lounge acts, the lowest rung in Vegas entertainment, charge only a drink minimum. All hotels have city-wide ticket booths in their lobbies.

Nightlife in Vegas gets rolling around midnight and keeps going until everyone drops or runs out of money. At Caesar's Palace (731-7110), **Cleopatra's Barge,** a huge ship-disco, is one boat that's made for rockin' (open Tues.-Sun. 10pm-4am; $5 cover Fri.-Sat.). Another popular disco, **Gipsy,** 4605 Paradise Rd. (731-1919), southeast of the Strip, may look deserted at 11pm, but by 1am the medium-sized dance floor packs in a gay, lesbian, and straight crowd (cover $4). Be forewarned that the Gipsy dancers go topless on Tuesdays. The **Comedy Stop at the Trop,** 3801 Las Vegas Blvd. South (739-2714 or 800-634-4000), inside the Tropicana, offers three comedians for $13 (includes 2 drinks); two shows nightly (8 and 10:30pm). Downtown, the **Fremont Street Blues and Reggae Club** (474-7209), at Fremont and 4th St., provides live music every night (open Sun.-Thurs. 7pm-3am, Fri-Sat. 7pm-5am).

Fans of classical music and kitsch will be delighted by the **Liberace Museum,** 1775 E. Tropicana Ave. (798-5595), devoted to the flamboyant late "Mr. Showmanship." Liberace's audacious uses of fur, velvet, and rhinestone boggle the rational mind. (Open Mon.-Sat. 10am-5pm, Sun. 1-5pm. $6.50, seniors $4.50, ages 6-12 $2.) **The Guinness World Records Museum,** 2780 Las Vegas Blvd. South (792-3766), showcases displays describing the most tattooed lady and the largest pizza, among other record-breakingly freaky stuff. (Open in summer 9am-8pm, off season 9am-6pm. $5; students, seniors, and military $4; ages 5-12 $3; under 5 free.)

The nearby city of Henderson offers a quartet of free factory tours and a break from casino craziness. All the factories have shops; most have free samples. **Kidd's Marshmallow Factory** (564-3878) is a standout; watch huge sheets of white gooey sugary stuff become the stuff of the StayPuft Marshmallow Man.

■■■ LAKE MEAD

The **Hoover Dam,** the brainchild of President Herbert Hoover and the Western Hemisphere's highest concrete dam, straddles Nevada and Arizona. Holding back the Colorado River, the dam creates **Lake Mead,** whose turquoise waters gleam in the distance as you approach through the Nevada desert on U.S. 93/95. The dam itself, made from 4.4 million cubic yards of concrete, is a testament to Depression-era dreams of a better world through engineering. On the Nevada side, two androgynous winged statues, arms thrust skyward, sit above an engraved tribute to the dam laborers. Guided 45-min. **tours** into the powerplant bowels of the dam begin continuously throughout the day at the **Hoover Dam Visitors Center** (293-8305; open 8:30am-6:30pm. $5, seniors and ages 10-16 $2.50, under 10 free. Wheelchairs available.) The **Lake Mead National Recreation Area** encompasses these sites.

The **Lake Mead Visitors Center** (293-8990) is on the Nevada half of the dam (open in summer daily 8:30am-6pm; off season 8:30am-4:30pm). Backcountry camping is permitted and free in most areas. Numerous National Park Service **campgrounds** lie within the recreation area as well (all sites $8 and first come, first served). The most popular is **Boulder Beach** (293-8906), accessible by Lakeshore Rd. off U.S. 93/95. The **Lake Shore Trailer Village** (293-2540) has RV sites with showers for around $15. (Reservations required Memorial Day, July 4th, and Labor Day weekends; all other times first come, first served.)

U.S. 93/95 runs right over Hoover Dam. There are several free parking lots at intervals along the highway; the lots are crowded, but less so on the Arizona side. Shuttle bus service is available from the more remote lots. Public transportation does not serve Hoover Dam, but **Gray Line** buses and **Ray and Ross Tours** offer rides from Las Vegas (see Las Vegas Practical Information p. 610).

■■■ RENO

Hypnotizing roulette wheels spin frantically around the clock and slot machines hungrily devour their shiny manna. Fuzzy blue dice bob down the Strip, hanging from the mirrors of well-worn speedsters. The kaleidoscope of casinos creates a non-stop hallucinatory daylight, but only a short drive away, Pyramid Lake and Lake Tahoe shine with the natural splendor of an evening full of stars.

Practical Information Only 14 mi. from the California border and 443 mi. north of Las Vegas, Reno sits at the intersection of **I-80** and **U.S. 395,** which runs along the eastern slope of the Sierra Mountains. For visitors information, check out the **Reno-Sparks Convention and Visitors Center,** 4590 Virginia St. (800-367-RENO/7366; open Mon.-Sat. 7am-8pm, Sun. 9am-6pm). The **Amtrak,** 135 E. Commercial Row and Lake St. (329-8638 or 800-872-7245), sells tickets daily 8am-4:45pm and 1-4:30pm for trains to San Francisco (1 per day, $58) and Chicago (1 per day, $217). **Greyhound,** 155 Stevenson St. (322-2970), has buses to San Francisco (14 per day, $34) and L.A. (10 per day, $42). The station is open 24 hrs. The local bus system, **Reno Citifare** (348-7433), at 4th and Center St., serves the Reno-Sparks area. Most routes operate 5am-7pm; those in the city center run 24 hrs. (Fare $1, seniors and disabled 50¢, ages 6-18 75¢.) Reno's **post office:** 50 S. Virginia St. (786-5523), at Mill; **ZIP code:** 89501; **area code:** 702.

Accommodations and Camping Downtown Reno is compact, with wide, well-lit, heavily-patroled streets. Be streetwise, though, and avoid walking in or near the northeast corner alone after dark. At the wonderfully clean **Windsor Hotel,** 214 West St. (323-6171), fans turn lazily overhead to compensate for the lack of A/C (singles $22, doubles $28). **Motel 6** has four locations in Reno: 866 N. Wells Ave. (786-0255), 1901 S. Virginia St. (827-0255), 1400 Stardust St. (747-7390), and 666 N. Wells Ave. (329-8681); all four live up to the chain's promise of clean, comfortable, and cheap rooms (singles $29, Fri.-Sat. $39). Those equipped to camp should make the drive to the woodland sites of **Davis Creek Park** (849-0684), 17 mi. south on U.S. 395 then ½ mi. west (follow the signs). Wrap yourself in a rustic blanket of pines and sage at the base of the Sierra Nevada's Mt. Rose. (63 sites $10 per vehicle; $1 per pet. All sites first come, first served. Picnic area open 8am-9pm.)

Food Eating in Reno is cheaper than yo' mama. To entice gamblers and to prevent them from wandering out in search of food, casinos offer a range of bland, all-you-can-eat cuisine at low, low prices. **Louis' Basque Corner,** 301 E. 4th St. (323-7203), is a local institution. The family-style dining and hearty full-course dinner with wine make the price ($15, under 10 $7) happily bearable. (Open daily 11:30am-2:30pm and 5-9:30pm.) Possibly the only restaurant in Reno without slot machines, **The Blue Heron,** 1091 S. Virginia St. (786-4110), offers hearty and healthy vegetarian cuisine. Filling entrees ($9) include soup or salad and deliciously fresh baked bread. (Open Mon.-Thurs. 11am-9pm, Fri.-Sat. 11am-10pm, Sun. 4-8pm.)

Sights and Entertainment Much of Reno's nightlife (and day life) revolves around the few dozen casinos downtown. Casinos provide live nighttime entertainment, but the schmaltzy performances target the Wayne Newton crowd and generally aren't worth the steep admission prices. Harrah's, 219 N. Center St. (786-3232), tries very hard to be hip with the recent addition of Planet Hollywood and a top-40 dance club (open 10pm-5am). Circus Circus, 500 N. Sierra (329-0711), has free 10- to 15-minute "big-top" performances (daily every ½ hr. 8am-midnight); the wacky atmosphere makes it a popular destination for families. In September, nearby Virginia City hosts Camel Races (847-0311), in which camels and ostriches actually race through town. To get to the site of this crazy festival, take U.S. 395S to Rte. 341 and follow Rte. 341 for about 25 mi.

Pyramid Lake Thirty mi. north of Reno off Pyramid Way on the Paiute Indian Reservation lies emerald green Pyramid Lake. Named for the pyramidal rock island which lies in its center, the lake is open for day use and camping. **Camping** is allowed anywhere on the lakeshore, but only designated areas have toilet facilities. A $5 **permit** is required for use of the park and the area is carefully patrolled by the Paiute tribe. Permits are available at the **Ranger Station** (476-1155; open Mon.-Sat. 9am-5pm). Surrounded by sagebrush-covered hills, this remnant of an ancient sea is a local escape from city life. It contains a hot spring and a series of rocks on the north shore which beg to be climbed. Those looking for solitude should try the south and east shores; the areas north of the ranger station are clogged with RVs.

Nevada Cathouse Etiquette

In 1967, Nevada legalized prostitution, and the Nevada cat house was born. Cat houses come in two flavors, parlor and bar. In a bar house, you are not obligated to do the dirty deed, but in a parlor house, sex is what it's all about. The most famous cat house in Nevada, the **Mustang Ranch,** awaits you in Reno. When you get there, ring the outside buzzer for admittance. The women will be lined up for your inspection. After you have selected, all arrangements take place in a private room, not at the bar or in the parlor. If you do not agree on terms, you may feel free to leave. Once a price is set, inspection takes place, money is paid, and the act takes place. Remember, though, no kissing on the mouth.

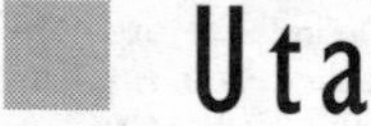

Utah

Beginning in 1848, persecuted Mormons settled on the land which is now Utah, intending to establish and govern their own theocratic state called Deseret. U.S. President James Buchanan quashed the Mormon rebellion in 1858, in a dispute which foreshadowed the states-rights conflicts leading up to the Civil War. Today the state's population is 70% Mormon—a religious presence felt particularly in Salt Lake City. Due to Mormon asceticism, you may have a hard time getting alcohol in Utah, but the marvelous landscapes will keep you intoxicated. From the vast, mountain-rimmed Salt Lake of the north to the redstone rock formations, river gorges, and crenellated cliffs in the southern parks, Utah's natural regions attest to the creative powers of wind and water. The quiet trails and cool mountain tops in the south and east are some of the state's least populated and most appealing sights.

PRACTICAL INFORMATION

Capital: Salt Lake City.

Utah Travel Council: 300 N. State St., Salt Lake City 84114 (801-538-1030), across the street from the capitol building. Distributes the free *Utah Vacation Planner,* with complete lists of motels, national parks, and campgrounds. Open Mon.-Fri. 9am-6pm, Sat.-Sun. 10am-5pm; off season Mon.-Fri. 8am-5pm, Sat.-Sun. 10am-5pm. **Utah Parks and Recreation,** 1636 W. North Temple, Salt Lake City 86116 (801-538-7220). Open Mon.-Fri. 8am-5pm.

Alcohol: Utah has weird alcohol laws. Alcohol may not be brought into Utah from another state. Only grocery and convenience stores may sell beer for take-out. Because licenses and zoning laws can split a room, drinkers may have to move a few ft. down the bar to get a mixed drink.

State Holiday: July 24 is Utah Day, and most places of business are closed.

Time Zone: Mountain (2hr. behind Eastern). **Postal Abbreviation:** UT

Sales Tax: 6.25%.

NORTHERN UTAH

■■■ SALT LAKE CITY

On July 24, 1847, Brigham Young saw the valley of the Great Salt Lake for the first time and said, "this is the right place." After more than five months of travel, Young knew that his band of Mormon pioneers had finally reached a haven where they could practice their religion free from the persecution they had faced in the east. Salt Lake City's "This is the Place" monument commemorates the famous utterance. The city is the spiritual center of the Church of Latter Day Saints, and home to the Mormon Temple and the Mormon Tabernacle Choir. Despite its commitment to preserving traditions, Salt Lake is a booming modern city whose proximity to the mountains makes it a favorite base for skiers and outdoor enthusiasts.

PRACTICAL INFORMATION

Tourist Office: Salt Lake Valley Convention and Visitors Bureau, 180 S. West Temple (521-2868), 2 blocks from Temple Sq. Open Mon.-Sat. 8am-6pm; Labor Day-Memorial Day Mon.-Sat. 8am-5pm. Distributes the *Salt Lake Visitors Guide.*

Airport: Salt Lake City International, 776 N. Terminal Dr. (575-2600), 4mi. west of Temple Sq. UTA bus #50 runs both ways between the terminal and downtown for 65¢. Taxi to Temple Sq. costs about $14.

Trains: Amtrak, 325 S. Río Grande (364-8562 or 800-872-7245), in a bad area. To: Las Vegas (3 per week, 8hr., $89); L.A. (3 per week, 15½hr., $111). Open 24 hrs.; tickets sold Mon.-Sat. 4-9:30am, 10am-12:30pm, and 4:15pm-1am, Sun. 4pm-1am.

Buses: Greyhound, 160 W. South Temple (800-231-2222), 1 block west of Temple Sq. To: Las Vegas (2 per day, 8hr., $42), L.A. (2 per day, 15hr., $69). Open daily 5:30am-midnight; tickets sold 5:30am-11pm.

Public Transportation: Utah Transit Authority (UTA), 600 S. 700 West (287-4636, until 7pm). Frequent service to University of Utah campus; buses to Ogden (#70/72 express), suburbs, airport, and east to the mountain canyons and Provo (#4 local or #1 express; fare $1.50). Buses every ½hr.-1hr. Mon.-Fri. 6am-11pm. Fare 65¢, seniors 30¢, under 5 free. Maps available at libraries and visitors bureau.

Taxis: Ute Cab, 359-7788. **Yellow Cab,** 521-2100. $1.25 base fare, $1.50 per mi.

Car Rental: Payless Car Rental, 1974 W. North Temple (596-2596). $28 per day, unlimited mi. within Utah, 200 free mi. outside the state. $135 per week, 1400

free mi. outside Utah. 16¢ per additional mi. Insurance $9 per day on sedans. Open Sun.-Fri. 6am-10pm, Sat. 6am-8pm. Must be 21 with a major credit card.

Bike Rental: Wasatch Touring, 702 E. 100 South (359-9361). 21-speed mountain bikes $20 per day. Open Mon.-Sat. 9am-7pm.

Crisis Lines: Rape Crisis, 467-7273. Operates 24 hrs.

Emergency: 911.

Post Office: 230 W. 200 South (974-2200), 1 block west of the visitors bureau. Open Mon.-Fri. 8am-5:30pm, Sat. 9am-2pm. **ZIP code:** 84101. **Area code:** 801.

Salt Lake's grid system makes navigation simple. Brigham Young designated **Temple Sq.** as the heart of downtown. Street names indicate how many blocks east, west, north, or south they lie from Temple Sq.; the "0" points are **Main St.** (north-south) and **South Temple St.** (east-west). Local address listings exclude the hundred at the end of each numbered street—825 E. 13 South means 825 E. 1300 South. Smaller streets and streets that do not fit the grid pattern often have non-numeric names. The downtown is equipped with audible traffic lights for the convenience of blind pedestrians.

ACCOMMODATIONS AND CAMPING

Ute Hostel (AAIH/Rucksackers), 19 E. Kelsey Ave. (595-1645). Young international crowd. Free pickups can be arranged from Amtrak, Greyhound, or the visitors information center. Free tea and coffee, parking, linen, and safe for valuables. Check-in 24 hrs. Dorm rooms $13-15. Cute doubles with futons $30-35.

The Avenues, 107 F St. (363-8137), 7 blocks east of Temple Sq. Blankets and linens provided. Kitchen and laundry available. Check-in daily 8am-2:30pm and 6-10pm. Dorm rooms with 4 bunks and shared bath $13 per person, nonmembers $15; singles with private bath $22, doubles $32.

Ken-del Motel, 667 N. 300 West (355-0293), 10 blocks northwest of Temple Sq. From the airport take bus #50 to N. Temple, then bus #70; from Greyhound or downtown catch bus #70. Huge dorm-style rooms with nice bath and kitchen $15 per person. Well-kept singles with kitchens, TV, and A/C $25, doubles $35.

The **Utah Travel Council** (538-1030) has detailed information on all campsites in the area. The **Wasatch-Cache National Forest** (524-5030) skirts Salt Lake City on the east, offering many established sites. Place reservations with MISTIX (800-283-2267). The terrain by the city is quite steep, making the best sites those on the far side of the mountains. Three of the closest campgrounds are in the **Mount Olympus Wilderness** (within the National Forest), off Rte. 210 east of the city: **Box Elder** (35 sites), **Terraces** (25 sites), and **Bigwater Trailhead** (45 sites). Four more campgrounds lie just north of the city on I-15, outside of the towns of Bountiful and Farmington: **Sunset** (32 sites), **Bountiful Park** (79 sites), **Buckland Flat** (26 sites), and **Mueller Park** (63 sites). On weekends, go early to ensure a space (sites $9-11). If you need a hookup, try **KOA,** 1400 W. North Temple (355-1192; 60 tent sites, 290 RV sites; $18, with water and electric $21, full hookup $23).

FOOD

Ethnic food clusters downtown, with cheap, slightly greasy eateries on the outer fringe. The two (literally) opposing main shopping malls, ZCMI Mall and Crossroads Mall on Main St., have food courts; the Cajun food stand at ZCMI is a cut above standard food court fare.

Salt Lake Roasting Company, 249 E. 400 South (363-7572). The cakes and pastries are the stuff of *Gourmet* magazine cover photos. Caters to twenty-somethings. Coffee 85¢; quiche $3; soup $1.50. Open Mon.-Sat. 6:45am-midnight.

Park Café, 604 E. 1300 South (487-1670), near Liberty Park. A classy little joint with a patio and a view of a park. Lunches about $6. Dinners $10-ish, but "light" meals (like chicken quesadillas) $6. Open Mon.-Thurs. 7am-3pm and 5-9pm, Fri. 7am-3pm and 5-10pm

Bill and Nada's Café, 479 S. 600 East (359-6984), by Trolley Sq. A locally revered café. Patsy Cline on the jukebox and paper placemats of U.S. presidents on the tables. Eggs, hash browns, and toast $3.60. Roast leg of lamb, salad, soup, vegetable, roll, and potatoes $5.50. Jell-O with whipped cream $1.20. Open 24 hrs.

SACRED SIGHTS

Followers of the **Church of Jesus Christ of Latter Day Saints** hold both the *Book of Mormon* and the *Bible* to be the word of God. The seat of the highest Mormon authority and the central temple, **Temple Sq.** (240-2534) is the symbolic center of the Mormon religion. Feel free to wander around the pleasant, flowery 10-acre square, but the sacred temple is off-limits to non-Mormons. Alighting on the highest of the building's three towers, a golden statue of the angel Moroni watches over the city. The square has two **visitors centers** (north and south); a 45-minute **Historical Tour** leaves from the south visitors center every 10 minutes. Thirty-minute **Book of Mormon** and **Purpose of Temple Tours** (alternately every 30min.) explain the significance of Temple Sq. (Centers open daily 8am-10pm; off season 9am-9pm.)

Visitors to Temple Sq. may visit the **Mormon Tabernacle,** which houses the famed Choir. Built in 1867, the structure is so acoustically sensitive that a pin dropped at one end can be heard 175 ft. away at the other end. Rehearsals on Thursday evenings (8pm) and Sunday morning broadcasts from the tabernacle are open to the public (9:30-10am; doors close at 9:15am). Of course, no matter how forcefully they sing, the choir can't quite match the size and sound of the 11,623-pipe organ which accompanies them. (Recitals Mon.-Sat. at noon; in summer also Sun. 2pm.) **Assembly Hall,** next door, hosts concerts almost every summer evening. The **Museum of Church History and Art,** 45 N. West Temple (240-3310), houses Mormon memorabilia from 1820 to the present (open Mon.-Fri. 9am-9pm, Sat.-Sun. and holidays 10am-7pm; free). The **Beehive House,** 67 E. South Temple (240-2671), at State St. 2 blocks east of Temple Sq., served as the official residence of Brigham Young while he served as "governor" of the Deseret Territory (unrecognized by the U.S. government) and president of the Church. (Open Mon.-Fri. 9:30am-6:30pm, Sat. 9:30am-4:30pm, Sun. 10am-1pm; Sept.-May Mon.-Sat. 9:30am-4:30pm, Sun. 10am-1pm. ½-hr. guided tours every 10-15 min. Closes 1pm on holidays. Free.)

The moment when Brigham Young and his band of Mormons first found the Great Salt Lake is commemorated at **"This is the Place" State Park,** 2601 Sunnyside Ave. (584-8391), in Emigration Canyon on the eastern end of town. Take bus #4 or follow 8th South St. until it becomes Sunnyside Ave., then take Monument Rd. The **"This is the Place" Monument** celebrates Brigham Young's decision to settle here. The **visitors center** has been demolished to make way for a larger facility. Tour **Brigham Young's forest farmhouse** (open Tues.-Sun. 11am-5pm), where the leader held court with his numerous wives. (Park open in summer daily 8am-8pm.

Baptisms for the Dead

Because they believe that only baptized Mormons can enjoy the highest level of heaven, the Church of Jesus Christ of Latter-Day Saints provides **Baptisms for the Dead.** Mormon doctrine holds that all those who died without a chance to accept Mormon doctrine be given a chance to accept the doctrine in the afterlife. The rites are performed on their behalf by proxies, which give deceased people a chance to accept the rites performed on their behalf. Those eligible for posthumous baptism include everyone who has not heard the Mormon doctrine and all those who lived before 1830. Baptisms were initially performed on behalf of members' ancestors; but beginning in 1961, lists of names for baptisms were drawn from parish records and oral histories. Jewish leaders were astonished to discover that over 380,000 Jewish Holocaust victims were baptized by the Mormon Church. Fifteenth president of the Mormon church, Gordon B. Hinckley, reiterated recently a committment to baptizing on behalf of only members' ancestors and reconfirming guidelines for selecting names.

Entrance $1 10:30am-4:30pm. Call ahead to double-check park hours; extensive construction is going on within the park.)

SECULAR SIGHTS AND ENTERTAINMENT

The gray-domed **capitol** (538-3000) lies behind the spires of Temple Sq. (tours Mon.-Fri. 9am-3pm). For more info, contact the **Council Hall Visitors Center** (538-1030), across from the main entrance (open Mon.-Fri. 8am-5pm, Sat.-Sun. and holidays 10am-5pm). **Pioneer Memorial Museum,** 300 N. Main St. (538-1050), next to the state capitol, has personal items from the earliest settlers in the valley and gives insight into two of the most prominent Mormon leaders: Brigham Young and his first counselor, Heber C. Kimball (open Mon.-Sat. 9am-5pm, Sun. 1-5pm; Sept.-May Mon.-Sat. 9am-5pm; free). While in the capitol area, hike up City Creek Canyon to **Memory Grove** and savor one of the city's best views, or ride up the **Church of Jesus Christ of Latter Day Saints Office Building,** 50 E. North Temple, to the 26th-floor **observation deck** (240-3789), to see the Great Salt Lake in the west and the Wasatch Mountain Range to the east (open Mon.-Sat. 9am-4:30pm). Also on capitol hill, the **Hansen Planetarium,** 15 S. State St. (538-2104), does fabulous free exhibits, in addition to their shows (open Sun.-Thurs. 9am-10pm, Fri.-Sat. 9am-1am).

Head for the **Children's Museum,** 840 N. 300 West (328-3383), to pilot a 727 jet or implant a Jarvik artificial heart in a life-sized "patient." (Open Mon. 9:30am-9pm, Tues.-Sat. 9:30am-5pm, Sun. noon-5pm. $3, ages 2-13 $2.15; Mon. after 5pm $1.50/ $1. Take bus #61.) Next to the Amtrak station, the **Utah State Historical Society,** 300 Río Grande (533-3500), hosts an interesting series of exhibits, including old photographs and quilts (open Mon.-Fri. 8am-5pm; free).

For happenings at the **University of Utah,** contact the **Information Desk** in the U. of Utah Park Administration Building (581-6515; open Mon.-Fri. 9am-4pm), or **Olpin Student Center** (581-5888; open Mon.-Sat. 8am-9pm).

The **Utah Symphony Orchestra** (533-6407) performs in Abravanel Hall, 123 W. South Temple (tickets in summer $10-25, in season $14-35; student rush $6). The neighboring **Salt Lake Art Center** (328-4201) stages dance and opera performances (open Tues.-Sat. 10am-5pm, Sun. 1-5pm; suggested donation $2).

ALCOHOL AND NIGHTLIFE

A number of hotels and restaurants have licenses to sell mini-bottles and splits of wine, but consumers must sometimes make drinks themselves. Most restaurants and all public bars serve only beer. Only private clubs requiring membership fees are allowed to serve mixed drinks. Some clubs sell two-week trial memberships for $5; others give free, temporary memberships to visitors in town for a night or two. In general, you need a sponsor to become a member or guest; many locals are aware that the laws of their state are unusual and offer their sponsorship to friendly strangers. The drinking age of 21 is well-enforced. There are six state liquor stores within 3 mi. of downtown Salt Lake City (open Mon.-Sat. 10am-10pm).

Despite the alcohol restrictions, several fun bars and clubs survive downtown. Pick up a free copy of *Private Eye Weekly* or *The Event,* both available at bars and restaurants, for local club listings and events. The **Dead Goat Saloon,** 165 S. West Temple (328-4628), attracts tourists and locals alike. (Open Mon.-Fri. 11:30am-2am, Sat. 6pm-2am, Sun. 7pm-1am. Beer served until 1am. Cover $1-5, Fri.-Sun. $5.) Head over to the **X Wife's Place,** 465 S. 700 East (532-2353), to shoot stick. There's no cover, but you'll need a club membership ($15 per yr.) or a member to sponsor you. (Open Mon.-Sat. 4pm-1am. Beer and mixed drinks served.) **Club DV8,** 115 S. West Temple (539-8400), deviates from the straight and narrow, with 25¢ drafts on Saturdays (9-10pm) and "modern music" on Thursday nights. (Open Thurs.-Sat. 9pm-1:30am. ½-price drafts 9-10pm. 2-wk. membership $5; guest cover $3, before 10pm $1.) **The Zephyr,** 79 W. 300 South (355-2582), blows with live rock and reggae nightly (open daily 7pm-1am; cover $3-20).

■ NEAR SALT LAKE CITY AND SKIING

The **Great Salt Lake,** 17 mi. west of town on I-80 (exit 104), a remnant of primordial Lake Bonneville, is a body of water so salty that only blue-green algae and brine shrimp can survive in it. The salt content varies from 5% to 15%, providing unusual buoyancy; in fact, no one has ever drowned in the Great Salt Lake. Due to its chemical make-up, the water smells...well, bad. It is nearly impossible to get to the lake without a car; bus #37 ("Magna") will take you within 4 mi., but no closer. Contact the visitors center (see Salt Lake City Practical Information p. 617) or **Great Salt Lake State Park** (250-1898) for directions. Flooding sometimes closes the state parks and beaches on the lakeshore, but you can still soak up rays at **Saltair Beach,** 17 mi. to the west, or head 40 minutes north to fresh-water **Willard Bay.**

In the summer, escape the heat with a drive or hike to the cool breezes and icy streams of the nearby mountains. One of the prettiest roads over the Wasatch Range, **Rte. 210** heads east from Sandy, 12 mi. southeast of the city, and goes up **Little Cottonwood Canyon** to the Alta ski resort. The **Lone Peak Wilderness Area** stretches south from Rte. 210, with peaks of over 11,000 ft. towering above.

Of the seven **ski areas** within 40 min. of Salt Lake City, **Snowbird** (521-6040; lift tickets $34-44) and **Park City** (649-8111; lift tickets $47), 30 mi. from Salt Lake on I-80E, host the classiest crowds. Nearby **Alta** provides a more economical alternative (742-3333; lift tickets $25); the **Alta Peruvian Lodge** (328-8589) offers a package for two people ($125 each) which includes a bed, all meals, service charges, tax, and lift tickets. **UTA** (see Salt Lake City Practical Information p. 617) runs buses from the city to the resorts in winter, with pickups at downtown motels. **Lewis Bros. Stages** (800-826-5844), one of many shuttle services which provide transport to Park City, departs the airport every ½ hour in winter and five times per day in summer ($19, $36 round-trip). **Breeze Ski Rentals** (800-525-0314), rents equipment at Snowbird and Park City ($16.60; 10% discount if reserved; lower rates for rentals over 3 days). Contact the Utah Travel Council (see Utah Practical Information p. 617) and request the free *Ski Utah* for listings of ski packages and lodgings.

Some resorts offer summer attractions as well. You can rent mountain bikes at **Snowbird** (see above) for $22 per day or $15 per ½-day. Snowbird's **aerial tram** climbs to 11,000 ft., offering a spectacular view of the Wasatch Mountains and the Salt Lake Valley below (open daily 11am-8pm; $8, ages 5-16 $6, seniors and under 5 free). When the snow has melted, mountain bikes are allowed on the tram (until 7pm; $8, $12 for a day pass). In the summer, **Park City** offers a thrilling ½ mi. of curves and drops on their **alpine slide.** (Open Mon.-Fri. noon-10pm, Sat.-Sun. 10am-10pm. $6, seniors and children $4.50, under 7 $1.75.)

■■■ DINOSAUR AND VERNAL

Dinosaur National Monument is more than just a heap of dinosaur bones. The Green and Yampa Rivers have created vast, colorful gorges and canyons here, and the harsh terrain evokes eerie visions of its reptilian past. Pittsburgh paleontologist Earl Douglass began scouring the area for bones in 1908; the quarry he excavated, not entirely depleted of fossil bones, lies at the west end of the park. The rest of Dinosaur features choice spots for hiking and boating, as well as a number of Indian petroglyphs. **Vernal,** 16 mi. west of Dinosaur on U.S. 40, is a popular base for exploring the Monument, Flaming Gorge, and the Uinta Mountains. Lest you forget how close Vernal is to Dinosaur, plastic brontosauruses lining the strip of highway that anchors the town will remind you.

Practical Information The park collects an **entrance fee** of $5 per car, and $3 per biker, pedestrian, or tour bus passenger. The Monument's more interesting west side lies along Rte. 149 off U.S. 40 just outside of **Jensen,** 30 mi. east of Vernal. The east side of the park is accessible only from a road off U.S. 40, outside **Dinosaur, CO.** The **Dinosaur National Monument Headquarters** (303-374-2216), at the inter-

THE SOUTHWEST

section of U.S. 40 and the park road in Dinosaur, CO, provides orientation for exploring the canyonlands of the park and also gives info on nearby river rafting. While you're there, pick up the Monument visitors guide *Echoes.* (Open daily 8am-4:30pm; Sept.-May Mon.-Fri. 8am-4:30pm.) The Monument Superintendent, P.O. Box 210, Dinosaur, CO 81610, has info on the east side of the park as well. For even more info and maps, call 800-845-3466. The **Dinosaur Quarry Visitors Center** (801-789-2115), 7 mi. from the intersection of U.S. 40 and the park road on the west side of the park, is accessible from the road by free shuttle bus or a fairly strenuous ½-mi. walk (cars prohibited in summer, although permitted after the center closes the rest of the year). A hill inside the center has been partially excavated to reveal the hulking skeletal remains of dinosaurs. Winter finds the park lonely, cold, and fossilized with neither shuttle service nor the possibility of self-guided tours. (Center open daily 8am-7pm, in winter 8am-4:30pm.) In Vernal, stop at the **visitors center** in the **Utah Fieldhouse of Natural History and Dinosaur Garden,** 235 W. Main St. (801-789-4002), which offers brochures and helpful advice for daytrips in the area (open daily 8am-9pm). The **Ashley National Forest Service,** 355 N. Vernal Ave. (801-789-1181), in Vernal, administers much of this area, including most campgrounds (open Mon.-Fri. 8am-5pm, Sat. 8am-4:30pm).

Greyhound (800-231-2222) makes daily runs east and west along U.S. 40 (4 or 5 per day each way), stopping in Vernal and Dinosaur, CO, en route from Denver and Salt Lake City. Jensen is a flag stop, as is Monument Headquarters, 2 mi. west of Dinosaur, CO. In an **emergency,** call 801-789-2115 (UT) or 303-374-2216 (CO). Vernal, UT's **post office:** 67 N. 800 West (801-789-2393; open Mon.-Fri. 9am-5pm, Sat. 10am-noon); **ZIP code:** 84078. Dinosaur, CO's **post office:** 198 Stegosaurus Dr. (303-374-2353; open Mon.-Fri. 8:30am-12:30pm and 1-5pm); **ZIP code:** 81610.

Camping, Accommodations, and Food For the low-down on campgrounds call the National Park Service at 801-789-2115. A few mi. beyond the Quarry Center on Rte. 149 you'll find the shady **Green River Campground** with flush toilets, drinking water, and sites for tents and RVs (80 sites $8; open late spring-early fall). There are also several free primitive campsites in and around the park; call the visitors center for details. A rugged 13 mi. east of Harper's Corner, on the park's east side, **Echo Campground** (9 free sites), provides the perfect location for a crystalline evening under the stars. Watch for signs near Harper's Corner leading to the dirt road into the valley below. For **backcountry camping,** obtain a free permit from the headquarters or from Quarry Center.

On the east side of the park, the **Hi-Vu (Park) Motel,** 105 E. Brontosaurus Blvd., Dinosaur, CO (303-374-2267), offers singles for $20, doubles for $22, and two beds for $26 (closed Nov. 15-April). Although the manager is friendly, Hi-Vu's location in a relatively unpopulated area might make single travelers nervous.

In Vernal, the **Sage Motel,** 54 W. Main St. (801-789-1442), has big, clean rooms, A/C, and cable TV (singles $35, doubles $42). A plastic dino out front wards off nightmares and intruders at the **Dine-A-Ville Motel,** 801 W. Main St. (801-789-9571), at the far west end of town. The attractive rooms feature color TV; some also have kitchenettes. (Singles $28-35, doubles from $39.) Camping in Vernal will satisfy a tighter budget, without forcing you to really rough it. **Campground Dina RV Park,** 930 N. Vernal Ave. (801-789-2148), about 1 mi. north of Main St. on U.S. 191, has shady sites and a convenience store (tent sites $6.50 per person, with water and electricity $17.50, with full hookup $19). **Vernal KOA,** 1800 W. Sheraton Ave. (801-789-8935), off U.S. 40 south of town, makes life easy with a store, laundry facilities, and a pool (tent sites $13, with water and electricity $17).

The **Open Hearth Donut Shop,** 360 E. Main St., Vernal (801-789-0274), makes home-style donuts (37¢ each, $3.70 per dozen) and large sub sandwiches ($2.75) for your dining pleasure (open Mon.-Fri. 5:30am-6pm, Sat. 6am-1pm). The **7-11 Ranch Restaurant,** 77 E. Main St., Vernal (801-789-1170), serves good food (how vivid!), including big breakfasts with two eggs, hashbrowns, and toast for $2.50 and dinners with a salad, a vegetable, and bread from $6 (open Mon.-Sat. 6am-10pm).

Sights and Activities Beyond the campgrounds on Rte. 149, just past the end of the road, you can see one of the best examples of the monument's many Native American **petroglyphs.** The most accessible rock art hangs at **Club Creek** (a few mi. east of Quarry Visitors Center), but **McKee Spring** displays the finest petroglyph panels. For 3-D relics, such as pot shards, visit **Jones Hole Trail** or **Yampa Canyon,** where the remains of granaries and other storage structures can be seen.

The 25-mi. road (closed in winter) to majestic **Harper's Corner,** at the junction of the Green and Yampa River gorges, begins 2 mi. east of Dinosaur. From the road's terminus, a 2-mi. round-trip nature hike leads to the corner itself. It's worth the sweat; the view of the Green River and the sculpted rocks is spectacular.

In Vernal, the **Utah Fieldhouse of Natural History and Dinosaur Garden,** 235 Main St. (801-789-3799), offers excellent displays on the state's geological and natural history. The dinosaur garden features life-size models. Check out the geological displays where fluorescent minerals make your shoelaces glow in the dark. (Open daily 8am-9pm; off season 9am-5pm. $1.50, ages 6-15 $1.)

■■■ FLAMING GORGE

Cutting across Utah's north border, **Flaming Gorge National Recreation Area** stretches from the cool mountains of Ashley National Forest to the south Wyoming desert, where wild horses roam. Fishing, boating, and hiking top the list of activities at Flaming Gorge. Each year, the 91-mi.-long **Flaming Gorge Reservoir,** created in 1963 by the construction of a dam on the Green River, is stocked with tons of doomed trout. Though Wyoming offers more recreation, Utah claims the most scenic and best-developed part of the park, at the base of the Uinta Mountains.

Practical Information From Wyoming travel the most scenic route to the gorge, **U.S. 191S** from I-80 (exit between Rock Springs and Green River). Rte. 530 closely parallels the reservoir's west shore, but the scenery won't blow you away; take this route only if you want to camp on the flat beaches of the reservoir's Wyoming section. From the south, take **U.S. 191N** from Vernal, over the gorgeous flanks of the Uinta Mountains (see below), to **Dutch John, UT.** The **Flaming Gorge Visitors Center** (885-3135), on U.S. 191 right on the top of Flaming Gorge Dam, offers free guided tours of the dam and maps of the area (open daily 8am-6pm; off season 9am-5pm). The **Red Canyon Visitors Center** (889-3713), a few mi. off U.S. 191 on Rte. 44 to Manila, hangs out 1360 ft. above Red Canyon and Flaming Gorge Lake (open daily 10am-5pm; closed in winter). Flaming Gorge, UT's **area code:** 801.

Camping and Accommodations Inexpensive **campgrounds** flourish in the Flaming Gorge area; ask for a pamphlet listing all the campgrounds at either visitors center. Reservations for large groups can be made by calling MISTIX (800-280-2267). Camp next to the Red Canyon Visitors Center in **Canyon Rim Campground** (18 sites $8; open mid-May to mid-Sept.), or in one of the numerous national forest campgrounds along U.S. 191 and Rte. 44 in the Utah portion of the park (2-week max. stay; sites $9-11). Farther north, **Buckboard Crossing** (307-875-6927; 68 sites $8) and **Lucerne Valley** (784-3293; 143 sites $10), tend to be drier and unshaded, but their location, close to the marinas on the reservoir, is a bonus (both open mid-April to mid-Oct.). A number of free primitive campgrounds hide in the high country. You do not necessarily have to camp at a developed site; just be sure to check with the rangers to make sure the spot you pick is kosher.

If you'd rather sleep indoors, **Red Canyon Lodge** (889-3759), west on Rte. 44 2 mi. before the Red Canyon Visitors Center, offers reasonably priced, rustic cabins. Frontier cabins share bath facilities (singles $28, doubles $38); deluxe cabins have private baths (singles $42, doubles $52; $5 for a roll-away). **Flaming Gorge Lodge,** near the dam in Dutch John (889-3773), charges upscale prices for upscale rooms with A/C and cable TV (singles $49, doubles $55; Nov.-Feb. $33/$39).

Sights and Activities Try your hand at **fishing** along the Green River Gorge below the dam. The lake teems with trout, and the Green River offers some of the best fly-fishing in the country. To fish, you must obtain a **permit** (available at Flaming Gorge Lodge, the marinas, and most stores in Manila). For more information, call the **Utah Department of Wildlife Resources,** 152 E. 100 North, Salt Lake City (789-3103; open Mon.-Fri. 8am-5pm). **Cedar Springs Marina** (889-3795), 3 mi. before the dam in Dutch John, rents out fishing rods and boats. (Fishing boats $40 for 3hr., $55 for 6hr., $65 per day; rods $5 with a boat. Pontoons also available. Open May-Sept. daily 8am-6:30pm.) At **Lucerne Valley Marina** (784-3483), 7 mi. east of Manila off Rte. 43, you can procure a small, 14-ft. fishing boat for $35 per day (open Mon.-Fri. 8am-6:30pm). **Dan River Hatch Expeditions,** 55 E. Main (789-4316 or 800-342-8243), in Vernal (see p. 621), arranges a wide variety of summer rafting trips for folks with money to burn (1-day voyage $60, under 12 $50).

The **Sheep Creek Geologic Loop,** an 11-mi. scenic drive off Rte. 44 just south of Manila, takes you past rock strata and wildlife. For a hide-out from tourists, the large valley of **Brown's Park,** 23 mi. east of Flaming Gorge, answers your prayers. Four-wheel drive is recommended. Nineteenth-century western outlaws Butch Cassidy and his Wild Bunch found the valley's isolation and its proximity to three state lines ideal for evading the law; today's visitors find the river's shore an idyllic place to camp or just stop for a while. Two free campsites (no water) lie within ¼ mi. of the park in either direction: **Indian Crossing,** just up the Green River, and **Indian Hollow,** just downstream. To get to Brown's Park from Dutch John, head north about 10 mi. on U.S. 191 until you reach Minnie's Gap; follow the signs to Clay Basin (13mi.) and to the park (23mi.).

SOUTHERN UTAH

■■■ MOAB

Moab first flourished in the 1950s due to an abundance of uranium in the area. Since then, the town has adapted itself to the industry of tourism; perhaps too well—the golden arches of McDonald's grace Main St. just as sandstone arches decorate the town's environs. Big Macs aside, Moab attracts a multitude of hippies and hyper-athletes alike. With its proximity to Arches (see p. 626) and Canyonlands (see p. 627), and its youthful, "crunchy" character, the town of Moab proves a great base for exploring southern Utah, either by car, mountain bike, or Green River raft.

Practical Information Inaccessible by public transportation, Moab sits 50 mi. southeast of I-70 on U.S. 191, 5 mi. south of Arches. **Amtrak** comes only as close as Thompson, 41 mi. northeast of town, and **Greyhound** plans its nearest stops in Green River, 52 mi. northwest—some buses will stop along I-70, in Crescent Junction, 30 mi. north of town. See if your hotel or hostel will pick you up from these distant points for a small fee; otherwise your best option is a taxi. Of course, **Redtail Aviation** (259-7421) does offer flights into Moab from the surrounding areas.

The **Moab Information Center,** 3 Center St. (259-2468), provides info on Moab and the nearby parks and monuments (open daily 8am-9pm, Nov.-Feb. 9am-5pm). Moab's **post office:** 50 E. 100 North (259-7427; open Mon.-Fri. 8:30am-4pm, Sat. 9am-noon); **ZIP code:** 84532; **area code:** 801.

Accommodations and Camping Though chain motels clutter Main St., Moab fills up fast in the summer, especially on weekends; call well ahead to guarantee a reservation. Off-season rates can drop as much as 50%; be willing to brave the cold. The owners of the **Lazy Lizard International Hostel (AAIH/Rucksackers),** 1213 S. U.S. 191 (259-6057; look for the "A1 Storage" sign when going north on U.S.

191), go out of their way to be helpful—they'll pick you up (usually for $10-15), and arrange rafting, bicycling, and horseback riding trips through local companies. The kitchen, VCR, laundry, and hot tub are at your beck and call. (Bunks $8; singles and doubles $22, triples $27; cabins for 1 or 2 $25, $5 per additional person up to 5; campsites, with water, $4 per person; teepees for 1 or 2 $10.)

A birdcage, bowling pins, and a moose serve as decorative accents in the quirky theme rooms of **Hotel Off Center,** 96 E. Center St. (259-4244 or 800-237-4685), ½ block off Main St. (Shared bathrooms. Dorm beds $12; singles $35, doubles $47, $5 per additional person.) **The Silver Sage Inn,** 840 S. Main (259-4420), operated by a Lutheran church, has sparse but clean rooms with cable TV, two of them equipped for disabled access (office closes 10pm; singles $40, doubles $45; $4 per additional person). **The Prospector Lodge,** 186 N. 1st West (259-5145), 1 block west of Main St., offers cool, comfy rooms with TV and free java. (Singles with a double bed $30, with queen-size $40, doubles $50, triples $60; $6 per additional person.)

Arches National Park (see p. 626) has the area's best **campground.** In town, the **Canyonlands Camp Park,** 555 S. Main St. (259-6848), provides well-shaded sites and a pool. (Sites $14, with water and electricity $17, with full hookup $19; $2 per additional person.) **Slickrock Campground,** 1302½ N. U.S. 191 (259-7660 or 259-4152), features a pool, 3 hot tubs, and laundry facilities. (Single sites $13.50, doubles $22; with full hookup $19.25; sparse cabins with A/C for 4 $27.)

Food **The Poplar Place Pub and Eatery,** 100 N. Main St. (259-6018; open daily 11:30am-11pm), serves great pizzas (from $8), Mexican dishes, and fresh salads (around $5). For retro diner decor, visit **The Moab Diner,** 189 S. Main St. (259-4006); try the veggie specials and the excellent french fries. (Burgers and sandwiches $4-5. Open Sun.-Thurs. 6am-10pm, Fri.-Sat. 6am-10:30pm.) **Eddie McStiff's,** 57 S. Main St. (259-BEER/2337), offers 12 homemade brews (pints $3), from "chestnut brown" to "passion fruit pale," to accompany salads, pizza ($6-10), and pasta (open daily 3-10pm). **Honest Ozzie's Café and Desert Oasis,** 60 N. 100 W. (259-8442), delivers breakfast combos, a plethora of fruity drinks ($3), and vegetarian dishes ($5-9)—no lie. (Open daily 6:30am-10:30pm.)

Eclectic dining establishments dot Moab's streets, but when you need a drink, the **Moab Liquor Store,** 260 S. Main St. (259-5314; open Mon.-Sat. 11am-9pm) is the only place to purchase alcohol above 3.2%. Mixed drinks without food can be had only at **The Rio,** 2 S. 100 West (259-6666), off Main St., a private club where you must be sponsored by a member or buy a 2-week pass for $5, good for up to 5 people (open Mon.-Fri. 11:30am-11pm, Sat. 5pm-1am, Sun. 10am-midnight).

Sights and Activities Although the nearby national parks are Moab's main event, the town has two museums worth a gander. Albert Christensen spent 12 years creating the weirder of the two, **Hole N" the Rock,** 15 mi. south of Moab on U.S. 191, a 14-room house carved out of a sandstone cliff. His wife Gladys kept the dream alive after his death in 1957 and opened the house to the public. Check out Christensen's nearby rendering of Franklin D. Roosevelt as well. (Open daily 9am-5pm. $2.) For a more traditional look at the history and geology of the area, peruse the **Dan O'Laurie Museum,** 118 E. Center St. (254-7445; open Mon.-Sat. 1-5pm and 7-9pm; off season Mon.-Thurs. 3-5pm and 7-9pm, Fri.-Sat. 1-5pm and 7-9pm).

Various outfitters in Moab arrange horseback, motorboat, raft, canoe, jeep, and helicopter rides. **Park Creek Ranch** (259-5505) offers **trail rides** into the La Sal Mountains (1hr. $15 per person; 2hr. $25) or the Arches (1hr. $20 per person; 2hr. $35). Raft, powerboat, and jeep tours into the Colorado River and canyons are the business of **Navtech Expeditions,** 321 N. Main St. (259-7983; $38-249 per person). **Trapax, Inc.** (259-5261) will take you for an evening boat ride along the Colorado River as their **Canyonlands by Night** sound and light show ricochets off the canyon walls ($20, ages 6-16 $10, under 6 free).

■ FINDING THE FAB FIVE

The five National Parks that cover this majestic area can be reached by several roads. From Moab, take U.S. 191N to **Arches.** Continue north on U.S. 191 to Rte. 313S, and this road will lead to the Islands in the Sky area of **Canyonlands** (60mi.). To reach **Capitol Reef,** take U.S. 191N to I-70W, leave I-70 at exit 147, and follow Rte. 24S to Hanksville and then west to the park. Route 24W runs to Torrey where scenic Rte. 12 branches south and west through **Dixie National Forest** to **Bryce Canyon.** If you're looking for **Zion,** continue on Rte. 12W to U.S. 89S through Mt. Carmel Junction and pick up Rte. 9W.

The two national forests in Southern Utah are divided into districts; some of which lie near the national parks and serve as excellent places to stay on a cross-country jaunt. **Manti-La Sal National Forest** has two sections near Arches and the Needles area of Canyonlands. **Dixie National Forest** stretches from Capitol Reef, through Bryce, all the way to the western side of Zion. Check below, in each park's Camping section, for additional information.

■■■ ARCHES

"This is the most beautiful place on earth," park ranger and novelist Edward Abbey wrote of **Arches National Park.** Abbey is not alone in that opinion; massive expanses of red rock spires, pinnacles, and, of course, arches overwhelm visitors and give testimony to the grandeur of nature. Arches National Park has more than 200 natural arches, structures so perfect in form that early explorers believed they had found the ruins of a lost civilization.

Practical Information The park entrance is on **U.S. 191,** 5 mi. north of Moab. Though no public transportation serves the park, **buses** running along I-70, stop in Crescent Junction. The **visitors center** (259-8161), to the right of the entrance station, distributes free Park Service maps (open daily 8am-6pm; off season 8am-4:30pm). An **entrance pass** covers admission for a week ($4 per carload, $2 per pedestrian or biker). For more info, write the Superintendent, Arches National Park, P.O. Box 907, Moab 84532 (259-8161). **Water** is available in the park. Moab makes an excellent **base town.** For more details on accommodations, food, and activities, see p. 624. **Emergency:** 911. **Area code:** 801.

Camping The park's only campground, **Devil's Garden,** has 54 sites (one reserved for disabled visitors) 18 mi. from the visitors center. Because Devil's Garden doesn't take reservations sites go quickly in season. Get there early; a line forms at the visitors center preparing for the rush at 7:30am. (No wood-gathering. Running water April-Oct. 2-week max. stay. Sites $8.) **Backcountry camping** in Arches is free, but not recommended. Register and pick up a map at the National Park Service office in Moab, 2 blocks west of the Ramada Inn on Main St. Bring plenty of water and bug spray, and avoid hiking on summer afternoons. For developed sites, Moab has several more campgrounds.

Escape the summer heat, crowds, and biting gnats by heading to the **Moab Range District** of the Manti-La Sal National Forest. Campgrounds (30mi. southeast of Moab off U.S. 191) sit about 4000 ft. higher than those at Arches. All sites cost $5, except the free sites at **Oowah Lake.** Oowah, 3 mi. down a dirt road, is a rainbow trout haven (fishing permits available at most stores in Moab and at the Forest Service office; $5 per day). For more info, contact the Manti-La Sal National Forest Service office in Moab, 125 W. 200 South 84532 (259-7155; open Mon.-Fri. 8am-4:30pm).

Sights and Activities Plenty of scenic wonders enliven the 18-mi. road between the visitors center and Devil's Garden. No matter how short your stay, be sure to see the **Windows** at **Panorama Point,** about halfway along the road. Cyclists enjoy the ride in spring or fall, but steep inclines make the trip almost unbearable in the summer heat. **Rim Cyclery,** 94 W. 100 North, Moab (259-5333), offers rimming bikes for $20 per ½-day or $28 per day, including a helmet and a water bottle (open daily 9am-6pm). At the end of the paved road, **Devil's Garden** boasts an astounding 64 arches. A challenging hike from the **Landscape Arch** leads across harrowing exposures to the secluded **Double O Arch.** The highlight of your visit should be the free-standing **Delicate Arch,** the symbol of the park; take the Delicate Arch turn-off from the main road, 2 mi. down a graded, unpaved road (impassable after rainstorms). Once you reach Wolfe Ranch, a 1½-mi. foot trail leads to the arch. Beyond, you can catch a glimpse of the Colorado River gorge and the La Sal Mountains. Visitors occasionally come across petroglyphs left on the stone walls by the Anasazi and Ute who wandered the area centuries ago.

Arches aren't the only natural wonders here. One of the most popular trails, the moderately strenuous 2-mi. **Fiery Furnace Trail,** leads down into the canyon bottoms, providing new perspective on the imposing cliffs and monoliths above. Only experienced hikers should attempt this trail alone. Rangers lead groups from the visitors center into the labyrinth twice daily in the summer. Tours tend to fill up the day before; reservations can be made 48 hours in advance.

■■■ CANYONLANDS

Those who make the trek to **Canyonlands National Park** are rewarded with a pleasant surprise: the absence of that overabundant, pestering species, *homo Winnebagiens.* The Green and Colorado Rivers divide the park into three sections, each with its own **visitors center.** (All three open daily 8am-5pm; hours subject to change off season; call ahead.) **The Needles** region (visitors center 259-4711) contains spires, arches, canyons, and Native American ruins, but is not as rough as the Maze area (see below). To get to the Needles, take Rte. 211W from U.S. 191, about 40 mi. south of Moab. Farther north, **Island in the Sky** (visitors center 259-4351), a towering mesa which sits within the "Y" formed by the two rivers, affords fantastic views of the surrounding canyons and mountains; take Rte. 313W from U.S. 191 about 10 mi. north of Moab. The most remote district of the park, the rugged **Maze** area (visitors center 259-4352), is a veritable hurly-burly of twisted canyons made for *über*-pioneers with four-wheel-drive vehicles only. Be certain which area you want to visit; once you've entered a section of the park, getting to a different section involves retracing your steps and re-entering the park, a tedious trip which can last from several hours to a full day.

Practical Information Two visitors centers lie outside the park. Monticello's **Interagency Visitors Center,** 117 S. Main. St. (587-3235), sells area maps ($3-6; open Mon.-Fri. 8am-5pm, Sat.-Sun 10am-5pm). The park collects **entrance fees** of $4 per car and $2 per hiker or cyclist. For more information, write to the Superintendent, Canyonlands National Park, 125 W. 200 South, Moab 84532 (259-7164). Moab makes an excellent base town from which to explore the park (see p. 624).

Neither gas nor water nor food services grace the park. Just outside the boundary in the Needles district, however, the **Needles Outpost** (979-4007 or 259-8545) houses a limited, expensive grocery store and gas pump (open daily 8am-7pm). Hauling in groceries, water, and first-aid supplies from Moab or Monticello makes the most sense for travelers on a budget.

Camping and Hiking Before **backcountry camping** or **hiking,** register at the proper visitors center for one of a limited number of permits ($10 for Needles or Island in the Sky). Four-wheel drivers should also register at the visitors center and inquire about fees and backcountry parking sites. The Maze area allows only 4WD vehicles (permit for vehicles and camping $25).

Each region has its own official **campground.** In the Needles district, **Squaw Flat's** 26 sites occupy a sandy plain surrounded by giant sandstone towers, 40 mi. west of U.S. 191 on Rte. 211. Avoid this area in June, when insects swarm. Bring fuel and water, although the latter is usually available from mid-March to October. (Sites $6; Oct.-March free.) **Willow Flat Campground,** in the Island in the Sky district, sits high atop the mesa on Rte. 313, 41 mi. west off U.S. 191. You must bring your own water and insect repellent. (12 free sites.) Willow Flat and Squaw Flat both provide picnic tables, grills, and pit toilets. The backcountry campground at the **Maze Overlook** offers no amenities. All campgrounds work on a first come, first served basis. (See Arches, p. 626, for more camping info.)

Each visitors center has a brochure of possible hikes including length and difficulty; pick one and start from there. With summer temperatures regularly climbing over 100°F, bring at least one gallon of water per person per day. Hiking options from the Needles area are probably the best developed, though Island in the Sky offers some spectacular views. In the Maze district, a six-hour, 6-mi. guided hike into Horseshoe Canyon leaves the visitors center at 8am on Fridays, Saturdays, and Sundays. If hiking in desert heat doesn't appeal to you, rent Jeeps or mountain bikes in Moab, or take a one-hour airplane flight from **Red Tail Aviation** (259-7421; $60 per person). Cyclists should check at the visitors centers for trails.

For some great overlooks at elevations above 8000 ft., head to the **Monticello District** of Manti-La Sal National Forest south of Needles. This section of the forest has two campgrounds on **Blue Mountain: Buckboard,** 6.5 mi. west of Rte. 191 (9 sites and 2 group areas), and **Dalton Springs,** 5 mi. west of Rte. 191 (9 sites). Both campgrounds operate from late May to late October and charge $5 per site. Reservations for areas in Buckboard can be made at the **visitors center** in Monticello, 117 S. Main St. (587-3235). From Moab, head south on U.S. 191 to Monticello and then west on Rte. 1S. For more info on the Monticello District, call the Manti-La Sal National Forest Service office in Monticello, 496 E. Central (587-2041), on U.S. 666 just east of town (open Mon. 8am-4:30pm).

Farther away, **Dead Horse Point State Park** (entrance fee $3), perches on the rim of the Colorado Gorge. The park, south of Arches and 14 mi. south of U.S. 191, accessible from Rte. 313, offers yet more camping, this time with modern restrooms, water, hookups, and covered picnic tables. (Sites Sun.-Thurs. $7, Fri.-Sat. $8; ½ are available on a first come, first served basis.) For more info, contact the Park Superintendent, Dead Horse Point State Park, P.O. Box 609, Moab 84532 (259-2614 or 800-322-3770; open daily 8am-6pm; call for off-season hours).

■■■ CAPITOL REEF

A geologist's fantasy and **Capitol Reef National Park's** feature attraction, the **Waterpocket Fold** bisects the park, presenting visitors with 65 million years of stratified natural history. This 100-mi. furrow in the earth's crust, with its rocky scales and spines, winds through Capitol Reef like a giant pre-Cambrian serpent. The sheer cliffs that border the fold were originally called a "reef," not for their oceanic origins, but because they posed a barrier to travel. Today, you can explore the Reef from the seat of your car on the 25-mi. **scenic drive,** a 90-min. (round trip) jaunt right out along the cliffs. Pause and ponder the bathroom-sized **Fruita Schoolhouse** built by Mormon settlers, and **Petroglyphs Panoramic Point** along Rte. 24 near the entrance to the park. When **hiking,** keep in mind that summer temperatures average 95°F, and most water found in seep springs and rain-holding water pockets can only be used if purified.

Backcountry hikers should load up with water and stop at the **visitors center** (801-425-3791), on Rte. 24, for waterproof topographical maps ($7), regular maps ($4), free brochures on the trails, and good ol' advice. The center also has general info on the park and daily activities such as ranger-led jaunts and campfire talks. (Open daily 8am-7pm; Sept.-May 8am-4:30pm.) The middle link in the Fab Five chain, east of Zion and Bryce Canyon and west of Arches and Canyonlands, Capitol Reef is unreachable by major bus lines. **Entrance** to the park costs $4 per vehicle, $2 per hiker, or $7 for overnight camping. For more info, contact the Superintendent, Capitol Reef National Park, Torrey 84775 (801-425-3791).

Backcountry campers must register at the visitors center; the park's campgrounds give out sites on a first come, first served basis. The main campground, **Fruita,** 1.3 mi. south off Rte. 24, provides 73 sites (one reserved for the disabled), drinking water, and toilets ($7). A nearby orchard lets you pick for a price. **Cedar Mesa Campground,** in the park's south end, and **Cathedral Valley,** in the north, have only five sites each; neither has water or a paved road—but hey, they're free. To get to Cedar Mesa, take Rte. 24 past the visitors center to Notom-Bullfrog Rd. and go about 25 mi. south. Cathedral Valley is accessible only by 4WD or on foot.

For accommodations in the region, head to **Torrey,** 11 mi. west of the visitors center on Rte. 24. **The Chuck Wagon Motel and General Store** (801-425-3288), in the center of Torrey on Rte. 24W, has a barbecue area, a beautiful pool, and attractive, wood-paneled rooms, in a new building (A/C and phone; from $47) and in the older building above the store (no A/C or phone; from $37). The store comes through with a good selection of groceries, sporting goods, baked goods and picnic goods (open daily 7am-10pm). **Rim Rock Motel and RV Park** (801-425-3843), also on Rte. 24, 3 mi. east of Torrey, perches dramatically atop a cliff (singles $45, doubles $50-55; sites $10, with full hookup $15). Treat yourself to a meal at the **Capitol Reef Inn and Café,** 360 W. Main St., Torrey (801-425-3271), which features local rainbow trout—smoked or grilled—and an enclosed-porch dining room that looks out on the russet hills. The grilled trout sandwich ($6) comes with a ten-vegetable salad. (Open April-Oct. daily for breakfast and dinner.) For a greasier repast, try **Brink's Burgers,** 165 E. Main St., Torrey (801-425-3710; various burgers $2-4; open daily 11am-9pm). **The Redrock Restaurant and Campground** (801-542-3235), in Hanksville 37 mi. from the visitors center on Rte. 24, provides both campsites and food. (Open daily 7am-10pm. Sites with water and electricity $8, with full hookup $12. Cheeseburgers $2.25; daily special $4.75.) For couples, **Joy's Bed and Breakfast,** 296 S. Center, Hanksville (801-542-3252 or 801-542-3255), accommodates with a room and bath (room for 2 $35, with breakfast $45).

Betwixt Boulder and Capitol Reef, a stretch of Dixie National Forest shelters three lovely campgrounds, off scenic Rte. 12 between Boulder and Torrey. All perch at elevations over 8000 ft. and have drinking water and toilets (sites $7; first come, first served; open May-Sept.). The **Oak Creek Campground** includes seven sites, and the **Pleasant Creek Campground** has 16 sites. **Single Tree Campground** offers 22 sites, with two group sites (800-280-CAMP/2267 for group reservations) and two family sites, one of which can be reserved ahead of time. For more info, call the **Interagency** in Escalante (801-826-5499).

THE SOUTHWEST

■■■ BRYCE CANYON

The fragile spires of pink and red limestone which pepper **Bryce Canyon National Park** often seem more like the subjects of surrealist painting than the results of nature's art. Carved by millennia of wind and water, the canyons made life difficult for the Anasazi, Fremont, and Paiute who first navigated the region. Ebenezer Bryce, a Mormon carpenter who settled here in 1875, called the area "one hell of a place to lose a cow." For a solitary experience, hike into the canyons or visit between mid-October and mid-April when accommodation rates drop to as low as ½-price.

Practical Information Approaching from the west, Bryce Canyon lies 1½ hr. east of Cedar City; take Rte. 14 to U.S. 89. From the east, take I-70 to U.S. 89, turn east on Rte. 12 at Bryce Junction (7mi. south of Panguitch), and drive 14 mi. to the Rte. 63 junction; go south 4 mi. to the park entrance. There is no public transportation to Bryce Canyon, but **shuttle buses** travel to developed areas of the park from Ruby's Inn on Rte. 63 (in summer daily 8am-7pm; $4, seniors and children $2). Bryce Canyon's **entrance fee** is $5 per car, or $3 per pedestrian.

Begin any tour at the **visitors center** (834-5322), on Rte. 63 inside the park. The free Bryce Canyon *Hoo Doo,* available here, lists all park services, events, suggested hikes, and sight-seeing drives. (Open daily 8am-8pm; April-May and Sept.-Oct. 8am-

6pm; Nov.-March 8am-4:30pm.) For more information, write the Superintendent, Bryce Canyon National Park, Bryce Canyon 84717. **Emergency:** 911 or 676-2411. Bryce Canyon's **post office** (834-5361), is in Bryce Lodge. **Area code:** 801.

Accommodations, Camping, and Food Though very expensive for single travelers, **Bryce Lodge** (834-5361 or 586-7686), open April through October, may be a good deal for a group. (Singles and doubles $77—heck, might as well get a double—triples $82, quads $88, quints $93.) The closest hostel is **Bryce Canyon International Hostel,** 190 Main St. in Panguitch, 21 mi from the park. From the park, take Rte. 12W to U.S. 89N. This hostel opened too late to be researched (kitchen facilities, $12). **Canyonlands International Youth Hostel (AAIH/Rucksackers)** (see p. 631), hosts travelers 60 mi. south of Bryce in **Kanab.**

North and **Sunset Campgrounds,** both within 3 mi. of the visitors center, offer toilets, picnic tables, potable water, and 210 sites on a first come, first served basis ($7; show up early in the morning to reserve). For free **backcountry camping,** obtain a permit from the ranger at the visitors center.

There are two campgrounds just west of Bryce on scenic Rte. 12, in the Dixie National Forest. At an elevation of 7400 ft., the **Red Canyon Campground** rents 36 sites on a first come, first served basis ($8, with Golden Age Passport $4). The **King Creek Campground,** 11 mi. from Bryce on a dirt road off Rte. 12 (look for signs to Tropic Reservoir), features lakeside sites surrounded by pine trees ($7). Group sites are available with reservations (800-280-2267). The **Panguitch District** of the Dixie National Forest has six campgrounds with toilets, running water, swimming, boating, and fishing, all within one hour's drive; of these, campers favor **TE-AH** (800-280-2264), **Spruces,** and **Navajo Lake** (only TE-AH accepts reservations; no fishing at Navajo Lake; sites at all campgrounds $9). Inquire at the visitors center or the forest service office in Panguitch, 225 E. Center St. (676-8815; open Mon.-Fri. 8am-4:30pm) for details. See Near Bryce below for more sites in the Bryce area.

The **grocery store** at Sunrise Point (831-5361) has the only reasonable in-park provisions (open mid-April-late Oct., 7am-7pm). Behind the store, there are **showers** ($1.75 for 10 min.; available 7am-10pm).

Sights and Activities Popular scenery surrounds the visitors center; sunrises here are particularly astounding. The trail between **Sunrise Point** and **Sunset Point** can be accessed in a wheelchair. The 3-mi. loop of the **Navajo** and **Queen's Garden** trails leads you into the canyon itself. If you feel up to a challenge, branch off onto the **Peek-A-Boo Trail,** a 4-mi. round-trip. **Trail to the Hat Shop** descends four extremely steep mi. (And if you think climbing down is tough...) Ask about these and other trails at the visitors center. The 15-mi. main road winds past spectacular look-outs such as Sunrise Point, Sunset Point, **Inspiration Point,** and **Bryce Point** (see Practical Information above for shuttle bus info). Due to construction, the park is closed south of **Farview Point.**

Reserve a **van tour** along the main road at Bryce Lodge ($4, under 13 $2), or arrange for a guided horseback tour through **Canyon Trail Rides** (834-5500, off season 679-8665; $25-35 per person). From Memorial Day to Labor Day, **Ruby's Inn Rodeo** (834-5341) pits human against beast again and again (Mon.-Sat. 7:30pm; $6, children $3). The **Fiddler's Association Contest** tunes up in early July.

Near Bryce Truly daring hikers taunt death in a network of sandstone canyons in the ominously named **Phipps Death Hollow Outstanding Natural Area,** just north of **Escalante.** (Actually, it's not so bad as all that.) The **Escalante Interagency Office,** 755 W. Main St., Escalante 84726 (826-5499), on Rte. 12 just west of town, has free maps and backcountry permits (open daily 7am-6pm; off season Mon.-Fri. 8am-5pm). **Calf Creek** camping grounds, 15 mi. east of Escalante on Rte. 12, has a great hike near a cascading waterfall (with drinking water and toilets, sites $7).

West on Rte. 14, the flowered slopes of the **Cedar Breaks National Monument** descend 2000 ft. into its chiseled depths. The rim of this giant amphitheater stands a lofty 10,350 ft. above sea level. (Entrance $4 per car, $2 per pedestrian.) A 30-site **campground** (sites $6) and the **visitors center** (586-0787; open in summer daily 8am-6pm) await at **Point Supreme.** For more information, contact the Superintendent, Cedar Breaks National Monument, 82 N. 100 E., Cedar City 84720 (586-9451).

■■■ ZION

Some 13 million years ago, sea waters flowed over the cliffs and canyons of **Zion National Park.** Over the centuries the sea subsided, leaving only the powerful **Virgin River** whose watery fingers still carve the russet sandstone. In the northwest corner of the park, the walls of Kolob Terrace tower thousands of feet above the river; elsewhere branching canyons and unusual rock formations show off erosion's unique artistry. In the 1860s, Mormon settlers came to the area and enthusiastically proclaimed that they had found the promised land. Brigham Young did not agree, however, and declared to his followers that the place was awfully nice, but "not Zion." The name "not Zion" stuck for years until a new wave of entranced explorers dropped the "not," giving the park its present name.

Practical Information The main entrance to Zion is in **Springdale,** on Rte. 9, which bounds the park to the south along the Virgin River. Approaching Zion from the west, take Rte. 9 from I-15 at Hurricane. In the east, pick up Rte. 9 from U.S. 89 at Mount Carmel Junction. The nearest **Greyhound** station (673-2933 or 800-231-2222) is in St. George (43mi. southwest of the park on I-15), in a McDonald's, 1235 S. Bluff St., at St. George Blvd. Buses run to Salt Lake City (2 per day, 6hr., $54), Provo (2 per day, 5hr., $44.50), Los Angeles (6 per day, 15hr., $59), and Las Vegas (6 per day, 2hr., $25). The main **Zion Canyons Visitors Center** (772-3256), in the southeast corner of the park ½ mi. off Rte. 9, has an introductory slide program and a small but interesting museum (open daily 8am-8pm; off season 8am-6pm). The **Kolob Canyons Visitors Center** (586-9548) lies in the northwest corner of the park, off I-15 (open daily 9am-5pm; off season 9am-4:30pm). The park charges an **entrance fee** of $5 per car, or $2 per pedestrian. For **emergency assistance,** call 772-3256 during the day, 772-3322 after hours. **Area code:** 801.

Camping and Accommodations Over 300 sites are available on a first come, first served basis (come early) in the **South** and **Watchman Campgrounds** at the south gate. Both sites have water, toilets, and a sanitary disposal station for trailers. (2-week max. stay. Sites $7. Always open.) The park's only other campground, a primitive area at **Lava Point,** can be accessed from a hiking trail in the mid-section of the park or from the gravel road which turns off Rte. 9 in **Virgin** (6 sites with toilets but no water; free; open May-Oct.).

One thousand ft. above the south entrance camping areas, **Mukuntuweep Campground** (644-5445 or 644-2154), near the east entrance, has altitude on its side. Not only is it cooler than the other sites, but a laundromat, toilets, showers, and a mountain backdrop enhance the area (70 tent sites $12.50, 30 full hookups $16.50).

Zion Canyon Campground, 479 Zion Park Blvd. (772-3237), in Springdale just south of the park, soothes the weary, hungry, and filthy with a convenience store, a restaurant, a grocery store (772-3402), showers, and a coin-op laundry. (Registration 24 hrs. Sites for 2 $14, full hookup $18; extra adult $3.50, extra child under 15 50¢. Store open daily 8am-9pm, off season 8am-5pm.) The **Zion Canyon Lodge** (772-3213, 586-7686 for reservations, 586-7624 for group reservations), along the park's main road, offers premium rooms at premium prices, with a snack shop (open daily 7am-9pm) and a dining room (772-3213 for required dinner reservations). (Singles and doubles $78, each additional person up to 5 $5. Cabin singles and doubles $81, each additional person up to 4 $5. Lodge suite singles and doubles $116, each additional person up to 4 $5.) For lodging alternatives, try **Springdale** or **Rockville,** 2-5 mi. south of the park.

You need a free permit from the visitors center for **backcountry camping.** Camping along the rim is *not* allowed, but a free map from the visitors center indicates where you may and may not pitch a tent. Zion campgrounds don't take reservations and often fill on holidays and summer weekends; if you don't get in, try one of the six campgrounds in Dixie National Forest (see Bryce Canyon p. 629). To the west of Zion lies another district of the Dixie National Forest—**Pine Valley.** Pine Valley, at an elevation of 6683 ft., offers 57 sites with water and toilets (entrance $9, open May-Sept.). Groups can reserve sites by calling 800-280-CAMP/2267; the National Forest Service for this district (673-3431) has more details.

Treat yourself to more than a roof at **O'Toole's,** 980 Zion Park Blvd., Springdale (772-3457), in a beautiful, recently-renovated stucco-and-sandstone house. The gorgeous rooms, with great windows and sumptuous beds, include hot tub access and full breakfast; make reservations early. (Rooms for 2 $60-120, $10 per additional person.) The nearest hostel is the **Canyonlands International Youth Hostel (AAIH/Rucksackers),** 143 E. 100 S., Kanab 84741 (801-644-5554), 40 mi. south in **Kanab.** The hostel's location, one hour north of the Grand Canyon on U.S. 89 and an equal distance south of Zion, Bryce, and Lake Powell, makes it a perfect base for exploring north Arizona and south Utah; roomy bunks, free linens, laundry facilities, TV, a kitchen, parking, and a bountiful but bizarre breakfast banquet make it worth a trip from any of the parks. ($9. Reservations recommended.)

Sights If you love to walk or hike, you're in the right place. Paved and wheelchair-accessible with assistance, the **Gateway to the Narrows Trail** stretches 1 mi. from the north end of Zion Canyon Dr. The refreshing **Emerald Pools** trail (1.2mi. round-trip) is accessible to the disabled along its lower loop, but not on its middle and upper loops. The **Angel's Landing** trail (5mi. round-trip) takes you 1488 ft. above the canyon; the last terrifying ½ mi. climbs a narrow ridge with guide chains blasted into the rock. Overnight hikers can spend days on the 27-mi. **West Rim Trail.** Even if you plan to visit **Kolob Canyon's** backcountry, be sure to make the pilgrimage to **Zion Canyon.** The 7-mi. dead-end road on the canyon floor rambles past the giant formations of **Sentinel, Mountain of the Sun,** and the overwhelming symbol of Zion, the **Great White Throne.** A shuttle from the lodge runs this route every hour on the hour in the summer (daily 9am-5pm; 1hr.; $3, children $2). Hikers enjoy the difficult trail to **Observation Point,** where steep switchbacks explore the unusually gouged canyon. Horseback tours arranged by **Canyon Trail Rides** (772-3967) leave from the lodge ($12-35 per person). To float down the ravishing Virgin River, rent an **inner tube** ($5) from the Canyon grocery store.

■■■ NATURAL BRIDGES AND HOVENWEEP

Natural Bridges National Monument Nearly 3000 years ago, the Paiutes who inhabited this region called it Ma-Vah-Talk-Tump "under the horse's belly." In 1909, President Taft renamed each bridge with a Hopi term like Sipapu "place of desolation" or Kachina "ghost dancer." Renamed once again in the less-imaginative present day, Utah's first national monument is simply called Natural Bridges. Despite the newer, blander moniker, these water-sculpted bridges which stretch up to 250 ft. high and across, still deserve a visit. Leave the overlooks and hike down to the bridges to truly appreciate the size of the monuments. (Hikes range from .4 to 1.5 mi. round-trip, except for the 8.6-mi. "loop" trail.)

To reach Natural Bridges from northern Utah, follow U.S. 191S from Moab to the junction with **Scenic Rte. 95W** (north of Bluff and 4mi. south of Blanding). From Colorado, Rte. 66 leads south from Cortez to U.S. 191S (the junction is in Monticello). Route 163N runs up through Monument Valley from Arizona; just past Mexican Hat, catch Rte. 261N to Scenic Rte. 95W.

The **visitors center** (259-5174), on Rte. 95E, offers a slide show, small bookstore, and exhibits, along with the usual resources. (Open daily 8am-6pm; Nov.-Feb. 9am-4:30pm; March-April 8am-5pm. Park entrance $4 per vehicle, $2 per hiker or bicyclist; good for 7 days.) Campfire ranger-talks take place in the amphitheater on summer evenings (Mon., Wed., and Fri.-Sat. 9pm), and ranger-led hikes set out from the visitors center on summer mornings (Tues. and Thurs. 10am). Sleep under the stars at the **campground** near the visitors center, where each of the 13 sites accommodates up to nine people with a grill, tent pad, and picnic table. Motorized campers must observe a 21-ft. combined length limit for RVs and vehicles with trailers. (Sites $5; first come, first served.) **Water** is available at the visitors center. For further info, contact the Superintendent, Natural Bridges, Box 1, Lake Powell 84533 (259-5174).

Hovenweep National Monument Hovenweep, from the Ute meaning "deserted valley" features six groups of Pueblo ruins dating back over 1000 years. The valley remains deserted today with only two rangers (one in Utah, one in Colorado) minding the monument's 784 acres. Immune to vacation swarms, or even small crowds, Hovenweep provides visitors plenty of space and time to ponder.

The best preserved and most impressive ruins, **Square Tower Ruins,** lie footsteps away from the visitors center (see below). The **Square Tower Loop Trail,** an easy 2-mi. round-trip, leads to the ruins in this section; the **Hovenweep Castle** and the two-story apartment houses called the **Twin Towers.** A shorter trail, the ½-mi. **Tower Point Loop,** accesses the ruins of a tower perched on a canyon. The outlying ruins—**Cujon Ruins** and **Huckberry Canyon** in Utah, and **Cutthroat Castle** and **Goodman Point Ruins** in Colorado—are isolated and difficult to reach. Inquire at the visitors center for more info on road conditions and access to these areas.

Desolate but beautiful roads usher you to Hovenweep. In Utah or Arizona, follow U.S. 191 to its junction with Rte. 262E (14mi. south of Blanding, 11mi. north of Bluff). After about 30 mi., watch for signs to the monument. Though unpaved for 2½ mi., the road in is accessible to all vehicles. From Cortez, CO, go south on U.S. 166/U.S. 160 to Country Rd. 6 (the airport road); follow the Hovenweep signs for 45 mi., including 15 mi. of gravel road. Call ahead to check road conditions at the **visitors center** (303-749-0510), accessible from both the Utah and Colorado sides (open daily 8am-5pm, except when the ranger is out on patrol). *There is no gasoline or telephone at the monument.* The 31-site **campground** near the center has drinking water and restrooms approximately March to mid-November (sites $6; without water free; first come, first served). For more info, contact the Superintendent, Hovenweep National Monument, McElmo Rte., Cortez, CO 81321 (303-749-0510).

Nearby Civilization Three small towns provide lodging and services for travelers to the monuments and the valley. In the agricultural town of **Blanding** (45mi. from Hovenweep, 60mi. from Natural Bridges), sleep at the **Prospector Motor Lodge,** 591 U.S. 191S (singles $35, doubles $39; off season $27/$32), or try the **Blanding Sunset Inn,** 88 W. Center St. (678-3323; basic rooms $27-$36). The **Elk Ridge Café,** 120 E. Center St. (678-3390), will pour your morning cup of Joe (1 egg, potatoes, and toast $3; open daily 6am-10pm). Saddle up to **The Cedar Pony** (678-2715), on U.S. 191N, for pizza (slices $1.50) and pasta dinners ($4-6; open Mon.-Sat. 11am-9:30pm).

Situated amidst the sandstone canyons, **Bluff** (40mi. from Hovenweep, 65mi. from Natural Bridges) welcomes the budget traveler. Several cheap motels line U.S. 191, including **The Recapture Lodge** (672-2281; singles $30-38, doubles $32-44). Try the Navajo's sheepherder sandwich ($5) at the **Turquoise Restaurant** (672-2219), on U.S.191S (open 7am-9pm; in winter 7am-8pm). The gigantic, austere sandstone sculptures of the **Valley of the Gods** provided the backdrop for some of the road scenes in *Thelma and Louise.* A tough but scenic 17-mi. drive departs from U.S. 163W, 15 mi. south of Bluff on the right side of the road, and runs right through the valley; if you have four-wheel drive, use it.

Mexican Hat, AZ (pop. 38; 60mi. from Hovenweep, 45mi. from Natural Bridges, 21mi. south of the Arizona border on U.S. 163), named for a rock formation that looks just like one, sits quietly by the San Juan River. Rest your head at the **Canyonlands Motel** (683-2230), on U.S. 163 (very basic rooms, no cable; $28-40). **The Old Bridge Bar and Grille** (683-2220), on U.S. 163, is the place for Navajo specialties and sandwiches ($4-6).

Arizona

Populated primarily by Native Americans through the 19th century, Arizona has been hit in the past hundred years by waves of settlers—from the speculators and miners of the late 1800s, to the soldiers who trained here during World War II and returned after the war, to the more recent immigrants from Mexico. Deserted ghost towns scattered through the area demonstrate the fast pace of urban development, while older monuments preserve settlements abandoned long before the existence of railroads or hamburgers. Traces of lost Indian civilizations remain at Canyon de Chelly, Navajo National Monument, and Wupatki and Walnut Canyons. (The descendants of these tribes, almost one-seventh of the United States's Native Americans, now occupy reservations on ¼ of the state's land.) However spectacular, neither ancient nor modern man-made memorials can overshadow Arizona's natural masterpieces—the Grand Canyon, Monument Valley, and the gorgeous landscapes seen from the state's highways.

PRACTICAL INFORMATION

Capital: Phoenix.
Arizona Tourism: 1100 W. Washington, Phoenix 85007 (602-542-8687 or 800-842-8257). Open Mon.-Fri. 7am-5pm. **Arizona State Parks,** 1300 W. Washington St., Phoenix 85007 (602-542-4174). Open Mon.-Fri. 8am-5pm.
Time Zone: Mountain (2hr. behind Eastern). Arizona (with the exception of the reservations) does not observe Daylight Savings Time; in the summer, it is 1hr. behind the rest of the Mountain Time Zone. **Postal Abbreviation:** AZ
Sales Tax: 6%.

NORTHERN ARIZONA

■■■ GRAND CANYON

Even the weariest of travelers snap to attention upon first sight of the Grand Canyon (277mi. long, 10mi. wide, and over 1mi. deep). King of natural wonders and mecca of the American family vacation, the canyon descends past looming walls of limestone, sandstone, and shale as mothers cling to their children and fathers wear out their video cameras. The U.S. began designating its most daunting wild regions as national park sites for two reasons—first, to compensate with natural grandeur for the country's lack of cultural tradition, and second, to preserve unfarmable lands for recreation. Both breathtaking and hell on a plow, the Grand Canyon exemplifies the national park as it was originally conceived. Hike down into the gorge to get a real feeling for the immensity and beauty of this natural phenomenon.

The **Grand Canyon National Park** is divided into three areas: the **South Rim,** including Grand Canyon Village; the **North Rim;** and the canyon gorge itself. The slightly lower, slightly more accessible South Rim draws 10 times as many visitors as the higher, more heavily forested North Rim. The 13-mi. trail that traverses the canyon floor makes a two-day adventure for sturdy hikers, while the 214 mi. perimeter road is a good five-hour drive for those who would rather explore from above. Despite commercial exploitation, the Grand Canyon is still untamed; every year several careless hikers take what locals morbidly call "the 12-second tour." Please observe all safety precautions and the rules of common sense.

■ SOUTH RIM

In summer, everything on two legs or four wheels converges on this side of the Grand Canyon. If you plan to visit during the mobfest, make reservations for lodging, campsites, or mules well in advance—and prepare to battle the crowds. That said, it's a lot better than Disney World—a friendly Park Service staff, well-run facilities, and beautiful scenery help ease crowd anxiety. During winter there are fewer tourists; however, the weather is brisk and many hotels and facilities close.

PRACTICAL INFORMATION

Tourist Office: The **visitors center** (638-7888), 6mi. north of the south entrance station. Open daily 8am-6pm, off season 8am-5pm. Ask for the *Trip Planner.* Free and informative, *The Guide* is available here, in case you somehow missed it at the entrance. Write the **Superintendent,** Grand Canyon National Park, P.O. Box 129, Grand Canyon, AZ 86023, for info before you go. **Travelers with disabilities** should call ahead (638-2631); free wheelchairs, *The Grand Canyon National Park Accessibility Guide,* and free permits for automobile access to the West Rim Drive (in summer only) are available. Ranger-led programs with wheelchair access are listed in the *The Guide*.

Buses: Nava-Hopi Bus Lines, 800-892-8687. Leaves Flagstaff Amtrak station for Grand Canyon daily 8am, 10:15am, 3:45pm; returns from Bright Angel Lodge 10:10am, 5:15pm, 6:45pm. $12.50, 14 and under $6.50; $4 canyon entrance fee not included. Times vary by season, so call ahead.

Transportation Information Desk: In **Bright Angel Lodge** (638-2631). Reservations for mule rides, bus tours, Phantom Ranch, taxis, everything. Open daily 6am-7pm. A **free shuttle bus** system rides the West Rim Loop (daily 7:30am-sunset) and the Village Loop (daily 6:30am-10:30pm) every 15min. A $3 **hiker's shuttle** runs between Grand Canyon village and the South Kaibab Trailhead near Yalci Point; leaves Bright Angel daily 6:30am, 8:30am, 11:30am.

Auto Repairs: Grand Canyon Garage (638-2631), east of the visitors center on the park's main road near Maswik Lodge. Garage open daily 8am-5pm. 24-hr. emergency service.

Equipment Rental: Babbit's General Store (638-2262 or 638-2234), in Mather Center, Grand Canyon Village near Yavapai Lodge and the visitors center. Rents comfortable hiking boots, socks included ($8 first day, $5 each additional); sleeping bags ($7-9/$5); tents ($15-16/$9); and other camping gear. Hefty deposits required on all items. Open daily 8am-8pm.

Weather and Road Conditions: 638-7888. 24 hrs.

Medical Services: Grand Canyon Clinic (638-2551 or 638-2469), several mi. south on Center Rd. Open Mon.-Fri. 8am-5:30pm, Sat. 9am-noon.

Emergency: 911.

Post Office: (638-2512), next to Babbit's. Open Mon.-Fri. 9am-4:30pm, Sat. 11am-1pm. **ZIP code:** 86023. **Area code:** 520.

There are two entrances to the park: the main **south entrance** lies on U.S. 180N, the eastern **Desert View** entrance lies on I-40W. From Las Vegas, the fastest route to the Canyon is U.S. 93S to I-40E, and then Rte. 64N. From Flagstaff, I-40E to U.S. 89N is the most scenic; from there, Rte. 64N takes you to the Desert View entrance. Straight up U.S. 180N is more direct.

The Grand Canyon's **entrance fee** is $10 per car and $4 for travelers using other modes of transportation—even bus passengers must pay. The pass lasts for one week. If you're coming from Flagstaff, check noticeboards in hotels and hostels; travelers who have moved on sometimes leave their valid passes behind. **Pets** are allowed in the park, provided they are on a leash. They may not go below the rim; the **kennel** (638-2631, ext. 6039) on the South Rim will keep them while you hike.

Inside the park, posted maps and signs make orienting yourself easy. Lodges and services concentrate in **Grand Canyon Village,** at the end of Park Entrance Rd. The east half of the Village contains the visitors center and the general store, while most of the lodges and the **Bright Angel Trailhead** lie in the west section. The south **Kaibab Trailhead** is off East Rim Dr., to the east of the village.

ACCOMMODATIONS AND CAMPING

Compared to the six million years it took the Colorado River to carve the Grand Canyon, the 11 months it will take you to get a room on the South Rim will pass in the blink of an eye. It is almost impossible to sleep indoors anywhere near the South Rim without reservations or a wad of cash. If you arrive unprepared, check at the visitors center and the Bright Angel Transportation Desk for vacancies (see above).

Most accommodations on the South Rim are very expensive. The campsites listed here usually fill early in the day. Campground overflow generally winds up in the **Kaibab National Forest,** along the south border of the park, where you can pull off a dirt road and camp for free. No camping is allowed within ¼ mi. of U.S. 64. Sleeping in cars is *not* permitted within the park, but is allowed in the Kaibab Forest. For more information, contact the Tusayan Ranger District, Kaibab National Forest, P.O. Box 3088, Grand Canyon 86023 (638-2443). Any overnight hiking or camping within the park requires a free **Backcountry Use Permit** which is available at the **Backcountry Office** (638-7875), ¼ mi. south of the visitors center (open daily 8am-noon; calls answered Mon.-Fri. 1-5pm). Permit requests are accepted by mail or in person only, up to four months in advance. The earlier you make your request the better. Call the Backcountry Office for a list of the information you must include in a mail-in permit request. Once reserved, the permit must be picked up *no later than 9am* on the day you plan to camp, or it will be cancelled. While you're hiking, extra luggage may be checked at Bright Angel Lodge for 50¢ per day. Reservations for **Bright Angel Lodge, Maswik Lodge, Trailer Village,** and **Phantom Ranch** can be made through Grand Canyon National Park Lodges, P.O. Box 699, Grand Canyon 86023 (638-2401; fax 638-9247). All rooms should be reserved 11 months in advance for the summer. For same-day reservations (usually not available), call the Grand Canyon operator at 638-2631 and ask to be connected with the proper lodge.

Bright Angel Lodge (638-2401), Grand Canyon Village. Rustic cabins with plumbing but no heat. Very convenient to Bright Angel Trail and shuttle buses. Singles or doubles $37-53, depending on how much plumbing you want; "historic" cabins for 1 or 2 people $61; $7 per additional person in rooms and cabins.

Maswik Lodge (638-2401), Grand Canyon Village. Small, clean cabins (singles or doubles) with showers $69; $7 per additional person.

Phantom Ranch (638-2401), on the canyon floor a 4-hr. hike down the Kaibab Trail. Dorm beds $22; cabins for 1 or 2 people $56; $11 per additional person. As usual, reservations required 11 months in advance for April-Oct., but the Bright Angel Transportation Desk (see above) lists last-minute cancellations. Don't show up without reservations—they'll send you back up the trail, on foot.

Camper Village (638-2887), 7mi. south of the visitors center in Tusayan. RV and tent sites $15-22. First come, first served tent sites; reservations required for RVs.

Cottonwood Campground (638-7888, for permit info and a planner), 16.6mi. from the Bright Angel trailhead on the North Kaibab trail. 14 free sites. Reservations recommended. Open May-Oct. The Backcountry Office (see above) may be of help for Cottonwood and Indian Garden.

Indian Garden (638-7888, for permit info and a planner), 4.6mi. from the South Rim Bright Angel trailhead and 3100ft. below the rim. 15 free sites, toilets, and water. Reservations recommended.

Mather Campground (MISTIX 800-365-2267), Grand Canyon Village, 1mi. south of the visitors center. 320 shady, relatively isolated sites with no hookups. 7-day max. stay. $10, with Golden Age Passport $5. For March-Nov. reserve through MISTIX up to 8 weeks in advance; Dec.-Feb. sites go on a first come, first served basis. Check at the office, even if the sign says the campground is full.

Trailer Village (638-2401), next to Mather Campground. Clearly designed with the RV in mind. Showers and laundry nearby. 7-day max. stay. Office open daily 8am-noon and 1-5pm. 84 sites with hookup $17 for 2 people; $1.50 per additional person. Reservations required 6-9 months in advance.

Desert View Campsite (638-7888, for permit info and a planner), 26mi. east of Grand Canyon Village. 50 sites with phone and restroom access, but no hookups, $8. No reservations; arrive early. Open mid-May to Oct.

Ten-X Campground (638-2443), in the Kaibab National Forest 10mi. south of Grand Canyon Village off Rte. 64. Shady sites surrounded by pine trees. Toilets, water, no hookups. Sites $10; with Golden Age Passport $5. Group sites for up to 100 people available with reservations. First come, first served. Open May-Sept.

FOOD

Fast food hasn't sunk its greasy talons into the rim of the Canyon, but you *can* find meals for fast-food prices. **Babbit's General Store** (638-2262), near the visitors center, has a deli counter (sandwiches $2-3.50) and a reasonably-priced supermarket. Stock up on trail mix, water, and gear. (Open daily 8am-8pm; deli open 8am-7pm.) **The Maswik Cafeteria,** in Maswik Lodge, puts out a variety of inexpensive grill-made options (hot entrees $5-7, sandwiches $2-3.50) served in a wood-paneled cafeteria atmosphere (open daily 6am-10pm). **Bright Angel Dining Room** (638-2631), in Bright Angel Lodge, serves hot sandwiches ($5.50-7.50; open daily 6:30am-10pm). The soda fountain at Bright Angel Lodge chills 16 flavors of ice cream (1 scoop $1.60) for hot hikers emerging from the trails (open daily 11am-9pm).

SIGHTS AND ACTIVITIES

From your first glimpse of the canyon, you will feel a compelling desire to see it from the inside, an enterprise which is much harder than it looks. Even the young-at-heart should remember that an easy downhill hike can become a nightmarish 100° incline on the return journey. Also keep in mind that the lower you go, the hotter it gets. Heat exhaustion, the second greatest threat after slipping, is marked by a monstrous headache and termination of sweating (*Let's Go* offers basic advice about heatstroke on p. 11.) You *must* take two quarts of water per person; it's absolutely necessary. A list of hiking safety tips can be found in *The Guide*. Don't overestimate your limits; parents should think twice about bringing children more than a mile down any trail—kids remember well and may exact revenge when they get bigger.

The two most accessible trails into the Canyon are the **Bright Angel Trail,** originating at the Bright Angel Lodge, and **South Kaibab Trail,** from Yaki Point. Bright Angel is outfitted for the average tourist, with rest houses strategically stationed 1½ mi. and 3 mi. from the rim. **Indian Gardens,** 4½ mi. down, offers the tired hiker restrooms, picnic tables, and blessed shade; all three rest stops usually have water in the summer. Kaibab is trickier, steeper, and lacking in shade or water, but it rewards the intrepid with a better view of the canyon. No matter which trail you take, hiking back up is much, *much* more arduous and takes *twice as long* as the hike down.

If you've made arrangements to spend the night on the canyon floor, the best route is the **South Kaibab Trail** (4-5hr., depending on conditions) and back up the Bright Angel (7-8hr.) the following day. Hikes down Bright Angel Trail to Indian Gardens and **Plateau Point,** 6 mi. out, where you can look down 1360 ft. to the river, make excellent daytrips (8-12hr.), but you must start early (around 7am).

If you're not up to descending into the canyon, follow the **Rim Trail** east to Grandeur Point and the **Yavapai Geological Museum,** or west to **Hermit's Rest,** using the shuttles. The Eastern Rim Trail swarms with sunset-watchers at dusk, and the observation deck at the Yavapai Museum, at the end of the trail, has a sweeping view of the canyon during the day. The Western Rim Trail leads to several vistas;

Hopi Point is a favorite for sunsets, and the **Abyss** overlooks an almost-vertical to the **Tonto Plateau** 3000 ft. below. To watch a sunset (or sunrise), check *The Guide* for the time. Show up at your chosen spot 45 min. beforehand and watch earth-tones and pastels melt into darkness.

The park service rangers present a variety of free, informative talks and hikes including a free talk at 8:30pm (in winter 7:30pm) in **Mather Amphitheater,** behind the visitors center. Listings are available at the visitors center.

■ NORTH RIM

If you are coming from Utah or Nevada or you simply want to avoid the crowds at the South Rim, the park's North Rim is a bit wilder, a bit cooler, and much more serene—all with a view as groovy as that from the South Rim. Unfortunately, because the North Rim is less frequented, it's hard to reach by public transportation.

PRACTICAL INFORMATION

Tourist Office: National Park Service Information Desk (638-2611; open daily 8am-5pm), in the lobby of Grand Canyon Lodge. Information on North Rim view-points, facilities, and some trails with **wheelchair access.**

Public Transportation: Transcanyon, P.O. Box 348, Grand Canyon 86023 (638-2820). Buses to South Rim depart 7am, arrive 11:30am; return 1:30pm, arrive 6:30pm. $60, $100 round-trip. Call for reservations. Open late May-Oct.

Medical Services: North Rim Clinic (638-2611 ext. 222), located in cabin #7 at Grand Canyon Lodge. Staffed by a nurse practitioner. Walk-in or appointment service. Open Tues. 9am-noon and 2-5pm, Fri. 9am-noon and 2-6pm, Sat.-Mon. 9am-noon and 3-6pm.

Emergency: 911.

Post Office: (638-2611), in Grand Canyon Lodge with everything else. Open Mon.-Fri. 8-11am and 11:30am-4pm, Sat. 8am-2pm. **ZIP code:** 86023. **Area code:** 520.

The **entrance fee** for the North Rim admits you to both rims for seven days ($10 per car, $4 per person on foot, bike, bus, or holy pilgrimage). From South Rim, take Rte. 64 east to U.S. 89N, which runs into Alt. 89; from Alt. 89, follow Rte. 67 south to the edge. Altogether, the drive is over 200 mi. long and stunningly beautiful. Snow closes Rte. 67 from the end of October to late May. Then, only a snowmobile can get you to the North Rim. Park visitor facilities close in winter as well.

ACCOMMODATIONS, CAMPING, AND FOOD

Since camping within the confines of the Grand Canyon National Park is limited to designated campgrounds, only a lucky minority of North Rim visitors get to spend the night "right there." Advance reservations can be made through **MISTIX** (800-365-2267 or 619-452-5956). Otherwise, mark your territory by 10am. If you can't get in-park lodgings, visit the **Kaibab National Forest,** which runs from north of Jacob Lake to the park entrance. You can camp for free, as long as you're ½ mi. from official campgrounds and the road. The nearest low-priced motels are an hour's drive to the north, in **Kanab, UT** and **Fredonia.** Hotel rooms in Kanab hover around $40; the **Canyonlands International Youth Hostel (AAIH/Rucksackers)** puts you in a dorm for $9 (see Zion National Park Camping and Accommodations p. 631).

Grand Canyon Lodge (638-2611), on the edge of the rim. Front desk open 24 hrs. Pioneer cabins shelter 4 people for $80, 5 for $85. Singles or doubles in frontier cabins $58. Western cabins and motel rooms cost more. Reservations 801-586-7686; calling hrs. daily 8am-7pm, late Oct. to mid-May Mon.-Fri. 8am-5pm.

Jacob Lake Inn (643-7232), 30mi. north of the North Rim entrance at Jacob Lake. Office open 6:30am-9pm. Cabins for 2 $65-70, for 3 $76-78, for 4 $81-84, for 5 $87, for 6 $92. Pricier motel units available. Reasonably priced dining room.

Jacob Lake RV Park (743-7804), ¼mi. south of the Inn. 50 tent sites $10, 60 sites with hookups for 2 people $20-22; $2 each additional person. Open May-Oct. 15.

North Rim Campground (MISTIX 800-365-2267), on Rte. 67 near the rim, the only campground in the park. You can't see into the canyon from the pine-covered site, but you know it's there. Near food store; has laundry facilities, recreation room, and showers. 7-day max. stay. 82 sites $10. Closes Oct. 21.

DeMotte Park Campground, 5mi. north of the park entrance in the Kaibab National Forest. 25 woodsy sites $10; first come, first served. For more information call Kaibab National Forest (643-7298).

Both feeding options on the North Rim are placed strategically at the **Grand Canyon Lodge** (638-2611). The restaurant serves dinners for $12 and up (reservations only) and breakfast for $4. A sandwich at the "buffeteria" costs $2.50. (Dining room open 6:30-10am, 11:30am-2:30pm, 5-9:30pm.) North Rim-ers are better off eating in Kanab or stopping at the **Jacob Lake Inn** for snacks and great milkshakes (lunch dishes about $5; open daily 6:30am-9pm).

SIGHTS AND ACTIVITIES

A ½-mi. paved trail takes you from the Grand Canyon Lodge to **Bright Angel Point,** which commands a seraphic view of the Canyon. **Point Imperial,** an 11-mi. drive from the lodge, overlooks **Marble Canyon** and the **Painted Desert.** The North Rim's *The Guide* lists trails in full. Only one trail, the **North Kaibab Trail,** leads into the Canyon from the North Rim; a shuttle runs to the trailhead from Grand Canyon Lodge (daily 6am-8pm; $5). Overnight hikers must get permits from the **Backcountry Office** in the Ranger Station (open daily 7:30am-noon), or write Backcountry Office, PO Box 129, Grand Canyon 86023; it may take a few days. Due to storm damage, cross-canyon hikes will not be possible until sometime in 1996.

The North Rim offers nature walks and evening programs at the North Rim Campground and at Grand Canyon Lodge. Check the info desk or campground bulletin boards for schedules. Half-day **mule trips** ($35) descend into the canyon from the lodge (638-2292; open daily 7am-8pm). If you'd rather tour the Canyon wet, pick up a *Grand Canyon River Trip Operators* brochure and select from among the 20 companies which offer trips.

On warm evenings, the Grand Canyon Lodge fills with an eclectic group of international travelers, U.S. families, and rugged adventurers. Thirsty hikers will find a bar and a jukebox at **The Tea Room,** within the lodge complex (open 11am-10pm). Others look to the warm air rising from the canyon, a full moon, and the occasional shooting stars for their intoxication at day's end.

■■■ NAVAJO AND HOPI RESERVATIONS

As late as the 1830s, federal policymakers planned to create a permanent Indian country in the west; by mid-century those plans had been washed away by the tide of American expansion. Indian reservations evolved out of the U.S. government's subsequent ad hoc attempts to prevent fighting between Native Americans and whites while facilitating white settlement. Originally conceived as a means to detribalize Native Americans and prepare them for assimilation into Anglo-American society, the reservation system imposed a kind of wardship on the Indians for over a century, until a series of Supreme Court decisions, beginning in the 1960s, reasserted the tribes' legal standing as semi-sovereign nations.

The largest reservation in America, the **Navajo Nation** covers 17 million acres of northeast Arizona, south Utah, and northwest New Mexico. Within its boundaries the smaller **Hopi Reservation** is home to 6,000 Hopi ("Peaceable People"). Ruins mark the dwellings of the Anasazi, Indians who inhabited the area until the 13th century. Over 140,000 Navajo, or Dineh ("the People"), live here, one-tenth of the Native Americans in the entire U.S. The Navajo Nation has its own police force and its own laws. *Possession and consumption of alcohol are prohibited* on the reservation. Do not remove anything from the reservation and always respect the privacy of the people who live here. Photography requires a permission fee, and tourist photography is not permitted among the Hopi. Lively reservation politics are written up in the local *Navajo-Hopi Observer* and *Navajo Times* and in regional sections of Denver, Albuquerque, and Phoenix newspapers. For a taste of the Dineh's language and some Native American ritual songs, tune your radio to 660AM, from Window Rock, "The Voice of the Navajo." Remember to advance your watch one hour during the summer; the Navajo Nation runs on **Mountain Daylight Time,** while the rest of Arizona remains on Mountain Standard Time.

Monument Valley, Canyon de Chelly, Navajo National Monument, Rainbow Bridge, and the roads which access these sights all lie on Navajo land. Driving off-road without a guide is considered trespassing. Fill up your gas tank before setting out to explore the reservation; stations are few and far between. *Discover Navajoland,* available from the **Navajoland Tourism Department,** P.O. Box 663, Window Rock 86515 (520-871-6436; open Mon.-Fri. 8am-5pm), has a full list of accommodations, jeep and horseback tours, and tourist info. *The Visitors' Guide to the Navajo Nation* ($3) includes a detailed map.

The "border towns" of **Gallup, NM,** and **Flagstaff** (p. 645) make good gateways to the reservations, with car rental agencies and frequent **Greyhound** service on I-40.

Window Rock, as well as being the seat of tribal government, features the geological formation for which the town is named. The limited lodging in town is expensive, but Navajo sights make Window Rock a good day trip. The **Navajo Tribal Museum** (520-871-6673), on Rte. 264, has small cultural exhibits (open Mon.-Fri. 8am-5pm; free). The **Navajo Council Tribal Chambers** (520-871-6417) offers free tours of the governing body's meeting place (open Mon.-Fri. 8am-noon and 1-5pm). The **Navajo Nation Zoo and Botanical Park** (520-871-6573), on Hwy. 264, ½ mi. east of Rte. 12, features wildlife native to the reservation (open daily 8am-5pm; free). The oldest trading post in the U.S. and a national historic site, the **Hubbell Trading Post** (520-733-3475), 30 mi. west of Window Rock on Rte. 264, has functioned as a store since 1876 and now houses a museum (open daily 8am-6pm).

For info on the **Hopi,** contact the Hopi Tribe at the **Hopi Cultural Preservation Office,** P.O. Box 123, Kykotsmovi 86039 (520-734-2244), or the **Hopi Cultural Center,** P.O. Box 67, Second Mesa 86043 (734-2401), on Rte. 264 in the community of **Second Mesa.** The center consists of a museum of pottery, photography, and handicrafts, along with four gift shops, a motel, and a restaurant (see below).

Inquire at the cultural center or at the Flagstaff Chamber of Commerce for the dates and sites of the **Hopi village dances.** Announced only a few days in advance, these religious ceremonies last from sunrise to sundown. While some have been closed to visitors, tourists may come to watch certain ceremonies. The dances are highly formal occasions; do not wear shorts, tank tops, or other casual wear. Photographs, recordings, and sketches are strictly forbidden.

Area hotels charge quite a lot; plan to camp at the national monuments or the Navajo campgrounds. The **hotel** at the Hopi Cultural Center (734-2401) is expensive but decent (singles $55, doubles $60; reservations required 2 weeks to a month in advance). The **restaurant** is surprisingly reasonable (open daily 7am-9pm). Alternatively, you can make your visit a hard-driving day trip from Flagstaff or Gallup.

■ CANYON DE CHELLY

When compared with the Grand Canyon, Canyon De Chelly (pronounced "Canyon de Shay") more than makes up in beauty what it lacks in size. Sandstone cliffs of 30 to 1000 ft. surround the sandy, fertile, and aptly-named **Beautiful Valley,** left by the Chelly River. Ruins in these eroded walls remind visitors of the advanced Anasazi civilization of the 12th century.

Canyon de Chelly National Monument lies on land owned by the Navajo Nation and administered by the National Park Service. (See Navajo and Hopi Reservations directly above for a brief explanation of reservation laws which affect tourists.) The park service offers **tours** three times per day during the summer (3-4hr., $10), or you can hire a private guide (min. 3hr., $10 per hr.). Reservations for both can be made through the visitors center, but are not required. To **drive** into the canyon with a guide, you must provide your own four-wheel-drive vehicle and acquire a free permit from the visitors center. Horseback tours can be arranged at **Justin's Horse Rental** (674-5678), on South Rim Dr., at the mouth of the canyon (open daily 9am-sundown; horses $8 per hr.; mandatory guide $8 per hr.).

The 1-mi. trail to **White House Ruin,** 7 mi. from the visitors center off South Canyon Rd., is *the only trail in the park which you can walk without a guide.* But what a trail—it winds down a 400-ft. face, past a Navajo farm and traditional *hogan* (a traditional log and clay shelter), through an orchard, and across a stream. In spring you can hike in the canyon heat with the cool stream swirling about your ankles. You can also take one of the paved **Rim Drives** (North Rim 44mi., South Rim 36mi.), which skirt the edge of the 300- to 700-ft. cliffs; the South Rim is more dramatic. **Spider Rock Overlook,** 16 mi. from the visitors center, is a narrow sandstone monolith towering hundreds of feet above the canyon floor. Native American lore says that the whitish rock at the top of Spider Rock contains bleached bones of victims of the *kachina* spirit, Spider Woman. Get booklets on the White House Ruin and Rim Drives (50¢) at the visitors center.

During the 1800s, Canyon de Chelly saw repeated conflict between Indians and whites. In 1805, dozens of Native American women and children were shot by the Spanish, in what is now called **Massacre Cave.** Kit Carson starved the Navajo out of the Canyon in the 1860s, but the land was eventually returned. Navajo farmers once again inhabit the canyon, cultivating the lush soil and living in Navajo *hogans.*

The most common route to the park is from Chambers, 75 mi. south, at the intersection of I-40 and U.S. 191; you can also come from the north via U.S. 191. Entrance to the monument is free. The **visitors center** (674-5500) sits 2 mi. east of **Chinle** on Navajo Rte. 64 (open daily 8am-6pm; Oct.-April 8am-5pm). One of the larger towns on the reservation, Chinle, located adjacent to U.S. 191, has restaurants and gas stations but no banks or ATMs. There is no public transportation to the park. For **emergencies,** contact the park ranger at 674-5523, the Navajo Police at 674-5291, or an ambulance at 674-5464.

Camp for free in the park's **Cottonwood Campground,** ½ mi. from the visitors center. This giant campground, in a pretty cottonwood grove, can get noisy with the din of the stray dogs who wander about the site at night. Sites are first come, first served, and facilities include restrooms, picnic tables, water (except in winter), and a dump station. (Max. RV length 35 ft.; 5-day max. stay. Group sites for 15-25 can be reserved 90 days in advance; 3-day max.; call 674-5500.) There are no budget accommodations anywhere in Navajo territory. **Farmington, NM,** and **Cortez, CO,** are the closest major cities with cheap lodging.

■ MONUMENT VALLEY AND NAVAJO MONUMENT

Monument Valley Navajo Tribal Park You may have seen the red rock towers of Monument Valley in one of the numerous westerns filmed here. Some years before John Wayne hung out in the valley, Anasazi Indians managed to sustain small communities here, despite the hot, arid climate. The park's sights, however, are natural rather than cultural; the breathtaking rust-hued sandstone formations can be seen from the park's looping 17-mi. **Valley Drive.** This dirt road winds in and out of the most dramatic monuments, including the famous pair of **Mittens** and the slender **Totem Pole.** The gaping ditches, large rocks, and mudholes on this road will do horrible things to your car—drive at your own risk, and hold your breath. Much of the valley can be reached only in a sturdy four-wheel-drive vehicle or by a long hike. In winter, snow laces the rocky towers, and most tourists flee. Inquire about snow and road conditions at the Flagstaff Chamber of Commerce (800-842-7293).

The park entrance is 24 mi. north on U.S. 163 from the town of **Kayenta,** at the intersection with U.S. 160. The **visitors center** (801-727-3287), at the end of Rte.

564 across the Utah border 9 mi. west of U.S. 160, has a craft shop as well as displays of pottery and artifacts. (Park and visitors center open daily 7am-8pm; Oct.-April 8am-5pm. Entrance $2.50, seniors $1, under 7 free.)

Mitten View Campground, ¼ mi. southwest of the visitors center, offers 99 sites ($10), showers, and restrooms. First come, first served; groups of 11 or more may make reservations. The Navajo National Monument has more camping (see below). Alternate lodging options await in the small town of **Mexican Hat, UT** (see p. 634).

Navajo National Monument Home to some of the best preserved ruins in the southwest, the park is located off U.S. 160, 20 mi. south of Kayenta. From the park entrance, Rte. 564 takes you 9 mi. to the Navajo National Monument. The site contains three Anasazi cliff-dwellings, though one, **Inscription House,** has been closed to visitors. The other two, Keet Seel and Betatakin, admit limited numbers of visitors. The stunning **Keet Seel** (open late May-early Sept.) requires a challenging 17-mi. hike round-trip or a $55 horseback ride from the visitors center. A free campground near Keet Seel allows hikers to stay overnight, but it has no showers or drinking water. Reservations for permits to visit Keet Seel must be made in advance through the **visitors center** (672-2366), up to two months prior to the date of visit; total reservations are limited to 20 people per day (open daily 8am-6pm, off season 8am-4:30pm). **Betatakin,** a 135-room complex, is limited to 25 people per ranger-led tour. (In summer 2 per day, May 1 per day. A challenging 5-mi. hike, 5-6 hr. Sign-up is first come, first served on the day of the tour.) If you're not up for the hike to the ruins, the paved, 1-mi. round-trip **Sandal Trail** lets you gaze down on Betatakin from a canyon-top overlook. The **Aspen Forest Trail,** another 1-mi. hike, overlooks canyons and aspens but no ruins. Write Navajo National Monument, HC 71 Box 3, Tonalea 86044 for more information.

The free campground, next to the visitors center, has 30 sites; an additional overflow campground nearby has no running water. Groups of 11 to 30 people may reserve spaces through the visitors center. Smaller groups or individuals must get sites on a first come, first served basis at either campground.

■■■ LAKE POWELL, PAGE, AND RAINBOW BRIDGE

In 1953, President Dwight Eisenhower said "dammit," and they did. Ten years and ten million tons of concrete later, Glen Canyon Dam, the second largest dam in the country, was completed. With no particular place to go, the Colorado River flooded a canyon in northern Arizona and southern Utah to form the 186-mi.-long Lake Powell. Named after John Wesley Powell, a one-armed Civil War veteran who led an exploratory expedition down the Colorado, the lake offers 1960 mi. of national recreation shoreline. The town of Page sits near the southwest tip of Lake Powell, at the U.S. 89/Rte. 98 junction, and serves as a gateway to Lake Powell. Now thriving with over 3 million visitors a year, Page has come a long way since its founding in 1957 as a construction camp for the federal government. To turn the Page from Utah, take U.S. 89 south and east, past Big Water and across into Arizona. From Flagstaff, take U.S. 89 north.

Practical Information Visitors can descend into the cool inner workings of Glen Canyon Dam alone, or let the **Carl Hayden Visitors Center** (645-8200), on U.S. 89N adjacent to the dam 1 mi. north of Page, take the lead with a guided tour. (Open daily 7am-7pm, off season 8am-5pm; free guided dam tours every hr. on the ½hr. 8:30am-5:30pm; off season 8:30am-3:30pm.) In **Page,** seek the **Chamber of Commerce,** 106 S. Lake Powell Blvd. (645-2741; open Mon.-Fri. 8am-9pm, Sat.-Sun. 8am-7pm; Dec.-Feb. Mon.-Fri. 9am-5pm). **Skywest** (645-4200) connects the Page airport to Phoenix, Las Vegas, St. George, and Salt Lake City, and the **Wahweep Marina Shuttle** (645-2333) runs from the airport to town (every hr. on the hr.; free).

Budget Rent-A-Car (645-3977), at the airport, rents cars for $39 per day (100 free mi., 30¢ each additional mi.) or $191 per week (700 free mi., 30¢ each additional mi.). Those under 25 pay a $5 surcharge per day, and must have a major credit card. **Emergency** in Page is 911. Lake Powell and Page's **area code:** 520.

Accommodations, Camping, and Food **Wahweep Campground,** 100 Lake Shore Dr. (645-2433 or 800-528-6154), adjacent to the exorbitant **Wahweep Lodge,** has 200 sites on a first come, first served basis ($8.50; group sites $2 per person, 9-person min.). The **Wahweep RV Park** next door takes care of the motorized set (sites with full hook-up $25, A/C or heater $2.30 extra, $2.50 per extra person). In Page, the **Lake Powell International Hostel (AAIH/Rucksackers),** 141 8th Ave. (645-3898), has free pickup and delivery to Lake Powell, free tea, coffee, linens, and blankets, a kitchen, a BBQ grill, TV, a volleyball court, an outdoor eating area, and bathrooms in every unit. The hostel also offers a $15 shuttle to Flagstaff. Ask Jeff, the host, to arrange tours for you. (No curfew. $12-15 a bunk, doubles $30, triples $40.) Under the same management, **Pension at Lake Powell,** next door to the hostel, has more upscale rooms with 4-6 person suites of 3 rooms with a bathroom, a living room with cable TV, and a kitchen for $50-70. If the hostel is full try **Uncle Bill's** (645-1224), 1 block farther down on 8th Ave., which boasts attractive rooms with kitchens adjoining, and a pretty patio out back (singles $33, doubles $40, 4-person apartment $64) or hit **Bashful Bob's Motel,** 750 S. Navajo Dr. (645-3919), where most rooms have kitchens and cable TV (doubles $43, triples $49).

For "calzones as big as your head ($6)," head to **Strombolli's Restaurant and Pizzeria,** 711 N. Navajo Dr. (645-2605; open Sun.-Thurs. 11am-10pm, Fri.-Sat. 11am-midnight). Gulp a margarita ($3) at **Salsa Brava** (645-9058) on Elm St. across from Page Plaza. (Open Mon.-Wed. 11am-10pm, Thurs.-Sun. 11am-11pm.)

Sights and Activities Lake Powell's man-made shores are rocky rather than sandy, with skimpy beaches that vanish when the water rises. However, recreation opportunities abound at **Wahweep Marina,** where you can swim, rent a boat (6-person skiff $63 per day), or take a boat tour ($9-72). Many companies lead **Jeep tours** to the side canyons including the kaleidoscopic **Antelope Canyon;** check pamphlets at the Page Chamber of Commerce (see above) for more information. Sacred to the Navajo, **Rainbow Bridge National Monument** takes its name from a Navajo word, Nonnezoshi, meaning "rainbow turned to stone." Rainbow Bridge, the world's largest natural stone bridge, can be reached by a hike or a boat-trip from Lake Powell. **ARA Leisure Services** (800-528-6154) conducts boat tours (full-day $65, under 12 $35; ½-day $52/$28). Call for reservations well in advance.

■■■ SUNSET CRATER, WUPATKI, AND WALNUT CANYON

Sunset Crater Volcano National Monument The volcanic crater encompassed by Sunset Crater Volcano National Monument (602-556-7042), 12 mi. north of Flagstaff on U.S. 89, appeared in 1065AD when molten rock spurted from a crack in the ground, then fell back to earth in solid form. Over the next 200 years, a 1,000-ft.-high cinder cone took shape as a result of periodic eruptions. The self-guided **Lava Flow Nature Trail** wanders 1 mi. through the surreal landscape surrounding the cone, 1½ mi. east of the visitors center, where gnarled trees lie uprooted amid the rocky black terrain. Lava tube tours have been permanently discontinued due to falling lava. The monument's **visitors center** is open daily 8am-5pm. (Entrance $4 per car, or $2 per person; includes Wupatki National Monument.) The **Bonito Campground** in the Coconino National Forest at the entrance to Sunset Crater provides the nearest camping (see p. 647).

Wupatki National Monument Eighteen mi. northeast of Sunset Crater, Wupatki National Monument possesses some of the Southwest's most scenic pueblo ruins, situated along a stunning road with views of the Painted Desert and the Grand Canyon. The Sinagua moved here in the late 11th century, after the Sunset Crater eruption forced them to evacuate the land to the south. In less than 200 years, however, droughts, disease, and over-farming led the Sinagua to abandon these stone houses perched on the sides of *arroyos* in view of the San Francisco Peaks. Five deserted pueblos front the 14-mi. road from U.S. 89 to the visitors center; another road to the ruins begins on U.S. 89 about 30 mi. north of Flagstaff. The largest and most accessible, **Wupatki Ruin,** located on a ½-mi. round-trip loop trail from the visitors center, rises three stories high; below the ruins, look for one of Arizona's two stone ballcourts. Get info and trail guide brochures (50¢, or borrow one and bring it back) at the **Wupatki Ruin Visitors Center** (556-7040; open daily 8am-5pm); **backcountry hiking permits** are also available. The monument stays open daily from dawn to dusk; admission to Sunset Crater includes Wupatki. The **Bonito Campground** (see p. 647) offers the nearest sites to Wupatki.

Walnut Canyon National Monument Constructed within a 400-ft.-deep canyon, 7 mi. east of Flagstaff off I-40, the ruins of more than 300 rooms in 13th-century Sinagua dwellings make up the Walnut Canyon National Monument (602-526-3367; open daily 7am-6pm; Labor Day to Memorial Day 8am-5pm). From a glassed-in observation deck in the **visitors center** you can survey the whole canyon and the stunning variety of plants which sprout from its striated walls. The steep, self-guided **Island Trail** snakes down from the visitors center past 25 cliff dwellings; markers along the 1-mi. trail describe aspects of Sinagua life and identify the plants the natives used for food, dyes, medicine, and hunting. Every Saturday morning, rangers lead 2-mi. hikes from the visitors center into Walnut Canyon, to the original Ranger Cabin and many remote cliff dwellings. Hiking boots and long pants are required for these challenging 2½-hour hikes. (Call ahead, hours change frequently. Free with entrance.) The monument charges an entrance fee of $4 per car or $2 per person.

■■■ PETRIFIED FOREST AND METEOR CRATER

Titanic and austere, **The Petrified Forest National Park** covers over 60,000 acres. This vast desert, dotted with tree logs which turned into rock some 225 million years ago, resembles no other forest. The park's showpiece is a scenic chunk of the **Painted Desert,** so named for the stunning colors which stripe its rock formations.

The park road winds past the logs in their native habitat and by **Newspaper Rock,** covered with Native American petroglyphs. At **Blue Mesa,** a hiking trail ventures into the desert. **Long Logs Crystal** and **Jasper Forest** contain some of the most exquisite pieces of petrified wood in the park. Picking up fragments of the wood is illegal and traditionally unlucky; if the demons don't getcha then the district attorney will. Those who *must* have a piece should buy one at a store along I-40.

You can enter the park either from the north or the south (open daily 7am-7pm; $5 per vehicle, $3 per pedestrian); a 27-mi. road connects the two entrances. To enter the North Forest section of the park, exit I-40 at Holbrook and take U.S. 180 west to the **Rainbow Forest Museum** (524-6228). The museum lets you look at petrified logs up close and serves as a visitors center (open daily 8am-7pm, off season 8am-5pm; free). There are no established campgrounds in the park, but **free backcountry camping** is allowed in several areas with a permit from the museum.

To enter the Painted Desert section of the park, take I-40 to exit 311 (107mi. east of Flagstaff). The **Painted Desert Visitors Center** (524-6228, ext. 236) is less than 5 mi. from the exit (open in summer daily 7am-7pm; off season 8am-5pm).

There is no public transportation to either part of the park. **Nava-Hopi Bus Lines, Gray Line Tours,** and **Blue Goose Backpacker Tours** offer services from Flagstaff (see Flagstaff Practical Information below). Lodging is available in **Holbrook** (27mi. from the museum), but prices are high. Budgeteers should return to Flagstaff.

Meteor Crater (774-8350), 35 mi. east of Flagstaff off I-40 on the Meteor Crater Rd. exit, is a great stop on the way from Flagstaff to the Petrified Forest. Originally thought to be a volcanic cone, the crater is now believed to be the impact site of a giant nickel-iron meteorite that fell to earth 50,000 years ago. Visitors cannot hike down into the crater, but must peer over the guard-railed edge. (Open daily 6am-6pm; in winter 8am-5pm. $7, seniors $6, ages 6-17 $2.) The site was used to train Apollo astronauts in the 1960s, and a museum in the building near the admission booth patriotically celebrates the U.S. space program, as well as the sciences of astronomy and mineralogy (free with entrance to the crater).

■■■ FLAGSTAFF

After a three-year stay among the Navajos and Apaches of south Arizona during the 1860s, Samuel Cozzens returned to New England and wrote *The Marvellous Country,* in which he promoted the *north* part of the territory as fertile, temperate, and ripe for settlement (despite never having been there). Colonists from Boston subsequently arrived in the San Francisco Mountains region and, having failed to find the rich farmland and gold veins they'd been led to expect, promptly departed. Before leaving, one group erected, as a marker for westward travelers, the stripped-pine flagpole from which Flagstaff takes its name. During the following decade, Flagstaff, designated a stop on the transcontinental railroad, became a permanent settlement; railroad tracks still cut through downtown. Flagstaff now provides a home for Northern Arizona University (NAU) students, retired cowboys, and earthy Volvo-owners and a base for Grand Canyon tourists (see Grand Canyon coverage p. 634).

PRACTICAL INFORMATION

Tourist Office: Flagstaff Visitors Center, 1 E. Rte. 66 (774-9541 or 800-842-7293), inside the Amtrak station. Courtesy phone. Open Mon.-Sat. 8am-7pm, Sun. 8am-5pm; Oct. 16-March 15 Mon.-Sat. 8am-6pm, Sun. 8am-5pm.

Tours: Blue Goose Backpacker Tours and Travels (774-6731 in AZ or 800-332-1944). Run from the Grand Canyon International Hostel, 19 S. San Francisco St. (see Accommodations below). Full-day round-trip guided tours to: the Grand Canyon ($36); Sedona and Oak Creek ($15); Page and Lake Powell ($25). Tours in summer only, starting in May or June; call for more information.

Trains: Amtrak, 1 E. Rte. 66 (774-8679 or 800-872-7245). To: Los Angeles (1 per day, 11hr., $87); Albuquerque (1 per day, 6hr., $82). Daily connecting shuttle bus to the Grand Canyon ($12). Open daily 6:15am-10:30pm; ticket office closed 6:30-7:30pm.

Buses: Greyhound, 399 S. Malpais Ln. (774-4573 or 800-231-2222), across from NAU campus, 5 blocks southwest of the train station on U.S. 89A. To: Phoenix (4 per day, 3hr., $20); Albuquerque (3 per day, 7hr., $47); Los Angeles (4 per day, 10-12hr., $59); Las Vegas (3 per day via Kingman, 6+hr., $43). Terminal open 24 hrs. **Gray Line/Nava-Hopi,** 144 W. Rte. 66, (774-5003 or 800-892-8687). Buses depart and arrive at both the Nava-Hopi terminal and Amtrak station. Use caution in this area at night. Shuttle buses to: the Grand Canyon (2 per day, $24 round-trip); Phoenix (3 per day, $43 round-trip).

Public Transportation: Pine Country Transit, 970 W. Rte. 66 (779-6624). Routes cover most of town. Buses once per hr.; route map and schedule available at visitors center. Fare 75¢. **Flagstaff Trolley** (774-5003) runs a hotel pickup route and a museum-shopping-history route (daily 8:45am-5pm). 1-day pass $4.

Taxis: Flagstaff Taxicab, 526-4123. 24 hrs. Airport to downtown about $12.

Car Rental: Budget Rent-A-Car, 100 N. Humphreys St. (774-2763), within walking distance of the hostels. Guarantees the lowest rates. Economy cars from $33 per day with 100 free mi., 25¢ per additional mi.; $145 per week with 1050 free mi. Insurance $12 per day. Must be 21 with major credit card or at least $200 for cash deposit. Under 25 surcharge $5 per day. Open daily 7am-9pm. Ask Tom for *Let's Go* discount rates.

Bike Rental: Cosmic Cycles, 113 S. San Francisco St. (779-1092), downtown. Mountain bikes $14 per ½day, $20 per day, $35 per weekend, $75 per week; with front-end suspension $25 per day. Open Mon.-Sat. 9am-6pm, Sun. 11am-4pm.

Camping Equipment Rental: Peace Surplus, 14 W. Rte. 66 (779-4521), 1 block from Grand Canyon Hostel. Daily rental of dome tents ($5-8; $100 deposit), packs ($5; $50 deposit), stoves ($3; $3 deposit), plus a good stock of cheap outdoor gear. 3-day min. rental on all equipment. Credit card or cash deposit required. Open Mon.-Fri. 8am-9pm, Sat. 8am-8pm, Sun. 8am-6pm.

Emergency: 911.

Post Office: 2400 N. Postal Blvd. (527-2440), for general delivery. Open Mon.-Fri. 9am-5pm, Sat. 9am-noon. **ZIP code:** 86004. **Area code:** 520.

Flagstaff sits 138 mi. north of Phoenix (take I-17), 26 mi. north of Sedona (take U.S. 89A), and 81 mi. south of the Grand Canyon's south rim (take U.S. 180). Downtown surrounds the intersection of **Beaver St.** and **Rte. 66** (formerly Santa Fe Ave.); both bus stations, the four youth hostels, the chamber of commerce, and a number of inexpensive restaurants lie within ½ mi. of this spot. Other commercial establishments line **S. San Francisco St.,** 2 blocks east of Beaver. As a mountain town, Flagstaff stays relatively cool and receives frequent afternoon thundershowers.

ACCOMMODATIONS AND CAMPING

When swarms of summer tourists descend on Flagstaff, accommodation prices shoot up. Thankfully, the town is blessed with excellent hostels. For cheap motels cruise historic Rte. 66. *The Flasgstaff Accommodations Guide*, available at the visitors center, lists all area hotels, motels, hostels, and B&Bs, with prices for each. If you're here to see the Grand Canyon, check the noticeboard in your hotel or hostel; some travelers leave their still-valid passes behind.

The Grand Canyon International Youth Hostel, 19 S. San Francisco St. (779-9421), in the 1930s Downtowner Motel just south of the train station. Sunny and clean. Free tea and coffee, breakfast, parking in a lot, and linen. Access to kitchen, TV room with cable, and laundry facilities. Free pickup from Greyhound and Amtrak stations. Shuttles to Page, Sedona, and Grand Canyon through Blue Goose Tours (see Practical Information above). Office open 6:30am-2am. Bunks $12; private doubles $30, $5 per additional person. Reservations accepted.

Motel Du Beau (AAIH/Rucksackers), 19 W. Phoenix St. (774-6731 or 800-332-1944), just behind the train station, which can make it noisy. Carpeted dorm rooms with private bathrooms and showers. Social atmosphere lasts into the wee hours. Tea and coffee, breakfast, linen, parking in a lot, and rides to and from the airport, train and bus stations are all gratis. Nameless café serves food 6-9pm ($1-4). Tours to Grand Canyon ($35), Sedona ($20), and Monument Valley (price varies) depending on interest. Office open 6am-midnight. Dorm beds $12; private rooms $25. Camping area out back $6 per person. Reservations accepted.

The Weatherford Hotel (HI-AYH), 23 N. Leroux St. (774-2731), downtown 1 block west of San Francisco St. Spacious rooms in a stately old hotel, with bay windows, bunk beds, and junk-store furniture. Convenient location. Dorm rooms have baths in rooms and halls. Access to kitchen. Open daily 7-10am and 5-10pm. Lockout 10am-5pm. Curfew 1am. Dorm beds $12; singles $30, Labor Day-Memorial Day $26; doubles $35/$28. Required sleepsheet $1. Guests pay no cover at **Charly's Pub,** downstairs, and receive discounts at **Charly's Restaurant.**

Hotel Monte Vista, 100 N. San Francisco St. (779-6971), also in the heart of downtown. Charmingly quirky decor, with a coffee shop and a bar (featuring pool tables, video games, and off-track betting) downstairs. Dorms sleep 16 as of June 1995; management plans to add beds in the coming months. Beds in dorms with private baths $12, Labor Day-Memorial Day $10; private rooms $40, Fri.-Sat. $45.

KOA, 5803 N. U.S. 89 (526-9926), 6mi. northeast of Flagstaff. Local buses stop near this beautiful campground. Showers, restrooms, and free nightly movies. Tent sites for 2 $22, "Kamping Kabins" $29; each additional person $4, under 18 $3.

Camping in the surrounding **Coconino National Forest** is a pleasant and inexpensive alternative, but you'll need a car to reach the designated camping areas. Pick up a forest map ($6) at the Flagstaff Visitors Center (see Practical Information above). Many campgrounds fill up quickly during the summer, particularly on weekends when Phoenicians flock to the mountains; those at high elevations close for the winter. All sites are handled on a first come, first served basis; stake out a site by 1pm. **Lake View,** 13 mi. southeast on Forest Hwy. 3 (U.S. 89A), has 30 sites ($10). **Bonito,** 10 mi. from downtown Flagstaff off U.S. 89 on Forest Rd. 545 at the entrance to Sunset Crater (see p. 643), rents 44 sites ($8). Both feature running water and flush toilets. (Both 14-day max. stay. Open mid-May to Sept.) Those who can live without amenities can camp free anywhere in the national forest outside the designated campsites, unless otherwise marked. For info on campgrounds and backcountry camping, call the **Coconino Forest Service** (527-3600; open Mon.-Fri. 7:30am-4:30pm). Privately owned **Fort Tuthill Park** (774-5139), 3 mi. south of Flagstaff on U.S. 89A, offers 335 acres of Ponderosa pines and the 100-site **Fort Tuthill Campground** (774-5130; open May-Sept.; $8, no hookups; reservations accepted).

FOOD, NIGHTLIFE, AND ENTERTAINMENT

Macy's, 14 S. Beaver St. (774-2243), behind Motel Du Beau. This hippy, happy, touristed, student hangout serves fresh pasta ($4-6), and a wide variety of vegetarian entrees ($3-6), sandwiches ($4-6), pastries ($1-2), and espresso-based drinks ($1-3). Open Sun.-Wed 6am-8pm, Thurs.-Sat. 6am-10pm; food served until 7pm.

Kathy's Café, 7 N. San Francisco St. (774-1951). Behind demure lace curtains, Kathy's prepares delicious breakfast entrees, accompanied by home fries and fresh fruit ($4-6). Also open for lunch. Open daily 6:30am-3pm.

Alpine Pizza, 7 Leroux St. (779-4109), and 2400 E. Rte. 66 (779-4138). A popular spot for beer, pool, and pizza. Large slices cooked-to-order ($2). Excellent, huge calzones $6; strombolis $7. Open Mon.-Sat. 11am-11pm, Sun. noon-11pm.

Main St. Bar and Grill, 4 S. San Francisco St. (774-1519), across from the Grand Canyon Hostel. When the vegetarian meals and non-alcoholic drinks of the cafés seem too healthy, try barbecued dishes ($6-14), complete with Buttery Texas Toast. Excellent selection of beers. Live music Tues.-Sat. 8pm; no cover. Open Mon.-Sat. 11am-midnight, Sun. noon-10pm.

Beer flows freely in downtown Flagstaff; a number of bars line S. San Francisco St. The **Mad Italian,** 101 S. San Francisco St. (779-1820), has pool tables and daily happy hours (4-7pm) with drink specials and ½-price munchies (open daily 11:30am-1am). Below the Weatherford Hotel, **Charly's,** 23 N. Leroux St. (779-1919), stages live music. Hostelers staying at the Weatherford get in free. (Open daily 11am-3pm and 5-9pm; bar open daily 11am-1am.) A little outside of town, the **Museum Club,** 3404 E. Rte. 66 (526-9434), caters to party animals with a taste for the wild west. Also known as the **Zoo,** the club rocks cowboys and cowgirls with live country-western (cover $3; open daily noon-1am).

In early June, the annual **Flagstaff Rodeo** comes to town with competitions, barn dances, a carnival, and the Nackard Beverage cocktail waitress race (call the visitors center, above, for more info). The season of the **Flagstaff Symphony** (774-5107) runs from October to May (tickets $11-22, students ½-price).

■ NEAR FLAGSTAFF

In 1894 Percival Lowell chose Flagstaff as the site for an astronomical observatory; he then spent the rest of his life here, culling data to support his theory that life exists on Mars. Though Lowell's theory has been discredited, **The Lowell Observatory,** 1400 W. Mars Hill Rd. (774-3358), just west of downtown off Rte. 66, now has eight telescopes used in breakthrough studies of Mars and Pluto. Visitors get a tour of the facility with hands-on astronomy exhibits. On clear summer nights, you can peer through the 99-year-old Clark telescope at some heavenly goodie selected by the staff. (Open daily 9am-5pm, night sky viewings Mon.-Wed. and Fri.-Sat. 8, 8:45, and 9:30pm; Nov.-March Mon.-Sat. 10am-5pm, Sun. noon-5pm. $2.50, ages 5-17 $1.)

The Museum of Northern Arizona (774-5211), on Fort Valley Rd. off U.S. 180 just north of town, houses a huge collection of Southwestern Native American art (open daily 9am-5pm; $5, college students $3, seniors $4). Nava-Hopi bus lines and the Flagstaff Trolley offer service to the museum (see Practical Information above.)

The huge, snow-capped mountains visible to the north of Flagstaff are the **San Francisco Peaks.** To reach the peaks, take U.S. 180 about 7 mi. north to the Fairfield Snow Bowl turnoff. Nearby **Mt. Agassiz** has the area's best skiing. The **Arizona Snow Bowl** (779-1951, daily 8am-5pm) operates four lifts from mid-December to mid-April; its 30 trails receive an average of 8½ ft. of powder each winter. Lift tickets cost $30. Call for information on ski conditions, transportation, and accommodations. During the summer, these peaks are perfect for hiking. The Hopi believe **Humphrey's Peak**—the highest point in Arizona at 12,670 ft.—to be the sacred home of the Kachina spirits. When the air is clear, you can see the North Rim of the Grand Canyon, the Painted Desert, and countless square miles of Arizona and Utah from the top of the peak. Reluctant hikers will find the vista from the top of the Snow Bowl's **chairlift** almost as stunning. (20-30min. Runs June 15-Labor Day daily 10am-4pm; Labor Day-April 15 Sat.-Sun. 10am-4pm. $9, seniors $6, ages 6-12 $5.) Picnic facilities and a cafeteria stay open May through October. Since the mountains occupy national forest land, camping is free, but there are no established campsites.

Old Route 66

Constructed in the 1920s along long-established trading routes, U.S. Highway 66, a modern manifestation of the desire to move west in search of opportunity, stretched from Chicago to Los Angeles. Over the years, Interstates have outdated the highway and the colorful road culture it created, leaving only disconnected patches. You can get your kicks on (a piece of) Rte. 66 in Arizona between **Kingman** and **Seligman,** a pleasurable 119-mi. detour from I-40. Despite the decay of mom-and-pop motels in the shadow of big chains, the mystique which sparked a million road-trips lives on. In the small town of **Hackberry,** less than 30 mi. east of Kingman, **The Old Route 66 Visitors Center and Preservation Foundation** (769-2605) makes its home in an old general store. Outside, elms and Joshua trees provide shade to travelers who sit on the old couches and chairs beneath them. (Center open daily 10am-dark; if no one's there, sit and wait a spell.)

■■■ JEROME

Perched on the side of Mingus Mountain, Jerome ranked as Arizona's third-largest city in 1920, populated by miners, speculators, saloon owners, and madams who came to the city following the copper boom of the late 1800s. The city never recovered from the stock market crash of 1929, however, and by mid-century Jerome was a ghost town. Now copperware boutiques and the hollow shells of stately old buildings vie for visitors' attention. Learn more about the area by heading over to **Jerome State Historic Park** (634-5381), ½ mi. off U.S. 89A just as you enter town. The park provides a panoramic view of the town, while helpful placards reveal the history of Jerome's decaying mansions. Inside the 80-year-old house of mine owner James Douglas, the park museum features exhibits on mining, minerals, and the early years of the town. (Open daily 8am-5pm; $2, ages 12-17 $1, under 12 free.) Enjoy period cars, trucks, machines, and props at **The Gold King Mine and Ghost Town** (634-0053), also on U.S. 89A just past Main St., even if it's not quite clear what period they're aiming to recreate. (Open daily 9am-5pm. $3, seniors $2.50, under 12 $2, under 5 free.) **The Mine Museum,** 200 Main St. (634-5477), displays a stock of rocks and old mining equipment (open daily 9am-4:30pm; 50¢).

U.S. 89A slinks its way to Jerome 30 mi. southwest of Sedona; the drive between the two is simply gorgeous. With no chamber of commerce, **The Station** (634-9621), on U.S. 89A across from the high school, serves as the unofficial visitors center (open daily 11am-6pm). Jerome's **area code:** 520.

Budget travelers should make Jerome a daytrip; lodging tends towards the expensive. **The Inn at Jerome,** 309 Main St. (634-5094 or 800-634-5094), is one of the lower-priced joints in town; rooms run about $55-75. The oldest restaurant in Arizona, **The English Kitchen,** 119 Jerome Ave. (634-2132), has a large array of salads and sandwiches for under $6 (open Tues.-Sun. 8am-3:30pm). **Marcy's,** 363 Main St. (634-0417), offers ice cream, soups, and sandwiches (under $4) in a pleasant ambience (open Fri.-Wed. 11am-5pm). At night, float over to **The Spirit Room** (634-8809), at Main St. and Jerome Ave., for live music and mayhem (open daily 10am-1am). **Paul and Jerry's Saloon** (634-2603), also on Main St., has been helping people get sloppy in Jerome for three generations (open daily 10:30am-1am).

■■■ SEDONA

The pines of the Coconino National Forest blanket Sedona's red sandstone formations, offering some of Arizona's most scent-sational scenery. Though a popular stopping point for vacationers, tourists, and the New Agers who believe the area to be a locus of "psychic vortices," the town itself consists of a cluster of gift shops and touring outfits. Ignore the upper-class shopping area and head for the state parks where the views, rather than the prices, will astound you.

Slide Rock Park (520-282-3034), 10 mi. north of Sedona on U.S. 89A, takes its name from a natural stone slide into the waters of Oak Creek. In the summer, locals swarm the slide. (Open in summer daily 8am-7pm; closes earlier off season. Entrance $5 per car, $1 per pedestrian.) An architectural wonder, **Chapel of the Holy Cross** (520-282-4069), on Chapel Rd., lies just outside a 1000-ft. rock wall in the middle of the red sandstone (call for hours). Meditate amidst the splendor of **Red Rock State Park** (520-282-6907), on U.S. 89A about 15 mi. southwest of town. Rangers lead day-hikes into the nearby red rocks, including nature and bird walks; inquire about times at the visitors center. (Visitors center open daily 8am-5pm. Park open daily 8am-6pm; Oct.-April 8am-5pm. Entrance $5 per car, $1 per pedestrian.)

The **Sedona Chamber of Commerce** (520-282-7722), at Forest Rd. and Rte 89A, distributes listings for accommodations and private campgrounds in the area (open Mon.-Sat. 8:30am-5pm, Sun. 9am-3pm). **The White House Inn** (520-282-6680) has singles ($38-50, depending on season and day of the week) and doubles ($40-75). Both under the same management, the **Star Motel,** 295 Jordan Rd. (520-282-0000), and **La Vista,** 500 N. Rte 89A (520-282-0000), can lodge you in comfy rooms with cable TV (1 bed $55-59, 2 beds $65-79). There are a number of **campgrounds** within **Coconino National Forest** (520-527-3600), along Oak Creek Canyon on U.S. 89A (sites $10 per vehicle). The largest, **Cave Springs,** 20 mi. north of town, administers 78 sites on a first come, first served basis. For more info on Coconino, visit the **ranger station,** 250 Brewer Rd. (520-282-4119); turn off U.S. 89A at Burger King (open Mon.-Sat. 7:30am-4:30pm; in winter Mon.-Fri. 7:30am-4:30pm). **Free backcountry camping** is allowed in the forest, anywhere outside of Oak Creek and more than 1 mi. from any official campground. **Hawkeye RV Park,** 40 Art Barn Rd. (520-282-2222), has full hookups, water, electric, and showers, as well as tent sites (sites $17, with water and electric $22.50, full hookup $27.50).

The **Coffee Pot Restaurant,** 2050 W. U.S. 89A (520-282-6626), dishes up 101 varieties of omelettes ($4-9; open daily 5:30am-9pm). **Cups Bistro and Gallery,** 1670 W. U.S. 89A (520-282-2531), in west Sedona, serves organic, karmic food in a garden setting. Breakfast dishes run $3-7, sandwiches $5-6. (Open in summer daily 8am-4pm; off season a bit later.)

Sedona lies 120 mi. north of Phoenix (take I-17 north to Rte. 179W) and 30 mi. south of Flagstaff (take I-17S to Rte. 179W or use U.S. 89A southwest). The **Sedona-Phoenix Shuttle** (520-282-2066) offers three trips daily ($30, $55 round-trip).

■ NEAR SEDONA

Montezuma Castle National Monument (567-3322), 10 mi. south of Sedona on I-17, consists of a 20-room adobe abode. The dwellings, built into a cliff recess, date back to the 12th century. Visitors view the "castle" from a path below. (Open daily 8am-7pm. $2, with Golden Age Passport free, under 16 free.) A beautiful lake formed by the collapse of an underground cavern, **Montezuma Well,** 11 mi. from the Castle off I-17 north of the Wall exit, once served as a source of water for the Sinagua who lived here (open daily 7am-7pm; free). Take U.S. 89A to Rte. 279 and continue through Cottonwood to reach **Tuzigoot National Monument** (634-5564), 20 mi. southwest of Sedona, a dramatic Sinaguan ruin overlooking the Verde Valley (open daily 8am-7pm; $2, with Golden Age Passport free, under 17 free.)

When finally completed, **Arcosanti** (632-7135), off I-17 at exit 262, will be a self-sufficient community embodying Italian architect Paolo Soleri's concept of an "arcology" (defined as "architecture and ecology working together as one integral process"). Budgetarians will appreciate the architect's vision of a city where cars are obsolete. The complete city, with its unusual geometric structures and subterranean parks, surprises even the most imaginative Legoland architects. (Tours daily every hr. 10am-4pm. Open to the public daily 9am-5pm. $5 donation.) For more info, contact Arcosanti, HC 74, P.O. Box 4136, Mayer 86333.

SOUTHERN ARIZONA

■■■ PHOENIX

Phoenix began as a small farming community in the late 1800s, but high tech jobs and shopping plazas have replaced wheatfields. Shiny high-rises crowd the business district, while a vast web of six-lane strip mall highways surrounds the downtown—don't come to Phoenix in search of the picturesque. Sun, sun, sun, and sun are the city's main attractions. During the balmy winter months, tourists, golfers, and business conventioneers flock to Phoenix; in the summer, the city crawls into its air-conditioned shell as temperatures climb to an average of 100°F and lodging prices drop by up to 70%. Summer visitors should carry water with them if they plan on walking for any length of time. On January 28, 1996, Phoenix will host the National Football League's Super Bowl. Plan well in advance if you wish to attend; rooms will be scarce, and those you find will cost three times the normal rates.

PRACTICAL INFORMATION

Tourist Office: Phoenix and Valley of the Sun Convention and Visitors Center, 400 E. Van Buren St. (254-6500), on the 6th floor of the Arizona Center. Open Mon.-Fri. 8am-5pm. **Weekly Events Hotline,** 252-5588. 24-hr. recording. **Gay/Lesbian Community Switchboard,** 234-2752. Operates daily 10am-10pm with recommendations for accommodations, restaurants, and entertainment.

Airport: Sky Harbor International (273-3300), only minutes southeast of downtown. Valley Metro bus #13 goes west into the city (5am-7pm). 24-hr. shuttle service to downtown $7.

Trains: Amtrak, 401 W. Harrison (253-0121 or 800-872-7245); follow 4th Ave. south 2 blocks past Jefferson St. *NOT safe at night.* To: Los Angeles (3 per week, 20hr., $109); San Antonio via El Paso (3 per week, 21hr., $168). Station and ticket office open Mon. and Wed. 5:45am-6:30pm, Tues. and Sun. 5:45am-1:15pm and 4:30pm-midnight, Thurs. 4:30pm-midnight.

Buses: Greyhound, 525 E. Washington St. (271-7425 or 800-231-2222). To: El Paso (15 per day, 8hr., $35); Los Angeles (12 per day, 8hr., $29); Tucson (13 per day, 2hr., $12); San Diego (4 per day, 8½hr., $34). Open 24 hrs. Lockers $2 for 6hr., $4 for 6-24hr.

Public Transportation: Valley Metro, 253-5000. Most lines run to and from the **City Bus Terminal,** Central and Washington. Most routes operate Mon.-Fri. 5am-8pm; really reduced service on Sun. Fare $1; disabled, seniors, and children 50¢. All-day $3, 10-ride pass $10; disabled and seniors ½-price. Pick up bus passes and free timetables and system maps at City Bus Terminal.

Taxis: Ace Taxi, 254-1999. $2.45 base fare, $1.10 per mi. **Yellow Cab,** 252-5252. $2.00 base fare, $1.35 per mi. Both 24 hrs.

Car Rental: Rent-a-Wreck, 2422 E. Washington St. (254-1000). Economy cars from $22 per day with 100 free mi.; 15¢ per additional mi. Must be 21 with credit card. Open Mon.-Fri. 7am-6:30pm, Sat.-Sun. 9am-5pm.

Auto Transport: Auto Driveaway, 3530 E. Indian School Rd. (952-0339). First tank of gas free. Must be 21 and pay $250 deposit. Open Mon.-Fri. 9am-4:30pm.

Crisis Lines: Center Against Sexual Assault, 241-9010. **Crisis Hotline,** 784-1500. Both 24 hrs. **Gay/Lesbian Hotline,** 234-2752. Open daily 10am-10pm.

Emergency: 911.

Post Office: 522 N. Central (407-2051), downtown. Open Mon.-Fri. 8:30am-5pm, Sat. 8:30am-noon. General Delivery, 1441 E. Buckeye Rd. (407-2049). Open Mon.-Fri. 8am-5pm. **ZIP code:** 85026. **Area code:** 602.

The bus terminal at **Central Ave.** and **Washington St.** marks the heart of downtown. **Central Ave.** runs north-south; "avenues" are numbered west from Central and "streets" are numbered east. **Washington St.** divides streets north-south. Parking is readily available downtown, for a price, at one of the many meters or garages. You'll need a car or a bus pass to see much of Phoenix; the city is a sprawler.

ACCOMMODATIONS AND CAMPING

Budget travelers should visit Phoenix in the summer. Almost all downtown motels have vacancies discounted up to 70% during July and August. In the winter, when temperatures and vacancy signs go down, prices go up; be sure to make reservations if possible. The reservationless should cruise the rows of motels on **Van Buren St.** and **Main St.** (a.k.a. Apache Trail) in the suburbs, Tempe and Mesa, east of downtown. The strips are full of 50s ranch-style motels with names like "Deserama," as well as the requisite modern chains. Be advised that parts of these areas *can be quite dangerous;* investigate a hotel thoroughly before checking in. **Bed and Breakfast Inn Arizona,** 8900 E. Via Linda, #101, Scottsdale 85258 (860-9338 or 800-266-STAY/7829), matches visitors with accommodations in homes in Phoenix and throughout Arizona. However, they will only return your call collect—which could be very expensive. (Preferred 2-night min. stay. Singles $30, doubles $40. Reservations recommended.)

Metcalf House (HI-AYH), 1026 N. 9th St. (254-9803), a few blocks northeast of downtown. From the City Bus Terminal, take bus #7 down 7th St. to Roosevelt St., walk 2 blocks east to 9th St., and turn left—the hostel is ½ block north. The manager has been known to turn off the A/C at night. Dorm-style rooms, wooden bunks, and common showers. Kitchen, porch, common room, and laundry facilities. Can also help you with car rentals. Check-in 7-10am and 5-10pm. Lockout 10am-5pm. $10, nonmembers $13. Linen $1.

Economy Inn, 804 E. Van Buren St. (254-0181), close to downtown. Standard rooms with TV and phones. Singles $27, doubles $35; in winter $30/$38.

The American Lodge, 965 E. Van Buren St. (252-6823). Another basic motel close to downtown. More TV, more phones—imagine! Pool. Singles $35, doubles $50; in winter $60/$85.

KOA Phoenix West (853-0537), 11 mi. west of Phoenix on Citrus Rd. Take I-10 to exit 124; go ¾mi. south to Van Buren St., then 1 mi. west to Citrus Rd. 285 sites, heated pool and jacuzzi, and other perks. Tent sites $14.50, RV sites $15.50, electric and water $3 extra.

FOOD

Aside from malls, you will rarely find several restaurants together amid Phoenix's expanse. Downtowners feed mainly at small coffeeshops, most of which close on weekends. For more variety, try **McDowell St.** The **Arizona Center** (271-4000), on 3rd and Van Buren St., boasts food venues, fountains, and palm trees. The *New Times* gives extensive restaurant recommendations.

Tacos de Juárez, 1017 N. 7th St. (258-1744), near the hostel. Mexican fare at rock-bottom prices. Specializes in tacos. All ala carte items under $3. Open Mon.-Thurs. 11am-9pm, Fri. 11am-10:30pm, Sat. 8am-10:30pm, Sun. 8am-8pm.

Mi Patio, 3477 N. 7th Ave. (277-4831), lures families and bargain-seekers with light, calming decor and filling dishes. Tacos and burritos $3-5; combination plates and specials $5-9. Open Mon.-Sat. 11am-10pm.

Bill Johnson's Big Apple, 3757 E. Van Buren St. (275-2107), and 3 other locations. A down-south delight with sawdust on the floor. Sandwiches $4-6; hearty soups $2-3. Open Mon.-Sat. 6am-11pm.

SIGHTS

The **Heard Museum,** 22 E. Monte Vista Rd. (252-8840), 1 block east of Central Ave. near the hostel, has outstanding collections of Navajo handicrafts. The museum also promotes the work of contemporary Native American artists, many of whom give free demonstrations, and sponsors occasional lectures and Native American dances. (Guided tours daily. Open Mon.-Tues. and Thurs.-Sat. 9:30am-5pm, Wed. 9:30am-9pm, Sun. noon-5pm. $5, students and seniors $4, ages 13-18 $3, ages 4-12 $2; free Wed. 5-9pm.) The **Phoenix Art Museum,** 1625 N. Central Ave. (257-1222), 3 blocks south, exhibits American folk art, as well as classical and modern European art. (Open Tues. and Thurs.-Sat. 10am-5pm, Wed. 10am-9pm, Sun. noon-5pm; $4, seniors $3, students $1.50, under 6 free; free Wed.) The **Pueblo Grande Museum and Cultural Park,** 4619 E. Washington St. (495-0900), features the remains of a Hohokam pueblo (open Mon.-Sat. 9am-4:45pm, Sun. 1-4:45pm; 50¢).

The **Desert Botanical Gardens,** 1201 N. Galvin Pkwy. (941-1225), in Papago Park 5 mi. east of the downtown area, grows a beautifully colorful collection of cacti and other desert plants. (Take bus #3 east to Papago Park. Open daily 7am-10pm; in winter 8am-sunset. $5, seniors $4, ages 5-12 $1.) Also within the confines of Papago Park, the **Phoenix Zoo** (273-1341), at 62nd and E. Van Buren St., presents exhibits and a children's zoo. Walk around or take a guided tour via tram. (Open daily 7am-4pm; Labor Day-April 9am-5pm. $7, seniors $6, children $3.50.) In summer, try to avoid outside attractions during the midday heat. The **Arizona Science Center,** 80 N. 2nd St. (256-9388), offers interactive science exhibits aimed at children (open Mon.-Sat. 9am-5pm, Sun. noon-5pm; $4.50, seniors and ages 4-12 $3.50.)

Taliesin West (860-8810 or 860-2700), on Frank Lloyd Wright Blvd. in nearby Scottsdale, served as the architectural studio and residence of Frank Lloyd Wright in his later years. Designed by Wright, the studio was meant to blend into the surrounding desert. (Guided tours only; open June-Sept. daily 8-11am. $10, students and seniors $8, children $3.) To see more of Wright's work, check out the **Arizona Biltmore** (955-6600), on 24th St. and Missouri.

South of Phoenix across the dry Salt River lie Tempe's **Arizona State University (ASU)** and its sunny college atmosphere. Cafés and art galleries abound in this area. Another Frank Lloyd Wright creation, the **Gammage Memorial Auditorium** (965-3434), at Mill Ave. on campus (take bus #60, or #22 on weekends), one of the last major buildings designed by the architect, wears the pink and beige tones of the surrounding desert (20-min. tours daily in winter).

NIGHTLIFE AND ENTERTAINMENT

The free *New Times Weekly* (271-0040), available on local magazine racks, lists club schedules for Phoenix's active scene. Gay and lesbian nightlife spots can be found in *The Western Front*, available in some bars and clubs. The *Cultural Calender of Events* guide covers three months of area entertainment.

Recently rated the nation's best country nightclub, **Toolie's Country Saloon and Dance Hall,** 4231 W. Thomas Rd. (272-3100), has country-western music nightly. (Free dance lessons Mon., Wed., and Sun. Open Mon.-Thurs. 8am-1am, Fri.-Sat. 7am-1am, Sun. 10am-1am. Cover Thurs. $5, Fri.-Sat. $4.) **Char's Has the Blues,** 4631 N. 7th Ave. (230-0205), is self-explanatory. Dozens of junior John Lee Hookers rip it up nightly. (Doors open 7pm; music starts 9pm. Cover $3 on weekends.) **Phoenix Live,** 455 N. 3rd St. (252-2112), at Arizona Center, quakes the complex with three bars and a restaurant. The $5 weekend cover (no cover on weeknights), buys access to the entire building. Tuesday through Saturday, **LTL Ditty's** gets someone to tickle the ivories for sing-alongs with wild fans. **Ain't Nobody's Biz,** 3031 E. Indian School, #7 (224-9977), is a spacious women's bar with Thursday night beer busts ($1.50 pitchers Thurs. 9pm-midnight; open daily 2pm-1am). **The Country Club,** 4428 N. 7th Ave. (264-4553), a gay bar, occupies a cute little house by the highway (happy hour Mon.-Sat. 11am-7pm; open daily 11am-1am).

Phoenix also has plenty for the sports-lover. Catch NBA action with the **Phoenix Suns** (379-7867), at the America West Arena, or root for the NFL's **Phoenix Cardinals** (379-0101). Phoenix also hosts professional indoor tennis tournaments, a professional baseball team, and a hockey team. Call the visitors center (see Practical Information above) for more info.

■ FROM PHOENIX TO TUCSON

Apache Junction and the Superstition Mountains A small mining town 40 mi. east of Phoenix at the junction of Rte. 88 and U.S. 60, **Apache Junction** serves as the "gateway to the **Superstition Mountains.**" Steep, gray, and haunting, the mountains derived their name from Pima Native American legends, but they could easily have gained the name from the legends of the **Apache Trail,** which follows Rte. 88 into the mountains. In the 1840s, a Mexican explorer found gold in these hills but was killed before he could reveal the location. In the 1870s, Jacob Waltz apparently found the mine and promptly died. As you drive, remember the lost gold of the Apache Trail, but think twice before trying to find it.

The trail loops back to the town and U.S. 60 after about 6-8 hrs. of driving. Along the way, the partly unpaved road passes cliff dwellings, caves, ghost towns, and the man-made **Lake Canyon, Lake Apache,** and **Lake Roosevelt.** Leave the driving to **Apache Trail Tours** (982-7662), a company which offers jeep tours along the trail (1½-hr. tours $25 per person, 8-hr. tours $75). For more info head to **Apache Junction Chamber of Commerce,** 1001 N. Idaho (982-3141; open Mon.-Fri. 8am-5pm).

Many attractions vie for your attention along the loop. Among the best, the **Goldfield Ghost Town Mine Tours** (983-0333), 3½ mi. north of the U.S. 60 junction on Rte. 88, offers tours of the nearby mines and some goldpanning from a refurbished ghost town (open daily 10am-6pm; mine tours $4, children $2; goldpanning $3). "Where the hell am I?" said Jacob Waltz when he came upon **Lost Dutchman State Park** (982-4485), 1½ mi. farther north on Rte. 88. At the base of the Superstitions, the park offers **nature trails, picnic sites,** and **campsites** (entrance $3 per vehicle; campsites $8, first come, first served). **Tortilla Flat** (984-1776), an old ghost town on Rte. 88 18 mi. north of the U.S. 60 junction, keeps its spirits up with a restaurant, ice cream shop, and saloon. The **Tonto National Monument** (467-2241), 5 mi. east of Lake Roosevelt on Rte. 88W, manages a 700-year-old masonry and pueblo ruin from the prehistoric Salado people (open daily 8am-5pm; entrance $4 per car).

Biosphere 2 In 1991, eight research scientists sealed themselves inside this giant greenhouse to cultivate their own food and knit their own socks with no aid from the outside world, as they monitored the behavior of seven man-made ecosystems—a savannah, a tropical rainforest, a marsh, a 25-ft. deep ocean and coral reef, a desert, an intensive agricultural area, and a 7-11. After two years, they found that farming and maintenance left little time for scientific research. Now no one lives in Biosphere 2, but teams of scientists still use it as a research facility.

The Biosphere is one hour from Tucson; take I-10 west to the "Miracle Mile" exit, follow the miracles to Oracle Rd., then go north until it becomes Rte. 77N. From Phoenix, take I-10 to exit 185, follow Rte. 387 to Rte. 79 (Florence Hwy.), and ride Rte. 79 to Oracle Juntio, where you'll turn left onto Rte. 77. The two-hour guided tours include two short films, a walk through the laboratory's research and development models for the Biosphere 2 ecosystems, and a stroll around Biosphere 2 itself. (Open daily 9am-5pm. $13, seniors $11, ages 5-17 $6. AAA discount.) The **Inn at the Biosphere** (825-6222) offers deluxe accommodations on the same ranch as the Biosphere. (Cable TV, giant beds, and huge patios overlooking the Catalina mountains. Rooms for 1 or 2 $49; Oct.-April $80. A hefty $20 for each additional person.) Guests are sealed into their rooms at 8pm and taken out the subsequent leap year. Also within the complex, the Canyon Café serves up sandwiches and salads ($6).

Aravaipa Canyon Looking for a true natural wonder off the beaten path? From the Biosphere, travel roughly 20 mi. north on Rte. 77. Just past the wooly town of **Mammoth,** take a right at the sign for Central Arizona College. **Aravaipa Canyon,** perfectly centered in a panorama of desert, mountains, and cacti, awaits about 11 mi. up this road (half of which is unpaved). Overseen by the Bureau of Land Management, the canyon takes only 50 visitors per day. Tourists must obtain **permits** ($1.50) in advance; call 428-4040 for reservations and permit pickup instructions. In 1993, winter storms knocked the road to the ranger station off the face of a cliff, so one must presently hike 3 mi. to the fee station and another mi. to the wilderness area. Construction of a new road began in July 1995; call for updated road reports. Some primitive **campsites** and backcountry camping areas are available (2-night max. stay, no more than 10 people). Take the posted warnings seriously: camp on high ground, beware of flash floods, don't camp on railroad tracks, and don't play with rattlesnake tails. Hydrate yourself frequently and with zeal.

■■■ TUCSON

Hohokam Indians inhabited the Tucson region some 1200 years ago; following their disappearance sometime later, Papago Indians settled in what is now west Tucson and gave the city its name. Between 1776 and 1848, the region fell under Spanish, then Mexican, and, finally, U.S. control. The genuine arrival of Western civilization became manifest in 1864, when locals ruled that pigs could no longer roam freely on city streets; they would have to be chained. Smaller and friendlier than Phoenix, Tucson is now struggling to preserve its attractive, pigless downtown, and it remains to be seen whether the small band of downtown cafés and artsy shops can compete with the city's suburban sprawl. Travelers can take advantage of Tucson's varied environments in the meantime—its walkable downtown, its restaurant-and-shop-crammed highways, and the national parks just outside the city.

PRACTICAL INFORMATION

Tourist Office: Metropolitan Tucson Convention and Visitors Bureau, 130 S. Scott Ave. (624-1817 or 800-638-8350). Ask for a bus map, the *Official Visitor's Guide,* and an Arizona campground directory. Open Mon.-Fri. 8am-5pm, Sat.-Sun. 9am-4pm. **Gay and Lesbian Community Center,** 422 N. 4th Ave. (624-1779).

Airport: Tucson International (573-8000), on Valencia Rd., south of downtown. Bus #25 runs every hr. to the Laos Transit Center; from there bus #16 goes downtown (last bus daily 7:48pm). **Arizona Stagecoach** (889-1000) will take you downtown for $12. Open 24 hrs. Reserve ahead.

Trains: Amtrak, 400 E. Toole (623-4442 or 800-872-7245), at 5th Ave., across from the Greyhound station. 3 trains per week to: Phoenix (3hr., $28); L.A. (12hr., $104). Open Sun.-Wed. 8am-8:30pm, Thurs. 1:15-8:30pm, Sat. 8am-3pm.

Buses: Greyhound, 2 S. 4th Ave. (882-4386 or 800-231-2222), between Congress St. and Broadway. To: Phoenix (11 per day, 2hr., $12); L.A. (7 per day, 10hr., $34); Albuquerque (6 per day, 12hr., $78); El Paso (7 per day, 7hr., $30). Ticket office and terminal open 5:30am-2am.

Taxis: Yellow Cab, 624-6611. 24 hrs. $1.10 base fare, $1.40 per mi.

Public Transportation: Sun-Tran (792-9222). Buses run from the Ronstadt terminal downtown at Congress and 6th. Service roughly Mon.-Fri. 5:30am-10pm, Sat.-Sun. 8am-7pm. Fare 75¢, students under 19 with ID 50¢, seniors 25¢.

Car Rental: Care Free, 1760 S. Craycroft Rd. (790-2655). For the car-free. $18 per day with 100 free mi.; within Tucson only. 2-day min. rental. Must be 21 with major credit card. Open Mon.-Fri. 9am-5pm, Sat. 9am-3pm.

Bike Rental: The Bike Shack, 835 Park Ave. (624-3663), across from the UA campus. $20 for 1 day, $30 for 2 days, $40 for 3 days. Open Mon.-Fri. 9am-7pm, Sat. 10am-5pm, Sun. noon-5pm.

Crisis Line: Rape Crisis, 327-7273. 24 hrs.

Emergency: 911.

Post Office: 141 S. 6th St. (622-8454). Open Mon.-Fri. 8:30am-5pm, Sat. 9am-noon. General Delivery, 1501 Cherry Bell (620-5157). **ZIP code:** 85726. **Area code:** 520.

Just east of I-10, Tucson's downtown area surrounds the intersection of **Broadway Blvd.** (running east-west) and **Stone Ave.,** 2 blocks from the train and bus terminals. The **University of Arizona** lies 1 mi. northeast of downtown at the intersection of **Park** and **Speedway Blvd.** Avenues run north-south, streets east-west; because some of each are numbered, intersections such as "6th and 6th" are possible—and probable. Speedway and Broadway Blvd. are the best east-west routes through town. To go north-south follow **Oracle Rd.** through the heart of the city, **Campbell Ave.** east of downtown, or **Swan Rd.** further east.

ACCOMMODATIONS AND CAMPING

When summer arrives, Tucson opens its arms to budget travelers. Motel row runs along **South Freeway,** the frontage road along I-10, north of the I-19 junction. **Old Pueblo Homestays Bed and Breakfast,** P.O. Box 13603, Tucson 85732 (800-333-9776), arranges stays in private homes. Singles run $45 and up, doubles $55 and up. (Open daily 8am-8pm. Winter reservations required 2 weeks in advance.)

The swank old **Hotel Congress and Hostel (AAIH/Rucksackers),** 311 E. Congress (622-8848), conveniently located across from the Greyhound and Amtrak stations, offers superb lodging to night-owl hostelers; Club Congress downstairs booms until 1am, making it a bit rough for early birds. Still, you get free earplugs and a real bed in a shared room with a private bath and a phone. The café downstairs serves great salads and some mean omelettes. ($12, nonmembers $14. Hotel singles $32, doubles $36; 20% discount for students. $3 more in winter or for renovated rooms.) **The Tucson Desert Inn** (624-8151), on I-10 at Congress, has the "largest pool in Tucson." Large rooms with large windows provide panoramic views of the interstate. (Singles $27, doubles $37; 10% senior discount. Light breakfast included.)

Mount Lemmon Recreation Area in the **Coronado National Forest** offers beautiful campgrounds and free off-site camping in certain areas. Campgrounds and picnic areas are two minutes to two hours outside Tucson via the Catalina Hwy. **Rose Canyon,** 33 mi. northeast of Tucson via Hitchcock Hwy., at 7000 ft., is heavily wooded and comfortably cool and has a small lake. Sites at higher elevations fill quickly on summer weekends. (Sites $8 at Rose and Spencer Canyons; General Hitchcock Campground free, but no water available.) For more info, contact the **National Forest Service,** 300 W. Congress Ave. (670-4552), 7 blocks west of the Greyhound station (open Mon.-Fri. 8am-4:30pm). Among the commercial campgrounds near Tucson, try **Cactus Country RV Park** (574-3000), 10 mi. southeast of

Tucson on I-10 off the Houghton Rd. exit, which has showers, restrooms, and a pool. (Sites for 1 or 2 $14, with full hookup $22. $2.50 per additional person.)

FOOD

Good cheap Mexican restaurants are everywhere in Tucson; pick up a free *Tucson Weekly,* or just follow your nose. **"Little" Café Poca Cosa,** 20 S. Scott St., the (less expensive) *niño* of the Café Poca Cosa on Broadway, prides itself on fresh ingredients and an ever-changing menu (lunch specials $5; open Mon.-Fri. 7:30am-2:30pm). The chef from one of Tucson's top restaurants moonlights making sumptuous (and less expensive) lunches at **Wild Johnny's Wagon,** 150 N. Main Ave. (884-9426), behind the art museum. (Grilled bluefish tacos $5.50; 2 salads, focaccia, and bean spread $4. Open Mon.-Fri. 11:30am-2pm.) **Two Pesos,** 811 N. Euclid (620-0306), may not be as cheap as its name implies, but it's pretty close—Mexican plates go for $3.50-5, margaritas for $1 (bottled beer $1.25; tacos $1-2; open Mon.-Sun. 10am-2am). When you've had it up to your sombrero with Mexican food, head for **India Oven,** 2727 N. Campbell (326-8635). The garlic nan ($2.65) is exquisite. (Vegetarian dishes $5. Tandoor meats and curries $5-8. Open daily 11am-10pm.)

SIGHTS

Many of the sights associated with Tucson lie outside of the city, so be sure to read Near Tucson, below. Lined with cafés, restaurants, galleries, and vintage clothing shops, **4th Ave.** is an alternative, artsy magnet and a great spot for a stroll. Between Speedway and Broadway Blvd., the street becomes a historic shopping district with more touristy shops. The **Tucson Museum of Art,** 140 N. Main Ave. (624-2333), downtown, shows an impressive collection of pre-Columbian art. (Open Tues.-Sat. 10am-4pm, Sun. noon-4pm; $2, students and seniors $1, under 12 free.)

Lovely for its varied—and elaborately irrigated—vegetation, the **University of Arizona's** "mall" sits where E. 3rd St. should be. **The Center for Creative Photography** (621-7968), on campus, houses the archives of major American photographers Ansel Adams and Richard Avedon. Exhibits come from the permanent collection and traveling shows. (Open Mon.-Fri. 11am-5pm, Sun. noon-5pm. Free.) Shops catering to students cluster along **University Blvd.** at the west end of campus.

The vibrant **mariachi mass** at **St. Augustine Church,** 192 S. Stone Ave. (623-6351), downtown, features singing and dancing, but is not intended as a tourist attraction (Sun. 8am mass in Spanish).

ENTERTAINMENT AND NIGHTLIFE

Tucson is a musical smorgasbord. While UA students rock and roll on Speedway Blvd., more subdued folks do the two-step in the country music clubs on N. Oracle. Pick up a copy of the free *Tucson Weekly* or the weekend sections of *The Star* or *The Citizen* for current entertainment listings. Throughout the year, the city of the sun presents **Music Under the Stars** (792-9155, for dates and times) a series of sunset concerts by the Tucson Symphony Orchestra. For milling and moseying head to **Downtown Saturday Night;** blockaded on the first and third Saturday of each month, Congress St. celebrates the arts with outdoor singers, crafts, and galleries. On the last Thursday of every month, **Thursday Night Art Walk** lets you mosey through downtown galleries and studios. Call the **Tucson Arts District** (624-9977) for info on Downtown Saturday Night or Art Walk.

An authentic Old West saloon, **Wild Wild West,** 4385 W. Ina Rd. (744-7744), plays continuous country-western music that will get you out on the largest dance floor (6000 sq. ft.) in Arizona. Bring the kids for family day on the second and fourth Sunday of each month (open 2pm-1am), and bring your two left feet for free dance lessons on Tuesday, Thursday, or Sunday. (Cover Fri.-Sat. $3; Wed. men pay $2, women get in free. Open Tues.-Fri. and Sun. 4pm-1am, Sat. and Mon. 5pm-1am.)

Club Congress, 311 E. Congress (622-8848), downstairs at the Hotel Congress, has DJs during the week and live bands (cover $3) on weekends. The friendly hotel staff and a cast of regulars make it an especially good time. (Drink specials $1.25.

Open daily 8pm-1am.) **The Rock,** 136 N. Park. (629-9211), caters to a college crowd with live shows and Friday-night Battles of the Bands (cover $3-8; open 8pm-1am when there's a show; call ahead). A good place for a quiet drink, **Bar Toma,** 311 N. Cart Ave. (622-5465), offers a wide selection of tequilas (open Sun.-Thurs. 11am-9pm, Fri.-Sat. 11am-10pm). For live blues and rock, try **Berky's on Fourth,** 424 N. 4th Ave. (622-0376; cover $1-3; open Mon.-Fri. 4pm-1am, Sat.-Sun. 11am-1am).

■ NEAR TUCSON

A museum, zoo, and nature preserve rolled into one, the **Arizona-Sonora Desert Museum,** 2021 N. Kinney Rd. (883-2702; follow Speedway Blvd. west of the city as it becomes Gates Pass Rd., then Kinney Rd.), recreates a range of desert habitats, from cave to mountain, and features over 300 kinds of animals including hummingbirds, ocelots, and rattlesnakes. Take at least two hours to see the museum—preferably in the cool morning hours when the animals have not yet begun their afternoon siesta. (Open daily 8:30am-5pm; Oct.-Feb. 7:30am-6pm. $9, ages 6-12 $2.)

Old Tucson Studios, 201 S. Kinney Rd. (883-0100), just south of the Desert Museum, a theme park originally built as a set for the movie *Arizona,* burned down in 1995 and was rebuilding at press time. Call for more information.

North of the museum, the western half of **Saguaro National Park,** also known as the Tucson Mountain District (883-6366), has limited hiking trails and an auto loop. The paved nature walk near the visitors center passes some of the best specimens of Saguaro cactus in the Tucson area. (Visitors center open daily 8am-5pm. Park open 24 hrs.) **Gates Pass,** on the way to the Tucson Mountain Unit and the Desert Museum, is an excellent spot for watching sunrises and sunsets.

Saguaro National Park East (733-5153), a.k.a. Rincon Mountain District, lies east of the city on the Old Spanish Trail; take I-10 east to exit 279 and follow Vail Rd. to the Old Spanish Trail. Within the park, 128 mi. of trails and an 8-mi. scenic drive lead through the cactus forest. (Open daily 8am-5pm. Entrance $4 per vehicle, $2 per pedestrian). Get a free permit from the visitors center for **backcountry camping.** The **Colossal Cave** (647-7275) on Vail Rd. is the only "dormant" cave in the U.S. Guided tours (45min.) involve flagstone walking and fluorescent lights. (Open Mon.-Sat. 8am-6pm, Sun. 8am-7pm; Sept. 15-March 16 Mon-Sat. 9am-5pm, Sun. 9am-6pm. $6.50, ages 11-16 $5, ages 6-10 $3.50.) In the shadow of the National Park, the cacti on Mt. Lemmon, just east of town, often go unsung; it's worth the time to drive up the mountain and see them.

Built around a deactivated missile silo, Pima's **Titan II Missile Museum,** 1580 W. Duvall Mine Rd. (791-2929), in Green Valley 25 mi. south of Tucson (take I-19 to exit 69), makes a chilling statement. (Open Wed.-Sun. 9am-4pm; Nov.-April daily 9am-5pm. $5, seniors and active military $4, ages 10-17 $3. Reservations advised.) Over 20,000 warplanes, from WWII fighters to Vietnam War jets, park in ominous, silent rows at the **Davis-Monthan Air Force Base** (750-4570), 15 mi. southeast of Tucson. Low humidity and sparse rainfall combine to preserve the relics. Take the Houghton exit off I-10, then travel west on Irvington to Wilmont. (Free tours Mon. and Wed. 9am; call ahead for reservations.) You can also view the 2-mi. long graveyard through the airfield fence.

North of Tucson, the cliffs and waterfalls of **Sabino Canyon** (749-2861) provide ideal scenery for picnics and day hikes (tram through the canyon daily every ½hr. 9am-4:30pm). Call the canyon folk for best directions. **Sabino Canyon Tours,** 5900 N. Sabino Canyon Rd. (749-2327), runs a shuttle bus through the canyon. (Mon.-Fri. every hr. on the hr. 9am-4pm; off season Sat.-Sun. every ½hr. 9am-4:30pm.)

■■■ TOMBSTONE

Founded in the wake of a gold and silver rush of the 1870s, Tombstone rebounded from two devastating fires before the failure of its mines spelled death for the town, but "the town too tough to die" has made yet another comeback. By inviting visitors to view the barnyard where Wyatt Earp and his brothers kicked butt, Tombstone has turned the minutes-long showdown at **The O.K. Corral** (520-457-3456), on Allen next to City Park, into a year-round tourist industry (open daily 8:30am-5pm; $2). The **Boothill Gunslingers,** the **Wild Bunch,** and the **Vigilantes/Vigilettes** perform **re-enactments** of famous gunfights (Mon.-Sat. 2pm at 4th and Toughnut; $2.50, ages 6-12 $1.50); call Lou at the Legends of the West Saloon (520-457-3055) to arrange with one of these groups to treat a friend or relative to a **public mock hanging.** The voice of Vincent Price narrates the town's history in the **Tombstone Historama** (520-457-3456), while a plastic mountain revolves onstage and a dramatization of the gunfight is shown on a movie screen—oh gee, did we give it away? (Shows daily every hr. on the ½hr. 9am-4pm. $2.) Marshals such as John Slaughter battled scores of outlaws at the **Tombstone Courthouse** (520-457-3311), at 3rd and Toughnut (open daily 8am-5pm; $2, ages 12-18 $1, under 12 free). See the **tombstones** of Tombstone—the result of all of this wanton gunplay—on Rte. 80 just north of town (open daily 7:30am-7pm; free). On an entirely different note, the **Rose Tree Museum** (520-457-3326), at 4th and Toughnut, houses the largest rose tree in the world (open daily 9am-5pm; $2, under 14 free). The **Tombstone Chamber of Commerce and Visitors Center** (520-457-3929), welcomes y'all at 4th and Allen St. (open Mon.-Fri. 9am-5pm, Sat.-Sun. 9am-4pm).

Hit the hay at the **Hacienda Huachuca Motel,** 320 Bruce St. (520-457-2201 or 800-893-2201), where John Wayne stayed (in room 4) during the 1963 shooting of *McLintock.* Behind the peeling-paint exterior lie cute little rooms with cute little televisions and mini-fridges. (Singles or doubles $27.) You no longer need to sleep with a pistol under your pillow at **Trail Rider's Inn,** 13 N. 7th St. (520-457-3573). Clean rooms complement decor à la late 20th century American motel. (Singles $27-35; $5 each additional person.) The **Round-up Trailer Ranch,** 201 W. Allen St. (520-457-3738), has tent sites for $10 and RV spots for $12.50.

Don Teodoro's, 15 N. 4th St. (520-457-3647), serves Mexican plates for less than $5 (open Mon.-Fri. 11am-2pm and 5-9pm, Sat.-Sun. 11am-9pm). Get some victuals at **Ol' Miner's BBQ and Cafe,** 10 S. 5th St. (520-457-3488), where burgers and other sandwiches run $3-5. (Fickle hours.) **Blake's Char-Broiled Burgers and BBQ Ranch,** 511B Allen St. (520-457-3646), slaps the cow on the bun starting at $3 (open Tues.-Sat. 11am-7pm, Sun.-Mon. 11am-6pm). For a bit of moonshine and country music, smell your way to **Big Nose Kate's Saloon** (520-457-3107), on Allen St., named for "the girl that loved Doc Holliday and everyone else too." Cowboy bartenders serve such specialty drinks as "sex in the desert." (Open daily 10am-midnight.)

To get to Tombstone, careen your Conestoga to the Benson exit off I-10, then go south on Rte. 80. The nearest **Greyhound** station (520-586-3141 or 800-231-2222), is in **Benson** at the Benson Flower Shop on 4th St.; **Amtrak** (800-872-7245) choo-choos stop across the street. **Mr. Reynolds Taxi** (520-457-3897), makes the trip from Benson to Tombstone ($20).

New Mexico

In 1540 an expedition led by Francisco Vasquez de Coronado left Mexico City for what is now New Mexico, hoping to conquer the legendary city of Cibola. There, it was said, silversmiths occupied entire streets, while gold, sapphires, and turquoise decorated every house. Coronado and his men found only Indian pueblos and none the richer, they returned to Mexico in 1542. Coronado may have failed in his quest, but he did start a trend—travelers have sought out New Mexico's riches ever since. Today, most explorers come in search of natural beauty and adobe architecture rather than gold; but the spirit of the conquistadors may live on in the purse-toting New Yorkers fingering turquoise jewelry in Taos Plaza.

New Mexico serves as a haven for hikers, backpackers, and mountain-climbers alike. Six national forests within the state provide miles and miles of beautiful and challenging opportunities for lovers of the outdoors, while Sandía, Mogollon, and Sangre de Cristo fulfill a mountain-climber's upward longings.

PRACTICAL INFORMATION

Capital: Santa Fe.
New Mexico Dept. of Tourism: 491 Old Santa Fe Trail, Santa Fe 87501 (800-545-2040). Open Mon.-Fri. 8am-5pm. **Park and Recreation Division,** Villagra Bldg., P.O. Box 1147, Santa Fe 87504 (505-827-7465). **U.S. Forest Service,** 517 Gold Ave. SW, Albuquerque 87102 (505-842-3292).
Time Zone: Mountain (2hr. behind Eastern). **Postal Abbreviation:** NM
Sales Tax: 5.7%.

NORTHERN NEW MEXICO

■■■ SANTA FE

Santa Fe lies at the convergence of the **Santa Fe Trail,** running from Independence, MO, and **El Camino Réal** ("Royal Road"), running from Mexico City. The settlers who traveled these trails have left an indelible imprint on Santa Fe. During the Mexican War, the Americans wrested control of the city from the Mexicans. But the Mexican influence has not died; a 1957 zoning ordinance required all downtown edifices to conform to Spanish Pueblo style. On certain buildings, adobe plaster fails to cover traces of formerly Victorian façades. In spite of the illiberal uniformity of its architecture, free-thinkers and artists have flocked to Santa Fe, where they coexist with Native Americans, retirees, tourists, and jewelry hawkers. A casual *paseo* down Canyon Rd., the local artist's turf, will give you a better feel for the town than a visit to Santa Fe's plaza and museums.

PRACTICAL INFORMATION

Tourist Office: The Santa Fe Convention and Visitors Bureau, 201 W. Mary St. (800-777-2489). Pick up the useful *Santa Fe Visitors Guide.* Open Mon.-Fri. 8am-5pm. There's an **Information Booth** at Lincoln and Palace, open in summer Mon.-Sat. 9am-4:30pm. Visitors from abroad should gallop on down to **Santa Fe Council on International Relations,** 100 E. San Francisco St., in the La Fonda Hotel #281. Open Mon.-Fri. 9am-noon.
Buses: Greyhound, 858 St. Michael's Dr. (471-0008 or 800-231-2222). To: Denver via Raton, NM (4 per day, $66); Taos (2 per day, 1½hr., $15); Albuquerque (4 per day, 1½hr., $10.50). Open Mon.-Fri. 7am-5:30pm and 7:30-9:35pm, Sat.-Sun. 7-9am, 12:30-1:30, 3:30-5, and 7:30-9:35pm.
Trains: Amtrak, nearest station in **Lamy** (466-4511 or 800-872-7245), 20mi. away on Country Rd. 41. Van shuttle to Santa Fe $14. Open daily 9am-5pm.
Public Transportation: Santa Fe Trails (984-6730) has 6 bus routes throughout the city (runs Mon.-Sat. 6:30am-7:30pm). Bus #6 leaves once every ½hr. from the downtown hub, on Sheridan Ave. 1 block from the plaza between Marcy St. and Palace Ave., going to the museums on Camino Lejo. 50¢, ages 6-12 25¢. **Shuttlejack** (982-4311) runs to the Albuquerque airport (13 per day, $20) and the opera (1 per day, $10 round-trip) from downtown hotels. Reserve 1 day in advance.
Car Rental: Budget Rent-a-Car, 1946 Cerrillos Rd. (984-8028). $39 per day, $146 per week. Must be 25 with major credit card. Open Mon.-Fri. 8am-6pm, Sat.-Sun. 8am-5pm.
Taxis: Capital City Taxi, 438-0000. $2 initial charge, $1.30 per mi.

New Age Referral Service: 474-0066. Information clearinghouse for holistic healing services and alternative modes of thought.
Crisis Line: Rape Abuse Help Line, 800-551-0008.
Emergency: 911.
Post Office: 120 S. Federal Pl. (988-6351), in the Montoya Office Bldg. next to the Courthouse. Open Mon.-Fri. 7:30am-5:45pm, Sat. 9am-1pm. **ZIP code:** 87501. **Area code:** 505.

Except for the museums southeast of the city center, most restaurants and important sights in Santa Fe cluster within a few blocks of the **downtown plaza** and inside the loop formed by the **Paseo de Peralta.** Narrow streets make driving troublesome; park your car and pad the pavement. You'll find **parking lots** behind Santa Fe Village, near Sena Plaza, and one block east of the Federal Courthouse near the plaza, or metered spaces on the streets just south of the plaza. Pick up a *Downtown Parking Guide* at the visitors center.

ACCOMMODATIONS AND CAMPING

For the low-down on budget accommodations call the **Santa Fe Detours Accommodations Hotline** (986-0038). Hotels in Santa Fe tend to be very expensive. As early as May, they become swamped with requests for **Fiesta de Santa Fe** week in early September and **Indian Market** the third week of August; make reservations early or plan to sleep standing up. At other times, look around the **Cerrillos Rd.** area for the best prices, but *use caution* and evaluate the motel before checking in. At many of the less expensive motels, bargaining is acceptable. The adobe **Santa Fe Hostel (AAIH/Rucksackers),** 1412 Cerrillos Rd. (988-1153), 1 mi. from the bus station and 2 mi. from the plaza, has a kitchen, a library, large dorm-style beds, and chores. (Office open daily 7am-11pm. $12, nonmembers $15; linen $2. B&B rooms $25-30. Reservations accepted with first night deposit.)

To camp around Santa Fe, you'll need a car. The **Santa Fe National Forest** (988-6940) has campsites and free backcountry camping in the beautiful Sangre de Cristo Mountains. The **Black Canyon Campground,** 8 mi. northeast of Santa Fe on Rte. 475, has 40 sites ($7). Four mi. farther, you can camp for free at one of **Big Tesuque's** seven sites; more free camping lurks at **Aspen Basin** (10 sites, 3mi. beyond Big Tesuque on Rte. 475). Neither Big Tesuque nor Aspen Basin has drinking water. (All 3 open May-Oct.; call the National Forest for info.) Or try **KOA Santa Fe** (982-1419), exit 290 on I-25N; follow the signs. (Sites $15, hookup $15.50-20. Open March-Oct.)

FOOD

Spicy Mexican food served on blue corn tortillas is the staple. The few vegetarian restaurants here are expensive. Better bistros near the plaza dish up their chilis to a mixture of government employees, well-heeled tourists, and local artistic types. Because many serve only breakfast and lunch, you should also look for inexpensive meals along **Cerrillos Rd.** and **St. Michael's Dr.** south of downtown. Or try the fragrant fajitas and fresh lemonade at one of the grill carts in the plaza.

Tomasita's Santa Fe Station, 500 S. Guadalupe (983-5721), near downtown. Locals and tourists line up for their blue corn tortillas and fiery green chili dishes ($4.50-5). Indoor and outdoor seating. Open Mon.-Sat. 11am-10pm.
Josie's, 225 E. Marcy St. (983-5311). The "J" is Spanish—say it like Hosie's. Incredible Mexican-style lunches and multifarious mouth-watering desserts worth the 20-min. wait. Specials $5.50-6.50. Open Mon.-Fri. 11am-3pm.
Tortilla Flats, 3139 Cerrillos Rd. (471-8685). Startlingly bland family atmosphere belies Mexican masterpieces ($4-8). *Huevos rancheros* ($5) make a good breakfast. Open daily 7am-10pm; in winter Sun.-Thurs. 7am-9pm, Fri.-Sat. 7am-10pm.
The Burrito Company, 111 Washington Ave. (98CHILE/982-4453). Excellent Mexican food at reasonable prices. Burrito plates $2.30-4. Open Mon.-Sat. 7:30am-7pm, Sun. 11am-5pm.

SIGHTS

The **Plaza de Santa Fe** is a good starting point for exploring the museums, sanctuaries, and galleries of the city. Since 1609, the plaza has held religious ceremonies, military gatherings, markets, cockfights, and public punishments.

The four museums run by **The Museum of New Mexico** (827-6465; 24 hrs.) have identical hours. A three-day pass bought at one museum admits you to all. (Open daily 10am-5pm; Jan.-Feb. closed Mon. Single visit $4.20, 3-day pass $5.25.) The **Palace of the Governors,** 100 Palace Ave. (827-6483), the oldest public building in the U.S., on the north side of the plaza, was the seat of seven successive governments after its construction in 1610. The *haciendas* palace is now a museum with exhibits on Native American, Southwestern, and New Mexican history. Bonus: the Native American craft and jewelry displays in front of the palace often have cheaper and better quality wares than you'll find in the "Indian Crafts" stores around town. Across Lincoln St., the **Museum of Fine Arts,** 107 W. Palace Ave. (827-4468), inhabits a large adobe building on the northwest corner of the plaza. Exhibits include works by major Southwestern artists, including Georgia O'Keeffe and Edward Weston, an amazing collection of 20th-century Native American art, and temporary exhibitions of more recent works. The other two museums lie southeast of town on **Camino Lejo,** just off Old Santa Fe Trail. The **Museum of International Folk Art,** 706 Camino Lejo (827-6350), 2 mi. south of the plaza, houses the Girard Collection of over 100,000 works of folk art from around the world. A gallery handout will help you to appreciate the fascinating, though jumbled, exhibit. Next door, the **Museum of American Indian Arts and Culture,** 710 Camino Lejo (827-6344), displays Native American photographs and artifacts.

The **Institute of American Indian Arts Museum,** 108 Cathedral Place (988-6281), downtown, houses an extensive collection of contemporary Indian art. (Open Mon.-Sat. 10am-5pm, Sun. noon-5pm; Oct. 1-April 30 Mon.-Fri. 10am-5pm, Sat.-Sun. noon-5pm. Closed Mon. in Jan. and Feb. $4, students and seniors $2, under 16 free.)

Across Palace Ave. from Sena Plaza at the eastern end of San Francisco St., adobe meets Gothic in the **San Francisco Cathedral** (982-5619); the blonde wood and stained glass interior fills with celebrants several times daily. About 5 blocks southeast of the Plaza lies the **San Miguel Mission** (983-3974), on the corner of DeVargas St. and the Old Santa Fe Trail. Built in 1710, the mission is the oldest functioning church in the U.S. Inside, glass windows at the altar look down upon the original "altar" built by Native Americans. (Open Mon.-Sat. 9am-4:30pm, Sun. 1-4:30pm; Nov.-April Mon.-Sat. 10am-4pm, Sun. 1-4:30pm. Free.) The United States' **Oldest House** (983-8206), just down DeVargas St. from the mission, dates from about 1200AD. The house, built by Pueblos, contains the remains of a certain Spaniard named Hidalgo, who allegedly bought a love potion from a woman who lived there and started kissing everything in sight; he was beheaded several days later—so much for free love. (Open Mon.-Sat. 9am-5pm. $1.) Enter through the ice cream parlor and dessert shop (cones $2).

ENTERTAINMENT AND NIGHTLIFE

Native American ceremonies, fairs, arts and crafts shows, rodeos, and tennis tournaments complement Santa Fe's active theater scene and the roster of world-famous musicians who often play in the city's clubs. The **El Farol,** 808 Canyon Rd. (983-9912), features up-and-coming rock and R&B musicians (shows nightly 9:30pm; cover $5). Find the *Santa Fe Reporter*, or *Pasatiempo* magazine, in the Friday *Santa Fe New Mexican,* for more nightlife information.

The **Santa Fe Opera,** P.O. Box 2408, Santa Fe 87504-2408 (982-3855), 7 mi. north of Santa Fe on Rte. 84, performs in the open, against a gorgeous mountain backdrop. Nights are cool here; bring a blanket. The downtown box office is at the El Dorado Hotel, 309 W. San Francisco St. (986-5900), in the gift and news shop. (July-Aug. Mon.-Sat. 9pm. Standing-room $6.) **Shuttlejack** has bus service from downtown for performances (see Practical Information p. 659). The **Santa Fe Chamber Music Festival** (983-2075) celebrates the works of great baroque, classical, and 20th-century composers in the St. Francis Auditorium of the Museum of Fine Arts. (July to mid-Aug. Mon.-Thurs. 8pm, Fri.-Sun. 6pm. Tickets $20-32.)

In August, the nation's largest and most impressive **Indian Market** floods the plaza, as tribes from across the U.S. put up over 500 exhibits of fine arts and crafts. The **Southwestern Association on Indian Affairs** (983-5220) has more info.

Don Diego De Vargas's peaceful reconquest of New Mexico in 1692 marked the end of the 12-year Pueblo Rebellion, now celebrated in the three-day **Fiesta de Santa Fe** (988-7575). Held in early September, the celebration reaches its height with the burning of the 40-ft. *papier-mâché* **Zozobra** "Old Man Gloom." Festivities include street dancing, processions, and political satires. Most events are free. The *New Mexican* publishes a guide and a schedule for the fiesta's events.

■ NEAR SANTA FE

Bandelier National Monument, 40 mi. northwest of Santa Fe (take U.S. 285 to Rte. 4, then follow signs), features some of the most amazing pueblos and cliff dwellings in the state (accessible by 50mi. of hiking trails), as well as 50 square mi. of dramatic mesas and tumbling canyons. The most accessible, **Frijoles Canyon,** is the site of the **visitors center** (672-3861 ext. 518; open daily 8am-6pm, in winter 9am-5:30pm). A 5-mi. hike from the parking lot to the Río Grande descends 600 ft. into the mouth of the canyon, past two waterfalls and fascinating mountain scenery. The **Stone Lions Shrine,** a 12-mi., eight-hour hike, round-trip from the visitors center, features two stone statues of crouching mountain lions and an unexcavated Yapashi pueblo. Unfortunately, the lions have been vandalized; the staff at the visitors center discourage hikers from making the trip, but the trail is still open. A two-day, 20-mi. hike leads from the visitors center past the stone lions to **Painted Cave,** decorated with over 50 Anasazi pictographs, then to the Río Grande. Both hikes are quite strenuous. Free permits are required for backcountry hiking and camping; pick up a topographical map ($9) of the monument area at the visitors center. A less taxing self-guided one-hour tour takes you through pueblo cliff dwellings near the visitors center. (Park entrance $5 per vehicle, $3 per pedestrian; good for 7 days.) The 95-site **Juniper Campground,** ¼ mi. off Rte. 4 at the entrance to the monument, has the area's only camping (sites $8, Golden Age passport ½-price; no reservations).

At the outset of World War II, the U.S. government selected **Los Alamos,** a small mountain village 10 mi. north of Bandelier on NM Loop 4, as the site of the nation's top-secret nuclear weapons development program, the Manhattan Project. Today, nuclear research continues at the **Los Alamos Scientific Laboratory,** a facility perched eerily atop several mesas connected by highway bridges. The public may visit the **Bradbury Museum of Science** (667-4444), at the corner of Central and 15th, for exhibits on the birth of the bomb, strategic nuclear balance, and the technical processes of nuclear weapons testing (open Tues.-Fri. 9am-5pm, Sat.-Mon. 1-5pm; free). The **Los Alamos County Historical Museum,** 1921 Juniper St. (662-6272 or 662-4493), off Central, lets the cat out of the bag on life in Los Alamos during the 1940s when the government's "secret city" was sealed. (Open Mon.-Sat. 9:30am-4:30pm, Sun. 1-5pm; Oct.-April Mon.-Sat. 10am-4pm, Sun. 1-4pm. Free.)

Pecos National Historical Park, located in the hill country 25 mi. southeast of Santa Fe on I-25 and Rte. 63, features ruins of a pueblo and a Spanish mission church. The small park includes an easy 1-mi. hike through various archaeological sites. Especially noteworthy are Pecos's renovated *kivas*—underground ceremonial chambers used in Pueblo rituals—built after the Rebellion of 1680. Off-limits at other ruins, the *kivas* in Pecos are open to the public. (Open daily 8am-dusk; Labor Day-Memorial Day 8am-5pm. Entrance $2 per person, $4 per car.) The monument's **visitors center** (757-6414 or 757-6032) has a small, informative museum and a 10-min. film shown every ½ hour (open daily 8am-6pm; Labor Day-Memorial Day 8am-5pm; free with park entrance). The park is not accessible by public transportation. If you make it there, you can pitch a tent in the backcountry of the **Santa Fe National Forest,** 6 mi. north on Rte. 63 (see Santa Fe Accommodations p. 660).

If you find yourself on the road to Taos, stop by **La Iguana** (852-4540), on Rte. 68 in the town of **Embudo.** The place functions as a café, a gift shop, and an Elvis memorial, serving up Love Me Tender Burrito Plates ($6) and velvet portraits of the King ($13). Forget Las Vegas: ¡Viva La Iguana! (Open daily April-Oct. 10am-6pm.)

■■■ TAOS

The many artists who now inhabit Taos are but the latest in a diverse series of settlers lured by the fertility and stark beauty of the Taos Valley region. First came the Native American tribes, whose pueblos still speckle the valley. In the 17th century, Spanish missionaries and farmers attempted to convert the Native Americans to Christianity while farming alongside them. The 20th century has seen the town invaded by artists, such as Georgia O'Keeffe, who have been captivated and inspired by Taos's untainted beauty. Aspiring artists still flock to the city, but recent trends indicate that the next generation of immigrants may be a mixed bag of pleasure-seekers and spiritualists who come to take advantage of Taos's natural surroundings. Each year a growing number of hikers and skiers infest the nearby mountains; more rafters brave the nearby whitewater of the Río Grande; and more New Agers get the vibe which draws them to the desert.

Practical Information In town, Rte. 68 becomes Paseo del Pueblo. Drivers should park on Placitas Rd., 1 block west of the plaza. Taos's **Chamber of Commerce,** 1139 Paseo del Pueblo Sur (758-3873 or 800-732-8267), just south of town at the Rte. 68/Rte. 64 junction, distributes maps and tourist literature from their office (open daily 9am-6pm; Nov.-April 9am-5pm) and from an information booth in the center of the plaza (no phone; hours vary by season and volunteer availability). **Greyhound** (758-1144 or 800-231-2222), on Paseo del Pueblo Sur near the Chamber of Commerce, provides two buses per day to Albuquerque (3hr., $20), Santa Fe (1½hr., $15), and Denver (8hr., $59). Buy tickets from the bus driver or in the shipping supply store (open Mon.-Sat. 8:30am-6pm). **Faust's Transportation** (758-3410) operates taxis daily 7am-6pm. In an **emergency,** call for the **police** (758-2216) or an **ambulance** (911). Taos's **post office:** 318 Paseo Del Pueblo Norte (758-2081), ¼ mi. north of the plaza (open Mon.-Fri. 8:30am-5pm, Sat. 12:30-2pm); **ZIP code:** 87571; **area code:** 505.

Accommodations and Camping The **Plum Tree Hostel (HI-AYH)** (758-0090 or 800-999-PLUM/7586), 15 mi. south of Taos on Rte. 68 in Pilar, hunkers down next to the Río Grande. Greyhound and airport shuttle buses between Santa Fe and Taos use the hostel as a flagstop. Kitchen facilities are available, as well as discounts on summer arts programs and Río Grande rafting trips; call ahead to reserve a spot. (Office open daily 8-10am and 5-9pm. Dorm beds $9, nonmembers $12. Private rooms with bath for 2 $26, for 3 $29. Bungalows for 1 $20, for 2 $24; must use shared bath in hostel.) A former hippie commune, made famous by the movie *Easy Rider,* **New Buffalo Bed and Breakfast Retreat Center,** P.O. Box 247, Arroyo Hondo 87513 (776-2015), 12 mi. north of Taos off Rte 522 (call for directions), has been reborn as a B&B (rooms $55-65). You can get back to New Buffalo's roots by sleeping in a teepee ($35-45), but no drugs or alcohol are permitted on these grounds where Timothy Leary and Janis Joplin once slept. Both rooms and teepees include a natural-foods breakfast. Relatively inexpensive motel rooms await at the **Taos Motel,** 1799 Paseo de Pueblo Sur (758-2524 or 800-323-6009), on Rte. 68 (singles $34-50, doubles $42-57). Next door, the **Taos RV Park** (758-2524 or 800-323-6009) offers tent sites ($13 for 2 people) and full hookups ($19 for 2 people).

Camping around Taos is easy for those with a car. Up in the mountains on wooded Rte. 64, 20 mi. east of Taos, the **Kit Carson National Forest** operates three campgrounds. **Las Petacas** is free but has no drinking water. **La Sombra** and **Capulin,** on the same road, charge $5. Additionally, four free campgrounds line Rte. 150 north of town. **Backcountry camping** requires no permit in the forest. For more info, including maps of area campgrounds, contact the **forest service office** (758-6200; open Mon.-Fri. 8am-4:30pm), or visit their visitors center (open daily 9am-4:30pm), on Rte. 64 west of town—next to an awesome campground near the **Río Grande Gorge Bridge** (758-8851; sites with water and porta-potty $7). At sunset, check out the incredible view from the bridge.

Food Restaurants congregate at Taos Plaza and Bent St. **El Patio de Taos Restaurant and Cantina** (758-2121), on Teresina Ln. between Taos Plaza and Bent St., serves excellent New Mexican and Mexican cuisine out of the oldest building in Taos (lunch entrees $7-12; dinner entrees $8-13; open daily 11:30am-10pm). **Murray's Deli and Takeout,** 115 E. Plaza St. (758-4205), in Taos Plaza, caters to the lover of kraut and potato pancakes (3 for $3), but the sandwich menu ($6.50-7.25) ranges well beyond the wurst (open Mon.-Sat. 8am-8pm, Sun. 9am-5pm). In the rear of **Amigo's Natural Foods,** 326 Pueblo Rd. (758-8493), across from Jack Donner's, lurks a small, holistic deli which serves such nutritionally correct dishes as tofu on polygranulated bread ($3.75; open Mon.-Sat. 9am-7pm, Sun. 11am-5pm).

Sights and Activities Many early Taos paintings hang at the **Harwood Foundation's Museum,** 238 Ledoux St. (758-9826), off Placitas Rd. (open Mon.-Fri. noon-5pm, Sat. 10am-4pm; free). Other galleries, with works by notable locals such as R.C. Gorman, can be found in the **Plaza**, on **Kit Carson Rd.** or **Ledoux St.,** and in the village of **El Prado,** just north of Taos. Taos's galleries range from high-quality operations of international renown to upscale curio shops. The **Taos Arts Festival** celebrates local art in early October each year.

Though not a part of the local-gallery circuit, the Mission of **St. Francis of Assisi,** Ranchos de Taos Plaza (758-2754), displays a "miraculous" painting that changes into a shadowy figure of Christ when the lights go out (open Mon.-Sat. 9am-4pm; $1 donation). Exhibits of Native American art, including a collection of beautiful black-on-black pottery, grace the **Millicent Rogers Museum** (758-2462), north of El Prado St., 4 mi. north of Taos off Rte. 522. (Open daily 10am-5pm; Nov.-March. closed Mon. $4, students and seniors $3, ages 6-16 $2, families $8.) A visit to the **Mabel Dodge Luhan Home** (758-9456) provides a quiet retreat from the tourist-packed plaza. The salon hostess drew such luminaries as D.H. Lawrence, Robinson Jeffers, and Jean Toomer to Taos. ($2.50 donation includes a cup of coffee or tea.)

Taos Pueblo (758-9593), remarkable for its five-story pink-and-white adobe mission church, and striking silhouette, is one of the last inhabited pueblos; thus much of the pueblo remains off-limits to visitors. (Open daily 8:30am-4:30pm. $5 per car, $3 per pedestrian, students $1, under 12 50¢. Camera permit $5, sketch permit $10, painting permit $15.) Feast days highlight beautiful tribal dances; **San Gerónimo's Feast Days** (Sept. 29-30) also feature a fair and races. Contact the **tribal office** (758-9593) for schedules of dances and other info. Best known for its sparkling pottery molded from mica and clay, **Picuris Pueblo** (587-2519), 20 mi. south of Taos on Rte. 75 near Peñasco, is smaller, less-touristed, and somewhat more accessible. Ask for a guide to Northern New Mexican Indian pueblos at the Taos Visitors Center (see Practical Information, above).

The state's premier ski resort, **Taos Ski Valley** (776-2291; 800-776-1111 for lodging info; 776-2916 for ski conditions), about 5 mi. north of town on Rte. 150, offers powder conditions in bowl sections and short but steep downhill runs which rival Colorado's. Reserve a room well in advance if you plan to come during the winter holiday season. (Lift tickets $38, equipment rental $12 per day.) In summer, the ski-valley area becomes a hiker's paradise.

Taos hums with every New Age service on earth: vibrasound relaxation, drum therapy, harmony massage, and cranial therapy for starters. **Taos Drums** (800-424-DRUM/3786), 5 mi. south of the plaza on Rte. 68, features the world's largest collection of Native American drums (open Mon.-Sat. 9am-6pm, Sun. 11am-6pm). A bulletin board outside **Merlin's Garden,** 127 Bent St. (758-0985), lists activities such as drum therapy and massage (open when Jupiter aligns with Mars).

■■■ ALBUQUERQUE

The Anasazi tribes settled here nearly 2000 years ago and created sophisticated transportation networks. Ever since, Albuquerque has been considered a stopover on the way to another destination. In search of the legendary seven cities of gold, the infamous Spaniard Coronado and his entourage camped here for the winter. Over the years, Spanish settlers and later the United States government routed major transportation lines through Albuquerque; Rte. 66 still splits the city in two. Smart travelers should linger long enough to enjoy the mellow neighborhood near the University, the adobe old town, and the dramatic Sandía Mountains.

PRACTICAL INFORMATION

Tourist Office: Albuquerque Convention and Visitors Bureau, 121 Tijeras N.E., 1st floor (243-3696 or 800-284-2282). Free maps and the useful *The Art of Visiting Albuquerque.* Open Mon.-Fri. 8am-5pm. After hours, call for recorded events info. **Old Town Visitors Center** (243-3215), at Plaza Don Luis on Romero N.W. across from the church. Open Mon.-Sat. 9am-7pm, Sun. 10am-5pm. They also have an information booth at the airport. Open Mon.-Sat. 9:30am-8pm. **Gay and Lesbian Information Line,** 266-8041. Open daily 7am-10pm.

Airport: Albuquerque International, 2200 Sunport Blvd. S.E. (842-4366), south of downtown. Take bus #50 from Yale Blvd. and Central Ave. **Checkered Airport Express** (765-1234) shuttles into the city (around $8). A taxi downtown costs under $10.

Trains: Amtrak, 214 1st St. S.W. (842-9650 or 800-872-7245). Open daily 9:30am-6pm. 1 train per day to: Los Angeles (13hr., $91); Kansas City (17hr., $157); Santa Fe (1hr. to Lamy, $22; 15min. shuttle to Santa Fe, $14); Flagstaff (5hr., $82). Reservations required.

Buses: Greyhound (247-0246 or 800-231-2222) and **TNM&O Coaches** (242-4998) run from 300 2nd St. S.W., 3 blocks south of Central Ave. Both lines go to: Santa Fe (4 per day, 1½hr., $10.50); Flagstaff (4 per day, 6hr., $55); Oklahoma City (4 per day, 12hr., $56); Denver (4 per day, 10hr., $61); Phoenix (4 per day, 9hr., $45); Los Angeles (4 per day, 18hr., $79).

Public Transportation: Sun-Tran Transit, 601 Yale Blvd. S.E. (843-9200; open Mon.-Fri. 7am-5pm). Most buses run Mon.-Sat. 6am-6pm. Pick up maps at visitors centers, the transit office, or the main library. Fare 75¢, seniors and ages 5-18 25¢.

Taxis: Albuquerque Cab, 883-4888. $3.60 first mi., $1.60 per additional mi.

Car Rental: Rent-a-Wreck, 501 Yale Blvd. S.E. (242-9556 or 800-247-9556). Cars with A/C from $25 per day with 150 free mi.; 20¢ per additional mi. $140 per week. Insurance $11 per day. Must be 21 with credit card; under 25 surcharge $3 per day. Open daily 8am-5pm.

Equipment Rental: Mountains & Rivers, 2320 Central Ave. S.E. (268-4876), across from the university. Rents camping equipment and canoes ($35 per day). Open Mon.-Fri. 9:30am-6:30pm, Sat. 9am-5pm. Deposit required; reservations recommended.

Crisis Lines: Rape Crisis Center, 1025 Hermosa S.E. (266-7711). Center open Mon.-Fri. 8am-noon and 1-5pm; hotline 24 hrs.

Emergency: 911.

Post Office: 1135 Broadway N.E. (245-9469). Open Mon.-Fri. 8am-6pm. **ZIP code:** 87104. **Area code:** 505.

Central Ave. and the **Santa Fe railroad tracks** create four quadrants used in city addresses: Northeast Heights (N.E.), Southeast Heights (S.E.), North Valley (N.W.), and South Valley (S.W.). The all-adobe campus of the **University of New Mexico (UNM)** stretches along Central Ave. N.E. from University Ave. to Carlisle St.

ACCOMMODATIONS AND CAMPING

Cheap motels line Central Ave., even near downtown—*use caution; many are dangerous.* Avoid decrepit motels or any place which seems to house transients; at night, look for bright, outdoor lighting. The **Route 66 Youth Hostel,** 1012 Central

Ave. S.W. (247-1813), at 10th St., offers bunks in sparse but clean rooms, as well as beautiful, newly-renovated private rooms. (Well-stocked kitchen; free food. Office open daily 7-11am and 4-11pm. Check-out 11am. Chores required. Bunks $11 with any affiliation. Private singles with shared bath $16, doubles $21. Linen $1. Key deposit $5. No reservations.) **University Lodge,** 3711 Central Ave. N.E. (266-7663), near campus, has your basic motel rooms and your basic motel pool (singles $24, doubles $30). **Lorlodge West Motel,** 1020 Central Ave. S.W. (247-4023), sets you up in a clean room with free local calls (singles $24.50, doubles $29.50).

Coronado State Park Campground (867-5589), 1 mi. west of Bernalillo on Rte. 44, about 20 mi. north of Albuquerque on I-25, provides a unique camping experience near the haunting Sandía Mountains. Adobe shelters on the sites provide a respite from the heat. (Toilets, showers, drinking water. 1-week max. stay. Open daily 7am-10pm. Sites $7, with hookup $11. No reservations.) The nearby **Albuquerque West Campground,** 5739 Ouray Rd. N.W. (831-1912), isn't scenic but it has a swimming pool. From downtown, take I-40W to the Coors Blvd. N. exit, or catch bus #15. (Tent sites for 2 $14.50, $2 per additional person.)

FOOD AND NIGHTLIFE

Tasty, inexpensive eateries border the University of New Mexico. Browse and graze at **Best Price Books and Coffee,** 1800 Central Ave. S.E. (842-0624), where you can chase pastries ($1-2.50), sandwiches ($3-5), and gourmet burritos ($2-3), with 12 different kinds of coffee ($1) or a mind-blowing "Psuper Psonic Psyber Tonic" ($3.50)—what's in this stuff, dude? (Open daily 7am-11pm.) With a soft-strumming guitarist and outdoor seating, **El Patio,** 142 Harvard St. S.E. (268-4245), beckons passersby to sit, relax, and down a few enchiladas (Mexican plates $3-6; open Mon.-Sat 11am-9:30pm, Sun. noon-9:30pm). The homemade ice cream at (hungry, hungry) **Hippo Ice Cream,** 120 Harvard St. S.E. (266-1997), could turn you into one. (1 scoop $1.10. Open Mon.-Thurs. 7:30am-10:30pm, Fri.-Sat. 7:30am-11:30pm, Sun. 9am-9pm.) **Olympia Café,** 2210 Central Ave. (266-5222), serves gyros and souvlaki (each $3.25), as well as vegetarian dishes and combination platters ($5-7); it's tasty, but greasy (open Mon.-Fri. 11am-10pm, Sat. noon-10pm). Crowds materialize for a clean lunch at the **M and J Sanitary Tortilla Factory,** 403 2nd St. S.W. (242-4890), at Lead St. (entrees $4-6; open Mon.-Sat. 9am-4pm).

Dig in your spurs at **Caravan East,** 7605 Central Ave. N.E. (265-7877), "where there is always a dancin' partner," and there's always live music. (Fri.-Sat. $3 cover. Drink specials for women daily 5:30-7:30pm. Open daily 4:30pm-2am.) Urban music lovers hear rock, blues, and reggae bands at **Dingo Bar,** 313 Gold St. S.W. (246-0663), where drafts run $2-3.50 (Fri.-Sat. after 8pm cover $2-8, depending on the band; open daily 4pm-1:30am). Get into the Dingo and five other bars for one $5 cover charge on the "Downtown Bar Crawl"; pay at any of the bars. **EJ's** (268-2233), at the intersection of Yale Blvd. and Silver St., satisfies late-night caffeine cravings in an airy coffeehouse with live music. (Open Mon.-Thurs. 7am-11pm, Fri. 7am-midnight, Sat. 8am-midnight, Sun. 8am-9:30pm.)

SIGHTS

Located just north of Central Ave. and east of Rio Grande Blvd., 1 mi. south of I-40, **Old Town** clusters around Albuquerque's Spanish plaza. In addition to shops, restaurants, and Native American art galleries, Old Town features three great museums. New Mexican art, Albuquerque history, and various temporary exhibits are displayed at the **Albuquerque Museum of Art and History,** 2000 Mountain Rd. N.W. (242-4600; open Tues.-Sun. 9am-5pm; free). The **Rattlesnake Museum,** 202 San Felipe N.W. (242-6569), houses the world's most diverse display of rattlesnakes (open daily 10am-8:30pm; $2.50, children $1). Spike and Alberta, two statuesque dinosaurs, greet you outside the **New Mexico Museum of Natural History,** 1801 Mountain Rd. (841-8837). Inside the museum, exhibits present the geologic and evolutionary history of New Mexico. (Open daily 9am-5pm. $4.20, students and seniors $3.15, children $1.) While in Old Town tour the beautiful adobe **San Felipe de Neri Church;** don't miss the Civil War cannons out back.

The **National Atomic Museum,** 20358 Wyoming Blvd. (845-6670), on Kirkland Air Force Base, tells the story of "Little Boy" and "Fat Man," the atomic bombs dropped on Hiroshima and Nagasaki. *Ten Seconds that Shook the World,* a 1-hour documentary on the making of the atomic bomb, shows daily; call for times. (Call to make tour arrangements. Open daily 9am-5pm. Free.) The Air Force base is a few mi. southeast of downtown, east of I-25. Ask at the visitor control gate on Wyoming Blvd. for a museum visitor's pass, and be prepared to show *several* forms of ID.

The **Indian Pueblo Cultural Center,** 2401 12th St. N.W. (843-7270), just north of I-40 (take bus #36 from downtown), provides a sensitive introduction to the Pueblo reservations (open daily 9am-5:30pm; $2.50, students $1, seniors $1.50). The center's cafeteria hosts Pueblo dance performances on weekends at 11am and 2pm; stay to eat authentic Pueblo food (fry-bread $1.75; open daily 7:30am-3:30pm).

■ NEAR ALBUQUERQUE

Located at the edge of suburbia on Albuquerque's west side, **Petroglyph National Monument** (897-8814) features over 15,000 images drawn on lava rocks by Native Americans and Spanish settlers over the course of centuries. Short paved trails access small sections of the park's **Boca Negra** Unit, but most of the area can be explored only by off-trail hiking. Take the Coors Blvd. exit on I-40 north to Atrisco Rd., or take bus #15 to Coors Blvd. and transfer to bus #93. (Open daily 9am-6pm; off season 8am-5pm. Entrance free. Parking $1, weekends and holidays $2.)

The **Sandía Peaks** were named by the Spanish for the pink color they turn at sunset (*sandía* means watermelon). Take Tramway Rd. from either I-25 or I-40 to the **Sandía Peak Aerial Tramway** (296-9585, or 298-8518 for recorded info), the world's longest aerial tramway. The thrilling ride to the top of **Sandía Crest** allows you to ascend the west face of Sandía Peak and gaze out over Albuquerque, the Río Grande Valley, and western New Mexico; the ascent is especially striking at sunset. (1½-hr. trip. Departs every 20-30min. daily 9am-10pm; Sept. 2-May 25 Mon.-Tues. and Thurs.-Sun. 9am-9pm, Wed. 5-9pm; during ski season Mon.-Tues. and Thurs.-Fri. 9am-9pm, Wed. noon-9pm, Sat.-Sun. 8am-9pm. Round-trip $13, seniors and ages 6-12 $9.50; combination chairlift and tram ticket $17/$13.50.) A 7-mi. toll-road (Rte. 536) leads to the summit of **Sandía Crest,** where the dazzling 1½-mi. ridge hike to **Sandía Peak** (10,678ft.) begins.

The **Sandía Ski Area** provides a beautiful 58-mi., day-long driving loop. Take I-40 east up Tijeras Canyon 17 mi., then turn north onto Rte. 44. The road winds through lovely forests of Piñon and Ponderosa pines, oaks, and spruce, then descends 18 mi. through a gorgeous canyon, to Bernalillo. Rangers lead guided hikes on Saturdays; you'll need reservations for the challenging winter snowshoe hikes (242-9052). During the summer, hiking and mountain-biking trails are often open to the public only during specific hours; call for details.

■■■ CHACO CANYON

Sun-scorched and water-poor, **Chaco Canyon** seems an improbable setting for the first great settlement of the Anasazi people. They imported most of their food, but also developed complex irrigation techniques and constructed five-story rock buildings while some Europeans were still living in wooden hovels. By the 11th century, the canyon residents had set up a major trade network with dozens of small satellite towns in the surrounding desert. However, around 1150AD the system collapsed; with no food and little water, the Chacoans left the canyon for greener pastures.

Chaco Canyon's ruins are the best-preserved sites in the Southwest. **Pueblo Bonito,** the canyon's largest town, demonstrates the skill of Anasazi masons. Among many low structures, one four-story-tall wall still stands. Nearby **Chetro Ketl** houses one of the canyon's largest *kivas,* a prayer room used in Chacoan religious rituals.

Chaco Canyon is now part of the **Chaco Culture National Historical Park.** The **visitors center** (505-988-6727 or 505-786-7014), at the east end of the canyon, contains an excellent free museum which exhibits Anasazi art and architecture and explains the sophisticated economic network by which the Chacoan Anasazi traded with the smaller Anasazi tribes of modern Colorado and northern Mexico. (Open daily 8am-6pm, Labor Day-Memorial Day 8am-5pm. $2 per person, $4 per carload.)

Camping in Chaco requires a backcountry permit and $8. Arrive by 11am; there are only 68 sites. You can also make Chaco a daytrip from **Gallup,** 92 mi. away, where cheap accommodations come easy. Bring water, since the visitors center occasionally runs dry. Be sure to fill up your car's tank; there is no gas in the park.

The canyon lies 160-mi. and a 3½-hr. drive northwest of Albuquerque and 120 mi. south of Durango, CO. At the turn of the century, it took a government archaeologist almost a year to get here from Washington, DC. Today's visitor takes **Rte. 57,** which covers 29 unpaved mi. to reach the park from the north (turn off Rte. 44 at the tiny town of **Nageezi**) and runs 60 mi. (40mi. paved!) from I-40 in the south.

Just west of the Continental Divide on Rte. 53, 12 mi. southeast of the Navajo town of **Ramah,** sits **Inscription Rock National Monument** (505-783-4226), where Native Americans, Spanish *conquistadores,* and later pioneers left their marks while traveling through the scenic valley. Self-guided trails allow access to the rock and ruins deeper in the park. The **visitors center** includes a small museum as well as several dire warnings against emulating the graffiti of old (open daily 9am-7pm; in winter 9am-5pm). For those unable to resist the urge to inscribe, an alternate boulder is provided. Trails close 1 hr. before the visitors center.

SOUTHERN NEW MEXICO

■■■ GILA CLIFF DWELLINGS AND SILVER CITY

The absolutely spectacular **Gila Cliff Dwellings National Monument** (536-9461), preserves over 40 stone and timber rooms carved into the cliff's natural caves by the Pueblo around 1200AD. Ten to 15 families lived here, farming the mesa top, until they mysteriously disappeared in the early 1300s. Accessible only by a 44-mi. drive on Rte. 15 from Silver City in the southwest part of the state, the stunning road to the park climbs up and down mountains to the canyon of the Gila River. The **visitors center** (536-9461), 1 mi. from the dwellings at the end of Rte. 15, has maps and information and serves as the trailhead for a picturesque 1-mi. round-trip hike to the dwellings (open daily 8am-5pm, off season 8am-4:30pm). The surrounding **Gila National Forest** (388-8201) supplies more great hiking, as well as **free backcountry camping.** For info before you go, write to the District Ranger, Rte. 11, Box 100, Silver City 88601.

Beds and restaurants await in **Silver City,** 80 mi. west of I-25 on Rte. 152W. The **Chamber of Commerce,** 1103 N. Hudson (538-3785), makes a good starting point for a trip to the area (open Mon.-Sat. 9am-5pm, Sun. noon-5pm). Twice daily, **Silver Stage Lines** (388-2586 or 800-522-0162) has bus service to Silver City from the El Paso airport ($33, home pickup $2 extra). **Las Cruces Shuttle Service** (800-288-1784) offers daily trips between Silver City and Deming (4 per day, $15), Las Cruces (4 per day, $25), and El Paso (3 per day, $32). Gila's and Silver City's **area code:** 505.

The squeaky-clean hostel at **Carter House (HI-AYH),** 101 N. Cooper St. (388-5485), has separate men's and women's dorms, a kitchen, and laundry facilities; a B&B occupies the upstairs. Check-in is officially 4-9pm; if you're going to be later than 9pm, call ahead. ($12, nonmembers $15. B&B doubles from $59.) The **Palace Hotel,** 106 W. Broadway (388-1811), has beautiful antique rooms (doubles from $33). Bring a healthy appetite to the **Red Barn Steakhouse,** 708 Silver Heights Blvd.

(538-5666), for sandwiches ($5) and an all-you-can-eat salad bar (open Mon.-Sat. 11am-10pm, Sun. 11am-9pm). The **Silver City Museum,** 312 W. Broadway (538-5921), houses excellent exhibits on the history of the town and an unusual collection of collections—local residents' treasure troves, past and present, include one man's post-WWII neckties, another couple's buttons, and the exhibit curator's Def Leppard paraphernalia (open Tues.-Fri. 9am-4:30pm, Sat.-Sun. 10am-4pm; free). The **New Mexico Cowboy Poetry Gathering** convenes in Silver City every August.

Truth or Consequences

In 1950, the popular radio show "Truth or Consequences" sought to celebrate its tenth anniversary by persuading a small town to change its name to that of the program. Surprisingly, several towns across the U.S. volunteered. The producers chose a town called Hot Springs, NM—T or C, NM was born. Although the town is not as entertaining as its story, the surrounding area includes a great collection of natural hot springs. T or C lies 60 mi. west of Gila Cliff Dwellings National Monument on I-25, an impressive 150-mi. drive south of Albuquerque. If you want to spend several days at the Monument, T or C's **Riverbend Hot Springs Hostel (HI-AYH),** 100 Austin St. (894-6183) offers a place to soak your weary bones and rest your weary head; the hostel's large earthen tubs on the balcony are filled twice daily with healing water from T or C's hot springs. Located on the banks of the Rio Grande, the hostel offers tours to the holy grounds of the Apache and rafting trips on the river. (Teepees $9, tent sites $7.50 per person, dorm beds $11. Rooms for couples $25, or for the same price try the "love boat" anchored on the river right outside the hostel.)

■■■ WHITE SANDS

Remember the sandbox? Located on Rte. 70, 15 mi. southwest of Alamogordo and 52 mi. northeast of Las Cruces, **White Sands National Monument** contains the world's largest gypsum sand dunes, covering 300 sq. mi. of beach without ocean. Located in the Tularosa Basin between the Sacramento and San Andres mountains, the dunes were formed when rainwater dissolved gypsum in a nearby mountain and then collected in the basin's Lake Lucero. As the desert weather evaporated the lake, the gypsum crystals were left behind and eventually formed the continually growing sand dunes. Hiking, walking, or just rolling through the dunes provides hours of mindless fun; the brilliant white sand is particularly awe-inspiring at sunset. Unfortunately, the basin is also home to a missile test range and the **Trinity Site,** where the world's first atomic bomb was detonated in July 1945. Although a visit to Trinity won't make your hair fall out, the road to the park is still subject to closure, usually for no more than two hours, when missiles are tested. You'll find the **visitors center,** P.O. Box 1086, Holloman AFB, 88330 (505-479-6124), as you enter the park from Rte. 70. (Open 8am-7pm; Labor Day-Memorial Day 8am-4:30pm. Dunes drive open 7am-9pm; off season 7am-sunset. $2, $4 per vehicle. Disabled access.)

To use the park's free backcountry **campsites,** you must register at the park headquarters. More free backcountry camping can be found at **Lincoln National Forest** (505-434-7200), 13 mi. to the east. **Aguirre Springs** (505-525-4300), 30 mi. to the west, claims to have free camping, but you pay $3 to enter. For info contact **Forest Supervisor,** Lincoln National Forest, 1101 New York Ave., Alamogordo 88310. **Oliver Lee Memorial State Park** (505-437-8284), 10 mi. south of Alamogordo on U.S. 54 then 5 mi. east on Dog Canyon Rd., has a campground at the canyon mouth on the west face of the Sacramento Mountains. (Sites $7, with wattage $11. Park open daily 6am-9pm; **visitor center** open daily 9am-4pm. Entrance $3 per vehicle.)

If you're not camping, make nearby **Alamogordo** your base. Several motels and restaurants front White Sands Blvd., including ol' faithful: **Motel 6,** 251 Panorama Blvd. (505-434-5970), off Rte. 70, with clean, sparse rooms, TV, HBO, a pool, free local calls, and a view (singles $26, doubles $32). **All American Inn,** 508 S. White

Sands Blvd. (505-437-1850), has clean rooms at reasonable prices, A/C, and a pool (singles $28, doubles $30). Reach for the stars at the **Space Center** (505-437-2840 or 800-545-4021), 2 mi. northeast of U.S. 54 in a glass building set against the mountains. (Open daily 9am-6pm; Sept.-May 9am-5pm. Museum and OmniMax theater $5.25, seniors and ages 6-12 $3.50, family rate $15.50.)

■■■ CARLSBAD CAVERNS

Imagine the surprise of the first Europeans to wander through southeastern New Mexico when 250,000 bats appeared at dusk. The legendary bat population of Carlsbad Caverns led to the discovery of the caverns at the turn of the century, when curious frontiersmen tracked the bats to their home. Once there, miners mapped the cave in search of bat *guano,* an excellent fertilizer found in 100-ft. deposits in the cave. By 1923, the caverns had been designated a national park, and herds of tourists were flocking to this desolate region. **Carlsbad Caverns National Park** marks one of the world's largest and oldest cave systems, and even the most jaded spelunker will stand in awe of the unusual creations beneath the surface.

Practical Information The **Carlsbad Visitors Center** (785-2232; 24-hr. recording 785-2107) has replaced dung-mining with a gift shop, nursery, and kennel. For 50¢ you can rent a small radio that transmits a guided tour. (Open daily 8am-7pm; Labor Day-Memorial Day 8am-5:30pm.) **White's City,** a tiny, expensive town, which seems to be run by Best Western, lies on U.S. 62/180 20 mi. southeast of Carlsbad and 7 mi. from the caverns along steep, winding mountain roads and serves as the access point to the park. Flash floods occasionally close the roads, so call ahead. El Paso, TX is the nearest major city, 150 mi. to the west past **Guadalupe Mountains National Park** (see p. 539), 35 mi. southwest of White's City. **Greyhound,** in cooperation with **TNM&O Coaches** (887-1108), runs two buses per day to White's City from El Paso ($29, $55.10 round-trip) or Carlsbad ($6.30 round-trip). Some of these routes use White's City only as a flag stop. White's City's **post office:** 23 Carlsbad Caverns Hwy. (785-2220), next to the Best Western Visitors Center (open Mon.-Fri. 8am-noon and 1-5pm); **ZIP code:** 88268; **area code:** 505.

Camping, Accommodations, and Food The **Park Entrance Campground** (785-2291), just outside the park entrance, provides water, showers, restrooms, and a pool (tent sites or full hookup $16; up to 6 people). Backcountry camping is free in the park; get a permit at the visitors center. For more nearby camping, see Guadalupe Mountains National Park, TX on p. 539. The **Carlsbad Caverns International Hostel** (785-2291), in White's City, has six-bed rooms, a pool, and a spa. HI-AYH membership is required (open 24 hrs.; $14.40). Drive to **Carlsbad,** 20 mi. north, for cheap motels. **La Caverna Motel,** 224 S. Canal (885-4151), requires reservations in summer (singles $22, doubles $24). Even less expensive motels lie farther down the road. If the bat *guano* hasn't ruined your appetite, feed it at **Lucy's,** 701 S. Canal (887-7714). Good, cheap Mexican dinners run $3-10. (Open Mon.-Sat. 11am-9:30pm.)

Sights Backcountry hiking is allowed in the Carlsbad Caverns National Park, but talk to rangers first. Most visitors take tours into the caves. The **Natural Entrance Tour** and the **Big Room Tour** are self-guided and take one hour each; plaques guide you along the way. The Big Room Tour, open 8:30am-5pm, has some wheelchair accessible sections. The Natural Entrance Tour, a more strenuous journey, is open 8:30am-3:30pm. ($5 each, Golden Age Passport holders $2.50, ages 6-15 $3.) The ranger-guided **King's Palace Tour** goes through four scenic rooms in one-and-a-half hours (tours on the hr.; $5, Golden Age Passport holders and ages 6-15 $2.50). Plan your visit to the caves for the late afternoon, and see the magnificent nightly **bat flight.** A ranger talk precedes the amazing ritual, in which an army of hungry bats pours out of the cave at a rate of 6000 per minute. (May-Oct. daily just before sunset.) Early-birds can catch them on the pre-dawn return.

For a rugged caving experience, visit the undeveloped **Slaughter Canyon Cave** (785-2232), formerly **New Cave.** Take a lot of energy and a car (there's no public transportation); the parking lot is 23 mi. down a dirt road off U.S. 62/180S, and the cave entrance is a steep, strenuous ½ mi. from the lot. Flashlight tours (bring your own flashlight) traverse the difficult and slippery terrain inside; there are no paved trails or handrails. Call to reserve at least two days in advance; the park limits the number of people allowed inside. (Tours 2hr., 1¼mi., 2 per day; Labor Day-Memorial Day Sat.-Sun. only. $8, Golden Age Passport holders and ages 6-15 $4.)

THE PACIFIC NORTHWEST

The drive of "manifest destiny" brought 19th-century pioneers to the Pacific Northwest, some of the most beautiful and awe-inspiring territory in the United States. Lush rainforests, snow-capped peaks, and the deepest lake on the continent all reside in this corner of the country. Oregon's Mt. Hood and Columbia River Gorge, Washington's Cascade Mountains, miles and miles of the Pacific Crest Trail, and a long, stormy coast inhabited by sea lions and giant redwoods draw rugged individualists and escapist urbanites. Moving up from California, Coastal Highway 101 hugs the Pacific Ocean, rising above the mist with over 200 miles of salty spray and breathtaking scenery.

Settled like jewels amid the wet and wild lands of the Pacific Northwest, the cities of this region sparkle with all the urban flair of their Northeastern counterparts. But unlike New York, Washington, DC, or Boston, the cosmopolitan communities of Seattle and Portland have spectacular mountain ranges in their backyards. The Northwestern traveler can hike the Cascade Range by day and club-hop by night, or eat breakfast at Pike Place Market in Seattle and have dinner deep in the rainforest of the Olympic Peninsula.

For more comprehensive coverage of the Pacific Northwest, consult the handsome and intrepid *Let's Go: Alaska & The Pacific Northwest*..

Pacific Specifics

Authors: Raymond Carver, Bernard Malamud, Alice Munro, Jack Kerouac (*The Dharma Bums*), John McPhee (*The Control of Nature*)
Artists: Emily Carr, Morris Graves, Mark Tobey, Kenneth Callahan.
Cuisine: dungeness crabs, salmon, any seafood, fruit, wine, berries.
Microbreweries: Fulton Pub and Brewery, Seattle Brewers, Full Sail, Widmer, BridgePort, Deschutes, Edgefield, Eugene City, Liberty, Mt. Hood, Oregon Trail, Portland, Star, Rainier, Redhook, Hale's Ales, Maritime Pacific, Onalaska, Pike Place, Roslyn, Thomas Kemper, Yakima Brewing and Malting Co., Pyramid Ales/Hart Brewing Co., Rogue Ales/Oregon Brewing Co.
Native Americans: Yakima, Chinook, Salish, Makah, Wasco, Tenino, Tillamook, Klamath, Coos.
Music: Jimi Hendrix, Seattle "grunge," Nirvana, Pearl Jam, Soundgarden.
Film and TV: *Sleepless in Seattle, Singles, Harry and the Hendersons, Frasier.*
Climate: Cool and rainy to the west of the Cascades, hot and dry to the east.
Geography: Pacific coast, rainforest, Cascade Mountains, high desert.

Washington

Geographically, politically, and culturally, Washington is divided by the Cascade Mountains. The personality difference between the state's eastern and western halves is pervasive and long-standing. To "wet-siders" who live near Washington's coast, the term "dry-siders" conjures images of rednecks tearing through the eastern deserts and farmlands in pickup trucks. In the minds of dry-siders, the residents of Seattle and the rest of western Washington might be yuppified, liberal freaks too wealthy to respect rural livelihoods or wildlife. These stereotypes are colorful, but fail to capture the full range of political views represented by Washingtonians, who are known for an independent frame of mind. Like its ideological spectrum, Wash-

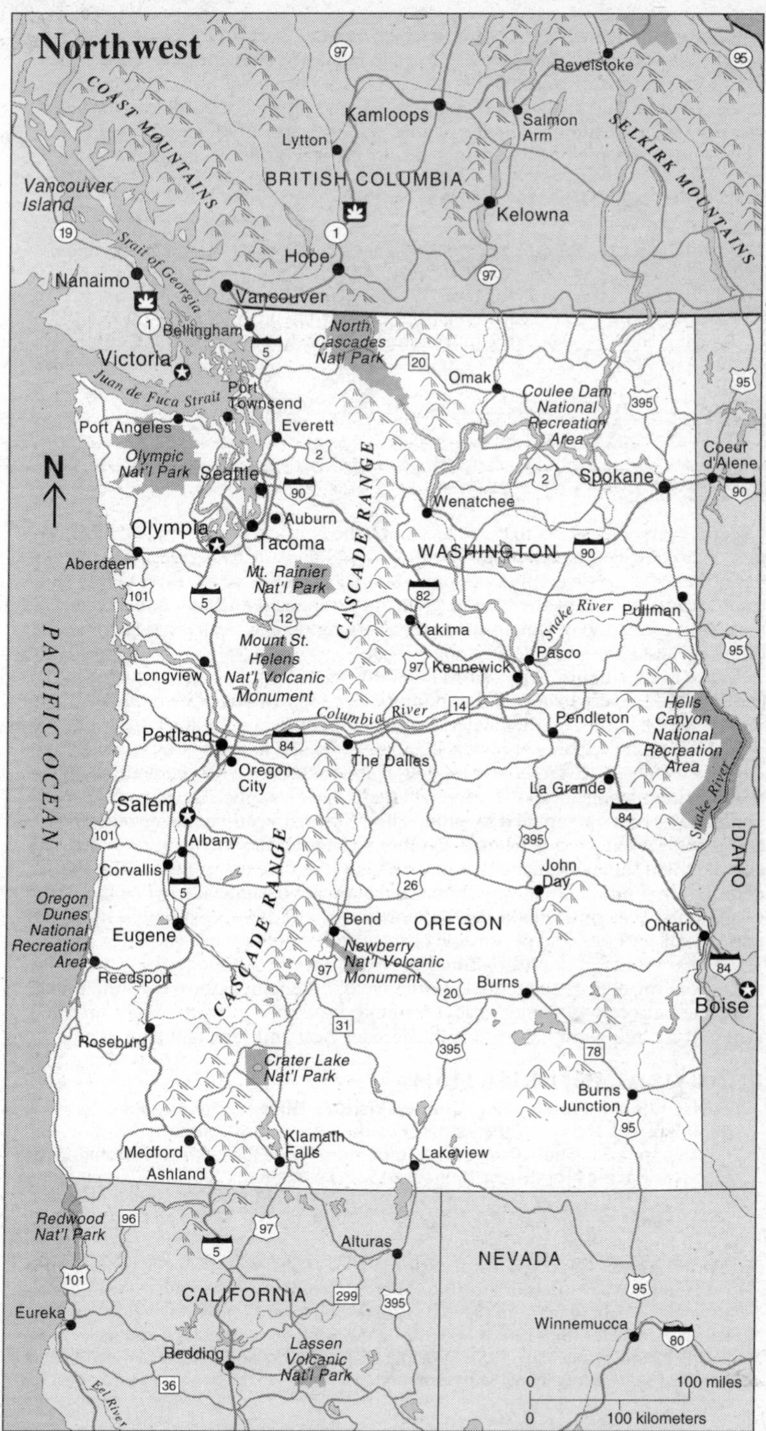
Northwest
COAST MOUNTAINS
Kamloops
Revelstoke
Salmon Arm
Lytton
BRITISH COLUMBIA
SELKIRK MOUNTAINS
Vancouver Island
Kelowna
Hope
Strait of Georgia
Nanaimo
Vancouver
Bellingham
North Cascades Nat'l Park
Victoria
Juan de Fuca Strait
Port Townsend
Omak
Coulee Dam National Recreation Area
Port Angeles
Everett
Olympic Nat'l Park
Seattle
Coeur d'Alene
Spokane
N
Wenatchee
Auburn
Olympia
Tacoma
CASCADE RANGE
WASHINGTON
Aberdeen
Mt. Rainier Nat'l Park
Snake River
Pullman
Yakima
PACIFIC OCEAN
Mount St. Helens Nat'l Volcanic Monument
Pasco
Kennewick
Longview
Columbia River
Hells Canyon National Recreation Area
Pendleton
Portland
The Dalles
Oregon City
La Grande
Salem
Albany
Corvallis
John Day
Oregon Dunes National Recreation Area
Bend
OREGON
Eugene
Ontario
Newberry Nat'l Volcanic Monument
Reedsport
Burns
Boise
IDAHO
Roseburg
Crater Lake Nat'l Park
Burns Junction
Medford
Klamath Falls
Lakeview
Ashland
Redwood Nat'l Park
Alturas
NEVADA
CALIFORNIA
Eureka
Winnemucca
Redding
Lassen Volcanic Nat'l Park
Eel River
0 100 miles
0 100 kilometers
97
95
19
1
5
20
395
2
90
101
82
12
14
84
26
31
78
96
299
36
80

ington's terrain is diverse: deserts, volcanoes, and the world's only non-tropical rain forest all lie within state boundaries. You can raft on Washington's rivers, sea kayak around the San Juan Islands, and build sand castles on the Olympic Peninsula. Mt. Rainier has fantastic hiking, while the Cascades boast perfect conditions for nearly every winter recreational activity. Seattle and Spokane are draped in handsome, green landscapes, proving that natural beauty can be its own selling point.

PRACTICAL INFORMATION

Capital: Olympia.

Washington State Tourism: Department of Community, Trade and Economic Development, P.O. Box 42500, Olympia 98504-2500 (360-586-2088 or 800-544-1800). Open Mon.-Fri. 9am-4pm. **Washington State Parks and Recreation Commission,** 7150 Cleanwater Lane, KY-11, Olympia 98504 (360-753-5755, May-Aug. in WA 800-562-0990). **Outdoor Recreation Information Center,** 915 2nd Ave., #442, Seattle 98174 (206-220-7450), has information on National Parks and Forests.

Time Zone: Pacific (3hr. behind Eastern). **Postal Abbreviation:** WA

Sales Tax: 6.5%

■■■ SEATTLE

It seems everybody wants to come to Seattle, the Northwest's largest and most cosmopolitan city. Glorified by films such as *Singles* and *Sleepless in Seattle*, the city has attracted a massive influx of young people in recent years. Even before they came, Seattle was blessed with a magnificent setting and a vibrant artistic community. With the arrival of legions of energetic young people, Seattle has become one of the liveliest cities in the United States.

Seattle is an isthmus, nearly surrounded by water, with mountain ranges to the east and west. Every hilltop offers an impressive view of Puget Sound, Lake Washington, Mt. Olympus, or Mt. Rainier. Residents spend as much time as possible outdoors, biking in the parks or hiking, climbing, or skiing in the nearby Cascades and Olympic Peninsula. Even those who do stay indoors do so with energetic abandon; Seattle is internationally known for its alternative music scene. The roar of the "Seattle Sound"—best exemplified by groups like Nirvana, Pearl Jam, Screaming Trees, and Soundgarden—has outshined all other recent developments in rock and roll, and outlasted the media hype that forced it into the national spotlight. The theater community supports Broadway shows and alternative vaudeville, while the opera consistently sells out. Seattle also supports a palette of large-scale museums and parks, small galleries, and personable bistros throughout downtown.

Whatever you do, don't be dismayed by the drizzle. Although the clouds may seem as permanent as the mountains they mask, the temperature is constant, too, hovering between 40°F and 70°F year-round. Especially in winter, light drizzle is standard; it rarely snows. Occasionally the skies clear and "the mountain is out."

PRACTICAL INFORMATION

Tourist Office: Seattle-King County Visitors Bureau, 8th and Pike St. (461-5840; fax 461-5855), on the 1st floor of the convention center. Open Mon.-Fri. 8:30am-5pm, Sat.-Sun. 10am-4pm; winter Mon.-Fri. 8:30am-5pm. **National Park Service, Pacific Northwest Region,** 915 2nd Ave. #442 (220-7450). Open Mon.-Fri. 8am-4:30pm. **Gay Information,** 1820 E. Pine (323-0220). Open Mon.-Fri. noon-9pm. **Lesbian Resource Center,** 1808 Belleview Ave. #204 (3322-3953). Open Mon.-Fri. 9am-7pm.

Airport: Seattle-Tacoma International (Sea-Tac) (431-4444 for general info) on Federal Way, south of Seattle proper. Metro buses #174 and 194 run downtown every ½hr. 6am-1am. ($1.10, $1.60 during peak hours).

Trains: Amtrak (382-4120 or 800-872-7245), King St. Station, 3rd and Jackson St. To: Portland (3 per day, $25); Spokane (4 per week, $67); San Francisco (1 per day, $153). Open daily 6:15am-8pm.

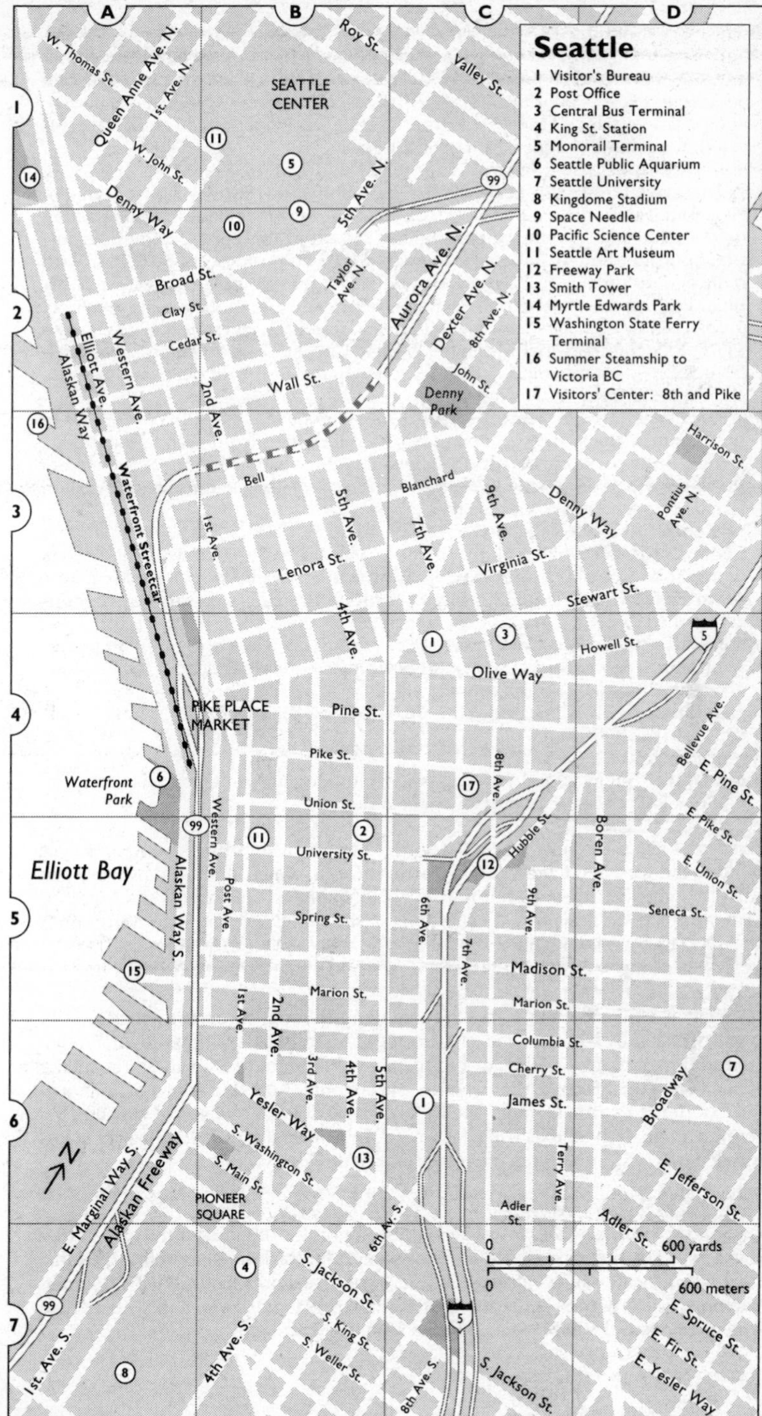
Seattle
1 Visitor's Bureau
2 Post Office
3 Central Bus Terminal
4 King St. Station
5 Monorail Terminal
6 Seattle Public Aquarium
7 Seattle University
8 Kingdome Stadium
9 Space Needle
10 Pacific Science Center
11 Seattle Art Museum
12 Freeway Park
13 Smith Tower
14 Myrtle Edwards Park
15 Washington State Ferry Terminal
16 Summer Steamship to Victoria BC
17 Visitors' Center: 8th and Pike
SEATTLE CENTER
PIKE PLACE MARKET
PIONEER SQUARE
Elliott Bay
Waterfront Park
Denny Park
Waterfront Streetcar
Alaskan Freeway
0 600 yards
0 600 meters

Buses: Greyhound (628-5526 or 800-231-2222), 8th Ave. and Stewart St. To: Sea-Tac Airport (7 per day, $4); Spokane (4 per day, $18-43); Vancouver, BC (8 per day, $25); Portland (9 per day, $19). Ticket office open daily 6:15am-9pm and 12:15-2am (324-7433 or 800-227-4766). **Green Tortoise** (324-7433 or 800-227-4766). To: Portland ($15); Berkeley, CA ($49); San Francisco ($49); Los Angeles ($89). Reservations required 5 days in advance.

Public Transportation: Metro Transit, 821 2nd Ave. (553-3000 for 24-hr. info; TTD service 684-1739), in the Exchange Building downtown. Open Mon.-Fri. 8am-5pm. Fares are based on a 2-zone system. Zone 1 includes everything within the city limits ($1.10 during peak hours, 85¢ off-peak); Zone 2 comprises anything outside the city limits ($1.60 peak, $1.10 off-peak). Ages 5-18 75¢. With reduced fare permits ($1), over 64 and disabled pay 25¢ to go anywhere at any time. Peak hours are generally Mon.-Fri. 6-9am and 3-6pm. Exact fare required. Transfers valid for 2hrs. and for Waterfront Streetcars. Weekend all-day passes $1.70. Ride free 4am-9pm within the **"Magic Carpet"** area downtown, bordered by Jackson St. on the south, 6th Ave. and I-5 on the east, Battery St. on the north, and the waterfront on the west.

Ferries: Washington State Ferries, (464-6400 or 800-84-FERRY/843-3779 in WA) Colman Dock, Pier 52, downtown. Service from downtown to Bainbridge Island, Bremerton in the Kitsap Peninsula, and Vashon Island. Service from Fauntleroy in West Seattle to Southworth in the Kitsap Peninsula and Vashon Island. Frequent ferries leave daily about 5am-2am.

Car Rental: A-19.95-Rent-A-Car, 804 N. 145th St. (365-1995). $20 per day, 100 free mi., 10¢ per additional mi. Under 25 surcharge $5. Free delivery. Drivers under 21 welcome, but must have verifiable auto insurance. Credit card required. **Auto Driveaway** (235-0880) hires people to drive cars to various locations across the U.S.

Bike Rentals: The Bicycle Center, 4529 Sand Point Way (523-8300). $3 per hr. (2-hr. min.), $15 per day. Credit card or license required as deposit. Open Mon.-Fri. 10am-8pm, Sat.-Sun. 10am-6pm.

Crisis Lines: Crisis Clinic, 461-3222. **Seattle Rape Relief,** 632-7273, 1905 S. Jackson St. #102. Both 24 hrs.

Emergency: 911.

Post Office: Union St. and 3rd Ave. (442-6340), downtown. Open Mon.-Fri. 8am-5:30pm. **ZIP code:** 98101. **Area code:** 206.

Seattle is a long, skinny city, stretched north to south on an isthmus between **Puget Sound** to the west and **Lake Washington** to the east, which are linked by locks and canals. Downtown, avenues run northwest to southeast and streets southwest to northeast. Outside downtown, everything is simplified: avenues run north-south and streets east-west, with few exceptions. The city is split into **quadrants:** 1000 1st Ave. NW is a long walk from 1000 1st Ave. S. Though logical and extremely helpful, the designation system takes getting used to.

The city is easily accessible via **I-5,** running north-south through the city, east of downtown; and by **I-90** from the east, ending at I-5 southeast of downtown. From I-5, get to downtown by taking any of the exits from James to Stewart St. (including **Pioneer Sq., Pike Place Market,** and the **waterfront**). Take the Mercer St./Fairview Ave. exit to the **Seattle Center.** The Denny Way exit leads to **Capitol Hill,** and farther north, the 45th St. exit will take you to the **University District. Rte. 99** is less crowded than I-5, and is often the better choice downtown.

ACCOMMODATIONS

The **Seattle International Hostel** is the best option for the budget traveler staying downtown. For those tired of the urban scene, the **Vashon Island Hostel** (sometimes called "Seattle B") is ideal (see Near Seattle: Vashon Island). **Pacific Bed and Breakfast,** 701 NW 60th St., Seattle 98107 (784-0539), can set you up with a single room in a B&B in the $45-70 range (open Mon.-Fri. 9am-5pm).

Seattle International Hostel (HI-AYH), 84 Union St. (622-5443), at Western Ave. Take Metro #174, 184, or 194 from the airport. 139 beds, 24-hr. common kitchen, immaculate facilities, modern amenities, and a friendly, knowledgeable staff. In summer, the hostel is always full and members receive priority. Make reservations early. In summer, there is a supplemental hostel for overflow. Offers discount tickets for Aquarium and Omnidome. Sleepsacks required (linen rental $2). 7-day max. stay in summer. Front desk open 7am-2am. Check-out 11am. Room lock-out 11am-2pm, but common room open at all times. No curfew. $16, nonmembers $19.

YMCA, 909 4th Ave. (382-5000), near Madison St. Good location; tight security. Small, well-kept rooms. TV lounges, laundry facilities, and swimming pool and fitness facilities. Bring your own bedding and lock. Men and women welcome; must be over 18. Check-out by 11am. No curfew. HI-AYH members: bunk in a 4-person room $16, singles and doubles $38-50. Nonmembers: singles $41, with bath $52, doubles $45/$57.

YWCA, 1118 5th Ave. (461-4888), near the YMCA. Take any 4th Ave. bus to Seneca St. Good, central location. Great security; front desk staffed 24 hrs. Shared kitchen facilities. Women only, under 18 requires advance arrangement. 2-week max. stay. No curfew. Singles $31, with bath $36, doubles $42. Weekly rates available. Health center use $5. Key deposit $2.

Green Tortoise Backpacker's Guesthouse, 715 2nd Ave. N. (322-1222; fax 282-9075), on the south slope of Queen Anne Hill, 3 blocks from the Space Needle. 40 beds in 11 rooms and a common kitchen with adjoining deck and garden. Can be loud and messy, depending on the crowd. No curfew. Quiet hours after 11pm. Beds $11; shared doubles $20, private doubles $30. Laundry $1. Call for pickup.

Commodore Hotel, 2013 2nd Ave. (448-8868), at Virginia. Nice, clean, feels safe. Singles $29, with bath $44, 2 beds and bath $49.

Moore Motel, 1926 2nd Ave. (448-4851 or 448-4852), at Virginia. Next to the historic Moore Theater. Big rooms include 2 beds, bath, and TV. Singles $34, doubles $39; HI members $4 off when the hostel is full.

Park Plaza Motel, 4401 Aurora Ave. N (632-2101). Just north of the Aurora bridge; take bus #6 to 46th Ave. or #5 to 43rd and Fremont. Friendly and surprisingly quiet. Bare rooms and halls. Singles $31, doubles from $37.

Nites Inn, 11746 Aurora Ave. N (365-3216). Take bus #6. One of the many motels that line Aurora north of 85th St., but the rooms are larger than most. Cable TV and free local calls. Singles $38, doubles $42.

FOOD

The best fish, produce, and baked goods can be purchased in the crowd-filled **Pike Place Market** (open Mon.-Sat. 6:30am-6pm, Sun. 6:30am-5pm). For excellent ethnic food, head for the **International District,** along King and Jackson St. between 5th and 8th Ave., which is packed with great eateries specializing in southeast Asian food. Fierce competition keeps prices low and quality high. Great food and interesting clubs abound in the **U District** near the University of Washington.

You can buy fish right off the boats at **Fisherman's Wharf,** at NW 54th St. and 30th Ave. NW in Ballard, along the route of bus #43. The wharf is usually open from 8am to 3 or 4pm. Seattle's cheapest food is available on University Ave. in the University district, where shops offer food from around the world for under $5. Or visit one of Seattle's active **food coops,** such as those at 6518 Fremont Ave. N (in Green Lake) and at 6504 20th NE (in the Ravenna District north of the university). Also in Ravenna is a fine produce stand, **Rising Sun Farms and Produce,** 6505 15th Ave. NE (524-9741; open daily 8am-8pm).

Seattlites are serious about their **coffee.** Fine java is available everywhere, including restaurants, drive-throughs, movie theaters, cafés, gas stations, etc. Most Seattlites develop strict loyalties to obscure street corner carts for their espresso. The dominant brands on the market are **Starbucks** and **SBC** ("Stuart Bros." or "Seattle's Best"). Fight the power and patronize independent shops, which probably tender the best cup anyway.

Soundview Café (623-5700), on the mezzanine level in the Main Arcade of Pike Place Market. This wholesome self-serve sandwich-and-salad bar offers fresh food. Get eggs and potatoes for $2.70, a hummus sandwich for $4, or bring a bag lunch: the café offers public seating. Open daily 7am-5pm.

Three Girls Bakery (622-1045), at Post and Pike Pl. Order to go or sit in the café. The rows of bread and pastry will make you drool, as will the aroma. A 2-lb. loaf of cinnamon-raisin bread goes for $4. Open Mon.-Sat. 7am-6pm, Sun. 8am-6pm.

Viet My Restaurant, 129 Prefontaine Pl. S. (382-9923), near 4th and Washington. Consistently delicious Vietnamese food at great prices. Try *bo la lot* (beef in rice pancakes, $3.50) or shrimp curry ($4.25). Avoid the lunch rush. Open Mon.-Sat. 11am-9pm.

Green Cat Café, 1514 E. Olive (726-8756). This small café is a favorite with locals, and for good reason. Its breakfast and lunch fare is incredible. Get down with the hobo scramble ($4). Open Mon.-Fri. 7am-7pm, Sat. 7:30am-7pm, Sun. 9am-7pm.

Café Paradiso, 1005 E. Pike (322-6960). A bit off the geographical beaten-path, this proud-to-be-alternative café gives you your RDA of both caffeine and counter-culture, but not much in the way of food. Muffin and croissant fare about does it. Open Mon.-Thurs. 6am-1am, Fri. 6am-4am, Sat. 8am-4am, Sun 8am-1am.

Asia Deli, 4235 University Way NE (632-2364). Quick service and generous portions of delicious Vietnamese and Thai food. Noodle central. Try the sauteed chicken and onions ($4). Few dishes over $5. No MSG. Open daily 11am-9pm.

Phnom Penh Noodle Soup House, 414 Maynard Ave. S (682-5690). Head to the tiny upstairs dining room for a view of the park and a large bowl of noodles. Try the Phnom Penh Noodle Special; some people come here weekly and never order anything else (well, there are only six items on the menu). Everything $3.90. Open Thurs.-Tues. 8:30am-6pm.

Taco Del Mar, 90 Yesler (467-5946). The cheapest eats in Pioneer Sq., and healthy too. Big burritos are a budget travelers godsend at $3.50 apiece. Open Mon.-Wed. 11am-10pm, Thurs.-Sat. 11am-11pm, Sun. 11am-8pm.

House of Hong Restaurant, 409 8th Ave. S. (622-7997), at Jackson on the border of the International district. The most popular *dim sum* in town at $2 per dish; served daily 11am-3pm. Open Mon.-Thurs. 11am-10pm, Fri. 11am-midnight, Sat. 10:30am-midnight, Sun. 10:30am-10pm. Reservations recommended.

Tandoor Restaurant, 5024 University Way (523-7477). The all-you-can-eat lunch buffet ($5) is a great deal. Dinner is more expensive. Open Mon.-Fri. 11am-2:30pm and 4:30-10pm, Sat.-Sun. 11am-10:30pm.

Un, Deux, Trois, 1329 First Ave. (233-0123). Very close to the Seattle Art Museum. Quiche ($5) and lunch salads ($5-7) make a good meal after a day at the gallery. Dinner is pricier. Open Mon.-Sat. 11am-3pm and 5:30 to 9:30pm.

SIGHTS AND ACTIVITIES

The best way to take in the city and its skyline is from one of the **ferries** that leave the waterfront at frequent intervals (see Practical Information, above). You can get a good look at most major sights in one frantic day—most are within walking distance of each other, within the Metro's free zone. You can explore Pike Place, the waterfront, Pioneer Sq., and the International District in one easy excursion. Or skip the downtown thing altogether and take a rowboat out onto Lake Union, bike along Lake Washington, or hike through Discovery Park.

The new **Seattle Art Museum,** 100 University Way (654-3100), near 1st and University Way, boasts a stunning design by Philadelphia architect Robert Venturi. There's art *inside* the building, too. (Call for free tour schedule. Open Fri.-Wed. 10am-5pm, Thurs. 10am-9pm. $6, students and seniors $4, under 12 free.) One block north of the museum on 1st Ave., inside the Alcade Plaza Building, is the **Seattle Art Museum Gallery,** featuring current art, sculpture, jewelry, and prints by local artists. Browse for free.

Lunatic fish- and produce-mongers bellow at customers and at each other while street performers offer their own entertainment to the crowds at **Pike Place Market.** Visit between 7 and 9am, when the fish are still flopping and the fruit is freshest. At **Pike Place Fish Co.** on the corner (you can't miss it), the famous fish flingers will sing your order in chorus and toss the fish amongst themselves—and you thought fish couldn't fly. For lots of info on Pike Place Market, pick up the free monthly *Pike Place Market News.* At the south end of the Market begins the **Pike Place Hillclimb,** a set of staircases leading down past chic shops and ethnic restaurants to Alaskan Way and the **waterfront.** (An elevator is also available.) The waterfront docks once accepted shiploads of gold from the 1897 Klondike gold rush. The excellent **Seattle Aquarium** (386-4320) sits at the base of the Hillclimb at Pier 59, near Union St. Outdoor tanks recreate the ecosystems of salt marshes and tide pools. Admission is steep, but worth it. (Open Memorial Day-Labor Day daily 10am-5pm. $7, seniors $5.50, ages 6-18 $4.50, ages 3-5 $2.25.)

Westlake Park, on Pike St. between 5th and 4th Ave., with its Art Deco patterns and Wall of Water, is a good place to kick back and listen to steel drums. This small park is bordered by the original **Nordstrom's** and the new **Westlake Center.** (Budget travelers may find **Nordstrom's Rack,** at 2nd and Pine, more appealing.) Take the **monorail** from the Westlake Center (90¢, ages 5-12 60¢, seniors 35¢) to the **Seattle Center,** every 15 minutes 9am-midnight. The center stretches between Denny Way and W. Mercer St., and 1st and 5th Ave., and has eight gates, each with a locating map. The **Pacific Science Center** (443-2001), within the park, houses a laserium (443-2850) and an IMAX theater (443-4629). Evening IMAX shows run Thursday through Sunday (tickets cover both IMAX and museum; $8.50, seniors and ages 6-13 $7, ages 2-5 $5.50). The evening laser shows quake to music by groups like Led Zeppelin and Nine Inch Nails (Tues. $2.50; Wed.-Sun. $5.50). Left over from the 1962 World's Fair, the **Space Needle** (443-2111) has an observation tower and an expensive, dizzying restaurant.

From the waterfront or downtown, it's just a few blocks to historic **Pioneer Sq.,** where 19th-century warehouses and office buildings were restored in the 1970s. "Doc" Maynard, a notorious early resident, gave a plot of land here to one Henry Yesler on the condition that he build a steam-powered lumber mill. Logs dragged down the steep grade of Yesler Way fed the mill, earning that street the epithet "Skid Road." Years later, the center of activity moved north, precipitating the decline of Pioneer Sq. and giving the term "skid row" its present meaning as a neighborhood of poverty and despair. The **Klondike Gold Rush National Historic Park,** 117 S. Main St. (553-7220), is merely an "interpretive center" that depicts the lives and fortunes of miners. To add some levity to this history of shattered dreams, the park has a free screening of Charlie Chaplin's 1925 classic, *The Gold Rush,* on the first Sunday of every month at 3pm. (Park open daily 9am-5pm.) While in Pioneer Sq., browse through the local art galleries, distributors for many of the Northwest's prominent artists. The first Thursday evening of each month, the art community sponsors **First Thursday,** a well-attended gallery walk; for info, call a Pioneer Sq. gallery. One of the galleries, **Flury and Co. Gallery,** 322 1st Ave. S (587-0260), has vintage photographic portraits of Native American life.

In 1889, a fire razed the Pioneer Sq. district; starting afresh, developers rebuilt the area twelve ft. above ground level, leaving the original streets intact. For decades, these streets in the **underground city** harbored Seattle's criminal community. Today, 90-minute tours of the subterranean rooms and passageways leave hourly from **Doc Maynard's Pub,** 610 1st Ave. (682-1511 for info or 682-4646 for reservations; $6, seniors and students $4, children $3).

Capitol Hill's leftist and gay communities set the tone for its nightspots. The hill's coffee shops and restaurants offer great people-watching. Explore Broadway and its cross streets, or stroll down the blocks east and north to see the Victorian homes of the hill's residential area. Bus #10 runs on 15th St.; #7 cruises Broadway.

University District

The immense **University of Washington** (colloquially known as "U-Dub"), north of downtown between Union and Portage Bays, supports a colorful array of funky shops, ethnic restaurants, and a slew of coffeehouses. Most of the good restaurants, jazz clubs, cinemas, and cafés are within a few blocks of **University Way.** Ask for

"University Way," however, and be prepared for puzzled looks; it's known around here as **"Th'Ave"** (one contracted syllable). To reach the University, take any one of buses #71-74 from downtown, or bus #7, 43, or 48 from Capitol Hill. Join the other 33,000 students milling around the **"U District,"** but first stop by the friendly, helpful **visitors center,** 4014 University Way NE (543-9198), to pick up a campus map and to obtain info about the University (open Mon.-Fri. 8am-5pm). At the northwest corner of campus, visit the **Thomas Burke Memorial Washington State Museum** (543-5590), at NE 45th St. and 17th Ave. NE, which exhibits a superb collection about the Pacific Northwest's Native nations (open daily 10am-5pm; suggested donation $3, seniors and students $2). The **UW Arts Ticket Office,** 4001 University Way NE (543-4880), has info and tickets for all events (open Mon.-Fri. 10:30am-4:30pm).

Students often cross town for drinks in the **Queen Anne** neighborhood; **Fremont,** the intervening neighborhood basks in the jovial atmosphere. Fremont is the home of **Archie McPhee's,** 3510 Stone Way (545-8344), a shrine to pop culture and plastic absurdity; people of the punk and funk persuasion make pilgrimages from the distant record stores of Greenwich Village in Manhattan just to handle its notorious **slug selection.** You can get to Archie's on the Aurora Hwy. (Rte. 99), or take bus #26. The store is east of the Hwy. between 35th and 36th, two blocks north of Lake Union (open Mon.-Fri. 9am-7pm, Sat. 10am-6pm).

The International District

Three blocks east of Pioneer Sq., up Jackson on King St., is Seattle's International District. Though sometimes still called "Chinatown" by Seattlites, this area is now home to immigrants from all over Asia and their descendants. Start off your tour of the district by ducking into the **Wing Luke Memorial Museum,** 414 8th St. (623-5124). This tiny museum houses a permanent exhibit on the different Asian nationalities in Seattle and temporary exhibits by local Asian artists. (Open Tues.-Fri. 11am-4:30pm, Sat.-Sun. noon-4pm. $2.50, seniors and students $1.50, ages 5-12 75¢; free Thurs.) Other landmarks include the **Tsutakawa sculpture** at the corner of S Jackson and Maynard St. and the gigantic dragon mural in **Hing Hay Park** at S King and Maynard St. The community gardens at Main and Maynard St. provide a peaceful and well-tended retreat from the downtown sidewalks.

Waterways, Parks and the Great Outdoors

A string of attractions festoon the waterways linking Lake Washington and Puget Sound. Houseboats and sailboats fill **Lake Union.** Here, the **Center for Wooden Boats,** 1010 Valley St. (382-2628; open daily 11am-6pm), rents rowboats ($8-12 per hr.), and sailboats ($10-15 per hr.).

Climb over to the **fish ladder** on the south side of the **Hiram M. Chittenden Locks** (783-7001) to boat-watch or to watch trout and salmon hurl themselves over 21 concrete steps on their journey from the sea. Take bus #43 from the U District or #17 from downtown. On the northwestern shore of the city lies the **Golden Gardens Park,** in the Loyal Heights neighborhood, between NW 80th and NW 95th St., an ideal spot for a picnic. Several expensive restaurants line the piers to the south, and unobstructed views of the Olympic Mountains almost justify the prices of their uniformly excellent seafood.

Directly north of Lake Union, run, ride, and skate around **Green Lake;** take bus #16 from downtown Seattle. Whoever named Green Lake wasn't kidding; even a quick dunk results in gobs of green algae clinging to your body. **Green Lake Rentals** (527-0171), on the lake's east side, rents rowboats ($6) and paddleboats, canoes, and kayaks ($8). Next to the lake lies **Woodland Park Zoo,** 5500 Phinney Ave. N (684-4800), best reached from Rte. 99 or N. 50th St.; take bus #5 from downtown. The park itself is shaggy, but the animals's habitats are realistic; the zoo is one of only three in the U.S. to receive the Humane Society's highest standard of approval. (Open daily 9:30am-6pm. $7, ages 6-17, seniors and disabled $5.25, ages 3-5 $4.)

Over 50 **whitewater rafting** outfitters are based in the Seattle area, even though the rapids are hours away by car. A good way to secure an inexpensive trip is to call outfitters and quote competitors' prices at them; they are often willing to undercut one another. Scour the "Guides" section in the Yellow Pages. Two trade organizations, **PRO (Professional Rafters Organizations)** (323-5485) and the **Washington State Outfitters and Guides Association** (392-6107), can provide advice and information. Whatever outfitter you use, be sure it lives up to basic safety standards. Don't hesitate to spend the extra dollars to ensure the highest level of safety.

The **Northwest Outdoor Center,** 2100 Westlake Ave. (281-9694), on Lake Union, holds instructional programs in **whitewater** and **sea kayaking** during the spring, summer, and fall (2-evening intro to sea kayaking, including equipment $45); the center also leads sea kayaking excursions through the San Juan Islands (open Mon.-Fri. 10am-8pm, Sat.-Sun. 9am-6pm).

Skiing near Seattle is every bit as good as the mountains make it look. **Alpental, Ski-Acres,** and **Snoqualmie** co-sponsor an information number (232-8182), which provides conditions and lift ticket rates for all three. **Crystal Mountain** (663-2265), the region's newest resort, can be reached by Rte. 410 south out of Seattle.

Since the Klondike gold rush, Seattle has been one of the foremost cities in the world for outfitting wilderness expeditions. Besides Army-Navy surplus stores and campers' supply shops, the city is home to many world-class outfitters. **Recreational Equipment Inc. Coop (REI Coop),** 1525 11th Ave. (323-8333), is the favored place to buy high-quality mountaineering and water recreation gear; take bus #10. For a few dollars you can join REI and receive a year-end rebate on your purchases. REI has a bulletin board where lone hikers advertise for hiking companions. The company offers its own backpacking and climbing trips and clinics, in addition to presenting free slide shows and lectures on topics such as trekking through Nepal, bicycling in Ireland, or improving your fly-fishing techniques (open Mon.-Fri. 10am-9pm, Sat. 10am-6pm, Sun. 11am-5pm).

PACIFIC NORTHWEST

ENTERTAINMENT

The **Seattle Opera** (389-7676, open Mon.-Fri. 9am-5pm; or TicketMaster at 292-2787) performs in the Opera House in the Seattle Center throughout the winter. Order tickets well in advance; rush tickets are sometimes available 15 min. before curtain ($8 and up). Write to the Seattle Opera, P.O. Box 9248, Seattle 98109. During lunch hours in the summertime, the free **Out to Lunch** series (623-0340) brings everything from reggae to folk dancing to the parks and squares of Seattle.

With the second-largest number of professional companies in the U.S., Seattle hosts an exciting array of first-run plays and alternative works. You can often get **rush tickets** at nearly half price on the day of the show (cash only) from **Ticket/Ticket** (324-2744). The award-winning **Seattle Repertory Theater,** 155 Mercer (443-2222), performs in the **Bagley Wright Theater** in Seattle Center. (Tickets $10-36; student and senior rush tickets 10 min. before show at substantial discount.) Other theaters to check out: **A Contemporary Theater (ACT),** 100 W. Roy St. (285-5110), at the base of Queen Anne Hill; the **Annex Theatre,** 1916 4th Ave. (728-0933); **The Empty Space Theatre,** 3509 Fremont Ave. N (547-7500).

Seattle is also a cinematic paradise. Most of the theaters that screen non-Hollywood films are on Capitol Hill and in the University District. Matinee shows (before 6pm) run $4; otherwise, expect to pay $6.75. **The Egyptian,** 801 E. Pine St. (323-4978), on Capitol Hill, shows artsy films and hosts the **Seattle Film Festival.** Half the fun of seeing a movie at **The Harvard Exit,** 807 E. Roy (323-8986), on Capitol Hill, is the theater itself, a converted residence—the lobby was once someone's living room. Arrive early for complimentary cheese and crackers over a game of chess, checkers, or backgammon (tickets at both $6.75, seniors and kids $4).

The Mariners play major-league baseball at the **Kingdome,** 201 S. King St. (622-3555 for info, or 622-4487 for tickets), down 1st Ave. Tickets $15 on the 3rd base line; Sunday is senior discount day. The **Seahawks** also play football here. The **Seattle Supersonics** (281-5800), the only Seattle team ever to win a national title, attract a religious following to their basketball games at the Coliseum in Seattle Center. The **University of Washington Huskies** football team has dominated the PAC-10 conference recently. Call (543-2200) for schedule and ticket info.

NIGHTLIFE

The best spot to go for guaranteed good beer, live music, and big crowds is **Pioneer Sq.** Most of the bars around the Sq. participate in a **joint cover** ($8) that will let you wander from bar to bar and sample the bands you like. **Fenix Café and Fenix Underground** (343-7740) and **Central Tavern** (622-0209) rock and roll, while **Larry's** (624-7665) and **New Orleans** (622-2563) feature great jazz and blues nightly. All the Pioneer Sq. clubs shut down at 2am Friday and Saturday nights, and at around midnight on weeknights. The Northwest produces a variety of local beers, some sold in area stores but most only on tap in bars. Popular brews include **Grant's, Imperial Russian Stout, India Pale Ale, Red Hook, Ballard Bitter, Black Hook,** and **Yakima Cider.**

Red Door Alehouse, 3401 Fremont Ave. N. (547-7521), at N. 34th St., across from the Inner-Urban Statue. Throbbing with yuppified university students who attest to the good local ale selection. Open daily 11am-2am. Kitchen closes at 11pm.

The Trolleyman Pub, 3400 Phinney Ave. N. (548-8000). In the back of the Red Hook Ale Brewery, which rolls the most popular kegs on campus to university students. Early hours make it a mellow spot to listen to good acoustic music and contemplate the newly made bubbles in a fresh pint. Open Mon.-Thurs. 9am-11pm, Fri. 9am-midnight, Sat. 11am-midnight, Sun. noon-7pm.

Kells, 1916 Post Alley (728-1916), at Pike Place. A lively Irish pub with nightly Irish tunes. Live music Wed.-Sat. Cover Fri. and Sat. $3. Open Wed.-Sat. 11:30am-2am.

Off Ramp, 109 Eastlake Ave. E. (628-0232). Among the most popular venues of the local music scene. Always loud; wild at times. Clear views of performers over a roiling mosh pit. Open 6pm-3am daily. Cover varies.

Under the Rail (448-1900), 5th and Battery. The largest downtown club offers local music (cover $5) and the occasional national tour. DJ and dancing on nights without concerts. Loud. Hours change nightly according to show times. Often open past 2am. Always open Sat. midnight-5am.

OK Hotel, 212 Alaskan Way S. (621-7903). One café, one bar, one building. Just below Pioneer Sq. toward the waterfront. Lots of wood, lots of coffee. Great live bands with hot alternative sound. Occasional cover charge up to $6. Open Sun.-Thurs. 6am-3am, Fri.-Sat. 8am-4am. Call 386-9934 for the coffee house.

Weathered Wall, 1921 5th Ave. (728-9398). An audience as diverse and artistic as its offerings (poetry readings to punk). The Weathered Wall is always interesting, and promotes audience interaction. Open Tues.-Sun. 9pm-2am. Cover $3-7.

Murphy's Pub (634-2110), at Meridian Ave. N. and N. 45th St., in Wallingford, west of the U District. Take bus #43. A classic Irish pub with a mile-long beer list. Popular with a young crowd. Open mic on Wed. Open daily 11:30am-2am.

Re-Bar, 1114 Howell (233-9873). A mixed gay and straight bar with a wide range of tunes and dancing on the wild side, depending on the night. Cover $4. Open daily 9:30pm-2am.

The Vogue, 2018 1st Ave. (443-0673). A rockin' danceteria for the black-clad and angst-ridden. Out of control. Open daily 9pm-2am.

■ NEAR SEATTLE: VASHON ISLAND

Only a short ferry ride from Seattle and an even shorter ferry hop from Tacoma, Vashon Island remains inexplicably invisible to most Seattlites—green forests of Douglas firs, rolling cherry orchards, strawberry fields, and wildflowers cover the island during the summer. Four different **Washington State Ferries** can get you to Vashon Island; call 464-6400 for all the details.

From Vashon Hwy. take Ellisburg to Dockton to Pt. Robinson Rd. for a picnic at **Point Robinson Park.** The island is wonderful for **biking.** More than 500 acres of hiking trails weave their way through the woods in the middle of the island, and several lovely walks start from the **Vashon Island Ranch/Hostel (HI-AYH)** 12119 SW Cove Rd. (463-2592). The hostel, sometimes called **"Seattle B,"** is really the island's only accommodation, and it is itself one of the main reasons to come here. It's easy to get to: jump on any bus at the ferry terminal, ride to Thriftway Market, and call from the free phone inside the store, marked with an HI-AYH label. Judy, the manager, will pick you up if the hour is reasonable, and she has never turned a hosteler away. "Seattle B" has free pancakes for breakfast, free use of old bikes, free campfire wood, free volleyball games in the afternoon, and a caring manager. When all beds are full, you can pitch a tent. (Open year-round; tents and beds $9, nonmembers $12). Most hostelers get creative in the kitchen with supplies from **Thriftway** downtown (open daily 8am-9pm).

■■■ SAN JUAN ISLANDS

The San Juan Islands are an accessible treasure. Bald eagles spiral above haggard hillsides, pods of orcas spout offshore, and despite what the lush vegetation might say, it rains half as much as in Seattle. Pick up the invaluable *The San Juan Islands Afoot and Afloat* by Marge Mueller ($10), available on the islands and in Seattle.

Ferries depart Anacortes on the mainland about nine times per day on a route that stops at **Lopez, Shaw, Orcas,** and **San Juan Islands.** Purchase ferry tickets in Anacortes. Foot passengers travel in either direction between the islands free of charge. Pay for a vehicle only on westbound trips to or between the islands; no charge is levied on eastbound traffic. Save money by traveling directly to the westernmost island on your itinerary, and then make your way back to the mainland island by island. For departure times and rates, call **Washington State Ferries** (464-6400). On peak travel days, arrive with your vehicle at least one hour prior to scheduled departure. The ferry authorities accept only cash. **Gray Line** (624-5077) runs a bus daily from Seattle to Anacortes ($15). San Juan Islands's **area code:** 206.

San Juan Island San Juan, may be the last stop on the ferry route, but it is still the most frequently visited island, combining the beauty of San Juan with the comforts of **Friday Harbor,** the largest town in the archipelago. Since the ferry docks right in town, this island is also the easiest to explore. The **Whale Museum,** 62 1st St. (378-4710), displays skeletons, sculptures, and information on new research. (Open daily 10am-5pm; in winter daily 11am-4pm. $3, seniors and students $2.50, under 12 $1.50.) **Lime Kiln State Park,** on West Side Rd., provides the best ocean vista for **whale-watching** of all of the islands. Part of the **San Juan National Historic Park** is the **British Camp,** which lies on West Valley Rd. on the sheltered **Garrison Bay** (take Mitchell Bay Rd. east from West Side Rd.). Here, four original buildings have been preserved from the days of the bizarre "Pig War," including the barracks, now used as an **interpretive center.** If you're eager to **fish** or **clam,** pick up a free copy of *Salmon, Shellfish, Marine Fish Sport Fishing Guide,* for details on regulations and limits at **Ace Hardware and Marine,** 270 Spring St. (378-4622; open Mon.-Sat. 8am-6pm, Sun. 9am-5pm). They also sell fishing licenses, which are required. For the low down on bike rentals, tours, and the island's sights check with the **chamber of commerce** (468-3663), in a booth on East St. up from Cannery Landing.

San Juan County Park, 380 Westside Rd. (378-2992), 10 mi. west of Friday Harbor on Smallpox and Andrews Bays, has cold water and flush toilets, but no RV hookups (vehicle sites $15, hiker/biker sites $4.50). **Lakedale Campgrounds,** 2627 Roche Harbor Rd. (378-2350), 4 mi. from Friday Harbor, has attractive grounds surrounded by 50 acres of lakes; boat rentals and swimming available. (Sites for 1-2 people with vehicle $16, July-Aug. $19, each additional person $3.50. Open April 1-Oct. 15.) **La Cieba,** 395 Spring St. (378-8666), is a small Mexican joint supported by locals; join the feast with a fantastic burrito ($4.50; open daily 11am-8pm).

Orcas Island **Mt. Constitution** overlooks Puget Sound from its 2409-ft. summit atop Orcas Island, the largest island of the San Juan group. In the mountain's shadow dwells a small population of retirees, artists, and farmers in understated homes surrounded by the red bark of madrona trees and greenery. Orcas has perhaps the best budget tourist facilities of all the islands. Unfortunately, the beach access is occupied by private resorts and is closed to the public. The trail to **Obstruction Pass Beach** is the best way to clamber down to the rocky shores. Because Orcas is shaped like a horseshoe, getting around is a chore. The ferry lands on the southwest tip. The island's main town, **Eastsound,** is 9 mi. northeast. Stop in a shop to get a free **map**. San Juan Transit (376-8887) provides bus service about every 90 minutes to most points on the island ($4-7).

Moran State Park, Star Rte. 22, Eastsound 98245 (376-2326), is Orcas's greatest attraction. Over 21 mi. of hiking trails cover the park, ranging in difficulty from a one-hour jaunt around Mountain Lake to a day-long constitutional up the south face of Mt. Constitution, the highest peak on the islands. Pick up a copy of the trail guide from the **registration station** (376-2837). From the summit of Constitution, you can see other islands, the Olympic and Cascade Ranges, Vancouver Island, and Mt. Rainier. Swim in two freshwater lakes easily accessible from the highway, or rent rowboats and paddleboats ($9 per hr.) from the park. **Camping** in the park offers all the best of San Juan fun: swimming, fishing, and hiking. There are four different campgrounds with a total of 151 sites. About 12 sites remain open year-round, as do the restrooms. Backcountry camping is prohibited. (Standard sites with hot showers $11; hiker/biker sites $5. Park open daily 6:30am-dusk; Sept.-March 8am-dusk. Camping reservations strongly recommended May-Labor Day.)

For **visitors information** call the Friday Harbor chamber of commerce (468-3663), or contact the Orcas Island **chamber of commerce** (376-2273). For **bike rental,** go to **Wildlife Cycle** (376-4708), A St. and North Beach Rd., in Eastsound (21-speeds $5 per hr., $21 per day; open Mon.-Sat. 10:30am-5pm). In an **emergency,** dial 911.

OLYMPIC PENINSULA

In the fishing villages and logging towns of the Olympic Peninsula, locals joke about having webbed feet and using Rustoleum instead of suntan oil. The Olympic Mountains wring the area's moisture out of the heavy Pacific air (up to 200 in. of rain per year fall on Mt. Olympus). While this torrent supports genuine rain forests in the peninsula's western river valleys, towns such as Sequim in the range's eastern rain shadow are among the driest in Washington.

Extremes of climate are matched by extremes of geography. The beaches along the Pacific strip are a hiker's paradise—isolated, windy, and wildly sublime. The seaports of the peninsula's northern edge crowd against the Strait of Juan de Fuca, hemmed in by the glaciated peaks of the Olympic range. Most visitors, however, come here for one reason: the spectacularly rugged scenery of Olympic National Park, which lies at the Peninsula's center. Though the park's network of trails now covers an area the size of Rhode Island, these rough and wooded mountains resisted exploration until well into the 20th century.

■■■ PORT TOWNSEND

The Victorian splendor of Port Townsend's buildings, unlike the salmon industry, has survived the progression of time and weather. The entire business district has been restored and declared a national landmark. Port Townsend is a cultural oasis on an otherwise untamed peninsula. Walk down Water Street, and you'll be lured by cafés, book shops, and an immense ice cream parlor.

Port Townsend has its share of Queen Anne and Victorian mansions. Of the over 200 restored homes in the area, some have been converted into bed and breakfasts; and two are open for tours. The 1868 **Rothschild House** (379-8076), at Franklin and Taylor St., has period furnishings and herbal and flower gardens (open daily 10am-

5pm; Oct.-March Sat.-Sun. 11am-4pm; requested donation $2). The **Ann Starret Mansion,** 744 Clay St. (385-3205), has nationally renowned Victorian architecture, including frescoed ceilings (tours daily noon-3pm, $2). **Point Hudson,** the hub of the small shipbuilding area, forms the corner of Port Townsend, where Admiralty Inlet and Port Townsend Bay meet. North of Point Hudson are several miles of beach in **Chetzemolka Park,** and the larger **Fort Worden State Park.** Port Townsend's **chamber of commerce,** 2437 E. Sims Way (385-2722), lies 10 blocks from the center of town on Rte. 20; ask the helpful staff for a map and visitors guide (open Mon.-Fri. 9am-5pm, Sat. 10am-4pm, Sun. 11am-4pm).

The Port Townsend area boasts two hostels. **Port Townsend Youth Hostel (HI-AYH),** Fort Worden State Park (385-0655), 2 mi. from downtown, is smack in the Fort. (Kitchen facilities. Check in 5-10pm; check-out 9:30am; no curfew. $11, nonmembers $14; cyclists $9-12. Family rates available. Open Feb.-Dec. 21; call ahead Nov.-Feb.) **Fort Flagler Youth Hostel (HI-AYH),** Fort Flagler State Park (385-1288), is on handsome Marrowstone Island, 20 mi. from Port Townsend. From Port Townsend head south on Rte. 19, which connects to Rte. 116 east and leads directly into the park. It's fantastic for cyclists and solitude-seekers. (Open reservation only. Check in 5-10pm, lockout 10am-5pm. $10, nonmembers $13. Cyclists $9-12.)

By land, Port Townsend can be reached either from **U.S. 101** or from the **Kitsap Peninsula** across the Hood Canal Bridge. Washington State Ferries serve Winslow on Bainbridge Island; from there, several bus transfers will get you to Port Townsend. Ask the chamber of commerce for details.

■■■ OLYMPIC PARK

Amid the august Olympic Mountains, **Olympic National Park** unites 900,000 acres of velvet-green rainforest, jagged snow-covered peaks, and dense evergreen woodlands. This enormous region at the center of the peninsula allows limited access to four-wheeled traffic. There is no scenic loop, and only a handful of secondary roads attempt to penetrate the interior. The roads that do exist serve as trailheads for over 600 mi. of hiking. The enormous amount of rain on the western side of the mountains supports rainforests dominated by Sitka spruce and western red cedars in the Hoh, Queets, and Quinault river valleys. The only people who seem not to enjoy this diverse and wet wilderness are those who come unprepared; a parka, good boots, and a waterproof tent are essential here.

Practical Information The **Olympic Visitors Center,** 3002 Mt. Angeles Rd., Port Angeles (452-0330), off Race St., fields questions about the whole park, including camping, backcountry hiking, and fishing, and displays a map of locations of other park ranger stations (open daily 9am-4pm). The park charges an **entrance fee** ($3 per car, $1 per hiker or biker) at the more built-up entrances, such as the Hoh, Heart o' the Hills, and Elwha—all of which have paved roads and toilet facilities. The entrance permit is good for 7 days. In an **emergency,** call 911. Olympic National Park's **area code:** 360.

The Park Service runs **interpretive programs** such as guided forest walks, tidal pool walks, and campfire programs out of its ranger stations (all free). For a schedule of events pick up the park newspaper from ranger stations or the visitors center. The map distributed at the park's gates is detailed and extremely helpful.

July, August, and September are the best months to visit Olympic National Park, since much of the backcountry often remains snowed-in until late June, and only the summer provides rainless days with any regularity. Be prepared for a potpourri of weather conditions at any time. Make sure hiking boots are waterproof and have good traction, because trails can transform into rivers of slippery mud. **Backcountry camping** requires a free **backcountry permit,** available at ranger stations.

Never drink the untreated **water** in the park. *Giardia,* a *very* nasty microscopic parasite, lives in all these waters, and causes severe diarrhea, gas, and abdominal cramps. Carry your own water supply, or boil local water for five minutes before drinking it. You can also buy water purification tablets at the visitors center (see above) or at most camping supply stores. **Dogs** are not allowed in the backcountry, and must be leashed at all times within the park.

Fishing within park boundaries requires no special permit, but you must obtain a state game department punch card for salmon and steelhead trout at outfitting and hardware stores locally, or at the game department in Olympia. The Elwha River is best for **trout,** and the Hoh is excellent for **salmon.**

Accommodations and Camping A roof can be a nice thing in the rainforest; find one at the **Rainforest Hostel,** 169312 U.S. 101 (374-2270), which has extremely knowledgable proprietors and $1.50 **showers** for non-guests (beds $11).

Olympic National Park, Olympic National Forest, and the State of Washington all maintain free campgrounds. Pick up an area **map** from a ranger station for comprehensive info. The free **National Park campgrounds** include **Deer Park, Ozette** (both with drinking water), and **Queets** (no water). In addition, the National Park has many standard campgrounds (sites $10). Fees in the **National Forest campgrounds** range from $4 to $12; six campgrounds in the Hood Canal Ranger District are free. Reservations can be made for three Forest Service campgrounds: **Seal Rock, Falls View,** and **Klahowga** by calling 800-280-CAMP/2267. Any ranger station can provide a list of both Park and Forest Service campgrounds, fees, and facilities. Several **State Parks** are scattered along Hood Canal and the eastern rim of the peninsula (sites generally $10-16; occasionally only $4-5). **Heart o' the Hills Campground** (452-2713; 105 sites), 5½ mi. from Port Angeles up Race Rd. inside Olympic National Park, is filled with vacationers poised to take **Hurricane Ridge** by storm the next day (sites $10, plus the $5 entrance fee), where interpretive programs and a ranger station await. Farther west on U.S. 101 are **Elwha Valley** (452-9191; 41 sites), 5 mi. south off U.S. 101, and nearby **Altaire** (30 sites). Both have drinking water (sites $10). **Fairholm Campground** (928-3380; 87 sites), 30 mi. west of Port Angeles at the western tip of Lake Crescent, has sites with drinking water ($10). **The Storm King Information Station** (928-3380) runs interpretive evening programs.

Farther west on U.S. 101, an entrance fee of $5 and 13 mi. of paved road will get you through to the **Sol Duc Hot Springs Campground** (327-3534), which has sites for $10. Get free backcountry permits at the **Eagle Ranger Station** (327-3534; open July-Aug. daily 8am-5pm). At nearby **Sol Duc Hot Springs** (327-3583; $5.50 per day, seniors $4.50), the cement docks, chlorine smell, and "shower before you enter" signs detract from this pristine source of naturally hot water (open mid-May to Aug. daily 9am-9pm; Sept. 9am-8pm; April and Oct. 9am-5pm). A better and less well-known way to harness the region's geothermal energy is to hike up to **Olympic Hot Springs.** Turn off at the Elwha River Road and follow it 12 mi. to the trailhead. The natural springs are about a 2½-mi. hike, but well worth it.

Outdoors Olympic National Park is home to one of the **world's only temperate rainforests.** Gigantic, thick old-growth trees, ferns, and mosses blanket the valleys of the Hoh, Queets, and Quinault Rivers, all on the west side of the Park. Although the forest floor is thickly carpeted with unusual foliage and fallen trees, rangers keep the many walking trails clear and well-marked. Many travelers seek out the **Hoh Rainforest Trail** for an incredible rainforest experience. The trail parallels the Hoh River for 18 mi. to Blue Glacier on the shoulder of Mt. Olympus. Shy Roosevelt elk and Northern spotted owl inhabit the area. The first two campgrounds along the Hoh River Rd., which leaves U.S. 101 13 mi. south of the town of Forks, are administered by the Department of Natural Resources (DNR), accept no reservations, and are free. Drinking water is available at the **Minnie Peterson** site only. DNR sites are usually uncrowded; stay at one and drive to the Hoh trailhead to get a map and begin your rainforest exploration. You can obtain a separate map of the Hoh-Clearwater Multiple Use Area from the DNR main office, just off U.S. 101 on the north side of Forks. The **Hoh Rainforest Visitors Center** (374-6925) provides posters and permits (open daily Sept.-June 9am-5pm).

Trailheads to seek out for relative solitude are **Queets, North Fork,** and **Graves Creek,** in the west and southwest of the Park. The Queets Trail follows the Queets River east from a free campground (20 sites for tents only; open June-Sept.). The Park and Forest Services and the Quinalt Reservation share the land surrounding **Quinault Lake.** The Forest Service operates a day-use beach and an information center in the **Quinault Ranger Station,** South Shore Rd. (288-2444; open daily 9am-4:30pm; in winter Mon.-Fri. 9am-4:30pm). From the Quinalt Ranger Station, it's 20 mi. to the North Fork trailhead; from there, enterprising hikers can journey 44 mi. north across the entire park, finishing up at Whiskey Bend.

Hurricane Ridge is 5½ mi. from Port Angeles up Race Rd. The road up the ridge is an easy drive for those short on time, but the curves make some queasy. Clear days bring splendid views of Mt. Olympus and Vancouver Island. The ridge can be crowded; the ideal time to go is sunrise. Many trails that originate here, including some for seniors and the disabled. On winter weekends the Park Service organizes **snowshoe walks** atop the ridge. Call the visitors center (452-0330) for details.

The Olympic Peninsula contains **Cape Flattery,** the northwesternmost point in the contiguous U.S. At the westernmost point on the strait is Neah Bay, the only town in the **Makah Reservation.** Rte. 112 leads there west from Port Angeles. In Neah Bay on Rte. 112, the **Makah Cultural and Research Center** (645-2711) houses artifacts from the archaeological site at Cape Alava, where a huge mudslide 500 years ago buried and preserved an entire settlement. The downstairs of a 70-ft.-long house, with a sloped roof ideally suited to the rainy environment, has been replicated at the museum. (Open daily 10am-5pm; Oct.-April Wed.-Sun. 10am-5pm. $4, seniors and students $3.)

Piles of driftwood, imposing sea stacks, sculptured arches, and abundant wildlife lie along 57 mi. of rugged and deserted beaches. Bald eagles are often out on windy days, and whales and seals tear through the sea. Where U.S. 101 hugs the coast between the Hoh and Quinault Reservations, the beaches are easily accessible. The 15-mi. stretch of beaches begins in the north with **Ruby Beach** near Mile 165 on U.S. 101. South of Ruby Beach at Mile 160 is **Beach #6,** a favorite whale-watching spot. Another 3 mi. south is **Beach #4,** with its beautiful tidepools. A unique 9-mi. loop trail starts at **Ozette Lake,** north of Ruby Beach, heading through the rainforest along boardwalks, then along the beach. It's a long day hike or a nice overnight. A permit is required to camp along the way; call 452-0300 to reserve one.

■■■ OLYMPIA

While still peaceful and easy-going, Olympia has moved smoothly from small fishing-and-oyster port to growing state capital. The sprawling Capitol Campus, with its whitewashed buildings and manicured lawns, dominates the downtown. The city draws on its natural environment for picturesque Japanese gardens and two wildlife refuges, one a haven for endangered wolves.

The focal point of Olympia is the **State Capitol Campus.** Take a free tour of the **Legislative Building** (586-8677) to sneak a peek of the public sphere. Only the tours can usher you in to the legislative chambers, which are otherwise off-limits. (45-min. tours daily 10am-3pm; building open Mon.-Fri. 8am-5pm, Sat.-Sun. 10am-4pm.)

Capitol Lake Park is a favorite retreat for runners, sailors, and swimmers. Or stroll on the boardwalk at **Percival Landing Park** (743-8379); various boats jam the Port, a reminder of Olympia's oyster-filled past. The **Yashiro Japanese Garden** (753-8380), near the chamber of commerce, is tiny but beautiful, a perfect spot for a picnic (open daily from 10am to dusk).

The **Nisqually National Wildlife Refuge** (753-9467), off I-5 between Olympia and Tacoma (at exit 114), has recently pitted environmentalists against developers in the quiet Nisqually delta. For the time being, you can still view the protected wildlife from blinds or walk the trails that wind through the preserve. Trails open daily during daylight hours (office open Mon.-Fri. 7:30am-4pm; $2). **Wolfhaven,** 3111 Offut Lake Rd. (264-4695 or 800-448-9653), 10 mi. south of Olympia, now preserves 40 wolves of six different species. Take a guided tour of the grounds ($5, children $2.50) or take part in the **Howl-In.** (May-Sept. Fri.-Sat. 7-9:30pm; $6, children $4. Haven open daily 10am-5pm; Oct.-April Wed.-Sun. 10am-4pm.)

Olympia's **Chamber of Commerce,** 1000 Plum St. (357-3362 or 800-753-8474), is next to the City Hall (open Mon.-Fri. 9am-5pm). **Emergency** is 911. Olympia's **post office:** 900 S. Jefferson SE (357-2286; open Mon.-Fri. 7:30am-6pm, Sat. 9am-4pm); **ZIP code:** 98501; **area code:** 360.

The motels in Olympia generally cater to lobbyists and lawyers rather than to budget tourists. Camping is the cheapest option. The **Bailey Motor Inn,** 3333 Martin Way (491-7515), exit 107 off I-5 has clean, comfortable rooms in a noisy location (singles from $35, doubles from $43). **Millersylvania State Park,** 12245 Tilly Rd. S (753-1519), lies 10 mi. south of Olympia; take Exit 99 off I-5, then head south on Rte. 121. The park offers 216 tree-shrouded, reasonably spacious sites with pay showers and flush toilets (standard sites $11, RV hookups $16). **Capital Forest Multiple Use Area,** 15 mi. southwest of Olympia, off I-5 exit 95, shelters 50 free campsites scattered among 6 campgrounds. The area is unsupervised; lone travelers and women might be better off paying the $11 for Millersylvania.

There is potential for good eating along bohemian 4th Ave., east of Columbia, especially when the pace picks up during the school year. The **Olympia Farmer's Market,** 401 N. Capitol Way (352-9096), has a great selection of in-season fruits and berries; you can buy a fantastic cheap lunch here. (Open May-Sept. Thurs.-Sun.10am-3pm; April Sat.-Sun. 10am-3pm; Oct. to mid-Dec. Fri.-Sun. 10am-3pm.) Try a grilled oyster sandwich or a Spar burger (both $6) at **The Spar Café & Bar,** 111 E. 4th Ave. (357-6444; open Mon.-Sat. 6am-9pm, Sun. 7am-8pm; bar open daily 11am-2am). Or, dig the deluxe burrito ($4.50) and the vegetarian and vegan options at the **Smithfield Café,** 212 W. 4th Ave. (786-1725; open Mon.-Fri. 7am-8pm, Sat.-Sun. 8am-8pm).

Amtrak, 6600 Yelm Hwy. (800-872-7245), toots from Olympia to Seattle ($14) and Portland ($18) three times per day. **Greyhound,** 107 E. 7th Ave. (357-8667), at Capitol Way, bounds to Seattle (8 per day, $6), Portland (8 per day, $12), and Spokane (3 per day, $27). (Open daily 7:30am-7:30pm.)

CASCADE RANGE

The Northwestern Native Americans summed up their admiration succinctly, dubbing the Cascades "The Home of the Gods." Intercepting the moist Pacific air, the Cascades have divided the eastern and western parts of Oregon and Washington into the lush green of the west and the high, dry plains of the east.

The tallest of these mountains—the white-domed peaks of Baker, Vernon, Glacier, Rainier, Adams, and Mt. St. Helens—have been made accessible by four major roads offering good trailheads and impressive scenery. **U.S. 12** through White Pass approaches Mt. Rainier most closely; **I-90** sends four lanes past the major ski resorts of Snoqualmie Pass; scenic **U.S. 2** leaves Everett for Stevens Pass and descends the Wenatchee River, a favorite of whitewater rafters; **Route 20,** the **North Cascades Hwy.,** provides access to North Cascades National Park. These last two roads are often traveled in sequence as the **Cascade Loop.**

Greyhound covers the routes over Stevens and Snoqualmie Passes to and from Seattle, while **Amtrak** cuts between Ellensburg and Puget Sound. Rainstorms and evening traffic can slow hitchhiking; locals warn against thumbing along Rte. 20, as a few hitchers apparently have vanished over the last few years. *Let's Go* does not recommend hitching anywhere, especially here. This corner of the world can only be explored properly with a car. The mountains are most accessible in July, August, and September; many high mountain passes are snowed in the rest of the year. The best source of information on the Cascades is the joint **National Park/National Forest Information Service,** 915 2nd Ave., Seattle 98174 (206-220-7450).

■■■ NORTH CASCADES REGION

A favorite stomping ground for deer, mountain goats, and bears, the North Cascades—an aggregation of dramatic peaks in the northern part of the state—remain one of the most rugged expanses of relatively untouched land in the continental U.S. The **North Cascades Hwy. (Rte. 20)** provides the major access to the area, as well as astounding views awaiting each twist in the road. Use the information below to follow the road eastward from Burlington (exit 230 on I-5) along the Skagit River to the Skagit Dams (whose hydroelectric energy powers Seattle), then across the Cascade Crest at Rainy Pass (4860 ft.) and Washington Pass (5477 ft.), finally descending to the Methow River and the dry Okanogan rangeland of eastern Washington. **Rte. 9** branches off of Rte. 20 and leads north through the rich farmland of **Skagit Valley,** offering roundabout access to **Mt. Baker** via forks at the Nooksack River and Rte. 542. Mt. Baker (10,778 ft.) has been belching since 1975, and in winter jets of steam often snort from its dome.

No public transportation lines run within the North Cascades National Park or along the North Cascades Highway. Avoid hitching in this area. Information on **North Cascades National Park** and **Ross Lake National Recreation Area** is available at 2105 Rte. 20, Sedro Wooley (206-856-5700; open daily 8am-4:30pm; Oct.-May Mon.-Fri. 8am-4:30pm). Find out more about **Wenatchee National Forest** go to 301 Yakima St., Wenatchee 98801 (509-662-4335).

PACIFIC NORTHWEST

North Cascades **Newhalem** is the first town on Rte. 20 as you cross into the Ross Lake National Recreation Area, a buffer zone between the highway and North Cascades National Park. A small grocery store and **hiking** trails to the dams and lakes nearby are the highlights of Newhalem. The **visitors center and ranger station** (386-4495), off Rte. 20, has information, exhibits, and a banana slug couch to chill on (open mid-April to mid-Nov. daily 8:30am-4:30pm; call for winter hours).

The artificial expanse of **Ross Lake,** behind Ross Dam, extends into the mountains as far as the Canadian border. The lake is ringed by 15 campgrounds, some accessible by trail, others only by boat. The trail along **Big Beaver Creek,** at Mile 134 on Rte. 20, leads from Ross Lake over Ross Dam into the Picket Range and eventually all the way to Mt. Baker. The **Sourdough Mountain** and **Desolation Peak lookout towers** near Ross Lake offer eagle-eye views of the range.

The National Park's **Goodell Creek Campground,** just south of Newhalem, has 22 sites for tents and trailers with drinking water and pit toilets, and a launch site for **whitewater rafting** on the Skagit River (sites $7; after Oct., no water, and sites are free). **Colonial Creek Campground,** 10 mi. to the east, is a fully developed, wheelchair-accessible campground with flush toilets, a dump station, and campfire programs every evening (open mid-May to Oct.; 164 sites, $10). **Newhalem Creek Campground,** near the visitors center, is another similarly developed National Park facility (129 sites, $10).

Diablo Lake lies southwest of Ross Lake; the foot of Ross Dam acts as its eastern shore. Diablo Lake is a major trailhead for hikes into the southern unit of the Park. The **Thunder Creek Trail** traverses Park Creek Pass to Stehekin River Rd., in Lake Chelan National Recreation Area south of the park. For some areas, a free **backcountry permit** is required, available from park ranger stations.

East to Mazama and Winthrop Leaving the basin of Ross Lake, Rte. 20 begins to climb, exposing the jagged, snowy peaks of the North Cascades. Thirty mi. of jaw-dropping views east on Rte. 20, the **Pacific Crest Trail** crosses **Rainy Pass** on one of the most scenic and difficult legs of its 2500-mi. Canada-to-Mexico route. The trail leads north through **Pasayten Wilderness** and south past **Glacier Peak** (10,541 ft.) in the **Glacier Peak Wilderness.** Near Rainy Pass, groomed **scenic trails** 1 to 3 mi. long can be hiked in sneakers, provided the snow has melted (about mid-July). An overlook at **Washington Pass** rewards a short hike with one of the state's most dramatic panoramas, a flabbergasting view of the red rocks exposed by upper Early Winters Creek in **Copper Basin.** The popular 2.2-mi. walk to **Blue Lake** begins just east of Washington Pass. An easier 2-mi. hike to **Cutthroat Lake** departs from an access road 4.6 mi. east of Washington Pass. From the lake, the trail continues 4 mi. further and almost 2000 ft. higher to **Cutthroat Pass,** giving the persevering hiker a breathtaking view of towering peaks. A spectacular, hair-raising 19-mi. gravel road snakes up to **Hart's Pass,** the highest pass crossed by any road in the state. The road begins at **Mazama,** 10 mi. east of Washington Pass. The narrow, rough road is open early July to late September and is closed to trailers.

The Forest Service maintains a string of campgrounds along Rte. 20 (sites $7), between Washington Pass and Mazama. The **Early Winters Visitor Center** (996-2534), just outside Mazama, is aflutter with information about the **Pasayten Wilderness,** an area whose rugged terrain and mild climate endear it to hikers and equestrians. Take yourself on a hard-core five-day backcountry excursion to really experience it. (Visitors center open daily 9am-5pm; closes Labor Day for winter.)

Winthrop to Twisp Farther east is the town of **Winthrop,** child of an unholy marriage between the old television series *Bonanza* and Long Island yuppies who would eagerly claim a rusty horseshoe as an antique. Find the **Winthrop Information Station** (996-2125), on the corner of Rte. 20 and Riverside (open early May to mid-Oct. daily 10am-5pm).

Late July brings the top-notch **Winthrop Rhythm and Blues Festival** (996-2148); 1995 featured Booker T. and the MGs, The Band, and Dorothy Moor. Tickets for the great three-day event cost around $35. You can take a guided trail ride at the **Rocking Horse Ranch** (996-2768), 9 mi. north of Winthrop on Rte. 20 ($20 per 1½ hrs.). Or, rent a bike ($5 per hr., $20 per day) at **Winthrop Mountain Sports,** 257 Riverside Ave. (996-2886). The **Winthrop Ranger Station,** P.O. Box 579 (996-2266), at 24 W. Chewuch Rd., off Rte. 20 in the west end of town, has information about campgrounds, hikes, and fishing spots (open Mon.-Fri. 7:45am-5pm, Sat. 8:30am-5pm; closed weekends in winter).

Flee Winthrop's prohibitively expensive hotels and sleep in **Twisp,** 9 mi. south of Winthrop on Rte. 20. This peaceful hamlet offers low prices and far fewer tourists than its neighbor. Stay at **The Sportsman Motel,** 1010 E. Rte. 20 (997-2911), a hidden jewel, where a barracks-like façade masks tastefully decorated rooms and kitchens (singles $31, two people $36, doubles $39). Stop by the **Cinnamon Twisp Bakery,** 116 N. Glover St. (997-5030), for wonderful fresh-baked breads, bagels, and muffins (open Mon.-Sat. 7am-5pm). For lunch, grab a gourmet sandwich ($5.25 with soup or salad) at the **Glover Street Café,** 104 N. Glover St. (997-1323).

Helpful employees at the **Twisp Ranger Station,** 502 Glover St. (997-2131), will pelt you with trail and campground guides (open Mon.-Sat. 7:45am-4:30pm; winter Mon.-Fri. 7:45am-4:30pm). From Twisp, Rte. 20 continues east to Okanogan, and Rte. 153 south to **Lake Chelan.**

■■■ MOUNT RAINIER

Rising 2 mi. above the surrounding foothills, 14,411-ft.-high Mt. Rainier (ray-NEER) presides regally over the Cascade Range. Native Americans once called it "Tahoma," meaning "mountain of God." Today, Rainier is simply "the mountain" to most Washingtonians. Rainier even creates its own weather, jutting up into the warm ocean air and pulling down vast amounts of snow and rain. Clouds mask the mountain up to 200 days per year. Some 76 glaciers patch the slopes and combine with sharp ridges and steep gullies to make Rainier an inhospitable place for the 3000 determined climbers who clamber to its summit each year. Even for those who don't feel up to scaling the peak, there is plenty to explore.

Practical Information Mt. Rainier is 70 mi. from Seattle. To reach the park from the west, drive south from Seattle on I-5 to Tacoma, then go east on Rte. 512, south on Rte. 7, and east on Rte. 706. **Rte. 706** is the only access road open throughout the year; snow usually closes all other park roads Nov.-May. The park **entrance fee** is $5 per car, $3 per hiker; the gates are open 24 hrs. For **visitor information,** stop in at the **Longmire Hiker Information Center,** which distributes backcountry permits (open Sun.-Thurs. 8am-4:30pm, Fri. 8am-7pm, Sat. 7am-7pm; closed in winter). **Paradise Visitors Center** (589-2275) offers lodging, food, and souvenirs (open daily 9am-7pm; late Sept. to mid-Oct. 9:30am-6pm; mid-Oct. to May 10am-5pm). The **Sunrise Visitors Center** contains exhibits, snacks, and a gift shop (open daily June 25 to mid-Sept. 9am-6pm). The **Ohanapecosh Visitors Center** offers information and wildlife displays (open daily 9am-6pm; May-June Sat.-Sun. 9am-6pm; closed mid-Oct. to April). All centers can be contacted by writing c/o Superintendent, Mt. Rainier National Park, Ashford 98304, or by calling 569-2211. **Rainier Mountaineering Inc. (RMI)** (569-2227), in Paradise, rents ice axes ($8), crampons ($8), boots ($16.50), packs ($15), and helmets ($5.50) by the day. Expert RMI guides also lead summit climbs, seminars, and special schools and programs. (Open May-Oct. daily 10am-5pm. Winter office: 535 Dock St. #209, Tacoma 98402; 627-6242.) In a park **emergency,** call 569-2211 or 911. Rainier's **area code:** 206.

Accommodations and Food **Longmire, Paradise,** and **Sunrise** offer hotels and food that are often very costly. Stock up and stay in **Ashford** or **Packwood.** The **Hotel Packwood,** 104 Main St. (494-5431), is an old motel with good prices (singles $20, with bath $38, doubles $30). The **Gateway Inn Motel,** 38820 Rte. 706, Ashford (569-2506), has cabins for two ($49; singles and doubles $35, with bath $40).

Camping at the auto-accessible campsites from June through September is on a first-come, first-camped basis ($6-10). There are five such campgrounds in the park. Go to **Ohanapecosh** (205 sites) for the serene high ceiling of old-growth trees, to **Cougar Rock** (200 sites) for the strict quiet hours, to **Isput Creek** (29 sites) for the lush vegetation, and to **White River** (117 sites) or **Sunshine Point** (18 sites) for the panoramas. Sunshine Point is the only auto site open year-round.

Alpine and **cross-country camping** require free permits year-round and are subject to restrictions. Be sure to pick up a copy of the *Wilderness Trip Planner* pamphlet at any ranger station before you set off. With a **backcountry permit,** cross-country hikers can use any of the free, well-established **trailside camps** scattered throughout the park's backcountry. Most camps have toilet facilities and a nearby water source, and some have shelters as well. *Fires are prohibited,* and the size of a party is limited. **Glacier climbers** and **mountain climbers** intending to go above 10,000 ft. must register in person at ranger stations to be granted permits.

Outdoors All major roads offering scenic views of the mountain have numerous roadside sites for viewing. The roads to Paradise and Sunrise are especially picturesque. **Stevens Canyon Road** connects the southeast corner of the national park with Paradise, Longmire, and the Nisqually entrance, unfolding spectacular vistas of Rainier and the rugged Tatoosh Range. The accessible roadside attractions of **Box Canyon, Bench Lake,** and **Grove of the Patriarchs** line the route.

Mt. Adams and Mt. St. Helens, not visible from the road, can be seen clearly from such **mountain trails** as **Paradise** (1½ mi.), **Pinnacle Peak** (2½ mi.), **Eagle Peak** (7 mi.), and **Van Trump Peak** (5½ mi.). For more information on these trails, pick up *Viewing Mount St. Helens* at one of the visitors centers.

A segment of the **Pacific Crest Trail (PCT),** running between the Columbia River and the Canadian border, crosses through the southeast corner of the park. The PCT is maintained by the U.S. Forest Service. Primitive **campsites** and **shelters** line the trail as it snakes through delightful wilderness areas.

A trip to the **summit** of Mt. Rainier requires special preparation and substantial expense. The ascent is a vertical rise of more than 9000 ft. over a distance of 8 or more mi.—usually taking two days. Experienced climbers may form their own expeditions upon completion of a detailed application; novices can sign up for a **summit climb** (around $400) with **Rainier Mountaineering, Inc. (RMI).** For more information, contact **Park Headquarters** or **RMI** (see Practical Information).

Hardcore hikers will also be thrilled by the 95-mi. **Wonderland Trail,** which circumscribes Rainier. The entire circuit takes 10 to 14 days and includes several brutal ascents and descents. Rangers can provide information on weather and trail conditions; they also can store food caches for you at ranger stations along the trail.

■■■ MOUNT ST. HELENS

On May 18, 1980, in a single cataclysmic blast, the summit of Washington's beautiful Mt. St. Helens exploded into dust, creating a hole 2 mi. long and 1 mi. wide in what had been a perfect cone. Ash blackened the sky for hundreds of miles and blanketed the streets of nearby towns with inches of soot. Debris from the volcano flooded Spirit Lake, choked rivers with mud, and sent house-sized boulders tumbling down the mountainside. The blast leveled entire forests, leaving a stubble of trunks on the hills and millions of trees pointing arrow-like away from the crater.

Mt. St. Helens National Volcanic Monument is steadily recovering from that explosion. Fifteen years later, the spectacle of disaster is freckled by signs of returning life—saplings push up past denuded logs, while insects and small mammals return to the blast zone. The mountain, like many other Cascade peaks, is still considered active and could erupt again, though risk is now low.

Practical Information Start any trip to the mountain at the **Mt. St. Helens National Volcanic Monument Visitors Center** (206-274-2100 or 206-274-2103 for 24-hr. recording), on Rte. 504 5 mi. east of Castle Rock (exit 49 off of I-5). Interpretive talks and displays recount the mountain's eruption and regeneration, and are augmented by a 22-min. film and many hands-on activities. The center also provides info on lodgings, camping, and mountain access. The **Pine Creek Information Center** in the south and the **Woods Creek Information Center** in the north are smaller than the main center, but are both within 1 mi. of excellent viewpoints. Both offer displays, maps, and brochures on the area. (All three centers open daily 9am-6pm; Oct.-March 9am-5pm). In an **emergency,** call 911.

The monument is roughly bounded on the north by U.S. 12, on the south by Forest Rd. 90, and on the east by Forest Rd. 25, which runs between Rd. 90 and U.S. 12. From the west, Rte. 504 and Rte. 503 offer access to the monument. **U.S. 12,** reached by Rte. 7 south from Tacoma or exit 68 off I-5, offers no direct mountain access but is the quickest way to Windy Ridge and offers stunning views of blasted forest. **Rte. 504** is the most scenic approach road. Rte. 504 can be reached by exiting I-5 at exit 49. Bear in mind that Rte. 504 dead-ends at Coldwater Lake; you must return to I-5. About 25 mi. farther south, **Rte. 503** runs east through Cougar, a center for hikers planning to tackle the peak, and connects with Rd. 90. *Drivers should fill up their gas tanks before starting the journey, as fuel is not sold within the park.* Mt. St. Helens's **area code:** 360.

Camping For those who want an early start touring the mountain, there are two primitive **campgrounds** relatively near the crater. **Iron Creek Campground,** on Forest Rd. 25 near the junction with Forest Rd. 76, has 98 sites ($8 each, call 800-283-2267 for reservations). **Swift Campground,** on Forest Rd. 90, has 93 sites ($8 each, no reservations). Just west of Swift Campground on Yale Reservoir lie **Beaver Bay** and **Cougar Campgrounds,** both of which have flush toilets and showers and are run by Pacific Power & Light (sites $8; for reservations call 503-464-5035). The monument itself contains no campgrounds, but there are many in the surrounding national forest, and free dispersed camping (in unmaintained, primitive sites) is allowed in the monument and national forest. Contact a ranger or the **Gifford Pinchot National Forest Headquarters,** 6926 E. Fourth Plain Blvd., Vancouver 98668 (696-7500), for information.

Outdoors **Forest Rd. 99** leads visitors along 17 mi. of curves, clouds of ash, and precipices, past **Spirit Lake,** to a point just 3½ mi. from the crater. Without stops it takes nearly an hour to travel out and back, but the numerous interpretive talks and walks, and the spectacular views along the way, are definitely worth exploring. Check with one of the visitors centers or in the free newsletters for times and meeting places of these interpretive activities. Continue 25 mi. south on Forest Rd. 25, 12 mi. west on Forest Rd. 90, then 2 mi. north on Forest Rd. 83 to **Ape Cave,** a broken, 2½-mi.-long lava tube formed in an ancient eruption, which is now open for visitors to explore. Be sure to wear a jacket and sturdy shoes; you can rent a lantern for $3.

The **Coldwater Ridge Visitors Center** (274-2131; fax 274-2129), 43 mi. east of Castle Rock and I-5 on Rte. 504, is an angular triumph of modern architecture, and practically a free museum unto itself. The deck, flooded with photographs, has a superb view of the cavity where the mountain's north side used to be and two lakes created by the eruption's aftermath. Check out the hiking and picnic areas, interpretive talks, snack bar, and gift shop. (Open daily 9am-6pm; Oct.-March 9am-5pm.).

Those with a taste for conquest and strong legs should scale the stunted crater for unmatched views of the eruption's destruction and its source. The route is not a technical climb, but is steep and covered in loose scree. Average hiking time up is 5 hours, down is 3 hours. Permits for the hike are required; contact **Monument Headquarters,** 42218 NE Yale Bridge Rd., Amboy 98601 (750-3900) for info and permit reservations. Some permits are distributed each day on a first come, first served basis; call Monument Headquarters for details.

It's big...and hairy!

You may have heard tales of mystery members of the hominid family whose existence remains shrouded in murky lore, inscrutable to the scientific community. Directly east of Mt. St. Helens lies the Dark Divide, the area most associated with the sightings of these large, hirsute creatures who lurk in the forests and eat nuts and twigs. This fearsome beast was known even before the white man got his grubby hands on the New World. The Salish called the creature *saskehavas*, from which comes the English term **"Sasquatch."** Many dismiss the possibility of any such mysterious **ape-man.** Why, they query, hasn't conclusive evidence of its existence been adduced? Cryptozoologists (scientists who study undiscovered species) reply that numerous sightings and photographs *are* conclusive, and that naysayers are deluded by their grouchy-gus skepticism. Regardless of your position in the debate, there are some basic facts you should know in case of a chance encounter with **Bigfoot.** First, it is easy to recognize. The **big galoot** stands roughly six to ten feet tall, weighs about 400 pounds, is covered in dark fur, and leaves behind a strong, fetid **odor.** Second, to assure that it does not attack and rip your head off, make the following sign of peace: cross your arms on your chest and pat your shoulders. Sasquatch will understand. Third, if you have serious evidence of a sighting, there are people who will listen. Call 800-BIGFOOT/2443668 in WA to speak to fellow believers.

EASTERN WASHINGTON

■■■ SPOKANE

Spokane was the first pioneer settlement in the Northwest, and is now one of the area's major trade centers. Spokane graces eastern Washington with inexpensive accommodations and lots of delicious, cheap food.

Spokane's best sights are the outdoors. **Riverfront Park,** N. 507 Howard St. (625-6600), just north of downtown, is Spokane's civic center and greatest asset. Developed for the 1974 World's Fair, the park's 100 acres are divided by the roaring rapids that culminate in Spokane Falls. There are few long waits for the fair's remaining attractions. The **Arbor Crest Estate,** N. 4705 Fruithill Rd. (927-9894), is a beautiful compound atop a breezy bluff with stunning vistas overlooking the gorgeous valley below. Sample excellent Washington wine for free. Take I-90 to exit 287, travel north on Argonne over the Spokane River, turn right on Upriver Dr., proceed 1 mi., and the bear left onto Fruithill Rd. Take a sharp left at the top of the hill.

Riverside State Park (456-3964) embroiders the Spokane River with 12 sq. mi. of volcanic outcroppings, hiking trails (especially good in **Deep Creek Canyon,** the fossil beds of a forest that grew seven million years ago), and equestrian trails in nearby Trail Town (horse rides $12.50 per hr., by appointment only; 456-8249). A July, 1994 wildfire charred much of the park, but the blackened trees blend in well with the volcanic rock, yielding a stark and beautiful effect. You can also camp at one of the 100 sites in Riverside ($11).

The **Spokane Area Convention and Visitors Bureau,** W. 926 Sprague Ave. (747-3230 or 800-248-3230), at Monroe, exit 280 off I-90, is overflowing with Spokane info (open Mon.-Fri. 8:30am-5pm). **Emergency** is 911. Spokane's **post office:** W. 904 Riverside (459-0230; open Mon.-Fri. 9am-5pm); **ZIP Code**: 99210; **area code:** 509.

Climb up Lincoln to **Hosteling International Spokane (HI-AYH),** S. 930 Lincoln (838-5968), a large Victorian house with a spacious porch, delightfully creaky wooden floorboards, kitchen, and laundry (22 beds; check-in 4-10pm; no curfew; $10, nonmembers $13).

The **Spokane County Market** (482-2627), on the north end of Riverside Park, sells fresh fruit, vegetables, and baked goods (open May-Oct. Wed. and Sat. 9am-5pm, Sun. 10am-5pm). A takeout burger phenom, **Dick's,** E. 10 3rd Ave. (747-2481), at Division, is in an inexplicably inflation-free pocket of Washington (burgers 55¢, fries 43¢, sundaes 65¢; open daily 9am-1:30am). Cyrus O'Leary's, W. 516 Main St. (624-9000), in the Bennetts Block complex at Howard St., is another Spokane legend; sandwiches are $5.75 and up (happy hour 4:30-6:30pm; open Mon.-Thurs. 11am-10pm, Fri.-Sun. 11am-11pm). For a bit of nightlife, Mother's Pub, W. 230 Riverside Ave. (624-9828), coddles with live rock Fri.-Sat. nights. (Cover charge $2-6; draft beer from $1.25; open Wed.-Sat. 7pm-2am.)

Spokane lies 280 mi. east of Seattle on I-90. Avenues in Spokane run east-west parallel to the river, streets north-south, and both alternate one-way. The city is divided north and south by **Sprague Ave.,** east and west by **Division St.** The **Spokane International Airport** (624-3218) is off I-90, 8 mi. southwest of town. **Amtrak,** W. 221 1st St. (624-5144, or 800-872-7245), at Bernard St., downtown, zips off to Chicago (1 per day, $217), Seattle (1 per day, $67), and Portland (1 per day, $67). (Station open 24 hrs. Ticket office open Mon.-Fri. 11am-5:30am, Sat.-Sun. 7:15pm-5:30am). **Greyhound,** (tickets 624-5251, info 624-5252 or 800-231-2222), runs from the train station to Seattle (5 per day, $19) and Portland (5 per day, $29). (Ticket office open daily 6am-7:30pm, 9:30-10:30pm, 1-2am.) **Northwestern Trailways** (838-5262 or 800-366-3830) also operates out of the train station, with service to other parts of Washington, Oregon, Idaho, and Montana.

Oregon

Have you ever wondered why, over 150 years ago, entire families liquidated their possessions and sank their life's fortunes into covered wagons, oxen, horses, flour, bacon, and small arms and trekked 1500 mi. from the edge of civilization across harsh, boundless, rugged, hostile, and totally unfamiliar country just to get to Oregon? Once you visit Oregon, you'll realize why. Thousands of visitors are drawn each year by the unparalleled natural beauty of this state. North America's deepest gorge and the towering Wallowa Mountains clash in the northeast, while the southeast's vast, desolate Steens country begs for outdoor exploration. With Crater Lake, Mt. Hood, and the Pacific Crest Trail, the forested peaks of the Cascade Range stun visitors with their splendor. The awesome Columbia River Gorge and the rugged coast with its brilliant tide pools beckon with shimmering blue waters. Hikers, cyclists, anglers, climbers, skiers, windsurfers, trekkers, and explorers all revel in Oregon.

The waves and cliffs of the gorgeous Oregon's Pacific coast are indeed amazing and constitute the state's primary tourist pull. However, you should also venture inland to see some of Oregon's greatest attractions—fabulous Mt. Hood, the volcanic cinder-cones near Crater Lake, the Shakespeare festival in Ashland, and world-class yet easy-going Portland.

At press time, the 503 area code was scheduled to split on November 5, 1995 to two area codes: 503 (Portland and the Willamette Valley) and 541 (the rest of the state). Check with the phone company to find out which area code should be used for the number you wish to call.

PRACTICAL INFORMATION

Capital: Salem.

Oregon Tourism Division: 775 Summer St. NE, Salem 97310 (800-547-7842; fax 503-986-0001). **Oregon State Parks,** 1115 Commercial St. NE, Salem 97310-1001 (378-6305). **Department of Fish and Wildlife,** P.O. Box 59, Portland 97207 (229-5404 or 229-5222 for recorded info).

Time Zone: Mountain and Pacific. **Postal Abbreviation:** OR

Sales Tax: 0%

■■■ PORTLAND

Casual and tolerant, Portland is the mellowest big city on the West Coast. Unhurried, uncongested, and without pretension, the downtown area is spotless, and building height is regulated to preserve views of the river, hills, and mountains. Funded by a one-percent tax on new construction, Portland's varied artistic scene is anchored by Portland's venerable Symphony Orchestra, the oldest in the country. On a July day you can ski Mt. Hood in the morning, watch the sun drop into the Pacific Ocean from the cool sand of an empty beach, and still return to town in time to catch an outdoor jazz concert at the zoo. Portland's first-rate flock of small breweries pump out barrels of some of the nation's finest ale.

The award-winning **Tri-Met bus system** weaves together Portland's districts and suburbs. In the transit mall, 31 covered passenger shelters serve as both stops and information centers. Southbound buses pick up passengers along SW 5th Ave.; northbound passengers board on SW 6th Ave. Bus routes fall into seven regional service areas, each with its own individual "Lucky Charm": orange deer, yellow rose, green leaf, brown beaver, blue snow, red salmon, and purple rain. Shelters and buses are color-coded for their regions. A few buses with black numbers on white backgrounds cross town north-south or east-west, ignoring color-coded boundaries.

PRACTICAL INFORMATION

Tourist Office: Portland/Oregon Visitors Association, 25 SW Salmon St. (222-2223 or 800-345-3214), at Front St. in the Two World Trade Center complex. From I-5, follow the signs for City Center. Pick up the *Portland Book.* Open Mon.-Fri. 8am-6:30pm, Sat. 8:30am-5pm; winter Mon.-Fri. 8:30am-5pm, Sat. 9am-3pm.

Airport: Portland International, 7000 NE Airport Way (335-1234). Take Tri-Met bus #12 (a 45-min. ride), which arrives going south on SW 5th Ave. (95¢). **Raz Tranz** (246-3301 for taped info) has a shuttle that stops at most major hotels downtown. Fare $7, ages 6-12 $1. Taxis to downtown $21-24.

Trains: Amtrak, 800 NW 6th Ave. (273-4866 or 800-USA-RAIL/872-7245, Union Station 273-4865), at Hoyt St. To: Seattle (4 per day, $23); Eugene (1 per day, $24); Spokane (1 per day, $67); Boise (1 per day, $83). Open daily 6:45am-6pm.

Buses: Greyhound, 550 NW 6th Ave. (243-2357 or 800-231-2222) at Glisan. To: Seattle (12 per day; $19); Eugene (9 per day, $15); Spokane (4 per day, $29). Lockers available, $2 for 6 hrs. Ticket window open daily 5am-midnight. Station open 24 hrs.

Public Transportation: Tri-Met, Customer Service Center, #1 Pioneer Courthouse Sq., 701 SW 6th Ave. (238-7433). Office open Mon.-Fri. 7:30am-5:30pm. Several 24-hr. recorded info lines; fare info 231-3198; updates, changes, and weather-related problems 231-3197; senior and disabled services 238-4952. Service generally 5am-midnight, reduced Sat.-Sun. Fare 95¢-$1.25, ages 7-18 70¢, over 65 and disabled 45¢; no fare downtown in the "Fareless Sq.," bounded by NW Irving St. in the north, I-405 in the west and south, and the Wilamette River in the east. All-day pass $3.25. All buses have bike racks ($5 2-year permit available at area bike stores) and are wheelchair-accessible. **MAX** (228-7246) is an efficient rail running between Gresham to the east and downtown. Same fare system as buses. Pick up monthly passes, bus maps, and schedules at the visitors center or at the customer service center.

Taxis: Broadway Cab, 227-1234. **Radio Cab,** 227-1212. Both 24 hrs.

Car Rental: Avis Rent-A-Car (800-331-1212 or 249-4950), at airport. $36 per day, $140 per week; unlimited free mi. Must be 25 with credit card.

Crisis Lines: Crisis Line, 223-6161. **Women's Crisis Line,** 235-5333. Both 24 hrs. **Phoenix Rising,** 223-8299. Gay and lesbian info and referrals. Open Mon.-Fri. 9am-5pm.

Emergency: 911.

Post Office: 715 NW Hoyt St. (294-2300). Open Mon.-Sat. 7am-6:30pm. **ZIP code:** 97208-9999. **Area code:** 503.

Portland is in the northwest corner of Oregon, near where the Willamette (wi-LAM-it) River flows into the Columbia River. By car, Portland lies about 70 mi. from the Pacific Ocean, 635 mi. north of San Francisco, and 170 mi. south of Seattle. **I-5** connects Portland with San Francisco and Seattle; **I-84** follows the route of the Oregon Trail through the Columbia River Gorge toward Boise.

Portland is divided into five districts. **Burnside St.** divides the city north and south; the Willamette River separates east and west. **Williams Ave.** cuts off a corner of the northeast which is called "North." All street signs are labeled by their districts: N, NE, NW, SE, and SW. **Southwest** district is the city's hub, encompassing the downtown area and the southern end of historic Old Town. The heart of downtown is between SW 5th and 6th Ave., where car traffic is prohibited. The **Northwest** district contains **Old Town** and the swanky **West Hills.** The **Southeast** is the hippest part of the city. The city's best ethnic restaurants line **Hawthorne Boulevard,** along with small cafés and theaters catering to the artsy crowd, mostly supported by nearby **Reed College's** students. The **North** and **Northeast** districts are chiefly residential, punctuated by a few quiet, small parks. Parking is plentiful but expensive: meters are 75¢ per hour.

ACCOMMODATIONS AND CAMPING

It's always wise to make reservations early, because places can fill in a flash, especially during the Rose Festival or a convention. Camping, though distant, is plentiful.

Portland International Hostel (HI-AYH), 3031 SE Hawthorne Blvd. (236-3380), at 31st Ave, is the place to meet cool folks. Take bus #14 "Brown Beaver." Sleep inside or on the back porch. Kitchen; laundromat across the street. Fills up early in the summer, so make reservations (credit card required) or plan to arrive at 5pm to get one of the 12-15 beds saved for walk-ins. Don't miss the all-you-can-eat pancakes every morning ($1). Open daily 7:30-10am and 5-11pm. No curfew. $12, nonmembers $15.

Ondine, 1912 SW 6th Ave. (725-4336), at Portland State University between College and Hall St. The budget travel experience of a lifetime. 5 clean, spacious rooms, each with 2 twin beds. Linen and towels provided. Private bathrooms. Microwaves available; no kitchen. Laundry facilities. The dormitory is in Fareless

Sq., so you can hop on the bus and be downtown in a minute. Parking nightmarish. Reservations required 1-2 wks. in advance. One person $20, two $25.

McMenamins Edgefield Hostel, 2126 SW Halsey St., Troutdale (669-8610 or 800-669-8610), 20 min. east of Portland off I-84. 2 vast rooms, single-sex, each with 12 beds. Showers down the hall in claw-footed tubs. $18 per night.

YWCA, 1111 SW 10th St. (223-6281). Women only. Clean and safe. Small rooms. Bathroom, shower, laundry, and small kitchen. Hostel has 4 beds ($10). Singles $22, with private bath $26, doubles $28/$31. Key deposit $2.

Ben Stark Hotel International Hostel (AAIH/Rucksackers), 1022 SW Stark St. (274-1223; fax 274-1033). Fantastic location, just blocks from downtown. Ascend the imposing, dark staircase to find 3 decent hostel rooms. Mostly international travelers. 12 beds. 24-hr. desk service. $15; in winter $12. Call for reservations.

Milo McIver State Park is 25 mi. southeast of Portland, off Rte. 211, 5 mi. west of the town of Estacada. Fish, swim, or bicycle along the Clackamas River. (Hot showers, flush toilets. Sites $15.) Hike, bike, or visit the historic home and log cabin museum at **Champoeg State Park,** 8239 Champoeg Rd. NE (678-1251; sites $15). **Ainsworth State Park,** 37 mi. east of Portland off I-84, in the Columbia Gorge, offers hot showers, flush toilets, hiking trails (sites with full hookup $19).

FOOD

Portland has more restaurants per capita than any other American city. You'll never get tired of eating out in Portland, and you'll also never go broke. Espresso bars are everywhere.

Chang's Mongolian Grill, 1 SW 3rd St. (243-1991), at Burnside. All-you-can-eat lunches ($6) or dinners ($9). Select your meal from a buffet of fresh vegetables, meat, and fish, mix your own sauce to taste, and watch your chef make a wild show of cooking it on a domed grill the size of a Volkswagen beetle. Rice and hot-and-sour soup included. Open daily 11:30am-2:30pm and 5-10pm.

Western Culinary Institute Chef's Corner, 1239 SW Jefferson (242-2422 or 800-666-0312). Testing ground for the cooking school's adventures. Students in tall white hats will whip up a delicious, cheap meal. All lunches under $6. For breakfast, try the gourmet hash browns. Open Mon. 8am-2:30pm, Tues.-Fri. 8am-6pm.

Brasserie Montmartre, 626 SW Park Ave. (224-5552). Paper tablecloths, crayons, and live jazz nightly offer diversions for dull dates and similarly awkward social situations. Lunch entrees around $6, dinner $9 for chicken or steak. Open Mon.-Thurs. 11:30am-2am, Fri. 11:30am-3am, Sat. 10am-3am, Sun. 10am-2am.

Food Front, 2375 NW Thurman St. (223-6819), offers a wonderland of natural foods, fruit, and baked goods. Open daily 9am-10pm; off-peak 9am-9pm.

Café Lena, 2239 SE Hawthorne Blvd. (238-7087), is known for its open-mike poetry every Tues. at 7:30pm. Live music accentuates an appetizing menu. Try the Birkenstock Submarine ($5). Open Tues.-Thurs. 7am-11pm, Fri.-Sat. 7am-midnight, Sun. 8am-2pm.

Old Town Pizza, 226 NW Davis St. (222-9999). Relax on a couch or at a table in this wood-lined former whorehouse. Ghost sightings have not affected staff's pizza-crafting abilities (small cheese, $4.55). Open daily 11am-11pm.

Kornblatt's, 628 NW 23rd Ave. (242-0055). Take bus #15 (red salmon). "What, you're not eating? You look so thin!" Sandwiches are expensive but huge ($5-8). Crowded, but worth the wait. Open Sun.-Wed. 7am-10pm, Thurs.-Sat. 7am-11pm.

Thanh Thao Restaurant, 4005 SE Hawthorne Blvd. (238-6232). Fabulous Thai. There's often a wait for dinner, so go early. Open Mon.-Fri. 11am-2:30pm and 5-10pm, Sat.-Sun. 11am-10pm.

SIGHTS

Shaded parks, magnificent gardens, innumerable museums and galleries, and bustling open-air markets beckon the city's tourists and residents alike. Catch the best of Portland's dizzying dramatic and visual arts scene on the first Thursday of each month when the small galleries in the Southwest and Northwest all stay open until

9pm. For information contact the **Metropolitan Arts Commission,** 1120 SW 5th Ave. (823-5111). Grab the *Art Gallery Guide* at the visitors center, which describes 65 art hot spots and pinpoints them on a map. Or go to **Portland Art Museum,** 1219 SW Park Ave. (226-2811), to latch onto a **Public Art Walking Tour**.

Portland's downtown area is centered on the pedestrian and bus **mall,** running north-south between 5th and 6th Ave., bounded on the north by W. Burnside St. and on the south by SW Madison St. At 5th Ave. and Morrison St. sits **Pioneer Courthouse,** a central downtown landmark. The monument is still a Federal courthouse and is the centerpiece for **Pioneer Courthouse Sq.,** 701 SW 6th Ave. (223-1613), which opened in 1983. Portlanders of every ilk hang out in this massive brick quadrangle that has a Starbucks in one corner and the travel branch of Powell's in the other. Area citizens purchased personalized bricks to support the construction of an amphitheater that hosts live jazz, folk, and international music. During the summer the **Peanut Butter and Jam Sessions** draw thousands to enjoy the music (Tues. and Thurs. noon-1pm).

Anyone who doubts that mega-corporations will soon rule the world need only visit **Niketown,** 930 SW 6th (221-6453). TVs in the floor, a life-sized Michael Jordan sculpture, and hypnotic signs have tourists wandering dazed (and loving it). Sports fans will enjoy the various artifacts: the jerseys and shoes of athletes, the balls they've played with, and even an autographed Jordan Wheaties Box. Advertising is art! Art is advertising! It's gotta be the shoes! (Open Mon.-Thurs. and Sat. 10am-7pm, Fri. 10am-8pm, Sun. 11:30am-6:30pm.) **The American Advertising Museum,** 524 NE Grand (226-0000 or 230-1090), chronicles the fast-paced, hopping world of advertising. The gallery shows temporary exhibits; summer 1995 showcased a fascinating and informative survey of AIDS posters. ($3, seniors and under 12 $1.50; open Wed.-Sun. 11am-5pm.)

The **Portland Art Museum,** 1219 SW Park (226-2811), at Jefferson St., houses Western painting and sculpture from the 1350s to the 1950s, as well as prints, photos, and contemporary works. The impressive collection of art from other cultures includes samples from Cameroon and Asia. The excellent Pacific Northwest Native American art exhibit includes masks, textiles, and sacred objects ($5, seniors $3.50, students $2.50; open Tues.-Sat. 11am-5pm, Sun. 1-5pm; 2 for 1 AAA discount; 1st Thurs. of each month free from 4-9pm; Thurs. seniors free). The **Pacific Northwest College of Art** (226-4391) and the **Northwest Film Center** (221-1156) are in the same building. The Film Center shows classics, documentaries, and off-beat flicks Thursdays through Sundays at 921 SW Morrison (tickets $6). **Museum After Hours** is a jazz and blues concert series (Oct.-April, 5:30-7:30pm) popular with execs and the after-work crowd (prices vary; call).

Old Town, north of the mall, resounded a century ago with the clamor of sailors whose ships filled the ports. The district has been revived by the large-scale restoration of store fronts, new "old brick," polished iron and brass, and a bevy of recently opened shops and restaurants. Old Town also marks the end of **Waterfront Park.** This 20-block-long swath of grass and flowers along the Willamette River provides locals with an excellent place to picnic, fish, stroll, and enjoy major community events. The eclectic, festive **Saturday Market,** 108 W. Burnside St. (222-6072), by the Skidmore Fountain between 1st and Front St., is overrun with street musicians, artists, craftspeople, chefs, and greengrocers clogging the largest open-air crafts market in the country. Many of these artists sell their work in the city's studios and galleries during the week. (March-Dec. Sat. 10am-5pm, Sun. 11am-4:30pm.)

Portland is the uncontested **microbrewery** capital of the United States and possibly the world, and Portlanders are proud of their beery city. The visitors center can give you a list of 26 metro area breweries, most of which will be happy to show you around their facilities. Henry Weinhard, a German brewmaster, started this tradition when he established the first brewery in the Northwest, outside of Fort Vancouver in 1856. Today, **Henry's** has become an Oregon standard, outgrowing its status as a microbrew. Visit the **Blitz Weinhard Brewery,** 1133 W. Burnside (222-4351), for a ½-hour tour and samples in the hospitality room (free; open weekday afternoons).

Less than 2 mi. west of downtown, the posh neighborhoods of **West Hills** form a manicured buffer zone between the soul-soothing parks and the turmoil of the city below. Take the animated "zoo bus" (#63) or drive up SW Broadway to Clay St. and turn right onto U.S. 26 (get off at zoo exit). **Washington Park** and its nearby attractions are perhaps the most soulful sites in Portland. The park's gates are open daily 7am to 9pm. **Hoyt Arboretum,** 4000 SW Fairview Blvd. (228-8733 or 823-3655), at the crest of the hill above the other gardens, features 200 acres of trees and trails. Free nature walks (April-Nov. Sat.-Sun. at 2pm) last 90 min. and cover 1-2 mi. The **Rose Garden,** 400 SW Kingston Ave., on the way to the zoo entrance, is a gorgeous place to stroll on a lazy day or cool evening. Clear days afford a spectacular view of the city and distant **Mount Hood.** Stunning views are also seen at the **Japanese Gardens,** 611 SW Kingston Ave., the most authentic outside Japan.

Below the Hoyt Arboretum stands Portland's favorite attractions. The **Washington Park Zoo,** 4001 SW Canyon Rd. (226-1561 or 226-7627), is renowned for its successful elephant-breeding and its scrupulous recreation of natural habitats. Take the #63 "Zoo" bus from the park to SW Morrison St. in the downtown mall. A miniature **railway** also connects the Washington Park gardens with the zoo. (Rail $2.50, seniors and ages 3-11 $1.75. Zoo open summer daily 9:30am-6pm. $5.50, seniors $4, children $3.50; second Tues. of each month free 3-6pm.) In June, July, or August, head to the Washington Park amphitheater to catch **Your Zoo and All That Jazz** (234-9695 or 226-1561), a nine-week series of open-air jazz concerts (Wed. 7-9pm), free with zoo admission. **Rhythm and Zoo Concerts** (234-9694) also features a series of concerts free with admission (Thurs. 7-9pm). The **World Forestry Center,** 4033 SW Canyon Rd. (228-1367), specializes in exhibits on Northwestern forestry and logging. Warning: the Forestry Center's 70-ft. "talking tree" *never shuts up*. (Open daily 9am-5pm, Labor Day-Memorial Day 10am-5pm. $3, students $2.)

The funky students in the cafés, theaters, and restaurants on Hawthorne Blvd. belong to **Reed College,** 3203 SE Woodstock (771-1112). Founded in 1909, Reed sponsors many cultural events. The ivy-draped grounds, which encompass a lake and a wildlife refuge, make up one of the most attractive campuses in the country. One-hour tours, geared to prospective students, leave Eliot Hall #220, 3203 Woodstock Blvd. at SE 28th, twice per day during the school year (Mon.-Fri. 10am and 2pm; individual tours are available by appointment in summer. Call 777-7511).

Farther southeast is **Mt. Tabor Park,** SE 60th Ave. and Salmon St., one of two city parks in the world on the site of an extinct volcano. Take bus #15 "Brown beaver."

Don't Expect to Play Frisbee in This Park

No one knew that a hole cut through the sidewalk at the corner of SW Taylor St. and SW Front St. in 1948 was destined for greatness. Indeed, it was expected to accommodate an inglorious lamp post. But the post was never installed, and the 24-inch circle of earth was left empty until Dick Fagan, a columnist for the Oregon Journal, noticed it. Fagan used his column, called "Mill Ends," to publicize the patch of dirt, pointing out that it would make a great, though microscopic park. After years of lobbying, the park was officially added to the city's roster in 1976. At 452.16 sq. in., **Mill Ends Park** is recognized by the *Guiness Book of World Records* as the **world's smallest park.** Locals have enthusiastically adopted the park, planting flowers and hosting a hotly contested **snail race** on St. Patrick's Day. Go, slug, go!

ENTERTAINMENT AND NIGHTLIFE

Once an uncouth and rowdy port town, Portland manages to maintain an irreverent attitude. Many waterfront pubs have evolved into upscale bistros and French bakeries. Nightclubs cater to everyone from the casual college student to the hardcore rocker. For entertainment listings, check the Friday edition of the *Oregonian* and in a number of free handouts: *Willamette Week* (put out each evening and catering to students), *Just Out* (catering to gay and lesbian interests), the *Main Event,* and the *Downtowner* are available in restaurants downtown and in boxes on street corners.

Portland has its share of good, formal concerts, but why bother with admission fees? The most exciting talent plays for free in various public facilities around the city. Call the Park Bureau (796-5193) for info, and check the *Oregonian* for **Brown Bag Concerts,** free public concerts given around the city in a six-week summer series (at noon during the week and Tues. evenings). The **Oregon Symphony Orchestra** plays classical and pop in **Arlene Schnitzer Concert Hall,** 1111 SW Broadway Ave. (228-1353 or 800-228-7343; Sept.-June; tickets $8-46; "Symphony Sunday" afternoon concerts $18.) **Chamber Music Northwest** performs summer concerts from late June through July at **Reed College Commons,** 3203 SE Woodstock Ave. (223-3202; Mon., Thurs., and Sat. at 8pm. $17, ages 7-14 $9).

Portland's many fine theaters produce everything from off-Broadway shows to experimental drama. **Portland Center Stage** (274-6588), at the Intermediate Theater of **Portland Center for the Performing Arts (PCPA)** (796-9293), at SW Broadway and SW Main. features classics from Oct.-April. (Tickets Fri.-Sat. $11-33, a little more Sun. and Tues.-Thurs.; ½-price tickets sometimes available at the Intermediate Theater 1hr. before showtime.)

Neighborhood taverns and pubs have the most character and best music, but are harder to find. The clubs closest to downtown are in Northwest Portland.

Produce Row Café, 204 SE Oak St. (232-8355), has 28 beers on tap, 72 bottled domestic and imported beers. Bus #6 "Red Salmon" to SE Oak and SE Grand, then walk west along Oak towards the river. Live music Sat.-Mon. Low, varying cover. Open Mon.-Fri. 11am-midnight or 1am, Sat. noon-1am, Sun. noon-midnight.

La Luna, 215 SE 9th Ave. (241-LUNA/5862). Take bus #20 "Purple Rain," get off at 9th, walk 2 blocks south. Live concerts, 2 bars and a Generation X crowd. Open Thurs.-Sat. 8pm-2:30am, concerts and special events other nights.

Bridgeport Brew Pub, 1313 NW Marshall (241-7179). Great beer and pizza. Open Mon.-Thurs. 11am-11pm, Fri. 11:30am-midnight, Sat. noon-midnight, Sun. 1-9pm.

Lotus Card Room and Café, 932 SW 3rd Ave. (227-6185), at SW Salmon St., plays techno, house, and hip-hop, attracting collegiate crowd Fri. and Sat. Dance floor Wed.-Sun. 10pm-2am. Cover $2-4, sometimes free. Open daily 7am-2am.

The Space Room, 4800 SE Hawthorne Blvd. (235-8303). Take bus #14 "Brown Beaver." Judy Jetson smoked way too many cigarettes inside this space-age joint. The cutting-edge crowd contemplate the vintage-clothing possibilities. One bloody mary ($3) will put you over the edge. Open daily 6am-2:30am.

Panorama, 341 SW 10th St. (221-RAMA/7262) at Stark St. Cavernous dance floor studded with elegant Mediterranean pillars. Thriving gay and straight crowd; dance till you drop. Walk into the connecting bars **Briggs** or **Boxes.** Panorama serves only beer and wine. Cover Fri.-Sat. $3; Sun. 50¢ draft beer. Open Thurs. and Sun. 9pm-2:30am, Fri.-Sat. 9pm-4am.

■ NEAR PORTLAND: THE COLUMBIA GORGE

Only an hour from Portland, close enough for a great daytrip, the spectacular Columbia River Gorge stretches 20 to 90 mi. east of Portland. Here the Columbia carves a canyon 1000 ft. deep through rumpled hills and sheer, rocky cliffs. The immense dams that choke the river look puny compared to the sheer expanse and depth of the gorge.

The famous **Vista House** (695-2240), completed in 1918 as a memorial to Oregon's pioneers, is now a visitors center in Crown Point State Park (open daily 9am-6pm). The house hangs on the edge of an outcropping high above the river. Crown Point is 3 mi. east of eastbound exit 22 off I-84. A string of waterfalls adorns the scenic highway east of Crown Point. The granddaddy of them all, **Multnomah Falls,** attracts two million visitors annually. The falls crash 620 ft. into a tiny pool which then drains into a lower falls. Exit 31, on I-84, is an island in the middle of the freeway from which you can see only the upper falls, but which provides access to walking trails through a pedestrian subway. A quick hike takes you to **Benson Bridge** wedged above the lower falls with views of the upper falls.

The wide Columbia and its 30mph winds make Hood River a **windsurfing** paradise. At **Duck Jibe Pete's,** 13 Oak St. (386-9434), you can rent a high-quality sailboard including a car rack for $35 a day (open 8am-8pm daily). If you catch windsurfing mania, a class at **Rhonda Smith Port Marina Park** (386-WIND/9463) will get you started or take you up a notch (classes at five different levels; 2½-3 hr.; $60-75). The visitors center at the **Dalles Lock and Dam** (296-1181), the longest concrete dam in America, offers free one-hour tours that include a train ride to the dam, an informative view of the fish ladder, a glimpse of the generator, and a look at old Indian pictographs (tours leave every ½hr.; visitors center open April-Sept., daily 9am-5pm). The Dalles is 19 mi. east of Hood River on I-84.

The town of Hood River, 76 mi. east of Portland on I-84, is the largest town in the gorge. The **Hood River County Chamber of Commerce** (386-2000 or 800-366-3530) in Port Marine Park has the scoop on the gorge. Pick up the free publications *Gorge Vistas* and *The Visitor's Guide to Gorge Fun.* (Open Mon.-Thurs. 9am-5pm, Fri. 9am-4pm, Sat.-Sun. 10am-4pm; mid-Oct. to mid-April Mon.-Fri. 9am-5pm).

The outdoorsy **Bingen School Inn Hostel** (509-493-3363), at Humbolt and Cedar St. in White Salmon, WA, 3 minutes away from Hood River across the Columbia on a 75¢ toll bridge, is a converted schoolhouse. (Bike rental $15 per day. Sailboard rental $40 per day. 42 hostel beds, $11. 18 private rooms, $29.) Campgrounds surround Hood River. **Ainsworth State Park** (695-2301), at exit 35 off I-84, caters to RVs but has many sites ($17). **Beacon Rock State Park,** across the Bridge of the Gods then 7 mi. west on Washington Rte. 14, has more secluded sites for $10.

To follow the gorge, which divides Oregon and Washington, take I-84 20 mi. east to the Troutdale exit onto the **Columbia River Scenic Hwy.** Take Greyhound from Portland ($10) or Seattle ($40) to Hood River; the **station** is at 1205 B Ave. (386-1212), between 12th and 13th St. (open Mon.-Sat. 8:30am-7pm). **Amtrak** also runs trains from Portland to the station at Cascade and 1st St. ($14). Unfortunately, public transportation is lacking in the gorge.

■■■ OREGON COAST

The renowned coastal highway **U.S. 101** hugs the shore, sometimes rising in elevation to lofty viewpoints. From **Astoria** in the north to **Brookings** in the south, the highway laces together the resorts and fishing villages that cluster around the mouths of rivers flowing into the Pacific. Its most breathtaking stretch lies between the coastal towns, where hundreds of miles of state parks allow direct access to the beach. Wherever the highway leaves the coast, look for a beach loop road—these quiet byways afford some of the finest scenery on the coast. **Greyhound** offers only two coastal runs from Portland per day; one of those takes place at night, when the coast's beautiful scenery is hidden. Gasoline and grocery **prices** on the coast are about 20% higher, so stock up and fill up before reaching the coastal highways.

Astoria Astoria was Lewis and Clark's final stop at the end of their transcontinental trek; they reached the Pacific here in 1805. Six years later, John Astor, scion of one of 19th-century America's most wealthy families, established a fur-trading post, making Astoria the first permanent U.S. settlement on the West Coast. Today Astoria is a scenic getaway for inlanders and city-dwellers. The **chamber of commerce,** 111 W. Marine Dr. (325-6311; fax 325-6311), just east of the bridge to Washington, is stocked with area info (open Mon.-Sat. 8am-6pm, Sun. 9am-5pm; Sept.-May Mon.-Fri. 8am-5pm, Sat.-Sun. 11am-4pm).

Astoria is the most convenient connection between the Oregon coast and Washington. Two bridges run from the city: the **Youngs Bay Bridge,** to the southwest, on which Marine Drive becomes U.S. 101, and the **Astoria Bridge,** a 4-mi. span over the Columbia River into Washington. The Astoria Bridge has extremely narrow and hazardous bike lanes. Motels are crowded and expensive. The great, almost unknown **Fort Columbia State Park Hostel (HI-AYH)** (360-777-8755), at Fort Columbia in Chinook, WA, within Fort Stevens State Park, is across the 4-mi. bridge into Washington, then 3 mi. north on U.S. 101. This hospital-turned-hostel has 50¢ stuff-your-face pancakes, coffee, tea, and snacks in the kitchen, and laundry and barbecue facilities. (Lockout 9:30am-5pm, check-in 5-10pm. $11, nonmembers $13, bicyclists $8, under 18 with parent $4.50. Open March 1-Oct. 3.) The area is also a haven for campers; U.S. 101, south of Astoria, is littered with campgrounds. **Fort Stevens State Park** is by far the best (sites $16-18).

Tillamook Ever seen a cheese factory at work? Some of Oregon's finest, most famous cheeses are cultured on the shore of Tillamook Bay, where cow pastures predominate. Most visitors hanker for a hunk at the **Tillamook Cheese Factory,** 4175 U.S. 101 N. (842-4481). Watch from glass windows of this temple to dairy delights as cheese is made, cut, weighed, and packaged. Sample a tidbit in the tasting room. Try their ice cream too. (Open daily 8am-8pm; Sept.-mid-June 8am-6pm.)

Tillamook lies 49 mi. south of Seaside and 44 mi. north of Lincoln City on U.S. 101. The most direct route from Portland is U.S. 26 to Rte. 6 (74 mi.). U.S. 101 is the main drag, and splits into two one-way streets in the downtown area. The Tillamook Cheese Factory is almost a downtown in itself, but is north of the major shops. The **visitors center** (842-7525), next to the cheese factory, has a map of all the camping spots in the area; it's worth a look. For a cheap bed try the **Tillamook Inn,** 1810 U.S. 101N (842-4413), between the center of town and the Tillamook Cheese Factory. (Singles $34, doubles $44; winter rates lower. Call a few days in advance.)

Newport Part tourist mill, part fishing village, and part logging town, Newport offers the sights and smells of a classic seaport with kitschy shops. Newport's **chamber of commerce,** 555 SW Coast Hwy. (265-8801 or 800-262-7844) has a helpful office (open Mon.-Fri. 8:30am-5pm, Sat.-Sun. 10am-4pm; Oct.-April no weekends).

The strip along U.S. 101 provides plenty of affordable motels, with predictably noisy consequences. The **Brown Squirrel Hostel (HI-AYH),** 44 SW Brook St. (265-3729), has a cavernous living room adjacent to the kitchen. You can be out the door and at the beach in 2 min. (22 beds. $12, couples $20. Couples should call ahead.) Campers should escape Newport to the many state campgrounds along U.S. 101. Just north of town lies the best option, **Beverly Beach State Park,** 198 N. 123rd St., (265-9278), which has 151 tent sites ($16) and 53 full hookup sites ($19); reserve ahead of time. **South Beach State Park,** 5580 S. Coast Hwy., South Beach 97366 (867-4715), 2 mi. south of town, has 254 electrical hookups ($18) and showers.

The Chowder Bowl, 728 NW Beach Dr. (265-7477), at Nye Beach, has renowned chowder ($3; open June-mid-Sept. daily 11am-9pm). After you've polished that off, head over to the **Oregon Coast Aquarium,** 2820 SE Ferry Slip Rd. (867-3474), a vast building featuring 2½ acres of exhibits. (Open daily 9am-6pm; winter 10am-4:30pm. $7.75, seniors and ages 13-18 $4.50, under 13 $3.30.)

Oregon is famous for its microbreweries. **Rogue Ale Brewery,** 2320 SE Oregon State University Dr. (867-3663), across the bay bridge, brews a local favorite. Request a tour. (Open daily 11am-8pm; call for winter hours.) The second week in October, the **Microbrew Festival** features beers of the Northwest.

Oregon Sand Dunes For 50 mi. between Florence and Coos Bay, the beach widens to form the **Oregon Dunes National Recreation Area.** Shifting hills of sand rise to 500 ft. and extend up to 3 mi. inland (often to the shoulder of U.S. 101), clogging streams and forming many small lakes. Hiking trails wind around the lakes, through the coastal forests, and up to the dunes.

Siuslaw National Forest administers the national recreation area. **Campgrounds** fill up early with dune buggy and motorcycle junkies, especially on summer weekends. The blaring radios, thrumming engines, and staggering swarms of tipsy tourists might drive you into the sands to seek eternal truth, or at least a quiet place to crash. The campgrounds that allow dune buggy access, **Spinreel, Lagoon,**

Waxmyrtle, parking-lot style **Driftwood II,** and **Horsfall** (with showers), are generally loud and rowdy in the summer. (Sites $10. Limited reservations for summer weekends are available; call 800-280-CAMP/2267 more than 10 days prior to arrival.) **Carter Lake** (22 sites) and **Tah Kenitch** (36 sites), both $10, are quiet sites for tenters and small RVs. The sites closest to Reedsport are in Winchester Bay and are either ugly, RV-infested, or both. The best campgrounds are 1-4 mi. south of the Bay.

The dunes' shifting grip on the coastline is broken only once along the expanse, when the Umpqua and Smith Rivers empty into Winchester Bay about 1 mi. north of town. **Reedsport,** 21 mi. south of Florence, is a typical small highway town of motels, banks, and flashy restaurants, neatly subdivided by U.S. 101 and Rte. 38. In Reedsport, the **National Recreation Area Headquarters** (271-3611), just south of the Umpqua River Bridge, will happily provide you with a map ($3) or *Sand Tracks,* the area recreation guide (open Mon.-Thurs. and Sat.-Sun. 8am-4:30pm, Fri. 8am-6pm; Sept.-May Mon.-Fri. 8am-4:30pm). **Winchester Bay,** just south of Reedsport, has inexpensive rooms. The **Harbor View Motel** (271-3352), on U.S. 101, has clean, comfortable rooms (singles $28; doubles $33; off season $24/$29).

Those with little time or low noise tolerance should at least stop at the **Oregon Dunes Overlook,** off U.S. 101, about halfway between Reedsport and Florence. Steep wooden ramps lead to the gold and blue swells of the dunes and the Pacific. Trails wander off from the overlook, as they do at several other points on U.S. 101. An excellent, easy trail is the **Taylor Dunes,** a gentle, ½-mi. trail that brings you to a good view of the dunes without the crowds.

For an authentically silence-shattering dune experience, venture out on wheels. Plenty of places rent and offer tours staring south of Florence and running almost to Coos Bay (see Practical Information). **Pacific Coast Recreation,** 4121 U.S. 101 (756-7183), in Hauser, has direct dune access and restored World War II army vehicles out front. Take a **sand dune tour** in an old transport ($12, under 14 $8) or rent ATVs ($20-25 per hr.). **Spinreel Dune Buggy Rentals,** 9122 Wild Wood Dr. (759-3313), on U.S. 101, 7 mi. south of Reedsport, rents Honda Odysseys ($18 ½hr., $30 first hr., $25 second hr.). They also have dune buggy rides, a good alternative to the monster dune tours ($15 ½hr., $25 per person per hr.). The chamber of commerce will provide a complete list of renting establishments.

Water enthusiasts can take a two-hour cruise of Winchester Bay with **Umpqua Jet Adventures,** 423 Riverfront Way (271-5694 or 800-3-JET-FUN/353-8386), in Reedsport ($15 a pop, ages 4-11 $8; two trips daily, departing at 10am and 1pm). In the same refurbished dock area is the **Umpqua Discovery Center,** 409 Riverfront Way (271-4816 or 800-247-2155). This interactive museum has exhibits on the local history and environment aimed at adults as well as children. You might find the neat gadgets aboard the *Hero,* an old Antarctic exploration vessel, more interesting. (Guided tours of the *Hero* leave every 45 min. Both open daily 10am-6pm, winter Wed.-Sun. 10am-4pm. Museum $3, *Hero* $3, both $5.) **Bird watching** and **whale watching** are also popular diversions.

CENTRAL AND EASTERN OREGON

■■■ ASHLAND

With an informal, rural setting near the California border, Ashland mixes hippiness and history, making it the perfect locale for the world-famous **Shakespeare Festival.** The brainchild of local college teacher Angus Bowmer, the festival began with two plays performed in the Chautauqua theater by schoolchildren as a complement to daytime boxing matches. Today, professional actors perform eleven plays. Shakespeare's share has shrunk to three; the other eight are classical and contemporary dramas. Performances run from mid-February through October on three Ashland stages—the **Elizabethan Stage,** the **Angus Bowmer,** and the **Black Swan.**

Due to the productions's popularity, ticket purchases are recommended six months in advance. General mail-order ticket sales begin in January, but phone orders are not taken until February ($19-37 spring and fall, $23-41 in summer). For complete ticket info, contact the Oregon Shakespeare Festival, P.O. Box 158, Ashland 97520 (482-4331; fax 482-8045). Though obtaining tickets can be difficult in summer, spontaneous theater-goers should not abandon hope. The **box office**, 15 S. Pioneer St., opens at 9:30am and releases any unsold tickets for the day's performances. Local patrons have been known to leave their shoes to hold their places in line; you should respect this tradition. **Backstage tours** provide a wonderful glimpse of the festival from behind the curtain leaving from the Black Swan (2 hr.; Tues.-Sun.10am-3pm; $8, ages 5-7 $6).

The **Ashland Hostel (HI-AYH),** 150 N. Main St. (482-9217), is well-kept, cheery, and run by a wonderful staff that is ready to advise you on the ins and outs of Shakespeare ticket-hunting. (Laundry facilities, game room. $11, nonmembers $13. Check-in 5-11pm. Curfew midnight. Lockout 10am-5pm. Reservations essential March-Oct.; large groups sometimes fill the hostel.) If you like your camping wet, try **Jackson Hot Springs,** 2253 Rte. 99N (482-3776), off exit 19 from I-5, down Valley View Rd. to Rte. 99N for about ½ mi. Jackson springs is campground nearest downtown, and also offers soothing mineral baths. (Laundry facilities, hot showers. Mineral baths $5 per person, $8 per couple. Sites $12, full hookup $17.)

■■■ EUGENE

Situated between the **Siuslaw** (see-YU-slaw) and the **Willamette** (wil-LAM-it) **National Forests,** Oregon's second-largest city sits astride the Willamette River. Home to the **University of Oregon,** Eugene teems with museums, pizza joints, and all the trappings of a college town. The fleet-footed and free-spirited have dubbed Eugene "the running capital of the universe." Only in this city could the annual **Bach Festival,** in late June, be accompanied by the **Bach Run.**

The Eugene-Springfield Visitors Bureau, 115 W. 8th (484-5307; outside OR 800-547-5445), at Olive St., has it all (open Mon.-Fri. 8am-5pm, Sat.-Sun. 10am-4pm; Sept.-April Mon.-Fri. 8:30am-5pm). Info on the area forests can be found at **Willamette National Forest,** 211 E. 7th Ave. (465-6522; open Mon.-Fri. 8am-4:30pm). Both **Amtrak,** 433 Willamette St. (800-USA-RAIL/872-7245), and **Greyhound,** 987 Pearl St. (344-6265 or 800-231-222; open daily 6am-10pm) roll through town.

Eugene is 111 mi. south of Portland on the I-5 corridor. The University of Oregon campus lies in the southeastern corner of town, bordered on the north by Franklin Blvd., which runs from the city center to I-5. **Willamette Ave.** is the main drag and is interrupted by the **pedestrian mall** on 7th, 8th, and 9th St. The city is a motorist's nightmare of one-way streets; free parking is virtually nonexistent downtown.

The cheapest motels are on E. Broadway and W. 7th St. **Lost Valley Educational Center (HI-AYH),** 81868 Lost Valley Ln. (937-3351; fax 937-3646), near Dexter, is an educational experience. Take Rte. 58 east for 8 mi. toward Oakbridge, turn right on Rattlesnake Creek Rd.; after 4 mi., turn right on Lost Valley Lane, and 1 mi. later you're there. Come in at night for the organic dinner. Call ahead for reservations. ($9, nonmembers $10. Campsites $6 per person. Dinner Mon.-Fri. $6.50.) Unfortunately, KOAs and RV-only parks monopolize the camping scene around Eugene, but farther east on Rte. 58 and 126, the immense **Willamette National Forest** is packed with forested campsites. The **Black Canyon Campground,** 28 mi. east of Eugene on Rte. 58 ($8-16), is another option.

If you just have an afternoon hour to spare, canoe or kayak the **Millrace Canal,** which parallels the Willamette for 3 mi. Head on down to **The Canoe Shack,** 1395 Franklin Blvd. (346-4386), run by University of Oregon students. (Open summer Mon.-Fri. 12:30-dusk, Sat.-Sun. 10:30am-dusk. $4 per hour, $14 per 24 hr. $30 deposit.) For a taste of the town, head to the **Saturday Market** (686-8885), at 8th and Oak, held weekly April through December (10am-5pm).

The granola crowd pirouettes brightly at **Sundance Natural Foods,** 748 E. 24th Ave. (343-9142), at 24th and Hilyard (open daily 7am-11pm). **Keystone Café,** 395 W. 5th St. (342-2075), is an eclectic co-op serving vegetarian and vegan food (open daily 7am-3pm). Locals also love **The Glenwood Restaurant,** 1340 Alder (687-0355), at 13th St. (open 24 hrs., except Sun. 9pm to Mon. 7am). For some mellow nightlife, head to the **High St. Brewery Café,** 1243 High St. (345-4905; open Mon.-Sat. 11am-1am, Sun. noon-midnight). **Doc's Pad,** 165 W. 11th St. (683-8101), has good (strong) drinks and live music (open daily 10am-2:30am).

■■■ CRATER LAKE

Mirror-blue Crater Lake, centerpiece of **Crater Lake National Park**, was regarded as sacred by Native American shamans, who forbade their people to look upon it. Iceless in winter and flawlessly circular, the lake plunges from its 6000-ft. elevation to a depth of nearly 2000 ft., making it the nation's deepest lake. This fantastic depth combined with the remarkable clarity of the water creates a serene, intensely beautiful effect.

Practical Information To get to the park from Portland, take I-5 to Eugene, then Rte. 58 east to U.S. 97 south for 18 mi., then west on Rte. 138. **Rte. 62** cuts through Crater Lake National Park's southwest corner and then heads southwest to **Medford** or southeast to **Klamath Falls,** 24 mi. south of the Rte. 62/U.S. 97 intersection. **Park admission** for cars is $5; hikers and bikers are charged $3 only in summer. The **William G. Steel Center** (594-2211), next to the park headquarters, provides free **backcountry camping permits,** details on the area, and road conditions (open daily 9am-5pm). Check out **Amtrak** at its S. Spring St. depot (884-2822 or 800-872-7245; open daily 7-10:30am and 8:45-10pm), and **Greyhound** at 1200 Klamath Ave. (882-4616; open Mon.-Fri. 6-10am and 11:30am-5:30pm, Sat. 6am-3pm). **Emergency** is 911.

Accommodations and Food The park contains two campsites: **Mazama Campground** (594-2511) has 200 sites with no hookups ($11). **Lost Creek Campground** (594-2211 ext. 402), at the southwest corner of the park, has only 16 sites ($5). You may be wise to make your foray to Crater Lake from the **Fort Klamath Lodge Motel** (381-2234), 6 mi. from the southern entrance to Crater Lake National Park on Rte. 62 (singles $30, doubles $40.)

Eating inexpensively in the Crater Lake area is difficult. Buying food at the **Old Fort Store** (381-2345; open summer daily 9am-7pm) in **Fort Klamath,** is the best bet. In Klamath Falls, shop at the 24-hr. grocery store **Safeway** (882-2660) at Pine and 8th St., or try the sandwiches ($4-6) at **Llao Rock Café,** in the Rim Village (open daily 8am-8pm). Upstairs, **The Watchman Eatery and Lounge** has burgers ($6 with potato salad) you can munch while looking out on the stillness of Crater Lake, plus a $6 all-you-can-eat salad bar (open June 10-Sept. 4 daily noon-10pm).

Sights About 7700 years ago, Mt. Mazama created this pacific scene through one of the Earth's most destructive cataclysms. A massive eruption buried thousands of square miles in the western U.S. under a thick layer of ash and left a deep caldera to be filled with the still waters of **Crater Lake.** This splendid lake is rightfully the center of attention and activity in the park.

Rim Drive, open only in summer, is a 33-mi. loop high above the lake and leads to some great trails, including **Discovery Point Trail** (1.3 mi. one way), where the first pioneer saw the lake in 1853, **Garfield Peak Trail** (1.7 mi. one way), and **Watchman Lookout** (.8 mi. one way). If pressed for time, walk the easy 100 yd. from the visitors center down to the **Sinnott Memorial Overlook.** The view is the area's most panoramic and accessible. The steep but rewarding hike up **Mt. Scott**

(2½mi. one way), the park's highest peak (a tad under 9000 ft.), begins from the drive near the lake's eastern edge. The **Cleetwood Trail,** a 1-mi. switchback, is the only route to the lake's edge. From here, the **Lodge Company** (594-2511) offers two-hour boat tours on the lake. (Tour schedule varies; 3-9 tours leave per day June 18-Sept. 17; fare $12, under 12 $6.50.) If you take an early tour, you can be left on **Wizard Island** to be picked up later. Picnics and fishing are allowed, as is swimming, but the surface temperature reaches a maximum of 50°F (10°C). Park rangers lead free walking tours daily in the summer and periodically during the winter. Call the Steel Center for schedules (see Practical Information).

■■■ BEND AND CENTRAL OREGON

Bordered by Mt. Bachelor, the Deschutes River, and a national forest, the city is an ideal focal point for hikers, bikers, rafters, and adventure-seekers. Put on the map in the 1820s by pioneers who found "Farewell Bend" a convenient river ford, the city has grown to become the state's largest urban population east of the Cascades. Bend's young, athletic crowd make the town one of the liveliest and most inexpensive in the Northwest.

Practical Information U.S. 97 (3rd St.) bisects Bend. The downtown area lies to the west along the Deschutes River; **Wall** and **Bond St.** are the two main arteries. **Central Oregon Welcome Center,** 63085 N. U.S. 97 (382-3221), has good info and free maps and coffee (open Mon.-Sat. 9am-5pm, Sun. 11am-3pm). **Deschutes National Forest Headquarters,** 1645 E. U.S. 20 (388-2715), can inform you on forests, recreation, and the wilderness (open Mon.-Fri. 7:45-4:30pm). **Greyhound,** 2045 E. U.S. 20 (382-2151), east of town, runs one bus per day to Portland ($21) and Klamath Falls ($20). (Open Mon.-Fri. 7:30-11:30am and 12:30-5pm, Sat. 7:30am-noon, Sun. 8-11:30am.) Bend's **post office:** 2300 NE 4th St. (388-1971), at Webster (open Mon.-Fri. 8:30am-5:30pm, Sat. 10am-1pm); **ZIP code:** 97701; **area code:** 503.

Accommodations Most of the cheapest motels are just outside town on 3rd St. **Bend Cascade Hostel,** 19 SW Century Dr., (389-3813) is a beautiful facility with great management, 2 blocks from ski and bike rentals and the free shuttle to Mt. Bachelor. From 3rd St., take Franklin west, and follow the Cascade Lakes Tour signs to Century Drive (14th St.). (Laundry and kitchen, linen rental available. Lockout 9:30am-4:30pm, curfew 11pm. $13, seniors and students $12, under 18 $6.50.) **Mill Inn,** 642 NW Colorado (389-9198), on the corner of Bond St., is a B&B in a recently rebuilt hotel and boarding house. $15 gets you a bunk in the dorm-style "Locker Room" (capacity 4), or splurge for a trim, elegant private room for $32 for one or $40 for two, with shared bath. Reservations are recommended. **Deschutes National Forest** maintains a huge number of campgrounds in the Cascades to the west of town. All have pit toilets; those with drinking water cost $8-12 per night; those without are free. Contact the **Bend/Ft. Rock Ranger District Office** at 1230 NE 3rd St.,#A266 (388-5664).

Food While downtown Bend offers many pleasant cafés, 3rd St. also proffers a variety of good eateries. **Devore's,** 1124 NW Newport (389-6588), stocks healthy groceries and snacks, plus wine and beer (open Mon.-Sat. 9:30am-6:30pm, Sun. noon-6pm). **West Side Bakery and Café,** 1005 NW Galveston (382-3426), is locally famous for its breakfasts and lunches. Virtually everything here is homemade, including the delicious bread. (Open Mon.-Sat. 7am-3pm, Sun. 7am-2pm.) **Pilot Butte Drive-In Restauarant,** 917 NE Greenwood/U.S. 20 (382-2972), is home of the 18-ounce "Pilot Butte Burger" ("It's BIG:" $9.50), and many of more manageable size; locals pack in for huge, great breakfasts (open daily 6am-9pm).

Sights and Outdoors The **High Desert Museum** (382-4754), 6 mi south of Bend on U.S. 97, is a sight for sore eyes, offering indoor and outdoor exhibits on the fragile ecosystem of the Oregon plateau, and dioramas of life in the West in days past. Coming early in the day is your only hope of beating the crowds. Allow at least a few hours for the visit. The price of admission is high, but it's well worth it. (Open daily 9am-5pm. $6.25, seniors and ages 13-18 $5.75, ages 5-12 $3.)

In November, 1990, **Newberry National Volcanic Monument** was established to link together and preserve the volcanic features south of Bend. For an introduction to the area, visit the **Lava Lands Visitor Center** (593-2421), 5 mi. south of the High Desert Museum on U.S. 97. The center has exhibits on the volcanism that created the Cascade Range and shaped the local geography. (Open March to mid-Oct. Wed.-Sun. 10am-4pm; Memorial Day-Labor Day daily 9am-5pm.) Immediately behind the visitor center is **Lava Butte**, a 500-ft. cinder cone from which many of the nearby lava flows and the high Cascades can be viewed. South of the visitor center on U.S. 97 is **Lava River Cave** (593-1456), a 1-mi.-long subterranean lava tube. The cave temperature hovers at 42°F (5°C) year-round, so come bundled in warm fuzzy clothes. (Open May-Oct. 10 daily 9am-6pm. $2, ages 13-17 $1.50, under 13 free. Lantern rental $1.50.) The central component of the monument is **Newberry Crater,** 18 mi. south of Lava Butte on U.S. 97, then about 15 mi. east on Rte. 21. This diverse volcanic region covers some 500 sq. mi. and contains two lakes, **Paulina Lake** and **East Lake.** Five campgrounds line the shores of the lakes.

West of Bend, the **Cascade Lakes Hwy.** (Century Drive in town; follow the signs throughout town) makes a dramatic 89-mi. loop past Mt. Bachelor, through the forest, and past the Crane Prairie Reservoir before rejoining U.S. 97. Thirty campgrounds, trout fishing areas, and hiking trails dot the countryside. Allow a full day for the spectacular drive, and pack a picnic lunch.

If you can ski the 9075-ft. **Mt. Bachelor,** with its 3100-ft. vertical drop, you're in good company; Mt. Bachelor is one of the home mountains of the U.S. Ski Team (daily lift passes $33, ages 7-12 $18; call 800-829-2442 for more info). Chairlifts are open for sightseers during the summer (open daily 10am-4pm; $9, kids $4.50, seniors $6.50) and in the summer a U.S. Forest Service naturalist gives free presentations on local natural history on the summit daily at 11:30am and 2:30pm.

Whitewater rafting, although costly, is the number one local recreational activity. Trips usually run around $65 per person per day, $25 per half day. Get a list of rafting outfits at the tourist office; one of the most highly regarded outfits is **Hunter Expeditions** (389-8370; ½ day $27, full day including lunch $60).

Yeeeeee-haw!

For most of the year, Pendleton is typical of Eastern Oregon's towns, offering little more than a quiet night's sleep for the weary traveler. During the day, porch swings are actually used here, and lawn care seems to be the primary recreation. At night, teens and wanna-bes slowly cruise the streets in jacked-up muscle cars, careful not to make too much noise, 'cause everybody knows everybody. All that changes in mid-September, however, when 50,000 yahoos descend on the town for the **Pendleton Round-Up.** Downtown, men gussied up in Stetson hats drink whiskey shots, swagger in dusty leather boots, and talk horses, as Pendleton becomes a macho town. The Round-Up is one of the premier events on the nation's rodeo circuit, drawing ranchers from all over the U.S. for "four glorious days and nights" (always the second full week in Sept.; Sept. 11-14, 1996; Sept. 10-13, 1997). Steer-roping, saddle-bronc riding, bulldogging, and bareback riding barely over-shadow the buffalo-chip tosses, wild cow milking, and greased-pig chases. Yippee-kai-yay! For information or tickets ($7-15), contact the Pendleton Round-Up Association, P.O. Box 609, Pendleton 97801 (276-2553 or 800-457-6336). While the 1996 event is already sold out and tickets for 1997 will probably be gone by the fall of 1996, have no fear: tickets for 1998 go on sale in November of 1996.

■■■ HELLS CANYON

"The government bet you 160 acres that you couldn't live there three years without starving to death," said one early white settler of the region. Hells Canyon's endearing name comes from its legendary inaccessibility and hostility to human inhabitants. It is North America's deepest gorge: in some places the walls drop 5500 ft. to **Snake River** below. The fault and fold lines in the canyon walls make the cliffs seem to melt into great wrinkles of grass and rock. **Hells Canyon National Recreation Area** is a dumbfoundingly beautiful, insanely remote, and astoundingly rugged corner of the northwest.

The only way to even get close to the canyon without taking at least a full day is to drive the **Hells Canyon National Scenic Loop Drive,** which will only give you only the vaguest conception of what Hells Canyon is all about. Still, this is the extent of most tourists' experiences of the area. The drive begins and ends in Baker City, following Rte. 86, Forest Rd. 39 and 350, Rte. 82, and finally I-84. Even this entirely paved route takes from six hours to two days to drive (and it covers nearly every mile of pavement in the area). Lookout points provide dramatic views of the rugged canyons. **Hells Canyon Overlook,** the most accessible (though least impressive), is reached by driving up Forest Rd. 3965. The road departs Rd. 39 about 5 mi. south of the Imnaha River crossing. The immense **Hells Canyon Dam** lies 23 mi. north of Oxbow on Rte. 86. The Snake's-eye views from the winding road become more dramatic the farther north you go. This drive is the only way to get near the bottom of the canyon by car.

Probably the easiest way to see a lot of the canyon is to zip through on a jet boat tour or float through on a raft. A panoply of outfitters run trips through the canyon; the Area Headquarters (see below) has a list. **Hells Canyon Adventures,** (503-785-3352, outside Oregon 800-422-3568), 1½ mi. from the Hells Canyon Dam in Oxbow, runs a wide range of jet boat and raft trips through the Canyon. You can take a full day ($70) or three hour ($30) jet boat tour. A full day of whitewater rafting ($90) includes a jet boat ride back upstream.

Hiking is perhaps the best way to fully comprehend the vast emptiness of Hells Canyon, but to really get into the canyon requires a backpacking trip of at least a few days. There are over 1000 mi. of trail in the canyon, only a fraction of which are maintained regularly by the Forest Service. A wide array of dangers lurk below the rim; discuss your plans with rangers before heading out.

The largest town and service center in the area is Enterprise, 65 mi. from La Grande on Rte. 82. The **Area Headquarters,** 88401 Rte. 82 (426-4978), is on the west side of Enterprise. Detailed **maps** are worth the $3 price. (Open Mon.-Sat. 8am-5pm, Sun. noon-5pm). There are also Recreation Area offices in Riggins, ID (208-628-3916), and Clarkston, WA (509-758-0616). For a recording of **road and trail conditions,** call 426-559. In an **emergency,** dial 911.

Camping in the region can be a spiritual experience for those who have made adequate preparations. If you must have a roof over your head, the **Indian Lodge Motel,** 201 S. Main (432-2651), on Rte. 82 in Joseph, 6 mi. south of Enterprise, has beautiful rooms with A/C (singles $35, doubles $45). The Hells Canyon area is covered with primitive campgrounds. Many have no drinking water, and none have showers. **Copperfield, McCormick,** and **Woodland** (all owned by Idaho Power) have tent and RV sites and restrooms, and are the only campgrounds open year round. These manicured campgrounds are located near Oxbow and Brownlee Dams, on Rte. 86 and Rte. 71 on the Snake (tent fee $5, RV fee $8).

Accessing the area without a vehicle or a horse is difficult. Some people hitchhike in from the gateway towns of Joseph or Halfway, and talk it up with people at campsites to get back out. *Let's Go* does not recommend hitchhiking.

California

For hundreds of years, settlers have come to California in search of the ephemeral and the unattainable. The Spanish conquistadors came for the mythical land of El Dorado, crusty 49ers hunted for the Mother Lode, while the naïve and beautiful still search for stardom. Those fleeing a world devoid of dreams still believe that California is a bastion of eternal opportunity.

California's status as a land of bewildering possibility stems from its uniquely divergent blend of cultural influences. The glare of headlights, the clang of a trolley, the soft vanilla scent of Jeffery pines, and the ghostly shimmer of the desert floor are all California. The breezy liberalism of the Bay Area, the consciously chic stylization of L.A., and the trendy traditionalism of San Diego are all California. It is not without conflict that these visions collide. The anti-war movement of the 60s and 70s, the political tensions of the 80s, and the race riots of the 90s are all testaments to the delicate balance which exists in California and to the strength of the forces that bring the state together.

Literally the movers of the world, the tectonic plates that rumble far below the surface reflect the Earth's change and growth. Californians have learned to live with this phenomenon and now almost revel in its power. The periodic shakes can be survived and California drifts ever farther from the rest of the continent. They bring with them the volatile mix of personalities that both creates and destroys. To the north and south, people build their monuments to themselves.

This book is cool and all, but for the hippest, funniest inside scoop on cheap tasty Mexican food, ostriches' dinky heads, screaming kids, and the whole wild, wet, 'n' wacky Cali scene, check out the red-hot *Let's Go: California 1996.*

CALIFORNIA

PRACTICAL INFORMATION

Capital: Sacramento.
California Office of Tourism: 801 K St. #1600, Sacramento 95814 (call 800-862-2543 to have a package of tourism materials sent to you).
Time Zone: Pacific (3hr. behind Eastern). **Postal Abbreviation:** CA
State Song: "I Love You, California."
Unofficial State Song: "California Über Alles."
Sales Tax: 7-8%, by county. .

California Clips

Authors: John Steinbeck, Bret Easton Ellis, Edward Abbey (*The Monkeywrench Gang*), Maya Angelou (*I know Why the Caged Bird Sings*), Joan Didion, Maxine Hong Kingston, Thomas Pynchon, Tom Robbins, Amy Tan, Armistead Maupin.
Artists: Richard Serra, Dorothy Lange, Frank Gehry, Christo, David Hockney.
Cuisine: Granola, wine and wine coolers, San Francisco sourdough bread, Ghirardelli chocolate, Rice-a-Roni, artichoke soup, citrus products, anything with sundried tomatoes, cilantro, polenta, avacados, or dates.
Microbreweries: Pacific Hop Exchange, Angeles, Etna, Golden Pacific, Hangtown, Mad River, Moonlight, Old Columbia, San Andreas, Tuscan Brewing Co.
Native Americans: Yuki, Pomo, Miwok, Costano, Chumash, Gabrielino, Luiseno, Tipai, Serrano, Mohave, Yuma.
Music: Beach Boys, Guns and Roses, The Go-Gos, Sheryl Crow, Michael Bolton.
Film and TV: Frankie Avalon and Annette Funicello movies, Down and Out in Beverly Hills, Gidget, CHiPs, Beverly Hills 90210, Melrose Place, and almost everything else you've ever seen on a screen of any size.
Climate: Excellent, Dude.
Geography: Beach, mountains, desert, you name it.

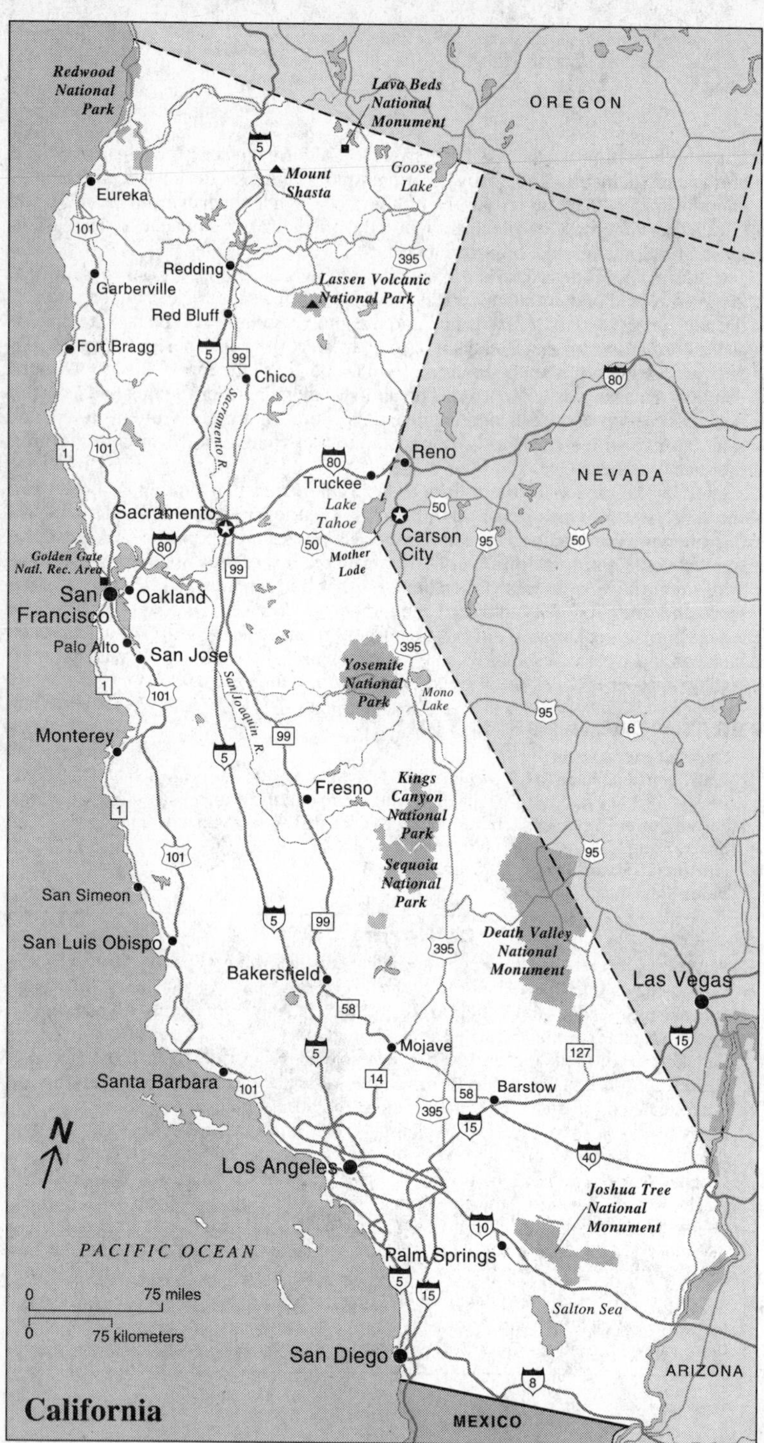
Redwood National Park
Lava Beds National Monument
OREGON
Mount Shasta
Goose Lake
Eureka
Redding
Lassen Volcanic National Park
Garberville
Red Bluff
Fort Bragg
Chico
Sacramento R.
Reno
NEVADA
Truckee
Lake Tahoe
Carson City
Sacramento
Mother Lode
Golden Gate Natl. Rec. Area
San Francisco
Oakland
Palo Alto
San Jose
San Joaquin R.
Yosemite National Park
Mono Lake
Monterey
Fresno
Kings Canyon National Park
Sequoia National Park
San Simeon
San Luis Obispo
Death Valley National Monument
Bakersfield
Las Vegas
Mojave
Santa Barbara
Barstow
N
Los Angeles
Joshua Tree National Monument
PACIFIC OCEAN
Palm Springs
0 75 miles
0 75 kilometers
Salton Sea
San Diego
ARIZONA
California
MEXICO

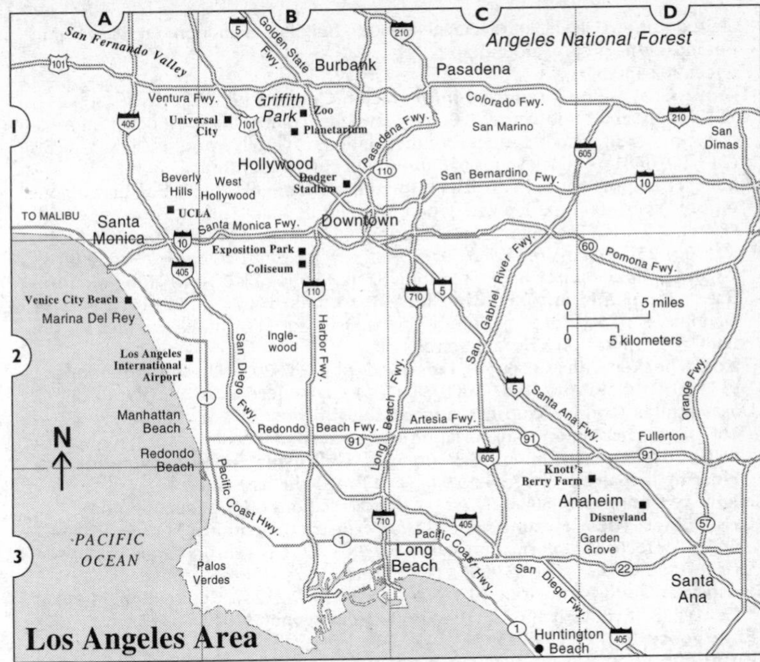

■■■ LOS ANGELES

Myth and anti-myth stand comfortably opposed in Los Angeles. Some see in its sweeping beaches and dazzling sun an extravagant demi-paradise, a bountiful land of opportunity where the most opulent dreams can be realized. Others point to its congestion, its smog, its increasing crime, and declare Los Angeles a sham, a converted wasteland where TV-numbed brain-dead masses go to wither in the sun.

Here is a wholly American urban phenomenon, one that developed not in the image and shadow of Europe, but contemporaneously with America's international ascendancy. It is this autonomy which gives L.A. its peculiar sense of pastlessness. In a city where nothing seems more than 30 years old, the latest trends curry more respect than the venerably ancient. Many come to this historical vacuum to make (or re-make) themselves. And what better place? Without the tiresome duty to kowtow to the gods of an established high culture, Angelenos are free to indulge not in what they must, but what they choose. The resulting atmosphere is deliciously rife with potential. Some savor L.A.'s image-bound culture, others may be appalled by the shallowness of its unabashed excess—but in any case, it's a hell of a show.

PRACTICAL INFORMATION

Tourist Office: Los Angeles Convention and Visitors Bureau, 685 S. Figueroa St. 90017 (624-7300), downtown. Hundreds of brochures. Staff speaks Spanish, Filipino, Japanese, French, and German. Publishes *Destination Los Angeles,* a free booklet including tourist information and a lodging guide. Open Mon.-Fri. 8am-5pm, Sat. 8:30am-5pm. In **Hollywood** at 6541 Hollywood Blvd. (213-624-7300). Open Mon.-Sat. 9am-5pm. In **Santa Monica,** 1400 Ocean Ave. (213-393-7593), in Palisades Park. Open daily 10am-5pm; winter 10am-4pm. **Gay and Lesbian Community Services Center,** 1625 Schrader Ave., Hollywood (993-7400), 1 block from Hollywood Blvd. Youth and senior groups, counseling, employment, housing, educational, legal, and medical services. Building open Mon.-Sat. 9am-10pm, but most offices close around 5pm.

Police: 202-4502.

Trains: Greyhound-Trailways Information Center: 1716 E. 7th St. (800-231-2222), at Alameda, downtown. Call for fares, schedules, and local ticket information. See neighborhood listings for other stations. In **Hollywood,** 1409 N. Vine St. (213-466-6381), 1 block south of Sunset Blvd.; in **Santa Monica,** at 4th.

Public Transportation: MTA Bus Information Line: 626-4455. You may be put on hold until the next ice age. Open Mon.-Fri. 8:30am-5pm. Customer Service Center at 5301 Wilshire Blvd. Free information, timetables, maps, fun. Fare $1.35, transfers 25¢. Open Mon.-Fri. 8:30am-5pm. Key buses: #1 along Hollywood Blvd., #2 and 3 along Sunset Blvd., #4 along Santa Monica Blvd., #10 along Melrose. **Santa Monica Municipal (Big Blue) Bus Lines:** 1660 7th St. (451-5444), at Olympic. Fare 50¢ for most routes, 25¢ transfer for MTA buses, transfer for Big Blue free! Open Mon.-Fri. 8am-5pm.

Taxis: Checker Cab (482-3456), **Independent** (385-8294), **United Independent** (653-5050), **Celebrity Red Top** (934-6700). If you need a cab, it's best to call.

Los Angeles County Commission on Disabilities: 500 W. Temple St. (974-1053). Information on transportation and recreational facilities for people with disabilities. Open Mon.-Fri. 8:30am-5pm. **California Relay Service for the Hearing Impaired:** 800-735-2929 (TTD/TTY). 24-hr. assistance.

Highway Conditions: 800-427-7623. AM radio stations offer frequent reports.

Crisis Lines: AIDS Hotline, 800-922-2437, or try the national hotline, 800-342-5971. For recorded information, call 976-4700. There is a small charge for this service. **Rape Crisis,** 310-392-9896. 24-hr. hotline.

Hospitals: Good Samaritan, 616 S. Witmer St. (977-2121). **Cedar-Sinai Medical Center,** 8700 Beverly Blvd. (310-855-5000, emergency 310-855-6517).

Emergency: 911. **Fire,** 485-5971.

Post Office: Centrally located branch at 900 N. Alameda, at 9th St. (310-431-6546). Open Mon.-Fri. 9am-5pm, Sat. 9am-noon. **ZIP code information:** 586-1737. **General Delivery ZIP code: 90086.** In Hollywood, at 1615 Wilcox Ave. (464-2194). Open Mon.-Fri. 8am-5pm, Sat. 8am-1pm. **General Delivery ZIP code:** 90028. In Santa Monica, at 1284 5th St. at Arizona (576-2626). Open Mon.-Fri. 9am-6pm, Sat. 9am-1pm. **General Delivery ZIP code: 90401. Area codes:** Downtown Los Angeles, Hollywood, Huntington Park, Santa Monica, and Montebello **213.** Malibu, Pacific Coast Highway, Westside, southern and eastern Los Angeles County **310.** Northern Los Angeles County, San Fernando Valley, and Pasadena **818.** Orange County **714.** San Diego County **619.** Eastern border of Los Angeles County **909.** Ventura County **805.**

CALIFORNIA

ORIENTATION

Los Angeles sprawls along the coast of Southern California, 127 mi. north of San Diego and 403 mi. south of San Francisco. You can still be "in" L.A. even if you're 50 mi. from downtown. Before you even think about navigating Los Angeles's 6500 mi. of streets and 40,000 intersections, get yourself a good **map**—Los Angeles defies all human comprehension otherwise. A sound investment is the *Thomas Guide: Los Angeles County Street Guide and Directory* ($25).

The predominately Latino section of L.A. known as **East L.A.** begins east of downtown's Western Ave., with the districts of **Boyle Heights, Montebello,** and **El Monte.** South of downtown are the **University of Southern California (USC), Exposition Park,** and the districts of **Watts** and **Compton,** home to a large concentration of African-Americans. The area south of downtown, known as **South Central,** suffered the brunt of the fires and looting that erupted in 1992. South Central and East L.A. are considered crime-ridden and have little to attract tourists.

Northwest of downtown is **Hollywood.** Sunset Boulevard, which runs from the ocean to downtown, presents a cross-section of virtually everything L.A. has to offer: beach communities, lavish wealth, famous nightclubs along "the strip," sleazy motels, the old elegance of Silver Lake, and Chicano murals. Hollywood Boulevard

L.A. Westside

Armand Hammer Museum of Art and Cultural Center, **1**
Barnsdall Park, **17**
Beverly Center, **7**
Beverly Hills Hotel, **4**
Century City, **2**
Pacific Design Center, **5**
Farmer's Market, **8**
Frederick's of Hollywood, **15**
Hollywood Wax Museum, **14**
I. Magnin BW Wilshire, **18**
La Brea Tar Pits, **10**
Los Angeles County Museum of Art, **9**
Mann's Chinese Theater, **13**
Max Factor Museum, **12**
Paramount Studios, **16**
Runyon Canyon Park, **11**
Schindler House, **6**
20th Century Fox Studios, **3**

runs just beneath the Hollywood Hills, where split-level buildings perched precariously on hillsides are home to screenwriters, actors, and producers.

The next major region, known informally as the **Westside,** encompasses West Hollywood, Westwood, Century City, Culver City, Crenshaw, Bel Air, Brentwood and (for our purposes) the independent city of **Beverly Hills.** The affluent Westside also is home to the University of California at Los Angeles and some trendy, off-beat Melrose Ave. hangouts. The area west of downtown is known as the **Wilshire District** after its main boulevard. **Hancock Park,** a green and affluent residential area, covers the northeast portion of the district.

The **Valley** spreads north of the Hollywood Hills and the Santa Monica Mountains. For most people, *the* valley is the **San Fernando Valley,** where more than a million people live in the suburbs of a basin bounded in the north and west by the Santa Susanna Mountains and the Simi Freeway, in the south by the Ventura Freeway, and to the east by the Golden State Freeway. The valleys also contain the suburb of **San Gabriel** and the city of **Pasadena.**

Eighty miles of beach line L.A.'s **Coastal Region. Zuma** is northernmost, followed by **Malibu,** which lies 15 mi. up the coast from **Santa Monica.** Just a bit farther south is the funky and famous beach community of **Venice.** The beach towns south of Santa Monica, comprising the area called the **South Bay,** are Marina del Rey, El Segundo, and Manhattan, Hermosa, and Redondo Beach. South across the **Palos Verdes Peninsula** is **Long Beach,** a port city of a half-million people. Finally, farthest south are the **Orange County** beach cities: Seal Beach, Sunset Beach, Huntington Beach, Newport Beach, and Laguna Beach. Confused yet? Invest in good maps.

GETTING AROUND

Nobody walks in L.A.

— Missing Persons

Public Transportation Nowhere in America is the automobile held in greater reverence than in L.A., though the **Metropolitan Transit Authority (MTA)** does work—sort of. The MTA was formerly known as the RTD (Rapid Transit District) and some older buses may still be labeled as such. Using the MTA to sightsee in L.A. can be frustrating simply because attractions tend to be spread out, and the system is nearly incomprehensible. Those determined to see *everything* in L.A. should get behind the wheel of a car. If this is not possible, base yourself in downtown or in Hollywood (where there are plenty of bus connections), make daytrips, and have plenty of change for the bus. Bus service is dismal in the outer reaches of the city, and two-hour journeys are not unusual.

To familiarize yourself with the MTA, write for a **Riders Kit,** MTA, Los Angeles 90001, or stop by one of the 10 **customer service centers.** There are three **downtown:** ARCO Plaza, 505 S. Flower St., Level C (open Mon.-Fri. 7:30am-3:30pm); 419 S. Main St. (open Mon.-Fri. 8am-4:30pm); and 1016 S. Main St. (open Tues.-Fri. 10am-6pm, Sat. 10am-6pm). The MTA prints **route maps** for the different sections of the city. You can also call 800-COMMUTE/266-6883 (TDD 800-252-9040; daily 5:30am-11:30pm) for transit information and schedules. Ninety percent of MTA's lines offer **wheelchair-accessible buses** (call 1 hr. in advance, 800-621-7828 daily 6am-10pm). Accessible bus stops are marked with the international symbol of disabled access.

The downtown **DASH shuttle** costs only 25¢ and serves numerous downtown points. DASH also operates a shuttle on Sunset Blvd. in Hollywood, as well as shuttles in Pacific Palisades, Watts, Fairfax, Midtown, Crenshaw, Van Nuys/Studio City, Venice, Warner Center, and Southeast L.A. Call 213-485-7201 for pickup points. (MTA's **basic fare** is $1.10, passengers with disabilities 45¢; transfers 25¢, 10¢ for seniors and disabled; exact change, bills accepted. 60 DASH coupons $15.) Transfers operate from one MTA line to another or to another transit authority. **All route numbers given are MTA unless otherwise designated.**

L.A. has recently begun work on a system of light-rail connections which are not yet very complete, but offer decent ways to reach a select few areas. For now the system serves spots in downtown, but is rapidly expanding. Call 800-2-LA-RIDE/252-7433 for updated information on stops, prices, and timetables. **Metrolink** is a train system which serves Orange County, San Bernardino, Riverside, Oxnard, and Lancaster. Call 808-LINK/5465 for information.

Freeways The freeway is perhaps the most enduring of L.A.'s images. When uncongested, these well-marked, 10- and 12-lane concrete roadways offer the ultimate in speed and convenience; the trip from downtown to Santa Monica can take as little as 20 minutes. A nighttime cruise along the I-10 past downtown—whizzing through the tangle of interchanges and on- and off-ramps, with the lights of L.A.'s skyscrapers providing a dramatic, futuristic backdrop—can be exhilarating.

The most frustrating aspect of driving is the sheer unpredictability of L.A. traffic. It goes without saying that rush hours, both morning and evening, are always a mess and well worth avoiding. But with construction performed at random hours there can be problems anytime. The solution? Patience. A little reminder: no matter how crowded the freeway is, it's almost always quicker and safer than taking surface streets to your destination. A good rule of thumb is that the same distance will take five times as long on surface streets as on the freeway.

Californians refer to their highways by names, numbers, or both. The names are little more than hints of a freeway's route, at best harmless, at worst misleading. For freeway information, call **CalTrans** (213-897-3693).

Do not hitchhike! In Los Angeles, it is tantamount to suicide. You could get picked up by a psycho, or run over by an absent-minded L.A. driver.

Abandon Hope, All Ye Who Attempt to Build Public Transportation Here

Any Angeleno will agree that the best way to traverse their city's urban sprawl is by using one of the numerous freeways which crisscross the L.A. area. Few that question the hegemony of the automobile culture bother to resist. This is, sadly, not true of the doomed attempts of the Metropolitan Transit Authority (MTA) to construct a subway system in downtown L.A. After revealing their grandiose plans in the early 80s, the MTA has met with disaster after disaster. A Green Line was supposed to transport workers to the industrial complex of El Segundo, but when most of these workers were laid off in post-Cold War retrenchments, the project was ceased, and now the Green Line is in search of passengers as much as cash. Estimates for constructing a Blue Line skyrocketed from $146 million in 1983 to $800 million in 1990; the track is still incomplete. The queen of fools, though, is the pathetic Red Line, which has already cost $5.8 billion—it's the most expensive public works program in U.S. history. Moreover, it has collapsed twice, created sinkholes along Hollywood Blvd., and incited irate citizens to sue the MTA for damage caused to their property by the project. Why is the L.A. subway so miserably doomed? The federal government would cite incompetence as the reason—they recently withheld $1.6 billion worth of funding for gross incompetence. However, natives suspect that kismet may have taken a hand. A system of mass transport is antithetical to the fiercely individualistic spirit that is one of the few common features shared by Angelenos. L.A. was built around a Byzantine maze of freeways and traffic jams, and dammit, that's just the way it was meant to be.

ACCOMMODATIONS

As in any large city, cheap accommodations in Los Angeles are often unsafe ones as well. Be suspicious of unusually low posted rates; they are rarely the bargains they seem. Ask to see a room before you plunk down any cash. Hotels in L.A. should cost at least $35 or they're probably not the kind of hotels most travelers would feel secure in. For those willing to share a room and a bathroom, hostels (see below) are a saving grace. However, many hostels require an international passport. Listed prices do not include L.A.'s 14% hotel tax.

Downtown

Though extremely busy and relatively safe by day, the downtown area empties and becomes dangerous when the workday ends and on weekends. But the savvy travelers who haggle and seek weekday discounts will be rewarded with good deals.

Hotel Stillwell, 838 S. Grand Ave. (627-1151 or 800-553-4774). Recently refurbished, this ultra-clean hotel is one of the most sensible downtown options. Rooms are bright and pleasantly decorated with new furniture and linens. A/C, color TV. Parking ($3). Singles $35, $175 per week; doubles $45, $225 per week.

Milner Hotel, 813 S. Flower St. (627-6981 or 800-827-0411). Central location and good upkeep make up for slightly shabby decor. Pub, grill, and pleasant lounge area in lobby. A/C, color TV with HBO. Singles $35; doubles $45.

Royal Host Olympic Motel, 901 W. Olympic Blvd. (626-6255). Standard budget motel, slightly threadbare, but clean. Singles $35, $175 weekly; doubles $40, $120 weekly. Offers student and weekend discounts

Park Plaza Hotel, 607 S. Park View St. (384-5281), on the west corner of 6th St. across from sometimes noisy MacArthur Park. Built in 1927, this grandiose Art Deco giant has a 3-story marble-floored lobby and a monumental staircase. Even if you don't plan to stay at the Park Plaza, check out the hotel for a reminder of an earlier era. A/C (in some rooms) and color TV in the clean but small newly renovated rooms. Olympic-size pool. Singles from $57; doubles $62.50.

CALIFORNIA

Hollywood and West Hollywood

Hollywood is well-connected to other areas of the city and contains the most famous sights, restaurants, and night spots. Exercise caution if scouting out one of the many budget hotels on Hollywood or Sunset Blvds.—especially east of the main strips, the area can be frightening, particularly at night. The hostels here are generally excellent, a much better value than anything else downtown.

Hollywood International Guest House and Hostel, 6561 Franklin Ave. (213-850-6287, 800-750-6561 in CA only), located in a residential area, 2 blocks north of Hollywood Blvd., at the corner of Whitley. A beautiful and cozy house somewhat hidden by trees and a high fence (look for the street number, not a sign). Shared rooms for four are clean, bright, and generously sized. The living room is well-furnished, quiet, and homey. Shuttle service to LAX, Amtrak, Greyhound, and various area attractions. Free coffee, full kitchen. Linen included. No curfew. $12 for shared room, $24 for double. Check-in 9am-8pm. Make reservations early.

Banana Bungalow Hollywood (AAIH/Rucksackers), 2775 Cahuenga Blvd. (213-851-1129 or 800-4-HOSTEL/467735), in Hollywood, just past the Hollywood Bowl. A bounty of attractions, an efficient, friendly staff, and a robust backpacker clientele. Free shuttle service from the airport, as well as to area beaches and attractions. Free nightly movies, arcade, and frequent parties with bouncy bodies bopping about. Pool, basketball court, weight room, and "snack-shack" on premises. Full restaurant serving breakfast ($2-4), lunch ($2-4.50), and dinner ($2-5.50) daily. 24-hr. check-in. Check-out 10:30am. Standard bunks in rooms for 6-10, with bathroom and color TV. Rooms are mostly mixed-sex, although some are women-only. Linen included. $15 per night; doubles $45. **Passport and international airline ticket required** for the dorm rooms.

Hollywood International Youth Hostel, 1553 N. Hudson Ave. (213-467-4161). This brand-spankin' new YMCA-operated hostel is well-appointed and clean throughout. $15 per night. 7-night max. stay. No kitchen, but free use of beautiful YMCA gym facilities. Single sex dorms. **Out of L.A. County I.D. required.** Lock-out 10am-4pm.

Hollywood Hills Hostel, 1921 Highland Ave. (213-876-6544). This hostel is found inside the Hollywood Terrace Hotel, two blocks south of the Hollywood Bowl. Fairly clean and comfortable. Shuttle to LAX, Amtrak, Greyhound. Linen provided. No curfew, 11am checkout. $15 for a shared room, doubles $30.

Westside: Beverly Hills, Westwood, Wilshire

The Westside is a snazzy and relatively safe part of town, but its room rates are out of sight. Call the **UCLA Off-Campus Housing Office** (310-825-4491; 350 Deneve Dr.; open Mon.-Fri. 8am-5pm) and see if they can put you in touch with students who have a spare room through their "roommate share board."

The Little Inn, 10604 Santa Monica Blvd. (310-475-4422), found on "Little Santa Monica," the smaller road paralleling the divided boulevard to the south. An unimpressive front, but step into the courtyard and you've reached budget-travel bliss. Rooms are sizable and very clean. A/C, TV, fridge. 24-hr. check-in. 11am check-out. Singles $40; doubles $45-55.

Stars Inn, 10264 Santa Monica Blvd. Several blocks east of the Little Inn, the Stars is managed by the same group, and delivers a similarly high level of quality. Spacious and clean, with sparkling bathrooms. Provides a glitzy view of Century City. A/C, cable, refrigerator. 11am check-out. Singles $40; doubles $45-55.

Crest Motel, 7701 Beverly Blvd. (213-931-8108), near Hollywood and Beverly Hills. An agreeable place with peachy-pink exterior. Bedspreads and carpets don't match, but do they ever in budget motels? All rooms have walk-in closets. Pool, TV with cable, and A/C. Singles $34; doubles $38. $5 key deposit.

Coastal: Santa Monica and Venice

The hostels at Venice Beach are havens for the young, sociable budget traveler whose highest priority is to meet other people and have an overtly "good time." You may miss the Sunset Strip (and L.A. traffic), but in return you'll find well-populated beaches, quirky architecture, and a mellow and unpretentious community devoted to worshiping the sun and cultivating its own eccentricities.

HI-Los Angeles/Santa Monica (HI-AYH), 1436 2nd St. (310-393-9913), two blocks from the beach and across from the Santa Monica promenade. Exquisite hostel with extremely tight security. Colossal kitchen, huge laundry facilities, two nightly movies, gorgeous library, and a hot breakfast (75¢-$2). Serves over 200 travelers. Safe deposit boxes and lockers available. 28-day max. stay. $15 per night, doubles $43; non-members $18, $46.

Venice Beach Cotel, 25 Windward Ave. (310-399-7649), Venice, ½-block off the beach. Caters mostly to an international crowd, **passport required.** Tidy modern rooms awash with cool ocean breezes. Free linen, towels, and soap. No curfew, but the security's tight. Free equipment with deposit. Shuttle from LAX ($5), trips to various attractions ($15-25). 3-6 people share rooms, from $13 (hall bath, no ocean view) to $16 (room bath, ocean view).

Venice Marina Hostel, 2915 Yale Ave. (310-301-3983), Marina del Rey. This homey hostel offers a respite from the manic pace closer to the shore. Free shuttle from LAX. TV room, laundry, and Brady Bunch-like kitchen. No curfew. 24-hr. check-in. Flexible check-out. Free linen, breakfast, and local phone calls. Friendly staff will admit U.S. travelers with out-of-state I.D. 10 people share rooms for $14.

Cadillac Hotel, 401 Ocean Front Walk (310-399-8876), Venice. Ab-fab art-deco landmark directly on the beachfront. Large, well-equipped gym, including sauna. Rooftop sundeck and available parking (a real find in Venice). International crowd. Bunk in a dorm-style room with bath for only $18-20. Rooms are pricey but luxurious (from $55). Mention *Let's Go* for a discount. Wheelchair accessible.

Share-Tel Apartments, 20 Brooks St. (310-392-0325). A clean hostel, not an apartment complex. **International passport required.** Some free food. Complementary airport pickup. City tours and shuttles to attractions ($12-20). Dorm rooms $18, $100 weekly. Parking available ($10 summer, $5 off season).

Inglewood

Inglewood is home to an excellent hostel, **Backpackers Paradise**, 4200 W. Century Blvd., Inglewood, CA 90304 (310-419-0999). This deluxe stop on the international hostel circuit boasts a courtyard with a heated pool, a pool table, ping pong, and video games. Room rates range from $12-32. Amenities include free shuttles to LAX and other area attractions as well as weekly service to San Diego ($12), bicycle and surfboard rentals (each $10 per day), free breakfast, and laundry facilities. However, Inglewood is an extremely dangerous area and is far from most sights and attractions. Visitors should not travel on foot or by public transportation.

FOOD

The range of culinary options in L.A. is directly proportional to the city's ethnic diversity—keep in mind that over 116 different languages are spoken here. Certain types of food are concentrated in specific areas. Jewish and Eastern European food is most prevalent in the **Fairfax** area; Mexican in **East L.A.;** Japanese, Chinese, Vietnamese, and Thai around **Little Tokyo** and **Chinatown;** and seafood along the coast. There are Hawaiian, Indian, Ethiopian, and Portuguese restaurants scattered throughout the city. There are restaurants where the main objective is to seen, and the food is secondary, as well as those where the food itself seems too beautiful to be eaten—it was here, after all, that 80s *nouvelle cuisine* reached its height.

For the optimal burger-and-fries experience, try **In 'n' Out Burger** (various locations, call 818-287-4377 for the one nearest you), a popular family-operated chain that sells ubiquitous t-shirts. **Johnny Rocket's** returns you to the lost era of American diners. **California Pizza Kitchen (CPK)** spawned the national interest in wood-fired, well-decorated pizza. Their pastas, salads, and desserts are also excellent.

Downtown

Lunch specials are easy to find in the financial district, but finding a reasonably priced and palatable dinner can be a challenge. Nearby **Chinatown** has restaurants with standard specials and inexpensive delis; **Weller Court** by the New Ofani Hotel surrounds several Japanese restaurants, a few of which are in budget range.

The Pantry, 877 S. Figueroa St. (213-972-9279). Open since the 20s, and it's easy to see why—the Pantry defies culinary trends. The restaurant seats only 84 yet serves 2500-3000 meals a day. Be prepared to wait for the giant breakfast specials ($6), especially on weekends. Sun. brunch is an L.A. tradition. Open 24 hrs.

Philippe's, The Original, 1001 N. Alameda (213-628-3781), north of Union Station. Bewildering variety of food, sizable portions, and low, low prices. The French-dip sandwiches are legendary; varieties include beef, pork, ham, turkey, or lamb ($3-4). Top it off with a large slice of pie ($1.90) and a 10¢ cup of coffee, and you've got a colossal meal at this L.A. institution. Open daily 6am-10pm.

La Luz Del Día, 1 W. Olvera St. (213-628-7495). This authentic and inexpensive Mexican restaurant is hidden amid the many tourist-trap Mexican joints along historic Olvera St. Tortillas are handmade on the premises, and the salsa's got some bite. Combination plates $4-5. Open Tues.-Sun. 11am-10pm.

Mon Kee Restaurant, 679 N. Spring St. (213-628-6717), in Chinatown. One of L.A.'s best restaurants, specializing in Chinese-style seafood. The menu is vast; the seafood is excellent. Dinner $10 and up. Open Sun.-Thurs. 11:30am-9:45pm, Fri.-Sat. 11:30am-10:15pm.

Wilshire District and Hancock Park

La Brea Ave. and Pico Blvd. deliver the goods with an assortment of fine restaurants.

The Apple Pan, 10801 W. Pico Blvd. (310-475-3585), in West L.A. From downtown, take bus #431. This nondescript but legendary little building has been open since 1927 and continues to draw crowds for large, juicy hamburgers ($3.60) and sandwiches ($3-5) with huge slices of apple pie for dessert ($2.50). Colorful local clientele. Open Sun. and Tues.-Thurs. 11am-midnight, Fri.-Sat. 11-1am.

Shalom Pizza, 8715 W. Pico Blvd. (271-2255). Kosher pizza in this pleasant Jewish neighborhood. Large cheese $11. Open Sun. and Thurs. 11am-10pm, Mon.-Wed. 10am-9pm, Fri. 11am-2 hrs. before sundown, Sat. 1 hr. after sunrise-2am.

Cassell's Hamburgers, 3266 W. 6th St. (213-480-8668), in the Wilshire District. Perhaps the finest burgers in the city. Basic 1/3-lb. burger $4.60, health-conscious turkey burger ($4.60) or chicken breast ($5). Open Mon.-Sat. 10:30am-4pm.

Hollywood

Forget those rumors about outrageously priced celebrity hangouts—they're here, but you can ignore them. Most of Hollywood and West Hollywood's residents are young, single, hungry, and near broke after paying the rent on their bungalows. As a result, Hollywood has the best budget dining in L.A. Hollywood and Sunset Blvd. offer a range of excellent and diverse cuisines, while Fairfax has Mediterranean-style restaurants and delis. Melrose is full of chic cafés and eateries, many with outdoor seating perfect for people-watching along the fabulous Blvd.

Lucy's El Adobe Café, 5536 Melrose Ave. (213-462-9421), 1 block east of Gower St., in Hollywood. Some of the best Mexican food in town. This family-run restaurant is a favorite among downtown politicians and Paramount executives from across the street. As you munch on your tostada ($7), glance at the celebrity photos or the commendation from the City Council adorning the walls. Full dinners $8-14. Open Mon.-Thurs. 11:30am-11pm, Fri.-Sat. 11:30am-11:30pm.

Duke's, 8909 Sunset Blvd. (310-652-3100), in West Hollywood. Where L.A.'s music industry bigwigs hang. Everyone reads *Ray Gun.* Try the "Revenge"—eggs scrambled with avocado, sour cream, onions, tomatoes, and peppers. Entrees $4-7. Open Mon.-Fri. 7:30am-9pm, Sat.-Sun. 8am-4pm.

Chin Chin, 8618 Sunset Blvd. (310-652-1818), in West Hollywood. Other locations in Brentwood, Studio City, and Woodland Hills. Way popular with the lunch set for its handmade "dim sum and then sum" (around $5). Sino-American cuisine is peculiar but successful; shredded chicken salad ($6) is a perfect example. Outdoor seating, take out, and special lite menu for the health-conscious. Open Sun.-Thurs. 11am-11pm, Fri.-Sat. 11am-midnight.

El Chavo, 4441 Sunset Blvd. (213-664-0871), in Hollywood. Big crowds at this out-of-the way joint testify to the quality of its divinely frothy margaritas ($3.75). Dimly lit; you'll have to rely on your sense of taste (no problem with any of these entrees, which range from $5.50-9.75). Try the *tostada con chorizo* ($7.75). Min. order $7.50. Live music Tues.-Sun. No credit cards. Open daily 11:30am-11pm.

Pink's Famous Chili Dogs, 711 N. La Brea Ave. (213-931-4223), in Hollywood. Despite self-conscious Hollywood air—not every hot dog stand calls itself "the best in the world"—this stand delivers the goods: mouth-watering chili dogs ($2.10). They've had lots of practice; Pink's has been serving up chili-slathered doggies since 1939. Open Sun.-Thurs. 8-2am, Fri.-Sat. 8-3am.

The Nature Club Café, 7174 Melrose Ave. (213-931-8994), in Hollywood. Next door to an herb shop, this cool, green restaurant has an expansive menu. Everything is made either vegan or lacto-ovo-vegetarian. Take advantage of the salad buffet ($8), which includes a choice of *farfaille,* herbed potato, spicy sesame, and more. Open daily 11:30am-10pm. Wheelchair accessible.

Beverly Hills

Don't expect too many bargains.

The Cheesecake Factory, 364 N. Beverly Dr. (278-7270), also in Brentwood (310-826-7111). Very, very popular—expect to stand in line. Once in, you'll be treated to ridiculously huge portions. A smart option is the half-sandwich with soup or salad ($6). Dessert here is the main event. The cheesecakes come in dozens of flavors and the strawberry shortcake is heavenly ($4.50-5.25). Open Sun. 10am-11pm, Mon.-Thurs. 11am-11pm, Fri.-Sat. 11-12:30am.

Ed Debevic's, 134 N. La Cienega Blvd. (659-1952), in Beverly Hills. By far the most mirthful of the phony 50s diners ("famous since 1984"). Always crowded. The atmosphere is relentlessly cheesy and the food affordable (dinner generally costs less than $7). The waitstaff dance as they serve. Full bar. Open Mon.-Thurs. 11:30am-3pm and 5:30-10pm, Fri.-Sat. 11:30am-midnight, Sun. 11:30am-10pm.

La Salsa: Tacos al Carbon, 9631 Santa Monica Blvd. (276-2373), in Beverly Hills. The prettiest taco stand you'll ever see. Where beautiful people come to feast on flour-dusted and not unhealthy tortillas, grilled chicken, and divine salsa (6 kinds). $5 should set you up. Mon.-Fri. 10:30am-9:30pm, Sat. 11am-7pm, Sun. 11am-8pm.

Westwood and UCLA

What do students want? Cheap food and beer. Both are found here in abundance.

Mongols B-B-Q, 1064 Gayley Ave. (310-824-3377). $5.45 buys a bowl which you can pile with raw meat, rice, and vegetables. The chefs sizzle up your creation over a glass-enclosed grill in the center of the restaurant. Come early to beat the line. Open Sun.-Thurs. 11:30am-10pm, Fri.-Sat. 11:30am-11pm.

Sphinx, 1779A Westwood Blvd. (310-477-2358). Only truly outstanding food at an even more outstanding price could compensate for the dumpy exterior. It does. The BBQ chicken ($3.50) is the best-prepared poultry around. Open Mon.-Fri. 10am-9:30pm, Sat. 11am-9:30pm.

Sak's Teriyaki, 1121 Glendon Ave. (310-208-2002), in Westwood. Excellent, low-priced Japanese plates including chicken and beef teriyaki ($3.70-5). Popular with students. Located in a courtyard off the street. Open Mon.-Wed. 10am-10pm, Thurs.-Fri. 10am-11pm, Sat. 11am-11pm, Sun. 11am-10pm.

Tacos Tacos, 1084 Glendon Ave. (310-824-6262), Westwood Village. And the specialty of the house *is*? A UCLA hangout with happy hour all Sat. and Thurs., a pool table, and beer. Combo plates $5. Student discounts. Open Mon.-Sat. 11am-10:30pm, Sun. 11am-9pm.

CALIFORNIA

Santa Monica, Venice, and Marina del Rey

Unfortunately, many of Santa Monica's eateries are quite expensive. The new **EATZ Café** in Santa Monica Place (at the end of the 3rd St. Promenade on Broadway) offers 17 different types of **mall food.** Some are actually good. Venetian cuisine runs the gamut from greasy to health-conscious, as befits its beachy-hippie population.

Wolfgang Puck's Express, 1315 3rd St. (310-576-4770), on the second level of an eating court on the 3rd St. Promenade. If you'd like to tell your pals that Wolfgang's pizza is simply divine, this is the cheapest way to have the quintessential California Cuisine experience. Garish interior. Salads, pizzas, and pastas range from $6-8.50. Open Sun.-Thurs. 11am-10pm, Fri.-Sat. 11am-11pm.

Noah's New York Bagels, 2710 Main St. (310-396-4339), Santa Monica. This divine San Francisco-based chain offers some of the best bagels west of the Mississippi. Open Mon.-Fri. 6:30am-7pm, Sat. 7am-7pm, Sun. 7am-6pm.

Tito's Tacos, 11222 Washington Place (310-391-5780), a bit out of the way in Culver City, virtually *beneath* the San Diego Fwy. (Rte. 410). The burrito, with its huge hunks of shredded beef, is the star attraction ($2.50). Tostadas and enchiladas $1.25, tacos $1. Plenty of parking. Open daily 9am(ish)-11:30pm.

Windward Farms Market, 105 Windward (310-392-3566), Venice. Whole grain breads and fresh fruit. Sells deli sandwiches (50¢-$3.50) and energy shakes ($2.50). Perfect picnic fare. Open daily 8am-7:30pm.

Café 50s, 838 Lincoln Ave. (310-399-1955), Venice. Retro diner with that rarity for retro diners—good food. *Huevos rancheros* ($4.25) are *muy bueno*—lakes of cheese and *frijoles* with lots of golden *huevos*. Open Sun.-Thurs. 7am-11pm, Fri.-Sat. 7am-midnight.

Sidewalk Café, 1401 Ocean Front Walk (310-399-5547), Venice. Popular spot on the boardwalk. Live music most nights. Omelettes $5.25-10. Sandwiches $5-9. Open Sun.-Thurs. 8am-midnight, Fri.-Sat. 8-1am.

On The Waterfront Café, 205 Ocean Front Walk (310-392-0322), Venice. This charming bar/café is a favorite with the international crowd. Warsteiner on tap. Salads and sandwiches and pasta to suit any palate. Best mussels on the beach ($12, serves two). Open Mon.-Fri. 10am-10pm, Sat.-Sun. 9am-11pm.

Aunt Kizzy's Back Porch, 4325 Glencoe Ave., C-9 (578-1005), Marina del Rey. Voted best soul food by L.A. Magazine and frequented by Magic Johnson. Chicken and dumplings or smothered pork chops crowd the plate with cornbread, rice, gravy, and 2 scoops of veggies ($7). Open Sun.-Thurs. 11am-10pm, Fri.-Sat. 11am-11pm. Sun. buffet brunch.

San Fernando Valley

Ventura Blvd. is filled with restaurants. Eating lunch near the studios in **Studio City** is your best stargazing opportunity. The famous are willing to dine outside the studios because of Studio City's unwritten law—you can stare all you want, but don't bother them, *and don't ask for autographs.* **Dalt's Grill,** 3500 W. Olive Ave. (818-953-7752) in Burbank, is a swank, busy grill next door to Warner Studios. Burgers and sandwiches cost about $4-5 (open Mon.-Thurs. 11am-11pm, Fri.-Sat. 11am-1am, Sun. 10am-midnight). Its stocked, lacquered oak bar stays open 'til 2am nightly. **Poquito Más,** 3701 Cahuenga Blvd. (818-760-8226), a wildly popular Mexican spot, is known for its fish tacos ($3.45-5 for two). Short on atmosphere, but fabulous *carnita* is only $1.85 (open Sun.-Thurs. 10am-midnight, Fri.-Sat. 10-1am). **Versailles,** 17410 Ventura Blvd. (818-906-0756), in Encino, serves Cuban food despite its name. Locals flock here for the roasted chicken dinner ($6.50), served with mojo sauce, black bean soup, rice, and fried banana. $4 lunch special (open Sun.-Thurs. 11am-10pm, Fri.-Sat. 11am-11pm).

SIGHTS

Downtown

The Los Angeles downtown area alone is larger than most cities. However, unless glassy skyscrapers get your juices a-flowin', there's not much to see.

To the north of the financial district is L.A.'s **Music Center,** 135 N. Grand Ave. (213-972-7211), comprised of the **Dorothy Chandler Pavillion** (site of the Oscars), the **Mark Taper Forum,** and the **Ahmanson Theatre.** The center is home to the Los Angeles Philharmonic Orchestra and the Joffrey Ballet. Local music-lovers hit Chinatown or Little Tokyo for dinner before a night at the opera.

Farther north lies the historic birthplace of L.A., bounded by Spring St., Arcadia St., and Macy St. In the place where the original city center once stood, **El Pueblo de Los Angeles State Historic Park** (213-680-2525) preserves a number of historically important buildings from the Spanish and Mexican eras (open daily 9am-9pm). Start out at the **visitors center,** 622 N. Main (213-628-1274), in the Sepulveda House, which offers free walking tours (Tues.-Sat. hourly 10am-1pm; call to check). Tours start at the **Old Plaza,** with its century-old Moreton Bay fig trees and huge bandstand, and wind their way past the **Avila Adobe,** 10 E. Olvera St., the oldest house in the city (the original adobe has been replaced with concrete in order to meet earthquake regulations), followed by **Pico House,** 500 N. Main St., once L.A.'s most luxurious hotel. Farther down, at 535 N. Main St., the **Plaza Church,** established in 1818, has an incongruously soft, rose adobe façade. The visitors center screens the film *Pueblo of Promise,* an 18-minute history of Los Angeles. **Olvera Street,** one of L.A.'s original roads, is now called Tijuana North by locals. The street is packed with touristy little stands selling Mexican handicrafts. Olvera St. is the sight of the Cinco de Mayo celebrations of L.A.'s Chicano population. Across Alameda St. from El Pueblo is grand old **Union Station.**

Chinatown lies north of this area, roughly bordered by Yale, Spring, Ord, and Bernard St. From downtown, take the DASH shuttle. Roman Polanski's *Chinatown* was filmed in this once vice-ridden neighborhood. **Little Tokyo** is centered on 2nd and San Pedro St. on the eastern edge of downtown. The **Japanese Village Plaza** (213-620-8861), in the 300 block of E. 2nd St., is the center of the district and is a florid fusion of American shopping mall and Japanese design. The **Japanese-American National Museum** was designed by Buckminster Fuller and Isamu Noguchi, who crafted a monumental sculpture for the courtyard. (Administrative offices open Mon.-Fri. 9am-5pm.)

Exposition Park

Exposition is one of the few areas in L.A. where worthwhile attractions are clustered together. *However, it is not a safe area, especially at night.* The park is southwest of downtown, just off the Harbor Fwy., and is bounded by Exposition Blvd.,

Figueroa St., Vermont Ave., and Santa Barbara Ave. From downtown, take bus #40 or 42 (from Broadway between 5th and 6th) to the park's southern edge. From Hollywood, take #204 down Vermont. From Santa Monica, take #20, 22, 320, or 322 on Wilshire, and transfer to #204 at Vermont.

Lovers and lovers of roses will enjoy the expansive, formal **rose garden** in the courtyard in front of the Museum of Science and Industry. More than 16,000 specimens of 190 varieties of roses surround walking paths, green lawns, and gazebos. The nearby **IMAX theater** has shown such classic films as live footage of those madcap tallywhackers, the Rolling Stones, on tour ($6, children and seniors $4).

The **University of Southern California (USC)** campus sits opposite Exposition Park on Exposition Blvd. The campus is generally safe, although caution should be exercised after dark. (213-740-2300. Walking tours available on the hr., Mon.-Fri. 10am-2pm.) The **Fisher Gallery,** 823 Exposition Blvd. (213-740-4561), displays portions of the Armand Hammer collection of 18th- and 19th-century Dutch paintings. (Open early Sept.-summer Tues.-Fri. noon-5pm, Sat. 11am-3pm. Free.)

South of Exposition Park, to the west, is the city of **Inglewood,** home to the **Great Western Forum,** where the **Los Angeles Kings** hockey team (with "The Great One," Wayne Gretzky), and the **Los Angeles Lakers** basketball team play; tickets to see both of these teams tend to be in demand. For Lakers and Kings tickets (and for tickets for other Forum events) call the **Forum Box Office** (Kings tickets 310-419-3160, Lakers tickets 310-419-3182; open daily 10am-6pm) or **Ticketmaster** (213-480-3232). Tickets range in price from $11 to $110.

CALIFORNIA

Wilshire District and Hancock Park

Wilshire Boulevard, especially the "Miracle Mile" between Highland and Fairfax Ave., played a starring role in Los Angeles's westward suburban expansion. The nearby residential neighborhoods and their 20s architecture are also worth touring by car. The streets south of Wilshire opposite Hancock Park are lined with Spanish-style bungalows and the occasional modernist manse. The **Los Angeles Conservancy** (213-623-2489) offers Saturday tours of downtown Art Deco sights for $5 (make reservations 1 week in advance).

A few miles farther down Wilshire, in **Hancock Park,** an acrid petroleum stench pervades the vicinity of the **La Brea Tar Pits,** one of the most popular hangouts in the world for fossilized early mammals. Many of the beasties who came, thousands of years ago, to drink from the pools here found themselves stuck in the tar that lurks below a thin film of water. Most of the bones recovered from the pits from 1913-1915 have found a new home in the **George C. Page Museum of La Brea Discoveries,** 5801 Wilshire Blvd. (recording 213-936-2230, operator 213-857-6311). The museum includes reconstructed Ice Age animals and murals of L.A. Ice Age life, a laboratory where paleontologists work behind plate-glass windows, and a display that shows what it's like to stick around in the tar. Check out the holographic transformation of the two-toed sloth. Archaeological digging continues in **Pit 91** behind the adjacent county art museum. (Open daily 10am-5pm. $5, seniors and students $3.50, ages 5-10 $2, under 5 free. Free 1st Tues. of month. Parking $7.50. Museum tours Wed.-Sun. 2pm; tours of grounds 1pm.)

About 3 mi. northeast of downtown is **Elysian Park;** with 525 acres of greenery, the park is ideal for picnicking. The park curves around the northern portion of Chavez Ravine, home of the well-designed and sparkling-clean **Dodger Stadium** (213-224-1400) and the perennially popular **Los Angeles Dodgers** baseball team. Tickets, which cost from $6-11 (all seats have good views of the field), are a hot commodity when the Dodgers are playing well; purchase in advance, if possible (tickets 213-964-6346). Scalpers sell them illegally and at a substantial mark-up outside.

Hollywood

Modern Hollywood is no longer the upscale home of movie stars and production studios. To catch a fleeting glimpse of the orange groves and farm lands that first lured movie men, travel through **Hollywood Hills,** north of the more urban and grittier world of central Hollywood. Here, beautiful homes, palm trees, and swimming pools are still abundant. Hollywood Boulevard and other thoroughfares, though still glittering and glamorous, are now home to prostitutes and porn shops as well. Hollywood is still a fascinating place, though not the Emerald City it once was.

The **Hollywood sign**—those 50-ft.-high, slightly erratic letters perched on Mt. Cahuenga north of Hollywood—stands with New York's Statue of Liberty and Paris's Eiffel Tower as a universally recognized symbol of its city. The original 1923 sign, which read HOLLYWOODLAND, was an advertisement for a new subdivision in the Hollywood Hills (a caretaker lived behind one of the "L"s). The sign has been a target of pranksters (USC frat boys and Cal Tech hackers) who have made it read everything from "Hollyweed" to "USCwood." For a closer look at the site, follow Beachwood Dr. up into the hills (MTA #208). Drive along the narrow, twisting streets of the Hollywood Hills for glimpses of the multi-colored homes and lifestyles of the rich and famous. **Hollywood Blvd.** itself, lined with souvenir shops, clubs, and theaters, is busy day and night. Most sights in this area now focus around the intersection of Highland Ave. and Hollywood Blvd., and then west down Hollywood. To the east, things turn seedier. The façade of **Mann's Chinese Theater** (formerly Grauman's), 6925 Hollywood Blvd. (213-464-8111), between Highland and La Brea, is a garish rendition of a Chinese temple. There's always a crowd of tourists in the courtyard, worshiping impressions made by movie stars in the cement outside the theater. Just across the street from Mann's is the newly-renovated **El Capitan Theatre,** 6838 Hollywood Blvd. (213-467-9545). This restored cinema house held the 1941 Hollywood premier of *Citizen Kane* and now shows only Disney flicks. If you plan to watch a movie anyway, bypass the mall theater and go to one of the famed theaters which are charmingly garish, and have mammoth screens and sound systems to satisfy the most die-hard movie buff.

If you want to stroll among the stars, have a look at the **Walk of Fame** along Hollywood Blvd. and Vine St. More than 2,500 bronze-inlaid stars are embedded in the sidewalk, inscribed with the names of the famous (including #2,032: Noriyuki "Pat" Morita). Many names will be meaningless to those under 40. To catch a glimpse of today's (or yesterday's) stars in person, call the Hollywood Chamber of Commerce (213-469-8311) for the times and locations of upcoming star-unveiling ceremonies.

Also two blocks east of Mann's is the **Hollywood Wax Museum,** 6767 Hollywood Blvd. (213-462-8860), where you'll meet 200 figures, from Jesus to Elvis (open daily 10am-midnight; $9, children $7). Down the street from the Wax Museum you'll find two touristy "Odd-itoriums," **Frederick's of Hollywood,** 6608 Hollywood Blvd. (957-5953), which includes the museum of lingerie with classic ads extorting you to "put your breasts on a shelf," and the **Max Factor Museum,** (463-6668), which features dozens of glamorous photos paying tribute to the most celebrated make-up artist of all time and some dramatic "before" and "after" photos proving that beauty is—or can be—constructed. Free admission makes it worth traipsing through these shrines to glam. (Frederick's open Mon.-Thurs. 10am-8pm, Fri. 10am-9pm, Sat. 10am-6pm, Sun. noon-5pm. Max Factor open Mon.-Sat. 10am-4pm.)

The **Hollywood Studio Museum,** 2100 N. Highland Ave. (213-874-2276), across from the Hollywood Bowl, provides a refreshing look at the history of early Hollywood film-making. Back in 1913, when it was a barn, famed director Cecil B. DeMille rented the building as a studio and shot Hollywood's first feature film, *The Squaw Man,* there. Antique cameras, costumes, props, vintage film clips, and other memorabilia clutter the museum. (Open Sat. and Sun. 10am-4pm. $4, seniors and students $3, ages 6-12 $2. Ample free parking.)

Music is another industry that, like film, finds a center in Los Angeles. The pre-eminent monument to the modern record industry is the 1954 **Capitol Records Building,** 1750 Vine St., just north of Hollywood Blvd. The building, which was designed to look like a stack of records, is cylindrical with fins sticking out at each floor (the "records") and a needle on top. At the corner of Hollywood and McCappen sits the massive inner sanctum of **Scientology**—the faith of the stars. The billboard on the side gives a count of the worldwide number of copies of Dianetics sold to date. Check out the district consisting of the two blocks of Franklin east of Tamarind. A group of coffeehouses and restaurants make this out of the way district one of the most trendy in the area. Stop in at the **Daily Planet,** 5931½ Franklin Ave. (213-957-0061), a bookstore which has a good "counterculture" section.

If you still haven't had enough showbiz glitz, visit the **Hollywood Memorial Park,** 6000 Santa Monica Blvd. (213-469-1181), between Vine and Western, a cemetery which has the remains of dead stars Rudolph Valentino, Douglas Fairbanks, Sr., and many, many more! (Open daily 8am-5pm. Mausoleums close at 4:30pm.)

West Hollywood

Once considered a no-man's land between Beverly Hills and Hollywood, West Hollywood was incorporated in 1985 and was one of the first cities in the country to be governed by openly gay officials. Although the famed thoroughfares of Melrose Ave. and Sunset Blvd. pass through both the city of West Hollywood and the neighboring Hollywood district, West Hollywood and Hollywood are distinct communities in every other sense.

In the years before incorporation, lax zoning laws gave rise to today's **Sunset Strip.** Long the nightlife center of L.A., the Strip was originally lined with posh nightclubs frequented by stars. Today the strip plays host to several rock clubs. The area's music scene is among the country's most fertile, and many world-famous bands from The Doors to Guns 'n' Roses got their start here. These days, much of the music on this stretch is heavy metal and hard rock, and weekend nights lead to tremendous crowds and traffic jams. Restaurants and comedy clubs flourish as well. The **billboards** on the Strip are often outrageous.

Melrose Avenue, running through the southern portion of West Hollywood, is lined with chi-chi restaurants, ultra-trendy boutiques, and superhip art galleries. The choicest stretch is between La Brea and Fairfax, but the entire 3-mi. stretch between Highland and Doheny is a fecund stomping ground for the stylized. The clothes here run the gamut from thrift to *haute,* but all styles are *de modo.* Who knows what hepcats will be sportin' next year, but it'll be available on Melrose. While much that is sold here is pre-owned ("vintage"), none of it is really cheap—expect to pay $15 for a pair of 501s. If you have old, funky clothes, you can make some cash by selling or exchanging your old duds. **Retail Slut,** 7308 Melrose, is a mecca for punks, goths, and sluts of all ilks. It's the place to find that fetish gear you've been searching for, or just a cool spot to browse a huge selection of ear- and body-rings, hang out with local club kids, and hear word-of-mouth about the dark side of L.A.'s alternative scene. If you plan on finding that special person to spend the rest of your night with, get ready at **Condom Mania,** 7306 Melrose. **Salvation Navy,** 7700 Melrose (open daily 11am-8pm) and **Aardvark's,** 7579 Melrose, are rad joints for used gear, from that pith helmet you can't go on safari without to corduroy sportshirts which weren't even popular in the 70s (open Mon.-Sat. 11am-9pm, Sun. 11am-7pm).

The massive **Beverly Center,** 8500 Beverly (310-854-0070), an expensive shopping complex, is found at the corner of Beverly and La Cienega. Escalators snake up the building's exterior, encased in transparent tubing. Inside lurks a dazzling maze of chic global merchandisers and funky specialty boutiques. Nothing's cheap, but even the most counter-culture mall-hater can enjoy a window-shopping stroll through the marvelously ostentatious Center. Its glass elevators, vast and vaulted open spaces, and bizarre sculpture make it more than just another retail complex—it is the Übermall.

Griffith Park

The L.A. Zoo, the Greek Theater, Griffith Observatory and Planetarium, Travel Town, a bird sanctuary, tennis courts, three golf courses, campgrounds, and 52 miles of hiking trails decorate the dry hills and mountains of Griffith Park (open daily 5:30am-10pm). This formidable recreational region stretches from the hills above North Hollywood to the intersection of the Ventura and Golden State Fwy.

The white stucco and copper domes of the Art Deco **Observatory and Planetarium** (213-664-1181, for a recording 664-1191) structure are visible from around the park. You might remember the planetarium from the denouement of the James Dean film *Rebel Without a Cause.* Even if you don't, the planetarium is a must-see. A telescope with a 12-in. lens is open to the public every clear night. (Open for viewing daily dusk-9:45pm; winter Tues.-Sun. 7-9:45pm. Sky report and information 213-663-8171.) The planetarium presents popular **Laserium** light shows (818-901-9405), a psychotronic romp through the strawberry fields of your consciousness. (Observatory open daily 12:30-10pm; winter Tues.-Sun. 2-10pm. Planetarium show Mon.-Fri. at 1:30, 3, and 7:30pm, Sat.-Sun. also 4:30pm; in winter Tues.-Fri. 3 and 7:30pm, Sat.-Sun. also 1:30 and 4:30pm. $4, seniors $3, under 12 $2, under 5 not admitted. Laser shows blaze Sun. and Tues.-Sat. 6 and 8:30pm, summer also Fri.-Sat. 9:45pm. $7, children $6.)

A large **bird sanctuary** at the bottom of the observatory hill serves its function well, but if you crave a wider assortment of fauna, you might prefer the **L.A. Zoo,** 5332 Western Heritage Way, at the park's northern end (213-666-4090). The zoo's 113 acres accommodate 2000 animals, and the facility is consistently ranked among the nation's best (open daily 10am-5pm; $8, seniors $5, ages 2-12 $3).

Beverly Hills

Boulevards are wider, palm trees healthier, and faces more surgically altered in Beverly Hills. This should surprise no one. Beverly Hills has long been a civic icon of wealth and glamour. Accordingly, this enclave of privilege is not the typical stomping ground of the budget traveler. But breathing the rarefied air of Rodeo Drive is still free, so take advantage of its beauty for a stroll. Don't worry about sticking out in the crowd, there will be plenty of other tourists.

The Beverly Hills Post Office (on Beverly Dr.) must be the only one in the country with valet parking. The heart of the city is in the **Golden Triangle,** a wedge formed by Wilshire and Santa Monica Blvd. centering on **Rodeo Drive,** known for its many opulent clothing boutiques and jewelry shops. The giant "Bulgari" sign reads "Vulgari" from certain angles: coincidence? The rich and powerful come to Rodeo to do what the rich and powerful do, but it is also a mecca for tourists who want to gawk at the opulent ones. Despite having cobbled streets and Cannes as its sister city, Beverly Hills is not really in Europe. Faking antiquity, the entire street of **Via Rodeo**—hill, lampposts and all—was constructed in the last decade, and it looks it. Across the way is the venerable **Beverly Wilshire Hotel** (310-275-5200), whose old and new wings are connected by **El Camino Real,** a cobbled street with Louis XIV gates. Inside, hall mirrors reflect the glitter of crystal chandeliers and marble floors.

The new **Beverly Hills City Hall** (310-285-1000) stands, looking a bit out of place, on Crescent Dr. just below Santa Monica Blvd. This Spanish Renaissance building was erected during the heart of the Great Depression, and is now engulfed by Beverly Hills' new **Civic Center.** Completed in September 1990, the Civic Center (which includes the Beverly Hills Fire Department, Police Station, and library) took nine years to build and cost $120 million. The **Beverly Hills Library,** 444 N. Rexford Dr. (213-228-2220), is a case study in the city's overriding concerns—the interior is adorned with marble imported from Thailand, but contains a paltry collection of books. As always, though, Beverly Hills coordinates well: the library's tiling matches the colors on City Hall's dome. Moving farther north, the **Beverly Hills Hotel,** 9641 Sunset Blvd. (310-276-2251), is a pink, palm-treed collection of poolside cottages. Howard Hughes established his infamous germ-free apartment in this jungle-bungalow mix of California cool, tropical paradise lushness, and Beverly Hills luxury.

Fans of *Beverly Hills 90210* should come to grips with the fact that West Beverly High, alas, is only a television construct. They can, however, cruise **Beverly Hills High** (located on Moreno, between Olympic and Spalding). Beverly Hills High must be the only high school in the country with its own **oil well.**

Westwood and UCLA

The gargantuan **University of California at Los Angeles** campus covers over 400 acres in the foothills of the Santa Monica Mountains. UCLA, described in *Let's Go: America 1969* as where "Playboy's pin-up beauties ripen," is not the one-dimensional, hedonistic colony of blond, deep-tanned party animals it was once may have been. Pick up a brochure describing the 15-minute **self-guided tour** of the campus.

The **Murphy Sculpture Garden,** which contains over 70 pieces scattered through five acres, lies directly in front of the Art Center. The collection includes works by such major artists as Rodin, Matisse, and Miró. Opposite the sculpture garden is **MacGowen Hall,** which contains the **Tower of Masks.** UCLA's **inverted fountain** is located between Knudsen Hall and Schoenberg Hall, directly south of Dickson Plaza. An innovation in the field of fountain design, the fountain spouts water from its perimeter that rushes down into the gaping hole in the middle. **Ackerman Union,** 308 Westwood Plaza (310-206-0833), stands southwest of the Quadrangle, at the bottom of the hill. A calendar lists the lengthy line-up of movies (first-runs often free), lectures, and campus activities. **Westwood Village,** just south of the campus, with its myriad movie theaters, trendy boutiques, and upscale bistros, is geared more toward the residents of L.A.'s Westside than UCLA students. Like most college neighborhoods, however, Westwood is humming on Friday and Saturday nights. Generally, the town is safe and usually overrun by the college crowd.

Directly across from UCLA is the opulent community of **Bel Air,** where Ronald Reagan has retired to become the new Fresh Prince. Farther west on Sunset Blvd., are the neighborhoods of **Brentwood** (former neighborhood of Nicole and O.J. Simpson) and beautiful **Pacific Palisades.** The cliffs give way to the ocean at the popular **Will Rogers State Beach,** on the 16000 block of Pacific Coast Highway.

Santa Monica

Beaches, bars, babes: Santa Monica's **3rd St. Promenade** has become the city's most popular nightspot, and the nearby beaches are jam-packed. Despite the resultant hassles (parking, prices, lines), there is much to do and see, especially at night.

There are much prettier and cleaner beaches to visit to the north and south, but at least Santa Monica Beach has public bathrooms. Santa Monica Beach may not be good for swimming, but a paved path stretching along the beach all the way to Venice is perfect for walking, in-line skating, and bicycling. (Rental shops are plentiful.) The colorful **Santa Monica Pier** is a nostalgic and popular spot. With the creation of the **3rd St. Promenade** in 1989 and the recent remodeling of **Santa Monica Place,** Santa Monica has become one of L.A.'s major walking, movie-seeing, and yuppie-gathering areas. The Third Street Promenade sports some cool cafés, a couple of L.A.'s better bookshops, popular bars and restaurants, and a variety of street artists (not to mention some water-spouting, ivy-lined, mesh dinosaur sculptures). The area really comes alive at night when the bars and cafés fill up.

Venice

Venice. A head bobs through the crowd, dredlocks flying, amp blaring. *Venice.* Street vendors sleep on benches near the beach—makes it easier to get to work in the morning. *Venice.* Originally meant to be a canal-crossed imitation of its Italian namesake, rife with mustachioed gondoliers. *Venice.* One of the most generative and intriguing places in the world. *Venice.* A life-long Dead concert. With sand.

Ocean Front Walk, Venice's main beachfront drag, is a dramatic demographic departure from Santa Monica's promenade. Street people converge on shaded clusters of benches, yelping evangelists drown out off-color comedians, and bodybuilders of both sexes pump iron in skimpy spandex outfits at the original **Muscle Beach** (1800 Ocean Front Walk, closest to 18th and Pacific Ave.). Fire-juggling cyclists, joggers, groovy elders (such as the "skateboard grandma"), and bards in Birkenstocks make up the balance of this playground population. Hang at a juice bar or coffeehouse for people-watching at its finest. During the day, things are relatively safe, but when the sun begins to fall, it's time to go. Venice's **street murals** are another free show. Don't miss the brilliant, graffiti-disfigured homage to Botticelli's *Birth of Venus* on the beach pavilion at the end of Windward Ave.: the Roman goddess of beauty rises from the foam of a SoCal beach, garbed in cut-off jeans and a Band-Aid top. L.A. to the max. To look at paintings indoors, you might want to stop by **L.A. Louver,** 77 Market St. and 55 N. Venice Blvd. (310-822-4955), a gallery showing the work of some hip L.A. artists (open Tues.-Sat. noon-5pm).

To get to Venice from downtown L.A., take bus #33 or 333 (or 436 during rush hour). From downtown Santa Monica, take Santa Monica bus #1 or 2. Drivers can avoid hourly meter-feedings by parking in the $5 per day lot at Pacific and Venice.

San Fernando Valley

The end of the Ventura Freeway marks the spiritual center of American suburbia—a long series of communities with tree-lined streets, cookie-cutter homes, lawns, and shopping malls. A third of L.A.'s population resides here. **Ventura Boulevard,** the main commercial thoroughfare, today combines business and recreation with its office buildings, restaurants, and shops. Once you've finished searching Ventura Blvd. for the ultimate valley hangout (try a Denny's on a weekend night between 2 and 4am), you may want to check out **Universal City,** which also boasts a number of restaurants, theaters, and clubs to waylay the traveler in search of a good time.

After about an hour's drive along the San Fernando Freeway you'll reach **Simi Valley,** home to the **Ronald Reagan Presidential Library,** 40 Presidential Dr. (805-522-8444). The museum traces Reagan's path from a poor childhood to movieland success, and finally his improbable jump to the governorship of California and eventually, the Presidency (open daily 10am-5pm; $4, seniors $2, under 15 free).

Museums

Los Angeles County Museum of Art (LACMA), 5905 Wilshire Blvd. (213-857-6000), Hancock Park. A distinguished, comprehensive collection which rebuts those who would argue that L.A.'s only culture is in its yogurt. Five major buildings cluster around the Times-Mirror Central Court, housing art and artifacts from all regions and all historical periods. For tours, check with the information desk in the Central Court (ticket office 857-6010) or contact the Docent Council at 857-6108. Open Mon. and Wed. 10am-5pm, Fri. 10am-9pm, Sat.-Sun. 11am-6pm. $6, seniors and students $4, ages 6-17 $1; free 2nd Wed. of each month.

Museum of Contemporary Art (MOCA), 250 S. Grand Ave. (213-626-6222), at California Plaza. A sleek and geometric architectural marvel, its excellent collection features works by artists such as Pollock, Miró, and Giacometti, focusing on abstract expressionism. Capacious interior illuminated by pyramidal skylights. Open Tues.-Wed. and Fri.-Sun. 11am-5pm, Thurs. 11am-8pm. $6, seniors and students with ID $4; under 12 free. Free Thurs. 5-8pm. Wheelchair accessible.

Huntington Library, Art Gallery, and **Botanical Gardens,** 1151 Oxford Rd., San Marino 91108 (818-405-2100, ticket information 818-405-2275), south of Pasadena. Bus #79 leaves from Union Station and takes you straight to the library. The stunning botanical gardens are home to 207 acres of rare plants. The library houses one of the world's most important collections of rare books and manuscripts, including a Gutenberg Bible. The art gallery is known for its 18th- and 19th-century British paintings. American art is on view in the Virginia Steele Scott Gallery. The Annabella Huntington Memorial Collection features Renaissance paintings and 18th-century French decorative arts. Open Tues.-Fri. 1-4:30pm, Sat.-Sun. 10:30am-4:30pm. $4.

J. Paul Getty Museum, 17985 PCH (310-458-2003). The collection of Greek and Roman sculpture, European paintings, and illuminated manuscripts is framed by a stunning setting of silver reflecting pools, stately marble, and graceful gardens. Each year the museum is required to purchase new artwork with Getty's $2.9 billion endowment (New York's MoMA has "only" $350 million). Access to the museum is tricky. The parking lot is small and reservations for drivers are needed well in advance in summer. Take MTA #434 to the museum, and ask for a free **museum pass** from the bus driver. Open Tues.-Sun. 10am-5pm. Free.

Norton Simon Museum of Art, 411 W. Colorado Blvd. (818-449-6840), in Old Pasadena. As sleek and glassy as the modernism to which it is a shrine, it houses numerous Rodin and Brancusi bronzes and paintings by Rembrandt, Raphael, and Picasso. Simon's eclectic, idiosyncratic taste, as well as the piquant descriptions of the works, make this museum more interesting than similar assemblages elsewhere. Don't miss the sculpture garden. Open Thurs.-Sun. noon-6pm. $4, seniors and students $2, under 12 free. Wheelchair accessible.

Armand Hammer Museum of Art and Cultural Center, 10899 Wilshire Blvd. (310-443-7000), in Westwood. A large array of European and American works from the 16th-20th century, including Van Gogh's striking *Hospital at Saint-Rémy* and the world's largest collection of works by Honoré Daumier. Open Tues.-Wed. and Fri.-Sat. 11am-7pm, Thurs. 11am-9pm, Sun. 11am-5pm. Tours daily at 1pm. $4.50, students and seniors $3, under 17 free; free Thurs. after 6pm.

L.A. Children's Museum, 310 N. Main St. (213-687-8800), in the L.A. mall. Interactive displays encourage children to overcome the confusion of a hyper-technological society by participating in demonstrations of scientific principles, and to create MOCA pieces of their own. Open to groups with pre-paid reservations Tues.-Fri. 9:15am-1pm and to everyone Sat.-Sun. 10am-5pm. $5, under 2 free.

Southwest Museum, 234 Museum Dr. (213-221-2163), just east of downtown. Take bus #83 along Broadway to Museum Dr. and trek up the hill, or take the Pasadena Fwy. (Rte. 110) to Ave. 43 and follow the signs. The museum's first-rate but under-appreciated collection of artifacts includes contemporary Native American art, housed in a palatial Hispano-Moorish home. Open Tues.-Sun. 11am-5pm. $5, seniors and students $3, ages 7-18 $2. Library open Wed.-Sat. 11am-5pm.

California Museum of Science and Industry, 700 State Dr. (213-744-7400), Exposition Park. IBM and Bell Telephone sponsor mathematics and communications, while McDonald's sponsors a display on nutrition. The Aerospace Building exhibits $8 million worth of aircraft, including the Gemini 11 space capsule. Open daily 10am-5pm. Free. Parking $3.

Natural History Museum, 900 Exposition Blvd. (213-744-3414), Exposition Park. Exhibits about pre-Columbian cultures, North American and African mammals, American history from 1472 to 1914, and dinosaurs. The **Hands-On Discovery Center** allows visitors to pet stuffed wild animals. Open Tues.-Sun. 10am-5pm; $8. Seniors and students $5.50, ages 5-12 $3, under 5 free.

Petersen Automotive Museum, 6060 Wilshire Blvd. (930-CARS/2277). Displays include dioramas illustrating the Californian fascination with the auto as well as row upon row of lovingly restored and preserved Jaguars, Porsches, Mercedes, and even a 1985 Indy car you can sit in. Parking $4 for the whole day (some park here and walk across the street to LACMA). Open Tues.-Sun. 10am-6pm. $7, students and seniors $5, kids $3.

Autry Museum of Western Heritage, 4700 Zoo Dr. (213-667-2000). The museum's collection covers both fact and fiction of the Old West, with exhibits on pioneer life and the history of Westerns, including costumes donated by Robert Redford, Gary Cooper, and Clint Eastwood. Open Tues.-Sun. 10am-5pm. $7.50, seniors and students $5, children $3.

Beit HaShoa Museum of Tolerance, 9786 W. Pico Blvd. (310-553-8043), just outside Beverly Hills. Includes displays on the Armenian and Native American genocides, as well as the Jewish Holocaust. One room features unseen voices that hurl insults at visitors! Tours leave between 10am and 4pm on Mon.-Thurs., noon and 3pm on Fri., and 10:30am-5pm on Sun. $8, seniors $6, students $5, ages 3-11 $3.

Route 1: The Pacific Coast Highway

Originating along the surfer beaches south of L.A., Rte. 1—or the Pacific Coast Highway (PCH)—sweeps grandly along the California coast. Across rolling hills dotted with extravagant mansions, past cow pastures and fruit orchards, inches from 100-ft. drop-offs, PCH traverses an admirably diverse cross-section of the state's landscape. Begun in 1920, the highway required $10 million and 17 years for completion. Many of the numerous bridges on the route were architectural wonders in their day; and some—such as the Bixby Creek Bridge, one of the longest single-span bridges in the world—still are. Some segments of the highway have been rebuilt more than once; earthquake damage forced a stretch of Rte. 1 in Marin County to close for nearly a year. But too much of California's identity is tied to this highway for locals to give it up. Beware: *many* Californians like to drive PCH, especially on weekends, when it can become an absolute parking lot.

After skirting the coastal communities of **Los Angeles,** including the celebrity colony of **Malibu,** PCH makes its sinuous way north from **Ventura** and **Oxnard** to breezy **Santa Barbara.** Rte. 1 twists and shouts past vineyards, fields of wildflowers, and miles of beach on the journey northward to **San Luis Obispo. San Simeon,** north of San Luis, anchors the southern end of **Big Sur,** the stately 90-mi. span of sparsely inhabited shoreline. Precariously navigating precipitous peaks, PCH inches motorists to the edge of jutting ocean cliffs on its way to the Monterey Peninsula. **Carmel** and **Monterey** sit stolidly ahead, catering to waves of genteel vacationers seeking placid diversion. Beyond, PCH rocks once again to the beat of a more lively drum machine, as it hops and bops through the youthful surfer-student burg of **Santa Cruz.** Finally, Rte. 1 takes a turn through the **Bay Area** and way-eclectic **San Francisco** before trundling on up the **North Coast,** terminating in **Garberville.**

ENTERTAINMENT

Film and Television Studios

Many tourists feel a visit to the world's entertainment capital is not complete without some exposure to the actual business of making a movie or TV show. Happily, most major production companies oblige. To find out what shows are available during your visit, send a SASE to either **Audiences Unlimited, Inc.,** 100 Universal City Plaza, Bldg. 153, Universal City, CA 91608 (818-506-0067), or **Paramount Pictures,** Paramount Guest Relations, 5555 Melrose Ave., Hollywood, CA 90038 (213-956-1777). These television tapings are often oversold—arrive early. **Hollywood Group Services,** 1918 W. Magnolia Blvd. #203, Burbank, CA 91506 (818-556-1516), offers guaranteed seating, but will charge $10 if you no-show.

Some networks also offer show tickets. **CBS** maintains a box office at 7800 Beverly Blvd., Los Angeles (213-852-2450; open Mon.-Fri. 9am-5pm). **NBC** has an office at 300 W. Alameda Dr., Burbank (recorded information, 818-840-3537; office open Mon.-Fri. 8am-5pm). The City/County Film Office maintains a list of what movies are filming in the area. Call 213-957-1000 to find out, but be aware that film crews may not share your enthusiasm about audience participation.

Universal Studios (818-508-9600), Universal City. Take Hollywood Fwy. to Lankershim or use bus #424. Visit the Bates Hotel from *Psycho*, watch Conan the Barbarian flex his pecs, be attacked by Jaws, experience an 8.3 earthquake, and witness a variety of special effects and other demonstrations of movie-making magic. Open summer and holidays daily 8am-8pm (last tram leaves at 5pm); Sept.-June 9am-6:30pm. $31, ages 3-11 and over 60 $25. Parking $6.

Paramount Studios Inc., 860 N. Gower St. (213-956-5000) in Hollywood. Guided 2-hr. historical walking tour. Mon.-Fri. 9am-2pm every hr. on the hr. $15.

Warner Bros. VIP Tour, 4000 Warner Blvd. (818-954-1744), Burbank. Personalized, unstaged tours (max. 12 people) through the Warner Bros. studios. These technical, 2-hr. treks chronicle the detailed reality of the movie-making craft. No children under 10. Tours every ½-hr. Mon.-Fri. 9am-4:30pm, additional tours in summer. Reservations recommended in advance. $27 per person.

Cinema

In the technicolor heaven of Los Angeles, you'd expect to find as many moviehouses as stars on the Walk of Fame. You won't be disappointed. Numerous theaters show films the way they were meant to be seen: in a big space, on a big screen, and with high-quality sound. Watching a movie at one of the **Universal City** or **Century City** theaters can be an amazing experience. The theaters in **Westwood Village** near UCLA are also incredibly popular, especially on weekends. You *will* wait in line at all the best theaters, especially for new releases, but the lively crowds, state-of-the-art sound systems, and large screens more than justify the wait. In Santa Monica, 22 theaters rest between Santa Monica Place and the Third St. Promenade. Foreign films play consistently at the six **Laemmle Theaters** in Beverly Hills, West L.A., Santa Monica, Pasadena, Encino, and downtown.

L.A.'s movie industry dwarfs any other, but it hosts no world-class film festival like Cannes or Sundance. Smaller festivals are plentiful, and have the virtue of being less expensive and more accessible. The **10th Annual Asian Pacific Film and Video Festival** (May, 206-8013), the **Annual L.A. International Gay and Lesbian Film Festival** (July, 213-951-1247), the **Annual Women in Film Festival** (Oct., 463-6040), are among the best of these small film showcases. The largest in the area is the **Annual AFI L.A. International Film Festival,** which features 150 shorts, documentaries, and features from around the world (Nov., 213-856-7707). For information on where anything in L.A. is playing, call 213-777-FILM/3456.

Theater and Concerts

Los Angeles has one of the most active theater circuits on the West Coast. One hundred and fifteen "equity waiver theaters" (under 100 seats) offer a dizzying choice for theater-goers, who can also take in small productions in museums, art galleries, universities, parks, and even garages. During the summer hiatus, TV stars frequently take parts in "legitimate theater" to hone their skills. The *L.A. Weekly* has comprehensive listings of L.A. theaters both big and small.

L.A.'s concert venues range from small to massive. The **Wiltern Theater** (213-380-5005) shows crunchy alterna-rock/folk acts. The **Hollywood Palladium** (213-962-7600) is of comparable size with 3500 seats. Mid-size acts head for the **Universal Amphitheater** (818-777-3931) and the **Greek Theater** (213-665-1927). Huge indoor sports arenas, such as the **Sports Arena** (213-748-6131) or the **Forum** (310-673-1300), double as concert halls for large shows. Few dare to play at the 100,000+ seat **L.A. Coliseum.** Only U2, Bruce Springsteen, the Rolling Stones, and Guns 'n' Roses have filled the stands in recent years.

Seasonal Events

Making a slumber party out of New Year's Eve at the **Tournament of Roses Parade** (Jan. 1; 818-449-7673) is a SoCal tradition. Some of the wildest New Year's Eve parties happen along Colorado Blvd., the parade route. The subsequent **Rose Bowl** football game is known as the "granddaddy of them all." **Grunion runs** occur throughout spring and summer. Watch slippery, silver fish squirm onto beaches (especially San Pedro) to mate. The fish can be caught by hand, but a license is required for those over 16. Obtain licenses from the Fish and Game Department (310-590-5132) for $10.50; they're valid until Dec. 31. The **Renaissance Pleasure Faire** (800-52-FAIRE/523-2473) takes place from late April to mid-June. From L.A., drive east along I-10 to I-15 north and look for signs as you draw near the city of Devore. Garbed in their best Elizabethan finery, San Bernardino teenagers are versed in the phrases of the bard before working at the Faire (open 10am-6pm; $16.50, seniors and students $13.50, children $7.50). On **Cinco de Mayo** (213-625-5045), May 5, huge celebrations mark Mexican Independence Day, especially downtown along Olvera St. **UCLA Mardi Gras** (310-825-8001), mid-May, has been billed as the world's largest collegiate activity (a terrifying thought). Proceeds benefit charity. In late June, the fabulous lesbian and gay community of L.A. celebrates **Gay Pride Week** in full force (213-656-6553). Art, politics, dances, and a big parade all center on the Pacific Design Center, 8687 Melrose Ave., Hollywood. Tickets cost $10.

NIGHTLIFE

Coffeehouses

Coffeehouses are L.A.'s new sizzlin' places to be, and have the added advantage of being open to the under-21 set. One popular chain is the **Coffee Bean and Tea Leaf.** There are locations in Santa Monica, Westwood (near UCLA), and Beverly

Hills. Buy ten beverages and get another free—you might scoff at this deal, but wait 'til you taste their Vanilla Ice Blended ($2.75). It won't take you long to down ten. Call 800-TEA-LEAF/832-5323 to find a location near you. For more eclectic and wacky café experience, try **Wednesday's House,** 2409 Main St. (310-452-4486; open daily 8-2am), frequented by the self-consciously Gen-X crowd; the hoity-toity **Living Room,** 110 S. La Brea (213-933-2933; open Mon.-Thurs. 9-1am, Fri.-Sat. 9am-3pm, Sun. 9am-2pm); **Bourgeois Pig,** 5931 Franklin Ave. (213-962-6366; open Mon.-Fri. noon-2am, Sat.-Sun. 8am-2am), perhaps the most dramatically gothic of the cafés. The **Highland Grounds,** 742 N. Highland Ave. (213-466-1507), features live entertainment which ranges from folk singer types to performance artists who beat themselves on the head with raw steak and shout "Absalom, it's time to boil the weenies!" (open Sun.-Thurs. 9-12:30am, Fri-Sat. 9-1am). The double cappuccino ("Tall Cappy") at **Anastasia's Asylum,** 1028 Wilshire Blvd. (310-394-7113), is amphetamine-esque (open Mon.-Thurs. 7-2am, Fri.-Sat. 8-3am, Sun. 8am-midnight).

Bars

Drink, scam, rock, dance, rage, puke, stumble home. Yeah. **Chiller's,** 1446 3rd St. (310-394-1993; open Sun.-Thurs. 11-1am, Fri.-Sat. 11-2am), on the Santa Monica Promenade, specializes in imaginative frozen drinks. The Suicide (151, light rum, dark rum, triple sec, vodka, and 5 fruit juices) is better than pills. The Purple Orgasm will come in your mouth. $4, 5, 6, for small, medium, and large cups with drink treat of your choice. Wed. night DJ and $1 drinks. One of L.A. nightlife's best-hidden secrets is **Al's Bar,** 305 S. Hewitt St. (213-625-9703; open daily 7pm-2am), in downtown. The wide range of nightly entertainment includes traditional rock 'n' roll, poetry, experimental bands, performance art and more. The **Atlas Bar and Grill,** 3760 Wilshire Blvd. (213-380-8400; open Mon.-Fri. 11-2am, Sat. 6pm-2am), in the Wilshire District, a glamorous nightspot with retro decor, offers jazz and cabaret. **The Snake Pit,** 7529 Melrose Ave. (213-852-9390; open Sun.-Thurs. 5pm-2am, Sat.-Sun. 11:30-2am), in W. Hollywood, is an unpretentious hole amid many poseur bars.

Clubs

With the highest number of bands per capita in the world, most clubs are able to book top-notch acts night after night. The distinction between music clubs and dance clubs is a bit sketchy in L.A.—most music clubs have DJs a couple times a week, and most dance clubs have bands a couple times a week. **Whisky A Go-Go,** 8901 Sunset Blvd. (310-652-4205), in W. Hollywood, is a venerable spot on the Strip, part of L.A.'s music history. You'll find no dancy techno here, only live bands on stage. Cover varies; no age restrictions. Beautiful people flock to Johnny Depp's small, dark, and infamous **Viper Room,** 8852 Sunset Blvd., (310-358-1880). Music genre changes nightly, as does the DJ. **Roxy,** 9009 Sunset Blvd. (310-276-2222), one of the best-known of L.A.'s Sunset Strip clubs, offers live bands playing rock, blues, alternative, and occasionally hip-hop. Many big and popular acts play here. Cover varies; no age restrictions. **The Palace,** 1435 N. Vine St. (213-462-3000), is a legendary Hollywood nightclub, where Rudy Vallee and the madcap Rolling Stones have performed. Cover varies, but hovers around $18. Ages 16 and over (usually). Open from 9pm. The 22,000 sq. ft. floor at **Arena,** 6655 Santa Monica Blvd. (213-462-0714), lends itself to frenzied techno, house, Latin beats, and even killer drag shows on occasion. Dance! Dance! Dance! **Club Lingerie,** 6507 Sunset Blvd., Hollywood (213-466-8557), offers enormously varied bookings and lots of indie rock. Come early; crowds can be formidable. Rock! Rock! Rock! **Kingston 12,** 814 Broadway (310-451-4423), Santa Monica, is L.A.'s only full-time reggae club; it presents both local and foreign acts. Dredlocks flow freely. Features Jamaican food, dance floor, and 2 bars. Cover varies; 21 and over. Rasta! Rasta! Rasta!

Gay and Lesbian Clubs

L.A.'s outrageous gay and lesbian scene is centered around Santa Monica Blvd. in W. Hollywood. However, many "straight" places have gay nights, and a genuinely tolerant atmosphere prevails at many joints, which are neither clearly gay nor straight. **The Palms,** 8572 Santa Monica Blvd. (310-652-6188; open until 2am daily), is W. Hollywood's oldest women's bar. Men are welcome, but may feel very alone. If you like rubber, you'll love **7969,** 7969 Santa Monica Blvd. (213-654-0280), in W. Hollywood. Sometimes a strip club, it sometimes presents drag and S&M shows. Get ready for lots of dancing and fetish gear—not for the faint-of-heart. **Rage,** 8911 Santa Monica Blvd. (310-652-7055), W. Hollywood, throbs with dance and R&B sounds for a gay male crowd. Some consider it the heart of W. Hollywood's gay community. Bartenders occasionally go shirtless! Cover varies. **Micky's,** 8857 Santa Monica Blvd. (657-1176; open daily noon-2am), is a large, popular wetspot filled with delectable men of all ages. On Thurs., male porno stars come to "hang around" and "dispense autographs." Tues. is 18 and up night, all others 21 and over only.

Comedy Clubs

L.A.'s comedy clubs are the world's best. The **Comedy Store,** 8433 Sunset Blvd. (213-656-6225), is like the shopping mall of comedy clubs, with 3 different rooms, each featuring a different type of comedy. Go to the Main Room for the big-name stuff and the most expensive cover charges ($10-12). The Original Room features mid-range comics for $7-8. The Belly Room has the real grab-bag material, with cover of $0-3. Beverages start at $4.50, and there's a 2-drink min. **The Improvisation,** 8162 Melrose Ave. (213-651-2583), offers L.A.'s best talent, including, on occasion, Robin Williams and Jerry "Jeri" Seinfeld. Cover $8-11, 2-drink min.; reservations recommended. **Groundling Theater,** 7307 Melrose Ave. (213-934-9700), is considered by many the best improv "forum" in town. Alums include Jon Lovitz, PeeWee Herman, and Noriyuki "Pat" Morita. Cover $10-17.50. Laff! Laff! Laff!

■■■ ORANGE COUNTY

Orange County is what many people associate with Southern California: beautiful beaches teeming with bronzed surfer dudes; boulevards of strip malls which stretch to the curve of the horizon and beyond; stunning homes perched high atop mottled hills; stately missions built by Spanish monks venturing north from Mexico; Walt Disney's expansive vision of what fun is and should be; and traffic snarls frustrating enough to make even the most jaded Angeleno weep. This most "typically Californian" of counties recently suffered perhaps a most "typically American" predicament: financial bankruptcy. Oh well—there's always Disneyland.

The **Anaheim Area Visitors and Convention Bureau,** 800 W. Katella Ave., Anaheim 92802 (999-8999), has free, glossy brochures, and is open Mon.-Fri. 8:30am-5pm. **Amtrak** stops 5 times in OC: 15215 Barranca (753-9713), in **Irvine;** 1000 E. Santa Ana (547-8389), in **Santa Ana;** Santa Fe Depot (240-2972), in **San Juan Capistrano;** 2150 E. Katella (385-1448), in **Anaheim** by the stadium; 235 S. Tremont (722-4622) in **Oceanside. Greyhound** has stations at 2080 S. Harbor (999-1256), in **Anaheim,** 3 blocks south of Disneyland (open daily 6:30am-8pm); 1000 E. Santa Ana Blvd. (542-2215), **Santa Ana** (open daily 7am-8pm); and 510 Avenida de la Estrella (492-1187), **San Clemente** (open Mon.-Thurs. 7:45am-6:30pm, Fri. 7:45am-8pm). **Orange County Transportation Authority (OCTA),** 550 S. Main St. (636-7433), in Garden Grove, allows you to subvert traffic snarls and lets locals navigate the Byzantine highway system. Bus #1 travels the coast from Long Beach down to San Clemente, once per hr. early morning-8pm (fare $1, transfers free). Call for specific times and routes. Anaheim's **post office:** 701 N. Loara (520-2600), Anaheim; **ZIP code:** 92803; **area code:** 714, 310 in Seal Beach.

ACCOMMODATIONS, CAMPING, AND FOOD

If you want to explore Disneyland or find yourself captivated by infinite strip malls, Anaheim is worth a visit; otherwise, try the coastal areas of Orange County for a less commercial experience. Cheap accommodations in California's bastion of conservatism and wealth are hard to come by. The hostels in the area have it all over the motels and campgrounds. Those roughin' it should make reservations through MISTIX (800-444-7275) a maximum of 8 weeks in advance, as soon as possible in the summer. There is a $6.75 *non-refundable* fee for every reservation made.

HI-Fullerton (HI-AYH), 1700 N. Harbor Blvd. (738-3721), in Fullerton, 15-min. drive north of Disneyland. Wonderfully refurbished hostel with an international clientele. Modern kitchen, clean communal bathrooms, and spiffy single- and mixed-sex accommodations. 5-day max. stay. No curfew. Registration daily 7:30-10:30am and 4-10pm (winter) or 5-11pm (summer). $14, nonmembers $17.

Huntington Beach Colonial Inn Youth Hostel, 421 8th St. (536-3315), in Huntington Beach, 4 blocks inland. Common showers, large kitchen, reading/TV room, and a lovable cat. Both the large deck and the surfboard shed out back are frequently used by the hostel's tan young guests. Free breakfast. Check-in 7am-11pm. No lockout. Multi-person dorms $12 per person; doubles $14. Must have picture ID. Call 2 days in advance for summer weekends.

Motel 6, 4 Anaheim locations, and 2 more in adjacent suburbs at 921 S. Beach Blvd. (220-2866), and 7450 Katella Ave. (891-0717), both within a 10-min. drive of Disneyland. Most rooms have HBO. All offer A/C and free local calls. The S. Beach Blvd. location is the best deal for groups ($32 for 1-4 persons). The Katella Ave. motel is in better shape and a steal: singles $25, doubles $29.

Mesa Motel, N. Newport Blvd. (646-3893). ½-mi. to the beach. Attractive location near many pricey establishments. Typical motel rooms. Singles $35, doubles $40.

Doheny (496-6172), Rte. 1 at the south end of Dana Point. Beachside location turns this place into a zoo. TVs, lounge furniture, play pens, aquariums, and more. Offers the only sites in the area with real beach sand (and yes, they go very fast). Beachfront sites $21, others $16. Off-season, beachfront sites $19, others $14.

For a break from the otherwise pervasive mini-mall fare, try one of the various inexpensive ethnic restaurants tucked into the strip malls that line Anaheim's streets.

■ DISNEYLAND

Disneyland is the self-described "happiest place on earth." Skeptical? Prepare to be convinced, or at least brainwashed. The rigidly enforced tone of carefree, wacky fun is inescapable, from the happy, happy tunes piped into every restaurant and ride to the relentlessly smiling Disney characters wandering about. You'll find the park populated almost exclusively by screaming kids and their harried parents, but with a sense of camp appreciation and some savvy, even the most jaded child of the 90s can have a good time in the Magic Kingdom.

Main Street, USA, a quaint, candied recreation of small-town American life, is the only entrance to the park and is lined with way-pricey boutiques—the Disney execs know the advantage of a captive market. However, a marvelous and **free** attraction is the nightly **Main Street Electrical Parade,** replete with fireworks and neon floats.

To the right of Main Street is **Tomorrowland,** where Disney meets the Jetsons in an imagination of the future which is sadly stuck in the 60s. This area houses some of the park's best rides, such as **Space Mountain** and **Star Tours.** While the attractions are indeed more titillating, you'll have to wait in much longer lines as a result.

Fantasyland is the geographical and spiritual center of the park. It contains the trademark castle as well as the scintillating **Matterhorn Bobsleds,** and numerous kiddie rides, such as **It's A Small World,** which will fiendishly burn its falsetto theme song into your brain if you are hearty enough to brave its treacherous waters.

Frontierland is home to the **Big Thunder Railroad** as well as the Mark Twain **riverboat,** whose hokey commercialism would have its namesake in stitches, or maybe in tears. On the shores of the "Rivers of America" is **Critter Country,** where the worthwhile **Splash Mountain** offers a wet ride in a log past singing rodents as well as a thrilling, though dousing, vertical drop. Nearby **New Orleans Sq.** includes the charmingly faux-creepy **Haunted Mansion,** and Michael Jackson's personal fave-rave, **Pirates of the Caribbean.**

The Unlimited Use Passport ($35) allows you to enter and exit as much as you want within a single day, as does the parking pass ($6 per day). Given the unimpressive and pricey nature of the food, you might want to consider leaving the park for lunch. Oh yes, and the lines for anything and everything are longer than Methuselah's beard. You'll wait for rides, food, even bathrooms. There is no escape.

The park may be approached by car via I-5 to Katella. From L.A., take MTA bus #460 from 4th and Flower (about 1-½ hrs.) to the Disneyland Hotel. The park is also served by Airport Service, OCTD, Long Beach Transit, and Gray Line (see Practical Information). The park's hours vary (call 999-4565 for exact information) but are approximately Sun.-Thurs. 9am-10pm, Fri.-Sat. 9-1am.

Consult the *Unofficial Guide to Disneyland* for further tips and descriptions.

■ COASTAL AREAS

Orange County **beaches** are generally cleaner, less crowded, and more charming than those in L.A. County. **Huntington Beach** served as a point of entry for the surfing **craze,** which transformed California coast life in the early 1900s. It's still a fun, crowded hotspot for wave-shredders, with a pristine pier for ogling. Newport Beach is the Beverly Hills of beach towns, though the beach itself displays few signs of ostentatious wealth; it is crowded with young, rowdy hedonists cloaked in neon.

The sands of Newport Beach run south onto the **Balboa Peninsula,** separated from the mainland by Newport Bay. The peninsula itself is only two to four blocks wide and can be reached from Pacific Coast Hwy. (PCH) by Balboa Blvd. **Ocean Front Walk** extends the length of the peninsula and provides excellent views of the ocean and numerous waterfront homes. At the end of the peninsula, **The Wedge,** seasonally pounded by storm-generated waves up to 20 ft. tall, is a **bodysurfing** mecca. Melt into the crowd on Newport Beach or the Balboa Peninsula by hopping on a bicycle or strapping on a pair of in-line skates. Ubiquitous stands offer just about anything the aspiring beach bum might crave.

Once you have reached the end of the peninsula, from the harbor side you can see **Balboa Island,** largest of the three islands sheltered by the peninsula. The island is expensive and covered with chic eateries, boutiques, and bikini shops. A vintage **ferry** (673-1070) will take you there from the peninsula. (Ferry every 3-5 min., Sun.-Thurs. 6:30am-midnight, Fri.-Sat. 6:30am-2am. Car and driver $1, passengers 35¢, children 15¢.) Balboa Island can also be reached from PCH by Jamboree Rd.

Back along the coast, **Laguna Beach,** 4 mi. south of Newport, is nestled between canyons. Back in the old days, Laguna was a Bohemian artists' colony, but no properly starving artists can afford to live here now. The surviving galleries and art supply stores nevertheless add a unique twist to the standard SoCal beach culture that thrives on Laguna's sands. **Main Beach** and the shops nearby are the prime parading areas, though there are other, less crowded spots as well. One accessible beach (with a sizable gay crowd) is **Westry Beach,** which spreads out south of Laguna just below **Aliso Beach Park.** Park on Pacific Coast Hwy. or residential streets to the east and look for "Public Access" signs between private properties.

Laguna Beach's artwork is displayed at the **Laguna Beach Museum of Art,** 307 Cliff Dr. (494-8971), which houses recent works by important Californian artists including an excellent collection of early 20th-century Impressionist works. Don't miss the early 20th-century photographs of industrial California. (Open Tues.-Sun. 11am-5pm. $5, students and seniors $4, children under 12 free. Docent tours Tues.-Wed. and Fri.-Sun. at 2pm.)

More tourists than swallows return every year to **Mission San Juan Capistrano** (248-2048), a half-hour south of Anaheim on I-5 (take Ortega Hwy. to Camino Capistrano). Established in 1776, it is somewhat run-down due to an 1812 earthquake—but, hey, what do you expect for a building that's been around for over 200 years? Father Junípero Serra, the mission's founder, officiated from inside the beautiful **Serra Chapel,** which at 218 years is the oldest building in the state. The dark chapel is warmed by the 17th-century Spanish cherrywood altar and the Native

American designs painted on walls and ceiling. It's still used by the Catholic Church, so enter quietly. (Open daily 8:30am-5pm. $4, seniors and ages 3-12 $3.)

San Onofre State Beach is a prime surf zone (particularly the famous "Trestles" area). The south end of the beach is frequented by nudists. (Drive down as far as you can go, and walk left on the trail for ¼-½ mi. There's both a gay and a straight area.) **Nude** bathing is illegal; you'll be fined if you're caught with your pants down.

■■■ BIG BEAR

Hibernating in the **San Bernardino Mountains,** the town of **Big Bear Lake** entertains visitors with winter skiing and summer boating. Call the **Big Bear Hotline** (909-866-7000) for recorded lodging and events information. To reach Big Bear Lake, take **I-10** to Junction 30/330. Follow **Rte. 30** to **Rte. 330,** also known as Mountain Rd., and continue to **Rte. 18.** Rim of the World Transit Bus runs a **bus service** between Big Bear and San Bernardino ($4.50) four times per day throughout the week and two times per day on weekends.

Big Bear has few budget accommodations, especially in the winter. The **Hillcrest Lodge,** 40241 Big Bear Blvd. (909-866-7330), offers cozy rooms an expensive feel at a budget price. The smallest rooms cost $32 in summer. Amenities include outdoor jacuzzi, free local calls, and HBO. Midweek chalet rates are not out of the budget traveler's reach, especially for groups of six or more. Camping is permitted at U.S. Forest Service sites throughout the area. Several of the grounds listed below accept reservations (800-280-2267). **Pineknot** (7000 ft.) is surprisingly isolated, with 48 heavily wooded spots, half of which accept reservations. It's wheelchair accessible, with flush toilets and water (sites $11). Tent campers can avoid crowds and fees by camping outside of designated campgrounds on U.S. Forest Service land. Sites must be at least 200 ft. from streams and lakes. Obtain maps and free permits from the Big Bear Ranger Station. **Food** is pricey in the mountains. Groceries are available at **Stater Bros.,** 42171 Big Bear Blvd. (909-866-5211; open 7am-10pm daily).

The **hiking** in Big Bear is both free and priceless. Stop at the Big Bear Ranger Station, Rte. 38 (909-866-3437) on opposite side of the lake. (Open Mon.-Sat. 8am-4:30pm in the summer, closed Sat. during winter.) Try the **Woodland Trail,** or for a more challenging hike, try the **Pineknot Trail,** which offers views of the lake. Beware of the high altitude and rarefied air here; expect to climb slowly.

Mountain biking is a popular activity in Big Bear when the snow melts. **Snow Mountain** operates lifts in summer so thrill-seeking bikers can plummet downhill without the grueling uphill ride. The chair lift costs $7 per ride or $16 for a day pass (helmet required). Save money and get a great workout by biking up yourself; trails are open and free to all riders. Beautiful national forest land to the east and west of ski country invites exploration.

Fishing, boating, and **horseback riding** are also popular Big Bear summer activities. No license is required at **Alpine Trout Lake** (909-866-4532), ¼ mi. off Big Bear Lake Blvd., a private, stocked lake where even the poorest anglers are virtually guaranteed to take something home ($3.50 entry fee and $4.70 per lb. of caught fish). Fishing boats can be rented at **Gray's Landing** (909-866-2443) on North Shore Dr., for $12 per hour or $25 per half-day. Call Big Bear Lake's **Fishing Association** (909-866-6260) for answers to your fishing questions. Inexpensive horseback tours are available in the evening from **Bear Mtn. Riding Stables** (909-565-1260) in Big Bear City (tours $15 per hour on weekdays, $20 weekends). When conditions are favorable, ski areas sell out lift tickets quickly. **Tickets** for the resorts listed below may be purchased over the phone with Visa or MasterCard through TicketMaster (213-480-3232 or 714-740-2000). Call 800-427-7623 for information on road conditions and closures. The **Bear Mountain Ski (and Golf) Resort** (909-585-2517), has 11 lifts, 250 acres of terrain, 100- to 1300-ft. vertical drops, snowmaking, and more expert runs than other area slopes. Lift tickets cost $38, $21 for ages 65 and over. Equipment rental is $16 for skis, $27 for boots and snowboards. New skier packages include lesson, lift ticket, and equipment rental for $29 on weekdays and $39 on weekends.

■■■ SAN DIEGO

San Diego is the sort of city that everyone—both residents and tourists—seems to like. A world-renowned zoo, Sea World, beautiful parks and beaches, fantastic weather without the L.A. smog, and affordable lodging all make it a Southern Californian version of Eden. Recently, many fed-up Angelenos and Easterners have discovered San Diego's charms. The question is not why so many, but why not more?

PRACTICAL INFORMATION

Tourist Office: International Visitors Information Center, 11 Horton Plaza (236-1212), downtown. Lots of information if you ask nicely. Multilingual staff. Open Mon.-Sat. 8:30am-5pm. Also Sun. 11am-5pm in summer.

Police: 531-2000.

Airport: San Diego International lies at the northwestern edge of downtown, across from Harbor Island. San Diego Transit bus #2 ("30th and Adams") goes downtown ($1.50); transfer to other routes. Cab fare to downtown $7.

Trains: Amtrak, Santa Fe Depot, 1050 Kettner Blvd. (239-9021, for schedules and information 800-872-7245), at Broadway. To L.A. (Mon.-Fri. 8 per day 5:05am-9pm; one way $24, round-trip $32). Ticket office open 5:15am-9pm.

Buses: Greyhound, 120 W. Broadway (239-8082), at 1st Ave. To L.A. Departures every hour on the hour, except last train which leaves at 8:30pm. One way $12, round-trip $24. Ticket office open 24 hrs.

Public Transportation: Call 233-3004 for information (Open Mon.-Fri. 5:30am-8:30pm. $1.50 for local routes and $1.75 for express buses; free transfers last for 1½ hrs. All buses wheelchair accessible. Exact change; most accept bills.) The **Day Tripper** pass allows unlimited rides on buses, ferries, and trollies for one day ($5). The **San Diego Trolley** consists of two lines leaving from downtown for El Cajon and San Ysidro, plus points in between. The El Cajon line leaves from 12th and Imperial; the San Ysidro line leaves from the Old Town Transit Center and goes to the border (5-1am daily, $1-1.75). **The Transit Store:** at 1st and Broadway (234-1060), has tickets, passes, and timetables for all public transport. Open Mon. and Fri. 8:30am-6pm, Tues.-Thurs. 8am-5:30pm.

Car Rental: Aztec Rent-A-Car, 2401 Pacific Hwy. (232-6117 or 800-231-0400). $22-50 per day with unlimited mileage. Must be 21 with major credit card. Open Mon.-Fri. 6am-8pm, Sat.-Sun. 8am-5pm.

Bike Rental: Rent-A-Bike, at 1st and Harbor Dr. (232-4700), offers a bike, helmet, and lock for $8 per hour, $28 per day or $70 per week. Open daily 8am-6pm.

Crisis Lines: Rape Hotline: 233-3088 (24 hrs). **Gay Crisis Line:** 692-4297, Mon.-Sat. 6am-10pm. **Crime Victims:** 236-0101. 24 hrs.

Emergency: 911.

Post Office: Main Branch, 2535 Midway Dr. (231-3119), between downtown and Mission Beach. **ZIP code:** 92138. **Area code:** 619.

San Diego rests in the extreme southwest corner of California, 127 mi. south of L.A. and 15 mi. north of the Mexican border. **I-5** runs south from Los Angeles and skirts the eastern edge of downtown. **I-15** runs northeast to Nevada. **I-8** runs east-west along downtown's northern boundary, connecting the desert to the east with Ocean Beach in the west. **Broadway** also runs east-west. On the northeast corner of downtown lies **Balboa Park.** Just northeast of the park are the cosmopolitan **Hillcrest** and **University Heights** areas, both centers for the gay community. The business district lies south and east of the park. South of downtown, between 4th and 6th St., is the newly energetic **Gaslamp District. Coronado Island** forms **San Diego Bay,** just south of the downtown area. The spit of land known as **Mission Beach,** which lies north of the airport and downtown areas, forms **Mission Bay,** home to a large park and **Sea World.** Farther north are **Pacific Beach** and **La Jolla.**

ACCOMMODATIONS AND CAMPING

Accommodations in San Diego can be incredible bargains. Rooms which go for $35 are comparable to $60 rooms in Los Angeles. For information on state park camping, call the enthusiastic people at San Elijo Beach (753-5091).

HI-Broadway (HI-AYH), 500 W. Broadway (525-1531), downtown, close to train and bus stations, as well as Horton Plaza and the Gaslamp District. Communal bathrooms, common room with TV. Laundry and game room (with pool table) downstairs. Good security. Desk open 8am-11pm. No curfew. $12, nonmembers $15. Doubles (with bunk) $26. Storage fee $1. IBN reservations available.

HI-Elliott (HI-AYH), 3790 Udall St. (223-4778), Point Loma. Take bus #35 from downtown; get off at the first stop on Voltaire and walk across the street. Or take I-5 to Sea World exit, then left to Sunset Cliffs Blvd.; go left on Voltaire, right on Warden and look for hostel sign painted on a remodeled church. The airy 2-story building is 1½mi. from Ocean Beach. Wooden bunks for 60, common room, large kitchen, and patio. 7-night max. stay. Check-out 10:30am. Office open 8-10pm. No curfew. $12, nonmembers $15. Reserve 48 hrs. in advance.

Banana Bungalow (AAIH/Rucksackers), 707 Reed Ave. (273-3060 or 800-5-HOSTEL/546-7835), just off of Mission Blvd., Mission Beach. Take bus #34 to Mission and Reed. A long list of amenities: great location on a beautiful beach, friendly staff, free breakfast, cheap keg parties ($3 all-you-can-drink), and bonfire BBQs on the beach. Also bike, boogie-board, and rollerblade rental. Near bars and restaurants. Check-out 10:15am. No curfew. Dorm $11-18, private double $45 (available in winter only). Linen included. Blankets and overnight key require $10 deposit. Call in advance.

Downtown Hotel at Baltic Inn, 521 6th Ave. (237-0687). Well-equipped, clean rooms (each has toilet, sink, microwave, mini-fridge, cable TV, closets). Clean communal showers. Great location for downtown connections. No curfew; 24-hr. security. Laundry facilities. Singles $15, doubles $27. Weekly rates from $73.

J Street Inn, 222 J St. (696-6922). Beautiful hotel located next to the Convention Center, among luxury hotels. For $35 (add $10 for a second person), you can enjoy a fab room. Super clean, with cable TV, microwave, refrigerator, sink, and private bath. Gym, reading room, and parking ($5 per day, $16 per week).

Jim's San Diego, 1425 C St. (235-0234), south of the park, 2 blocks from "City College" trolley. Spruce, hostel-type rooms for 4. Kitchen, sun deck, common room, laundry. Homey atmosphere, backpacker clientele. Check-out noon. $13 per night, $11 in winter, $77-80 per week. Breakfast and Sunday BBQ included.

Grand Pacific Hostel, 437 5th St. (232-3100). A fun, relaxed hostel in the center of the Gaslamp District. Free linen and breakfast, kitchen and coin-op laundry. Hostel offers tours to Tijuana ($10). Bunk $12-16, private room $30 per couple.

La Pacifica, 1546 2nd Ave. (236-9292), downtown. New European-style building with pretty, recently refurbished courtyard. Snappy rooms with phone, microwave, big refrigerator, cable TV and ceiling fan. Common room, laundry room. Singles $30, weekly $140-180; doubles $40, weekly $155-200.

South Carlsbad Beach State Park (431-3143), Rte. 21 near Leucadia, in north San Diego County. 226 sites, half for tents. On cliffs over the sea. Showers, laundry facilities. No hiking trails. Sites $16-21.

San Elijo Beach State Park (753-5091), Rte. 21 south of Cardiff-by-the-Sea. 271 sites (150 for tents) in a setting similar to that at South Carlsbad to the north. Strategic landscaping gives a secluded feel. Hiker/biker campsites too. Laundry and showers, but no hiking or biking trails. Oceanfront sites $21, inland $16.

FOOD

Machos, 1125 6th Ave. (231-1969). Excellent, cheap, authentic Mexican food. Endless chips and salsa. Daily specials. Two beef enchiladas $3. Freshly made iced tea. Open Mon.-Fri. 8am-7pm, Sat.-Sun. 8am-5pm.

Filippi's Pizza Grotto, 1747 India St. (232-5094), in Little Italy, is a local landmark. Serves up huge plates of pasta ($6-9) and delectable pizzas ($8-10). Eat in or take out. Always busy. Open Sun.-Thurs. 9am-10pm, Fri.-Sat. 9am-11pm.

Anthony's Fishette, 555 Harbor Ln. (232-2933), at the foot of Market St. on the bay. A downscale version of **Anthony's** restaurants. Quite a catch, with bay view and a bar. Dinners $5-10. Open Sun.-Thurs. 11am-8pm, Fri.-Sat. 11am-8:30pm.

Conora's, 3715 India St. (291-5938), in India St. Colony. Sandwich shop extraordinaire. Over 60 varieties, almost all $3.50-4.50. Call ahead if you're in a hurry, and Conora's will have your order ready. Open Mon.-Sat. 8am-6pm, Sun. 11am-4pm.

The Golden Dragon, 414 University Ave., (296-4119; delivery 275-7500), Hillcrest. Hugely varied menu offers over a hundred dishes and a special vegetarian menu. All you can eat buffet from 5:30 to 9:30 daily. Open daily 3pm-3am.

El Indio, 3695 India St. (299-0385), in India St. Colony. In operation since 1940. Counter-style service takes a while but is worth it. Sizable portions; combination plates around $3-5.50, à la carte tacos and burritos from $2. Open daily 7am-9pm.

SIGHTS

Downtown

Moored windjammers, cruise ships, and the occasional naval destroyer face the boardwalk shops and museums along the **Embarcadero** (Spanish for "dock"). The magnificently restored 1863 sailing vessel, *Star of India,* is docked in front of the touristy **Maritime Museum,** 1306 N. Harbor Dr. (234-9153). Alongside are anchored both the 1904 British steam yacht *Medea* and the 1898 ferryboat *Berkeley,* a bay ferry that slunk away from its mooring after the 1906 earthquake. (Ship open daily 9am-9pm. $6, ages 13-17 and over 55 $4, 6-12 $2, families $12.)

From Harbor Drive, the **Coronado Bridge** stretches westward from Barrio Logan to the Coronado Island. High enough to allow the Navy's biggest ships to pass underneath, the sleek, sky-blue arc rests upon spindly piers and executes a graceful, swooping turn over the waters of San Diego Bay before touching down in Coronado. When the bridge was built in 1969, its eastern end cut a swath through San Diego's largest Chicano community. In response, the community created **Chicano Park,** obtaining the land beneath the bridge and painting murals on the bridge's piers. The murals, best appreciated by a walk around the park, are heroic in scale and theme, drawing on Hispanic-American, Spanish, Mayan, and Aztec imagery. Take bus #11 or the San Ysidro trolley to Barrio Logan station.

South of Broadway, between 4th and 5th Ave., lie 16 blocks of antique shops, Victorian buildings, and trendy restaurants that comprise the historic **Gaslamp Quarter.** Gentrification has brought a number of new bars and bistros to the Quarter and the area is now well-frequented by upscale after-hours revelers. The area is a National Historic District, with several 19th-century landmarks worth a visit. The **Gaslamp Quarter Foundation** (233-4692) offers walking tours of the Quarter (Sat. 11am. 90-min. tours $5; seniors, students, ages 12-18 $3; under 12 free).

Balboa Park

Balboa Park was the creation of pioneering horticulturists whose plantings transformed a once-treeless pueblo tract into a botanical montage. Today, primitive Cycad and Coast Redwood trees tower above climbing roses and water lilies, and the city's population is over one million. Close to that number are drawn each year to Balboa Park for its concerts, cultural events, Spanish architecture, lush vegetation, and of course, the San Diego Zoo. Balboa Park is accessible by bus #7, or by driving east from downtown on Laurel St.

With over 100 acres of exquisite fenceless habitats, the **San Diego Zoo** (234-3153) deserves its reputation as one of the finest in the world. Joining the stunning **Tiger River** and **Sun Bear Forest** is the **Gorilla Tropics** enclosure, housing lowland gorillas and plant species imported from Africa. In addition to the usual elephants and zebras, the zoo houses such unusual creatures as Malay tapirs and everybody's favorite...koalas. The **Wings of Australasia Aviaries** is popular as well. New this year is **Hippo Beach,** where lovable behemoths Funani and Jabba swim and (sort of) frolic. The most efficient way to tour the zoo is to arrive as early as possible and take the 40-min. open-air **double-decker bus tour,** which covers

70% of the park. ($4, ages 3-11 $3. Sit on the left, given a choice.) Most of the zoo is wheelchair accessible, but steep hills make assistance necessary. (Open daily 9am-4pm. $13, ages 3-11 $6, military in uniform free.) Look for discount coupons for zoo entrance in guidebooks.

Balboa Park has the greatest concentration of museums in the U.S. outside of Washington, DC. Before exploring El Prado, stop by the **House of Hospitality** at 1549 El Prado St., which contains the park **visitors center** (239-0512; open daily 9am-4pm). The center sells simple maps of the park for a well-spent 65¢, and the **Passport to Balboa Park,** which contains coupons for a week's worth of entry to all of the park's museums ($18). Passports are also available at participating museums.

The star of the western axis of the Plaza de Panama is the **Museum of Man** (239-2001). Inside the much-photographed tower, human evolution is traced through permanent exhibits on primates and early man. Several displays focus on Native American societies. Half the museum is allotted to innovative temporary exhibits. (Open daily 10am-4:30pm. $4 or 2 coupons, ages 13-18 $2, 6-12 $1.)

Across the Plaza de Panama is the **San Diego Museum of Art** (232-7931), which maintains a comprehensive collection, ranging from ancient Asian to contemporary Californian. (Open Tues.-Sun. 10am-4:30pm. $6, seniors $5, military with ID $4, ages 6-17 $2, under 6 free. Free 3rd Tues. of each month.) Nearby is the outdoor **Sculpture Garden Court** (236-1725), with a sensuous Henry Moore piece presiding over other large abstract blocks. The **Timken Art Gallery,** 1500 El Prado (239-5548), features several superb portraits by David, Hals, Rubens, and others, and an excellent collection of large, abstract Russian church icons. (Open Oct.-Aug. Tues.-Sat. 10am-4:30pm, Sun 11am-4:30pm. Free).

Farther east along the plaza stands the **Botanical Building** (234-8901), a wooden Quonset structure accented by tall palms which threaten to burst through the roof. The scent of jasmine and the splash of fountains make this an authentic oasis (open Fri.-Wed. 10am-4pm; free). The same botanists run the **Desert and Rose Gardens** one block east at 2200 Park Blvd. (236-5717; free). Cacti and stunted desert vegetation in one building provide a striking contrast to the abundant roses next door.

At the east end of El Prado lies the **Natural History Museum** (232-3821). Life-size robotic dinosaurs enhance the standard fossils, and a recreated mine houses gem displays. (Open Fri.-Wed. 9:30am-5:30pm, Thurs. 9:30am-6:30pm. $5, seniors and military $4, ages 6-17 $2.) Across from the Natural History Museum is the **Reuben H. Fleet Space Theater and Science Center** (238-1233), with two **Omnimax** projectors, 153 speakers, and a hemispheric planetarium. (Sat. 10 and 11am shows are subtitled in Spanish. $6, senior citizens $4.50, ages 5-15 $3.50, military and students $4.80.) Tickets to the space theater include admittance to the Science Center, where visitors can play with a cloud chamber, light-mixing booth, and other gadgets. (Open Sun.-Tues. 9:30am-9:30pm, Sat. 9:30am-10:30pm. $2.50, ages 5-15 $1.25.)

Old Town

In 1769, a group of Spanish soldiers accompanied by Father Junípero Serra established the first European settlement on the United States' western coast. Today this area contains a number of museums, parks, and sundry attractions commemorating the historic settlement which gave rise to the modern metropolis of San Diego.

Presidio Park is most impressive of these historical areas. The park contains the **Serra Museum** (279-3258), open Tues.-Sat. from 10am-4:30pm, Sun. noon-4:30pm ($3, 12 and under free). Exhibits tell the story of the initial settlement and interactions with the native Americans who lived nearby. Apparently the Spanish soldiers were a rough and unholy bunch, because in 1774 the padres moved their mission some six miles away to its current location. **Mission Basilica San Diego de Alcalá** (281-8449) is still an active parish church where mass is held (daily 7am and 5:30pm). Mission San Diego has a chapel, a garden courtyard, a small museum of artifacts, and a reconstruction of the living quarters of boffo chap Junípero Serra.

West of the mission is **Jack Murphy Stadium,** home of the AFC champion **San Diego Chargers** football team and baseball's less successful **San Diego Padres.**

Sea World

Sea World is sort of like Disneyland plus fish and minus the rides. At **Shamu Stadium,** you can be amused and possibly drenched by cavorting orcas. If staying dry seems a little more appealing than the Shamu water treatment, consider the truly outstanding **Shark Encounter.** The highlight of this exhibit is the glass tunnel which leads you through the 700,000-gallon, shark-filled tank. New in 1995 is the **Baywatch at Sea World** ski show. Its lame plot is excused by exciting water and jet ski performances. Part of the event is narrated by none other than the international heartthrob **David Hasselhoff.** The hidden gem of the park is the **Anheuser-Busch Hospitality Tent,** which will give each (21 and over) guest up to **two free cups of beer.** Admission costs $29 for adults and $21 for children 3-11. It's open in summer Sun.-Thurs. 9am-10pm, Fri.-Sat. 9am-11pm. Hours are shorter off season.

NIGHTLIFE

Distinct pockets of action are scattered throughout the city. The Gaslamp Quarter is home to myriad upscale restaurants and bars that feature live music nightly. Hillcrest draws a young, largely gay crowd. The beach areas host tons of clubs and bars. The free *San Diego Reader* is the definitive source of entertainment information.

Pacific Beach Grill and Club Tremors, 860 Garnet Ave. (2-PB-PARTY/272-7277), in Pacific Beach. Attracts the young and unattached with a nightly DJ. Open nightly 8:30pm-2am. Cover varies ($1-5). The upstairs bar is more quiet and has an ever-changing menu of cheap food. Open 11-2am, kitchen 'til 11pm.

Dick's Last Resort, 345 4th Ave. (231-9100), in the Gaslamp Quarter. Buckets o' Southern grub and a wildly irreverent atmosphere. Beers from around the globe, like Dixieland Blackened Voodoo Lager. No cover for nightly rock or blues, but you'd better be buyin'! Burgers under $4, dinners $10-15. Open daily 11-1:30am.

Café Lu Lu, 419 F. St. (238-0114), in the Gaslamp Quarter. Funky vegetarian coffee house designed by local artists. See and be seen as you dine for under $5 and sip raspberry-mocha espresso ($3.50). Open Sun.-Thurs. 9-2am, Fri.-Sat. 9-4am.

Club Sevilla, 555 4th Ave. (233-5979). Nightly live bands include Brazilian, flamenco, and salsa. *Tapas* bar upstairs. Open daily 5pm-2am. 21 and over.

Velvet, 2812 Kettner Blvd. (692-1080), near Old Town. Live and loud, plays host to local rock 'n' roll up-and-comers, as well as established bands. Alterna-rock 6 nights a week. $5 cover Wed.-Sat. Pool table. 21 and over. Open daily 8pm-2am.

Chillers, 3105 Ocean Front Walk (488-2077), Mission Beach. Like an adults-only "7-11," this club offers intoxicating "slurpees." Everything from the mundane to the "Attitude Adjustment" (grain alcohol, vodka, pineapple juice, lemonade, and grenadine). Free samples. Boozy slushes $4-6. Open 11-2am daily.

Some of the more popular **lesbian** and **gay clubs** include: **The Flame,** 3780 Park Blvd. in Hillcrest (295-4163), a lesbian dance club; **West Coast Production Company,** 2028 Hancock St. in Middletown (295-3724), a lively gay club; **Bourbon Street,** 4612 Park Blvd. in University Heights (291-0173), a gay piano bar.

SEASONAL EVENTS

At the **Penguin Day Ski Fest** (276-0830), New Year's Day, De Anza Cove on Mission Bay, the object is to go water-skiing in the ocean or lie on a block of ice without a wet suit; those who do are honored with a "penguin patch." Those who fail come away with a "chicken patch" (festivities 8am-1pm). The **Ocean Beach Kite Festival** (531-1527), on the first Saturday in March, 4741 Santa Monica Ave. in Ocean Beach, is great for the kiddies. Kite-making materials are provided free, and judging at 1pm is followed by a parade to the beach for the kite-flying competition. On Fri.-Sat. nights from June 1-Labor Day, at San Diego State University's Mount Laguna Observatory, there's free **Summer Stargazing** (594-6182). **Surf, Sand, and Sandcastle**

Days (424-6663), mid-July at Imperial Beach, by the pier at 9:30am, features "Castles of the Mind" and "Creatures of the Sea," as well as a parade and fireworks.

Making Runs to the Border

The completion of the Transpeninsular Hwy. has made it quicker to travel the Baja peninsula by **car,** but be prepared to be cruising along at 60mph and suddenly careen into a rutted curve that can only be taken at 30mph. Remember that extra gas (unleaded) may be in short supply; don't pass a PEMEX station without filling your tank. If you will be driving in Baja for more than 72 hours, you need to get a free permit by showing vehicle title and proof of registration.

All major towns in Baja are served by **bus.** If you plan to navigate the peninsula by bus, be forewarned that you have to leave at inconvenient times, fight to procure a ticket, and then probably stand the whole way. A much better idea is to buy a reserved seat in Tijuana or Ensenada and traverse the peninsula in one shot while seated. Any way you cut it, Baja beaches and other points of interest off the main highway are often inaccessible on public transportation; buses don't stop at coastal spots between Tijuana and San Quintín.

If your travels in Mexico will be limited to Tijuana and Ensenada, you will probably not need to exchange your dollars for pesos; the vast majority of shops and restaurants in these cities are more than willing to take greenbacks. If you plan to travel farther into Baja, prices will be quoted in pesos and some establishments will not accept U.S. dollars, or if they do, will give you a bad exchange rate. The right rate fluctuates around 3.385 pesos per U.S. dollar. For extended forays into Mexico we use and endorse *Let's Go: Mexico* and Gibson guitars.

■ NORTH OF SAN DIEGO

La Jolla Pronounced "la HOY-a," this affluent locality houses few accommodations or eateries friendly to the budget traveler, but its beaches are largely open to the public and simply fabulous. The **La Jolla Cove** is popular with scuba divers, snorkelers, and brilliantly colored Garhibaldi Goldfish. Surfers are especially fond of the waves at **Tourmaline Beach** and **Windansea Beach.** These waves can be too much for non-surfers. **La Jolla Shores,** next to Scripps/UCSD, has gentler swells ideal for bodysurfers, boogie-boarders, and swimmers and is exceptionally clean. The few surfers who visit stay near the pier. **Black's Beach,** a public beach, is not officially a **nude beach,** but you wouldn't know it from the sun-kissed hue of most beachgoers' buns. The north end of the beach generally attracts gay patrons. To reach La Jolla, turn from I-5 and take a left at the Ardath exit or take buses #30 or 34 from downtown.

Escondido The **San Diego Wild Animal Park** (234-6541) is specifically dedicated to the preservation and display of endangered species. 800 of the park's 2200 acres have been landscaped to simulate four different geographical regions. A variety of African, European, and American animals range freely in their respective habitats. The entrance has shops, restaurants, and a 1¾-mi. trail—but most of the park is accessible only by the open-air **Wgasa Bush Line,** a 50-minute monorail tour through the four habitat areas. (Admission including 50-min. Wgasa Bush Line tour and animal shows is $17.50, seniors $15.50, ages 3-11 $10.50. Parking $3. Park open Mon.-Wed. 9am-7pm, Thurs.-Sun 9am-10pm.)

Visitors can poke through the late "wunnerful, wunnerful" champagne music conductor Lawrence Welk's personal barony, the **Welk Resort Center.** The lobby contains the **Lawrence Welk Museum,** 8860 Lawrence Welk Dr. (800-932-WELK/9355). All the majesty is open Sun.-Mon. and Wed. 10am-5pm, Tue.-Thurs. and Sat. 10am-1pm. It's all free. Those under the age of 60 may stand out in this crowd.

THE DESERT

Mystics, misanthropes, and hallucinogenophiles have long been fascinated by the desert—its vast open spaces, austere scenery, and brutal heat. In the winter the desert is a pleasantly warm refuge, in the spring, a technicolor floral landscape, and then in the summer, a blistering wasteland. A barren place of overwhelming simplicity, the desert's beauty lies not so much in what it contains, but in what it lacks—congestion, pollution, and crowds of visitors craning to see the same sights.

California's desert divides roughly into two zones. The **Sonoran,** or **Low Desert,** occupies southeastern California from the Mexican border north to Needles and west to the Borrego Desert; the **Mojave,** or **High Desert** spans the south central part of the state, bounded by the Sonoran Desert to the south, San Bernardino and the San Joaquin Valleys to the west, the Sierra Nevada to the north, and Death Valley to the east. As their names imply, the Low and High Deserts lie at different elevations, resulting in two different climates. The Low Desert, home of the **Anza-Borrego Desert State Park** and the fetid **Salton Sea,** is flat, dry, and barren. The oases in this area are essential to the existence of human, animal, and plant life, with the largest of them supporting the super-resort of Palm Springs.

In contrast, the **High Desert** consists of foothills and plains nestled within mountain ranges approaching 5,000 ft. Consequently, it is cooler (by about 10°F in summer) and wetter. Few resorts have been developed, but **Joshua Tree National Park** is a popular destination for campers. **Barstow** is the central city of the High Desert and an important rest station on the way from L.A. to Las Vegas or the Sierras. **Death Valley** represents the eastern boundary of the Mojave but could be considered a region unto itself, since it has both high and low desert areas. Major highways cross the desert east-west: I-8 hugs the California-Mexico border, I-10 goes through Blythe and Indio on its way to Los Angeles, and I-40 crosses Needles to Barstow, where it joins I-15, running from Las Vegas and other points west to L.A.

For important health and safety precautions concerning desert travel and recreation, see To Your Health, p. page 11, and By Car, p. page 31.

■■■ PALM SPRINGS

For years, the singularly lackadaisical brand of decadence offered by Palm Springs has attracted people from all walks of life. While Palm Springs is home to gaggles of retirees, it is also a popular spring break destination for students and a winter destination for middle-aged, fat cat golfers and hip, young scene-seekers from coastal communities. With relatively warm temperatures, ubiquitous golf courses, symmetrical rows of palm trees, and more pink than a Miami Vice episode, the desert city teems with those seeking a sunny respite from their everyday lives.

Go to the **Chamber of Commerce,** 190 W. Amado (325-1577), for friendly advice and sexy maps ($1). Pick up *The Desert Guide,* a free monthly magazine outlining attractions and entertainment (open Mon.-Fri. 8:30am-4:30pm). **Greyhound,** 311 N. Indian Canyon (800-231-2222), runs 7 buses per day to and from L.A. ($14 one way, $21 round trip). The local bus system, **Sun Bus** (343-3451), connects all Coachella Valley cities daily 6am-6pm. Fare is 75¢ with 25¢ transfers (exact change). Line #111 stays on a straight course along Palm Canyon Dr. and from there along Rte. 111 to Palm Desert (1 bus every ½ hr.). Lines #21 and #23 cover the downtown area. **Desert Cab,** 325-2868 and **Valley Cabousine,** 340-5845, both offer 24-hr. **taxi** service. **Emergency:** 911. Palm Springs' **post office:** 333 E. Amado Rd. (325-9631; open Mon.-Fri. 8am-5pm, Sat. 9am-1pm); **ZIP code:** 92263-9999; **area code:** 619.

The cheapest way to stay in Palm Springs is to find an outlying state park or national forest campground. If you've gotta stay in town, **Budget Host Inn,** 1277 S. Palm Canyon Dr. (325-5574 or 800-829-8099), has large, clean rooms with refrigerators, phones, pool/jacuzzi access, and continental breakfast. (Winter rates for two people $79 weekdays, $90 weekend; in the summer, $35, $45 weekend.).

Las Casuelas-The Original, 368 N. Palm Canyon Dr. (325-3213), has some of the best Mexican food around. Combos start at $7 (open Sun.-Thurs. 10am-10pm, Fri.-Sat. 10:30am-11pm). **Thai Smile,** 651 N. Palm Canyon Dr. (320-5503), offers tasty options for vegetarians. Vegetable soup goes for $2.50, tempura $5.25; spicy *pad thai* chicken is just $6.50 (open daily 11am-10pm). Bars offer nightly drink specials to lure revelers. **La Taquería,** 125 E. Tahquitz Way (778-5391), attracts customers by covering its tile patio with mist and serving Moonlight Margaritas for $2.25.

The **Palm Springs Aerial Tramway** (325-1391) climbs the cliffs of Mt. San Jacinto to an observation deck that has excellent views of the Coachella Valley. The tramway station is located on Tramway Dr., which intersects Rte. 111 just north of Palm Springs (round-trip $16, seniors $12, under 12 $10). A touch of true natural beauty has been marketed at the remarkable **Desert Museum,** 101 Museum Dr. (325-0189). The museum offers an impressive collection of Native American art, talking desert dioramas, and live animals. The **Living Desert Reserve** in Palm Desert, located 1½ mi. south of Rte. 111 at 47900 Portola Ave. (346-5694), houses Arabian oryces, iguanas, desert unicorns, and Grevy's zebras alongside indigenous flora in the **Botanical Gardens.** The twilight reptile exhibit is a must-see. (Open daily Sept.-mid-June 9am-5pm. $7, seniors $6, under 15 $3.50.)

The **Indian Canyons** (325-5673), once home to the Agua Caliente Cahuilla Indians, are oases that contain a wide variety of desert life and remnants of the human communities they once supported. All four canyons can be accessed at the end of S. Palm Canyon Dr., 5 mi. from the center of town. (Open daily fall/winter 8am-5pm, spring/summer 8am-6pm. $5 adults, seniors $2.50, children $1, students $3.50.)

Idiosyncracies abound at **Cabot's Old Indian Pueblo,** 67616 E. Desert View Ave. (329-7610), 1 mi. east of Palm Dr. in **Desert Hot Springs.** Take bus #19 from Palm Springs to Desert View Ave. The 35 rooms in the Hopi-style pueblo were built from materials found in the desert from 1941 to 1964. (Peruse the pueblo 10am-3pm Wed.-Sun.; July-Sept. Sat-Sun. only. $2.50, seniors $2, ages 5-16 $1.)

Let's Not Go: The Fetid Salton Sea

This man-made "wonder" was formed in 1905-1907 when the aqueduct from the Colorado River broke and flooded the Coachella Valley. The accident resulted in a stagnant 35 mi. by 15 mi. lake covering a patch of desert. The lake festered for a while until the 60s, when someone thought it was a great idea to market the area as a tourist attraction. Fresh and saltwater fish were stocked in the sea, and marinas were built in ill-fated anticipation of a thriving resort and vacation industry. Hopes were cruelly dashed when decaying vegetation in the still water produced a foul odor and high salt content killed all but a few hardy species of fish. The sea is now ringed by abandoned buildings and **Salton City** is a defunct resort town withering in the desert sun. For more information, call the **West Shores Chamber of Commerce,** P.O. Box 5185, Salton City, CA 92705.

■■■ JOSHUA TREE

When the Mormons crossed this desert area in the 1800s, they named the enigmatic desert tree they encountered after the Biblical prophet Joshua. Perhaps it was the heat, but the tree's crooked limbs reminded them of the Hebrew leader, who with his arms upraised, beckoned the weary traveler to the promised land. After crossing the more arid Arizona desert, finding the slightly cooler and wetter Mojave must have been like arriving in God's country. **Joshua Tree National Park** contains an eerie panoply of high and low desert landscapes and life forms. Piles of quartz monzonite boulders, some over 100 ft. high, punctuate the desert terrain. Desert winds and floods have created textures and shapes majestic to the viewer and irresistible to the climber; hardy fauna adapted to the unforgiving desert environment populate the park; and vestiges of past human occupation, like ancient rock petroglyphs, dams built in the 19th century to catch the meager rainfall for livestock, and the ruins of gold mines, still dot the park.

Practical Information Go to the **Headquarters and Oasis Visitor Center,** 74485 National Park Dr., Twentynine Palms 92277 (367-7511), ¼ mi. off Rte. 62, for displays, guidebooks, maps, access to water, and friendly rangers available to answer questions. Open daily 8am-4:30pm. Understanding the vicissitudes of **weather** is essential: summer highs 95-115°F; winter highs 60-70°F. It's warmer in the eastern area. The most comfortable places in summer are above 4000 ft.; in winter, stick to lower elevations. The **Hi-Desert Medical Center,** 6601 White Feather Rd. (366-3711) in Joshua Tree, provides 24-hr. emergency care. In case of an **emergency,** call 911, or 367-3523 for a **ranger.** For the **24-hr. dispatch center,** call 909-383-5651 collect. The nearest **post office:** 73839 Gorgonio Dr. (367-3501), in Twentynine Palms. It's open Mon.-Fri. 8:30am-5pm; **ZIP code:** 92277; **area code:** 619.

Joshua Tree National Park covers 558,000 acres northeast of Palm Springs, about 160 mi. east of L.A. The park is ringed by three highways: **I-10** to the south, **Rte. 62** to the west and north, and **Rte. 177** to the east. From I-10, the best approaches are via Rte. 62 from the west, or from the south entrance at Cottonwood Springs.

CALIFORNIA

Camping Most campgrounds in the park operate on a first-come, first-camped basis and accept no reservations. Exceptions are the group sites at Cottonwood, Sheep Pass, and Indian Cove and family sites at Black Rock Canyon. MISTIX (800-365-2267) will set you up for reservations there. The **backcountry** is also open for unlimited camping. All campsites have tables, fireplaces, and pit toilets, and are free unless otherwise noted. Water and flush toilets are available only at Black Rock Canyon and Cottonwood campgrounds. Bring your own firewood because burning anything you find in the park is a major offense. Tents in the backcountry must be pitched at least 500 ft. from a trail and 1 mi. from a road. Your camping stay is limited to 14 days between October and May and to 30 days in the summer. Be sure to register first at a backcountry board found along the park's main roads so park staff knows where you are. **Hidden Valley** (4200 ft.), in the center of the park, with secluded alcoves in which to pitch a tent, and shade provided by enormous boulders, is by far the best and most wooded of the campsites. The 39 sites in the Wonderland of Rocks fill quickly. Rock-climbers will be in heaven. **Jumbo Rocks** (4400 ft.) is located near Skull Rock Trail on the eastern edge of Queen Valley. 125 well-spaced sites (65 in summer) surround (you guessed it) jumbo rocks. Front spots have best shade and protection. **Indian Cove** (3200 ft.) has 107 sites (45 in summer) on the north edge of the Wonderland of Rocks. There are waterfalls after rain. Most of the 13 group sites are $15, but the two largest are $30.

Sights Over 80% of the park (mostly the southern and eastern areas) has been designated by Congress as a wilderness area—meaning trails but no roads, toilets, or campfires. For those seeking backcountry desert hiking and camping, Joshua Tree offers fantastic opportunities to explore truly remote territory. There is no water in the wilderness except when a flash flood comes roaring down a wash (beware your choice of campsite). Even then, it doesn't stay long. The most temperate weather is in late fall (Oct.-Dec.) and early spring (March-April). Temperatures in other months often span uncomfortable extremes.

Joshua Tree is world-renowned for **rock-climbing** and draws thousands of climbers each year. The visitors center can provide information on established top rope routes and will identify wilderness areas where placement of new bolts is restricted. The **Wonderland of Rocks** and **Hidden Valley** are particular hotspots. For instruction and equipment rentals contact **Ultimate Adventures,** Box 2072, Joshua Tree (366-4758) or **Wilderness Connection,** Box 29, Joshua Tree (366-4745).

A self-paced driving tour is an easy way to explore the magic of Joshua Tree without specialized equipment (although 4-wheel-drive wouldn't hurt). Paved roads branch through the park's varied sights, and roadside signs indicate points of interest scattered throughout the park. Some of the most outstanding scenic points can be reached by the side roads. One sight that must not be missed is **Key's View** (5185 ft.), 6 mi. off the park road just west of Ryan Campground. On a clear day, you can see to Palm Springs and the Salton Sea, and it's a fabulous spot to watch the sun rise. The **Cholla Cactus Garden,** off Pinto Basin Rd., also merits a visit. 4WD vehicles can access dirt roads, such as **Geology Tour Road,** which climbs through fascinating rock formations and ends in the Little San Bernardino Mountains.

Hiking through the park's trails is perhaps the best way to experience Joshua Tree. Hikers can tread through sand, scramble over boulders, and walk among the hardy Joshua trees themselves. Visitors will probably find the **Barker Dam Trail** packed with tourists. Painted petroglyphs and a tranquility that rises above the crowd make the reservoir worth a trip. Wildflowers, cooler temperatures, and the indelible picture of the encircling valleys reward the hardy hiker who climbs the 3 mi. to the summit of **Ryan Mountain** (5461 ft.). Bring plenty of water for this strenuous, unshaded climb. Information on many other hikes, ranging from a 15-minute stroll to the **Oasis of Mara** (wheelchair accessible) to a 35-mi. circumambulation of the park's **California Riding and Hiking Trail,** is available at the park center.

Joshua Tree teems with flora and fauna that you're unlikely to see anywhere else in the world. You can see adaptations that plants have made in order to survive the severe climate and admire their delicate blooms. More animals can be seen at dawn and dusk than at high noon, but watch for kangaroo rats and lizards at all times. Look for the cactus wren in the branches of **Pinto Basin's** cholla. You may meet an enormous swarm of ladybugs near the oases; be aware that enormous swarms of bees are equally common. Golden eagles and bighorn sheep also live near the oases while coyote and bobcats stalk their prey at night. If you come equipped with time, patience, and a sharp set of eyes, the desert's beauty will gradually reveal itself. **Wildflower season** (mid-March-mid-May) is an especially colorful season.

Hangin' with Christ

For a simply divine experience, picnic with Jesus and friends at Yucca Valley's **Desert Christ Park,** 57090 Twentynine Palms Hwy. This array of 10- to 15-ft. concrete figures depicting Biblical stories can be reached by turning north from Twentynine Palms Hwy, and proceeding reverently to the end of Mohawk Trail. (No phone, God has an unlisted number. Open dawn-dusk and free as air.)

■■■ BARSTOW

Do not expect to revel in this town. Barstow puts the "no" in "nowhere." It lies midway between Los Angeles and Las Vegas on I-15 and is the western terminus of I-40. The **California Desert Information Center,** 831 Barstow Rd., Barstow 92311 (255-8760), off I-15, has the best tourist information on the area, including the dirt on local off-road vehicle areas (open daily 9am-5pm). A ghostly silent and chilly **Amtrak** station lies at 7685 N. 1st St. (800-872-7245). Trains go to L.A. ($34), San Diego ($54), and Las Vegas ($45). **Greyhound,** 681 N. 1st St. (256-8757), has buses to L.A. (13 per day, $23) and Las Vegas (7 per day, $32). **Enterprise Car Rental,** 620 W. Main St. (256-0761), offers economy cars for $149 per week with 1050 free mi. Drivers must be 21 with credit card. In an **emergency** call 911. **Post office:** 425 S. 2nd Ave.; **ZIP code:** 92312; **area code:** 619.

What Barstow lacks in charm it makes up in utility with its abundant inexpensive motels and eateries. **Motel 6,** 150 N. Yucca Ave. (256-1752), is relatively close to Greyhound and Amtrak stations, and only a block from a 24-hr. grocery and drugstore. Standard, clean rooms have cable TV (singles $23, doubles $27). **Barstow/ Calico KOA** (254-2311), 7 mi. northeast of Barstow on north side of Outer Rte. 15, between Ft. Irwin Rd. and Ghost Town Rd. exits, caters to corporate campers with a pool, showers, and snack bar. It can get *very* crowded. (Tent sites for 2 $17; RVs $21 with electric and water hookup; sewer hookup $2 extra.)

Every restaurant chain this side of the Pecos has a representative on Main St. The **Barstow Station McDonald's,** 1611 E. Main St. (256-1233), made from old locomotive cars, is the busiest in the U.S., and is decked out with a kid's playground, gift shop, and **liquor store** (open Sun.-Thurs. 5am-10pm, Fri.-Sat. 5:30am-midnight). **Carlo's and Toto's,** 901 W. Main. St. (256-7513) is a favorite local diner. Huge platters of delicious Mexican cuisine $5-8. (Open Mon.-Thurs. 11am-10pm, Fri.-Sat. 11am-11pm, Sun. 9:30am-10pm.)

■■■ DEATH VALLEY

Dante and Milton could have found inspiration for further visions of hell in **Death Valley National Park.** No place in the Old World approaches the searing temperatures that are the summer norm here. The highest temperature ever recorded in the Western Hemisphere (134°F in the shade) was measured at the Valley's Furnace Creek Ranch on July 10, 1913. Of that day, the ranch caretaker Oscar Denton said, "I thought the world was going to come to an end. Swallows in full flight fell to the ground dead, and when I went out to read the thermometer with a wet Turkish towel on my head, it was dry before I returned."

Fortunately, the fatal threshold of 130°F is rarely crossed, and the region sustains a surprisingly intricate web of life. The elevation ranges from Telescope Peak at 11,049 ft. down to Badwater at 282 ft. below sea level. There are pure white salt flats on the valley floor, impassable mountain slopes, and enormous, shifting sand dunes. Nature focuses all of its extremes and varieties here at a single location, resulting in a landscape that is at once harshly majestic and improbably delicate.

Few venture to the valley floor during the summer and it is foolish to do so; the average high temperature in July is 116°F, with a nighttime low of 88°F. Ground temperatures hover near an egg-frying 200°F. When traveling through or visiting Death Valley in any season, follow the information given in the Health section, page 13, with care. In addition, check at the visitors center for the free pamphlet, *Hot Weather Hints.* To enjoy the park, visit in winter, *not* summer.

Practical Information For **Visitors Information,** traipse on over to the **Furnace Creek Visitor Center** (786-2331), on Rte. 190 in the east-central section of the valley (open daily summer 8am-4pm, winter 8am-7pm); or write the Superintendent, Death Valley National Park, Death Valley 92328. For **TTY information,** call 786-2471, daily 8am-5pm. **Ranger Stations** are located at **Grapevine,** junction of Rte. 190 and 267 near Scotty's Castle; **Stove Pipe Wells,** on Rte. 190; and **Shoshone,** outside the southeast border of the valley at the junction of Rtes. 178 and 127. Weather report, weekly naturalist program, and park information are posted at each station (open daily 8am-4pm). The $5 per vehicle entrance fee is collected only at the visitors center in the middle of the park. Resist the temptation not to pay; the Park Service needs all the money it can get. **Get tanked** outside Death Valley at Olancha, Shoshone, or Beatty, NV. Otherwise, you'll pay about 20¢ per gallon more across from the Furnace Creek Visitors Center (open 7am-7pm), in Stove Pipe Wells Village (open 7am-8pm), and at Scotty's Castle (open 9am-5:30pm). **Groceries** and supplies can be had at **Furnace Creek Ranch Store,** (786-2380), well-stocked and expensive (open daily 7am-9pm). **Stove Pipe Wells Village Store** (786-2578), is smaller but as pricey (open daily 7am-9pm). **Post Office:** Furnace Creek Ranch (786-2223); **ZIP code:** 92328; **area code:** 619.

Getting Around There is no regularly scheduled public transportation into Death Valley. Bus tours are monopolized by **Fred Harvey's Death Valley Tours** (786-2345, ext. 222). A two-hour tour of the lower valley costs $20 (children $12) and leaves at 9am, stopping briefly at Zabriskie Point, Mushroom Rock, Devil's Golf Course, Badwater, and Artists' Drive. The best tour is the five-hour excursion into hard-to-access Titus Canyon ($30, children $20). The best way to get around Death Valley is by car. The nearest agencies are in Las Vegas, Barstow, and Bishop.

Of the nine **park entrances,** most visitors choose Rte. 190 from the east. The road is well-maintained, the pass is less steep, and you arrive more quickly at the visitors center. But the visitor with a trusty vehicle will be able to see more of the park by entering from the southeast (Rte. 178 west from Rte. 127 at Shoshone) or the north (direct to Scotty's Castle via NV Rte. 267 from U.S. 95). Unskilled mountain drivers should not attempt to enter via Titus Canyon or Emigrant Canyon Drive roads; neither has guard rails to prevent your car from sliding over **precipitous cliffs.**

Eighteen-wheelers have replaced 18-mule teams, but driving in Death Valley still takes stubborn determination. **Radiator water** (*not* for drinking) is available at critical points on Rte. 178 and 190 and NV Rte. 374, but not on unpaved roads. Believe the signs that say "4WD Only." Those who *do* bound along the backcountry trails should carry chains, extra tires, gas, oil, radiator and drinking water, and spare parts.

Accommodations In Death Valley, enclosed beds and fine meals within a budget traveler's reach are as elusive as the desert bighorn sheep. During the winter months, camping out with a stock of groceries is a good way to save both money and driving time. **Stove Pipe Wells Village** (786-2387), will set you back $53 per night for one or two people, each additional person is $10.

The National Park Service maintains nine **campgrounds,** only two of which accept reservations. Call ahead to check availability and be prepared to battle for a space if you come during peak periods. Water availability is not completely reliable and supplies can at times be unsafe or unavailable; always pack your own. **Backcountry camping** is free and legal, provided you check in at the visitors center and pitch tents at least 1 mi. from main roads, 5 mi. from any established campsite, and ¼-mi. from any backcountry water source.

Sights Death Valley has hiking to bemuse the gentlest wanderer and to challenge the hardiest peregrinator. Backpackers and day hikers should inform the visitors center of their trip, and take along the appropriate topographic maps. The National Park Service recommends that valley floor hikers plan a route along roads where assistance is readily available, and outfit a party of at least two people. Do not wear sandals or lightweight footwear. Hiking in summer is a dumb-ass idea.

Artist's Drive is a one-way loop off Rte. 178, beginning 10 mi. south of the visitors center. The road snakes its sinuous way through craggy canyons on its way to **Artist's Palette,** a visually stunning array of green, yellow, and red mineral deposits in the hillside. 5 mi. south, you'll reach **Devil's Golf Course,** a plane of spiny salt crust composed of precipitate left from the evaporation of once-virile **Lake Manly.**

Three mi. south of Devil's Golf Course, on I-90, lies **Badwater,** an aptly named briny pool four times saltier than the ocean. The trek across the surrounding salt flat dips to the lowest point in the Western Hemisphere—282 ft. below sea level. Immortalized by Antonioni's film of the same name, **Zabriskie Point** is a marvelous place from which to view Death Valley's corrugated badlands. The view is particularly stunning when the setting sun fills the dried lake beds with burnt light. Perhaps the most spectacular sight in the entire park is the vista at **Dante's View,** reached by a 15-mi. paved road from Rte. 190. Just as the Italian poet stood with Virgil looking down on the damned, the modern observer gazes upon a vast inferno punctuated only by the perfect white expanse of the salt flats.

THE CENTRAL COAST

The spectacular stretch of coastline between L.A. and San Francisco known as the Central Coast may give you the sense of the awe felt by California's first settlers. The smogless sky meets the Pacific in a sweeping array of blue, while the shoreline runs the gamut from the dramatic plunge of Big Sur's cliffs to Carmel's white beaches.

Don't keep your fool head in the sand!

When you think weird-ass California wildlife, what springs to mind? Condors? Elephant seals? Dogs? Yes, yes, these are all titillating examples of Mother Nature's wackier side, but if you go out of your way just a little, you can find some funky fauna that aren't as readily associated with the Golden State. **Ostriches,** gentle readers, **ostriches** populate the desert and inland central coast regions of California. They're not wild, though. Rather, they've been imported by ranchers who want to market the lucrative flesh and hides of these sizable avian creatures (ostrich boots are all the rage among the line-dancin' crowd). If you happen upon an ostrich farm, you'll have a rare chance to observe some strange yet fabulous nine-foot fowl, but you should know some ostrich etiquette beforehand. It's safe to get out of your car and approach the birds' enclosure from a distance (provided that the owners don't object), but don't get too close, **don't try to pet their dinky heads** (irresistible though they might be), and *don't* act like a weenie and taunt these gallant, long-necked beasts. They may look like they have their heads in the sand, but they've got really bad tempers, too, so unless you want to be attacked, be cool. One particularly large concentration of ostrich ranches is located on Refugio Rd., off Rte. 246 in Santa Ynez. Enjoy!

■■■ SANTA BARBARA

Santa Barbara is obviously an enclave of wealth and privilege, but in a significantly less aggressive way then other Southern Californian enclaves of wealth and privilege. True to its soap opera image, the evening streets are thronged with lithe, thin-limbed young beauties walking hand in hand with guys named Rick or Stone. Yet the center of town, State St., is filled with inexpensive cafés and thrift stores as well as glamorous boutiques. The only common preoccupation here seems to be with perfecting the relaxed lifestyle.

PRACTICAL INFORMATION

Tourist Office: Chamber of Commerce, 504 State St. (965-3023). Open Mon.-Fri. 9am-5pm. Maps, brochures, and pamphlets abound.

Trains: Amtrak, 209 State St. (963-1015; for schedule and fares, 800-872-7245), downtown. Be careful around the station after dark. Open daily 7am-11pm. Tickets sold until 9:30pm. To L.A. ($20) and San Francisco ($67; reserve in advance).

Buses: Greyhound, 34 W. Cabrillo St. (962-2477), at Chapala. To L.A. ($12) and San Francisco ($38). Open Sun-Thurs. 6am-midnight; Fri.-Sat. 6am-8pm.

Taxis: Yellow Cab Company, (965-5111). 24 hrs.

Car Rental: U-Save Auto Rental, 510 Anacapa St. (963-3499). $20 per day with 100 free mi., $119 per week with 700 free mi.; 15¢ per additional mi. Must be 21 with major credit card. Open Mon.-Fri. 8am-6pm, Sat.-Sun. 8am-2pm.

Bike Rental: Cycles-4-Rent, 101 State St. (966-3804). 1-speed beach cruiser $4 per hr., $17 per day. Open Mon.-Fri. 9am-8pm, Sat.-Sun. 8am-8pm.

Emergency: 911.

Post Office: 836 Anacapa St. (564-2266), 1 block east of State St. Open Mon.-Fri. 8am-5:30pm, Sat. 10am-5pm. **ZIP code:** 93102. **Area code:** 805.

Santa Barbara is 96 mi. northwest of L.A. and 27 mi. past Ventura on **U.S. 101.** The beach lies at the south end of the city, and **State St.,** the main drag, runs northwest from the waterfront. All streets are designated east and west from State St. The major east-west arteries are U.S. 101 and **Cabrillo Blvd.**

Pick up **bus** route maps and schedules from the visitors center or the transit center behind the Greyhound station on Chapala. (75¢, disabled and over 61 30¢, under 5 free; free transfers.) A 25¢ **downtown-waterfront shuttle** runs along State St.

ACCOMMODATIONS AND CAMPING

A 10-minute drive north or south on U.S. 101 rewards you with cheaper lodgings than those in Santa Barbara proper.

Banana Bungalow Santa Barbara, 210 E. Ortega St. (963-0154), just off State St. Filled with a young, friendly group of revelers. For $15, you get a bunk in a dorm-style room; $12 gets you a bunk in a large, loud central area.

Hotel State Street, 121 State St. (966-6586), just off the beach. European travelers comprise most of the clientele. Occupants share hallway bathrooms but have private bedrooms which are small yet spruce. Cable TV. Continental breakfast included. $45 for one double bed, $55 for two.

New Faulding Hotel, 15 E. Haley St. (963-9191), near downtown. Many semi-permanent residents. Guests must sign in and present I.D. Singles $25-38.50.

The free *Santa Barbara Campsite Directory* lists prices, directions to sites, and reservation numbers for all campsites in the area, and is available at the visitors center. State campsites can be reserved through MISTIX (800-444-7275). **Carpinteria Beach State Park** (684-2811), 12 mi. southeast of Santa Barbara along U.S. 101, has 262 developed tent sites with hot showers (sites $16, $20-25 with hookups). There are three state beaches within 30 mi. of Santa Barbara, **El Capitan** (968-3294), **Gaviota** (968-3294), and **Refugio** (968-1350).

FOOD

Restaurants cluster on State, Milpas, and Cañon Perdido St.; State St. is more pricey.

Flavor of India, 3026 State St. (682-6561). Clean, friendly joint with astoundingly good tandoor and vegetarian dishes. All-you-can-eat lunch buffet ($6), Mon.-Sat. 11:30am-3pm. Open Sun.-Thurs. 5:30-10pm, Fri.-Sat. 5:30-10:30pm.

Esau's Coffee Shop, 403 State St. (965-4416). Fab blueberry wheat-germ pancakes ($5.75 for a stack of 6). Early birds (Mon.-Fri. 6-8am) get 2 pancakes, 2 eggs, and 2 strips of bacon for a mere $3.25. Open Mon.-Fri. 6am-1pm, Sat.-Sun. 7am-1:30pm.

La Super-rica Taquería, 622 N. Milpas (963-4940). The marinated pork tacos have been the deathbed request of many a Santa Barbarian. Dishes $1.30-5.10. Open Sun.-Thurs. 11am-9:30pm, Fri.-Sat. 11am-10pm.

R.G.'s Giant Hamburgers, 922 State St. (963-1654). Voted best burgers in S.B. 6 years running. Basic burger $3.11. Open Mon.-Sat. 7am-10pm, Sun. 7am-9pm.

SIGHTS

To get the full impact of the city's ubiquitous red tile motif, climb to the **observation deck** of the **Santa Barbara County Courthouse** at 1100 Anacapa St. (962-6464). The courthouse is one of the West's great public buildings (open Mon.-Fri. 8am-5pm, Sat.-Sun. 9am-5pm; tower closes at 4:45pm; free). Pick up *Santa Barbara's Red Tile Tour,* a map and walking tour guide, at the Chamber of Commerce.

The **Public Library** and the **Santa Barbara Museum of Art** also blend different styles of architecture into an tasteful ensemble. The library, 40E Anapamu St. (962-7653), and the museum, 1130 State St. (963-4364), are linked by a pedestrian plaza. Built as a post office in 1914, the art museum owns an outstanding collection of classical Greek, Roman, Asian, and European art, but prides itself on its American art and the portraits in the Preston Morton Gallery. (Open Tues.-Wed. and Fri.-Sat. 11am-5pm, Thurs. 11am-9pm, Sun. noon-5pm. Tours Tues.-Sun. 1pm. $4, seniors $3, ages 6-16 $1.50; free on Thurs.) The **Arlington Center for Performing Arts,** 1317 State St. (963-4408), is one of that rarest of movie theater species—a uniplex.

At the center of Montecito and Chapala Streets stands the famed **Moreton Bay Fig Tree.** Brought from Australia by a sailor in 1877, the tree's gnarled branches now span 160 ft., and can provide shade for upwards of 1,000 mostly transient people.

The beach west of State St. is called **West Beach;** to the east, **East Beach.** The latter is preferable because **Chase Palm Park** acts as a buffer between it and Cabrillo Blvd. The park threads nearly 2 mi. of bike and foot paths through green lawns and tall palms. **East Beach,** with volleyball and biking trails, is universally popular. The beach at **Summerland,** east of Montecito (bus #20), is frequented by the **gay** and **hippie** communities. **Rincon Beach,** 3 mi. southeast of Carpinteria, has the best surfing in the county. **Gaviota State Beach,** 29 mi. west of Santa Barbara, offers good surf, and the western end is a (sometimes) **clothing-optional** beach. Keep in mind, however, that **nude** sunbathing is illegal in Santa Barbara. You can **whale-watch** from late November to early April, as the grays migrate.

ENTERTAINMENT AND NIGHTLIFE

Even on Monday nights the clubs on State St. are packed. Be on the alert for happy hours, which often last from 5-8pm or 10-11pm and feature 50¢ drafts or 2-for-1 drink specials. Consult the *Independent* for the skinny on the S.B. scene.

Green Dragon Art Studio and Espresso Bar, 22 W. Mission (687-1902). Artsy joint inside an old church with open-mike fun on occasion. Open Sun.-Wed. 7am-11pm, Thurs. 7am-midnight, Fri.-Sat. 7-1am.

Joseppi's, 434 State St. (962-5516). Jazz and blues in a tiny club which sometimes overflows into the street. Cover $2-3. Open whenever owner Joe feels like it.

Alex's Cantina, 633 State St. (966-0032), downtown. The Happiest Hour in town, 3:30-8pm daily, with drink specials. Dancing nightly 9pm-2am. Live bands 6 nights per week, alternative music Sat. Cover varies, usually less than $5.

Calypso, 514 State St. (966-1388). Tropical theme. Crowded with local frat-types. Live performances every night: blues, jazz, rock, reggae. 2-for-1 drink specials from 10-11pm. No cover. Open daily 11am-2am.

The Gold Coast, 30 W. Cotu St. (965-6701). Polished and popular bar attracts a boisterous gay crowd. All-U-can-drink drafts Sun. 5-9pm $5. Open daily 4pm-2am.

■■■ BIG SUR

Upon beholding the startling scope of the Big Sur panorama, one might wish to say, "Golly, that *is* big, sir." Everyone will laugh. Your traveling companion may wish to interject, "It's big, sure." Everyone will laugh again. Frenchy friends may add, "Bien sûr!" They will be not nearly as funny. God will then smite you for your insolence. The locals will laugh their asses off and enjoy their little bit o' paradise alone.

Practical Information "Big Sur" signifies a coastal region bordered on the south by San Simeon and on the north by Carmel. For **Visitors Information,** go to the **Big Sur Station,** 667-2315, on Rte. 1, inside **Big Sur State Park,** a multi-agency that includes the **State Park Office,** the **U.S. Forest Service Office,** and the **CalTrans Office.** The station can provide information on all area State Parks, U.S. Forest Service campgrounds, and local transit (open daily 8am-6pm). Big Sur's **Post Office:** (667-2305), Rte. 1, next to the Center Deli in Big Sur Center; **ZIP code:** 93920; **area code:** 408.

Accommodations Camping in Big Sur is heavenly. The cheapest way to stay in Big Sur is to camp for free in the **Ventana Wilderness** (pick up a permit at Big Sur Station). Ventana, at the northern end of Los Padres National Forest, is a backpack-only area—no automobiles. **Big Sur Campgrounds and Cabins** (667-2322), 26 mi. south of Carmel, has campsites ($22, with hookup $25) and tent cabins in summer ($40), as well as a store, laundry, playground, volleyball courts, and hot showers. **Los Padres National Forest** hosts two U.S. Forest Service Campgrounds. **Plaskett Creek** (667-2315), south of Limekiln, has 43 sites. **Kirk Creek,** about 5 mi. north of Jade Cove, has 33 beautiful spots, but they're close to the highway. Both sites $15. **Pfeiffer Big Sur State Park** (667-2315), just south of Fernwood, is an inland park, but no less popular than those on the beach. The Big Sur River flows peacefully alongside the campground (hot showers; sites $16).

Food Grocery stores are located at River Inn, Ripplewood, Fernwood, Big Sur Lodge, Pacific Valley Center, and Gorda, but it's better to arrive prepared; prices are high. **Center Deli** (667-2225), beside the Big Sur Post Office, offers the most reasonably priced goods in the area (sandwiches $4) and a broad selection of groceries (open daily 8am-9pm; winter 8am-8pm). **Fernwood Burger Bar** (667-2422), Rte. 1, 2 mi. north of post office, has juicy burgers from $4 (open daily 11:30am-10pm).

Sights and Activities The **state parks** and **wilderness areas** are exquisite settings for dozens of outdoor activities. **Hiking** on Big Sur is fantastic: the state parks and **Los Padres National Forest** all have trails that penetrate redwood forests and cross low chaparral, offering even grander views of Big Sur than those available from Rte. 1. Within **Pfeiffer Big Sur State Park** are eight trails of varying lengths (50¢ map available at park entrance). Try the **Valley View Trail,** a short, steep path overlooking the valley below. **Buzzard's Roost Trail** is a rugged two-hour hike up tortuous switchbacks; if you can make it to the top, you'll be treated to a panorama of the Santa Lucia Mountains, the Big Sur Valley, and the Pacific Ocean.

Roughly at the midway point of Big Sur lies quiet **Julia Pfeiffer Burns Park** (day use only, $6), which features picnic tables among the redwoods and a chance to otter-watch in McWay Cove. Big Sur's most jealously guarded treasure is USFS-operated **Pfeiffer Beach,** 1 mi. south of Pfeiffer State Park. Turn off Rte. 1 at the "Narrow Road not suitable for trailers" sign. Follow the road 2 mi. to the parking area; take the footpath to the beach. The small cove, partially protected from the Pacific by an offshore rock formation, is replete with sea caves and sea gulls.

■ NEAR BIG SUR: HEARST CASTLE

Hearst San Simeon Historic Monument (927-2010), located off of Rte. 1, about 5 mi. east of Cambria, draws untold numbers of gawkers every year. It is an often graceful, always imposing building which sits atop a hill high above the Pacific, a testament to the wealth and ostentation of William Randolph Hearst. The park is run by the state parks department, and the only way to view the Castle is on a guided tour led by a docent. **Tour One** covers the gardens, pools, and main rooms of the house—it is the tour recommended for first-time visitors. Other tours cover smaller areas in more detail.

The building and grounds, the creation of Julia Morgan, are magnificent. Tours keep one moving along rather quickly, but the surroundings—natural and constructed—have a rarefied quality which only Hearst's millions and Morgan's gifts could bring to life. The four daytime tours cost $14 each (ages 6-12 $8), and last about 1¾ hours. Call MISTIX at 800-444-4445 for wheelchair accessible tours which must be reserved ten days in advance.

■■■ MONTEREY

In the 1940s, Monterey was a coastal town geared toward sardine fishing and canning. But the sardines disappeared in the early 50s, and when John Steinbeck revisited his beloved Cannery Row around 1960, he wrote scornfully of how the district had become a tourist trap. Today, few traces of the Monterey described in *Cannery Row* remain; along the famous Row and Fisherman's Wharf, packing plants have been converted to multiplex souvenir malls, and the old bars where sailors used to drink and fight now feature sad wax recreations.

Practical Information Motorists can approach Monterey from **U.S. 101** (Munras Ave. exit), or **Rte. 1,** the coastal highway. **Visitors Information** is available at the **visitors center,** 401 Camino El Estero (open Mon.-Sat. 9am-6pm, Sun. 9am-5pm, winter Mon.-Fri. 9am-5pm, Sat.-Sun. 9am-4pm). **Monterey-Salinas Transit (MST),** One Ryan Ranch Rd. (899-2555 or 424-7695, TTY available), serves the region. Fare per zone $1.25; ages 5-18, over 64, and people with disabilities 50¢

(each zone encompasses 1 or 2 towns, 4 zones total); exact change; transfers free. The free *Rider's Guide* to Monterey-Salinas Transit (MST) service contains complete schedules and route information. **Post Office:** 565 Hartnell (372-5803). Open Mon.-Fri. 8:45am-5:10pm; **ZIP code:** 93940; **area code:** 408.

Accommodations Reasonably priced hotels are found in the 2000 block of Fremont St. in Monterey and Lighthouse Ave. in Pacific Grove. The tidy **Paramount Motel,** 3298 Del Monte Blvd. (384-8674), in Marina, has singles for $25, doubles for $30. **Del Monte Beach Inn,** 1110 Del Monte Blvd. (649-4410), is close to downtown, across the street from the beach. This Victorian-style inn offers pleasant rooms (shared bath) and a hearty breakfast for $40-60. To get to **Veterans Memorial Park Campground** (646-3865), Via Del Rey, take Skyline Dr. off Rte. 68; or, from downtown, take Pacific St. south, turn right on Jefferson. It's perched on a hill with a view of the bay. 40 sites have hot showers (sites $15, hikers $3).

Food Although seafood is bountiful, it is often expensive—try chowing an early bird special (4-6:30pm or so). Head to **Fisherman's Wharf,** where the smoked salmon sandwiches ($5.50) are a local delicacy. **Casa de Gutiérrez,** 590 Calle Principal (375-0095), offers huge portions of traditional fare. A taco (big as 2) costs $2.75 (open Mon.-Thurs. 11am-9pm, Fri.-Sun. 10am-10pm). **London Bridge Pub,** Wharf II (625-2879), overlooks the Marina. Outstanding pub grub includes delicious fish and chips ($8) and an English breakfast of bacon, sausage, eggs, grilled tomato, and fried bread ($6). It's open Fri.-Sat. 11:30-2am, Sun.-Thurs. 11:30-1am, but food is served 'til 11pm. **Tillie Gort's,** 111 Central Ave. (373-0335), in nearby Pacific Grove, stocks vegetarian fare only, but the mushroom garden burger with jack cheese will satisfy even meativores (open Mon.-Fri. 11:30am-10:30pm, Sat.-Sun. 8am-10:30pm).

Sights The best reason to visit Monterey is the magnificent **Monterey Bay Aquarium,** 886 Cannery Row (648-4800). The facility allows visitors a window into the most curious and fascinating marine life of the Pacific, with interactive displays that provide opportunities to learn about, see, and even touch real sea-life. Highlights include the slithering frenzy of sea otters at feeding time, a living kelp forest housed in a two-story-tall glass case, and a titillating petting zoo of deep-sea denizens (ever think you'd pet a stingray?). Gaze through the **world's largest window** at an enormous marine habitat containing green sea turtles, 7-foot ocean sunfish, large sharks, and the oozingly graceful Portuguese Man-o'-War. ($11.75, over 65 $9.75, ages 3-12 $5.75, ages 13-18 $9.75. Open daily 10am-6pm.)

Cannery Row lies along the waterfront south of the aquarium. Once a depressed street of languishing sardine packing plants, this ¾-mi. row has been converted into glitzy mini-malls, bars, and discos. All that remains of the earthiness and gruff camaraderie celebrated by John Steinbeck in *Cannery Row* and *Sweet Thursday* are a few building façades: 835 Cannery Row once was the Wing Chong Market, the bright yellow building next door is where *Sweet Thursday* took place, and Doc Rickett's lab at 800 Cannery Row is now owned by a private men's club. For a stylized look at Steinbeck's Cannery Row, take a peek at the **Great Cannery Row Mural,** which stretches 400 ft. along the "700" blocks of Cannery Row. Fifty panels by local artists depict Monterey in the 30s.

Most of the town's historic buildings downtown now belong to the **Monterey State Historic Park.** If you plan to visit more than one of the houses that charge admission, you'll want to purchase a $5 pass that allows you to enter all historic park buildings and participate in any or all of the walking tours. Buy your ticket at the **visitors center** (649-7118) inside the Park Headquarters in the Customs House Plaza (open daily 10am-5pm, in winter 10am-4pm). The center sells the *Path of History* walking tour book ($2), and offers the Monterey Historic Park **House and Garden Tour** for history fans (daily 10:30am, 12:30, and 2:30pm).

You can find the **Monterey Peninsula Museum of Art,** 559 Pacific St. (372-5477), in the same neighborhood as the historic adobes. A new wing in La Mirada, 720 Via La Mirada (372-3689), houses exhibits on California history and regional art, Asian art, and art of the Pacific Rim. The Ralph K. Davies Collection of Western Art includes many of Charlie Russell's well-known bronze sculptures of bronco-busters (open Tues.-Sat. 10am-4pm, Sun. 1-4pm; $2).

17-Mile Drive meanders along the coast from Pacific Grove through **Pebble Beach** and the forests around Carmel. The Drive is rolling, looping, and often spectacular, though sometimes plagued by heavy tourist traffic and an outrageous $6.50 entrance fee. Save your money and bike it; bicyclists and pedestrians are allowed in at no cost. One point of interest along the drive is the **Lone Cypress**—an old, gnarled tree growing on a rock promontory; when viewed in the forgiving dimness of twilight, the tree is a silent testimony to perseverance and solitary strength.

■ NEAR MONTEREY: PINNACLES

If the banal farmland of the Salinas Valley is the "leafy and delicious salad bowl of the nation," the **Pinnacles National Monument** is the Bac-Os. The usual **Visitors Information** is at the **King City Chamber of Commerce and Agriculture,** 203 Broadway, King City, CA 93930 (385-3814). **Area code:** 408.

Towering dramatically over the chaparral east of Soledad, **Pinnacles National Monument** contains the spectacular remnants of an ancient volcano. The **High Peaks Trail** runs a strenuous 5.3 mi. across the park, and offers amazing views of the surrounding rock formations. For a less exhausting trek, try the **Balconies Trail,** a 1½-mi. promenade from the park's west entrance up to the Balconies Caves. Wildflowers bloom in the spring and Pinnacles offers excellent bird-watching all year long. Pinnacles also has the widest range of wildlife of any park in California, including a number of rare predators: mountain lions, bobcats, coyotes, golden eagles, and peregrine falcons ($4; parking free). The monument has a **campground** with fire-pits, restrooms, and picnic tables (sites $10). The park headquarters is located at the east side entrance (Rte. 25 to Rte. 146; 389-4485).

■■■ SANTA CRUZ

The city was born as one of foxy Father Junípero Serra's missions in 1791 (the name means "holy cross"), but today, Santa Cruz is nothing if not liberal. One of the few places where the old 60s catch-phrase "do your own thing" still applies, it simultaneously embraces macho surfers and a large lesbian community.

PRACTICAL INFORMATION

Tourist Office: Santa Cruz County Conference and Visitors Council, 701 Front St. (425-1234 or 800-833-3494). Publishes free *Visitors Guide, Dining Guide,* and *Accommodations Guide.* Open Mon.-Sat. 9am-5pm, Sun. 10am-4pm.

Buses: Greyhound/Peerless Stages: 425 Front St. (423-1800 or 800-231-2222). To San Francisco (2 per day, $14), and L.A. via Salinas (4 per day, $49). Luggage lockers. Open Mon.-Fri. 7am-noon, 1-6:45pm, Sat.-Sun. 7-11am, 1-6:15pm.

Public Transportation: Santa Cruz Metropolitan District Transit (SCMDT), 920 Pacific Ave. (425-8600 or 688-8600), in the middle of the Pacific Garden Mall. Pick up a free copy of *Headways* for route information. Bus fare is $1. Open Mon.-Fri. 8am-5pm.

Taxis: Yellow Cab, 423-1234. $1.75 plus $1.75 per mi. 24 hrs.

Bicycle Rental: The Bicycle Rental Center, 415 Pacific Ave. (426-8687), at Front St. First 2 hours $10, each additional hour $4. Helmets and locks provided. Summer open daily 10am-6pm. Winter open daily 10am-5pm.

Post Office: 850 Front St. (426-5200). **ZIP code:** 95060. **Area code:** 408.

Santa Cruz is about one hour south of San Francisco on the north lip of Monterey Bay. For a more scenic trip, take **U.S. 101** or **Rte. 1** from San Francisco. The Santa Cruz beach and its boardwalk run east-west, with Monterey Bay to the south.

ACCOMMODATIONS AND CAMPING

Like many a beach town, Santa Cruz gets crowded during the summer and on weekends and doubly crowded on summer weekends, when room rates skyrocket and availability plummets. Fortunately, a number of hotels, especially on San Lorenzo, East Cliff, Murry Dr. and on 2nd and 3rd St., hold an unreserved room or two.

Carmelita Cottage Santa Cruz Hostel (HI-AYH), 321 Main St. (423-8304), 4 blocks from Greyhound and 2 blocks from the beach. A 32-bed Victorian hostel with friendly staff. Kitchen, common room, cyclery; parking available. 11pm curfew. 3-day max. stay during summer. $12-14 per night. Reservations only via mail; write P.O. Box 1241, Santa Cruz 95061. Office open daily 8-10am and 5-10pm.

Salt Air, 510 Leibrant (423-6020). 2 blocks from the beach, the boardwalk, and the wharf. Swimming pool. Singles and doubles $39-50.

Harbor Inn, 645 7th Ave. (479-9731), near the harbor and a few blocks north of Eaton St. A small and beautiful hotel well off the main drag. 1 queen bed per room (1 or 2 people). Check-out 11am. Rooms $30, with bath $45. Weekends $45, with bath $70. In the winter, free breakfast is offered.

Santa Cruz Inn, 2950 Soquel Ave. (475-6322), located just off Rte. 1. Coffee and pastries for guests. Check-out 11am. Singles from $35, doubles from $45. $10 per additional person. Some rooms include private jacuzzis, A/C, and fireplaces.

Reservations for all state campgrounds can be made through MISTIX (800-444-7275). To get to **Manresa Uplands State Beach Park** (761-1795), take Rte. 1 and exit Larkin Valley; veer right and follow San Andreas Rd. for 4 mi. then turn right on Sand Dollar. The pretty area overlooks the ocean. There are 64 campsites for tents only ($16). **New Brighton State Beach** (475-4850 or 444-7275), is 4 mi. south of Santa Cruz off Rte. 1. Fall asleep to the murmur of the breakers in one of 112 campsites on a bluff overlooking the beach. Tall pines and shrubs maintain privacy. Showers get crowded from 7-9am (1-week max. stay; $16, winter $14).

FOOD

Santa Cruz offers the traveler an astounding number of restaurants in budget range. Fine local produce sells at the **Farmers Market,** at Pacific and Cathcart Ave. (open May-Sept. Wed. 3-7pm, Oct.-April Wed. 2-6pm).

Zachary's, 819 Pacific Ave. (427-0646). Bustling and happy breakfast joint. In the morning, locals crowd in for Mike's Mess: 3 scrambled eggs with bacon, mushrooms, and home fries topped with cheese, sour cream, tomatoes, and green onions served on toast ($5.50). Open Tues.-Sun. 7am-2:30pm.

The Jahva House, 120 Union St. (459-9876). Lush indoor and outdoor vegetation, live jazz, and high quality make this a standout among Santa Cruz's cafés. Cappuccino $1.80, or fresh apple pie $3. Open Mon.-Sat. 6am-midnight, Sun. 8am-8pm.

Cassanova Café, 922 Pacific Ave. (426-CAFE/2233). Self-described "gay-owned, hetero-friendly" joint offers live music and occasional poetry readings, pool ($1), as well as traditional café fare. Live music nightly. Espresso $1.90, beer $2.25-$2.75. Open Sun.-Mon. and Wed.-Thurs. noon-1am, Fri.-Sat. noon-3am.

Saturn Café, 1230 Mission St. (429-8505). A few blocks from downtown, but you'll be rewarded with vegetarian meals at their Santa Cruz best (generally under $4). Wheat germ is right-wing at this busy mixed hangout. Angry women's music Wed. 6:30-8:30pm. Open Mon.-Fri. 11:30am-midnight, Sat.-Sun. noon-midnight.

SIGHTS AND ACTIVITIES

The **Boardwalk,** is the most awesomely loud, fun, tacky thing on the Pacific this side of L.A. The three-block-long strip of over 25 amusement park rides, guess-your-weight booths, shooting galleries, and hot dog and caramel apple vendors provides a free diversion from the beach. Highly recommended is the Big Dipper, a 1924 wooden tower roller coaster ($3).

The **Santa Cruz Beach** (officially named Cowell Beach) itself is broad and sandy, and generally packed with students. If you're seeking solitude, try the banks of the San Lorenzo River immediately east of the boardwalk. If you've got a hankerin' to **get nekkid,** head for the **Red White and Blue Beach.** Take Rte. 1 north to just south of Davenport and look for the line of cars to your right ($7 per car).

The **Shroud of Turin Museum,** 1902 Ocean St. Extension (426-1601), is at St. Joseph's shrine. This famous piece of Jesus' burial shawl may just be a sham, but at least it's a religious sham (open Mon.-Fri. 1-4pm; donation requested). Just south of this museum lies the **Santa Cruz Surfing Museum** (429-3429). The main room of the lighthouse displays vintage wooden boards, early wetsuits, and surfing videos, while the tower contains the ashes of Mark Abbott, a local surfer who drowned in 1965 and to whom the museum is dedicated (open Wed.-Mon. noon-4pm, winter Thurs.-Mon. noon-4pm; $1).

The 2000-acre **University of California at Santa Cruz (UCSC)** campus lies 5 mi. northwest of downtown. The campus is accessible by public bus, auto, and bicycle. (From the Metro Center, bus #1 leaves every 15 to 30 minutes on Mon.-Fri. 6:30am-12:45am, Sat.-Sun. 7:30am-12:45am.) Then-governor Ronald Reagan's plan to make UCSC a "riot-proof campus" (i.e., without a central point where radicals could inflame a crowd), when it was built in the late 60s, resulted instead in a stunning, sprawling campus. Santa Cruz is famous for leftist politics supplemented by a curriculum offering such unique programs as "The History of Consciousness."

CALIFORNIA

ENTERTAINMENT AND NIGHTLIFE

Carding at local bars is stringent. The Boardwalk bandstand offers free Friday night concerts. *Good Times* and UCSC's *City on a Hill* are informative free weeklies.

Kuumbwa Jazz Center, 320-2 Cedar St. (427-2227). Great jazz, renowned throughout the region. Under 21derlings are welcome in this small and low-key setting. The big names play here on Mon. ($12-17); Fri. is the locals' turn (about $5). Rarely sold out. Most shows around 8pm.

Palookaville, 1133 Pacific Ave. (454-0600). The newest club in Santa Cruz, live music in an all-ages environment. Excellent wine and beer. Wide variety of shows and popular happy hour Fri. 4-7pm for $1.50 pints. Cover ranges from $0-20.

The Catalyst, 1011 Pacific Ave. (423-1336). This concert hall draws national acts, college favorites, and local bands. Boisterous, beachy bar and dance club with pool, grill, deli, and bar. Sandwiches ($2-5). Cover for local bands $1 until 9pm. Must be 21. Shows at 9:30pm. Open daily 9am-2am.

Blue Lagoon, 923 Pacific Ave. (423-7117). Relaxed gay bar. Giant aquarium contributes pleasantly flickering light. Sun.-Wed. videos, dancing; no cover. Thurs.-Sat. DJ; $1 cover. Drinks about $1.50. Open daily 4pm-2am.

SAN FRANCISCO BAY AREA

San Francisco—a city that evokes images of gold, cable cars, LSD, or gay liberation—began its life in 1776 as the Spanish mission of *San Francisco de Asis* (St. Francis of Assisi). The area remained sparsely populated until 1848, when gold was discovered in the Sierra Nevada's foothills. San Francisco's 800 or so residents realized that in addition to living a short river trip from the gold fields, they were also sitting on one of the greatest natural ports in the world. That year 10,000 people passed through San Francisco to get to the gold and a city was born.

The city's growth was neither smooth nor stable. Most famously, a massive 8.3 earthquake rocked the city on April 18, 1906, setting off three days of fire and looting. Unfazed, residents rebuilt their city within three years. The 1936 and '37 openings of the Golden Gate and Bay Bridges ended the city's isolation from the rest of the Bay Area. The city served as home to the Beat Generation in the 1950s; the 60s saw Haight-Ashbury become the hippie capital of the cosmos; and in the 70s, the gay population emerged as one of the city's most visible groups. To understand San Francisco one must get to know its neighborhoods, which pack an amazing level of diversity into a small area. Today, San Francisco continues to rest on mutual tolerance and appreciation of the different people who call this city home.

■■■ SAN FRANCISCO

PRACTICAL INFORMATION

Tourist Office: Visitor Information Center, Hallidie Plaza (391-2000), Market St. at Powell, beneath street level in Benjamin Swig Pavillion at the exit of the Powell St. BART stop. Italian, English, French, German, Japanese, and Spanish spoken. Open Mon.-Fri. 9am-5:30pm, Sat. 9am-3pm, Sun. 10am-2pm.

Airport: San Francisco International Airport (SFO; 761-0800) is located on a small peninsula in San Francisco Bay about 15 mi. south of the city center via U.S. 101. SFO has luggage lockers ($1 first day, $2 per additional day). **San Mateo County Transit (samTrans;** 800-660-4287) runs two buses from SFO to downtown. (Bus #7F; 35min.; runs 4am-1am, 9am-4pm less frequently; $2, under 18 85¢, over 64 60¢. Bus #7B; 55min.; same frequency; 85¢, under 18 35¢, over 64 25¢.) **Trains: Amtrak** (800-872-7245), 1707 Wood St., in Oakland (open daily 6:45am-10:45pm; to L.A. $75). They have a desk in the Transbay Terminal. **CalTrain** (800-660-4287) runs south to Palo Alto, San Jose, and Santa Cruz. The 4th St. and Townsend depot is served by **MUNI buses** #15, 30, 32, and 42.

Buses: Greyhound (800-231-2222) serves the **Transbay Terminal,** 425 Mission St. (495-1575), between Fremont and 1st downtown (open 5am-12:35am; to L.A. $39). The terminal is a regional transportation hub; buses from **Golden Gate Transit** (Marin County), **AC Transit** (East Bay), and **samTrans** (San Mateo County) all stop here. **Green Tortoise** (800-TORTISE/867-8647; in San Francisco 956-7500) offers overnight service complete with meals, beds, and a mellow attitude to destinations along the coast including L.A. ($30) and Seattle ($49).

Taxis: Yellow Cab, 626-2345. **Luxor Cabs,** 282-4141. For both, $1.70 plus $1.80 per additional mi. Rides to downtown from SFO cost about $25. Open 24 hrs.

Car Rental: Budget (415-875-6850) has several conveniently located branches, including Pier 39 and 321 Mason St. in Union Sq. Compacts are about $25 per day, $150 per week. Unlimited miles.

Ride Boards: Berkeley Ride Board (510-642-5259). **San Francisco State University** (469-1842, in the SFSU student union; open Mon.-Fri. 7am-10pm, Sat. 10am-4pm). **KALX Radio** (642-5259) broadcasts a ride list (Mon.-Sat. 10am and 10pm). Call them to put your name and number on the air for free.

Crisis Lines: Rape Crisis Center, 647-7273. **United Helpline,** 772-4357.

Emergency: 911

Post Office: 101 Hyde St., at Golden Gate Ave. Open Mon.-Fri. 7am-5:30pm, Sat. 7am-3pm. **ZIP code:** 94142. General Delivery open Mon.-Sat. 10am-2pm. **Area code:** 415.

ORIENTATION

San Francisco is 403 mi. north of Los Angeles and 390 mi. south of the Oregon border. The city proper lies at the north tip of the peninsula that separates San Francisco Bay from the Pacific Ocean. From the south, the city can be reached by car via **U.S. 101,** via **I-5** to **I-580,** or via **Rte. 1.** If approaching from the east on I-580 or I-80, go directly over the Bay Bridge into downtown. From the north, U.S. 101 leads directly into the city over the Golden Gate Bridge (toll $3).

San Francisco radiates outward from its docks (on the northeast edge of the peninsula just inside the lip of the bay). Most visitors' attention still gravitates to this area. Many of San Francisco's shining attractions are found within a wedge formed by **Van Ness Ave.** (running north-south), **Market St.** (running northeast-south-

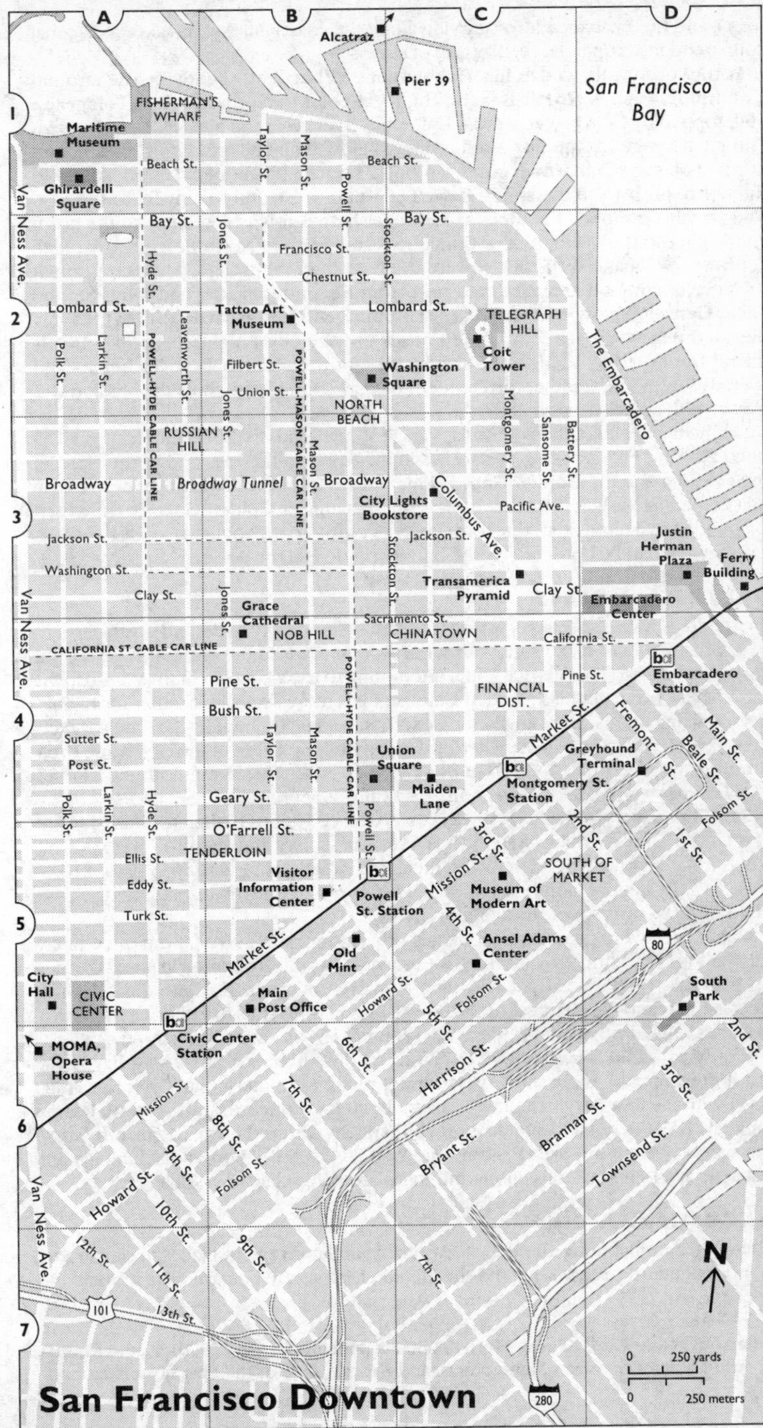
San Francisco Downtown
San Francisco Bay
Alcatraz
Pier 39
FISHERMAN'S WHARF
Maritime Museum
Ghirardelli Square
Beach St.
Bay St.
Francisco St.
Chestnut St.
Lombard St.
Tattoo Art Museum
TELEGRAPH HILL
Coit Tower
Washington Square
NORTH BEACH
RUSSIAN HILL
Broadway
Broadway Tunnel
City Lights Bookstore
Columbus Ave.
Pacific Ave.
Jackson St.
Washington St.
Clay St.
Transamerica Pyramid
Justin Herman Plaza
Ferry Building
Embarcadero Center
Grace Cathedral
NOB HILL
CHINATOWN
Sacramento St.
California St.
CALIFORNIA ST CABLE CAR LINE
POWELL-HYDE CABLE CAR LINE
POWELL-MASON CABLE CAR LINE
Pine St.
Bush St.
FINANCIAL DIST.
Embarcadero Station
Sutter St.
Post St.
Union Square
Maiden Lane
Montgomery St. Station
Greyhound Terminal
Geary St.
O'Farrell St.
Ellis St.
Eddy St.
Turk St.
TENDERLOIN
Visitor Information Center
Powell St. Station
Museum of Modern Art
SOUTH OF MARKET
Old Mint
Ansel Adams Center
City Hall
CIVIC CENTER
Main Post Office
Civic Center Station
MOMA, Opera House
South Park
Market St.
Mission St.
Howard St.
Folsom St.
Harrison St.
Bryant St.
Brannan St.
Townsend St.
The Embarcadero
Van Ness Ave.
Polk St.
Larkin St.
Hyde St.
Leavenworth St.
Jones St.
Taylor St.
Mason St.
Powell St.
Stockton St.
Montgomery St.
Sansome St.
Battery St.
Fremont St.
Beale St.
Main St.
1st St.
2nd St.
3rd St.
4th St.
5th St.
6th St.
7th St.
8th St.
9th St.
10th St.
11th St.
12th St.
13th St.
80
101
280
0 250 yards
0 250 meters
N
A B C D
1 2 3 4 5 6 7

CALIFORNIA

west), and the **Embarcadero** (curving along the coast). Market St. takes a diagonal course and interrupts the regular grid of streets.

At the top of this wedge lies **Fisherman's Wharf** and slightly below, around **Columbus Ave.,** is **North Beach.** The focal point of North Beach is **Telegraph Hill,** topped by Coit Tower. Across Columbus Ave. begin the **Nob Hill** and **Russian Hill** areas, home to the city's old money. Below Nob Hill and North Beach, and north of Market, **Chinatown** covers around 24 square blocks between Broadway to the north, Bush St. to the south, Powell St. to the west, and Kearny St. to the east. The heavily developed **Financial District** lies between Washington St. to the north and Market to the south, east of Chinatown and south of North Beach. Down Market from the Financial District, toward the bottom of the wedge, you pass through the core downtown area centered on **Union Sq.** and then, beyond Jones St., the **Civic Center.** Below Market St. lies the **South-of-Market Area (SoMa),** largely deserted during the day but home to much of the city's nightlife. SoMa extends inland from the bay to 10th St., at which point the **Mission District** begins and spreads south. The **Castro,** the center of the gay community, abuts the Mission District at 17th and also extends south.

On the north end of the peninsula, Van Ness Ave. leads to the commercially developed **Marina. Fisherman's Wharf** lies immediately to the east, and to the west lie the **Presidio** and the **Golden Gate Bridge**. Inland from the Marina rise the wealthy hills of **Pacific Heights.** Farther west is the rectangular **Golden Gate Park,** which is bounded by Fulton St. to the north and Lincoln St. to the south. At its east end juts a skinny panhandle bordered by the hippie-trippie **Haight-Ashbury** district.

GETTING AROUND

A **car** here is not the necessity it is in L.A. Parking in the city **sucks** and is very expensive. On steep hills, make sure your wheels point towards the curb. *Always* set the emergency brake. Think twice about attempting to use a **bike** to climb up and down San Francisco's many hills. Golden Gate Park is a more sensible location for biking. Even **walking** in this city is an exciting exertion—some of the sidewalks are so steep they have steps cut into them. There are many **walking tours** of the city; some even promise "no steep hills." **City Guides** (332-9601) has free summer tours. The $2 *San Francisco Street and Transit Map* is a valuable purchase.

San Francisco Municipal Railway, or **MUNI** (673-6864), operates buses, cable cars, and a subway/trolley system (bus fares $1, seniors and ages 5-17 35¢). MUNI passports valid on all MUNI vehicles, including cable cars (1 day, $6; 3 days, $10; 7 days, $15; 1 calendar month, $35). **MUNI buses** run frequently throughout the city. **MUNI Metro** runs streetcars along five lines.

Cable cars were named a national historic landmark in 1964. Of the three lines, the California (C) line is by far the least crowded; it runs from the Financial District up Nob Hill. The Powell-Hyde (PH) line, however, might be the best, for it has the steepest hills and the sharpest turns. Powell-Mason (PM) runs to Fisherman's Wharf. (All lines run daily 6:30am-12:30am. $2, seniors $1; 3-hr. unlimited transfers.)

Bay Area Rapid Transit (BART; 778-2288) does not serve the *entire* Bay Area, but it does operate modern, carpeted trains along four lines connecting San Francisco with the East Bay; including Oakland, Berkeley, Concord, and Fremont. Unfortunately, BART is not a local transportation system within the city (trains run Mon.-Sat. 6am-1:30am, Sun. 8am-1:30am; one way 80¢ to $3). Maps and schedules are available at all stations. All stations and trains are wheelchair accessible.

ACCOMMODATIONS

There are a tremendous number of reasonable and convenient places to stay in San Francisco, but the Tenderloin and the Mission District can be particularly unsafe.

Hostels

Pacific Tradewinds Guest House, 680 Sacramento St. (433-7970), in the **Financial District** between Montgomery and Kearny. One of the best hostels around.

No TV. Laundry ($4, they do it), kitchen, free tea and coffee. No smoking. Check-in 8am-midnight. Check-out 10:30am. No curfew. 14-day max. stay. $14 per night.

San Francisco International Hostel (HI-AYH), Bldg. 240, Fort Mason (771-7277), in the **Marina** west of Fisherman's Wharf. Beautiful location. Lockers supplied, locks aren't. Movies, walking tours, kitchens, dining room, laundry. No smoking. Registration 7am-2pm and 3pm-midnight daily. Come early. Be sure to have valid photo ID. IBN reservations available. $13 per night, $14 in the summer.

Green Tortoise Guest House, 494 Broadway (834-1000), at Kearney, in the colorful and relatively safe border of **North Beach** and **Chinatown**. Clean, fully-furnished rooms in an beautiful old Victorian building. Friendly atmosphere. Lockers under each bed; bring your own lock. Sauna, laundry room (wash $1.25, dry 75¢), internet access, kitchen, and complementary continental breakfast. 28-day max. stay. $12-14 per bed in shared room. Singles $19.50, doubles $29-30.

Hostel at Union Square (HI-AYH), 312 Mason St. (788-5604), 1 block from Union Sq. Third largest hostel in the country. Caution in this neighborhood is advised. Management is very safety-conscious and works hard to foster a sense of community. TV room, kitchen, big common rooms. $14 per night, nonmembers $17. Key deposit $5. IBN reservations available.

Globetrotter's Inn, 225 Ellis St. (346-5786), at Mason, in **Downtown.** On the border of the Tenderloin; caution is advised. Comfortingly small and intimate. Large kitchen, common room, piano, and TV. Washer/dryer and linen provided. Check-in summer 8am-11pm; winter 8am-1pm and 5-11pm; check-out 11am. No curfew. $12 per night; $75 per week. Call to reserve and confirm 2 days ahead.

San Francisco International Student Center, 1188 Folsom St. (255-8800), in **SoMa.** Bay windows, brick walls, and a big comfy couch. Only 17 rooms. Great massage showerheads. Free coffee and tea. 28-day max. stay. Registration 9am-11pm. No curfew. $13 per night. Pre-paid reservations required.

San Francisco International Guest House, 2976 23rd St. (641-1411), at Harrison, in the **Mission District.** In a beautiful Victorian house. Huge private rooms for couples. Free sheets and coffee. Two large kitchens. 5-day min. stay. All beds $13 per night; $11 per night after 10 days. **International passport required.**

Interclub Globe Hostel, 10 Hallam Place (431-0540), in **SoMa.** Catering to an adventurous Euro-crowd, the lobby blares "world music." Pool table, some fairly wild parties, and the Globe Café, which serves breakfast and dinner. Free sheets, blankets and pillows. $15 per night. A $10 deposit is required for a reservation. **International passport required.**

CALIFORNIA

Hotels

Many budget-range hotels in San Francisco are in unsavory areas. In terms of cleanliness and helpfulness, you often get what you pay for. It's best to call several weeks in advance to reserve a spot.

Adelaide Inn, 5 Isadora Duncan (441-2261), at the end of a little alley off Taylor near Post, 2 blocks west of Union Sq. One of the most charming of San Francisco's many "European-style" hotels. Large windows and kitchenettes. Continental breakfast included. Doors always locked. Office hours Tues.-Fri. 9am-1pm and 4-9pm, Sat.-Mon. flexible. 18 rooms. Shared hallway bathrooms. Singles $32-38; twin beds or doubles $42-48. Reservations encouraged.

Golden Gate Hotel, 775 Bush St. (392-3702), between Powell and Mason. Charming 1913 hotel. Beautiful rooms. Friendly, multi-lingual staff. Check-out noon. Rooms $59, with bath $89. Continental breakfast included.

Sheehan Hotel, 620 Sutter St. (775-6500 or 800-848-1529), at Mason. Excellent location. International students galore. Cable TV, phone. Swimming pool. Continental breakfast included. Economy singles $45, with bath $60; doubles $55, with bath $75. $10 per additional person. Children under 12 free with parents.

The Amsterdam, 749 Taylor St. (673-3277 or 800-637-3444). Beautiful rooms in a very central location. Some rooms have jacuzzi and private deck. Charming turn-of-the-century feel. Kitchen and patio. Check-out 11am. Continental breakfast included. Singles $45, with bath $60; doubles $50, with bath $69.

Allison Hotel, 417 Stockton St. (986-8737 or 800-628-6456). Lobby gleams with renovated opulence. The 25 rooms have shared baths. Cable TV, phones. Check-out 11am. Singles and doubles $29-49, with bath $69-89. Reserve ahead.

YMCA Chinatown, 855 Sacramento St., 94108 (982-4412). *Men over 18 only.* Convenient, central location. Pool and gym. Registration Mon.-Fri. 6:30am-10pm, Sat. 9am-5pm, Sun. 9am-3:30pm. Check-out 1pm. No curfew. Singles $28.70, with bath $39.25; doubles $37.40. 7th day free. Reserve by mail: send first day deposit.

Gum Moon Women's Residence, 940 Washington St. (421-8827), at Stockton. *Women only.* Truly beautiful. Piano, TV, and VCR. Kitchen and laundry facilities. Very secure. Call ahead for availability. Registration 9am-6pm. Check-out noon. Singles $25, per week $100; doubles $42, per week $166.

Grant Plaza, 465 Grant Ave. (434-3883 or 800-472-6899, within CA 800-472-6805), at Pine. Excellent location. Clean, bright rooms with bath, phones, and TV. Parking available for $8.50 per day. Check-in after 2:30pm. Check-out noon. Singles $39-42; doubles $47-57. Reservations advised 3 weeks in advance.

The Red Victorian Bed and Breakfast Inn, 1665 Haight St. (864-1978). The Red Vic is more a cosmic trip than a hotel. 18 wacky rooms. Check-in 3-6pm; check-out 11am. 2-night stay usually required on weekends. Discounts on stays longer than 3 days. Doubles $76-200, with discount $59-134. Reserve well in advance.

Harcourt Residence Club, 1105 Larkin St. (673-7720). One of the city's most popular residence clubs offers rooms by the week or by the month. Price includes maid service, 2 meals, Sunday brunch, and mailbox service. TV room, laundry room, and a sundeck. Office hours 9am-5pm. Weekly rates $130-200 per person.

Hotel Essex, 684 Ellis St. (474-4664, within CA 800-44-ESSEX/37739, outside CA 800-45-ESSEX), at Larkin. Newly renovated; one of the best budget hotels around. Free coffee and tea. Color TVs and phones. 24-hr. reception. Staff speaks French and German. Check-out noon. Singles $39, with bath $49; doubles $44, with bath $59. Weekly rates: singles $175, with bath $225; doubles $225, with bath $250.

YMCA Hotel, 220 Golden Gate Ave. (885-0460), at Leavenworth, on the edge of the infamous Tenderloin. Men and women allowed. Double locks on all doors and a policy requiring visitors to stay in the lobby enhance security. Pool, gym, and racquetball court. Breakfast included. Laundry. 24-hr. registration. No curfew. Singles $28, with bath $37.50; doubles $38; triples $60. Hostel beds ($15) for HI-AYH members only. $5 key deposit. 28-day max. stay.

FOOD

San Francisco's 4000 restaurants offer a bewildering array of culinary wonderment. Fear thee not; the best bets are broken down into easily digestible info-chunks.

Mission District

Even the most substantial appetites will be satisfied by the Mexican, Salvadoran, and other Latin American restaurants located on 24th St. After a burrito or some raw cuttlefish, nearby Castro St. is a great place for an evening coffee or drink.

La Cumbre, 515 Valencia St. (863-8205) between 16th and 17th. Mouth-watering steaks are grilled to perfection and deftly made into a superlative burrito ($2.75). Open Mon.-Sat. 11am-midnight, Sun. noon-midnight.

New Dawn Café, 3174 16th St., at Guerrero. An intense sensory experience prepared with care by a drag queen. Vegetable homefries $5.25, vegetarian chili $3.50. Open Mon.-Thurs. 8:30am-2:30pm, Wed.-Sun. 8:30am-8:30pm.

Café Macondo, 3159 16th St. (863-6517). Appetizing Central American food and coffee. Cappuccino ($1.65). Chicken tamale $3.75, pita bread sandwich $3.50. Open Mon.-Thurs. 11am-10pm, Fri.-Sun. 11am-11pm.

Mission Grounds, 3170 16th St. (621-1539). A popular café. Sit outside and enjoy a delicious Mexican drink ($1.65). Crepes in a variety of flavors, including cheddar and onion ($3.35) or brown sugar dessert ($1.75). Open daily 7am-10pm.

Manora, 3226 Mission St. (550-0856). This attractive Thai restaurant serves delicious food at reasonable prices. The red beef curry garners high praise ($6). Most vegetarian dishes $4-5, others can dine for about $5-6. Open Tues.-Sun. 5-10pm.

Chinatown

Chinatown is filled with downright cheap restaurants; in fact, their multitude and incredible similarity can make a choice nearly impossible.

House of Nanking, 919 Kearny St. (421-1429), between Columbus and Jackson. *Mu-shu* vegetables $5, onion cakes $1.75. Tsing Tao beer sauce is essential. Open Mon.-Sat. 11am-10pm, Sun. 4-10pm.

Sam Wo, 813 Washington St. (982-0596). The late hours and BYOB policy, not to mention the exceptionally cheap prices, make this restaurant a hit among students from all over the Bay Area. Most dishes $2-5. Shrimp noodle soup $2.75, chicken chow mein $3.60. Open Mon.-Sat. 11-3am.

North Beach

North Beach has excellent cafés, bakeries, and delis, but what truly sets it apart from other neighborhoods is its profusion of great Italian restaurants.

Tommaso's, 1042 Kearny St. (398-9696). Some of the best pizza anywhere. The super deluxe, piled high with mushrooms, peppers, ham, and Italian sausage, is enough for two ($18.50). Open Tues.-Sat. 5-10:45pm, Sun. 4-9:45pm.

U.S. Restaurant, 431 Columbus Ave. (362-6251). Once a hangout for Kerouac and pals, now popular with young San Franciscans. Calamari ($9, ½-portion $7), served Fri., is their most popular dish. Most dishes under $10. Open Tues.-Sat. 6:30am-9:30pm. Closed for 2-3 weeks in June or July.

Richmond

Some locals claim that the popular and authentic Chinese restaurants in Richmond are better than the ones in Chinatown.

The Red Crane, 1115 Clement St. (751-7226), between Park Presidio Blvd. and 12th, is an award-winning Chinese and seafood restaurant. The sweet and sour walnuts ($5.75) are divine. Open daily 11:30am-10pm.

Ernesto's, 2311 Clement St. (386-1446), at 24th. Dinners at this family-run Italian restaurant are reasonably priced (entrees $8-11.25, pizza $7.75-$15.50), and as authentic as anything in North Beach, if not Italy. Open Tues.-Sun. 4-10pm.

New Golden Turtle, 308 5th Ave. (221-5285), at Clement. Like the food in heaven, only with more ginger. Try the tender lemon grass chicken ($8) or flambé BBQ quail ($5). Open Tues.-Sun. 11am-11pm, Mon. 5-11pm.

Civic Center

Petite restaurants dot the entire Civic Center area, and Hayes offers an extensive selection of cafés. In the summer, load up on produce at the **Farmers Market** in the U.N. Plaza (every Wed. and Sun.). Use caution in this area at night.

Miss Pearl Jam's, 601 Eddy St. (775-5267), at Larkin. Reggae, jerk chicken, steel-drums, and a swimming pool make for a superb brunch ($5-11). Open Tues. 6-10pm, Wed. 11:30am-2:30pm and 6-10pm, Thurs.-Sat. 11:30am-2:30pm and 6-11pm, Sun. 11am-2:30pm and 5:30-10pm.

Nyala Ethiopian Restaurant, 39A Grove St. (861-0788), east of Larkin St. Nyala's Ethiopian and Italian cuisine is excellent. Buffet Mon.-Sat. 11am-3pm ($5) and 4pm-closing ($7). Open Mon.-Thurs. 11am-9pm, Fri.-Sat. 11am-10pm.

Haight-Ashbury

The Haight has many great bakeries and ethnic restaurants with reasonable prices. Select your restaurant carefully—quality varies greatly between establishments.

Cha Cha Cha, 1801 Haight St. (386-5758). The food is thought to be the best in the Haight. Fried bananas in black bean sauce are yum yum good ($5.25). Entrees $6.50-12.50. Open Mon.-Thurs. 11:30am-3pm and 5-11pm, Fri. 11:30am-3pm and 5-11:30pm, Sat. 9am-3pm and 5-11:30pm, Sun. 9am-3pm and 5-11pm.

Tassajara Bread Bakery, 1000 Cole St. (664-8947), at Parnassus. The scrumptious foccacia with pesto, artichoke hearts, feta, and garlic ($1.10) should not be missed. Sandwiches $4. Open Mon.-Sat. 7am-10pm, Sun. 8am-10pm.

Ganges, 775 Frederick St. (661-7290). Delicious vegetarian Indian food draws locals to this warm and intimate restaurant. Dinners $8.50-12.50. Live music Fri.-Sat. starting at 7:15pm. Open Tues.-Sat. 5-10pm. Reservations a good idea.

Marina and Pacific Heights

Pacific Heights and the Marina abound in high-quality restaurants serving tasty, fresh food. They love the ultra-chic, but anyone can find a great meal for under $12.

Leon's Bar*B*Q, 1911 Fillmore St. (922-2436), between Pine and Bush. At the southern end of yuppified Fillmore, Leon's has been serving up Cajun jambalaya ($5) and the like since 1963. Dinner plates with ribs or seafood and fixin's for $8-15.50. Open daily 11am-9:30pm for table service and for take out.

Jackson Fillmore Trattoria, 2506 Fillmore St. (346-5288). Great southern Italian cuisine and a lively atmosphere can always be counted on at this hip *trattoria*. Open Mon.-Thurs. 5:30-10:30pm, Fri.-Sat. 5:30-11pm, Sun. 5-10pm.

Sweet Heat, 3324 Steiner St. (474-9191). This spunky little place serves south-of-the-border food to a health-conscious crowd. Delicious grilled veggie burrito in whole wheat tortilla ($4). Eat in or take out. Open daily 11am-midnight.

SIGHTS

Any resident will tell you that this city is not made of landmarks or "sights," but of neighborhoods. If you blindly rush from the Golden Gate Bridge to Coit Tower to Mission Dolores, you'll be missing the point—the city itself. Whether defined by ethnicity, tax brackets, topography, or a shared spirit, these neighborhoods present off-beat bookstores, Chinatown *dim sum,* Pacific Heights architecture, SoMa's nightlife, Japantown folk festivals, Golden Gate Park's Strawberry Hill, North Beach's Club Fugazi, and Haight-Ashbury just being itself.

Downtown and Union Square

Now an established shopping area, **Union Sq.** has a rich and somewhat checkered history. During the Civil War, Unionists made the square their rallying ground. Their placards, reading "The Union, the whole Union, and nothing but the Union," gave the area its name. When the Barbary Coast (now the Financial District) was down and dirty, Union Sq.'s Morton Alley was dirtier. After the 1906 earthquake and fire destroyed most of the flophouses, a group of merchants moved in and renamed the area **Maiden Ln.** in hopes of changing the street's image. Surprisingly enough, the switch worked. Today Maiden Ln.—extending 2 blocks from Union Square's eastern side—is home to chi-chi shops and ritzy boutiques.

One of the Maiden Ln.'s main attractions is the **Circle Gallery** (989-2100), 140 Maiden Ln. The only Frank Lloyd Wright building in San Francisco, the gallery sells some of the city's most expensive art (open Mon.-Sat. 10am-6pm, Sun. noon-5pm; free). Take a free ride on the outside elevators of the **Westin St. Francis Hotel** on Powell St. at Geary. As you swiftly rise, the entire Bay Area spreads out before you. The "elevator tours" offer an unparalleled view of Coit Tower and the Golden Gate Bridge. Kitsch sinks in at the funky lobby of the **Hotel Triton,** 342 Granite St. (394-0500), where every room is decorated according to a different motif.

Financial District

It's only a mile from the Haight, but you'll find no trippin' hippies in the financial district; instead, business-suited bankers bustle buoyantly by boulevards bordered by the Bay Area's biggest buildings.

At the foot of Market St. is **Justin Herman Plaza** and its famous geodesic **Vallaincourt Fountain.** The area is often rented out by bands or for rallies during lunch from noon to 1:30pm. One such free lunchtime concert, performed by U2 in the fall of 1987, resulted in the arrest of lead singer and madcap non-conformist Bono for spray painting "Stop the Traffic—Rock and Roll" on the fountain.

Connected to the $300-million complex is the **Hyatt Regency** hotel (788-1234). Its 17-story atrium, dominated by a four-story geometric sculpture, is worth a peek. The glass elevator up the building's side leads to the 20th floor and the **Equinox Revolving Rooftop Restaurant and Lounge.** From the revolving cocktail lounge, you can catch a dazzling view the bay. Buy a drink and dawdling time for $3 (open Mon.-Fri. 4-11:30pm, Sat. noon-1am, Sun. 10am-11:30pm).

Designed by William Pereira and Associates as a show of architectural virtuosity, the 853-foot **Transamerica Pyramid,** on Montgomery St. between Clay and Washington St. (take MUNI bus #15), was never actually meant to be built. The Montgomery Block, a four-story brick building, once stood in its place. The Montgomery's in-house bar lured the likes of Mark Twain, Robert Louis Stevenson, and Jack London.

Golden Gate Ferries (332-6600) sends boats on the scenic voyage to Larkspur and Sausalito. (Fare to Sausalito $4.25, ages 6-12 $3.20, under 5 free; to Larkspur $2.50, ages 6-12 $1.90. Seniors and people with disabilities travel ½-price.)

South-of-Market (SoMa)

During the day the area fills with workers from the encroaching Financial District. At night, SoMa is the place for hip young professionals to dine at chic restaurants before hitting San Francisco's club scene. SoMa is one of the easiest areas of the city in which to park your car, but lock it securely, and don't leave valuables inside. Take samTrans bus #1A or 1L (weekends and holidays) or #1C, 22D, 10L, or 10T (8-10am and 4-6pm only) or take MUNI bus #9x, 12, 14, 15, 26, 27, 30, 45, or 71.

Civic Center

The Civic Center is a collection of gigantic buildings arranged around two massive plazas. Parking is easy on streets around the Civic Center. Take MUNI Metro to the "Civic Center/City Hall" stop or MUNI bus #5, 16X, 19, 21, 26, 42, 47, or 49. You can also take the J, K, L, M, or N lines to Van Ness station or Golden Gate Transit bus #10, 20, 50, or 70.

The palatial **San Francisco City Hall,** which was modeled after St. Peter's Cathedral, is the centerpiece of the largest gathering of Beaux Arts architecture in the U.S. The city hall was the site of the 1978 murder of Mayor George Moscone and City Supervisor Harvey Milk, the first openly gay politician to be elected to public office in the United States. At the eastern end are the library and UN Plaza, at the western end are the Opera House and Museum of Modern Art.

In the evenings, the **Louise M. Davies Symphony Hall,** 201 Van Ness Ave. (431-5400), at Grove, rings with the sounds of the **San Francisco Symphony** (open Mon.-Fri. 10am-6pm). Next door, the **War Memorial Opera House,** 301 Van Ness Ave. (864-3330), between Grove and McAllister, hosts the well-regarded **San Francisco Opera Company** (864-3330) and the **San Francisco Ballet** (621-3838 for information). Also in the block of Van Ness between Grove and McAllister is the **Veterans Building** (252-4000). Between the Opera House and the Veterans Building lies **Opera Plaza.** (Tours of these buildings leave every ½-hr. from the Grove St. entrance to Davies Hall at Mon. 10am-2pm. $3, seniors and students $2.)

Mission District

Founded by Spanish settlers in 1776, the Mission is home to some of the oldest structures in the city, as well as its newest cafés and clubs. Colorful **murals** celebrate Mexican and Latino history, while numerous *taquerías* and bakeries testify to today's prominent Latino presence. The area is also home to a significant lesbian community. A relatively safe district, the Mission is ideal for daytime walks—but exercise caution or travel in groups at night. The district, which lies south of the Civic Center area, is roughly bordered by 16th St. to the north, Noe St. to the west, Army St. to the south, and U.S. 101 to the east. The Mission District is laced with MUNI bus routes, including #9, 12, 22, 26, 27, 33, and 53.

Extant for over two centuries, **Mission Dolores,** at 16th St. and Dolores in the old heart of San Francisco, is considered the oldest building in the city. The mission was founded in 1776 by Father Junípero Serra and was named in honor of St. Francis of Assisi, as was San Francisco itself. The mission, however, sat close to a marsh known as *Laguna de Nuestra Señora de los Dolores* (Laguna of Our Lady of Sorrows) and despite Serra's wishes, gradually became known as *Misión de los Dolores.* Exotic bougainvillea, poppies, and birds-of-paradise bloom in the cemetery, which was featured in Hitchcock's *Vertigo.* (Open daily 9am-4:00pm, Nov.-April 9am-4pm. $1. Masses Mon.-Fri. 7:30am and 9am, Sun. 8am and 10am, Mass in Spanish Sun. noon.)

Women might enjoy the spiritual and physical rejuvenation of a plunge into the waters at **Osento,** 955 Valencia St. (282-6333), between 20th and 21st; a bathhouse which provides beautiful, clean, and very safe facilities to all women (as long as they're over 15), with wet and dry sauna, jacuzzi, and pool. (Entrance fee $7-11. $1 towel rental. Open daily 1pm-1am. Door closed after midnight.)

La Galeria de la Raza, 2857 24th St. (826-8009) at Bryant, is small but shows excellent exhibitions of Chicano and Latino art by local and international artists. The gift shop next door sells impressive pieces of folk art from Mexico and Latin America (open Tues.-Sat. noon-6pm; free). The **Mission Cultural Center,** 2868 Mission St. (821-1155), between 24th and 25th St., includes a theater, and often-stunning art exhibitions, as well as other cultural events throughout the year. (Gallery open Tues.-Fri. noon-6pm, Sat. 10am-4pm. Free. Box office 695-6970.)

Castro

Castro and the Mission District enjoy the city's best weather, often while fog blankets nearby Twin Peaks. Much of San Francisco's gay and lesbian community calls the area home. Some say that the scene has mellowed considerably from the wild days of the 70s, but Castro St. remains a proud and assertive emblem of gay liberation. Most of the action takes place along Castro St. to the south of Market St.

Perhaps the best way to see the Castro is in the reflection of a mug of cappuccino, but for a more conventional way around, **Cruisin' Castro** gives **walking tours** of Castro St. (daily 10am). Guide Trevor Hailey, a member of Castro's gay community since 1972, was named one of San Francisco's top tour guides in 1992. (Tours are $30, including brunch at the famed Elephant Walk Restaurant, at the "gayest four corners on earth." Call Trevor at 550-8110 for reservations.) MUNI bus #24 runs along Castro St. from 14th to 26th. Down the street, **The Names Project,** 2362 Market St. (863-1966), sounds a more somber note. This is the headquarters of an organization that has accumulated over 12,000 3 x 6 ft. panels from over 30 countries for the **AIDS Memorial Quilt.** Each panel is a memorial to a person who has died of AIDS. (Open Mon.-Fri. noon-5pm.)

West of Castro, the peninsula swells with several large hillocks. On rare fogless nights, you can get a breathtaking view of the city from **Twin Peaks,** between Portola Dr., Market St., and Clarendon Ave. South of the peaks on Portola Dr. is **Mount Davidson,** the highest spot in San Francisco (938ft.).

Haight-Ashbury

It's in the 60s and sunny every day in Haight-Ashbury. Originally a quiet lower-middle-class neighborhood, the Haight's large Victorian houses—perfect for communal living—and the district's proximity to the University of California in San Francisco (UCSF) drew a massive hippie population in the mid- and late-1960s. The hippie voyage reached its apogee in 1966-67 when Janis Joplin, the Grateful Dead, and the Jefferson Airplane all made love and music in the neighborhood. During 1967's "Summer of Love," young people from across the country converged on the grassy panhandle for the celebrated "be-ins." Today, many of the bars and restaurants are remnants of yesteryear, with faded auras and live-in regulars, though you're sure to run into some characters who don't know that the 60s are over, wandering the streets in various shades of purple haze. The Haight is great for browsing; bookstores are everywhere, as are vintage clothing stores and inexpensive cafés. MUNI buses #6, 7, 16x, 43, 66, 71, and 73 all serve the area, while Metro line N runs along Carl St., four blocks south.

The **Love 'n' Haight Tour** takes visitors past the **Psychedelic Shop** and the one-time Grateful Dead pad (2½hr.; $20; call to make reservations). Northeast of the Haight, at Hayes St. and Steiner, lies **Alamo Sq.,** the vantage point of a thousand postcards. Climb the gentle, grassy slope and you'll understand why it's a favorite with photographers—a string of lovely Victorian homes (the "Painted Ladies") is presented with the metropolitan skyline as a backdrop.

The **Red Victorian Movie House,** 1727 Haight St. (668-3994), between Cole and Shrader, is a collectively owned and operated theater that shows foreign, student, and recently run Hollywood films. **Wasteland,** 1660 Haight St. (863-3150), is an immense used clothing store, deserving of notice, if only for its wonderful façade and window displays (open daily 11am-7pm). Resembling a dense green mountain in the middle of the Haight, **Buena Vista Park** has, predictably, a reputation for free-wheeling lawlessness. Enter at your own risk, and once inside, be prepared for those "doing their own thing" and doing enough of it to kill a small animal.

LSD: From The Man to the People

Basel, Switzerland, 1938: A compound called **lysergic acid diethylamide (LSD)** is synthesized. Almost immediately, the medical community touts the effects of the new wonder drug, which is said to have a near-miraculous ability to cure psychoses with a minimum of therapeutic intervention. The U.S. government soon gets into the act. In the early 50s, the CIA attempts to use the hallucinogen as part of **"Operation MK-ULTRA,"** a series of cold-war mind control experiments. By the end of the next decade, LSD has been tested on some 1,500 military personnel in a series of ethically shady operations conducted by the U.S. Army Corps of Engineers on many unknowing subjects. However, by the early 60s, the effects of the drug are discovered by the burgeoning hippie population in San Francisco's Haight-Ashbury district. Soon, college students and prominent intellectuals advocate its use as a means of expanding one's consciousness. In 1965, the drug is made illegal, but it is too late. Once a pet tool of the military-industrial complex's oppression, **acid** had already become a key part of the massive counterculture of the late 60s, fueling anti-war protests and orgiastic love-ins across the Bay Area and the rest of America.

CALIFORNIA

Golden Gate Park

Frederick Law Olmsted—designer of New York's Central Park—said it couldn't be done when San Francisco's 19th-century elders asked him to build a park to rival Paris's Bois de Boulogne on their city's western side. But engineer William Hammond Hall and Scottish gardener John "Willy" McLaren proved him wrong. Hall designed the 1000-acre park—gardens and all—when the land was still just shifting sand dunes, and then constructed a mammoth breakwater along the oceanfront to protect the flora from the sea's burning spray.

To get to the park from downtown, hop on bus #5 or 21. Bus #44 passes right by the major attractions and serves 6th Ave. to California Ave. to the north and the MUNI Metro to the south. Most of the park is bounded by Fulton St. to the north, Stanyan St. to the east, Lincoln Way to the south, and the Pacific Ocean to the west. **Park Headquarters** (666-7200), where you can procure information and maps, is in McLaren Lodge at Fell St. and Stanyan, on the eastern edge of the park (open Mon.-Fri. 8am-5pm; inexplicably closed weekends and holidays).

The **Conservatory of Flowers** (752-8080), erected in 1879, is the oldest building in the park. The delicate and luminescent structure is modeled after Palm House in London's Kew Gardens and houses scintillating displays of tropical plants. (Open daily 9am-6pm; Nov.-April 9am-5pm. $1.50, seniors and ages 6-12 75¢, under 6 free. Free daily 9:30-10am and 5:30-6pm, on the 1st Wed. of month, and on holidays.) The **Strybing Arboretum,** on Lincoln Way at 9th (661-1316), southwest of the academy, is home to 5000 varieties of plants. The **Garden of Fragrance** is designed especially for the visually impaired; the labels are in Braille and the plants are chosen specifically for their texture and scent. (Open Mon.-Fri. 8am-4:30pm, Sat.-Sun. 10am-5pm. Tours daily 1:30pm, Thurs.-Sun. 10:30am. Free.) Near the Music Concourse on a path off of South Dr., the **Shakespeare Garden** contains almost every flower and plant ever mentioned by the herbalist of Stratford-upon-Avon (open daily dawn-dusk; in winter closed Mon.; free). In the middle of Stow Lake, **Strawberry Hill** is covered with strawberry fields forever. Rent a boat ($9.50-14.50 per hour), or cross the footbridge and climb the hill for a dazzling view of the San Francisco peninsula. At the intersection of Lincoln Way and South Dr., the **Japanese Cherry Orchard** blooms intoxicatingly during the first week in April.

Created for the 1894 Mid-Winter Exposition, the elegant **Japanese Tea Garden** is a serene collection of dark wooden buildings, small pools, graceful footbridges, and carefully pruned flora. Buy tea and cookies for $2.50 and watch the giant carp circle the central pond. (Open daily 9am-6:30pm; Oct.-Feb. 8:30am-dusk. $2, seniors and ages 6-12 $1, under 6 free. Free 1st and last ½-hr. and on holidays.)

What could be more American than a herd of **buffalo?** A dozen of the shaggy beasts roam a spacious paddock at the western end of John F. Kennedy Dr., near 39th Ave. On Sundays traffic is banned from park roads, and bicycles and in-line skates come out in full force. Rent bikes at **Stow Lake** ($7 per hour or $28 per day).

Richmond

Historically a neighborhood of first- and second-generation immigrants, the Richmond has served as a traditional home to the Irish-, Russian-, and Chinese-American communities. "Inner Richmond," the area east of Park Presidio Blvd., has a large Chinese population, earning it the nickname "New Chinatown."

Lincoln Park, at the northwest extreme of San Francisco, is Richmond's biggest attraction (MUNI bus #1 or 38). The grounds around the park also offer a romantic view of the Golden Gate Bridge. Take the **Land's End Path,** running northwest of the cliff edge, for an even better look. Southwest of Lincoln Park sits the precarious **Cliff House,** the third of that name to occupy this spot. The nearby **National Park Service Visitors Center** (556-8642), dispenses information on the wildlife of the cliffs area, as well as on the history of the present and previous Cliff Houses. (Open daily 10am-4:30pm. Free.)

Scope out **Seal Rocks,** often occupied by the sleek animals. Don't feed the coin-operated binoculars—simply have a free look at the visitor's center. **Ocean Beach,** the largest and most popular of San Francisco's beaches, begins south of Point Lobos and extends down the northwestern edge of the city's coastline. The undertow along the point is so strong that swimming is prohibited and even wading is dangerous. Swimming is allowed at **China Beach** at the end of Seacliff Ave. on the eastern edge of Lincoln Park. The water is COLD here too, but the views of the Golden Gate Bridge may be worth it (lifeguards on duty April-Oct.).

The Presidio and the Golden Gate Bridge

Established in 1776, the **Presidio** is a sprawling preserve that extends all the way from the Marina in the east to the wealthy Sea Cliff area in the west. The preserve also supports the southern end of San Francisco's world-famous Golden Gate Bridge, and used to support the troops of the U.S.'s 6th Army. (Take MUNI bus #28, 29, or 76 to the preserve.)

At the northern tip of the Presidio (and the peninsula), under the tower of the Golden Gate Bridge, **Fort Point** (556-1693) stands guard over the entrance to San Francisco Bay. The fort was built in 1853 as one of a series of bunker defenses designed to protect San Francisco from invasion by the British during the tense dispute over the Oregon boundary. (Museum open Wed.-Sun. 10am-5pm. Free 1-hr. **walks** with presentation 10:30am, 1:30 and 3:30pm with extra 12:30pm walk on weekends. Grounds open sunrise-sunset.)

The **Golden Gate Bridge,** the rust-colored symbol of the West's bounding confidence, sways above the entrance to San Francisco Bay. Built in 1937 under the direction of chief engineer Joseph Strauss, the bridge is almost indescribably beautiful from any angle on or around it. The bridge's overall length is 8981 ft.; the main span is 4200 ft. long. The stolid towers are 746 ft. high. Built to swing, the bridge was undamaged by the '89 quake. Just across the bridge, **Vista Point** is just that, providing a stunning view of the city.

Marina, Pacific Heights, and Presidio Heights

Hit hard by the '89 rumbler, yuppie-ville has been rebuilt quickly, with more well-kept gardens and aerobics studios than ever. **Fillmore, Union,** and **Chestnut St.** bustle in the evenings, but the area can be enjoyed best for its magnificent waterfront view of the Golden Gate Bridge during the day. Most everything is overpriced, but the beautiful parks, homes, and views warrant a glance.

Centered around Union and Sacramento St., Pacific Heights boasts the greatest number of **Victorian buildings** in the city as well as the best view of the Golden Gate Bridge. The **Octagon House,** 2645 Gough St. (441-7512), at Union, was built in 1861 with the belief that such architecture would bring good luck to its inhabitants; the house's survival of the many earthquakes and fires that have swept the city shows more than good fortune. (Open 2nd Sun. and 2nd and 4th Thurs. of all months except Jan. noon-3pm; group tours by arrangement available on any weekday.) The **Haas-Lilienthal House,** 2007 Franklin St. (441-3004), is another example of Victorian architecture run amok. (Open Wed. noon-4pm, Sun. 11am-4pm. $5, seniors and under 18 $3.)

To the east of Marina Green at Laguna and Marina lies **Fort Mason.** The army's former embarkation facility has been converted into a center for non-profit organizations. The Fort Mason Center houses many small museums with adjoining gift shops. The **African-American Historical and Cultural Society Museum** (441-0640), Building C, #165, focuses on contemporary African arts and crafts (open Wed.-Sun. noon-5pm; donation requested). **Museo Italo Americano** (673-2200), Building C #100, displays work created by artists with Italian heritage (open Wed.-Sun. noon-5pm; $2, students and seniors $1). The **Mexican Museum** (441-0404), Building D, offers free tours, exhibits, and educational workshops (open Wed.-Sun. noon-5pm; $4, seniors and students $2, under 10 free). The **Magic Theater** (441-8822), Building D, founded in 1967 by John Lion, is renowned for hosting Sam Shepard as its playwright-in-residence from 1975 to 1985. The Magic Theater continues to stage contemporary American plays (Oct.-July Wed.-Sun.).

To the east of Ft. Mason is Ghirardelli Sq. and to the west lies the **Palace of Fine Arts** (Baker St., between Jefferson and Bay St.). The beautiful domed structure and the two curving colonnades are reconstructed remnants of the 1915 Panama Pacific Exposition, which commemorated the opening of the Panama Canal and signalled San Francisco's recovery from the great earthquake. The grounds of the Palace of Art are some of the best picnic spots in the city. On summer days performances of Shakespeare are sometimes given in the colonnade section. Next to the domed building is the **Exploratorium,** 3601 Lyon St. (main line, 563-7337; recorded message, 561-0360). This way-cool warehouse is full of science projects turned fun. Displays range from the wonders of electricity to giant bubble-makers. Hundreds of interactive exhibits may teach even poets a thing or two about the sciences. (Open Sun.-Tues. and Thurs.-Sat. 10am-6pm, Wed. 10am-9:30pm. From Labor Day-Memorial Day, open Tues.-Sun.10am-5pm, Wed. 10am-9:30pm. $9, students and seniors $7, ages 6-17 $5. Free on the first Wed. of every month.) Within the Exploratorium dwells the **Tactile Dome** (561-0362), a pitch-dark maze of tunnels, slides, nooks, and crannies designed to help refine your sense of touch. The Dome is sometimes home to chemically-enhanced youths looking to expand their minds. Claustrophobes and those afraid of the dark should stay away (open Mon.-Fri. 10am-5pm; $10; advance reservations required—call to reserve).

Fisherman's Wharf and Ghirardelli Square

East along the waterfront is the most popular tourist destination in San Francisco. Stretching from Pier 39 in the east to Ghirardelli Sq. in the west is "Fisherman's Wharf," home to ¾-mi. of porcelain figurines, enough t-shirts to have kept Washington's army snug, and enough salt-water taffy to have made them all violently ill. **Pier 39** (981-7437), built on pilings that extend several hundred yards into the harbor, was designed to recall old San Francisco; in reality, it looks more like a Dodge City scene from a Ronald Reagan Western (shops open daily 10:30am-8:30pm). Toward the end of the pier is **Center Stage,** where mimes, jugglers, and magicians wow you with your frivolity. **Vlaho's Fruit Orchard** sells primo California produce (tangy cherries $4 per lb., juicy peaches $2 per lb., luscious strawberries $6 per lb.)

Tour boats and ferries dock just west of Pier 39. The **Blue and Gold Fleet** (705-5444) offers 1¼-hr. tours on 400-passenger sight-seeing boats. The tours cruise under both the Golden Gate and Bay Bridges, past Angel Island, Alcatraz, and Treasure Island, and provide sweeping views of the San Francisco skyline. (Tours begin at 10am, last boat 5:30pm. $15, seniors, ages 5-18, and military $8.) The **Red and White Fleet** (546-2700 for reservations, 546-2628 for recorded information within CA; also 800-BAY-CRUISE/229-2784) at Pier 41 offers both tours and ferry rides. The 45-minute Bay Cruise leaves from Piers 41 and 43½ and goes under the Golden Gate Bridge and past Alcatraz and Angel Island. ($15, over 62 and ages 12-18 $12, ages 5-11 $8; ask about the multi-lingual narratives.) Red and White boats also ferry passengers to Alcatraz (see below). Both cruises are fully narrated.

Easily visible from boats and the waterfront is **Alcatraz Island.** Named in 1775 for the *alcatraces* (pelicans) that flocked to it, this former federal prison looms over San Francisco Bay, 1½ mi. from Fisherman's Wharf. In 1934, Alcatraz was brought under federal purview and used to hold those who had wreaked too much havoc in other prisons. Of the 23 men who attempted to escape, all were recaptured or killed, except for five who were "presumed drowned" although their bodies were never found. The film *Escape from Alcatraz* relates the story of the most probable escape. Robert Stroud, "The Birdman of Alcatraz," spent 17 years in solitary confinement. Although sentenced to death for killing a prison guard, he was spared by President Wilson and went on to write two books on bird diseases. In 1962, Attorney General Robert Kennedy closed the prison, and the island's existence was uneventful until 1969, when about 80 Native Americans occupied it as a symbolic gesture, claiming the rock as their property under the terms of a broken 19th-century treaty. Alcatraz is currently a part of the **Golden Gate National Recreation Area,** the largest park in an urban area in the United States, administered by the National Park Service. The Red and White Fleet (see above) runs boats to Alcatraz from Pier 41. Once on Alcatraz, you can wander by yourself or take a 2-hr. audiotape-guided tour, full of clanging chains and the ghosts of prisoners past. (Boats depart every ½-hr. from Pier 41; summer 9:15am-4:15pm, winter 9:45am-2:45pm. $5.75, seniors $4.75, ages 5-11 $3.25; tours cost $3.25 extra, ages 5-11 $1.25 extra. Passengers can remain on the island until the final 6:30pm ferry departs.) Reserve tickets in advance through Ticketron (392-7469) for $1 extra or confront long lines and risk missing the boat.

The **Maritime National Historic Park** (929-0202), at the Hyde St. Pier where Hyde meets Jefferson, displays the *Balclutha,* a swift trading vessel that plied the Cape Horn route in the 1880s and 90s and was featured in the first Hollywood version of *Mutiny on the Bounty.* The vessel was recently restored with donated union labor. (Open daily 9am-6pm, last ticket sold at 5:30pm. $3, ages 12-17 $1, over 61 and under 12 free.)

Ghirardelli Sq. (GEAR-ah-deh-lee), 900 N. Point St. (information booth 775-5500; open daily 10am-9pm), is the most famous of the shopping malls in the area around Fisherman's Wharf and rightfully so—it houses some of the best chocolate in the world. Today, the only remains of the machinery from Ghirardelli's original **chocolate factory** (transformed from a uniform factory in the 1890s by Domingo Ghirardelli's family) are in the rear of the **Ghirardelli Chocolate Manufactory,** an old-fashioned ice-cream parlor. Ghirardelli Sq. is now a popular destination, with an elegant mermaid fountain. (Stores open Mon.-Sat. 10am-9pm, Sun. 10am-6pm.)

North Beach

As one walks along Stockton St. or Columbus Ave., there is a gradual transition from shops selling ginseng to those selling provolone. In the 50s this area was home to the bohemian Beats who moved in alongside the traditional Italian residents of the neighborhood. North Beach maintains a sense of serenity while being an entertaining, energetic, and popular place for locals and tourists both day and night.

Lying between Stockton and Powell is **Washington Sq.,** North Beach's *piazza* and the wedding site of Joe DiMaggio and Marilyn Monroe. Across Filbert, to the north of the square is the **Church of St. Peter and St. Paul** (421-0809), beckoning tired sight-seers to take refuge in its dark, wooden nave. In the square itself is the **Volunteer Firemen Memorial,** donated by Mrs. Lillie Hitchcock Coit, who was rescued from a fire as a girl. Coit's most famous gift to the city is **Coit Tower** (362-0808), also known as "the candle," which stands a few blocks to the east of the memorial. (Open daily 10am-7pm; Oct.-May 9am-4pm. Elevator fare $3, over 64 $2, ages 6-12 $1, under 6 free. Last ticket sold ½-hr. before closing.) There is very limited parking, so leave your car on Washington St. and walk up the **Filbert Steps** which rise from the Embarcadero to the eastern base of the tower. The walk is short, allows excellent views, and passes by many attractive Art Deco buildings.

North Beach Bohemianism came to national attention when Ferlinghetti's **City Lights Bookstore,** 261 Columbus Ave. (362-8193), published Allen Ginsberg's anguished and ecstatic dream poem *Howl.* Banned in 1956, the book was found "not obscene" after an extended trial, but the resultant publicity turned North Beach into a must-see for curious tourists. Says a clerk, "We're more than a bookstore—we're on to something." (Open Mon.-Sat. noon-9pm, Sun. noon-8pm.)

Nob Hill and Russian Hill

This is where the rich walk their foofy dogs. Before the earthquake and fire of 1906, Nob Hill attracted the mansions of the great railroad magnates. Today, Nob Hill remains one of the nation's most prestigious addresses. The streets are lined with many fine buildings, and the aura is that of idle and settled wealth. Sitting atop a hill and peering down upon the hoi polloi can be a pleasant afternoon diversion. **Grace Cathedral,** 1051 Taylor St. (776-6611), the biggest Gothic edifice west of the Mississippi, crowns Nob Hill. The castings for its portals are such exact imitations of Ghiberti's on the Baptistery in Florence that they were used to restore the originals.

Nearby Russian Hill is named after Russian sailors who died during an expedition in the early 1800s and were buried on the southeast crest. At the top of Russian Hill, the notorious snaking curves of **Lombard St.** (between Hyde St. and Leavenworth) afford a fantastic view of the city and harbor—that is, if you dare to allow your eyes to stray from the road. The switchbacks were installed in the 1920s by homesick Genoans to allow horse-drawn carriages to negotiate the extremely steep hill.

Nihonmachi (Japantown)

Since the Great Quake of 1906, Japanese have lived in this part of the city. Nihonmachi is less tourist-oriented than Chinatown, catering more to its 12,000 Japanese residents. This small neighborhood 1.1 mi. from downtown San Francisco is bounded on its east side by Fillmore St., on its west side by Laguna St., by Bush St. to the north, and by the Geary Expressway to the south. Take MUNI buses #2, 3, and 4 to Buchanan or #38 to Geary. Nihonmachi is centered around the **Japanese Cultural and Trade Center** at the corner of Post and Buchanan. Similar to the Tokyo Ginza, the five-acre center includes Japanese *udon* houses, sushi bars, and a massage center/bathhouse. Japan gave as a gift to the 12,000 Japanese-Americans of San Francisco the **Peace Pagoda,** a magnificent 100-ft. tall, five-tiered structure which graces the heart of Japantown. The **Kabuki Complex** (931-9800) at Post and Fillmore shows current films, and during early May it is the main site of the San Francisco International Film Festival (see p. page 772).

Chinatown

The largest Chinese community outside of Asia (over 100,000 people), Chinatown is also the most densely populated of San Francisco's neighborhoods. Chinatown was founded in the 1880s when, after the gold had been dug and the tracks laid, bigotry fueled by unemployment engendered a racist outbreak against what was then termed the "Yellow Peril." In response, Chinese-Americans banded together to protect themselves in a small section of the downtown area. As the city grew, speculators tried to take over the increasingly valuable land, especially after the area was leveled by the 1906 earthquake, but the Chinese were not to be expelled, and Chinatown, which has gradually expanded, remains almost exclusively Chinese. **Grant Avenue** is a sea of Chinese banners, signs, architecture, and tourist kitsch.

Watch fortune cookies being shaped by hand in the **Golden Gate Cookie Company,** 56 Ross Alley (781-3956; huge bag of cookies $2), between Washington and Jackson St., just west of Grant Ave. This famous alleyway, has been a filming site for many well-known movies including *Big Trouble in Little China, Karate Kid II,* and *Indiana Jones and the Temple of Doom.* Nearby **Portsmouth Sq.,** at Kearny St. and Washington, made history in 1848 when Sam Brennan first announced the discovery of gold at Sutter's Mill from the square. A stone bridge leads from this square to the **Chinese Culture Center,** 750 Kearny St., 3rd floor of the Holiday Inn (986-1822; open Tues.-Sat. 9am-5:30pm), which houses exhibits of Chinese-American art and sponsors two **walking tours** of Chinatown. The **Chinese Historical Society,** 650 Commercial St. (391-1188), between Kearny and Montgomery, relates the tale of the Chinese immigrants through informative tomes and some snappy artifacts, including a 1909 parade dragon head (open Tues.-Sat. noon-4pm; donation).

At Grant and Bush stands the ornate, dragon-crested **Gateway to Chinatown.** The dragon motif is continued on the lampposts that line Chinatown's streets. Some of Chinatown's noteworthy buildings include **Buddha's Universal Church** (720 Washington St.), the **Kong Chow Temple** (855 Stockton St.), and **Old St. Mary's,** (660 California St., at Grant), built in 1854 from granite cut in China.

Museums

California Academy of Sciences (221-5100; 750-7145 for a recording), in **Golden Gate Park** is one of the nation's largest institutions of its kind. The **Steinhart Aquarium** (home to members of over 14,000 aquatic species) is more lively than the natural history exhibits. The **Space and Earth Hall** lets you experience the great quake of 1906 firsthand, as an exhibit recreates the earthquake, which hit 5.7 on the Richter Scale. **Morrison Planetarium** (750-7138) re-creates the heavens ($2.50, seniors and students $1.25). Academy open daily 10am-5pm; Sept.-July 10am-5pm. $7, $5 with MUNI Fast Pass or transfer, seniors and ages 12-17 $3, 6-11 $1.50. Free 1st Wed. of month until 8:45pm.

San Francisco Museum of Modern Art, 151 3rd St., in **SoMa,** displays an impressive collection of both European and American 20th-century works. The museum's new site in the **Yerba Buena Gardens** was one of the largest building projects ever undertaken by an American museum. Open Tues.-Wed. and Fri.-Sun. 11am-6pm, Thurs. 11am-9pm. $7, students and those over 61 $3.50, under 13 free. Thurs. 5-9pm ½-price. 1st Tues. of month free.

Ansel Adams Center, 250 4th St. (495-7000), at Howard and Folsom, in **SoMa,** houses a permanent collection of the master's photographs, as well others' temporary shows. $4, students $3, over 64 and ages 13-17 $2, under 13 free. Open Tues.-Sun. 11am-5pm, and until 8pm on first Tues. of every month.

M. H. de Young Memorial Museum (750-3600), in **Golden Gate Park,** takes visitors through a 21-room survey of American painting, from the colonial period to the early 20th century. The **Asian Art Museum** (668-7855) in the west wing of the building is the largest museum outside Asia dedicated entirely to Asian artwork. The museum's beautiful collection includes rare pieces of jade and porcelain, in addition to 3000-year-old works in bronze. Both open Wed.-Sun. 10am-5pm. Admission $5, $3 with MUNI Fast Pass or transfer, seniors and ages 12-17 $2, under 12, 1st Wed. of month, and Sat. 11am-noon free.

The Martin Lawrence Gallery, 465 Powell St., in **Union Sq.,** sells and displays the works of pop artists like Andy Warhol as well as an impressive collection of Keith Haring's work. Open Mon.-Sat. 10am-9pm, Sun. 10am-6pm; free.

San Francisco Women Artists Gallery, 370 Hayes St. (552-7392), between Franklin and Gough, near the **Civic Center.** Exhibits women's photographs, paintings, prints, and crafts. Open daily 11am-6pm.

Cable Car Powerhouse and Museum, 1201 Mason St. (474-1887), at Washington, in **Nob Hill.** The building is the center of the cable-car system. Check out the operation from a gallery or view displays to learn more about the cars, some of which date back to 1873. Open daily 10am-6pm; Nov.-March 10am-5pm; free.

Tattoo Art Museum, 841 Columbus (775-4991), in **North Beach.** Tattoo memorabilia, including designs and exhibits on different techniques. $50 will buy a glowing rose on the hip. Open Mon.-Sat. noon-1pm, Sun. noon-8pm.

ENTERTAINMENT AND NIGHTLIFE

San Fran nightlife is the freshmaker. Call the **Entertainment Hotline** at 391-2001 or 391-2002. The *Bay Guardian* and *SF Weekly* always have a thorough listing of dance clubs and live music. **Sports** enthusiasts should see the **Giants** and the **49ers** play baseball and football at nearby **Candlestick Park** (467-8000), 8 mi. south of the city on the Bayshore Fwy. (U.S. 101).

Bars and Cafés

Nightlife in San Francisco is as varied as the city's personal ads. Everyone from "dominant duo looking for a third" to "shy first-timer" can find places to go on a Saturday (or even a Wednesday) night.

Café du Nord, 2170 Market St. (861-5016), between Church and Sanchez. Painfully hip. Huge and glamorous. Live music nightly. Beers $3.25. No cover before 9pm. Happy hour 4-7pm. Open daily 4pm-2am. Must be 21.

Noc Noc, 557 Haight (861-5811). Everyclub: hang with goths, raver-chicks, Haight hippies, and Eurotrash. Intimate corners make this a good place for a tête-a-tête. Never a cover. Pints $2.50 until 8pm. Open daily 5pm-2am.

The Elbo Room, 647 Valencia St. (552-7788), near 17th, in the Mission. Cover (usually $3) for funk, jazz, and indie music. Dancing upstairs only. It's becoming less roomy while getting more popular. Open daily 5pm-2am.

Café Istanbul, 525 Valencia St. (863-8854), between 16th and 17th, in the Mission. Traditional Middle Eastern music, coffees, teas, food, and low seating under the blue drapery ceiling. Sip *chai* ($1.50) or a rose syrup latté ($2). Frequent belly-dance shows. Open Fri.-Sat. 11am-4am, Sun.-Thurs. 11am-11pm.

Muddy Waters, 521 Valencia St. (863-8005), in the Mission. Go here to bitch about how trendy the Mission is becoming. Cappuccino $1.50, mocha $2. Open Mon.-Fri. 6:30am-midnight, Sat.-Sun. 7:30am-midnight.

Brainwash, 1122 Folsom St. (861-FOOD/3663 or 431-WASH/9274). Where to go to socialize while spinning your dirty Calvins. On the SoMa club A-list. Free live music Wed. and Sat. nights. Open Sun.-Thurs. 7:30am-11pm, Fri.-Sat. 7:30am-1am.

Vesuvio Café, 255 Columbus Ave. (362-3370), in North Beach. You can watch poets and chess players from a balcony in this beat bar or you can hide from them in some dark corner. Drinks average $3.25-6. Open daily 6am-2am.

Tosca, 242 Columbus Ave. (986-9651). No-frills, red vinyl bar with great cappuccino, opera on the juke, and a quietly cool attitude that makes other bars look like they're trying too hard. Swanky drinks. Open daily 5pm-2am.

Clubs

The San Francisco club scene rages hardcore. Unfortunately for young 'uns, most establishments admit only the 21+ crowd and card hard. For a direct line into local nightlife, pick up a *Guardian*, or try the **"be-at" line** (626-4087; 24hrs.).

DNA Lounge, 375 11th St. (626-1409), at Harrison, in SoMa. Both hip live music and funkalicious jammin'. The best night for dancing is Wed. Funk, house, and soul. Comfy couches. Cover varies but usually doesn't exceed $10. Open daily until 4am. Must be 21.

Club DV8, 540 Howard St. (957-1730), in SoMa. Three floors of sheer dance mania. Music from house to gothic, but the crowd is strictly hip-o-rama. For the best dancing, stick to the 3rd floor "osmosis." 18 and over on Tues.-Wed. Disco flashbacks on Thurs. Cover ranges from free to $10. Open Tues.-Sun. 8pm-4am.

The Paradise Lounge, 1501 Folsom St. (861-6906), at 11th, in SoMa. With 3 stages, 2 floors, 5 bars, and up to 5 different bands a night, this club is one of those unique places where you feel equally comfortable in spike heels or Birkenstocks. Pool tables upstairs. Open daily 3pm-2am. Minimal cover. Must be 21.

Cesar's Latin Palace, 3140 Mission St. (648-6611), in the Mission. *Huge* Latin dance hall. If you don't know what salsa is, this is the place to learn. Over 1000 people show up on weekends. Dance yo' ass off. Parking available. Open Thurs.-Sun. 'til dawn. Must be 18.

Slims, 333 11th St. (621-3330), between Folsom and Harrison, in SoMa. Epicenter of the big SoMa blues 'n' jazz scene. Legendary house for American roots music, rock, and "world beat." Open nightly. Must be 21.

El Río, 3158 Mission St. (282-3325), in SoMa. The featured entertainment here is the Latin music every Sun. night, but rock bands play regularly as well. "World beat" on Fri. Cover $5-7 when there's live music. Open Tues.-Sat. 3pm-2am, Sun.-Mon. 3pm-midnight. Food served Sun. from 4-8pm. Must be 21.

CRASH Palace, 628 Divisadero St. (931-1914). This hot new club features lots of jazz. "World beat" on Sun., speakeasy on Tues. Live music nightly. No cover Mon.-Tues., $5-10 otherwise. Open daily 5pm-2am.

Gay and Lesbian Clubs

Gay nightlife in San Francisco rocks. Most of the popular bars can be found in the city's two traditionally gay areas—the Castro and Polk St. Most "straight" dance clubs in San Francisco feature at least one gay night a week. Also consult the *Guardian* or staffers at the **Gay Switchboard** (510-841-6224). While a woman in a gay club may feel merely apathy, a man in a lesbian club may feel some hostility.

The Café, 2367 Market St. (861-3846), in the Castro. One of San Francisco's most popular dance spots, the Café is the only daily bar for women ("and a few good men"). 2 levels with pinball, pool tables, and sundeck. DJs lay down fierce music. No cover. $1.25 beers Mon. 5pm-2am. Open daily noon-2am.

The Stud, 399 9th St. (863-6623). A classic gay club with great dance music. Mon. night is funk night. Wed. night is oldies night and the cheap beer flows freely. Thurs. is women's night. Cover $2-4. Open daily 5pm-2am, Fri.-Sat. after hours.

The Phoenix, 482 Castro St. (552-6827), at Market St. International gay dance bar with non-stop jammin'. DJ Michael and DJ Bobby Keith play disco tunes and house music. Friendly to women. No cover. Open daily 1pm-2am. Must be 21.

Club Townsend, 177 Townsend St. (974-6020), in SoMa. The Pleasure Dome, at Club Townsend every Sun. night 8pm-dawn, is San Francisco's largest gay dance club. Fri. and Sat. nights are gay as well. Cover $7. Open daily 10pm-6am.

Seasonal Events

Chinese New Year Celebration (982-3000), late Feb. in Chinatown.

Cherry Blossom Festival (563-2313), 2 weekends in April; Japantown.

San Francisco International Film Festival (931-3456), mid-April-mid-May. The oldest film festival in North America.

San Francisco Examiner Bay to Breakers (777-7770), mid-May. The largest road race (7.1 mi.) in the United States, done in inimitable San Francisco style.

19th San Francisco International Lesbian & Gay Film Festival (703-8650), mid- to late June. The world's largest presentation of lesbian and gay media.

Lesbian-Gay Freedom Parade (864-3733), late June.

San Francisco Jazz Festival (864-5449), late Oct.-early Nov. Includes shows throughout the city, tributes to masters, and the Jazz Film Fest.

■■■ BERKELEY

Although the peak of its political activism occurred in the 60s and 70s, U.C. Berkeley still deserves it's funky, iconoclastic reputation. Telegraph Avenue—the Champs-Elysées of the 60s—remains the home of street-corner soothsayers, hairless hippies, countless cafés, and itinerant street musicians. Berkeley is also home to some of the best food in the Bay, thanks to the presence of a sizable professional population willing to pay for the freshest and tastiest seasonal ingredients. Alice Waters' Chez Panisse is the landmark home of California Cuisine.

PRACTICAL INFORMATION

Tourist Office: Berkeley Convention and Visitors Bureau, 1834 University Ave. (549-7040), at Martin Luther King, Jr. Way. Open Mon.-Fri. 9am-5pm. 24 hrs. **Visitor Hotline** 549-8710. **U.C. Berkeley Visitor Center,** 101 University Hall, 2200 University Ave. (642-5215). Open Mon.-Fri. 9am-5pm.

Public Transportation: Bay Area Rapid Transit (BART; 465-2278) stops at Shattuck Ave. and Center St., close to the western edge of the university, about 7 blocks from the Student Union. $2 to downtown San Francisco. The **Perimeter Shuttle** (642-5149; 25¢) connects the BART station with the university campus (shuttles run Sept.-June Mon.-Fri. 7am-7pm every 8min.). BART also stops at Virginia and Sacramento St. (north) and at Ashby St. (west). **Alameda County Transit (AC Transit;** 800-559-4636 or 839-2882) buses #15, 40, 43, and 51 all run from the BART stop to downtown Oakland. ($1.25; seniors, ages 5-12; and disabled 60¢; under 5 free; transfers (25¢) valid for 1hr.).

Taxis: Yellow A I Cab, 843-1111. Available 24hrs.

Emergency: 911.

Post Office: 2000 Allston Way (649-3100). Open Mon.-Fri. 8:30am-6pm, Sat. 10am-2pm. **ZIP code:** 94704. **Area code:** 510.

Berkeley lies across the bay northeast of San Francisco, just north of Oakland. Reach the city by BART from downtown San Francisco or by car (**I-80** or **Rte. 24**). Berkeley is sandwiched between a series of rolling hills to the east and San Francisco Bay to the west. The **University of California** campus stretches into the hills, but most of the university's buildings are on the west side of campus. **Telegraph Ave.,** which runs south from the Student Union, is the spiritual center of town. The **downtown** area, around the BART station, contains several businesses as well as the public library and central post office. The **Gourmet Ghetto** covers the area along Shattuck Ave. and Walnut St., between Virginia and Rose St. The **Fourth Street Center,** west of campus and by the bay, is home to great eats and window shopping. Northwest of campus, **Solano Ave.** offers countless ethnic restaurants and bohemian bounty. Avoid walking alone on Berkeley's streets at night.

Crossing the bay by **BART** ($2-2.20) is quick and easy; driving in the city is difficult and frustrating.

ACCOMMODATIONS

It is surprisingly difficult to sleep cheaply in Berkeley. The **Bed and Breakfast Network** (540-5123) coordinates 20 B&Bs in the East Bay. Do it as a daytrip.

Travel Inn, 1461 University Ave. (848-3840), 2 blocks from the North Berkeley BART station, 7 blocks west of campus. Newly redone rooms are clean and comfortable. All have TVs and phones. Free parking. Singles $32-40; doubles $45-50 depending on season and number of people. Key deposit $5.

YMCA, 2001 Allston Way (848-6800), at Milvia. Recently renovated. Prices include tax and use of pool, bed, linens, phone, and basic fitness facilities. All share hall baths. Registration daily 8am-9:30pm. Check-out noon. No curfew. 14-day max. stay. Singles $25, rooms for couples $30.

YMCA International Youth Hostel, 2001 Allston Way (848-6800), at Milvia. Open May-Aug. only. Same facilities as YMCA, but the tiny rooms provide low stretcher cots—no linens or beds. TV room, hall baths. Check-in 6:30pm, check-out 9am. Lockout 9am-6pm. Ages 18-30 only. $14-16 per night.

Golden Bear Motel, 1620 San Pablo Ave. (525-6770), at Cedar. Located further away from campus but has recently painted bedrooms and clean white bedspreads. Check-out noon. Room with queen-size bed (for 1 or 2) $41; room with 2 beds $46; room with 2 queen-size beds $49.

FOOD

Berkeley is a relatively small area with a wide range of excellent budget eateries. For Berkeley's best food, head downtown to **Shattuck Ave.** or north to **Solano Ave.**

Anne's Soup Kitchen, 2498 Telegraph Ave. (548-8885), at Dwight. *The* place for breakfast in Berkeley. Towering portions. Special includes 2 whole wheat pancakes with bacon and eggs or with homefries ($3.55). Open daily 8am-7pm.

Café Fanny, 1603 San Pablo Ave. (524-5447). Alice Waters' most recent venture. Lots of standing room and benches near the outdoor trellis. Famous for bowls of *café au lait* ($2). Open Mon.-Fri. 7am-3pm, Sat. 8am-4pm, Sun. 9am-3pm.

Plearn, 2050 University Ave.(841-2148), at Shattuck, 1 block west of campus. Constant winner of best Thai in the Bay Area. Curries $7. Plentiful vegetarian options. Lunch specials 11:30am-3:30pm for $4.25. Open daily 11:30am-10pm.

Blondie's Pizza, 2340 Telegraph Ave. (548-1129). Try this popular student hangout if only for the peace poppy atmosphere. Pizza and coke special $2. Open Mon.-Thurs. 10:30am-1am, Fri.-Sat. 10:30am-2am, Sun. noon-midnight.

The Blue Nile, 2525 Telegraph Ave. (540-6777). Winner of Best African food in *SF Focus* magazine, 1993. Huge portions of authentic Ethiopian food in a lavish setting. Customers eat with their hands. Multitudinous vegetarian dishes. Lunch around $5, dinner $6-7.50. Open Mon.-Sat. 11:30am-10pm, Sun. 4-10pm.

SIGHTS

In 1868, the private College of California and the public Agricultural, Mining, and Mechanical Arts College coupled to give birth to the **University of California.** Because Berkeley was the first of the nine University of California campuses, it is permitted the nickname "Cal." The school has an enrollment of over 30,000 students and more than 1000 full professors. Berkeley also boasts more Nobel laureates per capita than any other city. Berkeley's uniqueness has made it home to a student body of unparalleled diversity.

The staff at the **Visitor Information Center,** 101 University Hall, 2200 University Ave. (642-5215; open Mon.-Fri. 8:30am-4:30pm), provides free maps and information booklets (guided campus tours last 1½ hrs. Mon., Wed., Fri. 10am and 1pm.).

Sather Tower (much better known as the **Campanile,** Italian for "bell tower"), a 1914 monument to Berkeley benefactor Jane Krom Sather, is the most dramatic campus attraction. It was modeled after the clock tower in Venice's St. Mark's Sq. You can ride to the observation level of the 307-ft.-tall tower for a stupendous view (50¢). The tower's 61-bell carillon is played most weekdays, at 7:50am, noon, and 6pm. The **University Art Museum (UAM),** 2626 Bancroft Way (642-0808), at College, holds a diverse and enticing permanent collection and hosts different exhibits yearly. Check out the new galleries housing Asian art. Within the museum, the **Pacific Film Archives (PFA;** 642-1124), with one of the nation's largest film libraries, is a uniquely rich museum of cinematic art (open Wed. and Fri.-Sun. 11am-5pm, Thurs. 11am-9pm.; $6; students, over 64 and ages 6-17 $4. Free Thurs. 11am-noon and 5-9pm).

The **Lawrence Hall of Science** (642-5132), a concrete octagon standing above the northeast corner of campus, shares honors with San Francisco's Exploratorium as the finest science museum in the Bay Area. Take bus #8 or #65 from the Berkeley BART station; it's a 1-hr. walk from campus (open Mon.-Fri. 10am-5pm, Sat.-Sun. 10am-5pm; $5, seniors, students, and ages 7-18 $4, ages 3-6 $2).

The **Botanical Gardens** (642-3343), on Centennial Dr. in Strawberry Canyon, contain over 10,000 varieties of plant life. Berkeley's Mediterranean climate, moderated by coastal fog, provides an outstanding setting for this 33-acre garden (open daily 10am-4pm; free, parking permit $1 for 2 hrs.). The **Berkeley Rose Garden** on Euclid Ave. at Eunice St., north of campus contains a lovely collection of roses. Built by the WPA during the Depression, the garden spills from one terrace to another in a vast semicircular amphitheater (open May-Sept. dawn-dusk).

The **Judah Magnes Museum,** 2911 Russell St. (849-2710), displays a leading collection of Judaica (open Sun.-Thurs. 10am-4pm; free). The **Julia Morgan Theater,** 2640 College Ave. (box office 845-8542), is housed in a beautiful former church designed by its namesake and notable for its graceful and unusual mix of materials.

People's Park, on Haste St., one block off Telegraph, is a kind of unofficial museum. A mural depicts the 60s struggle between the city and local activists over whether to leave the park alone or to develop it commercially. During the conflict, then-governor Ronald Reagan sent in the National Guard, an action which led to the death of a Berkeley student. Three years ago, despite heated protests, the city and the university bulldozed part of the park to build beach volleyball courts, basketball courts, and restrooms. The park is patrolled by police officers 24 hrs.

Tilden Regional Park is part of the extensive East Bay park system. Hiking, biking, running, and riding trails crisscross the park and provide impressive views of the Bay Area. **Lake Anza** is a popular swimming spot and is overrun with screaming kids ($2, lake open 10am-dusk during summer).

ENTERTAINMENT

Hang out with procrastinating students in front of or inside the **Student Union** (642-4636). **The Underground** (642-3825) contains a ticket office, an arcade, bowling alleys, **fußball tables,** and pool tables (open Mon.-Fri. 8am-6pm, Sat. 10am-6pm; winter Mon.-Fri. 8am-10pm, Sat. 10am-6pm). The **Bear's Lair,** 2425 Bancroft (843-0373), is *the* popular campus hangout on sunny Friday afternoons, when quarts of beer are $2.75 (open Mon.-Thurs. 9am-10pm, Fri. 10am-midnight, Sat.-Sun. 10am-10pm; summer 10am-6pm daily). **Café Strada,** 2300 College Ave. (843-5282), at Bancroft, is the glittering jewel of the culinary-intellectual scene. Espresso drinks are $0.85-1.05, cappuccino $1.10, scones and large cinnamon rolls $1 (open Mon.-Fri. 7am-11pm, Sat. 7am-11:30pm, Sun. 8am-11:30pm). **Blakes,** 2367 Telegraph Ave. (848-0886), at Durant, was named "best bar in Berkeley" by the *Daily Californian,* Happy hour daily 4-6pm and 8-10pm. Beverages start at $2 (open Mon.-Fri. 11:30am-2am, Sat.-Sun. 9:30-2am; cover $2-5; be 21). **Jupiter,** 2181 Shattuck Ave. (843-8277), is across the street from the BART station. Table-bowling, beer garden, and terrific pizza ($6 for a loaded 8-in. pie) will keep you busy. International beers on tap (open Mon.-Thurs. 11:30am-1am, Fri. 11:30am-1:30am, Sat.-Sun. noon-1:30am; live music Fri.-Sun., no cover).

■■■ SAN MATEO COAST

Route 1, the **Pacific Coast Highway** winds along the San Mateo County Coast from San Francisco to the Big Basin Redwoods State Park. This expanse of shore is scattered with beautiful, isolated, sandy beaches. Although most people find it too cold for swimming (even in summer), the sands offer a royal stroll along the water's edge. State beaches charge $4, with admission valid for the entire day at all state parks—keep your receipt. About 2 mi. south of Pacifica (take samTrans bus #1L) is **Gray Whale Cove State Beach,** a privately owned nudist beach off Rte. 1. You must be 18 and pay $5 to join the fun (but where do you keep your ID???).

If you like pamphlets, you'll love the **San Mateo County Coast Convention and Visitors Center,** Seabreeze Plaza, 111 Anza Blvd., Suite 410 (800-28-VISIT/288-4748), in Burlingame (open Mon.-Fri. 8:30am-5pm). **San Mateo County Transit (samTrans),** 945 California Dr. (800-660-4287), has service from Burlingame to Half Moon Bay (85¢, seniors 25¢, ages 5-17 35¢). **Area code:** 415.

Half Moon Bay is an old coastal community 29 mi. south of San Francisco. Locals complain that it's becoming too commercialized, but visitors won't notice the change. The fishing and farming hamlet of **San Gregorio** rests 10 mi. south of Half Moon Bay. **San Gregorio Beach** is a delightful destination; walk to its southern end to find little caves in the shore rocks (open 8am-sunset; day use $4, seniors $3). To find a less-frequented beach, visit **Unsigned Turnout, Marker 27.35.** It's difficult to find without aid; keep an eye out for mysteriously vacant cars parked along the highway. A trip up Rte. 84 will take you into **La Honda,** where Ken Kesey lived with his merry pranksters in the 60s, before it got too small and they took off across the U.S. in a psychedelic bus. A few decades ago, residents of **Pescadero** created the **olallieberry** (oh-LA-la-behr-ee) by crossing a blackberry, a loganberry, and a youngberry. Pick a peck at **Phipp's Ranch,** 2700 Pescadero Rd. (879-0787), in Pescadero, (mid-June-July 10am-7pm. 85¢ per lb.) The **Pescadero Marsh** shelters such migratory birds as the elegant blue heron, often seen poised on its spindly legs.

Año Nuevo State Reserve (379-0595), 7 mi. south of Pigeon Point and 27 mi. south of Half Moon Bay, is the mating place of the 13-15-ft.-long **elephant seal.** December to March is breeding season, when males compete for beach space next to the more pleasingly hideous females. To see this unforgettable show (Dec. 15-Mar. 31), you must make reservations (8 weeks in advance recommended) by calling MISTIX (800-444-7275), since access to the park is limited. Tickets go on sale November 15 and are generally sold out by the end of the month, so plan ahead (The park is open daily 8am-sunset; last permits issued 4pm.)

The **Pigeon Point Lighthouse Hostel (HI-AYH;** 879-0633), 6 mi. south of Pescadero on the highway and 20 mi. south of Half Moon Bay, near the lighthouse, is almost an attraction in itself. This 52-bed beauty operates a hot tub in the old lightkeeper's quarters. (Check-in 4:30-9:30pm. Doors locked at 11pm. Check-out and chores completed by 9:30am. Hostel closed 9:30am-4:30pm. Dorm-style beds $11, nonmembers $14.) **Point Montara Lighthouse Hostel (HI-AYH;** 728-7177) is a wholesome 45-bed facility on windswept Lighthouse Point, 25 mi. south of San Francisco, 4 mi. north of Half Moon Bay. Laundry room will keep you squeaky clean. (Check-in 4:30-9:30pm. Curfew 11pm-7am. $9-11, nonmembers $12-14.)

3 Amigos, 200 N. Cabrillo Hwy. (Rte. 1; 726-6080), at Kelly, in Half Moon Bay, is wholeheartedly recommended for its savory Mexican fare. Casual atmosphere is perfect for a meal after a day beachcombing (quesadillas $1; jumbo vegetarian burrito $3; open daily 9am-midnight). **The Flying Fish Grill,** 99 San Mateo Road (712-1125), on Rte. 92 close to Rte. 1 at the southwest corner of Main St, in Half Moon Bay, is an inexpensive, tasty way to sample the delicious seafood of the coast. Fishburger and fries ($4.35) or a pint of clam chowder ($4.25) will satisfy a seafarer's appetite (open Tues.-Sun. 11am-8pm).

■■■ MARIN COUNTY

Home of Dana Carvey, 560 acres of spectacular redwood forest, and Jerry Garcia's eternal memory, Marin County (mah-RIN) boasts a bizarre blend of outstanding natural beauty, trendiness, liberalism, and wealth. Much of Marin can be explored in a daytrip from San Francisco by car, bus, or ferry. Muir Woods National Monument with its coastal redwoods, Marin Headlands, Mt. Tamalpais (tam-uhl-PAY-iss) State Park, and the Point Reyes National Seashore offer trails for mountain bikers and hikers looking for a day's adventure or a two week trek.

PRACTICAL INFORMATION

Tourist Office: Marin County Chamber of Commerce, 30 N. San Pedro Rd. #150 (472-7470). Open Mon.-Fri. 9am-5pm; phone hours Mon.-Fri. 1-5pm. **Sausalito Chamber of Commerce,** 333 Caledonia St. (332-7262). Open Mon.- Fri. 9am-5pm. **San Rafael Chamber of Commerce,** 818 5th Ave. (454-4163). Open Mon.-Fri. 9am-noon and 1-5pm.

Buses: Greyhound, 850 Tamalpais St. (453-0795), in San Rafael. To San Francisco: 2 buses per day, $5, leaving at 4:45am and 5pm.

Public Transportation: Golden Gate Transit (453-2100; 332-6600 in San Francisco). Daily bus service between San Francisco and Marin County via the Golden Gate Bridge, as well as local service in Marin. Buses #10, 20, 28, 30, and 50 provide service to Marin from San Francisco's Transbay Terminal at 1st St. and Mission. The **Golden Gate Ferry** (923-2000) provides transportation between Sausalito or Larkspur and San Francisco from the Ferry Bldg. at the end of Market St. Mon.-Fri. $2.50, Sat.-Sun. $4.25; seniors, youths, and disabled ½-price.

Taxis: Radio Cab (800-464-7234) serves all of Marin County.

Car Rental: Budget, 20 Bellam Blvd. (457-4282), San Rafael. $30 per day, unlimited mileage. Will rent to ages 21-25 at no extra charge.

Crisis Line: Rape Crisis, 924-2100. 24 hrs.

Emergency: 911.

Post Office: San Rafael Main Office, 40 Bellam Ave. (459-0944). Open Mon.-Fri. 8:30am-5pm, Sat. 10am-1pm. **ZIP code:** 94915. **Area code:** 415.

The Marin peninsula lies at the north end of San Francisco Bay, and is connected to the city by **U.S. 101** via the Golden Gate Bridge. **Rte. 1** creeps north along the Pacific to the Sonoma Coast. The Richmond-San Rafael Bridge connects Marin to the East Bay via **I-580.** The eastern side of the county cradles the settlements of **Sausalito, Larkspur, San Rafael, Terra Linda, Ignacio,** and **Novato.** These towns line U.S. 101, which runs north-south through Marin. West Marin is more rural, with rolling hills and fog-filled coastal valleys. Breathtaking **Rte. 1** runs through **Stinson Beach, Olema, Inverness,** and **Pt. Reyes National Seashore** (from south to north). **Sir Francis Drake Blvd.** runs from U.S. 101 in Larkspur west through the San Geronimo Valley. It passes through the towns of **Greenbrae, Kentfield, Ross, San Anselmo, Fairfax, Woodacre,** and **San Geronimo** on the way to Pt. Reyes and its rendezvous with Rte. 1.

ACCOMMODATIONS AND CAMPING

HI-Marin Highlands (HI-AYH), 331-2777. Located in historic 1907 buildings in the Marin Headlands, 6mi. south of Sausalito and 10mi. from downtown San Francisco. Those with cars coming from the north should take the Sausalito exit off U.S. 101 and follow the signs into the Golden Gate Recreation Area. From San Francisco, take U.S. 101 to the Alexander Ave. exit. Beautiful location. Game room, pool table, spacious kitchen, common room, and laundry facilities. Bring a lock for their lockers. Check in 9:30am-11:30pm. Curfew 12:30am. Linen rental $1. Members and nonmembers $11. Children under 13 ½-price.

Point Reyes Hostel (HI-AYH), 663-8811, sits 6mi. off Limantour Rd. in the Pt. Reyes National Seashore. By car, take the Seashore exit west from Rte. 1, then take Bear Valley Rd. to Limantour Rd. and drive 6mi. into the park. You're more likely to get a last-minute bed here than in the Golden Gate Hostel. The hostel is spread between two cabins on a spectacular site. Hiking, wildlife, bird-watching, and Limantour Beach are all within walking distance. Kitchen and cozy common room. Registration 4:30-9:30pm. Closed 9:30am-4:30pm. Sleep sheet and towel $1 each. Members and nonmembers $11. Chore expected.

Marin Headlands, northwest of the Golden Gate Bridge. 15 campsites; most are primitive. Two sites have running water; one site, Kirby Cove, has a cooking area. Reserve as much as 90 days in advance by calling the **visitors center** (331-1540; 9:30am-noon). Permits are required; sites are free. The Golden Gate Youth Hostel (see above) allows use of showers and kitchen ($2 each). Free outdoor cold showers available at Rodeo Beach (in the Headlands).

Mt. Tamalpais State Park, 801 Rte. 1 (388-2070). 16 walk-in campsites ($14; first come, first served), a group camp, and **Steep Ravine,** an "environmental camp" with cabins ($30 for up to 5 people) and tent sites ($9). Tent sites with fire pits, no showers. Cabins have wood-burning stoves but no running water or electricity. Make cabin reservations 90 days in advance (MISTIX 800-444-7275) or get there early. Reservation fee $6.75.

FOOD

Eco-head Marinites take their fruit juices, tofu, and non-fat double-shot cappuccino very seriously. A fun, cheaper option is to raid the area's many organic groceries and picnic in one of Marin's countless parks.

Mama's Royal Café, 387 Miller Ave. (388-3261), in Mill Valley. A local fave. Looks like gramma's attic after an explosion. Try the Enchilada El Syd ($6) or the Groove Burger ($5.45). Huge breakfast selection. Brunch with live music Sat. and Sun. Open Mon. 7:30am-3pm, Tues.-Fri. 7:30am-2:30pm, Sat.-Sun. 7:30am-3pm.

Stuffed Croissant, 43 Caledonia St. (332-7103), in Sausalito. Laid-back bakery-style sandwich shop (sandwiches $3-6). Sit at the counter or take it outside. Vegetarian options. Open Mon. 6:30am-3pm, Tues.-Sat. 7:30am-10pm, Sun. 7:30am-8pm.

The Town's Deli, 501 Caledonia St. (331-3311), in Sausalito. Sandwiches $2.50-3.75. Known for their roasted chicken (½-chicken $3). Killer picnic fare. Open Mon.-Sat. 8am-7pm, Sun. 8am-6pm.

SIGHTS

Marin's attractions range from the excellent hiking trails that criss-cross the county's parks and beaches to unique shopping and dining opportunities in the pleasant towns of Tiburon and Sausalito. **Sausalito** lies at the extreme southeastern tip of Marin. A complicated, bizarre, and somewhat showy houseboat community occupies the harbor, fostering such personalities as the **Pope of Soap,** a man who builds sculptures out of soap bubbles and then puts the unsuspecting inside of them.

The undeveloped, fog-shrouded hills just to the west of the Golden Gate Bridge comprise the **Marin Headlands.** The **Marine Mammal Center** (289-7325) offers a sobering look at the rehabilitation of beached marine mammals (open daily 10am-4pm; donation requested). Nearly all of the gorgeous headlands are open to hikers, and camping is allowed in designated areas.

Muir Woods National Monument, a 560-acre strand of primeval coastal redwoods, is located about 5 mi. west along Rte. 1 off U.S. 101. The **visitors center** (388-2595) will help you find a trail suited to your abilities. Nearby are **Muir Beach** and **Muir Beach Lookout** (open sunrise-9pm). Adjacent to Muir Woods is the isolated, largely undiscovered, and utterly beautiful **Mount Tamalpais State Park.** The heavily forested park has a number of challenging trails that lead to the top of **Mount Tam** (the highest peak in the county) and to a natural stone amphitheater.

Encompassing 100 mi. of coastline along most of the western side of Marin, the **Point Reyes National Seashore** juts into the Pacific from the eastern end of the submerged Pacific Plate. Sir Francis Drake Blvd. runs from San Rafael through Olema, where it crosses Rte. 1, all the way to Pt. Reyes itself. In summer an explosion of colorful wildflowers attracts surging crowds.

Limantour Beach, at the end of Limantour Rd., west of the seashore headquarters, is one of the area's best beaches. **San Rafael,** the largest city in Marin County, lies along U.S. 101 on the bay. Architecture buffs can check out the **Marin Civic Center,** 3501 Civic Center Dr. (499-7407), off U.S. 101. Frank Lloyd Wright designed this unusual but functional open-air building which looms over the highway. An information kiosk in the lobby supplies brochures and pamphlets; phone ahead for a tour (open Mon.-Fri. 9am-5pm).

■■■ WINE COUNTRY

Wine is what brings most visitors to the quiet vineyards of the Napa and Sonoma valleys, and with good reason—the area's wines are regarded highly by connoisseurs both in the U.S. and abroad. Napa is better known; Sonoma is older and less crowded. Green fields of gnarled grape vines stretch in all directions and scenic mountain views tower along the horizon.

PRACTICAL INFORMATION

Tourist Office: Napa Visitors Center, 1310 Town Center (226-7459), on 1st St. Eager staff has brochures, free tasting tickets, and the *California Visitors Review* (free). Open daily 9am-5pm, phones closed Sat.-Sun. **Sonoma Valley Visitors Bureau,** 453 E. 1st St. (996-1090), in the central plaza. Open daily 10am-7pm.

Buses: Greyhound, 2 per day through the valley. The bus stops in Napa at 9:45am and 6pm in front of Napa State Hospital, 2100 Napa-Vallejo Hwy. Also stops in Yountville, St. Helena, and Calistoga. Closest bus station is Vallejo (643-7661).

Public Transportation: Napa City Bus, 1151 Pearl St. (800-696-6443 or 255-7631; TDD 226-9722). Provides transport throughout the valley and to Vallejo. Fare 75¢, seniors and disabled 35¢, ages 13-18 50¢; 1 transfer free. Buses run Mon.-Fri. 6:45am-6:30pm, Sat. 7:45am-6pm. **Sonoma County Transit** (576-7433 or 800-345-7433) serves the entire county (Mon.-Fri., 3 on Sat.; $1.90, students $1.55, over 60 and disabled 95¢, under 6 free).

Car Rental: Budget, 407 Soscol Ave. (224-7845), in Napa. $29 per day. Must be 21 with credit card.

Bicycle Rental: St. Helena Cyclery, 1156 Main St. (255-3377), in Napa. Bikes $25 per day, including maps, helmet, lock, and picnic bag. Open Mon.-Sat. 9:30am-5:30pm, Sun. 10am-5pm.

Crisis Line: Sexual Assault Crisis Line, 258-8000. 24 hrs.

Emergency: 911.

Post Office: 1625 Trancas St. (255-1621). Open Mon.-Fri. 8:30am-5pm. **ZIP code:** 94558. **Sonoma,** 617 Broadway (996-2459), at Patten St. Open Mon.-Fri. 8:30am-5pm. **ZIP code:** 95476. **Area code:** 707.

CALIFORNIA

Rte. 29 runs through the middle of Napa valley from **Napa** at its southern end, to **Calistoga** in the north, passing **St. Helena** and **Yountville** in between. Napa is 25 min. away from Sonoma on **Rte. 12.** The best way to see Napa is by **bicycle** since the valley is dead level and only 30 mi. long. The Sonoma Valley runs between **Sonoma** and **Glen Ellen,** with **Rte. 12** traversing its length.

ACCOMMODATIONS AND CAMPING

B&Bs and most hotels are a budget-breaking $60-225 per night. If you have a car, it's better to stay in Santa Rosa, Sonoma, or Petaluma, where budget lodging is more plentiful. Or you could just get drunk, barf, and pass out in the street. (*Let's Go* does not recommend this, however.)

Triple S Ranch, 4600 Mountain Home Ranch Rd. (942-6730). Beautiful setting in the mountains above Calistoga. Take Rte. 29 toward Calistoga, and turn left past downtown onto Petrified Forest Rd. Pool, restaurant, and bar. Check-in 3pm. Singles $40; doubles $54. $7 per additional person. Call in advance. Open April-Dec.

Silverado Motel, 500 Silverado Trail (253-0892), in Napa near Soscol Ave. Clean, fresh, newly remodeled rooms with kitchenette, cable TV. Registration noon-6pm. Check-out 11am. Singles $40-45; doubles $40-48.

Motel 6, 5135 Montero Way (664-9090), in Petaluma. From San Francisco, take the Old Redwood/Petaluma Blvd. exit off U.S. 101. A/C, small pool, bed. Singles $32; second person $6, third and fourth person $3 each.

Sugarloaf Ridge State Park, 2605 Adobe Canyon Rd. (833-5712), near Kenwood. 50 sites. By far the most beautiful place to camp in Sonoma Valley. Flush toilets, running water, no showers. Sites $14. Call MISTIX (800-444-7275) to reserve.

Napa County Fairgrounds, 1435 Oak St. (942-5111), in Calistoga. First-come, first-camped. Shaded sites, with showers and electricity. $15 covers 2 adults. Closed June 28-July 5 for county fair. Check-out noon. Open 24hrs.

FOOD

Sit-down meals are often expensive here, but Napa and its neighboring communities support numerous delis where you can buy inexpensive picnic supplies. The **Sonoma Market,** 520 W. Napa St. (996-0563), in the Sonoma Valley Center, is an old-fashioned grocery store with deli sandwiches ($3-4.25) and very fresh produce.

Villa Corona, 3614 Bel Aire Plaza (257-8685), in Napa, off of Trancas, behind the Citibank building. Tiny, with a piñata-speckled ceiling. Large burrito with the works $4.50. Pastries 45-95¢. Open daily 9am-8pm.

Murphy's Irish Pub, 464 1st St. E. (935-0660 or 996-4359 events line), in Sonoma. Cozy place serving pub grub. Irish stew is made from Sonoma county lamb and comes with Sonoma French Bakery sourdough roll ($6.50). Live Irish music 8pm Thurs.-Sat., 6pm Sun. Open daily 11am-11pm.

Guigni's, 1227 Main St. (963-3421), in St. Helena. Friendly grocery store with sandwiches ($3.55). Lots of locals. Eclectic decorations on the walls. Open Mon.-Fri. 9am-5pm, Sat.-Sun. 9am-6pm.

WINERIES

There are more than 250 wineries in Napa County, nearly two-thirds of which are in Napa Valley. Many wineries now charge for wine tastings, but free tours and tastings are still available. The fee is usually small ($3-6), and includes a tour with three or four tastes. The majority of smaller wineries require that visitors phone ahead to ensure that someone is around to pour the wine. Visitors unfamiliar with U.S. drinking laws should be forewarned: you must be 21 or older to purchase or drink alcohol, which includes tastings at vineyards. And, yes, they do card.

Domaine Chandon, 1 California Dr. (944-2280), in Yountville. One of the finest tours in the valley. Owned by Moët Chandon of France. 45-min. tours hourly 11am-5pm. Tastings by the glass ($3-5; includes bread and cheese). Open daily 11am-6pm; Nov.-April Wed.-Sun. 11am-6pm.

Robert Mondavi Winery, 7801 St. Helena Hwy. (963-9611), 8mi. north of Napa in Oakville. The best free tour with tasting for the completely unknowledgeable. Spanish-style buildings, beautiful grounds. Tours 10am-4pm on the hour. It's a good idea to call ahead. Open daily 9am-5pm; Oct.-April 11am-4:30pm.

Sterling Vineyards, 1111 Dunaweal Lane (942-3344), 7 mi. north of St. Helena (go right on Dunaweal from Rte. 29 north), in Calistoga. Perhaps the most visually arresting of the valley's vineyards. Aerial tram to vineyard, tour, and tasting $6. Limited wheelchair access. Terrace for picnicking. Open daily 10:30am-4:30pm.

Hakusan Sake Gardens, 1 Executive Way (800-HAKUSAN/425-8726 or 258-6160). Take Rte. 29 south to the Rte. 12 intersection, turn left on North Kelly, then left onto Executive Way. A pleasant self-guided tour through the Japanese gardens provides a delightful respite from the power-chugging at the vineyards. Generous, free pourings of *Hakusan Sake,* known as *Haki Sake* to locals. Open daily 9am-6pm, Nov.-March 9am-5pm.

Beringer Vineyards, 2000 Main St. (963-4812), off Rte. 29, in St. Helena. The first vineyard to offer tours, and everyone's favorite. Free tours include Rhine House, a landmark mansion, and a tasting session.Try the reserve room on the second floor of the Rhine House. Generous samples cost $2-3. Open daily 9:30am-5pm.

Ravenswood, 18701 Gehricke Rd. (938-1960), off Lovall Valley Rd., in Sonoma. Produces some of the valley's best *vino,* strongly recommended by the locals. The picnic area and the view alone are worth the trip. Summer weekend BBQs ($4.75-8.75). Free tasting and tours by appointment. Open daily 10am-4:30pm.

NORTHERN CALIFORNIA

■■■ AVENUE OF THE GIANTS

About 6 mi. north of **Garberville** off U.S. 101, the **Avenue of the Giants** winds its way through a 31-mi.-long canopy of the largest living creatures this side of sea level. The tops of the mammoth trees cannot be seen from inside a car—pull over and get out to avoid straining your neck, wrecking your vehicle, and looking ridiculous. A slow meander through the forest is the best way to experience the redwoods' grandeur. The less crowded trails are found in the northern section of the park around **Rockefeller Forest,** which contains the largest grove of old-growth redwoods (200+ years) in the world. Be sure to pay your respects to the **Dyerville Giant,** located in the redwood graveyard at Founder's Grove, about midway through the Avenue of the Giants. It is difficult to appreciate the height of the trees while standing next to the upright trunk. However, because the Dyerville Giant rests on its side, over 60 human body-lengths long, it is possible to fully appreciate its size. Its **root ball** is three stories high. The **Garberville Chamber of Commerce,** 733 Redwood Dr. (923-2613; open daily 10am-5pm), will supply you with a free list of businesses on the Avenue, most of which you can safely dismiss as tourist traps. The **Eel River Redwoods Hostel,** 70400 U.S. 101 (925-6469), 16 mi. south on U.S. 101 in Leggett, is the place to hang your hat. This hosteling wonderland is located in an aromatic redwood grove right on the South Fork Eel River and provides access to a sauna, a jacuzzi, and a swimming hole (complete with inner tubes). If you're traveling by bus, ask the driver to stop at the hostel or get off at **Standish Hickey State Park (HI-AYH);** the hostel is a ½-mi. walk north from there ($12, nonmembers $14).

■■■ REDWOOD

While a simple tour of the appropriate sights and the Drive-thru Tree will certainly give visitors a few thrills and ample photo ops, it will also provide an overdose of fellow tourists. A less thorough, but more memorable way to experience **Redwood National Park** is to head down one of the less-travelled hiking paths into the quiet of the woods, where you can see the redwoods as they have been for thousands of years. As you listen to the quiet sounds of the creaking trees and burbling brooks, and inhale the wonderful mix of salty ocean air and trees, imagine a time when the only tourists were the wee furry forest animals.

PRACTICAL INFORMATION

Tourist Office: Redwood National Park Headquarters and Information Center, 1111 2nd St., Crescent City (464-6101; open daily 8am-5pm). **Redwood Information Center** (488-3461; open daily 9am-5pm), on U.S. 101, 1mi. south of Orick. **Crescent City Chamber of Commerce,** 1001 Front St., Crescent City (464-3174) provides cartloads of info. Open Mon.-Fri. 8am-7pm, Sat.-Sun. 9am-5pm; Labor Day-Memorial Day Mon.-Fri. 9am-5pm.

Buses: Greyhound, 1125 Northcrest Dr. (464-2807), in Crescent City. 2 buses per day going north and 2 going south. Buses can supposedly be flagged down at 3 places within the park: at the **Shoreline Deli** (488-5761), 1mi. south of Orick on U.S. 101; at **Paul's Cannery** in Klamath on U.S. 101; and in front of the **Redwood Hostel.** Beware, however, of capricious bus drivers who may decide to ignore you. Call the Greyhound station directly preceding your stop and ask the attendant to make the driver aware of your presence. Lockers available ($1 for 24hrs.). Open Mon.-Fri. 7-10am and 5-7:35pm, Sat. 7-10am and 7-7:45pm.

Emergency: 911.

Post Office: 751 2nd St. (464-2151), in **Crescent City.** Open Mon.-Fri. 8:30am-5pm, Sat. noon-3pm. **ZIP code:** 95531. Another office at 121147 U.S. 101 in **Orick.** Open Mon.-Fri. 8:30am-noon, 1-5pm. **ZIP code:** 95555. **Area code:** 707.

Crescent City, with park headquarters and a few basic services, stands at the park's northern end. The small town of Orick is situated at the southern limit and harbors an extremely helpful ranger station, a state park headquarters, and a handful of motels. **Rte. 101** connects the two, traversing most of the park. **Orick** in the south, **Klamath** in the middle, and **Crescent City** in the north, provide basic services and are home to a few motels.

ACCOMMODATIONS

The most pleasant pad is the **Redwood Youth Hostel (HI-AYH),** 14480 U.S. 101, Klamath 95548 (482-8265), at Wilson Creek Rd. This hostel, housed in the historic

Victorian DeMartin House, combines ultramodern facilities with a certain ruggedness. Its 30 beds and kitchen, dining room, and laundry facilities are all wheelchair accessible. There's a separate stove for vegetarians, a dozen recycling bins, two sundecks overlooking the ocean, staple foods for sale, and a laundry service. (Check-in 4:30-9:30pm. Curfew 11pm. Closed 9:30am-4:30pm, so you'll have to be an early riser. $10, under 18 with parent $5. Linen $1. Couples rooms available.) Reservations are recommended, and must be made by mail three weeks in advance.

Camp Marigold, 16101 U.S. 101 (482-3585 or 800-621-8513), in Klamath, has cabins with kitchens ($34 for 2 people) and is the best budget place in the area, after the Redwood Hostel. The well-kept, woodsy cabins are a pleasant alternative to the mundane budget-motel look. The **Park Woods Motel,** 121440 Rte. 101 (488-5175), in Orick, has clean, bare-bones rooms for the lowest prices in town ($35 for 1 or 2 people, and a 2-bedroom unit with full kitchen is only $40). **El Patio,** 655 H St. (464-5114), in Crescent City, offers decent rooms with wood-paneled early 70s look for a modest price. Some rooms have kitchenettes ($5 extra); all have TVs (singles $25, doubles $28; $2 key deposit).

FOOD

The best option for eating is probably to stop by the reasonably priced **Orick Market** (488-3225; open daily 8am-7pm), to stock up on supplies, and then find a spot by the ocean or the trees. **Alias Jones,** 983 3rd St. (465-6987), is known for serving hearty portions. For breakfast, try a cinnamon roll the size of a cake ($1.75) or a fruity muffin ($1.45; open Mon.-Fri. 7am-5:30pm, Sat. 7am-3pm). Your craving for buffalo meat can be satisfied at **Three Feathers Fry Bread,** 451 U.S. 101 (464-6003). These lean, tasty burgers will set you back $6, $4.50 for a regular cow burger. Forego the fries in favor of delicious, authentic fry bread $1.50 (open daily 11am-7pm). **Torero's,** 200 U.S. 101 (464-5712), dishes out filling, flavorful Mexican food in an not-so-authentic environment (lunch specials $5, entrees $4-8; open daily 11am-8pm). The **Palm Café,** Rte. 101 in downtown Orick (488-3381), dishes out basic diner food to local boys, but visitors are also welcome. Burgers with fries are $4.25. Homemade fruit pies ($2) are positively delicious.

SIGHTS

You can see Redwood National Park in just over an hour by car, but why rush? The park is divided into several regions, each of which have unique attractions and informations centers. Get out and stroll around—the redwoods should be experienced in person. The National Park Service conducts a symphony of organized activities for all ages. Pick up a detailed list of Junior Ranger programs and nature walks at any of the park's ranger stations or call the **Redwood Information Center** (488-3461) for details. Hikers should take particular care to wear protective clothing—**ticks** and **poison oak** thrive in these deep, dark places. Additionally, be on the lookout for the black bears and mountain lions that inhabit the southern region of the park.

Hiouchi Area This inland region sits in the northern part of the park along Rte. 199 and contains several excellent hiking trails. The **Stout Grove Trail** can be found by traveling 2 mi. north of Jedediah State Park on U.S. 101, and then 3 mi. along South Fork Rd., which becomes Douglas Park Dr. It's an easy ½-mi. walk, passing the park's widest redwood, (18ft. in diameter). The path is also accessible to people with disabilities; call 458-3310 for arrangements. Just 2 mi. south of Jedediah State Park on U.S. 101 lies the **Simpson-Reed Trail.** A tour map (25¢ from the ranger station) will guide you on this pleasant trek. The **Howland Hill Road** skirts the Smith River as it travels through redwood groves. This scenic stretch of road (no RVs or trailers allowed) begins near the Redwood Forest information center and ends at Crescent City.

Six Rivers National Forest lies directly east of Hiouchi. The Smith River rushes through rocky gorges as it winds its way from the mountains to the coast. This last wild and scenic river in California is the state's only major undammed river. Consequently, its salmon, trout, and steelhead fishing is heavenly.

Crescent City Area Crescent City calls itself the city "where the redwoods meet the sea." In 1964, a wrathful Mother Nature took this literally, when a *tsunami* caused by oceanic quakes brought 500mph winds and leveled the city. Nine blocks into the town, the powerful wave was still two stories high. The **Crescent City Visitors Center,** in the Chamber of Commerce at 1001 Front St. (464-3174), has lots o' brochures (open Mon.-Fri. 8am-7pm, Sat.-Sun. 9am-5pm; Labor Day-Memorial Day Mon.-Fri. 9am-5pm). Seven mi. south of the city lies the Del Norte Coast Redwoods State Park's **Mill Creek Campground** (464-9533), a state-level extension of the Redwood Forest. The park's magnificent ocean views—along with picnic areas, hiking trails, and nearby fishing—lure enough campers to fill the sites in summer (sites $14, primitive site free, day use $5.) The **Battery Point Lighthouse** (464-3089), on a causeway jutting out of Front St., houses a **museum** open only during low tide (open Wed.-Sun. 10am-4pm, tide permitting. $2, children 50¢).

Klamath Area To the north, the Klamath Area consists of a thin stretch of park land connecting Prairie Creek with Del Norte State Park. The main attraction here is the rugged and beautiful coastline. The **Klamath Overlook,** where Requa Rd. meets the Coastal Trail, is an excellent **whale-watching site.** The mouth of the **Klamath River** is a popular fishing spot (permit required) during the fall and spring when salmon spawn and during the winter when steelhead trout do the same. The town of Klamath has gone so far as to name itself the "Salmon and Steelhead Capital of the World." Sea lions in the spring and harbor seals in the summer congregate near the **Douglas Memorial Bridge,** or the part of it that survived a 1964 flood. Two golden bears guard each end of the bridge. **Coastal Drive** passes by the bridge and then continues along the ocean for 8 mi. of incredible views. The **Yurok Loop** (1mi.) is the best way for hikers to see the shoreline.

Prairie Creek Area The Prairie Creek Area, equipped with a **ranger station** and **state park campgrounds,** is perfect for hikers, who can experience 75 mi. of trails in the park's 14,000 acres. The **James Irvine Trail** (4.5 mi. one way) winds through magnificent redwoods, around clear and cold creeks, past numerous elk, through **Fern Canyon** (famed for its 50-ft. fern walls and crystalline creek), and by a stretch of the Pacific Ocean (wear shoes that you don't mind getting wet). The trail starts at the Prairie Creek Visitors Center. The less ambitious can elk-watch too, as elk love to graze on the meadow in front of the ranger station. The **Elk Prairie Trail** (1.4mi. one way) skirts the prairie and can be made into a loop by joining the nature trail. Elk may look peaceful, but they are best left unapproached. **Revelation** and **Redwood Access Trails** were designed to accommodate people with disabilities. **Big Tree Trail** is an easy walk, and its 306-ft. behemoth is a substitute for those who don't want to make the long trek to the tallest tree in the world.

Orick Area The Orick Area covers the southernmost section of the park. Its **visitors center** lies about 1 mi. south of Orick on U.S. 101 and ½ mi. south of the Shoreline Deli (the Greyhound bus stop). The main attraction is the tall trees grove, a 2½-mi. trail which begins 6 mi. from the ranger station. If you're driving, you'll need a **permit;** only 35 per day are issued on a first come, first served basis until 2pm. A minimum of three to four hours should be allowed for the trip. A **shuttle bus** ($7 donation per person) runs from the station to the tall trees trail (June 13-Sept. 7, 2 per day; May 23-June 12 and Sept. 8-20, 1 per day). From there, it's a 1.3-mi. hike down (about 30 min.) to the tallest redwoods in the park and, in fact, to the tallest known tree in the world (367.8 ft., one-third the height of the World Trade Center). If you're hiking in and hoping for a motorized return trip, book the shuttle before you go.

Orick itself (pop. 650) is a friendly town, overrun with souvenir stores selling "burl sculptures" (wood carvings pleasing to neither eye nor wallet). Nevertheless, the town provides some useful amenities. Along U.S. 101 are a **post office** and some motels. The market is open daily from 8am to 7pm and delivers groceries to Prairie Creek Campground at 7:30pm daily. Phone in your order before 6pm (minimum order $10; delivery free).

■■■ SACRAMENTO VALLEY AND THE CASCADES

Sleepy Sacramento is set in the heart of even sleepier farm country that extends northward for hundreds of miles. The quality of life here is vastly different than along the fast-paced coast, and such a Middle-America atmosphere comes as a welcome break to many who tire of the rigors of urban life. The expanse of farmland is interrupted to the northeast where both ancient and recent volcanic activity has left behind a surreal landscape of lava beds, mountains, lakes, waterfalls, caves, and recovering forest areas. The calm serenity of the lava beds matches that of the farm country, but its haunting beauty draws visitors in a way the Central Valley cannot.

Sacramento is the Rodney Dangerfield of California. As the indistinctive capital of a highly distinctive state, its residents don't give it no respect. In mock tribute of Sacramento's location in the middle of farm country, locals have dubbed it "Sacratomato" and "Excremento." Five major highways converge on the city: **I-5** and **Rte. 99** run north-south, **I-80** runs east-wes, and **U.S. 50** and **Rte. 16** bring traffic from Gold Country. Info! Get your fresh-roasted info at the **Sacramento Convention and Visitors Bureau,** 1421 K St. (264-7777; open daily 9am-5pm)! A 20 min. drive west will reveal **Davis,** a quaint town with 45,000 bicycles, a branch of the University of California, wonderful public transportation—and not much else. Don't go out of your way to come to **Chico.** You'll find the pervasive sense of tranquility refreshing, however, beneath the placidity lurks Chico State, where partying is the one true god.

Lassen Volcanic National Park is accessible by **Rte. 36** to the south, and **Rte. 44** to the north. In 1914, the earth radiated destruction as tremors, streams of lava, black dust, and a series of enormous eruptions ravaged the land, climaxing in 1915 when Mt. Lassen belched a 7-mi.-high cloud of smoke and ashes. Eighty-one years later, the destructive power of this eruption is still evident in the strange, unearthly pools of boiling water and the stretches of barren moonscape. **Lassen Volcanic National Park Headquarters,** in Mineral (595-4444), is an infogasm.

Those who live around **Mt. Shasta** (14,162ft.) will tell you that no one just visits the mountain—people are called to it. The Shasta Indians believed that a great spirit dwelled within the giant volcano, and modern day New Age spiritualists are drawn to the mountain by its mystical energy. Thousands of New Age believers converged here to witness the great event of Harmonic Convergence, which climaxed when a resident turned on her TV set and saw an angelic vision displayed on the screen. **Shasta-Trinity National Forest Service,** 204 W. Alma St. (926-4511 or 926-4596, TDD 926-4512), will charge your New Age info-crystals and give out maps.

Lava Beds National Monument has two entrances, both located off Rte. 139, south of the easily missed farming community of **Tulelake** (TOO-lee-lake). The southeast entrance (25 mi. south of town) is closer to the visitors center. Beneath an uncompromising lunar surface lies a complex web of lava-formed caves and otherworldly tunnels. Cool, quiet, and often eerie, caves range from 18-in. crawl spaces to 80-ft. awe-inspiring cathedrals. Pick up free maps from **Lava Beds Visitors Center,** (667-2282), 30 mi. south of Tulelake on Rte. 139; open daily 9am-6pm; Labor Day-June 15 8am-5pm. $4 per vehicle.) The **area code** for the region is 916.

■■■ GOLD COUNTRY

In 1848 California was a rural backwater of only 15,000 people. The same year, sawmill operator James Marshall wrote in his diary: "This day some kind of mettle...found in the tailrace...looks like goald." In the next four years some 90,000 49ers from around the world headed for California and the 120 mi. of gold-rich seams called the Mother Lode. Despite the hype, few of the prospectors struck it rich. Miners, sustained by dreams of instant wealth, worked long and hard, yet most could barely squeeze sustenance out of their fiercely guarded claims. Although gold remains in them thar hills, today the towns of Gold Country make their money mining the tourist traffic. Gussied up as "Gold Rush Towns," they solicit tourists traveling along the appropriately numbered Rte. 49, which runs through the foothills, connecting dozens of small Gold Country settlements.

Unsuspecting **Calaveras County** turned out to be literally sitting on a gold mine—the richest part of the Mother Lode—when the big rush hit. Over 550,000 pounds of gold were extracted from the county's earth. Calaveras County hops with small towns. **Angels Camp,** at the juncture of Rtes. 4 and 49, is the county hub and population center, but it isn't very big. Scattered throughout the rest of the county are **Alteville, Copperopolis, Sheep Ranch, San Andreas,** and other wee hamlets. Just south of Angels Camp is **Tuttletown,** Mark Twain's one-time home, now little more than a historic marker and a grocery store. **Mokelumne Hill,** 7 mi. north of San Andreas, is not a ghost town but rather a ghost story town—this town's modern claim to fame is an affinity for spooky tales.

About 20 mi. due east of Angels Camp lies **Calaveras Big Trees State Park** (795-3840; open dawn-dusk; day use $5). Here the *Sequoiadendron giganteum* (Giant Sequoia) reigns over all. **Mercer Caverns** (728-2101), 1 mi. north of Murphys off of Rte. 4, offers hour-long walking tours of its numerous internal spaces. ($5, children $2.50. Open daily Memorial Day-Sept. 9am-5pm. Oct.-May open weekends only 11am-4pm.)

The ravines and hillsides now known as **Sonora** were once the domain of the Miwok Indians, but the arrival of the 49ers changed this section of the Sierra foothills into a bustling mining camp. In its Gold Rush heyday, Sonora was a large and prosperous city that vied fiercely with nearby Columbia for the honor of being the richest city of the southern Mother Lode. The **visitors center** in Sonora, 55 W. Stockton Road (800-446-1333 or 533-4420), has guides to Columbia State Park and offers several local publications (open Mon.-Sat. 10am-5pm). **Columbia State Park** (532-0150) dedicates itself to the whole-hearted practice of thinly veiled artifice. The "miners" at this historical park peel off their beards at night, the outhouse is nailed shut, and the horse and buggy carriage spend the nights in a nearby parking lot. Entrance to the park and the **mining museum** (532-4301) within is free.

Stanislaus National Forest features 900,000 acres of the pine trees, craggy peaks, dozens of cool topaz lakes, and wildflower meadows. Here, peregrine falcons, bald eagles, mountain lions, and bears roam the hills and skies. In addition to great hiking trails, fishing, and campsites, Stanislaus offers a chance for a bit of solitude—some-

Pannin' fer Goald

It's easy and fun to pan for gold. Once you're in Gold Country, find one of many public stretches of river. You'll need a 12- or 18-inch gold pan, which will be easily found at local stores. Dig in old mine tailings, at turns in the river, around tree roots, and at the upstream ends of gravel bars where heavy gold may settle. Swirl water, sand, and gravel in a tilted gold pan, slowly washing materials over the edge. Be patient, and keep at it until you are down to black sand, and—hopefully—gold. Gold has a unique color. It's shinier than brassy-looking pyrite (Fool's Gold), and it doesn't break down upon touch, like mica, another common glittery substance.

thing its better-known neighbor, Yosemite, doesn't have. **Park headquarters** (532-3671) are located in Sonora at 19777 Greenly Rd. (open summer 8am-5pm).

Every gold miner's life was rough, but none had it rougher than those who worked the **northern** half of the Mother Lode. Here, granite peaks kept a rigid grip on the nuggets, while merciless winters punished persistent miners for their efforts. Today, the small towns of the Northern Gold Country are far removed from the less authentic "Main Street" scenes of the Southern Gold Country, and the natural beauty of this region handsomely rewards exploration. If you're lucky, you may catch a glimpse of a wiry prospector leading his donkey into the hills.

SIERRA NEVADA

The Sierra Nevada is the highest, steepest, and most physically stunning mountain range in the contiguous United States. Thrust skyward 400 million years ago by plate tectonics and shaped by erosion, glaciers, and volcanoes, this enormous hunk of granite stretches 450 mi. north from the Mojave Desert to Lake Almanor. The heart-stopping sheerness of Yosemite's rock walls, the craggy alpine scenery of Kings Canyon and Sequoia National Parks, and the abrupt drop of the Eastern Slope into Owens Valley are unparalleled sights.

Temperatures in the Sierra Nevada are as diverse as the terrain. Even in the summer, overnight lows can dip into the 20s. Check local weather reports. Normally, only U.S. 50 and I-80 are kept open during the snow season. Exact dates vary from year to year, so check with a ranger station for local road conditions, especially from October through June. Come summer, protection from the high elevations' ultraviolet rays is necessary; always bring sunscreen, and a hat is a good idea.

■■■ YOSEMITE

In 1868 a young Scotsman named John Muir arrived in San Francisco and asked for directions to "anywhere that's wild." He was pointed toward the Sierra Nevada and a lifetime of conservationism. In 1880 he succeeded in securing national park status for **Yosemite National Park.** Today, few of the park's 3.5 million annual visitors know of his efforts, but most leave with an appreciation and love for the awe-inspiring granite cliffs, thunderous waterfalls, lush meadows, and thick pine forests. The park covers 1189 sq. mi. of mountainous terrain. **El Capitán, Half Dome,** and **Yosemite Falls** lie in the Yosemite Valley, an area carved out by glaciers over thousands of years. Unless you like to hang out with mobs of Midwesterners and screaming kids, you should duck out of here quickly. Little Yosemite Valley, accessible by hiking trails, offers two spectacular waterfalls: **Vernal** and **Nevada Falls. Tuolumne Meadows** (pronounced ta-WALL-um-ee) in the northeastern corner of the park is an Elysian expanse of alpine meadows surrounded by granite cliffs and rushing streams. **Mariposa Grove** is a forest of giant sequoia trees at the park's southern end.

PRACTICAL INFORMATION

Tourist Office: A map of the park and a copy of the informative *Yosemite Guide* are available for free at visitors centers. Wilderness **permits** are available at all visitors centers; write ahead and reserve in advance. **General Park Information** (372-0265; 24-hr. recorded information 372-0200; TTY users 372-4726) Open Mon.-Fri. 9am-5pm. **Campground information:** 372-0200 (recorded). **Yosemite Valley Visitors Center,** Yosemite Village (372-0229). Open daily 8am-8pm; winter 8am-5pm.

Equipment Rental: Yosemite Mountaineering School, Rte. 120 (372-8344 or 372-1244), at Tuolumne Meadows. Sleeping bags $4 per day, backpacks $4 per day, snowshoes $11 per day. Climbing shoes rented to YMS students only. Driver's license or credit card required. Open daily 8:30am-5pm.

Post Office: Yosemite Village, next to the visitors center. Open June-Aug. Mon.-Fri. 8:30am-5pm, Sat. 10am-noon; Sept.-May Mon.-Fri. 8:30am-12:30pm and 1:30-5pm. **ZIP code:** 95389. **Area code:** 209.

Yosemite lies 200 mi. east of San Francisco and 320 mi. northeast of Los Angeles. It can be reached by taking **Rte. 140** from Merced, **Rte. 41** north from Fresno, and **Rte. 120** east from Manteca or west from Lee Vining.

Park Admission is $3 if you enter on foot, bicycle, or bus or $5 for a 7-day vehicle pass. Yosemite runs public **buses** that connect the park with Merced and Fresno. **Yosemite VIA,** 300 Grogan Ave., Merced 95340 (742-5211 or 800-VIA-LINE/842-5463), makes two round-trips per day from the Merced Amtrak station to Yosemite ($17, round-trip $30; discount for seniors). **Yosemite Gray Line** (YGL; 722-0366), connects with **Amtrak** (800-USA-RAIL/872-7245) in Merced. The free **shuttle bus** has knowledgeable drivers and broad viewing windows (daily at 10-min. intervals from 9am to 10pm, and every 20 min. from 7:30-9am).

ACCOMMODATIONS, CAMPING, AND FOOD

Lodgings in Yosemite Valley are monopolized by the **Delaware North Co. Room Reservations,** 5410 E. Home, Fresno 93727 (252-4848, TTY users 255-8345).

Yosemite Lodge, in Yosemite Valley west of Yosemite Village. Small, sparsely furnished cabins under surveillance by deer. To catch cancellations, inquire before 4pm. Singles and doubles $53, with bath $71.

Yosemite is camping country. Most of the valley's campgrounds are crowded, many choked with trailers and RVs. Reservations are required from April to November and must be made through MISTIX (800-436-4275) up to eight weeks ahead.

Backpacker's Camp, 1½mi. east of Yosemite Village across the river, behind North Pine Campground. Must have a wilderness permit and be a backpacker without a vehicle to camp here. Unadvertised. Low on facilities, high on camaraderie. Fishing is popular. 2-night max. stay. $3 per person. Open May-Oct.

Sunnyside, at the west end of Yosemite Valley past the Yosemite Lodge Chevron station. Near the climber's camp. Water, toilets, and tables. $3 per person. Often fills up early with reservation-less visitors. Open year-round.

Wawona, Rte. 41 in the southern end of the park. 100 sunny sites along the beautiful Merced River. Tables, toilets, and water. No showers. Pets allowed. Sites $10.

White Wolf, off Rte. 120 east. Water, toilets, tables, fire pits. Pets allowed. 87 sites. $10 per site. Open June or July-Sept., depending on snowpack.

Porcupine Flat, off Rte. 120 east. RV access to front section only. Pit toilets, potable stream water. 52 sites. $6 per site. Open June or July-Sept.

Hodgdon Meadow, on Rte. 120 near Big Oak Flat entrance. Suitable for winter camping or for finding solitude year-round. Water, tables, and toilets. Sites $12.

Lower Pines, in the busy eastern end of Yosemite Valley. This is the designated **winter camping** spot. Commercial, and crowded, the campground has toilets, water, showers, and tables. Sites $14.

Bring your own food for a campfire feast. Overpriced groceries are available from the **Yosemite Lodge, Wawona,** or the **Village Stores** (open daily 8am-10pm; Oct.-May 8am-9pm).

SIGHTS AND THE OUTDOORS

By Car or Bike You can see a large part of Yosemite from the bucket seat, but the view is better if you get out. The *Yosemite Road Guide* ($3.25 at every visitors center) is keyed to the roadside markers, and outlines a superb tour of the park—it's almost like having a ranger tied to the hood. The drive along **Tioga Road** (Rte. 120 east) reveals one panorama after another. Driving west from the Pass brings you to

Tuolumne Meadows, its open, alpine spaces, and shimmering **Tenaya Lake.** A drive into the heart of the valley leads to thunderous 2425-ft. **Yosemite Falls** (the highest in North America), **Sentinel Rock,** and **Half Dome.** For a different perspective on the valley, drive to **Glacier Point,** off Glacier Point Rd. Hovering 3214 ft. above the valley floor, this gripping overlook is guaranteed to impress the most jaded of travelers. Half Dome rests majestically across the valley, and the sight and sound of **Vernal Falls** and **Nevada Falls** shatter the silence.

A short hiking trail through the giant sequoias of **Mariposa Grove** begins off Rte. 41 at the **Fallen Monarch,** a massive trunk lying on its side, and continues to the 209-ft., 2700-year-old **Grizzly Giant,** and the fallen **Wawona Tunnel Tree.** Ancient Athens was in its glory when many of these trees were saplings.

Cyclists can pick up a brochure which indicates the safest roads at the visitors center. Roads are fairly flat near the villages, more demanding farther afield. Those near **Mirror Lake,** open only to hikers and bikers, guarantee a particularly good ride, and the valley roads, filled with traffic, are easily circumvented by the bike paths. For further information on bike routes, contact the bike rental stands at Yosemite Lodge (372-1208) or Curry Village (372-1200).

Day Hiking To experience Yosemite the way it was meant to be, travel on foot. Day-use trails are usually fairly busy, sometimes positively packed, and occasionally (i.e. July 4th weekend) the site of human traffic jams. A colorful trail map with difficulty ratings and average hiking times is available at the visitors center for 50¢. Misty **Bridalveil Falls** is an easy ¼-mi. walk from the shuttle bus stop. The **Mirror Lake Loop** is a level, 3-mi. walk to the glassy lake, which is slowly silting up to become a meadow. These two trails, as well as pretty **Lower Yosemite Falls,** are wheelchair accessible.

The wildflower-laden **Pohon Trail** starts from Glacier Point, crossing Sentinel River (spectacular Sentinel Falls, the park's second largest cascade, lies to the north) on its way to Taft Point and other secluded lookouts. For a taste of "real" rock-climbing without requisite equipment and training, Yosemite day hikers scramble up **Lembert Dome** above Tuolumne Meadows.

The world's best climbers come to Yosemite to test themselves at angles past vertical. If you've got the courage, you can join the stellar Yosemite rock climbers by taking a lesson with the **Yosemite Mountaineering School** (372-1335 or 372-8435; Sept.-May 372-1244; open 8:30am-5pm). The basic **rock-climbing classes,** offered daily in summer (usually mid-April to Oct.), teach you the basics on the ground, then take you 80 ft. up a cliff and introduce you to bouldering and rappelling (lesson prices depend on demand; $60 for three or more, $120 for individual courses).

■ BEYOND YOSEMITE VALLEY

Some folks never leave the valley, but a wilder, lonelier Yosemite awaits those who do. Preparation is key before an backcountry adventure; obtain a **topographical map** of the region you plan to explore and plan your route. **Backcountry camping** is prohibited in the valley (you'll get slapped with a stiff fine if caught), but it's generally permitted along the high-country trails with a free **wilderness permit** (call 372-0310 for general information). Each trailhead limits the number of permits available. Reserve by mail between March 1 and May 31 (write Wilderness Center, P.O. Box 577, Yosemite National Park 95389), or take your chances with the 50% quota held on 24-hr. notice at the Yosemite Valley Visitors Center, the Wawona Ranger Station, and Big Oak Flat Station. Popular trails like **Little Yosemite Valley, Clouds Rest,** and **Half Dome** fill their quotas regularly. To receive a permit, you must show a planned itinerary. Many hikers stay at the undeveloped mountain campgrounds in the high country for the company and for the **bear lockers,** used for storing food. Hikers can also store food in hanging bear bags or in rentable plastic **canisters** from the Yosemite Valley Sports Shop ($3 per day). Canisters may be mandatory on more popular hiking routes (check with rangers).

A free shuttle bus to **Tuolumne Meadows** will deposit you at the heads of several trails. **Lembert Dome** has a trail to its peak that is ideal for inexperienced hikers eager to test their skills. The **Pacific Crest Trail** follows a series of awe-inspiring canyons. South Yosemite is home to the **Giant Sequoia and Mariposa Grove,** the park's largest. Some trails continue as far as Washington State.

■■■ MONO LAKE

As fresh water from streams and springs drains into the "inland sea" of Mono Lake, it evaporates, leaving behind a mineral-rich, 13-mi. wide expanse that Mark Twain called "the Dead Sea of the West." The lake derives its lunar appearance from remarkable towers of calcium carbonate called *tufa,* which form when calcium-rich freshwater springs well up in the carbonate-filled salt water. At over 700,000 years old, this lake remains the Western Hemisphere's oldest enclosed body of water.

The town of **Lee Vining** provides the best access to Mono Lake and the ghost town of **Bodie.** Lee Vining is located 70 mi. north of **Bishop** on U.S. 395 and 10 mi. west of the Tioga Pass entrance to **Yosemite.** For tasty granola info-nuggets, see the **Mono Lake Visitors Center and Lee Vining Chamber of Commerce** (647-6595 or 647-6629; open daily 9am-9pm; Labor Day-Memorial Day 9am-5pm), on Main St. in Lee Vining. **Greyhound** (647-6301 or 800-231-2222; open daily 8am-9pm), in the Lee Vining Market, goes to L.A. ($42; 11:15am) and Reno ($30; 2:30am). Buy your ticket at the next stop, because they don't sell them here. **Area code:** 619.

Hotel accommodations are often scarce on Friday afternoons and holidays. At any time, lodging and meals are going to be expensive. There are six **Inyo National Forest campgrounds** ($0-8) within 15 mi. of town; these may fill quickly during peak times. Head west from town on Rte. 120. There are also two campgrounds less than 6 mi. north of town. **Sawmill** (free) and **Tioga Lake** ($8) are 9000 ft. up, at the edge of Yosemite. Make reservations for these campgrounds well in advance with the Lee Vining District Ranger. The **Lee Vining Market** is the town's closest thing to a grocery store (647-6301; next to the laundromat on Main St.; open daily 8am-9pm).

In 1984, Congress set aside 57,000 acres of land surrounding Mono Lake and called it the **Mono Basin National Forest Scenic Area** (647-6525). **South Tufa Grove,** 10 mi. from Lee Vining, harbors an awe-inspiring collection of calcium carbonate formations. (Take U.S. 395 south to Rte. 120, then go 4mi. east and take the Mono Lake Tufa Reserve turn-off 1mi. south of Tufa Grove.) The **Mono Lake Committee** offers excellent guided canoe tours of the lake that include a crash course on Mono Lake's natural history, ecology, and conservation. Arrange tours through the visitors center ($12, ages 4-12 $6). **June Lake,** a canyon carved by glaciers and now filled with water, is 10 mi. south of Lee Vining on U.S. 395. If you have time, take the scenic loop along Rte. 158. The sparkling lake and its surrounding ring of mountains are prized by visitors as a wayward slice of the Alps.

Tucked away in the high, God-forsaken desert, **Bodie** is a real ghost town, even if it does charge admission ($5; dogs $1; self-guide booklet $1). Described in 1880 as "a sea of sin, lashed by the tempests of lust and passion," the town was home to 10,000 people, 65 saloons, and one homicide per day. Bodie is accessible by a paved road off U.S. 395, 15 mi. north of Lee Vining, and by a dirt road from Rte. 167 out of Mono Inn (open daily 9am-7pm; Labor Day-Memorial Day 9am-4pm).

■■■ SEQUOIA AND KINGS CANYON

Though they may not attract the thunderous hordes of visitors that the "Big Three" (Yellowstone, Yosemite, and the Grand Canyon) do each summer, the twin parks of **Kings Canyon** and **Sequoia National Parks** can go sight-for-sight with any park in the U.S. Immense sequoia trees, found only on the western slope of the Sierra Nevada, thrive amid a panorama of cool waters, glacially chiseled rock, snowy mountains, and blooming meadows. Developed areas like Grant Grove and Giant Forest offer informative trails, lodging amenities, and paved vehicle access, while the backcountry offers only wilderness.

Practical Information The **Kings Canyon and Sequoia Main Line** (565-3134) offers 24-hr. direct contact with a park ranger in addition to dispatch service to any office within the parks. The **Parks General Information Line** is 565-3134. **Park Admission** is $5 for a 7-day vehicle pass valid in both parks Park **shuttle buses** operate out of Giant Forest in Sequoia National Park and go to and from Lodgepole, Moro Rock, Sherman Tree, and Crescent Meadow from 8am-6pm. (Single ride $1, $3 per family. Day pass $4, $6 per family.) There are many visitor's centers throughout the park. **Foothills Visitors Center** (565-3134), Three Rivers 93271, at the park headquarters 1 mi. beyond the Three Rivers entrance, on Rte. 198 out of Visalia (open daily 8am-5pm; Nov.-April 8am-4pm). **Grant Grove Visitors Center** (335-2856), Grant Grove Village, 2 mi. east of the Big Stump Entrance by Rte. 180 (open daily 8am-6pm, winter 9am-5pm). Sequioia's **post office** is at Lodgepole (open Mon.-Fri. 8:30am-1pm and 1:30-4pm); **ZIP code:** 93262. Kings Canyon's **post office** is in Grant Grove Village across from the Visitors Center (open June-Sept. Mon.-Sat. 9am-3pm); **ZIP code:** 93633.

The two parks are only accessible to vehicles coming from the west. From Fresno follow **Rte. 180** east into the foothills; it's about 60 mi. to the entrance of the detached **Grant Grove** section of Kings Canyon 30 more to **Cedar Grove.** The road into this region is closed in winter. From **Visalia,** take **Rte. 198** to Sequoia. **Generals Highway** (Rte. 198) connects the Ash Mountain entrance to the **Giant Forest** in Sequoia, and continues to Grant Grove in Kings Canyon. In summer, allow 2 hrs. for the treacherous road to **Mineral King** opens up the southern parts of Sequoia. From Visalia, take **Rte. 198;** the turnoff to Mineral King is 3 mi. past Three Rivers.

Accommodations, Camping, and Food **Sequoia Guest Services, Inc. (S.G.S.),** H.C. Box 500, Sequoia National Park, 93262-9601 (561-3314), monopolizes indoor accommodations and food in the parks. **Giant Forest** and **Grant Grove** offer "rustic sleeping cabins" with canvas tops during the summer season (May-Oct.) for $35.20; add $7 for a wooden roof. If you are desperate for electricity, the **Best Western,** (561-4119), and **Sierra Lodge,** (561-3681), in Three Rivers have rooms starting at about $58. Most campgrounds are open from mid-May to October.

For **camping** in Sequoia, try **Buckeye Flat,** past park headquarters, a few miles into the park from the Ash Mountain entrance on Rte. 198. Buckeye affords a truly unique camping experience (no RVs), with sites near a fabulous waterfall. Try **Lodgepole,** 4 mi. northeast of Giant Forest Village in the heart of Sequoia National Park by Kaweah River if you have no other option. (Both sites $10-12.) Reserve sites through MISTIX (800-365-2267) mid-May-mid-Sept.

In King's Canyon, **Sunset, Azalea,** and **Crystal Springs** are within a stone's throw of Grant Grove Village but are still relatively quiet. Azalea has a trailer dump station and Sunset features flat tenting spots, brilliant views of the San Joaquin Valley, and an amphitheater with daily programs. Crystal Springs is the smallest and the most quiet. All have restrooms and water and offer more privacy than most campgrounds. Sites $10. Azalea is open year-round; free in winter. **Sheep Creek, Sentinel, Canyon View,** and **Moraine,** at the Kings River near Cedar Grove. All have restrooms and water ($10). Canyon View accepts reservations from organized groups only. They fill on weekends. Access roads and campgrounds are closed from Oct.-May.

Park food is monopolized by SGS. Outside the park, in Three Rivers, the **Noisy Water Café** (561-4517), along Rte. 180, is the overwhelming favorite among the townfolk. Tasty sandwiches run from $4.50-6 (open daily 6am-10pm).

Sights **Giant Forest** is the center of activities in Sequoia and host to one of the world's greatest concentrations of giant sequoia trees. The tallest marvel is **General**

Sherman, standing 275 ft. tall and measuring 102 ft. around at its base; its trunk weighs in at 1385 tons. The 2-mi. **Congress Trail,** the park's most popular (and crowded) trail, boomerangs around General Sherman. Perhaps the most spectacular sight in the Giant Forest area is the view from atop **Moro Rock,** 1½ mi. from the village. A rock staircase winds ¼-mi. up this granite monolith to the top, which offers a stunning 360° view of the southern Sierras. Nine mi. from Giant Forest Village on Rte. 198 is **Crystal Cave,** one of the few caves on the western side of Sequoia open to the public. (Naturalists lead tours late June to Labor Day daily on the hour and ½-hr.; May-June and Sept. Fri.-Mon. on the hour. Cave open 10am-3pm. Admission $4, ages 6-12 $2. Buy tickets in advance at Lodgepole office between 8am-4pm.)

The most developed portion of Kings Canyon is **Grant Grove.** The **General Grant Tree,** the third-largest of the sequoias, gives the region its name. At 267.4 ft. tall, it is perhaps the most aesthetically pleasing, displaying "classic" sequoia form. Just north of the park entrance on Rte. 180 lies the **Big Stump Basin Trail,** a self-guided walk through an old logging camp. Here remain scars left by early loggers who erroneously viewed the enormous sequoia as a timber gold mine. They abandoned their efforts after assailing the unyielding trees with dynamite and hatchets.

Hidden in the visitors center parking lot behind the post office is the steep, switchback-riddled road to **Panoramic Point.** In addition to affording fantastic views of the nearby mountains, the point serves as the trailhead for **Park Ridge Trail,** one of the most scenic in the park. One of the more secluded regions of the two parks is the **Cedar Grove** area, which rests inside the towering granite walls of Kings Canyon. The drive on Rte. 180 is scenic and mountainous. **Road's End** brings you to the backcountry. The most popular foray is the **Rae Lakes Loop,** which traverses a sampling of the Sierra's best: glaciated canyons, gentle meadows, violent rapids, and inspiring lake vistas. Most hikers take a clockwise route to avoid an uphill grade. Well-spaced campgrounds pace the four- to five-day trek at about 7-mi. intervals. Obtain permits at the Cedar Grove Ranger Station or the Road's End Kiosk.

■■■ MAMMOTH LAKES

Home to one of the most popular ski resorts in the United States, the town of Mammoth Lakes is rapidly transforming itself into a giant, year-round playground. Mountain biking, rock-climbing, and hiking now complement the traditional wintertime pursuits. Mammoth is an outdoor lover's dream—spectacular peaks overlook a town where every establishment seems to exist solely for the excursionist's benefit.

Practical Information Mammoth Lakes is located on **U.S. 395** about 160 mi. south of Reno and 40 mi. southeast of the eastern entrance to Yosemite National Park. **Rte. 203** runs through the town as **Main St.** The **Visitors Center and Chamber of Commerce** (934-2712 or 800-367-6572), east off of U.S. 395, north of town at the National Forest Visitors Center, taps into Mammoth's big, hairy, info subculture (open Sat.-Thurs. 8am-6pm, Fri. 8am-8pm; winter daily 8am-6pm). **Greyhound** (213-620-1200) stops in the parking lot behind McDonald's on Main St. One bus daily to Reno ($32; 1:30am) and L.A. ($42; 12:30pm). The **post office** (934-2205) is on Main St., across from the visitors center (open Mon.-Fri. 8:30am-5pm); **ZIP code:** 93546; **area code:** 619.

Accommodations, Camping, and Food There are nearly 20 Inyo Forest public campgrounds in the area, at **Mammoth Lakes, Mammoth Village, Convict Lake,** and **Reds Meadow.** All sites have piped water. Call the Mammoth Ranger District (924-5500) for more information. Reservations taken for all group sites ($20-$55), as well at nearby Sherwin Creek, through MISTIX (800-280-2267). In-doorsy types need the **ULLR Lodge** (934-2454). Turn left from Main St. onto Minaret Rd. It's a chalet-esque place with sauna and a shared kitchen. Dorm style rooms run from $12-16. For a bite to eat, **Angel's** (934-7427), at Main St. and Sierra, is almost unanimously recommended among locals for da BBQ (open Mon.-Fri. 11:30am-10pm, Sat.-Sun. 5pm-10pm).

Sights There's plenty to see in Mammoth Lakes, but unfortunately most of it is accessible only by car. **Devil's Postpile National Monument,** an intriguing geological oddity, was formed when lava flows oozed through Mammoth Pass thousands of years ago and then cooled to form columns 40 to 60 ft. high. A pleasant 3-mi. walk away from the center of the monument is **Rainbow Falls,** where the middle fork of the San Joaquin River drops 140 ft. past dark cliffs into a glistening green pool. From U.S. 395, the monument can be reached by a 15-mi. drive past Minaret Summit on paved Rte. 203. To save the monument area from being completely trampled, rangers have introduced a shuttle service between a parking area and the monument center, which *all* visitors must use between 7:30am and 5:30pm. (Drivers have free access 5:30pm-7:30am. Shuttle lasts 30min. Round-trip $7, ages 5-12 $4.)

Although there are over 100 lakes near town (60 of them within a 5-mi. radius), not one actually goes by the name of "Mammoth Lake." The 1-mi. long **Lake Mary,** is popular for boating, fishing, and sailing. **Twin Lakes** is the closest lake to the village, only 3 mi. down Rte. 203. **Lake Mamie** has a picturesque picnic area, and many short hikes lead out to **Lake George,** where granite sheets attract climbers.

You can ride the **Mammoth Mountain Gondola** (934-2571) during the summer for a spectacular view of the area (open daily 9:30am-5:30pm; round-trip $10, children $5). **Obsidian Dome** lies 14 mi. north of Mammoth Junction and 1 mi. west of U.S. 395 on Glass Flow Rd. (follow the sign to "Lava Flow"). Hot-air balloons, climbing walls, mountain bike paths, and even dogsled trails attract visitors to Mammoth. You can evaluate your options at the **Mammoth Adventure Connection** (934-0606 or 924-5683), in the Mammoth Mountain Inn. Courageous cyclists can take the gondola to the top of **Mammoth Mountain Bike Park,** where the ride starts at 11,053 ft. and head straight down the rocky ski trails. Helmets are required. Get tickets and information at the **Mammoth Mountain Bike Center** at the base of the mountain (934-0606; bike rental including helmet $25 for 4hrs., $35 per 8-hr. day; open daily 9:30am-7pm). The gondola runs daily 9:30am-5:30pm ($20 per day for gondola ticket and trail use). Drop by the Mammoth Ranger Station (924-5500) for a map of bike trail networks on Forest Service land. A **ropes course** ($40 adults, $10 youth program) and **climbing wall** ($5 per climb or $15 per hr.) are the latest attractions at Mammoth (open July 1-Labor Day; call 924-5638 for reservations).

The **skiing** season extends from mid-Nov.-June; in a good year, alpine skiing can last through July. **Mammoth Mountain** lift tickets can be purchased at the **Main Lodge** at the base of the mountain on Minaret Rd. (934-2571; open Mon.-Fri. 8am-3pm, Sat.-Sun. 7:30am-3pm), at **Stormriders** at Minaret Rd. and Canyon Blvd. (open daily 8am-9pm), or at **Warming Hut II** at the end of Canyon Blvd. and Lakeview (934-0787; open Mon.-Fri. 8am-3pm, Sat.-Sun. and holidays 7:30am-3pm). A free **shuttle bus** transports skiers between lifts, town, and the Main Lodge. The Forest Service can provide information on the area's cross country trails.

■■■ LAKE TAHOE

In today's Lake Tahoe, both tall pines and high-rises are reflected in the crisp azure waters and silhouetted by the deep auburn glow of the setting sun.

PRACTICAL INFORMATION

Tourist Office: South Lake Tahoe Visitors Center, 3066 U.S. 50 (541-5255), at Lion's Ave. Open Mon.-Fri. 8:30am-5pm, Sat. 9am-4pm. **Lake Tahoe Visitor Center,** 4018 Lake Tahoe Blvd. (544-3133), 1 block from Stateline in the A-frame. **Visitors Bureau,** 950 North Lake Blvd. (581-6900), in Tahoe City.

Buses: Greyhound, 1098 U.S. 50 in Harrah's Hotel Casino (588-4645), by Raley's in S. Lake Tahoe. To San Francisco (5 per day, $20) and Sacramento (5 per day, $18). All rates subject to seasonal price changes. No lockers. Open daily 8am-noon, 2:30-6pm. **Tahoe Casino Express** (800-446-6128) provides shuttle service between Reno airport and Tahoe casinos (8am-12:30pm; $15).

Public Transportation: Tahoe Area Regional Transport (TART), 581-6365. Connects the west and north shores from Tahoma to Incline Village. 12 buses daily 6:30am-6:30pm ($1). **South Tahoe Area Ground Express (STAGE),** 573-2080. 24-hr. bus service around South Tahoe, service to the beach every hr.

Taxis: Sierra Taxi, 577-8888. Available 24 hrs.

Car Rental: Tahoe Rent-a-Car, (544-4500), U.S. 50 at Tahoe Keys Blvd. in S. Lake Tahoe. 100 free mi. Cars from $39 per day. Must be 25.

Bicycle Rental: Anderson's Bicycle Rental, 645 Emerald Bay Rd. (541-0500), convenient to the west shore bike trail. Mountain bikes $6 per hr., ½-day $18, full day $22. Deposit (usually ID) required. Open daily 8:30am-6:30pm.

Emergency: 911.

Post Office: Tahoe City, 950 N. Lake Blvd., in the Lighthouse Shopping Center (583-3936). Open Mon.-Fri. 8:30am-5pm, Sat. noon-2pm. **ZIP code:** 96145. **Area code:** 916 in CA, 702 in NV.

Lake Tahoe is located 118 mi. northeast of Sacramento and 35 mi. southwest of Reno. **U.S. 50** (also called Lake Tahoe Blvd.), **Rte. 89,** and **Rte. 28** overlap to form a ring of asphalt around the lake. The versatile Rte. 89 is also known as W. Lake Blvd. and Emerald Bay Rd. Rte. 28 masquerades as N. Lake Blvd. and Lakeshore Dr.

CALIFORNIA

ACCOMMODATIONS AND CAMPING

The strip off of U.S. 50 on the California side of the border supports the bulk of Tahoe's 200 motels. Others line Park Avenue and Pioneer Trail off of U.S. 50, which are quieter. The Forest Service provides up-to-date information on camping. **Bayview** is the only free campground (544-5994; 2-night max.; open June-Sept.). Advance reservations for all sites are essential. (Call MISTIX at 800-365-2267.)

El Nido, 2215 Lake Tahoe Blvd. (541-2711). Homey. TV, VCR, hot tub, pool, and casino shuttle to Stateline. Singles $30, $49 on weekends; add $10 Jun-.Aug.

Edwards Lodge (525-7207), along Rte. 89, in Tahoma. 11 cabins available during the summer, 7 during the winter. Large cabins with 2 stories, several beds, kitchen, big wooden deck, and TV. Cash only. Cabins $70-85.

Lake Shore Lodge, 3496 Lake Tahoe Blvd. (544-2834). Light, airy rooms are cheap, but beware of seasonal and weekend rate increases. TV, pool, and free breakfast. Mon.-Thurs.: singles $20, doubles $28. Fri.-Sat.: $35, $48.

Nevada Beach (573-2600), 1 mi. from Stateline on U.S. 50. Flush toilets and drinking water; no showers. Sites ($14-16) close to the shore. Open June-Labor Day.

D.L. Bliss State Park, (525-7277), Rte. 89, a few mi. west of Emerald Bay. Hot showers, blissful beach. 14-day max. stay. 168 sites; $14, near-beach sites $19. Open June to Labor Day. Arrive early to stake your claim.

FOOD

The casinos offer perpetually low-priced buffets, but there are restaurants along the lakeshore with reasonable prices, similar large portions, and much better food.

The Bridgetender, 30 West Lake Blvd. (583-3342), in Tahoe City. The specialty is a ½-lb. burger ($4-6), and there's no lack of variety. Festive atmosphere and late hours. Hoppin' at night. Open daily 11am-10pm. Bar open until 2am.

Red Hut Waffles, 2749 U.S. 50 (541-9024). Delicious home-style cooking. Young local crowd. Friendly staff. Plate-size waffle with fruit, whipped cream ($4). Boasts a 4-egg omelette for $5. Bottomless coffee 50¢. Open daily 6am-2pm.

Cantina Los Tres Hombres, (544-1233), Rte. 89, at 10th St. and Rte. 28, in Kings Beach (546-4052). Margarita pitchers ($9.25), free nachos during happy hour (4-6pm). Dinners from $7. Open daily 11:30am-10:30pm; bar open until 2am.

ACTIVITIES

Lake Tahoe supports numerous beaches. On the south shore, **Pope Beach,** off Rte. 89, is wide and shaded by pines (less traffic on the east end). **Nevada Beach** is close to the casinos off U.S. 50, offering a quiet place to reflect on your losses. **Zephyr Cove Beach** is a favorite spot for the younger well-oiled college crowd. On the west side, **Chambers Beach** draws the same bouncy types. **Meeks Bay,** 10 mi. south of Tahoe City, is more quiet. The North Shore offers **Hidden Beach** (just south of Incline Village) and **Kings Beach** (just across the California border on Rte. 28). The **nude beach** near Hidden is said to be a local gay and lesbian hangout.

Would-be **cyclists** without wheels are requited in the Tahoe-Truckee area. Bike rental places give all sorts of good advice. Rentals run $5 per hour, $20 per full day. Several paved bike trails circle the lake. **Angora Ridge** (4 mi.) is a moderate mountain bike trail accessible from Rte. 89 that meanders past Fallen Leaf Lake to the Angora Lakes. For serious mountain bikers, **Mr. Toad's Wild Ride** (3 mi.) is a strenuous, winding trail that climbs to 9000 ft. It can be reached from U.S. 50 or Rte. 89, with parking located off the major roads.

Hiking is one of the best ways to explore the beautiful Tahoe Basin. Detailed information, including trail maps for all types of hikes, is available at the visitors center. The **Lake of the Sky Trail** (0.6 mi. round-trip) leads to the **Tallac Historic Site,** which features a look at turn-of-the-century Tahoe life. More experienced hikers may want to try the West and the South Shore trails. Backcountry users must obtain a free **Wilderness Permit** for any hike into the Desolation Wilderness. Magnificent **Emerald Bay,** in the lake's southwest corner, has Tahoe's only island, **Fannette** (the most photographed sight in the area).

River rafting is an exciting and refreshing way to appreciate the Tahoe scenery. Unfortunately, the quality (and existence) of rafting on the American and the Truckee Rivers depends on the amount of snowfall during the preceding winter. Consequently, late spring and early summer are the best times to hit the rapids. If water levels are high, keep a look out for raft rental places along the Truckee. (For more information, call 800-466-RAFT/7238). If California droughts make conventional rafting scarce, all need not be lost. Floating around in an **inner tube** is popular with many **would-be rafters.** Make sure tubes are permitted on the body of water you select, don't go alone, and always know what lies downstream before you shove off.

In the summer, **Windsurf Fantasies,** 3411 U.S. 50, in South Lake Tahoe (541-SAIL/7215), rents windsurfing equipment ($15). They also offer lessons for even the most timorous first-timers. Rent a wetsuit: the average temperature of the lake remains a chilly 39°F year-round. Most drowned bodies are never recovered, one tourist leaflet cheerfully reveals, because the cold prevents the decomposition that usually makes corpses float to the surface. In fact, the Native Americans who used to live around Lake Tahoe "buried" their dead in the lake; changes in water temperature and current movements have, on occasion, brought these perfectly preserved bodies to the surface.

Tahoe is a **skiing** mecca and there are approximately 20 ski resorts in the Tahoe area. Check the visitors center for prices and maps. Pick up a copy of *Ski Tahoe* (free) at visitors centers for valuable coupons and more information. **Alpine Meadows** (583-4232), **Squaw Valley** (583-6985), and **Heavenly** (702-547-SKII/7544), are all modern classics. For **nordic** enthusiasts **Royal Gorge** (426-3871) on Old Hwy. 40 just below Donner Summit, is the nation's largest cross-country ski resort, with 80 trails totalling 300km in length (trail fee $17.50; children $8.50).

Alaska

Alaska's beauty is born of extremes. By far the largest of the 50 states, it comprises fully one-fifth of the land mass of the United States. The 33,000-mi. coastline stretches 11 times the distance from New York to San Francisco. Nineteen Alaskan peaks reach over 14,000 ft. and several glacial ice fields occupy areas larger than the state of Rhode Island. Alaska has the highest mountain in North America (20,320-ft. Mt. McKinley, or "Denali"), the largest American National Park (13-million-acre Wrangell-St. Elias National Park), the hugest carnivore in North America (the Kodiak brown bear), and the greatest collection of bald eagles in the world. At the height of summer, Alaska becomes the "Land of the Midnight Sun," where you can play volleyball at 2am; in spring and fall, shimmering curtains of spectral color—the *aurora borealis*—dance like smoke over the dark horizon; in the depths of winter Alaska is land of the noonday moon, and large portions of the state never see the sun.

The first humans to colonize North America crossed the Bering Strait into Alaska via a now-sunken land bridge. Russian-sponsored Danish navigator Vitus Bering was the first European to arrive, bringing in his wake a wave of Russian fur traders who exhausted the fur supply within a century. When Secretary of State James Seward negotiated the United States's acquisition of the territory from Russia for a trifling $7,200,000 (about 2¢ per acre) in 1867, he became the laughingstock of the nation. The purchase of seemingly worthless frozen land was commonly called "Seward's Folly," but within 20 years Alaska showed its worth in a series of massive gold strikes. In 1968, long after the gold rush had slowed to a trickle, the state's fortunes rebounded yet again, with the discovery of "black gold" (oil) on the shore of the Arctic Ocean. By 1981, $7,200,000 worth of crude oil flowed through the Trans-Alaska pipeline from the Arctic oil field every 4½ hours.

The rough 'n' ready *Let's Go: Alaska & The Pacific Northwest* covers the entire state of Alaska in depth. Get yours today!

Alaskan Attributes

Authors: Jack London, Tom Bodett, John McPhee (*Coming into the Country*).
Artists: Sydney Lawrence, Diana Tillion.
Cuisine: Salmon, salmon, and more salmon…oh, and some caribou.
Microbreweries: Alaska Brewing Co., Bird Creek Brewery.
Native Americans: Eskimo, Ingalik, Koyukon, Tanana, Ahtna, Eyak, Chugach, Aleut, Tlingit, Haida, Tsimshian.
Music: Down 'n' dirty bar bands, traditional music of indigenous peoples.
Film and TV: *Northern Exposure, White Fang, Salmonberries.*
Climate: Really cold in winter, with a lot of mosquitoes in the summer.
Geography: Tundra, rainforest, glaciers, and some mighty tall mountains.

PRACTICAL INFORMATION

Capital: Juneau.

Alaska Division of Tourism: 33 Willoughby St., P.O. Box 110801, Juneau 99811-0801 (907-465-2010). Open Mon.-Fri. 8am-4:30pm. **Alaska Public Lands Information Center,** 605 W. 4th Ave.; #105, Anchorage 99501 (907-271-2737; 907-258-PARK/7275 for a recording). Info on all public lands in Alaska. Open daily 9am-5:30pm. **Alaska State Division of Parks,** 3601 C St., #200, Anchorage 99510 (907-762-2617). Open Mon.-Fri. 11am-5pm.

Time Zones: Alaska (most of the state; 4hr. behind Eastern); Aleutian-Hawaii (westernmost Aleutian Islands; 6hr. behind Eastern). **Postal Abbreviation:** AK

Sales Tax: 0%

CLIMATE

No single climatic zone covers the whole state. Fairbanks, the Interior, and parts of the Bush experience Alaska's most extreme weather, with 95°F hot spells in summer, -50°F temperatures in winter, and less than eight in. of precipitation annually. The Japanese Current creates a moderating effect on the climate of Anchorage and other southcentral costal towns; average temperatures for Anchorage range from 13°F in January to 57°F in July. In the southeast, temperatures are even milder and rain even more frequent; a cold-temperate rainforest covers the region.

TRAVEL

Driving in Alaska is not for the faint of heart. Roads reach only a quarter of the state's area, and many of the major ones remain in deplorable condition. "Frost heaves" from melting and contracting permafrost cause dips and surreal "twists" in the road. Radiators and headlights should be protected from flying rocks with wire screens, and a full-size spare tire and a good set of shocks are essential. Winter can actually offer a smoother ride. At the same time, the danger of avalanches and ice is cause for major concern. Anyone venturing onto Alaska's roads should own a copy of *The Milepost,* available for $18 from **Vernon Publications, Inc.,** 300 Northrup Way, #200, Bellevue, WA 98004 (800-726-4707).

Given Alaska's size, **air travel** is often a necessity, albeit an exorbitantly expensive one (the hourly rate exceeds $100). Several intrastate airlines, based almost exclusively at the Anchorage airport, transport passengers and cargo to virtually every village in Alaska: **Alaska Airlines** (to larger Bush towns and Cordova; 800-426-0333); **Mark Air** (to larger Bush towns, Kodiak, and the Aleutians; 800-627-5247); **ERA Aviation** (southcentral; 907-243-6633); **Southcentral Air** (southcentral; 907-243-2761); **Reeve Aleutian Airways** (the Aleutians; 907-243-4700); and **Ryan Air Service** (practically anywhere in the Bush; 907-561-2090). Many other charters and flightseeing services are available. Write **Ketchum Air Service Inc.,** P.O. Box 190588, Anchorage 99519 (243-5525), on the North Shore of Lake Hood, to ask about their charters. One-day flights and overnight or weekend trips to isolated lakes, mountains, and tundra usually range from $165 up.

AlaskaPass offers unlimited access to Alaska's railroad, ferry, and bus systems; a 15-day pass sells for $569, a 30-day pass for $799. The pass, valid from Bellingham, WA to Dutch Harbor on the Aleutian Islands, is a good deal for those who want to see a lot of Alaska in a short amount of time. Call 800-248-7598 for details.

■■■ KETCHIKAN

Near Alaska's southeasternmost point, Ketchikan marks the first Alaskan stopping point for northbound cruise ships and ferries. The boats disgorge loads of tourists in search of an Alaskan experience and hordes of students looking for the big summer bucks offered by area canneries. No matter what they're expecting, there's one thing people who arrive in Ketchikan inevitably find: rain. "People don't tan in Ketchikan," according to a local proverb, "they rust." If the locals didn't learn to ignore the rain in this gussied-up fishing and lumber town, they would scarcely step outside. Fourteen feet of rain per year explain the ubiquitous awnings projecting over city streets.

Practical Information The **Southeastern Alaska Visitors Center (SEAVC)** (228-6219), on the waterfront next to the Federal building, has info on Ketchikan and the entire Panhandle, especially good on the outdoors (open daily 8:30am-4:30pm; Oct.-April Tues.-Sat. 8:30am-4:30pm). The **Ketchikan Visitors Bureau,** 131 Front St. (225-6166 or 800-770-3300), is on the cruise ship docks downtown (open Mon.-Fri. 7:30am-4:30pm, Sat.-Sun. depending on cruise ship arrival times). **Alaska Marine Highway** ferries (225-6181) dock north of town on Tongass Hwy. Ketchikan's **airport** floats across from the city on Gravina Island. A small ferry runs from

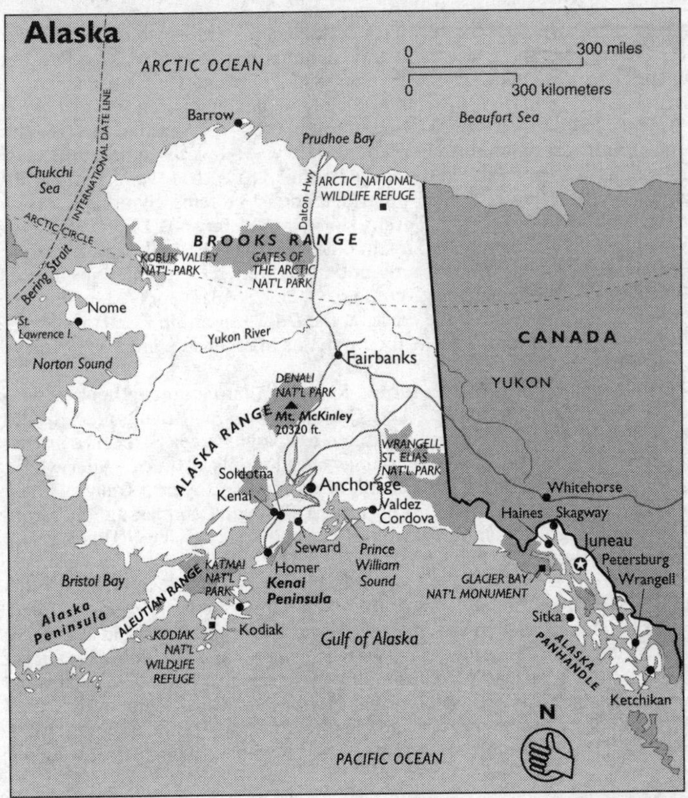

the airport to just above the state ferry dock ($3). **Alaska Airlines** (225-2141 or 800-426-0333) provides flight info; daily flights to Juneau cost $124 (open Mon.-Fri. 9:30am-5pm). Ketchikan's **post office:** (225-9601), next to the ferry terminal (open Mon.-Fri. 8:30am-5pm); **ZIP code:** 99901; **area code:** 907.

Accommodations and Food Besides hostels, rooms here are relatively expensive. The **Ketchikan Reservation Service** (225-3273) provides bed and breakfast rooms from $65-75. The **Ketchikan Youth Hostel (HI-AYH),** P.O. Box 8515 (225-3319), at Main and Grant St. in the basement of the First Methodist Church has no beds, but the 4-in.-thick foam mats on the floor are comfortable if you have a sleeping bag. Expect a clean kitchen, a common area, two showers, tea, and coffee. (3-day max. stay subject to availability. Lockout 9am-6pm. Lights out 10:30pm, on 7am. Curfew 11pm; call ahead if arriving on a late ferry. $7, nonmembers $10. Reservations advisable. Open June-Aug.) If you plan in advance, camping provides an escape from Ketchikan's high prices. **SEAVC** (228-6219) has information on several Forest Service campgrounds, including the **Signal Creek Campground** 6 mi. north of the ferry terminal on Tongass Hwy., which has 25 units on the shores of Ward Lake with water and pit toilets (sites $5; open in summer). The supermarket most convenient to downtown is **Tatsuda's,** 633 Stedman (225-4125), at Deermount St., just beyond the Thomas Basin (open daily 7am-11pm). The **5 Star Cafe,** 5 Creek St. (247-7827), has savory salads and sandwiches for $5-10 (open Mon.-Wed. and Sat.-Sun. 7am-6pm, Thurs.-Fri. 7am-8pm).

Sights and the Outdoors Pick up the guided walking totem tour at the visitors bureau to see the fine ancient and contemporary totems which adorn Ketchikan and the surrounding area. World-renowned totem carver Nathan Jackson lives here; his work stands in front of the Federal Building. If you can see only one thing in Ketchikan, visit the largest totem park in Alaska—the **Saxman Native Village,** 2½ mi. southwest of Ketchikan on Tongass Hwy. ($8 by cab), where artisans carve new totems in an open studio (open daily 9am-5pm). Also, 13½ mi. north of Ketchikan on Tongass Hwy. is **Totem Bight,** featuring 13 totems. (Both parks open during daylight hours. Free.) The **Totem Heritage Center,** 601 Deermount St. (225-5900), houses 33 well-preserved totem poles from Tlingit, Haida, and Tsimshian villages, the largest collection of authentic pre-commercial totem poles in the U.S. (Not all poles displayed at any given time. Open daily 8am-5pm. $2, under 18 free; free Sun. afternoon.) Across the creek, at the **Deer Mountain Fish Hatchery** (225-6760), a self-guided tour unlocks the mysteries of artificial salmon sex (open daily 8am-4:30pm; free).

Fortune-seeking prospectors turned Ketchikan into a mining boom-town, and some of this history is preserved on **Creek St.,** once a thriving red-light district where sailors and salmon went upstream to spawn. Creek St. itself consists of a shop-lined wooden boardwalk on pilings over Ketchikan Creek. Older women in black fishnets and red-tasseled silk still beckon passersby into **Dolly's House,** 24 Creek St. (225-6329), a former brothel turned museum. Countless antiques from the 1920s and 30s are set amidst bawdy colors and secret caches. (Hours vary with cruise ship arrivals; call ahead. $3.)

Deer Mountain (3100ft.) is a good day-hike from Ketchikan. Walk past the city park on Fair St. up the hill towards the town dump; the trail branches off left just behind the dump. A steep ascent leads 2½ mi. up the mountain and above treeline along a sometimes steep-sided ridge with great views of the town and sea beyond.

Many of the boats and planes continually buzzing through Ketchikan's harbor travel to nearby **Misty Fiords National Monument.** Only 20 mi. from Ketchikan, this region of narrow waterways and old-growth forests, home to both whales and mountain goats, invites hikers and kayakers to play in its huge, rugged wilderness.

■■■ JUNEAU

Accessible only by water or air, Alaska's capital was not founded for the convenience of its location but instead for its proximity to lucrative mineral deposits. In 1880, Tlingit Chief Kowee led Joe Juneau and Richard Harris to the gleaming "mother lode" in the hills up Gold Creek. Within 25 years, Juneau replaced Sitka as capital of the Alaska territory. Today, this tiny strip of land at the base of imposing Mt. Juneau offers jumbled architecture and a wharf-side tourist mecca, which have garnered it the nickname "Little San Francisco."

Practical Information **Davis Log Cabin,** 134 3rd St., 99801 (586-2284 or 586-2201; fax 586-6304), at Seward St., serves as the visitors center (open Mon.-Fri. 8:30am-5pm, Sat.-Sun. 9am-5pm; Oct.-May Mon.-Fri. 8:30am-5pm). **National Forest and National Park Services,** 101 Egan Dr. (586-8751), in Centennial Hall, provide info on hiking and fishing in the area (open daily 8am-5pm; in winter Mon.-Fri. 8am-5pm). **Juneau International Airport,** 9 mi. north of Juneau on Glacier Hwy., is serviced by Alaska Airlines (789-0600), Delta, and local charters. **Alaska Marine Highway,** 1591 Glacier Ave., P.O. Box 25535, 99802-5535 (465-3941 or 800-642-0066; fax 277-4829), docks its ferries at the Auke Bay terminal 14 mi. from the city on the Glacier Hwy. Call **MGT Ferry Express** (789-5460) from 6-8pm to reserve a ride from any major hotel to the airport or ferry for $5. MGT also offers a 2½-hour tour of Mendenhall Glacier ($12.50). Juneau's **post office:** 709 W. 9th St. (586-7138; open Mon.-Fri. 8:30am-5pm, Sat. 1-3pm); **ZIP code:** 99801; **area code:** 907.

Accommodations and Food If you can't get into Juneau's hostel, the **Alaska Bed and Breakfast Association,** P.O. Box 3/6500 #169, 99802 (586-2959), provides info on rooms. **Juneau International Hostel (HI-AYH),** 614 Harris St. (586-9559), at 6th atop a steep hill, is a spotless, efficient hostel. Clean up with the free showers and laundry (wash $1.25, dry 75¢). (Chores assigned. 48 beds. Will store packs during the day. Small charges for sheets, towels, soap, and detergent. 3-day max. stay if beds are full. Lockout 9am-5pm. Strict curfew 11pm. Beds $10. Popular; make reservations by May for July-Aug.) For sleeping under the stars, try the **Mendenhall Lake Campground,** Montana Creek Rd. Take Glacier Hwy. north 9 mi. to Mendenhall Loop Rd.; continue 3½ mi. and take the right fork. If asked, the bus driver will let you off within walking distance (2 mi.) of camp. (60 sites. Fireplaces, water, pit toilet, picnic tables, free firewood. 14-day max. stay. Sites $8. Reserve for an extra $7.50 by calling 800-280-2267.) **Auke Village Campground,** on Glacier Hwy., 15 mi. from Juneau, has 12 sites near a scenic beach, 1½ mi. west of ferry terminal. (Fireplaces, water, flush toilets, picnic tables. 14-day max. stay. Sites $8. No reservations.) Call the Forest Service, Juneau Ranger District (586-8800) for information about both campgrounds.

The **Armadillo Tex-Mex Café,** 431 S. Franklin St. (586-1880), packs in locals and tourists alike for heaps of fantastic food. Try *chalupa* for $8 (open Mon.-Sat. 11am-9pm, Sun. 4-9pm). The **Channel Bowl Café** (586-6139) is a right-rockin' breakfast joint with great pancakes ($5.50; open daily 7am-2pm). Buy groceries at the **Foodland Supermarket,** 631 Willoughby Ave. (586-3101; open daily 7am-9pm).

Sights The **Alaska State Museum,** 395 Whittier St. (465-2901), leads you through the history, ecology, and culture of Alaska's four major indigenous groups (Tlingit, Athabascan, Aleut, and Inuit). It also houses the famous "First White Man" totem pole, a carved likeness of Abraham Lincoln. (Open Mon.-Fri. 9am-6pm, Sat.-Sun. 10am-6pm; Sept. 18-May 17 Tues.-Sat. 10am-4pm. $3, students and seniors free.) Check out the impressive gold-onion-domed 1894 **St. Nicholas Russian Orthodox Church,** on 5th St. between N. Franklin and Gold St. Services Saturday at 6am and Sunday at 10am, are conducted in English, Old Slavonic, and Tlingit. Tours are open to the public. (Open daily 9am-5pm. $1 donation requested.) In Marine Park, rambunctious children play as tourists picnic and watch the approach of ships to the clogged docks (free concerts mid-June to mid-Aug. Fri. 7-8:30pm). The **Alaska Brewing Co.,** 5429 Shaune Dr. (780-5866), offers free tours complete with a free sample of its award-winning brew. Take the hourly city bus to Lemon Creek, turn onto Anka Rd. from the Glacier Hwy., and Shaune Dr. is the first right. (Tours Tues.-Sat. on the ½hr. 11am-4:30pm; Oct.-April Thurs.-Sat. on the ½hr. 11am-4:30pm.)

Juneau is a hiking center in southeast Alaska. If you're willing to hike for the best view of Juneau, go to the end of 6th St. and up the steep, 4-mi. trail to the summit of **Mt. Roberts (3576ft.).** In winter, the slopes of **Eaglecrest Ski Area,** 155 S. Seward St., 99801, on Douglas Island, offer decent **alpine skiing** (586-5284 or 586-5330).

The 38 glaciers of the **Juneau Icefield** cover an area larger than Rhode Island. The most visited glacier is the **Mendenhall Glacier,** about 10 mi. north of downtown Juneau. The **Glacier Visitors Center** (789-0097), will explain everything about the glacier (open daily late May to mid-Sept. 8:30am-5:30pm). The rangers also give an interesting walking tour Sunday through Friday at 9:30am, beginning from the flagpole. The 3½-mi. **West Glacier Trail** has the best view of the glacier. If pressed for time, the 3½-mi. **East Glacier Loop Trail** affords a way to catch a side view of the glacier. Take the local public bus down Glacier Hwy. and up Mendenhall Loop Rd. until it connects with Glacier Spur Rd. ($1.25). From there it's less than a ½-hr. walk to the visitors center.

■■■ WRANGELL-ST. ELIAS

Wrangell-St. Elias National Park and Preserve is Alaska's best-kept secret. If you have any time at all to spend in Alaska, come *here.* The largest national park in the

U.S., it could swallow more than 14 Yosemites. Four major mountain ranges converge in the park:, and nine peaks tower at more than 14,000 ft. within the park, including the second highest mountain in the U.S. (18,008-ft. **Mt. St. Elias**). The park is located in the southeast corner of Alaska's mainland, accessible by two roads: the **McCarthy Rd.,** which enters the heart of the park, and the **Nabesna Rd.,** which enters from the northern park boundaries. The **visitors center** (822-5234) can be found 1 mi. off the Richardson Hwy. on the side road toward **Copper Center** (open daily 8am-6pm; in winter Mon.-Fri. 8am-5pm). There are also **ranger stations** in **Chitina** (CHIT-na; 907-823-2205; open Fri.-Mon. 9:30am-4:30pm) and in **Slana,** on the northern park boundary (907-822-5238; open daily 8am-5pm).

OUTDOORS

Most travelers head to McCarthy, a small town in the middle of the park. To drive to McCarthy, turn onto the Edgerton Hwy. from the Richardson Hwy. 33 mi. south of Glenallen, and head east for 34 mi. to the town of **Chitina,** which has a single café (open daily 6am-10pm), a general store (907-823-2111; open daily June-Aug. 8am-11pm; in spring and fall 9am-8pm; in winter 10am-7pm), and a ranger station (see above). From Chitina, the **McCarthy Rd.** follows the old roadbed of the **Copper River and Northwestern Railway** for 58 mi. to the Kennicott River. This road is arguably the roughest state road in Alaska. The road terminates on the western edge of the Kennicott River, a silt-laden river originating within the Kennicott Glacier. The only way across the river is by a hand-operated **tram** (a metal "cart" with two seats, running on a cable). McCarthy is an easy ½-mi. walk from the far side of the river.

McCarthy, 5 mi. south of Kennicott, was developed for miners' recreation. From 1900-38, both women and alcohol were prohibited in Kennicott and abundant in McCarthy. Today, McCarthy retains a distinctive, if less bawdy, charm.

Getting to McCarthy isn't too difficult. Drive on your own if you want to test your car's suspension. **Backcountry Connections** (907-822-5292; 800-478-5292 in AK) will take you aboard their roomy, comfortable vans complete with friendly and knowledgeable drivers. (From Glenallen $69, from Chitina $35.) Vans depart Monday through Saturday from Glenallen (7:15am) and Chitina (8:30am) and return from McCarthy (4:30pm). **Wrangell Mountain Air** (see below) flies to McCarthy daily from Chitina ($60 each way).

Beds in the bunk house at the **McCarthy Lodge** (907-333-5402) cost $20. **Camping** is free on the west side of the Kennicott River (no water, pit toilets). Artifacts and documents from the mining days repose at the **McCarthy-Kennicott Historical Museum** (free; open daily 8am-6pm). Get general info about the area here and pick up a walking tour map ($1).

If you go **flightseeing** anywhere in Alaska, do it here. **Wrangell Mountain Air** (800-478-1160 for reservations), based in downtown McCarthy, has several flights over the area ($40-100). There is a three-person minimum on all flights. **McCarthy Air** (800-245-6909), also in McCarthy, offers similar flights and rates. The two companies are very competitive, so compare rates before you sign on.

The Bike Shop rents bikes ($8 per hr., $20 per day) with which you can explore some of the many old, obscure roads around town. **Copper Oar** (907-522-1670), at the end of the McCarthy Rd., offers a two-hour whitewater trip down the Kennicott River for $40. For those on a serious shoestring, just walking around McCarthy and Kennicott is plenty interesting. A **shuttle bus** runs out to Kennicott from McCarthy on a regular schedule ($8 round-trip). It's a 5-mi. hike between the two towns. Most **hikers and trekkers** use the McCarthy Rd. or McCarthy as a base. The park maintains no trails, but miners and other travelers from decades past have established various pathways. The most common route, a hike out past Kennicott to the Root Glacier, takes one to three days for the 16-mi. round-trip following roadbed and glacial moraine with three moderate stream crossings. For any overnight trip, the park service requests a written itinerary; though it's not required, it's in your own best interest.

■■■ ANCHORAGE

Only 80 years ago, cartographers wasted no ink on what is now Alaska's major metropolis, located in southcentral Alaska. Approximately half the state's population lives in "Los Anchorage," the term that rural Alaskans use to mock the city's urban affectations. Beyond its decentralized jumble of fast-food joints and liquor stores, Anchorage supports semi-professional baseball and basketball teams, performances by internationally known orchestras and music stars, theater, and opera. Still, moose and bear not only occasionally wander downtown but are hunted legally within the municipality—this is as close to "big city" as Alaska gets.

Practical Information The **Log Cabin Visitor Information Center,** W. 4th Ave. (274-3531), at F St., has plenty of maps and brochures (open daily 7:30am-7pm; Sept. and May 9am-6pm; Oct.-April 9am-4pm). The **Alaska International Airport,** P.O. Box 190649-VG, 99519-0649 (266-2525), is serviced by 8 international carriers and 15 domestic carriers, including **Delta** (249-2110 or 800-221-1212) and **Mark Air** (266-6802 or 800-627-5247). Nearly every airport in Alaska can be reached from Anchorage, either directly or through Fairbanks. **Alaska Railroad,** 411 W. 1st Ave., 99510-7500 (265-2494; 800-544-0552 out of state), runs to Denali ($88), Fairbanks ($129), and Seward ($50). (In winter, 1 per week to Fairbanks; no service to Seward.) For more info write to Passenger Service, P.O. Box 107500. (Office open daily 7am-5:30pm; ticket sales Mon.-Fri. 5:30am-5pm, Sat. 5:30am-2pm, Sun. 5:30am-2pm.)

Alaska Backpacker Shuttle (344-8775) has van service to towns and trailheads in the vicinity. Buses into Denali ($35, $60 round-trip; bike $5) leave at 8am daily from the youth hostel. Buses also go to Talkeetna ($30), Girdwood ($15), Portage Train Station ($17.50), and trailheads north and south of Anchorage ($5-10 depending on distance); call to arrange pick-up. **Fireweed Express** (452-0521) runs to Denali ($25, $45 round-trip; bike $5 bike); call for reservations. **Homer and Kenai Peninsula Bus Lines** (800-478-8280) sends one bus per day to Seward ($30) and Homer ($38). Leaves from the Alaskan Samovar Inn, 720 Gambell St. **Alaskon Express** (800-544-2206) heads to Valdez (leaves daily 8am, $61) and Haines (leaves Sun., Tues., and Fri. 7am, $200). **Alaska Direct** (277-6652) goes to Whitehorse, YT (Mon., Wed., and Sat. 6am, $145). **Alaska Marine Highway,** 333 W. 4th St. (272-7116), in the Post Office Mall, has no terminal, but sells ferry tickets and reservations (open Mon.-Fri. 8am-4:30pm). **Affordable Car Rental,** 4707 Spenard Rd. (243-3370), rents cars across from the Regal Alaskan Hotel ($29 per day, with 50 free mi.; 30¢ per additional mi.). **Gay/Lesbian Helpline:** 258-4777. **24-hr. Crisis Line:** 272-4048. **Emergency:** 911. Anchorage's **post office:** W. 4th Ave. and C St. (279-3062), in the lower level in the mall (open Mon.-Fri. 10am-5:30pm, Sat. 10am-4pm); **ZIP Code:** 99510; **area code:** 907.

The hub of southcentral Alaska, Anchorage sports a well-organized downtown grid. Numbered avenues run east-west; addresses are designated East or West from **C St.** North-south streets are lettered alphabetically west of A Street, and named alphabetically east of **A St.** The rest of Anchorage spreads out—way out—along the major highways.

Accommodations, Camping, and Food Although Anchorage is blessed with affordable lodgings, few can be found downtown. The best option is the **Anchorage International Youth Hostel (HI-AYH),** 700 H St. (276-3635), at 7th, one block south of the Transit Center downtown. (3 kitchens, 2 balconies, and scads of info on traveling throughout the state. Frequently filled in summer; write or call for reservations. Wheelchair accessible. Lockout noon-5pm. Curfew midnight; watchman can check you in until 3am. 4-day max. stay in summer. $15, nonmembers $18; photo ID required. Bag storage $1 per bag per day.) The quiet, comfortable **Spenard Hostel,** 2845 W. 42nd Pl. (248-5036), has kitchens, common rooms, and free local phone calls. Take bus #7 or 36 out Spenard to Turnagain; 42nd Pl. is the first left off Turnagain. (No curfew, no lockout. Chore requested. $12.)

Among the best of the state campgrounds near Anchorage, **Eagle River** (688-0998; $15) and **Eklutna** (694-2108; $10), are 12.6 mi. and 26.5 mi. northeast of Anchorage, respectively, along Glenn Hwy. For more information on these and other campsites, contact the **State Parks Service** (762-2261). **Centennial Park,** 5300 Glenn Hwy. (333-9711), lies north of town off Muldoon Rd.; look for the park sign. Take bus #3 or 75 from downtown. (90 sites for tents and RVs. Showers, dumpsters, fireplaces, pay phones, and water. 7-day max. stay. Check-in daily 7am-midnight. Flexible noon check-out. Sites $13. Open May-Sept.) **Lions' Camper Park,** 800 Boniface Pkwy. (333-9711), south of the Glenn Hwy. in Russian Jack Springs Park four blocks from the Boniface mall. Take bus #12 or 45 to the mall and walk. (50 campsites with showers, dumpsters, fireplaces, pay phones, and water. Office at Centennial Park. 7-day max. stay. Sites $13. Open June 15-Sept.)

Anchorage presents budget travelers with the most affordable and varied culinary fare in the state. **Blondie's Café** (279-0698), at the corner of 4th and D St., has a bizarre, eclectic decor and all-day breakfast including 3 hotcakes for $4.25 (ham and cheese sandwich $5; open daily 5am-11pm). **Twin Dragon,** 612 E. 15th Ave. (276-7535), near Gambell, offers one of the town's finest treats: a lunch buffet of marinated meats and vegetables, lightly barbecued on a giant, circular grill ($6.25). This new spot has become a favorite among Anchorage's knowledgeable diners. (Buffet served Mon.-Sat. 11am-3:30pm, Sun. 1-3:30pm. Open daily 11am-midnight.)

Sights and Nightlife Watching over Anchorage from Cook Inlet is **Mt. Susitna,** known to locals as the "Sleeping Lady." For a view of Susitna, head about 4 mi. from downtown to **Point Warzenof,** on the western end of Northern Lights Blvd. **Earthquake Park** recalls the 1964 Good Friday earthquake, a day Alaskans refer to as "Black Friday." The quake was the strongest ever recorded in North America, registering 9.2 on the Richter scale. For a little less shakin', drive, walk, skate, or bike along the **Tony Knowles Coastal Trail,** an 11-mi. paved track that skirts Cook Inlet on one side and the backyards of Anchorage's upper-crust on the other.

A four-hour **walking tour** of downtown Anchorage begins at the visitors center. The **Anchorage Museum of History and Art,** 121 W. 7th Ave. (343-4326), at A St., features exhibits of Alaskan Native artifacts and art. Native dance performances take place three times per day in the summer ($4). The gallery gives free tours daily at 10, 11am, 1, and 2pm. (Open daily 9am-6pm; Sept. 16-May 14 Tues.-Sat. 10am-6pm, Sun. 1-5pm. $4, seniors $3.50, under 18 free.) The **Alaska Aviation Heritage Museum,** 4721 Aircraft Dr. (248-5325), provides a fun look at Alaska's pioneer aviators (open daily 9am-6pm; $5.75, seniors $4.50, youths $2.75).

To counteract urban claustrophobia, hike to the summit of **Flattop Mountain** in the "Glenn Alps" of the Chugach Range near Anchorage. The view of the city and, if it's clear, sun-soaked Denali, is well worth the hour-long hike. To reach the trailhead, jump on bus #92 to the intersection of Hillside and Upper Huffman Rd. From

The Iditarod: A Pretty Long Race

And you thought walking to school in winter was rough. For the first three weeks of March each year, dog mushers race their teams 1100 mi. from Anchorage to Nome in the **Iditarod Trail Sled Dog Race.** The trail, made famous in 1925 when mushers ferried life-saving diphtheria serum to stave off an epidemic in Nome, crosses two mountain ranges, the Yukon River, and the frozen Bering Sea. The race, once a rollicking good time Alaska-style, has come under fire in recent years by animal-rights activists because of the hardships suffered by sled dogs, some of which inevitably die en route to Nome. Still, the city turns out in force for the ceremonial start of the race in Anchorage on March 3 (just outside town, the teams are unceremoniously loaded onto trucks and shuttled to the actual starting line). For more information, contact the Iditarod Trail Committee, Pouch X, Wasilla, AK 99687 (376-5155).

there walk ¾ mi. along Upper Huffman Rd. and take a right on Toilsome Hill Dr. Proceed for 2 mi. Trail signs point the way up the 4500-ft. mountain.

Six bars and a rockin' dance floor fill **Chilkoot Charlie's,** 2435 Spenard Rd. (272-1010), at Fireweed. Take bus #7 or 60. (Open Mon.-Thurs. 10am-2:30am, Fri.-Sat. 10am-3am, Sun. noon-2:30am.) Less crowded and more interesting is **Mr. Whitekey's Fly-by-Night Club,** 3300 Spenard Rd. (279-7726). Mr. Whitekey's serves "everything from the world's finest champagnes to a damn fine plate of Spam." Try Spam nachos or Spam on a bagel ($3-7). Nightly music ranges from rock to jazz to blues. (Take bus #7. Bar open Tues.-Sat. 4pm-2:30am.) Anchorage's leading gay and lesbian bar is the **Blue Moon,** 530 E. 5th Ave. (277-0441; open Mon.-Thurs. 1pm-2am, Fri. 1pm-3am, Sat. 3pm-3am, Sun. 3pm-2am).

■■■ DENALI

Established in 1917 to protect wildlife, **Denali National Park** also preserves the land on which the wildlife thrives. Denali (Athabascan for "The Great One"), also known as **Mt. McKinley,** is the tallest mountain in North America, boasting the greatest vertical relief in the world from base to summit; even mighty Mt. Everest rises only 10,000 ft. from its base on the Tibetan Plateau. Denali's 18,000 ft. of rock and ice scrape toward the sky without interruption, and its mass creates cloud formations that obscure the peak, only visible for about 20% of the summer. Even if you can't see the peak, you can still experience the park's tundra, taiga, and wildlife.

Practical Information All travelers stop at the **Denali Visitor Center** (683-1266), one mi. from Rte. 3 for orientation. At the center, pick up **maps,** shuttle-bus schedules, free permits for backcountry camping, and the indispensable (free!) publication *Alpenglow.* (Center open summer daily 7am-8pm. Lockers outside 50¢.) The center is also headquarters of the **shuttle-bus** which runs to **Eielson Visitors Center,** 66 mi. into the park (staffed by helpful rangers; open summer daily 9am-dusk). **Shuttle buses** leave the Denali Visitors Center daily (5:30am-2:30pm). The park **entrance fee** is $3, families $5. For info, write to **Denali National Park and Preserve,** P.O. Box 9, Denali Park 99755 (683-1266).

Only the first 14 mi. of the park road is accessible by private vehicle; the remaining 71 mi. of dirt road can be reached only by the shuttle bus. Go for the less frequent Wonder Lake bus if you can, as the best views of Denali are beyond Eielson. Some shuttle bus tickets may be reserved in advance (272-7275 or 800-622-7275), but more become available each day on a first come, first served basis. **Camper buses** ($15) move faster, transporting *only* people with **campground permits** and **backcountry permits.** You can get on and off these buses **anywhere along the road;** flag the next one down when you want to move on or back. This is a good strategy for dayhiking and convenient for Park explorers since they will also stop to pick up dayhikers along the road. Camper buses leave the visitors center five times per day. The final bus stays overnight at Wonder Lake and returns at 7:10am.

Denali National Park can be easily reached by air, road, or rail. The best place to catch a flightseeing tour is **Talkeetna.** The **George Parks Hwy.** (Rte. 3), connects Anchorage (240mi. south of Denali) and Fairbanks (120mi. north), and offers direct access to the Denali Park Rd. Several bus companies have service between Denali, Anchorage, and Fairbanks: **Parks Highway Express** (479-3065) charges $20 per person from Anchorage or Fairbanks to Denali; **Moon Bay Express** (274-6454) has one bus daily to Anchorage ($35, $60 round-trip); **Fireweed Express** (452-0251) provides daily van service to Fairbanks ($25). The **Alaska Railroad,** P.O. Box 107500, Anchorage 99510 (683-2233; 800-544-0552 out of state), makes stops at Denali station 1½ mi. from the entrance.

In an **emergency** call 683-9100. Denali's **post office:** (683-2291), next to the Denali Hotel, one mi. from the visitors center (open Mon.-Fri. 8:30am-5pm, Sat. 10am-1pm; Oct.-May Mon.-Sat. 10am-1pm); **ZIP code:** 99755; **area code:** 907.

Accommodations, Camping, and Food The **Denali Hostel,** P.O. Box 801, Denali Park 99755 (683-1295), waits 9.6 mi. north of the park entrance with bunks, showers, kitchen facilities, and morning shuttles into and out of the park ($22). Take a left on Otto Lake Rd.; it's the second house on the right.

Six **campgrounds** line Denali Park Rd. within the park. Most have water and some form of toilet facilities (sites $6-12) and all require permits. Only 30% of campsites can be reserved in advance (907-272-7275 or 800-622-7275); the remainder are issued daily on a first come, first served basis—arrive early. Backpackers waiting for a backcountry permit or a campsite can find a space in **Morino Campground** ($6), next to the Denali National Park Hotel. Food in Denali is expensive; try to bring groceries in with you. Meager provisions in the park are available at **Mercantile Gas and Groceries,** 1½ mi. along Denali Park Rd. (683-2215; open daily 7am-10pm). The **Lynx Creek Grocery** (683-2548) 1 mi. north of the park entrance, has similarly priced items (open 24 hrs.). **Lynx Creek Pizza** (683-2547), dishes up imposing Italian and Mexican favorites ($7-8.25) and good pizza (open daily 11am-11:30pm).

Exploring the Backcountry Denali National Park has no trails and cannot be covered in one day. Although dayhiking is unlimited, only 2-12 hikers can camp at one time in each of the park's 44 units; select a few different areas in the park in case your first choice is booked. The taiga forest and tundra of the first third of the park is hellish to hike—imagine walking on old wet mattresses with bushes growing out of them. The last third of the park swarms with mosquitoes in July and biting "no-see-ums" in August. For prime hiking and back-country camping, stick to the middle third. Although rangers at the backcountry desk will not give recommendations for specific areas (they want to disperse hikers as widely as possible), especially good locations are along the **Toklat River, Marmot Rock,** and **Polychrome Pass.** You'll want to take the 10-hr. round-trip bus ride to Wonder Lake Campground for your best chance at a glimpse of Denali *sans* clouds,; reserve the last bus out to the campground and the first bus back in the morning, and bring protective netted head gear (available in the convenience store). Beware of bears.

■■■ THE ALASKA HIGHWAY

Built during World War II, the Alaska Highway maps out an astonishing 2647-km route between Dawson Creek, BC, and Fairbanks, AK. After the Pearl Harbor attack in 1941, War Department officials became convinced that an overland route was necessary to supply the U.S. Army bases in Alaska. The U.S. Army Corps of Engineers completed the daunting task in just eight months and 12 days.

Travelers on the highway should be prepared for heavy-duty driving. For much of the route, pavement gives way to chip-seal, a layer of packed gravel held in place by hardened oil. In summer, dust and rocks fly freely, guaranteeing shattered headlights and a chipped windshield. Drivers should fit their headlights with plastic or wire-mesh covers. Most locals protect their radiators from bug splatter with large screens mounted in front of the grill. Travel with at least one full-size **spare tire** and some **spare gas;** if you're crazy enough to drive the highway in winter, bring along a full set of arctic clothing and prepare your vehicle for subzero conditions.

Before setting out on your epic journey, pick up a copy of the free pamphlet *Help Along the Way* at a visitors bureau, or contact the Department of Health and Social Services, P.O. Box H-06C, Juneau 99811 (907-465-3027); the pamphlet includes an exhaustive listing of Emergency Medical Services and phone numbers throughout Alaska, the Yukon, and British Columbia, plus tips on preparation and driving.

■■■ FAIRBANKS

If E.T. Barnette hadn't gotten stuck with his load of trade goods at the junction of the Tanana and Chena Rivers just when Felix Pedro, Italian immigrant-turned-prospector, unearthed a golden fortune nearby, and if territorial judge James Wickersham hadn't been trying to woo political favors from an Indiana senator (Charles Warren Fairbanks), then this town might never even have existed—and it certainly wouldn't have been named for somebody who never even set foot in Alaska.

Practical Information Fairbanks lies 358 mi. north of Anchorage via the **George Parks Hwy.** The **Convention and Visitors Bureau** (456-5774 or 800-327-5774) gives out info at 550 1st Ave. (open daily 8am-8pm; Sept.-May Mon.-Fri. 8am-5pm). The **Alaska Public Lands Information Center (APLIC),** 250 Cushman St., #1A (456-0527), has info on parks and protected areas of Alaska (open daily 9am-6pm; in winter Tues.-Sat. 10am-6pm). Fairbanks is headquarters for **Gates of the Arctic National Park,** 201 1st Ave. (456-0281; open Mon.-Fri. 8am-5pm) and the **Arctic National Wildlife Refuge,** 101 12th St., #266 (456-0250; open Mon.-Fri. 8am-4:30pm).

Fairbanks's **airport** lands them 5 mi. from downtown on Airport Way. **Alaska Air** (452-1661) flies to Anchorage ($109) and Juneau ($222). The **Alaska Railroad,** 280 N. Cushman (456-4155), has one train per day May through September to Nenana ($20), Anchorage ($129), and Denali National Park ($47). Ages 2-11 ride ½-price. During the winter, a train leaves for Anchorage every Sunday ($70). (Depot open Mon.-Fri. 7:30am-4:30pm, Sat.-Sun. 7:30am-noon.) **Parks Highway Express** (479-3065) speeds six buses per week to Denali ($20) and Anchorage ($40). **Alaskon Express** (800-544-2206) runs four times a week to Haines ($174). Fairbanks's **post office:** 315 Barnette St. (452-3203; open Mon.-Fri. 9am-6pm, Sat. 10am-2pm); **ZIP code:** 99707; **area code:** 907.

Accommodations, Camping, and Food For information on bed and breakfasts, go to the visitors bureau or write **Fairbanks B&B,** 902 Kellum St., Anchorage (452-4967). At **Grandma Shirley's Hostel,** 510 Dunbar St. (451-9816), Grandma fixes you up with bedding, kitchen, showers, and a free bike. Men and women share a room with nine beds ($15; call for directions). **Billie's Backpackers Hostel (AAIH/Rucksackers),** 2895 Mack Rd. (479-2034), has four beds in a simple, clean cabin and 8 beds in the main house. Take Westridge Rd. one block off College to Mack Rd. Look for the "Billie's B&B" sign. (Kitchen. Train and airport pickup available. $13.50.) **Tanana Valley Campground,** 1800 College (456-7956), next to the Aurora Motel and Cabins, though somewhat noisy, is the closest campground to the downtown. (Free showers, coin laundry. Tent sites $6, with vehicle $10.) Just about every fast-food chain in existence stakes a claim along Airport Way and College Rd. **The Whole Earth,** 1157 Deborah St. (479-2052), behind College Corner Mall, puts together a health food store, deli, and restaurant all in one. (Store and seating open Mon.-Sat. 8am-8pm, Sun. noon-6pm. Hot food served 11am-3pm and 5-7pm.) **Souvlaki,** 112 N. Turner (452-5393), across the bridge from the visitors center, stuffs three succulent grape leaves for $1.15. (Salad in a pita $3. Open Mon.-Fri. 10am-9pm, Sat. 10am-6pm; in winter Mon.-Sat. 10am-6pm.)

Sights and a Bar The **University of Alaska-Fairbanks** sits at the top of a hill overlooking the flat cityscape. Both bus lines stop at the **Wood Campus Center** (474-7034). The **University of Alaska Museum** (474-7505), a 10-min. walk up Yukon Dr. from the Campus Center, houses exhibits ranging from Russian Orthodox vestments to an impressive mummified prehistoric bison. (Open daily 9am-8pm; May and Sept. 9am-5pm; Oct.-April noon-5pm. $4, students and seniors $3, families $12.50; free Fri. Oct.-April.) View a technological wonder of the world, the **Trans-Alaska Pipeline,** at Mile 8 of Steese Hwy. heading out of Fairbanks. Supercooled posts elevate the Pipeline to protect the tundra's frozen ecosystem from the 108°F oil. With nothing but black spruce to keep them company, Fairbanksians turn to bars at night. UAF students and everyone else head for the legendary **Howling Dog Saloon** (457-8780), 11½ mi. down Steese Hwy., for live rock-and-roll and midnight volleyball (open May-Oct. Tues.-Sun. noon–5am).

■■■ EAGLE

Eagle sits on the banks of the Yukon River, alone at the end of the Taylor Hwy., and on the brink of vast stretches of wilderness. Like most towns along the Yukon River, Eagle exists because of the Klondike gold rush. Established in 1898 as a permanent mining community, Eagle's central location in the Interior led the Secretary of War to establish an adjacent military base in 1899; in 1901, Eagle became the first incorporated city in the Interior. The end of the Gold Rush marked the beginning of Eagle's decline as a military and mining center, but extensive restoration work by the BLM and Eagle Historical Society has returned many of the town's buildings to their original condition. To outsiders, Eagle mainly exists as a point of historical interest and a friendly launching point for canoe trips on the Yukon.

Eagle has, arguably, more square feet of museum space per capita than any other town, city, or village in Alaska; the only way to access all of the town's historic buildings and displays and get the full dope while you're at it, a daily 3-hr. walking tour ($3, under 12 free) leaves at 9am from the **Courthouse Museum** on Berry St. The courthouse is also open to the general public throughout much of the day. **Amundsen Park,** on 1st St. at Amundsen, honors the Norwegian explorer who hiked into Eagle in the *winter* of 1905 from Canada's Arctic Coast. He used Eagle's telegraph to inform the world that he had successfully navigated the Northwest Passage. Two months later, Amundsen mushed back to his ship, frozen in the ice floes of the Arctic Ocean. Nine months later, he completed the first successful journey from the Atlantic to the Pacific via the Arctic Ocean.

The Department of the Interior's **visitors center** (547-2233), on the west end of 1st St., can provide detailed information on the geography and wildlife of the area as well as the town itself (open daily 8am-5pm). In case of a **medical emergency** call 547-2300. Eagle's **post office:** (547-2211), on 2nd St. at Jefferson (open Mon.-Fri. 8:30am-4:30pm); **ZIP code:** 99738; **area code:** 907.

The **Yukon Adventure Bed and Breakfast** (547-2221), about ½ mi. east of town, sets a new standard for B&B amenities with a sun deck, TVs, VCRs in doubles, and a nice movie selection. With your back to the river, take a left on 1st Ave., pass the Village Store, and follow the signs for the boat launch. (Singles $50, doubles $60.) Campers will clap their hands and rejoice upon finding **Eagle BLM Campground,** a 1-mi. hike from town past Fort Egbert (free; no water, pit toilets). Several hiking trails start at the campground. The **Eagle Trading Co.** (547-2220), in the "mall" on Front St., has it all: groceries, showers ($4), RV hookups ($15), and rooms for rent (singles $50, doubles $60; open daily 9am-8pm; no credit cards accepted). The adjacent **Riverside Café** (547-2250) constitutes Eagle's restaurant industry, serving standard hotel food at reasonable (by Bush standards) prices (burgers with fries or salad $5; open daily 7am-8pm).

The Float from Eagle to Circle The **visitors center** (see above) is a good starting place for detailed information on the popular 158-mi. float down the Yukon River through **Yukon-Charley Rivers National Preserve** from Eagle to Circle. The full trip takes four to six days and passes through some of Alaska's wildest country. Bear, moose, and beaver abound, as do mosquitoes, though campers can generally avoid them by camping on the numerous gravel bars in the river. Canoes and inflatable rafts are the most common forms of transportation. **Eagle Canoe Rentals** (547-2203) sets you afloat for a five-day trip to Circle for $160 (paddles, life jackets, and canoe return included). Get information from the **Park Service** by writing Superintendent, P.O. Box 167, Eagle, AK 99738.

Hawaii

Hawaii, 2400 mi. off mainland America, is both physically and psychologically set apart from the rest of the United States. Here, as nowhere else, you will find lush vegetation, expansive beaches, towering surf, and sultry breezes. Acres of untainted tropical forest border luxurious resort areas while active volcanoes release billows of grey into the air. With no clear racial majority, Hawaii's cultural geography is as varied as that of the land, and the state is one of the most ethnically diverse regions in the world.

Hawaii is comprised of 132 islands, though only seven are inhabited. Honolulu resides on the island of **Oahu,** as do most of the state's residents and tourists. Oahu is the most accessible island in the chain, but as a consequence, there are few unexplored and unexploited places. The **Big Island** (officially called **Hawaii**) is famed for its Kona coffee, macadamia nuts, black sand beaches, open space and Volcanoes National Park. **Maui's** strong winds have made it one of the premier windsurfing destinations in the world, and with the windsurfers comes a hopping nightlife. Maui also boasts the historic whaling village of Lahaina, fantastic surfing, and the dormant volcanic crater of Haleakala. The green isle of **Kauai,** at the northwestern end of the inhabited islands, ranks first for sheer beauty. **Molokai,** with 6,000 inhabitants, is for the solitude-seeking traveler. The "Friendly Isle" still moves to the slow, quiet rhythms of the Pacific. On tiny **Lanai** exclusive resorts have replaced pineapples as the primary commodity. The seventh most populated isle, **Niihau,** is closed to most visitors, supporting just a few hundred plantation families who still converse in the Hawaiian language. Together, the Hawaii islands present, in the words of Mark Twain, "the loveliest fleet of islands that lies anchored in any ocean.

For more in depth coverage of Hawaii purchase *Let's Go: California 1996,* wherever fine books are sold."

Hawaiian Happenings

Authors: Isabella Bird, James Michener, Robert Louis Stevenson.
Artists: Madge Tennant, Jean Chalet, Robert Lyn Nelson.
Cuisine: *kim chee, katsu,* pineapple, *kalua* pig, *lay lau, lomi lomi* salmon, *haupia, poi, pupus, sashimi,* passion fruit.
Microbreweries: Primo Brewing & Malting Co.
Music: Don Ho.
Film and TV: *Hawaii Five-O,* everything with Pat Morita.
Climate: Even nicer than California.
Geography: Volcanic.

PRACTICAL INFORMATION

Capital: Honolulu.

Hawaii Visitors Bureau: 2270 Kalakaua Ave., 7th floor, Honolulu 96815 (923-1811).The ultimate source for information on Hawaii. Open Mon.-Fri. 8am-4:30pm. The other islands staff offices at major towns, as listed in the appropriate sections. **Camping and Parks: Department of Land and Natural Resources,** 1151 Punchbowl St., Room 310, Honolulu 96813 (587-0301). Open Mon.-Fri. 8am-4pm. Information and permits for camping in state parks and trail maps. **National Park Service,** Prince Kuhio Federal Bldg., #6305, 300 Ala Moana Blvd., Honolulu 96850 (541-2693). Permits are given at individual park headquarters. Open Mon.-Fri. 7:30am-4pm.

Time Zone: Hawaii (6hr. behind Eastern in spring and summer; 5hr. otherwise). **Postal Abbreviation:** HI

Area Code: 808 for all of Hawaii.

Sales Tax: 4.167%; hotel rooms 10.167%. **Road Tax:** $2 per day for rented cars.

GETTING AROUND AND SLEEPING AROUND

From Los Angeles round-trip tickets on many major carriers start at $300. **Cheap Tickets** (947-3717 in Hawaii, 800-234-4522 on the mainland) in Honolulu, offers low fares. Regular **ferry** service exists only between Maui, Molokai, and Lanai. **Airlines** are faster, cheaper, and often offer special deals on car rentals. The major inter-island carriers, **Hawaiian, Mahalo,** and **Aloha Airlines,** can jet you quickly (about 40 min.) from Honolulu to any of the islands. Travel agents, such as **Pali Tour and Travel, Inc.,** 1300 Pali Hwy. Suite 1004, Honolulu 96813 (533-3608), sell Hawaiian Air inter-island coupon books that are convenient for island-hopping (6 flights for $312). Hawaiian Airlines also sells **passes** offering unlimited inter-island flights (5-15 days; $169-269). Travel agents, such as Pali Tour and Travel, Inc. 1304 Pali Hwy. Suite 1004, Honolulu, 96813 (533-3608), sell inter-island coupon books that are extremely convenient for island-hopping (Hawaiian Air, 6 flights for $234; Aloha, 5 flights for $188). Most local travel agents carry Mahalo Air coupons for $34-38.

Sands and Seaside Hotels, (800-451-6754 from the islands, 800-367-7000 from the mainland), manages some of the cheapest (and only locally owned) resort hotels ($54 and up). For B&B reservations, try **B&B Hawaii** (822-7771 on Kauai; 800-733-1632 on the other islands), **B&B Honolulu (Statewide)** (595-7533; fax 595-2030), and **All Islands B&B** (800-542-0344 or 263-2342). **Camping** will save you money and bring you closer to natural beauty. The national campgrounds on Maui and The Big Island require no permit, but they do enforce a three-day maximum stay. Free **camping permits** are required (applicants must be at least 18 years old; available from the Dept. of State Parks in Honolulu). Camping is limited to five nights per 30 days. Sites are open Friday through Wednesday on Oahu, daily on the other islands.

OAHU

At the time of explorer Captain Cook's landing, Oahu was untouched by the West. Oahu's importance increased as Honolulu's commercial traffic expanded and the U.S. Navy acquired exclusive rights to the inlet at Pearl Harbor. Oahu can be roughly divided into four sections. **Honolulu** is a vibrant city inhabited by native Hawaiians, Caucasians, Japanese, Chinese, Samoans, Koreans, and Filipinos, and the metropolitan heart of the island. **Waikiki Beach,** 3 mi. from downtown Honolulu, extends outward toward the volcanic crater of **Diamond Head,** the island's southernmost extremity. The **North Shore,** from Kahuku to Kaena Point, is the home of the winter swells of which surfers around the world dream. The **Windward Coast** (on the east), especially around Hanauma Bay, is rife with tropical fish and coral reefs. The **Leeward Coast** (on the west) is raw and rocky. The slopes of two now-extinct volcanic mountain ridges, **Waianae** in the west and **Koolau** in the east, run parallel from northwest to southeast and make up the bulk of Oahu's 600 square mi.

■■■ HONOLULU

Honolulu is the cultural, commercial, and political locus of Hawaii. Its industrial-strength harbor and concrete-and-glass business district attest to its status as a capital city (pop. 370,000) and major Pacific seaport. At the same time, acres of white sand beaches make it one of the world's premier tropical vacation getaways. Waikiki, the quintessential tourist haven, boasts an abundance of glitzy restaurants and nightclubs interspersed among 70,000 hotel rooms. Honolulu offers a varied nightlife and bargains are available from establishments competing fiercely for your dollar.

Practical Information Visitors information is available at the **Hawaii Visitors Bureau,** 2270 Kalakaua Ave., 8th Floor, Honolulu 96815 (923-1811; open Mon.-Fri. 8am-4:30pm; closed holidays). **Buses** (848-5555) cover the entire island, but differ-

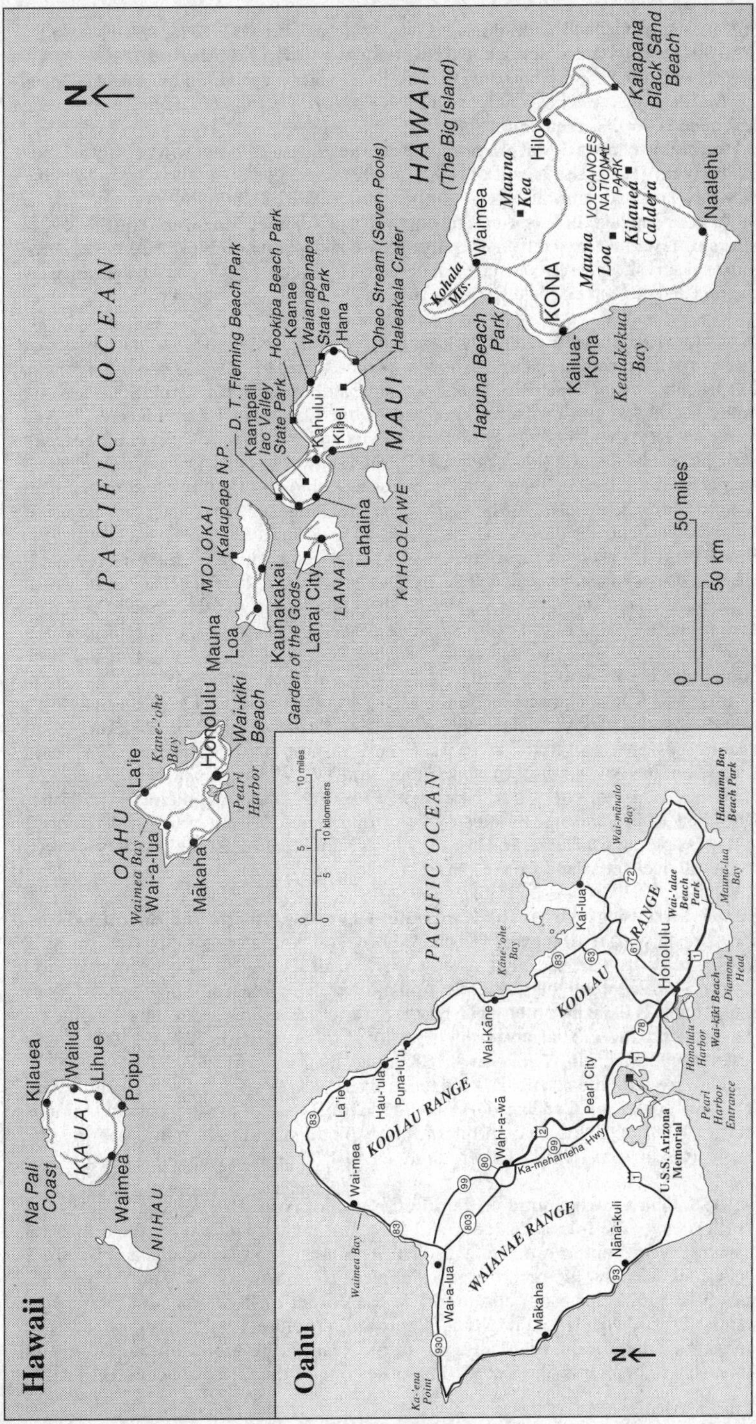

Hawaii
PACIFIC OCEAN
N
Na Pali Coast
Kilauea
Wailua
Lihue
Poipu
KAUAI
Waimea
NIIHAU
OAHU
Waimea Bay
Wai-a-lua
Mākaha
La'ie
Kane-'ohe Bay
Honolulu
Wai-kiki Beach
Pearl Harbor
MOLOKAI
Kalaupapa N.P.
Mauna Loa
Kaunakakai
Garden of the Gods
Lanai City
LANAI
Lahaina
KAHOOLAWE
Kaanapali
Iao Valley State Park
D. T. Fleming Beach Park
Kahului
Kihei
Hookipa Beach Park
Keanae
Waianapanapa State Park
Hana
Oheo Stream (Seven Pools)
Haleakala Crater
MAUI
HAWAII
(The Big Island)
Kohala Mts.
Waimea
Hapuna Beach Park
Mauna Kea
Hilo
VOLCANOES NATIONAL PARK
Kilauea Caldera
Mauna Loa
KONA
Kailua-Kona
Kealakekua Bay
Naalehu
Kalapana Black Sand Beach
0
50 miles
0
50 km
Oahu
PACIFIC OCEAN
0
5
10 miles
0
5
10 kilometers
N
Ka-'ena Point
930
Wai-a-lua
Waimea Bay
Mākaha
WAIANAE RANGE
93
Nānā-kuli
83
Wai-mea
803
99
80
Wahi-a-wā
Ka-mehameha Hwy
2
99
KOOLAU RANGE
83
La'ie
Hau-'ula
Puna-lu'u
Wai-Kāne
Pearl City
U.S.S. Arizona Memorial
1
Pearl Harbor Entrance
1
Honolulu Harbor
78
Wai-kiki Beach
Diamond Head
KOOLAU
Kāne-'ohe Bay
83
63
Honolulu
61
1
Kai-lua
RANGE
Wai-'alae Beach Park
Mauna-lua Bay
72
Wai-mānalo Bay
Hanauma Bay Beach Park

HAWAII

ent lines start and stop running at different times (fare $1). **Sida,** 439 Kalewa St. (836-0011), runs a taxi service. **Discover Rent-a-Car,** 1920 Ala Moana Blvd. (949-4767), rents for $25 per day (drivers must be 21 and older). Honolulu's **post office** is at 3600 Aolele Ave. (423-3990; open Mon.-Fri. 8am-7:30pm, Sat. 8am-2:30pm); the **ZIP code** is 96813; **area code:** 808.

Honolulu International Airport is 20 minutes west of downtown, off the Lunalilo Freeway (H-1). The **Nimitz Hwy.** (Rte. 92) will take you all the way to Waikiki. Buses #19 and 20, among others, go the 9 mi. to Waikiki, but you won't be able to bring your luggage unless it can fit on your lap. **Airport Motorcoach** (839-0911) offers continuous service from the airport to Waikiki and hotels ($7). 24-hr. advance return reservations are required (call 6:30am-10:30pm). **EM Tours and Transportation** (836-0210) will pick up at any time ($7).

Accommodations Honolulu, especially Waikiki, caters to affluent tourists, but there *are* bargains. Guests must show an airline ticket to stay at **Interclub Waikiki,** 2413 Kuhio Ave. (924-2636. Female or mixed dorms. Laundry, refrigerators, and outdoor grill. No curfew; reception open 24 hrs. Check-out 10am. Bunks $15, doubles $45. Key deposit $10.) Single-sex rooms and free use of snorkeling gear are available at **Hale Aloha (HI-AYH),** 2417 Prince Edward St. (926-8313), in Waikiki, 2 blocks from the beach. Take Waikiki #8 bus to Kuhio and Uluniu. (Beds guaranteed 3 nights although you might be allowed to stay longer. 24-hr. check-in. Check-out 11am. No lockout or curfew. Dorm bunks $15, doubles $35. Sleep sack rental $1. Key deposit $5. Make reservations.) Small and peaceful, though somewhat remote is **Honolulu International (HI-AYH),** 2323A Seaview Ave. (946-0591). 1½ mi. north of Waikiki. Take bus #6 from Ala Moana Shopping Center to Metcalf and University Ave. (Kitchen, locker, and clean single-sex facilities. Windows are netting; watch your belongings. Beds guaranteed for 3 nights. Reception open 7:30-10am and 5pm-midnight. Check-out 10am. Lights out 11pm; rooms locked noon-4:30pm. $12, nonmembers $15. Reservations recommended.) A converted hostel now houses **Kim's Island Hostel,** 1946 Ala Moana Blvd., Suite 130 (942-8748). Take bus #19 or #20 to the Hilton Hawaiian Village, cross Ala Moana, turn right and go about half a block. Each room has A/C, bathroom, sink, fridge, and TV. Cooking facilities available. (24-hr. check-in. 10am check-out. First night $11, each additional night $15; $95 per week, $350 per month. Singles $45 per night or $275 per week. $20 deposit includes linens.) **B&B Pacific Hawaii,** 19 Kai Nani Place (262-6026), will book B&B rooms all over the island from $45 per couple.

Food and Nightlife The **Kapahulu, Kaimuki, Moiliili,** and **downtown** districts are all within 10 min. of Waikiki by bus, and with a good map, you can walk from one district to the next quite easily. Small Chinese and other Asian food counters serve excellent, authentic, and affordable lunches and *dim sum* all over Chinatown, especially on **Hotel Street.** A variety of ethnic restaurants, including Hawaiian, Japanese, Thai, and French, are located between the 500 and 1000 blocks of **Kapahulu Avenue. The Wave,** 1877 Kalakaua Ave. (941-0424), on the edge of Waikiki, has loud music and dancing for a mixed crowd (open daily 9pm-4am; cover for live bands). **Pink Cadillac,** 478 Ena (942-5282), is one of the few dancing options for the 18-21 set. Neo-rave and neon lights blend with hip-hop and progressive music. (Open 9pm-1:45am. Cover: under 21 $10; 21 and over $5, Fri.-Sat. $3.)

Sights **Chinatown,** found at the intersection of Nuuanu Ave. and Hotel St., is worth seeing. The **Iolani Palace** (538-1471), at King and Richard St., the only royal residence ever built in America, was first the home of King Kalakaua and his sister Queen Liliuokalani. (45-min. tours begin every 15 min. Wed.-Sat. 9am-2:15pm. $6, ages 5-12 $1. Under 5 not admitted.) At the corner of Beretania and Richard St. stands Hawaii's postmodern **State Capitol,** an architectural mosaic of Hawaii's landscape (open Mon.-Fri. 9am-4pm; free). Nearby, the **Honolulu Academy of Arts,** 900 S. Beretania St. (532-8701), houses one of the finest collections of Asian art in the U.S. (Open Tues.-Sat. 10am-4:30pm, Sun. 1-5pm. Tours Tues.-Sat. 11am, Sun. 1pm. $5, students and seniors $3.)

On December 7, 1941 a stunned nation listened to the reports of the Japanese bombing of the U.S. Pacific Fleet in **Pearl Harbor.** Today, the **U.S.S. Arizona National Memorial** (422-2771) commemorates that event. The **visitors center** is open Monday through Sunday 7:30am to 5pm with the last commemorative program starting at 3pm. Take the #20 bus from Waikiki, the #50, 51, or 52 bus from Ala Moana, or the $2 shuttle from the major Waikiki hotels (839-0911). Tickets to the memorial are free, but 2-hr.+ waits are not unusual.

Visitors of all ages flock to the Waikiki Beach area for rest, relaxation, sun, surf, nightlife, tacky souvenirs, and romance. Originally a marshy swampland and hideaway for Hawaiian royalty, Waikiki's wetlands were drained into the Ala Canal to launch the island's tourist industry. Farthest to the east is the **Sans Souci Beach,** in front of the Kaimona Otani Hotel. The **Queen's Surf Beach,** closer to downtown, attracts swimmers, skaters, and an increasing number of in-line roller-skaters. If you seek more secluded beaches, head east on Diamond Head Rd. (a moped will do) until you hit Kahala Ave. For a break from sun and surf, hike the 1 mi. into the **Diamond Head Crater.** To get there, take bus #58 from Waikiki. Bring a flashlight to guide you through a pitch-dark section of the tunnel. The view of Waikiki is spectacular, and if you go on the right day, you might catch a rainbow arching over the U.S. military base in the center of the crater.

Miles of beaches and rural towns span the 40-mi. coast, running from Laie in the north to Mokapu Point in the south; the result is the most scenic drive on the island. The Koolau Range rises out of the ocean and the highway slices through the mountains, skirting the cliffs along the sea. Farther south, Kalanianaole Hwy. wraps around a rugged 2-mi. stretch to Koko Head, the eastern boundary of Honolulu.

Fruit vendors, plate lunches, and shaved ice are plentiful on the Windward Coast. Try the **Bueno Nalo,** 41-865 Kalanianaole Hwy. (259-7186), in Waimanalo, the best restaurant for miles. Delicious Mexican meals are the specialty ($6-9). Try the absolutely incredible cheese enchiladas (open daily 11:30am-9pm). **Ahi's,** (293-5650), just off Kamehameha Hwy. in Kahuku, is also a good choice. Look for the rusted circa-1940 pickup truck with the sign in the back. This popular local establishment features an $8.25 shrimp special (open Tues.-Sat. 11am-9pm).

MAUI

Maui has sun, sand, waves, and more than 2 million visitors each year. The island's resort areas are crowded and the beaches and waters are filled with families on vacation. But with a little effort (and a car), one can find unspoiled stretches of sand.

Maui is like several islands in one. The **West Maui Mountains** slope down to an arid coastline of drowsy little towns (including **Kaanapali,** the resort haven). A land bridge between two ancient volcanoes supports the **Wailuku-Kahului** sprawl (pop. 63,000), as well as acres of wind-blown sugarcane. Home of the mystifying **Haleakala volcano,** the **East Mountains** contain an imperiled native ecosystem, while Paia's aggressively 60s feel foreshadows the laid-back lushness of the **Hana coast.** The island's western side is dry and mountainous. The east is a rainforest enveloped by the famous Hana Highway. A large, semi-permanent population of windsurfers provides a more youthful, laid-back alternative to Maui's tourists.

Practical Information Visitors should visit the **Visitor Information Kiosk** (877-3893), at the Kahului Airport terminal. (Open daily 6am-9pm.) **Trans Hawaiian** (877-7308) offers hourly service between Kahului Airport and the major Lahaina-Kaanapali for $13; reservations are necessary only for return (runs on the hr. daily 7am-7pm). The **Lahaina Express** provides free transport between the Kaanapali Resorts and Lahaina. Get the schedule in the *Lahaina Historical Guide* (available at the tourist stands in Lahaina). **Department of Parks and Recreation,** War Memorial Gym, 1580 Kaahumanu Ave. (243-7389), between Kahului and Wailuku, has information and permits ($3) for county parks. (Open Mon.-Fri. 8am-4pm. You may have to knock on the window.) **Ferries** are an ideal way to go from Maui to Molokai and Lanai. Going by boat is more exciting and cheaper than flying. The **Maui Princess** (661-8397) runs daily from Lahaina to Kaunakakai (Molokai) at 7am and from Molokai, to Lahaina at 3:55pm. Crossing takes about 1¾ hr. and costs $25 each way. **Expeditions** (661-3756) runs daily between Lahaina and Manele, Lanai, $25 one way. **Resort Taxi** (661-5285) offers a $9 ride into Kahului or Wailuku from the airport. **Rent a car** at **Regency,** Kahului Airport (871-6147); it's the only option for those under 21. ($24 per day, $5 per day extra if under 25. Open daily 8am-8pm.)

Maui consists of two mountains joined at an isthmus. The highways follow the shape of the island in a broken figure-eight pattern. **Rte. 30** leads to hot and dry **Lahaina** and **Kaanapali,** the major resort area. **Rte. 34** leads counterclockwise around the same loop from the isthmus to where the paved road ends at **Kapuna.** Circling the slopes of Haleakala southbound along the eastern loop, **Rte. 31** runs past **Kihei** and **Wailea. Rte. 36** winds through rainy terrain, over 54 one-lane bridges and 600 hairpin curves, to **Hana.**

Accommodations The **Banana Bungalow Hotel and International Hostel,** 310 N. Market St., Wailuku (244-5090 or 800-846-7835), is a basic hostel supercharged with youthful energy. Windsurfers and international guests will plug you into the local tourist subculture with daytrips, night trips to clubs, athletic games, or dart tournaments. (TV room with A/C, VCR. Laundry. Kitchen. Airport pick-up. Bunks $15, singles with double bed $32, doubles $39. Key deposit $5.) Another option is the **Northshore Inn,** 2080 Vineyard St. (242-8999), which is secure and clean. There's a fan and fridge in each room, a full kitchen, laundry, and occasional barbecues. (Hostel bunks $13, singles $27, doubles $37. $10 key deposit.)

Haleakala Featuring a fantastic volcanic crater, **Haleakala National Park** is open 24 hrs. and costs $4 per car for a seven-day pass. The **Park Headquarters** (572-9300), about 1 mi. up from the entrance, provides camping **permits,** displays on Haleakala wildlife, and funky postcards (open daily 7:30am-4pm). **Haleakala Visitors Center** (572-9172), near the summit, has a few exhibits on the region's geology, archaeology, and ecology, and one of the best views of the crater. **Haleakala Crater Campground** (572-9306), 4 mi. from Halemauu parking lot, has camping and cabins within the crater. The park allocates cabins by a highly competitive lottery. You must apply three months prior to your visit. Holua and Paliku areas also serve as campgrounds. Free camping permits are issued at park headquarters (1 mi. up from park entrance; 2-night max. stay in cabins, 3 in campgrounds).

Hana The **Hana Coast** spans from the Keanae Peninsula to Kaupo. The **Hana Highway,** leading to the Hana coast, may be the world's most beautiful stretch of road; carved from cliff faces and valley floors, its alternate vistas of smooth sea and lush terrain are made only somewhat less enjoyable by its tortuous curves. Be prepared to spend an entire day on the trip. Wild ginger plants and fruit trees laden with mangos, guavas, and bananas perfume the air of the twisted drive.

THE BIG ISLAND

The Big Island, officially known as Hawaii, emerged from the confluence of five major volcanoes on top of a hot spot in the Pacific Plate. Two are still active: "Long Mountain," **Mauna Loa** (13,677ft.), and **Kilauea** (4000ft.), home of **Halemaumau Crater.** Kilauea is currently in its 51st phase of eruption without showing any signs of exhaustion, and crowds flock daily to the island to tread on newly created earth.

Although the eruptions are powerful, the volcanoes do not emit dangerous ash clouds. The lava flow is quick only near the summit and in underground lava tubes. **Hilo** and **Kailua-Kona,** on opposite sides of the island, are the main tourist towns.

The two mountains in **Volcanoes National Park** continue to spout and grow, adding acres of new land each year. **Kilauea Caldera,** with its steaming vents, sulfur fumes, and periodic "drive-in" eruptions, is the star of the park, although the less active **Mauna Loa** and its dormant northern neighbor, **Mauna Kea,** are in some respects more amazing. Each towers nearly 14,000 ft. above sea level and drops some 16,000 ft. to the ocean floor. Mauna Loa is the largest volcano in the world, while Mauna Kea, if measured from its ocean floor base, would be the tallest mountain on earth (park entrance $5 per car, valid for 7 days). At the **visitors center** in **Kilauea** (967-7311) Crater Rim Rd., receive bulletins of the latest volcanic activity. Trails of varying difficulty lead around Kilauea and to the summit of Mauna Loa; speak to a ranger before setting out (open daily 7:45am-5pm).

Staying in the volcano area is expensive because of the limited number of hotels. From Hilo, take Rte. 11 almost to the National Park, turn right at Haunani Rd. in Volcano Village, then left on Kalani Holua Rd, 2 mi. from the visitors center, to the **Holo Holo Inn,** 19-4036 Kalani Holua Rd., (967-7950), which offers several large, clean rooms (bunk $15; call after 4:30pm and reserve in advance). **Volcano House,** in the Hawaii Volcanoes National Park 96718 (967-7321), is expensive, but you can sleep on the rim of an active volcano ($79 and up). Also try the **Namakani Paio** cabins, 3 mi. behind the Volcano House in an *ohia* forest (check-in after 3pm; singles or doubles $32). In **Volcanoes National Park** (967-7311), find free campsites at **Kipuka Nene, Namakani Paio** (near Kilauea Crater), and **Kamoamoa** (on the coast)—each with shelters and fireplaces, but no wood (7-day max; no reservations).

The Pele's The Thing

The Volcano area is the home of Pele, the powerful Hawaiian volcano goddess. Cognizance of superstitions will keep you safe from vexing evil omens and such.

1) When driving, if you see an old woman by the side of the road, pick her up; it may be Pele. (*Let's Go* does not recommend hitchhiking.)

2) If there is a black dog by the side of the road, do not ignore it; superstitious Hawaiians carry a raw piece of meat with them in the car to feed the dog if they see it. Failure to comply results in nausea, illness, and a slow death.

3) If you notice there is an old woman in the back of your car, ignore her; this is just Pele. She is benign if left alone.

4) Avoid Saddle Rd., since many Hawaiians believe it is haunted.

5) Offerings to Pele in the volcanoes (and at trailheads) include *leis,* fruit, or sweets, rocks wrapped in *ti* leaves, and the occasional virgin. You will see stacks of rocks a few feet high dotting the strange landscape of the lava flows.

6) If you truly want to appease Pele, take a bottle of gin with you and pour it into one of the lava lakes; Pele will then smile on your adventure.

KAUAI

Anything nature does, Kauai can do better. The splendor of the Garden Isle is unsurpassed anywhere in the Hawaiian archipelago. The beaches are more graceful, the mountains more outrageous, and the waterfalls have more water and fall. When producers of such films as *Raiders of the Lost Ark, King Kong,* and *Jurassic Park* sought out a primeval paradise, they ended up on Kauai. **Lihue** is the hub of the island, and the home of the island.

The land of **Hanalei,** on the north coast, was made famous in by Peter, Paul, and Mary in their fattie-fueled song "Puff the Magic Dragon." If you squint, you may be able to make out the shape of a dragon from Hanalei Beach. **Lumahai Beach,** is probably on the postcard you'll send home. After visiting it, you'll see that pictures can't do it justice. The northwest side of the island, the **Na Pali Coast** is a true natural wonder. Sheer cliffs are interrupted only by empty white sand beaches washed by the bright blue seas. **Hanakapiai Beach** lies 2 mi. in and a marvelous waterfall lies another 2 mi. up Hanakapiai Valley. The mind-blowing **Kalalau Valley** lies at the end of 11 steep and cliffside miles but is said to be the most beautiful place on earth. The wild coastal areas beyond Haena are accessible only by hiking or by kayak.

The **Hawaii Visitors Bureau,** Lihue Plaza Bldg., 3016 Umi St. #207, Lihue (245-3971), at Rice St., is an info-bonnie good time. Stop by to pick up the fun and informative "Kauai Illustrated Pocket Map." Write for their vacation planner, a directory of services, events, and coupons: 3016 Umi St., Lihue 96766. (Open Mon.-Fri. 8am-4pm.) Camping is the best option on Kauai. Evaluate your options at the **Kauai County Parks Office,** 4193 Hardy St., Lihue (241-6670). The office is located behind the convention center in a long building by the parking lot. Information and permits for camping in county parks ($3; open Mon.-Fri. 7:45am-4:15pm). Permits also available from rangers on-site ($5). The **Division of State Parks,** 3060 Eiwa St. #306, Lihue 96766 (241-3444), at Hardy St., in the State Office Bldg., has even more info on camping in state parks. (Permits issued Mon.-Fri. 8am-4pm.)

If you can't stand to camp, try another island or try the **Kauai International Hostel,** 4532 Lehua St., Kapaa (823-6142 or 800-858-2295). This popular hostel—located across the street from the beach and several restaurants—has full kitchen, cable TV, laundry facilities, co-ed and single-sex dorms. Fantastic, choose-your-own-adventure day trips to many of Kauai's hidden spots ($10-15.) Terrific location, but can be noisy. (7 night max. stay. Bunk $15 per night, private room $40 per night. Office open daily 8am-10pm.)

CANADA

O Canada! The second largest country in the world, Canada covers almost 10 million square km (3.85 million square mi.); only Russia looms larger. Despite its size, Canada's population is relatively small. Twenty-six million people inhabit Canada's vast lands, and well over half of the population resides in Ontario and Québec. The rest of the population spreads over the eight remaining provinces. Framed by the Atlantic coastline in the east and the Pacific Ocean in the west, Canada also extends from fertile southern farmlands to frozen northern tundra.

The name Canada is thought to be derived from the Huron-Iroquois word "kanata," meaning "village" or "community." This etymology reveals the dependence of early settlers on the Native Canadians as well as the country's origins in a few small, isolated, trading villages. The early colonists, the French and English, were relatively distant and culturally distinct. Each population has fought to retain cultural and political dominance, but it is only in the 20th century that ethnic and linguistic differences between the two communities have flared into quasi-terrorist acts of violence. Native Canadian concerns have also become intertwined with the struggle of the dominant French and English cultures. Tensions between areas have been exacerbated by the different economic foundations on which the provinces are built: fishing feeds the Maritime provinces while the oil industry sustains Alberta. Canadian national propagandists have recognized the diversity within the federation of provinces and have tried to portray it in a positive light, teaching school children that Canada is a mixed salad, not an American melting pot.

The interchange between Canada and the U.S. has contributed to Canadian history. The U.S.-Canadian border is the longest undefended border in the world. The similarities between Canadian and American geography and history have led to certain similarities in culture. Some Canadian nationalists have become concerned that American culture is threatening indigenous attributes, but fundamental differences between the countries remain. The maintenance of distinct national identities will be strongly challenged by the North American Free Trade Agreement (NAFTA) involving the United States and Canada (as well as Mexico).

Much crucial information concerning Canada can be found in the Essentials section in the front of the book.

Canadian Culture

HISTORY

NATIVE CANADIANS

Canada was first settled around 25,000 years ago when a stream of Siberian hunter-nomads flowed over the Asian-Alaskan land bridge in search of better lands. Their descendants flooded the continent, breaking up into the various tribes that met European settlers upon their arrival. Dominant tribes in the Great Lakes region included the Five Nations of the Iroquois, composed of the Seneca, Mohawk, Onondaga, Oneida, and Cayuga tribes, and the Hurons, who normally opposed these people in almost continuous warfare. The Ojibwa, Blackfoot, and Cree settled in the Prairies, while the Inuit peoples remained in the North. The Tlingit and the Salish settled the Pacific Coast. After European contact, these nations often traded furs for guns, which intensified inter-tribal warfare. Tribes entered into alliances with would-be colonial powers, trading their vast knowledge of the land for aid in preexisting tribal conflicts. In the area around Niagara Falls, Indians helped the British annihilate the Americans in a decisive battle during the War of 1812, just as the Dutch had helped the Five Nations, by supplying firepower, to eradicate the Huron midway through the 17th century.

The tribes' bargains did not pay off. As the English and French became more familiar with the land, they squeezed the Indians out by force and by less-than-desirable land agreements. Natives found themselves confined to large settlements such as Moose Factory in Ontario or Oka in Québec. In 1951 a new Indian Act increased the autonomy of the tribes, and in 1959 the Act was amended to increase Indian influence in federal decisions concerning them. The federal government finally extended the franchise to all Indians in 1960. Recently, the Assembly of First Nations, an aboriginal organization, has taken legal action to secure compensation for lands that were taken from the tribes. The Inuit tribes have been granted a homeland in the Northwest Territories as a result of AFN negotiations.

EUROPEAN BEGINNINGS

The earliest evidence of European exploration of North America can be found at L'Anse aux Meadows in northern Newfoundland. The Norse apparently settled here around the year 1000. England came next; John Cabot sighted Newfoundland in 1497. But Jacques Cartier claimed the mainland for the French crown in 1534 when he landed on the gulf of the St. Lawrence River. In 1608 the French explorer Champlain established a fort at Québec. France wished to colonize and exploit the fur trade in the New World. The Company of New France was created for this purpose, and in 1663 the Company was declared a colony of France. England wanted a part of the fur trade action, and formed the Hudson Bay Company in 1670 to gain the mid-continent trade by way of the Hudson Bay. A rivalry for land persisted for a century until the Seven Years War, when the British captured Québec in 1759. In 1763 all of French North America east of the Mississippi was ceded to the English. Britain came to possess a colony populated almost entirely by colonists of alien descent.

On the heels of this acquisition came the American Revolution, in which Britain lost her more southern colonies. Thousands of Tory loyalists fled to Canada and settled along the St. John River, north of the Bay of Fundy. The settlers soon decided that the government in Halifax was too far away to meet their needs; when they complained, the British government rewarded their loyalty in 1784 by creating a province, New Brunswick. Loyalist sentiment was also instrumental in the Constitutional Act of 1791, which divided Québec into separate French and English provinces, Upper and Lower Canada. After an open rebellion by the French Canadians in 1837, the two halves were joined as the United Province of Canada in 1841. In 1846, the colonies were granted responsible government, which made the colonial executive responsible to the popularly elected assembly. A step towards sovereignty had been taken.

THE DOMINION OF CANADA

After the American Civil War, the U.S. informed Canada that it wished to abrogate the Reciprocity Treaty of 1854, which had provided a substantial trade market for Canada. Canadian politicians believed they could provide a substitute market by unifying the British North American colonies. Further motivation was provided by growing fears of U.S. military power and a desire to annex the northwest. For many, greater Canadian unity was an imperative. The Colonial Secretary struggled to establish the Confederation, working quickly to oust reluctant colonial leaders. The first Confederation proposal (1865) was nixed by New Brunswick. Over the next two years, though, sufficient support gathered, and in 1867 Nova Scotia, New Brunswick, and the United Province of Canada (now Québec and Ontario) were united as the Dominion of Canada (British Columbia waited until 1871, Prince Edward Island held out until 1873). The British North America (BNA) Act, as it was called, was signed by Queen Victoria on March 29, 1867, and proclaimed on July 1, Canada Day. Canada had its country but was still a dominion of the British throne.

WESTWARD HO!

Following the passage of the BNA Act, Conservatives rode the crest of the consolidation wave into power; Sir John MacDonald came to power in the English colonies, Sir George-Etienne Cartier in Québec. The government worked to expand the nation in three ways. It pumped money into economic growth, encouraged mass settlement in the west, and created high protective tariffs. As a result, Canada quickly grew to encompass most of the land it covers today; Manitoba and the Northwest Territories were molded in 1870 from Rupert's Land, a purchase from the Hudson Bay Company. By 1885, there was a railway to the Pacific and the economy boomed. Increased wheat production and immigration to the west sparked the division of the Northwest Territories into Alberta and Saskatchewan in 1905.

The expanding railroad displaced many Native Canadians, except for the Arctic Inuit, who were largely left alone while their lands were tacitly incorporated into the growing Canadian territory. Western tribes and the Metis (mixed-blood children of Native Canadian women and French fur-traders who inhabited Manitoba) faced a far greater challenge. Many of these people had earned their living by providing boat and cart transport, but the railroad superseded these services. At the same time, the buffalo herds they relied on for food were disappearing. Only Louis Riel, a Metis educated in Montréal, organized against the encroachment, but his armed resistance was crushed in 1885 and Riel was hanged. From then on, Western land acquisition went unchallenged.

TURN OF THE CENTURY POLITICS AND WWI

Newfound imperialism drove Prime Minister Sir Wilfrid Laurier, leader of the Liberal Party and Canada's first French-speaking Prime Minister, to send troops to aid Britain in the Boer War from 1899-1902 and in 1910 to create a Canadian navy, to be placed under British control in times of war. Nationalists in Québec bitterly opposed this move fearing that conscription to the British army would follow. Along with a proposed reciprocal trade agreement with the U.S. which would have lowered Canada's high trading tariffs, Laurier's naval policy cost him the election of 1911.

The tide of imperialism did not abate after Laurier's fall, and the Dominion sent troops to aid Britain in the Great War. By 1917, Canada was being torn apart by the issue of conscription. French Canadians, never enthusiastic about the war, were overruled by the Conservatives, a pro-conscription party, who won the wartime election of 1917. Though her sacrifice was great, Canada gained significantly from the Great War. The Dominion acquired new international status as a signator of the Treaty of Versailles and a charter member of the League of Nations. Further, women made headway on account of their war efforts, receiving the right to vote in 1918, two years before their American sisters received the same right.

THE INTER-WAR YEARS

Vets returning from the war and post-war slumps in production fueled high inflation and unemployment; protesting farmers ousted governments in the west and in Ontario, and the provincial economies collapsed. In 1919 over 4 million working days were lost due to strikes, the most famous of which was the six-week Winnipeg General Strike. Almost the entire labor force responded to aid the ailing metal-trades workers who had been denied wage increases. The government stepped in with police and troops, and the strike collapsed. By 1921, the labor revolts subsided as the economic downturn caused a virtual collapse of union power.

The labor disputes of the 20s were part of the painful transition from an agricultural to an industrial economy. As the population swelled in the cities, so did mass unemployment. The economy continued its long, slow downturn, and the 30s brought the Great Depression. Unemployment skyrocketed to 20% in 1933. Provincial governments tried to assist the troubled farmers, but relief was limited and drought exacerbated the problems of the agricultural community. The Liberals returned to power in 1935 under Mackenzie King. The government initiated direct relief programs and regulated businesses; both the Bank of Canada and the Canadian

Wheat Board were established during the Depression. King believed that stimulating international trade would pull Canada out of the Depression, but his schemes were interrupted by the conflict erupting in Europe. Canada dragged itself out of the Depression with the assistance of World War II.

COLD WAR PARTY-HOPPING

Louis St. Laurent took the helm of the Liberal party in 1948, just after the war. Newfoundland finally joined the Dominion a year later. The Liberals held office from 1935 to 1957, largely due to the success of their relief programs of the late 30s and later to the prosperity of the early Cold War years. Political decisions which would have otherwise irked the populace were deemed permissible because of the Cold War; thus, Canada joined the United Nations in 1945, hopped into the North Atlantic Treaty Organization in August, 1949, and sent troops to Korea in 1950 to solidify its commitment to the UN. With inspiring visions of a "new" Canada, the Conservatives, led by John Diefenbaker, grabbed precarious control in June 1957. Diefenbaker hoped to open up the north, diversify international trade, and to end corrupt Liberal rule. He was indecisive in reacting to the Cuban Missile Crisis, however, and Canadians were dismayed by their government's response. In 1963 Lester Pearson, leader of the Liberal party, defeated Diefenbaker's government. Although Pearson never achieved a majority, Canada gained a national flag, a national social security system, and a national health insurance program under his rule.

Pearson recognized that the main problem the federation would face in the coming years was an emergent French nationalism and separatism. In an attempt to unite Québec with the rest of the Dominion, Pierre Trudeau was selected to head the Liberal party in 1968. Trudeau espoused official bilingualism and biculturalism and brought many *Québécois* to his government. But he did not show similar sensitivity to other regional concerns, and problems with Québec remained. On October 5, 1970, the Front de Libération du Québec (FLQ) kidnapped the British trade commissioner while he was visiting Montréal. On October 10, Québec's Minister of Labor, Pierre Laporte, was seized. The Québec government turned to Trudeau, who took draconian measures. Local police rounded up 468 people, and there was a massive deployment of troops. The next day, Laporte was found strangled in a car trunk. After a slow and inept search, the British diplomat and Laporte's killers were located, but in the end, many Canadians resented Trudeau more than the terrorists. As a result, Liberal victory in 1972 was slim, and the New Democratic Party (NDP) held the deciding votes in Parliament. The Liberals shifted left to secure their support, permanently changing the party's policies.

The drive for French separatism strengthened in the late 70s. Under the banner of the *Parti Québécois,* separatist René Lévesque gained power in Québec in 1976, stunning Canadians across the country. With Bill 101, the *Parti Québécois* established French as the only official language seen and heard in Québec. Trudeau told Canadians, "I say to you with all the certainty I can command that Canada's unity will not be fractured." The crisis relaxed in 1977 as Lévesque postponed the independence referendum. In May 1979, Québec voted for Trudeau, but the rest of the nation backed the Conservative head, Joe Clark, who won the election. Clark floundered early, and with the defeat of his budget and a no-confidence motion in December, Trudeau and the Liberals returned in early 1980. This election marked perhaps the greatest national division of the century; the Liberals swept Québec but won no seats west of Manitoba. That year, the independence referendum was finally held in Québec. The *Québécois* decided not to sever their ties with Canada, and the country remained united if torn through early 1982.

THE CANADA ACT OF 1982

In his speeches against the Québec referendum, Trudeau had promised Canada a new constitution. After lengthy debates, a preliminary agreement was reached in Vancouver, where all the provincial premiers (including Lévesque) agreed on an amendment procedure in which no province had a veto. At a midnight meeting on

November 5, 1981, a compromise was reached that combined Trudeau's charter of rights with the Vancouver amendment formula. The nine premiers agreed to the terms while Lévesque slept across the river in Hull, Québec. He had refused to spend the night in Ottawa. On March 25, 1982, Canada's constitution was ratified by the British Parliament. Queen Elizabeth II gave her royal assent on April 17. Canada was released from the legal bonds of England. The constitution includes an unusual Charter of Rights and Freedoms, akin to the Bill of Rights, but more tepid in its provisions—in order to preserve parliamentary supremacy, individual rights may be superseded by federal Parliament or provincial legislatures via "notwithstanding clauses" for periods of up to five years. The document also institutionalized bilingualism in Canada. Québec tried to claim veto power over the constitution, but was rejected by courts at every level and still has not formally assented to the constitution that presently governs it.

MULRONEY, MEECH LAKE, AND NAFTA

In 1983 the Conservatives chose a new leader, the president of the Iron Ore Company of Canada, Brian Mulroney. Conservative support rose as Mulroney pronounced social programs "a sacred trust" and supported an NDP attempt to provide bilingual support in Manitoba. When Trudeau resigned in 1984 and John Turner took his place, the stage was set for a Conservative comeback. Turner buckled under pressure from Mulroney and lost money and support. Mulroney rolled to a landslide victory, claiming 211 of 281 seats in the Parliament, a clear mandate for Conservative change. Mulroney had promised in his campaign to restore a sense of community to Canada. He also supported privatization, increased armed forces, and reduction of the deficit. The freshman government had trouble achieving these goals, and Mulroney could do little to rally support in the west. By 1986, Mulroney lagged last in the polls as elections neared. In order to recapture the nation's attention, Mulroney's government embarked on two massive endeavors—rolling the dice for the Meech Lake Accord and the North American Free Trade Agreement (NAFTA). Mulroney got reelected, but the results of these two projects were mixed.

The Meech Lake Accord would have provided constitutional protection for the French language and culture in Québec. An attempt to keep Québec in Canada and to gain *québécois* support for the Conservatives, the Accord was designed to gain Québec's approval of the Canada Act of 1982. English Canadians feared that Québec would gain too much power over the Charter of Rights and Freedoms, while not guaranteeing similar powers for other minority groups. The Accord was defeated in June 1990, when Newfoundland and Manitoba failed to approve it. A patchwork replacement went to national referendum in 1993, but failed miserably.

NAFTA lowered trade tariffs between the economic giants of the western hemisphere and promises to allow the economy to thrive in a free-market system. Mulroney had greater success here; after years of negotiations (the roots for NAFTA stretch back to 1987), the central agreement was signed in May, 1992, and approved by the U.S. Senate in 1994.

THE END OF A CONSERVATIVE ERA

Even the promise of the benefits of free trade was not enough to prevent Mulroney's fall from popularity in 1992. As he finished up NAFTA, the country finished with him. In a cloud of incompetence and distrust, Mulroney was ousted from power in April 1993, and Kim Campbell was selected to lead the party. The first woman Prime Minister of Canada, Campbell's tenure was short—unrealistic expectations and campaign gaffs reduced the Conservatives from a majority government to a two seat presence in the House of Commons. Though Jean Chrétien and his Liberal Party won power, two new parties caught all the attention: the far-right Reform Party, led by former evangelist Preston Manning, blitzed Campbell's Tories in the West; and in Québec, the new opposition, the *Bloc Québécois* won a mandate to wrest their province from Canada's clutches.

■■■ GOVERNMENT AND POLITICS

Canada's government operates on a parliamentary system. The Queen, who reigns over both England and Canada, appoints a Governor General. However, both of these leaders' functions are mostly symbolic. There are 295 ridings, determined by population, whose residents elect representatives to the House of Commons. The leader of the majority then becomes the Prime Minister and leader of the country; members of Parliament from the ruling party form the Cabinet. The Governor General is selected based on the Prime Minister's recommendation to the Queen. Unlike the U.S., there is no separation of the executive and legislative branches of the government. Elected governments have a five-year maximum term. The Prime Minister can call an election any time before the end of the term. This is usually done to determine the country's sentiment about a major political issue, when the governing party believes such a vote would be advantageous to them.

There are presently five major political parties in Canada. Historically, the Conservatives, the Liberals, and the New Democratic Party (NDP) held substantial positions in the Parliament (although the NDP was a perpetual third behind the other parties). The Conservatives held power through much of the eighties, but in the 1993 election, the Liberals finally won a majority, after almost a decade as the opposition party. The Conservative and NDP presence was recently decimated by two new parties, the Reform and the *Bloc Québécois,* a change which exploded the balance of political power in Canada.

■■■ LANGUAGE

Canada officially has two languages, English and French, but there are numerous other native languages. Inuktitut is widely spoken in the Northwest Territories, but most Natives also speak English. *Québécois* pronunciation of French can be perplexing, but most natives are sympathetic to attempts to speak their language. The *Québécois* are also less formal than European French-speakers, and you might be corrected if you use the formal *vous.*

■■■ THE ARTS

LITERATURE

Canadian literature began as a colonial literature reflecting its French and English heritages. Marc Lescarbot's *Histoire de la Nouvelle France* (1609) was one of the first major French contributions. Interestingly, the first English Canadian novel, *History of Emily Montague*, was written by a woman, Frances Brooke in 1769. These early works were few and far between; most Canadian literature has been written since 1867. The opening of the northwest and the Klondike Gold Rush (1898) led the way for the blossoming of the adventure story. Jack London penned stories of wolves and prospectors based on his experiences of the Rush, while the Bard of the Yukon, Robert Service, composed the ballad "The Cremation of Sam McGee." Back East, L.M. Montgomery authored *Anne of Green Gables* (1908), to the delight of youngsters around the world. The onset of the 20th century brought a shift in emphasis to the cities and led to works exposing the dark side of urban conditions. Novelist and playwright Robertson Davies chronicled the roving Canadian identity in the *Deptford Trilogy,* and Margaret Laurence detailed the difficult lives of prairie women in such novels as *A Jest of God* and *The Stone Angel.* Two of Canada's most noteworthy authors, Malcolm Lowry and Hugh McLellan, also produced significant works, *Under the Volcano* and *Barometer Rising* (respectively), during this period. On the critical side, Canada boasted three of the world's most prominent cultural and literary authorities: Northrop Frye, Hugh Kenner, and Marshall McLuhan. Prominent contemporary authors include Margaret Atwood, best known for the futuristic bestseller *The Handmaid's Tale,* Alice Munro *(Lives of Girls and Women),* and Sri

Lankan-born poet and novelist Michael Ondaatje, who recently won the prestigious Booker Prize for *The English Patient.*

MUSIC

Canada's contribution to the world of popular music includes a range of artists such as Anne Murray, Neil Young, Joni Mitchell, Bruce Cockburn, Rush, Cowboy Junkies, Bare Naked Ladies, k.d. lang, Bryan Adams, Crash Test Dummies, and Sarah McLachlan. Tragically Hip is the band of choice for generation Xers. Today, Much-Music, the Canadian version of MTV, has been inspiring bands all over the country to capture the national identity on vinyl and on video. Canada is also home to world-class orchestras, including the Montréal, Toronto, and Vancouver Symphonies.

FILM

While Canadian films have yet to achieve the commercial success of Canadian literature, the National Film Board, which finances many documentaries, has gained world-wide acclaim. Claude Jutras's *Mon Oncle Antoine* (1970) was judged Canada's best movie ever by an international panel of film critics. Since then *québécois* filmmakers have captured the world's attention, producing Oscar-nominated movies like *Le declin de l'empire americain,* directed by Denys Arcand, who also directed the striking *Jesus de Montréal;* art-flick *Léolo* was deemed a classic by critics. François Girard has made audiences gasp with his recent *Thirty-two Short Films about Glenn Gould,* and actress Sheila McCarthy shone in *I Have Heard the Mermaids Singing*. Jim Carrey has recently achieved comedic super-stardom for his acting in *The Mask* and *Batman Forever.*

■■■ THE MEDIA

TELEVISION

The publicly owned Canadian Broadcasting Corporation (CBC) provides two national networks for both radio and television, one in English and one in French. The CBC has become strongly associated with Canadian national identity; most of the baby-boomer generation grew up on "Hockey Night" broadcasts which brought families together in front of the radio. Now the television version has replaced the radio show, but Canadians are still unified by CBC's influence. Canadians can now tune in to a third national network, the private network CTV, and several other private networks which broadcast in limited areas. Cable and satellite make access to U.S. television networks possible as well.

Many famous television actors and comedians are of Canadian origin, including Dan Aykroyd, Mike Myers of *Saturday Night Live* and *Wayne's World* fame, Michael J. Fox (*Family Ties, Back to the Future*), newscaster Peter Jennings, *Jeopardy* host Alex Trebek, and William Shatner (Captain James T. Kirk himself). The Canadian comedy troupe SCTV spawned the careers of many famous comedians, such as Martin Short, John Candy, Rick Moranis, Eugene Levy, and more. In an effort to hold down production costs, many American TV shows shoot in Canadian cities, such as Toronto and Vancouver.

PRINT MEDIA

The Toronto *Globe and Mail* calls itself Canada's national newspaper and is distributed six days a week across the entire country. In every Canadian city there is a daily newspaper, and in larger cities there is usually more than one. The weekly news magazine is *Maclean's*.

■■■ SPORTS

Canada is best known for sports appropriate to its northern latitudes. Winter sports include curling, ice skating, skiing, and, of course, the ultimate winter sport in Canada, ice hockey. Canadian players dominate the National Hockey League and most (good) collegiate teams in the U.S. Some of Canada's other popular sports are derived from those of the aboriginal peoples. Lacrosse, which is Canada's national game, was played by Native Canadians across the country and adopted by later immigrants. Finally, sports played in the United States have crossed the border—there is a Canadian Football League (CFL) which plays a game similar to that played in the U.S. Some American players have used the CFL as a springboard to better salaries in the American leagues. Recently Rocket Ismail accepted an $18 million contract with the CFL Argos, despite heavy recruiting from American teams. Canadians are even beating Americans at their own game, baseball. The Toronto Blue Jays won the 1992 and 1993 World Series.

■■■ THIS YEAR'S NEWS

This year could be a major turning point in Canada's history. The *Bloc Québécois* won a large number of seats in the Commons in 1993 on promises to work at a federal level for a sovereign Québec. In Québec, the separatist *Parti Québécois* has taken over the provincial government. These two parties have been coordinating a province-wide referendum on separation. The result of the referendum, even if positive, would face many international and legal problems of legitimacy. Further, a Native Canadian group within Québec has threatened to separate from the province if the province separates from Canada. This would create a country within a country within a country; for many Canadians, this would be an intolerable situation.

A major nickel deposit was discovered in Labrador. This discovery should have a major impact on the economy of the province of Newfoundland and Labrador.

On the international front, in the spring of 1995, Canada became embroiled in a "fish war" with Spain. Overfishing of the cod stocks in Canadian waters had led the national government to prohibit cod fishing. Many fishermen in Newfoundland lost their life's work and began receiving welfare, but the government claimed to have no choice, as it attempted to save the remaining stocks. Spain continued to fish these waters despite Canadian law; as a result, the Canadians became enraged, and a major international brouhaha ensued.

Canadians everywhere have been dismayed by the government's decision to remove human attendants from Canada's many lighthouses and replace the lighthouse masters by computers. This move will save the government money, but many who have been saved from the sea by the intervention of these workers believe that their salaries are money well-spent.

Nova Scotia

Four distinct geographies dominate Nova Scotia: the rugged Atlantic coast, the lush agricultural Annapolis Valley, the calm coast of the Northumberland Strait, and the magnificent highlands of Cape Breton Island. Each offers uniquely breathtaking scenery, and all are complemented by the province's equally diverse cultural landscape. Nova Scotia's population represents the Canadian ideal of a cultural "mixed salad," perhaps better than that of any other province. Around 1605, French colonists joined the indigenous Micmac Indians in the Annapolis Valley and on the shores of Cape Breton Island. During the American Revolution, Nova Scotia declined the opportunity to become the 14th American state and established itself as a refuge for fleeing British loyalists, despite trading ties with Massachusetts. The strong Scottish identity preserved in Pictou and Antigonish Counties derives from subsequent immigration which brought both Scottish and Irish settlers into the mix.

PRACTICAL INFORMATION

Capital: Halifax.

Economic Renewal Agency, Tourism Nova Scotia: Historic Properties, P.O. Box 456, Halifax B3J 2R5. The impressive, free *Doer's and Dreamer's Complete Guide* lists over 300 pages of Nova Scotia accommodations, restaurants, sights, and scenic drives. Call **Check-in Nova Scotia,** at 800-565-0000 (from Canada or the continental U.S.) to get tourist info or make reservations in many of the province's accommodations.

Drinking Age: 19.

Time Zone: Atlantic (1hr. ahead of Eastern). **Postal Abbreviation:** NS

Provincial Sales Tax: 11%, plus 7% GST (for details on obtaining a refund of the GST, see Essentials, p. 7).

■■■ ANNAPOLIS VALLEY

French Acadian farmers settled this area in the 17th century. Their expulsion by the British in 1755 was commemorated by Henry Wadsworth Longfellow's tragic epic poem "Evangeline"; although Longfellow himself never actually visited this "forest primeval," the title "Land of Evangeline" stuck. (For more on the story of the French expulsion, see Acadiana, p. 381.) Countless eponymous motels, a few historical dramas, and many a tourist brochure recall the haunting romantic tale.

Verdant and fertile, the Annapolis River Valley stretches along the **Bay of Fundy** between **Yarmouth** and the **Minas Basin.** Running slightly inland, but parallel to the coast, the valley is flanked by the imaginatively named North and South Mountains. Calm, sunny weather and many natural and historical attractions draw harried city-folk to the charming towns which scatter along the length of the Valley, connected by scenic Hwy. 1. Rushing from sight to sight is not the most satisfying method of exploring the Valley—if you want to blend in, stop and smell the aromatic pink apple blossoms which perfume area orchards in the spring. Bicycling provides an ideal means of transport between the towns, but beware of long, twisting, uninhabited stretches which look deceptively shorter on a map.

Northern Coast Home of the famous Digby scallops and one of the world's largest scallop fleets, **Digby** hosts the annual **Scallop Days** festival in the second week in August. About 104km up the coast from Yarmouth, Digby is connected by the **Marine Atlantic Ferry** (902-245-2116 or 800-341-7981 from the Continental U.S.), to Saint John, NB, which lies across the Bay of Fundy. (1-3 per day; 3hr.; \$21.50, seniors \$16.25, ages 5-12 \$10.75, car \$47, bike \$10.50; off season \$16.25/\$12.25/\$8.25/\$41.25/\$5.25.) Terminal open 24 hrs. for tickets and info.

The peninsula and islands of Digby Neck stretch 60km south from Digby on Hwy. 217; **Brier Island,** the home of Joshua Slocum (the first person to sail around the world solo), floats at the tip of the Neck. Whale watching is so successful in this area that **Brier Island Whale and Seabird Cruises** (902-839-2995), in Westport, guarantees whale sightings or you go again free. (Trips last 4hr., weather permitting. $35, seniors $31.50, ages 6-12 $16, under 6 free. Reserve at least 1 week in advance.) From **Westport,** it takes two ferries to get to Brier Island ($1 each): the first ferry sets out every ½-hour for **Freeport,** and the second leaves Freeport every hour for Brier Island. Both run 24 hrs.

French explorer Samuel de Champlain founded the earliest permanent European settlement in North America north of Florida at **Habitation Port-Royal** in 1605. The capital of French Acadia for nearly a century, Port-Royal capitulated to the British in 1710 and was renamed Annapolis Royal in honor of Queen Anne. Though it fell into ruin soon after changing hands, the town has been restored in the form of the **Port-Royal National Historical Park** (902-532-2898), 12km from modern-day Annapolis Royal across the Annapolis Basin. The restoration affords a rare glimpse of the wooden palisades and stone chimneys typical in early French fur-trading posts. To reach the Habitation, turn off Hwy. 1 at the Granville Ferry and go 10 km. (Open May 15-Oct. 15 daily 9am-6pm. $2.50, seniors $2, ages 6-16 $1.25, kids under 5 free.) The immaculate grounds of the **Annapolis Royal Historic Gardens** (902-532-7018) satisfy horticulturalist's wildest dreams and soothe the nerves of tourists and ducks alike; **Marsh Lookoff** (on the grounds) looks onto the **Ducks Unlimited Sanctuary,** noted for its variety and productivity. For laid-back lodging, try the **Sandy Bottom Lake Hostel (HI-C)** (902-532-2497), 20 min. outside Annapolis Royal off Rte. 8; turn off in South Milford onto Virginia/Bear River Rd. and look for the Hostel Rd. sign, on the right after 3km. (8 beds, kitchen facilities, spic-n-span shared bath; spitting distance from the waterfront. $12, nonmembers $14. Canoe rentals $2 per hr., $12 per day.) Relatively close by, **Kejimkujik National Park,** or "Keji" (902-682-2772), on Hwy. 8 about 60km inland from Annapolis Royal and 160km west of Halifax, includes dense woods, a liberal peppering of small lakes, and unspoiled waterways best explored by canoe. The park's **information center** lies in the northeast corner on the Mersey River. (Open daily 8:30am-9pm; Sept. 6 to mid-June 8:30am-4:30pm. Park use fee $2.25 per day, seniors $1.75, ages 6-16 $1.25, under 6 free; 4 days $6.75/ $5.25/$3.75.) The park has a **campground** with showers and 329 sites ($10.50) but no hookups. Rent canoes from **Jake's Landing** (902-682-2817; open mid-June to Sept. daily 9am-9pm; $3 per hr., $15 per day).

For amusement park fun, head to **Upper Clements Theme Park** (902-532-7557), 6km west of Annapolis Royal on Hwy. 1. Along with the requisite roller coasters, water rides, and mini-golf course, you'll find petting farms, artisans, storytellers, and craftspeople. (Open late June-early Sept. daily 10am-7pm. 2-day admission $5, pass for attractions $12; kids under 6 free.) Of note to engineers and "tidophiles": the 20,000kW **Annapolis Tidal Generating Station** (902-532-5454), just off Hwy. 1, marks the first attempt to generate electrical energy by harnessing the powerful Bay of Fundy tides. (Open daily 8am-8pm; off season 9:30am-5:30pm. Free—but then, who would pay?) For more thrills, there's a Provincial **visitors center** (same hours).

Eastern Annapolis Valley **Wolfville,** north of Annapolis Royal, was renamed in 1830 at the urging of postmaster de Wolf, whose nieces were ashamed of saying that they were from the town of Mud Creek. The town still commemorates its muckier appellation with **Mud Creek Days** (902-542-7000; Oct.-May 902-542-2400), a small party with fireworks, sidewalk sales, soap slides, general hoopla—the works—around the beginning of August. The **Atlantic Canada Theatre Festival** (902-542-1515) presents a number of plays in Wolfville mid-June to August (matinees $24, students and seniors $22). The most panoramic view of the Valley can be seen from the mountaintop of **The Lookoff,** Hwy. 358 20km north of Hwy. 1 (sorry, no wise sage awaits you).

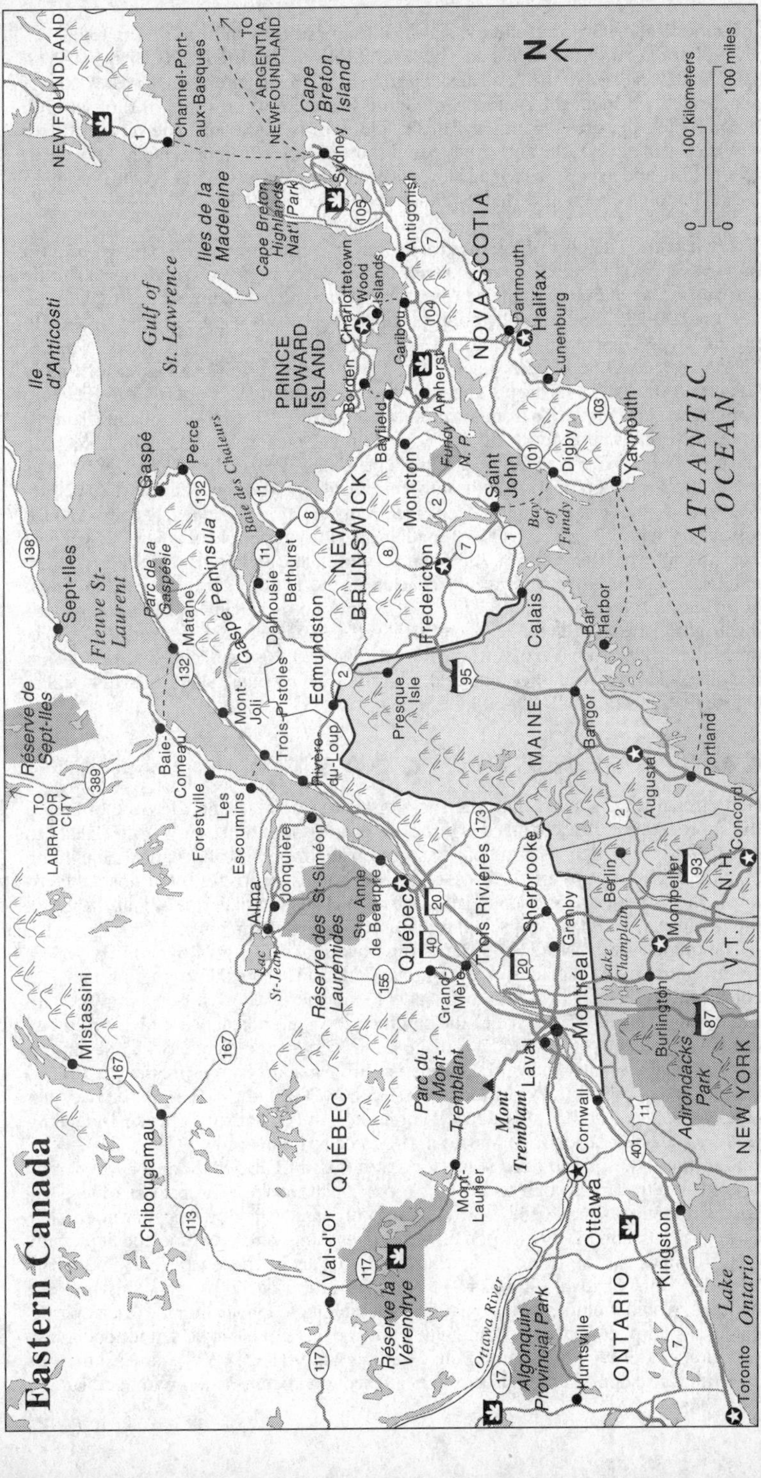
Eastern Canada
NEWFOUNDLAND
Channel-Port-aux-Basques
TO ARGENTIA NEWFOUNDLAND
Cape Breton Island
Sydney
Iles de la Madeleine
Cape Breton Highlands Nat'l Park
Antigonish
NOVA SCOTIA
Dartmouth
Halifax
Lunenburg
Gulf of St. Lawrence
Charlottetown
Wood Islands
Caribou
PRINCE EDWARD ISLAND
Borden
Amherst
Ile d'Anticosti
Bayfield
Fundy N. P.
Moncton
Saint John
Digby
Yarmouth
Bay of Fundy
ATLANTIC OCEAN
Gaspé
Percé
Baie des Chaleurs
Parc de la Gaspésie
Gaspé Peninsula
NEW BRUNSWICK
Bathurst
Dalhousie
Fredericton
Calais
Bar Harbor
Sept-Iles
Fleuve St-Laurent
Matane
Mont-Joli
Trois-Pistoles
Edmundston
Presque Isle
MAINE
Bangor
Augusta
Portland
Réserve de Sept-Iles
Baie-Comeau
Forestville
Les Escoumins
Rivière-du-Loup
TO LABRADOR CITY
Jonquière
St Siméon
Alma
Lac St-Jean
Ste Anne de Beaupré
Québec
Réserve des Laurentides
Trois Rivières
Sherbrooke
Granby
Berlin
Montpelier
N.H.
Concord
Lake Champlain
V.T.
Mistassini
Chibougamau
Grand-Mère
Montréal
Laval
Burlington
Adirondacks Park
NEW YORK
Parc du Mont-Tremblant
Mont Tremblant
Cornwall
QUÉBEC
Mont-Laurier
Ottawa
Kingston
Val-d'Or
Réserve la Vérendrye
Ottawa River
Algonquin Provincial Park
ONTARIO
Huntsville
Lake Ontario
Toronto
100 kilometers
100 miles
N
138
389
167
113
117
155
40
20
132
11
8
2
7
1
95
173
93
87
401
17
104
105
101
103

Grand Pré, or **Great Meadow,** stands at the northeastern head of Annapolis Valley, 100km northwest of Halifax. The **Grand Pré National Historic Site** (902-542-3631) memorializes to the Acadians deported in 1755. After refusing to take oaths of allegiance to Britain, the Acadians of Grand Pré were imprisoned in their church before being deported from the British colony of Nova Scotia. The refugees later resettled further south, and established communities in modern-day Louisiana, where time and accents have transformed "Acadians" into "Cajuns." (Grounds open 24hrs. Buildings open mid-May to mid-Oct. daily 9am-6pm. Free.)

Yarmouth The port of **Yarmouth,** 339km from Halifax on the southwestern tip of Nova Scotia, has a major **ferry terminal,** 58 Water St., from which boats shuttle across the **Bay of Fundy** to Maine (open daily 8am-5pm). **Marine Atlantic** (902-742-6800 or 800-341-7981 from the continental U.S.) provides service to Bar Harbor, ME (1 per day; 6-7hrs.; $50.75, seniors $38.75, ages 5-12 $27, under 5 $5, car $62.25, bike $8.50; early Sept.-early June $35/$27/$19/$5/$56/$5.75.) **Prince of Fundy Cruises** (800-341-7540 from Canada or the continental U.S.; open Mon.-Fri. 9am-9pm, Sat. 10am-9pm) sails from Yarmouth to Portland, ME. (May-Oct. daily 10am; 10 hrs.; early May to mid-June and mid-Sept. to mid-Oct. US$60, ages 5-14 US$31.50, car US$80, bike US$7; mid-June to mid-Sept. US$80/US$41.50/US$98/US$10.) Car rental agencies keep busy in Yarmouth; reserve ahead. **Avis,** 42 Starr's Rd. (902-742-3323), and at a desk in the ferry terminal, rents cars for $43 per day (plus $10 for insurance) with 200 free km (15¢ per additional km) to people of at least 21 years of age. The **information center,** 288 Main St., uphill and visible from the ferry terminal, houses both **Nova Scotia Information** (902-742-5033) and **Yarmouth Town and County Information** (902-742-6639; both open daily 8am-7pm). If you're staying around, crash at the **Ice House Hostel (HI-C)** (902-649-2818), overlooking Darling Lake 15km from Yarmouth on Rte. 1; take Old Post Rd. The small two-story building will give you a genuine feel for cabin life. (4 beds, shared bath, kitchen. $8.50, nonmembers $10. Open June-Sept.)

■■■ ATLANTIC COAST

Gulf Stream waters crash onto the rocky Atlantic Coast, setting the pace of life on the shore. Follow Nova Scotia's **Lighthouse Route** south on Hwy. 3 from Halifax to coastal villages which boast all of the picturesque trappings of oceanside life; here, boats and lobster traps are the tools of a trade, not just props for the tourists. **MacKenzie Bus Lines** (902-543-2491) runs between Halifax and Yarmouth, at the tip of the peninsula, with few stops (call for details Mon.-Sat. 9am-5pm).

The quintessential Nova Scotia lighthouse overlooks **Peggy's Cove,** off Hwy. 333, 43km southwest of Halifax. No public transportation serves the town, but most bus companies offer packages which include a stop there. These buses, coupled with the throngs of cars that arrive in the summer and the cruise lines which bring visitors on Wednesdays and Sundays, make a mockery of the cove's declared population of 60. Arrive early to avoid the crowds, and wake up with espresso ($1.25) and fresh baked goods from **Beal's Bailiwick** (902-823-2099); the café is on the back terrace (open May-Oct. daily 9am-dusk). For info on the cove, stop in at the **DeGarthe Gallery** (902-823-2256; open May to mid-Oct. daily 10am-6pm).

Return to Hwy. 3 and head south for about 50km to find **Mahone Bay,** a slightly larger town quaint enough to attract proportional crowds. The **tourist office,** 165 Edgewater St. (902-624-6151), provides info on area attractions, accommodations, campgrounds, and beaches (open July-Aug. daily 9am-7pm; May-June and Sept.-early Oct. 10am-6pm). Mahone Bay's big event comes at the end of July with the **Wooden Boat Festival** (902-624-8443), a celebration of the region's ship-building heritage, which includes a combination boat-building contest and race (lucky participants are supplied with wood and glue), and a parade of old-style schooners. Avast, ye scurvey dog! **Mug & Anchor Pub,** 634 Main St. (902-624-6378), tames a matey's appetite for seafood and draft beer beneath wooden beams laden with a collection of coasters. Specialties include the meat pie ($8), fish and chips ($4), and seafood pasta dishes ($8). (Open Sun.-Thurs. 11am-9pm, Fri.-Sat. 11am-10pm.)

The legendary, undefeated racing schooner Bluenose, which graces the back of the Canadian dime and the Nova Scotia license plate, saw its start in the shipbuilding center of **Lunenburg,** 11km east of Mahone Bay on Hwy. 3. Explore the schooner and trowler docked at the **Fisheries Museum of the Atlantic** (902-634-4794), on Bluenose Dr. by the harborfront, then see the fishing industry come alive in the museum's exhibits. (Open daily 9:15am-5:30pm; Oct. 15-May Mon.-Fri. by appointment. $4.50, ages 5-16 $1, under 5 free, families $10.) Several bed and breakfasts dot the roadsides in this area, but don't bother looking for the bargain of the century; **Margaret Murray's Bed and Breakfast,** 20 Lorne St., (902-634-3974), is as reasonable as it gets. (Singles $30, doubles $40. Includes full breakfast and parking. Reservations recommended). For info on camping, accommodations, and attractions, visit the **tourist office** (902-634-8100), in the faux lighthouse on Blockhouse Hill Rd. (open mid-June to early Oct. daily 9am-8pm; late May to mid-June 10am-6pm).

From Lunenburg, follow the signs 16km to **Ovens Natural Park** (902-766-4621), west on Hwy. 3 then south and east on Hwy. 332. The park features a spectacular trail along a cliff to a set of natural seacaves, the "ovens" from which the area takes its name, as well as the region's best **campground.** Steeped in lore that extends from Native Canadian legends to tales of the Nova Scotia Gold Rush, the park attains an almost spiritual quality, assisted by efforts not to overpackage it for tourists. The campground consists of 65 sites (some overlook the ocean) with access to the caves, free hot showers, a heated saltwater swimming pool, flush toilets, a restaurant, and a general store; half are kept unreserved to be allotted on a first come, first served basis. (Day use $3, kids 5-12 $2.50. Sites $16, with water and electricity $18, with full hookup $20. Open mid-May to mid-Oct.)

Hwy. 332 continues along the shore and into the town of **East LaHave,** where an unbelievably cheap **ferry** runs across the LaHave River into **LaHave** (on the ½hr. 6am-midnight, by demand midnight-6am; 50¢ fare per car or person). The **LaHave Bakery** (902-688-2908) beckons about 1000 ft. from the ferry dock on the left. Follow the mouthwatering smell of cheese-and-herb bread ($2.50) inside to check in for a night at the **LaHave Marine Hostel (HI-C).** Located upstairs in an apartment with a wood-burning stove, the hostel is run by the bakery proprietor; call ahead or arrive during bakery hours. (Bakery open daily 9am-6:30pm; mid-Sept to June 10am-5pm. Hostel has 9 beds $9, nonmembers $10; open June-Oct.)

■■■ HALIFAX

The British erected the Halifax Citadel in 1749 to counter the French Fortress of Louisbourg (see p. 832) on the northeastern shoulder of Cape Breton Island. Never captured or even attacked during the era of the colonial empires, the Citadel has seen more French tourists in its lifetime than it has French soldiers. Only one horrific event mars Halifax's placid history—in 1917, miscommunication between a Belgian relief ship and a French ship carrying picric acid and 400,000 tons of TNT resulted in a collision in Halifax Harbor, hurling sparks into the picric acid. One hour later, the largest man-made explosion before the advent of the atomic bomb rocked the city. Approximately 11,000 people were killed or injured, north Halifax was razed, and windows were shattered up to 50 mi. away. Long recovered from the disaster, Halifax (pop. 320,000) has grown to be the largest city in Atlantic Canada. The city's universities and active nightlife draw young people from throughout the province and beyond.

PRACTICAL INFORMATION

Tourist Office: Halifax Tourist Information (421-8736), in City Hall on the corner of Duke and Barrington St., and another branch (421-2772), at Sackville and S. Park St. across from the Public Garden. Both open June-Labor Day Mon.-Wed. 8:30am-7pm, Thurs.-Fri. 8:30am-8pm, Sun. 9am-6pm; City Hall location early

Sept.-May Mon.-Fri. 9am-5pm. **Tourism Nova Scotia,** 1869 Lower Water St. (424-4247), in a red building on the downtown harbor boardwalk. Open daily 8:30am-7pm; mid-Oct. to early June Mon.-Fri. 8:30am-4:30pm.

Student Travel Office: Travel CUTS (494-2054), on the 1st floor of the Dalhousie University Student Union Building. Open Mon.-Fri. 9am-4pm. **Rideboard** posted near Travel CUTS, near the cafeteria.

Airport: Halifax International, 40km from the city on Hwy. 102. The **Airbus** (873-2091) runs to downtown (18 per day 7:45am-10:45pm; $11, round-trip $18; under 10 free with adult). **Ace Y Share-a-cab** (429-4444) coordinates shared cab-rides to the airport 5am-9pm. Phone 3hr. ahead of pick-up time. Fare $18 ($30 for 2) from anywhere in Halifax. From the airport to town $20.

Trains: VIA Rail, 1161 Hollis St. (429-8421), at South St. in the South End near the harbor. To: Montréal ($160, student or senior $140, under 12 $80; discounts Sept. to mid-Dec. and mid-Jan. to mid-June). Open daily 8am-5:30pm.

Buses: Acadian Lines and **MacKenzie Bus Line** share a terminal at 6040 Almon St. (454-9321), near Robie St. To get downtown, take bus #7 or #80 on Robie St., or any of the 6 buses running on Gottingen St. 1 block east of the station. MacKenzie travels down the Atlantic coast to Yarmouth (1 per day, 6hr., $40); ask about stops at small towns en route. Acadian covers most of the remainder of Nova Scotia and Canada: Annapolis Royal (2 per day, 3-5hr., $25); Charlottetown, PEI (2 per day, 8½hr., $47); North Sydney (3 per day, 6-8hr., $47). 25% senior discounts, 50% discount for kids 5-11, under 5 free with adult. Station open Sun.-Fri. 6:30am-midnight, Sat. 6:30am-11pm; ticket office daily 7am-7pm.

Public Transportation: Metro Transit (421-6600; open Mon.-Fri. 7:30am-10pm, Sat.-Sun. 8am-10pm). Efficient and thorough. Pick up route maps and schedules at any info center. Fare $1.25, seniors 90¢, ages 5-15 75¢; fare from Sackville St. $1.50. Buses run daily roughly 7am-midnight.

Ferries: Dartmouth-Halifax Ferry (421-6600; 421-6594 for parking info), on the harborfront. 15-min. crossings depart from both terminals every 15-30min. Mon.-Thurs. 6:30am-midnight, Fri. 6:30am-3am; every 30min. Sat. 6:30am-3am, Sun. noon-5:30pm. Fare $1.10, ages 5-12 75¢.

Taxi: Aircab, 456-0373. **Ace Y Cab,** 429-4444. $2.40 base fee, $1.50 per mi.

Car Rental: Rent-a-Wreck, 2823 Robie St. (454-2121), at Almon St. $30 per day with 200 free km; 12¢ per additional km. Insurance $13 per day, ages 21-25 $15. Must be 21 with credit card. Open Mon.-Fri. 8am-5pm, Sat. 8am-1pm.

Bike Rental: Pedal and Sea, 1253 Barrington St. (471-1616), outside the hostel. Mountain bikes $6 per hr., $5 for HI members; $13/$11 per ½day; $22/$15 per day; $80/$60 per week. Open mid-May to mid-Oct. daily 9am-6pm (weather permitting).

Driver/Rider Services: Alternative Passage, 5224 Blower St., #202 (429-5169), matches member passengers with drivers. To: Montréal ($50); North Sydney ($21); Fredericton ($28); Cape Tourmentine ($16). Annual membership $7; 3 character references and positive I.D. required. Open Mon.-Sat. noon-4pm.

Crisis Lines: Sexual Assault, 425-0122. **Crisis Centre,** 421-1188. Both 24 hrs. **Gayline:** 423-7129. Operates Thurs.-Sat. 7-10pm.

Emergency: 4105.

Post Office: Station A, 6175 Almon St. (494-4712), in the North End 2½km from downtown. Open Mon.-Fri. 8am-5:15pm. **Postal code:** B3K 5M9. **Area code:** 902.

Barrington St., the major north-south thoroughfare, runs straight through downtown. Approaching the Citadel and the Public Garden, **Sackville St.** cuts east-west parallel to **Spring Garden Rd.,** Halifax's shopping thoroughfare. Downtown is flanked by the less affluent **North End** and the mostly quiet and arboreal **South End,** on the ocean. Downtown traffic doesn't get too hectic, but parking is difficult.

ACCOMMODATIONS AND CAMPING

You'll have no trouble finding affordable summer accommodations in Halifax, except during major events, such as the Tattoo Festival or the Moosehead Grand Prix (see Entertainment below). Plan well in advance for those times.

Halifax Heritage House Hostel (HI-C), 1253 Barrington St. (422-3863), a 3-min. walk from the heart of downtown 1 block from the train station. Clean rooms and access to a lounge with TV, a kitchen, and laundry facilities. Ask for a 1st-floor room where fewer people share each bathroom. No curfew, but ask for the security access code if you'll be out past 10pm. Office closed noon-3pm. Check-in 3-11pm. $13.75, nonmembers $16.75, non-Canadian nonmembers $17.75. Free linen. IBN reservations available.

Technical University of Nova Scotia, M. M. O'Brien Bldg., 5217 Morris St. (422-2495), at Barrington St. Refinished dorms right downtown. Free laundry facilities and parking in a lot. Kitchen access. Check-in 8am-midnight. Singles $23, doubles $36; students with ID $18/$32; under 14 $10/$16. Reservations recommended July-Aug. Open May-Aug.

Dalhousie University (494-3401; 494-2108 after 8pm), Howe Hall on Coburg Rd. at LeMarchant 3km southwest of downtown. "Dal" is usually packed; arrive early. Laundry and recreation facilities extra. Open 24 hrs. Singles $29, doubles $43 (breakfast and parking included); students $20/$32 ($5 extra for breakfast); under 11 free. July-Aug. make reservations 1 week in advance. Open early May-late Aug.

Gerrard Hotel, 1234 Barrington St. (423-8614), between South and Morris St. Subdued live-in clientele and elaborate rooms. Kitchen access and free parking. Check-in Mon.-Fri. 8am-8:30pm, Sat. 8am-7:30pm. Singles $30, with private bath $44; doubles $39/$49. $5 per extra person.

Hammond's Plain, a 20-minute drive north on Hwy. 102, has the closest campsites in the Halifax area. Take exit 3 from Rte. 213 and follow the signs to **Wood Havens Park** (835-2271; 95 sites; $14, with hookup $17-18.50; open May-Oct.).

FOOD

Downtown venues provide many options for appeasing the demons of hunger. Pubs peddle cheap grub and inner peace (see Entertainment and Nightlife below for suggestions), but their kitchens often close down around 10pm. For fresh local produce and baked goods, visit the **farmer's market** (492-4043), in the old brewery on Lower Water St. (open May-Sept. Sat. 7am-1pm.)

Granite Brewery, 1222 Barrington St. (423-5660). A microbrewery with some of the best pub food around. Produces 3 labels; the Old Peculiar is strangely appealing (9-oz. glass $2.30). Try it with the smoked salmon club sandwich ($7) or the beef and beer stew ($5). Open Mon.-Sat. 11:30am-12:30am, Sun. noon-11pm. Watch for a second location opening downtown early in 1996.

Lawrence of Oregano, 1726 Argyle St. (425-8077). Unlike his Arabian cousin, this Lawrence never made it to the silver screen. Called "Larry O's" by the regulars. Satisfying Italian and seafood dishes around $5; daily specials $3-4. Open daily 11am-3:30am. Kitchen closes at 10pm.

Mediterraneo Café, 1571 Barrington St. (423-6936), where somber, long-haired students engage in obviously profound conversation over Middle Eastern dishes. Coffee's filled twice for 80¢, so relax and stay a while. Tabouli with 2 huge pita pockets $2.50; falafel sandwich $3; filling daily specials $3.25-5. Open Mon.-Fri. 6am-8pm, Sat.-Sun. 7:30am-8pm.

SIGHTS

The star-shaped **Halifax Citadel National Historic Park** (426-5080), in the heart of Halifax, and the old **Town Clock,** at the foot of Citadel Hill, are Halifax traditions. A walk along the fortress walls affords a fine view of the city and harbor. Small exhibits and a one-hour film inside the fortress will fill you in on the relevant history. Come any day between June 15 and Labor Day at 11:40am to see the pageantry of preparation for the **noonday cannon firing.** (Open June 15-Labor Day daily 9am-6pm; Labor Day-Oct. and mid-May to mid-June10am-5pm. In summer $5, seniors $3.75, ages 6-16 $2.50; off season $3/$2.25/$1.50; under five free with adult.)

The **Halifax Public Gardens,** across from the Citadel near the intersection of South Park and Sackville St., make a relaxing spot for a lunch break. The Roman statues, Victorian bandstand, gas lamps, exquisite horticulture, and overfed loons on the pond are very properly British in style. (Open daily 8am-sunset.) From July through September, watch for concerts on Sunday afternoons at 2pm.

Chat with the mayor and fellow tourists over free tea and food at **Tea with the Mayor** (421-8736), inside City Hall on the corner of Duke and Barrington St. (July-Aug. Mon.-Thurs. 3:30-4:30pm; free). Filling your bag with finger sandwiches is generally frowned upon—to say the least.

Reconstructed early-19th-century architecture covers the **Historic Properties** district (429-0530), downtown on lower Water St. Unfortunately, the charming stone-and-wood façades are only sheep's clothing disguising wolfishly overpriced boutiques and restaurants. Museums in Halifax don't stack up to the competition elsewhere in Nova Scotia. However, die-hard museum-goers might enjoy the **Maritime Museum of the Atlantic,** 1675 Lower Water St. (424-7490), which has an interesting display on the Halifax Explosion. (Open Mon. and Wed.-Sat. 9:30am-5:30pm, Tues. 9:30am-8pm, Sun. 1-5:30pm; mid-Oct. to May. $2.25, under 17 50¢. Free Tues. 5:30-8pm and mid-Oct. to May.)

Point Pleasant Park, 186 car-free wooded acres at the southern tip of Halifax (take bus #9 from Barrington St. downtown), remains one of England's last imperial holdings, leased to the city of Halifax for 999 years at the bargain rate of 1 shilling per year. Inside the park, the **Prince of Wales Martello Tower,** an odd fort built by the British in 1797, stands as testimony to one of Prince Edward's two fascinations: round buildings and his mistress—both of which he kept in Halifax.

ENTERTAINMENT AND NIGHTLIFE

The **Neptune Theatre,** 5216 Sackville St. (429-7070, for info or tickets Mon.-Fri. 10am-5pm), presents the area's most noteworthy professional stage productions. The theater's season features classics as well as contemporary selections. (Performances Sept. to mid-May. Tickets $20-30.) At **Wormwood's Dog and Monkey Cinema,** 2015 Gottingen St. (422-3700), Canadian and international art films have been known to prompt sell-outs and sizable lines; get there early to beat the intellectual masses. (Tickets $7. Shows daily around 7 and 9:30pm; matinees on Sun.)

The Nova Scotia International Tattoo Festival (420-1114; 451-1221 for tickets), is possibly Halifax's biggest summer event. Presented by the Province of Nova Scotia and the Canadian Maritime Armed Forces, the festival runs through the first week of July, featuring international musicians, bicyclists, dancers, acrobats, gymnasts, and military groups. At noon, the Metro area overflows with free entertainment. Later, a two-hour show, featuring over 2000 performers, takes place in the Halifax Metro Centre. (Show tickets $11-25, seniors and kids under 13 $2 off.) The **DuMaurier Atlantic Jazz Festival** (492-2225 or 800-567-5277) fests for a week in mid-July with both ticketed and free concerts throughout the city. For ten days in mid-August, **Buskerfest** (429-3910) brings street performers to Halifax from around the world. The **Atlantic Film Festival** (422-3456) wraps up the festival season with a showcase of Canadian and international films at the end of September.

There's no need to beat around the bush: Halifax boasts one of Canada's most intoxicating nighttime scenes. Numerous pubs and clubs pack the downtown area, making bar-hopping common and recommended. The mammoth structure known as **The Dome** (that's the **Liquordome** to locals) houses four establishments which draw young people like a magnetic field to daily drink specials and dancing. Inside, **Lawrence of Oregano's, My Apartment, Cheers,** and **The Atrium** each strive to attain a distinct flavor, mainly through musical preference; walk-through access connects them all. (Cover $2-4. Open daily noon-3:30am.) At the **Seahorse Pub,** 1665 Argyle St. (423-7200), purple-haired students meet lawyers in a dark basement room with carved woodwork (open Mon.-Wed. noon-1am, Thurs.-Sat. 11:30am-2am). The **Lower Deck** (425-1501), in the Historic Properties, offers excellent Irish folk music along with nautical pub decor. (Cover $2-4; Sun. no music and no cover. Open Mon.-Sat. 11am-12:30am, Sun. 11am-11pm.) Huge and always packed, **Peddler's**

Pub (423-5033), in Barrington Place Mall on Granville St., is favored for good pub food, including wings ($4.50) and steamed mussels ($4), but there's no question it's a pub. (99¢ food specials Fri. after 4pm. Open Mon.-Sat. 11am-11pm, Sun. noon-10pm.) **J.J. Rossy's,** 1887 Granville St. (422-4411), across the street from Peddler's, attracts nocturnal crowds with a dance floor and tremendous drink specials—during the "power hours" (Wed.-Sat. 10-11pm and midnight-1am) a draft falls to 70¢ and shots plummet to $1.25. Rossy's also offers a $4.50 all-you-can-eat lunch special on Fridays from noon to 2pm. (Cover Thurs.-Sat. after 8pm $2.50. Open Mon.-Sat. 11am-2am; kitchen until 10pm.) **Birdland,** 2021 Brunswick St. (425-0889), caters to an alternative crowd with live bands three or four nights per week. Depending on the band, cover ranges $3-6. (Open Mon.-Sat. noon-3:30am.) **The Studio** (423-6866), at Barrington St. and Spring Garden Rd., is an unrestricted gay and lesbian club, with some of the city's best dance music. (Cover Thurs.-Sat. after 10pm $2-3. Open Mon.-Sat. 4pm-2am, Sun 6pm-2am.)

■■■ CAPE BRETON ISLAND

Alexander Graham Bell believed Cape Breton Island to be the most beautiful place he'd ever seen and backed that belief by building Bein Bhreagh, the estate where he spent the waning years of his life, on Cape Breton. The breathtaking coastline, loch-like finger-lakes, dramatic cliffs, and lush hills which compel thousands of visitors to drive the island's Cabot Trail each year have also prompted people to call Cape Breton Scotland's missing west coast. But this reference runs deeper than geography; immigrants from the Scottish Highlands began settling the area in 1805, and their cultural imprint on the island is indelible. Today, the Gaelic College of Celtic Arts and Crafts in St. Ann's is the only institution in North America where students can major in bagpiping, Highlands dancing, or Gaelic song. However, the Scots were not the only people attracted by Cape Breton's inviting highlands; a healthy French Acadian population thrives in and around the town of Cheticamp. Set aside ample time to savor both the island's rich cultural heritage and its legendary beauty.

Practical Information Northeast of mainland Nova Scotia, Cape Breton Island connects to the rest of the province by the **Trans-Canada Highway** across the **Canso Causeway,** 280km north of Halifax. The **Bras d'Or Lake,** an 80km-long inland sea, divides Cape Breton roughly in two. The larger western section includes the scenic Cape Breton Highlands and the Cabot Trail. The depressed industrial centers of the eastern section, including the island's largest cities, **Sydney** and **Glace Bay,** were developed with revenues mined from steel and coal. **Port Hastings,** the first town you'll encounter in Cape Breton, supports a **Provincial Tourism Nova Scotia** center (625-1717), just across the causeway on the right (open July-Aug. daily 8:30am-8pm, May 15-June and Sept.-Oct. 15 9am-5pm). Buses from **Acadian Lines,** 99 Terminal Drive, Sydney (564-5533), drive to Halifax with stops in many small towns along Rte. 4. Call to find out where, when, and for how much the bus stops. If you flag down the bus in a town near you, be prepared to stop the driver when you want to get off. (Open daily 7am-midnight.) Cape Breton's **area code:** 902.

The Cabot Trail and Cape Breton Highlands National Park Named after English explorer John Cabot, who landed in the Highlands in 1497, the **Cabot Trail** tops the list as Canada's most scenic marine drive. The 300km-long loop winds precipitously around the perimeter of northern Cape Breton. Wedged within the north loop of the Cabot Trail, the **Cape Breton Highlands National Park** encompasses 950 sq. km of highlands and ocean wilderness stretched across the north end of Cape Breton (entrance $6 per vehicle, $18 for 4 days). A photographer's dream, the Trail takes seven to 10 hours to enjoy (allowing for a lunch break, Kodak moments, and slow traffic). For a more relaxing experience, drive or bike the park's trail clockwise, shying away from the sheer cliffs. One **park information center** (224-2306) greets visitors at the southwest park entrance, 5 km north of **Cheti-**

camp on the Cabot Trail, while another (285-2535) waits at the southeast entrance in **Ingonish Beach**. (Both centers open daily 8am-8pm; Sept. to mid-Oct. and mid-May to June 8am-6pm; mid-Oct. to mid-May for phone inquiries only Mon.-Fri. 8am-4pm.) **Les Amis Du Plein Air** (224-3814) handles **bike rentals;** call or inquire at the bookstore in the southwest park information center ($5 per hr., $25 per day; nearby bike trail takes 2hrs).

Lodging is expensive along the Trail, generally $50-60 for a double. The **Glenmore International Hostel (HI-C)** (258-3622; call for directions), in Twin Rock Valley on Rte. 395 west of Whycocomagh, provides the only reasonably priced lodging within 140km. A 20-minute drive from the shore, the hostel occupies a rough but comfortable cabin near a large lake in beautiful hiking and mountain biking country. (Full kitchen; $10, nonmembers $12; tent sites $7; linen $2.) The park operates six **campgrounds** with 548 first come, first served sites.; weekdays yield the best selection. (Sites $13, with full hookup $19. Open mid-May to mid-Oct.)

The resort village of **Baddeck** lies on the shore of Lake Bras d'Or on the south loop of the Cabot Trail. **The Alexander Graham Bell National Historic Site** (295-2069), Chebucto St. (Rte. 205), in the east end of Baddeck, enjoys a spectacular view of the lake from its roof gardens. Inside the building, a fascinating museum commemorates the life and inventions of Bell. Along with his masterpiece the telephone, Bell's creations include innovative work on medical tools, hydrofoils, airplanes, and methods for educating the deaf to speak. Informative talks on his life and his projects provide all of the details. (Open daily 9am-8pm; Sept. 9am-6pm; Oct.-June 9am-5pm, exhibits only. Accessible to disabled-16 $1.25, under 5 free.)

Louisbourg The **Fortress of Louisbourg** was the King of France's most ambitious military project in the Colonies, his "New World Gibraltar"—the launching pad from which France would regain the Americas. Sadly for him, a small band of New Englanders laid siege to, and quickly captured, Louisbourg in 1745. Though a treaty soon returned the fortress to France, the British took it back in 1758 with even greater ease. The $25 million rebuilding of Louisbourg, the largest historic reconstruction in North America, has resulted in **Fortress of Louisbourg National Historic Park** (733-2280), 37km southeast of Sydney on Rte. 22. Far more successful as a tourist attraction than it ever was as a military outpost, the fort offers 2-4 guided walking tours daily, in English or French. Purchase tickets and park your car at the **Louisbourg Tourist Bureau** (733-2720), off Rte. 22 near the fortress (open May-Oct. daily 9am-7pm); a shuttle bus will take you to the fortress gates. Every attempt has been made to recreate the atmosphere of 1744. The buildings feature period rooms, staffed by costumed actors doing their 1744 thing; the scope is startling, and the re-creation provides an almost disturbingly convincing experience. (Open July-Aug. 9am-6pm; June and Sept. 9:30am-5pm; May and Oct. 9am-5pm. $7.50, seniors $6, students and youths $4.25, families $19.25, under 5 free.)

The **Hôtel de la Marine** within the fortress prepares full-course meals ($9) from authentic 1744 French recipes—lots of fun, but be forewarned that the 18th century had no Cordon Bleu chefs. Peek at the kitchen, if you can skirt the actors. The 80% whole wheat/20% rye bread ($2.50) from the **King's Bakery** looks like a cannonball and feels almost as hard.

Glace Bay The grimy, industrial city of **Glace Bay** proves that not all of Cape Breton is scenic. The town, which once drew innumerable immigrants for hazardous jobs in the Sydney coalfields, now preserves its history at the **Miners' Museum** 42 Birkley St. (849-4522), off South St. east of downtown. Exhibits on coal mining and the plight of organized labor, along with a reconstructed miners' village and films on life as a coal miner, set the background for the museum's big attraction, a ¼-mi. tour of an underground coal mine. The experienced miners who guide the tours paint a bleak picture of their hard days' toil; the result is a fascinating eye-opener. (Open Wed.-Mon. 10am-6pm, Tues. 10am-7pm; early Sept.-early June Mon.-Fri. 9am-4pm museum only. $3.25, with tour $6; kids $1.75/$3.) Don't miss the **Men of the**

Deeps, the local miners singing group, who perform at the museum Tuesday evenings at 8pm during July and August ($5.50, under 14 $3.50).

North Sydney North Sydney, Sydney Mines, Sydney River, and Sydney all conglomerate within a 20-km radius, 430km northeast of Halifax at the northeast end of Cape Breton Island. The Marine Atlantic Ferry Terminal at the end of the Trans-Canada Hwy. in **North Sydney** stands out as the departure point for ferries to **Newfoundland** (see Newfoundland Island Getting There and Getting Around p. 834). The **North Sydney Tourist Bureau,** 1 Purves St. (794-7719), next to the terminal, answers tourism and accommodation queries in a little house appropriately decorated with question marks (open July-early Sept. daily 8am-8pm). **Blue & White Taxi** (794-4767) charges $3.25 from any point in town to the ferry terminal for one or two passengers ($1 per additional person; kids under 13 free).

Make reservations to stay in North Sydney before you arrive, especially on those nights preceding the departure of the ferry to Argentia, NF, when the whole area gets booked solid. The Sydney area is no exception to the rule of expensive lodging on Cape Breton; the town's two B&Bs ask $45 for a single and $55 for a double. The area's best bargain, the **Seaview Inn,** 30 Seaview Dr. (794-3066), 2km from the ferry terminal, rents clean singles with shared baths for $28, doubles for $35.

Newfoundland and Labrador

Humans have been "discovering," settling, and rediscovering Newfoundland and Labrador for millenia. Inuit presence stretches back some 9000 years on both the island and the mainland, and confirmed European exploration dates to around 1000AD, when Norse Vikings settled briefly at L'Anse aux Meadows on the island's northern tip. Of course, relative newcomer John Cabot, who sailed into present-day St. John's harbor in 1497, has long been credited with finding Newfoundland. To this day, Newfoundland and Labrador remain relatively unknown except to their hardy inhabitants and the few very rich travelers for whom the vast, largely undeveloped regions become a wilderness playground. Be wary of blurring the distinction between the two regions which make up the province; residents of the considerably colder, less inhabited Labrador are quick to remind you of the difference.

PRACTICAL INFORMATION

Capital: St. John's.

Department of Tourism and Culture: P.O. Box 8730, St. John's A1B 4K2 (709-729-2830 or 800-563-6353). Open Mon.-Fri. 9:30am-6:30pm; answering service 24 hrs. Request the comprehensive, town-by-town *Newfoundland & Labrador Travel Guide* and the *Newfoundland and Labrador Official Highway Map,* which provides inset town maps and campsite info. For info specific to Labrador, contact **Destination Labrador,** 118 Humphrey Rd., Bruno Plaza, Labrador City A2V 2J8 (709-944-7788; fax 709-944-7787).

Time Zones: Labrador, except for the coast south of Cartwright, runs on Atlantic (1hr. ahead of Eastern). Newfoundland island and Labrador's southern coast use Newfoundland time (1½hr. ahead of Eastern). **Postal Abbreviation:** NF

Drinking Age: 19.

Provincial Sales Tax: 12%, plus 7% GST (for details on obtaining a refund of the GST, see Essentials, p. 7).

NEWFOUNDLAND ISLAND

The mountains of Newfoundland rise unexpectedly from the Atlantic to tower above rocky shores and waters that were once blessed with the earth's most plentiful cod stocks. Formed by collisions of the earth's tectonic plates, Newfoundland's breathtaking, if daunting, landscape is a natural wonder, alternately featuring deep fjords and granite cliffs, barren rock and gentle forests. The central region, hardly accessible and scarcely inhabited, combines lowlands, boggy forests, and rolling hills. In Gros Morne National Park and Terra Nova National Park diverse wildlife populations from the land, sea, and air live among geological formations which date back to the Earth's Precambrian period.

The people of "the rock" are strong, weathered by the ocean which isolates and nourishes them, and characterized by a sense of humor and friendliness virtually unparalleled on the mainland. Their notorious food and drink are equally unpretentious, hearty, sturdy, and in the case of "screech," the locally made rum, downright overwhelming. Newfoundlanders may speak in a deep, often incomprehensible drawl which combines both accent and idiom with an Irish or western English quality. Visitors should be advised not to employ the moniker "Newfie" at will; limit its use to situations where someone mentions it first, and then remember that it features prominently in numerous insulting jokes told in other parts of Canada.

Getting There and Getting Around There are only two ways to reach Newfoundland: boat or plane. Boats go a bit easier on the budget. **Marine Atlantic** (800-341-7981 from the Continental U.S.; 902-794-5700 from North Sydney or Nova Scotia; 709-695-7083 from Port-aux-Basques; 506-636-4048 from St. John's) ferries depart from North Sydney to Port-aux-Basques (1-4 per day, 5-7½hr., $17.75, ages 5-12 $9, seniors $13, cars $55) and Argentia (mid-June to Sept. 1 per day Tues. and Fri., $49, ages 5-12 $24.50, seniors $36.75, cars $107). Reservations are required, especially for the Argentia Ferry. Carless travelers who show up at the terminal at least two hours in advance can usually get on without a reservation.

CN Roadcruiser, 495 Water St., St. John's (709-737-5912), serves the whole island, running from Port-aux-Basques to St. John's. (1 per day, 14hr.; $80, 10% discount for students and seniors, ages 5-11 ½price, under 5 free.) The bus leaves early in the morning; try taking a night ferry if you don't want to be stranded overnight in barren Port-aux-Basques. **G and J Transportation** (709-682-6245) provides minibus service between Argentia and St. John's, a route unserviced by CN Roadcruiser. Call and the owner will pick you up anywhere in either town for the trip. (Departs St. John's daily 9am, returns 5pm. $12.) The **Coffey House Bed and Breakfast** (709-227-2262 or 709-227-7303), a convenient 6km from the Argentia ferry landing on Rte. 100 in Freshwater, makes a nice stopover between an evening ferry arrival and a next-day bus to St. John's (singles $38, doubles $45; breakfast included, other meals available). Newfoundland's limited transportation and formidable size severely impair exploration without a car.

■■■ ST. JOHN'S

St. John's, an oasis of civilization amidst Newfoundland's picturesque expanses of caribou and conifers, sits on the southeastern coast of the island's Avalon Peninsula. Most of the city's claims to fame relate to its location on the continent's easternmost point, almost halfway between Montréal and Europe; Marconi received the first trans-Atlantic wireless signal here in 1901, and the first successful nonstop trans-Atlantic flight took off from St. John's in 1919. However, Newfoundland's capital has more to offer than important dates; St. John's brims over with rugged, friendly locals and a distinct seaside culture.

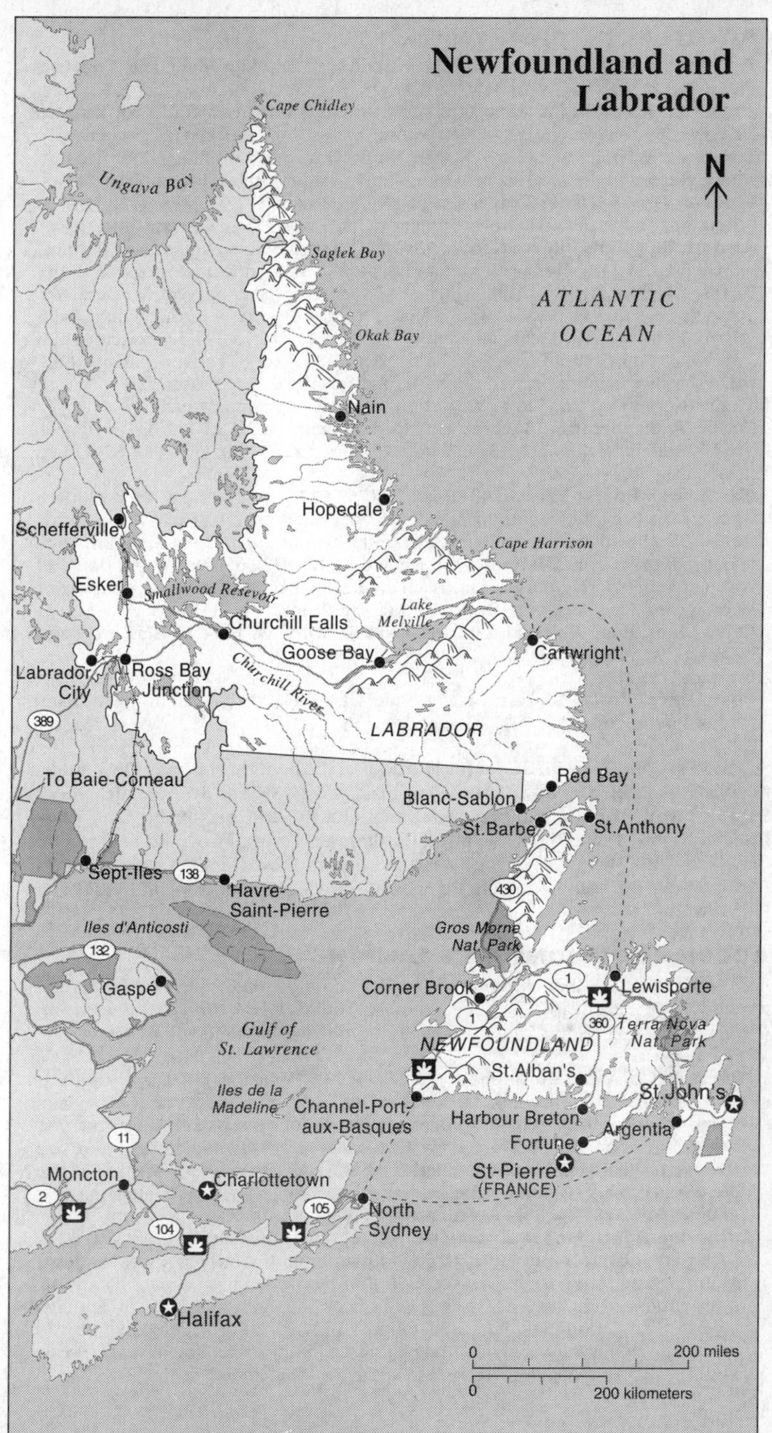

Newfoundland and Labrador
N
Cape Chidley
Ungava Bay
Saglek Bay
ATLANTIC OCEAN
Okak Bay
Nain
Hopedale
Schefferville
Cape Harrison
Esker
Smallwood Reservoir
Lake Melville
Churchill Falls
Goose Bay
Cartwright
Labrador City
Ross Bay Junction
Churchill River
389
LABRADOR
Red Bay
To Baie-Comeau
Blanc-Sablon
St.Barbe
St.Anthony
Sept-Iles
138
Havre-Saint-Pierre
430
Iles d'Anticosti
Gros Morne Nat. Park
132
Gaspé
Corner Brook
1
Lewisporte
1
360
Terra Nova Nat. Park
Gulf of St. Lawrence
NEWFOUNDLAND
St.Alban's
Iles de la Madeline
Channel-Port-aux-Basques
St.John's
Harbour Breton
Argentia
11
Fortune
St-Pierre (FRANCE)
Moncton
Charlottetown
2
105
North Sydney
104
Halifax
0
200 miles
0
200 kilometers

PRACTICAL INFORMATION

Tourist Office: The City of St. John's Economic Development and Tourism Division (576-8106 or 576-8455), on New Gower St. across from City Hall. Open Mon.-Fri. 9am-4:30pm, early Sept.-May Mon.-Fri. 9am-5pm. **Rail Car Tourist Chalet** (576-8514), on Harbor Dr. (you can't miss it, it's the only rail car in town). Open early June-Labor Day 8:30am-6:30pm. **Gay Info Line,** 753-4297. Tips on bars, clubs, and the local scene. Open Thurs. 7-10pm; answering machine 24 hrs.

Student Travel Office: Travel CUTS (737-7926 or 737-7936; fax 737-4743), in Memorial University's Thomson Student Center. Open Mon.-Fri. 9am-5pm.

Airport: St. John's International (726-7888), 10km from downtown off Portugal Cove Rd. (Rte. 40). No buses go to the airport; a taxi to downtown costs $11-13.

Buses: CN Roadcruiser, 495 Water St. (737-5912), serves the entire island. To: Port-aux-Basques (1 per day 8am, 14hr., $80); Lewisporte (1 per day, 6hr., $45). 10% discount for students and seniors, ages 5-11 ½price, under 5 free. Open Mon.-Fri. 7am-5:30pm, Sat.-Sun. 7am-4:30pm. **G and J Transportation** (682-6245) runs a minibus between Argentia and St. John's (1 per day, $12).

Taxis: Bugdon's Taxi, 726-4400. $2 base fare, $1.60 per mi. 24 hrs.

Public Transportation: Metrobus, 245 Freshwater Rd. (722-9400). Transportation throughout the city daily 6:30am-11:30pm. Fare $1.50, kids 4-18 $1. Office open daily 7am-11pm.

Car Rental: Rent-a-Wreck, 43 Pippy Pl. (753-2277). $32 per day with 100 free km; 12¢ per additional km. Insurance $12 per day, ages 21-24 pay $14 per day. Must be 21 with major credit card or $300 cash deposit. Open Mon.-Fri. 8am-5pm, Sat. 9am-1pm. **Discount,** 350 Kenmount Rd. (722-6699). $36 per day, 130 free km; 14¢ per additional km. Insurance $8 per day. Must be 21 with major credit card. Open Mon.-Fri. 8am-5pm, Sat. 9am-1pm.

Crisis Lines: Rape Crisis and Information Center, 726-1411. **Crisis Line Telecare,** 579-1601. Both 24 hrs.

Emergency: 911.

Post Office: Postal Station C, 354 Water St. (758-1003). Open Mon.-Fri. 8am-5pm. **Postal code:** A1C 5H1. **Area code:** 709.

St. John's sits on a hill with **St. John's Harbour** at the bottom. **Harbour Dr.** borders the water, paralleled by downtown's two main streets, **Water St.** and **Duckworth St. Freshwater Rd.** (which becomes Kenmount Rd. and, eventually, the **Trans-Canada Highway**) and **New Cove Rd.** (farther out, Portugal Cove Rd.) extend up the hill towards Memorial University and the airport. Prince Phillip Pkwy. connects Portugal Cove Rd. with Kenmount Rd., passing directly in front of the university and Pippy Park.

ACCOMMODATIONS AND CAMPING

B&Bs tend to be cheaper ($40-60 for a single) and more enjoyable than hotels and motels. However, cheaper lodgings do exist. The *St. John's Tourist Information Guide,* available in visitors centers, contains complete accommodations listings.

Memorial University Residences (737-7933; 737-7590 Mon.-Fri. 9am-4:30pm), at Hatcher House off Elizabeth Ave. From downtown take bus #3 or walk 45min. Clean dorm rooms with basic student amenities. Rooms reputedly never run out. Open 24 hrs., but the phone is rarely answered. Go directly to Hatcher house and find the on-guard clerk's phone number on the conference office booth. Call the clerk if necessary. Definitely the best prices around—singles $16, students $13; doubles $25/$20. Open mid-April to late Aug.

Catherine Booth House Traveler's Hostel, 18 Springdale St. (738-2804). Off Water St. 3min. from the heart of downtown. From the bus station, walk down Water St. and turn left on Springdale St. Run by the Salvation Army, this caring, sharing hostel functions like a B&B and offers 32 comfortable beds in spotless rooms. Free parking and laundry facilities. Must be 20 or accompanied by an adult. Curfew, closing, and quiet time 12:30am. Singles $36, doubles $42. Breakfast (7:30-9:30am) and late night snack (8:30-10pm) included.

Southcott Hall, 100 Forest Rd. (737-6448), a 10-min. walk from downtown. This nurses' residence at St. John's General Hospital rents 30 singles ($32) in a spartan 12-story highrise with a great view. Laundry and kitchen facilities. Open 24 hrs.

A Gower Street House B&B, 180 Gower St. (800-563-3959), 1 block from the St. John's Cathedral in the center of the old city. Close to downtown shopping and nightlife. Private rooms, telephones, A/C, off-street parking, and separate lounge. Singles $45, off season $35; includes full breakfast.

Pippy Park Trailer Park (737-3669), on Nagles Pl. off Prince Philip Pkwy. 180 nicely wooded campsites. Popular picnic and barbecue areas, hiking, fishing, and a convenience store within the park. $5.50, RV sites $11-15. Open May-Sept.

FOOD

Don't leave before having sampled traditional "Newfie" foods, such as jigg's dinner or fish 'n' brewis (basically fish mixed with soaked and boiled hardbread—it's much better than it sounds), scrunchions, and hot fried-dough toutons with blackstrap molasses. **House of Hayne's,** 207 Kenmount Rd. (754-4937), will set you up with plentiful portions of any of these delicacies. (Jigg's dinner $6; fish 'n' brewis with scrunchions $6.30; touton $1.50. Open daily 6:15am-10pm.)

Ches's, 9 Freshwater St. (722-4083). Great fish & chips ($5-6, depending on cod availability) are superbly greased and fried. Don't be put off by the fast-food setting; the food is good. Open Sun.-Thurs. 9am-2am, Fri.-Sat. 9am-3am.

Classic Cafe, 364 Duckworth St. (579-4444). Generous portions at all hours of the day. Great breakfast selection ($3-6) and inexpensive dinner fare. The "No Shame Burger" ($7) suits the laid back atmosphere. Open 24 hrs.

Magic Wok Eatery, 402 Water St. (753-6907), pulls Szechuan, Cantonese, and Peking dishes out of its wok at friendly prices. Lunch specials $5.50-7; dinner specials $5-6; and entrees $7-9. Open Mon.-Sat. noon-midnight, Sun. 3pm-midnight.

Cafe Duckworth, 190 Duckworth St. (722-1444). The place for coffee-sipping long-haired musicians drawing long puffs from imported cigarettes, blue-haired women reading *The New Yorker,* sandwiches ($4-6), breakfast specials ($4-6.50), and coffees. Open Mon.-Sat. 8am-9pm, Sun. 10am-8pm.

SIGHTS

One of the oldest cities in North America, St. John's is steeped in history. Architectural landmarks fill the downtown area. Among the most prominent, **St. John the Baptist Anglican Cathedral** (726-5677), on Gower St. at Church Hill, stands as one of the finest examples of ecclesiastical Gothic architecture in North America (tours May to mid-Oct. Mon.-Sat. 10am-5pm, Sun. noon-5pm). **Commissariat House** (729-6730), on King's Bridge Rd., displays late Georgian style as guides in period costumes show you around (open June to mid-Sept. daily 10am-6pm).

Signal Hill and the **Cabot Tower** perch above the city, uphill and to the east of the waterfront. The fuss about this place dates back to French and English struggles for control of the hill and an episode involving a man named Marconi and the first trans-Atlantic cable transmission in 1901. If none of this means much to you, at least take time to enjoy the hill's fantastic view of St. John's, the water (look for icebergs May -Aug.), and **Cape Spear,** the easternmost point of land in North America (to the south). During July and August, the **Military Tatoo** recreates the everyday drills and procedures of the fort's heyday (Wed.-Thurs. and Sat.-Sun. 3 and 7pm). The **Visitor Information and Interpretation Center** (772-5367) sheds some light on the history of the hill (open June daily 8:30am-8pm; July-Labor Day 8:30am-9pm).

Museum junkies get their fix at the **Newfoundland Museum,** 285 Duckworth St. (729-2329), where displays chronicle 900 years of Newfoundland history. An amazing display of stuffed animals (no, not teddy bears) represents Newfoundland's wildlife. (Open daily 10am-5:45pm; Labor Day-June Mon.-Fri. 9am-4:45pm, Sat.-Sun. 12:30-4:45pm.) During July and August, local musicians perform concerts at the museum in both modern and traditional styles (Sun. 2:30-4pm).

ENTERTAINMENT AND NIGHTLIFE

Theatrical productions, a permanent art gallery, and performances by local troupes make the small but lively **LPSU Hall Theatre and Resource Center for the Arts,** 3 Victoria St. (752-4531), the center of high culture in St. John's (free).

For a taste of Newfoundlander fun, head to the waterfront, where **Adventure Tours** (726-5000) combines whale watching, cod-jigging, drinking screech rum, and cod-kissing for a ceremony which earns the brave paticipant a genuine screechers certificate. Don't forget to pet Bosun, the enormous Newfoundland dog. (Tours 2½hr. Open daily 10am-5pm; additional hours Thurs.-Sat. for the Moonlight Tour at 9:30pm, $15. Day tours $20, students $15, seniors $10 on Mon., under 12 $10.)

The **George Street Festival** (576-8106) lets contemporary and traditional local musicians strut their stuff on Prince Edward Plaza the last weekend in July. On the first Wednesday of August, the city shuts down while everyone gathers at Quidi Vidi Lake (weather permitting) for the annual **St. John's Regatta,** North America's oldest continuing sporting event (since 1825); call the **Regatta Museum** (576-8058), in the boathouse at Quidi Vidi Lake for details.

St. John's transforms with the setting of the sun, and quiet streets come alive with the vibrancy of a young, partying crowd. **George St.** in particular becomes one continuous strip of clubs where loud music plays and drinking youths congregate. To avoid the long lines, show up before 10pm. Initiate yourself with an official screeching-in ceremony at **Trapper John's Museum and Pub,** 2 George St. (579-9630); the complimentary ceremony includes a gullet-warming belt of screech, a smooch from a puffin, and a certificate attesting your honorary Newfoundlander status. (Cover Fri. and when bands play $2. Open Mon.-Sat. 10am-2am, Sun 10am-midnight.) **The Sundance Saloon,** 33 George St. (753-7822), has noteworthy food and drink specials and an active dance floor. Go Thursday for 9¢ wings and Friday for Karaoke (5-9pm). Get there early—the line at the door can be more than 200 people long. (Cover Fri.-Sat. 8pm-1am $3. Open Mon.-Sat. noon-2am, Sun. noon-midnight.) For live entertainment every night of the week, including a Wednesday-night talent show and the area's best Irish folk music, stop in at **Erin's Pub,** 186 Water St. (722-1916). Bands strike up at 10:30pm to the delight of locals ranging in age from 19 to 90. You can get Guiness and Harp on tap, but not cheap. ($5 per pint. Cover Wed.-Sun. $1-3. Open Mon-Sat. noon-2am, Sun. noon-midnight.)

■■■ THE REST OF THE ISLAND

Caribou and moose, rather than people, roam Newfoundland's interior and pose a serious hazard to motorists; *watch the areas along the roadside carefully.* Communities and roads tend to concentrate along the island's rugged coast. Heading west from St. John's, charming villages speckle the coastline of Cape Bonavista and draw travelers away from the beaten path. Central Newfoundland's industrial towns present an unglamorized view of the logger lifestyle. After St. John's, **Corner Brook,** in the west, and **Gander,** east of center, rank as the island's main towns.

Passing directly through Terra Nova and within ½ hour of Gros Morne, the **Trans-Canada Highway (Rte. 1)** provides convenient access to Newfoundland's two sensational national parks. Both parks extract a car entrance fee ($5 per day, $10 for 4 days, $20 for the season mid-June to Labor Day), but only when you stop to use the park facilities; driving through and staring in awe are free of charge.

Terra Nova National Park Along the shores of Newman Sound and the beaches of Sandy Pond, and throughout the forests inbetween, Terra Nova's 400 square km prove ample room for lynx, moose, ospreys, and eagles; whales pass just off the coast. If you want to meet these locals, try one of the park's 16 hiking trails (45min.-6hr. long). Less strenuous enjoyment lies on the fine sands of Sandy Pond, where visitors swim, picnic, or rent canoes and kayaks ($5). **Twin Rivers Visitors Center** (543-2354) can direct you to rentals (open mid-June to early Sept. daily

10am-6pm). Another visitors center (533-2801; same hours) guards the entrance to the main **campground** at **Newman Sound** (387 sites, showers, laundry facilities, bike rentals, convenience store. Sites $11; $66 per week). Use of the **primitive campgrounds** at Minchin Cove, South Broad Cove, Overs Island, and Dumphy's Pond requires a permit ($7 per person per night); register at a visitors center before staking your claim. The Trans-Canada Highway crosses through Terra Nova, northwest of St. John's and about 400km east of Gros Morne.

Gros Morne National Park Long ago, receding glaciers gouged the spectacular cliffs and fjords for which Gros Morne was designated a UNESCO World Heritage Site. Though animals and vegetables thrive in the park, minerals are its claim to fame; spectacular and unique formations of ancient rock have earned the park the appellation "the Galapagos of geology." In the southwest corner of the park near Woody Point, a flat-topped mountain known as the **Serpentine Tableland** rises from the land, thrust up by powerful forces in the earth's mantle; due to its unusual mineral composition, the mountain glows with a golden hue when viewed from a distance. The dazzling 16-km James Callaghan Trail ascends Gros Morne Mountain and rewards the weary with a mind-blowing panorama at the top. Be warned—the hike is strenuous, steep, and saturated with black furry spiders; the park advises allotting seven to eight hours to make the trek (trail open July-first snowfall, usually mid-Oct.). Pick up a **backcountry camping** pass if you want to take a more leisurely pace ($2 per person per night). The **visitors center** (458-2417), 3km west of Rocky Harbor on Rte. 430 (1hr. from the Trans-Canada Highway), distributes camping passes, free trail guides, and information on other attractions (open daily 9am-5pm; late June to Labor Day 9am-10pm).

Five **campgrounds** bless Gros Morne with a total of 296 sites: Berry Hill, Green Point, Lomond, Shallow Bay, and Trout River (sites $7.25-11.25; no electrical hookups). **Berry Hill,** the most popular, has fuller service sites, three hiking trails within the campground, and a great location near Gros Morne Mountain. (156 wooded sites, showers, kitchen shelters, fireplaces. Sites $11.25. Open mid-May to Oct.) **Woody Point (HI-C)** (453-2442), in Woody Point, puts a roof over your head in a prime location—the Ritz it ain't. (10 beds, parking, kitchen without refrigerator, no showers. Open June-Sept. daily 10am-10pm; after hours call the manager at 453-2470. $10, nonmembers $12.).

New Brunswick

In the warm waters of the South Indian Ocean, powerful ocean currents sweep around the tip of Africa and ripple thousands of miles through the Pacific before coming to a spectacular finish on the coasts of New Brunswick. Here, the powerful Bay of Fundy tides ebb and flow as the world's highest tides, sometimes reaching a staggering 48 ft. Inland, away from the ocean's violent influence, vast unpopulated stretches of forest swathe the land in timeless wilderness. Over two centuries ago, British Loyalists, fleeing in the wake of the American Revolution, came to rest on the shores of the bay. Disgruntled by the distant government in Halifax, the colonists complained and were granted self-government by the Crown, and the province of New Brunswick was born. Much earlier, in the 17th century, French pioneers established the farming and fishing nation of *l'Acadie* on the northern and eastern coasts; today, the traditions of the French and British cultures live on in everything from cuisine to language. Although over a third of the province's population is French-speaking, English is far more widely used throughout most of the province.

PRACTICAL INFORMATION

Capital: Fredericton.

Department of Economic Development and Tourism, P.O. Box 12345, Fredericton E3B 5C3, distributes free publications including the *Official Highway Map, Outdoor Adventure Guide, Craft Directory, Fish and Hunt Guide,* and *Travel Guide* (with accommodation and campground directory). Call **Tourism New Brunswick** (800-561-0123) from anywhere in Canada Mon.-Fri. 8am-9pm, Sat.-Sun. 9am-6pm.

Drinking Age: 19.

Time Zone: Atlantic (1hr. ahead of Eastern). **Postal Abbreviation:** NB

Provincial Sales Tax: 11%.

■■■ SAINT JOHN

The city of Saint John was founded literally overnight on May 18, 1783, by the United Empire Loyalists, a band of about 10,000 American colonists loyal to the British crown. Saint John's long Loyalist tradition shows through in its architecture, festivals, and institutions; the walkways of King and Queen Squares in central Saint John (never abbreviated so as to prevent confusion with St. John's, Newfoundland) were laid out to resemble the Union Jack. The city rose to prominence in the 19th century as a major commercial and shipbuilding port. Now home to 125,000 people, Canada's oldest incorporated city maintains a small-town atmosphere uncharacteristic of a city its size. Saint John's location on the Bay of Fundy ensures cool summers and mild winters, though it often makes the city foggy and wet; locals joke that Saint John is where you go to get your car, and yourself, washed for free.

PRACTICAL INFORMATION

Tourist Office: Saint John Visitors and Convention Bureau, 15 Market Sq. (658-2990), on the 11th floor of City Hall at the foot of King St. Open Mon.-Fri. 8:30am-4:30pm. The **City Center** information center, alias **The Little Red Schoolhouse** (658-2855), offers info in Loyalist Plaza by the Market Slip uptown. Open early June-Labor Day daily 9am-7pm; Labor Day to mid-Oct. and mid-May to early June 9am-6pm.

Trains: Via Rail (642-2916), has a station in Moncton; take an SMT bus from Saint John, then catch a train in Moncton. A train ticket to Saint John or a Canrail pass will cover bus fare. Call for prices and schedules.

Buses: SMT, 300 Union St. (648-3555), provides service to: Moncton (2 per day, 2hr., $20); Montréal (2 per day, 14hr., $80); Halifax (2 per day, 8hr., $52). Station and ticket office open daily 9am-6pm.

Public Transportation: Saint John Transit (658-4700), runs until roughly 11:30pm. Fare $1.25, under 14 $1. Their 3-hr. guided tour of historic Saint John leaves from Loyalist Plaza and Reversing Falls (June 15-Sept.). $15, ages 6-14 $5.

Ferry: Marine Atlantic (636-4048 or 800-341-7981 from the continental U.S.), on the Lancaster St. extension in West Saint John near the mouth of Saint John Harbor; take the "West Saint John" bus, then walk 10 min. Crosses to Digby, NS (1-3 per day; 3hr.; $21.50, seniors $16.25, ages 5-12 $10.75, bike $10.50, car $47; mid-Sept. to May $16.25/$12.25/$8.25/$5.25/$41.25.)

Taxi: Royal Taxi, 800-561-8294. **Diamond,** 648-8888; disabled access minivans available. Both open 24 hrs.

Car Rental: Downey Ford, 10 Crown St. (632-6000). $20 per day with 100 free km; 10¢ per additional km. Insurance $10; ages 21-24 must be able to cover a hefty $1500 deductible. Must be 21 with major credit card. Open Mon.-Fri. 7am-6pm, Sat. 8am-5pm, Sun. 9am-5pm.

Weather: 636-4991. **Dial-a-Tide:** 636-4429. Both 24 hrs.

Crisis Lines: Provincial Crisis Line, 800-667-5005. **Rape Crisis Line,** 658-1791.

Emergency: 911.

Post Office: Main Office, 125 Rothesay Ave. (800-565-0726). Open Mon.-Fri. 7:30am-5:15pm. **Postal code:** E2L 3W9. **Area code:** 506.

Saint John's busy downtown (Saint John Centre) is bounded by **Union St.** to the north, **Princess St.** to the south, **King Sq.** on the east, and **Market Sq.** and the harbor on the west. Find free three-hour parking outside the city's malls. Fort Latour Harbor Bridge (toll 25¢) on Hwy. 1 connects Saint John to West Saint John, as does a free bridge on Hwy. 100.

ACCOMMODATIONS AND CAMPING

Finding lodging for under $35 per night is difficult, especially in summer. In West Saint John, a number of nearly identical motels on the 1100 to 1300 blocks of **Manawagonish Rd.** charge $35-45 for a single. Call Saint John Transit for directions by bus (see Practical Information above); by car, avoid the bridge toll by taking Hwy. 100 into West Saint John, turn right on Main St., and head west until it turns into Manawagonish Rd.

Saint John YMCA/YWCA (HI-C), 19-25 Hazen Ave. (634-7720); from Market Sq., it's 2 blocks up Union St. on the left. Drab, bare, but clean rooms. Access to YMCA recreational facilities, pool, and work-out room. Open daily 5:30am-11pm; guests arriving on the evening ferry can check in later. $25, nonmembers and nonstudents $30. Reservations recommended in summer.

Hillside Motel, 1131 Manawagonish Rd. (672-1273), in a quiet residential neighborhood within 10min. of downtown. Standard motel comforts include TV and private baths. 1 bed $38, 2 beds $50; Sept.-April $35/$45.

O'Neill's Bed and Breakfast, 982 Manawagonish Rd. (672-0111). Exudes Irishness. Few frills, but clean and well-kept. 3 doubles available (1 has twin beds) $49. Includes full breakfast.

Rockwood Park Campground (652-4050), at the southern end of Rockwood Park 2km north of uptown off Hwy. 1; take the "University" bus to the Mount Pleasant stop, then walk 5min. Tents in a partly wooded area; RV sites in cramped parking spaces. Showers included. Sites $13, with hookup $15; weekly $60/$80. Open mid-May to Sept.

FOOD

For cheap food, fresh from the butcher, baker, fishmonger, produce dealer, or cheese merchant, visit **City Market**, 47 Charlotte St. (658-2820), between King and Brunswick Sq. The market may also be the best place to look for **dulse,** a local specialty not found outside New Brunswick, which consists of sun-dried seaweed from the Bay of Fundy; it can best be described as "ocean jerky." A $1 bag is more than a sample. (Market open Mon.-Thurs. 7:30am-6pm, Fri. 7:30am-7pm, Sat. 7:30am-5pm.) **Reggie's Restaurant,** 26 Germain St. (657-6270), provides fresh, homestyle renditions of basic North American fare. The sandwiches, made with famous smoked meat from Ben's Deli in Montréal, may not fill you up, but the breakfast special will: two eggs, sausage, homefries, toast, and coffee for $3.25, served 6-11am. (Open daily 6am-9pm; Nov.-May Mon.-Wed. 6am-6pm, Thurs.-Fri. 6am-7pm, Sat. 6am-5pm, Sun. 7am-3pm.)

SIGHTS AND ENTERTAINMENT

Saint John's main attraction is **Reversing Falls,** a natural phenomenon caused by the powerful Bay of Fundy tides (for more on the tides see Fundy National Park, p. 845). Though the name may suggest 100-ft. walls of gravity-defying water, the "falls" are actually beneath the surface of the water; at high tide, patient spectators see the flow of water at the nexus of the Saint John River and Saint John Harbor slowly halt and change direction. More amazing than the event itself may be the number of people captivated by it. The **Reversing Falls Tourist Centre** (658-2937), at the west end of the Hwy. 100 bridge (take the west-bound "East-West" bus), distributes tide schedules and shows a thrill-a-minute 12-min. film on the phenomenon; unfortunately, the film does not show the Big Event. (Screenings every ½hr.; $1.25, kids under 12 free. Center open May-Oct. daily 8am-8pm.)

The oldest independent brewery in Canada, **Moosehead Breweries,** 49 Main St. (635-7020), in West Saint John, waits at the end of many a devoted enthusiast's pilgramage. (Free 1-hr. tours with samples mid-June to Aug. 9:30am and 2pm. Tours limited to 25 people; avoid heartbreak by making reservations 2-3 days in advance.)

Pick up a brochure at any tourist info center for the city's three self-guided **walking tours** (each about 2hr.). **The Victorian Stroll** roams past some of the old homes in Saint John, most dating to the late 1800s; **Prince William's Walk** details commerce in the port city; **The Loyalist Trail** traces the places frequented by the Loyalist founders. All three heavily emphasize history, architecture, and nostalgia. **Trinity Church,** 115 Charlotte St. (693-8558), on the Loyalist Trail tour, displays amazing stained-glass windows and the Royal Coat of Arms of George III's House of Hanover which was stolen ("rescued") from the old Boston Council Chamber by Loyalists fleeing the American Revolution (tours and viewing Mon.-Fri. 9am-4pm).

Fort Howe Lookout, originally erected to protect the harbor from dastardly American privateers, affords an impressive view of the city and its harbor. To visit the lookout, walk a few blocks in from the north end of the harbor and up the hill; look for the wooden blockhouse atop the hill. (Open 24 hrs. Free.)

In the second week of July, the unique **Loyalist Days** festival (634-8123) celebrates the historic arrival of the Tories, complete with a re-enactment, costumes, and a street parade. The **Festival By the Sea** (632-0086), August 9-18 in 1996, is a national performing arts festival with a number of stage and musical productions.

■■■ FREDERICTON

In the early 1780s, some 2000 British Loyalists fleeing from upstart American patriots to the south made a run for the border, journeying up the St. John River Valley and eventually coming to rest at Ste. Anne's Point. There, they renamed the settlement "Fredericstown" in honor of the second son of King George III. Two years later, the village was selected provincial capital because of its ready access to the Atlantic Ocean via the St. John River and its defensible location in the heart of New Brunswick. Despite its status as New Brunswick's governmental and administrative center, Fredericton still maintains a small size and small-town atmosphere. Amidst quiet residential areas and fast-food joints, shops and bars cater to the young crowd which inhabits the University of New Brunswick and St. Thomas College; termtime nightlife allegedly never wanes, a phenomenon that spills into the summer.

Practical Information Getting around Fredericton is easy; traffic congestion downtown is rare and almost all areas of interest can be easily reached on foot. Stop by the **Visitor's Information Centre** (452-9500), at City Hall on the corner of Queen and York, for the *Street Index Map/Transit Guide* and the invaluable *Fredericton Visitor's Guide* (both free). Visitors with out-of-province license plates should also grab a free 3-day, in-town parking pass. (Open daily 8am-8pm; Sept. to mid-May 8:30am-4:30pm.) **VIA Rail** (368-7818 or 800-561-3952), on Hwy. 101 in Fredericton Junction, comes close but quite not all the way to Fredericton; a shuttle runs between the station and the Sheraton Inn, 225 Woodstock Rd. (457-7000), in Fredericton. Buy the shuttle ticket along with your VIA Rail fare and it will cost less than the lone shuttle fare of $10.70 (students $9.70). Buses go to Montréal (3 per week, 11½hrs., $98, students $88); Halifax (3 per week, 9hrs., $70/$63). These prices do not include the shuttle. (Open Mon., Thurs., Sat. 6:30-10pm, Sun., Tues., Fri. 6:30-10am.) **SMT,** 101 Regent St. (458-6000), provides on-time service to Saint John (2 per day, 1½hr., $15), Edmunston (2 per day, 3½hr., $35), and Moncton (2 per day, 2-3hr., $25); connections to Halifax and Charlottetown can be made in Moncton (open Mon.-Fri. 7:30am-8:30pm, Sat.-Sun. 9am-8:30pm.) **Fredericton Transit,** 470 St. Mary's St. (454-6287), offers local transportation; all buses stop downtown on King St. in front of King's Place. Taxi cabs run around $3 within downtown: **Student,** 454-0000; **Budget,** 450-1199. **Savage's,** 449 King St. (458-8985), rents bikes. ($3 per hr., $15 per day. Open Mon.-Wed. 8:30am-6pm, Thurs.-Fri. 8:30am-9pm,

Sat. 9am-5pm.) **Emergency:** 911. Fredericton's **post office:** 527 Queen St. (452-3345), next to Officer's Sq. Open Mon.-Fri. 8am-5:15pm; **postal Code:** E3B 4Y1; **area code:** 506.

Accommodations, Camping, Food, and Nightlife For inexpensive summer accomodations, the clean dorm rooms of the **University of New Brunswick** are perhaps the best deal in town. Follow University St. to the campus; once there, look for the Residential Administration Building (453-4835), on Baily Dr. (Free local phone, laundry facilities. Student Hotel is open to students: $12.75 per day, $69 per week. Tourist Hotel is open to all: singles $28, doubles $41. Open May-late Aug.) For year-round lodging, try the motels outside of town. The **Norfolk Motel** (472-3278), 3 km east of downtown on the Trans-Canada Hwy. on the north shore of the river, has standard motel-issue rooms with clean, private bathrooms. Bus #15 North passes by near the end of the route. (Singles $29, doubles $32.) **Hartt Island Campground** (450-6057), hidden in the **Bucket Club** amusement park on the Trans-Canada Hwy., 5km west of town, rents 125 riverside sites with access to a pool, laundry, and showers. (Sites $15, with hookup $17-20; $2 per additional person after 4. Reservations highly recommended July-Aug. Open May-Oct.)

Those with a bottomless pit to fill should not pass up the **Hilltop Pub,** 152 Prospect St. (458-9057), for heaping portions of steak ($8-14), an ample lunch buffet ($6.50; offered Mon.-Fri 11am-2pm), or a cheap draft ($1.90). (Open Mon. and Wed. 11am-1am, Tues., Thurs., Fri. 11am-2am, Sat. 10am-2am; dining room closes at 9pm.) At **Whitney's Coffee,** 349 King St. (454-2233), check out the free public internet terminal while consuming coffees ($1-3), bagels ($1.75), or samosas ($3; open Mon.-Wed. 8am-6pm, Thurs.-Sat. 8am-9pm, Sun. noon-5pm). After dark, the **Lunar Rogue Pub,** 625 King St. (450-2065), warms up with eclectic live Irish, contemporary, and folk music, plus almost 40 varieties of scotch (open Mon.-Sat. 11am-1pm, Sun. noon-midnight). For the information of those who want to shake their soul thangs, the **Chestnut Pub,** 440 York St. (450-1230), is one of the few establishments in Fredericton that qualifies as a club, not a pub (open Mon.-Fri. 11am-1am, Sat. 10am-1am, Sun. 11:30am-11pm).

Sights Just inside the entrance to the **Beaverbrook Art Gallery,** 703 Queen St. (458-8545), hangs Salvador Dali's largest masterpiece (13x10ft.), the awe-inspiring **Santiago el Grande.** (Open Sun.-Wed. 10am-5pm, Thurs.-Sat. 10am-7pm; Sept.-June Sun.-Mon. noon-5pm, Tues.-Sat. 10am-5pm. $3, students $1, seniors $2). The quirky **York-Sunbury Historical Society Museum** (455-6041) operates within the Old Officer's Quarters in Officer's Sq. Exhibits highlight aspects of New Brunswick life from early Micinae natives through modern times; the most intriguing is perhaps the famous **42-16 Coleman Frog,** which reportedly had a strange liking for scotch, rum, and gin. (Open Mon.-Sat. 10am-6pm; Labor Day to mid-Oct. Mon.-Fri. 9am-5pm, Sat. noon-4pm; mid-Oct. to April Mon., Wed., Fri. 11am-3pm or by appointment. $2, students and seniors $1, families $4.) **King's Landing Historical Settlement,** 37 km west of Fredericton off exit 259 from the Trans-Canada Highway, is an amazing recreation of rural New Brunswick life. Period actors carry out their chores using techniques long since abandoned. Mr. Wizards should inquire about efforts to introduce period crop strains and livestock into the settlement.

■■■ FUNDY

Fundy National Park, occupying 260 sq. km of New Brunswick's coast an hour's drive southeast of Moncton on Hwy. 114, is characteristically New Brunswickian in that its main attractions are its natural wonders. Approximately every 12 hrs., the world's largest tides draw back over 1 km into the Bay of Fundy, allowing visitors to explore the vast territory uncovered by the ebbing tide. Don't get caught too far out without your running shoes though; the water rises 1 ft. per minute when the tide comes in. When you're not fleeing the surf, Fundy's extensive hiking tails, forests, campgrounds, and recreational facilities should keep you occupied.

Practical Information **Park Headquarters** (887-6000), P.O. Box 40, Alma, E0A 1B0, consists of a group of buildings in the southeastern corner of the Park facing the Bay, across the Upper Salmon River from the town of Alma. The area includes the administration building, the assembly building, an amphitheater, and the **Visitors Reception Center,** which sits at the park's east entrance (open daily 8am-9pm; mid-Sept.-late May Mon.-Fri. 8:15am-4:30pm). **Wolfe Lake Information** (432-6026), the other visitors center, lurks at the northwest entrance off Hwy. 114 (open mid-June to Sept. Sat.-Thurs. 10am-6pm, Fri. 9am-9pm). No public transportation serves Fundy; the nearest bus depots are in Moncton and Sussex. The park extracts a car entrance fee of $6 per day or $18 for four days from mid-June to Labor Day, but bicyclists and hikers enter for free year-round. The free and invaluable park newspaper *Salt and Fir,* available at the entrance stations and info centers, includes a map of hiking trails and campgrounds, and a schedule of programs and activities.

Fundy weather can be unpleasant for the unprepared. Evenings are often chilly, even when days are warm. It's best to always bring a wool sweater or jacket, as well as a can of insect repellent for the warm, muggy days. **Weather** forecasts are available from the info centers by calling 887-6000. **Area code:** 506.

Camping, a Hostel, and Food The park operates four **campgrounds** totalling over 600 sites. Getting a site is seldom a problem, but landing one at your campground of choice may be a little more difficult. The park accepts no reservations; all sites are first-come, first-grabbed. Due to its proximity to facilities, **Headquarters Campground** is in highest demand. When the campground is full, put your name on the waiting list, and sleep somewhere else for the night. Return the next day at noon when the names of those admitted for the night are read. (Sites $11, with hookup $16. Open mid-May to Labor Day.) The only other campground with facilities, **Chignecto North Campground,** off Hwy. 114, 5 km inland from the headquarters, puts the forest and distance between campsites for more privacy (sites $9, with varying degrees of hook-up $14-16. Open mid-June to mid-Oct.). **Point Wolfe Campground,** scenically located along the coast 7 km west of Headquarters, stays cooler and more insect-free than the inland campgrounds (sites $9; open July-Aug.). All three campgrounds have showers and washrooms. The **Wolfe Lake Campground** offers primitive sites, with no showers or washrooms, near the northwest park entrance about a minute's walk from the lake (sites $7; open late May-early Oct.). Year-round wilderness camping is also available in some of the most scenic areas of the park, especially **Goose River** along the coast. The campsites, all with fireplaces, wood, and an outhouse, carry a $2 per person per night permit fee. Call 887-6000, to make the required reservations one or two weeks in advance.

The **Fundy National Park Hostel (HI-C)** (887-2216), near Devil's Half Acre about 1 km south of the park headquarters, has a full kitchen, *cold* showers, and a common room with TV, although in separate buildings from the bunkrooms. Ask the staff for the lowdown on park staff nightlife. (Check-in 8am-noon and 5-10pm. $8.50, nonmembers $10; open June-Aug. Wheelchair-accessible.) For a cheap, home-cooked meal, try **Harbor View Market and Coffee Shop** (887-2450), on Main St. in Alma, where you can let the owner cook for you or get the groceries to cook for yourself. The breakfast special of two eggs, toast, bacon, and coffee runs $3; top it off with a scrumptious strawberry shortcake ($2; open daily 7am-10pm; Sept.-May daily 7:30am-8pm).

Activities The park maintains about 104km of park trails year-round, and about 35km are open to mountain bikes. You can hoof it or rent a bike from the youth hostel (887-2216; $7 for 1hr., $15 for 5hr.). *Salt and Fir* contains detailed descriptions of all trails, including where you'll find waterfalls and ocean views. Though declining in numbers, deer are still fairly common, and thieving raccoons run thick around the campsites. Catching a glimpse of a peregrine falcon will require considerable patience, but the moose come out to be seen around dusk.

Most recreational facilities operate only during the summer season (mid-May to early Oct.), including free daily interpretive programs designed to help visitors get to know the park. Park staff lead beach walks, evening programs (in the Amphitheater), and weekly campfire programs. Visit the park in September and October to catch the fall foliage and avoid the crush of vacationers. Those seeking quiet, pristine nature would be wise to visit in the chillier off season.

■ NEAR FUNDY: KOUCHIBOUGUAC

Unlike Fundy's rugged forests and the high tides along the Loyalist coast, **Kouchibouguac National Park** shows off warm lagoon waters, salt marshes, peat bogs, and white sandy beaches. Bask in the sun along the 25km stretch of barrier islands and sand dunes, or swim through canoe waterways that were once highways for the Micmacs. Rent canoes ($6.50 per hr., $27 per day), kayaks ($4.75 per hr.), and bikes ($5 per hr., $22 per day) at **Ryans Rental Center** (876-3733), in the park between the South Kouchibouguac Campground and Kellys Beach (open early June-early Sept. daily 8am-9pm; late May-early June Sat.-Sun. 9am-5pm). The park operates two campgrounds in the summer, neither with hookups (sites $8-11.75). **South Kouchibouguac** has 219 sites with showers, and **Côte-à-Fabien** has 32 sites and no showers. Off-season campers take advantage of primitive sites within the park and several commercial campgrounds just outside of the park. Kouchibouguac (meaning "river of the long tides" in Micmac) charges a vehicle permit fee of $6 per day, $18 per four days, or $30 per year. The **Park Information Centre** sits at the Park Entrance, on Hwy. 117 just off Hwy. 11, 90km north of Moncton. (Open mid-June to early Sept. 10am-6pm; early Sept. to mid-Oct. and mid-May to mid-June 8am-8pm.) The park administration (876-2443) is open year-round (Mon.-Fri. 8:15am-4:30pm).

Prince Edward Island

Prince Edward Island, now more commonly called "P.E.I." or "the Island," began as St. John's Island. In 1799, residents renamed the area for Prince Edward, son of King George III, in thanks for his interest in the territory's welfare. Almost too conveniently, the change cleared up the exasperating confusion between the island and St. John's, Newfoundland; St. John, Labrador; and Saint John, New Brunswick.

The smallest province in Canada attracts visitors hoping to share in the relaxing beauty made famous by Lucy Maud Montgomery's novel *Anne of Green Gables.* The fictional work did not exaggerate the wonders of natural life on the island; the soil, made red by its high iron-oxide content, complements the ubiquitous green crops and shrubbery, azure skies and turquoise waters, and purple roadside lupin. On the north and south shores, some of Canada's finest beaches extend for miles alternately displaying red and white sands. Inevitably small and quaint, Island towns seem to exist more for visitors than for residents and consist mainly of restaurants and shopping areas. The largest "city" is Charlottetown, the provincial capital, with a whopping 15,000 residents. Effusively hospitable, the Island's population is 17% Acadian French and 80% British.

It is a common misconception that P.E.I can be covered on foot. The island's diminutive size is perfect for short drives or comfortable bike rides, but don't expect to get from Charlottetown to Cavendish by your own locomotion.

PRACTICAL INFORMATION

Capital: Charlottetown.

Drinking Age: 19.

Time Zone: Atlantic (1hr. ahead of Eastern time). **Postal Abbreviation:** P.E.I.

Provincial Sales Tax: 10%.

Tourist Office: P.E.I. Visitor Information Centre, P.O. Box 940, C1A 7M5 (368-4444 or 800-463-4734), on the corner of University Ave. and Summer St. in Charlottetown. Courtesy calls for reservations. Open daily 9am-10pm; Sept.-May 9am-5pm. The **Charlottetown Visitors Bureau,** 199 Queen St. (566-5548), hides inside City Hall. Open Mon.-Fri. 9am-9pm.

Tours: Abegweit Tours, 157 Nassau St. (894-9966). Sightseeing tours on a London double-decker bus depart from Confederation Center in Charlottetown, at the corner of Grafton and Queen's. Tours of town (6 per day, 1hr., $8, under 12 $1), the North Shore including Green Gables (1 per day, 7hr., $40/$20), and the South Shore (1 per day, 5hr., $30/$15). Tours run June-Sept.

Buses: SMT, 330 University Ave., Charlottetown (566-9744; open 8am-6pm). To: Moncton (1-2 per day, 4hr., $29); Amherst (2 per day, 4-7hr., $23); Halifax (2 per day, 10hr., $49), via **Acadian Lines** connections in Amherst. Station open daily 9:30pm-10pm, also Mon.-Fri. 7am-6:15pm, Sat. 7am-1pm and 5:30-6:30pm, Sun. 7-8am, 11:30am-1pm, and 5:30-6:30pm. **Trius Lines** (566-5664), on Garfield St., runs 1 bus per day to Summerside (departs 6:45am; $7 1-way or round-trip).

Beach Shuttles: Sherwood Beach Shuttle, 566-3243. Picks up at the P.E.I. Visitor Information Centre and drops off in Cavendish. 2 per day June and Sept., 4 per day July-Aug.; 45min.; $8, $12 round-trip. Call for departure times.

Ferries: Marine Atlantic (855-2030; 800-341-7981 from U.S.), in Borden, 56km west of Charlottetown on the TCH. To: Cape Tormentine, NB (every hr. on the ½-hr. 6:30am-1am, 45min., round-trip $7.75, seniors $5.75, ages 5-12 $4, cars $18.75, not including driver). **Northumberland Ferries** (566-3838 or 800-565-0201 from P.E.I. and Nova Scotia), in Wood Islands 61km east of Charlottetown on TCH. To: Caribou, NS (15 per day, 1½hr., $9/$6.50/$4.25/$28.50). Both ferries collect only round-trip fares and only when leaving P.E.I. Thus, it is cheaper to leave from Borden than from Wood Islands, no matter how you come over.

Taxis: City Cab, 892-6567. **Star Cab,** 892-6581. Both open daily 24 hrs; no credit cards accepted. Service from Borden ferry to downtown Charlottetown $45.

Car Rental: Rent-a-Wreck, 57A St. Peter's Rd. (566-9955). $35 per day with 200km free, 12¢ per additional km. Damage waiver $9 per day. Must be 21 with credit card or $250 deposit. Under 25 surcharge $12 per day. Open Mon.-Fri. 8:30am-5:30pm, Sat. 8:30am-1pm, Sun. on call. **Hillside Autohost,** 207 Mt. Edward Rd. (894-7037). $43 per day (Sept.-June $30 per day) with 250 free km; 15¢ per additional km. Insurance $11 per day. Must be 21 with major credit card. Open Mon.-Fri. 8:30am-5pm; July-Aug. also Sat.-Sun. 9am-5pm.

Bike Rental: MacQueens, 430 Queen St. (368-2453). Road and mountain bikes, $20 per day, $80 per week. Must have credit card or $75 deposit. Open Mon.-Sat. 8:30am-5pm.

Crisis Line: Crisis Centre, 566-8999. 24 hrs.

Emergency: Charlottetown Police, 368-26778. **Royal Canadian Mounted Police,** 566-7111.

Post Office: 135 Kent St. (566-4400). Open Mon.-Fri. 8am-5:15pm. **Postal code:** C1A 7N1. **Area code:** 902.

Queen St. and **University Ave.** are Charlottetown's main thoroughfares, straddling **Confederation Centre** along the west and east, respectively. The most popular beaches, **Cavendish, Brackley,** and **Rustico Island,** lie on the north shore in the middle of the province, opposite but not far from Charlottetown. Hamlets and fishing villages dot the Island landscape of **Kings County** on the east and **Prince County** on the west. Acadian communities thrive on the south shore of Prince County. **Rte. 1/Trans-Canada Highway (TCH)** follows the southern shore from ferry terminal to ferry terminal, passing through Charlottetown.

ACCOMMODATIONS AND CAMPING

B&Bs and **country inns** crowd every nook and cranny of the province; many are open year-round. Rates are generally around $28 for singles and $35 for doubles.

Twenty-six farms participate in a provincial **Farm Vacation** program, in which tourists spend some time with a farming family. Call the **Tourist Industry Association of P.E.I.** (566-5008) for info, or pick up a brochure at the visitor information center.

P.E.I. has one hostel, the **Charlottetown International Hostel (HI-C),** 153 Mt. Edward Rd. (894-9696), across the yard from the University of P.E.I. in a large green barn 1 long block east of University Ave., a 45-minute walk from the bus station. Watch for the green and white sign marking the turnoff. (Neat, spacious rooms, friendly staff, diverse clientele. Kitchen facilities, showers, TV lounge. Bike rentals $8.50. 3-night max. stay. Check-in 7-10am and 4pm-midnight. Curfew midnight. $12.50, nonmembers $15. Blanket rental $1. Open June-Labor Day.) The **University of Prince Edward Island,** 550 University Ave. (566-0442), in **Blanchard Hall** in the southwest end of campus overlooking Belvedere St., offers fully serviced and furnished two-bedroom apartments with dorm rooms, kitchen, living room, and hall laundry room—a great value for four people. ($60, nonstudents $55 plus tax for up to 4 people; extra cot $5. Weekly and monthly rates available. Open May-Aug.) The University also runs a B&B in **Marion Hall** (singles $28.50/$22.50, doubles $37/$30; breakfast included; open July-Aug.). **Bernadine Hall,** open for most of the summer, is another option (singles $34.50/$27.50, doubles $42/$35). Check-in for all locations takes place at Blanchard Hall (2pm-midnight).

Prince Edward Island National Park (672-6350 or 963-2391) operates 3 campgrounds during the summer (148 primitive, secluded sites $10; 330 sites with showers, toilets, kitchen access, laundry facilities $15; 94 sites with hookup $19) and one off season campground (primitive sites $8). The many other provincial parks that offer camping, as well as the plentiful private campgrounds scattered throughout the Island, ensure that there will always be a campsite available. (Open seasons vary, but expect to find a campground open open mid-June to Sept.)

FOOD

The quest for food on P.E.I. boils down to the search for a cheap **lobster.** At market, the the coveted crustaceans go for $4-5 per lb. at canning quality, or $5-6 per lb. for the larger restaurant quality lobsters. Boiling them at home is not difficult, especially since any local you meet should have considerable experience. Try boiling lobsters in salt water for easy seasoning and delicious results. Die-hard bargain hunters take note: tourists tell tales of days spent on a lobster boat, a unique experience in itself, which can also yield several of the day's catch free of charge. There's no organized "Tourist goes Lobstering" program; just ask around at the waterfront if you're interested. Another option is the traditional **lobster supper,** usually thrown by churches and community centers. These feasts generally include all-you-can-eat extras. The P.E.I. Visitor Information Center (see Practical Information, above) has brochures on this year's dinners; be ready to pay $18-26, depending on the size of the lobster.

Fresh seafood, including the world famous **Malpeque oysters,** is sold along the shores of the island, especially in North Rustico on the north shore. **Fisherman's Catch,** near the Stanley Bridge west of Cavendish, peddles incredibly fresh, cheap seafood from a shack across the lake from the Fiddle 'n' Vittles restaurant. Ask the staff about oyster-shucking supplies and for a demo. (Lobster cooked or uncooked from $6 per lb. Oysters in the shells $2.50 per lb. Open mid-June to early Sept. daily 10am-8pm.) The back of the *P.E.I. Visitor's Guide* lists fresh seafood outlets. For the freshest food around, shop the **Charlottetown Farmers' Market** (368-4444), on Belvedere St. opposite U.P.E.I. (open July-Sept. Sat. 9am-2pm and Wed. 10am-5pm).

For non-aquatic fare, stop in at **Cedar's Eatery,** 81 University Ave., Charlottetown (892-7377), a local favorite that serves Lebanese and Canadian cuisine. Lunch specials (11am-5pm) are an ample meal at $5. (Open Mon.-Thurs. 10am-midnight, Fri.-Sat. 10am-1am, Sun. 4-10pm; bar open Mon.-Sat. 5pm-2am.) The cosmopolitan young clientele at **Café Soleil,** 52 University Ave., Charlottetown (368-8098), takes time out from postulating to partake of U-build deli sandwiches ($3.25; open Mon.-Fri. 7am-7pm, Sat. 9am-7pm, Sun. 9am-6pm).

SIGHTS AND ENTERTAINMENT

The Island at Large

Popularized by Lucy Maud Montgomery's novel, *Anne of Green Gables,* **Green Gables House** (672-6350), off Rte. 6 in Cavendish near Rte. 13, has become a mecca for adoring readers—a surprising number make the pilgrimage all the way from Japan. Green Gables can get very crowded between late July and September, so it's best to arrive in the early morning or the evening (peak hours 11am-4pm). Tours are available in English and French. (Open daily 9am-8pm; mid-May to late July and early Sept.-Oct. daily 9am-5pm; Nov. to mid-May by request, 894-4246. $2.50, seniors $2, ages 6-16 $1.25, under 6 free, families $6.)

Prince Edward Island National Park (672-2259 or 963-2391), the most popular Canadian national park east of Banff, consists of a 32-km coastal strip embracing some of Canada's finest beaches and over a fifth of P.E.I.'s northern coast. Along with the beaches, wind-sculpted sand dunes and salt marshes rumple the park's terrain. The park is home to many of the Island's 300-odd species of birds, including the endangered **piping plover;** birdwatchers should pick up the *Field Check List of Birds* (free) from any National or Provincial Park office. Park campgrounds, programs, and services operate mid-June to Labor Day; **Cavendish campground** stays open until late September. (Sites $15, entrance fees $4 per day, seniors $3, ages 6-16 $2, families $6.) Pick up a copy of the park guide *Blue Heron* at the entrance kiosks.

Woodleigh (836-3401), just off Rte. 234 in Burlington midway between Cavendish and Summerside, satisfies atent monarchists with cute miniature, but still sizeable, replicas of British architectural landmarks. The buildings include St. Paul Cathedral, the Tower of London (with replicated Crown Jewels inside), and Lord Nelson's Trafalgar Square statue—all strikingly crafted and available for exploration. Visit early in the week to avoid tour buses that roll in on Wednesday. (Open late June-early Sept. daily 9am-6pm; late May-late June and early Sept.-Columbus Day daily 9am-5pm. $8, seniors $7, 6-15 $4.50, under 6 free.)

Near the Island's northwest point, an unusual and fleeting sight known as **Elephant Rock** can be found off the shores of the town of Norway. Here wind and tides have carved a massive replica of an elephant in PEI's soft coastal rocks. The elephant is expected to be destroyed by the same natural forces which created it, and within a few years it should be indistinguishable.

The stretches of beach on the **eastern coast** of PEI are considerably less touristed than those in the west. **Lakeside,** a beach 35km east of Charlottetown on Rte. 2, is often almost deserted on weekdays during July and August (unsupervised). For the romantic equestrian in you, trot along the surf atop a sturdy steed from **Gun Trail Ride** (961-2076), located right beside the golf course ($8 per hr., with trail guide $9, June-Labor Day daily 9am-6pm). **Basin Head Beach,** 95km east of Charlottetown, makes a relaxing day-trip; over seven mi. of white sand ensures that you won't have to rumble with other visitors for turf (unsupervised).

Charlottetown

The province's capital prides itself on being the "Cradle of Confederation." Delegates from the British North American colonies met in 1864, inside the brownstone **Province House** (566-7626), on the corner of Great George and Richmond St., to discuss the union which would become the Dominion of Canada in 1867. Both the modern and the historical chambers of the legislature are open for viewing. (Open daily 9am-8pm; mid-Oct. to June Mon.-Fri. 9am-5pm. Free.) Adjoining the Province House, the modern performing arts complex at **Confederation Centre for the Arts** (628-1864), on the corner of Queen and Grafton St., contains theaters, exhibits, a library, and an art gallery. The Centre conducts hour-long guided tours July to August. (Box office open daily 9am-9pm; Sept.-June daily noon-5:30pm.) Every summer, a musical production of **Anne of Green Gables** (see below) takes the Mainstage as part of the Charlottetown Festival. (Performances July-early Sept. Mon and Wed.-Fri. 8pm; tickets $22-30. Matinees Wed. and Sat. 1:30pm; tickets $17-25. For ticket info, call 566-1267 or 800-565-0278). Proof that some Islanders aren't so reverent when it comes to *her*, **Annekenstein 6** (566-1267) gibes the girl and the island; call for details. In the summer, moving **P.E.I. House Parties** (800-461-4734) are all the rage; local musicians perform traditional music across the island for anyone who will pay to party ($5, kids under 12 $2; refreshments included).

Québec

Home to 90% of Canada's French-speaking citizenry, Québec continues to fight for political and legal recognition of its separate cultural identity. Originally populated by French fur trading settlements along the St. Lawrence River, Québec was ceded to the British in 1759. Ever since, anti-federalist elements within *québecois* society have rankled under control of the largely Anglicized national government. French is spoken by 95% of Québec's population; all signs are printed in French, as required by provincial law. The failure of the 1990 Meech Lake Accord to recognize Québec as a "distinct society" and the more recent election of the Bloc Québecois, a separatist party, to the status of official opposition in the federal government signal uncertain times ahead for the province. Visitors will likely never notice these underlying tensions—the majority of the struggle goes on behind closed doors in Ottawa— but the entire country wonders if this province will choose to stay a part of the whole.

PRACTICAL INFORMATION

Capital: Québec City.

Tourisme Québec: C.P. 20,000, Québec G1K 7X2 (800-363-7777; 514-873-2015 in Montréal). Open daily 8:30am-7:30pm; Labor Day to mid-June 9am-5pm. **Canadian Parks Service, Québec Region,** 3 Buade St., P.O. Box 6060, Québec GIR 4V7 (800-463-6769; 418-648-4177 in Québec City).

Time Zone: Eastern. **Postal abbreviation:** QU

Drinking Age: 18.

Sales Tax: 8% on goods and 4% on services, plus a 7% GST (for details on obtaining a refund of the GST, see Essentials, p. 7).

ACCOMMODATIONS INFORMATION

For assistance in locating accommodations throughout the province, try the following organizations.

Vacances-Familles, 1291, bd. Charest Ouest, Québec JIR 2C9 (418-682-5484; 514-251-8811 in Montréal). A lodging network with discounts of 10-40% on lodgings throughout Canada, primarily in Québec. Membership ($40 for the first year) applies to the household.

Camping: Association des terrains du camping du Québec, 2001, rue de la Metropole, Bureau 700 Longueil, Québec J4G 1S9 (514-651-7396), and **Fédération québecoise du camping et de caravaning,** 4545, ave. Pierre-de-Coubertin, Stade Olympique, C.P. 1000, succursale "M," Montréal H1V 3R2 (514-252-3003). Mon.-Fri. 8:30.

Hostels: Regroupement Tourisme Jeunesse (HI-C), at the Féderation address (514-252-3117). For reservations in any Québec hostel and a few in neighboring Ontario call 800-461-8585 at least 24 hrs. in advance, with a credit card.

■■■ MONTRÉAL

This island city, named for the Mont-Royal in its midst, has been coveted territory for over 300 years. Wars and sieges have brought governments in and out like the tide, including a brief takeover by American revolutionaries in late 1775. Amidst it all,

Montréal has grown into a diverse city with a cosmopolitan air seen in few other cities on the continent. Above and beyond the Québecois and English cultures which often still chafe, the city hosts large enclaves of Chinese, Italians, and Greeks. Whether you credit the international flavor or the large student population of the city, it is hard not to be swept up by the energy, vibrancy, and fun which course through Montréal's *centre-ville.*

PRACTICAL INFORMATION

Tourist Office: Infotouriste, 1001, rue de Square-Dorchester (873-2015 or outside Montréal 800-363-7777), on Dorchester Sq. between rue Peel and rue Metcalfe. Metro: Peel. Free city maps and guides, and extensive food and housing listings. Open daily 8:30am-7:30pm; Labor Day-June 9am-6pm. A branch office in **Old Montréal,** 174, rue Notre-Dame Est at Place Jacques Cartier. Open daily 9am-7pm; early Sept.-Oct. 9 9am-5pm; Oct. 10-Easter Tues.-Sun. 9am-5pm; Easter-late June daily 9am-5pm.

Youth Travel Office: Boutique Temps Libre, 3063, rue St-Denis (252-3117). Métro: Sherbrooke. Free maps; youth hostel info, travel gear, and advice available. A non-profit organization that inspects and ranks all officially recognized youth hostels in Québec. Open Mon.-Wed. 10am-6pm, Thurs.-Fri. 10am-9pm, Sat. 10am-5pm. Mailing address: c.p. 1000, Succursale "M," Montréal P.Q., H1V 3R2. **Travel CUTS,** McGill Student Union, 3480, rue McTavish (398-0647). Métro: McGill. Specializes in budget travel for college students. Open Mon.-Fri. 9am-5pm.

Consulates: U.S., 1155, rue St-Alexander (398-9695). Open for passports Mon.-Fri 8:30am-1pm; for visas Mon.-Fri. 8:30am-noon. **U.K.,** 1155, rue de l'Université, suite 901 (866-5863). Open for info Mon.-Fri. 9am-5pm; for consular help Mon.-Fri. 9am-12:30pm and 2-4:30pm. **France,** Place Ville-Marie, 26th (878-4281). Open 8:30am-1pm.

Currency Exchange: Currencies International, 1230, rue Peel (392-9100). Métro: Peel. Open Mon.-Fri. 8:30am-6pm, Sat.-Sun. 9am-5pm. **Thomas Cook,** 625, bl. René-Lévesque Ouest (397-4029). Métro: Square-Victoria. Open Mon.-Fri. 9am-5pm. **FORESCO,** 1250, rue Peel at Ste-Catherine (879-1300). Métro: Peel. Open Mon.-Fri. 8:30am-6pm. Another office at 382, rue St-Jacques (843-6922). Métro: Square-Victoria. Open Mon.-Fri. 8am-6pm, Sat. 8:30am-5pm. Although many cafés will take U.S. dollars, currency exchange agents offer better deals. Most **bank machines** are on the PLUS system and charge only the normal transaction fee for withdrawals in foreign countries; ask yor bank about fees.

Airports: Dorval (633-3105 for info), 20-30min. from downtown by car. From the Lionel Groulx Métro stop, take bus #211 to Dorval Shopping Center, then transfer to bus #204; total fare $1.75. **Connoisseur Grayline** (934-1222) runs daily bus service to Dorval from the Queen Elizabeth Hotel, at René-Lévesque and Mansfield, stopping at the Château Champlain, the Sheraton Center, and the Voyageur Terminal. Buses run Mon.-Fri. every ½hr. 5:20-7:20am and every 20min. 7:20am-11:20pm, Sat.-Sun. every ½hr. 7am-1am. $9; under 5 free. Taxi from downtown $24. **Mirabel International** (476-3010), 45min. from downtown by car. Handles all flights from outside North America. Grayline buses service Mirabel daily 1, 4, 6, and 8am, hourly 9am-noon, every ½hr. noon-8pm, every hr. 8pm-1am. $14.50. Taxi downtown $60.

Trains: Central Station, 895, rue de la Gauchetière under the Queen Elizabeth Hotel. Métro: Bonaventure. Served by **VIA Rail** (871-1331). To: Québec City (3 per day, 2½hr., $43), Ottawa (4 per day, 2½hrs., $36), Toronto (6 per day, 5hr., $83). Ticket counter open Mon.-Fri., Sun. 5:45am-9pm, Sat. to 11pm. Also, **Amtrak** (800-872-7245). To: New York (1 per day, 10hr., $178), Boston (2 per day, 15hr., $106). Amtrak ticket counter open Mon.-Sat. 7:30am-7:30pm, Sun. 8am-7:30pm. Baggage check $2; station open 24 hrs. for baggage pick-up.

Buses: Terminus Voyageur, 505, bd. de Maisonneuve Est (242-2281 for reservations). Métro: Berri-UQAM. Voyage to: Toronto (5 per day, 6½hr., $64.50); Ottawa (17 per day, 2½hr., $26.60); Québec City (17 per day, 3hr., $35). The Ottawa Bus also leaves from **Dépanneur Beau-soir,** 2875, bl. St-Charles (630-4836). **Greyhound** (287-1580) serves New York City (7 per day, 8¾hr., $91).

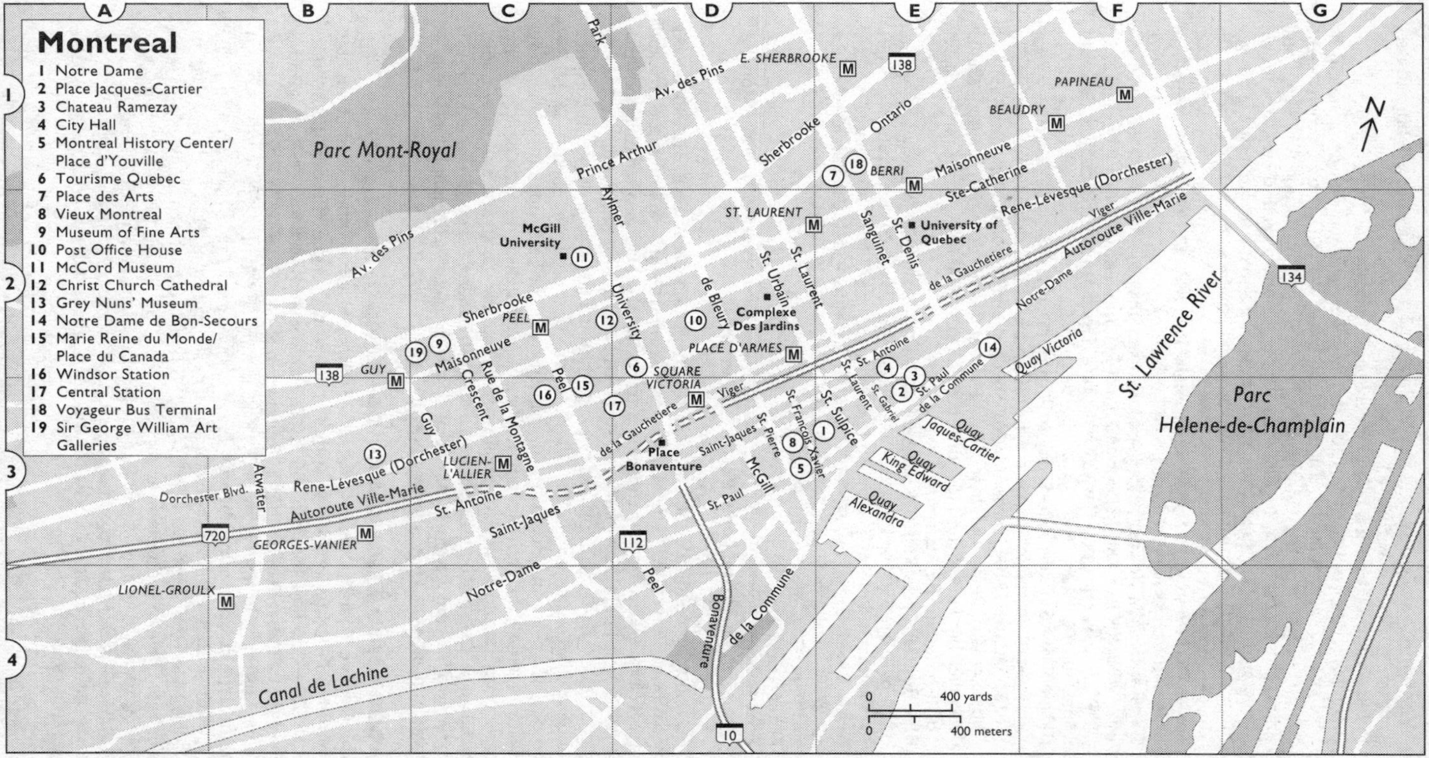
Montreal
1 Notre Dame
2 Place Jacques-Cartier
3 Chateau Ramezay
4 City Hall
5 Montreal History Center/ Place d'Youville
6 Tourisme Quebec
7 Place des Arts
8 Vieux Montreal
9 Museum of Fine Arts
10 Post Office House
11 McCord Museum
12 Christ Church Cathedral
13 Grey Nuns' Museum
14 Notre Dame de Bon-Secours
15 Marie Reine du Monde/ Place du Canada
16 Windsor Station
17 Central Station
18 Voyageur Bus Terminal
19 Sir George William Art Galleries
A
B
C
D
E
F
G
1
2
3
4
N
Parc Mont-Royal
Park
Av. des Pins
E. SHERBROOKE
138
PAPINEAU
BEAUDRY
Ontario
Sherbrooke
Prince Arthur
BERRI
Maisonneuve
Ste-Catherine
Rene-Lévesque (Dorchester)
Viger
Autoroute Ville-Marie
ST. LAURENT
Aylmer
McGill University
University of Quebec
Sanguinet
St. Denis
St. Urbain
St. Laurent
de la Gauchetiere
de Bleury
Complexe Des Jardins
University
PLACE D'ARMES
Notre-Dame
St. Lawrence River
134
Quay Victoria
St. Antoine
St. Paul
de la Commune
St. Gabriel
GUY
Crescent
Rue de la Montagne
Peel
PEEL
SQUARE VICTORIA
St. Sulpice
St. Francois Xavier
St. Pierre
Saint-Jacques
Place Bonaventure
Quay Jaques-Cartier
Quay King Edward
Quay Alexandra
Parc Helene-de-Champlain
Guy
LUCIEN-L'ALLIER
McGill
St. Paul
Atwater
Dorchester Blvd.
St. Antoine
Saint-Jaques
720
GEORGES-VANIER
112
LIONEL-GROULX
Bonaventure
de la Commune
Canal de Lachine
10
0 400 yards
0 400 meters

Vermont Transit (842-2281) serves Boston (2 per day, 8½hr., $77.60) and Burlington, VT (2 per day, 3hr., $31.70).

Public Transportation: STCUM Métro and Bus, 288-6287. A generally safe and extremely efficient network. The four Métro lines and most buses operate daily 5:30am-12:30am; some have night schedules as well. Get network maps at the tourist office, or at any Métro station booth. Maps have locations of shops and malls as well, especially useful for navigating the **underground city.** Downtown ticketing is rampant so take the Métro. Buses are a well integrated part of the system; transfer tickets from bus drivers are good as subway tickets. Fare for trains or bus $1.75, 6 tickets $7.

Taxis: Taxi Pontiac, 761-5522. **Champlain Taxi Inc.,** 273-2435. Both operate 24 hrs. at the city's regulated rates. $2.45 base fare.

Car Rental: Via Route, 1255, rue MacKay at Ste-Catherine (871-1166). $29 per day with 200 free km; 12¢ per additional km. Insurance $16 per day, ages 21-24 $19 per day. Must be 21 with credit card. Open Mon.-Fri. 8am-7pm, Sat. 8am-5pm, Sun. 9am-5pm.

Driver/Rider Service: Allo Stop, 4317, rue St-Denis (985-3032). Matches passengers with member drivers; part of the rider fee goes to the driver. To: Québec City ($15), Ottawa ($10), Toronto ($26), Sherbrooke ($9), New York City ($50), or Boston ($42). Riders and drivers fix their own fees for rides over 1000mi. Annual membership fee required ($6, drivers $7). Open Mon.-Tues. 8am-6pm, Wed.-Fri. 8am-7pm, Sat.-Sun. 9am-6pm.

Bike Rental: Cycle Pop, 978, Rachel Est (524-7102). Métro: Mont-Royal. 21-speeds $20 per day, $50 for the weekend. Open Mon.-Wed. 9:30am-6pm, Thurs.-Fri. 9:30am-9pm, Sat.-Sun. 9:30am-5pm. Credit card or $250 depositrequired.

Crisis Lines: Tel-aide, 935-1101. **Sexual Assault,** 934-4504. **Suicide-Action,** 723-4000. All three open 24 hrs. **Rape Crisis,** 278-9383. Open Mon.-Fri. 9:30am-4:30pm. **Gay Info,** 768-0199. Open Fri.-Sat. 7:30-10:30pm.

Emergency: 911.

Post Office: Succursale "A," 1025, St-Jacques Ouest (846-5390). Open Mon.-Fri. 8am-5:45pm. **Postal code:** H3C 1T1. **Area code:** 514.

Two major streets divide the city, making orientation convenient. The **boulevard St-Laurent** (also called "The Main") stretches north-south, splitting the city and streets east-west (traffic here runs one way: north). The Main also serves as the unofficial French/English divider; English **McGill University** lies to the west while slightly east is **St-Denis,** a parallel two-way thoroughfare which defines the **French student quarter** (also called the *quartier latin* or the student ghetto). **Rue Sherbrooke** which is paralleled by de Maisonneuve and Ste-Catherine downtown, runs east-west almost the entire length of Montréal. Parking is often difficult in the city, particularly during winter when snowbanks narrow the streets and slow traffic. Meters cost 25¢ for 10 min. downtown and $30 parking tickets are common. Take the **Métro** to avoid the hassle. Montréal's population is 85% Francophone, but most are bilingual. Speak French if you know it.

ACCOMMODATIONS AND CAMPING

The **Québec Tourist Office** is the best resource for info about hostels, hotels, and *chambres touristiques* (rooms in private homes or small guest houses). B&B singles cost $25-40, and doubles run $35-75. The most extensive B&B network is **Bed & Breakfast à Montréal,** P.O. Box 575, Snowdon St., H3X 3T8 (738-9410), which recommends that you reserve by mail. (Singles from $35, doubles from $55; $15 per night deposit upon confirmation. Leave a message if the owners are out.) The **Downtown Bed and Breakfast Network,** 3458, ave. Laval, H2X 3C8 (289-9749 or 800-267-5180), at Sherbrooke, lists about 80 homes downtown. (Singles $40, doubles $55. Open in spring and summer daily 9am-9pm; in fall and winter 9am-6pm.) For cheaper B&B listings, check with the **Marbel Guest House,** 3507, boul. Décarie, H4A 3J4. (486-0232; Métro: Vendôme; singles $25, doubles $30; breakfast $5). Make reservations by sending a check for the first night as a deposit. Virtually all B&Bs have bilingual hosts.

Many of the least expensive *maisons touristiques* and hotels cluster around rue St-Denis, ranging from quaint to seedy. The area flaunts lively nightclubs, a number of funky cafés and bistros, and abuts Vieux Montréal. Two blocks east of St-Denis, **Hotel Le Breton,** 1609, rue St-Hubert (524-7273; Métro: Berri-UQAM), is a gem in this set of accommodations. Though the neighborhood is not particularly wholesome, the 13 rooms are clean and comfortable and have TV and A/C. Around the corner from bus station. (Singles $30-55, doubles $55-70.) The hotel fills up quickly—make reservations.

Montréal Youth Hostel (HI-C), 1030, rue MacKay (843-3317). Métro: Lucien-L'Allier. Airport shuttle drivers will stop here if asked. Relatively new, large, and extremely convenient location in a hotel, compelemented by great service. The friendly, upbeat staff will give you the nightlife lowdown in addition to their own free tours and outings. Rooms have 2-6 beds (250 total). Kitchen, laundry facilities, carpet, A/C, and extensive ride board. Some parking. 1-week max. stay; in winter 10 days. Open 24 hrs. $16, Canadian nonmembers $18, non-Canadian nonmembers $20.56. Continental breakfast special $2.25. Linen $1.75. Reservations by credit card accepted with 24-hr. notice. IBN reservations available.

Résidences "Quartier Latin," 3475, St-Urbain (288-3366). Rents small, bare apartments with full kitchenettes right off of rue Sherbrooke. Rooms are clean and have private baths. No singles, but a great deal for groups of 3 or 4 who aren't concerned with meeting other travelers. Parking available. Pool and sauna. June-Aug. 55 beds in rooms of 2-4; Aug.-June 260 beds. Office open Mon.-Fri. 1-6pm, Sat. 1-4pm, Sun. 9am-noon by appt. $12.50 per person, $15.50 each for a double. Reservations recommended.

Collège Français, 5155, ave. de Gaspé, H2T 2A1 (495-2581). Métro: Laurier, then walk west on Laurier and ½ block north on Gaspé. Clean and well-located. Young clientele. Free parking during off-school hours. Open July-Aug. 24 hrs.; Sept.-June Mon.-Fri. 7:30am-1am, Sat.-Sun. 7:30am-2am. Prices vary from $13, depending on the number of beds in the room (4-7) and whether or not there's a private shower. Summer breakfast $3.25. More beds inconveniently located at 1391, rue Beauregard Longueuil (Métro: Longueuil, then take bus #71 up Tascherau and Ségin) Open July-Aug.

McGill University, Bishop Mountain Hall, 3935, rue de l'Université, H3A 2B4 (398-6367). Métro: McGill. Follow Université through campus (bring your hiking boots; it's a long haul). Ideally located singles. Desk open Mon.-Fri. 7am-10:30pm, Sat.-Sun. 8am-10pm; a guard will check you in late at night. Kitchenettes and payphones on each floor. Common room with TV and laundry facilities. Ask for Gardner building, where the views are best. $28, non-students $36.75. $51.50 per 2 nights. Weekly $150. Full breakfast $5, served Mon.-Fri. 7:30-9am. Reservations by mail (1-night deposit) needed July- Aug. Open May 15-Aug. 15.

Université de Montréal, Residences, 2350, rue Edouard-Montpetit, H2X 2B9, off Côte-des-Neiges (343-6531). Métro: Edouard-Montpetit. Located on the edge of a beautiful campus; try the East Tower for great views. Laundry facilities. Phone and sink in each room. Desk open 24 hrs. Singles $35, students $24. Cafeteria open Mon.-Fri. 7am-7pm. Open early May to mid-Aug.

YWCA, 1355, rue René-Lévesque Ouest (866-9941). Métro: Lucien l'Allier. Clean, safe rooms in the heart of downtown. Women only. Newly renovated. Access to Y facilities. Kitchen, TV on every floor. Doors lock at 10pm but the desk will buzz you in all night. Singles $35, with shared bathroom $40, with private bath $45; doubles $50, with semi-private bath $60. Key deposit $5. Reservations accepted.

YMCA, 1450, rue Stanley (849-8393), downtown. Métro: Peel. 331 rooms. Co-ed. Access to Y facilities. TV and phone in every room. Singles for men $35, for women $38; doubles $54; triples $62; quads $71. Students and seniors $2 off. Cafeteria open daily 7am-8pm. Usually fills up June-Aug.; make reservations

Maison André Tourist Rooms, 3511, rue Université (849-4092). Métro: McGill. Mme. Zanko will spin great yarns for you in her old, well-located house—but only if you don't smoke. Guests have been returning to this bastion of European cleanliness and decor for over 30 years. Singles $26-35, doubles $38-45; $10 per additional person. Reservations recommended.

Manoir Ambrose, 3422, rue Stanley (288-6922), just off of Sherbrooke in an old Victorian mansion. Somewhat upscale both in price and decor. 22 rooms, with TV and A/C, most with private baths. Singles from $40, doubles from $50. Continental breakfast included.

Those with a car and time can camp at **Camping Parc Paul Sauvé** (479-8365), 45 min. from downtown; take Autoroute 20 west to 13 north to 640 west and follow the signs to the park. There are 850 beautiful sites on the **Lac des Deux Montagnes.** (Sites $17, beachside $18, with hookup $22.) For private sites, try **KOA Montréal-South,** 130, bl. Monette, St-Phillipe J0L 2K0 (659-8626), a 15-min. drive from the city; follow Autoroute 15 south over Pont Champlain, take exit 38, turn left at the stop sign, and go straight for about 1 mi. (1.6km)—it's on your left (sites for 2 $17, with hookup $21; $3 per each additional person up to 6). If these don't wet your camping whistle try **Camping Pointe-des-Cascades,** 2 ch. du Canal, Pte. des Cascades (455-9953); take Autoroute 40 west, exit 41 at Ste. Anne de Bellevue, junction 20, and west to Dorion. In Dorion, follow "Théâtre des Cascades" signs. (140 sites, many near water. Sites $16, with hookup $20.)

FOOD

Restaurants pack in along **bd. St-Laurent** and on the western half of **Ste-Catherine,** with prices ranging from affordable to astronomical. While in the Latin Quarter, scout out energetic **rue Prince Arthur,** which vacuum-packs Greek, Polish, and Italian restaurants into a tiny area. Here maître-d's stand in front of their restaurants and attempt to court you toward their cuisine. The accent changes slightly at **ave. Duluth,** where Portuguese and Vietnamese establishments prevail. **Rue St-Denis,** the main thoroughfare in the French student quarter, has many small restaurants and cafés, most of which cater to student pocketbooks. If you want wine with your meal, you can save money by buying your own at a *dépanneur* or at the **SAQ** (Sociéte des alcohols du Québec) and bringing it to one of the unlicensed restaurants, concentrated on the **bd. St-Laurent,** north of Sherbrooke, and on the pedestrian precincts of **rue Prince Arthur** and **rue Duluth**.

French-Canadian cuisine is unique but generally expensive. When on a tight budget, look for *tourtière,* a traditional meat pie with vegetables and a thick crust, or *crêpes québecois,* stuffed with everything from scrambled eggs to asparagus with *béchamel* (a cream sauce). Wash it down with *cidre* (hard cider). Other Montréal specialties include French bread (the best on the continent), smoked meat, Matane salmon, Gaspé shrimp, lobster from the Iles de la Madelene, and *poutine,* a gooey concoction of French fries *(frites),* cheese curds, and gravy, which you can find everywhere. For *québecois* food in an authentic atmosphere, try **La Planéte Bleue,** 361 rue St.-Paul Est. (879-1278; traditional dinners $8-10; open daily noon-1am).

Montréal offers many ethnic options. See Sights (p. 856) for details on finding Chinese, Italian, and Greek neighborhoods. The Jewish community around bd. St-Laurent offers a few delis and bagel bakeries north of downtown. Don't leave without savoring a bagel from the brick ovens at **La Maison de l'Original Fairmount Bagel,** 74, rue Fairmount Ouest (272-0667; Métro: Laurier; open 24 hrs.).

You'll be charged 13% tax for meals totaling more than $3.25. All restaurants are required by law to post their menus outside, so shop around. Consult the free *Restaurant Guide,* published by the Greater Montréal Convention and Tourism Bureau (844-5400), which lists more than 130 restaurants by type of cuisine (available at the tourist office; see Practical Information, above). When preparing your own grub, look for produce at the **Atwater Market** (Metro: Lionel-Groulx); the **Marché Maisonneuve,** 4375, rue Ontario Est (Métro: Pie-IX); the **Marché St-Jacques** (Metro: Berri-UQAM, at the corner of Ontario and Amherst); or the **Marché Jean-Talon** (Métro: Jean Talon). For info on the markets, call 277-1873. (Call Mon.-Wed. and Sat. 7am-6pm, Thurs. 7am-8pm, Fri. 7am-9pm, Sun. 7am-5pm. All markets open Sat.-Wed. 8am-6pm, Thurs.-Fri. 8am-9pm.)

Café Santropol, 3990, rue Duluth (842-3110), at St-Urbain. Métro: Sherbrooke, then walk north on St-Denis and west on Duluth. *"Bienvenue à la planète Santropol!"* A student hangout, complete with an aquarium and an outdoor terrace for schmoozing. Cream cheese, cottage cheese, yogurt, and nuts are staples on the eclectic menu. Huge veggie sandwiches with piles of fruit $6-8. Open Mon.-Thurs. 11:30am-midnight, Fri.-Sat. noon-3am, Sun. noon-midnight.

Etoile des Indes, 1806, Ste-Catherine Ouest (932-8330), near St-Matthieu. Métro: Guy-Concordia. Split-level dining room with tapestries covering the walls. The best Indian fare in town. Dinner entrees $7-17; daily lunch specials $7 (11:30am-2:30pm). The brave should try their bang-up *bangalore phal* dishes. Open Mon.-Sat. 11:30am-2:30pm and 5-11pm, Sun. 5-11pm.

Dunn's, 892, Ste-Catherine Ouest (866-3866). Arguably the best smoked meat in town, served in monstrous slabs tucked between bread and slathered with mustard. Sandwiches $4.50; larger meat plates $7.10. Well-known for its strawberry cheesecake ($4). Open 24 hrs.

Peel Tavern, 1107, rue Ste-Catherine Ouest (844-6769). The consummate pub food. 99¢ buys a huge plate of spaghetti or, perhaps the best breakfast deal in town, 2 eggs, toast, bottomless coffee before 11am. Another location at 1106, bd. de Maisonneuve (845-9002.) Both open daily 11am-3am.

El Zaziummm, 51 Roy Est (844-0893), up the St. Laurent way. Spicy Mexican cuisine and sly, sweet alcoholic beverages; the food distracts you while the drinks strike silently with a kick like a mule. Funky, out-of-the-way location. Entrees $7-11. Open daily 4pm-midnight.

Wilensky's, 34, rue Fairmount Ouest (271-0247). Métro: Laurier. A great place for a quick lunch. Pull out a book from Moe Wilensky's shelf, note the sign warning "We always put mustard on it," and linger. Hot dogs $1.60; sandwiches $1.85. Open Mon.-Fri. 9am-4pm.

La Muraille Chine, 1017, boul. St-Laurent (875-8888). Canton and Szechuan in the heart of Chinatown. More expensive than some, but quality is above average. Dinner around $10. Open daily 10am-11pm.

Da Giovanni, 572, Ste-Catherine Est (842-8851). Métro: Berri. Serves generous portions of fine Italian food; don't be put off by the lines or the diner atmosphere. The sauce and noodles are cooked up right in the window. Open daily 7am-2am.

Au Pain Doré, 6850 Marquette, just off St. Catherines Ouest. An answer to the question "Oh where, oh where can I get some French baked goods?" Also offers a selection of cheeses (brie, havarti, cheddar, and more). Baguette $1.50-4; havarti $4.50 per ½kg. Open Mon.-Wed. 8am-6:30pm, Thurs.-Fri. 8am-7:30pm, Sat. 8:30am-5:30pm, Sun. 8:30am-4pm.

SIGHTS

On the Streets

Montréal has matured from a riverside settlement of French colonists into a hip metropolis. Museums, Vieux Montréal (Old Montréal), and the new downtown are fascinating, but Montréal's greatest asset is its cultural vibrancy. Wander aimlessly and often—and *not* through the high-priced boutiques touted by the tourist office. A small **Chinatown** orients itself along rue de la Gauchetière, near Vieux Montréal's Place d'Armes. Between 11:30am and 2:30pm, most of its restaurants offer mouth-watering Canton and Szechuan lunch specials ranging from $3.50 to $5. Baklava abounds in **Little Greece,** a bit farther than you might care to walk from downtown just southeast of the Outremont Métro stop around rue Hutchison between ave. Van Horne and ave. Edouard-Charles. At the northern edge of the town's center, **Little Italy** occupies the area north of rue Beaubien between rue St-Hubert and Louis-Hémon. Walk east from Métro Beaubien and look for pasta. For a **walking tour** approach to the city, stick to the downtown area. Many attractions between Mont Royal and the Fleuve St-Laurent are free, from parks (Mont Royal and Lafontaine, see below) and universities (McGill, Montréal, Concordia, Québec at Montréal) to architectural spectacles of all sorts.

Walk or bike down **bd. St-Laurent,** north of Sherbrooke. Originally settled by Jewish immigrants, this area now functions as a sort of multi-cultural welcome wagon, home to Greek, Slavic, Latin American, and Portuguese immigrants. **Rue St-Denis,** home to the city elite at the turn of the century, still serves as the **Latin Quarter's** mainstreet (Metro: Berri-UQAM). Jazz fiends command the street at the beginning of July during the annual **Montréal International Jazz Festival** (871-1881), June 27-July 7, 1996, with over 350 free outdoor shows. Also visit **rue Prince-Arthur** (Métro: Sherbrooke), which has street performers in the summer, **Carré St-Louis** (Métro: Sherbrooke), with its fountain and sculptures, and **Le Village,** a gay village in Montréal from rue St-Denis Est to Papineau along rue Ste-Catherine Est.

Museums

The **McGill University** campus (main gate at the corner of rue McGill and Sherbrooke; Métro: McGill) runs up Mont Royal and boasts Victorian buildings and pleasant greens in the midst of downtown. More than any other sight in Montréal, the university illustrates the impact of British tradition in the city. The campus also contains the site of the 16th-century Native-American village of Hochelaga and the **Redpath Museum of Natural History** (398-4086), with rare fossils and two genuine Egyptian mummies. (Open Mon.-Thurs. 9am-5pm; Sept.-June Mon.-Fri. 9am-5pm. Free.) Guided tours of the campus are available (daily 9am-4pm with 1-day advance notice; 398-6555).

About 5 blocks west of the McGill entrance, Montréal's **Musée des Beaux-Arts** (Fine Arts Museum), 1379 and 1380, rue Sherbrooke Ouest (285-1600; Métro: Peel or Guy-Concordia), houses a small permanent collection that touches upon all major artistic periods and includes Canadian and Inuit work; inquire about their impressive visiting exhibits. (Open Tues.-Mon. 11am-6pm, Wed. 11am-9pm. Permanent collection free. Temporary exhibits $12, students and seniors $7, under 12 $3; ½-price Wed. 5:30-9pm) The **McCord Museum of Canadian History,** 690, rue Sherbrooke Ouest (398-7100; Métro: McGill), presents textiles, costumes, paintings, prints, and 700,000 pictures spanning 133 years in their photographic archives. (Archives open by appointment only; contact Nora Hague. Open Tues.-Wed. and Fri. 10am-6pm, Thurs. 10am-9pm, Sat.-Sun. 10am-5pm; $5, students $2, seniors $3. Free Thurs. 6-9pm.) Opened in May 1989, the **Centre Canadien d'Architecture,** 1920, ave. Baile (939-7026; Métro: Guy-Concordia), houses one of the world's most important collections of architectural prints, drawings, photographs, and books. (Open Tues.-Sun. 11am-6pm, Thurs. 11am-8pm; Oct.-May Wed., Fri. 11am-6pm, Thurs. 11am-8pm, Sat., Sun. 11am-5pm; $5, students and seniors $3, under 12 free. Students free all day on Thurs., everyone free Thurs. 6-8pm.) **Musée d'Art Contemporain** (Museum of Contemporary Art), 185, Ste-Catherine Ouest at Jeanne-Mance (847-6226; Métro: Place-des-Arts), has the latest by *québecois* artists, as well as textile, photography, and avant-garde exhibits. (Open Tues.-Sun. 11am-6pm, Wed. also 6-9pm; $8, seniors $5, students $4, under 12 free; Wed. 6-9pm permanent exhibits free, temporary exhibits ½-price.) Outside of the downtown museum circuit, the **Montréal Museum of Decorative Arts,** 2929, rue Jeanne-d'Arc (259-2575; Metro: Pie-IX), houses innovatively designed decorative pieces dating from 1935 to the present and from the functional to the ridiculous (open Wed.-Sun. 11am-5pm; $3, students under 26 $1.50, under 12 free)

Great Big Green Places

Olympic Park, 4141, ave. Pierre-de-Coubertin (252-4737; Métro: Viau), hosted the 1976 Summer Olympic Games. Its daring architecture, uncannily reminiscent of the *U.S.S. Enterprise,* includes the world's tallest inclined tower and a stadium with one of the world's only fully retractable roofs. Despite this, baseball games *still* get rained out because the roof cannot be put into place with crowds in the building (small goof, really). (Guided tours in English daily 12:40 and 3:40pm; more often May-Sept. $5.25, ages 5-17 $4.25, under 5 free.) Take the *funiculaire* to the top of the tower for a panoramic view of Montréal and a guided tour of the observation deck. (Every 10min. Mon.-Thurs. 10am-9pm, Fri.-Sun. 10am-11pm; off season daily 10am-6pm. $10.25, kids $7.50.) The most recent addition to the attractions at the Olympic Park is the **Biodôme,** 4777, ave. Pierre-de-Coubertin (868-3000). Housed in the building which was once the Olympic Vélodrome, the Biodôme is a "living museum" in which four complete ecosystems have been reconstructed: the Tropical Forest, the Laurentian Forest, the St-Laurent marine ecosystem, and the Polar World. The goal is environmental awareness and conservation; the management stresses repeatedly that the Biodôme is *not* a zoo; rather, it is intended to be a means for people to connect themselves with the natural world. (Open daily 9am-8pm. $9.50, students and seniors $7, ages 6-17 $5, under 6 free.) In the summer, a train will take you across the park to the **Jardin Botanique** (Botanical Gardens), 4101, rue Sherbrooke Est (872-1400; Métro: Pie-IX), one of the most important gardens in the world. The Japanese and Chinese areas house the largest *bonsai* and *penjing* collections outside of Asia. (Gardens open daily 9am-8pm; Sept.-April daily 9am-4:30pm. $7, students and seniors $5, ages 6-17 $3.50, under 6 free; 30% less Sept.-April.) Package tickets for the Biodôme and the Gardens allow you to save money and split a visit up over a two-day period. Parking in the complex starts at $5.

Montréal's more natural approach to a park, **Parc du Mont-Royal,** Centre de la Montagne (844-4928; Métro: Mont-Royal), climbs up to the mountain from which the city took its name. From rue Peel, hardy hikers can take a foot path and stairs to the top, or to the lookouts on Camillien-Houde Pkwy. and the Mountain Chalet. The 30-ft. cross at the top of the mountain commemorates the 1643 climb by de Maisonneuve, founder of Montréal. In winter, *montréalais* congregate here to ice-skate, toboggan, and cross-country ski. In summer, Mont-Royal welcomes joggers, cyclists, picnickers, and amblers. (Officially open 6am-midnight.) **Parc Lafontaine** (872-2644; Métro: Sherbrooke), bordered by Sherbrooke, Rachel, and Papineau ave., has picnic facilities, an outdoor puppet theater, seven tennis courts (hourly fee), ice-skating in the winter, and an international festival of public theater in June.

The Underground City

Montréal residents aren't speaking cryptically of a sub-culture or a hideout for dissidents when they rave about their Underground City. They literally mean *under the ground:* 29km of tunnels link Métro stops and form a subterranean village of climate-controlled restaurants and shops—a haven in Montréal's sub-zero winter weather. The ever-expanding network connects railway stations, two bus terminals, restaurants, banks, cinemas, theaters, hotels, two universities, two department stores, 1700 businesses, 1615 housing units, and 1600 boutiques. Somewhat frighteningly hailed by the city as "the prototype of the city of the future," these burrows give the word "suburban" a whole new meaning. Enter the city from any Métro stop, or start your adventure at the **Place Bonaventure,** 901, rue de la Gauchetière Ouest (397-2205; Métro: Bonaventure), Canada's largest commercial building. Inside, the **Viaduc** shopping center contains a mélange of shops, each selling products imported from a different country. The tourist office supplies city guides that include treasure maps of the tunnels and underground attractions. (Shops open Mon.-Wed. 9:30am-6pm, Thurs.-Fri. 9:30am-9pm, Sat. 9:30am-5pm, Sun. 9am-noon.) Poke your head above ground to see **Place Ville-Marie** (Métro: Bonaventure), a 1960s office-shopping complex. Revolutionary when first built, the structure triggered Montréal's architectural renaissance.

Back in the underworld, ride the train that made it all happen, the Métro, to the McGill stop and enjoy some of the underground city's finest offerings. Here, beneath the Christ Church Cathedral, 625, Ste-Catherine Ouest, waits **Promenades de la Cathédrale** (849-9925), where you can not only shop but enjoy theatrical presentations in the complex's central atrium (call for details). Three blocks east, passing through **Centre Eaton,** of grand department store fame, the **Place Montréal Trust** is famous for its modern architecture and decadently expensive shopping area. Still, there's no charge for an innocent peek around.

Vieux Montréal (Old Montréal) and Fleuve St-Laurent Islands

In the 17th century, the city of Montréal struggled with Iroquois tribes for control of the area's lucrative fur trade, and erected walls circling the settlement for defense. Today the remnants of those ramparts do no more than delineate the boundaries of Vieux Montréal, the city's first settlement, on the stretch of river bank between rues McGill, Notre-Dame, and Berri. The fortified walls that once protected the quarter have crumbled, but the beautiful 17th- and 18th-century mansions of politicos and merchants retain their splendor. Take the Métro to Place d'Armes, or get off at Bonaventure and check out **Cathédrale Marie Reine du Monde (Mary Queen of the World Cathedral),** at the corner of René-Lévesque and Mansfield (866-1661), before walking to the port. A scaled-down replica of St. Peter's in Rome, the church was built in the heart of Montréal's Anglo-Protestant area. (Open daily 7am-7:30pm; off season Sun.-Fri. 9:30am-7:30pm, Sat. 8am-8:30pm.)

The 19th-century church **Notre-Dame-de-Montréal,** 116, rue Notre-Dame Ouest (842-2925), towers above the Place d'Armes and the memorial to de Maisonneuve. Historically the center for the city's Catholic population, the neo-Gothic church once hosted separatist rallies. It seats 4000 and is one of the largest and most magnificent churches in North America. (Shuffle around silently for free; concerts are held here throughout the year.) After suffering major fire damage, the **Wedding Chapel** behind the altar re-opened in 1982, complete with an enormous bronze altar. (Open daily 7am-8pm; Labor Day-June 24 7am-6pm. Free guided tours 8:30am-4:30pm.)

From Notre-Dame walk next door to the **Sulpician Seminary,** Montréal's oldest building (built in 1685) and still a functioning seminary. The clock over the facade is the oldest public timepiece in North America and has recorded the passage of over 9.3 billion seconds since it was built in 1700 (do the math). A stroll down rue St-Sulpice will bring you to the old docks along the **rue de la Commune,** on the banks of the Fleuve St-Laurent. Proceed east along rue de la Commune to **rue Bonsecours.** At the corner of rue Bonsecours and the busy rue St-Paul stands the 18th-century **Notre-Dame-de-Bonsecours,** 400, rue St-Paul Est (845-9991; Métro: Champ-de-Mars), founded on the port as a sailors' refuge by Marguerite Bourgeoys, leader of the first congregation of non-cloistered nuns. Sailors thankful for their safe pilgrimages presented the nuns and priests with the wooden boat-shaped ceiling lamps in the chapel. The church also has a museum in the basement and a bell tower with a nice view of Vieux Montréal and the Fleuve St-Laurent. (Chapel open Mon.-Sat. 9am-5pm, Sun. 9am-6pm; Nov.-April Mon.-Fri. 10am-3pm, Sat. 10am-5pm, Sun. 10am-6pm. Free. Tower and museum open the same hours. $4, under 4 50¢.)

Opening onto rue St-Paul is **Place Jacques Cartier,** site of Montréal's oldest market. Here the modern European character of Montréal is most evident; cafés line the square and street artists strut their stuff during the summer. Visit the grand **Château Ramezay,** 280, rue Notre-Dame Est (861-3708; Métro: Champ-de-Mars), built in 1705 to house the French viceroy, and its museum of Québecois, British, and American 18th-century artifacts. (Open Tues.-Sun. 10am-6pm. $5, students and seniors $3, families $10. Guided tours available Wed. and Sun. noon and 2pm.) The **Vieux Palais de Justice,** built in 1856 in Place Vaugeulin, stands across from **City Hall. Rue St-Jacques** in the Old City, established in 1687, is Montréal's Wall Street.

There are many good reasons to venture out to **Ile Ste-Hélène,** an island in the Fleuve St-Laurent just off the coast of Vieux Montréal. The best is **La Ronde** (872-6222; bus #167), Montréal's popular amusement park. It's best to go in the afternoon and buy an unlimited pass. From late May to July on Wednesday and Saturday, stick around La Ronde until 10pm to watch the **International Fireworks Competition** (872-8714; open June-Labor Day Sun.-Thurs. 11am-11pm, Fri.-Sat. 11am-midnight. $18, under 12 $9, families $42). If you don't want to pay admission to the park, watch the fireworks from people-packed Pont Jacques-Cartier.

Le Vieux Fort ("The Old Fort," also known as the **David M. Stewart Museum;** 861-6701), was built in the 1820s to defend Canada's inland waterways. Now primarily a military museum, the fort displays artifacts and costumes detailing Canadian colonial history. (Open Wed.-Mon. 10am-6pm; Sept.-April Wed.-Mon. 10am-5pm. 3 military parades daily June-Aug. $5, students, seniors, and ages 7-17 $3, under 6 free, families $10.) Take the Métro under the St-Laurent to the Ile Ste-Hélène stop.

The other island in Montréal's Parc des Iles is **Ile Notre-Dame,** where the recently opened **Casino de Montréal,** 1, ave. de Casino (392-2746 or 800-665-2274), awaits those who wish to push their luck. Don't bet against the house sticking to its dress code. T-shirts and running shoes are allowed only between June 1 and Labor Day; no athletic wear or jeans in any size, shape, or color, ever. (Open daily 11am-3am. Admission free. *Minimum age 18 to enter and to gamble.* Parking free, with shuttles from the parking lot every 10-15min.)

Whether swollen with spring run-off or frozen over during the winter, the **Fleuve St-Laurent** (St. Lawrence River) can be one of Montréal's most thrilling attractions, though the whirlpools and 15-ft. waves of the **Lachine Rapids** once precluded river travel. No longer—now St-Laurent and Montréal harbor cruises depart from Victoria Pier (842-3871), in Vieux Montréal (mid-May to mid-Oct. 3 per day, 2hr., $18.75). Tours of the Lachine Rapids (284-9607) leave five times per day (May-Sept. 10am-6pm; 1½-hr. cruise $48, seniors $43, ages 13-19 $38, ages 8-12 $28). For a close-up and personal introduction to the river, contact **Rafting Montréal,** 8912, boul. LaSalle (983-3707). Two 1½-hr. (2-hr. with preparation and travel) white water trips are available, at differing levels of shock-induction. Reservations are necessary. ($34, students and seniors $28, kids 6-12 $17. Open May-late Sept. daily 9am-5:30pm.Trip frequency decreases off season.)

ENTERTAINMENT

Like much of the city, Vieux Montréal is best seen at night. Street performers, artists, and *chansonniers* in various *brasseries* set the tone for lively summer evenings of clapping, stomping, and singing along. The real fun goes down on St-Paul, near the corner of St-Vincent. For a sweet Sunday in the park, saunter over to **Parc Jeanne-Mance** for bongos, dancing, and handicrafts (May-Sept. noon-7pm).

The city has a wide variety of theatrical groups: the **Théâtre du Nouveau Monde,** 84, Ste-Catherine Ouest (866-8667; Métro: Place-des-Arts) and the **Théâtre du Rideau Vert,** 4664, rue St-Denis (844-1793), stage *québecois* works (all productions in French). For English language plays, try the **Centaur Theatre,** 453, rue St-François-Xavier (288-1229; 288-3161 for ticket info; Métro: Place-d'Armes), which performs its season mainly October to June. The city's exciting **Place des Arts,** 260, boul. de Maisonneuve Ouest (842-2112 for tickets), houses the **Opéra de Montréal** (985-2258), the **Montréal Symphony Orchestra** (842-9951), and **Les Grands Ballets Canadiens** (849-8681). **The National Theatre School of Canada,** 5030, rue St-Denis (842-7954), stages excellent student productions during the academic year. **Théâtre Saint-Denis,** 1594, rue St-Denis (849-4211), hosts traveling productions like *Cats* and *Les Misérables.* Check the *Calendar of Events* (available at the tourist office and reprinted in daily newspapers), or call **Ticketmaster** (790-2222; open Mon.-Sat. 9am-9pm, Sun. noon-6pm) for ticket info. **Admission Ticket Network** (790-1245 or 800-361-4595) also has tickets for various events (open daily 8am-11pm; credit card number required).

Montréalais are rabid sports fans, and their home team support runs deep. In order to see professional sports, call well in advance to reserve tickets. The **Expos,** Montréal's baseball team, swing in Olympic Stadium (see Sights, above; for Expos info call 846-3976). Between October and April, be sure to attend a **Montréal Canadiens** hockey game: the **Montréal Forum,** 2313, Ste-Catherine Ouest (Métro: Atwater), is the shrine to hockey and **Les Habitants** (nickname for the Canadiens) are its acolytes. Be advised, however, that these are turbulent times at the Forum. The Habs have gone from a league championship in 1993 to missing the playoffs (virtually unheard of) only two seasons later. Games usually sell out; call for tickets as early as possible. Dress at games can be unusually formal; jackets and ties are not uncommon. The T-shirt-clad, jeans-ripped, hat-on-backwards, beer drinking American-style fan is somewhat unwelcome here. (For ticket info, call 790-1245.) *Mon-*

tréalais don't just like to watch: the one-day **Tour de l'île,** consisting of a 64-km circuit of the island, is the largest participatory cycling event in the world with 45,000 mostly amateur cyclists pedaling their wares. (Call 521-8356 if you wanna be a player. Registration for the ride in early June must be completed in April.) During the second weekend in June, the **Circuit Gilles-Villeneuve** on the Ile Notre-Dame hosts the annual **Molson Grand Prix,** a Formula One race (392-0000 or 800-567-8687), and in August, **Tennis Canada** brings the world's best tennis players to Jarry Park. The tournament features men and women in alternating years and will host women in 1996. (Metro: De Castelnau; 273-1515 ticket info.)

NIGHTLIFE, NIGHTLIFE, AND NIGHTLIFE

Montréal has some hip, hop, happening nightlife. Even in the dead of winter, the bars are full. Should you choose to ignore the massive neon lights flashing "films érotiques" and "Château du sexe," you can find lots and lots of nightlife in Québec's largest city—either in **brasseries** (with food as well as beer, wine, and music), in **pubs** (with more hanging out and less eating), or in the multitude of **dance clubs.** In the gay village of Montréal there are plenty of clubs for both women and men. (Métro: Papineau or Beaudry).

Though intermingled with some of the city's hottest dance venues, the establishments of **rue Ste-Catherine Ouest** and the near-by side streets tend to feature drink as the primary entertainment (Metro: Peel). Downstairs at 1107, rue Ste-Catherine Ouest, the **Peel Pub** (844-6769), provides live rock bands and good, cheap food nightly, but more noted are its exceptional drink prices. Here waiters rush about with three pitchers of beer in each hand to keep up with the mötley crüe of university students and suited types. Happy hour (Mon.-Fri. 2-8pm) floods the joint with $6 pitchers. Another location is at 1106, boul. de Maisonneuve (845-9002.) (Both open daily 11am-3am.) For slightly older and more subdued drinking buddies, search the side streets and the touristy English strongholds around **rue Crescent** and **rue Bishop** (Métro: Guy), where bar-hopping is a must. **Déjà-Vu,** 1224, Bishop near Ste-Catherine (866-0512), has live bands each night at 10pm (happy hour 3-10pm; no cover; open daily 3pm-3am). Set aside Thursday for a night at **D.J.'s Pub,** 1443, Crescent (287-9354), when $12 gets you drinks for the night after 9pm (open noon-3am). **Sir Winston Churchill's,** 1459, Crescent (288-0616), is another hotspot (no cover; open daily 11:30am-3am).

Rue Prince Arthur at St-Laurent is devoted solely to pedestrians who mix and mingle at the outdoor cafés by day and clubs by night. **Café Campus,** 57, Prince Arthur (844-1010), features live rock and other genres (cover up to $3; open Sun.-Fri. 8pm-1am). **The Shed Café,** 3515, St-Laurent (842-0220; open Mon.-Fri. 11am-3am, Sat.-Sun. 10am-3am), the **Zoo Bar,** 3556, St-Laurent (848-6398; open daily 9pm-3am; Wed. is the night here), and **Angel's,** 3604, St-Laurent (282-9944; open Thurs.-Sat. 8pm-3am) all host a young student clientele, charge little or no cover, and cluster within a few blocks around **St-Laurent** (Métro: St-Laurent or Sherbrooke). Farther up St-Laurent on the corner of rue Bernard (farther than most people care to walk), lies **Eugene Patin,** 5777, St-Laurent (278-6336), one of the city's hidden jewels (cover until 2am $5; open Wed.-Sat. 10pm-3am).

French nightlife also parleys in the open air cafés on **rue St-Denis** (Métro: UQAM). Rockin' dance club by night, **Bar Passeport,** 4156, rue St-Denis (842-6063), at Rachel, doubles as a store by day (no cover; open daily 10am-3am).

■■■ QUÉBEC CITY

Called the "Gibraltar of America" because of the stone escarpments and military fortifications protecting the port, Québec City sits high on the rocky heights of Cape Diamond where the Fleuve St-Laurent narrows and joins the St. Charles River. Passing through the portals of North America's only walled city is like stepping into the past. Narrow streets and horse-drawn carriages greet visitors to the Old City; there are enough sights and museums to satisfy the most voracious history buff. Along

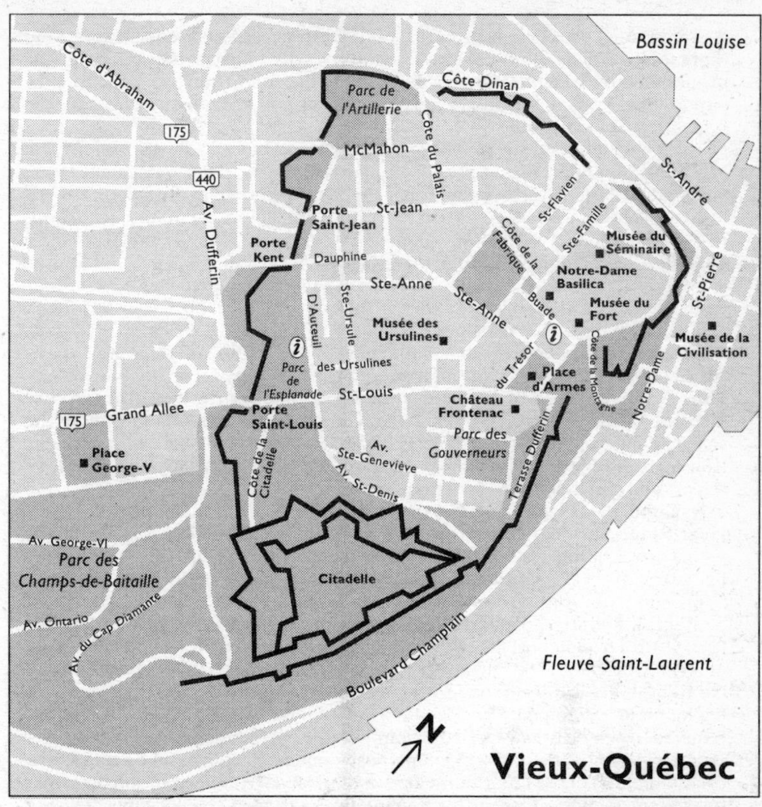

with the historical attachment, Canada's oldest city boasts a thriving French culture—never assume that the locals speak English. Acutely aware of their history and intensely devoted to their culture, local Québecois exude an energetic, cosmopolitan spirit and a refreshingly positive, upbeat outlook on life.

PRACTICAL INFORMATION

Visitor Information: Centre d'information de l'office du tourisme et des congrés de la communauté urbaine de Québec, a.k.a. "that place with an uncommonly long name," 60, rue d'Auteuil (692-2471), in the Old City. Accommodations listings, brochures, free maps, and friendly bilingual advice. Ask for the annual *Greater Québec Area Guide.* Free local calls. Open June-Labor Day daily 8:30am-8pm; April-May and Sept.-Oct. Mon.-Fri. 8:30am-5:30pm; Nov.-March Mon.-Fri. 8:30am-5pm. **Maison du tourisme de Québec,** 12, rue Ste-Anne (800-363-7777), deals specifically with provincial tourism, distributing accommodations listings for the entire province and free road and city maps. Some bus tours and Budget Rent-a-Car have desks here. Open daily 8:30am-7:30pm; Labor Day to mid-June 9am-5pm.

Youth Travel Office: Boutique Temps-Libre of Regroupement tourisme jeunesse, a.k.a. "another place with an uncommonly long name," 2700, bd. Laurier (800-461-8585), in Ste-Fo, in the Place Laurier. Sells maps, travel guides, ISICs and HI-C memberships, and health insurance. Makes reservations at any hostel in the province of Québec. (Open Mon.-Wed. 10am-6pm, Thurs.-Fri. 10am-9pm, Sat. 9am-5pm, Sun. noon-5pm.)

Airport: The airport is far out of town and inaccessible by public transport. Taxi to downtown $22. By car, turn right onto Rte. de l'aéroport and then take either bd.

Wilfred-Hamel or, beyond it, Autoroute 440 to get into the city. **Maple Leaf Sightseeing Tours** (649-9226) runs a shuttle service between the airport and the major hotels of the city. (Mon.-Fri. 5 per day to the airport and 8 per day from the airport, 8am-5:30pm; Sat.-Sun. 4 per day to the airport and 5 per day from the airport, 10am-3pm. $8.50.)

Trains: VIA Rail, 450, rue de la Gare du Palais in Québec City (524-6452). To: Montréal (3 per day; 3hr., $41). Open Mon.-Fri. 6am-8:45pm, Sat. 7am-8:45pm, Sun. 9am-8:45pm. Nearby stations at 3255, ch. de la Gare in Ste-Foy (658-8792; open same hours as Québec City station) and 5995, St-Laurent Autoroute 20 Lévis (833-8056). Open Thurs.-Mon. 4-5am, 8:15-10:45pm, Tues. 4-5am, Wed. 8:15-10:45pm. Reservations 800-361-5390 in Canada or the U.S.

Buses: Voyageur Bus, 320 Abraham Martin (525-3000). Open daily 5:30am-1am. Outlying stations at 2700, ave. Laurier, in Ste-Foy (651-7015; open daily 6am-1am), and 63, Hwy. Trans-Canada Ouest (Hwy. 132), in Lévis (837-5805; open 24 hrs). To Montréal (every hr. 6am-9pm and 11pm, 3hrs., $35.50) and Ste-Anne-de-Beaupré (2 per day, 25min., $5). Connections to U.S. via Montréal or Sherbrooke.

Public Transportation: Commission de transport de la Communauté Urbaine de Québec (CTCUQ), 270, rue des Rocailles (627-2511 for route and schedule info; open Mon.-Fri. 6:30am-10pm, Sat.-Sun. 8am-10pm. Buses operate daily 5:30am-12:30am although individual routes vary. Fare $1.95, students $1.45, seniors and children $1.25, under 6 free.

Taxis: Coop Taxis Québec, 525-5191. $2.25 base, $1 each additional km.

Driver/Rider Service: Allo-Stop, 467, rue St-Jean (522-0056), will match you with a driver heading for Montréal ($15) or Ottawa ($29). Must be a member ($6 per year, drivers $7). Open Mon.-Wed. 9am-5pm, Thurs.-Fri. 9am-7pm, Sat. 10am-5pm, Sun. 10am-7pm.

Car Rental: Pelletier, 900, bd. Pierre Bertrand (681-0678). $39 per day; 500 km free, 50¢ each additional km, $15 insurance. Must be 25 with credit card deposit of $350. Open Mon.-Fri. 7:30am-8pm, Sat.-Sun. 8am-4pm.

Bike Rental: Promo-Vélo (687-3301), located in a tent in the tourist center parking lot on Rue d'Auteuil. 1hr. $6, 4hr. $14, 1 day $23; credit card deposit of $40 required. Open daily May-Oct. 8am-9pm, weather permitting.

Crisis Lines: Tél-Aide, 683-2153. Open daily noon-midnight. **Viol-Secours** (sexual assault line), 522-2120. Counselors on duty Mon.-Fri. 9am-4pm and on call 24 hrs. for emergencies. **Center for Suicide Prevention,** 522-4588. Open 24 hrs.

Emergency: Police, 911 (city); 623-6262 (province). **Info-santé,** 648-2626. 24-hr. service with info from qualified nurses.

Post Office: 3, rue Buade (694-6102); also at 300, rue St-Paul (694-6175). **Postal code:** G1R 2J0. **Postal code:** G1K 3W0. Both open Mon.-Fri. 8am-5:45pm. **Area code:** 418.

Québec's main thoroughfares run though both the Old City (*Vieux Québec*) and outside it, generally parallel in an east-west direction. Within **Vieux Québec,** the main streets are **St-Louis, Ste-Anne,** and **St-Jean.** Most streets in Vieux Québec are one way, the major exception being rue d'Auteuil, which borders the walls and which is the best bet for parking during the busy times of day. Outside the walls of Vieux Québec, both St-Jean and St-Louis continue (St-Jean eventually joins Chemin Ste-Foy and St-Louis becomes **Grande Allée**). **Bd. René-Lévesque,** the other major street outside the walls, runs between St-Jean and St-Louis. The Basse-ville (lower town) is separated from the Haute-ville (upper town, Old Québec) by an abrupt cliff which is roughly paralleled by rue St-Vallier Est.

ACCOMMODATIONS AND CAMPING

Gîte Québec is Québec City's only referral service. Contact Thérèse Tellier, 3729, ave. Le Corbusier, Ste-Foy, Québec G1W 4P5 (651-1860). Singles run $30-40, doubles $60-65. (Call 8am-1pm or after 6pm.) Hosts are usually bilingual and the service inspects the houses for cleanliness and convenience of location. If parking is a problem (and it most often is in Old Quebec) and you have to make use of the underground parking areas, make sure you ask your host about discount parking passes. Most places offer them, which means paying $6 rather than $10 for a 24-hr. pass.

You can obtain a list of nearby campgrounds from the Maison du Tourisme de Québec (see Practical Information), or by writing tourisme Québec, c.p. 20,000 Québec, Québec G1K 7X2 (800-363-7777; open daily 9am-5pm).

Auberge de la Paix, 31, rue Couillard (694-0735). While it lacks many facilities, the friendly staff and big, clean mattresses make it worthwhile. Offers great access to the restaurants and bars on rue St.-Jean. Roomy co-ed rooms. 56 beds, 2-8 beds per room, but most have 3-4. Curfew 2am with all-day access. $17. Breakfast of toast, cereal, coffee, and juice included (8-10am). Kitchen open all day. Linen $2 for entire stay. Reservations necessary July-Aug.

Centre international de séjour (HI-C), 19, rue Ste-Ursule (694-0755), between rue St-Jean and Dauphine. Follow Côte d'Abraham uphill from the bus station until it joins ave. Dufferin. Turn left on St-Jean, pass through the walls, and walk uphill, to your right, on Ste-Ursule. If you're driving, follow St-Louis into the Old City and take the second left past the walls onto Ste-Ursule. The rooms are cramped, but a diverse, youthful clientele and a fabulous location make it a solid choice. Overly casual linen policy means that one should *definitely* cover the mattress with sheets and a blanket; cleanliness of mattresses is questionable at times. 300 beds. Laundry, microwave, TV, pool, ping-pong tables, living room, kitchen (open 7:30am-11pm), cafeteria in basement. Breakfast served 7:30-10am ($3.75). Check-out 10am, check-in starting at noon. Doors lock at 11pm, but front desk will let you in if you flash your key. One bed in a 2-bed room $17, in a 4-to 8-person room $15, in an 8- to 16-person room $13; nonmembers pay $3 more; ages 8-13 $8; kids under 8 free. HI-C memberships sold. Usually full July-Aug., so make reservations or arrive early. IBN reservations available.

Montmartre Canadien, 1675, ch. St-Louis, Sillery (681-7357), on the outskirts of the city, in the Maison du Pelerin; a small white house behind the main building at 1671. Take bus 25 or 1. Clean house in a religious sanctuary overlooking the Fleuve St-Laurent run by Assumptionist monks. Relaxed, almost ascetic setting—don't expect to meet tons of exciting new people here. Mostly used by groups. Common showers. Dorm-style singles $15. Doubles $26. Triples $36. Bed in 7-person dormitory $11; groups of 20 or more $13 per person. Breakfast (eggs, cereal, bacon, and pancakes…mmm!) $3.50. Reserve 2-3 weeks in advance.

Manoir La Salle, 18, rue Ste-Ursule (692-9953), opposite the youth hostel. Clean private rooms fill up quickly, especially in the summer. Reservations necessary. Cat-haters beware: felines stalk the halls. Singles $25-30; doubles $40-55 depending on bed-size and status of facilities.

Au Petit Hôtel, 3, ruelle des Ursulines (694-0965), just off of rue Ste-Ursule. This tidy little hotel is a great deal for two people, with a TV, free local phone, private bath, and refrigerator in each room. Audaciously combines a downtown location with free parking. May-Oct. $50 for 1 or 2 occupants; Nov.-May $40-45.

Maison Demers, 68, rue Ste-Ursule, GIR 4E6 (692-2487), up the road from the youth hostel. Clean, comfortable rooms with TV and live conversation with Jean-Luc Demers; all rooms have a sink, some have a private bath. Singles $33-35, doubles with shower $45-65; 2-bed, 4-person room $70. Breakfast of coffee and fresh croissants included. Parking available. Reservations recommended.

Camping Canadien, 6030, rue Ancienne-Lorette (872-7801). 17 sites. $17.50, with hookup $18.50. Showers, laundry. Open May 15-Oct. 15. Take Autoroute 173 out of the city to bd. Wilfred-Hamel and follow the signs.

Municipal de Beauport, Beauport (666-2228). Take Autoroute 40 east, exit #321 at rue Labelle onto Hwy. 369, turn left, and follow the signs marked "camping." Bus 800 will also take you to this campground overlooking the Montmorency River. Swimming pool and canoes ($6 per hr.) are available. Showers, laundry. 135 sites. $15, with hookup $20; weekly $85/$120. Open June-Labor Day.

FOOD

In general, rue Buade, St-Jean, and Cartier, as well as the **Place Royale** and **Petit Champlain** areas offer the widest selection of food and drink. The **Grande Allée,** a

2km-long strip of nothing but restaurants on either side, might seem like heaven to the hungry, but its steep prices make it a place to visit rather than to eat. Still, there are a few exceptions; see the Vieille Maison below.)

Traditional Québecois food is usually affordable and appetizing. One of the most filling yet inexpensive meals is a *croque-monsieur,* a large, open-faced sandwich with ham and melted cheese (about $5), usually served with salad. Be sure to try *québecois* French onion soup, slathered with melted cheese and generally served with bats of French bread or *tourtière,* a thick meat pie. Other specialties include the *crêpe,* stuffed differently to serve as either an entree or a dessert. The **Casse-Crepe Breton,** 1136, St-Jean, offers many choices of fillings in their "make your own combination" crepes for dinner ($3-5), as well as scrumptious dessert options ($2.25-$2.50; open daily 7:30am-1am). Finally, seek out the French-Canadian "sugar pie," made with brown sugar and butter. Don't be fooled into thinking that your best bet for a simple and affordable meal is to line up behind one of the many fast-food joints which proliferate throughout the city. Instead experience culinary excellence at the **Pâtisserie au Palet d'Or,** 60, rue Garneau (692-2488), a quaint French bakery where $2.75 will get you a salmon sandwich and $1.50 a crisp, golden baguette. (Open daily 8am-10pm.) Remember that some of these restaurants do not have non-smoking sections.

For those doing their own cooking, **J.A. Moisan,** 699, rue St-Jean (522-8268) sells groceries in an old country-style store (open daily 8:30am-10pm). **Dépanneurs** are like corner stores, selling milk, bread, snack food, and booze.

Café Mediterranée, 64, bd. René Lévesque (648-1849). Take the bus #25 or walk for about 10min. outside the walls. Elegant surroundings for a Mediterranean buffet. Enjoy vegetable platters, *couscous,* spicy chicken dishes—or all three: the ideal, filling lunch. Soup, dessert, coffee, and all-you-can-eat entrees for $8. Open Mon.-Fri. noon-2pm, Sat. noon-2pm. Arrive early for the best of the buffet. Reservations recommended.

Kyoto, 560, Grande Allée (529-6141). By night an expensive Japanese restaurant with authentic garden decor; by day a cheap buffet with authentic garden decor. Buffet $6.50 Mon.-Fri. 11:30am-2pm. Also open daily 5:30-9pm.

La Fleur de Lotus, 38, Côte de la Fabrique (692-4286), across from the Hôtel de Ville. Cheerful and unpretentious. Thai, Cambodian, Vietnamese, and Japanese dishes $8.75-14. Open Mon.-Wed. 11:30am-10:30pm, Thurs.-Fri. 11:30am-11pm, Sat. 5-11pm, Sun. 5-10:30pm.

Chez Temporel, 25, rue Couillard (694-1813). Stay off the tourist path while remaining within your budget at this genuine *café québecois,* discreetly tucked in a side alley off rue St-Jean. Besides the usual café staples, it offers exotic coffee and liquor drinks ($4.50). Linger as long as you like. Open Sun.-Thurs. 7am-1:30am, Fri.-Sat. 7am-2:30am.

Restaurant Liban, 23, rue d'Auteuil (694-1888), off rue St-Jean. Great café for lunch or a late-night bite. Tabouli and hummus plates $3.50, both with pita bread. Excellent falafel ($4) and baklava ($1.75). Open 11am-4am.

SIGHTS

Inside the Walls

Confined within walls built by the English, *Vieux Québec* (Old City) contains most of the city's historic attractions. Though monuments are clearly marked and explained, you'll get more out of the town if you consult the tourist office's *Greater Québec Area Tourist Guide,* which contains a walking tour of the Old City (available from all 3 tourist offices listed in Practical Information, above). It takes one or two days to explore Vieux Québec on foot, but you'll learn more than on the many guided bus tours and you'll tone those legs on the roller coaster roads to boot.

Begin your walking tour of Québec City by climbing to the top of **Cap Diamant** (Cape Diamond) to see what you can see. Just north is **Citadelle,** the largest North American fortification still guarded by troops—who knows why? Anyway, don't attack it. Visitors can witness the **changing of the guard** (mid-June to Labor Day daily 10am) and the **beating of the retreat** (July-Aug. Tues., Thurs., and Sat.-Sun. 7pm). Tours are given every 55 min. (Citadelle open daily 9am-6pm; Labor Day-Oct. and May-June 9am-4pm; mid-March to April 10am-3pm; Nov. to mid-March by reservation only. $4, ages 7-17 $2, disabled and under 7 free.)

Beat your own retreat from Citadelle by taking **Promenade des Gouverneurs** downhill to **Terrasse Dufferin.** Built in 1838 by Lord Durham, this popular promenade offers excellent views of the Fleuve St-Laurent, the Côte de Beaupré (the "Avenue Royale" Highway), and Ile d'Orléans across the channel. The promenade passes the landing spot of the European settlers, marked by the **Samuel de Champlain Monument,** where Champlain secured French settlement by building Fort St-Louis in 1620. Today, the promenade offers endless fascinating performers of all flavors—clowns, bagpipers, and banjo and clarinet duos.

At the bottom of the promenade, towering above the *terrasse* next to rue St-Louis, sits immense, baroque **le Château Frontenac** (692-3861), built in 1893 on the ruins of two previous châteaux and named for Comte Frontenac, governor of *Nouvelle-France*. The château was the site of two historic meetings between Churchill and Roosevelt during World War II, and is now a luxury hotel. The hotel is the budget traveler's nemesis, but you can still take a guided tour of Québec's pride and joy. (Tours leave daily on the hour 9am-6pm. $4, seniors $3, children 6-16 $2, children under 6 free.)

Near Château Frontenac, between rue St-Louis and rue Ste-Anne, lies the **Place d'Armes.** *Calèches* (horse-drawn buggies) that congregate here in summer provide a certain air that grows especially strong in muggy weather. A carriage will give you a tour of the city for $56, but your feet will do the same for free. From the Place d'Armes, the pedestrian and artist-choked rue du Trésor leads to rue Buade and the **Notre-Dame Basilica** (692-2533). The clock and outer walls date back to 1647; the rest of the church has been rebuilt twice, most recently after a fire in 1922. (Open daily 6:30am-6pm. Tours in multiple languages, mid-May to mid-Oct. daily 9am-4:30pm.) In addition to the ornate gold altar and impressive religious artifacts (including a chancel lamp given to the congregation by the cheery Louis XIV), the basilica is home to a 3D historical **Sound and Light show** (692-3200; daily 6:30, 7:45, and 9pm, also Tues. and Fri. 4 and 5:15pm; Oct.-May twice a week; $5, ages 12-17 $3, under 12 free). Notre-Dame, with its odd mix of architectural styles, contrasts sharply with the adjacent **Seminary of Québec,** an excellent example of 17th-century *québecois* architecture. Founded in 1663 as a Jesuit training ground, the seminary became the *Université de Laval* in 1852. The **Musée du Séminaire,** 9, rue de l'Université (692-2843), lies nearby. (Open daily 10am-5:30pm; Oct.-May Tues.-Sun. 10am-5pm; $3, seniors $2, students $1.50, under 16 $1.)

The **Musée du Fort,** 10, rue Ste-Anne (692-2175), presents a sound and light show that narrates the history of Québec City and the series of six battles fought between 1629 and 1775 for control of it (open June-Sept. daily 10am-6pm; $4.75, seniors $3.75, students 7-25 $2.75). Ask at the tourist office for their sporadic schedule.

The all-too-exciting **post office,** 3, rue Buade, now called **the Louis St-Laurent Building** (after Canada's second French Canadian Prime Minister), was built in the late 1890s and towers over a statue of Monseigneur de Laval, the first bishop of Québec. Across the Côte de la Montagne, a lookout park provides an impressive view of the Fleuve St-Laurent. A statue of Georges-Etienne Cartier, one of the key French-Canadian fathers of the Confederation, presides over the park.

Outside The Walls

From the old city, the **promenade des Gouverneurs** and its 310 steps lead to the **Plains of Abraham** (otherwise known as the **Parc des Champs-de-Bataille**). General James Wolfe's British troops and General de Montcalm's French forces clashed here in 1759; both leaders died during the decisive 15-min. confrontation, won by the British. The Plains now serve as drill fields and the site of the **Royal Québec Golf Course.** A **tourist reception center** (648-4071) at 390, ave des Bernières, offers maps and pamphlets about the park. (Open Thurs. and Tues. 10am-5:45pm, Wed. 10am-9:45pm; the park is accessible to the disabled.)

At the far end of the Plains of Abraham you'll find the **Musée du Québec,** 1, ave. Wolfe-Montcalm, parc des Champs-de-Bataille (643-2150), which contains (surprise!) a collection of *québecois* paintings, sculptures, decorative arts, and prints. The **Gérard Morisset pavilion,** greeting you with the unlikely *ménage à trois* of Jacques Cartier, Neptune, and Gutenberg, houses the Musée's permanent collection. The renovated old "prison of the plains," the **Baillarce Pavilion,** incarcerates temporary exhibits. (Open Thurs.-Tues. 10am-5:45pm, Wed. 10am-9:45pm; Labor Day to mid-May Tues. and Thurs.-Sun. 10am-6pm, Wed. 10am-10pm. $5.50, seniors $4.25, students and disabled persons $3, under 16 free. Free Wed.) At the corner of la Grande Allée and rue Georges VI, right outside Porte St-Louis, stands **l'Assemblée Nationale** (643-7239), built in the style of French King Louis XIII's era and completed in 1886. View debates from the visitors gallery. Anglophones and Francophones both have recourse to simultaneous translation earphones. (Free 30-min. tours daily 9am-4:30pm; Labor Day to late June Mon.-Fri. 9am-4:30pm. Call ahead to ensure a space.)

For the Stairmaster-less, a *funiculaire* (cable car) connects Upper Town with Lower Town and **Place Royale,** the oldest section of Québec (692-1132; operates June-Labor Day daily 8am-midnight; $1, under 6 free). This way leads to **rue Petit-Champlain,** the oldest road in North America. Many old buildings along the street have been restored or renovated and now house craft shops, boutiques, cafés, and restaurants. The **Café-Théâtre Le Petit Champlain,** 68, rue Petit-Champlain (692-2613), presents *québecois* music, singing, and theater. From here, just continue west (right, from the bottom of the *funiculaire)* to reach the Plains of Abraham.

From the bottom of the *funiculaire* you can also take rue Sous-le-Fort and then turn left to reach **Place Royale,** built in 1608, where you'll find the small but beautiful **l'Eglise Notre-Dame-des-Victoires** (692-1650), the oldest church in Canada, dating from the glorious year of 1688. (Open Mon.-Sat. 9am-4:30pm, closed on Sat. if a wedding is being held; Oct. 16-April Mon.-Sat. 9am-noon, Sun. 7:30am-1pm. Free.) The houses surrounding the square have been restored to late 18th-century styles. Considered one of the birthplaces of French civilization in North America, the Place Royale is now the site of fantastic outdoor summer theater and concerts. Giant phone booths, satellites, videos, and recreated moon landings celebrate Québec's past, present, and future at the recently opened **Musée de la Civilisation,** 85, rue Dalhousie (643-2158), also along the river. This thematic museum targets French Canadians, though English tours and exhibit notes are available. (Open daily 10am-7pm; early Sept.-late June Tues.-Sun. 10am-5pm, Wed. 10am-9pm. $5, students $3, seniors $4, under 7 free.)

ENTERTAINMENT AND NIGHTLIFE

The raucous **Winter Carnival** (626-3716) breaks the tedium of northern winters and lifts spirits in mid-February; the **Summer Festival** (692-4540) boasts a number of free outdoor concerts in mid-July. The **Plein Art** (694-0260) exhibition of arts and crafts takes over the Pigeonnier on Grande-Allée in early August. **Les nuits Black** (849-7080), Québec's rising jazz festival, bebops the city for two weeks in late June. But the most festive day of the year is June 24, **la Fête nationale du Québec** (Saint-Jean-Baptiste Day) (681-7011), a celebration of *québecois* culture with free concerts, a bonfire, fireworks, and five million roaring drunk francophones.

The Grande Allée's many restaurants are interspersed with a number of *Bar Discothèques,* where the early 20s mainstream crowd gathers. **Chez Dagobert,** 600 Grande Allée (522-0393), saturates its two dance floors while plentiful food and drink pour onto the streetside patio; it is *the* place to be seen (no cover; open daily 11am-3am). Down the block at **O'Zone,** 564 Grande Allée (529-7932), the tempo is a little slower and more pub-like (open daily 10am-3am).

Quebéc City's visible, young punk contingent clusters around rue St-Jean. **La Fourmi Atomik,** 33, rue d'Auteuil (694-1463), features underground rock. Monday is reggae only and Wednesday is rap only. (No cover. Open daily 10am-3am; Oct.-May 2pm-3am.) At **L'Ostradamus,** 29, rue Couillard (694-9560), you can listen to live jazz and intellectual conversations in a smoke-drenched pseudo-spiritual ambience and artsy Thai decor ($1-3 cover when band is playing; open daily 4pm-3am; Oct.-May 5pm-3am). A more traditional Québec evening can be found at **Les Yeux Bleux,** 1117½, rue St-Jean (694-9118), a local favorite where *chansonniers* perform nightly (no cover; open daily 8pm-3am).

The gay scene in Québec City isn't huge but also isn't hard to find. **Le Ballon Rouge,** 811, St-Jean (647-9227), near the walls of the Old City, is a popular dance club (no cover; open daily 10:30pm-3am). Farther from downtown at 157 Chemin Ste-Foy, **Studio 157** (529-9958), caters to a crowd of women only.

■ NEAR QUÉBEC CITY

Ile-d'Orléans on the St-Laurent is untouched by Québec City's public transport system, but its proximity to Québec (about 10km downstream) makes it an ideal side trip by car or bicycle (see Practical Information for rentals, p. 851). Take Autoroute 440 Est., and cross over the only bridge leading to the island (Pont de l'Ile). A tour of the island covers 64km. Originally called *Ile de Bacchus* because of the plethora of wild grapes fermenting here, the Ile-d'Orléans remains a sparsely populated retreat of several small villages and plentiful strawberry crops. The **Manoir Mauvide-Genest,** 1451, ch. Royal (829-2630), dates from 1734, and is now a private museum housing crafts and traditional colonial furniture. (Open June daily 10am-5pm; July-Aug. 10am-8pm; Sept.-Oct. weekends by reservation. $3, ages 10-18 $1.50.)

Exiting Ile-d'Orléans, turn right (east) onto Hwy. 138 (bd. Ste-Anne) to view the splendid **Chute Montmorency** (Montmorency Falls), which are substantially taller than Niagara Falls. In winter, vapors from the falls freeze completely to form a frozen shadow of the running falls. About 20 km along 138 lies **Ste-Anne-de-Beaupré** (Voyageur buses link it to Québec City, $5). This small town's entire *raison d'être* is the famous **Basilique Ste-Anne-de Beaupré,** 10018, ave Royale (827-3781). Since 1658, this double-spired basilica has contained a Miraculous Statue and the alleged forearm bone of Saint Anne (mother of the Virgin Mary). Every year, more than one million pilgrims come here in the hopes that their prayers will be answered, and legend has it that some have been quite successful. (Open early May to mid-Sept. daily 8:30am-5pm.) In the winter months (Nov.-Apr.), go to Ste-Anne for some of the best skiing in the province (lift tickets $38 per day). Contact **Parc du Mont Ste-Anne,** P.O. Box 400, Beaupré, G0A IE0 (827-4561), which has a 625-m/2050-ft. vertical drop and night skiing to boot.

Ontario

First claimed by French explorer Samuel de Champlain in 1613, Ontario soon became a center of English influence within Canada. Hostility and famine in Europe drove hordes of Scottish and Irish immigrants to this territory. They asserted control with a takeover of New France in 1763 during the Seven Years War; twenty years later, a flood of Loyalist emigres from the newly formed United States streamed into the province, fortifying its Anglo character. Now serving as a political counterbalance to French Québec, this populous central province tends to raise the ire of peripheral regions of Canada due to its high concentration of power and wealth. In the south world-class Toronto shines—multicultural, enormous (3 million plus, by *far* the largest city in sparse Canada), vibrant, clean, and safe. Yuppified suburbs, an occasional college town, and farms surround this sprawling megalopolis. In the east, national capital Ottawa sits on Ontario's border with Québec. To the north, layers of

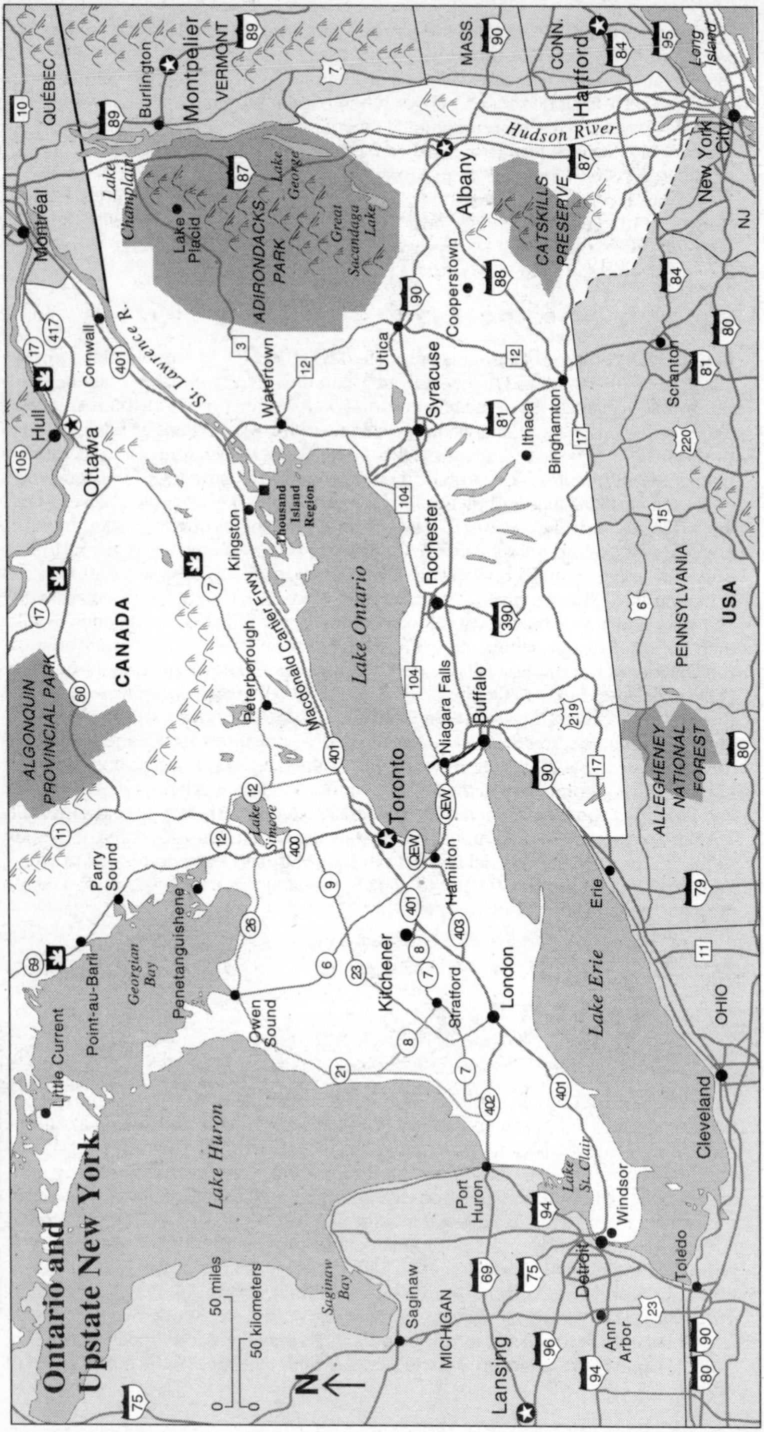

Ontario and Upstate New York
50 miles
50 kilometers
N
CANADA
USA
QUÉBEC
VERMONT
MASS.
CONN.
NJ
PENNSYLVANIA
OHIO
MICHIGAN
Montréal
Hull
Ottawa
Cornwall
Kingston
Peterborough
Toronto
Hamilton
Kitchener
Stratford
London
Windsor
Owen Sound
Parry Sound
Penetanguishene
Point-au-Baril
Little Current
Niagara Falls
Buffalo
Rochester
Syracuse
Utica
Watertown
Ithaca
Binghamton
Cooperstown
Albany
Lake Placid
Burlington
Montpelier
Hartford
New York City
Scranton
Erie
Cleveland
Toledo
Detroit
Ann Arbor
Port Huron
Saginaw
Lansing
Lake Huron
Georgian Bay
Saginaw Bay
Lake St. Clair
Lake Erie
Lake Ontario
Lake Simcoe
Lake Champlain
Lake George
Great Sacandaga Lake
Long Island
Hudson River
St. Lawrence R.
Thousand Island Region
Macdonald Cartier Fwy
ALGONQUIN PROVINCIAL PARK
ADIRONDACKS PARK
CATSKILLS PRESERVE
ALLEGHENY NATIONAL FOREST

CANADA

cottage country and ski resorts give way to a pristine wilderness that is as much French and Native Canadian as it is British.

PRACTICAL INFORMATION

Capital: Toronto.

Ontario Ministry of Culture, Tourism, and Recreation: Customer Service Branch, 800-668-2746. Open Mon.-Sat. 9am-8pm, Sun. 10am-5pm; Sept.-May Mon.-Fri. 9am-6pm, Sat.-Sun. 10am-5pm). Send written requests to Ontario Travel, Queen's Park, Toronto, ONT M7A 2E5. Free brochures, guides, maps, and info on special events.

Drinking Age: 19.

Time Zone: Eastern. **Postal Abbreviation:** ONT

Sales Tax: 8%, plus 7% GST (for details on obtaining a refund of the GST, see Essentials, p. 7).

■■■ TORONTO

Once a prim and proper Victorian city where even window-shopping was prohibited on the Sabbath, the city dubbed the world's most multicultural by the United Nations is today one of the hippest and most accessible urban areas in North America. Toronto has spent millions in recent decades on spectacular public works projects: the world's tallest "free-standing" structure (the CN tower), the biggest retractable roof (the Sky Dome), outstanding lakefront development, and significant sponsorship of arts and museums. Cosmetically, Toronto's skyscrapers and neatly gridded streets are strikingly reminiscent of New York, a resemblance which has not gone unnoticed—or unexploited—by Hollywood. But New York it's not, and, legend has it, two film crews learned this the hard way. One crew, after dirtying a Toronto street to make it look more like a typical "American" avenue, went on coffee break and returned only to find their set spotless again, swept by the ever-vigilant city maintenance department. Another crew, filming an attack scene, was twice interrupted by Torontonians hopping out of their cars to "rescue" the actress.

PRACTICAL INFORMATION

Tourist Office: Metropolitan Toronto Convention and Visitors Association (MTCVA), 207 Queens Quay W (203-2500 or 800-363-1990), at Harbourfront Centre. Open Mon.-Fri. 8:30am-6pm, Sat.-Sun. 9:30am-6pm; in winter Mon.-Fri. 8:30am-5pm, Sat. 9am-5pm, Sun. 9:30am-5pm. **Ontario Travel** (800-668-2746) has info on all of Ontario. Enter Eaton, 220 Yonge St. at Dundas St., go down to level 1, exit the store, and it's on the right. Open Mon.-Fri. 10am-9pm, Sat. 10am-6pm, Sun. noon-5pm.

Student Travel Office: Travel CUTS, 187 College St. (979-2406), just west of University Ave. Subway: Queen's Park. Smaller office at 74 Gerrard St. E. (977-0441). Subway: College. Both open Mon.-Fri. 9am-5pm.

Consulates: U.S., 360 University Ave. (595-1700). Subway: St. Patrick. Consular services Mon.-Fri. 8:30am-1pm. **Australia,** 175 Bloor St. E., #314-6 (323-1155). Subway: Bloor St. Open for info Mon.-Fri. 9am-5pm; visas 9am-1pm and 2-4pm. **U.K.,** 2800 Bay St. (593-1267). Subway: College. Open Mon.-Fri. 8:30am-5pm.

Currency Exchange: Toronto Currency Exchange, 313 Yonge St. (598-3769; open 9am-7pm), and 2 Walton (599-5821; open 8:30am-5:30pm), gives the best rates around, with no service fee. **Royal Bank of Canada,** 200 Bay St. (974-5151 for info; 974-5535 for foreign exchange), has exchange centers at Pearson Airport (676-3220; 24 hrs.) and throughout the city. **Money Mart,** 688 Younge St. (924-1000), has 24-hr. service with fees for some transactions. Subway: Bloor/Younge.

Airport: Pearson International (247-7678), about 20km west of Toronto via Hwy. 427, 401, or 409. Take Bus #58 west from Lawrence W. subway. **Pacific Western Transportation** (905-672-0293) runs buses every 20min. directly to downtown hotels ($11.45, $19.70 round-trip) and every 40min. to Yorkdale ($6.90), York Mills ($7.95), and Islington ($6.40) subway stations (all buses

6:05am-12:05pm). **Hotel Airporter** (798–2424) transports to select downtown hotels ($11, $19 round-trip).

Trains: All trains chug from **Union Station,** 65 Front St. (366-8411), at Bay and York. Subway: Union. **VIA Rail** (366-8411) cannonballs to: Montréal (4-6 per day, 5hr., $83); Vancouver (3 per week, 3 days, $483); Windsor (4-5 per day, 4hr., $62). **Amtrak** (800-872-7245) blasts off to: New York City (1 per day, 12hr. US$61-93); Chicago (6 per week, 11hr., US$93). Ticket office open Mon.-Sat. 6:45am-9:30pm, Sun. 8am-8:30pm; station open daily 6am-midnight.

Buses: Voyageur (393-7911) and **Greyhound** (367-8747) operate from 610 Bay St., just north of Dundas. Subway: St. Patrick or Dundas. Voyageur has service to Montréal (5-6 per day, 7hr., $64). Greyhound goes to Calgary (3 per day, 48hr., $242), Vancouver (3 per day, 2½ days, $284), or New York City (3 per day, 11hr., $79). No reservations; show up 30min. prior to departure. An advance-purchase, unlimited ticket can be used anywhere in Canada for 7 days ($212); a 15-day pass sells for $277. Ticket office open daily 5:30am-1am.

Ferries: Toronto Island Ferry Service (392-8194, 392-8193 for recording). Ferries to Centre Island, Wards Island, and Hanlans Point leave from Bay St. Ferry Dock at the foot of Bay St. Service daily approximately every ½hr.-1hr. 8am-midnight. $3 round-trip, seniors, students, and ages 15-19 $1.50, under 15 $1.

Public Transportation: Toronto Transit Commission (TTC) (393-4000). A network of 2 subway lines and numerous bus and streetcar routes. Free pocket maps at all stations. After dark, buses are required to stop anywhere along a route at a female passenger's request. Subway 6am-2:25am; then, buses cover subway routes. Some buses 24 hrs. Free transfers among subway, buses, and streetcars, but only at stations. Fare $2 (5 tokens $6.50), seniors with ID ½-price, under 13 50¢ (8 for $2.50). Mon.-Sat. 1-day unlimited travel pass $5; monthly pass $67.

Taxis: Co-op Cabs, 504-2667. $2.20 base fee, $1.10 per km. 24 hrs.

Car Rental: Wrecks for Rent, 77 Nassau St. (585-7782). Subway: Spadina or Bathurst. $29 per day with 100km free, 9¢ each additional km. Ages 23-25 pay $3 per day surcharge, ages 21-23 $5. Open Mon.-Fri. 8am-6pm, Sat. 9am-4pm.

Driver/Rider Service: Allo-Stop, 609 Bloor St. W (531-7668). Matches riders with drivers; part of the fee goes to the driver. Membership for passengers $6, for drivers $7. To: Ottawa ($24), Montréal ($26), Québec City ($41), New York ($40). Open Mon.-Wed. 9am-5pm, Thurs.-Fri. 9am-7pm, Sat.-Sun. 10am-5pm.

Bike Rental: Brown's Sports and Bike Rental, 2447 Bloor St. W. (763-4176). $17 per day, $34 per weekend, $44 per week. $200 deposit or credit card required. Open Mon.-Wed. 9:30am-5pm, Thurs.-Fri. 9:30am-8pm, Sat. 9:30am-5:30pm.

Crisis Lines: Rape Crisis, 597-8808. 24 hrs. **Services for the Disabled,** Ontario Travel, 314-0944. **Toronto Gay and Lesbian Phone Line,** 964-6600. Open Mon.-Sat. 7-10pm.

Emergency: 911.

Post Office: Toronto Dominion Centre (360-7105), at King and Bay St. **Postal Code:** M4P 2E0. General Delivery at Postal Station A, 25 the Esplanade, Toronto M5W 1A0 (365-0656). Open Mon.-Fri. 8am-5:45pm. **Area Code:** 416 (city), 905 (outskirts).

ORIENTATION

The city maps available at tourism booths only show major streets and may prove inadequate for getting around. A better bet is to buy the indispensable *Downtown and Metro Toronto Visitor's Map Guide* in the yellowish-orange cover ($2.95), available in drug stores or tourist shops. The *Ride Guide,* free at all TTC stations and tourism information booths (see Practical Information above), shows the subway and bus routes for the metro area.

Toronto's streets lie in a grid pattern. Addresses on north-south streets increase towards the north, away from Lake Ontario. **Yonge St.** is the main north-south route, dividing the city and the streets perpendicular to it into east and west. Numbering for both sides starts at Yonge St. and increases as you move away in either direction. West of Yonge St., the main arteries are **Bay St., University Ave., Spadina**

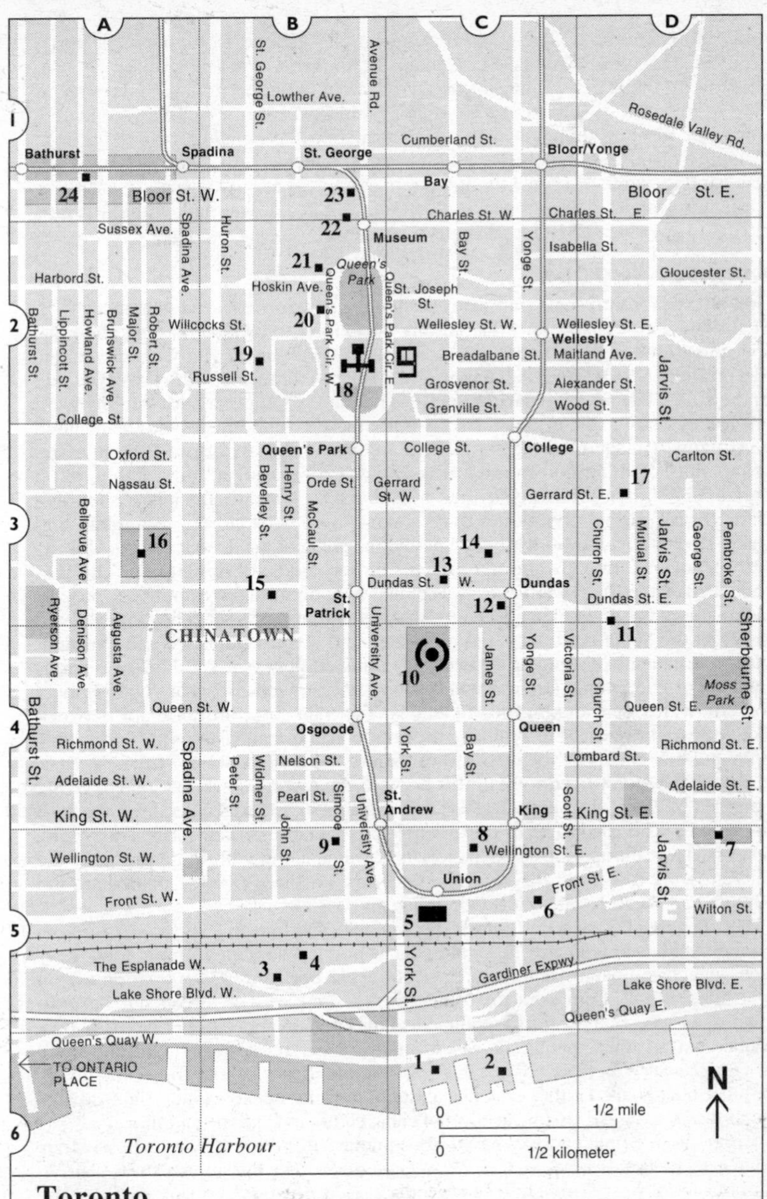

Toronto

1 Harbour Square
2 Toronto Island Ferry Terminal
3 Skydome
4 CN Tower
5 Union Station
6 O'Keefe Centre
7 St. Lawrence Market
8 Post Office
9 Roy Thomson (concert) Hall
10 Toronto City Hall
11 Toronto International Hostel
12 Infobooth
13 Bay Street Bus Terminal
14 World's Biggest Bookstore
15 Art Gallery of Ontario
16 Kensington Market
17 Neill-Wycik College-Hotel
18 Ontario Provincial Parliament Building
19 Knox College
20 Hart House
21 Trinity College
22 McLaughlin Planetarium
23 Royal Ontario Museum (ROM)
24 The Annex

Subway Line and Station

Ave., and **Bathurst St.** The major east-west routes include, from the water north, **Front St., Queen St., Dundas St., College St., Bloor St.,** and **EdlingtonSt.**

Toronto's traffic gets crowded—avoid rush hour (4-7pm). Parking on the street is hard to find and usually carries a one-hour limit, except on Sundays when street spaces are free and abundant. You can also park for free at night, but your car must be gone by 7am. Parking officials enforce regulations zealously—don't tempt them. Day parking generally costs inbound day-trippers $2-4 at outlying subway stations; parking overnight at the subway stations is prohibited. If you park within the city, expect to pay at least $12 for 24 hours (7am-7am).

NEIGHBORHOODS

Downtown Toronto splits into many distinctive and decentralized neighborhoods. Thanks to zoning regulations that require developers to include housing and retail space in commercial construction, many people live downtown. **Chinatown** centers on Dundas St. W. between Bay St. and Spadina Ave. Formerly the Jewish market in the 1920s, **Kensington Market,** on Kensington Ave., Augusta Ave., and the western half of Baldwin St., is now a largely Portuguese neighborhood with many good restaurants, vintage clothing shops, and an outdoor bazaar of produce, luggage, spices, nuts, clothing, and shoes. A strip of old factories, stores, and warehouses on **Queen St. West,** from University Ave. to Bathurst St., contain a fun mix of shopping from upscale, uptight boutiques to reasonable used book stores, restaurants, and cafés. The ivy-covered Gothic buildings and magnificent quadrangles of the **University of Toronto** occupy about 200 acres in the middle of downtown. The law-school cult-flick *The Paper Chase* was filmed here because the campus supposedly looked more Ivy League than Harvard, where the movie was set. **The Annex,** Bloor St. W. at the Spadina subway, has an artistic and literary ambiance and excellent budget restaurants dishing up a variety of ethnic cuisines (see Food below). This is the best place to come at night when you're not sure exactly what you're hungry for; afterwards, stay and hit the nightclubs. **Yorkville,** just north of Bloor between Yonge St. and Avenue Rd., was once the crumbling communal home of flower children and folk guitarists; today, if you can afford the upscale shops (Tiffany's, etc.), you probably don't need to read this book. **Cabbagetown,** just east of Yonge St., bounded by Gerrard St. E., Wellesley, and Sumach St., takes its name from the Irish immigrants who used to plant the green, leafy vegetable in their yards. Today, professionals inhabit its renowned Victorian housing, along with quite probably the only crowing rooster in the city. The **Gay and Lesbian Village,** located around Church and Wellesley St., offers fine dining and outdoor cafés.

The **Theatre District,** on Front St. between Sherbourne and Yonge St., supports enough venues to feed anyone's cultural and physical appetites. Music, food, ferry rides, dance companies, and art all dock at the **Harborfront** (973-3000 for info), on Queen's Quay W. from York to Bathurst St., on the lake. The three main **Toronto Islands,** all accessible by ferry (see Practical Information above), offer beaches, bike rentals, and an amusement park. East from the harbor, the **beaches** along and south of Queen's St. E. between Woodbine and Victoria boast tons of shops and a very popular boardwalk. Farther east still, about 5km from the city center, the **Scarborough Bluffs,** a rugged, 16-km. section of cliffs, climb up from the lakeshore.

Three more ethnic enclaves lie 30 to 40 minutes from downtown by public transit. **Corso Italia** surrounds St. Clair W. at Dufferin St.; take the subway to St. Clair W. and bus #512 west. You'll find **Little India** at Gerrard St. E. and Coxwell; ride the subway to Coxwell, then take bus #22 south to the second Gerard St. stop. Better known as **"the Danforth," Greektown** is on Danforth Ave. at Pape Ave. (subway: Pape). All three have bilingual street signs, cater to locals, and are worth the ride.

ACCOMMODATIONS AND CAMPING

Avoid the cut-rate hotels concentrated around Jarvis and Gerrard St. The University of Toronto provides cheap quality sleep for budget travelers; contact the **U. of Toronto Housing Service,** 214 College St. (978-8045), for $30-45 rooms (open Mon.-Fri.

8:45am-5pm; reservations recommended). You can call the Visitors Bureau or one of two B&B agencies to obtain a B&B room; the **Downtown Association of Bed and Breakfast Guest Houses** (690-1724) places guests in renovated Victorian homes (singles $40-60), while the **Metropolitan B&B Registry** (964-2566) handles locations all over the city (singles from $35). Because it is difficult to regulate these registries, you should always visit a B&B before you commit.

Toronto International Hostel (HI-C), 90 Gerrard St. West (971-4440; fax 368-6499), a few blocks from the bus station. Subway: College or Queen's Park. This newly relocated hostel occupies several floors of a hospital residence. Great central location with a kitchen, laundry facilities, a pool, and a fitness center, but no real common space or homey hostel atmosphere. Rooms have 2 beds each. 24-hr. access. $21, nonmembers $25; linen provided.

Leslieville Home Hostel, 185 Leslie St. (461-7258 or 800-280-3965; fax 469-9938). Subway: Queen. Take any Queen streetcar from the subway and get off at Leslie St.; walk left to hostel. Inviting home setting; friendly owners work hard to place all comers. No smoking. Check-out 10am, but travelers are welcome to hang out in the common area all day. Dorm-style beds in mixed and single sex rooms $13. Singles $32, doubles $39; in winter $27/$34. Linens, towels and soap included; breakfast $2. Reserve ahead in summer and for arrivals after midnight.

Knox College, 59 St. George St. (978-0168, Mon.-Fri. 9am-5pm). Subway: Queen's Park. U of T's most coveted residence has huge rooms with wood floors around an idyllic courtyard in the heart of campus. Many rooms refinished by the crew of TV's *Class of '96;* some, though, are a little ragged. Common rooms and baths on each floor. Singles $28, students $22.40; doubles $45/$40. Call to reserve months in advance, or chance it on short notice. Open June-Aug.

Neill-Wycik College Hotel, 96 Gerrard St. E. (800-268-4358 or 977-2320). Subway: College. Small, clean rooms, some with beautiful views of the city. Kitchen on every floor, but no utensils. Check-in after 4pm (lockers are available); check-out 10am. Singles $31.50, doubles $38. Family rooms available. Students, seniors, and HI members get a 20% discount. Open early May-late Aug.

Trinity College and St. Hilda's College Residences, 6 Hoskin Ave. (978-2523); check-in at bursar's office on U of T campus. Subway: Museum. Rooms from $28. Office open Mon.-Fri. 9am-4pm. Available late May-late Aug.

Karabanow Guest House and Tourist Home, 9 Spadina Rd. (phone and fax 923-4004), at Bloor St. Subway: Spadina; located near subway stop. Small and intimate; 9 rooms (mostly doubles) in a renovated Victorian house. TV, shared bath, free parking and local calls. Office open Mon.-Tues. 10am-8pm, Wed. and Sat. 10am-9pm, Sun. 10am-6pm. Check-out 11am. Singles $46, doubles $56; in winter $41/$51. Key deposit $10. No kids under 12 please. Reservations recommended.

The Allenby Bed and Breakfast, 223 Strathmore Blvd. (461-7095). Subway: Greenwood. Spacious, pristine rooms with private-use kitchens and bathrooms in a quiet neighborhood. Subway stop next door adds convenience, not noise. Light breakfast. Long-term and group stays encouraged. Singles $45, doubles $55.

Hotel Selby, 592 Sherbourne St. (921-3142 or 800-387-4788). Subway: Sherbourne. A registered historic spot and a thriving guest house, Hotel Selby has seen some changes since Hemingway knew it. Totally refurbished, including cable TV, A/C, laundry facilities, and phones. Special period suites are set up to capture the splendor of the 1920's Selby. Some private baths. Singles from $49; Jan.-April $40.

YWCA-Woodlawn Residence, 80 Woodlawn Ave. (923-8454), off Yonge St. Subway: Summerhill. In a nice neighborhood, 115 rooms for women only, with breakfast, TV lounges, and laundry facilities. Small, neat singles $44, doubles $59; private bath available. Beds in subterranean dormitory $18; linen $3. 10% seniors discount. Office open Mon.-Fri. 7:30am-11:30pm, Sat.-Sun. 7:30am-7:30pm.

Indian Line Tourist Campground, 7625 Finch Ave. W. (905-678-1233; off season 661-6600, ext. 203), at Darcel Ave. Follow Hwy. 427 north to Finch Ave. and go west. The closest campground (30min.) to metropolitan Toronto; near Pearson Airport. Showers, laundry. Gatehouse open 8am-9pm. Unwooded sites $15, with hook-up $19. Open May 10-early Oct. Reservations recommended July-Aug.

Glen Rouge Provincial Park, 7450 Hwy. 2, a.k.a. Kingston Rd. (392-2541), 30min. east of Toronto in the suburbs. Accessible by public transportation; call for directions. 127 sites. Showers, toilets. Nearby hiking, pool, tennis courts, and beach. $16, with water and electricity $22.

FOOD

A burst of immigration has made Toronto a haven for good international food rivaled in North America only by New York City. Over 5000 restaurants squeeze into metropolitan Toronto; you could eat out at a different place every night for the next 15 years. Some of the standouts can be found on **Bloor St. W.** and in **Chinatown.** For fresh produce, go to **Kensington Market** or the **St. Lawrence Market** at King St. E. and Sherbourne, 6 blocks east of the King subway stop. See Neighborhoods (above) for directions to these and other areas which offer ethnic or specialty fare. **Village by the Grange** (598-1414), at the corner of McCaul and Dundas near the Art Gallery of Ontario, is a vast collection of super-cheap restaurants and vendors—Chinese, Thai, Middle Eastern, you name it (generally open 11am-7pm). "L.L.B.O" posted on the window of a restaurant means that it has a liquor license.

Shopsy's, 33 Yonge St. (365-3333), at Front St. 1 block from Union Station. *The* definitive Toronto deli. 300 seats, snappy service. If you're feelin' frisky, try the "Hot and Topless" Reuben ($7.75). Shopsy's Hot Dog $3.85. Open Sun. 8am-11pm, Mon.-Wed. 7am-11pm, Thurs.-Fri. 7am-midnight, Sat. 8am-midnight.

Country Style Hungarian Restaurant, 450 Bloor St. W. (537-1745). Hearty stews, soups, and casseroles. Meals come in small (more than enough) and large (stop, lest I burst) portions. Entrees $3-8. Open daily 11am-10pm.

Real Peking Restaurant, 355 College St. (920-7952), at Augusta Ave. The effort many Chinese restaurants put into decorations goes into the food here. Understanding servers will explain the menu. Entrees $6.50-8.50. Lunch specials $4.25 (noon-3pm). Open Mon.-Thurs. noon-10pm, Sat. 5-11pm, Sun. 4-10pm.

Bagelworks, 326 Bloor St. W. (92-BAGEL/922-2435), at Spadina St. Fast becoming a Toronto institution, the original Bagelworks (other locations at 1946 Queen St. E. and 1450 Yonge St.) serves up gourmet bagels in a stylishly decorated café close to U. of T. and swingin' Spadina. Specialty bagels like Sourdough, Potato & Dill, or "The Bathurst," as well as old favorites (60¢, 6 for $3.25). Fruit smoothies $1.90. Open in summer Mon.-Fri. 7am-6pm, Sat. 7am-5pm, Sun. 8am-5pm.

Forkchops Noodle House, 1440 Yonge St. (944-8501), south of St. Clair St., and 730 Yonge St. (964-8410), south of Bloor St. Tasty, inexpensive noodles in chic Eurasian decor. Ramen, udon, or soba noodles in broth $3.99; shrimp shumai dumplings $1.99. Open Mon.-Thurs. and Sun. 11am-9pm, Fri.-Sat. 11am-9:30pm.

Mr. Greek, 568 Danforth Ave. (461-5470), at Carlaw. Subway: Pape. A friendly, bustling café serving shish kabobs, salads, steak, chicken, Greek music, and wine. Family atmosphere, fast service. Gyros or souvlaki $6.70. Open Sun.-Thurs. 10am-1am, Fri.-Sat. until 3am.

Future's Bakery and Café, 483 Bloor St. W. (922-5875). Have an espresso and hang out on the popular outdoor patio. Sinful desserts like the phantom cake ($3.35) follow earthy lunches such as pierogies ($5.40). Open daily 7:30am-3pm.

By The Way Café, 400 Bloor St. W. (967-4295). Subway: Spadina. Formerly vegetarian, this Mediterranean restaurant and café now apologizes for its use of chicken, but they need not apologize for the food. Outdoor patio seating available. Veggie burger $6.95. Open Mon.-Fri. 11am-1am, Sat.-Sun. 10am-2am.

Saigon Palace, 454 Spadina Ave. (963-1623), at College St. Subway: Queen's Park. Popular with locals. Great spring rolls. Beef, chicken, or vegetable dishes over rice or noodles $4-7. Open Mon.-Thurs. 9am-10pm, Fri.-Sat. 9am-10pm.

Mövenpick Marché (366-8986), in the BCE Place at Yonge and Front St. A 22,000-sq.-meter market/restaurant. Browse through and pick a meal from the various culinary stations, including a bakery, a wine shop, pasta, seafood, and salad counters, and a grill. Yuppie extravagance at its finest, and not too hard on the budget; entrees run $5-8. Open daily 9am-2am.

Chez Cappuccino, 3 Charles St. E. (925-6142). Subway: Yonge/Bloor. Jazz music provides the backdrop for this 24-hr. café. Quiches $4.35; 3 or 4 soups $2.95; scrumptious muffins $1.50. Live jazz Sun. 1-3pm. Upper Canada beer on tap.

The Old Fish Market Restaurant, 12 Market St. (363-FISH/3474), just off the Esplanade. Somewhat pricey but excellent seafood (lunch $6-14, dinner $10-30). Look for special deals: daily noon-2pm ½-price oyster special, 6 for $3.50; Mon. night all-you-can-eat mussels $8; ½-price menu after 9pm. Open Mon.-Thurs. 11:45am-2:30pm and 5-10pm, Fri. 11:45am-2:30pm and 5-11pm, Sat. 8:30-11am, 11:30am-3pm, and 4:30-11pm, Sun. noon-3pm and 4-10pm.

The Organ Grinder, 58 the Esplanade (364-6517). Subway: Union. Jingles dance forth from the 1925 theater pipe organ, assembled from pieces of over 50 pipe organs. Pizzas $7-9. Open Sun.-Thurs. 11:30am-10pm, Fri.-Sat. 11:30am-midnight.

The Midtown Café, 552 College St. W. (920-4533), sounds alternative music while you play pool or just relax and eat from the large *tapas* menu ($2.50-3.50). Sandwiches ($3.50-5). Open daily 10am-2am.

Bar Italia, 584 College St. W. (535-3621), at Clinton St. Excellent Italian food in a jazzy ambiance. Try the *panino terracina* sandwich ($6). Open daily 8am-1am.

SIGHTS

A walk through the city's diverse **neighborhoods** can be one of the most rewarding (and cheapest) activities in Toronto. Signs and streetside conversations change languages; an endless stream of food aromas wafts through the air; locals go about their business. For a more organized expedition, the **Royal Ontario Museum** (586-5513 or 556-55140) operates seven free **walking tours.** (Tours June Wed. 6pm, July-Aug. Wed. 6pm and Sun. 2pm. Destinations and meeting places vary; call for specific information.) The **University of Toronto** (978-5000) conducts free one-hour walking tours of Canada's largest university (and alma mater of David Letterman's band leader, Paul Schaffer). The tours, available in English, French, Portuguese, or Hindi (call ahead for the last two), meet at the Map Room of Hart House. (Tours June-Aug. Mon.-Fri. 10:30am, 1pm, and 2:30pm.) Other guided trips within the city revolve around architectural themes, sculptures, or ghost-infested Toronto haunts (contact the Visitors Bureau for info; tours $10).

Modern architecture aficionados should visit the curving twin towers and 2-story rotunda of **City Hall** (392-7341), at the corner of Queen and Bay St. between the Osgoode and Queen subway stops; pick up a brochure for a self-guided tour (open 8:30am-4:30pm). In front of City Hall, **Nathan Phillips Square** is home to a reflecting pool (which becomes a skating rink in winter) and numerous special events. Call the **Events Hotline** (392-0458) for information. A few blocks away, the **Toronto Stock Exchange,** 2 First Canadian Place (947-4676), on York between Adelaide St. W. and King St. W., exchanges over $250 million daily as Canada's leading stock exchange. (Presentations Tues.-Fri. 2pm. Visitors center with viewing gallery open Mon.-Fri. 9am-4:30pm.) The Ontario government legislates in the **Provincial Parliament Buildings** (325-7500; subway: Queen's Park), at Queen's Park in the city center. (Building open Mon.-Fri. 8:30am-6pm, Sat.-Sun. 9am-4pm; chambers close 4:30pm. Parliament in session March-June and Oct.-Dec. Mon.-Wed. 1:30-6pm, Thurs. 10am-noon and 1:30-6pm. Free guided tours Mon.-Fri. by request, Sat.-Sun. every ½hr. 9am-4pm except during lunch. Free gallery passes available at main lobby info desk 1:30pm.) At 553m, the **CN Tower** (360-8500; subway: Union, follow the skywalk) towers as the tallest free-standing structure in the world. The ride to the top is pricey ($12, seniors $9, children $7; open daily 10am-10pm), but those heading for the Horizons bar, or who claim to be heading there get free passage at night. Straight out of a fairy tale, the 99-room **Casa Loma** (923-1171 or 923-1172), Davenport Rd. at 1 Austin Terrace, near Spadina a few blocks north of the Dupont subway stop, is a classic tourist attraction. Secret passageways and an underground tunnel add to the magic of the only real turreted castle in North America. (Open daily 10am-5pm; box office 10am-4pm. $8, seniors and ages 5-16 $4.50, under 5 free with parent.)

Check out an autopsy of a mummified Egyptian at the **Royal Ontario Museum (ROM),** 100 Queen's Park (586-5551; subway: Museum), which houses artifacts from ancient civilizations (Greek, Chinese, and Egyptian), a bat cave (not *the* Bat-Cave), and preserved, stuffed animals. (Open Mon. and Wed.-Sat. 10am-6pm, Tues. 10am-8pm, Sun. 11am-6pm. $8, seniors, students, and children $4; free Tues. for seniors, and Tues. after 4:30pm for everyone. Includes the **George M. Gardiner Museum of Ceramic Art** across the street.) Also in the museum complex, the **McLaughlin Planetarium** (586-5736) showcases presentations on astronomy and laser shows. (Call for showtimes. Tickets $5.50, seniors and students $3.50, children $3. Planetarium discounted with ROM entrance.) There was an old lady who lived in a shoe, but it probably wasn't the shoe-shaped glass-and-stone edifice that is the **Bata Shoe Museum,** 327 Bloor St. W. (979-7799; subway: St. George). Even the shoe-indifferent will find the collection of footwear from many cultures and ages fascinating: Hindu ivory stilted sandals, Elton John's sparkling silver platform boots, and two-inch slippers once worn by Chinese women with bound feet. (Open Tues.-Wed. and Fri.-Sat. 10am-5pm, Thurs. 10am-8pm, Sun. noon-5pm. $6, seniors and students $4, 5-14 $2, families $12.) The **Art Gallery of Ontario (AGO),** 317 Dundas St. W. (979-6648; subway: St. Patrick), 3 blocks west of University Ave., houses an enormous collection of Western art from the Renaissance to the 1990s, concentrating on Canadian artists. (Open Tues.-Sun. 10am-5:30pm, Wed. until 10pm; early Sept.-late May Wed.-Sun. 10am-5:30pm, Mon., holidays 10am-5:30pm. $7.50, students and seniors $4, families $15, under 12 free. Wed. 5-10pm free. Seniors free Fri.)

The **Hockey Hall of Fame,** 30 Yonge St. (360-7765), on the concourse level of BCE at Front St., celebrates Canada's favorite sport. Head first to the Bell Great Hall, where plaques of hockey greats such as Bobby Orr and Bobby Clarke grace the walls; then be sure to catch the exhibits, including the evolution of skates, uniforms, and sticks, a goalie mask collection, and a replica dressing room. Flick a few pucks or test your goal-tending on the interactive video games. (Open Mon.-Sat. 9am-6pm, Sun. 10am-6pm. $8.75, seniors and children $5.75. Wheelchair accessible.)

The **Holocaust Education and Memorial Center of Toronto,** 4600 Bathurst St. (635-2283), on the Bathurst bus route near the Joseph Latimer Library, runs a museum and two audio-visual presentations portraying the lives of Jews in Europe before, during, and after WWII. The collection soberly commemorates the six million Jews murdered by Germany's Nazi regime. (Open daily 9am-4pm. Free.) Toronto offers several smaller museums as well. Visit the **Marine Museum of Upper Canada,** Exhibition Place (392-1765; open Tues.-Fri. 10am-5pm, Sat.-Sun. noon-5pm; $3.50, students and seniors $2.75, children $2.50), the **Museum for Textiles,** 55 Center Ave. (599-5515), 1 block east of the University (open Tues. and Thurs.-Fri. 11am-5pm, Wed. 11am-8pm, Sat.-Sun. noon-5pm), or the **Redpath Sugar Museum,** 95 Queens Quay E. (366-3561; open Mon.-Fri. 10am-1pm and 2-3pm; free. Subway: Union, then take the #6 Bay bus to the Toronto Star Building).

The **Upper Canada Brewing Company,** 2 Atlantic Ave. (534-9281; Subway: King or St. Andrews, then take the King streetcar west to Atlantic and Jefferson), gives free tours and tastings. (Tours Mon.-Sat. 1, 3, and 5:30pm, Sun. 1 and 3pm; reservations required. Open Mon.-Sat. 10am-8pm, Sun. 10am-6pm.)

Toronto crawls with **biking** and **hiking** trails. For a map of the trails, write the **Metro Parks and Property Department,** 55 John St., 24th Floor, station 1240, M5V 3C6 or call 392-8186. Call the **Parks and Recreation Department** at 392-1111 for info on local facilities and activities (open Mon.-Fri. 8:30am-4:30pm). It might not be the Caribbean, but the **beaches** on the southeast end of Toronto now support a permanent community in what was once a summer resort. The **Toronto Islands Park** is a 4-mi. strip of connected islands just opposite downtown. A popular "vacation-land," they have a boardwalk, bathing beaches, canoe and bike rentals, a Frisbee golf course, and an amusement park. Ferries leave from the Bay Street Ferry Dock at Bay St. (15-min. ferry trip; 392-8193 for ferry info, see Practical Information).

The **Ontario Science Center,** 770 Don Mills Rd. (696-3127), at Eglington Ave. E., presents more than 650 interactive exhibits, showcasing man's greatest innovations; an Omnimax theater will open summer 1996. Though farther from downtown than most sights, the center is still within the range of public transportation; call for directions. (Open Sat.-Thurs. 10am-6pm, Fri. 10am-9pm. $7.50, youths 11-17 $5.50, seniors and children $3.) The **Metro Toronto Zoo** (392-5900), Meadowvale Rd. off exit 389 on Hwy. 401N, houses over 6400 animals in a 710-acre park containing sections representing the world's seven geographic regions. (Open late May-late June 9am-7pm, late June-Labor Day 9am-7:30pm; call for off season hours. Last entry 1hr. before closing. $9.95, seniors and ages 12-17 $7, ages 4-11 $5; parking $5.)

ENTERTAINMENT

The monthly *Where Toronto,* available free at tourism booths, gives a good arts and entertainment run-down. Before you buy tickets, give a call to **T.O. Tix** (596-8211), which sells ½-price tickets for theater, music, dance, and opera on performance day. Their booth at Dundas and Yonge in front of Eaton Centre (Subway: Dundas) opens at noon; arrive before 11:45am for first dibs. (Open Tues.-Sat. noon-7:30pm, Sun. 11am-3pm.) Eddie Vedder's nemesis **Ticketmaster** (870-8000) also supplies tickets for many Toronto venues, but don't expect a discount price.

Ontario Place, 955 Lakeshore Blvd. W. (314-9811, 314-9900 for a recording), features cheap entertainment in the summer. Top pop artists like R.E.M. perform here in the new **Molson Amphitheatre** (260-5600); Ticketmaster handles tickets. ($17.50-50. Park open mid-May to early Sept. daily 10:30am-midnight. Call for events schedule.) Be ready to crane your neck for the IMAX movies of the six-story **Cinesphere** (870-8000; $6-9, seniors and kids $3-6; call for screening schedule).

Roy Thomson Hall, 60 Simcoe St. (872-4255; subway: St. Andrews), at King St. W., is both Toronto's premier concert hall and the home of the **Toronto Symphony Orchestra** (593-4828). Buy tickets ($19-50) at the box office or by phone. (Mon.-Fri. noon-6pm; off season Mon.-Fri. 8:45am-8pm, Sat. noon-5pm; year-round Sun. 2hr. before performances. Ask about discounts.) Rush tickets for the symphony ($10) are available at the box office on concert days (Mon.-Fri. 11am, Sat. 1pm). The same ticket office serves **Massey Hall,** 178 Victoria St. (593-4828; Subway: Dundas), near Eaton Centre, a great hall for rock and folk concerts and musicals. The opera and ballet companies perform at **O'Keefe Centre,** 1 Front St. E. (393-7469 or 872-2262; ballet from $55, opera from $27), at Yonge. Rush tickets for the last row of orchestra seats go on sale at 11am (from $10); a limited number of ½-price tickets are available for seniors and students. Seats at student dress rehearsals for selected shows go for $12. (Box office open Mon.-Sat. 11am-6pm, or until 1hr. after curtain.) Next door, **St. Lawrence Centre,** 27 Front St. E. (366-7723), stages excellent drama and chamber music recitals in two different theaters. Ask for possible student and senior discounts. (Box office open Mon.-Sat. 10am-6pm; in winter Mon.-Fri. 10am-8pm.) **Canadian Stage** (367-8243) puts up superb performances of summer Shakespeare amid the greenery of **High Park,** on Bloor St. W. at Parkside Dr. (Subway: High Park). Year-round performances include new Canadian works and time-honored classics. Bring something to sit on or perch yourself on the 45° slope which faces the stage. ($5 donation requested. Call for schedule.)

Film fans looking for good classic and contemporary cinema choose the **Bloor Cinema,** 506 Bloor St. W. (532-6677), at Bathurst, or the **Cinématheque Ontario,** 317 Dundas St. W. (923-3456), at McCaul St. Fans of Asian film should check out the **Golden Classics Cinema,** 186 Spadina Ave. (504-0585), for retrospectives.

Shinier, happier activities await at **Canada's Wonderland,** 9580 Jane St. (832-7000), about one hour from downtown but accessible by public transportation, Canada's answer to Disneyland. Splash down the water rides or try your stomach on the backwards, looping, and suspended roller coasters. (Open late June-Labor Day daily 10am-10pm; open in fall Sat.-Sun. and in May daily, but closing times vary. $33.50, seniors and ages 3-6 $16.50.)

Groove to the rhythms of old and new talents—in all, more than 1500 artists from 17 countries—at the ten-day **du Maurier Ltd. Downtown Jazz Festival** (363-5200), at Ontario Place in late June. Also in June, the **Toronto International Dragon Boat**

Race Festival (364-0046) continues a 2000-year-old Chinese tradition. The race finishes at Toronto's Center Island; the celebration includes traditional performances, foods, and free lunchtime and outdoor concerts. From mid-August through Labor Day, the **Canadian National Exhibition (CNE)** (393-6050), the world's largest annual fair, brings a country carnival atmosphere to Ontario Place. (Open daily 10am-midnight. $9.50, seniors $4.50, children $3; call for info on discount days.)

From April to October, the **Toronto Blue Jays** (341-1111, 341-1234 for tickets) play ball at the **Sky Dome,** Front and Peter St. (Subway: Union, follow the signs). Most games sell out, but the box office usually has some obstructed view seats before the game. (Tickets $6-23.) Scalpers sell tickets for far beyond face value; latecomers wait until the game starts and then haggle like mad. To get a behind-the-scenes look at the modern, commercialized Sky Dome, take the tour (341-2770; Mon.-Fri. 10am-6pm, Sept.-June Mon.-Fri. 10am-4pm, event schedule permitting; $9, seniors and under 16 $6). For information on concerts and other Sky Dome events, call 341-3663. Hockey fans should head for **Maple Leaf Gardens,** 60 Carlton St. (977-1641; Subway: College), to see the knuckle-crackin', puck-smackin' **Maple Leafs.** Tours of the gardens leave daily at 11am, 1, 2:30, and 4pm. Tickets required. Call for details.

NIGHTLIFE

Some of Toronto's clubs and pubs remain closed on Sundays because of liquor laws. The city shuts down alcohol distribution at 1am, so most clubs close down then. Some more formal clubs even maintain a dress code. The most interesting new clubs are on trendy **Queen St. W., College St. W.,** and **Bloor St. W.** The gay scene centers around **Wellesley** and **Church St.** Two comprehensive free entertainment magazines, *Now* and *Eye,* come out every Thursday.

Brunswick House, 481 Bloor St. W. (964-2242), between the Bathurst and Spadina subway stops. Reeling with students. Beer hall atmosphere, with long benches and little round tables. Beer $2.95—ouch! Thurs. means $5.50 pitchers; Fri. $1.50 domestic bottles. Open Mon.-Sat. noon-1am.

Lee's Palace, 529 Bloor St. W. (532-7383), just east of the Bathurst subway stop. Crazy creature art depicts a rock'n'roll frenzy. Live music nightly downstairs; DJ dance club, the **Dance Cave,** upstairs. Pick up a calendar of bands. Box office opens 8pm, shows begin 10pm. Downstairs open daily noon-1am; cover $3-12. Upstairs open Tues. and Thurs.-Sat. 8pm-3am; cover after 10pm $4.

The Madison, 14 Madison Ave. (927-1722), at Bloor. Subway: Spadina. Blonde wood, 2 patios, 4 floors, 17 beers on tap. Victorian interior. Pints $4.60. Giant nachos $7.45. Open 365 days a year; Mon.-Sat. 11am-1am, Sun. noon-1am.

Second City, 110 Lombard St. (863-1111), in The Old Firehall at Jarvis St., 2 blocks east and 2 short blocks south of Queen's Park subway stop. One of North America's wackiest, most creative comedy clubs. Spawned comics Dan Akroyd, John Candy, Gilda Radner, Martin Short, a hit TV show (SCTV), and the legendary "Great White North." Free improv sessions Mon.-Thurs. 10:15pm. Mon.-Thurs. dinner 6pm, show 8:30pm; Fri.-Sat. dinner 5 and 8:30pm, shows 8 and 11pm. Dinner and theater from $33, students $30. Theater only $13-20/$10; first come, first served behind the dinner tables. Sun. "best of" 8pm $11. Reservations required.

Sneaky Dee's, 431 College St. W. (368-3090 or 603-1824), at Bathurst. A hip Toronto hotspot tapping the most inexpensive brew (60oz. pitcher of Ontario microbrewery draught $8.50). Mon.-Fri. before 6pm, domestic beer goes for $2.50 per bottle. Pool tables in back. DJ and dancing upstairs daily 9:30pm. Open Mon.-Fri. 4pm-1am, Sat.-Sun. noon-1am.

College St. Bar, 574 College St. W. (533-2417), with its brick interior, has a mellow atmosphere. Live music; Wed. night jazz and Sun. night blues/funk pack the place (10:30pm both nights). Mostly Italian food; dinner entrees $8-10. Open Mon.-Fri. noon-1am, Sat. 4pm-1am, Sun. 11:30am-1am.

Bistro 422, 422 College St. W. (963-9416). A small (often cramped) downstairs bar catering to the Doc Martens crowd. Typical bar food, with daily specials $4.99. Open daily 4pm-1am.

Woody's/Sailor, 465-467 Church St. (972-0887), by Maitland. *The* established gay bar in the Church and Wellesley area. Neighborhood atmosphere; walls are lined with art nudes and photos of locals. Come to relax and hang out before heading to the clubs, but don't miss the raunchy weekend Mr. Woody (and now Miss Woody) contests. Bottled beer $2.75 before 4pm, $4 after. Open daily noon-2am.

Aztec, 2 Gloucester St. (975-8612), at Yonge. Subway: Wellesley or Bloor/Yonge. Toronto's premier gay dance club offers disco music beneath two huge bronze suns for a mixed crowd of men and women. Thurs.-Sun. 9pm-1am cover $5. **Tango,** the women's club downstairs, has pool tournaments, live performances, and a cozier bar atmosphere. Drinks in either bar run $2.50-$5.

■ NEAR TORONTO

As beautiful as its name is strange, **Onation's Niagara Escarpment** passes west of Toronto as it winds its way from Niagara Falls to Tobermory at the tip of the Bruce Peninsula. Along this rocky 724-km ridge, the **Bruce Trail** snakes through parks and private land; hikers are treated to spectacular waterfalls, the breathtaking cliffs along **Georgian Bay,** and unique flora and fauna, including an old growth forest. Because the escarpment is registered as a UN world biosphere reserve, future land development is limited to that which can exist symbiotically with the natural environment. For maps and Escarpment info, write or call the **Niagara Escarpment Commission,** 232 Guelph St., Georgetown L7G 4B1 (905-877-5191). Specifics on the Bruce Trail can be obtained by contacting the **Bruce Trail Association,** P.O. Box 857, Hamilton L8N 3N9 (905-529-6821). The area is unreachable by public transportation, but **The Canadian Experience** (368-1848 or 800-668-4487) organizes phenomenal escapes into the Ontarian countryside. Guides Kellie and Larry Casey Shaw, an Olympic skier and a former pro-hockey player respectively, take small groups on a 2½-day journey along the Bruce Trail and the Escarpment, with stops at Niagara Falls, Elora (home of limestone Elora Gorge), Sante Marie (a native Huron settlement), St. Jacobs (a Mennonite community), and Wasaga Beach (the world's largest freshwater beach). The price of $195 per person includes all food and transportation (including pick-up and drop-off at the Toronto International Hostel), along with a two-night stay at their 70-acre farm. (2 trips per week: Mon. 8am-Wed. 2pm, and Wed. 2pm-Fri. 8pm. 1-night trip $65. Bookings must be made by 10pm the night before through Toronto International Hostel; see Accommodations above.)

■■■ STRATFORD

Filling the coffers since 1953, the **Stratford Shakespeare Festival** has proven to be the lifeblood of this picturesque town. Stratford-born scribe Tom Patterson founded the festival, which opened its inaugural season with Sir Alec Guiness in the title role of *Richard III.* Since then, the town and the festival have become inextricably intertwined. The **Shakespeare Festival** runs from May, when previews begin, through late October. In the very midsummer madness (July-Aug.), up to six different shows play per day (none on Mon.). Matinees begin at 2pm and evening performances at 8pm in each of three theaters: the crown-shaped **Festival Theatre,** the **Avon Theatre,** once a vaudeville house, and the intimate **Tom Patterson Theatre.** Complete information about casts, performances, and other aspects of the Festival can be obtained by phone (363-4471 free from Toronto, 800-567-1600 from elsewhere) or by writing the **Stratford Festival,** P.O. Box 520, Stratford N5A 6V2. Tickets are expensive ($30-60), but a few good deals lower the stakes. For every performance, a number of **rush tickets** are sold at 9am on the morning of the show at the Festival Theatre Box Office, or ½ hour before the show by phone or at the appropriate theater ($15-40). Seniors and students enjoy discounts at certain designated mid-week matinee performances ($16.75-20). However, students can also purchase $20 tickets two weeks prior to any performance for any day except Saturday. During previews, seniors can claim unsold seats for $20. Tickets to some theater performances go for ½-price on Tuesdays. (Box office open Mon.-Sat. 9am-8pm, Sun. 9am-5pm.)

When you've had it with the Bard, look for free **Jazz on the River** (mid-June to early Sept. Mon.-Fri. 6:30-8pm), or stretch your legs on the **Avon Trail,** which crosses Stratford at the T.J. Dolan Natural Area, near the intersection of John and Centre St.

The **Tourism Stratford Information Center,** 30 York St. (273-3352 or 800-561-7926), on the river, will send a free visitors guide if you call ahead, and they're just as willing to help walk-ins (open Mon.-Sat. 9am-8pm, Sun. 9am-5pm). Stratford's **post office:** 34 Wellington St. (271-5712; open Mon.-Thurs and Sat. 9am-5:30pm, Fri. 9am-8pm), in Blowes Stationary; **postal code:** N5A 7M3; **area code:** 519.

The **Festival Accommodations Bureau** (273-1600) can tell you where to go when now spurs the lated traveler apace to gain the timely inn, guest home ($31-45), or B&B ($50-120). The **Burnside Guest Home,** 139 William St., Stratford N5A 4X9 (271-7076), is the budget traveler's best bet for lodging and a view of Lake Victoria. The room charge includes a hearty breakfast. (B&B rooms $40-60; student rooms $25. Reserve in advance.) Campsites at the **Wildwood Conservation Area** (519-284-2292), on Hwy. 7, 11km SW of Stratford, may have a few bugs, but they also have access to a beach, a pool, and a marina. The area can get a little cramped; trailers often outnumber tents 30 to one. (430 sites. $17, with hook-up $21.50.)

To get to Stratford, take **VIA Rail** (273-3234 or 800-361-1235) or **Cha-Co Trails** (271-7870), a bus company owned by Greyhound; both operate out of a depot on Shakespeare St. Service to Toronto (2hr., $25), London (1hr., $12), or Kitchener (½hr., $10) costs the same and takes an equal amount of time by train or bus.

■■■ OTTAWA

Legend has it that Queen Victoria chose this capital for Canada by closing her eyes and poking her finger at a map. But perhaps political savvy and not blind chance guided the Queen to this once-remote logging town, which, as a stronghold for neither French nor English interests, became a perfect compromise capital. Today, faced with the increasingly tricky task of forging national unity while preserving local identities, Ottawa continues to play cultural ambassador to its own country.

At the turn of the century, then-Prime Minister Sir Wilfred Laurier called on urban planners to polish Ottawa into a "Washington of the North." The carefully groomed and cultured façade which resulted has contributed to Ottawa's reputation for being somewhat boring; an evening stroll through Byward Market will challenge this notion. Rest assured that, behind the theaters, museums and parks, there is plenty of action both before and after quitting time in the capital.

PRACTICAL INFORMATION

Tourist Office: National Capital Commission Information Center, 14 Metcalfe St. (239-5000 or 800-465-1867 in Canada), at Wellington opposite the Parliament Buildings. Open daily 8:30am-9pm; early Sept.-early May Mon.-Sat. 9am-5pm, Sun. 10am-4pm. **Ottawa Tourism and Convention Authority Visitor Information Centre,** National Arts Centre, 65 Elgin St. (237-5158). Open daily 9am-9pm; early Sept.-April Mon.-Sat. 9am-5pm, Sun. 10am-4pm. Both provide free maps and the helpful *Ottawa Visitors Guide.* Free 30-min. parking in the Arts Centre lot with ticket validation. For info on Hull and Québec province, contact the **Association Touristique de l'Outaouais,** 103 rue Laurier, Hull (819-778-2222), at rue St. Laurent. Open mid-June to Sept. Mon.-Fri. 8:30am-8pm, Sat.-Sun. 9am-5pm; off season Mon.-Fri. 8:30am-5pm, Sat.-Sun. 8:30am-4pm. **Gayline-Telegai,** 238-1717. Info on local bars and special events. Open daily 7-10pm.

Police: Ontario Provincial Police, 592-4878; infoline 800-267-2677. **Ottawa Police,** 230-6211; infoline 236-0311.

Student Travel Agencies: Travel CUTS, 1 Stewart St., #203 (238-8222), at Waller, just east of Nicholas 2 blocks north of the Université d'Ottawa; also on the 1st level of the Unicentre, Carleton Univ. (238-5493). Experts in student travel, youth hostel cards, cheap flights, and VIA Rail. Open Mon. and Wed.-Fri. 9am-5pm, Tues. 9am-4pm. **Hosteling International-Canada (HI-C), Ontario East**

Region, 18 Byward Market (569-1400). Youth hostel passes, travel info, and equipment. Open Mon.-Fri. 9:30am-5:30pm, Sat. 9:30am-5pm (see Hostels, p. 39).

Embassies: U.S., 100 Wellington St. (238-5335), directly across from Parliament. Open daily 8:30am-5pm. **U.K.,** 80 Elgin St. (237-1530), at the corner of Queen St. Open Mon.-Fri. 9am-5pm. **Australia,** 50 O'Connor St., #710 (236-0841), at Queen St. Open for visas and info Mon.-Fri. 9am-noon and 2-4pm. **New Zealand,** 99 Bank St., #727 (238-5991). Open Mon.-Fri. 8:30am-4:30pm. **Ireland,** 170 Metcalfe St. (233-6281). Open Mon.-Fri. 10am-1pm and 2:30-4pm. **France,** 42 Sussex Dr. (789-1795). Open for information Mon.-Fri. 9:30am-1:30pm.

American Express: 220 Laurier W. (563-0231), between Metcalfe and O'Connor in the heart of the business district. Open Mon.-Fri. 8:30am-5pm.

Airport: Ottawa International (998-3151), 20min. south of the city off Bronson Ave. Take bus 96 from the MacKenzie King Bridge. **Tourist info** available daily 9am-9pm in arrival area. Express airport **Pars Transport** (736-6689) buses between the airport and 11 hotels, including Lord Elgin Hotel, 100 Elgin Blvd., at Slater and Hotel Novotel, 1 block north of Ottawa Int'l Hostel; call for pick-up from 14 other hotels. Daily every ½hr. 5am-midnight; call for later pick-up and schedule specifics. Fare $9, ages 7-12 $5, under 7 free, seniors 10% off.

Trains: VIA Rail, 200 Tremblay Rd. (244-8289 or 800-561-3949), off Alta Vista Rd. To: Montréal (4 per day, 2hr., $36, student $32); Toronto (4 per day, 4hr., $76/68); Québec City via Montréal (3 per day, 7hr., $66/59). Ticket office open Mon.-Fri. 5am-9pm, Sat. 6:30am-9pm, Sun. 8:30am-9pm.

Buses: Voyageur, 265 Catherine St. (238-5900), between Kent and Lyon. Service throughout Canada. To: Montréal (on the hr. 6am-10pm, 2½hr., $25); Toronto (7 per day, 4½hr., $55); Québec City (13 per day, 6hr., $59). For service to the U.S. you must first go to Montréal or Toronto; connections made through Greyhound. Open daily 5am-midnight. Purchase tickets at station or Ottawa Int'l Hostel.

Public Transportation: OC Transport, 1500 St. Laurent (741-4390). Excellent bus system. Buses congregate on either side of Rideau Centre. $1.60; peak hours (Mon.-Fri. 3-5:30pm) $2.10; express routes (green buses) $2.70; seniors $1.60, under 5 free. For info on the blue **Hull City Buses,** call 819-770-3242.

Taxis: Blue Line Taxi, 238-1111. $2 base fare, $1.90 per km. 24 hrs.

Driver/Rider Service: Allostop, 238 Dalhousie (562-8248), at St. Patrick. To: Toronto ($24), Québec City ($29), Montréal ($10), and New York City ($50). Membership ($6 yearly, drivers $7) required. Open Mon.-Wed. 9am-5pm, Thurs.-Fri. 9am-7pm, Sat.-Sun. 10am-5pm. There is also an active **rideboard** on the 2nd floor of the University of Ottawa's University center.

Bike Rental: Rent-A-Bike-Vélocationo, 1 Rideau St. (241-4140), behind the Château Laurier Hotel. $7 per hr., $16 per day. Tandems $15 per hr., $50 per day. Maps, locks, helmets free. 2-hr. escorted tours $10. In-line skates $12 for 2hr., $25 per day. Family deals available. Open mid-May to Oct. daily 9am-7:30pm. Credit card required. All new roads in Ottawa are required to have a bicycle lane.

Crisis Lines: Ottawa Distress Centre, 238-3311, English-speaking. **Tel-Aide,** 741-6433, French-speaking. **Rape Crisis Centre,** 729-8889. All 3 open 24 hrs. **Gayline-Telegai,** 238-1717, for counseling. Open daily 7-10pm.

Emergency: 911.

Post Office: Postal Station "B," 59 Sparks St. (844-1545), at Elgin St. Open Mon.-Fri. 8am-6pm. **Postal code:** K1P 5A0. **Area code:** 613 (Ottawa); 819 (Hull).

ORIENTATION

Rideau Canal divides Ottawa into the eastern lower town and the western upper town. West of the canal, Parliament buildings and government offices line **Wellington St.,** one of the city's main east-west arteries, which runs directly into the heart of downtown and crosses the canal. **Laurier** is the only other east-west street which permits traffic from one side of the canal to the other. East of the canal, Wellington St. becomes **Rideau St.,** surrounded by a fashionable shopping district. North of Rideau St. lies the **Byward Market,** a shopping area which hosts a summertime open-air market and much of Ottawa's nightlife. **Elgin St.,** a primary north-south artery, stretches from the **Queensway** (Hwy. 417) to the War Memorial just south of Wellington in front of **Parliament Hill. Bank St.,** parallel to Elgin three blocks to the east, services the town's older shopping area. The canal itself is a major access route: in winter, thousands of Ottawans skate to work on this, the world's longest skating rink; in summer, power boats breeze by regularly. Bike paths and pedestrian walkways also line the canals. Parking is painful downtown; meters often cost 25¢ for 10 min. Residential neighborhoods east of the canal have longer limits and the police ticket less often than on main streets.

Hull, Québec, across the Ottawa River, is most notable for its less strict drinking laws and 18 year old drinking age. Many bars and clubs rock nightly until 3am. Close to Gatineau Provincial Park, Hull connects to Ottawa by several bridges and the blue Hull buses from downtown Ottawa (see Practical Information).

ACCOMMODATIONS AND CAMPING

Clean, inexpensive rooms and campsites are not difficult to find in Ottawa except during May and early June, when student groups and conventioneers come to claim their long-reserved rooms, and during the peak of the tourist season in July and August. A complete list of B&Bs can be found in the *Ottawa Visitors Guide;* **Ottawa Bed and Breakfast** (563-0161), represents ten B&Bs in the Ottawa area and a way to find an affordable room (singles $45, doubles $55).

Ottawa International Hostel (HI-C), 75 Nicholas St., K1N 7B9 (235-2595), in downtown Ottawa. The site of Canada's last public hanging, this trippy hostel now "incarcerates" travelers in the cells of the former Carleton County Jail. Rooms contain 4-8 bunks and minimal storage space. Communal showers (hot only in the thermal sense), kitchen, laundry facilities, large and comfortable lounges, and a cast of friendly, personable regulars. Centrally located, funky international crowd, many organized activities (biking, canoeing, tours). IBN reservations available. 153 beds. Doors locked 2-7am. $14, nonmembers $18.

University of Ottawa Residences, 100 University St. (564-5400), in the center of campus directly across from the University Center, an easy walk from downtown. From the bus station, take bus #1, 7, or 11 on Bank St. to Rideau Centre and walk up Nicholas to the U of O campus. From the train station, catch bus #95 west. Clean dorm rooms in a concrete jungle. Hall showers. Free local hall phone. Access to University Center (with bank machines). Check-in 4:30pm; they'll store luggage until then. Singles $36, doubles $44; students with ID $21.50/$39. Continental breakfast $2. Free linen, towels. Open early May-late Aug.

YMCA/YWCA, 180 Argyle St. (237-1320), at O'Connor. Close to the bus station; walk left on Bank and right on Argyle. Nice-sized (though unattractively decorated) rooms in a modern high-rise. Free local phones in every room. Kitchen with microwave available until midnight. Guests can use gym facilities. Front desk open Mon.-Thurs. 7am-midnight, Fri.-Sat. 24 hrs. Singles with shared bath $42, with private bath $48.50, doubles $49. Weekly and group rates available. Payment must be made in advance. Cafeteria open daily 7am-2:30pm; breakfast $4. Indoor parking evenings 4:30pm-8:30am $2.75; day parking available.

Centre Town Guest House Ltd., 502 Kent St. (233-0681), just north of the bus station, a 10- to 15-min. walk from downtown. Clean rooms in an aging but comfortable house. Free breakfast (eggs, cereal, bacon, toast) in a cozy dining room. Singles from $25, doubles from $35, 2 twin beds $50. Monthly rates from $400. Reservations recommended. Parking available.

Camp Le Breton (943-0467), at the corner of Fleet and Booth. Urban tent-only camping within sight of Parliament, a 10-min. walk from downtown. Washrooms, showers, free wood. 5-day max. stay. Check-in 24 hrs. Sites $7.50 per person, seniors $3.75, under 12 free. No reservations—they'll squeeze you in.

Gatineau Park (456-3016 for reservations; 827-2020 for info), northwest of Hull, has three rustic campgrounds within 45min. of Ottawa: **Lac Philippe Campground,** 248 sites with facilities for family camping, trailers, and campers; **Lac Taylor Campground,** with 34 "semi-wilderness" sites; and **Lac la Pêche,** with 36 campsites accessible only by canoe. Camping permits for Taylor and Philippe ($16, seniors $8) are available at the entrance to the campground. Pay for a site at La Pêche ($13) on Eardley Rd. All sites available mid.-May to mid.-Oct. All the campgrounds are off Hwy. 366 northwest of Hull; watch for signs; map available at visitors center (open daily 9am-6pm; in winter Sat.-Sun. 9am-6pm). From Ottawa, take the Cartier-MacDonald Bridge, follow Autoroute 5 north to Scott Rd., turn right onto Hwy. 105 and follow it to 366. To reach La Pêche continue on Hwy. 366 to Eardley Rd. on your left.

FOOD

Fans of the cholesterol-rich breakfast find friends in Ottawa; the ubiquitous greasy spoon scene revolves around the worship of eggs, potatoes, meat, toast, and coffee. **Copacabano,** 380 Dalhousie St. (241-9762), offers a particularly artery-wrenching rendition of this stand-by: homefries, 3 pieces of bacon, ham, 2 eggs, toast, and coffee with refills ($2.35; open 24 hrs.). During the summer, occasional street music surrounds the fresh fruit, vegetables, and flowers of the lively open-air **Byward Market,** on Byward St. between York and Rideau St. (open daily 8am-6pm). After eating, relax and linger at the Dutch **Café Wim,** 537 Sussex Dr. (241-1771), which serves sumptuous Colombian brown coffee ($1.45) and decadent desserts ($2-6; open daily 9:30am-1am). To satisfy your sweet tooth, choose from 40 types of homemade Italian gelati at **Belmondo,** 381 Dalhousie St. (746-2983). **Dunn's,** 126 George St. (562-3866), a popular 24-hour deli provides even later nourishment for the after-clubbing crowd (deli fare $3.50-9).

Sunset Grill, 47 Clarence St. (241-9497). Sit on the huge outdoor terrace and grapple with an infamously large club sandwich ($8). Bright, lively colors and a perky staff melt the worries away. Open Sun.-Mon. 11am-11pm, Tues.-Sat. 11am-1am.

Las Palmas, 111 Parent Ave. (241-3738). Outstanding Mexican grub heaped high. Bring a garden hose—when they say hot, they mean *hot*. Dinners $7-13. Open Mon.-Thurs. and Sat. 11:30am-10:30pm, Fri. 11:30am-midnight.

Royal Star, 99 Rideau St. (562-2772), in the Byward Market Mall (entrance at 96 George St.). Killer lunch buffet ($7.25) with over 100 selections of Szechuan, Cantonese, Polynesian, and Canadian favorites. Open for lunch Mon.-Fri. 11am-3pm.

Mamma Grazzi's Kitchen, 25 George St. (241-8656). Quiet, intimate quarters bathed in the aroma of Italian specialties and thin-crust pizza ($7-9). Be patient; it's worth the wait. Open Mon.-Fri. 11:30am-10pm, Sat.-Sun. 11am-10pm.

The International Cheese and Deli, 40 Byward St. (241-5411). Deli and Middle Eastern sandwiches to go. Vegetable *samosa* $1.25; turkey and cheese $4; falafel on pita $2.30. Open Sat.-Thurs. 8am-6pm, Fri. 8am-8pm.

Father and Sons, 112 Osgoode St. (233-6066), at the eastern edge of the U of O campus. Student favorite for a menu of tavern-style food with some Lebanese dishes thrown in. Try the falafel platter ($6.50) or a triple-decker sandwich ($6.50). Spicy specials daily 8-11pm; Mon. after 7pm and Sat. all day 15¢ wings. Open Mon.-Fri. 7am-1am, Sat.-Sun. 8am-1am. Kitchen open until midnight.

SIGHTS

Although overshadowed by Toronto's size and Montréal's cosmopolitan color, Ottawa's status as capital of Canada is shored up by its cultural attractions. Since the national museums and political action pack tightly together, most sights can be reached on foot. **Parliament Hill,** on Wellington St. at Metcalfe, towers over downtown as the city's focal point, set apart by its Gothic architecture. Warm your hands and your heart over the **Centennial Flame** at the south gate, lit in 1967 to mark the 100th anniversary of the Dominion of Canada's inaugural session of Parliament. The Prime Minister can occasionally be spotted at the central parliament structure, **Centre Block,** which contains the House of Commons, the Senate, and the Library of Parliament. On display behind the library, the original bell from Centre Block is the only part of the original 1859-66 structure to survive the 1916 fire; according to legend, the bell crashed to the ground after chiming at midnight on the night of the fire. The carillon of 53 bells that replaced the old bell hangs in the **Peace Tower.** The bells range from ½ ounce to several tons; the tower is currently under renovation, and the bells hang mute. Free, worthwhile tours of Centre Block (in English or

French) depart every 30 minutes from the white **Infotent** in front of the visitor's center. (Group reservations, 996-0896. Public information, 992-4793. Open Mon.-Fri. 9am-8:30pm, Sat.-Sun. 9am-5:30pm; early Sept. to mid-May daily 9am-4:30pm. Last tour begins 40min. before closing time.) When Parliament is in session, you can watch Canada's Prime Minister and his government squirm on the verbal hot seat during the official **Question Period** in the **House of Commons** chamber (Mon.-Thurs. 2:15-3pm, Fri. 11:15am-noon). Those interested in trying to make a number of statuesque soldiers giggle should attend the **Changing of the Guard** (993-1811), on the broad lawns in front of Centre Block (late June-late Aug. daily 10am, weather permitting). At dusk, Centre Block and its lawns transform into the set for *Sound and Light,* which relates the history of the Parliament Buildings and the development of the nation (mid-May to July 9:30 and 10:30pm, Aug.-early Sept. 9 and 10pm; performances alternate between French and English). A five-minute walk west along Wellington St., the nine judges of the **Supreme Court of Canada** (995-5361) share a building with the Federal Court (free 30-min. tours every ½hr; open daily 9am-5pm; Sept.-April hours vary).

One block south of Wellington, the recently renovated **Sparks Street Mall,** hailed as an innovative experiment in 1960 when it was one of North America's first pedestrian malls, now houses many of Ottawa's banks and upscale retail stores. The **Rideau Centre,** south of Rideau St. at Sussex Dr., is the city's primary shopping mall as well as one of the main OC Transport stations. Glass encloses the sidewalks in front of Rideau Street's stores to make them bearable during the winter months.

East of the Parliament Buildings at the junction of Sparks, Wellington, and Elgin stands **Confederation Sq.** with its enormous **National War Memorial,** dedicated by King George VI in 1939. The towering structure symbolizes the triumph of peace over war, an ironic message on the eve of World War II. **Nepean Point,** several blocks northwest of Rideau Centre and the Byward Market behind the National Gallery of Canada, provides a panoramic view of the capital.

The Governor-General, the Queen's representative in Canada, resides at **Rideau Hall** (998-7113). Free tours leave from the main gate at One Sussex Dr. (998-7114; 800-465-6890 for tour info). Dress up nicely for the open house on New Year's Day or Canada Day and they'll even let you see the interior. Gawk from afar at nearby **24 Sussex Dr.,** the Prime Minister's residence.

Ottawa's reputation for respecting cultural difference extends beyond the conflict between French and English. Many nationalities integrate well here, leaving ethnically-grouped neighborhoods somewhat sparse. There is a small **Chinatown** clustered around Somerset St. between Kent St. and Bronson Ave. From downtown, walk south on Elgin St. until you reach Somerset; go west on Somerset until fruit stands line the streets and signs change from French and English to Chinese and English (about a 20min. walk). **Little Italy** is just around the corner on Bronson Ave., stretching south from Somerset to the Queensway (Hwy. 417).

Museums and Parks

Ottawa contains many of Canada's huge national museums. Most are wheelchair accessible; call for details. **The National Gallery,** 380 Sussex Dr. (990-1985), a spectacular glass-towered building adjacent to Nepean Point, holds the world's most comprehensive collection of Canadian art as well as outstanding European, American, and Asian works. The building's exterior is a parody of the neo-Gothic buttresses of the facing Library of Parliament. (Open Wed.-Mon. 10am-6pm, Tues. 10am-8pm; Oct.-May. Wed.-Sun. 10am-5pm, Tues. 10am-8pm. Permanent collection free; special events $8, students and under 18 free, seniors $5.) The **Canadian Museum of Contemporary Photography,** 1 Rideau Canal (990-8257), between the Chateau Laurier and the Ottawa Locks, allows a frozen glimpse of modern Canadian life. (Open Fri.-Tues. 11am-5pm, Wed. 4-8pm, Thurs. 11am-8pm; mid-Oct. to April Wed.-Thurs. 11am-8pm, Fri.-Sun. 11am-5pm. Free.)

A sand-dune-like structure across the river in Hull houses the **Canadian Museum of Civilization,** 100 Laurier St. (776-7000). Admire the architecture but be wary of overly ambitious exhibits that attempt to put perspective on 1000 years of Canadian history. Don't miss the breathtaking films shown in **CINEPLUS** (776-7010 for show-times), capable of projecting both IMAX and OmniMax. (Open Sat.-Wed. 9am-6pm, Thurs.-Fri. 9am-9pm; Sept.-late June Tues.-Sun. 9am-5pm, Thurs. 9am-8pm. Museum $5, seniors and ages 13-17 $3, under 13 free; free Sun. 9am-noon. CINEPLUS $7, students and seniors $5.) The **Canadian Museum of Nature,** 240 McLeod St. (996-3102), at Metcalf, explores the natural world from dinosaur skeletons to minerals through multi-media displays. (Open Fri.-Wed. 9:30am-5pm, Thurs. 9:30am-8pm; Oct.-April Fri.-Wed. 10am-5pm, Thurs. 10am-8pm. $4, students $3, seniors and ages 6-16 $2, under 6 free; Thurs. ½-price until 5pm, free 5-8pm.)

Canadian history buffs could easily lose themselves in the **National Library Archives,** 395 Wellington St. (995-5138), at Bay St., which houses oodles of Canadian publications, old maps, photographs, letters, and historical exhibits (open daily 9am-9pm). Liberal Prime Minister William Lyon Mackenzie King governed Canada from the elegant **Laurier House,** 335 Laurier Ave. E. (992-8142), for most of his lengthy tenure. Admire at your leisure the antiques King accumulated, as well as the crystal ball he used to consult his long-dead mother on matters of national importance. (Open Tues.-Sat. 9am-5pm, Sun. 2-5pm; call for hours Oct.-March. Free.)

Farther out of town, the **National Museum of Science and Technology,** 1867 St. Laurent Blvd. (991-3044), at Smyth, lets visitors explore the developing world of tech and transport with touchy-feely exhibits. The museum entrance is on Lancaster, 200m east of St. Laurent; take bus #85 or 148 from downtown. (Open daily 9am-5pm, Thurs. 9am-9pm; Sept.-April closed Mon. $4.30, students and seniors $3.50, ages 6-15 $1.50, under 6 free; free Thurs. 5-9pm.) The **National Aviation Museum** (993-2010), at the Rockcliffe Airport off St. Laurent Blvd. north of Montréal St., illustrates the history of human flight and displays more than 100 aircraft; take bus #95 and transfer to #198. (Open daily 9am-5pm, Thurs. 9am-9pm; Labor Day-April closed Mon. $5, students and seniors $4, ages 6-15 $1.75; free Thurs. 5-9pm.)

Ottawa has managed to skirt the traditional urban vices of pollution and violent crime; the multitude of parks and recreation areas may make you forget you're in a city at all. A favorite destination for Ottawans who want to cycle, hike, or fish, **Gatineau Park** (see Accommodations, above) extends 356 sq. km into the northwest. Man-made **Dow's Lake** (232-1001), accessible by the Queen Elizabeth Driveway, extends off the Rideau Canal 15 minutes south of Ottawa. **Dow's Lake Pavilion,** 101 Queen Elizabeth Driveway, near Preston St., rents pedal boats, canoes, and bikes. (Open daily 11:30am-1am. Rentals by the ½hr. and the hr.; prices vary.)

ENTERTAINMENT

The **National Arts Centre,** 53 Elgin St. (996-5051; 755-1111 for tickets), at Albert St., houses an excellent small orchestra and theater company and frequently hosts international entertainers (box office open Mon.-Sat. noon-9pm). **Odyssey Theatre** (232-8407) puts on open-air comedy at **Strathcona Park,** at the end of Laurier Ave. at Charlotte St., well east of the canal. The shows are bawdy enough that they don't recommend using the children's discount. (Shows July to mid-Aug. Tues.-Sun. 8:30pm; $15, students and seniors $12, under 12 $6.)

Ottawans seem to have a celebration for just about everything, even the bitter Canadian cold. During the first three weekends of February, **Winterlude** (239-5000) lines the Rideau Canal with a number of ice sculptures which illustrate how it feels to be an Ottawan in the winter—frozen. For a week in mid-May, the **Tulip Festival** (567-5757) explodes in a colorful kaleidoscope around Dow's Lake with more than 100,000 blooming tulips. Summer brings music to Ottawa both in the form of the **Dance Festival** (237-5158), in mid-June, and the **Jazz Festival** (594-3580), in mid-July. Performers come from all over the country to perform in free recitals and concerts, along with pricier events. Labor Day weekend, the folks on Parliament Hill lend some of their bombast to the **Hot Air Balloon Festival** (243-2330), which sends to the sky hundreds of beautiful balloons from Canada, the U.S., and Europe.

For an escape from the city hubbub, seek out the **beaches,** west of town by way of the Ottawa River Pkwy. (follow the signs). **Mooney's Bay,** one popular strip of river bank, is 15 minutes from Ottawa by car.

NIGHTLIFE

Hull, Québec remains the place for the dedicated nightlifer. Right across the border, where the legal drinking age is 18, establishments grind and gnash until 3am every day of the week. Over 20 popular nightspots pack the **Promenade du Portage** in Hull (a.k.a The Strip), just west of the huge government office complex **Place Portage.** But don't run from the capital just yet; Ottawa does have its own share of excitement, especially in the **Byward Market** area. Though Ottawa clubs close at 1am (many at 11pm on Sun.), many offer free admission, making them worth more than a look. **Château Lafayette,** 42 York St. (241-4747), the oldest tavern in Ottawa, lures the budgeteer with $3 pints; regulars are the kind of hard-core beer drinkers who pound a beer, slam the mug down on the bar, and say "Mr. Keeper, I'll hava 'nuther" (open daily noon-1am). **Heart & Crown,** 67 Clarence St. (562-0764), packs in a rowdier crowd eager to open wallets and gullets for the Harp and Guiness on tap (pints $4.50; open daily 11am-1am). If you're on a mission and are willing to forego the frills of a decorated establishment, **On Tap,** 160 Rideau Ave. (241-6827), is the place for absurdly cheap drinks (draft beer and shooters 99¢ Wed., $2.25 Fri.).

Ottawa's musical offerings cater to both listeners and dancers. Land on the **Blue Planet,** 18 York St. (241-8955), for bright lights and funky dance music (open daily 4pm-1am). Gat a taste of life, the universe, and a bit of everything else at **Zaphod Beeblebrox,** 27 York (562-1010), in Byward Market, a popular alternative club famous for their $5.50 Pangalactic Gargle Blasters. (Cover as much as $10 on Tues. or Thurs.–Sat. when live bands play. Open daily noon-1am.) **Cock Robin Deli Ltd.,** 56 Byward Mkt. (241-5404), offers something for the druid in you with Celtic music Thursdays and Sundays at 9pm (no cover; open daily 11am-1pm). The show must go on, and it has done so every single night for the last ten years at **The Rainbow Bistro,** 76 Murray St. (241-5123). This dark, smoky blues joint often draws major acts from Chicago and New Orleans. (Music starts 9pm; cover $5-10. Sun. afternoon matinee 3:30-7pm; $1. Open daily 11am-1pm.) A popular gay pub, **The Market Station,** 15 George St. (562-3540), sits above a happening, subterranean dance cavern known as **The Well.** (No cover. Market Station open Mon.-Tues. 3pm-1am, Wed.-Sun. noon-1am; Well Wed.-Sat. 9pm-1am. 19+.)

A slightly older crowd (25-35) congregates in the bars on Elgin St. Three establishments here stand out: **Bulldog,** 380 Elgin St. (567-9021), and **Maxwells,** 340 Elgin St. (232-5771), work solely with liquids (both open daily 11am-1am), while the **Indigo Café,** 360 Elgin St. (232-5771), pumps out high-energy music (bar and music Thurs.-Sat. 9pm–1am; open daily 11am-1am).

■■■ ALGONQUIN PROVINCIAL PARK

The wilder Canada of endless rushing rivers and shimmering lakes awaits in Algonquin Provincial Park, about 250km west of Ottawa. From the city, take Hwy. 417 (the Queensway) west to Renfrew exit, then follow Hwy. 60 west to the park. For information and camping permits, visit the **East Gate Information Center** (705-633-5572; open daily 7am-10pm; Labor Day-May 9am-6pm). Tents and trailers crowd the Hwy. 60 Corridor (permits $15.25 per person per night). To experience the "essence of Algonquin," pierce the park interior (permits $25 per person per night). **Algonquin Reservation Network** (705-633-5538), handles reservations for 1200 sites on the corridor (free showers, bathrooms, no hookups) and limitless primitive campsites in the interior accessible only by hiking or canoe. Several outfitting stores in the park area rent backcountry gear; closest to the eastern entrance,

Opeongo Algonquin Outfitters (613-637-2075), on Rte. 60 near Opeongo Lake, is about 15 minutes into the park. (Tents $6-10 per night, sleeping bags $3.50-5.50, canoes $15-25. Open daily 8am-8pm; Sept.-June 8am-6pm.)

Prairie Provinces

■■■ MANITOBA

Manitoba marks the beginning of the Canadian West. Though frontier prairie dominates this vast land, tens of thousands of lakes diversify the terrain. To the north, tundra and lush forests spread out from the wooded park lands of the central region. Farther west, rolling mountains carpeted with grain-rich fields also belie the misconception that Manitoba is a flat prairie.

What Manitoba lacks in sophistication it makes up for with a particular "midwestern" charm. The province's largest city and capital, **Winnipeg,** combines cosmopolitan elements with a folksy local atmosphere; the Royal Winnipeg Ballet is one of the best in North America, and its museums and art galleries are celebrated nationally. Contact **Tourism Winnipeg,** 302-25 Forks Market Rd., R3C 4S8 (800-665-0204 or 204-943-1970), or **Travel Manitoba** (800-665-0040 or 204-945-3777). Two youth hostels lodge in Winnipeg, **Ivey House International Hostel (HI-AYH),** 210 Maryland St. (204-772-3022; $12, nonmembers $16) and **Guest House International,** 168 Maryland St. (204-772-1272; $11).

Farther north, the prairie areas are still largely inhabited by Native Canadians. Taking the train north from Winnipeg, you'll reach **Churchill,** on **Hudson Bay,** which is worth the trip. Churchill's summer seaport becomes the "Polar Bear Capital of the World" in winter. Beluga whales, seals, and caribou live on and along Churchill's coast. The northern lights here are fabulous.

Around Winnipeg, **Lake Manitoba** offers excellent facilities, and **Riding Mountain National Park** displays forest, open grassland, meadows, prairies, and mountains. The fishing is superb and you are guaranteed to see bison, moose, and bears. Call **Wasagaming Visitors Center** (204-848-2811; open daily 9am-9pm) for details.

Manitoba is on Central time (1hr. behind Eastern). **Drinking Age:** 18. **Postal Abbreviation:** MAN **Sales Tax:** 7% plus a 7% GST (for deatils on obtaining a refund of the GST, see Essentials, p. 7).

■■■ SASKATCHEWAN

Saskatchewan, "the river that flows swiftly," produces over 60% of Canada's wheat; still, mountains, badlands, and more diversify the wheatfields of the "Heartland of North America." In the southwest, the mountains of Cypress Hills—insane, got no brain!—top Banff, Alberta; lakes, gardens, and parks nestle in the Qu'Apelle Valley to the southeast. To the north, Prince Albert National Park (*not* in a can) rests among nearly 100,000 lakes, 80 million acres of forests, and deserts. Saskatchewan's capital and Queen City of the plains, Regina (pronounced like angina) is home to the **Canadian Mounties' training academy** (306-780-5900). Unlike the francophone eastern provinces, Regina's second language is Ukrainian.

For more info, contact **Tourism Regina** (306-789-5099; open May-Sept. Mon.-Fri. 8am-7pm, Sat.-Sun. 10am-6pm, Oct.-April Mon.-Fri. 8:30am-4:30pm). In Regina, stay at the **Turgeon International Hostel (IYHF-CHA),** 2310 MacIntyre St. (306-791-8165), in a beautifully restored old mansion. (Kitchen, lockers. 50 beds. $12, nonmembers $17. Check-in summer 8am-midnight; otherwise 7-10am and 5-midnight.)

Saskatchewan is on Mountain Time (2 hr. behind Eastern). **Drinking Age:** 19. **Postal Abbreviation:** SK. **Sales Tax:** 9%, plus a 7% GST (for details on obtaining a refund of the GST, see Essentials, p. 7).

The Assman Cometh

In July 1995, *The Late Show with David Letterman* received a clipping of an ad for a gas station in Regina, Saskatchewan, featuring a 61-year-old pump attendant named Dick Assman. Dave contacted the man and set out to make Dick and the gas station the most popular tourist attraction in Canada. Dick Assmania spread like a bad case of hives, and the gas station was inundated with calls. In August 1995, *Let's Go* was unable to reach Mr. Assman since he had begun a tour of Eastern Canada. When he's not busy filming commercials or making guest appearances at monster truck rallies, Dick pumps away at **Petro Canada,** 2233 Victoria Ave. E., in Regina. Though his publicist Bob Bray swears that he hasn't changed a bit, it is safe to say that Dick has the whole world in his pants.

Alberta

Alberta's glitter is concentrated in the west of the province; the icy peaks and turquoise lakes of Banff and Jasper National Parks reign as Alberta's most prominent landscapes. To the east, less sublime vistas of farmland, prairie, and oil fields fill the yawning expanses. Alberta boasts thousands of prime fishing holes, world-renowned fossil fields, and centers of Native American culture. Calgary caught the world's eye when it hosted the XV Winter Olympics in 1988, and is annual host to the wild and woolly Stampede.

Alberta receives even more complete coverage in *Let's Go: Alaska & The Pacific Northwest.* Check it out!

PRACTICAL INFORMATION

Capital: Edmonton.

Visitors Information: Alberta Tourism, 10155 102 St., Third Floor, Edmonton T5J 4L6 (427-4321 or 800-661-8888). **Provincial Parks Information,** 10405 Jasper Ave., Eighth Floor, Edmonton T5J 3N4 (944-0313). **Parks Canada,** 220 4th Ave. SE, Room 552, Calgary T2P 3H8 (292-4401).

Drinking Age: 18.

Time Zone: Mountain (2hr. behind Eastern). **Postal Abbreviation:** AB

■■■ EDMONTON

Beyond Edmonton's superficial drabness, there is plenty to see and do. Edmonton boasts one of the few existing shops devoted exclusively to budget travel, and a funky conservatory which exhibits a large collection of tropical and desert plants north of 53°N latitude. Toss in a toy museum and a great alternative music festival, and it shouldn't take long for Edmonton to lose its dull image.

Practical Information Edmonton Tourism, City Hall, 1 Sir Winston Churchill Square (426-4715), at 102A Ave. west of 99 St. has info, maps, brochures, and directions (open Victoria Day-Labor Day Mon.-Fri. 9am-4pm, Sat.-Sun. 11am-5pm). **Greyhound,** 10324 103 St. (420-2412), runs to Calgary (nearly every hr., 8am-8pm, $33), Jasper (4 per day, $45) and Vancouver (5 per day, $113). (Open daily 5:30am-midnight. Locker storage $1.50 per 24 hrs.) **VIA Rail,** 10004 104 Ave. (422-6032 or 800-561-8630), in the CN Tower, thunders away to Jasper and Vancouver.

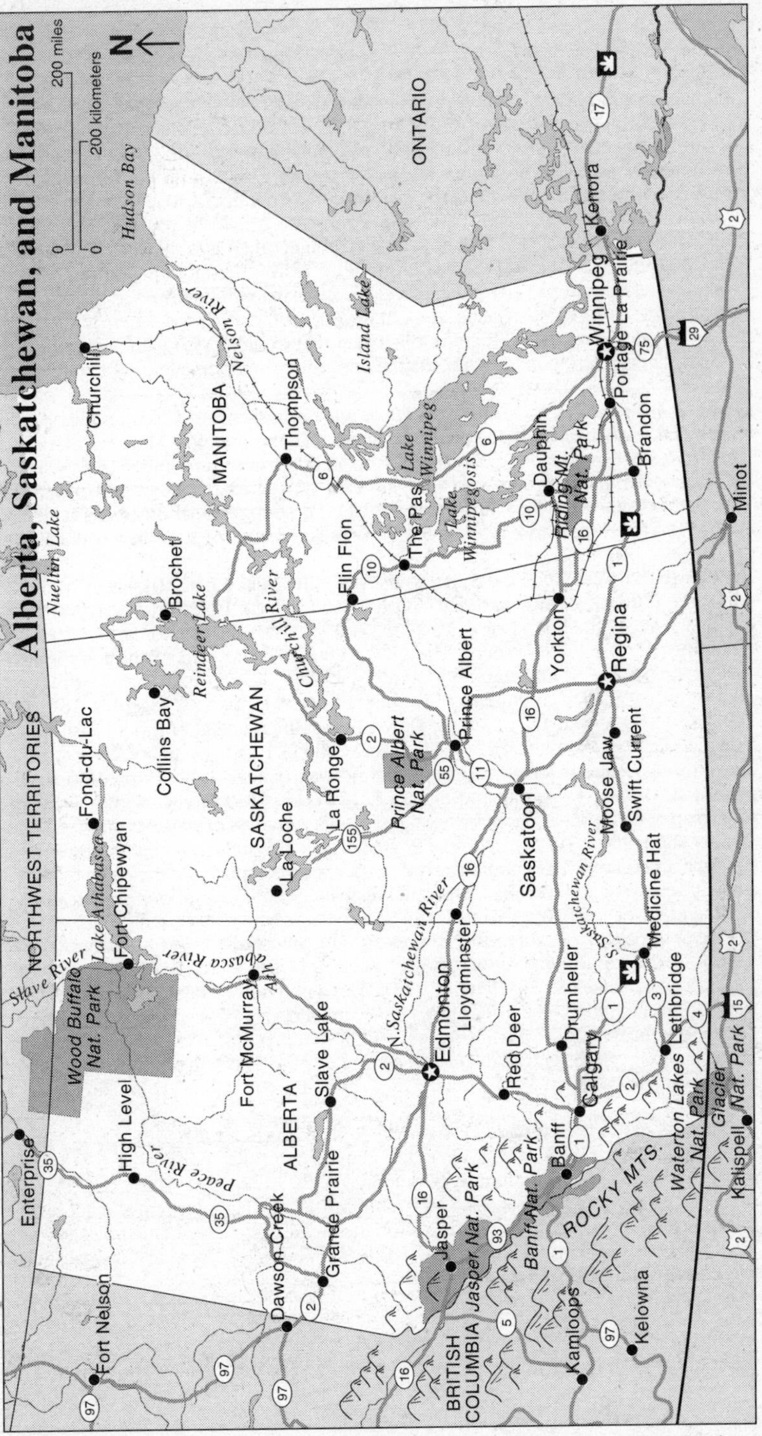
Alberta, Saskatchewan, and Manitoba
0 200 miles
0 200 kilometers
N
Hudson Bay
NORTHWEST TERRITORIES
ONTARIO
MANITOBA
SASKATCHEWAN
ALBERTA
BRITISH COLUMBIA
Churchill
Nueltin Lake
Nelson River
Island Lake
Thompson
Brochet
Reindeer Lake
Churchill River
Flin Flon
The Pas
Lake Winnipeg
Lake Winnipegosis
Dauphin
Riding Mt. Nat. Park
Winnipeg
Portage La Prairie
Kenora
Brandon
Minot
Yorkton
Regina
Prince Albert
Prince Albert Nat. Park
Collins Bay
Fond-du-Lac
Lake Athabasca
Fort Chipewyan
La Ronge
La Loche
Saskatoon
Moose Jaw
Swift Current
Medicine Hat
S. Saskatchewan River
N. Saskatchewan River
Lloydminster
Edmonton
Athabasca River
Fort McMurray
Slave River
Wood Buffalo Nat. Park
Slave Lake
Red Deer
Drumheller
Calgary
Lethbridge
Banff
Banff Nat. Park
Waterton Lakes Nat. Park
Glacier Nat. Park
Kalispell
ROCKY MTS.
Jasper
Jasper Nat. Park
Grande Prairie
Dawson Creek
Peace River
High Level
Enterprise
Fort Nelson
Kamloops
Kelowna
97
35
2
16
93
1
5
155
55
11
10
6
17
75
29
3
4
15

CANADA

That's Obscenely Huge

Capitalism's mother ship, the **West Edmonton Mall** (444-5200 or 800-661-8890) envelopes the general area of 170 St. and 87 Ave. Inside the Milky Way's largest assembly of retail stores, consumerism reigns unchecked. When It first landed, Its massive sprawl of boutiques and eateries seized 30% of Edmonton's retail business, choking the life out of the downtown shopping district. Encompassing a water park, an amusement park, and dozens of pathetically caged exotic animals, The World's Biggest Mall appears even Bigger than It is thanks to the mirrors plastered on nearly every wall. Among Its many attractions, The Über-Mall boasts over 800 stores, 110 eating places, twice as many submarines as the Canadian Navy, a full-scale replica of Columbus's *Santa Maria,* a 14-story roller coaster, and **Lazermaze,** the world's first walk-through video game. Take bus #10 to The Mall. (Open Mon.-Fri. 10am-9pm, Sat. 10am-6pm, Sun. noon-5pm.)

Edmonton Transit (496-1611 for schedule info) runs frequent buses and light rail transit **(LRT)** all over this sprawling metropolis. (Transit operates Mon.-Fri. 6:30am-10:30pm, Sat. 8am-5pm, Sun. 9am-5pm. Fare $1.60, over 65 and under 15 80¢. The LRT is free in the downtown area Mon.-Fri. 9am-3pm and Sat. 9am-5pm.) For a **taxi,** call **Yellow Cab** (462-3456). **Emergency** is 911. Edmonton's **post office:** 9808 103A Ave. (495-4105; open Mon.-Fri. 8am-5:45pm); **postal code:** T5J 2G8; **area code:** 403.

Accommodations, Food, and Sights The liveliest place to stay in Edmonton is the **Edmonton International Youth Hostel (HI-C),** 10422 91 St. (429-0140), off Jasper Ave. Take bus #1 or 2; it's a long walk from the bus station. The area surrounding the hostel is a bit seedy. The air-conditioned hostel offers common rooms, snack bar, showers, kitchen, and laundry facilities. (Open daily 8am-midnight. $12.50, non-Canadian members $17, nonmembers $17.50.) **St. Joseph's College** (492-7681), 89 Ave. at 114 St., in the University of Alberta neighborhood, has small, quiet, and cheap rooms. Take bus #43, or take the LRT and get off at University. In the summer, make reservations; rooms fill up fast. (Check-in desk open Mon.-Fri. 9am-5pm. Library, TV, pool table. Singles $21, weekly $130. Singles with full board $34, or pay for meals separately: breakfast $3.25, lunch $4.50, dinner $6.50.) **The Travel Shop,** 10926 88 Ave. (travel 439-3096, retail 439-3089), is the regional office for **Alberta Hostels.** The shop is a travel agency with camping and hiking gear, serving youth and student travelers. The staff will make hostel reservations. (Open Mon.-Wed. and Fri.-Sat. 9am-6pm, Thurs. 9am-8pm.)

One of the oldest restaurants in Edmonton, **The Silk Hat,** 10251 Jasper Ave. (428-1551), sits beside the Paramount theater, serving hearty food: two eggs with two monstrous pancakes $2.50, Hamburger Deluxe with choice of fries or potato salad $4.25. (Everything 10% off after 5pm. Open Mon.-Fri. 6:30am-10pm, Sat. 8am-9pm, Sun. and holidays 11am-7pm.) **Veggies,** 10331 82nd Ave. (432-7560), in Old Strathcona, serves creative vegetarian cuisine. (Hummus plate $6.75, grilled tofu and vegetable satay $6.75. Open Mon.-Thurs. 11am-10pm, Fri.-Sat. 11am-11pm, Sun. 11am-9pm.)

Take bus #51 to the **Muttart Conservatory,** 9626 96A St. (496-8755), where plant species from around the world live in the climate controlled comfort of four ultramodern glass and steel pyramids. (Open Sun.-Wed. 11am-9pm, Thurs.-Sat. 11am-6pm. $4.25, seniors and youths $3.25, children $2.) After sampling the achievements of late 20th-century malls, the Victorian era will seem a welcome relief as you head for **Fort Edmonton Park** (496-8787), off Whitemud Dr. near the Quesnell Bridge; take bus #123 or 32.

■■■ CALGARY

Calgary was founded in 1875 as a summer outpost of the Northwest Mounted Police. The discovery of oil in 1947 transformed this cowtown into a wealthy, cosmopolitan city, and in 1988, Calgary hosted the Winter Olympics. The oil may be crude, but the city is refined. Skyscrapers overshadow oil derricks, business people scurry about, and a modern transport system threads soundlessly through immaculate downtown streets. In July, Calgarians forget the oil business and get all gussied up in cowboy boots, jeans, Western shirts, and ten-gallon hats for the "Greatest Outdoor Show on Earth," the Calgary Stampede.

PRACTICAL INFORMATION

Tourist Office: Calgary Convention and Visitors Bureau, 237 8th Ave. SE, Calgary, AB T2G 0K8 (263-8510). Open daily 8am-5pm.

Airport: Calgary International (735-1200 or 735-1372), about 5km northwest of the city center. Bus #57 provides sporadic service to the city. The **Airporter Bus** (531-3907) offers frequent and friendly service for $8.50.

Buses: Greyhound, 877 Greyhound Way SW (265-9111 or 800-661-8747). Frequent service to Edmonton ($33) and Banff ($17). **Brewster Tours** (221-8242) runs buses to: Banff (3 per day, $30); Jasper (1 per day, $53).

Public Transportation: Calgary Transit, 240 7th Ave. SW. Schedules, passes, and maps. Open Mon.-Fri. 8:30am-5pm. Fare $1.50, ages 6-14 90¢, under 6 free. Exact change required. Day pass $4.50, children $2.50. **Information line,** 262-1000. Open Mon.-Fri. 6am-11pm, Sat.-Sun. 8:30am-9:30pm.

Taxi: Checker Cab, 299-9999. **Yellow Cab,** 974-1111. Both 24 hrs.

Car Rental: Rent-A-Wreck, 112 5th Ave, SE (228-1660). Cars start at $40 per day, 200km free, 12¢ per additional km. Under 25 surcharge $15 per day. Open Mon.-Fri. 8am-6pm, Sat.-Sun. 9am-5pm. Most companies raise rates during summer, especially during the Stampede; call for exact rates.

Bike Rental: Sports Rent, 9250 Macleod Trail (292-0066). $20 per day.

Help Lines: Crisis Line: 266-1605. **Sexual Assault Centre:** 237-5888. **Gay Lines Calgary:** 234-8973. Open daily 7-10pm.

Emergency: 911.

Post Office: 207 9th Ave. SW (974-2078). Open Mon.-Fri. 8am-5:45pm. **Postal Code:** T2P 180. **Area Code**: 403.

Calgary is divided into quadrants: **Centre Street** is the east-west divide; the **Bow River** divides the north and south sections. The rest is simple: avenues run east-west, streets run north-south.

ACCOMMODATIONS AND FOOD

Cheap lodging in Calgary is rare only when packs of tourists Stampede into the city's hotels. Contact the **B&B Association** of Calgary (531-0065) for info on B&Bs. Prices for singles begin around $30, doubles around $45. The **Calgary International Hostel (HI-C),** 520 7th Ave. SE (269-8239), is conveniently located several blocks east of downtown with access to the 3rd St. SE C-Train station and public buses. Facilities include snack bar, meeting rooms, barbecue, laundry, and a cycle workshop. Make reservations for the Stampede *way* in advance. (Wheelchair accessible. Open 24 hrs., but front desk closes at midnight. $14, nonmembers $19.) The **University of Calgary,** in the NW quadrant, is out of the way, but easily accessible via bus #9 or the C-Train. U of C was the Olympic Village home to 1988 competitors and offers clean, inexpensive rooms. Booking for all rooms is through **Kananaskis Hall,** 3330 24th Ave. (220-3203), a 12-min. walk from the University C-Train stop. (Open 24 hrs. 22 rooms are set aside for those with student ID: singles $30, doubles $38; these rooms may be reserved, and are often booked solid. Rooms available May-Aug. only.) **St. Regis Hotel,** 124 7th Ave. SE (262-4641) offers comfortable rooms in a classic old downtown building (doubles $37-58).

Ethnic and cafe-style dining spots line the **Stephen Avenue Mall,** 8th Ave. S between 1st St. SE and 3rd St. SW. If you're at the University, the **MacEwen Student Centre** has a food court on the 2nd floor with every kind of cheap, quick food imaginable. Fresh fruits, vegetables, seafood, and baked goods grace the upscale **Eau Claire Market** (264-6450), on 3rd St. SW near Prince's Island Park. **4th Street Rose,** 2116 4th St. SW (228-5377), is a fashionable eatery south of downtown. The house specialty is the "pro-size" Caesar salad ($4.25), served in a large Mason jar. (Open Mon.-Thurs. 11am-1am, Fri.-Sat. 11am-2am, Sun. 10am-midnight.) Island **Experience,** 314A 10th St. NW (270-4550), serves Caribbean treats borrowed from India, including *rotis* (open Mon.-Thurs. 11am-9pm, Fri.-Sat. 11am-10pm, Sun. noon-9pm).

SIGHTS AND THE STAMPEDE

Don't just gaze at the **Calgary Tower,** 101 9th Ave. SW (266-7171); ride an elevator to the top for a spectacular view of the Rockies (open daily 7am-midnight; $5, seniors $3, ages 13-18 $3.25, ages 3-12 $2; HI discount available). The **Glenbow Museum,** 130 9th Ave. SE (268-4100), is just across the street. From rocks and minerals to Native American lifestyles to the art of Asia to the history of the Canadian West, the Glenbow has it all. (Open Tues.-Sun. 10am-6pm. $5, seniors, students and children $3.50; under 7 free.) Fifty ft. straight up on the fourth floor of 317 7th Ave. SW are the 2.5-acre indoor **Devonian Gardens,** a cool, quiet oasis in an often hot and noisy city (open daily 9am-9pm, free).

Prince's Island Park can be reached by footbridges from either side of the Bow River. Many summer evenings at 7pm, Mount Royal College puts on free Shakespeare plays in the park. Calgary's other island park, **St. George's Island,** is accessible by the river walkway to the east and is home to the marvelous **Calgary Zoo** (232-9300). No matter how strongly you might disapprove of caging wild animals, you'll be impressed by the habitats's authenticity, the variety of animals, and how cute a baby hippo can be. ($7.50, seniors $5.50, children $3.75; Tues. seniors $2. Gates

Head-Smashed-In Buffalo Jump

Coveted as a source of fresh meat, sustenance, tools, and shelter, the buffalo was the victim of one of history's most innovative forms of mass slaughter: the buffalo jump. For 0ver 5500 years, Native Americans in Southern Alberta maneuvered the herd into position, while a few extremely brave young men, disguised in coyote skins among the buffalo, would spook hundreds of nearly-blind bison into a fatal stampede over a 10m cliff. Usually highly successful, though occasionally grotesquely fatal, this created an instant all-you-can-eat-or-use buffet at the bottom of the cliff. The area earned its name 150 years ago in memory of a young thrill-seeker who was crushed against the cliff by a pile of buffalo as he watched the event from the base.

Although UNESCO will fine you $50,000 if you forage for souvenirs in the 10m-deep beds of bone, you can learn about buffalo jumps and local Native culture at the **Interpretive Centre** (553-2731), a $10-million, 7-story facility built into the cliff itself. Two km of walking trails lead to the top of the cliff and the kill site below. Head-Smashed-In Buffalo Jump is in Southern Alberta, west of Lethbridge and Fort Macleod on Secondary Rte. 785, about 30km west off Hwy. 2.

open daily 9am-6:30pm, winter daily 9am-4pm; grounds open until 8:30pm, winter until 5:30pm.) The **Energeum,** 640 5th Ave. SW (297-4293), is Calgary's shrine to oil (open Sun.-Fri. 10:30am-4:30pm; free).

Stampede lovers join Calgarians in their "Greatest Outdoor Show on Earth." The Stampede draws millions from across the province, the country, and the world to don ten-gallon hats and yell "yahoo" in the least likely of circumstances. The Stampede will take place July 5-14 in 1996 and July 4-13 in 1997. Make the trip out to **Stampede Park,** southeast of downtown, for a glimpse of steer wrestling, bull riding, wild cow milking, and the famous chuckwagon races. For information and ticket order forms, contact the **Calgary Exhibition and Stampede,** Box 1860, Station M, Calgary T2P 2L8 (261-0101 or 800-661-1260; tickets are $16-42; inquire about rush tickets, available for $8; youth $7, seniors and children $4).

■■■ BANFF

Banff National Park is Canada's best-loved and best-known natural preserve, 2543 sq. mi. (6600 sq. km) of peaks and canyons, white foaming rapids, brilliant turquoise lakes, dense forests, and open meadows. Yet it was not simple love of natural beauty that motivated Prime Minister Sir John MacDonald to establish Canada's first national park in 1885. Rather, officers of the Canadian Pacific Railroad convinced him of Banff's potential for "large pecuniary advantage," and were quick to add, "since we can't export the scenery, we shall have to import the tourists."

PRACTICAL INFORMATION

Tourist Office: Banff Information Centre, 224 Banff Ave. (762-1550). Open daily 8am-8pm; Oct.-May daily 9am-5pm. **Lake Louise Information Centre** (522-3833). Open mid-May to mid-June daily 10am-6pm; mid-June to Aug. 8am-8pm; Sept.-Oct. 10am-6pm; winter 9am-5pm.

Buses: Greyhound, 100 Gopher St. (762-6767). From the Brewster terminal to: Lake Louise (4 per day, $9); Calgary ($17); Vancouver ($96). **Brewster Transportation,** 100 Gopher St. (762-6767), near the train depot. To: Jasper (1 per day, $37); Lake Louise (2 per day, $11.50); Calgary (5 per day, $30). Does not honor Greyhound Ameripasses. Depot open daily 7:30am-10pm.

Emergency: Banff Warden Office, 762-4506. **Lake Louise Warden Office,** 522-3866 . Open 24 hrs. **Police,** 762-2226. On Railway St. by the train depot.

Post Office: 204 Buffalo St. (762-2586). Open Mon.-Fri. 9am-5:30pm. **Postal Code:** T0L 0C0. **Area Code:** 403.

Banff National Park hugs the Alberta-British Columbia border, 120 km west of Calgary. The **Trans-Canada Hwy.** (Hwy. 1) runs east-west through the park; **Icefields Parkway** (Hwy. 93) connects Banff to Jasper National Park in the north. Civilization centers around the towns of Banff and **Lake Louise,** 55 km northwest on Hwy. 1.

ACCOMMODATIONS, CAMPING, AND FOOD

Finding a cheap place to stay is easy in Banff. Check the list of B&Bs in the back of the *Banff and Lake Louise Official Visitor's Guide,* available free at the tourist office. There's a chain of hostels stretching from Calgary to Jasper, anchored by the ones at Banff and Lake Louise. The **Pika Shuttle** (762-4122) offers transport among these hostels. To reserve a shuttle spot, you must have a reservation at your destination hostel. Shuttle rates vary from $5 to $51.

Banff International Hostel (HI-C), Box 1358, Banff T0L 0C0 (762-4122), 3 km from Banff townsite on Tunnel Mountain Rd. BIH has the look and setting of a ski lodge. Clean rooms with 2-4 bunk beds. Cafeteria, laundry facilities, TVs, hot showers. Wheelchair accessible. Accommodates 154. Open all day. No curfew; front desk closes at midnight. $17, nonmembers $22. Linen $1.

Castle Mountain Hostel (HI-C), on Hwy. 1A, 1.5km east of the junction of Hwy. 1 and Hwy. 93 between Banff and Lake Louise. Accommodates 36. Call Banff International Hostel (see above) for reservations. $11, nonmembers $16.

Lake Louise International Hostel (HI-C), Village Rd. (522-2200), ½km from Samson Mall in Lake Louise townsite. Accommodates 100. Cafeteria, full-service kitchen, hot showers. Wheelchair accessible. $17.50, nonmembers $24. Private rooms $21.50/$28.

Mosquito Creek Hostel (HI-C), 103km south of the Icefield Centre and 26km north of Lake Louise. Accommodates 38. Fireplace, sauna, full-service kitchen. $10, nonmembers $15. Call BIH for reservations.

Rampart Creek Hostel (HI-C), 34km south of the Icefield Centre. Accommodates 30 in rustic cabins. Sauna, full-service kitchen, wood-heated bathtub. $9, nonmembers $14. Call BIH for reservations.

Hilda Creek Hostel (HI-C), 8.5km south of the Icefield Centre on the Icefields Pkwy. Full-service kitchen. Accommodates 21. Excellent hiking and skiing nearby at Parker's Ridge. $9, nonmembers $14. Call BIH for reservations.

None of the park's popular camping sites accepts reservations, so arrive early. Many campgrounds reserve sites for bicyclists and hikers; inquire at the office (sites $10-15). Park facilities include (listed from north to south): **Waterfowl** (116 sites), **Lake Louise** (220 sites), **Protection Mountain** (89 sites), **Johnston Canyon** (132 sites), **Two Jack Main** (381 sites) and **Tunnel Mountain Village** (620 sites). Each site holds a maximum of two tents and six people.

Restaurants in Banff generally serve expensive, mediocre food. Luckily, the Banff **(Café Aspenglow)** and Lake Louise **(Bill Peyto's Cafe)** International Hostels serve wholesome, affordable for $3 to $7. Shop at **Safeway** (762-5378), at Marten and Elk St., just off Banff Ave. (open daily 8am-10pm; winter 9am-9pm). If you're 18, some of the bars in the Banff townsite offer daily specials at reasonable prices.

OUTDOORS

Hike to the **backcountry** for privacy, beauty, and over 1600km of trails. For info on day and overnight hikes in the Lake Louise and Banff areas, get the free pamphlet *Drives and Walks*, available at the Information Centers. Also available at the centers are backcountry **permits** ($5-35), which are required for overnight stays. Also bring a campstove; no wood may be chopped in the parks. The Park Information Center has the *Canadian Rockies Trail Guide,* with excellent information and maps.

Two easy but rewarding trails lie within walking distance of the townsite. **Fenland** winds 2 km through an area creeping with beaver, muskrat, and waterfowl. Follow Mt. Norquay Rd. out of Banff and look for signs. About 25km out of Banff toward Lake Louise, **Johnston Canyon** offers a popular ½-day hike. The 1.1-km hike to the canyon's lower falls and the 2.7-km trip to the canyon's upper falls consist mostly of a catwalk along the edge of the canyon. Don't stop here, though; continue along the trail for another 3.1 km to seven blue-green cold-water springs known as the **Inkpots.**

Your car will find **Tunnel Mountain Drive** and **Vermilion Lakes** particularly scenic places to cough fumes into the clear air. Turn right onto Tunnel Mountain Rd. to see the **hoodoos,** long, finger-like projections of limestone once part of the cliff wall and thought by Native Americans to encase sentinel spirits.

The **Sulphur Mountain Gondola** (762-5438), next to the Upper Hot Springs pool, lifts you 700m to a view of the Rockies normally reserved for birds and mountain goats. You can hike all the way back down on a 6-km trail that deposits you right back at the parking lot. (Open daily 8am-9pm; $9, kids 5-11 $5, under 5 free.) The **Summit Restaurant** (Canada's highest), perched atop Sulphur Mountain, serves an "Early Morning Lift" breakfast special for $4. Grab a table by the window.

Brewster Tours (762-6767) offers an extensive array of bus tours with knowledgeable and entertaining guides. If you don't have a car, these tours may be the only way to see some of Banff's main attractions, such as the Athabasca Glacier. (9½ hr. sightseeing trip to Jasper $60; 2-day round-trip $90).

Fishing is legal virtually anywhere you can find water, but you must hold a National Parks fishing permit, available at the Information Centre (7-day permit $6, annual permit $13). Those who prefer more vigorous water sports can **raft** the park's white waters. A particularly good deal is offered by the Banff International Hostel—a full day of rafting on the **Kicking Horse River** for $44.

■■■ JASPER

Before the Icefields Parkway was built, few travelers dared venture north from Banff into the untamed wilderness of **Jasper National Park.** But those bushwhackers who returned came back with stunning reports, and the completion of the Parkway in 1940 paved the way for everyone to appreciate Jasper's astounding beauty. In contrast to its glitzy southern peer, Jasper townsite maintains the feel of a small town.

Practical Information **Jasper townsite** lies near the center of the park, 362 km west of Edmonton and 287 km northwest of Banff. **Hwy. 16** crosses the northern reaches of the park, while the **Icefields Parkway** (Hwy. 93) connects to Banff National Park in the south. The **Park Information Centre,** 500 Connaught Dr. (852-6176), will pack you with info (open daily 8am-8pm; early Sept.-late Oct. and late Dec. to mid-May 9am-5pm; mid-May to mid-June 8am-5pm). **VIA Rail,** 314 Connaught Dr. (800-561-8630), runs to: Vancouver ($147); Edmonton ($87); and Winnipeg ($232). **Greyhound,** 314 Connaught Dr. (852-3926), in the VIA station, runs buses to: Edmonton (4 per day; $45); Vancouver ($86). **Brewster Transportation,** 314 Connaught Dr. (852-3332), in the VIA station, journeys to: Banff (daily; 4¼hr.; $40); Calgary (daily; 8hrs.; $53). Jasper's **post office:** 502 Patricia St. (852-3041; open Mon.-Fri. 9am-5pm); **postal code:** T0E 1E0; **area code:** 403.

Accommodations and Camping Hotels in Jasper are expensive, but you may be able to stay cheaply at a **B&B** (singles $25-35, doubles $30-45). If you have a car, head for one of Jasper's hostels (listed below from north to south). Reservations are made through the Edmonton-based **Northern Alberta Hostel Association** (439-3139; fax 433-7781), or through the **Whistlers Mountain Hostel** (852-3215).

Maligne Canyon Hostel (HI-C), (852-3584), 11km east of the townsite on Maligne Canyon Rd. Small, recently renovated cabins on the bank of the Maligne River. Accommodates 24. $9, nonmembers $14. Winter closed Wed.

Whistlers Mountain Hostel (HI-C), (852-3215), on Sky Tram Rd., 7km south of the townsite. Closest to the townsite, this is the park's most modern (and crowded) hostel. Accommodates 69. Curfew midnight. $14, nonmembers $19.

Mt. Edith Cavell Hostel (HI-C), on Edith Cavell Rd., off Hwy. 93A. The road is closed in winter, but the hostel welcomes anyone willing to ski 11km from Hwy. 93A; see reservations number above. Accommodates 32. $9, nonmembers $14. Open mid-June to early Oct., "key system" in winter.

Athabasca Falls Hostel (HI-C), on Hwy. 93 (852-5959), 30km south of Jasper townsite, 500m from Athabasca Falls. Huge dining/recreation room with wood-burning stove. Accommodates 40. $9, nonmembers $14. Closed Tues. in winter.

Beauty Creek Hostel (HI-C), on Hwy. 93, 78km south of Jasper townsite. Next to the stunning Sunwapta River. Accommodates 24. "Key system" in winter (groups only). $9, nonmembers $14. Open May-mid to Sept. Thurs.-Tues.

For camping updates, tune to **1450 AM** near Jasper Townsite. The park has sites at 10 campgrounds, including (north to south): **Pocahontas** (140 sites), **Snaring River** (56 sites), **Whistlers** (781 sites), **Wapiti** (366 sites), **Wabasso** (238 sites), **Columbia Icefield** (33 sites), and **Wilcox Creek** (46 sites). Sites run $10-19.

Food For grocery supplies at any time of night or day, stop at **Wink's Food Store,** 617 Patricia St. (852-4223), or **Super A Foods,** 601 Patricia St. For bulk grains, nuts, and dried fruits, try **Nutter's,** 622 Patricia St. (852-5844; open Mon.-Sat. 9am-10pm, Sun. 10am-8pm). **Mountain Foods and Cafe,** 606 Connaught Dr. (852-4050), has both hot and cold sandwiches ($3), soups, and desserts (open daily 8am-10pm). **Smitty's,** 109 Miette Ave. (852-3111) is a diner with all-day breakfast (open daily 6:30am-10pm; winter 6:45am-6:45pm).

Outdoors An extensive network of trails weaves through Jasper; many paths start at the townsite. Information Centres distribute *Day Hikes in Jasper National Park* (free) and a summary of longer hikes. **Mt. Edith Cavell** will shake you to the bone with the thunderous roar of avalanches off the Angel Glacier. Take the 1.6-km loop trail Path of the Glacier to the top or the 8-km hike through **Cavell Meadows.** Edith rears her enormous head 30 km south of the townsite on Mt. Edith Cavell Rd. If you only have time for a quickie, try the **Parker Ridge Trail.** The 2.4-km hike (one-way) guides you away from the parkway, past treeline, and over Parker Ridge, to an amazing view of the Saskatchewan Glacier. **Maligne Lake,** the largest glacier-fed lake in the Canadian Rockies, is located 50 km southeast of the townsite at the end of Maligne Lake Rd. Farther north in the valley and 30 km east of the townsite, the Maligne River flows into **Medicine Lake.** The water escapes underground through tunnels, re-emerging 16 km downstream in the **Maligne Canyon,** 11 km east of the townsite on Maligne Canyon Rd. This is the longest known underground river in North America. **Whitewater Rafting (Jasper) Ltd.** (852-7238) offers several rafting trips (from $40; 2-hr. trip down the Maligne River $48). Register by phone or stop at the Esso station in the townsite.

Trout abound in Jasper's spectacular lakes during the month of May—but so do anglers. **Beaver Lake,** however, located about 1km from the main road at the tip of Medicine Lake, is never crowded, and even novice fisherfolk can hook themselves a dinner. Rent equipment at **Currie's,** in **The Sports Shop** at 414 Connaught Dr. (852-3654; rod, reel, and line $10; one-day boat rental $25, $18 if rented after 2pm).

British Columbia

Larger in area than California, Oregon, and Washington combined, British Columbia attracts so many visitors that tourism has become the province's second largest industry after logging. Although skiing is excellent year-round, most tourists arrive in summer, flocking to Vancouver and Victoria, and the sprawling lakes and long beaches of the hot, dry Okanogan Valley.

As you head north, clouds begin to replace the crowds. Temperate BC receives even more rain than the American Northwest, and little snow. Thick forests, low mountains, and occasional patches of high desert are interrupted only by such supply and transit centers as Prince George and Prince Rupert. Farther north, even these outposts of civilization defer to thick spruce forests. BC's extensive and accessible park system allows for an affordable escape from every trace of civilization.

For even more thorough coverage of British Columbia, refer to *Let's Go: Alaska & The Pacific Northwest,* carried by reputable booksellers worldwide.

PRACTICAL INFORMATION

Capital: Victoria.

Tourism British Columbia: 1117 Wharf St., Victoria, BC V8W 2Z2 (604-387-1642 or 800-663-6000) **Parks Canada,** 220 4th Ave. SE #520, P.O. Box 2989, Station M, Calgary, AB T2P 3H8 (403-292-4401). **BC Parks,** 800 Johnson St., 2nd Floor, Victoria, BC V8V 1X4 (604-387-5002).

Drinking Age: 19.

Time Zone: Pacific and Mountain.

Postal Abbreviation: BC

■■■ VANCOUVER

Canada's third-largest city will thrill even the most jaded metropolis-hopping traveler. Vancouver has a seamless public transit system, spotless sidewalks, and a good

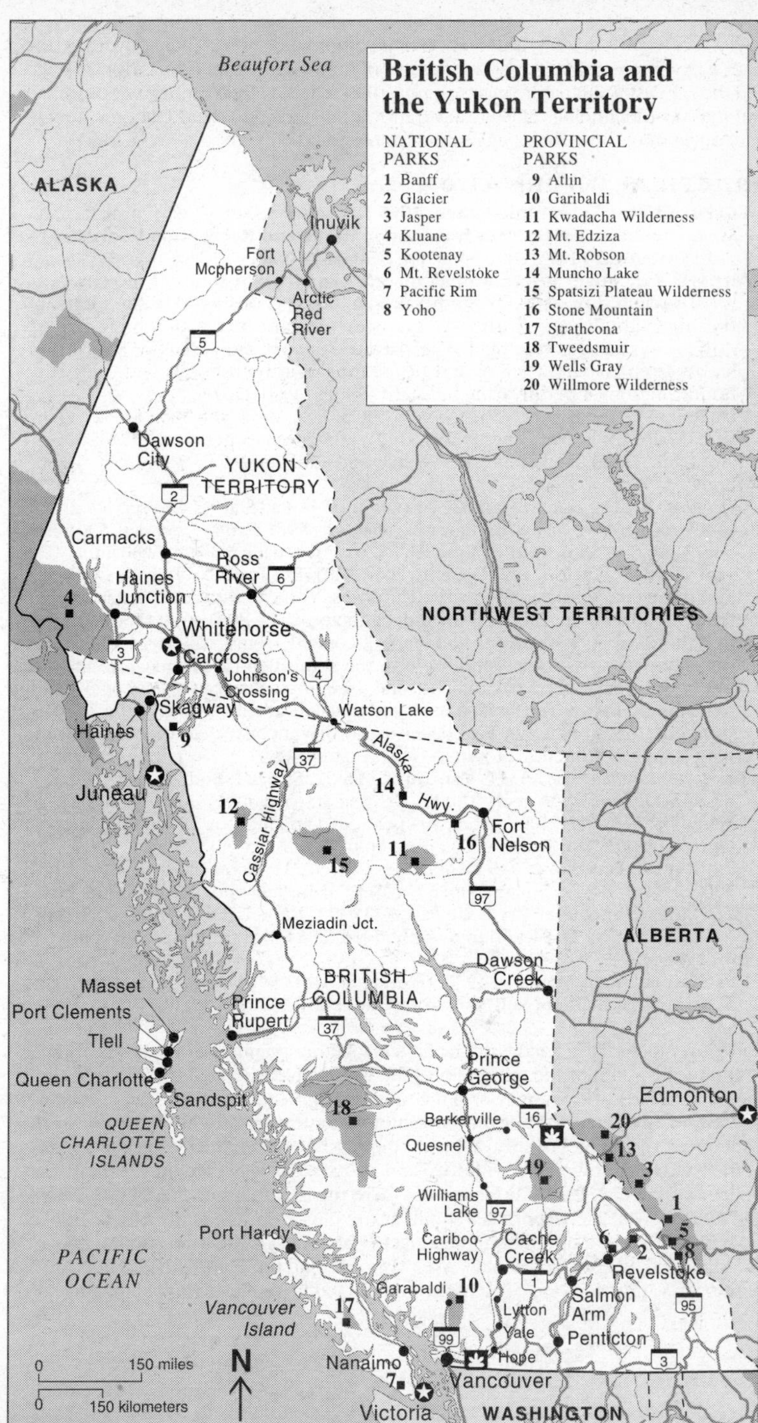
British Columbia and the Yukon Territory
NATIONAL PARKS
1 Banff
2 Glacier
3 Jasper
4 Kluane
5 Kootenay
6 Mt. Revelstoke
7 Pacific Rim
8 Yoho
PROVINCIAL PARKS
9 Atlin
10 Garibaldi
11 Kwadacha Wilderness
12 Mt. Edziza
13 Mt. Robson
14 Muncho Lake
15 Spatsizi Plateau Wilderness
16 Stone Mountain
17 Strathcona
18 Tweedsmuir
19 Wells Gray
20 Willmore Wilderness
Beaufort Sea
ALASKA
Inuvik
Fort Mcpherson
Arctic Red River
Dawson City
YUKON TERRITORY
Carmacks
Ross River
Haines Junction
Whitehorse
Carcross
Johnson's Crossing
Skagway
Haines
Watson Lake
Alaska Hwy.
Juneau
Cassiar Highway
Fort Nelson
NORTHWEST TERRITORIES
ALBERTA
Meziadin Jct.
Dawson Creek
BRITISH COLUMBIA
Masset
Port Clements
Tlell
Queen Charlotte
Sandspit
Prince Rupert
Prince George
Edmonton
QUEEN CHARLOTTE ISLANDS
Barkerville
Quesnel
Williams Lake
Cariboo Highway
Cache Creek
Revelstoke
Port Hardy
PACIFIC OCEAN
Garabaldi
Salmon Arm
Lytton
Yale
Hope
Penticton
Vancouver Island
Nanaimo
Vancouver
Victoria
WASHINGTON
0 150 miles
0 150 kilometers
N

CANADA

safety record rare in a city this size. A multi-ethnic metropolis, Vancouver is Canada's gateway to the Pacific, hosting scores of immigrants from China, Hong Kong, and the Far East. With nature walks among 1000-year-old virgin timber, windsurfing, and the most technologically advanced movie theater in the world all downtown, Vancouver offers an astounding range of things to do.

PRACTICAL INFORMATION

Tourist Office: Travel Infocentre, 1055 Dunsmuir St. (683-2000), near Burrard St., in the West End. Open daily 8am-6pm. **Parks and Recreation Board,** 2099 Beach Ave. (681-1141). Open Mon.-Fri. 8:30am-4:30pm.

Airport: Vancouver International, on Sea Island, 11km south of the city center. To reach downtown from the airport, take BC bus #100 to the intersection of Granville and 70th Ave. Transfer there to bus #20, which arrives downtown at Granville Mall. The private **Airport Express** (273-9023) bus leaves from airport level #2 and heads for downtown hotels and the Greyhound station (4 per hr. 6am-midnight; $8.25 per person).

VIA Rail, 1150 Station St. (669-3050 or 800-561-8630), at the Main St. Sky Train stop. Trains to: Jasper (3 per week, $147); Edmonton (3 per week, $204). Open Mon. and Thurs. 8am-8pm, Tues.-Wed., Fri., and Sun. 8am-3:30pm, Sat. 12:30-8pm.

Greyhound, 1150 Station St. (662-3222), in the VIA Rail Station. Bus service to the south and across Canada. To: Calgary (6 per day, $98); Banff (5 per day, $96); Jasper (3 per day, $86); Seattle (5 per day, $26). Open daily 5:30am-12:30am.

Local Transportation: BC Transit (261-5100). BC Transit subdivides the city into three concentric zones for fare purposes. You can ride in BC Transit's central zone for 90min. for $1.50 (seniors and ages 5-11 80¢) at all times. During peak hours (6:30-9:30am and 3-6:30pm), it costs $2 (seniors and ages 5-11 $1) to travel between two zones, and $2.75 to travel through three zones. During off-peak hours, passengers pay only the one-zone price. **Day passes** are $4.50, and transfers are free. Single fares, passes, and transfers are also good for the **SeaBus** (running from downtown Vancouver to North Vancouver) and **SkyTrain** (running southeast from downtown to New Westminster).

Taxis: Yellow Cab, 681-3311. **Vancouver Taxi,** 255-5111. Both 24 hrs.

Car Rental: Rent-A-Wreck, 180 W. Georgia St. (688-0001). Also 340 W. 4th at Manitoba. $33 a day; 300km free, 10¢ per added km. Must be 19 with credit card. Open Mon.-Fri. 7am-7pm, Sat.-Sun. 8am-5pm.

Bike Rental: Bayshore, 745 Denman St. (689-5071). Good bikes $5.60 per hr., $20 for 8 hrs., $25 overnight. Open May-Sept. daily 9am-9pm. Winter hours vary.

Help Lines: Vancouver Crisis Center, 733-4111. **Rape Crisis Center,** 255-6344. Both 24 hrs. **Gay and Lesbian Switchboard,** 684-6869. Open daily 7-10pm.

Emergency: 911.

Post Office: Main branch, 349 W Georgia St. (662-5725). Open Mon.-Fri. 8am-5:30pm. **Postal Code:** V6B 3P7. **Area Code:** 604.

Vancouver looks like a hand with the fingers together pointing west, and the thumb to the north. South of the mitten flows the Fraser River. Beyond the fingertips lies the Georgia Strait. Downtown is on the thumb. At the thumb's tip lie the residential **West End** and **Stanley Park.** Burrard Inlet separates the downtown from North Vancouver; the bridges over False Creek (the space between the thumb and the rest of the hand) link downtown with **Kitsilano** ("Kits"), **Fairview, Mount Pleasant,** and the rest of the city. East of downtown, where the thumb is attached, lie **Gastown** and **Chinatown.** The **airport** lies south, at the pinkie-tip; the University of British Columbia lies at the tip of the index finger (**Point Grey**). Kitsilano and Point Grey are separated by north-south Alma Ave., Hwy. 99, and the Trans-Canada Hwy. Most of the city's attractions are concentrated on the thumb peninsula and in the fingers.

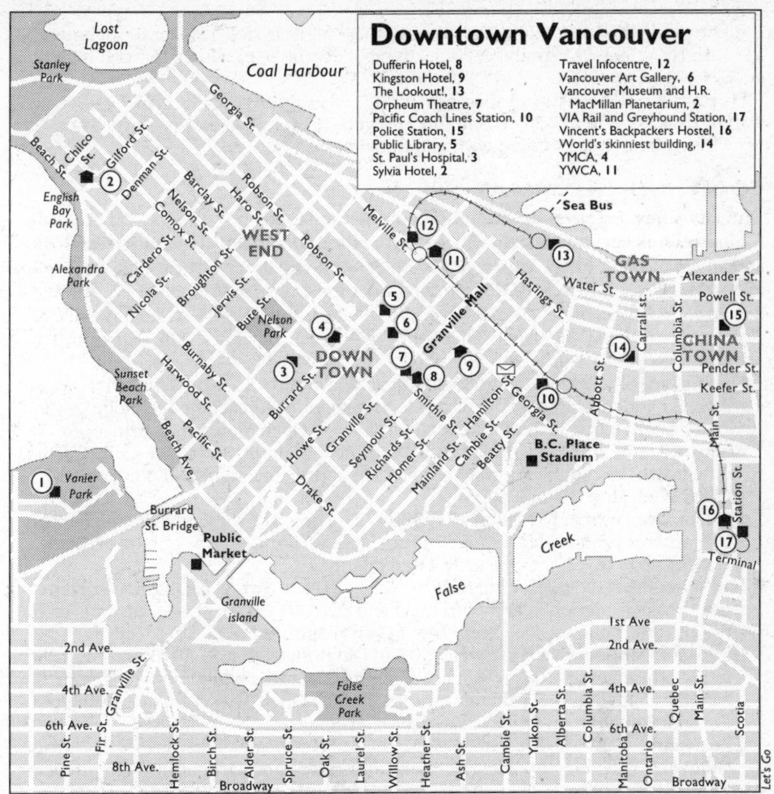

ACCOMMODATIONS AND CAMPING

Greater Vancouver offers many B&Bs. Rates average about $45 to $60 for singles and $55 to $75 for doubles. The visitors bureau has a list of B&Bs, or contact **Town and Country Bed and Breakfast** (731-5942) or **Best Canadian** (738-7207).

Vancouver International Hostel (HI-C), 1515 Discovery St. (224-3208), in Jericho Beach Park. Turn north off 4th Ave., following signs for Marine Dr., or take bus #4 from Granville St. downtown. 285 beds in dorm rooms and 9 family rooms. Kitchen, TV room, laundry. Rent top-quality mountain bikes for $20 per day. In summer 5-day max. stay. Registration 7am-midnight. Linen $1.50. $15, nonmembers $19. Reserve 2 weeks ahead during summer.

University of British Columbia Conference Centre, 5959 Student Union Mall, Walter Gage Residence (822-1010), at the end of Point Grey; take bus #4 or 10 from the Granville Mall. Dorm-style rooms available May-Aug. Check-in after 2pm. Dorm-style singles with shared bath $20, doubles $40; B&B-style singles with shared bath $24, doubles $48; private singles $56, doubles $76.

Paul's Guest House, 345 W. 14th Ave. (872-4753), at Alberta. Take bus #15. Shared baths. Complimentary full breakfast. If Paul's is booked, they can arrange a stay at another B&B. Check-in before 10pm. Call ahead for reservations. Singles $40, doubles $60; winter $35/$55.

Vincent's Backpackers Hostel, 927 Main St. (682-2441), next to the VIA Rail station. Take bus #3 "Main St" or #8 "Fraser". Super cheap. Kitchen, TV, laundry. Mountain bikes $18 per day. Office open 8am-midnight. Shared rooms $10. Singles with shared bath $20, Doubles with shared bath $20. Weekly shared rooms $60, singles $120, doubles $160. $1 off with ISIC student ID card.

Richmond RV Park, 6200 River Rd. (270-7878), near Holly Bridge in Richmond. Take Hwy. 99 to Westminster Hwy., then follow the signs. Sites $16, with hookup $21. Open April-Oct.

Hazelmere RV Park and Campground, 18843 8th Ave. (538-1167), in Surrey. Off Hwy. 99A, head east on 8th Ave. Showers 25¢ for 4½ min. Sites for 1-2 people $16, with hookups $19-22; each additional person $2.

FOOD

The city's best eateries are the ethnic and natural-foods restaurants. Vancouver's **Chinatown** is second in size only to San Francisco's in North America, and the Indian areas along Main, Fraser, and 49th St. serve up spicy dishes. The **Granville Island Market,** southwest of downtown under the Granville Bridge, off W. 4th Ave. across False Creek, offers countless produce stands. Take bus #50 from Granville St. downtown. (Open daily 9am-6pm; Labor Day-Victoria Day Tues.-Sun. 9am-6pm.)

Frannie's Deli, 325 Cambie (685-2928), at W. Cordova St. near Gastown. Doesn't look like much from outside, or inside, but let your stomach be the judge. A variety of sandwiches, including vegetarian ($3.40). Open Mon.-Sat. 6:30am-6pm.

Phnom Penh, 244 E. Georgia (682-1090), near Main St. Take bus #3 or 8 from downtown. Exceptionally tasty Cambodian and Vietnamese food. Entrees $5-10. Open Wed.-Mon. 10am-9:30pm.

Slice of Gourmet, 1152 Denman (689-1112). The place for tantalizing pizza with inventive toppings. Try a huge, filling slice of the peppery potato or Devil's Delight pizza ($3.25). Open daily 11am-midnight.

Nuff-Nice-Ness, 1861 Commercial Dr. (255-4211), at 3rd. Vegetable and meat patties ($2 each). Jerk chicken with salad and rice ($6.25). Daily specials offered in the late afternoon for $5. Open daily 11:30am-8pm.

Isadora's Cooperative Restaurant, 1540 Old Bridge Rd. (681-8816), on Granville Island. This natural foods restaurant sends its profits to community service organizations. Sandwiches $7, dinner entrees $10-13. Open Mon.-Thurs. 7:30am-9pm, Fri.-Sun. 9am-9pm. In winter closed Mon. evenings.

The Naam, 2724 W. 4th Ave. (738-7151), at MacDonald. Take bus #4 or 7 from Granville. Vancouver's oldest natural foods restaurant. Delightful. Tofu-nut-beet burgers ($6.75), spinach enchiladas ($7) Live music nightly 7-10pm. Open 24 hrs.

Nirvana, 2313 Main St. (872-8779), at 7th. Take bus #8, 3, or 9. Come as you are. Smells like authentic, savory, and possibly spiritual Indian cuisine. Chicken curry ($6), vegetable *thali* ($9). Open Mon.-Fri. 11:30am-11pm, Sat.-Sun. noon-11pm.

SIGHTS AND ACTIVITIES

The remaining downtown landmark of the Expo '86 World's Fair is a 17-story, metallic, geodesic sphere which houses **Science World,** 1455 Québec St. (268-6363), at Terminal Ave., which in turn houses an **Omnimax Theatre.** The Canada Pavilion, now called **Canada Place,** is about ½ km away and can be reached by SkyTrain from the main Expo site. The shops are expensive, but the promenades are terrific vantage points for gawking at one of the 200 luxury liners that dock here annually. At 8 W. Pender St. is squeezed the **world's skinniest building**.

The **Lookout!** at 555 W. Hastings St. (689-0421), offers fantastic 360° views of the city. Tickets are expensive!, but they're good for the whole day ($7!, seniors $6!, students $4!; open daily 8:30am-10:30pm, in winter 8:30am-9pm; 50% off with HI membership or receipt from the Vancouver International Hostel)!

Gastown, named for "Gassy Jack" Deighton, the con man who opened Vancouver's first saloon, is a tourist snare disguised as a restored turn-of-the-century neighborhood. Listen for the continent's only steam-powered clock on the corner of Cambie and Water St.—it whistles every 15 minutes. **Chinatown,** replete with restaurants and shops, also lies within walking distance of downtown, but you can take bus #22 on Burrard St. northbound to Pender St. at Carrall St. and return by bus #22 westbound along Pender St.

One of the city's most alluring sites is **Stanley Park,** on the western end of the city-center peninsula; take bus #19. Surrounded by a seawall promenade, this thickly wooded park is crisscrossed with cycling and hiking trails. Within the park's boundaries lie various restaurants, tennis courts, the **Malkin Bowl** (an outdoor theater), and equipped beaches. Cavort alongside beluga whales at the **Vancouver Aquarium** (682-1118), on the eastern side of the park near the entrance (open daily 9:30am-8pm; $11, seniors and students $8.50, under 12 $6.50).

During the summer, a tiny ferry, the **Aquabus** (684-7781), carries passengers from the Aquatic Centre across False Creek to **Vanier** (van-YAY) **Park** and its museum complex (ferries daily every 15min. 10am-8pm; fare $1.25, youth 50¢). Another **ferry** runs from the Maritime Museum in Vanier Park to **Granville Island** ($2.50). Vanier Park can also be reached by bus #22, which heads south on Burrard St. from downtown. Once you reach the park, visit the circular **Vancouver Museum,** 1100 Chestnut St. (736-4431), which displays artifacts from Native Canadian and American cultures in the Pacific Northwest as well as several rotating exhibits. (Open daily 10am-9pm, Oct.-April Tues.-Sun. 10am-5pm. $5, students, seniors, and under 18 $2.50, families $10.)

For a large city, Vancouver has remarkably clean beaches. Follow the western side of the Stanley Park seawall south to **Sunset Beach Park** (738-8535). At the southern end of Sunset Beach is the **Aquatic Centre,** 1050 Beach Ave. (665-3424), a public facility with a 50m indoor saltwater pool, sauna, gymnasium, and diving tank. (Open Mon.-Thurs. 7am-10pm, Sat. 8am-9pm, Sun. 11am-9pm; call for public swim times. Gym and pool use $3.55.)

Kitsilano Beach (731-0011), known to residents of Vancouver as "Kits," on the other side of Arbutus St. from Vanier, is a local favorite. Its heated outdoor saltwater pool has lockers and a snack bar. (Pool open June.-Sept. Mon.-Fri. 7am-8:30pm, Sat.-Sun. 10am-8:30pm. $3.55, seniors $1.75, children $2.30.)

Students hang at **Jericho Beach,** to the west, which tends to be less heavily used than Kits Beach. Jericho has free showers. North Marine Dr. runs along the beach, and a great cycling path at the edge of the road leads to the westernmost edge of the **University of British Columbia (UBC)** campus. Bike and hiking trails cut through the campus and crop its edges. From the UBC entrance, several marked trails lead down to the unsupervised, inauspicious **Wreck Beach.** The high point of a campus visit is the **Museum of Anthropology,** 6393 NW Marine Dr. (822-3825 for a recording, 822-5087 for an operator). Be sure to find the renowned work "The Raven and the First Man," by Bill Reid, an artistic allusion to the Haida creation myth. (Open Tues. 11am-9pm, Wed.-Mon. 11am-5pm. Sept.-June closed Mondays. $6, seniors and students $3.50, families $15, under 6 free; Tues. after 5pm free.) To reach the campus, take bus #4 or 10 from Granville Mall downtown.

With pseudo-European delicatessens and shops, the **Robsonstrasse** shopping district, on Robson St. between Howe and Broughton St., tempts tourists to throw around their money under kaleidoscopic awnings. For more reasonable prices and "idiosyncratic" offerings, stroll down Commercial Dr., or browse through the numerous boutiques lining 4th Ave. and Broadway. **Granville Mall,** on Granville Ave. between Smithe and Hastings St., is Vancouver's pedestrian and bus mall. From Hastings St. to the Orpheum Theatre, most shops and restaurants on the mall cater to young professionals and business executives on their power-lunch hours.

ENTERTAINMENT AND NIGHTLIFE

To keep abreast of the entertainment scene, pick up a copy of the weekly *Georgia Straight* or the monthly *AF Magazine,* both free at newsstands and record stores. The **Vancouver Symphony Orchestra (VSO)** (684-9100) plays in the refurbished **Orpheum Theater,** 884 Granville St. (280-4444; ticketline 280-3311).

Vancouver theatre is renowned throughout Canada. The **Arts Club Theatre** (687-1644) hosts big-name theatre and musicals, and the **Theatre in the Park** program (687-0174 for ticket info), in Stanley Park's Malkin Bowl, plays a summer season of musical comedy. The annual **Vancouver Shakespeare Festival** (734-0194), held

June through August in Vanier Park, often needs volunteer ticket-takers and program-sellers, who work for free admission to the acclaimed shows. **UBC Summer Stock** (822-2678) puts on four plays in summer at the **Frederick Wood Theatre.**

The famed **Vancouver Folk Music Festival** (879-2931) jams in mid-July in Jericho Park. For three days the best acoustic performers in North America give concerts and workshops. Tickets can be purchased for each day or for the whole weekend. (Tickets $26 per day, $70 per weekend. Prices increase at the gate.) Enjoy ten days of hot jazz at the annual **Du Maurier International Jazz Festival Vancouver** (682-0706) in the third week of June. Call or write to 435 W. Hastings, Vancouver V6V 1L4 for details. Ask about the free concerts at the Plaza, in Gastown, and on Granville Island. All kinds of music is enjoyed in Vancouver's pubs and clubs. Most shut down at 2am.

The Roxy, 932 Granville St. (684-7699). Vampire-free, since you have to get here before 8pm to avoid the lines. Live local and national rock makes the Roxy the talk of the town. Variable cover. Open Mon.-Sat. 7pm-2am, Sun. 7pm-midnight.

The Town Pump, 66 Water St. (683-6695), in Gastown. Large pub-style club featuring progressive bands. Variable cover. Open Mon.-Sat. noon-2am.

Luv-A-fair, 1275 Seymour St. (685-3288), downtown. Trendy dance space pipes alternative music into the ears of black-clad clubsters. Experiment with the live underground bands Wed. night. Open Mon.-Sat. 9pm-2am, Sun. 9am-midnight.

Celebrities, 1022 Davie St. (689-3180), downtown. Very big, very hot, and very popular with the gay community. Open Mon.-Sat. 9pm-2am, Sun. 9pm-midnight.

Graceland, 1250 Richards St. (688-2648), at Drake downtown. Warehouse space pulses to house music on Fri. and Sat. nights, reggae on Wed. Open Mon.-Sat. noon-2am, Sun. noon-midnight.

■■■ VICTORIA

Set among the rough-hewn logging and fishing towns of Vancouver Island, the capital of British Columbia demonstrates a reserve and propriety worthy of its name. On warm summer days, Anglophile residents sip their teas on the lawns of Tudor-style homes in the suburbs, while downtown, horse-drawn carriages clatter in the streets.

Practical Information Ferries and buses connect Victoria to most cities in British Columbia and Washington. The city of Victoria enfolds the Inner Harbour; **Government Street** and **Douglas Street** are the main north-south thoroughfares. **Tourism Victoria,** 810 Wharf St., (382-2127), at the corner of Government St., has the low-down (open daily 9am-9pm; winter daily 9am-5pm). **Pacific Coast Lines (PCL)** and its affiliate, **Island Coach Lines,** 700 Douglas St. (385-4411), at Belleville, connect all major points and most minor ones, running to Vancouver (16 per day, $22.50) and Seattle (1 per day, $28.60). **BC Ferry,** (656-0757 for a recording, 386-3431 for an operator 7am-10pm), runs between Swartz Bay (Victoria) and Tsawwassen (Vancouver). (20 per day 5:30am-10pm. $6.50, bikes $2.50, cars $25.) **Washington State Ferries,** (381-1551) makes waves from Sidney, BC to Anacortes, WA via the San Juan Islands, running twice daily in summer, once daily in winter. Fares vary; call for rates and schedules. Take bus #70 ($2) to reach the ferry terminal. **BC Transit** (382-6161) provides city bus service, with connections downtown at the corner of Douglas and Yates St. Travel in the single-zone area costs $1.50, in the multi-zone (north to Sidney and the Butchart Gardens) $2.25. Daily passes for unlimited single-zone travel are available at 7-11 and Shoppers Drug stores for $5 (over 65 and under 12 $4). **Emergency** is 911. Victoria's **post office:** 714 Yates (953-1351; open Mon.-Fri. 8:30am-5pm); **postal code:** V8W 1L0; **area code:** 604.

Accommodations, Camping, and Food **Victoria Youth Hostel (HI-C),** 516 Yates St., (385-4511), at Wharf St. downtown, has 104 beds in the newly remodeled Victoria Heritage Building. (Kitchen, laundry. Desk open 7am-midnight; curfew

2:30am. $15, nonmembers $19.) The **Renouf House Bunk and Breakfast,** 2010 Stanley Ave. (595-4774), is in a 1912 home close to downtown; rooms come with linen and an all-you-can-eat buffet breakfast (bunks, 2-4 to a room, from $18.25; singles $33.25; doubles $45.50). **Thetis Lake Campground,** 1938 Trans-Canada Hwy. (478-3845), 10 km north of the city center, has peaceful and removed sites ($15 for 2 people; 50¢ per additional person). **Fort Victoria Camping,** 340 Island Hwy. (479-8112), is 7 km northwest of downtown off the Trans-Canada Hwy. (Free hot showers. Laundromat. Sites $19 for 2 people, full hookups $24.)

John's Place, 723 Pandora St. (389-0711), is a locally favored diner with a Thai twist on the menu (open Mon.-Thurs. 7am-10pm, Sat. 7am-11pm, Sun. 5-10pm). **Eugene's,** 1280 Broad St. (381-5456), serves vegetarian souvlaki ($3). *Rizogalo* or *bougatsa* is a nice change for breakfast ($2). (Open Mon. 8am-6pm, Tues.-Fri. 8am-8pm, Sat. 10am-5pm.) The **Sally Café,** 714 Cormorant St. (381-1413), is *the* sophisticated meeting place, and dishes up a tasty curried chicken and apricot ($5.50). (Open Mon.-Fri. 7am-5pm, Sat. 8am-5pm.) **Ferris' Oyster and Burger Bar,** 536 Yates St. (360-1824), next to the hostel, has smoked oysters ($2 each) along with traditional pub fare and a number of vegetarian options. (Open Mon.-Thurs. 9am-10pm, Fri.-Sat. 9am-11pm, Sun. 9am-8pm. HI members discount.)

Sights and Nightlife Victoria is a small city; you can wander the **Inner Harbour,** watch the boats come in, and take in many of the city's main attractions, all on foot. The first stop for every visitor should be the **Royal British Columbian Museum,** 675 Belleville St. (387-3014 for a recording, 387-3701 for an operator). One of the best museums in Canada, it chronicles the geological, biological, and cultural history of the province, and showcases detailed exhibits on logging, mining, and fishing. (Open daily 9:30am-7pm; Sept. 11-June 10:30am-5pm. $5; seniors, disabled, and students with ID or HI card $3; ages 6-18 $2. Free after 5:45pm and Oct.-April Mon. Ticket is good for 2 days.) Behind the museum, **Thunderbird Park** is a striking thicket of totems and longhouses.

Across the street from the museum are the imposing **Parliament Buildings,** 501 Belleville St. (387-3046), home of the Provincial government since 1898. The 10-story dome and vestibule are gilded with almost 50 oz. of gold. Free tours leave from the main steps daily 9am to 5pm (20-23 times a day; in winter on the hour. Open Mon.-Fri. 8:30am-5pm, on weekends for tours only.)

South of the Inner Harbour, **Beacon Hill Park** surveys the Strait of Juan de Fuca; take bus #5. East of the Inner Harbour, **Craigdarroch Castle,** 1050 Joan Crescent (592-5323; take bus #11 or 14), was built in 1890 by Robert Dunsmuir, a coal and railroad tycoon, to lure his wife from their native Scotland to Victoria. (Open daily 9am-7pm; Sept. 6-June 14 10am-4:30pm. $6, students $5, ages 6-12 $2, under 6 $1.)

The stunning **Butchart Gardens,** 800 Benvenuto (652-5256 for a recording or 652-4422 for an operator Mon.-Fri. 9am-5pm), 22 km north of Victoria, are a maze of pools and fountains. Take bus #75 from Douglas and View St. northbound right into the Gardens. Motorists should consider approaching Butchart Gardens via the **Scenic Marine Drive,** following the coastline. (Gardens open 9am; call for closing times. $13, ages 13-17 $10, ages 5-12 $3.50; winter $7.50/$5.50/$2.50. Hang on to your ticket: readmission within 24 hrs. is only $1.)

You can get an exhaustive listing of what's where when in the free weekly *Monday Magazine.* For an eclectic mix of music, check out **Harpo's Cabaret,** 15 Bastion Sq. (385-5333), at Wharf St. (open Mon.-Sat. 9pm-2am, Sun. 8pm-midnight; cover around $5). **The Forge,** 919 Douglas St. (383-7137), in the Strathcona Hotel, specializes in loud 70s rock (open daily 9pm-3am). **Rumors,** 1325 Government St. (385-0566), has a lively gay and lesbian clientele (open Mon.-Sat. 9pm-3am).

■■■ GLACIER

For a $5000 salary bonus and immortality on the map, Major A.B. Rogers discovered a route through the Columbia Mountains which finally allowed Canada to build its first transcontinental railway. Completed in 1885, the railway was a dangerous enterprise; more than 200 lives were lost to avalanches during its first 30 years of operation. Today, Rogers Pass lies in the center of **Glacier National Park,** and 1350 sq. km commemorate the efforts of Rogers and other hardy explorers who bound British Columbia to the rest of Canada.

Practical Information Glacier lies on the Trans-Canada Hwy., 262 km west of Calgary and 723 km east of Vancouver. The Trans-Canada Hwy.'s many **scenic turn-offs** offer picnic facilities, bathrooms, and historical plaques. For a detailed description of the park's 19 hiking trails, talk to the rangers or buy a copy of *Footloose in the Columbias* ($1.50) at the **Rogers Pass Information Centre** (837-6274), on the highway in Glacier. The Centre has enough computerized information, scale models, and exhibits to warrant a visit. (Open daily 7am-7pm; in winter hours vary.) **Park passes** are required if you don't drive straight through ($5 per day, $10 for 4 days, $30 per year, good in all Canadian national parks). For more info about Glacier National Park, write the Superintendent, P.O. Box 350, Revelstoke V0E 2S0. **Greyhound** (837-5874) makes four trips daily from Revelstoke to Glacier ($10). In an emergency, call the **Park Warden Office** (837-6274; open daily 7am-11pm; winter daily 24 hrs.). The **area code** is 604.

Camping and Food There are two campgrounds in Glacier: **Illecillewaet** (ill-uh-SILL-uh-watt) and **Loop Brook.** Both offer flush toilets, kitchen shelters with cook stoves, drinking water, and firewood (open mid-June-Sept.; sites for both $13). Illecillewaet stays open in winter without plumbing; winter guests must register at the Park Administration Office at Rogers Pass. **Backcountry campers** must pitch their tents at least 5 km from the pavement and register with the Administration Office beforehand. For **food,** you'd do well to drop by a supermarket in Golden or Revelstoke before you enter the park.

Outdoors A century after Rogers's discovery, Glacier remains an unspoiled and remote wilderness. The jagged peaks and steep, narrow valleys of the Columbia Range prevent development. One would literally have to move mountains to build here. The Trans-Canada Highway cuts a thin ribbon through the park, affording spectacular views of over 400 glaciers. More than 140 km of challenging trails lead away from the highway, inviting rugged mountain men and women to penetrate the near-impenetrable. Try to visit the park in late July or early August, when brilliant explosions of mountain wildflowers offset the deep green of the forests. Glacier receives measurable precipitation every other day in summer, but the clouds of mist that encircle the peaks and blanket the valleys only add to the park's beauty. Unless you're Sir Edmund Hillary, avoid the park in winter, as snowfalls and the constant threat of avalanches often restrict travel to the Trans-Canada Hwy.

Eight popular **hiking trails** begin at the Illecillewaet campground, 3.4 km west of Rogers Pass. The relaxing, 1-km **Meeting of the Waters** trail leads to the confluence of the Illecillewaet and Asulkan Rivers. The 4.2-km **Avalanche Crest** trail offers spectacular views of Rogers Pass, the Hermit Range, and the Illecillewaet River Valley; the treeless slopes below the crest testify to the destructive power of winter snowslides. From early July to late August, the Information Centre runs daily **interpretive hikes** through the park beginning at 9am. Come prepared for one of these four- to six-hour tours with a picnic lunch, a rain jacket, and a sturdy pair of walking shoes. Regulations prohibit biking on the trails in Glacier.

■■■ PRINCE RUPERT

Most visitors come to Prince Rupert either for fishing or ferries. An afternoon in a guided fishing boat costs upwards of $100; pass the hours before your ship comes in browsing the 15 downtown blocks. The **Travel Infocentre** (624-5637), at 1st Ave. and McBride St., has maps for a self-guided tour, including the Infocentre's free museum, a cornucopia of totem poles, the manicured Sunken Gardens, and a Native Canadian carving shed (open May 15-Labor Day daily 9am-9pm; winter Mon.-Sat. 10am-5pm). The only major road into town is **Hwy. 16,** or McBride at the city limits, which curves left and becomes 2nd Ave. downtown. **Prince Rupert Bus Service** (624-3343) provides local service downtown Mondays through Saturdays (fare $1, seniors 60¢, students 75¢; day pass $2.50, seniors and students $2). The #52 bus runs from 2nd Ave. and 3rd St. to within a five-minute walk of the ferry terminal; you can also try **Skeena Taxi,** (624-2185; open 24 hrs.).

The **Alaska Marine Highway** (627-1744), at the end of Hwy. 16 (Park Ave.), runs ferries north from Prince Rupert to Ketchikan (US$38, car US$75) and Juneau (US$104, car US$240). **BC Ferries** (624-9627) serves the Queen Charlotte Islands (6 per week, $22, car $83) and Port Hardy (4 per week; $98, car $202; vehicle reservations required 3 wks. in advance). Ferrygoers may not leave cars parked on the streets of Prince Rupert. Some establishments charge a daily rate for storage; pick up a list at the Infocentre (see above). In an **emergency,** call 911. Prince Rupert's **post office:** 2nd Ave. and 3rd St. (624-2136; open Mon.-Fri. 8:30am-4:30pm); **postal code:** V8J 3P3; **area code:** 604.

Nearly all of Prince Rupert's hotels are within the six-block area defined by 1st Ave., 3rd Ave., 6th St., and 9th St. Everything fills when the ferries dock, so call a day or two ahead. **Pioneer Rooms,** 167 3rd Ave. E (624-2334) is a turquoise house with laundry facilities, floors clean enough to eat from, and great management (singles with shared bath $15-20, doubles $25-30; showers $3). The **Eagle Bluff Bed and Breakfast,** 201 Cow Bay Rd. (627-4955 or 800-833-1550) is a step up in quality and price (singles $40, doubles $50; reservations recommended). Camp at **Park Ave. Campground,** 1750 Park Ave. (624-5861 or 800-667-1994), less than 2 km east of the ferry terminal (tent sites $9; RV sites $16). Scarf some serious seafood at **Smiles Seafood Café,** 113 George Hills Way (624-3072), on the waterfront; the heaping fish 'n'chips platter ($8.75) is a feed (open daily 10am-10pm). Get your own raw fish at **Safeway** (624-2412) at 2nd. St. and 2nd. Ave. (open daily 9am-10pm).

The grassy hills of **Service Park,** off Fulton St., offer a panoramic view of downtown Prince Rupert and the harbor beyond. **Diana Lake Park,** 16 km east of town along Hwy. 16, provides a picnic area set against an enticing lake.

Yukon Territory

Native Americans recognized the majesty of this land when they dubbed the Yukon River "Yuchoo," or Big River. Gold-hungry white settlers streamed in at the end of the 19th century, interested in the yellow metal turned up by the Big River's tributaries, and left almost as quickly when the rushes didn't pan out. Although the Yukon and Northern British Columbia were the first regions of North America to be settled some 20,000 years ago, today they remain largely untouched and inaccessible. With an average of only one person per 15 sq. km, the loneliness of the area is overwhelming—as is its sheer physical beauty, a reward for those willing to deal with unpredictable winter weather and poor road conditions.

Let's Go: Alaska & The Pacific Northwest has golden info on the Yukon.

■■■ WHITEHORSE

Named for the once-perilous Whitehorse Rapids, whose crashing whitecaps were said to resemble a galloping herd of white mares before they were tamed by a dam, Whitehorse marks the highest navigable point on the Yukon. Capital of the Yukon since 1953, Whitehorse is developing a cosmopolitan outlook while staying fully aware and proud of its century-old Klondike history. Whitehorse is a good base for exploring the surrounding country.

Practical Information The **Whitehorse Visitor Reception Centre,** on the Alaska Hwy. next to the Transportation Museum (667-2915), has an entire forest's worth of free brochures and maps (open mid-May to mid-Sept. daily 8am-8pm). Or, get info by writing **Tourism Yukon,** P.O. Box 2703, Whitehorse, YT Y1A C26.

Canadian Airlines (668-4466, for reservations 668-3535) soars to Calgary (daily, $541), Edmonton (3 per day, $541), and Vancouver (3 per day, $457). **Greyhound** runs buses from 2191 2nd Ave. (667-2223) to Vancouver ($293), Edmonton ($227), and Dawson Creek ($162; open Mon.-Fri. 8:30am-5:30pm, Sat. 8am-noon, Sun. 5-9pm). **Alaskon Express** operates from the Westmark Hotel (668-3225), at 2nd Ave. and Wood St. Buses run from late May to mid-September to Anchorage (3 per week, US$190), Haines (3 per week, US$82), and Fairbanks (3 per week, US$160). In an **emergency,** call 911. There is no main **post office** in Whitehorse. For general services, go to 211 Main St. (668-5847; open Mon.-Fri. 8am-6pm, Sat. 9am-5pm). For general delivery, head for 3rd and Wood, in the Yukon News Bldg. (668-3824; open Mon.-Sat. 7am-7pm). General Delivery **Postal Code** for last names beginning with the letters A-L is Y1A 3S7; for M-Z it's Y1A 3S8. Whitehorse's **area code:** 403.

Accommodations, Camping, and Food Call the **Northern Network of Bed and Breakfasts** (993-5649), in Dawson City, to reserve a room in a Klondike household (singles from $50, doubles from $60). **High Country Inn,** 4051 4th Ave. (667-4471), offers long- and short-term housing. This residence boasts cooking and laundry facilities, and good security. (Shared doubles $18, private singles $50; call to reserve a bed.) **Roadhouse Inn,** 2163 2nd Ave. (667-2594), adjacent to the Roadhouse Saloon, has good, cheap rooms. (Shared rooms $18 per person; Private singles $50, private doubles $55.) Camping in Whitehorse is a problem: there is only one RV campground and one tenting park near the downtown area. **Robert Service Campground,** 1km from town on South Access Rd. on the Yukon River, is convenient for tenters, but has no RV sites (open late May-early Sept.; 40 sites, $14). RVs should head for **High-Country RV Park** (668-4500, 800-661-0539 for reservations), at the intersection of the Alaska Hwy. and South Access Rd., which has lots of amenities and a Good Sam discount (RV sites $13-18 for 2 people, $3 each added person).

No Pop Sandwich Shop, 312 Steele (668-3227), is popular with Whitehorse's small suit-and-tie crowd; have a Beltch (BLT and cheese, $4.50; open Mon.-Thurs. 8am-9pm, Fri. 8am-10pm, Sat. 10am-8pm, Sun. 10am-3pm). **Talisman Café,** 2112 2nd Ave. (667-2736) delivers good food in a nondescript environment (burgers from $5 and breakfasts around $5.50; open daily 6am-10pm).

Sights The restored *Klondike,* on South Access Rd. (667-4511), is a dry-docked sternwheeler that recalls the days when the Yukon River was the city's sole artery of survival. Pick up a ticket for a fascinating guided tour from the info booth at the parking lot entrance ($3, kids $2, families $7; open June 1-Sept. 15 daily 9am-7:30pm). The **Whitehorse Rapids Fishway** (633-5965), at the end of Nisutlin Dr., 2 km southeast of town, allows salmon to bypass the dam and continue upstream in the world's longest salmon migration (open daily mid-June to mid-Sept. 8am-10pm; free). **Miles Canyon** whispers 2 km south of town on Miles Canyon Rd. off of South Access Rd. Once the location of the feared Whitehorse rapids, this dammed stretch of the Yukon now swirls silently under the first bridge to span the river's banks. The **MacBride Museum** (667-2709), at 1st Ave. and Wood St., features memorabilia from the early days of the Yukon. (Open daily May and Sept. noon-4pm; June and Aug. 10am-6pm; July 9am-6pm. $3.50, seniors and students $2.75, families $8.50.) Many outfitters will get you out on the river. The **MV Schwatka** (668-2042), on Miles Canyon Rd. off South Access Rd., floats you through Miles Canyon for $17, ages 6-11 $8.50, under 6 free (2-hr. cruises leave daily at 2 and 7pm).

The Strange Saga of the Sourtoe

When most people run across an amputated body part, they avoid it. But for some inexplicable reason, Capt. Dick Stevenson decided to make a cocktail with the **human toe** he found in a cabin in the Yukon. Not surprisingly, the drink became famous and spawned the **Sourtoe Cocktail Club,** an institution with a history as peculiar as its name would suggest. Would-be members buy a drink of their choice and pay a small fee ($5) to Bill "Stillwater Willie" Boone (Dick's replacement as keeper of the toe), who proceeds to drop the chemically preserved (read: pickled) toe in the drink. Then it's bottoms up, and the moment the toe touches your lips, you've become one of the club's 12,000-plus proud members. "You can drink it fast, you can drink it slow—but the lips have gotta touch the toe." Listening to Stillwater Willie explain the club's sordid history and philosophize about life in the Yukon is itself worth the $5, but the fee includes a certificate, membership card, and pin. All the fun takes place in Dawson City, 533 km north of Whitehorse on the Klondike Hwy. (except when the toe is on one of its many publicity tours). Inquire at the Pleasure Island Restaurant (993-5482), on Front St. between King and Queen in Dawson City, for initiation times and locations.

■■■ CARCROSS

The 404 inhabitants of Carcross, short for "Caribou Crossing," live on the narrows between Bennet and Nares Lakes, completely surrounded by snow-capped peaks. Native Tagish people hunted caribou at the crossing until the early 1900s when the herds were obliterated. Since then, Carcross has survived off mining and tourists, drawn by the Yukon's pristine southern lakes district. On the Klondike Hwy. (Hwy. 2), Carcross is 74km south of Whitehorse and 106km north of Skagway, AK.

Practical Information Old photographs, displays, and a laser-disc presentation trace the history of the White Pass and Yukon Railroad at the **Carcross Visitor Reception Centre** (821-4431), inside the depot (open mid-May to mid-Sept. daily 8am-8pm). Tune in to **visitors information** on 96.1 FM. **Atlin Express** (604-651-7617) runs buses from Carcross to Atlin, BC ($21, seniors $18, ages 5-11 $10.50, under 5 free), Whitehorse ($15/$13/$7.50/free), and Tagish ($5/$4/$2.50/free). The two-story red building in Carcross houses the **health station** (821-4444). **Emergency numbers** include: **ambulance,** 821-3333; **fire,** 821-2222; **police,** 821-5555 (if no answer call 403-667-5555). The **post office** is the white building with red trim on Bennett Ave. (Open Mon., Wed., Fri. 8:30am-noon and 1-2pm, Tues. and Thurs. 10-11:45am); **postal Code:** Y0B 1B0; **area code:** 403.

Accommodations, Camping, and Food Carcross's **Caribou Hotel** (821-4501), stands as the oldest operating hotel in the Yukon. The original structure was destroyed in a 1909 fire; the present building was erected shortly thereafter. Insiders whisper that "she was rebuilt after the fire, but she's still old enough to have a ghost." (No phones, no TVs, shared bath; singles and doubles $35.) **Spirit Lake Lodge** (821-4337), 7km north of town on Hwy. 2, maintains forested tent sites overlooking the lake (sites $6; showers $3; firewood $3 per bundle) and rooms (singles $50; $5 per additional person). The Yukon Government maintains 14 secluded sites ($8) with drinking water, firewood, and pit toilets at **Carcross Campground,** 1km north of town on Hwy. 2.

Pirogies (Russian dumplings) are a local specialty. The restaurant at the Caribou Hotel serves standard food at standard prices; burgers cost $6.25 and up; dinners begin at $9.50 (open daily 7am-8pm). Herbivores seek out the cheese and potato *pirogies* ($5-9) at the **Spirit Lake Restaurant** (821-4337), in the Spirit Lake Lodge (open daily 7am-10pm). If you've brought your grandma's own *pirogi* recipe from Russia, look for the needed ingredients (or buy frozen *pirogies*—for shame!) at

Montana Services (821-3708), at the Chevron station on Hwy. 2 (open May-Sept. daily 7am-11pm; Oct.-April 8am-8pm).

Sights and Outdoors South of town an old, rough mining road reaches part-way up Montana Mountain. Legs and lungs carry the stalwart the rest of the way past the lichen, snow, and boulders to a spectacular view. Follow Hwy. 2 south, take the first right after crossing the bridge, then the first left, then follow until the road becomes impassable; from there, walk up to gain an astounding **view** of the Yukon. Anglers can cast for lake trout and grayling from the footbridge that spans the river, or check at the Reception Center for information on local lakes.

Souvenir-hunters sniff out **The Barracks** (821-4372), just across the railroad tracks from the Reception Center (open daily 9am-5pm). Be warned: shoppers mistaken for **Claim-Jumpin' Jim** may be thrown in the store's jail before they get a chance to browse through the local crafts, jewelry, and artwork.

Once the sandy bottom of a large glacial lake, the **Carcross Desert,** 2km north of town on Hwy. 2., was exposed by glacial retreat; harsh winds from Lake Bennett have discouraged plant growth since. At **Emerald Lake,** 8km farther north, light reflecting off a white sediment called marl creates a mottled blue-green effect. The **Spirit Lake Lodge** (821-4337), 7km north of town on Hwy. 2, rents out canoes ($5 per hr., $25 per day).

Frontierland (667-1055), 1km north of the desert, contains a wildlife gallery of mounted animals in life-like settings, including the largest bear ever mounted, a Heritage Park, featuring live Yukon wildlife such as lynxes and dall sheep, and some great **birdwatching** opportunities. (Open mid-May to mid-Sept. daily 8am-5:30pm; museum and park $6, children $4; one attraction $3.50/$2.50.)

■■■ KLUANE

On St. Elias' Day 1741, Vitus Bering, a Danish captain in the Russian service, sighted the mountains of what is now **Kluane National Park.** "Kluane" (kloo-AH-nee) is a Tutchone Native word, meaning "place of many fish." Kluane is Canadian wilderness at its most rugged, unspoiled, and beautiful. The "Green Belt" along the eastern park boundary, at the foot of the Kluane Range, supports the greatest diversity of plant and animal species in northern Canada. To the west loom the glaciers of the Icefield Range, home to Canada's highest peaks, including the tallest, 19,850-ft. Mt. Logan. The Alaska Highway, near the northeastern boundary of the park, provides generally convenient park access.

Practical Information Kluane's 22,015 sq. km are bounded by Kluane Game Sanctuary and the Alaska Hwy. to the north, and the Haines Hwy. (Hwy. 3) to the east. The town of **Haines Junction** is at the eastern park boundary, 158 km west of Whitehorse. Pick up plenty of free information at the **Haines Junction Visitor Centre,** on Logan St. in Haines Junction (Canadian Park Service 634-7207; Tourism Yukon 634-2345; open mid-May to mid-Sept. daily 8am-8pm), or at the **Sheep Mountain Visitor Centre,** at Alaska Hwy. Km 1707 (open June to mid-Sept. daily 9am-5pm). Visitors may also write to Superintendent, Kluane National Park and Preserve, Haines Junction, YT Y0B 1L0 for information. **Alaska Direct** (668-4833 or 800-770-6652) runs three buses per week from Haines Junction to Anchorage (US$125), Fairbanks (US$100), Whitehorse (US$20), and Skagway (US$55). The **visitor radio** station is FM 96.1. **Emergency numbers** in Haines Junction include: **medical,** 634-2213; **fire,** 634-2222; and **police,** 635-5555 (if no answer, call 1-403-667-5555). Kluane's **post office:** (634-2706) in Madley's General Store (open Mon., Wed., and Fri. 9-10am and 1-5pm, Tues. 9am-1pm, Thurs. 9am-noon, 1-5pm); **postal code:** Y0B 1L0; **area code:** 403.

Camping, Accommodations, and Food **Kathleen Lake Campground** (634-2251), 27 km south of Haines Junction off Haines Rd., is close to good hiking and fishing and features water, flush toilets, fire pits, firewood, and occasional "campfire talks" (sites $9; open June-Oct.). The Yukon government runs four campgrounds, all with hand-pumped cold water and pit toilets (sites $8; call Tourism Yukon at 634-2345 for more information): **Pine Lake,** 7 km east of Haines Jct. on the Alaska Hwy.; **Congdon Creek,** 85 km west of Haines Jct. on the Alaska Hwy.; **Dezadeash Lake,** 50 km south of Haines Junction on Haines Rd.; and **Million Dollar Falls,** 90 km south of Haines Jct. on Haines Rd., near the BC border. Beautiful indoor accommodations can be found at **Laughing Moose Bed and Breakfast,** 120 Alsek Crescent (634-2335; singles $55, doubles $65; shared bath).

Haines Junction restaurants offer (yawn) standard highway cuisine; for groceries, head for **Madley's General Store,** at Haines Rd. and Bates (634-2200; open daily 8am-9pm; Oct.-April 8am-6:30pm). Satiate your sweet tooth with a cinnamon bun ($1) or carbo-load with a tasty sourdough loaf ($2.25) from the **Village Bakery and Deli** (634-2867), on Logan St. across from the visitor centre (open May-Sept. daily 9am-9pm).

Outdoors in the Park There are few actual trails in the park; the major ones are the 4-km **Dezadeash River Loop** (dez-a-DEE-ush), beginning at the Haines Junction Visitor Centre, the 15-km **Auriol Trail** starting from Haines Hwy. (an excellent overnight hike), and the 85-km **Cottonwood Trail,** a four- to six-day trek beginning either 27 or 55 km south of Haines Junction on Haines Hwy. Cottonwood is a loop trail offering 25 km of trail above tree-line and a short detour up an adjacent ridge providing a view of the Icefield Ranges and Mount Logan on clear days.

The park also offers many **"routes"** following no formal trail and not maintained by the park. These are reserved for more experienced hikers, since route finding, map reading, and compass skills may all be called for. Perhaps the most popular are the **Slims East** and **Slims West** routes, both beginning 3 km south of the Sheep Mountain Information Center (see above); both follow the Slims River (each on its respective side) for 23-30km (one-way) to ridges overlooking the mighty **Kaskawalsh Glacier.** Both routes take from three to five days; due to increased bear activity in this area, the park mandates the use of **bear canisters** for the storage of food on all overnight trips. All trekkers camping in the backcountry must register at one of the visitor centres and purchase a permit ($10 per person per trip). The park strongly encourages day hikers to register, especially in the **north end** and **Slims Valley** section of the park where trails are not as well marked and bear activity is more frequent. For the less adventurous, the park offers shorter **day-hikes** and **walks** led by park interpreters concentrating on specific themes from bear habitats to the park's wildflowers.

The **Kluane Park Adventure Center** (634-2313) is the central booking office for outdoor activities going on in and around the park (open daily noon-8pm). The center has **mountain bikes** ($15 per ½ day, $25 for 24 hrs.) and canoes ($25 per day) for rent. For $100, you can ride the class III and IV rapids on the Tatshenshini River from Copper Mine, BC to Dalton Post, YT. The center also offers a more serene two-hour scenic float trip illustrating the park's ecology, fauna, and geology for $25.

At the junction of the Alaska Hwy. and Haines Hwy., your gaze will become uncontrollably fixed on Haines Junction's horrific wild-animal monument. Known locally as "the muffin," the gigantic faux-mountain landscape looks just like...well, a wild-animal muffin. In the most dramatic display of irony since O. Henry's "Gift of the Magi," the monument was actually constructed as part of a town beautification project in 1988.

INDEX

D

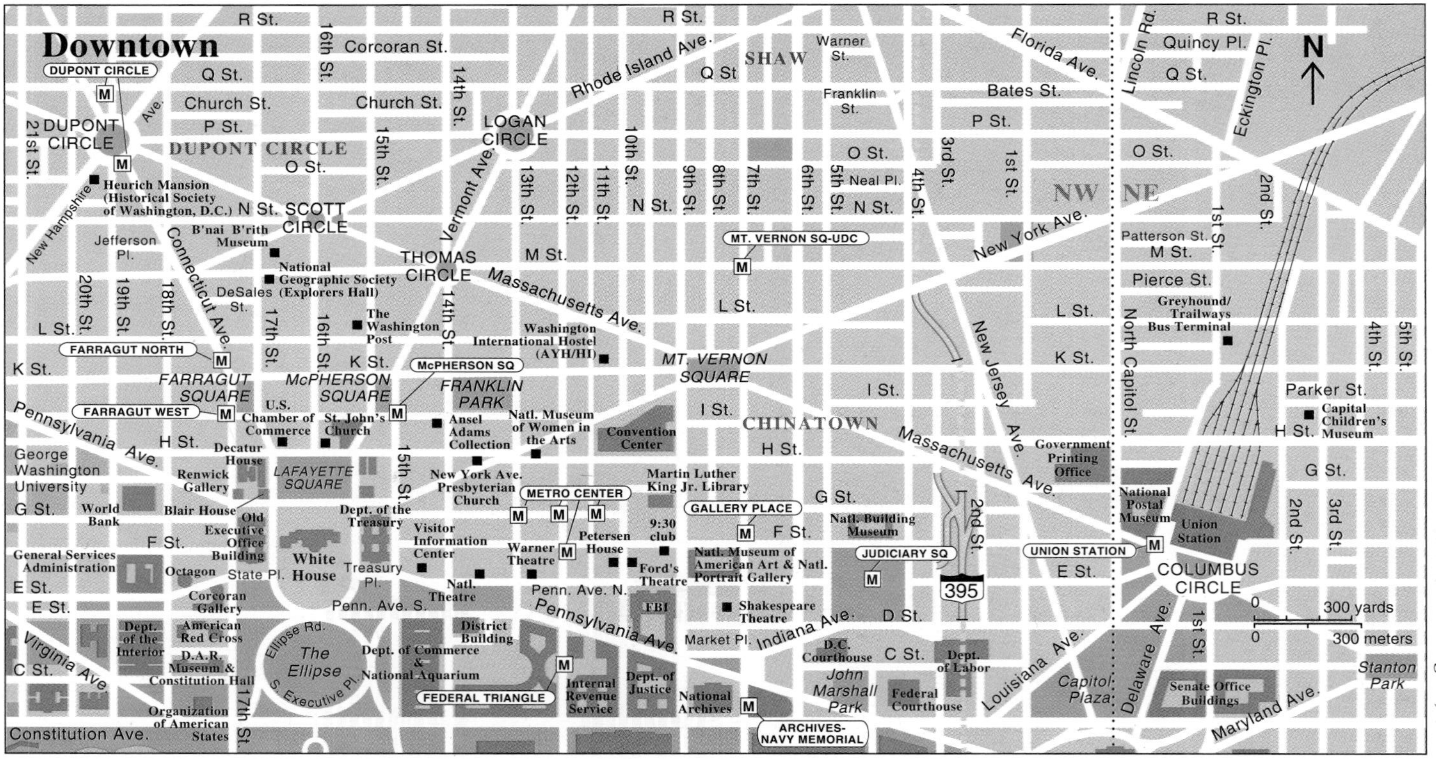

Downtown
N
DUPONT CIRCLE
DUPONT CIRCLE
SCOTT CIRCLE
THOMAS CIRCLE
LOGAN CIRCLE
SHAW
NW
NE
CHINATOWN
MT. VERNON SQUARE
FRANKLIN PARK
McPHERSON SQUARE
FARRAGUT SQUARE
LAFAYETTE SQUARE
COLUMBUS CIRCLE
FARRAGUT NORTH
FARRAGUT WEST
McPHERSON SQ
METRO CENTER
GALLERY PLACE
JUDICIARY SQ
UNION STATION
MT. VERNON SQ-UDC
FEDERAL TRIANGLE
ARCHIVES-NAVY MEMORIAL
Heurich Mansion (Historical Society of Washington, D.C.)
B'nai B'rith Museum
National Geographic Society (Explorers Hall)
The Washington Post
Washington International Hostel (AYH/HI)
Natl. Museum of Women in the Arts
Ansel Adams Collection
New York Ave. Presbyterian Church
Convention Center
Martin Luther King Jr. Library
9:30 club
Ford's Theatre
Petersen House
Warner Theatre
Natl. Theatre
Visitor Information Center
Natl. Museum of American Art & Natl. Portrait Gallery
Natl. Building Museum
Shakespeare Theatre
FBI
Dept. of Justice
Internal Revenue Service
National Archives
District Building
Dept. of Commerce & National Aquarium
Dept. of the Treasury
White House
The Ellipse
Old Executive Office Building
Blair House
Renwick Gallery
Decatur House
U.S. Chamber of Commerce
St. John's Church
Corcoran Gallery
Octagon
American Red Cross
D.A.R. Museum & Constitution Hall
Dept. of the Interior
Organization of American States
General Services Administration
World Bank
George Washington University
Government Printing Office
National Postal Museum
Union Station
Greyhound/Trailways Bus Terminal
Capital Children's Museum
Senate Office Buildings
Dept. of Labor
Federal Courthouse
D.C. Courthouse
John Marshall Park
Capitol Plaza
Stanton Park
395
0 300 yards
0 300 meters
Connecticut Ave.
Massachusetts Ave.
New York Ave.
New Jersey Ave.
Pennsylvania Ave.
Rhode Island Ave.
Vermont Ave.
New Hampshire Ave.
Florida Ave.
Virginia Ave.
Constitution Ave.
Indiana Ave.
Louisiana Ave.
Delaware Ave.
Maryland Ave.
North Capitol St.
Lincoln Rd.
Eckington Pl.
Quincy Pl.
Penn. Ave. N.
Penn. Ave. S.
Ellipse Rd.
S. Executive Pl.
State Pl.
Treasury Pl.
Market Pl.
Jefferson Pl.
DeSales St.
Corcoran St.
Church St.
Bates St.
Warner St.
Franklin St.
Neal Pl.
Patterson St.
Pierce St.
Parker St.
R St.
Q St.
P St.
O St.
N St.
M St.
L St.
K St.
I St.
H St.
G St.
F St.
E St.
D St.
C St.
1st St.
2nd St.
3rd St.
4th St.
5th St.
6th St.
7th St.
8th St.
9th St.
10th St.
11th St.
12th St.
13th St.
14th St.
15th St.
16th St.
17th St.
18th St.
19th St.
20th St.
21st St.

Central Washington, D.C.

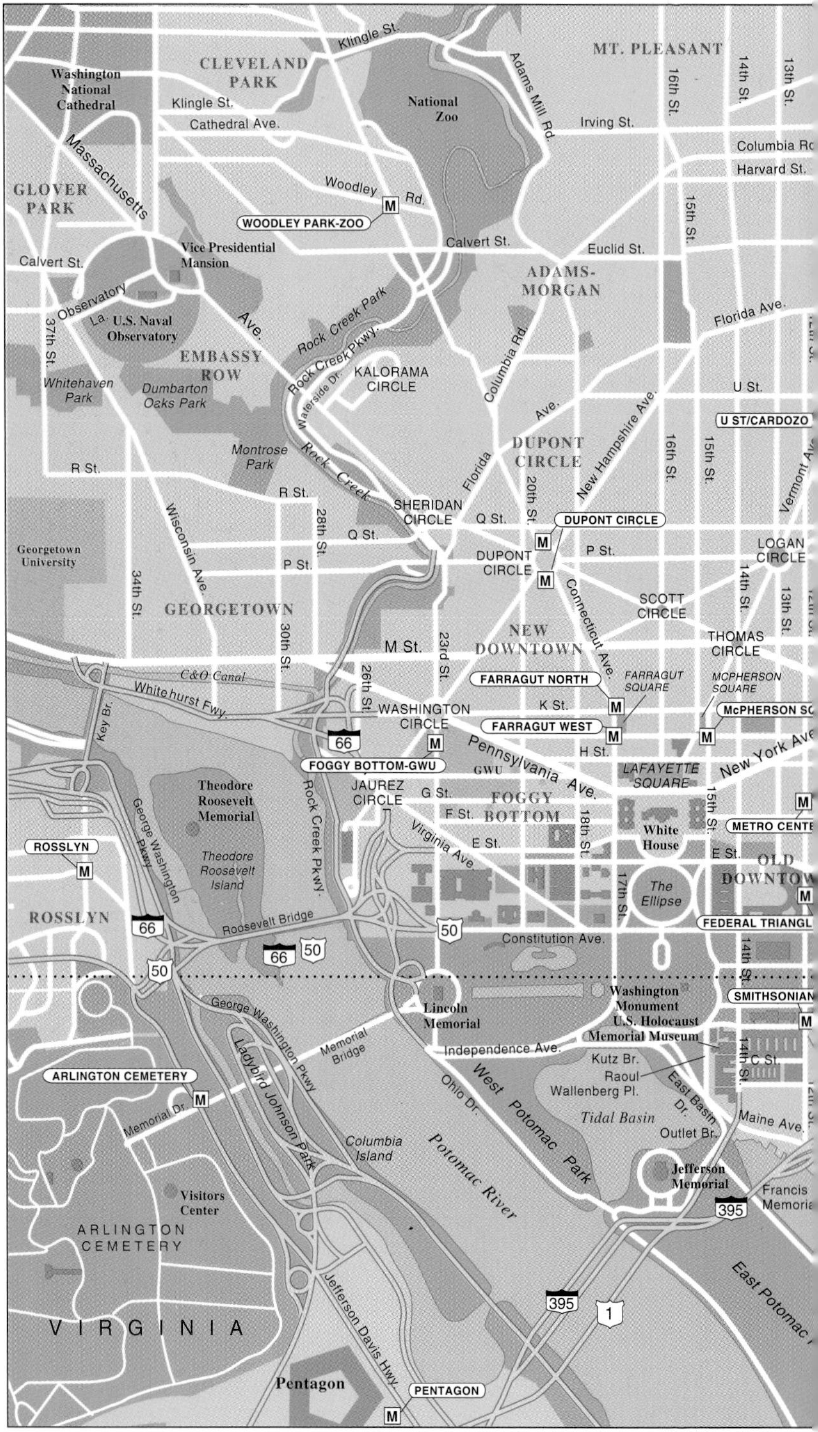

Klingle St.
CLEVELAND PARK
MT. PLEASANT
Washington National Cathedral
Klingle St.
Cathedral Ave.
National Zoo
Adams Mill Rd.
Irving St.
16th St.
14th St.
13th St.
Columbia Rd
Harvard St.
Massachusetts
GLOVER PARK
Woodley Rd.
WOODLEY PARK-ZOO
15th St.
Vice Presidential Mansion
Calvert St.
Euclid St.
Calvert St.
ADAMS-MORGAN
Observatory La.
U.S. Naval Observatory
Ave.
Rock Creek Park
Florida Ave.
37th St.
EMBASSY ROW
Rock Creek Pkwy.
Waterside Dr.
KALORAMA CIRCLE
Columbia Rd.
Whitehaven Park
Dumbarton Oaks Park
U St.
Ave.
New Hampshire Ave.
U ST/CARDOZO
DUPONT CIRCLE
16th St.
15th St.
Montrose Park
Rock Creek
Florida
Vermont Ave.
R St.
R St.
SHERIDAN CIRCLE
20th St.
Wisconsin Ave.
28th St.
Q St.
Q St.
DUPONT CIRCLE
Georgetown University
P St.
DUPONT CIRCLE
P St.
LOGAN CIRCLE
34th St.
GEORGETOWN
Connecticut Ave.
SCOTT CIRCLE
14th St.
13th St.
NEW DOWNTOWN
THOMAS CIRCLE
30th St.
23rd St.
M St.
C&O Canal
26th St.
Whitehurst Fwy.
FARRAGUT NORTH
FARRAGUT SQUARE
MCPHERSON SQUARE
K St.
WASHINGTON CIRCLE
McPHERSON SQ
Key Br.
FARRAGUT WEST
66
Pennsylvania Ave.
H St.
New York Ave
FOGGY BOTTOM-GWU
GWU
LAFAYETTE SQUARE
Theodore Roosevelt Memorial
Rock Creek Pkwy.
JAUREZ CIRCLE
G St.
FOGGY BOTTOM
15th St.
George Washington Pkwy
F St.
18th St.
METRO CENTER
ROSSLYN
Theodore Roosevelt Island
Virginia Ave.
E St.
White House
E St.
OLD DOWNTOWN
17th St.
The Ellipse
ROSSLYN
66
Roosevelt Bridge
50
FEDERAL TRIANGLE
Constitution Ave.
66
50
14th St.
50
Washington Monument
SMITHSONIAN
George Washington Pkwy
Lincoln Memorial
U.S. Holocaust Memorial Museum
Ladybird Johnson Park
Memorial Bridge
Independence Ave.
Kutz Br.
14th St.
C St.
ARLINGTON CEMETERY
Ohio Dr.
West Potomac Park
Raoul Wallenberg Pl.
East Basin Dr.
Memorial Dr.
Tidal Basin
Maine Ave.
Columbia Island
Potomac River
Outlet Br.
Visitors Center
Jefferson Memorial
Francis Memorial
395
ARLINGTON CEMETERY
Jefferson Davis Hwy
395
1
East Potomac
VIRGINIA
Pentagon
PENTAGON

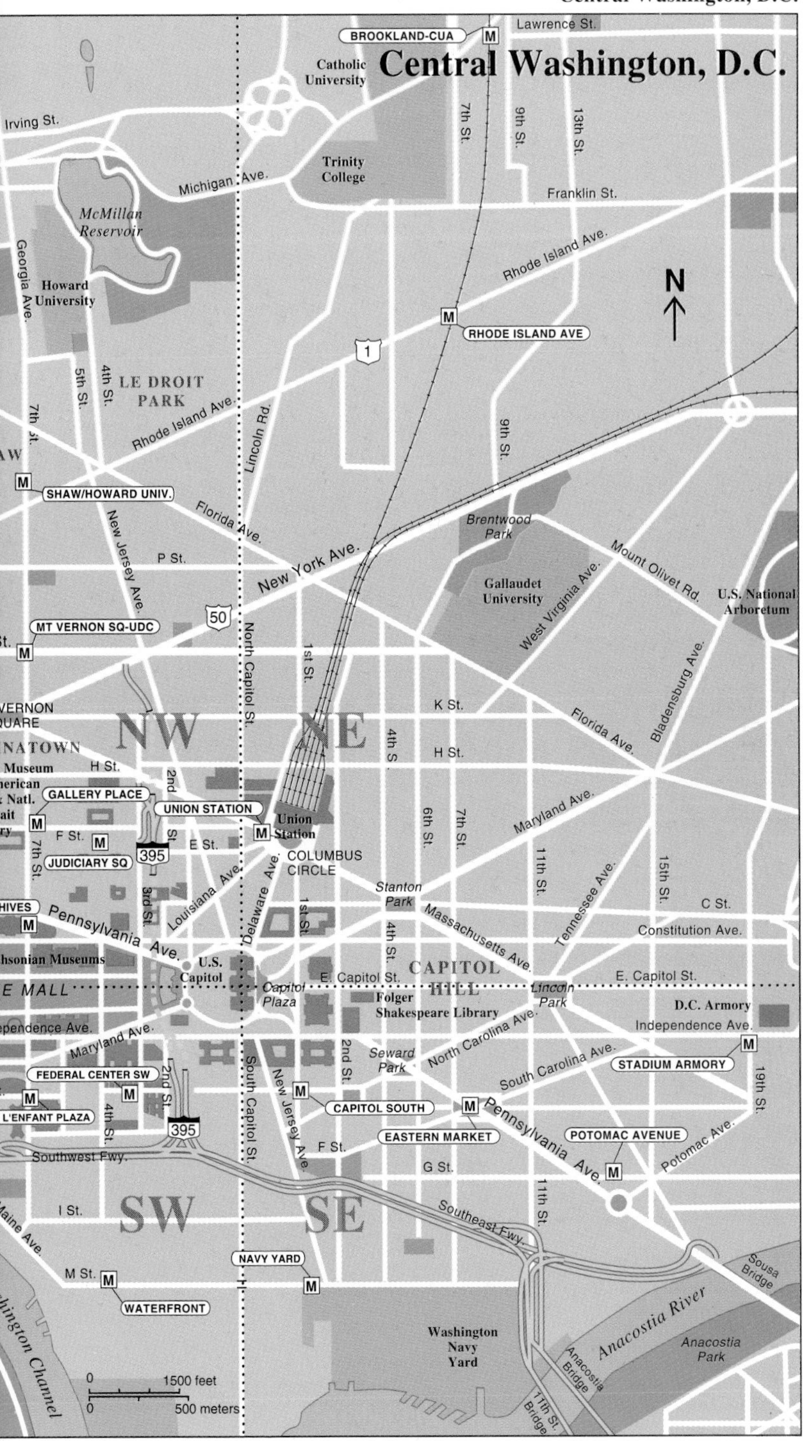
Central Washington, D.C.
BROOKLAND-CUA
Catholic University
Trinity College
McMillan Reservoir
Howard University
LE DROIT PARK
RHODE ISLAND AVE
SHAW/HOWARD UNIV.
MT VERNON SQ-UDC
Brentwood Park
Gallaudet University
U.S. National Arboretum
NW
NE
SW
SE
GALLERY PLACE
UNION STATION
Union Station
JUDICIARY SQ
COLUMBUS CIRCLE
Stanton Park
U.S. Capitol
Capitol Plaza
CAPITOL HILL
Lincoln Park
Folger Shakespeare Library
D.C. Armory
Seward Park
FEDERAL CENTER SW
L'ENFANT PLAZA
CAPITOL SOUTH
EASTERN MARKET
STADIUM ARMORY
POTOMAC AVENUE
NAVY YARD
WATERFRONT
Washington Navy Yard
Anacostia River
Anacostia Park
Sousa Bridge
Anacostia Bridge
11th St. Bridge
Southwest Fwy.
Southeast Fwy.
Lawrence St.
Irving St.
Michigan Ave.
Franklin St.
Rhode Island Ave.
Georgia Ave.
Lincoln Rd.
Florida Ave.
New York Ave.
Mount Olivet Rd.
West Virginia Ave.
Bladensburg Ave.
New Jersey Ave.
North Capitol St.
South Capitol St.
P St.
K St.
H St.
F St.
E St.
C St.
G St.
I St.
M St.
Maryland Ave.
Louisiana Ave.
Delaware Ave.
Pennsylvania Ave.
Massachusetts Ave.
Tennessee Ave.
Constitution Ave.
E. Capitol St.
Independence Ave.
North Carolina Ave.
South Carolina Ave.
Potomac Ave.
Maine Ave.
1
50
395
N
0 1500 feet
0 500 meters

The Mall Area, Washington, D.C.

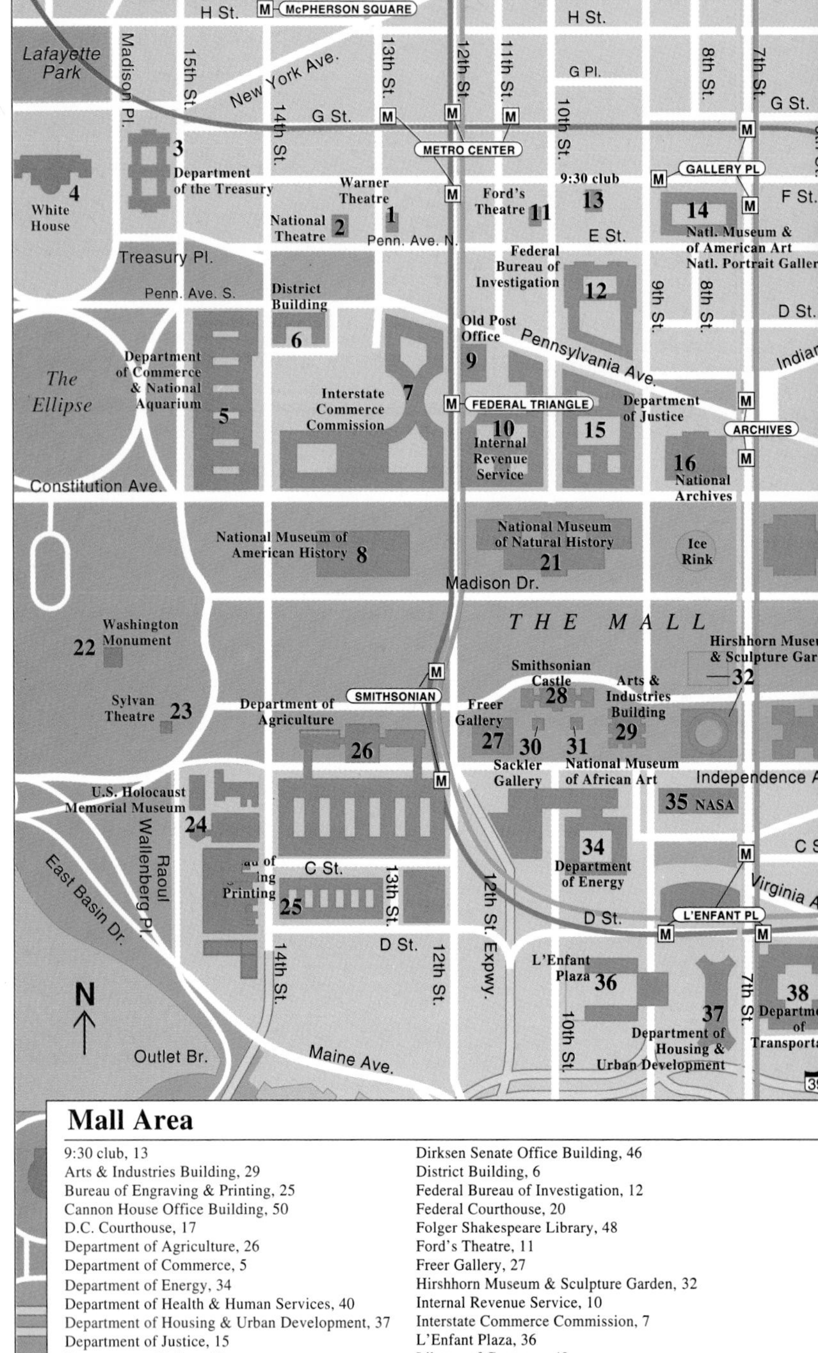

Mall Area

9:30 club, 13
Arts & Industries Building, 29
Bureau of Engraving & Printing, 25
Cannon House Office Building, 50
D.C. Courthouse, 17
Department of Agriculture, 26
Department of Commerce, 5
Department of Energy, 34
Department of Health & Human Services, 40
Department of Housing & Urban Development, 37
Department of Justice, 15
Department of Labor, 19
Department of Transportation, 38
Department of the Treasury, 3
Dirksen Senate Office Building, 46
District Building, 6
Federal Bureau of Investigation, 12
Federal Courthouse, 20
Folger Shakespeare Library, 48
Ford's Theatre, 11
Freer Gallery, 27
Hirshhorn Museum & Sculpture Garden, 32
Internal Revenue Service, 10
Interstate Commerce Commission, 7
L'Enfant Plaza, 36
Library of Congress, 49
Longwoth House Office Building, 51
National Aquarium, 5

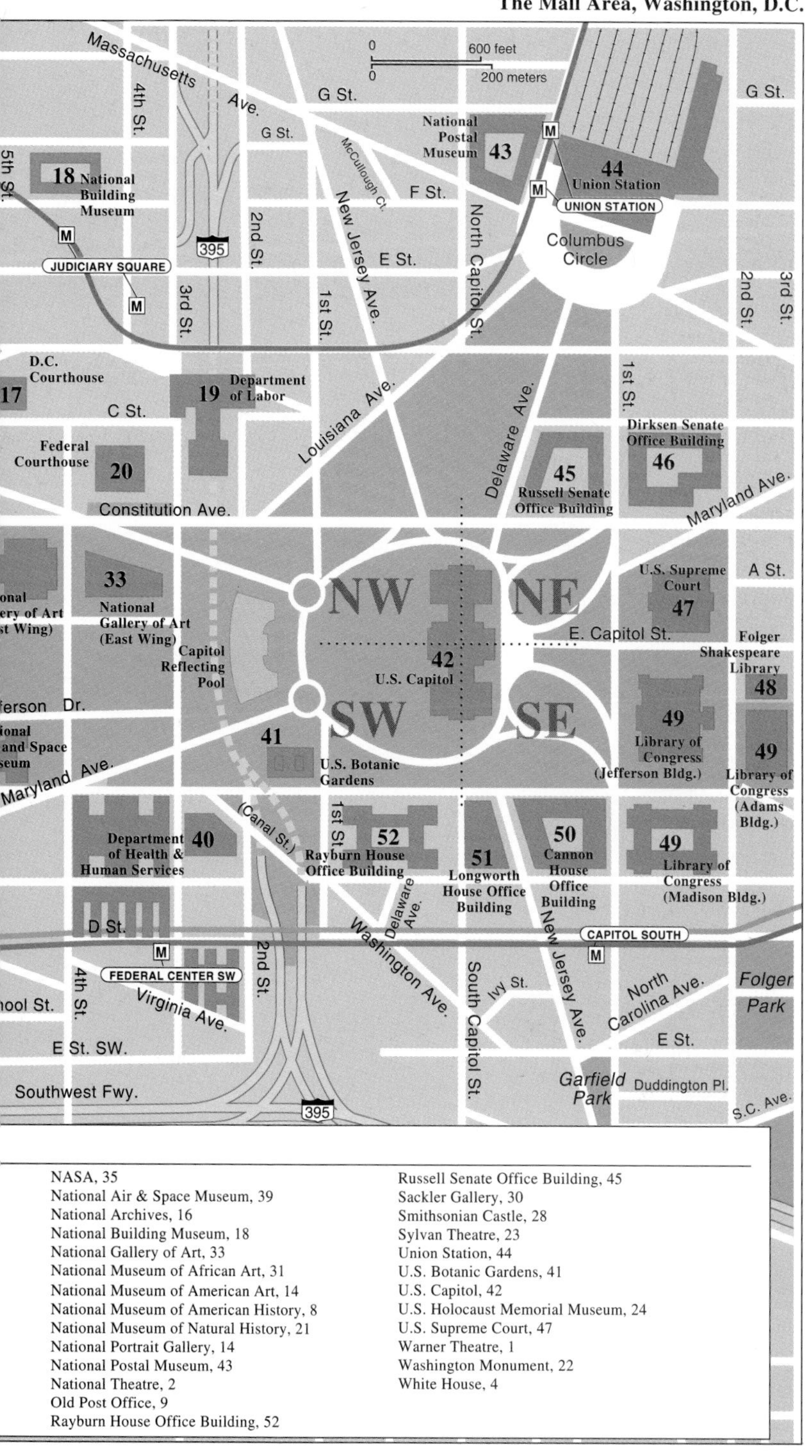

NASA, 35
National Air & Space Museum, 39
National Archives, 16
National Building Museum, 18
National Gallery of Art, 33
National Museum of African Art, 31
National Museum of American Art, 14
National Museum of American History, 8
National Museum of Natural History, 21
National Portrait Gallery, 14
National Postal Museum, 43
National Theatre, 2
Old Post Office, 9
Rayburn House Office Building, 52
Russell Senate Office Building, 45
Sackler Gallery, 30
Smithsonian Castle, 28
Sylvan Theatre, 23
Union Station, 44
U.S. Botanic Gardens, 41
U.S. Capitol, 42
U.S. Holocaust Memorial Museum, 24
U.S. Supreme Court, 47
Warner Theatre, 1
Washington Monument, 22
White House, 4

White House Area, Foggy Bottom, and Nearby Arlington

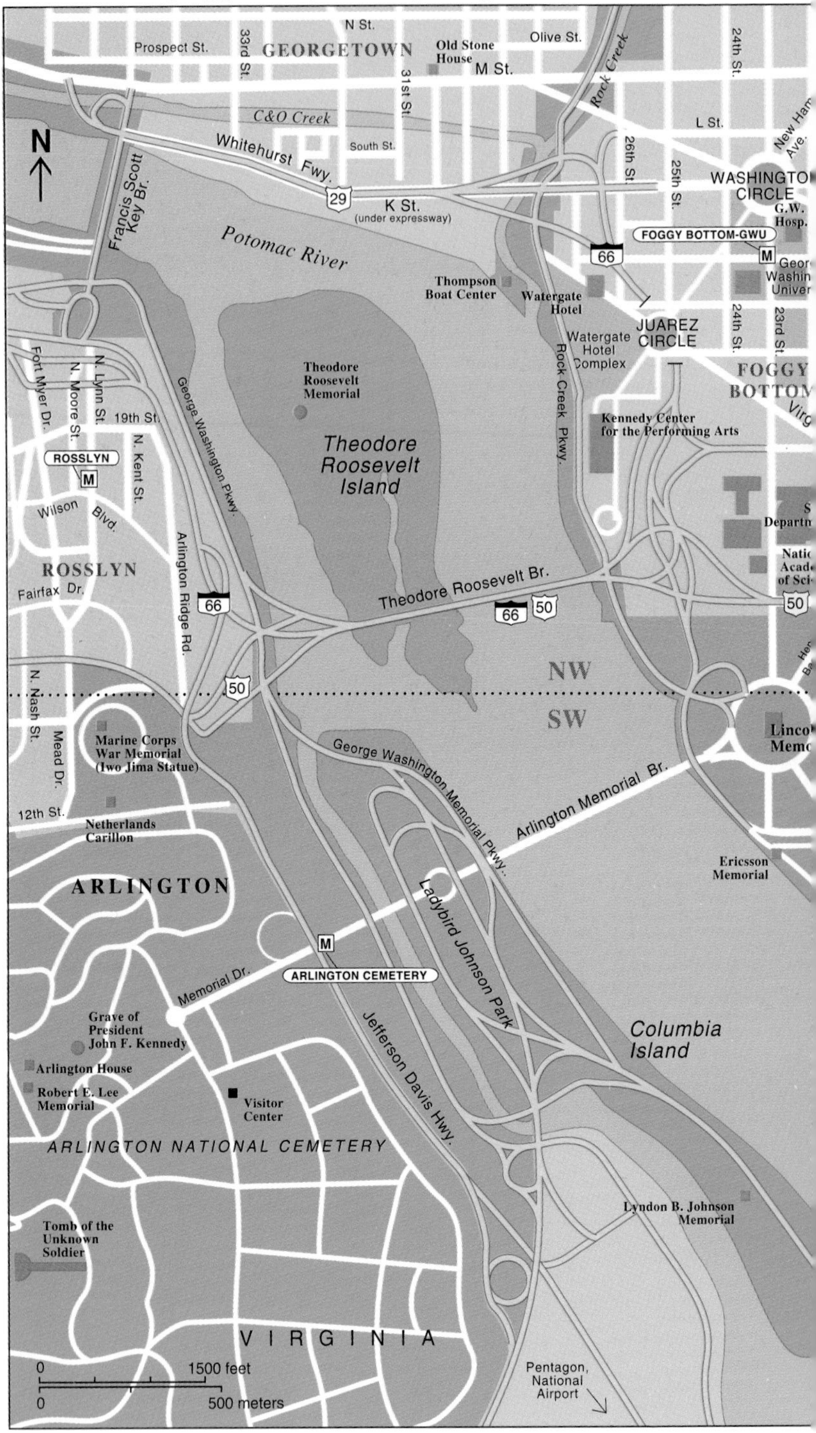

N St.
Prospect St.
33rd St.
GEORGETOWN
Old Stone House
M St.
Olive St.
31st St.
Rock Creek
24th St.
C&O Creek
L St.
New Hampshire Ave.
N
Whitehurst Fwy.
South St.
26th St.
25th St.
WASHINGTON CIRCLE
29
K St.
(under expressway)
G.W. Hosp.
Francis Scott Key Br.
Potomac River
FOGGY BOTTOM-GWU
M
66
George Washington University
Thompson Boat Center
Watergate Hotel
JUAREZ CIRCLE
Watergate Hotel Complex
24th St.
23rd St.
Fort Myer Dr.
N. Moore St.
N. Lynn St.
George Washington Pkwy.
Theodore Roosevelt Memorial
Rock Creek Pkwy.
FOGGY BOTTOM
Virginia Ave.
19th St.
Kennedy Center for the Performing Arts
ROSSLYN
M
N. Kent St.
Theodore Roosevelt Island
Wilson Blvd.
State Department
Arlington Ridge Rd.
ROSSLYN
National Academy of Sciences
Fairfax Dr.
66
Theodore Roosevelt Br.
66
50
50
NW
50
SW
N. Nash St.
Mead Dr.
Marine Corps War Memorial (Iwo Jima Statue)
George Washington Memorial Pkwy.
Lincoln Memorial
Arlington Memorial Br.
12th St.
Netherlands Carillon
Ericsson Memorial
ARLINGTON
Ladybird Johnson Park
M
ARLINGTON CEMETERY
Memorial Dr.
Jefferson Davis Hwy.
Columbia Island
Grave of President John F. Kennedy
Arlington House
Robert E. Lee Memorial
Visitor Center
ARLINGTON NATIONAL CEMETERY
Lyndon B. Johnson Memorial
Tomb of the Unknown Soldier
VIRGINIA
0
1500 feet
0
500 meters
Pentagon, National Airport

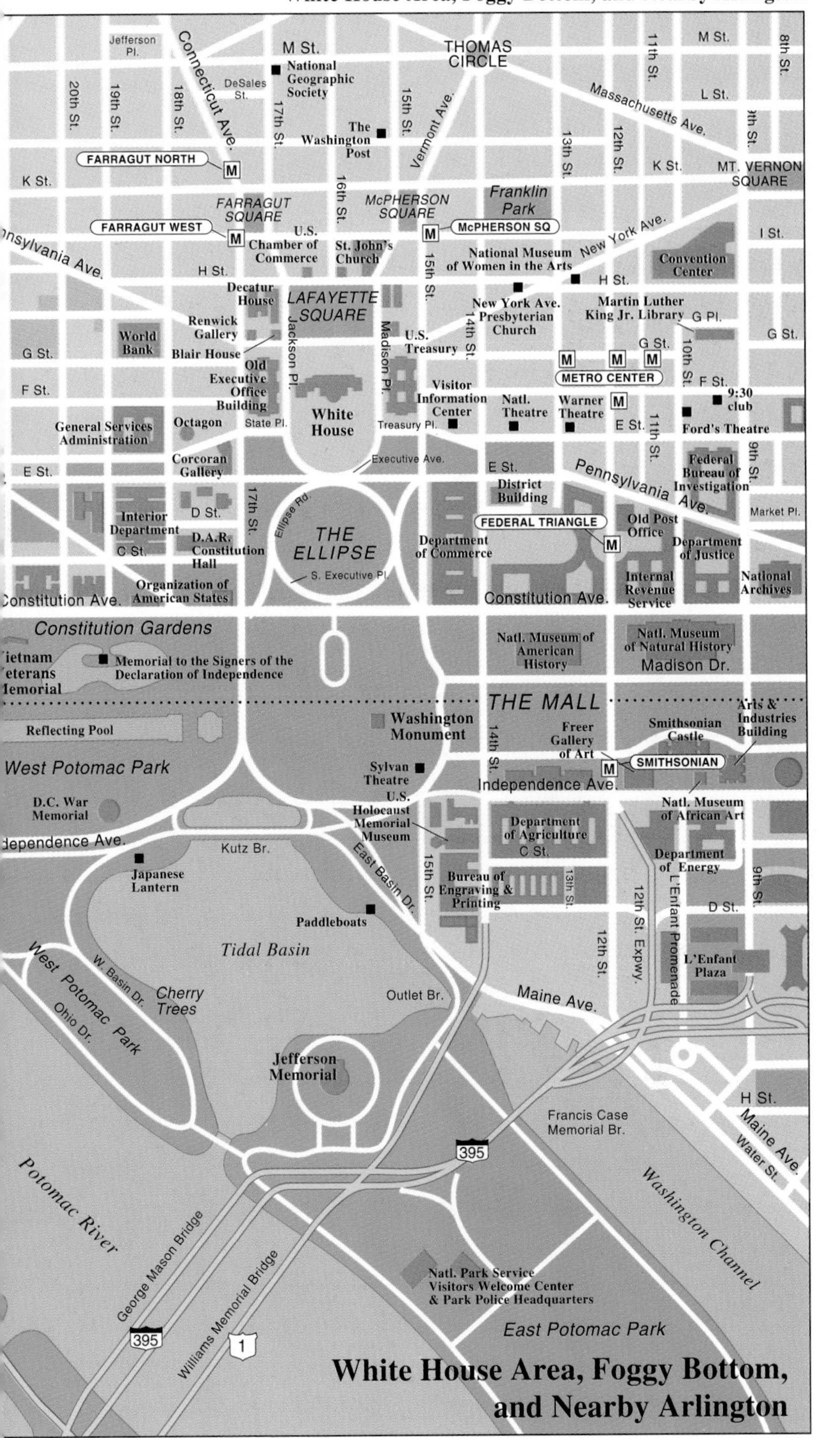

White House Area, Foggy Bottom, and Nearby Arlington

Metrorail System, Washington, D.C.

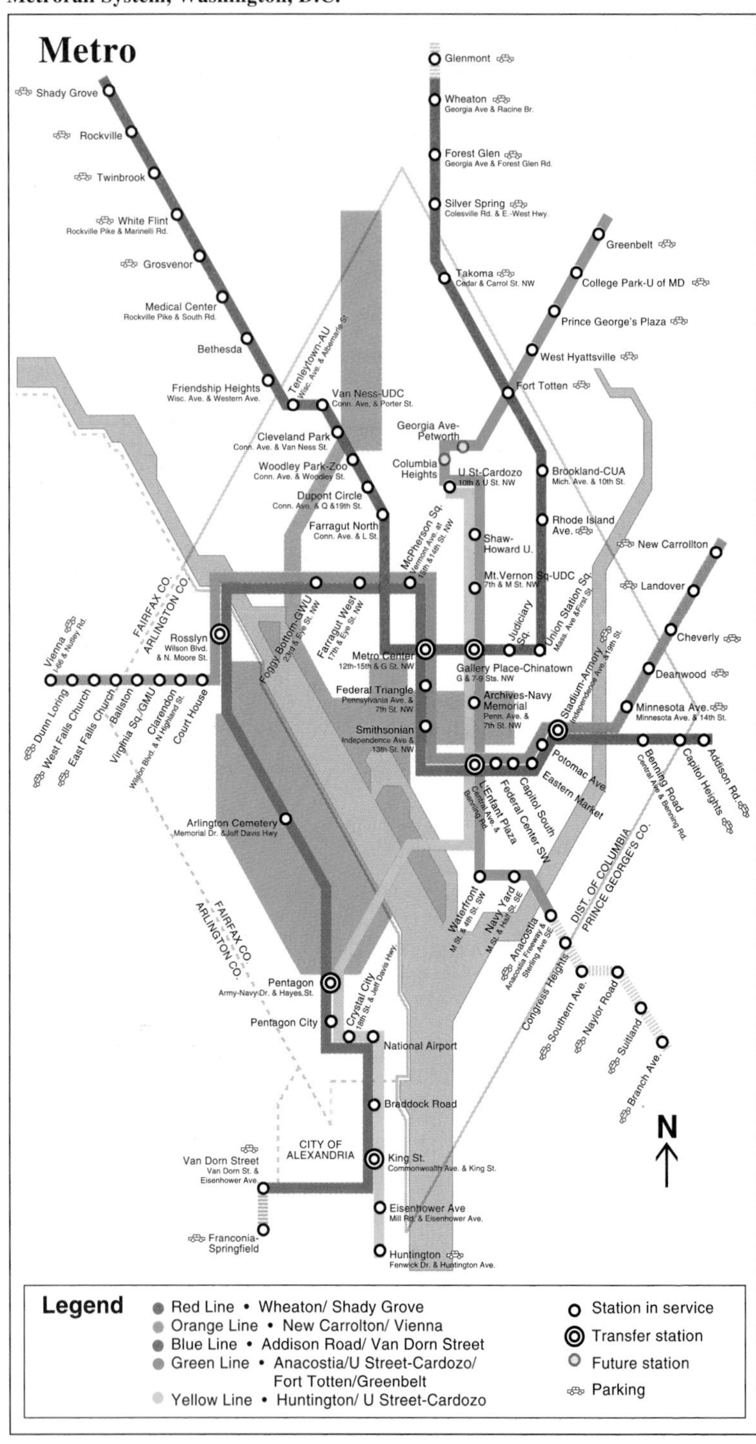

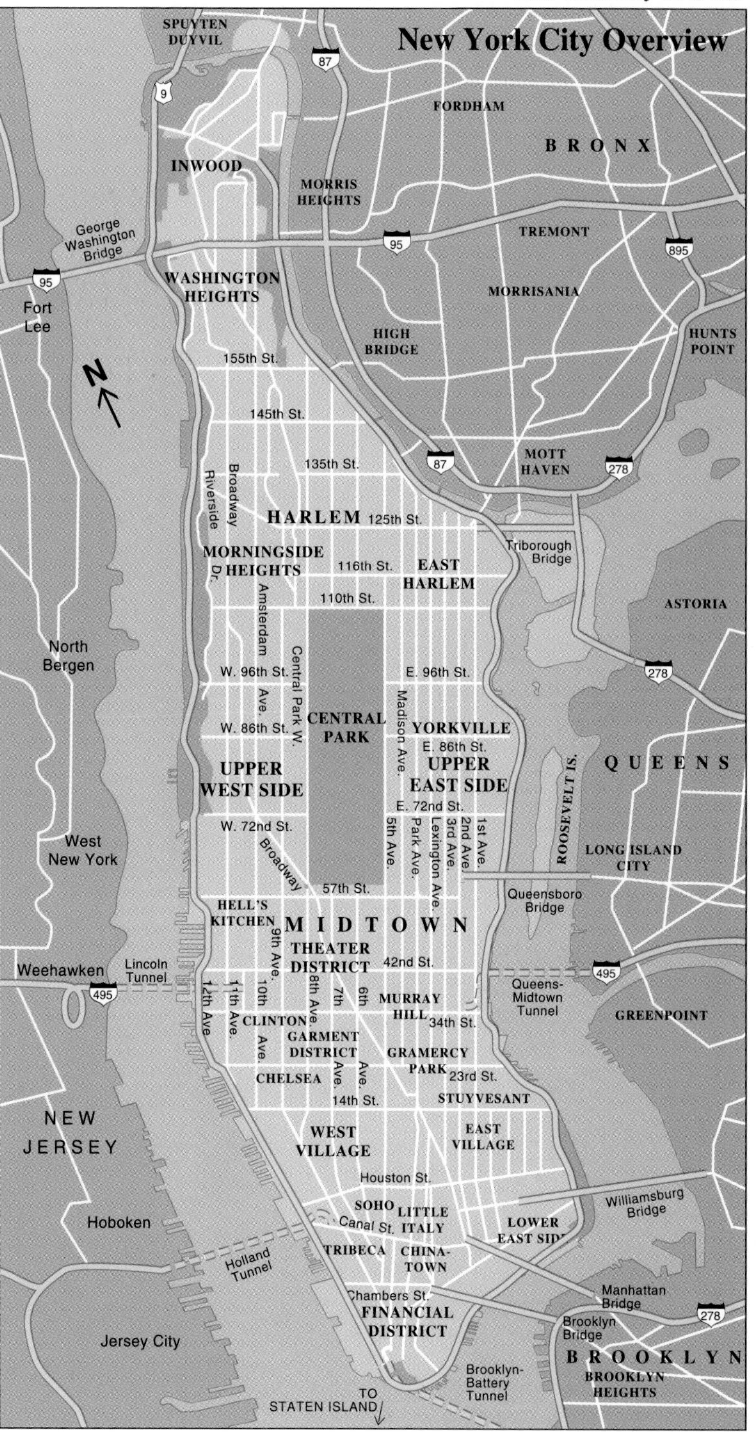
New York City Overview
SPUYTEN DUYVIL
INWOOD
MORRIS HEIGHTS
FORDHAM
BRONX
TREMONT
MORRISANIA
HIGH BRIDGE
HUNTS POINT
MOTT HAVEN
George Washington Bridge
Fort Lee
WASHINGTON HEIGHTS
155th St.
145th St.
135th St.
Riverside Dr.
Broadway
HARLEM
125th St.
MORNINGSIDE HEIGHTS
116th St.
EAST HARLEM
110th St.
Triborough Bridge
ASTORIA
North Bergen
Amsterdam Ave.
Central Park W.
W. 96th St.
E. 96th St.
W. 86th St.
CENTRAL PARK
Madison Ave.
YORKVILLE
E. 86th St.
UPPER WEST SIDE
UPPER EAST SIDE
ROOSEVELT IS.
QUEENS
E. 72nd St.
W. 72nd St.
Broadway
5th Ave.
Park Ave.
Lexington Ave.
3rd Ave.
2nd Ave.
1st Ave.
LONG ISLAND CITY
West New York
57th St.
Queensboro Bridge
HELL'S KITCHEN
MIDTOWN
9th Ave.
THEATER DISTRICT
42nd St.
Weehawken
Lincoln Tunnel
12th Ave.
11th Ave.
10th Ave.
8th Ave.
7th Ave.
6th Ave.
MURRAY HILL
34th St.
Queens-Midtown Tunnel
GREENPOINT
CLINTON
GARMENT DISTRICT
GRAMERCY PARK
23rd St.
CHELSEA
14th St.
STUYVESANT
NEW JERSEY
WEST VILLAGE
EAST VILLAGE
Houston St.
SOHO
LITTLE ITALY
Canal St.
Williamsburg Bridge
Hoboken
LOWER EAST SIDE
TRIBECA
CHINA-TOWN
Holland Tunnel
Chambers St.
FINANCIAL DISTRICT
Manhattan Bridge
Brooklyn Bridge
Jersey City
BROOKLYN
BROOKLYN HEIGHTS
Brooklyn-Battery Tunnel
TO STATEN ISLAND
N
9
87
95
895
278
495

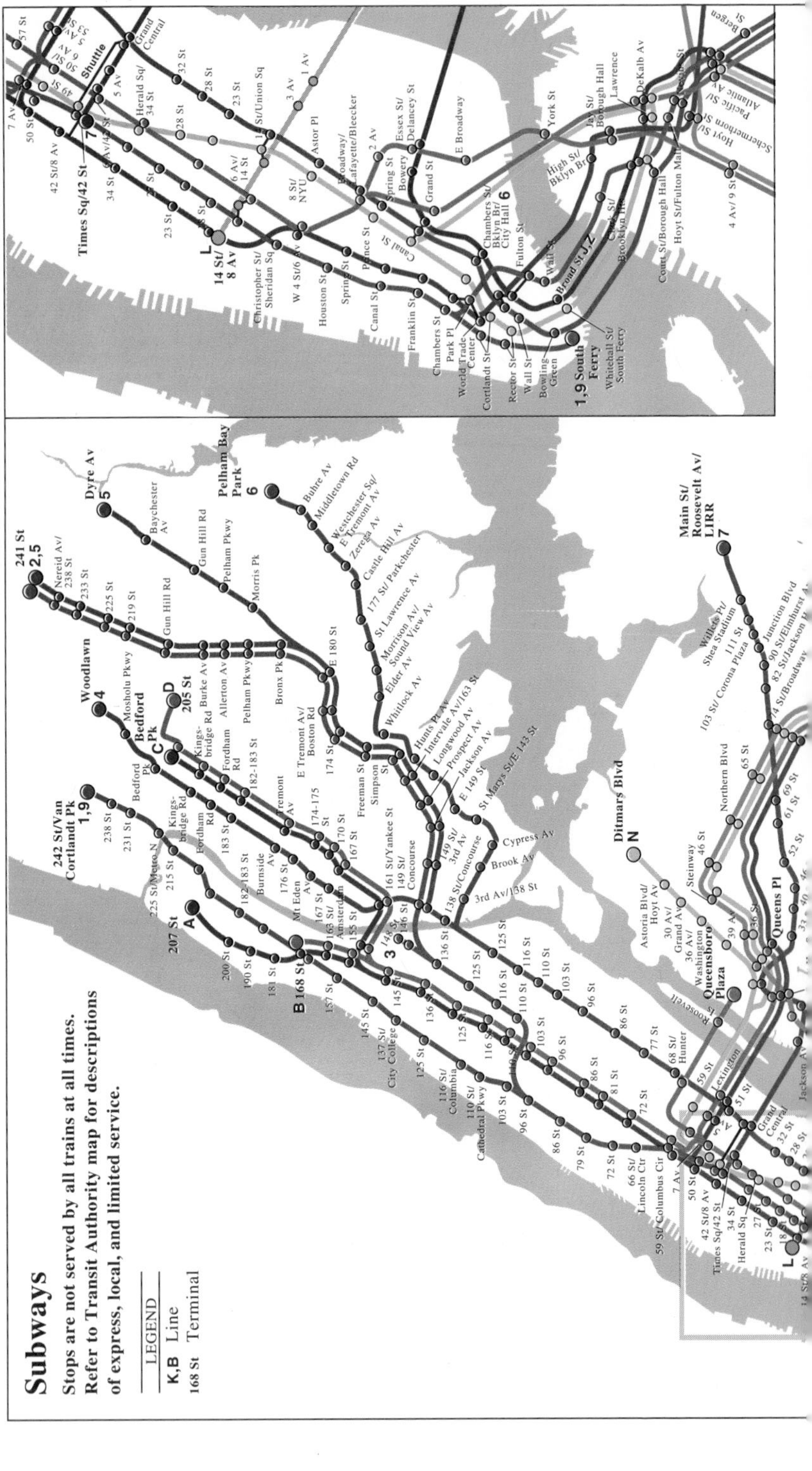

Subways

Stops are not served by all trains at all times. Refer to Transit Authority map for descriptions of express, local, and limited service.

LEGEND	
K,B	Line
168 St	Terminal

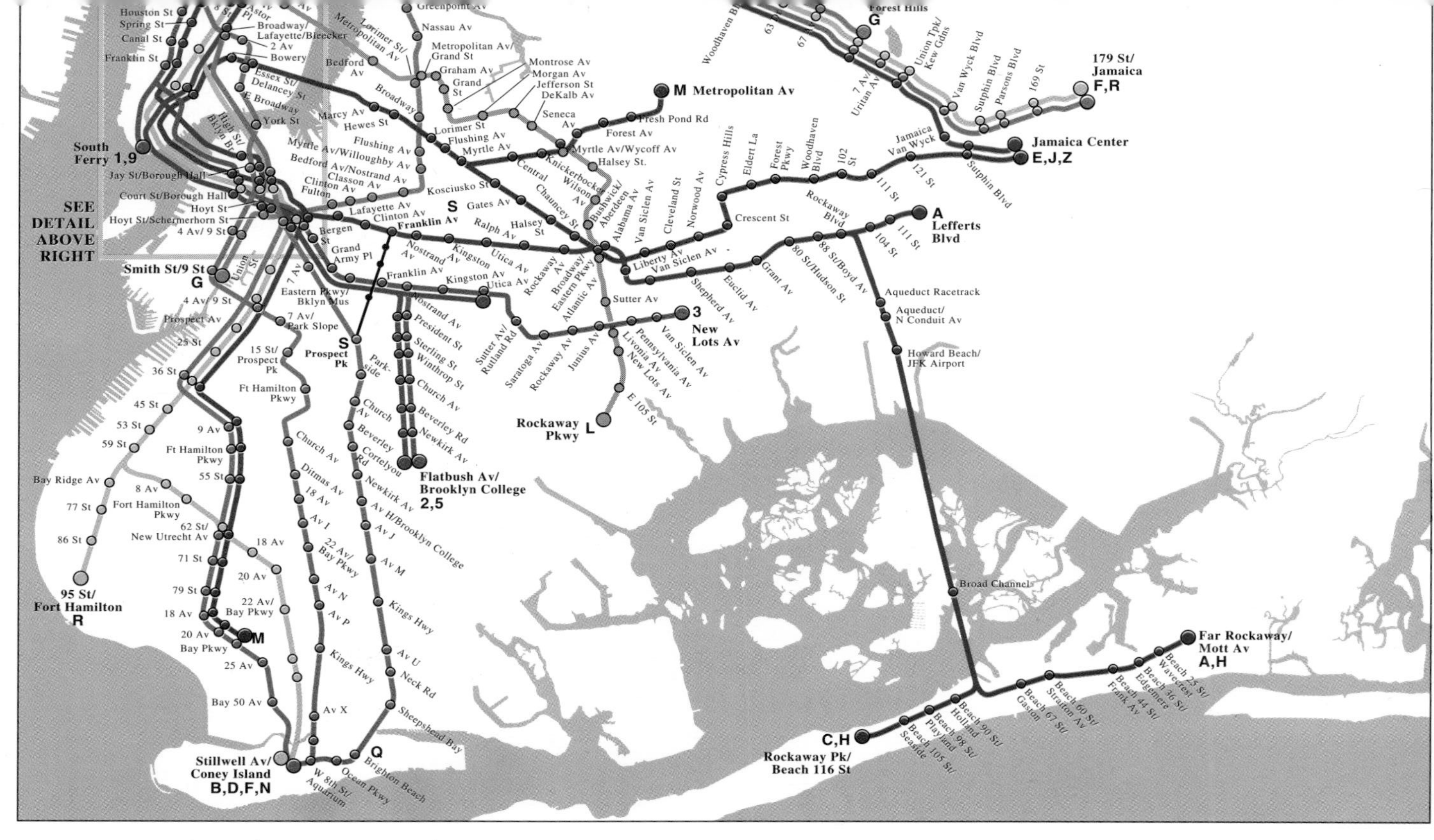
Greenpoint Av
Nassau Av
Forest Hills G
7 Av
Uritan Av
Union Tpk/ Kew Gdns
Van Wyck Blvd
Sutphin Blvd
Parsons Blvd
169 St
179 St/ Jamaica F,R
Jamaica Center E,J,Z
Jamaica Van Wyck
121 St
Sutphin Blvd
111 St
102 St
Woodhaven Blvd
Forest Pkwy
Eldert La
Cypress Hills
Crescent St
Norwood Av
Cleveland St
Van Siclen Av
A Lefferts Blvd
111 St
104 St
Rockaway Blvd
88 St/Boyd Av
80 St/Hudson St
Grant Av
Euclid Av
Shepherd Av
Liberty Av
Van Siclen Av
Aqueduct Racetrack
Aqueduct/ N Conduit Av
Howard Beach/ JFK Airport
Broad Channel
Far Rockaway/ Mott Av A,H
Beach 25 St/ Wavecrest
Beach 36 St/ Edgemere
Beach 44 St/ Frank Av
Beach 60 St/ Stratton Av
Beach 67 St/ Gaston
Beach 90 St/ Holland
Beach 98 St/ Playland
Beach 105 St/ Seaside
C,H Rockaway Pk/ Beach 116 St
M Metropolitan Av
Fresh Pond Rd
Forest Av
Myrtle Av/Wycoff Av
Halsey St.
Seneca Av
Knickerbocker
Wilson Av
Bushwick/ Aberdeen
Alabama Av
Broadway/ Eastern Pkwy
Atlantic Av
Sutter Av
3 New Lots Av
Van Siclen Av
Pennsylvania Av
Livonia Av
New Lots Av
E 105 St
Rockaway Pkwy L
Junius Av
Rockaway Av
Saratoga Av
Sutter Av/ Rutland Rd
Montrose Av
Morgan Av
Jefferson St
DeKalb Av
Central
Chauncey St
Halsey St
Ralph Av
Utica Av
Rockaway Av
Gates Av
Kosciusko St
Myrtle Av
Flushing Av
Lorimer St
Graham Av
Grand St
Metropolitan Av/ Grand St
Lorimer St/ Metropolitan Av
Broadway
Bedford Av
Marcy Av
Hewes St
Flushing Av
Myrtle Av/Willoughby Av
Bedford Av/Nostrand Av
Classon Av
Clinton Av
Fulton
Lafayette Av
Clinton Av
S Franklin Av
Nostrand Av
Kingston Av
Utica Av
Franklin Av
Kingston Av
Utica Av
Nostrand Av
President St
Sterling St
Winthrop St
Church Av
Beverley Rd
Newkirk Av
Flatbush Av/ Brooklyn College 2,5
Bergen St
Grand Army Pl
Eastern Pkwy/ Bklyn Mus
7 Av
S Prospect Pk
Parkside
Church Av
Beverley
Cortelyou Rd
Newkirk Av
Av H/Brooklyn College
Av J
Av M
Kings Hwy
Av U
Neck Rd
Sheepshead Bay
Q Brighton Beach
Ocean Pkwy
W 8th St/ Aquarium
Church Av
Ditmas Av
18 Av
Av I
22 Av/ Bay Pkwy
Av N
Av P
Kings Hwy
Av X
7 Av/ Park Slope
15 St/ Prospect Pk
Ft Hamilton Pkwy
Stillwell Av/ Coney Island B,D,F,N
Bay 50 Av
25 Av
20 Av
Bay Pkwy
18 Av
79 St
71 St
62 St/ New Utrecht Av
55 St
Ft Hamilton Pkwy
9 Av
18 Av
20 Av
22 Av/ Bay Pkwy
M
Houston St
Spring St
Canal St
Franklin St
Astor Pl
Broadway/ Lafayette/Bleecker
2 Av
Bowery
Essex St/ Delancey St
E Broadway
York St
High St/ Bklyn Br
South Ferry 1,9
Jay St/Borough Hall
Court St/Borough Hall
Hoyt St
Hoyt St/Schermerhorn St
4 Av/ 9 St
Union St
Smith St/9 St G
4 Av/ 9 St
Prospect Av
25 St
36 St
45 St
53 St
59 St
Bay Ridge Av
77 St
86 St
95 St/ Fort Hamilton R
8 Av
Fort Hamilton Pkwy
SEE DETAIL ABOVE RIGHT

Downtown Manhattan

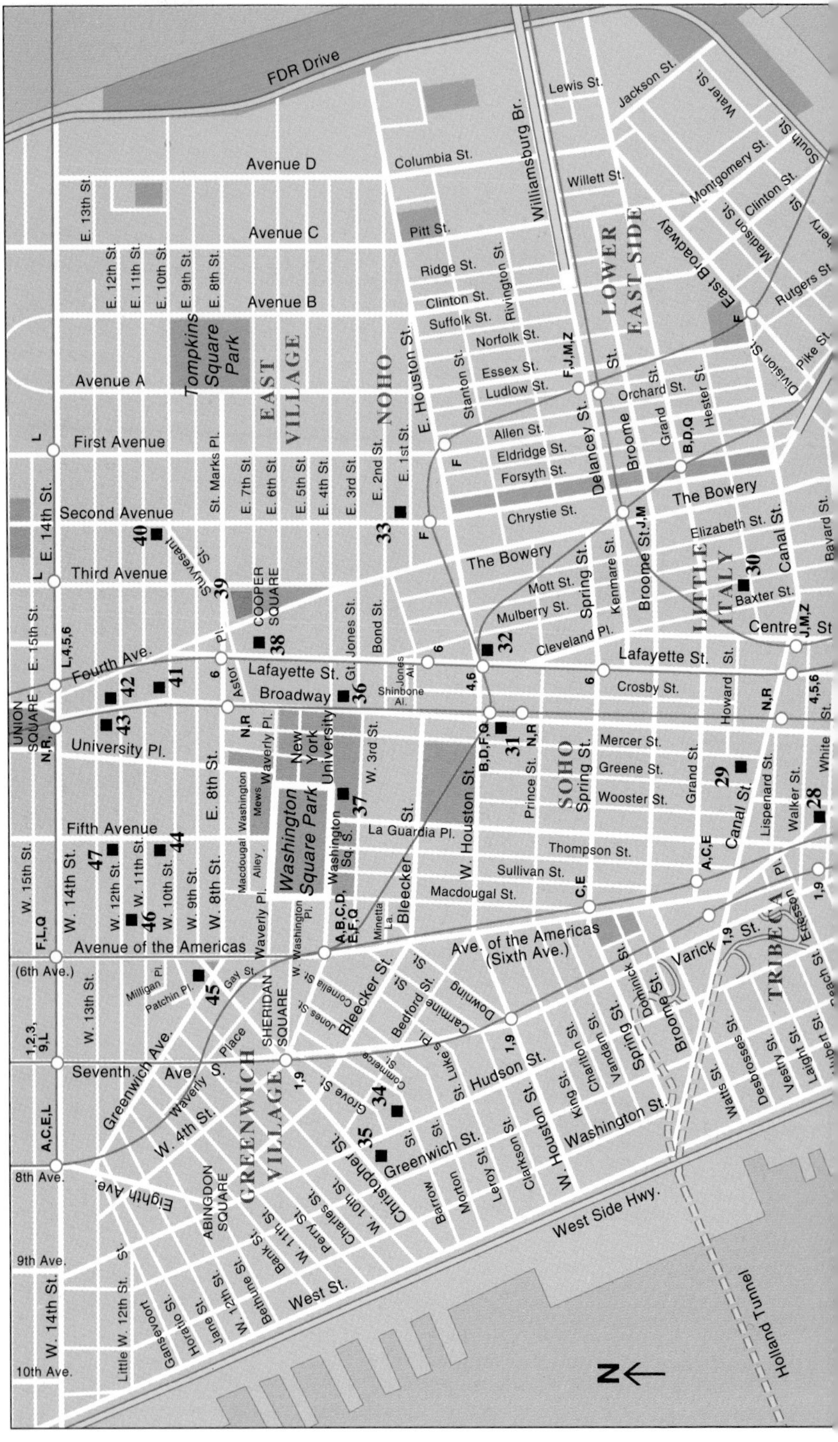

Downtown
Alternative Museum, 28
Anthology Film Archives, 33
Buddhist Temple, 27
Castle Clinton, 1
Cherry Lane Theatre, 34
Chinatown Fair, 26
Church of the Ascension, 44
Church of Our Lady of the Rosary, 8
City Hall, 24
Clocktower Gallery, 25
Cooper Union, 39
Downtown Heliport, 9
East Coast Memorial, 2
Federal Hall, 15
Federal Reserve Bank, 16
Forbes Magazine Galleries, 47
Forbidden Planet, 43
Fraunces Tavern, 10
Fulton Fish Market, 17
Grace Church, 41
Jefferson Market Library, 45
Joseph Papp Public Theater, 38
Morgan Guaranty Trust Company, 13
Museum of Holography, 29
New Museum of Contemporary Art, 31
New School of Social Research, 46
New York Stock Exchange, 14
New York University, 37
Puck Building, 32
St. John's Episcopal Methodist Church, 19
St. Luke's Chapel, 35
St. Mark's in the Bowery Church, 40
St. Paul's Chapel, 20
South Street Seaport Museum, 18
Staten Island Ferry Terminal, 7
Statue of Liberty and Ellis Island Ferry Terminal, 3
Strand Bookstore, 42
Tower Records, 36
Trinity Church, 12
Umberto's Clam House, 30
U.S. Customs House, 11
Woolworth Building, 23
World Financial Center, 22
World Trade Center, 21
East River
Manhattan Bridge
Brooklyn Bridge
South Street Seaport
Federal Plaza
FOLEY SQUARE
CHATHAM SQUARE
City Hall Park
World Trade Center
World Financial Center
BATTERY PARK CITY
Battery Park
Brooklyn-Battery Tunnel
0 yards 550
0 meters 500

Midtown Manhattan

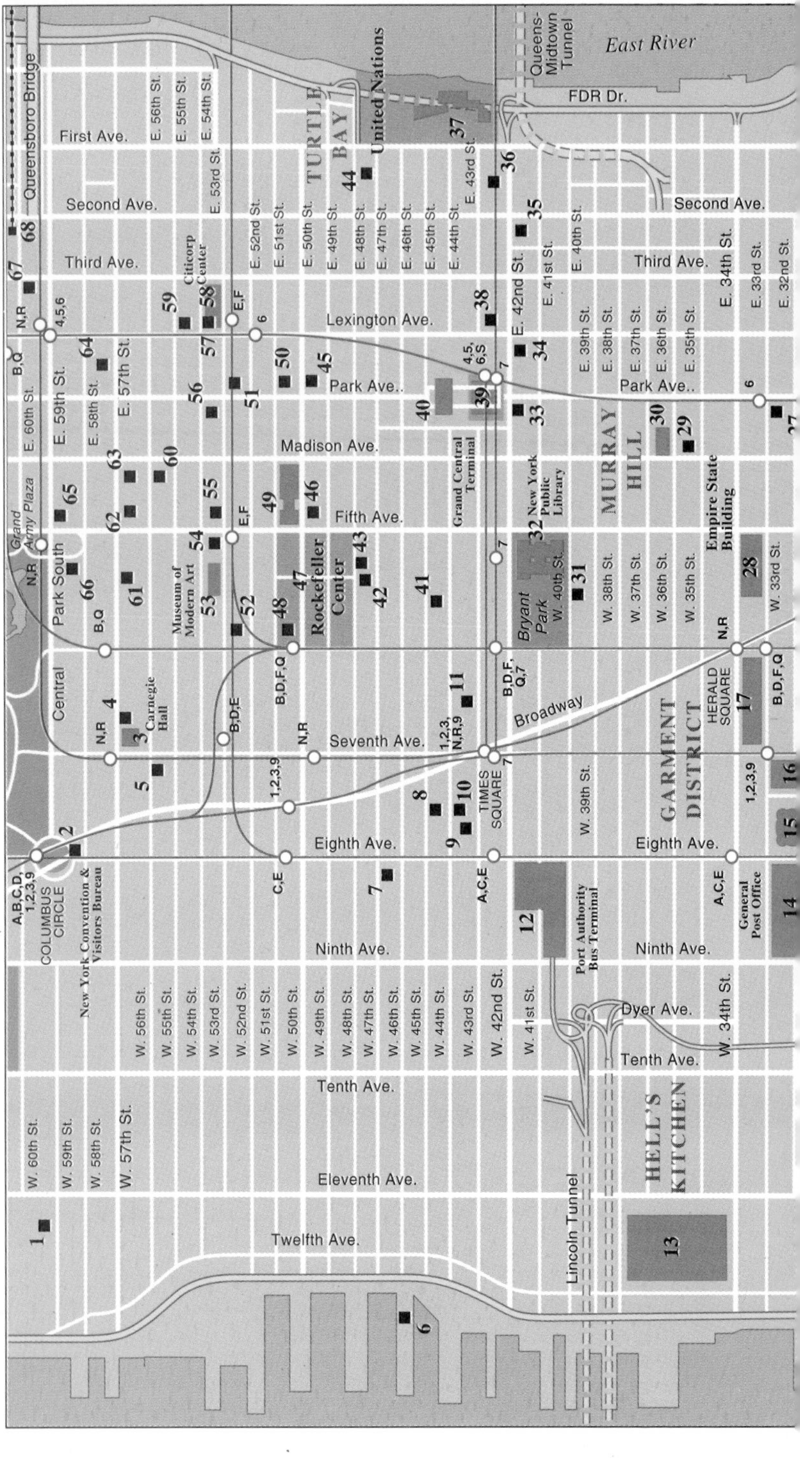

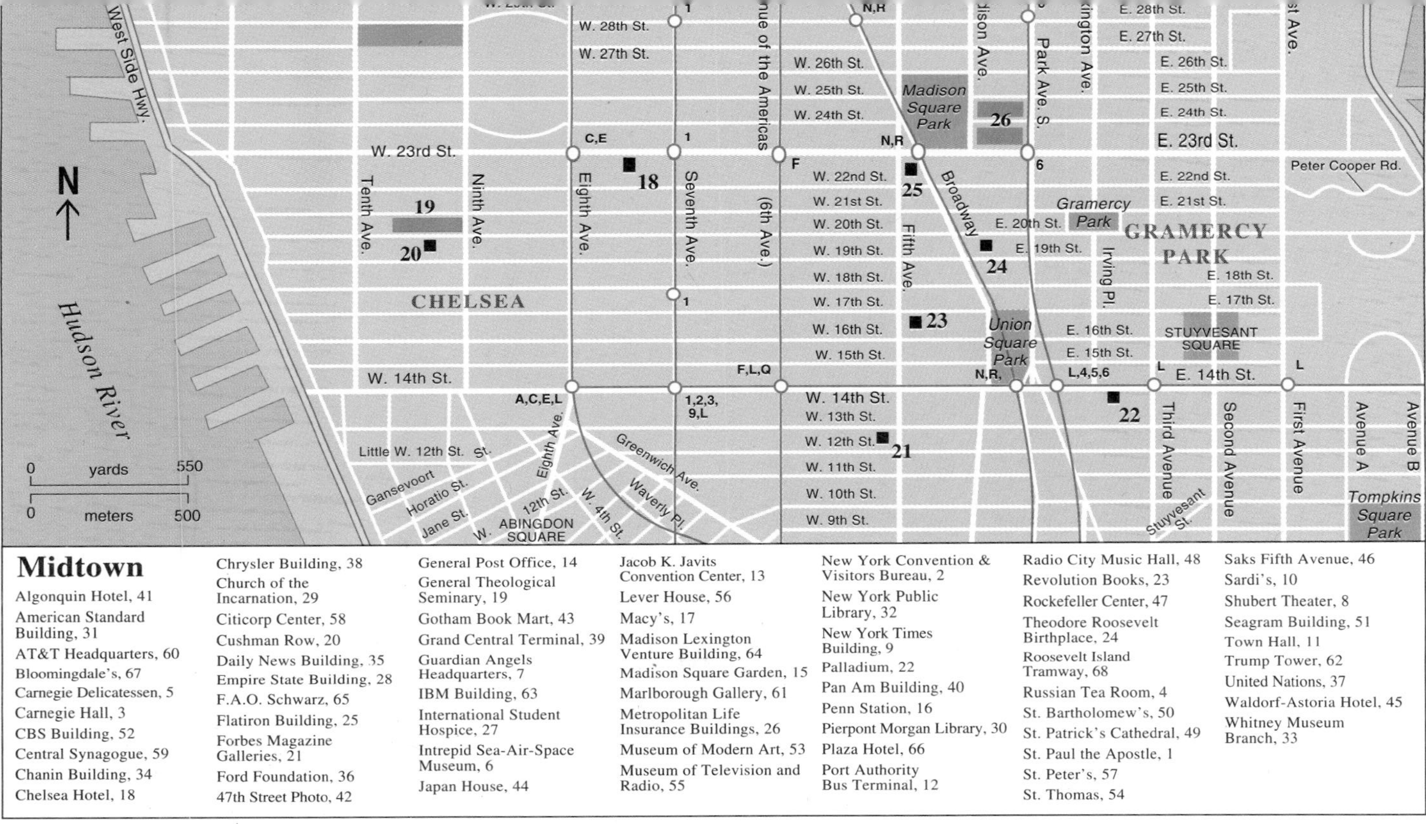
Midtown
Algonquin Hotel, 41
American Standard Building, 31
AT&T Headquarters, 60
Bloomingdale's, 67
Carnegie Delicatessen, 5
Carnegie Hall, 3
CBS Building, 52
Central Synagogue, 59
Chanin Building, 34
Chelsea Hotel, 18
Chrysler Building, 38
Church of the Incarnation, 29
Citicorp Center, 58
Cushman Row, 20
Daily News Building, 35
Empire State Building, 28
F.A.O. Schwarz, 65
Flatiron Building, 25
Forbes Magazine Galleries, 21
Ford Foundation, 36
47th Street Photo, 42
General Post Office, 14
General Theological Seminary, 19
Gotham Book Mart, 43
Grand Central Terminal, 39
Guardian Angels Headquarters, 7
IBM Building, 63
International Student Hospice, 27
Intrepid Sea-Air-Space Museum, 6
Japan House, 44
Jacob K. Javits Convention Center, 13
Lever House, 56
Macy's, 17
Madison Lexington Venture Building, 64
Madison Square Garden, 15
Marlborough Gallery, 61
Metropolitan Life Insurance Buildings, 26
Museum of Modern Art, 53
Museum of Television and Radio, 55
New York Convention & Visitors Bureau, 2
New York Public Library, 32
New York Times Building, 9
Palladium, 22
Pan Am Building, 40
Penn Station, 16
Pierpont Morgan Library, 30
Plaza Hotel, 66
Port Authority Bus Terminal, 12
Radio City Music Hall, 48
Revolution Books, 23
Rockefeller Center, 47
Theodore Roosevelt Birthplace, 24
Roosevelt Island Tramway, 68
Russian Tea Room, 4
St. Bartholomew's, 50
St. Patrick's Cathedral, 49
St. Paul the Apostle, 1
St. Peter's, 57
St. Thomas, 54
Saks Fifth Avenue, 46
Sardi's, 10
Shubert Theater, 8
Seagram Building, 51
Town Hall, 11
Trump Tower, 62
United Nations, 37
Waldorf-Astoria Hotel, 45
Whitney Museum Branch, 33
Hudson River
West Side Hwy.
CHELSEA
GRAMERCY PARK
Gramercy Park
Madison Square Park
Union Square Park
STUYVESANT SQUARE
Tompkins Square Park
ABINGDON SQUARE
Broadway
Fifth Ave.
(6th Ave.)
Seventh Ave.
Eighth Ave.
Ninth Ave.
Tenth Ave.
Park Ave. S.
Irving Pl.
Third Avenue
Second Avenue
First Avenue
Avenue A
Avenue B
Peter Cooper Rd.
Greenwich Ave.
Waverly Pl.
W. 23rd St.
E. 23rd St.
W. 14th St.
E. 14th St.
0 yards 550
0 meters 500
N

Uptown Manhattan

Uptown

American Museum of Natural History, 53
The Ansonia, 55
The Arsenal, 25
Asia Society, 14
Belvedere Castle, 36
Bethesda Fountain, 33
Blockhouse No. 1, 42
Bloomingdale's, 22
Bridle Path, 30
Cathedral of St. John the Divine, 47
Central Park Zoo, 24
Chess and Checkers House, 28
Children's Museum of Manhattan, 51
Children's Zoo, 26
China House, 19
Cleopatra's Needle, 38
Columbia University, 46
Conservatory Garden, 2
Cooper-Hewitt Museum, 7
The Dairy, 27
Dakota Apartments, 56
Delacorte Theater, 37
El Museo del Barrio, 1
Fordham University, 60
Frick Museum, 13
Gracie Mansion, 10
Grant's Tomb, 45
Great Lawn, 39
Guggenheim Museum, 9
Hayden Planetarium (at the American Museum of Natural History), 53
Hector Memorial, 50
Hotel des Artistes, 57
Hunter College, 16
International Center of Photography, 5
Jewish Museum, 6
The Juilliard School (at Lincoln Center), 59
Lincoln Center, 59
Loeb Boathouse, 34
Masjid Malcolm Shabazz , 43
Metropolitan Museum of Art, 11
Mt. Sinai Hospital, 4
Museum of American Folk Art, 58
Museum of American Illustration, 21
Museum of the City of New York, 3
National Academy of Design, 8
New York Convention & Visitors Bureau, 61
New York Historical Society, 54
New York Hospital, 15
Plaza Hotel, 23
Police Station (Central Park), 40
Rockefeller University, 20
7th Regiment Armory, 17
Shakespeare Garden, 35
Soldiers and Sailors Monument, 49
Strawberry Fields, 32
Studio Museum in Harlem, 44
Symphony Space, 48
Tavern on the Green, 31
Temple Emanu-El, 18
Tennis Courts, 41
Whitney Museum of American Art, 12
Wollman Rink, 29
Zabar's, 52

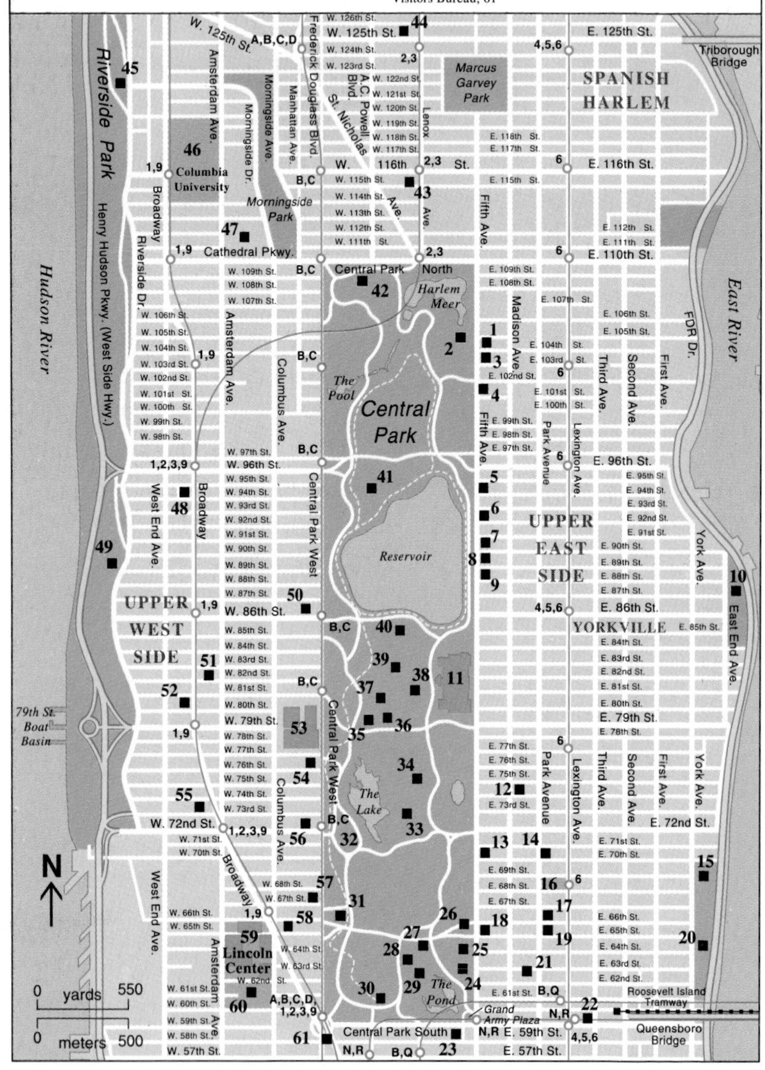